INFORMATION RIGHTS

A PRACTITIONER'S GUIDE TO DATA PROTECTION, FREEDOM OF INFORMATION & OTHER INFORMATION RIGHTS

Fifth edition

VOLUME 1

COMMENTARY

INFORMATION RIGHTS

A PRACTITIONER'S GUIDE TO DATA PROTECTION, FREEDOM OF INFORMATION & OTHER INFORMATION RIGHTS

Fifth edition

by

Philip Coppel QC

Contributors

Paul Bowen QC
Isabella Buono
Richard Clayton QC
Gerry Facenna QC
James Findlay QC
John Fitzsimons
Henry King QC
Jacqueline Lean
James Maurici QC
Gavin Millar QC
Julianne Morrison
Aidan O'Neill QC
Oliver Sanders QC
His Honour Judge Shanks
Bankim Thanki QC
Martin Westgate QC
Antony White QC
Gemma White QC

•HART•
OXFORD • LONDON • NEW YORK • NEW DELHI • SYDNEY

HART PUBLISHING

Bloomsbury Publishing Plc

Kemp House, Chawley Park, Cumnor Hill, Oxford, OX2 9PH, UK

1385 Broadway, New York, NY 10018, USA

HART PUBLISHING, the Hart/Stag logo, BLOOMSBURY and the Diana logo are trademarks of Bloomsbury Publishing Plc

First published in Great Britain 2020

Reprinted 2020

First published 2004
Second edition 2007
Third edition 2010
Fourth edition 2014

A catalogue record for this book is available from the British Library.

ISBN: HB: 978-1-50992-159-1 (Volume 1)
978-1-50992-163-8 (Volume 2)
978-1-50992-224-6 (2 Volume set)
ePDF: 978-1-50992-248-2
ePub: 978-1-50992-247-5

Typeset by Compuscript Ltd, Shannon
Printed and bound in Great Britain by CPI Group (UK) Ltd, Croydon CR0 4YY

To find out more about our authors and books visit www.hartpublishing.co.uk. Here you will find extracts, author information, details of forthcoming events and the option to sign up for our newsletters.

PHILIP COPPEL QC
Cornerstone Barristers

PAUL BOWEN QC
Brick Court Chambers

ISABELLA BUONO
Cornerstone Barristers

RICHARD CLAYTON QC
Ely Place Chambers

GERRY FACENNA QC
Monckton Chambers

JAMES FINDLAY QC
Cornerstone Barristers

JOHN FITZSIMONS
Cornerstone Barristers

HENRY KING QC
Fountain Court

JACQUELINE LEAN
Landmark

JAMES MAURICI QC
Landmark

GAVIN MILLAR QC
Matrix

JULIANNE MORRISON
Monkton Chambers

AIDAN O'NEILL QC
Matrix

OLIVER SANDERS QC
1 Crown Office Row

HIS HONOUR JUDGE SHANKS
A Judge of the Crown Court and of the First-tier Tribunal

BANKIM THANKI QC
Fountain Court

MARTIN WESTGATE QC
Doughty Street Chambers

ANTONY WHITE QC
Matrix

GEMMA WHITE QC
Blackstone Chambers

Preface

Almost six years have elapsed since the last edition. In that time, there have been well publicised changes to the data protection regime. From much of what is written one could be excused for thinking that the General Data Protection Regulation (GDPR) supplanted domestic legislation. The position is rather different, with the Data Protection Act 2018 (DPA 2018) supplementing the GDPR's general processing regime, as well as defining the regime for law enforcement and intelligence services purposes. Despite the reams of legislative provisions, the changes are evolutionary, rather than revolutionary. Indeed, many of the central principles in the current regime can be readily traced to the 1981 Convention for the Protection of Individuals with regard to the Automatic Processing of Personal Data.

The legislative changes have been taken as an opportunity to extend the scope of this work to provide a comprehensive treatment of data protection law in the United Kingdom. Having for years been the poor relation in the protection of personal privacy – dull and technical next to glittering human rights conceptions that for a while enjoyed official favour – data protection has come to assume increased importance. Controlling the use and abuse of personal information is no less an 'information right' than eliciting information from public authorities. Where data protection differs from freedom of information is that its reach is not confined to public authorities. Given that the GDPR/DPA 2018 regime has evolved from the predecessor regime, the work includes a detailed account of the DPA 1998. The case law in relation to that Act, as well as Directive 2003/4/EC which it implemented, provides useful guidance to the current regime.

On the topic of data protection guidance, the Information Commissioner is under a statutory duty to publish various codes and guidance documents, some of which require Parliamentary approval. Of significance in the preparation of a text such as this work, it is regrettable that almost 2 years after coming into force, there has been only part performance. Despite the centrality of the journalism code (s 124) and media redress guidance (s 177) to counterbalance the disapplication of the data protection regime to that industry, not so much as a draft of either mandatory publication has emerged. Correcting regulatory indifference to the data processing activities of this particular industry was one of the recommendations of the *Report of the Leveson Inquiry* (2102, Part L paras 58-66). Moreover, it is not readily apparent from the Commissioner's website which statutory codes have been published. While there is statutory guidance about regulatory action including penalties – the importance of which is evident from the detail that Parliament has specified in s 160 of the DPA 2018 – this has been mixed up with guidance about privileged communications and non-payment of fees. The guidance is to be found in a document entitled *Regulatory Action Policy*, but it gives no clue whether or when it was approved by Parliament or when it came into force. This is despite a foreword that proclaims:

> "Organisations should be able to predict how [the Commissioner's] office will carry out its regulatory activity."

Although the document states that the Commissioner will use sanctions proportionately, it is notable that the financial impact on the controller is not listed as one of the factors that will be taken into account in setting penalties. Applying this policy, the Commissioner has notified businesses of her intention to impose penalties, some exceeding £100 million, sufficient to collapse the entire business. None of this is easy to reconcile with the Commissioner's stated first goal: "increase the public's trust and confidence."

In relation to freedom of information, the Independent Commission on the Freedom of Information Act 2000 has come and gone (2016). In no small part due to the press, the attempt to reverse FOIA's modernising influence on the business of government has been successfully resisted. Nevertheless, it would be naive to think that the natural inclination to governmental secrecy has vanished. It has instead been more attractively re-packaged as 'blue-sky thinking' and other metaphors to cloud the issue.

Most of the main principles in relation to freedom of information have now been settled by tribunal decisions. As many of the recent First-tier Tribunal decisions are simply the application of these principles, I have not attempted in this edition to list them all. Rather, I have limited the notation of new FTT decisions to those that either establish a principle or provide a good illustration of established principles. There does remain a more general question – by no means unique to FOI cases – as to the true role of the FTT when re-making non-monetary administrative decisions such as the entitlement to information. While it is said that the FTT exercises a full merit-review function 'standing in the shoes of the decision-maker,' that function is bedevilled by a reluctance to accept the concept of a tribunal charged with making the right decision on the facts as they are using all the information before it. The standstill approach – looking at matters as they stood at the moment that the decision-maker happened to put pen to paper – should be the preserve of judicial review. Although the standpoint is not always significant, in some cases the passage of years before the matter comes before the FTT can make a profound difference to what falls to be evaluated. It is to be hoped that one day this will be corrected, in the process clearing the convolutions and inconsistencies that attend it.

All this said, this work remains as it started – a practitioner's text. Its object is to provide a comprehensive and authoritative statement of legal principles, referenced to statute and case-law.

I have taken the opportunity in this edition to invigorate the work with new contributors. Here I have deliberately cast the net wide, with pre-eminence my only guiding principle. I have been amply rewarded. I am grateful for the expertise that they have brought into the text. It is easy to fall back on simply adding new citations between editions. My contributors have protected me from this. Existing text has been considered afresh, citations checked, new material has been introduced and old material excised. All the while, the strengths of earlier editions have been kept. Chapters not having a contributor named in the table of contents are written by me.

I am grateful too for those who have written to me with comments, criticisms or suggestions. Regardless of whether I have adopted them, they have invariably been both thoughtful and helpful. They are always welcomed.

I record my particular indebtedness to Dr Roberta Bassi at Hart Publishing for her enthusiasm for and support of this publication. To my father and my brother Nicholas go many thanks for their acuity and tireless proof-reading.

I have stated the law in light of the material available to me at 1 February 2020. In light of legal uncertainties remaining after the withdrawal of the United Kingdom from the EU, I have not attempted to guess what changes might result in the fields of data protection and environmental information. Once these changes do become clear, they will be absorbed and reflected in the text, either by way of a supplement or in a new edition (depending on the scale of the changes).

Philip Coppel QC
1 May 2020

CONTENTS

Chapter 6 – Prejudice and the public interest

Isabella Buono

Part II Data protection

Chapter 7 – Data protection: introduction

Isabella Buono (section 5)

Chapter 8 – GDPR and DPA 2018: introduction

Chapter 9 – General processing: continuing obligations

Chapter 10 – General processing: data subject rights

Chapter 11 – General processing: exemptions etc

Part V Exemptions

Chapter 41 – Common law rights and controls

Gavin Millar QC

Chapter 42 – Court-held documents

Martin Westgate QC

Chapter 43 – Information held by EU bodies

Aidan O'Neill QC

Part VII Appeals, remedies and enforcement

Chapter 44 – The Information Commissioner and the tribunals

HHJ Murray Shanks

Chapter 45 – FOIA and EIR appeals

HHJ Murray Shanks

Chapter 46 – The Scottish Information Commission and FOI(S)A etc appeals

James Findlay QC

Chapter 47 – Freedom of information: regulatory enforcement

HHJ Murray Shanks & James Findlay QC

Chapter 48 – GDPR and DPA 2018: private remedies and regulatory enforcement

Part VIII Comparative law

Index

Tables of Cases

United Kingdom

CJEU and ECtHR

United States of America

Australia

Canada

New Zealand

Aldous v Auckland City Council [1990] DCR 385 1241
Attorney General and Gow v Leigh [2011] NZSC 106 753
Attorney General for England and Wales v Television New Zealand Ltd (1999) 44 IPR 123 (CA).......... 634
Attorney General for England and Wales v 'R' [2002] 2 NZLR 91 (CA).......... 634, 635
Attorney General for the United Kingdom v Wellington Newspapers Limited [1988] 1 NZLR 129 ..... 108, 858
Attorney-General v Davidson [1994] 3 NZLR 143 (CA) 1246
Auckland Regional Council v North Shore City Council [1995] 3 NZLR 18 782
In the matter of C [2005] NZLR 56 1241
Chief Executive of the Ministry of Social Development v Holmes [2013] NZHC 672.......... 1242
Commissioner of Police v District Court at Manukau [2007] NZHC 101 1243
Commissioner of Police v Ombudsman [1985] 1 NZLR 578.......... 80, 82, 511, 1241
Commissioner of Police v Ombudsman [1988] 1 NZLR 385.......... 80, 82, 85, 122, 512, 1241, 1244
Cornelius v Commissioner for Police [1998] 3 NZLR 373 1241
Director of Human Rights Proceedings v Commissioner of Police [2008] NZHC 1286 1240
Gravatt v Auckland Coroner's Court [2013] NZHC 390 1245
Herewini v Ministry of Transport [1992] 3 NZLR 482.......... 1241
Kelsey v Minister of Trade [2015] NZHC 2497, [2016] 2 NZLR 218.......... 1241, 1244
Leach v Ministry of Transport [1993] 1 NZLR 106 1241
Mafart and anor v Television New Zealand [2006] NZCA 183 1245
Nicholl v Chief Executive of the Department of Work and Income [2003] 3 NZLR 426 1244
Police v Keogh [2000] 1 NZLR 736 1241
R v Craig [1975] 1 NZLR 597.......... 762, 766
R v Harvey [1991] 1 NZLR 242 .... 512, 1241
R v Uljee [1982] 1 NZLR 561 at 576–577 763
Ross v Tarnaki City Council [1990] DCR 11 1241
Television New Zealand Ltd v Ombudsman [1992] 1 NZLR 106 1244
Wyatt Co (NZ) Ltd v Queenstown-Lakes District Council [1991] 2 NZLR 180 .... 85, 571, 1245

Republic of Ireland

Attorney General v Hamilton [1993] 2 IR 250 789
Deely v Information Commissioner [2001] IEHC 91 .... 1254, 1259
EH v Information Commissioner [2001] IEHC 58, [2001] 2 IR 463.......... 777, 1255-1257
FP v Information Commissioner & Ors [2016] IEHC 771 .... 1257, 1258
Health Service Executive v Information Commissioner [2008] IEHC 298 .... 87, 1257
Kruse v Information Commissioner [2009] IEHC 286.......... 1259
Minister for Agriculture and Food v Information Commissioner [2000] 1 IR 309.......... 87, 1257, 1259
Minister for Communications Energy and Natural Resources v Information Commissioner [2017] IEHC 222 1256
Minister for Communications, Energy and Natural Resources v Information Commissioner & ors [2019] IECA 68 1258
Minister for Education & Science v Information Commissioner [2008] IEHC 279.......... 1257
Minister for Education and Science v Information Commissioner [2001] IEHC 116 .... 1258, 1259
Minister for Enterprise Trade and Employment v Information Commissioner [2006] IEHC 39 1254
P v Information Commissioner [2009] IEHC 574 1257
Rotunda Hospital v Information Commissioner [2009] IEHC 315 .... 777, 1257, 1259

TABLES OF LEGISLATION

Westminster Primary Legislation

Westminster Secondary Legislation

International Instruments

Glossary

Art 29WP	Article 29 Working Party, an advisory body made up of a representative from the data protection authority of each EU Member State, the EDPS and the European Commission, replaced on 25 May 2018 by the EDPB
AG	Advocate General
CFR	Charter of Fundamental Rights of the European Union, proclaimed 7 December 2000 by the European Parliament, Council and Commission, and taking legal effect on 1 December 2009
CJEU	Court of Justice of the European Union
Council of Europe	founded on 5 May 1949 by the Treaty of London, currently comprising 47 member states including the United Kingdom
Convention 108	Convention for the Protection of Individuals with regard to Automatic Processing of Personal Data, drawn up by the Council of Europe and opened for signature on 28 January 1981, currently signed and ratified by 54 parties, including the United Kingdom on 15 May 1981 and 26 August 1987 (respectively)
Convention 108 Mod	Convention 108 as amended by amending Protocol, opened for signature on 11 October 2108
COPR	Court of Protection Rules 2017 (SI 2017/1035)
CPR	Civil Procedure Rules 1998 (SI 1998/3132)
Crim PR	Criminal Procedure Rules 2015 (SI 2015/1490)
DCA	Department of Constitutional Affairs
DEFRA	Department for Environment, Food and Rural Affairs
Directive 95/46/EC	Directive of the European Parliament and of the Council of 24 October 1995 on the Protection of Individuals with Regard to the Processing of Personal Data and on the Free Movement of Such Data, implemented in the United Kingdom by the DPA 1998, and repealed by GDPR Art 94(1) with effect from 25 May 2018
DPA 1998	Data Protection Act 1998, which implemented Directive 95/46/EC in the United Kingdom and was repealed with effect from 25 May 2018
DPA 2018	Data Protection Act 2018
DP (Fees) Regs	Data Protection (Subject Access) (Fees and Miscellaneous Provisions) Regulations 2000 (SI 2000/191)
DPP	data protection principle, as set out in Part 1 of Schedule 1 to the DPA 1998
DPPECR	Data Protection, Privacy and Electronic Communications (Amendments etc) (EU Exit) Regulations 2019 (SI 2019/419)
EC	European Community, established by the TEU with effect from 1 November 1993, replacing the EEC, and re-named as the EU with effect from 1 December 2009
ECHR	Convention for the Protection of Human Rights and Fundamental Freedoms, commonly called the European Convention on Human Rights, which entered into force on 3 September 1953 and to which all members states of the Council of Europe are party
ECtHR	European Court of Human Rights, established on 21 January 1959

under ECHR Article 19

EDPB	European Data Protection Board, established by Article 68 of the GDPR on 25 May 2018, comprising the EDPS and representatives of the national data protection authorities of the member states of the EEA, and replacing the A29WP
EDPS	European Data Protection Supervisor, established by Article 41 of Regulation (EC) 45/2001 (on the protection of individuals with regard to the processing of personal data by the Community institutions and bodies and on the free movement of such data), with effect from 17 January 2004
EEA	European Economic Area, comprising the 27 EU Member States, the EFTA Member States (excluding Switzerland) and Croatia
EEC	European Economic Community, established by the Treaty of Rome and replaced on 1 November 1993 with the EC
EEC Treaty	the Treaty of Rome (*qv*)
EFTA	European Free Trade Association, established on 12 January 1960, currently comprising Switzerland, Iceland, Norway and Liechtenstein
EIR	Environmental Information Regulations 2004 (SI 2004/3391)
EI(S)R	Environmental Information (Scotland) Regulations 2004 (SSI 2004/520)
EU	European Union, being the EC as re-named by the Treaty of Lisbon, signed on 13 December 2007 and entering into force on 1 December 2009
EU(W)A	EU (Withdrawal) Act 2018
EU(WA)A	EU (Withdrawal Agreement) Act 2020
Fees Regs 2004	Freedom of Information and Data Protection (Appropriate Limit and Fees) Regulations 2004 (SI 2004/3244)
Fees (Scot) Regs	Freedom of Information (Fees for Required Disclosure) (Scotland) Regulations 2004 (SSI 2004/467)
Fees (s 13) Regs	Freedom of Information (Fees for Disclosure under Section 13) (Scotland) Regulations 2004 (SSI 2004/376)
FOIA	Freedom of Information Act 2000
FOI (Time) Regs	Freedom of Information (Time for Compliance with Request) Regulations 2004 (SI 2004/3364)
FOI(S)A	Freedom of Information (Scotland) Act 2002
FPR	Family Procedure Rules 2010 (SI 2010/2955)
FTT	First-tier Tribunal, established by the Tribunals, Courts and Enforcement Act 2007 s 3(1), and into which the functions of the IT transferred with effect from 18 January 2010
FTT Rules	Tribunal Procedure (First-tier Tribunal) (General Regulatory Chamber) Rules 2009 (SI 2009/1976)
GDPR	Regulation (EU) 2016/679 of the European Parliament and of the Council, generally known as the General Data Protection Regulation, which applied from 25 May 2018
HC	House of Commons
HL	House of Lords
HRA	Human Rights Act 1998

IC	Information Commissioner, established as a corporation sole as the Data Protection Commissioner by DPA 1998 s 6(1) and Sch 5, re-named as the Information Commissioner by FOIA s 18(1), and continued by DPA 2018 s 114(1) and Sch 12
ICCPR	International Covenant on Civil and Political Rights, adopted by the General Assembly of the United Nations General Assembly on 16 December 1966, and in force from 23 March 1976
ICO	Information Commissioner's Office, comprising the IC and the officers and staff thereof
IT	Information Tribunal, being the Data Protection Tribunal (established by DPA 1983 s 3(1) and continued by DPA 1998 s 6(3)) as re-named by FOIA s 18(2), the functions of which were transferred into the FTT by The Transfer of Tribunal Functions Order 2010 with effect from 18 January 2010
LED	Directive (EU) 2016/680 of the European Parliament and of the Council, commonly known as the Law Enforcement Directive, which entered into force on 5 May 2016
MoJ	Ministry of Justice
OECD	Organisation for Economic Co-operation and Development, formed on 30 September 1961 to supersede the Organisation for European Economic Co-operation which had been formed on 16 April 1948, and now comprising 36 member states
PD	Practice Direction made under the CPR
s 45 Code of Practice	Secretary of State for Constitutional Affairs' Code of Practice On the Discharge of Public Authorities' Functions under Part I of the Freedom of Information Act 2000. Presented to Parliament by the Secretary of State for Constitutional Affairs pursuant to section 45(5) of the FOIA, 25 November 2004.
s 46 Code of Practice	Lord Chancellor's Code of Practice on the Management of Records issued under section 46 of the Freedom of Information Act 2000. Presented to Parliament by the Lord Chancellor pursuant to section 46(6) of the FOIA, 16 July 2009
TEU	Treaty Establishing the European Union, also known as the Maastricht Treaty, signed on 7 February 1992, and re-naming the EEC as the EC with effect from 1 November 1993
TFEU	Treaty on the Functioning of the European Union, being the Treaty of Rome as amended and re-named by the Treaty of Lisbon, signed on 13 December 2007 and entering into force on 1 December 2009
Treaty of Rome	Treaty establishing the European Economic Community, signed on 25 March 1957 and entering into force on 1 January 1958
UT	Upper Tribunal, established by the Tribunals, Courts and Enforcement Act 2007 s 3(2)
UT Rules	Tribunal Procedure (Upper Tribunal) Rules 2008 (SI 2008/2698)

Part I

Overview

CHAPTER 1

Introduction

1. OVERVIEW OF INFORMATION RIGHTS

1–001 The meaning of information rights

Information rights may be said to be of two kinds. First, rights of an individual to obtain access to information held by a governmental body. Secondly, rights of an individual to limit the use that is made of that individual's personal information. Whereas the first relates solely to information held by governmental bodies, the second applies to the use of information relating to an individual by any legal person, whether a governmental body, a company, an organisation or another individual. The first kind of right most commonly arises through FOIA or FOI(S)A. Those two Acts are not, however, the only sources of such rights: there is an array of other legislation providing rights of access to governmental information. And, it would seem, the common law has discovered that it, too, may be willing to recognise such rights.[1] The second kind of right most commonly arises through the GDPR as supplemented by the Data Protection Act 2018. But again, those are not the only sources, with both the common law and the ECHR busying themselves in this area. These, then, are what this work terms 'information rights.' Unlike intellectual property rights – many of which also revolve around information – 'property' concepts do not animate information rights. Rather, their concern is the use and misuse of information – in the broadest sense of the word 'use' – referenced by individual, business, governmental and public interests. Although it may be considered to be a right in relation to information, save to the extent that the preceding rights are shaped by it, this work does not concern itself with the law of confidentiality, whether arising by contract or in equity.

1–002 Early rights to official information

The four decades leading to 2000 saw within the United Kingdom a gradual increase in the rights of an individual to elicit information from public authorities. The Public Bodies

[1] *Kennedy v Charity Commission* [2014] UKSC 20, [2015] AC 455. Indeed, such is the fecundity of the common law in this area that the Supreme Court has shown itself willing to find such a right despite the parties not having made any submissions that one existed.

(Admission to Meetings) Act 1960 marked the first step in that process.[2] The Act had been introduced into Parliament as a private Member's Bill. The Member sponsoring the Bill spoke of a 'right to know'[3] and set out the purpose of that right:

> The public has the right...to know what its elected representatives are doing.... Unless the Press, which is to report to the public, has some idea from the documents before it what is to be discussed, the business of allowing the Press in becomes wholly abortive...The Press must have some idea from the documents what is the true subject to be discussed at a meeting to which its representatives are entitled to be admitted...I hope that hon. Members will think fit to give this Bill a Second Reading, and to consider that the paramount function of this distinguished House is to safeguard civil liberties rather than to think that administrative convenience should take first place in law.[4]

The novelty of the Act lay in the conferral of a right to obtain access to official documents.[5] Although the scope of the right was narrow, to some its mere existence made the Act 'a very controversial piece of legislation'.[6] Its potential for extension, in particular to the ministries of central government, was immediately recognised.[7] Indeed, apart from the right of access to documents, there was little in the Act that was new:

> As the Hon Member for Islington North said, unless the spirit of the Bill is observed, it will do little more than the existing legislation. It will, however, do one thing more, and that is the most important feature to have come out of the Bill. It is not so much the admission of the public, curiously enough, but the provisions relating to the distribution of documents, that may well turn out to be the most important part of the Bill.[8]

The rationale for this early legislation and its identification of the competing considerations for and against disclosure of official information were to anticipate the preoccupations of Parliament 40 years later.

1–003 Freedom of Information Act 2000

The enactment of FOIA represented a significant step in the process that had begun with the Public Bodies (Admission to Meetings) Act 1960. For the first time in the United Kingdom,

---

2 The Act applies to local authorities, education committees, parish meetings of rural parishes, various NHS boards, bodies and executive councils, as well as their committees. It makes the meetings of all such bodies open to the public, except where publicity 'would be contrary to the public interest'. Section 1(4)(b) provides that where the meeting is required to be open to the public, a newspaper can request, and on payment of postage must be supplied with, the agenda of the meeting '...together with such further statements or particulars, if any, as are necessary to indicate the nature of the items included or, if thought fit in the case of any item, with copies of any reports or other documents supplied to members of the body in connection with the item'. The Act is considered further at §§37–043 to 37–044.

3 In a speech by Lord Falconer (Constitutional Affairs Secretary and Lord Chancellor) to the International Conference of Information Commissioners, Manchester, 22 May 2006, he stated: 'Freedom of Information demands extra of our public officials, it requires cultural change within Governments and among public officials – a shift in mindset from the "need to know" to the "right to know".'

4 Hansard HC vol 616 cols 1350-1358 (5 February 1960) (Margaret Thatcher, Finchley, Second Reading Speech. This was her maiden speech).

5 The provision of a right for the press to attend meetings of local authorities had been introduced by The Local Authorities (Admission of the Press to Meetings) Act 1908, passed in consequence of the judgment in *Tenby Corp v Mason* [1908] 1 Ch 457. Section 3 of the 1908 Act provided that it was not to extend to any meeting of a committee of a local authority, other than education committees. The efficacy of the Act was reduced by the Local Government Act 1933 s 85, which empowered local authorities to appoint any committees they chose. As a result of this, many authorities went into committee of the full council in order to be able to exclude the press. Its efficacy was further reduced by the Education Act 1944, which removed education committees from the operation of the Act.

6 Hansard HC vol 616 col 1366 (5 February 1960) (Mr GW Reynolds, Islington North).

7 'How Parliament would get on in those circumstances I really dread to think.' — Hansard HC vol 616 col 1384 (5 February 1960) (Mr Arthur Skeffington, member for Hayes and Harlington, quoting from the Official Report of the Standing Committee D on the Local Government Bill in 1958).

8 Hansard HC vol 617 col 830 (13 May 1960) (Mr Peter Kirk, Gravesend).

Parliament conferred an entitlement to official information that was not confined either by its permissible subject matter or by reference to the persons who enjoy that entitlement. Its starting point is an entitlement, described without reference to a subject-matter, conferred upon every person to have disclosed all information answering the terms of a request held by the requested public authority. Up until FOIA, every right to elicit official information had been limited. The limitation had been generally referable to information answering a particular description or emanating from a particular source. But it had also been limited by reference to the persons on whom the right was conferred. In some cases, it was limited in both such respects. The entitlement conferred by the 2000 Act has no such limitation: it is given to every person, irrespective of that person's interest in the information; and it applies to all information, irrespective of its subject-matter. The entitlement is, however, shaped by a series of specific exemptions.[9] To the extent that the requested information does not fall within one or more of those exemptions, it must be disclosed. There are two types of exemption. If information falls within the terms of a provision conferring 'absolute exemption' the entitlement is thereby disapplied.[10] If information falls within the terms of a provision conferring exemption, but not 'absolute exemption', then only if the public interest in maintaining that exemption outweighs the public interest in disclosure of the information will the entitlement to disclosure be disapplied. The breadth of FOIA gives it greater significance than the earlier legislation conferring subject-specific rights of access.

1–004 Other rights to official information

Although the earlier patchwork of rights initiated by one paragraph in the Public Bodies (Admission to Meetings) Act 1960 has been eclipsed by FOIA, it remains largely intact.[11] From the perspective of an individual seeking to elicit official information, the paramount concern will be the existence of a right to obtain that information, rather than the statutory provenance of that right. From the perspective of a public authority responding to a request for information under FOIA, the existence of an alternative statutory right of access to the information will result in the displacement of the entitlement to that information under the 2000 Act.[12] The earlier legislation thus remains significant. In this work, subject-specific rights of access have been considered thematically in Chapters 5, 6 and 8.

1–005 Relationship between main statutes

On the same day that FOIA came fully into force (1 January 2005), the EIR also came into force. The Regulations impose a duty to make available on request 'environmental information' held by public authorities. FOIA, whilst unrestricted in its breadth, expressly acknowledges the proscriptions and the disclosure regimes of both the data protection regime and the Regulations. Both of these implement European Directives that had to be accommodated by the draftsman of FOIA. This requirement was secured by routeing the treatment of requested information through the data protection regime or the Regulations according to whether that information related to the applicant or was 'environmental

---

[9] See FOIA s 1(2); FOI(S)A s 1(6). These make the entitlements or entitlement, respectively, subject to (most importantly) s 2, thereby bringing in the provisions of Pt II of the Act.

[10] The verb 'disapply' in relation to the entitlements is used throughout this work to signify that one or both of the entitlements do not apply. It is recognised that the creation of express relationships between ss 1(1), 1(2), 2 and Pt II of the FOIA is simply a legislative technique for delineating the bounds of those entitlements. In other words, these provisions shape the scope of the entitlements, rather than remove or negate a entitlement already given. For a similar technique used elsewhere, see *Matthews v Ministry of Defence* [2003] 1 AC 1163, esp at [20], in relation to the Crown Proceedings Act 1947.

[11] Some rights were repealed by the DPA 1998, namely: the Access to Personal Files Act 1987; parts of the Access to Health Records Act 1990.

[12] FOIA s 21; FOI(S)A s 25.

information' (respectively). So far as personal information is concerned, an applicant's right of access to information of which he is the data subject is governed by the data protection regime. Where an applicant seeks personal information of which he is not the data subject, then the applicant's right of access is governed by the Freedom of Information Act. In this case, however, disclosure under the Act will constitute a processing of personal data, which is a matter governed by the data protection regime. The legislative regime reconciles the competing interests of the applicant and the subject of the personal information by importing into FOIA the protection given by certain of the data protection principles.[13] Where a request is for, or includes, environmental information, the request (or that part of the request) is governed by the EIR. This routeing is necessary in order to implement the more generous disclosure regime applicable to environmental information under European Parliament's Directive 2003/4/EC. Disclosure of environmental information is considered in Chapter 6.

1–006 Wales

Although the Government of Wales Act 1998 created a National Assembly for Wales, it was an administrative body rather than a legislative body. It had no power to make laws with respect to the granting of access to official information. The Government of Wales Act 2006 replaced the National Assembly with the Welsh Assembly Government, but did not alter the position in relation to the making of laws with respect to access rights to official information.[14] Accordingly, FOIA applies equally to public authorities in Wales as it does to public authorities in England.[15] Schedule 1 to the Act, which lists public authorities for the purposes of the Act, includes the National Assembly for Wales, Welsh county councils, borough councils and community councils, health authorities, maintained schools and other educational institutions, police authorities, and various other bodies ranging from the Ancient Monuments Board for Wales to the Welsh Optometric Committee. The National Assembly for Wales has its own Code of Practice on Public Access to Information,[16] which, like all such codes,[17] does not confer rights but merely states intent. It contemplates a more generous provision of information than the minimum that may be provided under FOIA and EIR. Since the initial coming into force of the Act, certain public authorities have been removed from its operation.[18]

1–007 Northern Ireland

The Freedom of Information Act 2000 extends to Northern Ireland[19] and specifically captures public authorities whose functions are exercisable only or mainly in or as regards Northern Ireland and relate only or mainly to transferred matters.[20] Schedule 1 to the Act includes the

13 Disclosure of personal information is considered in detail in Chapters 10, 13 and 14 (right of access under the general processing, law enforcement processing and intelligence service processing regimes, respectively) and Chapter 33 (the freedom of information exemption).

14 As is evident from The Freedom of Information (Parliament and National Assembly for Wales) Order 2008 SI 2008 1967. Certain amendments to FOIA consequential upon the creation of the Welsh Assembly were effected by the Government of Wales Act 2006 (Consequential Modifications and Transitional Provisions) Order 2007 SI 2007/1388 Sch 1 para 80.

15 The only difference is that where the Secretary of State for Justice proposes to add a body or office-holder to the list of public authorities in the Act and that body or office-holder is one whose functions are exercisable only or mainly in or as regards Wales, he must consult the National Assembly before doing so: FOIA s 4(7). The Secretary of State for Justice is not required to consult where he intends to add a police authority to the list.

16 www.assemblywales.org/abthome/abt-nafw/abt-foi/abt-foi-cop-pub.htm

17 See §21–008.

18 Freedom of Information (Excluded Welsh Authorities) Order 2002 SI 2002/2832.

19 FOIA s 88(2). The specific reference to Northern Ireland is, strictly speaking, superfluous, but simply accords with a drafting convention.

20 FOIA s 84. 'Transferred matters' are defined in the Northern Ireland Act 1998 s 4(1).

Northern Ireland Assembly, district councils, health and social services boards, schools and universities, the police authority, and various other bodies ranging from the Advisory Committee on Pesticides for Northern Ireland to the Northern Ireland Pig Production Development Committee.

2. TERMINOLOGY

1–008 **Basic concepts**

It is convenient at this point to set out the principal terms that will be used in this work.

(1) When this work refers to the 'FOI Acts', it generally means both FOIA and FOI(S)A. Footnotes identify the different section numbers, as well as differences between the two Acts. Where those differences are more substantive than can properly be set out in a footnote, they are treated separately in the main text.

(2) When this work refers to the 'data protection regime', it means the GDPR as supplemented by the DPA 2018 (in the case of general processing) and the DPA 2018 (in relation to law enforcement processing by a competent authority and in relation to intelligence service processing). The data protection regime applies equally to Scotland.

(3) The EIR apply to public authorities and the EI(S)R apply to Scottish public authorities. Footnotes identify the different regulation numbers as well as differences between the two regimes. Footnotes also indicate the provenance of the regulations, both from Directive 2003/4/EC and the Aarhus Convention from which it was derived.

(4) The FOI Acts confer on every person two distinct but interrelated entitlements:

(a) First, an entitlement to be informed in writing by a public authority whether it holds information of the description specified in a request.[21] The FOI Acts label the duty of a public authority to comply with this entitlement as the *duty to confirm or deny*.[22] In shorthand, this may be called the *divulgence duty*. From the perspective of the person who made the request for the information, this may be called the *existence right*.

(b) Secondly, but more importantly, if the public authority does hold information of the description specified in a request, an entitlement to have that information communicated to him.[23] The FOI Acts[24] refer to this at various points as *disclosure*. In this work, this duty has been variously called the *disclosure duty* or the *duty to communicate*. From the perspective of the person requesting the information, this may be called the *access right*. Although the FOI Acts locate this right after the existence right, it is better considered first: the existence right is academic if a decision has been made to disclose the information.[25]

(5) The EIR and the EI(S)R confer a similar access right, but confined to 'environmental information'. There are significant differences in the breadth of the

---

21 FOIA s1(1)(a). This does not exist as a discrete entitlement under the FOI(S)A.

22 FOIAs1(6).

23 FOIA s 1(1)(b); FOI(S)A s 1(1).

24 FOIA ss 9(5), 13(3), 17(4), 22, 23(5), 26(1), 27(1) and (4), 28(1), 29(1), 33(2), 35(4), 36(2) and (7), 38(1), 40(3), 41(1), 42(2), 43(1), 44(1), 45(2), 53(7), 77(1), and 81(2); FOI(S)A ss 9(7), 13(4), 16(2), 26, 27, 28, 29(3), 30, 31(4), 32(1), 33(1) and (2), 35(1), 36(2), 38(2), 39(1), 40, 45, 50(7), 52(3), 60(2), 62(4), 64(1), 65(1).

25 As is implicitly recognised by the FOIA s 1(5).

rights conferred by the FOI Acts and the right conferred by the Regulations. Generally, but not always, the Regulations provide a more liberal disclosure regime than the FOI Acts.

(6) The data protection regime confers on every person a right to be informed whether personal data of which the applicant is the data subject is being held and a right to have communicated to him those data. The data protection regime speaks of 'data' rather than of 'information', but the definition of 'data' makes it clear that data are simply information that has certain routine characteristics.

1– 009 Exemptions and exceptions

Part II of the FOI Acts enumerate a series of provisions, which in this work are called *exemptions.* Part 3 of the EIR and of the EI(S)R employ the term *exceptions* rather than *exemptions.* Nothing turns on the different terminology. Each of the provisions of Part II of the FOI Acts, in describing one or more types of information, renders it *exempt information.*[26] This designation is significant for the disclosure duty: the designation is a requirement for disapplication of that duty and, in relation to some of the provisions, is sufficient for disapplication of that duty. In relation to the duty to confirm or deny, each of the provisions in Part II (with two exceptions),[27] after describing a type of exempt information, is followed by a closely corresponding provision preventing that duty from arising. The FOI Acts sometimes speak of the latter as an *exclusion* of the duty to confirm or deny,[28] and that term is used in this work.

1– 010 Absolute exemptions

Some provisions in Part II of the FOI Acts confer what that Act calls *absolute exemption.*[29] The remaining provisions[30] in Part II of the FOI Acts confer what this work terms *qualified exemption.* The EIR do not employ these terms, although the exceptions may be similarly divided. Where information falls within the terms of a provision that confers absolute exemption, the disclosure right does not apply and the public authority is thereby relieved from the duty to communicate. Similarly, where confirmation or denial of a holding would fall within one of the provisions in Part II under which the duty to confirm or deny is said not to arise and that provision confers absolute exemption, the right does not apply and the public authority is thereby relieved from the duty to confirm or deny. The Act speaks of an 'exclusion' of the duty to confirm or deny and of an 'exemption' from the duty to communicate.[31] Those duties may be said to be *disapplied.*[32] For information that falls within the terms of a provision that confers qualified exemption, the public authority may or may not be relieved from the duty to confirm or deny and from the duty to communicate depending upon a consideration of the public interest.[33]

1– 011 Procedural terms

The person who seeks the information under the FOI Acts or the EIR is called the *applicant.*[34]

---

26 A term recognised throughout the FOI Acts: see FOIA s 84; FOI(S)A s 73. There are some specific sections in Pt II that are simply supportive of other provisions in that Part, eg FOIA s 25.

27 FOIA ss 21 and 43(1).

28 FOIA ss 2(1)(a), 15(2)(a) and 17(3)(a).

29 FOIA s 2(3); FOI(S)A s 2(2). These provisions are listed at §5– 016.

30 Excluding the provisions that are purely supportive, such as s 25. The remaining provisions are listed at §5– 017.

31 FOIA s 2(1), (2)(b).

32 FOIA s 2(1) and (2); FOI(S)A s 2(1). See n 10.

33 See §§6– 010 to 6– 019.

34 FOIA s 84; FOI(S)A s 1(2); EIR reg 2(1); EI(S)R reg 2(1).

Under both Acts and the Regulations, information is sought by a *request*.[35] A request under the FOI Acts and the Regulations is addressed to a *public authority*, which may be a government department, one of the Houses of Parliament, any emanation of local government or the National Health Service, any number of specifically named public bodies or officers, or a publicly owned company.[36] A request under the data protection regime is addressed to a *controller*, which includes each government department as if it were a separate individual.[37] Under both Acts and the Regulations, once the public authority receives a valid request, it may give the applicant a *fees notice*, in which it sets out the amount it will charge the applicant for complying with the request.[38] Where a public authority decides that some or all of the information sought should not be disclosed to the applicant, it must give the applicant notice of this, which this work calls a *refusal notice*. A public authority may decide to mask parts of a document disclosed to an applicant on the basis that it is not obliged to disclose those blanked out parts of the document. That blanking out process is called *redaction* and the document is said to be *redacted*.[39]

1– 012 Review, etc

The FOI Acts provide for two codes of practice. The *section 45 Code of Practice* is issued by the Secretary of State and provides guidance on the handling of requests for information.[40] The *section 46 Code of Practice* is issued by the Lord Chancellor and relates to the keeping, management and destruction of records.[41] The EIR provide for one code of practice, similar to that issued under s 45.[42] An applicant who is dissatisfied with the way in which a public authority has dealt with his request under the FOI Acts may complain to that authority and seek *internal review* under the *section 45 Code of Practice*. If the applicant remains dissatisfied with the response, he may pursue what in this work is called a *2nd stage appeal* by making an *application* to the *Information Commissioner*.[43] At this point the applicant becomes a *complainant*.[44] If the Information Commissioner needs more information in order to determine an application, he may serve on the public authority an *information notice*.[45] If the Information Commissioner decides that the public authority has not complied with its disclosure duty or the duty to confirm or deny, he must serve a *decision notice* on the public authority and on the complainant.[46] If the Information Commissioner decides that the public authority has not otherwise properly complied with its duties in relation to a request, he may serve an *enforcement notice* on the public

---

35 In the FOIA, called a 'request for information': ss 8 and 84. In Scotland, see FOI(S)A s 8.

36 Public authorities are considered in detail at §§20– 018 to 20– 033. The definition is wider in the case of the EIR: see §18– 003.

37 DPA 2018 s 209(2).

38 FOIA s 9(1): FOI(S)A s 9(1).

39 Although not strictly a correct use of the word, this is the meaning it has come to assume in this and related areas of the law.

40 FOIA s 45; FOI(S)A s 60. The Code is reproduced in the Appendix to this work.

41 FOIA s 46; FOI(S)A s 61. The Code is reproduced in the Appendix to this work.

42 EIR reg 18; EI(S)R reg 16.

43 Similarly, under the EIR reg 18(1), EI(S)R reg 17. The Information Commissioner is simply a new name for the Data Protection Commissioner: FOIA s 18(1). In Scotland, the application is made to the Scottish Information Commissioner, who is referred to in the FOI(S)A s 73 as 'the Commissioner'.

44 FOIA s 50(1); EIR reg 18(1); EI(S)R reg 17.

45 FOIA s 50(1); FOI(S)A s 50(1); EIR reg 18; EI(S)R reg 17.

46 FOIA s 50(3)-(4); EIR reg 18. In Scotland the function of decision notices is absorbed within enforcement notices: FOI(S)A s 51; EI(S)R reg 17.

authority and on the complainant.[47] Either the complainant or the public authority may appeal against the Information Commissioner's decision to the *Tribunal*.[48] In this work, such an appeal is called a *3rd stage appeal*. In most cases, the tribunal will be the First-tier Tribunal, but in more significant cases it may go directly to the Upper Tribunal. The tribunal re-determines the issues based on its own evaluation of the evidence (including the requested information) before it. If a party is not satisfied with the decision of the tribunal, that party needs permission to have the tribunal's decision reviewed, either by the Upper Tribunal or, if the third-stage appeal was heard by the Upper Tribunal, by the Court of Appeal.

1– 013 Miscellaneous terms

The FOI Acts, the data protection regime and the EIR enable a *conclusive certificate* to be issued in certain circumstances by a Minister of the Crown or like official.[49] There are two types of conclusive certificate. An *exemption conclusive certificate* certifies either that a particular exemption or that a particular harm required for exemption is applicable, and the certificate stands as conclusive evidence of that 'fact', irrespective of what the reality might be.[50] A *compliance conclusive certificate* certifies that the person signing it has on reasonable grounds formed the opinion that the public authority has not failed to comply with the duty to disclose or the duty to confirm or deny,[51] irrespective of what the reality might be. The effect of both types of certificate is to remove altogether or cut down substantially an applicant's rights of appeal, either by express provision[52] or because of the deeming effect of the certificate. Although the FOI Acts, the data protection regime and the EIR may excuse a public authority from disclosing certain information, the public authority may nevertheless decide to voluntarily disclose that information. In this work such disclosure is called *discretionary disclosure*. Legislation providing for access to official information exists in many other jurisdictions. In this work, where it has been thought enlightening, reference has been made to the jurisprudence of those jurisdictions whose legal systems and official information access legislation bear the closest resemblance to that of the United Kingdom: the United States of America, the Commonwealth of Australia, New Zealand, Canada and the Republic of Ireland. In this work, these are called *the comparative jurisdictions*.

3. THE RATIONALE FOR OFFICIAL INFORMATION ACCESS LEGISLATION

1– 014 Introduction

The Freedom of Information Act 2000 confers a right to secure the disclosure of certain information and imposes a correlative duty to disclose it. The short title of each of the FOI Acts tends to mask its compulsive character. The benefits typically attributed to the dissemination of official information, namely:[53]

---

47 FOIA s 52; EIR reg 18. In Scotland, an enforcement notice is employed wherever the Information Commissioner decides that the public authority has not properly complied with its duties in relation to a request: FOI(S)A s 51; EI(S)R reg 17.

48 FOIA s 57(1); EIR reg 18. There is no such right of appeal in Scotland.

49 FOIA ss 23(2), 24(3)-(4), 25, 34(3), 36(7), 53(2)-(3) and (6); FOI(S)A ss 31(2)-(3) and 52(2); EIR reg 15; EI(S)R reg 12.

50 FOIA ss 23(2), 24(3)-(4), 25, 34(3) and 36(7); FOI(S)A s 31(2)-(3); EIR reg 15; EI(S)R reg 12.

51 FOIA s 53(2)-(3) and (6); FOI(S)A s 52(2); EIR reg 18(6); EI(S)R reg 17.

52 FOIA s 60; EIR reg 18(1) and 18(7).

53 'This principle allows the public and the media to exercise scrutiny of the State, the municipalities and other parts of the public sector which, in turn, contributes to the free exchange of opinions and ideas and to efficient and correct management of public affairs and, thereby, to maintaining the legitimacy of the democratic system': *Gillberg*

— increased information in relation to the making of official decisions; and

— an electorate informed as to what its Government is or has been doing,

do not, in theory, require compulsion for their efficacy. The Act is not one that merely enables a public authority to do what otherwise it could not lawfully do for lack of statutory authority. Other than in limited circumstances,[54] it is and always has been perfectly open for a public authority to volunteer any information that it holds to anyone who requests it.[55] Such voluntary disclosure would, moreover, have been consistent with the spirit and letter of the Code of Practice on Access to Government Information.[56] A public authority owes its life to the public: unlike a private company or an individual, it has no interests that do not ultimately derive from that public. The compulsion that is at the heart of the FOI Acts recognises that a public authority to which a request for information has been made may be disinclined to disclose it. There is no deference in the Act to that disinclination. Disapplication of the duties under the Act only results where one or more of the statutory exemptions apply and, in some cases, the balance of specific facets of the public interest requires it.

1–015 The mischief

It is conventional to speak of Parliament intending that an enactment remedy a particular mischief or vice.[57] From that convention, it is presumed that Parliament intends that courts and those administering an enactment should do so in such a manner that promotes the remedy: a purposive construction.[58] The task is of particular significance for a statute such as the FOI Acts.[59] The existence of a public authority's obligation to disclose or not to disclose

v Sweden (2012) 34 BHRC 247 at [39]; 'The basic purpose of [the] FOIA is to ensure an informed citizenry, vital to the functioning of a democratic society, needed to check against corruption and to hold the governors accountable to the governed.': *National Labor Relations Board v Robbins Tire & Rubber Co* 437 US 214, 242 (1978). Or, put another way, 'to reinforce "the three basic principles of democratic government, namely, openness, accountability and responsibility."': *Commissioner of Police v District Court of New South Wales* (1993) 31 NSWLR 606 at 612; *Osland v Secretary to the Department of Justice* [2008] HCA 37, (2008) 234 CLR 27 at [62].

54 For example: confidential information received by a public authority from a third party; information subject to a statutory or contractual proscription on disclosure; or personal information relating to a third person. See §§20–034 to 20–038.

55 In *Reynolds v Times Newspapers Ltd* [2001] 2 AC 127 at 200, a case concerning qualified privilege, Lord Nicholls of Birkenhead said that 'the high importance of freedom to impart and receive information and ideas has been stated so often and so eloquently that this point calls for no elaboration in this case.'

56 The Code ceased to operate on 31 December 2004. The Code only applied to central government departments and agencies.

57 *Heydon's case* (1584) 3 Co Rep 7a. And, more recently: *Malloch v Aberdeen Corp* [1971] 1 WLR 1578 at 1583-1584 (Lord Reid); *Black-Clawson International Ltd v Papierwerke Waldhof-Aschaffenburg* AG [1975] AC 591 at 614 (Lord Reid); *AG ex rel Yorkshire Derwent Trust Ltd v Brotherton* [1992] 1 AC 425 at 442 and 447; *Attorney-General v Associated Newspapers Ltd* [1994] 2 AC 238 esp at 259 (Lord Lowry); *R v Secretary of State for the Environment, Transport and the Regions, ex p Spath Holme Ltd* [2001] 2 AC 349 at 362, 376, 391 and 397; *R (Quintavalle) v Secretary of State for Health* [2003] UKHL 13, [2003] 2 AC 687 at [21]; *Wilson v First County Trust* [2004] 1 AC 816 at [56] '...no legislation is enacted in a vacuum...'

58 *Pepper v Hart* [1993] AC 593 at 617, 'The days have long passed when the courts adopted a strict constructionist view of interpretation which required them to adopt the literal meaning of the language. The courts now adopt a purposive approach which seeks to give effect to the true purpose of legislation and are prepared to look at much extraneous material that bears upon the background against which the legislation was enacted' (Lord Griffiths) and 635 (Lord Browne-Wilkinson); *Inland Revenue Commissioners v McGuckian* [1997] 1 WLR 991 at 999 (Lord Steyn) 'During the last 30 years there has been a shift away from literalist to purposive methods of construction'; *Macniven (HM Inspector of Taxes) v Westmoreland Investments Ltd* [2001] UKHL6, [2003] 1 AC 311 at [6] (Lord Nicholls). In relation to those administering the Act: *Padfield v Minister of Agriculture, Fisheries & Food* [1968] AC 977 at 1039 'Where some legal right or entitlement is conferred or enjoyed, and for the purpose of effectuating such right or entitlement a power is conferred upon someone, then words which are permissible in character will sometimes be construed as involving a duty to exercise the power. The purpose and the language of any particular enactment must be considered' (Lord Morris); *Crédit Suisse v Allerdale Borough Council* [1995] 1 Lloyd's Rep 315 at 345; *R v Secretary of State for the Environment, Transport and the Regions, ex p Spath Holme Ltd* [2001] 2 AC 349 at 362, 376, 397 and 400.

59 Lord Falconer (Constitutional Affairs Secretary and Lord Chancellor), in a formal address to the International

information, as well as its obligation to confirm or deny that the information requested is held, is in many instances made to depend upon a balancing of competing facets of the public interest.[60] Whilst it is not unusual for the operation of a statutory provision to be part dependent upon the public interest,[61] it is unusual to ascribe to it an overriding importance about which an interested party[62] is given the adjudicative role. Identification of the purposes of the Act moderates the ability of the decision-maker to assess the public interest by undue reference to the interests of the public authority or to the idiosyncratic views of the decision-maker. Equally, an identification of purpose guides the exercise of the discretions conferred by the Act,[63] including that of whether or not a public authority should rely on an exemption.[64] The method for discerning the purpose of an Act or group of provisions in a statute is well known enough:

> In the absence of [looking at the legislative history and preparatory works] the courts have five principal avenues of approach to the ascertainment of the legislative intention: (1) examination of the social background, as specifically proved if not within common knowledge, in order to identify the social or juristic defect which is the likely subject of remedy; (2) a conspectus of the entire relevant body of the law for the same purpose; (3) particular regard to the long title of the statute to be interpreted (and, where available, the preamble), in which the general legislative objectives will be stated; (4) scrutiny of the actual words to be interpreted in the light of the established canons of interpretation; (5) examination of the other provisions of the statute in question (or of other statutes in pari materia) for the light which they throw on the particular words which are the subject of interpretation.[65]

1–016 The legislative background

The White Paper[66] that anticipated introduction of an FOI Bill spelled out the purpose of the

---

Conference of Information Commissioners, Manchester, 22 May 2006, said: '...unless FOI is consciously and carefully maintained, and its purposes are understood by people making requests, and by public officials, FOI can be perceived as a bureaucratic hassle, without any short-term benefit. The public become cynical, and officials fail to see FOI as part of public service and public communication.' The significance was addressed by Kirby J in *Osland v Secretary to the Department of Justice* [2008] HCA 37, (2008) 234 CLR 27 at [66] where he said: 'In the present setting, that purpose is a radical one. It assigns very high importance to a public interest in greater openness and transparency in public administration. Given the historical background, the attitudinal shift that FOI legislation demanded of Ministers, departments, agencies and the public service is nothing short of revolutionary. The courts ought not to obstruct that shift. On the contrary, they should strive to interpret FOI legislation in a manner harmonious with its objectives, doing so to the fullest extent that the text allows.' Although *Osland* was concerned with the Freedom of Information Act 1982 (Vic), the reasoning is equally applicable to all such legislation, including the FOI Acts.

60 FOIA s 2(1) and (2); FOI(S)A s 2(1).

61 Even though enactments may be seen as an expression of the public interest: *Bombay Province v Bombay Municipal Corp* [1947] AC 58 at 62-63.

62 Namely, the public authority to whom a request for information has been made.

63 'Hansard has frequently been referred to with a view to ascertaining whether a statutory power has been improperly exercised for an alien purpose or in a wholly unreasonable manner': *Pepper v Hart* [1993] AC 593 at 639; *R v Northumbrian Water Ltd, ex p Newcastle and North Tyneside Health Authority* [1999] Env LR 715 at 727 (Collins J). See further: *Assange v Swedish Prosecution Authority* [2012] UKSC 2, [2012] 2 AC 471.

64 See FOIA s 17(1); FOI(S)A s 16(1).

65 *Ealing London Borough Council v Race Relations Board* [1972] AC 342 at 361, [1972] 1 All ER 105 at 114 (Lord Simon of Glaisdale). Similarly: *Black Clawson International Ltd v Papierwerke Waldhof-Aschaffenburg AG* [1975] AC 591 at 647, [1975] 1 All ER 810 at 844 (Lord Simon of Glaisdale).

66 Cabinet Office, *Your Right to Know. The Government's Proposals for a Freedom of Information Act. White Paper* (Cm 3818, 1997): www.archive.official-documents.co.uk/document/caboff/foi/foi.htm
As to the permissibility of considering a White Paper, etc for the purpose of ascertaining the mischief and for drawing inferences as to Parliamentary intention, see: *Pepper v Hart* [1993] AC 593 at 630 and 635 (Lord Browne-Wilkinson); *R v Northumbrian Water Ltd, ex p Newcastle and North Tyneside Health Authority* [1999] Env LR 715 at 727 (Collins J); *R (on the application of Heather) v Leonard Cheshire Foundation* [2002] EWCA Civ 366, [2002] 2 All

legislation. In the preface by the Prime Minister it was said:

> This White Paper explains our proposals for meeting another key pledge—to legislate for freedom of information, bringing about more open Government. The traditional culture of secrecy will only be broken down by giving people in the United Kingdom the legal right to know. This fundamental and vital change in the relationship between government and governed is at the heart of this White Paper.

The Minister in charge of the Bill declared in his foreword:

> Openness is fundamental to the political health of a modern state. This White Paper marks a watershed in the relationship between the government and people of the United Kingdom. At last there is a government ready to trust the people with a legal right to information. This right is central to a mature democracy.

The opening paragraphs gave a straightforward statement of purpose:

> 1.1 Unnecessary secrecy in government leads to arrogance in governance and defective decision-making. The perception of excessive secrecy has become a corrosive influence in the decline of public confidence in government. Moreover, the climate of public opinion has changed: people expect much greater openness and accountability from government than they used to.
>
> 1.2 ......The purpose of the Act will be to encourage more open and accountable government by establishing a general statutory right of access to official records and information.[67]

1– 017 Legislative purpose

Official information access legislation has been variously considered to serve the following purposes:

(1) To enable members of the public to be more informed as to the way in which administrative decisions are made and the basis for such decisions. The House of Commons Select Committee considered that this would improve the quality of government decision-making.[68]

(2) To enable the curious to find out what information the instruments of government hold about themselves and others.[69]

(3) To hold government and other bodies to account by drawing out information revealing maladministration.[70] Put another way, to supplement the operation of responsible government.[71]

(4) To impose the discipline of potential revelation upon public authorities in their recording of information.

(5) To counteract undue secrecy in the making of decisions and the formulation of

ER 936 [2002] HRLR 30; *Wilson v First County Trust* [2004] 1 AC 816 at [56] and [64]; *R (G) v London Borough of Barnet* [2004] 2 AC 208 at [84]-[85].

67 See also para 2.5 of the White Paper.

68 House of Commons, *Public Administration—Third Report* (Cm 4355, 1999) para 12: www.publications.parliament.uk/pa/cm199899/cmselect/cmpubadm/570/57007.htm
For judicial support, see *London Regional Transport v Mayor of London* [2001] EWCA Civ 1491 [2003] EMLR 4 at [40], quoting Sullivan J with approval. In *Kuijer v Council of the European Union* (No 2) [2002] 1 WLR 1941 at [52] the Court of First Instance, dealing with Council Directive 93/731/EC, said: 'It is first necessary to point out that the principle of transparency is intended to secure a more significant role for citizens in the decision-making process and to ensure that the administration acts with greater propriety, efficiency and responsibility *vis-à-vis* the citizens in a democratic system. It helps strengthen the principle of democracy and respect for fundamental rights.' See, further: Case C-64/05 *IFAW gGmbH v European Commission* [2008] QB 902 (Opinion of Advocate General Maduro, 18 July 2007) at [53].

69 House of Commons, *Public Administration—Third Report* (Cm 4355, 1999) para 12 (see n 68).

70 *United States Department of Justice v Reporters Committee for Freedom of the Press*, 489 US 749 at 773.

71 *Osland v Secretary to the Department of Justice* [2008] HCA 37, (2008) 234 CLR 27 at [62]; *Egan v Willis* [1998] HCA 71 at [42] (High Court of Australia).

policy.[72]

(6) For any number of commercial ends.

(7) As a form of pre-action disclosure or disclosure in judicial review or in connection with tribunal proceedings and the like.

The 'mischief' or 'vice' giving rise to the need for FOIA was acknowledged as a matter of public record by the Minister in introducing the Bill that became the Act:

> Unnecessary secrecy in Government and our public services has long been held to undermine good governance and public administration, ...the Bill will not only provide legal rights for the public and place legal duties on Ministers and public authorities, but will help to transform the culture of Government from one of secrecy to one of openness. It will transform the default setting from "this should be kept quiet unless" to "this should be published unless." By doing so, it should raise public confidence in the processes of government, and enhance the quality of decision making by the Government.[73]

And, a little later:

> The Bill will lead to cultural change throughout the public sector. There will be more information about how health authorities, local councils and the police deliver services. It will give citizens a right to know and a right to appeal to the commissioner if they do not get the information that they have sought. That is a fundamental change in the relationship between the citizens and the state.[74]

It is implicit in the above statements that the voluntary code to which the same public sector had been subject for the preceding eight years had not effected the 'cultural' or 'fundamental' change hoped for the FOI Acts.[75] The most significant dissimilarity between the Code and the FOI Acts is the replacement of voluntariness with compulsion.[76] This dependence upon compulsion to secure the cultural change from the regime which pervaded under the voluntary Code gives support to the proposition that notions of due deference to a public authority's claims of exemption should play little or no part in the determination of claims of exemption save to the extent that they are substantiated by objective evidence. Domestic jurisprudence since the Act has come into force has recognised its basic objectives and significance:

> FOIA introduced a radical change to our law, and the rights of the citizen to be informed

---

72 House of Commons, *Public Administration—Third Report* (Cm 4355, 1999) para 12 (see n 68).

73 Hansard HC vol 340 col 714 (7 December 1999) (Mr Jack Straw). In the construction of a statute, reference may be made to Parliamentary materials 'where (a) legislation is ambiguous, obscure or leads to an absurdity; (b) the material relied upon consists of one or more statements by a minister or other promoter of the Bill together if necessary with such other Parliamentary material as is necessary to understand such statements and their effect; (c) the statements relied upon are clear...': *Pepper v Hart* [1993] AC 593 at 640 (Lord Browne-Wilkinson). Satisfaction of these three conditions is critical to the entitlement to refer to the material: *R v Secretary of State for the Environment, Transport and the Regions, ex p Spath Holme Ltd* [2001] 2 AC 349 at 391-392 (Lord Bingham) and at 398-399 (Lord Nicholls). It has been said that the true purpose in referring to Hansard is to 'preven[t] the executive from placing a different meaning on the words used in legislation from that which they attributed to those words when promoting the legislation in Parliament...': *R v A (No 2)* [2001] UKHL 25, [2002] 1 AC 45 at [81] (Lord Steyn). Similarly stated in Johan Steyn, '*Pepper v Hart*: A re-examination' (2001) 21 *Oxford Journal of Legal Studies*, 59.

74 Hansard HC vol 340 col 725 (7 December 1999) (Mr Jack Straw). Similarly, cols 728, 738-739; 744-745 ('the legislation transforming the relationship between citizen and state'); 754-755; 771-772; Hansard HL vol 612 cols 830, 831, 835, 837, 847, 849, 853, 858-859, 862 (20 April 2000); Hansard HL vol 618 col 440 (25 October 2000).

75 Thus, Lord Phillips in *The BSE Inquiry—The Report* (2000) found that there had been 'positive censorship' (vol 3, para 2.175) in relation to information relating to zoonotic qualities of bovine spongiform encephalopathy (BSE); that there was a 'clear policy of restricting the disclosure of information about BSE' (vol 3, para 2.189); and he spoke of a policy of secrecy rather than one of openness (vol 3, para 2.191). Similarly, Sir Richard Scott's *Report of the Inquiry into the Export of Defence Equipment and Dual-Use Goods and Related Prosecutions* (1996): 'in circumstances where disclosure might be politically or administratively inconvenient, the balance struck by the government came down, time and time again, against full disclosure' (para D1.165). The unlikelihood of cultural change and the importance of compulsion were adverted to by the House of Commons, Constitutional Affairs Committee, *Freedom of Information—One Year On*, Seventh Report of Session 2005-06, HC 991 at paras 112-113: www.publications.parliament.uk/pa/cm200506/cmselect/cmconst/991/991.pdf

76 At any rate, so far as concerns central government departments and agencies.

about the acts and affairs of public authorities.[77]

And, from the Supreme Court:

> It is common ground that the 2000 Act was enacted in order to promote an important public interest in access to information about public bodies. There are ... thousands of public authorities, large and small, which are paid for out of public funds, and whose actions or omissions may have a profound effect on citizens and residents of the United Kingdom. There is a strong public interest in the press and general public having the right, subject to appropriate safeguards, to require public authorities to provide information about their activities. It adds to parliamentary scrutiny a further and more direct route to a measure of public accountability.[78]

And again from the Supreme Court:

> The Freedom of Information Act 2000 was a landmark enactment of great constitutional significance for the United Kingdom. It introduced a new regime governing the disclosure of information held by public authorities. It created a prima facie right to the disclosure of all such information, save in so far as that right was qualified by the terms of the Act or the information in question was exempt.[79]

And a little later:

> Without freedom to receive certain information, there is no freedom to proceed to express it; and a person's freedom to express the information is likely to carry much greater value for the public if the person holding the information is unwilling to impart it to him. In his illuminating and appropriately cautious discussion of these tensions in *Freedom of Speech*, 2nd ed (2005), Professor Barendt states, at p 110, that the link between freedom of expression and freedom of information is undeniable. Indeed, if efficacy is to be given to the right to freedom of expression, there is no reason to consider that information held by a public authority (whether relevant to itself or to a private person or, as in the present case, to both) is of lesser significance to it than information held by a private person. On the contrary.[80]

1–018 Purpose of exemptions

There is a corresponding need to understand the purpose of the exemptions. The White Paper described long-recognised interests which fell to be substantially prejudiced by disclosure. It proposed seven such interests.[81] It characterised the Code of Practice as being too restrictive:

> We believe the 15 exemptions in the Code of Practice can be substantially reduced. Indeed, we do not propose that the Act should contain exempt categories at all, but rather that disclosure should be assessed on a 'contents basis', records being disclosed in partial form with any necessary deletions, rather than being completely withheld...We have provisionally identified seven 'specified interests' in place of the Code's exemptions.

1–019 Legislative purpose: comparative

The US Supreme Court summarised the object of such legislation:

> The basic purpose of [the Freedom of Information Act] is to ensure an informed citizenry, vital to the functioning of a democratic society, needed to check against corruption and to hold the governors accountable to the governed.[82]

The Supreme Court of Canada expressed it as follows:

> The [Access to Information] Act is concerned with securing values of participation and

---

77 *OGC v IC* [2008] EWHC 774 (Admin), [2010] QB 98, [2008] ACD 54 at [68].

78 *BBC v Sugar (No 2)* [2012] UKSC 4, [2012] 1 WLR 439, [2012] EMLR 17, [2012] 2 All ER 509 at [76] per Lord Walker of Gestingthorpe JSC.

79 *Kennedy v Charity Commission* [2014] UKSC 20, [2015] AC 455 at [153].

80 *Kennedy v Charity Commission* [2014] UKSC 20, [2015] AC 455 at [178].

81 White Paper para 3.11.

82 *National Labor Relations Board v Robbins Tire & Rubber Co* (1978) 437 US 214 at 242. Similarly: *National Archives and Record Administration v Favish*, 541 US 157 (2004) at 171-72.

> accountability in the democratic process. The overarching purpose of access to information legislation is to facilitate democracy by helping to ensure that citizens have the information required to participate meaningfully in the democratic process and that politicians and bureaucrats remain accountable to the citizenry…Rights to state-held information are designed to improve the workings of government; to make it more effective, responsive and accountable.[83]

Most recently, in the High Court of Australia, Kirby J, after a consideration of the evolution of such legislation in Australia, said:[84]

> The basic purpose of the introduction of freedom of information legislation is the same in all jurisdictions. It is to reinforce "the three basic principles of democratic government, namely, openness, accountability and responsibility". The central objective is to strengthen constitutional principles of governance not always translated into reality because of a lack of material information available to electors. Fundamentally, the idea behind such legislation is to flesh out the constitutional provisions establishing the system of representative government; to increase citizen participation in government beyond a fleeting involvement on election days; and to reduce the degree of apathy and cynicism sometimes arising from a lack of real elector knowledge about, or influence upon, what is going on in government.

And in Ireland:[85]

> The passing of the Freedom of Information Act 1997 constituted a legislative development of major importance. By it, the Oireachtas took a considered and deliberate step which dramatically alters the administrative assumptions and culture of centuries. It replaces the presumption of secrecy with one of openness. It is designed to open up the workings of government and administration to scrutiny. It is not designed simply to satisfy the appetite of the media for stories. It is for the benefit of every citizen. It lets light in to the offices and filing cabinets of our rulers. The principle of free access to publicly held information is part of a world-wide trend. The general assumption is that it originates in the Scandinavian countries. The Treaty of Amsterdam adopted a new Art 255 of the EC Treaty providing that every citizen of the European Union should have access to the documents of the European Parliament, Council and Commission.

1– 020 Long title - purpose clause

It is unusual for an Act of Parliament to have a purpose clause.[86] To the extent permitted by a single sentence, the purpose of an Act is normally only expressly articulated within a statute by its long title. For the reasons noted above, ascertainment of the purpose of the Act is of particular importance in statutes such as the FOI Acts.[87] An amendment to the Bill that would have seen a purpose clause included in the Act was defeated.[88] Instead, it was considered that changing the preposition *about* in the long title of the Bill to *for* would adequately articulate the

---

83 *Dagg v Canada (Minister of Finance)* [1997] 2 SCR 403 at 432-433 and 450. Similarly, *Canada Post Corp v Canada (Minister of Public Works)* [1995] 2 FC 110 (FCA) at 124.

84 *Osland v Secretary to the Department of Justice* [2008] HCA 37 at [62].

85 *Sheedy v Information Commissioner* [2005] 2 IR 272 at 275

86 But not unknown, see eg: Health and Safety at Work, etc Act 1974 s 1; Proceeds of Crime Act 2002 s 240; Education Act 2002 s 1; Pollution Prevention and Control Act 1999 s 1.

87 The inclusion of a purpose clause was recommended by the House of Commons, *Public Administration-Third Report* (Cm 4355, 1999) para 59 (see n 68). A purpose clause is to be found in: Freedom of Information Act 1982 (Cth of Australia) s 3 (substituted by the Freedom of Information Amendment (Reform) Act 2010); Official Information Act 1982 (NZ) s 4; Access to Information Act (1982)(Canada) s 2. The Freedom of Information Act 1997 (Ireland), although not including a purpose clause, includes a comprehensive statement of purpose in its long title.

88 Hansard HC vol 347 col 830 (4 April 2000) (Amendment No 100). For discussion on the proposed purpose clause, see: Hansard HC vol 347 cols 830-855 (4 April 2000); Hansard HL vol 617 cols 886-888 and 892-900 (17 October 2000). It was opposed on the basis that it was 'pointless' because it would add nothing to what was explained 'more comprehensively' in the long title and that it would cause confusion to those minded to compare the long title with the purpose clause: Hansard HC vol 347 col 844 (4 April 2000) (Mr Mike O'Brien); Hansard HL vol 617 col 894 (17 October 2000) (Lord Brennan).

purpose of the Act.[89] Although not having the status of a purpose clause, the following formal statement by the then Constitutional Affairs Secretary and Lord Chancellor, Lord Falconer, describes the aim more clearly than would be possible in a statute:

> FOI regimes, wherever they may be, are usually established from common principles. Governments have been motivated by citizen empowerment; by the desire to drive more democratic engagement; by the need to fight corruption; and by the simple notion that openness is a public good. More recently, Freedom of Information has been introduced in many countries because it is seen as a standard part of a liberal democracy.[90]

[89] An amendment proposed by Lord Archer: Hansard HL vol 617 col 890 (17 October 2000)

[90] Speech by Lord Falconer (Constitutional Affairs Secretary and Lord Chancellor) to the International Conference of Information Commissioners, Manchester, 22 May 2006.

CHAPTER 2
Westminster legislation

1. BACKGROUND TO FREEDOM OF INFORMATION LEGISLATION

2– 001 Early legislative efforts

As noted above,[1] rights of access to official information in the United Kingdom increased in a piecemeal fashion in the 40 years prior to the enactment of the FOI Acts. It may fairly be observed that in that period Parliament showed a greater disposition to impose duties of disclosure upon the emanations of local government than it did upon central government departments or agencies. Notable increases in the right of access came with:

— the Local Government Act 1972 Part VA (ss 100A-100K) s 228, Sch 12A,[2]
— the DPA 1984,[3]
— the Health Service Joint Consultative Committees (Access to Information) Act 1986,[4]
— the Access to Personal Files Act 1987,[5]

[1] See §1– 002.

[2] These provisions were inserted by the Local Government (Access to Information) Act 1985. They are considered in greater detail at §§37– 011, 37– 011 to 37– 031.

[3] Section 21 of the DPA 1984 introduced the concept of a 'subject-access request' in which a person could seek access to information held by an organisation (which included private organisations as well as governmental organisations) about himself. The right was re-enacted and broadened by s 7 of the DPA 1998.

[4] Repealed by the Health Act 1999 s 65, Sch 4 para 72 and Sch 5, with effect from 1 April 2000 (in England) and 1 January 2001 (in Wales).

[5] Repealed by the DPA 1998 s 74(2) Sch 16 Pt I, as from 1 March 2000. Similarly the Access to Personal Files (Social Services) Regulations 1989 and the Access to Personal Files (Housing) Regulations 1989 made under it. The purpose of this Act was to catch personal information that was recorded in 'manual files' and which, accordingly, fell outside the ambit of the DPA 1984. The Act came into force on 15 May 1987 and provided a

— the Community Health Councils (Access to Information) Act 1988 (which applied, with modifications, the provisions of Part VA of the Local Government Act 1972 to community health councils established under s 20 of the National Health Service Act 1977), and

— the Access to Health Records Act 1990.[6]

Where central government departments or agencies found themselves having to disclose information, this was generally the result of outside obligations.[7]

2–002 Attempts at comprehensiveness

From 1974 onwards, the Labour Party would before each General Election state a commitment to 'freedom of information'. The first indication of any realisation of that commitment was a directive issued in 1977 by the head of the Civil Service.[8] This promised to release more of the background detail and information behind Ministerial decisions. In March 1979 the Labour Government published a Green Paper on Open Government, which proposed a non-statutory code for the release of official information.[9] At about the same time a private member's Bill that would have compelled disclosure of official documents was introduced by Sir Clement Freud MP.[10] Both the non-statutory code and private Member's Bill did not survive the General Election of May 1979. In 1981 another freedom of information Bill, also drafted by the Outer Circle Policy Unit, was introduced by Frank Hooley MP. The Bill was opposed by the Conservative Government and defeated at second reading.

2–003 The Data Protection Act 1984

In 1981 the Council of Europe opened for signature and ratification its Convention for the Protection of Individuals with regard to the Automatic Processing of Personal Data. This ultimately led to the DPA 1984. Although this gave an individual a right of access to information relating to himself provided that it was held as part of a data processing system, the focus of the Act was not the extraction of information from governmental bodies: the right given by the Act applied to personal information irrespective of the identity of the body that held it. In 1984 a freedom of information Bill drafted by the Campaign for Freedom of Information was introduced by David Steel MP. At the same time the Campaign for Freedom of Information also pressed for the introduction of subject-specific legislation establishing more limited rights of access to information. Legislation receiving its support included the Local Government (Access to Information) Act 1985,[11] the Access to Personal Files Act 1987,[12] and

---

right of access to personal information (which was defined in the same way as in the DPA 1984) falling within defined categories and held by 'Housing Act local authorities' and by 'local social services authorities'.

6 This establishes a right of access to health records held by, inter alia, 'health service bodies' (ie a health authority, a health board, a special health authority or a National Health Service trust) for the individuals to whom the record relates and certain other persons. The Act is considered in greater detail at §38–007.

7 Such as the Environmental Information Regulations 1992, which implemented Council Directive 90/313/EEC on the freedom of access to information on the environment, and the DPA 1998, which implemented Directive 95/46, adopted by the European Parliament and European Council on 24 October 1998. These are considered in detail in chs 6 and 5 respectively.

8 The Directive was actually a confidential memorandum from the Head of the Civil Service, Sir Douglas Allen, who became Lord Croham. It was published officially after it was leaked to *The Times*. The directive became known as the 'Croham directive'.

9 *Open Government* (Cmnd 7520).

10 Then Mr Clement Freud MP, Isle of Ely.

11 It was introduced as a private member's Bill promoted by the Community Rights Project and introduced by Robin Squire MP. It gave the public wider rights of access to council meetings, reports and papers. See §§37–011, 37–011 to 37–031.

12 This was also the result of a private member's Bill promoted by the Campaign for Freedom of Information and

the Access to Medical Reprts Act 1988.[13] The Campaign for Freedom of Information made another attempt at a comprehensive information access Bill in January 1991, but it only lasted 45 minutes in Parliament and did not get a second reading.[14] In the following year the Environmental Information Regulations 1992 were adopted to implement the Access to Environmental Information Directive of the European Community. On 7 February 1992 the Final Act of the Treaty of the European Union was signed at Mastricht. Declaration No 17 annexed to it recited the importance of transparency of the decision-making process.[15] In that same year, Roy Hattersley MP, the then shadow Home Secretary, promised that a freedom of information act would be the first piece of Home Office legislation if Labour were to win the election. The Conservatives won the election and William Waldegrave was given responsibility for implementing an 'open government' policy. In early 1993 a private member's Bill entitled The Right to Know Bill was introduced[16] into Parliament. This Bill had its second reading in the House of Commons and completed its Committee stage, but it failed to receive the necessary support.

2. THE OPEN GOVERNMENT CODE OF PRACTICE

2–004 The Code of Practice

In July 1993 the Conservative Government issued a White Paper which proposed a Code of Practice on Access to Government Information. In 1994 that Government issued a Code of Practice on Access to Government Information.[17] This was the first true attempt at a comprehensive scheme for the release of official information. But it was voluntary in nature, conferring no enforceable right of access. In 1996 the Select Committee on the Parliamentary Commissioner for Administration published its report on the operation of the voluntary scheme. It recommended that a freedom of information act be introduced. The Government rejected the recommendation and instead issued a slightly revised version of the Code in February 1997.

2–005 Application

The Code applied to bodies falling within the jurisdiction of the Parliamentary Commissioner for Administration, and it was the Commissioner who enforced the Code.[18] These bodies included almost all central government departments and their agencies, as well as many other public bodies. The Code contained a non-statutory, discretionary regime. It did not confer rights of access to information of any kind upon any person or class of persons. Nor did it

---

introduced by Archy Kirkwood MP. It gave people the right to see manually held social work and housing records about themselves. The Bill originally also included access to school records, but this was later brought in under existing legislation by agreement with the Government.

13 This was another private member's Bill drafted by the Campaign for Freedom of Information and introduced by Archy Kirkwood MP. It gives people the right to see any report produced by their own doctor for an employer or insurance company. See §38– 007.

14 This was introduced by Archy Kirkwood MP.

15 The declaration is reproduced at §43– 002. Its importance was noted in *Common Services Agency v IC* [2008] UKHL 47, [2008] 1 WLR 1550 at [3].

16 This was introduced by Mark Fisher MP.

17 The code was revised in 1997 and remained in effect until 1 January 2005: `www.foi.gov.uk/ogcode981.htm`
The Cabinet Office also published *Open Government Code of Practice on Access to Government Information: Guidance on Interpretation*, 2nd edn (1997).

18 *Code of Practice*, paras 3 and 6.

override any statutory prohibitions upon the release of information or documents. Where information that fell, in principle, within the scope of the Code was also available pursuant to a statutory right of access, that right took precedence and the release of the information in question was governed thereby.[19] In particular, the Code expressly stated that it was not intended to override statutory provisions on access to public records, whether over or under 30 years old. The reason for this lay in the fact that the Ombudsman was not required, under s 12(3) of the Parliamentary Commissioner Act 1967, to question the merits of a decision if it had been taken without maladministration by a government department or other body in the exercise of a discretion vested in it; and decisions made in England and Wales with respect to public records by the Lord Chancellor, or in Scotland and Northern Ireland by the corresponding Secretary of State were such discretionary decisions.[20]

2–006 Code's main commitments

The Code's five main commitments were to supply facts and analysis with major policy decisions; to open up internal guidelines about departments' dealings with the public; to supply reasons for administrative decisions; to provide information about public services, what they cost, targets, performance, complaints and redress; and to respond to requests for information.

2–007 Purpose and aims of the Code

The Code was intended to give effect to the Government's stated policy of extending access to official information. The approach to the release of information that it embodied rested on an explicit assumption that information should be disclosed, except where its release would not be in the public interest.[21] Cases where the release of information would not be in the public interest were described in Part II of the Code. Exemptions under the Code may therefore be seen as the articulation of those circumstances where it was considered to have been not in the public interest (at least in the view of the Cabinet Office) to disclose information. The Code had three aims, subsidiary to its overall purposes.[22] These were: to improve policy-making and the democratic process by extending access to the facts and analyses which provide the basis for the consideration of proposed policy; to protect the interests of individuals and companies by ensuring that reasons are given for administrative decisions, except where there is statutory authority or established convention to the contrary; and to support and extend the principles of public service established by the Citizen's Charter.

2–008 Privacy and confidentiality

The Code recognised that these objectives had to be balanced against the need to keep information private or confidential in certain circumstances. In particular, it expressly recognised that the aims of the Code had to be balanced against two countervailing requirements: namely, the need to maintain high standards of care in ensuring the privacy of personal and commercially confidential information, and the need to preserve confidentiality where disclosure would not be in the public interest or would breach personal privacy or the confidences of a third party in accordance with statutory requirements and Part II of the Code.[23]

---

19 *Code of Practice*, para 8. The bodies in question are listed in Sch 2 to the Parliamentary Commissioner Act 1967.

20 *Code of Practice*, para 9.

21 *Code of Practice*, para 1.

22 *Code of Practice*, para 2.

23 *Code of Practice*, para 2.

2–009 **Code released information**

Subject to the exemptions contained in Part II, the Code committed Government departments and applicable public bodies to publishing the facts and analyses that the Government considered relevant and important in framing major policy proposals and decisions, and, ordinarily, to making such information available once those policies and decisions had been announced. The second Code commitment was to publish, or otherwise make available, explanatory material on departments' dealings with the public (including such rules, procedures, internal guidance to officials, and similar administrative manuals as would assist better understanding of departmental action in dealing with the public) except where publication could prejudice any matter which should properly be kept confidential under Part II of the Code. Thirdly, the Code enshrined a commitment on behalf of the bodies to which it applied to give reasons for administrative decisions to those affected, and to publish in accordance with the Citizen's Charter full information about how public services were run, how much they cost, who was in charge, and what complaints and redress procedures were available; and full and (where possible) comparable sets of information about what services were being provided, what targets were set, what standards of service were expected and the results that had been achieved. The final Code commitment was to release, in response to specific requests, information relating to the policies of the bodies covered, as well as information relating to their actions and decisions and other matters related to their areas of responsibility.[24] The Code did not require the release of information that the relevant public bodies did not themselves possess, or to provide information that had already been published, or to provide information which was provided as part of an existing service other than through that service.[25]

2–010 **Exempted bodies**

The Security and Intelligence Services were not within the scope of the Code, and information obtained from or relating to them was not covered by it.[26] The Code did not apply to or affect information held by courts or tribunals or inquiries, or information contained in the documents of such bodies.[27]

2–011 **Excluded information**

Part II of the Code excluded fifteen categories of information from the commitment of disclosure set out in Part I. These categories of information were variously subject to two kinds of exemption from the assumption that information was to be disclosed, namely an exemption which applied in cases where a 'harm' or 'prejudice' test was satisfied, and an exemption that was absolute in the sense that no harm or prejudice test applied. 'Harm' and 'prejudice', for the purposes of Part II of the Code, included actual harm and prejudice and a risk or reasonable expectation of harm or prejudice. The Code explained that in such cases, consideration should be given to whether any harm or prejudice arising from disclosure was outweighed by the public interest in making the information available.[28] The Ombudsman interpreted the 'harm' test under the Code as allowing for a balancing of public interests, such that information should be disclosed when the public interest was best served thereby.[29] The categories of exempt information that were subject to a 'harm' test under Part II of the Code

---

24 *Code of Practice*, para 3.

25 *Code of Practice*, para 4.

26 *Code of Practice*, para 6.

27 *Code of Practice*, para 10.

28 *Code of Practice*, Pt II.

29 Case A8/00 HC 494 (1999-00), Case A31/99 HC 21 (1999-00).

included information relating to defence,[30] security[31] and international relations;[32] and information whose disclosure would harm the frankness and candour of internal discussion.[33] The Code gave as examples of the latter kind of information: the proceedings of Cabinet and Cabinet committees; internal opinion, advice, recommendations, consultation and deliberation; projections and assumptions relating to internal policy and analysis, analysis of alternative policy options and information relating to rejected policy options; and confidential communications between departments, public bodies and regulatory bodies. The categories of information that were subject to an absolute exemption included information relating to confidential communications with the Royal Household;[34] and information relating to public employment and public appointments and honours.[35] Most of the fifteen categories of excluded information were, however, subject to a 'harm' or 'prejudice' test of some form or other.

2–012 Code procedure

Information that was made available by the Code could be obtained simply by writing to the relevant department, agency or body and explaining what information was required. It was not necessary to specify particular files or documents. The Code specified that departments should reply to most requests within 20 working days, and should inform the maker of the request that they need longer to reply, if that was the case. Most information had to be provided free of charge, especially where it was needed to explain such matters as benefits, grants and entitlements; the standards and performances of services; the reasons for administrative decisions made with respect to the person requesting information; the way in which the person requesting information might exercise rights to appeal or complain about a decision; or regulatory requirements bearing upon the business of the person making the request. If the request did not fall within any one or more of the above categories, however, then a charge could be imposed for supplying it.

2–013 Code enforcement

As noted above, the Code did not confer rights of access to information upon anyone. If a department did not comply with a request for information the matter might be taken up by the Ombudsman, who could, however, only instigate an investigation upon the referral of a complaint from an MP. The Ombudsman could then recommend disclosure or uphold the department's decision not to disclose. The Ombudsman's recommendations were not legally binding, although in practice most departments complied with them.

2–014 The Code and FOIA

It will be noted from the above outline that the Code bore some resemblance to FOIA in its structure. Once the Act came fully into force (1 January 2005), the Code ceased to operate. Despite the absence of an enforceable right, the Code was an important step in the evolution of information rights in the United Kingdom. Given the continued official acknowledgment of a 'culture of secrecy' after its implementation, the attributes distinguishing FOIA from it may be seen as critical to countering that culture.[36] Most notable is the conferral of an enforceable

---

[30] See now FOIA s 26, FOI(S)A s 31.

[31] See now FOIA ss 23, 24, FOI(S)A s 31.

[32] See now FOIA s 27, FOI(S)A s 32.

[33] See now FOIA ss 35, 36, FOI(S)A ss 29, 30.

[34] See now FOIA s 37, FOI(S)A s 41.

[35] See now FOIA s 37, FOI(S)A s 41.

[36] The difficulty of effecting a cultural change and the importance of the enforceable right was acknowledged by the House of Commons, Constitutional Affairs Committee, *Freedom of Information — One Year On*, Seventh Report of

right of access and the imposition of a correlative duty to disclose. The Code also provides valuable insight into the public interest in disclosure of information held by a public authority and in the public authority maintaining the various exemptions under FOIA. It is to be noted that the Act provides a qualified exemption in respect of information that the Code did not exempt, so that the Code's treatment of that information could be of some relevance to the consideration of the public interest under s 2 of FOIA.

2– 015 The Data Protection Act 1998

The DPA 1998 implemented an EC Directive on the protection of individuals with regard to the processing of personal data and on the free movement of such data.[37] It replaced the DPA 1984. The Act, and subordinate legislation made under it, effected major changes to the data protection regime, including access to personal data. The Act removed the limitation on subject-access rights to computerised records, extending it to most manual records. It widened the definition of 'processing' so that it included obtaining, storing and disclosing of data. It remained in force until 25 May 2018 when a replacement data protection regime, comprising the GDPR and the DPA 2018, came into force.

3. ENACTMENT OF THE FREEDOM OF INFORMATION ACT 2000

2– 016 Parliamentary history of FOIA

Before the May 1997 General Election, both the Labour Party and Liberal Democrat party had promised to introduce freedom of information legislation if elected. The former secured election in May 1997, and in December 1997 a White Paper[38] was published, setting out its proposals for legislation. On 19 May 1998 the House of Commons Select Committee reported on the proposals,[39] stating in its Introduction:

> Freedom of Information Act is a major plank in the Government's proposals for constitutional reform, and a radical advance in open and accountable government. It will help to begin to change for good the secretive culture of the public service.
>
> Lack of openness and transparency in British government have featured in tribunals and inquiries as a contributory factor in many cases where things have gone seriously wrong ... [M]aking government more open is something which should have a serious impact on the daily lives of ordinary people. In other countries with Freedom of Information laws, most requests for information are for "my own file." Public authorities keep a vast amount of information about individuals. Some of this they can now get access to, under a patchwork of statutes and codes of practice. Some of it they still cannot get. Many people may want access to their files in order to pursue a dispute with a government department or other public authority. Individuals who are unhappy with the way they have been dealt with by, for example, the Child Support Agency or the Benefits Agency, or local Housing Authorities and Social Services Departments have a strong need to see how the authority concerned has handled their case...
>
> Freedom of Information should change the culture within the public sector so that the sort of obstruction that members of the public experienced in these cases no longer happens. We believe that the proposals, if implemented as presented in the White Paper, will have three

Session 2005-06, HC 991 at paras 112-113 (see n 75).

[37] Directive of the European Parliament and of the Council of 24 October 1995 on the Protection of Individuals with Regard to the Processing of Personal Data and on the Free Movement of Such Data 95/46/EC [1995] OJ L281/31.

[38] *Your Right to Know—The Government's Proposals for a Freedom of Information Act* (Cm 3818, 1997): see n 66. The document was prepared by the Chancellor of the Duchy of Lancaster, Dr David Clark.

[39] *Third Report of the Select Committee on Public Administration: Your Right to Know—The Government's Proposals for a Freedom of Information Act*, HC (1997-1998) 398-I.

purposes and effects. Increased access to information will:

— Make it easier for members of the public to find out what information government holds about themselves.
— Make it easier for politicians, journalists and members of the public to hold the government to account by making government cover-ups more difficult.
— Make it easier for members of the public to participate in an informed way in the discussion of policy issues, and improve the quality of government decision-making because those drafting policy advice know that they must be able, ultimately, to defend their reasoning before public opinion. We believe that Dr Clark's proposals will begin to bring about a significant change in the culture of the UK Government.

The Report made a total of 44 recommendations and observations. In July 1998 responsibility for the Bill was transferred from the Cabinet Office to the Home Office. The Government officially responded to the Report.[40] The Minister then responsible, Dr David Clark, said:

> The Government's commitment to a radical Freedom of Information Act is clear, and has already been set out in Your Right to Know…FOI is a key part—and in my view a central part—of the Government's programme to modernise British politics through radical constitutional change. The Prime Minister has said that freedom of information is not some isolated constitutional reform, but a change that is absolutely fundamental to how we see politics developing in this country...

2–017 Consultation paper and draft Bill

On 24 May 1999 the Government published a consultation paper with its proposals for freedom of information legislation, including a draft Bill.[41] The consultation paper was followed by a process of pre-legislative scrutiny by committees in both Houses of Parliament and a period of further public consultation. The House of Commons Select Committee on Public Administration reported on 29 July 1999,[42] summarising its conclusions and recommendations:

> 1. We welcome the fact that the Government has published a draft Freedom of Information Bill. Legislation on the information rights of citizens is a historic moment for our democracy. However, we believe that the present form of the Bill has significant deficiencies which, if not remedied, will undermine its potential. In particular we recommend that:
> — There should be a purpose clause stating a clear presumption in favour of disclosure as a right of citizenship;
> — The public interest in disclosing particular information in each case should be balanced against the prospect of harm in so doing; the information should be released if the public interest is greater; and decisions about where the balance lies in particular cases should be transparent, and reviewable by an Information Commissioner, whose decisions are enforceable;
> — The right of access to information should apply as broadly as possible, and exemptions to it should be drawn as narrowly and precisely as possible with a more demanding harm test;
> — A statutory freedom of information regime should contain, as much as possible, enforceable rights of access to information; not undertakings to consider the discretionary release of information,...
>
> We believe that this will make the draft Bill better, our democracy stronger, and the information rights of citizens more effective.

The House of Lords appointed its own select committee on 17 June 1999, which reported on

40 The Government's reply to the Report was the *Fourth Special Report of the Select Committee on Public Administration: Government Response to the Third Report from the Select Committee on Public Administration (Session 1997-1998) on Your Right to Know—The Government's Proposals for a Freedom of Information Act*, HC (1997-1998) 1020: www.parliament.the-stationery-office.co.uk/pa/cm199798/cmselect/cmpubadm/1020/102002.htm

41 Home Office, *Freedom of Information: Consultation on draft legislation* (Cm 4355, May 1999): www.nationalarchives.gov.uk/ERORecords/HO/421/2/foi/dfoibill.htm

42 *House of Commons, Public Administration—Third Report* (Cm 4355, 1999) (see n 68).

27 July 1999.[43] Its recommendations included:

> 63. The draft Bill should provide a framework for transforming the "culture of secrecy" in British government....
>
> 64. If the draft Bill is to conform to true Freedom of Information principles, the most important single amendment needed is to give the Information Commissioner a public interest override power in clause 44 to overrule a ministerial decision under clause 14, and to order disclosure.
>
> ....
>
> 82. The draft Bill does not need a purpose clause but the Long Title should be amended by leaving out the words "make provision about the disclosure of information" and substituting "facilitate the disclosure of information." This would clarify the draft Bill's purpose of providing a framework for transforming the "culture of secrecy" in British government.

The Government's response to the Report of the House of Commons Select Committee was published on 27 October 1999.[44] The document said that it agreed with the bulk of the Select Committee's recommendations. The Government's response to the Report of the House of Lords Select Committee was published on 17 January 2000.[45] That document, too, said that it agreed with the bulk of the Select Committee's recommendations.

2– 018 Freedom of Information Bill

The Freedom of Information Bill was introduced into the House of Commons on 18 November 1999, and received its second reading on 7 December 1999. It enjoyed a close Parliamentary scrutiny before receiving Royal Assent on 30 November 2000.[46]

2– 019 Implementation of FOIA

The Act was brought into force incrementally over the next four years. The initial implementation of the Act was concerned with publication schemes, the establishment of the Information Commissioner and the introduction of concepts basic to the operation of the Act.[47] A few further such provisions came into force on 1 February 2001.[48] The renaming of the Data Protection Tribunal took effect from 14 May 2001.[49] On 13 November 2001, the Lord Chancellor announced in Parliament an implementation plan for the Act:

> The Act will be fully implemented by January 2005, 11 months before the timetable set out

---

43 *Draft Freedom of Information Bill—First Report* (Select Committee Report HL 97), Session 1998-1999, 27 July 1999: www.parliament.the-stationery-office.co.uk/pa/ld199899/ldselect/ldfoinfo/97/9701.htm

44 www.publications.parliament.uk/pa/cm199899/cmselect/cmpubadm/831/83102.htm

45 www.nationalarchives.gov.uk/ERORecords/HO/421/2/foi/dfoilsc.htm

46 The stages and dates of the Act's progress are as follows:
In the House of Commons: (1) Introduction, 18 November 1999, Hansard vol 339 col 124; (2) Second Reading, 7 December 1999, Hansard vol 340 cols 714-798; Committee, 1st Sitting, 21 December 1999; 2nd Sitting, 11 January 2000; 3rd Sitting, 11 January 2000; 4th Sitting, 18 January 2000; 5th Sitting, 18 January 2000; 6th Sitting, 20 January 2000 [Pt I]; 6th Sitting 20 January 2000 [Pt II]; 7th Sitting, 25 January 2000; 8th Sitting, 25 January 2000; 9th Sitting, 27 January 2000; 10th Sitting, 1 February 2000; 11th Sitting, 1 February 2000; 12th Sitting, 8 February 2000; 13th Sitting, 8 February 2000; 14th Sitting, 10 February 2000; (4) Report and Third Reading, 4 April 2000, Hansard vol 1857 cols 830-935; 5 April 2000, Hansard vol 1857 cols 981-1123; (5) Royal Assent, 30 November 2000 vol 1877 col 1231.
In the House of Lords: (1) Introduction, 6 April 2000, vol 1802, col 1490; (2) Second Reading, 20 April 2000, Hansard vol 612 cols 823-893; (3) Committee, 17 October 2000, Hansard vol 617 cols 883-954 and 971-1020; 19 October 2000, Hansard vol 617 cols 1208-1300; 24 October 2000, Hansard vol 618 cols 273-314; 25 October 2000, Hansard vol 618 cols 407-476; (4) Report, 14 November 2000, Hansard vol 1824 cols 134-158 and 173-266; (5) Third Reading, 22 November 2000, Hansard vol 1825 cols 817-852; (6) Royal Assent, 30 November 2000, Hansard vol 1826 col 1492.

47 These provisions came into force on 30 November 2000: FOIA s 87(1).

48 FOIA s 87(2).

49 FOIA (Commencement No 1) Order 2001 SI 2001/1637. The Order also brought into force provisions relating to the appointment of members to the Tribunal and certain provisions relating to the Information Commissioner.

in the Act itself. The publication scheme provisions will be implemented first, on a rolling programme, starting with central government in November 2002. I am today placing a full schedule of organisations and dates of implementation in the Libraries of both Houses. This roll-out [ie of publication scheme provisions] will be completed in June 2004, and the individual right of access to information held by all public authorities, including government departments, will be implemented in January 2005.

The requirement on each public authority to produce a publication scheme began with named public authorities on 30 November 2002, widening over the course of 2003.[50] The requirement for the Lord Chancellor to issue a Code of Practice and for the Information Commissioner to issue practice recommendations and to promote good practice also took effect on that date. The publication scheme requirements were extended to smaller public authorities over the course of the first half of 2004.[51] The remainder of the Act, including the enforceable right of access to information held by public authorities, came into force on 1 January 2005.[52] On that same day, the EIR came into force.

4. DEVELOPMENTS SINCE 1 JANUARY 2005

2– 020 Legislative developments

The principal changes to the freedom of information regime since 1 January 2005 have been:

(1) Numerous additional public authorities have been made subject to the Act.[53]

(2) With effect from 18 January 2010, the Information Tribunal ceased to exist and its functions were assumed by the First-tier Tribunal and the Upper Tribunal.[54]

(3) The Constitutional Reform and Governance Act 2010 extended the types of Royal communications enjoying exemption (s 37(1)) and added those to the list of absolute exemptions. It also reduced from 30 years to 20 years the period after which a record becomes a 'historical record' under s 62, with a resultant falling away of exemptions through s 63. At the same time, it removed from that list ss 28 (relations within the United Kingdom), 36 (prejudice to conduct of public affairs), 37(1)(a) (Royal communications) and 43 (prejudice to commercial interests), but restored all but s 37(1)(a) to the 30-year regime. In relation to s 37(1), the period was made into the later of 5 years after the death of the Royal member concerned or 20 years.

(4) The Protection of Freedoms Act 2012 widened the range of publicly owned companies subject to the 2000 Act by including companies owned 'by the wider

---

[50] FOIA (Commencement No 2) Order 2002 SI 2002/2812.

[51] FOIA (Commencement No 3) Order 2003 SI 2003/2603.

[52] FOIA (Commencement No 4) Order 2004 SI 2004/1909, dealing with environmental information. FOIA (Commencement No 5) Order 2004 SI 2004/3122, dealing with everything else.

[53] Most notably, through:
Freedom of Information (Additional Public Authorities) Order 2002 SI 2002/2623;
Freedom of Information (Additional Public Authorities) Order 2003 SI 2003/1882;
Freedom of Information (Additional Public Authorities) Order 2004 SI 2004/938;
Freedom of Information (Additional Public Authorities) Order 2005 SI 2005/3593;
Freedom of Information (Additional Public Authorities) Order 2008 SI 2008/1271;
Freedom of Information (Additional Public Authorities) Order 2010 SI 2010/937;
Freedom of Information (Additional Public Authorities) Order 2011 SI 2011/1041.
Some public authorities have since been removed from the scope of the Act. See:
Freedom of Information (Removal of References to Public Authorities) Order 2003 SI 2003/1883;
Freedom of Information (Removal of References to Public Authorities) Order 2004 SI 2004/1641;
Freedom of Information (Removal of References to Public Authorities) Order 2005 SI 2005/3594;
Freedom of Information (Removal of References to Public Authorities) Order 2010 SI 2010/939;
Freedom of Information (Removal of References to Public Authorities) Order 2011 SI 2011/1042 .

[54] The changes are considered further at §§44– 008 to 44– 019.

public sector' (s 6). It also allowed an applicant that he or she wanted the information to be communicated electronically in a re-usable form (s 11) and to provide for the imposition of a licence fee in order to re-use copyright material in that information (ss 11A and 11B). Finally, it enabled enhancement of the publication scheme provisions in s 19.

2–021 Proposals

On 18 December 2006 David Maclean MP introduced a Private Members Bill to amend FOIA so as to remove the House of Commons and the House of Lords as public authorities and to declare as exempt information correspondence between a Member of Parliament and a public authority.[55] On 19 January 2007 the Bill received an unopposed second reading in the House of Commons and on 7 February 2007 passed its Public Bill Committee stage. The Bill received backing from the Parliamentary Labour Party's committee, which urged Labour backbenchers to support it.[56] On 18 May 2007 the Bill was passed with a large majority by the House of Commons. However, the Bill did not survive in the House of Lords, with its Select Committee on the Constitution reporting that ' the Bill does not meet the requirements of caution and proportionality in enacting legislation of constitutional importance.'[57]

2–022 Reviews

On 3 July 2012 the House of Commons Justice Select Committee published its first post-legislative scrutiny of FOIA.[58] It summarised its conclusions:

> The Freedom of Information Act has been a significant enhancement of our democracy. Overall our witnesses agreed that the Act was working well. The right to access information has improved openness, transparency and accountability. The principal objectives of the Act have therefore been met, but we are not surprised that the unrealistic secondary expectation that the Act would increase public confidence in Government and Parliament has not been met. We do not believe that there has been any general harmful effect at all on the ability to conduct business in the public service, and in our view the additional burdens are outweighed by the benefits. There is some risk-based on perception as much as reality-that policy discussions at the highest levels may be inhibited or not properly recorded because of fear of early disclosure under the Act. This was never intended to be the effect of the Act, and we believe that it can be dealt with by the proper application of the protection provided in section 35 of the Act, firm guidance to senior civil servants about the extent of the protections provided and, where necessary and appropriate, by the use of the ministerial veto to protect the 'safe space' for such discussions. We also note that disclosure of such discussions is as likely to occur through major public inquiries or court proceedings as it is under the Freedom of Information Act.[59]

In relation to openness, it specifically recorded:

> We agree with the Ministry of Justice that the Act has contributed to a culture of greater openness across public authorities, particularly at central Government level which was previously highly secretive. We welcome the efforts made by many public officials not only to implement the Act but to work with the spirit of FOI to achieve greater openness. Our evidence shows that the strength of the new culture of openness is, however, variable and depends on both the type of organisation and the approach to freedom of information of the

---

55 The Freedom of Information (Amendment) Bill 2006-07. A copy of the Bill is at: www.publications.parliament.uk/pa/cm200607/cmbills/039/2007039.pdf

56 See: www.cfoi.org.uk/pdf/PLP.pdf

57 See: www.publications.parliament.uk/pa/ld200607/ldselect/ldconst/127/127.pdf

58 See: www.publications.parliament.uk/pa/cm201213/cmselect/cmjust/96/9602.htm

59 At para 242.

individual public authority.[60]

The claimed 'chilling effect' of the legislation preoccupied the Select Committee, but its conclusions were tentative:

> We are not able to conclude, with any certainty, that a chilling effect has resulted from the FOI Act. On the one hand, [University College of London's] Constitution Unit's research – the most in- depth available – suggests it has only a marginal effect. On the other hand, a range of distinguished participants who are, or who have been recently, at the heart of the policy-making process attest that it is a problem. We see no reason why former senior ministers and officials in particular would flag this up as a concern if they did not genuinely believe it to be so, and we think their views are of value. However, so too of value is the increased openness introduced by the Act and, especially, the power of individuals to exercise their right to information proactively, rather than having public authorities decide what they will disclose, when and to whom, even when acting with the best intentions. Equally, there are other reasons why some officials and politicians may be increasingly reluctant to create paper records, not least the increasing possibility that some form of public inquiry may lead to the subsequent publication of minutes and records. That is why we are cautious about restricting the rights conferred in the Act in the absence of more substantial evidence.
>
> Given the uncertainty of the evidence we do not recommend any major diminution of the openness created by the Freedom of Information Act, but, given the clear intention of Parliament in passing the legislation that it should allow a "safe space" for policy formation and Cabinet discussion, we remind everyone involved in both using and determining that space that the Act was intended to protect high-level policy discussions. We also recognise that the realities of Government mean that the ministerial veto will have to be used from time to time to protect that space.[61]

2– 023 Independent Commission

In July 2015, the Minister for the Cabinet Office and Paymaster General, Mr Matthew Hancock MP, appointed Lords Burns, Carlile of Berriew and Howard of Lympne, Dame Patricia Hodgson and the Rt Hon Jack Straw to review FOIA. In March 2016 they reported:

> It is the conclusion of the Independent Commission on Freedom of Information ("the Commission") that the Act is generally working well, and that it has been one of a number of measures that have helped to change the culture of the public sector. It has enhanced openness and transparency. The Commission considers that there is no evidence that the Act needs to be radically altered, or that the right of access to information needs to be restricted. In some areas, the Commission is persuaded that the right of access should be increased. More generally, the Commission would like to see a significant reduction in the delays in the process whereby without good reason requests can go unresolved for several years. We have not been persuaded that there are any convincing arguments in favour of charging fees for requests and therefore we make no proposals for change.[62]

Given its commissioning body, it not surprising concentrated on the exemptions in sections 35 and 36 of FOIA (Cabinet material, policy formulation, public affairs etc). Reflecting Cabinet Office preoccupations, it summarised its conclusions:

> that sections 35 and 36 are clarified so that material relating to collective Cabinet agreement is protected under a single exemption instead of being spread across two different exemptions. In relation to the public interest test that is applied under section 35, we recommend that the Act is clarified so that it is clear that the need for safe space is not diminished simply because a decision has been taken (although it may be diminished for other reasons), and that section 35 is amended so that when a public interest assessment is made some weight is given to the need to protect collective Cabinet responsibility, and the

---

[60] Paragraph 17.

[61] Paragraphs 200-201.

[62] *Independent Commission on Freedom of Information Report*, March 2016, Cabinet Office, Foreword.

need to protect frank exchanges of views or advice for the purposes of deliberation.[63]

The recommendations came to nothing, and the Cabinet Office continued appealing Information Commissioner decisions, repeatedly taking the same point in order to secure the same outcome.

2–024 Data protection changes

On 25 May 2018 a new data protection regime took effect, with the old regime – represented by the DPA 1998 – being brought to an end. The new regime split the regulation of data protection into three separate streams:

- intelligence service processing of personal data;
- law enforcement processing of personal data by competent authorities; and
- all other processing of personal data, called 'general processing.'

The first stream is regulated exclusively by its own regime – Part 4 of the DPA 2018. The second stream is the subject of an EU Directive, which is implemented in the UK by Part 3 of the DPA 2018. The third stream is governed by an EU regulation having direct effect – 'the GDPR' – supplemented by Part 2 of the DPA 2018. The Act also has the effect of making subject to the general processing regime data processing that its outwith the legislative competence of the EU – this is called 'applied GDPR.' In this way, between the GDPR and DPA 2018, the field of data protection in the UK was covered. As a result of freedom of information legislation (ie FOIA, EIR and their Scottish public authority cousins) using the DPA 1998 as the normative touchstone to determine when personal information relating to a third party should be exempted from disclosure, the 25 May 2018 data protection regime change necessitated amendments to the personal information exemptions.

[63] *Independent Commission on Freedom of Information Report*, March 2016, Cabinet Office, Executive Summary.

CHAPTER 3
Scottish legislation

3–001 Scotland: the demarcation

The applicability of the FOIA and of the DPA 2018 to Scotland, as well as the scope of the FOI(S)A, reflect the settlement of legislative powers effected by the Scottish devolution in 1998. Section 1(1) of the Scotland Act 1998 established a Scottish Parliament, which has a limited, devolved power to make laws with respect to certain matters in Scotland.[1] It does not have the power to make laws with respect to 'reserved matters', which remain within the exclusive competence of Westminster.[2] Moreover, Westminster retains its plenary power to make laws with respect to Scotland,[3] but it is recognised that it will not normally exercise that power in relation to devolved matters without the consent of the Scottish Parliament.[4] In relation to the right of access to official information, the legislative competence of the Scottish Parliament is limited to public authorities that operate purely in or as regards Scotland.[5]

3–002 Background

In July 1999 the Scottish Executive published a Code of Practice on Access to Scottish Executive Information. The Code stated its aims and purpose as being:

> 1. This Code of Practice supports Scottish Ministers' policy of extending access to official information, and responding to reasonable requests for information. The approach to release of information should in all cases be based on the assumption that information should be released except where disclosure would not be in the public interest, as specified in Part II of this Code.
>
> 2. The aims of the Code are:
>
> — to facilitate policy-making and the democratic process by providing access to the facts

1 Scotland Act 1998 ss 28-29. Its statutes are known as Acts of the Scottish Parliament: s 28(1).

2 Scotland Act 1998 ss 29(2)(b) and 30(1). Reserved matters are listed in Sch 5. Specifically reserved at Pt II s B13 is 'public access to information held by public bodies or holders of public offices (including Government departments and persons acting on behalf of the Crown).' An exception to this reservation is made in relation to information held by the Scottish Parliament, any part of the Scottish Administration, the Scottish Parliamentary corporation and any Scottish public authority with mixed functions or no reserved functions, unless supplied by a Minister of the Crown or Government department and held in confidence. For an instance of a reserved matter relating to Scotland being covered by FOIA, rather than FOI(S)A, see *Scotland Office v IC*, IT, 8 August 2008.

3 Scotland Act 1998 s 28(7).

4 Scotland Act 1998 s 28(5).

5 Scotland Act 1998 s 29(2)(a). The Scottish devolution settlement was reformed by the Scotland Acts of 2012 and 2016, passed either side of the Scottish independence referendum held on 18 September 2014 under the Scotland Act 1998 (Modification of Schedule 5) Order SI 2013/242 and the Scottish Independence Referendum Act 2013 (Scottish Act). The Scotland Act 2012 implemented certain recommendations contained in the report of the independent Calman Commission on Scottish Devolution, Serving Scotland Better: Scotland and the UK in the 21st Century. Final Report of Commission on Scottish Devolution dated June 2009. The Scotland Act 2016 implemented the all-party Smith Commission Agreement published in Report of the Smith Commission for further devolution of powers to the Scottish Parliament dated 27 November 2014.

and analyses which form the basis for the consideration of proposed policy;
— to protect the interests of individuals and companies by ensuring that reasons are given for administrative decisions, except where there is statutory authority or established convention to the contrary; and

...

These aims are balanced by the need:
— to maintain high standards of care in ensuring the privacy of personal and commercially confidential information; and
— to preserve confidentiality where disclosure would not be in the public interest or would breach personal privacy or the confidences of a third party, in accordance with statutory requirements and Part II of the Code.

Like the Code for England and Wales issued in 1994 and revised in 1997,[6] it conferred no enforceable rights.

3–003 FOI(S)A

On 24 April 2002 FOI(S)A was passed by the Scottish Parliament.[7] As noted above, the Act only applies to public authorities that operate purely in or as regards Scotland.[8] Westminster-established bodies, government departments, offices and office-holders when operating in Scotland, including what are termed cross-border public authorities,[9] are in any event not susceptible to coverage by FOI(S)A.[10] Difficult issues arise as to whether some of the exemptions in the FOI(S)A are outside the legislative competence of the Scottish Parliament on the basis that they represent provisions that relate to reserved matters.[11]

3–004 Implementation of FOI(S)A

The Act was brought into force incrementally over the course of three years. The initial implementation of the Act brought into force those provisions that specified which bodies were to be subject to the Act, that provided for publication schemes and for the establishment of the Scottish Information Commissioner, and that effected certain amendments to public records legislation.[12] The remaining provisions for publication schemes, the Scottish Information Commissioner and immunity from suit were brought into force on 31 October 2003.[13] The remaining administrative provisions took effect from 30 April 2004.[14] Finally, the enforceable

---

6 See §2–004.

7 It received Royal Assent on 28 May 2002.

8 These are listed in Sch 1 to FOI(S)A.

9 Cross-border authorities are listed in the Scotland Act 1998 (Cross-Border Public Authorities) (Specification) Order 1999 SI 1999/1319. These include the Criminal Injuries Compensation Board and the Meat and Livestock Commission.

10 See §3–001. When operating in Scotland, these public authorities will be governed by the FOIA.

11 An Act of the Scottish Parliament is not law in so far as any provision of it is outside the legislative competence of the Scottish Parliament: Scotland Act 1998 s 29(1). A provision will be outside the legislative competence of the Scottish Parliament if it relates to 'reserved matters': Scotland Act 1998 s 29(2)(b). Reserved matters are defined in Sch 5 to the Scotland Act 1998. Significantly, in light of the exemptions in the FOI(S)A, these include: international relations, including relations with territories outside the United Kingdom, the European Communities (and their institutions) and other international organisations; the defence of the realm and the naval, military or air forces of the Crown; data protection; national security, etc; social security; health and safety. The phrase 'relates to' indicates more than a loose or consequential connection or a touching upon the matter: *Martin v Most* [2010] UKSC 10, 2010 SC (UKSC) 40 at [49], [159]. And similarly: *Imperial Tobacco Ltd v Lord Advocate* [2012] UKSC 61, 2013 SLT 2 at [16]; *Re Agricultural Sector (Wales) Bill* [2014] UKSC 43, [2014] 1 WLR 2622 at [50]; *Recovery of Medical Costs for Asbestos Diseases (Wales) Bill* [2015] UKSC 3, [2015] AC 1016 at [25]; *Christian Institute v Lord Advocate* [2016] UKSC 51, [2016] HRLR 19 at [29] (concerning the DPA 1998).

12 FOI(S)A (Commencement No 1) Order 2002 SSI 2002/437.

13 FOI(S)A (Commencement No 2) Order 2003 SSI 2003/477.

14 FOI(S)A (Commencement No 3) Order 2004 SSI 2004/203.

right of access was brought into force with effect from 1 January 2005.[15] On that same day, the EI(S)R came into force. Since that day, various additional Scottish public authorities have been made subject to the Act[16] and those that no longer exist have been taken out of the Act.

3– 005 Differences between the two Acts

Although closely modelled on FOIA, the Scottish Act treats a number of matters differently:

(1) The scheme for responses that neither confirm nor deny that the public authority holds information answering the terms of the request. FOIA spells out a separate duty on a public authority to inform an applicant whether it holds information of the description specified in the request.[17] In relation to all but one of the heads of exemption, that duty is disapplied where, or to the extent that, confirming or denying that the public authority holds the requested information would, or would be likely to, prejudice the matter protected by the head of exemption and, if the exemption is a qualified one, to do so would be contrary to the public interest.[18] FOI(S)A creates no separate duty to confirm or deny that the information requested is held by the public authority. Instead, more elegantly, it provides that a refusal notice must, amongst other things, disclose that the public authority holds the information sought;[19] this requirement in relation to a refusal notice is then disapplied where information answering the terms of the request would be exempt under certain exemptions[20] and the public authority considers that it would be contrary to the public interest to reveal whether such information exists or is so held.[21]

(2) To the extent that there is an onus in engaging the public interest override in relation to the qualified exemptions, it is reversed. Under FOIA, the duty to disclose exempt information is disapplied where, in all the circumstances of the case, the public interest in maintaining the exemption outweighs the public interest in disclosing the information.[22] Under FOI(S)A, the duty to disclose non-absolute exempt information only applies to the extent that, in all the circumstances of the case, the public interest in disclosing the information is not outweighed by the public interest in maintaining the exemption.[23] Guidance from the Scottish Information Commissioner suggests that the verbal reversal has little, if any, significance.[24]

(3) The harm level required to engage the prejudice-based exemptions is higher under

---

15 FOI(S)A (Commencement No 3) Order 2004 SSI 2004/203.

16 For example: The Scottish Further and Higher Education Funding Council; Bòrd na Gàidhlig; and the Office of the Scottish Charity Regulator.

17 FOIA s 1(1)(a). This is termed 'the duty to confirm or deny': s 1(6).

18 FOIA ss 2(1), 22(2), 23(5), 24(2), 26(3), 27(4), 28(3), 29(2), 30(3), 31(3), 32(3), 33(3), 34(2), 35(3), 36(3), 37(2), 38(2), 39(3), 40(5), 41(2), 42(2), 43(3) and 44(2). The sole head of exemption that does not have a disapplication of the duty to confirm or deny is s 21.

19 FOI(S)A s 16(1)(a).

20 The exemptions to which the duty to confirm or deny is disapplied are more limited than those under the FOIA: namely, ss 28-35, 39 and 41. The Scottish equivalents to the FOIA ss 22, 32, 33, 40, 41, 42 and 44 do not ground a refusal to confirm or deny under the FOI(S)A.

21 FOI(S)A s 18.

22 Section 2(2)(b).

23 Section 2(1)(b).

24 *FOI in the UK. Differences between the Scottish and UK FOI Acts, 2017.*

FOI(S)A ('would, or would be likely to, substantially prejudice')[25] than it is under FOIA ('would or might prejudice').[26] In light of the assurances given during the introduction into Parliament of FOIA[27] the differences in practice ought to be less significant than the language might suggest.

(4) Under FOIA, information held by a public authority is absolutely exempt if it was directly or indirectly supplied to the public authority by one of the security bodies or if it relates to one of the security bodies.[28] Moreover, a Minister of the Crown can sign a conclusive certificate certifying that the information to which the certificate applies was directly or indirectly supplied by, or relates to, any of the security bodies.[29] In Scotland, there is no such exemption,[30] although the exemption in respect of national security and defence may apply.[31]

(5) In England, Wales and Northern Ireland, information the disclosure of which would be a breach of parliamentary privilege enjoys an absolute exemption.[32] There is no such exemption under the Scottish Act.

(6) The exemption in respect of confidentiality of communications in legal proceedings provided for by s 36 of FOI(S)A is more broadly expressed than that which applies to public authorities under FOIA.[33]

(7) There are fewer grounds for issuing an exemption conclusive certificate under FOI(S)A[34] than there are under FOIA.[35]

(8) The preconditions for the issue of a compliance conclusive certificate are more onerous under FOI(S)A than they are under FOIA. In both jurisdictions, where the Information Commissioner is satisfied that a public authority has failed to comply with any of the requirements of Part I of the Act, he may serve on that public authority an enforcement notice specifying the steps that the public authority must take.[36] In both jurisdictions, limited provision[37] is made for a high-ranking official to give the Information Commissioner, within a certain time, a certificate that causes the enforcement notice to cease to have effect.[38] Under FOIA, the

---

25 FOI(S)A ss 27(2), 28(1), 30, 31(4), 32(1), 33(1), 33(2), 35(1) and 40.

26 FOIA ss 26(1), 27(1), 28(1), 29(1), 31(1), 33(2), 36(2), 38(1) and 43(2).

27 See §6– 021.

28 FOIA s 23(1). The security bodies are those listed in s 23(3).

29 FOIA s 23(2). The effect of a conclusive certificate is considered in §5– 040(1).

30 This raises a serious issue in relation to the FOI(S)A. The exemption in the FOIA s 23 does not, of course, operate to render exempt information requested under the FOI(S)A.

31 FOI(S)A s 31.

32 FOIA s 34(1).

33 FOIA s 42.

34 The only ground is national security: FOI(S)A s 31(2).

35 The grounds are: security body information, s 23(2); national security, s 24(3); parliamentary privilege, s 34(3); and deliberative or cabinet information held by either House of Parliament, s 36(7).

36 FOIA s 52(1); FOI(S)A s 51(1).

37 Under the FOIA, the power to issue a certificate is confined to where the enforcement notice relates to: (a) a failure to inform an applicant that it holds information of the description specified in the request in circumstances where s 2(1) does not operate to disapply the duty to confirm or deny; (b) a failure to communicate information to an applicant in circumstances where s 2(2) does not operate to disapply the duty to disclose: FOIA s 53(1)(b). In Scotland, the power to issue a certificate is confined to where the enforcement notice relates to a failure to give information to an applicant in circumstances where s 2(1) does not operate to disapply the duty to disclose and the information is exempt information by virtue of s 29, 31(1), 32(1)(b), 34, 36(1) or 41(b): FOI(S)A s 52(1)(b).

38 Under the FOIA, that high-ranking official is the 'accountable person' (itself defined in s 53(8)) and the time allowed is 20 working days: s 53(2). In Scotland that high-ranking official is the First Minister of the Scottish

precondition for the high-ranking official issuing the certificate is that on reasonable grounds he has formed the opinion that, in respect of the request or requests concerned, there was no relevant[39] failure to comply with the Act.[40] In Scotland, the high-ranking official must also form the opinion that the information requested is of exceptional sensitivity.[41]

(9) FOI(S)A gives no express right of review in relation to the decision to issue a conclusive certificate.[42]

(10) FOI(S)A has no equivalent to s 81(1) of FOIA, which treats each government department as a person separate from any other government department.

FOI(S)A establishes the office of the Scottish Information Commissioner.[43] This is independent of the office of the Information Commissioner, who is responsible for policing FOIA. The Scottish Information Commissioner does not have responsibility for the enforcement of the DPA 2018 in Scotland or in relation to Scottish public authorities: these are the responsibility of the Information Commissioner. The Scottish Information Commissioner has produced a briefing paper on the main differences between Scotland's 2002 Act and Westminster's 2000 Act. As well as the points covered above, it lists a number of other detailed differences of approach, including destruction of information, disability rights, fees, information for future publication, publication schemes and settlement.[44]

3– 006 Environmental information

In relation to 'environmental information', Scottish public authorities are subject to the EI(S)R. Apart from their applying to Scottish public authorities, these Regulations are very similar to the EIR which apply to Westminster public authorities. Both regimes are considered in Chapters 17-19 of this work. Appeal provisions are dealt with in Chapter 46: they closely follow the regime under FOI(S)A.

3– 007 Data protection

Data protection is a reserved matter. Responsibility for enforcement of the GDPR and the DPA 2018 lie with the Information Commissioner: the Scottish Information Commissioner does not have responsibility for enforcing the GDPR or the DPA 2018. Thus a request by an individual for information about himself will be exempt under FOI(S)A and will instead be treated as a subject access request under the GDPR/DPA 2018, save to the extent that it also involves the disclosure of personal information about a third party.[45] Similarly:

— other rights enjoyed by individuals and exercised by notice on the controller so as to result in a duty, and

— complaints by an individual about the misuse or over-use of his or her personal information by a controller (ie breach of the data protection principles),

are provided for exclusively by the GDPR/DPA 2018. These are enforceable both by an individual bringing a private court action against the controller and by the Information Commissioner (not the Scottish Information Commissioner) through regulatory provisions.

Executive and the time allowed is 30 working days: FOI(S)A s 52(2).

39 In other words, a failure of the sort set out in fn 37.

40 FOIA s 53(2).

41 FOI(S)A s 52(2).

42 Either on national security or exceptional sensitivity grounds: FOI(S)A ss 31(2) and 52(2).

43 FOI(S)A s 42(1).

44 See further: Karen McCullagh, 'Information Access Rights in FOIA and FOISA - fit for purpose?', *Edin LR*, vol 21(1), 2017, 55-87.

45 See chs 7-16.

3–008 Codes of practice

Section 60 of FOI(S)A makes provision for Codes of Practice by the Scottish Ministers. The current Code of Practice on Discharge of Functions by Scottish Public Authorities under FOI(S)A and the EI(S)R is dated 1 December 2016. There is a further Code on Records Management issued on 16 December 2011 under section 61 of FOI(S)A.

3–009 Developments since 2005

In January 2012 the Scottish Information Commissioner submitted his Special Report to the Scottish Parliament.[46] This presented a generally positive picture of the operation of the Act, with increasing public awareness of the Act. One concern expressed was the failure to include private organisations which had been contracted to carry out public functions, eg prisons. Following on from his recommendations, the Scottish Parliament enacted the Freedom of Information (Amendment) (Scotland) Act 2013. This imposed a requirement on the Scottish Ministers to consult before designating a public authority for the purposes of the Act. It also enabled the Scottish Ministers to alter the period after which a record becomes a 'public record.' On 13 June 2018 the Scottish Information Commissioner published a report on the Scottish Government's FOI practice and performance, and made seven recommendations for specific improvements to performance. He required an action plan to be developed for his approval by 13 September 2018. In particular, his report highlighted that journalists, MSPs and political researchers were made subject to a different process for clearance than other groups, which he considered to be inconsistent with the applicant-blind principle of the legislation. Following revisals, on 13 November 2018 a final Action Plan was published by Scottish Ministers. Its implementation will now be kept under review by the Scottish Information Commissioner until November 2019. He will then undertake an assessment as to the success of the action plan in achieving improvements.

[46] Entitled *Informing the Future* Laid before Parliament under s 46(3) of FOI(S)A. Available at www.itspublicknowledge.info/home/SICReports/OtherReports/SpecialReport2012.aspx

CHAPTER 4

The influence of the European Convention on Human Rights etc

1. THE ECHR AND INFORMATION RIGHTS

4–001 Positive obligations

The provisions of the European Convention on Human Rights – the ECHR – impose primarily negative obligations on States to refrain from taking steps that infringe the fundamental rights and obligations described in the Convention. The Convention, however, has increasingly been interpreted to impose positive obligations on States to take steps that protect the enjoyment of those fundamental rights from interference from other sources. In assessing whether States are under an obligation to take a particular positive measure, the European Court of Human Rights – the ECtHR – examines whether, in the absence of that positive measure, the essence of the right has been destroyed or its effective exercise is barred.[1]

[1] *Artico v Italy* (1980) 3 EHRR 1 at [47]; *Cudak v Lithuania* (2010) 30 BHRC 157, 51 EHRR 418 at [55]; *Goodwin v United Kingdom* (1996) 22 EHRR 123 at [101]; *Centrum för Rättvisa v Sweden* (2019) 68 EHRR 2 at [166].

The ECtHR also examines whether a fair balance has been struck between the interests of the individual and those of the wider community. The imposition of positive obligations is most apparent in relation to Article 8.[2]

4– 002 Balancing of considerations

Once it is established that there is an interference with a right under Article 8(1) or 10(1), a court must go on to consider whether the interference is justified and proportionate by reference to one or more of the legitimate aims identified in Articles 8(2) and 10(2), that is:

— national security;
— public safety;
— the economic well-being of the country;
— the prevention of disorder or crime;
— the protection of health or morals; and
— the protection of rights and freedoms of others.

4– 003 Accessing official information

Although the principal human rights instruments do not directly address the right of access to officially-held information, a consensus is developing that the right to freedom of expression confers a right of access to information held by emanations of the state.[3] Article 19 of the International Covenant on Civil and Political Rights[4] includes the 'freedom to seek, receive and impart information', which has been interpreted to embrace a right of access to information held by public bodies.[5] Article 10 of the ECHR[6] is framed in narrower terms than Art 19 of the ICCPR, and includes the freedom to receive and impart information.[7] There has been an emerging line of ECtHR jurisprudence that, in certain circumstances, the notions of 'freedom of expression' and 'freedom to receive information' embrace a right of access to information held by emanations of the state, at least where disclosure is in the public interest.[8] In 2017 the

---

[2] But it is also apparent in the interpretation of ECHR Arts 2, 3, 10 and 11.

[3] See, for example, Report to the General Assembly by the UN Special Rapporteur on the Promotion and Protection of the Right to Freedom of Opinion and Expression (A/68/362, 4 September 2013) at [38]; Council of Europe Report *Implementation of the Declaration of the Committee of Ministers on measures to promote the respect of Article 10 of the European Convention on Human Rights* CM(2013)29 (3 April 2013) at p 3; Human Rights Committee General Comment 34 CCPR/C/GC/34 (12 September 2011) at [18].

[4] Article 19 of the ICCRP, para 2 provides that: 'Everyone shall have the right to freedom of expression: this right shall include freedom to seek, receive and impart information and ideas of all kinds, regardless of frontiers, either orally, in writing or in print, in the form of art or through any other media of his choice.' This is based on Art 19 of the UN Universal Declaration of Human Rights, 1948.

[5] §4– 024 below.

[6] Article 10 of the ECHR provides:

1. Everyone has the right to freedom of expression. This right shall include freedom to hold opinions and to receive and impart information and ideas without interference by public authority and regardless of frontiers. This article shall not prevent States from requiring the licensing of broadcasting, television or cinema enterprises.
2. The exercise of these freedoms, since it carries with it duties and responsibilities, may be subject to such formalities, conditions, restrictions or penalties as are prescribed by law and are necessary in a democratic society, in the interests of national security, territorial integrity or public safety, for the prevention of disorder or crime, for the protection of health or morals, for the protection of the reputation or rights of others, for preventing the disclosure of information received in confidence, or for maintaining the authority or impartiality of the judiciary.

[7] In the late 1970s a draft additional protocol to the ECHR was discussed which expressly extended the right to freedom of expression protected under Art 10 of the ECHR to include the freedom to seek information. This draft protocol failed to secure widespread support and was abandoned. See Malinverni, 'Freedom of Information in the European Convention on Human Rights and the International Covenant on Civil and Political Rights' (1983) 4 *Human Rights Law Journal* 443.

[8] See §§4– 019 to 4– 020 below. See also C J S Knight 'Article 10 and a Right of Access to Information' [2013] PL 468.

Grand Chamber confirmed that freedom of expression entails a right of access to official information, whilst defining the scope of this right narrowly, namely:

— where disclosure of the information has been imposed by a judicial order which has gained legal force; or

— in circumstances where access to the information is instrumental for the individual's exercise of his or her right to freedom of expression, in particular 'the freedom to receive and impart information' and where its denial constitutes an interference with that right.[9]

A right of access to official information has, in certain contexts, also been recognised under the rubric of other human rights: in particular, the right to a fair trial protected by Art 6 of the ECHR and the right to life protected by Art 2 of the ECHR.

4–004 Protecting personal information

Article 8 of ECHR provides:

1. Everyone has the right to respect for his private and family life, his home and his correspondence.
2. There shall be no interference by a public authority with the exercise of this right except such as is in accordance with the law and is necessary in a democratic society in the interests of national security, public safety or the economic well-being of the country, for the-prevention of disorder or crime, for the protection of health or morals, or for the protection of the rights and freedoms of others.

Although Article 8 does not specifically refer to 'privacy' it has been successfully deployed to protect facets of 'personal privacy.'[10] A satisfactory definition of 'personal privacy' has proved elusive.[11] Although potentially overlapping in operation, the protection of personal privacy may be conceptually divided between the protection against intrusions on what a person is doing or how a person lives (eg by peeping on an individual or into an individual's home or other private sphere, without making any form of record of or disseminating what is peeped upon) and the protection of information that is about aspects of an individual the dissemination of which that individual wishes to restrict – sometimes termed 'informational privacy.' The first can readily provide the opportunity for the second. For the purposes of this work, it is only 'informational privacy' that is treated as an 'information right.' The ECHR Article 8 protection of informational privacy spawned a domestic creation – what has become termed the tort of misuse of private information. Mothered from the protection that equity gave against a breach of confidence where there was no contract, fathered by the growing jurisprudence of Article 8 of the ECHR, the infant tort disowned its parents, claiming instead a common law pedigree.[12]

[9] *Magyar Helsinki Bizottság v Hungary* [2016] ECHR 18030/11.

[10] See further §4–011.

[11] See §7–003 and: R Wacks, 'The poverty of "Privacy"', (1980) 96 LQR 73; Richard Hixson, *Privacy in a Public Society: Human Rights in Conflict*, OUP 1987; Daniel Solove, *Understanding Privacy*, Harvard University Press, 2008.

[12] In *Campbell v Mirror Group Newspapers Ltd* [2004] UKHL 22, [2004] 2 AC 457 Lord Nicholls declared that it had 'changed its nature' so that formulation based on a breach of confidence in equity had become 'awkward' and 'not altogether comfortable' at [14]. As to its status as a 'common law right', see: *Various Claimants v Morrison Supermarkets plc* [2018] EWCA Civ 2339, [2019] QB 772 at [31], [126], [160]; *NT1 v Google LLC* [2018] EWHC 799 (QB), [2019] QB 344 at [13(7)], [49], [165]; *PJS v News Group Newspapers Ltd* [2016] UKSC 26, [2016] AC 1081 at [42]. See further §4–014 and §41–009.

2. ARTICLE 8: ACCESSING INFORMATION

4– 005 Introduction

Whilst Article 8 of the ECHR[13] does not provide for a generalised right of access to official information, in certain circumstances Article 8 imposes on the State authorities a positive obligation to supply information of particular significance to an individual or group of individuals.[14] Early case law focused on the right of access to personal information (ie information relating to the person seeking it). In *Gaskin v United Kingdom*,[15] the applicant successfully relied upon Article 8 of the ECHR in challenging a local authority's refusal to supply information held relating to him.[16] The applicant had been fostered as a child. He sought access to his own records, which included contributions from a number of professionals, some of whom objected to disclosure. The ECtHR concluded that the right to access his file fell within the ambit of Article 8 of the ECHR and that the local authority's blanket refusal to disclose the applicant's records unjustifiably interfered with his right.[17] Following *Gaskin*, the United Kingdom Government enacted legislation providing access to one's own 'personal data.'[18] This right was later embodied within the DPA 1998,[19] and is now in the GDPR.[20] The existence of a right to appeal to an independent authority against the non-disclosure of certain records under the DPA 1998 was held to be sufficient to discharge the State's positive obligation to supply personal information under Article 8 of the ECHR.[21] The Court has left open the

---

13 See §4– 004.

14 Information encompasses images and photographs: *Von Hannover v Germany (No 2)* [2012] ECHR 228, (2012) 55 EHRR 15 at [96].

15 *Gaskin v United Kingdom* (App no 10454/83) (1989) 12 EHRR 36, [1990] 1 FLR 167.

16 Similarly *R (Rose) v Secretary of State for Health* [2002] EWHC 1593, [2002] 2 FLR 962, [2002] 3 FCR 731, [2002] UKHRR 1329, where the Claimant, who had been born by artificial insemination, sought judicial review of decisions of the Secretary of State and the Human Fertilisation and Embryology Authority which refused her requests for access to non identifying information and, where possible, identifying information in respect of anonymous sperm donors and for the establishment of a voluntary contact register. In partly granting the application, the Court held that respect for private and family life under Art 8 required that persons should be able to establish details of their identity as human beings. This included establishing their origins and the opportunity to understand them. It also embraced their physical and social identity. The Court held that this included the right to obtain information concerning a biological parent who inevitably had contributed to the identity of the child.

17 Contrast *Odièvre v France* (App no 42326/98) (2004) 38 EHRR 43, where the Grand Chamber concluded ten votes to seven that there was no positive obligation under Art 8 to disclose to an applicant the identity of her mother who had, under domestic law, been permitted to give birth anonymously. The majority of the Grand Chamber held that, unlike in *Gaskin*, there were competing Art 8 rights: the child had a right to know where she came from, but the mother also had a right under Art 8 to remain 'anonymous in order to protect her health by giving birth in appropriate medical conditions' (at [44]). The majority concluded that the balance struck between those competing interests by France was within the state's margin of appreciation.

18 The Access to Health Records Act 1990. Although the DPA 1984 s 21 provided for a right of access to personal data, it was confined to data recorded in a form in which it could be processed by equipment operating automatically in response to instructions given for that purpose: it thus did not include paper records. The DPA 1984 did not have its origins in a European Directive.

19 DPA 1998, s 7. The definition of 'data' in the DPA 1998 was significantly wider than it had been in the DPA 1984. The DPA 1998 repealed most of the Access to Health Records Act 1990.

20 Article 15. A subject access request involves a determination of the requester's civil rights and obligations: *R (Michael) v HMP Whitemoor* [2020] EWCA Civ 29 at [31].

21 See *MG v United Kingdom* (App no 39393/98) [2002] 3 FCR 289, (2003) 36 EHRR 3, 13 BHRC 179 (however, the European Court found a violation of Art 8 of the ECHR from 1995 to 1 March 2000 prior to the coming into force of the DPA 1998); *cf Martin v United Kingdom* (App no 27533/95) (1996) 21 EHRR CD112, where the European Commission of Human Rights declared inadmissible an application under Art 8 of the ECHR for records relating to an intermittent period of mental health treatment for four years. The Court in *MG* distinguished *Martin* on the

question whether Article 8 includes a right for an individual to prevent an emanation of the state imparting confidential information.[22]

4–006 Health etc risks

The ECtHR has developed the positive obligation under Article 8 to hold that the state is under a positive obligation to provide access to information which enables individuals to assess risks to health and life, and that this duty may extend to providing such information concerning both the risks that have materialised and the preventative measures that have been taken.[23]

4–007 Medical records

The ECtHR takes a particular approach in relation to access to an individual's own medical records. In *KH v Slovakia*[24] the Court held that the right of effective access to information concerning a person's own health and reproductive status was a positive right protected by Art 8. The positive obligation in such cases extended to making available to an individual a physical copy of his or her medical records.[25]

4–008 Police etc records

The ECtHR has also considered a number of cases concerning the individual's right to access the information about him held secretly by police or security services. In *Leander v Sweden*,[26] the applicant sought access under domestic legislation to a secret file containing information relating to himself which had been consulted by his employer, a Naval Museum, in deciding what position the applicant could hold. The ECtHR held that the state's refusal to allow Mr Leander to see the information amounted to an interference with his right to respect for his private life, as guaranteed by Article 8(1).[27] The court went on to find that the aim of the legislative regime by which a file on security risks could be maintained, including the extensive suite of safeguards against abuse, meant that the interference with Mr Leander's Article 8(1) right could not be considered disproportionate. On that basis there was no violation of Article 8.[28] In *Rotaru v Romania*, however, the Grand Chamber held that the storing of information about the appellant by the Romanian secret police, and their use of it, coupled with a refusal to allow the applicant an opportunity to refute it, breached Article 8, as the system employed by the Romanian secret police was not in accordance with law, nor did it have proper safeguards or supervision procedures.[29] The Grand Chamber held that public information

basis that, in *MG* the requested social service records contained the principal source of information for a significant part of the applicant's formative years, whereas the records in *Martin* were for a limited and intermittent period.

22 *Gillberg v Sweden* [2012] ECHR 569, 34 BHRC 247 at [64].

23 *Vilnes v Norway* (52806/09) (2013) 36 BHRC 297, (2013) 139 BMLR 199.

24 (App no 32881/04) (2009) 49 EHRR 34. This concerned a group of women who, through their lawyers, tried to obtain copies of their medical files concerning their childbirths.

25 At [47]-[56].

26 (App no 9248/81) (1987) 9 EHRR 433.

27 At [48].

28 See also *Haralambie v Romania* (App no 21737/03) ECHR 21 January 2010 (only available in French), in which the Court emphasised that public authorities had a duty to provide an effective procedure for obtaining access to personal files and found a breach of Art 8 where the applicant had been unable to obtain his personal security files within a reasonable time; *Segerstedt-Wiberg v Sweden* (App no 62332/00) (2007) 44 EHRR 2 at [69]-[104], where the Court concluded that the state's refusal of full access to a national security police register when the state legitimately feared that the provision of such information might jeopardise the efficacy of a secret surveillance system designed to protect national security and combat terrorism was permissible under Art 8; *Brinks v Netherlands* (App no 9940/04) (2005) 41 EHRR SE5, where the Court declared inadmissible a complaint by an academic for access to all information possibly held on him by the Dutch Secret Service.

29 *Rotaru v Romania* (2000) 8 BHRC 449 at [45]-[46] and [59]-[62]. A concurring judgment, criticising the 'national

(such as publication of political pamphlets or a criminal conviction) can fall within the scope of private life where it is systematically collected and stored in files held by authorities, particularly where the information concerns a person's distant past.[30]

4–009 Third-party information

The ECtHR has relied on Article 8 to support access to information concerning a third party, provided that there is a close relationship between the third party and the person requesting the information. In *TP and KM v United Kingdom*,[31] which concerned information relied upon by a local authority in taking the appellant's child into protective care, the Grand Chamber held that it was essential that such information be made available to the parent, even where it had not been directly requested. However, that right to information had to be curtailed where required by the interests of the child, and the decision as to what information should be released should be made by a court.

4–010 Public information

Whilst initially it was thought that Article 8 of the ECHR was limited to granting a right to information that was about the applicant (eg medical records, adoption records, employment records), the ECtHR has adopted a broader interpretation and extended the right of access to include environmental information that has an impact on an individual's private life or home life. In *Guerra v Italy*,[32] the Court concluded that the state authorities were under a positive obligation to collect and disseminate information about the dangers of a local chemical factory to local residents so that they could assess the extent of the risk and take steps to reduce that risk.[33] In *Roche v United Kingdom*[34] the Grand Chamber unanimously found a violation of Article 8 arising from the Government's failure to provide an effective and accessible procedure enabling the applicant to have access to all relevant and appropriate information which would allow him to assess any risk to which he may have been exposed during his participation in tests at Porton Down.[35] Where there are effective and accessible procedures for obtaining

---

security' justification for indiscriminate storing of information relating to individuals' private lives, was given by the President of the Grand Chamber and concurred in by six further judges.

30 At [43]. See also: *Copland v United Kingdom* (App no 62617/00) (2007) 45 EHRR 37 at [43]-[44]; *S v United Kingdom* (App nos 30562/04 and 30566/04) [2008] ECHR 1581; but compare *Chief Constable of Humberside Police & ors v IC and SSHD* [2009] EWCA Civ 1079, [2010] 1 WLR 1136, where the Court of Appeal was equivocal about whether Art 8 was applicable to the retention on the Police National Computer of old criminal convictions (at [50] and [78]-[81]). The Information Tribunal had explicitly held that processing included retention of information and that retention would breach Art 8(1) unless it could be justified: *Chief Constable of Humberside and ors v IC*, IT, 21 July 2008 at [173]-[180]. The Court of Appeal has, however, been clear that the disclosure of cautions held on the Police National Computer does engage Art 8. In *(T) v Chief Constable of Greater Manchester* [2013] EWCA Civ 25, [2013] 1 WLR 2515 the Court made a declaration of incompatibility, finding that the blanket statutory regime requiring disclosure of old cautions in certain circumstances breached Art 8 (at [33]-[54]).

31 *TP and KM v United Kingdom* (App no 28945/95) (2002) 34 EHRR 2 at [80]-[82].

32 *Guerra v Italy* (App no 14967/89) (1998) 26 EHRR 357, 4 BHRC 63 at [56]-[60]. Note that in this case although domestic legislation conferred a right to request information, the applicants had not exercised that right ([O32]-[O37]). The case was thus concerned with an obligation upon a public authority, on its own motion, to collect and disseminate information.

33 See also: *Lopez Ostra v Spain* (App no 16798/90) (1995) 20 EHRR 277; *McGinley and Egan v United Kingdom* (App nos 21825/93 and 23414/94) (1999) 27 EHRR 1, 4 BHRC 421, (1998) 42 BMLR 123, where the court concluded, by a majority of five to four, that although there was a positive obligation pursuant to Art 8 of the ECHR to supply information about nuclear tests at Christmas Island to individuals present in the area, this obligation was discharged in relation to the applicants by r 6 of the Pensions Appeals Tribunals (Scotland) Rules; *Taskin v Turkey* (App no 46117/99) (2006) 42 EHRR 50, where the court held that there was a violation of Art 8 in relation to lack of information relating to operation of a goldmine using cyanide extraction methods that allegedly threatened the health of local residents.

34 *Roche v United Kingdom* (App no 32555/96) (2006) 42 EHRR 30, 20 BHRC 99.

35 At [164], the Grand Chamber distinguished the earlier decision in *McGinley and Egan v United Kingdom* (App no

information, then Article 8 may not encompass a broader right of access to information than that provided for by the domestic procedures.[36]

3. ARTICLE 8: PERSONAL INFORMATION

4–011 Informational privacy

Although Article 8 of the ECHR does not include the term 'privacy,' in its interpretation of that Article the ECtHR has gradually developed principles that serve to protect different facets of personal privacy. It has developed these principles on the basis that in certain circumstances Article 8 requires the adoption of measures designed to secure respect for private life in the sphere of relations between individuals.[37] As part of this, the ECtHR has shown an increasing preparedness to recognise that uses of personal information may, depending on their intensity and nature, amount to an interference to an individual's Article 8 right and that the State is required to provide a remedy for such uses of personal information. Although in each case highly fact-specific, the ECtHR has in certain circumstances found each of the following uses of personal information to be an interference with an individual's Article 8 right:

- the collection of personal information;[38]
- the storage of personal information;[39]
- the transmission of personal information;[40]
- the collateral use of personal information;[41] and
- the publication of personal information.[42]

The intensity and nature of the use will be critical to a determination whether that use constitutes an interference with the Article 8(1) right.[43]

4–012 Justification

21825/93) (1999) 27 EHRR 1, 4 BHRC 421, (1998) 42 BMLR 123, on the basis that Mr McGinley and Mr Egan's search for documents was 'inextricably bound up with their domestic applications for pensions', whereas Mr Roche had made numerous attempts to obtain the relevant records independently of any litigation.

36 In *Hardy and Maile v United Kingdom* (App no 31965/07) (2012) 55 EHRR 28, the Court held that Art 8 had been complied with in circumstances where environmental information about the risks arising from the construction and operation of two liquefied natural gas terminals at Milford Haven Harbour had been provided during the planning process, as a result of the requirements of the regulatory regime and through the Information Commissioner (as a result of a request under the Environmental Information Regulations): see [233]-[250].

37 See, for example: *Von Hannover v Germany* (2004) 43 EHRR 139, 40 EHRR 1 at [57]; *Goodwin v United Kingdom* (2002) 13 BHRC 120 at [90]; *Smirnova v Russia* (2004) 39 EHRR 450 at [95]; *Avram v Moldova* (2011) 31 BHRC 543 at [36]; *Bărbulescu v Romania* [2017] IRLR 1032, (2017) 44 BHRC 17 at [70]; *Couderc v France* [2016] EMLR 19, (2016) 40 BHRC 436 at [83]; *Ismayilova v Azerbaijan* [2019] ECHR 65286/13 at [112]-[116].

38 *Uzun v Germany* (2010) 53 EHRR 852, 30 BHRC 297 (GPS data); *LH v Latvia* (2014) 61 EHRR 466; *Klass v Germany* (1979-80) 2 EHRR 214 (interception of communications); *Malone v United Kingdom* (1985) 7 EHRR 14 (telephone interception and metering of calls); *RE v United Kingdom* (2015) 63 EHRR 55, 41 BHRC 1 (covert surveillance record); *Bărbulescu v Romania* [2017] IRLR 1032, (2017) 44 BHRC 17 (monitoring of computer use); *Peck v United Kingdom* (2003) 36 EHRR 41, 13 BHRC 669 (video surveillance).

39 *Marper v United Kingdom* [2008] ECHR 1581, (2009) 48 EHRR 50 at [67] (indefinite retention of fingerprints and DNA samples); *Dimitrov v Bulgaria* (2011) 62 EHRR 850 (applicant's name in a police register); *MM v United Kingdom* [2012] ECHR 1906 (indefinite retention of a caution); *Rotaru v Romania* (2000) 8 BHRC 449 (retention of information about the applicant on a file kept by the intelligence service).

40 *LL v France* (2006) 50 EHRR 834 (conveyance of an individual's medical record to a court for use in proceedings).

41 *Vukota-Bojić v Switzerland* [2017] IRLR 94 (use in court of covert surveillance); *LL v France* (2006) 50 EHRR 834 (conveyance of an individual's medical record to a court for use in proceedings).

42 *Z v Finland* (1997) 25 EHRR 371 (disclosure of applicant's identity and HIV infection in the text of a judgment).

43 *Couderc v France* [2016] EMLR 19, (2016) 40 BHRC 436 at [84]-[86].

Once it is established that the collection, storage or disclosure etc of personal information constitutes an interference with an individual's Article 8(1) right, it is then necessary to go on to consider whether that interference is justified within the meaning of Article 8(2).[44] This requires that it be in accordance with the law, that it pursue one or more legitimate aims and that it is necessary in a democratic society to achieve those aims:

(1) In accordance with the law. A legal basis for the collection, storage and disclosure of personal information must lay down the limits of these powers and, in particular, the necessary safeguards against abuse and disproportionate uses.[45]

(2) Legitimate aim. Article 8(2) identifies which aims are legitimate, namely the interests of national security, public safety, the economic well-being of the country, the prevention of disorder or crime, the protection of health or morals, and the protection of the rights and freedoms of others.

(3) Necessary in a democratic society. Whether the interference is necessary in a democratic society requires that the interference be supported by relevant and sufficient reasons and that it be proportionate to the legitimate aim or aims pursued. This will often involve (and, where the Press is concerned, will always involve) a consideration of a competing right under ECHR Article 10(1). The starting point is that the rights in Articles 8 and 10 are of equal value and that these should be weighed according to:
   — whether the publication constitutes a contribution to a debate of general interest;
   — how well known the person concerned is and the subject-matter of the publication;
   — prior conduct of the person concerned, including the extent to which he or she has previously courted publicity;
   — the person's consent and the extent and nature of that consent;
   — the content, form and consequences of the publication; and
   — the circumstances and manner in which the information was acquired.[46]

4–013 Differences with data protection

Although the data protection regime can be similar to the protection given by ECHR Article 8, there are some notable differences:

(1) Article 8 of the ECHR will not protect all information about an identified or identifiable individual, whereas the data protection regime will protect it provided that it is processed automatically or in a structured filing system.

(2) Article 8 of the ECHR is less likely to protect information about an individual who is a public figure,[47] whereas the data protection regime is generally indifferent to

---

[44] See §4–002. At a general level, in order for an interference with an Article 8(1) right to be justified, it must meet a four-part test, namely: (1) whether the objective of the measure pursued is sufficiently important to justify the limitation of a fundamental right; (2) whether it is rationally connected to the objective; (3) whether a less intrusive measure could have been used without unacceptably compromising the objective; and (4) whether, having regard to these matters and to the severity of the consequences, a fair balance has been struck between the rights of the individual and the interests of the community: *Bank Mellat v Her Majesty's Treasury* [2013] UKSC 38, [2014] AC 700. In this specific context, see *Perincek v Switzerland* (2015) 40 BHRC 313, (2016) 63 EHRR 6 at [198].

[45] *Rotaru v Romania* (2000) 8 BHRC 449 at [57]-[62]; *Liberty v United Kingdom* (2009) EHRR 1 at [59]-[69]; *Association for European Integration and Human Rights and Ekimzhiev v Bulgaria* [2007] ECHR 62540/00 at [75]-[77]; *Marper v United Kingdom* [2008] ECHR 1581, (2009) 48 EHRR 50, 25 BHRC 557 at [99]; *Shimovolos v Russia* (2011) 31 BHRC 506, (2014) 58 EHRR 26 at [68]; *Zakharov v Russia* (2015) 39 BHRC 435, (2016) 63 EHRR 17 at [227]-[234].

[46] *Axel Springer AG v Germany* [2012] ECHR 227, (2012) 55 EHRR 6 at [90]-[95]; *Von Hannover v Germany (No 2)* [2012] ECHR 228, (2012) 55 EHRR 15 at [108]-[115]; *Couderc v France* [2016] at EMLR 19, (2016) 40 BHRC 436 at [92]-[93]; *Brčko v Bosnia and Herzegovina* (2017) 43 BHRC 535 at [80]-[88].

[47] *Craxi v Italy* (2003) 38 EHRR 995 at [65]; *Ageyevy v Russia* (2013) 34 BHRC 449 at [221].

such considerations.

(3) The protection given by ECHR Article 8 will usually not apply where the information has entered the public domain, but that will not normally diminish the data protection right.

(4) The sorts of use of personal information that constitute an interference for ECHR Article 8 right are narrower than the range of uses that constitute 'processing' and so enjoy the protection afforded by the data protection regime.[48]

(5) The data protection regime places a greater emphasis on consent than does ECHR Article 8, with an absence of consent more likely to be determinative under the data protection regime.

4– 014 Misuse of private information

The cause of action now labelled 'misuse of private information' is a domestic, private law manifestation of the positive obligation under ECHR Article 8 for measures that secures a respect for private life by placing limits on the use that bodies can make of information that is private to an individual.[49] The cause of action has two elements:[50]

(1) The information must be, or must at the relevant time have been, sufficiently private in nature to engage Article 8 of the ECHR. This involves a consideration of whether there was a reasonable expectation of privacy, the attributes of the claimant, the nature of the activity recorded in the information, where the activity was occurring, the absence of consent (including the manner in which the information was acquired) and the effect of the use upon the claimant.[51]

(2) The claimant's Article 8 rights in that information must not be outweighed by the defendant's rights in making use of that information, particularly those that the defendant may have under Article 10 of the ECHR. Here, the court will consider the legitimate public interest in the information and whether it would contribute to a debate of general interest,[52] the prior conduct of the claimant (including publicity in respect of the same subject matter), interests of third parties, and the matters that contributed to the conclusion that Article 8 was engaged (including the age and vulnerability of the claimant).[53]

---

48 For example: *Rechnungshof v Österreichischer Rundfunkat* (C-465/00) [2003] 3 CMLR 10, where it was held that the mere recording by an employer of data by name relating to the remuneration paid to his employees could not constitute an interference with private life (which would constitute the processing of personal data).

49 See also §41– 009.

50 *McKennitt v Ash v* [2006] EWCA Civ 1714, [2008] QB 73 at [11]; *HRH the Prince of Wales v Associated Newspapers Ltd* [2006] EWCA Civ 1776, [2008] Ch 57 at [65]-[68].

51 *Murray v Express Newspapers Ltd* [2007] EWHC 1908, [2007]EMLR 22 at [35]; *CC v AB* [2006] EWHC 3083 (QB), [2007] EMLR 312; *Mosley v News Group Newspapers Ltd* [2008] EWHC 687 (QB), [2008] EMLR 679; *Lord Browne of Madingley v Associated Newspapers Ltd* [2007] EWCA Civ 295, [2008] QB 103; *PJS v News Group Newspapers Ltd* [2016] UKSC 26, [2016] AC 1081. Surreptitious acquisition of the information will inform both the private nature of the information and the second element of the cause of action, and appears to be particularly significant.

52 This is sometimes the decisive factor: *Von Hannover v Germany* (2004) 43 EHRR 139, 40 EHRR 1; *K v News Group Newspapers Ltd* [2011] EWCA Civ 439, [2011] 1 WLR 1827.

53 *Lord Browne of Madingley v Associated Newspapers Ltd* [2007] EWCA Civ 295, [2008] QB 103 at [46]-[62]; *X v Persons Unknown* [2006] EWHC 2783 (QB), [2007] EMLR 290 at [22]-[39], [42]-[46]; *Ferdinand v MGN Ltd* [2011] EWHC 2454 (QB) at [84]-[102]; *McClaren v News Group Newspapers Ltd* [2012] EWHC 2466 (QB), [2012] EMLR 729 at [34]; *AAA v Associated Newspapers Ltd* [2013] EWCA Civ 554 at [21]-[37]; *Weller v Associated Newspapers Limited* [2015] EWCA Civ 1176, [2016] 1 WLR 1541 at [29]-[30]; *Various 3rd Wave Claimants v MGN Ltd* [2019] EWHC 2122 (Ch).

4. ARTICLE 10: ACCESSING INFORMATION

4–015 Early jurisprudence

Article 10 of the ECHR confers on everyone 'the right to freedom of expression' and this right expressly includes the right 'to hold opinions and to receive and impart information and ideas without interference.' Initially, it appeared that the right would be interpreted broadly to include some form of right of access to information held by States. In *X v Federal Republic Germany*[54] the European Commission on Human Rights stated:

> it follows from the context in which the right to receive information is mentioned…that it envisages first of all access to general sources of information…the right to receive information may under certain circumstances include a right of access by the interested person to documents which although not generally accessible are of particular importance.[55]

Subsequent case law from the ECtHR indicated that Article 10 of the ECHR did not form the basis of a generalised right of access to information in circumstances where there was no 'willing speaker.' In *Leander v Sweden*[56] the ECtHR held, in relation to the State's refusal to reveal secret information:

> [T]he right to freedom to receive information basically prohibits a Government from restricting a person from receiving information that others wish or may be willing to impart to him. Article 10 does not, in circumstances such as the present case,[57] confer on the individual a right of access to a register containing information on his personal position, nor does it embody an obligation on the Government to impart such information to the individual.[58]

A similar approach was adopted in *Gaskin v United Kingdom*[59] where the applicant complained that a local authority had refused him access to a case record relating to him created when he was a minor. The ECtHR found that there was no violation of Article 10 of the ECHR although it again limited that finding to the particular facts of the case.[60] In both *Leander*[61] and *Gaskin*,[62] the information sought related to a specific individual and its disclosure could not be said to be in the wider public interest. The Court restricted its judgments on Article 10 to those cases and did not consider the broader question of a general right of access to non-personal information in the public interest.

---

54 *X v Federal Republic Germany* (App no 8383/78) (1979) 17 DR 227.

55 At 228-229.

56 *Leander v Sweden* (App no 9248/81) (1987) 9 EHRR 434.

57 'The circumstances of the case' are those of a claim made for the freedom to receive information and the circumstances set out in [9]-[17] of the judgment.

58 At [74]. Contrast *Brown v Executors of the Estate of HM Queen Elizabeth the Queen Mother* [2008] EWCA Civ 56, [2008] 1 WLR 2327 at [41], where the Court of Appeal acknowledged that the question of the extent to which there can be justification for sealing a will in order to give effect to the desire of beneficiaries for privacy (in that case, the Royal family), might 'engage' both Art 8 and Art 10 ECHR. *Leander* was cited to the Court but was not discussed in the judgment.

59 (1989) 12 EHRR 36, [1990] 1 FLR 167.

60 However, the ECtHR concluded that the applicant was entitled to the information sought under Art 8 of the ECHR: see §4– 005. The incongruity of this, given that Art 8 does not mention 'information' whereas Art 10 explicitly includes the 'freedom to receive…information,' was highlighted by Sir Stephen Sedley in 'Information as a Human Right' in J Beatson and Y Cripps (eds), *Freedom of Expression and Freedom of Information: Essays in Honour of Sir David Williams* (Oxford, OUP, 2000) at 245.

61 *Leander v Sweden* (App no 9248/81) (1987) 9 EHRR 434.

62 *Gaskin v United Kingdom* (1989) 12 EHRR 36.

4– 016 Later jurisprudence

The disclosure of information in the public interest was considered in *Guerra v Italy*,[63] which concerned the collection and dissemination (without a request being made) of information relating to the dangers of a chemical factory. The residents contended that the authorities were obliged under each of Arts 8 and 10 of the ECHR to inform them about the hazards of the activity undertaken at the factories and about major accident procedures. The European Commission of Human Rights had expressed the view that both Article 8 and Article 10 of the ECHR not only placed states under an obligation to make environmental information accessible to the public, but also under a positive obligation to collect, process and disseminate information which, by its very nature, is not directly accessible and which cannot be known to the public unless the authorities act accordingly. However, the ECtHR, having found a violation of Article 8 resulting from the non-dissemination of information,[64] considered that Article 10 of the ECHR 'cannot be construed as imposing on a State, in circumstances such as those of the present case, positive obligations to collect and disseminate information of its own motion.'[65] The Court distinguished the situation in *Guerra* from cases concerning the right to receive information as a corollary of the function of the press to impart information and ideas on matters of public interest.[66] Article 10 was again briefly considered and held not to be applicable by the Grand Chamber in *Roche v United Kingdom*,[67] which concerned personal information relating to the effect on the applicant of tests conducted at Porton Down.

4– 017 The emerging jurisprudence

From 2006 there were indications of a broadening of the ECtHR's approach to the right to receive information. The first indication came in the admissibility decision of *Sdruženi Jihočeské Matky v Czech Republic*.[68] The Court recognised that the refusal by the Czech authorities to provide the applicant ecological NGO with access to documents regarding a nuclear power station amounted to an interference with the right to receive information under Article 10. After referring to its traditional case law, including *Leander*,[69] *Guerra*[70] and *Roche*,[71] and

---

[63] *Guerra v Italy* (App no 14967/89) (1998) 26 EHRR 357, 4 BHRC 63. Similarly: *Oneryildiz v Turkey* (App no 48939/99) (2004) 39 EHRR 12 at [108]. Contrast *R (Furness) v Environment Agency* [2001] EWHC (Admin) 1058, [2002] Env LR 26.

[64] At [60]. See further §4– 010.

[65] At [53], citing *Leander v Sweden* (App no 9248/81) (1987) 9 EHRR 434. Although the concurring opinion of Judge Palm, joined by five others, indicated that in certain circumstances there may be a positive obligation to make available to the public information which by its nature could not otherwise come to the attention of the public. Similarly, in his concurring opinion, Judge Walsh observed that 'on the particular facts of this case Article 8 is the more appropriate Article to examine than Article 10. The Convention and its Articles must be construed harmoniously.' See also the Grand Chamber decision in *Roche v United Kingdom* (App no 32555/96) (2006) 42 EHRR 30, 20 BHRC 99 where the Grand Chamber, although finding a violation of Art 8 ECHR, unanimously concluded (at [172]) that there was no violation of Art 10.

[66] At [53], citing *Observer and Guardian v United Kingdom* (App no 13585/88) (1992) 14 EHRR 153 (the 'Spycatcher' case) and *Thorgeirson v Iceland* (App no 13778/88) (1992) ECHR 51. See also *Romanenko v Russia* (App no 11751/03) [2006] ECHR 877 at [42] and *Eerikäinen v Finland* (App no 3514/02) [2009] ECHR 255 at [68].

[67] *Roche v United Kingdom* (App no 32555/96) (2006) 42 EHRR 30, 20 BHRC 99, (2006) 42 EHRR 30 at [170]. The case did not involve a request for any non-personal information. The Court's treatment of Art 8 occupied the bulk of the judgment (from [139]-[169]), with the Court concluding that there had been a violation of Art 8 through the state's non-provision of the information that Mr Roche sought. The Court's treatment of Art 10 was very much shorter (at [170]-[173]).

[68] *Sdruženi Jihočeské Matky v Czech Republic* (App no 19101/03) [2006] ECHR 1205 (French only).

[69] *Leander v Sweden* (App no 9248/81) (1987) 9 EHRR 434.

[70] *Guerra v Italy* (App no 14967/89) (1998) 26 EHRR 357, 4 BHRC 63.

[71] *Roche v United Kingdom* (App no 32555/96) (2006) 42 EHRR 30, 20 BHRC 99, (2006) 42 EHRR 30.

commenting that it was 'difficult to derive from [Article 10] a general right to access to data and documents of an administrative character,' the Court went on to recognise that the particular refusal in issue was an interference with the applicant's right to receive information and that it was one that had to be justified under Article 10(2).[72] In *Társaság Szabadságjogokért (Hungarian Civil Liberties Union) v Hungary*,[73] the Court cited the *Matky* decision as indicative of a recent advance towards 'a broader interpretation of the notion of "freedom to receive information" ... and thereby towards the recognition of a right of access to information.'[74] *Társaság* concerned the refusal to allow the applicant NGO access to the text of a constitutional complaint challenging amendments to drug-related offences in the Criminal Code. The applicant was active in the field of drug policy. The Court held that, in seeking to publicise the information gathered from the constitutional complaint, the applicant's activities amounted to an essential element of informed public debate on a matter of public importance. The applicant could therefore be characterised, like the press, as a social 'watchdog', and the Constitutional Court's refusal to provide information in which it had a monopoly amounted to a form of censorship which interfered with Article 10(1).[75] The Court went on to find that the interference was not justified under Article 10(2).[76] *Társaság* itself has been recognised as a 'landmark decision' by the advisory constitutional law body to the Council of Europe.[77] The above authorities marked the start of a move by the ECHR towards recognising that Article 10 confers a right of access to information which, in the public interest, should be disseminated. The trend continued[78] in decisions following *Társaság*:

— *Kenedi v Hungary*;[79]

— *Gillberg v Sweden*;[80]

---

72 The Court held the refusal was justified in the interests of protecting the rights of others (industrial secrets), national security (risk of terrorist attacks) and public health. The Court also held that the request for technical information about the nuclear power station did not reflect a matter of public interest. The application was therefore declared inadmissible. The Court's reasoning is not easy to discern. Two elements appear to have been important: the appellant NGO needed the information in order to disseminate it as part of its public role in debating the desirability of the nuclear power station; and the information was of the type that could usually be accessed through the Czech law on freedom of information (although the request for access had failed).

73 *Társaság a Szabadságjogokért v Hungary* (2011) 53 EHRR 3.

74 At [35].

75 At [26]-[28].

76 At [36]. In so doing the Court noted that the information sought by the applicant was 'ready and available' and did not require the collection of any data by the government, unlike the situation in *Guerra*.

77 Venice Commission Opinion *Draft Law about Obtaining Information of the Courts of Azerbaijan* (Opinion No 548/2009) at [13]-[21]. The evolution in Strasbourg case law was recognised by Advocate General Kokott in her opinion in *Commission of the European Communities v Technische Glaswerke Ilmenau GmbH* (C-139/07) [2011] 1 CMLR 3, [2010] ECR I-5885, [2011] Bus LR D81 at fn18 to [AG47]. But contrast the CJEU's approach in Case T-590/10 *Thesing v European Central Bank* [2013] 2 CMLR 8 at [65] to [81], which concerned the ECB's refusal to grant a journalist access to documents concerning the Greek government's use of derivative transactions to finance the country's deficit and manage government debt. For an assessment of the evolving Strasbourg case law, as well as its effects on CJEU jurisprudence, see A O'Neill, *EU Law for UK Lawyers*, (Oxford, Hart, 2011) at Ch 16.

78 For an early critique of the piecemeal nature of these developments, see K Steyn and H Slarks 'Positive Obligations to Provide Access to Information under the European Convention on Human Rights' [2012] 17 JR 308.

79 *Kenedi v Hungary* (31475/05) [2009] ECHR 78, (2009) 27 BHRC 335. See §4– 020 below.

80 *Gillberg v Sweden* [2012] ECHR 569, 34 BHRC 247 at [86]. This case concerned a professor at the University of Gothenberg, who had headed a large 15-year study into neuropsychiatric disorders in children, who destroyed university documents (research material) in order to prevent the university from complying with rulings by the domestic courts that the research material be provided to two researchers ('K' and 'E') outside the university. Effectively, Professor Gillberg claimed that the ECHR gave him a personal right to maintain a reverse-FOI position (ie an entitlement to prevent a public authority from complying with a FOI request for information held by it). In rejecting Professor Gillberg's claim, the Court made the important observation (at [93]) that such a reverse-FOI right in Professor Gillberg 'would also impinge upon K's and E's rights under article 10, as granted by the Administrative Court of Appeal, to receive information in the form of access to the public documents concerned...' The 'public documents concerned' had earlier (at [87]) been identified as the information they had

— *Shapovalov v Ukraine*;[81]
— *Youth Initiative v Serbia*;[82]
— *Austrian Agricultural Land Association*;[83] and
— *Guseva v Bulgaria*.[84]

It culminated in the Grand Chamber judgment in *Magyar Helsinki Bizottság v Hungary*.[85]

4– 018 Summary of current position

The position reached is as follows:

(1) Article 10 does not in terms confer a right of access to State-held information.[86]

(2) Where an applicant has under domestic law an established right[87] to requested information, but the public authority has failed to give effect to that right, that will constitute an interference with a right protected by Article 10(1) of the Convention.[88]

(3) Further, notwithstanding there being no domestic law entitlement (whether generally or because of limitations to entitlement or applicable exemptions), where an applicant is involved in the legitimate gathering of information on a matter of public importance with the intention of imparting that information (or information relying upon it) so as to contribute to public debate on that matter, that individual has under Article 10(1) of the Convention an individual right of access to state-held information relating to that matter.[89] The sorts of applicants who fit this role is

---

requested and held by the university, ie information that was not personal information relating to the requesters.

81 *Shapovalov v Ukraine* [2012] ECHR 1665. See §4– 019 below.

82 *Youth Initiative for Human Rights v Serbia* (App no 48135/06) [2013] ECHR 584. See §4– 019 below.

83 *Österreichische Vereinigung zur Erhaltung v Austria* (2013) 36 BHRC 697 (ie Austrian Association for the Preservation, Strengthening and Creation of an Economically Sound Agricultural and Forestry Land Ownership).

84 *Guseva v Bulgaria* (6987/07), 17 February 2015. The applicant was a member of the Board of Directors of the Animal Protection Society in Vidin who was authorised to act for the Society. The applicant made three requests to the mayor of Vidin for access to information about an agreement, concluded between the municipality and the municipal company Cleanliness EOOD, for the collecting of stray animals on the territory of Vidin municipality, about animals held in an animal shelter called 'Municipal Care' and about a public procurement procedure which had been organised by the mayor and aimed at reducing the number of stray dogs in Vidin. The matter fell to be determined by the Access to Public Information Act 2000. As required by the Act, in relation to the first two requests the mayor sought the consent of a third party for its disclosure, but that consent was refused, resulting in the mayor refusing to disclose, and in relation to the third it was withheld on the basis of it being commercial information. The applicant successfully appealed all three refusals, but the mayor refused to comply.

85 *Magyar Helsinki Bizottság v Hungary* [2016] ECHR 18030/11. The applicant was a non-governmental organisation that monitored the implementation of international human rights standards in Hungary, provided legal representation to victims of alleged human rights abuses etc. From its research it concluded that the system of ex officio appointed defenders did not operate adequately, as the police were free to choose defence counsel from a list compiled by the relevant bar associations. As part of its research, the applicant requested under s 20(1) of Hungarian Act no LXIII of 1992 various police departments to provide the names of the public defenders selected in 2008 and the number of assignments given to each lawyer. Two police departments refused on the basis that the information requested was not public interest data, nor information subject to disclosure in the public interest. This stance was upheld by the Hungarian Supreme Court.

86 *Magyar Helsinki Bizottság v Hungary* [2016] ECHR 18030/11 (Grand Chamber) at [117], [126].

87 That is, where a domestic court has determined that the public authority is required under domestic 'freedom of information' legislation (however termed) to disclose the requested information to the applicant.

88 *Magyar Helsinki Bizottság v Hungary* [2016] ECHR 18030/11 (Grand Chamber) at [131], [156]; *Kenedi v Hungary* (31475/05) [2009] ECHR 78, (2009) 27 BHRC 335 at [43]; *Youth Initiative for Human Rights v Serbia* [2013] ECHR 584, (2013) 36 BHRC 687 at [24]; *Guseva v Bulgaria* (6987/07), 17 February 2015 at [55].

89 *Magyar Helsinki Bizottság v Hungary* [2016] ECHR 18030/11 (Grand Chamber) at [132]-[133], [156]; *Társaság a Szabadságjogokért v Hungary* (2011) 53 EHRR 3 at [26]-[28]; *Österreichische Vereinigung zur Erhaltung v Austria* (2013) 36 BHRC 697 at [36].

considered in detail below,[90] but what unifies applicants under this principle is that they all request the information for the purpose of performing a 'social watchdog' role – journalists, civil society organisations, researchers, public interest groups and the like. In other words, the information is requested for the purpose of receiving and imparting information and ideas to others.[91] No particular formality or arrangement is required for such an applicant: an applicant working on his or her own particular matter of public interest may fit the role as well as an investigative journalist.[92] What unifies the character of the information sought is that it relates to the particular 'social watchdog' subject (which must be a matter of public interest)[93] with which the applicant is concerned and withholding that information would hinder or impair the individual's exercise of his or her right to freedom of expression.[94] The reasoning behind this principle is that to starve a social watchdog of the official information needed by it to carry out its social watchdog function is to impede its right to freedom of expression, including its ability to impart information and ideas.

(4) Article 10 of the Convention does not oblige a public authority to collect information.[95] In other words, the right is to information that is 'ready and available' (ie it applies only to recorded information that is held by the public authority).[96]

(5) Article 10 of the Convention does not oblige a public authority to disseminate information of its own motion (ie without having received a request for that information).[97]

(6) Where the public authority has already disclosed sufficient, though not all, information on the subject matter such that the requester is not impaired in carrying out its watchdog or research functions and there are grounds (eg cost) for not disclosing the balance, it may be that a refusal to provide the balance will not

---

90 §§4–019 to 4–020.

91 *Magyar Helsinki Bizottság v Hungary* [2016] ECHR 18030/11 (Grand Chamber) at [158], [164]-[168]. See further §§4–019-4–020 below.

92 But in all cases it is subject to the proviso that the applicant is acting in good faith in order to provide accurate and reliable information in accordance with the ethics of journalism: *Magyar Helsinki Bizottság v Hungary* [2016] ECHR 18030/11 (Grand Chamber) at [159].

93 As to the meaning of 'a subject of public interest,' this (at [162]):

> will depend on the circumstances of each case. The public interest relates to matters which affect the public to such an extent that it may legitimately take an interest in them, which attract its attention or which concern it to a significant degree, especially in that they affect the well-being of citizens or the life of the community. This is also the case with regard to matters which are capable of giving rise to considerable controversy, which concern an important social issue, or which involve a problem that the public would have an interest in being informed about. The public interest cannot be reduced to the public's thirst for information about the private life of others, or to an audience's wish for sensationalism or even voyeurism.

Magyar Helsinki Bizottság v Hungary [2016] ECHR 18030/11 (Grand Chamber) at [160]-[163].

94 *Magyar Helsinki Bizottság v Hungary* [2016] ECHR 18030/11 (Grand Chamber) at [159].

95 *Magyar Helsinki Bizottság v Hungary* [2016] ECHR 18030/11 (Grand Chamber) at [156].

96 *Társaság a Szabadságjogokért v Hungary* (2011) 53 EHRR 3 at [36]; *Österreichische Vereinigung zur Erhaltung v Austria* (App 39534/07) 28 November 2013 at [44]; *Magyar Helsinki Bizottság v Hungary* [2016] ECHR 18030/11 (Grand Chamber) at [170]. In *Bubon v Russia* (63898/09), 7 February 2017, the ECtHR held that the fact that the information requested is ready and available constitutes an important criterion in the overall assessment of whether a refusal to provide the information can be regarded as an interference with the freedom to receive and impart information as protected by Art 10. In that case the applicant had not sought the primary statistical material (which the public authority held) but 'essentially asked the domestic authorities to process and summarise information using specific parameters', with the effect that since it was not information 'ready and available' to the public authority, there was no interference with Art 10 in declining the applicant's request.

97 *Magyar Helsinki Bizottság v Hungary* [2016] ECHR 18030/11 (Grand Chamber) at [156].

be disproportionate for the purposes of Article 10(2).[98]

4–019 Social watchdogs

The right of access to official information by journalists was considered in *Shapovalov v Ukraine*,[99] where the Court held that 'the gathering of information is an essential preparatory step in journalism and is an inherent, protected part of press freedom.'[100] The ECtHR stated that obstacles which hinder access to information of public interest could discourage those working in the media or related fields from pursuing such matters, undermining their 'vital role as "public watchdogs," and [adversely affecting] their ability to provide accurate and reliable information.'[101] A different type of public watchdog was considered in *Youth Initiative for Human Rights v Serbia*,[102] which concerned an NGO that monitored the implementation of transitional laws in Serbia with a view to ensuring respect for human rights, democracy and the rule of law. The Government argued that the NGO's application to the European Court was inadmissible on the basis that Article 10 did not guarantee a general right to freedom of information.[103] The Court rejected that argument, holding that 'the notion of "freedom to receive information" embraces a right of access to information,' and that the NGO's activities as 'a public watchdog of similar importance to that of the press' warranted similar Convention protection.[104] The Court found that there had been a breach of Article 10.[105] A concurring opinion went on to point out that any individual seeking information which is not of a personal nature but is in the public interest is acting as a public watchdog.[106]

4–020 Research

Article 10 of the ECHR has been relied upon in cases relating to the right of access to official information required for research. In *Kenedi v Hungary*[107] the ECtHR held that 'access to original

---

98 *Österreichische Vereinigung zur Erhaltung v Austria* (App 39534/07) 28 November 2013 at [47].

99 *Shapovalov v Ukraine* [2012] ECHR 1665. The applicant had sought access to official information under domestic FOI legislation. The public authority, an electoral commission, refused and the refusal was upheld in the domestic courts (at [28]). Although the ECtHR found no violation of Art 10, that was because the public authority had subsequently provided the applicant with the great majority of the information he sought (at [71]-[75]).

100 At [68].

101 At [68], following *Dammann v Switzerland* (no 77551/01), ECtHR, 25 April 2006 at [52]. Endorsed in *Österreichische Vereinigung zur Erhaltung v Austria* (App 39534/07) 28 November 2013 at [34].

102 *Youth Initiative for Human Rights v Serbia* (App no 48135/06) [2013] ECHR 584. Using Serbia's FOI legislation, an NGO requested information from the Intelligence Agency about the number of people it had subjected to electronic surveillance. The Agency relied on an exemption to refuse, but, following a complaint by the NGO, was ordered to make the information available by the Serbian Information Commissioner. The Agency had then denied holding any information.

103 At [17].

104 At [20].

105 At [24]-[26]. The Court examined the facts and found the Intelligence Agency's denial of holding the information 'unpersuasive' and that its actions amounted to arbitrary defiance of domestic law. The decision in *Youth Initiative for Human Rights* was cited in the Report of the UN Special Rapporteur on the Promotion and Protection of the Right to Freedom of Opinion and Expression (A/68/362, 4 September 2013) at [38] as support for the Rapporteur's conclusion that the right to receive information 'comprises the right of individuals to access general information and, more particularly, information of public interest that can contribute to public debate.'

106 Joint Concurring Opinion of Judges Sajó and Vučinić, who added: 'We are in full agreement with the conclusions and reasoning of this judgment. It is of particular importance for those countries where, even today, long lasting habits make it difficult to have access to data which, in the days of totalitarianism, were used for oppressive purposes by secret services. However, we write this concurring opinion in particular to highlight the general need to interpret Art 10 in conformity with developments in international law regarding freedom of information, which entails access to information held by public bodies. We refer, in particular, to Human Rights Committee, General Comment No 34 (document CCPR/C/GC/34 of 12 September 2011, §18).'

107 *Kenedi v Hungary* (App no 31475/05) [2009] ECHR 78, (2009) 27 BHRC 335. This case concerned a historian specialising in the functioning of secret services of dictatorships, whose statutory request for access to documents

documentary sources for legitimate historical research was an essential element of the exercise of the applicant's right to freedom of expression.'[108] The Grand Chamber in *Gillberg v Sweden*[109] characterised researchers' rights of access to the results of a research study conducted through a university as 'rights under Article 10.'[110] In the Austrian Agricultural Land Association case,[111] where the applicant was an association for agricultural land preservation which was involved in the legitimate gathering of information of public interest and whose aims were to carry out research and submit comments on draft laws, the ECtHR held that it contributed to public debate and enjoyed rights under Article 10.[112]

4–021 Disclosure obligations

As noted above, the failure of a public authority to adhere to statutory requirements to disclose information may itself represent a breach of Article 10:

— In *Kenedi v Hungary* the state accepted that there had been an interference with the applicant's right to freedom of expression, since access to original documentary sources for legitimate historical research was an essential element of exercising the right to freedom of expression. The reluctance of the state to comply with the execution orders was in defiance of domestic law and was tantamount to arbitrariness and was not 'prescribed by law.'[113]

— In *Affaire Roşiianu v Roumanie* the ECtHR decided that the applicant's access to information that he had requested was necessary for him to work as a journalist. Based on the evidence before it, the Court found that the failure to execute three final judicial decisions ordering the national authorities to disclose that information to the applicant was not prescribed by law or proportionate.[114]

— In *Guseva v Bulgaria* the ECtHR held that the mayor's failure to enforce three final administrative court judgments ordering him to provide public information to the applicant breached her right to freedom of expression, since she had sought the information in order to contribute to public debate in the field of animal protection.[115]

— In *Satakunnan Markkinapörssi Oy v Finland* the ECtHR held that prohibiting the publication of taxation data which was publicly accessible required it to decide whether the correct balance was struck by the national courts in assessing whether the applicants' right to impart information as guaranteed by Article 10 as against the right to privacy as embodied in domestic data protection and access to

held by the Hungarian State Security Service had been refused, despite court decisions in his favour mandating that access be given.

108 At [43].

109 *Gillberg v Sweden* [2012] ECHR 569, 34 BHRC 247. See fn 80 above.

110 At [93].

111 *Österreichische Vereinigung zur Erhaltung v Austria* (App 39534/07) (2013) 36 BHRC 697, where the applicant sought information (namely, a request of the Regional Property Transactions Commissions, for all land transactions approvals given by it from 1 January 2000 to mid 2005, anonymised), the applicant sought the information to further its aim of researching and studying past and present transfers of agricultural land. The Commissions refused to disclose any details, arguing that Art 10 did not impose any obligation to provide access to information (at [3]). The ECtHR held that the interference was not justified since the Commissions had refused to give the applicant any information, making its task impossible (at [47]).

112 See [36].

113 *Kenedi v Hungary* (31475/05) [2009] ECHR 78, (2009) 27 BHRC 335.

114 *Affaire Roşiianu v Roumanie* (27329/06), 24 June 2014.

115 *Guseva v Bulgaria* (6987/07), 17 February 2015.

information legislation.[116] The Grand Chamber concluded that the interference with Article 10 was 'prescribed by law'[117] and that the national court's decision was in the circumstances proportionate and necessary.[118]

5. OTHER ECHR ARTICLES

4–022 Article 6

In certain circumstances, a request for access to information may engage Art 6(1)[119] of the ECHR. The concept of a 'civil right' has an autonomous meaning under the Convention, such that the classification of the right under domestic law is not decisive.[120] Public law matters are not excluded from being 'civil rights and obligations' if they are directly decisive of private law rights.[121] The Court has expressly recognised that the majority of the Convention rights, including those of non-pecuniary nature, are 'civil rights' for the purposes of Art 6(1).[122] So far as enforcing rights of access to information held by public authorities, there has been an evolution in Convention jurisprudence:

(1) The European Commission of Human Rights in *Barry v France*[123] rejected an argument that Art 6 of the ECHR applied to a refusal of an application for access to information relating to steps being taken by the French Foreign Ministry to inquire about and support political prisoners.

(2) The Commission dismissed a similar application in relation to a rejection of a request by an individual who was seeking access to redacted parts of his police file which disclosed the identity of members of the security services.[124] In both cases, the Commission dismissed the applications because the information sought could not be considered personal to the applicant.

(3) In *Kenedi v Hungary*,[125] the ECtHR 'recalled' that the right to freedom of expression constituted a 'civil right' and went on to characterise the applicant's domestic statutory right to access information as a civil right.[126]

---

116 *Satakunnan Markkinapörssi Oy v Finland* (931/13) (2018) 66 EHRR 8.

117 At [142]-[154].

118 At [160]-[199].

119 Article 6(1) of the ECHR provides:

> In the determination of his civil rights and obligations or of any criminal charge against him, everyone is entitled to a fair and public hearing within a reasonable time by an independent and impartial tribunal established by law. Judgment shall be pronounced publicly but the press and public may be excluded from all or part of the trial in the interests of morals, public order or national security in a democratic society, where the interests of juveniles or the protection of the private life of the parties so require, or to the extent strictly necessary in the opinion of the court in special circumstances where publicity would prejudice the interests of justice.

120 *König v Germany* (1978) 2 EHRR 170 at [89].

121 R Clayton and H Tomlinson, *The Law of Human Rights* (Oxford, OUP, 2009) at 11.329 and 11.346-350. See also, in the context of access to information, *Taskin v Turkey* (App no 46117/99) (2006) 42 EHRR 50 at [128]-[138].

122 See the discussion in *Shapovalov v Ukraine* [2012] ECHR 1665 at [45]. cf §4– 019.

123 *Barry v France* (App no 14497/89) 14 October 1991. But see now: *Syndicat CFDT des Etablissements et Arsenaux du Val-de-Marne and Vesque v France* (App no 11678/85) 7 December 1987; *Loiseau v France* (App No 46809/99) ECHR 18 November 2003; *Micallef v Malta* (App no 17056/06) ECHR 15 January 2008 at [39].

124 See *Schaller Volpi v Switzerland* (App no 25147/94) 84 DR 106.

125 *Kenedi v Hungary* (App no 31475/05) [2009] ECHR 78, (2009) 27 BHRC 335. cf §4– 020.

126 At [33]-[34]. The Court went on at [35]-[39] to find a breach of Art 6(1) in circumstances where a period of over 10 years had passed from the applicant making request for information, including a lengthy period in which he had been unable to enforce a court decision in his favour.

(4) In *Shapovalov v Ukraine*[127] the ECtHR conducted an extensive analysis of the applicability of Art 6(1) to proceedings concerning access to information, and concluded that a number of factors are relevant to whether the right will be engaged, including whether a right to obtain information is recognised in domestic law and where the information is required for the applicant to practise a profession.[128]

(5) In *Affaire Roşiianu v Roumanie* the ECtHR held that where an applicant had successfully pursued a right of access conferred by domestic legislation by securing a court order requiring the state body to disclose the requested information, the refusal of that state body to obey that order constituted a violation of Art 6(1) of the ECHR.[129]

Article 6(1) has also successfully been relied upon to require disclosure of documents that may be relevant to litigation.[130]

4–023 Other articles of the ECHR

Article 5(4) of the ECHR, which concerns the right of access to a court to test the lawfulness of detention, includes the right to access documents and information.[131] Article 2 of the ECHR, which protects the right to life, may in certain circumstances require provision of information relating to matters concerning health and safety.[132] Article 2 of the ECHR also imposes positive obligations on states to establish effective mechanisms to investigate deaths in certain situations.[133] The Tribunal has not been open to arguments in support of access to information based on Art 9 of the ECHR, which protects freedom of thought, or Art 11 of the ECHR, which protects freedom of association.[134]

---

[127] *Shapovalov v Ukraine* (App no 45835/05) [2012] ECHR 1665. cf §4– 019.

[128] At [42]-[49].

[129] *Affaire Roşiianu v Roumanie* (27329/06), 24 June 2014, where the Court held that the public authority, by refusing to implement three judicial decisions ordering the disclosure of requested information, had deprived the applicant of effective access to a court.

[130] See *KH v Slovakia* (App no 32881/04) (2009) 49 EHRR 34, 27 BHRC 373 at [59]-[69] (disclosure of medical records prior to institution of civil proceedings); *McGinley and Egan v United Kingdom* (App nos 21825/93 and 23414/94) (1999) 27 EHRR 1, 4 BHRC 421, (1998) 42 BMLR 123 (disclosure of documents relating to nuclear tests for the purposes of litigation before the Pensions Appeals Tribunal). See also *Edwards v United Kingdom* (App no 13071/87) (1992) 15 EHRR 417 (defendants in criminal cases have the right to disclosure of information relevant to their trial). Cf Case C-450/06 *Varec v Belgium* [2008] 2 CMLR 24 at [43]-[55] in the context of access to documents under EU law in litigation to review the award of contracts. For consideration by domestic courts see: *Re B (Disclosure to other Parties)* [2001] 2 FLR 1017, [2002] 2 FCR 32, [2001] Fam Law 798; *R (Ann S) v Plymouth City Council and C* [2002] EWCA Civ 388, [2002] 1 WLR 2583, [2002] 1 FLR 1177; *Roberts v Nottingham Healthcare NHS Trust*, IT, 1 August 2008 at [19]-[25].

[131] See *Weeks v United Kingdom* (App no 9787/82) (1988) 10 EHRR 293 at [66]-[67]; *Roberts v Nottingham Healthcare NHS Trust* [2008] EWHC 1934 (QB), [2009] FSR 4 at [19].

[132] See *Osman v United Kingdom* (2000) 29 EHRR 245, [1999] 1 FLR 193, (1999) 11 Admin LR 200. See also *Oneryildiz v Turkey* (App no 48939/99) [2004] 39 EHRR 12 where the Court found that the Government had violated Art 2 of the Convention because it did not provide inhabitants living near an unsafe rubbish tip with information 'enabling them to assess the risks they might run as a result of the choices they had made'. In this context there is likely to be an overlap with Art 8 of the ECHR. See, for example, *Guerra v Italy* (App no 14967/89) (1998) 26 EHRR 357, 4 BHRC 63 at [61]-[62] and *Taskin v Turkey* (App no 46117/99) (2006) 42 EHRR 50 at [139]-[140].

[133] See *R v SSHD, ex p Amin* [2003] UKHL 5, [2004] 1 AC 653, [2003] 4 All ER 1264, [2004] HRLR 3, [2004] UKHRR 75.

[134] *Ritchie v IC*, FTT, 26 July 2011 at [60]-[67], which concerned a request for access to an alleged blacklist of workers in the construction industry who engaged in trade union activities.

6. INTERNATIONAL INSTRUMENTS

4–024 ICCPR

The Human Rights Committee, which interprets and applies the International Covenant on Civil and Political Rights – the ICCPR – has held in two individual cases that the right to freedom of expression in Art 19(2)[135] guarantees a right to access to information: *Gauthier v Canada*,[136] a complaint brought by a journalist, and *Toktakunov v Kyrgyzstan*,[137] a complaint brought by an NGO. The Human Rights Committee has since issued General Comment 34,[138] in which it declared that Art 19(2) 'embraces a right of access to information held by public bodies.'[139] The Human Rights Committee has also observed in General Comment 16,[140] that the right to privacy in Art 17 of the Covenant[141] includes an individual right of access to personal information held by public authorities or private individuals or bodies.[142]

4–025 Inter-American Commission

The Inter-American Court of Human Rights has concluded that Art 13 of the Convention[143]

---

135 Set out in fn 4 above.

136 Communication 633/1995, CCPR/C/65/D (5 May 1999) at [13.5]. This case concerned the publisher of a newspaper. He had applied for membership of the Canadian Parliamentary Press Gallery, a private association administering accreditation for access to the precincts of the Parliament. He was provided with a temporary pass but his repeated requests for equal access on the same terms as other reporters and publishers were refused. The temporary pass meant he was denied access to the press facilities of Parliament and so was not allowed to take notes during Parliamentary debates, although he could watch from the public gallery. The Human Rights Committee held that the complainant's rights under Art 19(2) had been violated, because the restriction on his right of access to information was not proportionate. See [13.6]-[13.7].

137 Communication 1470/2006, CCPR/C/101/D/1470/2006 (21 April 2011). This case concerned a human rights NGO which requested the Kyrgyz Ministry of Justice and Central Department of Corrections to provide it with information on the number of individuals sentenced to death in Kyrgyzstan as of 31 December 2003, as well as on the number of individuals sentenced to death and detained in the penitentiary system. The request was refused on the basis that the information was classified. The Committee held that the State party had an obligation to provide the requested information and that the refusal to do so was not justified, resulting in a breach of Art 19. See [7.4]-[7.8].

138 CCPR/C/GC/34 (12 September 2011). General Comments are authoritative interpretative instruments which give rise to a normative consensus on the meaning and scope of particular human rights: see Conway Blake, 'Normative Instruments in International Human Rights Law: Locating the General Comment' (2008) Centre for Human Rights and Global Justice Working Paper No 17.

139 At [18]. This was cited by the ECtHR in *Youth Initiative for Human Rights v Serbia* (App no 48135/06) [2013] ECHR 584 at [13].

140 HRI/GEN/1/Rev.9 (8 April 1988).

141 Article 17(1) provides: 'No one shall be subjected to arbitrary or unlawful interference with his privacy, family, home or correspondence, nor to unlawful attacks on his honour and reputation.'

142 At [10].

143 Article 13 of the American Convention on Human Rights, entitled 'Freedom of Thought and Expression', provides:

1. Everyone has the right to freedom of thought and expression. This right includes freedom to seek, receive, and impart information and ideas of all kinds, regardless of frontiers, either orally, in writing, in print, in the form of art, or through any other medium of one's choice.
2. The exercise of the right provided for in the foregoing paragraph shall not be subject to prior censorship but shall be subject to subsequent imposition of liability, which shall be expressly established by law to the extent necessary to ensure:
    1. respect for the rights or reputations of others; or
    2. the protection of national security, public order, or public health or morals.
3. The right of expression may not be restricted by indirect methods or means, such as the abuse of government or private controls over newsprint, radio, broadcasting frequencies, or equipment used in the dissemination of information, or by any other means tending to impede the communication and

includes a right of access to information. The Inter-American Commission in *Claude Reyes v Chile*[144] was of the view that the free expression rights guaranteed by Art 13 includes a general right to access state-held information and a corresponding obligation for states to ensure that the information is available. The information sought in *Claude Reyes* concerned a major logging project. The Commission's view was affirmed by the American Court of Human Rights on 11 October 2006. The Court stated:

> With respect to the facts of the present case, the Court concludes that article 13 of the Convention, which specifically establishes the rights to "seek" and "receive" information protects the right of all persons to request access to information held by the State, with the exceptions permitted by the restrictions regime of the Convention. As a result, this article supports the right of persons to receive such information and the positive obligation on the State to supply it, so that the person may have access to the information or receive a reasoned response when, on grounds permitted by the Convention, the State may limit access to it in the specific case. The said information should be provided without a need to demonstrate a direct interest in obtaining it, or a personal interest, except in cases where a legitimate restriction applies. Disclosure to one person in turn permits it [the information] to circulate in society in such a way that it can be known, obtained and evaluated. In this way, the right to freedom of thought and of expression contemplates protection of the right of access to information under State control.[145]

The approach in *Reyes* was followed by the Court in *Lund v Brazil*,[146] in which the failure of the Brazilian state to provide access to information requested by the next of kin of 'disappeared persons' was held to breach Art 13.[147] The Inter-American Commission has also found a number of breaches of Art 13 on the basis of failures by states to provide access to information.[148] It remains to be seen whether the *Claude Reyes v Chile* line of cases will have any influence on the ECtHR's thinking on the issue.[149] It is possible that the Strasbourg Court may

---

circulation of ideas and opinions.

4. Notwithstanding the provisions of paragraph 2 above, public entertainments may be subject by law to prior censorship for the sole purpose of regulating access to them for the moral protection of childhood and adolescence.
5. Any propaganda for war and any advocacy of national, racial, or religious hatred that constitutes incitements to lawless violence or to any other similar action against any person or group of persons on any grounds including those of race, color, religion, language, or national origin shall be considered as offenses punishable by law.

The Convention was adopted by the nations of the Americas in 1969 and came into operation on 18 July 1978. As at the date of writing, 24 of the 35 members of the Organization of American States are parties to the Convention.

144 Inter-American Commission on Human Rights, Report 31/05, Case 12.108.

145 At [77]. The Court ordered Chile to provide the information requested about the logging project or adopt a reasoned decision as to why it was not providing it (at [157]-[158]. The Court further required the State to train public officials on the right of access to information (at [164]).

146 Series C No 219 (24 November 2010).

147 At [197]-[200].

148 See, for example, *Kichwa People of Sarayaku v Ecuador*, Report 138/09, Case 12.465 (right of access to information concerning exploration and exploitation activities for natural resources in the territory of indigenous communities); *José Miguel Gudiel Álvarez ("Diario Militar") v Guatemala*, Report 116/10, Case 12.590 (right of access to information concerning human rights violations; where national security is raised against disclosure, the state is required to demonstrate to an impartial authority that disclosing the information could have a serious, real, objective, and immediate impact on the defence of a democratic state).

149 *Reyes* has been cited once by the Court, in *Stoll v Switzerland* (App no 69698/01) ECHR 10 December 2007 (Grand Chamber), but not in the context of the right to receive information. The case concerned the criminal prosecution of a journalist who published a leaked confidential memo sent from the Swiss Ambassador to the US head of a team conducting highly sensitive negotiations about repatriation of unclaimed assets held in Swiss banks by those presumed killed during the Holocaust. The Grand Chamber relied on *Reyes* in finding that press freedom assumes even greater importance in circumstances in which state activities and decisions escape democratic or judicial scrutiny on account of their confidential or secret nature (at [111]). However, the Court held that the prosecution was justified because the sensationalist and truncated nature of the news report was likely to mislead the public.

seek to distinguish such case law on the basis that Art 13 of the Inter-American Convention on Human Rights, unlike Article 10 of the ECHR, includes the right to 'seek information' rather than merely receive and impart information.

7. HUMAN RIGHTS ACT 1998

4–026 Introduction

Prior to the coming into force of FOIA and the EIR[150] on 1 January 2005, attempts were made in various contexts to rely upon the Human Rights Act in order to secure official information. Although the conferral of an entitlement to information under FOIA and the EIR has diminished the need to found a right upon the Human Rights Act, the existence of a suite of exemptions and the public interest balancing exercise required for qualified exemptions mean that pre-entitlement authorities retain significance both in the interpretation of exemptions (so that, as far as possible, they are read consistently with Convention rights) and in the procedural mechanisms by which rights of access to public body information may be enforced.

4–027 Background

In introducing the second reading of the Freedom of Information Bill in the House of Commons, Jack Straw (the then Home Secretary), acknowledged that the Bill and the Human Rights Act 1998 were interrelated. He stated:

> The 1998 Act sets out the European Convention's statement of basic rights. Some of those rights are absolute, such as that provided in Article 3, guaranteeing freedom from torture or degrading treatment. The rights which we have had to wrestle in the Freedom of Information Bill are not absolutes, but have to be balanced one with another. Article 10 gives a right to freedom of expression, but that has to be set against Article 8 on the right to respect for a private life. We have therefore sought in the Bill to secure a balance between the right to information needed for the proper exercise of freedom of expression and the directly conflicting right of individuals to protection of information about themselves; the rights that institutions, including commercial companies should have to proper confidentiality; and the need for any organisation, including the Government, to be able to formulate its collective policies in private.[151]

All the bodies that are subject to the duties imposed by s 1 of FOIA are likely to be public authorities within the meaning of s 6 of the Human Rights Act 1998. Equally, the bodies that are responsible for enforcing FOIA, including the Information Commissioner, the FTT, the Upper Tribunal and the Courts, are also public authorities within the meaning of s 6 of the Human Rights Act 1998. All such bodies are required to act compatibly with the provisions of the ECHR. In most cases under FOIA, no issues will arise under the ECHR. However, in certain cases the ECHR may have an impact. Such an impact is likely to occur in two areas: (a) the information sought engages a substantive provision of the Convention; (b) Article 6 of the ECHR may be relevant to the fairness of a hearing before the Information Commissioner, the FTT, the Upper Tribunal or the Courts.

4–028 Interpretational significance

Public authorities holding information and equally the Information Commissioner and the Tribunals have a duty, pursuant to section 3 of the Human Rights Act 1998, to interpret FOIA so far as possible in a way that is compatible with the provisions of the ECHR incorporated into domestic law by the Human Rights Act 1998.

---

[150] And their Scottish public authority equivalents.

[151] Hansard HC cols 719-720 (7 December 1999).

- In cases concerning personal information, and environmental information that may have an impact on an individual's private or home life, Article 8 of the ECHR may well be of relevance to the interpretation of the provisions of FOIA.[152]
- Article 2 will be relevant to investigations of deaths in custody.[153]
- Article 10 is likely to be engaged in cases concerning access to information by a 'public watchdog' or access to information necessary for the applicant to practice a profession or to conduct academic research.[154]

If a right under the ECHR is engaged this may require the public authority, the Commissioner or tribunals to adopt a restrictive approach to the exemptions permitting the withholding of the information sought and may impinge on the public interest balancing exercise (in relation to qualified exemptions). For example, where the information sought relates to environmental issues that could have an impact on the applicant's health or well being, the public authority holding the information is likely to be required to consider the impact of Article 8 of the ECHR when deciding whether a particular exception applies and, if it is a qualified exemption, whether the public interest favours disclosure. Equally, if the public authority refuses disclosure and the applicant appeals to the Information Commissioner or the tribunals, these bodies will also have to have regard to the rights of the applicant under Article 8 and Article 10 of the ECHR to such information when interpreting the scope of exceptions and whether the public interest is in favour of disclosure. The ECHR may also be invoked in support of any argument that the public interest favours withholding the information sought. Indeed, it is in this context that the ECHR has been invoked most often before the tribunals. Respondents seeking to resist disclosure of information that is protected by legal professional privilege[155] and confidentiality[156] have invoked the ECHR in support of their arguments that the material sought should not be disclosed.

4–029 Procedural significance

As noted above,[157] in certain circumstances a request for information may engage Art 6(1) of the ECHR.[158] Applications for access to personal information under Art 15 of the GDPR are likely to engage Art 6 of the ECHR because the information sought is, by definition, of a personal nature.[159] Applications for non-personal information under FOIA or the EIR may engage Art 6 where compliance with the access right is important for the applicant's personal or professional interests – such as a journalist making a request for information in order to practise his profession – on the basis that that request will fall within the applicant's freedom of expression and constitute a 'civil right' for the purposes of Art 6(1) of the ECHR.[160] Hearings

---

152 See §§4–005 to 4–010 above.

153 See §4–023 above.

154 See §§4–015 to 4–020 above.

155 See, eg *Bellamy v Information Commissioner and DTI*, IT, 4 April 2006 at [11]; *Kitchener v Information Commissioner*, IT, 20 December 2006 at [16]-[17].

156 See, eg: *Bustin v Information Commissioner*, IT, 16 December 2005 at [35]; *Veolia ES Nottinghamshire Ltd v Nottinghamshire County Council & ors* [2010] EWCA Civ 1214, [2012] PTSR 185 at [141].

157 §4–022.

158 Article 6(1) is set out in fn 119 above.

159 See Chapters 10 and 12 on access to personal information.

160 *Kenedi v Hungary* (31475/05) [2009] ECHR 78, 27 BHRC 335 at [33]-[34]; *Shapovalov v Ukraine* [2012] ECHR 1665 at [42]-[49]. Lord Brown in *Sugar v BBC (No 2)* [2012] UKSC 4, [2012] 1 WLR 439, [2012] EMLR 17, [2012] 2 All ER 509 at [94], dealing with the disapplication of the Act to information held by the BBC for journalistic purposes, considered that Art 10 does not create a 'general right to freedom of information,' noting that the applicant's position would not have been any better had he been a journalist. The Upper Tribunal in *Browning v Information Commissioner and DBIS* [2013] UKUT 236 (AAC) (20 May 2013) at [82] (a case involving a journalist)

before the FTT and Upper Tribunal will be subject to the domestic law requirements of natural justice, which raises similar issues to Art 6 of the ECHR.[161]

4– 030 Personal information

Article 8 of the ECHR has been relied upon in a number of cases relating to personal information although, so far, its impact on access rights has been limited. In *Linda Gunn-Russo v Nugent Care Society and The Secretary of State for Health*[162] the claimant sought disclosure of her adoption records held by a voluntary adoption agency. The High Court concluded that in that context Article 8 of the ECHR added nothing to the common law. The Court rejected the claimant's argument, based on *Gaskin*, that the voluntary adoption agency could not have the last word and there must be some form of appeal to an independent authority: unlike *Gaskin*[163] the information sought included private information relating to others, namely the adoptive family, rather than just the claimant. However, the courts have permitted access to third party information in the context of guardianship proceedings and care proceedings.[164]

4– 031 Environmental information

Article 8 was deployed to support a right to public information in *R (Furness) v Environment Agency*,[165] where the claimants cited *Guerra*[166] in relation to an alleged failure to protect their right to information affecting their homes. The claimants had been challenging the grant of an authorisation for incineration of municipal waste to take place at an industrial estate near their homes. Although the challenge failed,[167] the court appeared to accept that Article 8 could require the provision of information if there were a substantial threat to health or property. Article 8 and the *Guerra/Roche* line of cases is yet to be properly considered by the Tribunal.[168]

4– 032 Police etc information

Article 8 has also been relied on in relation to access to information held by the Security

---

doubted that the entitlement conferred by FOIA constituted a 'civil right', but did so without considering the decision in *Shapovalov v Ukraine* [2012] ECHR 1665. See further *Társaság a Szabadságjogokért v Hungary* (2011) 53 EHRR 3. The CJEU, when considering the right of access to Community institution information (see Chapter 4), has acknowledged the development in ECHR jurisprudence: *Commission of the European Communities v Technische Glaswerke Ilmenau GmbH* (C-139/07P) [2011] 1 CMLR 3, [2010] EUECJ C-139/07, [2011] Bus LR D81 at fn 18.

161 In *BBC v Sugar* [2007] EWHC 905 (Admin), [2007] 1 WLR 2583 at [45] the Court rejected an argument that Art 6 was offended by the appeal system under the FOIA. This was upheld by the Court of Appeal ([2008] EWCA Civ 191, [2008] 1 WLR 2289 at [38]-[47]. The point was not appealed to the House of Lords: [2009] UKHL 9. [2009] 1 WLR 430.

162 [2001] EWHC (Admin) 566, [2002] 1 FLR 1, [2001] UKHRR 1320.

163 *Gaskin v United Kingdom* (1989) 12 EHRR 36.

164 See *R (Ann S) v Plymouth City Council and C* [2002] EWCA Civ 388, [2002] 1 WLR 2583, [2002] 1 FLR 1177, which concerned the disclosure to the appellant's mother and nearest relative of certain information contained in social service files concerning her adult but mentally incapacitated son, C. The Court of Appeal concluded, relying in part on Art 8, that disclosure was appropriate. And similarly *Re B (Disclosure to other Parties)* [2001] 2 FLR 1017, [2002] 2 FCR 32 and *Re R (a child) (disclosure)* [2004] EWHC 2085 (Fam), which concerned disclosure of documents in care proceedings. But compare *FL v Registrar General* [2010] EWHC 3520 (Fam), [2011] 2 FLR 630, where the court rejected an application for disclosure of the adoption records of the applicant's father. Article 8 was relied on, but was dismissed at [49]-[52] without much analysis.

165 *R (Furness) v Environment Agency* [2001] EWHC (Admin) 1058, [2002] Env LR 26.

166 *Guerra v Italy* (App no 14967/89) (1998) 26 EHRR 357, 4 BHRC 63.

167 At [25]-[27].

168 See *Civil Aviation Authority v Information Commissioner and Kirkaldie*, IT, 22 January 2010 at [48]. Art 10 was considered in *Kennedy v Charity Commission*, FTT, 18 November 2011 and the *Guerra/Roche* line of cases was cited at [25]-[28], but the Tribunal did not engage in any analysis based on Art 8.

Service. In *Baker v SSHD*,[169] the appellant challenged the Security Service's refusal to confirm or deny (NCND) that it kept records about him, and the SSHD's certificate purporting to exempt the Security Service from the provisions of Part II of the DPA 1998. The Information Tribunal held that Article 8 was engaged, as NCND removed one of the preconditions of action by the data subject: knowledge as to whether his data was held.[170] However, NCND was justifiable in appropriate cases. The Tribunal went on to quash the certificate as it was found to be wider than necessary to protect national security.[171] In *MacMahon's (Aine) Application*[172] the High Court in Northern Ireland left open the possibility that Article 8 may require the police or the prosecution to allow victims of crime (or their families) access to information available to the investigating authorities, although the court recognised that this had to be balanced against the 'obvious interest in preserving confidentiality.'[173]

4–033 **Article 10: pre-FOIA cases**

There has been little domestic case law successfully relying on Article 10 of the ECHR to found an entitlement to information held by a public authority. The early cases considered by the English Courts related to government inquiries. In *R (Wagstaff) v Secretary of State for Health*[174] the claimant successfully relied upon Article 10 to require that the inquiry into Dr Shipman's activities be held in public. The *Wagstaff* decision was a high watermark, not least because it pre-dated the coming into force of the Human Rights Act. Later cases concerning inquiries have been more reluctant to apply Article 10. In *Persey v Secretary of State for Environment, Food and Rural Affairs*,[175] which concerned the inquiry into the outbreak of foot and mouth disease, the High Court held that Article 10 was not engaged by a decision to hold a closed public inquiry.[176] The Court stated that Article 10 does not impose a positive obligation on government to provide, in addition to existing means of communication, 'an open forum to achieve the yet wider dissemination of views.'[177] The Court was critical of the analysis of Article 10 in *Wagstaff*, noting that the decision was not supported by the Strasbourg authorities.[178] Similar criticism was voiced in *R (Howard) v Secretary of State for Health*,[179] with Scott Baker J noting that Article 10 'does not confer a right on individuals to receive information that others are not willing to impart.'[180]

---

169 *Baker v SSHD* [2001] UKHRR 1275.

170 At [67]. See also *Gosling v SSHD*, Data Protection Tribunal, 1 August 2003 and *Hitchens v SSHD*, Data Protection Tribunal, 4 August 2003, which challenged the use of NCND permitted by the revised certificate.

171 At [113]-[116].

172 *MacMahon's (Aine) Application* [2012] NIQB 60.

173 At [66]-[88] and [110].

174 [2001] 1 WLR 292, [2000] HRLR 646, [2000] UKHRR 875.

175 [2002] EWHC 371 (Admin), [2003] QB 794.

176 See also *R (Howard) v Secretary of State for Health* [2002] EWHC 396 (Admin), [2003] QB 803, which held that Art 10 was not engaged in a decision not to hold a public inquiry into circumstances surrounding the serious misbehaviour of a doctor.

177 At [53]. Similarly, in *R (Pelling) v Bow County Court (No 2)* [2001] UKHRR 165, [2001] ACD 1 (at [36]), the Divisional Court, after quoting from *Guerra v Italy* (App no 14967/89) (1998) 26 EHRR 357, 4 BHRC 63 said: 'The point does not arise in this case, but it seems to me very pertinent that the Strasbourg court does not recognise an absolute right to receive information in the absence of willingness on the part of those holding that information to give it to him. ...If the state makes arrangements to prevent that information flowing it does not, in my judgment, by that step alone, involve itself in any breach of Article 10.'

178 At [48]-[54].

179 [2002] EWHC 396 (Admin), [2003] QB 803 at [99]-[112].

180 In *Higher Education Funding Council for England v Information Commissioner & anor*, IT, 13 January 2010 at [28], the Information Tribunal considered itself bound by *Howard*.

4– 034 Article 10 since FOIA

By 2010 the Court of Appeal had recognised the development in Strasbourg jurisprudence regarding Article 10 rights of access to information held by public authorities.[181] In *Independent News and Media Ltd v A*,[182] the Court examined the case law culminating in *Társaság* and observed that Article 10 was developing a wider scope, concluding that cases where the media is involved and a genuine public interest is raised might in any event be outside the *Leander*[183] approach.[184] In *R (Guardian News and Media Ltd) v City of Westminster Magistrates' Court*,[185] the Court surveyed the Strasbourg cases up to *Kenedi*[186] and characterised them as 'leading in the same direction' as the common law principle of open justice, which the Court held required that the media be given access to various documents referred to in the course of an extradition hearing.[187] However, the Supreme Court in *BBC v Sugar (No 2)*[188] was not prepared to accept that the case law culminating in *Kenedi* established that an individual's Article 10 freedom to receive information would be interfered with 'whenever, as in the present case, a public authority, acting consistently with the domestic legislation governing the nature and extent of its obligations to disclose information, refuses access to documents.'[189] The Supreme Court maintained this posture in *Kennedy v Charity Commission*, where it: (a) rejected the submission that the exemption in FOIA s 32 should be interpreted in accordance with s 3 of the HRA so as to be in line with Article 10 decisions of the ECtHR; (b) held that Article 10 did not contain any right to receive information held by a public authority, whether sought by a 'public watchdog' or otherwise.[190] The ratio in *Kennedy* is irreconcilable with the subsequent Grand Chamber decision in *Magyar Helsinki Bizottság v Hungary*[191] and is more notable for its invention of a common law right of access to information held by public authorities[192] than for its preparedness to acknowledge developments in Convention jurisprudence.[193]

---

[181] See §4– 017 above.

[182] *Independent News & Media Ltd & ors v A* [2010] EWCA Civ 343, [2010] 1 WLR 2262.

[183] *Leander v Sweden* (App no 9248/81) (1987) 9 EHRR 434.

[184] At [39] and [41]. See also *Sugar v British Broadcasting Commission & anor* [2010] EWCA Civ 715, [2010] 1 WLR 2278 at [76], where Moses LJ described *Társaság* as 'a landmark decision on freedom of information'. Following *Independent News and Media Ltd v A*, the First-tier Tribunal held that Art 10 was engaged in *Cobain v IC and Crown Prosecution Service*, FTT, 8 February 2012 at [55]-[58], which concerned a request by a journalist for information held by the CPS.

[185] *R (Guardian News and Media Ltd) v City of Westminster Magistrates' Court* [2012] EWCA Civ 420, [2013] QB 618.

[186] *Kenedi v Hungary* (31475/05) [2009] ECHR 78, (2009) 27 BHRC 335.

[187] At [89].

[188] *Sugar v BBC (No 2)* [2012] UKSC 4, [2012] 1 WLR 439.

[189] Per Lord Brown at [95]-[98], per Lord Mance at [113] and per Lord Wilson, with some diffidence, at [58]. This pre-dated *Gillberg v Sweden* [2012] ECHR 569, 34 BHRC 247, *Shapovalov v Ukraine* [2012] ECHR 1665 and *Youth Initiative for Human Rights v Serbia* (App no 48135/06) [2013] ECHR 584.

[190] *Kennedy v Charity Commission* [2014] UKSC 20, [2015] AC 455, on appeal from *Kennedy v Charity Commission* [2012] EWCA Civ 317, [2012] 1 WLR 3524.

[191] *Magyar Helsinki Bizottság v Hungary* [2016] ECHR 18030/11 (Grand Chamber), summarised above at §4– 018. Indeed, it was irreconcilable with the authorities as they were in 2014.

[192] See the dissenting judgments of Lord Wilson at [198]-[199] and of Lord Carnwath at [230]-[231] and [247].

[193] This has spawned a new chapter in this work – Chapter 41, dealing with common law rights of access to information held by public authorities. One possibility is that the common law right (the existence of which was not argued by any party in *Kennedy* nor adverted to by the Court during the hearing) was invented to forestall the ECtHR entertaining proceedings that would have questioned the reasoning and conclusions of the Supreme Court: see further *Times Newspapers Ltd and Kennedy v United Kingdom* (64367/14), ECtHR, 6 December 2018, where the Court declined to entertain Mr Kennedy's application to the ECtHR on the basis that he had not exhausted his alternative remedies, namely seeking judicial review of the Charity Commission's refusal to grant access to the requested information which Mr Kennedy had sought after the Supreme Court's judgment relying on his newly-

CHAPTER 5

Exemptions: general principles

1. THE UNIT OF EXEMPTION

5– 001 Information, not documents

As noted later,[1] under the freedom of information regimes[2] both the existence and the access entitlements attach to 'information' rather than to documents or records.[3] Although the

minted common law right of access.

[1] See §20– 001.

[2] That is, the FOIA, the FOI(S)A, the EIR, the EI(S)R, the GDPR and DPA 2018.

[3] FOIA s 1(1); FOI(S)A s 1(1); EIR regs 6(1), 12(6); EI(S)R regs 6(1), 10(8). The GDPR Art 15 and DPA 2018 s 45(1) give a right to 'personal data', with GDPR Art 4(1) and DPA 2018 s 3(2) defining 'data' to mean 'information' possessing certain characteristics.

distinction is narrowed by 'information' being defined to mean 'recorded information',[4] the terms are not synonymous: a document or record may contain any number of discrete pieces of information. Similarly, engagement of each of the exemptions and consideration of the public interest both turn upon the quality or characteristics of the particular 'information', rather than of the document or record containing that information.[5] It is information that has that quality or characteristic, rather than the document or record containing it, which disapply the existence entitlement and the access entitlement.[6]

5–002 Exempt information

Information that falls within one or other of the exemptions in Part II of FOIA is termed 'exempt information'.[7] Only 'exempt information' is capable of being excused from the duty to disclose. If information falls within one of the 'absolute exemptions'[8] within Part II, then that will be sufficient to disapply the duty to communicate that information. If it does not fall within one of the absolute exemptions, disapplication of the duty to communicate will depend upon a consideration of the public interest. Similarly, under the environmental information regime, only 'environmental information' that falls within one of the exceptions in Part 3 (regs 12-15) is excused from the duty to disclose.[9] Apart from environmental information that includes personal data, disapplication of the duty to make such information available will depend upon a consideration of the public interest.[10]

5–003 Partial disclosure

A single document or record may contain some information that (or the existence of which) need not be disclosed and other information that (or the existence of which) must be disclosed. Where the information in a document is segregable then, provided that the information in the remainder of the document or record falls within the terms of a request, a public authority remains under its two duties in relation to that information. The use of 'information' as the unit of disclosure and of exemption makes it unnecessary for there to be a specific provision requiring a public authority to redact and disclose a document of which only a part contains information that is excused from disclosure.[11] An amendment to the Freedom of Information

---

4 FOIA s 84; FOI(S)A s 73. In the environmental information regime, information means 'information in written, visual, aural, electronic or any other material form': EIR reg 2(1); EI(S)R reg 2(1). Note that for the Commissioner's purposes in serving an information notice under s 51, information extends to unrecorded information: FOIA s 51(8); FOI(S)A s 50(9); EIR reg 18; EI(S)R reg 17. Unlike DPA 1998 s 1(1)(b)-(c), in the GDPR and DPA 2018 'personal data' is not defined by reference to whether the information is recorded: GDPR Art 2(1) and DPA 2018 s 3(2).

5 With the possible exceptions in FOIA s 32 and FOI(S)A s 37, which focus on the type of document within which the information is contained – court records etc – rather than the content or subject matter of the information itself.

6 FOIA s 2(1) and (2); FOI(S)A ss 2(1) and 18(1); EIR regs 5(1) and 12(1); EI(S)R regs 5(1) and 10(1). *DBERR v IC and Friends of the Earth*, IT, 29 April 2008 at [28]-[30].

7 FOIA s 84, referring to ss 21(1), 22(1), 22A(1), 23(1), 24(1), 26(1), 27(1), 28(1), 29(1), 30(1) and (2), 31(1), 32(1) and (2), 33(2), 34(1), 35(1), 36(2), 37(1), 38(1), 39(1), 40(1) and (2), 41(1), 42(1), 43(1) and (2), and 44(1). FOI(S)A s 73, referring to ss 25(1), 26, 27(1) and (2), 28(1), 29(1), 30, 31(1) and (4), 32(1), 33(1) and (2), 34(1)-(4), 35(1), 36(1) and (2), 37(1), 38(1), 39(1) and (2), 40 and 41.

8 FOIA s 2(2); FOI(S)A s 2(1). Absolute exemptions are considered at §5– 016.

9 EIR reg 5(1); EI(S)R reg 5(1). But see EIR reg 3(4)-(4) and EI(S)R reg 3(2).

10 EIR reg 12(1); EI(S)R reg 10(1).

11 See *IPSA v IC* [2015] EWCA Civ 388, [2015] 1 WLR 2879, where the Court of Appeal made clear that the requested is entitled only to the relevant recorded information, not the record itself. The potential for partial disclosure of a document or record is made explicit in the environmental information regime: EIR reg 12(11); EI(S)R reg 10(7). This is the approach taken in most of the comparative regimes: Freedom of Information Act 1982 (Cth of Aust) s 22(1) (substituted in 2010); The Official Information Act 1982 (NZ) s 17; Access to Information Act, (1982) (Canada) s 25; Freedom of Information Act 2014 (Ireland) s 18.

Bill that would have compelled a public authority to consider partial disclosure[12] was withdrawn following this explanation:

> We have been discussing whether the Bill in effect permits partial disclosure. It will in fact require that when some of the information that is requested is exempt but other information is not. The right of access in Clause 1 involves information that is recorded in any form. That means that the right of access attaches to the content of documents or records rather than to the documents or records themselves. When a document contains a mixture of disclosable and non-disclosable information, the disclosable information must be communicated to the applicant.[13]

5– 004 The relevant standpoint

In many cases it will make no difference whether determination of the applicability of an exemption and the public interest balancing test are carried out at the moment of receipt of the request or at the time that the request is decided. However, in some circumstances even a small amount of time may effect a significant difference: for example, where in the intervening period information on the same topic as the requested information is formally released. The Tribunal's approach had originally been that the applicability of an exemption and the public interest balancing exercise were to be determined by reference to the facts and circumstances as they stood at the time that the request should have been answered.[14] Later Tribunal decisions have held that both matters should be determined by reference to the facts and circumstances as they stood at the moment when the request was actually answered. This applies not just to the public authority making the original decision, but also those making merit-review decisions – that is, the Information Commissioner and the First-tier Tribunal.[15]

---

12 Amendment no 25, moved by Lord Lucas: Hansard HL vol 617 col 930 (17 October 2000); withdrawn, col 932.

13 Hansard HL vol 617 col 931 (17 October 2000) (Lord Falconer of Thoroton).

14 In ordinary circumstances, the 20-day working limit is merely the endstop date, so that normally responses should be given before then. The date for consideration can normally be approximated as being within a short period after receipt of the request for information. See: *Bellamy v IC and DTI*, IT, 4 April 2006 at [6]; *DTI v IC*, IT, 10 November 2006 at [44], [46]; *DWP v IC*, IT, 5 March 2007 at [30]; *Campaign against the Arms Trade v IC and MoJ*, IT, 26 August 2008 at [43]-[53] (where it was held that the public authority had to consider matters as at the date at which it was obliged to respond to the request); *DCLG v IC*, IT, 22 July 2008; *Dept of Culture, Media and Sport v IC*, IT, 29 July 2008 at [4].

15 *Maurizi v IC and CPS* [2019] UKUT 262 (AAC) at [156]-[185]; *All Party Parliamentary Group on Extraordinary Rendition v IC and FCO* [2015] UKUT 0377 (AAC) at [48]-[52]; *IC v HMRC and Gaskell* [2011] UKUT 296 (AAC) at [15]-[30]; *All Party Parliamentary Group on Extraordinary Rendition v IC and Ministry of Defence* [2011] UKUT 153 (AAC) at [9], [109], [116], [121]; *British Union for the Abolition of Vivisection v IC and Newcastle University*, FTT, 13 July 2011 at [21]; *Sittampalam v IC and BBC*, FTT, 4 July 2011at [53]-[61]; *Chagos Refugees Group v IC and FCO*, FTT, 4 September 2012 at [26]; *DfES v IC and The Evening Standard*, IT, 19 February 2007 at [20(iv)]; *Baker v IC and Cabinet Office*, IT, 28 February 2007 at [25]; *Evans v IC and MoD*, IT, 26 October 2007 at [23]; *DBERR v IC and Friends of the Earth*, IT, 29 April 2008 at [104]; *Campaign against the Arms Trade v IC and MoJ*, IT, 26 August 2008 at [37]-[53]; *DBERR v IC and Friends of the Earth*, IT, 29 April 2008 at [104]-[111]; *Bellamy v IC and DBIS*, FTT, 23 February 2010 at [38(iii)]). So far as the decision by the primary decision-maker (ie the public authority), this approach is undoubtedly correct. Similarly, the Tribunal is correct in relation to the identification of the information that answers the terms of the request (FOIA s 1(4); FOI(S)A s 1(4), and see §20– 011). However, it is difficult to see why those making a merit-review decision (ie the Information Commissioner and the First-tier Tribunal) should not decide the applicability of an exemption or the public interest balance on the basis of the facts and circumstances as they exist when each of those bodies makes its decision. As with any administrative decision, unless statute otherwise provides, satisfaction of statutory requirements is decided on the basis of the facts known to the decision-maker at the time that the decision is made. On an appeal to a merit-review tribunal, that tribunal should, unless statute otherwise provides, determine an appeal based on the facts known to it at the time that it makes its decision: *Saber v SSHD* [2008] UKHL 97, [2008] 3 All ER 97 at [2] ('common sense indicates that the final decision, whenever it is made, should be based on the most up to date evidence that is available,' dealing with an asylum-seeker who was in need of international protection, although the common sense is not unique to that jurisdiction); *Mucelli v Government of Albania (Criminal Appeal from Her Majesty's High Court of Justice)* [2009] UKHL 2, [2009] 1 WLR 276. This is the position that has been taken in other jurisdictions when dealing with requests under freedom of information legislation and having a provision similar to FOIA s 1(4): *Re Radar Investments and Health Insurance Commission* (2004) 80 ALD 733 at [30]-[42]. The Tribunal's power under FOIA s 58(2) is ample for this purpose. The FOIA does not confer an accrued right to information; nor does it impose an accrued liability to communicate information. In these circumstances, the taking of evidence in order to make findings so as to confirm or overturn

However, the decision-maker (whether the public authority, the Information Commissioner or the First-tier Tribunal) may properly take into account circumstances or matters that come to light after the date of the request where those subsequent circumstances or matters shed light on the public interest at the time that it falls to be decided.[16] If an applicant is disadvantaged by this approach, the disadvantage can be circumvented by lodging a fresh request in identical terms.[17]

2. THE DUTY TO CONFIRM OR DENY

5–005 Exemption – FOIA

Under FOIA, dispensation from the duty to confirm or deny turns upon the purpose for which the information is held, the nature of the information sought or, most commonly, the effect that confirmation or denial of holding the sought information would have. In the last case, the effect required in order to trigger dispensation varies according to the ground of exemption. In summary:

(1) Where the information sought:

(a) has at any time been held for the purposes of a criminal investigation or is confidential information obtained for the purposes of the authority's functions relating to such an investigation;

(b) has at any time been held as part of court or arbitral proceedings;

(c) is held by a government department and relates to[18] the formulation of policy or to Ministerial communications;

(d) relates to communications with the Royal Family or Royal Household or the conferring of honours or dignities;

(e) is required to be made available under the access to environmental information provisions; or

(f) constitutes personal data of which the requester is the data subject,

---

an evaluative conclusion on a state of facts as they existed long before is not a fruitful exercise. In *OGC v IC* [2008] EWHC 774 (Admin), [2010] QB 98, [2008] ACD 54 at [98], the High Court doubted whether the Tribunal's approach (ie deciding the matter by reference to the facts and circumstances at the time of the public authority's decision) was correct. To the extent that the Upper Tribunal in *Maurizi v IC and CPS* [2019] UKUT 262 (AAC) at [100]-[101] and *All Party Parliamentary Group on Extraordinary Rendition v IC and FCO* [2015] UKUT 0377 (AAC) at [48]-[52] has considered this question to have been conclusively decided by the Supreme Court in *R (Evans) v Attorney-General* [2015] UKSC 21, [2015] AC 1787, its reasoning is questionable: the passage in Lord Neuberger's judgment alighted upon ([73]) is obiter and does not squarely address the issue.

16 *IC v HMRC and Gaskell* [2011] UKUT 296 (AAC) at [28]; *DTI v IC*, IT, 10 November 2006 at [46]-[47].

17 If the facts and circumstances have truly changed, this should render the interval between the requests a 'reasonable' one, so that the applicant should not fall foul of the proscription against repeat requests: see §§23–017 to 23–019.

18 In the context of considering the Scotland Act 1998 (which it has been said is to be interpreted on ordinary principles), the Supreme Court has held that the phrase 'relates to' indicates more than a loose or consequential connection or a touching upon the matter: *Martin v Most* [2010] UKSC 10, 2010 SC (UKSC) 40 at [49], [159]. And similarly: *Imperial Tobacco Ltd v Lord Advocate* [2012] UKSC 61, 2013 SLT 2 at [16]; *Re Agricultural Sector (Wales) Bill* [2014] UKSC 43, [2014] 1 WLR 2622 at [50]; *Recovery of Medical Costs for Asbestos Diseases (Wales) Bill* [2015] UKSC 3, [2015] AC 1016 at [25]; *Christian Institute v Lord Advocate* [2016] UKSC 51, [2016] HRLR 19 at [29] (concerning the Data Protection Act 1998). In the context of FOIA the meaning of the phrase 'relates to' has been considered in: *Home Office v IC and Cobain*, FTT, 30 January 2013 at [15]-[19]; *Callus v IC and Home Office*, FTT, 6 May 2014 at [39]-[41]; *University and Colleges Admissions Service v IC and Lord Lucas* [2014] UKUT 0557 (AAC) at [44]-[46] (meaning of 'relates to' in FOIA s 7(5)); *Home Office v IC and Cobain* [2014] UKUT 0306 (AAC) at [39]; *All Party Parliamentary Group on Extraordinary Rendition v IC and FCO* [2015] UKUT 0377 (AAC) at [14]-[33]; *Reprieve v IC and FCO*, FTT, 26 April 2016 at [37]-[39]; *Corderoy and Ahmed v IC and Attorney General* [2017] UKUT 0495 (AAC) at [51] [54] and [59]-[62]; *Department of Health v IC and Lewis* [2017] EWCA Civ 374, [2017] 1 WLR 3330 at [13] (Sir Terence Etherton MR) (meaning of 'relates to' in FOIA s 35(1)).

then the public authority is excused from the duty to confirm or deny that such information is held.[19]

(2) Where, or to the extent that, exemption from confirmation or denial of a holding of the information sought is required:
(a) to safeguard national security;
(b) to avoid an infringement of the privileges of either House of Parliament;
(c) to avoid an actionable breach of confidence;
(d) to maintain the possibility of a claim of legal professional privilege; or
(e) to avoid contravention of an enactment or of an EU obligation, or to avoid a contempt of court,

then the public authority is excused from the duty to confirm or deny that any information answering the request is held.[20]

(3) Where the information sought:
(a) is intended for future publication;
(b) is supplied by, or relates to, bodies dealing with security matters; or
(c) is confidential information obtained from the Government of any state other than the United Kingdom or from an international organisation or court,

then the duty to confirm or deny does not arise if, or to the extent that, confirmation or denial that the requested public authority holds the information sought would itself involve the disclosure of any information so exempted from disclosure.[21]

(4) Where confirmation or denial that the public authority holds the information sought would, or would be likely to, prejudice:
(a) a programme of research which is continuing with a view to publication;
(b) the defence of the nation or the effectiveness of the armed forces;
(c) relations between the United Kingdom and another state or an international organisation or the interests of the United Kingdom abroad;
(d) relations between administrations within the United Kingdom;
(e) the economic interests of the United Kingdom or the financial interests of any administration within the United Kingdom;
(f) the efficacy of law enforcement;
(g) the exercise of an auditing body's functions;
(h) the collective responsibility of Cabinet, the frank provision of advice or the effective conduct of public affairs;
(i) the physical or mental health or safety of an individual; or
(j) the commercial interests of a person,

then the duty to confirm or deny is, to that extent, disapplied.[22]

(5) Where the information sought constitutes personal data of which the requester is not the data subject and where confirmation or denial that the public authority holds the information requested would contravene one of the data protection principles or Article 21 of the GDPR or the information is exempt under ss 15, 16, 26, 45(4) of or Schedules 2-4 to the DPA 2018, then the duty to confirm or deny is, to that extent, disapplied.[23]

(6) In relation to:

---

[19] FOIA ss 30(3), 32(2), 35(3), 37(2), 39(2) and 40(5A), respectively.

[20] FOIA ss 24(2), 34(2), 41(2), 42(2) and 44(2), respectively.

[21] FOIA ss 22(2), 23(5) and 27(4)(b), respectively.

[22] FOIA ss 22(A)(2), 26(3), 27(4)(a), 28(3), 29(2), 31(1), 33(3), 36(3), 38(2) and 43(3), respectively.

[23] FOIA s 40(5B).

(a) information accessible to a requester by other means; or
(b) information that constitutes a trade secret,

there is no disapplication of the duty to confirm or deny the existence of such information.[24]

The existential regime in relation to 'environmental information'[25] is simpler and more limited. To the extent that confirmation or denial that the public authority holds the requested information would involve the disclosure of information that would adversely affect international relations, defence, national security or public safety, and that disclosure would not satisfy the public interest balancing test, then the public authority may issue a notice neither confirming nor denying that it holds the requested information.[26] Under the data protection regime, exemption from the duty to advise that personal data answering the terms of the request are being processed by the public authority[27] turns generally on whether the exemption is a necessary and proportionate means of safeguarding one of the protected interests listed in Article 23(1) of the GDPR.[28]

5– 006 Exemption – FOI(S)A

There is no discrete duty in FOI(S)A to confirm or deny the existence of information answering the terms of a request. A Scottish public authority nevertheless can, in certain circumstances, reply to a request for information by neither confirming or denying the existence of the information, or some of the information, sought.[29] The ability to do so does not, of course, depend upon the existence of the information sought: to so confine it would rob the provision of its efficacy. The exercise involves assuming that the sought information exists (irrespective of whether or not it does). If, on that assumed basis, the public authority could give a refusal notice on the basis that that information would be exempt by virtue of:

— its disclosure substantially prejudicing relations between administrations within the United Kingdom;
— it relating to the formulation of Scottish Administration policy, Ministerial communications, the provision of advice by Law Officers or the operation of any Ministerial private office;
— its disclosure substantially prejudicing the effective conduct of public affairs;
— its exemption being required to safeguard national security;
— its disclosure being substantially prejudicial to the defence of the nation or the effectiveness of the armed forces;
— its disclosure being substantially prejudicial to relations between the United Kingdom and another state or an international organisation, or the interests of the United Kingdom abroad;
— it constituting a trade secret;
— its disclosure being substantially prejudicial to commercial interests of any person, the economic interests of the United Kingdom or any part of it, or to the financial interests of any administration within the United Kingdom;
— it having been held for the purposes of a criminal investigation;
— its disclosure being substantially prejudicial to law enforcement;
— its disclosure endangering the physical or mental health or safety of an individual;

24 FOIA ss 21 and 43(1), respectively.

25 As to the meaning of which, see §17– 011.

26 EIR reg 12(6).

27 That is, GDPR Art 15 and DPA 2018 s 45(1)(a).

28 See further DPA 2018 ss 26, 45(4) and Schs 2-4.

29 FOI(S)A s 18(1); EI(S)R reg 10(8).

or

— it relating to communications with Her Majesty or other members of the Royal Family, or the Royal Household, or to the conferring of honours by the Crown,[30]

then the public authority may proceed to consider whether confirming or denying the existence of the information would be contrary to the public interest.[31] If confirmation or denial would be so contrary to the public interest, the public authority is permitted to give the applicant a refusal notice that neither discloses that it holds the sought information nor sets out its reasoning in relation to the public interest.[32] Under the EI(S)R, to the extent that a confirmation or denial that the public authority holds the requested information would involve the disclosure of information that would adversely affect international relations, defence, national security or public safety, and that disclosure would not satisfy the public interest balancing test, then the public authority may issue a notice neither confirming nor denying that it holds the requested information.[33]

3. THE DISCRETION TO MAINTAIN AN EXEMPTION[34]

5– 007 Introduction

The Freedom of Information Act 2000 opens by describing an unrestricted entitlement to be informed as to the existence of, and to have communicated, information held by a public authority.[35] These broadly-described entitlements are shaped by a series of exemptions, some of which involve a consideration of the public interest. Provided that it has power to disclose information that it holds, the applicability of an exemption, whether an absolute one or a qualified one, does not preclude the public authority from otherwise disclosing the information: a 'discretionary disclosure'. It simply means that the applicant has no entitlement under FOIA to the disclosure of that information. The Act expressly affirms this position.[36] In relation to central government departments it has occasionally been suggested that they may disclose and disseminate information under a prerogative power of the Crown.[37] Alternatively, the power to disclose and disseminate information may be seen as a common law power possessed by the Crown by virtue of its legal personality as a corporation sole.[38] Regardless of Crown status, all

---

30 FOI(S)A ss 28, 29, 30, 31(1), 31(4), 32, 33(1)(a), 33(1)(b) and 33(2), 34, 35, 39(1) and 41 respectively.

31 FOI(S)A s 18(1).

32 FOI(S)A s 18(2).

33 EI(S)R reg 10(8).

34 See further §§20– 036 to 20– 038.

35 FOIA s 1(1). And similarly: FOI(S)A s 1(1), in relation to information held by Scottish public authorities; EIR reg 5(1), in relation to environmental information; EI(S)R reg 5(1), in relation to environmental information held by Scottish public authorities. Under the GDPR Art 15 and DPA 2018 s 45(1)(b), the entitlement is to personal data of which the applicant is the data subject.

36 FOIA s 78; FOI(S)A s 66. This provision overtly recognises that the Act is not a complete code but applies in conjunction with other rules of English law dealing with disclosure: *Kennedy v Charity Commission* [2014] UKSC 20, [2015] AC 455 at [156] per Lord Sumption See also FOIA s 17, and FOI(S)A s 16(1), which speak of 'relying' on a 'claim' that information is exempt information, that the duty to confirm or deny does not arise and that the public interest is against disclosure. The EIR, the EI(S)R and the GDPR contain no equivalent. The FOIA resembles, in this respect, the Freedom of Information Act 1982 (Cth of Aust) and Official Information Act 1982 (New Zealand), but differs from those in the Access to Information Act, (1982) (Canada) and the Freedom of Information Act 2014 (Ireland) which spell out circumstances in which a request may be refused and circumstances in which a request must be refused.

37 *Jenkins v AG* (1971) *The Times*, August 14 (issue of a pamphlet on the common market); *R v Secretary of State for the Environment, ex p Greenwich London Borough Council* [1989] COD 530 (DC) (publication of a leaflet about the 'poll tax').

38 *Malone v Metropolitan Police Commissioner* [1979] Ch 344, sub nom *Malone v Metropolitan Police Commissioner (No 2)* [1979]

public authorities will also have power to disclose information where this is expressly provided for by statute or is necessarily incidental or conducive to the exercise of another statutory, prerogative or common law function:[39] subject, of course, to any countervailing restrictions on disclosure:

(a) Some legislative provisions *prohibit* the disclosure of certain information to certain people at certain times.[40]

(b) Some statutory regimes provide that disclosure is *unlawful* outside the circumstances mandated by the legislation. The most significant such regime is that imposed by the GDPR and DPA 2018.[41]

(c) Disclosure may interfere with a person's private life and, if not justified, may contravene Article 8 of the ECHR.[42]

(d) Disclosure may be unlawful because it would breach some common law or equitable duty, such as respecting confidentiality, whether arising under contract or otherwise.

The power to make a voluntary disclosure may be precluded by a statutory bar or by a comprehensive statutory regime which provides for similar disclosures subject to specific requirements and which must be read as displacing any more general power to act outside that regime.[43]

5–008 Nature of discretion

Other than perhaps through its long title, the Act does not expressly encourage the discretionary disclosure of information.[44] Some encouragement can be found in the statutory recognition of a public interest in disclosing exempt information, at least in relation to qualified exemptions.[45] The decision to provide discretionary disclosure of information is distinct from the conclusion that results from weighing the public interest in maintaining a qualified exemption against the public interest in disclosing the information.[46] Other than in relation to

---

2 All ER 620; *R v Secretary of State for Health, ex p C* [2000] 1 FLR 627 (CA); *Shrewsbury & Atcham Borough Council & anor v Secretary of State for Communities & Local Government & anor* [2008] EWCA Civ 148, [2008] 3 All ER 548 at [44]-[48]; *R (New London College Ltd) v Secretary of State for the Home Department* [2013] UKSC 51, [2013] 1 WLR 2358 at [28].

39 *Electoral Commission v Good Law Project* [2019] EWCA Civ 1938 at [21]-[28]; *R (W, X, Y, Z) v Secretary of State for Health* [2015] EWCA Civ 1034, [2016] 1 WLR 698 at [68].

40 See further §20–037.

41 See, generally, Chapters 7 to 16 and 33.

42 See further §20–037.

43 *R v Liverpool City Council, ex p Baby Products Association* [2000] BLGR 171, 2 LGR 689; *AG v De Keyser's Royal Hotel Ltd* [1920] AC 508; *R v SSHD, ex p Fire Brigades Union* [1995] 2 AC 513.

44 Compare EIR reg 12(2); EI(S)R reg 10(2). Compare also Freedom of Information Act 1982 s 3A (Cth of Aust), which expressly records that the Act is not intended to discourage the disclosure of information otherwise than under the Act, including information that is exempt under the Act.

45 FOIA s 2(2); FOI(S)A s 2(1). Amendments to the Bill that would have recorded that the purpose of the Act was to encourage the provision of information by public authorities to the public were unsuccessful: Hansard HL vol 617 cols 886-888 (17 October 2000). Lord Falconer of Thoroton (the Minister of State, Cabinet Office) said that a purpose clause was not 'appropriate': Hansard HL vol 617 col 898 (17 October 2000). He later said: 'We make it clear, and made it clear in Committee, that what we are interested in seeking to achieve is a change of culture in relation to freedom of information... [the Government's amendments] put beyond doubt the Government's resolve that information must be disclosed except where there is an overriding public interest in keeping specific information confidential. Perhaps I may repeat that: information must be disclosed except where there is an overriding public interest in keeping specific information confidential.' — Hansard HL vol 619 col 143 (14 November 2000). See §1–016.

46 See FOIA ss 17 and FOI(S)A s 16(1), from which it is tolerably clear that a public authority makes a decision whether to rely both on the applicability of a provision in Pt II and on the result of the public interest weighing exercise.

information the disclosure of which is unlawful,[47] a public authority does not require a statutory mandate to disclose information held by it.[48] It is an ordinary incident of holding information that the person holding it may choose to disclose it to others. A public authority may, however, be constrained by other considerations, most notably the effect of any disclosure upon either the public generally or specific individuals.[49]

5–009 Discretionary disclosure - scope

It is nevertheless difficult to see much scope for discretionary disclosure under FOIA, certainly in relation to information that is not required to be disclosed on the basis of a qualified exemption: the public authority will necessarily already have concluded that the public interest in maintaining the exemption outweighs the public interest in disclosing the information.[50] In relation to environmental information, although the regime provides express encouragement to make it available to the public by electronic means which are easily accessible and for public authorities to 'take reasonable steps to organise the information relevant to [their] functions with a view to the active dissemination to the public of the information', that general duty only applies to information that would be required to be disclosed if a request were made.[51]

5–010 Discretionary disclosure - waiver

A discretionary disclosure of information may impinge upon the subsequent ability of a public authority to rely on a claim[52] of exemption or exclusion in relation to similar requests for information. Elsewhere it has been held that a decision not to maintain any of the available grounds of exemption and to release information that could properly be withheld does not prevent the subsequent maintenance of grounds of exemption.[53] In the United States, the starting-point is that an agency may make a discretionary disclosure of material that is exempt under FOIA without undue concern that it will be impairing its ability subsequently to invoke applicable exemptions in relation to like information. Notions of waiver have usually been resisted on the basis that they would tend to thwart the purpose of the Act:

> Implying such a waiver could tend to inhibit agencies from making any disclosures other than those explicitly required by law because voluntary release of documents exempt from disclosure requirements would expose other documents [of a related nature] to risk of disclosure. An agency would have an incentive to refuse to release all exempt documents if it wished to retain an exemption for any documents...[R]eadily finding waiver of confidentiality for exempt documents would tend to thwart the [FOI Act's] underlying statutory purpose, which is to implement a policy of broad disclosure of government records.[54]

---

[47] Whether because it is defamatory, a breach of copyright, a breach of confidentiality, a breach of privacy rights, a breach of the GDPR or DPA 2018 or contravenes a statutory proscription against disclosure.

[48] *AG v Guardian Newspapers Ltd (No 2)* [1990] 1 AC 109 at 256: 'The general rule is that anyone is entitled to communicate anything he pleases to anyone else, by speech or in writing or in any other way.'

[49] See further §§20– 036 to 20– 038.

[50] The House of Commons Select Committee appeared to consider that there was scope for discretionary disclosure in relation to purely class-based exemptions: House of Commons, *Public Administration — Third Report* (Cm 4355, 1999) para 60 (see Ch 1 n 68).

[51] EIR reg 4; cf EI(S)R reg 3(3).

[52] See FOIA s 17 and FOI(S)A s 16(1). See *Mitchell v IC*, IT, 10 October 2005 at [22].

[53] *Re Lordsvale Finance Ltd v Department of Treasury* (1985) 9 ALD 16, 3 AAR 301 (Australia).

[54] *Mobil Oil Corp v Environmental Protection Agency*, 879 F 2d 698 (9th Cir 1989), where the applicant argued that by making a discretionary disclosure of certain records that could have been withheld under the FOI Act, the agency had waived its right to invoke that exemption for a group of related records. The Court did hold that the release of the documents amounted to a waiver of the exemptions for those documents so released. Similarly: *Nationwide Building Maintenance Inc v Sampson*, 559 F 2d 704 at 712 (DC Cir 1977) ('The FOI Act should not be construed so as to put the federal bureaucracy in a defensive or hostile position with respect to the Act's spirit of open

Although it is possible for a claim of waiver to meet with success, such claims have been met with a preliminary requirement that the applicant establish that the exempt information sought duplicates or sufficiently matches the information that previously has been voluntarily disclosed.[55] Moreover, in order to found a waiver, the previous disclosure must have been an authorised one[56] and it must have been made voluntarily.[57]

5– 011 Discretionary disclosure - effect

There is a distinction between the effect of discretionary disclosure upon the subsequent invocation of a purely class-based exemption and the subsequent invocation of a prejudice-based exemption. In the former case, previous disclosure of like information does not impede subsequent information from falling within the terms of the exemption. In the latter case, the exemption requires that disclosure 'would or would be likely to' cause some prejudice. The requirement that it 'cause' or 'be likely to cause' prejudice may be lost by the earlier disclosure of like information.[58] Similarly, discretionary disclosure may impinge upon a subsequent weighing of the public interest in maintaining an exemption in respect of like information.

5– 012 Other consequences

In granting discretionary disclosure, a public authority will not enjoy any protection should that disclosure represent a publication of defamatory matter. That protection only applies to publication effected by a communication of information under FOIA.[59] Other statutory protections may also only be engaged where disclosure is pursuant to the statutory duty imposed by s 1.[60] Where a public authority decides to give discretionary disclosure it may charge for the cost of the communication of that information.[61]

5– 013 Review of discretionary disclosure

A decision not to effect a voluntary disclosure will not engage the appeal structure set out in FOIA.[62] Such a decision is theoretically justiciable by judicial review, but other than in relation to an unjustifiably selective discretionary disclosure of exempt information, it is questionable whether there is much scope for judicial review of a refusal to provide discretionary disclosure.

---

government and liberal disclosure of information.'); *Mehl v Environmental Protection Agency*, 797 F Supp 43 at 47 (DDC 1992) ('A contrary rule would create an incentive against voluntary disclosure of information.'); *Greenberg v United States Department of Treasury*, 10 F Supp (2d) at 23-24 (DDC 1998).

55 *Public Citizen v Department of State*, 276 F 3d 634 at 645 (DC Cir 2002); *Afshar v Department of State*, 702 F 2d 1125 at 1132 (DC Cir 1983).

56 *Public Citizen Health Research Group v FDA*, 953 F Supp 400 (DDC 1996) (no waiver where material accidentally released); *Simmons v United States Department of Justice*, 796 F 2d 709 (4th Cir 1986) (unauthorised disclosure does not constitute waiver); similarly *Medina-Hincapie v Department of State*, 700 F 2d 73 (DC Cir 1983).

57 *Lead Industry Association v OSHA*, 610 F 2d 70 (2d Cir 1979).

58 As, eg, in *John Connor Press Associates v IC*, IT, 25 January 2006, where the disclosure of certain commercial information relating to a particular transaction precluded exemption under FOIA s 43(2), for the remaining commercial information relating to that transaction.

59 FOIA s 79; FOI(S)A s 67.

60 See further §§20– 034 to 20– 035.

61 FOIA s 13(1)(b); FOI(S)A s 13(1)(b). The provisions do not enable the public authority to charge for the cost of locating the information, determining whether the information is exempt information or considering the public interest: see §§22– 015 to 22– 017. A voluntary disclosure of environmental information is not a disclosure under the EIR (because of regs 4(3) and 5(1)), but constitutes the disclosure of exempt information under the FOIA (because of s 39). In relation to environmental information held by Scottish public authorities, a voluntary disclosure will be under the EI(S)R reg 3(3). There is no power to charge for the provision of such information.

62 And similarly: FOI(S)A; EIR; EI(S)R. So held in Australia in relation to the analogous s 14 Freedom of Information Act 1982: *Re Waterford and Department of Treasury* (1983) 5 ALD 193; *Re Waterford and Department of Health* (1983) 5 ALN N139. Section 14 has since been repealed, but see now s 3A.

5– 014 Non-reliance upon an exemption

Where there is more than one ground upon which a public authority can rely for the disapplication of its duty to confirm or deny or of its duty to disclose information, it may when giving a refusal notice choose not to rely on one or more of those grounds of exemption.[63] The distinction between this and discretionary disclosure is that here the public authority maintains that confirmation or denial, or that disclosure, of the information should be resisted. The public authority, in choosing not to rely on a particular exemption, makes no concession other than as to its assessment of the most convenient or apposite exemption. Moreover, by having not disclosed the information, it will remain open for the disclosure of the information to have, or to be likely to have, a prescribed prejudicial effect. Accordingly, the decision of a public authority not to invoke a potential ground of exemption does not preclude a subsequent invocation of that ground of exemption, either in relation to a subsequent like request or in the enforcement or appeal procedure.[64]

4. CLASSIFICATION OF EXEMPTIONS

5– 015 Introduction

Part II of FOIA enumerates discrete grounds upon which a public authority is excused both from its duty to confirm or deny that it holds the information sought and from its duty to disclose that information.[65] A classification of the different grounds for dispensation from the duty to confirm or deny has been considered above.[66] More generally and in relation to both duties, FOIA divides each of the exemptions into absolute exemptions and qualified exemptions. Each exemption can also be characterised either as being a purely class-based exemption or as being a prejudice-based exemption. Depending on the circumstances, the applicability of an exemption will be either a question of law or a question of mixed fact and law.[67]

5– 016 Absolute exemptions

Absolute exemptions are defined in FOIA[68] to be those conferred in respect of:

— information that is reasonably accessible to the applicant otherwise than under FOIA;[69]

— information held by the requested public authority that was directly or indirectly supplied to it by, or that relates to, any of the defined security bodies;[70]

---

63 FOIA s 17(1); FOI(S)A s 16(1).

64 In relation to a public authority relying in a Tribunal appeal upon an exemption not previously relied upon, see §45– 016.

65 FOIA ss 21-44; FOI(S)A ss 25-41. Pt 2 of the latter Act relates only to exemption from the duty to disclose information. In relation to the circumstances in which a Scottish public authority is excused from revealing in a refusal notice whether the information sought exists, see §3– 005(1). In relation to the classification of exceptions under the environmental information regime, see §19– 001. In relation to the classification of exemptions under the data protection regime, see Chapters 9, 10 and 16.

66 See §5– 005.

67 *DWP v IC*, IT, 5 March 2007 at [16].

68 FOIA s 2(3); FOI(S)A s 2(2).

69 FOIA s 21(1); FOI(S)A s 25(1).

70 FOIA s 23(1). This does not constitute an absolute exemption in relation to information held by a Scottish public authority.

- information held by the requested public authority only by virtue of that information being contained in a formal document filed with a court or tribunal, in a formal document served for the purposes of court or tribunal proceedings, or in a formal document created by a court or by staff of a court;[71]
- information held by the requested public authority only by virtue of it being contained in a document placed in the custody of a person conducting an inquiry or arbitration, or in a document created by a person conducting an inquiry or arbitration, for the purposes of the inquiry or arbitration;[72]
- information for which exemption is required for the purpose of avoiding an infringement of the privileges of either House of Parliament;[73]
- information held by the House of Commons or the House of Lords that, in the reasonable opinion of the Speaker of the House of Commons or the Clerk of the Parliaments respectively, if disclosed under FOIA, would or would be likely to:
  - prejudice the convention of the collective responsibility of Ministers of the Crown, etc;
  - inhibit the free and frank provision of advice or exchange of views for the purposes of deliberation; or
  - otherwise prejudice the effective conduct of public affairs;[74]
- information relating to communications with the Sovereign or the heir to or person second in line to the Throne;[75]
- information that constitutes personal data of which the applicant is the data subject;[76]
- information that is not unstructured manual data but which constitutes personal data of which the applicant is not the data subject, the disclosure of which would contravene a data protection principle;[77]
- information that is unstructured manual data and constitutes personal data of which the applicant is not the data subject, the disclosure of which would contravene one of the data protection principles disregarding the exemptions from the data protection principles granted by s 24(1) of the DPA 2018;[78]
- information obtained by the public authority from any other person (including another public authority) the disclosure of which would constitute an actionable breach of confidence by the public authority;[79] and
- information the disclosure of which is prohibited by or under an enactment, is incompatible with any EU obligation or would constitute a contempt of court.[80]

Under the environmental information regime, there is only an absolute exception to the extent

[71] FOIA s 32(1); FOI(S)A s 37(1)(a).

[72] FOIA s 32(2); FOI(S)A s 37(1)(b).

[73] FOIA s 34(1). This does not constitute an absolute exemption in relation to information held by a Scottish public authority.

[74] FOIA s 36(2). This does not constitute an absolute exemption in relation to information held by a Scottish public authority.

[75] FOIA s 37(1)(a)-(ab). This does not constitute an absolute exemption in relation to information held by a Scottish public authority.

[76] FOIA s 40(1); FOI(S)A s 38(1)(a). In relation to information held by a Scottish public authority, personal census information and a deceased person's health record are also absolute exemptions: s 38(1)(c) and (d).

[77] FOIA s 40(3A)(a); FOI(S)A s 38(2A)(a).

[78] FOIA s 40(3A)(b); FOI(S)A s 38(2A)(b).

[79] FOIA s 41(1); FOI(S)A s 36(2).

[80] FOIA s 44(1); FOI(S)A s 26.

that the requested information includes personal data or where disclosure would involve an infringement of the privileges of a House of Parliament.[81] None of the exemptions under the data protection regime involves an express consideration of the public interest. Where information satisfies a provision conferring absolute exemption, that will be sufficient to disapply both the duty to confirm or deny the existence of that information and the duty to disclose that information.[82] Subject to any proscription against disclosure, a public authority may, in its discretion, nevertheless decide to disclose the information.[83]

5– 017 Qualified exemptions

The remaining exemptions, which may for convenience be termed 'qualified exemptions', are those conferred in respect of:

— information whose disclosure would or would be likely to prejudice a programme of research which is continuing with a view to publication;[84]
— information intended for future publication;[85]
— information for which exemption from the duties is required for the purpose of safeguarding national security;[86]
— information whose disclosure would or would be likely to prejudice the defence of the British Isles;[87]
— information whose disclosure would or would be likely to prejudice relations between the United Kingdom and any other state or international organisation or to prejudice the interests of the United Kingdom abroad;[88]
— confidential information obtained from a foreign state or from an international organisation or court;[89]
— information whose disclosure would or would be likely to prejudice relations between administrations within the United Kingdom;[90]
— information the disclosure of which would or would be likely to prejudice the economic interests of the United Kingdom or any part of it or the financial interests of any administration within the United Kingdom;[91]
— information held by a public authority for the purposes of a criminal investigation or proceedings;[92]
— information the disclosure of which would or would be likely to prejudice the prevention or detection of crime, etc;[93]

81 EIR regs 3(4), 5(3), 12(1) and 12(3). In Scotland, there is an absolute exemption only for personal data: EI(S)R regs 10(1), 10(3) and 11(1).

82 FOIA ss 2(1)(a) and 2(1)(b); FOI(S)A s 2(1)(a)EIR reg 12(6)-(7); EI(S)R reg 10(7)-(8). In relation to information held by a Scottish public authority it will not automatically lead to that public authority being excused from revealing in a refusal notice whether the information sought exists: see §5– 006.

83 See §§20– 034 to 20– 035 and 5– 007 to 5– 009.

84 FOIA s 22A; FOI(S)A s 27(2).

85 FOIA s 22(1); FOI(S)A s 27(1).

86 FOIA s 24(1); FOI(S)A s 31(1).

87 FOIA s 26(1); FOI(S)A s 31(4).

88 FOIA s 27(1); FOI(S)A s 32(1)(a).

89 FOIA s 27(2); FOI(S)A s 32(1)(b).

90 FOIA s 28(1); FOI(S)A s 28(1).

91 FOIA s 29(1); FOI(S)A s 33(2).

92 FOIA s 30(1); FOI(S)A s 34(1).

93 FOIA s 31(1); FOI(S)A s 35(1).

— information that would or would be likely to prejudice the exercise of an auditing body's audit functions;[94]
— information relating to government policy, Ministerial communications, the provision of advice by Law Officers, or the operation of any Ministerial private office;[95]
— information, other than that held by the House of Commons or the House of Lords that, in the reasonable opinion of a qualified person, if disclosed under FOIA, would or would be likely to:
  — prejudice the convention of the collective responsibility of Ministers of the Crown, etc;
  — inhibit the free and frank provision of advice or exchange of views for the purposes of deliberation; or
  — otherwise prejudice the effective conduct of public affairs;[96]
— where held by a Scottish public authority, information relating to communications with Her Majesty or the Royal Household;[97]
— where held by a non-Scottish public authority, information relating to communications with members of the Royal Family other than the Sovereign or the heir or second in line to the Throne, or with the Royal Household, or to the conferring of honours by the Crown;[98]
— information the disclosure of which would or would be likely to endanger the physical or mental health of an individual or endanger an individual's safety;[99]
— environmental information;[100]
— information in respect of which a claim to legal professional privilege could be maintained;[101]
— information that constitutes a trade secret or the disclosure of which would or would be likely to prejudice the commercial interests of any person.[102]

In relation to environmental information held by a public authority, each of the exceptions set out in reg 12(4)-(5) is qualified.[103]

5– 018 Principal significance

As noted above, where information satisfies a provision conferring absolute exemption, that will be sufficient to disapply the duty to disclose that information.[104] And similarly a provision conferring absolute exclusion from the duty to confirm or deny the existence of information. Where information satisfies a provision conferring qualified exemption then:

(a) the duty to confirm or deny will be disapplied where, in all the circumstances of the

---

94 FOIA s 33(2); FOI(S)A s 40.

95 FOIA s 35(1); FOI(S)A s 29(1).

96 FOIA s 36(2). FOI(S)A s 30.

97 FOI(S)A s 41.

98 FOIA s 37(1).

99 FOIA s 38(1); FOI(S)A s 39(1).

100 FOIA s 39(1); FOI(S)A s 39(2).

101 FOIA s 42(1); FOI(S)A s 36(1).

102 FOIA s 43(1) and (2); FOI(S)A s 33(1).

103 EIR reg 12(1). In relation to environmental information held by a Scottish public authority, similarly under EI(S)R regs 10(1), (4) and (5).

104 FOIA ss 2(1) and (2); FOI(S)A s 2(1); EIR reg 12(1); EI(S)R reg 10(1). Scottish public authorities are not under a separate duty to confirm or deny the existence of information sought under FOI(S)A.

case, the public interest in maintaining the exclusion of the duty to confirm or deny outweighs the public interest in disclosing whether the public authority holds the information; and

(b) the duty to disclose will be disapplied where, in all the circumstances of the case, the public interest in maintaining the exemption outweighs the public interest in disclosing the information.

That which is being balanced thus differs according to the duty being disapplied. Although the public interest in 'maintaining the exclusion of the duty to confirm or deny' may be thought to be less pressing than the public interest in 'maintaining the exemption', the counterbalancing public interest in 'disclosing whether the public authority holds the information' may be thought to be correspondingly less compelling than the public interest in 'disclosing the information'. The public interest in maintaining the exclusion of the duty to confirm or deny will involve a consideration of the terms of the request. A highly specific request is more likely than a general request to result in the public interest in maintaining the exclusion of the duty to confirm or deny outweighing the public interest in disclosing whether the public authority holds the information: answering a highly specific request can effectively amount to a disclosure of the information sought. The public interest in maintaining the exemption from disclosure will, on the other hand, involve a greater emphasis on the information itself, rather than on the terms of the request.

5–019 Time-limit ramifications

The distinction between the two categories of exemption has significance for the time within which a public authority must reply to a request. The time-limit for complete compliance with a request under FOIA varies according to whether there are any qualified grounds of exemption applicable to the information sought. To the extent that a public authority, in claiming a disapplication of the duty to confirm or deny or to communicate particular information, relies exclusively upon one or more absolute exemptions, the public authority must give notice of its refusal within 20 working days.[105] To the extent that a public authority, in claiming a disapplication of the duty to confirm or deny or to communicate particular information, relies upon one or more qualified exemptions, the public authority must first, within 20 working days, give notice specifying the exemption relied upon and the reason it applies, but advising the applicant that no decision in relation to the weighing of the public interest has yet been reached and giving an estimate of when it expects that exercise to be completed.[106] The public authority then has a reasonable time within which to carry out the exercise of weighing the public interest[107] and a further reasonable time to give the applicant notice of that decision.[108] In relation to environmental information held by a public authority, the time limit is set at 20 working days regardless of whether a consideration of the public interest is involved.[109]

5–020 Enforcement ramifications

The distinction between the two categories of exemption also has significance for the ability of certain public authorities to shield themselves from decision notices and enforcement notices.

---

105 FOIA ss 17(1) and 10(1)); FOI(S)A ss 17(1) and 10(1). See §22–026.

106 FOIA ss 17 and 10(1). No additional time for responding is provided under the FOI(S)A. See further §§22–020 to 22–027.

107 FOIA s 10(3).

108 FOIA s 17(3).

109 EIR reg 5(2); EI(S)R reg 5(2). The environmental information regime does, however, provide for an extension of time from 20 to 40 working days, but availability of this extension depends upon the complexity of the request and the amount of environmental information requested: EIR reg 7(1); EI(S)R reg 7(1).

Certain core, central government public authorities, when served with a decision notice or an enforcement notice, may give the Information Commissioner a certificate under s 53(2).[110] In general terms, the effect of the certificate is to shield that public authority from its duty to comply with a decision notice or an enforcement notice.[111] In relation to the communication obligation, the ability to serve such a notice is confined to where there has been a failure to comply with the duty to communicate in respect of exempt information. In relation to the duty to confirm or deny, the ability to serve such a notice is confined to where there has been a failure to comply with the duty to confirm or deny in respect of information falling within any provision of Part II stating that that duty does not arise. In those circumstances, the 'accountable person' of the public authority can give the Information Commissioner a certificate stating that he has on reasonable grounds formed the opinion that, in respect of the request, there has been no failure to comply with the s 1 duty. Because certification can only apply to a decision notice or an enforcement notice that relates to a failure to comply with the s 1 duty, the issue of whether the information falls within any provision of Part II is outside the certification process under s 53. The s 53(2) certificate is directed to the accountable person's opinion in relation to the weighing of the public interest: it is only that weighing which can reasonably induce an accountable person to form the opinion that there has been no failure to comply with the s 1(1) duties where the information is exempt information. In short, the effect of a s 53(2) certificate is confined to shielding certain central government public authorities from the Information Commissioner's determination that information falling within a qualified exemption ought to be disclosed in the public interest.[112]

5–021 Implicit ramifications

Underlying each of the exemptions in Part II of FOIA is a public interest against the disclosure of information falling within the terms of the exemption. It is implicit in the creation of the qualified exemptions that the public interest in a public authority confirming or denying that it holds certain information and in it communicating that information are each capable of outweighing the underlying public interest in maintaining each of the exemptions. Approximately half of the qualified exemptions, in order to be engaged, expressly require that disclosure of the information under the Act would cause, or would be likely to cause, some form of prejudice.[113] The existence of that prejudice or of the likelihood of that prejudice will not automatically represent an adequate counterbalancing public interest against disclosure, as that would effectively elevate the exemption into an absolute exemption.[114] FOIA recognises that

---

110 FOI(S)A s 52(2); EIR regs 15(1), 18(2)-(3); EI(S)R regs 12(1), 17(2).

111 See §19–005.

112 As is confirmed in *Explanatory Notes to the FOIA*, para 180. This was also confirmed to Parliament by Lord Falconer of Thoroton (the Minister of State, Cabinet Office) who said: 'Contrary to what my noble friend Lord Brennan said, it is worth noting that the effect of this provision is not that any decision of the information commissioner can be overridden: the only decision of the information commissioner that can be overridden is one on the balance of the public interest under cl 13. If, for example, the information commissioner determined that something was not covered by an exemption, then the ministerial override would never apply. Once it is not exempt, disclosure is automatic. The ministerial override under cl 13 applies only where something is exempt and the Minister or the public authority concerned has refused to override the exemption in the public interest." — Hansard HL vol 618 cols 445-446 (25 October 2000). See also: Hansard HL vol 619 col 258 (14 November 2000) (Lord Falconer of Thoroton).

113 FOIA ss 22A(1), 24(1), 26(1), 27(1), 28(1), 29(1), 31(1), 33(2) and (3), 36(2), 38(1) and 43(2); FOI(S)A ss 28(1), 30, 31(1), 31(4), 32(1)(a), 33(1)(b), 33(2), 35(1), 39(1) and 40; EIR reg 12(5); EI(S)R reg 10(5). The requirement in relation to information held by a Scottish public authority is that the prejudice be a 'substantial' one before the exemption is engaged and before considering whether nevertheless the public interest in disclosing the information is not outweighed by the public interest in maintaining the exemption.

114 See generally: Hansard HL vol 617 cols 901-905, 912-913, and 923-924 (17 October 2000) (Lord Falconer of Thoroton, the Minister of State at the Cabinet Office, during Committee Stage of the FOI Bill in the House of Lords and introducing the amendment that resulted in s 2). Questioned as to what a public official was to do when

where a qualified exemption is engaged, the public interest in the maintenance of that exemption is not of fixed weight, but that it will vary according to 'all the circumstances of the case'. Similarly, FOIA recognises that whilst there always exists a public interest in disclosing whether a public authority holds information and in disclosing that information, the weight to be afforded to this interest will vary according to 'all the circumstances of the case'.[115]

5–022 Purely class-based exemptions

Independently of the statutory distinction between absolute and qualified exemptions, it is possible to characterise some of the exemptions as purely class based,[116] whereas others require some form of prejudice before the exemption is engaged. Purely class-based exemptions are those conferred in respect of:

— information that is reasonably accessible to the applicant otherwise than under FOIA;[117]
— information intended for future publication;[118]
— information held by the requested public authority that was directly or indirectly supplied to it by, or that relates to, any of the defined security bodies;[119]
— confidential information obtained from a foreign state or from an international organisation or court;[120]
— information held by a public authority for the purposes of a criminal investigation or proceedings;[121]
— information held by the requested public authority only by virtue of that information being contained in a formal document filed with a court or tribunal, in a formal document served for the purposes of court or tribunal proceedings, or in a formal document created by a court or by staff of a court;[122]
— information held by the requested public authority only by virtue of it being contained in a document placed in the custody of a person conducting an inquiry or arbitration, or in a document created by a person conducting an inquiry or arbitration, for the purposes of the inquiry or arbitration;[123]
— information for which exemption is required for the purpose of avoiding an

required to weigh the competing public interests, he said (col 921): 'As far as public interest between disclosure on the one hand and the maintenance of exemption on the other is concerned, it has to be looked at objectively. One looks at the impact of disclosure, that is, making it public. What is the impact of the exemption being maintained? That should be looked at objectively rather than in terms of whatever the motive may be of the person applying. That does not mean that the motive of the person applying may not coincide with factors that could be relevant to what damage may be done and what assistance could be served by making the matter public. But individual motives will not be relevant to that.. The FOI Bill as originally introduced (cl 14, later cl 13) required a public authority to consider 'discretionary disclosure' of exempt information: see House of Commons, *Public Administration — Third Report,* (Cm 4355, 1999) para 60 (see Ch 1 n 68).

115 The necessity of carrying out this exercise on a case-by-case basis was acknowledged by Lord Falconer of Thoroton: Hansard HL vol 619 col 831 (22 November 2000).

116 Although the term 'class-based exemption' is not used in the Act, they were so described in the *Explanatory Notes, FOI Act 2000* (see paras 12 and 85) and in House of Commons, *Public Administration — Third Report,* (Cm 4355, 1999) para 60. The following categorisation is consistent with that given in the *Explanatory Notes, FOI Act 2000* and in the *Public Administration — Third Report.*

117 FOIA s 21(1); FOI(S)A s 25(1).

118 FOIA s 22(1); FOI(S)A s 27(1).

119 FOIA s 23(1). This does not constitute an absolute exemption in relation to information held by a Scottish public authority.

120 FOIA s 27(2); FOI(S)A s 32(1)(b).

121 FOIA s 30(1); FOI(S)A s 34(1).

122 FOIA s 32(1); FOI(S)A s 37(1)(a).

123 FOIA s 32(2); FOI(S)A s 37(1)(b).

infringement of the privileges of either House of Parliament;[124]

- information relating to government policy, Ministerial communications, the provision of advice by Law Officers, or the operation of any Ministerial private office;[125]
- information relating to communications with Her Majesty or other members of the Royal Family, or with the Royal Household, or the conferring by the Crown of any honour;[126]
- environmental information;[127]
- information that constitutes personal data;[128]
- information obtained by the public authority from any other person (including another public authority) the disclosure of which would constitute an actionable breach of confidence by the public authority;[129]
- information in respect of which a claim to legal professional privilege could be maintained;[130]
- information that constitutes a trade secret;[131] and
- information the disclosure of which is prohibited by or under an enactment, is incompatible with any EU obligation or would constitute a contempt of court.[132]

A small number of exceptions in the environmental information regime are class-based.[133] In relation to each of these exemptions and exceptions, the fact that the disclosure of the information would be demonstrably harmless will not detract from it being 'exempt information'. Where the exemption is a qualified exemption, that harmlessness may, however, impinge upon the public interest in maintaining the exemption.

5–023 Prejudice-based exemptions

The remaining exemptions all require 'prejudice' in order for the exemption to be engaged; or, in the case of Scotland, 'substantial prejudice'. Prejudice-based exemptions are those conferred in respect of:

- information whose disclosure would or would be likely to prejudice a programme of research which is continuing with a view to publication;[134]
- information for which exemption from the duties is required for the purpose of safeguarding national security;[135]
- information whose disclosure would or would be likely to prejudice the defence of the nation or the effectiveness of the armed forces;[136]

---

124 FOIA s 34(1). This does not constitute an absolute exemption in relation to information held by a Scottish public authority.

125 FOIA s 35(1); FOI(S)A s 29(1).

126 FOIA s 37(1); FOI(S)A s 41.

127 FOIA s 39(1); FOI(S)A s 39(2).

128 FOIA s 40(1); FOI(S)A s 38(1)(a). In relation to information held by a Scottish public authority, personal census information and a deceased person's health record are also absolute exemptions: FOI(S)A s 38(1)(c) and (d).

129 FOIA s 41(1); FOI(S)A s 36(2).

130 FOIA s 42(1); FOI(S)A s 36(1).

131 FOIA s 43(1); FOI(S)A s 33(1)(a).

132 FOIA s 44(1); FOI(S)A s 26.

133 EIR regs 3(4), 5(3), 12(3), 12(4)(d) and 12(4)(e); EI(S)R regs 10(3), 10(4)(d), 10(4)(e) and 11(1).

134 FOIA s 22A(1); FOI(S)A s 27(2).

135 FOIA s 24(1); FOI(S)A s 31(1).

136 FOIA s 26(1); FOI(S)A s 31(4).

- information whose disclosure would or would be likely to prejudice relations between the United Kingdom and any other state or international organisation or to prejudice the interests of the United Kingdom abroad;[137]
- information whose disclosure would or would be likely to prejudice relations between administrations within the United Kingdom;[138]
- information the disclosure of which would or would be likely to prejudice the economic interests of the United Kingdom or any part of it, or the financial interests of any administration within it;[139]
- information the disclosure of which would or would be likely to prejudice the prevention or detection of crime, etc;[140]
- information that would or would be likely to prejudice the exercise of an auditing body's audit functions;[141]
- information held by the House of Commons or the House of Lords that, in the reasonable opinion of the Speaker of the House of Commons or the Clerk of the Parliaments respectively, if disclosed under FOIA, would or would be likely to:
    - prejudice the convention of the collective responsibility of Ministers of the Crown, etc;
    - inhibit the free and frank provision of advice or exchange of views for the purposes of deliberation; or
    - otherwise prejudice the effective conduct of public affairs;[142]
- information the disclosure of which would or would be likely to endanger the physical or mental health of an individual or endanger an individual's safety;[143] and
- information the disclosure of which would or would be likely to prejudice the commercial interests of any person.[144]

The majority of exceptions in the environmental information regime are prejudice-based.[145]

5. INTERPRETATION OF EXEMPTIONS AND ONUS

5–024 Introduction

The Freedom of Information Act 2000 does not explicitly specify whether it is for the applicant to show that he has a right to the information requested or for the public authority to show that it is excused from disclosing the information requested; or whether there is a shifting 'onus' of some sort.[146] In this, the Act is no different from most statutes that confer upon an individual a right against a public authority.[147] The environmental information regime does specifically

[137] FOIA s 27(1); FOI(S)A s 32(1)(a).

[138] FOIA s 28(1); FOI(S)A s 28(1).

[139] FOIA s 29(1); FOI(S)A s 33(2).

[140] FOIA s 31(1); FOI(S)A s 35(1).

[141] FOIA s 33(2); FOI(S)A s 40.

[142] FOIA s 36(2); FOI(S)A s 30. This does not constitute an absolute exemption in Scotland.

[143] FOIA s 38(1); FOI(S)A s 39(1).

[144] FOIA s 43(1); FOI(S)A s 33(1)(b).

[145] EIR reg 12(5); EI(S)R reg 10(5).

[146] However, FOIA s 10(3), in speaking of 'if the condition in section 2(1)(b) were satisfied' implies some sort of a burden on the authority. Similarly, FOIA s 17 and FOI(S)A s 16(1), in referring to 'relying on a claim' that any of the provisions in Pt II applies.

[147] The freedom of information legislation of most comparative jurisdictions does specifically state that the onus of

provide that a public authority is to apply a presumption in favour of disclosure.[148] It is unlikely that the difference will make any operative difference.[149] It has been held in the context of a confidentiality claim:

> it is incumbent upon the Crown, in order to restrain disclosure of Government secrets, not only to show that the information is confidential, but also to show that it is in the public interest that it should not be published .... The reason for this additional requirement in cases concerned with Government secrets appears to be that, although in the case of private citizens there is a public interest that confidential information should as such be protected, in the case of Government secrets the mere fact of confidentiality does not alone support such a conclusion, because in a free society there is a continuing public interest that the workings of government should be open to scrutiny and criticism. From this it follows that, in such cases, there must be demonstrated some other public interest which requires that publication should be restrained.[150]

And, in relation to adoption information held by a local authority:

> the bias, if any, should be in favour of allowing access to information rather than concealing information.[151]

These statements predate FOIA. It may be thought that their sentiments are sufficiently embodied within the Act as not to require the application of any gloss to its provisions.

5–025 Onus: exemption information

The scope of the rights given by s 1(1) of FOIA is shaped by whether the information to which a request relates is or is not 'exempt information'. To be exempt information, the information must fit within one or more of the descriptions of exempt information given by the provisions of Part II of the Act. Some of these descriptions involve an identification of some specific sort of prejudice or likely prejudice: matters on which there will often be legitimate differences of view. It is generally considered inappropriate to speak of a formal 'onus of proof' in the exercise of an administrative duty or discretion.[152] The convention is that a public authority is presumed to have properly and duly performed its statutory duties:[153]

> The legal, as contrasted with the evidential, burden being on the applicant to establish his entitlement to relief, [the courts] are entitled and are very willing to assume that the authority has acted in accordance with law, until the contrary is shown. But authorities assist

---

establishing an exemption lies upon the recipient public authority or agency: Freedom of Information Act 1982 ss 3, 55D and 61 (Cth of Australia); Access to Information Act, (1982) (Canada) s 48; Freedom of Information Act 2014 (Ireland) s 22(12)(b). In New Zealand there is a general statement of principle: Official Information Act 1982 (NZ) s 5. This has been held not to create an onus upon the agency seeking to rely upon an exemption: *Commissioner of Police v Ombudsman* [1988] 1 NZLR 385 (CA), on appeal from [1985] 1 NZLR 578. In debate on the FOI Bill, it was thought to be 'seriously defective' in not having a clear presumption in favour of disclosure, with most debate as to presumption concerned with the presumption in relation to the weighing of the aspects of the public interest, rather than the presumption in relation to whether information falls within one or other of the provisions of Pt II of FOIA: Hansard HL vol 619 col 136 (14 November 2000) (Lord Lester of Herne Hill).

148 EIR reg 12(2); EI(S)R reg 10(2)(b).

149 *Guardian Newspapers Ltd and Heather Brooke v IC and BBC*, IT, 8 January 2007 at [82], where the Information Tribunal spoke of a default setting of disclosure. However, there is no such presumption in favour of the release of personal information (*Common Services Agency v IC* [2008] UKHL 47, [2008] 1 WLR 1550 at [7], [68]) and, by parity of reasoning, in any other circumstance where disclosure might impinge upon the rights of a third party.

150 *AG v Guardian Newspapers (No 2)* [1990] 1 AC 109 at 283 (Lord Goff). See also the quotation at §34–028 from *A-G (UK) v Heinemann Publishers Pty Ltd* (1987) 10 NSWLR 86 at 191, 75 ALR 353 at 454.

151 *Birmingham City District Council v O* [1983] 1 AC 578 at 596.

152 *Pye (Oxford) Estates Ltd v Secretary of State for the Environment* [1982] JPL 575 (in relation to a planning appeal). The point has been considered elsewhere at length: *McDonald v Director General of Social Security* (1986) 6 ALD 6; *Lodkowski v Comcare* (1998) 53 ALD 371 at 386; *Re VBN and Prudential Regulatory Authority (No 5)* (2006) 92 ALD 259 at 328-31.

153 *Point of Ayr Collieries Ltd v Lloyd-George* [1943] 2 All ER 546; *Wilover Nominees Ltd v Inland Revenue Commissioners* [1973] 1 WLR 1393 at 1389; *R v Inland Revenue Commissioners, ex p Rossminster* [1980] AC 952 at 1009, 1013; *R v Inland Revenue Commissioners, ex p TC Coombs & Co* [1991] 2 AC 283 at 300.

> neither themselves nor the courts, if their response is a blanket assertion of having acted in accordance with law or one which begs the question. If the issue is whether an authority took a particular factor into account, it will be a sufficient response to show that it did. But if the allegation is that a decision is prima facie irrational and that there are grounds for inquiring whether something immaterial may have been considered or something material omitted from consideration, it really does not help to assert baldly that all relevant matters and no irrelevant matters were taken into consideration without condescending to mention some at least of the principal factors on which the decision was based.[154]

Where a public authority is required to be satisfied of something or to form some opinion, then, absent evidence to the contrary, in public law its say-so that it was satisfied or formed that opinion will generally suffice.[155] The transposition of this principle to the prejudice-based exemptions in the freedom of information regime requires a public authority to make a disinterested assessment of those wider interests, uncoloured by its disinclination to disclose. Although official material leading to the passage of the Act spoke of 'a presumption of openness', there is no such presumption expressed in the Act itself.[156] The short title of FOIA might suggest some sort of presumption of openness, although as an interpretative tool it is of limited use.[157] Nevertheless, the basic scheme of the Act and the language employed suggest that it is for a public authority to demonstrate the applicability of a provision in Part II of the Act before it may rely on that provision.[158] The Tribunal has noted:

> The FOIA, in s 1, conferred an important new fundamental right to information held by public bodies. It is a right subject to exceptions, or conditions as they were termed by Lord Turnbull. Where such an exception is relied on by a public authority, it is for that authority to justify such reliance. If it says there is an absolute exemption, it must demonstrate it. If prejudice is a requisite factor, it must prove it.[159]

The specifying of 'exemptions' from 'a general right of access' implies a requirement that the

---

[154] *R v Lancashire County Council, ex p Huddleston* [1986] 2 All ER 941 at 945-946 (Donaldson MR).

[155] *Wilover Nominees Ltd v Inland Revenue Commissioners* [1973] 1 WLR 1393 at 1389; *Stoke-on-Trent City Council v B&Q (Retail) Ltd* [1984] Ch 1; *R v Inland Revenue Commissioners, ex p TC Coombs & Co* [1991] 2 AC 283 at 299-302.

[156] Cabinet Office, *Your Right to Know. The Government's Proposals for a FOI Act. White Paper* (Cm 3818, 1997) para 3.1. In *R (Rose) v Secretary of State for Health* [2002] 2 FLR 962, [2002] UKHRR 13 at [47] Scott Baker J (in the context of an application by an individual conceived through artificial insemination for information about the donor) said: 'We live in a much more open society than even 20 years ago. Secrecy nowadays has to be justified where previously it did not.'

[157] *Re Vexatious Actions Act 1886, Re Boaler* [1915] 1 KB 21 at 40; *R v Wheatley* [1979] 1 WLR 144 at 147; *Lonrho Ltd v Shell Petroleum Co Ltd (No 2)* [1982] AC 173 at 187.

[158] As noted above, this is expressly required by the environmental information regime: EIR reg 12(2); EI(S)R reg 10(2)(b). See further: *Lin v Commissioner of Police for the Metropolis* [2015] EWHC 2484 (QB), where Green J held that, under the DPA 1998 s 19(1), the burden was on the data controller to show its entitlement to refuse access on the basis of 'significant and weighty grounds and evidence (at [85] and [101]); *Guriev v Community Safety Development (UK) Ltd* [2016] EWHC 643 (QB) at [45].

[159] *DfES v IC and The Evening Standard*, IT, 19 February 2007 at [61]. See further: *Boam v IC*, FTT, 16 May 2016 at [26]. In *Toms v IC*, IT, 19 June 2006 at [2] the Information Tribunal stated that 'the 2000 Act contains a presumption in favour of disclosure.' Similarly: *DTI v IC*, IT, 10 November 2006 at [54]; *Guardian Newspapers Ltd and Heather Brooke v IC and BBC*, IT, 8 January 2007 at [82]-[83]; *DWP v IC*, IT, 5 March 2007 at [25]; *Reith v IC and LB Hammersmith & Fulham*, IT, 1 June 2007 at [41]; *Scotland Office v IC*, IT, 8 August 2008 at [77]; *Bellamy v IC and DBIS*, FTT, 23 February 2010 at [38]; *Dedalus Ltd v IC and Arts Council of England*, FTT, 21 May 2010 at [74(1)] (default setting is in favour of disclosure); *DEFRA v IC and Portman*, FTT, 13 November 2012 at [38(1)]; *Arts and Humanities Research Council v IC and Bimmler*, FTT, 4 December 2012 at [33(1)]. Similarly, the President of the Scottish Court of Session has held that 'as each [provision in Part II] is an exemption to a general entitlement it is for the public authority relying on it to demonstrate that the exemption is engaged.' — *Scottish Ministers v Scottish IC* [2007] CSIH 8, 2007 SCLR 253 at [12]. Where, however, statute precludes disclosure of certain information, there is no presumption in favour of the release of that information: see *Common Services Agency v IC* [2008] UKHL 47, [2008] 1 WLR 1550 at [7], dealing with third party personal data. In relation to exceptions in the environmental information regime, see: *Friends of the Earth v IC and ECGD*, IT, 20 August 2007 at [53]. In *Burgess v IC and Stafford Borough Council*, IT, 7 June 2007 at [43] the Tribunal considered that the express presumption in favour of disclosure in the EIR made them 'significantly different' from the FOIA: see further §19– 003.

operative words of any of those exemptions must be satisfied in order for it to be triggered[160] on the basis of:

> the orthodox principle (common to both the criminal and the civil law) that exceptions, etc are to be set up by those who rely on them.[161]

The exemptions do not, however, set up a threshold of the harm that must be caused.[162]

5– 026 Onus: elsewhere

In the analogous regime in New Zealand, the courts have held[163] that the ombudsman, to whom an appeal against an agency's decision lies, has no pre-determined starting point and that the agency withholding the information is under no obligation to establish affirmatively each element of the exemption. Nevertheless, despite avoiding use of terms such as 'onus', the courts there have held that the withholding agency bears an obligation:

> to justify its refusal to disclose ... with sufficient particularity for the ombudsman to make his or her decision and recommendation.[164]

5– 027 Onus: public interest

Having established that information answering the terms of the request falls within one of the provisions of Part II, if those provisions do not confer absolute exemption it will be necessary to weigh the competing aspects of the public interest to determine if the duty to acknowledge and the duty to communicate are disapplied.[165] When the public interest override was first introduced in the FOI Bill, it provided that, if information fell within one of the qualified exemptions, then it would only be required to be communicated to the applicant if:

> in all the circumstances of the case, the public interest in disclosing the information outweighs the public interest in maintaining the exemption.[166]

In the face of criticism,[167] the section was modified to its present form, which reversed the order. In moving the amendments, it was specifically stated:

> the starting point is the public right of access and the public interest in disclosure, and it is for the public authority to justify non-disclosure on the basis that public disclosure is

---

160 Similarly, when refusing a request, it is for the public authority to rely upon a claim that one of the provisions of Pt II applies: FOIA s 17(2); FOI(S)A s 16(2). In Canada, the view taken is that since the basic principle of the statute is to codify the right of public access to government information two things follow: first, that such public access ought not to be frustrated by the Courts except upon the clearest grounds so that doubt ought to be resolved in favour of disclosure; secondly, the burden of persuasion must rest upon the party resisting disclosure whether it be a private corporation, citizen or the Government: *Maislin Industries Limited v Minister for Industry, Trade & Commerce* [1984] 1 FC 939; *Rubin v Canada (Canada Mortgage and Housing Corp)* [1989] 1 FC 265 (CA) ('the general rule is disclosure, the exception is exemption and the onus of proving the entitlement to the benefit of the exception rests upon those who claim it.'); *Canada (Information Commissioner) v Canada (Minister of External Affairs)* [1990] 3 FC 665; *Rubin v Canada (Solicitor General)* (2000) 187 DLR (4th) 675. Note, however, that the Access to Information Act, (1982) (Canada) has both a purpose clause (s 2) and an onus provision in relation to appeals (s 48).

161 *Nimmo v Alexander Cowan & Sons Ltd* [1968] AC 107 at 130 (Lord Wilberforce). Similarly: *R v Hunt* [1987] AC 352 at 373-375 (Lord Griffiths).

162 *ECGD v Friends of the Earth* [2008] EWHC 638 (Admin), [2008] Env LR 40, [2008] JPL 1813 at [31]-[37], criticising the Tribunal for requiring a public authority to specify clearly and precisely the harm or harms that would be caused were disclosure to be ordered.

163 *Commissioner of Police v Ombudsman* [1988] 1 NZLR 385 (CA), on appeal from [1985] 1 NZLR 578.

164 *Commissioner of Police v Ombudsman* [1988] 1 NZLR 385 at 406.

165 FOIA s 2(1)(b) and 2(2)(b); FOI(S)A s 2(1)(b). In Canada the two-stage burden, ie that the information falls within the exemption and that the public interest is against disclosure, is recognised: *Rubin v Canada (Solicitor General)* (2000) 187 DLR (4th) 675.

166 Under this, it was recognised that if evenly-balanced, there should be no disclosure: Hansard HL vol 617 col 914 (17 October 2000) (Lord Falconer of Thoroton).

167 It was described as turning the burden the wrong way round: Hansard HL vol 617 col 907 (17 October 2000) (Lord Goodhart). And, later on, as making the balance to be in favour of concealment: Hansard HL vol 619 col 134 (14 November 2000) (Lord Archer).

> outweighed in the circumstances of the case by the public interest in non-disclosure .... The burden of proof, as lawyers would say, is placed upon the public authority to show that there is some pressing need for non-disclosure and that the restriction on the public right of access is necessary in the sense of being a proportionate way of meeting that need.[168]

The suggested amendments were accepted by the Minister in charge of the Bill in the House of Lords, saying they:

> will result in an important and significant shift towards greater openness. They will put beyond doubt the Government's resolve that information must be disclosed except where there is an overriding public interest in keeping specific information confidential. Perhaps I may repeat that: information must be disclosed except where there is an overriding public interest in keeping specific information confidential .... They significantly contribute to the change in culture. They contribute significantly to ensuring that the public authority must make out the case for non-disclosure before there is non-disclosure. That is why we have agreed to accept them.[169]

Section 2, in speaking of the acknowledgement and communication duties being disapplied where 'the public interest in maintaining the exemption outweighs the public interest in disclosing the information', posits a starting position of disclosure.[170] This was acknowledged by the Tribunal in *Hogan v Oxford City Council and Information Commissioner*:

> [The Act] does not include any general provision that there is a presumption in favour of the disclosure of information held by public authorities. However in one important respect FOIA does contain a presumption in favour of disclosure. The duty to communicate under s 1(1)(a) [*sic*] is displaced by a qualified exemption under s 2(2)(b) only if the public interest in maintaining the exemptions *outweighs* the public interest in disclosure of the information sought. So if the interests are equally balanced, then the public authority, in our view, must communicate the information sought.[171]

Similarly, in *Dept for Education and Skills v Information Commissioner and The Evening Standard* the Tribunal held:

> Section 2(2)(b) is clear: the authority must disclose unless the public interest in withholding the information outweighs the public interest in disclosure. If the scales are level, it must disclose. Such an equilibrium may not be a purely theoretical result: there may be many cases where the apparent interests in disclosure and in maintaining the exemption are equally slight. The weighing exercise begins with both pans empty and therefore level. Disclosure follows if that remains the position.[172]

These views have been endorsed by the High Court:

> In my judgment, it is both implicit and explicit in FOIA that, in the absence of a public

---

168 Hansard HL vol 619 col 137 (14 November 2000) (Lord Lester of Herne Hill).

169 Hansard HL vol 619 cols 143-144 (14 November 2000) (Minister of State, Cabinet Office, Lord Falconer of Thoroton). See also: Hansard HC vol 357 cols 719, 721-72 (27 November 2000), where, in introducing the amendment that led to s 2, the Parliamentary Under-Secretary of State for the Home Department (Mr O'Brien), said: 'the amendment also reverses the way in which the test works, so that the public interest in disclosing the information must be outweighed by the public interest in maintaining an exemption before any information can be withheld.'

170 Similarly, EIR reg 12(1)(b); EI(S)R reg 10(1)(b). The position under the FOI(S)A is slightly different. The duty to disclose non-absolute exempt information only applies to the extent that, in all the circumstances of the case, the public interest in disclosing the information is not outweighed by the public interest in maintaining the exemption: s 2(1)(b). The provision is couched as part of the circumscription of the parameters of the right of access, rather than as an exception to be invoked in order to disapply the right of access.

171 IT, 17 October 2006 at [56]. Similarly, *Kitchener v IC and Derby City Council*, IT, 20 December 2006 at [13]; *Dept of Culture, Media and Sport v IC*, IT, 29 July 2008 at [22]; *DBERR v IC and Friends of the Earth*, IT, 29 April 2008 at [112(a)]; *Scotland Office v IC*, IT, 8 August 2008 at [77]; *Galloway v IC and NHS*, IT, 20 March 2009 at [69]; *ECGD v IC and Campaign Against Arms Trade*, IT, 21 October 2009 at [50(i)].

172 *DfES v IC and The Evening Standard*, IT, 19 February 2007 at [64]-[65]. Similarly: *DTI v IC*, IT, 10 November 2006 at [54]; *Arts and Humanities Research Council v IC and Bimmler*, FTT, 4 December 2012 at [33(ii)]; *DEFRA v IC and Portman*, FTT, 13 November 2012 at [38(ii)]; *Dedalus Ltd v IC and Arts Council of England*, FTT, 21 May 2010 at [74(ii)]; *Evans v IC and DBIS* [2012] UKUT 313 (AAC) at [27].

> interest in preserving confidentiality, there is a public interest in the disclosure of information held by public authorities. That public interest is implicitly recognised in section 1, which confers, subject to specified exceptions, a general right of access to information held by public authorities...
> The public interest in disclosure is explicitly recognised and affirmed in section 19(3). Section 19(1) imposes on every public authority a duty to adopt and to maintain a scheme for the publication of information by it....[173]

5–028 Onus: even balance

The Court of Appeal has now also held that, whilst there is no general presumption in favour of disclosure when carrying out the public interest balancing exercise, if the competing public interests for and against disclosure are found to be evenly balanced, a decision-maker cannot properly conclude that the public interest in maintaining the exemption outweighs the public interest in disclosing the information.[174] Put another way, the mere fact that information falls within a qualified exemption does not necessarily mean that disclosure would damage the interest protected by that exemption.[175] Accordingly, it is for a public authority that does not wish to communicate or acknowledge the existence of information falling within one of the provisions of Part II, other than one conferring absolute exemption, to demonstrate that in all the circumstances that stance is supported by a weighing of the relevant aspects of the public interest.[176] The Tribunal has rejected the notion that certain qualified exemptions have an inherently greater public interest against disclosure than others.[177]

5–029 Standard of proof

In administrative matters, to the extent that there is any standard of proof, the civil standard of proof applies.[178] In other spheres where the courts have had to consider the public interest in disclosing and in not disclosing information, a mere say-so of harm, other than in cases involving national security, has not sufficed.[179]

5–030 Special interpretative principles

Applying the ordinary principles of administrative law, a public authority must exercise its discretion so as to promote the policy and objects of FOIA, and not so as to frustrate that policy

---

173 *OGC v IC* [2008] EWHC 774 (Admin), [2010] QB 98, [2008] ACD 54 at [69]-[70]. See also [78]-[79] and *Home Office and MoJ v IC* [2009] EWHC 1611 (Admin) at [35].

174 *Dept of Health v IC and Lewis* [2017] EWCA Civ 374, [2017] 1 WLR 3330 at [46].

175 *DfES v IC and The Evening Standard*, IT, 19 February 2007 at [60], [62]; approved in *OGC v IC* [2008] EWHC 774 (Admin), [2010] QB 98, [2008] ACD 54 at [79].

176 *DfES v IC and The Evening Standard*, IT, 19 February 2007 at [64]-[67]; *DWP v IC*, IT, 5 March 2007 at [27]-[29].

177 The argument has been run repeatedly before the Tribunal despite judicially approved decisions of the Tribunal: *DfES v IC and The Evening Standard*, IT, 19 February 2007 at [60]-[63]; *OGC v IC* [2008] EWHC 774 (Admin), [2010] QB 98, [2008] ACD 54 at [79]; *DBERR v IC and Friends of the Earth*, IT, 29 April 2008 at [103]. On the other hand, the Tribunal has itself repeatedly countenanced the suggestion: *Bellamy v IC and DBIS*, FTT, 23 February 2010; *People for the Ethical Treatment of Animals Europe v IC and University of Oxford*, FTT, 18 January 2010 at [68]; *All Party Parliamentary Group on Extraordinary Rendition v IC and Ministry of Defence* [2011] UKUT 153 (AAC) at [77]; *Home Office v IC*, FTT, 8 June 2010 at [47]; *Ritchie v IC*, FTT, 26 July 2011 at [89]; *British Union for the Abolition of Vivisection v IC and Newcastle University*, FTT, 11 November 2011 at [54].

178 *R v SSHD, ex p Khawaja* [1984] AC 74.

179 *AG v Guardian Newspapers (No 2)* [1990] 1 AC 109 at 263 and 283. Although the standard remains the civil one, if the predicted consequence is inherently unlikely that will affect the cogency of the evidence required to satisfy the civil standard: *Re D* [2008] UKHL 33, [2008] 1 WLR 1499; *Re H (minors) (sexual abuse: standard of proof)* [1996] AC 563 at 586, [1996] 1 All ER 1 at 16 (Lord Nicholls); *SSHD v Rehman* [2001] UKHL 47, [2003] 1 AC 153 at [55] (Lord Hoffmann); *R (AN) v Mental Health Review Tribunal (Northern Region)* [2005] EWCA Civ 1605, [2006] QB 468 at [60], [62]-[71] (where it is said that the more serious the allegation or the more serious the consequences if the allegation is proved, the stronger must be the evidence before a court will find the allegation proved on the balance of probabilities).

and those objects.[180] In the comparative jurisdictions, it has sometimes been argued that the nature of freedom of information legislation calls for any ambiguity to be decided in favour of wider disclosure. Underlying this argument is the notion that legislation providing for access to official information is akin to a constitutional instrument and that special principles of interpretation apply.[181] Whilst support can be found in judgments from comparative jurisdictions for the idea that official information access legislation may rank as a constitutional measure, those same judgments have not taken the additional step of giving the legislation a benevolent interpretation as a result of it.[182]

5–031 General interpretative principles

Putting to one side characterisation of 'freedom of information' legislation as a constitutional measure, an issue that has arisen elsewhere is whether ambiguities in freedom of information legislation should as a rule be resolved so as to favour disclosure.[183] In relation to FOI(S)A, Lord Marnoch in the Court of Session expressed the view:

> …that the statute, whose whole purpose is to secure the release of information, should be construed in as liberal a manner as possible and, as long as individual and other rights are respected, and the cost limits are not exceeded, I do not myself see any reason why the Commissioner should not be accorded the widest discretion in deciding the form and type of information which should be released in furtherance of its objectives.[184]

This was given qualified approval by the House of Lords on appeal:[185]

> [4] There is much force in Lord Marnoch's observation in the Inner House 2007 SC 231, para 32 that, as the whole purpose of the 2002 Act is the release of information, it should be construed in as liberal a manner as possible. But that proposition must not be applied too widely, without regard to the way the Act was designed to operate in conjunction with the [DPA 1998]. It is obvious that not all government can be completely open, and special consideration also had to be given to the release of personal information relating to individuals. So while the entitlement to information is expressed initially in the broadest terms that are imaginable, it is qualified in respects that are equally significant and to which appropriate weight must also be given....
>
> [7] In my opinion there is no presumption in favour of the release of personal data under the general obligation that the 2002 Act lays down. The references which that Act makes to provisions of the 1998 Act must be understood in the light of the legislative purpose of that Act, which was to implement Council Directive 95/46/EC.
>
> [68] Where the legislature has thus worked out the way that the requirements of data protection and freedom of information are to be reconciled, the role of the courts is just to apply the compromise to be found in the legislation. The 2002 Act gives people, other than

---

180 *Padfield v Minister of Agriculture, Fisheries and Food* [1968] AC 997 at 1030; *London Boroughs Transport Committee v Freight Transport Assocn Ltd* [1991] 1 WLR 828 at 836. See further J Auburn, J Moffett and A Sharland, *Judicial Review. Principles and Procedure* (OUP, Oxford, 2013) Ch 16. As to the purpose of the FOIA, see §§1– 014 to 1– 020.

181 In relation to the principles of construction of a true constitutional instrument, see *Minister of Home Affairs v Fisher* [1980] AC 319 at 329; *Riley v AG of Jamaica* [1983] 1 AC 719. In *Thoburn v Sunderland City Council* [2002] EWHC 195 Admin, [2003] QB 151 at [62] Laws LJ spoke of a hierarchy of 'ordinary' and 'constitutional' statutes, with the former being amenable to implied repeal and the latter not: 'In my opinion a constitutional statute is one which (a) conditions the legal relationship between citizen and State in some general, overarching manner, or (b) enlarges or diminishes the scope of what we would now regard as fundamental constitutional rights.'

182 *Commissioner of Police v Ombudsman* [1988] 1 NZLR 385 (CA) at 391, 402 and 411; *Wyatt Co Ltd v Queenstown Lakes District Council* [1991] 2 NZLR 180.

183 Directive 2003/4 Art 4(2) expressly provides that the grounds for refusing requests for environmental information are to be 'interpreted in a restrictive way,' in line with Art 4(4) of the Aarhus Convention. The EIR, which implement that Directive, make mention of any such rule of restrictive interpretation. On the other hand, EI(S)R reg 10(2)(a) does.

184 *Common Services Agency v Scottish IC*, 2006 CSIH 58, 2007 SLT 7 at [32].

185 *Common Services Agency v IC* [2008] UKHL 47, [2008] 1 WLR 1550, per Lord Hope at [4] and [7], and Lord Rodger at [68].

> the data subject, a right to information in certain circumstances and subject to certain exemptions. Discretion does not enter into it. There is, however, no reason why courts should favour the right to freedom of information over the rights of data subjects. If Lord Marnoch's observations [32], were intended to suggest otherwise, I would respectfully disagree.

Similarly, two members of the Supreme Court in *BBC v Sugar (no 2)* spoke of the Act reflecting values to be attached to transparency and openness in the workings of public authorities in a modern society 'and its provisions should be construed in as liberal a manner as possible.'[186] Thus, where there is no countervailing third party interest against disclosure, the principle of liberal construction (and, hence, of confined interpretation of exemptions) would appear to survive and enjoy endorsement from the highest court.[187]

5– 032 Interpretation elsewhere

In Australia, the High Court has said:

> In the light of [s 3 and s 16] it is proper to give to the relevant provisions of the Act a construction which would further, rather than hinder, free access to information.[188]

More recently, Kirby J, in considering the Victorian Freedom of Information Act, stated:[189]

> The starting point for resolving the issues presented by the present appeal is an appreciation of the duty of this Court, in this context, to do what we are constantly instructing other courts to do in giving effect to legislation. This is to read the legislative text in its context (including against the background of the significant change that the legislation introduces) and, so far as the text and context permit, to give effect to the legislative purpose.
>
> In the present setting, that purpose is a radical one. It assigns very high importance to a public interest in greater openness and transparency in public administration. Given the historical background, the attitudinal shift that FOI legislation demanded of Ministers, departments, agencies and the public service is nothing short of revolutionary. The courts ought not to obstruct that shift. On the contrary, they should strive to interpret FOI legislation in a manner harmonious with its objectives, doing so to the fullest extent that the text allows.

In Canada, the view taken is that public access ought not to be frustrated by the Courts except upon the clearest grounds, so that doubt ought to be resolved in favour of disclosure.[190] The European Court of Justice has consistently stated that exceptions to the right of access to documents under Article 4 of Regulation 1049/2001 are to be interpreted strictly, given that they each depart from the principle that members of the public should have the widest possible access to documents held by EU institutions.[191] In Ireland a similar view has been expressed:

---

186 *BBC v Sugar (No 2)* [2012] UKSC 4, [2012] 1 WLR 439 per Lord Mance at [110] and similarly per Lord Walker at [77]. Both referred to Lord Hope's qualification in *Common Services Agency v IC* [2008] UKHL 47, [2008] 1 WLR 1550, ie that this proposition must not be applied too widely.

187 On the basis that since any such third party interest weighs against disclosure (resulting in an even opening public interest balance), where there is no such countervailing interest against disclosure, the opening public interest balance should be in favour of disclosure.

188 *Victorian Public Service Board v Wright* (1986) 160 CLR 145 at 153, considering the FOI Act of the State of Victoria. Similarly: *Accident Compensation Commission v Croom* [1991] 2 VR 322; *Sobh v Police Force of Victoria* [1994] 1 VR 41, although these decisions are in part based on an objects section in the legislation. See also: *Commissioner of Police v District Court of NSW and Perrin* (1993) 31 NSWLR 606; *Re Eccleston and Dept of Family Services and Aboriginal and Islander Affairs* (1993) 1 QAR 60. Contrast decisions of the Federal Court, considering the Commonwealth Act: *Kavvaadias v Commonwealth Ombudsman* (1984) 1 FCR 80 at 85; *News Corporation Ltd v National Companies & Securities Commission* (1984) 1 FCR 64; *Attorney-General's Department v Cockcroft* (1986) 10 FCR 180 at 195; *Commissioner of Taxation v Swiss Aluminium Australia Ltd* (1986) 10 FCR 321 at 327; *Searle Australia Pty Ltd v Public Interest Advocacy Centre* (1992) 36 FCR 111 at 114-115; cf *Arnold v Queensland* (1987) 13 ALD 195 at 205.

189 *Osland v Secretary to the Department of Justice* [2008] HCA 37 at [65]-[66].

190 *Maislin Industries Limited v Minister for Industry, Trade & Commerce* [1984] 1 FC 939.

191 *ClientEarth v European Commission* (C-57/16) [2019] 1 CMLR 37, [2019] Env LR 11 at [77]-[78] and [80]; *Saint-Gobain Glass Deutschland GmbH v European Commission* (C-60/15) [2018] Env LR 8 at [61]-[63]; *Sweden v My Travel*

> (In) the light of the preamble, it seems to me that there can be no doubt but that it was the intention of the legislature when enacting the provisions of the Freedom of Information Act 1997, that it was only in exceptional cases that members of the public at large should be deprived of access to information in the possession of public bodies and this intention is exemplified by the provision of s 34(12)(b) of the Act which provides that a decision to refuse to grant access to information sought shall be presumed not to have been justified until the contrary is shown.[192]

And later:

> … given the policy and object of the Act to give wide and generous access to the documents held by public bodies, any exemptions or restrictions, such as those contained in Part III of the Act (ss. 19 to 32) ought to be given a narrow restrictive interpretation so as to derogate as little as possible from the main purpose of the Act.[193]

6. CONCLUSIVE CERTIFICATES

5–033 Introduction

FOIA, the DPA 2018 and the EIR all provide for the signing and issuing of 'conclusive certificates'. The effect of a conclusive certificate is evidential: the certificate stands as conclusive evidence of the 'facts' certified in it, irrespective of the reality. The 'facts' that may be so certified are:

(1) that particular information was directly or indirectly supplied by, or relates to, any of the security bodies specified in s 23(3) of FOIA;[194]
(2) that exemption from s 1(1)(b) (the disclosure duty) or s 1(1)(a) and (b) (the existence duty and the disclosure duty) of FOIA, is, or at any time was, required for the purpose of safeguarding national security;[195]
(3) that exemption from the disclosure duty, or from the existence duty and the disclosure duty, under FOIA is required for the purpose of avoiding an infringement of the privileges of either House of Parliament;[196]
(4) that disclosure of information held by either House of Parliament would, or would be likely to, have any of the effects mentioned in s 36(2) of FOIA (in other words, it would be prejudicial to the maintenance of the convention of the collective responsibility of Ministers of the Crown; it would be prejudicial to the work of the Executive Committee of the Northern Ireland Assembly or the work of the Cabinet

---

Group plc (C-506/08) [2011] ECR I-6237, [2012] All ER (EC) 968, [2011] 5 CMLR 18 at [73]-[75]; *Sweden and API v European Commission* (C-514/07, C-528/07, C-532/07) [2011] 2 AC 359, [2010] ECR I-8533 at [69]-[70] and [72]-[73]; *IFAW GmbH v European Commission* (C64/05) [2007] ECR I-11389, [2008] QB 902 at [66]; *Sison v Council of the European Union* (C-266/05) [2007] ECR I-1233, [2007] 2 CMLR 17 at [61]-[63].

192 *Minister for Agriculture and Food v Information Commissioner* [2000] 1 IR 309 at 319. The Freedom of Information Act 1997 (Ireland) has since been repealed and replaced by the Freedom of Information Act 2014 (Ireland). Section 22(12)(b) of the 2014 Act is materially the same as s 34(12)(b) of the 2997 Act.

193 *Health Service Executive v Information Commissioner and Another* [2008] IEHC 298.

194 FOIA s 23(2). Neither the certificate provision nor the underlying exemption exists in FOI(S)A. In the context of FOIA the meaning of the phrase 'relates to' has been considered in: *Home Office v IC and Cobain*, FTT, 30 January 2013 at [15]-[19]; *Callus v IC and Home Office*, FTT, 6 May 2014 at [39]-[41]; *University and Colleges Admissions Service v IC and Lord Lucas* [2014] UKUT 0557 (AAC) at [44]-[46] (meaning of 'relates to' in FOIA s 7(5)); *Home Office v IC and Cobain* [2014] UKUT 0306 (AAC) at [39]; *All Party Parliamentary Group on Extraordinary Rendition v IC and FCO* [2015] UKUT 0377 (AAC) at [14]-[33]; *Reprieve v IC and FCO*, FTT, 26 April 2016 at [37]-[39]; *Corderoy and Ahmed v IC and Attorney General* [2017] UKUT 0495 (AAC) at [51] [54] and [59]-[62]; *Department of Health v IC and Lewis* [2017] EWCA Civ 374, [2017] 1 WLR 3330 at [13] (Sir Terence Etherton MR) (meaning of 'relates to' in FOIA s 35(1)).

195 FOIA s 24(3); FOI(S)A s 31(2).

196 FOIA s 34(2). Neither the certificate provision nor the underlying exemption exists in FOI(S)A.

of the Welsh Government; it would inhibit the free and frank provision of advice or the free and frank exchange of views for the purposes of deliberation; or it would otherwise prejudice the effective conduct of public affairs);[197]

(5) that the exemption of personal data from all or any of the provisions listed in s 26(2) or mentioned in s 110(2) of the DPA 2018 is, or at any time was, required for the purpose of safeguarding national security;[198]

(6) that a restriction on the provision of information to a data subject under ss 44(2), 45(1), 48(1)(b)(i) or 68(1) of the DPA 2018 - imposed by a competent authority carrying out law enforcement processing subject to Part 3 of that Act - is a necessary and proportionate measure to protect national security for the purposes of ss 44(4), 45(4), 48(3) or 68(7);[199]

(7) that a refusal to disclose information under reg 12(1) of the EIR is because the disclosure would adversely affect national security and would not be in the public interest under reg 12(1)(b).[200]

Section 53 of FOIA[201] also sets out circumstances in which the duty to comply with a decision notice or enforcement notice may be excepted through the issue of a certificate.[202] A certificate under s 53 has a prescribed statutory effect and operates as a 'statutory override or veto':[203] it is not a conclusive evidential certificate as such. Certificates under s 53 are considered elsewhere in this work.[204]

5– 034 General effect

Each of the seven types of conclusive certificate effectively deems that a prerequisite to the application of a particular exemption is satisfied, thereby facilitating the application of that exemption for the purposes of the relevant enactment.[205] These conclusive certificates fall into two categories: appealable ministerial 'national security certificates' under ss 23(2) and 24(3) of FOIA, ss 27(1), 79(1) and 111(1) of the DPA 2018 and reg 15(1) of the EIR; and non-appealable 'Parliamentary certificates' under ss 34(3) and 36(7) of FOIA. The former may be signed by certain Ministers of the Crown[206] and the latter may be signed by the Speaker of the House of Commons or the Clerk of the Parliaments ('the House Authorities').[207] Each of the underlying exemptions can nevertheless operate independently of conclusive certificates: the issue of an appropriate certificate is a sufficient but not a necessary condition for the engagement of each one.[208] Indeed, as a matter of practice, central government public authorities have tended not

---

[197] FOIA s 36(7). Although the underlying exemption is provided for by FOI(S)A s 30, it does not provide for conclusive certificates to facilitate its engagement.

[198] DPA 2018 ss 27(1), 111(1). See previously DPA 1998 s 28(2).

[199] DPA 2018 s 79(1).

[200] EIR reg 15(1); EI(S)R reg 12.

[201] FOI(S)A s 52(2).

[202] EIR reg 18 incorporates the certification power contained in FOIA s 53 into the regime applicable to requests for environmental information: see *R (Evans) v Attorney-General* [2013] EWHC 1960 (Admin) at [40].

[203] *R (Evans) v Attorney-General* [2015] UKSC 21, [2015] AC 1787, considered in *Roszkowski v SSHD* [2017] EWCA Civ 1893, [2018] 1 WLR 2848 at [21]-[30].

[204] See §45– 011.

[205] Both Acts confer power to 'sign' such certificates but talk in terms of their being 'issued' in relation to appeals. See also FOI(S)A s 31(2)-(3).

[206] FOIA s 25(3); DPA 2018 ss 27(10), 79(12), 110(10); EIR reg 15(6). EIR reg 15(2) further provides that a Minister of the Crown may designate a person to certify the matters in reg 15(1) on his behalf.

[207] FOIA ss 34(4) and 36(5)(d)-(e) and (7).

[208] *Beam v IC and FCO*, IT, 12 May 2009, where the Tribunal upheld reliance upon FOIA s 23(1), (3)(b) without the

to rely on certificates when invoking the exemptions in s 23 or 24 of FOIA and the issue of certificates thereunder is the exception, rather than the norm.

5– 035 Types of ouster clause

Statutory provisions which seek to confer finality on determinations of the executive by excluding judicial review of those determinations are often referred to as 'preclusive clauses' or 'ouster clauses' because they seek to preclude or oust the supervisory jurisdiction of the courts over the executive.[209] Such clauses can take the form of 'finality' clauses, 'no certiorari' clauses, 'as if enacted' clauses, 'shall not be questioned' clauses and 'conclusive evidence' clauses.[210] An ouster clause which seeks to preclude judicial review other than by way of an exclusive statutory appeal or a review mechanism is known as a 'partial' ouster clause and, where the prescribed mechanism must be invoked within a particular limitation period, as a 'time-limited' clause.[211] The provisions in FOIA, the DPA 2018 and the EIR allowing for the issue of conclusive certificates thus contain a species of conclusive evidence clause.[212] In relation to ss 23(2) and 24(3) of FOIA, ss 27(1), 79(1) and 111(1) of the DPA 2018 and reg 15(1) of the EIR these are partial ouster clauses because national security certificates signed thereunder are appealable. In relation to ss 34(3) and 36(7) of FOIA, they are absolute as there is no scope for challenging parliamentary certificates.

5– 036 Judicial approach to ouster

In very general terms, the courts have been prepared to enforce partial and time-limited ouster clauses on the basis that they do not altogether preclude judicial oversight.[213] By contrast, the

need for a ministerial certificate under FOIA s 23(2). The FCO had stated in its evidence that 'we did not feel it necessary or helpful to the parties concerned to take up ministerial time by going down that line in this case' (at [11]) and the Tribunal made it clear that production of a ministerial certificate is not always necessary and may be disproportionate (at [15]).

[209] See further J Auburn, J Moffett and A Sharland, *Judicial Review. Principles and Procedure* (OUP, Oxford, 2013) §§2.100-2.113. H Woolf, J Jowell, A Le Sueur, C Donnelly and I Hare, *De Smith's Judicial Review*, 8th edn (London, Sweet & Maxwell, 2018) paras 4-016 to 4-057; W Wade and C Forsyth, *Administrative Law*, 11th edn (Oxford, Oxford University Press, 2014) pp 608-629.

[210] See further J Auburn, J Moffett and A Sharland, *Judicial Review. Principles and Procedure* (OUP, Oxford, 2013) §§2.103-2.110. H Woolf, J Jowell, A Le Sueur, C Donnelly and I Hare, *De Smith's Judicial Review*, 8th edn (London, Sweet & Maxwell, 2018) paras 4-019 to 4-026; W Wade and C Forsyth, *Administrative Law*, 11th edn, (Oxford, Oxford University Press, 2014) pp 608-613; M Fordham, *Judicial Review Handbook*, 6th edn (Oxford, Hart Publishing, 2012) Ch P28.

[211] See further J Auburn, J Moffett and A Sharland, *Judicial Review. Principles and Procedure* (OUP, Oxford, 2013) §§2.107-2.108. H Woolf, J Jowell, A Le Sueur, C Donnelly and I Hare, *De Smith's Judicial Review*, 8th edn (London, Sweet & Maxwell, 2018) paras 4-027 to 4-029, and 4-042 and 4-046; W Wade and C Forsyth, *Administrative Law*, 11th edn (Oxford, Oxford University Press, 2014) pp 605-608 and 619-625; M Fordham, *Judicial Review Handbook*, 6th edn (Oxford, Hart Publishing, 2012), Ch P36.

[212] For examples of traditional certificate-based conclusive evidence clauses see: the Race Relations Act 1976, ss 42 and 69 as originally enacted (subsequently amended by the Employment Rights Act 1996 and the Race Relations (Amendment) Act 2000 and repealed by the Equality Act 2010); and the Fair Employment (Northern Ireland) Act 1976 s 42 (subsequently repealed and replaced by the Fair Employment and Treatment (Northern Ireland) Order 1998 SI 1998/3162 (NI 21)). Both sets of provisions were amended or replaced so as to allow, inter alia, for appeals to be brought against the relevant type of ministerial national security certificate following the decision of the European Court of Human Rights in *Tinnelly and Sons Ltd v United Kingdom* (1999) 27 EHRR 249 (ECtHR). For further examples see: Parliamentary Commissioner Act 1967 s 8(4) allowing the Secretary to the Cabinet to issue a certificate with the approval of the Prime Minister certifying conclusively that any information, question, document or part of a document relates to proceedings of the Cabinet or any committee of the Cabinet and is thus immune from compulsory disclosure or production under that Act (such a certificate was issued in the *Court Line* case: HC 498, 1974-1975, para 9: W Wade and C Forsyth, *Administrative Law*, 11th edn (Oxford, Oxford University Press, 2014) p 82); Trade Union and Labour Relations (Consolidation) Act 1992 s 183; Northern Ireland Act 1998, ss 90-91; International Criminal Court Act 2001 s 39; Privacy and Electronic Communications (EC Directive) Regulations 2003 SI 2003/2426 reg 28; Civil Contingencies Act 2004 s 12A.

[213] *Smith v East Elloe RDC* [1956] AC 736 (HL); *R v Secretary of State for the Environment, ex p Ostler* [1977] QB 122 (CA); *R v Cornwall CC, ex p Huntington* [1992] 3 All ER 566; *R v Dacorum DC, ex p Cannon* [1996] 2 PLR 45 (DC); *R (Privacy*

courts have had a long-standing reluctance to give full literal effect to absolute ouster clauses, eventually leading to a complete unwillingness to read 'shall not be questioned' clauses as ousting their supervisory jurisdiction over subordinate authorities in particular.[214] In modern times, the domestic courts have upheld conclusive evidence clauses[215] and accepted that they cannot go behind or scrutinise non-appealable national security certificates unless and in so far as obtained or issued in bad faith.[216] However, recent decisions of the CJEU and the ECtHR founded on human rights principles have, in effect, declared certain conclusive evidence clauses precluding any judicial oversight to be incompatible with fundamental rights.[217]

5– 037 Human rights

Human rights issues[218] are therefore potentially important to the application and effectiveness of the conclusive evidence clauses in FOIA, the DPA 2018 and the EIR. If it can be shown that a conclusive certificate issued under one of these Acts has interfered with the enjoyment or exercise of a 'Convention right' within the meaning of the Human Rights Act 1998[219] or a right under European Community law that can be relied upon before the domestic courts,[220] this will

---

International) v Investigatory Powers Tribunal [2017] EWCA Civ 1868, [2018] 1 WLR 2572; cf *Anisminic Ltd v Foreign Compensation Commission* [1969] 2 AC 147 (HL) at 171 (Lord Reid), 200 (Lord Pearce), 210 (Lord Wilberforce).

214 *Anisminic Ltd v Foreign Compensation Commission* [1969] 2 AC 147; *R v Hull University Visitor, ex p Page* [1993] AC 682; *Boddington v British Transport Police* [1999] 2 AC 143; *R v SSHD, ex p Fayed* [1998] 1 WLR 763 (CA). See also the debate on the abandoned ouster clause originally included in the Asylum and Immigration (Treatment of Claimants, etc) Bill 2003, cl 11: H Wade and C Forsyth, *Administrative Law*, 11th edn (Oxford, Oxford University Press, 2014) pp 615-616, n 265; Jowell, 'Heading for Constitutional Crisis?' (2004) 154 *New Law Journal* 401; Le Sueur, 'Three Strikes and It's Out? The UK Government's Strategy to Oust Judicial Review from Immigration and Asylum Decision Making' [2004] *Public Law* 225; Rawlings, 'Review, Revenge and Retreat' (2005) 68 *Modern Law Review* 378; Thomas, 'After the Ouster: Review and Reconsideration in a Single Tier Tribunal' [2006] *Public Law* 674; Craig, 'Ouster clauses, separation of powers and the intention of Parliament: from Anisminic to Privacy International' [2018] *Public Law* 570.

215 *R v Registrar of Companies, ex p Central Bank of India* [1986] QB 1114 (CA); cf *R v Preston Supplementary Benefits Appeal Tribunal, ex p Moore* [1975] 1 WLR 624 (CA). See also the Tribunals and Inquiries Act 1958 s 11, Tribunals and Inquiries Act 1971 s 14 and Tribunals and Inquiries Act 1992 s 12.

216 See the references to the various unreported judicial review proceedings in the Northern Ireland High Court before Nicholson and McCollum JJ which preceded *Tinnelly and Sons Ltd v United Kingdom* (1999) 27 EHRR 249 (ECtHR) at [18]-[32], [64], [66]-[67] and [74]-[75] and before Kerr J which preceded *Devlin v United Kingdom* (2002) 34 EHRR 43 (ECtHR) at [12]-[14]. See also: *R v Secretary of State for Foreign and Commonwealth Affairs, ex p Vidler* [1993] COD 305 (national security certificate under the Employment Protection (Consolidation) Act 1978, Sch 9, para 2); *R v Secretary of State for Transport, ex p Evans and Commission for Racial Equality* [1992] COD 196 (national security certificate under the Race Relations Act 1976, ss 42 and 69); and *R v Secretary of State for Northern Ireland, ex p Gilmore* (unreported, 10 April 1987) referred to in White, 'Security Vetting, discrimination and the right to a fair trial' [1999] *Public Law* 406.

217 Case 222/84 *Johnston v Chief Constable of the Royal Ulster Constabulary* [1987] QB 129 (CJEU); *Tinnelly and Sons Ltd v United Kingdom* (1999) 27 EHRR 249 (ECtHR); *Devlin v United Kingdom* (2002) 34 EHRR 43 (ECtHR); *Devenney v United Kingdom* (2002) 35 EHRR 24 (ECtHR). See further §5– 037.

218 For the role of the ECHR in relation to FOIA generally, see Chapter 4.

219 Human Rights Act 1998 s 1(1)-(3), Sch 1 define 'the Convention rights' for the purposes of that Act as the rights and fundamental freedoms set out in Arts 2-12 and 14 of the Convention for the Protection of Human Rights and Fundamental Freedoms (Cmd 8969, 1953), Arts 1-3 of the First Protocol and Arts 1-2 of the Sixth Protocol. The ECHR, Arts 1 and 13 are notable omissions from 'the Convention rights'. Primary and subordinate legislation must, so far as possible, be read and given effect in a way which is compatible with the Convention rights (s 3) and it is unlawful for public authorities (including courts) to act in a way which is incompatible with them unless left with no alternative by primary legislation (s 6).

220 In this regard, reliance can be placed on Community law in accordance with the doctrine of direct effect including the subsidiary or related doctrines of vertical, indirect and incidental direct effect: P Craig and G De Búrca, *EU Law: Text, Cases and Materials*, 6th edn (Oxford, Oxford University Press, 2015) chs 7-9; D Wyatt and A Dashwood, *European Union Law*, 6th edn (Oxford, Hart, 2011) Ch 8. In particular, the doctrine of incidental direct effect requires that national law implementing Directives is interpreted and applied in accordance with Community law and norms and is therefore relevant to DPA 2018 (insofar as it supplements the GDPR and the LED) and the EIR (implementing European Community Public Access to Environmental Information Directive 2003/4/EC): Case 14/83 *Von Colson v Land Nordrhein-Westfalen* [1984] ECR 1891 (CJEU); Case C-106/89 *Marleasing SA v La Comercial*

have two important consequences. First, the Tribunal and the courts will need to be persuaded that there is sufficient judicial control over the operation of the relevant provisions when reading and giving effect to them generally and when considering whether it is possible and appropriate to intervene in relation to decisions taken thereunder.[221] Secondly, the Tribunal and the courts will apply a more intensive proportionality-based standard of scrutiny if and when called upon to review any such decisions.[222] Whether any relevant Convention or

Internacional de Alimentacion SA [1990] ECR I-4135 (CJEU); Cases C-240-244/98 *Océano Grupo Editorial v Rocio Murciano Quintero* [2000] ECR I-449 (CJEU); P Craig, 'Directives: Direct Effect, Indirect Effect and the Construction of National Legislation' (1997) 22 EL Rev 519. In relation to the interpretation of DPA 1998 see in particular: *Campbell v MGN Ltd* [2002] EWCA Civ 1373, [2003] QB 633 (CA) at [96] (Phillips MR); *Durant v Financial Services Authority* [2003] EWCA Civ 1746, [2004] FSR 28 (CA) at [3]-[4] (Auld LJ); *Common Services Agency v IC* [2008] UKHL 47, [2008] 1 WLR 1550 at [7], [20]-[27] (Lord Hope), [82] (Lord Rodger), [91] (Baroness Hale); *South Lanarkshire Council v Scottish IC* [2013] UKSC 55, [2013] 1 WLR 2421 at [7]-[8] (Baroness Hale, giving the judgment of the Court); *Vidal Hall v Google Inc* [2015] EWCA Civ 311, [2016] QB 1003. Where Community law can be relied upon, the legality of acts done by European Community member states in the exercise of powers conferred or reserved by Community law falls to be determined by reference to the 'general principles of Community law' which include principles of administrative or procedural fairness: J Usher, *General Principles of EC Law*, (London, Longmans, 1998); T Tridimas, *The General Principles of EU Law*, 3rd edn (Oxford, Oxford University Press, 2018); P Craig and G De Búrca, *EU Law: Text, Cases and Materials*, 6th edn (Oxford, Oxford University Press, 2015), Ch 11. In relation to procedural fairness, these principles can confer a right to a fair hearing (Case 17/74 *Transocean Marine Paint Association v EC Commission* [1974] ECR 1063 (CJEU) at 1080) and to judicial oversight and control (Case 222/84 *Johnston v Chief Constable of the Royal Ulster Constabulary* [1987] QB 129 (CJEU) at 147 (although note that the decision itself rested on 'the principle of effective judicial control laid down in article 6 of Council Directive (76/207/EEC) of 9 February 1976': see 155)).

221 The scope for appealing national security certificates issued under FOIA ss 23(2) and 24(3), DPA 2018 ss 27(1), 79(1) and 111(1) and EIR reg 15(1) should suffice for these purposes but questions may nevertheless arise as to the grounds and intensity of the review thereby allowed (cf the non-appealability of parliamentary certificates issued under FOIA ss 34(3) and 36(7). In *Tinnelly and Sons Ltd v United Kingdom* (1999) 27 EHRR 249 (ECtHR) two non-appealable certificates had been signed by the Secretary of State under the Fair Employment (Northern Ireland) Act 1976 s 42 certifying conclusively that certain decisions were acts done for the purpose of safeguarding national security, etc. The European Court of Human Rights held that: civil rights under the ECHR Art 6(1) were engaged (at [61]-[63]); the scope for judicial review of the certificates was limited to a review of whether they had been obtained or issued in bad faith and could not entail 'full scrutiny' of their factual basis (at [74]-[75]); and the exclusion of a judicial determination of the merits of the complaints constituted a disproportionate interference with the applicants' rights under the ECHR, Art 6(1) (at [77] and [79]). In Case 222/84 *Johnston v Chief Constable of the Royal Ulster Constabulary* [1987] QB 129 (CJEU) a non-appealable certificate had been signed by the Secretary of State under the Sex Discrimination (Northern Ireland) Order 1976 SI 1976/1042 (NI 15) Art 53(2) certifying conclusively that Mrs Johnston had been refused employment on the grounds of national security, etc. The CJEU held that the exclusion of judicial review was contrary to Community law: 'The requirement of judicial control stipulated by [article 6 of the Equal Treatment Directive] reflects a general principle of law which underlies the constitutional traditions common to the member states. That principle is also laid down in articles 6 and 13 of the [ECHR]' (at 147); and 'The principle of effective judicial control laid down in article 6 of Council Directive (76/207/EEC) of 9 February 1976 does not allow a [national security certificate]...to exclude the exercise of any power of review by the courts' (at 155).

222 The traditional standard of review for reasonableness is that enunciated in *Associated Provincial Picture Houses Ltd v Wednesbury Corp* [1948] 1 KB 223 (CA) and *Council of Civil Service Unions v Minister for the Civil Service* [1985] AC 374 at 410 (Lord Diplock). As a matter of common law principle, a heightened standard of review will be applied where 'fundamental rights' are engaged (*R v Ministry of Defence, ex p Smith* [1996] QB 517 (CA) at 554 (Bingham MR)) and where 'Convention rights' are engaged for the purposes of the Human Rights Act 1998 a yet more intensive proportionality-based standard of review is appropriate (*R (Daly) v SSHD* [2001] UKHL 26, [2001] 2 AC 532 at [26]-[27] (Lord Steyn)); *Kennedy v Charity Commission* [2014] UKSC 20, [2015] AC 455 at [51]-[55]; *R (Lord Carlile of Berriew QC) v SSHD* [2014] UKSC 60, [2015] AC 915 at [31]-[34]; *Pham v SSHD* [2015] UKSC 19, [2015] 1 WLR 1591 at [59]-[60], [98], [108]-[110]. In the light of these principles, the Information Tribunal adopted a proportionality-based standard of review in *Baker v SSHD* [2001] UKHRR 1275 in an appeal under DPA 1998 s 28(4) against a certificate issued by the Home Secretary which effectively conferred a blanket exemption allowing the Security Service to respond with a 'neither confirm nor deny' reply to every request made to it under DPA 1998 s 7(1)(a) without considering each request on its individual merits (at [83]). Having referred in general terms to the Council of Europe Convention for the Protection of Individuals with Regard to Automatic Processing of Personal Data dated 28 January 1981, the European Community Data Protection Directive 95/46/EC dated 24 October 1995 and the Human Rights Act 1998 ss 1, 3 and 6, the Tribunal asked itself whether the issue of the certificate was 'reasonable in the extended sense of proportionate by reference to the precepts of the ECHR' (at [63]) and concluded that the certificate had an 'unnecessarily wide effect' and should be quashed accordingly (summary, [14]). See also *Gosling v SSHD*, IT, 1 August 2003; *Hitchens v SSHD*, IT, 4 August 2003; *Hilton v FCO*, IT, 28 June 2005; *Stevenson v SSHD*, IT, 30 April 2009. Whether or not human rights are engaged for these purposes, it remains the case that the courts will show 'considerable deference' to the executive's assessment of

Community rights will be engaged by the issue of conclusive certificates for these purposes is another matter[223] but the rights which are most likely to be relied upon in this regard are: rights to procedural fairness and judicial oversight under Art 6 of the ECHR and the general principles of Community law;[224] rights to privacy and data protection rights under Article 8 of the ECHR, Arts 7-8 of the CFR, the GDPR and the LED,[225] and rights to freedom of expression under Article 10 of the ECHR and Art 11 of the CFR.[226]

5– 038 Legislative history

The policy and consultation documents which preceded and underlay FOIA contain very little discussion of its conclusive evidence clauses.[227] Section 28 of the DPA 1998 was plainly the model for s 24 of FOIA[228] and thus provided a template for adopting a certification procedure in relation to the national security exemption.[229] So far as parliamentary debate is concerned, Mr O'Brien, the Home Office Minister, made the following points during the Report and Third Reading debate in the House of Commons in relation to the clauses which became ss 23-24 of FOIA:

---

national security matters whilst bearing in mind that they must do so 'in a manner appropriate to the national security context': *Baker v SSHD* [2001] UKHRR 1275 at [76]; *Gosling v SSHD*, IT, 1 August 2003 at [44] and [48]; *SSHD v Rehman* [2001] UKHL 47, [2003] 1 AC 153 at [50] and [62] (Lord Hoffmann) and at [16] (Lord Slynn); *A v SSHD* [2004] UKHL 56, [2005] 2 AC 68, 'Safeguarding national security is (with the possible exception of some questions of macro-economic policy and allocation of resources) the area of policy in which the courts are most reluctant to question or interfere with the judgment of the executive or (a fortiori) the enacted will of the legislature' at [192] (Lord Walker dissenting). Although these cases pre-date the creation of the new tribunal system, in these situations consideration does not appear to have been given to the appointment of an independent assessor to assist the tribunal evaluate matters. Section 27(1) of the Tribunals Courts and Enforcement Act 2007 provides:

> 'If it appears to the First-tier Tribunal or the Upper Tribunal that a matter before it requires special expertise not otherwise available to it, it may direct that in dealing with that matter it shall have the assistance of a person or persons appearing to it to have relevant knowledge or experience.'

For more recent discussion of judicial scrutiny and 'deference' in the national security context see: *Bank Mellat v Her Majesty's Treasury* [2013] UKSC 38, [2014] AC 700 at [21]; *R (Lord Carlile of Berriew QC) v SSHD* [2014] UKSC 60, [2015] AC 915 at [19]-[34].

223 See §§5– 043 to 5– 046.

224 See §5– 044. See, generally, §4– 023.

225 See §5– 045. See, generally, §§4– 005 to 4– 030.

226 See §5– 046. See, generally, §§4– 015 to 4– 034.

227 As already mentioned, the use of conclusive certificate provisions is by no means unprecedented, particularly in the national security context, and once an exemption has been settled on as a matter of principle, the technicalities of its application are much less likely to generate political or public interest or debate.

228 'The clause [which became FOIA s 24] is drafted in similar terms to section 28 of the DPA 1998. The two provisions have the same purpose. It is therefore sensible for them to be drafted in similar language. Any difference of approach between the provisions could lead to them being interpreted differently. Clearly, that is not the intention' (Mr O'Brien, the Home Office Minister, Report and Third Reading debate on the Freedom of Information Bill in the House of Commons: Hansard HC vol 347 col 1060 (5 April 2000).

229 DPA 1998 s 28 was itself preceded by the national security exemption in the DPA 1984 s 27 which provided that, 'Any question whether the exemption mentioned in subsection (1) above is or at any time was required for the purpose there mentioned [ie the purpose of safeguarding national security] in respect of any personal data shall be determined by a Minister of the Crown; and a certificate signed by a Minister of the Crown certifying that the exemption is or at any time was so required shall be conclusive evidence of that fact.' — DPA 1984 s 27(2), see also s 27(3). The 'required for the purpose of safeguarding national security' test was therefore the same under both Acts, the key difference being the addition of an appeal mechanism in DPA 1998 s 28. This was explained during the parliamentary passage of the 1998 Data Protection Bill as follows: 'This is broadly familiar from the 1984 provision, but it contains two important changes. First, it allows a certificate confirming the need for the exemption to be expressed in general terms and to be prospective, and, secondly, it allows a limited right of appeal to the Data Protection Tribunal for individuals who are affected by such a certificate.' — Hansard HL vol 585 col 441 (2 February 1998) (Home Office Minister, Lord Williams, Second Reading). Similarly: 'The right of appeal against a national security certificate is an important new safeguard. It represents an advance on the 1984 Act, which offered no appeal rights.' — Hansard HC vol 315 col 586 (2 July 1998) (Home Office Minister, Mr Howarth, Report and Third Reading).

— information covered by certificates signed under these provisions will be 'extremely sensitive' and should not therefore be seen by the Information Commissioner or his staff;
— such certificates can only be signed 'at the highest level'; and
— they will not operate as 'ministerial vetoes' because they are 'nothing more than evidential certificates' subject to challenge before the Tribunal.[230]

During Committee Stage in the House of Lords, Lord Falconer of Thoroton, the Cabinet Office Minister, said he could not conceive that a conclusive certificate issued under the clause which became s 23 of FOIA could ever be subject to an exemption itself or be anything other than a public document.[231]

5–039 Comparative jurisdictions

At the time that FOIA was enacted, the Freedom of Information Act 1982 (Cth of Aust) and the Freedom of Information Act 1997 (Ireland) both[232] provided for the issue of conclusive certificates as a means of activating certain exemptions:[233]

(1) Under the Freedom of Information Act 1982 (Cth of Aust), conclusive certificates could be issued by ministers under s 33(2) and (4) (documents affecting national security, defence or international relations), s 33A(2) and (4) (documents affecting relations with States) and s 36(3) (internal working documents),[234] by the Secretary to the Department of the Prime Minister and Cabinet under s 34(2) and (4) (Cabinet documents) and by the Secretary to the Executive Council (or a person performing his or her duties) under s 35(2) and (4) (Executive Council documents). Such certificates were required, where appropriate, to identify the part or parts of the document covered by the relevant exemption[235] and they had to make clear the particular kind of document in respect of which the exemption had been claimed.[236] While they remained in force,[237] such certificates were conclusive in their effect subject to the relevant review procedures in Part VI of the Freedom of Information Act 1982 (Cth of Aust). In this latter regard, the Administrative Appeals Tribunal, on an application under s 55, could not review the decision to give the certificate but could review 'whether there existed reasonable grounds' for claiming that the relevant exemption applies.[238] It had been held 'that it is a heavy thing for the Tribunal to reject

230 Hansard HC vol 347 col 1060 (5 April 2000).

231 Hansard HL vol 617 col 1259 (19 October 2000). See also J Wadham and J Griffiths, *Blackstone's Guide to the Freedom of Information Act 2000*, 4th edn (Oxford, Oxford University Press, 2011) para 7.3.2 contending that the minister's assertion is 'open to question.'

232 As to the position under the Access to Information Act (1982) (Canada) see §§51– 025 to 51– 030.

233 Official Information Act 1982 s 31 (NZ) allows for certificates to be issued preventing an Ombudsman from recommending the disclosure of information where this would be likely to prejudice: (a) security, defence or international relations (power conferred on Prime Minister); or (b) the prevention, investigation or detection of offences (power conferred on Attorney-General). These are not 'conclusive certificates' as such but they operate in a similar way and demonstrate a common approach in relation to the provision of executive override mechanisms in areas generally regarded as being particularly sensitive. See §51– 021.

234 Ministerial certificates were required to specify the relevant ground of exemption: Freedom of Information Act 1982, ss 33(2) and (4), 33A(2) and (4) and 36(3) (Cth of Aust). In relation to certificates under Freedom of Information Act 1982 s 36(3) (Cth of Aust), see *McKinnon v Secretary, Department of Treasury* [2006] HCA 45, (2006) 229 ALR 187. These were abolished by the Freedom of Information (Removal of Conclusive Certificates and Other Measures) Act 2009.

235 Freedom of Information Act 1982 ss 33(3), 33A(3), 34(3), 35(3), 36(4) (Cth of Aust).

236 *Department of Industrial Relations v Forrest* (1990) 21 FCR 93, 11 AAR 256, 91 ALR 417 (certificate under Freedom of Information Act 1982 s 34 (Cth of Aust) invalid for uncertainty).

237 Freedom of Information Act 1982 s 36A (Cth of Aust).

238 Freedom of Information Act 1982 s 58(3), (4), (5) and (5A) (Cth of Aust). The issue for the Tribunal under s 58(4), (5) and (5A) had been whether the view expressed in the certificate was reasonably open to the Minister and not

a certified claim.'[239] However, the above-mentioned provisions were all repealed with effect from 7 October 2009 by the Freedom of Information (Removal of Conclusive Certificates and other Measures) Act 2009 (Cth of Aust),[240] thereby removing conclusive certificates entirely from the scheme of the Freedom of Information Act 1982 (Cth of Aust).

(2) In relation to the Freedom of Information Act 1997 (Ireland), conclusive certificates could be issued by ministers under s 25 in order to declare that a record was exempt by virtue of s 23 (law enforcement and public safety) or s 24 (security, defence and international relations).[241] Such certificates could only be issued where access to a record had been refused in reliance on one of these exemptions and the minister was satisfied that the record was of 'sufficient sensitivity or seriousness' to 'justify' the issue of a certificate.[242] While they remained in force,[243] such certificates were conclusive in their effect[244] subject to appeal to the High Court on a point of law under s 42(2) of the Freedom of Information Act 1997 (Ireland). The Act also establishes various mechanisms for monitoring, controlling and publicising the use of such certificates.[245] These provisions were re-enacted in substantially the same terms in ss 32-34 of the Freedom of Information Act 2014 (Ireland).

5–040 National security certificates

Appealable ministerial national security certificates may be issued under FOIA, the DPA 2018[246] and the EIR as follows:

---

whether it was reasonable to release the document: *Re Bracken and Minister of State for Education and Youth Affairs* (1984) 2 AAR 406, (1985) 7 ALD 243; *Re Waterford and the Treasurer of the Commonwealth (No 2)* (1985) 8 ALN N37; *Re Porter and Department of Community Services* (1988) 8 AAR 335, 14 ALD 403; *Department of Industrial Relations v Burchill* (1991) 33 FCR 122, 14 AAR 408, 105 ALR 327; *Re Cleary and Department of the Treasury* (1993) 18 AAR 83; *Australian Doctors Fund Ltd v Commonwealth* (1994) 49 FCR 478, 34 ALD 451; *McKinnon v Secretary, Department of Treasury* [2006] HCA 45, (2006) 229 ALR 187. Specific provision was made regarding the constitution of the Tribunal and its hearings in cases where a conclusive certificate had been issued: Freedom of Information Act 1982, ss 58B, 58C and 58E (Cth of Aust). Where the Tribunal determined that there did not exist reasonable grounds for claiming that an exemption applied, the appropriate minister had 28 days either to revoke the certificate or follow the special procedure for deciding not to do so: Freedom of Information Act 1982 s 58A (Cth of Aust). The existence of these review procedures did not oust the scope for judicial review of the issue of conclusive certificates: *Shergold v Tanner* [2002] HCA 19, (2002) 188 ALR 302.

239 *Re Porter and Department of Community Services and Health* (1988) 14 ALD 403 at 405-406.

240 Section 1, Sch 3.

241 M McDonagh, *Freedom of Information Law in Ireland*, 2nd edn (Dublin, Thomson Round Hall, 2006), pp 154-158. See now Freedom of Information Act 2014 ss 32-34 (Ireland).

242 Freedom of Information Act 1997 s 25(1)(a) (Ireland). See now Freedom of Information Act 2014 s 34(1)(a) (Ireland).

243 Freedom of Information Act 1997 s 25(9), (10) and (13) (Ireland). See now Freedom of Information Act 2014 s 32-34(9), (10) and (13) (Ireland).

244 Freedom of Information Act 1997 s 25(3) (Ireland). The issue of a certificate could not therefore be subject to internal review or review by the Information Commissioner: Freedom of Information Act 1997 s 25(3)(b) (Ireland). See now Freedom of Information Act 2014 s 34(3) (Ireland).

245 Under the Freedom of Information Act 1997 s 25(6)(b) (Ireland) the Taoiseach (and prescribed ministers) were provided with a copy of every certificate and a statement explaining why it was issued and, under s 25(7), they were required to carry out periodic reviews of the operation of s 25(1). The Taoiseach also had power under s 25(8) to conduct specific reviews of the operation of s 25(1) in relation to particular ministers or certificates. In accordance with s 25(9), both periodic and specific reviews could result in requests that a certificate be revoked which had to be complied with. Each minister was also required to provide the Information Commissioner with a written annual return detailing the number of conclusive certificates issued by him or her in the preceding year and these were then appended to the Commissioner's annual report to the Houses of the Oireachtas: ss 25(11) and 40(1)(b). See now Freedom of Information Act 2014 ss 34, 47(2) (Ireland).

246 DPA 2018 s 130 requires all national security certificates issued under ss 27, 79 and 111 to be copied to the Information Commissioner who must then publish a record setting out the name of the issuing Minister and the

(1) Under s 23(2) of FOIA a Minister of the Crown may sign a certificate certifying that the information to which it applies was directly or indirectly supplied by, or relates to, any of the 'security bodies' specified in s 23(3). Such a certificate will then stand as conclusive evidence of that fact, thus confirming the engagement of the s 23 exemption, unless and until withdrawn or revoked[247] or quashed on an appeal under s 60(1) of FOIA. The coincidence between what is certified by a s 23(2) certificate and what is required to engage the s 23(1) exemption is not perfect. The certificate will not certify whether the information was directly or indirectly supplied *to* the public authority *by* any of the s 23(3) bodies. It is possible that a public authority's holding of information to which a certificate applies may not result, directly or indirectly, from a supply by any of the bodies specified in s 23(3). For example, where a public authority has acquired the information independently or where it has acquired it from a third party that has itself acquired it independently.[248] There is no provision allowing such a certificate to identify the information to which it applies by means of a general description or to be expressed to have prospective effect.[249] Such a certificate may only be signed by a Minister who is a member of the Cabinet or by the Attorney-General, the Advocate General for Scotland or the Attorney-General for Northern Ireland.[250] While a s 23(2) certificate facilitates the rendering of information as exempt information and the disapplication of the disclosure duty, it is not determinative of the separate question whether the duty to confirm or deny arises, although it will undoubtedly bear on this issue.

(2) Under s 24(3) of FOIA a Minister of the Crown may sign a certificate certifying that exemption from the disclosure duty in s 1(1)(b), or from the divulgence and disclosure duties in s 1(1)(a) and (b), is, or at any time was, required for the purpose of safeguarding national security.[251] Such a certificate will then stand as conclusive

date and text of each certificate, save for any text whose publication would, in the Minister's opinion, be against the interests of national security or contrary to the public interest or a risk to the safety of any person.

247 There is no obvious reason for construing FOIA ss 23(2), 24(3), 34(3) or 36(7), DPA 2018 ss 27(1), 79(1) or 111(1), or EIR reg 15(1) as preventing the withdrawal or revocation of certificates or rendering their signatories *functus officio*. Changes in circumstances may very well make the withdrawal or revocation of a certificate appropriate without the need (where this route is open) for an appeal to the Upper Tribunal. The existence of an implied power of revocation is confirmed by the language of the DPA s 130(6) and Sch 20 para 17(3). See also: *Al Fayed v SSHD*, IT, 28 February 2002 at [9] and [15]-[16]; W Wade and C Forsyth, *Administrative Law*, 11th edn (Oxford, Oxford University Press, 2014) pp 191-194; and the Interpretation Act 1978 s 12.

248 Always assuming, of course, that it does not relate to any of the s 23(3) bodies.

249 Compare FOIA s 24(4), on the one hand, and DPA 1998 s 28(3) and DPA 2018 ss 27(2)(b), 79(4) and 111(2)(b), on the other.

250 FOIA s 25(3). The continued inclusion of the Attorney-General for Northern Ireland in s 25(3) as a 'Minister of the Crown' able to exercise the power to issue certificates under ss 23(2) and 24(3) is curious and open to question following the devolution of justice matters to the Northern Ireland Executive on 12 April 2010. Up to that point, the Attorney-General for England and Wales was also ex officio the Attorney-General for Northern Ireland. However, this state of affairs ended with the entry into force of the Justice (Northern Ireland) Act 2002 Pt 2 on 12 April 2010 and the Attorney-General for Northern Ireland is now a (devolved) 'Northern Ireland Minister' appointed and funded by the Northern Ireland First Minister and deputy First Minister acting jointly (s 22). FOIA s 84 (read with the Ministers of the Crown Act 1975 s 8(1)) provides that 'Minister of the Crown' means 'the holder of an office in Her Majesty's Government in the United Kingdom, and includes the Treasury, the Board of Trade and the Defence Council.' Furthermore, it is clear that this expression does not ordinarily include 'Northern Ireland Ministers' when used in FOIA (cf ss 4(9) and 6(3)). The Attorney-General for Northern Ireland has no particular responsibilities in relation to securities bodies, national security or the subject matter of FOIA ss 23-24 and he would appear not to be a Minister of the Crown for the purposes of FOIA. Accordingly, it would appear arguable that a reference to the new (non-devolved) Advocate General for Northern Ireland (who is also the Attorney-General for England and Wales by virtue of the Justice (Northern Ireland) Act 2002 s 27) should be substituted for the reference to the Attorney-General for Northern Ireland in FOIA s 25(3).

251 FOI(S)A s 31(2)-(3). Under FOI(S)A s 31(2) a certificate may be signed by a member of the Scottish Executive and

evidence of that fact, thus confirming the engagement of the s 24 exemption, unless and until withdrawn or revoked or quashed on an appeal under s 60(1) or (4) of FOIA. If a s 24(3) certificate is confined to exemption from s 1(1)(b), determination of the existence duty will be decided on the ordinary basis, unaffected by the certificate. A s 24(3) certificate may not deem that the public interest in maintaining the exemption outweighs the public interest in divulgence or disclosure but may identify the information to which it applies by means of a general description and may be expressed to have prospective effect.[252] Such a certificate may only be signed by a Minister who is a member of the Cabinet or by the Attorney-General, the Advocate General for Scotland or the Attorney-General for Northern Ireland.[253]

(3) Under s 27(1) of the DPA 2018 a Minister of the Crown may sign a national security certificate certifying that exemption from all or any of the provisions of the applied GDPR or the DPA 2018 listed in s 26(2) of that Act is, or at any time was, required in relation to any personal data for the purpose of safeguarding national security.[254] Such a certificate will then stand as conclusive evidence of that fact, thus confirming the engagement of the national security exemption in s 26(1)(a) of the DPA 2018, unless and until withdrawn or revoked or quashed on an appeal under s 27(3) or (5). Such a certificate may identify the personal data to which it applies by means of a general description and may be expressed to have prospective effect.[255] Such a certificate may only be signed by a Minister who is a member of the Cabinet or by the Attorney-General or the Advocate General for Scotland.[256]

(4) Under s 79(1) of the DPA 2018 a Minister of the Crown may sign a national security certificate certifying that a restriction on the provision of information to a data subject under ss 44(2), 45(1), 48(1)(b)(i) or 68(1) – imposed by a competent authority carrying out law enforcement processing subject to Part 3 of that Act – is a necessary and proportionate measure to protect national security for the purposes

---

will stand as being conclusive of the fact certified (ie exemption from s 1(1) is required for the purpose of safeguarding national security): FOI(S)A does not expressly provide or allow for any appeal or review. Under FOI(S)A s 31(3), such a certificate may identify the information to which it applies by means of a general description and may be expressed to have prospective effect.

252 FOIA s 24(4). Pursuant to FOIA s 60(4) a public authority may claim in proceedings under or by virtue of that Act that a certificate issued under s 24(3) which identifies the information to which it applies by means of a general description applies to particular information and, subject to any contrary determination by the Upper Tribunal on appeal, the certificate will be conclusively presumed so to apply.

253 FOIA s 25(3). See fn 250 above in relation to the questionable inclusion of the Attorney-General for Northern Ireland in s 25(3).

254 Prior to the entry into force of the GDPR and the DPA 2018 - and the repeal of the DPA 1998 - DPA 1998 s 28(2) allowed a Minister of the Crown to sign a national security certificate certifying that exemption from all or any of the provisions of the data protection principles provided for by Pts II, III or V or ss 54A or 55 of the DPA 1998 (which included the subject access rights conferred by s 7) was, or at any time had been, required for the purpose of safeguarding national security in respect of any personal data. Such a certificate then stood as conclusive evidence of that fact, thus confirming the engagement of the exemption in DPA 1998 s 28, unless and until withdrawn or revoked or quashed on an appeal under s 28(4) or (6). Such a certificate could: identify the personal data to which it applied by means of a general description and be expressed to have prospective effect (DPA 1998 s 28(3)); and be signed only by a Minister who was a member of the Cabinet or by the Attorney-General or the Advocate General for Scotland (DPA 1998 s 28(10)). DPA 2018 Sch 20, paras 17-18 and 40 contain transitional provisions: saving the effect of the DPA 1998 s 28 and any certificates made thereunder with respect to the processing of personal data to which that Act applies (para 17); and continuing the effect of any such certificate as if it were a certificate made under one or more of the DPA 2018 ss 27, 79 and 111 for one year following the entry into force of the repeal of the DPA 1998 s 28 (para 18).

255 DPA 2018 s 27(2). Pursuant to DPA 2018 s 27(5)-(7) a data controller may claim in proceedings under or by virtue of the applied GDPR or the DPA 2018 that a certificate under s 27(1) which identifies the personal data to which it applies by means of a general description applies to any personal data and, subject to any contrary determination of the Upper Tribunal on appeal, the certificate will be conclusively presumed so to apply.

256 DPA 2018 s 27(10).

of ss 44(4), 45(4), 48(3) or 68(7).[257] Such a certificate will then stand as conclusive evidence of that fact, thus confirming the engagement of the national security limb of the relevant provision, unless and until withdrawn or revoked or quashed on an appeal under s 79(5) or (7). Such a certificate may relate to a specific restriction or proposed restriction or identify any restriction to which it relates by means of a general description and may be expressed to have prospective effect.[258] Such a certificate may only be signed by a Minister who is a member of the Cabinet or by the Attorney-General or the Advocate General for Scotland.[259]

(5) Under s 111(1) of the DPA 2018 a Minister of the Crown may sign a national security certificate certifying that exemption from all or any of the provisions of Part 4 - on intelligence service processing - mentioned in s 110(2) of that Act is, or at any time was, required for the purpose of safeguarding national security in respect of any personal data. Such a certificate will then stand as conclusive evidence of that fact, thus confirming the engagement of the national security exemption in s 110(1) of the DPA 2018, unless and until withdrawn or revoked or quashed on an appeal under s 111(3) or (5). Such a certificate may identify the personal data to which it applies by means of a general description and may be expressed to have prospective effect.[260] Such a certificate may only be signed by a Minister who is a member of the Cabinet or by the Attorney-General or the Advocate General for Scotland.

(6) Under reg 15(1) of the EIR a Minister of the Crown may certify that a refusal to disclose information under reg 12(1) is required because the disclosure would adversely affect national security and would not be in the public interest under reg 12(1)(b).[261] For these purposes, Ministers of the Crown may designate persons to certify these matters on their behalf and a refusal to disclose information under reg 12(1) includes a neither confirm nor deny response under reg 12(6).[262] A certificate issued in accordance with reg 15(1) will then stand as conclusive evidence of the fact that disclosure would adversely affect national security and would not be in the public interest, unless and until withdrawn or revoked or quashed on an appeal under s 60 of FOIA.[263] A national security certificate under reg 15(1) of the EIR may identify the information to which it relates in general terms but there is no express provision allowing for such certificates to be expressed to have prospective effect.[264] The power to sign such a certificate or to designate another

[257] Restrictions imposed under the DPA 2018 ss 44(4), 45(4), 48(3) or 68(7) may restrict the provision of information in whole or in part and to the extent that and for so long as necessary and proportionate having regard to the fundamental rights and interests of the data subject. DPA 2018 s 79(13) further provides that none of the enforcement powers conferred by Pt 6 of that Act may be exercised in relation to the imposition of a specific restriction in a s 79(1) certificate or a restriction falling within a general description in such a certificate.

[258] DPA 2018 s 79(2) and (4). Pursuant to DPA 2018 s 79(7)-(9) a data controller may claim in proceedings under or by virtue of the DPA 2018 that a restriction under ss 44(4), 45(4), 48(3) or 68(7) falls within a general description in a certificate under s 79(1) and, subject to any contrary determination of the Upper Tribunal on appeal, the restriction will be conclusively presumed so to fall.

[259] DPA 2018 s 79(12).

[260] DPA 2018 s 111(2). Pursuant to DPA 2018 s 111(5)-(7) a data controller may claim in proceedings under or by virtue of the DPA 2018 that a certificate under s 111(1) which identifies the personal data to which it applies by means of a general description applies to any personal data and, subject to any contrary determination of the Upper Tribunal on appeal, the certificate will be conclusively presumed so to apply.

[261] See also EI(S)R reg 12.

[262] EIR reg 15(2).

[263] FOIA s 60 is applied for the purposes of the EIR with modifications by EIR reg 18(1), (3)-(4), (7). As to appeals, see §45– 026.

[264] Compare FOIA s 24(4) and DPA 2018 ss 27(1), 79(1) and 111(1).

person to certify the relevant matters is only exercisable by a Minister who is a member of the Cabinet or by the Attorney-General, the Advocate General for Scotland or the Attorney-General for Northern Ireland.[265]

5– 041 National security appeals

The appeals procedure is considered in detail later in this work.[266] In summary, certificates issued under ss 23(2) and 24(3) of FOIA, ss 27(1), 79(1) and 111(1) of the DPA 2018 and reg 15(1) of the EIR may be appealed to the Upper Tribunal under a common appeal mechanism provided for by ss 60-61 of FOIA, ss 27, 79 and 111 of the DPA 2018 and reg 18 of the EIR.

(1) In relation to certificates issued under ss 23(2) and 24(3) of FOIA and reg 15(1) of the EIR, such an appeal may be brought by the Information Commissioner or any applicant whose request for information is affected and, in relation to certificates issued under ss 27(1), 79(1) and 111(1) of the DPA 2018, such an appeal may be brought by any person directly affected.[267] The Tribunal may allow the appeal and quash the certificate if it finds: in relation to a certificate under s 23(2) of FOIA, that the information referred to in the certificate was not exempt information by virtue of s 23(1);[268] or, in relation to a certificate under s 24(3) of FOIA, s 27(1), 79(1) or 111(1) of the DPA 2018 or reg 15(1) of the EIR, that, applying the principles applied by the court on an application for judicial review, the Minister or the person designated by him did not have reasonable grounds for issuing the certificate.[269]

---

265 EIR reg 15(6) giving the term 'Minister of the Crown' in reg 15(1)-(2) and (5) the same meaning as in FOIA s 25(3). See fn 250 above in relation to the questionable inclusion of the Attorney-General for Northern Ireland in s 25(3).

266 See §§45– 026 to 45– 020 and 49– 016 to 49– 017.

267 FOIA s 60(1) and EIR reg 18(7)(a); DPA 2018 ss 27(3), 79(5) and 111(3). FOIA s 60 is applied for the purposes of the EIR with modifications by EIR reg 18(1), (3)-(4), (7). Appeals under FOIA s 60, DPA 2018 ss 27(1), 79(1) and 111(1) and EIR reg 18(7) are governed by UT Rules. Where a national security certificate is issued under DPA 2018 ss 27(1) and 111(1) in response to an assessment by the Information Commissioner under DPA 2018 s 146 and/or the issue by the Information Commissioner of an information notice under DPA 2018 s 142, the Information Commissioner will be a 'person directly affected' by the issuing of that certificate for the purposes of DPA 2018 s 27(3) or 111(3) who will therefore be able to appeal to the Upper Tribunal against the certificate (see *R (SSHD) v Information Tribunal* [2006] EWHC 2958 (Admin), [2007] 2 All ER 703 (DC) at [41] (Latham LJ), in relation to the equivalent provisions in DPA 1998 ss 28 and 42-43).

268 FOIA s 60(2). The Tribunal is thus given full appellate jurisdiction to review the matter, unconstrained by any caveat that it 'apply the principles applied by the court on an application for judicial review' and assess only whether the minister had 'reasonable grounds for issuing the certificate' (cf FOIA s 60(3), DPA 2018 ss 27(4), 79(6) and 111(4), and EIR reg 18(7)).

269 FOIA s 60(3); DPA 2018 ss 27(4), 79(6) and 111(4); EIR reg 18(7). In determining whether the minister did or did not have reasonable grounds for issuing the certificate, the Tribunal will inevitably have to assess whether the minister did or did not have reasonable grounds for concluding: in relation to FOIA s 24(3) and DPA 2018 ss 27(1) and 111(1), that exemption from the relevant provision is, or at any time was, required for the purpose of safeguarding national security; in relation to DPA 2018 s 79(1), that the relevant information is a necessary and proportionate measure to protect national security; or, in relation to EIR reg 15(1), that disclosure would adversely affect national security and would not be in the public interest. See the discussion of the analogous 'reasonable grounds' provision in FOIA s 53(2) in *R (Evans) v Attorney-General* [2015] UKSC 21, [2015] AC 1787. It would appear that the Tribunal is thus confined to applying only one of the three heads of judicial review identified in *Council of Civil Service Unions v Minister for the Civil Service* [1985] AC 374 at 410 (Lord Diplock) (ie irrationality but not illegality or procedural impropriety): if the minister took into account an irrelevant consideration or failed to take into account a relevant consideration, made an error of law or failed to act fairly in a procedural sense this will only be relevant if and in so far as it led or contributed to him not having reasonable grounds for issuing the certificate. So far as concerns 'the principles applied by the court on an application for judicial review' in relation to 'reasonable grounds', the Tribunal will review whether the minister's decision was reasonable or so unreasonable that no reasonable minister could have taken it (*Associated Provincial Picture Houses Ltd v Wednesbury Corp* [1948] 1 KB 223 (CA)) and the intensity of its scrutiny will increase if it can be shown that 'fundamental rights' are engaged (*R v Ministry of Defence, ex p Smith* [1996] QB 517 (CA) at 554 (Bingham MR)). If satisfied that a 'Convention right' as defined by the Human Rights Act 1998 has also been affected by the minister's decision and the appellant may have been the 'victim' of this for the purposes of that Act, the Tribunal will also need to go further and determine whether the decision to issue a certificate was compatible with that Convention right and would thus have to apply

(2) A second type of appeal may be brought under s 60(4) of FOIA or s 27(7), 79(7) or 111(5) of the DPA 2018 by a party to any proceedings under or by virtue of the relevant Act if it is claimed by a public authority or a data controller that a certificate issued under s 24(3) of FOIA or s 27(1), 79(1) or 111(1) of the DPA 2018 which identifies the information, personal data or restriction to which it applies by means of a general description applies to particular information or personal data or a particular restriction. It is arguable that such an appeal may also be brought under s 60(4) of FOIA by a party to any proceedings under the EIR where similar claims are made by a public authority in relation to a certificate issued under reg 15(1) of the Regulations.[270] Appeals of this type are also dealt with elsewhere in this work,[271] but it should be noted here that the Tribunal has power to determine that the certificate in question does not apply to the information, personal data or restriction referred to by the public authority or data controller.[272]

5– 042 Parliamentary certificates

Non-appealable parliamentary certificates may be issued under FOIA as follows:

(1) Under s 34(3) of FOIA, the 'appropriate authority' may sign a certificate certifying that exemption from the disclosure duty in s 1(1)(b), or from the divulgence and disclosure duties in s 1(1)(a) and (b), is, or at any time was, required for the purpose of avoiding an infringement of the privileges of either House of Parliament.[273] Such

---

a more intensive proportionality-based standard of review: *R (Daly) v SSHD* [2001] UKHL 26, [2001] 2 AC 532 at [26]-[27] (Lord Steyn); *Baker v SSHD* [2001] UKHRR 1275, at [63]; *Gosling v SSHD*, IT, 1 August 2003 at [48]. See also: *Kennedy v Charity Commission* [2014] UKSC 20, [2015] AC 455 at [51]-[55]; *R (Lord Carlile of Berriew QC) v SSHD* [2014] UKSC 60, [2015] AC 915 at [31]-[34]; *Pham v SSHD* [2015] UKSC 19, [2015] 1 WLR 1591 at [59]-[60], [98], [108]-[110]. The language used in FOIA s 60(3) and DPA 2018 ss 27(4), 79(6) and 111(4) might also be thought to suggest that the Tribunal must focus solely on the grounds which the minister had in his mind at the time he issued the certificate (to the exclusion of other grounds which he might now wish to rely upon). However, this will not affect the eventual outcome because there is nothing to prevent a minister from issuing a fresh certificate on new grounds to replace one that has been quashed.

270 EIR reg 18(1), (3), (4)(a)-(b) and (7)(a). This assumes that EIR reg 18(7)(a) operates to apply FOIA s 60(4) as if the reference therein to a certificate under FOIA s 24(3) were substituted by a reference to a certificate issued in accordance with EIR reg 15(1). The interaction between these provisions is not perfect, however, as EIR reg 18(7)(a) refers to 'the reference' in FOIA s 60 to a certificate under FOIA s 24(3) when there are three such references. Moreover, EIR reg 15(3)(b) allows for a certificate to 'identify the information to which it relates in general terms' while FOIA s 60(4) applies to a certificate 'which identifies the information to which it relates by means of a general description.'

271 See §45– 026.

272 The Tribunal is thus given full appellate jurisdiction to review such matters unconstrained by any caveat that it 'apply the principles applied by the court on an application for judicial review' and assess only whether the minister had 'reasonable grounds for issuing the certificate' (cf FOIA s 60(3), DPA 2018 ss 27(4), 79(6) and 111(4) and EIR reg 18(7)). The explanation for this is no doubt that the minister can issue a new certificate with a much clearer application if dissatisfied with a determination made by the Tribunal under FOIA s 60(5) or DPA 2018 s 27(7), 79(9) or 111(7). In *Nasresfahani v SSHD and Data Controller* [2014] UKUT 0487 (AAC), the Upper Tribunal nevertheless took a more restrictive approach to the construction of its powers under the equivalent appeal provision in DPA 1998, s 28(6) given the wording of the relevant certificate under s 28(2). See at [27]: 'However, as under the certificate it is for the Security Services [sic] to determine whether or not the exemption is required for the purpose of safeguarding national security, in effect it is in our judgment a question whether the Security Services [sic] have lawfully made that determination. That is therefore also a question that is in effect to be determined on administrative law principles and in particular whether the determination failed to have regard to material considerations or was perverse or otherwise unlawful.' FOIA s 60(4) or DPA 2018 s 27(7), 79(7) or 111(5) only provide for the resolution by way of appeal of a dispute over a certificate's applicability where it arises, in relation to FOIA, 'in any proceedings under this Act', in relation to DPA 1998, 'in any proceeding under or by virtue of this Act' and, in relation to EIR, 'in any proceedings under these Regulations.' — see EIR, reg 18(4)(a)(i). The reason for the different formulations is unclear and their effect depends on whether the need for 'proceedings' is given a strict or generous construction; the latter would expand the scope for having disputes over a certificate's applicability resolved by the Tribunal without the procedural need for separate 'proceedings'.

273 A certificate under FOIA s 34(3) was not signed in *House of Commons v IC and Brooke, Leapman, Ungoed-Thomas* [2008] EWHC 1084 (Admin), [2009] 3 All ER 403 at [2]. See also DPA 2018 Sch 2, para 13, Sch 11, para 4, exempting

a certificate will then stand as conclusive evidence of that fact, thus confirming the engagement of the s 34 exemption, unless and until withdrawn or revoked or (in so far as this is possible given that parliamentary privilege should be in play and there is no scope for an appeal under FOIA) quashed on an application for judicial review.[274] The 'appropriate authority' for these purposes is, in relation to the House of Commons, the Speaker of that House, and in relation to the House of Lords, the Clerk of the Parliaments.[275] If a s 34(3) certificate is confined to exemption from s 1(1)(b), determination of the existence duty will be decided on the ordinary basis, unaffected by the certificate.

(2) Under s 36(7) of FOIA, a 'qualified person' may sign a certificate certifying that, in his reasonable opinion, disclosure of information held by either House of Parliament or compliance with the divulgence duty in s 1(1)(a) by either House would, or would be likely to, have any of the effects mentioned in s 36(2) of FOIA (in other words, it would be prejudicial to the maintenance of the convention of the collective responsibility of Ministers of the Crown; it would be prejudicial to the work of the Executive Committee of the Northern Ireland Assembly or the work of the Cabinet of the Welsh Government; it would inhibit the free and frank provision of advice or the free and frank exchange of views for the purposes of deliberation; or it would otherwise prejudice the effective conduct of public affairs). Such a certificate will then stand as conclusive evidence of the 'fact' that disclosure or divulgence would, or would be likely to, produce any of those effects, thus facilitating application of the s 36 exemption. The certificate is not determinative of the application of the exemption, as it will also be necessary to demonstrate that the information satisfies the description in s 36(1). The certificate stands unless and until withdrawn or revoked or (in so far as this is possible given that parliamentary privilege may be in play and there is no scope for an appeal under FOIA) quashed on an application for judicial review.[276] The 'qualified person' for these purposes is, in relation to information held by the House of Commons, the Speaker of that House, and in relation to information held by the House of Lords, the Clerk of the Parliaments.[277] If a s 36(7) certificate is confined to exemption from s 1(1)(b), determination of the existence duty will be decided on the ordinary basis, unaffected by the certificate.

5– 043 Certificates: challenges

As mentioned above, certificates issued by the House Authorities under ss 34(3) and 36(7) of FOIA are not subject to any express appeal procedure. The following factors tend to suggest that the courts would probably be disinclined to intervene if an attempt were made to challenge such a certificate by way of judicial review: the wording of the relevant conclusive evidence clauses follows a format which has previously been given full effect as a matter of statutory construction without any consideration of human rights;[278] the clear intention not to provide

personal data from certain provisions of the GDPR and DPA 2018 Pt 4 where this is required for the purpose of avoiding an infringement of the privileges of either House of Parliament.

274 FOIA ss 2(3) and 34 confer an 'absolute exemption'.

275 FOIA s 34(4).

276 FOIA ss 2(3) and 36 (so far as relates to information held by the House of Commons or the House of Lords) confer an 'absolute exemption'.

277 FOIA s 36(5)(d)-(e) and (7).

278 See: §5– 036; *Tinnelly and Sons Ltd v United Kingdom* (1999) 27 EHRR 249 (ECtHR) at [18]-[32], [64], [66]-[67] and [74]-[75]; *Devlin v United Kingdom* (2002) 34 EHRR 43 (ECtHR) at [12]-[14]; *R v Secretary of State for Foreign and Commonwealth Affairs, ex p Vidler* [1993] COD 305; *R v Secretary of State for Transport, ex p Evans and Commission for Racial*

for any oversight by way of an appeal to the Upper Tribunal;[279] and the fact that considerations of parliamentary privilege will inevitably be engaged in circumstances where the courts will not as a matter of constitutional principle interfere with the affairs of Parliament.[280] As already explained, were it possible to establish that a parliamentary certificate had interfered with the enjoyment or exercise of a Convention or Community right, the courts might be more inclined to intervene.[281] The scope for relying on such arguments is limited in this context, however, and the very strong constitutional and policy reasons which inhibit the courts from interfering with the affairs of Parliament would probably be enough to establish that any infringement of rights was necessary and proportionate in any event or, at least, unsuited to judicial scrutiny or interference.

5–044 Procedural fairness

Article 6(1) of the ECHR confers a right of access to a fair and effective hearing before an independent and impartial tribunal in relation to 'the determination of civil rights and obligations' and Community law can also require a similar level of judicial oversight and effective judicial protection in relation to the exercise, enjoyment and implementation of Community rights. Such rights only guarantee a certain level of procedural protection, however, and they cannot confer, or alter the substantive extent of, any freestanding rights of access to information or personal data.[282] Having said this, the relevance of such rights to procedural fairness and judicial oversight in relation to conclusive certificates issued under FOIA, the DPA 2018 or the EIR is not without question. There is an argument that Art 6 of the ECHR cannot be relied upon in this context in relation to any of these enactments, although the argument is more tenuous in relation to the DPA 2018 and the EIR:

(1) So far as concerns Art 6 of the ECHR, a question may arise whether the rights of access to information and personal data conferred by FOIA, the DPA 2018 or the EIR have the requisite 'private law' character to count as 'civil rights' for the purposes of Art 6(1). In this regard: 'Art 6(1) is engaged where the decision which is to be given is of an administrative character, that is to say one given in an exercise of a discretionary power, as well as a dispute in a court of law regarding the private rights of the citizen, provided

---

Equality [1992] COD 196.

279 Compare FOIA ss 23(2), 24(3) and 60(1) and (4), DPA 2018 ss 27(3), (7), 79(5), (7) and 111(3), (5), and EIR reg 18.

280 *Prebble v Television New Zealand Ltd* [1995] 1 AC 321 (PC) at 332: 'wider principle... that the courts and Parliament are both astute to recognise their respective constitutional roles. So far as the courts are concerned they will not allow any challenge to be made to what is said or done within the walls of Parliament in performance of its legislative functions and protection of its established privileges.' (Lord Browne-Wilkinson). See also: the Bill of Rights 1689 art IX; *Bradlaugh v Gossett* (1884) 12 QBD 271 (DC); *Pickin v British Railways Board* [1974] AC 765; *Hamilton v Al Fayed* [2001] 1 AC 395; *R v Parliamentary Commissioner for Standards, ex p Al Fayed* [1998] 1 WLR 669 (CA); *OGC v IC* [2008] EWHC 774 (Admin), [2010] QB 98. Support for this can also be found in H Woolf, J Jowell, A Le Sueur, C Donnelly and I Hare, *De Smith's Judicial Review*, 8th edn (London, Sweet & Maxwell, 2018) para 4-031 where it is suggested, in relation to statutory formulae purporting to exclude judicial review by general but comprehensive language, that in the context of the working of the parliamentary system there is a much stronger probability that the courts will give the words prohibiting judicial review a literal interpretation (referring to the Parliament Act 1911 s 3). See also the Ministerial and other Salaries Act 1975 s 2(2). See further J Auburn, J Moffett and A Sharland, *Judicial Review. Principles and Procedure* (OUP, Oxford, 2013) §§22.09-22.10.

281 See §5–037.

282 ECHR Art 6 can itself confer a subsidiary right of access to information but only where it has already been established that Art 6 is engaged and it is then shown that access to the information in question is essential to the exercise of the right to a fair trial: *McGinley and Egan v United Kingdom* (1998) 27 EHRR 1 (ECtHR); *R (S) v Plymouth City Council* [2002] EWCA Civ 388, [2002] 1 WLR 2583; *Roche v United Kingdom* (2006) 42 EHRR 30 (ECtHR). In general terms, the rules and procedures on disclosure and witness summonses in domestic civil and criminal proceedings (eg CPR 31 and CPR 34, Employment Tribunals Rules of Procedure para 31 at Employment Tribunals (Constitution and Rules of Procedure) Regulations 2013 SI 2013/1237 Sch 1 and Criminal Procedure Rules 2015 SI 2015/1490 Pts 15 and 17) can be seen as satisfying Art 6 for these purposes and FOIA need not be seen as contributing to this: *McGinley and Egan v United Kingdom* (1998) 27 EHRR 1, 4 EHRC 421 (ECtHR) at [86] and [90].

that it directly affects civil rights and obligations and is of a genuine and serious nature.'[283] If it were possible to show that Art 6(1) is prima facie engaged through the presence of a relevant 'civil right', it would next be necessary to show that the issue of a conclusive certificate or the operation of the relevant exemption has interfered with the exercise or enjoyment of that right.[284] In other words, it would have to be shown that the certificate or the exemption has operated to 'defeat' or 'cut off' an otherwise enforceable entitlement to the information or personal data in question rather than having acted simply to define and confirm the substantive bounds of a right which never extended further.[285] If these hurdles can be overcome, non-appealable national security certificates have been found to operate as procedural bars to the judicial resolution of disputes in contravention of Art 6(1), unless justified by reference to principles of proportionality.[286] However, the context and structure of FOIA, the DPA 2018 and the EIR are very different and there is an argument that the relevant exemptions (whether or not engaged via the issue of a conclusive certificate) do not infringe rights to information or personal data whose non-disclosure is required for the purpose of safeguarding national security but rather confirm the total absence of any such right.[287]

(2) Community law has no bearing on the application or enforcement of FOIA but it is relevant to the DPA 2018, which in part supplements the GDPR and implements the LED, and the EIR, which implement European Community Public Access to Environmental Information Directive 2003/4/EC. The DPA 2018 (to some extent) and the EIR must therefore be construed and given effect in accordance with the terms of their parental Directives, the CFR and the general principles of Community law.[288] As

---

283 *R (Alconbury Developments Ltd) v Secretary of State for the Environment, Transport and the Regions* [2001] UKHL 23, [2003] 2 AC 295, [2001] 2 All ER 929 at [150] (Lord Clyde) and [79]-[80] (Lord Hoffmann); *Ringeisen v Austria (No 1)* (1979-80) 1 EHRR 455 (ECtHR) at [94]; *König v Germany* (1978) 2 EHRR 170 (ECtHR); *Le Compte, Van Leuwen and De Meyere v Belgium* (1981) 4 EHRR 1 (ECtHR) at [46] and [49]; *H v France* (1990) 12 EHRR 74 (ECtHR) at [47]; *Shapovalov v Ukraine* [2012] ECHR 1665 at [42]-[57]. The right must be a private law right or it must be 'decisive for private rights and obligations'. In *Tinnelly and Sons Ltd v United Kingdom* (1999) 27 EHRR 249 (ECtHR) it was held that the right not to be discriminated against conferred by the Fair Employment (Northern Ireland) Act 1976 was a 'civil right' for the purposes of the ECHR Art 6(1) 'having regard to the context in which it applied and to its pecuniary nature' and that s 42 of that Act did not define the scope of that substantive right *in limine* but provided a respondent with a defence to a complaint of unlawful discrimination (at [61]-[63]). The same reasoning was applied and the same conclusion reached in the employment context in *Devlin v United Kingdom* (2002) 34 EHRR 43 (ECtHR) at [26] and *Devenney v United Kingdom* (2002) 35 EHRR 24 (ECtHR).

284 *Matthews v Ministry of Defence* [2003] UKHL 4, [2003] 1 AC 1163 at [3] (Lord Bingham); *Wilson v First County Trust Ltd (No 2)* [2003] UKHL 40, [2004] 1 AC 816 at [32]-[35] (Lord Nicholls), [103]-[105] (Lord Hope), [132] (Lord Hobhouse) and [165] (Lord Scott); *Golder v United Kingdom* (1979-80) 1 EHRR 524 (ECtHR); *König v Germany* (1978) 2 EHRR 170 (ECtHR); *Fayed v United Kingdom* (1994) 18 EHRR 393 (ECtHR) at [65]-[67]; *Tinnelly and Sons Ltd v United Kingdom* (1999) 27 EHRR 249 (ECtHR) at [72]-[79]; *Z v United Kingdom* [2001] 2 FLR 612 (ECtHR) at [87].

285 *Matthews v Ministry of Defence* [2003] UKHL 4, [2003] 1 AC 1163 at [141] (Lord Walker).

286 *Tinnelly and Sons Ltd v United Kingdom* (1999) 27 EHRR 249 (ECtHR); *Devlin v United Kingdom* (2002) 34 EHRR 43 (ECtHR); *Devenney v United Kingdom* (2002) 35 EHRR 24 (ECtHR). However, note the emphasis on the context and the pecuniary nature of the right not to be discriminated against.

287 While FOIA s 1(1) does enact what is described in the side-note as a 'general right of access to information held by public authorities' this is immediately qualified by s 1(2) which brings in the remainder of s 1, ss 2, 9, 12 and 14 and, in turn, Pt II. It is made clear in s 1(2) that s 1(1) 'has effect' throughout and is at all times 'subject to' these provisions (see also the language of 'section 1(1)(a) does not apply' and 'section 1(1)(b) does not apply' (in s 2) and 'the duty to confirm or deny does not arise' (throughout)). See especially the ultimate conclusion reached by the House of Lords on whether ECHR, Art 6(1) was engaged in *Matthews v Ministry of Defence* [2003] UKHL 4, [2003] 1 AC 1163.

288 See §5– 037. Although GDPR art 23(1)(a) permits the imposition of legislative restrictions on certain rights and obligations provided for therein in the interests of safeguarding national security, the provisions of the GDPR should, in practice, rarely, if ever, apply in connection with personal data, processing or subject access requests raising national security issues. This is because, first, the GDPR does not apply to the processing of personal data in the course of an activity which falls outside the scope of EU law or within the scope of the LED and, secondly, national security is outside the scope of EU law by virtue of the TEU Art 4(2) and the LED (see recital (14)). Accordingly: the processing of personal data in connection with national security activities is not within scope of

a consequence, there may be greater scope for relying on Community rights to effective judicial protection by this route in relation to s 79 of the DPA 2018 and regs 15 and 18 of the EIR. In any event, limited practical consequences would flow from being able to show that rights to procedural fairness and judicial oversight are engaged and arguably infringed in relation to the issue of conclusive certificates under FOIA, the DPA 2018 or the EIR. In this regard, the scope for appealing national security certificates issued under ss 23(2) and 24(3) of FOIA, ss 27, 79 and 111 of the DPA 2018 and reg 18 of the EIR arguably provides a respectable measure of judicial oversight[289] that should justify the restrictions entailed, bearing in mind the importance of national security matters and the fact that the executive is generally considered better qualified and equipped to judge related issues.[290] As a consequence, the successful invocation of Community rights is unlikely to go further than encouraging the Upper Tribunal to apply a more intensive proportionality-based standard of scrutiny when considering this type of appeal.

5– 045 Privacy and data protection

The right to respect for private and family life contained in Article 8 of the ECHR can confer a right of access to personal information where this is essential to the exercise and enjoyment of that right.[291] Although it is not inconceivable that information falling within this category might be sought under FOIA or the EIR, it is much more likely that requests under the DPA 2018 will seek such information. So far as concerns conclusive certificates issued under ss 27, 79 and 111 of the DPA 2018, Convention rights under Article 8 may therefore be engaged in a very direct way and Community rights may also come into play by virtue of the fact that the DPA 2018 supplements the GDPR and implements the LED.[292] Of course, Article 8 of the ECHR, the GDPR, the LED and DPA 2018 do not confer absolute rights and all four expressly allow, where necessary and proportionate, for the curtailment and denial of these rights in the interests of national security.[293] The rights of appeal under ss 27, 79 and 111 of the DPA 2018

---

the GDPR or the LED (DPA 2018 s 15(5)); such processing will instead be subject to DPA 2018 Pt 2 Ch 3 (the applied GDPR), Pt 3 (law enforcement processing) or Pt 4 (intelligence services processing); and DPA 2018 ss 27, 79 and 111 on national security certificates do not give effect to Community law or take effect within a Community law context.

289 Questions may nevertheless arise as to the grounds and intensity of the review thereby allowed (cf the non-appealability of Parliamentary certificates issued under FOIA ss 34(3) and 36(7)).

290 It is important to note that the right of access to the courts secured by the ECHR Art 6(1) is not absolute and may be subject to limitations provided they do not restrict or reduce the access left to the individual in such a way or to such an extent that the very essence of the right is impaired, provided that they pursue a legitimate aim and provided that there is a reasonable relationship of proportionality between the means employed and the aim sought to be achieved: *Fayed v United Kingdom* (1994) 18 EHRR 393 (ECtHR) at [65]-[67]; *Tinnelly and Sons Ltd v United Kingdom* (1999) 27 EHRR 249 (ECtHR) at [74]; *Lithgow v United Kingdom* (1986) 8 EHRR 329 (ECtHR) at [194].

291 *Gaskin v United Kingdom* (1989) 12 EHRR 36 (EctHR) at [60]; *Botta v Italy* (1998) 26 EHRR 241 (ECtHR); *Guerra v Italy* (1998) 26 EHRR 357 (EctHR) at [60]; *McGinley and Egan v United Kingdom* (1998) 27 EHRR 1 (ECtHR) at [101] and [103]; *R (S) v Plymouth City Council* [2002] EWCA Civ 388, [2002] 1 WLR 2583; *MG v United Kingdom* (2003) 36 EHRR 3, [2002] 3 FCR 289 (ECtHR); *Craxi v Italy (No1)* (2004) 28 EHRR 47 (ECtHR); *Roche v United Kingdom* (2006) 42 EHRR 30, (2006) BHRC99. Note that in *MG v United Kingdom* it was held that ECHR Art 8 required only the establishment of a procedure facilitating access to local authority care records relating to significant periods of the applicant's formative years and that the violation of Art 8 therefore ceased on entry into force of the DPA 1998. Similarly, in *Hardy and Maile v United Kingdom* (2012) 55 EHRR 28 it was held that FOIA and EIR provided an effective and accessible procedure enabling individuals to seek relevant and appropriate information about potential risks to their health which fulfilled the positive obligation under ECHR Art 8 to make this available (at [245]-[250]). See further Ch 3.

292 Indeed, the connection between rights to privacy (including under the ECHR Art 8) and data protection was strongly emphasised throughout the recitals to the European Community Data Protection Directive 95/46/EC and in Art 1, and it is similarly emphasised throughout the GDPR. See §§5– 037 to 5– 045 and especially 5– 044 on the way in which the Community law connection can engage rights to effective judicial oversight.

293 ECHR Art 8(2); European Community Data Protection Directive 95/46/EC, recital (16) and Art 13(1); DPA 1998 s 28.

and the adequacy of the judicial oversight they provide will therefore be crucial if it is to be demonstrated that the use of national security certificates thereunder, and the application of the exemption therein, is compatible with Convention rights and Community law. In this regard, it is notable that in relation to the first substantive decision taken by the Information Tribunal under the equivalent predecessor provisions of the DPA 1998, a more intensive proportionality-based standard of review was applied and the certificate in question was quashed for having an 'unnecessarily wide effect'.[294]

5– 046 Rights to freedom of expression

Although expressed to include 'the right to receive and impart information and ideas without interference' the right to freedom of expression guaranteed by Article 10 to the ECHR has until recently not been held to confer or entail a general right of access to information.[295] Although there has been some development in the jurisprudence on this point,[296] as a result of the subject matter of certificates being aligned with the interests in Article 10(2), it remains unlikely that there could be a successful invocation of Article 10 rights in order to bring or enhance a challenge to the issue of a conclusive certificate under ss 23-24, 34 or 36 of FOIA, s 27, 79 or 111 of the DPA 2018 or reg 15 of the EIR or to the application of one of the exemptions whose engagement may be certified thereunder.

---

[294] *Baker v SSHD* [2001] UKHRR 1275. Note the emphasis on Convention and Community rights at [50]-[64] and, more generally, see §5– 037. In *Gosling v SSHD*, IT, 1 August 2003 a replacement certificate whose application depended upon a consideration of the requirements of national security in relation to the need for particular exemptions in each individual case was subsequently upheld by the Information Tribunal albeit upon limited grounds (at [28]) and the Tribunal again emphasised the relevance of Convention and Community rights when considering the appropriate intensity of its review (at [48]). This decision was followed in *Hitchens v SSHD*, IT, 4 August 2003, *Hilton v FCO*, IT, 28 June 2005, *Stevenson v SSHD*, IT, 30 April 2009 and *Nasresfahani v SSHD and Data Controller* [2014] UKUT 0487 (AAC).

[295] *R (Persey) v Secretary of State for the Environment, Food and Rural Affairs* [2002] EWHC 371 (Admin), [2003] QB 794 (DC) at [52]-[53] (Simon Brown LJ); *R (Howard) v Secretary of State for Health (Note)* [2002] EWHC 396 (Admin) at [103] (Scott Baker J); *Leander v Sweden* (1987) 9 EHRR 433 (ECtHR); *Gaskin v United Kingdom* (1989) 12 EHRR 36 (ECtHR); *Guerra v Italy* (1998) 26 EHRR 357 (ECtHR); *BBC, Petitioners (No 2)* 2000 JC 521; *cf R (Wagstaff) v Secretary of State for Health* [2001] 1 WLR 292 (DC). See further Ch 4.

[296] See Ch 3.

CHAPTER 6

Prejudice and the public interest

1. THE PUBLIC INTEREST

6–001 Introduction

The Freedom of Information Act 2000 implicitly recognises a public interest underlying each of the grounds of exemption, as well as a public interest in divulging whether information is held and in disclosing that information.[1] Indeed, most of the exemptions simply articulate a public interest in non-disclosure that has been well recognised in other contexts, most notably national security, law enforcement, public interest immunity, confidentiality and the protection of privacy and personal data.[2] Where information falls within one of the qualified exemptions within Part II of the Act, the competition between the relevant aspects of the public interest is determinative of whether the duty to confirm or deny and the duty to communicate are disapplied or not. In requiring such a balancing exercise, the FOI Acts also recognise that the force of an aspect of the public interest will vary according to the information sought and 'all the circumstances of the case'. This latter phrase requires that for each request a public authority should take account of all the circumstances that bear upon the public interest in maintaining the applicable exemptions and upon the public interest in disclosing the

[1] FOIA s 2(1) and (2). Similarly: FOI(S)A s 2(1); EIR reg 12(1)(b); EI(S)R s 10(1)(b).

[2] The public interest in disclosing official information has itself been long recognised: *British Steel Corporation v Granada Television Ltd* [1981] AC 1096 at 1129, (Lord Denning). Similarly: *X v Morgan-Grampian (Publishers) Ltd* [1991] 1 AC 1 at 40 ('The courts have always recognised an important public interest in the free flow of information'); *Camelot Group plc v Centaur Communications Ltd* [1999] QB 124 at 139 (the 'general public interest in access to information'); *Hyde Park Residence Ltd v Yelland* [2001] Ch 143 at 170 ('the public interest in knowing the truth' (Mance LJ)).

information sought.[3] A blanket approach by a public authority to requests of a particular sort will not take into account all the circumstances of the case.[4]

6–002 **Aggregating facets**

In relation to the disclosure of exempt information under a qualified exemption, the task under s 2 is not to 'weigh'[5] the public interest in non-disclosure against the public interest in disclosure: the task is to weigh the public interest 'in maintaining the exemption'[6] that renders it exempt information against the public interest in disclosing that information. Only if the weighing process favours maintenance of the applicable exemptions is the duty to communicate disapplied. Accordingly, the balancing exercise does not involve a consideration of all aspects of the public interest that weigh against disclosure.[7] The consideration of the public interest, so far as it weighs against disclosure, is focused upon the public interest embodied in the exemptions by which the information sought is rendered exempt information. Previously, the Tribunal, and earlier editions of this work, had interpreted s 2(2) as requiring the public interest in maintaining each exemption applicable to an item of information to be weighed singly against the public interest in disclosing that information: only if there was a qualified exemption in the maintenance of which the public interest outweighed the public interest in disclosure would s 2(2)(b) disapply the s 1(1)(b) duty to communicate that information.[8] In relation to the EIR,[9] that approach was rejected by the Court of Appeal in *R (Office of Communications) v Information Commissioner*.[10] The Court of Appeal held that in carrying out the balancing exercise, the public interest in all exceptions applicable to a particular item of information must be aggregated and that it is that aggregated public interest which must be weighed against the public interest in disclosing that information.[11] This was upheld on a reference to the European

---

3 *OGC v IC* [2008] EWHC 774 (Admin), [2010] QB 98, [2008] ACD 54 at [87].

4 *Hogan and Oxford City Council v IC*, IT, 17 October 2006 at [57]; *Galloway v IC and NHS*, IT, 20 March 2009 at [70(c)]; *ECGD v IC and Campaign Against Arms Trade*, IT, 21 October 2009 at [50(iv)].

5 The FOI Acts employ the term 'outweigh', although it has been observed that 'this is a metaphor that does not reveal the nature of the process,' namely 'a comparative analysis of the importance or significance of the factors on either side,' which 'in turn, requires an analysis of the values underlying the different public interests': *Kirkhope v IC* [2016] UKUT 0344 (AAC) at [10]. See, to the same effect: *LO v IC* [2019] UKUT 34 (AAC) at [15]. It was similarly observed in relation to public interest immunity that a balance is 'a rough metaphor' and that it involves 'a more complex process than merely using the scales': *Science Research Council v Nassé* [1980] AC 1028 at 1067 (Lord Wilberforce).

6 'Exemption' here cannot mean exemption from the duty to communicate, as that only arises after the weighing process: it cannot, at this stage, be said to be being 'maintained'. The same phraseology is used in the environmental information regime: EIR reg 12(1)(b); EI(S)R reg 10(1)(b). See, also, DPA 2018 s 26 and Schs 2-4, which similarly uses the term 'exemption.'

7 *R (Office of Communications) v IC* [2009] EWCA Civ 90, [2009] ACD 48 at [35].

8 *Bellamy v IC and DTI*, IT, 4 April 2006 at [5]; *Toms v IC*, IT, 19 June 2006 at [5]-[7]; *Hogan and Oxford City Council v IC*, IT, 17 October 2006 at [59]-[60]; *ECGD v IC and Campaign Against Arms Trade*, IT, 21 October 2009at [50] and [52]-[54].

9 There is no good reason for a different view being taken in relation to FOIA, as the FTT has recognised: *Bowden Consulting Ltd v IC and Cabinet Office*, IT, 26 August 2009 at [57]; *ECGD v IC and Campaign Against Arms Trade*, IT, 21 October 2009 at [51]; *Dept for Culture, Media & Sport v IC*, FTT, 22 February 2010 at [13(5)]; *DEFRA v IC and Portman*, FTT, 13 November 2012 at [38(x)].

10 *R (Office of Communications) v IC* [2009] EWCA Civ 90, [2009] ACD 48. An appeal to the Supreme Court saw the matter being referred to the European Court of Justice, but with an indication that the majority favoured the view expressed in the Court of Appeal: *Office of Communication v Information Commissioner* [2010] UKSC 3. In *South Gloucestershire Council v IC and Bovis Homes Ltd*, IT, 20 October 2009 the FTT was critical of the reasoning of the Court of Appeal, observing (with good reason) that 'Richards LJ dealt with the aggregation issue in theoretical terms, without giving an example of how aggregation might make a difference in practice.' One obvious, practical difficulty is that unless the qualified exemptions are the same for all the information answering the terms of a request, the aggregate public interest in upholding the exemptions will not be the same for all that information.

11 See further n 49.

Court of Justice.[12] The applicability of this approach to the balancing exercise under FOIA has been confirmed by the High Court.[13] Whether the aggregation of public interest considerations will make much practical difference remains to be seen.[14] Public interest considerations against disclosure but not relevant to maintaining the applicable exemptions remain outside the balancing exercise.[15] Similarly, public interest considerations relating to exemptions that have not been invoked are not included in the aggregated public interest.[16] Thus it remains important to identify the public interest in maintaining each particular exemption.[17] Where there is a variety of information captured by a request with different combinations of exemptions applicable to different items of information, the aggregated public interest in maintaining those exemptions may vary according to the different combinations of applicable exemptions.[18]

6–003 The balancing exercise

The public interest balancing exercise does not involve the exercise of discretion.[19] It is an issue of mixed law and fact,[20] and the Tribunal may substitute its judgment for that of the Commissioner.[21] The required approach is to identify the actual harm or prejudice that the

---

12 *OFCOM v IC* (C-71/10) [2011] PTSR 1676, [2012] Env LR 7 at [32].

13 *Home Office and MoJ v IC* [2009] EWHC 1611 (Admin) at [25], [38]. The Tribunal does, however, sometimes still maintain that an aggregated approach should not be taken under FOIA: *European Raelian Movement v IC*, FTT, 6 December 2013 at [52]; cf *Dept of Health v IC and Lewis*, FTT, 17 March 2014 at [57] (only overlapping interests should be aggregated). The Information Commissioner also considers that when considering the public interest in maintaining an exemption, arguments that relate to other exemptions are irrelevant (at [21]-[22]): `www.ico.uk/media/for-organisations/documents/1183/the_public_interest_test.pdf`

14 As the FTT observed when the matter returned to it after its journey through the appeal courts:

> This Tribunal would respectfully agree with the Commissioner that in addressing the question of aggregation, a Tribunal cannot simply apply a simplistic mathematical approach to the subject. It is simply not possible to ascribe what is called an artificial or numerical value to the public interest in disclosure and then ascribe the same or corresponding value to the different interests against disclosure and then adding the two to find some form of total value. As the Commissioner rightly says, the weighing process is of necessity 'more impressionistic.' It requires consideration of the degree of weight each individual interest should be accorded. However, it is also important to note the prescription afforded to the exercise in the reported case law and referred to above. There is no obligation on this Tribunal at least in this case to aggregate: this exercise is merely as it was put, permissive.

OFCOM v IC and Everything Everywhere Ltd, FTT, 12 December 2012 at [69].

15 *R (Office of Communications) v IC* [2009] EWCA Civ 90, [2009] ACD 48 at [35].

16 *ECGD v IC and Campaign Against Arms Trade*, IT, 21 October 2009 at [52]-[53].

17 *ECGD v IC and Campaign Against Arms Trade*, IT, 21 October 2009 at [50(v)].

18 The practical difficulties that this interpretation presents to those charged with carrying out the exercise has been touched upon in a number of Tribunal decisions: *South Gloucestershire Council v IC and Bovis Homes Ltd*, IT, 20 October 2009 at [49]-[52]; *SS for Transport v IC*, IT, 5 May 2009 at [103].

19 *Common Services Agency v IC* [2008] UKHL 47, [2008] 1 WLR 1550 at [68].

20 In *Currie v Commissioners of Inland Revenue* [1921] 2 KB 332 at 339, Scrutton LJ, in considering the question whether a particular person carried on a 'profession' within the meaning of a Finance Act, said:

> I rather agree with what Lord Parker said in *Farmer v Cotton's Trustees* [1915] AC 922 at 932 "It may not always be easy to distinguish between questions of fact and questions of law for the purpose of the Taxes Management Act, 1880, or similar provisions in other Acts of Parliament. The views from time to time expressed in this House have been far from unanimous." I think the reason is, as has been suggested by the Master of the Rolls, that there has been a very strong tendency, arising from the infirmities of human nature, in a judge to say, if he agrees with the decision of the Commissioners, that the question is one of fact, and if he disagrees with them that it is one of law, in order that he may express his own opinion the opposite way.

Where there is a question of mixed law and fact, whether the facts in issue are *capable* of falling within the statutory condition is the question of law (since it requires a determination of the bounds of the condition), and whether the facts *actually* fall within those bounds is a question of fact.

21 See: *Bellamy v IC and DTI*, IT, 4 April 2006 at [34]; *Hogan and Oxford CC v IC*, IT, 17 October 2006 at [55]; *Hemsley v IC and Chief Constable of Northamptonshire*, IT, 10 April 2006 at [18]; *Toms v IC*, IT, 19 June 2006; *DWP v IC*, IT, 5 March 2007 at [22]; *CPS v IC*, FTT, 25 March 2010 at [14].

proposed disclosure would (or would be likely to or may) cause and the actual benefits its disclosure would (or would be likely or may) confer or promote. It equates to the approach taken in public interest immunity claims and requires an appropriately detailed identification, explanation and examination of the harm or prejudice and the benefits of the proposed disclosure.[22]

6–004 The nature of the public interest

The 'public interest', whether unlimited in its scope or focused upon a particular matter, is not a reference to something that is of interest to the public.[23] It signifies something that is in the interests of the public; that is, for the common welfare.[24] Thus:

> The public are interested in many private matters which are no real concern of theirs and which the public have no pressing need to know.[25]

And:

> There is a wide difference between what is interesting to the public and what it is in the public interest to make known.[26]

Thus, there may be a public interest in obtaining access to information on an issue even though the number of individuals affected by that issue is numerically low.[27] Where a statute speaks of a decision-maker being able to do something when that is in the public interest, that operates as a device by which the discretion vested in the decision-maker is directed away from matters of narrower or immediate concern to the decision-maker and to matters which are not necessarily of direct interest to the decision-maker:

> [T]he expression "in the public interest", when used in a statute, classically imports a discretionary value judgment to be made by reference to undefined factual matters, confined only "in so far as the subject matter and the scope and purpose of the statutory enactments may enable…given reasons to be [pronounced] definitely extraneous to any objects the legislature could have had in view".[28]

---

22 *APPGER v IC and FCO* [2013] UKUT 0560 (AAC) at [149], and see further [152].

23 *DTI v IC*, IT, 10 November 2006 at [50]; *Mersey Tunnel Users Association v Information Commissioner and Halton BC*, IT, 11 January 2010 at [48(vii)]; *Bellamy v IC and DBIS*, FTT, 23 February 2010 at [38(viii)]; *Metropolitan Police v IC*, FTT, 9 July 2010 at [71(vi)]; *DEFRA v IC and Portman*, FTT, 13 November 2012 at [38(ix)]; *Arts and Humanities Research Council v IC and Bimmler*, FTT, 4 December 2012at [33(x)]; *Dedalus Ltd v IC and Arts Council of England*, FTT, 21 May 2010 at [74(x)]. Some Tribunal decisions have appeared to suggest otherwise: *Cabinet Office v IC*, IT, 27 January 2009 at [14]; *Pugh v IC and MoD*, IT, 17 December 2007 at [48]; *Barrett v IC and Office for National Statistics*, IT, 23 April 2008 at [26]; *ECGD v IC and Campaign Against Arms Trade*, IT, 21 October 2009 at [50(xi)]. The first three may be thought the product of loose language rather than of loose thought.

24 The definition given to it in the *Shorter Oxford English Dictionary*, 2nd edn, (Oxford, Oxford University Press, 1993).

25 *Lion Laboratories Ltd v Evans* [1985] QB 526 at 537, [1984] 2 All ER 417 (CA). In *Francome v Mirror Group Newspapers Ltd* [1984] 1 WLR 892 (at 898) the Court of Appeal spoke of the newspapers as being 'peculiarly vulnerable to the error of confusing the public interest with their own interest.'

26 *Hyde Park Residences Ltd v Yelland* [2001] Ch 143 at 164; *Reynolds v Times Newspapers Ltd* [2001] 2 AC 127 at 202; *Douglas v Hello!* [2001] QB 967 at 997-998; *British Steel Corporation v Granada Television Ltd* [1981] AC 1096 at 1168 (Lord Wilberforce). Similarly: *R v Inhabitants of the County of Bedfordshire* (1855) 24 LJQB 81 at 84; *Sinclair v Mining Warden at Maryborough* (1975) 132 CLR 473 at 480; *Director of Public Prosecutions v Smith* [1991] 1 VR 63 at 75. Similarly in *AG for the United Kingdom v Wellington Newspapers Limited* [1988] 1 NZLR 129 at 178-179, McMullin J said: 'By public interest is meant something more than that which catches one's curiosity or merely raises the interest of the gossip. It is something which may be of real concern to the public.' On FOIA specifically, see: *Guardian Newspapers Ltd and Brooke v IC and BBC*, IT, 8 January 2007 at [34].

27 *Bellamy v IC and DTI*, IT, 4 April 2006 at [35]; *DTI v IC*, IT, 10 November 2006 at [50]; *Cabinet Office v IC and Aitchison* [2013] UKUT 0526 (AAC) at [73]; cf *Szucs v IC*, FTT, 16 August 2011 at [54]; *O'Keefe v IC*, FTT, 2 June 2015 at [34]-[35].

28 *O'Sullivan v Farrer* (1989) 168 CLR 210 at 216, cited with approval in *McKinnon v Secretary, Department of Treasury* [2006] HCA 45, (2006) 229 ALR 187 at [55].

6– 005 The relevant standpoint

The public interest is not immutable.[29] In some circumstances even a small amount of time may effect a significant difference: for example, where in the intervening period information on the same topic as the requested information is formally released. As already noted,[30] the Tribunal's approach had originally been that the applicability of an exemption and the public interest balancing exercise were to be determined by reference to the facts and circumstances as they stood at the time that the request should have been answered.[31] Later Tribunal decisions have held that both matters should be determined by reference to the facts and circumstances as they stood at the moment when the request was actually answered. This applies not just to the public authority making the original decision, but also those making merit-review decisions – that is, the Information Commissioner and the First-tier Tribunal.[32] However, the decision-maker (whether the public authority, the Information Commissioner or the First-tier Tribunal) may properly take into account circumstances or matters that come to light after the date of the request where those subsequent circumstances or matters shed light on the public interest at the time that it falls to be decided.[33] If an applicant is disadvantaged by this approach, the disadvantage can be circumvented by lodging a fresh request in identical terms.[34] Any change in those circumstances may influence the outcome of the balancing exercise. Accordingly, while a public authority may properly refuse to disclose information subject to a qualified exemption, where a subsequent request is made for the same information a change in the surrounding circumstances may result in the public authority being obliged to disclose that information.

6– 006 Evidence as to the public interest

Both the identification of relevant aspects of the public interest and the balancing of those aspects are evaluative matters exclusively for the public authority in the first instance, the Information Commissioner on a complaint, and the Tribunal on an appeal.[35] The Tribunal should, of course, receive evidence of anticipated consequences of disclosure or non-disclosure of the requested information so far as it is relevant to the claimed exemptions.[36] That evidence should include bringing forward facts that validate any expression of opinion by a public

29 *AG v Times Newspapers Ltd* [1974] AC 273 at 320.

30 §5– 004.

31 In ordinary circumstances, the 20-day working limit is merely the endstop date, so that normally responses should be given before then. The date for consideration can normally be approximated as being within a short period after receipt of the request for information. See: *Bellamy v IC and DTI*, IT, 4 April 2006 at [6]; *DTI v IC*, IT, 10 November 2006 at [44], [46]; *DWP v IC*, IT, 5 March 2007 at [30]; *Campaign against the Arms Trade v IC and MoJ*, IT, 26 August 2008 at [43]-[53] (where it was held that the public authority had to consider matters as at the date at which it was obliged to respond to the request); *DCLG v IC*, IT, 22 July 2008; *Dept of Culture, Media and Sport v IC*, IT, 29 July 2008 at [4]. Contrast: *Scotland Office v IC*, IT, 8 August 2008 at [77] (determined on the basis of facts and circumstances at the moment of the request); *Easter v IC and New Forest National Park Authority*, FTT, 14 May 2010 at [65(vii)] (determined on the basis of the facts and circumstances at the time that the request is refused by the public authority); *Dedalus Ltd v IC and Arts Council of England*, FTT, 21 May 2010 at [74(ix)]; *DEFRA v IC and Portman*, FTT, 13 November 2012 at [38(vii)]; *Arts and Humanities Research Council v IC and Bimmler*, FTT, 4 December 2012 at [33(ix)].

32 The authorities and competing arguments are considered at §5– 004.

33 *IC v HMRC and Gaskell* [2011] UKUT 296 (AAC) at [28]; *DTI v IC*, IT, 10 November 2006 at [46]-[47].

34 If the facts and circumstances have truly changed, this should render the interval between the requests a 'reasonable' one, so that the applicant should not fall foul of the proscription against repeat requests: see §§23– 017 to 23– 019.

35 *HM Treasury v IC* [2009] EWHC 1811 (Admin) at [39], [62].

36 *Guardian Newspapers Ltd v IC and BBC*, IT, 8 January 2007 at [92]; *Reith v IC*, IT, 1 June 2007 at [32]-[33] and [37]-[38]; *HM Treasury v IC* [2009] EWHC 1811 (Admin) at [41]; cf *England and LB of Bexley v IC*, IT, 10 May 2007 at [62].

authority as to type and likelihood of harm that would result from disclosure of the requested information. The evidence given to the Tribunal will inform its conclusions whether the predicted adverse effects to protected interests are likely to result from disclosure of the requested information (in the case of harm-based exemptions) and the strength of the evidential underpinning for the relevant public interest considerations (particularly in the case of public interest considerations that express a predicted harm resulting from disclosure). The Tribunal should not defer to the views of a public authority or those employed by it, either as to the likely effects of disclosure of information (whether upon an interest protected by an exemption or upon a matter that a recognised public interest is designed to protect) or as to what the outcome of the public interest balancing exercise should be.[37] It is the Tribunal which is charged with the task of evaluating the evidence.[38] Relevant evidence from a public authority will, however, be useful to identify and explain matters of recognised public interest, including putting before the Tribunal facts that support any predictions of the effect of disclosing the requested information. Similarly, evidence from a requester of the public curiosity in the subject matter of the request is unlikely to be relevant:

> ...the public interest is a matter for the judgment of the Commissioner or a tribunal in the light of the background facts. It is not a subject for "proper evidence", which I take to mean some sort of trawl through the views of others either in the published media...or perhaps general trawls of the internet.[39]

6– 007 Weight of the public interest

A decision-maker must take into account all considerations that are relevant to the public interest balancing exercise and not take into account any that are irrelevant to that exercise. On an appeal to the Tribunal, it is required to take the same approach. It is well established that while a decision-maker may be required to take certain matters into account in making a decision in exercise of a function, unless otherwise required the weight to be given to such material considerations is quintessentially one for the decision-maker.[40] This has been acknowledged by the High Court in relation to the s 2(2) exercise.[41] There is nothing in FOIA stipulating the particular weight to be given to the applicable aspects of the public interest in maintaining the qualified exemptions. The statutory bifurcation of exemptions into those that are absolute and those that are not, together with the requirement that in the latter case regard is to be had to 'all the circumstances', is not without significance to the character of the public interest balancing exercise that is to be carried out. Nevertheless, the High Court has on occasions maintained that it is 'incumbent' on the Tribunal to give 'significant weight' to the public interest built in to certain exemptions.[42]

---

37 *Home Office and MoJ v IC* [2009] EWHC 1611 (Admin) at [29]; *Dept of Health v IC and Lewis*, FTT, 17 March 2014 at [41]; *Dept of Health v IC and Lewis* [2015] UKUT 0159 (AAC) at [66]-[68].

38 Moreover, the appeal will generally be against the decision of the public authority.

39 *Cabinet Office v IC and Aitchison* [2013] UKUT 0526 (AAC) at [75].

40 *Tesco Stores v SSE* [1995] 1 WLR 759 (HL) at 764, 770 and 780; *R (von Brandenburg) v East London and The City Mental Health NHS Trust* [2001] EWCA Civ 239, [2002] QB 235 at [41] ('The principle that the weight to be given to such facts is a matter for the decision-maker, moreover, does not mean that the latter is free to dismiss or marginalise things to which the structure and policy of the Act attach obvious importance'). The nature of the right that stands to be affected by the decision will colour a court's preparedness to interfere on the basis of the weight given by a decision-maker: *R (Samaroo) v SSHD* [2001] EWCA Civ 1139, [2001] UKHRR 1150 at [39].

41 *ECGD v Friends of the Earth* [2008] EWHC 638 (Admin), [2008] Env LR 40, [2008] JPL 1813 at [38]; *Home Office and MoJ v IC* [2009] EWHC 1611 (Admin) at [29 and [32]. See further: *Cabinet Office v IC and Aitchison* [2013] UKUT 0526 (AAC) at [62]; *Cabinet Office v IC* [2014] UKUT 0461 (AAC) at [51]-[54].

42 *DBERR v O'Brien and IC* [2009] EWHC 164 (QB) at [41], [51], [53], [54]; *HM Treasury v IC* [2009] EWHC 1811 (Admin) at [42]-[43], [51]. See further the various Tribunal decisions which suggest that the public interest in maintaining certain exemptions is weightier than for others, eg: *All Party Parliamentary Group on Extraordinary Rendition v IC*, FTT, 24 January 2011 at [146]; *British Union for the Abolition of Vivisection v IC and Newcastle University*, FTT, 11

6– 008 The two balancing exercises

The FOI Acts distinguish the public interest in disclosing whether a public authority holds certain information from the public interest in disclosing that information. Although the FOI Acts place the balancing exercise for the purpose of disclosure after the balancing exercise for the purpose of the duty to confirm or deny,[43] the former is better considered before the latter. If it is in the public interest for a public authority to disclose certain information, it follows that it will be in the public interest for that public authority to disclose that it holds that information. Logically, then, the need to carry out the weighing exercise set out in s 2(1) of the FOI Acts will only arise if the result of carrying out the separate weighing exercise in s 2(2) is a decision not to disclose the information.

6– 009 Comparative jurisprudence

This focused approach to the public interest in the FOI Acts distinguish them from the freedom of information legislation of comparative jurisdictions. The FOI Acts of Australia, New Zealand and Ireland all require the decision-maker, if he is to rely on certain exemptions, to be satisfied that the disclosure of the document would be contrary to 'the public interest'.[44] This generalised reference to the public interest enables a broad range of matters to be taken into account as part of the balancing exercise.[45] But it also means that despite a superficial similarity with the regime in the United Kingdom,[46] their jurisprudence on this issue is limited in its comparative value.

2. WEIGHING THE PUBLIC INTEREST: DISCLOSURE

6– 010 Interest in the exemption

As noted above,[47] where information is covered by a qualified exemption, displacement of the duty to communicate that information involves weighing the public interest in maintaining the

November 2011 at [53]-[54]; *Keane v IC* [2016] UKUT 461 (AAC) at [58]; *Arthurs v IC*, FTT, 15 January 2017 at [97]. There has, however, been criticism of this approach: *Cabinet Office v IC and Aitchison* [2013] UKUT 0526 (AAC) at [62]; *Cabinet Office v IC* [2014] UKUT 0461 (AAC) at [52]-[54]; *Dept of Health v IC and Lewis* [2015] UKUT 0159 (AAC) at [22]-[24].

43 That is, FOIA ss 2(2) and 2(1), respectively. In relation to information held by a Scottish public authority, FOI(S)A ss 18(1) and 2(1) respectively. In relation to a request made under the environmental information regime, there is no discrete duty on a public authority to disclose whether or not it holds the requested information.

44 Freedom of Information Act 1982 (Cth of Australia), ss 11A(5), 11B, 47B, 47C, 47E, 47F, 47G, 47H and 47J, which require considering whether disclosing the documents would be contrary to the public interest, but do not require a general or focused weighing of it; Official Information Act 1982 (NZ) s 9(1); Freedom of Information Act 2014 (Ireland), ss 28(5), 29(1), 30(2), 31(4), 32(3)(b), 35(3), 36(3), 39(2), 40(3); cf 37(5). The Access to Information Act (1982) (Canada) does not involve consideration of the public interest, except where the request relates to 'third party information', in which case the decision-making involves a focused treatment of the public interest: s 20(6). Within the terms of the Freedom of Information Act 1966 (USA) itself, the role of the public interest is confined to considering whether the information requested should be provided free of charge: 5 USC 552(a)(4)(A)(iii). In relation to declassification decisions, Executive Order 13,526 3.1(d) authorises agencies to apply a balancing test: namely, to determine 'whether the public interest in disclosure outweighs the damage to national security that might reasonably be expected from disclosure.'

45 See, eg: *Re Howard and the Treasurer* (1985) 7 ALD 626, 3 AAR 169; *Director of Public Prosecutions v Smith* [1991] 1 VR 63. The absence of any such focus led the Australian Law Reform Commission and the Administrative Review Council in their joint review of the operation of the Freedom of Information Act 1982 to recommend that the FOI Commissioner issue guidelines listing the factors that are relevant and that are irrelevant when weighing the public interest: Australian Law Reform Commission and Administrative Review Council, *Open Government: a review of the Federal Freedom of Information Act 1982* (Canberra, 1995) para 8.14, recommendation 37.

46 That is, the FOIA, FOI(S)A, EIR and EI(S)R.

47 §§6– 001 to 6– 002.

applicable exemptions, rather than all aspects of the public interest that are against disclosure of that information:

> The public authority's assessment of the public interest in maintaining the exemption should focus on the public interest factors specifically associated with that particular exemption, rather than on a more general consideration of the public interest in withholding the information: see the decision of the Tribunal in *Hogan and Oxford City Council v Information Commissioner* at [59]. This exercise requires the public authority to stand back and abnegate its own interests except and in so far as those interests are properly viewed as part of the public interest.[48]

The public interest in all exceptions applicable to a particular item of information must be aggregated and it is that aggregated public interest which must be weighed against the public interest in disclosing that information.[49] It will never be enough for a public authority simply to rely upon the public interest against disclosure that is inherent in the particular qualified exemption that applies to the information sought without a consideration of the particular circumstances relating to the information.[50] To allow this would effectively be to elevate a qualified exemption into an absolute exemption. Nevertheless, it is legitimate to take into account the public interest in avoiding the harm sought to be protected by the exemption and the likelihood of that harm eventuating from disclosure of the requested information.[51] Section 2(2) contemplates instances in which information rendered exempt information by a qualified exemption will be required to be disclosed. The specific aspect of the public interest that underlies each of the qualified exemptions is considered in more detail in the chapters that deal with particular exemptions. The only 'internal' indication of the public interest in maintaining the exemptions comes from the provisions reducing the exemptions in relation to historical records.[52] Implicit in the removal of those exemptions is that if the information is without contemporaneity there is no significant public interest served by the exemption. With all qualified exemptions, the public interest balancing exercise will often be time sensitive.[53] In

---

48 *DWP v IC*, IT, 5 March 2007 at [24]. Similarly: *Bellamy v IC and DTI*, IT, 4 April 2006 at [5]; *Hogan and Oxford City Council v IC*, IT, 17 October 2006 at [55]; *Office of Commerce v IC*, IT, 2 May 2007 at [51]; *Student Loans Company Ltd v IC*, IT, 17 July 2009 at [53]; *Scotland Office v IC*, IT, 8 August 2008 at [77]; *Easter v IC and New Forest National Park Authority*, FTT, 14 May 2010 at [65(iv)]; *Dedalus Ltd v IC and Arts Council of England*, FTT, 21 May 2010at [74(v)]; *DEFRA v IC and Portman*, FTT, 13 November 2012 at [38(v)]; *Arts and Humanities Research Council v IC and Bimmler*, FTT, 4 December 2012 at [33(v)].

49 Although the Court of Appeal was concerned with the public interest weighing exercise expressed in the EIR, its reasoning is equally applicable to the FOIA: the phraseology used in the EIR mimics that used in the FOIA, and not vice versa. This appears to be confirmed by *Home Office and MoJ v IC* [2009] EWHC 1611 (Admin) at [25]. The Tribunal does, however, sometimes still maintain than an aggregated approach should not be taken under FOIA: *European Raelian Movement v IC*, FTT, 6 December 2013 at [52]; cf *Dept of Health v IC and Lewis*, FTT, 17 March 2014 at [57] (only overlapping interests should be aggregated). The Information Commissioner also considers that, when assessing the public interest in maintaining an exemption, arguments that relate to other exemptions are irrelevant (at [21]-[22]):
`www.ico.uk/media/for-organisations/documents/1183/the_public_interest_test.pdf`
The treatment of the public interest in FOIA differs markedly from that which had originally been proposed in cl 14(3) of the original FOI Bill. Some indication of this change appears from Hansard HL vol 617 cols 901-902 (17 October 2000) (Minister of State, Cabinet Office, Lord Falconer of Thoroton), when introducing the amendment that led to s 2, and in Hansard HL vol 617 col 1265 (19 October 2000), Lord Falconer of Thoroton gave an example of how it should work in practice. For a fuller consideration of the genesis of the public interest balancing exercise, see Philip Coppel, 'The public interest and the Freedom of Information Act 2000' *Judicial Review*, vol 10, issue 4, December 2005.

50 *DfES v IC and The Evening Standard*, IT, 19 February 2007 at [63]; *OGC v IC* [2008] EWHC 737 (Admin), [2010] QB 98, [2008] ACD 54 at [79]; *Bellamy v IC and DBIS*, FTT, 23 February 2010 at [38(iv)].

51 *DTI v IC*, IT, 10 November 2006 at [48]-[49].

52 FOIA s 63; FOI(S)A s 58. See §§36– 010 to 36– 012. Under the environmental information regime, the exceptions are the same for information contained in historical records as for information not so contained: EIR reg 17; EI(S)R reg 15.

53 *Hogan and Oxford City Council v IC*, IT, 17 October 2006 at [58] and [71]; *Guardian Newspapers Ltd and Brooke v IC and BBC*, IT, 8 January 2007 at [57(3)]; *Pugh v IC*, IT, 17 December 2007 at [53]; *Dept of Health v IC*, IT, 18 November

carrying out the public interest balancing exercise, the First-tier Tribunal must articulate the competing public interests and explain why it struck the balance as it did.[54]

6–011 Interest in disclosure

The FOI Acts describe at various points a public interest in disclosing information.[55] In introducing the Bill and in commending its provisions, the objectives and aspirations for it were said to be:

> ... the Bill will not only provide legal rights for the public and place legal duties on Ministers and public authorities, but will help to transform the culture of Government from one of secrecy to one of openness. It will transform the default setting from "this should be kept quiet unless" to "this should be published unless." By doing so, it should raise public confidence in the processes of government, and enhance the quality of decision making by the Government'[56]

It may be thought that the public interest in disclosure lies partly in the attainment of those stated objectives. The significance of the public interest was described by those supporting the Bill in these terms:

> The duty to disclose information in the public interest is one of the most important aspects of the Bill. It is the key to creating the new culture of openness in the public sector with which the Government intend to replace the secrecy that, as everyone accepts, permeates Whitehall and too much of the public sector. We are introducing the Bill because we want to change that. The question is how to achieve the necessary balance between opening up the public sector and recognising that openness does not always have a monopoly on righteousness. It needs to be balanced against the need for personal privacy, commercial confidentiality and effective government.[57]

A consideration of the provisions and structure of the Act reveals that it is the disclosure of information that animates it.[58] The purposes of the FOI Acts, although not recited within their provisions, guide the public interest in disclosure.[59] To the extent that discernment of the public interest in disclosure is left in the hands of the courts, it may be thought that some guidance may be found in this underlying philosophy of the Act:

> Where over a period of years there can be discerned a steady trend in legislation which reflects the view of successive Parliaments as to what the public interest demands in a particular field of law, development of the common law in that part of the same field which has been left to it ought to proceed upon a parallel rather than a diverging course.[60]

2008 at [78]; *Savic v IC and Attorney General* [2016] UKUT 534, 535 (AAC) at [52], [77], [80] and [122]. That is underscored in relation to the exemptions listed in s 63 (which fall away after a specified number of years): see *Cabinet Office v IC and Aitchison* [2013] UKUT 0526 (AAC) at [40]-[43]. But see *Beggs v Scottish IC* [2014] CSIH 10 at [11], where the Court of Session held that the public interest in maintaining the exemption under FOI(S)A s 34(1) does not diminish with the passage of time, as that exemption is not included in s 58 as one which falls away entirely after a specified number of years: a questionable conclusion that confuses the statutory disapplication of an exemption with the weight to be afforded to the public interest in an exemption.

54 *O'Hanlon v IC* [2019] UKUT 34 (AAC) at [15].

55 FOIA ss 2(2)(b), 17(3)(b), 19(3), 35(4) and 46(3); FOI(S)A ss 2(1)(b), 16(2), 23(3), 29(3) and 61(3). See also §§5– 024 and 5– 028 in relation to the presumption of openness in the FOI Acts.

56 Hansard HC vol 340 (7 December 1999) (Mr Jack Straw, second reading speech).

57 Hansard HC vol 357 col 719 (27 November 2000) (Parliamentary Under-Secretary of State for the Home Department, Mr O'Brien, introducing amendments to the public interest provisions of the Bill).

58 See: *Common Services Agency v Scottish IC*, 2006 CSIH 58, 2007 SLT 7 at [32].

59 The purposes of the FOI Acts are considered in Ch 1.

60 *Erven Warnink Besloten Vennootschap v J Townend & Sons (Hull) Ltd* [1979] AC 731 at 743 (Lord Diplock). See also the quotation at §34– 028 from *A-G (UK) v Heinemann Publishers Pty Ltd* (1987) 10 NSWLR 86 at 191, 75 ALR 353 at 454.

6–012 Tribunal approach

The approach taken by the Tribunal has been to start from a position that assumes a public interest in disclosure of requested information.[61] Absent any public interest against maintaining an applicable qualified exemption, the public interest in disclosure will prevail, requiring the information to be disclosed. In assessing the harm that might result from disclosure (and, connected to that, the public interest in maintaining an exemption), the Tribunal is not bound to follow the views expressed by public officials:

> Mr Crow argued, in effect, that the Tribunal had no real alternative to accepting the evidence of the eminent witnesses that he called on these matters, in the absence of any evidence to refute them. We accept without question their assertions as to the vital importance of the principles listed in the last paragraph and others which they cited. Indeed, as we have already said, nobody cast doubt upon them. When it comes to the effects of disclosure, however, we have listened with care and respect to their warnings but remain entitled, indeed under a duty, to reach our own conclusions, applying our commonsense and, as to the lay members, our experience to our decision.[62]

The appeals decided by the Tribunal have recognised a particular public interest in disclosure in various circumstances:

- There is a public interest in the accountability and transparency of the decision-making process of a public authority, including the provision of reasons for those decisions.[63]
- There is a public interest in the proper conduct of investigative processes and procedures carried out by public authorities, particularly those which might lead to criminal proceedings.[64]
- There is a strong public interest in understanding how government negotiates with the opposition and makes a decision to allow a free vote.[65]
- There is a strong public interest in knowing about the involvement of privileged lobbyists and how they influence government.[66]
- There is a public interest in ensuring the accountability of a public authority, including its decision to launch care proceedings[67] and to take enforcement action in support of planning control.[68] However, there must be some link between the attainment of this objective and the disclosure of the information sought.[69]
- There is a public interest in divulging a current policy that is used by a public

[61] *Hogan and Oxford City Council v IC*, IT, 17 October 2006 at [56]; *DTI v IC*, IT, 10 November 2006 at [42]-[43], [45] and [54]; *Reith v IC and LB Hammersmith & Fulham*, IT, 1 June 2007 at [41]; *Bellamy v IC and DBIS*, FTT, 23 February 2010 at [38(i)]. Similarly the Scottish Court of Session: *Scottish Ministers v Scottish IC* [2007] CSIH 8, 2007 SCLR 253 at [11]. See further §5–027.

[62] *DfES v IC and The Evening Standard*, IT, 19 February 2007 at [72]. Similarly *Cabinet Office v IC and Aitchison* [2013] UKUT 0526 (AAC) at [75].

[63] *Burgess v IC and Stafford Borough Council*, IT, 7 June 2007 at [45]; *Ministry of Defence v IC and Evans*, IT, 20 July 2007 at [14]-[68]; *OGC v IC*, IT, 19 February 2009 at [146]-[147], [149], [162]; *Galloway v IC and NHS*, IT, 20 March 2009 at [70(d)]; *Mersey Tunnel Users Association v Information Commissioner and Halton BC*, IT, 11 January 2010 at [64].

[64] *DTI v IC*, IT, 10 November 2006 at [57]. However, it is necessary to bear in mind whether existing systems and procedures provide sufficient means of ensuring the proper conduct of such processes and procedures (at [62]); *McTeggart v IC*, IT, 4 June 2007 at [44].

[65] *CPS v IC*, FTT, 25 March 2010 at [87].

[66] *CPS v IC*, FTT, 25 March 2010 at [86].

[67] *Kitchener v IC and Derby City Council*, IT, 20 December 2006 at [13]-[14].

[68] *Archer v IC and Salisbury District Council*, IT, 9 May 2007 at [60].

[69] *ECGD v IC and Campaign Against Arms Trade*, IT, 21 October 2009 at [50(ix)]; *Dept of Culture, Media and Sport v IC*, IT, 29 July 2008 at [28].

authority to make decisions.[70]

- There is a public interest in the disclosure of information if it would disclose a cause of action legitimately open to the applicant.[71]
- There is a public interest in disclosing the workings of a public body, particularly one that is in receipt of public funds[72] or one in relation to a matter where government does not have a good track record.[73]
- There is a public interest in a disclosure that would promote public debate and meaningful participation in any aspect of the democratic process,[74] including upon important government decisions (eg introduction of an ID card).[75]
- There is a public interest in being able to test whether the assessments of a minister are robust or where disclosure of information will allow the public to better judge the Government's performance in a particular sphere.[76]
- There is a public interest in disclosing information that reveals corruption, illegality or mismanagement on the part of public officials.[77]
- There is a legitimate public interest in ensuring the security of the postal system.[78]
- There is a public interest that all persons or parties subject to a Companies Act investigation be acquainted with the reasons for the investigation.[79]
- Where the decision is the product of a quasi-judicial function (eg whether to refer something to the Monopolies Commission), then there is a public interest in knowing the arguments for and against those decisions.[80]

---

70 *Kitchener v IC and Derby City Council*, IT, 20 December 2006 at [15]; *Kalman v IC and Dept for Transport*, FTT, 6 July 2010 at [65]-[66]. In *Department of Economic Policy and Development of the City of Moscow and another v Bankers Trust Co and another* [2004] EWCA Civ 314, [2005] QB 207 at [39] Mance LJ spoke of 'the public interest in ensuring appropriate standards of fairness in the conduct of arbitrations militates in favour of a public judgment in respect of judgments given on applications under section 68 [of the Arbitration Act 1996]. The desirability of public scrutiny as a means by which confidence in the courts can be maintained and the administration of justice made transparent applies here as in other areas of court activity under the principles of *Scott v Scott* [1913] AC 417 and Art 6.'

71 *Alcock v IC and Chief Constable of Staffordshire Police*, IT, 3 January 2007 at [41]. In *AG's Reference No 5* [2004] UKHL 40, [2005] 1 AC 167 at [20] Lord Bingham spoke of the 'obvious public interest' in the disclosure of information that would reveal that a telephone intercept was unlawful.

72 *Guardian Newspapers Ltd and Heather Brooke v IC and BBC*, IT, 8 January 2007 at [120]-[121]. In *Archer v IC and Salisbury District Council*, IT, 9 May 2007 at [60] the IT identified a public interest in knowing why public money has been used abortively. This public interest is conventionally recognised in freedom of information regimes: *Harris v Australian Broadcasting Corporation* (1983) 78 FLR 236, 50 ALR 551.

73 *OGC v IC*, IT, 19 February 2009 at [152] (the procurement of large information technology projects, such as the ID card system).

74 *Dept of Culture, Media and Sport v IC*, IT, 29 July 2008 at [28]; *Galloway v IC and NHS*, IT, 20 March 2009 at [70(d)].

75 *DWP v IC*, IT, 5 March 2007 at [97]; *OGC v IC*, IT, 19 February 2009 at [152]-[162].

76 *DWP v IC*, IT, 5 March 2007 at [99]-[101].

77 *Mitchell v IC*, IT, 10 October 2005 at [6]. This reflects the stance taken in other areas of the law: *Beloff v Pressdram Ltd* [1973] 1 All ER 241 at 260 ('disclosure justified in the public interest, of matters carried out or contemplated, in breach of the country's security, or in breach of law, including statutory duty, fraud, or otherwise destructive of the country or its people, including matters medically dangerous to the public; and doubtless other misdeeds of similar gravity.'); *AG v Guardian Newspapers (No 2)* [1990] 1 AC 109 ('possibly the public interest in the exposure of iniquity in the Security Service' at 212 (Dillon LJ); also, 268-269 (Lord Griffiths) and at 282-283 (Lord Goff); Lord Salmon in *British Steel Corporation v Granada Television Ltd* [1981] AC 1096 at 1185; *Sankey v Whitlam* (1978) 142 CLR 1; *Director of Public Prosecutions v Smith* [1991] 1 VR 63; *Cochran v United States*, 770 F 2d 949 (11th Cir 1985); *Columbia Packing Co v USDA*, 563 F 2d 495.

78 *Toms v IC*, IT, 19 June 2006 at [18] and [22].

79 *DTI v IC*, IT, 10 November 2006 at [51]; *FCO v IC*, IT, 22 January 2008 at [27]-[28].

80 *Cabinet Office v IC and Aitchison* [2013] UKUT 0526 (AAC) at [90].

6–013 Information already public

If the Tribunal, having examined the requested information, is of the view that it will add little to what is already in the public domain, the public interest in the disclosure of that information may be diminished.[81] On the other hand, to the extent that relevant aspects of the public interests are directed to protecting an interest from harm arising from disclosure, the fact that the requested information is already in the public domain will generally mean that no harm will be caused by the release of the requested information.[82] It will matter not that the original release did cause harm, as what is required is that the disclosure in answer to the request be causative of harm. On the other hand, the relevant aspects of the public interest in maintaining an exemption or in disclosing the requested information (or both) may be substantially restored if the same information, although in the public domain, has not been officially released and the official releasing of the information would have significance.[83]

6–014 Relevance of information use

In assessing the public interest in disclosing the requested information, it is permissible to take into account a use that would be made of that information, even though that use would involve an unlawful act.[84] If the cumulative effect of similar requests gives rise to a well-founded fear of misuse of the information, that may be a legitimate factor to be taken into account in maintaining an exemption.[85]

6–015 Applicant identity and motive

Although the identity of and motive for the applicant seeking access to information provide no separate grounds for declining to answer a request,[86] these can impinge upon the public interest in disclosing the information[87] (as well as whether the request for information is vexatious).[88]

---

81 See eg: *FCO v IC and Friends of the Earth*, IT, 29 June 2007; *Metropolitan Police v IC*, FTT, 9 July 2010 at [75]-[76]; *BBC and One Transport Ltd v IC and Davis*, FTT, 11 April 2011 at [30]; *Savic v IC and Attorney General* [2016] UKUT 534, 535 (AAC) at [126]-[127]. It will be necessary to consider the similarity between the information that falls within the terms of the request and that which is in the public domain. If it is identical, a public authority should generally be relying upon FOIA s 21(1) if it does not wish to release the requested information. A public authority must be careful not to deploy the principle that effectively requires an applicant to have a legitimate motive for making the request for information.

82 See: *John Connor Press Associates v IC*, IT, 25 January 2006 at [16]; *FCO v IC*, IT, 22 January 2008 at [26], [28]; *Cabinet Office v IC and Lamb*, IT, 27 January 2009 at [78].

83 See: *S v IC and General Register Office*, IT, 9 May 2007 at [80]; *Gilby v IC and FCO*, IT, 22 October 2008 at [42]-[48]; *People for the Ethical Treatment of Animals Europe v IC and Oxford University*, IT, 13 April 2010 at [49], [53].

84 *R (Office of Communications) v IC* [2009] EWCA Civ 90, [2009] ACD 48 at [54]-[59] (breach of a third party's copyright).

85 *Hemsley v IC and Chief Constable of Northamptonshire*, IT, 10 April 2006 at [23]. The appellant had sought detailed information relating to speed offences recorded by a particular speed camera. The Tribunal found that the information fell within FOIA s 31(1). In considering the public interest balancing exercise, it held (at [23]): '...we are impressed by the argument as to setting a precedent. Whilst every request must be dealt with on its merits, if this request were granted, it is not hard to envisage the difficulties faced by police authorities in dealing with future requests for such information, justified more or less plausibly, as designed to test the efficacy of signs, the hazards posed by weather conditions or the vigilance of drivers at particular times of day. It might be difficult to distinguish between the public spirited motivation of such as the appellant and others whose purpose was less admirable, eg the creation of a commercial website selling forecasts on the operation of safety cameras.'

86 As was stated in *Durns v Bureau of Prisons*, 804 F 2d 701 at 706 (DC Cir 1986), 'Congress granted the scholar and the scoundrel equal rights of access to agency records.' More prosaically: *Dept of Culture, Media and Sport v IC*, IT, 29 July 2008 at [4]; *Armstrong v IC and HMRC*, IT, 14 October 2008 at [75], [96]; *MoD v IC and Evans*, IT, 20 July 2007 at [50]-[51]; *S v IC and General Register Office*, IT, 9 May 2007 at [19], [80]; *O'Brien v IC and DBERR*, IT, 20 July 2009 at [38]; *East Riding of Yorkshire Council v IC and Stanley Davis Group Ltd*, FTT, 15 March 2010 at [28]. This reflects the basic proposition of English law that a bad motive for exercising a right does not invalidate its exercise: *Bradford Corp v Pickles* [1895] AC 587 at 594.

87 In *Hogan and Oxford City Council v IC*, IT, 17 October 2006 at [32], the IT considered that the motive of an applicant

Case law in most comparative jurisdictions recognises that the public interest in disclosure embraces the right of an individual to have disclosed documents that relate to him or that may affect his interests.[89] Under the FOI Acts, where what is requested amounts to personal information relating to the applicant, the information enjoys absolute exemption under the FOI Acts,[90] so that the public interest in its disclosure need not be considered.[91] The issue may, nevertheless, arise in other circumstances. Information, although not personal information, may be of especial interest to, or significance for, the applicant: for example, where it does touch upon the applicant, albeit falling short of having the biographical requirement of personal information;[92] or information relating to an institution with which the applicant is associated.[93]

6–016 Universal public interest factors

The precursor to FOIA, the *Code of Practice on Access to Government Information*,[94] stated that its aims were:

- to improve policy-making and the democratic process by extending access to the facts and analyses which provide the basis for the consideration of proposed policy;
- to protect the interests of individuals and companies by ensuring that reasons are given for administrative decisions, except where there is statutory authority or established convention to the contrary; and
- to support and extend the principles of public service established under the Citizen's Charter.[95]

The 2000 Act was intended to represent a development from the Code of Practice, but there is nothing to suggest that its core purpose was materially different from that of the Code.[96]

6–017 Public interest irrelevancies

The Tribunal has rejected as a relevant consideration the possibility that members of the public might be confused by the information disclosed: if a public authority entertains that fear, it can always volunteer information that will redress any imbalance.[97] On the other hand, where only

could be relevant for the purposes of determining the degree of prejudice likely to result from disclosure. See also: *Ferguson v IC*, FTT, 4 November 2010 at [65].

88 As to which, see Chapter 23.

89 *Burns v Australian National University (No 1)* (1984) 6 ALD 193, 1 AAR 456; *Burns v Australian National University (No 2)* (1985) 7 ALD 425. The courts in the US have been generally less receptive to this notion, taking the view that although the public interest may affect the priority of processing requests, it has no bearing on an individual's rights of access under the FOI Act: *EPA v Mink*, 410 US 73 (1973) (the FOI Act 'is largely indifferent to the intensity of a particular requester's need'); *United States Department of Justice v Reporters Committee for Freedom of the Press*, 489 US 749 (1989); *Forsham v Califano*, 587 F 2d 1128 (DC Cir 1978). Thus, it has been held that a convicted criminal's wish to establish his own innocence through the requested documents does not create a FOI Act-recognised public interest: *Landano v United States Department of Justice*, 956 F 2d 422 (3d Cir 1991); *Hale v United States Department of Justice*, 973 F 2d 894 (10th Cir 1992); *Neely v FBI*, 208 F 3d 461 (4th Cir 2000).

90 FOIA s 40(1); FOI(S)A s 38(1); EIR regs 5(3) and 12(3); EI(S)R regs 10(3) and 11(1). It is instead normally accessible under the GDPR Art 15(1) and DPA 2018 s 45(1). The ability of the data subject to rectify, etc such information under GDPR Art 16 and DPA 2018 s 46 would serve to enhance the public interest in that individual being granted access to it.

91 Equally, where the request is made by a third party in the data subject's interests or on his behalf, the public interest in an individual seeing information about himself will be given minimal weight, if any: *Maurizi v IC and CPS* [2019] UKUT 262 (AAC) at [203].

92 See §§15–020 to 15–023.

93 As in *Burns v Australian National University (No1)* (1984) 6 ALD 193, 1 AAR 456.

94 In relation to information held by Scottish public authorities, see §§3–003 to 3–005.

95 2nd edn 1997, para 2.

96 The most significant distinction between the Act and the Code is that the former imposes an enforceable duty to disclose in certain circumstances, whereas the latter merely exhorted disclosure in certain circumstances.

97 *Kitchener v IC and Derby City Council*, IT, 20 December 2006 at [19]; *Hogan and Oxford City Council v IC*, IT, 17 October

part of the information will be disclosed (because the remainder is absolutely exempt), if the part that stands to be disclosed would result in speculation which 'could cause problems', then that will be a public interest factor against disclosure.[98] There is a public interest in the disclosure of information that is needed to disclose the full picture: in other words, where there has been a partial disclosure of information upon a particular matter the selection of which is unrepresentative of the whole.[99] Similarly, there is a public interest in the disclosure of information where that would correct misinformation that is in the public domain, particularly where the origin of the misinformation is the public authority to whom the request has been made.[100]

3. WEIGHING THE PUBLIC INTEREST: CONFIRMATION AND DENIAL

6–018 Interest in the exemption

As noted above,[101] the need to undertake the weighing exercise set out in subs 2(1)[102] will only arise if the result of carrying out the separate weighing exercise in subs 2(2) is a decision not to disclose the information.[103] Unlike the weighing exercise in relation to the duty to communicate, under subs 2(1) there is no focussing of the public interest upon the particular provision of Part II by which the duty to confirm or deny does not arise. The identified public interest is the maintenance of 'the exclusion of the duty to confirm or deny'. The public interest in maintaining the exclusion of the duty to confirm or deny will vary with the specificity of the request: the more specifically the request identifies the information sought, the more readily may it be determined that the public interest in maintaining the exclusion of the duty to confirm or deny outweighs the public interest in disclosing whether the public authority holds the information. Authorities from the USA illustrate the types of request that have there been held entitle a public authority in the name of the public interest neither to confirm nor deny

---

2006; *DWP v IC*, IT, 5 March 2007, argument at [92] not accepted; *OGC v IC*, IT, 2 May 2007 at [75]; *House of Commons v IC and Leapman, Brooke and Thomas*, IT, 26 February 2008 at [79(e)]; *SSHD v IC*, IT, 15 August 2008 at [15] ('the right under the Act is to information which is held, not to information which is accurate'); *Dept of Health v IC and Lewis*, FTT, 17 March 2014 at [94] (burden of publishing additional explanation to correct actual or potential misunderstanding would be modest); cf *McIntyre v IC and University of East Anglia*, FTT, 7 May 2013 at [31(iii)-(iv)] (exception under EIR reg 12(4)(d) maintained where disclosure would 'likely result in further confusing and fuel controversy' in a 'complex and controversial area'); *OGC v IC*, IT, 19 February 2009 at [161], [182].

[98] *FCO v IC and Plowden* [2013] UKUT 0275 (AAC) at [16].

[99] *Woodward v Hutchins* [1977] 1 WLR 760 at 764 ('If the image which they fostered was not a true image, it is in the public interest that it should be corrected. In these cases of confidential information it is a question of balancing the public interest in knowing the truth.' (Lord Denning)). Significant doubts have been expressed about this authority: it was said to be 'framed in astonishingly wide terms' in *Douglas v Hello! Ltd* [2001] QB 967 at [96]; and it was doubted by Lightman J at first instance in *Campbell v Frisbee* [2002] EWHC 328 (Ch), [2002] EMLR 656 at [40]-[41] and the Court of Appeal (reversing his decision) said his doubts 'may well be right', [2002] EWCA Civ 1374, [2003] ICR 141 at [34]. Moreover, Australian courts have expressly departed from it in favour of a narrower approach: *Castrol Australia Pty Ltd v Emtech Associates Pty Ltd* (1980) 33 ALR 31 at 56 (Rath J). Less controversially, in *AG v Guardian Newspapers (No 2)* [1990] 1 AC 109 at 196 Lord Donaldson MR spoke of 'the legitimate public interest in being fully informed.'

[100] *Hyde Park Residence Ltd v Yelland* [2001] Ch 143 at 170 ('the public interest in knowing the truth' (Mance LJ)).

[101] See §6–008.

[102] In relation to information held by Scottish public authorities, see s 18(1).

[103] In relation to information held by Scottish public authorities, see s 2(1). The exemptions to which the duty to confirm or deny is disapplied are more limited than those under the FOIA: namely, ss 28-35, 39 and 41. The Scottish equivalents to the FOIA ss 22, 32, 33, 40, 41, 42 and 44 do not ground a refusal to confirm or deny under the FOI(S)A. In relation to the differences between the approach taken to the duty to confirm or deny in the FOIA and that which is taken in the FOI(S)A, see §3–005(1). Where the request is made under the environmental information regime, there is no discrete obligation on a public authority to disclose whether or not it holds the requested information.

holding any documents of the sort requested.[104]

6–019 Interest in informing

This public interest is analogous to the public interest in disclosing the information. However, as the applicant is not receiving the information requested but only an acknowledgment that it is or is not held by a particular public authority, it may be thought that the public interest in it is generally less compelling than the public interest in communicating the information requested. The analogy, moreover, has its limitations. In order to be effective, disapplication of the duty to confirm or deny must be invoked consistently to requests of a particular type, whether or not the public authority holds information of the precise sort requested. Unless this is done, a response neither confirming or denying that the sought information is held by the public authority will be understood to represent an acknowledgment that that information is in fact held. The public interest in disclosing whether an authority holds the information sought thus involves a consideration of the public interest in generally disclosing whether that authority holds information of the type requested. For example:[105] an applicant may request all information received by a public authority from X that contributed to the public authority's decision to discontinue benefits to the applicant; the public authority holds no such information received from X; the public authority nevertheless declines to disclose whether it holds the information sought on the basis that unless it uniformly so declines all requests for information on informants, irrespective of the identity or existence of the informant, its ability to conceal the identity of its informants will be prejudiced. The public interest here is that of protecting the anonymity of informants.

4. ASCERTAINING AND WEIGHING PREJUDICE

6–020 Introduction

With the exception of the national security and health and safety exemptions, under each of the prejudice-based exemptions[106] information only becomes exempt information if its disclosure under the FOI Acts 'would, or would be likely to, prejudice' that which the particular exemption seeks to protect.[107] If a public authority is to refuse a request for information, it must specify the exemption relied on and the reason it applies.[108] Where a prejudice-based exemption is specified in the refusal notice, that will involve, if it is not otherwise apparent, stating the basis upon which disclosure 'would, or would be likely to, prejudice' that which the particular exemption seeks to protect.

---

[104] *Frugone v CIA*, 169 F 3d 772 (DC Cir 1999) (where it was upheld that the CIA's refusal to confirm or deny whether plaintiff was ever employed by CIA on the basis that disclosure could cause 'diplomatic tension between Chile and the United States' or could 'lessen the burden facing a foreign intelligence agency attempting to track the CIA's covert activities abroad'); *Miller v Casey*, 730 F 2d 773 (DC Cir 1984) (upholding a refusal to confirm or deny holding any record reflecting any attempt by western countries to overthrow the Albanian government); *Gardels v CIA*, 689 F 2d 1100 (DC Cir 1982) (upholding a refusal to confirm or deny holding any record revealing any covert CIA connection with the University of California). In the United States, this is often called a 'Glomar response'.

[105] The example is loosely based on the Australian case of *Department of Community Services v Jephcott* (1987) 15 FCR 122, 73 ALR 493 (Federal Court on appeal from the Administrative Appeals Tribunal to which the matter had previously been remitted by the Federal Court – see (1985) 8 FCR 85, 62 ALR 421).

[106] FOIA ss 26(1), 27(1), 28(1), 29(1), 31(1), 33(2), 36(2), 38(1) and 43(2); FOI(S)A ss 27(2), 28(1), 30, 31(4), 32(1), 33(1), 33(2), 35(1) and 40.

[107] In Scotland the requirement is to show 'serious prejudice'.

[108] FOIA s 17(1); FOI(S)A s 16(1).

6–021 The meaning of 'prejudice'

Some indication of what was said to be intended by the word 'prejudice' appears from the Second Reading speech in the House of Lords:

> I want to emphasise the strength of the prejudice test. Prejudice is a term used in other legislation relating to the disclosure of information. It is a term well understood by the courts and the public. It is not a weak test. The commissioner will have the power to overrule an authority if she feels that any prejudice caused by a disclosure would be trivial or insignificant. She will ensure that an authority must point to prejudice which is "real, actual or of substance." We do not think that reliance on undefined terms such as "substantial" or "significant" is a sensible way forward. We do not know how they will be interpreted by the commissioner or the courts. We can never deliver absolute certainty, but we can avoid making uncertainty worse by adding ill-defined terminology into the Bill.[109]

In rejecting a proposed amendment that would have required the prejudice to be 'substantial' or 'probable', it was said:

> .. qualification of the term is unnecessary. The Government have consistently stated their views that prejudice means prejudice that is actual, real or of substance.[110]

And similarly in the House of Lords:

> There were also complaints about the "harm" test. A number of noble Lords said that the reference should be to "substantial harm". That was the kind of test they were looking for. The word that was chosen where we are dealing with a harm test is "prejudice". To all lawyers present—there are depressingly few—"prejudice" will mean some real harm to government, or whatever the reference is in a particular part of the Bill. It is something real, and it is harm. Should it be "substantial harm", or should it be "prejudice"? That sounds like the kind of discussion that a lawyer would like to enter into, but it does not cut to the heart of the debate. It sounds much more theological, if I may use that word in this context, rather than cutting to the fundament of the Bill.[111]

This has been endorsed by the Tribunal:

> An evidential burden rests with the decision maker to be able to show that some causal relationship exists between the potential disclosure and the prejudice and that the prejudice is, as Lord Falconer of Thoroton has stated, "real, actual or of substance" (Hansard HL vol 162 col 827 (20 April 2000)). If the public authority is unable to discharge this burden satisfactorily, reliance on "prejudice" should be rejected. There is therefore effectively a *de minimis* threshold which must be met.[112]

---

[109] Hansard HL vol 162 col 827 (20 April 2000) (Minister of State, Cabinet Office, Lord Falconer of Thoroton). When the Lord Chancellor (Lord Irvine) announced in the House of Lords the publication of the *White Paper, Your Right to Know* (Cm 3818, 1997) Hansard HL vol 584 col 245 (11 December 1997), he identified as one of the key features of the proposed FOI regime: 'Thirdly, fewer exemptions. ...Significantly, in most cases information could only be withheld if its disclosure would cause "substantial" harm – a further important advance on the Code.' The House of Lords, *Draft FOI Bill – First Report*, (Select Committee Report HL 97), Session 1998-99, 29 July 1999, had recommended that prejudice be qualified by 'substantial.' — para 32 (see Ch 1 n 43).

[110] Hansard HC vol 347 col 1067 (5 April 2000) (Mr Mike O'Brien). The Government advised the House of Commons Select Committee that the formula required 'probable prejudice, not just possible prejudice': House of Commons, *Public Administration — Third Report* (Cm 4355, 1999) para 65-71 (see Ch 1 n 68); Annex 6, para 47-48. The Home Secretary specifically invited reliance upon his explanation in Parliament as a tool of interpretation in the Courts: para 68.

[111] Hansard HL vol 612 col 889 (20 April 2000) (Minister of State, Cabinet Office, Lord Falconer of Thoroton). See also: Hansard HL vol 617 col 1267 (19 October 2000) – the harm must be 'real'. The House of Commons, *Public Administration — Third Report* (Cm 4355, 1999) para 65, although considering them to be synonymous, preferred the word 'prejudice' to 'harm' on the basis that it was 'more common in other legislation', citing the Local Government Act 1972 Sch 12A, para 4, Taxes Management Act 1970 s 20(8H), Drug Trafficking Act 1994 s 53(2)(b) (since repealed), and DPA 1998 ss 29, 30 and 31.

[112] *Hogan and Oxford City Council v IC*, IT, 17 October 2006 at [30]. Similarly: *Hemsley v IC and Chief Constable of Northamptonshire*, IT, 10 April 2006 at [17] ('some prejudice' is sufficient); *Ministry of Defence v IC and Evans*, IT, 20 July 2007 at [73]; *OGC v IC*, IT, 19 February 2009 at [131]. As to the requisite causal relationship between disclosure and the prejudice see: *Reith v IC*, IT, 1 June 2007 at [37]-[38]; *England and LB of Bexley v IC*, IT, 10 May 2007 at [62].

It has also been affirmed by the Court of Appeal.[113] The statutory formulation 'would be likely to prejudice...' embodies protection against 'risks,'[114] spelling out the precise probability and consequence that will engage the exemption.[115] In this way, it can properly be said that the identified risks constitute a prejudice that is 'real, actual and of substance.'

6– 022 Required degree of likelihood

With the exception of the national security exemption, each of the prejudice-based exemptions employs the formula 'would, or would be likely to prejudice' (or 'endanger' in the case of the health and safety exemption, and 'inhibit' in the case of the exemption concerning public affairs advice).[116] The range of meaning that might be given to the phrase was noted by the House of Commons Select Committee, which quoted one witness before it:

> I think the words "likely to prejudice" are ones which are not the most desirable to have in this field because there is a very considerable risk of conflict as to what the word "likely" means. Does it mean "likely to rain," as in the possibility that it is going to rain, or does it mean "it is more likely than that," in other words that it is more probable than that. ...If "prejudice" is the appropriate word, surely the issue is whether some interest would be prejudiced, and the word "likely" can be somewhat weasel.[117]

In *R (Lord) v Secretary of State for the Home Department*[118] Munby J had cause to consider the meaning of the phrase 'would be likely to prejudice' for the purpose of considering certain exemptions under the DPA 1998. In the course of judgment, he said:

> I accept that "likely" in section 29(1) [of the Data Protection Act 1998] does not mean more probable than not. But on the other hand, it must connote a significantly greater degree of probability than merely "more than fanciful". A "real risk" is not enough. I cannot accept that the important rights intended to be conferred by section 7 are intended to be set at nought by something which measures up only to the minimal requirement of being real, tangible or identifiable rather than merely fanciful. Something much more significant and weighty than that is required....In my judgment "likely" in section 29(1) connotes a degree of probability where there is a very significant and weighty chance of prejudice to the identified public interests. The degree of risk must be such that there "may very well" be prejudice to those interests, even if the risk falls short of being more probable than not.

This passage has been quoted with approval by the Tribunal when considering the phrase as used in FOIA:

> We interpret the expression "likely to prejudice" as meaning that the chance of prejudice being suffered should be more than a hypothetical or remote possibility; there must have been a real and significant risk.[119]

---

113 *Dept for Work and Pensions v IC and Zola* [2016] EWCA Civ 758, [2017] 1 WLR 1 at [22], [27].

114 It is suggested that to the extent that *Campaign against the Arms Trade v IC and MoJ*, IT, 26 August 2008, at [81], and *Gilby v IC and FCO*, IT, 22 October 2008, at [23], consider that a 'risk of harm' to a protected interest is synonymous with harm to that protected interest, they are wrong.

115 Indeed, consideration should be had both to the nature of the harm and the likelihood of its occurrence: an important factor in determining the weight to be given to the risk of harm is the gravity of the harm should it occur, irrespective of the likelihood of its occurrence: *All Party Parliamentary Group on Extraordinary Rendition v IC and FCO* [2015] UKUT 0377 (AAC) at [101].

116 FOIA ss 22A(1), 24(1), 26(1), 27(1), 28(1), 29(1), 31(1), 33(2), 36(2), 38(1) and43(2). In Scotland, the formula 'would or would be likely to prejudice substantially' (or 'inhibit substantially' or merely 'endanger') is used: FO(S)A ss 27(2), 28(1), 30, 31(1), 31(4), 32(1), 33(1)(b), 33(2), 35(1), 39(1) and 40.

117 Lord Woolf, quoted in House of Commons, *Public Administration — Third Report* (Cm 4355, 1999) para 66 (see Ch 1 n 68). The Government had argued before the Committee that the phrase required the prejudice to be at least 'likely' or 'probable', rather than merely 'possible': *Public Administration — Third Report* (Cm 4355, 1999) para 68.

118 [2003] EWHC 2073 (Admin) at [99]-[100].

119 *John Connor Press Associates v IC*, IT, 25 January 2006 at [15]. Similarly: *Hogan and Oxford City Council v IC*, IT, 17 October 2006 at [34]; *McIntyre v IC and MoD*, IT, 4 February 2008 at [40]; *Craven v IC*, IT, 13 May 2008 at [14], [19], [24]; *Keene v IC and Central Office of Information*, IT, 14 September 2009 at [36]; *Bangar v IC and Transport for London*, IT, 23 November 2009 at [5]; *University of Central Lancashire v IC and Colquhoun*, IT, 8 December 2009 at [32];

And similarly:

> It means that inhibition would probably occur (ie, on the balance of probabilities, the chance being greater than 50%) or that there would be a "very significant and weighty chance" that it would occur. A "real risk" is not enough; the degree of risk must be such that there "may very well be" such inhibition, even if the risk falls short of being more probable than not.[120]

The correctness of this approach has been accepted by the Court of Appeal.[121] The mere assertion of inhibition resulting from disclosure, while not necessarily fatal to a claim for exemption, will be an important consideration.[122] The Tribunal has indicated that it expects to receive evidence of the likelihood, severity, extent or frequency of the claimed inhibition.[123] There must also be evidence of a causal link between potential disclosure and the prejudice claimed.[124]

6– 023 Approach elsewhere

Similar formulae of likelihood of harm are used in the prejudice-based exemptions of other FOI Acts. In Australia, the phrase 'would or could reasonably be expected to' has been consistently been held to mean that the decision-maker must have real and substantial grounds for the expectation that harm will occur: it requires more than a possibility, risk or chance of the event occurring.[125] In New Zealand, the phrase 'likely to prejudice' has been held to mean no more than a distinct or significant possibility, and that it is enough if there is a serious or real and substantial risk to a protected interest or that a risk might well eventuate.[126] In Canada, in order to rely on a prejudice-based exemption,[127] it has been held that the agency need not prove

BBC and One Transport Ltd v IC and Davis, FTT, 11 April 2011 at [22]-[23]; *Dept for Work and Pensions v IC and Zola* [2014] UKUT 0334 (AAC) at [26]; *Dept of Business, Innovation & Skills v IC and Whyte*, FTT, 20 April 2015 at [25] and [50]; *Baker v IC and LB Lambeth*, FTT, 31 October 2019 at [12]-[13]. An attack on the applicability of *R (Lord) v SSHD* to the FOIA was rejected by the Tribunal in *Office of Commerce v IC*, IT, 2 May 2007 at [48].

120 *Guardian Newspapers Ltd v IC and BBC*, IT, 8 January 2007 at [53]. Similarly: *Evans v IC and MoD*, IT, 26 October 2007 at [21]; *Galloway v IC and NHS*, IT, 20 March 2009 at [93]. For the interpretation given to the word 'likely' in s 12(3) of the Human Rights Act 1998, see *Cream Holdings Ltd v Banerjee* [2003] EWCA Civ 103, [2003] 2 All ER 318 at [12(i)] and [83] and, on appeal, *Cream Holdings Ltd v Banerjee* [2004] UKHL 44, [2005] 1 AC 253 at [16] and [22]. For the interpretation given to the word 'likely' in s 1(1) of the Defamation Act 2013 see *Lachaux v Independent Print Media Ltd* [2019] UKSC 27, [2019] 4 All ER 485, [2019] 3 WLR 18 at [14].

121 *Dept for Work and Pensions v IC and Zola* [2016] EWCA Civ 758, [2017] 1 WLR 1 at [22], [27].

122 *Guardian Newspapers Ltd and Heather Brooke v IC and BBC*, IT, 8 January 2007 at [78].

123 *Guardian Newspapers Ltd and Heather Brooke v IC and BBC*, IT, 8 January 2007 at [99]-[102].

124 *Reith v IC*, IT, 1 June 2007 at [37]-[38]; *England and LB of Bexley v IC*, IT, 10 May 2007 at [62].

125 *News Corporation v National Companies and Securities Commission* (1984) 5 FCR 88, 57 ALR 550, where (at ALR 561) a distinction was drawn between the two phrases 'would or could reasonably be expected to prejudice' and 'would or might prejudice', with the former requiring more than the latter; *Attorney-General's Department v Cockcroft* (1986) 10 FCR 180, 64 ALR 97; *Arnold v Queensland* (1987) 13 ALD 195 at 215; *Re Binnie and Department of Agriculture and Rural Affairs* [1989] VR 836; *Searle Australia Pty Ltd v Public Interest Advocacy Centre and Department of Community Services and Health* (1992) 108 ALR 163; *George v Rocket* (1990) 170 CLR 104. See Freedom of Information Act 1982 (Cth of Australia), ss 33, 37, 47B, 47E, 47G, 47H and 47J.

126 *Commissioner of Police v Ombudsman* [1988] 1 NZLR 385 at 391, 404 and 411, which considered the various possible shades of meaning that could be given to the word 'likely'. The Official Information Act 1982, ss 6 and 7 render information exempt from disclosure where that disclosure 'would be likely to prejudice/endanger/damage seriously' one of the protected interests. Exemption is also granted where that 'is necessary to protect/avoid prejudice/maintain the constitutional conventions which would protect/maintain the effective conduct of public affairs/enable a Minister to carry out/prevent the disclosure of use of official information for improper gain' (s 9).

127 Section 20(1)(c) of the Access to Information Act 1985 creates a mandatory exemption for 'information the disclosure of which could reasonably be expected to result in material financial loss or gain to, or could reasonably be expected to prejudice the competitive position of, a third party.' See also: ss 14-18, which use 'could reasonably be expected to be injurious' (ss 14-16), 'could reasonably be expected to facilitate the commission of an offence' (s 16(2)), 'could reasonably be expected to threaten' (s 17), 'could reasonably be expected to prejudice' (s 18(b)) and 'could reasonably be expected to result in an undue benefit' (s 18(d)).

direct causation between disclosure and harm: indirect causality will suffice.[128] However, in order to uphold non-disclosure on an appeal, the Courts have required evidence to justify the apprehension of prejudice: evidence that describes in a most general way certain consequences that could ensue from disclosure has been held to fall short of meeting the burden of proving the harm that disclosure would cause.[129] Similarly, mere affirmations that the disclosure would cause the harm required by the section will not suffice where the expectation of the harm is not self-evident.[130] European case law in relation to Regulation 1049/2001 Article 4 requires that 'the risk of the interest being undermined must be reasonably foreseeable and must not be purely hypothetical.'[131]

6– 024 Cumulative prejudice

Although disclosure of particular information, when considered in isolation, may fail to satisfy the prejudice requirement, consideration of the prejudice caused by the disclosure of that information together with that caused by the disclosure of other similarly non-prejudicial information may yield a different result. This is variously termed 'jigsaw', 'mosaic' or 'cumulative' prejudice. There is nothing in the FOI Acts requiring such an exercise to be carried out. A provision in the FOI Bill specifically enabling such an exercise was criticised by both the House of Commons Select Committee and the House of Lords Select Committee, and did not find its way into the statute.[132] The Tribunal and the Commissioner have, however, said that 'mosaic' effects can be taken into account.[133]

6– 025 Cumulative prejudice elsewhere

Freedom of information legislation in comparative jurisdictions invariably prescribes certain exemptions on the basis of anticipated prejudice or harm resulting from disclosure. The concept of 'mosaic' or cumulative prejudice has been accepted as capable of constituting that prejudice or harm, albeit only in particular spheres of governmental activity. In the United States, mosaic prejudice is well-recognised in relation to intelligence gathering activities,[134] and is now explicitly recognised by Executive Order.[135] In Australia, security and criminal investigation agencies have usually been able to sustain claims of exemption founded upon

---

[128] *Canada Packers Inc v Canada (Minister of Agriculture)* [1989] 1 FC 47.

[129] *Ottawa Football Club v Canada (Minister of Fitness and Amateur Sports)* [1989] 2 FC 480; *Merck Frosst Canada Inc v Canada (Minister of Health and Welfare)* (1988), 20 FTR 73 30 CPR (3d) 473; *Canada Post Corp v Canada (Minister of Public Works)* [1993] 3 FC 320, affirmed (1993) 64 FTR 62.

[130] *Canadian Broadcasting Commission v National Capital Commission* (1998) 147 FTR 264.

[131] *ClientEarth v European Commission* (C-57/16 P) [2019] Env LR 19 at [51]; *Council of the European Union v in't Veld* (C-350/12) [2015] 1 CMLR 11 at [53]; *Council of the European Union v Access Info Europe* (C-280/11) [2014] 2 CMLR 6 at [31]; *European Commission v Agrofert Holding AS* (C-477/10) [2012] 5 CMLR 9 at [79]; *Sweden v My Travel Group plc* (C-506/08) [2011] ECR I-6237, [2012] All ER (EC) 968, [2011] 5 CMLR 18 at [76]; *Sweden and Turco v Council* (C-39/05, C-52/05) [2009] QB 269, [2009] 2 WLR 867, [2008] 3 CMLR 17 at [43].

[132] House of Commons, *Public Administration—Third Report* (Cm 4355, 1999) paras 113-116; Annex 6, paras 70-72; House of Lords, *Draft FOI Bill—First Report*, (Select Committee Report HL 97), Session 1998-99, 29 July 1999, paras 36-37, referring to cl 37 (see Ch 1 n 43). In relation to mosaic prejudice and intelligence and national security matters, see §26– 036(1).

[133] *All Party Parliamentary Group on Extraordinary Rendition v IC and FCO*, FTT, 3 May 2012 at [166] and [177]-[179]. See also the Information Commissioner's Guidance on Information in the Public Domain at [63]-[65]: `www.ici.org/media/for-organisations/documents/1204/information-in-the-public-domain-for-eir-guidance.pdf`

[134] *Halperin v CIA*, 629 F 2d 144 (DC Cir 1980), 'each individual piece of intelligence information, much like a piece of a jigsaw puzzle, may aid in piecing together other bits of information even when the individual piece is not of obvious importance in itself'; *Salisbury v United States*, 690 F 2d 966; *Taylor v Department of the Army*, 684 F 2d 99; *ACLU v Dept of Justice*, 681 F 3d 61, 71 (2d Cir 2012).

[135] Executive Order 13,526, 1.7(4)(e).

prejudice to the integrity of their intelligence from incremental disclosure.[136] In Canada, there is less authority on the point: it has on one occasion received passing acceptance in relation to police information.[137]

6–026 Information already public

Each of the prejudice-based exemptions requires that disclosure 'would, or would be likely to, prejudice' a particular protected interest.[138] If that anticipated prejudice has already resulted from an earlier disclosure, it will be difficult to attribute any material prejudice[139] to a later disclosure of the same or like information.[140] The fact that there has been an earlier disclosure of the same or like information does not, however, necessarily mean that the anticipated prejudice has already occurred. The manner in which information is disclosed can impinge upon the prejudice resulting from that disclosure. In particular, the prejudice resulting from an unintentional or unauthorised disclosure of information may, in some circumstances, be different from that resulting from an official disclosure of the same information.[141] Official confirmation carries with it secondary information as to the accuracy of the earlier disclosure: this secondary information can turn theory into fact and render others more likely to act upon it. In the United States the courts have held that, in asserting a claim of prior public disclosure, the applicant bears the initial burden of pointing to specific information in the public domain that appears to duplicate that being withheld.[142] If the public authority itself has made the information available to certain quarters of the public, it will be difficult to sustain a prejudice-based exemption.[143]

---

[136] *Re Low and Department of Defence* (1984) 2 AAR 142 at 149; *Re Actors' Equity Association of Australia and Australian Broadcasting Tribunal (No 2)* (1985) 7 ALD 584 (information sought relating to commercial television licensees); *Re Robinson and Department of Foreign Affairs* (1986) 11 ALN N48; *Re Throssell and Australian Archives* (1986) 10 ALD 403 at 406 and 407; *Re Throssell and Department of Foreign Affairs* (1987) 14 ALD 296; *Re Slater and Cox (Director General, Australian Archives)* (1988) 15 ALD 20 at 27; *Re McKnight v Australian Archives* (1992) 28 ALD 95 at 112; *Re Ewer and Australian Archives* (1995) 38 ALD 789.

[137] *Ruby v Canada (Royal Canadian Mounted Police)* [1998] 2 FC 351 (TD). The Court of Appeal appeared less enthusiastic about it: *Ruby v Canada (Solicitor General)* [2000] 3 FC 589 (CA) at [89] *et seq.*

[138] Apart from the exemptions from disclosure that would, or would be likely to, 'inhibit' the provision of advice in the context of the conduct of public affairs or 'endanger' the physical or mental health or safety of any individual: FOIA ss 22A(1), 26(1), 27(1), 28(1), 29(1), 31(1), 33(2), 36(2), 38(1) and 43(2). 'Endanger' and 'prejudice' come to essentially the same thing: *People for the Ethical Treatment of Animals Europe v IC and Oxford University*, IT, 13 April 2010 at [30]. In Scotland, the requirement is for 'substantial prejudice' (and the 'substantial inhibition' of advice, but only the mere endangerment of health or safety: FOI(S)A ss 27(2), 28(1), 30, 31(4), 32(1), 33(2), 35(1), 39(1) and 40.

[139] See §6–021 for the meaning of 'prejudice'.

[140] See, for example: *FCO v IC*, IT, 22 January 2008 at [26], [28]; *Cabinet Office v IC and Lamb*, IT, 27 January 2009 at [78].

[141] *S v IC and The General Register Office*, IT, 9 May 2007 at [80]; *People for the Ethical Treatment of Animals Europe v IC and Oxford University*, IT, 13 April 2010 at [49] and [53]; *Ministry of Defence v IC and Evans*, IT, 20 July 2007 at [57]; *Gilby v IC and FCO*, IT, 22 October 2008 at [42]-[44]. In Australia, in *Ascic v Australian Federal Police* (1986) 11 ALN N184, it was held that the mere fact that information in respect of which an agency claimed exemption may have been 'leaked' did not necessarily prejudice the merits of the exemption claimed: disclosure by order under the Act being considered a very different thing with very different consequences to unauthorised access. In Canada the jurisprudence indicates that once information is public from another source the release of the same information by the Government will be less likely to cause harm; the courts have required the Government to show specific reasons why its release of the same information would cause harm: *Canada (IC) v Canada (Prime Minister)* [1993] 1 FC 427 (TD); *Cyanamid Canada Inc v Canada (Minister of Health and Welfare)* (1992) 45 CPR (3d) 390 (FCA).

[142] *Afshar v Department of State*, 702 F 2d 1125 (DC Cir 1983); *Assassination Archives & Research Centre v CIA*, 177 F Supp 2d 1 (DDC 2001) (holding that the CIA's prior disclosure of some intelligence methods employed in Cuba does not oblige it to disclose all forms of intelligence gathering in Cuba); *Billington v Department of Justice*, 11 F Supp 2d 45 (DDC 1998) (holding that because the release of similar types of information by the FBI in one case did not warrant disclosure in the instant case); *Hunt v CIA*, 981 F 2d 1116 (9th Cir 1992) (held that although some information about subject of request may have been made public by other governmental agencies, the CIA's 'neither confirm nor deny' response was warranted).

[143] *Kuijer v Council of the European Union (No 2)* [2002] 1 WLR 1941 at paras 73-74 (Court of First Instance of the

6–027 Use of disclosed information

Once the access right is engaged, it not having been disapplied by any provision in the Act, the duty on a public authority is to communicate the requested information in one of the ways specified in the Act. There is nothing in the FOI Acts enabling a public authority when communicating information to place restrictions on the use of that information.[144] The unqualified nature of any disclosure required under the Act is shared by the FOI legislation in comparative jurisdictions. Attempts in the USA and Australia to impose restrictions on the use of disclosed information have been held unlawful.[145]

6–028 Significance of potential uses

The inability of a public authority to restrict the use made of information disclosed under the Act is of particular significance in the determination of the prejudice-based exemptions. The prejudice that is to be measured is that resulting from an unrestricted disclosure, and not just a disclosure to the applicant.[146] There is nothing in the FOI Acts to prevent a person when requesting information and who anticipates that the public authority may claim that disclosure would prejudice a protected interest, to reduce the scope for prejudice by offering to limit use of the information so disclosed.[147] Such undertakings have, however, been rejected in the US.[148]

European Communities). For an example of how disclosure by a public authority of some of the requested information can make a claim for a prejudice-based exemption unsustainable, see *John Connor Press Associates v IC*, IT, 25 January 2006, where the disclosure of certain commercial information relating to a particular transaction precluded exemption under FOIA s 43(2), for the remaining commercial information relating to that transaction. See also *Hogan and Oxford City Council v IC*, IT, 17 October 2006 at [42]-[50] and [71].

144 *Hogan and Oxford City Council v IC*, IT, 17 October 2006 at [31]; *S v IC and The General Register Office*, IT, 9 May 2007 at [80].

145 *Schiffer v FBI* 78 F 3d 1405 (9th Cir 1996). The FOI Act (US) does not provide for limited disclosure; rather, it 'speaks in terms of disclosure and nondisclosure [and] ordinarily does not recognize degrees of disclosure, such as permitting viewing, but not copying, of documents' — *Julian v United States Department of Justice*, 806 F 2d 1411 at 1419 n.7 (9th Cir 1986). In Australia, *Re Dwyer and Department of Finance* (1985) 8 ALD 474.

146 *Hogan and Oxford City Council v IC*, IT, 17 October 2006 at [31]; *Guardian Newspapers Ltd and Brooke v IC and BBC*, IT, 8 January 2007 at [52]. Similarly, in relation to the EIR: *R (Office of Communications) v IC* [2009] EWCA Civ 90, [2009] ACD 48.

147 The Information Commissioner's Guide to Freedom of Information affirms that public authorities can 'restrict the release of information to a specific individual or group at [their] discretion, outside the provisions of the Act' www.ico.org.uk/for-organisations-guide-to-freedom-of-information/receiving-a-request

148 *Maricopa Audobon Society v United States Forest Service*, 108 F 3d 1082 at 1088-89 (9th Cir 1997) on the basis that the 'FOI Act does not permit selective disclosure of information to only certain parties, and that once the information is disclosed to [the plaintiff], it must be made available to all members of the public who request it.'

Part II

Data Protection

CHAPTER 7

Data protection: introduction

1. ORIGINS OF DATA PROTECTION LAW

7–001 Meaning of data protection

The essence of data protection is the legislative control over the extent to which and the manner in which information about an individual may be used by others, and the correlative extent and manner that those others are permitted to use information about an individual. The word 'use' here covers the complete life-cycle of information: acquisition, storage, organisation, retrieval, consultation, reliance, adaptation, copying, dissemination, publication, blocking, erasure and destruction. The legislative control seeks to accommodate and, so far as possible, reconcile the two interests that are within the concept of data protection: (a) the interest of an individual that information relating to him or herself should not be misused or over-used; and (b) the interest of a user of that personal information in being permitted due use of it. The need for and nature of data protection reflect information not in itself being a species of property, with the consequence that the panoply of rights and correlative obligations attaching to property and enforceable at law are inapplicable to personal information.[1] For this reason, it is an unhelpful distraction to look to property law for answers to issues in data protection law.

7– 002 Approach of data protection law

Data protection law aims to protect the rights of identifiable living individuals ('data subjects') as regards anything done ('processing') with information relating to them ('personal data') by or on behalf of persons who determine how and for what purposes that information is used ('controllers'). It does so by imposing a range of continuing obligations on controllers and those acting on their behalf ('processors') in respect of all processing of personal data ('principles'), as well as by conferring specific rights that data subjects can assert against a data controller. Although these rights will often overlap with the ordinary conception of a right to personal privacy, there is no requirement that personal privacy be infringed in order for data protection obligations or rights to be infringed: the obligations and rights are inherent in the processing of personal data. Thus, data protection law recognises that where, for example, a controller has, without the consent of a data subject, abstracted his or her personal data, that data subject will have an actionable claim against the controller without needing to support that claim with an allegation of resultant pecuniary loss or resultant distress.[2] The rights and obligations are legislatively shaped in order not to impede recognised interests making legitimate use of that information.

7– 003 In the beginning

Until well into the 1990s, courts in the United Kingdom, while occasionally acknowledging shortcomings in the common law's protection of personal privacy,[3] invariably declined to protect a person from aspects of his or her personal life being watched, recorded or disseminated to others unless there was something more to it — eg a confidential relationship.[4]

1 That data is not per se regarded as a species of property has been repeatedly recognised: *OBG Ltd v Allan* [2007] UKHL 21, [2008] 1 AC 1 at [275]-[276]; *Phillips v News Group Newspapers Ltd* [2012] UKSC 28, [2013] 1 AC 1 at [30]; *Your Response Ltd v Datateam Business Media Ltd* [2014] EWCA Civ 281, [2015] QB 41; *Environment Agency v Churngold Recycling Ltd* [2014] EWCA Civ 909, [2015] Env LR 13 at [16]-[19]; *Computer Associates UK Ltd v Software Incubator Ltd* [2018] EWCA Civ 518, [2018] 2 All ER (Comm) 398; *Various Claimants v Morrison Supermarkets plc* [2018] EWCA Civ 2339, [2019] QB 772 at [44]-[45]; *Lloyd v Google LLC* [2019] EWCA Civ 1599, [2020] EMLR 2 at [46]; *Ramsden v HMRC* [2019] EWHC 3566 (QB) at [99]. See also the authorities cited at §20– 038.

2 See *Lloyd v Google LLC* [2019] EWCA Civ 1599, [2020] EMLR 2 at [45]-[70]. Although in that case the wrong suffered was labelled a 'loss of control' of the personal data, whether a data subject ever had, or wished to exert, that control should make no difference to the existence of the wrong: the true wrong lies in the misuse and over-use of the data subject's personal data, regardless of resultant pecuniary loss, regardless of resultant distress and regardless of whether the data subject ever had or exerted control. In this respect it is like trespass to goods or land, neither of which require loss and both of which take account of the extent of the interference and the benefit had by the defendant in assessing the damages to be awarded. Other authorities have recognised that mere interference with personal data is sufficient to provide the data subject with a basis for claim: *Re EU-Canada Passenger Name Record (PNR) Agreement* [2018] 1 CMLR 1083 at [124] ('it does not matter whether the information in question relating to private life is sensitive or whether the persons concerned have been inconvenienced in any way on account of that interference'); *Schrems v Data Protection Commissioner* (C-362/14) [2016] QB 527, [2016] 2 CMLR 2 at [87]; *Digital Rights Ireland Ltd v Minister for Communications, Marine and Natural Resources* (C-293/12 and C-594/12) [2015] QB 127, [2014] 3 CMLR 44 at [33].

3 For example: *Turner v Spooner* (1861) 30 LJ Ch 801 at 803; *Monson v Tussauds Ltd* [1894] 1 QB 671 at 687; *Tolley v Fry Ltd* [1930] 1 KB 467 at 478 per Greer LJ; reversed on appeal [1931] AC 333; *Victoria Park Racing v Taylor* (1937) 58 CLR 479 at 505, per Rich J (diss); *Bernstein v Sky Views* [1978] QB 479 at 483; *Kaye v Robertson* [1991] FSR 62 at 70 (CA); *R v Khan (Sultan)* [1997] AC 558 at 582-583; *Mills v News Group Newspapers Ltd* [2001] EWHC Ch 412 ('But the day may not be far off when this deficiency will be remedied'); *A v B plc* [2002] EWCA Civ 337, [2003] QB 195; *Douglas v Hello! Ltd* [2003] EWHC 786, [2003] 3 All ER 996 at [229]; cf *Morris v Beardmore* [1981] AC 446 at 465.

4 In *Prince Albert v Strange* (1849) 1 Mac & G 25, 41 ER 1171, (1849) 1 De G & Sm 652 Knight-Bruce VC referred to a 'sordid spying into the privacy of domestic life' (DeG & Sm at 698) and, on appeal, Lord Cottenham LC spoke of privacy as the right being invaded (1 Mac & G at 47). However, the Court did treat the case as one of an interference with the plaintiff's property, namely his right to publish the etchings (DeG & Sm at 697). While it is

This contrasted with the position in the USA. An article by Warren and Brandeis published in 1890[5] had proved seminal in the development of a legal right of privacy. By 1960 the common law in that country had sufficiently developed to recognise that 'privacy' was not a unitary concept:

> The law of privacy comprises four distinct kinds of invasion of four different interests of the plaintiff, which are tied together by a common name, but otherwise have almost nothing in common except that each represents an interference with the right of the plaintiff....to be let alone.[6]

Such concepts remained alien in the United Kingdom: without any external impetus, there was no need to pretend that the common law was vibrant or adapted to the needs of the age. In February 1961 Lord Mancroft introduced a Right of Privacy Bill into the House of Lords.[7] The stated object of the Bill was:

> to give every individual such further protection against invasion of his privacy as may be desirable for the maintenance of human dignity while protecting the right of the public to be kept informed in all matters in which the public may be reasonably concerned.[8]

The method used to achieve this was to confer on a person a right of action:

> against any other person who without his consent publishes of or concerning him in any newspaper or by means of cinematograph exhibition or any television or sound broadcast any words relating to his personal affairs or conduct if such publication is calculated to cause him distress or embarrassment.

The Bill then provided for various defences. The Bill did not survive the Parliamentary Session. In an article in1962, Brian Neill pressed for legal protection for privacy, observing that it was expressly provided for in Art 12 of the Universal Declaration of Human Rights and Article 8(1) of the European Convention on Human Rights.[9] Between 1967 and 1980 the lack of legal protection for privacy had been the target of five parliamentary bills,[10] two parliamentary reports,[11] two White Papers[12] and a Law Commission working paper. The sentiments expressed within them remained just that.

7–004 International instruments

At the international level, the right to a private domain had been recognised in Art 12 of the Universal Declaration of Human Rights, adopted and proclaimed by the United Nations on 10 December 1948. Although a non-binding declaration, the Universal Declaration has always

---

possible that the identity of the parties informed the outcome, for the next 150 years equity and the common law rested.

5 'The Right to Privacy', *Harvard Law Review*, vol 4, 1890, 193.

6 Prosser, 'Privacy' *California Law Review*, vol 48, 1960, 383 at 389. Professor Prosser taxonimised 'privacy' into four classes: (1) an intrusion upon the plaintiff's physical solitude or seclusion (including unlawful searches, telephone tapping, long-distance photography and telephone harassment); (2) a public disclosure of private facts; (3) publicity putting the plaintiff in a false light; and (4) an appropriation, for the defendant's advantage, of the plaintiff's name or likeness. The taxonomy does not provide an ideal fit with English jurisprudence. It is partly shaped by the premium placed on free speech under the US Constitution. 'Data protection' is principally concerned with (1) and (2), with (3) being protected through the law of defamation and (4) being protected through various intellectual property rights. Class (1) may also give rise to a claim in private nuisance: see *Fearn v Tate Gallery* [2019] EWHC 246 (Ch), [2019] Ch 369 at [133]-[179].

7 *Hansard* HL vol 229, col 660.

8 Explanatory memorandum.

9 'The Protection of Privacy', *Modern Law Review*, vol 25, 1962, 393. The author subsequently became Neill LJ.

10 Introduced by: Mr Lyon, 1967; Mr Walden, 1968; Mr Kenneth Baker, 1969; Mr Huckfield, 1971; Lord Manocroft, 1971.

11 *Report on the Committee on Privacy* – called 'the Younger Report' – (Cmnd 5012, 1972), which established 10 principles for the handling of personal data, and the *Report on the Committee on Data Protection* – called 'the Lindop Committee Report' – (Cmnd 7341, 1978).

12 *Computers and Privacy*, Cmnd 6353, 1975; and *Computers: Safeguards for Privacy*, Cmnd 6354, 1975.

had considerable status as the foundational instrument of international human rights law. On 16 December 1966 the General Assembly of the United Nations resolved to adopt the International Covenant on Civil and Political Rights, Art 17 of which reproduced Art 12 of the Universal Declaration:

> 1. No one shall be subjected to arbitrary or unlawful interference with his privacy, family, home or correspondence, nor to unlawful attacks on his honour and reputation.
> 2. Everyone has the right to the protection of the law against such interference or attacks.

The United Kingdom signed the Covenant on 16 September 1968 and ratified it on 20 May 1976.

7–005 Council of Europe

The Council of Europe was founded on 5 May 1949 by the Treaty of London.[13] It has the stated aim of upholding human rights, democracy and the rule of law in Europe. It currently has 47 Member States, of which 28 are Member States of the EU. It does not make binding laws, but it does enforce select international agreements to which its Member States are parties. The ECHR is an instance of such an international agreement, and the ECtHR is a body of the Council which enforces the ECHR. The Council's three statutory bodies are the Committee of Ministers (comprising the foreign ministers of each Member State), the Parliamentary Assembly (composed of members of the national parliaments of each Member State and which adopts resolutions and makes recommendations to all Member States). and the Congress of Local and Regional Authorities (currently comprising 648 members holding elective regional, mayoral or municipal office in the different Member States). In 1968, the Parliamentary Assembly addressed Recommendation 509 to its Committee of Ministers, asking it to examine whether the ECHR and the domestic law of the Member States offered adequate protection to the right of personal privacy vis-à-vis modern science and technology. A study carried out on instruction of the Committee of Ministers in response to that Recommendation showed that national legislation gave insufficient protection to individual privacy and other rights and interests of individuals with regard to automated data banks. It was the first recognition that regulation of the use of personal information need not always be coincident with the protection of personal privacy and of an individual's elemental right to limit other's use of personal information about him or herself. On the basis of these findings, the Committee of Ministers adopted in 1973 and 1974 two resolutions on data protection. The first – Resolution (73) 22 – established principles of data protection for the private sector. The second – Resolution (74) 29 – did the same for the public sector. Within five years after the passing of the second resolution, general data protection laws had been enacted in seven Member States (Austria, Denmark, France, Federal Republic of Germany, Luxembourg, Norway and Sweden).[14] For its part, the United Kingdom turned its face against such regulation. In 1974, its status as a so-called 'data haven' (ie a country with no legal control over or regulation of the use of personal data) resulted in the Swedish Data Inspector Board banning the export of Swedish personal data to the United Kingdom under the terms of that country's Data Act 1973. This forced the United Kingdom to re-visit its position, in the first instance by commissioning what became the Lindop Committee. It proved to be a slow business, with an institutional reluctance to participate, let alone assist.[15] Meanwhile, in three Member States, data protection had been

---

13 The original signatories were Belgium, Denmark, France, Ireland, Italy, Luxembourg, Netherlands, Norway, Sweden and the United Kingdom. The idea of such a body had been urged by Sir Winston Churchill in an address to the University of Zurich on 19 September 1946.

14 In 1970 the German state of Hesse adopted the world's first data protection law: Hessisches Datenschutzgesetz. It applied only to that state. in 1973 Sweden adopted the Datalagen. In 1976 Germany adopted the Bundesdatenschutzgestez. And in 1977 France adopted the Loi relatif à l'informatique, aux fichiers et aux libertés.

15 For a fuller account, see: Warren and Dearnley 'Data Protection Legislation in the United Kingdom from development to statute 1969-84', *Information, Communication & Society*, vol 8, no 2, June 2005, pp 238-263.

incorporated as a fundamental right in the Constitution (Article 35 of the 1976 Constitution of Portugal; Article 18 of the 1978 Constitution of Spain; Article 1 of the 1978 Austrian Data Protection Act: Fundamental Right of Data Protection).

7–006 OECD

Developments in data protection were not confined to Europe. On 23 September 1980 the Council of the Organisation for Economic Co-operation and Development – the OECD – adopted a 'Recommendation concerning Guidelines on the Protection of Privacy and Transborder Flows of Personal Data.'[16] The paramount concern of the recommended guidelines was to prevent adverse economic consequences of different national standards governing the processing of personal information, which the OECD characterised as a barrier to trade and which it recognised was acutely significant for the rapidly growing processing of data by computers.[17] The OECD guidelines accommodated the competition of interests between the member countries advocating the greatest freedom in transborder data flows (principally the USA) and those member countries placing greater emphasis on the protection of individual rights (principally certain European countries). The Guidelines defined terms that were to become familiar in the field – 'data controller'[18] and 'personal data'[19] – and set out eight 'basic principles of national application'[20] and four 'basic principles of international application.'[21] On 11 July 2013 the OECD Council adopted a revised Recommendation Concerning Guidelines Governing the Protection of Privacy and Transborder Flows of Personal Data – 'The OECD Privacy Guidelines' – the first revision since the 1980 guidelines.

7–007 Council Convention 108

On 28 January 1981 the Council of Europe opened the Convention for the Protection of Individuals with regard to the Automatic Processing of Personal Data – 'Convention 108.' The Convention applies to all data processing carried out, whether in the private sector or in the public sector, including data processing by the judiciary and law enforcement agencies. The Convention remains in force. Article 1 states that its purpose is to secure for every individual:

> respect for his rights and fundamental freedoms, and in particular his right to privacy, with regard to automatic processing of personal data relating to him ('data protection').

---

[16] Organisation for Economic Co-operation and Development, *Guidelines on the Protection of Privacy and Transborder Flows of Personal Data*, adopted 23 September 1980. The background to the OECD involvement is summarised in an article by the Chairman of the expert group that was tasked with preparing its guidelines: Michael Kirby, 'The history, achievement and future of the 1980 OECD guidelines on privacy', *International Data Privacy Law*, 2011, vol 1, no 1, 6-14.

[17] 'One normally thinks of the OECD as a body of sober economists, statisticians, and technologists. One does not normally expect such people to be dripping with human rights sentiments.': Michael Kirby, 'The history, achievement and future of the 1980 OECD guidelines on privacy', *International Data Privacy Law*, 2011, vol 1, no 1, at p 6.

[18] The Guidelines defined 'data controller' for the purposes of the Guidelines to mean 'a party who, according to domestic law, is competent to decide about the contents and use of personal data regardless of whether or not such data are collected, stored, processed or disseminated by that party or by an agent on its behalf.'

[19] The Guidelines defined 'personal data' for the purposes of the Guidelines to mean 'any information relating to an identified or identifiable individual.'

[20] These were: (1) a collection limitation principle; (2) a data quality principle; (3) a purpose specification principle; (4) a use limitation principle; (5) a security safeguards principle; (6) an openness principle; (7) an individual participation principle; and (8) an accountability principle.

[21] These were: (1) each Member country taking into consideration the implications for other Member countries of domestic processing and re-export of personal data; (2) each Member country taking reasonable and appropriate steps to ensure that transborder flows of personal data were uninterrupted and secure; (3) each Member country refraining from restricting transborder flows of personal data between itself and another Member country, with certain limitations; and (4) each Member country avoiding developing laws, policies and practices in the name of protecting privacy that created obstacles to the transborder flow of personal data that would exceed the requirements for such protection.

Although its stated purpose places the use of personal information within the concept of the right to privacy, the scope of the Convention (Art 3) is unrelated to privacy and the statement of basic principles (Arts 4 to 11) is similarly unrelated.[22] This was an even clearer recognition of an individual's elemental right to limits on the use made of private information relating to him or herself than the Council of Europe's Recommendation 509.

7– 008 Convention 108 content

The Convention provides definitions of 'personal data,'[23] 'data subject' and 'controller of the [automated data file].' Article 5 provides the central set of principles governing the processing of personal data:

Personal data undergoing automatic processing shall be:
(a) obtained and processed fairly and lawfully;
(b) stored for specified and legitimate purposes and not used in a way incompatible with those purposes;
(c) adequate, relevant and not excessive in relation to the purposes for which they are stored;
(d) accurate and, where necessary, kept up to date;
(e) preserved in a form which permits identification of the data subjects for no longer than is required for the purpose for which those data are stored.

The Convention recognises that certain categories of personal data are particularly sensitive, requiring special safeguards for their processing.[24] The Convention provides that a data subject should be able to request information to establish the existence of 'an automated personal data file' and to secure a copy of it and, where it has not been processed in accordance with the principles, to rectify or erase it.[25] Various exceptions on the usual basis – protecting State security, public safety and the rights and freedoms of others etc – are provided for.[26] Reflecting the OECD's other concern, the Convention also provides that transborder flows of personal data are not to be prohibited or subject to special authorisation for the sole purpose of protecting privacy.[27] The United Kingdom signed the Convention on 14 May 1981 and ratified it on 26 August 1987. As at January 2020, 55 parties have signed and ratified the Convention, including Mexico, Uruguay, all EU countries, Switzerland, Russia, Turkey and other Member States of the Council of Europe. Amendments made to the Convention in 2018 have not yet been ratified or come into force.[28]

7– 009 DPA 1984

By signing Convention 108, the United Kingdom had signified its willingness to enact data protection legislation. In April 1982 a White Paper[29] was published. It said that legislation was needed because of the threat to privacy posed by the rapid growth in the use of computers. But, in a nod to the earlier troubles with Sweden,[30] it also recognised that when the Convention came into force those countries with data protection legislation in place would be able to refuse

---

22 The reference to privacy in Art 9(3) is confined to use of personal data for statistics or scientific research purposes.

23 Identical to the OECD's definition.

24 Article 6.

25 Article 8.

26 Article 9.

27 Article 12.

28 Effected by Protocol amending the Convention for the Protection of Individuals with regard to Automatic Processing of Personal Data, ETS no 223.

29 *Data Protection: the Government's Proposals for Legislation* (Cmnd 8539).

30 See §7– 005 above.

to allow personal data to be sent to countries that did not have such legislation in place. In December 1982 a data protection bill was introduced in the House of Lords but, after passing in the House of Commons, it failed to achieve enactment before Parliament was dissolved in 1983. A new bill was introduced in the House of Lords and, after being passed by both Houses, on 12 July 1984 it received Royal Assent. The Data Protection Act 1984 drew on the principles fashioned by the OECD Recommendation and the Council of Europe's Convention, as well as the Younger Report and Lindop Committee Report. The DPA 1984 did not once use the word 'privacy.' Although the DPA 1984 did not adopt all the reports' recommendations on the protection of privacy, it did provide a measure of protection against the mishandling of personal, private information. The individual was given limited rights to bring a claim against a data controller, with most non-compliance to be dealt with by the data protection registrar.[31] That the Act's dual object was to protect against the misuse and over-use of personal information as well as to ensure the free movement of data was recognised in the only authority on the DPA 1984 to reach the House of Lords:[32]

> My Lords, one of the less welcome consequences of the information technology revolution has been the ease with which it has become possible to invade the privacy of the individual. No longer is it necessary to peep through keyholes or listen under the eaves. Instead, more reliable information can be obtained in greater comfort and safety by using the concealed surveillance camera, the telephoto lens, the hidden microphone and the telephone bug. No longer is it necessary to open letters, pry into files or conduct elaborate inquiries to discover the intimate details of a person's business or financial affairs, his health, family, leisure interests or dealings with central or local government. Vast amounts of information about everyone are stored on computers, capable of instant transmission anywhere in the world and accessible at the touch of a keyboard. The right to keep oneself to oneself, to tell other people that certain things are none of their business, is under technological threat.
>
> English common law does not know a general right of privacy and Parliament has been reluctant to enact one. But there has been some legislation to deal with particular aspects of the problem. The Data Protection Act 1984, with which this appeal is concerned, is one such statute....The Act was therefore intended not only to protect the privacy of our own citizens but to provide sufficient safeguards for the protection of computerised personal information to satisfy other member states that such information could safely be exported to the United Kingdom.

Such insight was the exception, with ignorance, impatience and hostility being the norm. In 1990 a further report on privacy was laid before Parliament.[33]

2. DIRECTIVE 95/46/EC & DPA 1998 REGIME

7–010 The Maastricht Treaty (TEU)

On 25 March 1957 the six founder members of the European Economic Community had signed the Treaty Establishing the European Economic Community (also known as the Treaty

---

[31] See: *Lord Ashcroft v AG* [2002] EWHC 1122 (QB).

[32] *R v Brown* [1996] 1 All ER 545 at 555-556 (Lord Hoffmann).

[33] *Report of a Committee on Privacy and Related Matters*, chaired by Sir David Calcutt QC (Cm 1102). It concluded that an overwhelming case for introducing a statutory tort of infringement of privacy had not so far been made out (§12.5). In 1992 Sir David Calcutt carried out a review of the Press Complaints Commission. In his report (Cm 2135, published in January 1993), he recommended that the Government should give further consideration to the introduction of a tort of infringement of privacy. In July 1993 the Lord Chancellor's Department and the Scottish Office issued a consultation paper called Infringement of Privacy, inviting responses on the proposal to create a tort of infringement of privacy. In July 1995 the Government published its response (Privacy and Media Intrusion, Cmnd 2918), concluding that no persuasive case had been made for statutory regulation of the press and announcing that it had no plans to introduce a statutory right to privacy.

of Rome), which came into force on 1 January 1958.[34] On 7 February 1992 the Treaty on European Union – the TEU – (also known as 'The Maastricht Treaty') was signed. The TEU re-named the European Economic Community as 'the European Community' – the EC – and it established the European Union – the EU. The TEU introduced the principle of subsidiarity (which delineated the spheres in which action was best taken at Community or national level) and the concept of citizenship of the EU, added areas of competence and dealt with various other matters.

7–011 Convention 108: ratification

Although by 1990 seven Member States of the EEC had ratified Convention 108 (1981),[35] they had done so in significantly differing ways. What these differences had made apparent was the need to harmonise the laws to ensure effective protection of individual's data whilst at the same time securing the free flow of personal data amongst the Member States. The free movement of goods, capital, services and people within the internal market required the free flow of personal data; and that could not be achieved unless Member States were bound by a uniform level of data protection. As a result, in that year the European Commission issued a communication on the protection of individuals in relation to the processing of personal data. The proposals were subjected to scrutiny in the UK Parliament.[36] A report of the House of Lords Select Committee on the European Communities, published on 30 March 1993, outlined the concepts of the right to privacy and to freedom of expression, and the tension which could exist between them.[37] After five years of negotiations, a common position on the Directive was adopted by the European Council in February 1995.

7–012 Directive 95/46/EC

On 24 October 1995 the European Parliament formally adopted Directive 96/45/EC. The Directive, inspired by Convention 108, represented an evolution of data protection principles up to then contained in national laws. The Directive was based on Article 95 of the then-EC Treaty – the general harmonisation Article for the internal market.[38] The Directive established

34 This was amended by: the Single European Act 1986, which came into effect on 1 July 1987; by the Treaty on European Union 1992 (also known as the Maastricht Treaty), which came into force on 1 November 1993; and by the Treaty of Amsterdam 1997, which came into force on 1 May 1999; the Treaty of Nice 2001, which came into force on 1 February 2003.

35 Namely: Denmark, France, Germany, Luxembourg, Ireland, Spain, and the United Kingdom.

36 Drafts of the Directive were reported on by the Commons Select Committee on European Legislation in December 1990 (HC 291-v of 1990/91), debated in Commons European Standing Committee B on 5 June 1991 (European Standing Committee B, *Official Report*, cols 1-32) and reported on by the Commons Select Committee on European Legislation on 25 November 1992 (HC 79-x of 1992/93). The House of Lords Select Committee on the European Communities reported in detail on the draft proposals and issues underlying them (*Protection of Personal Data*, HL 75-I of 1992/93). This report was debated in the Lords on 11 October 1993 (HL Deb, vol 549, cols 9-44). The Commons Select Committee on European Legislation further reported on the draft Directive on 6 July 1994 (HC 4x-xxiv of 1993/94) and again on 30 November 1994 (HC 70-1 of 1994/95), when further consideration in European Standing Committee B was recommended. This debate took place on 7 December 1994 (European Standing Committee B, *Official Report*, cols 3-32).

37 *Protection of Personal Data*, HL 75-I of 1992-93.

38 Now TFEU Art 114. The CJEU held that the fact that it was an internal market measure did not mean that the Directive could apply only to processing of personal data involving some facet of free movement: *Rechnungshof v Österreichischer Rundfunkat* (C-465/00) [2003] 3 CMLR 10. The Advocate General had counselled that the Court find the processing not within the Directive's scope since it had been 'carried out in the course of activities entirely unrelated to the establishment and functioning of the internal market' (at [AG53]). The same Advocate General pointed out in *Re Lindqvist (Approximation of Laws)* [2004] QB 1014 that protecting fundamental rights of the individual could not constitute independent objectives of the Directive (at [AG42]). While, at the time, the EU possessed competence to ensure that fundamental rights were respected when the EU or Member States acted within the scope of EU law (ie a negative duty not to breach fundamental rights), the EU did not possess competence to legislate so as to further the protection of fundamental rights (ie a positive duty): *Internationale Handelsgesellschaft mbH v Einfuhr und Vorratsstelle für Getreide und Futtermittel* (11/70) [1972] CMLR 255; *Nold Kohlen und*

a detailed and comprehensive data protection system in the EU. The Directive applied to personal data processed wholly or partly by automatic means, and to manual data held in filing systems structured by reference to individuals. As it was a Directive, it did not apply directly in Member States. Rather, each Member State had to transpose the Directive into its national laws, with each of them having a legislative latitude in the manner in which it implemented the Directive's provisions into those national laws.

7–013 UK response to Directive

The United Kingdom had abstained from the vote on the Directive.[39] Nonetheless, the Directive was an internal market harmonisation measure.[40] The Directive required implementation by 24 October 1998.[41] In March 1996 the Home Office issued a Consultation Paper on the Directive. This recorded that the Government did not see the need for the Directive:

> The Government believes that the United Kingdom's data protection regime should be the least burdensome for business and other data users, whilst affording the necessary protection for individuals. The Government has long recognised the importance of effective data protection controls: that is why it enacted the 1984 Act and ratified the Council of Europe Data Protection Convention. It believes, however, that those provisions are sufficient, both for the protection of individuals, and as a means of ensuring the free flow of data between European partners......Over-elaborate data protection threatens competitiveness, and does not necessarily bring additional benefits for individuals. It follows that the Government intends to go no further in implementing the Directive than is absolutely necessary to satisfy the UK's obligations in European law. It will consider whether any additional changes to the current data protection regime are needed so as to ensure that it does not go beyond what is required by the Directive and the Council of Europe Convention.[42]

7–014 Treaty of Amsterdam

On 2 October 1997 the Treaty of Amsterdam was signed. It:

— amended the TEU and the EC Treaty;
— inserted in the TEU principles of openness and transparency;[43]
— declared that the EU was founded on respect for human rights and fundamental freedoms, democracy and the rule of law;[44]
— gave EU citizens a right of access to documents held by EU institutions;[45] and
— guaranteed safeguards in relation to the protection of the personal data of EU citizens.[46]

The Treaty of Amsterdam entered into force on 1 May 1999.

Baustoffgrosshandlung v EC Commission (4/73) [1975] ECR 985; *Johnston v Chief Constable of the Royal Ulster Constabulary* (C-222/84) [1987] QB 129, [1986] 3 All ER 135 at [18]; *Wachauf v Federal Republic of Germany* (C-5/88) [1991] 1 CMLR 328 at [19]; *Elliniki Radiophonia Tileorass v Pliroforissis* (C-260/89) [1991] ECR I-2925, [1994] 4 CMLR 540 at [41]-[44].

[39] The original proposal for this Directive had been welcomed, with reservations, by the Select Committee appointed by the House of Lords to consider it. The Committee's report opened by acknowledging that the right of privacy was a matter of concern in the 20th Century: *Protection of Personal Data: Report of the Select Committee on the European Communities.* HL Paper 75-1, March 1993.

[40] That is, under what is now Art 114 of the TFEU.

[41] Content of the Directive is considered in §15– 005.

[42] Consultation Paper §1.2.

[43] Article 1(4).

[44] Article 1(8).

[45] Article 2(45).

[46] Article 2(54).

7–015 DPA 1998

In the same year (1997), the Secretary of State for the Home Department presented proposals for new data protection legislation to Parliament. On 2 February 1998 Lord Williams of Mostyn gave the Data Protection Bill its second reading speech, opening:

> I recognise that data protection does not sound like a subject to attract obsessive interest; witness the general exodus from your Lordships' House as I start to introduce this Second Reading. Data protection is redolent in many ways of computers and electronic processing: necessary but essentially technical providers of services. In fact it affects our well-being in a much more general way. It shares common ground to that extent with the Human Rights Bill. That Bill will improve the position of citizens of this country by enabling them to rely on the wide range of civil and political rights contained in the European Convention on Human Rights. Those rights include the right to respect for private and family life. The Data Protection Bill also concerns privacy, albeit a specific form of privacy; personal information privacy. The subject matter of the Bill is, therefore, inherently important to our general social welfare.[47]

Thereafter the Bill was subjected to close analysis by Committee and to lengthy debate. With certain amendments, the Bill was passed and on 1 March 2000 the DPA 1998 came into force. The DPA 1998 is considered in detail in Chs 15-16. Under ordinary principles of EU law, the freedom to choose the ways and means of ensuring that a directive is implemented did not affect the obligation imposed on the United Kingdom, as a Member State to which the Directive was addressed, to adopt all the measures necessary to ensure that the Directive was fully effective in accordance with the objective which it pursued.[48] Moreover, the principle of effective judicial protection required that the UK courts provided the legal protection which individuals derived from the Directive and to ensure effective protection of the rights conferred.[49]

7–016 HRA 1998

The decade 1995-2005 saw the courts waking to the possibility of finding a relationship of non-commercial confidentiality sufficient to attract legal protection.[50] This awakening was prompted by the imminent Human Rights Act 1998.[51] Initially the courts sought precedent for this in the law of confidentiality, bending its principles to fashion a law of privacy, and so give it the appearance of evolution rather than revolution. But within a decade the House of Lords had come out, acknowledging in *OBG Ltd v Allan* a distinct cause of action for breach of privacy:

> As the law has developed breach of confidence, or misuse of confidential information, now covers two distinct causes of action, protecting two different interests: privacy, and secret

---

47 *Hansard*, HL 5th series, vol 585, col 436.

48 Article 4(3) of the TEU, following earlier case law: *Impact v Minister for Agriculture and Food* (C-268/06) [2008] ECR I-2483, [2008] 2 CMLR 47 at [40]; *Von Colson v Land Nordrhein-Westfalen* (14/83) [1984] ECR 1891, [1986] 2 CMLR 430 at [15], [26].

49 *Pfeiffer v Deutsches Rotes Kreuz Kreisverband Waldshut eV* (C-397/01) [2004] ECR I-8835, [2005] 1 CMLR 44 at [111]; *Unibet (London) Ltd v Justitiekanslern* (C-432/05) [2007] 2 CMLR 30 at [37]; *Bozzetti v Invernizzi SpA* (179/84) [1985] ECR 2301, [1986] 2 CMLR 246 at [17]; *Dorsch Consult Ingenieurgesellschaft mbH v Bundesbaugesellschaft Berlin mbH* (C-54/96) [1997] ECR I-4961, [1998] 2 CMLR 237 at [40]; *Impact v Minister for Agriculture and Food* (C-268/06) [2008] ECR I-2483, [2008] 2 CMLR 47 at [41]-[45].

50 *Hellewell v Chief Constable of Derbyshire* [1995] 1 WLR 804; *R v The Department of Health, ex p Source Informatics Ltd* [2000] 1 All ER 786 (CA); *Barrymore v News Group Newspapers* [1997] FSR 600; *Mills v News Group Newspapers Ltd* [2001] EWHC Ch 412; *Theakston v MGN Ltd* [2002] EWHC 137, [2002] EMLR 22; *Douglas v Hello! Ltd* [2001] QB 967 esp at [122], [166]; *Douglas v Hello! Ltd* [2003] EWHC 786, [2003] 3 All ER 996 esp at [66], but see *Douglas v Hello! Ltd (No 3)* [2006] EWCA Civ 595, [2006] QB 125; *Campbell v Mirror Group Newspapers* [2002] EWHC 499 (QB); *Campbell v Mirror Group Newspapers Ltd* [2002] EWCA Civ 1373, [2003] QB 633; *Campbell v Mirror Group Newspapers Ltd* [2004] UKHL 22, [2004] 2 AC 457.

51 *Campbell v Mirror Group Newspapers Ltd* [2004] UKHL 22, [2004] 2 AC 457 at [11], [16]-[17], [49]-[52], [86], [105]-[111].

> ('confidential') information. It is important to keep these two distinct. In some instances information may qualify for protection both on grounds of privacy and confidentiality. In other instances information may be in the public domain, and not qualify for protection as confidential, and yet qualify for protection on the grounds of privacy. Privacy can be invaded by further publication of information or photographs already disclosed to the public. Conversely, and obviously, a trade secret may be protected as confidential information even though no question of personal privacy is involved.[52]

With this, earlier denials of a right of privacy[53] were magicked away. To no small degree, this judicial creativity – which would have had much to commend it at any time in the preceding 150 years – had become unnecessary. The assemblage of case law by which a law of privacy was constructed was, for the greater part, protecting interests that had recently been given protection by the DPA 1998. The Act did so in a structured and coherent way that incremental case law could not match. Moreover, the DPA 1998 was liberated from the need to show an interference with personal privacy, with focus instead being on a legal entity's misuse and over-use of an individual's personal information. But, helped by the then-sparkling HRA 1998, this autochthonous creation attracted judicial attention, while the DPA 1998, with its Continental parentage, was relegated to the sidelines.[54]

7–017 Regulation 45/2001

Directive 95/46/EC could apply only to EU Member States, and not to the EU institutions and bodies. These had to be covered by a separate legal instrument. This was achieved by Regulation 45/2001.[55] The stated object of the Regulation is:

> In accordance with this Regulation, the institutions and bodies set up by, or on the basis of, the Treaties establishing the European Communities, hereinafter referred to as 'Community institutions or bodies', shall protect the fundamental rights and freedoms of natural persons, and in particular their right to privacy with respect to the processing of personal data and shall neither restrict nor prohibit the free flow of personal data between themselves or to recipients subject to the national law of the Member States implementing Directive 95/46/EC.[56]

The scope of the Regulation is:

> 1. ...the processing of personal data by all Community institutions and bodies insofar as such processing is carried out in the exercise of activities all or part of which fall within the scope of Community law.
> 2. This Regulation shall apply to the processing of personal data wholly or partly by automatic means, and to the processing otherwise than by automatic means of personal data which form part of a filing system or are intended to form part of a filing system.[57]

Apart from the scope of the Regulation, in terms it was substantially the same as Directive 95/46/EC.

7–018 Data protection: ECHR link

When founded in 1957, the European Economic Community was envisaged as a regional organisation focussed on economic integration and the establishment of a common market. Accordingly, the original treaties of the European Community did not contain any reference

52 [2007] UKHL 21, [2008] 1 AC 1 at [255].

53 *Wainwright v Home Office* [2003] UKHL 53, [2004] 2 AC 406 at [35]; *R v Brown* [1996] 1 All ER 545 at 556.

54 See, for example: *Campbell v Mirror Group Newspapers Ltd* [2004] UKHL 22, [2004] 2 AC 457 at [10], [32], [130].

55 Of the European Parliament and of the Council on the protection of individuals with regard to the processing of personal data by the Community institutions and bodies and on the free movement of such data.

56 Article 1.1.

57 Article 3.

to human rights or their protection. The institutions of the European Economic Community only had such competence as had been collectively conferred on them by the Member States, as articulated in the Treaty of Rome. In contrast to the Council of Europe, the Treaty of Rome, and its successor the Maastricht Treaty, included no explicit competence on fundamental rights matters. However, from time to time cases came before the European Court of Justice – the CJEU – alleging human rights violations in areas within the scope of European Community law. In order to give individuals protection, the CJEU absorbed fundamental rights into the general principles of European law. It did this by holding that where laws of the EC were capable of more than one interpretation, it should choose the interpretation that did not prejudice fundamental rights protection.[58] For the purposes of identifying the content of 'fundamental rights' the CJEU drew inspiration from international human rights treaties, including the ICCPR, but most notably from the ECHR.[59] In this way a link was made between the enforcement of European Community law and the principles of the ECHR.

7–019 Charter of Fundamental Rights

The EU decided to bring within a single text the various existing personal, civic, political, economic and social rights enjoyed by each individual, whether those rights were declared in case law, the ECHR, international instruments or common constitutional traditions of EU countries. The result was the Charter of Fundamental Rights of the EU – 'the Charter.' It was proclaimed in 2000 by the EU institutions, originally only as a political, rather than a legally-binding, document. The Charter was not intended to create new rights, but rather to reaffirm rights that already existed in EU law and to make them more 'visible.'[60] Prior to the entry into force of the Lisbon Treaty there was no explicit legal basis for the adoption of data protection rules other than in the third pillar areas.[61] The Charter became legally binding as EU primary law when the Lisbon Treaty came into force on 1 December 2009. The provisions of the Charter are addressed to EU institutions and bodies, obliging them to respect the rights described in it while fulfilling their duties. The provisions of the Charter also bind Member

[58] Starting with: *Stauder v City of Ulm* [1970] CMLR 112, [1969] ECR 419; *Internationale Handelsgesellschaft mbH v Einfuhr und Vorratsstelle für Getreide und Futtermittel* (11/70) [1972] CMLR 255.

[59] *Nold Kohlen und Baustoffgrosshandlung v EC Commission* (4/73) [1975] ECR 985; *Orkem v EC Commission* (374/87) [1989] ECR 3283, [1991] 4 CMLR 502 (right not to give evidence against oneself or to confess guilt, derived from Art 14 ICCPR, applying by analogy as a fundamental principle of the Community legal order to impliedly limit the Commission's powers of investigation); *Kremzow v Austria* (C-299/95) [1997] ECR I-2629, [1997] 3 CMLR 1289, where it was held:

> ....fundamental rights form an integral part of the general principles of Community law whose observance the Court ensures. For that purpose, the Court draws inspiration from the constitutional traditions common to the Member States and from the guidelines supplied by international treaties for the protection of human rights on which the Member States have collaborated or of which they are signatories. The [ECHR] has special significance in that respect. As the Court has also held, it follows that measures are not acceptable in the Community which are incompatible with observance of the human rights thus recognised and guaranteed (at [14]).

[60] Preamble to Charter.

[61] The 'three pillar' structure of the EU had its origins in the attempt of the Maastricht Treaty to enlarge the range of matters with which the EU was concerned. Some Member States took objection to the new matters being added to the EU's competencies (on the basis that they were properly matters of individual Member State concern), and the compromise was that they would be dealt with by means of intergovernmental cooperation. The matters over which the EU had full competency belonged to the first pillar. The second pillar (common foreign and security policy) and the third pillar (police and judicial cooperation in criminal matters) were to be dealt with by intergovernmental cooperation. This conception of three pillars vanished with the Lisbon Treaty. That treaty replaced it with a tripartite competency scheme comprising: (i) exclusive competence, ie where the EU has exclusive competence to make regulations and directives and conclude international agreements; (ii) shared competence, ie where the EU has competence and that either covers the field or can co-exist with Member State competency; and (iii) supporting competence, where the EU has competence but only to support, coordinate or supplement Member State action.

States when they implement EU law.

7–020 Nature of the Charter

The rights and freedoms are grouped into chapters (termed 'Titles') under six topics or themes (entitled dignity, freedoms, equality, solidarity, citizens' rights, and justice) plus a set of general provisions in a seventh chapter/Title. The Charter binds Member States only when they are implementing EU law.[62] To the extent that the Charter contains rights that stem from the ECHR, their meaning and scope are the same. The DPA 1998 represented an implementation of EU law, with the effect that the Charter has direct effect in relation to data protection.[63] The Charter applies to the EU and its institutions in all areas.

7–021 Privacy and data protection

Chapter II (Arts 6-19) of the Charter is entitled 'Freedoms.' Article 7 describes a right to privacy:

> Everyone has the right to respect for his or her private and family life, home and communications.

Consistent with the Charter being a re-affirmation of existing rights in EU law, Article 7 of the Charter more-or-less copied over Article 8 of the ECHR.[64] Article 8 of the Charter describes a separate right to data protection:

> 1. Everyone has the right to the protection of personal data concerning him or her.
> 2. Such data must be processed fairly for specified purposes and on the basis of the consent of the person concerned or some other legitimate basis laid down by law. Everyone has the right of access to data which has been collected concerning him or her, and the right to have it rectified.
> 3. Compliance with these rules shall be subject to control by an independent authority.

Article 8 of the Charter distilled Article 286 of the EC Treaty,[65] Directive 95/46/EC and the 1981 Council of Europe Convention. But in removing any express reference to the internal market and harmonisation, until the entry into force of the Treaty of Lisbon (1 December 2009),[66] it reflected the contemporeaneous position that it was a political, rather than a legally-binding, document.

7–022 Articles 7 and 8 of the Charter

The two rights separately described by Articles 7 and 8 of the Charter differ in their formulation and scope. Article 7 consists of a general prohibition on interference, subject to certain public interest criteria that can justify interference in certain cases. Article 8 of the Charter is a more modern and active right,[67] putting in place a systems of checks and balances

---

62 Article 51. The phrase 'implementing EU law' is to be interpreted broadly and, in effect, means whenever a Member State is acting within the material scope of EU law: *Rugby Football Union v Viagogo Ltd* [2012] UKSC 55, [2012] 1 WLR 3333 at [28]; *R (Bashir) v SSHD* [2018] UKSC 45, [2018] 3 WLR 573 at [67].

63 *NT1 v Google LLC* [2018] EWHC 799 (QB), [2019] QB 344 at [13(8)].

64 The protection to personal information afforded by ECHR Art 8 is considered at §4–011.

65 Article 286 of the EC Treaty was introduced by the Treaty of Amsterdam, which was signed on 2 October 1997 and entered into force on 1 May 1999: see further §7–014. Article 286 provided:

> 1. From 1 January 1999, Community acts on the protection of individuals with regard to the processing of personal data and the free movement of such data shall apply to the institutions and bodies set up by, or on the basis of, this Treaty.
> 2. Before the date referred to in paragraph 1, the Council, acting in accordance with the procedure referred to in Article 251, shall establish an independent supervisory body responsible for monitoring the application of such Community acts to Community institutions and bodies and shall adopt any other relevant provisions as appropriate.

66 See further §7–028.

67 *Volker und Markus Schecke GbR v Land Hessen* (C-92/09) [2012] All ER (EC) 127, [2012] IP & T 513, opinion of AG Sharpston at [71].

to protect an individual's right to the protection of personal data concerning him or herself. The description of a right in Article 8, distinct from the right of privacy, underscores that it has its own work to do, unconstrained by a requirement that there be an infringement of privacy.[68] Since 1 December 2009 EU institutions and bodies must guarantee and respect this right, as must Member States when implementing EU law.[69] A legal person can claim the protection of Articles 7 and 8 only in so far as the information relates to a natural legal person who is identified by or is identifiable from that information.[70]

7–023 Article 52 of the Charter

Within Chapter VII (General Provisions), Art 52(1) of the Charter provides:

> Any limitation on the exercise of the rights and freedoms recognised by this Charter must be provided for by law and respect the essence of those rights and freedoms. Subject to the principle of proportionality, limitations may be made only if they are necessary and genuinely meet objectives of general interest recognised by the Union or the need to protect the rights and freedoms of others.

Thus, under Article 52(1), a limitation on the exercise of the right to the protection of personal data (being one of the rights and freedoms recognised by the Charter) is permissible only if it:

— is provided for by law;[71]

— respects the essence of the right to data protection;[72]

---

68 Judicial recognition of it as a right distinct from the ECHR privacy right first came in *Productores de Musica de Espana (Promusicae) v Telefonica de Espana SAU* (C-275/06) [2008] 2 CMLR 17, [2008] IP&T 746 at [61]-[65]. That the one did not require the other was recognised in: *Re EU-Canada Passenger Name Record (PNR) Agreement* [2018] 1 CMLR 1083 at [124] ('it does not matter whether the information in question relating to private life is sensitive or whether the persons concerned have been inconvenienced in any way on account of that interference'); *Schrems v Data Protection Commissioner* (C-362/14) [2016] QB 527, [2016] 2 CMLR 2 at [87]; *Digital Rights Ireland Ltd v Minister for Communications, Marine and Natural Resources* (C-293/12 and C-594/12) [2015] QB 127, [2014] 3 CMLR 44 at [33]. See also fn 2 above.

69 Charter Art 51.

70 *Volker und Markus Schecke GbR v Land Hessen* (C-92/09) [2012] All ER (EC) 127, [2012] IP & T 513 at [53].

71 In other words, any limitation must be based on a legal basis that is adequately accessible and foreseeable and formulated with sufficient precision to enable individuals to understand their obligations and regulate their conduct: *Knauf Gips KG v European Commission* (C-407/08P) [2010] 5 CMLR 12 at [81]. The phrase 'prescribed by law' is used in ECHR Arts 9(2), 10(2) and 11(2). The equivalent phrase in ECHR Art 8(2) is 'in accordance with the law.' There are two elements to the ECHR concept of 'prescribed by law:' see *R v Shayler (David)* [2002] UKHL 11, [2003] 1 AC 247 at [56]. First, it requires that the measure complained of must have some basis in domestic law, whether in statute, international law or through the common law: *Sunday Times v United Kingdom* [1979] ECHR 1, (1979) 2 EHRR 245 at [48]-[49]; *Malone v United Kingdom* (1985) 7 EHRR 14 (ECtHR) at [66]; *Chappell v United Kingdom* (1990) 12 EHRR 1 at [56]; *R (Munjaz) v Ashworth Hospital Authority* [2005] UKHL 58, [2006] 2 AC 148 (a code of practice provided sufficient basis); *R (Matthias Rath) v Advertising Standards Authority* [2001] HRLR 22, [2001] EMLR 22 at [22]; cf *Herczegfalvy v Austria* (1993) 15 EHRR 437 at [91]. Secondly, the domestic law must be sufficiently precise and accessible for an individual to be able to foresee with a reasonable degree of certainty the consequences of his or her actions, or the cirumstances in which and the conditions on which authorities may take particular steps: *Silver v United Kingdom* (1983) 5 EHRR 347 at [85]-[88]. The level of precision required will depend upon the subject area: *Olsson v Sweden* (1988) 11 EHRR 259 at [62].

72 In other words, limitations that are so extensive or intrusive as to empty a fundamental right of its basic content will be impermissible. Thus:

(1) Legislation not providing for any possibility for an individual to pursue legal remedies in order to have access to personal data relating to him, or to obtain the rectification or erasure of such data, does not respect the essence of the fundamental right to effective judicial protection, as enshrined in article 47 of the Charter: *Schrems v Data Protection Commissioner* (C-362/14) [2016] QB 527, [2016] 2 CMLR 2 at [95].

(2) Directive 2006/24/EC (Data Retention Directive), which obliged electronic communication providers to retain traffic and location data for at least 6 months and up to 24 months (including IP addresses) in order to assist crime detection, did not adversely affect the essence of the right to data protection as the Directive did not permit the acquisition of knowledge of the content of the electronic communications: *Digital Rights Ireland Ltd v Minister for Communications, Marine and Natural Resources* (C-293/12 and C-594/12) [2015] QB 127, [2014] 3 CMLR 44 at [39]. See also: *Tele2 Sverige AB v Post- och telestyrelsen* (C-203/15) [2017] QB 771, [2017] 2 CMLR 30; *Proceedings brought by Ministerio Fiscal* (Case C-207/16) [2019] 1 WLR 3121, [2019] 1 CMLR 31; *R (Watson) v SSHD* [2018] EWCA Civ 70, [2018] QB 912.

— subject to the principle of proportionality, is necessary;[73] and
— genuinely meets objectives of general interest recognised by the EU or the need to protect the rights and freedoms of others.[74]

In relation to the right to the protection of personal data recognised in Article 8, the limitation allowed for by Art 52(1) resembles the limitation to rights tolerated by Articles 8(2), 9(2), 10(2) and 11(2) of the ECHR.[75] Article 52(3) of the Charter provides:

> In so far as this Charter contains rights which correspond to rights guaranteed by the Convention for the Protection of Human Rights and Fundamental Freedoms, the meaning and scope of those rights shall be the same as those laid down by the said Convention. This provision shall not prevent Union law providing more extensive protection.

The CJEU will thus take account of, but not necessarily follow, the case law of the ECtHR.[76]

7–024 Treaty of Lisbon

The Treaty of Lisbon was signed on 13 December 2007 and entered into force on 1 December 2009. It:

— amended further the TEU and re-numbered its provisions;

---

[73] This requires that the measure be appropriate for attaining the objective pursued and that it not go beyond what is necessary to achieve it: *Volker und Markus Schecke GbR v Land Hessen* (C-92/09) [2012] All ER (EC) 127, [2012] IP & T 513 at [74]; *Digital Rights Ireland Ltd v Minister for Communications, Marine and Natural Resources* (C-293/12 and C-594/12) [2015] QB 127, [2014] 3 CMLR 44 at [46]. The criterion to be applied is not whether a measure adopted in such an area was the only or the best possible measure – rather, the question is whether the measure is manifestly inappropriate having regard to the objective which the competent institution is seeking to pursue: *R (Vodafone Ltd) v Secretary of State for Business, Enterprise and Regulatory Reform* (C-58/08) [2010] 3 CMLR 44, [2010] All ER (EC) 741 at [52]. The choice must be based on objective criteria, weighing the benefits against the burdens: at [53]. Where interferences with fundamental rights are at issue, the extent of the legislative latitude may prove to be limited, depending on the nature of the right at issue guaranteed by the Charter, the nature and seriousness of the interference and the object pursued by the interference: *Digital Rights Ireland* at [47]. Limitations may be imposed on the exercise of rights and freedoms only if they are necessary and if they genuinely meet objectives of general interest recognised by the European Union or the need to protect the rights and freedoms of others: *Tele2 Sverige AB v Post-och telestyrelsen* (C-203/15) [2017] QB 771, [2017] 2 CMLR 30 at [94]. In relation to the fundamental right to private life (Article 7 of the Charter), derogations from and limitations on the protection of personal data should apply only in so far as is strictly necessary: *Tietosuojavaltuutettu v Satakunnan* (C-73/07) [2010] All ER (EC) 213 at [56]; *Volker und Markus* at [77]; *Digital Rights Ireland* at [52]; *Schrems v Data Protection Commissioner* (C-362/14) [2016] QB 527, [2016] 2 CMLR 2 at [92]; *Tele2 Sverige* at [96].

[74] Thus:

(1) A provision in Council Regulation (EC) 1290/2005 (on the financing of the common agricultural policy) setting detailed rules on the publication of information on beneficiaries was held to genuinely meet an objective of general interest, namely that citizens be able to participate more closely in the decision-making process and that the administration enjoy greater legitimacy and be more effective and more accountable to the citizen in a democratic system: *Volker und Markus Schecke GbR v Land Hessen* (C-92/09) [2012] All ER (EC) 127, [2012] IP & T 513 at [67]-[71] (the provision was held invalid on the grounds of proportionality).
(2) A provision enabling the retention and communication of electronic communications data for the purpose of fighting crime was held to genuinely meet an objective of general interest: *Tele2 Sverige AB v Post-och telestyrelsen* (C-203/15) [2017] QB 771, [2017] 2 CMLR 30 at [103] (the provision was held invalid on the grounds of proportionality).
(3) A provision safeguarding the freedoms protected under Art 11 of the Charter (freedom of expression) will clearly constitute a legitimate aim: *Sky Österreich GmbH v Österreichischer Rundfunk* (C-283/11) [2013] 2 CMLR 25, [2013] IP&T 672 at [52].
(4) Where tax authorities drew up a list of those who, according to the authorities, were front men suspected of tax fraud, for the purpose of collecting tax and combatting tax fraud, civil code provisions that required a person to exhaust available administrative remedies before going to court 'increase[d] the efficiency of judicial proceedings' and thereby pursued a legitimate aim: *Puškár v Finančné riaditeľstvo Slovenskej* (C-73/16) [2017] 4 WLR 209, [2018] 1 CMLR 44 at [65].
(5) A provision that has as its objective the protection of national security and public order will satisfy this requirement: *N v Staatssecretaris voor Veiligheid en Justitie (Case C-601/15)* [2016] 1 WLR 3027, [2017] 1 CMLR 42 at [53].

[75] *Volker und Markus Schecke GbR v Land Hessen* (C-92/09) [2012] All ER (EC) 127, [2012] IP & T 513 at [52].

[76] *McB v E* (C-400/10) [2011] Fam 364, [2010] ECR I-8965; *CK v Republika Slovenija* (C-578/16) [2017] 3 CMLR 283. In other cases the CJEU has simply quoted ECtHR case law: *MP v Secretary of State for the Home Department* (C-353/16) [2018] 1 WLR 5585.

— amended the EC Treaty and re-named it 'The Treaty on the Functioning of the European Union' – the TFEU; and

— made the Charter of Fundamental Rights legally binding.[77]

The effect of the Treaty of Lisbon was that the TEU, the TFEU and the Charter of Fundamental Rights were given equal legal value and, combined, constituted the legal basis of the EU. The parties to the Treaty of Lisbon also appended 37 protocols, each specific to one or more Member States.

7–025 **TFEU Article 16**

Article 16 of the TFEU provides:

> 1. Everyone has the right to the protection of personal data concerning them.
> 2. The European Parliament and the Council, acting in accordance with the ordinary legislative procedure, shall lay down the rules relating to the protection of individuals with regard to the processing of personal data by Union institutions, bodies, offices and agencies, and by the Member States when carrying out activities which fall within the scope of Union law, and the rules relating to the free movement of such data. Compliance with these rules shall be subject to the control of independent authorities. The rules adopted on the basis of this Article shall be without prejudice to the specific rules laid down in Article 39 of the Treaty on European Union.[78]

Thus, not only did the Treaty of Lisbon elevate the Charter to the status of a binding legal document at the level of primary EU law, but it conferred on the European Parliament and the Council a competency in relation to data protection, both as regards data processing by the European Institutions[79] and by Member States. The latter was an important development. Up until the Treaty of Lisbon, EU data protection rules (such as Directive 95/46/EC) had been based on the internal market legal basis and on the need to approximate national laws so that the free movement of personal data within the EU was not inhibited. Article 16 now provided an independent legal basis for a treatment of data protection on matters of EU competence.

7–026 **TEU Article 39**

Chapter 2 of Title V of the TEU (Articles 21 - 46) contains specific provisions dealing with common foreign and security policy matters. Article 39 of the TEU introduced a specific legal basis for data processing by Member States when acting on those matters:

> In accordance with Article 16 of the Treaty on the Functioning of the European Union and by way of derogation from paragraph 2 thereof, the Council shall adopt a decision laying down the rules relating to the protection of individuals with regard to the processing of personal data by the Member States when carrying out activities which fall within the scope of this Chapter, and the rules relating to the free movement of such data. Compliance with these rules shall be subject to the control of independent authorities.

Between them, Article 16 of the TFEU and Article 39 of the TEU supplied the mandates for making, respectively, the GDPR and the Law Enforcement Directive.

---

[77] Article 6.1 of the TEU provides:

> The Union recognises the rights, freedoms and principles set out in the Charter of Fundamental Rights of the European Union of 7 December 2000, as adopted at Strasbourg, on 12 December 2007, which shall have the same legal value as the Treaties...

[78] See also Declarations 20-21 annexed to the Lisbon Treaty. Protocol 21 to the Lisbon Treaty provided that the United Kingdom would not be bound by the rules adopted on the basis of TFEU Art 16 'which relate to the processing of personal data by the Member States when carrying out activities which fall within the scope of Chapter 4 or Chapter 5 of Title V of Part Three of that Treaty where the United Kingdom ... [is] not bound by the rules governing the forms of judicial cooperation in criminal matters or police cooperation which require compliance with the provisions laid down on the basis of Article 16.' In other words, if the United Kingdom does not participate in particular aspects of police and judicial cooperation, it does not have an obligation pursuant to Article 16.

[79] Which had formerly been dealt with in the EC Treaty Art 286.

7–027 Protocol 21

Protocol 21 is specific to the United Kingdom and Ireland and is concerned with 'the area of freedom, security and justice.' By this Protocol, it was agreed that the United Kingdom and Ireland would not take part in the adoption by the Council of proposed measures pursuant to Title V of Part Three of the TFEU (Articles 67 - 89), dealing with freedom, security and justice. As one of the measures to give effect to that, Article 6a of Protocol 21 provides:

> The United Kingdom and Ireland shall not be bound by the rules laid down on the basis of Article 16 of the Treaty on the Functioning of the European Union which relate to the processing of personal data by the Member States when carrying out activities which fall within the scope of Chapter 4 or Chapter 5 of Title V of Part Three of that Treaty where the United Kingdom and Ireland are not bound by the rules governing the forms of judicial cooperation in criminal matters or police cooperation which require compliance with the provisions laid down on the basis of Article 16.

Chapter 4 of Title 5 (Articles 82 - 86) deals with judicial cooperation in criminal matters and Chapter 5 of Title 5 (Articles 87 - 89) deals with police cooperation.

7–028 Protocol 30

Protocol 30, which applies only to the United Kingdom and Poland, concerns the application of the Charter to the United Kingdom and Poland. Article 1 of Protocol 30 provides:

> 1. The Charter does not extend the ability of the Court of Justice of the European Union, or any court or tribunal of Poland or of the United Kingdom, to find that the laws, regulations or administrative provisions, practices or action of Poland or of the United Kingdom are inconsistent with the fundamental rights, freedoms and principles that it reaffirms.
> 2. In particular, and for the avoidance of doubt, nothing in Title IV of the Charter creates justiciable rights applicable to Poland or the United Kingdom except in so far as Poland or the United Kingdom has provided for such rights in its national law.[80]

The Protocol does not call into question the applicability of the Charter in the United Kingdom nor exempt the United Kingdom from the obligation to comply with the Charter's provisions or prevent a United Kingdom court from ensuring compliance with them.[81]

3. GDPR, DIRECTIVE 2016/680 & DPA 2018 REGIME

7–029 Background

Although Directive 95/46/EC was intended to provide complete harmonisation,[82] in practice its transposition varied between the Member States. This resulted in diverse data protection rules across the EU, with the definitions and rules interpreted differently in national laws, as well as varying levels of enforcement. Moreover, Directive 95/46/EC was limited in its scope to activities relating to the internal market and to activities of public authorities other than law enforcement. Accordingly, it had been necessary to adopt special instruments to deal with certain sectors. This included:

(1) Council Framework Decision 2007/977/JHA on the protection of personal data processed in the framework of police and judicial cooperation in criminal matters. Its rules applied only to police and judicial data when exchanged between Member

[80] Title IV is headed 'Solidarity' and concerns certain economic, social and cultural rights.

[81] *R (NS) v SSHD* (C-411/10) [2013] QB 102, [2012] All ER (EC) 1011 at [119]-[122].

[82] *Asociacion Nacional de Establecimientos Financieros de Credito v Administracion del Estado* (Case C-468/10) [2012] 1 CMLR 48 at [29].

States.[83]

(2) Directive 2002/58/EC concerning the processing of personal data and the protection of privacy in electronic communications. This is sometimes called the 'ePrivacy Directive.'

Article 16 of the TFEU entered into force on 1 December 2009.[84] With its entry into force, the European Parliament and Council were no longer constrained when legislating with respect to data processing by having to link it to the internal market and notions of equivalence and approximation.[85] Article 16 of the TFEU gave the European Parliament and Council free-standing competence to lay down the rules relating to data processing by EU institutions and 'by Member States when carrying out activities which fall within the scope of Union law, and the rules relating to the free movement of such data.'

7–030 The proposal

Liberated from its constraints, between 9 July 2009 and 15 January 2011 the European Commission undertook extensive consultations on the legal framework for the right to the protection of personal data in the EU. This produced over 450 responses from individuals, business organisations, associations and public authorities. In the first half of 2011 the Commission undertook various studies. The principal criticisms of the Directive 95/46/EC and other data protection measures that emerged from the consultations revolved around fragmentation of the regime and complexity of the rules on international transfers of personal data. It was business interests who in particular asked for increased legal certainty and harmonisation of the rules. On 6 July 2011 the European Parliament resolved to support the Commission's approach to reforming the data processing framework. Three different options were considered, and the impact and efficacy of each was assessed. Following the conclusion of this, in January 2012 the European Commission published a proposal for a general data protection regulation.[86] The Commission explained:

> A Regulation is considered to be the most appropriate legal instrument to define the framework for the protection of personal data in the Union. The direct applicability of a Regulation in accordance with Article 288 TFEU will reduce legal fragmentation and provide greater legal certainty by introducing a harmonised set of core rules, improving the protection of fundamental rights of individuals and contributing to the functioning of the Internal Market.

In October 2013 the European Parliament Committee on Civil Liberties, Justice and Home Affairs voted on a compromise text. In December 2015 the text of the GDPR was agreed. On 14 April 2016, the Council and the European Parliament adopted the 'data protection package,' comprising the General Data Protection Regulation – the GDPR – and the Law Enforcement Directive – the LED.[87] These required implementation at Member level by 25 May 2018.

7–031 Modernised Convention 108

In 2011 the Council of Europe carried out a public consultation into the operation of Convention 108.[88] This confirmed the need to enhance the protection of personal privacy in

[83] This is considered in detail in A Fiordorova, *Information Exchange and EU Law Enforcement*, Routledge, Oxford, 2018.

[84] See §§7–025 to 7–028.

[85] Contrast Directive 95/46/EC recitals (3), (5), (8), (9) and (10).

[86] European Commission, *Proposal for a Regulation of the European Parliament and of the Council on the protection of individuals with regard to the processing of personal data and on the free movement of such data (General Data Protection Regulation)*, 25 January 2012.

[87] Directive (EU) 2016/680.

[88] As to the original Convention 108, see §§7–007 to 7–008.

data and to strengthen the enforcement mechanisms in the Convention. The ensuing drafting exercise strove to ensure consistency and compatibility with the new EU data protection regulation then being drafted. On 10 May 2018 the Council of Europe adopted an amending protocol to Convention 108. The Convention as amended retains the basic structure of the original version, but provides new rights to individuals and increases the responsibilities of controllers and processors. It also provides for the supervisory authorities to be vested with enhanced powers and functions. On 10 October 2018 the UK signed the protocol.[89] The Convention as amended by the protocol is generally called 'modernised Convention 108.' A treaty such as Convention 108 (whether as amended or in its original form) does not take direct effect in municipal law.[90] Nevertheless, where a statute embodies the provisions of a treaty reference should be had to the treaty and applicable interpretational principles when construing that statute and in deciding which available meaning to prefer.[91] The DPA 2018, when referring to the 'Data Protection Convention,' is referring to the modernised Convention 108.[92]

7–032 GDPR

The GDPR took effect on 25 May 2018.[93] The GDPR applies to personal data processed by automated means and, where personal data is processed by other than automated means, where the personal data forms part of a filing system.[94] The GDPR preserves and develops the core principles of Directive 95/46/EC and the rights which the Directive conferred on data subjects. In addition, the GDPR has introduced new obligations requiring organisations to implement data protection by design and by default; to appoint a data protection officer in certain circumstances; to comply with a new right to data portability; and to comply with the principle of accountability. Although, as a Regulation, the GDPR is directly applicable, it provides a significant measure of legislative latitude in prescribed areas.[95] The GDPR applies to businesses established in the EU, as well as to controllers and processors not established in the EU that offer goods or services to data subjects in the EU or that monitor their behaviour.[96]

7–033 Law Enforcement Directive

While the GDPR lays down general rules to protect individuals in relation to the processing of their personal data and to ensure the free movement of personal data within the EU, the LED lays down specific rules for data protection in the fields of judicial cooperation in criminal matters and police cooperation. Where a competent authority processes personal data for the purposes of the prevention, investigation, detection or prosecution of criminal offences, the LED will apply. Where a competent authority processes personal data for other purposes, the GDPR will apply. The LED is not limited to exchanges of personal data between Member States, but applies to purely domestic processing of personal data for law enforcement purposes.

---

89 Council of Europe Convention for the Protection of Individuals with regard to Automatic Processing of Personal Data (CETS No 223). As at October 2019, no state had ratified modernised Convention 108 and it had not entered into force.

90 *Fothergill v Monarch Airlines Ltd* [1981] AC 251 at 271.

91 *Salomon v Customs and Excise Commissioners* [1967] 2 QB 116 at 143; *Corocraft Ltd v Pan American Airways Ltd* [1969] 1 QB 616, [1969] 1 All ER 82. As to the approach to the interpretation of international treaties, see: *Warner v Scapa Flow Charters* [2018] UKSC 52, [2019] 2 All ER 1042.

92 DPA 2018 s 3(13).

93 GDPR Art 99(2).

94 As to the meaning of these terms, see §§8–040 to 8–041.

95 See Recital (10) and, for example, the Art 23 restrictions.

96 GDPR Art 3(2).

7–034 DPA 2018

The DPA 2018 also took effect on 25 May 2018.[97] It replaced the DPA 1998. In conjunction with the GDPR and the LED, it seeks to cover the field of data protection in the UK. The three legislative measures are considered in detail in Chapters 8-14 of this work.

4. INTERPRETATIONAL PRINCIPLES

7–035 EU legislation

When interpreting EU law, domestic courts must apply the same principles of interpretation as the CJEU.[98] Domestic law that implements EU law, such as the DPA 1998 and the DPA 2018 (to the extent that it supplements the GDPR and implements the LED), is also to be construed as a matter of EU law.[99] Those principles may be arranged into three groups: the hierarchy of norms; over-arching principles of interpretation; and general principles of interpretation.

7–036 Hierarchy of norms

The sources of EU law are arranged in a hierarchy, called a 'hierarchy of norms.'[100] At the apex of the hierarchy are the TEU, the TFEU, the Charter of Fundamental Rights and the general principles of EU law – collectively termed 'primary law.' Next in rank are regulations and directives (ie EU legislation) – collectively termed 'secondary law.' All sources of EU law are generally to be interpreted in accordance with this hierarchy of norms. Accordingly, regulations and directives are to be interpreted, so far as possible, so as to be consistent with primary law.[101]

7–037 Overarching principles

There are a number of overarching principles devised by the CJEU to assist with the interpretation of EU law. These include:

(1) The principle of legal certainty. This has a number of facets to it. First, it requires that rules be clear, precise and predictable in their effects – in particular, where those rules may have negative consequences on an individual or undertaking.[102] Secondly, it requires that every person concerned by EU legislation be able to

---

97 DPA 2018 s 212; Data Protection Act 2018 (Commencement No 1 and Transitional and Saving Provisions) Regulations 2018 (SI 2018/625) reg 2.

98 European Communities Act 1972 s 3(1). And see: *Bulmer v Bollinger* [1974] Ch. 401, [1974] 2 All ER 1226.

99 In particular, the doctrine of incidental direct effect requires that national law implementing Directives is interpreted and applied in accordance with Community law and norms: Case 14/83 *Von Colson v Land Nordrhein-Westfalen* [1984] ECR 1891; *Marleasing SA v La Comercial Internacional de Alimentacion SA* (C-106/89) [1990] ECR I-4135, [1992] 1 CMLR 305; *Océano Grupo Editorial v Rocio Murciano Quintero* (C-240-244/98) [2000] ECR I-4491; Craig 'Directives: Direct Effect, Indirect Effect and the Construction of National Legislation' (1997) 22 EL Rev 519. In relation to the interpretation of DPA 1998 see in particular: *Campbell v MGN Ltd* [2002] EWCA Civ 1373, [2003] QB 633 at [96] (Phillips MR); *Durant v Financial Services Authority* [2003] EWCA Civ 1746, [2004] FSR 28 at [3]-[4] (Auld LJ); *Common Services Agency v IC* [2008] UKHL 47, [2008] 1 WLR 1550 at [7], [20]-[27] (Lord Hope), [82] (Lord Rodger), [91] (Baroness Hale); *South Lanarkshire Council v Scottish IC* [2013] UKSC 55, [2013] 1 WLR 2421 at [7]-[8] (Baroness Hale, giving the judgment of the Court); *Vidal Hall v Google Inc* [2015] EWCA Civ 311, [2016] QB 1003; *Lloyd v Google LLC* [2019] EWCA Civ 1599, [2020] EMLR 2 at [40]-[42].

100 The term 'norm' is used to indicate setting a standard of general application, as opposed to an individual decision.

101 *Rauh v Hauptzollamt Nürnberg-Fürth* (C-314/89) [1991] ECR I-1647, [1993] 1 CMLR 171 at [17]; *EC Commission v Germany* (C-61/94) [1996] ECR I-3989, [1997] 1 CMLR 28 at [52]; *Bertelsmann AG v Independent Music Publishers and Labels Association (Impala)* (C-413/06) [2008] ECR I-4951, [2008] 5 CMLR 17, [2010] All ER (EC) 377 at [174].

102 *Förster v Hoofddirectie van de Informatie Beheer Groep* (C-158/07) [2008] ECR-I 8507, [2009] 1 CMLR 32 at [67].

acquaint him or herself with the precise extent of the obligations which are imposed on him or her by that legislation: this requires that EU law be published adequately and in a timely manner.[103] Thirdly, it generally precludes EU legislation being applied retroactively.[104] Fourthly, it requires that reasonable time-limits are laid down in advance for the bringing of proceedings under EU legislation.[105] And fifthly, it requires that EU law is applied uniformly by national courts.[106] This includes a requirement that where provisions of EU law permit derogations from a directive or regulation, those derogations must be implemented with the requisite degree of precision and clarity necessary to satisfy the requirements flowing from the principle of legal certainty.[107]

(2) The principle of proportionality. At the EU level, this requires that the content and form of EU action not exceed what is necessary to achieve the objectives of the Treaties.[108] Thus, measures implemented through the provisions of EU law should be appropriate for attaining the legitimate objectives pursued by the legislation at issue and must not go beyond what is necessary to achieve those objectives.[109] Where there is a choice between several appropriate measures, the least onerous one should be selected and the disadvantages must not be disproportionate to the aims pursued. The principle of proportionality also applies to a Member State when acting within the scope of EU law. When considering proportionality in relation to a measure taken by a Member State, a three-stage inquiry is undertaken: does the measure pursue a legitimate aim; is the measure appropriate for achieving that aim; and could the aim have been achieved by less restrictive measures?[110]

(3) The principle of effective judicial protection. This principle prohibits Member States from rendering the exercise of rights conferred by the EU legal order impossible in practice or excessively difficult.[111]

(4) The principle of natural justice. In all proceedings in which sanctions may be imposed, it is a fundamental principle of EU law that a person who is affected (in particular, by being subject to a fine or other penalty) be accorded natural justice.[112] This means: being informed in good time of the case upon which the proceedings are founded;[113] being given a reasonable opportunity to examine the evidence on

---

[103] *Proceedings Brought by Heinrich* (C-345/06) [2009] CR-I 1659 [2010] QB 521, [2009] 3 CMLR 7 at [44]; *Firma A Racke v Hauptzollamt Mainz* (98/78) [1979] ECR 69 at [15].

[104] *Kauer v Pensionsversicherungsanstalt der Angestellten* (C-28/00) [2002] ECR-I 1343, [2002] 1 CMLR 51.

[105] See, for example: *Test Claimants in the FII Group Litigation v HMRC* [2012] UKSC 19, [2012] 2 AC 337; *FMX Food Merchants Import Export Co Ltd v HMRC* [2018] EWCA Civ 2401, [2019] 1 WLR 2841; *Akzo Nobel Chemicals Ltd v European Commission* (C-550/07) [2011] 2 AC 338, [2011] All ER (EC) 1107; *R (PJSC Rosneft Oil Co) v HM Treasury* (C-72/15) [2018] QB 1, [2017] 3 CMLR 23.

[106] *Air Transport Association of America v Secretary of State for Energy and Climate Change* (C-366/10) [2013] PTSR 209, [2012] 2 CMLR 4 at [47]-[48].

[107] *Accardo and Others v Comune di Torino* (C-27/09) [2010] ECR I-10273, [2011]1 CMLR 44 at [55].

[108] TEU Art 5(4) and Protocol (No 2) and Charter of Fundamental Rights Art 52.

[109] *R (ABNA Ltd) v Secretary of State for Health* (C-453/03) [2005] ECR I-10423, [2006]1 CMLR 48 at [68]; *R (Vodafone Ltd) v Secretary of State for Business, Enterprise and Regulatory Reform* (C-58/08) [2010] 3 CMLR 44, [2010] All ER (EC) 741 at [51].

[110] See, for example: *Ingeniørforeningen I Danmark v Region Syddanmark* (C-499/08) [2011] 1 CMLR 35, [2012] All ER (EC) 342.

[111] *Littlewoods Retail Ltd v HMRC* (C-591/10) [2012] STC 1714, [2012] STI 2359 at [28]; *Germany GmbH and Arcor AG & Co KG* (C-392/04) [2006] ECR-I 8559, [2007] 1 CMLR 10 at [57].

[112] *Hoffmann La Roche & Co AG v Commission of the European Communities* (85/76) [1979] ECR 461, [1979] 3 CMLR 211 at [9]; *Akzo Nobel Chemicals Ltd v European Commission* (C-550/07) [2011] 2 AC 338, [2011] All ER (EC) 1107 at [92].

[113] *Hoffmann La Roche & Co AG v Commission of the European Communities* (85/76) [1979] ECR 461, [1979] 3 CMLR 211

which it is based;[114] being given a reasonable opportunity to make submissions; and being permitted legal representation.

7–038 General principles

The third group of principles is directed to discerning the meaning and operation of specific provisions of an EU legislative measure:

(1) The provisions are to be construed in the light of the spirit, general scheme, wording and overall legal context of the legislative measure, the words used being given their usual meaning in everyday language unless the regulation or directive expressly defines them otherwise or expressly leaves their meaning to be determined by national law.[115]

(2) The legislative measure must be construed so as to give effect to its objectives.[116]

(3) Recitals are an aid to interpretation but do not constitute a legal rule: they cannot alter the scope of a provision where the provision does not endorse them.[117]

(4) When interpreting a provision, account must be taken of the purpose and general structure of the legislation itself,[118] the meaning and purpose of the Treaty provisions on which the legislation is based,[119] the relationship between that provision and other provisions in the legislation, the wording of the provision to be construed (in all its different language versions)[120] and any relevant general principles of EU law. No priority is given to any one of those elements of interpretation, and the general approach is to find an interpretation that reconciles them.[121]

(5) Where a legislative measure supersedes an earlier measure covering the same topic, it is permissible to construe the later measure by reference to case law on the earlier measure. Given that the purpose of the GDPR is the same as that of Directive 95/46/EC, it is permissible to take into account judgments of the CJEU construing similar provisions in that Directive.[122]

---

at [10].

[114] *Hoffmann La Roche & Co AG v Commission of the European Communities* (85/76) [1979] ECR 461, [1979] 3 CMLR 211 at [11].

[115] *Denmark v EC Commission* (Case 349/85) [1988] ECR 169 at [9]; *P DIR International Film v EC Commission* (C-164/98) [2000] ECR I-447, [2000] 1 CMLR 619 at [26]; *Re Massachusetts Institute of Technology* (C-431/04) [2006] ECR I-4089, [2006] RPC 34 at [17].

[116] *R (Catt) v ACPO* [2015] UKSC 9, [2015] AC 1065 at [8] (referring to the DPA 1998).

[117] *Toshiba Europe GmbH v Katun Germany GmbH* (C-112/99) [2001] ECR I-7945, [2002] 3 CMLR 7 at [36]; *Casa Fleischhandel v Bundesanstalt für Landwirtschaftliche Marktordnung* (215/88) [1989] ECR 2789 at [31]; *Societe d'importation Edouard Leclerc-Siplec v TF1 Publicite SA* [1995] ECR I-179, [1995] 3 CMLR 422 at [45]-[47]; *British Steel plc v EC Commission* (C-1/98) [2000] ECR I-10349 at [29].

[118] *Austria Asphalt GmbH v Bundeskartellanwalt* (C-248/16) [2018] Bus LR 462, [2017] 5 CMLR 21 at [20]; *Landeskreditbank Baden-Württemberg v European Central Bank* (T-122/15) [2018] 1 CMLR 7 at [40]; *Trijber (trading as Amstelboats) v College van burgemeester en wethouders van Amsterdam* (C-340/14) [2016] 1 CMLR 38 at [46]; *HMRC v Isle of Wight Council* (C-288/07) [2008] ECR I-7203, [2009] 1 CMLR 135 at [25], [41].

[119] *Witzemann v Hauptzollamt München-Mitte* (C-343/89) [1990] ECR I-4477, [1993] STC 108 at [20] (Advocate General).

[120] For example: *Maio Marques da Rosa v Varzim Sol* (C-306/16) [2018] 2 CMLR 8, [2018] IRLR 470 at [40]; *Vinyls Italia SpA (in liquidation) v Mediterranea di Navigazione SpA* (C-54/16) [2018] 1 WLR 543, [2018] 2 CLC 558 at [3].

[121] See, for example: *Wightman and others v Secretary of State for Exiting the European Union* (C-621/18) [2019] QB 199, [2019] 1 CMLR 29 at [137] (Adv Gen); *Mahamdia v People's Democratic Republic of Algeria* (C-154/11) [2014] All ER (EC) 96, [2013] CEC 452 at [35].

[122] *Anonymi Geniki Etairia Tsimenton Iraklis (AGET Iraklis) v Ypourgos Ergasias* (C-201/15) [2017] 2 CMLR 32, [2017] IRLR 282 at [29]-[32]. In relation to the replacement of Directive 95/46/EC with the GDPR, see: *R (CL) v Chief Constable of Greater Manchester Police* [2018] EWHC 3333 (Admin).

(6) Preparatory or working documents, declarations and so forth that form part of the legislative history of the provision to be construed are not normally taken into account when interpreting a provision.[123]

(7) International agreements to which the EU is a party may also be relied upon to inform the meaning to be given to a provision of EU law.[124]

(8) Provisions conferring power on a Member State to carve out exemptions and derogations are to be strictly construed.[125]

(9) Where a term is not defined, it may be construed by reference to its usual sense,[126] the purpose and aim of the measure,[127] the wording, context and aim of the provision,[128] or the general context in which the word is used and its usual meaning in ordinary language.[129] The general tendency is to give words used in European Union legislation an 'autonomous' or 'EU' meaning: that is, a meaning appropriate to the context within which the word is used and to the purpose of the provision containing it, rather than the meaning that may typically be given to the word in the context of the legal system of a particular Member State.[130]

(10) Where a provision derogates from or restricts a 'fundamental right', that derogation or restriction must be construed narrowly, such that the individual's right is only weakened insofar as is strictly necessary.[131] In this regard, it should be noted that data protection rights have the status of fundamental rights.[132]

7–039 Domestic legislation

To the extent that the DPA 2018 supplements the GDPR or implements the LED, the DPA 2018 must be interpreted by UK courts in conformity with the GDPR and the LED, as well

---

123 *Arbeitsgemeinschaft Deutscher Rundfunkanstalten (ARD) v PRO Sieben Media AG* (C-6/98) [1999} ECR I-7599, [1999] 3 CMLR 769 at [27]; *Inuit Tapiriit Kanatami and others v European Parliament* (C-583/11P) [2014] QB 648, [2014] 1 CMLR 54 at [59], [66], [70].

124 *Rizeni Letoveho Provozu CR v Bundesamt fur Finanzen* (C-335/05) [2007] ECR I-4307, [2007] 3 CMLR 13 at [16]-[21]. The GDPR expressly refers in recital (105) to the requirement to take into account obligations arising under multilateral or regional systems for the protection of personal data, specifically the Council of Europe Convention of 28 January 1981 for the Protection of Individuals with regard to the Automatic Processing of Personal Data and its Additional Protocol.

125 *Muhlleitner v Usufi* (C-190/11) [2013] CEC 595, [2013] Bus LR D42 at [27]; *European Commission v Ireland* (C-82/10) [2012] CEC 229 at [44]; *Inuit Tapiriit Kanatami and others v European Parliament* (C-583/11P) [2014] QB 648, [2014] 1 CMLR 54 at [130]; *European Commission v Republic of Malta* (C-557/15) 21 June 2018 at [47]; *Buccioni v Banca d'Italia* (C-594/16) [2018] Bus LR 2236 at [37].

126 *United Kingdom v EC Commission* (C-209/96) [1998] ECR I-5655, [1999] 1 CMLR 236 at [30]-[37].

127 *Veedfald v Arhus Amtskommune* (C-203/99) [2001] ECR I-3569, [2003] 1 CMLR 41 at [14].

128 *Pharos SA v Commission of the European Communities* (C-151/98), 18 November 1998 at [19]; *Reliance Industries Ltd v European Council* (T-45/06) [2008] ECR II-2399 at [101].

129 *P DIR International Film v EC Commission* (C-164/98) [2000] ECR I-447, [2000] 1 CMLR 619 at [26].

130 See, for example: *Ville de Nivelles v Matzak* (C-518/15) [2018] 2 CMLR 37, [2018] ICR 869 at [28], [45]; *English Bridge Union Ltd v HMRC* (C-90/16) [2017] STC 2317, [2017] BVC 53 at [43]; *Re Eurofood IFSC Ltd* (C-341/04) [2006] ECR I-3813, [2006] Ch 508 at [31].

131 This has repeatedly been held applicable to derogations and limitations in relation to the protection of personal data: *Tietosuojavaltuutettu v Satakunnan* (C-73/07) [2010] All ER (EC) 213 at [56]; *Volker und Markus Schecke GbR v Land Hessen* (C-92/09) [2012] All ER (EC) 127, [2012] IP & T 513 at [77], [86]; *IPI v Englebert* (C-473/12) [2014] 2 CMLR 9, [2014] CEC 719 at [39]; *Tele2 Sverige AB v Post- och telestyrelsen* (C-203/15) [2017] QB 771, [2017] 2 CMLR 30 at [96]; *Valsts policijas Rīgas reģiona pārvaldes Kārtības policijas pārvalde v Rīgas pašvaldības SIA* (Case C-13/16) [2017] 4 WLR 97, [2017] 3 CMLR 39 at [30].

132 GDPR recitals (1) (referring to Charter of Fundamental Rights of the EU Art 8(1) and TFEU Art 16(1)), (2), (3), (4), (10), (16), (47), (51), (52), (53), (69), (102), (109), (111), (113), (114), (153), (166), (173), and Arts 1(2), 6(1)(f), 9(2)(b), 9(2)(g), 9(2)(j), 23(1), 45(2)(a), 50(b), 51(1) and 88(2).

as the remainder of EU law, including the Charter of Fundamental Rights.[133] To the extent that the DPA 2018 otherwise deals with data protection, ordinary principles of interpretation of domestic legislation apply.

5. POST-EU MEMBERSHIP

7–040 Background

The UK ceased to be a Member State of the EU at 23:00hrs GMT on 31 January 2020 – 'exit day.'[134] This started a period of legal change, albeit one not principally to be felt until the end of the 'implementation period' – defined to be 23:00hrs GMT on 31 December 2020.[135] Until that moment, EU law continues to apply to and in the UK, producing the same effects as it would in relation to, and being interpreted and applied in the same manner as it would by, a Member State.[136] This work is written to reflect the law as it stands on 1 February 2020 and as it is likely to continue to stand until at least 23:00hrs GMT on 31 December 2020. Nevertheless, since the legal changes that will occur on and after that moment will be relevant to data protection law, this section provides an introduction to the provenance and nature of those changes.

7–041 EU (Withdrawal) Act 2018

The primary instrument for the UK's domestic process of disengagement from the EU legal order is the EU (Withdrawal) Act 2018 – the 'EU(W)A.'[137] In an attempt to ensure that the statute book continued to function on and after exit day,[138] the EU(W)A made, and will make, certain structural changes to the UK's constitutional architecture:

(1) The European Communities Act 1972 – the 'ECA' – was repealed on exit day,[139] but its effect is preserved until the end of the implementation period.[140] It is not until that time, therefore, that the 'conduit pipe' through which EU law flows into UK law will be closed.[141]

---

133 See: *Zarraga v Pelz* (C-491/10) [2011] ILPr 32 at [75]; *Tele2 Sverige AB v Post- och telestyrelsen* (C-203/15) [2017] QB 771, [2017] 2 CMLR 30 at [91]; *NT1 v Google LLC* [2018] EWHC 799 (QB), [2019] QB 344 at [13(8)], [162].

134 As defined in EU(W)A s 20(1).

135 Otherwise termed 'IP completion day', as defined in the EU(WA)A 2020 s 39(1). The implementation period can, under Art 132 of the re-revised Withdrawal Agreement (19 October 2019), be extended by consent. As a matter of UK law, however, Ministers are prohibited from agreeing to such an extension: EU(W)A s 15A.

136 This is established, as a matter of EU and international law, by Arts 126-127 of the Agreement and, as a matter of UK law, by the EU(W)A ss 1A and 1B.

137 As amended by the EU(WA)A 2020.

138 See Explanatory Notes §10 ('The principal purpose of the Act is to provide a functioning statute book on the day the UK leaves the EU. As a general rule, the same rules and laws will apply on the day after exit as on the day before') and White Paper, *Legislating for the United Kingdom's withdrawal from the European Union* (Cm 9446) §1.12 ('In order to achieve a stable and smooth transition… as a general rule, the same rules and laws will apply after we leave the EU as they did before'). Exceptions to this general policy choice in favour of legal continuity, including in respect of the non-retention of the Charter of Fundamental Rights and Freedoms, general principles of EU law, and *Franconvich* damages, are discussed at §§7–041 to 7–044 below.

139 EU(W)A s. 1.

140 EU(W)A ss 1A (ECA 1972 will continue to have effect despite its repeal, with references to 'the Treaties' being read so as to include Part 4 of the Withdrawal Agreement (on the implementation period)) and 1B (EU-derived domestic legislation will continue to have effect, subject to certain glosses, including that references to 'EU law' be read as references to EU law so far as it applies to the UK under Part 4 of the Withdrawal Agreement (on the implementation period)).

141 On the 'conduit pipe' metaphor, see *R (Miller) v Secretary of State for Exiting the European Union* [2017] UKSC 5, [2018] AC 61 at [65], [80] and [84].

(2) At the end of the implementation period, the EU(W)A will create a new body of 'retained EU law', by preserving EU-derived UK law[142] and by converting the existing body of 'direct' EU law into UK law.[143] The latter conversion exercise is subject to a notable exception:[144] the Charter of Fundamental Rights will not form part of UK law after the end of the implementation period.[145]

(3) The EU(W)A gives Ministers wide-ranging powers to 'prevent, remedy or mitigate' any 'failure of retained EU law to operate effectively' or any 'deficiency in retained EU law' arising from the UK's withdrawal from the EU.[146] This power can be used by Ministers to amend or repeal primary legislation,[147] and has been exercisable since the EU(W)A was passed.[148]

7–042 Status of retained EU law

The legal status of the new body of retained EU law will be governed by an inchoate group of rules and principles:

(1) The principle of the supremacy of EU law will continue to apply to the interpretation, disapplication or quashing of any enactment or rule of law passed

---

[142] EU(W)A s 2. This category of 'preserved legislation' is broadly defined so as to include any enactment which 'relates to' the EU or EEA: s 2(2)(d). Primary legislation which is not dependent for its existence on the ECA 1972 therefore can fall within the scope of EU(W)A s 2: see Explanatory Notes §23, fn 6.

[143] EU(W)A s 3; s, 4 and Sch 8, para 38. Directly applicable EU legislation (including EU regulations, decisions and tertiary legislation) and directly effective EU rights and obligations (including those contained in EU treaties, and EU directives if recognised as such by an EU or UK court or tribunal before the end of the implementation period, or by a UK court or tribunal in a case begun before that date but decided thereafter) are captured, respectively. During the Act's passage through Parliament, the Government repeatedly described this as taking a 'snapshot' of the existing body of EU law: see *Hansard*, HC, 14 November 2017, vol 631, cols 287-289; HC, 21 November 2017, vol 631, cols 894, 900, 975; HL, 30 January 2018, vol 788, col 1373; HL, 28 February 2018, vol 789, col 688; HL, 7 March 2018, vol 789, col 1213; HL, 19 March 2018, vol 790, col 19; HL, 18 April 2018, vol 790, col 1211; HL, 23 April 2018, vol 790, col 1452.

[144] There are other exceptions to the EU(W)A's general maintenance of the status quo, namely the principle of supremacy, the general principles of EU law, challenges to the validity of EU instruments, the preliminary reference procedure, and *Francovich* damages. To the extent that these exclusions affect the status and interpretation of, and remedies and rights of action available in relation to, the new body of retained EU law, they are discussed at §§7–042 to 7–044 below.

[145] EU(W)A s 5(4). This exclusion will apply in respect of matters which occurred before the end of the implementation period, as well as matters occurring thereafter, except where proceedings were begun before a UK court or tribunal before that day but decided thereafter: EU(W)A Sch 8, para 39(1)-(3). The consequent loss of Art 8 of the Charter (right to protection of one's personal data) is particularly significant in the present context and was lamented by members of both Houses of Parliament during the passage of both the EU(W)A and the DPA 2018: see *Hansard*, HC, 7 September 2017, vol 628, col 413; HC, 5 March 2018, vol 637, col 84; HL, 30 October 2017, vol 785, col 1162-1163; HL, 31 January 2018, vol 788, cols 1551 and 1670-1671; HL, 5 March 2018, vol 789, col 917; HL, 23 April 2018, vol 790, cols 1364-1365. The Government's repeated assertion, both during the parliamentary debates and in its *Charter of Fundamental Rights of the EU: Right by Right Analysis* (5 December 2017), that rights protection in the UK would not be weakened was widely criticised and remains patently incorrect. The erstwhile Secretary of State for Exiting the EU, David Davis, himself recognised that the Charter provides greater substantive protection for the right to one's personal data than is otherwise available under UK law by bringing his successful challenge to s 1 of the Data Protection and Investigatory Powers Act 2014 on grounds of its contravention of Arts 7, 8 and 11 of the Charter and not by reference to the HRA 1998: *R (Watson) v SSHD* [2018] EWCA Civ 70, [2018] QB 912. That the Charter provides for stronger remedial protection than the HRA, through the disapplication of inconsistent primary legislation, is demonstrated by the decision in *Benkharbouche v Sudan and FCO* [2017] UKSC 62, [2019] AC 777.

[146] EU(W)A s 8. 'Deficiency' is defined so as to include provisions which are rendered 'substantially redundant', which confer functions on EU entities which no longer have functions in relation to the UK, or which make provision for reciprocal arrangements between the UK and the EU or a Member State which no longer exist: s 8(2). This power is subject to a two-year sunset clause, running from the end of the implementation period: s 8(8).

[147] EU(W)A s 8(5). It is thus said to constitute a 'Henry VIII power.' There are exceptions to its scope of application, namely the HRA 1998, the Scotland Act 1998, the Government of Wales Act 2006 or the Northern Ireland Act 1998: s 8(7)(f) and (g). An amendment which would have precluded use of the s 8 power to amend or repeal the DPA 2018 was proposed but ultimately withdrawn: see *Hansard*, HL, 12 March 2018, vol 789, cols 1370-1378.

[148] EU(W)A s 25(1).

or made before the end of the implementation period[149], including where such an enactment or rule of law is modified on or after that date, provided that this accords with the intention of the modification.[150] The principle of supremacy will not apply, however, to any enactment or rule of law passed or made on or after the end of the implementation period.[151]

(2) EU-derived UK laws which are preserved by s 2 of the EU(W)A will retain their pre-exit classification as primary legislation of a particular kind, subordinate legislation of a particular kind, or another enactment of a particular kind.[152]

(3) No legal status is expressly afforded to the laws converted under ss 3 and 4 of the EU(W)A.[153] General inferences could, however, be drawn from the provisions which govern the manner in which these laws can be amended,[154] or from the manner in which they are treated for the purposes of the HRA 1998.[155]

7–043 **Interpretation of retained EU law**

At the end of the implementation period, the new body of retained EU law is to be interpreted in accordance with the following rules and principles:

(1) Case law decided by the CJEU before the end of the implementation period will continue to bind domestic courts and tribunals other than the Supreme Court[156] and, in respect of criminal matters in Scotland, the High Court of Justiciary,[157] so far as is relevant to their determination of any question as to the validity, meaning

---

149 EU(W)A s 5(2). Accordingly, if a conflict arises between pre-exit domestic legislation and retained EU law, the latter will take precedence over the former: Explanatory Notes §103.

150 EU(W)A s 5(3).

151 EU(W)A s 5(1). Accordingly, if an Act of Parliament is passed after the end of the implementation period which is inconsistent with any retained EU law, the former will take precedence over the latter: Explanatory Notes §102.

152 EU(W)A s 7(1).

153 This gives rise to considerable legal uncertainty. The relative status of one legal norm relative to another is determinative of a number of important questions, including which norm prevails in the event of a conflict, whether the norm can be challenged and if so on what grounds, and what remedies are available in the event that a challenge is successful. The recommendation of the Select Committee of the House of Lords that all retained direct EU law be treated as primary legislation, deemed to have been enacted on exit day, was ultimately rejected: see *European Union (Withdrawal) Bill*, 9th Report of Session 2017-2019, 29 January 2018, §§45-52; *Hansard*, HL, 5 March 2018, vol 789, cols 884-886 and 895-897; *Hansard*, HL, 16 May 2018, vol 791, cols 712-717. An amendment which would have afforded a presumptive legal status to retained direct EU law according to its origins was debated but not moved to a vote: *Hansard*, HC, 16 January 2018, vol 634, cols 744-745; see also *Hansard*, HL, 5 March 2018, vol 789, cols 885 and 889-890.

154 For the purposes of amendment, direct EU law retained under s 4 is treated akin to primary legislation, insofar as it can be modified by delegated legislation only if made under the EU(W)A itself, or a pre-existing Henry VIII power, unless the modification is supplementary, incidental or consequential: EU(W)A s 7(4) and Sch 8, paras 3, 5, 8 and 10-12. For the purposes of amendment, direct EU legislation retained under s 3 is divided into two novel categories: 'retained direct principal EU legislation', comprising EU Regulations and Annexes to EEA Agreements referring to or amending such Regulations, which is treated akin to primary legislation, insofar as it can be modified by delegated legislation only if made under the EU(W)A itself, or a pre-existing Henry VIII power, unless the modification is supplementary, incidental or consequential; and 'retained direct minor EU legislation', comprising all other direct EU legislation retained under s 3, which is treated akin to subordinate legislation, as it can be modified by any existing or future power to make, confirm or approve subordinate legislation: EU(W)A s 7(2)-(3) and Sch 8 paras 3, 5, 8 and 10-12.

155 For the purposes of the HRA 1998, 'retained direct principal EU legislation' is to be treated as primary legislation, and 'retained direct minor EU legislation' is to be treated as primary legislation so far as it amends any primary legislation, but otherwise as subordinate legislation: EU(W)A Sch 8, para 30. No mention is made of how direct EU law retained under EU(W)A s 4 is to be treated for the purposes of the HRA 1998.

156 EU(W)A s 6(4)(a).

157 Where it is sitting as a court of appeal otherwise than in relation to a compatibility issue under the Criminal Procedure (Scotland) Act 1995, s 288ZA(2), or a devolution issue under the Scotland Act 1998, Sch 6, para 1, or sitting on a reference under the Criminal Procedure (Scotland) Act 1995, s 123(1): EU(W)A s 6(4)(b).

or effect of any retained EU law, provided that retained law is unmodified after the end of the implementation period, or has been modified with the intention that this case law should continue to apply.[158] Regard must be had to the pre-exit limits of EU competence in this context.[159] In deciding whether to depart from the existing body of CJEU case law, the Supreme Court and High Court of Justiciary must each apply the same test as it would in deciding whether to depart from its own case law.[160]

(2) Domestic case law decided before the end of the implementation period will continue to bind domestic courts and tribunals in accordance with the ordinary rules of precedent, so far as is relevant to their determination of any question as to the validity, meaning or effect of any retained EU law, provided that retained law is unmodified, or has been modified with the intention that this case law should continue to apply.[161] Regard must be had to the pre-exit limits of EU competence in this context.[162]

(3) Case law decided by the CJEU after the end of the implementation period will not be binding, but domestic courts and tribunals may have regard to it so far as is relevant to any matter before them.[163]

(4) The duty to interpret domestic law so far as possible in a manner consistent with EU law will apply only to domestic law passed or made before the end of the implementation period, and only if that domestic law is either unmodified after that date or modified with the intention that the interpretative obligation will continue to apply.[164]

(5) General principles of EU law, which were recognised as such by the CJEU before the end of the implementation period,[165] must be followed by domestic courts and tribunals so far as is relevant to their interpretation of any retained EU law, provided that retained law is unmodified, or has been modified with the intention that the general principles should continue to apply.[166] Regard must be had to the

158 EU(W)A ss 6(3)(a), 6(6), 6(7).

159 EU(W)A s 6(3)(b).

160 EU(W)A s 6(5).

161 EU(W)A s 6(3)(a), 6(4)(c), 6(6), 6(7).

162 EU(W)A s 6(3)(b). This includes CJEU case law which sets out principles of interpretation, including that a purposive approach should be taken where the meaning of an interpretation is unclear: Explanatory Notes §111.

163 EU(W)A s 6(1)-(2). The EU (Withdrawal) Bill, as introduced, would have given domestic courts and tribunals a discretion to have regard to post-exit CJEU case law if 'appropriate' to do so. With concern that this provided inadequate guidance and risked involving the judiciary in matters of political controversy, an alternative formulation ('shall have regard… if relevant') was proposed, in line with s 2(1) of the HRA 1998: see House of Lords Select Committee on the Constitution, *European Union (Withdrawal) Bill*, 9th Report of Session 2017-2019, 29 January 2018, §§132-142. EU(W)A s 6, as enacted, is a halfway house between these proposals – a discretion not a duty, qualified by reference to what is relevant rather than what is appropriate – which still leaves uncertainty as to when and how post-exit CJEU case law should be taken into account.

164 This duty of consistent construction, as established in cases including *Marleasing SA v La Comercial Internacional de Alimentacion SA* (C-106/89) [1990] ECR I-4135, [1992] 1 CMLR 305 and *Impact v Minister for Agriculture and Food* (C-268/06) [2008] ECR I-2483, [2008] 2 CMLR 47, is taken to constitute an element of the principle of the supremacy, as governed by EU(W)A s 5(1)-(3): see Explanatory Notes §104.

165 Examples include the principles of proportionality, non-retroactivity, equivalence and effectiveness: see Explanatory Notes §§59 and 209. It will also include fundamental rights which find expression in, but are not dependent for their existence on, the Charter of Fundamental Rights, as is recognised in EU(W)A s 5(5).

166 EU(W)A ss 6(3)(a), 6(6), s 6(7) and Sch 1, para 3(1). These general principles will form part of domestic law at the end of the implementation period, but as no right of action can be based on non-compliance with them, their role will merely be as an aid to interpretation: EU(W)A s 4(1) and Sch 1, paras 2-3.

pre-exit limits of EU competence in this context.[167]

(6) The meaning or effect in EU law of any EU Treaty or treaty relating to the EU, or the validity, meaning or effect in EU law of any EU instrument, is to be treated as a question of law and not as a question of fact.[168]

(7) Preliminary references can no longer be made to the CJEU.[169]

These rules and principles – in particular (1), (2), (4) and (5) – will apply subject to the exercise by Ministers of their power to make regulations setting out the circumstances in which domestic courts and tribunals may depart from CJEU and domestic case law decided before the end of the implementation period.[170] Such regulations may designate courts and tribunals other than the Supreme Court and the High Court of Justiciary as having the power to depart from such case law.[171]

7– 044 **Excluded rights and remedies**

At the end of the implementation period, certain rights of action and remedies will no longer be available in domestic law:

(1) There will be no right to challenge any retained EU law on the basis that, immediately before the end of the implementation period, the corresponding EU instrument was invalid.[172]

(2) There will be no right of action based on a failure to comply with any of the general principles of EU law.[173]

---

167 EU(W)A s 6(3)(b).

168 EU(W)A Sch 5, para 3. This continues the position under s 3 of the ECA 1972, but departs from the general rule by which the meaning or effect of the law in other jurisdictions is treated as a question of fact, to be proved in legal proceedings by evidence: see Explanatory Notes §§278-279. Ministers have the power to make provision about judicial notice and the admissibility of evidence concerning retained EU law, EU law and the EEA Agreement: EU(W)A Sch 5, para 4.

169 EU(W)A s 6(1)(b). Under the re-revised Withdrawal Agreement (19 October 2019), the preliminary reference procedure is, however, preserved for an eight-year period for questions concerning the interpretation of the citizens' rights provisions (Art 158) and for an indefinite period for certain questions relating to EU budgetary matters (Arts 136, 138 and 160).

170 EU(W)A ss 6(4)(ba) and 6(5A)-(5D). This law-making power can be sub-delegated to persons including the President of the Supreme Court, the Senior President of Tribunals, and the Lord Chief Justice of England and Wales: EU(W)A s 6(5B)(d). These provisions, inserted by the EU (Withdrawal) Agreement Act 2020, constitute a clear affront to the principle of the separation of powers. They were, unsurprisingly, criticised in strong terms by the House of Lords Select Committee on the Constitution: *European Union (Withdrawal Agreement) Bill*, 1st Report of Session 2019-2021, 14 January 2020, §§104-108. For further criticism of these provisions, dubbed 'Henry VIII on steroids' during the parliamentary debates, see: *Hansard*, HC, 8 January 2020, cols 414-416; HL, 15 January 2020, cols 679-691; HL, 20 January 2020, cols 981-984.

171 EU(W)A s 6(5A)(a). In departure from the usual system of hierarchy and precedent, lower courts could thus be given power to depart from earlier decisions of domestic (and non-domestic) higher courts. Amendments which would have removed the Ministerial power to allow lower courts to depart from retained EU case law, or alternatively would have required lower courts minded to depart from such case law to refer the matter to the Supreme Court or High Court of Justiciary, were agreed by the House of Lords but ultimately rejected by the House of Commons: see *Hansard*, HC, 22 January 2020, cols 338-346.

172 EU(W)A Sch 1, para 1(1). This exclusion will not apply where the CJEU decided before the end of the implementation period that the EU instrument is invalid, or where there is secondary legislation allowing for such a challenge: EU(W)A Sch 1, para 1(2)-(3). There is now secondary legislation which allows for the continuation of challenges that were begun but not finally decided in a domestic court or tribunal before the end of the implementation period: Challenges to Validity of EU Instruments (EU Exit) Regulations 2019, reg 3, read alongside the EU(WA)A 2020, Sch 5, para 1(1). The EU(W)A Sch 1, para 1(1) exclusion will also not apply in relation to proceedings begun, but not finally determined, before a domestic court or tribunal before the end of the implementation period, or in relation to conduct which occurred before that date which gives rise to criminal liability: EU(W)A Sch 8, para 39(3)-(4).

173 EU(W)A Sch 1, para 3(1). A three-year grace period is, however, given for proceedings relating to matters that occurred before the end of the implementation period, provided they are not for the disapplication or quashing of Act of Parliament or rule of law, or anything else which could not have been different, or which gives effect to or enforces, an Act of Parliament or rule of law: EU(W)A Sch 8, para 39(5). The exclusion also will not apply in

(3) No court or tribunal may disapply or quash any enactment or other rule of law, or quash any conduct or otherwise decide that it is unlawful, because it is incompatible with any of the general principles of EU law.[174]

(4) There will be no right to *Francovich* damages in respect of a public body's failure to comply with EU law.[175]

7–045 Retained data protection law

At the end of the implementation period, although the GDPR will no longer apply directly to and in the UK,[176] the new body of retained EU law will include the GDPR,[177] as well as Chapters 2 and 3 of Part 2 and Part 3 of the DPA 2018.[178] Without modification, these retained laws would make little sense, not least because they would refer to EU institutions, procedures and decisions that will no longer be directly relevant to the UK's data protection regime.[179]

7–046 DPPEC Regulations 2019

The Data Protection, Privacy and Electronic Communications (Amendments etc) (EU Exit) Regulations 2019 – the DPPECR – were made on 28 February 2019 pursuant to powers conferred by s 8 of the EU(W)A, s 211(2) of the DPA 2018 and s 2(2) of the ECA 1972. At the end of the implementation period,[180] the Regulations will make the following changes in an

---

relation to proceedings begun, but not finally determined, before a domestic court or tribunal before the end of the implementation period, or in relation to conduct which occurred before day which gives rise to criminal liability: EU(W)A Sch 8, para 39(3)-(4). General principles will still have a bearing on the interpretation of retained EU law: see §7–043 above.

174 EU(W)A Sch 1, para 3(2). This exclusion will not apply in relation to decisions that are a necessary consequence of a decision made before the end of the implementation period, or of a decision made on or after that day on this basis: EU(W)A Sch 8, para 39(6). It also will not apply in relation to proceedings begun, but not finally determined, before a domestic court or tribunal before the end of the implementation period, or in relation to conduct which occurred before that day which gives rise to criminal liability: EU(W)A Sch 8, para 39(3)-(4). General principles will still have a bearing on the interpretation of retained EU law: see §7–043 above.

175 EU(W)A Sch 1, para 4. A two-year grace period is given, however, for claims relating to matters that occurred before the end of the implementation period: EU(W)A Sch 8, para 39(1), (7). The exclusion also will not apply in relation to proceedings begun, but not finally determined, before a domestic court or tribunal before the implementation period, or in relation to conduct that occurred before that date which gives rise to criminal liability: EU(W)A Sch 8, para 39(3)-(4).

176 The full and final repeal of the ECA 1972, by EU(W)A ss 1A and 1B, will remove the domestic basis for the GDPR's effect in UK law. As a matter of EU law, the GDPR will cease to apply to the UK by virtue of the operation of Art 50(3) TEU, as augmented by Arts 126-127 of the re-revised Withdrawal Agreement (19 October 2019).

177 During the passage of the DPA 2018 through Parliament, the Government indicated that the EU(W)A is intended to capture the 'full text' of the GDPR, including its recitals: *Hansard*, HL, 13 November 2017, vol 785, col 1907; HL, 13 December 2017, vol 787, col 1658. The Government's assertion that the EU(W)A will 'firmly entrench' the GDPR in UK law is somewhat misleading, given that retained EU law can be repealed or amended by Government ministers in exercise of the powers conferred by s 8: see *Hansard*, HC, 13 March 2018, col 12; HL, 11 December 2017, vol 787, col 1385.

178 As direct EU legislation under EU(W)A s 3 and as EU-derived UK law under EU(W)A s 2, respectively. The latter is an example of 'preserved legislation' which is not dependent for its existence on the ECA 1972, or indeed the EU(W)A, as referred to in §7–041(2) above. It will retain its status as primary legislation under EU(W)A s 7(1). The GDPR constitutes 'retained direct principal EU legislation' for the purposes of amendment, under EU(W)A s 7(2) and (6).

179 During the implementation period, these issues are resolved by the glosses in EU(W)A s 1B and EU (Withdrawal Agreement) Act 2020, Sch 5.

180 The Data Protection, Privacy and Electronic Communications (Amendments etc) (EU Exit) Regulations 2019 ('DPPECR'), reg 1(2), provides that the relevant regulations come into force on exit day. The EU (Withdrawal Agreement) Act 2020, Sch 5, para 1(1) provides that, where subordinate legislation made before exit day under the EU(W)A which provides that all or part of the legislation is to come into force on exit day, this is to be read instead as providing that the legislation comes into force on 'IP completion day' (defined in s 39(1) of that Act to mean 31 December 2020at 23:00hrs GMT).

effort to ensure that the UK data protection regime continues to function correctly on and after that date:[181]

(1) They will 'merge' the two existing regimes for general processing, namely (i) the EU GDPR, which will be retained in UK law by s 3 of the EU(W)A and (ii) the applied GDPR, as established in Chapter 3 of Part 2 of the DPA 2018.[182] Together, these regimes will be termed the 'UK GDPR.'[183] Substantial divergences between the two regimes will remain, however, as the applied GDPR is presently outside the scope of EU competences, and thus EU case law and general principles will not be relevant to its interpretation and application.[184]

(2) They will correct deficiencies in the UK GDPR and the DPA 2018, and make consequential changes to other primary and secondary legislation, including by replacing references to EU Member States, institutions, procedures and decisions with references to UK equivalents[185] and by replacing references to the GDPR with references to the UK GDPR.[186]

(3) They will revoke certain directly applicable EU instruments, including Commission decisions on the adequacy of third countries and on standard contractual clauses, and Regulation 2018/1725 on the processing of personal data by EU institutions, which would otherwise be retained under s 3 of the EU(W)A.[187]

This work has dealt with data protection law as it stands on 1 February 2020. Substantial changes are supposed to take effect on 31 December 2020 at 23:00hrs GMT.[188]

---

181 Explanatory Memorandum §2.1. In addition to this, on 29 March 2019, the DPPECR regs 1(3) and 8 inserted into the Privacy and Electronic Communications Regulations 2003 the definition of 'consent' currently used in the GDPR, as defined in s 3(10) of the DPA 2018.

182 DPPECR Schs 1-2.

183 DPA Sch 21, as inserted by DPPECR Sch 2, para 102.

184 DPPECR reg 5; EU(W)A s 6.

185 References to 'Union or Member State law' will be changed to 'domestic law', 'supervisory authority' to 'the Commissioner', and 'Member States' to 'the UK:' DPPECR Schs 1-2. Functions conferred on the European Commission by the GDPR will be transferred to the Secretary of State and/or the Information Commissioner: see eg DPPECR Sch 1, paras 38 (decisions on the adequacy of third countries) and 39 (approval of standard data protection clauses). The Information Commissioner's various obligations to cooperate with the supervisory authorities of other Member States will also be removed: DPPECR Sch 1, para 55.

186 DPPECR Sch 3, Pts 2-4.

187 DPPECR Sch 3, Pt 1. The power to make adequacy decisions, and to approve standard data protection clauses, will be transferred to the Information Commissioner and the Secretary of State, respectively: DPPECR Sch 1, paras 38 and 39. The UK Government has said that it will endeavour to adopt its adequacy decisions as soon as possible, and in any event by the end of 2020: Political Declaration on the Future Relationship between the EU and the UK (19 October 2019) §9.

188 See the final paragraph of the Preface to this work.

CHAPTER 8

GDPR and DPA 2018: introduction

1. OVERVIEW

8–001 Introduction

With effect from 25 May 2018, the legislative regime in the United Kingdom governing data protection ceased to be Directive 95/46/EC and the DPA 1998 and became the GDPR, the Law Enforcement Directive ('the LED')[1] and the DPA 2018.[2] The GDPR is a regulation of the European Parliament and of the Council.[3] Being a regulation of the EU, the GDPR is directly

---

[1] Directive 2016/680.

[2] GDPR Art 99(2); DPA 2018 s 212; Data Protection Act 2018 (Commencement No 1 and Transitional and Saving Provisions) Regulations 2018 (SI 2018/625) reg 2.

[3] The source of the power to make the GDPR is Art 16 of the TFEU, which provides:
'1. Everyone has the right to the protection of personal data concerning them.
2. The European Parliament and the Council, acting in accordance with the ordinary legislative procedure, shall lay down the rules relating to the protection of individuals with regard to the processing of personal data by Union institutions, bodies, offices and agencies, and by the Member States when carrying out activities which fall within the scope of Union law, and the rules relating to the free movement of such data. Compliance with these rules shall be subject to the control of independent authorities.

applicable in Member States.[4] A regulation does not always require a Member State to pass legislation to give its provisions legal effect within that Member State. A regulation may, however, contain provisions empowering each Member State to pass its own implementing measures or conferring on each Member State legislative latitude – which may be limited to derogations – on specific aspects covered by the regulation.[5] The GDPR adopted the permissive approach, conferring on each Member State a considerable degree of legislative latitude on a range of matters covered by it.[6]

8– 002 The new regime

Under the new regime, the processing of personal data in the United Kingdom is divided into four separate regulatory sectors:

(1) Intelligence services processing of personal data. This sector is governed by Part 4 of the DPA 2018 (ss 82-108). The GDPR has no role. This is dealt with in Chapters 8 and 14.

(2) Processing of personal data by competent authorities for law enforcement purposes. This is governed by Part 3 of the DPA 2018 (ss 29-81), which implements the LED in the United Kingdom. The GDPR has no role. This sector is dealt with in Chapters 8, 12 and 13.

Processing of personal data that is not within (1) or (2) is termed 'general processing.' There are two separate sectors dealing with general processing:

(3) Processing of personal data that falls within the GDPR.[7] This sector is governed by the GDPR as supplemented by Chapters 1-2 of Part 2 of the DPA 2018 (ss 4-20). This is dealt with in Chapters 8-11.

(4) Processing of personal data that falls outside the GDPR. The GDPR has no direct role, but it is applied with modifications by Chapter 3 of Part 2 of the DPA 2018 (ss 21-28). This sector, too, is dealt with in Chapters 8-11.

Most processing of personal data within the United Kingdom is general processing and falls within the third of the above sectors. It follows that the GDPR, as supplemented by the DPA 2018, governs most processing of personal data in the United Kingdom.

8– 003 Objectives of the GDPR

The objectives of the GDPR are stated to be:

> ...to protect the fundamental rights and freedoms of natural persons and in particular their right to the protection of personal data and to ensure the free movement of personal data within the [European] Union[8]

The rules adopted on the basis of this Article shall be without prejudice to the specific rules laid down in Article 39 of the Treaty on European Union.'

4 TFEU Art 288. By contrast, a directive, such as 95/46/EC, while binding as to the result to be achieved and requiring the Member State to legislate within a prescribed period to give effect to the directive, leaves to each Member State the choice of the most suitable form and method of doing so. Upon incorporation into the EEA Agreement (6 July 2018), the GDPR became applicable in Iceland, Liechtenstein and Norway.

5 These are often termed 'opening clauses.'

6 See especially GDPR Art 23(1) (restricting the rights of data subjects in certain circumstances), but also Arts 4(7) (definition of 'controller'), 6(2) (allowing a Member State to determine when processing is necessary in the public interest or to carry out a statutory function), 8(1), 9(2)(a), (g), (h), (i), (j), 9(4), 10, 14(5)(c), 17(1)(e), 17(3)(b), 18(2), 22(2)(b) (allowing a Member State to limit controls on automated decision-making and profiling), 26(1), 28(3)(a), (g), 29, 32(4), 35(10), 36(5), 37(4) (dealing with data protection officers), 38(5) and 88 (data processing under employment contracts).

7 The GDPR applies to personal data processed by automated means and, where personal data is processed by other than automated means, where the personal data forms part of a filing system. As to the meaning of these terms, see §§8– 040 to 8– 041.

8 GDPR recital (166).

and

> to ensure an equivalent level of protection of natural persons and the free flow of personal data throughout the [European] Union[9]

Article 1 of the GDPR further provides for its subject-matter and objectives:

> 1. This Regulation lays down rules relating to the protection of natural persons with regard to the processing of personal data and rules relating to the free movement of personal data.
> 2. This Regulation protects fundamental rights and freedoms of natural persons and in particular their right to the protection of personal data.
> 3. The free movement of personal data within the Union shall be neither restricted nor prohibited for reasons connected with the protection of natural persons with regard to the processing of personal data.

The GDPR is thus the confluence of two objectives: the rights and freedoms of natural persons to the protection of their personal data;[10] and the removal of impediments to the free movement of the personal data. Notably, the GDPR aims to ensure a 'high'[11] level of protection for the former. Those fundamental rights and freedoms are enshrined in Article 8(1) of the Charter of Fundamental Rights[12] and in Article 16(1) of the TFEU.[13]

8–004 Continuing obligations

The GDPR imposes on each 'controller'[14] a continuing obligation to comply with six principles relating to the processing of personal data:[15]

(1) Personal data must be processed lawfully, fairly and in a transparent manner in relation to the data subject – 'lawfulness, fairness and transparency.'[16]

(2) Personal data shall be collected only for specified, explicit and legitimate purposes, and not further processed in a manner that is incompatible with those purposes – 'purpose limitation.'[17]

(3) Personal data shall be adequate, relevant and limited to what is necessary in relation to the purposes for which they are processed – 'data minimisation.'[18]

(4) Personal data processed shall be accurate and, where necessary, kept up to date – 'accuracy.'[19]

(5) Personal data shall be kept in a form which permits identification of data subjects for no longer than is necessary for the purposes for which the personal data are processed – 'storage limitation.'[20]

(6) Personal data shall be processed in a manner that ensures appropriate security of the personal data, including protection against unauthorised or unlawful processing and against accidental loss, destruction or damage, using appropriate technical or

---

9 GDPR recital (170).

10 As to the meaning of 'rights and freedoms of natural persons' in this context, see §8– 006.

11 GDPR recitals (6) and (10).

12 As to which, see §§7– 019 to 7– 023.

13 As to which, see §7– 025.

14 The equivalent of the 'data controller' in the DPA 1998. As to the meaning of 'controller,' see further §8– 019.

15 GDPR Art 5.

16 Considered further at §§9– 006 to 9– 022.

17 Considered further at §§9– 023 to 9– 027.

18 Considered further at §9– 028.

19 Considered further at §§9– 029 to 9– 030.

20 Considered further at §§9– 031 to 9– 033.

organisational measures – 'integrity and confidentiality.'[21]

The obligation to comply with these six processing principles is called 'accountability.'[22] In addition to the obligation to comply with these processing principles, there are three other sets of continuing obligations which may or may not arise according to the type of processing being carried out and to the type of organisation that is the controller or processor:

— Additional obligations imposed on a controller processing sensitive personal information.[23]
— Obligations relating to the set up and internal organisation of a controller or processor.[24] These depend on the size of the controller or processor.
— Obligations engaged by the international transfer of personal data.[25]

Non-compliance with, or an inability to demonstrate compliance with, any of these obligations exposes the controller both to regulatory action (through the Information Commissioner)[26] and to a private law claim from the individual to whom the personal data relates.[27]

8– 005 Data subject rights

In addition to the continuing obligations, the GDPR confers on every individual seven conditional rights in respect of processing of his or her personal data, all but one of which is engaged by the individual giving a notice to the controller, who then becomes subject to a correlative obligation to comply with that notice:[28]

(1) A right of access, which comprises confirmation by the controller whether or not personal data concerning the data subject are being processed and, if so, being informed of the purposes of the processing, the categories of personal data concerned, the recipients to whom the personal data have been or will be disclosed, the period for which the personal data will be stored, the source of the data (if it is not the data subject) and certain other information.[29]

(2) A right of rectification, which comprises the right to obtain from a controller rectification of inaccurate personal data concerning the data subject, including completion of incomplete personal data.[30]

(3) A right of erasure (sometimes termed 'the right to be forgotten'), which comprises the right to obtain from a controller the erasure of personal data concerning the data subject.[31]

(4) A right to restrict processing (other than storage) of personal data.[32]

(5) A right to data portability, which comprises a right to receive personal data relating to the data subject in a machine-readable format and the right to transmit that data

---

21 Considered further at §§9– 034 to 9– 039.

22 GDPR Art 5(2) and recital (85).

23 Considered further at §§9– 040 to 9– 047. As to the meaning of 'sensitive personal information' see §9– 040.

24 Considered further at §§9– 048 to 9– 056.

25 Considered further at §§9– 057 to 9– 064.

26 GDPR Art 77. Regulatory enforcement is considered at §§48– 014 to 48– 055.

27 GDPR Art 79. Private law claims are considered at §§48– 005 to 48– 013.

28 GDPR Art 12. The exception is the right against automated decision-making. This does not require a notice but subsists whenever a controller is processing the personal data of a data subject.

29 GDPR Art 15. Considered further at §§10– 014 to 10– 017.

30 GDPR Arts16 and 19. Considered further at §§10– 018 to 10– 022.

31 GDPR Arts 17 and 19. Considered further at §§10– 023 to 10– 028.

32 GDPR Arts18 and 19. Considered further at §§10– 029 to 10– 034.

to another controller.[33]

(6) A right to object to processing of a data subject's personal data and to compel cessation of that processing.[34]

(7) A right to prevent automated decision-making, including profiling.[35]

Non-compliance with the obligation triggered by engagement of the right exposes the controller both to regulatory action and to a private law claim from the individual.[36]

8–006 **Rights and freedoms of persons**

The original treaties of the European Economic Community did not contain any references to fundamental rights and their protection.[37] As the objectives of the EEC were primarily economic, it was unnecessary to do so. Moreover, the ECHR appeared to offer adequate protection. However, the CJEU gradually absorbed elements from various international treaties, including the ECHR, to produce a body of 'fundamental rights and freedoms' upon which it asserted the Community legal order was premised. From this stems the characterisation of the central objective of the GDPR – like Directive 95/46/EC before it[38] – namely, to protect fundamental rights and freedoms of natural persons, and in particular their right to the protection of personal data.[39] This central objective is now independent of, and is not coincident with, the right to the protection of personal privacy. Although a set of facts and circumstances may contravene both the right to privacy and the right to the protection of personal data, the obligations imposed and rights conferred by the GDPR do not turn on there being a breach of personal privacy.[40] The existence of an individual's right to the protection of personal data concerning him or her that is separate from the right to respect for an individual's private and family life, home and communication – which embodies a right to personal privacy that includes personal information[41] – is acknowledged in the Charter.[42] The

---

33 GDPR Art 20. Considered further at §§10–035 to 10–039.

34 GDPR Art 21. Considered further at §§10–040 to 10–044.

35 GDPR Art 22. Considered further at §§10–045 to 10–048.

36 GDPR Arts 77 and 79. Regulatory enforcement is considered at §§48–014 to 48–055. Private law claims are considered at §§48–005 to 48–013.

37 See further §7–018.

38 Directive 95/46/EC had used the same phrase and balancing device, expressly recognising 'the right to privacy' as one of those rights and freedoms: see Arts 1(1), 7(f), 18(2), 20(1), 28(4) and 30(1)(c) and recitals (2), (7), (8), (9), (10), (11), (30), (46), (49), (53) and (68). That Directive expressly linked 'rights and freedoms' of natural persons to the ECHR Art 8 and general principles of Community law and to Convention 108: see recitals (10) and (11) respectively.

39 GDPR Art 1(2). The centrality of protecting fundamental rights and freedoms of natural persons and in particular their right to the protection of personal data is borne out by the repeated reference to this concept in the GDPR recitals: see (2), (9), (10), (16), (47), (51), (54), (68), (69), (73)-(81), (84)-(86), (89), (91), (94), (98), (113), (137), (156), (162), (166) and (173). And see also: *Google Spain SL v Agencia Espanola de Proteccion de Datos* (C-131/12) [2014] QB 1022 at [53]; *Puškár v Finančné riaditeľstvo Slovenskej* (C-73/16) [2017] 4 WLR 209, [2018] 1 CMLR 44 at [38]; *Buivids v Latvia* (C-345/17) [2019] 1 WLR 4225, [2019] 2 CMLR 24 at [45]; *Tietosuojavaltuutettu v Jehovan todistajat* (C-25/17) [2019] 4 WLR 1, [2019] 1 CMLR 5 at [35]; *Unabhangiges Landeszentrum fur Datenschutz Schleswig-Holstein v Wirtschaftsakademie Schleswig-Holstein GmbH* (C-210/16) [2018] 3 CMLR 32, [2019] 1 WLR 119 at [87]; *Fashion ID GmbH & Co KG v Verbraucherzentrale NRW eV* (C-40/17), CJEU, 29 July 2019 at [50].

40 The GDPR does not once use the word 'privacy.' In this way, the protection afforded by the GDPR may be seen to be more extensive than that afforded by ECHR Art 8 (which, in this sphere, is concerned with the protection of personal privacy).

41 And similarly under ECHR Art 8, see for example: *Klass v Germany* (1979-80) 2 EHRR 214 (interception of communications); *A v France* (1993) 17 EHRR 462 (interception of telephone); *Peck v United Kingdom* (2003) 36 EHRR 41, 13 BHRC 669 (CCTV images); *Perry v United Kingdom* (2003) 39 EHRR 76 (covert surveillance at police station during interview with montage); *Rotaru v Romania* (2000) 8 BHRC 449 (retention of old surveillance records); *Z v Finland* (1997) 25 EHRR 371 (uninvited disclosure of medical records); *Malone v United Kingdom* (1985) 7 EHRR 14 (interception of mail and telephone and numbers called); *Szabo v Hungary* (2016) 63 EHRR 102 (legislation permitting personal surveillance); *Big Brother Watch v United Kingdom* [2018] ECHR 58170/13 (retention of personal

GDPR repeatedly uses this conception of the rights and freedoms of the individual, embodying the right to the protection of personal data, as a touchstone by which to measure the acceptability of specific issues and measures in the processing of personal data.[43]

8– 007 Risks to rights and freedoms

Many of the obligations imposed on controllers and processors by the GDPR involve a consideration of 'risks' to the 'rights and freedoms of natural persons,' with those rights and freedoms including their right to the protection of personal data.[44] The risks to those rights and freedoms from processing include physical, material and non-material damage.[45] Such damage expressly includes:

— resultant discrimination, identity theft or fraud, financial loss, damage to the reputation, loss of confidentiality of personal data protected by professional secrecy, unauthorised reversal of pseudonymisation, or any other significant economic or social disadvantage;
— where data subjects might be deprived of their rights and freedoms or prevented from exercising control over their personal data;
— where personal data are processed which reveal racial or ethnic origin, political opinions, religion or philosophical beliefs, trade union membership, and the processing of genetic data, data concerning health or data concerning sex life or criminal convictions and offences or related security measures;
— where personal aspects are evaluated, in particular analysing or predicting aspects concerning performance at work, economic situation, health, personal preferences or interests, reliability or behaviour, location or movements, in order to create or use personal profiles;
— where personal data of vulnerable natural persons, in particular of children, are processed; and
— where processing involves a large amount of personal data and affects a large number of data subjects.[46]

The 'risk' to the rights and freedoms of natural persons is the combination of the severity of impact of an occurrence upon the rights and freedoms of natural persons and the likelihood of that occurrence. Risk is to be measured on the basis of an objective assessment.[47]

8– 008 European Data Protection Board

data for law enforcement purposes); *In re Gallagher* [2019] UKSC 3, [2019] 2 WLR 509 (disclosure of spent convictions to employer); *Segerstedt-Wiberg v Sweden* (2006) 44 EHRR 14, 21 BHRC 155 at [72] (information recording participation of an individual at a public demonstration); *MM v United Kingdom* [2012] ECHR 1906 at [188] (record of conviction); *B v General Medical Council* [2018] EWCA Civ 1497, [2019] 2 All ER219 (professional criticism of individual); *R (C) v Secretary of State for Work and Pensions* [2017] UKSC 72, [2017] 1 WLR 4127 (computer record of individual's gender history). But contrast: *In Re JR38* [2015] UKSC 42, [2016] AC 1131.

42 As to the Charter, see further §§7– 019 to 7– 033. It is for this reason that the authorities speak of the fundamental rights (plural) to privacy and to the protection of personal data: *GC v Commission nationale de l'informatique et des liberté* (C-136/17) [2019] All ER (D) 66 (Sep) at [37], [44], [46], [59], [67], [68]; *Tietosuojavaltuutettu v Jehovan todistajat* (C-25/17) [2019] 4 WLR 1, [2019] 1 CMLR 5 at [18]; *Puškár v Finančné riaditeľstvo Slovenskej* (C-73/16) [2017] 4 WLR 209, [2018] 1 CMLR 44 at [30]; *Tele2 Sverige AB v Post-och telestyrelsen* (C-203/15) [2017] QB 771, [2017] 2 CMLR 30 at [93].

43 GDPR Arts 5(1)(e), 6(1)(f), 9(2)(i), 10, 14(5)(b), 15(4), 20(4), 21(1), 22(2)(b), (3), (4), 23(1), (2), 24(1), 25(1), 27(2)(a), 30(5), 32(1), 33(1), 34(1), (3)(b), 35(1), 35(7)(c), 36(3)(c), 49(1), 50(b), 51(1), 57(1)(c), 66(1), (3), 80(1), 87, 88(1) and 89(1).

44 GDPR Art 1(2) and recitals (2) and (9).

45 GDPR recital (75).

46 GDPR recital (75).

47 GDPR recital (76).

Up to 25 May 2018 the Article 29 Working Party – 'Art 29 WP' – had been the independent European working party that dealt with issues relating to the protection of privacy and personal data. It was an advisory body made up of a representative from the data protection authority of each EU Member State, the European Data Protection Supervisor and the European Commission. The Art 29 WP produced various working papers that dealt with issues arising in data protection. On 25 May 2018, with the coming into force of the GDPR, the Art 29 WP was replaced by the European Data Protection Board – 'the EDPB.' During its first plenary meeting the EDPB endorsed all of the Art 29 WP working papers, which serve as guidance on the operation of the GDPR.

8–009 DPA 2018

The DPA 2018 supplements the processing of personal data that is covered by the GDPR, implements the Law Enforcement Directive – the LED – in the UK, and deals with processing of personal data that is not covered by the GDPR. The combined effect of the DPA 2018 and the GDPR is to create a regime that covers the field of data protection in the United Kingdom. In summary, the DPA 2018 splits the field of data protection into four sectors, each of which it treats separately. Starting with the most specific, these four sectors are:

(1) Processing of personal data by the intelligence services – 'intelligence services processing.' This is a topic that is not within the legislative competence of the EU legislator, hence not covered by either the GDPR or the LED. The principal provisions dealing with processing of personal data by the intelligence services are in Part 4 of the DPA 2018 (ss 82-108). This is the sector in which an individual's rights are most abbreviated and, correlatively, the controller is most free to process personal data without legislative constraint.[48]

(2) Processing of personal data by competent authorities for law enforcement purposes – 'law enforcement processing.' The GDPR is inapplicable to this processing. The principal provisions in the DPA 2018 dealing with this processing are in Part 3 (ss 29-81). These provisions represent the domestic implementation of the LED, which was required to be transposed into domestic law by 6 May 2018.[49] Although an individual's rights are abbreviated, their reduction is not as marked as in relation to processing of personal data by the intelligence services.[50]

(3) General processing (ie processing that is not within (1) or (2) above) that:
   (a) is outside the scope of EU law; and
   (b) that is processing by a Member State when carrying on an activity that falls within the EU's common foreign and security policy,[51]

   or that involves processing by a public authority without using automated means or a filing system – 'applied GDPR processing.' For this processing, the DPA 2018 applies a modified GDPR, which it terms the 'applied GDPR.'[52] The principal provisions are ss 21-28 of the DPA, together with the applicable Schedules.[53]

(4) Processing governed by the GDPR: in other words, all processing of personal data not within (1), (2) or (3) above – 'general processing.' As previously noted, most processing of personal data falls within this sector. In this sector, the DPA 2018 exercises for the United Kingdom the legislative latitude conferred on each Member

48 See Chapter 14.

49 LED Art 63.

50 See Chapters 12-13.

51 That is, within Chapter 2 of Title V of the TEU: see GDPR Art 2(2)(b).

52 DPA 2018 s 3(11).

53 See Chapters 9-11.

State by the GDPR. The Act does not displace, supplant or override the GDPR. To the extent that processing of personal data is governed by the GDPR, the DPA 2018 supplements, and must be read with, the GDPR.[54] The principal provisions are ss 4-20 of the DPA 2018, together with the applicable Schedules. In practice, for most controllers that are not public authorities, general processing covered by the GDPR will be the only processing with which they will be concerned.[55]

Collectively, the four sectors may be called 'the data protection regime.' The DPA 2018 also deals with the Information Commissioner and with the enforcement – by the Information Commissioner and the courts – of the GDPR and DPA 2018.[56]

2. TERMINOLOGY

8–010 Introduction

As with the DPA 1998, the data protection regime employs a number of key terms that are critical to an understanding of its operation:

— The *individual* whose interests are protected by the regime is the 'data subject,' who is an 'identified or identifiable natural person.'

— The *activity* regulated by the regime is called 'processing.'

— The *matter* the processing of which is regulated by the regime is called 'personal data,' being 'information relating to' a data subject.

— The principal *person* whose activity is regulated by the regime is called the 'controller.'[57] This is the person who determines the processing carried out on the personal data. A lesser degree of regulation is imposed on a 'processor,' being the person who processes personal data as instructed by the controller.

— The *standard* of processing required by the regime is prescribed by a set of continuing 'obligations' which persist throughout the processing. The obligations include adherence to a set of 'processing principles.'

— A data subject has *rights* which, apart from enforcing adherence to the obligations and requirements in relation to automated decision-making, are triggered by giving notice to the controller.

The definition given to these and other terms varies according to the applicable regulatory sector: that is, whether the processing in question constitutes 'general processing,' 'law enforcement processing,' or 'intelligence services processing.' In addition, within each of the four sectors certain terminology is used that is unique to that sector. The terms considered below are common to two or more of the sectors, with any differences footnoted. Terminology that is unique to a particular sector in the relevant chapter.[58]

8–011 Identified or identifiable persons

The obligations imposed and the rights conferred by the data processing regime are imposed and conferred for the benefit of 'identified or identifiable natural persons' only.[59] Accordingly,

---

54 DPA 2018 s 4(2)(b).

55 See Chapters 9-11.

56 DPA 2018 Parts 5 and 6.

57 Called the 'data controller' in the DPA 1998.

58 In relation to law enforcement processing, see §§12– 006 to 12– 010. In relation to intelligence services processing, see §§14– 002 to 14– 003.

59 GDPR Art 4(1) and recital (26) and DPA s 3(5), applying to all sectors. This is also the approach taken in Convention 108 Mod. A different approach is taken by the ePrivacy Directive, Art 1(2) and recital (7).

the obligations are not imposed and the rights are not conferred for the benefit of deceased natural persons nor for the benefit of non-natural persons such as companies or other corporate legal persons.[60] An 'identified natural person' is a person who, from the information in question, is revealed with sufficient particularity – a person's name with postal address is the most obvious means. An 'identifiable natural person' is

> one who can be identified, directly or indirectly, in particular by reference to an identifier such as a name, an identification number, location data, an online identifier or to one or more factors specific to the physical, physiological, genetic, mental, economic, cultural or social identity of that natural person.[61]

The definition does not expressly identify by whom the person must be capable of being identified. It is not necessary that all the information enabling the identification of the person be in the hands of one person.[62] Whether a person is or is not capable of being identified is decided at a practical, rather than theoretical, level.[63] Thus, if assembling the separate items of information that is needed to identify the individual is prohibited by law or is

> practically impossible on account of the fact that it requires a disproportionate effort in terms of time, cost and man-power, so that the risk of identification appears in reality to be insignificant

then the individual will not be identifiable from those separate items of information.[64] On the other hand, where a controller assembles items of data, none of which individually enables identification of an individual, but which is nominally attributed to a single person, at some point that assemblage will individuate to an individual: in other words, the assemblage will attain sufficient specificity to be able to be linked to an individual and, by having been added to the assemblage, each of the items of the information in it will be so linked.[65] Thus, in much the same way as a picture emerges as pieces are added to a jigsaw puzzle, information that might start out as not being information from which a natural person is identifiable may achieve that status that as further information is acquired even though the individual is not identifiable from any single item of the information.[66] A video image of an individual, with no other information identifying that individual but with sufficient clarity to make it possible to

---

60 GDPR recital (14) confirms that the GDPR applies to natural persons, ie individuals, only. GDPR recital (27) makes clear that the GDPR does not apply to deceased individuals, but expressly leaves up to Member States the ability to provide data protection law for the deceased.

61 GDPR Art 4(1) and DPA 2018 s 3(3), applying to all sectors.

62 GDPR recital (26); *Breyer v Federal Republic of Germany* (C-582/14) [2017] 1 WLR 1569 at [43].

63 GDPR recital (26) provides:

> To determine whether a natural person is identifiable, account should be taken of all the means reasonably likely to be used, such as singling out, either by the controller or by another person to identify the natural person directly or indirectly. To ascertain whether means are reasonably likely to be used to identify the natural person, account should be taken of all objective factors, such as the costs of and the amount of time required for identification, taking into consideration the available technology at the time of the processing and technological developments.

The language of 'all the means reasonably likely to be used… by the controller or by another person' also appeared in Directive 95/46/EC recital (26).

64 *Breyer v Federal Republic of Germany* (C-582/14) [2017] 1 WLR 1569 at [46]. Thus in *R (Department of Health) v Information Commissioner* [2011] EWHC 1430 (Admin), [2011] ACD 97 statistics about the grounds for the termination of pregnancies were held not to constitute personal data where the prospect of identification by a third party was 'extremely remote' (at [59]). See also: *IC v Magherafelt DC* [2012] UKUT 263 (AAC) at [37]-[40], [87]-[89]; *Craigdale Housing Association & ors v Scottish Information Commissioner* [2010] CSIH 43, 2010 SLT 655; *Information Commissioner v Miller* [2018] UKUT 229 (AAC) at [50]-[52].

65 *Vidal Hall v Google Inc* [2015] EWCA Civ 311, [2016] QB 1003 at [115], where browser generated information about an individual's internet usage, that neither named nor explicitly identified an individual, was collected by the search company and given a unique identifier based on the user's IP address, and where the court held that the collection was personal data.

66 See, for example: *R (Bridges) v Chief Constable of South Wales Police* [2019] EWHC 2341 (Admin) at [122]-[125].

identify the individual, will be information relating to an identifiable natural person.[67] Fingerprints, facial images, DNA information and other biometric data each individually constitute information from which a natural person is identifiable.[68] An internet protocol address[69] does not of itself identify a natural person but it may make the person 'identifiable,' particularly where it is fixed or static rather than dynamic.[70]

8– 012 **Anonymised data**

The data protection regime does not apply to 'anonymised' data.[71] Anonymised data is data that previously related to an identified or identifiable person but which, by a process being applied to that data, can no longer be related to an identified or identifiable person. Data may be anonymised so far as one person is concerned, but not so far as concerns another. For example, if A redacts names and all other identifying information from a copy of a document that A supplies to B, the information in that document is likely to be anonymous in the hands of B but not anonymous in the hands of A.[72] Whether a process has or has not been successful in anonymising what was personal data turns on whether that data, after the process has been completed, still relates to an identified or identifiable person.[73] Where personal data is anonymised for a particular purpose but the unanonymised version is retained, the former will remain information relating to an identifiable person, at least so far as concerns any person having access to the unanonymised information.[74]

8– 013 **Pseudonymised data**

The GDPR introduced the concept of 'pseudonymisation', which it defines to mean:

> the processing of personal data in such a manner that the personal data can no longer be attributed to a specific data subject without the use of additional information, provided that such additional information is kept separately and is subject to technical and organisational measures to ensure that the personal data are not attributed to an identified or identifiable

67 *Rynes v Urad pro ochranu osobnich udaju* (C-212/13) [2015] 1 WLR 2607, [2015] CEC 732 at [19]-[22]; *Buivids v Latvia* (C-345/17) [2019] 1 WLR 4225, [2019] 2 CMLR 24 at [31]-[32].

68 *Schwarz v Stadt Bochum* (C-291/12) [2013] 2 CMRL 5 at [27]-[30], [49]; *R (Bridges) v Chief Constable of South Wales Police* [2019] EWHC 2341 (Admin) at [58]-[62]; *S v United Kingdom* (30562/04) (2009) 48 EHRR 50, (2009) 25 BHRC 557 at [104].

69 An internet protocol address ('IP address') is a sequence of binary numbers which, when allocated to a device (a computer, a tablet or a smartphone), identifies it and allows it to access that electronic communications network. Internet service providers (generally, telephone companies) assign to their clients 'dynamic IP addresses' on a temporary basis, for each internet connection, and change them when subsequent connections are made. Those same companies keep a record of which IP address has been assigned, at any one time, to a particular device. Thus, it is possible for the individual's internet service provider, but no-one else, to link the IP address to an individual, unless, of course, the internet service provider gives that information to another person: *Productores de Musica de Espana (Promusicae) v Telefonica de Espana SAU* (C-275/06) [2008] 2 CMLR 17, [2008] IP&T 746 at [45].

70 *Scarlet Extended SA v Société belge des auteurs* (C-70/10) (2012) 31 BHRC 558, [2012] ECDR 4 at [51]; *Breyer v Federal Republic of Germany* (C-582/14) [2017] 1 WLR 1569 at [56]; *Benedik v Slovenia* [2018] ECHR 62357/14; *G v Wikimedia Foundation Inc* [2009] EWHC 3148, [2010] EMLR 14; *R (British Telecommunications plc & ors) v Secretary of State for Business, Innovation and Skills* [2011] EWHC 1021 (Admin), [2012] 3 CMLR 98 at [156].

71 GDPR recital (26). This accords with the approach taken by equity to protecting confidential information: *R v The Department of Health, ex p Source Informatics Ltd* [2000] 1 All ER 786, [2001] QB 424 at [34], [44]-[45].

72 *Common Services Agency v IC* [2008] UKHL 47, [2008] 1 WLR 1550; *R (Department of Health) v Information Commissioner* [2011] EWHC 1430 (Admin), [2011] ACD 97, [2011] Med LR 363 at [44]-[56].

73 As to which, see §8– 011. See also: *IC v Magherafelt DC* [2012] UKUT 263 (AAC). *R (Department of Health) v Information Commissioner* [2011] EWHC 1430 (Admin), [2011] ACD 97, [2011] Med LR 363 is better understood as a pseudonymized data case decided before the GDPR. *Common Services Agency v IC* [2008] UKHL 47, [2008] 1 WLR 1550 and *Information Commissioner v Miller* [2018] UKUT 229 (AAC) look at identifiability from the perspective of members of the public receiving the information.

74 *All Party Parliamentary Group on Extraordinary Rendition v IC and Ministry of Defence* [2011] UKUT 153 (AAC) at [127].

natural person.[75]

The technique is one in which a controller or processor with a body of data relating to a person separates that body of data into two parts, with one part having nothing within it that identifies that person but having within it a link (eg a unique number) to the other part, and the other part having the data from which the person is or can be identified. The first part is the pseudonymised personal data. For the purposes of the data processing regime, the pseudonymised personal data is still personal data in the hands of the controller or processor holding or having access to the other part.[76] As such, the GDPR applies to the pseudonymised personal data held by the controller or processor that holds or has access to the linked body of information. The process of pseudonymisation is intended to be a security measure so as to help controllers and processors comply with their data-protection obligations.[77] It achieves this where the first part – ie the pseudonymised personal data – is used for day-to-day processing and is more readily accessible, while the second part is made particularly secure. It follows from the description that the controller or processor will be able to reverse the process by re-joining the pseudonymised personal data to the linked personal data.[78] Whether or not pseudonymised personal data when held by a person other than the controller or processor with or without access to the linked information is personal data will depend on the thoroughness with which the pseudonymised personal data has been stripped of identifiers and the quantity of the pseudonymised personal data. These will determine the ease with which another person holding or having access to the pseudonymised personal data will be able to infer the identity of the person to whom it relates by correlating it with other data.

8–014 Meaning of 'relating to'

Personal data is defined to mean any information 'relating to' an identified or identifiable natural person.[79] Information will be relating to an identified or identifiable natural person 'where the information, by reason of its content, purpose or effect, is linked to a particular person.'[80]

---

75 This applies to general processing: GDPR Art 4(5) and DPA 2018 s 5(1). In relation to law enforcement processing, the same definition is in LED Art 3(5). This had been referred to in Art 29 WP Opinion 4/2007 (WP 136) at p 18. The process is one most common in medical research, an instance of which is the 'barnardisation' referred to in *Common Services Agency v IC* [2008] UKHL 47, [2008] 1 WLR 1550. There is a wealth of information about the process in the medical sphere: see, for example, T Neubauer and B Riedl, 'Improving Patient Privacy with Pseudonymization' in *Studies in Health Technology and Informatics*, vol 106, 2008, 691-698.

76 GDPR recital (26).

77 GDPR Arts 6(4)(e), 25(1), 32(1)(a), 40(2)(d), 89(1) and recitals (28)-(29), (78).

78 As is recognised in GDPR recitals (75), (85), (156).

79 GDPR Art 4(1). The DPA 1998 s 1(1) similarly defined 'personal data' to mean 'data which relate to a living individual.' This spawned a body of inconsistent domestic case law: *Durant v Financial Services Authority* [2003] EWCA Civ 1746, [2004] FSR 28; *Edem v IC and FSA* [2014] EWCA Civ 92; *Ittihadieh v 5-11 Cheyne Gardens RTM Co Ltd* [2017] EWCA 121, [2018] QB 256. For an analysis of these and other authorities under the DPA 1998, see §§15–023 to 15–026.

80 *Nowak v Data Protection Commissioner* (C-434/16) [2018] 1 WLR 3505, [2018] 2 CMLR 21 at [35]. See also *Ittihadieh v 5-11 Cheyne Gardens RTM Co Ltd* [2017] EWCA 121, [2018] QB 256 at [60]. The CJEU approach stems from Art 29 WP Opinion 4/2007 (WP 136) under which the requirement that the information 'relate to' an individual could be satisfied by a content element, a purpose element or a result element. The content element was satisfied if the content of the information on its face related to an individual. The purpose element was satisfied if the information was or was likely to be used with the specific purpose of evaluating, treating in a certain way or influencing the status or behaviour of an individual. The result element was satisfied when the use of information was likely to have an impact on an individual's rights or interests. *Nowak* concerned exam scripts: the exam questions were not the personal data of the candidate, but both completed scripts and examiner comments were: at [37]-[43] and [58].

8–015 Data subject

'Data subject' means the identified or identifiable living person to whom personal data relates.[81]

8–016 Personal data

Information is 'personal data' if it relates to an identified or identifiable living individual.[82] The scope of the definition is very wide. By way of example:

— a person's name and address will generally be personal data;[83]

— subject to questions of identification, a photographic image of an individual will be personal data;[84]

— information about an individual's date of birth, nationality, sex, ethnicity, religion and language, salary, an injury he has suffered, his working conditions or hobbies will be personal data;[85]

— information about an individual's bank account, including allegedly suspicious transactions, the reasons for those suspicions and information about meetings and decisions concerning the individual banking customer will be personal data.[86]

But it has been held that legal analysis of an individual's case was not personal data.[87]

8–017 Sensitive personal data

Over and above the general protections for personal data conferred by the GDPR and DPA 2018, two categories of personal data attract heightened protection by virtue of their sensitivity and potential impact on data subjects and their privacy.

(1) For the purposes of general processing, Article 9 of the GDPR defines 'special categories' of personal data:[88]

> personal data revealing racial or ethnic origin, political opinions, religious or philosophical beliefs, or trade union membership, and the processing of genetic data, biometric data for the purpose of uniquely identifying a natural person, data concerning health or data concerning a natural person's sex life or sexual orientation.[89]

'Genetic data', 'biometric data' and 'data concerning health' all have specific definitions.[90] The processing of special category personal data is prohibited[91] unless one of the lawful processing conditions under Article 9(2) of the GDPR or Schedule 1 to the DPA 2018 is satisfied.[92]

---

81 GDPR Art 4(1) and DPA 2018 s 3(5), applicable to all sectors of processing. In relation to law enforcement processing, see also LED Art 3(1). As to the meaning of 'data subject' under the DPA 1998, see §15– 033.

82 GDPR Art 4(1) and DPA 2018 s 3(2), applicable to all sectors of processing. In relation to law enforcement processing, see also LED Art 3(1). The definition of 'personal data' in the DPA 1998 had a like requirement. For the case law under the DPA 1998, see §§15– 020 to 15– 026.

83 *College van burgemeester en wethouders van Rotterdam v Rijkeboer* (C-553/07) [2009] 3 CMLR 28.

84 *Rynes v Urad pro ochranu osobnich udaju* (C-212/13) [2015] 1 WLR 2607, [2015] CEC 732.

85 *Ittihadieh v 5-11 Cheyne Gardens RTM Co Ltd* [2017] EWCA 121, [2018] QB 256 at [62]; *Rechnungshof v Österreichischer Rundfunk* (C-465/00) [2002] ECR I-4989, [2003] 3 CMLR 10; *Re Lindqvist (Approximation of Laws)* [2004] QB 1014.

86 *Lonsdale v National Westminster Bank Plc* [2018] EWHC 1843 (QB), [2019] Lloyd's Rep FC 94.

87 *YS v Minister voor Immigratie, Integratie en Asiel* (C-141/12) [2015] 1 WLR 609, [2015] 1 CMLR 18.

88 Article 9 is the successor to Article 8 of Directive 95/46/EC and s 2 DPA 1998 and the concept of 'sensitive personal data.' See §15– 028.

89 GDPR Art 9(1); see also recital (51).

90 GDPR Arts 4(13)-(15). See also recital (51).

91 GDPR Art 9(1).

92 See further DPA 2018 s 10(1)-(3).

(2) For the purposes of general processing, personal data 'relating to criminal convictions and offences or related security measures' is afforded special treatment by Article 10 of the GDPR. In the UK, such data includes data relating to 'the alleged commission of offences by the data subject' as well as data relating to 'proceedings for an offence committed or alleged to have been committed by the data subject or the disposal of such proceedings, including sentencing.'[93] Processing of such criminal convictions data may only be carried out 'under the control of official authority or when the processing is authorised by Union or Member State law providing for appropriate safeguards for the rights and freedoms of data subjects.'[94] In the UK, the lawful conditions for processing such data are set out in Schedule 1 DPA 2018.[95] Article 10 GDPR also provides that 'any comprehensive register of criminal convictions shall be kept only under the control of official authority.'

Determining whether personal data falls within these categories of heightened protection is a question of fact based on the circumstances of any given case.[96] The data must speak for itself in its immediate context; information which on the face of it is 'ordinary' personal data is not rendered special category personal data by virtue of other information which is in the public domain or by how some people would construe or misconstrue it.[97]

8–018 Processing

'Processing' means:

> any operation or set of operations which is performed on personal data or on sets of personal data, whether or not by automated means, such as collection, recording, organisation, structuring, storage, adaptation or alteration, retrieval, consultation, use, disclosure by transmission, dissemination or otherwise making available, alignment or combination, restriction, erasure or destruction.[98]

'Processing' is thus sufficiently wide to include passive activities, such as retaining, storing or holding information. In analysing compliance with data protection obligations, it is important

---

93 DPA 2018 s 11(2).

94 As to the meaning of 'rights and freedoms of natural persons' in this context, see §8– 006.

95 See further DPA 2018 s 10(5).

96 See *IC v Colenso-Dunne* [2015] UKUT 471 (AAC) at [37] as regards the DPA 1998.

97 *IC v Colenso-Dunne* [2015] UKUT 471 (AAC) at [45]-[46].

98 GDPR Art 4(2) and DPA 2018 s 3(4), applicable to all sectors of processing. In relation to law enforcement processing, see also LED Art 3(2). See also Convention 108 Mod Art 2(b). As to the meaning of 'processing' under DPA 1998, see §15– 029. Thus:
(1) In *Rynes v Urad pro ochranu osobnich udaju* (C-212/13) [2015] 1 WLR 2607, [2015] CEC 732, under the earlier regime, recording and storage of video surveillance footage was held to constitute 'processing.'
(2) In *Camera di Commercio, Industria, Artigianato e Agricoltura di Lecce v Manni* (C-398/15) [2018] Bus LR 25, [2017] 3 CMLR 18 each of transcribing, holding and communicating on request information on a company's register was held to constitute 'processing.'
(3) In *Re Lindqvist (Approximation of Laws)* [2004] QB 1014 each of referring on an internet page to an individual and giving that person's telephone number was held to constitute 'processing.'
(4) In *Google Spain SL v Agencia Espanola de Proteccion de Datos* (C-131/12) [2014] QB 1022 each of a search engine's automatic scouring of the internet and collecting of information, its organisation of that information, its retrieval and its making available of that information was held to constitute 'processing.'
(5) In *Campbell v Mirror Group Newspapers Ltd* [2002] EWCA Civ 1373, [2003] QB 633 the Court of Appeal observed that 'the definition of processing [in the DPA 1998] is so wide that it embraces the relatively ephemeral operations that will normally be carried out by way of the day-to-day tasks, involving the use of electronic equipment, such as the laptop and the modern printing press, in translating information into the printed newspaper' (at [122]).
(6) In *Tietosuojavaltuutettu v Satakunnan Markkinaporssi Oy* (C-73/07) [2008] ECR I-9831, [2010] All ER (EC) 213 at [35]-[49], the CJEU held that 'processing' includes collating information from publicly available documents held by a public authority, the provision of information on a CD-ROM and the provision of information via text message.

to identify the particular acts of processing in question. Although processing by automated means will form the great majority of processing of personal data, the GDPR also covers processing other than by automated means where the personal data forms part of a filing system or is intended to form part of a filing system.[99]

8–019 Controllers

A 'controller' is a:

> person or body which, alone or jointly with others, determines the purposes and means of the processing of personal data.[100]

The phrase 'purposes and means' is used in the GDPR as a composite phrase: thus, the regulatory regime cannot be escaped by allocating to one person the purposes of processing of personal data, and to another person the means of processing that personal data.[101] The obligations imposed under the data protection regime fall primarily on 'controllers' of personal data. Accordingly, whenever personal data is processed it is essential to identify the controller(s) for the relevant acts of processing. A controller may process personal data itself, or through a person or body acting on its behalf, eg by using a 'processor.' Individual employees and directors of companies (or other entities with separate legal personality) will not themselves be controllers, even where they in fact undertake the processing or make decisions about the processing. In those circumstances, the controller will be the company or other body, rather than the individual within the company or other body.[102] The same is true of administrators overseeing a liquidation.[103] Where personal data is processed only for the purposes and using the means required under an enactment, the person on whom the enactment imposes the requirement will be the controller.[104] Otherwise, the identification of a controller requires an assessment of the factual and legal arrangements by which personal data is processed. This is based on a factual rather than a formal analysis.[105] The term 'controller' must be construed broadly, so as to ensure effective protection of personal data.[106] A person can delegate the determination of the 'means' of processing to someone else, without ceasing to be a controller – at least as regards the technical and organisational measures (including data security measures) applied to the processing. Such 'means' of processing can be determined by processors rather than controllers. However, substantial questions that go to the heart of compliance with data protection obligations – such as what data is to be processed and how long it should be retained – are questions for controllers rather than processors. In its guidance[107] under the DPA 1998, the Information Commissioner expressed the view that the controller exercises overall control over the 'why' and the 'how' of a data processing activity.

---

99 GDPR Art 2(1). This definition is identical to the definition in Directive 95/46/EC Art 3(1). Under GDPR Art 4(6) a 'filing system' is any structured set of personal data which is accessible according to specific criteria, whether centralised, decentralised or dispersed on a function or geographical basis. See further §8– 028 and GDPR recital (15).

100 GDPR Art 4(7) and DPA 2018 s 5(1) in relation to general processing. In relation to law enforcement processing, a similar definition applies: DPA 2018 ss 3(6) and 32(1)-(2), and see LED Art 3(8). In relation to intelligence services processing a similar definition applies: DPA 2018 ss 3(6) and 83(1)-(2). See also Convention 108 Mod Art 2(d). Under the DPA 1998, the equivalent of the 'controller' was called a 'data controller.' As to the meaning of 'data controller' under the DPA 1998, see §§15– 030 to 15– 032.

101 See GDPR Arts 4(16), 26(1), 28(10) and 36(3)(b) and recitals (36) and (79). Such a split would result in the two persons being joint controllers: GDPR Art 26.

102 *Ittihadieh v 5-11 Cheyne Gardens RTM Co Ltd* [2017] EWCA 121, [2018] QB 256 at [70].

103 As regards the DPA 1998, see *Re Southern Pacific Personal Loans Ltd* [2013] EWHC 2485 (Ch), [2014] Ch 426 at [19].

104 DPA 2018 s 6(2).

105 Article 29 WP *Opinion 1/2010 on the concepts of 'controller' and 'processor'* (WP 169).

106 *Google Spain SL v Agencia Espanola de Proteccion de Datos* (C-131/12) [2014] QB 1022 at [34].

107 *Data controllers and data processors: what the difference is and what the governance implications are* (May 2014).

The Information Commissioner gave examples of the kinds of decisions that can only be taken by controllers and the kinds that can be delegated to processors.[108] Notable examples include the following:

(1) Google was held to be a controller as regards the processing of personal data through the delivery of search results through its search engine.[109] Google's search engine activities were distinct from the processing activities undertaken by the publishers whose websites were identified through Google searches about individuals. Google's search engine played a decisive role in the overall dissemination of the personal data available on the internet.

(2) A holder of a Facebook 'fan page' was held to be a controller of personal data processed by Facebook (including through the use of cookies placed by Facebook), even though the page holder had no access to that data.[110] This was because the fan page holder set processing parameters that influenced or contributed to the purposes and manner of Facebook's processing.

(3) The Jehovah's Witnesses Community was held to be a controller (jointly with its members who engage in preaching) with regard to the processing of personal data carried out by its members in the context of door-to-door preaching. The Jehovah's Witnesses Community had no access to the majority of that data and gave no written guidelines or instructions to its members, but it organised, coordinated and encouraged the preaching activities that entailed the processing of personal data.[111]

As appears from the above cases and from the definition of 'controller', a processing activity can have more than one controller. In circumstances of pluralistic control, the controllers may be 'joint controllers' who devise arrangements for the joint discharge of their data protection duties, or they may be independent controllers who each discharge their own duties. Pluralistic control does not, however, imply equality of responsibility: different controllers may be involved at different stages of the processing and to different degrees, giving rise to obligations that do not fully overlap.[112]

8– 020 Shared data processing

The processing of personal data for which a controller is responsible may, in practice, be carried out by or in conjunction with other parties with whom the controller works, rather than by the controller alone.[113] There are, broadly speaking, three types of arrangement by which the processing of particular personal data may be shared:

(1) First, a controller may sometimes share personal data with a third-party controller for use by the latter for its own legitimate purposes (albeit in many cases subject to restrictions on what the third party can do with that data). This may usefully be thought of as disclosure to an 'independent controller,'[114] because – provided the transfer itself is lawful – the disclosing controller's data protection duties end once the data is in the hands of the recipient controller. For the purposes of general

[108] *Data controllers and data processors: what the difference is and what the governance implications are* (May 2014) paras 16-18. Guidance documents issued under Directive 95/46/EC and the DPA 1998 remains relevant under the GDPR and DPA 2018. The same is true of cases decided under the old regime.

[109] *Google Spain SL v Agencia Espanola de Proteccion de Datos* (C-131/12) [2014] QB 1022.

[110] *Unabhangiges Landeszentrum fur Datenschutz Schleswig-Holstein v Wirtschaftsakademie Schleswig-Holstein GmbH* (C-210/16) [2018] 3 CMLR 32.

[111] *Tietosuojavaltuutettu v Jehovan todistajat* (C-25/17) [2019] 4 WLR 1, [2019] 1 CMLR 5 at [75].

[112] *Unabhangiges Landeszentrum fur Datenschutz Schleswig-Holstein v Wirtschaftsakademie Schleswig-Holstein GmbH* (C-210/16) [2018] 3 CMLR 32 at [43].

[113] In relation to joint processing under the DPA 1998, see §15– 031.

[114] This is not a statutory term, but may be useful for distinguishing this scenario from one of joint controllership.

processing, neither the GDPR nor the DPA 2018 imposes any specific governance arrangements on such disclosures. That is not to say, however, that disclosures to third party controllers can be made without regard to data protection principles. The disclosing controller must be able to demonstrate that its disclosure complies with the principles under Article 5(1) of the GDPR, including lawfulness, fairness and transparency. The disclosing controller's privacy notices must include information about any recipients or categories of recipients. Where the disclosure is justified by reference to the legitimate interests of the disclosing controller or the receiving controller, those interests must be identified.[115]

(2) Secondly, controllers very often use the services of processors[116] who undertake data processing activities on their behalf. A processor essentially processes personal data as an agent of the controller, rather than on its own terms or for its own purposes.[117] A controller is thus liable for the processing undertaken by its processor: for example, a subject access or erasure request made to a controller can encompass personal data being processed by processors on the controller's behalf, and a data subject can sue a controller for the acts and omissions of its processor.[118]

(3) Thirdly, a controller may sometimes share personal data with a third-party controller in circumstances where *both* remain to some extent in control of how that data is processed. In this situation, they are termed 'joint controllers.' Each of the three data protection regimes – general processing, law enforcement processing and security services processing – makes special provision for joint controllers.

8–021 Joint controllers

Article 26(1) of the GDPR provides that where two or more controllers jointly determine the purposes and means of processing, they are 'joint controllers.'[119] Unless their processing activities are dictated by EU or Member State law, joint controllers must determine their respective responsibilities as regards relationships with data subjects (including by the designation of a point of contact where appropriate) and for compliance with the GDPR (including the provision of transparency information).[120] Those responsibilities must be reflected in 'arrangements.' The joint controllers' arrangements need not be contractual, but they must be 'transparent', including by making them available to data subjects. Irrespective of those arrangements, however, data subjects remain entitled to exercise their rights against either or both controllers.[121] Thus, for example, if joint controllers decide that one controller will take responsibility for responding to subject access requests, this does not preclude a data subject from making a subject access request to the other controller.

8–022 Processors

A 'processor' is a:

> natural or legal person, public authority, agency or other body which processes personal data

---

[115] GDPR Arts 13(1)(d) and 14(2)(d).

[116] As to the meaning of a 'processor,' see §8– 022.

[117] See GDPR recitals (36) and (81).

[118] GDPR Art 82(1)-(2). In relation to applied GDPR processing, this is modified by DPA 2018 Sch 6 para 62.

[119] GDPR Art 26(1), which applies to general processing: DPA 2018 s 5(1). This is the also definition that applies for the purposes of law enforcement processing and the intelligence services processing: DPA 2018 ss 58(1) and 104, respectively.

[120] As to the transparency information, see §9– 017.

[121] GDPR Art 26(3). In relation to applied GDPR processing, this is modified by DPA 2018 Sch 6 para 22.

on behalf of the controller.[122]

A processor is effectively the agent of the controller: the latter – as principal – bears primary responsibility under data protection law.[123] The previous data protection regime imposed no duties on processors themselves. In contrast, the GDPR imposes certain duties on processors and exposes them to potential enforcement action.[124] A processor may only process personal data on instructions from the controller, unless the EU or Member State law requires the processor to do so.[125] There must be a contract governing the relationship between the controller and the processor.[126] The contract must include in particular the subject matter, nature, purpose and duration of the processing, the type of personal data and the categories of data subjects. It must also stipulate the controller's and the processor's obligations and rights, such as requirements regarding confidentiality and security.[127] Where a processor exceeds its authority to process personal data as set by the controller, the processor will become a controller – at the very least to the extent that it has exceeded its authority.[128] In this situation, the processor will almost certainly not have complied with the obligations that will apply to it as a controller. And the proper controller will be under an obligation to explain how it was possible for the processor to breach its mandate.[129] Guidance issued by the Information Commissioner under the previous regime suggests that a processor's activities:

> must be limited to the more 'technical' aspects of an operation, such as data storage, retrieval or erasure. Activities such as interpretation, the exercise of professional judgement or significant decision-making in relation to personal data must be carried out by a data controller.[130]

8–023 Controller-processor relationship

A controller may only use a processor who has provided sufficient guarantees to implement appropriate technical and organisational measures to ensure that personal data is processed in accordance with the requirements of the GDPR and to ensure the protection of the rights of the data subjects whose personal data will be processed.[131] In practice, a controller will need to have undertaken, and to be able to demonstrate having undertaken, due diligence of the data protection arrangements of every processor that it is using. The controller will need to ensure that that due diligence is current and to be able to demonstrate that it is current. A processor must not permit another processor to process personal data on behalf of a controller without prior written authorisation of the controller. The prior written authorisation may be specific or general.[132] A 'specific authorisation' means an authorisation identifying the other processor and the processing that that processor may carry out. A general authorisation does not require

122 GDPR Art 4(8) and DPA 2018 s 5(1) in relation to general processing. In relation to law enforcement processing, a similar definition applies: DPA 2018 ss 3(6) and 32(3), and see LED Art 3(9). In relation to intelligence services processing a similar definition applies: DPA 29018 ss 3(6) and 83(3). See also Convention 108 Mod Art 2(f).

123 If a processor exceeds its mandate, it will become a controller: GDPR Art 28(10).

124 See §9–005. Where a controller and a processor are involved in the same processing and are responsible for any damage caused by processing, each controller and processor will be liable for the entire damage: GDPR Art 82(4).

125 GDPR Art 29.

126 GDPR Art 28(3). The failure to have a contract is an infringement of the controller's obligation to keep written documentation of mutual responsibilities.

127 GDPR Art 28(3).

128 GDPR Art 28(10).

129 GDPR Art 82(2).

130 *Data controllers and data processors: what the difference is and what the governance implications are'* (May 2014), para 10.

131 GDPR Art 28(1) and DPA 2018 s 5(1) in relation to general processing.

132 GDPR Art 28(2).

that specificity, but before engaging a replacement or additional processor the existing processor must inform the controller of the identity of that additional or replacement processor in sufficient time for the controller to object to the engagement of that processor. Where a processor engages an additional or replacement processor, that engagement must be governed by a contract or some other 'legal act' enforceable by the controller.[133] That contract or other 'legal act' must stipulate that the processor will:[134]

(a) process the personal data only on documented instructions from the controller (unless there is a statutory or EU law requirement to process the personal data);[135]

(b) ensure that individuals authorised to process the personal data have either committed themselves to confidentiality or are under a statutory obligation of confidentiality;[136]

(c) implement appropriate technical and organisational measures to ensure a level of security appropriate to the risk, and will also take steps to ensure that any individual acting on the authority of the processor who has access to personal data does not process them except on instructions from the controller (unless there is a statutory or EU law requirement to process them);[137]

(d) not engage another processor without prior specific or general written authorisation of the controller and without the contract with that other processor similarly stipulating (a)-(h);[138]

(e) assist the controller in responding to requests from data subjects (including subject access and erasure requests);[139]

(f) assist the controller in ensuring compliance with the obligations relating to security of processing operations,[140] notification of personal data breaches,[141] and data protection impact assessments;[142]

(g) as directed by the controller, delete or return all the personal data to the controller after the end of the provision of the processing services (unless there is a statutory or EU law requirement to keep the data);[143] and

(h) make available to the controller all information necessary to demonstrate compliance with the obligations in Article 28, including inspections conducted by the controller.[144]

Where a processor engages another processor, the original processor remains liable for the acts and omissions of the later processor.[145] Controller-processor contracts may take standard

[133] GDPR Art 28(3). Effectively, the controller will either need to be made a party to the contract or the contract will have to comply with the requirements of the Contracts (Rights of Third Parties) Act 1999 s 1. The interaction of s 5 of the 1999 Act and the GDPR is uncertain.

[134] GDPR Art 28(3). In relation to applied GDPR processing, this is modified by DPA 2018 Sch 6 para 24(a)-(b).

[135] GDPR Art 28(3)(a). Where the processor is required by a statutory or EU law requirement to process the personal data, the processor must first inform the controller (unless proscribed by that law on important grounds of public interest).

[136] GDPR Art 28(3)(b).

[137] GDPR Arts 28(3)(c) and 32.

[138] GDPR Art 28(3)(d), in conjunction with Arts 28(2) and (4).

[139] GDPR Art 28(3)(e).

[140] That is, the obligations under GDPR Art 32. See further §§9– 034 to 9– 039.

[141] That is, the obligations under GDPR Arts 33-34. See further §§9– 037 to 9– 039.

[142] GDPR Art 28(3)(f). The obligations are those under GDPR Arts 33-34. See further §9– 050.

[143] GDPR Art 28(3)(g).

[144] GDPR Art 28(3)(h).

[145] GDPR Art 28(4).

forms, as approved, for example, by the European Commission or by the Information Commissioner.[146]

8– 024 Consent

For the purposes of general processing, 'consent' (so far as it is from the data subject) is defined to mean:

> any freely given, specific, informed and unambiguous indication of the data subject's wishes by which he or she, by a statement or by a clear affirmative action, signifies agreement to the processing of personal data relating to him or her.[147]

The same definition is used in relation to intelligence services processing.[148] Although the term 'consent' is used in relation to law enforcement processing, there is no definition of it.[149] Consent given under the repealed DPA 1998 is effective for the current regime provided that that consent complies with the requirements of the current regime.[150]

8– 025 Third party

A 'third party' is:

> a natural or legal person, public authority, agency or body other than the data subject, controller, processor and persons who, under the direct authority of the controller or processor, are authorised to process personal data[151]

The definition of 'third party' excepts: (a) the data subject, the controller and the processor; and (b) persons who, under the direct authority of the controller or processor, are authorised to process personal data. Thus, in the case of a company, public authority or other body with employees whose jobs require them to process personal data for their employer, those employees are not 'third parties.'[152] In the case of a group of companies or related companies, in respect of particular personal data one company (A) will be the controller or processor. Each of the other companies in the group will be a 'third party' apart from those companies in the group that are under the direct authority of the controller and are authorised by it to process that personal data.

8– 026 Recipient

A 'recipient' is:

> a natural or legal person, public authority, agency or another body, to which the personal data are disclosed, whether a third party or not[153]

Excluded from the definition of 'recipient' are public authorities receiving personal data in the

---

146 GDPR Art 28(4)-(8). In relation to applied GDPR processing, this is modified by DPA 2018 Sch 6 para 24(c)-(e). The ICO has published guidance entitled *Contracts and liabilities between controllers and processors*.

147 GPDR Art 4(11) and DPA 2018 s 5(1). See also GDPR Arts 7 and 8, and recitals (32), (33), (42), (43) and (112). See further §9– 008.

148 DPA 2018 s 84(2).

149 DPA 2018 ss 35 and 42.

150 GDPR recital (171), in relation to general processing.

151 GDPR Art 4(10) and DPA 2018 s 5(1) in relation to general processing. The term is not defined for the purposes of law enforcement processing, whether in the DPA 2018 or the LED. It is defined for the purposes of intelligence services processing only in relation to the conditions needed to satisfy the first data protection principle: DPA 2018 s 86(2) and Sch 9 para 6(1).

152 Were such employees 'processors' they would have imposed on them personally all the responsibilities of a processor, eg GDPR Art 30(2). That such employees are not 'third parties' is borne out by GDPR Arts 6(1)(f), 13(1)(d), 14(2)(b) and recitals (47) and (69), which suggest that a third party has legitimate interests independently of and separate from those of the controller or processor.

153 GDPR Art 4(9) and DPA 2018 s 5(1) in relation to general processing. In relation to law enforcement processing, a similar definition applies: DPA 2018 ss 3(6) and 33(5), and see LED Art 3(10). In relation to intelligence services processing a similar definition applies: DPA 29018 ss 3(6) and 84(5).

context of a particular inquiry that is part of its statutory functions. Implicit in the definition of 'recipient' is that a recipient may be a person within a public authority or corporate person that is a controller or processor, and through that a public authority or corporate person acts. Where a 'recipient' is within a public authority or corporate person that is a controller or processor and properly receives personal data in that capacity, there is no additional regulatory requirement.

8–027 Establishment

The GDPR contemplates that a controller or a processor may have a 'main establishment' in one EU Member State as well as one or more other 'establishments' in other EU Member States. The existence of an 'establishment' is important to the operation of the territorial scope of the GDPR.[154] Identification of the location of the 'main establishment' determines which EU Member State's supervisory authority will be the lead supervisory authority to deal with the controller or processor in data protection matters that straddle more than one Member State. As to the meaning of those terms:

(1) The term 'establishment' is not defined in the GDPR. In that Regulation it appears to mean any premises occupied – more than just spasmodically – by a controller or processor at which it carries out a part of its business activities.[155] An establishment can be shown by 'any real and effective activity – even a minimal one – exercised through stable arrangements.'[156] The presence of a single representative or a bank account in an EU Member State can be sufficient in certain circumstances.[157] The fact that the undertaking responsible for the data processing does not have a branch or subsidiary in a Member State does not preclude it from having an establishment there.[158] But mere accessibility of the undertaking's website in a Member State, with the ability to conclude contracts on that website, does not constitute an establishment in that Member State.[159] In order for processing to fall within the territorial scope of the GDPR on the basis of an establishment of a controller or processor in the EU, it will also be necessary to show the processing of the personal data was 'in the context of the activities' of that establishment.[160]

(2) The term 'establishment' is given an inclusive definition in the DPA 2018 for the purposes of the territorial application of that Act:

> ...references to a person who has an establishment in the United Kingdom

---

[154] See §§8–042 to 8–045.

[155] GDPR recital (22).

[156] *Verein fur Konsumenteninformation v Amazon EU Sarl* (C-191/15) [2017] QB 252, [2017] 2 WLR 19 at [75]; *Weltimmo sro v Nemzeti Adatvédelmi és Információszabadság Hatóság* (Case C-230/14) [2016] 1 WLR 863 at [28]-[29]; *Unabhangiges Landeszentrum fur Datenschutz Schleswig-Holstein v Wirtschaftsakademie Schleswig-Holstein GmbH* (C-210/16) [2018] 3 CMLR 32, [2019] 1 WLR 119 at [54].

[157] *Weltimmo sro v Nemzeti Adatvédelmi és Információszabadság Hatóság* (Case C-230/14) [2016] 1 WLR 863 at [30]-[31].

[158] *Verein fur Konsumenteninformation v Amazon EU Sarl* (C-191/15) [2017] QB 252, [2017] 2 WLR 19 at [76]. Both the degree of stability of the arrangements and the effective exercise of activities in the Member State must be interpreted in the light of the specific nature of the economic activities and the provision of services concerned, and this is particularly true for undertakings offering services exclusively over the internet: *Weltimmo sro v Nemzeti Adatvédelmi és Információszabadság Hatóság* (Case C-230/14) [2016] 1 WLR 863 at [29].

[159] *Verein fur Konsumenteninformation v Amazon EU Sarl* (C-191/15) [2017] QB 252, [2017] 2 WLR 19 at [76], AG [120]. Nor, seemingly, would an after-sales service such as a complaints service, be sufficient to give the undertaking an establishment in the Member State: AG at [121]. But in *Weltimmo sro v Nemzeti Adatvédelmi és Információszabadság Hatóság* (Case C-230/14) [2016] 1 WLR 863 a company that had its registered office in Slovakia but with a website in Hungarian, advertising and dealing with Hungarian properties for a fee, with a representative in Hungary (who was responsible for recovering advertising fees and receiving complaints), with a Hungarian bank account and with a letter-box there for the management of its everyday business affairs, had an establishment in Hungary.

[160] GDPR Art 3(1). This is dealt with below at §8–043.

include the following—
(a) an individual who is ordinarily resident in the United Kingdom,
(b) a body incorporated under the law of the United Kingdom or a part of the United Kingdom,
(c) a partnership or other unincorporated association formed under the law of the United Kingdom or a part of the United Kingdom, and
(d) a person not within paragraph (a), (b) or (c) who maintains, and carries on activities through, an office, branch or agency or other stable arrangements in the United Kingdom,

and references to a person who has an establishment in another country or territory have a corresponding meaning.[161]

(3) The term 'main establishment' is defined to mean the place of a controller or processor's central administration in the EU or, if the decisions on the purposes and means of processing of personal data are taken in another establishment of that controller or processor within the EU, then that establishment.[162] In the case of a corporate controller or processor, the central administration will normally be the EU Member State in which it is incorporated. Where a controller has establishments in multiple Member States, the supervisory authorities in those Member States can conduct joint operations including investigations and enforcement measures.[163] The definition of 'main controller' does not apply to applied GDPR processing.[164]

8–028 Filing system

A 'filing system' is defined to mean:

> any structured set of personal data which are accessible according to specific criteria, whether centralised, decentralised or dispersed on a functional or geographical basis.[165]

The significance of this definition is that the GDPR applies to the processing of personal data other than by automated means where that personal data forms part of a 'filing system' or is intended to form part of a filing system.[166] The definition is materially different from its equivalent in the DPA 1998 but identical to that which appeared in Directive 95/46/EC.[167] It is difficult to see how the judicial activism which was brought to bear on the definition in the DPA 1998 may legitimately be carried over to the GDPR definition.[168] More useful is CJEU jurisprudence on the identically-worded definition in Directive 95/46/EC, which indicates:

(1) The content of a filing system must be structured in order to allow easy access to personal data. The requirement that the set of personal data must be 'structured according to specific criteria' is simply intended to enable personal data to be easily retrieved.[169]

---

161 DPA 2018 s 207(7).

162 See GDPR Art 4(16) and recitals (36), (124). The Article 29 Working Party has issued guidelines for identifying a controller or processor's lead supervisory authority, which include the criteria for identifying the main establishment: *Guidelines for identifying a controller or processor's lead supervisory authority*, WP 244, Brussels, 13 December 2016, revised on 5 April 2017.

163 GDPR Art 62(1).

164 DPA 2018 Sch 6 para 9(c).

165 GDPR Art 4(6) and DPA 2018 s 3(7), in relation to all sectors of processing. See also GDPR recitals (15), (31) and (67). In relation to law enforcement processing, see LED Art 3(6).

166 GDPR Art 2(1).

167 DPA 1998 s 1(1), definition of 'relevant filing system'; Directive 95/46/EC Art 2(c).

168 See §15–013.

169 *Tietosuojavaltuutettu v Jehovan todistajat* (C-25/17) [2019] 4 WLR 1, [2019] 1 CMLR 5 at [57].

(2) There is no prescribed practical means by which a filing system is be structured or the form in which it is to be presented. It is not necessary that the personal data at issue must be contained in data sheets or specific lists or in another search method.[170]

(3) A physical set of examination scripts in paper form ordered alphabetically or according to other criteria will be a structured set of personal data.[171]

8–029 Profiling

'Profiling' is defined to mean:

> any form of automated processing of personal data consisting of the use of personal data to evaluate certain personal aspects relating to a natural person, in particular to analyse or predict aspects concerning that natural person's performance at work, economic situation, health, personal preferences, interests, reliability, behaviour, location or movements.[172]

A data subject has a right to object to profiling in certain circumstances, to be informed about the existence of profiling and to be provided with information about the logic involved , as well as the significance and envisaged consequences of the profiling.[173]

8–030 Personal data breach

'Personal data breach' is defined to mean:

> a breach of security leading to the accidental or unlawful destruction, loss, alteration, unauthorised disclosure of, or access to, personal data, personal data transmitted, stored or otherwise processed.[174]

8–031 Restriction of processing

'Restriction of processing' is defined to mean:

> the marking of stored personal data with the aim of limiting their processing in the future.[175]

---

170 *Tietosuojavaltuutettu v Jehovan todistajat* (C-25/17) [2019] 4 WLR 1, [2019] 1 CMLR 5 at [58], where data was collected in the course of door-to-door preaching and, to facilitate the organisation of subsequent visits to persons who had already been contacted, was structured on the basis of an allocation by geographical sector. The data included not only information relating to the content of conversations concerning the beliefs of the person contacted, but also his name and address. The data, or at least a part of it, was used to draw up lists kept by the congregations of the Jehovah's Witnesses Community of persons who no longer wish to receive visits by members who engage in the preaching of that community. The CJEU concluded that there was a 'personal data filing system':

> 60. ...the personal data collected in the course of the door-to-door preaching... are structured according to criteria chosen in accordance with the objective pursued by that collection, which is to prepare for subsequent visits and to keep lists of persons who no longer wish to be contacted. Thus, as it is apparent from the order for reference, those criteria, among which are the name and address of persons contacted, their beliefs or their wish not to receive further visits, are chosen so that they enable data relating to specific persons to be easily retrieved.
>
> 61. ...the specific criterion and the specific form in which the set of personal data collected by each of the members who engage in preaching is actually structured is irrelevant, so long as that set of data makes it possible for the data relating to a specific person who has been contacted to be easily retrieved, which is however for the referring court to ascertain in the light of all the circumstances of the case...

171 *Nowak v Data Protection Commissioner* (C-434/16) [2018] 1 WLR 3505, [2018] 2 CMLR 21 at AG [69].

172 GDPR Art 4(4) and DPA 2019 s 5(1) in relation to general processing, and see GDPR recitals (60), (63) and (70)-(73). In relation to law enforcement processing, a similar definition applies: DPA 2018 ss 3(6) and 33(4) and see LED Art 3(4).

173 GDPR Arts 13(2)(f), 14(2)(g), 15(1)(h), 21, 22. It also impinges on data protection impact assessments (Art 35(3)(a)), and binding corporate rules (Art 47(2)(f)).

174 GDPR Art 4(12) and DPA 2018 s 5(1) in relation to general processing. In relation to law enforcement processing, a similar definition applies: DPA 2018 ss 3(6) and 33(6), and see LED Art 3(11). In relation to intelligence services processing a similar definition applies: DPA 29018 ss 3(6) and 84(6).

175 GDPR Art 4(3) and DPA 2018 s 5(1) in relation to general processing. In relation to law enforcement processing, a similar definition applies: DPA 2018 ss 3(6) and 32(3), and see LED Art 3(3). In relation to intelligence services processing a similar definition applies: DPA 29018 ss 3(6) and 83(3).

Restriction of processing is one of the data subject rights, with the definition signifying rather less than the glossed words might suggest.[176]

8– 032 **Third country**

'Third country' although not defined (for general processing purposes) means any country outside the European Economic Area.[177] For the purposes of law enforcement processing, a third country is defined to mean a country or territory other than a EU member State.[178] The GDPR and DPA 2018 recognise that a particular 'third country' may have within it 'territories,' each of which may have legislative competence in relation to data protection so as to produce a different data protection regime in each of them.[179] The term 'third country' is not used in relation to intelligence services processing.[180]

8– 033 **International organisation**

'International organisation' is defined to mean:

> an organisation and its subordinate bodies governed by public international law, or any other body which is set up by, or on the basis of, an agreement between two or more countries.[181]

Beyond this general definition, the phrase is likely to be the meaning given to it in public international law.[182]

8– 034 **Meaning of 'necessary'**

Throughout the GDPR, obligations imposed and rights conferred are made to turn on something being 'necessary.' The word 'necessary' has a specific meaning within EU jurisprudence, both as regards ECHR rights and as regards EU regulations and directives.[183] Accordingly, when the term is used in Directive 95/46/EC or in the GDPR it must be understood as it has been interpreted in this body of jurisprudence.[184] Where the term is used in the context of justification (as opposed to being used in support of derogation) the standard is 'reasonable necessity': that is, something more than 'desirable' or 'useful', but less than

---

176 GDPR Arts 15(1)(e), 18(1) and 19 and recitals (67) and (156). Similarly, in relation to law enforcement processing, DPA 2018 s 47(2)-(4); and in relation to intelligence services processing DPA 2018 s 100(3)-(5).

177 In other words, any country outside: Austria, Belgium, Bulgaria, Croatia, Cyprus, Czech Republic, Denmark, Estonia, Finland, France, Germany, Greece, Hungary, Ireland, Italy, Latvia, Lithuania, Luxembourg, Malta, Netherlands, Poland, Portugal, Romania, Slovakia, Slovenia, Spain, Sweden and the United Kingdom, as well as Iceland, Norway and Liechtenstein. The question whether a territory is to be regarded as a third country is context specific and will depend on whether, under the relevant Treaty of Accession and supplementary measures, the relevant provisions of EU law apply to that territory: *Routier v HMRC* [2019] UKSC 43, [2019] 3 WLR 757 at [35].

178 DPA 2018 s 33(7).

179 For example, the 50 states of the United States, the six states and 10 territories of Australia, and the 10 provinces and 3 territories of Canada.

180 This is because any transfer of personal data to a country outside the United Kingdom (regardless of the country or territory or an international organisation is treated the same: DPA 2018 s 109.

181 GPDR Art 4(26) and DPA s 5(1) in relation to general processing. And, in relation to all sectors of processing, DPA 2018 s 205(1). In relation to law enforcement processing, see also LED Art 3(16).

182 As to that meaning, see §27– 005.

183 Its meaning in English-language jurisprudence involves a greater stringency: see *Re an inquiry under the Companies Securities (Insider Dealing) Act 1985* [1988] AC 660, [1988] 1 All ER 203 (which suggests that the word 'necessary' has a meaning somewhere between 'indispensable' on the one hand and 'useful' or 'convenient' on the other); *Hogan v Australian Crime Commission* [2010] HCA 21, (2010) 240 CLR 651 at [30].

184 *Huber v Germany* (C-524/06) [2009] 1 CMLR 49, [2009] All ER (EC) 239 at [52]; *South Lanarkshire Council v Scottish IC* [2013] UKSC 55, [2013] 1 WLR 2421 at [22]; *House of Commons v IC and Brooke, Leapman, Ungoed-Thomas* [2008] EWHC 1084 (Admin), [2009] 3 All ER 403 at [43].

'indispensable' or 'absolutely necessary.'[185] Thus, EU regulations, directives and jurisprudence draw a distinction between 'necessary' and 'strictly necessary,' with only the latter connoting indispensability or absolute necessity and being generally used in the context of derogations.[186] For an activity such as processing to be 'necessary' simpliciter the particular processing to which the word 'necessary' is linked must be proportionate to the aim pursued by that processing.[187] That is, it must serve a pressing social need and it must be the least intrusive way of achieving that aim.[188] If the processing involves an interference with a data subject's ECHR right to respect for his or her private life, then the requirements of ECHR Article 8(2) must be fulfilled.[189] By way of examples:

(1) A publicly-available database giving *all* the details of a recipient of public funds went beyond what was necessary for the performance of public tasks.[190]
(2) A centralised government system holding details of foreign nationals provided that it was available only to those bodies that had a legitimate need to consult it and that the details did not go beyond what was necessary for the statutory purposes.[191]
(3) Disclosing personal information pursuant to an obligation in a freedom of information regime (subject to any exemption in that regime) will be processing that is 'necessary.'[192]
(4) A police database with the fingerprints and DNA samples of those arrested but never convicted of offences, which extended to offences that were not punishable by imprisonment and that was retained indefinitely, was held to be a disproportionate interference with the right to private life that could not be regarded as 'necessary' in a democratic society.[193]
(5) The retention of traffic and location data of all subscribers and registered users and all means of electronic communication as well as metadata without differentiation, limitation or exception according to the objective pursued was not 'necessary' for

---

185 *Sunday Times v United Kingdom* [1979] ECHR 1, (1979) 2 EHRR 245 at [59]; *R v Shayler (David)* [2002] UKHL 11, [2003] 1 AC 247 at [23]; *House of Commons v IC and Brooke, Leapman, Ungoed-Thomas* [2008] EWHC 1084 (Admin), [2009] 3 All ER 403 at [43]; *South Lanarkshire Council v Scottish IC* [2013] UKSC 55, [2013] 1 WLR 2421 at [8] and [19]-[27]; *Cooper v National Crime Agency* [2019] EWCA Civ 16 at [89]-[93]. cf *Valsts policijas Rīgas reģiona pārvaldes Kārtības policijas pārvalde v Rīgas pašvaldības SIA* (Case C-13/16) [2017] 4 WLR 97, [2017] 3 CMLR 39 at [30]-[32].

186 GDPR recitals (47) and (49); LED Arts 10 and 39(1)(a), recital (72); *Tietosuojavaltuutettu v Satakunnan* (C-73/07) [2010] All ER (EC) 213 at [56]; *Volker und Markus Schecke GbR v Land Hessen* (C-92/09) [2012] All ER (EC) 127, [2012] IP & T 513 at [77]; *Digital Rights Ireland Ltd v Minister for Communications, Marine and Natural Resources* (C-293/12 and C-594/12) [2015] QB 127, [2014] 3 CMLR 44 at [52]; *Rynes v Urad pro ochranu osobnich udaju* (C-212/13) [2015] 1 WLR 2607, [2015] CEC 732 at [28]; *Schrems v Data Protection Commissioner* (C-362/14) [2016] QB 527, [2016] 2 CMLR 2 at [92]-[93]; *Tele2 Sverige AB v Post-och telestyrelsen* (C-203/15) [2017] QB 771, [2017] 2 CMLR 30 at [96], [108]-[119]; *Staatssecretaris van Justitie en Veiligheid v A and others* (C-79/18) [2019] 4 WLR 129 at [29], [56]. Similarly, Directive 2002/58/EC (Directive on privacy and electronic communications) Art 5(2).

187 *Leander v Sweden* (App no 9248/81) (1987) 9 EHRR 434 at [58]; *South Lanarkshire Council v Scottish IC* [2013] UKSC 55, [2013] 1 WLR 2421 at [25]. By contrast, in *Homer v Chief Constable of West Yorkshire Police* [2012] UKSC 15, [2012] ICR 704 it was held that 'to be proportionate, a measure has to be both an appropriate means of achieving the legitimate aim and (reasonably) necessary in order to do so' (at [22]).

188 See, for example: *Sunday Times v United Kingdom* [1979] ECHR 1, (1979) 2 EHRR 245 at [59]-[62]; *R v Shayler (David)* [2002] UKHL 11, [2003] 1 AC 247 at [23]. This has been applied in the context of data protection law in the UK, for example in: *House of Commons v IC and Brooke, Leapman, Ungoed-Thomas* [2008] EWHC 1084 (Admin), [2009] 3 All ER 403 at [43].

189 *South Lanarkshire Council v Scottish IC* [2013] UKSC 55, [2013] 1 WLR 2421 at [25].

190 *Volker und Markus Schecke GbR v Land Hessen* (C-92/09) [2012] All ER (EC) 127, [2012] IP & T 513 at [79]-[86].

191 *Huber v Germany* (C-524/06) [2009] 1 CMLR 49, [2009] All ER (EC) 239 at [49]-[68].

192 *European Commission v Bavarian Lager Co Ltd* [2010] EUECJ C-28/08, [2010] ECR I-06055, [2011] Bus LR 867 at [24], [47].

193 *Marper v United Kingdom* [2008] ECHR 1581, (2009) 48 EHRR 50. Contrast: *Schwarz v Stadt Bochum* (C-291/12) [2013] 2 CMRL 5 at [46]-[53].

the purpose of fighting against serious crime.[194]

Where processing is carried out in the performance of a task entrusted to a public authority in the public interest, then 'a certain amount of discretion' is to be afforded in determining the extent to which it was necessary to forward data to third parties.[195]

3. SCOPE AND LIMITS

8–035 Introduction

It is theoretically possible for data protection legislation to seek to regulate all processing of personal data, regardless of the manner of that processing, regardless of where that processing takes place and regardless of the nationality or residency of the data subject. Most legislation, regardless of topic, does not attempt to exert such an extravagant legislative reach, not least because it would offend the comity of nations, might exceed the competency of the legislative body and would result in rights and obligations that prove unenforceable. Both the GDPR and the DPA 2018 recognise this, with both limiting the scope of the processing of personal data to which they apply.

8–036 Limits of the GDPR

The reach of the GDPR is significantly less than that of the DPA 2018. Specifically, the GDPR does not apply to processing of personal data:

(a) where it is in the course of an activity that is outside the scope of EU law, most notably intelligence services processing, and processing for defence or national security purposes;[196]

(b) where it is by a Member State when carrying out an activity that falls within GDPR Art 2(2)(b) (ie the foreign and security policy of the EU);[197]

(c) where it is by a natural person in the course of a purely personal or household activity;[198]

(d) where it is by a competent authority for any of the law enforcement purposes;[199]

(e) by EU institutions, bodies, offices and agencies;[200]

---

194 *Tele2 Sverige AB v Post-och telestyrelsen* (C-203/15) [2017] QB 771, [2017] 2 CMLR 30.

195 *Oikonomopoulos v European Commission* (T-483/13) CJEU 20 July 2016 at [58]-[60].

196 GDPR Art 2(2)(a) and recital (16). Defence and national security are matters outside the competence of the EU: TEU Art 4. For case-law in this area, see: *Spain v Eurojust* (C-160/03) 15 March 2005; *Sayn-Wittgenstein v Landeshauptmann von Wien* (C-208/09) [2010] ECR I-13693, [2011] 2 CMLR 738; *Runevic-Vardyn v Vilniaus miesto savivaldybes administracija* (C-391/09) [2015] 1 CMLR 853.

197 GDPR Art 2(2)(b) and recital (16). Chapter 2 of Title 5 of the TEU (Arts 23-46) is entitled 'Specific Provisions on the Common Foreign and Security Policy.' As to whether an activity is within the foreign and security policy of the EU, see: *European Parliament v Council of the European Union* (C-263/14) [2016] QB 1123, [2017] 1 CMLR 10; *R (PJSC Rosneft Oil Co) v HM Treasury* (C-72/15) [2018] QB 1, [2017] 3 CMLR 23. Article 39 TEU provides:

> 'In accordance with Article 16 of the Treaty on the Functioning of the European Union and by way of derogation from paragraph 2 thereof, the Council shall adopt a decision laying down the rules relating to the protection of individuals with regard to the processing of personal data by the Member States when carrying out activities which fall within the scope of this Chapter, and the rules relating to the free movement of such data. Compliance with these rules shall be subject to the control of independent authorities.'

As at the date of publication, no decision had been adopted by the Council. Instead, this processing is governed by Ch 3 of Part 2 of the DPA 2018: see s 21(1)(b). This is dealt with in Chapter 14.

198 GDPR Art 2(2)(c) and recital (18). See §8–038.

199 GDPR Art 2(2)(d). This has its own regulatory regime: see Chapters 12 and 13.

200 GDPR Art 2(3). These are governed by their own regulatory regime which mirrors the GDPR, namely Regulation (EU) 2018/1725. This repealed Regulation (EC) No 45/2001 and Decision No 1247/2002/EC.

(f) that does not involve either any automated means or a filing system;[201] or

(g) that is not within the 'territorial scope' of the GDPR.[202]

Collectively, (a)-(f) are referred to as the 'material scope' of the GDPR. So far as (a), (b) and (f) are concerned, these types of processing of personal data are regulated by the DPA 2018 without any EU law input.[203] So far as (c) is concerned, this type of processing is not subject to any form of regulation, whether under the GDPR or the DPA 2018. So far as (d) is concerned, this type of processing is dealt with by the DPA 2018 in its implementation of the Law Enforcement Directive.[204] So far as (e) is concerned, this type of processing is dealt with by Regulation 45/2001, either directly or as applied by other EU acts.

8– 037 Limits of the DPA 2018

In so far as the DPA 2018 deals with processing that is covered by the GDPR, its scope coincides with that of the GDPR. Specifically, in so far as the DPA 2018 regulates general processing it is subject to the same 'territorial scope' as the GDPR.[205] In so far as the DPA 2018 governs general processing of personal data that is not covered by the GDPR,[206] its territorial scope is more limited: it applies only to the processing of personal data in the context of activities of an establishment of a controller or processor in the United Kingdom, whether or not the processing takes place in the United Kingdom.[207]

8– 038 Personal or household activity

Neither the GDPR nor the DPA 2018 applies to the processing of personal data by a natural person in the course of a purely personal or household activity.[208] The processing of personal data by a natural person in the course of a purely personal or household activity is thus unregulated. Directive 95/46/EC provided for an exemption for such processing. This was implemented through the DPA 1998 with a similarly (but not identically) worded exemption.[209] Given the identical language used, case law under Directive 95/46/EC remains relevant. The CJEU has held that activity cannot be regarded as being purely personal or domestic where its purpose is to make personal data widely accessible (such as on the internet)[210] or where that activity extends even partly to a public space directed beyond that person's private setting.[211]

---

201 GDPR Art 2(1). As to the meaning of these terms, see §§8– 040 to 8– 041.

202 GDPR Art 3. As to the territorial scope of the GDPR, see §§8– 042 to 8– 045.

203 In relation to (a), this is dealt with in DPA 2018 Pt 4 (ss 82-113) and is termed 'intelligence services processing.' This is dealt with in Chapter 14. In relation to (b) and (f), these are dealt with in DPA 2018 ss 21-28 and are termed 'other general processing.' This is dealt with in Chapters 12 and 13.

204 This is dealt with in DPA 2018 Pt 3 (ss 29-81).

205 DPA s 207(2)-(3). See §§8– 042 to 8– 045.

206 That is: (a) automated or structured processing of personal data in the course of an activity that is either outside the scope of EU law or that falls within the scope of GDPR Art 2(2)(b), but which is not law enforcement processing or intelligence service processing; and (b) processing that does not involve either any automated means or a filing system: see DPA 2018 s 21. As to the meaning of these terms, see §§8– 040 to 8– 041.

207 DPA 2018 s 207(2). As to the meaning of 'a person who has an establishment in the United Kingdom,' see DPA 2018 s 207(7). See further §8– 027.

208 GDPR Art 2(2)(c); DPA 2018 s 21(3). Recital (18) records that 'personal or household activities could include correspondence and the holding of addresses, or social networking and online activity undertaken within the context of such activities.' As this is an exception rather than a rule, it will be interpreted restrictively.

209 The purely personal or household activity exemptions under Directive 95/46/EU and under the DPA 1998 are considered at §16– 030.

210 *Re Lindqvist (Approximation of Laws)* [2004] QB 1014 at [47].

211 *Satakunnan Markkinapörssi and Satamedia* (C-73/07) [2008] ECR I-9831, [2010] All ER (EC) 213 at [44]; *Rynes v Urad pro ochranu osobnich udaju* (C-212/13) [2015] 1 WLR 2607, [2015] CEC 732 at [31], [33]. In relation to the similarly worded exemption in the DPA 1998, the Court of Appeal held that a balance had to be struck between two

The Information Commissioner may serve an information notice on any person for the purpose of determining whether the processing of personal data is carried out by an individual in the course of a purely personal or household activity.[212]

8– 039 Applicable processing

The GDPR applies to two categories of processing:

(a) 'the processing of personal data wholly or partly by automated means'; and

(b) 'the processing other than by automated means of personal data which form part of a filing system or are intended to form part of a filing system.'[213]

Processing of personal data outside both (a) and (b) is termed 'manual unstructured processing of personal data' and is governed by the DPA 2018.[214]

8– 040 Processing by automated means

The first class of processing to which the GDPR applies[215] is the processing of personal data wholly or partly by automated means.[216] Most processing of personal data will fall within this class. The act of referring to identifiable individuals on an internet page constitutes 'the processing of personal data wholly or partly by automatic means.'[217]

8– 041 Processing by filing system

The second class of processing to which the GDPR applies[218] is the processing of personal data, other than by automated means, which forms part of a filing system or are intended to form part of a filing system.[219] 'Filing system' means any structured set of personal data which is accessible according to specific criteria, whether held by automated means or manually and whether centralised, decentralised or dispersed on a functional or geographical basis.[220] Jurisprudence concerning 'relevant filing system' – the term used under Directive 95/46/EC and the DPA 1998 – is likely to remain applicable.[221] The touchstone is that the processing of personal data other than by automated means will be subject to the GDPR if the data is structured in such a way that information about particular individuals can be readily located.

8– 042 Territoriality: introduction

The extent of the rights conferred and the obligations imposed by the GDPR and the DPA 2018 depends upon:

— the nationality and residence of the data subject;

— whether the controller or processor has an establishment in the EU in the context of which the processing of the personal data takes place;

— whether the processing is related to the offering of goods and services to data

---

competing entitlements to privacy, ie that of the data subject and that of the individual data controller: *Ittihadieh v 5-11 Cheyne Gardens RTM Co Ltd* [2017] EWCA 121, [2018] QB 256 at [76].

212 DPA 2018 s 142(1)(b)(ii).

213 GDPR Art 2(1).

214 DPA 2018 s 21(2), (4).

215 And to which Part 2, Ch 2 of the DPA 2018 (ss 6-20) similarly applies.

216 GDPR Art 2(1).

217 *Re Lindqvist (Approximation of Laws)* [2004] QB 1014 at [27].

218 And to which Part 2, Ch 2 of the DPA 2018 (ss 6-20) similarly applies.

219 GDPR Art 2(1). See also GDPR recital (15).

220 GDPR Art 4(6); DPA 2018 s 3(7). See further §8– 028.

221 See §§15– 012 to 15– 015.

subjects in the EU or to the monitoring of the behaviour of data subjects in the EU so far as it takes place in the EU; and

— whether the controller is established in a place to which the law of a Member State applies by virtue of public international law.

Collectively, these variables define what is termed the 'territorial scope' of the GDPR and the 'territorial application' of the DPA 2018.[222] To be within the territorial scope of the GDPR, the processing of personal data must be within one or more of the three limbs described in Article 3. To the extent that the DPA 2018 deals with general processing by supplementing the GDPR, its territorial application is identical to the territorial scope of the GDPR.[223] To the extent that the DPA 2018 deals with general processing that is not covered by the GDPR, its territorial application is limited to processing of personal data that is within the first limb of the territorial scope of the GDPR.[224] Where a data subject claims that a controller or processor has not complied with its obligations in the processing of his or her personal data or has infringed his or her rights, that data subject has a choice in relation to the jurisdiction in which to bring an action on that claim: he or she may bring it either in the Member State in which the controller or processor has an establishment or in the Member State in which the data subject has his or her habitual residence.[225]

8–043 Territoriality: establishment limb

The first limb of the territorial scope of the GDPR is sometimes termed the 'establishment criterion.' It provides that the GDPR applies to:

> the processing of personal data in the context of the activities of an establishment of a controller or a processor in the Union, regardless of whether the processing takes place in the Union or not.[226]

This limb is indifferent to the nationality or residence of the data subject[227] and to the jurisdiction in which the processing takes place. The predecessor provision under Directive 95/46/EC referred to the establishment of a controller only.[228] The reach of the first limb is thus more extensive, encompassing the establishment of a processor as well as that of a controller. The first limb entails a determination of:

(a) whether the controller or processor has an 'establishment' in the EU; and
(b) if so, whether the processing in question takes place 'in the context of the activities' of that establishment.

Those questions are, it seems, to be construed expansively rather than restrictively.[229] Determining whether a controller or processor has an 'establishment' in the EU has been

---

[222] GDPR Art 3; DPA 2018 s 207. The detailed legislative treatment of territoriality in the DPA 2018 s 207 displaces the common law interpretive presumptions on territoriality, as to which see: *Clark v Oceanic Contractors Inc* [1983] 2 AC 130 at 145, 152; *Lawson v Serco* [2006] UKHL 3, [2006] ICR 250 at [6]; *R (Al-Skeini) v SS for Defence* [2007] UKHL 26, [2008] 1 AC 153 at [11], [38], [86], [137]; *Duncombe v SS for Children etc (no 2)* [2011] UKSC 36, [2011] ICR 495; *Ravat v Halliburton* [2012] UKSC 1, [2012] ICR 389; *Cox v Ergo Verischerung AG* [2014] UKSC 22, [2014] AC 1379 at [27], [29].

[223] DPA 2018 s 207(2)-(3).

[224] DPA 2018 s 207(2), (6).

[225] GDPR Art 79(2),

[226] GDPR Art 3(1). Similarly, DPA 2018 s 207(2).

[227] GDPR recital (2).

[228] Directive 95/46/EC Art 4(1)(a).

[229] See, under Directive 95/46/EC: *Google Spain SL v Agencia Espanola de Proteccion de Datos* (C-131/12) [2014] QB 1022 at [50]-[54]; *Weltimmo sro v Nemzeti Adatvédelmi és Információszabadság Hatóság* (Case C-230/14) [2016] 1 WLR 863 at [25]-[28]; *Unabhangiges Landeszentrum fur Datenschutz Schleswig-Holstein v Wirtschaftsakademie Schleswig-Holstein GmbH* (C-210/16) [2018] 3 CMLR 32, [2019] 1 WLR 119 at [56]; *CG v Facebook Ireland Ltd* [2016] NICA 54, [2017] 2 CMLR 29 at [90].

addressed above.[230] In relation to the second question, the requirement is not that the processing of the personal data in question be carried out 'by' the establishment: it is enough that the processing of the personal data is carried out 'in the context of the activities of an establishment.'[231] Thus it has been held in relation to a US parent company (with a number of EU subsidiaries who collectively had exclusive responsibilities within the group for collecting and processing personal data) and a Spanish subsidiary which was responsible for the promotion and sale of advertising and marketing on the search engine and which oriented the engine towards Spanish inhabitants:

> that processing of personal data [by the Spanish subsidiary] is carried out in the context of the activities of an establishment of the controller on the territory of a member state, within the meaning of that provision, when the operator of a search engine sets up in a member state a branch or subsidiary which is intended to promote and sell advertising space offered by that engine and which orientates its activity towards the inhabitants of that member state[232]

Processing of data in the context of the activities of an establishment is governed by the law of the Member State in whose territory that establishment is situated.[233]

8–044 Territoriality: targeting limb

The second limb of the territorial scope of the GDPR is sometimes referred to as the 'targeting criterion.' It provides that the GDPR applies to:

> the processing of personal data of data subjects who are in the Union by a controller or processor not established in the Union, where the processing activities are related to
> (a) the offering of goods or services, irrespective of whether a payment from the data subject is required, to such data subjects in the [EU]; or
> (b) the monitoring of their behaviour as their behaviour takes place within the

230 As to the meaning of 'establishment' see §8–027.

231 *Google Spain SL v Agencia Espanola de Proteccion de Datos* (C-131/12) [2014] QB 1022 at [52]; *Verein fur Konsumenteninformation v Amazon EU Sarl* (C-191/15) [2017] QB 252, [2017] 2 WLR 19 at [75]; *Unabhangiges Landeszentrum fur Datenschutz Schleswig-Holstein v Wirtschaftsakademie Schleswig-Holstein GmbH* (C-210/16) [2018] 3 CMLR 32, [2019] 1 WLR 119 at [57].

232 *Google Spain SL v Agencia Espanola de Proteccion de Datos* (C-131/12) [2014] QB 1022 at [60]. It was critical to this conclusion that the establishment in Spain was 'intended to promote and sell, in that member state, advertising space offered by the search engine which serves to make the service offered by that engine profitable' at [55]. Similarly, in *Unabhangiges Landeszentrum fur Datenschutz Schleswig-Holstein v Wirtschaftsakademie Schleswig-Holstein GmbH* (C-210/16) [2018] 3 CMLR 32, [2019] 1 WLR 119 the fact that Facebook Germany was responsible for promoting and selling advertising space and carried on activities addressed to persons residing in Germany meant that there was an inextricable link between its activities and the processing of personal data carried out by Facebook Inc jointly with Facebook Ireland sufficient to mean that that processing was carried on in the context of the establishment in Germany (at [56]-[60]). And similarly *Weltimmo sro v Nemzeti Adatvédelmi és Információszabadság Hatóság* (Case C-230/14) [2016] 1 WLR 863 at [34]-[38], where the Court concluded that there was no doubt that a Slovakian company that had a Hungarian-language website advertising properties for sale in Hungary was carrying out processing in the context of activities of its establishment in Hungary. It is for the court of a Member State to determine whether the undertaking carries out the data processing in question in the context of the activities of an establishment of that Member State: *Verein fur Konsumenteninformation v Amazon EU Sarl* (C-191/15) [2017] QB 252, [2017] 2 WLR 19 at [79]-[81]. And in *CG v Facebook Ireland Ltd* [2016] NICA 54, [2017] 2 CMLR 29 it was held that Facebook was a controller within the meaning of the DPA 1998 because a company called Facebook (UK) Ltd had been established for the sole purpose of promoting the sale of advertising space offered by Facebook, it conducted its activities within the United Kingdom, it was responsible for those in the United Kingdom who sought to use the Facebook service for advertising and it held relevant date on behalf of Facebook in respect of advertising customers:

> [Although there] is no direct evidence of its connection with Facebook but there is an irresistible inference in the absence of any further explanation that Facebook (UK) Ltd was established to service Facebook and is part of the wider Facebook group of companies...Facebook (UK) Ltd plainly engages in the effective and real exercise of activity through stable arrangements in the United Kingdom and having regard to the importance of those activities to Facebook's economic enterprise the processing of data by Facebook was carried out in the context of the activities of that establishment. (at [90]-[91])

233 *Verein fur Konsumenteninformation v Amazon EU Sarl* (C-191/15) [2017] QB 252, [2017] 2 WLR 19 at [74], [80]-[81].

[EU].[234]

The first requirement of this limb is that the data subject whose personal data is being processed be in the EU. Satisfaction of the requirement falls to be answered at the moment of the processing of the data subject's personal data. It is suggested that the requirement that the data subject be 'in the EU' means a physical presence in the EU, regardless of nationality, citizenship, residency or other legal status.[235] The second requirement of this limb is that the data subject's personal data be processed by a controller or processor which is not established in the EU. Although this limb refers to 'established' in the EU, whereas the first limb refers to 'an establishment' in the EU, it would appear that the second limb is directed to controllers and processors that, because of the establishment requirement, fall outside the first limb. On this basis, where a controller or processor has an establishment both inside and outside the EU, it will not meet the second requirement of this limb. The third requirement of this limb is that the processing activities are related to (a) or (b) – what is sometimes termed a 'trigger activity.' The European Data Protection Board's draft guidance provides examples of and considerations relevant to the two types of 'trigger activity'. As regards the 'offering of goods and services', indicators include: the use of contact details and delivery information within the EU; the use of EU web domains, languages and currencies; references to EU-based clients (for example through testimonials) and the international nature of the goods or service on offer. Examples of behavioural monitoring include targeted advertising, the use of cookies or pixels, and geolocation activities.[236] It is unlikely that the mere provision of access to a website or publishing an email address will suffice to satisfy paragraph (a).[237]

8–045 Territorial scope: diplomacy limb

The third limb of the territorial scope of the GDPR captures:

> the processing of personal data by a controller not established in the Union, but in a place where Member State law applies by virtue of public international law.[238]

Examples include processing of personal data by diplomatic missions and consular posts[239] and by international organisations.[240]

---

[234] GDPR Art 3(2). And see GDPR recitals (23)-(24). Contrast the use of the phrase 'main establishment' in GDPR Art 4(16) and recital (36).

[235] GDPR recital (2); draft EDPB territoriality guidance, p 13. Thus, a data subject who is present in the EU but neither a resident nor a citizen of a Member State will satisfy the requirement, but a citizen of a Member State who, at the relevant time, is physically outside the EU will not.

[236] GDPR recital (24).

[237] In light of the requirements in GDPR Arts 27(3), 35(6) and recital (80). See: *Pammer v Reederei Karl Schluter GmbH & Co KG* (C-585/08) [2011] 2 All ER (Comm) 888, [2012] Bus LR 972.

[238] GDPR Art 3(3).

[239] GDPR recital (25).

[240] See GDPR Art 4(26). As to the meaning of 'international organisations,' see §8– 033.

CHAPTER 9

General processing: continuing obligations

1. INTRODUCTION

9– 001 Meaning of general processing

General processing comprises all processing of personal data other than:

(a) processing of personal data by any of the intelligence services;[1]

(b) processing of personal data by a competent authority for a law enforcement purpose;[2]

(c) processing of personal data by a natural person in the course of a purely personal or household activity;[3]

(d) processing of personal data that is not:

  (i) by automated means;[4]

  (ii) of data that forms, or is intended to form, part of a filing system;[5] and

  (iii) of personal data held by a public authority;[6] and

(e) processing that is outside the territorial scope of the GDPR and the DPA 2018.[7]

Unless otherwise stated, in this Chapter 'processing' means general processing and does not include any of (a)-(e) above.

9– 002 Types of general processing

General processing of personal data divides into two types:

(1) General processing that is directly governed by the GDPR – 'GDPR processing.' This is the more common of the two types of general processing. The regime for GDPR processing is supplemented by the DPA 2018.[8]

(2) General processing that is not directly governed by the GDPR but to which a modified version of the GDPR has been applied by the DPA 2018 – 'applied GDPR processing.'[9] This covers:

  (a) general processing of personal data in the course of an activity which is

---

1 The 'intelligence services' comprise the Security Service, the Secret Intelligence Service and the Government Communication Headquarters: DPA 2018 s 82(2). The intelligence services for data protection purposes is a subset of the excluded security bodies specified in FOIA s 23(3) but coincides with the three bodies excluded from FOIA by s 84. The identity of these three bodies is considered further in §26– 015. Processing of personal data by the intelligence services is governed by Part 4 of the DPA 2018 (ss 82-113) and Schs 9-11. This is dealt with in Chapter 14 of this work.

2 The 'competent authorities' are the bodies listed in Sch 7, as well as any other person if and to the extent that the person has a statutory function for any of the law enforcement purposes other than any of the intelligence services: DPA 2018 s 30(1)-(2). The 'law enforcement purposes' are the purposes of the prevention, investigation, detection or prosecution of criminal offences or the execution of criminal penalties, including the safeguarding against and prevention of threats to public security: DPA 2018 s 31. Processing of personal data by competent authorities for law enforcement purposes is governed by the LED and Part 3 of the DPA 2018 (ss 29-81) and Schs 7 and 8. Processing of personal data by competent authorities for law enforcement purposes is dealt with in Chs 11-12 of this work.

3 See further §8– 038.

4 See further §8– 040.

5 See further §8– 041.

6 That is, a legal person that is neither a public authority within the meaning of FOIA nor a Scottish public authority within the meaning of FOI(S)A: DPA 2018 s 21(5). Public authorities within the meaning of FOIA are considered at §§20– 018 to 20– 025. Scottish public authorities within the meaning of FOI(S)A are considered at §§20– 027 to 20– 032. As to when information is 'held' by a public authority, see §§20– 009 to 20– 012.

7 See further §§8– 042 to 8– 045.

8 Specifically by Chapter 2 of Part 2 of the DPA 2018 (ss 6-20) and Schs 1-5.

9 DPA 2018 s 22.

outside the scope of EU law,[10] provided that the processing is by automated means[11] or is of data that forms, or is intended to form, part of a filing system;[12]

(b) general processing of personal data in the course of an activity which falls with the scope of Article 2(2)(b) of the GDPR (common foreign policy and security policy activities),[13] provided that the processing is by automated means[14] or is of data that forms, or is intended to form, part of a filing system;[15] and

(c) general processing of manual unstructured personal data held by a public authority.[16] 'Manual unstructured personal data' means personal data that is not processed by automated means,[17] does not form part of, and is not intended to form part of, a filing system.[18]

The obligations on a processor are much the same for the two types of general processing. Unless otherwise stated, the analysis in this chapter applies equally to the two types of general processing.

9–003 Continuing obligations

The obligations on a controller associated with the general processing of personal data divide into two types:

— Obligations that persist whenever there is general processing of personal data – 'continuing obligations.' These are considered in this chapter.

— Obligations that are triggered by the data subject of that personal data exercising a right conferred by the GDPR, usually by the data subject giving the controller a notice. These are considered in Chapter 10.

The main continuing obligation – 'accountability'[19] – requires that whenever personal data is processed, the controller is responsible for, and must be able to demonstrate, compliance with six processing principles.[20] In addition to the accountability obligation, the other continuing obligations are:

(1) Obligations imposed on a controller processing personal information that, by its very nature, is acutely personal – which in this work is termed 'sensitive personal information.'[21] When processing sensitive personal information a controller must

---

10 DPA 2018 s 21(1)(a). For example, activities concerning national security. See further §8–036(a).

11 See further §8–040.

12 See further §8–041.

13 DPA 2018 s 21(1)(b). See further §8–036(b).

14 See further §8–040.

15 See further §8–041.

16 DPA 2018 s 21(2). That is, a public authority within the meaning of FOIA or a Scottish public authority within the meaning of FOI(S)A: DPA 2018 s 21(5). Public authorities within the meaning of FOIA are considered at §§20–018 to 20–025. Scottish public authorities within the meaning of FOI(S)A are considered at §§20–027 to 20–032. As to when information is 'held' by a public authority, see §§20–009 to 20–012.

17 As to the processing of personal data by automated means, see §8–040.

18 As to the meaning of personal data which forms part of a filing system or which is intended to form part of a filing system, see §8–041.

19 GDPR Art 5(2). See also GDPR recital (85).

20 GDPR Art 5(1)-(2). In relation to applied GDPR processing, DPA 2018 s 22(1).

21 Although both the GDPR and DPA 2018 recognise this class of acutely personal information, neither defines the term. It was, however, so defined in DPA 1998. As to what falls within this category of 'sensitive personal information' see §9–040. The obligations imposed on a controller when processing 'sensitive personal information' is considered further at §§9–040 to 9–047.

comply with these obligations in addition to complying with the accountability obligation.

(2) Obligations relating to the set up and internal organisation of a controller or processor.[22] These obligations cover the internal systems that a controller and processor must have, data protection impact assessments, record-keeping requirements, data protection officers, co-operation with the Information Commissioner and payment of annual charges and fees.

(3) Obligations engaged by the international transfer of personal data.[23]

Non-compliance with any of these obligations exposes the controller both to regulatory action (through the Information Commissioner)[24] and to a private law claim from the individual to whom the personal data relates.[25]

9– 004 The processing principles

The six processing principles embodied in the accountability obligation for which the controller is responsible and must be able to demonstrate are:[26]

(1) Personal data must be processed lawfully, fairly and in a transparent manner in relation to the data subject.[27]

(2) Personal data must be collected only for specified, explicit and legitimate purposes, and not further processed in a manner that is incompatible with those purposes.[28]

(3) Personal data must be adequate, relevant and limited to what is necessary in relation to the purposes for which they are processed.[29]

(4) Personal data processed must be accurate and, where necessary, kept up to date.[30]

(5) Personal data must be kept in a form which permits identification of data subjects for no longer than is necessary for the purposes for which the personal data are processed.[31]

(6) Personal data must be processed in a manner that ensures appropriate security of the personal data, including protection against unauthorised or unlawful processing and against accidental loss, destruction or damage, using appropriate technical or organisational measures.[32]

Of the above processing principles, (1), (2), (5) and (6) are directed to an activity of processing, while (3) and (4) are directed to the quality of the personal data. The onus is on the controller

---

22 Considered further at §§9– 048 to 9– 056.

23 Considered further at §§9– 057 to 9– 064.

24 GDPR Art 77. In relation to applied GDPR processing, this is modified by DPA 2018 Sch 6 para 50. Regulatory enforcement is considered at §§48– 014 to 48– 055.

25 GDPR Art 79. In relation to applied GDPR processing, this is modified by DPA 2018 Sch 6 para 52. Private law claims are considered at §§48– 005 to 48– 013.

26 GDPR Art 5(2). Similarly, Convention 108 Mod Art 10(1). See also: OECD, *Guidelines on governing the Protection of Privacy and transborder flows of personal data*, 2013 Art 14.

27 GDPR Art 5(1)(a). In relation to applied GDPR processing (for which, see §8– 009(3)), DPA 2018 s 22(1). Considered further at §§9– 006 to 9– 022.

28 GDPR Art 5(1)(b). In relation to applied GDPR processing, DPA 2018 s 22(1). Considered further at §§9– 023 to 9– 027.

29 GDPR Art 5(1)(c). In relation to applied GDPR processing, DPA 2018 s 22(1). Considered further at §9– 028.

30 GDPR Art 5(1)(d). In relation to applied GDPR processing, DPA 2018 s 22(1). Considered further at §§9– 029 to 9– 030.

31 GDPR Art 5(1)(e). In relation to applied GDPR processing, DPA 2018 s 22(1). Considered further at §§9– 031 to 9– 033.

32 GDPR Art 5(1)(f). In relation to applied GDPR processing, DPA 2018 s 22(1). Considered further at §§9– 034 to 9– 039.

not merely to comply with the six processing principles but to be able to demonstrate compliance with these principles.[33]

9–005 Duties on processors

By definition, a processor should be confining itself to processing personal data on behalf of a controller.[34] A processor should not be determining the purposes or means of the processing of personal data: these are the exclusive domain of the controller.[35] Where a processor does stray into the domain of the controller by determining the purposes and means of processing, the processor will be treated as a controller in respect of that processing and will be subject to the six processing principles.[36] Provided that a processor does not so stray, it will not be required to comply with the six processing principles.[37] There are, however, other duties and liabilities imposed on processors:[38]

(1) A processor that is not established in the EU must designate in writing a representative in the EU.[39]

(2) Processing by a processor must be governed by a contract or statutory instrument conferring on the controller control over processing by the processor as well as compelling the processor to ensure security of processing and confidentiality of the data.[40]

(3) A processor must not engage another processor without prior written authorisation of the controller, with the controller necessarily being given an opportunity to object to the addition or replacement of a processor.[41] The additional or replacement processor must be bound by the same terms as are required of the original processor, with the original processor remaining liable for the performance of an additional or replacement processor.[42]

(4) A processor must ensure that no person under its authority with access to personal

---

33 GDPR Art 5(2). See also GDPR recital (85).

34 GDPR Art 4(8).

35 GDPR Art 4(7)-(8).

36 GDPR Art 28(10).

37 GDPR Art 5(2).

38 The duties apply only where the processing is in the context of an establishment of a controller or processor in the EU. See further §§8–042 to 8–045. As to the meaning of a 'processor,' see §8–022. In terms of the duties imposed on processors, the GDPR differs from the previous regime. Neither Directive 95/46/EC nor the DPA 1998 imposed duties on processors – all liabilities and duties (including the duty to comply with the data protection principles) were borne by data controllers.

39 GDPR Art 27(1). See also recital (22). The obligation to appoint a representative in the EU does not apply where: (a) the processing is occasional, does not include large-scale processing of special category data (ie data revealing racial or ethnic origins, political opinions, religious beliefs etc – see GDPR Art 9(1)), or personal data revealing criminal convictions and offences, and that is unlikely to result in a risk to the rights and freedoms of an individual; or (b) the processor is a public authority or body: GDPR Art 27(2). As to the meaning of 'rights and freedoms of natural persons' in this context, see §8–006. Adherence to an approved code of conduct under GDPR Art 40 or an approved certification mechanism under GDPR Art 42 may be used to demonstrate sufficient guarantees under GDPR Art 28(1): see GDPR Art 28(5). In relation to applied GDPR processing, this is modified by DPA 2018 Sch 6 para 23.

40 GDPR Art 28(3). In relation to applied GDPR processing, this is modified by DPA 2018 Sch 6 para 24(a)-(b). Provision is made for the European Commission and for the Information Commissioner to lay down standard contractual clauses covering these matters: GDPR Art 28(7)-(8).

41 GDPR Art 28(2). See also recital (109).

42 GDPR Art 28(4). Provision is made for the European Commission and for the Information Commissioner to lay down standard contractual clauses covering these matters: GDPR Art 28(7)-(8). Adherence to an approved code of conduct under GDPR Art 40 or an approved certification mechanism under GDPR Art 42 may be used to demonstrate sufficient guarantees under GDPR Art 28(4): see GDPR Art 28(5). In relation to applied GDPR processing, this is modified by DPA 2018 Sch 6 para 24(d).

data processes that data except on instructions from the controller, unless required to do so by EU or UK law.[43]

(5) The purposes and means of processing must be determined by the controller. If, in practice, a processor determines those purposes and means, it will be a *de facto* controller and will be subject to the full range of a controller's duties and liabilities.[44]

(6) A processor employing more than 250 persons must retain records of its processing activities and make them available to the Information Commissioner on request.[45]

(7) A processor must co-operate with the Information Commissioner.[46]

(8) A processor must comply with the conditions laid down for the transfer of personal data to third countries.[47]

(9) A processor is under the same duty as a controller in relation to ensuring the security of personal data.[48] A processor must notify the controller without delay after becoming aware of a personal data breach.[49]

(10) A processor is under the same duty as a controller to designate a person as a data protection officer.[50]

(11) Where a processor has infringed the GDPR and, as a result, a person has suffered material or non-material damage, the processor will be liable, but only if: (a) the processor has not complied with an obligation under the GDPR that is specifically directed to processors; or (b) the processor has acted outside or contrary to lawful instructions of the controller.[51] It will be a defence for the processor to prove that it was not in any way responsible for the event giving rise to the damage.[52] Administrative fines can also be imposed on processors.[53]

2. LAWFULLY, FAIRLY AND TRANSPARENTLY

9–006 First processing principle

The first processing principle is that personal data shall be:

---

43 GDPR Art 29. See also recital (81).

44 GDPR Art 28(10).

45 GDPR Art 30(2)-(5). This obligation will apply to a processor employing fewer than 250 employees where: (a) the processing that it carries out is likely to result in a risk to the rights and freedoms of data subjects; (b) the processing is not occasional; or (c) the processing is of special category data (ie data revealing racial or ethnic origins, political opinions, religious beliefs etc – see GDPR Art 9(1)) or relates to criminal convictions and offences referred to in GDPR Art 10: GDPR Art 30(5). As to the meaning of 'rights and freedoms of natural persons' in this context, see §8– 006. In relation to applied GDPR processing, this is modified by DPA 2018 Sch 6 para 25(d)-(g).

46 GDPR Art 31. See also GDPR Art 58 and recitals (36), (77) and (95). In relation to applied GDPR processing, this is modified by DPA 2018 Sch 6 paras 26 and 47.

47 GDPR Arts 44, 46(1), 49(6).

48 GDPR Art 32. See also recital (83).

49 GDPR Art 33(2). A 'personal data breach' means a breach of security leading to the accidental or unlawful destruction, loss, alteration, unauthorised disclosure of, or access to, personal data transmitted, stored or otherwise processed: GDPR Art 4(12).

50 GDPR Art 37. See also recital (80). As to the role of the data protection officer, see §9– 052. In relation to applied GDPR processing, this is modified by DPA 2018 Sch 6 paras 29-30.

51 GDPR Art 82(2). Private law claims are considered at §§48– 005 to 48– 013.

52 GDPR Art 82(3).

53 Neither GDPR Art 77 (right to complain to a supervisory authority) nor GDPR Art 83 (administrative fines) is confined to controllers. In relation to applied GDPR processing, this is modified by DPA 2018 Sch 6 paras 50, 56

processed lawfully, fairly and in a transparent manner in relation to the data subject.[54]

This is termed the 'lawfulness, fairness and transparency' principle. The first processing principle embodies three distinct requirements:

(1) Personal data must be processed 'lawfully.'[55] The GDPR circumscribes where processing will be lawful, providing that it will be 'lawful' if and to the extent that at least one of six bases apply.[56]

(2) Personal data must be processed 'fairly.'[57] The GDPR does not specify what is meant by this, although it is possible to piece together factors and circumstances that will point to personal data being processed fairy or not fairly.

(3) Personal data must be processed 'in a transparent manner.' The GDPR separately imposes specific transparency requirements.[58]

9–007 Processed lawfully: six bases

The first requirement of the first processing principle is that personal data be processed 'lawfully....in relation to the data subject.' For the purposes of this requirement, processing of personal data will be lawful only if and to the extent that one or more of the following bases applies:[59]

(a) The data subject has given consent to the processing of his or her personal data for one or more specific purposes.

(b) The processing is necessary for the performance of a contract to which the data subject is party or in order to take steps at the request of the data subject prior to entering into a contract.

(c) The processing is necessary for compliance with a legal obligation to which the controller is subject.

(d) The processing is necessary in order to protect the vital interests of the data subject or of another natural person.

(e) The processing is necessary for the performance of a task carried out in the public interest or in the exercise of official authority vested in the controller.

(f) The processing is necessary for the purposes of the legitimate interests pursued by the controller or by a third party, except where such interests are overridden by the interests or fundamental rights and freedoms of the data subject[60] which require protection of personal data, in particular where the data subject is a child.

Each of these is described as a 'basis' for lawful processing.[61]

9–008 Basis 1 - with consent

The first basis for lawful processing of personal data is where:

the data subject has given consent to the processing of his or her personal data for one or

---

54 GDPR Art 5(1)(a). See also Convention 108 Mod Art 5(3)-(4). Regulatory enforcement is considered at §§48–014 to 48–055. Private law claims are considered at §§48–005 to 48–013.

55 Under the DPA 1998, the first data protection principle required that personal data be processed 'lawfully.' Neither the DPA 1998 nor Directive 95/46/EC specified what was meant by 'lawfully.' See further §15–039.

56 GDPR Art 6(1).

57 Under the DPA 1998, the first data protection principle required that personal data be processed 'fairly.' Part II of Sch 1 to the DPA 1998 spelt out certain minimum requirements for personal data to have been processed 'fairly' but otherwise did not specify the criteria by which that was to be determined. See further §15–038.

58 GDPR Arts 12-15. See §§9–016 to 9–022.

59 GDPR Art 6(1).

60 As to the meaning of 'rights and freedoms of natural persons' in this context, see §8–006.

61 See GDPR recitals (40), (50), (68) and (155) and Art 6(3).

more specific purposes.[62]

Consent is defined to mean any freely given, specific, informed and unambiguous indication of the data subject's wishes by which he or she, by a statement or by a clear affirmative action, signifies agreement to the processing of personal data relating to him or her.[63] The requirement is slightly more stringent than was required under Directive 95/46/EC and significantly more prescriptive that the equivalent provision in the DPA 1998.[64] The burden is on the controller to be able to demonstrate that the data subject has given consent to the processing of his or her personal data.[65] In relation to the above four elements in the definition of consent:

(1) *Freely given.* Consent is unlikely to be 'freely given' where imbalances of power mean the data subject has no genuine choice or is unable to refuse or withdraw consent without detriment. Reliance on consent should thus be approached with caution in contexts such as employment and the provision of services by public authorities. Similarly, where the performance of a contract is conditional upon consent to the processing of personal data that is not necessary for the performance of that contract, the consent is very unlikely to be treated as having been freely given.[66] Significant economic duress will render consent not 'freely given.'[67] Consent is unlikely to be 'freely given' if it is unnecessarily imposed as a condition of the performance of a contract, including for services.[68] Consent will not be 'freely given' if the data subject's declaration of consent is pre-formulated and the data subject must actively object to the processing.[69]

(2) *Specific.* Where processing is for multiple purposes, 'specific' consent entails data subjects being free to choose which purposes they accept, rather than having to consent to a bundle of processing purposes. Where a request for consent forms part of a document, whether electronic or in print, also concerning other matters, the request for consent must be presented in a manner that is clearly distinguishable from those other matters; it must also be presented in an intelligible and easily accessible form, using clear and plain language.[70]

(3) *Informed.* For consent to be 'informed', the data subject should be aware at least of the identity of the controller and the purposes of the intended processing. It is, however, the purpose of the processing that must be consented to, rather than the identity of the controller who is carrying out that processing.[71] The data subject must be advised that he or she has the right to withdraw that consent at any time.[72]

---

62 GDPR Art 6(1)(a).

63 GDPR Art 4(11). See also Convention 108 Mod Art 5(2). A consent from someone other than the data subject will not amount to consent for GDPR purposes.

64 Directive 95/46/EC Arts 2(h) and 7(a); DPA 1998 Sch 2, condition 1, as read down by the Court of Appeal in *Cooper v National Crime Agency* [2019] EWCA Civ 16. See further §15– 041. Consents given before 25 May 2018 will only be effective as consents if they meet the requirements of the GDPR: recital (171).

65 GDPR Art 7(1).

66 GDPR Art 7(4).

67 *Volker und Markus Schecke GbR v Land Hessen* (C-92/09) [2012] All ER (EC) 127, [2012] IP & T 513 at [82].

68 Explanatory Report on Convention 108 Mod §42.

69 *Planet49 GmbH v Bundesverband der Verbraucherzentralen und Verbraucherverbände – Verbraucherzentrale Bundesverband eV* (C-673/17), 21 March 2019 (Adv Gen Szpunar) at [61]-[62].

70 GDPR Art 7(2). If the request for consent does not meet these requirements it will not be binding.

71 *Deutsche Telekom AG v Bundesrepublik Deutschland* (C-543/09) [2011] ECR I-3441at [61]-[65], dealing with Art 12 of the Directive on Privacy and Electronic Communications; *Tele2 (Netherlands) BV and Others v Autoriteit Consument en Markt (ACM)* (C-536/15), CJEU, 15 March 2017 at [36].

72 GDPR Art 7(3).

It must be as easy to withdraw consent as to give consent.

(4) *Unambiguous*. In order to be 'unambiguous', consent must involve a clear affirmative action. 'Opt-out' or pre-ticked 'opt-in' models will not suffice. Acknowledging prior notice that publication of some kind will happen is not 'unambiguous' consent to a particular kind of detailed publication.[73]

Where consent is relied upon to process the data in relation to the offer of 'information society services'[74] directly to a child under the age of 13, that consent must be given or authorised by the holder of parental responsibility for the child.[75] Controllers cannot swap from consent to another basis for lawful processing. Thus, if consent is relied upon in order for the processing to be lawful, and then that consent is withdrawn, the processing must cease.

9– 009 Basis 2 - contractual necessity

The second basis for lawful processing of personal data is where:

> processing is necessary for the performance of a contract to which the data subject is party or in order to take steps at the request of the data subject prior to entering into a contract.[76]

The second basis is substantially the same as was provided for under the previous data protection regime.[77] The second basis has two limbs:

(i) processing necessary for the performance of a contract to which the data subject is party; and

(ii) processing necessary to take steps at the request of the data subject prior to entering into a contract.

In both limbs it is not necessary that the controller or processor is a party to the contract with the data subject. The word 'necessary' carries a specific meaning in this context.[78] In relation to the first limb, 'necessary' means that the processing must be proportionate to the contractual obligation in support of which the processing is being carried out: the processing will not be 'necessary' where the contractual obligation could be performed without processing the personal data of the data subject or with processing of that personal data that was less intensive or invasive. In relation to the second limb, 'necessary' means that the processing must be proportionate to the step requested by the data subject prior to entering into the contract: the processing will not be 'necessary' where the step could be performed without processing the personal data of the data subject or with processing of that personal data that was less intensive or invasive. The second basis may overlap with the first basis (data subject consent) in that a contract may provide that making the contract signifies or constitutes consent to the processing of a party's personal data.[79] However, where a controller seeks to process personal data that are in fact necessary for the performance of a contract, then the appropriate basis for lawful processing is 'performance of a contract' rather than 'consent.' Guidance on this condition[80] issued by the Article 29 Working Party and adopted by the EDPB states that this basis should

---

73 *Volker und Markus Schecke GbR v Land Hessen* (C-92/09) [2012] All ER (EC) 127, [2012] IP & T 513 at [79].

74 By GDPR Art 4(25), 'information society service' means a service as defined in Directive (EU) 2015/1535 Art 1(1)(b), ie 'any service normally provided for remuneration, at a distance, by electronic means and at the individual request of a recipient of services.'

75 GDPR Art 8, as varied by DPA 2018 s 9.

76 GDPR Art 6(1)(b).

77 Under the DPA 1998, the first data protection principle required at least one of the conditions in Sch 2 to be met. The second condition in Sch 2 was in more-or-less identical terms to GDPR Art 6(1)(b). Thus, the overall effect of the condition being met under the former data protection regime was the same as the second basis applying under the current regime. As to the second condition in DPA 1998 Sch 2, see §§15– 040 and 15– 041(2).

78 See further §8– 034.

79 See, for example: *Cooper v National Crime Agency* [2019] EWCA Civ 16 at [103].

80 Opinion 06/2014 of WP29.

be interpreted strictly. There must be a 'direct and objective link' between the processing and the execution of the contract. The basis may apply, where, for example, address and credit card details are processed in order to deliver goods and take payment, or where bank account details are processed for the payment of salaries.

–010 Basis 3 - legal obligations

The third basis for lawful processing of personal data is where:

> processing is necessary for compliance with a legal obligation to which the controller is subject.[81]

The third basis is substantially the same as was provided for under the former data protection regime.[82] In relation to controllers, the phrase 'legal obligation' is used in the GDPR to signify a duty, as opposed to the term 'task' which is used to signify a power.[83] The relevant obligation must be laid down by EU or Member State law.[84] This does not include obligations imposed by contract.[85] The obligation does not necessarily need to come from legislation, but it must be clear and precise and its application should be foreseeable to persons subject to it.[86] The word 'necessary' carries a specific meaning in this context.[87] For the purposes of Basis 3, 'necessary' means that the processing must be proportionate to the legal obligation in support of which the processing is being carried out: the processing will not be 'necessary' where the legal obligation could be performed without processing the personal data of the data subject or with processing of that personal data that was less intensive or invasive. The lawful basis for processing must thus accord with EU law principles of legal certainty and proportionality.[88] There does not need to be a specific obligation to process personal data.

–011 Basis 4 - protecting vital interests

The fourth basis for lawful processing of personal data is where:

> processing is necessary in order to protect the vital interests of the data subject or of another natural person[89]

The fourth basis is substantially the same as was provided for under the former data protection regime.[90] 'Vital interests' means an interest which is essential for the life of the data subject or

---

81 GDPR Art 6(1)(c).

82 Under the DPA 1998, the first data protection principle required at least one of the conditions in Sch 2 to be met. The third condition in Sch 2 was in more-or-less identical terms to GDPR Art 6(1)(c). Thus, the overall effect of the condition being met under the former data protection regime was the same as the third basis applying under the current regime. As to the third condition in DPA 1998 Sch 2, see §§15–040 and 15–041(3).

83 This appears from GDPR recitals (5), (10), (45), (51), (65) and (68), as well as Arts 17(3)(b) and 43(2)(e). When it comes to supervisory authorities, the meaning of the terms 'tasks' and 'powers' is more clearly set out: GDPR Arts 57 and 58.

84 GDPR Art 6(3).

85 See, for example: *R (British Telecommunications plc & ors) v Secretary of State for Business, Innovation and Skills* [2011] EWHC 1021 (Admin), [2012] 3 CMLR 98 at [152]; *CN v European Parliament* (T-343/13) 3 December 2015 at [35]; *R (Hussain) v Sandwell MBC* [2017] EWHC 1641 (Admin), [2018] PTSR 142 at [231]-[233] (duty in s 27 of Localism Act 2011 on a local authority to promote and maintain high standards said to justify publishing critical report of an elected member of that authority). Judicial activism under the former regime stretched it to cover public law obligations on a public sector data controller created by its own policies: *Cooper v National Crime Agency* [2019] EWCA Civ 16 at [104].

86 GDPR recitals (41) and (45).

87 See further §8–034.

88 *Rechnungshof v Österreichischer Rundfunkat* (C-465/00) [2003] 3 CMLR 10 at [91].

89 GDPR Art 6(1)(d).

90 Under the DPA 1998, the first data protection principle required at least one of the conditions in Sch 2 to be met. The fourth condition in Sch 2 was in more-or-less identical terms to GDPR Art 6(1)(d). Thus, the overall effect of the condition being met under the former data protection regime was the same as the fourth basis applying

that of another natural person.[91] It requires more than that the processing is likely to benefit the well-being of the data subject or another person: the most obvious example is a medical emergency.[92] The word 'necessary' carries a specific meaning in this context.[93] For the purposes of Basis 4, 'necessary' means that the processing must be proportionate to the vital interest that is being protected by the processing: the processing will not be 'necessary' where the vital interest could be equally well protected without processing the personal data of the data subject or with processing of that personal data that was less intensive or invasive. This basis should only be relied on where the processing cannot be manifestly based on another legal basis.[94]

9– 012 Basis 5 - public interest tasks

The fifth basis for lawful processing of personal data is where:

> processing is necessary for the performance of a task carried out in the public interest or in the exercise of official authority vested in the controller.[95]

The fifth basis is, in general terms, similar to what was provided for under the previous data protection regime.[96] In relation to controllers and processors, the word 'task' is used in the GDPR to signify a power, as opposed to the phrase 'legal obligation' which is used to signify a duty.[97] Although Basis 5 has two limbs:

(i) processing necessary for the performance of a task carried out in the public interest; and

(ii) processing of a task carried out in the exercise of official authority vested in the controller,

the two limbs are largely overlapping. The first limb is capable of independent operation where a private-sector processor is processing personal data on behalf of a public authority in the performance of the authority's functions. Basis 5 is thus most relevant to public authorities, but it can apply to any controller carrying out tasks in the public interest or exercising official authority.[98] The relevant task or authority must be laid down by EU or Member State law.[99] The task or authority does not necessarily need to come from legislation, but it must be clear

---

under the current regime. As to the fourth condition in DPA 1998 Sch 2, see §§15– 040 and 15– 041(4).

91 GDPR recitals (46) and (112).

92 *Christian Institute v Lord Advocate* [2016] UKSC 51, [2016] HRLR 19 at [48], [50].

93 See further §8– 034.

94 GDPR recital (46).

95 GDPR Art 6(1)(e).

96 Under the DPA 1998, the first data protection principle required at least one of the conditions in Sch 2 to be met. The fifth condition in Sch 2, which had five limbs, achieved a similar outcome as, but with greater specificity than, GDPR Art 6(1)(e). The fifth condition in Sch 2 was supposed to give effect to Art 7(e) of Directive 95/46/EC. That Article was not limited to those having a function conferred on them by an enactment and, as such, had a further reach than the fifth condition in Sch 2 and more closely resembled GDPR Art 6(1)(e). The overall effect of the condition being met under the former data protection regime was substantially the same as the fifth basis applying under the current regime. As to the fifth condition in DPA 1998 Sch 2, see §§15– 040 and 15– 041(5).

97 This appears from GDPR recitals (5), (10), (45), (51), (65) and (68), as well as Arts 17(3)(b) and 43(2)(e). When it comes to supervisory authorities, the meaning of the terms 'tasks' and 'powers' is more clearly set out: GDPR Arts 57 and 58.

98 See DPA 2018 s 7(2). An example of a private body performing a task in the public interest could be a privatised water or sewage company, provided that the processing is in support of the supply of water or the collection of sewage. The GDPR contradistinguishes tasks carried out in the public interest from tasks carried out for commercial gain. Examples of tasks carried out in the public interest are given in GDPR recitals (45), (46), (50), (52), (53), (54), (62), (65), (73), (112) and (156): safeguarding public security, public health, social protection, humanitarian purposes, natural and man-made disasters, prevention, investigation and prosecution of criminal offences, breach of ethics by regulated professions, the collection of taxes, and maintaining official archives.

99 GDPR Art 6(3).

and precise and its application should be foreseeable to persons subject to it. The word 'necessary' carries a specific meaning in this context.[100] For the purposes of Basis 5, 'necessary' means that the processing must be proportionate to the task being carried out by the processing: the processing will not be 'necessary' where the task could equally well be carried out without processing the personal data of the data subject or with processing of that personal data that was less intensive or invasive.[101] The requirement that the task be one carried out in the public interest or in the exercise of official authority may not be satisfied where a public authority relies on common law powers or implied statutory powers for the task for which the processing of personal data is being carried out. Under the equivalent provision in the former data processing regime, once the function had been carried out, it did not automatically follow that processing (eg retaining the personal data) thereafter was necessary.[102] The qualified right to object to processing can be exercised in respect of processing undertaken in reliance on this basis.[103]

9– 013 Basis 6 - legitimate interests

The sixth basis for lawful processing of personal data is where:

> processing is necessary for the purposes of the legitimate interests pursued by the controller or by a third party, except where such interests are overridden by the interests or fundamental rights and freedoms of the data subject which require protection of personal data, in particular where the data subject is a child.[104]

This basis does not apply to 'processing carried out by public authorities in the performance of their tasks.'[105] For the purposes of the GDPR, with certain exceptions 'public authorities' or 'public bodies' are those listed as 'public authorities' under FOIA or FOI(S)A.[106] The reason for excepting public authorities in the performance of their tasks is that processing necessary for the performance of a task carried out in the exercise of official authority is covered by the fifth basis. Apart from this exception, the sixth basis is substantially the same as was provided for under the previous data protection regime.[107] The word 'necessary' carries a specific meaning in this context.[108] For the purposes of Basis 6, 'necessary' means that the processing must be proportionate to the legitimate interests pursued by the controller or a third party that are being served by the processing: the processing will not be 'necessary' where those legitimate interests could be equally well pursued without processing the personal data of the data subject or with processing of that personal data that was less intensive or invasive.

---

100 See further §8– 034.

101 GDPR recitals (41) and (45). See *R (SXM) v Disclosure and Barring Service* [2020] EWHC 624 (Admin) at [72].

102 See: *Camera di Commercio, Industria, Artigianato e Agricoltura di Lecce v Manni* (C-398/15)[2018] Bus LR 25, [2017] 3 CMLR 18 at [42]-[46]; and, by analogy, *NT1 v Google LLC* [2018] EWHC 799 (QB), [2018] 3 All ER 581 at [102].

103 GDPR Art 21.

104 GDPR Art 6(1)(f).

105 GDPR Art 6(1) coda. As to the meaning of 'rights and freedoms of natural persons' in this context, see §8– 006.

106 DPA 2018 s 7(1). The exceptions are a parish council in England, a community council in Wales or Scotland, a parish meeting constituted under LGA 1972 s 13, a community meeting constituted under LGA 1972 s 192 and certain statutorily constituted charter trustees: DPA 2018 s 7(3).

107 Under the DPA 1998, the first data protection principle required at least one of the conditions in Sch 2 to be met. The sixth condition in Sch 2 was in more-or-less identical terms to GDPR Art 6(1)(f). Thus, the overall effect of the condition being met under the former data protection regime was the same as the sixth basis applying under the current regime. As to the second condition in DPA 1998 Sch 2, see §§15– 040 and 15– 041(6).

108 See further §8– 034.

9–014 Basis 6 - the 3-step process

The existence of a legitimate interest must be carefully assessed in each specific case.[109] Reliance on this basis involves a three-step process: (i) identifying the legitimate interest being pursued; (ii) assessing whether the processing of personal data is 'necessary' for that purpose;[110] and (iii) determining whether the data subject's interests override those of the controller or third party.[111] In terms of 'legitimate interests pursued by the controller or by a third party' these have been held to include:

(a) The economic interest that a search engine operator (such as Google) has in ensuring that the search engine is effective.[112]

(b) The interests of users of a search engine in having free access to information about things and people.[113]

(c) The interest of a member of the public in receiving information about local environmental health risks.[114]

(d) The provision by a public authority of a comprehensive database for consultation by the public.[115]

(e) The investigation and prevention of crimes, the disclosure of an individual's criminal record, and the investigation of facts needed to bring a civil claim.[116]

(f) Protection of life, limb and property.[117]

(g) Matters of social concern, such as equal pay.[118]

(h) Ensuring that a public authority has performed its functions properly.[119]

(i) Ensuring the openness and transparency of a body responsible for regulating a profession.[120]

---

109 GDPR recital (47). Touched on in *R (SXM) v Disclosure and Barring Service* [2020] EWHC 624 (Admin) at [72].

110 As to the meaning of 'necessary,' see §8–034.

111 This is the same procedure that was used in relation to the equivalent provision in the previous data protection regime: *South Lanarkshire Council v Scottish IC* [2013] UKSC 55, [2013] 1 WLR 2421 at [18]; *Valsts policijas Rīgas reģiona pārvaldes Kārtības policijas pārvalde v Rīgas pašvaldības SIA* (Case C-13/16) [2017] 4 WLR 97, [2017] 3 CMLR 39 at [28], where the CJEU set out three sequential conditions that must be fulfilled for personal data to be lawful on the legitimate interest ground, namely (i) the third party to whom the personal data are disclosed must be pursuing a legitimate interest, eg to be able to sue a person, (ii) the processing of the personal data must be necessary for the purposes of the legitimate interest being pursued, and (iii) the fundamental rights and freedoms of the data subject must not overwhelm the legitimate interests of the controller or of the third party; *Asociacion Nacional de Establecimientos Financieros de Credito v Administracion del Estado* (Case C-468/10) [2012] 1 CMLR 48, which held that the significance of the rights and freedoms of the data subject is informed by the seriousness of the infringement. See also *Rodriguez-Noza v IC and Nursing and Midwifery Council* [2015] UKUT 449 (AAC) at [19]. Further guidance on the equivalent basis under Article 7 of Directive 95/46/EC was issued by the Article 29 Working Party: WP29 Opinion 06/2014 (9 April 2014).

112 *Google Spain SL v Agencia Espanola de Proteccion de Datos* [2014] QB 1022 at [81]; *NT1 v Google LLC* [2018] EWHC 799 (QB), [2019] QB 344 at [115], [134]; *Townsend v Google Inc* [2017] NIQB 81 at [46], [61].

113 *Google Spain SL v Agencia Espanola de Proteccion de Datos* [2014] QB 1022 at [81], [91]; *NT1 v Google LLC* [2018] EWHC 799 (QB), [2019] QB 344 at [115], [134], [168]; *Campbell v Mirror Group Newspapers Ltd* [2002] EWCA Civ 1373, [2003] QB 633 at [40].

114 *Common Services Agency v IC* [2008] UKHL 47, [2008] 1 WLR 1550 at [32].

115 *Breyer v Federal Republic of Germany* (C-582/14) [2017] 1 WLR 1569 at [60].

116 *R (Bridges) v Chief Constable of South Wales Police* [2019] EWHC 2341 (Admin) at [127]; *Holyoake v Candy* [2017] EWHC 3397 (Ch) at [464]; *Valsts policijas Rīgas reģiona pārvaldes Kārtības policijas pārvalde v Rīgas pašvaldības SIA* (Case C-13/16) [2017] 4 WLR 97, [2017] 3 CMLR 39 at [29]. See also GDPR recital (47).

117 *Rynes v Urad pro ochranu osobnich udaju* (C-212/13) [2015] 1 WLR 2607, [2015] CEC 732 at [34].

118 *South Lanarkshire Council v Scottish IC* [2013] UKSC 55, [2013] 1 WLR 2421.

119 *Beggs v Scottish Information Commissioner* [2016] CSIH 23, 2016 SC 615, 2016 GWD 11-225.

120 *DB v General Medical Council* [2016] EWHC 2331 (QB), [2019] 1 WLR 4044 at [22]-[23] and [81]-[83].

(j) Direct marketing.[121] Care should be taken here to ensure that direct marketing is conducted in accordance with Privacy and Electronic Communications law,[122] as an interest is unlikely to qualify as 'legitimate' if it is unlawful.[123]

(k) The pursuit of any legitimate business, including ensuring its smooth operation.[124]

In terms of 'the interests or fundamental rights and freedoms of the data subject which require protection of personal data, in particular where the data subject is a child'[125] these have been held to include:

(a) The reasonable expectation of the data subject, at the time and in the context of the collection of their data, as to how his or her data would be used.[126]

(b) Protection of a data subject's private life.[127]

For GDPR purposes, the EDPB has adopted and retained the guidance and opinions issued by the Article 29 Working Party.[128] Where controllers contend that the sixth basis applies, the information that they provide under their transparency duties must identify the legitimate interest(s) being pursued.[129] The qualified right to object to processing can be exercised in respect of processing undertaken in reliance on this basis.[130]

9–015 Processed fairly

The second requirement of the first processing principle is that personal data be processed 'fairly....in relation to the data subject.'[131] The content of the requirement that personal data be processed 'fairly' is not expressly spelled out by the GDPR, with the Regulation allowing a Member State to identify the measures required in order for there to be fair processing.[132] The DPA 2018 has not taken that opportunity. Certain factors do, however, emerge from the text of the GDPR itself:

(1) The requirement that personal data be processed fairly overlaps with the requirement that it be processed 'in a transparent manner.' Specifically, the provision of information to a data subject on the identity of the controller, the purposes of the processing and 'further information' about the processing relate both to the requirement to process fairly and to the requirement to process in a transparent manner.[133]

(2) The requirement that personal data be processed fairly also impinges upon consent, seemingly adding a requirement that any consent not contain unfair terms.[134]

---

121 GDPR recital (47).

122 That is, the Privacy and Electronic Communications (EC Directive) Regulations 2003.

123 *Google Spain SL v Agencia Espanola de Proteccion de Datos* [2014] QB 1022 at [74].

124 *Townsend v Google Inc* [2017] NIQB 81 at [46]; *NT1 v Google LLC* [2018] EWHC 799 (QB), [2018] 3 All ER 581 at [115]; *Murray v Express Newspapers Ltd* [2007] EWHC 1908, [2007] EMLR 22 at [76]; *Bărbulescu v Romania* [2017] IRLR 1032, (2017) 44 BHRC 17 at [127].

125 As to the meaning of 'fundamental rights and freedoms of the data subject' in this context, see §8– 006.

126 GDPR recital (47).

127 *Nowak v Data Protection Commissioner* (C-434/16) [2018] 1 WLR 3505, [2018] 2 CMLR 21 at [50].

128 That is, WP29 Opinion 06/2014 (9 April 2014).

129 GDPR Art 13(1)(d).

130 GDPR Art 21.

131 GDPR Art 5(1).

132 GDPR Art 6(2)-(3) and recital (45).

133 GDPR Arts 13(2) and 14(2) and recitals (39), (60) and (71).

134 GDPR recital (42). This is in addition to the requirement for due consent under GDPR Ar 6(1)(a) in conjunction with Art 4(11).

The statutory allocation of requirements to the duty to process 'lawfully' and to the duty to process 'fairly' differs from the allocation of requirements in the previous regime's first data protection principle. As a result, jurisprudence on the meaning of the content of those terms under the previous regime provides no safe guide to their meaning for the purposes of the first processing principle in the GDPR.[135] Nevertheless, the Information Commissioner considers that processing personal data fairly entails:[136]

(a) ensuring that data subjects are not deceived or misled when their personal data is collected;
(b) processing data in accordance with data subjects' reasonable expectations (unless a departure from those expectations can be justified); and
(c) avoiding causing adverse effects to data subjects (unless those adverse effects can be justified).

9– 016 Processed transparently

The third requirement of the first processing principle is that personal data be processed in 'a transparent manner in relation to the data subject.'[137] Although the GDPR does not for the purposes of the first processing principle expressly specify the content of the requirement that personal data be processed in a transparent manner, that content is tolerably clear from the various references to transparency in the GDPR:

(1) Articles 12-14 spell out specific information that a controller must provide in relation to the processing of personal data.[138] It is suggested that compliance with these Articles will usually suffice to show that personal data has been or is being processed in a transparent manner in relation to the data subject and thus satify the third requirement of the first processing principle.[139]
(2) Underscoring Articles 12-14, recital (39) provides:

> ...The principle of transparency requires that any information and communication relating to the processing of those personal data be easily accessible and easy to understand, and that clear and plain language be used. That principle concerns, in particular, information to the data subjects on the identity of the controller and the purposes of the processing and further information to ensure fair and transparent processing in respect of the natural persons concerned and their right to obtain confirmation and communication of personal data concerning them which are being processed....[140]

(3) Where there are joint controllers, they must 'in a transparent manner determine their respective responsibilities for compliance with the obligations' under the

---

135 See §15– 038. While, under that regime, the minimum requirements of processing personal data 'fairly' were spelled out, the requirements of processing personal data 'lawfully' were not. The sum of their contents plus those in Schedule 2 was similar to those of the first processing principle under GDPR.

136 Information Commissioner, *Guide to the GDPR*. The Guide does not have any special status.

137 GDPR Art 5(1). See also recital (39). Transparency duties were imposed under Directive 95/46/EC Arts 10-12 and DPA 1998 s 7 and Sch 1 Part II para 2.

138 See §§9– 018 to 9– 021.

139 This is borne out by GDPR Art 5(1)(a) defining 'transparency' to mean its requirement that personal data be 'processed in a transparent manner in relation to the data subject' and the title of GDPR Chapter III section 1 (Art 12), ie 'Transparency and modalities.' GDPR Art 12 imposes a duty on a controller to take:

> '....appropriate measures to provide any information referred to in Articles 13 and 14 and any communication under Articles 15 to 22 and 34 relating to processing to the data subject in a concise, transparent, intelligible and easily accessible form, using clear and plain language, in particular for any information addressed specifically to a child.'

This links GDPR Arts 13 and 14 to the requirement in Art 5(1)(a) to process personal data 'in a transparent manner.'

140 To similar effect, see also GDPR recitals (58), (60), (78).

GDPR.[141]

9–017 Transparency obligations

By its nature, most processing of personal data will be done without the knowledge of the individual to whom the data relates. Indeed, throughout the entire life-cycle of information about an individual – from its acquisition, through all its uses, modification, transfers, storage, and ending with its destruction or erasure – that individual, while suffering the consequences, may be oblivious to any of that processing, including the uses to which that personal information is being put. The rights of an individual may thus be diminished, if not emptied, without a mechanism by which that individual is informed of the uses to which information about him or her is being processed. The GDPR further recognises that, without a continuing obligation on a controller to reveal the processing of an individual's personal information, processing, both in kind and in scale, may remain undetected by the individual to whom it relates. The GDPR addresses these closely related matters in two ways:

(1) In defined circumstances, it imposes on a controller a continuing duty to provide a data subject with particular information relating to the controller's processing of that data subject's personal data.[142] The existence of this duty does not depend on the data subject having requested the information or even being aware of its existence: the duty is spontaneous. The scope of the duty and the moment at which it arises depends on whether the personal data has or has not been collected from the data subject.[143] It is this spontaneous duty to which the first processing principle is linked. The duty is subject to disapplications and to exemptions, under the GDPR and under the DPA 2018 respectively. The GDPR disapplications are specific to the continuing transparency obligation. The reach of these disapplications varies according to whether the personal data has or has not been collected from the data subject.[144] The DPA 2018 exemptions are largely the same as those applicable to the data subject rights (and the resultant controller and processor obligations).[145]

(2) An individual may request a controller to provide him or her with information on that controller's processing of his or her personal data.[146] In this situation, it is the individual's request that triggers the obligation on the controller. While serving a similar objective to the spontaneous duty, it is not part of the transparency requirement within the first processing principle. This distinct, additional duty is considered separately.[147] This right, with the duty that results for the controller, is subject to exemptions under the DPA 2018 that are largely the same as those applicable to other data subject rights.[148]

9–018 Subject sourced data

Where personal data relating to a data subject are collected from the data subject, the

---

141 GDPR Art 26(1).

142 GDPR Arts 13 and 14.

143 GDPR Arts 13 and 14 respectively.

144 These are considered at §9–022.

145 These are considered in Chapter 11.

146 GDPR Art 15.

147 See §§10–014 to 10–017.

148 These are considered in Ch 11.

transparency obligation arises at the time 'when personal data are obtained.'[149] The obligation is iterative, arising each time the controller obtains further personal data relating to the data subject. For the purposes of this obligation, it is not necessary that the controller is the person who collected the personal data from the data subject: the obligation will, for example, arise where a controller obtains the personal data from a source and it is that source that has collected the personal data from the data subject. In this way, the obligation will not be circumvented by separating the controller from the activity of collecting personal data relating to the data subject.

9–019 Notification: subject sourced

In relation to personal data collected from a data subject, the controller must provide that data subject with certain specific information, as well as with certain other information to the extent that that information is 'necessary to ensure fair and transparent processing.'[150] The specific information is:

- (a) the identity and the contact details of the controller and, where applicable, of the controller's representative;[151]
- (b) the contact details of the controller's data protection officer, where the controller is required to have one;[152]
- (c) the purposes of the processing for which the personal data are intended as well as the legal basis for the processing;[153]
- (d) where the processing is based on it being necessary for legitimate interests pursued by the controller or by a third party, the legitimate interests pursued by the controller or by a third party;[154]
- (e) the recipients or categories of recipients of the personal data, if any;
- (f) where the controller intends to transfer personal data to a third country or international organisation:[155]
  - (i) the fact of that intention;
  - (ii) the existence or absence of an adequacy decision by the European Commission;[156] and
  - (iii) in the case of a transfer to a third country or international organisation where there is no adequacy decision, reference to the appropriate or

---

149 GDPR Art 13(1).

150 GDPR Art 13(1)-(2).

151 An email address is a contact detail: GDPR recital (23).

152 GDPR Art 37 imposes a requirement on certain controllers to designate a data protection officer: see §9–052.

153 The 'legal basis' does not necessarily require a legislative act adopted by a legislature, but such a basis must be clear and precise and its application should be foreseeable to persons subject to it: GDPR recital (41). The legitimate interests of a controller, including those of a controller to which the personal data may be disclosed, or of a third party, may provide a legal basis for processing, provided that the interests or the fundamental rights and freedoms of the data subject are not overriding: GDPR recital (47). As to the meaning of the 'fundamental rights and freedoms of the data subject' in this context, see §8–006. Subordinate legislation may specify a legal basis for processing: DPA 2018 Sch 6 para 10(b). Where the controller intends to further process the personal data for a purpose other than that for which the personal data were collected, the controller shall provide the data subject prior to that further processing with information on that other purpose: GDPR Art 13(3).

154 As to what might constitute a 'legitimate interest', see GDPR recitals (47)-(51) and (88). See further §9–014.

155 As to the meaning of 'third country,' see §8–032. As to the meaning of 'international organisations,' see §8–033.

156 A transfer of personal data to a third country or an international organisation may take place where the European Commission has decided that the third country, a territory or one or more specified sectors within that third country, or the international organisation in question ensures an adequate level of protection. The decision of the Commission is called an 'adequacy decision.' The European Commission publishes a list of countries and territories for which it has made an adequacy decision in the Official Journal of the European Union and on its website: GDPR Art 45.

suitable safeguards and the means by which the data subject can obtain a copy of them or where they have been made available.[157]

The other specified information that the controller must provide the data subject,[158] but only so far as necessary to ensure fair and transparent processing, is information as to:

(g) the period for which the personal data will be stored, or if that is not possible, the criteria used to determine that period;[159]

(h) the existence of the right to request from the controller access to and rectification or erasure of personal data or restriction of processing concerning the data subject or to object to processing as well as the right to data portability;[160]

(i) where the processing is based on the data subject having given consent to the processing of his or her personal data for one or more specific purposes or, in the case of sensitive personal information, it is based on the data subject having given 'explicit consent' to the processing of his or her personal data for one or more specific purposes, the existence of the right to withdraw consent at any time;

(j) the right to lodge a complaint with the Information Commissioner;[161]

(k) whether the provision of personal data is a statutory or contractual requirement, or a requirement necessary to enter into a contract, as well as whether the data subject is obliged to provide the personal data and of the possible consequences of failure to provide such data; and

(l) the existence of automated decision-making, including profiling,[162] and meaningful information about the logic involved, as well as the significance and the envisaged consequences of such processing for the data subject.

The controller must take appropriate measures to provide the data subject with the above information in a concise, transparent, intelligible and easily accessible form, using clear and plain language.[163] The information must be provided free-of-charge and may include machine-readable icons.[164]

9–020 Non-subject sourced data

Where personal data relating to a data subject is not obtained from the data subject – for example, where the controller has itself generated that personal data or has obtained it from another source that has generated it – the transparency obligation on the controller is less categorical than it is in relation to data obtained from the data subject.[165] The moment at which the transparency obligation arises depends upon the use to which the controller intends

---

[157] GDPR Arts 46-47 and 49(1). As to the meaning of 'third country,' see §8– 032. As to the meaning of 'international organisations,' see §8– 033.

[158] GDPR Art 13(2).

[159] Courts have considered the proportionality of retention periods in terms of compliance with Article 8 ECHR and the DPA 1998: see, for example, *R (Catt) v ACPO* [2015] UKSC 9, [2015] AC 1065.

[160] Rectification and erasure are provided for by GPDR Arts 16-17. As to the meaning of 'restriction of processing,' see §8– 031.

[161] The Information Commissioner is the 'supervisory authority' in the UK for the purposes of the GDPR: DPA 2018 s 115(1).

[162] 'Profiling' means any form of automated processing of personal data evaluating the personal aspects relating to a natural person, in particular to analyse or predict aspects concerning the data subject's performance at work, economic situation, health, personal preferences or interests, reliability or behaviour, location or movements: GDPR Art 4(4) and recital (71).

[163] GDPR Art 12(1). See also GDPR recital (60).

[164] GDPR Art 12(5) and (7).

[165] See the disapplications of the obligation in §9– 022. These disapplications are more extensive than the single disapplication for subject-sourced data.

to put that personal data:[166]

(a) where the personal data are to be used for communication with the data subject — no later than at the time of the first communication to that data subject;
(b) where a disclosure to another recipient is envisaged — no later than when the personal data are first disclosed;
(c) otherwise — within a reasonable period after obtaining the personal data, but at the latest within one month, having regard to the specific circumstances in which the personal data are processed.[167]

9–021 Notification: non-subject sourced

In relation to personal data not collected from a data subject, the controller must provide that data subject with certain specific information, as well as with certain other information to the extent that that information is 'necessary to ensure fair and transparent processing.'[168] The specific information is:

(a) the identity and the contact details of the controller and, where applicable, of the controller's representative;[169]
(b) the contact details of the controller's data protection officer, where the controller is required to have one;[170]
(c) the purposes of the processing for which the personal data are intended as well as the legal basis for the processing;[171]
(d) the categories of personal data concerned;
(e) the recipients or categories of recipients of the personal data, if any;
(f) where the controller intends to transfer personal data to a third country or international organisation:[172]
    (i) the fact of that intention;
    (ii) the existence or absence of an adequacy decision by the European Commission;[173] and
    (iii) in the case of a transfer to a third country or international organisation where there is no adequacy decision, reference to the appropriate or suitable safeguards and the means by which the data subject can obtain

166 GDPR Art 14(1), (3).

167 GDPR Art 14(3).

168 GDPR Art 14(1)-(2).

169 An email address is a contact detail: GDPR recital (23).

170 GDPR Art 37 imposes a requirement on certain controllers to designate a data protection officer: see §9–052.

171 The 'legal basis' does not necessarily require a legislative act adopted by a legislature, but such a basis must be clear and precise and its application should be foreseeable to persons subject to it: GDPR recital (41). The legitimate interests of a controller, including those of a controller to which the personal data may be disclosed, or of a third party, may provide a legal basis for processing, provided that the interests or the fundamental rights and freedoms of the data subject are not overriding: GDPR recital (47). As to the meaning of the 'fundamental rights and freedoms of the data subject' in this context, see §8–006. Subordinate legislation may specify a legal basis for processing: DPA 2018 Sch 6 para 10(b). Where the controller intends to further process the personal data for a purpose other than that for which the personal data were collected, the controller shall provide the data subject prior to that further processing with information on that other purpose: GDPR Art 14(4).

172 As to the meaning of 'third country,' see §8–032. As to the meaning of 'international organisations,' see §8–033.

173 A transfer of personal data to a third country or an international organisation may take place where the European Commission has decided that the third country, a territory or one or more specified sectors within that third country, or the international organisation in question ensures an adequate level of protection. The decision of the Commission is called an 'adequacy decision.' The European Commission publishes a list of countries and territories for which it has made an adequacy decision in the Official Journal of the European Union and on its website: GDPR Art 45.

a copy of them or where they have been made available.[174]

The other specified information that the controller must provide the data subject,[175] but only so far as necessary to ensure fair and transparent processing, is information as to:

(g) the period for which the personal data will be stored, or if that is not possible, the criteria used to determine that period;[176]

(h) where the processing is based on it being necessary for legitimate interests pursued by the controller or by a third party, the legitimate interests pursued by the controller or by a third party;[177]

(i) the existence of the right to request from the controller access to and rectification or erasure of personal data or restriction of processing concerning the data subject or to object to processing as well as the right to data portability;[178]

(j) where the processing is based on the data subject having given consent to the processing of his or her personal data for one or more specific purposes or, in the case of sensitive personal information, it is based on the data subject having given 'explicit consent' to the processing of his or her personal data for one or more specific purposes, the existence of the right to withdraw consent at any time;

(k) the right to lodge a complaint with the Information Commissioner;[179]

(l) the source from which the personal data originate, and if applicable, whether it came from publicly accessible sources;[180] and

(m) the existence of automated decision-making, including profiling,[181] and meaningful information about the logic involved, as well as the significance and the envisaged consequences of such processing for the data subject.

The controller must take appropriate measures to provide the data subject with the above information in a concise, transparent, intelligible and easily accessible form, using clear and plain language.[182] The information must be provided free-of-charge and may include machine-readable icons.[183]

9– 022 Transparency: disapplication

In limited circumstances the GDPR disapplies the two transparency obligations. These disapplications are in addition to exemptions created by the DPA 2018. The exemptions apply to the data subject rights as well as the transparency obligations, whereas the disapplications are confined to the transparency obligations.[184] The scope of the disapplications under the

---

[174] GDPR Arts 46-47 and 49(1). As to the meaning of 'third country,' see §8– 032. As to the meaning of 'international organisations,' see §8– 033.

[175] GDPR Art 14(2).

[176] Courts have considered the proportionality of retention periods in terms of compliance with Article 8 ECHR and the DPA 1998: see, for example, *R (Catt) v ACPO* [2015] UKSC 9, [2015] AC 1065.

[177] As to what might constitute a 'legitimate interest', see GDPR recitals (47)-(51) and (88).

[178] Rectification and erasure are provided for by GPDR Arts 16-17. As to the meaning of 'restriction of processing,' see §8– 031.

[179] The Information Commissioner is the 'supervisory authority' in the UK for the purposes of the GDPR: DPA 2018 s 115(1).

[180] Under GDPR Art 13, this information need not be provided in relation to data subject-sourced personal data.

[181] 'Profiling' means any form of automated processing of personal data evaluating the personal aspects relating to a natural person, in particular to analyse or predict aspects concerning the data subject's performance at work, economic situation, health, personal preferences or interests, reliability or behaviour, location or movements: GDPR Art 4(4) and recital (71).

[182] GDPR Art 12(1). See also GDPR recital (60).

[183] GDPR Art 12(5) and (7).

[184] Despite being a regulation, a Member State is entitled to pass laws restricting the scope of obligations provided

GDPR depends on whether the personal data has or has not been collected from the data subject:

(1) Where the personal data being processed has been collected from the data subject (whether by the controller or someone else), then, to the extent that the data subject already has the information, the transparency obligation is disapplied.[185]

(2) Where the personal data being processed has not been collected from the data subject (whether by the controller or someone else) – for example, where it has been generated by the controller or someone else – then the transparency obligation[186] is disapplied:

(a) to the extent that the data subject already has the information;[187]

(b) where the provision of that information proves impossible or would involve a disproportionate effort;[188]

(c) where the provision of that information is already expressly covered by EU or domestic legislation;[189] or

(d) where the provision of that information would breach a confidentiality obligation either imposed or regulated by statute and the provision of that information would conflict with a legal obligation of secrecy.[190]

Save to the extent provided above, cost does not provide a basis under the GDPR for non-compliance with the transparency obligations.[191]

3. PURPOSE LIMITATION

9–023 Second processing principle

The second processing principle is that personal data shall be:

> collected for specified, explicit and legitimate purposes and not further processed in a manner that is incompatible with those purposes; further processing for archiving purposes in the public interest, scientific or historical research purposes or statistical purposes shall, in accordance with Article 89(1), not be considered to be incompatible with the initial purposes.[192]

---

for in Arts 13-14: GDPR Art 23(1). Such restrictions must respect 'the essence of the fundamental rights and freedoms and [be] a necessary and proportionate measure in a democratic society to safeguard national security, defence, public security, crime detection and prosecution, other important objectives of general public interest, the protection of the judicial independence and judicial proceedings, upholding ethical standards in the professions, protection of the rights of a data subject or others, or the enforcement of civil law claims': GDPR Art 23(1). As to the meaning of the 'fundamental rights and freedoms of the data subject' in this context, see §8–006. In the United Kingdom, the DPA 2018 s 15 lays claim to have done so, as set out in Schs 2, 3 and 4. This work has not sought to measure those exemptions against the competency limits set by GDPR Art 23(1). The exemptions under the DPA 2018 are considered in Ch 11.

185 In other words, the transparency obligation imposed by GDPR Art 13 is disapplied: GDPR Art 13(4).

186 In other words, the transparency obligation imposed by GDPR Art 14.

187 GDPR Art 14(5)(a).

188 Special allowance is made in relation to processing for archiving purposes in the public interest, scientific or historical research purposes or statistical purposes: GDPR Arts 14(5)(b) and 89 and recital (62), and DPA 2018 s 15 and Sch 2 paras 27-28. In relation to these purposes, see further §§11–051 to 11–052.

189 GDPR Art 14(5)(c).

190 GDPR Art 14(5)(d).

191 To the extent that GDPR Art 12(5) allows a controller to charge a fee or to refuse to act, it is confined to requests made in respect of data subject rights, and is not concerned with the continuing obligations.

192 GDPR Art 5(1)(b). Regulatory enforcement is considered at §§48–014 to 48–055. Private law claims are considered at §§48–005 to 48–013.

As part of the transparency obligation, a controller must communicate to a data subject the purposes of the processing for which the personal data are intended.[193]

– 024 Processing for other purposes

As a corollary of the second processing principle, where a controller intends to process personal data for a purpose other than the specified, explicit purpose for which it was collected, the controller must give the data subject prior notice of the proposed further processing.[194] The person who collected the personal data being processed by the controller may be someone other than the controller: for example, where a controller obtains the personal data from a source and it is that source that has collected the personal data from the data subject.

– 025 Compatible purposes

Regardless of any notification advising the data subject of processing for other purposes, the controller must not further process that personal data in a manner that is incompatible with the purposes for which the data was collected from the data subject.[195] In assessing whether the subsequent purpose is 'compatible' with the purposes for which the data was collected, the following factors are relevant:

- the links between those purposes;
- the context in which the data was collected;
- the reasonable expectations of the data subjects about the use of their data;
- the nature of the data; and
- the consequences of the intended further processing and the existence of safeguards for data subjects.[196]

– 026 Deemed compatible purposes

Provided that it is carried out in accordance with applicable safeguards, further processing that is necessary:

- for archiving purposes in the public interest,
- for scientific or historical research purposes, or
- for statistical purposes

is deemed not to be incompatible with the initial purposes.[197] There are two situations where processing of personal data for any of the above purposes will not meet the safeguards:

(1) Where the processing is likely to cause substantial damage or substantial distress to a data subject.[198]

(2) Where the processing is carried out for the purposes of measures or decisions with respect to a particular data subject, unless the purposes for which the processing is necessary include the purposes of approved medical research.[199]

---

193 GDPR Arts 13(1)(c) and 14(1)(c). See §§9–017 to 9–021.

194 GDPR Arts 13(3) and 14(4), and recitals (61), (70). See §§9–017 to 9–021.

195 GDPR Art 5(1)(b). The comparator is the purpose for which the personal data was collected. The person who collected the personal data being processed by the controller may be someone other than the controller.

196 GDPR recital (50).

197 GDPR Arts 5(1)(b) and 89(1), and see recitals (50), (73), (156) and (158).

198 DPA 2018 s 19(2).

199 DPA 2018 s 19(3). 'Approved medical research' means medical research carried out by a person who has approval to carry out that research from a research ethics committee recognised or established by the Health Research Authority under the Care Act 2014 or a body appointed for the purpose of assessing the ethics of research. The latter body must be one involving individuals appointed by the Secretary of State, the Scottish Ministers, the Welsh Ministers, or a Northern Ireland department, a relevant NHS body; United Kingdom Research and Innovation or a body that is a Research Council for the purposes of the Science and Technology Act 1965, an institution that

Provided that neither of these is applicable, further processing of personal data for any of the above purposes will meet the applicable safeguards and thus be deemed not incompatible with the initial purposes.[200]

9–027 Incompatible purposes

Where the other purposes for which a controller is processing, or intends to process, a data subject's personal data are incompatible with the specified, explicit and legitimate purposes for which that data was collected, the processing of that personal data for those other purposes may take place only:

(a) with the data subject's consent;

(b) pursuant to proportionate Union or Member State laws for important objectives of general public interest, or

(c) in order to report possible criminal acts or threats to public security to competent authorities, subject to a legal, professional or other binding obligation of secrecy.[201]

4. DATA MINIMISATION

9–028 Third processing principle

The third processing principle is that personal data shall be:

> adequate, relevant and limited to what is necessary in relation to the purposes for which they are processed.[202]

This is termed 'data minimisation.' This principle is directed to the quality and quantity of the personal data being processed. The specified, explicit and legitimate purposes for which the personal data has been collected – whether by the controller or another person – and provided for by the second processing principle, supplies the yardstick against which to measure the adequacy, relevance and necessity of the personal data. In providing that the personal data shall be limited to what is necessary in relation to the purposes for which they are processed, the third processing principle sets a quantitative limit on the personal data. The fifth processing principle adds a temporal limit on the keeping of that personal data.[203]

5. ACCURACY

9–029 Fourth processing principle

The fourth processing principle is that personal data shall be:

> accurate and, where necessary, kept up to date; every reasonable step must be taken to ensure that personal data that are inaccurate, having regard to the purposes for which they

---

is a research institution for the purposes of the Income Tax (Earnings and Pensions) Act 2003 s 457 of that Act. A 'relevant NHS body' means an NHS trust or NHS foundation trust in England, an NHS trust or Local Health Board in Wales, a Health Board or Special Health Board constituted under the National Health Service (Scotland) Act 1978 s 2, the Common Services Agency for the Scottish Health Service, or any of the health and social care bodies in Northern Ireland falling within the Health and Social Care (Reform) Act (Northern Ireland) 2009 s 1(5).

200 DPA 2018 s 19

201 GDPR recital (50).

202 GDPR Art 5(1)(c). Regulatory enforcement is considered at §§48–014 to 48–055. Private law claims are considered at §§48–005 to 48–013.

203 The link between the third and fifth processing principles is recognised in GDPR recital (39).

are processed, are erased or rectified without delay.[204]

This is termed 'accuracy.' In common with the third processing principle, this principle is concerned with the quality of the personal data rather than with the activity of its processing. The principle is concerned with the accuracy of the data itself and not simply whether that data has been accurately recorded. Thus, even if a controller or processor has accurately recorded personal data provided by a data subject or a third party, but the data itself is inaccurate, the principle engages.[205] For the purposes of this principle, there is no definition of 'accurate' or 'inaccurate' and, in particular, nothing limiting it to matters of fact as opposed to evaluative conclusions. The DPA 2018 specifically confines 'inaccurate' to matters of fact that are incorrect or misleading.[206]

9– 030 Supporting rights

The continuing obligation arising from the fourth processing principle is supported by two rights conferred on data subjects:

(1) A data subject's right to temporarily restrict a controller's processing of his or her personal data where the accuracy of that personal data is challenged by the data subject. The restriction is for a period that enables the controller to verify the accuracy of the data.[207]

(2) A data subject's right to compel a controller to rectify inaccurate personal data concerning him or herself.[208]

The Information Commissioner may serve an enforcement notice for failure to comply with the fourth processing principle.[209] In addition to the usual requirements for an enforcement notice, an enforcement notice in respect of a failure to comply with the fourth processing principle may require the controller to rectify or erase not just the inaccurate personal data but also any other data that contains an expression of opinion which appears to the Commissioner to be based on the inaccurate personal data.[210] Unlike the other processing principles, the fourth processing principle does not apply to manual unstructured data held by public authorities.[211]

6. STORAGE LIMITATION

9– 031 Fifth processing principle

The fifth processing principle is that personal data shall be:

> kept in a form which permits identification of data subjects for no longer than is necessary for the purposes for which the personal data are processed; personal data may be stored for longer periods insofar as the personal data will be processed solely for archiving purposes in the public interest, scientific or historical research purposes or statistical purposes in

[204] GDPR Art 5(1)(d). See also GDPR recitals (39), (71). Regulatory enforcement is considered at §§48– 014 to 48– 055. Private law claims are considered at §§48– 005 to 48– 013.

[205] This is implicitly acknowledged by DPA 2018 s 151(3).

[206] DPA 2018 s 205(1).

[207] GDPR Art 18(1)(a). The controller must notify the data subject before lifting the restriction: GDPR Art 18(3). The right is considered further in §§10– 029 to 10– 034. As to the meaning of 'restriction of processing,' see §8– 031.

[208] GDPR Art 16. The right is considered further in §§10– 018 to 10– 022.

[209] DPA 2018 s 149(2)(a).

[210] DPA 2018 s 151(2). For the purposes of the DPA 2018 (but not the GDPR) 'inaccurate' means incorrect or misleading as to any matter of fact: DPA s 205.

[211] DPA 2018 ss 24-25.

> accordance with Article 89(1) subject to implementation of the appropriate technical and organisational measures required by this Regulation in order to safeguard the rights and freedoms of the data subject.[212]

This is termed 'storage limitation.' Whereas the third processing principle is directed to the quality and quantity of the personal data being processed, the fifth processing principle imposes a temporal limit on the keeping of that personal data. Within the context of the ECHR, it has been held that indefinite retention of fingerprints, cell samples and DNA profiles may be disproportionate and unnecessary in a democratic society.[213] Where personal data has been pseudonymised it will necessarily cease to have been kept in a form that permits identification of the data subject.[214]

9–032 Supporting obligations

The fifth processing principle is supported by the requirement of the transparency obligations that the controller provide the data subject with information as to the period for which personal data will be stored or, if that is not possible, the criteria used to determine that period.[215] Unless these obligations are disapplied or an exemption applies, the fifth processing principle will in practice require a controller to keep personal data no longer than its stated retention period.

9–033 Supporting rights

The continuing obligation arising from the fifth processing principle is also supported by two rights conferred on data subjects:

(1) The right to erasure, also known as the 'right to be forgotten.'[216] One of the circumstances where the right to erasure arises is where the personal data are no longer necessary in relation to the purposes for which they were collected or otherwise processed.[217] The right is subject to certain qualifications.[218]

(2) A data subject's right to restrict a controller's processing of his or her personal data where the controller no longer needs the personal data for the purposes of the processing, but they are required by the data subject for the establishment, exercise or defence of legal claims.[219]

7. DATA SECURITY

9–034 Sixth processing principle

---

[212] GDPR Art 5(1)(e). See further GDPR recitals (65) and (156). As to the meaning of 'the rights and freedoms of the data subject' in this context, see §8–006. Regulatory enforcement is considered at §§48–014 to 48–055. Private law claims are considered at §§48–005 to 48–013.

[213] *MM v United Kingdom* [2012] ECHR 1906; *S and Marper v United Kingdom* [2008] ECHR 1581, (2009) 48 EHRR 50. In those cases criminal proceedings against the applicant had been terminated by an acquittal and a discontinuance. See also: *Digital Rights Ireland Ltd v Minister for Communications, Marine and Natural Resources* (C-293/12 and C-594/12) [2015] QB 127, [2014] 3 CMLR 44 (dealing with the Data Retention Directive which is directed at harmonising national provisions on the retention of personal data generated by electronic communication services for the purpose of dealing with crime).

[214] GDPR Art 4(5).

[215] GDPR Arts 13(2)(a) and 14(2)(a). The transparency obligations, including the disapplications and exemptions, are considered at §§9–016 to 9–022.

[216] GDPR Art 17. The right is considered further in §§10–023 to 10–028.

[217] GDPR Art 17(1)(a).

[218] GDPR Art 17(3).

[219] GDPR Art 18(1)(c). The controller must notify the data subject before lifting the restriction: GDPR Art 18(3). The right is considered further in §§10–029 to 10–034. As to the meaning of 'restriction of processing,' see §8–031.

The sixth principle is that personal data shall be:

> processed in a manner that ensures appropriate security of the personal data, including protection against unauthorised or unlawful processing and against accidental loss, destruction or damage, using appropriate technical or organisational measures.[220]

This is termed 'integrity and confidentiality' but it is essentially a data security duty. The requirements of the principle include:

(1) The controller taking measures to prevent unauthorised access to or use of equipment used for the processing of personal data.[221] It requires consideration to be given to the risks presented by accidental or unlawful destruction, loss, alteration, unauthorised disclosure of, or access to, personal data transmitted, stored or otherwise processed.[222] This is termed a 'personal data breach.'[223]

(2) Requiring that a network or system is able to resist accidental events or malicious actions that compromise the availability, authenticity, integrity and confidentiality of stored or transmitted personal data.[224]

(3) A continuing obligation to update security measures to follow developments in the area and to meet newly-identified risks.[225]

(4) Similarly, a continuing obligation to evaluate the risks inherent in the processing and implementing measures to mitigate those risks, such as encryption.[226] This involves taking into account the state of the art and the costs of implementation in relation to the risks and the nature of the personal data to be protected.

(5) When entrusting a processor to carry out processing activities, ensuring that the processor provides sufficient guarantees so that that processing will meet the data security requirements.[227]

As a general rule, higher standards are to be expected for larger organisations processing substantial volumes of personal data.[228]

9–035 Supporting obligations

The sixth processing principle is supported by a set of inter-connected data security obligations.[229] Although principally resting on the controller, the first of these obligations – the security measures obligation – also applies to processors.

9–036 Security measures obligation

Both controllers and processors must implement appropriate technical and organisational measures to ensure a level of security that is appropriate to the risk.[230] The appropriateness of

---

220 GDPR Art 5(1)(f). See also GDPR recitals (39), (49), (78), (81) and (83).

221 GDPR recital (39).

222 GDPR recital (83).

223 GDPR Art 4(12).

224 GDPR recital (49).

225 GDPR recital (78).

226 GDPR recital (83).

227 GDPR recital (81).

228 *Various Claimants v Wm Morrisons Supermarket plc* [2017] EWHC 3113 (QB), [2018] 3 WLR 691 at [70].

229 GDPR Arts 32-34. Regulatory enforcement is considered at §§48– 014 to 48– 055. Private law claims are considered at §§48– 005 to 48– 013.

230 GDPR Art 32(1). In the case of a processor, see also GDPR Art 28(3)(c). This obligation does not apply to applied GDPR processing to the extent that the controller or the processor is processing personal data for the purpose of safeguarding national security or defence purposes: DPA 2018 s 28(2). However, where this obligation is disapplied, the controller or the processor must still:

(a) implement security measures that are appropriate to the risks arising from the processing of the personal

measures will be informed by the 'state of the art, the costs of implementation and the nature, scope, context and purposes of processing.'[231] The 'risk' is the product of the severity of the impact of that occurrence upon the rights and freedoms of natural persons and the likelihood of that occurrence.[232] In assessing the appropriate level of security account must be taken of the risks from accidental or unlawful destruction, loss, alteration or unauthorised access or disclosure of personal data.[233] Examples of measures that fall to be considered for the purposes of this obligation include:

(a) the pseudonymisation and encryption of personal data;
(b) the ability to ensure the ongoing confidentiality, integrity, availability and resilience of processing systems and services;
(c) the ability to restore the availability and access to personal data in a timely manner in the event of a physical or technical incident;
(d) a process for regularly testing, assessing and evaluating the effectiveness of technical and organisational measures for ensuring the security of the processing.

Compliance with this obligation can be demonstrated by adherence to an approved code of conduct or an approved certification mechanism.[234] Depending on the size of the enterprise, a controller must keep a record of the security measures implemented.[235]

9–037 Obligation to notify ICO

Where there has been a breach of security leading to the accidental or unlawful destruction, loss, alteration, unauthorised disclosure of or access to personal data – in other words 'a personal data breach' – the controller and the processor must each notify the Information Commissioner.[236] Notification must be given without delay, and in any event within 72 hours of the controller becoming aware of the breach. In the case of a controller, where notification is not made within 72 hours, it must be accompanied by an explanation for the delay. As a minimum, the notification must:

(a) describe the nature of the personal data breach including where possible, the categories and approximate number of data subjects concerned and the categories and approximate number of personal data records concerned;

---

data: DPA 2018 s 28(3); and
(b) where the processing of personal data is carried out wholly or partly by automated means, the controller or the processor must, following an evaluation of the risks, implement measures designed to: (i) prevent unauthorised processing or unauthorised interference with the systems used in connection with the processing, (ii) ensure that it is possible to establish the precise details of any processing that takes place, (iii) ensure that any systems used in connection with the processing function properly and may, in the case of interruption, be restored, and (iv) ensure that stored personal data cannot be corrupted if a system used in connection with the processing malfunctions: DPA 2018 s 28(4).

231 GDPR Art 32(1).

232 As to the meaning of 'rights and freedoms of natural persons' in this context, see §8–006. And see the discussion in *Various Claimants v Wm Morrisons Supermarket plc* [2017] EWHC 3113 (QB), [2018] 3 WLR 691 at [67]-[68]. That case concerned the DPA 1998, but the discussion is equally applicable to data security principles under the GDPR and DPA 2018.

233 GDPR Art 32(2).

234 GDPR Art 32(3). Codes of conduct are provided for by GDPR Art 40 and DPA 2018 ss 121-128 (in which they are called 'codes of practice'). A failure by a person to act in accordance with a code of practice does not of itself make that person liable to legal proceedings: DPA 2018 s 127(1). But a code is admissible as evidence in legal proceedings, though it is not clear as to what it is evidence of: DPA 2018 s 127(2).

235 See §§9–036 and 9–051.

236 GDPR Arts 33(1)-(2). The controller is excused from the notification obligation were the breach is unlikely to result in a risk to the rights and freedoms of individuals. As to the meaning of 'rights and freedoms of natural persons' in this context, see §8–006. This obligation does not apply to applied GDPR processing to the extent that the controller or the processor is processing personal data for the purpose of safeguarding national security or defence purposes: DPA 2018 s 26(2)(c)(i).

(b) communicate the name and contact details of the data protection officer or other contact point where more information can be obtained;
(c) describe the likely consequences of the personal data breach; and
(d) describe the measures taken or proposed to be taken by the controller to address the personal data breach, including, where appropriate, measures to mitigate its possible adverse effects.[237]

9– 038 Obligation to notify data subject

Where there has been a personal data breach that is likely to result in a high risk to the rights and freedoms of individuals,[238] then, unless:

(a) the controller has implemented appropriate technical and organisational protection measures, and those measures were applied to the personal data affected by the personal data breach, in particular those that render the personal data unintelligible to any person who is not authorised to access it, such as encryption;
(b) the controller has taken subsequent measures which ensure that the high risk to the rights and freedoms of data subjects is no longer likely to materialise; or
(c) it would involve disproportionate effort,[239]

the controller must, in addition to notifying the Information Commissioner, also notify the data subject without delay.[240] The notification must:

(i) describe in clear and plain language the nature of the personal data breach;
(ii) give the name and contact details of the data protection officer or other contact point where more information can be obtained;
(iii) describe the likely consequences of the personal data breach; and
(iv) describe the measures taken or proposed to be taken by the controller to address the personal data breach, including, where appropriate, measures to mitigate its possible adverse effects.[241]

9– 039 Obligation to limit access

Every controller and every processor must take steps to ensure that any natural person acting under its authority who has access to personal data does not process that personal data except on instructions from the controller unless that person is required to do so by domestic or EU

237 GDPR Art 33(3).

238 As to the meaning of 'rights and freedoms of individuals' in this context, see §8– 006.

239 Where it would involve a disproportionate effort and on that basis the controller does not notify the data subject(s), the controller must give some form of public notification or similar measure whereby the data subjects are informed in an equally effective manner: GDPR Art 34(3)(c).

240 GDPR Arts 34(1), (3). This obligation does not apply to:
(a) applied GDPR processing to the extent that the controller or the processor is processing personal data for the purpose of safeguarding national security or defence purposes: DPA 2018 s 26(2)(c)(ii);
(b) GDPR processing for the purposes of the prevention or detection of crime, the apprehension or prosecution of offenders, or the assessment or collection of a tax or duty or an imposition of a similar nature, to the extent that compliance with the obligation would be likely to prejudice any of those purposes: DPA 2018 Sch 2 para 2(1);
(c) GDPR processing where non-compliance with the obligation is required for the purposes of avoiding an infringement of the privileges of either House of Parliament: DPA 2018 Sch 2 para 13; and
(d) GDPR processing where the processing is for the purposes of journalism, academic purposes, artistic purposes or literary purposes and the controller reasonably believes that compliance with the obligation is incompatible with those purposes: DPA 2018 Sch 2 para 26.

Regulatory enforcement is considered at §§48– 014 to 48– 055.

241 GDPR Art 34(2)-(3). Where a a controller has not already given notification to the data subject and the Information Commissioner considers that none of (a)-(c) applies, the Commissioner, having considered the likelihood of the personal data breach resulting in a high risk, may require the controller to notify the data subject: GDPR Art 34(4).

law.[242] By creating a primary obligation on controllers and processors, the general exemption from liability enjoyed by a controller or processor that proves that it is not in any way responsible for an event giving rise to damage does not protect that controller or processor where someone under its authority has processed personal data without instruction.[243]

8. SENSITIVE PERSONAL DATA

9–040 Introduction

Two classes of personal data attract a more stringent control on processing:

(1) Personal data revealing racial or ethnic origin, political opinions, religious or philosophical beliefs, or trade union membership, and the processing of genetic data, biometric data for the purpose of uniquely identifying a natural person, data concerning health or data concerning a natural person's sex life and sexual orientation.[244] This is termed 'special category data.'

(2) Personal data relating to criminal convictions and offences or related security measures.[245] This includes data relating to 'the alleged commission of offences by the data subject' as well as data relating to 'proceedings for an offence committed or alleged to have been committed by the data subject or the disposal of such proceedings, including sentencing.'[246] For convenience, this is called 'criminal offence data,' although it also includes conviction data. The controls over the processing of criminal offence data are less stringent than those over special category data.

Under the DPA 1998, data answering these descriptions was called 'sensitive personal data'[247] and it, too, was subject to more stringent control. The main differences between the DPA 1998 regime and the current regime are:

(1) Under the former regime, the greater rigour was achieved by adding a further requirement to the first data protection principle in the case of sensitive personal data, rather than through the imposition of a freestanding prohibition on

---

242 GDPR Art 32(4). In the case of a processor, see also GDPR Art 28(3)(c). This obligation does not apply to applied GDPR processing to the extent that the controller or the processor is processing personal data for the purpose of safeguarding national security or defence purposes: DPA 2018 s 28(2). However, where this obligation is disapplied, the controller or the processor must still:

(a) implement securing measures that are appropriate to the risks arising from the processing of the personal data: DPA 2018 s 28(3); and

(b) where the processing of personal data is carried out wholly or partly by automated means, the controller or the processor must, following an evaluation of the risks, implement measures designed to: (i) prevent unauthorised processing or unauthorised interference with the systems used in connection with the processing, (ii) ensure that it is possible to establish the precise details of any processing that takes place, (iii) ensure that any systems used in connection with the processing function properly and may, in the case of interruption, be restored, and (iv) ensure that stored personal data cannot be corrupted if a system used in connection with the processing malfunctions: DPA 2018 s 28(4).

Regulatory enforcement is considered at §§48–014 to 48–055.

243 GDPR Art 82(3).

244 GDPR Art 9(2); see also recital (51). 'Genetic data', 'biometric data' and 'data concerning health' all have specific definitions: GDPR Arts 4(13)-(15).

245 GDPR Art 10.

246 DPA 2018 s 11(2).

247 DPA 1998 s 2. The first six classes of 'sensitive personal data' were equivalent to the classes of 'special category personal data' in the GDPR. In including convictions, s 2(h) went further than Directive 95/46/EC: see further §15–028.

processing.[248]

(2) Under the former regime, no distinction was drawn between what is now special category data and conviction data: all of these were labelled 'sensitive personal data.'

(3) The current regime gives Member States a greater legislative latitude in setting the reach of the heightened control and the extent of that heightened control. In the case of the United Kingdom, that legislative latitude has been exercised in the DPA 2018.

Taking into account the adjustments made by the DPA 2018 to the GDPR provisions, the similarities between the current regime and the DPA 1998 regime are significantly greater than the differences. It is convenient to refer collectively to special category data and criminal offence data as 'sensitive personal data' even though this is not a term used in the current data protection regime.

– 041 Special category data

To the extent that personal data is special category data its processing is prohibited.[249] Where, however, any of paragraphs (a)-(j) in GDPR Article 9(2) applies, that prohibition is disapplied.[250] Where that prohibition is disapplied, processing of that special category data must still comply with the six processing principles applicable to other personal data.[251]

– 042 Permitted processing

Where any of paragraphs (a)-(j) below applies, the Article 9 prohibition on the processing of special category data is disapplied.[252]

(a) The prohibition on processing does not apply where:

> the data subject has given explicit consent to the processing of those personal data for one or more specified purposes, except where Union or Member State law provide that the prohibition referred to in paragraph 1 may not be lifted by the data subject.[253]

This exception allows a Member State to provide that the explicit consent of a data subject will not disapply the prohibition of processing of special category data.[254] The term 'explicit' refers to the way consent is expressed by the data subject. Explicit consent can be obtained by written or signed statements, the completion of electronic forms, the use of digital signatures or online verification links or by documenting explicit consent provided orally.[255]

(b) The prohibition on processing does not apply where:

---

248 In the case of sensitive personal data, the first data protection principle required that at least one of the conditions in Sch 3 was also met: DPA 1998 Sch 1, Pt 1, para 1. See further §§15– 042 to 15– 043.

249 GDPR Art 9(1). Regulatory enforcement is considered at §§48– 014 to 48– 055. Private law claims are considered at §§48– 005 to 48– 013.

250 GDPR Art 9(2), which lists the ten bases. In relation to certain of these bases, Member States are given legislative latitude in describing their reach and application. In addition, GDPR Art 9(4) provides that Member States may maintain or introduce further conditions, including limitations, with regard to the processing of genetic data, biometric date or data concerning health.

251 That is, the processing principles listed at §9– 004: GDPR Art 5 and recital (51).

252 GDPR Art 9(2).

253 GDPR Art 9(2)(a). This is essentially the same as under the previous regime: see DPA 1998 Sch 3 para 1. As to the nature of consent required under the GDPR, see Arts 4(11), 7, 13(2)(c), 14(2)(d) 17(1)(b) and 20(1)(a), and recitals (32), (42), (43). In relation to consent by children, see GDPR Art 8 and recitals (38) and (65). In relation to reliance on consent given under the former data protection regime, see GDPR recital (171).

254 See further GDPR recital (51).

255 A29 GDPR Consent Guidance, as adopted by EDPB, revised 10 April 2018.

processing is necessary for the purposes of carrying out the obligations and exercising specific rights of the controller or of the data subject in the field of employment and social security and social protection law in so far as it is authorised by Union or Member State law or a collective agreement pursuant to Member State law providing for appropriate safeguards for the fundamental rights and the interests of the data subject.[256]

The processing will be necessary for these purposes where, and only where, it meets one of the employment, health and research etc conditions in Part 1 of Schedule 1 to the DPA 2018.[257]

(c) The prohibition on processing does not apply where:

processing is necessary to protect the vital interests of the data subject or of another natural person where the data subject is physically or legally incapable of giving consent.[258]

(d) The prohibition on processing does not apply where:

processing is carried out in the course of its legitimate activities with appropriate safeguards by a foundation, association or any other not-for-profit body with a political, philosophical, religious or trade union aim and on condition that the processing relates solely to the members or to former members of the body or to persons who have regular contact with it in connection with its purposes and that the personal data are not disclosed outside that body without the consent of the data subjects.[259]

(e) The prohibition on processing does not apply where:

processing relates to personal data which are manifestly made public by the data subject.[260]

(f) The prohibition on processing does not apply where:

processing is necessary for the establishment, exercise or defence of legal claims or whenever courts are acting in their judicial capacity.[261]

(g) The prohibition on processing does not apply where:

processing is necessary for reasons of substantial public interest, on the basis of Union or Member State law which shall be proportionate to the aim pursued, respect the essence of the right to data protection and provide for suitable and specific measures to safeguard the fundamental rights and the interests of the data subject.[262]

The processing will be necessary for these reasons where, and only where, it meets one of the 'substantial public interest conditions' listed in Part 2 of Schedule 1 to the DPA 2018.[263]

(h) The prohibition on processing does not apply where:

processing is necessary for the purposes of preventive or occupational medicine,

---

256 GDPR Art 9(2)(b). See also GDPR recitals (52) and (155) and DPA 2018 s 10(1)(a) and (2). This is essentially the same as under the previous regime: see DPA 1998 Sch 3 para 2 (employment).

257 DPA 2018 s 10(2). These conditions are considered in §9– 043.

258 GDPR Art 9(2)(c). See also GDPR recitals (46) and (112). This is essentially the same as under the previous regime: see DPA 1998 Sch 3 para 3. In relation to 'vital interests,' see §9– 011.

259 GDPR Art 9(2)(d). See also GDPR recital (51). This is essentially the same as under the previous regime: see DPA 1998 Sch 3 para 4.

260 GDPR Art 9(2)(e). This is essentially the same as under the previous regime: see DPA 1998 Sch 3 para 5.

261 GDPR Art 9(2)(f). This is essentially the same as under the previous regime: see DPA 1998 Sch 3 paras 6 and 7(1)(a).

262 GDPR Art 9(2)(g) and DPA 2018 s 10(1)(b) and (3). The approach taken under the previous regime, while similar in outcome, gave greater definition to the circumstances in which the processing would be proportionate to the aim pursued by identifying those aims: see DPA 1998 Sch 3 para 10 and Data Protection (Processing of Sensitive Personal Data) Order 2000 SI 2000/417 art 2 and Schedule.

263 DPA 2018 s 10(3). These conditions are considered in §9– 044.

> for the assessment of the working capacity of the employee, medical diagnosis, the provision of health or social care or treatment or the management of health or social care systems and services on the basis of Union or Member State law or pursuant to contract with a health professional and subject to the conditions and safeguards referred to in paragraph 3.[264]

The processing will be necessary for these purposes where, and only where, it meets one of the employment, health and research etc conditions in Part 1 of Schedule 1 to the DPA 2018.[265] Special category data may be processed for these purposes when they are processed by or under the responsibility of a health professional or a social work professional, or by another person who in the circumstances owes a duty of confidentiality under an enactment or rule of law.[266]

(i) The prohibition on processing does not apply where:

> processing is necessary for reasons of public interest in the area of public health, such as protecting against serious cross-border threats to health or ensuring high standards of quality and safety of health care and of medicinal products or medical devices, on the basis of Union or Member State law which provides for suitable and specific measures to safeguard the rights and freedoms of the data subject, in particular professional secrecy.[267]

The processing will be necessary for these reasons where, and only where, it meets one of the employment, health and research etc conditions in Part 1 of Schedule 1 to the DPA 2018.[268]

(j) The prohibition on processing does not apply where:

> processing is necessary for archiving purposes in the public interest, scientific or historical research purposes or statistical purposes in accordance with Article 89(1) based on Union or Member State law which shall be proportionate to the aim pursued, respect the essence of the right to data protection and provide for suitable and specific measures to safeguard the fundamental rights and the interests of the data subject.[269]

The processing will be necessary for these purposes where, and only where, it meets one of the employment, health and research etc conditions in Part 1 of Schedule 1 to the DPA 2018.[270] The processing will not be in accordance with Article 89(1) – and hence paragraph (j) will not disapply the prohibition on processing – if it is likely to cause substantial damage or substantial distress to a data subject.[271] Where the processing is carried out for the purposes of measures or decisions with respect to a particular individual, then that processing will not be in accordance with Article 89 unless the purposes for which the processing is necessary includes the purposes

---

264 GDPR Art 9(2)(h). The conditions in paragraph 3 are that the data is processed by or under the responsibility of a professional subject to the obligation of professional secrecy under EU or Member State law or rules established by national competent bodies or by another person also subject to a like obligation.

265 DPA 2018 s 10(2). These conditions are considered in §9– 043.

266 GDPR Art 9(3) and DPA 2018 ss 10(1)(c), (2) and 11(1). A 'health professional' is defined in DPA 2018 s 204(1), (3) and (4), a 'social work professional' is defined in DPA 2018 s 204(2). As to the meaning of 'enactment', see DPA 2018 s 205(1).

267 GDPR Art 9(2)(i) and DPA 2018 s 10(1)(d), (2). This is similar to what was provided under the previous regime: see DPA 1998 Sch 3 para 8. As to the meaning of the 'fundamental rights and freedoms of the data subject' in this context, see §8– 006.

268 These conditions are considered in §9– 043.

269 GDPR Art 9(2)(j) and DPA s 10(1)(e), (2). There was no equivalent to this under the previous regime, although some elements were picked up by DPA 1998 Sch 3 para 9 and Data Protection (Processing of Sensitive Personal Data) Order 2000 SI 2000/417 Sch para 9.

270 DPA 2018 s 10(2). These conditions are considered in §9– 043.

271 DPA 2018 s 19(2).

of 'approved medical research.'[272]

9–043 Employment etc conditions

The employment, health and research etc conditions referred to in paragraphs (b), (h), (i) and (j) are set out in Part 1 of Schedule 1 to the DPA 2018.[273] These conditions are:

(1) The processing is necessary for the purposes of performing or exercising obligations or rights which are imposed or conferred by law on the controller or the data subject in connection with employment, social security or social protection, and, when the processing is carried out, the controller has an appropriate policy document in place.[274]

(2) The processing is necessary for health or social care purposes.[275] 'Health or social care purposes' means the purposes of preventive or occupational medicine, the assessment of the working capacity of an employee, medical diagnosis, the provision of health care or treatment, the provision of social care, or the management of health care systems or services or social care systems or services.[276]

(3) The processing is necessary for reasons of public interest in the area of public health, and is carried out by or under the responsibility of a health professional,[277] or by another person who in the circumstances owes a duty of confidentiality under an enactment or rule of law.[278]

(4) The processing is necessary for archiving purposes, scientific or historical research purposes or statistical purposes, is carried out in accordance with the technical and organisational safeguards prescribed by the Information Commissioner,[279] and is in the public interest.[280]

9–044 Public interest conditions

The requirement in GDPR Art 9(2)(g) that processing be necessary for reasons of substantial public interest will only be met if the processing meets one or more of the substantial public interest conditions that are listed in Part 2 of Sch 1 to the DPA 2018.[281] Save in relation to (e), (h) and (x) below, a pre-requisite for meeting one of those substantial public interest conditions is that, throughout the time that the processing is being carried out, the controller has an appropriate policy document in place.[282] The substantial public interest conditions are:

---

272 DPA 2018 s 19(3). 'Approved medical research' means medical research carried out by a person who has approval to carry out that research from: (a) a research ethics committee recognised or established by the Health Research Authority under Chapter 2 of Part 3 of the Care Act 2014, or (b) a body appointed by any of the persons specified in DPA 2018 s 19(4).

273 DPA 2018 s 10(2).

274 DPA 2018 Sch 1 para 1(1). 'Social security' and 'social protection' are defined in DPA 2018 Sch 1 para 1(3). The nature of an 'appropriate policy' is set out in DPA 2018 Sch 1 para 39. See further §9–045. In so far as the processing is necessary for employment obligations, this resembles the previous regime: see DPA 1998 Sch 3 para 2.

275 DPA 2018 Sch 1 para 2(1).

276 DPA 2018 Sch 1 para 2(2).

277 'Health professional' means a registered medical practitioner, nurse, midwife, dentist, optometrist, osteopath, chiropractor, pharmacist, a dispensing optician, and various others: DPA 2018 s 204(1).

278 DPA 2018 Sch 1 para 3.

279 As provided for by GDPR Art 89(1) supplemented by DPA 2018 s 19.

280 DPA 2018 Sch 1 para 4.

281 DPA 2018 s 10(3).

282 DPA 2018 Sch 1 para 5. Paragraphs (e), (h) and (v) below equate to paragraphs 10, 13 and 27 of DPA 2018 Sch 1. As to the meaning of an 'appropriate policy document,' see §9–045.

(a) *Statutory etc & government purposes*. The processing is necessary both: (i) for the exercise of functions conferred by enactments or rules of law, or the functions of the Crown, Ministers of the Crown or government departments; and (ii) for reasons of substantial public interest.[283]

(b) *Administration of justice parliamentary purposes*. The processing is necessary for the administration of justice or for the exercise of a function of either House of Parliament.[284]

(c) *Equality of opportunity or treatment*. The processing is necessary for the purposes of identifying or keeping under review the existence or absence of equality of opportunity or treatment between persons of different racial or ethnic origins, people holding different religious or philosophical views, people with different states of physical or mental health or people of different sexual orientation, with a view to enabling that equality to be promoted or maintained.[285] The condition is limited to personal data revealing racial or ethnic origin, religious or philosophical beliefs, health, or sexual orientation, respectively. This condition does not apply to processing carried out for the purposes of measures or decisions with respect to a particular data subject. Nor does it apply if it is likely to cause substantial damage or substantial distress to an individual. And it does not apply if the individual has given the controller a written notice to stop processing his or her personal data.[286]

(d) *Racial & ethnic diversity*. The processing is of personal data revealing racial or ethnic origins which is carried out as part of a process of identifying suitable individuals to hold senior positions[287] in an organisation, and the processing is necessary for the purposes of promoting or maintaining diversity in the racial and ethnic origins of individuals who hold senior positions in organisations, provided that it can reasonably be carried out without the consent of the data subject.[288] This condition does not apply where the processing is likely to cause substantial damage or substantial distress to an individual, whether that individual is the data subject or someone else.[289]

(e) *Preventing unlawful acts*. The processing is necessary for the purposes of preventing or detecting an unlawful act, must be carried out without the consent of the data subject so as not to prejudice those purposes and is necessary for reasons of substantial public interest.[290] Where the processing consists of disclosing the personal data to a law enforcement body, an appropriate policy document is not required.[291]

(f) *Protecting the public against dishonesty*. The processing is necessary for the exercise of a protective function, must be carried out without the consent of the data subject so

---

283 DPA 2018 Sch 1 para 6.

284 DPA 2018 Sch 1 para 7.

285 DPA 2018 Sch 1 para 8.

286 DPA 2018 Sch 1 para 8(3)-(5).

287 A 'senior position' means: a director, secretary or other similar officer of a body corporate; a member of a limited liability partnership; a partner in a partnership; and a senior manager of an organisation, that is to say someone who plays a significant role in the making of decisions about how the whole or a substantial part of the organisation's activities are to be managed or organised or the actual managing or organising of the whole or a substantial part of those activities: DPA 2018 Sch 1 para 9(4)-(7).

288 DPA 2018 Sch 1 para 9.

289 DPA 2018 Sch 1 para 9(3).

290 DPA 2018 Sch 1 para 10(1).

291 DPA 2018 Sch 1 para 10(2).

as not to prejudice that protective function and is necessary for reasons of substantial public interest.[292]

(g) *Regulatory requirements to avoid dishonesty etc.* The processing is necessary for the purposes of complying with, or assisting other persons to comply with, a regulatory requirement which involves a person taking steps to establish whether another person has committed an unlawful act, or been involved in dishonesty, malpractice or other seriously improper conduct. Two further requirements are: the controller cannot reasonably be expected to obtain the consent of the data subject; and the processing is necessary for reasons of substantial public interest.[293]

(h) *Journalism in connection with unlawfulness etc.* The processing consists of the disclosure of personal data for the purposes of journalism or for academic, artistic or literary purposes, it is carried out in connection with alleged or proven unlawful acts, dishonesty, malpractice, unfitness, incompetence, mismanagement or failures, by a body (as opposed to a person), it is necessary for reasons of substantial public interest and it is carried out with a view to the publication of personal data by any person.[294] The controller must reasonably believe that publication would be in the public interest. An appropriate policy document is not required.[295]

(i) *Preventing fraud.* The processing is necessary for the purposes of preventing fraud and the processing consists of the disclosure of personal data by a person as a member of an 'anti-fraud organisation.'[296]

(j) *Terrorist financing and money laundering.* The processing is necessary for the purposes of making a disclosure in good faith under certain legislation concerned with terrorist financing or money laundering.[297]

(k) *Support for person with disability or medical condition.* The processing is necessary for the purposes of: (i) raising awareness of a particular disability or medical condition; or (ii) providing support to individuals with that particular disability or medical condition, or enabling them to provide support to each other.[298] The condition applies only to certain types of personal data, namely personal data revealing racial or ethnic origins, genetic or biometric data, data concerning health or personal data concerning an individual's sex life or sexual orientation. Moreover, the condition applies only where the processing: (i) is carried out by a not-for-profit body which provides support to individuals with a particular disability or medical condition; (ii) can reasonably be carried out without the consent of the data subject; and (iii) is necessary for reasons of substantial public interest.

(l) *Counselling.* The processing is necessary both for the provision of confidential counselling, advice or support or of another similar service provided confidentially

---

292 DPA 2018 Sch 1 para 11(1). A 'protective function' means a function that is intended to protect members of the public against: dishonesty, malpractice or other seriously improper conduct; unfitness or incompetence; mismanagement in the administration of a body or association; or failures in services provided by a body or association: DPA 2018 Sch 1 para 11(2).

293 DPA 2018 Sch 1 para 12(1). A 'regulatory requirement' means a requirement imposed by legislation or by a person in exercise of a function conferred by legislation, or a requirement forming part of generally accepted principles of good practice relating to a type of body or an activity: DPA 2018 Sch 1 para 12(2).

294 DPA 2018 Sch 1 para 13.

295 DPA 2018 Sch 1 para 13(3).

296 DPA 2018 Sch 1 para 14. 'Anti-fraud organisation' is defined in the Serious Crime Act 2007 s 68.

297 DPA 2018 Sch 1 para 15. The legislation is the Terrorism Act 2000 s 21CA and the Proceeds of Crime Act 2002 s 339ZB.

298 DPA 2018 Sch 1 para 16. 'Disability' has the same meaning as in the Equality Act 2010 s 6 of and Sch 1. 'Carer' means an individual who works or intends to provide care for another individual other than under or by virtue of a contract or as voluntary work.

and for reasons of substantial public interest.[299] The condition is only available where the processing is carried without the consent of the data subject because the data subject cannot give that consent, the controller cannot reasonably be expected to obtain that consent, or the processing must be carried out without that consent because obtaining it would prejudice the confidential counselling, advice or support.

(m) *Safeguarding children and vulnerable persons.* The processing is necessary both for the purposes of protecting an individual from neglect or physical, mental or emotional harm and for reasons of substantial public interest.[300] The condition is only available where the individual is either aged under 18, or aged 18 or over and at risk.[301] The condition is only available where the processing is carried out without the consent of the data subject because the data subject cannot give that consent, the controller cannot reasonably be expected to obtain that consent, or the processing must be carried out without that consent because obtaining it would prejudice the protection of the individual.

(n) *Safeguarding finances of vulnerable person.* The processing is necessary both for the purposes of protecting the economic well-being of an individual at economic risk who is aged 18 or over, and for reasons of substantial public interest.[302] The condition applies only to data concerning health. The condition is only available where the processing is carried out without the consent of the data subject because the data subject cannot give that consent, the controller cannot reasonably be expected to obtain that consent, or the processing must be carried out without that consent because obtaining it would prejudice the protection of the individual's economic well-being.

(o) *Insurance.* The processing is necessary both for an insurance purpose and for reasons of substantial public interest.[303] The condition applies only to personal data revealing racial or ethnic origin, religious or philosophical beliefs or trade union membership, genetic data or data concerning health. Where the processing is not carried out for the purposes of measures or decisions with respect to the data subject and the data subject does not have and is not expected to acquire rights or obligations against an insured person under an insurance contract to which that insurance purpose relates, then the condition will not be satisfied unless the processing can reasonably be carried out without the consent of the data subject.

(p) *Occupational pensions.* The processing is necessary for the purpose of making a determination in connection with eligibility for, or benefits payable under, an occupational pension scheme and can reasonably be carried out without the consent of the data subject.[304] The condition applies only to data concerning health which

---

299 DPA 2018 Sch 1 para 17.

300 DPA 2018 Sch 1 para 18. Similarly, this paragraph will apply where the processing is necessary for the purposes of protecting the physical, mental or emotional well-being of an individual.

301 An individual is 'at risk' where the controller has reasonable cause to suspect that the individual has needs for care and support, is experiencing, or at risk of, neglect or physical, mental or emotional harm, and, as a result of those needs is unable to protect himself or herself against the neglect or harm or the risk of it: DPA 2018 Sch 1 para 18(3).

302 DPA 2018 Sch 1 para 19. An 'individual at economic risk' means an individual who is less able to protect his or her economic well-being by reason of physical or mental injury, illness or disability.

303 DPA 2018 Sch 1 para 20. 'Insurance purpose' means advising on, arranging, underwriting or administering an insurance contract, administering a claim under an insurance contract, or exercising a right, or complying with an obligation, arising in connection with an insurance contract, including a right or obligation arising under an enactment or rule of law. 'Insurance contract' means a contract of general insurance or long-term insurance.

304 DPA 2018 Sch 1 para 21. As to the meaning of 'occupational pension scheme' see Pension Schemes Act 1993 s 1.

relates to a data subject who is the parent, grandparent, great-grandparent or sibling of a member of the scheme. And the condition applies only where the processing is not carried out for the purposes of measures or decisions with respect to the data subject.

(q) *Political parties.* The processing is carried out by an organisation or person included in the Electoral Commission's register of political parties and is necessary for the purposes of the political activities of that organisation or person.[305] The condition applies only to personal data revealing political opinions. The condition will not be met where it is likely to cause substantial damage or substantial distress to a person. The condition is also not met where an individual who is the data subject (or one of the data subjects) gave written notice to the controller requiring the controller not to process the personal data of which he or she is the data subject.

(r) *Elected representative responses.* The processing is carried out by or on behalf of a member of the House of Commons, the National Assembly for Wales, a member of the Scottish Parliament, a member of the Northern Ireland Assembly, a UK member of the European Parliament and certain local authority members. The condition applies only where the processing is in connection with the discharge of that elected representative's functions and in response to a request by an individual that that elected representative take action on behalf of the individual.[306] Where the request is made by an individual other than the data subject, the condition applies only where the absence of the data subject's consent is because the data subject cannot give it, the elected representative cannot reasonably be expected to obtain it or obtaining it would prejudice the action taken by the elected representative, or the processing is necessary in the interests of another individual and the data subject has withheld consent unreasonably.

(s) *Disclosure to elected representatives.* The processing consists of the disclosure of personal data to an elected representative and is in response to a communication to the controller from that representative or person, which was itself made in response to a request from an individual.[307] The condition applies only where the personal data is relevant to the subject matter of that communication and the disclosure is necessary for the purpose of responding to that communication.

(t) *Elected representatives and prisoners.* The processing consists of the processing of personal data about a prisoner for the purpose of informing a member of the House of Commons, a member of the National Assembly for Wales or a member of the

---

[305] DPA 2018 Sch 1 para 22. The register of political parties is maintained by the Electoral Commission under the Political Parties, Elections and Referendums Act 2000 s 23. 'Political activities' include campaigning, fund-raising, political surveys and case-work: DPA 2018 Sch 1 para 22(4).

[306] DPA 2018 Sch 1 para 23. The local authority members to which the condition applies are: (a) an elected member of a local authority within the meaning of the Local Government Act 1972 s 270(1); (b) an elected mayor of a local authority within the meaning of Part 1A or 2 of the Local Government Act 2000; (c) a mayor for the area of a combined authority established under Local Democracy, Economic Development and Construction Act 2009 s 103; (d) the Mayor of London or an elected member of the London Assembly; (e) an elected member of the Common Council of the City of London, or the Council of the Isles of Scilly; (f) an elected member of a council constituted under the Local Government etc (Scotland) Act 1994 s 2; (g) an elected member of a district council within the meaning of the Local Government Act (Northern Ireland) 1972; and (h) a police and crime commissioner.

[307] DPA 2018 Sch 1 para 24. 'Elected representative' has the same meaning as in (q) above: DPa 2018 Sch 1 para 23(3)-(5). Where the request to the elected representative came from an individual other than the data subject, the condition is met only if the disclosure must be made without the consent of the data subject because consent to the processing cannot be given by the data subject, the elected representative cannot reasonably be expected to obtain the consent of the data subject to the processing, obtaining the consent of the data subject would prejudice the action taken by the elected representative or the processing is necessary in the interests of another individual and the data subject has withheld consent unreasonably.

Scottish Parliament about the prisoner and the member is under an obligation not to further disclose the personal data.[308]

(u) *Publication of legal judgments.* The processing consists of the publication of a judgment or other decision of a court or tribunal or the processing is necessary for the purposes of publishing such a judgment or decision.[309]

(v) *Anti-doping in sport.* The processing is necessary for the purposes of measures designed to eliminate doping which are undertaken by or under the responsibility of a body or association that is responsible for eliminating doping in a sport, at a sporting event or in sport generally or it is necessary for the purposes of providing information about doping, or suspected doping, to such a body or association.[310] Where the processing consists of the disclosure of personal data to such a body or association, then an appropriate policy document is not required.

(w) The processing is necessary for the purposes of measures designed to protect the integrity of a sport or a sporting event, must be carried out without the consent of the data subject so as not to prejudice those purposes, and is necessary for reasons of substantial public interest.[311]

– 045 Appropriate policy document

For the purposes of Schedule 1 to the DPA 2018, a controller will have an appropriate policy document in place in relation to the processing of personal data if the controller has produced a document:

(a) that explains the controller's procedures for securing compliance with the six processing principles in Art 5 of the GDPR in connection with the processing under the applicable condition in Schedule 1 to the DPA 2018; and

(b) that explains the controller's policies as regards the retention and erasure of personal data under that condition, giving an indication of how long that personal data is likely to be retained.[312]

Throughout the period when the controller carries out the processing in reliance on that condition, the controller must retain and review (and if appropriate update) the appropriate policy document.[313] Throughout that period, the controller must also, if requested, volunteer it to the Information Commissioner.[314]

– 046 Criminal offence data

The second class of personal data attracting a more stringent control on processing is personal data relating to criminal convictions and offences or related security measures – 'criminal offence data.'[315] This includes data relating to 'the alleged commission of offences by the data subject' as well as data relating to 'proceedings for an offence committed or alleged to have

---

[308] DPA 2018 Sch 1 para 25. 'Prisoner' means a person detained in a prison. And a 'prison' includes a young offender institution, a remand centre, a secure training centre or a secure college: DPA 2018 Sch 1 para 25(3).

[309] DPA 2018 Sch 1 para 26.

[310] DPA 2018 Sch 1 para 27.

[311] DPA 2018 Sch 1 para 28. 'Measures designed to protect the integrity of a sport or a sporting event' mean measures designed to protect a sport or a sporting event against dishonesty, malpractice or other seriously improper conduct, or failure by a person participating in the sport or event in any capacity to comply with standards of behaviour set by a body or association with responsibility for the sport or event.

[312] DPA 2018 Sch 1 para 39.

[313] DPA 2018 Sch 1 paras 40-41.

[314] DPA 2018 Sch 1 paras 40-41.

[315] GDPR Art 10.

been committed by the data subject or the disposal of such proceedings, including sentencing.'[316] The approach taken by the GDPR to the processing of criminal offence data is to impose a separate proscription on it that is relaxed in only two situations:

(1) Where the processing is carried out only under the control of official authority.[317] Further detail of what is meant by processing under the control of official authority is not provided by the DPA 2018. It would appear to be confined to processing carried out by a public authority in the exercise of a statutory function that requires the processing for its due performance. Processing of personal data that involves the maintenance of a comprehensive register of criminal convictions can only be carried out only under the control of official authority.[318]

(2) Where the processing is authorised by EU or Member State law, and that law provides appropriate safeguards for the rights and freedoms of data subjects.[319] In the United Kingdom, that law is the DPA 2018. Processing of criminal offence data is authorised by the DPA 2018 only where that processing meets:[320]
   (a) one of the employment, health, research etc conditions;[321]
   (b) one of the substantial public interest conditions;[322] or
   (c) one of the specific criminal offence data conditions.[323]

   Since meeting one of the conditions in (a) and (b) is also one of the avenues for disapplying the separate prohibition on the processing of special category data, the preceding analysis of those conditions is equally applicable to the processing of criminal offence data. The specific criminal offence data conditions are considered below.

Where the separate proscription against the processing of criminal offence data is relaxed under one of the above, that processing must still comply with the six processing principles generally applicable to personal data.[324]

9–047 Criminal offence data conditions

By providing a further nine conditions any of which, if met, relaxes the additional prohibition against the processing of criminal offence data, control over the processing of criminal offence data is made less stringent than it is over the processing of special category data. Some of these nine conditions are no more than a relaxation of the employment, health, research etc conditions or the substantial public interest conditions applicable to special category data. The criminal offence data conditions are:

(a) The data subject has given consent to the processing.[325] Unlike with special

---

316 DPA 2018 s 11(2).

317 In order to be 'carried out under the control of official authority' the processing should have a basis in the law of the EU or the UK: GDPR recital (45). The GDPR leaves it up to the law of a Member State to determine whether the requirement that it be carried out under the control of official authority requires that it be carried out by a public authority: GDPR recital (45). What is clear is that in order for 'official authority' to exist, it must be 'vested' in the controller: GDPR Arts 6(1)(e), 6(3)(b), 17(3)(b) and 20(3) and recitals (50), (51), (65), (68) and (69); DPA 2018 s 7(2).

318 GDPR Art 10.

319 GDPR Art 10. As to the meaning of 'rights and freedoms of data subjects' in this context, see §8–006.

320 DPA 2018 s 10(4)-(5).

321 Set out in DPA 2018 Sch 1 Part 1. This is dealt with at §9–043.

322 Set out in DPA 2018 Sch 1 Part 2. This is dealt with at §9–044.

323 Set out in DPA 2018 Sch 1 Part 3.

324 That is, the processing principles listed at §9–004.

325 DPA 2018 Sch 1 para 29.

category data, consent need not be 'explicit.'

(b) The processing is necessary to protect the vital interests of an individual, and the data subject is physically or legally incapable of giving consent.[326]

(c) The processing is carried out in the course of its legitimate activities with appropriate safeguards by a foundation, association or other not-for-profit body with a political, philosophical, religious or trade union aim, and on condition that the processing relates solely to the members or to former members of the body or to persons who have regular contact with it in connection with its purposes, and the personal data is not disclosed outside that body without the consent of the data subjects.[327]

(d) The processing relates to personal data which is manifestly made public by the data subject.[328]

(e) The processing is necessary for the purpose of, or in connection with, any legal proceedings (including prospective legal proceedings), is necessary for the purpose of obtaining legal advice, or is otherwise necessary for the purposes of establishing, exercising or defending legal rights.[329]

(f) The processing is necessary when a court or tribunal is acting in its judicial capacity.[330]

(g) The processing is of personal data about a conviction or caution for offences involving indecent photographs of children and the processing is necessary for the purpose of administering an account relating to the payment card used in the commission of the offence or cancelling that payment card.[331] An appropriate policy document is required.[332]

(h) The processing would, but for the requirement that the processing be necessary for reasons of substantial public interest, meet any of the substantial public interest conditions in Part 2 of Schedule 1.[333]

(i) The processing would, but for the requirement that the processing be of personal data revealing racial or ethnic origin, religious or philosophical beliefs or trade union membership, genetic data or data concerning health, meet the insurance condition in Part 2 of Schedule 1 by being necessary for an insurance purpose.[334] The requirement in that condition that the processing be necessary for reasons of substantial public interest need not be satisfied.

9. ORGANISATIONAL OBLIGATIONS

– 048 Introduction

The processing principles and supporting obligations are complemented by organisational

[326] DPA 2018 Sch 1 para 30. 'Vital interests' include a person's physical integrity or life: GDPR recital (112).

[327] DPA 2018 Sch 1 para 31.

[328] DPA 2018 Sch1 para 32.

[329] DPA 2018 Sch 1 para 33.

[330] DPA 2018 Sch 1 para 34. 'Tribunal' means any tribunal in which legal proceedings may be brought: DPA 2018 s 205(1).

[331] DPA 2018 Sch 1 para 35. The specific offences are listed in para 35(2).

[332] As to the meaning of an 'appropriate policy document', see §9– 045.

[333] DPA 2018 Sch 1 para 36. As to the substantial public interest conditions, see §9– 044.

[334] DPA 2018 Sch 1 para 37. As to the insurance condition, see §9– 044(o).

obligations which are applicable to controllers and, to a lesser extent, to processors. These organisational obligations require every controller and every processor to set itself up so as to comply, and be able to demonstrate compliance, with the GDPR regime and, specifically, to undertake impact assessments, to maintain records, to have a specific responsible officer and to co-operate with the Information Commissioner.[335] These obligations are additional to related obligations that are triggered by events (for example, the obligation on a controller to notify the Information Commissioner where there has been a personal data breach)[336] and obligations that impinge upon the processing itself (for example, the security measures obligation).[337]

9– 049 Internal systems obligation

A controller is under three inter-related obligations to have internal systems in place to maximise the likelihood of processing being in accordance with the GDPR regime and to be able to demonstrate adherence to that regime. These are all characterised as 'technical and organisational' measures that a controller must implement.

(1) A controller must implement technical and organisational measures to ensure, and to be able to demonstrate, that processing is performed in accordance with the GDPR regime.[338] The measures taken need only be proportionate to the nature, scope, context and purposes of processing, as well as to the risk to individuals. The 'risk' is the product of the severity of an occurrence adverse to the rights and freedoms of individuals and the likelihood of that occurrence.[339] Where it is proportionate to the processing activities, these measures may require a controller to implement data protection policies that are appropriate to the processing of personal data.[340] Where necessary, the controller must review and update these measures.[341] Compliance with a code of conduct[342] approved by the Information Commissioner or with an approved certification mechanism[343] may be used to help demonstrate that this obligation has been met.[344]

(2) A controller must implement technical and organisational measures that are designed to give effect to the processing principles and to integrate necessary safeguards into the processing so as to meet the regulatory requirements and to

335 Regulatory enforcement is considered at §§48– 014 to 48– 055.

336 See §9– 037.

337 See §9– 036.

338 GDPR Art 24(1). In imposing an obligation that requires the measures ensure and demonstrate 'that processing is performed' in accordance with the GDPR – as opposed to ensuring and demonstrating that the controller is processing in accordance with the GDPR – the obligation extends to where processing is carried out on behalf of the controller by a processor. The Information Commissioner does not have power to serve an enforcement notice for failure to comply with this obligation: DPA 2018 s 149(2).

339 As to the meaning of 'rights and freedoms of natural persons' in this context, see §8– 006. See the discussion in *Various Claimants v Wm Morrisons Supermarket plc* [2017] EWHC 3113 (QB), [2018] 3 WLR 691 at [67]-[68]. That case concerned the DPA 1998, but the discussion is equally applicable to data security principles under the GDPR and DPA 2018.

340 GDPR Art 24(2).

341 GDPR Art 24(1).

342 Codes of conduct are provided for by GDPR Art 40 and DPA 2018 ss 121-128 (in which they are called 'codes of practice'). A failure by a person to act in accordance with a code of practice does not of itself make that person liable to legal proceedings: DPA 2018 s 127(2).

343 GDPR Art 25(3). As to approved certification mechanisms, see: GDPR Arts 42-43 and recitals (77), (81), (100) and (168); DPA 2018 ss 17, 115(8)(b), 149(4), 155(3)(j) and Sch 5.

344 GDPR Art 24(3).

protect the rights of data subjects.[345] The measures need only be proportionate to the state of the art, the cost of implementation and the nature, scope, context and purposes of processing, as well as to the risk for the data subject from the processing. The 'risk' is the product of the severity of an occurrence adverse to the rights and freedoms of natural persons and the likelihood of that occurrence.[346] The obligation is engaged both at the time at which the controller determines the means for processing and at the time of the processing itself. Organisational measures may include pseudonymisation. Compliance with an approved certification mechanism may be used to help demonstrate that this obligation has been met.[347]

(3) A controller must implement technical and organisational measures for ensuring that only personal data that is necessary for each specific purpose of the processing is processed.[348] This obligation will impinge upon the amount of personal data collected, the extent of their processing, the period of their storage and their accessibility. In particular, the measures must ensure that by default personal data is not made accessible without the individual's intervention to an indefinite number of individuals. Compliance with an approved certification mechanism may be used to help demonstrate that this obligation has been met.[349]

9– 050 Impact assessments

Where a type of processing is likely to result in a high risk to the rights and freedoms of natural persons,[350] the controller must carry out an assessment of the impact of the envisaged processing operations on the protection of personal data.[351] This is termed a 'data protection impact assessment.' Although the trigger for the obligation normally depends on the risk evaluation, wherever there is:

(a) a systematic and extensive evaluation of personal aspects relating to natural persons which is based on automated processing, including profiling, and on which decisions are based that produce legal effects concerning the natural person or similarly significantly affect the natural person;
(b) processing of sensitive personal information[352] on a large scale; or
(c) the systematic monitoring of a publicly accessible area on a large scale,

a data protection impact assessment is required.[353] The controller must carry out the data

---

345 GDPR Art 25(1). Where the Information Commissioner is satisfied that a person has failed, or is failing, to comply with this obligation, the Commissioner may issue an enforcement notice: DPA 2018 s 149(2)(c).

346 As to the meaning of 'rights and freedoms of data subjects' in this context, see §8– 006. See the discussion in *Various Claimants v Wm Morrisons Supermarket plc* [2017] EWHC 3113 (QB), [2018] 3 WLR 691 at [67]-[68]. That case concerned the DPA 1998, but the discussion is equally applicable to data security principles under the GDPR and DPA 2018.

347 GDPR Art 25(3). As to approved certification mechanisms, see: GDPR Arts 42-43 and recitals (77), (81), (100) and (168); DPA 2018 ss 17, 115(8)(b), 149(4), 155(3)(j) and Sch 5.

348 GDPR Art 25(1). The specific purposes for which personal data are processed should be explicit and legitimate and determined at the time of the collection of the personal data: GDPR recital (39). Where the Information Commissioner is satisfied that a controller has failed, or is failing, to comply with this obligation, the Commissioner may serve an enforcement notice: DPA 2018 s 149(2)(c). See further Chapter 48.

349 GDPR Art 25(3). As to approved certification mechanisms, see: GDPR Arts 42-43 and recitals (77), (81), (100) and (168); DPA 2018 ss 17, 115(8)(b), 149(4), 155(3)(j) and Sch 5.

350 As to the meaning of 'rights and freedoms of natural persons' and 'risk' in this context, see §§8– 006 to 8– 007.

351 GDPR Art 35(1). Unless otherwise provided, the obligation does not arise where the processing is carried out in order to comply with a requirement of domestic or EU law regulating the specific processing operations and in respect of which a data protection impact assessment has already been carried out: GDPR Art 35(10).

352 As to the meaning of 'sensitive personal information' see §9– 040.

353 GDPR Art 35(3). The Information Commissioner must publish a list of the kind of processing operations for which

protection impact assessment before embarking on the processing, but one assessment may suffice for a set of similar processing operations that present similar high risks.[354] Where a controller has a data protection officer, the controller must seek the advice of that officer when carrying out the data protection impact assessment.[355] As a minimum, a data protection impact assessment must contain:

— a systematic description of the envisaged processing operations and the purposes of the processing, including, where applicable, the legitimate interest pursued by the controller;
— an assessment of the necessity and proportionality of the processing operations in relation to the purposes;
— an assessment of the risks to the rights and freedoms of data subjects; and
— the measures envisaged to address the risks, including safeguards, security measures and mechanisms to ensure the protection of personal data and to demonstrate compliance with the GDPR taking into account the rights and legitimate interests of data subjects and other persons concerned.[356]

Compliance with a code of conduct approved by the Information Commissioner may be used to help demonstrate that this obligation has been met.[357] Where a data protection impact assessment indicates that 'the processing would result in a high risk in the absence of measures taken by the controller to mitigate the risk', the controller must consult with and seek the advice of its supervisory authority.[358]

9–051 **Record keeping**

Where an enterprise with 250 or more employees processes personal data, it will be under a record-keeping obligation.[359] An enterprise with fewer employees will also be under a record-keeping obligation where the processing it carries out is likely to result in a risk to the rights and freedoms of data subjects, the processing is not occasional, or the processing includes sensitive personal information.[360] Where the enterprise under a record-keeping obligation is a controller,

---

a data protection impact assessment is required and may also publish a list of the kind of processing operations for which no data protection impact assessment is required: GDPR Art 35(4)-(5). The list publication requirement does not apply to applied GDPR processing: DPA 2018 Sch 6 para 27.

354 GDPR Art 35(1). Where there is a change to the risk represented by the processing operation, the controller must carry out a review to assess if processing is performed in accordance with the data protection assessment: GDPR Art 35(11).

355 GDPR Art 35(2).

356 GDPR Art 35(7). As to the meaning of 'rights and freedoms of data subjects' and 'risk' in this context, see §§8–006 to 8–007.

357 GDPR Art 35(8). Codes of conduct are provided for by GDPR Art 40 and DPA 2018 ss 121-128 (in which they are called 'codes of practice'). A failure by a person to act in accordance with a code of practice does not of itself make that person liable to legal proceedings: DPA 2018 s 127(2). The EDPB has adopted guidance issued by the Article 29 Working Party on data protection impact assessments: namely, A29 Guidelines WP/248 (revised 4 October 2017). Annex 1 to that guidance provides links to model examples; annex 2 sets out criteria for an acceptable data protection impact assessment. The guidance also looks at when processing is likely to result in a 'high risk.

358 GDPR Art 36(1). The information that the controller must provide the Information Commissioner when consulting and seeking advice is set out in GDPR Art 36(3). The consultation obligation does not apply to high risk processing for the purposes of journalism, academic purposes, artistic purposes or literary purposes: DPA 2018 Sch 2 para 26(9)(c)(ii).

359 GDPR Art 30(5). An 'enterprise' means a natural or legal person engaged in an economic activity, irrespective of its legal form, including partnerships or associations regularly engaged in an economic activity: GDPR Art 4(18). The notion of an 'enterprise' is informed by Commission Recommendation 2003/361/EC Annex Art 2: GDPR recital (13). In relation to applied GDPR processing, the references to the controller's representative and the processor's representative are removed: DPA 2018 Sch 6 para 25.

360 GDPR Art 30(5). As to the meaning of 'rights and freedoms of data subjects' and 'risk' in this context, see §§8–006 to 8–007. As to the meaning of 'sensitive personal information' see §9–040.

the record must contain:

— the name and contact details of the controller and, where applicable, the joint controller, the controller's representative and the data protection officer;
— the purposes of the processing;
— a description of the categories of data subjects and of the categories of personal data;
— the categories of recipients to whom the personal data have been or will be disclosed, including recipients outside the EU or international organisations;[361]
— where applicable, details of transfers of personal data to a country outside the EU or to an international organisation, including the identification of that country or international organisation and, in the case of such transfers that are exceptional,[362] the documentation of suitable safeguards;
— where possible, the envisaged time limits for erasure of the different categories of data; and
— where possible, a general description of the measures taken under the security measures obligation.[363]

In the case of sensitive personal information, the record must also contain the appropriate policy document.[364]

Where the enterprise under a record keeping obligation is a processor, the record must contain:

— a record of all categories of processing activities carried out on behalf of a controller;
— the name and contact details of the processor or processors and of each controller on behalf of which the processor is acting, and, where applicable, of the controller's or the processor's representative, and the data protection officer;
— the categories of processing carried out on behalf of each controller;
— where applicable, details of transfers of personal data to a country outside the EU or an international organisation, including the identification of that country or international organisation and, in the case of such transfers that are exceptional,[365] the documentation of suitable safeguards; and
— where possible, a general description of the measures taken under the security measures obligation.[366]

Where requested, a controller or processor must make the record available to the Information Commissioner.[367]

9–052 Data protection officers

Where:

(1) processing of personal data is carried out by a public authority (other than a court

[361] As to the meaning of 'international organisations,' see §8– 033.

[362] That is, a transfer that is not repetitive, concerns only a limited number of data subjects, is necessary for the purposes of compelling legitimate interests pursued by the controller which are not overridden by the interests or rights and freedoms of the data subject, and where the controller has assessed all the circumstances surrounding the data transfer and has on the basis of that assessment provided suitable safeguards with regard to the protection of personal data: GDPR Art 49(1).

[363] GDPR Art 30(1). As to the security measures obligation, see §9– 036.

[364] DPA 2018 Sch 1 paras 40-41, excluding the situations listed in §9– 044(e), (h) and (v). As to the appropriate policy document, see §9– 045. The record must include which condition in DPA 2018 Sch 1 is relied upon, how the processing satisfies the first requirement of the first processing principle – ie lawfulness (see §9– 007) – and whether the personal data is retained and erased in accordance with the controller's retention policies set out in its appropriate policy document and, if it is not, the reasons for not following those policies.

[365] As to the meaning of 'exceptional transfers' see fn 362. As to the meaning of 'international organisations,' see §8– 033.

[366] GDPR Art 30(2). As to the security measures obligation, see §9– 036.

[367] GDPR Art 30(4).

acting in its judicial capacity);

(2) the core activities of a controller or a processor consist of processing operations which, by virtue of their nature, their scope and/or their purposes, require regular and systematic monitoring of data subjects on a large scale; or

(3) the core activities of the controller or the processor consist of processing on a large scale of sensitive personal information,

then that controller and that processor must designate a data protection officer.[368] A data protection officer may be an existing employee of the controller or processor, with or without other responsibilities, or may be an individual in an outside body formally engaged by the controller or processor and provided with all the necessary support and access.[369] A single data protection officer may be shared between a group of undertakings.[370] Similarly, where the controller or the processor is a public authority, a single data protection officer may be designated for several such authorities.[371] A data protection officer must have expert knowledge of data protection law and practices and be able to fulfil the tasks required under the regulatory regime.[372] A controller and a processor must provide details of its data protection officer:

(a) upon appointment – to the Information Commissioner;[373]

(b) where personal data is collected about a data subject – to that data subject;[374]

(c) where there has been a personal data breach – to the Information Commissioner and, depending on the gravity of that breach, to the data subject;[375] and

(d) where it is under a record-keeping obligation – in its formal record.[376]

A benefit to a controller and to a processor of designating a data protection officer is that fees that the Information Commissioner could impose for providing services to a controller or processor cannot be imposed where the Commissioner provides those services to a data protection officer of that controller or processor.[377]

9–053 Data protection officer tasks

Where a controller or a processor is required to designate a data protection officer, then that officer must, as a minimum, be tasked with:

(a) informing and advising the controller or the processor of their obligations under the

368 GDPR Art 37(1). As to the meaning of 'sensitive personal information' see §9–040.

369 GDPR Arts 37(6), 38(6) and recital (97). That the data protection officer must be an individual, as opposed to a corporate person, is apparent from a reading of all the provisions of the GDPR relating to data protection officers, and especially Art 37(5).

370 GDPR Art 37(2). Each establishment in the group must have easy access to the data protection officer. The notion of a 'group of undertakings' implies that there is one undertaking in the group that exerts a dominant influence over the others in relation to the processing of personal data and that there are binding data protection policies to be adhered to by all members of the group: GDPR Art 4(19)-(20) and recital (37). The approved binding corporate rules governing every member of the group must specify the tasks of any data protection officer: GDPR Art 47(2)(h). An affiliated central body would appear not to be part of the group, even if engaged in a joint economic activity: GDPR recitals (48) and (110).

371 GDPR Art 37(3).

372 GDPR Art 37(5).

373 GDPR Art 37(7). An email address is a contact detail: GDPR recital (23).

374 GDPR Arts 13(1)(b) and 14(1)(b). See §§9–019 and 9–021. This is a facet of the transparency obligation. A data subject may contact the data protection officer in relation to all issues relating to the processing of his or her personal data and to the exercise of GDPR rights: GDPR Art 38(4).

375 GDPR Arts 33(3)(b) and 34(2). See §§9–037 to 9–038.

376 GDPR Arts 30(1)(a) and 30(2)(a). See §9–051.

377 GDPR Art 57(3) and DPA 2018 s 134. Where the Information Commissioner provides the service in response to a request from a data protection officer, then if the Commissioner can show that the request is manifestly unfounded or excessive the Commissioner may either refuse to act on the request or charge a reasonable fee for dealing with it: GDPR Art 57(4) and DPA 2018 s 135(1), (3).

data protection regime;
(b) monitoring compliance with the data protection regime;
(c) monitoring compliance with the data protection policies of the controller or processor in relation to the protection of personal data;
(d) informing the employees who carry out processing for a controller or processor of their obligations under the data protection regime, raising their awareness of those obligations and training them;
(e) carrying out audits; and
(f) co-operating with the Information Commissioner and acting as the contact point with the Commissioner.[378]

Where a controller is carrying out a data protection impact assessment, the controller must seek the advice of its data protection officer.[379] More generally, where a controller or a processor is required to designate a data protection officer, that controller or processor must ensure that the data protection officer:

— is properly and punctually involved in all issues relating to the protection of personal data;[380]
— is allowed to carry out the functions required by the data protection regime without deviation by instructions or by threat of dismissal or any other sanction;[381]
— is supported in the performance of the tasks at (a)-(f) above through the provision of the necessary resources and access to personal data and processing operations;[382] and
— reports to the highest management level of the controller or processor (which will usually be the board of directors of a company or the like).[383]

A data protection officer will be bound by such confidentiality as is required by domestic or EU law.[384]

9– 054 Cooperation with Commissioner

Both controllers and processors are under a general obligation to cooperate with the Information Commissioner where so requested.[385] Where a controller or processor has a data protection officer, that officer should be tasked with meeting this general obligation to

378 GDPR Art 39(1). The 'data protection regime' means the GDPR, the DPA 2018 and subordinate legislation made thereunder. The EDPB has adopted guidance issued by the Article 29 Working Party on data protection officers: see A29 Guidelines WP/243 (revised 5 April 2017).

379 GDPR Arts 35(2) and 36(3)(d). See §9– 050.

380 GDPR Art 38(1).

381 GDPR Art 38(3).

382 GDPR Art 38(2).

383 GDPR Art 38(3). Since 1 October 2009, companies are incorporated under the Companies Act 2006. Such a company must have articles of association prescribing its regulations, which are either those registered by it or the applicable Model Articles, which also apply in default of registering articles: Companies Act 2006 ss 18-20. Model Articles are prescribed by the Companies (Model Articles) Regulations 2008, with those in Schedule 1 applicable to private companies limited by shares, those in Schedule 2 applicable to private companies limited by guarantee and those in Schedule 3 applicable to public companies. Article 4 of Schedule 1 provides: 'Subject to the articles, the directors are responsible for the management of the company's business, for which purpose they may exercise all the powers of the company.' Article 3 of Schedule 2 and Article 3 of Schedule 3 are in the same terms. For the position in relation to companies limited by shares and incorporated under the Companies Act 1985 using Table A: see regulation 70.

384 GDPR Art 38(5).

385 GDPR Art 31. The Information Commissioner is the 'supervisory authority' in the UK for the purposes of the GDPR: DPA s 115(1). See also GDPR Arts 57 and 58, which enumerate the tasks and powers of the Information Commissioner, and recitals (80), (82), (86), (124). In relation to GDPR processing (but not applied GDPR processing), this includes, where applicable, their representatives: DPA 2018 Sch 6 para 26.

cooperate.[386] In addition to the general obligation to cooperate, there are specific obligations:

— to notify the Information Commissioner of any personal data breach;[387]
— where a data protection impact assessment indicates that the processing would result in a high risk, to consult the Information Commissioner prior to processing and to provide the necessary information;[388]
— to notify the Information Commissioner of the contact details of the data protection officer, if there is one;[389] and
— to inform the Information Commissioner of transfers of personal data outside the EU in certain circumstances.[390]

The degree of co-operation with the Information Commissioner is one of the matters that the Commissioner must take into account when deciding whether to give a penalty notice and in determining the amount of a penalty.[391]

9–055 Multi-state processing

Controllers and processors that process data in more than one EU Member State or whose processing affects data subjects in more than one EU Member State[392] will generally be regulated by their 'lead supervisory authority.'[393] The lead supervisory authority is the supervisory authority in the country where that controller or processor has its 'main establishment' or only establishment.[394] The rationale for this is that a controller or a processor processing personal data in more than one EU Member State should generally be obliged to deal with only one supervisory authority.[395] A lead supervisory authority is required to cooperate and consult supervisory authorities in other Member States concerned with the processing activity in question so as to reach mutually agreeable decisions so far as possible, with disagreements between supervisory authorities being resolved by the European Data Protection Board.[396] This is consistent with the objective of harmonising data protection standards across the EU.[397]

9–056 Regulatory charge

Every controller must, unless all its processing is 'exempt processing,' pay the Information

---

386 GDPR Art 39(1)(d).

387 GDPR Art 33(1). See §9–037.

388 GDPR Art 36(1)-(3). See §9–050.

389 GDPR Art 37(7). See §9–052.

390 GDPR Art 49(1).

391 DPA 2018 s 155(2)(b) and (3)(f). And see GDPR Art 83(2)(f). Regulatory enforcement is considered at §§48–014 to 48–055.

392 This is termed 'cross-border processing' and is defined in GDPR Art 4(23).

393 GDPR Art 56.

394 GDPR Art 4(16). The main establishment of a controller in the Union should be the place of its central administration in the Union, unless the decisions on the purposes and means of the processing of personal data are taken in another establishment of the controller in the Union, in which case that other establishment should be considered to be the main establishment....': GDPR recital (36). The lead supervisory authority is competent to act as the lead supervisory authority for cross-border processing. The Information Commissioner is the 'supervisory authority' in the UK for the purposes of the GDPR: DPA s 115(1).

395 GDPR recitals (127)-(128).

396 GDPR Arts 60-61. The EDPB has adopted guidance on lead supervisory authorities issued by the Article 29 Working Party in preparation for the GDPR: *Guidelines on the Lead Supervisory Authority*, WP244, 13 December 2016.

397 See GDPR recitals (3), (10), (13), (53), (123), (129), (130), (133), (135), (139), (150) and (152).

Commissioner an annual charge.[398] The charge is either £40, £60 or £2,900, depending on whether the controller is in tier 1 (micro organisations), tier 2 (small and medium organisations) or tier 3 (large organisations).[399] The tier into which a controller falls, depends upon its annual turnover, the number of staff it has, whether it is a charity, whether it is a small occupational pension scheme and whether it is a public authority. The Information Commissioner must publish a document specifying the penalty for non-payment of the annual charge.[400] In addition to the annual charge, the Information Commissioner may also impose a fee for a service under data protection legislation provided to a person, other than where that service is provided to a data subject or data protection officer.[401]

10. INTERNATIONAL TRANSFERS

9–057 Introduction

The transfer of personal data to a 'third country' or 'international organisation' is an instance of processing that gives rise to additional obligations on a controller and on a processor.[402] The objective of these additional obligations is to ensure that the destination to which the personal data is sent provides a comparable level of protection (including data subject rights) in relation to the processing of personal data.[403] A destination will provide a comparable level of protection where:

(a) the destination has been assessed by the European Commission as providing a comparable level of protection;[404] or

(b) the controller or processor provides the data subject with adequate safeguards and enforceable rights.[405]

9–058 Restricted destinations

The area of free data flow has been extended by the Agreement on the European Economic Area (EEA) so as to bring Iceland, Liechtenstein and Norway into the internal market. Those three countries are thus also subject to the GDPR.[406] Although not expressly defined in the

---

398 Data Protection (Charges and Information) Regulations 2018 reg 2(2). The power to impose the charge is provided by DPA 2018 s 137. 'Exempt processing' is defined in the Data Protection (Charges and Information) Regulations 2018 Sch para 2.

399 Data Protection (Charges and Information) Regulations 2018 reg 3(1).

400 The Information Commissioner's duty to produce, publish and modify the schedule of fees is imposed by DPA 2018 s 158(1). The manner of performance of the duty is constrained by statutory requirements: DPA 2018 ss 158-159.

401 DPA 2018 s 134. 'Data protection legislation' means the GDPR and the DPA 2018: DPA 2018 s 3(9). Where the request from a data subject or data protection officer is manifestly unreasonable, the Information Commissioner may either refuse to act on the request or charge a reasonable fee for dealing with it: DPA 2018 s 135(1) and GDPR Art 57(4). All fees received by the Information Commissioner are paid over to the Secretary of State and then paid into the Consolidated Fund: DPA 2018 Sch 12 para 10.

402 These obligations are set out in GDPR Ch V, Arts 44-50. They are additional to the other obligations on those processing – which includes transferring – personal data: GDPR Art 44 ('...subject to the other provisions of this Regulation...'). See also DPA 2018 s 18 on the power of the Secretary of State to regulate the reach of the transfer provisions. Regulatory enforcement is considered at §§48– 014 to 48– 055. Private law claims are considered at §§48– 005 to 48– 013. As to the meaning of 'third country,' see §8– 032. As to the meaning of 'international organisations,' see §8– 033.

403 GDPR Art 44.

404 See §9– 061.

405 See §§9– 062 to 9– 064.

406 Decision of the Council and the Commission of 13 December 1993 on the conclusion of the Agreement on the

Regulation, where the term 'third country' is used, it means a country outside the EEA.[407] An 'international organisation' is defined to mean an organisation and its subordinate bodies governed by public international law, or any other body which is set up by, or on the basis of an agreement, between two or more countries.[408] Collectively, third countries and international organisations are here referred to as 'restricted destinations.'

9–059 The transfer restriction

Neither a controller nor a processor may send personal data to a restricted destination other than where:

(a) the transfer is an excepted transfer;

(b) the transfer is in compliance with a current 'adequacy decision' of the European Commission; or

(c) the controller or processor has provided 'appropriate safeguards' and the data subject has enforceable rights and effective remedies.

The transfer restriction also applies to onward transfers of personal data from the restricted destination.[409] Where a transfer is not authorised by an adequacy decision, the Secretary of State may by regulations restrict the transfer of a category of personal data to a third country or international organisation.[410] In this way, a transfer that meets (a) or (c), but not (b), may be restricted. Sending personal data to a controller or processor in a restricted destination in electronic or hard copy form, or making personal data available to such recipients, is a restricted transfer. If personal data is uploaded to a website within the EEA and it is anticipated that the website may be accessible to persons in a restricted destination, that will be treated as a restricted transfer. However, if data is transferred from one EEA country to another via a server in a restricted destination without it being accessed in that restricted destination, that should not be treated as a restricted transfer.

9–060 Excepted transfers

The transfer restriction does not apply where:[411]

(a) after having been informed of the possible risks to the data subject of the proposed transfer, the data subject has explicitly consented to the proposed transfer;[412]

(b) the transfer is necessary for the performance of a contract between the data subject and the controller or for the implementation of pre-contractual measures taken at the data subject's request;[413]

(c) the transfer is necessary for the conclusion or performance of a contract concluded

European Economic Area between the European Communities, their Member States and the Republic of Austria, the Republic of Finland, the Republic of Iceland, the Principality of Liechtenstein, the Kingdom of Norway, the Kingdom of Sweden and the Swiss Confederation, OJ 1994 L 1.

407 In other words, any country outside: Austria, Belgium, Bulgaria, Croatia, Cyprus, Czech Republic, Denmark, Estonia, Finland, France, Germany, Greece, Hungary, Ireland, Italy, Latvia, Lithuania, Luxembourg, Malta, Netherlands, Poland, Portugal, Romania, Slovakia, Slovenia, Spain and Sweden, as well as the United Kingdom, Iceland, Norway and Liechtenstein.

408 See further §8–033.

409 GDPR Art 44.

410 DPA 2018 s 18(2)(a). As to the meaning of 'third country,' see §8–032. As to the meaning of 'international organisations,' see §8–033.

411 GDPR Art 49(1). See also GDPR recital (111). The EDPB has issued guidelines on derogations: Guidelines 2/2018 on derogations of Article 49 GDPR.

412 This does not apply to public authorities in the exercise of their public powers: GDPR Art 49(3).

413 This does not apply to public authorities in the exercise of their public powers: GDPR Art 49(3).

in the interest of the data subject between the controller and another legal person;[414]

(d) the transfer is necessary for important reasons of public interest;[415]

(e) the transfer is necessary for the establishment, exercise or defence of legal claims;[416]

(f) the transfer is necessary in order to protect the vital interests of the data subject or other persons where the data subject is physically or legally incapable of giving consent; or

(g) the transfer is made from a register which by law is intended to provide information to the public and that is open to consultation (either generally or limited to those showing a legitimate interest).[417]

A transfer on any of the above bases may take place only where the transfer:

— is not repetitive;
— concerns only a limited number of data subjects;
— is necessary for the purposes of compelling legitimate interests pursued by the controller which are not overridden by the interests or rights and freedoms of the data subject; and
— the controller has assessed all the circumstances surrounding the data transfer and has on the basis of that assessment provided suitable safeguards with regard to the protection of personal data.[418]

The controller must inform the Information Commissioner of the transfer. The controller must also inform the data subject of the transfer and of the compelling legitimate interest that the controller is pursuing through the transfer.[419]

9–061 Transfers: adequacy decision

A controller or a processor may, without requiring any specific authorisation, send personal data to a restricted destination where the transfer is in compliance with a current 'adequacy

414 This does not apply to public authorities in the exercise of their public powers: GDPR Art 49(3).

415 The public interest must be one that is recognised in the law of the United Kingdom or the EU: GDPR Art 49(4). The GDPR does not equate the public interest with the exercise of official authority: see GDPR recitals (10), (45), (50) and (51). The following are recognised as being carried out in the public interest:
(a) Processing of personal data by official authorities for the purpose of achieving the aims, laid down by constitutional law or by international public law, of officially recognised religious associations, is carried out on grounds of public interest: recital (55).
(b) The compilation by political parties of personal data on people's political opinions in the course of electoral activities: recital (56).
(c) An important economic or financial interest of a Member State: recital (73).
(d) International data exchange between competition authorities, tax or customs administrations, between financial supervisory authorities, between services competent for social security matters, or for public health, for example in the case of contact tracing for contagious diseases or in order to reduce and/or eliminate doping in sport: recital (112).
(e) Public access to official documents: recital (154).
In addition, the Secretary of State may, by regulation specify the circumstances in which a transfer of personal data to a third country or international organisation is to be taken to be necessary for important reasons of public interests and the circumstances in which a transfer of person data to a third country or international organisation that is not required by an enactment is not to be taken to be necessary for important reasons of public interest: DPA 2018 s 18(1).

416 Legal claims includes proceedings in court, administrative tribunals and out-of-court procedures: GDPR recital (52).

417 The transfer must not involve the entirety of the register: GDPR Art 49(2). Where the register is intended for consultation by persons having a legitimate interest, the transfer can only be made at the request of a person having such a legitimate interest or where a person having that legitimate interest is to be the recipient: GDPR Art 49(2).

418 GDPR Art 49(1). These requirements do not apply to public authorities in the exercise of their public powers: GDPR Art 49(3). The controller or processor must document the assessment as well as the suitable safeguards under its record-keeping obligation: GDPR Art 49(6).

419 GDPR Art 49(1).

decision' of the European Commission.[420] An 'adequacy decision' is a decision by the European Commission that a third country, a territory or one or more specified sectors within a third country or an international organisation ensures an adequate level of protection of what is guaranteed by the GDPR – that is, the continuing obligations imposed on controllers and processors, and the rights conferred on data subjects.[421] An adequacy decision must be reviewed at least every four years, and it may at any time and to any extent be repealed, amended or suspended. The European Commission publishes all adequacy decisions, including revocations. To date, the European Commission has made adequacy decisions in respect of: Andorra, Argentina, Canada (for commercial organisations), the Faroe Islands, Guernsey, Israel, the Isle of Man, Japan, Jersey, New Zealand, Switzerland and Uruguay. The European Commission has also made an adequacy decision in respect of the USA, but it applies only to recipients registered as part of the 'Privacy Shield' framework.'[422] An adequacy decision by the European Commission is not determinative: despite an adequacy decision, the Information Commissioner, as the supervisory authority, may examine the claim of a person who complains that the level of protection given in a third country to which his or her personal data has been transferred is inadequate.[423]

9– 062 Transfers: appropriate safeguards

A controller or processor may send personal data to a restricted destination provided that:

(a) the controller or processor has provided 'appropriate safeguards;' and
(b) enforceable data subject rights and effective legal remedies for data subjects are available.[424]

The manner in which the appropriate safeguards are provided will determine whether or not specific authorisation for the transfer will be required from the Information Commissioner. Appropriate safeguards should:

— ensure compliance with data protection requirements and the rights of the data subjects appropriate to processing within the Union, including the availability of enforceable data subject rights and of effective legal remedies, including to obtain effective administrative or judicial redress and to claim compensation, in the Union or in a third country; and
— relate in particular to compliance with the general principles relating to personal data processing, the principles of data protection by design and by default.[425]

9– 063 Authorisation not required

In order to transfer personal data to a restricted destination without specific authorisation from the Information Commissioner, the appropriate safeguards must be provided by one or more

420 GDPR Art 45(1).

421 GDPR Art 45(1). The process of assessing the adequacy of the level of protection, and of reviewing at least every four years, is set out in GDPR Art 45(2)-(7). As to the meaning of 'third country,' see §8– 032. As to the meaning of 'international organisations,' see §8– 033.

422 'Privacy Shield' is a framework for transatlantic data transfers introduced following a judgment of the European Court of Justice in C-362/14 (6 October 2015), which struck down the predecessor framework known as 'Safe Harbor'. Under the Privacy Shield, US entities register, self-certify as to the adequacy of their data protection arrangements, with their self-certification then being verified and monitored by the US Department of Commerce.

423 *Schrems v Data Protection Commissioner* (C-362/14) [2016] QB 527, [2016] 2 CMLR 2 at [63]-[66].

424 GDPR Art 46(1). See also recital (108). Given that the Commission, when making an adequacy decision, must take account of the existence in the destination of 'effective and enforceable data subject rights and effective administrative and judicial redress for the data subjects whose personal data are being transferred' (GDPR Art 45(2)(a)), those adequacy decisions may provide a useful measure of what will suffice for the purposes of the analogous requirement for transfers under GDPR Art 46(1).

425 GDPR recital (108). As to the meaning of 'third country,' see §8– 032.

of the following:[426]

(a) A legally binding and enforceable instrument between public authorities or bodies. The expectation here is that the public authorities or bodies have corresponding duties or functions, and that there might be provisions inserted into their administrative arrangements to secure the safeguards.[427]

(b) In relation to transfers between members of a group of undertakings, or a group of enterprises engaged in a joint economic activity, binding corporate rules that have been approved by the Information Commissioner.[428] 'Binding corporate rules' means personal data protection policies that are adhered to by a controller or processor established in a Member State for transfers or a set of transfers of personal data to a controller or processor in one or more third countries within a group of undertakings, or group of enterprises engaged in a joint economic activity.[429] In order for corporate rules to be approved by the Information Commissioner, those rules must expressly confer enforceable rights on data subjects with regard to the processing of their personal data.[430]

(c) Standard data protection clauses adopted by the European Commission.[431]

(d) Standard data protection clauses adopted by the Information Commissioner and approved by the European Commission.

(e) An approved code of conduct, together with binding and enforceable commitments of the controller or processor in the third country to apply the appropriate safeguards, including as regards data subjects' rights.[432]

(f) An approved certification mechanism, together with binding and enforceable commitments of the controller or processor in the third country to apply the appropriate safeguards, including as regards data subjects' rights.[433]

–064 Authorisation required

Subject to authorisation from the Information Commissioner, the appropriate safeguards required for a transfer of personal data to a restricted destination may be provided by one or more of the following:[434]

(a) Contractual clauses between the controller or processor and the controller, processor or recipient of the personal data in the third country or international organisation.[435]

(b) Provisions to be inserted into administrative arrangements between public authorities or bodies which include enforceable and effective data subject rights.

426 GDPR Art 46(2).

427 GDPR recital (108).

428 See also GDPR recital (110). An 'undertaking' is a non-natural legal person: GDPR recital (14). A 'group of undertakings' means a controlling undertaking and its controlled undertakings: GDPR Art 4(19) and recital (37). An 'enterprise' means a natural or legal person engaged in an economic activity, irrespective of its legal form, including partnerships or associations regularly engaged in an economic activity: GDPR Art 4(18). 'Enterprises engaged in a joint economic activity' could include joint venturers.

429 GDPR Art 4(20).

430 The rules must fulfil the requirements in GDPR Art 47(2).

431 Standard data protection clauses must follow the examination procedure in GDPR Art 93(2).

432 A code of conduct is approved under GDPR Art 40. As to the meaning of 'third country,' see §8– 032.

433 A certification mechanism is approved under GDPR Art 42.

434 GDPR Art 46(3).

435 As to the meaning of 'third country,' see §8– 032. As to the meaning of 'international organisations,' see §8– 033.

CHAPTER 10

General processing: data subject rights

1. OVERVIEW

10–001 Introduction

In addition to data subject rights that enure from the obligations on controllers and processors whenever undertaking general processing of personal data,[1] the GDPR confers on every data subject seven separate rights exercisable against a controller directly or indirectly processing the

[1] That is, the obligations dealt with in Chapter 9.

data subject's personal data. Six of these rights are exercised by giving a notice to the controller: the seventh (automated decisions) requires no notice. Upon receiving a notice the controller becomes under a correlative duty to comply. The correlative duty on the seventh right subsists at all times. The GDPR provides limited exemptions, leaving Member States latitude to specify other exemptions subject to the constraints set by the GDPR.[2] The DPA 2018 acknowledges these GDPR rights,[3] supplementing them with a detailed suite of exemptions.[4] Where the correlative duty does arise, non-compliance will expose the controller both to regulatory action from the Information Commissioner and to a private law claim from the data subject.[5]

10– 002 Background

The DPA 1998 provided a similar system of notice-triggered duties. Indeed, for many, the DPA 1998 regime was synonymous with one facet of the duty arising from one such notice – the 'subject access request' – and not much more. Although the nomenclature has evolved and while some of these rights are now more easily engaged than under the DPA 1998, five of the six notice-exercisable rights conferred on data subjects can be traced to the previous regime.

10– 003 Summary of the rights

The seven rights conferred by the GDPR and supplemented by the DPA 2018 are as follows:

(1) A 'right of access.'[6] This is a multi-faceted right that entitles a data subject to obtain from the controller:
   (a) confirmation whether or not personal data about the data subject are being processed;
   (b) if personal data about the data subject are being processed, certain information about the personal data being processed, the purposes of the processing, the period for which that personal information will be stored, the persons to whom that personal data have or will be disclosed, the source of the personal data and a statement of the data subject's rights; and
   (c) a copy of the personal data.

(2) A 'right to rectification.'[7] A data subject can require a controller to rectify inaccurate personal data concerning the data subject and to complete incomplete personal data.

(3) A 'right to erasure.'[8] This is sometimes called the 'right to be forgotten.' A data subject can, in some circumstances, require a controller to erase such personal data as the controller holds about the data subject.

(4) A 'right to restrict processing.'[9] In certain circumstances a data subject can restrict temporarily the uses for which a controller may process personal data about the data subject.

---

2 GDPR Art 23.

3 DPA 2018 s 2(1)(b).

4 DPA 2018 s 15 and Schs 2, 3 and 4.

5 Regulatory enforcement is considered at §§48– 014 to 48– 055. Private law claims are considered at §§48– 005 to 48– 013.

6 GDPR Art 15.

7 GDPR Art 16.

8 GDPR Art 17.

9 GDPR Art 18. As to the meaning of 'restriction of processing,' see §8– 031.

(5) A 'right to data portability.'[10] In certain circumstances a data subject may require the controller to provide the data subject with the personal data concerning him or herself in a structured, commonly-used and machine readable format and to transmit that data to another controller.

(6) A 'right to object.'[11] In relation to processing of personal data carried out by a controller because it is necessary either for the purpose of performing a public function or in order to pursue some legitimate interest of the controller or of a third party, a data subject may object to that processing and the controller must, unless able to demonstrate compelling legitimate grounds for the processing that override the data subject's interests, desist from the processing.

(7) A right not to be subject to automated decision-making.[12] Subject to exceptions, the default position is that a data subject is not to be made subject to a decision based solely on automated processing which produces legal effects concerning the data subject. This right does not require a notice from the data subject.

In order to exercise the rights in (2)-(6) effectively, a data subject will very often need to serve first a notice under (1) and receive the results.[13] The response to a notice under (1) will often be useful to dispel any suggestion that a notice under (2)-(6) is manifestly unfounded: for example, where the response to a notice under (1) reveals inaccuracies in the data subject's personal data being processed by the controller.

10–004 Rights against processors

Where a processor is processing personal data, that processor will, by definition, be carrying out that processing on behalf of a controller.[14] The seven rights are exercisable against a controller, and not against a processor processing on behalf of that controller. The controller is responsible for all processing of personal data carried out on its behalf by a processor, including in respect of the correlative duties that arise where a data subject exercises any of the above rights. A controller is under a statutory obligation to use only processors that provide sufficient guarantees to implement measures that will ensure the protection of the rights of the data subject.[15] The relationship between controller and processor must be governed by a binding contract, which must include provisions to assist the controller in fulfilling its duties where a data subject exercises his or her rights.[16]

10–005 Joint controllers

Where two or more controllers jointly determine the purposes and means of processing – with the result that they are joint controllers – then regardless of how the controllers have divided their responsibilities, a data subject may exercise his or her rights against each of those controllers.[17]

---

10 GDPR Art 20.

11 GDPR Art 21.

12 GDPR Art 22.

13 That is implicitly recognised in GDPR Art 15(1)(e).

14 GDPR Art 4(8).

15 GDPR Art 28(1).

16 GDPR Art 28(3)(e).

17 GDPR Art 26(3).

10–006 Facilitating requests

A controller must facilitate the exercise of these data subject rights.[18] This includes providing means for requests to be made electronically.[19] A controller's data protection officer must be available to respond to a data subject in relation to all issues relating to the processing of his or her data, including the exercise of a data subject's rights.[20]

10–007 Form of notice

There is no specified form for a notice exercising any of the data subject rights. However, it is implicit in the GDPR that the notice should provide sufficient information that the controller is able to identify the data subject in a way that leaves no reasonable doubt.[21] In practice, to avoid legitimate doubt and facilitate engagement with the issues, a notice should give:

- the full name and address of the controller to whom it is addressed, including any email address;
- the date of the notice;
- an identification of the right(s) that the data subject is exercising;
- the full name, postal address and date of birth of the data subject;[22]
- the format in which the data subject wishes to receive any response (ie electronic, printed or oral); and
- the address to which the data subject wishes the controller to send the response.

Depending on the right being exercised, a notice may need to include other information.[23] If at all possible, it is prudent for a data subject to restrict the reach of the request, for example by date range, or at least invite the controller to request the data subject to refine the request if the controller estimates that compliance will impose an excessive amount of work.[24] If the data subject anticipates that non-compliance by the controller with the requirements of the notice will result in loss, damage or distress of any kind, it is prudent to spell that out in the notice, together with a statement of the kinds of loss and damage anticipated and how they might result. A notice should be addressed to the data protection officer of the controller.[25]

10–008 Requiring further details

The only explicit basis on which a controller can refuse to act on a notice from a data subject is if the controller cannot identify the data subject.[26] A controller is expected to take all reasonable measures to identify a data subject, in particular where an access request is made

---

18 GDPR Art 12(2).

19 GDPR recital (59).

20 GDPR Art 38(4).

21 GDPR Art 12.

22 To avoid needless correspondence, it is sensible to include a photocopy of identification documentation (such as a passport and utilities or bank statement).

23 The other information required is dealt with below under the individual rights.

24 This will pre-empt any claim by the controller that the burden of complying with the request is manifestly unfounded or excessive in character. The GDPR contemplates that where a controller processes a large quantity of information concerning the data subject and the controller receives a right of access notice under Art 15 , the controller should be able to request that, before the information is delivered, the data subject should specify the information or processing activities to which the request relates: GDPR recital (63).

25 GDPR Art 38(4).

26 GDPR Art 12(2). A person may be identifiable directly or indirectly by reference to, for example, identifiers such as a name, an identification number, location data, an online identifier or to one or more factors specific to the physical, physiological, genetic, mental, economic, cultural or social identity of that person: GDPR Art 4(1). A person may be identified through biometric data: GDPR Art 4(14). Identifiers include national identification numbers and any other identifiers of general application: GDPR Art 87.

under Article 15.[27] Where a controller is unable to identify the data subject, the controller must within one month of receiving the notice advise the data subject of that fact.[28] Where a controller has reasonable doubts concerning the identity of the person giving notice, the controller may within one month of receiving the notice request additional information in order to confirm the identity of the data subject.[29] Once a controller has satisfactorily identified a data subject, the controller must act on the request by considering its terms, deciding whether it is manifestly unfounded or excessive and, if not, whether the claimed right has been disapplied or falls within exemptions, and otherwise by doing as requested and advising the data subject of what has been done.

10– 009 Time for compliance

The standard time for compliance is 'without undue delay' but in any event within one month of receipt of the notice.[30] Where, taking into account the complexity of a notice and the number of notices received, the controller needs more time, that period can be extended by up to two further months.[31] Where the period is so extended, the controller must within one month of receiving the notice notify the data subject of the extra time required by the controller together with a statement of the reasons for the controller needing the extra time.[32]

10– 010 Fees

A controller must normally comply with a notice without charge to the data subject.[33] This includes the provision of a copy of the data subject's personal information on a notice under Article 15.[34] The normal position is displaced and a controller may charge a reasonable fee where:

(a) the controller demonstrates that requests from the data subject are manifestly unfounded or excessive, in particular because they are repetitive;[35] or

(b) the data subject requires more than one copy of his or her personal information on a notice under Article 15.[36]

The quantum of the fee is to take account of the administrative costs of providing the information or taking the action requested in the notice.[37]

---

27 GDPR recital (64). Reasonable measures will include resorting to online identifiers such as internet protocol addresses, cookie identifiers and radio frequency identification tags: GDPR recital (30).

28 GDPR Arts 11(2) and 12(3).

29 GDPR Arts 12(3) and (6).

30 GDPR Arts 12(3), 16 and 17 and recital (59).

31 GDPR Art 12(3).

32 GDPR Art 12(3) and recital (59).

33 GDPR Art 12(5).

34 GDPR Art 15(3).

35 GDPR Art 12(5). Alternatively, in this situation the controller may refuse to act on the notice. The use of the plural in Art 12(5), and the singular elsewhere in Art 12, implies that a controller may not charge a fee for a first request from a particular data subject. This is consistent with the approach to copies in GDPR Art 15(3). A similar choice of language is made in GDPR Art 57(4) dealing with a data subject's complaints to the supervisory authority, ie the Information Commissioner.

36 GDPR Art 15(3).

37 GDPR Arts 12(5)(a) and 15(3). Searching for the information captured by the terms of a notice, identifying the processing of that information, and considering applicable exemptions are all antecedent to providing that information and taking the action requested in a notice. As such, it should not be included within the 'reasonable fee.' Contrast the basis for fees under FOIA: see §22– 016.

10– 011 Unfounded/excessive requests

Where a controller can demonstrate that a request made by notice is 'manifestly unfounded or excessive' (in particular, because it is unduly repetitive),[38] the controller may refuse to act on the request.[39] Where a controller refuses to act on a request for this reason, the controller must notify the data subject of this within one month of the controller's receipt of the request.[40] The refusal notice must set out the reasons for refusal and must also advise the data subject of his or her right both to lodge a complaint with the Information Commissioner and to bring a private law claim.[41]

10– 012 Refusal response

Where a controller refuses to comply with a request on grounds other than that the request is 'manifestly unfounded or excessive' – in other words, because the controller contends that a restriction or exemption is applicable – the controller must notify the data subject of this within one month of the controller's receipt of the notice.[42] Where a controller can accommodate a disapplication or exemption by a part refusal, the controller should do what is possible to comply with the request.[43] The refusal notice must set out the reasons for refusal and must also advise the data subject of his or her right both to lodge a complaint with the Information Commissioner and to bring a private law claim.[44]

10– 013 Compliant response

Where a controller complies with a request, the controller must notify the data subject in a concise, transparent, intelligible and easily accessible form, using clear and plain language.[45] Where the data subject's request was made electronically, then, unless otherwise requested, the controller's response should be sent electronically.[46] Where the controller is providing the data subject with a copy of information, this should be provided with the response and in the same format as the response.[47]

---

38 The GDPR nevertheless recognises that a data subject should be able to exercise his or her right 'at reasonable intervals,' at least in relation to the right of access: GDPR recital (63).

39 GDPR Art 12(5). The GDPR contemplates that where a controller processes a large quantity of information concerning the data subject and the controller receives a right of access notice under Art 15 , the controller should be able to request that, before the information is delivered, the data subject should specify the information or processing activities to which the request relates: GDPR recital (63).

40 GDPR Art 12(4).

41 GDPR Art 12(4). Regulatory enforcement is considered at §§48– 014 to 48– 055. Private law claims are considered at §§48– 005 to 48– 013.

42 GDPR Art 12(4).

43 GDPR recital (63) ('...the result of those considerations should not be a refusal to provide all information to the data subject') dealing with an access request, but equally applicable to the other data subject rights.

44 GDPR Art 12(4). Regulatory enforcement is considered at §§48– 014 to 48– 055. Private law claims are considered at §§48– 005 to 48– 013.

45 GDPR Art 12(1) and recital (58).

46 GDPR Art 12(1).

47 GDPR Art 15(3), ie printed, electronic etc.

2. RIGHT OF ACCESS

10–014 Introduction

Article 15(1) of the GDPR confers on every data subject a right to obtain from a controller confirmation whether or not that controller (or a processor processing personal data on behalf of that controller)[48] is processing personal data concerning him or her. A similar right existed under the previous regime, with such notices commonly called 'subject access requests.'[49] The Article 15(1) right is attenuated where the controller is a credit reference agency.[50] The provision in the GDPR allowing a controller to refuse to act on a 'manifestly unfounded' request does not allow a controller to avoid its duty to comply with the request by questioning the purpose for which a data subject has made a request under Article 15(1).[51]

10–015 The right

Where a data subject exercises the Article 15(1) right by giving the controller a notice, the controller must, in the time and manner prescribed,[52] respond confirming that it (or a processor acting on its behalf) is or is not processing personal data concerning the data subject.[53] Where the controller (or a processor on behalf of the controller) is processing personal data concerning the data subject, then the controller must in its response also give the data subject access to the personal data by providing a copy of it[54] as well as a written statement. The written statement must contain the following information:[55]

---

[48] The obligation is cast in the passive voice in order to capture both the controller and a processor acting on behalf of the controller: see GDPR Art 4(8).

[49] DPA 1998 s 7 and Directive 95/46/EC Arts 10-12. See further §15–053. A subject access request under that Act was held to involve a determination of the requester's civil rights and obligations: *R (Michael) v HMP Whitemoor* [2020] EWCA Civ 29 at [31].

[50] That is, a credit reference agency within the meaning of the Consumer Credit Act 1974 s 145(8): see DPA 2018 s 13(1). In the case of such an agency, the controller's obligations apply only to personal data relating to the data subject's financial standing, unless the data subject has indicated a contrary intention.

[51] In relation to 'manifestly unfounded' requests, see §10–011. Early judicial activism by the Court of Appeal in relation to the corresponding right under the DPA 1998 expressly to give it a narrow construction, inserted a purpose limitation: namely, that DPA 1998 s 7 entitled a data subject to have access to his or her personal data only to enable him or her to check whether the data controller's processing of it unlawfully infringed the data subject's privacy, and that it did not provide the data subject with 'automatic key to any information...of matters in which he may be named or involved': *Durant v Financial Services Authority* [2003] EWCA Civ 1746, [2004] FSR 28 at [27]-[29]; *Johnson v Medical Defence Union* [2007] EWCA Civ 262, [2007] 3 CMLR 9, (2007) 96 BMLR 99 at [16] ('...it is not easy to extract from this Directive any purpose other than the protection of privacy' – surprising given that the European Parliament had no legislative competence to pass a directive on privacy.) Later Court of Appeal authority shifted away from this reading down of DPA 1998 s 7: *Dawson-Damer v Taylor Wessing LLP* [2017] EWCA Civ 74, [2017] 1 WLR 3255; *Re Southern Pacific Personal Loans Ltd* [2013] EWHC 2485 (Ch), [2014] Ch 426. Whether or not it was ever correct under the DPA 1998, there is no basis for its transposition into the GDPR regime, which does not tie data protection to personal privacy: see §§8–003 and 8–006 to 8–007. Thus, the GDPR specifically recognises that a data subject may require personal data for the establishment, exercise or defence of legal claims: GDPR Arts 18(1)(c) and 21(1). Furthermore, the GDPR expressly contemplates that an Article 15(1) request may be made in order to determine whether to make a request for rectification, erasure, restriction of processing or objection to processing: GDPR Art 15(1)(e) and recital (63). As to the meaning of 'restriction of processing,' see §8–031.

[52] As to the time and manner prescribed, see §§10–009 and 10–013.

[53] GDPR Art 15(1). The controller must respond to the request even though it is not processing personal data concerning the data subject.

[54] GDPR Art 15(2).

[55] GDPR Art 15(1).

(a) the purposes of the processing;[56]
(b) the categories of personal data concerned;[57]
(c) the recipients or categories of recipient to whom the personal data have been or will be disclosed, in particular recipients in third countries or international organisations;[58]
(d) where possible, the envisaged period for which the personal data will be stored, or, if not possible, the criteria used to determine that period;
(e) the existence of the right to request from the controller rectification or erasure of personal data or restriction of processing of personal data concerning the data subject or to object to such processing;[59]
(f) the right to lodge a complaint with a supervisory authority;[60]
(g) where the personal data are not collected from the data subject, any available information as to their source;[61] and
(h) the existence of automated decision-making, including profiling, referred to in Article 22(1) and (4) and, at least in those cases, meaningful information about the logic involved, as well as the significance and the envisaged consequences of such processing for the data subject.

The controller must answer the request and provide the information from the standpoint of the personal information that the controller is processing at the moment that the notice is received.[62] Within the same period a controller must inform the data subject of the action taken on the request.[63] Where supplying a copy of the information would adversely affect the rights and freedoms of other individuals, then the information supplied should be redacted in order that the adverse effects are tempered or avoided.[64]

10–016 Searches

Domestic case law under the previous data protection regime conceived a notion that a controller's obligation to search for personal data relating to the data subject was limited to what was 'proportionate.'[65] There is nothing in the GDPR to support writing such a limitation into the current data protection regime. In allowing a controller to refuse to act on requests

---

56 The purposes of the processing should normally not have strayed outside of those purposes for which the controller secured the data subject's consent or a compatible purpose: GDPR Art 6(1)(a), 6(4), recitals (32), (39), (42), (45), (47), (48), (50) and (60).

57 The 'categories' of personal data is a reference to personal data the processing of which is attended by a higher level of protection, ie 'sensitive personal data' (see §9–040): GDPR Arts 6(4)(c), 9. Where the controller obtained the personal data from someone other than the data subject, the controller should have provided the data subject with information about the categories of personal data: GDPR Art 14(1)(d). In the record of processing activities that a controller with 250 or more employees is required to maintain, this must include a description of the categories of personal data and the time within which it will be erased: GDPR Art 30(1)(c), (f).

58 As to the meaning of 'third country,' see §8–032. As to the meaning of 'international organisations,' see §8–033. Where the personal data have been transferred to a third country or an international organisation, the controller must also inform the data subject of the appropriate safeguards relating to the transfer. As to the meaning of 'appropriate safeguards' see §§9–062 to 9–064.

59 That is, the rights under GDPR Arts 16, 17, 18 and 21 respectively.

60 That is, the right to lodge a complaint with the supervisory authority under GDPR Art 77(1). In the United Kingdom, the supervisory authority is the Information Commissioner: DPA 2018 ss 115(1) and 165(1).

61 This should comprise no less than the details prescribed in GDPR Art 14(1)(a) and (b).

62 GDPR Art 15(3). Contrast the position under DPA 1998, see §15–068.

63 GDPR Art 12(3).

64 GDPR Art 15(4) and recital (63). This will include protecting the trade secrets and intellectual property of those third parties. The redaction should not prevent the data subject from being made aware of or verifying the lawfulness of the processing.

65 *Ittihadieh v 5-11 Cheyne Gardens RTM Co Ltd* [2017] EWCA 121, [2018] QB 256; *Dawson-Damer v Taylor Wessing LLP* [2017] EWCA Civ 74, [2017] 1 WLR 3255; *Ezsias v Welsh Ministers* [2007] EWHC B15 (QB). Given that there were no words so limiting the obligation in either the DPA 1998 or in the Directive 95/46/EC, it appears to have been immaculate in conception.

that are 'manifestly unfounded or excessive,'[66] the GDPR has confined its attention to the requests themselves, rather than to the amount of effort in complying with a request that is the result of the system (or lack of system) by which the controller has arranged its collection of personal data. The GDPR places responsibility on the controller to organise itself – including by acquiring and keeping only such personal data as it needs for its purposes – so that it can comply with Article 15 requests efficiently. A controller that amasses personal data unnecessarily or that fails to organise properly the personal data that it holds will assume for itself the cost of finding all the personal data that concerns a data subject when complying with requests made by data subjects. In this way the GDPR further encourages a controller to collect and to retain only so much personal data as is necessary for its purposes[67] – a policy object underpinning the third and fifth processing principles.[68]

10– 017 Exemptions and refusals

The GDPR gives Member States a qualified right to impose legislative restrictions to the scope of the access right,[69] as well as to provide derogations from it.[70] This right has been exercised by various exemptions provided for in the DPA 2018.[71] Where or to the extent that a controller refuses to comply with a notice requiring access, the controller must give the data subject a compliant refusal notice.[72] Where a controller does not have good grounds for not complying with a notice under Article 15, the data subject may bring a private claim against the controller, invite the Information Commissioner to take regulatory action, or both.[73]

3. RIGHT TO RECTIFICATION

10– 018 Introduction

The GDPR confers on every data subject a right to rectification exercisable against a controller processing personal data concerning the data subject.[74] The right provides data subjects with a direct means of compelling a controller to comply with one facet of the accuracy principle, and to do so without having to go through the process of establishing a breach of that principle.[75] Under the previous regime provision for rectification existed, albeit exercisable on application by the data subject to a court rather than as a right exercisable on notice to the

---

66 GDPR Art 12(5). See further §10– 011 and GDPR recital (63).

67 See, for example, GDPR recital (64).

68 That is, data minimisation and storage limitation. See §9– 028 and §9– 031.

69 GDPR Art 23(1). The restrictions must both respect the essence of the fundamental rights and freedoms and be a necessary and proportionate measure in a democratic society to safeguard any of the matters listed in GDPR Art 23(1). As to the 'fundamental rights and freedoms', see GDPR Arts 1(2) and 6(1)(f) and recitals (2), (10), (16), (47), (51), (69), (113) and (166).

70 GDPR Art 89(2)-(3).

71 See Chapter 11.

72 As to the content of a refusal notice, see §10– 012.

73 Regulatory enforcement is considered at §§48– 014 to 48– 055. Private law claims are considered at §§48– 005 to 48– 013.

74 GDPR Art 16. See also recitals (39) and (65). The right also applies where the personal data is being processed by a processor on behalf of the controller.

75 'Accuracy' is one of the six processing principles in GDPR Art 5(1) that constitute the 'accountability obligation' for which the controller is responsible and must be able to demonstrate compliance. See further §§9– 004 and §§9– 029 to 9– 030.

controller.[76] A data subject does not need to disclose a purpose in making a request to rectify.[77] Pending a controller determining whether it must comply with a rectification notice, a data subject may also serve a notice restricting processing of the data subject's personal data.[78] The latter right is attenuated by fewer conditions and exemptions than the right to rectification.

10– 019 The right

The rectification right has two limbs:

> ...the right to obtain from the controller without undue delay the rectification of inaccurate personal data concerning him or her.

and

> ...taking into account the purposes of the processing, the right to have incomplete personal data completed, including by means of providing a supplementary statement.[79]

'Inaccurate' means incorrect or misleading as to any matter of fact.[80] An opinion – even if wrong-headed or devoid of factual basis – cannot be 'inaccurate': but it may be incomplete and it may be inaccurately recorded. In determining whether personal data is 'incomplete,' regard must be had to the purposes of the processing. Given that a controller must at all times comply with the third processing principle (data minimisation), personal data will not be 'incomplete' where further personal data concerning a data subject is not necessary in relation to the purposes for which the controller is processing that data subject's personal data.[81]

10– 020 The notice

The right is exercised by notice to the controller.[82] In addition to the usual requirements for a notice exercising rights under the GDPR,[83] a rectification notice will generally need to identify which of the personal data relating to the data subject that is held by the controller is inaccurate, and to specify in what respects it is inaccurate or incomplete and how it should read in order not to be inaccurate (including any supplementary statement). It is unlikely that a data subject will be able to prepare an adequate rectification notice without having first served a notice under Article 15 and received a response. At the same time as exercising the rectification right, the data subject may include a notice under Article 18 requiring the controller to restrict processing of the data subject's personal data pending the controller's verification of the accuracy of the personal data.[84] The controller must comply with any notice 'without undue delay' and in any event within one month.[85] Within the same period a controller must inform the data subject of the action taken on the request.[86] A controller is not entitled to charge a fee

---

76 DPA 1998 s 14(1). Given that a data subject would normally be expected to forewarn a controller of a court application and enable the controller to rectify without the need for a court order, the difference between the previous regime and the current is one more apparent than real.

77 Given the free-standing continuing obligation in GDPR Art 5(1)(d), that is self-evident.

78 GDPR Art 18(1)(a). See further §§10– 029 to 10– 034. As to the meaning of 'restriction of processing,' see §8– 031.

79 The controller should at the time of obtaining the data subject's personal data have informed the data subject of the purposes of the processing: GDPR Arts 13(1)(c) and 14(1)(c). A controller should also, when answering an Article 15 request, have informed the data subject of the purposes of the processing: GDPR Art 15(1)(a).

80 DPA 2018 s 205(1).

81 GDPR Art 5(1)(c). See further §9– 028.

82 As to the form of the notice, see §10– 007.

83 As to which, see §10– 007.

84 GDPR Art 18(1)(a) and see further §§10– 029 to 10– 034. As to the meaning of 'restriction of processing,' see §8– 031.

85 On time for compliance, see further §10– 009.

86 GDPR Art 12(3).

for compliance.[87]

10– 021 Supplementary obligations

The rectification right is supplemented by Article 19 of the GDPR, which requires:

(a) the controller to communicate any rectification of personal data carried out to each recipient to whom the personal data have been disclosed,[88] unless this proves impossible or involves disproportionate effort; and

(b) if the data subject has requested it, to inform the data subject of each recipient to whom the personal data have been disclosed.

The implication is that a controller must do (a) regardless of whether the data subject has requested it.

10– 022 Exemptions and refusals

The GDPR gives Member States a qualified right to impose legislative restrictions to the scope of the rectification right,[89] as well as to provide derogations from it.[90] This right has been exercised by various exemptions provided for in the DPA 2018.[91] Where or to the extent that a controller refuses to comply with a notice requiring rectification, the controller must give the data subject a refusal notice.[92] Where, on the basis of impossibility or disproportionate effort, the controller has not notified every recipient of the personal data of the rectification, that should also be stated in the refusal notice, including details of the recipients, or class of recipients, that have not been notified.[93] Where a controller does not have good grounds for not complying with a rectification notice under Article 16, the data subject may bring a private claim against the controller, invite the Information Commissioner to take regulatory action, or both.[94]

4. RIGHT TO ERASURE

10– 023 Introduction

The GDPR confers on every data subject a qualified right of erasure – otherwise called a 'right to be forgotten' – exercisable against a controller processing personal data concerning the data subject.[95] The right provides data subjects with a direct means of compelling a controller to comply with three of the processing principles embodied in the accountability obligation, and

87 See further §10– 010.

88 Although not expressly stated, this would appear to mean disclosed by the controller or by a processor on behalf of that controller.

89 GDPR Art 23(1). The restrictions must both respect the essence of the fundamental rights and freedoms and be a necessary and proportionate measure in a democratic society to safeguard any of the matters listed in GDPR Art 23(1). As to the 'fundamental rights and freedoms', see GDPR Arts 1(2) and 6(1)(f) and recitals (2), (10), (16), (47), (51), (69), (113) and (166).

90 GDPR Art 89(2)-(3).

91 See Chapter 11.

92 As to the content of a refusal notice, see §10– 012.

93 In order that the Information Commissioner can effectively exercise the corrective powers provided for in GDPR Art 58(2)(g).

94 Regulatory enforcement is considered at §§48– 014 to 48– 055. Private law claims are considered at §§48– 005 to 48– 013.

95 GDPR Art 17(1). See also recitals (39), (59), (65), (66), (68), (73) and (156). The right also applies where the personal data is being processed by a processor on behalf of the controller.

to do so without having to go through the process of establishing a breach of those principles.[96] The right is one of a data subject's rights that a controller, upon obtaining personal data concerning a data subject, must inform that data subject.[97] A controller must also inform a data subject of the right in responding to an access request under Article 15.[98] Under the previous regime provision for personal data erasure existed, albeit exercisable on application by the data subject to a court rather than as a right exercisable on notice to the controller.[99] Although a data subject does not need to disclose a purpose in making a request to a controller to erase, a request that addresses the grounds founding the right and that forestalls possible bases for exemption should expedite the process and improve the prospects for a correct outcome.

10– 024 The grounds

Subject to disapplications and exemptions, a data subject has a right to require a controller to erase personal data concerning him or her where one or more of the following grounds applies:

(a) The personal data are no longer necessary in relation to the purposes for which they were collected or otherwise processed.[100] The word 'necessary' means 'reasonably necessary' as adjudged by the precepts of EU law.[101]

(b) The data subject has withdrawn the consent on which the processing is based[102] and there is no other legal ground for the processing.[103]

(c) The data subject has objected to the processing:
— pursuant to Article 21(1) and there are no overriding legitimate grounds for the processing, or
— pursuant to Article 21(2).[104]

Article 21(1) is concerned with where a data subject has given the controller a notice

---

96 The three principles in the GDPR all compel the controller to limit the purposes of processing of personal data:
(1) Art 5(1)(b) provides that personal data must be collected only for specified, explicit and legitimate purposes, and not further processed in a manner that is incompatible with those purposes. In relation to applied GDPR processing, see DPA 2018 s 22(1) (as to the meaning of 'applied GDPR processing', see §9– 002). Considered further at §§9– 023 to 9– 027.
(2) Art 5(1)(c) provides that personal data must be adequate, relevant and limited to what is necessary in relation to the purposes for which they are processed. In relation to applied GDPR processing, see DPA 2018 s 22(1). Considered further at §9– 028.
(3) Art 5(1)(e) provides that personal data must be kept in a form which permits identification of data subjects for no longer than is necessary for the purposes for which the personal data are processed. In relation to applied GDPR processing, see DPA 2018 s 22(1). Considered further at §§9– 031 to 9– 033.

97 GDPR Arts 13(2)(b) and 14(2)(c).

98 GDPR Art 15(1)e).

99 DPA 1998 s 14(1). Given that a data subject would normally be expected to forewarn a controller of a court application and enable the controller to rectify without the need for a court order, the difference between the previous regime and the current is one more apparent than real.

100 GDPR Art 17(1)(a). And see recital (65). The controller should at the time of obtaining the data subject's personal data have informed the data subject of the purposes of the processing: GDPR Arts 13(1)(c) and 14(1)(c). A controller should also, when answering an Article 15 request, have informed the data subject of the purposes of the processing: GDPR Art 15(1)(a). As to the technique under the former regime, see *Google Spain SL v Agencia Espanola de Proteccion de Datos* (C-131/12) [2014] QB 1022. This considered a data subject's request to Google to be removed from the list of results displayed following a search on the basis of the data subject's name. The results displayed links reporting details of a repossession order that had been made against the data subject 16 years earlier. The CJEU, having identified a list of factors relevant to the determination, held that this was excessive and no longer relevant, requiring Google to remove these results.

101 See §9– 004.

102 In other words under GDPR Art 6(1)(a) and, in relation to special category personal data, under Art 9(2)(a).

103 GDPR Art 17(1)(b). For personal data that is not sensitive personal data, the other legal grounds for processing are those set out in GDPR Art 6(1): see further §§9– 007 to 9– 013. In the case of sensitive personal data, the other legal grounds for processing are those set out in Arts 9(2) and 10: see further §§9– 040 to 9– 047.

104 GDPR Art 17(1)(c).

objecting to processing of personal data relating to him or her, the lawfulness of which processing is based on that processing being necessary for the performance of a statutory function or being necessary for the purposes of the legitimate interests pursued by the controller or a third party.[105] Article 21(2) is concerned with where personal data are being processed for direct marketing purposes and a data subject has given the controller a notice objecting to the processing of personal data concerning him or her for those purposes.[106]

(d) The personal data have been unlawfully processed.[107]

(e) The personal data have to be erased in order to comply with a legal obligation in Union or Member State law to which the controller is subject.[108]

(f) The personal data have been collected in relation to the offer of information society services referred to in Article 8(1): that is, where 'information society services' have been collected from a child under the age of 16 years and consent was not secured from the holder of parental responsibilities over the child.[109]

10–025 The notice

The right is exercised by notice given to the controller.[110] In addition to the usual requirements for a notice exercising rights under the GDPR,[111] an erasure notice will generally need to identify:

(a) which (if not all) of the personal data relating to the data subject that is held by the controller should be erased; and

(b) which of the six grounds for erasure in Article 17(1) is applicable,[112] setting out the basis for its application.

Where a data subject is of the view that the controller should also inform other controllers of the erasure notice so that they too erase the data,[113] it is good practice for the notice to spell that out. A data subject will generally be better placed to prepare an adequate erasure notice after having first served a notice under Article 15 and received a response. The controller must comply with the notice 'without undue delay' and in any event within one month.[114] Within the same period a controller must inform the data subject of the action taken on the request.[115] A controller is not entitled to charge a fee for compliance.[116]

---

105 In relation to notices under Art 21(1), see §§10–040 to 10–043. In relation to the meaning of 'necessary' see §9–004.

106 In relation to notices under Art 21(2), see §§10–040 to 10–043.

107 GDPR Art 17(1)(d). For personal data that is not sensitive personal data, personal data will have been unlawfully processed if none of the grounds set out in GDPR Art 6(1) is applicable: see further §§9–007 to 9–013. In the case of sensitive personal data, personal data will have been unlawfully processed where none of the grounds for processing in Art 9(2) or 10 is applicable: see further §§9–040 to 9–047.

108 GDPR Art 17(1)(e).

109 GDPR Art 17(1)(f). 'Information society service' means any service normally provided for remuneration, at a distance, by electronic means and at the individual request of a recipient of services: GDPR Art 4(25), picking up the definition in Directive EU 2015/1535 Art 1(1). Annex I of that Directive provides an indicative list of services that are not included in the definition.

110 As to the form of the notice, see §10–007.

111 As to which, see §10–007.

112 See §10–024.

113 See GDPR Art 17(2).

114 On time for compliance, see further §10–009.

115 GDPR Art 12(3).

116 See further §10–010.

10– 026 Supplementary obligations

Where the controller has made public the personal data and is obliged to erase the personal data, then the controller must also take reasonable steps to inform other controllers that are processing that personal data that the data subject has requested erasure.[117] The erasure right is further supplemented by Article 19 of the GDPR, which requires:

(a) the controller to communicate any erasure of personal data carried out to each recipient to whom the personal data have been disclosed,[118] unless this proves impossible or involves disproportionate effort; and

(b) if the data subject has requested it, to inform the data subject of each recipient to whom the personal data have been disclosed.

The implication is that a controller must do (a) regardless of whether the data subject has requested it.

10– 027 Disapplication of right

The GDPR excludes from the right of erasure processing of personal data that is necessary:[119]

(a) For exercising the right of freedom of expression and information.[120]

(b) For compliance with a legal obligation which requires processing by Union or Member State law to which the controller is subject[121] or for the performance of a task carried out in the public interest or in the exercise of official authority vested in the controller.[122]

(c) For reasons of public interest where the processing is necessary for the purposes of:

(i) preventive or occupational medicine, assessment of employee working capacity, medical diagnoses, the provision of health or social care, or the management of health or social care systems and services, on the basis of EU or UK law, or pursuant to contract with a health professional who is subject to obligations of professional secrecy; or

(ii) public health, such as protecting against serious cross-border threats to health or ensuring high standards of quality and safety of health care and of medicinal products or medical devices, on the basis of EU or UK law which provides for suitable and specific measures to safeguard the rights of freedoms of data subjects.[123]

---

[117] GDPR Art 17(2). See also recital (66). Although it is not clear what is meant by 'has made the personal data public,' this would appear to include placing the information on any web-based forum available to the public. See also GDPR Art 9(2)(e).

[118] Although not expressly stated, this would appear to mean disclosed by the controller or by a processor on behalf of that controller.

[119] As to the meaning of 'necessary' see §9– 004.

[120] GDPR Art 17(3)(a). This is a reference to Article 11 of the CFR: see GDPR recitals (4) and (153). The disapplication is supportive of GDPR Art 85. Article 11 of the CFR, entitled 'Freedom of expression and information' provides:

1. Everyone has the right to freedom of expression. This right shall include freedom to hold opinions and to receive and impart information and ideas without interference by public authority and regardless of frontiers.
2. The freedom and pluralism of the media shall be respected.

It is distinct from the rights protected by Articles 7 and 8: see further §§7– 019 to 7– 033.

[121] The formula of words is the same as is used in GDPR Art 6(1)(c), which is considered at §9– 010. See also GDPR recitals (10), (31), (45), (51) and (68).

[122] GDPR Art 17(3)(b): see also recital (65). The formula of words in the second half is the same as is used in GDPR Art 6(1)(e), which is considered at §9– 012, and Arts 6(3), 20(3) and 23(1)(h). See also GDPR recitals (10), (45), (50), (51), (65) and (69).

[123] GDPR Art 17(3)(c), which expressly adopts Art 9(2)(h) and (i).

(d) For archiving purposes in the public interest, scientific or historical research purposes or statistical purposes in accordance with Article 89(1) in so far as the right referred to in paragraph 1 is likely to render impossible or seriously impair the achievement of the objectives of that processing.[124]

(e) For the establishment, exercise or defence of legal claims.[125]

10– 028 Exemptions and refusals

The GDPR also gives Member States a qualified right to impose legislative restrictions to the scope of the erasure right,[126] as well as to provide derogations from it.[127] This right has been exercised by various exemptions provided for in the DPA 2018.[128] Where or to the extent that a controller refuses to comply with a notice requiring erasure, the controller must give the data subject a refusal notice.[129] Where, on the basis of impossibility or disproportionate effort, the controller has not notified every recipient of the personal data of the erasure, that should also be stated in the refusal notice, including details of the recipients, or class of recipients, that have not been notified.[130] Where a controller does not have good grounds for not complying with an erasure notice under Article 17, the data subject may bring a private claim against the controller, invite the Information Commissioner to take regulatory action, or both.[131]

5. RIGHT TO RESTRICT PROCESSING

10– 029 Introduction

The GDPR confers on every data subject a qualified right to restrict a controller's processing of personal data concerning the data subject.[132] The 'restriction of processing' is defined to mean the marking of stored personal data with the aim of limiting their processing in the future.[133] The right provides data subjects with a direct means of compelling a controller to comply with three of the processing principles embodied in the accountability obligation, and to do so without having to go through the process of establishing a breach of those principles.[134]

---

[124] GDPR Art 17(3)(d). The exemption adopts the same formula of words as GDPR Arts 5(1)(b), 5(1)(e), 9(2)(j), 14(5)(b) and 21(6). As to the special status accorded to 'archiving' and 'scientific or historical research purposes or statistical purposes' see GDPR Art 89 and recitals (26), (50), (52), (53), (62), (65), (73), (113), (153), (156), (158) and (162).

[125] GDPR Art 17(3)(e). This applies to administrative or out-of-court procedures: GDPR recital (52). The formula of words is the same as is used in GDPR Arts 9(2)(f), 18(1)(c), 18(2), 21(1) and 49(1)(e).

[126] GDPR Art 23(1). The restrictions must both respect the essence of the fundamental rights and freedoms and be a necessary and proportionate measure in a democratic society to safeguard any of the matters listed in GDPR Art 23(1). As to the 'fundamental rights and freedoms', see GDPR Arts 1(2) and 6(1)(f) and recitals (2), (10), (16), (47), (51), (69), (113) and (166).

[127] GDPR Art 89(2)-(3).

[128] See Chapter 11.

[129] As to the content of a refusal notice, see §10– 012.

[130] In order that the Information Commissioner can effectively exercise the corrective powers provided for in GDPR Art 58(2)(g).

[131] Regulatory enforcement is considered at §§48– 014 to 48– 055. Private law claims are considered at §§48– 005 to 48– 013.

[132] GDPR Art 18(1). See also recitals (67) and (156). The right also applies where the personal data is being processed by a processor on behalf of the controller.

[133] GDPR Art 4(3).

[134] The three principles in the GDPR all compel the controller to limit the purposes of processing of personal data:
(1) Art 5(1)(b) provides that personal data must be collected only for specified, explicit and legitimate purposes, and not further processed in a manner that is incompatible with those purposes. In relation to applied GDPR processing, see DPA 2018 s 22(1). Considered further at §§9– 023 to 9– 027.

The right is supportive of the right to rectification, enabling a data subject to restrict processing pending a controller checking the accuracy of the personal data relating to the data subject.[135] The right is one of a data subject's rights that a controller, upon obtaining personal data concerning a data subject, must inform that data subject.[136] A controller must also inform a data subject of the right in responding to an access request under Article 15.[137] Under the previous regime a data subject could serve a notice requiring a controller to cease processing personal data relating to him or her where the data subject claimed that that processing was or would be likely to cause substantial harm or damage, and was unwarranted.[138] Although a data subject does not need to disclose a purpose in making a request to a controller to restrict processing, a request that addresses the grounds founding the right and that forestalls possible bases for exemption should expedite the process and improve the prospects for a correct outcome.

10– 030 The grounds

Subject to domestic exemptions, a data subject has a right to require a controller to restrict the processing of personal data concerning him or her in each of the following situations.

(1) Where the accuracy of the personal data is contested by the data subject. In this case the restriction will be for a period enabling the controller to verify the accuracy of the personal data.[139]

(2) Where the processing is unlawful and the data subject opposes the erasure of the personal data and requests the restriction of their use instead.[140]

(3) Where the controller no longer needs the personal data for the purposes of the processing, but they are required by the data subject for the establishment, exercise or defence of a legal claim.[141] The controller's need for the personal data for the purposes of the processing is determined objectively, measured against the controller's previously-stated purposes of the processing of that personal data.[142]

(4) Where the data subject has objected to the processing pursuant to Article 21(1) pending verification and the legitimate grounds of the controller override those of

---

(2) Art 5(1)(c) provides that personal data must be adequate, relevant and limited to what is necessary in relation to the purposes for which they are processed. In relation to applied GDPR processing, see DPA 2018 s 22(1). Considered further at §9– 028.

(3) Art 5(1)(e) provides that personal data must be kept in a form which permits identification of data subjects for no longer than is necessary for the purposes for which the personal data are processed. In relation to applied GDPR processing, see DPA 2018 s 22(1). Considered further at §§9– 031 to 9– 033.

135 The right to rectification is conferred by GDPR Art 16. See further §§10– 018 to 10– 022.

136 GDPR Arts 13(2)(b) and 14(2)(c).

137 GDPR Art 15(1)e).

138 DPA 1998 s 10(1).

139 GDPR Art 18(1)(a). Thus, where a data subject exercises the right to rectification under GDPR Art 16, pending verification of the accuracy of the personal data the data subject can also require the controller to restrict processing of that personal data.

140 GDPR Art 18(1)(b). Unlike Art 17(1)(d), which only looks to whether personal data have been unlawfully processed, Art 18(1)(b) also looks to whether the processing of the personal data is unlawful. For personal data that is not sensitive personal data, personal data will be unlawfully processed if none of the grounds set out in GDPR Art 6(1) is applicable: see further §§9– 007 to 9– 013. In the case of sensitive personal data, personal data will be unlawfully processed where none of the grounds for processing in Art 9(2) or 10 is applicable: see further §§9– 040 to 9– 047.

141 GDPR Art 18(1)(c). This applies also to administrative or out-of-court procedures: GDPR recital (52). The formula of words is the same as is used in GDPR Arts 9(2)(f), 17(3)(e), 21(1) and 49(1)(e).

142 The controller should at the time of obtaining the data subject's personal data have informed the data subject of the purposes of the processing: GDPR Arts 13(1)(c) and 14(1)(c). A controller should also, when answering an Article 15 request, have informed the data subject of the purposes of the processing: GDPR Art 15(1)(a).

the data subject.[143] Article 21(1) is concerned with where a data subject has given the controller a notice objecting to processing of personal data relating to him or her, the lawfulness of which processing is based on that processing being necessary for the performance of a statutory function or being necessary for the purposes of the legitimate interests pursued by the controller or a third party.[144]

10– 031 The notice

The right is exercised by notice given to the controller.[145] In addition to the usual requirements for a notice exercising rights under the GDPR,[146] a notice restricting processing will generally need to identify the period for which the data subject wishes to restrict processing and which of the four bases in Article 18(1) is said to apply and the grounds relied upon, namely:

(a) that the personal data about the data subject held by the controller is inaccurate;
(b) that the processing of the data subject's personal data is unlawful and that the data subject does not want the controller to erase it;
(c) that the controller no longer needs the personal data for the purposes of the processing, but the data is required by the data subject for the establishment, exercise or defence of legal claims; or
(d) that the data subject has given a notice of objection under Article 21 and is awaiting the outcome of the balancing exercise.

It is prudent for the data subject to specify the number of days notice required before the controller lifts the restriction.[147] The notice should also make clear that during the period of restriction, the controller will not have the data subject's consent to process his or her personal data unless that consent has been given in writing in advance of the processing. It is unlikely that a data subject will be able to prepare an adequate restriction notice without having first served a notice under Article 15 and received a response. The controller must comply with the notice 'without undue delay' and in any event within one month.[148] Within the same period a controller must inform the data subject of the action taken on the request.[149] A controller is not entitled to charge a fee for compliance.[150]

10– 032 Effect of restriction notice

Where a data subject has the right to restrict a controller's processing of his or her personal data and serves a notice, the controller may, until the lifting of the restriction, only carry out the processing in the following situations:

— where the processing consists solely for the storage of the data subject's personal data;
— where the processing of the data subject's personal data is with the data subject's consent;
— where the processing of the data subject's personal data is for the establishment, exercise or defence of a legal claim;[151] or

143 GDPR Art 18(1)(d).

144 In relation to notices under Art 21(1), see §10– 043. In relation to the meaning of 'necessary' see §9– 004.

145 As to the form of the notice, see §10– 007.

146 As to which, see §10– 007.

147 That is, where lifted under GDPR Art 18(3).

148 On time for compliance, see further §10– 009.

149 GDPR Art 12(3).

150 See further §10– 010.

151 This applies also to administrative or out-of-court procedures: GDPR recital (52). The formula of words is the

— where the processing of the data subject's personal data is for the protection of the rights of another natural or legal person or for reasons of important public interest of the Union or of a Member State.[152]

The methods by which a controller may restrict the processing of personal data include:

— temporarily moving the selected data to another processing system,
— making the selected personal data unavailable to users, and
— temporarily removing published data from a website.[153]

In automated filing systems, the restriction of processing should generally be ensured by technical means in such a manner that the personal data are not subject to further processing operations and cannot be changed.[154] The fact that the processing of personal data is restricted should be clearly indicated in the system.[155] Where the controller decides it wishes to lift the restriction, it must notify the data subject before doing so.[156]

10– 033 Supplementary obligations

The restriction right is also supplemented by Article 19 of the GDPR, which requires:

(a) the controller to communicate any restriction of processing of personal data carried out to each recipient to whom the personal data have been disclosed,[157] unless this proves impossible or involves disproportionate effort; and
(b) if the data subject has requested it, to inform the data subject of each recipient to whom the personal data have been disclosed.

The implication is that a controller must do (a) regardless of whether the data subject has requested it.

10– 034 Exemptions and refusals

The GDPR gives Member States a qualified right to impose legislative restrictions to the scope of the restriction right,[158] as well as to provide derogations from it.[159] This right has been exercised by various exemptions provided for in the DPA 2018.[160] Where or to the extent that a controller refuses to comply with a notice requiring restriction, the controller must give the data subject a refusal notice.[161] Where, on the basis of impossibility or disproportionate effort, the controller has not notified every recipient of the personal data of the restriction, that should also be stated in the refusal notice, including details of the recipients, or class of recipients, that have not been notified.[162] Where a controller does not have good grounds for not complying

same as is used in GDPR Arts 9(2)(f), 17(3)(e), 21(1) and 49(1)(e).

152 GDPR Art 18(2).

153 GDPR recital (67).

154 GDPR recital (67).

155 GDPR recital (67).

156 GDPR Art 18(3).

157 Although not expressly stated, this would appear to mean disclosed by the controller or by a processor on behalf of that controller.

158 GDPR Art 23(1). The restrictions must both respect the essence of the fundamental rights and freedoms and be a necessary and proportionate measure in a democratic society to safeguard any of the matters listed in GDPR Art 23(1). As to the 'fundamental rights and freedoms', see GDPR Arts 1(2) and 6(1)(f) and recitals (2), (10), (16), (47), (51), (69), (113) and (166).

159 GDPR Art 89(2)-(3).

160 See Chapter 11.

161 As to the content of a refusal notice, see §10– 012.

162 In order that the Information Commissioner can effectively exercise the corrective powers provided for in GDPR Art 58(2)(g).

with a notice under Article 18, the data subject may bring a private claim against the controller, invite the Information Commissioner to take regulatory action, or both.[163]

6. RIGHT TO DATA PORTABILITY

10–035 Introduction

Where a data subject has provided a controller with personal data relating to him or herself, that data subject has a qualified right to receive from the controller, and the controller is under a correlative duty to provide to the data subject, that personal data in a structured, commonly-used and machine-readable format.[164] The GDPR terms this 'data portability.' The right is one of the data subject rights that a controller, upon obtaining personal data concerning a data subject, must inform him or her.[165] Given that the right under Article 15 includes entitlement to receive from the controller a copy of the personal data undergoing processing and that 'processing' includes storing, the right of data portability does not add much to the rights elsewhere conferred by the GDPR. The main use of the right is where a data subject is changing the organisation that provides him or her with a particular service, for example banking or telephone services. The previous data protection regime did not include a specific right of data portability.[166] Although a data subject does not need to disclose a purpose in making a request to a controller to be provided with this data or to have his or her data transferred, a request that addresses the grounds founding the right and that forestalls possible bases for exemption should expedite the process and improve the prospects for a correct outcome.

10–036 The grounds

Subject to exemptions, where:

(a) a controller's processing of a data subject's personal data is based on:
  - (i) the data subject's consent (in so far as the personal data is not sensitive personal data);[167]
  - (ii) the data subject's express consent (in so far as the personal data is special category personal data);
  - (iii) a contract;[168]

(b) that processing is carried out by automated means;[169] and

(c) that processing is not necessary for the performance of a task:
  - (i) carried out in the public interest;[170] or

---

163 Regulatory enforcement is considered at §§48–014 to 48–055. Private law claims are considered at §§48–005 to 48–013.

164 GDPR Art 20(1). See also recitals (68), (73) and (156). The data subject is entitled to transmit those data to another controller without hindrance from the first controller. Recital (68) makes clear that paragraphs (a) and (b) in Art 20(1) condition the entire right, and not just the right to transmit.

165 GDPR Arts 13(2)(b) and 14(2)(c).

166 Although a 'subject access request' under DPA 1998 s 7(1), in conjunction with s 8(2), yielded a similar outcome.

167 That is, consent under GDPR Art 6(1)(a). As to what is meant by 'consent' for these purposes, see §9–008. As to the meaning of 'sensitive personal data' see §8–017.

168 That is, express consent under GDPR Art 9(2)(a). As to what is meant by 'express consent' for these purposes, see §9–042. As to the meaning of 'sensitive personal data' see §8–017.

169 As opposed to the processing of personal data that forms part of, or is intended form part of, a filing system: see GDPR Arts 2(1) and 4(2) and recitals (15) and (68).

170 GDPR Art 20(3). Where the processing is necessary for the performance of a task 'carried out in the public interest' that processing should have a basis in EU or UK law: GDPR recital (45), and see also recitals (50), (51),

(ii) in the exercise of official authority vested in the controller,[171]

a data subject has a right to require a controller to provide, in the required format, him or her with the personal data that he or she provided the controller.[172] The right is confined to the information that the data subject provided to the controller. Accordingly, it does not cover information about the data subject that the controller acquired from elsewhere. Nor does it cover information that the controller has itself generated about the data subject, even if based on information that the data subject provided to the controller.

10– 037 Supplementary obligations

The data subject may, when exercising his or her right to portability, require the controller to transmit the personal data directly to another controller.[173] Provided that it is technically feasible, the controller is under a correlative obligation to transmit to the other controller the personal data that the data subject supplied to the controller. The data portability right does not create an obligation on controllers to adopt or maintain processing systems that are technically compatible, although they are encouraged to do so.[174]

10– 038 The notice

In addition to the usual requirements for a notice exercising rights under the GDPR,[175] a data portability notice under Article 20 will generally need to:

(a) specify which of the bases in Article 20(1) is said to apply;
(b) specify the machine-readable format by which the controller should communicate the data to the data subject; and
(c) if the data subject wishes the controller to transmit his or her personal data directly to another controller, the data subject should identify that controller and an address to which the data should be transmitted.

Beyond this it is not necessary for a data subject to be more specific than to ask to be given all personal data that he or she has at any time provided the controller.

10– 039 Exemptions and refusals

In complying with a data portability notice, the controller must not adversely affect the rights and freedoms of other data subjects: for example, where a certain set of personal data concerns more than one data subject.[176] The GDPR gives Member States a qualified right to impose legislative restrictions to the scope of the data portability right,[177] as well as to provide derogations from it.[178] This right has been exercised by various exemptions provided for in the

(65), (68) and (69). This is the same formula of words as used in GDPR Arts 6(1)(e) (see §9– 012), 6(3), 17(3)(b) and 86.

171 GDPR Art 20(3). Where the processing is necessary for the performance of a task 'carried out in the exercise of official authority vested in the controller' that processing should have a basis in EU or UK law: GDPR recital (45), and see also recitals (50), (51), (65), (68) and (69). This is the same formula of words as used in GDPR Arts 6(1)(e) (see §9– 012), 6(3), 17(3)(b)and 23(1)(h).

172 GDPR Art 20(1).

173 GDPR Art 20(2).

174 GDPR recital (68).

175 As to which, see §10– 007.

176 GDPR Art 20(4), and see recital (68). As to the meaning of the 'rights and freedoms of others' see §8– 006.

177 GDPR Art 23(1). The restrictions must both respect the essence of the fundamental rights and freedoms and be a necessary and proportionate measure in a democratic society to safeguard any of the matters listed in GDPR Art 23(1). As to the 'fundamental rights and freedoms', see GDPR Arts 1(2) and 6(1)(f) and recitals (2), (10), (16), (47), (51), (69), (113) and (166).

178 GDPR Art 89(2)-(3).

DPA 2018.[179] Where or to the extent that a controller refuses to comply with a data portability notice, the controller must give the data subject a refusal notice.[180] Where a controller does not have good grounds for not complying with a notice under Article 20, the data subject may bring a private claim against the controller, invite the Information Commissioner to take regulatory action, or both.[181]

7. RIGHT TO OBJECT

10–040 Introduction

The GDPR confers on every data subject two separate rights to object to a controller's processing of personal data concerning the data subject:

(a) a general right of objection, with certain exemptions;[182] and
(b) a specific right of objection where personal data are processed for direct marketing purposes,[183]

collectively called a 'right to object.' A data subject may exercise these rights at any time that the conditions for their exercise are met. The right to object is one of the data subject rights that a controller, upon obtaining personal data concerning an individual, must inform that data subject.[184] A controller must also inform a data subject of the right to object in responding to an access request under Article 15.[185] Where a data subject has a right to object and exercises it, that provides the data subject with a free-standing basis for requiring the controller to erase his or her personal data[186] and to restrict processing of it.[187] Under the previous regime a data subject could serve a notice requiring a controller to cease processing personal data relating to him or her where the data subject claimed that that processing was or would be likely to cause substantial harm or damage, and was unwarranted.[188] Although a data subject does not need to disclose a purpose in giving a notice exercising the right to object, a notice that addresses the grounds founding the right and that forestalls possible bases for exemption should expedite the process and improve the prospects for a correct outcome.

10–041 The general right

Subject to exemptions, where processing of personal data concerning a data subject is based on it being necessary:[189]

(a) for the performance of a task carried out in the public interest or in the exercise of official authority vested in the controller;[190] or

179 See Chapter 11.

180 As to the content of a refusal notice, see §10–012.

181 Regulatory enforcement is considered at §§48–014 to 48–055. Private law claims are considered at §§48–005 to 48–013.

182 GDPR Art 21(1). See also recitals (50), (59), (65), (73) and (156). The right also applies where the personal data is being processed by a processor on behalf of the controller.

183 GDPR Art 21(2).

184 GDPR Arts 13(2)(b) and 14(2)(c).

185 GDPR Art 15(1)e).

186 GDPR Art 17(1)(c).

187 GDPR Art 18(1)(d). As to the meaning of 'restriction of processing,' see §8–031.

188 DPA 1998 s 10(1).

189 As to the meaning of 'necessary' in this context, see §8–034.

190 That is, processing based on the fifth basis for lawful processing: GDPR Art 6(1)(e), as to which see §9–012.

(b) for the purposes of the legitimate interests pursued by the controller or by a third party that are not overriden by the interests or fundamental rights and freedoms of the data subject which require protection of personal data, in particular where the data subject is a child,[191]

that data subject may object to that processing of his or her personal data.[192] Unless the controller demonstrates:

— compelling, legitimate grounds for the processing that override the interests, rights and freedoms of the data subject, or

— that the processing is necessary for the establishment, exercise or defence of legal claims,[193]

the controller must no longer process that personal data.[194] Where the controller has, or comes to have a basis other than (a) or (b) for processing the data subject's personal data, that will negate the right to object.

10– 042 The direct marketing right

Where a controller, or a processor on behalf of a controller, processes personal data concerning a data subject for direct marketing purposes, that data subject may at any time object to the processing for that purpose.[195] This right is not qualified by the requirements of the general right. Where a data subject gives such a notice, the controller must cease processing his or her personal data for that purpose.[196]

10– 043 The notice

In addition to the usual requirements for a notice exercising rights under the GDPR,[197] where a data subject is exercising the general right the notice of objection should identify his or her particular situation so that the controller fully appreciates how continued processing of the data subject's personal data impinges upon his or her interests or fundamental rights and freedoms. A data subject will usually be better placed to prepare a notice of objection exercising the general right after having first served a notice under Article 15 and received a response. Where a data subject is exercising the right to object in relation to direct marketing, the notice should specify that. If the applicant is a child, the notice should say so. A notice of objection may also include:

---

191 That is, processing based on the sixth basis for lawful processing: GDPR Art 6(1)(f), as to which see §9– 013. As to the meaning of 'third party' see § 8– 025. As to the meaning of 'fundamental rights and freedoms' see §8– 006. In relation to this sort of processing, child will mean a person under 13 years of age: see DPA 2018 ss 9, 208 (Scotland).

192 GDPR Art 21(1).

193 It is necessary to insert the words 'is necessary' in the second sentence of GDPR Art 21(1) to give it grammatical sense. 'Defence of legal claims' applies also to administrative or out-of-court procedures: GDPR recital (52). The formula of words is the same as is used in GDPR Arts 9(2)(f), 17(3)(e), 18(1)(c) and 49(1)(e).

194 GDPR Art 21(1).

195 GDPR Art 21(2), and see recital (70). Under the GDPR, direct marketing is a legitimate interest of a controller: recital (47). Although neither the GDPR nor the DPA 2018 defines 'direct marketing' generally, the definition in DPA 2018 s 122(5) (which is only for the purposes of that s 122), and which is repeated in Financial Guidance and Claims Act 2018 s 26(1) and repeats what was in DPA 1998 s 11(3), is as good as any:

> 'direct marketing' means the communication (by whatever means) of advertising or marketing material which is directed to particular individuals.

Similarly, although Directive 2002/58/EC (Directive on privacy and electronic communications) does not define 'direct marketing' it provides numerous examples of what will constitute direct marketing. The Directive is implemented in the United Kingdom by the Privacy and Electronic Communications (EC Directive) Regulations 2003 (SI 2003/2426).

196 GDPR Art 21(3).

197 As to which, see §10– 007.

— a notice of erasure, requiring the controller to erase the data subject's personal data;[198] and
— a notice of restriction, restricting processing of the data subject's personal data by or on behalf of the controller.[199]

10–044 Exemptions and refusals

The GDPR gives Member States a qualified right to impose legislative restrictions to the scope of the right to object,[200] as well as to provide derogations from it.[201] This right has been exercised by various exemptions provided for in the DPA 2018.[202] Where or to the extent that a controller refuses to comply with a notice exercising the right to object, the controller must give the data subject a refusal notice.[203] Where a controller does not have good grounds for not complying with a notice under Article 21, the data subject may bring a private claim against the controller, invite the Information Commissioner to take regulatory action, or both.[204]

8. RIGHT AGAINST AUTOMATED DECISIONS

10–045 Introduction

Every data subject has a qualified right not to be subject to a decision that produces legal effects concerning him or her, or that similarly significantly affects him or her, where that decision is based solely on automated processing.[205] The right subsists without any need for a notice from the data subject to the controller. At the time when a controller obtains personal data about a data subject, the controller must advise the data subject of the existence of any automated decision-making concerning the data subject, providing meaningful information about the logic involved, as well as the significance and the envisaged consequences of that processing for the data subject.[206] A controller must similarly inform a data subject when responding to an access request under Article 15.[207] Automated decisions give rise to a requirement on the controller to carry out a data protection impact assessment.[208] Where a controller is subject to binding corporate rules, those rules must cover a right against automated decisions.[209]

10–046 The right

The right is to be not subject to a decision that is based solely on automated processing and

[198] GDPR Art 17(1)(c). In relation to the requirements of the notice in this regard, see §10–025.

[199] GDPR Art 18(1)(d). In relation to the requirements of the notice in this regard, see §10–031. As to the meaning of 'restriction of processing,' see §8–031.

[200] GDPR Art 23(1). The restrictions must both respect the essence of the fundamental rights and freedoms and be a necessary and proportionate measure in a democratic society to safeguard any of the matters listed in GDPR Art 23(1). As to the 'fundamental rights and freedoms', see GDPR Arts 1(2) and 6(1)(f) and recitals (2), (10), (16), (47), (51), (69), (113) and (166).

[201] GDPR Art 89(2)-(3).

[202] See Chapter 11.

[203] As to the content of a refusal notice, see §10–012.

[204] Regulatory enforcement is considered at §§48–014 to 48–055. Private law claims are considered at §§48–005 to 48–013.

[205] GDPR Art 22(1), and see recital (71).

[206] GDPR Arts 13(2)(f) and 14(2)(g).

[207] GDPR Art 15(1)(h).

[208] GDPR Art 35(3)(a). As to data protection impact assessments, see §9–050.

[209] GDPR Art 47(2)(e). As to binding corporate rules, see §9–063.

which produces legal effects concerning the data subject[210] or that similarly significantly affects him or her. Examples of such decisions include:

— automatic refusal of an online credit application;
— e-recruiting practices without any human intervention;
— 'profiling' that consists of any form of automated processing of personal data evaluating the personal aspects relating to a natural person, in particular to analyse or predict aspects concerning a data subject's performance at work, economic situation, health, personal preferences or interests, reliability or behaviour, location or movements.[211]

Examples given by the EDPB are decisions that:

— significantly affect the individual's circumstances, behaviour or choices;
— have a prolonged or permanent impact on the individual;
— lead to exclusion or discrimination against an individuals; and
— affect an individual's financial circumstances (such as eligibility for credit), access to health services or employment or educational opportunities (such as university admission).

10– 047 Disapplication

The right is disapplied in three situations:

(1) Where the decision is necessary for entering into, or performance of, a contract between the data subject and a data controller.[212] In this situation the controller must implement suitable measures to safeguard the data subject's rights and freedoms and legitimate interests, at least the right to obtain human intervention on the part of the controller, to express his or her point of view and to contest the decision.[213]

(2) Where the decision is authorised by EU or UK law to which the controller is subject and which also lays down suitable measures to safeguard the data subject's rights and freedoms and legitimate interests.[214]

(3) Where the decision is based on the data subject's explicit consent to the making of a fully automated decision that will produce legal effects on him or her (or that will otherwise similarly significantly affect the data subject).[215] In this situation the controller must implement suitable measures to safeguard the data subject's rights and freedoms and legitimate interests, at least the right to obtain human intervention on the part of the controller, to express his or her point of view and to contest the decision.[216]

All the above are subject to the proviso that the decision is not made on the basis of special category personal data, unless either the data subject has given express consent for that data to be used in that way or the processing is necessary for reasons of substantial public interest, and in either case suitable measures to safeguard the data subject's rights and freedoms and legitimate interests are in place.[217]

---

210 Examples given by the EDPB of 'legal effects' include the cancellation of a contract, a decision about entitlement to a social security benefit or the refusal of citizenship or entry into a country.

211 GDPR recital (71).

212 GDPR Art 22(2)(a).

213 GDPR Art 22(3). As to the meaning of 'rights and freedoms' of a person, see §8– 006.

214 GDPR Art 22(2)(b). As to the meaning of 'rights and freedoms' of a person, see §8– 006.

215 GDPR Art 22(2)(c). As to the meaning of 'consent' see §9– 008.

216 GDPR Art 22(3). As to the meaning of 'rights and freedoms' of a person, see §8– 006.

217 GDPR Art 22(4). As to the meaning of 'necessary' see §8– 034. As to the meaning of 'consent' see §9– 008.

10– 048 Exemptions and refusals

The GDPR gives Member States a qualified right to impose legislative restrictions to the scope of the right to object,[218] as well as to provide derogations from it.[219] This right has been exercised by various exemptions provided for in the DPA 2018.[220] Where a controller has made a decision in breach of a data subject's right under Article 22, the data subject may bring a private claim against the controller, invite the Information Commissioner to take regulatory action, or both.[221]

9. ANCILLARY RIGHTS AND OBLIGATIONS

10– 049 Introduction

In addition to the seven main rights, data subjects have a number of other rights that are supportive of these main rights and the continuing obligations.

10– 050 Withdrawal of consent

A data subject has, at all times, the right to withdraw his or her consent to a controller's processing of his or her personal data.[222] At the time of acquiring personal data about the data subject, the controller should have advised the data subject of the right to withdraw consent.[223] The data subject does not need to have or to supply any reason for withdrawing consent.[224] Withdrawing consent should be as easy as it was to give that consent.[225] Where a data subject withdraws consent, that will often provide the foundation for exercising the right to erasure.[226] It may also remove the basis for automated decision-making.[227]

10– 051 International transfers

Where a controller transfers the personal data of a data subject to a third country or to an international organisation, the data subject has the right to be informed of the appropriate safeguards relating to the transfer.[228]

10– 052 Scientific etc processing

In relation to personal data that is processed for scientific or historical research purposes or for statistical purposes the GDPR makes special provision for the EU and Member States to

---

218 GDPR Art 23(1). The restrictions must both respect the essence of the fundamental rights and freedoms and be a necessary and proportionate measure in a democratic society to safeguard any of the matters listed in GDPR Art 23(1). As to the 'fundamental rights and freedoms', see GDPR Arts 1(2) and 6(1)(f) and recitals (2), (10), (16), (47), (51), (69), (113) and (166).

219 GDPR Art 89(2)-(3).

220 See Chapter 11.

221 Regulatory enforcement is considered at §§48– 014 to 48– 055. Private law claims are considered at §§48– 005 to 48– 013.

222 GDPR Art 7(3).

223 GDPR Arts 13(2)(c) and 14(2)(d).

224 See, by implication, GDPR recital (42).

225 GDPR Art 7(3).

226 GDPR Art 17(1)(b), and see recital (65).

227 GDPR Art 22(2)(c).

228 GDPR Art 15(2). As to the meaning of 'third country,' see §8– 032. As to the meaning of 'international organisations,' see §8– 033. As to the 'appropriate safeguards' on such a transfer see §9– 062.

derogate from the data subject rights.[229] As a counterbalance, where personal data is processed for those purposes pursuant to such derogations, the data subject has a qualified right to object to the processing of personal data relating to him or her.[230] The controller should have advised the data subject of this right.[231] The only qualification to the right is that the processing is necessary for the performance of a task carried out for reasons of public interest.[232] The data subject exercises the right by giving a notice to the controller. Unless the processing is necessary for the performance of a task carried out for reasons of public interest, the controller must cease processing the data subject's personal data.[233] Where a controller does not have good grounds for not complying with a notice to cease processing, the data subject may bring a private claim against the controller, invite the Information Commissioner to take regulatory action, or both.[234]

229 GDPR Art 89, and see recital (156).

230 GDPR Art 21(6).

231 GDPR Arts 13(2)(b) and 14(2)(c).

232 GDPR Art 21(6). It is for the controller to demonstrate that the processing is necessary for the performance of a task carried out for reasons of public interest: GDPR recital (69).

233 GDPR recital (65).

234 Regulatory enforcement is considered at §§48– 014 to 48– 055. Private law claims are considered at §§48– 005 to 48– 013.

CHAPTER 11

General processing: exemptions etc

1. GENERAL PRINCIPLES

11–001 Introduction

The GDPR is intended to set the principles of and rules on the protection of individuals with regard to the general processing of their personal data and on the free movement of such data.[1]

[1] The EU has exclusive competence on these matters only in so far as concerns the processing of personal data by Member States when carrying out activities that fall within the scope of Chapter 2 of Title V (Arts 23-46) of the TEU (dealing with common foreign and security policy): TEU Art 39. The EU has shared competence on the processing of personal data by Member States when carrying out activities which fall within the scope of EU law and on the rules relating to the free movement of personal data: TFEU Art 16(2). By imposing general obligations on controllers and processors, and conferring rights on data subjects, the GDPR has laid down rules relating to

The GDPR itself provides certain exemptions from and restrictions to the continuing obligations and data subject rights it imposes and confers.[2] Although a Regulation – and thus having direct effect in Member States – the GDPR expressly allows each Member State legislative latitude by allowing both derogations from and further restrictions to those obligations and rights, subject to certain criteria.[3] Each Member State has a qualified right:

(a) to restrict the scope of the data subject rights, and the correlative obligations imposed on controllers and processors; and

(b) to restrict the scope of the continuing obligation on controllers and processors to comply with the processing principles, but only in so far as those principles 'correspond' to the rights and obligations in (a).[4]

Any restriction must be effected by legislative measure.

11–002 Qualified restrictions

Article 23 of the GDPR imposes a three-fold qualification on the power of a Member State to restrict the scope of the rights conferred on data subjects and the correlative obligations on controllers.

(1) First, the restriction must respect 'the essence of the fundamental rights and freedoms.'[5]

(2) Secondly, the restriction must be a necessary[6] and proportionate measure in a democratic society to safeguard:

  (a) national security;
  (b) defence;
  (c) public security;
  (d) the prevention, investigation, detection or prosecution of criminal offences or the execution of criminal penalties, including the safeguarding against and the prevention of threats to public security;
  (e) other important objectives of general public interest of the Union or of a Member State, in particular an important economic or financial interest of the Union or of a Member State, including monetary, budgetary and taxation matters, public health and social security;
  (f) the protection of judicial independence and judicial proceedings;
  (g) the prevention, investigation, detection and prosecution of breaches of ethics for regulated professions;
  (h) a monitoring, inspection or regulatory function connected, even occasionally, to the exercise of official authority in the cases referred to in points (a) to (e) and (g);
  (i) the protection of the data subject or the rights and freedoms of others; or
  (j) the enforcement of civil law claims.

---

the free movement of personal data and covered the field.

2 GDPR Arts 9(2), 17(3), 20(3), 21(1) and 22(2).

3 Principally GDPR Art 23(1), but also Arts 6(2), (3) and 9(4). The difference between 'restrictions' and 'derogations' would appear to be that a Member State is required to notify the Commission of a derogation, but not of a restriction: GDPR Arts 49(5) and 85(3), although there is no such requirement in relation to derogations under Art 89. In relation to restrictions, see GDPR Art 23 and recitals (8) and (73). In relation to derogations, see GDPR Arts 49, 85(2) and 89 and recitals (51), (52), (107), (112), (153) and (156).

4 GDPR Art 23(1). The data subject rights are those dealt with in Chapter 10. The processing principles are set out in GDPR Art 5 and are dealt with in Chapter 9: see further §9–004.

5 As to the meaning of this, see §8–006.

6 As to the meaning of 'necessary' in this context, see §8–034.

(3) Thirdly, where relevant the legislative measure must contain specific provisions as to:
   (a) the purposes of the processing or categories of processing;
   (b) the categories of personal data;
   (c) the scope of the restrictions introduced;
   (d) the safeguards to prevent abuse or unlawful access or transfer;
   (e) the specification of the controller or categories of controllers;
   (f) the storage periods and the applicable safeguards taking into account the nature, scope and purposes of the processing or categories of processing;
   (g) the risks to the rights and freedoms of data subjects; and
   (h) the right of data subjects to be informed about the restriction, unless that may be prejudicial to the purpose of the restriction.

11–003 Derogations

In addition to the power to introduce restrictions, the GDPR provides for derogations in four specific situations:

(1) For processing for journalistic purposes or the purpose of academic artistic or literary expression, Member States are required to provide for exemptions or derogations from Articles 5-76 and 85-91, provided that those exemptions or derogations are necessary to reconcile the right to the protection of personal data with the freedom of expression and information.[7] The provision is unique in requiring, rather than merely empowering, Member States to provide such derogations.
(2) Where personal data are processed for scientific or historical research purposes or for statistical purposes, Member States have a qualified power to provide for derogations from a data subject's access, rectification, restriction and objection rights.[8] Any such derogations must contain appropriate safeguards for the rights and freedoms of the data subject and ensure that technical and organisational measures are in place in particular in order to ensure respect for the principle of data minimisation.
(3) Where personal data are processed for archiving purposes in the public interest, Member States have a qualified power to provide for derogations from a data subject's access, rectification, restriction, objection and data portability rights.[9] Any such derogations must contain appropriate safeguards for the rights and freedoms of the data subject and ensure that technical and organisational measures are in place in particular in order to ensure respect for the principle of data minimisation.
(4) In relation to transfers of personal data to third countries and international organisations for which there has not been an adequacy decision and there are no appropriate safeguards, there is a limited power to derogate.[10] Although Article 49 is entitled 'derogations,' it actually describes specific situations in which such transfers may take place, rather than being a provision enabling Member State law

[7] GDPR Art 85(2). The exclusion of GDPR Arts 77-84 (dealing with remedies, liability and penalties) from the power of Member States to provide derogations and exemptions implies that those derogations and exemptions must leave such processing sufficiently regulated as to be capable of requiring remedies, liability and penalties.

[8] GDPR Art 89(2). There is no power to derogate from the right to erasure or the right to data portability.

[9] GDPR Art 89(3). There is no power to derogate from the right to erasure.

[10] GDPR Art 49. As to the meaning of 'third countries' see §9–058. As to the meaning of 'international organisations,' see §8–033. As to the meaning of an 'adequacy decision' see §9–061. As to the meaning of 'appropriate safeguards' see §9–062.

to provide derogations from rules established by the GDPR. The only derogation, in the conventional sense of the word, is where, for important reasons of public interest, a Member State expressly sets limits to the transfer of specific categories of personal data to a third country or an international organisation.[11]

11–004 Non-regulated processing

Quite apart from derogations, restrictions and exemptions, certain processing of personal data is outside the reach of the general processing regime established by the GDPR as supplemented by the DPA 2018:

(1) Intelligence services processing of personal data. This is governed by Part 4 of the DPA 2018 (ss 82-108).[12] The GDPR and the exemptions provided for in Schedules 2, 3 and 4 to the DPA 2018 have no role in relation to processing of personal data by the intelligence services.

(2) Processing of personal data by competent authorities for law enforcement purposes.[13] This is governed by Part 3 of the DPA 2018 (ss 29-81), which implements the LED in the United Kingdom. The GDPR and the exemptions provided for in Schedules 2, 3 and 4 to the DPA 2018 have no role in relation to processing of personal data by competent authorities for law enforcement purposes.

(3) Processing of personal data by a natural person in the course of a purely personal or household activity.[14] This is unregulated.

(4) Processing of personal data that does not involve either any 'automated means' or a 'filing system.'[15] In the case of personal data held by an FOI Act public authority, this is regulated through a modified, but domestic, version of GDPR – that is the 'applied GDPR.'[16] Otherwise, this processing is unregulated.

(5) Processing of personal data where that processing is not within the 'territorial scope' of the GDPR.[17] This is not regulated by either the GDPR or the DPA 2018, but may be regulated by the law of another jurisdiction.

In relation to such processing, it will not be necessary to consider the exemptions and derogations considered in this Chapter.

11–005 Operation of exemptions etc

The exemptions, derogations, limitations etc provided for by the GDPR and the DPA 2018 operate in relation to one or more of the data subject rights and, in some cases, one or more of the processing principles that apply whenever a controller or processor is processing personal data. Where an exemption etc operates but applies to certain data subject rights only, the other data subject rights and unconnected continuing obligations are unaffected in their operation. Although the exemptions introduced by the DPA 2018 disapply 'listed GDPR provisions,' the engagement of an exemption – and the consequent disapplication of a data subject right – falls to be decided by reference to the specific data subject right from which exemption is claimed.[18]

---

[11] GDPR Art 49(5). As to the meaning of 'third country,' see §8– 032. As to the meaning of 'international organisations,' see §8– 033.

[12] Dealt with in Chapter 14.

[13] Dealt with in Chapters 12 and 13.

[14] GDPR Art 2(2)(c) and recital (18). See §8– 038.

[15] GDPR Art 2(1). As to the meaning of these terms, see §§8– 040 to 8– 041.

[16] DPA 2018 ss 21-28.

[17] GDPR Art 3. As to the territorial scope of the GDPR, see §§8– 042 to 8– 045.

[18] To disapply all rights in the 'listed GDPR provisions' on the basis that one right in the list satisfies the requirements of the exemption would neither 'respect the essence of the fundamental rights and freedoms' nor be 'a necessary

As such, the fact that a controller satisfies the requirement of an exemption on the basis of one of the rights in the 'listed GDPR provisions,' does not mean that the requirements of that exemption are necessarily satisfied so far as it relates to other rights in that list: many will depend principally on whether compliance with that other right would prejudice the interest protected by the exemption.[19]

11–006 Multiple purpose processing

The engagement of each exemption in section 3 of this Chapter turns on the purpose for which the controller (or processor on its behalf) is processing the personal data, rather than the attributes of the personal data itself. In considering whether such an exemption is engaged, it is necessary to identify the purpose or purposes for which the controller or processor is, or was at the relevant time, processing the personal data. The controller, being the person who determines the purpose(s) of the processing of personal data,[20] should at the start of processing have specified and recorded this purpose (or, if there is more than one, these purposes)[21] and should normally have notified the data subject of that purpose or those purposes.[22] Where a controller (or a processor on behalf of that controller) processes personal data for more than one purpose, it will be necessary to consider each exemption in section 3 of this Chapter by reference to each of those purposes.

11–007 Interpretative principles

The principles of and rules on general processing are required to respect the fundamental rights and freedoms of individuals.[23] In allowing Member States legislative latitude to specify some of the detail of those rules, including restrictions to data subject rights, the GDPR did not permit the essence of those rights and freedoms to be overridden.[24] Where there is more than one reasonable interpretation of an exemption, limitation, restriction or derogation, the interpretation that affords the greatest respect for the fundamental rights and freedoms of individuals is to be preferred.[25]

---

and proportionate measure in a democratic society' to safeguard any of the matters listed in GDPR Art 23(1).

19 Thus many of the exemptions are stated to apply only 'to the extent that the application' of the rights 'would be likely to prejudice' any of the interests protected by the exemption.

20 By definition, a controller is the person or body who determines the purposes of processing personal data, or where the purposes are defined by law, the person provided for in that law: GDPR Arts 4(7) and 26(1).

21 GDPR Arts 5(1)(b), 30(1)(b). The controller is required to maintain this record, so that if further purposes are subsequently added, these should be added to the record. See also GDPR Arts 25(1)-(2), 35(1), (7), 36(3)(b) and 39(2). Where the controller engages a processor to carry out processing of personal data, that engagement must be in a contract that sets out the purposes of the processing: GDPR Art 28(3). If the processor goes beyond its remit and determines the purpose of processing, the processor becomes a controller: GDPR Art 29(10).

22 GDPR Arts 13(1)(c), 13(3), 14(1)(c) and 14(4).

23 GDPR Art 1(2) and recitals (4) and (10). As to the meaning of those rights and freedoms, see §8–006.

24 GDPR Art 23(1) and recitals (47), (51) and (113).

25 This was the approach taken by the CJEU in relation to Directive 95/46/EC which similarly referred to data protection principles and rules respecting fundamental rights and freedoms: *IPI v Englebert* (C-473/12) [2014] 2 CMLR 9, [2014] CEC 719 at [39] ('the protection of the fundamental right to privacy requires that derogations and limitations in relation to the protection of personal data must apply only in so far as is strictly necessary'); *Tietosuojavaltuutettu v Satakunnan* (C-73/07) [2010] All ER (EC) 213 at [56]; *Volker und Markus Schecke GbR v Land Hessen* (C-92/09) [2012] All ER (EC) 127, [2012] IP & T 513 at [77], [86]; *Digital Rights Ireland Ltd v Minister for Communications, Marine and Natural Resources* (C-293/12 and C-594/12) [2015] QB 127, [2014] 3 CMLR 44 at [52]; *Lin v Commissioner of Police for the Metropolis* [2015] EWHC 2484 (QB) at [80]; *Schrems v Data Protection Commissioner* (C-362/14) [2016] QB 527, [2016] 2 CMLR 2 at [92]; *Tele2 Sverige AB v Post-och telestyrelsen* (C-203/15) [2017] QB 771, [2017] 2 CMLR 30 at [96]; *Valsts policijas Rīgas reģiona pārvaldes Kārtības policijas pārvalde v Rīgas pašvaldības SIA* (Case C-13/16) [2017] 4 WLR 97, [2017] 3 CMLR 39 at [30].

11–008 Onus

The controller bears the burden of demonstrating that an exemption etc applies. This follows from the accountability obligation, which requires the controller to be responsible for and be able to demonstrate compliance with the processing principles.[26] The first of the processing principles includes a requirement that personal data be processed 'in a transparent manner,' and that requirement is itself linked to compliance with the data subject rights.[27]

11–009 Likelihood of prejudice

Many of the exemptions in the DPA 2018 require for their engagement that application of the applicable provision of the GDPR 'would be likely to prejudice' the subject matter of the exemption. This formula – 'would be likely to prejudice' a protected interest – is the same formula and approach that was used in the DPA 1998. Under that legislation, it had been interpreted to mean 'a significantly greater degree of probability than merely "more than fanciful."'[28] There is nothing to suggest that different principles should apply to the determination of the likelihood of prejudice for the purposes of the DPA 2018.[29]

11–010 Public interest exemptions

In addition to limiting in certain respects the reach of the DPA 2018,[30] the public interest is a constituent element of various restrictions and exemptions, both within the GDPR and the DPA 2018.[31] Sometimes 'public interest' is qualified by 'substantial' or 'important,' but mostly it is left unqualified. Regardless of any qualification, the notion of the 'public interest' is the same.[32]

11–011 DPA 2018 approach

The approach taken in the DPA 2018 is to deal collectively with derogations from, and restrictions and adaptations of, the rules provided by the GDPR by a suite of provisions in Schedules 2, 3 and 4.[33] These provisions divide as follows:

(1) Restrictions to the data subject rights: Schedule 2, Parts 1 and 2 (paragraphs 1-15).

(2) Restrictions specifically to the access right, so as to protect the rights of third parties: Schedule 2, Part 3 (paragraphs 16-17).

---

26 GDPR Art 5(2). In other words, the principles in GDPR Art 5(1). See also GDPR recital (69). This was also the position in proving the applicability of exemptions in DPA 1998: *R (Lord) v SSHD* [2003] EWHC 2073 (Admin) at [94], [99]; *Lin v Commissioner of Police for the Metropolis* [2015] EWHC 2484 (QB) at [84]-[85].

27 GDPR Art 12(1)

28 *R (Lord) v SSHD* [2003] EWHC 2073 (Admin) at [99]; *Lin v Commissioner of Police for the Metropolis* [2015] EWHC 2484 (QB) at [84]-[85]. This is the same meaning that is given to 'likely' in other statutory contexts: *Three Rivers District Council v Bank of England (Disclosure) (No 4)* [2002] EWCA Civ 1182, [2003] 1 WLR 210 at [32]. See further §6–022.

29 As to the method of ascertaining and measuring prejudice, see §6–020. As to the meaning of 'would be likely to prejudice,' see §6–022.

30 DPA 2018 ss 7(2), 16(1) and 18(1)-(2).

31 GDPR Arts 5(1)(b), (e), 6(1)(e), (3), 9(2)(g), (i), (j), 14(5)(b), 17(3), 18(2), 20(3), 21(6), 23(1)(e) and 28(3)(a), and DPA 2018 ss 8 and 19 and Sch 1 paras 3, 4, 6, 10, 11, 12, 13, 16, 17, 18, 19, 20 and 28, Sch 2 paras 7, 26 and 17.

32 As to the meaning of the 'public interest' see §6–004. As to the evidence that may be used to ascertain the public interest, see §6–006. And in relation to the 'public interest' generally, see §§6–007 to 6–017.

33 The Schedules are given effect to by DPA 2018 s 15. As noted in §11–005, although individual exemptions are drafted to disapply a list of GDPR provisions, engagement of an exemption and the consequent disappliction of a right falls to be determined by the specific right in the list of GDPR provisions. A general disapplication of all the rights in the list of GDPR provisions would be irreconcilable with 'respect[ing] the essence of the fundamental rights and freedoms' nor be 'a necessary and proportionate measure in a democratic society' to safeguard any of the matters listed in GDPR Art 23(1).

(3) Restrictions to the requirement on controllers to notify data subjects of data collection, and further restrictions to the access right: Schedule 2, Part 4 (paragraphs 18-25).
(4) Derogations from most obligations and rights 'for reasons relating to freedom of expression': Schedule 2, Part 5 (paragraph 26).
(5) Derogations from all of the data subject rights (apart from the rights to erasure and against automated decision-making): Schedule 2, Part 6 (paragraphs 27-28).
(6) Restriction of the data subject rights (apart from the right against automated decision-making), as well as to the requirement on controllers to notify data subjects of data collection, in respect of data concerning health, social work, education and child abuse: Schedule 3.
(7) Restriction of the data subject rights (apart from the right against automated decision-making), as well as to the requirement on controllers to notify data subjects of data collection, in respect of data the disclosure of which is prohibited or restricted by enactment: Schedule 4.

Whether all the restrictions and exemptions are mandated by the GDPR, in particular the effective entire removal of rights effected by Schedule 2, Part 5, remains to be seen.

2. GROUPS OF DISAPPLIED PROVISIONS

11–012 Introduction

The drafting technique adopted by the DPA 2018 is to arrange the GDPR rights and obligations into overlapping groups of provisions, with the engagement of an exemption disapplying one or other group of provisions. The application of an exemption to one provision in a group does not necessarily result in the exemption disapplying all the other provisions in that group. Rather, most exemptions look to the extent to which the application of provisions in the group would be likely to prejudice the interests protected by the exemption.[34] Given that each right and obligation within a group of provisions is different in kind and may result in a different impact upon the interest protected by an exemption, a right or obligation within the group will be disapplied only if its application would have the result against which the exemption protects.

11–013 The first group

The first group of provisions comprises:[35]

(a) all the data subject rights (apart from the right against automated decision-making);[36]
(b) where a controller obtains personal data about a data subject (whether directly from the data subject or from someone else), the obligation on a controller to provide a data subject with certain information about the controller, the purposes of the controller's processing, the legitimate interests being pursued in processing the data and the recipients of the personal data;[37]

---

[34] See further §11–005.

[35] DPA 2018 Sch 2 para 1.

[36] GDPR Arts 15, 16, 17, 18, 19, 20 and 21(1), as to which see §§10–014 to 10–017 (access), §§10–018 to 10–022 (rectification), §§10–023 to 10–028 (erasure), §§10–029 to 10–034 (restriction), §§10–035 to 10–039 (data portability), and §§10–040 to 10–044 (objection).

[37] That is, a data subject's entitlement to be provided by the controller with the information listed in GDPR Arts 13 and 14, as to which see §§9–017 to 9–021.

(c) the processing principles, but only so far as the obligations in those principles correspond to the rights and obligations arising under (a) and (b);[38] and
(d) the first processing principle other than the lawfulness requirement (that is, the requirement that processing be fair and transparent) and the second processing principle (that is, the purpose limitation).[39]

The first group does not include the following rights and obligation, which subsist where this group of provisions is disapplied:

— The prohibition on processing of sensitive personal data: this is because exemptions from that prohibition are dealt with separately in Schedule 1 to the DPA 2018.[40]
— The obligations that arise on transfers of personal data to a third country or an international organisation: these are dealt with separately in the GDPR.[41]
— The right against automated decisions: this has its own disapplication in the GDPR.[42]
— The obligation on a controller and processor to comply with the processing principles (other than as set out in (c)-(d) above, including lawfulness).[43]

1–014 The second group

The second group of provisions comprises:[44]

(a) the data subject's access right, right to erasure, right to restrict processing and right to object to processing;[45]
(b) where a controller obtains personal data about a data subject (whether directly from the data subject or from someone else), the obligation on a controller to provide a data subject with certain information about the controller, the purposes of the controller's processing, the legitimate interests being pursued in processing the data and the recipients of the personal data;[46] and
(c) the processing principles, but only so far as the obligations in those principles correspond to the rights and obligations arising under (a) and (b).[47]

The second group does not include the following rights and obligation, which subsist where this group of provisions is disapplied:

— The prohibition on processing of sensitive personal data: this is because exemptions from that prohibition are dealt with separately in Schedule 1 to the DPA 2018.[48]

---

38 That is, the principles in GDPR Art 5(1), as to which see §§9–006 to 9–039.

39 That is, the principles in GDPR Art 5(1)(a) and (b), as to which see §§9–006 to 9–016 and §§9–023 to 9–027.

40 These exemptions are dealt with in §§9–042 to 9–045 (special category data) and in §§9–046 to 9–047 (criminal offence data).

41 As to the obligations that arise on transfers of personal data to a third country or an international organisation, see §§9–057 to 9–064. As to the meaning of 'third country,' see §8–032. As to the meaning of 'international organisations,' see §8–033.

42 GDPR Art 22, as to which see §§10–045 to 10–048.

43 That is, the principles in GDPR Art 5(1) (as to which see §§9–006 to 9–039), but only so far as its provisions correspond to the rights and obligations provided for in DPA 2018 Sch 2 para 4(2)(a)-(f). By implication from DPA 2018 Sch 2 para 1(b) this does not cover all the obligations within GDPR Art 5(1).

44 DPA 2018 Sch 2 para 4(2).

45 GDPR Arts 15, 17, 18 and 21, as to which see §§10–014 to 10–017 (access), §§10–023 to 10–028 (erasure), §§10–029 to 10–034 (restriction) and §§10–040 to 10–044 (objection).

46 That is, a data subject's entitlement to be provided by the controller with the information listed in GDPR Arts 13 and 14, as to which see §§9–017 to 9–021.

47 That is, the principles in GDPR Art 5(1), as to which see §§9–006 to 9–039.

48 These exemptions are dealt with in §§9–042 to 9–045 (special category data) and in §§9–046 to 9–047 (criminal offence data).

— The obligations that arise on transfers of personal data to a third country or an international organisation: these are dealt with separately in the GDPR.[49]
— The right against automated decisions: this has its own disapplication in the GDPR.[50]
— The right to rectification, the notification obligation and the right to data portability.[51]
— The obligation on a controller and processor to comply with the processing principles (other than as set out in (c) above).[52]

11–015 The third group

The third group of provisions comprises:[53]

(a) all the data subject rights (apart from the right against automated decision-making);[54]

(b) where a controller obtains personal data about a data subject (whether directly from the data subject or from someone else), the obligation on a controller to provide a data subject with certain information about the controller, the purposes of the controller's processing, any legitimate interests being pursued in processing the data and recipients of the personal data;[55] and

(c) the processing principles, but only so far as the obligations in those principles correspond to the rights and obligations arising under (a) and (b).[56]

The third group does not include the following rights and obligation, which subsist where this group of provisions is disapplied:

— The prohibition on processing of sensitive personal data: this is because exemptions from that prohibition are dealt with separately in Schedule 1 to the DPA 2018.[57]
— The obligations that arise on transfers of personal data to a third country or an international organisation: these are dealt with separately in the GDPR.[58]
— The right against automated decisions: this has its own disapplication in the

---

49 As to the obligations that arise on transfers of personal data to a third country or an international organisation, see §§9–057 to 9–064. As to the meaning of 'third country,' see §8–032. As to the meaning of 'international organisations,' see §8–033.

50 GDPR Art 22, as to which see §§10–045 to 10–048.

51 That is, the rights under GDPR Arts 16, 19 and 20, as to which see §§10–018 to 10–022 (rectification), §§10–021 and 10–026 (notification) and §§10–035 to 10–039 (data portability).

52 That is, the principles in GDPR Art 5(1), as to which see §§9–006 to 9–039. Given that in relation to the first group, the first and second processing principles are expressly excluded without the requirement for the obligations in those principles to correspond to the rights and obligations in (a) and (b), the absence in the second group of any such exclusion of the processing principles suggests that the second group to some extent leaves the processing principles in place. Thus the words in parentheses in DPA 2018 Sch 2 para 4(2) give paramountcy to para 4(2)(g) over the provisions of GDPR Art 5 listed in DPA 2018 Sch 2 para 1(b)

53 DPA 2018 Sch 2 para 6.

54 GDPR Arts 15, 16, 17, 18, 19, 20 and 21, as to which see §§10–014 to 10–017 (access right), §§10–018 to 10–022 (rectification), §§10–023 to 10–028 (erasure), §§10–029 to 10–034 (restriction), §§10–035 to 10–039 (data portability), and §§10–040 to 10–044 (objection).

55 That is, a data subject's entitlement to be provided by the controller with the information listed in GDPR Arts 13 and 14, as to which see §§9–017 to 9–021.

56 As to which, see §§9–006 to 9–039.

57 These exemptions are dealt with in §§9–042 to 9–045 (special category data) and in §§9–046 to 9–047 (criminal offence data).

58 As to the obligations that arise on transfers of personal data to a third country or an international organisation, see §§9–057 to 9–064. As to the meaning of 'third country,' see §8–032. As to the meaning of 'international organisations,' see §8–033.

GDPR.[59]

— The obligation on a controller and processor to comply with the processing principles (other than as set out in (c) above).[60]

11–016 The fourth group

The fourth group of provisions comprises:[61]

(a) the data subject's access right;[62]

(b) where a controller obtains personal data about a data subject (whether directly from the data subject or from someone else), the obligation on a controller to provide a data subject with certain information about the controller, the purposes of the controller's processing, the legitimate interests being pursued in processing the data and the recipients of the personal data;[63] and

(c) the processing principles, but only so far as those obligations correspond to the rights and obligations arising under (a) and (b).[64]

The fourth group does not include the following rights and obligation, which subsist where this group of provisions is disapplied:

— The prohibition on processing of sensitive personal data: this is because exemptions from that prohibition are dealt with separately in Schedule 1 to the DPA 2018.[65]

— The obligations that arise on transfers of personal data to a third country or an international organisation: these are dealt with separately in the GDPR.[66]

— The data subject's right to rectification, right of erasure, right to restrict processing, right to portability of data, right to object to processing or the right against automated decisions.[67]

— The obligation on a controller and processor to comply with the processing principles (other than as set out in (c) above).[68]

---

59 GDPR Art 22, as to which see §§10–045 to 10–048.

60 That is, the principles in GDPR Art 5(1), as to which, see §§9–006 to 9–039. Given that in relation to the first group, the first and second processing principles are expressly excluded without the requirement for the obligations in those principles to correspond to the rights and obligations in (a) and (b), the absence in the second group of any such exclusion of the processing principles suggests that the second group to some extent leaves the processing principles in place.

61 DPA 2018 Sch 2 para 18.

62 GDPR Art 15, as to which see §§10–014 to 10–017.

63 That is, a data subject's entitlement to be provided by the controller with the information listed in GDPR Arts 13 and 14, as to which see §§9–017 to 9–021.

64 That is, the principles in GDPR Art 5(1), as to which see §§9–006 to 9–039.

65 These exemptions are dealt with in §§9–042 to 9–045 (special category data) and in §§9–046 to 9–047 (criminal offence data).

66 As to the obligations that arise on transfers of personal data to a third country or an international organisation, see §§9–057 to 9–064. As to the meaning of 'third country,' see §8–032. As to the meaning of 'international organisations,' see §8–033.

67 GDPR Arts 16, 17, 18, 19, 20, 21 and 22, as to which see §§10–018 to 10–022 (rectification), §§10–023 to 10–028 (erasure), §§10–029 to 10–034 (restriction), §§10–035 to 10–039 (data portability), §§10–040 to 10–044 (objection), and §§10–045 to 10–048 (automated decisions).

68 That is, the principles in GDPR Art 5(1), as to which see §§9–006 to 9–039. Given that in relation to the first group, the first and second processing principles are expressly excluded without the requirement for the obligations in those principles to correspond to the rights and obligations in (a) and (b), the absence in the second group of any such exclusion of the processing principles suggests that the second group to some extent leaves the processing principles in place.

11–017 The fifth group

The fifth group of provisions comprises:[69]

(a) all the data subject rights (apart from the right against automated decision-making);[70]

(b) where a controller obtains personal data about a data subject (whether directly from the data subject or from someone else), the obligation on a controller to provide a data subject with certain information about the controller, the purposes of the controller's processing, any legitimate interests being pursued in processing the data and recipients of the personal data;[71] and

(c) the processing principles, but only so far as the obligations in those principles correspond to the rights and obligations arising under (a) and (b).[72]

The fifth group does not include the following rights and obligation, which subsist where this group of provisions is disapplied:

— The prohibition on processing of sensitive personal data: this is because exemptions from that prohibition are dealt with separately in Schedule 1 to the DPA 2018.[73]

— The obligations that arise on transfers of personal data to a third country or an international organisation: these are dealt with separately in the GDPR.[74]

— The right against automated decisions: this has its own disapplication in the GDPR.[75]

— The obligation on a controller and processor to comply with the processing principles (other than as set out in (c) above).[76]

11–018 The sixth group

The sixth group of provisions comprises:[77]

(a) the data subject's access right;[78] and

(b) the processing principles, but only so far as those obligations correspond to the rights and obligations arising under (a).[79]

The sixth group does not include the following rights and obligation, which subsist where this group of provisions is disapplied:

---

69 DPA 2018 Sch 3 para 1.

70 That is, the rights conferred on a data subject by GDPR Arts 15 (access), 16 (rectification), 17 (erasure), 18 (restriction of processing), 20 (data portability) and 21 (objection), as to which see §§10–014 to 10–044.

71 That is, a data subject's entitlement to be provided by the controller with the information listed in GDPR Arts 13 and 14, as to which see §§9–017 to 9–021.

72 As to which see §§9–006 to 9–039.

73 These exemptions are dealt with in §§9–042 to 9–045 (special category data) and in §§9–046 to 9–047 (criminal offence data).

74 As to the obligations that arise on transfers of personal data to a third country or an international organisation, see §§9–057 to 9–064. As to the meaning of 'third country,' see §8–032. As to the meaning of 'international organisations,' see §8–033.

75 GDPR Art 22, as to which see §§10–045 to 10–048.

76 That is, the principles in GDPR Art 5(1), as to which see §§9–006 to 9–039. Given that in relation to the first group, the first and second processing principles are expressly excluded without the requirement for the obligations in those principles to correspond to the rights and obligations in (a) and (b), the absence in the second group of any such exclusion of the processing principles suggests that the second group to some extent leaves the processing principles in place.

77 DPA 2018 Sch 4 para 1.

78 GDPR Art 15, as to which see §§10–014 to 10–017.

79 That is, the principles in GDPR Art 5(1), as to which see §§9–006 to 9–039.

- The prohibition on processing of sensitive personal data: this is because exemptions from that prohibition are dealt with separately in Schedule 1 to the DPA 2018.[80]
- The obligations that arise on transfers of personal data to a third country or an international organisation: these are dealt with separately in the GDPR.[81]
- The data subject's right to rectification, right of erasure, right to restrict processing, right to portability of data, right to object to processing or the right against automated decisions.[82]
- Where a controller obtains personal data about a data subject (whether directly from the data subject or from someone else), the obligation on a controller to provide a data subject with certain information about the controller, the purposes of the controller's processing, the legitimate interests being pursued in processing the data and the recipients of the personal data.[83]
- The obligation on a controller and processor to comply with the processing principles (other than as set out in (b) above).[84]

11–019 The seventh group

The seventh group of provisions comprises[85] all the data subject rights (apart from the right to erasure and the right against automated decision-making).[86] The seventh group does not include the following rights and obligation, which subsist where this group of provisions is disapplied:

- The prohibition on processing of sensitive personal data: this is because exemptions from that prohibition are dealt with separately in Schedule 1 to the DPA 2018.[87]
- The obligations that arise on transfers of personal data to a third country or an international organisation: these are dealt with separately in the GDPR.[88]
- The right to erasure.[89]
- The right against automated decisions: this has its own disapplication in the

80 These exemptions are dealt with in §§9–042 to 9–045 (special category data) and in §§9–046 to 9–047 (criminal offence data).

81 As to the obligations that arise on transfers of personal data to a third country or an international organisation, see §§9–057 to 9–064. As to the meaning of 'third country,' see §8–032. As to the meaning of 'international organisations,' see §8–033.

82 GDPR Arts 16, 17, 18, 19, 20, 21 and 22, as to which see §§10–018 to 10–022 (rectification), §§10–023 to 10–028 (erasure), §§10–029 to 10–034 (restriction), §§10–035 to 10–039 (data portability), §§10–040 to 10–044 (objection), and §§10–045 to 10–048 (automated decisions).

83 That is, a data subject's entitlement to be provided by the controller with the information listed in GDPR Arts 13 and 14, as to which see §§9–017 to 9–021.

84 That is, the principles in GDPR Art 5(1), as to which see §§9–006 to 9–039. Given that in relation to the first group, the first and second processing principles are expressly excluded without the requirement for the obligations in those principles to correspond to the rights and obligations in (a) and (b), the absence in the second group of any such exclusion of the processing principles suggests that the second group to some extent leaves the processing principles in place.

85 DPA 2018 Sch 2 para 28(2).

86 That is, the rights conferred by GDPR Arts 15, 16, 18, 19, 20 and 21, as to which see §§10–014 to 10–017 (access), §§10–018 to 10–022 (rectification), §§10–029 to 10–034 (restriction), §§10–035 to 10–039 (data portability) and §§10–040 to 10–044 (objection).

87 These exemptions are dealt with in §§9–042 to 9–045 (special category data) and in §§9–046 to 9–047 (criminal offence data).

88 As to the obligations that arise on transfers of personal data to a third country or an international organisation, see §§9–057 to 9–064. As to the meaning of 'third country,' see §8–032. As to the meaning of 'international organisations,' see §8–033.

89 That is, the right conferred by GDPR Art 17, as to which see §§10–023 to 10–028.

GDPR.[90]

— Where a controller obtains personal data about a data subject (whether directly from the data subject or from someone else), the obligation on a controller to provide a data subject with certain information about the controller, the purposes of the controller's processing, the legitimate interests being pursued in processing the data and the recipients of the personal data.[91]

— The obligation on a controller and processor to comply with the processing principles.[92]

11–020 The eighth group

The eighth group of provisions comprises[93] the access right, the right to rectification, the right to restrict processing and the right to object to processing.[94] The eighth group does not include the following rights and obligations, which subsist where this group of provisions is disapplied:

— The prohibition on processing of sensitive personal data: this is because exemptions from that prohibition are dealt with separately in Schedule 1 to the DPA 2018.[95]

— The obligations that arise on transfers of personal data to a third country or an international organisation: these are dealt with separately in the GDPR.[96]

— The right to erasure and the right to object to processing.[97]

— Where a controller obtains personal data about a data subject (whether directly from the data subject or from someone else), the obligation on a controller to provide a data subject with certain information about the controller, the purposes of the controller's processing, any legitimate interests being pursued in processing the data and recipients of the personal data.[98]

— The right against automated decisions: this has its own disapplication in the GDPR.[99]

— The obligation on a controller and processor to comply with the processing principles.[100]

11–021 The ninth group

The ninth group of provisions is the most comprehensive and comprises:[101]

(a) all the processing principles (apart from 'integrity and confidentiality'), as well all the

---

90 GDPR Art 22, as to which see §§10–045 to 10–048.

91 That is, a data subject's entitlement to be provided by the controller with the information listed in GDPR Arts 13 and 14, as to which see §§9–017 to 9–021.

92 That is, the principles in GDPR Art 5(1), as to which see §§9–006 to 9–039.

93 DPA 2018 Sch 2 para 27(2).

94 That is, the rights conferred by GDPR Arts 15, 16, 18 and 21, as to which see §§10–014 to 10–017 (access), §§10–018 to 10–022 (rectification), §§10–029 to 10–034 (restriction) and §§10–040 to 10–044 (objection).

95 These exemptions are dealt with in §§9–042 to 9–045 (special category data) and in §§9–046 to 9–047 (criminal offence data).

96 As to the obligations that arise on transfers of personal data to a third country or an international organisation, see §§9–057 to 9–064. As to the meaning of 'third country,' see §8–032. As to the meaning of 'international organisations,' see §8–033.

97 That is, the right conferred by GDPR Arts 17 and 20, as to which see §§10–023 to 10–028 (erasure) and §§10–035 to 10–039 (data portability).

98 That is, a data subject's entitlement to be provided by the controller with the information listed in GDPR Arts 13 and 14, as to which see §§9–017 to 9–021.

99 GDPR Art 22, as to which see §§10–045 to 10–048.

100 That is, the principles in GDPR Art 5(1), as to which see §§9–006 to 9–039.

101 DPA 2018 Sch 2 para 26(9).

requirements for lawfulness and consent (including a child's consent);[102]

(b) all the restrictions on the processing of sensitive personal data;[103]

(c) all the data subject rights (apart the rights against automated decision-making and to object to direct marketing);[104]

(d) all the obligations that arise on transfers of personal data to a third country or an international organisation;[105] and

(e) all the Information Commissioner reporting and consultative requirements, and all the obligations for co-operation and consistency.[106]

The only right left remaining is the right against automated decisions, which has its own disapplication in the GDPR anyway.[107]

3. PURPOSE-BASED EXEMPTIONS

11–022 National security

The GDPR allows a Member State to restrict the scope of data subject rights, as well as the processing principles in so far as they correspond to those rights, when such a restriction respects the essence of the fundamental rights and freedoms and is a necessary and proportionate measure in a democratic society to safeguard national security.[108] In so providing, the GDPR recognises that processing that is necessary and proportionate to safeguard national security is outside the legislative competence of the EU.[109] Being an activity that is outside the scope of EU law, processing of personal data in order to safeguard national security is 'other general processing' – that is, processing that is covered by the DPA 2018 and the applied GDPR.[110] Apart from:

(a) the first processing principle so far as it requires processing of personal data to be lawful;[111] and

(b) the principles relating to the processing of special category data,[112]

the obligations imposed on controllers and processors and the rights conferred on data subjects are disapplied where exemption from them is 'required for the purpose of safeguarding national

---

102 As to which see §§9–006 to 9–039. Integrity and confidentiality is provided for in GDPR Art 5(1)(f).

103 These exemptions are dealt with in §§9–042 to 9–045 (special category data) and in §§9–046 to 9–047 (criminal offence data).

104 GDPR Arts 15, 16, 17, 18, 19, 20 and 21, as to which see §§10–014 to 10–017 (access), §§10–018 to 10–022 (rectification), §§10–023 to 10–028 (erasure), §§10–029 to 10–034 (restriction), §§10–035 to 10–039 (data portability), and §§10–040 to 10–044 (objection).

105 As to the obligations that arise on transfers of personal data to a third country or an international organisation, see §§9–057 to 9–064. As to the meaning of 'third country,' see §8–032. As to the meaning of 'international organisations,' see §8–033.

106 As to which, see GDPR Arts 34, 36, 60, 61, 62, 63, 64, 65, and 67.

107 GDPR Art 22, as to which see §§10–045 to 10–048.

108 GDPR Art 23(1)(a). A similar exemption applies under DPA 2018 s 28.

109 TEU Art 4(2).

110 Specifically, it is covered by Chapter 3 of Part 2 of the DPA 2018 (ss 21-28) by virtue of DPA 2018 ss 21(1) and 22(1). 'The applied GDPR' means the GDPR as applied by Chapter 3 of Part 2: DPA s 3(11).

111 As to which, see §§9–007 to 9–014.

112 As to the meaning of 'special category data' and the principles applicable to its processing, see §§9–040 to 9–045. However, applied GDPR Art 9(1) does not prohibit the processing of personal data to the extent that the processing is carried out for the purposes of safeguarding national security and with appropriate safeguards for the rights and freedoms of the data subject: DPA 2018 s 28(1).

security.'[113] Although 'national security' is not defined, its meaning is likely to be the same as given in other legislative spheres.[114] The DPA 2018 permits a Minister of the Crown to certify that exemption from provisions of the applied GDPR is or was required in relation to any personal data for the purpose of safeguarding national security, with that certificate being conclusive evidence of that fact.[115]

11–023 Defence

The GDPR allows a Member State to restrict the scope of data subject rights, as well as the processing principles in so far as they correspond to those rights, when such a restriction respects the essence of the fundamental rights and freedoms and is a necessary and proportionate measure in a democratic society to safeguard defence.[116] In so providing, the GDPR recognises that processing that is necessary and proportionate to safeguard defence is outside the legislative competence of the EU.[117] Being an activity that is outside the scope of EU law, processing of personal data in order to safeguard the defence of the United Kingdom is 'other general processing' – that is, processing that is covered by the DPA 2018 and the applied GDPR.[118] Apart from:

(a) the first processing principle so far as it requires processing of personal data to be lawful;[119] and

(b) the principles relating to the processing of special category data,[120]

the obligations imposed on controllers and processors and the rights conferred on data subjects are disapplied where exemption from them is 'required for defence purposes.'[121] Although the defence purposes are not defined, consistent with the comity of nations those purposes will be limited to defence of the British Islands and colonies.[122] Defence purposes will cover the armed forces of the Crown and their capabilities.[123]

11–024 Law enforcement purposes

The GDPR does not apply to the processing of personal data by 'competent authorities' for law enforcement purposes: such processing is governed instead by Part 3 of the DPA 2018.[124] In relation to a controller or processor that is not a 'competent authority' which processes personal data, the GDPR allows a Member State to restrict the scope of data subject rights, as well as the processing principles in so far as they correspond to those rights, when such a restriction

113 DPA 2018 s 26(1)(a).

114 As to which, see §§26–050 to 26–054.

115 As to the operation of national security certificates, see §§26–057 to 26–061.

116 GDPR Art 23(1)(b).

117 TEU Art 4(2).

118 Specifically, it is covered by Chapter 3 of Part 2 of the DPA 2018 (ss 21-28) by virtue of DPA 2018 ss 21(1) and 22(1). 'The applied GDPR' means the GDPR as applied by Chapter 3 of Part 2: DPA s 3(11).

119 As to which, see §§9–007 to 9–014.

120 As to the meaning of 'special category data' and the principles applicable to its processing, see §§9–040 to 9–045. However, applied GDPR Art 9(1) does not prohibit the processing of personal data to the extent that the processing is carried out for defence purposes and with appropriate safeguards for the rights and freedoms of data subject: DPA 2018 s 28(1).

121 DPA 2018 s 26(1)(b).

122 As to the meaning of which, see §26–074.

123 See further §§26–075, 26–077 and 26–078.

124 This is dealt with in Chapters 12 and 13. As to the meaning of 'competent authorities' see §12–007. The 'law enforcement purposes' are the purposes of the prevention, investigation, detection or prosecution of criminal offences or the execution of criminal penalties, including the safeguarding against and the prevention of threats to public security: DPA 2018 s 31.

respects the essence of the fundamental rights and freedoms and is a necessary and proportionate measure in a democratic society for 'the law enforcement purposes.'[125] The DPA 2018 has exercised this power.

(1) Where a controller or processor processes personal data for the law enforcement purposes, the DPA 2018 disapplies the first group of provisions to the extent that the application of those provisions would be likely to prejudice any of the law enforcement purposes.[126]

(2) Where personal data consists of a classification applied to a data subject as part of a risk assessment system operated by a government department, local authority or another authority administering housing benefit, and that system is operated for the purpose of collecting or imposing a tax or duty or for the purpose of enforcement of a law involving the unlawful use or payment of public money, the DPA 2018 disapplies the fourth group of provisions to the extent that the application of those provisions would prevent the risk assessment system from operating effectively.[127]

(3) Where a controller is processing personal data for any of the law enforcement purposes, and a second controller obtains that personal data from that controller for the purpose of the second controller discharging a statutory function, the DPA 2018 disapplies the fourth group of provisions in relation to the second controller to the same extent that the first controller is exempt from those obligations on the basis that their application would be likely to prejudice any of the law enforcement purposes.[128]

11–025 Taxation purposes

The GDPR allows a Member State to restrict the scope of data subject rights, as well as the processing principles in so far as they correspond to those rights, when such a restriction respects the essence of the fundamental rights and freedoms and is a necessary and proportionate measure in a democratic society to safeguard important objectives of general public interest of the EU or of a Member State, in particular an important economic or financial interest of the EU or of a Member State, including taxation matters.[129] The DPA 2018 has exercised this power.

(1) Where a controller or processor processes personal data for the assessment of a tax or duty or an imposition of a similar nature – 'the taxation purposes' – the DPA 2018 disapplies the first group of provisions to the extent that the application of those provisions would be likely to prejudice any of the taxation purposes.[130]

(2) Where a controller is processing personal data for any of the taxation purposes, and a second controller obtains that personal data from that controller for the purpose of the second controller discharging a statutory function, the DPA 2018 disapplies the fourth group of provisions in relation to the second controller to the same extent that the first controller is exempt from those obligations on the basis that their application would be likely to prejudice any of the taxation purposes.[131]

---

125 GDPR Art 23(1)(d). See also GDPR recitals (19), (50), (73) and (104).

126 DPA 2018 Sch 2 para 2(1). As to the meaning of 'the first group of provisions,' see §11–013.

127 DPA 2018 Sch 2 para 3. As to the meaning of 'the fourth group of provisions,' see §11–016.

128 DPA 2018 Sch 2 para 2(2)-(3). As to the meaning of 'the fourth group of provisions,' see §11–016.

129 GDPR Art 23(1)(e).

130 DPA 2018 Sch 2 para 2(1). As to the meaning of 'the first group of provisions,' see §11–013.

131 DPA 2018 Sch 2 para 2(2)-(3). As to the meaning of 'the fourth group of provisions,' see §11–016.

11– 026 Immigration control

Although immigration control is not specifically mentioned as a basis for restriction or derogation in the GDPR, the DPA 2018 provides exemptions where personal data is processed for the purpose of maintaining effective immigration control or for the purpose of investigating or detecting activities that would undermine the maintenance of effective immigration control – 'the immigration control purposes.'[132]

(1) Where a controller or processor processes personal data for the immigration control purposes, the DPA 2018 disapplies the second group of provisions to the extent that the application of those provisions would be likely to prejudice any of the immigration control purposes.[133]

(2) Where a controller is processing personal data for any of the immigration control purposes, and a second controller obtains that personal data from that controller for the purpose of the second controller discharging a statutory function, the DPA 2018 disapplies the fourth group of provisions in relation to the second controller to the same extent that the first controller is exempt from those obligations on the basis that their application would be likely to prejudice any of the immigration control purposes.[134]

11– 027 Legal proceedings

The GDPR allows a Member State to restrict the scope of data subject rights, as well as the processing principles in so far as they correspond to those rights, when such a restriction respects the essence of the fundamental rights and freedoms and is a necessary and proportionate measure in a democratic society to safeguard the protection of legal proceedings.[135] The DPA 2018 has exercised this power in relation to legal proceedings.

(1) Where a controller is obliged by an enactment to make personal data available to the public, the DPA 2018 disapplies the first group of provisions to the extent that the application of those provisions would prevent the controller from complying with that obligation.[136]

(2) Where a controller is obliged by an enactment, a rule of law or an order of a court or tribunal to disclose personal data, the DPA 2018 disapplies the first group of provisions to the extent that the application of those provisions would prevent the controller from giving disclosure of that personal data.[137]

(3) Where disclosure of personal data by a controller is necessary for the purpose of, or in connection with, legal proceedings (including prospective proceedings), or is necessary for the purpose of obtaining legal advice, or is otherwise necessary for the purposes of establishing, exercising or defending legal rights, the DPA 2018 disapplies the first group of provisions to the extent that the application of those provisions would prevent the controller from making the disclosure.[138]

11– 028 Public protection functions

The GDPR allows a Member State to restrict the scope of data subject rights, as well as the

---

[132] DPA 2018 Sch 2 para 4(1).

[133] DPA 2018 Sch 2 para 2(1). As to the meaning of 'the second group of provisions,' see §11– 014.

[134] DPA 2018 Sch 2 para 2(2)-(3). As to the meaning of 'the fourth group of provisions,' see §11– 016.

[135] GDPR Art 23(1)(f).

[136] DPA 2018 Sch 2 para 5(1). As to the meaning of 'the first group of provisions,' see §11– 013.

[137] DPA 2018 Sch 2 para 5(2). As to the meaning of 'the first group of provisions,' see §11– 013.

[138] DPA 2018 Sch 2 para 5(3). As to the meaning of 'the first group of provisions,' see §11– 013.

processing principles in so far as they correspond to those rights, when such a restriction respects the essence of the fundamental rights and freedoms and is a necessary and proportionate measure in a democratic society to safeguard important objectives of general public interest of the EU or of a Member State, in particular an important economic or financial interest, or public health or social security objectives.[139] So far as this mandates exemptions where personal data is being processed for taxation purposes, this is dealt with above. So far as concerns processing of personal data for the purposes of discharging other statutory functions, the DPA 2018 provides exemptions for certain emanations of the Crown and public authorities. The Act disapplies the third group of provisions in relation to the processing of personal data for specific functions (specified by the object of the function), but only to the extent that the application of the third group of provisions would be likely to prejudice the proper discharge of those functions.[140]

11– 029 Audit functions

Where an enactment confers a function on the Comptroller and Auditor General (or the equivalents for Scotland, Wales or Northern Ireland), the DPA 2018 disapplies the third group of provisions in relation to the processing of personal data for those functions, but only to the extent that the application of the third group of provisions would be likely to prejudice the proper discharge of those functions.[141]

11– 030 Bank of England functions

In relation to limited functions of the Bank of England, the DPA 2018 disapplies the third group of provisions in relation to the processing of personal data for those functions, but only to the extent that the application of the third group of provisions would be likely to prejudice the proper discharge of those functions.[142]

11– 031 Complaint handling functions

In relation to functions of the Legal Services Board, legal complaints under Part 6 of the Legal Services Act 2007 and specific other complaint procedures,[143] the DPA 2018 disapplies the third group of provisions in relation to the processing of personal data for those functions, but only to the extent that the application of the third group of provisions would be likely to prejudice

139 GDPR Art 23(1)(e).

140 DPA 2018 Sch 2 para 7. As to the meaning of 'the third group of provisions,' see §11– 015. Statutory functions are those functions provided for in an enactment. 'Enactment' includes an enactment comprised in subordinate legislation, in subsequently passed legislation, in Measures or Acts of the National Assembly for Wales, in Acts or subordinate instruments of the Scottish Parliament and in instruments made under Northern Ireland legislation: DPA 2018 s 205(1).

141 DPA 2018 Sch 2 para 8. As to the meaning of 'the third group of provisions,' see §11– 015. 'Enactment' includes an enactment comprised in subordinate legislation, in subsequently passed legislation, in Measures or Acts of the National Assembly for Wales, in Acts or subordinate instruments of the Scottish Parliament and in instruments made under Northern Ireland legislation: DPA 2018 s 205(1).

142 DPA 2018 Sch 2 para 9. As to the meaning of 'the third group of provisions,' see §11– 015. The functions are those which it discharges as a monetary authority (as defined in the Banking Act 2009 s 244), as a public function (within the meaning of the Financial Services and Markets Act 2000 s 349) and those conferred on the Prudential Regulation Authority under an enactment. 'Enactment' includes an enactment comprised in subordinate legislation, in subsequently passed legislation, in Measures or Acts of the National Assembly for Wales, in Acts or subordinate instruments of the Scottish Parliament and in instruments made under Northern Ireland legislation: DPA 2018 s 205(1).

143 Namely: NHS Redress Act 2006 s 14; Health and Social Care (Community Health and Standards) Act 2003 ss 113(1) or (2) and 114(1) or (3); Children Act 1989 ss 24D and 26; Public Services Ombudsman (Wales) Act 2005 Part 2A; Social Services and Well-being (Wales) Act 2014 Pt 10 Ch 1. As to the meaning of 'the third group of provisions,' see §11– 015.

the proper discharge of those functions.[144]

11– 032 Other regulatory functions

In relation to certain functions conferred on the Information Commissioner, the Scottish Information Commissioner, the Pension Ombudsman (and cognate office holders), the Financial Conduct Authority, the Financial Ombudsman (and certain financial investigators), the Charity Commissioner, and the monitoring officer of a relevant authority, the DPA 2018 disapplies the third group of provisions in relation to the processing of personal data for those functions, but only to the extent that the application of the third group of provisions would be likely to prejudice the proper discharge of those functions.[145]

11– 033 Judicial functions etc

The DPA 2018 disapplies the third group of provisions:[146]

(1) Where a controller or processor is processing personal data for the purposes of assessing a person's suitability for judicial office or the office of Queen's Counsel.
(2) Where personal data is being processed by an individual acting in a judicial capacity or a court or tribunal acting in its judicial capacity.
(3) In relation to personal data that is outside (1) and (2), to the extent that the application of the third group of provisions would be likely to prejudice judicial independence or judicial proceedings.

11– 034 Crown honours, etc

The DPA 2018 disapplies the third group of provisions:[147]

(1) Where a controller or processor is processing personal data for the purposes of the conferring by the Crown of any honour or dignity.[148]
(2) Where a controller or processor is processing personal data for the purposes of assessing a person's suitability for various church and specified offices.

11– 035 Protecting others' rights

Where compliance with the access right would disclose information relating to another individual who can be identified from that information, the DPA 2018 disapplies the access right (and the processing principles so far as the obligations in those principles correspond to the access right).[149] However, there is no disapplication of the access right where:

(a) the other individual has consented to the disclosure of the information to the data subject; or
(b) it is reasonable, having regard to all the circumstances, to disclose the information

144 DPA 2018 Sch 2 para 10. As to the meaning of 'the third group of provisions,' see §11– 015.

145 DPA 2018 Sch 2 paras 11-12. The functions are those conferred by the means set out in the second column of the table in para 11. As to the meaning of 'the third group of provisions,' see §11– 015.

146 DPA 2018 Sch 2 para 14. As to the meaning of 'the third group of provisions,' see §11– 015.

147 DPA 2018 Sch 2 para 15. As to the meaning of 'the third group of provisions,' see §11– 015. The offices include the Provost of Eton, the First and Second Church Estates Commissioners, the Poet Laureate, the Astronomer Royal, and the Masters of Trinity College and Churchill College, Cambridge.

148 As to the meaning of 'honour or dignity,' see §35– 010. As to the process of conferral of an honour or dignity, see §35– 011.

149 DPA 2018 Sch 2 paras 16-17. The access right is provided for by GDPR Art 15, as to which see §§10– 014 to 10– 017. 'Information relating to another individual' includes information identifying the other individual as the source of information: DPA 2018 Sch 2 para 16(4)(a). An individual can be identified from information to be provided to a data subject by a controller if the individual can be identified from that information or from that information and any other information that the controller reasonably believes that the data subject is likely to possess or obtain: DPA 2018 Sch 2 para 16(4)(b).

to the data subject without the consent of the other individual.[150]

In certain health, social work and educational settings, it will be deemed reasonable to disclose the information to the data subject without the consent of the other individual.[151]

11–036 Corporate finance service

Provided certain requirements are met, where a controller or processor processes personal data for the purposes of or in connection with a corporate finance service, the DPA 2018 disapplies the fourth group of provisions.[152] The requirements for disapplication are:

(a) the corporate finance service satisfies the statutory definition;[153]

(b) the corporate finance service is provided by a 'relevant person' as defined;[154] and

(c) (i) the application of the fourth group of provisions would be likely to affect the 'price' of an 'instrument';[155] or

(ii) – the 'relevant person' reasonably believes that application of the fourth group of provisions in relation to the personal data in question could affect the decision of a person whether to deal in, subscribe to or issue an instrument or whether to act in a way that is likely to have an effect on a business activity; and

– the application of the fourth group of provisions would have a prejudicial effect on the orderly functioning of financial markets or the efficient allocation of capital within the economy.[156]

11–037 Management forecasts

Where a controller or processor processes personal data for the purposes of management forecasting or management planning in relation to a business or other activity, then the DPA 2018 disapplies the fourth group of provisions but only to the extent that the application of those provisions would be likely to prejudice the conduct of the business or the activity concerned.[157]

11–038 Exam marking

Where personal data consists of marks or other information processed by a controller for the purposes of determining the results of an exam or in consequence of the determination of the results of an exam, the DPA delays the obligation on a controller to notify the data subject of the action that the controller has taken upon the access request of the data subject.[158]

---

150 DPA 2018 Sch 2 para 16(2). All the circumstances will include: (a) the type of information that would be disclosed; (b) any duty of confidentiality owed to the other individual; (c) any steps taken by the controller with a view to seeking the consent of the other individual; (d) whether the other individual is capable of giving consent; and (e) any express refusal of consent by the other individual.

151 DPA 2018 Sch 2 para 17. Whether it is deemed reasonable will depend on the identity of the other individual. Deemed reasonableness will usually require that the other individual is the person who was employed or otherwise engaged to prepare the document in which the information is recorded.

152 DPA 2018 Sch 2 para 21(1). As to the meaning of the 'fourth group of provisions,' see §11–016.

153 The definition is in DPA 2018 Sch 2 para 21(4).

154 The definition is in DPA 2018 Sch 2 para 21(4).

155 Both 'price' and 'instrument' are defined in DPA 2018 Sch 2 para 21(4).

156 DPA 2018 Sch 2 para 21(3).

157 DPA 2018 Sch 2 para 22. As to the meaning of the 'fourth group of provisions,' see §11–016.

158 DPA 2018 Sch 2 para 25(2)-(3), referring to the obligation imposed by GDPR Art 12(3)-(4). The term 'exam' is defined in DPA 2018 Sch 2 para 25(4).

4. DATA TYPE EXEMPTIONS

11– 039 Parliamentary proceedings

Although the GDPR does not expressly allow a Member State to restrict the scope of its rules so as to exclude Parliamentary proceedings, the privileges that attach to those proceedings are part of the fundamental political and constitutional structures of the nation, with the effect that they are outside the legislative competence of the EU.[159] Being an activity that is outside the scope of EU law, processing of personal data in the course of Parliamentary proceedings is 'other general processing' – that is, processing that is covered by the DPA 2018 and the applied GDPR.[160] The DPA 2018 disapplies the third group of provisions, as well as the controllers obligation to communicate any data breach to a data subject,[161] where that disapplication is required in order to avoid an infringement of the privileges of either House of Parliament.[162]

11– 040 Legal professional privilege

The DPA 2018 disapplies the fourth group of provisions to personal data that consists of:

(a) information in respect of which a claim to litigation privilege (or its Scottish equivalent) could be maintained;[163] or

(b) information in respect of which a duty of confidentiality is owed by a professional legal adviser to a client of the adviser.[164]

11– 041 Self-incrimination

The DPA 2018 disapplies the fourth group of provisions to the extent that compliance with an obligation in those provisions would, by revealing evidence of the commission of an offence, expose the person to proceedings for that offence.[165]

11– 042 Confidential references

Where personal data consists of a reference given, or to be given, in confidence for the purposes of:

(a) the education, training or employment (or prospective education, training or employment) of the data subject;

(b) the placement (or prospective placement) of the data subject as a volunteer;

(c) the appointment (or prospective appointment) of the data subject to any office; or

(d) the provision (or prospective provision) by the data subject of any service,

the DPA 2018 disapplies the fourth group of provisions.[166]

159 TEU Art 4(2). See further §8– 036.

160 Specifically, it is covered by Chapter 3 of Part 2 of the DPA 2018 (ss 21-28) by virtue of DPA 2018 ss 21(1) and 22(1). 'The applied GDPR' means the GDPR as applied by Chapter 3 of Part 2: DPA s 3(11).

161 GDPR Art 34.

162 DPA 2018 Sch 2 para 13. As to the privileges of the Houses of Parliament, see §30– 003. As to the meaning of 'the third group of provisions,' see §11– 015.

163 DPA 2018 Sch 2 para 19(a). As to the meaning of the 'fourth group of provisions,' see §11– 016. As to the circumstances in which litigation privilege arises, see §§30– 014 to 30– 016.

164 DPA 2018 Sch 2 para 19(b). As to the meaning of the 'fourth group of provisions,' see §11– 016. As for the circumstances in which such a duty of confidentiality arises, see §§30– 014 to 30– 016.

165 DPA 2018 Sch 2 para 20(1). As to the meaning of the 'fourth group of provisions,' see §11– 016. Offences under the DPA 2018 and the Perjury Act 1905 s 5 (and its Scottish and Northern Ireland equivalents) are not covered by the exemption: DPA 2018 Sch 2 para 20(2).

166 DPA 2018 Sch 2 para 24. As to the meaning of the 'fourth group of provisions,' see §11– 016.

11–043 Negotiations

The DPA disapplies the fourth group of provisions in relation to personal data that consists of records of the intentions of the controller in relation to any negotiations with the data subject, but only to the extent that the application of those provisions would be likely to prejudice those negotiations.[167]

11–044 Exam papers

The DPA 2018 disapplies the fourth group of provisions in relation to personal data that consists of information recorded by a candidate during an exam.[168]

11–045 Health data

In relation to personal data concerning health:[169]

(1) Where that data is being processed by a court, it consists of information supplied in a report or other evidence given to the court in the course of certain proceedings and, in accordance with court rules, the personal data may be withheld in part or in whole from the data subject, the fifth group of provisions is disapplied.[170]

(2) Where that data is sought in the exercise of a power conferred by an enactment or rule of law, and:

  (a) the data subject is aged under 18 and the request is made by a person having parental responsibility for the data subject; or

  (b) the data subject is incapable of managing his or her own affairs and the request is made by a person appointed by the court to manage the data subject's affairs,

  the fifth group of provisions is disapplied to data concerning health, but only to the extent that it would disclose information:

  – that was provided by the data subject in the expectation that it would not be disclosed to the person making the request;

  – that was obtained as a result of an examination or investigation to which the data subject consented in the expectation that it would not be disclosed to the person making the request, or

  – that the data subject has expressly indicated should not be disclosed to the person making the request.[171]

(3) The access right is disapplied to the extent that the application of that right to the personal data would be likely to cause serious harm to the physical or mental health of the data subject or another individual.[172]

---

167 DPA 2018 Sch 2 para 23. As to the meaning of the 'fourth group of provisions,' see §11–016.

168 DPA 2018 Sch 2 para 25(1). As to the meaning of the 'fourth group of provisions,' see §11–016. The term 'exam' is defined in DPA 2018 Sch 2 para 25(4).

169 'Data concerning health' is defined in DPA 2018 s 205(1) to mean 'personal data relating to the physical or mental health of an individual, including the provision of health care services, which reveals information about his or her health status.'

170 DPA 2018 Sch 3 para 3(1). As to the meaning of the 'fifth group of provisions.' see §11–017. As to the applicable court rules, see DPA 2018 Sch 3 para 3(2)

171 DPA 2018 Sch 3 para 4. As to the meaning of the 'fifth group of provisions.' see §11–017. In Scotland, it is age 16 rather than age 18. 'Enactment' includes an enactment comprised in subordinate legislation, in subsequently passed legislation, in Measures or Acts of the National Assembly for Wales, in Acts or subordinate instruments of the Scottish Parliament and in instruments made under Northern Ireland legislation: DPA 2018 s 205(1).

172 DPA 2018 Sch 3 para 5(1). But a controller who is not a health professional cannot rely on this exemption unless that controller has obtained an opinion (not more than 6 months' old) from the person who appears to be the 'appropriate health professional' (defined in DPA 2018 Sch 3 para 2(1)) to the effect that the serious harm

(4) Where the controller is not a health professional, the access right is further disapplied in respect of personal data concerning health, unless that controller has obtained an opinion from the person who appears to the controller to be 'the appropriate health controller' to the effect that the application of the access right to that personal data would be likely to cause serious harm to the physical or mental health of the data subject or another individual.[173]

11–046 Social work data

The DPA 2018 lists a large number of public authorities having social work functions (including National Health Service trusts), as well as voluntary organisations such as the National Society for the Prevention of Cruelty to Children – 'social work bodies.'[174] The Act provides a number of exemptions that are principally concerned with personal data that is neither 'education data' nor 'data concerning health'[175] where it is being processed by social work bodies for the purposes of their social work functions or services – 'social work data.'[176]

(1) The access right is disapplied to social work data where the application of that right to the personal data would be likely to prejudice carrying out social work because it would be likely to cause serious harm to the physical or mental health of the data subject or another individual.[177]

(2) Where social work data is sought in the exercise of a power conferred by an enactment or rule of law, and:

(a) the data subject is aged under 18 and the request is made by a person having parental responsibility for the data subject; or

(b) the data subject is incapable of managing his or her own affairs and the request is made by a person appointed by a court to manage the data subject's affairs,

the fifth group of provisions is disapplied to the social work data, but only to the extent that it would disclose information:

– that was provided by the data subject in the expectation that it would not be disclosed to the person making the request;
– that was obtained as a result of an examination or investigation to which the data subject consented in the expectation that it would not be disclosed to the person making the request, or
– that the data subject has expressly indicated should not be disclosed.[178]

---

requirement is met with the respect to the personal data: DPA 2018 Sch 3 para 5(2). The access right is provided by GDPR Art 15, as to which see §§10–014 to 10–017.

173 DPA 2018 Sch 3 para 6(1). But a controller cannot rely on this exemption unless that opinion is not more than 6 months' old. 'Appropriate health professional' is defined in DPA 2018 Sch 3 para 2(1). The access right is provided by GDPR Art 15, as to which see §§10–014 to 10–017.

174 DPA 2018 Sch 3 para 8.

175 'Education data' is defined in DPA 2018 Sch 3 para 17 to mean 'personal data which constitutes an educational record but is not data concerning health,' 'educational record' is defined in DPA 2018 Sch 3 para 13 to mean a record to which paragraph 14, 15 or 16 of that Schedule applies, and 'data concerning health' is defined in DPA 2018 s 205(1) to mean 'personal data relating to the physical or mental health of an individual, including the provision of health care services, which reveals information about his or her health status.'

176 DPA 2018 Sch 3 para 7(1).

177 DPA 2018 Sch 3 para 11 in conjunction with the definition of 'serious harm test' in para 7(2). The access right is provided by GDPR Art 15, as to which see §§10–014 to 10–017.

178 DPA 2018 Sch 3 para 10. As to the meaning of the 'fifth group of provisions.' see §11–017. In Scotland, it is age 16 rather than age 18. 'Enactment' includes an enactment comprised in subordinate legislation, in subsequently passed legislation, in Measures or Acts of the National Assembly for Wales, in Acts or subordinate instruments of the Scottish Parliament and in instruments made under Northern Ireland legislation: DPA 2018 s 205(1).

(3) Where personal data that is neither 'education data' nor 'data concerning health'[179] is processed by a court and that data consists of information supplied in a report or other evidence given to the court in the course of proceedings to which specified court rules apply and in accordance with which the data may be withheld from the data subject, then the fifth group of provisions is disapplied to the extent of that data.[180]

11–047 Education data

The DPA 2018 provides a number of exemptions for proprietors of and teachers at schools when processing a record of information relating to an individual who is or has been a pupil at the school, where that information originates from, or was supplied by or on behalf of, the local education authority, a teacher at the school, the pupil or the pupil's parent – 'education data.'[181] 'Data concerning health' is excluded from education data.[182]

(1) The access right is disapplied to education data where the application of that right to the personal data would be likely to cause serious harm to the physical or mental health of the data subject or another individual.[183]

(2) Where education data is processed by a court and that data consists of information supplied in a report or other evidence given to the court in the course of proceedings to which specified court rules apply and in accordance with which the data may be withheld from the data subject, then the fifth group of provisions is disapplied to the extent of that data.[184]

11–048 Child abuse data

The DPA 2018 disapplies the access right where a request for 'child abuse data' is made in the exercise of a power conferred by an enactment or rule of law and:

(a) the data subject is aged under 18 and the access request is made by a person having parental responsibility for the data subject; or

(b) the data subject is incapable of managing his or her own affairs and the access request is made by a person appointed by a court to manage the data subject's affairs.[185]

---

179 'Education data' is defined in DPA 2018 Sch 3 para 17 to mean 'personal data which constitutes an educational record but is not data concerning health,' 'educational record' is defined in DPA 2018 Sch 3 para 13 to mean a record to which paragraph 14, 15 or 16 of that Schedule applies, and 'data concerning health' is defined in DPA 2018 s 205(1) to mean 'personal data relating to the physical or mental health of an individual, including the provision of health care services, which reveals information about his or her health status.'

180 DPA 2018 Sch 3 para 9(1). As to the meaning of the 'fifth group of provisions.' see §11–017. The court rules are specified in DPA 2018 Sch 3 para 9(2).

181 DPA 2018 Sch 3 para 14. The types of school to which the exemption applies are listed in para 14(3) and the full list of persons to which the exemption applies are listed in para 14. There are variants for Scotland (para 15) and Northern Ireland (para 16). The terms 'pupil', 'school', 'teacher', and 'education authority' are all defined in para 17(1).

182 'Data concerning health' is defined in DPA 2018 s 205(1) to mean 'personal data relating to the physical or mental health of an individual, including the provision of health care services, which reveals information about his or her health status.'

183 DPA 2018 Sch 3 para 19 in conjunction with the definition of 'serious harm test' in para 17(2). The access right is provided by GDPR Art 15, as to which see §§10–014 to 10–017.

184 DPA 2018 Sch 3 para 18(1). As to the meaning of the 'fifth group of provisions,' see §11–017. The court rules are specified in DPA 2018 Sch 3 para 18(2).

185 DPA 2018 Sch 3 para 21. 'Child abuse data' is defined to mean personal data consisting of information as to whether the data subject is or has been the subject of, or may be at risk of, child abuse; and child abuse includes non-accidental physical injury to, and physical and emotional neglect, ill-treatment and sexual abuse of, an individual aged under 18. The exemption does not apply in relation to Scotland.

11– 049 Statutory prohibitions etc

The DPA 2018 disapplies the sixth group of provisions in respect of personal data consisting of information the disclosure of which is prohibited by specific statutory provisions.[186]

5. DEROGATIONS

11– 050 Journalistic etc purposes

The GDPR requires each Member State to provide for 'exemptions or derogations' from various of its provisions where processing is 'carried out for journalistic purposes or the purposes of academic, artistic or literary expression...if they are necessary to reconcile the right to the protection of personal data with the freedom of expression and information.'[187] The DPA 2018 defines 'the special purposes' to mean one or more of the purposes of journalism, academic purposes, artistic purposes and literary purposes.[188] Where:

(a) the processing of personal data is being carried out with a view to the publication by a person of journalistic, academic, artistic or literary material; and

(b) the controller reasonably believes that the publication of the material would be in the public interest,

then the ninth group of provisions is disapplied 'to the extent that the controller reasonably believes that the application of those provisions would be incompatible with the special purposes.'[189] Given that Member States are obliged to:

> reconcile the right to the protection of personal data pursuant to this Regulation with the right to freedom of expression and information, including processing for journalistic purposes and the purposes of academic, artistic or literary expression...[190]

the unqualified disapplication of all the rights conferred and obligations imposed by the GDPR that go to constitute the right to the protection of personal data is questionable.[191] In relation

---

186 DPA 2018 Sch 4 paras 2-6. The statutory provisions concern, in general terns, information in relation to: (a) human fertilisation and embryology; (b) adoption; (c) special educational needs; (d) parental orders; and (e) in Scotland, information provided by the Principal Reporter for children's hearings. As to the meaning of the 'sixth group of provisions,' see §11– 018.

187 GDPR Art 85(2). The requirement of a reconciliation of the individual's right to the protection of personal data with the right to freedom of expression is reiterated in the recital (153):

> Member States law should reconcile the rules governing freedom of expression and information, including journalistic, academic, artistic and or literary expression with the right to the protection of personal data pursuant to this Regulation. The processing of personal data solely for journalistic purposes, or for the purposes of academic, artistic or literary expression should be subject to derogations or exemptions from certain provisions of this Regulation if necessary to reconcile the right to the protection of personal data with the right to freedom of expression and information, as enshrined in Article 11 of the Charter....Therefore, Member States should adopt legislative measures which lay down the exemptions and derogations necessary for the purpose of balancing those fundamental rights...

188 DPA 2018 Sch 2 para 26(1). Neither the Act nor the GDPR indicates if, when determining whether processing of personal data is carried out for the special purposes, the focus is on the occupation held by the person carrying out the activity that is said to be part of the special purposes, on the nature of that activity, on the objective of that activity or on some combination of them.

189 DPA 2018 Sch 2 para 26(2)-(3). As to the meaning of 'the ninth group of provisions' see §11– 021. In determining whether publication would be in the public interest, the controller must take into account the special importance of the public interest in the freedom of expression and information: DPA 2018 Sch 2 para 26(4). Journalistic, academic, artistic and literary expression are included within 'freedom of expression and information': GDPR recital (153). The DPA 2018 omits any balancing requirement on the controller to take into account the protection of personal data: cf GDPR Arts 2(1) and 85(1) and recitals (1), (2), (4), (11) and (153).

190 GDPR Art 85(1).

191 See also Charter of Fundamental Rights Arts 8, 47 and 52. Labelling DPA 2018 Sch 2 para 26 as a 'limitation' rather than a 'derogation' is a linguistic stunt.

to general processing, the DPA 2018 also introduces procedural obstacles to both regulatory enforcement and private claims which are placed in the way of the Information Commissioner and a data subject upon the say-so of a controller that its processing of personal data for the special purposes.[192]

11–051 Archiving purposes

Provided that the controller is processing personal data for archiving purposes in the public interest, then the seventh group of provisions is disapplied, but only to the extent that the application of those provisions would prevent or seriously impair the achievement of those archiving purposes.[193] The disapplication will not apply where the processing is likely to cause substantial damage or substantial distress to a data subject.[194]

11–052 Research and statistics

Provided that the controller has appropriate safeguards for the rights and freedoms of the data subject, where personal data is being processed for personal data for scientific or historical research purposes, or for statistical purposes, the eighth group of provisions is disapplied, but only to the extent that the application of those provisions would prevent or seriously impair the achievement of those purposes.[195] The disapplication will not apply where:

(a) the processing is likely to cause substantial damage or substantial distress to a data subject;[196]

(b) the processing is carried out for the purposes of measures or decisions with respect to a particular data subject, unless the purposes for which the processing is necessary include the purposes of approved medical research;[197] or

(c) in the case of the access right, the results of the research or any resulting statistics are made available in a form that identifies a data subject.[198]

192 See further §§48–056 to 48–059.

193 DPA 2018 Sch 2 para 28(1). As to the meaning of 'seventh group of provisions,' see §11–019.

194 DPA 2018 s 19(2).

195 DPA 2018 Sch 2 para 27 and GDPR Art 89(1). As to the meaning of 'the eighth group of provisions,' see §11–020. Appropriate safeguards may include encryption or pseudonymisation: GDPR Art 6(4)(e). In relation to appropriate safeguards, see also GDPR Art 40(3), (5), 41(4), 42(2) and 46.

196 DPA 2018 s 19(2).

197 DPA 2018 s 19(3). 'Approved medical research' is defined in DPA 2018 s 19(4).

198 DPA 2018 Sch 2 para 27(3).

CHAPTER 12

Law enforcement processing: continuing obligations

1. INTRODUCTION

2–001 Background

The processing of personal data by competent authorities for law enforcement purposes is not governed by the GDPR. This reflects the European Union's acknowledgment at the time of the Lisbon Treaty that specific rules on the protection of personal data and the free movement of personal data in the fields of judicial co-operation in criminal matters and police co-operation were likely to be necessary because of the specific nature of those fields.[1] Instead, simultaneously with the adoption of the GDPR, the European Parliament and the Council of the European Union adopted a directive

> on the protection of natural persons with regard to the processing of personal data by competent authorities for the purposes of the prevention, investigation, detection or prosecution of criminal offences or the execution of criminal penalties, and on the free movement of such data.[2]

This directive is generally termed the 'Law Enforcement Directive' – the 'LED.' The processing of personal data by 'competent authorities' for those purposes is generally termed 'law enforcement processing.'

2–002 Law Enforcement Directive

Within the United Kingdom the LED only applies to criminal justice processing falling within the scope of EU law to which the United Kingdom has opted-in.[3] Parliament could have enacted different rules governing domestic law enforcement processing falling outside the scope of the LED. However, it chose not to do so. Rather, it opted for a single, universal data processing regime, covering all domestic and trans-national law enforcement processing.[4] As such, the LED is a legitimate aid to the interpretation of the law enforcement processing provisions of the DPA 2018.[5]

---

1 Declaration No 21 on the protection of personal data in the fields of judicial co-operation in criminal matters and police co-operation, annexed to the final act of the intergovernmental conference which adopted the Treaty of Lisbon. Directive 95/46/EC did not apply to the processing of personal data in the course of an activity falling outside the scope of what was European Community law, including, for example, the 'activities of the State in areas of criminal law': Art 3(2). Nevertheless, the DPA 1998, which implemented the Directive 95/46/EC, applied to all data controllers, including the police and security bodies. There was one specific set of circumstances in which the DPA 1998 did not apply. Part 4 of the Criminal Justice and Data Protection (Protocol No 36) Regulations 2014 applied to processing within the scope of Council Framework Decision 2008/977/JHA. That Council Framework Decision governed processing of personal data in the areas of judicial cooperation in criminal matters and police cooperation. The scope of application of that Framework Decision was limited to the processing of personal data transmitted or made available between Member States. The Framework Decision had a limited scope of application to the United Kingdom because the United Kingdom had the right to decide whether to opt-in to EU measures in this area, pursuant to Protocol No 21 on the position of the United Kingdom and Ireland in respect of the area of freedom, security and justice, annexed to the TEU and to the TFEU. Under Article 6a of that Protocol, the United Kingdom and Ireland are not bound by the rules laid down in the LED when their processing of personal data is carried out in the context of activities which: (a) fall within the scope of Chapter 4 or Chapter 5 of Title V of Part Three of the TFEU, and (b) are forms of judicial cooperation in criminal matters or police cooperation that are governed by EU instruments that the UK and Ireland have not opted into. The 2014 Regulations disapplied the DPA 1998 but incorporated many of the components of that regime.

2 The need for this resulted from the scope of EU law having expanded to encompass judicial cooperation in criminal matters and police cooperation. The EU legislature recognised the need for specific legislation to harmonise the protection of rights in relation to the processing of personal data by competent authorities in the area of criminal justice, having regard to the growth of activity in that area, and increasing use of new technologies.

3 LED Art 2(3) and recital (99); *R (El Gizouli) v SSHD* [2019] EWHC 60 (Admin), [2019] 1 WLR 3463 at [172]-[174] (a point not in dispute on appeal).

4 Explanatory Notes to DPA 2018 paras 38-40.

5 *R (El Gizouli) v SSHD* [2020] UKSC 10 at [8], [208]. However, the Divisional Court held that questions arising

12–003 Data Protection Act 2018

Part 3 of the DPA 2018[6] implements the LED in the United Kingdom and otherwise makes provision about law enforcement processing.[7] In accordance with the Government's Transposition Guidance, the approach taken in Part 3 of the DPA 2018 is broadly to copy-out the LED wherever possible and only to elaborate where such elaboration is necessary to reflect UK-drafting style, clarify the legal effect of a provision or take advantage of flexibility afforded by the terms of the LED.[8]

12–004 LED and GDPR: differences

The obligations on a competent authority when processing for the law enforcement purposes divide into:

— Obligations that persist whenever there is law enforcement processing of personal data – 'continuing obligations.' These are considered in this chapter.

— Obligations that are triggered by the data subject exercising a right conferred by Part 3 of the DPA 2018, usually by the data subject giving the controller a notice. There are considered in Chapter 13.

The main continuing obligation is the requirement on the controller to be responsible for, and be able to demonstrate, compliance with six data protection principles.[9] In this general arrangement of obligations, the regime governing law enforcement processing and the regime governing general processing are much the same. There are, however, certain differences. Most notably:

(1) The continuing obligations imposed on a competent authority when engaged in law enforcement processing are less burdensome.

(2) The rights conferred on a data subject when his or her personal data is the subject of law enforcement processing are fewer and less extensive than those for general processing.

(3) The impact of the dilution of the continuing obligations and data subject rights is ameliorated by enhanced obligations on controllers and processors to record and log their processing activities, with the records and logs being made available to the Information Commissioner.[10]

This difference reflects the particular importance that is attached to the accomplishment of security and justice, and the recognition that processing of personal data is essential for its attainment.

12–005 Scope of processing

For the purposes of law enforcement processing, the term 'processing' covers the same activities and states as it does for general processing.[11] In order for such an activity or state to constitute 'processing' either:

---

under Part 3 of the 2018 Act not governed by EU law should not be analysed by reference to the EU Charter (at [178], a point not commented on by the Supreme Court on appeal).

6 Sections 29-81 and Schs 7 and 8.

7 DPA 2018 s 1(4). For an overview of the splitting of the field of data protection into four regulatory sectors, see §8–002 and §8–010.

8 Explanatory Notes to the DPA 2018 para 57.

9 DPA 2018 s 34(3). In relation to general processing, this is called the 'accountability principle': see §9–003.

10 See in particular DPA 2018 ss 61 and 62 and §§12–040 to 12–041. The efficacy of this counter-balance depends on the Information Commissioner initiating requests to controllers and processors for records and logs to be made available, and for those records and logs then to be scrutinised.

11 See §8–018.

— that processing must be wholly or partly by automated means; or
— the personal data must form part of a filing system or be intended to form part of a filing system.[12]

In order to constitute 'law enforcement processing,' such processing must be by a 'competent authority.'[13] Further, each of the continuing obligations and each of the rights applies only to the processing of personal data for a 'law enforcement purpose.'[14]

12– 006 Law enforcement purposes

The phrase 'the law enforcement purposes' is defined to mean the purposes of the prevention, investigation, detection or prosecution of criminal offences or the execution of criminal penalties, including the safeguarding against and the prevention of threats to public security.[15] The DPA 2018 does not indicate whether 'criminal offences,' 'criminal penalties' and 'public security' extends to criminal offences against and criminal penalties under the law of any country in the world and threats to public security in any part of the world.[16] The Directive suggests that it is not confined to 'criminal offences' etc within the meaning of the law of any Member State, but that it will extend to criminal offences against and criminal penalties under the law of any country in the world and threats to public security in any part of the world.[17]

12– 007 Competent authorities

A person is a 'competent authority' for the purposes of law enforcement processing either because that person falls within the statutory description of competent authorities (which are listed in Schedule 7 to the DPA 2018) or because that person has statutory functions for any of the law enforcement purposes.[18] In relation to the statutory description of competent

---

[12] DPA 2018 s 29(1); LED Art 2(2). As to the meaning of a 'filing system,' see §8– 028.

[13] DPA 2018 s 29(1); LED Art 2(2).

[14] DPA 2018 ss 35(1), 36(1), 37, 38(1), 39(1), 40, 41(1) and 43(2). There is nothing to suggest that the obligations and rights applicable to law enforcement processing arise only where a law enforcement purpose is the sole purpose for which a competent authority processes the personal data.

[15] DPA 2018 s 31. These purposes form the recurrent theme of the LED: see Art 1(1) and recitals (3), (4), (7), (11), (12), (15), (26), (27), (29), (34), (35), (44), (64) and (72).

[16] General principles of statutory interpretation point against such a wide-reaching meaning: *Clark v Oceanic Contractors Inc* [1983] 2 AC 130 at 145, 152; *Lawson v Serco* [2006] UKHL 3, [2006] ICR 250 at [6]; *R (Al-Skeini) v SS for Defence* [2007] UKHL 26, [2008] 1 AC 153 at [11], [38], [86], [137]; *Duncombe v SS for Children etc (no 2)* [2011] UKSC 36, [2011] ICR 495; *Ravat v Halliburton* [2012] UKSC 1, [2012] ICR 389; *Cox v Ergo Verischerung AG* [2014] UKSC 22, [2014] AC 1379 at [27], [29]; *R (XH and AI) v SSHD* [2017] EWCA Civ 41, [2018] QB 355 at [97]. See also DPA 2018 ss 38(3), 44(4), 45(4), 48(3), 68(7), 72-78 and 80. Applying this principle, references in the DPA 2018 to, for example, 'national security' are to be read as the national security of the United Kingdom, and not that of other countries. Where there is a nexus between an offence against the law of a foreign state and the United Kingdom, it may be that the prevention, investigation, detection or prosecution of a criminal offence under the law of that foreign state might prevent a threat to public security in the United Kingdom, thus causing processing for that purpose to fall within the definition of a 'law enforcement purpose.' Given that there is a proscription on any transfer of personal data to a third country or an international organisation unless the transfer is 'necessary for any of the law enforcement purposes,' the point is of particular importance to transfers: see DPA 2018 s 73(2). The point appears to have been assumed, rather than argued, in *R (El Gizouli) v SSHD* [2020] UKSC 10 at [152], [226]-[227]. Various provisions in Part 3 of the Act point to it having the wide-reaching meaning, see eg DPA 2018 s 73(7).

[17] LED recital (13) provides: 'A criminal offence within the meaning of this Directive should be an autonomous concept of Union law as interpreted by the Court of Justice of the European Union....' Other recitals support this extension to 'third countries': LED recitals (4), (11), (12), (15), (26), (72) and (82). This would then leave it to the other conditions in DPA 2018 s 73 and other instruments, such as the ECHR, to control transfers on the basis of the nature of the offence, the penalty, the criminal procedures and so forth.

[18] DPA 2018 s 30(1); LED Art 3(7). 'Statutory function' means a function under or by virtue of an enactment: DPA 2018 s 30(7). The term 'enactment' includes enactments comprised in subordinate legislation, enactments and subordinate legislation of the Scottish Parliament, Northern Ireland legislation and Measures and Acts of and under the National Assembly for Wales: DPA 2018 s 205(1).

authorities, the list includes:

— all United Kingdom government departments, other than a non-ministerial government department;
— the Scottish Ministers;
— all Northern Ireland departments;
— the Welsh Ministers;
— the chief constable of a police force or police service;
— the Commissioners for Her Majesty's Revenue and Customs;
— the Director General of the National Crime Agency;
— the Director of the Serious Fraud Office;
— the Financial Conduct Authority;
— the Health and Safety Executive;
— the Food Standards Agency;
— the Director of Public Prosecutions;
— the Information Commissioners; and
— all courts and tribunals,

as well as various other similar bodies.[19] In relation to persons having statutory functions for any of the law enforcement purposes, this will mainly (but not exclusively) be public authorities of one sort or another, but in all cases are persons having a statutory power or duty in relation to the prevention, investigation, detection or prosecution of criminal offences etc.[20] The intelligence services are excluded from the term 'competent authorities.'[21]

12– 008 Data subject categories

In processing personal data for any of the law enforcement purposes, a clear distinction must, where relevant and as far as possible, be made between personal data relating to different categories of data subject, such as:

(a) persons suspected of having committed or being about to commit a criminal offence;
(b) persons convicted of a criminal offence;
(c) persons who are or may be victims of a criminal offence;
(d) witnesses or other persons with information about offences.[22]

This distinction informs various continuing obligations on controllers and processors.[23]

---

19 These are listed in DPA 2018 Sch 7.

20 A sewerage undertaker is an example of a person that is not a public authority that has powers to investigate and prosecute criminal offences: see Water Industry Act 1991 s 211.

21 DPA 2018 s 30(2). These are the Security Service, the Secret Intelligence Service and the Government Communications Headquarters: DPA 2018 s 30(7).

22 DPA 2018 s 38(3); LED Art 6.

23 DPA 2018 ss 59(5), 61(2) and 67(4)(a). It is arguable that DPA 2018 s 38 implements Article 6 by requiring a distinction to be drawn between different types of data subject, so that the section applies only in the specific context of compliance with the obligations imposed by the fourth data protection principle. This contention is supported by the Explanatory Notes to DPA 2018 para 187:

> In the law enforcement context, the principle of accuracy of data must take account of the circumstances in which data is being processed. It is accepted that, for example, statements by victims and witnesses containing personal data will be based on the subjective perceptions of the person making the statement. Such statements are not always verifiable and are subject to challenge during the legal process. In such cases, the requirement for accuracy would not apply to the content of the statement but to the fact that a specific statement has been made. Section 38(2) recognises the distinction between personal data based on facts (for example, the details relating to an individual's conviction for an offence) and data based on personal assessments, such as a witness statement. The requirement to keep personal data up to date must also be viewed in this context. If an individual's conviction is overturned on appeal, police records must be amended to reflect that fact. However, this principle would not require the retrospective alteration of a witness statement which the appellate court found to be unreliable.

2–009 Joint controllers

Where two or more controllers act together as controllers to decide the purpose and means of any data processing they are known as 'joint controllers.'[24] Other than where specified by statute, joint controllers must, in a transparent manner, determine their respective responsibilities for compliance with the law enforcement data processing requirements by means of an arrangement between them.[25] The arrangements put in place by the controllers must designate which controller is to be the contact point for data subjects.[26] The objective is to avoid data subjects being 'passed around' by different controllers that are engaged in processing their data.

2–010 Other terminology

For the purposes of law enforcement processing, certain terms bear the same meaning, or a similar meaning, as they bear for the purposes of general processing.[27] The following terms have a particular meaning in relation to law enforcement processing:

(1) 'Controller.' For the purposes of law enforcement processing, the 'controller' means the competent authority that, whether alone or jointly with others:
    (a) determines the purposes and means of the processing of personal data; or
    (b) where the personal data is processed only for purposes required by an enactment to be processed and by means by which it is required to be processed, is the competent authority on which the obligation to process the data is so imposed.[28]

    Accordingly, if a competent authority outsources processing which by enactment it is obliged to undertake, it will remain the controller for the purposes of law enforcement processing.
(2) 'Third country.' For the purposes of law enforcement processing, 'third country' means a country or territory other than an EU Member State.[29]
(3) 'Recipient.' For the purposes of law enforcement processing, 'recipient' does not include a public authority to whom disclosure is or may be made in the framework of a particular inquiry in accordance with the law.[30]
(4) 'Consent.' For the purposes of law enforcement purposes, the term 'consent' is undefined.[31]

2–011 Data protection principles

In relation to the processing of personal data by a competent authority for the law enforcement purposes, there are six data protection principles that the controller is responsible for and with

---

24 DPA 2018 s 58(1); LED Art 21. For example, the Police National Computer is managed on behalf of all police forces in the UK with individual chief constables jointly determining the purposes and means of the processing of the personal data held on the database, and in that situation the chief constables will be acting as joint controllers: see Explanatory Notes to the DPA 2018 para 177.

25 DPA 2018 s 58(2).

26 DPA 2018 s 58(3).

27 See §§8–010 to 8–034.

28 DPA 2018 s 32(1)-(2).

29 DPA 2018 s 33(7). Unlike for general processing, 'third country' does not cover Iceland, Norway and Liechtenstein: see §8–032.

30 DPA 2018 s 33(5); LED Art 3(10). Contrast the position in relation to general processing: see §8–026.

31 Contrast the position in relation to both general processing and intelligence services processing: DPA 2018 s 84(2); GDPR Art 4(11); cf LED recital (35); and see §8–024.

which the controller must be able to demonstrate compliance:[32]

(1) The processing of personal data for those purposes must be lawful and fair.[33]

(2) The law enforcement purpose for which personal data is collected must be specified, explicit and legitimate, and thereafter it must not be processed in a manner that is incompatible with the purpose for which it is collected.[34]

(3) Personal data processed for any of the law enforcement purposes must be adequate, relevant and not excessive in relation to the purpose for which it is processed.[35]

(4) Personal data processed for any of the law enforcement purposes must be accurate and, where necessary, kept up-to-date and every reasonable step must be taken to ensure that personal data that is inaccurate, having regard to the law enforcement purpose for which it is processed, is rectified without delay.[36]

(5) Personal data processed for any of the law enforcement purposes must be kept for no longer than is necessary for the purpose for which it is processed.[37]

(6) Personal data processed for any of the law enforcement purposes must be processed in a manner that ensures appropriate security of the personal data.[38]

Non-compliance with the data protection principles exposes the controller both to regulatory action (through the Information Commissioner)[39] and to a private law claim from the individual to whom the personal data relates.[40]

12–012 Other controller obligations

In addition to responsibility for, and ability to demonstrate, compliance with the six data protection principles, there are other continuing obligations imposed on a competent authority when processing personal data for law enforcement purposes:

(1) Obligations imposed on a controller when processing sensitive personal data.[41] These are additional to the obligation to comply with the six data protection principles.

(2) Obligations relating to the set up and internal organisation of controller or processor.[42] These obligations cover the internal systems that a controller and a processor must have, data protection impact assessments, record-keeping requirements, data protection officers, co-operation with the Information

32 DPA 2018 s 34(3). In relation to the comparable position in respect of general processing, see §9–004.

33 DPA 2018 s 35(1); LED Art 4(1)(a). See further §§12–014 to 12–022. In relation to the comparable position in respect of general processing (which has, in addition, a requirement of transparency), see GDPR Art 5(1)(a).

34 DPA 2018 s 36(1); LED Art 4(1)(b). See further §§12–023 to 12–025. In relation to the comparable position in respect of general processing, see GDPR Art 5(1)(b).

35 DPA 2018 s 37 ; LED Art 4(1)(c). See further §§12–026 to 12–027. In relation to the comparable position in respect of general processing, see GDPR Art 5(1)(c).

36 DPA 2018 s 38(1); LED Art 4(1)(d). See further §§12–028 to 12–031. In relation to the comparable position in respect of general processing, see GDPR Art 5(1)(d).

37 DPA 2018 s 39(1); LED Art 4(1)(e). See further §§12–032 to 12–033. In relation to the comparable position in respect of general processing, see GDPR Art 5(1)(e).

38 DPA 2018 s 40; LED Art 4(1)(f). See further §§12–034 to 12–036. In relation to the comparable position in respect of general processing, see GDPR Art 5(1)(f).

39 DPA 2018 ss 2(1)(c), 2(2), 116(2) and Sch 13 paras 1 and 2. Regulatory enforcement is considered at §§48–014 to 48–055.

40 LED Art 54. The claim would be one in tort for breach of statutory duty. Private law claims are considered at §§48–005 to 48–013.

41 DPA 2018 ss 35(3)-(8), 42 and Sch 8; LED Art 10. This is considered at §§12–016 to 12–021. 'Sensitive personal data' is not a term used in the DPA 2018 or the LED, but conveniently describes the data the processing of which constitutes 'sensitive processing' as defined in DPA 2018 s 35(8).

42 DPA 2018 ss 55-71, 81. This is considered at §§12–037 to 12–047.

Commissioner and so forth.

(3) Obligations engaged by the international transfer of personal data.[43]

Non-compliance with any of these obligations exposes the controller both to regulatory action (through the Information Commissioner)[44] and to a private law claim from the individual to whom the personal data relates.[45]

12– 013 Processor obligations

By definition, a processor is a person who processes personal data on behalf of a controller, other than someone who is the employee of the controller.[46] A controller may use a processor to carry out processing of personal data on behalf of the controller only where the processor has provided guarantees to implement appropriate technical and organisational measures that are sufficient to secure that the processing will meet the requirements of the law enforcement processing regime.[47] The relationship between a controller and a processor must be governed by a prior written contract that sets out the subject-matter and duration of the processing, the nature and purpose of the processing, the type of personal data and categories of data subject involved, and the obligations and rights of the controller and processor.[48] Given the record-keeping obligations on a processor,[49] the contract should stipulate that the controller must provide the processor with sufficient information about the processing that the processor is to carry out such that the processor is able to comply with those record-keeping obligations. A processor who has access to personal data may not process that data except on instruction from the controller or in order to comply with a legal obligation.[50] If a processor over-steps the mark and determines the purposes and means of processing, then for the purposes of the law enforcement provisions of the DPA 2018 that processor is treated as a controller in respect of that processing, with all the attendant obligations and liabilities.[51] A controller may use a processor to carry out processing of personal data on behalf of the controller only where the processor has provided guarantees to implement appropriate technical and organisational measures that are sufficient to secure that the processing will meet the requirements of the law enforcement processing regime.[52]

---

43 DPA 2018 ss 72-79. Considered further at §§12– 048 to 12– 058.

44 DPA 2018 ss 2(1)(c), 2(2), 116(2) and Sch 13 paras 1 and 2. Regulatory enforcement is considered at §§48– 014 to 48– 055.

45 LED Art 54. The claim would be one in tort for breach of statutory duty. Private law claims are considered at §§48– 005 to 48– 013.

46 DPA 2018 s 32(3); LED Art 3(9).

47 DPA 2018 s 59(1)-(2). See further §§12– 034 to 12– 038.

48 DPA 2018 s 59. The contract must, in particular, provide that the processor must: (a) act only on instructions from the controller; (b) ensure that the persons authorised to process personal data are subject to an appropriate duty of confidentiality; (c) assist the controller by any appropriate means to ensure compliance with the rights of the data subject under DPA 2018 Part 3; (d) at the end of the provision of services by the processor to the controller either delete or return to the controller (at the choice of the controller) the personal data to which the services relate, and delete copies of the personal data unless subject to a legal obligation to store the copies; (e) make available to the controller all information necessary to demonstrate compliance with DPA 2018 s 59; and (f) comply with the requirements of s 59(3)-(4) for engaging sub-processors: DPA 2018 s 59(6).

49 See §12– 040.

50 DPA 2018 s 60.

51 DPA 2018 s 59(8); LED Art 22(5).

52 DPA 2018 s 59(1)-(2). The requirements of the law enforcement processing regime means the obligations and rights covered in Chapters 12 and 13 of this work.

2. LAWFULLY AND FAIRLY

12–014 First data protection principle

The first data protection principle, which the controller is responsible for and must be able to demonstrate, is that:

> the processing of personal data for any of the law enforcement purposes must be lawful and fair.[53]

Unlike the equivalent principle for general processing of personal data, the first data protection principle does not include a requirement that the processing be 'transparent.'[54] Neither the DPA 2018 nor the LED spells out what is meant by 'fair' in processing personal data for law enforcement purposes.[55]

12–015 Lawfully

The Act does spell out what is meant by 'lawful' for the purposes of law enforcement processing:

> The processing of personal data for any of the law enforcement purposes is lawful only if and to the extent that it is based on law and either:
>
> (a) the data subject has given consent to the processing for that purpose, or
>
> (b) the processing is necessary for the performance of a task carried out for that purpose by a competent authority.[56]

There are thus two requirements, with the second requirement capable of being satisfied in either of two ways. The first requirement – that the processing is based on law – requires that the processing for the law enforcement purpose be mandated by statute or some other externally imposed legal obligation: a contractual obligation will not by itself suffice.[57] In relation to the first way of satisfying the second requirement – the consent of the data subject to the processing for that purpose – this requires that the data subject has given consent to the processing of his or her personal data 'for that [law enforcement] purpose.' Thus, while the word 'consent' is not qualified by the epithet 'explicit,'[58] a general consent or a consent that otherwise does not specify the particular law enforcement purpose for which the personal data is being processed will not suffice.[59] Whether that specificity must go beyond the description

---

53 DPA 2018 s 35(1); LED Art 4(1)(a). The responsibility for compliance with the first data protection principle and ability to demonstrate compliance with that principle rests exclusively with the controller: DPA 2018 s 34(3); LED Art 4(4).

54 Although LED recital (26) refers to the need for processing to be transparent, that requirement is not included in LED Art 4(1)(a). DPA 2018 Explanatory Notes para 180 acknowledges this omission. In relation to the transparency requirement for general processing, see §9–006 and §§9–016 to 9–022.

55 LED recital (26) makes clear that 'fairly' does not in itself prevent the law-enforcement authorities from carrying out activities such as covert investigations or video surveillance. Such activities can be done for the purposes of the prevention, investigation, detection or prosecution of criminal offences or the execution of criminal penalties, including the safeguarding against and the prevention of threats to public security, as long as they are laid down by law and constitute a necessary and proportionate measure in a democratic society with due regard for the legitimate interests of the natural person concerned. In relation to the first processing principle for general processing, neither the DPA 2018 nor the GDPR spells out what is meant by 'fairly': see §9–015.

56 DPA 2018 s 35(2); LED Art 8(1). Although consent is not provided for in LED Art 8(1), recital (35) indicates that Member States may provide by law that data subjects can consent to the processing of their data for the purposes of the Directive. The LED identifies two potential examples where consent could be relied upon to process personal data for law enforcement purposes: (a) DNA tests in criminal investigations; or (b) the monitoring of the location of a data subject with electronic tags for the execution of criminal penalties.

57 LED Art 8(1), recital (35), ie 'based on [EU] or Member State law.' This is the equivalent of the fifth basis of 'lawful' processing for general processing: see §9–012 As to the meaning of 'necessary' in this context, see §8–034.

58 Contrast the comparable requirement for general processing: see §9–008.

59 For the purposes of law enforcement processing, 'consent' is not defined: see §8–024.

in the definition of 'law enforcement purposes' – ie that the processing is for the purposes of the prevention, investigation, detection or prosecution of criminal offences or the execution of criminal penalties, including the safeguarding against and the prevention of threats to public security[60] – is not clear.[61] The second way of satisfying the second requirement – the processing is necessary for the performance of a task carried out for that purpose by a competent authority – is similar to the fifth basis for 'lawfully' in relation to general processing, except that in relation to law enforcement processing the task must be 'carried out for [the law enforcement] purpose, rather than 'carried out in the public interest.'[62]

2– 016 Sensitive processing proscription

Supplementing the first data protection principle is a qualified proscription against the processing for law enforcement purposes of:

(a) personal data revealing racial or ethnic origin, political opinions, religious or philosophical beliefs or trade union membership;
(b) genetic data,[63] or of biometric data,[64] for the purpose of uniquely identifying an individual;
(c) data concerning health;[65]
(d) data concerning an individual's sex life or sexual orientation.

The processing of such personal data for law enforcement purposes is termed 'sensitive processing.'[66] Sensitive processing for any of the law enforcement purposes is permitted in only two situations.[67]

2– 017 First permitted situation

The first situation in which sensitive processing is permitted for any of the law enforcement purposes is where:

(a) the data subject has given consent to the processing for the law enforcement purpose; and
(b) at the time when the processing is carried out, the controller has an appropriate policy document in place.[68]

The consent required to be given is the same consent required as a way of satisfying the second

---

60 DPA 2018 s 31.

61 It might be that it is sufficient that the purposes are described in the same way as is required for compliance with DPA 2018 ss 44(1)(c), 45(2), 58(1), 59(5)(b) and 61(2)(d).

62 In relation to the analogous provision for general processing, see §9– 012. As to the meaning of 'necessary', see §8– 034.

63 Defined to mean 'personal data relating to the inherited or acquired genetic characteristics of an individual which gives unique information about the physiology or the health of that individual and which results, in particular, from an analysis of a biological sample from the individual in question': DPA 2018 s 205(1).

64 Defined to mean 'personal data resulting from specific technical processing relating to the physical, physiological or behavioural characteristics of an individual, which allows or confirms the unique identification of that individual, such as facial images or dactyloscopic data': DPA 2018 s 205(1). As to the requirement for 'unique identification,' see *R (Bridges) v Chief Constable of South Wales Police* [2019] EWHC 2341 (Admin), [2020] 1 WLR 672 at [130]-[132].

65 Defined to mean 'personal data relating to the physical or mental health of an individual, including the provision of health care services, which reveals information about his or her health status': DPA 2018 s 205(1).

66 DPA 2018 s 35(8). The processing of such data is, by its nature, considered to be particularly sensitive in relation to fundamental rights and freedoms so as to merit specific protection on the basis that the context of their processing could create significant risks to the fundamental rights and freedoms: LED Art 10 and recitals (37) and (51).

67 DPA 2018 s 35(3); LED Art 10, recitals (37), (51).

68 DPA 2018 s 35(4). This situation does not have provenance in the LED: under Art 10 an indispensable precondition for sensitive processing is that that processing is 'strictly necessary.'

requirement of the first data protection principle.[69] In this first permitted situation, the critical safeguards for sensitive processing are the requirements for there to be an 'appropriate policy document'[70] and for the controller's record of processing activities to include information as to how the sensitive processing is lawful.[71]

12–018 Second permitted situation

The second situation in which sensitive processing is permitted for any of the law enforcement purposes is where:

(a) the processing is strictly necessary for the law enforcement purpose;
(b) the processing meets at least one of the conditions specified in Schedule 8 to the DPA 2018; and
(c) at the time when the processing is carried out, the controller has an appropriate policy document in place.[72]

In this second permitted situation, the absence of data subject consent to the processing for the law enforcement purpose is remedied by the twin requirements of the processing being 'strictly necessary' for the law enforcement purpose and satisfaction of one of the conditions in Schedule 8. Given that where there is no data subject consent, the first data protection principle already requires the processing to be 'necessary' for the law enforcement purpose:[73] the insertion of 'strictly' appears to take out the balancing considerations that are otherwise legitimate in determining what is 'necessary.'[74] The conditions specified in Schedule 8 are extensive and resemble those in the previous data protection regime.[75] As in the first permitted situation, the critical safeguards for sensitive processing are the requirements for there to be an 'appropriate policy document'[76] and for the controller's record of processing activities to include information as to how the sensitive processing is lawful.[77]

12–019 Schedule 8 conditions

The second situation in which sensitive processing is permitted has as one of its requirements that one of the conditions in DPA 2018 Schedule 8 is satisfied. These conditions are:

(1) The processing:
  (a) is necessary for the exercise of a function conferred on a person by an enactment or rule of law, and
  (b) is necessary for reasons of substantial public interest.[78]

---

69 See §12–015.

70 As to the meaning of this, see §12–020.

71 As to the specific requirements for the record of processing in relation to sensitive processing, see §§12–016 to 12–021.

72 DPA 2018 s 35(5); LED Art 10.

73 DPA 2018 s 35(2)(b).

74 This is supported by the requirement of 'strictly necessary' deriving from LED Art 10 and the conventional EU law interpretation of the term 'necessary' simpliciter: see §8–034. See further: *TK v Asociatia de Proprietari bloc M5A-ScaraA* (C-708/18), CJEU, 28 January 2020 at [47]-[49]; *Staatssecretaris van Justitie en Veiligheid v A and others* (C-79/18) [2019] 4 WLR 129 at [56]-[70]; cf *R (Bridges) v Chief Constable of South Wales Police* [2019] EWHC 2341 (Admin), [2020] 1 WLR 672 at [136].

75 That is, under DPA 1998 Sch 3: see §§15–042 to 15–043. The conditions in DPA 2018 Sch 8 are set out below in §12–019.

76 As to the meaning of this, see §12–020.

77 As to the specific requirements for the record of processing in relation to sensitive processing, see §12–021.

78 This is similar to DPA 1998 Sch 3 para 7(1)(b), except that the substantial public interest requirement has been introduced. The Data Protection (Processing of Sensitive Personal Data) Order 2000 (SI 2000/417) added a further series of purposes for which sensitive personal data could be processed under the DPA 1998, and each of these had a requirement that the processing be 'in the substantial public interest.'

(2) The processing is necessary for the administration of justice.[79]

(3) The processing is necessary to protect the vital interests of the data subject or of another individual.[80]

(4) The processing:

(a) is necessary for the purposes of protecting an individual from neglect or physical, mental or emotional harm, or protecting the physical, mental or emotional well-being of an individual, being an individual who is either aged under 18 or is aged 18 or over and at risk;

(b) is carried out without the consent of the data subject, either because the data subject cannot give it, or it cannot reasonably be expected to be obtained, or it would prejudice protecting the data subject from neglect etc; and

(c) is necessary for reasons of substantial public interest.[81]

(5) The processing relates to personal data which is manifestly made public by the data subject.[82]

(6) The processing:

(a) is necessary for the purpose of, or in connection with, any legal proceedings (including prospective legal proceedings);

(b) is necessary for the purpose of obtaining legal advice; or

(c) is otherwise necessary for the purposes of establishing, exercising or defending legal rights.[83]

(7) The processing is necessary when a court or other judicial authority is acting in its judicial capacity.[84]

(8) The processing is necessary for the purposes of preventing fraud or a particular kind of fraud, and consists of:

(a) the disclosure of personal data by a competent authority as a member of an anti-fraud organisation;

(b) the disclosure of personal data by a competent authority in accordance with arrangements made by an anti-fraud organisation; or

(c) the processing of personal data disclosed as described in either of the above two sub-paragraphs.[85]

(9) The processing is necessary:

(a) for archiving purposes in the public interest;

(b) for scientific or historical research purposes; or

---

79 This is the same as DPA 1998 Sch 3 para 7(1)(a).

80 This is similar to DPA 1998 Sch 3 para 3, but with the requirement of inability to secure consent now removed.

81 This is a paraphrasing: for the exact terms, see DPA 2018 Sch 8 para 4. The phrase 'at risk' is defined in DPA 2018 Sch 8 para 4(3). A roughly similar provision was provided for under DPA 1998 by the Data Protection (Processing of Sensitive Personal Data) Order 2000 (SI 2000/417) Sch para 4.

82 This is similar to DPA 1998 Sch 3 para 5.

83 This is identical to DPA 1998 Sch 7 para 6.

84 This is novel. Whether it adds anything to (2) remains to be seen.

85 An 'anti-fraud organisation' means 'any unincorporated association, body corporate or other person which enables or facilitates any sharing of information to prevent fraud or a particular kind of fraud or which has any of these functions as its purpose or one of its purposes:' Serious Crime Act 2007 s 68(8), applied by DPA 2018 Sch 8 para 8(2). Section 68(1) of the Serious Crime Act 2007 provides: 'A public authority may, for the purposes of preventing fraud or a particular kind of fraud, disclose information as a member of a specified anti-fraud organisation or otherwise in accordance with any arrangements made by such an organisation.' There was an equivalent provision in DPA 1998 Sch 3 para 7A.

(c) for statistical purposes.[86]

12–020 Appropriate policy document

Sensitive processing is permitted for any of the law enforcement purposes only where, at the time when the processing is carried out, the controller has an 'appropriate policy document' in place.[87] This means a document that the controller has produced that:

(a) explains the controller's procedures for securing compliance with the six data protection principles in connection with sensitive processing; and

(b) explains the controller's policies as regards the retention and erasure of personal data processed, giving an indication of how long such personal data is likely to be retained.[88]

An 'appropriate policy document' must differentiate the controller's procedures and policies on (a) and (b) according to whether the sensitive processing relies upon the consent of the data subject (ie the first permitted situation) or the meeting of a Schedule 8 condition (ie the second permitted situation). Throughout the period when the controller is carrying out sensitive processing up until 6 months after its conclusion, the controller must retain the appropriate policy document, review and update it from time to time, and make it available to the Information Commissioner.[89]

12–021 Record of sensitive processing

One of the continuing obligations on both a controller and a processor is for each of them to maintain a record of all categories of processing activities for which each is responsible.[90] In addition to the information that such a record must contain regardless of whether there is sensitive processing,[91] where sensitive processing is being carried out that record must also include the following information:

(a) whether the sensitive processing is carried out in reliance on the consent of the data subject or, if not, which condition in Schedule 8 is relied on;

(b) how the processing otherwise satisfies the first data protection principle, including the other requirements that must be satisfied for sensitive processing to be permitted; and

(c) whether the personal data is retained and erased in accordance with the policies described in an appropriate policy document and, if it is not, the reasons for not following those policies.[92]

A processor will only need to include the above information in its record of processing where the processor is carrying out sensitive processing on behalf of the controller.[93]

86 This was formerly achieved through an exemption in DPA 1998 s 33, provided for in Directive 95/46/EC Art 6(1)(b). Note, however, that where this paragraph applies, processing of personal data will nevertheless not be permitted where: (a) it is carried out for the purposes of, or in connection with, measures or decisions with respect to a particular data subject; or (b) it is likely to cause substantial damage or substantial distress to a data subject: DPA 2018 s 41(2).

87 DPA 2018 s 35(4)-(5).

88 DPA 2018 s 42(2), alluding to LED Art 19(2).

89 DPA 2018 s 42(3), (5). The Information Commissioner has published an 'Appropriate Policy Document Template' as a guideline to the content of this document.

90 DPA 2018 s 61(1), (3).

91 As to which, see §12–040.

92 DPA 2018 s 42(4).

93 DPA 2018 s 42(4).

2– 022 Infringement consequence

Where a controller's processing of personal data would infringe the first data protection principle, that controller must, without having to be requested, erase the personal data without undue delay.[94] Where the controller has, at the time of erasing, already disclosed the personal data, the controller must notify the recipients and those recipients must similarly erase the personal data.[95] These erasure obligations are automatic and are additional to enforcement procedures instigated by the Information Commissioner for breach of the first data protection principle or private remedies sought by the data subject.[96]

3. SPECIFIC, EXPLICIT & LEGITIMATE PURPOSE

2– 023 Second data protection principle

The second data protection principle, which the controller is responsible for and must be able to demonstrate, is that:

(a) the law enforcement purpose for which personal data is collected on any occasion must be specified, explicit and legitimate; and

(b) personal data so collected must not be processed in a manner that is incompatible with the purpose for which it was collected.[97]

The second data protection principle centres upon the law enforcement purpose for which the personal data was collected. The principle resembles the second processing principle that applies to general processing.[98] The data protection regime contemplates that a controller may process personal data that has been collected for law enforcement purposes without the knowledge of the data subject.[99] The data subject's lack of knowledge may be absolute in the sense that the data subject does not know that any person has collected his or her personal data for law enforcement purposes; or it may be limited in the sense that the data subject, while knowing that his or her personal data has been collected, does not know that it was collected for law enforcement purposes, or does not know the law enforcement purposes for which it was collected, or does not know by which particular controllers his or her personal data has been collected. This may arise, for example, where a first controller has, unbeknownst to the data subject, transmitted the personal data to a second controller. The infringement of the data subject's right to the protection of his or her personal data that might result from its undisclosed collection are tempered by the requirement that the controller (or, where it acts on behalf of a controller, the processor) keep a log of the collection of personal data in order to verify the lawfulness of the processing.[100] This requirement, linked to the second data protection

---

94 DPA 2018 s 47(1)(a), (4). If the personal data must be maintained for the purposes of evidence, instead of erasing the data the controller must restrict its processing: DPA 2018 s 47(2).

95 DPA 2018 s 48(9).

96 In relation to regulatory enforcement by the Information Commissioner see §§48– 014 to 48– 055; in relation to private remedies sought by a data subject see §§48– 005 to 48– 013.

97 DPA 2018 s 36(1); LED Art 4(1)(b). This is a variation on the second data protection principle under DPA 1998 Sch 1 Pt 1 para 2; Directive 95/46/EC Art 6(1)(b). In relation to that provision, see §15– 044. The principle originates from Convention 108 Art 5(4)(b). In relation to Convention 108 generally, see §§7– 007 to 7– 008.

98 GDPR Art 5(1)(b). See §§9– 023 to 9– 027.

99 DPA 2018 s 44(3).

100 DPA 2018 s 62(1)(a), (4)(a). The controller or processor must make the log available to the Information Commissioner on request: DPA 2018 s 62(5). The right to the protection of personal data, which is a facet of the fundamental rights and freedoms of natural persons, lies at the heart of what the LED is intended to protect: see LED Art 1(2)(a).

principle, imposes a check on controllers and processors, enabling breaches of the continuing obligations on controllers and processors to be more readily identified and enforced.

12–024 Personal data collection

The 'collection' of personal data is not synonymous with the 'receipt' of personal data. The law enforcement processing regime recognises that personal data being processed by a controller may have been collected by another controller.[101] The necessary implication is that a controller is able to process the personal data without having 'collected' it – for example, where the controller that has collected personal data has 'made available' that personal data to another controller.[102] The second data protection principle accommodates this by permitting personal data collected for a law enforcement purpose (whether by one controller or by another controller) to be processed for another law enforcement purpose provided that:

(a) the controller is authorised by law to process the data for the other purpose; and
(b) the processing is necessary and proportionate to that other purpose.[103]

Where this applies, the requirement that the personal data not be processed in a manner that is incompatible with the purpose for which the personal data was collected falls away.[104] Personal data collected for any of the law enforcement purposes may not be processed for a purpose that is not a law enforcement purpose unless the processing is authorised by law.[105]

12–025 Infringement consequence

Where a controller's processing of personal data:

(a) would be for a law enforcement purpose other than that for which it was collected but the controller is not authorised by law to process for that other purpose or the processing is not necessary or proportionate to that other purpose; or
(b) would be in a manner that is incompatible with the purpose for which the personal data was collected,

that controller must, without having to be requested, erase the personal data without undue delay.[106] Where the controller has, at the time of erasing, already disclosed the personal data, the controller must notify the recipients and those recipients must similarly erase the personal data.[107] These erasure obligations are automatic and are additional to enforcement procedures instigated by the Information Commissioner for breach of the second data protection principle or private remedies sought by the data subject.[108]

4. ADEQUATE, RELEVANT AND NOT EXCESSIVE

12–026 Third data protection principle

The third data protection principle, which the controller is responsible for and must be able to

---

101 DPA 2018 s 36(3).

102 See DPA 2018 ss 38(4), (5), 73(1), 78(4) and 80.

103 DPA 2018 s 36(3); LED Art 4(2).

104 DPA 2018 s 36(2).

105 DPA 2018 s 36(4); LED Art 4(2)(a).

106 DPA 2018 s 47(1)(a), (4). If the personal data must be maintained for the purposes of evidence, instead of erasing the data the controller must restrict its processing: DPA 2018 s 47(2).

107 DPA 2018 s 48(9).

108 In relation to regulatory enforcement by the Information Commissioner see §§48–014 to 48–055; in relation to private remedies sought by a data subject see §§48–005 to 48–013.

demonstrate, is that:

> personal data processed for any of the law enforcement purposes must be adequate, relevant and not excessive in relation to the purpose for which it is processed.[109]

The third data protection principle resembles the third processing principle that applies to general processing.[110] The third data protection principle is in the same terms as the third data protection principle under the previous regime.[111]

12– 027 Infringement consequence

Where a controller's processing of personal data would infringe the third data protection principle, that controller must, without having to be requested, erase the personal data without undue delay.[112] Where the controller has, at the time of erasing, already disclosed the personal data, the controller must notify the recipients and those recipients must similarly erase the personal data.[113] These erasure obligations are automatic and are additional to enforcement procedures instigated by the Information Commissioner for breach of the third data protection principle or private remedies sought by the data subject.[114]

5. ACCURATE AND UP-TO-DATE

12– 028 Fourth data protection principle

The fourth data protection principle, which the controller is responsible for and must be able to demonstrate, has two aspects. The first is that:

> (a) personal data processed for any of the law enforcement purposes must be accurate and, where necessary, kept up to date.[115]

'Inaccurate' for these purposes means incorrect or misleading as to any matter of fact.[116] The second aspect of the principle spells out the obligation that arises whenever personal data is inaccurate:

> (b) every reasonable step must be taken to ensure that personal data that is inaccurate, having regard to the law enforcement purpose for which it is processed, is erased or rectified without delay.[117]

The fourth data protection principle closely resembles the fourth processing principle that applies to general processing.[118] The fourth data protection principle is in the same terms as the third data protection principle under the previous regime.[119] The principle is concerned

---

109 DPA 2018 s 37; LED Art 4(1)(c).

110 GDPR Art 5(1)(c), recital (39). See §9– 028.

111 DPA 1998 Sch 1 para 3; Directive 95/46/EC Art 6(1)(c). In relation to that provision, see §15– 045. The principle originates from Convention 108 Art 5(4)(c). In relation to Convention 108 generally, see §§7– 007 to 7– 008.

112 DPA 2018 s 47(1)(a), (4). If the personal data must be maintained for the purposes of evidence, instead of erasing the data the controller must restrict its processing: DPA 2018 s 47(2).

113 DPA 2018 s 48(9).

114 In relation to regulatory enforcement by the Information Commissioner see §§48– 014 to 48– 055; in relation to private remedies sought by a data subject see §§48– 005 to 48– 013.

115 This is very similar to the fourth data protection principle under DPA 1998 Sch 1 Pt 1 para 4; Directive 95/46/EC Art 6(1)(d). In relation to that provision, see §15– 046. The principle originates from Convention 108 Art 5(4)(d). In relation to Convention 108 generally, see §§7– 007 to 7– 008.

116 DPA 2018 s 205(1).

117 DPA 2018 s 38(1); LED Art 4(1)(d).

118 GDPR Art 5(1)(d), recital (39). See §9– 029.

119 DPA 1998 Sch 1 para 3; Directive 95/46/EC Art 6(1)(c). In relation to that provision, see §15– 045. The principle originates from Convention 108 Art 5(c). In relation to Convention 108 generally, see §§7– 007 to 7– 008.

with the accuracy of the data itself and not simply with whether that data has been accurately recorded.[120] In requiring accuracy, the fourth data protection principle also requires a clear distinction to be kept between personal data relating to different categories of data subject.[121]

12–029 Facts and assessments

In processing personal data for any of the law enforcement purposes, personal data based on facts must, so far as possible, be distinguished from personal data based on personal assessments.[122] Although a personal assessment is a fact (in the sense that it records what is the assessment of the person making it), in relation to 'accuracy' the Act is concerned only with the actualities of personal data, rather than with what an evaluation of that personal data might yield.[123]

12–030 Consequential obligations

Whenever personal data processed by a controller is inaccurate – that is, incorrect or misleading as to any matter of fact – every reasonable step must be taken to erase it or rectify it without delay.[124] This obligation arises without the need for any request from the Information Commissioner or the data subject to whom the personal data arises. In addition, all reasonable steps must be taken to ensure that personal data which is inaccurate, incomplete or no longer up to date is not transmitted or made available for any of the law enforcement purposes.[125] This requires that:

(a) the quality of personal data must be verified before it is transmitted or made available;
(b) in all transmissions of personal data, the necessary information enabling the recipient to assess the degree of accuracy, completeness and reliability of the data and the extent to which it is up to date must be included; and
(c) if, after personal data has been transmitted, it emerges that the data was incorrect or that the transmission was unlawful, the recipient must be notified without delay.[126]

12–031 Infringement consequence

Where a controller's processing of personal data would infringe the fourth data protection principle, that controller must, without having to be requested, erase the personal data without undue delay.[127] Where the controller has, at the time of erasing, already disclosed the personal data, the controller must notify the recipients and those recipients must similarly erase the personal data.[128] These erasure obligations are automatic and are additional to enforcement procedures instigated by the Information Commissioner for breach of the fourth data protection principle or private remedies sought by the data subject.[129]

---

120 This is implicit in DPA 2018 s 151(3).

121 DPA 2018 s 38(3). See §12–008.

122 DPA 2018 s 38(2); LED Art 7(1).

123 DPA 2018 s 205(1), definition of 'inaccurate.'

124 DPA 2018 s 38(1)(b).

125 DPA 2018 s 38(4).

126 DPA 2018 s 38(5).

127 DPA 2018 s 47(1)(a), (4). If the personal data must be maintained for the purposes of evidence, instead of erasing the data the controller must restrict its processing: DPA 2018 s 47(2).

128 DPA 2018 s 48(9).

129 In relation to regulatory enforcement by the Information Commissioner see §§48–014 to 48–055; in relation to private remedies sought by a data subject see §§48–005 to 48–013.

6. STORAGE LIMITATION

2–032 Fifth data protection principle

The fifth data protection principle, which the controller is responsible for and must be able to demonstrate, is that:

> personal data processed for any of the law enforcement purposes must be kept for no longer than is necessary for the purpose for which it is processed.[130]

The fifth data protection principle is an abbreviation of the fifth processing principle that applies to general processing.[131] Where it is no longer necessary to keep the personal data for the law enforcement purpose for which it is processed, the controller must, without having to be requested, erase the personal data without undue delay.[132] Where the controller has, at the time of erasing, already disclosed the personal data, the controller must notify the recipients and those recipients must similarly erase the personal data.[133] These erasure obligations are automatic and are additional to enforcement procedures instigated by the Information Commissioner for breach of the fifth data protection principle or private remedies sought by the data subject.[134]

2–033 Periodic reviews

The controller is under a continuing obligation to establish appropriate time limits for the periodic review of the need for the continued storage of personal data for any of the law enforcement purposes.[135]

7. PROCESSED SECURELY

2–034 Sixth data protection principle

The sixth data protection principle, which the controller is responsible for and must be able to demonstrate, is that:

> personal data processed for any of the law enforcement purposes must be so processed in a manner that ensures appropriate security of the personal data, using appropriate technical or organisational measures (and, in this principle, "appropriate security" includes protection against unauthorised or unlawful processing and against accidental loss, destruction or damage).[136]

This is a variation of the sixth processing principle that applies to general processing.[137] Where

---

130 DPA 2018 s 39(1); LED Art 4(1)(e). This is very similar to the fifth data protection principle under DPA 1998 Sch 1 Pt 1 para 5; Directive 95/46/EC Art 6(1)(e). In relation to that provision, see §15–047. The principle originates from Convention 108 Art 5(4)(e). In relation to Convention 108 generally, see §§7–007 to 7–008.

131 GDPR Art 5(1)(e). See §9–031.

132 DPA 2018 s 47(1)(a), (4). If the personal data must be maintained for the purposes of evidence, instead of erasing the data the controller must restrict its processing: DPA 2018 s 47(2).

133 DPA 2018 s 48(9).

134 In relation to regulatory enforcement by the Information Commissioner see §§48–014 to 48–055; in relation to private remedies sought by a data subject see §§48–005 to 48–013.

135 DPA 2018 s 39(2); LED Art 5.

136 DPA 2018 s 40 ; LED Art 4(1)(f). This resembles the seventh data protection principle under DPA 1998 Sch 1 Pt 1 para 7; Directive 95/46/EC Art 17. In relation to that provision, see §15–046. The principle originates from Convention 108 Art 7. In relation to Convention 108 generally, see §§7–007 to 7–008.

137 GDPR Art 5(1)(f). See §9–034.

there is a breach of security and that breach leads to the accidental or unlawful destruction, loss, alteration, unauthorised disclosure of or access to personal data, that will constitute a 'personal data breach.'[138] As part of its record of all categories of processing activities, a controller's record must contain a general description of the technical and organisational security measures that it has adopted.[139] A controller's logs of processing operations may be used to ensure the integrity and security of personal data.[140] The controller's data protection impact assessment must include the security measures and mechanisms in place to ensure the protection of personal data.[141]

12–035 Infringement consequence

Where personal data is not processed in a manner that ensures appropriate security of that personal data, the controller must, without having to be requested, erase the personal data without undue delay.[142] Where the controller has, at the time of erasing, already disclosed the personal data, the controller must notify the recipients and those recipients must similarly erase the personal data.[143] These erasure obligations are automatic and are additional to enforcement procedures instigated by the Information Commissioner for breach of the sixth data protection principle or private remedies sought by the data subject.[144]

12–036 Other security obligations

In addition to the obligation to comply with the sixth data protection principle, each controller and each processor must implement appropriate technical and organisational measures to ensure a level of security appropriate to the risks arising from the processing of personal data.[145] In the case of automated processing, each controller and each processor must, following an evaluation of the risks, implement measures designed to:

(a) prevent unauthorised processing or unauthorised interference with the systems used in connection with it;

(b) ensure that it is possible to establish the precise details of any processing that takes place;

(c) ensure that any systems used in connection with the processing function properly and may, in the case of interruption, be restored; and

(d) ensure that stored personal data cannot be corrupted if a system used in connection with the processing malfunctions.[146]

8. ORGANISATIONAL OBLIGATIONS

138 DPA 2018 s 33(3). A 'personal data breach' carries specific notification consequences: DPA 2018 ss 67-68, and see §§12–045 to 12–046.

139 DPA 2018 s 61(2)(k). And similarly the processor's record: DPA 2018 s 61(4)(f). These records must be made available to the Information Commissioner: DPA 2018 s 61(5).

140 DPA 2018 s 62(4)(c).

141 DPA 2018 s 64(3)(d).

142 DPA 2018 s 47(1)(a), (4). If the personal data must be maintained for the purposes of evidence, instead of erasing the data the controller must restrict its processing: DPA 2018 s 47(2).

143 DPA 2018 s 48(9).

144 In relation to regulatory enforcement by the Information Commissioner see §§48–014 to 48–055; in relation to private remedies sought by a data subject see §§48–005 to 48–013.

145 DPA 2018 s 66(1).

146 DPA 2018 s 66(2); LED Art 29.

12– 037 Introduction

The data protection principles are complemented by organisational obligations which are applicable to controllers and, to a lesser extent, to processors. These organisational obligations require every controller and every processor to establish and conduct itself so as to comply, and be able to demonstrate compliance, with the law enforcement processing regime. Specifically, controllers are required to undertake impact assessments, to take and follow advice from and otherwise cooperate with the Information Commissioner, to maintain records and logs, and to have a qualified, independent officer responsible for data protection.[147] These obligations are additional to related obligations that are triggered by events (for example, the obligation on a controller to notify the Information Commissioner where there has been a personal data breach)[148] and obligations that impinge upon the processing itself (for example, the security measures obligation).[149] The organisational obligations resemble those applicable to general processing, but place greater emphasis on the recording and logging of processing activities: this enables the Information Commissioner to detect more readily deviations from the requirements of the law enforcement processing regime.[150]

12– 038 Internal systems obligation

A controller is under three inter-related obligations to have internal systems in place to maximise the likelihood of processing being in accordance with the law enforcement processing regime and to be able to demonstrate adherence to that regime.[151] These are all characterised as 'technical and organisational' measures that a controller must implement.

(1) A controller must implement appropriate technical and organisational measures to ensure, and to be able to demonstrate, that processing complies with the law enforcement processing requirements imposed by the DPA 2018.[152] In deciding what technical and organisational measures are appropriate, the controller must take into account: the latest developments in technology; the cost of implementation; the nature, scope, context and purposes of processing; and the risks for the rights and freedoms of individuals arising from the processing.[153] The 'risk' is the product of the severity of an occurrence adverse to the rights and freedoms of individuals and the likelihood of that occurrence.[154] Where it is proportionate to the processing activities, these measures may require a controller to implement data protection policies that are appropriate to the processing of personal data.[155] Where

---

147 DPA 2018 ss 55, 56(1), 57(1), 58(2), , 61(1), (3), 62(1), 63, 64(1), 66(1), (2), 67(1), 68(1), 69(1), 70, and 71(1). Regulatory enforcement is considered at §§48– 014 to 48– 055.

148 See §12– 045. As to the meaning of 'personal data breach,' see §12– 034.

149 See §12– 034.

150 See §9– 048 to 9– 054.

151 These are similar, but not identical, to those apply to general processing: see §9– 049.

152 DPA 2018 s 56(1); LED Art 19(1). For the purposes of law enforcement processing, the requirements are set out in DPA 2018 ss 29-81. The general processing equivalent is GDPR Art 24(1). In imposing an obligation that requires the measures ensure and demonstrate 'that processing complies with the requirements' of DPA 2018 Part 4 (ss 29-81) – as opposed to ensuring and demonstrating that the controller is processing in accordance with those provisions – the obligation extends to where processing is carried out on behalf of the controller by a processor. The Information Commissioner does not have power to serve an enforcement notice for failure to comply with this obligation: DPA 2018 s 149(2).

153 DPA 2018 s 55(3). As to the meaning of 'rights and freedoms of natural persons' in this context, see §8– 006.

154 See the discussion in *Various Claimants v Wm Morrisons Supermarket plc* [2017] EWHC 3113 (QB), [2018] 3 WLR 691 at [67]-[68]. That case concerned the DPA 1998, but the discussion is equally applicable to data security principles under the DPA 2018.

155 DPA 2018 s 56(2).

necessary, the controller must review and update these measures.[156] Compliance with a code of practice[157] approved by the Information Commissioner may be used to help demonstrate that this obligation has been met.[158]

(2) A controller must implement appropriate technical and organisational measures that are designed to implement the data protection principles in an effective manner and to integrate into the processing itself the safeguards necessary for that purpose.[159] In deciding what technical and organisational measures are appropriate, the controller must take into account the same matters taken into account for the purposes of (1).[160] The 'risk' is the product of the severity of an occurrence adverse to the rights and freedoms of natural persons and the likelihood of that occurrence.[161] The obligation is engaged both at the time at which the controller determines the means for processing and at the time of the processing itself.[162]

(3) A controller must implement technical and organisational measures for ensuring that the processing is limited to just so much of the personal data that is necessary for each specific purpose.[163] This duty applies to: (a) the amount of personal data collected; (b) the extent of its processing; (c) the period of its storage; and (d) its accessibility.[164] Specifically, the controller must implement measures to ensure that, by default, personal data is not made accessible to an indefinite number of people without an individual's intervention.[165]

12– 039 Impact assessments

Where a type of law enforcement processing is likely to result in a high risk to the rights and freedoms of natural persons,[166] the controller must first carry out an assessment of the impact of the envisaged processing operations on the protection of personal data.[167] This is termed a 'data protection impact assessment.' The controller's data protection officer must provide advice on the carrying out of the data protection impact assessment and monitor compliance

---

[156] DPA 2018 s 56(3).

[157] The only code of conduct potentially applicable to law enforcement processing is the one provided for in DPA 2018 s 121. A failure by a person to act in accordance with a code of practice does not of itself make that person liable to legal proceedings: DPA 2018 s 127(1).

[158] DPA 2018 s 127(3)-(5).

[159] DPA 2018 s 57(1); LED Art 20(1). For the general processing equivalent, see GDPR Art 25(1). Unlike the position in relation to general processing, in relation to law enforcement processing failure to comply with this obligation does not entitle the Commissioner to issue an enforcement notice: DPA 2018 s 149.

[160] DPA 2018 s 55(3). As to the meaning of 'rights and freedoms of natural persons' in this context, see §8– 006.

[161] As to the meaning of 'rights and freedoms of data subjects' in this context, see §8– 006. See the discussion in *Various Claimants v Wm Morrisons Supermarket plc* [2017] EWHC 3113 (QB), [2018] 3 WLR 691 at [67]-[68]. That case concerned the DPA 1998, but the discussion is equally applicable to data security principles under the GDPR and DPA 2018.

[162] DPA 2018 s 57(2).

[163] DPA 2018 s 57(3); LED Art 20(2). The general processing equivalent is GDPR Art 25(1). The law enforcement purposes for which personal data is collected must be specified, explicit and legitimate (ie the second data protection principle): DPA 2018 s 36(1)(a). But there may be processing for other law enforcement processes thereafter: DPA 2018 s 36(3). See further §§12– 023 to 12– 024.

[164] DPA 2018 s 57(4).

[165] DPA 2018 s 57(5).

[166] As to the meaning of 'rights and freedoms of natural persons' and 'risk' in this context, see §§8– 006 to 8– 007.

[167] DPA 2018 s 64(1)-(2); LED Art 27(1), recitals (53) and (58). A data protection impact assessment is intended to be prophylactic rather than aetiological. The general processing equivalent is GDPR Art 35(1).

with the statutory requirements.[168] In deciding whether a type of law enforcement processing is likely to result in a high risk to the rights and freedoms of individuals, the controller must take into account the nature, scope, context and purposes of the processing.[169] The requirements of a data protection impact assessment for law enforcement processing are significantly less than those required for general processing.[170] For law enforcement processing, a data protection impact assessment must as a minimum contain:

— a general description of the envisaged processing operations;
— an assessment of the risks to the rights and freedoms of data subjects;
— the measures envisaged to address those risks; and
— the safeguards, security measures and mechanisms to ensure the protection of personal data and to demonstrate compliance with the requirements of the law enforcement data processing regime, taking into account the rights and legitimate interests of data subjects and other persons concerned.[171]

Where a controller has failed to carry out a data protection impact assessment, the Information Commissioner may serve an enforcement notice.[172] Where a data impact protection assessment indicates that, in the absence of measures to mitigate the risk, the processing of the data would result in a high risk to the rights and freedoms of individuals, the controller must prior to the processing consult the Information Commissioner.[173]

2– 040 Record-keeping

One aspect of the law enforcement processing regime that is more rigorous than that of the general processing regime is the record keeping obligation. The record keeping obligation applies to all controllers and all processors processing personal data for a law enforcement purpose, regardless of size.[174] The obligation on a controller and a processor is for each of them to 'maintain' a record: in other words, it is a continuing obligation that requires the record to be kept up-to-date.[175] A controller's record must contain:[176]

— a record of all categories of law enforcement processing activities for which the controller is responsible;[177]
— the name and contact details of the controller and, where applicable, the joint controller and the data protection officer;
— the purposes of the processing;
— a description of the categories of data subjects and of the categories of personal data;
— the categories of recipients to whom the personal data have been or will be

168 DPA 2018 s 71(1)(b).

169 DPA 2018 s 64(4).

170 In relation to data protection impact assessments for the purposes of general processing, see §9– 050.

171 DPA 2018 s 64(3); LED Art 27(2). As to the meaning of 'rights and freedoms of data subjects' and 'risk' in this context, see §§8– 006 to 8– 007.

172 DPA 2018 s 149(2)(c). In relation to enforcement notices and other regulatory measures available to the Information Commissioner, see §§48– 014 to 48– 055.

173 DPA 2018 s 65(2); LED Art 28(1). In relation to that consultation, see §12– 044.

174 DPA 2018 s 61; LED Art 24. For general processing, the record-keeping obligation arises where the enterprise processing personal data has 250 or more employees or, where it has fewer employees, where the processing it carries out is likely to result in a risk to the rights and freedoms of data subjects, the processing is not occasional, or the processing includes sensitive personal information: GDPR Art 30(5) and see further §9– 051.

175 On the duty to 'maintain' records, see: *R (English Democrats Party) v Electoral Commission* [2018] EWHC 251 (Admin), [2018] 4 WLR 54.

176 DPA 2018 s 61(2); LED Art 24(1).

177 DPA 2018 s 61(1).

disclosed, including recipients in third countries or international organisations;[178]
— where applicable, details of the use of profiling;[179]
— where applicable, the categories of transfers of personal data to a third country or to an international organisation;[180]
— an indication of the legal basis for the processing operations, including transfers, for which the personal data is intended;
— where possible, the envisaged time limits for erasure of the different categories of data; and
— where possible, a general description of the technical and organisational security measures required for law enforcement processing.[181]

In the case of sensitive personal information, the controller's record must also contain certain other information.[182] The processor's record must contain:[183]
— a record of all categories of law enforcement processing activities carried out on behalf of a controller;[184]
— the name and contact details of the processor and any sub-processor[185] and of the controller on behalf of which the processor is acting, and, where applicable, of the controller's data protection officer;
— the categories of processing carried out on behalf of the controller;
— where applicable, details of transfers of personal data to a third country or an international organisation where explicitly instructed to do so by the controller, including the identification of that country or international organisation;[186] and
— where possible, a general description of the technical and organisational security measures required for law enforcement processing.[187]

Where requested, a controller or processor must make the record available to the Information Commissioner.[188]

12– 041 Processing operations logs

A further, related aspect of the law enforcement processing regime that is more rigorous than that of the general processing regime is the obligation on controllers and processors to keep logs of certain law enforcement processing operations.[189] Where personal data is processed on behalf of the controller by a processor, it is the processor that must keep the logs: otherwise, it is the controller that must keep the logs.[190] A separate log must be kept for each of the six

178 As to the meaning of 'third countries,' see §8– 032. As to the meaning of 'international organisations,' see §8– 033. As to the meaning of 'recipients,' see §8– 026.

179 As to the meaning of 'profiling,' see §8– 029.

180 As to the meaning of 'third country,' see §8– 032. As to the meaning of 'international organisations,' see §8– 033.

181 As to these measures, see §§12– 034 to 12– 036.

182 See §12– 021.

183 DPA 2018 s 61(4); LED Art 24(2).

184 DPA 2018 s 61(3).

185 Where a processor engages another processor with the prior written authorisation of the controller, the processor so engaged is called 'a sub-processor': DPA 2018 s 59(3).

186 As to the meaning of 'third countries,' see §8– 032. As to the meaning of 'international organisations,' see §8– 033.

187 As to these measures, see §§12– 034 to 12– 036.

188 DPA 2018 s 61(5).

189 DPA 2018 s 62; LED Art 25. Under the general processing regime, there is no requirement on a controller or a processor to keep any logs of processing operations.

190 DPA 2018 s 62(1).

specified processing operations. The processing operations that require a log to be kept are:[191]

(1) The collection of personal data. The details of this log are not expressly specified, but other requirements of the law enforcement processing regime would suggest that it should include the date of collection,[192] the basis on which the collection was lawful,[193] the law enforcement purpose for which the personal data was collected,[194] whether the personal data was collected without the knowledge of the data subject[195] and the amount of personal data collected.[196]
(2) Alteration of personal data. The details of this log are not expressly specified, but other requirements of the law enforcement processing regime would suggest that it should include the equivalent details required for collection of personal data, as well as whether the alteration resulted from a personal data breach.[197]
(3) Consultation of the personal data. The consultation logs must make it possible to establish the justification for, and date and time of, the consultation, and, so far as possible, the identity of the person who consulted the data.[198]
(4) Disclosure, including transfers, of the personal data. The disclosure logs must make it possible to establish the justification for, and date and time of, the disclosure, and, so far as possible the identity of the person who disclosed the data and the identity of the recipients of the data.[199]
(5) Combination of the personal data. The details of this log are not expressly specified, but other requirements of the law enforcement processing regime would suggest that it should include the equivalent details required for collection of personal data.[200]
(6) Erasure of the personal data. The details of this log are not expressly specified, but other requirements of the law enforcement processing regime would suggest that it should include the equivalent details required for collection of personal data, as well as whether the erasure resulted from the personal data having been inaccurate, whether it was sensitive processing, what animated the erasure, and the recipients notified of the erasure.[201]

The only purposes for which a log may be used are:

(a) to verify the lawfulness of processing;
(b) to assist with self-monitoring by the controller or the processor, including the conduct of internal disciplinary proceedings;
(c) to ensure the integrity and security of personal data; and
(d) criminal proceedings.[202]

---

191 DPA 2018 s 62(1); LED Art 25(1).

192 DPA 2018 s 39(1).

193 DPA 2018 s 39.

194 DPA 2018 s 36(1)(a).

195 DPA 2018 s 44(3).

196 DPA 2018 s 57(3)-(4).

197 DPA 2018 s 33(3). As to the meaning of 'personal data breach,' see §12– 034.

198 DPA 2018 s 62(2). In relation to consultation, see LED Art 3(2) and 25(1) and recital (57).

199 DPA 2018 s 62(3).

200 'Combination' is a processing operation: DPA 2018 s 3(4)(e).

201 DPA 2018 ss 38(1)(b), 42(2)(b), 47(1) and 48(9) respectively. The log will not need to repeat the information required to be kept in the record under DPA 2018 s 42(4)(c).

202 DPA 2018 s 62(4); LED Art 25(2).

The controller or the processor must make the logs available to the Commissioner on request.[203]

12– 042 Data protection officers

A controller (other than a court or other judicial authority) must designate a person as its data protection officer, publish the contact details of that data protection officer and communicate those details to the Information Commissioner.[204] A data protection officer must have expert knowledge of data protection law and practices and be able to fulfil the tasks required under the law enforcement processing regime.[205] Although it is the controller who is required to entrust specific tasks to a data protection officer,[206] it is the data protection officer who is statutorily tasked to perform them. Performance of the tasks is not subordinated to contractual obligations that the data protection officer might owe to the controller. Rather, the controller must facilitate the due performance of the data controller's statutory tasks.[207] Thus, the controller:

(a) must ensure that the data protection officer is involved, properly and in a timely manner, in all issues which relate to the protection of personal data;
(b) must provide the data protection officer with the necessary resources and access to personal data and processing operations to enable the data protection officer to perform the statutory tasks and maintain his or her expert knowledge of data protection law;
(c) must ensure that the data protection officer does not receive any instructions regarding the performance of the statutory tasks;
(d) must ensure that the data protection officer does not perform a task or fulfil a duty other than the statutory tasks where such task or duty would result in a conflict of interests; and
(e) must not dismiss or penalise the data protection officer for performing the statutory tasks.[208]

Consistent with the data protection officer's tasks not being subordinated to employer instructions, the officer is statutorily mandated to report to 'the highest management level of the controller.'[209] The controller must implement effective mechanisms to encourage the data protection officer to report infringements of the law enforcement processing regime.[210]

12– 043 DPO statutory tasks

The controller must entrust the data protection officer with at least the following tasks:

(a) monitoring compliance with the data protection regime;
(b) monitoring compliance with the controller's data protection policies in relation to the protection of personal data, including assigning responsibilities under those

---

203 DPA 2018 s 62(5); LED Art 25(3).

204 DPA 2018 ss 44(1)(b), 61(2)(c), 67(4)(b), 68(2)(b), 69; LED Art 32(1), (4). In this regard, too, the requirements of the law enforcement processing regime are more stringent than in relation to general processing: see GDPR Art 37(1) and §9– 051. The same person may be designated as a data protection officer by more than one controller: DPA 2018 s 69(3); LED Art 32(3), recital (63).

205 DPA 2018 s 69(2); LED Art 32(2). There is a similar requirement in relation to general processing: GDPR Art 37(5).

206 DPA 2018 s 71(1).

207 See further §12– 047.

208 DPA 2018 s 70(2)-(3); LED Art 33.

209 DPA 2018 s 70(5).

210 DPA 2018 s 81(1). Although this requirement is not limited to the data protection officer and applies generally to those employed by the controller, it is of particular significance for the data protection officer. In so reporting an infringement, the data protection officer will not be breaching any obligation of confidence owed by the officer nor breaching any other restriction on the disclosure of information, howsoever that may arise: DPA 2018 s 81(4).

policies, raising awareness of those policies, training staff involved in processing operations and conducting audits required under those policies;[211]

(c) informing and advising the controller, any processor engaged by the controller and any employee who carries out law enforcement processing of personal data, of their obligations under the law enforcement processing regime;

(d) providing advice on the carrying out of a data protection impact assessment and monitoring compliance with the obligation to carry out those assessments and their implementation;[212] and

(e) co-operating with the Information Commissioner.[213]

In performing these tasks, the data protection officer must have regard to the risks associated with processing operations, taking into account the nature, scope, context and purposes of processing.[214] Where there has been a personal data breach, the data protection officer will be the contact point for the Information Commissioner and the data subject.[215] A data subject may contact the data protection officer with regard to all issues relating to the processing of that data subject's personal data or the exercise of that data subject's rights.[216]

2–044 Cooperation with Commissioner

When requested, each controller and each processor must co-operate with the Information Commissioner in the performance of the Commissioner's tasks.[217] As a general rule, it is the task of the data protection officer to act as the contact point for the Commissioner on issues relating to law enforcement processing.[218] Quite apart from general co-operation, where a data protection impact assessment indicates that the processing of the data would result in a high risk to the rights and freedoms of individuals (in the absence of measures to mitigate the risk), the controller must consult the Information Commissioner prior to the processing of personal data and, as part of that consultation, must give the Commissioner the data protection impact assessment and any other information requested by the Commissioner to enable the Commissioner to make an assessment of the compliance of the processing with the requirements of the law enforcement processing regime.[219] On being so consulted, if the Commissioner is of the opinion that the controller's intended processing of personal data would infringe any of the requirements of the law enforcement processing regime, the Commissioner must, within 6 weeks of the consultation request, provide written advice to the controller and, where the controller is using a processor, to the processor.[220] In providing that advice, the

---

[211] Where proportionate in relation to the processing, the measures implemented to comply with the duty to ensure compliance with the requirements of the law enforcement processing regime must include appropriate data protection policies: DPA 2018 s 56(2).

[212] The obligation to carry out data protection impact assessments is imposed by DPA 2018 s 64. See §12–039.

[213] DPA 2018 s 71(1)-(2); LED Art 34. This is slightly less than the comparable provision in relation to general processing: GDPR Art 39(1) and §9–053.

[214] DPA 2018 s 71(3).

[215] DPA 2018 ss 67(4)(b) and 68(2)(b). As to the meaning of 'personal data breach,' see §12–034.

[216] DPA 2018 s 70(4).

[217] DPA 2018 s 63; LED Art 26. There is a similar obligation in relation to general processing: GDPR Art 31, and see §9–054.

[218] DPA 2018 s 71(1)(d).

[219] DPA 2018 s 65(1)-(4); LED Art 28(1), (4). This, too, falls to the data protection officer: DPA 2018 s 71(1)(d). As to the meaning of 'rights and freedoms of data subjects' and 'risk' in this context, see §§8–006 to 8–007. As to the requirement on a controller to prepare a data protection impact assessment, see §12–039.

[220] DPA 2018 s 65(4)-(5); LED Art 28(5). There is an analogous requirement in relation to general processing: GDPR Art 36(1). The Commissioner may extend the period of 6 weeks by a further period of 1 month, taking into account the complexity of the intended processing and, where the Commissioner does so, the Commissioner must

Commissioner must have regard to the importance of securing an appropriate level of protection for personal data, taking account of the interests of data subjects, controllers and others and matters of general public interest.[221]

12–045 Obligation to notify ICO

Where a controller becomes aware of a personal data breach in relation to personal data for which the controller is responsible, then, unless the personal data breach is unlikely to result in a risk to the rights and freedoms of individuals, the controller must notify the breach to the Information Commissioner without undue delay and, where feasible, not later than 72 hours after becoming aware of it.[222] The notification must include:

(a) a description of the nature of the personal data breach including, where possible, the categories and approximate number of data subjects concerned and the categories and approximate number of personal data records concerned;
(b) the name and contact details of the data protection officer or other contact point from whom more information can be obtained;
(c) a description of the likely consequences of the personal data breach;
(d) a description of the measures taken or proposed to be taken by the controller to address the personal data breach, including, where appropriate, measures to mitigate its possible adverse effects; and
(e) the facts relating to the personal data breach, its effects and the remedial action taken, all recorded in such a way as to enable the Commissioner to verify compliance with the notification requirement.[223]

Where a processor becomes aware of a personal data breach in relation to personal data being processed by it, the processor is not under any obligation to notify the Information Commissioner. Instead, the processor must notify the controller without undue delay, and it then falls on the controller to notify the Commissioner.[224]

12–046 Obligation to notify data subject

Where a personal data breach is likely to result in a high risk to the rights and freedoms of individuals, the controller must, in addition to informing the Information Commissioner, also inform the data subject of the breach without undue delay.[225] The controller will, in the first

inform the controller and, where applicable, the processor of any such extension before the end of the period of 1 month beginning with receipt of the request for consultation, and provide reasons for the delay: DPA 2018 s 65(6)-(7).

[221] DPA 2018 s 2(2). 'Interests of data subjects' is given expression to in DPA 2(1), and include the requirement that personal data be processed lawfully and fairly, on the basis of a data subject's consent or another specified basis, that data subjects have rights to obtain information about the processing of personal data and to require inaccurate personal data to be rectified. See also DPA 2018 Sch 13 para 1(1).

[222] DPA 2018 s 67(1)-(2); LED Art 30(1). As to the meaning of 'personal data breach,' see §12–034. As to the meaning of 'rights and freedoms of data subjects' and 'risk' in this context, see §§8–006 to 8–007. Where the notification to the Commissioner is not made within 72 hours, the notification must be accompanied by reasons for the delay: DPA 2018 s 67(3); LED Art 30(1). There is a similar provision in relation to general processing: GDPR Art 33(1)-(2), and see §9–037.

[223] DPA 2018 s 67(4)-(7); LED Art 30(3), (5). The 'facts relating to the breach, its effect and the remedial action taken' (which, under DPA 2018 s 67(6), constitute 'information relating to a personal data breach,' form part of the 'description of the nature of the personal data breach' in DPA 2018 s 67(4)(a). Where a personal data breach involves personal data that has been transmitted by or to a person who is a controller under the law of another member State, the information in (e) must be communicated to that person without undue delay: DPA 2018 s 67(8); LED Art 30(6).

[224] DPA 2018 s 67(9); LED Art 30(2).

[225] DPA 2018 s 68(1); LED Art 31(1). As to the meaning of 'data protection breach,' see §12–034. As to the meaning of 'rights and freedoms of data subjects' and 'risk' in this context, see §§8–006 to 8–007. There is a similar provision in relation to general processing: GDPR Art 34(1), (3), and see §9–038.

instance, be excused from so informing the data subject where:

(a) the controller has implemented appropriate technological and organisational protection measures which were applied to the personal data affected by the breach;[226]

(b) the controller has taken subsequent measures which ensure that the high risk to the rights and freedoms of data subjects is no longer likely to materialise; or

(c) notification would involve a disproportionate effort.[227]

But the Information Commissioner, after considering the likelihood of the breach resulting in a high risk to the rights and freedoms of individuals, may require the controller to notify the data subject of the breach.[228] Where the controller is required to notify the data subject of the breach, the notification must normally include:

(a) a description of the nature of the breach;

(b) the name and contact details of the data protection officer or other contact point from whom more information can be obtained;

(c) a description of the likely consequences of the personal data breach;

(d) a description of the measures taken or proposed to be taken by the controller to address the personal data breach, including, where appropriate, measures to mitigate its possible adverse effects.[229]

The controller may, however, restrict wholly or partly the information notified to the data subject where and to the extent that that is a necessary and proportionate measure:[230]

— to avoid obstructing an official or legal inquiry, investigation or procedure;
— to avoid prejudicing the prevention, detection, investigation or prosecution of criminal offences or the execution of criminal penalties;
— to protect public security;
— to protect national security; or
— to protect the rights and freedoms of others.[231]

2– 047 Whistleblowing

The controller must implement effective mechanisms to encourage the reporting to the controller or the Commissioner of an infringement of the requirements of the law enforcement processing regime.[232] This encouragement must include raising awareness of the employment law protections attaching to such reporting.[233] Any person so reporting an infringement will not be breaching an obligation of confidence owed by that person nor breaching any other restriction on the disclosure of information howsoever that obligation may arise.[234]

---

226 In other words, complied with the sixth data protection principle: see §12– 034. Although DPA 2018 s 55(3) uses the word 'technical' rather than 'technological' as used in DPA 2018 s 68(3)(a), it seems unlikely that anything turns on this. Accordingly, the controller is required to take into account the latest developments in technology, the cost of implementation, the nature, scope, context and purposes of processing, and the risks for the rights and freedoms of individuals arising from the processing: DPA 2018 s 55(3).

227 DPA 2018 s 68(3); LED Art 31(3). Where it would involve a disproportionate effort, the controller must instead make the information available to the data subject in an equally effective way, eg a public communication: DPA 2018 s 68(5).

228 DPA 2018 s 68(6); LED Art 31(4).

229 DPA 2018 s 68(2); LED Art 31(2).

230 DPA 2018 s 68(7); LED ARts 13(3) and 31(5).

231 As to the scope of these five overriding interests, see §13– 003.

232 DPA 2018 s 81(1)-(2); LED Art 48.

233 DPA 2018 s 81(3).

234 DPA 2018 s 81(4).

9. International transfers

12–048 Introduction

The transfer or transmission of personal data is an instance of processing of personal data[235] that carries additional restrictions and obligations. Within the law enforcement processing regime, a competent authority may not transfer or transmit personal data outside the United Kingdom other than in prescribed circumstances. Where the transfer or transmission of the personal data is to a recipient in a 'third country' (ie not an EU Member State) or an 'international organisation,' the prescribed circumstances are more limited than where the recipient is in an EU Member State.[236] The objective of these restrictions is to ensure that the transfer itself is for law enforcement purposes and that the person, body or organisation receiving the personal data meets certain criteria. In addition to these restrictions, the transfer or transmission of personal data outside the United Kingdom is attended by additional obligations on the controller. The importance of these restrictions and additional obligations is reflected by a proscription on a processor making any particular transfer of personal data to a third country or international organisation unless instructed by the controller under a provision in the contract between the controller and processor.[237] Unlike transfers to a third country or an international organisation in the course of general processing, the law enforcement provisions are not directly concerned with ensuring that the destination to which the personal data is sent provides comparable, or any, data subject rights.[238] On the other hand, unlike transfers to a third country or an international organisation in the course of general processing, the law enforcement provisions are concerned with the attributes of the intended recipient, rather than just of the country in which the intended recipient is located.[239] In addition to the conditions that must be met before a competent authority may transfer or transmit personal data outside the United Kingdom and the obligations that are the consequence of such transfers, there are overarching conditions of transfer, both for outgoing personal data and incoming personal data.[240]

12–049 Third country conditions

A controller may not transfer personal data to a third country or to an international organisation unless three conditions are met:

(1) The transfer is necessary for any of the law enforcement purposes.[241]

(2) The transfer:

(a) is based on an 'adequacy decision';

(b) if not based on an adequacy decision, is based on there being

[235] DPA 2018 s 3(4)(d), 61(2)(i), 62(1)(d).

[236] These restrictions are set out in DPA 2018 ss 72-78. For the purposes of law enforcement processing, the term 'third country' means a country or territory other than a Member State. Thus, unlike in relation to general processing it does not include Iceland, Norway, Liechtenstein or the Swiss Confederation: see further §8–032. As to the meaning of 'international organisations,' see §8–033. The LED gives Member States considerable latitude in setting the conditions for law enforcement international transfers: LED Arts 9(3)-(4) and 39.

[237] DPA 2018 s 59(7).

[238] In relation to international transfers in general processing, see §§9–057 to 9–064.

[239] DPA 2018 s 73(4), ie the 'third condition,' and s 77.

[240] DPA 2018 s 80. See further §12–058.

[241] DPA 2018 s 73(2). As to the meaning of 'necessary,' see §8–034. As to the meaning of the law enforcement purposes, see §12–006.

'appropriate safeguards'; or

(c) if not based on an adequacy decision or on there being appropriate safeguards, is based on 'special circumstances.'[242]

(3) Either:

(a) the intended recipient is a 'relevant authority' in a third country or an international organisation that is a 'relevant international organisation'; or

(b) the controller is a specific sort of competent authority, and the intended recipient is not a relevant authority, and certain additional conditions are met.[243]

Where the conditions are met, the controller must, in transferring personal data to a third country or to an international organisation, impose a 'subsequent transfer condition' on the recipient.[244] Where the personal data was originally transmitted or otherwise made available to the controller or another competent authority in Member State B by a competent authority in Member State A, there is a fourth condition that must also be met, namely:

(4) A competent authority in Member State A must authorise the transfer from Member State B in accordance with the law of Member State A.[245] However, authorisation is not required where the transfer is necessary for the prevention of an immediate and serious threat either to the public security of a Member State or a third country or to the essential interests of a Member State, and the authorisation cannot be obtained in good time.[246]

12–050 Adequacy decision

The first method of satisfying the second condition is for the transfer to be based on an 'adequacy decision.' This means that:

(a) the European Commission has decided, in accordance with Article 36 of the Law Enforcement Directive, that the recipient third country (or a territory or one or more specified sectors within that third country) or the recipient international organisation ensures an adequate level of protection of personal data; and

(b) that decision has not been repealed or suspended, or amended in a way that demonstrates that the Commission no longer considers there to be an adequate level of protection of personal data.[247]

---

242 DPA 2018 s 73(3). As to the meaning of an 'adequacy decision,' see §12–050. As to the meaning of 'appropriate safeguards,' see §12–051. As to the meaning of 'special circumstances,' see §12–052. As to the relationship between these three bases and their application, see *R (El Gizouli) v SSHD* [2020] UKSC 10 at [8]-[15], [154]-[158] and [209]-[227].

243 DPA 2018 s 73(4). In relation to this condition, see §12–054 below.

244 DPA 2018 s 78(1). As to the meaning of a 'subsequent transfer condition,' see §12–056.

245 DPA 2018 s 73(1)(b). The sub-section as drafted does not make sense, but the intended meaning can be worked out from LED Art 35(1)(e).

246 DPA 2018 s 73(5). Where a transfer is made without the authorisation, the authority in the Member State which would have been responsible for deciding whether to authorise the transfer must be informed without delay: DPA 2018 s 73(6). Where the fourth condition applies, the 'subsequent transfer condition' is more onerous: see §12–056.

247 DPA 2018 s 74; LED Art 36(1). In assessing the adequacy of the level of protection for the purposes of an adequacy decision, the Commission will take into account:

(a) the rule of law, respect for human rights and fundamental freedoms, relevant legislation, both general and sectoral, including concerning public security, defence, national security and criminal law and the access of public authorities to personal data, as well as the implementation of such legislation, data protection rules, professional rules and security measures, including rules for the onward transfer of personal data to another third country or international organisation, which are complied with in that country or international organisation, case-law, as well as effective and enforceable data subject rights and effective administrative and judicial redress for the data subjects whose personal data are

An adequacy decision is effected by the adoption of an implementing act of the European Commission.[248] The implementing act must specify its territorial and sectoral application. It must also provide a mechanism for periodic review of not more than 4 years.[249] Where a transfer is based on an adequacy decision, there are no specific procedural obligations that attend the transfer.

12–051 Appropriate safeguards

The second method of satisfying the second condition is only available where the recipient country is not covered by an adequacy decision. The second method relies on there being 'appropriate safeguards.' This means either:[250]

(1) that there is a legal instrument containing appropriate safeguards for the protection of personal data and that that instrument binds the intended recipient of the data; or

(2) that the controller, having assessed all the circumstances surrounding transfers of that type of personal data to the third country or international organisation, concludes that appropriate safeguards exist to protect the data. In this case, the controller must inform the Commissioner about the categories of data transfers that take place.[251]

Where a transfer is based on appropriate safeguards, the controller making the transfer must document the transfer and must provide that documentation to the Commissioner on request. The documentation must include: the date and time of the transfer; the name of and any other pertinent information about the recipient; the justification for the transfer; and a description of the personal data transferred.[252]

12–052 Special circumstances

The third method of satisfying the second condition is only available where the recipient country is not covered by an adequacy decision and the transfer is not based on there being appropriate safeguards. The third method of satisfying the second condition requires that the transfer be based on 'special circumstances.' A transfer of personal data to a third country or international organisation is based on special circumstances where the transfer is necessary in any one or more of the following circumstances:[253]

(1) To protect the vital interests of the data subject or another person.[254]

---

transferred;

(b) the existence and effective functioning of one or more independent supervisory authorities in the third country or to which an international organisation is subject, with responsibility for ensuring and enforcing compliance with data protection rules, including adequate enforcement powers, for assisting and advising data subjects in exercising their rights and for cooperation with the supervisory authorities of the Member States; and

(c) the international commitments the third country or international organisation concerned has entered into, or other obligations arising from legally binding conventions or instruments as well as from its participation in multilateral or regional systems, in particular in relation to the protection of personal data: LED Art 36(2).

[248] Regulation (EU) No 182/2011, Art 5. The Commission is required to publish in the Official Journal of the European Union and on its website a list of the third countries, territories and specified sectors within a third country and international organisations for which it has decided that an adequate level of protection is or is no longer ensured: LED Art 36(8).

[249] LED Art 36(3).

[250] DPA 2018 s 75(1); LED Art 37(1).

[251] DPA 2018 s 75(2).

[252] DPA 2018 s 75(3).

[253] DPA 2018 s 76(1); LED Art 38.

[254] As to the meaning of the 'vital interests' of the data subject or another person, see LED recital (35), (37) and (72)

(2) To safeguard the legitimate interests of the data subject.[255]
(3) For the prevention of an immediate and serious threat to the public security of a member State or a third country.
(4) In individual cases for any of the law enforcement purposes, but only provided that the controller determines that fundamental rights and freedoms of the data subject override the public interest in the transfer.
(5) In individual cases for a 'legal purpose,' but only provided that the controller determines that fundamental rights and freedoms of the data subject override the public interest in the transfer. A transfer is necessary for a legal purpose only where:
   (a) it is necessary for the purpose of, or in connection with, any legal proceedings (including prospective legal proceedings) relating to any of the law enforcement purposes;
   (b) it is necessary for the purpose of obtaining legal advice in relation to any of the law enforcement purposes; or
   (c) it is otherwise necessary for the purposes of establishing, exercising or defending legal rights in relation to any of the law enforcement purposes.[256]

Where a transfer is based on appropriate safeguards, the controller making the transfer must document the transfer and must provide that documentation to the Commissioner on request. The documentation must include: the date and time of the transfer; the name of and any other pertinent information about the recipient; the justification for the transfer; and a description of the personal data transferred.[257]

12– 053 Relevant authorities etc

The first method of satisfying the third condition is for the intended recipient of the personal data to be either a 'relevant authority' in a third country or a 'relevant international organisation.'[258] These are defined terms:

— 'relevant authority' means any person based in a third country that has, in that country, functions comparable to those of a competent authority;[259] and
— 'relevant international organisation' means an international organisation that carries out functions for any of the law enforcement purposes.[260]

Where a competent authority relies on this method of satisfying the third condition, there are no additional procedural obligations that the competent authority must meet in carrying out the transfer.

12– 054 Additional conditions

The second method of satisfying the third condition is very narrow in operation. First, it is

---

and GDPR recitals (46) and (112).

255 As to the meaning of the 'legitimate interests' of the data subject, see §8– 006.

256 DPA 2018 s 76(4).

257 DPA 2018 s 76(3).

258 DPA 2018 s 73(4)(a). As to the meaning of a 'third country,' see §8– 032.

259 DPA 2018 s 72(2). Given that the functions of the competent authorities listed in DPA 2018 Sch 7 cover the range of governmental activity (other than purely local or parochial) and given that the requirement is that the relevant authority has functions comparable to those of 'a' competent authority, it should not be difficult for a competent authority to find a person in a third country with comparable functions, whether to its own functions or those of another competent authority.

260 DPA 2018 s 73(7). As to the meaning of 'international organisation,' see §8– 033.

applicable to only some of the competent authorities.[261] Secondly, that limited class of competent authorities will satisfy the third condition only if three requirements are met, namely:

(a) the intended recipient is in a third country (ie the recipient is not in a EU Member State);

(b) the intended recipient is not a 'relevant authority' (ie the recipient is *not* a person that has in the third country functions comparable to those of a competent authority); and

(c) all four 'additional conditions' are met.[262]

The four additional conditions are:

(1) The transfer is strictly necessary in a specific case for the performance of a task of the transferring controller as provided by law for any of the law enforcement purposes.

(2) The transferring controller has determined that there are no fundamental rights and freedoms of the data subject concerned that override the public interest necessitating the transfer.

(3) The transferring controller considers that the transfer of the personal data to a relevant authority in the third country would be ineffective or inappropriate (for example, where the transfer could not be made in sufficient time to enable its purpose to be fulfilled).

(4) The transferring controller informs the intended recipient of the specific purpose or purposes for which the personal data may, so far as necessary, be processed.

Where a competent authority relies on this method of satisfying the third condition for transfer of personal data, it must without undue delay inform a relevant authority in the third country to which the personal data has been transferred of the transfer.[263] The transferring controller must document the transfer and must inform the Information Commissioner about the transfer.[264]

12–055 Subsequent transfer condition

In transferring personal data to a third country or to an international organisation on any of the above bases, the transferring controller must make it a condition of the transfer that the data is not to be further transferred to a third country or international organisation without the authorisation of the transferring controller or another competent authority.[265] The transferring controller may only give an authorisation (whether to the first third country recipient or other recipients down the line) where the further transfer is necessary for a law enforcement purpose.[266] In deciding whether to give the authorisation, the transferring controller must take

[261] Namely, the competent authorities specified in paragraphs 5 to 17, 21, 24 to 28, 34 to 51, 54 and 56 of DPA 2018 Sch 7. In general terms, these are the chief constables of the various police forces, the revenue authorities (including HMRC), the Financial Conduct Authority, the Health & Safety Executive, various bodies with parole functions, and bodies whose principal function is the prosecution of offences regardless of subject-matter. This second method of meeting the third condition does not constrain the operation of international agreements in force between Member States and third countries in the field of judicial cooperation in criminal matters and police co-operation: DPA 2018 s 77(8).

[262] DPA 2018 s 73(4)(b). DPA 2018 s 77(1)-(4). The requirement to meet all four, rather than just one or more, is evident from the requirement in DPA 2018 s 73(4)(b)(ii) that the 'additional conditions in s 77 *are* met.'

[263] DPA 2018 s 77(6). The competent authority is relieved of this obligation where it would be 'ineffective or inappropriate,' whatever that might mean.

[264] DPA 2018 s 77(7). The obligation to inform the Information Commissioner does not depend on a request from the Commissioner.

[265] DPA 2018 s 78(1). The proscription on further transfer is not limited to the person receiving the personal data from the transferring controller: the obligation in DPA 2018 s 78(1) is cast in the passive voice, making it clear that the condition must be imposed on every person down the line receiving the personal data.

[266] DPA 2018 s 78(2).

into account the seriousness of the circumstances leading to the request for authorisation, the purpose for which the personal data was originally transferred, and the standards for the protection of personal data that apply in the third country or international organisation to which the personal data would be transferred.[267] Where, because of the origins of the personal data, the transferring controller must meet the fourth condition, [268] the transferring controller must normally refuse an authorisation unless that member State, or any person based in that member State which is a competent authority for the purposes of the Law Enforcement Directive, has authorised the transfer in accordance with the law of the member State.[269]

12–056 Overarching transfer obligations

In addition to the conditions and obligations imposed on a controller where that controller transfers or transmits personal data to a third country or an international organisation, there are overarching obligations that apply whenever for a law enforcement purpose a controller transmits or otherwise makes available personal data to a person, body or organisation outside the United Kingdom.[270] These obligations apply to transfers to persons, bodies and organisations in third countries, as well as to those in EU Member States. The starting requirement is that whenever a controller transmits or otherwise makes available personal data to such persons, bodies or organisations:

> the controller must consider whether, if the personal data had instead been transmitted or otherwise made available within the United Kingdom to another competent authority, processing of the data by the other competent authority would have been subject to any restrictions by virtue of any enactment or rule of law.[271]

Given that any transfer for law enforcement purposes of personal data by one competent authority in the United Kingdom to another competent authority will constitute 'processing' of that personal data, whenever there are restrictions of processing arising under Part 3 of the DPA 2018, the transmitting controller will be required to give consideration to these restrictions. 'Restriction of processing' does not mean the regulatory constraints universally applicable to law enforcement processing of personal data by a competent authority: it means the formal marking of personal data by which its processing has been limited.[272] Where there is such a restriction on processing, the transmitting controller must inform the:

> ...recipient that the data is transmitted or otherwise made available subject to compliance by that person with the same restrictions (which must be set out in the information given to that person).[273]

Where the controller is transmitting the personal data to an EU recipient, the controller may not impose other restrictions on the processing of the personal data transmitted or otherwise made available by the controller.[274] Where the transmission of personal data is in the opposite direction – in other words, where a competent authority in the United Kingdom receives

---

[267] DPA 2018 s 78(3).

[268] See §12–049.

[269] DPA 2018 s 78(4); LED Art 35(1)(c). Refusal of authorisation is not required where the transfer is necessary for the prevention of an immediate and serious threat either to the public security of a Member State or a third country or to the essential interests of a Member State, and the authorisation cannot be obtained in good time: DPA 2018 s 78(5). In this situation, the authority in the Member State which would have been responsible for deciding whether to authorise the transfer must be informed without delay: DPA 2018 s 78(6).

[270] DPA 2018 s 80.

[271] DPA 2018 s 80(3).

[272] DPA 2018 s 33(6). The restriction on processing may arise under DPA 2018 s 46(4), 47(2)-(4), 48(9)-(10), 51(4)(b), 79(1) or 151(1)(b).

[273] DPA 2018 s 80(4); LED Art 9(3)-(4), recital (36).

[274] DPA 2018 s 80(5). See further Council Framework Decision 2008/977/JHA in relation to judicial cooperation in criminal matters and police cooperation.

personal data for a law enforcement purpose from a competent authority in an EU Member State – and the competent authority in the EU Member State advises the UK competent authority that the data is transmitted or otherwise made available subject to compliance with restrictions, the UK competent authority must comply with the restrictions set out by the EU competent authority.[275] Where the controller is transmitting the personal data to a non-EU recipient, the controller may, having regard to the considerations such as those in the 'additional conditions,' transmit the personal data with further conditions on its processing by the recipient.[276]

12–057 Ancillary obligations

A controller's record of the categories of processing activities must include the categories of transfers of personal data to a third country or an international organisation.[277] A processor's record of the categories of processing activities carried out on behalf of a controller must include details of transfers of personal data to a third country or an international organisation, including the identification of that third country or international organisation.[278] The logs of processing operations that a controller and processor are required to keep include a log of transfers.[279]

12–058 Non-compliance

Where a controller or processor has failed, or is failing, to comply with the principles for transfers of personal data to third countries or international organisations, the Information Commissioner may serve an enforcement notice.[280]

10. ENFORCEMENT AND REMEDIES

12–059 Overview

The Information Commissioner is the 'supervisory authority' for the purposes of the Law Enforcement Directive.[281] The Commissioner's monitoring and enforcement of the provisions of the law enforcement processing regime is statutorily linked to the protection of individuals with regard to the processing of personal data.[282] In carrying out functions under the Act, the Commissioner must have regard to the importance of securing an appropriate level of protection for personal data, taking account of the interests of data subjects, controllers and matters of general public interest.[283] Specifically, the Commissioner must:

(a) monitor and enforce the provisions of the law enforcement processing regime;
(b) promote public awareness and understanding of the risks, rules, safeguards and rights in relation to processing of personal data under the law enforcement

---

275 DPA 2018 s 80(6)-(7); LED Art 9(3)-(4).

276 DPA 2018 s 77; LED recital (36). See further §12–055.

277 DPA 2018 s 61(2)(h). In relation to the controller's record, see §12–040.

278 DPA 2018 s 61(4)(e). Given that the terms of the required contract between controller and processor must include a term that the processor may transfer personal data to a third country or international organisation only if instructed by the controller to make the particular transfer (DPA 2018 s 59(7)), the words 'where explicitly instructed to do so by the controller' in s 61(4)(e) should not restrict the operation of the recording requirement. In relation to the processor's record, see §12–040.

279 DPA 2018 s 62(1)(d). In relation to logs, see §12–041.

280 DPA 2018 s 149(2)(e). In relation to enforcement notices, see further §§48–034 to 48–038.

281 DPA 2018 s 116(1)(a); LED Art 41.

282 DPA 2018 ss 2(1)(c) and 116.

283 DPA 2018 s 2(2).

processing regime;

(c) advise Parliament, the government and other institutions and bodies on legislative and administrative measures relating to the protection of individuals' rights and freedoms with regard to processing of personal data under the law enforcement processing regime;

(d) promote the awareness of controllers and processors of their obligations under the law enforcement processing regime;

(e) on request, provide information to a data subject concerning the exercise of the data subject's rights under the law enforcement processing regime; and

(f) conduct investigations on the application of the law enforcement processing regime.[284]

12– 060 Regulatory enforcement

In relation to the law enforcement processing regime, the Information Commissioner has the power:

(a) to notify a controller or a processor of an alleged infringement of any of the obligations imposed on a controller or processor;

(b) to issue a warning to a controller or processor that intended processing operations are likely to infringe those obligations;

(c) to issue reprimands to a controller or processor where processing operations have infringed those obligations; and

(d) to issue, whether on request or on the Commissioner's initiative, opinions to Parliament, the government or other institutions as well as the public on any issue related to the protection of personal data.[285]

Where an individual considers that the controller is not complying with its obligations, the individual may complain to the Information Commissioner. The Commissioner must investigate the complaint and enforce the obligations.[286] If the Commissioner is satisfied that the controller has failed, or is failing, to comply with any of the continuing obligations, the Commissioner may serve an enforcement notice.[287]

12– 061 Private remedies

Non-compliance by a competent authority with the continuing obligations may give rise to a cause of action actionable by the data subject in whose favour the obligation has been imposed.[288] This is additional to regulatory action that may be taken by the Information Commissioner in respect of such breaches.

[284] DPA 2018 s 116 and Sch 13 para 1(1).

[285] DPA 2018 Sch 13 para 2. In relation to the Information Commissioner generally, see Chapter 44.

[286] DPA 2018 Sch 13 para 1(1)(a), (e), (g). See further §48– 004.

[287] DPA 2018 s 149(2)(a). Regulatory enforcement is considered at §§48– 014 to 48– 055.

[288] Private remedies are considered further in §§48– 005 to 48– 013.

CHAPTER 13

Law enforcement processing: data subject rights

1. OVERVIEW

13–001 Introduction

In addition to data subject rights that enure from the obligations on competent authorities whenever processing personal data for the law enforcement purposes,[1] Part 3 of the DPA 2018 (ss 29-81) confers on every data subject five separate rights exercisable against such a controller when processing his or her personal data for law enforcement purposes:

(1) a right of access;
(2) a right to rectification;
(3) a right to erasure;
(4) a right to restrict processing; and
(5) a right not to be subject to automated decision-making.

---
[1] That is, the obligations dealt with in Chapter 12.

The first four rights are exercised by giving a notice to the controller. Upon receiving a notice the controller comes under a correlative duty to comply. The fifth right and the correlative duty subsist whenever a controller is processing personal data for the law enforcement purposes and requires no notice. To facilitate a data subject exercising these rights, there is a further, continuing obligation on every competent authority processing personal data to make available basic information about its processing activities – 'the information obligation.'[2] The first right (ie the right of access) and the information obligation may be restricted where required to secure overriding interests.[3] The controller may not so restrict the second to fifth rights. Non-compliance with a duty will expose the controller both to regulatory action from the Information Commissioner and to a private law claim from the data subject.[4]

13–002 Differences from GDPR regime

As with the continuing obligations imposed on competent authorities when processing personal data for the law enforcement purposes, the rights conferred on data subjects vis-à-vis those authorities are a diluted version of those imposed on controllers and conferred on data subjects under the general processing regime.[5] Two of the rights conferred on data subjects in relation to processing of personal data under the general processing regime have no equivalent in relation to law enforcement processing of personal data by a competent authority:

— the right to portability of data;[6] and
— the right to object.[7]

Most of the data subject rights in the law enforcement regime can be traced to the previous data processing regime – the DPA 1998 – with the similarities to that regime being greater than the differences.[8]

13–003 The overriding interests

The information obligation and the right of access may be restricted in order to secure a set of defined, overriding interests.[9] Whenever the controller is under a duty to comply with the information obligation or the right of access, the controller may restrict, wholly or partly, compliance with the duty to the extent that and for so long as the restriction is, having regard to the fundamental rights and legitimate interests of the data subject,[10] a necessary and proportionate measure:[11]

(a) to avoid obstructing an official or legal inquiry, investigation or procedure;
(b) to avoid prejudicing the prevention, detection, investigation or prosecution of criminal offences or the execution of criminal penalties;

---

2 See §13–004.

3 See §13–003.

4 Regulatory enforcement is considered at §§48–014 to 48–055. Private law claims are considered at §§48–005 to 48–013.

5 For that reason, jurisprudence on the correlative provision in the general processing regime will often illuminate, but not dictate, the meaning and operation of its law enforcement processing counterpart.

6 GDPR Art 20(1). As to this right, see §§10–035 to 10–039.

7 GDPR Art 21(1)-(2). As to this right, see §§10–040 to 10–044. There is a right to object to processing of personal data under the intelligence services regime: DPA 2018 s 99(1). See further §14–033.

8 Again, for that reason the jurisprudence on the correlative provision under the DPA 1998 can be helpful. However, some of the earlier authorities from the Court of Appeal dealing with the DPA 1998 should be approached with caution.

9 DPA 2018 ss 44(4) and 45(4); LED Art 13(3).

10 As to the meaning of 'the fundamental rights and legitimate interests of the data subject,' see §8–006 and LED Art 1(2)(a) and recitals (2), (25), (37), (38), (93) and (104).

11 In relation to the meaning of 'necessary' in this context, see §8–034.

(c) to protect public security;[12]
(d) to protect national security;[13] or
(e) to protect the rights and freedoms of others,[14]

– 'the overriding interests.' Although the second to fourth rights may not themselves be so restricted, where or to the extent that a controller refuses a request exercising the second, third or fourth right, with a resultant obligation on the controller to give reasons for that refusal, the controller may restrict what information is given in those reasons where it is a necessary and proportionate measure to protect the overriding interests.[15] Although in the first instance it is the controller who evaluates whether restriction of compliance with the obligation or the right is a necessary and proportionate measure to protect an overriding interest, this must be objectively justified.

13– 004 The information obligation

The absence of any manifestation of the processing of a data subject's personal data does not empty or lessen that data subject's right to protection against misuse or over-use of his or her personal data. The processing of personal data for the law enforcement purposes is, in particular, liable to be submerged. Unless a controller makes certain information available to a data subject (without prompting by the data subject), a data subject may be oblivious to the controller's processing of his or her personal data. To make effective the rights conferred on data subjects, the law enforcement processing regime imposes on each competent authority processing personal data for the law enforcement purposes a continuant, qualified obligation to make certain information available to data subjects – 'the information obligation' – namely:[16]

— the identity and the contact details of the controller;
— where applicable, the contact details of the data protection officer;[17]
— the purposes for which the controller processes personal data;[18]
— the existence of the rights of data subjects to request from the controller access to personal data, rectification of personal data and erasure of personal data or the restriction of its processing;[19]
— the existence of the right to lodge a complaint with the Commissioner and the contact details of the Commissioner;[20]
— information about the legal basis for the processing;[21]
— information about the period for which the personal data will be stored or, where

---

12 The term 'public security' is conventionally used in EU measures: see, for example, Directive 95/46/EC Art 13(1)(c), Directive 2003/4/EC (Environmental Information) Art 4(2)(b) and Regulation 1049/2001 Art 4(1)(a). As to the meaning of 'public security,' see §16– 014, §17– 002, §19– 015 and §43– 040.

13 As to the meaning of 'national security,' see §26– 050.

14 In relation to rights and freedoms of others, see §8– 007.

15 DPA 2018 s 48(3). The controller is under a duty to record the reasons for a decision to restrict the provision of information when supplying reasons for refusing to comply with these duties: DPA 2018 s 48(6)(a). The data subject may request the Information Commissioner to check that a refusal to comply with such a duty was lawful and, where so requested by the data subject, the Commissioner is entitled to examine the unrestricted reasons for the refusal: DPA 2018 ss 48(6) and 51(1)-(2). In any refusal notice, the controller must inform the data subject of the right to make such a request to the Information Commissioner: DPA 2018 s 48(1)(b)(ii).

16 DPA 2018 s 44(1)-(2); LED Art 13(1)-(2).

17 As to data protection officers, see §12– 042.

18 This is linked to the second data protection principle: see §§12– 023 to 12– 025.

19 That is, the rights under DPA 2018 ss 45, 46 and 47.

20 That is, the right under DPA 2018 s 165(2). In relation to complaints, see further §48– 004.

21 This is linked to the first data protection principle: see §§12– 014 to 12– 022.

that is not possible, about the criteria used to determine that period;[22]

— where applicable, information about the categories of recipients of the personal data (including recipients in third countries or international organisations);[23] and

— such further information as is necessary to enable the exercise of the data subject's rights.[24]

The obligation is disapplied in relation to the processing of personal data contained in a judicial decision or other court-created documents that relate to a criminal investigation or criminal proceedings, including proceedings for the purpose of executing a criminal penalty.[25] The obligation to make information available may be restricted where that is required to secure the overriding interests.[26] Where the controller restricts compliance with the information obligation, whether in whole or in part, the controller must inform the data subject in writing and without undue delay:[27]

(a) that the provision of information has been restricted;
(b) of the reasons for the restriction;
(c) of the data subject's right to make a request to the Information Commissioner to check that the restriction was lawful;[28]
(d) of the data subject's right to lodge a complaint with the Commissioner;[29] and
(e) of the data subject's right to apply to a court.[30]

If a data subject is dissatisfied with a restriction on the information provided, a data subject should normally in the first instance request the Information Commissioner to check whether the restriction was lawful and await the outcome of the Commissioner's investigation.[31]

13–005 Summary of the rights

The five rights conferred on data subjects by Part 3 of the DPA 2018 are as follows:

(1) A 'right of access.'[32] This is a multi-faceted right that entitles a data subject to obtain from the controller:
   (a) confirmation whether or not personal data about the data subject are being processed;
   (b) if personal data about the data subject are being processed, certain information about the personal data being processed, the purposes of the processing, the period for which that personal information will be

---

[22] This is linked to the fifth data protection principle: see §§12–032 to 12–033.

[23] In relation to international transfers, the controller will need to refer to satisfaction of the third country conditions: see §12–049.

[24] The further information might relate to the third data protection principle ('adequate, relevant and not excessive,' as to which see §§12–026 to 12–027), the fourth data protection principle ('accurate and up-to-date,' as to which see §§12–028 to 12–031) and the sixth processing principle ('processed securely,' as to which see §§12–034 to 12–036). An example of where further information may be necessary is when the personal data being processed was collected without the knowledge of the data subject: DPA 2018 s 44(3).

[25] DPA 2018 s 43(3)-(4).

[26] DPA 2018 s 44(4). As to the overriding interests, see §13–003.

[27] DPA 2018 s 44(5). The obligation to inform the data subject is disapplied where provision of the information would undermine the purpose of the restriction: DPA 2018 s 44(6). This does not, however, disapply the obligation to record the reasons for the restriction, which must be made available to the Information Commissioner on request: DPA 2018 s 44(7).

[28] Under DPA 2018 s 51(1)-(2). See further §13–032.

[29] That is, the right under DPA 2018 s 165(2). In relation to complaints, see further §48–004.

[30] That is, the right under DPA 2018 s 167. In relation to private law claims, see further §13–034.

[31] DPA 2018 s 51(1)-(2). See further §13–032.

[32] DPA 2018 s 45; LED Art 14.

stored, the persons to whom that personal data have or will be disclosed, the source of the personal data and a statement of the data subject's rights; and

(c) a copy of the personal data.

The right of access may be restricted to the extent that that is required to secure the overriding intersts.[33]

(2) A 'right to rectification.'[34] A data subject can require a controller to rectify inaccurate personal data concerning the data subject and to complete incomplete personal data. The right to rectification is not subject to the overriding interests.

(3) A 'right to erasure.'[35] This is sometimes called the 'right to be forgotten.' Where a controller is in breach of a data protection principle in the law enforcement processing of a data subject's personal data, that data subject may require the controller to erase such personal data as the controller holds about the data subject. The right to erasure is not subject to the overriding interests.

(4) A 'right to restrict processing.'[36] Where a controller is in breach of a data protection principle in the law enforcement processing of a data subject's personal data, that data subject may require the controller to restrict processing personal data about him or her. The right to restrict processing is not subject to the overriding interests.

(5) A right not to be subject to automated decision-making.[37] The default position is that a data subject is not to be made subject to a decision based solely on automated processing which produces legal effects concerning the data subject. This right does not require a notice from the data subject. The right to not be subject to automated decision-making is not subject to the overriding interests.

In order to exercise the rights in (2)-(4) effectively, a data subject will very often need first to ascertain the extent to which, and manner in which, his or her personal data is being processed for law enforcement purposes and secure access to it by making a request under (1).[38] The response to a request under (1) will often be useful to dispel any suggestion that a request under (2)-(4) is manifestly unfounded: for example, where the response to a request under (1) reveals inaccuracies in the data subject's personal data being processed by the controller or that there are other breaches of the data protection principles.

13– 006 Rights against processors

Where a processor is processing personal data, that processor will, by definition, be carrying out that processing on behalf of a controller.[39] The five rights are exercisable against a controller, and not against a processor processing on behalf of that controller. The controller is responsible for all processing of personal data carried out on its behalf by a processor, and this includes the correlative duties that arise where a data subject exercises any of the above rights. A controller is under a statutory obligation to use only processors that provide sufficient guarantees to implement measures that will ensure the protection of the rights of the data subject.[40] The relationship between controller and processor must be governed by a binding

---

[33] See further §13– 003 and §13– 017.

[34] DPA 2018 ss 46, 48; LED Art 16(1).

[35] DPA 2018 ss 47(1) , (4) and 48; LED Art 16(2).

[36] DPA 2018 ss 47(2)-(4) and 48; LED Art 16(3). As to the meaning of 'restriction of processing,' see §8– 031.

[37] DPA 2018 ss 49-50; LED Art 11.

[38] That is implicitly recognised in DPA s 45(2)(e).

[39] DPA 2018 s 32(3); LED Art 3(9).

[40] DPA 2018 s 59(2); LED Art 22(1).

contract, which must include provisions to assist the controller in fulfilling its duties where a data subject exercises his or her rights.[41]

13–007 Facilitating exercise of rights

A data subject may contact a controller's data protection officer in relation to all issues relating to the exercise of his or her rights.[42] The controller must facilitate the exercise of a data subject's rights.[43] The Information Commissioner, too, is under a general obligation to provide on request information to data subjects concerning the exercise of their rights.[44] In addition, where a data subject exercises his or her rights (ie information, access, rectification, erasure or restriction), but the controller claims reliance on one or more of the exemptions to restrict the response or refuse the request, the data subject may request the Commissioner to check that the restriction or refusal was lawful.[45] If so requested, the Commissioner must take such steps as appear to the Commissioner 'to be appropriate' to respond, which may include serving an information notice or an assessment notice.[46] The Commissioner must inform the data subject of the outcome of that exercise, as well as the data subject's right to apply to the County Court or the High Court for a compliance order.[47]

13–008 Form of request

There is no specified form for a request exercising any of the data subject rights. However, it is implicit in the DPA 2018 that the request should provide sufficient information that the controller is able to identify the data subject in a way that leaves no reasonable doubt.[48] In practice, to avoid legitimate doubt and facilitate engagement with the issues, a request should give:

- the full name and address of the controller to whom it is addressed, including any email address;
- the date of the request;
- an identification of the right(s) that the data subject is exercising;
- the full name, postal address and date of birth of the data subject;[49]
- the format in which the data subject wishes to receive any response (ie electronic, printed or oral); and
- the address to which the data subject wishes the controller to send the response.

It is prudent for a data subject to include in the request a requirement that the controller contact the data subject immediately should the controller have any doubts about the identity of the data subject. Depending on the right being exercised, a request may need to include other information.[50] If at all possible, it is prudent for a data subject to restrict the reach of the

---

41 DPA 2018 s 59(6)(c); LED Art 22(3)(c).

42 DPA 2018 s 70(4). In relation to the role of the data protection officer and how the officer must perform the functions allocated to the office, see §§12–042 to 12–043.

43 DPA 2018 s 52(6); LED Art 12(2).

44 DPA 2018 s 116, Sch 13 para 1(1)(e).

45 DPA 2018 s 51(1)-(2); LED Art 17(1).

46 DPA 2018 s 51(3); LED Art 17(3). In relation to information notices, see §§48–018 to 48–024; in relation to assessment notices, see §§48–025 to 48–033.

47 DPA 2018 s 51(4)-(6); LED Art 17(3). In relation to appeals to the County Court and the High Court, see §48–007 to 48–013. As to compliance orders, see §48–012.

48 DPA 2018 s 52(4); LED Art 12(5).

49 To avoid needless correspondence, it is sensible to include a photocopy of identification documentation (such as a passport and utilities or bank statement).

50 The other information required is dealt with below under the individual rights.

request, for example by date range, or at least invite the controller to ask the data subject to refine the request if the controller estimates that compliance will impose an excessive amount of work.[51] If the data subject anticipates that non-compliance by the controller with the requirements of the request will result in loss, damage or distress of any kind, it is prudent to spell that out in the request, together with a statement of the kinds of loss and damage anticipated and how they might result. A request may be addressed to the data protection officer of the controller.[52]

13– 009 Requiring further details

The only explicit basis on which a controller can refuse to act on a request from a data subject is if the controller has reasonable doubts about the identify of the data subject.[53] Although requesting additional information to confirm the data subject's identity is not expressed as a duty on the controller, declining to act on a request on the basis of identity doubt without asking for confirmatory information would breach the duty to facilitate exercise of the data subject's rights.[54] On the other hand, acting on a request in relation to which there are reasonable doubts as to the data subject's identity risks the controller breaching various continuing obligations. Once a controller has satisfactorily identified a data subject, the controller must:

— act on the request by considering its terms;
— decide whether it is manifestly unfounded or excessive;
— if it is not manifestly unfounded or excessive, comply with the request save to the extent (if at all) that a restriction of the right is necessary to protect an overriding interest;
— notify the data subject of what has been done (including the results); and
— in the event of a restriction having been applied, notify the data subject of its extent and the reasons for its application.

13– 010 Fees

A controller must normally comply with a data subject request without charge to the data subject.[55] This includes the provision of a copy of the data subject's personal information under the access right. The normal position is displaced and a controller may charge a reasonable fee where the controller demonstrates that a request from the data subject is manifestly unfounded or excessive, in particular because it repeats the substance of previous requests.[56] The fee should take account of the administrative costs of providing the information or communication or taking the action requested.[57]

13– 011 Unfounded or excessive request

Where a request from a data subject is manifestly unfounded[58] or excessive, the controller has

51 This will pre-empt any claim by the controller that the burden of complying with the request is manifestly unfounded or excessive in character.

52 DPA 2018 s 70(4).

53 DPA 2018 s 52(4); LED Art 12(5).

54 DPA 2018 s 52(6); LED Art 12(2)-(3).

55 DPA 2018 s 52(5); LED Art 12(4).

56 DPA 2018 s 53(1)-(2). Alternatively, in this situation the controller may refuse to act on the notice.

57 LED Art 12(4).

58 In relation to 'manifestly unfounded' requests, see §10– 011. Early judicial activism by the Court of Appeal in relation to the subject access right under the DPA 1998 expressly sought to give it a narrow construction, and introduced a purpose limitation: namely, that DPA 1998 s 7 entitled a data subject to have access to his or her

three options:

(1) charge the data subject a reasonable fee for the administrative costs of providing the information or taking the action requested and not act on the request until the charge is paid;[59]

(2) refuse to act on the request;[60] or

(3) overlook the shortcomings in the request and deal with it as if it were not manifestly unfounded or excessive.[61]

The burden is on the controller to show that a request from a data subject is manifestly unfounded or excessive.[62]

13–012 Time for compliance

The standard time for compliance is one month from the latest of:

— the controller receiving the request;

— the controller receiving requested additional information to confirm the identity of the individual making the request; and

— the individual making the request paying the fee required where the request is manifestly unfounded or excessive.[63]

Unlike the general processing regime, there is no provision for an extension of time.[64]

13–013 Mode of response

The controller must take reasonable steps to ensure that any information that is required to be provided to the data subject is provided in a concise, intelligible and easily accessible form, using clear and plain language.[65] Unless it is impractical to do so, the controller should provide the information in the same form (including electronic) as the data subject's request.[66]

---

personal data only to enable him or her to check whether the data controller's processing of it unlawfully infringed the data subject's privacy, and that it did not provide the data subject with 'automatic key to any information...of matters in which he may be named or involved': *Durant v Financial Services Authority* [2003] EWCA Civ 1746, [2004] FSR 28 at [27]-[29]; *Johnson v Medical Defence Union* [2007] EWCA Civ 262, [2007] 3 CMLR 9, (2007) 96 BMLR 99 at [16]. Later Court of Appeal authority shifted away from this reading down of DPA 1998 s 7: *Dawson-Damer v Taylor Wessing LLP* [2017] EWCA Civ 74, [2017] 1 WLR 3255; *Re Southern Pacific Personal Loans Ltd* [2013] EWHC 2485 (Ch), [2014] Ch 426. Whether or not it was ever correct under the DPA 1998, there is no basis for its transposition into the law enforcement processing regime, which does not tie data protection to personal privacy: see DPA 2018 s 2 and the LED (which does not at any point use the word 'privacy,' though it does, in recital (104) refer to respect for private life).

59 DPA 2018 ss 45(3)(b), 48(2)(b), 54(1)-(3).

60 DPA 2018 s 53(1). Although there is no express obligation on the controller to notify the data subject that it is refusing to act on the request, such stonewalling would contravene the duty on a controller to facilitate the exercise of a data subject's rights: DPA 2018 s 52(6).

61 Where there is a risk that the data subject will not share the controller's assessment, a controller's refusal to act may prompt the data subject to make a complaint to the Information Commissioner, and all that follows: DPA 2018 s 165(2)-(6). Should the Information Commissioner not share the controller's assessment, the Commissioner may take enforcement action: see Chapter 48. A data subject may also make an application to a court for a compliance order, with all that might follow: DPA 2018 s 167.

62 DPA 2018 s 53(3); LED Art 12(4).

63 DPA 2018 s 54.

64 GDPR Art 12(3).

65 DPA 2018 s 52(1); LED Art 12(1).

66 DPA 2018 s 52(2)-(3); LED Art 12(1).

2. RIGHT OF ACCESS

13–014 Scope

Every data subject has a restrictable right to obtain from a controller – ie a controller that is a competent authority – confirmation whether or not that controller (or a processor processing personal data on behalf of that controller)[67] is for a law enforcement purpose processing personal data concerning him or her.[68] The right is disapplied in relation to the processing of personal data contained in a judicial decision or other court-created documents that relate to a criminal investigation or criminal proceedings, including proceedings for the purpose of executing a criminal penalty.[69] The controller may also restrict the access right to the extent and for so long as that restriction is a necessary and proportionate measure to secure the overriding interests.[70] A similar right existed under the previous regime (undifferentiated between general processing and law enforcement processing), with such notices commonly called 'subject access requests.'[71]

13–015 Mode of compliance

Where a data subject exercises this right, the controller must, without undue delay and in any event before the end of the prescribed period,[72] respond confirming that it (or a processor acting on its behalf) is or is not processing for a law enforcement purpose personal data concerning the data subject.[73] Where the controller (or a processor on behalf of the controller) is for a law enforcement process processing personal data concerning the data subject, then, subject to any restrictions,[74] the controller must in its response also give the data subject a written statement containing the following information:[75]

(a) the [law enforcement] purposes of and legal basis for the processing;[76]
(b) the categories of personal data concerned;[77]
(c) the recipients or categories of recipient to whom the personal data have been or will be disclosed (including recipients or categories of recipients in third countries or international organisations);[78]

---

67 The entitlement is cast in the passive voice in order to capture both the controller and a processor acting on behalf of the controller.

68 DPA 2018 s 45(1)(a) in conjunction with ss 29(1)-(2) and 43(2); LED Art 14. A similar right is conferred on data subjects in relation to personal data processed by a controller under the general processing regime established by the GDPR and supplemented by the DPA 2018: see §§10–014 to 10–017.

69 DPA 2018 s 43(3)-(4).

70 DPA 2018 s 44(4). As to the overriding interests, see §13–003 and §13–017.

71 DPA 1998 s 7 and Directive 95/46/EC Arts 10-12. See further §15–053.

72 DPA 2018 s 45(3). As to the 'prescribed period,' see §13–012.

73 DPA 2018 s 45(1)(b) in conjunction with ss 29(1)-(2) and 43(2); LED Art 14. The controller must respond to the request if it is processing personal data concerning the data subject, even though it is not doing so for law enforcement purposes.

74 See §13–017.

75 DPA 2018 s 45(2); LED Art 14. This is analogous to the statement that a controller must provide to a data subject where such a request is made in relation to general processing of personal data: see §10–015.

76 The purposes for the processing is linked to the second data protection principle: see §§12–023 to 12–025. The legal basis for the processing is linked to the first data protection principle: see §§12–014 to 12–022.

77 The 'categories' of personal data is a reference to personal data the processing of which is attended by a higher level of protection, ie 'sensitive personal data': see §12–016; DPA 2018 ss 33(4), and 35(8); LED Art 10.

78 As to the meaning of 'third country,' see §8–032. As to the meaning of 'international organisations,' see §8–033.

(d) the period for which it is envisaged that the personal data will be stored or, where that is not possible, the criteria used to determine that period;
(e) the existence of the data subject's right to request from that controller:
  (i) rectification of personal data, and
  (ii) erasure of personal data or the restriction of its processing;[79]
(f) the existence of the data subject's right to lodge a complaint with the [Information] Commissioner and the contact details of the Commissioner;[80]
(g) communication of the personal data undergoing processing and of any available information as to its origin.

Subject to restrictions necessary to secure the overriding interests, the controller must give the data subject access to the personal data being processed for law enforcement purposes.[81] Where an access request is made and the data subject would have been entitled to receive information in response to that request, it is an offence for the controller and any employee or officer of the controller to alter, deface, block, erase, destroy or conceal information with the intention of preventing disclosure of all or part of the information to which the data subject would have been entitled.[82]

3– 016 Searches

Domestic case law under the previous data protection regime conceived a notion that a controller's obligation to search for personal data relating to the data subject was limited to what was 'proportionate.'[83] There is nothing in Part 3 of the DPA 2018 to support writing such a limitation into the law enforcement processing regime. In allowing a controller to refuse to act on requests that are 'manifestly unfounded or excessive,'[84] the Act and the Directive it implements have confined their attention to the requests themselves, rather than to the amount of effort required to comply with a request. The effort will in part be the result of the system (or lack of system) by which the controller has arranged its collection of personal data. The Act and the Directive place responsibility on the controller to organise itself – including by acquiring and keeping only such personal data as it needs for its purposes – so that it can comply with access requests efficiently. A competent authority that amasses personal data for law enforcement purposes unnecessarily or that fails to organise properly the personal data that it holds will assume for itself the cost of finding all the personal data that concerns a data subject when complying with requests made by that data subject. In this way the Act and the Directive further encourage a controller to collect and to retain only so much personal data as is necessary for its purposes – a policy objective underpinning the third data protection principle.[85]

3– 017 Restriction and refusal

To the extent that, having regard to the fundamental rights and legitimate interests of the data subject, it is a necessary and proportionate measure to restrict the access right to avoid harm

---

79 That is, the rights under DPA 2018 ss 46(1), 47(1) and 47(2) respectively.

80 That is, the right to lodge a complaint with the Information Commissioner under DPA 2018 s 165(2). As to complaints to the Information Commissioner, see §48– 004.

81 DPA 2018 s 45(1)(b) in conjunction with ss 29(1)-(2) and 43(2); LED Art 14. As to the format of response, see §13– 013. In relation to restrictions to secure the overriding interests, see §13– 003 and §13– 017.

82 DPA 2018 s 173. The penalty for the offence is set by DPA 2018 s 196(1). As to the prosecution of this offence, see DPA 2018 s 197. In relation to an offence committed by a body corporate and the liability of directors, see DPA 2018 s 198.

83 *Ittihadieh v 5-11 Cheyne Gardens RTM Co Ltd* [2017] EWCA 121, [2018] QB 256; *Dawson-Damer v Taylor Wessing LLP* [2017] EWCA Civ 74, [2017] 1 WLR 3255; *Ezsias v Welsh Ministers* [2007] EWHC B15 (QB).

84 DPA 2018 s 53; LED Arts 12(4) and 46(4), recital (40). See further §13– 011.

85 See §12– 026.

to or to protect the overriding interests, the controller may restrict the access right.[86] Other than where there is only a single item of personal data being processed for law enforcement purposes, the requirement that any restriction be 'to the extent' required to avoid harm to or to protect the overriding interests will, for that purpose, generally require items of personal data and the kinds of processing of those items to be considered singly or thematically. This also requires a controller to consider which facets of the access right would disproportionately impair the overriding interests: self-evidently, mere confirmation that a controller is processing personal data concerning a data subject is less likely to disproportionately impair the overriding interests than giving access to all of that information. Where the controller restricts compliance with the access right, whether in whole or in part, the controller must inform the data subject in writing and without undue delay:[87]

(a) that the rights of the data subject have been restricted;
(b) of the reasons for the restriction;
(c) of the data subject's right to make a request to the Information Commissioner to check that the restriction was lawful;[88]
(d) of the data subject's right to lodge a complaint with the Commissioner;[89] and
(e) of the data subject's right to apply to a court.[90]

Where a data subject's rights are restricted or a request is refused, if dissatisfied with that restriction or refusal a data subject should normally in the first instance request the Information Commissioner to check whether the restriction or refusal was lawful and await the outcome of the Commissioner's investigation.[91] Where a controller does not have good grounds for not complying with an access request, the data subject may bring a private claim against the controller, invite the Information Commissioner to take regulatory action, or do both.[92]

3. RIGHT TO RECTIFICATION

13– 018 Scope

Every data subject has a right to require a controller – ie a controller that is a competent authority processing personal data for law enforcement purposes – to rectify inaccurate personal data relating to him or herself.[93] 'Inaccurate' means incorrect or misleading at to any

[86] DPA 2018 s 45(4). As to the meaning of 'the fundamental rights and legitimate interests of the data subject,' see §8– 006 and LED Art 1(2)(a) and recitals (2), (25), (37), (38), (93) and (104). As to the meaning of 'the overriding interests,' see §13– 003. As to the meaning of 'necessary' in this context, see §8– 034.

[87] DPA 2018 s 45(5). The obligation to inform the data subject that his or her rights have been restricted and the reasons therefor is disapplied where provision of the information would undermine the purpose of the restriction: DPA 2018 s 45(6). This does not, however, disapply the obligation to record the reasons for the restriction, which must be made available to the Information Commissioner on request: DPA 2018 s 45(7).

[88] Under DPA 2018 s 51(1)-(2). See further §13– 032.

[89] That is, the right under DPA 2018 s 165(2). In relation to complaints, see further §48– 004.

[90] That is, the right under DPA 2018 s 167. In relation to private law claims, see further §§48– 006 to 48– 013.

[91] DPA 2018 s 51(1)-(2). See further §13– 032.

[92] The controller is under a duty to record the reasons for a decision to restrict the right of access: DPA 2018 s 45(7)(a). The data subject may request the Information Commissioner to check that a refusal to comply with the right of access was lawful and, where so requested by the data subject, the Commissioner is entitled to examine the unrestricted reasons for the refusal: DPA 2018 ss 45(7)(b) and 51(1)-(2). In any refusal notice, the controller must inform the data subject of the right to make such a request to the Information Commissioner: DPA 2018 s 45(1)(c). Regulatory enforcement is further considered at §§48– 014 to 48– 055. Private law claims are considered at §§48– 005 to 48– 013.

[93] DPA 2018 ss 2(1)(b) and 46(1); LED Art 16(1), recital (47).

matter of fact.[94] Where a data subject contests the accuracy of personal data (by whatever means), if the controller is unable to ascertain whether or not the personal data is accurate, the controller must restrict its processing.[95] The right to rectification provides data subjects with a direct means of compelling a controller to comply with the fourth data protection principle, and to do so without having to go through a prior process of establishing a breach of that principle – that is, by contesting accuracy rather than establishing inaccuracy.[96] The rectification right is disapplied in relation to the processing of personal data contained in a judicial decision or other court-created documents that relate to a criminal investigation or criminal proceedings, including proceedings for the purpose of executing a criminal penalty.[97] Where a data subject exercises the right to rectification, the correlative duty on the controller to rectify is not restricted by the overriding interests. Under the previous regime provision for rectification existed, albeit exercisable on application by the data subject to a court rather than as a right exercisable on notice to the controller.[98] A data subject does not need to disclose a purpose in making a request to rectify.[99]

13–019 Mode of compliance

Where a data subject requests a controller to rectify his or her personal data, the controller must inform the data subject in writing whether the request has been granted or refused (in whole or in part).[100] The controller must respond to a rectification request without undue delay, but in any event before the standard time for compliance.[101] Where personal data is inaccurate because it is incomplete, the controller may rectify it by providing a supplementary statement.[102] Where a data subject has requested rectification, but the controller is unable to ascertain whether the personal data is inaccurate, the controller must restrict its processing.[103] Where, despite the inaccuracy, the personal data must be maintained for the purposes of evidence, instead of rectifying the inaccurate data the controller must restrict its processing.[104] When rectifying personal data, the controller may also need to notify others of the rectification:

(1) Where the controller received the inaccurate personal data from another competent authority, the controller must notify that other competent authority of the rectification of the personal data.[105] 'Competent authority' here includes any person that is within the meaning of the LED a competent authority in a Member State

---

94 DPA 2018 s 205(1). Personal data may be 'inaccurate' because it is incomplete: DPA 2018 s 46(2). Under the enforcement notice powers, the Information Commissioner may require a controller or processor to rectify personal data that contains an expression of opinion which appears to the Commissioner to be based on the inaccurate personal data – ie regardless of whether the expression of opinion has itself been accurately recorded: DPA 2018 s 151(2)(b).

95 DPA 2018 s 47(3). See §13–025.

96 As to the fourth data protection principle, see DPA 2018 ss 34(1)(d) and 38 and §§12–028 to 12–031.

97 DPA 2018 s 43(3)-(4).

98 DPA 1998 s 14(1). Given that a data subject would normally be expected to forewarn a controller of a court application and enable the controller to rectify without the need for a court order, the difference between the previous regime and the current is more apparent than real.

99 Given the free-standing continuing obligation in DPA 2018 s 38(1), that is self-evident.

100 DPA 2018 s 48(1), (4); LED recital (47).

101 DPA 2018 s 48(2). As to 'standard time for compliance,' see §13–012. Where the controller restricts the rights of the data subject, the controller must respond without undue delay and is not entitled to fall back on the standard time for compliance: DPA 2018 s 48(4).

102 DPA 2018 s 46(3); LED Art 16(1).

103 DPA 2018 s 47(3).

104 DPA 2018 s 46(4); LED Art 16(3)(a), recital (47).

105 DPA 2018 s 48)7).

other than the United Kingdom.[106] Although there is no separate obligation on the originating competent authority to rectify the personal data upon receiving that notification, the application of the fourth data protection principle will achieve the same thing. Where the controller received the inaccurate personal data from a person who is not a competent authority, there is no obligation on the controller to notify that person of the rectification.

(2) Where the controller has forwarded the inaccurate personal data to another person, the controller must notify that other person of the rectification of that inaccurate personal data.[107] The other person need not be a competent authority. That other person must then similarly rectify the inaccurate personal data.[108]

13– 020 Refusal

Where the controller refuses a request for rectification of personal data, the controller must in its refusal response inform the data subject:[109]

(a) of the reasons for the refusal;[110]

(b) of the data subject's right to ask the Information Commissioner to check that the refusal was lawful;[111]

(c) of the data subject's right to lodge a complaint with the Information Commissioner;[112] and

(d) of the data subject's right to apply to a court for a compliance order.[113]

If a data subject is dissatisfied with a refusal notice, that data subject should normally in the first instance request the Information Commissioner to check whether the refusal was lawful and await the outcome of the Commissioner's investigation.[114] Where a controller does not have good grounds for refusing to comply with a rectification request, the data subject may bring a private claim against the controller, invite the Information Commissioner to take regulatory action, or do both.[115] Where the Commissioner gives the controller an enforcement notice in respect of a failure to comply with a data subject's request to rectify personal data, that enforcement notice may require the controller to rectify other data held by the controller or to erase any such data.[116]

---

106 DPA 2018 s 48(8); LED Art 16(5), recital (47).

107 DPA 2018 s 48(9)(a); LED Art 16(6), recital (47).

108 DPA 2018 s 48(9)(b); LED Arts 7(3) and 16(6). The separate obligation is needed here because that person may not be a competent authority and, as such, will not be subject to the fourth data protection principle.

109 DPA 2018 s 48(1); LED Art 16(4).

110 To the extent that, having regard to the fundamental rights and legitimate interests of the data subject, it is a necessary and proportionate measure to avoid harm to or to protect the overriding interests, the controller may restrict the reasons for refusal given to the data subject: DPA 2018 s 48(3). In this situation, the controller must record the reasons for these restrictions and, on request from the Information Commissioner, make the record of reasons for these restrictions available to the Commissioner: DPA 2018 s 48(6).

111 See §13– 032.

112 Under DPA 2018 s 165(2). See further §48– 004.

113 Under DPA 2018 s 167. See further §48– 012.

114 DPA 2018 s 51(1)-(2). See further §13– 032.

115 Regulatory enforcement is considered at §§48– 014 to 48– 055. Private law claims are considered at §§48– 005 to 48– 013.

116 DPA 2018 s 151(2). The Information Commissioner may also require a controller or processor to rectify personal data that contains an expression of opinion which appears to the Commissioner to be based on the inaccurate personal data – ie regardless of whether the expression of opinion has itself been accurately recorded: DPA 2018 s 151(2)(b).

4. RIGHT TO ERASURE

3– 021 Scope

Where the law enforcement processing by a controller – ie a controller that is a competent authority processing personal data for law enforcement purposes – of a data subject's personal data would infringe:

(a) any of the data processing principles;[117] or

(b) any of the obligations applicable to the processing of sensitive personal data,[118]

that data subject has a right to require the controller to erase that personal data.[119] This erasure right provides data subjects with a direct means of ending an infringement of the data protection principles. The erasure right is disapplied in relation to the processing of personal data contained in a judicial decision or other court-created documents that relate to a criminal investigation or criminal proceedings, including proceedings for the purpose of executing a criminal penalty.[120] Where a data subject exercises the right to erasure, the correlative duty on the controller to erase is not restricted by the overriding interests. Under the previous regime, provision for erasure of personal data existed, albeit exercisable on application by the data subject to a court rather than as a right exercisable on notice to the controller.[121] A data subject does not need to disclose a purpose in making a request to erase.[122]

3– 022 Mode of compliance

Where a data subject requests a controller to erase his or her personal data, the controller must inform the data subject in writing whether the request has been granted or refused (in whole or in part).[123] The controller must respond to an erasure request without undue delay, but in any event before the standard time for compliance.[124] Where, despite the basis for erasure having been made out, the personal data must be maintained for the purposes of evidence, instead of erasing the data the controller must restrict its processing.[125] Where the controller has previously forwarded the erased personal data to another person, the controller must notify that other person of the erasure of that personal data.[126] The other person need not be a competent authority. That other person must then similarly erase the personal data.[127]

117 As to the data protection principles, see §12– 011.

118 As to which, see §§12– 016 to 12– 021.

119 DPA 2018 s 47(4).

120 DPA 2018 s 43(3)-(4).

121 DPA 1998 s 14(1) and (4). The power to make an erasure order under DPA 1998 was conditional on either the personal data being inaccurate or the data subject having suffered damage from contravention of the data protection principles.

122 Given the free-standing continuing obligation in DPA 2018 to comply with the data protection principles, that is self-evident.

123 DPA 2018 s 48(1), (4); LED recital (47).

124 DPA 2018 s 48(2). As to the 'standard time for compliance,' see §13– 012. Where the controller restricts the rights of the data subject, the controller must respond without undue delay and is not entitled to fall back on the standard time for compliance: DPA 2018 s 48(4).

125 DPA 2018 s 47(2).

126 DPA 2018 s 48(9)(a); LED Art 16(6), recital (47).

127 DPA 2018 s 48(9)(b); LED Arts 7(3) and 16(6).

13–023 Refusal

Where the controller refuses a data subject's request for erasure of his or her personal data, the controller must in its refusal response inform the data subject:

(a) of the reasons for the refusal;[128]

(b) of the data subject's right to ask the Information Commissioner to check that the refusal was lawful;[129]

(c) of the data subject's right to lodge a complaint with the Information Commissioner;[130] and

(d) of the data subject's right to apply to a court for a compliance order.[131]

If a data subject is dissatisfied with a refusal notice, that data subject should normally in the first instance request the Information Commissioner to check whether the refusal was lawful and await the outcome of the Commissioner's investigation.[132] Where a controller does not have good grounds for refusing to comply with an erasure request, the data subject may bring a private claim against the controller, invite the Information Commissioner to take regulatory action, or do both.[133] Where the Commissioner gives the controller an enforcement notice in respect of a failure to comply with a data subject's request to erase personal data, that enforcement notice may require the controller to erase other data held by the controller or to rectify any such data.[134]

5. RIGHT TO RESTRICT PROCESSING

13–024 Scope

Where the law enforcement processing by a controller – ie a controller that is a competent authority processing personal data for law enforcement purposes – of a data subject's personal data would infringe:

(a) any of the data processing principles;[135] or

(b) any of the obligations applicable to the processing of sensitive personal data,[136]

that data subject has a right to require the controller to restrict the processing of that personal data.[137] The 'restriction of processing' means the marking of stored personal data with the aim

128 DPA 2018 s 48(1)(b)(i). To the extent that, having regard to the fundamental rights and legitimate interests of the data subject, it is a necessary and proportionate measure to avoid harm to or to protect the overriding interests, the controller may restrict the reasons for refusal given to the data subject: DPA 2018 s 48(3). In this situation, the controller must record the reasons for these restrictions and, on request from the Information Commissioner, make the record of reasons for these restrictions available to the Commissioner: DPA 2018 s 48(6).

129 See §13–032.

130 Under DPA 2018 s 165(2). See further §48–004.

131 Under DPA 2018 s 167. See further §48–012.

132 DPA 2018 s 51(1)-(2). See further §13–032.

133 Regulatory enforcement is considered at §§48–014 to 48–055. Private law claims are considered at §§48–005 to 48–013.

134 DPA 2018 s 151(2). The Information Commissioner may require a controller or processor to erase personal data that contains an expression of opinion which appears to the Commissioner to be based on the inaccurate personal data – ie regardless of whether the expression of opinion has itself been accurately recorded: DPA 2018 s 151(2)(b).

135 As to the data protection principles, see §12–011.

136 As to which, see §§12–016 to 12–021.

137 DPA 2018 s 47(4); LED Art 16(3).

of limiting its processing for the future.[138] The right to restrict law enforcement processing of a data subject's personal data provides data subjects with a direct means of ending or lessening the extent of an infringement of the data protection principles. The right to restrict processing is disapplied in relation to the processing of personal data contained in a judicial decision or other court-created documents that relate to a criminal investigation or criminal proceedings, including proceedings for the purpose of executing a criminal penalty.[139] Where a data subject exercises the right to restrict processing, the correlative duty on the controller to restrict the processing – namely, to mark stored personal data with the aim of limiting its processing for the future – is not restricted by the overriding interests. Under the previous regime, provision for blocking the processing of personal data existed, albeit exercisable on application by the data subject to a court rather than as a right exercisable on notice to the controller.[140] A data subject does not need to disclose a purpose in making a request to restrict processing.[141]

3– 025 Other bases for restrictions

Quite apart from where a data subject makes a request to restrict processing, there are two situations where a controller will be under an automatic duty to restrict the processing of personal data for law enforcement purposes:

(1) Where a controller has received a request to erase, but the controller must maintain the personal data for the purposes of evidence. In this situation, the controller must, instead of erasing the personal data, restrict its processing.[142]

(2) Where a data subject contests the accuracy of personal data, but it is not possible to ascertain whether it is accurate or not. In this situation, the controller must restrict its processing.[143]

3– 026 Mode of compliance

Where a data subject requests a controller to restrict the law enforcement processing of his or her personal data, the controller must inform the data subject in writing whether the request has been granted or refused (in whole or in part).[144] The controller must respond to a request to restrict processing without undue delay, but in any event before the standard time for compliance.[145] Where the controller has previously forwarded the personal data to another person, the controller must notify that other person of the restriction of processing of that personal data.[146] The other person need not be a competent authority. That other person must then similarly restrict the processing of that personal data.[147]

---

138 DPA 2018 s 33(6).

139 DPA 2018 s 43(3)-(4).

140 DPA 1998 s 14(1) and (4). The power to make a blocking order under DPA 1998 was conditional on either the personal data being inaccurate or the data subject having suffered damage from contravention of the data protection principles.

141 Given the free-standing continuing obligation in DPA 2018 to comply with the data protection principles, that is self-evident.

142 DPA 2018 s 47(2).

143 DPA 2018 s 47(3).

144 DPA 2018 s 48(1), (4); LED recital (47).

145 DPA 2018 s 48(2). As to the 'standard time for compliance,' see §13– 012. Where the controller restricts the rights of the data subject, the controller must respond without undue delay and is not entitled to fall back on the standard time for compliance: DPA 2018 s 48(4).

146 DPA 2018 s 48(9)(a); LED Art 16(6), recital (47).

147 DPA 2018 s 48(9)(b); LED Arts 7(3) and 16(6).

13– 027 Refusal

Where the controller refuses a data subject's request to restrict the processing of his or her personal data, the controller must in its refusal response inform the data subject:

(a) of the reasons for the refusal;[148]

(b) of the data subject's right to ask the Information Commissioner to check that the refusal was lawful;[149]

(c) of the data subject's right to lodge a complaint with the Information Commissioner;[150] and

(d) of the data subject's right to apply to a court for a compliance order.[151]

If a data subject is dissatisfied with a refusal notice, that data subject should normally in the first instance request the Information Commissioner to check whether the refusal was lawful and await the outcome of the Commissioner's investigation.[152] Where a controller does not have good grounds for refusing to comply with a request to restrict processing, the data subject may bring a private claim against the controller, invite the Information Commissioner to take regulatory action, or do both.[153]

6. RIGHT AGAINST AUTOMATED DECISIONS

13– 028 Scope

In processing personal data for law enforcement purposes, limitations are placed on a controller – ie a controller that is a competent authority – taking certain types of decisions based 'solely on automated processing' of personal data. These limitations are described as an individual's right not to be subject to automated-decision making.[154] The nature of the right differs according to whether or not the decision is required or authorised by law. The right arises and is restricted to where all the following requirements are met:

(1) The decision is a 'significant decision' in relation to the data subject. A decision is a 'significant decision' if, in relation to a data subject, it produces an adverse legal effect concerning the data subject or it significantly affects the data subject.[155]

(2) The decision is based solely on automated processing of that data subject's personal data.[156] Personal data will be processed by automated means other than where it forms part of a filing system or is intended to form part of a filing system.[157]

[148] DPA 2018 s 48(1)(b)(i). To the extent that, having regard to the fundamental rights and legitimate interests of the data subject, it is a necessary and proportionate measure to avoid harm to or to protect the overriding interests, the controller may restrict the reasons for refusal given to the data subject: DPA 2018 s 48(4). In this situation, the controller must record the reasons for these restrictions and, on request from the Information Commissioner, make the record of reasons for these restrictions available to the Commissioner: DPA 2018 s 48(6).

[149] See §13– 032.

[150] Under DPA 2018 s 165(2). See further §48– 004.

[151] Under DPA 2018 s 167. See further §48– 012.

[152] DPA 2018 s 51(1)-(2). See further §13– 032.

[153] Regulatory enforcement is considered at §§48– 014 to 48– 055. Private law claims are considered at §§48– 005 to 48– 013.

[154] DPA 2018 s 49.

[155] DPA 2018 s 49(2).

[156] DPA 2018 s 49(1).

[157] DPA 2018 s 29(1)(b). As to the meaning of a 'filing system,' see §8– 028. Profiling is a paradigm instance of automated decision-making involving automated processing. As to the meaning of profiling, see DPA 2018 s 33(4)

13–029 Decision not authorised by law

In relation to decisions that are not required or authorised by law, there is a blanket proscription against a controller making decisions based solely on automated processing of personal data for law enforcement purposes.[158] The data subject is not entitled to ask the Information Commissioner to check whether a controller has infringed this proscription.[159] Where a controller has infringed the proscription against making decisions based solely on automated processing of personal data, the data subject may bring a private claim against the controller, invite the Information Commissioner to take regulatory action, or do both.[160]

13–030 Decision authorised by law

Where the decision is one that is required or authorised by law, that decision is termed a 'qualifying significant decision.'[161] Where a controller takes a qualifying significant decision in relation to a data subject based solely on automated processing:

(a) the controller must, as soon as reasonably practicable, notify the data subject in writing that a decision has been taken based solely on automated processing; and

(b) the data subject may, before the end of the period of 1 month beginning with receipt of the notification, request the controller to reconsider the decision, or to take a new decision that is not based solely on automated processing.[162]

If a data subject asks the controller to reconsider the 'qualifying significant decision' or to take a new one that is not based solely on automated processing, the controller must, before the end of the period of 1 month beginning with receipt of the request:

— consider the request, including any information provided by the data subject that is relevant to it,
— comply with the request, and
— by notice in writing inform the data subject of the steps taken to comply with the request, and the outcome of complying with the request.[163]

The data subject is not entitled to ask the Information Commissioner to check whether a controller has complied with the request.[164] Where a controller has not complied with the request, the data subject may bring a private claim against the controller, invite the Information Commissioner to take regulatory action, or do both.[165]

---

and §8–029.

158 DPA 2018 s 49(1).

159 That is, under DPA 2018 s 51(1)-(2).

160 Regulatory enforcement is considered at §§48–014 to 48–055. Private law claims are considered at §§48–005 to 48–013.

161 DPA 2018 s 50(1).

162 DPA 2018 s 50(2).

163 DPA 2018 s 50(3). Where the controller provides information in response to the data subject's request, the controller must, so far as practicable, provide the information in the same form as the request: DPA 2018 s 52(3).

164 That is, under DPA 2018 s 51(1)-(2).

165 Regulatory enforcement is considered at §§48–014 to 48–055. Private law claims are considered at §§48–005 to 48–013.

7. ENFORCEMENT AND REMEDIES

13– 031 Overview

The Information Commissioner is the 'supervisory authority' for the purposes of the Law Enforcement Directive.[166] The Commissioner's monitoring and enforcement of the provisions of the law enforcement processing regime is statutorily linked to the protection of individuals with regard to the processing of personal data.[167] In carrying out functions under the Act, the Commissioner must have regard to the importance of securing an appropriate level of protection for personal data, taking account of the interests of data subjects, controllers and matters of general public interest.[168] Specifically and directly relevant to the rights conferred on data subjects and the correlative duties on controllers, the Commissioner must:

(a) monitor and enforce the provisions of the law enforcement processing regime;
(b) promote the awareness of controllers and processors of their obligations under the law enforcement processing regime;
(c) on request, provide information to a data subject concerning the exercise of the data subject's rights under the law enforcement processing regime; and
(d) conduct investigations on the application of the law enforcement processing regime.[169]

13– 032 Commissioner-exercised rights

The Information Commissioner has an enlarged role in relation to the rights of data subjects under Part 4 of the DPA 2018. Specifically, where a controller restricts information provided to a data subject under the information obligation, restricts a data subject's right of access or refuses a request to rectify, a request to erase or a request to restrict processing, a data subject may request the Information Commissioner to check that the restriction or refusal was lawful.[170] The data subject is said to be exercising his or her rights 'through the Commissioner.' The enlarged role counterbalances the abbreviation of a data subject's entitlement to be informed of the basis for a restriction or refusal of a request; and it recognises that the Commissioner may be safely informed of the full reasons for that restriction or refusal.[171] In performing this role, the Commissioner thus stands in a role that is protective of a data subject's interests.[172] Where a data subject makes such a request of the Information Commissioner, the Commissioner must take appropriate steps to respond, including giving the controller an information notice and an assessment notice.[173] After taking the steps, the Commissioner must inform the data subject whether the restriction or refusal was lawful.[174]

---

166 DPA 2018 s 116(1)(a).

167 DPA 2018 ss 2(1)(c) and 116.

168 DPA 2018 s 2(2).

169 DPA 2018 s 116 and Sch 13 para 1(1).

170 DPA 2018 s 51(1)-(2). The 'information obligation' is the obligation imposed by DPA 2018 s 44 (see §13– 004); a data subject's right of access is that conferred by DPA 2018 s 45 (see §§13– 014 to 13– 017); a data subject's right to rectification is that conferred by DPA 2018 s 46(1) (see §§13– 018 to 13– 020); a data subject's right to erasure is that conferred by DPA 2018 s 47(1) (see §§13– 021to 13– 023); a data subject's right to restrict processing is that conferred by DPA 2018 s 47(3) (see §§13– 024 to 13– 026).

171 DPA 2018 ss 44(7)(b), 45(7)(b) and 48(6)(b).

172 See, generally, DPA 2018 ss 2(2) and 116, Sch 13 paras 1(1)(a), (e) and 2.

173 DPA 2018 s 51(3). In relation to information notices and assessment notices, see §§48– 018 to 48– 033.

174 DPA 2018 s 51(4). Although not statutorily specified, as a matter of public law the Commissioner must give

13– 033 Regulatory enforcement

Whether or not a data subject has requested the Information Commissioner to check that a controller's decision was lawful, the Commissioner has a free-standing power:

(a) to notify a controller or a processor of an alleged infringement of any of the obligations imposed on a controller or processor;
(b) to issue a warning to a controller or processor that intended processing operations are likely to infringe those obligations;
(c) to issue reprimands to a controller or processor where processing operations have infringed those obligations; and
(d) to issue, whether on request or on the Commissioner's initiative, opinions to Parliament, the government or other institutions as well as the public on any issue related to the protection of personal data.[175]

Where an individual considers that the controller is not complying with its obligations, the individual may complain to the Information Commissioner. The Commissioner must investigate the complaint and enforce the obligations.[176] If the Commissioner is satisfied that the controller has failed, or is failing, to comply with any of the continuing obligations, the Commissioner may serve an enforcement notice.[177]

13– 034 Private remedies

Where a controller restricts information provided to a data subject under the information obligation, restricts a data subject's right of access or refuses a request to rectify, a request to erase or a request to restrict processing, a data subject will normally first request the Information Commissioner to check that the restriction or refusal was lawful.[178] The outcome of that checking should normally expose whether the restriction or non-compliance was or was not justified.[179] Unjustified non-compliance by a controller with a request by a data subject exercising any of those four rights may give rise to a cause of action actionable by the data subject.[180] Breach of the proscription against automated decision-making may also give rise to a cause of action actionable by the data subject. This is additional to other regulatory action that may be taken by the Information Commissioner in respect of that non-compliance.[181]

13– 035 National security certificates

A Minister of the Crown may issue a certificate certifying that, for the purpose of the information obligation, the right of access or the provision of information when notifying a data subject of the reasons for refusing the right to rectify, to erase or to restrict processing, a

sufficient reasons to enable the data subject to determine whether or not there has been an infringement of his or her rights and thus make an informed decision whether or not to apply to a court for a compliance order under DPA 2018 s 167.

[175] DPA 2018 Sch 13 para 2. In relation to the Information Commissioner generally, see Chapter 44.

[176] DPA 2018 Sch 13 para 1(1)(a), (e), (g). See further §48– 004.

[177] DPA 2018 s 149(2)(a). Regulatory enforcement is considered at §§48– 014 to 48– 055.

[178] DPA 2018 s 51(1)-(2). The 'information obligation' is the obligation imposed by DPA 2018 s 44 (see §13– 004); a data subject's right of access is that conferred by DPA 2018 s 45 (see §§13– 014 to 13– 017); a data subject's right to rectification is that conferred by DPA 2018 s 46(1) (see §§13– 018 to 13– 020); a data subject's right to erasure is that conferred by DPA 2018 s 47(1) (see §§13– 021to 13– 023); a data subject's right to restrict processing is that conferred by DPA 2018 s 47(3) (see §§13– 024 to 13– 026).

[179] The Information Commissioner must, at the end of the checking exercise, inform the data subject whether the restriction or refusal was lawful: DPA 2018 s 51(4)-(5).

[180] Private remedies are considered further in §§48– 005 to 48– 013.

[181] DPA 2018 s 51(6).

restriction is a necessary and proportionate measure to protect national security.[182] The certificate is conclusive evidence that the restriction is a necessary and proportionate measure to protect national security.[183] Where a conclusive certificate has been issued, the Information Commissioner's enforcement powers are disapplied in relation to the restriction in the certificate.[184] A person directly affected by the issuing of a certificate may appeal to the First-tier tribunal.[185]

[182] DPA 2018 s 79(1). The Minister must be a member of the Cabinet or the Attorney-General: DPA 2018 s 79(12). As to the meaning of 'national security,' see §26– 050.

[183] As to the operation of conclusive certificates, see §§5– 033 to 5– 037 and §§26– 057 to 26– 059.

[184] DPA 2018 s 79(13).

[185] DPA 2018 s 79(5). As to the nature of an appeal against a conclusive certificate and the grounds of appeal, see §26– 061, §45– 013 and §§49– 016 to 49– 017.

CHAPTER 14
Intelligence services processing

1. INTRODUCTION

14–001 Introduction

Neither the GDPR nor the Law Enforcement Directive applies to processing of personal data concerning national security, activities of agencies or units dealing with national security issues or the processing of personal data by Member States when carrying out activities which fall within the scope of Chapter 2 of Title V of the Treaty on European Union.[1] Such processing of personal data is within the exclusive legislative domain of each EU Member State. The approach taken in the United Kingdom to such processing has been to exclude the processing of personal data by the intelligence services from the general processing regime,[2] and instead

[1] GDPR Art 2(2)(a) and recital (16); LED Art 2(3)(a) and recital (14).

[2] In other words, the regime established by the GDPR and supplemented by the DPA 2018 Part 2 (ss 4-28) and Schs

regulate it by a separate regime. That separate regime forms Part 4 (ss 82-113) of the DPA 2018.[3] Although certain concepts and the structure are similar to those applicable to general processing, the GDPR has no role to play in relation to processing of personal data by the intelligence service agenies. As with general processing, this special regime comprises a set of continuing obligations imposed on each controller as an incident of the controller processing personal data, as well as a set of rights conferred on the data subject which are normally triggered by notice to the controller. An additional and more stringent set of requirements apply where the personal data that is being processed is sensitive in nature.[4] There are exemptions which reduce the scope of the obligations and rights.

14– 002 Intelligence services

Part 4 of the DPA 2018 applies only to processing by an intelligence service, which means:

(a) the Security Service;
(b) the Secret Intelligence Service;
(c) the Government Communications Headquarters.[5]

As with general processing, the special regime applies only to processing of personal data where that processing is wholly or partly by 'automated means'[6] or where the personal data forms part of a filing system or is intended to form part of a filing system.[7]

14– 003 Other terminology

Most of the terms used in relation to intelligence services processing bear the same meanings that they have in relation to general processing,[8] but specific meanings are given to the following terms:

(1) 'Controller' is defined to mean:
    (a) the intelligence service that, alone or jointly with others, determines the purposes and means of the processing of personal data; or
    (b) where the personal data is processed only for purposes for which it is required by an enactment to be processed and by means by which it is required by an enactment to be processed, the intelligence service on which the obligation to process the data is imposed.[9]
(2) 'Processor' is defined to mean any person who processes personal data on behalf of the controller (other than a person who is an employee of the controller).[10]
(3) 'Consent' is given a different definition from that applicable to general processing.[11] For the purposes of Part 4, 'consent' means a 'freely given, specific, informed and

1-6.

3 The DPA 1998 applied to the intelligence services in the same way as other data controllers. However, in enacting the DPA 2018, the Government decided not to apply the same data protection regimes to the intelligence services as law enforcement competent authorities and/or other data controllers subject to the GDPR/the applied GDPR. Instead, Part 4 DPA 2018 is intended to build on the DPA 1998 regime by seeking to adopt the standards of the modernised Convention 108 (which does apply to national security data processing). In relation to Convention 108 generally, see §§7– 007 to 7– 008.

4 For the purposes of DPA 2018 Part 4, this is termed 'sensitive processing': DPA 2018 s 86(7).

5 DPA 2018 s 82.

6 DPA 2018 s 82(1)(a). As to the meaning of this, see §8– 040.

7 DPA 2018 s 82(1)(b). As to the meaning of forming part of a filing system, see §8– 028.

8 As to which, see §§8– 011 to 8– 028.

9 DPA 2018 s 83(1)-(2).

10 DPA 2018 s 83(3).

11 As to its meaning in relation to general processing, see §9– 008.

unambiguous indication of the individual's wishes by which the individual, by a statement or by a clear affirmative action, signifies agreement to the processing of the personal data.'[12]

(4) 'Employee' is defined to include an individual who holds a position (whether paid or unpaid) under the direction and control of that person.[13]

(5) 'Recipient' is defined to mean any person to whom the data is disclosed, whether a third party or not, but it does not include a person to whom disclosure is or may be made in the framework of a particular inquiry in accordance with the law.[14]

4–004 Sensitive processing

As with the general processing regime, additional, more stringent requirements apply to processing of certain sorts of personal data by the security services. The categories of personal data to which these more stringent requirements apply resemble those for general processing,[15] but the trigger for the application of the requirements is 'sensitive processing' rather than by reference to the data type.[16] 'Sensitive processing' is defined to mean:

(a) the processing of personal data revealing racial or ethnic origin, political opinions, religious or philosophical beliefs or trade union membership;

(b) the processing of genetic data for the purpose of uniquely identifying an individual;

(c) the processing of biometric data for the purpose of uniquely identifying an individual;

(d) the processing of data concerning health;

(e) the processing of data concerning an individual's sex life or sexual orientation;

(f) the processing of personal data as to

  (i) the commission or alleged commission of an offence by an individual, or

  (ii) proceedings for an offence committed or alleged to have been committed by an individual, the disposal of such proceedings or the sentence of a court in such proceedings.[17]

'Sensitive processing' impinges on the first data protection principle and reduces the exemptions from the data subject rights.[18]

4–005 Deemed controller

To ensure that controllers and processors are identified properly, and in order that applicable obligations are complied with, a processor (and any person acting under the authority of a controller or processor) who has access to personal data may not process the data except on instructions from the controller or to comply with a legal obligation.[19] The controller may use only a processor who undertakes:

(1) to implement appropriate measures that are sufficient to secure that the processing complies with Part 4 of the DPA 2018; and

(2) to provide to the controller such information as is necessary for demonstrating that

---

12 DPA 2018 s 84(2).

13 DPA 2018 s 84(3).

14 DPA 2018 s 84(5). Contrast the definition for the purposes of general processing: see §8–026.

15 As to which, see §8–017.

16 DPA 2018 s 86(7). The difference comes to nothing, since each of the six classes of 'sensitive processing' opens with the same words ('the processing of') with the differences in the classes all being in the data type being processed.

17 DPA 2018 s 86(7).

18 DPA 2018 s 86(2)(b) and Sch 11 para 1(a).

19 DPA 2018 s 106.

the processing complies with Part 4.[20]

Where a processor in fact determines the purposes and means of processing, then the processor is treated as a controller in respect of that processing.[21]

14– 006 Joint controllers

Where two or more intelligence services jointly determine the purposes and means of processing personal data, they are 'joint controllers.'[22] As such, they must, in a transparent manner, determine their respective responsibilities for compliance with Part 4 of the DPA 2018 by means of an arrangement between them, except to the extent that those responsibilities are determined under or by virtue of an enactment.[23] They must designate the controller which is to be the contact point for data subjects.[24] They should also identify which of them will, if the requirement arises, be responsible for carrying out any rectification, erasure or restriction of processing, whether sought by a data subject or ordered by a court.[25]

2. THE CONTINUING OBLIGATIONS

14– 007 Introduction

As with general processing, the regime governing the processing of personal data by an intelligence service revolves around an obligation on the controller to adhere to a set of principles when processing personal data. These are termed 'data protection principles' rather than just 'processing principles,' but nothing turns on the nomenclature. There are six data protection principles:

(1) The processing of personal data must be:
  (a) lawful; and
  (b) fair and transparent.[26]

(2) The purpose for which personal data is collected on any occasion must be specified, explicit and legitimate, and it must not be processed in a manner that is incompatible with the purpose for which it is collected.[27]

(3) The personal data must be adequate, relevant and not excessive in relation to the purpose for which it is processed.[28]

(4) Personal data undergoing processing must be accurate and, where necessary, kept up to date.[29]

---

20 DPA 2018 s 105(2).

21 DPA 2018 s 105(3).

22 DPA 2018 s 104(1).

23 DPA 2018 s 104(2).

24 DPA 2018 s 104(3).

25 DPA 2018 s 100(5). As to the meaning of 'restriction of processing,' see §8– 031.

26 DPA 2018 s 86. See §§14– 009 to 14– 010. For the equivalent data protection principle under the general processing regime, see §§9– 006 to 9– 022. For the equivalent data protection principle under the law enforcement processing regime, see §§12– 014 to 12– 022.

27 DPA 2018 s 87. See §14– 011. For the equivalent data protection principle under the general processing regime, see §§9– 023 to 9– 027. For the equivalent data protection principle under the law enforcement processing regime, see §§12– 023 to 12– 025.

28 DPA 2018 s 88. See §14– 012. For the equivalent data protection principle under the general processing regime, see §9– 028. For the equivalent data protection principle under the law enforcement processing regime, see §§12– 026 to 12– 027.

29 DPA 2018 s 89. See §14– 013. For the equivalent data protection principle under the general processing regime,

(5) Personal data must be kept for no longer than is necessary for the purpose for which it is processed.[30]

(6) Personal data must be processed in a manner that includes taking appropriate security measures as regards risks that arise from processing personal data.[31]

Each controller must implement appropriate measures to ensure that the processing of personal data complies with the data protection principles.[32] In addition, the controller must implement appropriate measures to be able to demonstrate – in particular to the Information Commissioner – that the processing of personal data complies with the data protection principles.[33]

4– 008 Lawful

The first of the two requirements of the first data protection principle – that the processing of the personal data be 'lawful' – is satisfied only if and to the extent that one or more of the following six conditions is met:[34]

(1) The data subject has given consent to the processing.[35]

(2) The processing is necessary—
  (a) for the performance of a contract to which the data subject is a party, or
  (b) in order to take steps at the request of the data subject prior to entering into a contract.

(3) The processing is necessary for compliance with a legal obligation to which the controller is subject, other than an obligation imposed by contract.

(4) The processing is necessary in order to protect the vital interests of the data subject or of another individual.

(5) The processing is necessary—
  (a) for the administration of justice,
  (b) for the exercise of any functions of either House of Parliament,
  (c) for the exercise of any functions conferred on a person by an enactment or rule of law,
  (d) for the exercise of any functions of the Crown, a Minister of the Crown or a government department, or
  (e) for the exercise of any other functions of a public nature exercised in the public interest by a person.

(6) The processing is necessary for the purposes of legitimate interests pursued by—
  (a) the controller, or
  (b) the third party or parties to whom the data is disclosed.

This condition does not apply where the processing is unwarranted in any particular

see §§9– 029 to 9– 030. For the equivalent data protection principle under the law enforcement processing regime, see §§12– 028 to 12– 031.

30 DPA 2018 s 90. See §14– 014. For the equivalent data protection principle under the general processing regime, see §§9– 031 to 9– 033. For the equivalent data protection principle under the law enforcement processing regime, see §§12– 032 to 12– 033.

31 DPA 2018 s 91. See §14– 015. For the equivalent data protection principle under the general processing regime, see §§9– 034 to 9– 039. For the equivalent data protection principle under the law enforcement processing regime, see §§12– 034 to 12– 036.

32 DPA 2018 s 102(a).

33 DPA 2018 s 102(b). Regulatory enforcement is considered at §§48– 014 to 48– 055. Private law claims are considered at §§48– 005 to 48– 013.

34 DPA 2018 s 86(2)(a) and Sch 9.

35 As to the meaning of 'consent' see §14– 003(3).

case because of prejudice to the rights and freedoms or legitimate interests of the data subject.[36]

These conditions resemble the conditions in DPA 1998 Schedule 2, so that the jurisprudence in relation to the latter is likely to inform the understanding and application of the former.[37]

14– 009 Fair and transparent

The second of the two requirements of the first data protection principle is that the processing of the personal data be 'fair and transparent.'[38] Whilst there is a similar requirement in the first processing principle for general processing,[39] the prescribed content of that requirement is not carried over or replicated in relation to processing by the security services. For the purposes of processing of personal data by the security services, one of the factors that must be taken into account when evaluating whether that processing is 'fair and transparent' is the method by which that personal data was obtained.[40] Personal data is deemed to have been obtained 'fairly and transparently' if it consists of information obtained from a person who is authorised by an enactment to supply it or who is required to supply it by an enactment or by an international obligation of the United Kingdom.[41] The explanatory notes to the DPA 2018 suggest that the concept of fair processing should be interpreted and understood within the context of the work of the intelligence services.[42] Outside of processing that is deemed to be 'fair and transparent,' it is doubtful that substitute epithets shed much light on their meaning.[43] It is enough to observe that the DPA 2018 having clearly specified two mandatory requirements ('lawful' and 'fair and transparent'), the second requirement must involve something more than satisfying what is statutorily prescribed for the first requirement.

14– 010 Sensitive personal data

In relation to 'sensitive processing,'[44] in addition to meeting the 'lawful' and 'fair and transparent' requirements, it must also meet one of a further set of conditions.[45] The conditions are:[46]

(1) The data subject has given consent to the processing.[47]

(2) The processing is necessary for the purposes of exercising or performing any right or obligation which is conferred or imposed by an enactment or rule of law on the controller in connection with employment.

(3) The processing is necessary:

(a) in order to protect the vital interests of the data subject or of another person, in a case where:

---

36 DPA 2018 Sch 9 para 6(2). As to the meaning of 'prejudice to the rights and freedoms or legitimate interests of the data subject' see §§8– 006 to 8– 007.

37 As to the conditions in DPA 1998 Sch 2, see §15– 040.

38 DPA 2018 s 86(1)(b). The second requirement – 'fair and transparent' – is better characterised as a composite requirement rather than as containing two separate requirements.

39 As to which, see §§9– 015 to 9– 016.

40 DPA 2018 s 86(5).

41 DPA 2018 s 86(6).

42 Paragraphs 249-250.

43 See *Brutus v Cozens* [1973] AC 854, [1972] 2 All ER 1297; *R v Golds* [2016] UKSC 61, [2016] 1 WLR 5231 at [37].

44 As to the meaning of which, see §14– 004.

45 DPA 2018 s 86(2)(b).

46 DPA 2018 Sch 10.

47 As to the meaning of 'consent' see §14– 003(3).

(i) consent cannot be given by or on behalf of the data subject; or

(ii) the controller cannot reasonably be expected to obtain the consent of the data subject; or

(b) in order to protect the vital interests of another person, in a case where consent by or on behalf of the data subject has been unreasonably withheld.

(4) The processing is necessary for the purposes of:

(a) protecting an individual from neglect or physical, mental or emotional harm or protecting the physical, mental or emotional well-being of an individual;

(b) the individual is aged under 18, or aged 18 or over and at risk;

(c) the processing is carried out without the consent of the data subject for specified reasons;[48] and

(d) the processing is necessary for reasons of substantial public interest.

(5) The information contained in the personal data has been made public as a result of steps deliberately taken by the data subject.

(6) The processing:

(a) is necessary for the purpose of, or in connection with, any legal proceedings (including prospective legal proceedings);

(b) is necessary for the purpose of obtaining legal advice; or

(c) is otherwise necessary for the purposes of establishing, exercising or defending legal rights.

(7) The processing is necessary:

(a) for the administration of justice;

(b) for the exercise of any functions of either House of Parliament;

(c) for the exercise of any functions conferred on any person by an enactment or rule of law; or

(d) for the exercise of any functions of the Crown, a Minister of the Crown or a government department.

(8) The processing is necessary for medical purposes[49] and is undertaken by a health professional, or a person who in the circumstances owes a duty of confidentiality which is equivalent to that which would arise if that person were a health professional.

(9) The processing:

(a) is of sensitive personal data consisting of information as to racial or ethnic origin,

(b) is necessary for the purpose of identifying or keeping under review the existence or absence of equality of opportunity or treatment between persons of different racial or ethnic origins, with a view to enabling such equality to be promoted or maintained, and

(c) is carried out with appropriate safeguards for the rights and freedoms of data subjects.[50]

These further conditions bear a resemblance to those that had to be met for the processing of

---

48 The reasons are specified in DPA 2018 Sch 10 para 4(2). As to the meaning of 'at risk' see DPA 2018 Sch 10 para 4(3). As to the meaning of 'consent' see §14–003(3).

49 'Medical purposes' includes the purposes of preventative medicine, medical diagnosis, medical research, the provision of care and treatment and the management of healthcare services: DPA 2018 Sch 10 para 8(2).

50 As to the meaning of 'the rights and freedoms of data subjects' see §§8–006 to 8–007.

sensitive personal data under the DPA 1998.[51]

14–011 Purpose limitation

The second data protection principle is that:

(a) the purpose for which personal data is collected on any occasion must be specified, explicit and legitimate, and
(b) personal data so collected must not be processed in a manner that is incompatible with the purpose for which it is collected.[52]

In so far as satisfying the requirement in (a), personal data collected by a controller for one purpose may be processed for any other purpose of the controller that collected the data or any purpose of another controller provided that the controller is authorised by law to process the data for that purpose, and the processing is necessary and proportionate to that other purpose.[53] In so far as satisfying the requirement in (b), processing of personal data is deemed to be compatible with the purpose for which it is collected if the processing consists of:

— processing for archiving purposes in the public interest,
— processing for the purposes of scientific or historical research, or
— processing for statistical purposes, and

is subject to appropriate safeguards for the rights and freedoms of the data subject.[54]

14–012 Data minimisation

The third data protection principle is that personal data must be adequate, relevant and not excessive in relation to the purpose for which it is processed.[55] The Act does not prescribe any mandatory considerations in evaluating whether the third data protection principle is being complied with.[56]

14–013 Accuracy

The fourth data protection principle is that personal data undergoing processing must be accurate and, where necessary, kept up to date.[57] The Act does not prescribe any mandatory considerations in evaluating whether the fourth data protection principle is being complied with.[58] The content of the principle will be part informed by the powers conferred on the security service in making use of that personal data.

14–014 Storage limitation

The fifth data protection principle is that personal data must be kept for no longer than is necessary for the purpose for which it is processed.[59] The Act does not prescribe any mandatory considerations in evaluating whether the fifth data protection principle is being complied with.[60] As with the DPA 1998, the principle does not prescribe the minimum or

---

51 As to which, see §§15–042 to 15–043.

52 DPA 2018 s 87(1). In relation to general processing, this has its analogue in the second processing principle: see §§9–023 to 9–027, but without the detail provided for by the GDPR.

53 DPA 2018 s 87(3).

54 DPA 2018 s 87(4). As to the meaning of 'the rights and freedoms of data subjects' see §§8–006 to 8–007.

55 DPA 2018 s 88.

56 In relation to general processing, this has its analogue in the third processing principle: see §9–028.

57 DPA 2018 s 89.

58 In relation to general processing, this has its analogue in the fourth processing principle: see §§9–029 to 9–030.

59 DPA 2018 s 90.

60 In relation to general processing, this has its analogue in the fifth processing principle: see §§9–031 to 9–033.

maximum periods for the retention of data. In general, in order to comply with this principle, controllers should establish time limits for automatic erasure of data, and/or for the periodic review of data held to establish whether it is appropriate or not to retain it. In practice, this will involve controllers considering the purpose or purposes for which they hold information in deciding whether, and if so for how long, to retain it; updating or archiving information and securely deleting information that is no longer needed for those purposes.[61]

14–015 Data security

The sixth data protection principle is that personal data must be processed in a manner that includes taking appropriate security measures as regards risks that arise from processing personal data.[62] Although not expressly linked to the sixth data protection principle, DPA 2018 s 107 in specifying certain security measures appears to set the parameters of the sixth data protection principle:

(1) Each controller and each processor must implement security measures appropriate to the risks arising from the processing of personal data.

(2) In the case of automated processing, each controller and each processor must, following an evaluation of the risks, implement measures designed to:

- (a) prevent unauthorised processing or unauthorised interference with the systems used in connection with it;
- (b) ensure that it is possible to establish the precise details of any processing that takes place;
- (c) ensure that any systems used in connection with the processing function properly and may, in the case of interruption, be restored; and
- (d) ensure that stored personal data cannot be corrupted if a system used in connection with the processing malfunctions.

14–016 Data protection by design

Where a controller proposes that a particular type of processing of personal data be carried out by or on behalf of the controller, the controller must, prior to the processing, consider the impact of the proposed processing on the rights and freedoms of data subjects.[63] Having undertaken such consideration, the controller must implement appropriate technical and organisational measures that are designed to ensure that the processing complies with the data protection principles and that the risks to the rights and freedoms of data subjects are minimised.[64] As part of the 'general obligations' imposed on a controller,[65] the controller must both implement appropriate measures to ensure, and be able to demonstrate, that the processing of personal data complies with these requirements.[66] The obligation is not subject to the exemptions.[67]

---

[61] The Investigatory Powers Act 2016 requires the retention and examination of a bulk personal dataset by an intelligence service to be authorised by a warrant issued by a Secretary of State and approved by a Judicial Commissioner.

[62] DPA 2018 s 91(1). The risks include accidental or unauthorised access to, or destruction, loss, use, modification or disclosure of personal data: DPA 2018 s 91(2). In relation to general processing, this has its analogue in the sixth processing principle: see §§9–034 to 9–039.

[63] DPA 2018 s 103(1). The person carrying out processing on behalf of a controller is the processor. As to what is meant by the 'rights and freedoms of data subjects,' see §§8–006 to 8–007.

[64] DPA 2018 s 103(2).

[65] See DPA 2018 s 101(a).

[66] DPA 2018 s 102.

[67] DPA 2018 ss 110 and 112.

14–017 Breach notification duty

Where a controller becomes aware of a serious personal data breach in relation to personal data for which the controller is responsible, the controller must notify the Commissioner of the breach without undue delay.[68] The obligation is subject to the exemptions.[69] There is no obligation to notify the data subject.[70] A serious personal data breach is one that seriously interferes with the rights and freedoms of a data subject.[71] Where a processor under the instruction of a controller that is part of an intelligence service becomes aware of a personal data breach when it is processing personal data, the processor must notify the controller without undue delay.[72]

14–018 International transfers

A controller must not transfer personal data to a country or territory outside the United Kingdom or to an international organisation unless:

(a) that transfer is a necessary and proportionate measure carried out for the purposes of the controller's statutory functions; or

(b) that transfer is a necessary and proportionate measure carried out for the prevention or detection of serious crime or for the purpose of any criminal proceedings, the interests of national security or the functions of GCHQ.[73]

The proscription on transfers is not subject to exemptions.[74]

14–019 Regulatory enforcement

The Information Commissioner has a general duty to monitor and enforce the provisions of the DPA 2018 and, in so doing, to have regard to the importance of securing an appropriate level of protection for personal data, taking account of the interests of the data subject, controllers and matters of general public interest.[75] In relation to the above obligations in the processing of personal data, the Information Commissioner has the power:

(a) to notify a controller or a processor of an alleged infringement of the above obligations;

(b) to issue warning to a controller or processor that intended processing operations are likely to infringe those obligations;

(c) to issue reprimands to a controller or processor where processing operations have

---

68 DPA 2018 s 108(1). The analogous provision in relation to general processing is GDPR Art 33. 'Personal data breach' is defined by DPA 2018 s 84(4) to mean:

> a breach of security leading to the accidental or unlawful destruction, loss, alteration, unauthorised disclosure of, or access to, personal data transmitted, stored or otherwise processed.

This is the same definition given to 'personal data breach' for the purposes of law enforcement processing: DPA 2018 s 33(3). The matters that must be included in the notification are specified by DPA 2018 s 108(3) and, where the notification is not made within 72 hours, the reasons for the delay must be given.

69 DPA 2018 ss 110(2)(c) and 112, Sch 11 para 1(c). However, the obligation to communicate a personal data breach does not arise in relation to a personal data breach where the breach also constitutes a relevant error within the meaning given by section 231(9) of the Investigatory Powers Act 2016. The disapplication of the notification obligation is designed to avoid the double reporting of breaches. A relevant error under the Investigatory Powers Act means an error made by a public authority in complying with any requirement over which the Investigatory Powers Commissioner has oversight.

70 Contrast GDPR Art 34 (general processing) and DPA 2018 s 68 (law enforcement processing).

71 DPA 2018 s 108(7). As to what is meant by the 'rights and freedoms of data subjects,' see §§8–006 to 8–007.

72 DPA 2018 s 108(5). The controller will then become responsible for reporting that breach to the Information Commissioner.

73 DPA 2018 s 109(2); Security Service Act 1989 s 2(2)(a); Intelligence Services Act 1994 ss 2(2)(a) and 4(2)(a).

74 DPA 2018 ss 110 and 112. As to the meaning of 'international organisations,' see §8–033.

75 DPA 2018 s 2 and Sch 13 para 1(1).

infringed those obligations; and

(d) to issue, whether on request or on the Commissioner's initiative, opinions to Parliament, the government or other institutions as well as the public on any issue related to the protection of personal data.[76]

Where an individual considers that the controller is not complying with its obligations, the individual may complain to the Information Commissioner. The Commissioner must investigate the complaint and enforce the obligations.[77] If the Commissioner is satisfied that the controller has failed, or failing, to comply with any of the continuing obligations, the Commissioner may serve an enforcement notice.[78]

14–020 Private remedies

Where an intelligence service controller fails to comply with the data protection principles in respect of its processing of the personal data of a data subject, the only private remedy expressly provided for is an application to the court by the data subject for an order that the controller erase that data without undue delay and, in the case of the fourth data protection principle (accuracy), an order for rectification.[79] Although the power of the court to make such an order is expressed in discretionary terms, the remedy is equally expressed as a right of the data subject.[80] Given that the DPA 2018 imposes a duty on such controllers to 'implement appropriate measures to ensure...that the processing of personal data complies with the requirements' of Part 4 and that the six data protection principles are described as 'requirements,'[81] there is an argument that non-compliance with that duty gives rise to a private law cause of action – namely, breach of statutory duty[82] – actionable at the suit of the data subject.[83] Although the argument has the usual difficulties in trying to establish whether a breach of a statutory duty gives rise to a cause of action,[84] the DPA 2018 does not expressly

---

[76] DPA 2018 Sch 13 para 2. In relation to the Information Commissioner generally, see Chapter 44. For further treatment of private remedies and regulatory enforcement under the DPA 2018, see Chapter 48.

[77] DPA 2018 Sch 13 para 1(1)(a), (e), (g). See further §48–004.

[78] DPA 2018 s 149(2)(a). Regulatory enforcement is considered at §§48–014 to 48–055.

[79] DPA 2018 s 100(1)-(2). The jurisdiction is exercisable by the High Court or, in Scotland, the Court of Session: DPA 2018 s 100(6). Where there are joint controllers, see §14–006.

[80] See DPA 2018 ss 100(2) and 92(1)(f) respectively.

[81] DPA 2018 ss 102 and 85(1) respectively.

[82] The common law treats actionable breach of statutory duty as a species of tort: *Thornton v Kirklees Metropolitan Borough Council* [1979] QB 626, [1979] 2 All ER 349 at 642.

[83] Where a breach of statutory duty to an individual (as opposed to a statutory duty to members of the public generally) gives rise to a cause of action, that cause of action arises at common law rather than being conferred by statute: *Butler (or Black) v Fife Coal Co Ltd* [1912] AC 149 at 165; *Cutler v Wandsworth Stadium Ltd* [1949] AC 398 at 413.

[84] Whether Parliament intends that a breach of statutory duty to an individual should not give rise to a common law cause of action involves looking at the statutory scheme. The courts will readily read in an intention that a breach of statutory duty does not give rise to a common law cause of action where the statute provides a curial route for a person adversely affected by non-performance of statutory obligations to secure some form of relief: *Institute of Patent Agents v Lockwood* [1894] AC 347; *Pasmore v Oswaldtwistle Urban District Council* [1898] AC 387 at 394 per Earl of Halsbury; *Cutler v Wandsworth Stadium Ltd* [1949] AC 398 at 407, [1949] 1 All ER 544 per Lord Simonds; *Lonrho Ltd v Shell Petroleum Co Ltd (No 2)* [1982] AC 173 at 185, [1981] 2 All ER 456 per Lord Diplock; *X (Minors) v Bedfordshire County Council* [1995] UKHL 9, [1995] 2 AC 633 at 731; *Campbell v Peter Gordon Joiners Ltd* [2016] UKSC 38, [2016] AC 1513. *Sovar v Henry Lane Pty Ltd* (1967) 116 CLR 397 per Kitto J

> The intention that such a private right shall exist is not...conjured up by judges to give effect to their own ideas of policy and then 'imputed' to the legislature. The legitimate endeavour of the courts is to determine what inference really arises, on a balance of considerations, from the nature, scope and terms of the statute, including the nature of the evil against which it is directed, the nature of the conduct prescribed, the pre-existing state of the law, and, generally, the whole range of circumstances relevant upon a question of statutory interpretation...It is not a question of the actual intention of the legislators, but of the proper inference to be perceived upon a consideration of the document in the light of all its

exclude such a claim and does not provide a criminal sanction for non-compliance.[85] If such a cause of action does exist, a claim on the cause of action could, if resultant loss were proved, lead to an award of damages.[86]

3. DATA SUBJECT ACCESS RIGHT

14– 021 Introduction

In addition to the continuing obligation on an intelligence service controller to comply with the data protection principles, Part 4 of the DPA 2018 confers five rights on every data subject whose personal data is being processed by an intelligence service controller:

(1) An access right.
(2) A right of rectification.
(3) A right of erasure.
(4) A right of objection.
(5) Various rights in relation to automated decision-making.

The first right complements the others. It will often need to be exercised and satisfied in order to decide which, if any, of the other rights should be exercised and in what manner they should be exercised. As the gateway to the other four rights, the first right has foundational importance to the rights and freedoms of the data subject.

14– 022 General information

Intelligence service controllers must give data subjects certain basic information about their processing of personal data:

(a) the identity and the contact details of the controller;
(b) the legal basis on which, and the purposes for which, the controller processes personal data;
(c) the categories of personal data relating to the data subject that are being processed;
(d) the recipients or the categories of recipients of the personal data (if applicable);
(e) the right to lodge a complaint with the Information Commissioner and the contact details of the Commissioner;
(f) how to exercise the data subject rights;
(g) any other information needed to secure that the personal data is processed fairly and transparently.[87]

The controller may comply with this duty by making the information generally available.[88] The

---

surrounding circumstances.

85 Contrast FOIA s 56(1). For the relevance of such provisions, see: *Boyce v Paddington Borough Council* [1903] 1 Ch 109; *Lonrho Ltd v Shell Ltd (no 2)* [1982] AC 173 at 185. Where an intelligence service controller invokes the national security exemption (DPA 2018 s 110), that leaves in place the requirement that the controller implement measures to ensure that the processing of personal data is 'lawful' (DPA 2018 ss 86(1)(a) and (2) and 102), but disapplies the erasure right (DPA 2018 s 100(2)) and all the Information Commissioner's enforcement powers (DPA 2018 ss 110(2)(e), 142-154), with the result that without a common law action for breach of statutory duty there would be no remedy, regulatory or otherwise, for a breach of the residual statutory obligation (ie DPA 2018 s 102 in conjunction with s 86(1)(a) and (2)).

86 The principle is ubi jus, ibi remedium (where there is a right, the law provides a remedy): *Pasmore v Oswaldtwistle UDC* [1898] AC 387; *Cutler v Wandsworth Stadium Ltd* [1949] AC 398 at 407, [1949] 1 All ER 544 at 548; *Booth & Co (International) Ltd v National Enterprise Board* [1978] 3 All ER 624; *Thornton v Kirklees Metropolitan Borough Council* [1979] QB 626, [1979] 2 All ER 349. Private law claims are considered at §§48– 005 to 48– 013.

87 DPA 2018 s 93(1).

88 DPA 2018 s 93(2). The duty may, for example, be complied with by a general notice on a website.

controller is not required to give a data subject information that the data subject already has.[89] To the extent that the controller has collected the personal data from a person other than the data subject, the duty is disapplied where either the processing is authorised by an enactment or giving the information to the data subject would be impossible or involve disproportionate effort.[90]

14–023 Right of access

Every individual has a three-fold right to learn of the processing of his or her personal data by an intelligence service.[91] The right is subject to exemptions. Subject to satisfying certain procedural requirements and to the exemptions, an individual is entitled to obtain from a controller:

(1) Confirmation whether or not the controller, or a processor on its behalf, is processing personal data concerning that individual.[92]

(2) Where the controller, or a processor on its behalf, is processing personal data concerning that individual, communication in intelligible form of the personal data of which that individual is the data subject.[93]

(3) Where the controller, or a processor on its behalf, is processing personal data concerning that individual, the following information:[94]
   - (a) the purposes of and legal basis for the processing;
   - (b) the categories of personal data concerned;
   - (c) the recipients or categories of recipients to whom the personal data has been disclosed;
   - (d) the period for which the personal data is to be preserved;
   - (e) the existence of a data subject's rights to rectification and erasure of personal data;
   - (f) the right to lodge a complaint with the Information Commissioner and the contact details of the Commissioner; and
   - (g) any information about the origin of the personal data concerned.

Unless there are time constraints, it may well be prudent for an individual to exercise the three aspects of the access right separately.[95]

14–024 Procedural requirements

Before being obliged to respond to a request for access, the controller may require further information from the individual:

(a) to satisfy itself of the identity of the individual making the request; and

(b) to locate the information that the individual seeks.[96]

---

89 DPA 2018 s 93(3).

90 DPA 2018 s 93(4). In relation to processing authorised by enactment, this will cover, for example, where data is being processed as a result of surveillance conducted under an authorisation issued under the Regulation of Investigatory Powers Act 2000. In relation to the second option, given that the controller may satisfy the duty by making the information generally available – for example, posting on a website – impossibility and disproportionate effort might seem not easily satisfied.

91 DPA 2018 s 94(1). The right is given to every 'individual' rather than to every 'data subject' in recognition that the right arises even where the controller has no personal data relating to the individual: see DPA 2018 s 3(5).

92 DPA 2018 s 94(1)(a).

93 DPA 2018 s 94(1)(b)(i).

94 DPA 2018 s 94(1)(b)(ii).

95 It will be beneficial to the individual so far as the fees that the controller can reasonably charge and the application of the exemptions.

96 DPA 2018 s 94(5).

The controller may also require the individual to pay a reasonable fee.[97] Where a controller has previously complied with a request by an individual, that controller is not obliged to comply with a subsequent identical or similar request by that individual unless a reasonable interval has elapsed between compliance with the previous request and the making of the later request.[98]

14–025 Time for compliance

The controller must comply with a request promptly and, in any event, within one month of receiving the request, the fee or the required identity details (whichever is the later).[99]

14–026 Mixed personal data

Where compliance with the request would disclose information relating to another individual, the controller should redact so much of the information as would disclose the identity of that other individual.[100] To the extent that a controller cannot comply with the request without disclosing information relating to another individual who can be identified from that information,[101] the controller is not obliged to comply with the request unless:

(a) the other individual has consented to the disclosure of the information to the individual making the request; or

(b) it is reasonable in all the circumstances to comply with the request without the consent of the other individual.[102]

14–027 Response

The controller must answer the request by reference to the data in question at the time that the request is received.[103] Where the individual requests communication in intelligible form of the personal data of which that individual is the data subject then, subject to any exemption or the individual otherwise agreeing, the controller must (unless it is impossible or would involve disproportionate effort) supply the individual with a copy of the information in writing.[104] There are no prescribed requirements for a refusal.

14–028 Enforcement and remedies

Where an individual is not satisfied with the controller's response to an access request, the

97 DPA 2018 s 94(3).

98 DPA 2018 s 95(2). In determining whether requests are made at reasonable intervals, regard is had to: (a) the nature of the data; (b) the purpose for which the data is processed; and (c) the frequency with which the data is altered: DPA 2018 s 95(3). Where an individual has in an earlier request merely sought confirmation whether or not personal data concerning him or her is being processed, a later request exercising just the rights under s 94(1)(b) will be neither 'identical' nor 'similar.'

99 DPA 2018 s 94(10), (14). The Secretary of State may specify by regulations a longer period: DPA 2018 s 94(14).

100 DPA 2018 s 94(6), (8).

101 An individual can be identified from information to be disclosed to a data subject by a controller if the individual can be identified from: (a) that information, or (b) that and any other information that the controller reasonably believes the data subject making the request is likely to possess or obtain: DPA 2018 s 95(5).

102 DPA 2018 s 94(6). The reference to information relating to another individual includes a reference to information identifying that individual as the source of the information sought by the request: DPA 2018 s 94(7). In determining whether it is reasonable in all the circumstances to comply with the request without the consent of the other individual concerned, regard must be had, in particular, to: (a) any duty of confidentiality owed to the other individual; (b) any steps taken by the controller with a view to seeking the consent of the other individual; (c) whether the other individual is capable of giving consent; and (d) any express refusal of consent by the other individual: DPA 2018 s 94(9). As to the meaning of 'consent' see §14–003(3).

103 DPA 2018 s 95(4). The response may nevertheless take account of any amendment or deletion made between that time and the time when the information is supplied, being an amendment or deletion that would have been made regardless of the receipt of the request.

104 DPA 2018 s 95(1). Where the information is expressed in terms that are unintelligible to the individual without an explanation, the controller must also provide an explanation of those terms.

individual may bring a claim in the High Court or, in Scotland, in the Court of Session.[105] Where the court is satisfied that the controller has failed to comply with the individual's request, the court may order the controller to comply with the request.[106] In addition, the individual may complain to the Information Commissioner. The Commissioner must investigate the complaint and enforce the access right.[107] If the Commissioner is satisfied that the controller has failed, or is failing, to comply with the right of access conferred by the DPA, the Commissioner may serve an enforcement notice on the controller.[108]

14–029 Supplementary right

Where an intelligence service controller processes personal data relating to a data subject and the results produced by the processing are applied to that data subject, he or she is entitled to obtain from the controller knowledge of the reasoning underlying the processing.[109] In practice, a data subject is unlikely to know of the processing and use of results without having first made an access request.[110] Apart from requesting that the controller provide the data subject with the knowledge of the reasoning underlying the processing, there are no formal requirements in exercising the right: nor is there any fee payable. The controller must comply with the request without undue delay.[111] No private law remedy is provided for non-compliance with such a request. The data subject may, however, complain to the Information Commissioner. The Commissioner must investigate the complaint and enforce the supplementary right.[112] If the Commissioner is satisfied that the controller has failed, or is failing, to comply with this right, the Commissioner may serve an enforcement notice on the controller.[113]

4. OTHER DATA SUBJECT RIGHTS

14–030 Introduction

As well as the access right, a data subject has four other rights exercisable against a controller in respect of personal data about him or herself that is being processed by the controller or by a processor on behalf of the controller. In order for these rights to be effectively exercised, a data subject will normally have first exercised the access right and from that learnt what personal data relating to him or her is being processed by the controller and the manner in which it is being processed.

14–031 Right to rectification

Where personal data relating to a data subject is inaccurate, the data subject to whom that

105 DPA s 94(11)-(13).

106 DPA 2018 s 94(11).

107 DPA 2018 Sch 13 para 1(1)(a), (e), (g). See further §48–004.

108 DPA 2018 s 149(2)(b). In relation to enforcement notices, see further §§48–034 to 48–038.

109 DPA 2018 s 98(1).

110 Under DPA 2018 s 94(1)(b), where a data subject makes an access request that includes a request that the controller provide the information set out in s 94(2), that will include 'the purposes of the processing' from which it should emerge whether the controller is applying results produced by the processing to the data subject.

111 DPA 2018 s 98(2).

112 DPA 2018 Sch 13 para 1(1)(a), (e), (g). See further §48–004.

113 DPA 2018 s 149(2)(b). In relation to enforcement notices, see further §§48–034 to 48–038. The Information Commissioner also has the investigative, corrective, authorisation and advisory powers listed in §14–019 above: DPA 2018 Sch 13 para 2.

personal data relates has a qualified right to require the controller to rectify it.[114] 'Inaccurate' means incorrect or misleading as to any matter of fact.[115] The right is subject to exemptions. There are no formal requirements in exercising the right, and there is no power on the controller to impose a fee for complying with a rectification request.[116] No time-limit is prescribed for compliance, but delayed compliance may be treated as tantamount to refusal. Where a controller refuses a request by a data subject to rectify his or her personal data that is inaccurate, that data subject may apply to the High Court for a coercive order that the controller rectify that data without undue delay.[117] Where on such an application the court is satisfied that the personal data relating to the data subject is inaccurate, the court may order the controller to rectify that data without undue delay.[118] Where the court is satisfied that the controller is not able to ascertain whether the personal data is accurate or not, the court may order the controller to restrict its processing of that data, rather than order its rectification.[119] A court may also order restriction of processing instead of rectification where the personal data must be maintained for the purposes of evidence.[120]

14– 032 Right to erasure

Where an intelligence service controller in processing personal data concerning a data subject is infringing any of the data protection principles, that data subject may seek a court order that the controller erase that data without undue delay.[121] The right is subject to exemptions. A data subject may exercise this right in either of two ways:

(1) As the relief in a private law claim by the data subject that the controller is breaching its obligation to comply with the data protection principles.

(2) Where the Information Commissioner has issued an enforcement notice stating that the controller has breached its duty to comply with the data protection principles in respect of its processing of personal data concerning one or more data subjects. In this situation, any such data subject can request the controller to erase the personal data relating to him or her being processed by the controller. There are no formal requirements in exercising the right, and there is no power on the controller to impose a fee for complying with a rectification request.[122] No time-limit is prescribed for compliance, but delayed compliance may be treated as

---

114 DPA 2018 ss 94(2)(f), 100(1).

115 DPA 2018 s 205(1).

116 Plainly, the data subject will need to specify which of the personal data being processed by the controller is inaccurate, in what respects it is inaccurate and the changes that are required to be made to it in order to render it accurate. A data subject will normally need to have received the results of an access request in order to be able to do so. In order to maximise the prospects of the data being rectified, rather than a court merely ordering under DPA 2018 s 100(4) a restriction of processing, it will be prudent for the data subject to provide the controller with as much material as possible to demonstrate that the data is inaccurate.

117 DPA 2018 s 100(1), (6). In Scotland, it is the Court of Session that has jurisdiction. See further §§48– 005 to 48– 013. Where there are joint controllers of the personal data, the order will be made against the controller responsible for rectification (as determined under DPA 2018 s 104(2)). Alternatively or additionally, the data subject may request the Information Commissioner to take enforcement action: see further §§48– 014 to 48– 055.

118 DPA 2018 s 100(1).

119 DPA 2018 s 100(4).

120 DPA 2018 s 100(3). A 'restriction of processing' simply means the marking of stored personal data with the aim of limiting its processing for the future: DPA 2018 s 84(6). See further §8– 031.

121 DPA 2018 ss 94(2)(f), 100(2).

122 Plainly, the data subject will need to know how his or her personal data is being processed by the controller in order to exercise this right. A data subject will normally need either to have received the results of an access request in order to be able to do so or to have learnt the outcome of enforcement action by the Information Commissioner.

tantamount to refusal. Where a controller refuses a request by a data subject to erase his or her personal data, that data subject may apply to the High Court for a coercive order that the controller erase that data without undue delay.[123]

Where on such an application the court is satisfied that the personal data relating to the data subject is inaccurate, the court may order the controller to rectify that data without undue delay.[124] A court may order restriction of processing instead of erasure where the personal data must be maintained for the purposes of evidence.[125]

4–033 Right to object

A data subject has a right to require an intelligence service controller:

(a) not to process personal data relating to him or her; or

(b) not to process personal data relating to him or her for a specified purpose or in a specified manner,

on the basis that for specified reasons relating to the situation of the data subject, the processing in question is an unwarranted interference with the rights or interests of the data subject.[126] The right is subject to exemptions. The right is exercised by notice to the controller and it may be exercised at any time.[127] Where the controller reasonably requires further information in order for it to be satisfied as to the identity of the individual giving the notice or to locate the data to which the notice relates, the controller may notify the data subject of the further information it requires. Where the controller does so notify the data subject, the obligation on the controller to comply with the notice does not commence unless the controller is supplied with that further information.[128] The controller must within 21 days of receiving the notice (or of the notice becoming effective) notify the data subject either:

(a) that it has complied or intends to comply with the data subject's notice; or

(b) that it does not intend to comply with the notice (and, if only partially not comply, the extent to which it will comply), setting out its reasons for not complying with the notice.[129]

To the extent that a controller does not comply with a notice of objection, the data subject may apply to a court for an order that the controller take steps to comply with the notice.[130] Where the court is satisfied that the controller should comply with the notice (or should comply to any extent), the court may order the controller to take such steps for complying with the notice (or for complying with it to that extent) as it thinks fit.[131]

---

123 DPA 2018 s 100(2), (6). In Scotland, it is the Court of Session that has jurisdiction. See further §§48–005 to 48–013. Where there are joint controllers of the personal data, the order will be made against the controller responsible for rectification (as determined under DPA 2018 s 104(2)). Alternatively or additionally, the data subject may request the Information Commissioner to take enforcement action: see §14–019, §14–035 and §§48–014 to 48–055.

124 DPA 2018 s 100(1).

125 DPA 2018 s 100(3). A 'restriction of processing' simply means the marking of stored personal data with the aim of limiting its processing for the future: DPA 2018 s 84(6). See further §8–031.

126 DPA 2018 s 99(1). The phrase 'interests or rights of the data subject' is wider than 'rights or freedoms of the data subject': see §§8–006 to 8–007 on the meaning of the latter.

127 DPA 2018 s 99(1).

128 DPA 2018 s 99(2).

129 DPA s 99(3).

130 DPA 2018 s 99(4). Private law claims are considered at §§48–005 to 48–013. Alternatively or additionally, the data subject may request the Information Commissioner to take enforcement action: see §14–019 and §14–035. Regulatory enforcement is considered at §§48–014 to 48–055.

131 DPA 2018 s 99(5). The jurisdiction is conferred on the High Court or, in Scotland, on the Court of Session. Private law claims are considered at §§48–005 to 48–013. A court may make an order in relation to a joint controller whose responsibilities are determined in an arrangement only if the controller is responsible for

14– 034 Automated decisions right

Every data subject has a qualified right not to be subject to a decision by an intelligence service controller significantly affecting him or her that is based solely on automated processing of personal data relating to the data subject.[132] A decision that has legal effects as regards an individual will be regarded as significantly affecting the individual.[133] In addition to exemptions, the right is qualified in that it does not prevent the controller making such a decision where:

(a) the decision is required or authorised by law;
(b) the data subject has given consent to the decision being made on that basis; or
(c) the decision is a decision taken in the course of steps taken:
  (i) for the purpose of considering whether to enter into a contract with the data subject;
  (ii) with a view to entering into such a contract; or
  (iii) in the course of performing such a contract.[134]

Where such a decision is required or authorised by law, but neither (b) nor (c) applies, the controller must as soon as reasonably practicable notify the data subject that such a decision has been made.[135] Once the data subject has been so notified, he or she may request the controller either to reconsider the decision or to take a new decision that is not based solely on automated processing.[136] Such a request must be made within one month of the data subject receiving notification of the decision.[137] If the data subject makes such a request, the controller must within one month consider it and inform the data subject of the outcome of that consideration.[138] No private law remedy is provided for non-compliance with such a request.[139] The data subject may, however, complain to the Information Commissioner. The Commissioner must investigate the complaint and enforce the data subject's right.[140] If the Commissioner is satisfied that the controller has failed, or is failing, to comply with this right, the Commissioner may serve an enforcement notice on the controller.[141]

5. EXEMPTIONS

14– 035 Introduction

The DPA 2018 provides a number of exemptions from the obligations and data subject rights in respect of processing of personal data by an intelligence service. The most significant exemption is the exemption for national security. Where engaged, this disapplies all of the data

compliance with the obligation to which the order relates (as determined under DPA 2018 s 104(2)).

132 DPA 2018 s 96(1).

133 DPA 2018 s 96(3).

134 DPA 2018 s 96(2). As to the meaning of 'consent' see §14– 003(3).

135 DPA 2018 s 97(1)-(3).

136 DPA 2018 s 97(4).

137 DPA 2018 s 97(4).

138 DPA 2018 s 97(5).

139 As to whether this would give rise to a common law right for breach of statutory duty, see §14– 020.

140 DPA 2018 Sch 13 para 1(1)(a), (e), (g). See further §48– 004.

141 DPA 2018 s 149(2)(b). In relation to enforcement notices, see further §§48– 034 to 48– 038. The Information Commissioner also has the investigative, corrective, authorisation and advisory powers listed in §14– 019 above: DPA 2018 Sch 13 para 2.

subject's rights, disapplies all but one of the continuing obligations on the controller, empties the Information Commissioner of any enforcement powers and disapplies the criminal provisions.[142] The other exemptions resemble those applicable to general processing of personal data. Some of these exemptions are prejudice-based: that is, in order to be engaged there must be a likelihood of prejudice to the interest protected by the exemption. The other exemptions are purely data-type exemptions: that is, to the extent that the data being processed is of the type described, the exemption will be engaged. Where engaged, these exemptions disapply all of the data subject's rights and disapply all but one of the continuing obligations on the controller, but leave intact the Information Commissioner's enforcement powers and the criminal provisions.[143] The same principles in relation to onus and likelihood of prejudice applicable to general processing apply to processing by an intelligence service.[144]

14– 036 National security

To the extent that exemption from:

(a) the continuing obligation to comply with the data protection principles;[145]
(b) any of the data subject rights;[146]
(c) the duty to report personal data breaches to the Information Commissioner;[147]
(d) the Information Commissioner's enforcement powers;[148]
(e) the criminal sanctions,[149]

is required for the purpose of safeguarding national security, that obligation, right, power or sanction is disapplied.[150] The exemption does not have the effect of disapplying the continuing obligation on an intelligence service controller to implement measures to ensure that the processing of personal data is at all times 'lawful.'[151] The disapplication is not monolithic, so that in each case it is only where exemption from a particular provision is required for the purposes of safeguarding national security that that provision (but not necessarily the other provisions) will be disapplied.[152] The phrase 'required for the purpose of safeguarding national security' is the same as is used in relation to general processing.[153] Although 'national security' is not defined, its meaning is likely to be the same as given in other legislative spheres.[154] The DPA 2018 permits a Minister of the Crown to certify that exemption from all or any of the

---

142 DPA 2018 s 110(2).

143 DPA 2018 Sch 11 para 1.

144 See §§11– 008 and 11– 009 respectively. Given that the intelligence services provisions do not have their basis in EU law, the interpretative principles applicable to exemptions from general processing are inapplicable to processing of personal data by the intelligence services: see §11– 007.

145 That is, the six data protection principles in DPA 2018 ss 86-91.

146 That is, the rights conferred on data subject by DPA 2018 ss 92-100.

147 That is, the duty imposed by DPA 2018 s 108.

148 That is, the duties and powers imposed and conferred on the Information Commissioner by DPA 2018 ss 142-154, including the power to serve information notices, assessment notices, enforcement notices and the power of entry and inspection.

149 That is, the offences relating to the unlawful obtaining of personal data (DPA 2018 s 170), the re-identification of de-identified personal data (DPA 2018 ss 171-172) and the alteration of personal data to prevent disclosure to the data subject (DPA 2018 s 173).

150 DPA 2018 s 110(1)-(2),

151 DPA 2018 s 110(2)(a), which leaves intact ss 86(1)(a) and (2) and 102. As to the scope of the 'lawful' obligation, see §14– 008.

152 DPA 2018 s 110(1).

153 DPA 2018 ss 26(1)(a), 27(1) and 28(1)-(2). See further §11– 022.

154 As to which, see §§26– 050 to 26– 054.

provisions in (a)-(e) above is or was required in relation to any personal data for the purpose of safeguarding national security, with that certificate being conclusive evidence of that fact.[155]

14– 037 Scope of other exemptions

The scope of the other exemptions is:

(a) the continuing obligation to comply with the data protection principles;[156]

(b) the data subject rights;[157] and

(c) the duty to report personal data breaches to the Information Commissioner,[158]

collectively 'the listed provisions.'[159] Disapplication of the listed provisions is not monolithic, so that in each case it is only to the extent to which a particular provision in (a)-(c) satisfies the requirements of the exemption that that provision (but not necessarily the other provisions) will be disapplied. Engagement of any of these exemptions also leaves intact:

— the continuing obligation on an intelligence service controller to implement measures to ensure that the processing of personal data is at all times 'lawful';[160]

— the Information Commissioner's enforcement powers;[161] and

— the criminal sanctions.[162]

14– 038 Law enforcement purposes

The DPA 2018 provides a prejudice-based exemption to cover an intelligence service controller that is processing personal data for the purpose of:

(a) the prevention or detection of crime; or

(b) the apprehension or prosecution of offenders.

Where an intelligence service controller is processing personal data for that purpose, then, to the extent that the application of the listed provisions would be likely to prejudice (a) or (b), the listed provisions are disapplied.[163]

14– 039 Legal proceedings

The DPA 2018 describes four separate exemptions relating to legal proceedings:

(1) It provides a prejudice-based exemption in respect of personal data consisting of information that the controller is obliged by enactment to make available to the public. To the extent that the application of the listed provisions would prevent the controller from complying with its obligation to make that information available to

---

155 DPA 2018 s 111(1). There is a limited right of appeal to the First-tier Tribunal against the issue of a certificate by any person affected by it: DPA 111(2)-(3). As to the operation of national security certificates, see §§26– 057 to 26–061. As to the nature of appeals against national security certificates, see §§48– 060 to 48– 062.

156 That is, the six data protection principles in DPA 2018 ss 86-91.

157 That is, the rights conferred on data subject by DPA 2018 ss 92-100.

158 That is, the duty imposed by DPA 2018 s 108.

159 DPA 2018 Sch 11 para 1.

160 DPA 2018 s 110(2)(a), which leaves intact ss 86(1)(a) and (2) and 102. As to the scope of the 'lawful' obligation, see §14– 008.

161 That is, the duties and powers imposed and conferred on the Information Commissioner by DPA 2018 ss 142-154, including the power to serve information notices, assessment notices, enforcement notices and the power of entry and inspection.

162 That is, the offences relating to the unlawful obtaining of personal data (DPA 2018 s 170), the re-identification of de-identified personal data (DPA 2018 ss 171-172) and the alteration of personal data to prevent disclosure to the data subject (DPA 2018 s 173).

163 DPA 2018 Sch 11 para 2. As to the meaning of 'the listed provisions,' see §14– 037. This is similar, but not identical, to the definition of 'law enforcement purposes' in DPA 2018 s 31. As to the meaning of likelihood of prejudice, see §11– 009.

the public, the listed provisions are disapplied.[164]

(2) It provides a prejudice-based exemption in respect of personal data that is required to be disclosed by an enactment, a rule of law or an order of a court. To the extent that the application of the listed provisions would prevent the controller from complying with its obligation to disclose that personal data, the listed provisions are disapplied.[165]

(3) Where the disclosure of personal data:
   (a) is necessary for the purpose of, or in connection with, legal proceedings (including prospective legal proceedings);
   (b) is necessary for the purpose of obtaining legal advice; or
   (c) is otherwise necessary for the purposes of establishing, exercising or defending legal rights,

   the listed provisions are disapplied to the extent that those provisions would prevent the controller from making the disclosure.[166]

(4) To the extent that the application of the listed provisions would be likely to prejudice judicial proceedings, the listed provisions are disapplied.[167]

14– 040 Parliamentary privilege

The listed provisions do not apply to personal data where this is required for the purpose of avoiding an infringement of the privileges of either House of Parliament.[168] This is the same as an exemption which applies to general processing.[169]

14– 041 Crown honours etc

The listed provisions do not apply to personal data processed for the purpose of the conferring by the Crown of any honour or dignity.[170]

14– 042 Armed forces

The listed provisions do not apply to personal data to the extent that the application of the listed provisions would be likely to prejudice the combat effectiveness of any of the armed forces of the Crown.[171] This is less wide than the comparable exemption which applies to general processing.[172]

14– 043 Economic well-being

The listed provisions do not apply to personal data to the extent that the application of the

---

164 DPA 2018 Sch 11 para 3(1). As to the meaning of 'the listed provisions,' see §14– 037.

165 DPA 2018 Sch 11 para 3(2).

166 DPA 2018 Sch 11 para 3(3).

167 DPA 2018 Sch 11 para 5. It is not clear what the difference is between 'legal proceedings' and 'judicial proceedings.' but possibly the latter is a subset of the former and does not cover tribunal proceedings, arbitral proceedings or the like, nor legal proceedings of which the hearing has not commenced: see DPA 2018 Sch 2 para 14.

168 DPA 2018 Sch 11 para 4. As to the meaning of 'the listed provisions,' see §14– 037. As to the privileges of the Houses of Parliament, see §30– 003.

169 See §11– 039.

170 DPA 2018 Sch 11 para 6. As to the meaning of 'the listed provisions,' see §14– 037. As to the meaning of 'honour or dignity,' see §35– 010. As to the process of conferral of an honour or dignity, see §35– 011. A like exemption applies to general processing: see §11– 034.

171 DPA 2018 Sch 11 para 7. As to the meaning of 'armed forces of the Crown,' see §§26– 075 to 26– 076. As to the meaning of 'combat effectiveness,' see §26– 078. As to the meaning of 'the listed provisions,' see §14– 037.

172 See §11– 023.

listed provisions would be likely to prejudice the economic well-being of the United Kingdom.[173]

14–044 Legal professional privilege

The listed provisions do not apply to personal data that consists of:

(a) information in respect of which a claim to legal professional privilege or, in Scotland, confidentiality of communications, could be maintained in legal proceedings;[174] or

(b) information in respect of which a duty of confidentiality is owed by a professional legal adviser to a client of the adviser.[175]

14–045 Negotiations

The listed provisions do not apply to personal data that consists of records of the intentions of the controller in relation to any negotiations with the data subject to the extent that the application of the listed provisions would be likely to prejudice the negotiations.[176] There is a similar exemption in relation to general processing of personal data.[177]

14–046 Confidential references

The listed provisions do not apply to personal data consisting of a reference given (or to be given) in confidence by the controller for the purposes of:

(a) the education, training or employment (or prospective education, training or employment) of the data subject;

(b) the appointment (or prospective appointment) of the data subject to any office; or

(c) the provision (or prospective provision) by the data subject of any service.[178]

There is a similar exemption in relation to general processing of personal data.[179]

14–047 Exam papers

The listed provisions do not apply to personal data consisting of information recorded by candidates during an exam.[180] Where personal data consists of marks or other information processed by a controller for the purposes of determining the results of an exam or in consequence of the determination of the results of an exam, the obligation to respond to the right of access is deferred until after the results are announced.[181] There are similar exemptions in relation to general processing of personal data.[182]

---

173 DPA 2018 Sch 11 para 8. As to the meaning of 'the listed provisions,' see §14–037.

174 As to the circumstances in which litigation privilege arises, see §§30–014 to 30–016.

175 DPA 2018 Sch 11 para 9. As to the meaning of 'the listed provisions,' see §14–037. As for the circumstances in which such a duty of confidentiality arises (ie legal advice privilege), see §§30–014 to 30–016.

176 DPA 2018 Sch 11 para 10. As to the meaning of 'the listed provisions,' see §14–037.

177 See §11–043.

178 DPA 2018 Sch 11 para 11. As to the meaning of 'the listed provisions,' see §14–037.

179 See §11–042.

180 DPA 2018 Sch 11 para 12(1). As to the meaning of 'the listed provisions,' see §14–037. The word 'exam' is defined to mean an academic, professional or other examination used for determining the knowledge, intelligence, skill or ability of a candidate and may include an exam consisting of an assessment of the candidate's performance while undertaking work or any other activity.

181 DPA 2018 Sch 11 para 12(2)-(5).

182 See §11–044.

14– 048 Research and statistics

In relation to personal data processed for scientific or historical research purposes, or for statistical purposes, where:

(a) the personal data is processed subject to appropriate safeguards for the rights and freedoms of data subjects; and

(b) the results of the research or any resulting statistics are not made available in a form which identifies a data subject,

then the listed provisions do not apply to the extent that the application of those provisions would prevent or seriously impair the achievement of the purposes in question.[183]

14– 049 Archiving purposes

In relation to personal data processed for archiving purposes in the public interest, where the personal data is processed subject to appropriate safeguards for the rights and freedoms of data subjects, then the listed provisions do not apply to the extent that the application of those provisions would prevent or seriously impair the achievement of those purposes.[184]

[183] DPA 2018 Sch 11 para 13. As to the meaning of 'the listed provisions,' see §14– 037. As to the meaning of 'the rights and freedoms of data subjects' see §§8– 006 to 8– 007. For the purposes of general processing, there is a more extensive derogation for research and statistical purposes: see §11– 052.

[184] DPA 2018 Sch 11 para 14. As to the meaning of 'the listed provisions,' see §14– 037. As to the meaning of 'the rights and freedoms of data subjects' see §§8– 006 to 8– 007. For the purposes of general processing, there is a more extensive derogation for archiving purposes: see §11– 051.

CHAPTER 15

DPA 1998: concepts, rights and duties

1. INTRODUCTION

5–001 Introduction

Notwithstanding its repeal by the DPA 2018, the DPA 1998 continues to apply:

— to subject access requests and other notices received prior to its repeal, and
— to claims for breach of the duty to comply with the data protection principles arising out of acts or omissions prior to its repeal.

Moreover, although the organisation and provenance of the DPA 1998 are very different from the GDPR and DPA 2018, the concepts, principles, rights and duties are remarkably similar. It is therefore to be expected that the jurisprudence developed under the DPA 1998 will inform and illuminate the interpretation and application of the GDPR and DPA 2018. For these reasons, an understanding of the DPA 1998 remains important.

5–002 Purpose of DPA 1998

The DPA 1998[185] served two related purposes:

(1) to protect the data privacy of every individual by regulating the use that others could make of information relating to each such individual through the setting of limits and the imposition of conditions on that use; and
(2) to delimit the permitted uses of information relating to individuals, varying the extent of those permitted uses according to the identity of the user, the nature of the information, the purpose for which the information was being used, the type of use and the knowledge and consent of the individual to that use.

These two purposes reflected the provenance of the DPA 1998, stemming on the one hand from the right to a private domain recognised in Art 12 of the Universal Declaration of Human Rights (adopted and proclaimed by the United Nations in 1948) and, on the other hand, from guidelines on transborder data flows developed in 1978-1980 by the Organisation for Economic Co-operation and Development (OECD) so as to facilitate trade.[186]

5–003 Transitional arrangements

The DPA 1998 was repealed by the DPA 2018.[187] The GDPR repealed Directive 95/46/EC.[188] Both repeals took effect from 25 May 2018, being the date on which the DPA 2018 and the GDPR came into force. Transitional provisions mean that the DPA 1998 continues to apply as follows:

(1) In relation to subject access requests received before 25 May 2018 – see para 2 of Sch 20 DPA 2018.
(2) In relation to notices given under the DPA 1998 s 10 before 25 May 2018 – see para 3 of Sch 20 DPA 2018.

---

185 The DPA 1998 applied equally to England, Northern Ireland, Scotland and Wales. Data protection is a reserved matter under the Scotland Act 1998 and, accordingly, is outside the legislative competence of the Scottish Parliament: see Scotland Act 1998 s 27(2)(b) and Sch 5, and §3–001. As a matter of drafting convention rather than necessity, the DPA 1998 was expressly stated to apply to Northern Ireland: s 75(5) and (6).

186 These two purposes were reflected in Art 1 of Directive 95/46/EC.

187 DPA 2018, Sch 19, Pt 1, para 44.

188 GDPR Art 94.1.

(3) In relation to notices given under the DPA 1998 s 11 before 25 May 2018 – see para 4 of Sch 20 DPA 2018.
(4) In relation to notices given under the DPA 1998 s 12 before 25 May 2018 – see para 5 of Sch 20 DPA 2018.
(5) In relation to a breach of the duty imposed on a data controller by DPA 1998 s 4(4) to comply with the data protection principles, where the breach took place before 25 May 2018 (whether in whole or in part), the data subject will be able to institute and continue a claim in respect of that breach as if the DPA 1998 had not been repealed.[189]
(6) In circumstances where the provisions of the DPA 1998 continue to apply as set out in (1)-(5) above, the exemptions in Part 4 of the Act likewise continue to apply – see para 9 of Sch 20 DPA 2018

Given this continued application and given the similarities with its successor regime (as established by the GDPR and the DPA 2018), the way in which the DPA 1998 operated and had been interpreted are important to an understanding of information rights. Those elements of the DPA 1998 that are no longer of current concern have been removed or receive abbreviated treatment in this work.

15–004 DPA 1984

The predecessor to the DPA 1998 was the DPA 1984. It had been more limited in scope than the DPA 1998, in particular being confined to 'automated data'.[190] The DPA 1984 had its origins, in part, in the Convention for the Protection of Individuals with regard to Automatic Processing of Personal Data, adopted by the Council of Europe in 1981.[191]

15–005 Data Protection Directive

In 1995 the European Council issued what became generally termed the 'Data Protection Directive'.[192] This Directive applied not only to automated data[193] but also to certain types of manually stored data.[194] Member States were required to implement the Directive within three years of its adoption.[195] The Directive required Member States:

— to provide for certain principles relating to the processing of personal data;[196]
— to provide for higher regulatory standards in relation to the processing of certain sorts of personal data;[197]
— to provide an individual with a right of access to data relating to him or herself;[198]
— to provide an individual with a right to object to certain sorts of processing;[199]
— to enable an individual to restrict automated individual decisions relating to him or

189 Interpretation Act 1978, s 16(1). The DPA 2018 expressly preserves the remedies provided for by DPA 1998 ss 13 and 14: DPA 2018 Sch 20 paras 6, 7.

190 Effectively, information falling within either paragraph (a) or (b) of the definition of 'data' in DPA 1998 s 1(1).

191 Convention for the Protection of Individuals with regard to Automatic Processing of Personal Data, 28 January 1981, ETS No 108.

192 Council Directive 95/46/EC, [1995] OJ L281/31.

193 Effectively, information falling within either paragraph (a) or (b) of the definition of 'data' in DPA 1998 s 1(1). The DPA 1984 was only concerned with 'automated data.'

194 Council Directive 95/46/EC Art 2(c) and 3(1).

195 Article 32.

196 Articles 6 and 7.

197 Article 8.

198 Article 12.

199 Article 14.

herself;[200] and

— to provide for remedies, liability and sanctions in the case of non-compliance.[201]

15– 006 Directive-based interpretation

Implementation of the Directive in the United Kingdom was by the enactment of the DPA 1998, which was brought fully into force on 1 March 2000. In light of its origins in Directive 95/46/EC, the DPA 1998 had to be construed in a purposive fashion, having regard to the aims of the Directive.[202] The Directive was specifically linked to the need to respect 'fundamental rights and freedoms, notably the right to privacy' and it referred in that respect to the ECHR.[203] The European Court of Human Rights repeatedly noted that under the Directive the object of national laws on the processing of personal data was to protect the right to privacy as recognised both in Art 8 of the ECHR and in the general principles of Community law.[204] As the Court noted:

> There are various crucial stages at which data protection issues under Article 8 of the Convention may arise, including during collection, storage, use and communication of data. At each stage, appropriate and adequate safeguards which reflect the principles elaborated in applicable data protection instruments and prevent arbitrary and disproportionate interference with Article 8 rights must be in place.[205]

15– 007 Extra-territoriality

The rights enjoyed by individuals under the DPA 1998 were not expressly limited to individuals of British nationality or residence: rather, the beneficiaries of the rights conferred by the DPA 1998 fell to be determined by ordinary principles of statutory interpretation relating to extra-territoriality.[206] So far as the duties imposed on data controllers,[207] the Act applied:

(1) To data controllers established in the United Kingdom[208] in respect of data processed in the context of that establishment.[209] Establishment in the United

---

200 Article 15.

201 Articles 22, 23 and 24.

202 *Campbell v Mirror Group Newspapers Ltd* [2002] EWCA Civ 1373, [2003] QB 633 at [97] (the decision of the Court of Appeal was overturned on different grounds by the House of Lords: *Campbell v Mirror Group Newspapers* [2004] UKHL 22, [2004] 2 AC 457); *Durant v Financial Services Authority* [2003] EWCA 1746, [2004] FSR 28 at [3]; *R (Lord) v SSHD* [2003] EWHC 2073 (Admin) at [90]-[93]; *Johnson v Medical Defence Union* [2007] EWCA Civ 262, [2007] 3 CMLR 9, (2007) 96 BMLR 99 at [88]-[93]; *South Lanarkshire Council v Scottish IC* [2013] UKSC 55, 2013 GWD 25-508, 2013 SLT 799, [2013] 1 WLR 2421 at [7]; *Asociacion Nacional de Establecimientos Financieros de Credito v Administracion del Estado* (C-468/10) [2012] 1 CMLR 48; *R (Catt) v ACPO* [2015] UKSC 9, [2015] AC 1065 at [8]. For a summary of the interpretative principles applicable to a directive, see §§7– 035 to 7– 038.

203 Preambles (2) and (10).

204 *MM v United Kingdom* [2012] ECHR 1906 at [145]. See further *Marper v United Kingdom* [2008] ECHR 1581, (2009) 48 EHRR 50. Similarly, the European Court of Justice repeatedly noted that 'the protection of the fundamental right to privacy requires that derogations and limitations in relation to the protection of personal data must apply only in so far as is strictly necessary': Case C-473/12 *Institut professionnel des agents immobiliers v Geoffrey Englebertat* [2013] ECR at [39]; *Tietosuojavaltuutettu v Satakunnan Markkinaporssi Oy* (C-73/07) [2008] ECR I-9831, [2010] All ER (EC) 213 at [56]; *Volker und Markus Schecke GbR v Land Hessen* (C-92/09) [2012] All ER (EC) 127, [2012] IP & T 513 at [77], [86].

205 *MM v United Kingdom* [2012] ECHR 1906 at [195].

206 As to which, see: *Clark v Oceanic Contractors Inc* [1983] 2 AC 130 at 145, 152; *Lawson v Serco* [2006] UKHL 3, [2006] ICR 250 at [6]; *R (Al-Skeini) v SS for Defence* [2007] UKHL 26, [2008] 1 AC 153 at [11], [38], [86], [137]; *Duncombe v Secretary of State for Children etc (no 2)* [2011] UKSC 36, [2011] ICR 495; *Ravat v Halliburton* [2012] UKSC 1, [2012] ICR 389; *Cox v Ergo Verischerung AG* [2014] UKSC 22, [2014] AC 1379 at [27], [29]; *R (XH and AI) v SSHD* [2017] EWCA Civ 41, [2018] QB 355 at [97].

207 DPA 1998 s 5.

208 That is, England, Wales, Scotland and Northern Ireland: see Interpretation Act 1978, Sch 1.

209 DPA 1998 s 5(1)(a), based on Art 4(1)(a) of the Directive. In a key decision which brought many large companies within the EU data protection regime, the CJEU held in *Google Spain SL v Agencia Espanola de Proteccion de Datos*

Kingdom covered:
- individuals ordinarily resident in the United Kingdom;
- bodies incorporated, and partnerships or unincorporated associations formed, under the law of any part of the United Kingdom; and
- persons who maintained offices, branches or agencies in the United Kingdom through which they carried on any activity, or who maintained a regular practice there.[210]

(2) To data controllers established neither in the United Kingdom nor elsewhere in the European Economic Area, but who used equipment in the United Kingdom for processing data, other than for the purposes of transit through the United Kingdom.[211] A transit exemption meant that data merely passing through the United Kingdom, for instance emails routed through a United Kingdom server, were not caught by the Act. A data controller had to nominate a representative established in the United Kingdom for the purposes of the DPA1998.[212]

Where a data subject with rights under the DPA 1998 was resident abroad in a country which was a party to the 1981 Convention for the Protection of Individuals with regard to Automatic Processing of Personal Data, the Information Commissioner was under certain obligations to assist that person in exercising his or her subject access rights; for instance, by notifying him or her of the data controller's address and of his or her rights in respect of subject access.[213]

15– 008 Terminology

Five terms were central to the DPA 1998:[214]
- The *matter* whose activity was regulated by the DPA 1998 was called 'personal data.'
- The *activity* regulated by the DPA 1998 was called 'processing.'
- The *person* whose activity was regulated by the DPA 1998 was called the 'data controller.'
- The *standard* of processing required by the DPA 1998 was set by the 'data protection principles.'
- The *individual* whose interests were protected by the DPA 1998 was the 'data subject.'

Of these terms, it was 'personal data' that occasioned the greatest difficulty. The obligations imposed on a data controller, and the correlative rights conferred on an individual, by the DPA 1998 were confined to 'personal data' of which that individual was the 'data subject'.[215] Whether data 'relates to' or is 'about' an individual is conceptually fraught with difficulty.[216]

[2014] QB 1022 that this applied where a search engine operator set up in a member state a branch or subsidiary to promote and sell advertising oriented towards inhabitants of that state. This was followed by the Northern Ireland Court of Appeal in *CG v Facebook Ireland Ltd* [2016] NICA 54, [2017] 2 CMLR 29 in the case of a social media platform which operated through a similar structure.

210 DPA 1998 s 5(3).

211 DPA 1998 s 5(1)(b).

212 DPA 1998 s 5(2).

213 Data Protection (Functions of Designated Authority) Order 2000 SI 2000/186 Art 4; Convention for the Protection of Individuals with regard to Automatic Processing of Personal Data, Arts 8, 13 and 14. In relation to duties to give assistance, see Ch 21.

214 As noted by the Court of Appeal in *Stunt v Associated Newspapers Ltd* [2018] EWCA Civ 1780, [2018] 1 WLR 6060 at [12]-[18].

215 DPA 1998 s 7.

216 The phrase 'relates to' indicates more than a loose or consequential connection or a touching upon the matter: *Martin v Most* [2010] UKSC 10, 2010 SC (UKSC) 40 at [49], [159]. And similarly: *Imperial Tobacco Ltd v Lord Advocate* [2012] UKSC 61, 2013 SLT 2 at [16]; *Re Agricultural Sector (Wales) Bill* [2014] UKSC 43, [2014] 1 WLR 2622 at [50]; *Recovery of Medical Costs for Asbestos Diseases (Wales) Bill* [2015] UKSC 3, [2015] AC 1016 at [25];

It depends on identifying the unit against which that evaluative judgment is to be made, what else is known about the individual and the extent to which that other information is taken into account in making the evaluation, and subjective notions of the significance of information about an individual. The difficulty is a variation of the difficulty that can arise in determining whether something constitutes 'information.'[217]

2. THE REGULATED MATTER: PERSONAL DATA

5–009 Meaning of 'data'

Although it employed the term 'data', the manner in which that term was defined and employed in the DPA 1998 revealed that 'data' essentially meant grouped information obtained, recorded, held or used in a particular way or by a particular body. Thus, the Act spoke of 'information contained in the data',[218] suggesting that data involved some grouping of information. The Act identified five classes of information that constituted 'data' for the purposes of the Act:[219]

(1) information being processed by equipment operating automatically in response to instructions;
(2) information recorded with the intention that it should be so processed;
(3) information recorded as part of a 'relevant filing system' or with the intention that it should form part of such a system;
(4) information forming part of an 'accessible record'; and
(5) any other recorded information held by a public authority.

These are considered separately below. The first three classes of data reflected the coverage of the Data Protection Directive.[220] The fifth class of data applied only to information held by a public authority. It had been added by FOIA to ensure that an applicant's right of access to information relating to him or herself was not, on the ground of the manner of its holding, less than that given by FOIA.[221] Whilst this fifth class invariably meant that all recorded information held by a public authority was 'data' for the purposes of the DPA 1998, whether the information fell into one of the first four data classes could nevertheless be important in terms of the format of the request,[222] the charging regime,[223] the exemptions available[224] and certain other matters.[225]

Christian Institute v Lord Advocate [2016] UKSC 51, [2016] HRLR 19 at [29] (concerning the Data Protection Act 1998). In the context of FOIA the meaning of the phrase 'relates to' has been considered in: *Home Office v IC and Cobain*, FTT, 30 January 2013 at [15]-[19]; *Callus v IC and Home Office*, FTT, 6 May 2014 at [39]-[41]; *University and Colleges Admissions Service v IC and Lord Lucas* [2014] UKUT 0557 (AAC) at [44]-[46] (meaning of 'relates to' in FOIA s 7(5)); *Home Office v IC and Cobain* [2014] UKUT 0306 (AAC) at [39]; *All Party Parliamentary Group on Extraordinary Rendition v IC and FCO* [2015] UKUT 0377 (AAC) at [14]-[33]; *Reprieve v IC and FCO*, FTT, 26 April 2016 at [37]-[39]; *Corderoy and Ahmed v IC and Attorney General* [2017] UKUT 0495 (AAC) at [51] [54] and [59]-[62]; *Department of Health v IC and Lewis* [2017] EWCA Civ 374, [2017] 1 WLR 3330 at [13] (Sir Terence Etherton MR) (meaning of 'relates to' in FOIA s 35(1)).

217 See §20– 023,

218 DPA 1998 s 1(2). See also, ss 14(2), 40(4) and Sch 1 Pt II paras 3(2)(b) and 7.

219 DPA 1998 s 1(1). The five classes were there labelled (a)-(e).

220 Council Directive 95/46/EC Art 3(1).

221 This was underscored by DPA 1998 s 1(5).

222 DPA 1998 s 9A(2).

223 DPA 1998 s 9A(3)-(6).

224 DPA 1998 s 33A.

225 DPA 1998 Sch 8 para 14A, dealing with exemptions available during the period up to 24 October 2001 and up

15– 010 Automatically processed data

The first class of information that constituted 'data' for the purposes of the DPA 1998 was information 'being processed by means of equipment operating automatically in response to instructions given for that purpose'. As noted below,[226] 'processing' was very broadly defined in the Act.[227] Most significantly for subject access rights, it included 'holding' the information. Information held on computer-based storage (eg on hard disks, flash memory, tape drives, CD-ROMs) was information held by means of equipment operating automatically in response to instructions given for the purpose of processing that information.[228] The class was sufficiently wide to include word-processed documents, electronically scanned documents and emails to the extent that they were being stored electronically, whether in live, archive or back-up systems. It also included such information in a 'deleted' form where it could still technically be recovered.[229] The phrase was also wide enough to include information gathered and automatically processed by website operators. However, this class required that the information was being processed by the automatically operating equipment. Information that was held on computer-based storage satisfied the requirement; on the other hand, information that was once so held but was no longer so held did not satisfy the requirement. Thus, for example, where the electronic copy of a word-processed document had been irretrievably deleted but a paper copy had been retained, the paper copy did not constitute data within this class.[230]

15– 011 Intended automatic processing

The second class of information that constituted 'data' for the purposes of the DPA 1998 was information recorded with the intention that it should be processed by means of equipment operating automatically in response to instructions given for that purpose. Unlike the first data class, the information need not have been 'processed' by automatically operating equipment: it was enough that it had been recorded with that intention. For example, information recorded by hand on paper but with the intention that it be transferred to a computer based storage system (eg by being keyed in or by being scanned) fell within the second data class but not the first.

15– 012 Relevant filing system data

The third class of information that constituted 'data' for the purposes of the DPA 1998 was information recorded as part of a 'relevant filing system' or with the intention that it should form part of such a system. A 'relevant filing system' was defined to mean:

> any set of information relating to individuals to the extent that, although the information is not processed by means of equipment operating automatically in response to instructions

---

to 24 October 2007. Also, in relation to public authorities to which the FOIA had only limited application, by virtue of s 7 of that Act, an applicant would only have subject access rights in relation to information falling within the first four data classes: DPA 1998 s 1(6).

226 §15– 029.

227 DPA 1998 s 1(1). But it did not include the manual selection of data the results of which were then, as part of the same operation, recorded or transmitted in electronic form. That decision-making process preceded the processing, which would ordinarily begin with the entry of the manually selected information onto a computer: *Johnson v Medical Defence Union* [2007] EWCA Civ 262, [2007] 3 CMLR 9 at [44]-[48].

228 Computer-based storage media are blank to begin with. Information is not stored on them without, ultimately, some instruction for that purpose.

229 Information Commissioner, Subject access to personal data contained in emails, DPA Compliance advice. See also *Harper v Information Commissioner*, IT, 15 November 2005 at [21] and §20– 008. In the case of a public authority, any paper copy will almost certainly fall within data class 5.

230 *Johnson v Medical Defence Union* [2004] EWHC 347 (Ch) at [34], not overruled in *Johnson v Medical Defence Union* [2007] EWCA Civ 262; *Smith v Lloyds TSB Bank plc* [2005] EWHC 246 (Ch) at [17]-[18].

given for that purpose, the set is structured, either by reference to individuals or by reference to criteria relating to individuals, in such a way that specific information relating to a particular individual is readily accessible.[231]

The starting-point for the third data class was that it be information not processed by automatically operating equipment. Most commonly, the third class thus excluded information held on computer-based storage. To fall in the third data class, this information had to be structured, either by reference to individuals or by reference to criteria relating to individuals, in such a way that specific information relating to a particular individual was readily accessible.

15–013 Early jurisprudence

In *Durant v Financial Services Authority* [232] the Court of Appeal held that it was only to the extent that a manual filing system was, in terms of its accessibility to relevant information capable of constituting personal data, broadly equivalent to a computerised system that it would be within the system of data protection.[233] The Court held that 'relevant filing system' was to be restrictively interpreted, so as not to impose a disproportionate burden on a data controller, and that it was limited to a system:

(1) in which the files forming part of it were structured or referenced in such a way as clearly to indicate at the outset of the search whether specific information capable of amounting to personal data about the individual requesting it was held within the system and, if so, in which files; and

(2) which had as part of its own structure or referencing mechanism, a sufficiently sophisticated and detailed means of readily indicating whether and where in an individual file or files specific criteria or information about the applicant could be readily located.

Therefore it was not enough that a filing system lead a searcher to a file containing documents mentioning the data subject. The file itself had to be so structured and/or indexed as to enable easy location within it, or any sub-files, of specific information about the data subject that he or she had requested. Thus a set of manual personnel files arranged alphabetically by employee name, each of which related to a particular individual and contained, in no particular order, every document relating to that individual's employment, did not fall within the third data class. This interpretation was consistent with the Government's view, which had been expressed by Lord Williams of Mostyn during the passage of the Data Protection Bill through Parliament.[234] It also appeared to reflect the intentions of the Data Protection Directive itself. The Directive defined the equivalent concept — a 'personal data filing system' — as 'any structured set of personal data which were accessible according to specific criteria...'.[235] Recital 27 made clear that the Directive was to apply only to filing systems, not to unstructured files, and that individual files, not simply the whole filing system, had to be structured according to criteria

[231] DPA 1998 s 1(1). The definition in Council Directive 95/46/EC Art 2(c) states that the relevant filing system can be 'centralised, decentralised or dispersed on a functional or geographical basis'. DPA 1998 s 1(1) does not reproduce this part of the Directive, but should nevertheless be purposively interpreted to accord with it, particularly when dealing with decentralised or dispersed data sets.

[232] [2003] EWCA Civ 1746, [2004] FSR 28 at [34], [45]-[50].

[233] While the restrictive interpretation held for other data protection purposes, the addition of the fifth class of 'data' in section 1(1) largely undid this aspect of the Court of Appeal's judgment in relation to public authorities. At the time of *Durant v Financial Services Authority*, this fifth class of 'data' was not in force. However, *Smith v Lloyds TSB Bank plc* [2005] EWHC 246 (Ch) illustrated the effect of *Durant*, where a former client of Lloyds Bank was refused access to manual records in the form of unstructured bundles kept in boxes, which he maintained would evidence an oral agreement to provide him with substantial long-term finance.

[234] Hansard HL vol 587 cols 467-468 (16 March 1998).

[235] Council Directive 95/46/EC Art 2(c).

relating to individuals.[236] In *Johnson v Medical Defence Union*,[237] the Court held that the definition of data referred to information which 'is' being processed or recorded, so the question as to whether information was data within the meaning of the 1998 Act had to be determined at the time when the data subject made his or her data request.[238] The fact that data might at a prior stage have been held as part of an electronic filing system thus did not avail an applicant if, at the time of the request, the data was held only in an unstructured manual filing system.

15–014 Later jurisprudence

The narrow interpretation place on 'relevant filing system' by the Court of Appeal in *Durant v FSA*[239] appears to have been unduly restrictive. The Grand Chamber of the CJEU held that the concept of a 'filing system' in the Directive was broadly defined and appeared to treat easy retrieval (rather than any internal system of organisation) as the touchstone, with the structure of the files regarded as 'irrelevant.'[240] The questions which must be asked are the following. First, are the files a 'structured set of personal data'? Secondly, are the data accessible according to specific criteria? Thirdly, are those criteria 'related to individuals'? Fourthly, do the specific criteria enable the data to be easily or readily retrieved?[241]

15–015 Examples

The requirement in the definition of 'relevant filing system' that the set of information be structured in such a way that specific information relating to a particular individual was 'readily' accessible reflected the reference to 'easy' access in recital 27. Because the definition of 'data' included information recorded with the intention that it should form part of a relevant filing system, it included documents that would eventually form part of a structured set, but had not been filed: for example an employer's note of a conversation with an employee who phoned in sick, intended, eventually, for his or her personnel file. The Data Protection Directive also made clear that the structured set of personal data need not be held in one place: they might be centralised, decentralised or dispersed on a functional or geographical basis.[242] Thus, wage records held in one place and sickness records in another would still fall within the third data class.

15–016 Accessible records

The fourth class of information that constituted 'data' for the purposes of the DPA 1998 was information that did not fall within any of the preceding classes but was 'data' that formed part of an 'accessible record'. There were three specific categories of accessible record:

— health records;
— educational records; and
— accessible public records.[243]

Each was defined in some detail in the Act.[244] Broadly speaking, a health record was a record

---

236 Council Directive 95/46/EC recital 27.

237 [2007] EWCA Civ 262, [2007] 3 CMLR 9, (2007) 96 BMLR 99.

238 At [30]-[34]. See also *Smith v Lloyds TSB Bank plc* [2005] EWHC 246 (Ch) at [12]-[17].

239 *Durant v Financial Services Authority* [2003] EWCA Civ 1746, [2004] FSR 28.

240 *Tietosuojavaltuutettu v Jehovan todistajat* (C-25/17), 10 July 2018 at [56]-[61]. Followed in *Dawson-Damer v Taylor Wessing LLP* [2020] EWCA Civ 352 at [100], rejecting *Durant* as too narrow.

241 *Dawson-Damer v Taylor Wessing LLP* [2020] EWCA Civ 352 at [90].

242 Council Directive 95/46/EC Art 2(c).

243 DPA 1998 s 1(1) s 68. See further IC Guidance Data Protection - Subject Access Request to Health Records (13 November 2001) Appendix 1 'Who is a "health professional"?'

244 DPA 1998 ss 68(1)(a), (2), 69 (health record); DPA 1998 s 68(1)(b), Sch 11 (educational record); DPA 1998 s 68(1)(c),

of information relating to an individual's health made by a health professional, and an 'educational record' was a record of specified information relating to a present or former pupil at a maintained or special school. The term 'health professional' included a wide range of professionals, from doctors, dentists and opticians to clinical psychologists and certain therapists.[245] Accessible public records were defined by reference to particular bodies or authorities. In England and Wales they were: a record of information held by a Housing Act local authority for the purpose of any of its tenancies and a record of information held by a local social services authority for any purpose of its social services functions.[246]

5– 017 Jurisprudence

The fourth class of data (and the associated exemption and access provisions dealt with below) had its origins in the decision of the European Court of Human Rights in *Gaskin v United Kingdom*.[247] There an individual had been denied access by a local authority in whose care he had been to certain records relating to him, in order to protect the confidence of individuals who had contributed to those records. The European Court upheld the domestic approach of striking a balance between an individual's right to respect for his private life (and access to the records in question) and the public interest in maintaining the confidence of those who contributed to such records, so as to ensure frankness in such contributions. The special regime in relation to 'accessible records' was secured through the inclusion of the fourth data class, together with special exemptions for each of the three categories.[248]

5– 018 Other recorded information

The final class of information, 'any other recorded information held by a public authority', was introduced into the DPA 1998 by FOIA.[249] For a public authority, any recorded information held by it, but not falling within the preceding classes, would fall within this fifth data class. For the purposes of the DPA 1998, 'public authority' had the same meaning as it had under FOIA.[250] Likewise, the reference to information 'held' by a public authority was to be construed in accordance with s 3(2) of FOIA.[251] The term 'recorded' was not defined.[252] In respect of some public authorities, FOIA had effect only in relation to specified information.[253] Where that was the case, other information held by the public authority was deemed not to fall within the final limb of the definition of data in the DPA 1998.[254] As noted above, the addition

---

Sch 12 (accessible public record).

245 DPA 1998 s 69.

246 DPA 1998 s 68(1)(c) Sch 12 paras 1(a) and 2. In Scotland accessible public records are records of information held by a local authority for any purpose of its tenancies and records of information held by a social work authority for any purpose of specified social work functions: DPA 1998 s 68(1)(c) Sch 12 paras 1(b) and 4.

247 (1989) 12 EHRR 36. Special transitional provisions applied (up until 24 October 2001) to 'accessible records': DPA 1998 Sch 8 para 3. See also DPA 1998 Sch 8 paras 14 and 14A for the period up to 24 October 2007.

248 Data Protection (Subject Access Modification) (Health) Order 2000 SI 2000/413; Data Protection (Subject Access Modification) (Education) Order 2000 SI 2000/414; Data Protection (Subject Access Modification) (Social Work) Order 2000 SI 2000/415.

249 DPA 1998 s 1(1); FOIA ss 68(1), (2), 86, Sch 8 Pt III. For the meaning of 'public authority' see §§20– 018 to 20– 026.

250 DPA 1998 s 1(1). For detailed consideration of the meaning of 'public authority' see §§20– 018 to 20– 026.

251 DPA 1998 s 1(5). For detailed consideration of the meaning of 'held' see §20– 009.

252 The reference in the DPA 1998 to 'recorded information' mirrors the FOIA, which only applies to recorded information: see the definition of 'information' in the FOIA s 84 and in the FOI(S)A s 73. See further §§20– 001 to 20– 008.

253 FOIA s 7, Sch 1. See further §§20– 022 and 20– 030.

254 DPA 1998 s 1(6).

of the fifth class of 'data', in relation to local authorities, largely undid one aspect of the Court of Appeal's judgment in *Durant v Financial Services Authority*.[255] Thus, so far as a public authority is concerned, any recorded information held by it constituted 'data' for the purposes of the DPA 1998.[256]

15– 019 Archived and deleted data

The fact that a data controller had placed data in some form of archive, whether physical or electronic, did not make the data any less subject to a subject access request.[257] The Information Commissioner maintained that where an applicant had specifically requested backed-up data, the data controller might consider whether that data materially differed from the live data held on the data subject and, if there was no such difference, provide only the latter.[258] According to the Information Commissioner, information was 'deleted' when the data controller tried to permanently discard it and had no intention of ever trying to access it again.[259] The Information Commissioner took the view that where data was so deleted, the fact that technical expertise might enable that information to be restored did not mean that the data controller must go to those efforts in answering a subject access request:

> The Commissioner does not require organisations to expend time and effort reconstituting information that they have deleted as part of their general records management.[260]

15– 020 Meaning of 'personal data'

The subject access rights were conferred only in relation to 'personal data'. Section 1(1) of the DPA 1998 provided:

> 'personal data' means data which relate to a living individual who can be identified—
> (a) from those data, or
> (b) from those data and other information which is in the possession of, or is likely to come into the possession of, the data controller,
>
> and includes any expression of opinion about the individual and any indication of the intentions of the data controller or any other person in respect of the individual.

The definition was not identical to that in the Directive.[261] The inclusion of any expression of opinion about the individual and any indication of the intentions of the data controller or any other person in respect of the individual represented a change from the position under the DPA 1984. It covered, for example, employee appraisals and assessments of their promotion prospects (provided that they fell within the definition of 'data'). The first two required characteristics of 'personal data' were straightforward. The data had to relate to a human being, rather than to a corporate person. And that individual had to be alive, rather than

---

255 [2003] EWCA Civ 1746, [2004] FSR 28 at [34], [45]-[50].

256 But see the final sentence of §15– 010. As an example of its operation in relation to public authorities, see *A v Information Commissioner*, IT, 11 July 2006.

257 Information Commissioner, *Subject access code of practice*, August 2013, p 24.

258 Information Commissioner, *Subject access code of practice*, August 2013, p 24.

259 Information Commissioner, *Subject access code of practice*, August 2013, p 25.

260 Information Commissioner, *Subject access code of practice*, August 2013, p 25.

261 Set out in Art 2(a). On 20 June 2007 the Working Party on the Protection of Individuals with regard to the Processing of Personal Data (constituted under Art 29) adopted Opinion 4/2007 on the concept of personal data: `http://ec.europa.eu/justice/policies/privacy/docs/wpdocs/2007/wp136_en.pdf` It identifies four elements to the definition of 'personal data': (1) That it be 'information'. (2) That it 'relate to' an individual. Information that was 'about' an individual would 'relate to' that individual. Data that might be used or have a result in relation to an individual would also relate to that individual: 'This means also that it is not necessary that the data "focuses" on someone in order to consider that it relates to him.' (3) That the individual be identified or identifiable. (4) That the person be a natural person.

dead[262] or unborn. Thus, information about the business of a sole trader and about a specific individual in a partnership would be personal information, whereas information solely about a legal entity would not.[263] The third required characteristic – that the individual to whom the data relate could be identified from the data or information described in paragraph (a) or (b) – proved less straightforward. One difficulty was whether the phrase 'data which relate to a living individual' did more than link the word that is qualified to the words that qualify and, if so, what the phrase required.

15–021 Identifiable individual

Whether an individual could be identified from data was a matter of fact and degree. The greater the number of an individual's attributes that were included in the data (name, date of birth, place of birth, residential address, account numbers, telephone numbers etc), the more likely it was that an individual could be identified from the data. The fewer the individuals that shared the data's value (eg a National Insurance number, as opposed to a forename) or the collection of values (eg name plus date of birth plus residential postcode) that are the data, the more likely it was that an individual could be identified from the data. Data such as a sound recording, a photograph or another image made of an individual might have the specificity needed to identify the individual. DNA, fingerprints or similar information were recognised as personal data.[264] In order to be able to identify an individual from data it was not necessary that the data be unique to a single individual. It was sufficient that the data left no reasonable doubt as to the identity of the individual. A set of data might relate itself to other data by some sort of cross-reference within the set of data. The relation might be express or might be derived from the ordering of data according to a set of rules (which are themselves data). Where the particular set of data identified a living individual or related itself to other data that identified a living individual, then the set of data would 'relate to a living individual' – paragraph (a) of the definition of 'personal data' applied.

15–022 Part-identifiable data

Where a set of data neither identified a living individual nor related itself to other data that identified a living individual, but the data controller held (or was likely to hold) other data or information that related to the particular data and from which a living individual could be identified, then the set of data would 'relate to a living individual' – paragraph (b) of the definition of 'personal data' applied.[265] The set of data might be related to other data by the latter data or by yet further data. The latter gave effect to Art 2 of the Data Protection Directive. This defined personal data as information relating to an 'identified or identifiable' natural person, and provided that an identifiable person was:

> one who can be identified, directly or indirectly, in particular by reference to an identification number or to one or more factors specific to his physical, physiological, mental, economic, cultural or social identity.[266]

---

262 For a case where this was significant, see *Etchells v IC*, FTT, 31 March 2010 at [7] - information collected under the National Registrations Act 1939 which related to deceased persons ordered to be disclosed by the NHSIC.

263 See *Smith v Lloyds TSB Bank plc* [2005] EWHC 246 (Ch) at [31]-[33].

264 *S and Marper v United Kingdom* [2008] ECHR 1581, (2009) 48 EHRR 50 at [63] and [68]. The ECHR held that the blanket and indiscriminate retention of fingerprint and DNA information breached the right to privacy.

265 A similar example was given in *Common Services Agency v IC* [2008] UKHL 47, [2008] 1 WLR 1550 at [75]. Thus in *England and LB of Bexley v Information Commissioner*, IT, 10 May 2007 at [98] it was held that addresses of empty residential properties constituted 'personal data' because that information was held together with ownership details from the Council Tax register.

266 Council Directive 95/46/EC Art 2(a). In *Alcock v IC and Chief Constable of Staffordshire Police*, IT, 3 January 2007 at [25] the Information Tribunal held that information could identify an individual, even if not mentioning him by name.

Both the characteristics of the data controller and of the data processing (eg its location) could be taken into account in determining whether an individual could be identified from the data. These characteristics were 'other information' within the meaning of paragraph (b) of the definition of 'personal data'.[267] However, the fact that the data controller knew the derivation of a set of data did not itself link that set of data to information within the derived source.[268] It was not clear what information was 'likely to come into the possession of [a] data controller'. Recital 26 to the Data Protection Directive provided that in order to determine whether a person was identifiable, account was to be taken of 'all the means likely reasonably to be used' either by the data controller or by any other person to identify the individual.[269] Thus, taking into account that a Norwich Pharmacal order could be obtained to identify the users of devices connected to the internet, IP addresses were treated as 'personal data.'[270] This implied that it was not simply identification by the data controller that was important, but that identification by any other person would also count. On that basis it did not matter whether the data controller took steps to avoid information coming into his possession, if that information was reasonably likely to be used by a third party to identify the individual. This was probably beyond the scope of the definition in the DPA 1998, which was concerned only with identification by the data controller.[271]

15–023 Durant identification

On one reading of the definition of 'personal data', the phrase 'which relate to' did no more than link the word 'data' to the qualifying requirements which follow. However, another reading was that, in addition to its linking function, the phrase imposed its own qualitative requirement. In *Durant v Financial Services Authority*[272] the Court of Appeal interpreted the phrase to require a direct connection between the individual and the subject matter of the data:

> As a matter of practicality and given the focus of the Act on ready accessibility of the information – whether from a computerised or comparably sophisticated non-computerised system – it is likely in most cases that only information that names or directly refers to him will qualify. In this respect, a narrow interpretation of "personal data" goes hand in hand with a narrow meaning of "a relevant filing system".[273]

The Court of Appeal identified what would and would not suffice:

> It follows from what I have said that not all information retrieved from a computer search against an individual's name or unique identifier is personal data within the Act. Mere mention of the data subject in a document held by a data controller does not necessarily amount to his personal data. Whether it does so in any particular instance depends on where it falls in a continuum of relevance or proximity to the data subject as distinct, say, from

267 In the same way in which the country code of a telephone number can often be inferred from these.

268 Thus in *Common Services Agency v IC* [2008] UKHL 47, [2008] 1 WLR 1550 at [26]-[27] Lord Hope contemplated that the agency could create a new set of data from the original set (which was personal data) and, provided that there was nothing linking the new set to the original set and that the new set did not itself identify individuals, the new set of data would not constitute personal data. See also *R (Department of Health) v Information Commissioner* [2011] EWHC 1430 (Admin), [2011] ACD 97, [2011] Med LR 363 at [52].

269 Council Directive 95/46/EC, recital 26.

270 *R (British Telecommunications plc & ors) v Secretary of State for Business, Innovation and Skills* [2011] EWHC 1021 (Admin), [2012] 3 CMLR 98 at [152]-[157], on appeal *R (British Telecommunications plc & ors) v Secretary of State for Culture, Olympics, Media and Sport* [2012] EWCA Civ 232, [2012] 2 CMLR 23, [2012] Bus LR 1766 at [75].

271 Note that in *Collie and CSA* Scottish Information Commissioner decision 021/2005 at [63]-[65] it is suggested (based on guidance from the OIC) that s 8(7) of the DPA 1998 applies in these circumstances. However, this seems on the face of it to be inconsistent with the terms of the DPA 1998. Section 8(7) is concerned with subject access requests under s 7 and not with the definition of personal data in s 1(1).

272 [2003] EWCA Civ 1746, [2004] FSR 28 at [27]-[28]. See also *Johnson v Medical Defence Union* [2004] EWHC 347 (Ch) at [37]-[49].

273 At [27] (Auld LJ).

> transactions or matters in which he may have been involved to a greater or lesser degree. It seems to me that there are two notions that may be of assistance. The first is whether the information is biographical in a significant sense, that is, going beyond the recording of the putative data subject's involvement in a matter or an event that has no personal connotations, a life event in respect of which his privacy could not be said to be compromised. The second is one of focus. The information should have the putative data subject as its focus rather than some other person with whom he may have been involved or some transaction or event in which he may have figured or have had an interest, for example, as in this case, an investigation into some other person's or body's conduct that he may have instigated. In short, it is information that affects his privacy, whether in his personal or family life, business or professional capacity.[274]

There were practical and legal difficulties with the analysis in *Durant*. First, paragraph (b) of the definition of 'personal data' recognised that particular data might 'relate to' an individual even though it was not possible to identify the individual from those data alone.[275] Paragraph (b) drew on the distinction between 'data' and 'information'. More often than 'information', 'data' might not have a self-contained intelligibility with which to carry out the exercise required in *Durant*.[276] A particular set of data might – and in a computer typically would – 'relate to' an individual by only a single unique identifier, such as a number.[277] Analysis of that particular data set was unlikely to satisfy the *Durant* requirements. If, however, that particular data set and other data and information possessed by the data controller were assembled – in the way required by paragraph (b) – it might become clear that the former related to an identifiable individual. Secondly, although the purpose of s 7 of the DPA 1998 was to uncover the extent of a data controller's processing of personal data relating to an individual and to do so as a precursor to procedures under the Act (including making a claim for breach of the s 4(4) duty), that object was impeded by dividing the total data held by a data controller relating to an individual into separate 'documents' and analysing the latter one-by-one for 'proximity' and the like. Thirdly, the Court of Appeal did not consider the impact that its approach had on the exemption in s 40(2) of FOIA. That exemption preserves the high degree of protection which the DPA 1998 gives an individual against any disclosure by a public authority to another person of data relating to the individual held by that public authority.[278] That protection was weakened by the *Durant* approach. And fourthly, there was the House of Lords' judgment in *Common Services Agency v IC* [2008] UKHL 47, [2008] 1 WLR 1550.[279] Although not expressly stated, that judgment did not follow the premise in *Durant* that the phrase 'relate to' did more

---

274 At [27] (Auld LJ). The Court of Appeal (Auld LJ) held (at [30]) that documents concerning Mr Durant's complaint to the FSA about Barclays Bank and concerning the FSA's own investigation of that complaint did not constitute 'personal data' relating to Mr Durant: 'Just because the FSA's investigation of the matter emanated from a complaint by him does not, it seems to me, render information obtained or generated by that investigation, without more, his personal data. For the same reason, either on the issue as to whether a document contains "personal data" or as to whether it is part of a "relevant filing system", the mere fact that a document is retrievable by reference to his name does not entitle him to a copy of it under the Act.' See also *Ezsias v Welsh Ministers* [2007] EWHC B15 (QB) at [65]-[66]. In *Common Services Agency v IC* [2008] UKHL 47, [2008] 1 WLR 1550 Lord Hope appears to suggest at [19]-[20] that the remark of Auld LJ that 'mere mention of the data subject in a document [does] not necessarily amount to his personal data' was concerned with references to persons other than the applicant, which might otherwise disentitle the applicant from access: ss 7(4) and 8(7).

275 As Lord Hope in *Common Services Agency v IC* [2008] UKHL 47, [2008] 1 WLR 1550 at [24] expressed it: 'The formula which this part of the definition uses indicates that each of these two components must have a contribution to make to the result.'

276 Thus, fingerprint images are personal data: *Marper v United Kingdom* [2008] ECHR 1581, (2009) 48 EHRR 50, 25 BHRC 557, 48 EHRR 50, [2009] Crim LR 355; *Schwarz v Stadt Bochum* (C-291/12) [2014] 2 CMLR 5 at [27].

277 This is the example given by Lord Rodger of Earlsferry in *Common Services Agency v IC* [2008] UKHL 47, [2008] 1 WLR 1550 at [76].

278 *Common Services Agency v IC* [2008] UKHL 47, [2008] 1 WLR 1550 at [5], [29], [63] and [67].

279 [2008] UKHL 47, [2008] 1 WLR 1550.

than link 'data' to the requirements that follow in the remainder of the definition.

15– 024 Post-Durant guidance

As a result of the impact of *Durant* on the scope of the DPA 1998, the Information Commissioner issued guidance concerning the case.[280] The guidance pre-dated the House of Lords' judgment in *Common Services Agency*. The guidance recognised the central role played by the concept of privacy in the definition of personal data and from this concluded that the ability of particular information to have an adverse impact on the individual should form part of the determination of whether it amounted to personal data.[281] The guidance and decisions following *Durant* took the view that information about matters such as an individual's medical history, salary,[282] tax details[283] and spending preferences would be likely to amount to personal data; by contrast with mere reference to his name,[284] his attendance at a business meeting[285] or his receipt of a document or email, which would be unlikely to do so.[286] Reference to a person's name, when combined with another identifier such as an address[287] or a telephone number, would generally amount to personal information.[288] On this approach it was recognised that it was not necessary that data identify the data subject by name in order to constitute personal data relating to that person.[289] The Guidance suggested that an individual would be capable of being identified if the data controller was able to process the data so as to distinguish the data

---

280 Information Commissioner, *The 'Durant' case and its impact on the interpretation of the DPA*. In *Harcup v IC*, IT, 5 February 2008, the Tribunal commented at [23]: 'The Court of Appeal's approach in Durant was significantly to narrow the concept of personal data as it had been widely understood and applied. The attempt in the IC's Guidance to apply Durant in practice restores much of the previous width.'

281 Information Commissioner, *The 'Durant' case and its impact on the interpretation of the DPA*. See also *England v IC*, IT, 10 May 2007 at [95]-[98]; *Kelway v IC and Northumbria Police*, IT, 14 April 2009 at [58]-[61]; *Guardian News & Media Ltd v IC and MoJ*, IT, 10 June 2009 at [83]-[85].

282 In *Rechnungshof v Österreichischer Rundfunk* [2002] ECR I-4989 the CJEU confirmed that data concerning salaries and pensions of employees of the State, generated in the course of their employment and held by the State, were personal information (see [64]).

283 The CJEU has accepted that information on income, wealth and taxes can amount to personal data: *Tietosuojavaltuutettu v Satakunnan Markkinaporssi Oy* (C-73/07) [2008] ECR I-9831, [2010] All ER (EC) 213. See also *Kirkhope v IC and National Archives*, FTT, 15 January 2013 at [72].

284 In *Harcup v IC*, IT, 5 February 2008 at [18]-[27], the names of attendees of a public authority's hospitality events, listed without any reference to the organisations they worked for, were held not to be personal data. But cf *DBERR v IC and Friends of the Earth*, IT, 29 April 2008, which held at [91] that a list of names of individuals who attended meetings between ministers and/or senior civil servants (Grade 5 or above) and employees from the Confederation of British Industry (CBI) was personal data, as it would have 'biographical significance for the individual in that [the minutes of the meetings] record his/her employer's name, whereabouts at a particular time and that he/she took part in a meeting with a government department which would be of personal career or business significance.' In *European Commission v Bavarian Lager Co Ltd* [2010] EUECJ C-28/08, [2010] ECR I-06055, [2011] Bus LR 867 the Grand Chamber of the CJEU held that a list of attendees at a meeting was personal data since it allowed the persons participating in the meeting to be identified. See also *Squier v IC and Metropolitan Police Commissioner*, FTT, 13 November 2012 at [45].

285 *O'Connell v IC and CPS*, IT, 17 September 2009 at [9]; *Brett v IC and FCO*, IT, 21 August 2009 at [43].

286 Information Commissioner, *The 'Durant' case and its impact on the interpretation of the DPA*. In *Corporate Officer of the House of Commons v Information Commissioner and Baker*, IT, 16 January 2007 at [38] the Information Tribunal held that a breakdown of MPs' travel expenses by name, mode of travel and amount, constituted 'personal data'.

287 A person's residential address has been held to be personal data: *House of Commons v IC and Leapman, Brooke and Thomas*, IT, 26 February 2008 at [41], upheld at *House of Commons v IC and Brooke, Leapman, Ungoed-Thomas* [2008] EWHC 1084 (Admin), [2009] 3 All ER 403; *Exeter City Council v IC and Guagliardo*, FTT, 24 September 2012 at [4]. A full postcode may be personal data: *MacFarlane v IC and Dept of Energy and Climate Change*, FTT, 30 November 2012 at [38]-[44].

288 This was accepted by the CJEU in the first case on the Directive, *Re Lindqvist (Approximation of Laws)* [2004] QB 1014 at [24]. See also Case C-553/07 *College van burgemeester en wethouders van Rotterdam v Rijkeboer* [2009] 3 CMLR 28 at [42] and the references cited therein. In the domestic context, see *Benford v IC and DEFRA*, IT, 14 November 2007 at [48]-[51].

289 *A v Information Commissioner*, IT, 11 July 2006 at [11].

subject from any other individual, and that this would be the case if the data subject could be treated differently from other individuals.[290] Thus, personal data would include, for example:

— closed-circuit television recordings of an individual from which he or she could be visually identified by reference to a photograph, physical description or physical features;[291]
— many email addresses, such as those including the individual's name and workplace;[292]
— in the context of the internet, 'browser-generated information' transmitted by an internet user can be personal data since it 'individuates' such a user in the sense of singling out that user and distinguishing the individual from others, even if it does not enable the individual to be named;[293] and
— similarly, personalised user profiles developed by website operators (eg through the use of 'cookies'), which are capable of being linked to an individual, through his or her email address or IP address, for example, would also amount to personal data.[294]

The identifying information need not be in the possession of the data controller: it would be enough that it is likely to come into the possession of the data controller. The Information Commissioner's view was that information might be in the possession of a data controller not simply when it was in his physical control but also, for example, when it was in the physical control of his contracted data processor.[295] Information in publicly-available sources could also be relevant.[296]

5– 025 Common Services approach

It is not clear to what extent, if any, the *Durant* approach survived the House of Lords' judgment in *Common Services Agency v Information Commissioner*.[297] In denying that the lower court's application of the *Durant* principles had any relevance when resolving whether the data was 'personal data' and in suggesting that the above passages from *Durant* were made in the context of third party identification, Lord Hope of Craighead put its continued significance into

290 Information Commissioner, *Determining what is personal data*, pp 7-8. The approach in the Guidance has been criticised for being at odds with the broad approach to identifiability in the Directive: see R Jay, *Data Protection Law and Practice*, 4th edn (London, Sweet & Maxwell, 2012) at p 173, para 4-07.

291 See also Council Directive 95/46/EC, recitals 14 and 26.

292 Information Commissioner, *Determining what is personal data*, p 9.

293 *Vidal Hall v Google Inc* [2015] EWCA Civ 311, [2016] QB 1003.

294 Information Commissioner, *Determining what is personal data*, p 9. A dynamic IP address registered by an online media services provider when a person accesses a website that the provider makes accessible to the public constitutes 'personal data' within the meaning of that provision, in relation to that provider, where the latter has the legal means which enable it to identify the data subject with additional data which the internet service provider has about that person: *Breyer v Federal Republic of Germany* (C-582/14) [2017] 1 WLR 1569 at [49].

295 See further §§20– 009 to 20– 010.

296 In *McIntosh v IC and BBC*, FTT, 23 October 2014, it was held that a postcode (at least when it relates to a relatively small number of premises) is personal data since individuals living at premises at that postcode can be identified from publicly-available sources.

297 The leading speech was given by Lord Hope, with whom Lord Hoffmann agreed. Lord Hope focused on paragraph (b) of the definition of 'personal data'. Lord Rodger of Earlsferry held that paragraph (a) of the definition of 'personal data' was applicable, but said that if he were wrong about this he would agree with Lord Hope's approach. Lord Mance said that it was not necessary to decide which paragraph was applicable, but that he preferred Lord Hope's reasoning. Baroness Hale of Richmond gave separate reasons. Thus, Lord Hope's speech constitutes the majority view: *R (Department of Health) v Information Commissioner* [2011] EWHC 1430 (Admin), [2011] ACD 97, [2011] Med LR 363 at [45]; cf *All Party Parliamentary Group on Extraordinary Rendition v IC and Ministry of Defence* [2011] UKUT 153 (AAC) at [125]. Although *Durant* was referred to by Lord Hope and by Lord Rodger, they neither expressly supported nor rejected the approach taken by the Court of Appeal. Their analyses are, however, irreconcilable with an endorsement of the *Durant* approach. The barnardised statistics were not 'biographical in a significant sense;' nor did they have a particular individual as their focus: cf *Durant v Financial Services Authority* [2003] EWCA Civ 1746, [2004] FSR 28 at [27], quoted at §15– 023.

question.[298] Lord Hope restored the breadth of the definition of 'personal data':

> [The data controller] cannot exclude personal data from the duty to comply with the data protection principles simply by editing the data so that, if the edited part were to be disclosed to a third party, the third party would not find it possible from that part alone without the assistance of other information to identify a living individual. Paragraph (b) of the definition of "personal data" prevents this. It requires account to be taken of other information which is in, or is likely to come into, the possession of the data controller.[299]

The position that appears to have been reached was that the requirement that the data 'relate to' a living individual did not involve an evaluation of the 'relevance' or the 'proximity' or the 'biographical significance' of the data to the data subject. Nor did the definition of 'personal data' require them to be evaluated to see whether the individual is the 'focus' of those data. The requirement that data 'relate to' an individual was not separate from or additional to the requirement that the individual be able to be identified from the data, whether alone or in conjunction with other data. What was important was a sufficiently definite identification of the individual within those data.[300]

15– 026 The ultimate approach

Later cases further distinguished or diminished the importance of the *Durant*[301] approach to 'personal data.' Thus:

— In *Edem v IC*[302] the Court of Appeal held that the *Durant* approach was irrelevant where the information in question plainly concerned an individual or individuals, such as a name (or, in the case of a very common name, the name in conjunction with other identifying information).

— In *YS v Minister*[303] the Court of Justice explained that data relating to an applicant in an application for a resident's permit – such as the applicant's name, date of birth, nationality, sex etc is personal data, even if legal analysis of the applicant's situation is not.

---

298 At [20] and [19] respectively. Similarly, Lord Rodger of Earlsferry at [76]-[77]: 'Paragraph (b) of the definition of "personal data"...applies where the individual to whom data relate is identifiable not from the data themselves but from "other information", ie information which does not count as "data" because it does not fall under any of paragraphs (a) to (e) in the definition of data...and that information will make it possible to identify a living individual to whom existing data relate....It could [also] include, for instance, a single sheet of paper containing the key which identified the individual to whom data...related. The data would be "personal data" if the person to whom they related could be identified from the "information" on that sheet of paper.'

299 At [22]. Lord Rodger of Earlsferry agreed with Lord Hope's approach on this issue (at [75]). He added (at [76]): 'So, if one asks what data the agency holds on an individual, it is all the information which it has relating to that individual. If the individual to whom all the information relates is identifiable from some information in the data, then all the data count as "personal data".'

300 In other words, following the approach set out in §§15– 021-15– 022 above. The point is underscored by Lord Hope's contemplation that data, despite being barnardised, could still fall within the definition of 'personal data' (at [17]-[28]). In remitting the matter back to the Scottish Information Commissioner for his reconsideration, Lord Hope indicated that satisfaction of the definition would turn on whether the barnardised data 'becomes data from which a living individual can no longer be identified...If [the data controller] is unable to say that [the data] would in that form be fully anonymised he will then need to consider whether disclosure of this information by the agency would be in accordance with the data protection principles and in particular would meet any of the conditions in Schedule 2' (at [27]). And similarly Lord Rodger at [79]-[81], in considering that 'aggregate data' setting out the incidence of childhood leukaemia covering 'a large geographical area' would 'undoubtedly relate to living individuals' if those individuals 'could be identified' from the aggregate data. Notably, neither Lord Hope nor Lord Rodger saw the need to consider whether the barnardised 'aggregate data' had an individual as their 'focus' or whether those aggregate data were of 'biographical significance' to that individual. The Scottish Information Commissioner, in reconsidering the matter following the House of Lords' judgment, concluded that individuals could be identified from the barnardised data alone, and that those barnardised data were accordingly 'personal data': Decision 021 of 2005, dated 26 May 2010.

301 *Durant v Financial Services Authority* [2003] EWCA Civ 1746, [2004] FSR 28.

302 *Edem v IC and FSA* [2014] EWCA Civ 92.

303 *YS v Minister voor Immigratie, Integratie en Asiel* (C-141/12) [2015] 1 WLR 609, [2015] 1 CMLR 18.

— Lastly, in *Ittihadieh v 5-11 Cheyne Gardens*[304] the Court of Appeal reviewed all the authorities and acknowledged the limits of the *Durant* approach - names (with or without other identifying information), dates of birth, nationality, ethnicity and image are all personal data. The 'notions' proclaimed in *Durant* are only relevant when considering whether *other* information in a document is also personal data.

5–027 Anonymised data

The DPA 1998 and the Data Protection Directive did not apply to data anonymised in such a way that the data subject was no longer identifiable.[305] However, care had to be taken in anonymising the data.[306] If the data controller separated the personal identifiers from the rest of the data, it might be possible to process the anonymised data (eg by publishing it) even though the identifying material was information in the possession of the data controller.[307]

5–028 Sensitive personal data

Article 8 of the Directive provided for special categories of data which were subject to a blanket prohibition on processing, subject to certain exemptions:

> Member States shall prohibit the processing of personal data revealing racial or ethnic origin, political opinions, religious or philosophical beliefs, trade-union membership, and the processing of data concerning health or sex life.

Article 8 was implemented in the DPA 1998 by a definition of 'sensitive personal data' provided by section 2, together with additional controls on its processing imposed by DPP1 and the requirement to meet one of the conditions in Schedule 3 to the Act.

3. THE REGULATED ACTIVITY: PROCESSING

5–029 'Processing'

'Processing' was an extremely broad concept under the DPA 1998. It was used as both a stative verb and as a dynamic verb, covering the holding information or data, as well as carrying out any operation or set of operations on it.[308] The carrying out of an operation received a similarly

---

304 *Ittihadieh v 5-11 Cheyne Gardens RTM Co Ltd* [2017] EWCA 121, [2018] QB 256.

305 *R v The Department of Health, ex p Source Informatics Ltd* [2000] 1 All ER 786 (CA); Directive 95/46/EC, recital 26. The Information Commissioner has issued a code of practice under DPA 1998 s 51: *Anonymisation: managing data protection risk. Code of Practice*, November 2012.

306 In *Common Services Agency v IC* [2008] UKHL 47, [2008] 1 WLR 1550 the House of Lords considered the disclosure control method known as 'barnardisation' (named after Professor George Alfred Barnard (1915-2002), a professor of mathematical statistics at the University of Essex), which is used to render statistical information anonymous by randomly subtracting or adding 1 to some values in a table of statistics. It was considered that barnardisation might be able to render the data sufficiently anonymous that the data controller could publish it in a form which meant it was no longer possible to identify a living individual from that data, even though the data controller still held the original information on which the barnardised information was based (see [17]-[27] and [73]-[88]). Whether that was actually possible was left as a question of fact for the Scottish IC. See also *Craigdale Housing Association & ors v Scottish Information Commissioner* [2010] CSIH 43, 2010 SLT 655 where a similar issue was remitted.

307 See *R (Department of Health) v Information Commissioner* [2011] EWHC 1430 (Admin), [2011] ACD 97, [2011] Med LR 363 at [52] – anonymised abortion statistics published by the Department of Health were not personal data even though the Department of Health held the patient details. The critical question was whether the public could identify a living individual from the published data. This approach was followed in *Beckles v IC*, FTT, 7 September 2011 at [31]; *Smith v IC and Devon and Cornwall Constabulary*, FTT, 15 September 2011 at [19]-[20]; *OFSTED v IC*, FTT, 20 February 2012 at [32]-[37]; *IC v Magherafelt DC* [2012] UKUT 263 (AAC) at [51]; *All Party Parliamentary Group on Extraordinary Rendition v IC and Ministry of Defence* [2011] UKUT 153 (AAC) at [109], focusing on the 'relevant communities' in which the published information might be used to identify the individuals in question.

308 DPA 1998 s 1(1). In *Campbell v Mirror Group Newspapers Ltd* [2002] EWCA Civ 1373, [2003] QB 633, the Court of Appeal held that the publication of material in hard copy, where it had previously been automatically processed, fell within the definition of 'processing'.

broad (non-exhaustive) definition, including the organisation, adaptation or alteration of the information or data; their retrieval, consultation, use and disclosure; and their alignment, combination, blocking, erasure or destruction.[309] This reflected the definition of 'processing' in the Data Protection Directive.[310] Recital 14 to the Directive made it clear that the capture, transmission, manipulation, recording, storage and communication of sound and image data were intended to be covered.[311] For the avoidance of doubt, in relation to personal data, obtaining or recording the data included obtaining or recording the information to be contained in the data; and using or disclosing the data included using or disclosing the information to be contained in the data.[312] Given the breadth of these definitions, there was little if any interaction with data that did not amount to processing.[313] Thus, for example, the activities of internet intermediaries was held to amount to processing within the meaning of the Directive.[314]

4. THE REGULATED PERSON: THE DATA CONTROLLER

15–030 'Data controller'

The rights given to an individual by the DPA 1998 were rights as against the data controller.[315] The 'data controller' was defined to be a person who determined the purposes for which and the manner in which personal data were processed.[316] Where personal data were processed pursuant to an obligation imposed by or under an enactment, the person on whom the obligation to process the data was imposed was the data controller.[317] For example, where a local authority engaged a contractor to acquire, hold or otherwise process personal data that it was under a statutory obligation to acquire, hold or otherwise process, the local authority would be the data controller of those data even though it was the contractor who carried out the processing. The definition of data controller followed fairly closely that in the Data

309 DPA 1998 s 1(1). It does not cover a verbal disclosure: *Scott v LGBT Foundation* [2020] EWHC 483 (QB) at [61].

310 Council Directive 95/46/EC Art 2(b).

311 Council Directive 95/46/EC recital 14. In *Tietosuojavaltuutettu v Satakunnan Markkinaporssi Oy* (C-73/07) [2008] ECR I-9831, [2010] All ER (EC) 213 at [35]-[49], the CJEU held that 'processing' includes collating information from publicly available documents held by a public authority, the provision of information on a CD-ROM and the provision of information via text message.

312 DPA 1998 s 1(2). *A v Information Commissioner*, IT, 11 July 2006 at [14] and *R v Rooney* [2006] EWCA Crim 1841 at [12]-[13].

313 In *Johnson v Medical Defence Union* [2007] EWCA Civ 262, [2007] 3 CMLR 9, (2007) 96 BMLR 99 an individual took the central role in processing, rather than it being automated. The processing revolved around a risk assessment of the claimant, performed by a risk manager creating a new data set by selecting information from computerised files (which fell within the DPA 1998) and from various manual and microfiche files (which did not fall within the DPA 1998), adding information to some of the computerised files and then adding new observations and allocating scores. The claimant alleged that the defendant had unfairly processed his personal data by 'selecting the information contained in the personal data and thereby presenting a false picture of the situation'. The Court of Appeal held by a majority that the operation did not fall within the s1(1) DPA 1998. The majority of the court focused on the fact that the relevant activities were conducted wholly by the human agent and involved an exercise of judgment (at [21]-[54] and [154]-[156]). Arden LJ dissented, holding that the manual selection and presenting of information into automated form fell within s1(1) DPA 1998 (at [120]-[136]).

314 *Google Spain SL v Agencia Espanola de Proteccion de Datos* [2014] QB 1022.

315 DPA 1998 s 7.

316 DPA 1998 s 1(1). It does not include the liquidator of a company in respect of the personal data held by the company: *Re Southern Pacific Personal Loans Ltd* [2013] EWHC 2485 (Ch). For the meaning of processing see §15–029.

317 DPA 1998 s 1(4).

Protection Directive.[318] The definition in the Data Protection Directive expressly included public authorities, but covered all other natural or legal persons, agencies and other bodies.[319]

15–031 Multiple data controllers

There could be more than one data controller in respect of the same personal data — the Act made clear that a data controller might act alone, or jointly or in common with others.[320] Thus, in the context of the internet, a search engine operator was held to be a data controller even though it processed data posted on the internet by others (who would be likely also to be data controllers of that personal data).[321] Similarly, those operating social media platforms and those who operate specific pages on social media platforms were held to be data controllers of personal data on those platforms.[322]

15–032 Data controller: guidance

The Information Commissioner issued advice on the meaning of 'data controller'. The view expressed was that where one person determined the purposes for which personal data were processed, but that person delegated responsibility for determining the manner in which they were processed to someone else, it was the person who determined the purposes who was the data controller.[323] In the Commissioner's view, a decision as to the manner in which the data were to be processed was implicit in that determination, and thus determination of the purposes of processing took precedence in identifying the data controller.[324] In relation to personal data held by staff on their own devices (eg personal computers and mobile telephones) but used for work purposes, the Commissioner's view was that if the data controller permitted its staff to so use their own computers, then personal data so held might fall within the scope of a subject access request made of the data controller.[325]

15–033 'Data subject'

A data subject was defined as being the individual who was the subject of personal data.[326] The data subject had be a living individual.[327] In the Data Protection Directive, reference was made to 'natural persons' rather than to living individuals.[328] There was no age restriction — children of any age enjoyed the rights conferred by the DPA 1998 as well as the protection secured by the s 4(4) duty imposed on the data controller.

---

318 Council Directive 95/46/EC Art 2(d).

319 Council Directive 95/46/EC Art 2(d).

320 DPA 1998 s 1(1).

321 *Google Spain SL v Agencia Espanola de Proteccion de Datos* [2014] QB 1022.

322 *Unabhangiges Landeszentrum fur Datenschutz Schleswig-Holstein v Wirtschaftsakademie Schleswig-Holstein GmbH* (C-210/16) [2018] 3 CMLR 32 (Grand Chamber).

323 Information Commissioner, *Identifying 'data controllers' and 'data processors'*.

324 This appears to be at odds with the DPA 1998 and Council Directive 95/46/EC, neither of which indicate that one part of the definition should be given precedence over the other.

325 Information Commissioner, *Subject access code of practice*, August 2013, p 26. In practice, unless the data controller acknowledges that that data is held by the member of staff on behalf of the data controller (and thus within the scope of the subject access request made of the data controller), the data controller is likely to have breached the data protection principles in allowing the information to be sent to the member of staff.

326 DPA 1998 s 1(1). For the meaning of 'data controller' see §15–030.

327 Information Commissioner, *Determining what is personal data*.

328 Council Directive 95/46/EC Art 2(a).

5. THE REQUIRED STANDARD: THE DATA PROTECTION PRINCIPLES

15–034 The central duty

The central, continuing duty on a data controller under the DPA 1998 was to comply with the data protection principles.[329] Unlike the other duties that might befall a data controller under the DPA 1998 (eg compliance with a data subject request), the duty to comply with the data protection principles did not require a request or notice from the data subject for the duty to arise. Rather, the duty to comply with the data protection principles was a duty that subsisted whenever a data controller was processing personal data: it was continuing. Non-compliance with that duty exposed the data controller to a claim by the data subject and to regulatory action by the Information Commissioner. This duty is considered below. The exemptions from the duty are dealt with in Chapter 16.

15–035 Non-compliance

Non-compliance with the data protection principles exposed the data controller to:

(a) a private action by the data subject for breach of statutory duty. The remedies available included compensation for distress and for damage, as well as coercive orders such as erasure and correct; and

(b) regulatory enforcement action by the Information Commissioner, including mandatory orders and monetary penalties.

Both are dealt with in Chapter 49.

6. THE AUTOMOUS DUTY: COMPLIANCE WITH THE PRINCIPLES

15–036 Introduction

One of the core concepts of the DPA 1998 was that data controllers, in their processing of personal data, were under a statutory duty imposed by s 4(4) to comply with the eight data protection principles ('the DPPs') set out in Part 1 of Schedule 1 to that Act.[330] The data protection principles derived from the standards originally set out in the Convention for the Protection of Individuals with regard to Automatic Processing of Personal Data.[331] The eight data protection principles were:

1. Personal data shall be processed fairly and lawfully and, in particular, shall not be processed unless—
   (a) at least one of the conditions in Schedule 2 is met, and
   (b) in the case of sensitive personal data, at least one of the conditions in Schedule 3 is also met.
2. Personal data shall be obtained only for one or more specified and lawful purposes, and shall not be further processed in any manner incompatible with that purpose or those purposes.
3. Personal data shall be adequate, relevant and not excessive in relation to the purpose

---

[329] DPA 1998 s 4(4). The principles were listed in Part 1 of Schedule 1 to the DPA 1998.

[330] *Stunt v Associated Newspapers Ltd* [2018] EWCA Civ 1780, [2018] 1 WLR 6060 at [12]-[16].

[331] Opened for signature on 28 January 1981. This was signed by the United Kingdom on 14 May 1981, ratified on 26 August 1987 and entered into force on 1 December 1987. It has been signed and ratified by all other members of the Council of Europe, as well as six countries that are not members of the Council of Europe. The treaty formed the basis of the Data Protection Act 1984. The Directive was said to give substance to and amplify the principles in the Convention: see recital (11) in the Directive.

or purposes for which they are processed.

4. Personal data shall be accurate and, where necessary, kept up to date.
5. Personal data processed for any purpose or purposes shall not be kept for longer than is necessary for that purpose or those purposes.
6. Personal data shall be processed in accordance with the rights of data subjects under this Act.
7. Appropriate technical and organisational measures shall be taken against unauthorised or unlawful processing of personal data and against accidental loss or destruction of, or damage to, personal data.
8. Personal data shall not be transferred to a country or territory outside the European Economic Area unless that country or territory ensures an adequate level of protection for the rights and freedoms of data subjects in relation to the processing of personal data.

Breach of this statutory duty was, like any other actionable breach of statutory duty, a tort.[332] It is notable that until the final years of the DPA 1998, there were very few reported cases in UK courts for claims alleging a breach of this duty. This appears partly to have been because of a preference by data subjects to complain to the regulator, leaving the Information Commissioner to use her enforcement powers to secure the wished outcome and without exposing the data subject to legal costs. For those to whom the latter was of little concern and for those who advised them, an analogue in the form of a claim under the Human Rights Act 1998 and Art 8 of the ECHR[333] – whether as the newly minted tort of misuse of private information or otherwise – had a sparkle that never quite made it to the DPA 1998.[334] Others found the Protection from Harassment Act 1997 less intimidating. Claims for breach of the s 4(4) duty were often presented as a fallback. Wider recognition of the free-standing importance of claims for breach of the statutory duty only came in the last years of the 1998 Act, as its particular suitability to securing relief against misuse of personal information through the

---

332 *Vidal Hall v Google Inc* [2015] EWCA Civ 311, [2016] QB 1003. The DPA 1998 did not leave the remedies at large, but specified the remedies that could be sought by private action, as well as a suite of regulatory enforcement provisions exercisable by the Information Commissioner: these are considered in Ch 49.

333 Paradoxically, compliance with the data protection principles gave the data controller the comfort of knowing that its handling of personal data was in accordance with the law for the purposes of Art 8(2) of the ECHR: *R (Catt) v ACPO* [2015] UKSC 9, [2015] AC 1065 at [11]-[17], [47], [57], [60]; *R (AB) Chief Constable of Hampshire Constabulary* [2015] EWHC 1238 (Admin), [2015] 1 WLR 5250 at [73]; *R (W, X, Y, Z) v Secretary of State for Health* [2015] EWCA Civ 1034, [2016] 1 WLR 698.

334 See, for example: *R (TD) Commissioner of Metropolitan Police & SSHD* [2013] EWHC 2231 (Admin), [2014] ACD 7; *R (Segalov) v Chief Constable of Sussex Police* [2018] EWHC 3187 (Admin); *Murray v Express Newspapers plc* [2008] EWCA Civ 446, [2009] Ch 481 (contrast the claim in the High Court: *Murray v Express Newspapers Ltd* [2007] EWHC 1908, [2007]EMLR 22). In *Campbell v Mirror Group Newspapers* [2002] EWHC 499 (QB) at [77], Morland J said: 'Mr Desmond Browne QC for the defendant likened the Act to a thicket. I hope that I have been able to thread a path through it. If I have lost my way, it will not be due to Mr Antony White QC whose submissions for the claimant in respect of this part of her case were admirably lucid and educative.' On appeal, the Court of Appeal referred to his description with no evident disapproval: *Campbell v Mirror Group Newspapers Ltd* [2002] EWCA Civ 1373, [2003] QB 633 at [72]. On appeal to the House of Lords, the parties agreed that the data protection claim 'stood or fell with the main claim,' ie the claim for breach of Ms Campbell's rights under Art 8 of the ECHR: *Campbell v Mirror Group Newspapers Ltd* [2004] UKHL 22, [2004] 2 AC 457 at [32]. Baroness Hale described the claim for breach of s 4(4) of the DPA 1998 as 'add[ing] nothing to the claim for breach of confidence' (at [130]). The judicial distaste for the DPA 1998 remained until almost the end: *In Re JR38* [2015] UKSC 42, [2016] AC 1131 at [70]; *R (T) v Chief Constable of Greater Manchester* [2014] UKSC 35, [2015] AC 49; *R (L) v Commissioner of Police of the Metropolis* [2007] EWCA Civ 168, [2008] 1 WLR 681; cf *R (Catt) v ACPO* [2015] UKSC 9, [2015] AC 1065. Particular judicial hostility to the DPA 1998, evident in decisions such as *Durant v Financial Services Authority* [2003] EWCA Civ 1746, [2004] FSR 28, *Grow with Us Ltd v Green Thumb (UK) Ltd* [2006] EWCA Civ1201 and *Johnson v Medical Defence Union* [2007] EWCA Civ 262, [2007] 3 CMLR 9, (2007) 96 BMLR 99, began to abate in later appellate judgments with a differently constituted Court of Appeal: see *Vidal Hall v Google Inc* [2015] EWCA Civ 311, [2016] QB 1003; *Gulati v MGN Ltd* [2015] EWCA Civ 1291, [2017] QB 149; *Dawson-Damer v Taylor Wessing LLP* [2017] EWCA Civ 74, [2017] 1 WLR 3255; *Ittihadieh v 5-11 Cheyne Gardens RTM Co Ltd* [2017] EWCA 121, [2018] QB 256; *Stunt v Associated Newspapers Ltd* [2018] EWCA Civ 1780, [2018] 1 WLR 6060. The trend was not universal: see *Cooper v National Crime Agency* [2019] EWCA Civ 16, in particular for the court's willingness to countenance the circumvention of the requirement that the data subject give his or her consent to processing of his or her personal data.

internet and social media became apparent.[335]

15–037 DPP1: introduction

The first data protection principle provided:

> Personal data shall be processed fairly and lawfully and, in particular, shall not be processed unless—
> (a) at least one of the conditions in Schedule 2 is met, and
> (b) in the case of sensitive personal data, at least one of the conditions in Schedule 3 is also met.

The first data protection principle represented the domestic implementation of Arts 6.1(a), 10 and 11 of the Directive. In the case of personal data that was not sensitive data, DPP1 imposed three requirements ('fairly,' 'lawfully' and meeting at least one of the conditions in Schedule 2). And, in the case of personal data that was sensitive data, DPP1 imposed a fourth requirement of meeting at least one of the conditions in Schedule 3. Of the eight data protection principles, DPP1 imposed the most wide-ranging, continuing obligation upon the data controller.

15–038 DPP1: 'fairly'

Part II of Sch 1 to the DPA 1998[336] spelt out certain minimum requirements of fairness and also identified certain behaviour as necessarily being not fair processing. It directed attention to the method by which the personal data was obtained,[337] but otherwise did not supply criteria by which fair processing was to be adjudged.[338]

(1) Paragraph 2 of Part II set a mandatory, minimum requirement for fair processing, which varied according to whether or not the data was obtained from the data subject.
  (a) In the case of data obtained from the data subject, fair processing required that the data controller 'ensure so far as practicable' that the data subject was given, or had made available to him or her, information as to:
    (i) the identity of the data controller,
    (ii) the purpose(s) for which the data were intended to be processed,[339] and
    (iii) any further information necessary 'having regard to the specific circumstances in which the data [were or were being] processed, to enable processing in

---

[335] See, for example: *Google Spain SL v Agencia Espanola de Proteccion de Datos* [2014] QB 1022; *Vidal Hall v Google Inc* [2015] EWCA Civ 311, [2016] QB 1003; *AY (a minor acting by FY as next friend) v Facebook (Ireland) Ltd & others* [2016] NIQB 76; *CG v Facebook Ireland Ltd* [2016] NICA 54, [2017] 2 CMLR 29; *Townsend v Google Inc* [2017] NIQB 81; *Galloway v Frazer* [2016[NIQB 7 (YouTube); *NT1 v Google LLC* [2018] EWHC 799 (QB), [2018] 3 All ER 581; *Unabhangiges Landeszentrum fur Datenschutz Schleswig-Holstein v Wirtschaftsakademie Schleswig-Holstein GmbH* (C-210/16) [2018] 3 CMLR 32; *Schrems v Facebook Ireland Ltd* (C-498/16) [2018] 1 WLR 4343, [2018] IL Pr 11; *Sabados v Facebook Ireland* [2018] EWHC 2369 (QB).

[336] DPA 1998 s 4(2) provided that the data protection principles were to be interpreted in accordance with Part II of Sch 1.

[337] With particular emphasis on whether *any* person from whom the personal data had been obtained had been deceived or misled as to the purposes for which the data would be processed: DPA 1998 Sch 1 Pt II, para 1(1). This provision picked up both the original acquisition of personal data and any data controller to whom the personal data was transferred. Covertly photographing a child was not considered a deception: *Murray v Express Newspapers Ltd* [2007] EWHC 1908, [2007]EMLR 22 at [73].

[338] In *R (Hussain) v Sandwell MBC* [2017] EWHC 1641 (Admin), [2018] PTSR 142 at [237] the court seemed to think that there was an overarching fairness judgment to be made (as opposed to the directed enquiry demanded by Part II of Sch 1 to the DPA 1998): this is questionable. In *McGuffick v Royal Bank of Scotland plc* [2009] EWHC 2386 (Comm), [2010] 1 All ER 635 it was held that the processing of the data by sharing it with other financial institutions through credit reference agencies, pursuant to the Principles of Reciprocity, was 'clearly in the legitimate interests of the bank, the CRAs and other financial institutions, for all of whom the governing principle is that the sharing of data has the aim of promoting responsible lending' and was thus both lawful and fair (at at [113]).

[339] As to which, see *López Ribalda and others v Spain* [2018] IRLR 358 at [69].

respect of the data subject to be fair.'[340]

Although paragraph 2 of Part II did not specify the time at which the data subject was to be given this information, the clear implication was that it had to be before or at the moment that the data controller obtained the information from the data subject.[341]

(b) In the case of data not obtained from the data subject, fair processing required that the data controller 'ensure so far as practicable' the same information as in (a), except that:

(i) it specified the time at which the data controller had to provide or make readily available this information, namely: (a) the time when the data controller first processed the data; or (b) where the data controller envisaged disclosure of the data to a third party within a reasonable period, when the data was so disclosed or when the controller became aware that it was no longer likely to be disclosed; and

(ii) there was a disapplication where the provision of the information would have involved a disproportionate effort[342] or where the disclosure was required to comply with a non-contractual legal obligation.

(2) Paragraph 1(2) of Part II deemed processing to be fair, insofar as the processing was obtaining the data, if it consisted of information obtained from a person who was authorised by or under any enactment to supply it or who was required to supply it by enactment or international obligation.

If the processing did not offend (1) but was not deemed fair under (2), then satisfaction of the requirement that personal data be processed 'fairly' was left open, to be decided from the perspective of the data subject having regard to, amongst other things, the method by which the data were obtained (whether by the data controller or a data controller 'up the chain'), whether anybody had been misled as to the purpose(s) for which the data were to be processed, the intensity of the processing, the proximity between the data controller and the data subject, and the foreseeability to the data subject of the processing.[343]

15–039 DPP1: 'lawfully'

The DPA 1998 did not specify the content of the requirement that personal data be processed 'lawfully.'[344] Any processing proscribed by statute would certainly not have been lawful

---

340 This would include informing the data subject of the transfer of their data to another data controller: *Bara and others v Presedintele Casei Nationale de Asigurari de Sanatate and others* (C-201/14) [2016] 1 CMLR 41 at [34].

341 Since the information to be provided included 'the purpose or purposes for which the data *are intended to be processed*.': para 2(3)(c). Also, the distinction with data not so obtained, which was subject to the precepts of 'the relevant time.'

342 In addition, the data controller had to record his reasons for his view that it would involve a disproportionate effort: SI 2000/185.

343 See para 1(1) of Part II of Sch 1. For a detailed consideration of how the fairness requirement operated in practice, see: *AB v A Chief Constable* [2014] EWHC 1965 (QB), [2014] IRLR 700; *Chief Constable of Humberside Police & ors v IC and SSHD* [2009] EWCA 1079, [2010] 1 WLR 1136 at [48], [100]-[105]; *R (Ali & anor) v Minister for the Cabinet Office the Statistics Board* [2012] EWHC 1943 (Admin); *Johnson v Medical Defence Union* [2004] EWHC 347 (Ch) on appeal *Johnson v Medical Defence Union* [2007] EWCA Civ 262, [2007] 3 CMLR 9, (2007) 96 BMLR 99; *Law Society & ors v Kordowski* [2011] EWHC 3185 (QB), [2014] EMLR 2; *R (Ellis) v Chief Constable of the Essex Police* [2003] EWHC 1321 (Admin) (DC), [2003] 2 FLR 566.

344 CJEU jurisprudence made clear that Art 7 of Directive 95/46 set out an exhaustive and restrictive list of cases in which the processing of personal data could be regarded as lawful: *Asociacion Nacional de Establecimientos Financieros de Credito v Administracion del Estado* (C-486/10) [2012] 1 CMLR 48 at [30]-[32]; *Breyer v Federal Republic of Germany* (C-582/14) [2017] 1 WLR 1569 at [57]. The list in Art 7 of the Directive was more-or-less replicated in Sch 2 to the DPA 1998. Accordingly, the requirement of the first data protection principle that personal data be processed 'lawfully' may not have added anything to the requirement in that principle that at least one of the conditions in Sch 2 had to be met.

processing – for example hacking,[345] processing indecent images[346] or receipt or disclosure of personal data without the consent of the data controller.[347] Similarly, any processing by a public authority that was incompatible with a Convention right would not have been lawful.[348] Disclosure where a data controllers knew that the disclosed data would be used for direct marketing purposes would have been unlawful if the data subject had made an objection under section 11 of the DPA 1998.[349] The case law suggested that any processing that gave rise to a civil liability (eg because it was a breach of confidence, libellous or harassment) did not constitute lawful processing.[350]

15– 040 Schedule 2: general

The third requirement of the first data protection principle was satisfaction of at least one of the conditions in Schedule 2. The conditions were:

1. The data subject has given his consent to the processing.
2. The processing is necessary—
   (a) for the performance of a contract to which the data subject is a party, or
   (b) for the taking of steps at the request of the data subject with a view to entering into a contract.
3. The processing is necessary for compliance with any legal obligation to which the data controller is subject, other than an obligation imposed by contract.
4. The processing is necessary in order to protect the vital interests of the data subject.
5. The processing is necessary—
   (a) for the administration of justice;
   (aa) for the exercise of any functions of either House of Parliament;
   (b) for the exercise of any functions conferred on any person by or under any enactment;
   (c) for the exercise of any functions of the Crown, a Minister of the Crown or a government department; or
   (d) for the exercise of any other functions of a public nature exercised in the public interest by any person.
6.(1) The processing is necessary for the purposes of legitimate interests pursued by the data controller or by the third party or parties to whom the data are disclosed, except where the processing is unwarranted in any particular case by reason of prejudice to the rights and freedoms or legitimate interests of the data subject.
   (2) The Secretary of State may by order specify particular circumstances in which this condition is, or is not, to be taken to be satisfied.

Engagement of most of the conditions thus turned on whether the processing was 'necessary' for one or other particular purpose. In each of these conditions, 'necessary' meant 'reasonably necessary,' and not absolutely or strictly necessary.[351] Necessity was considered to be part of

---

345 See Computer Misuse Act 1990 ss 1, 2 and 3.

346 See: Criminal Justice Act 1988 s 160; Protection of Children Act 1978 s 1; *R v Smith* [2002] EWCA Crim 683, [2003] 1 Cr App R 13.

347 ie in breach of DPA s 55(1).

348 See: Human Rights Act 1998 s 6(1); *Dept of Health v IC and Pro-Life Alliance*, IT, 15 October 2009 at [71]-[72]; *Rechnungshof v Österreichischer Rundfunk* [2002] ECR I-4989, [2003] 3 CMLR 10 at [68] and [73]-[75].

349 *Robertson v Wakefield DC and SSHD* [2001] EWHC Admin 915, [2002] QB 1052. This case concerned a challenge under DPA 1998 and HRA 1998 to the practice of making information on the electoral register available to organisations, some of which would use the names and addresses on the register for the purposes of direct marketing. The claimant succeeded on all his grounds, including breach of his Art 8 right to private life and the right to free elections under Art 3 of Protocol 1 ECHR.

350 *Campbell v Mirror Group Newspapers* [2002] EWHC 499 (QB); *Murray v Express Newspapers Ltd* [2007] EWHC 1908, [2007]EMLR 22 at [72]; *Law Society & ors v Kordowski* [2011] EWHC 3185 (QB), [2014] EMLR 2 at [78], [101].

351 *South Lanarkshire Council v Scottish IC* [2013] UKSC 55, [2013] 1 WLR 2421 at [8] and [19]-[27]; *Cooper v National Crime Agency* [2019] EWCA Civ 16 at [89]-[93]; *House of Commons v IC and Brooke, Leapman, Ungoed-Thomas* [2008]

the proportionality test and required the minimum interference with the Art 8 rights of the data subject that would achieve the legitimate aim pursued.[352]

5–041 Schedule 2: conditions

In relation to the specific conditions:

(1) Condition 1 gave effect to Art 7(a) of the Directive. This provided that personal data could be processed only if 'the data subject has unambiguously given his consent.' The DPA 1998 itself did not spell out what 'consent' required. Art 2(h) of the Directive provided that the data subject's consent meant 'any freely given, specific and informed indication of his wishes by which the data subject signifies his agreement to personal data relating to him being processed.' The contrast with condition 1 in Schedule 3 suggested that consent need not be explicit for the purpose of condition 1 in Schedule 2. Nevertheless, consent by its very nature involves something more than not objecting, whether that something more is written, oral or by conduct.[353] A person cannot consent to something about which he or she is unaware.[354] But the data subject did not have to be informed about every aspect of the processing for the consent to be effective.[355] The importance of consent was recognised by the Supreme Court, which called for guidance on the issue.[356]

(2) Condition 2 gave effect to Art 7(b) of the Directive.[357] The condition was restricted to contracts to which the data subject was a party.[358]

(3) Condition 3 gave effect to Art 7(c) of the Directive. The imposition of a statutory duty on the data controller requiring the particular processing sufficed for the purposes of condition 3.[359] But obligations could arise elsewhere[360] or be far more general.[361]

EWHC 1084 (Admin), [2009] 3 All ER 403 at [43]; cf *Valsts policijas Rīgas reģiona pārvaldes Kārtības policijas pārvalde v Rīgas pašvaldības SIA* (Case C-13/16) [2017] 4 WLR 97, [2017] 3 CMLR 39 at [30]-[32].

352 *Christian Institute v Lord Advocate* [2016] UKSC 51, [2016] HRLR 19 at [56]; *R (Ali & anor) v Minister for the Cabinet Office the Statistics Board* [2012] EWHC 1943 (Admin) at [76]. This is the longstanding meaning that it has had in ECtHR jurisprudence: *Sunday Times v United Kingdom* [1979] ECHR 1, (1979) 2 EHRR 245 at [59].

353 *AG v Jonathan Cape Ltd* [1976] QB 752; *Bell v Alfred Franks & Bartlett Co Ltd* [1980] 1 WLR 340, [1980] 1 All ER 356; *Zino Davidoff SA v A&G Imports Ltd* (C-414/99) [2002] Ch 109, [2002] 1 CMLR 1.

354 *Re Caughey, ex p Ford* (1876) 1 Ch D 521 at 528.

355 *Johnson v Medical Defence Union (No 2)* [2006] EWHC (Ch) 321, (2006) 89 BMLR 43 at [103]; cf *Volker und Markus Schecke GbR v Land Hessen* (C-92/09) [2012] All ER (EC) 127, [2012] IP & T 513 at [76]-[78]; *Re Baronetcy of Pringle of Stichill* [2016] UKPC 16, [2017] 1 All ER 106 at [74]. Thus, a term in an employment contract giving general consent could suffice even though the particular use had not been in the contemplation of the parties: *Cooper v National Crime Agency* [2019] EWCA Civ 16 at [98]-[102], [116].

356 *Christian Institute v Lord Advocate* [2016] UKSC 51, [2016] HRLR 19.

357 See also Recital (30).

358 *Grow With Us Ltd v Green Thumb (UK) Ltd* [2006] EWHC 379 (QB) at [43]. It could cover application of an employer's contractual disciplinary policy with the data subject: *Cooper v National Crime Agency* [2019] EWCA Civ 16 at [103].

359 *Christian Institute v Lord Advocate* [2016] UKSC 51, [2016] HRLR 19 at [56]; *Worten - Equipamentos para o Lar SA v Autoridade para as Condicoes de Trabalho (ACT)* (C-342/12) [2013] ICR D29. This could include an obligation to disclose under freedom of information legislation: *European Commission v Bavarian Lager Co Ltd* [2010] EUECJ C-28/08, [2010] ECR I-06055, [2011] Bus LR 867 at [24], [47].

360 See, for example: *R (British Telecommunications plc & ors) v Secretary of State for Business, Innovation and Skills* [2011] EWHC 1021 (Admin), [2012] 3 CMLR 98 at [152]; *CN v European Parliament* (T-343/13) 3 December 2015 at [35].

361 *R (Hussain) v Sandwell MBC* [2017] EWHC 1641 (Admin), [2018] PTSR 142 at [231]-[233] (duty in s 27 of Localism Act 2011 on a local authority to promote and maintain high standards said to justify publishing critical report of an elected member of that authority). Apparently, it could even include public law obligations for a public sector data controller to comply with legitimate expectations created by the terms of its policies and with the duty of reasonable inquiry: *Cooper v National Crime Agency* [2019] EWCA Civ 16 at [104].

Embedded in the condition was a requirement of proportionality.[362]

(4) Condition 4 gave effect to Art 7(d) of the Directive. This required more than that the processing was likely to benefit the well-being of the data subject.[363]

(5) Condition 5, broadly speaking, gave effect to Art 7(e) of the Directive. The wording of Art 7(e) was more general: 'necessary for the performance of a task carried out in the public interest or in the exercise of official authority vested in the controller or in a third party to whom the data are disclosed.' By not being limited to those having a function conferred on them by an enactment, Art 7(e) had a further reach than condition (5).[364] The 'public interest' limb covered, for example, processing of data so as to list people who, according to public authorities, were suspected of being 'front men' for those associated with tax fraud.[365] In practice, the courts readily found this condition satisfied by public authorities.[366] Under both Art 7(e) and condition (5), whether processing was 'necessary' for the performance of a function depended to a significant degree upon the function being performed and the circumstances in which it was being performed.[367] Disclosing personal information pursuant to an obligation in a freedom of information regime (subject to any exemption in that regime) would satisfy this condition.[368] Once the function in sub-paras (a)-(d) had been carried out, it did not automatically follow that processing (eg retaining the personal data) thereafter was necessary.[369]

(6) Condition 6 gave effect to Art 7(f) of the Directive. The condition required three questions to be answered: (i) was the data controller, or the third party to whom the data had been disclosed, pursuing a legitimate interest or interests?; (ii) was the processing in question necessary for the purposes of the pursuit of that legitimate interest?; and (iii) was the processing unwarranted by reason of prejudice to the rights and freedoms or

---

[362] *Rechnungshof v Österreichischer Rundfunkat* (C-465/00) [2003] 3 CMLR 10 at [91].

[363] *Christian Institute v Lord Advocate* [2016] UKSC 51, [2016] HRLR 19 at [48], [50].

[364] See, for example: *Satakunnan Markkinapörssi Oy v Finland* (931/13) (2018) 66 EHRR 8.

[365] *Puškár v Finančné riaditeľstvo Slovenskej* (C-73/16) [2017] 4 WLR 209, [2018] 1 CMLR 44 at [106]-[117].

[366] *R (Hussain) v Sandwell MBC* [2017] EWHC 1641 (Admin), [2018] PTSR 142 at [234]-[235] where the 'functions' of promoting and maintaining high standards of member, securing adherence to the Nolan principles of accountability, to ensure financial integrity, were thought to be well within the grasp of 5(b) and of 5(d). The reasoning is questionable. In *Cooper v National Crime Agency* [2019] EWCA Civ 16 at [122] the Court of Appeal was ready to find this condition engaged by the 'function' of a public sector employer engaging staff, managing them and implementing staffing policies, notwithstanding that the rights, liabilities and obligations of the parties arose from a contract; and further see [105]-[113].

[367] *R (Castle) v Metropolitan Police Commissioner* [2011] EWHC 2317 (Admin), [2012] 1 All ER 953 at [51], applied in a data protection context in *R (CL) v Chief Constable of Greater Manchester Police* [2018] EWHC 3333 (Admin) at [92]-[93]; *Chief Constable of Humberside Police & ors v IC and SSHD* [2009] EWCA 1079, [2010] 1 WLR 1136 at [72], in relation to retention of police records. Where the processing was carried out in the performance of a task entrusted to a public authority in the public interest, then 'a certain amount of discretion' was to be afforded in determining the extent to which it was necessary to forward data to third parties: *Oikonomopoulos v European Commission* (T-483/13) CJEU 20 July 2016 at [58]-[60]. Similarly at *Worten - Equipamentos para o Lar SA v Autoridade para as Condicoes de Trabalho (ACT)* (C-342/12) [2013] ICR D29 at [43]-[45], condition satisfied by an employer making available for immediate consultation by the national authority responsible for monitoring working conditions a record of working time of employees; *Volker und Markus Schecke GbR v Land Hessen* (C-92/09) [2012] All ER (EC) 127, [2012] IP & T 513 at [79]-[86] where it was held that a publicly-available database giving *all* the details of a recipient of public funds went beyond what was necessary; cf *Huber v Germany* (C-524/06) [2009] 1 CMLR 49, [2009] All ER (EC) 239 at [49]-68] where the court upheld a centralised government system holding details of foreign nationals provided that it was available only to those bodies that had a legitimate need to consult it and that the details did not go beyond what was necessary for the statutory purposes.

[368] *European Commission v Bavarian Lager Co Ltd* [2010] EUECJ C-28/08, [2010] ECR I-06055, [2011] Bus LR 867 at [24], [47]. The court in *Chung v FCO* [2011] EWCA Civ 541 at [21] doubted whether 'administration of justice' was confined to the administration of justice in the United Kingdom.

[369] See: *Camera di Commercio, Industria, Artigianato e Agricoltura di Lecce v Manni* (C-398/15)[2018] Bus LR 25, [2017] 3 CMLR 18 at [42]-[46]; and, by analogy, *NT1 v Google LLC* [2018] EWHC 799 (QB), [2018] 3 All ER 581 at [102].

legitimate interests of the data subject.[370] It involved a balancing of the opposing rights and interests concerned, in the context of which account had to be taken of the data subject's rights arising from Articles 7 and 8 of the Charter.[371] The legitimate interests of a data controller could include that of running a business using data.[372] The legitimate interests of a data subject included protection of his or her private life.[373] The outcome of that exercise itself depended upon the intensity and intrusiveness of the processing.[374] Thus, for example:

— A professional examining body in its capacity as a data controller had a legitimate interest in storing the exam papers of a candidate and the examiner's comments on them, but the candidate's legitimate interest in protecting his private life would preclude that body sending that information to a third party or publishing it.[375]
— While there was a legitimate interest in a data subject's criminal record receding into the past, there was a stronger public interest in open justice.[376]
— An employer's legitimate interest in ensuring the smooth running of the company by monitoring its staff's emails outweighed the privacy interests of the employee[377] And an employer's legitimate interest in maintaining high standards of conduct by its employees.[378]
— The inclusion of a person's name on a list of those considered by a government department to be front-men for others involved in tax avoidance could be justified processing if the list were confidential and internal to the department, but not insofar as the processing involved disclosing that list more widely.[379]
— A domestic CCTV system that recorded images whilst pursuing the controller's legitimate interests of protecting his property and the health and life of his family, went beyond what was legitimate by including images of persons on the adjacent public footpath and entrance to the opposite house.[380]
— The interest of a third party in obtaining from police records information about a person who damaged their property in order for that third party to be able sue that person for damages qualified as a legitimate interest that was not overriden by those of the data subject.[381]
— The inclusion in a publicly-accessible companies register of the details of a director's involvement in a struck-off company could be justified long after the

370 *South Lanarkshire Council v Scottish IC* [2013] UKSC 55, [2013] 1 WLR 2421 at [18]; *Valsts policijas Rīgas reģiona pārvaldes Kārtības policijas pārvalde v Rīgas pašvaldības SIA* (Case C-13/16) [2017] 4 WLR 97, [2017] 3 CMLR 39 at [28]; *Rodriguez-Noza v IC and Nursing and Midwifery Council* [2015] UKUT 449 (AAC) at [19].

371 *Google Spain SL v Agencia Espanola de Proteccion de Datos* [2014] QB 1022 at [74].

372 *Townsend v Google Inc* [2017] NIQB 81 at [46]; *NT1 v Google LLC* [2018] EWHC 799 (QB), [2018] 3 All ER 581 at [115].

373 *Nowak v Data Protection Commissioner* (C-434/16) [2018] 1 WLR 3505, [2018] 2 CMLR 21 at [50].

374 *South Lanarkshire Council v Scottish IC* [2013] UKSC 55, [2013] 1 WLR 2421 at [25], [27].

375 *Nowak v Data Protection Commissioner* (C-434/16) [2018] 1 WLR 3505, [2018] 2 CMLR 21 at [50].

376 *Townsend v Google Inc* [2017] NIQB 81 at [61].

377 *Bărbulescu v Romania* [2017] IRLR 1032, (2017} 44 BHRC 17 at [127].

378 *Cooper v National Crime Agency* [2019] EWCA Civ 16 at [114]-[115].

379 *Puškár v Finančné riaditeľstvo Slovenskej* (C-73/16) [2017] 4 WLR 209, [2018] 1 CMLR 44 at [92]-[93].

380 *Rynes v Urad pro ochranu osobnich udaju* (C-212/13) [2015] 1 WLR 2607, [2015] CEC 732.

381 *Valsts policijas Rīgas reģiona pārvaldes Kārtības policijas pārvalde v Rīgas pašvaldības SIA* (Case C-13/16) [2017] 4 WLR 97, [2017] 3 CMLR 39 at [29]-[34].

striking off as the legitimate interest in allowing those dealing with the director to know his business history so as to make informed decisions.[382]

— The legitimate interest of internet users in having access to personal information about a data subject had to be balanced against its intrusiveness into the data subject's life, and would also depend upon the interest of the public in having the information, the quantity of information and the role played by the subject in public life.[383]

— A data subject who was not a party to a legal dispute between two others could be entitled to be informed of a prospective order disclosing his details so that the data subject could identify reasons why his identity should not be disclosed.[384]

15–042 Schedule 3: general

The fourth requirement of the first data protection principle applied only where the processing was of sensitive personal data.[385] The processing of sensitive personal data also had to satisfy at least one of the conditions in Schedule 2. Those conditions were:

1. The data subject has given his explicit consent to the processing of the personal data.

2(1). The processing is necessary for the purposes of exercising or performing any right or obligation which is conferred or imposed by law on the data controller in connection with employment.

(2) .....

3. The processing is necessary—
   (a) in order to protect the vital interests of the data subject or another person, in a case where—
      (i) consent cannot be given by or on behalf of the data subject; or
      (ii) the data controller cannot reasonably be expected to obtain the consent of the data subject; or
   (b) in order to protect the vital interests of another person, in a case where consent by or on behalf of the data subject has been unreasonably withheld.

4. The processing–
   (a) is carried out in the course of its legitimate activities by any body or association which–
      (i) is not established or conducted for profit, and
      (ii) exists for political, philosophical, religious or trade-union purposes,
   (b) is carried out with appropriate safeguards for the rights and freedoms of data subjects,
   (c) relates only to individuals who are either members of the body or association or have regular contact with it in connection with its purposes, and
   (d) does not involve disclosure of the personal data to a third party without the consent of the data subject.

5. The information contained in the personal data has been made public as a result of steps deliberately taken by the data subject.

---

382 *Camera di Commercio, Industria, Artigianato e Agricoltura di Lecce v Manni* (C-398/15) [2018] Bus LR 25, [2017] 3 CMLR 18.

383 *Google Spain SL v Agencia Espanola de Proteccion de Datos* [2014] QB 1022 at [80]-[81].

384 *Totalise plc v The Motley Fool Ltd & anor* [2001] EWCA Civ 1897, [2002] 1 WLR 1897 at [24]-[26].

385 That is, data consisting of information as to the data subject's racial or ethnic origin, political opinions, religious or like beliefs, union membership, health, commission or alleged commission of an offence and proceedings for the same: DPA 1998 s 2.

6. The processing—
   (a) is necessary for the purpose of, or in connection with, any legal proceedings (including prospective legal proceedings);
   (b) is necessary for the purpose of obtaining legal advice; or
   (c) is otherwise necessary for the purposes of establishing, exercising or defending legal rights.

7(1). The processing is necessary—
   (a) for the administration of justice;
   (aa) for the exercise of any functions of either House of Parliament;
   (b) for the exercise of any functions conferred on any person by or under an enactment; or
   (c) for the exercise of any functions of the Crown, a Minister of the Crown or a government department.

(2) ....

8(1). The processing is necessary for medical purposes and is undertaken by—
   (a) a health professional, or
   (b) a person who in the circumstances owes a duty of confidentiality which is equivalent to that which would arise if that person were a health professional.

(2) In this paragraph 'medical purposes' includes the purposes of preventative medicine, medical diagnosis, medical research, the provision of care and treatment and the management of healthcare services.

9(1). The processing–
   (a) is of sensitive personal data consisting of information as to racial or ethnic origin,
   (b) is necessary for the purpose of identifying or keeping under review the existence of equality of opportunity or treatment between persons of different racial or ethnic origins, and
   (c) is carried out with appropriate safeguards for the rights and freedoms of data subjects.

(2). ...

10. The personal data are processed in circumstances specified in an order made by the Secretary of State for the purposes of this paragraph.

As with most of the conditions in Schedule 2, most of the conditions in Schedule 3 turned on whether the processing was 'necessary' for one or other particular purpose. And as with Schedule 2, in each of these conditions, 'necessary' meant 'reasonably necessary,' and not absolutely or strictly necessary.[386] Necessity was considered to be part of the proportionality test and required the minimum interference with the Art 8 rights of the data subject that would achieve the legitimate aim pursued.[387]

5–043 Schedule 3: conditions

These conditions were supposed to be narrowly construed, on the basis that their object was to restrict the purposes for which sensitive personal data could be processed.[388] There was some issue – not ultimately resolved – whether the requirement to satisfy one of the conditions in Schedule 3 needed to be disapplied if that requirement was irreconcilable with the Directive in relation to specific processing.[389] In relation to the specific conditions:

---

386 *South Lanarkshire Council v Scottish IC* [2013] UKSC 55, [2013] 1 WLR 2421 at [8] and [19]-[27]; *Cooper v National Crime Agency* [2019] EWCA Civ 16 at [89]-[93]. cf *Valsts policijas Rīgas reģiona pārvaldes Kārtības policijas pārvalde v Rīgas pašvaldības SIA* (Case C-13/16) [2017] 4 WLR 97, [2017] 3 CMLR 39 at [30]-[32].

387 *Christian Institute v Lord Advocate* [2016] UKSC 51, [2016] HRLR 19 at [56]; *R (Ali & anor) v Minister for the Cabinet Office the Statistics Board* [2012] EWHC 1943 (Admin) at [76].

388 *R (T) v The Commissioner of Police for the Metropolis* [2012] EWHC 1115 (Admin), [2012] 1 WLR 2978 at [72].

389 See *NT1 v Google LLC* [2018] EWHC 799 (QB), [2018] 3 All ER 581 at [103]-[105].

(1) Condition (1) gave effect to Art 8.2(a) of the Directive. By adding 'explicit' to the analogous condition (1) in Schedule 2, it removed the possibility of consent being implied in relation to sensitive personal data: for example, by the data subject entering or continuing to be in an area in which the data controller had placed a notice imputing consent from those entering or remaining in the area. It would also seem that the data controller, in obtaining consent from the data subject, had to have given the data subject greater specifics of the particular types of processing that would be carried out and to have spelled out that the processing would include sensitive personal data for that consent to be 'explicit consent to the processing of the personal data.'[390]

(2) Condition (2) gave effect to Art 8.2(b) of the Directive. The condition was a sub-set of condition (2) in Schedule 2, confined to rights and obligations conferred or imposed by law and having to be in connection with employment.[391] Voluntary work was outside the scope of the condition.[392]

(3) Condition (3) gave effect to Art 8.2(c) of the Directive. A 'vital interest' was one that concerned a matter of life or death.[393]

(4) Condition (4) gave effect to Art 8.2(d) of the Directive.

(5) Condition (5) gave effect to one part of Art 8.2(e) of the Directive. This did not require a deliberate decision or step by the data subject to make the information public, but rather the taking of a deliberate decision or step by the data subject as a result of which the information was made public. Thus where a data subject committed a crime, that carried with it the consequence that it might result in a trial at which that would become public.[394] So, too, an individual's walking in a public place meant that the information contained in a photograph of that individual had been made public by steps taken by that individual.[395]

(6) Condition (6) gave effect to the other part of Art 8.2(e) of the Directive. This could cover processing taking place well before the instigation of legal proceedings.[396] But it did not cover disciplinary proceedings by an employer.[397]

(7) Other than in relation to processing of convictions and the like,[398] condition (7) did not have any express mandate from the Directive.[399] The language of condition (7) replicated

[390] Despite this, in *Cooper v National Crime Agency* [2019] EWCA Civ 16 at [98]-[102], [116] the Court of Appeal held that a term in an employment contract giving general consent would suffice even though the particular use had not been in the contemplation of the parties.

[391] In *Cooper v National Crime Agency* [2019] EWCA Civ 16 at [118] the Court of Appeal suggested that rights under a contract were rights 'conferred or imposed by law.' The suggestion is questionable.

[392] *Re Lindqvist (Approximation of Laws)* [2004] QB 1014 at [44].

[393] *Heath v IC*, IT, 16 September 2009 at [15]. For an application, see *Scott v LGBT Foundation* [2020] EWHC 483 (QB).

[394] *Townsend v Google Inc* [2017] NIQB 81 at [62]; *NT1 v Google LLC* [2018] EWHC 799 (QB), [2018] 3 All ER 581 at [110]-[113].

[395] *Murray v Express Newspapers Ltd* [2007] EWHC 1908, [2007]EMLR 22 at [81]. Although this judgment was reversed on appeal, a claimed breach of Art 8 of the ECHR formed the basis for that decision, with little consideration of the DPA 1998: *Murray v Express Newspapers plc* [2008] EWCA Civ 446, [2009] Ch 481.

[396] Reliance on this was rejected in *NT1 v Google LLC* [2018] EWHC 799 (QB), [2018] 3 All ER 581 at [107]; but it was accepted in: *R (British Telecommunications plc & ors) v Secretary of State for Culture, Olympics, Media and Sport* [2012] EWCA Civ 232, [2012] 2 CMLR 23, [2012] Bus LR 1766 at [76]-[77]; *Valsts policijas Rīgas reģiona pārvaldes Kārtības policijas pārvalde v Rīgas pašvaldības SIA* (Case C-13/16) [2017] 4 WLR 97, [2017] 3 CMLR 39 at [29].

[397] *Cooper v National Crime Agency* [2019] EWCA Civ 16 at [119]-[121].

[398] See Art 8.5 of the Directive.

[399] Other than, possibly, Art 8.4 of the Directive, albeit condition (7) did not have any of the safeguards and was difficult to reconcile with the presence of Art 8.5. In *Stone v South East Coast Strategic Health Authority* [2006] EWHC 1668 (Admin), [2007] UKHRR 137 at [64]-[65], the court rejected the contention that the qualification 'subject to the provision of suitable safeguards' should be read into paragraph 7 of Schedule 3, in order to construe it

that of condition (5) in Schedule 2.[400]

(8) Condition (8) gave effect to Art 8.3 of the Directive. The term 'medical purposes' was given a wide meaning.[401]

(9) Condition (9) did not have specific mandate from the Directive, but, given that it did provide safeguards, was justifiable under Art 8.4 of the Directive.

(10) In providing for further circumstances in subordinate legislation, condition (10) relied upon Art 8.4 of the Directive. A further 11 circumstances in which processing would satisfy the fourth requirement of DPP1 were added through three separate statutory instruments, each of which was of narrow scope.[402]

15–044 DPP2: specified purposes

The second data protection principle provided:

> Personal data shall be obtained only for one or more specified and lawful purposes, and shall not be further processed in any manner incompatible with that purpose or those purposes.

The second data protection principle represented the domestic implementation of Art 6.1(b) of the Directive.[403] Paragraphs 5-6 of Part 2 of Sch 1 to the DPA 1998 provided two methods for specifying the purpose for which personal data was obtained, including notification to the Information Commissioner.[404] Incompatibility in the manner of processing had a high threshold, certainly so far as processing by public authorities was concerned.[405]

15–045 DPP3: not excessive

The third data protection principle provided:

> Personal data shall be adequate, relevant and not excessive in relation to the purpose or purposes for which they are processed.

The third data protection principle represented the domestic implementation of Art 6.1(c) of the Directive.[406] This principle recognised that initially compliant processing could, over the course of time, become incompatible with the Directive where the data was no longer necessary

consistently with Art 8(4) of the Directive. This conclusion was questionable: see *S v United Kingdom* (30562/04) (2009) 48 EHRR 50, (2009) 25 BHRC 557. The requirement of adequate safeguards appears to have been implicitly accepted in *R (T) v The Commissioner of Police for the Metropolis* [2012] EWHC 1115 (Admin), [2012] 1 WLR 2978.

400 In *Cooper v National Crime Agency* [2019] EWCA Civ 16 at [122] the Court of Appeal was ready to find this condition engaged by the 'function' of a public sector employer engaging staff, managing them and implementing staffing policies, notwithstanding that the rights, liabilities and obligations of the parties arose from a contract.

401 In *Stone v South East Coast Strategic Health Authority* [2006] EWHC 1668 (Admin), [2007] UKHRR 137, the court held that the publication of a report produced by an Inquiry into the psychiatric and medical care, treatment and supervision of a man convicted of a notorious double murder fell within the ambit of 'medical purposes', as relating to 'the management of healthcare services'.

402 The Data Protection (Processing of Sensitive Personal Data) Order 2000, SI 2000/417 added nine. The Data Protection (Processing of Sensitive Personal Data) (Elected Representatives) Order 2002, SI 2002/2905 added one to cover certain processing by elected representatives. And the Data Protection (Processing of Sensitive Personal Data) Order 2006, SI 2006/2068 added a very specific one.

403 See also Art 23.1 and Recital (28).

404 It seems that these two methods were exhaustive.

405 See, for example: *Chung v FCO* [2011] EWCA Civ 541 at [21]; *Cooper v National Crime Agency* [2019] EWCA Civ 16 at [128]-[132] (where it was held that when considering the purpose limitation of the second data protection principle, one had to look at the purpose for which the data had been obtained by the controller in question, and not any purpose of another controller from whom that controller had earlier obtained the personal data); *Puškár v Finančné riaditeľstvo Slovenskej* (C-73/16) [2017] 4 WLR 209, [2018] 1 CMLR 44. But this generosity did not extend to individuals making video recordings of data subjects that were published on an internet site: *Buivids v Datu valsts inspekcija* (C-345/17) (Adv General, 27 September 2018) at [70]. Breach of DPP2 was alleged in *Vidal Hall v Google Inc* [2015] EWCA Civ 311, [2016] QB 1003.

406 See also Recital (28).

in light of the purposes for which it had been collected or initially processed.[407] The purposes for which personal data was processed were taken from those that were registered with the Information Commissioner.[408] The processing of criminal convictions, even by a commercial organisation, was treated as a consequence of the open justice principle.[409]

15–046 DPP4: accurate

The fourth data protection principle provided:

> Personal data shall be accurate and, where necessary, kept up to date.

The fourth data protection principle represented the domestic implementation of Art 6.1(d) of the Directive.[410] Paragraph 7 of Part 2 of Sch 1 to the DPA 1998 explained that a data controller did not offend the principle if it annotated a record with a claim of inaccuracy. The Act provided that data was inaccurate if it was incorrect or misleading as to any matter of fact.[411] In relation to a reporting or an account given to a public authority (eg the police), being 'accurate' did not require that what had been reported be accurate: only that the fact of what had been reported was accurate.[412] In relation to findings about a data subject made in a document, the view seemed to be that provided that they were genuinely held, it did not matter that they were subsequently renounced.[413] Although this fourth data protection principle did not require continuous checking for currency and accuracy, it did require reasonable steps to be taken, with the burden being on the data controller to show that that had been done.[414] Thus, a lender registering with credit referencing agencies a default by a data subject in respect of a hire purchase agreement that was inaccurate in amount and description and that did not record that the agreement was unenforceable under the Consumer Credit Act 1974 was a breach of the fourth principle even though the registration system did not have provision for recording that the default related to an unenforceable agreement.[415] In assessing whether personal data was sufficiently inaccurate to constitute a breach of the fourth principle, the words had to be read and interpreted in context, and it was necessary to identify the single natural and ordinary meaning which the words complained of would convey to the ordinary reasonable reader.[416] The extent of the inaccuracy informed the court's identification of the appropriate remedy for a breach of this principle.[417] It was permissible to link a claim of breach of the fourth principle to a defamation claim.[418]

---

407 *Google Spain SL v Agencia Espanola de Proteccion de Datos* [2014] QB 1022 at [93].

408 *Chief Constable of Humberside Police & ors v IC and SSHD* [2009] EWCA 1079, [2010] 1 WLR 1136 at [32]-[36], where it was held that police retention of convictions over 30 years' old served the registered purpose of supplying accurate records of convictions. cf *R (T) v The Commissioner of Police for the Metropolis* [2012] EWHC 1115 (Admin), [2012] 1 WLR 2978; *Woolley v Akram* 2017 SLT (Sc Ct) 175, 2017 SCLR 647.

409 *Townsend v Google Inc* [2017] NIQB 81 at [63].

410 See also Art 12(b).

411 DPA 1998 s 70(2).

412 *Lyons v Chief Constable of Strathclyde* [2012] CSOH 45, 2012 Rep LR 108 at [57] (no breach where police disclosed letter received from a third party without endorsing its contents).

413 *R (Hussain) v Sandwell MBC* [2017] EWHC 1641 (Admin), [2018] PTSR 142 at [238]. Like most of the treatment of the DPA 1998 in this judgment, this is questionable. The better analysis is that although it breached the principle, the correct remedy was not destruction or erasure, but annotation.

414 *Smeaton v Equifax plc* [2013] EWCA Civ 108, [2013] 2 All ER 959 at [44], [80]-[81]. cf the court at first instance: *Smeaton v Equifax plc* [2012] EWHC 2322 (QB), [2012] 4 All ER 460 at [106], [113]-[125].

415 *Grace v Black Horse Ltd* [2014] EWCA Civ 1413, [2015] 3 All ER 233 at [37]-[44].

416 *NT1 v Google LLC* [2018] EWHC 799 (QB), [2018] 3 All ER 581 at [80]-[82], [93]-[94].

417 *NT1 v Google LLC* [2018] EWHC 799 (QB), [2018] 3 All ER 581 at [191], [223]-[228].

418 *Prince Moulay Hicham Ben Abdullah Al Alaoui of Morocco v Elaph Publishing Ltd* [2017] EWCA Civ 29, [2017] 4 WLR 28.

5–047 DPP5: duration

The fifth data protection principle provided:

> Personal data processed for any purpose or purposes shall not be kept for longer than is necessary for that purpose or those purposes.

The fifth data protection principle represented the domestic implementation of Art 6.1(e) of the Directive. Where the purpose of processing was to maintain a complete record or register of certain matters, eg of convictions or of memberships, the fifth principle would not be contravened.[419]

5–048 DPP6: compliant

The sixth data protection principle provided:

> Personal data shall be processed in accordance with the rights of data subjects under this Act.

The sixth data protection principle represented the domestic implementation of Art 22 of the Directive.[420] Paragraph 8 of Part 2 of Schedule 1 to the DPA 1998 explained that this principle would only be contravened where there had been non-compliance with one of the duties that resulted from service of a notice by the data subject.[421]

5–049 DPP7: security

The seventh data protection principle provided:

> Appropriate technical and organisational measures shall be taken against unauthorised or unlawful processing of personal data and against accidental loss or destruction of, or damage to, personal data.

The seventh data protection principle represented the domestic implementation of Arts 17.1 and 17.2 of the Directive.[422] Paragraphs 9-12 of Part 2 of Schedule 1 to the DPA 1998 fleshed out what the seventh principle required. The seventh data protection principle did not impose an absolute duty to prevent misuse of data.[423] What was 'appropriate' took its measure from contemporaneous technical norms, the cost of implementation, the nature of the data to be protected and the likelihood of unauthorised or unlawful processing of that data.[424] Breaches of this principle could arise from lack of secure systems, lack of precautions or internal checks and so forth.[425]

5–050 DPP8: transfers

The eighth data protection principle provided:

> Personal data shall not be transferred to a country or territory outside the European Economic Area unless that country or territory ensures an adequate level of protection for the rights and freedoms of data subjects in relation to the processing of personal data.

The eighth data protection principle represented the domestic implementation of Arts 25-26

---

[419] *Chief Constable of Humberside Police & ors v IC and SSHD* [2009] EWCA 1079, [2010] 1 WLR 1136 at [98]; *Johnson v Medical Defence Union (No 2)* [2006] EWHC (Ch) 321, (2006) 89 BMLR 43 at [204]-[206].

[420] See also Recitals (20) and (55).

[421] ie under s 7, 10, 11, 12 or 12A of the DPA 1998.

[422] See also Recitals (25) and (46).

[423] *CLG v Chief Constable of Merseyside Police* [2015] EWCA Civ 836 at [46].

[424] *College van burgemeester en wethouders van Rotterdam v Rijkeboer* (C-553/07) [2009] 3 CMLR 28 at [62]; *Tietosuojavaltuutettu v Satakunnan Markkinaporssi Oy* (C-73/07) [2008] ECR I-9831, [2010] All ER (EC) 213 at [108]; *Worten - Equipamentos para o Lar SA v Autoridade para as Condicoes de Trabalho (ACT)* (C-342/12) [2013] ICR D29 at [24].

[425] *Various Claimants v Wm Morrisons Supermarket plc* [2017] EWHC 3113 (QB), [2018] 3 WLR 691 at [67]-[120]. Upheld on appeal: *Wm Morrisons Supermarket plc v Various Claimants* [2018] EWCA Civ 2339.

of the Directive.[426] Paragraphs 13-15 of Part 2 of Schedule 1 to the DPA 1998 gave detail of what was required and provided for exemptions – specifically where an otherwise proscribed transfer was necessary for reasons of substantial public interest or in connection with legal proceedings.[427] Transfer of personal data to a third country outside the EEA could take place only if the European Commission had, pursuant to Art 25(6) of the Directive, adopted a Decision finding that that third country ensured an 'adequate level of protection' by reason of its domestic law or its international commitments.[428]

15– 051 Remedies and enforcement

Breach of a data protection principle was actionable at the suit of the data subject. Jurisdiction was conferred on the High Court and the County Court to hear a claim, and on the Court or Session and the sheriff in Scotland.[429] Remedies for breach included compensation for damage and for distress, as well as coercive remedies of rectification, blocking, erasure and destruction order.[430] These are considered in detail in Chapter 49. In addition, the Information Commissioner, in her capacity as regulator, could take enforcement measures against a data controller for breach of the data protection principles. These are also considered in Chapter 49.

7. THE NOTICE-BASED RIGHTS AND RESULTANT DUTIES

15– 052 Introduction

In addition to giving a data subject the right to enforce the duty to comply with the data protection principles, the DPA 1998 gave the data subject four other rights. Where a data subject wished to exercise any of those four rights, the data subject had to serve a notice on the data controller, which then resulted in a specific duty on the data controller. The four rights were:

(1) A right to know what personal data the data controller was processing on the data subject and to obtain a copy of it - the so-called 'subject access right.'
(2) A right to require a data controller to cease processing personal data about the data subject on the ground that it was causing or would be likely to cause substantial and unwarranted damage or distress.
(3) A right to require a data controller to cease processing personal data about the data subject for the purposes of directing marketing of his or her personal data.
(4) A right to require a data controller to ensure that the controller took no decision significantly affecting the data subject that was based solely on the automatic processing of the data subject's personal data.

Each of these rights is considered below. Of these four rights, it was the first – the 'subject

---

426 See also Recitals (56)-(59).

427 Relied on in *Re Bernard L Madoff Investment Securities LLC* [2009] EWHC 442 (Ch), [2009] 2 BCLC 78.

428 The term 'adequate level of protection' required the third country to ensure, by reason of its domestic law or its international commitments, a level of protection of fundamental rights and freedoms which was essentially equivalent, although not necessarily identical, to that guaranteed under European Union law by virtue of Parliament and Council Directive 95/46/EC, read in the light of the Charter of Fundamental Rights of the European Union: *Schrems v Data Protection Commissioner* (C-362/14) [2016] QB 527, [2016] 2 CMLR 2 at [73]. In *Schrems* the CJEU ruled that a safe harbour decision of the Commission, applying to transfers to the USA, was invalid. On 12 July 2016 the Commission adopted the EU-US Privacy Shield Decision for the purposes of Art 25(6).

429 DPA 1998 s 15(1).

430 DPA 1998 ss 13-14.

access right' – that assumed greatest interest. The others attracted little attention.

5– 053 Subject access right

The subject access right was conferred by the DPA 1998 s 7(1). Although often characterised as solely a right to obtain a copy of the information held by the data controller relating to the data subject, there were four separate facets to the subject access right:

(1) A right to be informed by any data controller whether such data was being processed by or on behalf of the data controller.[431]

(2) If such data was being processed by or on behalf of the data controller, a right to be given by the data controller a description of the data, the purposes for which they are being or are to be processed, and the recipients or classes of recipients to whom they are or may be disclosed.[432]

(3) A right to have communicated in an intelligible form the information constituting the personal data and any information available to the data controller as to the source of those data.[433]

(4) Where such data were automatically processed in order to evaluate matters relating to the individual, such as the individual's work performance, creditworthiness, reliability or conduct, and such processing constituted or was likely to constitute the sole basis for any decision significantly affecting the individual, a right to be informed by the data controller of the logic involved in that decision-taking.[434]

The subject-access right implemented Art 12(a) of the Data Protection Directive.

5– 054 Relationship with FOIA

In passing freedom of information legislation, Parliament created exemptions so as to make the subject access right the sole means by which an individual could access information about him or herself.[435] However, because the DPA 1998 was restricted to information held by an automated system or in a file referable to the individual,[436] it was necessary to amend the DPA 1998 in order to make it apply to all manually stored data held by a public authority.[437] Although a single request for information made to a public authority could straddle any combination of these regimes, the statutory source of an applicant's right of access to information held by a public authority defined the scope of the right, the available exemptions and the applicant's right of appeal. In summary:

(1) In relation to personal data[438] that related to the applicant himself and no one else, the right of access to that information fell to be determined by the DPA 1998.[439]

---

431 DPA 1998 s 7(1)(a).

432 DPA 1998 s 7(1)(b).

433 DPA 1998 s 7(1)(c).

434 DPA 1998 s 7(1)(d).

435 FOIA s 40(1); FOI(S)A s 38(1)(a); EIR reg 13(1); EI(S)R reg 11(1).

436 That is, information forming part of a 'relevant filing system' as defined by DPA 1998 s 1(1) or in an 'accessible record' as defined by DPA 1998 s 68.

437 Thus, the FOIA ss 68-73 effected the following amendments to the DPA 1998: (1) the definition of 'data' was enlarged to include all recorded information held by a public authority; (2) 'held' was given the same meaning as in the FOIA; (3) 'public authority' was given the same meaning as in the FOIA; (4) a special provision, s 9A, was introduced to deal with unstructured personal data held by public authorities; (5) a limited ground of exemption, s 33A, was introduced to protect certain types of manual data held by a public authority; and (6) a further exemption, s 35A, was introduced to protect from disclosure where that was required to avoid an infringement of the privileges of either House of Parliament.

438 As to the meaning of which, see §§15– 020 to 15– 033.

439 If a request were made for this sort of information under the FOIA, the public authority would be entitled to refuse

Neither FOIA nor the EIR impinged upon the applicant's right of access to that information.[440]

(2) In relation to personal data that related both to the applicant and another individual, to the extent that the information could be disclosed without revealing the identity of that other individual or the individual has consented to disclosure or it would be reasonable not to secure that consent, the right of access to that information fell to be determined by the DPA 1998.[441] To the extent that these conditions could not be met, FOIA, or in respect of 'environmental information', the EIR, governed the applicant's right of access to that information.[442]

(3) In relation to personal data that related to an individual (other than the applicant), the applicant's right of access to that information fell to be determined by FOIA or, to the extent that that personal data was also 'environmental information',[443] by the EIR.[444] The Act and the Regulations each provided a specific exemption for certain sorts of personal data relating to an individual other than the applicant.[445] This exemption is considered in Chapter 33.

(4) In relation to information that was not personal data relating to an individual, the applicant's right of access fell to be determined by FOIA or, to the extent that that information was 'environmental information',[446] by the EIR.[447]

(5) Where the request for information is made by a corporate entity, its right of access fell to be determined by FOIA or, to the extent that 'environmental information'[448] was captured by the request, by the EIR 2004.[449] A corporate entity had no right of access to information under the DPA 1998. To the extent that the request captures information relating to an individual, the Act and the Regulations each provided a specific exemption for certain sorts of personal data.[450]

15–055 Access right: purpose

The principal purpose of the subject access right was to make known to an individual the use that was being made of his or her personal data so that that individual could make an informed decision as to what response, if any, he or she should take in relation to that use:

> The data subject's ability to make use of the safeguards given to him by ss 10-14 are dependent upon him knowing what personal data relating to him is controlled, and how it has been and will be processed or used, by the data controller. However, in the majority of

---

the request without any consideration of the public interest: see s 40 of that Act; FOI(S)A s 38.

440 FOIA s 40(1); EIR reg 5(3). See *Wise v Information Commissioner*, First-Tier Tribunal, 3 February 2010. Nor, in relation to a request for information made of a Scottish public authority, will the FOI(S)A or the EI(S)R impinge upon the applicant's right of access: FOI(S)A s 38(1)(a); EI(S)R reg 11(1).

441 DPA 1998 ss 7(4)-(6) and 8(7). See further §15–066.

442 FOIA s 40(1); EIR reg 5(3). Nor, in relation to a request for information made of a Scottish public authority, will the FOI(S)A or the EI(S)R impinge upon the applicant's right of access: FOI(S)A s 38(1)(a); EI(S)R reg 11(1).

443 As to the meaning of which, see §17–011.

444 Where the request for information is made to a Scottish public authority, it will fall to be determined by the FOI(S)A and the EI(S)R, respectively.

445 FOIA s 40(2)-(4); FOI(S)A s 38(1)(b), (2), (3); EIR regs 12(3), 13; EI(S)R reg 10(3), 11(2)-(5).

446 As to the meaning of which, see §17–011.

447 Where the request for information is made to a Scottish public authority, it will fall to be determined by the FOI(S)A and the EI(S)R, respectively.

448 As to the meaning of which, see §17–011.

449 Where the request for information is made to a Scottish public authority, it will fall to be determined by the FOI(S)A and the EI(S)R, respectively.

450 FOIA s 40(2)-(4); FOI(S)A s 38(1)(b), (2), (3); EIR regs 12(3), 13; EI(S)R reg 10(3), 11(2)-(5).

> cases the data subject will have little or no knowledge of these matters. He may not even know whether any personal data are held by the data controller. To overcome this, the DPA provides individuals with a mechanism by which they can find out what data, if any, are held by data controllers and, where such data are held, to what use they have been or will be put.[451]

This did not mean that a data subject could not legitimately use the subject access right for other purposes, in particular to obtain information or documents for use in other litigation against the data controller or against others.[452] A data subject could also legitimately make a subject access request for personal information that he or she already had: the true purpose of a subject access request was to ascertain what use the data controller was making or had made of that information.[453]

5–056 Access right: first facet

The first facet was straightforward. If personal data about the data subject was not being processed, the data controller simply informed the applicant of that fact, and the remaining rights were inapplicable. Typically, the first right would be satisfied by the data controller informing the data subject that the data controller held personal data relating to the data subject. The first right was analogous to the 'existence right' in FOIA.[454]

5–057 Access right: second facet

The second facet only arose where the data controller was processing personal data relating to the data subject. Where this was the case, the data subject had a right to be given by the data controller a description of the data, the purposes for which they were being or were to be processed, and the recipients or classes of recipients to whom they are or might be disclosed. As a necessary corollary to this right, information on the recipients or categories of recipient of data and on the content of data disclosed had to be stored for an appropriate period of time, in order that it could be provided when requested.[455] The DPA 1998 did not make clear the level of detail to which a data subject was entitled under the second facet. So far as the description of the data was concerned, the data subject's entitlement under the Data Protection Directive was to information as to 'the categories of data concerned'.[456] This indicated that the description of the data might be confined to a statement of the categories of data being processed, rather than anything more detailed. The data controller did not have to name the recipients of the data; he could simply describe the categories into which they fell. A recipient was anyone to whom the data was disclosed, including employees or agents of the data controller to whom they were disclosed in the course of processing.[457] However, someone to

---

451 *Johnson v Medical Defence Union Ltd* [2004] EWHC 2509 (Ch), [2005] 1 All ER 87 at [19]. Similarly, *YS v Minister voor Immigratie, Integratie en Asiel* (C-141/12) [2015] 1 WLR 609, [2015] 1 CMLR 18 at [44] where the CJEU explained that the purpose of the subject access right was to enable an individual to establish whether the personal data held by a data controller was correct and was being processed in a lawful manner. Exercise of that right could lead to the data subject obtaining remedies such as rectification, erasure or blocking of data.

452 *Dawson-Damer v Taylor Wessing LLP* [2017] EWCA Civ 74, [2017] 1 WLR 3255; *Ittihadieh v 5-11 Cheyne Gardens RTM Co Ltd* [2017] EWCA 121, [2018] QB 256 at [82]-[89].

453 *Ittihadieh v 5-11 Cheyne Gardens RTM Co Ltd* [2017] EWCA 121, [2018] QB 256 at [46].

454 FOIA s 1(1) (a), arising from the duty to confirm or deny.

455 C-553/07 *College van burgemeester en wethouders van Rotterdam v Rijkeboer* [2009] 3 CMLR 28, where the CJEU held that the appropriate period will depend on the period for which the 'basic data' (ie the personal information of or from which disclosure is made) is stored, tempered by the burden that storage places on the data controller (see [66]). The United Kingdom intervened in the *Rijkeboer* case, arguing that the right of access in Art 12(a) exists only in the present and not the past (see [37]). The CJEU rejected that proposition (see [53]-[54]).

456 Council Directive 95/46/EC Art 12(a).

457 DPA 1998 s 70(1).

whom the data was (or might have been) disclosed as a result of, or with a view to, a particular inquiry made in the exercise of a legal power was not classed as a recipient.[458] So an employer would have to include, for example, the category of payroll employees to whom an individual's personal data were disclosed, but not the Inland Revenue, if those data were disclosed pursuant to a specific inquiry.

15–058 Access right: third facet

The third facet invariably proved the most important for a data subject. It was the right of the data subject to have communicated in an intelligible form the information constituting the personal data and any information available to the data controller as to the source of those data. Unless it was impossible or would have involved disproportionate effort, compliance with the correlative duty required the data controller to provide the data subject with a copy of the information in permanent form.[459] The right to have the information relating to the data subject had been present in DPA 1984. It was the equivalent to the main right conferred by FOIA.[460] The right of the data subject also to be provided with any available information as to the source of the data was new to the 1998 Act and had no equivalent in FOIA. It was derived directly from the Data Protection Directive and adopted the same wording.[461] However, neither the Directive nor the DPA 1998 provided any indication as to the level of detail to be supplied, nor as to what information was to be classed as 'available'.[462] Data controllers were obliged only to provide such information as was available at the time of the request. Requests for information as to the source of personal data could involve information relating to other identifiable individuals, and as such was subject to the third-party disclosure provisions.[463]

15–059 Access right: fourth facet

The fourth facet only arose in limited cases. Where personal data relating to the data subject was automatically processed in order to evaluate matters relating to the individual, such as the individual's work performance, creditworthiness, reliability or conduct, and such processing constituted or was likely to constitute the sole basis for any decision significantly affecting the individual, the data subject had the right to be informed by the data controller of the logic involved in that decision-taking. This right, which was derived directly from the Data Protection Directive,[464] was linked to rights to object to such automated decisions being taken about oneself on important matters. It enabled the individual to inform himself or herself in order properly to exercise those rights.[465] The DPA 1998 did not define the term 'logic'. This right only applied to data processed automatically in order to evaluate matters relating to the individual such as conduct, reliability and the like. So, for example, a system that rejected job applicants under the age of 18 would not be caught, whereas an automated psychometric testing system would. The decision-taker was not required to provide information as to the

458 DPA 1998 s 70(1).

459 DPA 1998 s 8(2) and see *Ittihadieh v 5-11 Cheyne Gardens RTM Co Ltd* [2017] EWCA 121, [2018] QB 256 at [93].

460 FOIA s 1(1)(b).

461 Council Directive 95/46/EC Art 12(a).

462 It is to be narrowly construed. It does not include 'every hand through which the data have passed', such as secretarial or administrative personnel: *Johnson v Medical Defence Union* [2004] EWHC 347 (Ch) at [55].

463 DPA 1998 s 7(4), (5). See §15–066.

464 Council Directive 95/46/EC Art 12(a).

465 DPA 1998 s 12; Council Directive 95/46/EC Art 15.

logic involved in any decision-taking if the information constitutes a trade secret.[466] Again, 'trade secret' was not defined.[467]

15–060 Access right: formalities

Under the DPA 1998 a data controller was not obliged to supply any of the information identified above unless he had received a written request.[468] A request sent by electronic means, which was received in legible form and was capable of being used for subsequent reference, satisfied the requirement that the request be in writing.[469] A data controller could not request that a subject access request be made using a particular form.[470] What mattered was that the writing made clear that the recipient was being asked to comply with the statutory duty in section 7.[471] The breadth of the request was to be interpreted by the usual principles applied in construing written communications: it had to be read fairly and as a whole.[472] Generally a request sent to a director of a company was, unless clearly stated to be directed to the director in his or her personal capacity, treated as being a request to the company.[473] The DPA 1998 expressly allowed an individual in prescribed cases to limit his request to personal data of any prescribed description.[474] A request in relation to one of the first three rights was deemed to include a request in relation to the other two such rights.[475] However, the fourth right (information as to the logic involved in automated decision-taking) was treated separately. A general request was not deemed to include a request in respect of the fourth right unless it showed an express intention to that effect.[476] Similarly, a request in respect of the fourth right was not deemed to include a request in respect of the other rights unless it showed an express intention to that effect.[477]

15–061 Particularising a request

Under the DPA 1998 a data controller could ask for further information from a person making a subject access request in certain circumstances, and was not obliged to comply with the request unless he was supplied with that further information.[478] The further information had to be reasonably required by the data controller to enable him to satisfy himself as to the identity of the person making the request and to locate the information sought, and the data

---

466 DPA 1998 s 8(5).

467 As to its meaning under the FOIA, see §§34–049 to 34–054.

468 DPA 1998 s 7(2)(a). Query whether the obligation to submit a written request is a 'constraint' contrary to Art 12(a) of the Data Protection Directive.

469 DPA 1998 s 64. Unless the contrary intention appears, 'writing' includes other modes of representing or reproducing words in a visible form: see the Interpretation Act 1978 s 5. This covered communications by email or social media: *Ittihadieh v 5-11 Cheyne Gardens RTM Co Ltd* [2017] EWCA 121, [2018] QB 256 at [79]-[80].

470 Information Commissioner, *Subject access code of practice*, August 2013, p 9.

471 *Ittihadieh v 5-11 Cheyne Gardens RTM Co Ltd* [2017] EWCA 121, [2018] QB 256 at [80].

472 *Ittihadieh v 5-11 Cheyne Gardens RTM Co Ltd* [2017] EWCA 121, [2018] QB 256 at [80]. The Data Protection (Subject Access) (Fees and Miscellaneous Provisions) Regulations 2000 Art 2(1) provided that a request under any provision of DPA 1998 s 7(1)(a), (b) or (c) was to be treated as extending also to information under all the other provisions of s 7(1)(a), (b) and (c). This was generally observed in the breach, with data controllers simply providing a copy of the information held by them of which the requester was the data subject. Few data subjects appear to have complained about this.

473 See *Ittihadieh v 5-11 Cheyne Gardens RTM Co Ltd* [2017] EWCA 121, [2018] QB 256.

474 DPA 1998 s 7(7).

475 DP (Fees) Regs reg 2(1).

476 DP (Fees) Regs reg 2(2).

477 DP (Fees) Regs reg 2(3).

478 DPA 1998 s 7(3).

controller had to inform the individual of this requirement.[479]

15– 062 Unstructured personal data

'Unstructured personal data' was defined to mean:

> any personal data falling within paragraph (e) of the definition of "data" in section 1(1), other than information which is recorded as part of, or with the intention that it should form part of, any set of information relating to individuals to the extent that the set is structured by reference to individuals or by reference to criteria relating to individuals.[480]

As noted above,[481] the fifth class of data had been introduced into the DPA 1998 by FOIA. It expanded the subject access right conferred by the DPA to give it equivalence (in relation to information held by a public authority) with the right of access conferred by FOIA. The amendment of the definition was principally a measure related to freedom of information, rather than to data protection. This was reflected in the expanded right under the DPA 1998 being given only in relation to data held by a public authority.[482] Information falling within the fifth data class was not conventionally within the grasp of data protection legislation. Because information in paragraph (e) fell outside the first four data classes, there was less scope for such information to impinge upon a data subject's privacy. Some information falling within paragraph (e) of the definition of 'data' did not constitute 'unstructured personal data', namely information that formed part of a set of information structured by reference to individuals or by reference to criteria relating to individuals. This brought in such information even though the set was structured in such a way that specific information relating to a particular individual was readily accessible.[483] This was illustrated by the examples given in the explanatory notes to FOIA (which implemented this provision).[484] While incidental personal information on a policy file or in loose papers would amount to unstructured personal data, a case file about an individual containing correspondence about a number of matters relating to that individual and indexed by reference only to correspondence dates would be structured personal data for these purposes.

15– 063 Public authority extension

To the extent that the subject access request related to unstructured personal data, a public authority was not obliged to comply with the request unless it contained a description of the data.[485] The authority was therefore allowed to look to the data subject for help in identifying the data. Secondly, if the authority estimated that the cost of complying with the request so far as it related to the unstructured personal data would exceed the relevant prescribed limit, it was not obliged to comply with it.[486] However, the public authority's obligation to comply with the first access related right, ie to inform the individual whether unstructured personal data in respect of which the applicant is the data subject are being processed by or on behalf of the data

---

479 DPA 1998 s 7(3). Information Commissioner, *Subject access code of practice*, August 2013, p 23.

480 DPA 1998 s 9A(1). As to paragraph (e), see §15– 018.

481 §§15– 009 and 15– 018.

482 It is also reflected in DPA 1998 s 33A.

483 DPA 1998 s 9A(1).

484 Explanatory Notes 215 and 216.

485 DPA 1998 s 9A(2).

486 DPA 1998 s 9A(3). The limit is prescribed by the Secretary of State for Justice by regulations and he may prescribe different amounts in relation to different cases: s 9A(5). The Fees Regs 2004 prescribe a limit of £600 for public authorities listed in Pt I of Sch 1 to the FOIA and a limit of £450 in the case of any other public authority. In relation to fees, see §§22– 012 to 22– 019.

controller,[487] also had to be considered separately. Only if the estimated cost of complying with that obligation alone would have exceeded the appropriate limit was the public authority relieved of the requirement of doing so.[488] When estimating the cost of compliance with the request, the public authority had to comply with regulations made under FOIA.[489] In making its estimate, the public authority could only take account of costs it reasonably expects to incur in determining whether it holds the information, locating the information (or a document that may contain it), or retrieving the information (or such a document and extracting the information from it).[490]

5–064 Access request: fees

The general position under the DPA 1998 was that a data controller was not obliged to comply with a subject access request unless he had received such fee as he might require, provided that the fee did not exceed the maximum prescribed by the Secretary of State for Justice.[491] The Secretary of State for Justice also had the power to prescribe cases in which no fee is payable.[492] In most cases the normal maximum subject access fee prescribed was £10, except in the case of certain educational and health records.[493] The data controller had to require the fee: neither payment of a fee nor an inquiry by the data subject of the data controller about what (if any) fee was required was a pre-condition of the making of a valid subject access request.[494] If payment was not received with a subject access request, the data controller was required to contact the requester seeking payment.[495] In the case of educational records, no fee could be charged, unless a permanent copy of the information is to be provided, in which case the maximum fee varied from £1 to £50, according to the type and number of the copies in question.[496] In the case of health records, the maximum that could be charged for a copy of a non-automated record was £50. Where the request was restricted solely to data forming part of a health record that had been created, at least in part, within the 40 days preceding the request, no fee could be charged, provided that no permanent copy of the information was to be supplied.[497] Requests could be specifically limited to conform to these circumstances.[498] Where the request related to unstructured personal data held by a public authority, it was not required to comply with the request if it estimated that the cost of doing so would exceed either £450 or £600.[499]

5–065 Third party information

As noted above, to the extent that a request for information captured personal information

---

487 See §15–056.

488 DPA 1998 s 9A(4).

489 DPA 1998 s 9A(6), FOIA s 12(5). The relevant regulations are the Fees Regs 2004. See further §22–016.

490 Fees Regs 2004 reg 4.

491 DPA 1998 s 7(2)(b), (10). The fee is set by the DP (Fees) Regs reg 3.

492 DPA 1998 s 7(2)(b), (10).

493 For the definition of educational and health records, see §15–016.

494 *Ittihadieh v 5-11 Cheyne Gardens RTM Co Ltd* [2017] EWCA 121, [2018] QB 256 at [79].

495 Information Commissioner, *Subject access code of practice*, August 2013, p 17.

496 DP (Fees) Regs reg 5 and schedule.

497 DP (Fees) Regs reg 6.

498 DP (Fees) Regs reg 6.

499 Effectively, this puts a request for unstructured personal data on the same basis as a request for information under FOIA. The reasoning for this is that a request for unstructured personal data, though handled through the DPA 1998, is outside the scope of the Directive.

about a third party, the applicant's right of access to that information was governed by FOIA and not by the DPA 1998. In broad terms, the provisions of FOIA were designed to ensure that such information was only provided under that Act if it could have been disclosed under the DPA 1998 both to the data subject and to the person making the request. Thus, information was exempt from disclosure under FOIA if:

(a) disclosure to a member of the public would have breached any of the data protection principles;[500]

(b) in the case of most types of personal data[501] disclosure would have contravened the individual's right under s 10 of the DPA 1998 to prevent processing likely to cause damage or distress;[502] or

(c) the information was exempt from the subject access rights of the DPA 1998.[503]

In Scotland, there were also exemptions under FOI(S)A in respect of personal census information and a deceased person's health record.[504]

15– 066 Mixed personal information

The right conferred by s 7(1)(c) was a right to have communicated in an intelligible form the information constituting the personal data and any information available to the data controller as to the source of those data. As just noted, once a proper request had been received, and if there was no applicable exemption, the data controller ordinarily had to provide the data subject with all the data held by the data controller relating to the data subject. Where a data controller could not comply with a subject access request without disclosing information relating to another individual[505] who could be identified from that information, the data controller was not obliged to comply with the request unless that other individual had consented to the disclosure or it was reasonable in all the circumstances for him to have complied with the request without such consent.[506] Another individual could be identified from the information being disclosed if he could be identified from that information alone, or from that disclosed information in conjunction with any other information that, in the reasonable belief of the data controller, was likely to be in, or to come into, the possession of the data subject making the request.[507] On its own, s 7(4) had the potential to defeat the subject access rights of many data subjects according to whether or not information relating to them also happened to relate to another person. To overcome this, s 7(5) provided that s 7(4):

> is not to be construed as excusing a data controller from communicating so much of the information sought by the request as can be communicated without disclosing the identity of the other individual concerned, whether by the omission of names or other identifying particulars or otherwise.

In relation to the data that disclosed the identity of the other individual concerned, the Court of Appeal emphasised that the data controller is only required to carry out that balancing act if the information about the third party was necessarily part of the data subject's personal data; otherwise the third-party information should simply be redacted.[508] The DPA 1998 specified

---

500 FOIA s 40(2), (3)(a)(i), (3)(b); FOI(S)A s 38(1)(b), (2)(a)(i), (2)(b).

501 As to which see §§15– 020 to 15– 023.

502 FOIA s 40(3)(b); FOI(S)A s 38(2)(b).

503 FOIA s 40(4); FOI(S)A s 38(3).

504 FOI(S)A s 38(1)(c), (d).

505 This includes information identifying an individual as the source of the information sought by the request: DPA 1998 s 7(5).

506 DPA 1998 s 7(4).

507 DPA 1998 s 8(7).

508 *Durant v Financial Services Authority* [2003] EWCA Civ 1746, [2004] FSR 28 at [64]-[66].

a number of factors to be taken into account in determining whether it was reasonable to comply with the request without such consent.[509] In a mixed-data case there was no presumption, or even starting point, that the information relating to the third party should not be disclosed without consent; the rights of the data subject and of the third party were of equal presumptive value, with neither having priority.[510] It was no objection in a mixed-data case that the data subject intended to use the data in litigation against the third party.[511]

15– 067 Access request: time limit

A data controller was required to comply with a subject access request promptly and in any event within a prescribed period (40 days)[512] from the day on which he received the request or, if later, the day on which he had both the required fee and any further information required by him pursuant to s 7(3).[513]

15– 068 Temporal standpoint

Under the DPA 1998, the information supplied pursuant to a subject access request had to be supplied by reference to the data in question at the time when the request had been received, except that it could take account of any subsequent amendment or deletion provided that amendment or deletion would have been made regardless of the receipt of the request.[514] This meant that data controllers could carry on with their routine processing despite the receipt of a subject access request. What they could not do was make special deletions or amendments in response to the request. The Information Commissioner advised that it would be reasonable for a data controller to supply a requester with the information it held when it sent out the response, even if that was different from the information held at the time that the request had been received.[515]

15– 069 Copy of the information

Specific requirements were imposed by the DPA 1998 as to the manner of compliance for certain of the access-related rights. In particular, in order to comply with the obligation to communicate to the data subject in an intelligible form the information constituting any personal data of which he was the subject, the data controller had to supply the data subject with a copy of the information in permanent form, unless that would be impossible or would involve disproportionate effort or the data subject agreed otherwise.[516] A copy of the information in permanent form covered a photocopy, printout or video recording. If any of the information was expressed in terms that are not intelligible without explanation, the copy had to be accompanied by an explanation of those terms.[517] The data controller was also under

[509] DPA 1998 s 7(6).

[510] *B v General Medical Council* [2018] EWCA Civ 1497.

[511] *B v General Medical Council* [2018] EWCA Civ 1497.

[512] DPA 1998 s 7(10). In relation to subject access requests wholly or partly relating to personal data forming part of an accessible record which is an educational record within the meaning of Sch 11 to the Act, a period of 15 school days is allowed: DP (Fees) Regs reg 5(4).

[513] DPA 1998 s 7(8), (10).

[514] DPA 1998 s 8(6). In relation to the possibility of making a request for future information, see §20– 011.

[515] Information Commissioner, *Subject access code of practice*, August 2013, p 27.

[516] DPA 1998 ss 7(1)(c)(i), 8(2). *Ezsias v Welsh Ministers* [2007] EWHC B15 (QB) at [95]-[97]. The Information Commissioner takes the view that the data controller may elect not to provide a copy of the information but instead provide the information 'in the form of transcripts of relevant documents...or by providing a print-out of the relevant information from your computer systems": Information Commissioner, *Subject access code of practice*, August 2013, p 35.

[517] DPA 1998 s 8(2).

an obligation to disclose sources of information.[518] There was no obligation to maintain records of such sources, only to supply them if they were available in recorded form.[519] If the data controller held no information answering the terms of the subject access request, the data controller had to so advise the requester.[520]

15– 070 Use of the information

The DPA 1998 imposed no restriction on the use that might be made of information supplied to a data subject pursuant to a subject access request.[521] There was nothing to stop the data subject from using the information supplied in support of proceedings, whether civil, criminal or administrative, against the organisation supplying the information or any other organisation. Nor did the DPA 1998 prevent a data subject from volunteering the information received under a subject access request to a third party. Although in the earlier cases the courts took the view that the underlying purpose of s 7 was not to assist a data subject, for example, to obtain discovery of documents that might assist him in litigation or complaints against third parties,[522] this view did not prevail. The position reached was that there was no rule that a data subject could not use a subject access request to obtain information for use in litigation against the data controller or others.[523]

15– 071 Repeat requests

Where a data controller had previously complied with a subject access request, it was not obliged to comply with a subsequent identical or similar request made by the same individual unless a reasonable interval had elapsed between compliance with the previous request and the making of the later request.[524] This 'reasonable interval' limitation reflected the wording of the Data Protection Directive.[525] In determining whether a reasonable interval had elapsed, regard had to be had to the nature of the data, the purpose for which they were being processed and the frequency with which they were altered.[526]

15– 072 Cost of compliance

The principle of proportionality – a general principle of EU law – applied to all stages of the analysis of a subject access request.[527] In so far as a subject access request related to unstructured personal data,[528] the public authority was not obliged to comply with it if it

---

518 DPA 1998 s 7(1)(c)(ii). The entitlement was to a copy of the information, and not to a copy of the entire document in which the information was recorded: *B v General Medical Council* [2018] EWCA Civ 1497 at [93].

519 *Ezsias v Welsh Ministers* [2007] EWHC B15 (QB) at [77]-[78]. See also Council Directive 95/46/EC Art 12(a), which specifies that 'any available information' as to the source of the data has to be provided.

520 Information Commissioner, *Subject access code of practice*, August 2013, p 34.

521 As to the ability of a data controller to impose such a condition, see §6– 027.

522 *Durant v Financial Services Authority* [2003] EWCA Civ 1746, [2004] FSR 28 at [27]. So far as a claim by the data subject that the data controller had breached its duty under DPA 1998 s 4(4), this is plainly wrong: the central object of the subject access right was to enable the data subject to know what processing of his or her personal data was being carried out by the data controller and, on the basis of that knowledge, decide whether or not to commence proceedings for breach of the s 4(4) duty and frame the claim and the relief sought.

523 *Dawson-Damer v Taylor Wessing LLP* [2017] EWCA Civ 74, [2017] 1 WLR 3255; *Valsts policijas Rīgas reģiona pārvaldes Kārtības policijas pārvalde v Rīgas pašvaldības SIA* (Case C-13/16) [2017] 4 WLR 97, [2017] 3 CMLR 39; *Ittihadieh v 5-11 Cheyne Gardens RTM Co Ltd* [2017] EWCA 121, [2018] QB 256 at [82]-[89].

524 DPA 1998 s 8(3).

525 Directive 95/46/EC Art 12(a). There is a corresponding provision in the FOIA s 14(2); FOI(S)A s 14(2).

526 DPA 1998 s 8(4). Information Commissioner, *Subject access code of practice*, August 2013, p 38.

527 *Dawson-Damer v Taylor Wessing LLP* [2017] EWCA Civ 74, [2017] 1 WLR 3255 at [76].

528 As to the meaning of 'unstructured personal data', see §15– 062.

estimated that the cost of doing so would exceed the relevant prescribed limit.[529] In this context, the public authority's obligation to comply with the first access related right, ie to inform the individual whether unstructured personal data in respect of which he or she is the data subject are being processed by or on behalf of the data controller, had to be considered separately. Only if the estimated cost of complying with that obligation alone would have exceeded the appropriate limit was the public authority relieved of the requirement of doing so.[530] When estimating the cost of compliance with the request, the public authority had to comply with regulations made under FOIA.[531] In making its estimate, the public authority could only take account of costs it reasonably expected to incur in: determining whether it held the information, locating the information or a document that might contain it, retrieving the information or such a document and extracting the information from such a document.[532]

15–073 Remedies and civil enforcement

A failure by a data controller to comply with the duty resulting from a data subject serving one of the above notices constituted a breach of the sixth data protection principle and, as such, actionable at the suit of the data subject. In addition to the remedies generally available for breach of the data protection principles – compensation for damage and for distress, as well as coercive remedies of rectification, blocking, erasure and destruction order[533] – the DPA 1998 conferred on the courts power to make orders specific to the notices:

— compelling an answer to a subject access request;[534]
— compelling compliance with a notice under s 10 to prevent processing likely to cause distress or damage;[535]
— compelling compliance with a notice under s 11 to prevent processing for the purposes of direct marketing;[536]
— compelling compliance with a notice under s 12 requiring the person to reconsider the automatically made decision;[537]
— compelling compliance with a notice under s 12A to destroy etc manual data.[538]

Jurisdiction was conferred on the High Court and the County Court to hear a claim, and on the Court or Session and the sheriff in Scotland.[539] With one exception, the task of the court was to determine the rights of the parties to reach what was the right decision based on the evidence before it – it was not confined to a consideration of the correctness of the data controller's decision-making methodology. The exception was where the data controller had refused a subject access request in a mixed data case: here alone the court's role was one of supervisory review (rather than taking the decision afresh), since the data was exercising a

529 DPA 1998 s 9A(3). The limit was prescribed by the Secretary of State for Justice by regulations and he could prescribe different amounts in relation to different cases: s 9A(5). The Fees Regs 2004 prescribe a limit of £600 for public authorities listed in Pt I of Sch 1 to the FOIA and a limit of £450 in the case of any other public authority. There is a parallel provision in the FOIA s 13(1); FOI(S)A s 12. In relation to fees, see §22–016.

530 DPA 1998 s 9A(4).

531 DPA 1998 s 9A(6), FOIA s 12(5). See the Fees Regs 2004.

532 Fees Regs 2004 reg 4. For a case where the cost limit would have been exceeded and the public authority would have been entitled to refuse to comply with the request, see *Roberts v IC and DBIS*, FTT, 26 May 2010 at [40].

533 DPA 1998 ss 13-14.

534 DPA 1998 s 7(9).

535 DPA 1998 s 10(4).

536 DPA 1998 s 11(2).

537 DPA 1998 s 12(8).

538 DPA 1998 s 12A(3).

539 DPA 1998 s 15(1).

discretion and there could be room for reasonable people to disagree.[540] Although if a breach was established, a remedy would be expected to follow, given the role of proportionality running throughout the DPA, the significance of the matter to the data subject and the cost to the data controller of compliance could inform the relief granted by the courts.[541] Remedies are considered in detail in Chapter 49. In addition, the Information Commissioner, in her capacity as regulator, could take enforcement measures against a data controller for breach of the data protection principles. These are also considered in Chapter 49.

15–074 Notice to cease

Section 10 of the DPA 1998 conferred on every data subject two notice-based entitlements. First, an entitlement to send a notice to a data controller requiring the data controller within a reasonable period to cease, or not to begin, processing the data subject's personal data. Secondly, an entitlement to send a notice to a data controller to cease, or not to begin, processing the data subject's personal data for a specified purpose or in a specified manner.[542] Where the data subject exercised that entitlement but the data controller did not comply with the notice, the data subject could seek a court order compelling the data controller to comply.[543] This provision implemented in domestic law (with certain limitations[544]) Art 14(a) of the Data Protection Directive, which referred to a right to object to the processing of data on 'compelling legitimate grounds.' Parliament gave effect to Art 14(a) by introducing the requirements of 'substantial damage' and 'substantial distress,' with a view to setting a high threshold. If actual or likely substantial distress was made out, the Court had to go on to consider whether the substantial distress was unwarranted. This necessarily involved a balancing exercise[545] requiring a 'broad consideration of the competing rights at play.[546] Article 14(a) of the Directive was one of the provisions on which the CJEU based the 'right to be forgotten.'[547]

15–075 Cease notice procedure

Unlike a subject access request, the data subject, in giving a data controller a notice under s 10 of the DPA 1998, was obliged to specify upon what basis: (a) the processing of the data subject's personal data was causing or was likely to cause substantial damage or substantial distress to the data subject or to someone else; and (b) that damage or distress was or would be unwarranted.

> The whole point of requiring the person in the position of the claimant to specify reasons for his complaint is so that the data controller knows exactly what the complaint is and can respond to it within the 21-day period under s 10(3). There can then be a constructive

---

540 *B v General Medical Council* [2018] EWCA Civ 1497. The Court also considered whether in a mixed-data case the data controller or the court could make disclosure conditional upon undertakings limiting the use that the data subject could make of the data.

541 *Ittihadieh v 5-11 Cheyne Gardens RTM Co Ltd* [2017] EWCA 121, [2018] QB 256and [108]-[110].

542 This was in part fulfilment of the rights guaranteed by Articles 7 and 8 of the Charter: *Camera di Commercio, Industria, Artigianato e Agricoltura di Lecce v Manni* (C-398/15) [2018] Bus LR 25, [2017] 3 CMLR 18 at [40].

543 DPA 1998 s 10(4).

544 The wording of Art 14(a) of the Directive ("save where otherwise provided by national legislation"), and recital 45 ("whereas Member States may nevertheless lay down national provisions to the contrary"), make clear that national legislation can impose limitations on (or even exclude altogether) the right provided by Art 14(a).

545 *Townsend v Google Inc* [2017] NIQB 81 at [54]; *Camera di Commercio, Industria, Artigianato e Agricoltura di Lecce v Manni* (C-398/15) [2018] Bus LR 25, [2017] 3 CMLR 18 at [47]. The outcome of that balancing exercise can change over time – thus, for example, if a company has dissolved, the court could order that processing in the form of making the information available to third parties could be limited to those who could demonstrate a specific interest: *Camera di Commercio, Industria, Artigianato e Agricoltura di Lecce v Manni* (C-398/15) [2018] Bus LR 25, [2017] 3 CMLR 18 at [60]-[61].

546 *Townsend v Google Inc* [2017] NIQB 81 at [46].

547 *Google Spain SL v Agencia Espanola de Proteccion de Datos* (C-131/12) [2014] QB 1022.

discussion as to how the individual's concerns might be addressed and, if the parties cannot agree, the court may have to make an order under s 10(4).[548]

The data subject was required to demonstrate both (a) and (b) before the court would consider any relief.[549] There was a disapplication of the data subject's entitlement if any of the conditions in paragraphs 1 to 4 of Schedule 4 was met.[550] Even if both were demonstrated, relief under the section was in the court's discretion.[551] This discretion was exercised on all the available material.[552] There were few reported cases on the provision.[553]

5–076 Direct marketing notice

Section 11 of the DPA 1998 gave every individual an entitlement to serve a notice on a data controller requiring the data controller at the end of a reasonable period to cease, or not to begin, processing that person's personal data for the purposes of direct marketing.[554] The notice could be given at any time. Upon receipt of that notice, the data controller was under a resultant duty (unless an exemption applied) to cease the processing the person's personal data for direct marketing purposes. Where the data controller did not comply with the notice, the data subject could seek a court order compelling the data controller to comply, with the court being given a discretion as to what steps it ordered the controller to take in order to comply with the notice.[555] The section gave effect to Art 14(b) of the Directive. There was very little case law on the provision.[556]

5–077 Automated decision notice

Section 12 of the DPA gave every individual an entitlement to serve a notice on a data controller requiring the data controller to ensure that no decision taken by or on behalf of the data controller that significantly affected that individual was based solely on the processing by automatic means of that individual's personal data where it was for the purpose of evaluating matters relating to that individual – for example, credit worthiness. The individual could give the notice at any time. The provision resulted in no recorded case law. It may be that the reason for this was that where a notice had not been given but an automatic decision was made, the data controller had to inform the individual concerned and that individual could require the data controller to reconsider the decision.

---

548 *McGuffick v Royal Bank of Scotland plc* [2009] EWHC 2386 (Comm), [2010] 1 All ER 635 at [109].

549 *AB v A Chief Constable* [2014] EWHC 1965 (QB), [2014] IRLR 700 at [84].

550 DPA 1998 s 10(2). The disapplication was successfully relied upon in *Re Doran's Application for Judicial Review* [2017] NIQB 24.

551 *NT1 v Google LLC* [2018] EWHC 799 (QB), [2018] 3 All ER 581 at [85]-[86].

552 *AB v A Chief Constable* [2014] EWHC 1965 (QB), [2014] IRLR 700 at [84].

553 In *Mosley v Google Inc* [2015] EWHC 59 (QB), [2015] 2 CMLR 22 the court allowed a claim against a data search engine operator to proceed under DPA 1998 s 10 in which the data subject sought order requiring the removal from search results of links to photographs of the data subject. See also: *Law Society & ors v Kordowski* [2011] EWHC 3185 (QB), [2014] EMLR 2 at [76]-[92] (order made against data controller); *Al-Ko Kober Ltd v Sambhi (t/a Torquebars)* [2017] EWHC 2474 (QB) (order made against data controller).

554 'Direct marketing' was defined to mean the communication (by whatever means) of any advertising or marketing material which was directed to particular individuals: DPA 1998 s 11(3).

555 DPA 1998 s 11(2).

556 *Robertson v Wakefield DC and SSHD* [2001] EWHC Admin 915, [2002] LGR 286.

CHAPTER 16

DPA 1998: exemptions

1. INTRODUCTION

16–001 Introduction

Part IV (ss 27-39) of the DPA 1998 contained a series of exemptions. For the most part, each exemption was engaged by reference to the purpose for which personal data was processed, with or without a requirement of likely harm to a protected interest. The object of each exemption was to protect a particular use of personal data by lessening the restrictions that would otherwise attend that use. For most (but not all) of the exemptions, engagement did not disapply all of the duties and rights under the DPA 1998. Rather, engagement had the effect of disapplying one or more of the data protection principles (or a part of one data protection principle) and/or one or more of the rights conferred by ss 7, 10, 11 and 12. Central to an understanding of the exemptions were two definitions in DPA 1998 s 27:

— the 'subject information provisions'
— the 'non-disclosure provisions.'

These provided a shorthand method of listing the disapplied principles or parts of principles.

6– 002 Terminology

The 'subject information provisions' was defined to mean:

(a) the first data protection principle to the extent that it required compliance with paragraph 2 of Part II of Schedule 1 (a paragraph that deemed personal data not to have been processed fairly – and thus in breach of the first data protection principle – unless certain requirements were met); and

(b) section 7 (ie the subject access right).

The 'non-disclosure provisions' was defined to mean:

(a) the lawfulness and fairness requirements of the first data protection principle (in other words, compliance with the conditions in Schedules 2 and 3 remained);

(b) the second, third, fourth and fifth data protection principles;

(c) section 10 (ie the right to prevent processing likely to cause substantial damage or distress); and

(d) section 14(1)-(3) (ie the remedy of rectification, blocking, erasure and/or destruction of personal data, but leaving intact that remedy where it had caused damage to the data subject and there was a substantial risk of further contravention by the data controller).

2. THE MAIN EXEMPTIONS

6– 003 Introduction

Part IV of the DPA 1998 (ss 27-39) contained ten classes of processing that contained the main exemptions from the rights conferred and duties imposed by the Act:

- national security (s 28);
- crime and taxation (s 29);
- health, education and social work (s 30);
- regulatory activity (s 31);
- journalism, literature and art (s 32);
- research, history and statistics (s 33);
- information available to the public by or under enactment (s 34);
- disclosures required by law or made in connection with legal proceedings (s 35);
- parliamentary privilege (s 35A); and
- domestic purposes (s 36).

Most of the ten classes contained more than one exemption, some referable to the 'subject information provisions,' others to the 'non-disclosure provisions'[1] and others to one or more of the four rights conferred on a data subject.[2] In each case, the effect of the exemption was to allow the data controller a greater freedom to process personal data and, correspondingly, to reduce the data subject's right to limit the use by others of his or her personal information. Each of those adjustments to the extent to which an individual's personal information could be used by others reflected a recognition that the individual's legitimate interest in restricting that use was to be subordinated to another, higher interest served by that use of that information.

6– 004 National security

The Directive entitled Member States to adopt national measures restricting the rights and duties otherwise applicable to the processing of personal data where that was necessary to

---

[1] In relation to both terms, see §16– 002.

[2] That is, the four rights referred to at §§15– 053, 15– 074, 15– 076 and 15– 059.

safeguard national security.[3] The exception was to be interpreted strictly.[4] Section 28 of DPA 1998 provided a single, wide-ranging disapplication of the rights conferred and the duties imposed by the Act where that was 'required for the purpose of safeguarding national security.'[5] The phrase 'required for the purpose of safeguarding national security' was the same as that used in the national security exemption in FOIA, and in this work the meaning of the phrase is considered under the FOIA exemption.[6]

16– 005 Conclusive certificates

A claim for exemption on the grounds of safeguarding national security could be made the subject of a conclusive certificate signed by a Minister of the Crown.[7] A conclusive certificate stood as conclusive evidence of the 'fact' that exemption from the subject access rights was or at any time had been required for the purpose of safeguarding national security.[8] The certificate could identify the personal data to which it applies by means of a general description; it could also be expressed to have prospective effect.[9] The principal effect of a conclusive certificate was to change the right of appeal against a decision to refuse access from one of independent merit-review, in which the Upper Tribunal made a fresh decision unconstrained by the original decision, to one in which the Upper Tribunal merely determined whether the Minister was reasonable in his decision to issue a certificate.[10] If a data controller claimed that the terms of a conclusive certificate employing a general description applied to particular personal data, the certificate was presumed so to apply.[11] That presumption was itself capable of challenge by any party to proceedings before the Upper Tribunal, which could determine

---

3 Directive Arts 3.2 and 13.1(a). See also recitals (16) and (43).

4 *Buivids v Latvia* (C-345/17) [2019] 1 WLR 4225, [2019] 2 CMLR 24 at [41]; *Puškár v Finančné riaditeľstvo Slovenskej* (C-73/16) [2017] 4 WLR 209, [2018] 1 CMLR 44 at [38]; *Tietosuojavaltuutettu v Jehovan todistajat* (C-25/17), 10 July 2018 at [37].

5 The rights and duties disapplied by s 28(1) were: (a) the data protection principles; (b) all the provisions in Parts II (which included the rights conferred by ss 7, 10, 11 and 13, as well as the remedies provided for in ss 13 and 14), III and V of the Act; and (c) ss 54A and 55.

6 FOIA s 24 and FOI(S)A s 31(1). In relation to the meaning of the phrase, see §§26– 002 and 26– 047 to 26– 072. National security is a qualified exemption under the FOIA, so that it may be disengaged upon a consideration of the public interest. There is no such potential public interest override where the national security exemption is engaged under the DPA 1998.

7 DPA 1998 s 28(2). The only Ministers that may issue a certificate are those who are members of the Cabinet or the Attorney-General or the Advocate General for Scotland: DPA 1998 s 28(10).

8 A conclusive certificate could also be issued for purpose of defeating any of the other provisions of the DPA 1998 mentioned in s 28(1).

9 DPA 1998 s 28(3).

10 Appeals against non-certificated claims of exemption under the DPA 1998 are considered at §§49– 004 to 49– 014; appeals against certificated exemptions under the DPA 1998 are considered at §§49– 016 to 49– 017. In *Norman Baker MP v SSHD* [2001] UKHRR 1275 the Data Protection Tribunal (as the Tribunal was then known) held that a national security exemption certificate applying effectively a blanket exemption to files held by MI5 was unreasonably wide. A revised form of the certificate was considered by the High Court in *Re Ewing* [2002] EWHC 3169 (QB), where it was held that the criticisms of the Information Tribunal had been addressed: '...a general [neither confirm nor deny] policy, in response to requests for personal data, including as to the existence (or non-existence) of personal data, is in principle justifiable and cannot be criticised as unreasonable or unnecessary' (at [60]). The Information Tribunal expressed the view in *Hitchens v SSHD*, IT, 4 August 2003 at [49] and *Gosling v SSHD*, IT, 1 August 2003 at [56] that the Investigatory Powers Tribunal established pursuant to the Regulation of Investigatory Powers Act 2000 had power to consider whether the Security Services were justified in claiming that a neither confirm nor deny policy was necessary in a particular case and, for this reason, found that the revised form of national security exemption certificate issued in those two cases had been issued on reasonable grounds. *Gosling* was followed in *Stevenson v SSHD*, IT, 30 April 2009. See also *Nasresfahani v SSHD and Data Controller* [2014] UKUT 0487 (AAC) at [21] and *Hilton v FCO*, IT, 28 June 2005, which applied the same reasoning in relation to GCHQ.

11 DPA 1998 s 28(6).

that the certificate did not apply to the personal data in question.[12] The Information Commissioner also had a role to play in relation to national security exemptions, as he had to determine whether an exemption under section 28 of the Act has been properly claimed.[13] In any case where s 28 was relied upon (either through the issue of a certificate or otherwise), the Information Commissioner was entitled to satisfy himself that the requested material was indeed exempt, and in so doing he was entitled to request to see the material. If refused, the Commissioner could serve a notice under s 43 of the Act requiring the data controller to furnish him with the requested material.

6– 006 Crime and tax

The Directive entitled Member States to adopt national measures restricting the rights and duties otherwise applicable to the processing of personal data where that was necessary to safeguard the prevention, investigation, detection and prosecution of criminal offences; and the Directive was stated not to apply to 'the activities of the State in areas of criminal law.'[14] Section 29 of the DPA 1998 provided four related exemptions covering processing that was for the purposes of:

(a) the prevention or detection of crime;[15]
(b) the apprehension or prosecution of offenders; or
(c) the assessment or collection or any tax or duty or of any imposition of a similar nature

('the crime and tax collection purposes').[16]

6– 007 Crime and tax exemption

As to the reach of the four exemptions:

(1) Where personal data was being processed for any of the crime and tax collection purposes, DPA 1998 s 29(1) exempted that personal data from:
   – the first data protection principle (except to the extent that it required compliance with the conditions in Schedules 2 and 3), and
   – section 7,

---

12 DPA 1998 s 28(6).

13 DPA 1998 s 51, construed in light of Articles 13 and 28 of the Directive. See *R (SSHD) v Information Tribunal* [2006] EWHC 2958 (Admin), [2007] 2 All ER 703, where the Court upheld a decision by the Information Tribunal to quash a national security certificate which was made on the basis that the IC had no statutory role within the context of s 28 exemptions.

14 Directive Arts 3.2 and 13.1(d). See also recitals (13), (16) and (43).

15 'The proper definition of the word "crime" is an offence for which the law awards punishment': *Mann v Owen* (1829) 9 B & C 595 at 602, per Littledale J. See also: *Treacy v DPP* [1971] AC 537 at 560C-D per Lord Diplock; Sir J.F. Stephen defined a crime as 'an act or omission in respect of which legal punishment may be inflicted on the person who is in default either by acting or omitting to act': *History of the Criminal Law of England* (1883), vol 1, p 1. In *Re Martin* [2002] NIQB 67 the High Court in Northern Ireland held that information held by the Health & Social Services Trust obtained by it when investigating allegations of sexual abuse by the applicant represented data processed for the purposes of the prevention or detection of crime. In *R (A) v Chief Constable of C* [2001] 1 WLR 461, [2001] 2 FCR 431 it was held that non-conviction information following a police vetting enquiry in respect of the applicant's application for the post of head-teacher represented data processed for the prevention and detection of crime. See also *Chief Constable of Humberside Police & ors v IC and SSHD* [2009] EWCA 1079 and *R (AB) Chief Constable of Hampshire Constabulary* [2015] EWHC 1238 (Admin), [2015] 1 WLR 5250 in relation to the retention of old criminal convictions on the police national computer.

16 DPA 1998 s 29(1). Equivalent provisions are found in the FOIA s 31(1)(a), (b) and (d), and in the FOI(S)A s 35. These are considered in detail at §29– 014ff. Law enforcement is a qualified exemption under the FOIA, so that it may be disengaged upon a consideration of the public interest. There is no such potential public interest override where the law enforcement exemption is engaged under the DPA 1998.

to the extent that their application would be likely to prejudice[17] any of the crime and tax collection purposes.

(2) Where personal data was processed for the purpose of discharging statutory functions and it consisted of information obtained for that purpose from a person who had it in his possession for any of the crime and tax collection purposes, DPA 1998 s 29(2) exempted that personal data from the subject information provisions[18] to the extent to which the application of the subject information provisions to that information would be likely to prejudice any of the crime and tax collection purposes.

(3) Where disclosure of personal data was for any of the crime and tax collection purposes and the application of the non-disclosure provisions would be likely to prejudice any of the crime and tax collection purposes, DPA 1998 s 29(3) exempted that personal data from the non-disclosure provisions.[19]

(4) Where the data controller was a government department or a local authority (or any other authority administering housing benefit or council tax benefit)[20] ('the administering authority'), to the extent that that personal data:

(a) consisted of a classification applied to the data subject as part of a risk assessment operated by the administering authority either for the purpose of assessing or collecting any tax or the like or for the prevention or detection of crime or prosecution of offenders, where the offence involved any unlawful claim for payment out of public funds;[21] and

(b) was processed for any of the purposes in (a),

then DPA 1998 s 29(4) exempted that personal data from the subject access right (s 7) to the extent that that exemption was required in the interests of the operation of the classification system.

16–008 Health information

The Directive required Member States to prohibit the processing of personal data concerning health, but then carved out of that requirement processing for certain purposes.[22] The DPA 1998 met the restrictive requirements of the Directive by including information as to a person's physical or mental health within the definition of 'sensitive personal data.'[23] Although not required by the Directive to do so, in relation to an individual accessing his or her own medical records the DPA 1998 generally favoured the individual's right over processing controls. So as to facilitate an individual's right to gain access to information relating to his or her own health, certain health records were specifically brought within the definition of an 'accessible record'.[24] The DPA 1998 did not itself provide any exemption from the subject access right

17 As to the meaning of 'would be likely to prejudice', see §§6–020 to 6–028.

18 As to the meaning of the 'subject information provisions' see §16–002.

19 As to the meaning of 'non-disclosure provisions' see §16–002.

20 See DPA 1998 s 29(5) definition of 'relevant authority.'

21 'Public funds' was defined to include funds provided by any EU institution: DPA 1998 s 29(5). 'EU institution' means any institution of the European Union: see the European Communities Act 1972, Sch 1, Pt II, as applied by the Interpretation Act 1978, s 5, Sch 1.

22 Article 8. See also recitals (33), (34) and (42).

23 DPA 1998 s 2(e), with the effect that any processing had to satisfy one of the conditions in Schedule 3, unless that processing was exempted.

24 DPA 1998 s 68. Information Commissioner, *Subject access code of practice*, August 2013, p 48.

for information relating to the health of a person.[25] Section 30 of the Act did, however, empower the Secretary of State to exempt or modify the subject access rights in relation to personal data consisting of information as to the physical or mental health of the data subject.[26] The Secretary of State made an order[27] under this power.

16–009 Health exemptions

The order defined three circumstances in which information as to the physical or mental health of the data subject would be exempt from the subject access rights:

(1) Where the information was held by a court and it consisted of information supplied to it in a report or other evidence given by certain bodies or individuals.[28]

(2) Where application of the rights would be likely[29] to cause serious harm to the physical or mental health or condition of the data subject or any other person.[30] Where the data controller was not a health professional, the controller had to consult (or to have consulted) the appropriate health professional before withholding information on this ground.[31] However, the obligation to consult did not arise where the data controller was satisfied that the information requested had previously been seen by the data subject or was known to the data subject.[32]

(3) Where a request was made on behalf of the data subject by the person with parental responsibility for the data subject (if the data subject was a child) or by the person appointed by the court to manage his affairs (if the data subject was incapable of doing so) and granting access would disclose information:
   (i) that the data subject had provided in the expectation that it would not be disclosed to the applicant;
   (ii) that was obtained as a result of an examination or investigation to which the data subject consented in the expectation that the information would not be so disclosed; or
   (iii) that the data subject had expressly indicated should not be so disclosed.[33]

---

25 Limited exemptions for certain health information exist under the FOIA ss 31(2)(i), (j) and 38(1)(a) and the FOI(S)A ss 35(2)(i) and 39(1). Free-standing information access rights to certain medical information are given by other legislative provisions: see §38–001ff.

26 DPA 1998 s 30(1). The Information Commissioner has issued detailed guidance in this area: Use and Disclosure of Health Data: Guidance on the Application of the DPA 1998 (May 2002).

27 The Data Protection (Subject Access Modification) (Health) Order 2000 SI 2000/413.

28 The Data Protection (Subject Access Modification) (Health) Order 2000 SI 2000/413 Art 4. The bodies and persons were: a local authority; a Health and Social Services Board; a Health and Social Services Trust; a probation officer; and other persons who gave evidence in the course of any proceedings to which the Family Proceedings Courts (Children Act 1989) Rules 1991, the Magistrates' Courts (Children and Young Persons) Rules 1992, the Magistrates' Courts (Criminal Justice (Children)) Rules (Northern Ireland) 1999, the Act of Sederunt (Child Care and Maintenance Rules) 1997 or the Children's Hearings (Scotland) Rules 1996 apply provided that under those rules the information could be withheld by the court in whole or in part from the data subject.

29 In *Roberts v Nottingham Healthcare NHS Trust* [2008] EWHC 1934 (QB), [2009] FSR 4, [2008] MHLR 294, Cranston J adopted the meaning of 'likely' expounded in *R (Lord) v SSHD* [2003] EWHC 2073: the question is whether there may very well be a risk of harm to health even if the risk falls short of being more probable than not (at [7]-[9]).

30 The Data Protection (Subject Access Modification) (Health) Order 2000 SI 2000/413 Art 5. This is similar to the exemption granted by the FOIA s 38(1)(a) and the FOI(S)A s 39(1).

31 The Data Protection (Subject Access Modification) (Health) Order 2000 SI 2000/413 Arts 5(2) and 7. As to the meaning of 'health professional' see the DPA 1998 s 69.

32 The Data Protection (Subject Access Modification) (Health) Order 2000 SI 2000/413 Art 6(2).

33 The Data Protection (Subject Access Modification) (Health) Order 2000 SI 2000/413 Art 5(3)-(4). See Information Commissioner, *Subject access code of practice*, August 2013, p 49.

16–010 Educational records

The Directive did not differentiate educational information from other personal data relating to an individual. The reach of the DPA 1998 in relation to educational information was extended by educational records[34] being specifically brought within the definition of an 'accessible record'.[35] Save in relation to the subject access right, the DPA 1998 did not treat the processing of educational information differently from the processing of other information relating to an individual. In relation to the subject access right, the DPA 1998 did not itself exempt educational records from the s 7 right. Instead, s 30 of the Act empowered the Secretary of State to exempt or modify the subject access rights in relation to certain sorts of educational information.[36] The Secretary of State made an order under this power.[37]

16–011 Educational exemptions

The order defined three circumstances in which personal data consisting of information that constituted an 'educational record'[38] were made exempt from the subject access provisions:

(1) where the data had been provided to a court in specified proceedings, and was information that the court might withhold from the data subject;[39]

(2) where the disclosure of the data would be likely to cause serious harm to the physical or mental health or condition of the data subject or any other person;[40]

(3) where the request was made on behalf of the data subject by a person with parental responsibility for the data subject (in the case of a child) or by a person appointed by the court to manage the data subject's affairs (in the case of a person incapable of doing so) and the request related to information as to whether the data subject had been the subject of or may be at risk of child abuse. In such circumstances, the subject access rights did not apply in any case to the extent to which their application would not have been in the best interests of the data subject.[41]

These exemptions did not apply to data to which the health exemption applied.[42]

---

34 Defined in the DPA 1998 Sch 11.

35 DPA 1998 s 68(1).

36 DPA 1998 s 30(2)(a). The exemption was restricted to data in respect of which the data controller is the proprietor of, or a teacher at, a school and which consisted of information relating to persons who were or had been pupils at the school. The proprietor of a school was the person or body responsible for its management, generally the governing body: DPA 1998 s 30(5) and Education Act 1996 s 579.

37 The Data Protection (Subject Access Modification) (Education) Order 2000 SI 2000/414.

38 As defined in the DPA 1998 Sch 11, para 1.

39 The Data Protection (Subject Access Modification) (Education) Order 2000 SI 2000/414 Art 4. The proceedings to which it applied were those under the Family Proceedings Courts (Children Act 1989) Rules 1991, the Magistrates' Courts (Children and Young Persons) Rules 1992, the Magistrates' Courts (Criminal Justice (Children)) Rules (Northern Ireland) 1999, the Act of Sederunt (Child Care and Maintenance Rules) 1997 or the Children's Hearings (Scotland) Rules 1996, provided that under those rules the information may be withheld by the court in whole or in part from the data subject.

40 The Data Protection (Subject Access Modification) (Education) Order 2000 SI 2000/414 Art 5(1). For an example of where it did not apply, see: In *A v Information Commissioner*, IT, 11 July 2006 at [17b]. In Scotland, where an education authority received a request relating to relevant education information it believed to have originated from the Principal Reporter, it had to notify the Principal Reporter of that request and could not communicate the information to the data subject unless the Principal Reporter had given his opinion that this ground of exemption (serious harm to the physical or mental health or condition of the data subject or any person) did not apply: Art 6. This was similar to the exemption granted by the FOIA s 38(1)(a) and the FOI(S)A s 39(1).

41 The Data Protection (Subject Access Modification) (Education) Order 2000 SI 2000/414 Art 5(2)-(5). This exemption did not apply in Scotland.

42 The Data Protection (Subject Access Modification) (Education) Order 2000 SI 2000/414 Art 3(2)(a). See Information Commissioner, *Subject access code of practice*, August 2013, p 50. As to the health exemption, see §16–008.

6– 012 Social work exemption

The Directive did not differentiate social work records from other personal data relating to an individual. Save in relation to the subject access right, the DPA did not deal differently with social work records from other personal data relating to an individual. In relation to the subject access right, the Secretary of State had power to exempt or modify that right in relation to social work records.[43] The power to exempt applied to a much broader category of personal data than that to which the relevant accessible public record provisions applied (ie information held by a local social services authority for any purpose of its social services functions).[44] It applied to personal data consisting of information processed by government departments, local authorities, voluntary organisations or other bodies designated by the Secretary of State, where that information appeared to him to be processed in the course of, or for the purposes of carrying out, social work in relation to the data subject or other individuals.[45] The power to exempt or modify the subject access provisions was only exercisable where the Secretary of State considered that the application of those provisions would be likely to prejudice the carrying out of social work.[46]

6– 013 Social work order

The Secretary of State exercised his power of exemption by the making of an order.[47] The order applied:

(1) to personal data processed by a diverse range of authorities and bodies pursuant to a variety of social services and other functions specified in the order, including information processed by local authorities in connection with their social services functions, and also, for example, data processed by probation committees, special health authorities, any court-appointed children's guardian and the National Society for the Prevention of Cruelty to Children in connection with specified functions;[48] and

(2) to personal data processed by a court in specified proceedings.[49]

The data was made exempt:

(1) In the case of the former, where disclosure of the information would be likely to prejudice the carrying out of social work by reason of the fact that serious harm to the physical or mental health or condition of the data subject or any other person would be likely to be caused.[50] The two elements had to be satisfied before the second exemption could be relied upon: not only was it required that the application of the relevant access rights would be likely to cause serious harm to physical or mental health, but, in turn, this had to be likely to prejudice the carrying

43 DPA 1998 s 30(3).

44 DPA 1998 s 68(1)(c) Sch 12.

45 DPA 1998 s 30(3).

46 DPA 1998 s 30(3).

47 The Data Protection (Subject Access Modification) (Social Work) Order 2000 SI 2000/415 as amended.

48 The Data Protection (Subject Access Modification) (Social Work) Order 2000 Art 3(1) and sch para 1.

49 The Data Protection (Subject Access Modification) (Social Work) Order 2000 Art 3(1) and sch para 2.

50 The Data Protection (Subject Access Modification) (Social Work) Order 2000 Arts 3(1), 5(1)-(2) and Sch para 1. This exemption applied only to the second, third and fourth subject access rights: the data subject remained entitled to be informed whether personal data of which he or she was the subject were being processed by the data controller: The Data Protection (Subject Access Modification) (Social Work) Order 2000 SI 2000/415 Art 5(1); DPA 1998 s 7(1).

out of social work.[51]

(2) Again in the case of the former, where a request was made on behalf of the data subject and the information was provided by the data subject in the expectation that it would not be disclosed to the person making the request.[52]

(3) In the case of the latter, where the information had been provided to a court in specified proceedings, and was information that the court could withhold from the data subject.[53] The social work exemptions did not apply to data to which the health or education exemptions applied.[54]

16–014 Regulatory activity

The Directive entitled Member States to adopt national measures restricting the rights and duties otherwise applicable to the processing of personal data where that was necessary to safeguard: (a) the prevention, investigation, detection and prosecution of breaches of ethics for regulated professions, and (b) a monitoring, inspection or regulatory function connected, even occasionally, with the exercise of official authority in such cases or in cases of public security or an important economic or financial interest.[55] Section 31 of the DPA 1998 provided eight separate exemptions under the heading 'regulatory activity.' The first of these exemptions, contained in DPA 1998 s 31(1)-(3) ('the general regulatory exemption'), was not confined to named regulatory bodies. It is considered in this paragraph. The remaining seven exemptions, contained in DPA 1998 s 31(4)-(7), were directed to named regulatory bodies. They are considered in the following paragraphs. The general regulatory exemption was an exemption from the subject information provisions.[56] The exemption applied to:

(a) any function conferred on any person by or under any enactment,

(b) any function of the Crown, a Minister of the Crown or a government department,[57] and

(c) any other function which was of a public nature and was exercised in the public interest,[58]

where that function was designed for a specified purpose, but only to the extent that the application of the subject information provisions[59] to the personal data would be likely to

---

51 The Data Protection (Subject Access Modification) (Social Work) Order 2000 SI 2000/415 Art 5(1). This reflected the qualification to the Secretary of State's exemption power. In Scotland, where a social work authority received a request relating to relevant social work information it believed to have originated from the Principal Reporter, it had to notify the Principal Reporter of that request and could not communicate the information to the data subject unless the Principal Reporter had given his opinion that this ground of exemption (prejudice to social work because of serious harm to the physical or mental health or condition of the data subject or any other person) did not apply: Art 6.

52 The Data Protection (Subject Access Modification) (Social Work) Order 2000 SI 2000/415 Arts 3(1), 5(3)-(4) and Sch para 1.

53 DPA 1998 ss 3(1), 4 and Data Protection (Subject Access Modification) (Social Work) Order 2000 Sch para 2. The proceedings to which it applies are those to which the Family Proceedings Courts (Children Act 1989) Rules 1991, the Magistrates' Courts (Children and Young Persons) Rules 1992, the Magistrates' Courts (Criminal Justice (Children)) Rules (Northern Ireland) 1999, the Act of Sederunt (Child Care and Maintenance Rules) 1997, the Children's Hearings (Scotland) Rules 1996 or the Family Proceedings Rules 1991 apply provided that under those rules the information could be withheld by the court in whole or in part from the data subject.

54 The Data Protection (Subject Access Modification) (Social Work) Order 2000 SI 2000/415 Art 3(2)(a). As to the health exemption, see §16–008. As to educational records, see §16–010.

55 Article 13.1. And see recital (43).

56 As to the meaning of the 'subject information provisions', see §16–002.

57 Both 'Minister of the Crown' and 'government department' were defined in DPA 1998 s 70(1).

58 DPA 1998 s 31(3).

59 As to the meaning of the 'subject information provisions' see §16–002.

prejudice[60] the proper discharge of those functions. The functions were those designed:

(a) for protecting members of the public against–
  (i) financial loss due to dishonesty,[61] malpractice or other seriously improper conduct by, or the unfitness or incompetence of, persons concerned in the provision of banking, insurance, investment or other financial services or in the management of bodies corporate,
  (ii) financial loss due to the conduct of discharged or undischarged bankrupts,[62] or
  (iii) dishonesty, malpractice or other seriously improper conduct by, or the unfitness or incompetence of, persons authorised to carry on any profession[63] or other activity,
(b) for protecting charities[64] or community interest companies[65] against misconduct or mismanagement (whether by trustees, directors or other persons) in their administration,
(c) for protecting the property of charities or community interest companies from loss or misapplication,
(d) for the recovery of the property of charities or community interest companies,
(e) for securing the health, safety and welfare of persons at work, or
(f) for protecting persons other than persons at work against risk to health or safety arising out of or in connection with the actions of persons at work.

16–015 Ombudsman

The first of the specific regulatory exemptions was provided by DPA 1998 s 31(4). It was confined to personal data processed for the purpose of discharging any function which was conferred by or under any enactment on–

(i) the Parliamentary Commissioner for Administration,
(ii) the Commission for Local Administration in England,
(iii) the Health Service Commissioner for England,
(iv) the Public Services Ombudsman for Wales,
(v) the Assembly Ombudsman for Northern Ireland.
(vi) the Northern Ireland Commissioner for Complaints, or
(vii) the Scottish Public Services Ombudsman

('an ombudsman function'). The exemption was limited to such a body's processing of personal data for the purpose of discharging any of its functions that was designed for protecting members of the public against–

(i) maladministration by public bodies,
(ii) failures in services provided by public bodies, or
(iii) a failure of a public body to provide a service which it was a function of the body to provide.

Provided that those requirements were met, then that body was exempt from the subject

---

60 As to the meaning of the word 'prejudice' and the phrase 'would be likely to prejudice' see §§6– 020 to 6– 028.

61 As to the meaning of 'dishonesty', see: *Royal Brunei Airlines Sdn Bhd v Tan* [1995] 2 AC 378 at 389.

62 As to the meaning of a 'bankrupt', see Insolvency Act 1986 s 381(1).

63 As to the meaning of 'profession', see: *Inland Revenue Commissisoners v Maxse* [1919] 1 KB 647 at 657; *Currie v Inland Revenue Commissioners* [1921] 2 KB 332 at 340-341; *Carr v Inland Revenue Commissioners* [1944] 2 All ER 163 at 166-167.

64 As to the meaning of 'charity', see Charities Act 2011 s 1 (formerly Charities Act 2006 s 1).

65 Community interest companies are provided for in Part 2 (ss 26-63) of the Companies (Audit, Investigations and Community Enterprise) Act 2004.

information provisions to the extent to which the application of the subject information provisions[66] to the data would be likely to prejudice[67] the proper discharge of that function.

16–016 Financial conduct ombudsman

The second of the specific regulatory exemptions was provided by DPA 1998 s 31(4A). It was confined to personal data processed for the purpose of discharging any function which was conferred by or under Part XVI of the Financial Services and Markets Act 2000 on the body established by the Financial Conduct Authority for the purposes of Part XVI of that Act: in other words, the Financial Conduct Ombudsman provided for in Schedule 17 to that Act. Section 231 of that Act confers power on the Ombudsman to require information in relation to a complaint. The Ombudsman was exempted from the subject information provisions to the extent to which the application of the subject information provisions[68] to the data would be likely to prejudice[69] the proper discharge of the Ombudsman's functions.

16–017 Legal Services Board etc

The third was a pair of regulatory exemptions provided by DPA 1998 s 31(4B) and (4C). The first of the pair was confined to personal data processed for the purpose of discharging any function of the Legal Services Board. Under this, the Board was exempted from the subject information provisions to the extent to which the application of the subject information provisions to the data would be likely to prejudice the proper discharge of its functions. The second of the pair was confined to personal data processed for the purposes of the function of considering a complaint under the scheme established under Part 6 of the Legal Services Act 2007 (legal complaints). Where the processing was for the purpose of considering such a complaint, it was exempt from the subject information provisions in any case to the extent to which the application of the subject information provisions[70] to the data would be likely to prejudice[71] the proper discharge of the function.

16–018 Office of Fair Trading

The fourth of the specific regulatory exemptions was provided by DPA 1998 s 31(5). It was confined to personal data processed for the purpose of discharging any function which was conferred by or under any enactment on the Office of Fair Trading. Provided that the function for which the personal data was being processed was that one designed:

(i) for protecting members of the public against conduct which may adversely affect their interests by persons carrying on a business,
(ii) for regulating agreements or conduct which have as their object or effect the prevention, restriction or distortion of competition in connection with any commercial activity, or
(iii) for regulating conduct on the part of one or more undertakings which amounts to the abuse of a dominant position in a market,

then the Office of Fair Trading was exempted from the subject information provisions[72] to the extent to which the application of the subject information provisions to the data would be likely

[66] As to the meaning of the 'subject information provisions' see §16–002.

[67] As to the meaning of the word 'prejudice' and the phrase 'would be likely to prejudice' see §§6–020 to 6–028.

[68] As to the meaning of the 'subject information provisions' see §16–002.

[69] As to the meaning of the word 'prejudice' and the phrase 'would be likely to prejudice' see §§6–020 to 6–028.

[70] As to the meaning of the 'subject information provisions' see §16–002.

[71] As to the meaning of the word 'prejudice' and the phrase 'would be likely to prejudice' see §§6–020 to 6–028.

[72] As to the meaning of the 'subject information provisions' see §16–002.

to prejudice[73] the proper discharge of that function.

16– 019 Consumer protection

The Enterprise Act 2002 labels Regulation (EC) No 2006/2004[74] the 'CPC Regulation.'[75] That Act lists various bodies as 'CPC enforcers'[76] who are designated as enforcers of the CPC Regulation. Section 31(5A) of the DPA 1998 exempted a CPC enforcer from the subject information provisions[77] for personal data that it processed for the purpose of discharging any function conferred on it by or under the CPC Regulation, but the exemption was only to the extent to which the application of the subject information provisions to the data would be likely to prejudice[78] the proper discharge of that function.

16– 020 Health and child body

Section 113 of the Health and Social Care (Community Health and Standards) Act 2003 empowered the Secretary of State to make regulations to provide for the handling and consideration of complaints about NHS bodies in relation to their provision of health care.[79] Section 114 of that Act did the same in relation to the handling and consideration of complaints about the discharge by a local authority of social services functions etc.[80] The NHS Redress Act 2006 (which provided for the making by regulations of a redress scheme to deal with complaints against the NHS without the need for recourse to legal proceedings), including s 14, has never been brought into force. Section 24D of the Children Act 1989 provides that every local authority must establish a procedure for considering complaints from certain children about the discharge of its functions under Part III of that Act. Section 26 of that Act empowers the Secretary of State to make regulations for the review of any child who is being looked after by a local authority.[81] In relation to personal data processed for the purpose of the function of considering complaints to any such bodies, the DPA 1998 s 31(6) provided an exemption from the subject information provisions[82] to the extent to which the application of the subject

---

73 As to the meaning of the word 'prejudice' and the phrase 'would be likely to prejudice' see §§6– 020 to 6– 028.

74 That is, Regulation (EC) No 2006/2004 of the European Parliament and of the Council of 27 October 2004 on cooperation between national authorities responsible for the enforcement of consumer protection laws as amended by the Unfair Commercial Practices Directive.

75 Enterprise Act 2002 s 235A.

76 'CPC' means 'consumer protection cooperation.' Under the Enterprise Act 2002 s 212(5A), a 'CPC enforcer' means any of: (a) the Competition and Markets Authority; (b) the Civil Aviation Authority; (c) the Financial Conduct Authority; (d) the Secretary of State for Health and Social Care; (e) the Department of Health, Social Services and Public Safety in Northern Ireland; (f) the Office of Communications; (g) the Department of Enterprise, Trade and Investment in Northern Ireland; (h) every local weights and measures authority in Great Britain; (i) an enforcement authority within the meaning of section 120(15) of the Communications Act 2003 (regulation of premium rate services); and (j) the Information Commissioner.

77 As to the meaning of the 'subject information provisions' see §16– 002.

78 As to the meaning of the word 'prejudice' and the phrase 'would be likely to prejudice' see §§6– 020 to 6– 028.

79 The regulations in England are the Local Authority Social Services and National Health Service Complaints (England) Regulations 2009, SI 2009/309. The regulations in Wales are the National Health Service (Concerns, Complaints and Redress Arrangements) (Wales) Regulations 2011, SI 2011/704.

80 The regulations in England are the Local Authority Social Services and National Health Service Complaints (England) Regulations 2009, SI 2009/309. The regulations in Wales are the Social Services Complaints Procedure (Wales) Regulations 2014, SI 2014/1794.

81 The regulations so made include: Children Act 1989 Representations Procedure (England) Regulations 2006, SI 2006/1738; Care Planning, Placement and Case Review (England) Regulations 2010, SI 2010/959; Fostering Services (England) Regulations 2011, SI 2011/581; Adoption Agencies (Wales) Regulations 2005, SI 2005/1313; Special Guardianship (Wales) Regulations 2005, SI 2005/1513; and Representations Procedure (Wales) Regulations 2014, SI 2014/1795.

82 As to the meaning of the 'subject information provisions' see §16– 002.

information provisions to the data would be likely to prejudice[83] the proper discharge of that function.

16– 021 Welsh monitoring officer

Part 3 of the Local Government Act 2000 (ss 49-83) provided for local authority monitoring officers to investigate and report on certain matters. The provisions in relation to local authorities in England have been repealed. The provisions in relation to local authorities in Wales remain in force, together with the provisions providing for investigations by the Public Services Ombudsman for Wales (ss 68-70). In relation to the processing of personal data for the purpose of discharging any function conferred by or under Part 3 of the Local Government Act 2000 on the monitoring officer or the Public Services Ombudsman for Wales, DPA 1998 s 31(7) provided an exemption from the subject information provisions[84] to the extent to which the application of the subject information provisions to the data would be likely to prejudice[85] the proper discharge of that function.

16– 022 Journalism etc: Directive

The Directive expressly provided that its principles were to apply in a restricted manner in relation to processing of personal data carried out solely[86] for the purposes of journalism, or literary and artistic purposes.[87] The CJEU held that in order to take account of the importance of the right to freedom of expression in every democratic society, it was necessary to interpret notions relating to that freedom, such as journalism, broadly.[88] The Directive applied not only to media undertakings but also to every person engaged in journalism.[89] The CJEU interpreted 'journalistic activities' to mean those which have as their purpose the disclosure to the public of information, opinions or ideas, irrespective of the medium which is used to transmit them.[90] However, the Court also held that the derogation could be applied only where its was necessary in order to reconcile two fundamental rights, namely the right to privacy and the right to freedom of expression, meaning that the derogation could only apply only in so far as is strictly necessary.[91]

16– 023 Journalism etc: exemption

Section 3 of the DPA 1998 defined as 'the special purposes':

(a) the purposes of journalism,
(b) artistic purposes, and
(c) literary purposes.

Processing of personal data for the special purposes was exempted by DPA 1998 s 32(1) from

83 As to the meaning of the word 'prejudice' and the phrase 'would be likely to prejudice' see §§6– 020 to 6– 028.

84 As to the meaning of the 'subject information provisions' see §16– 002.

85 As to the meaning of the word 'prejudice' and the phrase 'would be likely to prejudice' see §§6– 020 to 6– 028.

86 If the processing was not 'solely' to disclose information, opinions or ideas to the public, it would not be held that the processing of the personal data at issue was carried out 'solely for journalistic purposes': *Buivids v Latvia* (C-345/17) [2019] 1 WLR 4225, [2019] 2 CMLR 24 at [62].

87 Article 9. And see recitals (17) and (37).

88 *Tietosuojavaltuutettu v Satakunnan Markkinaporssi Oy* (C-73/07) [2008] ECR I-9831, [2010] All ER (EC) 213 at [54]-[56]; *Buivids v Latvia* (C-345/17) [2019] 1 WLR 4225, [2019] 2 CMLR 24 at [51].

89 *Tietosuojavaltuutettu v Satakunnan Markkinaporssi Oy* (C-73/07) [2008] ECR I-9831, [2010] All ER (EC) 213 at [58]; *Buivids v Latvia* (C-345/17) [2019] 1 WLR 4225, [2019] 2 CMLR 24 at [52].

90 *Tietosuojavaltuutettu v Satakunnan Markkinaporssi Oy* (C-73/07) [2008] ECR I-9831, [2010] All ER (EC) 213 at [61]; *Buivids v Latvia* (C-345/17) [2019] 1 WLR 4225, [2019] 2 CMLR 24 at [53].

91 *Tietosuojavaltuutettu v Satakunnan Markkinaporssi Oy* (C-73/07) [2008] ECR I-9831, [2010] All ER (EC) 213 at [55]-[56]; *Buivids v Latvia* (C-345/17) [2019] 1 WLR 4225, [2019] 2 CMLR 24 at [63]-[64].

most of the duties imposed by the DPA 1998.[92] An individual had little, if any, recourse against a data controller processing his or her personal information where that processing was only for the special purposes. In so providing, DPA 1998 s 32(1) set a balance between the protection of individual privacy and the right to freedom of expression.[93] In order for the exemption to apply to the processing of personal data, four requirements had to be satisfied:

- the data was being processed only for the special purposes,
- the processing was undertaken with a view to the publication by any person of any journalistic, literary or artistic material,[94]
- the data controller had reasonably to believe that, having regard in particular to the special importance of the public interest[95] in freedom of expression,[96] publication would be in the public interest,[97] and
- the data controller had reasonably to believe that, in all the circumstances, compliance with the provision imposing a duty or conferring a right was incompatible with the special purposes.

If and to the extent that those requirements were met, the data controller was exempted from its s 4(4) duty to comply with the data protection principles (apart from the seventh data protection principle) and the rights conferred by ss 7, 10, 12 and 14(1)-(3) were disapplied. The nature and breadth of the s 32(1) exemption were considered in *Campbell v MGN Ltd*, where the Court of Appeal described it as a a 'widespread exemption from the duty to comply with the provisions that impose substantive obligations upon the data controller' subject only to 'simple conditions.'[98]

16– 024 Journalism etc: pre-publication

Quite apart from the special purposes exemption in s 32(1), the DPA 1998 also provided a further layer of protection for processing of personal data for the special purposes prior to publication and, correspondingly, weakened the position of an individual vis-a-vis processing of his or her personal information for those purposes. Under DPA 1998 s 32(4), where a data subject had initiated proceedings against a data controller for breach of the data protection principles or for non-compliance with a request under DPA 1998 s 7, 10 or 12 or otherwise seeking relief under s 13 or 14, the court was obliged to stay those proceedings if the data controller claimed or if it appeared to the court:

(a) that any personal data to which the proceedings related were being processed only for the special purposes, and

---

92 This reflected the restricted operation of the Directive in relation to processing for those purposes: see Recitals (17), (37) and Art 9. Under FOIA, public authorities that are involved in journalism (eg BBC) are only within the grasp of that Act in respect of information held for purposes other than those of journalism, art or literature.

93 *Sugar v BBC (No 2)* [2012] UKSC 4, [2012] 1 WLR 439, [2012] EMLR 17, [2012] 2 All ER 509 at [69]-[70].

94 This second requirement was readily satisfied in that: (a) the future publication with a view to which the data controller was processing the individual's personal information need not be a publication by the data controller or any specific person; (b) the future publication need not be of the personal information that the data controller was processing; (c) the timing of the future publication need not be fixed or even known; and (d) the fact that the personal information had itself already been published (or used for the purposes of a publication) did not preclude the s 32(4) claim being made on the basis that that personal information was thereafter being processed with a view to the publication of different journalistic material.

95 DPA 1998 s 32(1)(b). The public interest is treated in greater detail at §§6– 001 to 6– 019.

96 As to the influence of Arts 8 and 10 of the ECHR in this area, and to which the DPA 1998 s 32 exemption was supposed to give expression, see §4– 015ff.

97 In considering whether the belief of a data controller (ie the belief that publication would be in the public interest) had been or was a reasonable one, regard could be had to the data controller's compliance with any relevant code of practice designated by the Secretary of State: DPA 1998 s 32(3). The codes of practice were designated by the Data Protection (Designated Codes of Practice) (No 2) Order 2000, SI 2000/1864.

98 *Campbell v Mirror Group Newspapers Ltd* [2002] EWCA Civ 1373, [2003] QB 633 at [117].

(b) that any personal data to which the proceedings related were being processed with a view to the publication of any journalistic, literary or artistic material that had not previously been published by the data controller.

Thus, in order for the stay to be engaged:

- the data controller only had to claim, or it had to appear to the court, that (a) and (b) were met, with no requirement that the claim be reasonably made;[99]
- that claim only had to be made in respect of the first two requirements of the exemption in DPA 1998 s 32(1);
- it mattered not that there was no harm or likely harm to the data controller; and
- the harm to the interests of the data subject, including his or her privacy, was irrelevant.

Furthermore, as with the exemption in s 32(1):

- the future publication with a view to which the data controller was processing the individual's personal information need not have been a publication by the data controller or any specific person;
- the future publication need not have been of the personal information that the data controller was processing;
- the timing of the future publication need not have been fixed or even known; and
- the fact that the personal information had itself already been published (or used for the purposes of a publication) did not preclude the s 32(4) claim being made on the basis that that personal information was thereafter being processed with a view to the publication of different journalistic material.

The stay endured until the claim was withdrawn[100] or until the Information Commissioner made a determination either that the personal data was not being processed only for the special purposes or that the personal data was not being processed with a view to to the publication of any journalistic, literary or artistic material that had not previously been published by the data controller.[101] A challenge to the compatibility with EU law of the mechanism provided by s 32(4)-(5) was referred by the Court of Appeal to the CJEU.[102]

16– 025 Research etc purposes

Article 32.3 of the Directive allowed Member States to provide for derogations from Articles 6, 7 and 8 (compliance with data protection principles) in respect of personal data kept for the sole purpose of historical research.[103] Article 13.2 allowed Member States to restrict the subject access right where personal data was being processed solely for the purposes of scientific research or for the sole purpose of creating statistics.[104] The use of information for the purposes of legitimate historical research can constitute a breach of Art 10 of the ECHR[105] Cases under

---

99 *Steinmetz and ors v Global Witness Ltd* [2014] EWHC 1186 (Ch).

100 Presumably exposing the individual to the costs of the data controller.

101 That is, a determination under DPA 1998 s 45. A determination under s 45 gave rise to a right of appeal by the data controller to the FTT: DPA 1998 s 48(1). The individual who was the subject of the information being processed was a bystander in the s 45 procedure and any appeal therefrom. The DPA 1998 did not indicate who instigated the procedure for a determination under s 45. Nor did the DPA 1998 indicate what would happen to proceedings stayed under s 32(4) that were neither withdrawn nor made the subject of a s 45 determination.

102 *Stunt v Associated Newspapers Ltd* [2018] EWCA Civ 1780, [2018] 1 WLR 6060.

103 See also recital (34).

104 Article 11.2 also recognised that the subject access right was, in the case of processing of personal information for the purposes of historical or scientific research, particularly susceptible to resulting in an impossible or disproportionate effort on the data controller, and gave Member States latitude to disapply the subject access right in that situation provided that appropriate safeguards were in place.

105 See *Magyar Helsinki Bizottság v Hungary* [2016] ECHR 18030/11 (Grand Chamber) at [160] (Grand Chamber); *Wegrzynowski and another v Poland* (2013) 36 BHRC 573 at [59]; *Google Spain SL v Agencia Espanola de Proteccion de Datos*

Art 10 recognise that the term 'historical research' has a normative element that differentiates it from research the predominant objective of which is to justify an ideology and whose choice of technique and source is driven by a sought outcome.[106] Section 33 of the DPA 1998 provided three limited exemptions for processing of personal data only for 'research purposes' (defined as including statistical or historical purposes).[107] Each of the exemptions required that the processing complied with 'the relevant conditions', defined as meaning:

(a) that the data was not processed to support measures or decisions with respect to particular individuals; and

(b) that the data was not processed in such a way that substantial damage or substantial distress was, or was likely to be, caused to any data subject.

Provided that the processing was only for 'research purposes' and was compliant with those conditions, there was exemption:

– from the requirement in the second data protection principle that personal data not be further processed in any manner incompatible with any of the purposes for which the personal data had been obtained (s 33(2));
– from the requirement in the fifth data protection principle that personal data processed for any purpose not be kept for longer than is necessary for that purpose (s 33(3)); and
– from the entitlement to make and comply with a subject access request (s 7), provided that the results of the research or resulting statistics were not made available in a form that identified any data subject (s 33(4)).

16– 026 Otherwise available

Insofar as personal data consisted of information that the data controller was statutorily obliged (other than by or under an 'enactment[108] contained in' FOIA[109]) to make available to the public, whether by publishing it or by making it available for inspection,[110] under the DPA 1998 that personal data was exempt from:

(a) the subject information provisions,[111]
(b) the fourth data protection principle and s 14(1)-(3),[112] and
(c) the non-disclosure provisions.[113]

It is not clear which provision of the Directive mandated this exemption.

(C-131/12) [2014] QB 1022 at [123]; *Kenedi v Hungary* (31475/05) [2009] ECHR 78, (2009) 27 BHRC 335, seemingly supported in this by the Supreme Court in *Kennedy v Charity Commission* [2014] UKSC 20, [2015] AC 455 at [183].

106 See *Perincek v Switzerland* (App no 27510/08) (2015) 40 BHRC 313.

107 DPA 1998 s 33(5) provided that processing was not to be treated as being otherwise than for research purposes merely because the personal data was disclosed: (a) to any person for research purposes; (b) to the individual or any person acting on his or her behalf; (c) at the request or with the consent of the individual to another person; or (d) in circumstances in which the person making the disclosure had reasonable grounds for believing that the disclosure fell within one of (a), (b) or (c).

108 The word 'enactment' does not include an enactment comprised in, or in an instrument made under, an Act of the Scottish Parliament: Interpretation Act 1978, ss 5 and 23A and Sch 1.

109 The wording would appear to have been not sufficiently wide to cover information that the data controller was obliged to disclose under FOI(S)A, the EIR, the EI(S)R or other legislation referred to in this work.

110 Whether for or without a fee.

111 As to the meaning of the 'subject information provisions' see §16– 002.

112 Given that the fourth data protection principle and s 14(1)-(3) are included within the definition of the non-disclosure provisions (DPA 1998 s 27(4)), s 34(b) was unnecessary.

113 DPA 1998 s 34. As to the meaning of the 'non-disclosure provisions' see §16– 002.

16– 027 Disclosures required by law

Where disclosure of personal data was required by or under an enactment (other than FOIA),[114] by any rule of law[115] or by order of a court, that personal data was exempt from the non-disclosure provisions.[116] This covered personal data included in statutory registers open to the public[117] and personal data to which the public had some other statutory right of access.[118] The exemption did not cover uses of personal data other than disclosure.[119]

16– 028 Legal professional privilege

Where disclosure of personal data was necessary:

(a) for the purpose of, or in connection with, any legal proceedings (including prospective legal proceedings)[120],

(b) for the purpose of obtaining legal advice, or

(c) for the purposes of establishing, exercising or defending legal rights,[121]

that personal data was exempt from the non-disclosure provisions[122] and the subject information provisions.[123] The concept of establishing, exercising or defending legal rights has been widely interpreted.[124]

16– 029 Parliamentary privilege

Where it was necessary to avoid an infringement of the privileges of either House of Parliament,[125] personal data was exempt from:

(a) the first data protection principle, except to the extent that it required compliance with the conditions in Schedules 2 and 3;

---

114 The word 'enactment' does not include an enactment comprised in, or in an instrument made under, an Act of the Scottish Parliament: Interpretation Act 1978, ss 5 and 23A and Sch 1.

115 For example, under common law, EU law or prerogative.

116 DPA 1998 s 35(1). As to the meaning of the 'non-disclosure provisions' see §16– 002.

117 At any rate, to the extent that the statutory provision required the inclusion of the personal data in that register.

118 It thus did not include a right of access the existence of which depended upon the identity of the requester but included certain rights under Part VA of the Local Government Act 1972 (although those provisions have their own personal information exemption).

119 *Cooper v National Crime Agency* [2019] EWCA Civ 16 at [127].

120 Legal proceedings did not include internal disciplinary proceedings of an employer: *Cooper v National Crime Agency* [2019] EWCA Civ 16 at [119], [126].

121 Touched on by the Court of Appeal in *Totalise plc v The Motley Fool Ltd & anor* [2001] EWCA Civ 1897, [2002] 1 WLR 1897. In *Cooper v National Crime Agency* [2019] EWCA Civ 16 at [121], [126] this was held to extend to the disciplining of an employee.

122 DPA 1998 s 35(2). As to the meaning of the 'non-disclosure provisions' see §16– 002.

123 DPA 1998 s 37, Sch 7 para 10. As to the meaning of the 'subject information provisions' see §16– 002. The analogous provisions are the FOIA s 42(1) and FOI(S)A s 36(1). In relation to freedom of information legislation, exemption on the ground of legal professional privilege under freedom of information legislation is considered at §§30– 013 to 30– 024. Those paragraphs set out the principles relating to legal professional privilege. Whereas the exemption in FOIA and the EIR for legal professional privilege is qualified, there was no public interest override under DPA 1998 s 35 or Sch 7 para 10.

124 *R (British Telecommunications plc & ors) v Secretary of State for Culture, Olympics, Media and Sport* [2012] EWCA Civ 232, [2012] 2 CMLR 23, [2012] Bus LR 1766 at [77], where it was extended to the sending of letters encouraging online infringers of copyright to desist. However, in relation to foreign proceedings the exemption was held to be available to an English data controller only if it could resist disclosure on the grounds of legal professional privilege under English law principles were there to be legal proceedings to which it was a party in England: *Dawson-Damer v Taylor Wessing LLP* [2020] EWCA Civ 352 at [46].

125 In relation to freedom of information legislation, exemption on the ground of breaching the privileges of either House of Parliament is considered at §§19– 009, 30– 001 to 30– 012. Those paragraphs set out what constitutes a breach of the privileges of a House of Parliament.

(b) section 7 (the subject access right);
(c) section 10 (the right of a data subject to serve a notice requiring the data controller to stop processing his or her personal information where that was likely to cause unwarranted, substantial damage or distress); and
(d) section 14(1)-(3) (rectification, blocking, erasure and destruction of personal data on the ground of that data being inaccurate).[126]

16–030 Domestic purposes

The Directive provided that it was not to apply to the processing of personal data by a natural person in the course of a purely personal or household activity.[127] The exception was to be interpreted strictly.[128] This was implemented through DPA 1998 s 36, which provided that personal data processed by an individual for the purposes of that individual's personal, family or household affairs (including recreational purposes)[129] were exempt from the data protection principles and the provisions of Part II and III (ie all the rights conferred on a data subject by the DPA 1998).[130] The phrase 'personal, family or household affairs' was considered not to extend to CCTV coverage outside the boundaries of a domestic property[131] but sufficient to cover the management of a private block of flats where the data controller resided.[132] Where the processing results in an indeterminate number of people being able to view personal data, such as where an individual posts video to a website, that processing would not come within the exemption.[133]

3. THE MINOR EXEMPTIONS

16–031 Introduction

Apart from the exemptions contained within the body of Part IV of the DPA 1998, miscellaneous exemptions were contained in Schedule 7 and in statutory instruments made

126 DPA 1998 s 35A.

127 Article 3.2. See also recital (12). The words 'personal or household', within the meaning of that provision, refer to the activity of the person processing the personal data and not to the person whose data are processed: *Tietosuojavaltuutettu v Jehovan todistajat* (C-25/17), 10 July 2018 at [41].

128 *Buivids v Latvia* (C-345/17) [2019] 1 WLR 4225, [2019] 2 CMLR 24 at [41]; *Puškár v Finančné riaditeľstvo Slovenskej* (C-73/16) [2017] 4 WLR 209, [2018] 1 CMLR 44 at [38]; *Tietosuojavaltuutettu v Jehovan todistajat* (C-25/17), 10 July 2018 at [37].

129 As to the meaning of 'personal, family or household affairs' see: *L v L* [2007] EWHC 140 (QB), [2007] 2 FLR 171; *Law Society and others v Kordowski* [2011] EWHC 3185 (QB), [2014] EMLR 2; *Ittihadieh v 5-11 Cheyne Gardens RTM Co Ltd & ors* [2017] EWCA Civ 121, [2018] QB 256. On the footing that the phrase 'personal, family or household affairs' had been intended to bear a meaning analogous to the phrase 'private and family life' as used in Art 8 of the ECHR (and to which express reference was made in recitals (10), (22) and (60) of the Directive), it would appear that this meant not just the physical area of an individual's home but the quiet enjoyment of that individual's home, such as to capture unauthorised entry into the home and interferences such as noise, emissions, smells etc: see *Moreno Gomez v Spain* (2005) 41 EHRR 40 at [53]; *Dees v Hungary* (2013) 57 EHRR 12; *Maempel v Malta* (2016) 62 EHRR 13 at [36]. As to the meaning of 'personal affairs' in a freedom of information context, see *Colakovski v Australian Telecommunications Corpn* (1991) 100 ALR 111 at 118-119.

130 DPA 1998 s 36.

131 *Rynes v Urad pro ochranu osobnich udaju* (C-212/13) [2015] 1 WLR 2607, [2015] CEC 732.

132 *Ittihadieh v 5-11 Cheyne Gardens RTM Co Ltd* [2017] EWCA 121, [2018] QB 256. See further *Re Lindqvist (Approximation of Laws)* [2004] QB 1014 at [47].

133 *Buivids v Latvia* (C-345/17) [2019] 1 WLR 4225, [2019] 2 CMLR 24 at [43]; *Rynes v Urad pro ochranu osobnich udaju* (C-212/13) [2015] 1 WLR 2607, [2015] CEC 732 at [31]-[33]; *Tietosuojavaltuutettu v Satakunnan Markkinaporssi Oy* (C-73/07) [2008] ECR I-9831, [2010] All ER (EC) 213 at [44]; *Tietosuojavaltuutettu v Jehovan todistajat* (C-25/17), 10 July 2018 at [42].

under DPA 1998 s 38.[134] In addition, FOIA inserted an exemption that was confined to 'manual data'[135] held by a 'public authority.'[136]

16– 032 Public authority manual data

As a result of FOIA routing a request for information through the DPA 1998[137] (so far as the request captured information that constituted personal data of which the applicant was the data subject) and because FOIA was not limited to information processed automatically or forming part of a relevant filing system or an accessible record,[138] it was necessary to ensure that the routing did not result in a reduced right of access to information held by a public authority where the request captured personal data of which the applicant was the data subject.[139] To this end, paragraph (e) was added to the definition of 'data' in s 1(1) and s 33A was added as an exemption. Personal data falling within paragraph (e) of the definition of 'data' in the DPA 1998 was termed 'manual data.' The paragraph (e) definition applied only to recorded information held by a public authority. But in so doing, unless a specific exemption had been included, it would have brought to bear on that class of data all the duties imposed by the DPA 1998. To limit the reach of the DPA 1998 so that in respect of that class of data it merely gave equivalence to the right of access conferred by FOIA, the DPA 1998 included a specific exemption for 'manual data' held by public authorities – s 33A. In broad terms, this exemption operated by disapplying all the duties imposed by and rights conferred by the DPA 1998, apart from the subject access right (s 7).[140] In addition to this exemption, manual data recorded by a public authority and relating to certain personnel matters was exempted from the subject access right.[141] The types of personnel matters concerned included appointments and removals, pay, discipline and superannuation.[142] The exemption covered service in the armed forces, service in any office or employment under the Crown or a public authority, and service in any other office or employment or under any contract for services where the power to take action in respect of such personnel matters rested with Her Majesty, a Minister of the Crown, the National Assembly for Wales, a Northern Ireland Minister or any public authority.[143]

16– 033 Confidential references

Personal data was exempt from the subject access rights if they consisted of a reference given (or to be given) in confidence[144] by the data controller for the purposes of the education, training or employment of the data subject; his or her appointment to any office; or the provision by him or her of any service.[145] This exemption applied only to references given or

---

134 The power of the Secretary of State to make further exemptions by order was limited: see DPA 1998 s 38(1).

135 That is, data falling within paragraph (e) of the definition of 'data' in DPA 1998 s 1(1).

136 That is, a 'public authority' within the meaning of FOIA or FOI(S)A: DPA 1998 s 1(1).

137 See FOIA s 40(1); and similarly FOI(S)A s 38(1)(a).

138 In contrast to the DPA 1998: see paragraphs (a)-(d) of the definition of 'data' in s 1(1).

139 Being the reach of the right conferred by FOIA s 1(1) and FOI(S)A s 1. In so doing, this was conferring a right on a data subject that was additional to what was required by the Directive.

140 DPA 1998 s 33A.

141 As to which, see §15– 018.

142 DPA 1998 s 33A(2).

143 DPA 1998 s 33A(2).

144 As to the meaning of information given 'in confidence', see §§34– 001 to 34– 028. The FOIA s 41(1) and the FOI(S)A s 36, provide a general exemption for information acquired in confidence. The FOIA s 27(3) and the FOI(S)A s 32(1)(b) also deal with certain other information acquired by a public authority in confidence: see §27– 016.

145 DPA 1998 s 37, Sch 7 para 1.

to be given by the data controller. If the data controller had on file references provided by a previous employer, those did not fall within the scope of the exemption.[146]

16–034 Armed forces

Personal data was exempt from the subject information provisions in any case to the extent to which the application of those provisions would have been likely to prejudice the combat effectiveness of any of the armed forces of the Crown.[147]

16–035 Judicial appointments etc

Personal data processed for the purposes of assessing a person's suitability for judicial office or the office of Queen's Counsel, or for the purposes of the conferring by the Crown of any honour or dignity was exempt from the subject information provisions.[148]

16–036 Crown employment etc

The DPA 1998 conferred a power on the Secretary of State to exempt from the subject information provisions[149] personal data processed for the purposes of assessing a person's suitability for Crown employment or appointment to any office by Her Majesty, a Minister of the Crown or a Northern Ireland department.[150] This power was exercised in relation to a variety of Crown appointments, including archbishops, bishops and certain other clergy; Lord-Lieutenants; Masters of certain Cambridge colleges; the Provost of Eton; the Poet Laureate and the Astronomer Royal.[151]

16–037 Management forecasts

Personal data processed for the purposes of management forecasting or management planning to assist the data controller in the conduct of any business or other activity was exempt from the subject information provisions in any case to the extent to which the application of those provisions would be likely to prejudice the conduct of that business or activity.[152]

16–038 Corporate finance

Personal data processed for the purposes of, or in connection with, a corporate finance service was, in certain circumstances, exempt from the subject information provisions.[153] The concept of a 'corporate finance service' derived from the EC Directive on investment services in the

---

146 Information Commissioner, *Subject access code of practice*, August 2013, p 40.

147 DPA 1998 s 37, Sch 7 para 2. As to the meaning of the 'subject information provisions', see §16–002. The analogous provisions are the FOIA s 26(1), and the FOI(S)A s 31(4). These are qualified exemptions under the FOI Acts. These exemptions are considered in §§26–047 to 26–056, 26–059 to 26–062, 26–065 to 26–069 and 26–072. As to the meaning of the word 'prejudice' and the phrase 'would be likely to prejudice' see §§6–020 to 6–028.

148 DPA 1998 s 37, Sch 7 para 3. As to the meaning of the 'subject information provisions', see §16–002. The conferring of a life peerage is an 'honour or dignity': *Ranger v House of Lords Appointments Commission* [2015] EWHC 45 (QB), [2015] 1 WLR 4324. In relation to the making of a subject access request, an applicant could not circumvent the exemption by arranging for another person to request the information under the FOIA: see ss 40(2) and (4) of that Act and FOI(S)A ss 38(1)(b) and 38(3). Both are absolute exemptions under those Acts.

149 As to the meaning of the 'subject information provisions', see §16–002.

150 DPA 1998 s 37, Sch 7 para 4.

151 The Data Protection (Crown Appointments) Order 2000 SI 2000/416.

152 DPA 1998 s 37, Sch 7 para 5. As to the meaning of the 'subject information provisions' see §16–002. There is no analogous provision under either the FOIA or the FOI(S)A. As to the meaning of the word 'prejudice' and the phrase 'would be likely to prejudice' see §§6–020 to 6–028. A public authority may be a 'business': *Friends of the Earth v Information Commissioner and DTI*, IT, 4 April 2007.

153 DPA 1998 s 37, Sch 7 para 6. As to the meaning of the 'subject information provisions' see §16–002.

securities field.[154] It covered certain activities relating to issues of specified instruments, as well as the provision of advice to undertakings on matters such as capital structure, industrial strategy and mergers.[155] Where personal data was processed for the purposes of, or in connection with, a corporate finance service provided by a relevant person,[156] the data was exempt from the subject information provisions to the extent to which the application of those provisions could affect the price of any specified instrument (whether it already exists, or is to be or may be created).[157] This limb of exemption also extended to circumstances in which the data controller reasonably believed that the price of such an instrument could be so affected.[158] Such data was also exempt if exemption was required to safeguard an important economic or financial interest of the United Kingdom.[159] The Secretary of State had a power to specify matters to be taken into account in determining whether exemption on the latter ground is required, or circumstances in which exemption was (or was not) to be taken to be required.[160] This power was exercised in relation to personal data to which the application of the subject information provisions could affect decisions whether to deal in, subscribe for or issue instruments or decisions which are likely to affect any business activity.[161] In such cases, the matter to be taken into account was the inevitable prejudicial effect on the orderly functioning of financial markets or the efficient allocation of capital within the economy resulting from the application of the subject access rights.[162]

16– 039 Negotiations

Personal data comprising records of the data controller's intentions in relation to any negotiations with the data subject was exempt from the subject information provisions in any case to the extent to which the application of those provisions would be likely to prejudice those negotiations.[163]

16– 040 Examination scripts etc

A group of exemptions and modifications related to examination marks and scripts. In relation to 'examination marks'[164] and other information processed by a data controller for the purpose of determining the results of an academic, professional or other examination, the subject access right provisions were modified by delaying the moment at which those rights could be exercised.[165] The modifications effectively prevented a data subject from using his or her subject access rights to obtain examination results before they were announced by extending

154 Council Directive 93/22/EEC. See DPA 1998 Sch 7 para 6(3).

155 DPA 1998 Sch 7 para 6(3).

156 Defined in DPA 1998 Sch 7 para 6(3).

157 DPA 1998 Sch 7 para 6(1)(a)(i).

158 DPA 1998 Sch 7 para 6(1)(a)(ii).

159 DPA 1998 Sch 7 para 6(1)(b).

160 DPA 1998 Sch 7 para 6(2).

161 Data Protection (Corporate Finance Exemption) Order 2000 SI 2000/184 Art 2(3).

162 Data Protection (Corporate Finance Exemption) Order 2000 SI 2000/184 Art 2(2).

163 DPA 1998 s 37, Sch 7 para 7. As to the meaning of the 'subject information provisions' see §16– 002. As to the meaning of the word 'prejudice' and the phrase 'would be likely to prejudice' see §§6– 020 to 6– 028.

164 Defined in DPA 1998 Sch 7 para 8(5) to include any process for determining the knowledge, intelligence, skill or ability of a candidate by reference to his performance in any test, work or other activity. Answers written by a candidate at a professional examination will constitute personal information relating to that candidate, and hence fell within the grasp of the DPA 1998: *Nowak v Data Protection Commissioner* (C-434/16) [2018] 1 WLR 3505, [2018] 2 CMLR 21.

165 DPA 1998 Sch 7 para 8(1), (5).

the period for compliance with a subject access request.[166] Examination scripts, that is to say personal data consisting of information recorded by candidates during an academic, professional or other examination,[167] were exempt from the subject access rights.[168]

6–041 Legal professional privilege

Personal data was exempt from the subject information provisions where the data consisted of information in respect of which a claim to legal professional privilege (or, in Scotland, to confidentiality of communications) could be maintained in legal proceedings.[169] 'Legal proceedings' was interpreted to mean legal proceedings in the United Kingdom.[170] The exemption thus only applied when there was relevant privilege according to the law of any part of the United Kingdom.[171] The exemption was limited to legal professional privilege, and did not apply to other rights of non-disclosure such as certain rights of non-disclosure enjoyed by trustees.[172]

6–042 Self-incrimination

A person was not required to comply with a subject access request (or an order under s 7) to the extent that to do so would, by revealing evidence of the commission of any offence (other than an offence under the DPA 1998), have exposed him or her to proceedings for that offence.[173] Information disclosed by a person in compliance with such a request or order was not admissible against him in proceedings for an offence under the DPA 1998.[174]

6–043 Disclosure otherwise prohibited

In addition to the exemptions conferred by the DPA 1998 itself, there are additional exemptions from the subject access rights made pursuant to a further general power of exemption conferred on the Secretary of State by the Act in respect of information the disclosure of which is already prohibited or restricted by other legislation. The Secretary of State may exempt personal data consisting of such information, where he considers it necessary for safeguarding the interests of the data subject or the rights and freedoms of any other individual that the prohibition or restriction should prevail over the subject access rights.[175] Pursuant to this power, there are exemptions in respect of certain information relating to human fertilisation and embryology,[176] adoption records and reports,[177] statements of special

---

166 DPA 1998 Sch 7 para 8.

167 DPA 1998 Sch 7 para 8(5). Information Commissioner, *Subject access code of practice*, August 2013, p 52.

168 DPA 1998 s 37, Sch 7 para 9.

169 DPA 1998 Scch 7 para 10. As to the meaning of the 'subject information provisions' see §16– 002. Legal professional privilege is considered in detail in Chapter 30.

170 *Dawson-Damer v Taylor Wessing LLP* [2017] EWCA Civ 74, [2017] 1 WLR 3255 at [39].

171 *Dawson-Damer v Taylor Wessing LLP* [2017] EWCA Civ 74, [2017] 1 WLR 3255 at [45].

172 *Dawson-Damer v Taylor Wessing LLP* [2017] EWCA Civ 74, [2017] 1 WLR 3255 at [54].

173 DPA 1998 s 37 and Sch 7 para 11(1).

174 DPA 1998 Sch 7 para 11(2).

175 DPA 1998 s 38(1).

176 The Data Protection (Miscellaneous Subject Access Exemptions) Order 2000 SI 2000/419 Art 2 and sch Pt I.

177 The Data Protection (Miscellaneous Subject Access Exemptions) Order 2000 SI 2000/419 Art 2 and sch Pt II(a), III(a), IV(a) as amended by the Data Protection (Miscellaneous Subject Access Exemptions) (Amendment) Order 2000 SI 2000/1865. In Scotland information provided by a Principal Reporter for a children's hearing is also exempted: The Data Protection (Miscellaneous Subject Access Exemptions) Order 2000 SI 2000/419 Art 2 and sch Pt III(b).

educational needs[178] and parental order records and reports.[179]

[178] The Data Protection (Miscellaneous Subject Access Exemptions) Order 2000 SI 2000/419 Art 2 and Sch Pt II(b), III(c) (record of special educational needs in Scotland), Pt IV(b).

[179] The Data Protection (Miscellaneous Subject Access Exemptions) Order 2000 SI 2000/419 Art 2 and Sch Pt II(c), III(d), IV(c).

Part III

Environmental Information

CHAPTER 17

Environmental information – introduction

1. THE AARHUS CONVENTION

17– 001 The Aarhus Convention

On 25 June 1998, the UN Economic Commission for Europe (UNECE), at its Fourth Ministerial Conference in the 'Environment for Europe' process, adopted a Convention on Access to Information, Public Participation in Decision-Making and Access to Justice on Environmental Matters. This has become known as the 'Aarhus Convention'. The Convention entered into force on 30 October 2001. The UK and the European Community is each a signatory to the Aarhus Convention.[1] The Aarhus Convention establishes a number of rights of the public (citizens and their associations) with respect to the environment. It contains three broad themes or 'pillars': access to information, public participation, and access to justice.[2] The Convention recites as one of its goals the protection of the right of every person of present and future generations to live in an environment which is adequate to health and well-being. The UNECE has described the Aarhus Convention as 'a new kind of

[1] As to the status of the Convention in UK domestic law see *Morgan v Hinton Organics (Wessex) Ltd* [2009] EWCA Civ 107, [2009] Env LR 30 per Carnwath LJ at [19]-[34] and [47]. In relation to EU institution decision-making and legal processes, the three pillars of the Aarhus Convention have been implemented through Regulation 1367/2006/EC on the application of the provisions of the Aarhus Convention on Access to Information, Public Participation in Decision-Making and Access to Justice in Environmental Matters to Community Institutions and Bodies ("the Aarhus Regulation"). For a recent example of this Regulation in action in securing access to documentation held by the EU institutions, see *ClientEarth v European Commission* (C-57/16 P) [2019] Env LR 19, where the CJEU said:

> Regulation No 1367/2006 aims … to ensure the widest possible systematic availability and dissemination of environmental information (*Saint-Gobain Glass Deutschland GmbH v European Commission* (C-60/15) [2018] Env LR 8 at [64] and the case law cited). It follows, in essence, from recital 2 of that regulation that the purpose of access to that information is to promote more effective public participation in the decision-making process, thereby increasing, on the part of the competent bodies, the accountability of decision-making and contributing to public awareness and support for the decisions taken (*European Commission v Stichtung Greenpeace Nederland and another* (C-673/13) [2017] 2 CMLR 529 at [80]).

[2] Thus Art 1 of the Aarhus Convention provides: 'In order to contribute to the protection of the right of every person of present and future generations to live in an environment adequate to his or her health and well-being, each Party shall guarantee the rights of access to information, public participation in decision-making, and access to justice in environmental matters in accordance with the provisions of this Convention.'

environmental agreement', which links environmental rights and human rights, and government accountability and environmental protection. Thus, it is not only an environmental agreement, but also an agreement about government accountability, transparency and responsiveness.[3] The then Secretary of State for the Environment stated that the UK Government strongly supported the objectives of the Aarhus Convention, adding that the three areas in which it provides additional rights (namely, under the three 'pillars' referred to above) would allow the public[4] to be better informed and more involved in decision-making, and that 'more broadly based discussion can lead to better decisions and so make an important contribution to achieving sustainable development'.[5] The European Community ratified the Aarhus Convention on 17 February 2005. The United Kingdom ratified it on 24 February 2005, becoming a full party to the Convention 90 days thereafter. The UNECE has published an Implementation Guide to the Aarhus Convention which seeks to explain the meaning and purpose of the Convention.[6]

---

3 The Preamble to the Aarhus Convention states, inter alia, that the parties thereto agreed to its terms 'Affirming the need to protect, preserve and improve the state of the environment and to ensure sustainable and environmentally sound development; Recognising that adequate protection of the environment is essential to human well-being and the enjoyment of basic human rights, including the right to life itself; Recognising also that every person has the right to live in an environment adequate to his or her health and well-being, and the duty, both individually and in association with others, to protect and improve the environment for the benefit of present and future generations; Considering that, to be able to assert this right and observe this duty, citizens must have access to information, be entitled to participate in decision-making and have access to justice in environmental matters, and acknowledging in this regard that citizens may need assistance in order to exercise their rights; Recognising that, in the field of the environment, improved access to information and public participation in decision-making enhance the quality and the implementation of decisions, contribute to public awareness of environmental issues, give the public the opportunity to express its concerns and enable public authorities to take due account of such concerns; Aiming thereby to further the accountability and transparency in decision-making and to strengthen public support for decisions on the environment; Recognising the desirability of transparency in all branches of government and inviting legislative bodies to implement the principles of the Convention in their proceedings, [and] Recognising also that the public needs to be aware of the procedures for participation in environmental decision-making, have free access to them and know how to use them.'

4 'The public' is defined in Art 2(4) of the Aarhus Convention to mean 'one or more natural or legal persons, and, in accordance with national legislation or practice, their associations, organisations or groups'. In *R (Halebank Parish Council) v Halton Borough Council* (unreported, 30 April 2012) that HHJ Raynor QC decided (in considering a protective costs order application) that a Parish Council fell within the definition of the 'public' for the purposes of the Aarhus Convention. There is no transcript of this decision available. In findings adopted on 24 September 2013 the Aarhus Compliance Committee found in ACCC/C/2012/68, at [79]-[83], in relation to a communication from a Scottish community council, that it could be accepted as a member of the public by looking at its role and functions, and in particular that such councils 'have no regulatory decision-making functions and are essentially voluntary bodies established within a statutory framework.' In a determination issued on 7 August 2015 the Aarhus Compliance Committee found in ACCC/C/2012/68 that the London Borough of Hillingdon was a 'public authority' under Art 2, paragraph 2(a) of the Convention 'since [it] exercised administrative decision-making powers' and hence was not a 'member of the public' for the purposes of article 15 of the Convention.

5 Michael Meacher, Minister for the Environment, 6 October 2000 Explanatory Memorandum, Report from the Commission to the Council and the European Parliament on the experience gained in the application of Directive 90/313/EEC of 7 June 1990, on freedom of access to information on the environment and Proposal for a Directive of the European Parliament and of the Council on public access to environmental information, para 15.

6 Now in its second edition. The guide is available on the UNECE website. In *Solvay and ors v Region Wallone* (Case C-182/10) [2012] 2 CMLR 19 the Court of Justice of the European Union held (at [27]-[28]) that the implementation guide was to be regarded as an explanatory document, capable of being taken into consideration if appropriate among other relevant material for the purpose of interpreting the convention. See also *Flachglas Torgau GmbH*, C-204/09 [2013] QB 212, [2012] Env LR 26, [2012] EUECJ C-204/09, [2012] 2 CMLR 17 at [58], where the Court said that the Guide was 'not entirely valueless' as an aid to interpretation of the Aarhus Convention but was in no way 'decisive.' In *Fish Legal v Information Commissioner United Utilities, Yorkshire Water and Southern Water* (C-279/12) [2014] QB 521, [2014] 2 CMLR 36 (at [38]) the court characterised the guide as an 'explanatory document, capable of being taken into account, if appropriate, among other relevant material for the purpose of interpretation of the convention [but with] no binding force...' This was quoted with seeming approval by the Upper Tribunal in *Highways England v IC and Manisty* [2018] UKUT 423 (AAC) at [19]. For an annotated guide to case law on the Convention, see: A Andrusevych, S Kern (eds), *Case Law of the Aarhus Convention Compliance Committee (2004-2014)*, 3rd Edition (RACSE, Lviv 2016), available on the UNECE website. More recent decisions can be found at: `www.unece.org/env/pp/pubcom.html`

17–002 First pillar – information access

The Aarhus Convention provides for the right of everyone to receive environmental information that is held by public authorities. Within the United Kingdom, this pillar is implemented through Directive 2003/4/EC and the EIR.[7] The Convention provides an elaborate definition of 'environmental information'.[8] Having defined 'public authorities',[9] the Convention requires each Contracting Party to ensure that each public authority makes available, in response to a request and within the framework of national legislation, a copy of 'the actual documentation' containing or comprising the requested environmental information. The Convention expressly provides that the person making the request need not state an interest in the information sought.[10] The Convention requires a public authority to make the information available 'as soon as possible' and at the latest within one month after the request has been submitted.[11] The Convention permits a Contracting Party to make a charge 'for supplying information' according to a pre-published schedule of charges.[12] Charges must be reasonable.[13] A request for environmental information may be refused in the circumstances set out in Arts 4(3)-(4) of the Convention. Article 4.3 sets out procedural grounds for refusal: the information is not held by the recipient public authority, the request is manifestly unreasonable, or the information is deliberative material whose disclosure is customarily or expressly provided for. Article 4.4 sets out seven classes of protected interest. Under that Article, a public authority may refuse to disclose requested information to the extent that its disclosure would adversely affect:

— the confidentiality of the proceedings of public authorities, provided that such confidentiality is provided for under national law;[14]
— international relations, national defence or public security;[15]
— the course of justice, the ability of a person to receive a fair trial or the ability of a public authority to conduct an enquiry of a criminal or disciplinary nature;[16]
— the confidentiality of commercial and industrial information, where such confidentiality is protected by law in order to protect a legitimate economic interest;[17]

---

7 In relation to Scottish public authorities, it is implemented through the EI(S)R.

8 Article 2.3, considered in §§17–008 to 17–018.

9 'Public authority' is defined in Art 2.2 of the Aarhus Convention as meaning '(a) Government at national, regional and other level; (b) Natural or legal persons performing public administrative functions under national law, including specific duties, activities or services in relation to the environment; (c) Any other natural or legal persons having public responsibilities or functions, or providing public services, in relation to the environment, under the control of a person falling within subparagraphs (a) or (b) above; (d) the institutions of any regional economic integration organisation referred to in Art 17 which is a party to this Convention.' Article 2 further states that the above definition of 'public authority' does not include bodies or institutions acting in a judicial or legislative capacity.

10 Aarhus Convention Art 4.1.

11 Aarhus Convention Art 4.2. This requirement is subject to the proviso that this period may be extended, if the volume and complexity of the information justifies the extension, to up to two months after the request. The applicant for information must be informed of any extension and the reasons for it.

12 Aarhus Convention Art 4.8.

13 Aarhus Convention Art 4.8.

14 Aarhus Convention Art 4.4(a). See §19–022.

15 Aarhus Convention Art 4.4(b). See §19–015.

16 Aarhus Convention Art 4.4(c). See §19–018.

17 Aarhus Convention Art 4.4(d). This Article specifically provides that 'Within this framework, information on emissions which is relevant for the protection of the environment shall be disclosed.' See §19–024.

— intellectual property rights;[18]
— the confidentiality of personal data and/or files relating to a natural person, where that person has not consented to the disclosure of the information to the public and where such confidentiality is provided for in national law;[19]
— the interests of a third party which has supplied the information requested without that party being under or capable of being put under a legal obligation to do so, and where that party does not consent to the release of the material;[20] or
— the environment to which the information relates, such as the breeding sites of rare species.[21]

These grounds for refusal are not made subject to a public interest balancing test. Rather, the Convention provides that the grounds for refusal are to be interpreted in a restrictive way, taking into account the public interest served by the disclosure and taking into account whether the information requested relates to emissions into the environment.[22] The Convention imposes an obligation on a public authority that does not hold requested information to transfer the request to a public authority that it believes holds the requested information.[23] Alternatively, the public authority may inform the applicant that it believes that the other public authority holds the requested information. The Convention provides for redaction of exempt material.[24] Refusals must be in writing, must set out the reasons for refusal and must advise of the applicant's right of review.[25] The right of review must be determined by a court or an independent body established by law.[26] The procedure must be free of charge or 'inexpensive'.[27] Under the Convention, public authorities also have a separate obligation to actively disseminate environmental information in their possession.[28] The first pillar, as it has been implemented in the United Kingdom, is considered in this chapter.

7– 003 Second pillar — participation

Article 6 of the Aarhus Convention guarantees the right to participate from an early stage in environmental decision-making with respect to certain specified activities,[29] and with respect to activities that are not specified in the Aarhus Convention itself, but which may have a significant effect on the environment. Where the provisions of Art 6 are applicable, the public concerned[30] must be informed, either by public notice or individually as appropriate, early in

---

18 Aarhus Convention Art 4.4(e). See §19– 020.

19 Aarhus Convention Art 4.4(f). See §19– 032.

20 Aarhus Convention Art 4.4(g). See §19– 026.

21 Aarhus Convention Art 4.4(h). See §19– 028.

22 Aarhus Convention Art 4.4.

23 Aarhus Convention Art 4.5.

24 Aarhus Convention Art 4.6.

25 Aarhus Convention Art 4.7.

26 Aarhus Convention Art 9.1.

27 Aarhus Convention Art 9.1. The Convention implies that if the procedure would not be 'inexpensive' for the appellant, legal aid or some other form of assistance must be made available.

28 Aarhus Convention Art 5.

29 Namely, those listed in Annex I to the Aarhus Convention. These include activities carried out in the energy sector; in the course of the production and processing of materials; in the mineral and chemical industries; in waste management; by water treatment plants with a capacity exceeding 150,000 population equivalent; by industrial plants; in the construction of transport infrastructure such as railways, airports and roads; and other activities; as well as any activities not specifically mentioned where public participation is provided for under an environmental impact assessment procedure in accordance with national legislation.

30 Namely by Art 2.5, the public affected or likely to be affected by, or having an interest in, the environmental

the environmental decision-making procedure, and in an adequate, timely and effective manner, inter alia, of the proposed activity and the application on which a decision will be taken; the nature of the possible decisions or draft decision; the public authority responsible for making the decision, the envisaged decision-making procedure; and the fact that the activity is subject to a national or trans-boundary environmental impact assessment procedure.[31] Each party to the Convention must require the competent public authorities to give the public concerned access for examination, upon request where so required under national law, free of charge and as soon as it becomes available, all information relevant to the decision-making referred to in Art 6 that is available at the time of the public participation procedure, including at least a description of the site and the physical and technical characteristics of the proposed activity; a description of the significant effects of the proposed activity on the environment; a description of the measures envisaged to prevent and/or reduce the effects, including emissions; a non-technical summary of the above; an outline of the main alternatives studied by the applicant; and, in accordance with national legislation, the main reports and advice issued to the public authority at the time when the public concerned shall be informed in accordance with Art 2.[32] The procedure for public participation must then allow for the public to submit, in writing or, as appropriate, at a public hearing or inquiry with the applicant, any comments, information, analyses, or opinions that it considers relevant to the proposed activity;[33] and the parties to the Convention must ensure that in the decision due account is taken of the outcome of the public participation.[34]

17–004 Third pillar — access to justice

This pillar of the Aarhus Convention, which is set out in Art 9, aims to provide access to justice in three contexts, namely, review procedures with respect to information requests; review procedures with respect to specific decisions that are subject to the public participation requirements, and challenges to breaches of environmental law in general. So far as access to information appeals are concerned, the Convention provides that a person who considers that his Convention request for information has been ignored, wrongfully refused, inadequately answered, or otherwise not dealt with in accordance with the provisions of that Article, must be provided with access to a review procedure by a court or another independent and impartial body established by law.[35] The Convention further provides that, in the circumstances where a party provides for such a review by a court of law, it must ensure that a complainant also has access to an expeditious procedure established by law, that is free of charge or inexpensive, for reconsideration by a public authority or review by an independent and impartial body other than a court of law. Secondly, Art 9.2 provides that each party must, within the framework of

decision-making. Article 2.5 further provides that, for the purpose of the latter definition, non-governmental organisations promoting environmental protection and meeting any requirements under national law shall be deemed to have an interest.

31 Aarhus Convention Art 6.2.

32 Aarhus Convention Art 6.6. These provisions are without prejudice to the provisions of Art 4 of the Aarhus Convention: Aarhus Convention Art 6.6.

33 Aarhus Convention Art 6.7.

34 Further steps in the public participation procedure are provided for in Arts 6.8-6.11. In addition, requirements for public participation concerning plans, programmes and policies relating to the environment are set out in Art 7; while Art 8 provides for public participation during the preparation of executive regulations and/or generally applicable legally binding normative instruments. The above-mentioned provisions are already largely reflected in the Environmental Impact Assessment procedure that is provided for in England and Wales under the Town and Country Planning (Environmental Impact Assessment) (England and Wales) Regulations 2011, which were drafted with the Aarhus Convention in mind. Similar provision is made in various other regulations concerned with specific activities, eg pipelines and infrastructure planning. Similar regulations also exist in Northern Ireland and Scotland.

35 Aarhus Convention Art 9.1.

its national legislation, ensure that members of the public concerned having a sufficient interest, or, alternatively, maintaining impairment of a right, where the administrative procedural law of a party requires this as a precondition, have access to a review procedure before a court of law and/or another independent and impartial body established by law to challenge the substantive and procedural legality of any decision, act or omission subject to the provisions of Art 6 and, where so provided for under national law, of other relevant provisions of the Aarhus Convention.[36] Article 9.2 further provides that what constitutes a sufficient interest or impairment of a right shall be determined in accordance with the requirements of national law and consistently with the objective of giving the public concerned wide access to justice within the scope of the Convention. To this end, Art 9.2 states, the interest of any non-governmental organisation meeting the requirements referred to in Art 2.5 (namely non-governmental organisations which promote environmental protection and meeting any requirements under national law) shall be deemed sufficient; and that such organisations shall also be deemed to have rights capable of being impaired for the purposes of Art 9.2.[37]

7–005 Directive 2003/4/EC

On 28 January 2003 the European Parliament and the Council of the European Union adopted Directive 2003/4/EC on public access to environmental information ('the Directive').[38] The Directive repeals Council Directive 90/313/EEC,[39] which in Great Britain had been implemented through the Environmental Information Regulations 1992.[40] The recitals to the 2003 Directive record a general favouring of the disclosure of official information 'to the widest extent possible',[41] crediting increased public access to environmental information with:

> contribut[ing] to a greater awareness of environmental matters, a free exchange of views, more effective participation by the public in environmental decision-making and, eventually, to a better environment.[42]

The Directive records that its disclosure obligations are not intended to dissuade Member States from providing more extensive disclosure regimes than that which is required by the Directive.[43] The Directive imposes, in other words, the minimum acceptable level of disclosure of environmental information: it does not set the bounds of permissible disclosure.[44] Under the EU (Withdrawal) Act 2018 the Directive will be 'Retained EU law' on exit day.

---

36 This provision is subject to Art 9.3, which provides that in addition and without prejudice to the review procedures referred to in Arts 9.1 and 9.2, each Party shall ensure that, where they meet the criteria, if any, laid down in its national law, members of the public have access to administrative or judicial procedures to challenge acts and omissions by private persons and public authorities which contravene provisions of its national law relating to the environment.

37 See the discussion of Art 9 in *R (Evans) v Attorney-General* [2015] UKSC 21, [2015] AC 1787, considered further below.

38 The Directive entered into force on 14 February 2003. Article 10 of the Directive obliges the Member States of the European Union to have their legislation in place at the latest by 14 February 2004. For a summary of the interpretative principles applicable to a directive, see §§7–035 to 7–038.

39 With effect from 14 February 2005: Art 11. Recital (6) of the 2003 Directive records that 'it is appropriate in the interest of increased transparency to replace Directive 90/313/EEC rather than to amend it, so as to provide interested parties with a single, clear and coherent legislative text.'

40 SI 1992/3240. These were amended by the Environmental Information (Amendment) Regulations 1998 SI 1998/1447, which reduced the exceptions from disclosure so as to make the 1992 regulations properly align with Council Directive 90/313/EEC.

41 Directive 2003/4/EC Recital (9).

42 Directive 2003/4/EC Recital (1).

43 Directive 2003/4/EC Recital (24).

44 This is acknowledged in the Code of Practice, February 2005, issued under reg 16, para 7. See below for the status of the Code of Practice.

17– 006 The EIR 2004

Both the Parliament at Westminster and the Scottish Parliament have made regulations implementing the Directive. The EIR implement the Directive in relation to public authorities that owe their existence to the Parliament at Westminster,[45] including those operating or holding information in Scotland. The EI(S)R implement the Directive in relation to public authorities that owe their existence to the Scottish Parliament, ie Scottish public authorities.[46] The two sets of Regulations are very similar. The EIR may be invoked by a person in Scotland to seek information from a non-Scottish public authority. The EI(S)R may be invoked by a person in England, Wales or Northern Ireland to request information from a Scottish public authority. There is an obligation to interpret each set of Regulations 'as far as possible, in the light of the wording and the purpose of the Directive in order to achieve the result pursued by the latter'.[47] Although the Directive left it open for Member States to implement a more generous disclosure regime than the minimum prescribed by the Directive, there is nothing to indicate that the EIR intended to do more than introduce into domestic law exceptions matching in their terms and their extent those permitted by the Directive.[48]

17– 007 Inter-relationship with FOIA

Information to which a person has a right of access under the EIR is exempt information under FOIA.[49] In this way, the Act attempts to funnel requests for 'environmental information' through the Regulations.[50] The attempt is not entirely successful, as the exemption under FOIA is not absolute.[51] Accordingly, the right under the Act to environmental information is only disapplied to the extent that, in all the circumstances of the case, the public interest in maintaining the exemption outweighs the public interest in disclosing the information.[52] There is nothing to preclude an applicant making a composite request for specified information under both FOIA and the EIR. A public authority faced with such a request will need: (1) to determine which of the information captured by the request falls within the access right given by the Regulations (ie to determine which of that information falls within the definition of 'environmental information')[53]; (2) then, in relation to that 'environmental information',

---

45 These are the public authorities that are listed in Sch 1 of the FOIA or that are designated by order under s 5(1) of that Act.

46 These are the public authorities that are listed in Sch 1 of the FOI(S)A or that are designated by order under s 5(1) of that Act.

47 *ECGD v Friends of the Earth* [2008] EWHC 638 (Admin), [2008] Env LR 40, [2008] JPL 1813 at [20]; Case C-106/89 *Marleasing SA v La Comercial Internacional de Alimentación SA* [1992] 1 CMLR 305 at [8]; Case C-365/98 *Brinkmann Tabakfabriken GmbH v Hauptzollamt Bielefeld* [2002] 2 CMLR 36; *Perceval-Price v Department of Economic Development* [2000] IRLR 380, [2000] NI 141.

48 *Office of Communication v Information Commissioner* [2010] UKSC 3 at [3].

49 FOIA s 39(1)(a). And, similarly, information to which a person has a right of access under the EI(S)R is exempt information under the FOI(S)A s 39(2)(a). See further §§25– 012 to 25– 015.

50 The FTT has held that decisions as to which regime applies should not normally involve a minute analysis of each paragraph but appraisal of the document as a whole in the light of the broad definition of environmental information: see *Cabinet Office v IC*, FTT, 4 October 2010 at [18].

51 FOIA s 2(3); FOI(S)A s 2(2).

52 FOIA s 2(2); FOI(S)A s 2(1)(b).

53 A single document or electronic file, all of which falls within the terms of a request, may be made up partly of environmental information (access to which falls to be decided under the EIR) and the remainder of information that is not environmental information (access to which falls to be decided under FOIA). The practical difficulties which this presents for any public authority was acknowledged by the Tribunal in *DBERR v IC and Friends of the Earth*, IT, 29 April 2008 at [29]. *Department for Business, Energy and Industrial Strategy v Information Commissioner* [2015] UKUT 671 (AAC) has said been said to be a 'roadmap' for deciding if the EIR apply. See further the guidance on the correct approach in *Dept of Transport v IC and Hastings*, FTT, 6 July 2016 especially at [20] including on the

determine whether any of the exceptions in the Regulations applies, including a consideration of the public interest;[54] (3) in relation to the requested information that is 'environmental information' but which, under (2), need not be disclosed, consider whether in all the circumstances the public interest in maintaining the s 39 exemption outweighs the public interest in disclosing that information; and (4) in relation to the requested information that is not 'environmental information', determine whether any of the other exemptions in the Act applies (including, where necessary, a consideration of the public interest). The definition of 'public authority' in the Regulations is different from that in the Act. Where environmental information is sought of a body that is a public authority under the Act, but not under the Regulations, the request will fall to be determined solely by reference to the Act.[55]

2. ENVIRONMENTAL INFORMATION

17– 008 Introduction

The EIR establish a regime that overall confers a greater right of access than that conferred by FOIA. The special treatment afforded to environmental information gives effect to the recited objectives of the Aarhus Convention and Directive 2003/4/EC.[56] At their core is the belief that protection of the environment is a matter of legitimate individual concern and involvement. Each of the three pillars of the Convention require the Contracting Parties to bestow an individual right that enables that individual involvement. Each right partly depends on the two others for its efficacy. Informed public participation in the making of decisions relating to the environment requires access to information on the environment held by public authorities. Central to the regime established by the Directive, and faithfully reproduced in the Regulations, is the definition of 'environmental information'.[57] The definition of 'environmental information' in regulation 2(1) of the 2004 Regulations is expressly the same as that given in Article 2(1) of the Directive. The definition has six limbs. The term 'environmental information' is to be interpreted broadly.[58] However, that does not give a general and unlimited right of access to all information held by public authorities that has a connection, however minimal with one of the environmental factors mentioned in Article 2(1) of the Convention. To be covered by the right of access secured by the Convention, the information must fall within one or more of the categories set out in article 2(1).[59] If any of the information

---

predominant purpose test. See also *Ames v IC and Dept for Transport*, FTT, 18 July 2016; *Holland v IC and University of Cambridge* [2016] UKUT 260 (AAC) at [36]-[38]; *Crane v IC and Dept for Transport*, FTT, 16 January 2017; *LB of Haringey v IC*, FTT, 27 January 2017. See further *Dept for Transport v IC and Hastings* [2019] EWCA Civ 2241, overturning *IC v Dept for Transport and Hastings* [2018] UKUT 185 (AAC).

54 Under EIR reg 12(1)(b), or EI(S)R reg 10(1)(b).

55 See further §19– 008.

56 On which, see generally, *Department for Business, Energy and Industrial Strategy v Information Commissioner* [2017] EWCA Civ 844, [2017] PTSR 1644 at [14]-[15]; *Dept for Transport v IC and Hastings* [2019] EWCA Civ 2241 at [28].

57 EIR reg 2(1), reproducing Art 2.1 of the Directive. Similarly, EI(S)R reg 2(1). Their provenance is in Art 2.3 of the Aarhus Convention, although there are slight variations: see §17– 011. The meaning given to the phrase 'environmental information' is significantly wider than that given to it in the Town and Country Planning (Environmental Impact Assessment) (England and Wales) Regulations 1999, as to which see *R (Richardson) v North Yorkshire County Council* [2003] EWHC 764 (Admin).

58 See: *Department for Business, Energy and Industrial Strategy v Information Commissioner* [2017] EWCA Civ 844, [2017] PTSR 1644 at [16] citing, inter alia, *Glawischnig v Bundesminster für soziale Sicherheit und Generationen* (C-316/01) [2003] ECR I-5995, [2003] All ER (D) 147 (Jun) at [24] and *Venn v Secretary of State for Communities and Local Government* [2014] EWCA Civ 1539, [2015] 1 WLR 2328 at [10]-[12]; *Dept for Transport v IC and Hastings* [2019] EWCA Civ 2241 at [28].

59 *Glawischnig v Bundesminster für soziale Sicherheit und Generationen* (C-316/01) [2003] ECR I-5995, [2003] All ER (D) 147

sought by an applicant is outside the definition of 'environmental information', the right of access will fall to be decided principally by FOIA.

17– 009 'Any information on'

In order for information[60] to constitute 'environmental information' the nexus required between that information and the matters set out in regulation 2(1)(a)-(f) of the EIR is that the information be 'on' the matters set out in regulation 2(1)(a)-(f). The ICO's Guidance on Environmental Information states that this is to be interpreted broadly, and suggests that 'information that would inform the public about matters affecting the environment or enable them to participate in decision making, and help to achieve that purpose' is likely to be environmental information, even if the information itself does not directly mention the environment.[61] It also suggests that the test to be applied is 'whether the information is on or about something falling within the six limbs of the definition in regulations 2(1)(a)-(f), and not whether the information directly mentions the environment or any environmental matter.[62] By way of example, the FTT concluded that the names of mobile network operators were environmental information as:

> the name of a person or organisation responsible for an installation that emits electromagnetic waves falls comfortably within the meaning of the words 'any information…on….radiation.'[63]

Whilst it is debatable whether it is useful to synonymize a preposition, the Court of Appeal has held that information is 'on' a measure if 'it is about, relates to or concerns the measure in question.'[64] The fact that information provides something, originally emanating from a third party about (for example) a measure, does not make it information 'on' that measure.[65] Where it is borderline whether or not information is information 'on' one of the matters, the tribunal should adopt a cautious approach before finding that the information is to be disclosed.[66]

17– 010 State of the elements

The first limb of the definition of 'environmental information' is:

> (a) the state of the elements of the environment, such as air and atmosphere, water, soil, land, landscape and natural sites including wetlands, coastal and marine areas, biological diversity and its components, including genetically modified organisms, and the interaction among those elements;[67]

(Jun) at [25].

60 As to the meaning of 'information', see §§17– 018 and 20– 001 to 20– 008.

61 ICO, *What is environmental information? Regulation 2(1)) Environmental Information Regulations* at para 16.

62 ICO, *What is environmental information? Regulation 2(1)) Environmental Information Regulations* at para 17.

63 *OFCOM v IC and T-Mobile (UK) Ltd*, IT, 4 September 2007 at [31]. This decision does not sit altogether easily with the conclusion of the CJEU in *Glawischnig v Bundesminster für soziale Sicherheit und Generationen* (C-316/01) [2003] ECR I-5995, [2003] All ER (D) 147 (Jun) in which it upheld the public authority's refusal to answer a request to the extent that it sought the names and producers of genetically-modified products in respect of which the authority had received complaints or had imposed penalties for non-compliance with product labelling laws.

64 *Department for Business, Energy and Industrial Strategy v Information Commissioner* [2017] EWCA Civ 844, [2017] PTSR 1644 at [37]; *Dept for Transport v IC and Hastings* [2019] EWCA Civ 2241 at [30], [39]; *Department for Transport & ors v IC and Cieslik* [2018] UKUT 127 (AAC) at [21]-[27], [33] ('information which has only a minimal connection with the environment is not environmental information,' where it was held that throttle test results of a particular model of car for safety reasons were not environmental information).

65 *Dept for Transport v IC and Hastings* [2019] EWCA Civ 2241 at [39].

66 *Dept for Transport v IC and Hastings* [2019] EWCA Civ 2241 at [33].

67 Derived from Aarhus Convention Art 2.3(a) and Directive 2003/4/EC Art 2.1(a). In *R v British Coal Corporation, ex p Ibstock Building Products Ltd* [1995] Env LR 277, a case under the 1992 Regulations, Harrison J held that the name of an informant who had advised a local authority that naval munitions had been dumped down a mineshaft in 1947 (a matter which impinged upon the grant of planning permission) was information that was capable of relating to the state of the land.

In relation to these 'elements of the environment,' guidance issued by the ICO suggests[68] that:

— The use of the words both 'air' and 'atmosphere indicate that it includes air which is confined in some way as well as air outside.[69] The term also includes the various gases and particles comprised in air and atmosphere.
— 'Water' includes water in all forms (ie whatever form it may exist under different temperatures or conditions), and location of that water is immaterial (i.e underground, surface water, or in natural settings).[70]
— 'Soil' is taken to be the top layer of soil in which plants grow.
— 'Land' means 'the solid parts of the earth, whether at the surface or underground.' It is expressly distinguished from the definition of 'land' for the purposes of English property law. 'Landscape' means landscape as that term is 'commonly understood'. It may be in any location, or of any quality.
— 'Natural sites including wetlands, coastal and marine areas' covers any sites regarded as examples of sites supporting natural flora or fauna, or landscape in its natural condition. There is no need for the site to be formally designated.[71]
— 'Biological diversity and its components', is the 'balance between the various species on earth' and as such it is considered by the ICO that this would not encompass information about a single species, but that information about the balance between species, and how an individual species made up that balance, would fall within the definition. The United Nation's Implementation Guide cross-refers to the definition given to the phrase in Art 2 of the Convention on Biological Diversity:[72] namely, 'the variability among living organisms from all sources including, inter alia, terrestrial, marine and other aquatic ecosystems and the ecological complexes of which they are part; this includes diversity within species, between species and of ecosystems.' The Implementation Guide continues by stating that biodiversity 'includes, but is not limited to, ecosystem diversity, species diversity and genetic diversity. In addition, tangible entities identifiable as a specific ecosystem (a dynamic complex of plant, animal and micro-organism communities and their non-living environment interacting as a functional unit), are considered components of biodiversity.'

The list of 'elements of the environment' is non-exhaustive. The United Nations Implementation Guide considers that radiation, in addition to being a factor, is an element of the environment.[73] Information on or about the interaction between the elements of the environment is also environmental information within the meaning of regulation 2(1).[74] The requirement on signatories to the Aarhus Convention to report regularly on 'the state of the environment' might suggest that information on the state of the elements of the environment

68 ICO, *What is environmental information? Regulation 2(1)) Environmental Information Regulations.*

69 The same view is taken in J Ebbeson, H Gaugitsch, J Jendroska, F Marshall and S Stec, *The Aarhus Convention: an Implementation Guide* (2nd Edn) (New York, United Nations, 2014) p 51, which indicates that the term invites Parties to include 'indoor and workplace air.'

70 The ICO Guidance does not expressly refer to water held in man-made structures – cf the guidance provided in the (now archived) DEFRA Guidance, Ch 3, *What is covered by the Regulations?* (December 2006, para 3.5). However, such information would, clearly, be environmental information for the purposes of regulation 2(1).

71 J Ebbeson, H.Gaugitsch, J.Jendroska, F Marshall and S Stec, *The Aarhus Convention: an Implementation Guide* (2nd Edn) (New York, United Nations, 2014) p 51 suggest that the term would also include 'any objects of nature which are of specific value, including not only officially designated protected areas, but also, for example, a forest, a tree or a park that is of localised significance, having special natural, historic or cultural value.'

72 Concluded at Rio de Janeiro on 5 June 1992. J Ebbeson, H Gaugitsch, J Jendroska, F Marshall and S Stec, *The Aarhus Convention: an Implementation Guide* (2nd Edn) (New York, United Nations, 2014) p 51.

73 J Ebbeson, H Gaugitsch, J Jendroska, F Marshall and S Stec, *The Aarhus Convention: an Implementation Guide* (2nd Edn) (New York, United Nations, 2014) p 52.

74 EIR reg 2(1)(a); EI(S)R reg 2(1)(a).

is not concerned with the detail of information relating to each of these elements but with higher level analysis of them.[75]

17–011 Factors affecting the elements

The second limb of the definition of 'environmental information' is:

(b) factors, such as substances, energy, noise, radiation or waste, including radioactive waste, emissions, discharges and other releases into the environment, affecting or likely to affect the elements of the environment referred to in (a);[76]

The ICO considers that for the purposes of the Regulations a 'factor' is something physical that has an 'impact' or 'influence' on the environment.[77] The ICO also suggests that:

- 'substances' includes all physical materials or matter, whether natural or synthetic, and in any form (ie solid, liquid, gas);
- 'energy' includes all types of energy (thermal, chemical, electrical, nuclear, kinetic, sound, potential, light and gravitational);
- 'noise' is, essentially, unwanted sound – "a simple definition of noise is a sound, especially one that is loud, unpleasant, or disturbing";
- 'radiation' is energy transmitted as waves, rays or as sub-atomic particles, and can be either natural or man-made;
- 'waste' can be broadly interpreted, to mean anything discarded;
- 'emissions, discharges and other releases into the environment' may overlap. The ICO suggests that 'emissions' and 'discharges' indicate 'direct or indirect, accidental or deliberate release of substances, heat, radiation or noise into the air, water or land' whereas 'release' suggests 'liberation, or a change of state from confined to unconfined.'[78]

Information about a 'factor' is only 'environmental information' if it is about the factor 'affecting' or 'likely to affect' the environment. The ICO suggests that 'affecting' means 'there has already been an impact on the state of the environment, or that the impact is current or ongoing.'[79] As to whether a factor is 'likely to affect' the environment, the ICO suggests this means that there is a 'likelihood' that the factor will impact on the state of element of the environment. 'Likely', in this context, does not mean more probable than not, but does require some real and substantial possibility – more than a merely remote prospect.[80] The authors of the United Nations Implementation Guide draw attention to the difference between the English version of the Convention and the literal translation of the French and Russian versions (all of which are equally authentic under Article 22 of the Convention). In the French and Russian versions, the text translates as 'may affect' which the authors of the Guide consider to be a lower

---

75 See Aarhus Convention Art 5.4, and Directive 2003/4/EC Art 7.3. In *Archer v IC and Salisbury DC*, IT, 9 May 2007 (at [32]) it was held that para (a) covered a joint report to a committee of a local council from the head of development services and the head of legal and democratic services which identified breaches of planning control and recommended certain legal action.

76 Derived from Aarhus Convention Art 2.3(b), and Directive 2003/4/EC Art 2.1(b).

77 ICO, *What is environmental information? Regulation 2(1)) Environmental Information Regulations* at para 25.

78 In *OFCOM v IC and T-Mobile (UK) Ltd*, IT, 4 September 2007 the Tribunal rejected an argument that emission bore the narrow meaning given to it in Council Directive 96/6/EC and concluded that radiation emanating from mobile phone base stations are a type of 'emission' (at [25]). The Tribunal also concluded that the radio emissions were a form of energy or radiation that affected the elements of the environment (at [27]). The definition was found to be wide enough to cover the names of mobile network operators that owned the different base stations (at [31]).

79 ICO, *What is environmental information? Regulation 2(1)) Environmental Information Regulations* at para 27.

80 ICO, *What is environmental information? Regulation 2(1)) Environmental Information Regulations* at para 28. In *Uttlesford District Council v IC*, FTT, 6 June 2012 the Tribunal held that matters relating to the emails concerning the Council's code of conduct for members, albeit in a planning context, were too remote to be within the EIR (at [27]-[29]).

test than the English 'likely to affect.'[81] The point has not, as yet, been determined by a Meeting of the Parties.

17– 012 Measures affecting the elements

The third limb of the definition of 'environmental information' is:

> (c) measures (including administrative measures), such as policies, legislation, plans, programmes, environmental agreements, and activities affecting or likely to affect the elements and factors referred to in (a) and (b) as well as measures or activities designed to protect those elements;[82]

The ICO also identifies the regulatory measures such as Acts of Parliament, local by-laws, taxes, prosecutions, charges and voluntary agreements fall within reg 2(1)(c) and highlights that it is not only 'environmental policies' which fall within this provision, but any policies on development, transport or health if they are likely to affect the elements of the environment.[83] This limb would seem not to be concerned with routine information, but instead with information having sufficient formality for it to constitute a 'measure.'[84] It may be that documents recording the decision-making process leading to the passing of a measure are therefore outside the grasp of the paragraph. This would tend to explain the need for paragraph (e) of the definition, which might otherwise be superfluous. The ICO suggests, in this regard, that reg 2(1)(c) would cover not only the documents setting out the measures themselves, but also (1) any information on the way those measures have been developed and are applied, and (2) any information about the results of that application.[85] It is capable of covering officer reports to the committee of a local council.[86] The UN Implementation Guide considers that 'environmental agreements' applies to 'voluntary agreements such as those negotiated between government and industry, and may also apply to bilateral or multilateral environmental agreements among States... These agreements are sometimes published, and sometimes not published, and may be negotiated by committees dominated by either representatives of the regulated industry or by the officials who will be responsible for enforcing the regulations.'[87] As with paragraph (b) of the definition, this paragraph requires a nexus between the measure or activity and the elements in paragraph (a) or the factors in paragraph (b).

17– 013 Third limb – technique

The judicially-endorsed technique for determining whether information is on a measure affecting or likely to affect the elements and factors referred to in regulation 2(1)(a) and (b) involves three stages.[88] First, it is necessary to identify the 'measure' which the information is

---

[81] J Ebbeson, H Gaugitsch, J Jendroska, F Marshall and S Stec, *The Aarhus Convention: an Implementation Guide* (2nd Edn) (New York, United Nations, 2014) pp 52-53.

[82] Derived from Aarhus Convention Art 2.3(b), and Directive 2003/4/EC Art 2.1(c).

[83] ICO, *What is environmental information? Regulation 2(1)) Environmental Information Regulations* at para 40.

[84] That appears to be how the word is used elsewhere in the Aarhus Convention (Arts 3.1, 3.5, 5.5 and 5.6) and in Directive 2003/4/EC (recitals (2), (23) and (24) and Arts 7.3 and 10). Hence, building regulation documents and planning agreements under the Town and Country Planning Act 1990 s 10 are not within the scope of 'measures': *Spurgeon v IC and Horsham DC*, IT, 29 June 2007 at [21]. See also *Uttlesford District Council v IC*, FTT, 6 June 2012 at [27]-[28].

[85] ICO, *What is environmental information? Regulation 2(1)) Environmental Information Regulations* at para 41.

[86] *Archer v IC and Salisbury DC*, IT, 9 May 2007 at [32].

[87] J Ebbeson, H Gaugitsch, J Jendroska, F Marshall and S Stec, *The Aarhus Convention: an Implementation Guide* (2nd Edn) (New York, United Nations, 2014) pp 53-54.

[88] *Department for Business, Energy and Industrial Strategy v Information Commissioner* [2017] EWCA Civ 844, [2017] PTSR 1644. The information sought was the Project Assessment Review about the communications and data component of the United Kingdom Government's Smart Meter Programme. The Smart Meter Programme was introduced

'on.' Secondly, information is 'on' a measure if 'it is about, relates to or concerns the measure in question.' Thirdly, it is permissible to look beyond the precise issue with which the disputed information is concerned in identifying the relevant 'measure.' This does not mean that it is permissible to look at issues with which the information is not concerned, or at issues with which the information is merely connected: it means simply that the determining body (whether the public authority or the FTT) is not restricted by what the information is specifically, directly or immediately about. The question of where the line is to be drawn between information which qualifies as 'information… on' and that which does not will be fact and context specific.

17– 014 Reports on implementation

The fourth limb of the definition of 'environmental information' is:

(d) reports on the implementation of environmental legislation;[89]

The ICO Guidance suggests that this limb would include 'reports reviewing or monitoring the operation or performance of environmental legislation, or evaluating its success or failure.'[90]

17– 015 Cost-benefit etc analyses

The fifth limb of the definition of 'environmental information' is:

(e) cost-benefit and other economic analyses and assumptions used within the framework of the measures and activities referred to in (c);

It is conventional in freedom of information regimes that exempt policy formulation or 'deliberative' documents, nevertheless to make available the background statistical information or purely factual material that informed the policy decision taken.[91] By way of example, the ICO directed the Department for Transport to release information compiled as part of a modelling process to compare different combinations of property compensation schemes, which contained a common set of assumptions, including around property values, which the ICO concluded (contrary to the Department for Transport's submissions) fell within reg 2(1)(e).[92]

17– 016 Health etc matters

The sixth limb of the definition of 'environmental information' is:

(f) the state of human health and safety, conditions of human life, cultural sites and built structures inasmuch as they are or may be affected by the state of the elements of the environment referred to in (a) or, through those elements, by any of the matters referred to in (b) and (c)'.[93]

The ICO Guidance emphasises that, unlike other definitions in reg 2(1), reg 2(1)(f) does not take the form of an illustrative list of examples. It relates to three areas:

(1) the state of human health and safety;
(2) conditions and human life; and
(3) cultural sites and built structure.

According to the ICO Guidance, information on these matters is only environmental information to the extent that they are or may be affected by the state of the elements of the

---

pursuant to Direction 2009/72/EC, and sought to provide information about energy usage to consumers, suppliers, and network operators in near real time. Similarly: *Dept for Transport v IC and Hastings* [2019] EWCA Civ 2241.

89 This limb is not in the definition of 'environmental information' in the Aarhus Convention. See Aarhus Convention Arts 5.3(a) and 5.4, and Directive 2003/4/EC Arts 7.2(d) and 7.3.

90 ICO, *What is environmental information? Regulation 2(1)) Environmental Information Regulations* at para 43.

91 See, eg: FOIA s 35(2) and (4); FOI(S)A s 29(3). The Aarhus Convention Art 2.3(b), speaks of 'cost benefit and other economic analyses and assumptions used in environmental decision-making'. The words used in the Regulations derive from Directive 2003/4/EC Art 2.1(f).

92 ICO decision FS50498174.

93 Derived from Aarhus Convention Art 2.3(c), and Directive 2003/4/EC Art 2.1(f).

environment in reg 2(1)(a) or through those elements, or by any of the factors, measure or activities referred to in reg 2(1)(b) and (c).[94] By way of example, the ICO suggests that a report into public sickness which concludes that the sickness arose as a result of industrial waste being emptied into a river and entering the food chain through the fish in that river would be environmental information, whereas a report concluding that sickness arising as a result of a restaurant's poor food preparation processes would not.[95] Similar to its guidance on reg 2(1)b), the ICO suggests that 'are affected by' means that the effect 'has already occurred or is ongoing.'[96] However, a lower test is applied to 'may be affected by' than the 'likely to be affected by' test in reg 2(1)(b): merely meaning that there must be 'some possibility' of an effect.[97] It is not clear whether the limb is confined to information that itself links the state of human health and safety, etc to the state of the elements of the environment, etc; or whether it is sufficient that the information is on the state of human health and safety, etc and that it can be shown that the state of the elements of the environment, etc are or may be affecting them. In *OFCOM v IC and T-Mobile (UK) Ltd*, the Tribunal expressed the view that (f) was intended to apply to information on the state of human health (and not just information on factors that are suspected of possibly creating a risk to it) and that the information must be *on* the result of those factors affecting human health and not the factors themselves.[98]

7–017 Examples

The Tribunal has concluded that the following all constitute 'environmental information':

— pre-application planning advice and documents;[99]
— an application for planning permission;[100]
— legal advice which included the enforceability of an agreement under section 106 of the Town and Country Planning Act 1990;[101]
— legal advice on a planning inspector's decision and on the meaning of certain provisions of planning legislation;[102]
— an enforcement file in connection with a breach of planning control;[103]
— an appraisal prepared in connection with negotiations for an agreement under s 106 of the Town and Country Planning Act 1990;[104]
— submissions to a Minister on a 'called-in' planning inquiry;[105]

---

94 ICO, *What is environmental information? Regulation 2(1)) Environmental Information Regulations* at para 48.

95 ICO, *What is environmental information? Regulation 2(1)) Environmental Information Regulations* at p 17.

96 ICO, *What is environmental information? Regulation 2(1)) Environmental Information Regulations* at para 50.

97 ICO, *What is environmental information? Regulation 2(1)) Environmental Information Regulations* at para 51.

98 IT, 4 September 2007 at [29].

99 *St Albans City and District Council v IC*, FTT, 18 September 2014.

100 *Markinson v IC*, IT, 28 March 2006; *Robinson v IC and East Ridings of Yorkshire Council*, IT, 9 October 2007; cf *Spurgeon v IC and Horsham DC*, IT, 29 June 2007; *Bristol City Council v IC and Portland and Brunswick Square Association*, FTT, 24 May 2010; *Surrey Heath Borough Council v IC and McCullen*, FTT, 11 August 2010 at [19]-[20]. In *Venn v Secretary of State for Communities and Local Government* [2014] EWCA Civ 1539, [2015] 1 WLR 2328 the Secretary of State accepted (at [11]) that the Convention is arguably broad enough to catch most, if not all, planning matters.

101 *Kirkaldie v IC and Thanet DC*, IT, 4 July 2006. The actual request was for the legal advice that Thanet District Council had sought regarding the night-flying policy at Kent International Airport.

102 *Burgess v IC and Stafford BC*, IT, 7 June 2007.

103 *Young v IC and Dept for Environment for Northern Ireland*, IT, 12 December 2007; *Easter v IC and New Forest National Park Authority*, FTT, 14 May 2010 at [33]-[37].

104 *South Gloucestershire Council v IC and Bovis Homes Ltd*, IT, 20 October 2009.

105 *Lord Baker of Dorking v IC and DCLG*, IT, 1 June 2007, although all parties agreed that the information sought was environmental information.

— a river works licence;[106]
— information relating to land holdings of a public authority;[107]
— information about a local authority's liability to construct a sea defence;[108]
— information about the location, ownership and technical attributes of mobile phone cellular base stations;[109]
— statements in support of an application to modify a right of way shown on the definitive map under the Wildlife and Countryside Act 1981;[110]
— information on 'energy policy' in respect of 'supply, demand and pricing';[111]
— records of a meeting held to consider perceived 'climate change';[112]
— records of the quantity, origin and prices of mussels imported and exported from certain fishery areas;[113]
— a draft report jointly commissioned by the Chancellor of the Exchequer and the Secretary of State for Transport to examine the long-term links between transport, economic productivity and competitiveness;[114]
— information relating to the building of a bridge and its tolling;[115]
— certain information relating to an oil pipeline;[116]
— building control/traffic schemes abutting/highway schemes within 200m records necessary to complete a local search (CON 29);[117]
— information related to a highway crossover;[118]
— information related to a dispute over rights of way;[119]
— information related to a dispute on leaseholders having to pay service charges in respect of maintenance of footpaths and roads;[120]
— mineral sales and permitted reserves information provided by minerals operators to the mineral planning authority;[121]
— information related to the disposal land for development;[122]

---

106 *Port of London Authority v IC and Hibbert*, IT, 31 May 2007, although not disputed by any of the parties in that appeal.

107 *Perrins v IC and Wolverhampton City Council*, IT , 9 January 2007; and see also *Chichester District Council v IC and Friel*, FTT, 16 March 2011 (concerning valuation information related to public authority land holdings).

108 *McGlade v IC and Redcar and Cleveland BC*, IT, 23 November 2009.

109 *OFCOM v IC and T-Mobile (UK) Ltd*, IT, 4 September 2007, on appeal *R (Office of Communications) v IC*, [2008] EWHC 1445 (Admin), [2008] ACD 65, [2009] Env LR 1, then *R (Office of Communications) v IC* [2009] EWCA Civ 90, [2009] ACD 48, then *Office of Communication v IC* [2010] UKSC 3 and then *OFCOM v IC* (C-71/10) [2011] PTSR 1676, [2012] Env LR 7.

110 *Dainton v IC and Lincolnshire CC*, IT, 10 September 2007; see also *Woodford v IC*, FTT, 21 April 2010 at [6]-[7] and [26].

111 *DBERR v IC and Friends of the Earth*, IT, 29 April 2008 at [27].

112 *DBERR v IC and Friends of the Earth*, IT, 29 April 2008 at [27].

113 *North Western and North Wales Sea Fisheries Committee v IC*, IT, 8 July 2008.

114 *Secretary of State for Transport v IC*, IT, 5 May 2009.

115 *Mersey Tunnel Users Association v IC and Halton BC*, IT, 24 June 2009 at [54]-[70].

116 *ECGD v IC and Corner House*, IT, 11 August 2009.

117 *Easter v IC and New Forest National Park Authority*, FTT, 14 May 2010.

118 *Martyres v IC and Huntingdonshire District Council*, FTT, 6 July 2010.

119 *Plumbe v IC and Hampshire County Council*, FTT, 10 September 2010 at [12]-[13].

120 *West v IC*, FTT, 25 October 2010, the request in that case was made under FOIA; the Commissioner dealt with it under the EIR as did the FTT but with reservations as to this being correct, see [7].

121 *Staffordshire County Council v IC and Sibelco (UK) Ltd*, FTT, 20 December 2010 at [129]-[131].

122 *Little v IC and Welsh Assembly Government*, FTT, 30 December 2010; *Vale of White Horse District Council v IC, Gill and Doric Properties Ltd*, FTT, 17 June 2015 at [17]-[19].

— the national grid reference of a site sowing a trial crop of oilseed rape and found to be contaminated by genetically modified seed;[123]
— information related to the preparation of an equality impact assessment in respect of a decision by a council to dispose of land in order for it to be used to retain a memorial to IRA hunger strikers;[124]
— information related to flood risks from a watercourse;[125]
— information related to a Special Area of Conservation under the Directive 92/43/EEC, the Habitats Directive;[126]
— information related to the economic and financial costs of cutting greenhouse emissions in the context of the Copenhagen conference;[127]
— information related to an application for a certificate of lawful use or development;[128]
— information related to discussions between the Mayor of London and the Government on matters of air pollution and compliance with EU air quality legislation;[129]
— a number of decisions have proceeded on the basis that all of the information needed to answer personal search enquiries (Con29R) is environmental information;[130]
— information related to financial guarantee arrangements put in place by a landfill operator as a condition for obtaining a permit;[131]
— the Project Assessment Review (a high level review) about the communications and data component of the United Kingdom government's Smart Meter Programme;[132]
— a lightning risk assessment for a stadium;[133]
— information related to orders to carry out work to a pier;[134]
— information relating to the subsidence of a park, including hydrogeological reports;[135]
— information submitted on a consultation concerning plans which affected Hackney Marches;[136]
— information relating to a PFI contracts for the design, installation, operation and maintenance of street lighting[137] and for an energy from waste facility;[138] and

[123] *Freeze v IC and DEFRA*, FTT, 8 March 2011, in that case the Tribunal held the sowing of seed was not an 'emission': see [28]-[32].

[124] *Omagh District Council v IC*, FTT, 20 May 2011. The Tribunal held this to be environmental information despite having sympathy that the dispute information was 'more cultural than environmental': see [33]-[46].

[125] *Walker v IC*, FTT, 21 October 2011.

[126] *Bruton v IC and Duchy of Cornwall*, FTT, 3 November 2011.

[127] *Sinclair v IC and Department of Energy and Climate Change*, FTT, 8 November 2011.

[128] *Plumb v IC and Babergh District Council*, FTT, 29 November 2011.

[129] *DEFRA v IC and Birkett* [2011] UKUT 39 (AAC), [2011] UKUT 17 (AAC).

[130] See *East Riding of Yorkshire Council v IC and Stanley Davis Group Ltd*, FTT, 15 March 2010 and *Kirklees Council v IC and PALI* [2011] UKUT 104 (AAC) at [37]-[40].

[131] *Jones v IC and Environment Agency*, FTT, 27 April 2012 at [12]-[13]. Similarly: *Natural Resources Wales v Swansea Friends of the Earth and IC* [2013] UKUT 0473 (AAC).

[132] *Department for Business, Energy and Industrial Strategy v Information Commissioner* [2017] EWCA Civ 844, [2017] PTSR 1644.

[133] *Dransfield v IC and Olympic Delivery Authority*, FTT, 23 January 2014.

[134] *Willetts v IC and Conwy CBC*, FTT, 18 February 2014. The FTT concluded that orders to carry out work on a pier fell within reg 2(1)(f) information relating to 'the state of .. built structures inasmuch as they may be affected by the state of the elements of the environment referred to in (a).'

[135] *Knight v IC and Newbury Town Council*, FTT, 4 April 2015.

[136] *LB of Hackney v IC and Mudge*, FTT, 19 June 2015.

[137] *Turner v IC and Sunderland City Council*, FTT, 2 February 2016.

[138] *Gloucestershire CC v IC and Costas Ttofa*, FTT, 10 March 2017. See also *Worcestershire CC v IC and Mercia Waste*

— information on construction costs, and other information, relating to a major infrastructure project.[139]

The Tribunal has concluded that the following does not constitute 'environmental information':

— communications between UK and US authorities relating to decommissioned US warships containing toxic waste and to be dismantled in the United Kingdom;[140]
— information on the conditions related to internal refurbishment of a listed building;[141]
— meetings between the Chancellor of the Exchequer and a former Chancellor largely fiscal and about banking;[142] and
— within a planning context, emails concerning the Council's code of conduct for members.[143]

17–018 Format of information

The right given by the Regulations is to 'information in written, visual, aural, electronic or any other material form'.[144] The medium on which the information is recorded does not affect the existence of the right. Unlike FOIA, which defines 'information' as 'information recorded in any form',[145] there is no such requirement in the EIR or in Directive 2003/4/EC. Arguably, 'information' in the EIR extends to samples or specimens held by a public authority.[146] The form and format provision of the EIR[147] gives a public authority more flexibility in the method by which it meets a request than does the corresponding provision in FOIA.[148] The former provision would enable a public authority to meet a request by making samples or specimens available for inspection.[149] Environmental information accordingly includes information contained in documents, pictures and records, where records are taken to include registers, reports, returns, computer records, maps and other non-documentary records.

Management Ltd, FTT, 10 April 2017 at [15]-[24].

139 *Crane v IC and Dept for Transport*, FTT, 16 January 2017 at [67], [70]. This applied *Department for Energy and Climate Change v IC* [2015] UKUT 0671 (AAC), where the request related to HS2.

140 *FCO v IC and Friends of the Earth*, IT, 29 June 2007.

141 *Black v IC*, FTT, 16 September 2011. Information related to the conditions imposed by English Heritage to external works to that listed building was held to be environmental information.

142 *Montague v IC and HM Treasury*, FTT, 7 January 2014 at [29]-[31].

143 *Uttlesford District Council v IC*, FTT, 6 June 2012 at [27]-[29].

144 EIR reg 2(1); EI(S)R reg 2(1). Derived from Directive 2003/4/EC Art 2.1.

145 FOIA s 84; FOI(S)A s 73.

146 See Directive 2003/4/EC Art 8.2.

147 EIR reg 6(1); EI(S)R reg 6(1).

148 FOIA s 11(1); FOI(S)A s 11(2).

149 Compare the FOIA and FOI(S)A ss 1 and 11, which provide for the communication of the requested information.

CHAPTER 18

Environmental information – rights & appeals

1. THE RIGHT TO ENVIRONMENTAL INFORMATION

18– 001 Scope of the right

The Regulations are retrospective in that they apply to 'environmental information' irrespective of whether it was created or received before the Regulations came into effect.[1] The Regulations do not specifically include a provision to 'freeze' the information captured by a request to that information which is held at the time when the request is received. Nevertheless, there are indications in the Regulations that point to this being the intention.[2] The 'snapshot' approach is consistent with what is expressly provided for in FOIA.[3]

---

1 The position is the same under the FOIA and under the FOI(S)A. This retrospectivity was confirmed by the Home Secretary during the passage of the Bill through the House of Commons: Hansard HC vol 340 col 728 (7 December 1999). See further §20– 011.

2 See, eg EIR regs 10(2)-(3), 12(4)(a) and 19(1); but cf EIR reg 5(4). In Scotland, EI(S)R regs 12(4)(a), 14(2) and 19(1).

3 Compare FOIA s 1(4) and FOI(S)A s 1(4). See further §20– 011. In *Kirkaldie v IC and Thanet DC*, IT, 4 July 2006, the Tribunal said (at [17]) that the position was not clear, but that 'it would not make much sense for a public

18– 002 Persons enjoying the right

Save to the extent that it may be relevant to a consideration of the public interest, the motives of the person for making a request are irrelevant to the decision to disclose.[4] The Regulations speak of an applicant being a 'person'.[5] Consistently with the general position at law and with the Directive, this will extend to companies and other legal persons, corporate or unincorporate.[6] The Aarhus Convention states that the right should be exercisable by any person, irrespective of citizenship, nationality or domicile.[7] Although this did not find its way into either the Directive or the Regulations, it is questionable whether the right could be denied on the basis of any of these.[8] In particular, it is questionable whether a Scottish public authority could refuse a request made by a UK citizen resident in England.

18– 003 Bodies subject to the EIR

Under the EIR, the right of access is only exercisable against a 'public authority.'[9] Under the EI(S)R, the right of access is only exercisable against a 'Scottish public authority.'[10] Each of the terms is given a similar, but not identical, definition to that which it bears under the corresponding freedom of information Act.[11] The EIR expand the definition given to 'public authority' in FOIA by adding to it two additional limbs. First, by para (c) of the definition, 'public authority' also embraces 'any other body or other person that carries out functions of public administration'. Most bodies and persons that carry out functions of public administration are already captured under paras (a) and (b) through the incorporation of the Act's definition. Secondly, paragraph (d) of the definition in both Regulations adds any other body or person 'that is under the control of' a public authority (as defined in paras (a)-(c)) and that:

— has public responsibilities relating to the environment;
— exercises functions of a public nature relating to the environment; or

---

authority to respond that it did not hold the information when it had just received it before sending the response. Also the public authority would no doubt be under a duty to advise and assist the applicant under Regulation 9 EIR that the information was not in its possession at the time the request was received although knowing that it was about to be received so that the applicant could then make a new request, if necessary, when the information was then held by the public authority. Alternatively the public authority could take the sensible and pragmatic approach and accept the request under the EIR and deal with it accordingly.'

4 See recital (8) to and Art 3.1 of the Directive and Aarhus Convention Art 4.1. See further §20– 017.

5 Regulation 2(1).

6 Recital (8) to and Art 2.6 of the Directive. Similarly, Aarhus Convention Art 2.4. Interpretation Act 1978 s 5 and Sch 1. See further §20– 013.

7 Aarhus Convention Art 3.9. See: J Ebbeson, H Gaugitsch, J Jendroska, F Marshall and S Stec, *The Aarhus Convention: an Implementation Guide* (2nd Edn) (New York, United Nations, 2014) pp 55-58.

8 Article 3.1 of the Directive requires Member States to ensure that public authorities make available environmental information 'to any applicant' on request. See further: §20– 014; J Ebbeson, H Gaugitsch, J Jendroska, F Marshall and S Stec, *The Aarhus Convention: an Implementation Guide* (2nd Edn) (New York, United Nations, 2014) p 57, noting that in its findings on communication ACCC/C/2004/03 (Ukraine) the Committee observed that in the case of an activity that potentially crosses an international border, that 'foreign or international non-governmental environmental organisations that have similarly expressed an interest in or concern about the procedure would generally fall under these definitions as well.'

9 EIR reg 5(1).

10 EI(S)R reg 5(1).

11 EIR reg 2(2); EI(S)R reg 2(1). This is so that the definition of 'public authority' accords with Art 2.2 of the Directive. See also recital (11) of the Directive and Art 2.2 of the Aarhus Convention. The Implementation Report by the EU records at §15 that the definition in the Directive 'corresponds' to that in the Aarhus Convention. Thus, in requiring member states to make environmental information available in response to a request, the Directive limits this obligation to environmental information held by a 'public authority' as defined by it.

— provides public services relating to the environment.[12]

18–004 Bodies within reg 2(2)(c)

As noted above, in addition to capturing bodies that are 'public authorities' within the meaning of FOIA, reg 2(2)(c) defines 'public authority' to include:

> any other body or other person, that carries out functions of public administration[13]

The source for this definition is Article 2(2) of Directive 2003/4/EC, paragraph (b) of which provides that a 'public authority' means:

> any natural or legal person performing public administrative functions under national law, including specific duties, activities or services in relation to the environment;[14]

Thus, the definition in reg 2(2)(c), in referring to a body that carries out a function of public administration, omits two limiting qualifications in the corresponding definition in Art 2(2()b):

(a) that in carrying out functions of public administration, the person/body does so 'under national law'; and

(b) that the administrative functions that the person/body carries out are administrative functions 'in relation to the environment.'[15]

In relation to Article 2(2)(b), the CJEU has ruled that:[16]

– only entities that, by virtue of a legal basis specifically defined in the applicable national legislation, are empowered to perform public administrative functions are capable of falling within the definition;

– the question of whether a function is a 'public administrative function' for the purpose of Article 2(2)(b) must be examined under EU law, having regard to the Aarhus Convention, in order for there to be an autonomous and uniform definition of that context;

– public authorities under Article 2(2)(b) concerned administrative authorities:

---

12 This limb of the definition has no counterpart in the FOIA or in the FOI(S)A. This paragraph is derived from Directive 2003/4/EC, recital (11) and Art 2.2(c).

13 The EI(S)R reg 2(1) makes a like provision in relation to the definition of 'Scottish public authority.'

14 This limb of the definition is derived from Art 2(2)(c) of the Aarhus Convention. On a purely grammatical analysis, the absence of a comma after 'services' in paragraph (b) of the definition in the Directive (and similarly in the Aarhus Convention) results in the phrase 'in relation to the environment' not qualifying 'any natural or legal person performing public administrative functions under national law.' However, it is evident from recital (11) to the Directive that this was not the intention: the intention was that only natural or legal persons performing public administrative functions in relation to the environment under national law were to be within paragraph (b) of the definition in the Directive.

15 Given that the EIR is subordinate legislation, that it was made under s 2(2) of the *European Communities Act 1972* and that it is intended to implement the Directive, this leads to a question over the vires of the definition insofar as it exceeds that in the Directive. This was not a point that concerned the Court in *Fish Legal v Information Commissioner United Utilities, Yorkshire Water and Southern Water* (C-279/12) [2014] QB 521, [2014] 2 CMLR 36, [2015] All ER (EC) 795 or the UT in *Fish Legal and anor v IC and ors* [2015] UKUT 52 (AAC) since it was not in dispute that the water companies and the sewage companies were concerned with services that were 'services in the environmental field' and involving a number of environmental directives: see *Fish Legal v Information Commissioner United Utilities, Yorkshire Water and Southern Water* (C-279/12) [2014] QB 521, [2014] 2 CMLR 36, [2015] All ER (EC) 795 at [52]-[53]. It was noted in *A-G for Prince of Wales v IC and Bruton* [2016] UKUT 0154 (AAC) at [37] and [48] but the point appears to have been conceded. The Upper Tribunal regarded provision of services outside the environmental field as relevant to the issue of hybridity, but otherwise did not engage with the mismatch between the Directive and the EIR. Nor was the point taken in *Cross v IC and Cabinet Office* [2016] UKUT 0153 (AAC) : see [46]. In *Cross*, although the Upper Tribunal concluded that the Sovereign did not carry out functions of public administration (and thus was necessarily outside paragraph (c) of the definition in reg 2(2)), it appears to have accepted that paragraph (c) required the functions of public administration to relate to the environment: see [7], [90] and [113].

16 *Fish Legal v Information Commissioner United Utilities, Yorkshire Water and Southern Water* (C-279/12) [2014] QB 521, [2014] 2 CMLR 36, [2015] All ER (EC) 795 at [48]-[56]. The reference from the Upper Tribunal followed an earlier decision of the Upper Tribunal in *Smartsource v IC* [2010] UKUT 415 (AAC), [2011] JPL 455 which concluded that water companies were not public authorities, taking a multi-factorial approach considering (inter alia) that although appointed and licensed under statute, the water companies were not creatures of statute but fundamentally private companies independent of Government, and that the core regulatory functions rested not with the water companies but with the Secretary of State and Ofwat.

> defined in functional terms, namely entities, be they legal persons governed by public law or by private law, which are entrusted, under the legal regime which is applicable to the, with the performance of services of public interest, inter alia in the environmental field, and which are, for this purpose, vested with special powers beyond those which result from the normal rules applicable in relations between persons governed by private law; and

– that, in order to determine whether a body could be classified as a legal person performing 'public administrative functions' under article 2(2)(b):

> it should be examined whether those entities are vested, under the national law which is applicable to them, with special powers beyond those which result from the normal rules applicable in relations between persons governed by private law.

On those proceedings returning to the Upper Tribunal and in applying these principles to reg 2(2)(c) of the EIR, the Upper Tribunal found that it did not need to decide whether one 'special power' was sufficient to mean that a body was a public authority for the purposes of the EIR and found that water companies possess a number of special powers and, on this basis, concluded they are public authorities for the purposes of reg 2(2)(c).[17] Determining factors would appear to be:

– the extent to which a power conferred a potential advantage on the water companies that it would not otherwise enjoy in a purely commercial context;
– the extent to which an element of compulsion allowed companies 'effectively to override the individuality that can be a feature of the exercise of private law powers' (ie departing from the idea that private law rules operate 'on the basis of assumed consent or acquiescence'); and
– that some of the powers given to the companies operated outside any existing relationship and without any practical limit.[18]

As the Upper Tribunal has subsequently observed:

> So although … the Directive, and so the EIR, is intended to have a wide reach they nonetheless were not intended to give a right to request environmental information from anyone simply because they hold it. This is the case even if it can be said that the environmental information relates to the exercise of powers or responsibilities concerning an iconic building […] or a large estate in respect of which it can be said there is a strong public interest in favour of the disclosure of environmental information.[19]

17 *Fish Legal and anor v IC and ors* [2015] UKUT 52 (AAC) at [97]-[98], [105]-[107]. The powers discussed by the Upper Tribunal (and thus, presumably, regarded by them as 'special powers,' although they did not explicitly state as such in respect of each power) were:

> The compulsory purchase power in s.155 of the Water Industry Act 1990 (albeit subject to confirmation by the Secretary of State) (at [107]);
> The power to make by-laws – including provision for criminal sanction in the event of breach of those by-laws (at [110]);
> The power to lay pipes in land other than a street, under s.159 of the Water Industry Act 1990 (at [118]-[123]);
> The power to enter onto land for specified purposes, under s.168 of the Water Industry Act 1990 (at [125]); and
> The power to impose a 'hosepipe ban' (at [126]).

18 *Fish Legal and anor v IC and ors* [2015] UKUT 52 (AAC) at [107], [118]-[125].

19 *Cross v IC and Cabinet Office* [2016] UKUT 0153 (AAC) at [24]-[26]. In that case, Mrs Cross had applied to the Information Officer of the Royal Household, seeking minutes of meetings of the 'Social Responsibility Committee.' The Information Office declined on the basis that the Royal Household was not a 'public authority.' That refusal was upheld by the Upper Tribunal. In neither *Fish Legal* nor *Cross* was it argued that: (a) to be a public authority under the functional test the entity had to be entrusted with special powers for the purpose of the performance of services of public interest in the environmental field; or (b) that the reference in [52] of the CJEU judgment in *Fish Legal* to 'this purpose' linked to the need for special powers to only the services of public interest in the environmental field. The Upper Tribunal determined the appeal on the basis that it was 'common ground' between the parties that if a body is entrusted with 'special powers' for the performance of services of public interest, they can be a public authority under EIR. They do not have to be entrusted with 'special powers' for "the

8–005 Bodies within reg 2(2)(d)

As noted above, in addition to capturing bodies that are 'public authorities' within the meaning of FOIA, reg 2(2)(d) defines 'public authority' to include:

> any other body or other person, that is under the control of a person falling within sub-paragraphs (a), (b) or (c) and –
> (i) has public responsibilities relating to the environment;
> (ii) exercises functions of a public nature relating to the environment; or
> (iii) provides public services relating to the environment.[20]

The source for this definition is Article 2(2) of Directive 2003/4/EC, paragraph (c) of which provides that a 'public authority' means:

> any natural or legal person having public responsibilities or functions, or providing public services, relating to the environment under the control of a body or person falling within (a) or (b).[21]

The CJEU in *Fish Legal* characterised paragraph (c) of the definition in the Directive as intended to cover 'an entity controlled by the State.'[22] The court then proceeded to explain what it meant by that phrase:

> 68 Those factors lead to the adoption of an interpretation of "control", within the meaning of article 2(2)(c) of Directive 2003/4, under which this third, residual, category of public authorities covers any entity which does not determine in a genuinely autonomous manner the way in which it performs the functions in the environmental field which are vested in it, since a public authority covered by article 2(2)(a) or (b) of the Directive is in a position to exert decisive influence on the entity's action in that field.
>
> 69 The manner in which such a public authority may exert decisive influence pursuant to the powers which it has been allotted by the national legislature is irrelevant in this regard. It may take the form of, inter alia, a power to issue directions to the entities concerned, whether or not by exercising rights as a shareholder, the power to suspend, annul after the event or require prior authorisation for decisions taken by those entities, the power to appoint or remove from office the members of their management bodies or the majority of them, or the power wholly or partly to deny the entities financing to an extent that jeopardises their existence.
>
> 70 The mere fact that the entity in question is, like the water companies concerned, a commercial company subject to a specific system of regulation for the sector in question cannot exclude control within the meaning of article 2(2)(c) of Directive 2003/4 in so far as the conditions laid down in para 68 of the present judgment are met in the case of that entity.
>
> 71 If the system concerned involves a particularly precise legal framework which lays down a set of rules determining the way in which such companies must perform the public functions related to environmental management with which they are entrusted, and which, as the case may be, includes administrative supervision intended to ensure that those rules are in fact complied with, where appropriate by means of the issuing of orders or the imposition of fines, it may follow that those entities do not have genuine autonomy vis-à-vis the state, even if the latter is no longer in a position, following privatisation of the sector in question, to determine their day-to-day management.

On its return to the Upper Tribunal, it summarised this as meaning that a body is a public authority under paragraph (d) of the definition in the EIR 'if it does not provide its services in a genuinely autonomous manner.[23] This, the Upper Tribunal held, fell to be determined

---

performance of services of public interest in the environmental field': *Cross* at [46]. It is at least debatable whether the Upper Tribunal in *Cross* was wholly in agreement with this approach – not least in light of its later observations in [85]-[92].

20 The EI(S)R reg 2(1) makes a like provision in relation to the definition of 'Scottish public authority.' This limb of the definition is derived from Art 2(2)(c) of Directive 2003/4/EC and Art 2(2)(c) of the Aarhus Convention.

21 This limb of the definition is derived from Art 2(2)(c) of the Aarhus Convention.

22 *Fish Legal v Information Commissioner United Utilities, Yorkshire Water and Southern Water* (C-279/12) [2014] QB 521, [2014] 2 CMLR 36, [2015] All ER (EC) 795 at [67].

23 *Fish Legal and anor v IC and ors* [2015] UKUT 52 (AAC) at [94].

according to the 'control test'–

131 CJEU explained in the second paragraph of its Order that a person was under another's 'control':

> ... if they do not determine in a genuinely autonomous manner the way in which they provide those services since a public authority covered by Article 2(2)(a) or (b) of the directive is in a position to exert decisive influence on their action in the environmental field.
>
> For convenience, we call this the control test.

....

133 The control test distinguishes between the functions that a body performs and the manner in which it performs them. It has to be applied to the manner of performance, not to the functions themselves...

134 We read the [CJEU] judgment as laying down a single test with two elements that identify cause and effect: is a body performing its functions in 'a genuinely autonomous manner' (the effect) 'since a public authority ... is in a position to exert decisive influence on their action in the environmental field' (the cause)?

135 ....It is not sufficient merely to show the potential for influence. It is necessary to show that it has had an actual impact on the companies' decision-making. The test is only satisfied if they 'do not determine in a genuinely autonomous manner' how they provide their services.

136 As we read the control test, we have to take an overall view of whether in practice the companies operate in a genuinely autonomous manner in the provision of the services that relate to the environment. It is not sufficient to show that they do not do so in one or two marginal aspects of their business. Nor is it necessary to show that they do not do so in almost every aspect of their business. The CJEU has stated the test in a general way that excludes those extreme positions and requires an overview of the position in relation to environmental services.

....

141 ....autonomy has to be judged not by reference to absolute liberty, but against the normal background radiation of the constraints that limit the freedom of action for every business.

...

155 The control test is a demanding one that few commercial enterprises will satisfy.....

18–006 Hybrid bodies

A hybrid body is a body that in relation to certain of its activities is captured by one or more of the limbs of the definition of 'public authority' but falls outside all limbs in relation to its other activities. In relation to the definition of 'public authority' in Article 2(2) of Directive 2003/4/EC, the CJEU has held that if a body is captured by paragraph (b) of that definition, then it is a 'public authority' in relation to all of its activities (ie there is no scope for hybridity), but that if a body is captured only by paragraph (c) of that definition, it will be a 'public authority' for the purposes of the Directive only when it is providing public services in the environmental field and it is doing so under the control of an Article 2(2)(a) or (b) body.[24]

18–007 Judicial and legislative bodies

The Regulations do not apply to a public authority when it is acting in a judicial or legislative

---

[24] *Fish Legal v Information Commissioner United Utilities, Yorkshire Water and Southern Water* (C-279/12) [2014] QB 521, [2014] 2 CMLR 36, [2015] All ER (EC) 795 at [74]-[83]. This 'hybrid' approach had been previously adopted in FTT cases: *Port of London Authority v IC and Hibbert*, IT, 31 May 2007 at [44]. The treatment of the issue of hybridity by the UT in *A-G for Prince of Wales v IC and Bruton* [2016] UKUT 0154 (AAC) is confused. In that case it had been conceded that the Duchy was a public authority under reg 2(2)(c) (the equivalent of Art 2(2)(b) of the Directive). As such, the Duchy was not a public authority under reg 2(2)(d) (the equivalent of Art 2(2)(c) of the Directive): see [11]. In *Fish Legal v Information Commissioner United Utilities, Yorkshire Water and Southern Water* (C-279/12) [2014] QB 521, [2014] 2 CMLR 36, [2015] All ER (EC) 795 (at [76]-[83]) the CJEU held that if a body fell within para 2(2)(b) of the Directive's definition (ie the equivalent of EIR reg 2(2)(c)), then the EIR would apply to all that that body – in this case, the Duchy – did. In other words, hybridity only matters to a body that is a public authority because it falls within para (d) of the EIR definition of public authority.

capacity.[25] Thus, while environmental information held by a judge or other person while performing judicial functions is outside the grasp of the Regulations, the Courts Service in carrying out administrative functions will be within that grasp.

8– 008 The holding requirement

A public authority is only obliged to disclose environmental information that it 'holds'.[26] The corollary of this is that the right of access is conferred only in relation to environmental information that is 'held' by a public authority. Information 'held by a public authority' is defined to extend to information held by third parties on behalf of that public authority.[27] Thus, the Regulations extend to information held on behalf of a public authority by consultants or archival companies. The term 'hold' itself suggests that information that neither is nor has been created, sought, used or consciously retained by a public authority will not be information 'held' by it.[28] Thus, the private papers of a member of staff of a public authority that that staff member brings into work will not be information 'held' by the public authority.[29] The word 'held' also indicates that a public authority is not obliged to assemble and record what it knows nor to ascertain matters so as to produce information that answers a request. On appeal the question of whether the Commissioner was correct to hold that an authority was entitled to refuse a request on the basis that it did not hold information when an applicant's request was

---

25 EIR reg 3(3); EI(S)R reg 3(2). See further §19– 008. In *R v Secretary of State for the Environment, Transport and Regions, ex p Marson*, 23 March 1998, Jowitt J rejected an argument made in relation to the analogous reg 2(1)(b) of the 1992 Regulations that this disapplied the Regulations where the information related to any function carried out in pursuance of a power conferred by primary or secondary legislation. The disapplication, he held, referred to those things done in the preparation and enactment of legislation. This part of his ruling did not form part of a subsequent challenge to the Court of Appeal [1998] 3 PLR 90, (1999) 77 P&CR 202, [1998] JPL 869. In *Flachglas Torgau GmbH*, C-204/09 [2013] QB 212, [2012] Env LR 26, [2012] EUECJ C-204/09, [2012] 2 CMLR 17 the Court of Justice of the European Union held that the exception in Art 2(2) of Directive 2003/4/EC could be applied to ministries to the extent that they participate in the legislative process in particular by tabling laws or giving opinions to the legislature: see [33]-[51]. However, in *Deutsche Umwelthilfe eV v Bundesrepublik Deutschland* [2013] EUECJ (C-515/11) the Court of Justice of the European Union held that the exception 'may not be applied to ministries when they prepare and adopt normative regulations which are of a lower rank than a law'. In *Flachglas Torgau GmbH*, C-204/09 [2013] QB 212, [2012] Env LR 26, [2012] EUECJ C-204/09, [2012] 2 CMLR 17 the Court also held that the exception only applied during the legislative process and until the legislation as promulgated and could not be applied beyond that: see [52]-[58].

26 EIR regs 4(1) and 5(1); EI(S)R regs 4(1) and 5(1). This is also the requirement in the Directive: see Arts 1(a) and 3.1.

27 EIR reg 3(2); EI(S)R reg 2(2). This is consistent with the requirements of the recital (12) and Arts 1(a), 2.3, 2.4 and 3.1 of the Directive. This is acknowledged in DEFRA, *Code of Practice – Environmental Information Regulations*, February 2005, Foreword, para 14(iii). As to when information is held on behalf of a public authority: *Martyres v IC and Huntingdonshire District Council*, FTT, 6 July 2010 at [9] and [53]-[59] (considering whether information held by a County Council, a law firm or a contractor was held on behalf of the Borough Council); *Clyne v IC and London Borough of Lambeth*, FTT, 10 May 2012 at [42]-[45] (information held by external solicitors); *Chagos Refugees Group v IC and FCO*, FTT, 4 September 2012 at [55]-[74] (material held by consultants); *Holland v IC and University of East Anglia*, FTT, 29 April 2013 at [23]-[122] (whether information held by the Independent Climate Change E-mail Review set up by the University of East Anglia was held on behalf of the latter); *King v IC and Ceredigion CC*, FTT, 29 April 2013 at [12]-[16] and [30] (whether information held by contractors or subcontractors held by public authority). See also: *Sand v IC and FCO*, FTT, 28 July 2014 (holding that a company contracted to the US military was holding information on behalf of the British Indian Ocean Territory Government); *Baker v IC and Liverpool CC*, FTT, 20 April 2017 (holding that information held by a consultant pursuant to a contract with the Merseyside Passenger Transport Executive an executive body that was part of the Liverpool City Region Combined Authority was not held on behalf of Liverpool City Council).

28 'Hold' is similarly, but not identically, defined in s 3(2) of FOIA. See further §20– 009.

29 See *Shevlin v IC and Cornwall Council*, FTT, 15 January 2016 which concerned a request to the University of Cambridge to provide information about the Fifth Assessment Report by the Intergovernmental Panel on Climate Change ('IPCC') including reports of a Professor Wadhams (an employee of the University) as Review Editor of the IPCC. The Upper Tribunal held that the fact that something was received by means of electronic communication on an authority's computer system was not enough [45] and that reg 3(2)(a) required it to be considered whether the information was produced or received by means which were unconnected to the authority (such as an employee of the authority). The connection must be such that it could be said that the production or receipt of the information is attributable to ('by') the authority (at [47]-[49]).

received is a question of law.[30] The Tribunal may, on an appeal, review the adequacy of a public authority's search for information answering the terms of a request.[31] The question for the Tribunal is whether, on the balance of probabilities, the public authority held the requested information.[32] The Tribunal will answer this question by reference to: (i) the quality of the authority's initial search based on the request; (ii) the scope of that search; (iii) the rigour and efficiency of that search; and (iv) the discovery of materials elsewhere which point to there being more. The Tribunal may order deleted backup e-mail files to be restored and searched.[33]

18– 009 Historical records

Emulating FOIA rather than the Directive, the Regulations make special provision for 'historical records'.[34] A record becomes a historical record at the end of 20 years beginning with the year following that in which it was created.[35] The Regulations import various terms from the regime created by Part VI (ss 62-67) of FOIA.[36] The Regulation's treatment of historical records is simpler and less generous than that of the Act. Whereas the Act provides for certain exemptions to fall away according to the age of the record,[37] the Regulations maintain all the exceptions[38] whatever the antiquity of the information. Instead, the Regulations require the public authority holding the information to consult certain bodies before deciding whether it is in the public interest to maintain the exception.[39]

18– 010 Electronic reading rooms

The Directive exhorts public authorities to disseminate environmental information without specific request and to do so electronically.[40] While FOIA provides for publication schemes,[41] which serve a similar purpose, the Directive's emphasis on the use of electronic communications to achieve this takes its inspiration from the US Electronic Freedom of Information Act of 1996.[42] The Directive's exhortations find their way into the 2004 Regulations,[43] albeit they are not so emphatic. Although the availability of information through general dissemination does

---

30 *McGlade v IC and Redcar and Cleveland BC*, IT, 23 November 2009 at [33].

31 *Mersey Tunnel Users Association v IC and Halton BC*, IT, 24 June 2009 at [71]-[87]; *Martyres v IC and Huntingdonshire District Council*, FTT, 6 July 2010 at [42]-[44].

32 *Bromley v IC and Environment Agency*, IT, 31 August 2007; *Keiller v IC and University of East Anglia*, FTT, 18 January 2012 at [15]-[35] and *Clyne v IC and London Borough of Lambeth*, FTT, 10 May 2012 at [21]-[61].

33 As was done in *Clyne v IC and London Borough of Lambeth*, FTT, 10 May 2012.

34 EIR reg 17. 'Historical record' is given the same meaning as it has in section 62 of the 2000 Act: reg 2(1). In Scotland, EI(S)R reg 15, and FOI(S)A s 57. See further §36– 010.

35 See §36– 010. Note, the period used to be 30 years and there are transitional arrangement for records created between 1984 and 2001.

36 Thus: 'transferred public records' and 'open information'. In Scotland, FOI(S)A, Pt V (ss 57-59). As to the meaning of these, see §§36– 015 and 36– 018.

37 FOIA s 63. See further §36– 012.

38 What are termed 'exemptions' in the FOIA are termed 'exceptions' in the EIR. See further §19– 001.

39 See further Ch 36.

40 See recitals (9), (14), (15) and (21) and Arts 1(b) and 7. The Aarhus Convention similarly encourages public authorities: see Arts 5.3, 5.5 and 5.7.

41 FOI ss 19 and 20; FOI(S)A ss 23-24. See further §§21– 013 to 21– 017.

42 These amended the Freedom of Information Act 1966 by establishing a requirement for the electronic availability of 'reading room' records in what are referred to as 'electronic reading rooms': see 5 USC 552(a)(2) (D). Under these amendments, all federal agencies have FOI Act sites on the world wide web to serve this 'electronic reading room' function.

43 EIR reg 4; EI(S)R reg 4. This regulation is not made under the power conferred by the FOIA s 74, but under the European Communities Act 1972 s 2(2).

not remove the obligation to answer a request,[44] it does enable the public authority to decline to provide the applicant with the information in the particular form or format requested.[45] It would seem that the public authority may respond to the request by simply directing the applicant to its 'reading room' facility.

8–011 Information registers

Article 3(5)(c) of the Directive requires each Member State to ensure that practical arrangements are defined for ensuring that the right of access to environmental information can be exercised, including (by way of example) through the maintenance of registers or lists of the environmental information held by public authorities. The Environmental Information Unit of DEFRA created a central register, setting out where these registers could be found, but this was later archived, with no replacement.

8–012 Codes of practice etc

The Secretary of State may issue and revise a code of practice providing guidance to public authorities as to desirable practice in carrying out the Regulations.[46] Before issuing the code of practice, the Secretary of State is required to consult the Information Commissioner. The code of practice must be laid before each House of Parliament. The Secretary of State issued a Code of Practice in February 2005. It 'outlines to public authorities the practice that it would, in the opinion of the Secretary of State, be desirable for them to follow in connection with the discharge of their duties under' the Regulations.[47] The Department for Environment, Food and Rural Affairs also issued 'guidance' on the operation of the Regulations. The guidance was non-statutory, with neither the Regulations nor the Directive making provision for it, and it has since been relegated to archived status. As under FOIA, the Information Commissioner may give practice recommendations.[48]

8–013 Advice and assistance

Each public authority must provide applicants and prospective applicants with so much advice and assistance as would be reasonable.[49] The provision emulates FOIA[50] but has its provenance in the Aarhus Convention[51] and Directive 2003/4/EC.[52] Compliance with the guidance given in the Code of Practice in relation to advice and assistance is deemed to constitute due compliance with the duty to advise and assist.[53] Examples given in the Code of assistance that 'might be appropriate' include 'providing access to detailed catalogues and indexes, where these are available, to help the applicant ascertain the nature and extent of the information held by

---

44 Contrast FOIA s 21(1) and FOI(S)A s 25, which are absolute exemptions.

45 EIR reg 6(1); EI(S)R reg 6(1).

46 EIR r16(1). The Directive does not provide for a code of practice for public authorities. The only form of guidance it contemplates is for those seeking information: Art 3.5.

47 Foreword, para 9.

48 EIR reg 16; EI(S)R reg 18. These can be found on the ICO website: https://ico.org.uk/media/for-organisations/documents

49 EIR reg 9(1); EI(S)R reg 9(1). *Boddy v IC and North Norfolk DC*, IT, 23 June 2008 at [25].

50 FOI s 16, considered further at §§21–001 to 21–006. The provision derives from Art 3 of the Aarhus Convention. See further J Ebbeson, H Gaugitsch, J Jendroska, F Marshall and S Stec, *The Aarhus Convention: an Implementation Guide* (2nd Edn) (New York, United Nations, 2014) p 64.

51 Article 3.2 requires each Contracting Party to endeavour to ensure that officials and authorities 'assist and provide guidance to the public in seeking access to information'.

52 Article 3.5 provides that Member States are to ensure that 'officials are required to support the public in seeking access to information' and spells out certain specific requirements.

53 EIR reg 9(3); EI(S)R reg 9(3).

the authority'.[54] The Code requires public authorities to publish their procedures for dealing with requests for environmental information.[55] Where a request is inadequately particularised, the public authority is required to assist the applicant in providing the required detail.[56] Where a public authority proposes to charge for supplying an applicant with a copy of the information answering the terms of a request, the duty to advise and assist may require that public authority to offer the applicant an opportunity to inspect that information (without charge) in order to decide which of it he would like copied.[57] If a public authority fails to provide advice and assistance, it would appear that the public authority will not be able subsequently to refuse the request on the basis of that request being manifestly unreasonable.[58]

18– 014 The request

For a person to exercise his right of access to environmental information held by a public authority, that person must make a request.[59] The Regulations do not prescribe any formalities for the request.[60] There is nothing to preclude an applicant making a request orally.[61] Although there is no obligation for an applicant to state his name or address, a failure to do so may make it impossible for the public authority to comply properly with its obligations where the response would include personal data. Where a request does not describe the information sought with sufficient particularity, the recipient public authority must ask the applicant as soon as possible (and in any event not more than 20 working days after receipt of the request) to provide more particulars in relation to the request and it must help the applicant to do so.[62] The particularity of a request will impinge upon its reasonableness and upon the cost of compliance. What may be 'manifestly unreasonable' in a single compendious request (whether itemised or not), may be split between two or more requests, each of which is reasonable. Splitting a request may make it more difficult for a public authority to award itself an extra 20 working days within which to answer the request.[63]

18– 015 Fees

Article 5 of the Directive makes provision for a public authority imposing a reasonable charge

---

54 Code of Practice, February 2005, para 10.

55 Article 3.3 of the Aarhus Convention requires each Contracting Party to 'promote environmental education and environmental awareness among the public, especially on how to obtain access to information.' The requirements of the Code give effect to Art 3.5 of Directive 2003/4/EC.

56 Code of Practice, February 2005, paras 15-16. See further §18– 014.

57 *Keston Ramblers Association v IC and LB of Bromley*, IT, 26 October 2007 at [56]-[59].

58 *Mersey Tunnel Users Association v IC and Halton BC*, IT, 24 June 2009 at [95].

59 EIR reg 5(1); EI(S)R reg 5(1). See further §§22– 001 to 22– 009.

60 Cash flow. FOIA s 8(1); FOI(S)A s 8(1).

61 As is acknowledged in the Code of Practice, February 2005, Foreword, para 14(iii) and main text paras 1-2, 8 and 15. This is the approach taken in the Aarhus Convention: J Ebbeson, H Gaugitsch, J Jendroska, F Marshall and S Stec, *The Aarhus Convention: an Implementation Guide* (2nd Edn) (New York, United Nations, 2014) p 79.

62 EIR reg 9(2); EI(S)R, 9(2). Derived from Directive 2003/4/EC Art 3.3. See further §22– 009. See Code of Practice, February 2005, paras 15-18. If a public authority maintains that a request lacks sufficient particularity, it is prudent for that public authority to seek further details from the applicant. On an appeal, the Tribunal may not share the public authority's difficulty: *Mersey Tunnel Users Association v IC and Halton BC*, IT, 24 June 2009 at [36]-[53]. Similarly, the Tribunal may not share a public authority's narrow construction of a request, resulting in a finding by the Tribunal that the public authority has not identified all the information held by it answering the terms of that request: *Mersey Tunnel Users Association v IC and Halton BC*, IT, 24 June 2009 at [73], [81]-[83].

63 Under EIR reg 7(1) and EI(S)R reg 7(1), it is the impracticality of answering a particular request that enables a public authority to award itself an extension of time: it is not the volume of requests received. Contrast the FOIA s 14(2), and FOI(S)A s 14(7), which entitle a public authority to refuse to comply with a request on the ground of a 'substantially similar' request from the applicant within a reasonable interval before. There is nothing to stop an applicant side-stepping this by asking another person to put in later requests on his behalf.

for supplying environmental information, but requires that access *in situ* be free-of-charge.[64] The Regulations make provision for a public authority to charge an applicant 'for making the information available.'[65] There is no obligation on a public authority to charge any fee.[66] The 'supplying information' does not include the costs associated with maintaining registers or databases of information which the authority is obliged to provide access to under Article 3(5) of the Directive or to which the right of 'examination in situ' arises under Article 5(1).[67] But the term will cover not only photocopying and postal costs, but also the costs attributable to the time spent by staff on answering an individual request for information, including the time spent searching for information and putting it in the form required.[68] The ICO 'strongly discourages' public authorities from including costs of staff time spent in pondering potential exceptions and/or redactions.[69] In terms of evaluating whether the charge is a reasonable one, the key question is whether the charge may have a deterrent effect on the person seeking the information.[70] The charge must neither exceed the financial capability of the person requesting the information, nor appear objectively unreasonable.[71] The ICO considers the overall reasonableness of the charge to be the most important consideration, but notes that the context of the request may affect the reasonableness of the charge.[72] The ICO also highlights that the public authority must be prepared to demonstrate why it believes the charge is reasonable in an individual case – which may include providing a breakdown of the charges so the person requesting the information can understand the fees.[73] Further, the authority may only make a charge which is in line with a published schedule of charges.[74] Where a public authority requires advance payment of a charge, this has the effect of freezing the time for compliance with the request.[75] If the amount requested is not received within 60 working days of a notification of advance payment, the request effectively lapses.[76] An applicant may appeal to the Information Commissioner against the amount of any fees sought to be imposed.[77] In contrast to FOIA, a public authority is not excused from processing a request for environmental

---

64 See further recital (18). A public authority must publish a list of charges.

65 EIR reg 8(1), EI(S)R reg 8(1). This is consistent with recital (18) and Art 5.2 of the Directive and Art 4.8 of the Aarhus Convention. Article 4.8 of the Convention and Art 5.3 of Directive 2003/4/EC require public authorities to provide a schedule of the charges that may be levied and to set out the circumstances in which charges are to be levied or may be waived. See S Stec, S Casey-Lefkowitz & J Jendroska, *The Aarhus Convention: an Implementation Guide* (New York, United Nations, 2000) p 65.

66 Acknowledged in the *Code of Practice – EIR*, February 2005, para 28.

67 *East Sussex CC v IC & ors* (C-71/14) [2016] 2 CMLR 5, [2016] PTSR 179 at [29].

68 *East Sussex CC v IC & ors* (C-71/14) [2016] 2 CMLR 5, [2016] PTSR 179 at [31]-[39].

69 ICO *Charging for Environmental Information (regulation 8) Environmental Information Regulations* at para 16. Further guidance on 'staff costs' is provided at paras 20-25.

70 *East Sussex CC v IC & ors* (C-71/14) [2016] 2 CMLR 5, [2016] PTSR 179 at [42].

71 *East Sussex CC v IC & ors* (C-71/14) [2016] 2 CMLR 5, [2016] PTSR 179 at [43]. J Ebbeson, H Gaugitsch, J Jendroska, F Marshall and S Stec, *The Aarhus Convention: an Implementation Guide* (2nd Edn) (New York, United Nations, 2014) p 94 for further examples of costs found to be unreasonable.

72 ICO *Charging for Environmental Information (regulation 8) Environmental Information Regulations* at paras 11-12. By way of example, in *East Sussex*, the charge – for providing property search information – was only a small part of the wider costs associated with the property purchase transaction.

73 ICO *Charging for Environmental Information (regulation 8) Environmental Information Regulations* at para 17.

74 ICO *Charging for Environmental Information (regulation 8) Environmental Information Regulations* at paras 18, 45-51.

75 EIR reg 8(5)-(7); EI(S)R reg 8(5)-(6). There is no comparable provision in the Directive.

76 EIR reg 8(5); EI(S)R reg 8(6).

77 EIR reg 18(1)-(7) and FOIA s 50(1); EI(S)R reg 17. The Tribunal has held that the proper role of the Commissioner is not to substitute his view of what a reasonable fee would be, but to assess whether the fee imposed by the public authority was within the range that a public authority could reasonably impose: *Markinson v IC*, IT, 28 March 2006.

information on the basis that it will involve costs in excess of a specified limit.[78]

2. THE RESPONSE

18–016 Time for compliance

A public authority must make the requested information available 'as soon as possible and no later than 20 working days after the date of the receipt of the request.'[79] If further particulars of the request have been sought or if the public authority has notified the applicant that it requires advance payment of a charge, this has the effect of stopping the clock until these are received.[80] Where a public authority reasonably believes that the complexity or volume of information requested makes it impracticable to deal with a request, it may award itself a further 20 working days within which to deal with the request.[81] The Code of Practice suggests that in the latter case the public authority is expected to inform the applicant of this 'as soon as possible' and within 20 working days and that the public authority should also be as specific as possible in relation to the length of and reason for the delay.[82] In contrast to FOIA, the time limit is not extended where the public authority is required to carry out a public interest balancing exercise.[83]

18–017 Transferring the request

The Regulations provide for the transfer of a request for environmental information where the recipient public authority believes that another public authority holds the information requested.[84] The drafting of the provision seemingly only contemplates the situation where the recipient public authority holds no information answering the terms of the request, rather than where it holds some information but is aware that another public authority holds further information. The Code of Practice nevertheless contemplates that in this latter situation one of the options for the public authority is to transfer that part of the request that relates to information which is not held by it.[85] Given this arrangement, it is sensible for any applicant who considers that there is a prospect that information may also be held by other public authorities (bearing in mind that each government department is treated as a separate public authority)[86] to include in the request an express requirement that the public authority provide

---

78 As is acknowledged in the *Code of Practice — EIR*, February 2005, paras 8 and 20, and in the Foreword, para 14(vi).

79 EIR reg 5(2); EI(S)R reg 5(2). This roughly accords with the Directive, recital (13) and Art 3.2 (which allows normally one month), and the Aarhus Convention Art 4.2. 'Working day' is defined in FOIA, imported by reg 2(2). See further §22–023. The *Code of Practice — EIR*, February 2005, para 25 expressly reminds public authorities that 'they must not delay responding until the end of the 20 working day period…if the information could reasonably have been provided earlier.' This accords with the UN view: J Ebbeson, H Gaugitsch, J Jendroska, F Marshall and S Stec, *The Aarhus Convention: an Implementation Guide* (2nd Edn) (New York, United Nations, 2014).

80 FEIR regs 9(4) and 8(5)-(6) respectively; EI(S)R regs 9(4) and 8(6)-(7). See the *Code of Practice — EIR*, February 2005, Foreword, para 14(iv).

81 Regulation 7(1). This accords with Art 4.2 of the Aarhus Convention and with Art 3.2(b) of the Directive. See further §22–027.

82 *Code of Practice — EIR*, February 2005, para 26.

83 As is acknowledged in the *Code of Practice — EIR*, February 2005, paras 8 and 26, and in the Foreword, para 14(v).

84 EIR reg 10(1); EI(S)R reg 14(1). This is broadly consistent with Art 4.1(a) of the Directive and Art 4.5 of the Aarhus Convention. See J Ebbeson, H Gaugitsch, J Jendroska, F Marshall and S Stec, *The Aarhus Convention: an Implementation Guide* (2nd Edn) (New York, United Nations, 2014) pp 91-92. The FOIA has no such provision. However, the Act's Code of Practice, paragraph 25, requires a similar exercise. See further §22–034.

85 EIR reg 9(1); EI(S)R reg 9(1). See the *Code of Practice — EIR*, February 2005, paras 31, 34-35.

86 EIR reg 3(5). There is no comparable provision in the EI(S)R.

assistance by advising the applicant of any other public authorities it believes may also hold information of the kind requested.[87] The Code of Practice indicates that where such a transfer requirement is not included within the request, the public authority should first contact the applicant.[88] The Code also provides that all transfers of requests should take place 'as soon as possible'.[89] Where a request has been transferred to another public authority it becomes a new request received by that public authority, with time running afresh for answering the request.[90]

18– 018 Communicating information

Once a public authority decides that it will disclose information it must normally do so in the form or format requested by the applicant.[91] If it decides not to use the applicant's preferred format, it must explain its decision to the applicant. This decision gives rise to a right to appeal to the Information Commissioner.[92] Unlike FOIA,[93] the Regulations do not provide for communication of the requested information by means of the provision of a summary of that information. It is doubtful whether the provision of merely a summary of the information held would meet the obligation imposed by the Regulations.[94] The Code of Practice suggests that where the applicant requests that the information be provided by means of a summary, the public authority should generally comply with that request.[95]

18– 019 Refusal notices

To the extent that a public authority refuses a request for information, whether because an exception applies to any of the information and the public interest weighs in favour of maintaining that exception,[96] because the request is procedurally flawed, because the request involves personal data or because the public authority did not hold the information when the request was received, the public authority must serve a 'refusal notice' that complies with the requirements of the Regulations.[97] The Regulations spell out the detail of reasons that are

---

87 EIR reg 9(1); EI(S)R reg 9(1).

88 The *Code of Practice — EIR*, February 2005, para 36.

89 The *Code of Practice — EIR*, February 2005, para 38.

90 EIR reg 10(2); EI(S)R reg 14(2).

91 EIR reg 6(1); EI(S)R reg 6(1). These provisions are derived from: Directive, recital (14) and Arts 3.4 and 8.2, and Aarhus Convention Art 4.1. This is also the view expressed in J Ebbeson, H Gaugitsch, J Jendroska, F Marshall and S Stec, *The Aarhus Convention: an Implementation Guide* (2nd Edn) (New York, United Nations, 2014) pp 80-81. In *Rhondda Cynon Taff CBC v IC*, IT, 5 December 2007 at [26]-[27] the Tribunal expressed the view that there was no obligation under the EIR 'to communicate' (by which it meant supply a copy of) information answering the terms of a request: the public authority could simply make the information available for inspection by the applicant. The Tribunal considered that it was at that point that an applicant could specify the mode of access and, if that mode was refused, could appeal that decision. Further, in that situation, the public authority would need to consider whether the information was required to be disclosed under FOIA, as that Act does give a right to have information communicated. The decision is questionable. By allowing a person to inspect documents, the information in those documents is being communicated. That is recognised in FOIA s 11(1)(b). Moreover, a well drawn request for information will specify the preferred mode of communication for information captured by its terms.

92 eg *Bunton v IC*, FTT, 9 March 2012 at [20].

93 Section 11(1)(c); FOI(S)A s 11(2)(b).

94 Article 4.1 of the Aarhus Convention requires Contracting States to pass legislation conferring a right to 'copies of the actual documentation containing or comprising [the requested] information.' See also Directive 2003/4/EC Arts 3.1 and 3.4.

95 The *Code of Practice — EIR*, February 2005, para 23. Under the terms of the Aarhus Convention, it is the information that must be provided, rather than just a summary of it: J Ebbeson, H Gaugitsch, J Jendroska, F Marshall and S Stec, *The Aarhus Convention: an Implementation Guide* (2nd Edn) (New York, United Nations, 2014) pp 80-81. The UN authors consider that the applicant should be provided with 'the context' of the information.

96 What are termed 'exemptions' in the FOIA are termed 'exceptions' in the EIR. See further §19– 001.

97 EIR reg 14(1); EI(S)R reg 13(a). For the provenance of this provision, see: Directive, Arts 3.3 and 4.5; Aarhus

required in a refusal notice.[98] The refusal notice should not merely paraphrase the terms of an exception, but should state clearly the reasons why the public authority has decided to apply each particular exception to the information requested.[99] Where the exception is qualified, the refusal notice should specify the public interest factors for upholding the exception, and those for disclosure, that have been taken into account before reaching the decision (unless to do so would involve the disclosure of the excepted information).[100] A refusal notice should notify the applicant of the complaints (ie review) procedure.[101] A refusal notice must be served within 20 working days of the receipt of the request.[102] If neither a refusal notice nor the requested information is received within 20 working days (unless extended for one of the reasons described above), then:

(1) the applicant has 40 days within which to make representations to the public authority in relation to its failure to comply with its obligations;[103] and
(2) if, within 40 working days of receipt of the representations, the public authority either gives no response or gives a response with which the applicant is not satisfied, this will constitute non-compliance with Pt 2 of the Regulations, enabling the applicant to make a complaint to the Information Commissioner, who will look at the matter afresh.[104]

18– 020 Information not held

An authority may refuse to disclose information answering the terms of the request where it does not hold that information at the time at which that authority receives the applicant's request for information.[105] Information 'held' by a public authority means information in the possession of that public authority which has been produced or received by it.[106] Information held by another on behalf of a public authority will also be captured by a request for information addressed to the public authority.[107] In answering a request for information a public authority is not required to reduce to writing or to some other recorded form what is known or could be know to the authority: a person's entitlement, and the correlative obligation on the public authority, is limited to information recorded in some medium that is held by the

Convention, Arts 4.3(b), 4.5-4.7; J Ebbeson, H Gaugitsch, J Jendroska, F Marshall and S Stec, *The Aarhus Convention: an Implementation Guide* (2nd Edn) (New York, United Nations, 2014) pp 92-93. See further §24– 009. For an example of a failure to issue a proper refusal notice, see *Remington v IC*, FTT, 23 January 2013 at [7]-[11].

98 EIR reg 14(3); EI(S)R reg 13(c). The notice must also set out an applicant's right of representations and appeal: EIR reg 14(5); EI(S)R reg 13(e).

99 The *Code of Practice — EIR*, February 2005, para 56.

100 The *Code of Practice — EIR*, February 2005, para 56.

101 The *Code of Practice — EIR*, February 2005, para 56. Directive 2003/4/EC Art 4.5.

102 EIR reg 13(2); EI(S)R, 13(a). This is slightly less generous to the public authority than is contemplated under the Directive Art 4.5, and the Aarhus Convention Art 4.7.

103 EIR reg 11(1)-(2); EI(S)R reg 16(1)-(2).

104 EIR regs 11(4) and 18(1), and FOIA s 50; EI(S)R regs 16(4) and 17 (the time limit in Scotland is 20 days). See further §22– 020. Rights of appeal under the EIR are considered in Ch 45; rights of appeal under the EI(S)R are considered in Ch 46. Regulatory enforcement under both the EIR and EI(S)R is considered in Ch 47. Criminal sanctions under the EIR and under the EI(S)R are considered in Ch 50.

105 EIR reg 12(4)(a); EI(S)R reg 10(4)(a). This is derived from Art 4(1)(a) of Directive 2003/4/EC and Art 4(3)(a) of the Aarhus Convention. For a more detailed analysis of the holding requirement (as it applies under FOIA and FOI(S)A) see §§20– 009 to 20– 012.

106 EIR reg 3(2)(a); EI(S)R reg 2(2)(a). This is derived from Art 2(3) of Directive 2003/4/EC and from Art 4(3)(a) the Aarhus Convention.

107 EIR reg 3(2)(b); EI(S)R reg 2(2)(b). This is derived from Arts 2(4), 3(1), 3(4), 4(1)(a), 4(4) of Directive 2003/4/EC.

public authority.[108] Where a public authority acquires or generates information after receipt of a request, that public authority is not obliged to consider that information in responding to the request. A person may, of course, make a further request for information in the same terms as the earlier request, but limited to information received or generated by the public authority after the date of receipt of the earlier request.

8–021 Neither confirm nor deny

The Regulations enable a public authority to respond to a request by 'neither confirming or denying' that the information requested exists.[109] The Directive does not provide for such a response.[110] Such a notice can only be given under the Regulations where confirmation or denial that the public authority holds the requested information:

(1) would involve the disclosure of information that would adversely affect international relations, defence, national security or public safety; and

(2) in all the circumstances of the case, the public interest in not disclosing that information outweighs the public interest in disclosing the information.[111]

8–022 Unreasonable requests

A public authority may refuse to disclose environmental information to the extent that the request for information is 'manifestly unreasonable.'[112] The comparative epithet in FOIA is 'vexatious.'[113] For all intents and purposes, the difference between the two phrases is 'vanishingly small.'[114] Complexity alone does not make a request 'manifestly unreasonable.'[115] What is required under both regimes is that it be clear that there is no reasonable foundation for thinking that the requested information would be of value to the person requesting it or to any section of the public.[116] Whilst the test is objective, the motive of the person making the request for information may provide a basis for inferring that the request is manifestly unreasonable.[117] The environmental information regime does not set a financial limit to the cost of compliance with a request, beyond which a public authority is not obliged to deal with it.[118] A public authority will not be able to claim that a request has been manifestly unreasonable if the public authority itself has acted unreasonably in dealing with a request: for

---

108 See Directive 2003/4/EC Arts1(a) and recitals (7), (8), (12), (14) and (15). See further §20–007 and §20–011.

109 EIR reg 12(6); EI(S)R reg 10(8).

110 The Regulations seek to address this anomaly through a quasi-deeming provision: EIR reg 12(7); EI(S)R reg 10(9). Presumably the FOIA s 74(3)(b), and FOI(S)A s 62(3)(b), are relied upon in this regard. Paragraph 4(ix) of the *Explanatory Memorandum* to the Regulations recognises that the basis for a 'neither confirm nor deny' response is not to be explicitly found in the Directive, but states that 'it is believed to be implicit.'

111 EIR reg 12(6)-(7); EI(S)R reg 10(8)-(9). The scope for issuing a neither confirm nor deny response is thus considerably narrower than it is under the FOIA.

112 EIR reg 12(4)(b); EI(S)R, 10(4)(b). Derived from Art 4.1(b) of the Directive and Art 4.3(b) of the Aarhus Convention.

113 FOIA s 14; FOI(S)A s 14. See further §§23–012 to 23–016.

114 *Dransfield v IC and Devon CC* [2015] EWCA Civ 454, [2015] 1 WLR 5316 at [78].

115 J Ebbeson, H Gaugitsch, J Jendroska, F Marshall and S Stec, *The Aarhus Convention: an Implementation Guide* (2nd Edn) (New York, United Nations, 2014) p 84, citing the Compliance Committee findings in ACCC/S/200/1 (Ukraine) and ACCC/C/2004/3 (Ukraine).

116 *Dransfield v IC and Devon CC* [2015] EWCA Civ 454, [2015] 1 WLR 5316 at [78]. The Court of Appeal in *Dransfield* noted that it was possible that CJEU jurisprudence could develop in a different way in future, and that the public interest test could compel a different outcome under EIR and FOIA (at [78]). Some element of public interest is no automatic bar to a request being vexatious: *Parker v IC* [2016] UKUT 0427 (AAC) at [34], [78].

117 *Dransfield v IC and Devon CC* [2015] EWCA Civ 454, [2015] 1 WLR 5316 at [78]. Contrast recital (8) of Directive 2003/4/EC.

118 Compare FOIA s 12. See §23–002 and *Mersey Tunnel Users Association v IC and Halton BC*, IT, 24 June 2009 at [90].

example, by failing to comply with its duty to provide advice and assistance.[119] Tribunal cases illustrate that reliance upon the exception has met with some success.[120] It is possible for a request that has been properly adjudged to be 'manifestly unreasonable' to lose that quality over time by virtue of changed circumstances.[121]

18–023 Cost of compliance

Whilst the cost of compliance may be taken into account in concluding that the request is manifestly unreasonable, the particular financial limits set by regulations under FOIA do not represent an expression of the dividing line between requests that, on the basis of the cost of compliance, are and are not manifestly unreasonable.[122]

18–024 Vague requests

A public authority may also refuse to disclose environmental information to the extent that the request is formulated in too general a manner, but only provided that the public authority has complied with its obligation to provide reasonable advice and assistance to the applicant.[123] ICO guidance suggests that a request is too general if it has more than one possible interpretation or it is not specific enough to allow the public authority to identify what has been asked for. Before refusing to disclose the information, the public authority will have to satisfy itself that in all the circumstances of the case, the public interest in maintaining the particular exception outweighs the public interest in disclosure.[124]

18–025 Partial disclosure and redaction

The Regulations specifically require a public authority to treat discretely information that answers the terms of a request. Thus, the fact that a public authority is entitled to refuse to disclose a particular document relying on reg 12 does not detract from the obligation of the public authority to disclose all other information that it holds that answers the terms of the request, save to the extent that some exception applies to any of that remainder. Similarly, within any particular document, a public authority must consider whether it is possible to release part of the document, redacting, if necessary, parts that are excepted from disclosure.[125]

---

119 Under EIR reg 9 and EI(S)R reg 9: *Mersey Tunnel Users Association v IC and Halton BC*, IT, 24 June 2009 at [95]; *Little v IC and Welsh Assembly Government*, FTT, 30 December 2010 at [58]-[71].

120 Use of the exception was upheld in: *Easter v IC and New Forest National Park Authority*, FTT, 14 May 2010 at [43] and [61]-[62]; *Little v IC and Welsh Assembly Government*, FTT, 30 December 2010 at [32]-[42]; *Harding v IC and London Borough of Camden*, FTT, 17 October 2011 at [12]-[13]; *Walker v IC*, FTT, 21 October 2011; *Lavelle v IC and Stafford Borough Council*, FTT, 30 November 2011 at [17]-[37]; *Lancashire Constabulary v IC and Wise*, FTT, 15 March 2012 at [25]-[34] (in that case the Tribunal had regard in considering reasonableness to the local authority being small 'with limited resources to devote to information requests;' *Ainslie v IC and Dorset CC* [2012] UKUT 441. For examples of where use of the exception was not upheld: *Remington v IC*, FTT, 23 January 2013; *Harris v IC*, FTT, 23 January 2014; *Dept of Finance and Personnel for Northern Ireland v IC*, FTT, 31 July 2014.

121 *Thornton v IC*, FTT, 22 May 2017.

122 *Mersey Tunnel Users Association v IC and Halton BC*, IT, 24 June 2009 at [92]-[98] (by inference).

123 EIR reg 12(4)(c); EI(S)R reg 10(4)(c). Derived from Art 3.3 and 4.1 (c) of the Directive and Art 4.3(b) of the Aarhus Convention. As to the duty to give advice and assistance when a request is too vague, see §§18–013 to 18–014. Suggested meanings of the provision in the Aarhus Convention are given in J Ebbeson, H Gaugitsch, J Jendroska, F Marshall and S Stec, *The Aarhus Convention: an Implementation Guide* (2nd Edn) (New York, United Nations, 2014) p 84. The public authority must comply with its duty to provide reasonable advice and assistance before invoking this as a basis for refusing to disclose: *Mersey Tunnel Users Association v IC and Halton BC*, IT, 24 June 2009 at [100].

124 EIR reg 12(1)(b); EI(S)R reg 10(1)(b). In *Easter v IC and New Forest National Park Authority*, FTT, 14 May 2010 the Tribunal observed that reg 12(4)(b) appeared to envisage that a manifestly unreasonable request might need to be complied with because of the application of the public interest test and that this seemed 'logically absurd' [75]. The Tribunal considered that the exception had 'an in-built public interest' against disclosure which should be given significant weight (at [75]-[81]).

125 EIR reg 12(11); EI(S)R reg 10(7). Derived from Directive 2003/4/EC, recital (17) and Art 4.4, and Aarhus Convention Art 4.6. This is said to be required by the Aarhus Convention: J Ebbeson, H Gaugitsch, J Jendroska,

8– 026 Third party consultation

Information answering the terms of a request may have originated from a third party. Such information may have been volunteered to the public authority by the third party, it may have been supplied under compulsion or it may have been supplied in support of an application of some sort. A public authority is not obliged by the Regulations to consult the third party who supplied this information to it before communicating it to an applicant. The Code of Practice does not impose a requirement to consult the third party.[126] A public authority cannot contractually agree with a third party that it will not disclose information supplied by that third party to the public authority that subsequently falls within the terms of a request made under the Regulations. The Code of Practice exhorts public authorities against making agreements with such provisions.[127]

3. COMMISSIONERS, APPEALS, ENFORCEMENT ETC

8– 027 Information Commissioner

The main responsibility for enforcing the EIR lies with the Information Commissioner. The principal functions of the Commissioner under the EIR track the Commissioner's functions under FOIA.[128] In performing her functions, the Commissioner must comply with the requirements of confidentiality and the precepts of the Human Rights Act 1998.[129]

8– 028 EIR practice recommendations

The general functions of the Information Commissioner under sections 47 to 49 of FOIA apply under the EIR.[130] Under s 47 of FOIA (as applied to the EIR), the Information Commissioner has a duty to promote the observance by public authorities of the Code of Practice prepared under reg 16. If it appears to the Commissioner that the practice of a public authority in the exercise of its functions under the EIR does not conform with that proposed in the Code of Practice, the Commissioner may give the public authority a practice recommendation under s 48, specifying the steps which should, in the Commissioner's opinion, be taken to promote such conformity. Unless the public authority appeals against the decision of the Commissioner, the public authority must comply with the practice recommendation of the Commissioner. A practice recommendation must be given in writing and must refer to the particular provisions of the Code of Practice with which, in the Commissioner's opinion, the public authority's practice does not conform. A practice recommendation is simply a recommendation and cannot be directly enforced by the Commissioner. However, a failure to comply with a practice recommendation may lead to a failure to comply with the EIR. Further, a failure to take account of a practice recommendation may lead to an adverse comment in a report to Parliament by the Commissioner.

F Marshall and S Stec, *The Aarhus Convention: an Implementation Guide* (2nd Edn) (New York, United Nations, 2014) pp 91-92. See further §24– 014. Thus in *Archer v IC and Salisbury DC*, IT, 9 May 2007, the Tribunal ordered the disclosure of part of a joint report by officers of a local authority into planning control enforcement options whilst upholding a claim for exception in relation to other parts of that report.

[126] The *Code of Practice — EIR*, February 2005, paras 40-45.

[127] The *Code of Practice — EIR*, February 2005, paras 46-55.

[128] These are listed at §44– 003.

[129] See further at §§44– 006 to 44– 007.

[130] EIR reg 16(5).

18– 029 EIR appeals

The EIR include a four-tiered review structure which imports most of the review provisions of FOIA:

(1) The first stage is an internal, merit-based reconsideration of the decision.[131] In contrast to FOIA, it is mandatory for a public authority to have a complaints and reconsideration procedure to deal with representations complaining of a failure to comply with the EIR. A public authority is obliged to notify an applicant of his or her right of complaint.[132] The Code provides that this notification should set out details of the public authority's complaints procedure, how it may be invoked and the right to complain to the Information Commissioner under section 50 of FOIA if the applicant is still dissatisfied after the public authority's review.[133] The Code also provides that the complainant should be informed of the public authority's target date for determining the complaint.[134] Complaints must, in any event, be responded to within 40 working days from the time when the complaint was received.[135]

(2) If, after that, the applicant (who becomes a 'complainant'[136]) remains dissatisfied, an application can be made to the Information Commissioner.[137] The Commissioner is given a wide remit to deal with refusals, the level of fee charged, the time taken and so forth.[138] Unless a conclusive certificate has been issued, the Commissioner will undertake a merit review of the public authority's decision.[139] The Commissioner's review results in what is termed a 'decision notice.' For the purpose of carrying out her review, the Information Commissioner can issue an 'information notice' which requires a public authority to furnish the Commissioner with relevant information within such time as the Commissioner specifies.[140] Through this notice, the Commissioner is able to see the information that is being sought by the applicant in order to form a judgment as to whether it ought to be disclosed under the EIR.

(3) The third stage of the appeal process is an appeal to the FTT or the Upper Tribunal under section 57 of FOIA. The appeal is normally to the FTT but the appeal can, in suitable cases (eg where the appeal is of considerable public importance or involves complex or unusual issues), be transferred to the Upper Tribunal.[141] The grounds of appeal are the same as under FOIA.[142] It is not just the complainant who may appeal to the Tribunal: if a public authority does not care for the decision of the Information

---

[131] EIR reg 11. This meets the requirement of Art 6.1 of the Directive, which permits reconsideration by the same body.

[132] EIR reg 14(5).

[133] *Code of Practice — EIR*, February 2005, para 59.

[134] *Code of Practice — EIR*, February 2005, para 62.

[135] *Code of Practice — EIR*, February 2005, para 63.

[136] FOIA s 50(1).

[137] EIR reg 18(1) and FOIA s 50(1), imported by reg 18(3) and (4).

[138] See §§45– 005 to 45– 011. In relation to fees, the Tribunal has held that the proper role of the Commissioner is not to substitute his view of what a reasonable fee would be, but to assess whether the fee imposed by the public authority was within the range that a public authority could reasonably impose: *Markinson v IC*, IT, 28 March 2006.

[139] Directive 2003/4/EC Art 6.2, and Aarhus Convention Art 9.1, require a second-stage review process 'in which the acts or omissions of the public authority concerned can be reviewed and whose decisions may become final.'

[140] FOIA s 51(1) and (7).

[141] FTT Rules r 19(2)-(3). See further §44– 019.

[142] See further §45– 014.

Commissioner, it too may appeal to the Tribunal.[143] The Tribunal must allow the appeal if the notice is 'not in accordance with the law.' If the Information Commissioner's decision involved the exercise of discretion, the Tribunal can interfere if it takes the view that the Commissioner should have exercised her discretion differently.[144]

(4) Under section 11 of Tribunals, Courts and Enforcement Act 2007 any party to a case has a right of appeal to the Upper Tribunal on any point of law arising from a decision made by the FTT.[145]

(5) Section 13 of Tribunals, Courts and Enforcement Act 2007 provides for an appeal from the decision of the Upper Tribunal to the Court of Appeal (or, in Scotland, to the Court of Session). Again, decisions in relation to national security certificates are excluded.[146]

A public authority may, in an appeal to the FTT, rely on exceptions not invoked in the original decision, or in the internal review or on complaint to the Information Commissioner.[147] The Regulations do not make specific provision for a third party who may be affected by a proposed disclosure of information to be invited to participate in the appeal process.[148]

8–030 EIR regulatory enforcement

The EIR import, with limited modification, the regulatory enforcement provisions of FOIA.[149] Thus:

(1) Where the Information Commissioner has received a 'complaint', the Commissioner may serve an information notices on a public authority.[150]

(2) Where the Information Commissioner reasonably requires information for the purpose of determining whether a public authority has complied, or is complying, with the requirements of Part 2 and 3 of the EIR, or for the purpose of determining whether the practice of a public authority in relation to the exercise of its functions conforms with the code of practice, again the Commissioner may serve an information notice on a public authority.[151]

(3) Where the Information Commissioner is satisfied that a public authority has failed to comply with any of the statutory requirements in Parts 2 and 3 of the EIR, the Commissioner may serve the authority with an enforcement notice requiring the authority to take, within such time as may be specified in the notice, such steps as may be so specified for complying with those requirements.[152]

8–031 EIR offences, contempt etc

If a decision notice, enforcement notice or information notice issued by the Information Commissioner (and not successfully appealed against) is not complied with, she may certify that

143 See further §45–015.

144 FOIA s 58(1). See further §§45–014 to 45–019.

145 See further §45–020. Aarhus Convention Art 3.8, implies that this is the first point at which costs may be awarded against an applicant.

146 Tribunals, Courts and Enforcement Act 2007 s 13(8). See further §45–027.

147 *DEFRA v IC and Birkett* [2011] UKUT 39 (AAC), [2011] UKUT 17 (AAC). See further §45–016.

148 Directive 2003/4/EC Art 6.2, enables, but does not require, Member States to so provide.

149 EIR reg 18.

150 See further §47–002(1).

151 See further §47–002(2).

152 See further §47–003.

that is the case to the High Court.[153] The court may then inquire into the matter and, after hearing evidence and any statement which may be offered in defence, it may deal with the public authority 'as if it had committed a contempt of court.'[154] Where there are reasonable grounds for suspecting:

- non-compliance with the requirements of Part 2 or 3 of the EIR or with the requirements of a decision, information or enforcement notice, or
- that an offence under reg 19 of the EIR has been committed,

and there are grounds for suspecting that evidence of any of these is to be found on any premises, the Information Commissioner may seek a warrant from a circuit judge authorising her officers to enter and search premises, to inspect and seize documents or other material[155] which might be evidence of that non-compliance or offence, and to inspect, examine, operate and test equipment found there in which information may be recorded.[156] Where a request for environmental information has been received by a public authority and the applicant would have been entitled to the information, it is an offence for a person to alter, deface, block, destroy or conceal any record held by the recipient public authority with the intention of preventing the applicant from obtaining disclosure of some of or all the information requested.[157]

18– 032 EIR: private claims

The EIR provide that the Regulations do not confer any right of action in civil proceedings in respect of a failure to comply with a duty imposed by or under its provisions.[158]

18– 033 EIR: defamatory material

The EIR do not contain a provision conferring privilege in respect of defamatory material supplied to a public authority by a third person and published to a person making a request for information.[159]

18– 034 Scottish Commissioner

The main responsibility for enforcing the EI(S)R lies with the Scottish Information Commissioner. The principal functions of the Scottish Information Commissioner under the EI(S)R track the Commissioner's functions under FOI(S)A.[160] In performing her functions, the Scottish Information Commissioner must comply with the requirements of confidentiality and the precepts of the Human Rights Act 1998.[161]

18– 035 EI(S)R appeals

The EI(S)R include a three-tiered review structure which imports most of the review provisions of FOI(S)A:

---

153 EIR reg 18 (applying FOIA, Pt IV (ss 50-56), incl Sch 3).

154 EIR reg 18 (applying FOIA, Pt IV (ss 50-56), incl Sch 3). The Court's contempt jurisdiction and procedure is considered further in §§50– 002 to 50– 003.

155 In relation to the power of a magistrate under s 8 of the Police and Criminal Evidence Act 1984 to grant a warrant to a constable to enter and search the premises (containing a like power to 'seize documents and other material'), the phrase 'other material' has been held to be wide enough to cover a computer and its hard disk: *R (Faisaltex Ltd) v Preston Crown Court* 2008] EWHC 2832 (Admin), [2009] 1 Cr App R 37; *R (Cabot Global Ltd) v Barkingside Magistrates' Court* [2015] EWHC 1458 (Admin), [2015] 2 Cr App R 26.

156 EIR reg 18 (applying FOIA, Pt IV (ss 50-56), incl Sch 3). See further §§50– 004 to 50– 005.

157 EIR reg 19. Section 77 is the comparable provision in FOIA. See further §50– 006.

158 EIR reg 18 (applying FOIA Pt IV (ss 50-56), incl Sch 3). See further §50– 025.

159 Contrast FOIA s 79. See further §50– 026.

160 These are listed at §46– 002.

161 See further at §46– 003.

(1) An applicant who is dissatisfied with the way in which a Scottish public authority has dealt with his or her request for information may require that public authority to review its actions and decisions in relation to that request: this is called a 'requirement for review.'[162] An applicant cannot make an application to the Scottish Information Commissioner without having first sought a requirement for review.[163] The procedure, nature and time-limits for such a requirement for review are considered later in this work.[164]

(2) A person dissatisfied with the decision (or a failure or refusal[165] to take a decision) of a Scottish public authority on the first stage of review can apply to the Scottish Information Commissioner for a decision whether the request for information to which the requirement for review relates was dealt with in accordance with Part 1 of the EI(S)R.[166] The practice and procedure to be followed in such an application and the powers and functions of the Scottish Information Commissioner are considered later in this work.[167]

(3) Where an applicant or a public authority is unhappy with a decision of the Scottish Information Commissioner, each can appeal to the Court of Session but only on a point of law.[168] An appeal to the Court of Session is to the Inner House, in broad terms the equivalent of the English and Welsh Court of Appeal. The procedure and nature of such an appeal are considered later in this work.[169]

8– 036 EI(S)R regulatory enforcement

The EI(S)R import, with limited modification, the regulatory enforcement provisions of FOI(S)A.[170] Thus:

(1) Where the Scottish Information Commissioner has received an 'application,' the Commissioner may serve an information notice on a Scottish public authority.[171]

(2) Where the Scottish Information Commissioner reasonably requires information for the purpose of determining whether a public authority has complied, or is complying, with the requirements of Part 2 and 3 of the EI(S)R, or for the purpose of determining whether the practice of a public authority in relation to the exercise of its functions conforms with the codes of practice, again the Commissioner may serve an information notice on a public authority.[172]

(3) Where the Scottish Information Commissioner is satisfied that a public authority has failed to comply with any of the statutory requirements in Parts 2 and 3 of the EI(S)R, the Commissioner may serve the authority with an enforcement notice requiring the authority to take, within such time as may be specified in the notice, such steps as may

---

162 EI(S)R reg 16(2).

163 FOI(S)A s 47(1) as applied by EI(S)R reg 17(1).

164 See §§46– 008 to 46– 010.

165 That is, one on the ground that the request is vexatious or repeated or there has already recently been an answer to the same or substantially the same request for information.

166 FOI(S)A s 47(1) applied by EI(S)R reg 17(1) and (2)(b). The language is materially the same as the FOIA s 50(1): see §45– 005. The phrase 'dealt with in accordance with Part 1 of the Act' is sufficiently wide to cover a review decision dealing with any of the four types of reviewable responses identified in §46– 005.

167 See §§46– 011 to 46– 013.

168 FOI(S)A s 56 applied by EI(S)R reg 17.

169 See §§46– 015 to 46– 016.

170 EI(S)R reg 17.

171 FOI(S)A s 50(1)(a). See further §47– 008.

172 FOI(S)A s 50(1)(b). See further §47– 008.

be so specified for complying with those requirements.[173]

18– 037 EI(S)R offences, contempt etc

If a decision notice, enforcement notice or information notice issued by the Scottish Information Commissioner (and not successfully appealed against) is not complied with, he may certify that that is the case to the Court of Session.[174] The court may then inquire into the matter and, after hearing evidence and any statement which may be offered in defence, it may deal with the public authority 'as if it had committed a contempt of court.'[175] Where there are reasonable grounds for suspecting:

- non-compliance with the requirements of Part 2 or 3 of the EI(S)R or with the requirements of a decision, information or enforcement notice, or
- that an offence under reg 19 of the EI(S)R has been committed,

and there are grounds for suspecting that evidence of any of these is to be found on any premises, the Scottish Information Commissioner may seek a warrant from a sheriff authorising his officers to enter and search premises, to inspect and seize documents or other material[176] which might be evidence of that non-compliance or offence, and to inspect, examine, operate and test equipment found there in which information may be recorded.[177] Where a request for environmental information has been received by a public authority and the applicant would have been entitled to the information, it is an offence for a person to alter, deface, block, destroy or conceal any record held by the recipient public authority with the intention of preventing the applicant from obtaining disclosure of some of or all the information requested.[178]

18– 038 EI(S)R: private claims

The EI(S)R provide that the Regulations do not confer any right of action in civil proceedings in respect of a failure to comply with a duty imposed by or under their provisions.[179]

18– 039 EI(S)R: defamatory material

The EI(S)R do not contain a provision conferring privilege in respect of defamatory material supplied to a public authority by a third person and published to a person making a request for information.[180]

---

173 See further §47– 009.

174 EI(S)R reg 17 (applying FOI(S)A, Pt 4 (ss 47-56), incl Sch 3).

175 EI(S)R reg 17 (applying FOIA, Pt 4 (ss 47-56), incl Sch 3). The Court's contempt jurisdiction and procedure is considered further in §§50– 002 to 50– 003.

176 In relation to the power of a magistrate under s 8 of the Police and Criminal Evidence Act 1984 to grant a warrant to a constable to enter and search the premises (containing a like power to 'seize documents and other material'), the phrase 'other material' has been held to be wide enough to cover a computer and its hard disk: *R (Faisaltex Ltd) v Preston Crown Court* 2008] EWHC 2832 (Admin), [2009] 1 Cr App R 37; *R (Cabot Global Ltd) v Barkingside Magistrates' Court* [2015] EWHC 1458 (Admin), [2015] 2 Cr App R 26.

177 EI(S)R reg 17 (applying FOI(S)A, Pt 4 (ss 47-56), incl Sch 3). See further §50– 008.

178 EI(S)R reg 19. Section 65 is the comparable provision in FOI(S)A. See further §50– 009.

179 EI(S)R reg 17 (applying FOI(S)A Pt 4, specifically s 55(1). See further §50– 025.

180 Contrast FOI(S)A s 67. See further §50– 026.

CHAPTER 19

Environmental information – exceptions

1. GENERAL PRINCIPLES

19–001 Introduction

The Regulations set out the circumstances in which a public authority may or must refuse to disclose requested information.[1] These are called 'exceptions'. The exceptions may be divided into three categories:

(1) Refusals on procedural grounds: namely, where the request is vague, the request is manifestly unreasonable,[2] or the public authority does not hold the requested information;[3]

(2) Where the information falls within one of the three purely class-based exceptions, namely:

— information that includes personal data of which the applicant is not the data subject;[4]

---

1 EIR reg 12(3)-(5); EI(S)R reg 10(3)-(5).

2 For example, by making overlapping requests or by making further requests before awaiting the outcome of earlier requests: *Latimer v IC and Environment Agency*, IT, 3 August 2009; *Carpenter v IC and Stevenage BC*, IT, 17 November 2008.

3 EIR reg 12(4)(a)-(c); EI(S)R reg 10(4)(a)-(c). Derived from Art 4.1(a)-(c) of the Directive and Art 4.3(a)-(b) of the Aarhus Convention. See further §18–022. The Tribunal has jurisdiction to consider whether a public authority holds more information answering the terms of a request than it claims: *McGlade v IC and Redcar and Cleveland BC*, IT, 23 November 2009; *Latimer v IC and Environment Agency*, IT, 3 August 2009.

4 EIR reg 12(3); EI(S)R regs 10(3) and 11(1). Derived from Art 4.2(f) of the Directive and Art 4.4(f) of the Aarhus Convention. See further §19–032.

— where the request relates to incomplete material;[5] or
— where the request involves the disclosure of internal communications;[6]

(3) Where disclosure of the information would adversely affect one of a number of matters specifically protected.[7]

Apart from information that includes personal data of which the applicant is not the data subject, the applicability of any of the above exceptions is not by itself enough to enable a public authority to refuse to disclose the requested information. It must also be shown that in all the circumstances of the case the public interest in maintaining the exception outweighs the public interest in disclosing the information.[8]

19– 002 Comparison with FOIA

Apart from where the request would involve disclosure of 'internal communications',[9] the Regulations are more liberal in the disclosure of information than is FOIA. First, there are fewer exceptions under the Regulations than there are exemptions under the Act. The Regulations do not provide an express exception for:

— information available under an alternative access regime;[10]
— policy information;[11]
— information in respect of which a claim to legal professional privilege could be maintained;[12]
— information the disclosure of which would or would be likely to prejudice relations between any administrations within the United Kingdom;[13]
— information the disclosure of which would be or would be likely to be prejudicial to the economic or financial interests of the United Kingdom;[14] and
— information the disclosure of which is prohibited by or under any enactment or by rule of law (such as contempt of court).[15]

---

5 EIR reg 12(4)(d); EI(S)R regs 10(4)(d). Derived from Art 4.1(d) of the Directive and Art 4.3(c) of the Aarhus Convention. See further §19– 011.

6 EIR reg 12(4)(e); EI(S)R reg 10(4)(e). Derived from Art 4.1(e) of the Directive and Art 4.3(c) of the Aarhus Convention. See further §19– 013.

7 EIR reg 12(5); EI(S)R reg 10(5). Derived from Art 4.2 of the Directive and Art 4.4 of the Aarhus Convention. See further §§19– 015 to 19– 022 and 19– 026 to 19– 029.

8 EIR reg 12(1)(b); EI(S)R reg 10(1)(b). Loosely derived from Arts 4.1(e) and 4.2 (antepenultimate sentence) of the Directive and Art 4.4 (final sentence) of the Aarhus Convention. The Regulations differ from the Act in that refusal on procedural grounds under the Act does not involve any consideration of the public interest: FOIA ss 1(2)-(4) and 14; FOI(S)A ss 1 and 14.

9 EIR regs 12(4)(e) and 12(8); EI(S)R reg 10(4)(e). The Explanatory Memorandum to the EIR describes this exception as not being made under s 74 of the FOIA, but under s 2(2) of the European Communities Act 1972.

10 Compare FOIA s 21; FOI(S)A s 25. However, under the EIR regime a public authority is not required to make information available if it is already publicly available and easily accessible to the applicant: EIR reg 6(1)(b); EI(S)R reg 6(1)(b). This means publicly available in the format sought by the applicant in the request for information: *OFCOM v IC and T-Mobile (UK) Ltd*, IT, 4 September 2007 at [69].

11 Compare FOIA s 35(1); FOI(S)A s 29(1). Some policy information may be captured by EIR reg 12(4)(e) and the EI(S)R reg 10(4)(e). See further §19– 013 for the closest comparable provision.

12 Compare FOIA s 42(1); FOI(S)A s 36. Although similar protection is afforded by EIR reg 12(5)(b) and (d), and EI(S)R reg 10(5)(b) and (d). The Tribunal in *Kirkaldie v IC and Thanet DC*, IT, 4 July 2006, considered (at [21]) that reg 12(5) 'exists in part to ensure that there should be no disruption to the administration of justice, including the operation of the courts and no prejudice to the right of individuals or organisations to a fair trial. In order to achieve this it covers legal professional privilege, particularly where a public authority is or is likely to be involved in litigation.' A claim for exemption in respect of legal advice was similarly upheld in *Burgess v IC and Stafford BC*, IT, 7 June 2007.

13 Compare FOIA s 28(1); FOI(S)A s 32.

14 Compare FOIA s 29(1); FOI(S)A s 33.

15 Compare FOIA s 44(1); FOI(S)A s 26. The EIR reg 5(6), and the EI(S)R reg 5(3), specifically disapply any

Secondly, a number of the exceptions in the Regulations are more narrowly drafted than are the equivalent exemptions in the Act:

— confidential or commercial information;[16] and
— information relating to the detection of crime or to the conduct of criminal proceedings.[17]

Thirdly, many of the exceptions in the Regulations that approximate class-based exemptions under the Act differ in their additional requirement that disclosure 'adversely affect' the interest protected by the exception.[18] And fourthly, all exceptions, save one, in the Regulations involve a consideration of the public interest before the public authority can refuse to communicate the requested information.[19]

19–003 Onus

The more restrictive treatment of exceptions is further marked by a specific onus provision in the Regulations.[20] The presumption in favour of disclosure informs both the specific exceptions and the public interest weighing exercise.[21] The progenitors of the Regulations also include an interpretive provision that requires exceptions to be read restrictively:[22] no such provision is to be found in the Regulations.

19–004 Discretionary disclosure

The applicability of an exception merely means that an applicant has no entitlement under the Regulations to the disclosure of the information to which the exception applies. Other than in relation to personal data of which the applicant is not the data subject,[23] it does not mean that the public authority is unable to disclose the information.[24] In practice, there is a risk that voluntary disclosure of environmental information (other than of 'internal communications')

---

enactment or rule of law that would prevent the disclosure of information in accordance with the Regulations.

16 Compare FOIA ss 41(1) and 43 with EIR reg 12(5)(e) and (f) and FOI(S)A ss 36 and 33, EI(S)R reg 10(5)(e) and (f).

17 Compare FOIA ss 30(1) and 31(1) with EIR reg 12(5)(b), and FOI(S)A ss 34 and 35, EI(S)R reg 10(5)(b).

18 In other words, what in the FOIA is a purely class-based exemption becomes a prejudice-based exception in the EIR: see ss 27(2), 30(1), 32(1), 34(1), 35(1), 41(1), 42(1), 43(1) and 44(1). And similarly as between the FOI(S)A ss 25(1), 26, 27(1), 29(1), 31(1), 32(1)(b), 33(1)(a), 34, 36, 37(1), 38(1), 39(2) and 41, and the EI(S)R.

19 Namely, those exemptions not listed in the FOIA s 2(3), ie ss 21(1), 23(1), 32(1), 32(2), 34(1), 36(2), 40(1), 40(3)(a)(i,) 40(3)(b), 41(1) and 44(1). In Scotland, FOI(S)A ss 27, 28, 29, 30, 31, 32, 33, 34, 35, 36(1), 39, 40 and 41.

20 EIR reg 12(2), to which a public authority's power to refuse to disclose environmental information is made subject: reg 12(1). In *Burgess v IC and Stafford BC*, IT, 7 June 2007 at [43] the Tribunal regarded this as a significant difference from the FOIA. EI(S)R reg 10(2), is to similar effect. Directive 2003/4/EC, recital (16) states 'disclosure of information should be the general rule and...public authorities should be permitted to refuse a request for environmental information in specific and clearly defined cases.'

21 There is, at most, only an implication of onus in the FOIA: see further §5–025.

22 EI(S)R do include a requirement that exceptions be interpreted in a restrictive way. This derives from recital (16) to and Art 4.2 (penultimate sentence) of the Directive and the concluding words of Art 4.4 of the Aarhus Convention. This is consistent with the approach that the European Court of Justice has taken in relation to other freedom of information instruments: see *Hautala v Council of the European Union* [2002] 1 WLR 1930 at [25]. See further J Ebbeson, H Gaugitsch, J Jendroska, F Marshall and S Stec, *The Aarhus Convention: an Implementation Guide* (2nd Edn) (New York, United Nations, 2014) p 90 (the Aarhus Convention sets 'a floor, not a ceiling'). The Tribunal has recognised that recital (16) 'suggests that the grounds for refusal to disclose should be interpreted in a restrictive way' and that it followed that any rider to an exception (such as EIR reg 12(9)) should be given a broad interpretation: *OFCOM v IC and T-Mobile (UK) Ltd*, IT, 4 September 2007 at [25]. As to reading the exemptions in the Act restrictively, see §5–031.

23 EIR reg 12(3); EI(S)R regs 10(3) and 11(1). The matter here being protected is the privacy of a third person.

24 EIR reg 12(1); EI(S)R reg 10(1). In relation to discretionary disclosure, Directive 2003/4/EC, recital (24) and Art 4.1, are to the same effect. The Aarhus Convention is yet more emphatic in its support of discretionary disclosure: Arts 3.5-3.6. The FOIA s 78, affirms the position under the Act. See further §§20–036 to 20–038.

will expose the public authority to a claim for breach of copyright, breach of confidentiality or breach of the data protection principles.[25]

19– 005 Ministerial certificates

Both the EIR and the EI(S)R make provision for ministerial conclusive certificates on national security grounds.[26] The effect of a conclusive certificate is evidential: the certificate stands as conclusive evidence of the 'fact' certified in it, irrespective of the reality. Once a conclusive certificate is issued, the ordinary appeal provisions are displaced and review is confined to the reasonableness of the certificate.[27] There is no provision in the Directive for such a device. The Aarhus Convention does not provide any such exception to its specific requirement for independent review or reconsideration of refusals.[28] By a conclusive certificate a Minister of the Crown certifies that a refusal to disclose information under EIR reg 12(1)[29] is because the disclosure would adversely affect national security and the disclosure would not be in the public interest.[30] A Minister of the Crown may designate persons to certify these matters on his or her behalf. The power to sign such a certificate or to designate another person to certify the relevant matters is only exercisable by a Minister who is a member of the Cabinet or by the Attorney-General, the Advocate General for Scotland or the Attorney-General for Northern Ireland.[31] A refusal to disclose information includes a neither confirm nor deny response.[32] A conclusive certificate stands as conclusive evidence of the fact that disclosure would adversely affect national security and would not be in the public interest (irrespective of whether it would), unless and until the certificate is withdrawn or revoked or quashed on an appeal under s 60 of FOIA.[33] A conclusive certificate under the Regulations may identify the information to which it relates in general terms but there is no express provision allowing for such certificates to be expressed to have prospective effect.[34] A more detailed account of the effect of a conclusive certificate, whether under the Regulations or FOIA, when such a certificate may be issued,[35] and the means of challenging such a certificate are considered in detail elsewhere in this work.[36]

---

25 See further §20– 034.

26 EIR reg 15; EI(S)R reg 12. The FOIA allows for conclusive certificates to protect national security (s 24(3)), as well as certificates in relation to information from or relating to nominated security bodies (s 23(2)), information the disclosure of which would infringe a privilege of a House of Parliament (s 34(2)) and certain information held by either House of Parliament (s 36(7)). In Scotland, FOI(S)A s 31(2) provides for a conclusive certificate on national security grounds.

27 EIR reg 18(3) and (7). As with the FOI(S)A, the EI(S)R do not make provision for an appeal against a conclusive certificate.

28 Article 9.1. Article 6(1)(c) of the Aarhus Convention permits the Contracting Parties to deem public participation in environmental decision-making to be contrary to 'national defence purposes' but does not make analogous provision in relation to withholding the disclosure of environmental information.

29 EI(S)R reg 12.

30 Although the wording might suggest that a generalised appraisal of the public interest is all that is required, the reference to reg 12(1)(b) (reg 10(1)(b) in Scotland) indicates that it is the outcome of that balancing exercise which the Minister must certify.

31 EIR reg 15(6) giving the term 'Minister of the Crown' in reg 15(1)-(2) and (5) the same meaning as in FOIA s 25(3).

32 EIR reg 15(2).

33 FOIA s 60 is applied for the purposes of the EIR with modifications by EIR reg 18(1), (3)-(4) and (7).

34 Compare FOIA s 24(4) and DPA 1998 s 28(3).

35 The question of whether ministerial certificates are subject only to challenge by way of judicial review, would seem to be at least questionable, in light of *R (Evans) v Attorney-General* [2015] UKSC 21, [2015] AC 1787 at [105]-[108]. What is clear, from *Evans*, is that once a Tribunal or Court has determined that information should be disclosed, it would not, at that stage, be open to the Attorney-General to issue a ministerial certificate, the effect of which is to override that decision (at [102]-[103]).

36 As to the effect of a conclusive certificate generally, see §§5– 033 to 5– 039. As to national security certificates specifically, see §§5– 040 and 26– 057. As to certificate appeals generally, see §26– 061. As to national security

19– 006 The public interest

All the exceptions other than the personal data exception[37] are made subject to a weighing of the public interest.[38] Apart from where the personal data exception applies, the fact that particular environmental information falls within one of the exceptions in the regulations will not be enough to enable a public authority to refuse to disclose that information. What is also required is that in all the circumstances of the case the public interest in maintaining the exception must outweigh the public interest in disclosing the information.[39] In order for the public interest balancing exercise to have some independent function, it is implicit that there will be circumstances in which although it can be shown that disclosure would adversely affect one of the matters in the exceptions, there should nevertheless be disclosure of that information. The mere identification of the adverse effect that engages the exception cannot always be sufficient to outweigh the public interest in disclosure. As with FOIA, the public interest weighing exercise involves a focused consideration of the public interest:

— On one side is the public interest in *maintaining* the exception. This involves an identification of the public interest that is embodied in the exception.[40] In carrying out the balancing exercise, the public interest in all exceptions applicable to a particular item of information must be aggregated and that aggregated public interest must be weighed against the public interest in disclosing that information.[41] The CJEU, following a reference by the Supreme Court, held that 'where a public authority holds environmental information ... when weighing the public interests served by disclosure against the interests served by refusal to disclose, in order to assess a request for that information to be made available to a natural or legal person, take into account cumulatively a number of the grounds for refusal set out in that provision.'[42] The matter was eventually remitted to a Tribunal which found even applying an aggregated approach the public interest favoured disclosure.[43] Public interest considerations against disclosure but not relevant to maintaining the applicable exceptions remain outside the balancing exercise.[44] Thus it is important to identify the public interest in maintaining each particular exception. Where there is a variety of information captured by a request with different combinations of exceptions applicable to different items of information, the aggregated public interest in maintaining those exceptions will vary according to the combination of applicable exceptions.[45]

---

appeals specifically, see §5– 041. As to national security certificate appeals under the DPA 1998, see §§49– 016 to 49– 017. As to the role of Art 6 of the ECHR in national security certificate appeals, see §5– 044.

37 EIR reg 12(3); EI(S)R regs 10(3) and 11(1). The personal data exception involves a different and less focused consideration of the public interest: see §19– 032.

38 EIR reg 12(1); EI(S)R reg 10(1). The provision is derived from Directive 2003/4/EC Art 4.2 (penultimate paragraph). The 'public interest' is a composite phrase and it is unlikely that its meaning is modified by the definition of 'public' in the Directive Art 2.6, notwithstanding EIR reg 2(5), and EI(S)R reg 2(4).

39 See further §6– 001.

40 *Archer v IC and Salisbury DC*, IT, 9 May 2007 at [59]. The focused approach to the public interest balancing exercise is also employed in the FOIA s 2(2), and in the FOI(S)A s 2(1)(b): see further §6– 001 and 6– 010.

41 *R (Office of Communications) v Information Commissioner* [2009] EWCA Civ 90, [2009] ACD 48. On further appeal (*Office of Communication v Information Commissioner* [2010] UKSC 3), the Supreme Court referred the question to the European Court of Justice, pursuant to Art 267 of the Treaty on the Functions of the European Union (formerly Art 234 (EC)), with a 3-2 majority indicating a preference for the view expressed by the Court of Appeal.

42 *OFCOM v Information Commissioner* (C-71/10) [2011] PTSR 1676, [2012] 1 CMLR 184 at [21].

43 *OFCOM v IC and Everything Everywhere Ltd*, FTT, 12 December 2012 at [89].

44 *R (Office of Communications) v IC* [2009] EWCA Civ 90, [2009] ACD 48 at [35].

45 The practical difficulties that this interpretation presents to those charged with carrying out the exercise has been

— On the other side is the public interest 'in disclosing the information'. This imports the basic purpose of the Regulations,[46] together with any particular benefit in disclosure of the subject information that may be thought to arise in all the circumstances of the case. Facets of the public interest in disclosing information recognised by the Tribunal include: greater transparency and, through that, greater public confidence in official decision-making; greater accountability in official decision-making; better informed public debate; better public understanding of official decisions and the decision-making process (including the role played by lobbyists); more informed and meaningful public participation in the decision-making process; increased opportunity to challenge decisions; improved future decision-making; and satisfying those having a local or special interest in a particular decision.[47] In assessing this side of the public interest it is permissible to take into account a use that would be made of the information even though that use would involve an unlawful act.[48]

Early cases looked at the matter as at the date of the request[49] but it is clear now that the date which the public interest balance must be decided is the date of the primary decision refusing the request.[50] Given the stated objective of the Aarhus Convention to facilitate public participation in decisions whether to permit activities specified in Annex I to that Convention,[51] there may be a particularly compelling public interest in making available[52] environmental information conducive to that public participation. Depending on the information being considered and the exception being invoked, the result of the public interest balancing exercise may be time-sensitive. In carrying out the balancing exercise, it will also be necessary to consider the ECHR.[53] In particular, it has been held that Art 8 will, in certain circumstances, impose a positive obligation to disclose 'essential information' relating to environmental matters.[54] Thus, in *McGinley v United Kingdom*[55] the Court, dealing with information relating to

---

touched upon in a number of Tribunal decisions: *South Gloucestershire Council v IC and Bovis Homes Ltd*, IT, 20 October 2009 at [49]-[52]; *SS for Transport v IC*, IT, 5 May 2009 at [103].

46 Elements of which are articulated in recitals (1), (8), (9) and (16) to and Art 1(b) of the Directive and the recitals to and Art 5.1(c) of the Aarhus Convention.

47 *FCO v IC and Friends of the Earth*, IT, 29 June 2007 at [41]; *DBERR v IC and Friends of the Earth*, IT, 29 April 2008 at [132]-[133]; *Maiden v IC and King's Lynn and West Norfolk BC*, IT, 15 December 2008 at [42][-44]; *SS for Transport v IC*, IT, 5 May 2009 at [137]-254]; *Creekside Forum v IC and Dept for Culture Media and Sport*, IT, 28 May 2009 at [38]-[40]; *Mersey Tunnel Users Association v IC and Halton BC*, IT, 11 January 2010 at [49]; *Office of Communication v Information Commissioner* [2010] UKSC 3 at [6].

48 For example, breach of a third party's copyright: *R (Office of Communications) v IC* [2009] EWCA Civ 90, [2009] ACD 48 at [54]-[59].

49 *Creekside Forum v IC and Dept for Culture Media and Sport*, IT, 28 May 2009 at [36]; *SS for Transport v IC*, IT, 5 May 2009 at [102]; *ECGD v IC and Corner House*, IT, 11 August 2009 at [16]; *DBERR v IC and Friends of the Earth*, IT, 29 April 2008 at [104]-[111].

50 *R (Evans) v Attorney-General* [2015] UKSC 21, [2015] AC 1787 at [72]-[73]. See further *Vale of White Horse District Council v IC, Gill and Doric Properties Ltd*, FTT, 17 June 2015. Given that in EIR and FOIA appeals the FTT is a full merit-review body able to take evidence and reach its own findings of fact and its evaluative conclusions, and given that there is nothing to preclude a requester re-making the same request for information (on the basis that the facts informing the public interest balancing exercised have materially changed), this conclusion makes little policy-sense.

51 The list includes oil and gas refineries, power stations, various facilities for the production and processing of metals, various installations in the mineral and chemical industries, various facilities for waste management, most large transport facilities, pipelines, dams, large mines, and large pig or poultry farms.

52 See Art 6.6 of the Aarhus Convention.

53 Human Rights Act 1998 ss 3 and 6.

54 *Guerra v Italy* (1998) 26 EHRR 357, 4 BHRC 63, [1998] HRCD 277; *Roche v United Kingdom* (2006) 42 EHRR 30, 20 BHRC 99.

55 (1999) 27 EHRR 1, 4 BHRC 421, (1998) 42 BMLR 123.

the exposure of individuals to radiation, said:

> Where a government engages in hazardous activities, such as those at issue in the present case, which might have hidden adverse consequences on the health of those involved in such activities, respect for private and family life under Article 8 requires that an effective and assessable procedure be established which enables such persons to seek all relevant and appropriate information.

And in *Taskin v Turkey*[56] the European Court of Human Rights summarised its views in this area:

> Where a State must determine complex issues of environmental and economic policy, the decision-making process must firstly involve appropriate investigations and studies in order to allow them to predict and evaluate in advance the effects of those activities which might damage the environment and infringe individuals' rights and to enable them to strike a fair balance between the various conflicting interests at stake. The importance of public access to the conclusions of such studies and to information which would enable members of the public to assess the danger to which they are exposed is beyond question.

19– 007 Measuring prejudice

The degree of prejudice required by the prejudice-based exceptions is that 'disclosure would adversely affect' the matters protected by those exceptions.[57] This is in contrast to the prejudice-based exemptions in FOIA, which employ the formula 'disclosure would, or would be likely to, prejudice' any of the protected matters.[58] Given that consideration of a request necessarily involves speculation as to the effects that disclosing the sought information will have, a requirement of apparent certainty rather than likelihood constitutes a significant divergence from the regime established by the Act.[59]

2. SPECIFIC EXCEPTIONS

19– 008 Judicial/legislative body: reg 3(3)

Both the Aarhus Convention and the Directive exclude from the definition of a public authority 'bodies acting in a judicial or legislative capacity'.[60] This is carried through to the regulations.[61] This is not an 'exception' within the meaning of the Regulations. Rather, these are bodies that are outside the regime established by the Regulations such that, whether or not one of the exceptions applies, there is no right of access under the Regulations to information held by them. Accordingly, an applicant seeking environmental information held by such bodies or

---

56 (2006) 42 EHRR 50 at [119]. And similarly *Giacomelli v Italy* (2007) 45 EHRR 38 at [83].

57 Prejudice-based exceptions are those listed in the EIR reg 12(5), and in the EI(S)R reg 10(5). These are derived from Art 4.2 of the Directive and Art 4.4 of the Aarhus Convention.

58 Sections 26(1), 27(1), 29(1), 31(1), 33(2), 36(2), 38(1), 43(1) and (2). In Scotland, the FOI(S)A requires the same degree of likelihood but a higher degree of prejudice, employing the phrase 'would, or would be likely to, prejudice substantially' any of the protected interests: ss 27(2)(b), 28(1), 30, 31(4), 32(1)(a), 33(1)(b), 33(2), 35(1) and 40. See further §6– 022. Given that elsewhere in the Regulations (reg 2(1), paragraphs (b) and (c) of the definition of 'environmental information') the formula 'affect or likely to affect' is used, the exclusion of the latter limb is unlikely to have been an oversight. The deliberateness of the omission is supported by the terms of recital (10) and Arts 2.1(b), (c), 7.2(e) and 7.4 of the Directive. See also J Ebbeson, H Gaugitsch, J Jendroska, F Marshall and S Stec, *The Aarhus Convention: an Implementation Guide* (2nd Edn) (New York, United Nations, 2014) p 86.

59 *Archer v IC and Salisbury DC*, IT, 9 May 2007 at [51], after noting this and other differences from the FOIA, concluded: 'The result, in short, is that the threshold to justify non-disclosure is a high one.'

60 Aarhus Convention Art 2.2; Directive 2003/4/EC Art 2.2. Under Directive 2003/4/EC, this exemption is to be interpreted narrowly and only applies to those procedures that could result in the adoption of a law: *Deutsche Umwelthilfe eV v Bundesrepublik Deutschland* (C-515/11) [2013] 1 WLR 3764, [2014] Env LR 8 at [35]-[36]. In that case, the exemption did not apply to information obtained during consultation by the ministry which preceded the adoption of a regulation (which had a lower status than a law) on energy consumption labelling.

61 EIR reg 3(3); EI(S)R reg 3(2).

institutions will need to rely on the right of access given by FOIA. Because these bodies and institutions are neither obliged by the Regulations to disclose, nor would be so obliged but for any exception contained in the Regulations, section 39 of FOIA[62] is inapplicable: disclosure under the Act will fall to be determined by other exemptions in Part II of the Act.

19– 009 Parliamentary privilege: reg 3(4)

Each House of Parliament is a 'public authority' within the meaning of the EIR.[63] Each House is accordingly subject to the information disclosure regime provided by the EIR. However, the EIR provide that they do not apply to either House of Parliament 'to the extent required for the purpose of avoiding an infringement of the privileges of either House.'[64] There is no equivalent provision in the EI(S)R. What constitutes an infringement of the privileges of a House of Parliament is considered later in this work.[65] This exception is not subject to a public interest balance. Unlike the equivalent exemption in FOIA, the EIR do not provide for conclusive certificates in support of the exception.

19– 010 Otherwise accessible: reg 6(1)(b)

The Aarhus Convention does not expressly provide an exception for information that is otherwise accessible to an applicant. However, excluded from the requirement for each Contracting Party to ensure that public authorities make available requested information to members of the public in the form requested is information that is already available in another form.[66] Under the Regulations, a public authority may decline to provide an applicant with requested information where the information is already publicly available and easily accessible to the applicant in another form or format.[67] The implication is that if the information is available to the applicant in the *same* form or format, for example through some other access regime, that will not provide the public authority with a basis for refusing to provide it under the Regulations.[68]

19– 011 Unfinished material: reg 12(4)(d)

Subject to the public interest test, a public authority may refuse to disclose information to the extent that 'the request relates to material which is still in the course of completion, to unfinished documents or to incomplete data.'[69] The exception is purely class-based. The public authority may thus rely on the exception without having to show any harm or likelihood of harm which would result from disclosure. The comparable exemption in FOIA imposes a reasonableness requirement.[70] The focus of the exception does not appear to be the state of completion of the function, project or matter to which the information relates: rather, it is the

---

62 In relation to Scottish public authorities, FOI(S)A s 39.

63 FOIA Sch 1 Pt I. They are thereby public authorities for the purposes of the EIR: EIR reg 2(2). The DPA 2018 applies to personal data processed (including held or stored) by or on behalf of the Houses of Parliament: DPA 2018 s 210.

64 EIR reg 3(3). This is permitted by the Directive 2003/4/EC Art 2(2). Similarly the Aarhus Convention Art 2(2).

65 See §§19– 009, 30– 001 to 30– 010.

66 Aarhus Convention Art 4.1. This is reproduced in Directive 2003/4/EC, recital (14) and Art 3.4(a).

67 EIR reg 6(1)(b); EI(S)R reg 6(1)(b).

68 *OFCOM v IC and T-Mobile (UK) Ltd*, IT, 4 September 2007 at [69].

69 EIR reg 12(4)(d); EI(S)R reg 10(4)(d). Derived from Art 4.1(d) of the Directive and Art 4.3(c) of the Aarhus Convention. See the ICO's guidance *Material in the course of completion, unfinished documents and incomplete data (regulation 12(4)(d))*.

70 FOI s 22(1)(c); FOI(S)A s 27(1)(c). See further §25– 009.

state of completion of the material, documents or data with which it is concerned.[71] The exception will thus capture an incomplete draft of a document but not a finalised preliminary document.[72] However, a request for raw environmental data cannot be refused on the grounds that it has not yet been 'processed.'[73] Moreover, it has been held that a particular document may itself be finished, but still part of 'material' which is in the course of completion.[74] But the exception is not engaged when a piece of work may fairly be said to be complete in itself: whether the public authority treats the material as being complete is material but not decisive – 'a public authority cannot label its way out of its duty to disclose.'[75] 'Material' must have physical existence: it is not apt to describe something that is incorporeal, such as an exercise or project.[76] As with the internal communications exception, whereas the unit of exception is usually 'information' to the extent that its disclosure would adversely affect any of the identified matters, the unit of exception in relation to this exception appears to be all information covered by the terms of the request.[77]

19–012 Public interest: reg 12(4)(d)

Even where the terms of this exception are met, the public authority may only not disclose that part of the information in respect of which it is satisfied that in all the circumstances the public interest in maintaining this and other exceptions applicable to it outweighs the public interest

71 Thus a request for a draft version of a document that has been subsequently finalised will fall within the exception: *SS for Transport v IC*, IT, 5 May 2009 at [66]-[83]. Similarly: *Mersey Tunnel Users Association v Information Commissioner and Halton BC*, IT, 11 January 2010 at [20]-[23].

72 In *Maile v Wigan MBC* [2001] Env LR 11, [2001] JPL 193 the applicant made a request to Wigan MBC for access to a database held by the Council comprising raw data relating to potentially contaminated sites. The database was being prepared in advance of the implementation of forthcoming remediation obligations imposed upon the Council by the Environment Act 1995 s 57. At the time of the request and before completing it, the Council had put this exercise 'on hold'. The Council refused access, relying on both reg 4(2)(c) and (d) of the Environmental Information Regulations 1992, stating that the data was incomplete and had inaccuracies. On a challenge to the lawfulness of that decision, Eady J upheld the Council's decision on both grounds. He said that 'to reveal these purely speculative thoughts could cause unnecessary alarm and despondency among the local citizens or landowners.' In relation to reg 4(2)(c) Eady J said that 'any deliberations as to how the Council and its officers should prepare for fulfilling the anticipated obligations of "remediation" need to be conducted in confidence.' In relation to reg 4(2)(d), Eady J said that it 'would be highly unsatisfactory to reveal to the public material which has variously been described as inchoate, embryonic and hypothetical....The fact that an operation may have been put, as it were, "on ice" at a preliminary stage does not mean that it should therefore be regarded as having been completed.' See also *Eastleigh BC v IC*, FTT, 13 January 2014 at [21]-[24] where it was held that documents related to a draft development plan that had been published did not fall within this exception; a draft plan published for consultation was not by definition a draft document as it was a formal document decided to be ready for consultation.

73 J Ebbeson, H Gaugitsch, J Jendroska, F Marshall and S Stec, *The Aarhus Convention: an Implementation Guide* (2nd Edn) (New York, United Nations, 2014) p 85, citing the Committee findings in ACCC/C/2010/53 (United Kingdom) in which the Committee found that raw air pollution data which had not yet been subject to data correction was environmental information within the meaning of Art 2 paragraph 3(a) of the Convention, and advised that if the authority had concerns about disclosing the data, they should provide the data and advise that it had not yet been subject to processing in accordance with the regulated system for processing raw environmental data. The Committee also held that where processed data was provided, it should be accompanied by an explanation that it had been so processed.

74 See *Ames v IC and Dept for Transport*, FTT, 18 July 2016 at [38] and [42]. See also *Amin v IC and Dept of Energy and Climate Change*, FTT, 28 July 2016, applying this exception to a draft impact assessment. This is covered in the ICO's guidance at para 8: 'While a particular document may itself be finished, it may be part of material which is still in the course of completion. An example of this could be where a public authority is formulating and developing policy. In this case, an officer may create an "aide memoire" note which is not intended to be a formal record but is nevertheless part of the on-going process of developing a particular policy. If this aide memoire note is within the scope of a request, the exception may be engaged because the request relates to material which is still in the course of completion.'

75 *Highways England v IC and Manisty* [2018] UKUT 423 (AAC) at [31]-[32].

76 *Highways England v IC and Manisty* [2018] UKUT 423 (AAC) at [23].

77 It is not clear whether the words 'to the extent that' and EIR reg 12(9) will be sufficient to displace this interpretation.

in the information's disclosure.[78] Where there is no finished material on an environmental matter upon which a decision is to be made by the public authority, the stated public interest in disclosure of environmental information, namely public participation in that decision-making process, may in some circumstances compel the disclosure of unfinished material if that is required for effective public participation. Where a final version of a draft document has been published at the time that the request for the draft is made, the public interest in maintaining the exception may be heightened (on account of disclosure of a draft serving to confuse matters)[79] and the public interest in disclosure reduced (on account of the public interest in disclosure having been served by disclosure of the finalised document).[80] Where this exception is invoked as the basis for the refusal to disclose information, the public authority is required to specify, if known to the public authority, the name of any other public authority preparing the information and the estimated time within which the information will be finished or completed.[81]

19– 013 Internal material: reg 12(4)(e)

Subject to the public interest test, a public authority may refuse to disclose information to the extent that 'the request involves the disclosure of internal communications'.[82] 'Internal communications' can include communications[83] with an external advisor working under contract to a public authority. Whether communications by such an advisor are 'internal communications' will depend upon the facts in each case, in particular whether the advisor was physically located within the premises of the public authority, the extent to which the advisor received support from the staff of the public authority and the extent to which the advisor had the final word on any document he was commissioned to produce.[84] Under the Westminster regulations, the operation of the exception is enlarged by providing that internal communications include communications between government departments.[85] The exception

---

78 As to the public interest exercise in relation to 'unfinished material', see further §25– 009. For an example of the public interest test under this exception being applied, see *Burton v IC*, FTT, 14 April 2017 at [13].

79 It may legitimately be asked why in these circumstances the public authority retains the draft in its records, rather than destroying it. See *Amin v IC and Dept of Energy and Climate Change*, FTT, 28 July 2016 at [54]-[59].

80 See, eg: *SS for Transport v IC*, IT, 5 May 2009 at [127]-[160]; *Mersey Tunnel Users Association v Information Commissioner and Halton BC*, IT, 11 January 2010 at [27]; *Mersey Tunnel Users Association v Information Commissioner and Halton BC*, IT, 11 January 2010 at [24]-[29]; *DEFRA v IC and Portman*, FTT, 13 November 2012 at [28]-[50]; *Wirral MBC v IC*, FTT, 6 December 2012 at [16]-[38]. Note, however, that this reasoning will weaken with time, normally being strongest immediately after publication of the final report: *SS for Transport v IC*, IT, 5 May 2009 at [166]. The continued retention of the draft will serve to indicate that it has some enduring significance.

81 EIR reg 14(4); EI(S)R reg 13(d). Derived from Directive 2003/4/EC Art 4.1 (final sentence).

82 EIR reg 12(4)(e); EI(S)R reg 10(4)(e). Derived from Art 4.1(e) of the Directive and Art 4.3(e) of the Aarhus Convention. The Explanatory Memorandum describes this exception as not being made under s 74 of the FOIA but under s 2(2) of the European Communities Act 1972. Whether particular information falls within this description is a question of fact and law: *SS for Transport v IC*, IT, 5 May 2009 at [84].

83 The ICO website guidance on internal communications states: 'The concept of a communication is broad and will encompass any information someone intends to communicate to others, or even places on file (including saving it on an electronic filing system) where others may consult it. It will therefore include not only letters, memos, and emails, but also notes of meetings or any other documents if these are circulated or filed so that they are available to others … it will not include any information recorded simply to be used by its author, for example as an aide-memoire, unless this records the content of other communications (eg personal notes of an internal meeting or discussion).' (paras 14-15). The guidance also suggests that draft communications can fall within the exception (para 16).

84 *SS for Transport v IC*, IT, 5 May 2009 at [84]-[98]; *South Gloucestershire Council v IC and Bovis Homes Ltd*, IT, 20 October 2009 at [24]-[33]; *Cartwright v IC*, FTT, 6 September 2017 (holding that communications between a council and a company formed as a joint venture between the council and some private companies were 'internal' at [8]-[14], [37]).

85 EIR reg 12(8): cf reg 3(5). There is no equivalent provision in the EI(S)R. 'Government department' is not defined, although it may be inferred from reg 2(2) that it bears the same meaning as in the FOIA s 84. In *DEFRA v IC and*

potentially applies to much environmental information that answers the terms of a request.[86] The exception is purely class based. The public authority may thus rely on either exception without having to show any harm or likelihood of harm which would result from disclosure. The comparable exemption in FOIA imposes a likelihood of an identified prejudice.[87] The Act also requires that invocation of the exemption be founded upon the reasonable opinion of a 'qualified person', being a high-level official in the public authority: there is no comparable requirement in the Regulations. Moreover, whereas the unit of exception under the Regulations is usually 'information' to the extent that its disclosure would adversely affect any of the identified matters, the unit of exception under the internal communications exception appears to be all information covered by the terms of the request.[88] Other than what has been sent to it by, or sent by it to, third parties, most of the information held by a public authority will be an 'internal communication'.[89]

19– 014 Public interest: reg 12(4)(e)

Even where the terms of this exception are met, the public authority may only not disclose that part of the information in respect of which it is satisfied that in all the circumstances the public interest in maintaining this and other exceptions applicable to it outweighs the public interest in the information's disclosure.[90] Because disclosure of such information may well serve the interests described in the recitals to the Directive, the public interest balancing exercise will often prove determinative of disclosure.[91] There is no immediately obvious, universal public interest in maintaining an exception that entitles refusal on the basis that 'the request involves the disclosure of internal communications' without unpicking the objective of the Regulations.[92] The stated rationale for the exception is 'that it is often in the public interest that public

Portman, FTT, 13 November 2012, it was held that the Marine Management Organisation, an executive agency of Defra, was not 'internal' to Defra so that the exception could not be relied upon: see [18]-[27].

86 The UN Implementation Guide seems to suggest that the provision should have a narrower operation, excluding factual material or any material once it has been passed to a third party: J Ebbeson, H Gaugitsch, J Jendroska, F Marshall and S Stec, *The Aarhus Convention: an Implementation Guide* (2nd Edn) (New York, United Nations, 2014) pp 84-85.

87 FOI s 36(2). See further §§31– 026 to 31– 033.

88 It is not clear whether the words 'to the extent that' and EIR reg 12(10), will be sufficient to displace this interpretation.

89 In *R v Secretary of State for the Environment, Transport and Regions, ex p Marson*, 23 March 1998, Jowitt J considered (in a judicial review permission application) a challenge to the Secretary of State's refusal to produce under the 1992 Regulations a copy of a 'specific estimate' of the effects of a project on the environment as well as briefing documents, notes and appraisals. He upheld the Secretary of State's contention that the information was excepted under reg 4(1)(a) and 4(2)(c) ('confidential deliberation'): 'the Secretary of State is not required by the regulations to open up his files so as to make available the advice he has received from his officers and documents which record his own thinking about the matter leading up to his actual decision.' The Court of Appeal [1998] 3 PLR 90 at 98, (1999) 77 P&CR 202, [1998] JPL 869 merely accepted this part of the judgment. The Tribunal in *Archer v IC and Salisbury DC*, IT, 9 May 2007 at [72] had no difficulty in finding that an officer report to a local authority committee fell within the exception. The Tribunal's transposition to this exception of the public interest factors in maintaining the exception under reg 12(5)(b) is difficult to reconcile with its observations at [59].

90 As to the public interest exercise in relation to 'unfinished material', see further §25– 009.

91 The Tribunal in *Friends of the Earth v IC and ECGD*, IT, 20 August 2007 at [76] considered that disclosure of the requested information before the public authority made the decision to which it related would, 'if anything, [be] likely to improve the quality of the deliberative process.'

92 Namely, participation in the decision-making process: Principle 10 of the Rio Declaration on Environment and Development (1992). See further §31– 003. In other administrative law spheres, it is recognised that where consultation is required, it must be at a formative stage and it must be adequate: *R v North & East Devon Health Authority, ex p Pow* (1997-98) 1 CCL Rep 280, (1998) 39 BMLR 77; *R (Essex CC) v Secretary of State for Transport, Local Government and the Regions* [2002] EWHC 2516, [2003] JPL 583, [2002] 49 EGCS 123; *R (Montpeliers and Trevors Association) v Westminster City Council* [2005] EWHC 16, [2006] BLGR 304; *R (Capenhurst) v Leicester City Council* [2004] EWHC 2124; *R (Newsum) v Welsh Assembly (No 2)* [2005] EWHC 538, [2006] Env LR 1, [2005] 2 P & CR 32, [2005] JPL 1486; *R (Madden) v Bury MBC* [2002] EWHC 1882.

authorities have a space within which to think in private as recognised in the Aarhus Convention.'[93] The rationale is not uniformly applicable and the metaphor has its limitations. Mere thoughts are not manifested and leave no record; they have no external consequences. The recording of thoughts, however tentative, reflects a process of selection and an intention that the thoughts either be communicated to others or serve as a reminder. Where the record is intended only to remind the writer of a thought, the rationale is well founded. Where, however, the record is intended to be communicated to others or to rest on the file, able to be consulted by others, the rationale is weaker and the metaphor inapt. Moreover, internal communications may represent the only indication of an intention to make a decision on a matter affecting the environment before a public authority formally takes that decision. Where there is no publicly-available means, or only limited means, of discovering an intention to make a decision on a matter affecting the environment, the stated public interest in disclosure of environmental information (namely, public participation in that decision-making process) may in some circumstances compel the disclosure of internal communications that would reveal that intention and the bases for it. The Tribunal, while recognising the differences between the public interest in maintaining the exception in reg 12(4)(e) and the public interest in maintaining the exemption in s 36 of FOIA,[94] has adopted a broadly similar approach in both cases.[95] In *Lord Baker of Dorking v Information Commissioner and Department for Communities and Local Government*[96] both the public authority and the Information Commissioner argued that any disclosure of advice given by civil servants would present a risk that they would be less frank and impartial in their advice and less punctilious in recording it. The Tribunal rejected the argument, deciding the public interest issue upon the facts of the case.[97] Of significance to the Tribunal's conclusion were:

— that the decision, namely whether to grant or to refuse planning permission, based upon the advice sought had been taken;[98]
— that the advice related to an administrative decision, rather than general policy;[99] and
— that the requested information would provide 'the whole picture' for a controversial decision:

> It seems to us, however, that one reason for having a freedom of information regime is to protect Ministers and their advisers from suspicion or innuendo to the effect that the public is not given a complete and accurate explanation of decisions; that the outcome is in some way "spun" (to adopt the term whose very invention

93 DEFRA, *EIR Guidance*, Ch 7, July 2007, para 7.4.5.1. To similar effect, para 7.4.5.8: 'The rationale behind this exception is ensuring that the formulation and development of government policy and government decision making can proceed in the self-contained space needed to ensure that it is done well. The fact that this exception is subject to the public interest test ensures that the right balance is struck between disclosing information to enable proper public participation in policy debates and providing public authorities with the space they need in which to do their work best.' In fact, the Aarhus Convention, recital (17), acknowledges that 'public authorities hold environmental information in the public interest.' See: *DEFRA v IC and Badger Trust* [2014] UKUT 0526 (AAC) preferring to refer to a public authority having 'space to think in private' (at [49]-[53]); *Dept of Health v IC and Lewis* [2015] UKUT 0159 (AAC) at [31]; *Amin v IC and DECC* [2015] UKUT 527 (AAC) at [88]-[121]. See also the ICO web guidance on material in the course of completion at paras 8 and 15-16.

94 *Lord Baker of Dorking v IC and DCLG*, IT, 1 June 2007 at [18].

95 See §§31– 018 and 31– 032 to 31– 033. *Friends of the Earth v IC and ECGD*, IT, 20 August 2007, on app *ECGD v Friends of the Earth* [2008] EWHC 638 (Admin), [2008] Env LR 40, [2008] JPL 1813; *SS for Transport v IC*, IT, 5 May 2009 at [105].

96 *Lord Baker of Dorking v IC and DCLG*, IT, 1 June 2007 at [12].

97 Similarly: *Friends of the Earth v IC and ECGD*, IT, 20 August 2007 at [49]-[76]; *SS for Transport v IC*, IT, 5 May 2009 at [108]-[126].

98 *Lord Baker of Dorking v IC and DCLG*, IT, 1 June 2007 at [16], [22] and [29].

99 *Lord Baker of Dorking v IC and DCLG*, IT, 1 June 2007 at [17]. The Tribunal considered that in some cases the public interest in maintaining the exception in relation advice on an administrative decision would be greater than where the information sought related to general policy.

> illustrates this tendency towards cynicism and mistrust). Disclosure of internal communications is not therefore predicated by a need to bring to light any wrongdoing of this kind. Rather, by making the whole picture available, it should enable the public to satisfy itself that it need have no concerns on the point. ...We repeat that we believe that the strength of the argument in favour of disclosure and against maintaining the exemption is that disclosure will enable the public to form a view on what actually happened and not on what it can only guess at.[100]

The Tribunal has been similarly reluctant to find that the public interest in maintaining the exception is enhanced by related arguments that policy-making requires 'private space' and that that 'space' would be destroyed or polluted by disclosure, or that disclosure would send 'secondary signals.'[101] However, in *Cabinet Office v Information Commissioner* the Tribunal upheld the exception in relation to information connected with a speech by the Prime Minister on nuclear energy policy, commenting that the 'safe space' argument had some force because the policy was still under discussion in Government at the time of the request.[102]

19–015 National security etc: reg 12(5)(a)

Subject to the public interest test, a public authority may refuse to disclose information to the extent that its disclosure would adversely affect 'international relations, defence, national security or public safety'.[103] The Regulations give no guidance as to the meaning of any of these terms. There are analogues for each of the four in FOIA, which are slightly more informative as to their scope.[104] It is suggested that the phrase 'international relations' encapsulates the four matters described in s 27(1) of FOIA. The requirement in regulation 12(5)(a) that disclosure would 'adversely affect' international relations presents a higher threshold for successful invocation than the corresponding requirement in s 27(1) that disclosure 'would, or would be likely to, prejudice' any of the matters in paras (a)-(d). Although the EIR do not include an equivalent exception to the exemption in s 27(2) of FOIA, there will be instances where the disclosure of confidential information obtained from a foreign state or, less likely, from an international organisation or international court will adversely affect international relations.[105] The exception in reg 12(5)(a), unlike the exemption in s 27(1), is not confined to prejudice to relations between the United Kingdom and another country. Thus, resultant prejudice to international relations between two foreign states will suffice. The operation of this exception is further considered under the analogous provision of FOIA.[106]

19–016 National security etc examples

Examples of where the Tribunal has held that this exception applies include:

---

[100] *Lord Baker of Dorking v IC and DCLG*, IT, 1 June 2007 at [24] and [28].

[101] *DBERR v IC and Friends of the Earth*, IT, 29 April 2008 at [113]-[131]; *DEFRA v IC and Badger Trust* [2014] UKUT 0526 (AAC) at [61]-[64]; *Salford CC v IC and Redwater Development Ltd*, FTT, 4 July 2017 at [38]-[41].

[102] *Cabinet Office v IC*, FTT, 4 October 2010; *Eastleigh BC v IC*, FTT, 13 January 2014 at [30]; *Amin v IC and Dept of Energy and Climate Change*, FTT, 12 June 2014; *Amin v IC and Dept of Energy and Climate Change*, FTT, 28 July 2016 at [67]-[72]. See further ICO website guidance.

[103] EIR reg 12(5)(a); EI(S)R, 10(5)(a). Derived from Art 4.2(b) of the Directive and Art 4.4(b) of the Aarhus Convention. The term 'public security' in the Directive and Convention is converted by the Regulations into 'national security' and 'public safety.'

[104] FOI ss 27(1) (international relations), 26(1) (defence), 24(1) (national security) and 38(1)(b) (public safety), none of which is an absolute exemption. In Scotland, FOI(S)A ss 32(1), 31(4), 31(1) and 39(1), respectively.

[105] See §§27–007 to 27–010.

[106] For the international relations exemption, see §§27–001 to 27–016. For the defence exemption, see §§26–070 to 26–079. For the national security exemption, see §§26–047 to 26–069. For the health and safety exemption, see §§32–010 to 32–022. For an instance in which the exception has been applied: *FCO v IC and Friends of the Earth*, IT, 29 June 2007.

— Information setting out the details of mobile phone base stations, including their grid references. The Tribunal held that disclosure of the information would provide some assistance to criminals.[107]
— Information about an oil pipeline in Turkey. The Tribunal held that the disclosure of the information would harm international relations.[108]
— Information related to the international climate change negotiations at the Copenhagen conference undertaken in the context of the UN Framework Convention on Climate Change.[109]
— Information from the Met Office in relation to a meeting of the Inter-governmental Panel on Climate Change.[110]

19– 017 Public interest: reg 12(5)(a)

Even where the terms of this exception are met, the public authority may only not disclose that part of the information in respect of which it is satisfied that in all the circumstances the public interest in maintaining this and other exceptions applicable to it outweighs the public interest in the information's disclosure.[111]

19– 018 Justice interference: reg 12(5)(b)

Subject to the public interest test, a public authority may refuse to disclose information to the extent that its disclosure would adversely affect 'the course of justice, the ability of a person to receive a fair trial or the ability of a public authority to conduct an inquiry of a criminal or disciplinary nature.'[112] There is an issue whether the exemption applies where justice has run its course and the proceedings or investigation is concluded.[113] In the absence of any explicit exception for information in respect of which a claim to legal professional privilege could be

[107] *OFCOM v IC and T-Mobile (UK) Ltd*, IT, 4 September 2007 at [36]-[40]. Appeals at *R (Office of Communications) v IC*, [2008] EWHC 1445 (Admin), [2008] ACD 65, [2009] Env LR 1; *R (Office of Communications) v IC* [2009] EWCA Civ 90, [2009] ACD 48; *Office of Communication v Information Commissioner* [2010] UKSC 3.

[108] *ECGD v IC and Corner House*, IT, 11 August 2009.

[109] *Sinclair v IC and Department of Energy and Climate Change*, FTT, 8 November 2011 at [9] and [18]-[24].

[110] *Holland v IC and DBIS*, FTT, 26 July 2013. For a case where the public safety exception was considered but not upheld, see *DEFRA and Natural England v IC and Dale*, FTT, 9 November 2015.

[111] See §19– 006. For examples of the public interest balancing exercise being carried out with this exception, see: *OFCOM v IC and T-Mobile (UK) Ltd*, IT, 4 September 2007 at [41]-[42]; *FCO v IC and Friends of the Earth*, IT, 29 June 2007 at [37]-[45].

[112] EIR reg 12(5)(b); EI(S)R reg 10(5)(b). Derived from Art 4.2(c) of the Directive and Art 4.f(c) of the Aarhus Convention. See *Turner v IC and Cheshire East BC*, FTT, 12 November 2014 as an example of this exemption being in play. In *ClientEarth v European Commission* (T-111/11) [2014] Env LR 11 the CJEU held that the Commission was entitled to maintain the confidentiality of documents assembled during an investigation relating to potential infringement proceedings, where their disclosure might damage that relationship of trust between the Commission and the Member State concerned (at [60]). The argument that that exemption, so applied, was contrary to the right of access to environment information afforded by the Convention was not upheld (at [92]-[99]).

[113] This is the view taken in relation to the Aarhus Convention provision itself: J Ebbeson, H Gaugitsch, J Jendroska, F Marshall and S Stec, *The Aarhus Convention: an Implementation Guide* (2nd Edn) (New York, United Nations, 2014) p 87. The Tribunal in *Archer v IC and Salisbury DC*, IT, 9 May 2007, while prepared to uphold the exception in relation to an officer report to a local council committee suggesting options for enforcement of planning control, inferred that the position might be otherwise where the possibility of enforcement had passed (at [57]). Although it was not necessary for the Tribunal to decide, it also noted (at [65]) that the currency of the advice might have impinged upon the public interest balancing exercise. In *Burgess v IC and Stafford BC*, IT, 7 June 2007 at [28] and [38] the Tribunal concluded that reg 12(5)(b) could apply to counsel's advice on a planning inspector's decision letter on an enforcement appeal notwithstanding that enforcement was no longer in contemplation by the local authority to which the advice was provided. Legal professional privilege will extend to communications by in-house lawyers: *Woodford v IC*, FTT, 21 April 2010. Legal professional privilege will extend to draft officer reports passing between the council and its legal advisers: *Uttlesford District Council v IC*, FTT, 6 June 2012 at [37]-[63].

maintained,[114] the Tribunal has upheld claims to protect such material on the basis that the disclosure of privileged material would interfere with the course of justice.[115] The fact that information is legally privileged may generally facilitate the conclusion that its disclosure would impinge upon the course of justice, but a careful assessment of whether that protected interest would be adversely affected is still required.[116] It is for the party asserting privilege to establish that the information is privileged.[117] The exception is not confined to what would be protected by legal professional privilege.[118] The exception may also be engaged by common interest privilege.[119] Information relating to civil investigations, other than those of a disciplinary nature, may fall within the grasp of the exception.[120] Information that is revelatory of a public authority's strategy for dealing with regulatory breaches, including an assessment by the public authority of the strengths and weaknesses of its position, may have the adverse effect upon the protected interest.[121] Official documents, which may not be held by the prosecution or by the public authority responsible for the prosecution, can be of considerable importance in an environmental prosecution. The Regulations provide an accused person with scope for securing information from both the prosecuting authority and other public authorities more quickly and extensively than under criminal disclosure rules. It is not readily obvious that earlier, rather than later disclosure, of such information can properly be characterised as 'adversely affecting' the course of justice. The exception differs from its equivalent in FOIA, the focus of which is prejudice to investigations and prosecutions.[122] It would seem that the exception has potentially wider operation than its equivalent under the Act in cases where a request for the information emanates from someone other than the person being investigated or prosecuted. In this situation, even if there is no prejudice to the investigation or prosecution from the disclosure, the Regulations provide a basis for non-disclosure where it would prejudice

[114] Cf FOIA s 42(1); FOI(S)A s 36. And see §§30–013 to 30–021.

[115] *DCLG v IC and WR* [2012] UKUT 103 (AAC) at [36]-[74], which followed a string of FTT and IT decisions to like effect: *Burgess v IC and Stafford BC*, IT, 7 June 2007 at [44]-[49]; *Boddy v IC and North Norfolk DC*, IT, 23 June 2008 at [33]-[37]; *Rudd v IC and Verderers of the New Forest*, IT, 29 September 2008 at [25]-[32]; *Maiden v IC and King's Lynn and West Norfolk BC*, IT, 15 December 2008 at [32]-[37]; *Creekside Forum v IC and Dept for Culture Media and Sport*, IT, 28 May 2009 at [29]-[34]; *Mersey Tunnel Users Association v Information Commissioner and Halton BC*, IT, 11 January 2010 at [38]-[44]; *Mersey Tunnel Users Association v Information Commissioner and Halton BC*, IT, 11 January 2010 at [30]-[53]; *Woodford v IC*, FTT, 21 April 2010 at [26]-[35]; *Plumbe v IC and Hampshire County Council*, FTT, 10 September 2010 at [14]-[32]; *West v IC*, FTT, 25 October 2010 at [9]-[17]; *Skinner v IC and North Somerset Council*, FTT, 1 March 2011 at [27]-[31]; *McCullough v IC and Northern Ireland Water*, FTT, 6 November 2012 at [21]-[54] and *Hartles v IC*, FTT, 27 February 2013 at [17]-[44]; *Willetts v IC and Conwy CBC*, FTT, 18 February 2014; *GW v Local Government Ombudsman and ors* [2014] UKUT 0130 (AAC).

[116] See: *GW v Local Government Ombudsman and ors* [2014] UKUT 0130 (AAC) at [43], considering legal advice privilege; *Knight v IC and Newbury Town Council*, FTT, 4 April 2015, considering litigation privilege.

[117] See *Knight v IC and Newbury Town Council*, FTT, 4 April 2015 at [20], referring to *West London Pipeline and Storage v Total UK* [2008] EWHC 1729 (Comm), 2 CLC 258. On the possibility of waiver of privilege, see, for example: *Fenning v IC and Christchurch BC*, FTT, 27 April 2015.

[118] *McCullough v IC and Northern Ireland Water*, FTT, 6 November 2012 at [3], [10]; but see the conclusion in that case on the public interest at [11]-[23].

[119] *Salford CC v IC and Redwater Development Ltd*, FTT, 4 July 2017 at [42]-[46].

[120] See, for example: *GW v Local Government Ombudsman and ors* [2014] UKUT 0130 (AAC) concerning a Local Government Ombudsman investigation; *Williamson v IC and City University*, FTT, 7 September 2017, holding that reg 12(5)(b) was applicable to a criminal investigation being carried out by the HSE; *Carrabino v IC*, FTT, 27 November 2017, where the exception was held to apply in the context of noise abatement proceedings that were under appeal in the Magistrates Court. See, though, what is said in J Ebbeson, H Gaugitsch, J Jendroska, F Marshall and S Stec, *The Aarhus Convention: an Implementation Guide* (2nd Edn) (New York, United Nations, 2014) p 87.

[121] *Archer v IC and Salisbury DC*, IT, 9 May 2007 at [56].

[122] FOIA s 31(1); FOI(S)A s 35(1). This exception is considered further at §§29–014 to 29–018.

the rights of the accused to receive a fair trial or otherwise interfere with the course of justice.[123]

19–019 Public interest: reg 12(5)(b)

Even where the terms of this exception are met, the public authority may only not disclose that part of the information in respect of which it is satisfied that in all the circumstances the public interest in maintaining this and other exceptions applicable to it outweighs the public interest in the information's disclosure.[124] Where this exception is relied upon on the basis that the information is subject to legal professional privilege, the Tribunal has tracked the approach which it has used when considering the express exemption in FOIA for information subject to legal professional privilege.[125] The qualified nature of the exception acknowledges that there will be circumstances in which material subject to legal professional privilege must be disclosed.[126] That said, the Tribunal has shown itself ready to find that the public interest in maintaining the exception outweighs the public interest in disclosure.[127] In particular, if the information evidences malfeasance, fraud or corruption, the public interest in disclosure will be heightened.[128] In considering where the balance of the public interest lies, the age of the information and the existence of current legal proceedings that relates to the information will both be relevant.[129]

19–020 Intellectual property: reg 12(5)(c)

Subject to the public interest test, a public authority may refuse to disclose information to the extent that its disclosure would adversely affect 'intellectual property rights'.[130] Conventionally, 'intellectual property rights' comprise rights for the protection of patents, secret processes, copyright, registered designs, plant breeders' rights, trade marks and any related or similar kinds of rights. The Copyright, Designs and Patents Act 1988 provides that a disclosure 'specifically authorised by an Act of Parliament' does not infringe copyright.[131] The fact that

---

[123] See §29–018.The Tribunal in *Kirkaldie v IC and Thanet DC*, IT, 4 July 2006, considered (at [21]) that reg 12(5) 'exists in part to ensure that there should be no disruption to the administration of justice, including the operation of the courts and no prejudice to the right of individuals or organisations to a fair trial. In order to achieve this it covers legal professional privilege, particularly where a public authority is or is likely to be involved in litigation.' Similarly: *Archer v IC and Salisbury DC*, IT, 9 May 2007 at [61]; *Burgess v IC and Stafford BC*, IT, 7 June 2007 at [33]; *Young v IC and Dept for Environment for Northern Ireland*, IT, 12 December 2007; but cf *Watts v IC*, IT, 20 November 2007. See §19–002.

[124] See §19–006.

[125] See §§30–020 to 30–021: *Creekside Forum v IC and Dept for Culture Media and Sport*, IT, 28 May 2009 at [36]-[46]; *Mersey Tunnel Users Association v Information Commissioner and Halton BC*, IT, 11 January 2010 at [46]-[53]; *Boddy v IC and North Norfolk DC*, IT, 23 June 2008 at [38]-[47]; *Salmon v IC and King's College Cambridge*, IT, 17 July 2008 at [55]; *Rudd v IC and Verderers of the New Forest*, IT, 29 September 2008 at [35]-[42]; *Mersey Tunnel Users Association v Information Commissioner and Halton BC*, IT, 11 January 2010 at [39]-[40].

[126] See *GW v Local Government Ombudsman and ors* [2014] UKUT 0130 (AAC), concerning legal advice provided by a local authority to the Local Government Ombudsman during an investigation. And, by way of example, *Crawford & Co Adjusters (UK) Ltd v IC and Cheshire East CC*, FTT, 17 June 2017 at [31]-[36].

[127] See, for example: *Knight v IC and Newbury Town Council*, FTT, 4 April 2015 at [55]-[61]; *Fenning v IC and Christchurch BC*, FTT, 27 April 2015 at [37]-[44]; *Holmes v IC and Cumbria CC*, FTT, 9 May 2017 at [24]-[31].

[128] *Creekside Forum v IC and Dept for Culture Media and Sport*, IT, 28 May 2009 at [40]; *Woodford v IC*, FTT, 21 April 2010 at [33].

[129] *Creekside Forum v IC and Dept for Culture Media and Sport*, IT, 28 May 2009 at [45]; *Maiden v IC and King's Lynn and West Norfolk BC*, IT, 15 December 2008 at [38]-[47]; *Mersey Tunnel Users Association v Information Commissioner and Halton BC*, IT, 11 January 2010 at [46]-[53]; *Woodford v IC*, FTT, 21 April 2010 at [32]; *Cabinet Office v IC*, FTT, 16 August 2010 at [46]-[69]; *DCLG v IC and WR* [2012] UKUT 103 (AAC) at [49]-[55].

[130] EIR reg 12(5)(c); EI(S)R reg 10(5)(c). Derived from Art 4.2(e) of the Directive and Art 4.4(e) of the Aarhus Convention. None of the instruments defines what is meant by 'intellectual property rights'.

[131] Section 50(1). As the FOIA s 74(3), empowers the Secretary of State to make regulations 'for the purpose of implementing the information provisions of the Aarhus Convention' and as the Regulations constitute that implementation, it is suggested that a disclosure under the Regulations constitutes a disclosure 'specifically

a disclosure under the Regulations would otherwise be a breach of copyright will thus not of itself be sufficient to engage the exception.[132]

19– 021 Public interest: reg 12(5)(c)

Even where the terms of this exception are met, the public authority may only not disclose that part of the information in respect of which it is satisfied that in all the circumstances the public interest in maintaining this and other exceptions applicable to it outweighs the public interest in the information's disclosure.[133]

19– 022 Agency confidences: reg 12(5)(d)

Subject to the public interest test,[134] a public authority may refuse to disclose information to the extent that its disclosure would adversely affect 'the confidentiality of the proceedings[135] of that or any other public authority where such confidentiality is provided by law'.[136] It is not for a public authority to unilaterally determine that confidentiality applies.[137] This would appear to be directed to *in camera* proceedings of one sort or another.[138] It is capable of applying to meetings of a local authority.[139] Provided that such proceedings enjoy legal protection of their confidentiality and that maintenance of it outweighs the public interest in disclosure, that protection is not disturbed by the Regulations.[140] There is no direct equivalent in FOIA. This exception does not apply to information on emissions.[141]

---

authorised by an Act of Parliament'. This is reinforced by EIR reg 5(6) and EI(S)R reg 5(3). See, by way of example: *Vehicle Certification Agency v IC and ClientEarth*, FTT, 12 July 2017 at [61]-[69].

132 The Tribunal has held that this exception will exempt the complete data set of mobile phone base stations, which the public authority had compiled from data supplied to it by the mobile phone operators: *OFCOM v IC and T-Mobile (UK) Ltd*, IT, 4 September 2007 at [43]-[58]. See also *LB of Southwark v ICO and Lend Lease (Elephant and Castle) Ltd*, FTT, 9 May 2014, applying this exception to a financial model in a viability assessment.

133 EIR reg 12(1)(b); EI(S)R reg 10(1)(b). See §19– 006. By way of example, see: *OFCOM v IC and T-Mobile (UK) Ltd*, IT, 4 September 2007 at [59]-[62]; and *Worcestershire CC v IC and Mercia Waste Management Ltd*, FTT, 10 April 2017 at [85]-[94].

134 See §19– 006.

135 See *Saint-Gobain Glass Deutschland GmbH v European Commission* (C-60/15) [2018] Env LR 8 on the meaning of 'proceedings' for these purposes.

136 EIR reg 12(5)(d); EI(S)R reg 10(5)(d). Derived from Art 4.2(a) of the Directive and Art 4.4(a) of the Aarhus Convention. The exception does not apply to information on (or, possibly, relating to) emissions: EIR reg 12(9); EI(S)R reg 10(6).

137 *Flachglas Torgau GmbH* (C-204/09) [2013] QB 212, [2012] Env LR 26, [2012] EUECJ C-204/09, [2012] 2 CMLR 17 at [63].

138 For other suggestions, see J Ebbeson, H Gaugitsch, J Jendroska, F Marshall and S Stec, *The Aarhus Convention: an Implementation Guide* (2nd Edn) (New York, United Nations, 2014) pp 86-88.

139 *Archer v IC and Salisbury DC*, IT, 9 May 2007 at [68]. A document referred to at such a meeting will only fall within the exception, it would seem, if it was prepared exclusively for the discussions at that meeting (at [70]); *Chichester District Council v IC and Friel*, FTT, 16 March 2011 at [17]-[19]. The requirement that the confidentiality be provided for by law can be satisfied by a rule which 'provides, generally, that the confidentiality of the proceedings of public authorities is a ground for refusing access to information held by those authorities, in so far as national law clearly defines the concept of "proceedings"': *Flachglas Torgau GmbH* (C-204/09) [2013] QB 212, [2012] Env LR 26, [2012] EUECJ C-204/09, [2012] 2 CMLR 17 at [65].

140 *Gore v IC and Local Government Ombudsman*, FTT, 23 March 2012 at [1]-[26] where the Tribunal upheld a refusal to disclose under reg 12(5)(d) documents held by the Local Government Ombudsman because of the statutory restriction on disclosure in s 32(2) of the Local Government Act 1974 and which exists to protect people required to provide the Ombudsman with information under compulsion.

141 EIR reg 12(9); EI(S)R reg 10(6). Derived from Directive 2003/4/EC Art 4.2 (penultimate paragraph) and, more loosely, from the Aarhus Convention Art 4.4(d) (last sentence) and the last sentence of Art 4.4 itself. See *GW v Local Government Ombudsman and ors* [2014] UKUT 0130 (AAC), applying reg 12(5)(d) to information obtained in the course of a Local Government Ombudsman investigation.

19– 023 Public interest: reg 12(5)(d)

Where disclosure of information satisfies this exception, unless the public interest in maintaining the exception outweighs the public interest in disclosure, the information will, unless another exception applies, have to be disclosed.[142]

19– 024 Business confidences: reg 12(5)(e)

Subject to the public interest test,[143] a public authority may refuse to disclose information to the extent that its disclosure would adversely affect 'the confidentiality of commercial or industrial information where such confidentiality is provided by law to protect a legitimate economic interest.'[144] In order for information to be captured by the exception:[145]

(1) First, the information in question must be commercial or industrial in kind.
(2) Secondly, the information must be subject to confidentiality provided by law.[146] In broad terms, the law provides three means by which confidentiality is attached to information: (i) By statute.[147] (ii) By agreement between the parties.[148] (c) In equity (ie without their necessarily being any agreement covering confidentiality).[149] In order for

---

142 By way of illustration, see: *GW v Local Government Ombudsman and ors* [2014] UKUT 0130 (AAC).

143 See §19– 006.

144 EIR reg 12(5)(e); EI(S)R reg 10(5)(e). Derived from Art 4.2(d) of the Directive and Art 4.4(d) of the Aarhus Convention. The exception does not apply to information on (or, possibly, relating to) emissions: EIR reg 12(9); EI(S)R reg 10(6). In *R v Secretary of State for the Environment, Transport and the Regions, ex p Alliance against Birmingham Northern Relief Road (No 1)* [1999] Env LR 447, [1999] JPL 231, the applicant sought access under the 1992 Regulations to a concession agreement, made under s 1 of the *New Roads and Street Works Act 1991* between Midland Express Motorway Ltd and the Secretary of State, by which Midland Express was to design, build, finance and operate a motorway. After the agreement had been made, the required public inquiry concluded with the Secretary of State deciding to make the necessary orders. The applicant was concerned that the Secretary of State, in deciding to make the orders, might have been influenced by the prospect of having to pay compensation to Motorway Express if he decided otherwise. The Secretary of State refused to disclose the agreement, citing commercial confidentiality and reg 4(1)(a) and 4(2)(e) and the applicant challenged that refusal by way of judicial review. Sullivan J held that the issues of whether information was 'environmental information' and whether it was 'confidential' were objective issues to be determined in an objective manner (JPL at 247). He found that the concession agreement was not intrinsically confidential (JPL at 253) and rejected a submission that because it was a commercial document having financial implications all of it was confidential (JPL at 254). He accepted that information in the agreement relating to prices, costs, payment, compensation events and trade secrets should attract confidentiality (JPL at 255).

145 See, for example: *Turner v IC and Sunderland City Council*, FTT, 2 February 2016; *Gloucestershire CC v IC and Costas Ttofa*, FTT, 10 March 2017; *Vehicle Certification Agency v IC and ClientEarth*, FTT, 12 July 2017.

146 As to which, see §§34– 015 to 34– 020. The mere stamping of a document with the words 'confidential' (or the like) does not transform its contents into confidential information. The duty of confidence may be owed to the body that supplied the information or to a third party: *South Gloucestershire Council v IC and Bovis Homes Ltd*, IT, 20 October 2009 at [39]-[42]; *Mersey Tunnel Users Association v Information Commissioner and Halton BC*, IT, 11 January 2010 at [54]-[62]; *Bristol City Council v IC and Portland and Brunswick Square Association*, FTT, 24 May 2010 at [8]-[14]; *Staffordshire County Council v IC and Sibelco (UK) Ltd*, FTT, 20 December 2010 at [132]-[152]. Or it may arise through a contractual provision: *Mersey Tunnel Users Association v Information Commissioner and Halton BC*, IT, 11 January 2010 at [58]-[61]. In *Chichester District Council v IC and Friel*, FTT, 16 March 2011 at [20]-[24] the Tribunal held that confidentiality under reg 12(5)(d) required a duty of confidence to be owed to a third party and could not be 'self-generated' in respect of information created in-house, not containing third party information and not intended to be shared. In *Jones v IC and Environment Agency*, FTT, 27 April 2012 at [33]-[39] the Tribunal rejected a claim for confidentiality in respect of documents (namely an agreement and bond) provided to the Environment Agency because it was not communicated by one party to the other but generated via negotiation.

147 See, for example: *Natural Resources Wales v Swansea Friends of the Earth and IC* [2013] UKUT 0473 (AAC). This may operate to protect limited information within a document, rather than the entire document. Thus, where FoE had sought access to a complete copy of the financial bond required by regulations of a landfill site operator in order to secure a landfill permit, the figures in the bond (which were defined by the landfill regulations as being commercially confidential) were excepted by EIR reg 12(5)(e). See further: *Natural Resources Wales v Swansea Friends of the Earth and IC* [2013] UKUT 0473 (AAC).

148 See, for example: *Gloucestershire CC v IC and Costas Ttofa*, FTT, 10 March 2017 at [46]-[50].

149 For more detail, see §34– 010.

equity to attach confidentiality to information the information must enjoy the quality of confidentiality (ie not be common knowledge) and must have been imparted in circumstances that most would understand carried an expectation that the information not to be further disseminated.[150] Confidentiality arising in equity is subject to certain limiting principles.[151]

(3) Thirdly, the purpose of that confidentiality must be to protect legitimate economic interests. Thus, personal e-mails will not ordinarily be within the exception.[152]

(4) Fourthly, disclosure of the information would adversely effect the confidentiality.[153]

The exception in the Regulations straddles three separate exemptions in FOIA.[154] While all trade secrets will be covered, non-confidential commercial information will not be covered.[155] Nor will non-commercial or non-industrial confidential information be covered. The Directive provision from which it derived confirms its more limited scope, providing for refusal of a request for environmental information where disclosure would adversely affect 'the confidentiality of commercial or industrial information where such confidentiality is provided for by national or Community law to protect a legitimate economic interest, including the public interest in maintaining statistical confidentiality and tax secrecy.'[156]

9– 025 Public interest: reg 12(5)(e)

Even where the terms of this exception are met, the public authority may only not disclose that part of the information in respect of which it is satisfied that in all the circumstances the public interest in maintaining this and other exceptions applicable to it outweighs the public interest in the information's disclosure.[157] Reflecting the limiting equitable principles (and instances where a court will not uphold contractual confidentiality), this exception is acutely sensitive to countervailing public interest considerations.[158] The Tribunal has on occasions concluded that the public interest in the disclosure of viability assessments and similar commercially confidential documents submitted to local authorities in support of proposed developments (which is information that is generally captured by the exception) outweighs the public interest

[150] For more detail, see §§34– 012 to 34– 021, 35– 021.

[151] For more detail, see §§34– 022 to 34– 029.

[152] *Montague v IC and Liverpool John Moores University*, FTT, 13 December 2012 applying *University of Newcastle upon Tyne v Information Commissioner and BUAV* [2011] UKUT 185 (AAC).

[153] This is different from adverse effects on economic interests, see: *Gloucestershire CC v IC and Costas Ttofa*, FTT, 10 March 2017 at [45].

[154] FOIA ss 41(1), 43(1) and 43(2); FOI(S)A ss 36 and 33(1). In *Natural Resources Wales v Swansea Friends of the Earth and IC* [2013] UKUT 0473 (AAC) it was held that this exception should be considered without reference to s 41 of FOIA (at [45], [50]).

[155] For example, in *St Albans City and District Council v IC*, FTT, 18 September 2014 the Tribunal held that it was not correct that all pre-application information submitted by a developer to a planning authority benefited from the exemptions in reg 12(5)(e) or (f) and that the sensitivity of what was submitted varied according to its content.

[156] Directive Art 4.2(d). In *Krizan v Slovenska inspekcia zivotneho prostredia* (C-416/10) [2013] Env LR 28 the CJEU held that Directive 96/61/EC (IPPC) did not allow the competent national authorities to refuse the public concerned access to a planning decision on the location of a landfill site for which a permit was then sought under Directive 96/61, on the basis of reliance on commercial confidentiality (at [74]-[91]).

[157] EIR reg 12(1)(b); EI(S)R reg 10(1)(b). See §19– 006.

[158] For examples of the public interest being applied for this exception, see: *Natural Resources Wales v Swansea Friends of the Earth and IC* [2013] UKUT 0473 (AAC) (where the information in issue was financial guarantees on a landfill site, was confidential and was required to be provided under the Pollution Prevention Control (England and Wales) Regulations 2000); *Guildford BC v IC and Extreme Oyster Ltd*, FTT, 14 November 2016; *Gloucestershire CC v IC and Costas Ttofa*, FTT, 10 March 2017; *Crane v IC and Dept for Transport*, FTT, 16 January 2017; *Worcestershire CC v IC and Mercia Waste Management Ltd*, FTT, 10 April 2017 at [72]-[81]; *Bergen v IC and LB of Lewisham*, FTT, 29 August 2017 at [105], [133]-[141], [149]-[150] and [152]-[167].

in upholding the exception, and in other cases reached the opposite conclusion.[159] This tends to be a time-sensitive judgment. Disclosure of third-party confidential information may constitute a breach of Art 1 of Protocol 1 of the ECHR, and thus be against the public interest.[160] This exception does not apply to information on emissions.[161]

19–026 External material: reg 12(5)(f)

Subject to the public interest test,[162] a public authority may refuse to disclose information to the extent that its disclosure would adversely affect:

the interests of the person who provided the information where that person:

(i) was not under, and could not have been put under, any legal obligation to supply it to that or any other public authority,

(ii) did not supply it in circumstances such that that or any other public authority is entitled apart from these Regulations to disclose it, and

(iii) has not consented to its disclosure.[163]

The exception attempts to provide some protection for information held by a public authority that has been supplied to it by a third party. The list of conditions required for the exception to engage gives it a limited operation. First, the disclosure must adversely affect the interests of the person who provided the information. A mere likelihood of harm is not sufficient. Secondly, it must be information that was not supplied under compulsion, nor could have been legally required to be supplied. This is particularly limiting. There is little information that at

---

159 In *Bristol City Council v IC and Portland and Brunswick Square Association*, FTT, 24 May 2010 the Tribunal held that the public interest favoured disclosure of a viability report submitted with a planning application in respect of a listed building despite having been provided in confidence. The Tribunal emphasised the decision turned on the facts and did not set a precedent such that 'every piece of commercially sensitive information which is provided in confidence by a developer to a local planning authority in the course of a planning application must be disclosed to the public on request' [23]. Of particular importance to the decision in favour of disclosure was: (i) the fact that the building the subject of the application was owned by the council; and (ii) the information was submitted to satisfy national planning policy criteria [23]. See also *Bath and North East Somerset Council v IC*, FTT, 5 October 2010 at [39]-[89]. More recent decisions have tended to favour disclosure of viability reports provided in connection with planning applications and other development proposals: *Hughes v IC*, FTT, 10 March 2014; *Randle v IC and Poole Harbour Commissioners*, FTT, 27 March 2014; *LB Greenwich v IC*, FTT, 30 January 2015; *Waltho v IC*, FTT, 16 June 2015; *Clyne v IC and LB Lambeth*, FTT, 14 June 2016. The approach in the context of the EIR is materially different from that taken by the High Court in judicial review proceedings, see: *R (Bedford) v LB Islington and Arsenal FC* [2002] EWHC 2044 (Admin) (where the court held that a local planning authority 'needs to be able to examine matters in a confidential matter with applicants.'); *R (Perry) v LB Hackney* [2014] EWHC 3499 (Admin) (where the Court referred to such reports as being 'clearly matters of the utmost commercial sensitivity' – the doubtfulness of *Perry* is considered further in Ch 37); *Turner v SSCLG* [2015] EWHC 375 (Admin). In *LB of Southwark v ICO and Lend Lease (Elephant and Castle) Ltd*, FTT, 9 May 2014 the Upper Tribunal upheld reliance on reg 12(5)(c) for that part of viability assessment which consisted of a proprietary financial model which allowed dynamic costs assessments to be made during build (at [55]). It also accepted that information about sales and rentals were matters of great sensitivity and risked prejudicing the developer in negotiations (at [56]) but that this did not apply to private purchasers (para 57). The viability assessment was required in part to be disclosed (at [59]).

160 In *Veolia ES Nottinghamshire Ltd v Nottinghamshire County Council & ors* [2010] EWCA Civ 1214, [2012] PTSR 185 (a case dealing with commercially confidential information produced by a waste disposal company and where an elector sought to inspect under s 15(1) of the Audit Act 1998) the Court of Appeal used the ECHR to read in an exception to the statutory right of inspection conferred. The Court of Appeal also recognised 'that there is a strong public interest in the maintenance of valuable commercial confidential information' (at [126]).

161 EIR reg 12(9); EI(S)R reg 10(6). Derived from Directive 2003/4/EC Art 4.2 (penultimate paragraph) and, more loosely, from the Aarhus Convention Art 4.4(d) (last sentence) and the last sentence of Art 4.4 itself. See the discussion of reg 12(9) in: *Worcestershire CC v IC and Mercia Waste Management Ltd*, FTT, 10 April 2017 at [82]-[84]; *Vehicle Certification Agency v IC and ClientEarth*, FTT, 12 July 2017 at [58]-[60].

162 See §19–006.

163 EIR reg 12(5)(f); EI(S)R reg 10(5)(f). Derived from Art 4.2(g) of the Directive and Art 4.4(g) of the Aarhus Convention. In *R v Secretary of State for the Environment, Transport and the Regions, ex p Alliance against Birmingham Northern Relief Road (No 1)* [1999] Env LR 447, [1999] JPL 231, (summarised in §17–008) Sullivan J held that parts of the concession agreement fell within reg 4(3)(c). See *McIntyre v IC and University of East Anglia*, FTT, 7 May 2013 considering this exception and refusing to apply it because there was no adverse effect. The exception does not apply to information on (or, possibly, relating to) emissions: EIR reg 12(9); EI(S)R reg 10(6).

least one public authority, if it so wishes, cannot compel an individual to supply to it. Moreover, information supplied under compulsion (or that could be legally required to be supplied) is often that which is most sensitive to the person supplying it: for example, tax and business information.[164] It is not clear whether information required to be supplied to a public authority in order to secure a licence, permission, consent and so forth, would be treated as having been supplied under an obligation.[165] Thirdly, few are the circumstances in which information, other than personal information, held by a public authority may not be disclosed by it or any other public authority: subject to proscriptions arising by statute or common law, a person (including a public authority) holding information may generally disclose it as it likes.[166]

19–027 Public interest: reg 12(5)(f)

Even where the terms of this exception are met, the public authority may only not disclose that part of the information in respect of which it is satisfied that in all the circumstances the public interest in maintaining this and other exceptions applicable to it outweighs the public interest in the information's disclosure.[167] Instances in which the Tribunal has held that the public interest in maintaining the exception outweighs the public interest in the disclosure include:

— Where disclosure of the information would weaken a public authority's ability to negotiate with a developer and so increase the cost to the public purse.[168]

— Where disclosure of a forensic accountant's report would damage the public authority's economic interests.[169]

This exception does not apply to information on emissions.[170]

19–028 Environment: reg 12(5)(g)

Subject to the public interest test, a public authority may refuse to disclose information to the extent that its disclosure would adversely affect the protection of the environment to which the information relates.[171] There is no equivalent exemption in FOIA. The Regulations, the Directive and the Convention all expressly presuppose that disclosure of environmental information should work to assist protecting the environment.[172]

---

164 For an example of the exception being successfully relied on, see *Brain v IC and MoJ*. FTT, 15 September 2014 (where the information sought related to the money paid to a local authority for a lease to a developer).

165 J Ebbeson, H Gaugitsch, J Jendroska, F Marshall and S Stec, *The Aarhus Convention: an Implementation Guide* (2nd Edn) (New York, United Nations, 2014) pp 88-89.

166 Unless proscribed from doing so, a public authority needs no explicit statutory power to disclose information. See §20–036. See: *Vale of White Horse District Council v IC, Gill and Doric Properties Ltd*, FTT, 17 June 2015 (holding that the exception applied to various information related to a public authority land disposal but not the contract price).

167 EIR reg 12(1)(b); EI(S)R reg 10(1)(b). See §19–006.

168 *South Gloucestershire Council v IC and Bovis Homes Ltd*, IT, 20 October 2009 at [46].

169 *Salmon v IC and King's College Cambridge*, IT, 17 July 2008 at [57]-[58]; *Vale of White Horse District Council v IC, Gill and Doric Properties Ltd*, FTT, 17 June 2015 (where the disclosure in relation to a local authority land sale included the purchase price, the profit sharing mechanism and material relating to market demand).

170 EIR reg 12(9); EI(S)R reg 10(6). Derived from Directive 2003/4/EC Art 4.2 (penultimate paragraph) and, more loosely, from the Aarhus Convention Art 4.4(d) (last sentence) and the last sentence of Art 4.4 itself.

171 EIR reg 12(5)(g); EI(S)R reg 10(5)(g). Derived from Art 4.2(h) of the Directive and Art 4.4(h) of the Aarhus Convention.

172 See the recitals to the Aarhus Convention and the recitals to the Directive. In *DEFRA v IC and Portman*, FTT, 13 November 2012 at [51]-[65] DEFRA relied on this exemption, arguing that disclosure of the information requested risked undermining the enforcement of laws designed to ensure environmentally sound scallop fishing. The Tribunal ruled that the public interest in that case favoured disclosure. See also: *DEFRA and Natural England v IC and Dale*, FTT, 9 November 2015 (where the exception was found to be inapplicable in the context of information being sought on badger culling).

19– 029 Public interest: reg 12(5)(g)

Even where the terms of this exception are met, the public authority may only not disclose that part of the information in respect of which it is satisfied that in all the circumstances the public interest in maintaining this and other exceptions applicable to it outweighs the public interest in the information's disclosure.[173] This exception does not apply to information on emissions.[174]

19– 030 Personal information: reg 13

To the extent that information captured by a request for information includes 'personal data,' the Regulations either permit or require the public authority not to disclose that personal data. In the case of personal data of which the applicant is the data subject (ie, the information relates to the applicant), the objective of the Regulations is to route through the GDPR all requests for information concerning the applicant him or herself.[175] In the case of personal data of which the applicant is not the data subject (ie the information relates to a third party), the objective of the Regulations is generally – but not universally – to subordinate the applicant's right of access to information to the privacy rights of that third party. The terms 'personal data' and 'data subject' all have the meanings that are given to them in the DPA 2018.[176] These definitions are considered in Chapter 8 of this work. Although the Directive provides that this exception does not apply to information on emissions, the Regulations do not so provide.[177]

19– 031 Applicant information: reg 13

To the extent that the information requested includes 'personal data' of which the applicant is the data subject, the applicant has no right under the Regulations to that personal data.[178] No consideration of the public interest is involved. The disentitlement effected by the Regulations is limited to the personal data within the requested information. Accordingly, insofar as a public authority identifies 'documents' answering the terms of a request, it is only to the extent that those documents include 'personal data' that the duty to disclose is disapplied. Unless another exception applies, the public authority will remain under a duty to disclose the remainder of the information in those documents. The Regulations do not preclude a public authority from volunteering personal data relating to the applicant. Where only parts of a document falling with the terms of a request is personal data relating to the applicant, volunteering that personal data saves the public authority from the effort of redacting that personal data from the documents to be disclosed, only to have to supply the redacted personal

---

173 EIR reg 12(1)(b); EI(S)R reg 10(1)(b). See §19– 006.

174 EIR reg 12(9); EI(S)R reg 10(6). Derived from Directive 2003/4/EC Art 4.2 (penultimate paragraph) and, more loosely, from the Aarhus Convention Art 4.4(d)(last sentence) and the last sentence of Art 4.4 itself.

175 In practice, to avoid receiving multiple requests – one under the EIR and the other under the GDPR – most public authorities take the sensible strategy of treating a single request as being under both regimes, at least so far as concerns a request by an applicant to be supplied with copies of the information held by the public authority answering the terms of the request.

176 EIR reg 2(4); EI(S)R reg 2(3). Each of these terms is defined in s 1(1) of that Act.

177 EIR reg 12(9); EI(S)R reg 10(6). Derived from Directive 2003/4/EC Art 4.2 (penultimate paragraph) and, more loosely, from the Aarhus Convention Art 4.4(d) (last sentence) and the last sentence of Art 4.4 itself. For examples of the Tribunal's treatment of this exception, see: *Turner v IC and Cheshire East BC*, FTT, 12 November 2014; *Turner v IC and Sunderland City Council*, FTT, 2 February 2016 at [21]-[52] (concerning names of persons attending a meeting); *LB of Hackney v IC and Mudge*, FTT, 19 June 2015(concerning IP addresses); *Bartram v IC*, FTT, 2 February 2016 (concerning the addresses and postcodes of properties affected by a subsidence claim, with the Tribunal ruling the former but not the latter should be withheld); *Dept of Transport v IC and Hastings*, FTT, 6 July 2016 (also concerning names of those attending a meeting); *Wells v IC*, FTT, 29 September 2016(holding that matters relevant to business as opposed to personal activities can still be personal in nature ([25])).

178 EIR reg 5(3); EI(S)R reg 11(1). The applicant will, however, have a right of access to that information under s 7 of the DPA 1998, subject to the exemptions in that Act. The DPA 1998 does not have an equivalent of s 39 of the FOIA. This exception is not found in Directive 2003/4/EC: see Art 4.2(d).

data in response to a request from the applicant made under the GDPR.

9– 032 Third-party information: reg 13

To the extent that the information requested includes 'personal data' of which the applicant is not the data subject, then in most – but not all – circumstances the public authority must not disclose that person data.[179] The rationale for this is the protection of third-party privacy rights.[180] This exception is unique in that non-disclosure where the exception applies is mandatory.[181] The exception mimics s 40(2)-(4) of FOIA, but in certain circumstances adds onto it a consideration of the public interest.[182] In summary, personal data of which the applicant is not the data subject must not be disclosed by a public authority under the Regulations in any of the four situations below:

(1) Where disclosure of that personal data would contravene any of the principles set out in:

(a) Article 5 of the GDPR (which sets out principles governing non-law enforcement and non-intelligence services processing of personal data);[183]

(b) section 34 of DPA 2018 (which sets out principles governing law enforcement processing of personal data); and

(c) section 85 of DPA 2018 (which sets out principles governing intelligence services processing of personal data)

There is no consideration of the public interest.

(2) In relation to:

(a) manual unstructured processing of personal data;[184] and

(b) the automated or structured processing of personal data[185] in the course of an activity that is outside the scope of EU law or in the course of an activity that falls within the scope of Art 2(2)(b) of the GDPR,

where disclosure of the information would contravene any of the principles set out in (1) above disregarding the exemptions in s 24(1) of the DPA 2018.[186] There is no

---

179 EIR reg 12(3); EI(S)R reg 10(3). Derived from Arts 4.2(f) and 4.4 (final sentence) of the Directive and Art 4.4(f) of the Aarhus Convention. The Regulations do not proscribe its disclosure should there be another right of access to some or all of the information. By way of example of this provision in operation (in relation to the DPA 1998), see: *Wells v IC*, FTT, 29 September 2016 (considering whether disclosure of personal data would contravene data protection principles.)

180 The Explanatory Memorandum notes: 'The handling of personal data is not covered explicitly under the Directive although Art 4(2) refers to compliance with Directive 95/46/EC on the protection of individuals with regard to the processing of personal data and on the free movement of such data (the Data Protection Directive). Regulations 5(3), 12(3) and 13 relating to personal data contain similar provisions to those in section 40 of the FOIA and are believed to be compatible with the Data Protection Directive.' The Directive is now replaced by the GDPR. For instances in which the exception has been applied: *Creekside Forum v IC and Dept for Culture Media and Sport*, IT, 28 May 2009 at [47]-[82]; *Surrey Heath Borough Council v IC and McCullen*, FTT, 11 August 2010 at [22]-[44], which considers redaction at [43]-[45]; *Plumb v IC and Babergh District Council*, FTT, 29 November 2011 at [17]-[25]; *Downs v IC and HSE*, FTT, 1 May 2013 at [43]-[96].

181 EIR regs 12(4) and 13(1); EI(S)R regs 10(4) and 11(2). Although Art 4.2(f) of the Directive does not make non-disclosure mandatory Art 4.4 (last sentence), in requiring compliance with Directive 95/46/EC, effectively makes mandatory non-disclosure of this class of information (on the basis of it not being a 'fair processing').

182 The principles relating to this exception are considered in detail in Ch 24.

183 EIR reg 13(2A)(a); EI(S)R reg 11(3)(a)(i). This exception is in the same terms as the FOIA s 40(3)(a)(i). For more detail as to its operation, see §33– 014 and: *Freeze v IC and DEFRA*, FTT, 8 March 2011 at [17]-[44]; *McIntyre v IC and University of East Anglia*, FTT, 7 May 2013 at [43]-[96].

184 Defined in DPA 2018 s 21(4).

185 Defined in DPA 2018 s 21(4).

186 EIR reg 13(2A)(b); EI(S)R reg 11(3)(b). In other words, processing to which Chapter 3 of Part 2 of the DPA 2018 applies. For all its needless complexity, this limb is of very narrow application. This exception is in the same terms as the FOIA s 40(3)(b). For more detail as to its operation, see §33– 014.

consideration of the public interest.

(3) In a case where the data subject has previously given a notice objecting to processing of his or her personal data under Art 21 of the GDPR or under s 99 of the DPA 2018 (in relation to intelligence services processing), where disclosure of the personal data would contravene Art 21 of the GDPR or s 99 of the DPA 2018.[187] In addition, in this situation, the reg 13 exception only applies if the public interest in not disclosing the information outweighs the public interest in disclosing it.

(4) Where, had the personal data been sought by the data subject in a request made by him or her under Art 15(1) of the GDPR,[188] the information would have been withheld in reliance upon an applicable exemption.[189] In addition, in this situation, the reg 13 exception only applies if the public interest in not disclosing the information outweighs the public interest in disclosing it.

The first three circumstances protect the interests or privacy of the data subject. The fourth circumstance ensures that an applicant under the Regulations has, subject to the public interest, no greater right of access than a data subject making a request under the GDPR for information of which he is the data subject. The public interest balancing exercise, which is different from that which applies to the other exceptions,[190] may serve to enlarge the right of an applicant under the Regulations over that of an applicant under the GDPR and the DPA 2018.

---

[187] EIR reg 13(2)(a)(ii); EI(S)R reg 11(3)(a)(ii). This exception only applies where the information is held or is intended to be held as part of a 'relevant filing system' (for the meaning of which, see §15– 012), or is held as part of an 'accessible record' (for the meaning of which, see §15– 016), or is processed or intended to be processed automatically (for the meaning of which, see §15– 011). The exception is in the same terms as the FOIA s 40(3)(a)(ii), FOI(S)A s 38(2)(a)(ii). Disclosure under it may, however, differ in that section 40(3)(a)(ii) is not an absolute exemption and, accordingly, the public authority may only not disclose the information to the extent that, in all the circumstances, the public interest in maintaining the exemption outweighs the public interest in disclosing it: s 2(3)(f)(ii). For more detail as to its operation, see §33– 024.

[188] Or, in relation to law enforcement processing, in a request under s 45(1)(b) of the DPA 2018, or, in relation to security services processing, in a request under or 94(1)(b) of the DPA 2018.

[189] This exception is in the same terms as the FOIA s 40(4) and FOI(S)A s 38(3).

[190] The public interest balancing exercise here involves balancing, on the one hand, the public interest in not disclosing the information (as opposed to the public interest in maintaining the exception) against the public interest, on the other hand, in disclosing the information: EIR reg 13(3); EI(S)R reg 11(4). The wording suggests that it is for the public authority to show that the public interest in non-disclosure outweighs the public interest in disclosure, rather than vice versa. The Directive does not differentiate between the exceptions in its treatment of the public interest: see Art 4.2 (penultimate paragraph).

Part IV

Freedom of Information

CHAPTER 20
The right to information

1. THE NATURE OF INFORMATION

20– 001 Introduction

The entitlements conferred by FOIA and the EIR are conferred in relation to 'information'.[1] Similarly, engagement of any of the provisions of Part II of the Act,[2] which render information exempt information, turns upon the attributes of the information in question or upon the likely effects of its disclosure: it does not turn upon the attributes of the document or record

[1] FOIA s 1; FOI(S)A s 1; EIR reg 5(1); EI(S)R reg 5(1). The entitlements in s 1(1) are satisfied by a communication of information that complies with s 11. The DPA 2018 employs the term 'data', which is defined in s 3(2) to mean 'information' having certain attributes: see further at §15– 009. It is suggested that the analysis below holds true for 'data' under that Act: see *Durant v Financial Services Authority* [2003] EWCA Civ 1746, [2004] FSR 28 at [65] in relation to the DPA 1998. Of the comparative jurisdictions, only New Zealand employs 'information' as the unit of disclosure: see §51– 018. In the United States, a person is entitled to access to 'records' of an agency: see §51– 003. In Australia, the right of access is to 'documents' of an agency: see §51– 011. In Canada, a person is given a right of access to 'records' under the control of a government institution: see §51– 026. And in the Republic of Ireland, a person is given a right of access to any 'record' held by a public institution: see §51– 035.

[2] Similarly EIR Pt 3 and EI(S)R regs 10-13.

containing the information sought nor upon the likely effects of disclosure of such a document or record. If a provision in Part II of the Act does apply, the information that caused it to apply will become exempt information. Only if the document or record is coincident with that information will it thereby be rendered exempt.[3] The unit of disclosure and of exemption may therefore be said to be 'information'.[4] Although information is at the heart of FOIA and of the EIR, in relation to the great majority of requests for information it is to be expected that there will be no real question whether that which falls within the terms of a request represents information. The mere ability to consider that a certain matter answers the terms of the request will normally be sufficient indication that that matter constitutes information. Thus, in most cases, the words appearing on the face of a document will represent recorded information capable of being the subject matter of a request. The simplicity of this part of the exercise in the vast majority of cases is deceptive. The word 'information' does not enjoy a clearly delineated, universal meaning, but varies according to the context in which it is used.[5] Subject to the qualification introduced by the limited definition of information in the Act,[6] it is suggested that so far as FOIA and the EIR are concerned, 'information' is any matter that is capable of being recorded and of being communicated from one person to another. This definition, which is consistent with the ordinary meaning of the word, avoids the intractable difficulties which attach to any narrower definition of the word.[7]

20–002 The meaning of 'information'

The term 'information' is defined in the Act to mean information recorded in any form,[8] implicitly recognising that information may also be unrecorded. The Court of Appeal has held that 'information' is an:

> ordinary English word and there is nothing to suggest that it is being used [in FOIA] in an unusual or narrow sense.[9]

The *New Shorter Oxford Dictionary* (1993) defines 'information' as:

> 1.[....]
> 2. Communication of the knowledge of some fact or occurrence.
> 3. a. Knowledge or facts communicated about a particular subject, event, etc; intelligence, news.

---

3 Subject to FOIA s 2; FOI(S)A s 2(1); EIR reg 12(1); EI(S)R reg 10(1). See §5–001.

4 That the distinction in the Act between 'information' and 'record' is both real and intentional is apparent from FOIA s 77 and FOI(S)A s 65. The significance of the distinction is discussed in: *DBERR v IC and Friends of the Earth*, IT, 29 April 2008 at [29]; *Glasgow City Council & anor v Scottish IC* [2009] CSIH 73 at [43]. Similarly in relation to 'data' under the DPA 1998: *Durant v Financial Services Authority* [2003] EWCA Civ 1746, [2004] FSR 28 at [65]. See further: *IPSA v IC* [2015] EWCA Civ 388, [2015] 1 WLR 2879 at [36].

5 Other fields of human endeavour have struggled to find a satisfactory definition of 'information', with the impetus largely originating with telecommunications and its need to identify the limits of message degradation before that which is received ceases to be information to the recipient. The starting point is generally considered to be found in CE Shannon, 'A mathematical theory of communication' (1948) 27 *Bell System Technical Journal* 379 and 623. There are many treatments of the subject: see, eg R Losee, 'A Discipline Independent Definition of Information' (1997) 48 *Journal of the American Society for Information Science* 254-269.

6 FOIA s 84; FOI(S)A s 73. Under the environmental information regime, 'information' is not defined, but 'environmental information' is defined: EIR reg 2(1); EI(S)R reg 2(1).

7 The Court of Appeal has in any event held that the term should be construed in a liberal manner: *IPSA v IC* [2015] EWCA Civ 388, [2015] 1 WLR 2879 at [33].

8 FOIA s 84; FOI(S)A s 73; cf EIR reg 2(1); EI(S)R reg 2(1). An exception is made for FOIA s 51(8), empowering the Information Commissioner to require a public authority to furnish him with information, whether recorded or not recorded, for the purpose of determining whether a public authority has complied or is complying with its duties under Part I of the Act, and for FOIA s 75(2), enabling the Secretary of State for Justice and the Minister for the Cabinet Office each to override a statutory proscription on the disclosure of information, whether recorded or unrecorded, in order to give full effect to FOIA s 1. The equivalent provisions in FOI(S)A, are ss 50(9) and 64(2), respectively.

9 *IPSA v IC* [2015] EWCA Civ 388, [2015] 1 WLR 2879 at [33].

b. [....]

c. Without necessary relation to a recipient: that which inheres in or is represented by a particular arrangement, sequence, or set, that may be stored in, transferred by, and responded to by inanimate things; Math. a statistically defined quantity representing the probability of occurrence of a symbol, sequence, message, etc as against a number of possible alternatives.

The dictionary definition does not turn upon the recipient's state of knowledge. While the extent, if any, to which material is informative will depend upon the knowledge of the recipient, even with the narrowest dictionary definition material will be 'information' if it is *capable* of being informative, irrespective of whether it is to the recipient. This accords with the nature of disclosure under FOIA and the EIR. As it is effectively disclosure to the world, the fact that certain material is wholly uninformative to the applicant does not cause that material to cease to be information.[10] Whether material constitutes information for the purposes of the Act should not, therefore, depend upon the state of knowledge of the applicant.[11] While the same issue may arise in relation to the state of knowledge of the public authority holding the information,[12] as a matter of practice it is difficult to imagine how a public authority could identify material as being information answering the terms of a request unless the nature of that material were understood by someone within the public authority.

20–003 The recording medium

The medium on which matter is recorded should not, in principle, impinge upon its characterisation as information.[13] Material stored on the hard disk of a computer or on a video tape is just as much capable of being information as words appearing on a document. So, too, the fact that a machine or an instrument may be required to render the matter intelligible or readable is of no greater significance to its being information than are the spectacles of a long-sighted applicant. This is confirmed by the White Paper that anticipated the introduction of the Act, which indicated that information should extend to computer data, drawings, maps,[14] plans, photographs,[15] images, video and sound recordings.[16]

20–004 Disinformation

On one view, information that is incorrect may be said not to be information at all. The Government appears to have taken the view during the passage of the Freedom of Information Bill through Parliament that issues about the accuracy of information are separate from the

10 Most people would, for example, recognise that the Rosetta Stone contains information, even if they were unable to read hieroglyphics, demotic or Greek.

11 *FCO v IC and Friends of the Earth*, IT, 29 June 2007 at [36(5)].

12 So that the inscriptions on the Rosetta Stone would represent information even if there were no-one in the British Museum who could read hieroglyphics, demotic or Greek. And, it may be added, the hieroglyphs were information even before Champollion completed his work.

13 *Glasgow City Council & anor v Scottish IC* [2009] CSIH 73 at [43], [47]; *DBERR v IC and Peninsula Business Services*, IT, 28 April 2009 at [50].

14 For an instance in which maps were requested: *OFCOM v IC and T-Mobile (UK) Ltd*, IT, 4 September 2007.

15 For instances in which photographs were requested: *Francis v IC and GMC*, IT, 15 January 2009; *Freebury v IC and Chief Constable of Devon and Cornwall Constabulary*, IT, 5 October 2009. See also *IPSA v IC* [2015] EWCA Civ 388, [2015] 1 WLR 2879 at [33] and [44] ('information includes visual as well as linguistic information such as logos, drawings and photographs').

16 See, eg Home Office, *Your Right to Know* (1997), para 85. These are no more than different means for the *storage* or *conveyance* of information. Information stored on a computer is no more than an array of binary digits, wholly unintelligible to an average person. Also included would be undeleted voice-box messages. The EIR specifically provide that 'environmental information' means information in written, visual, aural, electronic or any other material form: EIR reg 2(1) and EI(S)R reg 2(1).

rights of access to information under the Act.[17] In terms of sheer practicality, there is much sense in ignoring inaccuracies in material in deciding whether that material constitutes information. This approach has been taken elsewhere when considering whether material represents information. Thus, in *Win v Minister for Immigration and Multicultural Affairs* the Federal Court of Australia considered that the term was sufficiently wide to cover material that was completely worthless or that was bare assertion.[18]

20–005 Information – comparative law

Of the comparative jurisdictions, only New Zealand employs 'information' as the unit of disclosure. The jurisprudence of that country gives some indication of the scope that has been given to that word and of a general disinclination to refuse a request on the basis that what is sought does not constitute information. In *Commissioner of Police v Ombudsman*,[19] the applicant had been charged with various offences. His solicitors made a request under the Official Information Act 1982 for copies of the briefs of evidence of the witnesses that the police intended to call. This was refused. On appeal to the Ombudsman, he recommended that the information be made available. The police sought judicial review of the Ombudsman's decision. Although the police accepted that the briefs contained 'personal information', the High Court,[20] in a general overview of the Act, considered the meaning of the word 'information':

> Perhaps the most outstanding feature of the definition is that the word "information" is used which dramatically broadens the scope of the whole Act. The stuff of what is held by Departments, Ministers, or organisations is not confined to the written word but embraces any knowledge, however gained or held, by the named bodies in their official capacities. The omission, undoubtedly deliberate, not to define the word "information" serves to emphasise the intention of the Legislature to place few limits on relevant knowledge.[21]

---

17 During the Bill's passage through Parliament, Mr David Lock, The Parliamentary Secretary, Lord Chancellor Department, rejected a proposed amendment that would have required a public authority to make a judgment on whether the information is accurate, saying: 'The authority may not know whether the information is accurate, and the cost ceiling for charges made under the freedom of information regime is designed only to cover finding and retrieving the information. The public authority should not have to go to further unlimited lengths in verifying the accuracy of information. If information is disclosed by a public authority under the duty and is subsequently found to be inaccurate, the manufacturer could subject the decision to legal proceedings, thereby placing severe burdens on a range of public authorities on whom the duty was placed. I remind hon. Members that the provisions of clause 13 apply, and that those are the better route' — Hansard HC vol 347 col 909 (4 April 2000).

18 [2001] FCA 56 at [17]-[21], (2001) 105 FCR 212 at 217-218. The case concerned the Migration Act 1958 s 503A, which provides that information communicated in confidence to a migration officer by particular agencies is to be protected from disclosure, including disclosure under the Freedom of Information Act 1982. On the other hand, in *WAGP of 2002 v Minister for Immigration & Multicultural & Indigenous Affairs* (2002) 124 FCR 276 at [26]-[29] the Full Court of the Federal Court held that mere 'observations' did not constitute information. The court there was considering the Migration Act 1958 s 424A, which provides that the Refugee Review Tribunal must give an applicant to that tribunal particulars of any information that it considers would be a reason for affirming a decision, in this case refusing to grant the applicant a protection visa. The Court held that neither of two observations by the Tribunal: (a) that the applicant did not refer to a particular matter in his evidence; and (b) that there was inconsistency between two pieces of information, constituted information. Similarly: *Paul v Minister for Immigration and Multicultural Affairs* (2001) 113 FCR 396 at [99]-[100], [107]-[108] and [116]; *NAIH of 2002 v Minister for Immigration & Multicultural & Indigenous Affairs* (2002) 124 FCR 223; *VAF v Minister for Immigration and Multicultural and Indigenous Affairs* (2004) 206 ALR 471; *SZECF v Minister for Immigration and Multicultural and Indigenous Affairs* [2005] FCA 1200.

19 [1985] 1 NZLR 578.

20 Which held that the information was exempt on the grounds that substantial disclosure before trial would be likely to prejudice the maintenance of the law.

21 [1985] 1 NZLR 578 at 586. See also *Mecklenburg v Kreis Pinneberg der Landrat* (C-321/96) [1999] 2 CMLR 418, [1999] Env LR D6, [1999] All ER (EC) 166, where the ECJ showed a willingness to find that the Community legislature intended to make the concept of information in Directive 1990/313/EEC on freedom of access to information on the environment was a broad one (at [19]). The definition in that Directive was more detailed than that in FOIA. That Directive has since been repealed and replaced by Directive 2003/4/EC on public access to environmental information, Art 2(1) of which defines 'environmental information' in wider terms still: see

On appeal, the Court of Appeal[22] said:

> Information is not defined in the Act. From this it may be inferred that the draftsman was prepared to adopt the ordinary dictionary meaning of that word. Information in its ordinary dictionary meaning is that which informs, instructs, tells or makes aware. It is reasonable to suppose that, by their very nature, the police briefs contain information pointing to the commission of offences of the kind charged against the appellant and to the involvement of the appellant in them.[23]

In other legislative contexts, a similarly broad meaning has been given to the word. Thus, in relation to a trade descriptions offence, the mileage shown on the odometer of a car has been treated as information.[24] In relation to a defence of relying upon information supplied by another to a prosecution under the Consumer Credit Advertisements Regulations 1989, the Divisional Court has held that 'information' extended to advice as well as factual information.[25] And, in relation to the expenses to be borne by the purchaser of land where he requires verification of information not in the possession of the vendor[26] the Court of Appeal has said: '[t]he word "information" is as large as can be.'[27] The suggested definition[28] is sufficiently wide to avoid the need to inquire as to the intelligibility of what is sought to the applicant, or to any other person, or to ascertain its worth or reliability, whilst according with the dictionary meaning.[29]

20–006 Information must be recorded

As noted above, the entitlements under the Act and Regulations only apply to information that is 'recorded in any form'.[30] In practical effect, the requirement that information be recorded places FOIA regime closer to the comparative regimes that confer rights to 'documents' and 'records'[31] than to that in New Zealand, which requires only that the information be held, not that it be recorded.[32] The Act and the Regulations specifically do not limit or prescribe the medium on which the information must be recorded. It will cover handwritten or typed

Glawischnig v Bundesminster für soziale Sicherheit und Generationen (C-316/01) [2003] ECR I-5995, [2003] All ER (D) 147 (Jun) at [5].

22 Which allowed the appellant's appeal and found that the disclosure would not be likely to prejudice the maintenance of the law, including the prevention, investigation and detection of offences, and the right to a fair trial.

23 [1988] 1 NZLR 385 at 402. Considered further in *R v Harvey* [1991] 1 NZLR 242. Not followed in *Vice-Chancellor Macquarie University v FM* [2005] NSWCA 192 dealing with a request under the Privacy and Personal Information Act 1998 (NSW).

24 For the purposes of the Trade Descriptions Act 1968 s 24(1)(a): *Simmons v Potter* [1975] RTR 347, [1975] Crim LR 354.

25 *Coventry City Council v Lazarus* (1996) 160 JP 188, [1996] C CLR 5.

26 Now under the Law of Property Act 1925 s 45(4).

27 *Re Stuart and Seadon* [1896] 2 Ch 328 at 334.

28 See §20–001.

29 See definition 3c. at §20–002. That the FOIA recognises that something may be information even though not recorded suggests that, for the purposes of the Act, matter takes on the quality of information before its articulation in one form or another.

30 FOIA s 84; FOI(S)A s 73. Similarly EIR reg 2(1); EI(S)R reg 2(1).

31 These terms are given an expanded definition in each of the Acts to cover non-written material and so forth: see §§51–003, 51–011, 51–026 and 51–035. Similarly, UK legislation regularly gives the term 'document' an expanded definition in order to capture the different media upon which information may be recorded, eg: CPR 31.4; Civil Evidence Act 1995 s 13; Criminal Justice Act 2003 s 134(1); Police and Criminal Evidence Act 1984 s 118(1); Value Added Tax Act 1994 s 96(1); Charities Act 2011 s 353(2). A broad interpretation has been afforded to the word 'document' as used in FOIA s 32 so as to include audio recordings and electronic records: see §29–033.

32 See §20–001.

information, information stored in any computer storage device, maps, plans, models, any film and any form of magnetic storage such as tapes and videos.[33] The visual appearance of the information can itself constitute 'recorded information' – for example, the style or layout of an invoice or a person's signature on a document– which cannot necessarily be captured by a transcription of the words and numbers recorded on the invoice or other document.[34]

0– 007 No obligation to record

The purpose of the requirement that the information be recorded 'in any form' removes the need for a public authority to identify and record information held by it but unrecorded.[35] There is no obligation on a public authority to answer questions generally or to create information which is not held in recorded form at the time of the request.[36] Matters known to an officer or employee of a public authority but not recorded will thus be outside the scope of the Act.[37] Similarly, information that can be assembled from material held by a public authority but which has not been recorded at the time of the receipt of a request will not be information recorded in any form:[38]

> The only obligation under the Act is for the public authority to provide the information it holds of the description specified in the request.[39]

However, a request for information that would be answered by a public authority changing the form in which it holds that information will not involve the creation of new information.[40]

---

33 See §20– 003.

34 *IPSA v IC* [2015] EWCA Civ 388, [2015] 1 WLR 2879. The fact that these visual elements are capable of informing an inquiry into the genuineness of the document could be relevant to this assessment (at [45]), such that sometime disclosure of the actual record might be necessary to answer the request for information (at [36]).

35 Compare House of Commons, *Public Administration Third Report* (Cm 4355, 1999) Annex 6, para 3 (see Ch 1 n 68) where the Freedom of Information Unit, Home Office stated, 'we think that it would be unworkable to include information which had not been recorded in any form whatsoever within the scope of the statutory right because of the difficulty of establishing whether such information actually exists. There is a need for absolute clarity when creating statutory rights and obligations.'

36 *Home Office v IC and Cobain*, FTT, 30 January 2013 at [29].

37 Except for the purposes of FOIA ss 51(8) and 75(2). Even if officials of a public authority know more about the matter in respect of which an applicant has made a request for information, the public authority is not obliged to reduce what it knows into writing: *Reed v IC and Astley Abbotts Parish Council*, IT, 29 December 2008 at [12]; *Ingle v IC*, IT, 29 June 2007 at [8]. See, in the context of the DPA 1998, *Holyoake v Candy* [2017] EWHC 3397 (Ch) at [458] ('...the purpose of the Act is to regulate what a data controller does with information stored in a relevant record, and it does not seem consonant with that for the Act also to regulate what a person does with information in his own head that has not been derived from the records...'). Nor is the Tribunal concerned with whether a public authority should have recorded or held particular information: *Brigden v IC and North Lincolnshire and Goole Hospitals NHS Trust*, IT, 5 April 2007; *Commissioner of Police for the Metropolis v Information Commissioner and Mackenzie* [2014] UKUT 479 (AAC) at [42] ('FOIA is about the citizen's right to information...It is not a statute that prescribes any particular organisational structure or record-keeping practice in public authorities'). The position is the same under Council Regulation (EC) 1049/2001, with the entitlement being to recorded information and not to interrogate the organisation: *WWF European Policy Programme v European Union Council* (T-264/04) [2007] ECR II-911 at [75]-[76]. The Information Commissioner has, however, expressed an interest in the incorporation of a 'duty to document' into the UK regime: see Openness by Design: The Information Commissioner's Strategic Plan 2019/20-2021/22 (July 2019).

38 Thus, the fact that the information held by a public authority is inadequate for the purpose of its functions does not give rise to a right under the FOIA to more adequate information: *Simmons v IC*, IT, 16 December 2005.

39 *Prior v IC*, IT, 27 April 2006 at [22]. In *Johnson v IC and Ministry of Justice*, IT, 13 July 2007 at [47] the Tribunal held that if answering a request for information merely requires 'simple collation of the raw data [already held] to arrive at the total figures that the Applicant has sought' this does not mean that the requested information is not 'held' by the public authority. In that case the applicant requested statistics on an annual basis of claims allocated to and struck out by individual masters of the High Court. Similarly in *Benford v IC and DEFRA*, IT, 14 November 2007 at [57] the Tribunal held that the production of a redacted list from a computer database did not represent the production of new information.

40 *Common Services Agency v IC* [2008] UKHL 47, [2008] 1 WLR 1550, where the public authority was required to 'barnardise' the requested information (that is, add -1, 0 or 1 to very low values so as to make more difficult identification of the individuals reflected in those values) held by it. The House of Lords held that the process of

> Public authorities are frequently requested under FOIA for statistics. They may not previously have extracted the particular statistic from their records but may be able to do so easily. In that case, the authority would be regarded as holding the requested information. By contrast, where the requested statistic cannot be derived readily from the existing records (because, say, the request is for a level of detail which simply cannot be ascertained from existing records), then it would be regarded as a request, falling outside FOIA, for the public authority to create new information, and the authority would be entitled to respond that it did not hold the requested information. Determining whether a requested statistic is "held", by virtue of the public authority holding the "building blocks" of raw data from which the statistic can be derived, turns therefore on the complexity of the operations which need to be performed on the building blocks and the degree of skill and judgement necessary to ascertain whether a particular building block should be regarded as contributing to the statistic.[41]

The requirement to change the form may involve a considerable imposition on the public authority,[42] including the interrogation of a computer database using software to yield a bespoke output directed to answering the request.[43]

20–008 Computer-stored information

Computers, which are increasingly used to store the bulk of information held by a public authority, present three particular difficulties so far as the recording of information is concerned. First, any computer will typically store information in a variety of ways, principally according to the manner in which the computer needs to access the information at any given time. Its storage systems are conventionally divided into volatile and non-volatile.[44] Volatile memory may properly be said to lack the requisite degree of permanence to be described as having been 'recorded'. The position in relation to non-volatile memory is less straightforward, and this leads to the second difficulty. A computer ordinarily generates numerous temporary or working files during any session, without any specific intervention by the user. Some of these temporary files are stored in the volatile memory, but some are also written to the hard disk of the computer. The computer may automatically delete these files at the end of a session, after a set time, by overwriting them, or they may be left on the hard disk indefinitely. Information so stored can include accessed web pages, back-up files, unsaved documents, overflow files and so forth. These files are generally capable of being retrieved. The unifying feature of these files is that although they contain information, the information has been created and is stored within the computer without specific user intervention. It is arguable – but perhaps no more – that such information is not 'recorded' on the basis that that verb requires an animate subject or at least some conscious decision connected to the process.[45] Thirdly, most computer files, whether

---

barnardisation did not involve the creation of new information, but rather that it represented a change in the form in which the information might be provided. See further *Home Office v IC and Cobain*, FTT, 30 January 2013 at [31].

41 *Home Office v IC and Cobain*, FTT, 30 January 2013 at [32].

42 In *Common Services Agency v IC* [2008] UKHL 47, [2008] 1 WLR 1550 at [15] it was held that this part of the statutory regime should be construed in as liberal a manner as possible.

43 *SSHD v IC*, IT, 15 August 2008 at [12]. The Tribunal held that there is no difference between 'information' held by a public authority and 'raw data' held on a database held by a public authority. The fact that the public authority had to run an existing computer programme (which it routinely used for other reporting purposes) in order to interrogate the database and yield the output so as to answer the request did not represent creating new information held by the authority.

44 Volatile memory is 'held' by an electrical charge which requires regular 'refreshing' if it is not to be lost. Unless there is some other source of power, shutting down a computer will result in the loss of this memory. Non-volatile memory does not require such refreshing, and will be stored on devices such as the computer's hard disk. Once 'written' to the disk, it will remain accessible, unless deleted or overwritten.

45 The *New Shorter Oxford English Dictionary* (1993), gives as the meaning of the verb 'record': '4.a. Relate, tell, or narrate in writing; set down in writing or other permanent form; make a written record of. 4.b. Make an official record of (an action, decision, etc); set down officially or permanently.' In relation to information under the EIR

word processing and the like or the automatically generated variety, remain accessible for some time after 'deletion', whether deleted automatically or by human intervention.[46] On the footing that the file before its 'deletion' was recorded information, if such a file is deleted but remains accessible, it will continue to be subject to the Act and the Regulations.[47]

2. THE HOLDING REQUIREMENT

20– 009 When information is 'held'

For the purposes of FOIA, information is 'held' by a public authority if it is held by the authority otherwise than on behalf of another person, or if it is held by another person on behalf of the authority.[48] The Act has avoided the technicalities associated with the law of disclosure, which has conventionally drawn a distinction between a document in the power, custody or possession of a person.[49] The Act imposes a duty on a public authority to search for information answering the terms of a request.[50] Putting to one side the effects of s 3(2) (see §20–010 below), the word 'held' suggests a relationship between a public authority and the information akin to that of ownership or bailment of goods. It requires an appropriate connection between the information and the public authority.[51] Information:

---

and the EI(S)R, the argument is stronger as those regulations provide that information is held by a public authority 'if the information is in the authority's possession and has been produced or received by the authority': EIR reg 3(2); EI(S)R reg 2(2).

46 Deletion normally only removes the leading character of the filename, so that that file no longer appears in the list of files which is accessible to most programs. Provided that the file has not been overwritten, it is normally a comparatively simple task to restore the totality, or the better part, of the file by assigning a character to replace the missing one.

47 It may be that the restoration of the file will cause the cost of compliance to exceed the appropriate limit and enable the public authority to avoid answering the request. See FOIA s 12, FOI(S)A s 12 and §§23– 002 to 23–008. There is no equivalent let-out in the EIR or the EI(S)R. The Tribunal has taken a rigorous line: *Harper v IC and Royal Mail Group plc*, IT, 15 November 2005 at [17]-[27]. It is notable that certain public authorities, relying on their powers to have access to documents and other recorded information of, eg, taxpayers, will in the exercise of that power restore deleted files from a computer hard disk: see, generally, *R (Paul da Costa & Co (a firm)) v Thames Magistrates' Court* [2002] EWHC 40, [2002] STC 267, [2002] Crim LR 504. Parties to litigation are also required to give access to 'deleted' information on a computer: CPR PD 31A para 2A.

48 FOIA s 3(2). The position is the same under the FOI(S)A s 3(2), except for three differences: information is not held by an authority if it is held by the authority in confidence, having been supplied by a Minister of the Crown or by a department of the Government of the United Kingdom (s 3(2)(a)(ii)); the definition is subject to any qualification set out in Sch 1 (s 3(3)); and there is a particular exception relating to the Keeper of the Records of Scotland (s 3(4)). Differing approaches are taken in the comparative regimes. In the United States, the right attaches to 'agency records:' see §51– 003. In Australia, the right attaches to 'documents of an agency:' see §51–011. In New Zealand, the right attaches to information 'held' by a department, etc: see §51– 018. In Canada, the right attaches to a record 'under the control' of a government institution: see §51– 026. This phrase, too, is vague and the Federal Court in *Canada Post Corp v Canada (Minister of Public Works)* [1995] 2 FC 110, 30 Admin CR (2d) 242 (affirming [1993] 3 FC 320, 19 Admin CR (2d) 230) held that the notion of control was not limited to the power to dispose of a record, that there was nothing in the Act that indicated that the word 'control' should not be given a broad interpretation, and that a narrow interpretation would deprive citizens of a meaningful right of access under the Act. In the Republic of Ireland, the right attaches to any record 'held' by a public body: see §51–035.

49 This passage in the third edition of this book was approved by the UT in *University of Newcastle upon Tyne v Information Commissioner and BUAV* [2011] UKUT 185 (AAC) at [28]. See P Matthews and H Malek, *Disclosure*, 4th edn (London, Sweet & Maxwell, 2012) paras 5.44-5.60.

50 See further §24– 001.

51 *University of Newcastle upon Tyne v Information Commissioner and BUAV* [2011] UKUT 185 (AAC) at [29] approving *British Union for the Abolition of Vivisection v IC and Newcastle University*, FTT, 10 November 2010 at [47]. In that case the UT upheld the FTT's finding that information contained in two scientific project licences given to scientists employed by the university was information held by the university (rather than by the scientists): *University of Newcastle upon Tyne v Information Commissioner and BUAV* [2011] UKUT 185 (AAC) at [54]. 'Appropriate connection' is not, however, a strict legal test: *King's College Cambridge v IC and Lee*, FTT, 15 October 2013 at [38].

— that is, without request or arrangement, sent to or deposited with a public authority which does not hold itself out as willing to receive it and which does not subsequently use it;[52]
— that is accidentally left with a public authority;[53]
— that just passes through a public authority;[54] or
— that 'belongs' to an employee or officer of a public authority but which is brought[55] by that employee or officer onto the public authority's premises,[56]

will lack the requisite assumption by the public authority of responsibility for or dominion over the information that is necessary before it can be said that the public authority can be said to 'hold' the information.[57] Whether information is or is not held by a public authority is thus fundamentally a factual issue[58] The factual issue may involve consideration of the legal basis on which the public authority or someone else retains the information[59] and the legal relationship between the public authority and the third person.[60] The issue is decided on the balance of probabilities.[61] The position under the EIR is clearer, those regulations expressly providing that environmental information must have been produced or received by the public authority if it is to be information 'held' by that public authority.[62] Under both regimes, information sent to

---

52 By analogy with a gratuitous bailment by deposit: *Howard v Harris* (1884) 1 Cab & El 253. In the law of bailment, a slight assumption of control of the chattel so deposited will render the recipient a depositary: *Newman v Bourne and Hollingworth* (1915) 31 TLR 309. For further examples, see N Palmer, *Bailment*, 3rd edn (London, Sweet & Maxwell, 2009) pp 39-44, 619-621 and 712-4.

53 Also by analogy with a gratuitous bailment by deposit: *Mills v Brooker* [1919] 1 KB 555.

54 In *Information Commissioner for Western Australia v Ministry of Justice* [2001] WASC 3 at [20] it was held that 'It may be that mere transient physical custody will not suffice. There may arise sometimes questions of knowledge or of intention. For example, there may be inadvertent delivery of documents to an agency, or documents may be presented to an agency for the purpose of inspection (eg when a person presents their birth certificate for the purpose of identification) in circumstances where it is plainly not intended that the document form any part of the records of the agency.'

55 *Quaere* would this be the case if the employee or officer were to place the information on a computer of the public authority?

56 *McBride v IC and MOJ*, Information Tribunal, 27 May 2008 at [31]; *Digby-Cameron v IC*, IT, 16 October 2008 at [14]-[19]. This is also the approach that has been taken in the comparative jurisdictions: *Re Horesh and Ministry of Education* [1986] 1 VAR 143 (departmental inquiry concerning the professional relationship between the applicant and the principal of the school at which he had taught, notes taken by a friend of the principal who was also the secretary of the relevant teachers association and not used by the authority were personal to the principal and not disclosable under Australian legislation); *Re Mann and Capital Territory Health Commission* (1983) 5 ALN N368; *Re O'Sullivan and Family Court of Australia* (1997) 47 ALD 765 (dealing with the meaning of the 'documents of a court'); *Loughman v Altman* (1992) 39 FCR 90, 111 ALR 445 (document held to be 'of a court' even though possessed by another agency); *Re Barkhordar and Australian Capital Territory Schools Authority* (1987) 12 ALD 332 (personal documents can become documents of an agency); *Bureau of National Affairs, Inc v US Department of Justice* 742 F (2d) 1484 (DC Cir 1984); *Canada (Privacy Commissioner) v Canada (Labour Relations Board)* [1996] 3 FC 609, (1996) 118 FTR 1, approved on appeal (1996) 180 FTR 313, 25 Admin LR (3d) 305 (notes taken by members of the Canada Labour Relations Board in the course of quasi-judicial proceedings are not under the control of the Board itself).

57 *University of Newcastle upon Tyne v Information Commissioner and BUAV* [2011] UKUT 185 (AAC) at [23]-[28] approving *British Union for the Abolition of Vivisection v IC and Newcastle University*, FTT, 10 November 2010.

58 *University of Newcastle upon Tyne v Information Commissioner and BUAV* [2011] UKUT 185 (AAC) at [41]; *Voyias v IC and LB of Camden*, FTT, 24 January 2013 at [10]; *Whitehead v IC*, FTT, 29 April 2014 at [16]. The assessment must be made in relation to each piece of information, and not the document within which it is recorded taken as a whole: *Dept of Health v IC and Lewis* [2017] EWCA Civ 374, [2017] 1 WLR 3330 at [54].

59 *Chagos Refugees Group v IC and FCO*, FTT, 4 September 2012 at [61].

60 *Visser v IC and LB of Southwark*, FTT, 11 January 2013 at [29]. See, by way of example: *Dransfield v IC and Devon County Council*, FTT, 30 March 2011 at [17]; *Arkison v IC and Office of Fair Trading*, FTT, 29 September 2011 at [40]-[47]; *King's College Cambridge v IC and Lee*, FTT, 15 October 2013 at [24]-[28].

61 *Arkison v IC and Office of Fair Trading*, FTT, 29 September 2011 at [33].

62 EIR reg 3(2); EI(S)R reg 2(2). The information must thus be produced or received by means which are connected with the authority (such as by someone employed by the authority, acting in their professional rather than personal capacity) such that production or receipt is attributable to the authority: *Holland v IC and University of Cambridge*

a public authority without invitation and knowingly kept for any material length of time can probably be said to be held by the public authority. In short, information will not be 'held' by a public authority, it is suggested, where that information neither is nor has been created, sought, used or consciously retained by it. Thus, in the example given by the explanatory notes to the legislation,[63] a Minister's constituency papers would not be held by the department just because the Minister happens to keep them there.[64] It is quite possible for the same information to be held by more than one public authority. For example, if a document is sent by one public authority to another, but the first keeps a copy for itself, both public authorities will be holding the information comprised in the document. There is nothing to stop an applicant making a request to either or both public authorities for the same information.

20– 010 Held by or on behalf of others

Section 3(2) of the Act has two effects. First, to take out of the scope of 'documents held by a public authority' those documents which are held by it on behalf[65] of another person.[66] This issue arises in relation to personal emails that are sent through, but retained on, the server of a public authority.[67] Secondly, to bring within the scope of 'documents held by a public authority' information held by another person on behalf of that public authority.[68] Thus, where an authority uses a private data storage company to maintain its records,[69] or where information is processed by another on behalf of the authority,[70] that information will be treated as being held by the authority. The comparable provision in the EIR has the second effect, but not the first effect.[71] A third-party database capable of being accessed by a public authority, as

[2016] UKUT 260 (AAC) at [48].

63 Stationery Office, *Explanatory Notes, Freedom of Information Act 2000*, para 31.

64 This has been held to be the case in Australia: *Re Said and Dawkins* (1993) 30 ALD 242. The Court of Appeal has held, however, that a Ministerial diary can be held by the department even if the Minister himself is replaced in so far as such a diary is maintained by the department at least in part for its own benefit: *Dept of Health v IC and Lewis* [2017] EWCA Civ 374, [2017] 1 WLR 3330 at [55]-[57].

65 The phrase 'on behalf of' suggests an agency relationship between the public authority and the person for whom the information is held. Information held by a public authority on behalf of another person is only outside FOIA s 1 if it is held solely on behalf of the other person. If the information is held to any extent on behalf of the public authority itself, that public authority 'holds' the information within the meaning of FOIA: *University of Newcastle upon Tyne v Information Commissioner and BUAV* [2011] UKUT 185 (AAC) at [21]-[22], approving *British Union for the Abolition of Vivisection v IC and Newcastle University*, FTT, 10 November 2010. This results in FOIA s 3(2) having a very wide operation: *University of Newcastle upon Tyne v Information Commissioner and BUAV* [2011] UKUT 185 (AAC) at [41]. See further the Information Commissioner's Guidance on Information held by a public authority for the purposes of FOIA at paras 7-25.

66 Each government department is treated as a separate person: FOIA s 81(1); EIR reg 3(5).

67 In *Voyias v IC and LB of Camden*, FTT, 24 January 2013 the Tribunal held that emails received or sent by a local authority councillor on his local authority email address was held by the local authority solely on behalf of the councillor and to any extent on behalf of the local authority itself. Such information would be sufficiently connected to the local authority only where 'the emails arrive by virtue of a function the councillor performs by virtue of being a councillor' and this 'depends on whether the function is performed [by the Councillor] in any way on behalf of the Council.' at [23(e)]. Thus, emails that relate 'purely to private correspondence' or a councillor's trustee work was not held by the public authority [23].

68 As to which see *Jeffs v IC and Dept of Transport*, FTT, 12 August 2014 at [21]-[25] ('factors such as ownership of the information, control over it, access to it and responsibility for storing it may all be relevant considerations, but none of them, by themselves, are determinative, and there is no legal test as such to be applied'); *King's College Cambridge v IC and Lee*, FTT, 15 October 2013 at [24]-[28] (consideration of whether there was a legal or equitable basis for requiring the other person to supply the information). See further the Information Commissioner's Guidance on Information held by a public authority for the purposes of FOIA at paras 28-34.

69 See Stationery Office, Explanatory Notes, Freedom of Information Act 2000, para 31. See, for example: *Francis v IC and South Essex Partnership Foundation NHS Trust*, IT, 21 July 2008 at [21]-[38]; *Tuckley v IC and Birmingham City Council*, IT, 28 February 2008 at [24]-[32].

70 House of Commons, *Public Administration—Third Report* (Cm 4355, 1999) Annex 6, para 6 (see Ch 1 n 68).

71 EIR reg 3(2); EI(S)R reg 2(2).

well as by others, is not information held by the public authority.[72] The Act does not expressly deal with the situation of a public authority that has contracted with a person who is not a public authority for the provision of goods or services to that public authority. Such a contract may include the provision of services that would otherwise be carried out by the public authority itself: for example, occupational health services in connection with the public authority's employees. It is not a normal incident of the performance of such a contract that each party to the contract is obliged to share with the other party the information generated by that party in the performance of its contractual obligations. Information acquired or generated by a person with whom a public authority contracts will not, in the absence of some special contractual provision, be held 'on behalf of' the public authority.[73]

20– 011 The relevant moment

The information which is to be communicated, or to have its existence disclosed, is the information held at the time when the request is received, irrespective of the date at which the information was recorded or came to be held by the public authority.[74] FOIA and the EIR are to this extent retrospective.[75] In the case of a request under the Act, the public authority is not obliged when answering a request to consider information that is first held or recorded after the receipt of the request, even though this information answers the terms of the request.[76] It follows that a request under the Act which is specifically expressed to apply to information of a particular description that may, after receipt of the request, come to be held or recorded by the public authority, is ineffective.[77] In relation to a request under the Regulations, where a public authority first holds information answering the terms of the request after the request is received, the public authority may refuse to disclose that information only if in all the circumstances of the case the public interest in refusing to do so outweighs the public interest in disclosing the information.[78] Where an appeal is lodged against a decision of a public

72 *Marlow v IC*, IT, 1 June 2006 (Lexis Nexis Butterworths legal information database not information held by a public authority that had access to it).

73 *Chagos Refugees Group v IC and FCO*, FTT, 4 September 2012 at [55]-[68], dealing with draft prepared by an external consultant (see [14] and [64]), where the Tribunal held that:

> ... any copies of drafts which the consultants retained after the conclusion of their appointment would be for their own records, as would their copies of letters written. It is very common for professional advisers to keep their own copies of drafts, letters or final reports for a period of time, in case of any future dispute over fees or over the quality of the work. The consultants were free to destroy or delete such copies as they might wish, without asking the FCO. That there were restrictions on the consultants' right to use or disclose the information which they kept is not to the point. The existence of the restrictions does not mean that the information was kept on behalf of the FCO.

74 FOIA s 1(4); FOI(S)A s 1(4); EIR reg 12(4)(a); EI(S)R reg 10(4)(a). Under FOIA the Tribunal has no power on an appeal to require a public authority to disclose information first held by that public authority after its receipt of the request: *OGC v IC* [2008] EWHC 774 (Admin), [2010] QB 98 at [105]-[109]. Also, if a public authority has shredded the requested information before a request for that information is received, the request may be refused on that basis: *Mitchell v IC*, IT, 10 October 2005. Similarly, *Harper v IC and Royal Mail Group plc*, IT, 15 November 2005 at [17].

75 In relation to the FOIA, this was confirmed by the Home Secretary during the passage of the Bill through the House of Commons: Hansard HC vol 340 col 728 (7 December 1999). Beyond this, the Act is not retrospective: *Mitchell v IC*, IT, 10 October 2005 at [14]. The position is the same in Canada and New Zealand. Only limited retrospectivity is granted by the Freedom of Information Act 1982 (Cth of Aust) s 12(2) and the Freedom of Information Act 2014 (Ireland) s 11(4).

76 FOIA s 1(4); EIR reg 12(4)(a); EI(S)R reg 10(4)(a). The wording in the FOI(S)A s 1(4) is slightly different, stating that any such amendment or deletion may be made before the information is given. In addition, the Scottish Act provides that the requested information is not, by virtue of s 1(4), to be destroyed before it can be given unless the circumstances are such that it is not reasonably practicable to prevent such destruction from occurring: s 1(5).

77 As has been generally held under the Australian Act: *Murtagh v Federal Commissioner of Taxation* (1984) 1 AAR 419, 54 ALR 313; *Re Edelsten and Australian Federal Police* (1985) 4 AAR 220.

78 EIR reg 12(4)(a) in conjunction with reg 12(1)(a), and EI(S)R reg 10(4)(a) in conjunction with reg 10(1)(a). This does not permit an applicant to make ongoing requests, but will cover the situation where the public authority has first

authority, the appeal body will be concerned with the information held by the public authority at the time of the request, and not at the time of the appeal. The receipt of a request does not, however, require the public authority to take a 'snapshot' of the information held by it at the time of the receipt of the request. The Act specifically contemplates that a public authority might, in the time between receipt of a request and determination of that request, legitimately have sought to amend or delete information answering the terms of the request. Where such amendment or deletion has taken place, the public authority is not obliged to answer, but may answer, the request so far as the deleted or pre-amendment information is concerned.[79] Nevertheless, a public authority must be careful in amending or deleting information caught by the terms of a request. If a public authority deletes information as the result of its routine application of a pre-existing practice (eg the 6-monthly bulk deletion of email of more than a certain age), then, if that deletion occurs after receipt of a request but before the last date for compliance, that is a matter that may be taken into account under s 1(4) in deciding what information is held by the public authority.[80] If, on the other hand, a public authority, after receiving a request for information but before the date for compliance, decides to cull some of the information that it holds (which includes information covered by the terms of the request), the information deleted almost certainly cannot be taken into account under s 1(4) in deciding what information is held by the public authority.[81] Even in the former case, the deletion of information after receipt of the request may result in the public authority being required to make a greater effort to try to recover the 'deleted' information.[82]

20– 012 Alteration etc of records

The Freedom of Information Act 2000 does not impose an obligation on a public authority to keep information.[83] However, it is a criminal offence to alter, deface, block, erase, destroy or conceal any record[84] held by a public authority with the intention of preventing the disclosure by that authority of all or any part of the information, to the communication of which the applicant would have been entitled.[85] This applies to the public authority itself (but not a government department or the Welsh Government)[86] as well as to any person who is employed by, is an officer of, or is subject to the direction of that authority.[87] A prosecution for this offence, which is triable summarily only, can only be brought by the Information Commissioner

held information after receipt of the request but before making its decision or decision on review. It would also appear to permit the Commissioner and the Tribunal to deal with information that is first held by the public authority after it makes its decision.

79 There is no such let-out in the EIR.

80 *Harper v IC and Royal Mail Group plc*, IT, 15 November 2005 at [17].

81 *Harper v IC and Royal Mail Group plc*, IT, 15 November 2005 at [17].

82 *Harper v IC and Royal Mail Group plc*, IT, 15 November 2005 at [18], [27]. See further: *Whitehead v IC*, FTT, 29 April 2014 at [16].

83 *Babar v IC and British Council*, IT, 14 November 2007 at [33]. However, a public authority is under a duty to comply with the Code of Practice issued under FOIA s 46, Part 1 of which deals with records management.

84 Note the reference is to a 'record' rather than 'information'.

85 FOIA s 77; FOI(S)A s 65; EIR reg 19(1); EI(S)R reg 19(1). Destruction of material before the FOIA came into force will not offend this provision: *Mitchell v IC*, IT, 10 October 2005.

86 FOIA s 81(3). However, this only applies to the Government department itself. Section 77 applies to a person in the public service of the Crown as it does to any other person: s 81(3). In Scotland, the exemption is for the Scottish Parliament, the Parliamentary Corporation and the Scottish Administration, although again this immunity does not extend to members of staff of these entities or persons acting on their behalf: FOI(S)A s 68. In relation to environmental information, EIR reg 19(2), (5); EI(S)R reg 19(2), (4).

87 FOIA s 77(2); FOI(S) s 65(2); EIR reg 19(2); EI(S)R reg 19(2).

or with the consent of the Director of Public Prosecutions.[88] The maximum fine is level five on the standard scale.[89]

3. PERSONS WITH RIGHTS

20– 013 Types of legal person

The rights conferred by s 1 of FOIA are rights conferred upon any 'person'.[90] The term 'person' extends to any body of persons corporate or incorporate,[91] so that companies, clubs and associations are able to rely on the Acts.

20– 014 Territoriality of the rights

It is a principle of statutory interpretation that Parliament does not assert or assume jurisdiction that goes beyond the limits established by the common consent of nations. Provided that its language admits, an Act of Parliament is to be applied so as not to be inconsistent with the comity of nations or with the established principles of public international law.[92] The principle of comity between nations requires that each sovereign state should be left to govern its own territory.[93] Thus, while words in a statute may be expressed in universally applicable language, the rebuttable presumption is that Parliament is concerned with the conduct of persons taking place within the territories to which the Act extends, and with no other conduct.[94] In relation to rights conferred and obligations imposed by a statute, the presumption operates to limit these rights and obligations to those persons within the country at the time at which the right is sought to be exercised.[95] There is little within FOIA suggest that the presumption against extra-territoriality was intended to be rebutted.[96] While the extra-territorial application of the Act

---

88 FOIA s 77(4); EIR reg 19(4). In Northern Ireland, it is the consent of the Director of Public Prosecutions for Northern Ireland which is necessary. FOI(S)A and the EI(S)R contain no limitation.

89 FOIA s 77(3); FOI(S)A s 65(3); EIR reg 19(3); EI(S)R reg 19(3).

90 The position is the same under the FOI(S)A, the EIR and the EI(S)R.

91 'Person' includes a body of persons corporate or unincorporated: Interpretation Act 1978 s 5 and Sch 1. It can include a committee: *Davey v Shawcroft* [1948] 1 All ER 827.

92 See *Halsbury's Laws of England*, 2018, vol 96, para 757.

93 *AG v Prince Ernest Augustus of Hanover* [1957] AC 436 at 462; *Gaudiya Mission v Brahmachary* [1998] Ch 341.

94 *Lawson v Serco* [2006] UKHL 3, [2006] 1 All ER 823, [2006] ICR 250; *Clark (Inspector of Taxes) v Oceanic Contractors Inc* [1983] 2 AC 130 at 144-145; *Al Sabah v Grupo Torras SA* [2005] UKPC 1, [2005] 2 AC 333 at [13]; *Agassi v Robinson (Inspector of Taxes)* [2006] UKHL 23, [2006] 1 WLR 1380 at [16] and [20]; *R (Al-Skeini) v SS for Defence* [2007] UKHL 26, [2008] 1 AC 153 at [11] and [44]-[55].

95 *Jefferys v Boosey* (1854) 4 HL Cas 815 (copyright given by the Copyright Act 1709 to 'the author of any book' included only authors who were British subjects or were aliens resident in the country); *Tomalin v Pearson & Son Ltd* [1909] 2 KB 61 (where it was held that the Workmen's Compensation Act 1906, which provided for compensation to be paid 'if in any employment personal injury by accident arising out of and in the course of the employment is caused to any workman', did not apply to an English workman employed by an English company sent to carry out work in Malta); cf *Howgate v Bagnall* [1951] 1 KB 265, dealing with the Personal Injuries (Emergency Provisions) Act 1939.

96 In the United States, foreign citizens, partnerships, corporations, associations, states and state agencies, and foreign or domestic governments could until very recently apply: 5 USC 551(2): see §51– 003. In Australia, the Freedom of Information Act 1982 is expressed to give every person a right of access. This has been held to extend to a foreign corporation: *Re Lordsvale Finance Ltd and Department of the Treasury* (1985) 3 AAR 301, AAT: see §51– 011. Section 12(1) of the Official Information Act 1982 (New Zealand) enables citizens, permanent residents and persons in New Zealand and companies incorporated or with a place of business in New Zealand to make a request for official information: see §51– 018. Section 4 of the Access to Information Act 1985 (Canada) gives Canadian citizens and permanent residents a right of access to records under the control of a government institution: see §51– 026. The review of the Act recommended that the Act be amended to provide that any person has a right of access: Government of Canada, *Report of the Access to Information Review Task Force* (June 2002), p 19.

would not encroach upon the sovereignty of another state, it would confer rights on people all over the world who have little or no connection with the United Kingdom. Although FOIA will certainly extend to confer rights on a person in Scotland, it is doubtful whether FOI(S)A extends to confer rights on a person in England, Wales or Northern Ireland, as the territorial limits of the Acts of the Scottish Parliament are the boundaries of Scotland. Nevertheless, the presumption against extra-territoriality is unlikely to make much practical difference, as a foreign applicant can always engage an undisclosed local agent to make the request. Equally, in the case of a natural person, there is nothing to stop such a person coming into the jurisdiction for the purpose of making a request. It follows that a non-resident present in the United Kingdom, however fleetingly, is entitled to make a request under FOIA.[97]

20– 015 Convicted criminals

On the face of the Act, a convicted criminal and a law-abiding citizen are equally entitled to rely on the rights conferred by FOIA. Depending upon the terms of the request, however, it may be that a request from the former will be more readily characterised as vexatious. The position in the comparative jurisdictions, none of which excepts convicted criminals, varies. In the USA, exceptions to the right of access have sometimes,[98] but not always,[99] been made in the case of criminals. In Australia, it has been held that the fact that a person had convictions for rape and armed robbery did not prevent him from applying for access to documents under the legislation.[100]

20– 016 Children

The Freedom of Information (Scotland) Act 2002 provides that where a question falls to be determined as to the legal capacity of a person who has not attained the age of sixteen years to exercise any right conferred by any provision of this Act, any such person is to be taken to have that capacity who has a general understanding of what it means to exercise the right.[101] A child over 12 is presumed to have this understanding.[102] FOIA[103] does not make any mention of applications by children and the Interpretation Act 1978 is silent on the question whether a reference to a 'person' is confined to persons of full age and capacity.[104] In both cases, any

---

The Freedom of Information Act 2014 (Ireland) gives every person a right of access to records held by a public body: see §51– 035.

97 Examples of recently-arrived persons enjoying statutory rights include: *R v Inhabitants of Eastbourne* (1803) 4 East 103; *R v Hillingdon London Borough Council, ex p Streeting* [1980] 1 WLR 1425; *Re Islam* [1983] 1 AC 688. In a speech by Lord Falconer (Constitutional Affairs Secretary and Lord Chancellor) to the International Conference of Information Commissioners, Manchester, 22 May 2006, he stated: 'From its introduction on 1 January 2005 any individual, from anywhere in the world, can submit requests to public bodies in the UK.' He did not state whether those individuals had to be within the UK at the time of making the request.

98 *Doyle v US Department of Justice*, 668 F 2d 1365 (DC Cir 1981) (fugitive not entitled to enforcement of the Freedom of Information Act access provisions because he could not expect judicial aid in obtaining government records related to the sentence he was evading).

99 *O'Rourke v US Department of Justice*, 684 F Supp 716 (DDC 1988) and *Doherty v US Department of Justice*, 596 F Supp 423 (SDNY 1984) (convicted criminal and fugitive from his own country and undergoing US deportation proceedings qualified as 'any person').

100 *Re Ward and Secretary, Department of Industry and Commerce* (1983) 8 ALD 324.

101 FOI(S)A s 69(1). There is no equivalent in the EI(S)R.

102 FOI(S)A s 69(2).

103 And the EIR and the EI(S)R.

104 In *Wallace v Health Commission of Victoria* [1985] VR 403 the Supreme Court of Victoria held, in relation to a request made under the Freedom of Information Act 1982 (Vic) by a person lacking mental capacity, that it was a prerequisite to enforcement of the right of access that an application is made which is the conscious voluntary act of the person making it so that the person making it fully understood the nature and significance of the act and wished it to be done in order to obtain access to documents. Similarly, in a different context, see *R v Oldham*

limitation can readily be circumvented by the application being made by someone on the minor's behalf.

20– 017 Applicant's motives

An applicant's motives in making a request are irrelevant and so cannot be demanded by a public authority.[105] Nor does the absence of any actual or apparent motive for the request provide any basis for refusing it.[106] The Government considered an amendment to the Bill making this clear, but concluded that it was unnecessary:[107]

> It is perfectly legitimate for an official to have a discussion with the applicant with a view to helping the applicant to refine the request he or she is making so as to use better the provisions of the Bill. That is only for the purpose of assistance, not for examining motive with a view to determining whether to proceed with the request because that is quite irrelevant in the context of the Bill as drafted.[108]

Having said this, the absence of any apparent motive for a request may be relevant in considering whether a request is vexatious or in determining whether the public authority's response has been reasonable.[109] Where it is apparent that the applicant has a legitimate motive for making the request, that may be relevant in balancing the public interest for the purpose of qualified exemptions.[110]

4. BODIES SUBJECT TO FREEDOM OF INFORMATION ACT

20– 018 Exhaustive definition

The rights conferred by FOIA are only exercisable against 'public authorities'.[111] These are defined to mean:

Metropolitan Borough Council, ex p Garlick [1993] AC 509 at 520, although this may be explained on the basis that the wider interpretation of 'person' would have enabled a circumvention of restricted rights in the Housing Act 1985.

105 *S v IC and The General Register Office*, IT, 9 May 2007 at [80]; *Berend v Information Commission and LB of Richmond upon Thames*, IT, 12 July 2007 at [46]; *Betts v IC*, IT, 19 May 2008 at [29], [43]. This is conventional in freedom of information legislation. Thus, in the USA, see *United States Department of Justice v Reporters Committee for Freedom of the Press*, 489 US 749 (1989); *Durns v Bureau of Prisons*, 804 F 2d 701 (DC Cir 1986) ('Congress granted the scholar and the scoundrel equal rights of access to agency records'); *Forsham v Califano*, 587 F 2d 1128 (DC Cir 1978); *O'Rourke v Department of Justice*, 684 F Supp 716 (DDC 1988). In Australia, see *Re Green and Australian and Overseas Telecommunications Corp* (1992) 28 ALD 655; *Re Russell Island Development Association Inc and Department of Primary Industry and Energy* (1994) 33 ALD 683; *Re Collie and Deputy Commissioner of Taxation* (1997) 45 ALD 556. And in Canada, see *Canada (Information Commissioner) v Canada (Commissioner of the Royal Canadian Mounted Police)*, [2003] 1 SCR 66 at [33]; *Intercontinental Packers Ltd v Canada (Minister of Agriculture)* (1987) 14 FTR 142; *Prud'homme v Canada (Canadian International Development Agency)* (1994) 85 FTR 302.

106 A lack of motive does not make a request 'vexatious'. However, a reasonable motive may prevent a request that would otherwise be vexatious from being so: *Adair v IC*, IT, 14 January 2010 at [40]-[42]; *Gowers v IC and LB of Camden*, IT, 13 May 2008; *Craven v IC*, IT, 13 May 2008; *IC v Devon CC and Dransfield* [2012] UKUT 440 (AAC) at [34].

107 Hansard HL vol 617 col 921 (17 October 2000) (Minister of State, Cabinet Office, Lord Falconer).

108 Hansard HL vol 617 col 921 (17 October 2000) (Minister of State, Cabinet Office, Lord Falconer). See also the Information Commissioner's Guidance on the Duty to Provide Advice and Assistance (section 16), which at para 15 states that that duty 'is not a way for a public authority to establish a motive for the request.' See similarly the Information Commissioner's Guidance on the Consideration of the Identity or Motives of the Applicant at para 4.

109 For example, under the FOIA ss 17(3) and 22(1)(c); EIR reg 12(4)(b); EI(S)R reg 10(4)(b).

110 *DTI v IC*, IT, 10 November 2006 at [53]; *Hepple v IC and Durham CC*, FTT, 26 February 2014 at [36]-[37].

111 Similarly the EIR, although the definition extends further: see §20– 026. Those rights conferred by the FOI(S)A and the EI(S)R are only exercisable against Scottish public authorities. In the case of the EI(S)R, the definition of Scottish public authorities extends further: see §20– 033.

(1) any body,[112] person or office holder which or who is listed in Schedule 1 to the Act;[113]
(2) any body, person or office holder designated by order of the Secretary of State or the Minister for the Cabinet Office;[114] or
(3) a publicly owned company.[115]

These categories are exhaustive[116] and have been estimated to cover in excess of 50,000 bodies.[117]

20–019 Listed public authorities

Schedule 1 to FOIA[118] provides the core list of those bodies, persons and office-holders who are deemed to be public authorities and against whom the s 1 rights may be exercised. These bodies are also subject to the EIR.[119] The Schedule is divided into seven numbered parts:

(I) GENERAL: This includes all government departments,[120] both Houses of Parliament,[121] the Northern Ireland Assembly and the National Assembly for Wales, and most of the armed forces.[122] A Member of Parliament is not a public authority. Accordingly, information held by an individual Member of Parliament does not come within the scope of the Act (eg a Member's casework file). However, information held by departments within the House's administration service, by Select Committees, by the Parliamentary Archive or by the private office of Mr Speaker will be information held by the House of Commons.[123] A government department is defined to include any

112 Body includes an unincorporated association: FOIA s 84; FOI(S)A s 73.

113 FOIA s 3(1)(a)(i); FOI(S)A s 3(1)(a)(i). These are considered at §§20–019 and 20–027.

114 FOIA s 3(1)(a)(ii); FOI(S)A s 3(1)(a)(ii); EIR reg 2(2). These are considered at §§20–023 and 20–031.

115 FOIA s 3(1)(b); FOI(S)A s 3(1)(b). These are considered at §§20–024 and 20–032.

116 The Home Office Freedom of Information Unit stated during the passage of the Bill: 'Because FOI applications are made direct by a person to an organisation, there needs to be absolute clarity as to whether any particular organisation is covered by the legislation. It is therefore necessary to spell out either in the Bill itself, or in an order, those organisations which are public authorities for the purpose of the legislation.' — House of Commons, *Public Administration—Third Report* (Cm 4355, 1999) Annex 6, para 1 (see Ch 1 n 68). The importance of and rationale for this were acknowledged in *Sugar v BBC* [2009] UKHL 9, [2009] 1 WLR 430 at [56].

117 Government estimates have ranged from 50,000 (Hansard HC vol 347 col 883 (4 April 2000), Parliamentary Under-Secretary of State for the Home Department, Mr Mike O'Brien) to 88,000 (the Lord Chancellor's Advisory Group on Implementation of the Freedom of Information Act).

118 Which now includes those authorities added by various statutory instruments: see §20–020.

119 EIR reg 2(2)(b).

120 Each government department is to be treated as a person separate from any other government department: FOIA s 81; EIR reg 3(5). However, a government department cannot rely upon this to claim a duty of confidence arising with respect to another government department so as to rely upon the exemption in s 41 (information provided in confidence): FOIA s 81(2). There is no equivalent provision under the FOI(S)A, the EIR or the EI(S)R. For information provided in confidence, see Ch 25.

121 The Houses of Parliament are not bodies corporate or any other kind of legal person. When dissolved by Her Majesty (for example, before a general election), they cease to exist. Nevertheless, the Houses of Parliament do not suspend rights of access when Parliament has been dissolved: *House of Commons v IC*, IT, 9 August 2007 at [34], [38]. Proceedings under the Act are brought against The Corporate Officer of the House of Commons by virtue of The Parliamentary Corporate Bodies Act 1992 s 2: *House of Commons v IC*, IT, 9 August 2007 at [42].

122 The only exceptions are the special forces (meaning those units of the armed forces of the Crown the maintenance of whose capabilities is the responsibility of the Director of Special Forces or which are for the time being subject to the operational command of that Director: FOIA s 84) and any unit or part of a unit which is for the time being required by the Secretary of State to assist the Government Communications Headquarters in the exercise of its functions: FOIA Sch 1 Pt I para 6. As to the special exemption granted in relation to information supplied by these, and other, security bodies, to a public authority, see Ch 17.

123 *House of Commons v IC*, IT, 9 August 2007 at [38], [42]-[44]. The House of Commons, as a body of Members of Parliament, is distinct from The Corporate Officer of the House of Commons (established by the Parliamentary Corporate Bodies Act 1992 s 2) and from the Commission of the House of Commons (established by the House of Commons (Administration) Act 1978), although information held by them may, by virtue of s 3(2)(b), be treated

body or authority exercising statutory functions on behalf of the Crown,[124] so that information held by such bodies will be subject to the Act.[125] Notable examples are: HMRC, the Charity Commission, the Crown Estate, the Food Standards Agency, the Health and Safety Executive, ACAS, the Central Arbitration Committee, the Gas and Electricity Markets Authority, the Water Services Regulation Authority, the Statistics Board and the Civil Aviation Authority.[126] However, the Security Service, the Secret Intelligence Service, the Government Communications Headquarters, the National Crime Agency, the Welsh Government, the Scottish Parliament, any part of the Scottish Administration, the Scottish Parliamentary Corporate Body, and any Scottish public authority with mixed or no reserved functions (within the meaning of the Scotland Act 1998) are excluded from the definition[127] and are therefore exempt from the operation of the Act.[128] Courts are not public authorities within the meaning of the Act.[129] However, the Court Service is a public authority.[130]

(II) LOCAL GOVERNMENT: This Part contains a list of over 30 types of local government bodies in England and Wales, including the Greater London Authority, county

---

as being held by the House of Commons.

124 FOIA s 84.

125 This was confirmed by the Government during the Bill's passage by the Parliamentary Under-Secretary of State: Hansard HL vol 619 col 231 (14 November 2000) (Lord Bassam).

126 Commissioners for Revenue and Customs Act 2005 s 1(4); Charities Act 2011 s 13(3); Crown Estate Act 1961 s 1(1); Food Standards Act 1999 s 1(3); Health and Safety at Work etc Act 1974 s 10(3); Trade Union and Labour Relations (Consolidation) Act 1992 ss 247(3) and 259(2); Utilities Act 2000 s 1(2); Water Industry Act 1991 s 1A(2); Statistics and Registration Service Act 2007 s 2(1). The Civil Aviation Authority acts on behalf of the Crown in relation to only certain of its functions, and so FOIA will only apply to information held by it relating to those functions: Civil Aviation Act 1982 s 20(2). In the absence of express statutory provision, determining whether a body or authority exercises statutory functions on behalf of the Crown will turn on the degree of control which the Crown, through its ministers, may exercise over it in the performance of its duties: *Fox v Government of Newfoundland* [1898] AC 667 at 672; *Metropolitan Meat Industry Board v Sheedy* [1927] AC 899 at 905; *Bank voor Handel en Scheepvaart NV v Administrator of Hungarian Property* [1954] AC 584 at 616, [1954] 1 All ER 969 at 982. The fact that a minister of the Crown appoints the members of such a body or authority, is entitled to require them to give him information and is entitled to give them directions of a general nature, does not make that body or authority his agent. Similarly, the fact that the body or authority is controlled to some extent by a government department does not mean that it acts on behalf of the Crown: that is particularly so where that body or authority has commercial functions: *Tamlin v Hannaford* [1950] 1 KB 18, [1949] 2 All ER 327. However, it will be easier to conclude that a body or authority exercises statutory functions on behalf of the Crown where its functions are not commercial but are connected with matters which are conventionally the domain of government, such as the defence of the realm: *London County Territorial and Auxiliary Forces Association v Nichols* [1949] 1 KB 35 at 47, [1948] 2 All ER 432 at 434; *Territorial Forces Association v Philpot* [1947] 2 All ER 376.

127 FOIA s 84.

128 The Scottish Parliament, the Scottish Administration, the Scottish Parliamentary Corporate Body, and any Scottish public authority with mixed functions or no reserved functions are, of course, subject instead to the FOI(S)A.

129 *Mitchell v IC*, IT, 10 October 2005 at [31], although the point was not necessary for the decision. In *MoJ v IC*, IT, 29 July 2008 at [32], a differently constituted Information Tribunal held that *Mitchell v IC* was wrongly decided, though not on this point. In *DBERR v IC and Peninsula Business Services Ltd*, IT, 28 April 2009 at [47] the Information Tribunal held that an Employment Tribunal was not a "public authority."

130 As it falls within the definition of 'government department' in FOIA s 84 (by virtue of being a body that exercises statutory functions on behalf of the Crown) and, by virtue of Sch 1, Pt I. The courts, as the bodies exercising the judicial power of the State, have a personality distinct from that of the Court Service. Requests made of the Department of Constitutional Affairs for audio records of a criminal trial in the Crown Court and the Family Division of the High Court held by companies "as agents of HMCS and MoJ" were not rejected on the basis that the body holding the information was not a public authority: *Ministry of Justice v IC*, IT, 29 July 2008. Similarly, in *Institute of Chartered Accountants of England and Wales v IC and MoJ*, FTT, 8 December 2011 the Tribunal treated HMCS as being a public authority for the purposes of FOIA. Court files held by the Court Service (ie those holding pleadings, applications, witness statements, court orders, judgments etc) will generally be held by the Court Service on behalf of the court itself, and so (as an executive agency of a government department) will be within the operation of the Act: FOIA ss 3(2)(a) and 84 (definition of 'government department') and Sch 1 Part 1; FOI(S)A s 3(2)(a)(i).

councils, London borough councils, district councils, parish councils, county borough councils, community councils, fire authorities, National Parks authorities, Transport for London, as well as all Northern Ireland district councils.

(III) THE NATIONAL HEALTH SERVICE: This covers core NHS bodies in England, Wales and Northern Ireland, such as health authorities, special health authorities, NHS trusts, community health councils and so forth. It also extends to individual GPs, dentists, opticians and pharmacists, but only in respect of information relating to the provision of medical services under the NHS.

(IV) MAINTAINED SCHOOLS AND OTHER EDUCATIONAL INSTITUTIONS: Governing bodies of all maintained schools,[131] as well as further and higher education institutions, are all included in this Part. It was suggested by the Government in Parliament that information about institutions which do not have governing bodies, such as pupil referral units, will be accessible through the local education authority directly responsible for such institutions.[132] (The General Teaching Council for Wales, the Higher Education Funding Council for Wales, Her Majesty's Chief Inspector of Education and Training in Wales and the School Teachers Review Body are all listed in Part VI).

(V) POLICE: This Part covers all police authorities in England, Wales and Northern Ireland, the chief officer of police forces (including the Chief Constable of the Royal Police Service of Northern Ireland), the British Transport Police, the Ministry of Defence Police and any person (not otherwise covered by Sch 1) who has the statutory power to nominate individuals for appointment as special constables by magistrates (but only in respect of information relating to this function). (The Independent Office for Police Conduct listed in Part VI).

(VI) OTHER PUBLIC BODIES AND OFFICES: GENERAL: This Part enumerates over 400 miscellaneous public bodies and offices, ranging from the Advisory Committee on Conscientious Objectors and the Wool Marketing Board to the OSO Board and the Zoos Forum. Some are well known, such as the Health and Safety Executive, the Arts Council and the Environment Agency, whereas others such as the Unlinked Anonymous Serosurveys Steering Group, the Marshall Aid Commemoration Commission and the Spongiform Encephalopathy Advisory Committee are less so. The BBC, Channel 4 and Sianel Pedwar Cymru (S4C) are included (but only in respect of information held for purposes other than those of journalism, art or literature),[133] as well as the Broadcasting Standards Commission, the Independent Television Commission, the Theatres Trust and most of the country's main museums and galleries. The Bank of England is included, but information relating to its functions with respect to monetary policy, financial operations intended to support financial institutions for the purposes of maintaining stability, and the provision of private banking and related services is all excluded. Bodies omitted include the British Board of Film Classification, those running prisons under contract, the Press Complaints Commission, and those assigned responsibility for running the railways.

(VII) OTHER PUBLIC BODIES AND OFFICES: NORTHERN IRELAND: This is a very similar list to that in Part (VI) above, containing over 100 bodies and offices which relate to Northern Ireland.

---

131 Within the meaning of the School Standards and Framework Act 1998 s 20(7): FOIA Sch 1 Pt I para 52.

132 Hansard HL vol 617 col 946 (17 October 2000) (Lord Falconer, Minister of State, Cabinet Office); cf FOIA Sch 1 Pt IV para 54.

133 In relation to determining whether a request for information falls within or outside the limits of operation, see §20–022.

20– 020 Adding public authorities

The Secretary of State for Justice[134] and the Minister for the Cabinet Office each have the power[135] to add to Sch 1 any body or holder of any office which satisfies two specified conditions.[136] The first specified condition is that the body or office is either (a) established by virtue of royal prerogative, an enactment or subordinate legislation,[137] or (b) is established in any other way by a Minister of the Crown (in his capacity as such), a government department or the Welsh Ministers, the First Minister for Wales or the Counsel General for the Welsh Government.[138] The second condition is (in the case of a body) that the body is wholly or partly constituted by appointment made by the Crown, a Minister of the Crown, a government department or the Welsh Ministers, the First Minister for Wales or the Counsel General for the Welsh Government,[139] or (in the case of an office) that appointments to the office are made by one of the same.[140] However, this power may not be exercised to add the Scottish Parliament, any part of the Scottish administration, the Scottish Parliamentary Corporate Body, or any Scottish public authority with mixed functions or no reserved functions (within the meaning of the Scotland Act 1998).[141] An order adding a public authority to Sch 1 in this way may relate to a specified person or office or to persons or offices falling within a specified description[142] and may list the new entry only in relation to information of a specified description.[143]

20– 021 Removing public authorities

The Secretary of State for Justice and the Minister for the Cabinet Office each have the power to limit any entry on Sch 1 to information of a specified description, as well as to remove any

---

[134] The FOIA originally referred to the 'Secretary of State' but all his functions under the Act were first transferred to the Lord Chancellor by the Transfer of Functions (Miscellaneous) Order 2001 SI 2001/3500 and then to the Secretary of State for Constitutional Affairs by the Secretary of State for Constitutional Affairs Order 2003 SI 2003/1887 and on 9 May 2007 to the Secretary of State for Justice under The Secretary of State for Justice Order 2007 SI 2007/2128. The Chancellor of the Duchy was given power to exercise these functions concurrently by the Transfer of Functions (Information and Public Records) Order 2015 SI 2015/1897, but his power was transferred to the Minister for the Cabinet Office by the Transfer of Functions (Elections, Referendums, Third Sector and Information) Order 2016 SI 2016/997.

[135] FOIA s 4(1). Where such an order relates to a body or office-holder whose functions are exercisable only or mainly in or as regards Wales, or to a Northern Ireland public authority, the Secretary of State or Minister must consult either the Welsh Ministers or the First Minister and deputy First Minister in Northern Ireland respectively: FOIA s 4(7). 'Northern Ireland public authority' means any public authority, other than the Northern Ireland Assembly or a Northern Ireland department, whose functions are exercisable only or mainly in or as regards Northern Ireland and relate only or mainly to transferred matters: FOIA s 84. 'Transferred matter' has the meaning given by s 4(1) of the Northern Ireland Act 1998: FOIA s 84. Such an order is subject to annulment in pursuance of a resolution of either House of Parliament: FOIA s 82(3).

[136] Eight dedicated orders have been made: Freedom of Information (Additional Public Authorities) Order 2002 SI 2002/2623 Freedom of Information (Additional Public Authorities) Order 2003 SI 2003/1882; (Additional Public Authorities) Order 2004 SI 2004/938; Freedom of Information (Additional Public Authorities) Order 2005 SI 2005/3593; Freedom of Information (Additional Public Authorities) Order 2008 SI 2008/1271; Freedom of Information (Additional Public Authorities) Order 2010 SI 2010/937; Freedom of Information (Additional Public Authorities) Order 2011 SI 2011/1041; Freedom of Information (Additional Public Authorities) Order 2018 SI 2018/173. In addition, other bodies have been added to Sch 1. These are brought within the EIR by the limb of the definition of 'public authority' in reg 2(2)(b)(ii).

[137] FOIA s 4(2)(a).

[138] FOIA s 4(2)(b).

[139] FOIA s 4(3)(a).

[140] FOIA s 4(3)(b).

[141] FOIA s 80.

[142] FOIA s 4(6). An example of this is found in Sch 1, Pt VI, 'any housing action trust established under Pt III of the Housing Act 1988.'

[143] FOIA s 7(2). For such partly-affected public authorities, see §20– 022.

such limitation.[144] Whilst the removal of a limitation is unlikely to be controversial (at least outside the body in question), the power to introduce limits would allow the Government to cut down the Act's scope so far as rights of access to particular information are concerned. Concern about this was expressed during the Bill's passage through Parliament and in response to a proposed amendment removing this power, and a direct question asking what the Government's intention was in conferring this, Lord Bassam, the Parliamentary Under-Secretary of State, Home Office, replied as follows:

> The power to amend the entries in Schedule 1 so as to limit them to specific types of information is necessary in order to ensure that the bodies listed at Schedule 1 are covered by the Freedom of Information Act only in respect of those activities which should properly be the subject of the obligations in the Bill. It is not the Government's [intention] to apply the Bill to information held for purposes in respect of which it would be inappropriate and damaging to apply freedom of information principles. Journalistic information held by public sector broadcasters or private banking information held by the Bank of England are two current examples of such information. Where we have identified information which needs to be protected in this way, we have amended the entry in Schedule 1 accordingly. However, we cannot be certain that any of the bodies listed may not change their functions in the future. For that reason, we need to make provision for a power to amend the entry if this should be deemed necessary. To that extent, clause 7(3) is a just-in-case provision.
>
> The noble Lord asked for an example, hypothetical or otherwise, and I am happy to try to provide one. The entry in Schedule 1 relating to the Bank of England is already limited to certain information. Should the Bank decide to add, say, an insurance provision to the services it provides to its private customers, that private activity which would relate to private customers would be brought within the scope of the Freedom of Information Act, unless an order was made to limit the entry in Schedule 1 specifically to exclude it.
>
> That is why the power in clause 7(3) is necessary. I hope that the noble Lord will accept the example I have given and feel able to withdraw his amendment.[145]

The Act provides that all such orders must be approved by a resolution of each House of Parliament.[146] A body or office-holder listed in Pts VI and VII of Sch 1 automatically ceases to be a public authority by virtue of its entry in the Schedule if it ceases to satisfy either of the two conditions specified above.[147] Where this happens, or where the body or office ceases to exist, the Secretary of State for Justice and the Minister for the Cabinet Office each have the power to amend Sch 1 to reflect this change,[148] described in Parliament as a 'form of housekeeping... necessary so that the lists may be routinely updated to remove dead wood.'[149]

---

144 FOIA s 7(3). In other words, a public authority can be turned into a 'partly affected' public authority and vice versa: see §20– 022.

145 Hansard HL vol 619 cols 182-183 (14 November 2000). Lord Mackay, who had tabled the amendment and asked the question, replied as follows: 'I am reasonably grateful for the answer. [Lord Bassam] set out a clear scenario and I hope that if the Secretary of State decides to go a good deal further a clever lawyer will be able to prevent him by using the courts and quoting what the noble Lord said and the example he gave. I am pleased to beg leave to withdraw my amendment.' — Hansard HL vol 619 col 183 (14 November 2000). See also the debate in the House of Commons, with Government pronouncements on very similar lines: Hansard HC vol 347 cols 871-890 (4 April 2000) (Mr Mike O'Brien, Parliamentary Under-Secretary of State for the Home Department).

146 FOIA s 82(2).

147 FOIA s 4(4). The two conditions are those in s 4(2)-(3), as to which see §20– 020.

148 FOIA s 4(5). But this is not necessary as the removal occurs automatically under s 4(4).

149 Hansard HL vol 617 col 952 (17 October 2000) (Lord Falconer, Minister of State, Cabinet Office). In contrast to other powers to add to or amend Sch 1 (see §§20– 020, 20– 021 and 20– 023), the FOIA requires only that such an order be laid before Parliament after being made: s 82(4). Orders removing public authorities are: Freedom of Information (Removal of References to Public Authorities) Order 2003 SI 2003/1883; Freedom of Information (Removal of References to Public Authorities) Order 2004 SI 2004/1641; Freedom of Information (Removal of References to Public Authorities) Order 2005 SI 2005/3594; Freedom of Information (Removal of References to Public Authorities) Order 2010 SI 2010/939; Freedom of Information (Removal of References to Public Authorities) Order 2011 SI 2011/1042; Freedom of Information (Removal of References to Public Authorities) Order 2018 SI 2018/185.

So long as a body or office continues to fulfil the two specified conditions,[150] however, it can only be removed from Sch 1 by means of further primary legislation.

20– 022 Part-affected public authorities

Some public authorities are listed in Sch 1 only in relation to information of a specified description.[151] In these cases, the rights conferred by FOIA do not apply to any other information held by that authority.[152] A partly-affected public authority is a public authority within the meaning of FOIA whatever the nature of the information held by it.[153] Once a request for information is made under the Act to a partly-affected public authority, the fact that it claims that the information is excluded under Schedule 1 does not mean that it thereby ceases to be a public authority under the Act.[154] The obligation of a partly-affected public authority under section 1 is to ascertain the extent to which the requested information that it holds is excluded in Schedule 1. If it is excluded, the public authority is entitled to reply that that part of the requested information does not form part of the information it holds, followed by the description of excluded information specified in Schedule 1.[155] Whether requested information is or is not within the exclusion is a question of law, for which there is only one correct answer.[156] The specified descriptions in Sch 1 vary in nature: in some cases the limiting characteristic is the capacity in which the public authority holds the information; in other cases it is the subject matter to which the information relates; and in others it is the purpose for which the information is held. Information falling within the excepted aspect of a public authority is treated as enjoying disapplication of the s 1(1) duties. One public authority in respect of which the Act has a limited operation is the BBC. It is listed in Part VI of Sch 1 to the Act as follows:

> The British Broadcasting Corporation, in respect of information held for purposes other than those of journalism, art or literature.

The same limitation applies to other public broadcasters.[157] Where information is held for mixed purposes, some of which are for excepted aspects of a partly-affected public authority and some of which are not, if to any significant degree the authority holds the information for

---

150 That is, those in FOIA s 4(2)-(3): see §20– 020.

151 For example: the Common Council of the City of London, in respect of information held in its capacity as a local authority, police authority or port health authority (Sch 1 Pt II para 9); the Sub-Treasurer of the Inner Temple or the Under-Treasurer of the Middle Temple, in respect of information held in his capacity as a local authority (Sch 1 Pt II para 9); any person providing primary medical services, primary dental services, general medical services, general dental services, general ophthalmic services or pharmaceutical services, etc under the NHS Act 2006, in respect of information relating to the provision of those services (Sch 1 Pt III paras 43A-45A); the Bank of England, in respect of information held for purposes other than those of its functions with respect to: (a) monetary policy, (b) financial operations intended to support financial institutions for the purposes of maintaining stability, and (c) the provision of private banking services and related services (Sch 1 Pt VI); and the Traffic Commissioners, in respect of information held by them otherwise than as a tribunal (Sch 1 Pt VI).

152 FOIA s 7(1). The Secretary of State for Justice and the Minister for the Cabinet Office each have the power, in relation to any entry in Sch 1, to introduce, remove or amend any such limitation: FOIA s 7(3). If such an order relates to the National Assembly for Wales or a Welsh public authority, which is a subsidiary of the Assembly Commission, the Welsh Government or a Welsh public authority which is not a subsidiary of the Assembly Commission, the Northern Ireland Assembly, or a Northern Ireland department or a Northern Ireland public authority, the Secretary of State or Minister must consult the Presiding Officer of the National Assembly for Wales, the First Minister for Wales, the Presiding Officer of the Northern Ireland Assembly, or the First Minister and deputy First Minister in Northern Ireland respectively before making such an order: FOIA s 7(4). As to the meaning of a 'Welsh public authority', see FOIA s 83. In any event, a draft of such an order must be laid before and approved by a resolution of each House of Parliament before it is made: FOIA s 82(2).

153 *Sugar v BBC* [2009] UKHL 9, [2009] 1 WLR 430, [2009] 4 All ER 111.

154 *Sugar v BBC* [2009] UKHL 9, [2009] 1 WLR 430, [2009] 4 All ER 111 at [90].

155 *Sugar v BBC* [2009] UKHL 9, [2009] 1 WLR 430, [2009] 4 All ER 111 at [33].

156 *Sugar v BBC* [2009] UKHL 9, [2009] 1 WLR 430, [2009] 4 All ER 111 at [53].

157 That is, Channel Four Television Corporation and Sianel Pedwar Cymru.

excepted aspects then it is not required to disclose that information, even if that information was held for other, possibly more important, purposes.[158] In determining whether information is held for the purpose of journalism, it must be directly related to those purposes: an immediate object of the body holding that information must be to use it for one of those purposes.[159] The term 'journalism' has been described as having a 'striking elasticity'[160] but that in the Freedom of Information Act it is 'used primarily to refer to output on news and current affairs.'[161] The phrase 'journalism, art or literature' has been held to cover the whole of the BBC's output in its 'mission' to inform, educate and entertain the public.[162] Similarly, financial information held for 'operational purposes' of a broadcaster is, it seems, not subject to the obligation to disclose.[163] Regardless of whether the requested information is outside the description in Schedule 1, the Information Commissioner has power to review the question whether the information is within the excepted aspect of a public authority and may issue a decision notice under s 50.[164]

20– 023 Designated public authorities

An entity not listed in Sch 1 nor capable of being added to that list by an order under s 4(1) may be designated by order as a public authority for the purposes of the Act if it appears to the Secretary of State for Justice or Minister for the Cabinet Office to exercise functions of a public nature or is providing under a contract made with a public authority any service whose provision is a function of that authority.[165] It is not necessary in this latter case that the contractor itself should be performing functions of a public nature.[166] The determination of what is and is not a 'function of a public nature' is a familiar one for the courts, being central to both judicial review and the Human Rights Act 1998.[167] When exercising this power, the Secretary of State for Justice or Minister for the Cabinet Office may designate a specified

---

158 *Sugar v BBC (No 2)* [2012] UKSC 4, [2012] 1 WLR 439, [2012] 2 All ER 509. Put another way, the phrase 'held for purposes other than' means 'held for purposes apart from or in addition to': *BBC v IC* [2009] EWHC 2348 (Admin), [2010] EMLR 6 at [62]. The question is not resolved by a consideration of the predominant purpose for which the information is held: *BBC v IC* [2009] EWHC 2348 (Admin), [2010] EMLR 6 at [63]. See further: *University and College Admissions Service v IC and Lord Lucas* [2014] UKUT 0557 (AAC) at [53]-[55].

159 *BBC v Sugar (No 2)* [2012] UKSC 4, [2012] 1 WLR 439 at [42], [67], [83], [106]. See further: *Tomlinson v IC and BBC*, FTT, 6 July 2015.

160 *BBC v Sugar (No 2)* [2012] UKSC 4, [2012] 1 WLR 439 at [38].

161 *BBC v Sugar (No 2)* [2012] UKSC 4, [2012] 1 WLR 439 at [70].

162 *BBC v Sugar (No 2)* [2012] UKSC 4, [2012] 1 WLR 439 at [70]. It seems that no inquiry is necessary whether its output succeeds in any of those goals.

163 *BBC v IC* [2009] EWHC 2348 (Admin), [2010] EMLR 6 at [86]-[87]. This is a surprising outcome for a publicly-funded body given the objects of the FOIA. But see *BBC v Sugar (No 2)* [2012] UKSC 4, [2012] 1 WLR 439, [2012] EMLR 17, [2012] 2 All ER 509 at [42].

164 *Sugar v BBC* [2009] UKHL 9, [2009] 1 WLR 430, [2009] 4 All ER 111 at [23], [36]-[37], [73], [91].

165 FOIA s 5(1). A draft of such an order must be laid before and approved by a resolution of each House of Parliament before it is made: FOIA s 82(2). Such a draft is not to be treated for the purposes of the Standing Orders of either House of Parliament as a hybrid instrument: s 82(5). As with orders under s 4(1) (as to which see §20– 020) this power cannot be exercised in relation to the Scottish Parliament, any part of the Scottish Administration, the Scottish Parliamentary Corporate Body, or any Scottish public authority with mixed functions or no reserved functions (within the meaning of the Scotland Act 1998): ss 5(4) and 80. The Information Commissioner has called for this power to be used more widely in order to ensure that FOIA keeps pace with modern public service delivery: see Outsourcing Oversight? The case for reforming access to information law (January 2019).

166 House of Commons, *Public Administration—Third Report* (Cm 4355, 1999) Annex 6, para 9 (Notes by the Freedom of Information Unit, Home Office) (see Ch 1 n 68).

167 Human Rights Act 1998 s 6 makes it unlawful for public authorities to act incompatibly with rights under the ECHR and provides that 'public authority' includes (a) a court or tribunal and (b) any person certain of whose functions are 'functions of a public nature'.

person or office falling within a specified description.[168] Before making such an order the Secretary of State or Minister must consult every person to whom the order relates, or persons appearing to represent them.[169] An order of this type made in relation to a person who appears to exercise functions of a public nature[170] must specify the functions of the designated public authority with respect to which the order is to have effect. The general right of access under the Act to information held by the public authority does not apply to information held by the authority which does not relate to the exercise of those functions.[171] Similarly, where an order is made in relation to a person who is providing under a contract made with a public authority any service whose provision is a function of that authority,[172] it must specify the services provided under contract with respect to which the order is to have effect. The general right of access under the Act to information held by the public authority does not apply to information held by the authority which does not relate to the provision of those services.[173]

20– 024 Publicly owned companies

A company is a publicly owned company[174] and therefore a public authority under FOIA if it is wholly owned by either (1) the Crown; (2) the wider public sector, or (3) the Crown and the wider public sector.[175] For these purposes, a company is considered to be wholly-owned by the Crown if it has no members other than Ministers of the Crown,[176] government departments or companies wholly owned by the Crown, or persons acting on behalf of any of these.[177] A company is considered to be wholly owned by the wider public sector if it has no members except the wider public sector or companies wholly owned by the wider public sector, or persons acting on behalf of either of these.[178] A company is considered to be wholly owned by the Crown and the wider public sector if its members are comprised of companies wholly owned by the Crown, by the wider public sector and/or the Crown and wider public sector together, or else is solely comprised of companies wholly owned by the Crown and wider public sector together.[179] However, the general right of access to information under the Act does not

---

168 FOIA s 5(2).

169 FOIA s 5(3). It was also said by the Home Office that, 'as a matter of good administrative practice it is expected that the Secretary of State will consult other persons whom he believes have a legitimate and direct interest in the order.' — House of Commons, *Public Administration—Third Report* (Cm 4355, 1999) Annex 6, para 10 (Notes by the Freedom of Information Unit, Home Office) (see Ch 1 n 68).

170 That is, under FOIA s 5(1)(a).

171 FOIA s 7(5).

172 That is, under FOIA s 5(1)(b).

173 FOIA s 7(6).

174 'Company' includes any body corporate: FOIA s 6(3).

175 FOIA s 6(1).

176 Including a Northern Ireland Minister: FOIA s 6(3).

177 FOIA s 6(2)(a). Examples include: Northern Ireland Water; the Commonwealth Development Corporation. See further the Information Commissioner's Guidance on Public Authorities under FOIA at para 11.

178 FOIA s 6(2)(b). Although 'wider public sector' is not defined in the Act, it seems from the Explanatory Notes to the Protection of Freedoms Act 2012 at paragraphs 405-408 which inserted this provision into FOIA, that the 'wider public sector' means 'relevant public authority' as defined in s 6(3) (ie those in the Sch 1 list, excepting Government departments). See further the Information Commissioner's Guidance on public authorities under FOIA at paras 12-15 and 17.

179 FOIA s 6(2)(c), (2A). More fully, a company is wholly owned by the Crown and the wider public sector if:
(1) at least one member is wholly owned by the Crown, at least one member is wholly owned by the wider public sector, and every member is wholly owned in one of these two ways;
(2) at least one member is either wholly owned by the Crown or by the wider public sector, at least one member is wholly owned by the Crown and the wider public sector together, and every member is owned in one of these three ways; or
(3) all its members are wholly owned by the Crown and the wider public sector together.

apply to any information held by a publicly owned company which is defined by order of the Secretary of State for Justice or Minister for the Cabinet Office as 'excluded information' in relation to that company.[180]

20– 025 Welsh public authorities

Welsh public authorities are defined to mean any public authority listed in Pt II, III, IV or VI of Sch 1 whose functions are exercisable only or mainly in or as regards Wales, other than an 'excluded authority'.[181] These bodies will also fall within the scope of the EIR.[182] Welsh public authorities are also defined to include any public authority which is:

— a subsidiary of the Welsh Ministers (as defined by section 134(4) of the Government of Wales Act 2006);[183] or
— a subsidiary of the Assembly Commission (as defined by section 139(4) of the Government of Wales Act).[184]

20– 026 Environmental information

Under the EIR, the right of access is similarly exercisable against a 'public authority'.[185] However, the term is given a different definition from that which it bears under FOIA.[186] The EIR expand the definition given to 'public authority' in FOIA by adding to it two additional limbs. First, by para (c) of the definition, 'public authority' also embraces 'any other body or other person that carries out functions of public administration.' The Court of Justice has held that this applies to bodies that are vested, under national law, with special powers beyond those which result from the normal rules applicable in relations between persons governed by private law.[187] Secondly, para (d) of the definition adds any other body or person 'that is under the control of' a public authority (as defined in paras (a)-(c)) and that:

— has public responsibilities relating to the environment;
— exercises functions of a public nature relating to the environment; or

---

This means that a company's ownership can be shared between government departments and list authorities and still satisfy the s 6 test.

180 FOIA s 7(8).

181 FOIA s 83(1)(a). An excluded authority is a public authority which is designated by the Secretary of State or the Minister for the Cabinet Office by order as an excluded authority for the purposes of FIOA s 83(1)(a): FOIA s 83(2). By the Freedom of Information (Excluded Welsh Authorities) Order 2002 SI 2002/2832, the Lord Chancellor excluded four magistrates' court committees, the Advisory Committee on General Commissioners of Income Tax for certain areas, the Parliamentary Boundary Commission for Wales, and Sianel Pedwar Cymru, in respect of information held for purposes other than those of journalism, art or literature, and certain other bodies.

182 EIR reg 2(2)(b).

183 FOIA s 83(1)(b)(i). It is defined by s 134(4) to mean: (a) any body corporate or other undertaking in relation to which, if the Welsh Ministers were an undertaking, the Welsh Ministers would be a parent undertaking, (b) any trust of which the Welsh Ministers are settlors, or (c) any charitable institution of which the Welsh Ministers are founders but which is neither a body corporate nor a trust.

184 FOIA s 83(1)(b)(ii). It is defined by s 139(4) to mean: (a) any body corporate or other undertaking in relation to which the Assembly Commission is a parent undertaking, (b) any trust of which the Assembly Commission is settlor, or (c) any charitable institution of which the Assembly Commission is founder but which is neither a body corporate nor a trust.

185 EIR reg 5(1).

186 EIR reg 2(2). This is so that the definition of 'public authority' accords with Art 2.2 of the Directive. See also recital (11) of the Directive and Art 2.2 of the Aarhus Convention.

187 *Fish Legal v Information Commissioner United Utilities, Yorkshire Water and Southern Water* (C-279/12) [2014] QB 521, [2014] 2 CMLR 36, [2015] All ER (EC) 795 at [52]. When this case returned to the Upper Tribunal, the water companies at issue were found to have the requisite 'special powers,' those powers including the power to impose hosepipe bans and to make byelaws relating to waterways, the breach of either of which could constitute a criminal offence: *Fish Legal and anor v IC and ors* [2015] UKUT 52 (AAC). See further §18– 006.

— provides public services relating to the environment.

The Court of Justice has clarified that in order to fall within this limb of the definition, the 'control' must be such that the body is unable to determine in a genuinely autonomous manner the way in which it provides public services.[188]

5. BODIES SUBJECT TO FREEDOM OF INFORMATION (SCOTLAND) ACT

20– 027 Listed public authorities

Schedule 1 to FOI(S)A provides a similar list to that in Sch 1 to the Westminster Act. These bodies are also subject to the EI(S)R.[189]

(I) MINISTERS, THE PARLIAMENT: This comprises the Scottish Ministers, the Scottish Parliament and the Scottish Parliamentary Corporate Body.

(II) NON-MINISTERIAL OFFICER HOLDERS IN THE SCOTTISH ADMINISTRATION: This includes such persons as the Chief Dental Officer and Chief Medical Officer of the Scottish Administration, Her Majesty's various Chief Inspectors of Constabulary and of Prisons, Her Majesty's Inspector of Anatomy, of Fire and Rescue Services and inspectors of schools for Scotland, the Keepers of the Records and Registers of Scotland, procurators fiscal, the Queen's and Lord Treasurer's Remembrancer, the Queen's Printer for Scotland, the Registrars of Births, Deaths and Marriages and of Independent Schools, rent officers[190] and Revenue Scotland.

(III) LOCAL GOVERNMENT: This comprises Councils constituted, and assessors appointed, under the Local Government, etc (Scotland) Act 1994, joint boards within the meaning of s 235(1) of the Local Government (Scotland) Act 1973, licensing boards continued or established under the Licensing (Scotland) Act 2005 and the Strathclyde Passenger Transport Authority.

(IV) THE NATIONAL HEALTH SERVICE: This Part covers most NHS institutions in Scotland and, as with FOIA, includes individual GPs, dentists, opticians and pharmacists, but only in respect of information relating to their provision of services under the NHS.

(V) EDUCATIONAL INSTITUTIONS: This lists the board of management of colleges of further education, central institutions within the meaning of the Education (Scotland) Act 1980, and institutions in receipt of funding from the Scottish Further Higher Education Funding Council other than any institution whose activities are principally carried on outside Scotland.

(VI) POLICE: Listed here are the chief constables of Police Service of Scotland, joint police boards and the Police Negotiations Board for Scotland.

(VII) OTHERS: This is a general list of 70 other public bodies and offices, similar to that contained in Part VI of Sch 1 to FOIA.

20– 028 Adding public authorities

---

188 *Fish Legal v Information Commissioner United Utilities, Yorkshire Water and Southern Water* (C-279/12) [2014] QB 521, [2014] 2 CMLR 36, [2015] All ER (EC) 795 at [68]. When this case returned to the Upper Tribunal, the water companies at issue were found not to satisfy this test since, inter alia, each was run by an independent board of directors who were answerable to shareholders and not solely to the state: *Fish Legal and anor v IC and ors* [2015] UKUT 52 (AAC) at [141]-[151]. See also *Poplar Housing Association and Regeneration Community Association v IC & anor*, FTT, 20 February 2019. See further §18– 006. Contrast earlier authorities such as: *Network Rail Ltd v IC and Network Rail Infrastructure Ltd*, IT, 17 July 2007.

189 EI(S)R reg 2(2)(a)-(b).

190 Appointed under Rent (Scotland) Act 1984 s 43(3): FOI(S)A Sch 1 Pt 2 para 18.

The Scottish Ministers have the power[191] to add to Sch 1 any body or holder of any office which is either a part of the Scottish Administration or a Scottish public authority with mixed functions or no reserved functions.[192] The Act imposes no duty to consult before making such an order.[193] An order adding a Scottish public authority to Sch 1 in this way may relate to a specified person or office or to persons or offices falling within a specified description.[194] In addition, the order may list the new entry only in relation to information of a specified description, in which case nothing in the Act applies to any other information held by the authority.[195]

20– 029 Removing public authorities

The Scottish Ministers have the power to remove from Sch 1 any entry listed there.[196] There is no requirement for approval of such an order by the Scottish Parliament.[197]

20– 030 Part-affected public authorities

The Freedom of Information (Scotland) Act 2002 provides that any body listed in Sch 1 is considered a Scottish public authority for the purposes of that Act,[198] subject to any qualification in that Schedule.[199] Therefore, as with FOIA, there is no right of access to information held by such an authority if the information falls outside the description in the Schedule. The difference is really only conceptual: the effect of the Scottish approach is that such a body is not considered by the Act to be a Scottish public authority in such circumstances, whereas under FOIA such a body remains at all times a public authority under the statute, although not always subject to the Act's main provisions.[200] The Scottish Ministers have the power, in relation to any entry in Sch 1, to introduce, amend or remove any such limitation.[201]

20– 031 Designated public authorities

A person who is not listed in Sch 1 nor capable of being added to that list by an order under s 4(1)[202] may be designated by order as a Scottish public authority for the purposes of the Act if he: (a) appears to the Scottish Ministers to exercise functions of a public nature, or (b) is providing under a contract made with a Scottish public authority any service whose provision

---

191 FOI(S)A s 4(1). Such an order is subject to annulment in pursuance of a resolution of the Scottish Parliament: FOI(S)A s 72(2)(a). If the order is adding an authority only in relation to information of a specified description then a draft order must be laid before and approved by a resolution of that body before being made: FOI(S)A s 72(2)(b).

192 'Scottish public authority' has the meaning it has in the rest of the Act, as defined in FOI(S)A s 3(1), ie either a body or office which is listed in Sch 1 (although obviously that could not apply here, since this concerns adding a body or office to Sch 1), a body designated by the Scottish Ministers or a publicly-owned company. However, this reference to an authority with mixed functions or no reserved functions is to be construed in accordance with paras 1(4) and 2 of Pt III of Sch 5 to the Scotland Act 1998: FOI(S)A s 4(2).

193 Contrast the position under the FOIA s 4(7): see §20– 020 fn 135.

194 FOI(S)A s 4(3).

195 FOI(S)A, s 7(1).

196 FOI(S)A s 4(1)(b).

197 As there is when adding bodies in relation to specified information, or introducing such a limitation to a body on Sch 1: see §20– 031.

198 FOI(S)A s 3(1)(a)(i).

199 FOI(S)A s 3(3). For example, Pt 4 (the National Health Service) para 33 has the entry, 'A person providing primary medical services, general dental service, general ophthalmic services or pharmaceutical services, but only in respect of information relating to the provision of those services.'

200 That is, those in Pts I to V of the FOI(S)A. See §20– 022.

201 FOI(S)A s 7(2). Such an order must be laid before and approved by a resolution of the Scottish Parliament before being made: FOI(S)A s 72(2)(b).

202 See §20– 028.

is a function of that authority.[203] In such cases, the order must specify the functions of a public nature which appear to be exercised or the service being provided.[204] As with orders made under section 4(1) of FOIA,[205] such an order may designate a specified person or office or persons or offices falling within a specified description.[206] In contrast to the position under section 4(1) of FOIA,[207] however, before making this type of order the Scottish Ministers must consult every person to whom the order relates, or persons appearing to represent them, and such other persons as they consider appropriate.[208]

20– 032 Publicly owned companies

A company is a publicly owned company[209] and therefore a Scottish public authority under FOI(S)A if it is wholly owned by either (1) the Scottish Ministers; or (2) any other Scottish public authority listed in Sch 1 to the Act other than an authority listed only in relation to particular information.[210] For these purposes, a company is considered to be wholly owned by the Scottish Ministers if it has no members other than the Scottish Ministers or companies wholly owned by the Scottish Ministers, or persons acting on behalf of either of these.[211] A company is considered to be wholly owned by any other Scottish public authority if it has no members except that authority or companies wholly owned by that authority, or persons acting on behalf of either of these.[212] However, nothing in the Act applies to any information held by a publicly owned company which is of a description specified in relation to that company in an order made by the Scottish Ministers.[213]

20– 033 Environmental information

Under the EI(S)R, the right of access is similarly exercisable against a 'Scottish public authority'.[214] However, the term is given a different definition from that which it bears under FOI(S)A.[215] The EI(S)R expand the definition given to 'public authority' in FOI(S)A by adding to it two additional limbs. First, by para (c) of the definition, 'public authority' also embraces 'any other Scottish public authority with mixed functions or no reserved function (within the meaning of the Scotland Act 1998).' Secondly, para (d) of the definition adds any other body or person 'that is under the control of' a public authority (as defined in paras (a)-(c)) and that:

— has public responsibilities relating to the environment;
— exercises functions of a public nature relating to the environment; or
— provides public services relating to the environment.

---

203 FOI(S)A s 5(1)-(2). Such an order must be laid before and approved by a resolution of the Scottish Parliament before being made: FOI(S)A s 72(2)(b).

204 FOI(S)A s 5(4).

205 See §20– 023.

206 FOI(S)A s 5(3).

207 See §20– 028.

208 FOI(S)A s 5(3).

209 'Company' includes any body corporate: FOI(S)A s 6(3).

210 FOI(S)A s 6(1). For Scottish public authorities listed in Sch 1 only in relation to particular information see §20– 030.

211 FOI(S)A s 6(2)(a).

212 FOI(S)A s 6(2)(b).

213 FOI(S)A s 7(4). This is the equivalent of the 'excluded information' provision in s 7(7)-(8) of the FOIA.

214 EI(S)R reg 5(1).

215 EI(S)R reg 2(1). This is so that the definition of 'public authority' accords with Art 2.2 of the Directive. See also recital (11) of the Directive and Art 2.2 of the Aarhus Convention.

Paragraph (d) may be apt to cover private companies operating in certain regulated industries, such as water and public transport.[216]

6. CONSTRAINTS ON DISCLOSURE

20– 034 Confidentiality, copyright etc

A disclosure that for one person may represent 'freedom of information', may for another constitute an undue processing of personal data, a breach of confidence, a breach of copyright or a defamatory publication.[217] FOIA accommodates the first two of these competing interests by rendering information exempt information where it would offend either interest.[218] In these two cases, the right of access yields to another interest: to a person's right not to have personal data relating to himself unduly disclosed; and to a person's right not to have confidential information disclosed. Furthermore, the proscription against disclosure is left intact, such that the public authority must not disclose the information.[219] In the case of copyright and defamation, however, these interests generally yield to the right of access conferred by FOIA. Section 50(1) of the Copyright, Designs and Patents Act 1988 provides:

> Where the doing of a particular act is specifically authorised by an Act of Parliament, whenever passed, then, unless the Act provides otherwise, the doing of that act does not infringe copyright.

Disclosure of information where there is a duty to do so under FOIA or the EIR (because there is no exemption disapplying that duty) will be specifically authorised and so not constitute a breach of copyright.

20– 035 Defamatory material

Neither FOIA nor the EIR confers absolute privilege for the disclosure of information pursuant to the duty to disclose.[220] Generally, where a public authority is under a duty to disclose information to an applicant by reason of the Act or the EIR, that communication will attract qualified privilege.[221] Such a disclosure may be said to be a paradigm instance satisfying the duty-interest test. Information held by a public authority that is disclosed by it to a person where there is no obligation to do so (eg because an exemption applies), will, if it is defamatory, not automatically enjoy qualified privilege.[222] In relation to information that a public authority is required to disclose under s 1 of FOIA but which was supplied to the public authority by a third person, the Act specifically provides that the publication to an applicant of any defamatory material contained in that information will be privileged unless the publication is shown to have been made with malice.[223] While qualified privilege will, as just discussed, invariably protect the public authority in such circumstances, the statutory provision is required

---

216 See further §18– 003.

217 For the ability of an affected third party to participate in any decision to disclose information, see §§22– 036 to 22– 042.

218 Thus: processing of personal data is protected by FOIA s 40; FOI(S)A s 38; EIR reg 13; EI(S)R reg 11; confidentiality is protected by FOIA ss 41 and 43; FOI(S)A ss 33 and 36; EIR reg 12(5)(d)-(f); EI(S)R reg 10(5)(d)-(f).

219 See further §§20– 037 and 22– 036 to 22– 042.

220 Compare Parliamentary Commissioner Act 1967 s 10(5); Care Standards Act 2000 s 76(7); Competition Act 1998 s 57, and various other statutes.

221 See: *Adam v Ward* [1917] AC 309 at 334; *Moore v Canadian Pacific SS Co* [1945] 1 All ER 128.

222 *Wood v Chief Constable of the West Midlands* [2003] EWHC 2971, [2004] EMLR 17. But in *S v Newham LBC* [1998] 1 FLR 1061, [1999] EMLR 583 (CA) the defence was available to a local authority which, in accordance with ministerial guidelines, sent details concerning one of its social workers to the Department of Health for inclusion in an index of persons unsuitable for child care work.

223 FOIA s 79; FOI(S)A s 67. There is no equivalent provision in the EIR or the EI(S)R.

to protect the third party. But for the provision, if a public authority, in answer to a request for information under the Act, supplied a defamatory statement made to the public authority by a third party, that supply would constitute a further publication for which the third party could be liable:[224]

> The law would part company with the realities of life if it were held that the damage caused by the publication of a libel began and ended with publication to the original publishee. Defamatory statements are objectionable not least because of their propensity to percolate through underground channels and contaminate hidden springs.[225]

Because FOIA imposes a duty on a public authority to disclose requested information, the foreseeability of the republication will be higher than if it were a matter of pure discretion:

> Where an actual duty is cast upon the person to whom the slander is uttered to communicate what he has heard to some third person, as when a communication is made to a husband, such as, if true, would render the subject of it unfit to associate with his wife and daughters, the slander cannot excuse himself by saying: "True, I told the husband, but I never intended that he should carry the matter to his wife." In such a case... the originator of the slander, and not the hearer of it, is responsible for the consequences.[226]

Provided that the republication is without malice, it will be privileged, protecting both the public authority and the third party. The third party will, of course, remain potentially liable for the original publication to the public authority.

7. DISCRETIONARY DISCLOSURE OF INFORMATION[227]

20– 036 Discretionary disclosure

The Freedom of Information Act 2000 and the EIR do not set the limits of the information that a public authority may lawfully disclose.[228] Disclosure of information by a public authority where it is not under a duty to do so may be called *discretionary disclosure*. The Open Government Code of Practice, published in 1993 and applying to almost all central government bodies and their agencies, was a non-statutory, discretionary regime.[229] Implicit in the Code was an acknowledgment that the public authorities to which it applied could lawfully disclose information held by them despite the absence of a specific statutory provision empowering them to do so.

20– 037 Duties, powers and unlawfulness

In any consideration of discretionary disclosure by a public authority, three concepts should be kept distinct:

(1) Whether there is a *duty* on the public authority to disclose the particular information.
(2) Whether the public authority has *power* to disclose the particular information; and
(3) Whether it is *unlawful* for the public authority to disclose the particular information.

FOIA imposes a *duty* on public authorities to communicate information of the description

224 The republication may be treated either as a separate cause of action or (provided that it was not too remote) as part of the foreseeable damage resulting from the original publication to the public authority: *Toomey v Mirror Newspapers* (1985) 1 NSWLR 173 at 182-183; *Sims v Wran* [1984] 1 NSWLR 317.

225 *Slipper v BBC* [1991] 1 QB 283 at 300 (Bingham LJ). See further *McManus v Beckham* [2002] EWCA Civ 939, [2002] 1 WLR 2982; *Collins Stewart Ltd v Financial Times Ltd (No 2)* [2005] EWHC 262, [2006] EMLR 5.

226 *Derry v Handley* (1867) 16 LT 263 at 264 (Cockburn CJ).

227 See further §§5– 007 to 5– 014 in relation to the discretion to maintain a particular exemption.

228 FOIA s 78; FOI(S)A s 66.

229 See §§2– 004 to 2– 014.

specified in a request.[230] The exemptions in Part II of the Act do not make *unlawful* the disclosure of particular information: rather, they shape the *duty* imposed by s 1(1) of the Act.[231] Disclosure of information requested under the FOIA that is not required to be disclosed is effectively a discretionary disclosure. Other legislation similarly imposes a duty on certain public authorities to disclose certain information to certain people at certain times.[232] The limit of each of those duties does not of itself make *unlawful* the disclosure of information beyond that limit. In certain circumstances, however, disclosure of information in the absence of a statutory obligation to do so (whether from FOIA or otherwise) will be *unlawful*. Thus:

(a) Some legislative provisions *prohibit* the disclosure of certain information to certain people at certain times.[233] An exception to such a prohibition does not of itself give rise to a duty to disclose that information: it simply sets the limit of the prohibition. Similarly, disclosure may be prohibited by EU obligations.[234]

(b) Some statutory regimes provide that a disclosure is *unlawful* outside the circumstances mandated by the legislation. The most significant such regime is that imposed by the GDPR and DPA 2018.[235]

(c) Disclosure may interfere with a person's private life and, if not justified, may contravene Art 8 of the ECHR.[236] The more systematic the collection of the information, the longer that the information is held, the more it relates to things that are out of the public domain, the more likely that its disclosure will interfere with the subject's private life.[237]

(d) Disclosure may be unlawful because it would breach some common law or equitable duty, such as respecting confidentiality, whether arising under contract or otherwise. Public authorities hold large quantities of commercially sensitive information provided to them by third parties, whether under compulsion or in order for those third parties to carry out an activity regulated or supervised by public authorities.

In all cases where a request under FOIA captures information that *may* be subject to such constraints but which the public authority is minded to disclose (because it considers the constraint inapplicable), it is prudent for the public authority to take all reasonable steps to invite the views of the bodies whose interests are protected by the constraint before disclosing the information.[238] Where a public authority discloses information that it is not required to disclose and whose disclosure is constrained in any of the above ways, the public authority will have acted unlawfully.[239] The public authority will not necessarily be excused from civil liability by its genuine belief that it was obliged to disclose the information under FOIA.

---

230 FOIA,s 1(1)(b).

231 FOIA s 1(2) in conjunction with s 2(2).

232 See chs 5, 6 and 8.

233 For examples of statutory prohibitions, see § 35– 018. A statutory prohibition on the disclosure of information renders that information exempt information under the FOIA, but not under the EIR: FOIA s 44(1)(a); FOI(S)A s 26(a); EIR reg 5(6); EI(S)R reg 5(3).

234 For example, Council Directive 90/220 on the deliberate release into the environment of genetically modified organisms Art 19. See further §§35– 025 to 35– 026.

235 See, generally, Chapters 7-16.

236 *R (L) v Metropolitan Police Commissioner* [2009] UKSC 3, [2010] 1 All ER 113; *R v Chief Constable of North Wales Police, ex p Thorpe* [1999] QB 396 at 414, 416, 429. See further Chapter 4.

237 *R (L) v Metropolitan Police Commissioner* [2009] UKSC 3, [2010] 1 All ER 113 at [27], [71].

238 Applying the reasoning in *R (L) v Metropolitan Police Commissioner* [2009] UKSC 3, [2010] 1 All ER 113 at [46]. See further §§22– 036 to 22– 042.

239 And, in certain circumstances, potentially criminally.

20– 038 Power to disclose information

While a statute occasionally confers power on a public authority to disclose particular information, discretionary or voluntarily disclosure is not ordinarily specifically provided for. Nevertheless, it is an ordinary incident of a person (whether a natural person or a body corporate or public authority) holding information that that person may deal with that information (including disclosing it) as that person sees fit, subject to any prohibition, constraint or implied limitation.[240] The power of a public authority to voluntarily disclose information that it holds will be shaped by its functions. If there is no specific statutory power[241] to disclose particular information, a public authority will be acting lawfully in disclosing information that it holds provided that that voluntary disclosure is reasonably required to enable that public authority to properly carry out its functions, subject to any prohibition, limitation or constraint on that disclosure.[242] A power to disclose information may be impliedly limited where the disclosure of certain information would undermine a regulated statutory regime for the disclosure of that information.[243] It may also be limited where the disclosure would involve an interference with a person's private and family life, home or correspondence.[244] Defamation

---

240 This may in part no more than reflect the fact that without more there is no property in information as such. In *Boardman v Phipps* [1967] AC 46 at 127-128 Lord Upjohn said: 'In general, information is not property at all. It is normally open to all who have eyes to read and ears to hear. The true test is to determine in what circumstances the information has been acquired. If it has been acquired in such circumstances that it would be a breach of confidence to disclose it to another then courts of equity will restrain the recipient from communicating it to another. In such cases such confidential information is often and for many years has been described as the property of the donor, the books of authority are full of such references; knowledge of secret processes, "know-how," confidential information as to the prospects of a company or of someone's intention or the expected results of some horse race based on stable or other confidential information. But in the end the real truth is that it is not property in any normal sense but equity will restrain its transmission to another if in breach of some confidential relationship.' Similarly, *Federal Commissioner of Taxation v United Aircraft Corp* (1944) 68 CLR 525 at 534-6 and *Moorgate Tobacco Co Ltd v Philip Morris Ltd (No 2)* (1984) 156 CLR 414 at 438. And, more recently, see *Douglas v Hello! (No 3)* [2006] QB 125 at [127]; *OBG Ltd v Allan* [2007] UKHL 21, [2007] 2 WLR 920 at [275]-[277], [282], [286].

241 In the case of a local authority it may derive that power from the Local Government Act 1972 ss 142 and 111, or the Local Government Act 2000 s 2. As to the first provision, see: *Meek v Lothian Regional Council* [1983] SLT 494; *R v Inner London Education Authority, ex p Westminster City Council* [1986] 1 WLR 28, [1986] 1 All ER 19.

242 *R v Chief Constable of North Wales Police, ex p Thorpe* [1999] QB 396 at 410-411, 415 and 429; *R v Local Authority in the Midlands* [2000] 1 FCR 736; *Green v Police Complaints Authority* [2004] 1 WLR 725 (HL). The public authority might be empowered by statute to do anything calculated to facilitate, or which is incidental to, the carrying out of its functions. As to the permissibility of voluntary disclosure under such provisions, see: *Electoral Commission v Good Law Project* [2019] EWCA Civ 1938 at [21]-[28]; *R (W, X, Y, Z) v Secretary of State for Health* [2015] EWCA Civ 1034, [2016] 1 WLR 698 at [68].

243 In *R v Liverpool City Council, ex p Baby Products Association* [1999] LGLR 689 the court considered that a local authority did not have power to issue a press release identifying models of babywalkers that did not comply with safety standards. This conclusion was reached on the basis that the issue of consumer warnings was governed by section 13 of the Consumer Protection Act 1987, which granted the Secretary of State the power to require companies to issue warnings only where he considered the goods unsafe and statutory safeguards were complied with. The Court held: 'It is apparent that these provisions comprise a detailed and carefully-crafted code designed, on the one hand, to promote the very important objective of protecting the public against unsafe consumer products and, on the other, to give fair protection to the business interests of manufacturers and suppliers... Mr Fordham [appearing for the Baby Products Association] accepted that, generally speaking, it was open to local authorities to publish information relating to their activities, at any rate within their areas. Had the Council issued suspension notices in accordance with section 14 of the Act, that fact could (he accepted) have been announced to the public. Had the Council initiated any criminal proceedings that fact, and the outcome of such proceedings, could similarly have been announced to the public. Sections 142(2) and 111(1) gave authority to make such announcements if statutory authority was needed. What, however, was impermissible was to make a public announcement having an intention and effect which could only be achieved by implementation of clear and particular procedures prescribed in an Act of Parliament when the effect of the announcement was to deny the companies the rights and protections which Parliament had enacted they should enjoy. So to act was to circumvent the provisions of the legislation and to act unlawfully.'

244 *R (L) v Metropolitan Police Commissioner* [2009] UKSC 3, [2010] 1 All ER 113; *R v Chief Constable of North Wales Police, ex p Thorpe* [1999] QB 396 at 410-411, 415 and 429 (held lawful for Chief Constable to disclose information from the local press about T's convictions to a proprietor of a caravan site at which T (a married couple who had been released from prison after serving lengthy sentences for serious sexual offences against children) were staying); *R*

and data protection may constrain a public authority volunteering to a person information held by the public authority, whether that information was generated by it or was supplied by a third party. Where the information was supplied to the public authority by a third party, there may also be issues of breach of confidence and copyright that further constrain a voluntary disclosure. If the public authority obtained the information from a third party under some form of compulsion, fairness may require the public authority to notify that third party before voluntarily disclosing it.[245]

v Local Authority in the Midlands, ex p LM [2000] 1 FCR 736, [2000] UKHRR 143, (2000) 2 LGLR 1043 (held unlawful for a local authority and local police authority to disclose to a county council, with whom the claimant had contracted to supply school transport, allegations made 10 years earlier that the claimant had sexually abused his daughter and a child in his care). Although the two earlier decisions were questioned in *R (X) v Chief Constable of the West Midlands* [2004] EWCA Civ 1068, [2005] 1 WLR 65, in *R (L) v Metropolitan Police Commissioner* [2009] UKSC 3, [2010] 1 All ER 113 at [44], [63] it was held that the latter decision had tilted the balance too far against the person to whom the information relates. See also: *R (A) v Chief Constable of C* [2001] 1 WLR 461, [2001] 2 FCR 43 (held lawful for a Chief Constable to disclose sensitive non-conviction information to a local education authority on the basis that the LEA had a lawful interest in the information and a pressing need to receive it); *Re C (Sexual Abuse: Disclosure to Landlords)* [2002] EWHC 234, [2002] 2 FLR 375, [2002] 2 FCR 385 (Court granting permission to Chief Constable and Director of Social Services to disclose to a local housing association with whom C housed findings of child sexual abuse made against C in care proceedings, but refusing permission to disclose to housing authorities that might house C in the future); *R (L) v Metropolitan Police Commissioner* [2006] EWHC 482 (held lawful for the Commissioner to disclose information not amounting to criminal conduct or potentially criminal conduct as part of an enhanced criminal record certificate); *R (D) v Secretary of State for Health* [2006] EWCA Civ 989 [2006] Lloyd's Rep Med 457 (held lawful for the Secretary of State to issue an alert letter advising NHS bodies of allegations of indecent assault made against claimant doctor).

245 See *R (Kent Pharmaceuticals Limited) v SFO* [2004] EWCA Civ 1494, [2005] 1 All ER 449 (where the SFO did have an express statutory power to disclose to a government department information obtained from the claimant).

CHAPTER 21

The duty to advise and assist, codes of practice and publication schemes

1. THE DUTY TO ADVISE AND ASSIST

21–001 Introduction

Section 16(1) of FOIA imposes a duty upon a public authority to provide advice and assistance to any person who proposes to make, or who has made, a request for information to it.[1] The duty is not open-ended, but is stated to be a duty to provide advice and assistance 'so far as it would be reasonable to expect the authority to do'.[2] The duty was introduced on the basis that it represented an important step in achieving the cultural change stated to be sought by the legislation.[3] There had been an initial reluctance on the part of the government to impose such a duty, said to be because of difficulties in adequately describing the limits of the duty.[4] The

---

1 Similarly FOI(S)A s 15(1).

2 There are similar duties in three of the comparative jurisdictions: Freedom of Information Act 1982 (Cth of Aust) s 15(3); Official Information Act 1982 (NZ) s 13; Freedom of Information Act 2014 (Ireland), long title and s11(2); Access to Information Act 1982 (Canada) s4(2.1) (inserted by the Federal Accountability Act 2006). There is no provision in either the US or the Canadian Act requiring an agency to give assistance. In its review of the Freedom of Information Act 1982, the Australian Law Reform Commission noted that many agencies did not seem to have an adequate commitment to the obligation to give assistance. The Review declined to prescribe further what assistance had to be given, instead considering that the FOI Commissioner should encourage agencies to do more than the bare statutory minimum. The Commission concluded: 'if agencies take care to find out exactly what information an applicant requires they may ultimately save resources and avoid disputes': Australian Law Reform Commission and Administrative Review Council, *Open Government: a review of the Federal Freedom of Information Act 1982*, ALRC 77, ARC 40 (Canberra, 1995) para 7.5. See also paras 7.14, 8.14 and 10.9.

3 See Hansard HL vol 617 cols 940 and 942 (17 October 2000).

4 See House of Commons, *Public Administration—Third Report* (Cm 4355, 1999) Annex 6, para 24 (see Ch 1 n 68); House of Commons, *Select Committee on Public Administration, 5th Special Report*, Appendix, 27 October 1999, p 11; Hansard HC vol 347 cols 856-870 (4 April 2000); Hansard HL vol 617 cols 938-945 (17 October 2000). For the

expedient adopted was to leave the detail to one of the codes of practice.[5] A main object of providing such advice and assistance is to clarify the nature of the information required. Effective exercise of the rights conferred by the Act requires the person seeking information to know how most appropriately to describe what they are seeking. The Tribunal has emphasised the importance of providing as much practical assistance as possible to those making information requests.[6] There are limits, however. The Upper Tribunal has held, in the context of a case about application of the s12 costs limit,[7] that s16 does not require a public authority to 'exercise its imagination to proffer other possible solutions to the problem.'[8]

21– 002 Scope of the duty

Section 16(2) provides that a public authority which conforms with the Code of Practice issued under s 45 is to be taken to comply with the duty to advise and assist. That, however, does not mean that nothing less will suffice. The question, for the purposes of the s16(1) duty is what it is reasonable for the public authority to do. There are a number of notable features of the duty to advise and assist. First, there is no identification of the matters with respect to which the public authority is obliged to provide advice and assistance: it is to a class of persons to which the duty is owed.[9] Secondly, the duty is not only engaged where the applicant seeks advice or assistance: the public authority may be required to volunteer advice and assistance.[10] Thirdly, the duty relates to both an unformed request and to one already made.[11] The former means that the duty includes advising and assisting in the formulation of a request that meets the formal requirements of the Act.[12] Fourthly, the fact that the duty is not tied to advice and assistance in relation to FOIA suggests that a public authority may also be required to advise and assist where the request for information would be better made under other legislation, such as the GDPR and the DPA 2018 in relation to a request for personal information.[13] Fifthly, it is apparent from the wording of the section that the duty to advise and assist does not end with the receipt by the public authority of a properly formulated request. Thus the duty may require the giving of advice and assistance:

— where a public authority apprehends that the request is more likely to retrieve the information requested if directed to another public authority;
— where a public authority estimates that the cost of compliance with the request will exceed the appropriate limit, thereby removing the obligation upon the public authority to comply with the request[14] or, if it chooses to do so, to charge for

---

final acceptance by the Government of this, see Hansard HL vol 619 cols 194-197 (14 November 2000).

5 During the passage of the Bill, it had been suggested that rather more detail should be spelt out in the Act itself: House of Commons, *Public Administration–Third Report* (Cm 4355, 1999) para 52 (see Ch 1 n 68); House of Commons, *Select Committee on Public Administration 5th Special Report*, Appendix, 27 October 1999, p 5; Hansard HC vol 347 cols 868-870 (4 April 2000); Hansard HL vol 619 cols 250-252 (14 November 2000).

6 *Bellamy v IC and DTI*, IT, 4 April 2006 at [40]. Similarly, in relation to Scottish public authorities, *Common Services Agency v Scottish IC*, 2006 CSIH 58, 2007 SLT 7 at [16].

7 See §23– 001ff.

8 *Commissioner of Police for the Metropolis v Information Commissioner and Mackenzie* [2014] UKUT 479 (AAC) at [17].

9 Namely, 'persons who propose to make, or have made, requests for information': FOIA s 16(1).

10 *Barber v IC*, IT, 20 February 2006 at [17]-[19].

11 See, for example, *Hogan v IC and Oxford City Council*, IT, 17 October 2006, where Oxford City Council were held to have breached the duty to advise and assist in relation to what was held to be a modified request for information.

12 That is, the requirements set out in the FOIA s 8(1), and the FOI(S)A s 8(1). See *Lamb v IC*, IT, 16 November 2006 at [2]. In relation to requests for environmental information, see §18– 013.

13 A request for such information made under the FOIA could properly be refused by virtue of FOIA s 21, or FOI(S)A s 25.

14 FOIA s 12(1); FOI(S)A s 12(1). See, for example, *Cain v IC and LB Islington*, FTT, 10 April 2013 at [50].

meeting the request;[15]

— where a public authority considers that it requires further information in order to identify and locate the information requested by the applicant;[16]
— where a public authority considers that the request would be more successful if the applicant were to obtain the consent of a third party to disclosure and that could properly be suggested to the applicant without the disclosure of exempt information; and
— in relation to the applicant's appeal and enforcement rights.

And sixthly, the duty is one to give advice and assistance to the extent that it is reasonable to expect of the public authority. The size and resources of the public authority will therefore in part determine how much advice and assistance a public authority must give an applicant in the proper discharge of its duty.

21– 003 Limits of the duty

The Tribunal has made it clear that the duty does not extend to creating intelligible information from raw data held by the public authority. Nor does a public authority need to explain the information it discloses.[17] FOIA does not have an equivalent to the requirement in the GDPR/DPA 2018 that the holding body communicate information in an 'intelligible form.'[18] The Information Commissioner has previously expressed the view, accepted by the Tribunal,[19] that where a public authority comes to the objectively reasonable conclusion that a request is vexatious, it will not be held to have breached the duty to provide advice and assistance by not engaging in further communications with the applicant. However, neither the Information Commissioner's most recent guidance on the provision of advice and assistance nor the new Code of Practice under s 45 go this far and more recent Tribunal authority suggests that the position may be more nuanced.[20]

21– 004 Role of the Code of Practice

Section 45(1) of FOIA obliges the Minister for the Cabinet Office to issue a Code of Practice providing guidance to public authorities as to the practice which it would be desirable for public authorities to follow in connection with the discharge of their functions under Part I of the Act.[21] The section specifically requires the Code of Practice to cover the provision of advice and assistance by public authorities to persons who propose to make, or have made, requests

---

15 FOIA s 13(1); FOI(S)A s 13(1). If a request is refused on grounds of excessive cost of compliance, it may then be appropriate for the authority to provide advice and assistance to help the person who made the request to focus their request: see the Information Commissioner, *Duty to provide advice and assistance*, 23 June 2016, para 43; and *Requests where the cost of compliance exceeds the appropriate limit*, 9 September 2015, paras 59-62. But see *Roberts v IC*, IT, 4 December 2008 where it was held that a failure to advise and assist did not render a costs estimate invalid. See also *Garrard v IC and Home Office*, FTT, 6 September 2010 at [37].

16 FOIA s 1(3); FOI(S)A s 1(3).

17 *Innes v IC*, FTT, 5 May 2011 at [27]; *Innes v IC and Buckinghamshire County Council*, FTT, 26 August 2011 at [29]. Compare the position in relation to datasets: the section 45 Code of Practice recommends, at para 11.17, that datasets are accompanied by sufficient metadata and contextual information about how and why the dataset was compiled or created.

18 GDPR Art 12(1), (7) and recitals (420, (60); DPA 2018 ss 52(1), 94(1)(b). See *Evans v IC and MoD*, IT, 26 October 2007 at [48]-[50] (in relation to the like requirement in the DPA 1998).

19 *Billings v IC*, IT, 6 February 2008 at [13]-[14]; Information Commissioner, *Good Practice in Providing Advice and Assistance*, 17 December 2008.

20 See, for example, *McIrney v IC and Dept for Education* [2015] UKUT 47 (AAC) at [56].

21 Similarly FOI(S)A s 60.

for information.[22] The present Code of Practice under s 45 was published on 4 July 2018.[23] As noted above, the Act provides that conformity with the Code will constitute compliance with the duty to advise and assist, so that so far as this duty is concerned it may go beyond the minimum that is required of a public authority. Other Acts of Parliament may also be relevant to the way in which authorities provide advice and assistance to applicants or potential applicants, such as the Equality Act 2010.[24] The Code's requirements do not, of course, prevent an authority from offering additional assistance if it wishes.[25]

1– 005 Requirements of the Code

Chapter 2 of the Code of Practice sets out the requirements for providing advice and assistance which are summarised below. Like the rest of the Code, these requirements do not in themselves have statutory force. However, by virtue of s16(2) compliance with them will discharge a public authority's statutory duty to provide advice and assistance.

(1) Advice and assistance to prospective requesters. Pubic authorities should publish a postal address and email address (or other online alternative) to which requests for information or assistance can be sent.[26] Where an applicant asks for recorded information but does not mention FOIA the public authority should consider the request under FOIA and let the applicant know how the request is being handled. Where a request is made orally, the applicant should be advised to put the request in writing in accordance with s8(1)(a).[27] If a person is unable to frame a request in writing[28] the public authority should assist them to do so by, for example, referring them to a body such as a citizens advice bureau for advice, or by offering to take a note which is then sent to the applicant for confirmation.[29]

(2) Clarifying the request. The Code provides that if a public authority considers that the applicant has not provided their real name (for example because they appear to have used a pseudonym) the public authority can inform the applicant that it does not intend to respond to the request until further information is received.[30] Where a request is not clear enough to adequately describe the information sought, public authorities may ask for more detail in order to enable them to identify it.[31] In either case, the 20 day response period does not start until a satisfactory response constituting a valid request is received. The Code provides that letters should make clear that if no response is received the request will be considered closed, and that two months would be an appropriate period to wait.[32]

(3) Reducing the cost of a request. Where a public authority estimates that complying with the request would exceed the s12 costs limit, it should provide the applicant

22 FOIA s 45(2)(a); FOI(S)A s 60(2)(a).

23 It is reproduced in vol 2 of this work.

24 See the s 45 Code of Practice, para 2.2, and the Scottish Ministers Code of Practice on the Discharge of Functions by Public Authorities under the FOI(S)A, dated 1 December 2016, para 5.3.2.

25 See Hansard HL vol 619 col 196 (14 November 2000) (Lord Falconer, Minister of State, Cabinet Office).

26 Para 2.4.

27 Para 2.5.

28 For example because they have a disability.

29 Para 2.6.

30 Para 2.7. Care should be taken by a public authority to ensure that it has good reason for doubting the name provided by an applicant.

31 Para 2.8.

32 Para 2.9.

with advice and assistance to help them re-frame their request to bring it within the limit.[33] Chapter 6 of the Code of Practice provides further guidance on the costs limit.[34]

(4) Transferring requests for information. Where a public authority is unable to comply, or comply in full, with a request because it does not hold the information, but thinks that another public authority may hold it, it should inform the applicant. It should also provide the contact details of that authority where it can. If the public authority wishes to ask another public authority to deal with the request, by transferring it, it should only do so with the applicant's consent.

21– 006 Enforcement of the duty

There are two principal mechanisms contemplated in the Act for enforcement of the duty to advise and assist. First, a duty is imposed upon the Information Commissioner to promote the following of 'good practice', which is defined to include compliance with the requirements of the Act and the provisions of the Code of Practice.[35] Where it appears to the Information Commissioner that the practice of a particular public authority does not conform with the requirements laid out in the Code of Practice, the Information Commissioner can issue a 'practice recommendation' that specifies the steps which, in the opinion of the Information Commissioner, ought to be taken in order to promote conformity.[36] The second mechanism is applicant-driven. In addition to being able to apply to the Information Commissioner on the basis of non-disclosure of requested information, a person may apply to the Information Commissioner on the grounds that the advice and assistance that he was entitled to receive from the public authority after having made a request was not provided to him.[37] In order to be able to make the application, the person must have made a request for information that meets all the formal requirements.[38] However, once an applicant makes complaint to the Information Commissioner the applicant will normally be seeking the Commissioner's decision upon a refusal to disclose, irrespective of the level of help that might have been given. A complainant in person should not be expected to be familiar with s 16 of the Act, and even if such a complainant does not specify a breach of the duty to advise and assist in his complaint, the Commissioner may still be obliged to consider whether s 16 has been complied with.[39] The Commissioner may issue a decision notice that specifies whether the public authority has or has not breached its duty under s 16.[40] A party dissatisfied with that decision notice may appeal to the First-Tier Tribunal in relation to the finding as to the provision of advice and assistance.[41] The Tribunal has stated that non-compliance with s 16 'may go to the very nature of the request and that any exercise of discretion by the Commissioner which does not take this into

33 Para 2.10.

34 See §23– 001ff.

35 FOIA s 47(1); FOI(S)A s 43(1).

36 FOIA s 48(1); FOI(S)A s 44(1).

37 FOIA s 50(1). The position would appear to be otherwise in Scotland: see FOI(S)A s 47.

38 FOIA ss 8(1) and 50(1).

39 *Barber v IC*, IT, 11 November 2005 at [17]-[18]; cf *Johnson v IC*, IT, 28 April 2006 at [2].

40 See §45– 010.

41 See further §§45– 019 to 45– 019. For example: *Hogan and Oxford City Council v IC*, IT, 17 October 2006 at [17]-[21]; *Campsie v IC*, IT, 5 April 2007; *Lamb v IC*, IT, 16 November 2006 at [2]-[4] and [19]-[20], where the Information Tribunal found that a public authority should have asked the applicant to specify more precisely the information that was being requested. In *Urmenyi v IC and LB of Sutton*, IT, 13 July 2007, the Tribunal held that the public authority had failed in its duty to advise and assist where the cost of complying with the applicant's request for information would have exceeded the appropriate limit and the public authority did not suggest ways in which the applicant could reduce the scope of his request so as not to exceed that limit.

account may be flawed'; and that failure to consider compliance with s 16 may mean that the Commissioner has not complied with s 47 of the Act, which is the general duty to promote good practices.[42] In appropriate cases the Tribunal will direct that a public authority takes steps to remedy any breach of s16.[43]

2. THE CODES OF PRACTICE

21– 007 **Introduction**

The Freedom of Information Act 2000 requires two Codes of Practice to be issued: the first, to be issued by the Minister for the Cabinet Office,[44] providing guidance to public authorities on good practice in dealing with requests for information;[45] the second, to be issued by the Secretary of State,[46] providing guidance to relevant authorities[47] on good practice in keeping, managing and destroying records.[48] The Secretary of State for Justice and the Lord Chancellor may amend the respective codes from time to time.[49] The Information Commissioner is under a duty to promote observance of the codes by public authorities.[50] In response to a recommendation from the Independent Commission on Freedom of Information,[51] the government announced that it would review and update the section 45 Code of Practice. The new *Freedom of Information Code of Practice* was published, following consultation, on 8 July 2018. The Lord Chancellor's Code of Practice on the Management of Records under section 46,

42 *Barber v IC*, IT, 20 February 2006 at [17]-[18].

43 See, for example: *McGoldrick v IC*, FTT, 30 October 2017 at [19]; *Moss v IC*, FTT, 20 March 2017; cf *Howells v IC and Financial Ombudsman Service*, FTT, 9 October 2018 (in particular at [82]) in which the Tribunal found that s 16 had been breached but directed no further steps as a result of action which had subsequently been taken.

44 With effect from 9 November 2016: see Transfer of Functions (Elections, Referendums, Third Sector and Information) Order 2016/997 Sch.2(1) para.14(2)(k). The Act originally assigned the function to the Secretary of State, but that function was first transferred to the Lord Chancellor by the Transfer of Functions (Miscellaneous) Order 2001 SI 2001/3500 and then to the Secretary of State for Constitutional Affairs by the Secretary of State for Constitutional Affairs Order 2003 SI 2003/1887 and, from 9 May 2007, to the Secretary of State for Justice under The Secretary of State for Justice Order 2007 SI 2007/2128.

45 FOIA s 45; FOI(S)A s 60. In Scotland, the duty is cast upon the Scottish Ministers. These provisions set out what must be included in the code, and allow for different provisions to be made for different public authorities. The former also provides that before issuing or revising any code under this section, the Minister for the Cabinet Office must consult the Information Commissioner and then must subsequently lay any code or revised code before each House of Parliament.

46 The function was originally assigned to the Lord Chancellor but was transferred to the Secretary of State with effect from 9 December 2015 by the Transfer of Functions (Information and Public Records) Order 2015/1897 Sch.1 para.2(5)(b).

47 'Relevant authority' means: (a) any public authority, and (b) any office or body which is not a public authority but whose administrative and departmental records are public records for the purposes of the Public Records Act 1958 or the Public Records Act (Northern Ireland) 1923: FOIA s 46(7).

48 FOIA s 46; FOI(S)A s 61. In exercising his functions under this section the Secretary of State is required to have regard to the public interest in allowing public access to information held by relevant authorities. The code may make different provisions for different relevant authorities. Before issuing or revising any code under this section the Secretary of State must consult the Minister for the Cabinet Office, the Information Commissioner and (in relation to Northern Ireland), the appropriate Northern Ireland Minister, and then must subsequently lay any code or revised code before both Houses of Parliament.

49 The Minister for the Cabinet Office and Secretary of State must consult the Information Commissioner before revising a Code of Practice: FOIA ss 45(4) and 46(5). In Scotland, the Scottish Ministers must consult the Scottish Information Commissioner before revising a Code of Practice: FOI(S)A ss 60(4) and 61(5). Any revision to a Code of Practice must be laid before both Houses of Parliament: FOIA ss 45(5) and 46(6). In Scotland, revisions must be laid before the Parliament: FOI(S)A ss 60(5) and 61(6).

50 FOIA s 47(1); FOI(S)A s 43(1).

51 *Independent Commission on Freedom of Information Report*, March 2016, www.gov.uk/government/organisations/independent-commission-on-freedom-of-information

which was revised and re-issued on 16 July 2009, remains in force. There is also a Code of Practice relating to the Environmental Information Regulations.

21–008 Status of the codes

The Freedom of Information Act 2000 imposes no direct duty on public authorities to follow or even to have regard to the Codes. Instead, where it appears to the Information Commissioner that the practice of a public authority in relation to the exercise of its functions under FOIA does not conform with the codes of practice, the Commissioner can give the public authority a written 'practice recommendation' specifying the steps which in the Commissioner's opinion ought to be taken for promoting such conformity.[52] In contrast to non-compliance with a decision notice, information notice or enforcement notice issued by the Information Commissioner (which can amount to contempt of court), the Act does not specify the consequences of a failure to comply with a practice recommendation. The Government referred to this during the Bill's passage through Parliament, and commented as follows:

> [C]ompliance with the published codes of practice would not be enforceable in the courts in the same way that a statutory duty might be. We believe it would be an exceptional authority which ignored a [practice] recommendation, particularly given the commissioner's powers to name and shame in any report that she might make to Parliament. An additional point is that the code of practice could be referred to in any test case which was the subject of judicial review. The power of naming and shaming should not be underestimated in regard to public sector bodies keen to keep the confidence of the public they serve.[53]

21–009 Other compliance methods

In addition to making practice recommendations in the event of non-conformity with the Code the Information Commissioner can refer to non-compliance with the Code in decision and enforcement notices. Non-compliance with the codes could form part of a wider challenge to the discharge by a public authority of its duties under the Act, such as a failure in relation to the duty to advise and assist.[54] In these circumstances, the Information Commissioner could serve an enforcement notice. By itself, however, the failure of a public authority to comply with either of the codes of practice does not provide a basis for a disgruntled applicant to make an application to the Information Commissioner under s 50.[55]

21–010 Aims of the section 45 code

The s 45 code of practice provides guidance to public authorities as to the practice which it would, in the opinion of the Minister for the Cabinet Office, be desirable for them to follow in connection with the discharge of their functions under Part I of the Act.[56] In the foreword to the draft revised Code published for consultation on 15 November 2017 the Minister for the Constitution explained that the revised Code seeks to set a standard for all public authorities responding to requests, providing certainty for FOI practitioners and requesters. It would also go further in enhancing transparency than previous Codes by providing that certain information (for example information about the pay and benefits of senior staff) should be made

---

52 FOIA s 48(1); FOI(S)A s 44(1). The Information Commissioner is required to consult the Keeper of the Public Records (or the Deputy Keeper of the Records of Northern Ireland) before giving a practice recommendation relating to conformity with the Lord Chancellor's Code of Practice on record-keeping: FOIA s 48(3) and (4).

53 Hansard HL vol 617 col 944 (17 October 2000) (Lord Bassam of Brighton, Parliamentary Under-Secretary of State, Home Office).

54 This is suggested by the Foreword to the s 45 Code of Practice.

55 This is because compliance with the codes of practice is not a requirement of Pt I of the Act: see FOIA s 50(1). This is confirmed by FOIA s 51(1)(b), which contradistinguishes the requirements of Pt I of the Act from the codes of practice.

56 FOIA s 45.

routinely available. The Code of Practice published on 18 July 2018 is considerably more detailed than the previous version.

21– 011 Content of the section 45 code

The Code is divided into 11 Chapters as follows.

(1) Right of Access. The Code contains a succinct and accessible summary of a public authority's general obligations under the Act covering the right of access, the definition of 'information', whether information is 'held' for the purposes of the Act, the requirements of a valid request, fees which may be charged and the way in which information must be communicated. It also reminds public authorities to ensure that their staff are aware of the criminal offence of altering records with the intent to prevent disclosure, created by s77 of the Act.

(2) Advice and Assistance. This has been addressed in paragraph 21– 005 above.

(3) Consultation with Third Parties. The Code provides that there are circumstances in which public authorities should consult with third parties, which may include:

(a) requests for information which relates to a third party and

(b) requests for information the disclosure of which is likely to affect the interests of a third party.

Views of third parties are important, particularly where they have created the information, but they are not determinative: the decision on disclosure must be taken by the public authority.[57] Decisions to release information following consultation should be drawn to the attention of the third party as soon as possible.[58] If a large number of third parties are affected the Code suggests contacting a representative, or a sample.[59]

(4) Time limits for responding to requests. The Code addresses the statutory 20-day time limit and its extension by regulations in certain cases.[60] It also addresses the public interest test extension and provides that in general best practice is to extend for no more than 20 days but in any event to communicate new deadlines to the applicant.[61]

(5) Internal Reviews. The Code encourages public authorities to have in place an internal review procedure, in relation to their handling of requests for information. The Code encourages public authorities to respond to a request for an internal review within 20 days but in any event to inform the applicant of the target response date.[62] The review should be undertaken by someone other than the original decision-maker and should be a re-evaluation of the request paying particular attention to the applicant's concerns.[63] It may result in different exemptions being applied.[64]

(6) Cost limit. The Code summarises the statutory provisions relating to application of the cost limit and provides some guidance as to how they should be applied: public authorities do not need to search until the costs limit is reached, they must

57 Para 3.3 and 3.4.

58 Para 3.5.

59 Para 3.6.

60 Paras 4.1-4.3.

61 Paras 4.6 and 4.7.

62 Paras 5.4 and 5.5.

63 Para 5.9.

64 Para 5.8.

produce a 'sensible and realistic' estimate rather than a precise calculation, and may wish to consider a sample search.

(7) Vexatious requests. For the first time the Code provides detailed guidance on vexatious requests. It summarises the statutory provisions and the effect of the case law which has developed in this area, focussing on the factors which the tribunals and Court of Appeal have held should be taken into account.[65] It provides examples of cases in which public authorities might wish to consider whether a request is vexatious and directs public authorities to the Information Commissioner's website.[66] The Code addresses the interaction between the cost limit and vexatious requests,[67] repeated requests, and the statutory requirements as to the context of responses to vexatious requests.[68]

(8) Publication schemes. Another new area covered by the Code of Practice is publication schemes. After setting out the statutory obligation and referring public authorities to the Information Commissioner's model publication scheme and guidance,[69] the Code provides specific guidance on two areas. The first is compliance statistics. Public authorities with over 100 FTE employees should publish details of their performance in handling requests under the Act, to include specified minimum details. The second is data to deliver 'sufficient transparency' in relation to senior executive pay and benefits.[70]

(9) Confidentiality and transparency obligations in contracts and outsourced services. Where contractors hold information on behalf of a public authority the Code advises public authorities to make provision, in the contract or in a memorandum of understanding, for the arrangements for the public authority gaining access to the relevant information when a request is made. It recognises that public authorities may be asked to accept confidentiality clauses and advises that public authorities should carefully consider whether such clauses are compatible with their obligations under the Act and with public accountability.[71] Where they are, the Code suggests identifying the relevant information and the reasons for confidentiality.[72]

(10) Communicating with a requester. The Code provides some brief, common sense, guidance on ways to respond to requests, ensuring that the requirements of the Act are complied with.

(11) Datasets. Finally, the Code provides guidance on a public authority's obligations in relation to the release and re-use of datasets (as defined by s11(5) of the Act).[73] Datasets were previously addressed in a separate Code of Practice[74] made under s 45(3) of the Act, following its amendment by the Protection of Freedoms Act 2012 which introduced amendments to FOIA in relation to the provision of datasets. The Code summarises and explains a public authority's obligations under the Act,

65 See §§23– 012 to 23– 016.

66 Para 7.9.

67 Paras 7.12-7.15.

68 Paras 7.17-7.19.

69 Paras 8.1-8.3.

70 Paras 8.7-8.11.

71 Para 9.11.

72 Para 9.12.

73 See further §24– 019.

74 Secretary of State's Code of practice (datasets) on the discharge of public authorities' functions under Part I of the Freedom of Information Act, published on 24 July 2013.

it also recommends that public authorities comply with the Public Data Principles and provide sufficient metadata and contextual information about how and why the dataset was compiled or created.[75] Separate guidance in relation to re-use of datasets is provided in Annex B to the Code.

1– 012 The section 46 code

This Code of Practice was revised and re-issued on 16 July 2009.[76] Its aims are:

(1) To set out practices which public authorities, and bodies subject to the Public Records Act 1958 and the Public Records Act (NI) 1923, should follow in relation to the creation, keeping, management and destruction of their records (including specific provision for management of electronic records) (Part I of the Code); and

(2) To describe the arrangements which public record bodies should follow in reviewing public records and transferring them to The National Archives or to a place of deposit for public records or to the Public Record Office of Northern Ireland (Part II of the Code).

3. PUBLICATION SCHEMES

21– 013 Introduction

Public authorities should not be solely reactive to specific requests for information, but also take steps to ensure that some of their information is publicly available. FOIA does not limit the pre-existing powers of public authorities to disclose their information.[77] Every public authority must adopt and maintain a scheme, called a 'publication scheme'.[78] A publication scheme sets out the classes of information which the public authority intends to make available to the public as a matter of course. In that publication scheme, the public authority must specify the classes of information that it publishes or intends to publish, the manner in which it publishes each class of information, and state whether the material is available to the public free-of-charge or

---

75 Paras 11.17 and 11.18.

76 The code is reproduced in the Appendix. The original code was issued in November 2002.

77 FOIA s 78.

78 FOIA s 19(1); FOI(S)A s 23(1). In relation to environmental information, see §18– 010. The freedom of information legislation in each of the comparative jurisdictions includes the equivalent of a publication scheme. Most of the comparative regimes also require their statutory equivalent of a public authority to prepare and make available a statement that sets out the organisation, functions and adopted policies of the public authority. So far as equivalents of the publication scheme are concerned, in the United States, the Freedom of Information Act 1966 s 552(a)(2) requires that certain sorts of records, such as policy statements and certain administrative staff manuals, be routinely made available for public inspection in 'an electronic format.' In Australia, the Freedom of Information Act 1982 ss 8 - 8D include a comprehensive regime obliging agencies to publish a wide range of accurate, up-to-date information about themselves and their functions. The Information Commissioner may review information publication schemes: s 8F. In Canada, the Access to Information Act 1982 s 5(1) requires the designated Minister to publish at least once a year 'a description of all classes of records under the control of each government institution in sufficient detail to facilitate the exercise of the right of access under [the] Act.' The Minister must also prepare a bulletin at least twice a year, and both documents must be 'made available throughout Canada in conformity with the principle that every person is entitled to reasonable access thereto.' In New Zealand, the Official Information Act 1982 s 20 requires the Ministry of Justice to publish for each Department and organisation subject to the Act a general description of the categories of documents held by it, a description of the manuals containing policies by which decisions are made, as well as the officer to whom requests for information should be sent. Under s 21, a person is entitled to access to the latest edition of the publication, and there are various provisions giving a person an absolute right to particular documents. In Ireland, the Freedom of Information Act 2104 requires each public body to prepare and publish a 'reference book' containing, amongst other things, a general description of the classes of records held by it, giving such particulars as are reasonably necessary to facilitate the exercise of the right of access as well as the rules, procedures, etc used by the body for the purposes of any enactment or scheme administered by it.

on payment.[79] The publication scheme is not intended to be a list of information held by the authority.[80] The rationale for the scheme is two-fold: to spare a public authority from having to deal with standard requests under the Act which it may be anticipated will be sought; and to encourage a culture of openness within public authorities:[81]

> The Freedom of Information Act must be a catalyst for changes in the way that public authorities approach openness. Experience overseas consistently shows the importance of changing the culture through requiring active disclosure, so that public authorities get used to making information publicly available in the course of their activities. This helps ensure that FOI does not simply become a potentially confrontational arrangement under which nothing is released unless someone has specifically asked for it. We believe it is important that further impetus is given to the pro-active release of information. So, the Act will impose duties upon public authorities to make certain information publicly available, as a matter of course.[82]

There is a particular incentive for authorities to publish information under a publication scheme, as it grounds an absolute exemption under Part II of the Act[83] or, in the case of information intended to be published, a qualified exemption, as the information is already reasonably accessible to the applicant.[84] Under the Environmental Information Regulations, there is no requirement for publication schemes as such, but there is provision for dissemination of environmental information electronically.[85] Under section 19(2A)-(2F) of the Act,[86] publication schemes now include a requirement for a public authority to publish any datasets, and any updated version of a dataset, it holds where it is requested by an applicant unless the authority is satisfied that it is not appropriate for the dataset to be so published. Public authorities must, where reasonably practicable, publish any dataset under section 19(2A)(a) in an electronic form which is capable of re-use.[87] Subject to provisions on the charging of fees by public authorities for making datasets (where they contain relevant copyright works) available for re-use,[88] if the public authority is the only owner, it must make any relevant copyright work available for re-use in accordance with the terms of the specified licence[89].

21– 014 Duties of public authorities

The publication scheme requirement comprehends three discrete duties which are imposed upon a public authority:

(1) to adopt and maintain a publication scheme that is approved by the Information

[79] FOIA s 19(2); FOI(S)A s 23(2). Note that local authorities are only empowered to impose charges for such services where authorised by Parliament to do so (*McCarthy & Stone plc v London Borough of Richmond* [1992] 2 AC 48; *R (Stennett) v Manchester CC* [2002] UKHL 34, [2002] 4 All ER 124) and the provisions of the Freedom of Information legislation do not authorise such charging where the information is supplied under a publication scheme, particularly where the statutory scheme makes detailed provision for charges levied on information provided pursuant to specific requests.

[80] House of Commons, *Public Administration—Third Report* (Cm 4355, 1999) Annex 6, para 18 (see Ch 1 n 68).

[81] Hansard HL vol 612 col 826 (20 April 2000) (Minister of State, Cabinet Office, Lord Falconer).

[82] Cabinet Office, *Your Right to Know—The Government's Proposals for a FOI Act. White Paper* (Cm 3818, 1997) paras 2.17-2.18.

[83] FOIA s 21(1); FOI(S)A s 25(1).

[84] FOIA s 22(1); FOI(S)A s 27(1).

[85] See further §18– 010.

[86] Inserted by the Protection of Freedoms Act 2012, with effect from 1 September 2013.

[87] FOIA s 19(2A)(b).

[88] As to which, see §22– 016.

[89] FOIA s 19(8) provides definitions of the terms 'copyright owner', 'copyright work', 'database', 'database right', 'owner', 'relevant copyright work' and 'the specified licence.' The definition of a 'relevant copyright work' excludes a 'relevant Crown work' and a 'relevant Parliamentary work' which are separately defined.

Commissioner;

(2) to publish information in accordance with its publication scheme; and

(3) from time to time to review that publication scheme.[90]

However, nothing in section 19 prohibits or in any way prevents a public authority from relying on one or more exemptions contained in Part II of FOIA in response to a request for information – albeit that this may amount to a breach of section 19 if the authority refuses to publish information in accordance with its publication scheme.[91]

21– 015 Model publication schemes

In practice, rather than approving individual schemes for each public authority, the Information Commissioner has since 1 January 2009, used the power granted under s 20 of FOIA to prepare model publication schemes which public authorities are required to adopt. The current model publication scheme, dated 23 October 2015, includes revisions which take account of the amendments to the Act relating to datasets. There are two, near identical, versions: one of the majority of public authorities and another for public authorities for only part of their functions. The model publication schemes commit the public authority to making available to the public information within seven specified classes, where that information is held by the authority (and in the case of bodies where the information is about the functions for which the body is a public authority). The classes of information are:

(1) Who we are and what we do;

(2) What we spend and how we spend it;

(3) What our priorities are and how we are doing;

(4) How we make decisions;

(5) Our policies and procedures;

(6) Lists and registers; and

(7) The services we offer.

The model scheme provides that the authority will indicate clearly to the public what information is available to the public and how it can be obtained. It provides that any material provided on a website by the public authority will be made free of charges and that any other charges will be 'justified and transparent and kept to a minimum.' Any charges must be in accordance with a published schedule of fees which is accessible to the public. Thus public authorities must produce and publish the following documents to supplement the model scheme: a guide to information setting out what information (within the seven classes) they publish and how it is made available; and a schedule of fees charged. In order to assist public authorities with producing their guide to information the Information Commissioner has produced guidance in the form of 'definition documents' setting out the information that the Commissioner would normally expect public authorities in various different sectors to publish. The sectors covered by definition documents are: :

- Government departments;
- the House of Commons;
- the House of Lords;
- the Northern Ireland Assembly;
- Northern Ireland Government departments;
- Northern Ireland non departmental public bodies;
- Northern Ireland District Councils;
- Education and library boards Northern Ireland;
- the National Assembly for Wales;

[90] FOIA s 19(1); FOI(S)A s 23(1).

[91] *Wilson v IC*, FTT, 15 June 2010 at [32]-[42].

- Welsh Assembly Government;
- Welsh Assembly Government sponsored bodies;
- Principal local authorities;
- Joint authorities and boards;
- Inshore Fisheries and Conservation Authorities;
- National parks and Broads authorities and conservation boards;
- Charter Trustees;
- Health bodies in England;
- Health bodies in Wales;
- Community Health Councils, Wales;
- Health bodies, Northern Ireland;
- Health regulators;
- Patient and Client Care Council - Northern Ireland;
- Higher education institutions;
- Colleges of further education;
- Schools in England, Northern Ireland and Wales;
- Elected local policing bodies;
- Police authorities;
- Police forces;
- Armed forces;
- Museums, libraries, art galleries and historical collections;
- Non-departmental public bodies; and
- Wholly owned companies.

For some smaller public authorities (namely, for parish councils, parish meetings, Community Councils in Wales, dentists, general practitioners, opticians, pharmacists, and schools) the Information Commissioner has produced template guides to information which can simply be completed. The Information Commissioner has published guidance, entitled 'Model publication scheme: Using the definition documents,' which explains to public authorities how to fulfill their obligations to make certain information routinely available and how to make use of the definition documents. The Commissioner has also published guidance going into further detail on matters related to the model scheme: in order to help public authorities decided when they should publish the minutes and agendas of meetings and in which cases they can be edited;[92] explaining the provisions relating to datasets;[93] and fees.[94] There is also guidance on proactive dissemination under the EIRs

21–016 Publication schemes: Scotland

The position in Scotland is different. Until 2011, there was no single approved model publication scheme in Scotland. Bodies had to submit schemes to the Scottish Commissioner for approval. Since 2011, the Commissioner has been developing and approving a single model publication scheme, reviewed and updated each year, which is suitable for adoption by all authorities. The Scottish Commissioner produces guidance on adopting and using the model scheme. Authorities adopting the Model Publication Scheme are not required to submit a scheme for approval (as the model scheme is already approved by the Commissioner) but they must notify the Commissioner that they have adopted the model scheme. They must also produce and publish a guide to information setting out the information they make available through the scheme and explaining how to access it. In contrast to the position in England,

[92] *What should be published? Minutes and agendas.*

[93] *Datasets (section 11, 19 & 45).*

[94] *Charging for information in a publication scheme.*

Wales and Northern Ireland, the option is still available to authorities to submit a bespoke scheme of their own design to the Commissioner for approval.[95] However, the Scottish Commissioner strongly recommends that public authorities adopt the model publication scheme, and all Scottish public authorities have now done so.

1– 017 Enforcing publication schemes

Where a public authority breaches its statutory duty to to adopt a publication scheme approved by the Information Commissioner, the Commissioner can serve an enforcement notice on the authority requiring it to remedy this.[96] In England, Wales and Northern Ireland, the Information Commissioner has exercised control over the content of publication schemes by publishing a single approved model scheme which all public authorities are obliged to adopt. It is therefore most unlikely that the Commissioner would take action in respect of the content of the publication scheme itself. The model scheme does, however, require public authorities to produce supplementary documents, in particular the guide to information, and to make information available in accordance with the scheme. Enforcement notices could be served on public authorities who fail to comply with these obligations.[97] If a public authority fails to provide information under its publication scheme a standard request for information can be made with any refusal[98] appealable to the Information Commissioner and the Tribunal in the normal way. Furthermore, the Information Commissioner can also issue a Practice Recommendation where there has been non-conformity with the Code of Practice. The extension of the Code of Practice under s 45 of the Act to address publication schemes (and in particular the two specific categories of information to be provided)[99] provides scope for the Information Commissioner to issue Practice Recommendations in relation to a failure to comply with the requirements as to publication schemes.

4. GUIDANCE

21– 018 Sources of guidance

The Information Commissioner has a statutory obligation, pursuant to s 47(2) of FOIA, to disseminate, in such manner as the Commissioner considers appropriate, information to the public about the operation of the Act, good practice, and other matters within the scope of her functions under the Act. The Commissioner has issued an increasing volume of guidance, on the operation of the Act generally, on the application of individual exemptions and on a wide variety of specific issues which arise under the Act. The guidance is regularly updated in response to legal developments. A number of different government departments have also issued guidance on the application of the Act. Perhaps because of the volume and detail of the guidance now provided by the Information Commissioner, departmental guidance is rarer than in the early days of operation of the Act. The Information Commissioner has published a range of separate guidance documents in relation to environmental information.

---

95 FOI(S)A s 23.

96 Under FOIA s 52(1), or FOI(S)A s 51(1).

97 On the basis that a request for information has not been dealt with in accordance with Pt I of the Act. For enforcement notices, see FOIA s 52 and FOI(S)A s 52 discussed in §§47– 003 and 47– 009.

98 Which could not be on the basis of the exemptions usually application to publication scheme information, that the information was accessible by other means or intended for future publication: FOIA ss 21 and 22; FOI(S)A ss 25 and 27.

99 See §21– 011.

21– 019 Status of guidance

The guidance documents issued by the Information Commissioner and government departments do not have any statutory force.[100] FOIA neither provides for nor requires such guidance to be given.[101] Nor is there any statutory requirement upon a public authority either to follow or even to have regard to such guidance. The guidance documents are no more authoritative than any other statement of opinion by a public official. However, public authorities would be well advised to pay close attention to and, in the absence of good reason for departure from it, to follow the Information Commissioner's guidance. Not only does much of it contain a succinct summary of the requirements of the relevant legislative provisions as developed by Tribunal case law but it may provide a clear indication of the approach the Information Commissioner would take on an eventual application for a decision under s 50 of the Act.

21– 020 Practice recommendations

Where the Information Commissioner considers that the practice of a public authority in relation to the exercise of its functions under the Act does not conform with that proposed in the Codes of Practice, the Commissioner can give the public authority a written 'practice recommendation' specifying the steps which in the opinion of the Commissioner ought to be taken for promoting such conformity.[102] Non-compliance with a Code of Practice could form part of a wider challenge to the discharge by a public authority of its duties under the Act.[103]

---

[100] See, for example: *Dransfield v IC and Devon CC* [2015] EWCA Civ 454, [2015] 1 WLR 5316 at [32]; *Dept of Environment (Northern Ireland) v IC* [2016] UKUT 83 (AAC) at [22], the Upper Tribunal observing that it is nevertheless 'helpful in addressing the practical problems which can arise in particular cases...'

[101] Indeed, FOIA s 45-46 and 60-61 contemplate that any guidance that is to be given will find expression in the s 45 Code of Practice or the s 46 Code of Practice. The position is the same with FOI(S)A.

[102] FOIA s 48(1); FOI(S)A s 44(1). See §21– 008.

[103] See the discussion in §21– 009.

CHAPTER 22
The request

1. THE REQUEST FOR INFORMATION

22–001 Introduction

Under FOIA, for a person to exercise his right to information held by a public authority, he must first make a 'request for information'.[1] A 'request for information' is one that:[2]

— is made in writing;
— states the name of the applicant;
— states an address for correspondence; and

---

1 FOIA s 1(1). The FOI(S)A does not invoke the concept of a defined 'request for information' but gives an entitlement to 'a person who requests information': FOI(S)A s 1(1). Section 8(1) of the FOI(S)A provides that a reference in that Act to 'requesting' information is a reference to a request which, save for the requirement that it be in writing, has the same characteristics as a 'request for information' under the FOIA.

2 FOIA s 8(1).

— describes the information requested.

Quite apart from meeting the formal requirements of each statutory regime, the terms of a request are of fundamental importance. An applicant's description of the information sought will determine the efficacy of the request; the cost of compliance; the public authority's obligation to comply with the request on the grounds of particularity, repetitiveness, etc; the information yielded; and, thereafter, the applicable exemptions. It is suggested that, save for routine requests, it will generally be in the interests of both the applicant and the public authority for a request to describe the information sought by reference to one or more of the following attributes:

a) the date or period over which the information was created or first held by the public authority;
(b) the subject matter of the information, with as much precision as possible;
(c) the types of information sought (eg correspondence, reports, internal documents and so forth);
(d) the authorship or provenance of the information, if needs be by class;
(e) the original intended recipient of the information; and
(f) the manner in which the information is recorded (eg written or stored on a computer, etc).

This is not to say that an applicant should strive to guess precisely what information is held by a public authority: it is simply a matter of reflecting upon the attributes of the information that is being sought and attempting, so far as is reasonably practicable, to articulate those attributes. Whilst an applicant's motives for requesting information are irrelevant to a request,[3] where an applicant anticipates that some or all of the information may fall within a qualified exemption, it may be in the applicant's interests to set out in the request any facts and matters which may relate to the public interest in disclosing the information.[4] Finally, there will be circumstances in which it will be mutually advantageous for an applicant to take a staged approach to requesting information from a public authority. For example, a properly-drawn first request may be designed to elicit information that will assist in the subsequent identification of the information sought to be disclosed.[5]

22– 002 Must be in writing

A request made under FOIA must be made in writing.[6] 'Writing' means the representation or reproduction of words in a visible form.[7] A request is deemed to have been made in writing where it has been transmitted by electronic means, it has been received in legible form and it is capable of being used for subsequent reference.[8] Accordingly, a request made by way of a facsimile transmission or email qualifies as a request made in writing. The *Code of Practice* provides that a request submitted through social media will be valid where it meets the requirements of section 8 by providing an applicant's name and address for correspondence and a clear request for information provided that the public authority has a formal, monitorable

3 See §§20– 017, 23– 013 and 6– 015.

4 See §§6– 011, 6– 012 and 6– 018.

5 For example, a request for a list of files relating to a particular topic may, when answered, help the applicant to identify from which of those files a second request for information should be answered. If the second request does not yield the information expected, the applicant can make a third request identifying other files from the list, and so on.

6 FOIA s 8(1)(a); cf EIR reg 5; EI(S)R reg 5; and see further §18– 014. The FOI(S)A provides that although such a request may be made in writing, it may also be made in another form which has some permanency: see §22– 004.

7 Interpretation Act 1978 s 5 and Sch 1.

8 FOIA s 8(2); FOI(S)A s 8(2).

presence on the particular platform being used by an applicant.[9]

22–003 Oral requests

The requirement under the Acts that a request be made in writing means that an oral request will not be sufficient to give rise to an obligation on a public authority to communicate information.[10] However, where a person makes a request orally, they should be advised, pursuant to a public authority's duty to provide advice and assistance, to put their application in writing in accordance with the requirements of the Act.[11] The *Code of Practice* suggests that where a person is unable to put his request in writing, the public authority should provide appropriate assistance to enable that person to make a request for information, such as pointing him or her towards another person who could assist him (such as a Citizen's Advice Bureau) or, in exceptional circumstances, by taking a note of the person's request and then sending it to him for confirmation (in which case receipt of the confirmed note would constitute a written request).[12]

22–004 Scottish public authorities

For Scottish public authorities, a request need not be made in writing but may be made in another form which, by reason of it having some permanency, is capable of being used for subsequent reference.[13] FOI(S)A cites recordings made on audio or video tape as specific examples of such a form,[14] and a request by email would also clearly suffice.[15]

22–005 Name of applicant

A request made under FOIA or FOI(S)A must state the name of the applicant.[16] In this context, 'the applicant' is the person who is making the request.[17] As noted elsewhere,[18] the identity of the applicant will only be relevant to a public authority's obligation to communicate information in limited circumstances.[19] The fact that 'any person' may make a request for information means that there is no reason why one individual cannot apply on behalf of another,[20] there is no need for an applicant to have any particular standing to seek information and an applicant need not be a United Kingdom national or resident.[21] The *Code of Practice*

9 Section 45 Code of Practice, para 1.16.

10 In Scotland, an oral request recorded onto audio or video tape would be sufficient: see §22–004.

11 Section 45 Code of Practice, para 2.4.

12 Section 45 Code of Practice, para 2.5.

13 FOI(S)A s 8(1)(a).

14 FOI(S)A s 8(1)(a). Quite why anyone would wish to make a request by video tape is not obvious.

15 The Scottish Ministers code of Practice, para 4.4.2 advises that a sufficiently permanent voicemail message would be a valid request under the FOI(S)A.

16 FOIA s 8(1)(b); FOI(S)A s 8(1)(b). There is no such requirement in relation to a request for 'environmental information': EIR reg 5(1); EI(S)R reg 5(1); and see §18–014.

17 FOIA s 84; FOI(S)A s 1(2). In the House of Lords debate on this provision, it was suggested by the Parliamentary Under-Secretary of State for the Home Office that s 8(1)(b) of the FOIA did not require an applicant to give his real name: Hansard HL vol 619 col 184 (14 November 2000). However, the requirement in s 8(1)(b) to give '*the* name *of* the applicant rather than '*a* name *for*' the applicant suggests the contrary. The Section 45 Code of Practice provides, at para 1.14 concerning validity of requests, that applicants must provide their real name, not a pseudonym.

18 See §23–013.

19 For example, in the case of vexatious or repeated requests (see §§23–012 to 23–020).

20 As was recognised in the House of Commons' Public Administration Committee's *Third Report* (Cm 4355, 1999) Annex 6, para 14 (see Ch 1 n 68).

21 As is recognised in the *Explanatory Notes to the Freedom of Information Act 2000*, para 49. As to applications made by

provides that if a public authority considers the applicant has not provided their real name the public authority can make the applicant aware it does not intend to respond to the request until further information is received from the applicant. It provides as an example the case when an applicant appears to have used a pseudonym.[22]

22– 006 Address for correspondence

A request made under FOIA or FOI(S)A must state an address for correspondence.[23] Neither FOIA nor FOI(S)A specifies what is meant by 'an address for correspondence.' The *Code of Practice* provides that addresses for correspondence can take the form of an email address or a unique name or identifier on a social media platform (for example a Twitter handle), as well as postal addresses.[24]

22– 007 Information description

A request for information must describe the information requested.[25] There is no formal obligation on an applicant to describe the information sought in a particular way and, in particular, an applicant is not required to describe a particular record.[26] Conversely, the Upper Tribunal has held that a request for particular records (emails sent and received by particular individuals) constituted a valid request even though it did not describe the information sought within those emails.[27] It is questionable whether it would be sufficient for an applicant to request a random sample of information, as this does not identify the information requested but requires the intercession of an act of selection by the public authority.[28] Where a request does not describe the information requested with sufficient particularity, the recipient public authority ought to consider whether it should advise or assist the applicant in relation to the proper particularisation of his request, whether it should inform the applicant that it requires further particulars,[29] or both. Public authorities should take care to look beyond the language or tone of a request for information and should focus on the substance of what is being requested.[30] The mere fact that a public authority does not approve of the language used, or allegations made, in a request does not prevent such a request being a request for the purposes of the legislation.[31] The Tribunal takes a fairly liberal, rather than literal, approach to requests.[32] The scope of a request must, in general, be determined on an objective reading of the request itself in the light of any relevant background facts.[33]

---

persons outside the United Kingdom, see §20– 014.

22 Section 45 Code of Practice, para 2.7.

23 FOIA s 8(1)(b); FOI(S)A s 8(1)(b).

24 Section 45 Code of Practice , para 1.16.

25 FOIA s 8(1)(c); FOI(S)A s 8(1)(c).

26 As is recognised in the *Explanatory Notes to the Freedom of Information Act 2000*, para 23. But see §22– 001.

27 See *Dept of Environment (Northern Ireland) v IC* [2016] UKUT 83 (AAC), where the Upper Tribunal rejected the Department's argument that such a request was a request for a medium on which information was recorded rather than a request for information as required by s 8(1)(c).

28 See *Redfern v University of Canberra* (1995) 38 ALD 457 in relation to the comparable s 15(2)(b) of the Freedom of Information Act 1982 (Cth of Australia).

29 As to requiring particulars in order to identify and locate requested information, see §§22– 010 to 22– 011.

30 *Barber v IC*, IT, 20 February 2006 at [9] and [12]. The fact that the request is in accusatorial terms should not generally be used as a basis for refusing to treat the request as valid.

31 Subject, of course, to the provisions on vexatious requests: see §§23– 012 to 23– 016.

32 See, for example, *Alcock v IC and Chief Constable of Staffordshire Police*, IT, 3 January 2007 at [25].

33 *Dept for Culture, Media & Sport v IC*, FTT, 22 February 2010 at [16]; *Dedalus Ltd v IC and Arts Council of England*, FTT, 21 May 2010 at [35]-[37].

2– 008 Matters not required

There is no requirement in FOIA[34] for a request for information to make reference to the fact that it is being made under the Act. Nevertheless, as a public authority has a duty to provide advice and assistance to those who make requests under the Act, it is desirable that a request for information states that it is being made under FOIA. Further, as there is no requirement in the Act that a request for information be sent to a particular individual or department within a public authority, it will be necessary for public authorities to ensure that all staff who might receive such requests are aware of the appropriate procedures for dealing with them.[35]

22– 009 Advice and assistance

A public authority has a duty to provide advice and assistance, so far as it is reasonable to expect it to do so, to persons who have made or who propose to make requests for information to it pursuant to the Freedom of Information Acts.[36] Compliance with the relevant provisions of the *Code of Practice*[37] is deemed to be compliance with the duty to provide advice and assistance.[38] The terms of the Code of Practice indicate that there is a strong emphasis on public authorities providing advice and assistance to applicants and potential applicants and that public authorities will be discouraged from relying upon formal or procedural defects in would-be requests for information to avoid having to comply with requests which would otherwise have been valid.

2. PARTICULARISING THE REQUEST

22– 010 Introduction

Although a request for information under FOIA or FOI(S)A must describe the information requested,[39] both Acts make provision for the situation in which an applicant does not provide sufficient detail of the requested information to enable the public authority to identify and locate that information.[40]

22– 011 Insufficient particularity

Under FOIA, where a public authority reasonably requires further detail about the information requested in order to identify and locate that information, then, as long as it has informed the applicant of that requirement,[41] the public authority is not obliged to provide the information requested unless it is furnished with the further detail that it requires to identify and locate that information. In such a case, the time allowed for the public authority to comply with the

---

34 Or FOI(S)A, DPA 1998, EIR, or EI(S)R.

35 This is recommended by para 15 of the foreword to the s 45 Code of Practice.

36 FOIA s 16(1); FOI(S)A s 15(1). See §§21– 001 to 21– 006 and, in relation to 'environmental information', see §18– 013.

37 As to the s 45 Code of Practice, see §§21– 007 to 21– 011.

38 FOIA s 16(2); FOI(S)A s 15(2).

39 As to the requirement that a request for information must describe the information requested, see §22– 007.

40 In relation to a request for, or to the extent that a request includes, 'environmental information', see EIR reg 9(2); EI(S)R reg 9(2). As to the treatment of inadequately particularised requests under the EIR, see §18– 013.

41 The original version of s 1(3) of the FOIA did not feature the requirement that a public authority must inform an applicant that it requires further particulars before it is absolved of its obligations under s 1(1): Freedom of Information Bill 1999, cl 8(3).

request for information only starts to run from the date on which it receives the further details.[42] A public authority may only seek further details which are relevant to identifying the information sought by the applicant and not, for example, to the applicant or his motives.[43] Further, a public authority may not seek further details which an applicant could not reasonably be expected to have, such as a file number or the exact location of the information sought.[44] The *Code of Practice* recommends that, where a request for information is insufficiently clear, the public authority should ask for more detail to enable them to identify the information sought.[45] A failure to seek to elicit greater particularity may constitute a failure of the duty to advise and assist.[46]

3. FEES

22– 012 Introduction

Both FOIA and FOI(S)A establish a framework for the charging of fees by any public authority that receives a request for information.[47] Neither Act obliges a public authority to charge fees. In some cases, a public authority will have had the practice of voluntarily providing information pursuant to informal requests: there is nothing in FOIA to prevent such a practice continuing.[48] The level of fee is to be determined in accordance with regulations.[49] The relevant regulations are the Freedom of Information and Data Protection (Appropriate Limit and Fees) Regulations 2004 SI 2004/3244.[50] The *Code of Practice*[51] covers the charging of fees and the Information Commissioner has issued guidance on the regulations.[52]

22– 013 Fees notice: FOIA

Where a public authority receives a request for information, it may, within the period of time allowed for it to comply with its duties under s 1(1) of FOIA, give the applicant a fees notice. A fees notice is a notice in writing which states that a fee of the amount stated in the notice is

---

42 As to the time for compliance generally, see §22– 020. To the extent that a request for information captures 'environmental information', see §18– 016.

43 As to the irrelevancy of motives, see §20– 017. See also the House of Commons' *Public Administration –Committee's Third Report* (Cm 4355, 1999) Annex 6, para 25 (see Ch 1 n 68).

44 See the House of Commons' *Public Administration Committee's Third Report* (Cm 4355, 1999) Annex 6, para 25.

45 Section 45 Code of Practice, para 2.8.

46 See §§21– 001 to 21– 006. This may be the subject of complaint to the Information Commissioner and of appeal to the First-Tier Tribunal.

47 FOIA s 9; FOI(S)A s 9. The EIR also provide for the charging of fees: EIR reg 8; EI(S)R reg 8. As to the charging of fees under the EIR, see further §18– 015. It is suggested that where a request for information captures information some of which falls to be disclosed under the FOI/FOI(S)A regime and some of which falls to be disclosed under the EIR/EI(S)R regime, it is impermissible for a public authority to aggregate the two or deal with them other than under their respective regimes. This is because the right to each of the two classes of information has a distinct statutory provenance.

48 See §22– 013. Arguably, the disclosure remains one under FOIA, rather than a true discretionary disclosure: see §§20– 036 to 20– 038.

49 FOIA s 9(3); FOI(S)A s 9(4). This restriction does not apply where provision is made by or under another enactment for the charging of a fee by a public authority for the disclosure of the information (FOIA s 9(5); FOI(S)A s 9(7)).

50 In Scotland, the Fees (Scot) Regs.

51 *Section 45 Code of Practice*, paras 1.18-1.23. And in Scotland, the *Scottish Ministers Code of Practice*, section 5.6.

52 *Fees that may be charged when the cost of compliance does not exceed the appropriate limit.*

to be charged by the public authority for complying with its duties under s 1(1).[53] Section 9 gives a public authority a 'time window' within which to give an applicant a fees notice. The *Code of Practice* advises that the fees notice should include information about how the fee has been calculated. It should inform applicants that the 20 working-day period for responding is paused, how to pay the fee, and of their rights of complaint via internal review and to the Information Commissioner about the fee levied.

22– 014 Fees notice: FOI(S)A

In Scotland, a fees notice must set out the manner in which the fee has been calculated.[54] A fees notice in Scotland must also comply with the formal requirements prescribed by s 19 of FOI(S)A.[55] A fees notice in Scotland must therefore also contain particulars of the procedure provided by the public authority for dealing with complaints about the handling by it of requests for information[56] and about the rights of the applicant to apply for a review of the public authority's actions and to apply to the Commissioner for a decision as to whether the public authority has acted in accordance with Part I of the Act.[57]

22– 015 Determination of fees

Unless provision is made by or under some other enactment for the charging of fees by a public authority for the disclosure of information,[58] then any fee must be determined in accordance with the relevant regulations.[59] Accordingly, although the fees regime gives a public authority a discretion as to whether to give an applicant a fees notice, if it decides to give a fees notice, it has no discretion as to whether it applies the fees regulations. As will be seen, those regulations prescribe the maximum fee that may be charged but, subject to that upper limit, a public authority has a discretion as to the amount of fee that it charges.

22– 016 Amount of fees: FOIA

The Freedom of Information and Data Protection (Appropriate Limit and Fees) Regulations 2004 provide that the fee is not to exceed a maximum equivalent to the total costs that the public authority reasonably expects to incur in informing the person making the request whether it holds the information and in communicating the information.[60] The costs that the public authority may take into account when calculating the total costs that it expects to incur include the costs of complying with any obligation under s 11(1) as to the means or form of communicating the information, the costs of reproducing any document containing the information and the costs of postage and any other forms of transmitting the information.[61] However a public authority may not take into account any costs which are attributable to the time which persons undertaking the activities of informing the applicant whether the public authority holds the information or of communicating the information are expected to spend on

53 FOIA s 9(1); FOI(S)A s 9(1).

54 Fees (Scot) Regs reg 4(4).

55 FOI(S)A s 9(2).

56 FOI(S)A s 19(a).

57 FOI(S)A s 19(b).

58 FOIA s 9(3) and (5); FOI(S)A s 9(4) and (7).

59 FOIA s 9(3); FOI(S)A s 9(4). The relevant regulations are the Fees Regs 2004 (in relation to the FOIA) and the Fees (Scot) Regs (in relation to the FOI(S)A).

60 Fees Regs 2004 reg 6(1) and (2). In relation to fees for environmental information, see §18– 015.

61 Fees Regs 2004 reg 6(3).

those activities.[62] Nor may a public authority take into account what may prove to be the most time-consuming part of the exercise, ie ascertaining whether the information is exempt information and, if so, the public interest balancing exercise. The regulations do not prescribe a particular method for calculating the amount of any fee that is to be charged. Accordingly, where a public authority exercises its discretion to charge a fee, it has a further discretion as to the amount of the fee that it charges (provided always that it does not exceed the prescribed maximum). Nevertheless, a public authority exercising its discretion as to the amount of the fee to be charged must do so in accordance with normal public law principles.[63] Thus, improper discrimination between different types of requests or a lack of consistency in approach in relation to the amount of fees will be unlawful.

22– 017 Amount of fees: FOI(S)A

The Fees (Scot) Regs invoke the concept of 'projected costs' in the context of the amount of fees that may be charged.[64] In relation to a request for information, the 'projected costs' are the total costs, whether direct or indirect, which a public authority reasonably estimates that it is likely to incur in locating, retrieving and providing such information.[65] However, in estimating projected costs, no account may be taken of costs incurred in determining whether the public authority holds the information specified in the request or whether the person seeking the requested information is entitled to receive it (or, if not so entitled, whether he should nevertheless be provided with it or refused it).[66] Further, any estimate of the cost of staff time shall not exceed £15 per hour per member of staff.[67] Where the projected costs do not exceed £100, no fee shall be payable[68] and where the projected costs exceed £100 but do not exceed £600,[69] the fee shall not exceed ten per cent of the difference between the projected costs and £100.[70]

22– 018 Effect of fees notice

Where a public authority gives a fees notice to an applicant, it is not required to comply with s 1(1) of the relevant Act unless the applicant pays the fee within the period of three months beginning with the day on which the fees notice is given to the applicant.[71] Where a fees notice has been given to an applicant and he has paid the fee within the requisite period, the time taken for the applicant to pay the fee is to be disregarded when calculating the date on which the public authority is required to comply with s 1(1).[72] The combined effect of the provisions makes it prudent for a public authority to serve a fees notice as soon as possible after receipt of a request. In this way a public authority may lessen the possibility of abortive costs where an applicant subsequently indicates that he is not prepared to pay. The fact that a public authority

62 Fees Regs 2004 reg 6(4).

63 For an example of a case where the Tribunal held that the fees charged by a public authority were unreasonable (in the context of the EIR), see *Markinson v IC*, IT, 28 March 2006.

64 Fees (Scot) Regs reg 4.

65 Fees (Scot) Regs reg 3(1).

66 Fees (Scot) Regs reg 3(2)(a).

67 Fees (Scot) Regs reg 3(2)(b).

68 Fees (Scot) Regs reg 4(2).

69 That is, the amount prescribed under reg 5 of the Fees (Scot) Regs.

70 Fees (Scot) Regs reg 4(3). The intention may have been that, when projected costs exceed £600, the excessive cost provisions come into play. However, this is not necessarily the case: see §23– 005.

71 FOIA s 9(2); FOI(S)A s 9(3). This is a similar formulation to that used in other comparable legislation, such as s 111(2)(a) of the Employment Rights Act 1996.

72 FOIA s 10(2); FOI(S)A s 10(3).

gives a fees notice in which the fee is calculated on the basis of a prospective estimate of costs means that, should the actual cost of complying with the request for information be higher than the fee stated in the fees notice, the public authority cannot then claim that additional sum from the applicant: the public authority must bear the burden of any additional cost. The Information Commissioner recommends, as a matter of good practice, that if the actual cost of complying with the request is lower than the amount specified public authorities should refund the excess.[73]

22– 019 Excessive cost of compliance

In cases where a public authority is not obliged to comply with a request for information because the cost of complying with it is deemed to be excessive,[74] where the communication of the information is not otherwise required by law, and where no provision is made by or under another enactment for the charging of fees, if the public authority nevertheless decides to communicate the information it may charge a fee for doing so.[75] In such a case, it will be good practice for the public authority to provide an indication of what information could be provided within the costs ceiling or to advise the applicant that a reformulated request for information may result in information being supplied for a lower, or no, fee. The fee is to be determined by the public authority in accordance with regulations.[76]

4. TIME FOR COMPLIANCE

22– 020 Introduction

A public authority is required to comply with a request for information promptly and in any event not later than the twentieth working day following the 'date of receipt'.[77] Although the date of receipt is generally the date on which the public authority receives the request,[78] it is effectively postponed in cases where a public authority has sought further particulars of a request[79] and extended where a public authority has given a fees notice to an applicant.[80]

22– 021 Promptness

The primary obligation imposed on a public authority is to promptly comply with s 1(1) of the Act.[81] Accordingly, the requirement that a public authority comply in any event not later than the 20th working day following the date of receipt is an outer, or 'long-stop', time-limit:[82] the fact that a public authority complies within 20 working days will not necessarily mean that it

73 ICO Guidance, *Fees that may be charged when the cost of compliance does not exceed the appropriate limit.*

74 As to the situation where the cost of complying with a request for information would be excessive, see §§23– 001 to 23– 010.

75 FOIA s 13(1) and (3); FOI(S)A s 13(1) and (4).

76 FOIA s 13(1); FOI(S)A s 13(1). The relevant regulations are the Fees (s 13) Regs.

77 FOIA s 10(1). The FOI(S)A s 10(1) does not invoke a defined concept of 'date of receipt', but its effect is the same. The EIR require information to be made available 'as soon as possible and no later than 20 days after the date of receipt of the request': EIR reg 5(2). As to the time for compliance with requests for information under the EIR, see §18– 016.

78 FOIA s 10(6); FOI(S)A s 10(1)(a).

79 FOIA ss 1(3) and 10(6); FOI(S)A ss 1(3) and 10(1)(b).

80 FOIA s 10(2); FOI(S)A s 10(3).

81 FOIA s 10(1); FOI(S)A s 10(1).

82 This was the intention: see Hansard HC vol 347 col 858 (4 April 2000).

has complied promptly.[83] It is implicit[84] in the dual requirement that there will be instances in which compliance in 20 or fewer working days will not constitute prompt compliance. There is no provision in FOIA to deal with the situation where a request for information is particularly urgent.[85] However, the urgency or otherwise of a request is likely to be one of the factors relevant to an assessment of whether a public authority has promptly complied with its obligations under s 1(1).

22–022 Date of receipt

Ordinarily, the period for compliance with a request for information is calculated from the date of actual receipt, namely the day on which the public authority receives the request for information.[86] However, in a case where a public authority has sought further particulars about a request,[87] then the date of receipt is deemed to be the day on which the public authority receives the further particulars sought by it.[88]

22–023 Meaning of a 'working day'

A 'working day' is any day other than a Saturday, a Sunday, Christmas Day, Good Friday or a bank holiday 'in any part of the United Kingdom'.[89]

22–024 Effect of a fees notice

Where a public authority has given a fees notice to an applicant and the fee is paid within the specified period,[90] the working days in the period beginning with the day on which the fees notice is given to the applicant and ending on the day on which the fee is received by the public authority are to be disregarded when calculating the 20th working day following the date of receipt.[91]

22–025 Effect of a qualified exemption

To the extent that the requested information is exempt information by virtue of one of the qualified exemptions[92] in Part II of FOIA, then the ordinary 20-working-day time limit for compliance is extended, but only for the purpose of conducting the public interest balancing

83 This accords with the approach adopted to similar provisions in the former RSC Ord 53 r 3(4) (see now CPR 54.5(1)): *R v Independent Television Commission, ex p TV NI Ltd, The Times*, 30 December 1991 (CA).

84 On the basis that there is a strong presumption that every word in a statute must be given some effective meaning: *McMonagle v Westminster City Council* [1990] 2 AC 716 at 727; *Gubay v Kingston* [1984] 1 WLR 163 (HL) at 172.

85 Compare the Official Information Act 1982 (New Zealand) s 12(3), which provides that an applicant may inform the body of which he makes his request that the request is urgent and the reasons why it is urgent.

86 FOIA s 10(6)(a); FOI(S)A s 10(1)(a).

87 As to requiring particulars in order to identify and locate requested information, see §§22–010 to 22–011.

88 FOIA s 10(6)(b); FOI(S)A s 10(1)(b).

89 FOIA s 10(6); FOI(S)A s 73. The FOI(S)A only excludes bank holidays 'in Scotland' from the definition of a 'working day' and Good Friday is a working day for the purposes of the FOI(S)A. Because bank holidays under the Banking and Financial Dealings Act 1971 differ in the various parts of the United Kingdom, the effect of the FOIA referring to a bank holiday under the Banking and Financial Dealings Act 1971 'in any part' of the United Kingdom is to exclude each of the following days: New Year's Day (or if New Year's Day be a Sunday, 2 January, or if 2 January be a Sunday, 3 January), 17 March (or if 17 March be a Sunday, 18 March), Easter Monday, the first Monday in May, the last Monday in May, the first Monday in August, the last Monday in August, 25 December, 26 December (if it not be a Sunday) and 27 December (in a year in which 25 or 26 December is a Sunday): see Banking and Financial Dealings Act 1971 Sch 1.

90 As to the period within which fees must be paid, see §22–018.

91 FOIA s 10(2); FOI(S)A s 10(3). Where a request is for, or to the extent that a request includes, 'environmental information', see EIR reg 8(5)-(6); EI(S)R reg 8(6)-(7); and see further §18–015.

92 The qualified exemptions are listed at §5–017.

exercise.[93] For this exercise, the public authority is allowed 'such time as is reasonable in the circumstances'.[94] Some idea of what is meant by 'reasonable in the circumstances' can be deduced from the fact that where s 10(3) applies, the only addition to the public authority's burden in dealing with the request is the balancing exercise set out in s 2(1) and (2) of the Act. On the assumption that Parliament, in specifying the ordinary time limit in s 10(1), was not setting a time limit that it thought was or might be unreasonable in any circumstance, it is to be inferred that the 'reasonable time' permitted by s 10(3) can only exceed the time limit set by s 10(1) to the extent, if any, that is reasonably required to carry out the public interest balancing exercise. This reading is confirmed by the requirements of s 17, relating to the giving of a refusal notice. Section 10(3) expressly retains the obligation to give a refusal notice within the ordinary 20-working-day time limit, even where a qualified exemption is involved. Where s 10(3) applies, however, if the public interest balancing exercise has not been determined within that ordinary time limit, the refusal notice must state that an exemption applies and that no decision has been taken on the balancing exercise required by the Act, and must give an estimate of the date on which the public authority expects that such a decision will be taken.[95] Where a request for information relates to information, some of which is exempt information by virtue of one of the qualified exemptions and the rest of which is either not exempt or is exempt information by virtue of one of the absolute exemptions, the public authority must both disclose the non-exempt information and give a refusal notice (dealing with everything save for the public interest balancing exercise) within the ordinary time limit.

22–026 **Time limits: refusal notices**

If a public authority is required to give a refusal notice to an applicant,[96] then it must do so within the time allowed for compliance with s 1(1) of FOIA.[97] In other words, the back-stop time for compliance (save for the public interest balancing exercise) is the same whether a public authority is communicating the information to the applicant or whether it is giving the applicant a refusal notice, or a combination of the two. The special provisions that relate to cases where a public authority has sought further particulars of a request for information[98] or where a public authority has given a fees notice to an applicant[99] equally apply to extend the time given to a public authority for giving a refusal notice.

22–027 **Extensions of time**

There is power to modify by regulations references to the 20th working day to another working day not more than the 60th working day after the date of receipt.[100] To date, the Secretary of

93 *Prior v IC*, IT, 27 April 2006 at [24]. There is no such extension of time to the extent that a request is for or extends to 'environmental information'.

94 FOIA s 10(3). There is no comparable provision in the FOI(S)A. It is difficult to see what practical difference s 10(3)(a) makes to the operation of s 10(3). The public authority's consideration of whether it is obliged to communicate information logically precedes a discrete consideration of the obligation to confirm or deny: see §1–008(4)(b) and FOIA s 1(5). Exclusion of the duty to confirm or deny will at most be co-extensive with exemption from the duty to disclose. Accordingly, other than where information is exempt information by virtue of a qualified exemption in Pt II of the FOIA, there are no circumstances in which the duty to confirm or deny does not arise or apply, and extension of the ordinary time limit will already have been secured by s 10(3)(b).

95 FOIA s 17(2) and see Ch 13. In *Berend v IC and LB of Richmond upon Thames*, IT, 12 July 2007 at [61] the Tribunal criticised the use of a s 17 notice lacking identification of the invoked exemptions but claiming consideration of the public interest as a means of 'buying time'.

96 The requirements of a refusal notice are considered at §§24–008 to 24–014.

97 FOIA s 17(1); FOI(S)A s 16(1). In relation to 'environmental information', see: EIR reg 13(2); EI(S)R reg 13(a).

98 As to seeking further particulars of a request for information, see §§22–010 to 22–011.

99 As to fees notices, see §22–013.

100 FOIA s 10(4); FOI(S)A s 10(4).

State has made the following regulations:[101]

— Freedom of Information (Time for Compliance with Request) Regulations 2004 SI 2004/3364;
— Freedom of Information (Time for Compliance with Request) Regulations 2009 SI 2009/1369; and
— Freedom of Information (Time for Compliance with Request) Regulations 2010 SI 2010/2768.

These provided modified time limits for maintained schools, for archives, for armed forces and for information held outside the United Kingdom in certain circumstances. The Scottish Ministers have made the Freedom of Information (Scotland) Act 2002 (Time for Compliance) Regulations 2016/346. These provide for equivalent extensions of time in the case of Scottish grant-aided schools and independent special schools to those provided to maintained schools.

22– 028 Maintained schools

Under the FOIA (Time) Regs 2004, time for compliance for a request for information may be extended where the request is received by the governing body of a maintained school, or a maintained nursery school or it relates to information which is held by the recipient public authority only by virtue of the information being situated in a school which is maintained by the Secretary of State for Defence (and which provides primary or secondary education or both). The FOIA (Time) Regs 2009 provide that time for compliance for a request for information may be extended where the request is received by the managers of a controlled school, voluntary school or grant-maintained integrated school within the meaning of Art 2(2) of the Education and Libraries (Northern Ireland) Order 1986 or a pupil referral unit in Northern Ireland. The FOIA (Time) Regs 2010 similarly extend time for compliance for a request for information that is received by the proprietor of an Academy. In such cases, any references in s 10(1) and (2) of FOIA to the 20th working day following receipt of the request are to be read as either a reference to the 20th working day following receipt disregarding any working day which is not a school day[102] or a reference to the 6oth working day following the date of receipt, whichever occurs first.[103]

22– 029 Archives

Time for compliance with a request for information is extended where a request for information is received by an appropriate records authority[104] or by a person at an appointed place of deposit[105] and the request relates wholly or partly to information that may be contained in a transferred public record[106] and that has not been designated as open information.[107] In such a case, any references in s 10(1) and (2) of FOIA to the 20th working day following the date of

101 As to which, see §§22– 028 to 22– 031. The Parliamentary Secretary for the Lord Chancellor's Department told Parliament that such regulations would only be made in 'exceptional circumstances' — Hansard HC vol 347 col 858 (4 April 2000). It is difficult to envisage what new 'exceptional circumstances' might have been thought to have arisen since the enactment of the FOIA to necessitate the FOI (Time) Regs and its two successors.

102 In this context, a 'school day' means any day on which at the relevant school there is a session: FOI (Time) Regs 2004 reg 3(3); FOI (Time) Regs 2009 reg 2(3); FOI (Time) Regs 2010 reg 2(3).

103 FOI (Time) Regs 2004 reg 3(2); FOI (Time) Regs 2009 reg 2(2); FOI (Time) Regs 2010 reg 2(32.

104 That is, the Public Records Office, the Lord Chancellor or the Public Records Office of Northern Ireland: FOIA s 15(5). As to appropriate records authorities, see §36– 016.

105 That is, a place of deposit appointed under s 4(1) of the Public Records Act 1958: FOI (Time) Regs 2004 reg 4(1)(b). As to appointed places of deposit, see §36– 040.

106 That is, a public record which has been transferred to the Public Records Office, an appointed place of deposit, or the Public Records Office of Northern Ireland: FOIA s 15(4). As to transferred public records, see §36– 015.

107 That is, designated as open information for the purposes of s 66(1) of the FOIA. As to open information, see §36– 018.

receipt are to be read as references to the 30th working day following the date of receipt.[108]

22–030 Armed forces operations

Time for compliance with a request for information may be extended where the public authority cannot comply with s 1(1) of FOIA without obtaining information (whether or not that information is recorded) from any individual who is actively involved in an operation of the armed forces of the Crown or in the preparations for such an operation, whether or not that individual is himself a member of the armed forces.[109] In such a case, the public authority may apply to the Information Commissioner for, in effect, an extension of time for complying with the request for information.[110] Such an application is to be made within 20 working days following receipt of the request for information by the public authority.[111] If such an application is duly made, the Information Commissioner shall specify such a day as he considers reasonable in all the circumstances,[112] not later than the 60th working day following the date of receipt of the request for information.[113] Any reference in s 10(1) and (2) of FOIA is then to have effect as if any reference to the 20th working day following the date of receipt of the request for information were a reference to the day specified by the Information Commissioner.[114] Neither the Freedom of Information (Time for Compliance with Request) Regulations 2004 nor FOIA provide any definition of what is meant by an 'operation' in this context. However, assuming the word is to be given its ordinary dictionary meaning, it refers to 'a strategic movement of troops, ships, etc for military action'.[115]

22–031 Information outside the UK

Time for compliance with a request for information may be extended where the request may relate to information not held in the United Kingdom[116] or may require information[117] that is not held in the United Kingdom to be obtained in order to comply with it[118] and, for that reason, the public authority would not be able to obtain the information within such time as to comply with the request for information within the 20-working-day period.[119] In such a case, the public authority may apply to the Information Commissioner for, in effect, an extension of time for complying with the request for information.[120] Such an application is to be made within 20 working days following receipt of the request for information by the public authority.[121] If such an application is duly made, the Information Commissioner shall specify

108 FOI (Time) Regs 2004 reg 4(2). To the extent that the request is for 'environmental information', the time limit remains that provided by the EIR.

109 FOI (Time) Regs 2004 reg 5(1).

110 FOI (Time) Regs 2004 reg 5(2) and (3). To the extent that the request is for 'environmental information', the time limit remains that provided by the EIR.

111 FOI (Time) Regs 2004 reg 5(3)(b).

112 FOI (Time) Regs 2004 reg 5(3).

113 FOI (Time) Regs 2004 reg 5(2).

114 FOI (Time) Regs 2004 reg 5(2).

115 *New Shorter Oxford English Dictionary* (1993).

116 FOI (Time) Regs 2004 reg 6(1)(a)(i).

117 Whether or not that other information is held by a public authority: FOI (Time) Regs reg 6(1)(a)(ii).

118 FOI (Time) Regs 2004 reg 6(1)(a)(ii).

119 FOI (Time) Regs 2004 reg 6(1) (b). To the extent that the request is for 'environmental information', the time limit remains that provided by the EIR.

120 FOI (Time) Regs 2004 reg 6(2) and (3).

121 FOI (Time) Regs 2004 reg 6(3)(b).

such a day as he considers reasonable in all the circumstances,[122] not later than the 60th working day following the date of receipt of the request for information.[123] Any reference in s 10(1) and (2) of FOIA then has effect as if any reference to the 20th working day following the date of receipt of the request for information were a reference to the day specified by the Information Commissioner.[124] The provisions relating to information held outside the United Kingdom proceed on the basis of an unusual dichotomy. In effect, for them to apply, it need only be possible that the information is not held in the United Kingdom, or may require such information,[125] but it must be certain that that possibility would prevent compliance with the normal time limit.[126] It is difficult to see how a possibility could give rise to a certainty in such a way. Accordingly, the circumstances in which a public authority will actually be able to avail itself of the provisions relating to information held outside the United Kingdom may be limited to those where it can be certain that the information is not held in the United Kingdom.

22– 032 FOI(S)A extension

Under FOI(S)A, where the public authority of whom the request is made is the Keeper of the Records of Scotland and the request is one that relates to information which is contained in a record transferred to him by a public authority and which has not been designated by the public authority as open information,[127] then references to the 20th working day are to be read as references to the 30th working day.[128]

5. TRANSFERRING REQUESTS FOR INFORMATION

22– 033 Introduction

The Freedom of Information Act 2000 does not expressly deal with the situation where a public authority receives a request for information which it itself does not hold, but which it believes is held by a different public authority.[129] This is relegated to the Code of Practice issued under s 45 of the Act.[130]

22– 034 Code of Practice

The *Code of Practice* provides that where a public authority is not able to comply with a request because it does not hold the information requested and thinks that another public authority does, they should:

(a) respond to the applicant to inform them that the requested information is not held by them, and that it may be held by another public authority; and

---

[122] FOI (Time) Regs 2004 reg 6(3).

[123] FOI (Time) Regs reg 6(2).

[124] FOI (Time) Regs reg 6(2).

[125] By virtue of the word 'may' in reg 6(1)(a) of the FOI (Time) Regs.

[126] By virtue of the word 'would' in reg 6(1)(b) of the FOI (Time) Regs.

[127] FOI(S)A s 22(1). As to 'open information', see §36– 018.

[128] FOI(S)A s 10(2). To the extent that the request is for 'environmental information', the time limit remains that provided by the EIR.

[129] This is in contrast to the EIR, which do make provision for such situations: EIR reg 10. As to the transfer of requests under the EIR, see §18– 017. This is also in contrast to freedom of information legislation in other jurisdictions. See, eg Freedom of Information Act 1982 s 16 (Commonwealth of Australia); Official Information Act 1982 s 14 (New Zealand); Freedom of Information Act 2014 s 15(1)(a) (Republic of Ireland).

[130] In Scotland, under FOI(S)A s 60. For a general treatment of the s 45 Code of Practice, see Ch 21.

(b) provide the contact details for that public authority.[131]

If the public authority wishes to ask a different public authority directly to deal with the request by transferring it to them, this should only be done with the applicant's agreement.[132]

6. FAILURE TO LOCATE INFORMATION

22– 035 Search duty scope

The Freedom of Information Act 2000 does not deal expressly with what is required of a public authority before it may respond to a request by stating that it does not hold any information of the type requested by an applicant.[133] A failure to locate any information answering the terms of the request does not constitute a 'refusal' of that request and, accordingly, none of the notice requirements of s 17 is applicable.[134] The Code of Practice provides that searches should be conducted in a 'reasonable and intelligent way based on an understanding of how the public authority manages its records.' The Code advises that if a reasonable search in the areas most likely to hold the information does not reveal it, the public authority may consider that on the balance of probabilities the information is not held.[135] Since the duty to confirm or deny applies (subject to Part II and s 2(1)) irrespective of whether a public authority holds the information requested, it is to be deduced that any search must be completed within 20 working days[136] and that the minimum entitlement of the applicant is to be informed in writing that the public authority does not hold information of the description specified in the request.[137] In contrast, FOI(S)A does expressly provide for the giving of written notice that information is not held.[138] Where no information is found, the public authority is entitled to give an applicant a fees notice under s 9(1), but the amount required by that notice is, strictly speaking, confined to the costs of complying with s 1(1)(a): in other words, the cost of informing the applicant, and not the cost of the search.

131 Section 45 Code of Practice, paras 2.11-2.12.

132 Section 45 code of Practice, para 2.13. In Scotland, section 9.3 of the Scottish Ministers' Code of Practice (20106 deals with transferring requests. Paragraph 2.1 states that if the authority is aware that the information requested is instead held by another public authority, the authority should provide the applicant with contact details of the authority holding the information and suggest the applicant re-applies to that authority. For best practice under the Environmental Information Regulations, see paras 2.2-2.4.

133 In the USA, the yardstick used is that an agency must undertake a search that is 'reasonably calculated to uncover all relevant documents'— *Weisberg v United States Department of Justice*, 705 F 2d 1344 (DC Cir 1983). This involves a consideration of: (a) how the agency conducted its search in light of the scope of the request; (b) the applicant's description of the records sought; (c) the standards the agency used in determining where the records were likely to be found; and (d) whether the agency believes the records sought may exist.

134 Compare the Freedom of Information Act 1982 (Commonwealth of Australia) s 24A, which expressly provides for the refusal of a request for access to a document if all reasonable steps have been taken to find the document and the relevant public authority is satisfied that it cannot be found. The Information Commissioner can require further searches: s 55V. See also the similar provision in the Freedom of Information Act 2014 (Republic of Ireland) s 10(1)(a). In Canada, the Federal Court has suggested that a total failure to make a search or an adequate search might, if proven, be tantamount to a refusal to disclose: *X v Canada (Minister of National Defence)* (1992) 58 FTR 93.

135 Section 45 Code of Practice, para 1.12.

136 FOIA s 10(1). See §§22– 020 to 22– 027.

137 FOIA s 1(1)(a).

138 FOI(S)A s 17.

7. CONSULTATION WITH THIRD PARTIES

22– 036 Introduction

In addition to generating information themselves, public authorities are repositories of large amounts of third-party information, either collected by those public authorities or, more commonly, provided to them by members of the public, businesses, foreign governments and international organisations.[139] In some cases, the information will have been truly volunteered to a public authority. But in most cases, the information will have been provided either under compulsion (such as an income tax return) or by practical necessity in order to secure a licence, grant, permit, authorisation, dispensation or some other such advantage. The information may have been supplied with no thought or warning as to public rights of access to information held by the recipient public authority. Indeed, the information may have been supplied before such rights were put on the statute books. The person who supplied the information may have done so expecting that it, or at least some of it, should not be used by the recipient public authority other than for the purpose for which it was supplied. While sometimes the expectations and wishes of that person, and the reasons for them, will be self-evident to the recipient public authority, in other cases these will either not be obvious or not fully appreciated. Those expectations and wishes may moreover reflect a wider public interest in non-disclosure. Neither FOIA nor the EIR[140] makes express provision for third-party involvement in the determination of a request for information. There is no general legal obligation to notify or consult a third party whose interests would be affected by the disclosure of information. Nor do third parties have a statutory right to challenge or seek a review of decisions to disclose information. Thus, although many of the exemptions under the Acts are designed to protect third parties' interests, the Acts themselves do not provide procedural mechanisms for protecting those interests.

22– 037 Comparative jurisdictions

The differing approaches taken in the comparative jurisdictions are illuminating, showing the importance that has been attached to the rights of third parties.[141] Thus:

(1) In the USA, the Freedom of Information Act 1966 makes no provision for a third party to attempt to stop disclosure of information. In *Chrysler Corp v Brown*[142] the Supreme Court held that jurisdiction for a reverse FOI action cannot be based on the Freedom of Information Act itself 'because Congress did not design the FOIA exemptions to be mandatory bars to disclosure.' Instead, the Court found that review of an agency's decision to disclose requested records can be brought under the Administrative Procedure Act.[143] As a result, a third party will ordinarily argue that an agency's contemplated release would violate the Trade Secrets Act and thus would 'not be in accordance with law' or would be 'arbitrary and capricious' within the meaning of the Administrative Procedure Act. The third party's right of challenge is thus on judicial review grounds, and not one of merit review. On top of this, Executive Order 12,600 requires that notice be given to submitters of confidential

---

139 In addition, a person may have supplied information to one public authority and that public authority may, without reference to the person supplying the information, have supplied it to one or more other public authorities.

140 Similarly the FOI(S)A and the EI(S)R.

141 Given that the FOIA was the last of its comparators and that those comparators were the subject of close scrutiny (see §51– 001), it is a little surprising that its treatment of third parties' interests is the most primitive.

142 (1979) 441 US 281.

143 5 USC 701-706 (2000).

commercial information whenever an agency 'determines that it may be required to disclose' the requested information. When a third party is given notice, it must be given a reasonable period of time within which to object to disclosure of any of the requested material. If the third party's objection is not upheld by the agency, the third party must be notified in writing and given a brief explanation of the agency's decision. The notification must be provided a reasonable number of days before the disclosure date, so as to give the third party an opportunity to seek judicial relief.

(2) In Australia, the Freedom of Information Act 1982 provides that before an agency discloses documents containing information that originated from a state, that contain business information or contain personal information (each of which is an exemption), the agency holding the documents is required to give the potentially affected third party an opportunity to make representations as to whether the relevant exemption applies.[144] If, despite the representations, the agency intends to disclose the documents, the third party may request the Information Commissioner to review the decision and thereafter appeal to the Tribunal.[145] The third party is entitled to put forward any of the grounds of exemption, including those not relied upon by the agency holding the documents.[146] The Act is silent as to whether the third party should be advised of the identity of the applicant.[147]

(3) In New Zealand, the Official Information Act 1982 imposes no binding obligation upon an agency to consult with a third party before releasing information relating to that party. Instead, s 30(3) of the Official Information Act 1982 and s 18(3) of the Ombudsmen Act 1975 require an Ombudsman, before making any report or recommendation that may adversely affect any person, to give that person an opportunity to be heard.[148] Limited provision is also made by the Privacy Act 1993 in relation to personal information.

(4) In Canada, the Access to Information Act, deals methodically with the rights of third parties.[149] Section 20 provides a number of exemptions for records specifically relating to third parties: trade secrets; financial, commercial, scientific or technical information supplied by third parties in confidence; information disclosure of which might cause material financial loss or gain to, or prejudice the competitive position of, a third party; information disclosure of which might prejudice negotiations of a third party. Under s 27, where the institution intends to disclose a record that contains, or that the head of the institution has reason to believe might contain, matter specifically exempted by s 20, notice must be given to the third party giving

---

144 Sections 26A, 27 and 27A (substituted by the Freedom of Information (Amendment) Reform Act 2010). The third party can request internal review: ss. 53C and 54A(2).

145 Commissioner: ss 54M(3)(a), 54P, 54Q, 54S(2), 55A(1)(c) and 55D(2). Tribunal: ss 60AA, 60AB(2) and 61(2).

146 The third party may be made a party to the proceedings by the Administrative Appeals Tribunal Act 1975, ss 27(1) and 30(1A). But see *Mitsubishi Motors Australia Ltd v Department of Transport* (1986) 12 FCR 156, 68 ALR 626, where the Federal Court held that a third party could only apply to the Tribunal for review in respect of a decision that a document was not exempt under s 43: the Tribunal did not have jurisdiction to deal with the whole question of access to that document, including other grounds of exemption. The Federal Court expressly recognised that, where s 43 was not being relied upon, the third party could seek judicial review of the agency's decision to disclose a document. The decision must now be read in light of the Freedom of Information Reform (Amendment) Act 2010.

147 In its review of the Freedom of Information Act 1982, the Australian Law Reform Commission said that revealing the identity of the applicant to the third party was best left to the discretion of the agency, although it was sensible to consult the applicant before doing so: Australian Law Reform Commission and Administrative Review Council, *Open Government: a Review of the Federal Freedom of Information Act 1982*, ALRC 77, ARC 40 (Canberra, 1995) para 10.17.

148 See *Wyatt Co (NZ) Ltd v Queenstown-Lakes District Council* [1991] 2 NZLR 180.

149 Access to Information Act ss 20, 27, 28, 33, 37, 43 and 44.

him 20 days within which to make representations as to whether the record should be disclosed.[150] Section 28 deals with the manner in which a third party is required to make representations. Section 33 provides that a third party is to be given notice of a complaint against a non-disclosure decision, provided that notification under s 27 would have been required had it been intended to disclose. Section 35 gives a third party a right, where necessary, to make representations to the Information Commissioner and the third party will, in those circumstances, receive a copy of his report (s 37(2)). An affected, or potentially affected, third party is given a right to participate in a review application and is notified of the same (s 43). A third party may also itself apply for a review order to prevent disclosure of a record (s 44). The statutory scheme is said to give a third party a vested right to have its information withheld from unqualified requesters.[151] The courts have taken the view that a third party is not able to invoke exemptions with which it has no connections, such as injury to international relations, if the government institution has chosen not to invoke it.[152]

(5) In Ireland, there are two separate procedures in the Freedom of Information Act 2014 obliging a public body to consult with a third party before deciding to disclose records answering the terms of the request. The first applies where the records stand to fall within the scope of one of three particular exemptions: records obtained in confidence, commercially sensitive information and personal information about third parties.[153] Where a record answering the terms of a request falls within the scope of one or more of these exemptions but the head of the public body is nevertheless of the opinion that the public interest lies in favour of disclosure, that public body is required to inform a third party to whom the record relates of this fact.[154] The third party has a right to make written representations in relation to the access request.[155] The second procedure applies to certain categories of record relating to matters before government: the head of a public body may not release the record until he has consulted with the leader of each political party to which a member of the Government belonged that made any decision to which the record relates.[156] A person notified under the first procedure must be advised in writing of the decision and of his right of appeal.[157] The Act is silent as to whether the third party should be advised of the identity of the applicant.

22– 038 Third-parties & FOIA

The only recognition of the interests of a third party affected by disclosure under FOIA is a non-statutory statement of expectation that such a third party should in some circumstances be consulted before any such disclosure.[158] The absence of any statutory protection in the draft

[150] Outside the grounds specified in s 27, a third party has no right to be notified of a disclosure and, accordingly, no right of review under s 44: *Twinn v Canada (Minister of Indian Affairs and Northern Development)* [1987] 3 FC 368.

[151] *Glaxo Canada Inc v Canada (Minister of National Health and Welfare)* [1990] 1 FC 652.

[152] *Saint John Shipbuilding Ltd v Canada (Minister of Supply and Services)* (1988) 24 FTR 32; on appeal, (1990) 67 DLR (4th) 315.

[153] Freedom of Information Act 2014 ss 35, 36 and 37, respectively.

[154] Freedom of Information Act 2014 s 38.

[155] Freedom of Information Act 2014 s 38(4). The third party has three weeks in which to do so. The head is obliged to take the submissions into account before making his decision.

[156] Freedom of Information Act 2014 s 28(4).

[157] Freedom of Information Act 2014 s 38(4).

[158] Section 45 Code of Practice paras 3.1-3.6. There are similar provisions in the codes applying to FOI(S)A, EIR

freedom of information legislation drew considerable criticism during its passage through Parliament.[159] Businesses concerned about their commercial interests, as well as others concerned at the possible implications of the release of information about them (a striking example being the Research Defence Society, which expressed concerns about the implications for holders of licences for scientific research involving animals) argued that the protection afforded to third parties by a code of practice was inadequate, and there were recommendations that third parties should be given a legal right to be consulted and to challenge decisions to disclose information about them. However, professed concerns about the administrative burden and lack of flexibility to which such an approach would give rise, its cost to the public purse by comparison with reliance on third parties' existing legal rights (eg by way of action for breach of confidence) and its putative potential to undermine the very principle of access to information, were considered to defeat the concerns of third parties.[160]

22– 039 Code of Practice

Apart from any free-standing bases for controlling disclosure[161] all that remains for an affected third party is the s 45 Code of Practice.[162] Whereas the first version of the Code of Practice provided some concrete guidelines for the consultation of third parties before disclosure of information,[163] the current version is more flexible. So far as third party consultation is concerned, the Code of Practice advises that:

(1) There will be circumstance in which a public authority should consult third parties. These may include requests for information relating to persons or bodies who are not the applicant or public authority or requests for information likely to affect the interests of such persons.[164]
(2) A particular example is that of contractual obligations which require consultation before information is released
(3) In other circumstances such as where the information relates to third parties or release may affect their business interests, it may be good practice to do so.[165]
(4) Where the information affects a number of third parties, a public authority may consult representative organisations, or even representative samples of numbers of individuals.[166]

The Code of Practice emphasises that while reasonable views of third parties may be helpful, they are not determinative and it is for the public authority to take the decision as to release.[167]

---

and EI(S)R. The Information Commissioner has issued guidance in relation to requests for data under the DPA 1998 that contain third-party information.

159 Hansard, HL, vol 617, 17 October 2000, cols 983-990. An amendment was moved to impose a notification upon a public authority: col 983. Similarly, Hansard, vol 347, 4 April 2000, col 890. While the original White Paper (*Cabinet Office, Your Right to Know: The Government's Proposals for a Freedom of Information Act* (Cm 3818, 1997) invited views on whether a mechanism for protecting third parties was needed (at para 5.19), the draft bill contained no such mechanism.

160 See, eg *House of Commons Select Committee on Public Administration—Third Report* (Cm 355, 1999) paras 107-110; *Report from the House of Lords Select Committee appointed to consider the draft Freedom of Information Bill*, 27 July 1999, paras 40-47, 76; House of Commons, *Select Committee on Public Administration—Fifth Special Report*, Appendix, p 10, 27 October 1999; Hansard HC vol 347 cols 890-915 (4 April 2000); Hansard HL vol 617 cols 983-991 (17 October 2000).

161 See §22– 040.

162 In relation to the force of which, see §21– 008.

163 Paragraphs 34-38.

164 Section 45 Code of Practice, para 3.1.

165 Section 45 Code of Practice, para 3.2.

166 Section 45 Code of Practice, para 30.

167 Section 45 Code of Practice, paras 3.3-3.4.

If a decision is made to release following consultation it is good practice to give the third party advance notice or draw it to their attention as soon as possible.[168]

22– 040 Other third-party rights

Given the absence of any statutory provision or real, substantive provision in the Code of Practice requiring an invitation to or the participation of an affected third party, other means of influencing a public authority's decision to disclose come to assume greater importance. Those other means will almost certainly require an underlying and recognisable right, such as:

— a third party's rights under Art 8 of the ECHR;
— a third party's intellectual property in the information proposed to be disclosed;
— a right of confidentiality (including one arising out of a contract);
— a right arising out of the GDPR/DPA2018;
— rights arising out of the law of defamation; or
— parliamentary privilege.

A threatened breach of such a right may provide a direct basis upon which to seek injunctive relief. Alternatively, it may provide a basis for challenging by way of judicial review the decision or the proposed decision of a public authority. The facts and circumstances giving rise to the underlying right will often also result in the information falling within one of the exemptions in Part II of the Act.[169] If the exemption is absolute, or if not absolute but the public interest lies against disclosure, disclosure will not be required by the Act:[170] as such, it will be a voluntary disclosure.[171] Various statutory protections provided to a public authority where a disclosure is required by statute[172] will be thereby removed. In both cases, the real issue for most third parties will be knowing of the decision to disclose before the disclosure has been made. In all cases, a third party can improve its prospects of being invited for its views and in subsequent coercive proceedings by formally advising a public authority that it expects to be consulted should that public authority propose to disclose particular information to any other person, including another public authority. Such notification can accompany the provision of the information or can be given subsequently. In relation to personal data, a data subject may serve a notice under Art 21(1) of the GDPR objecting to the further processing of personal data concerning him or her.[173] Where a public authority has disclosed information in circumstances where an exemption could have been invoked and in breach of one of the above rights, an

168 Section 45 Code of Practice, para 3.6.

169 For example, s 34, 40, 41 or 43.

170 FOIA s 2(1)-(2).

171 As to which, see §§20– 036 to 20– 038.

172 For example: FOIA s 79; Copyright, Designs and Patents Act 1988 s 50; DPA 1998 Sch 2. And see further §§20– 034 to 20– 035.

173 Under Art 21(1) of the GDPR, a data subject has the right to object at any time, on grounds relating to his or her personal situation, to processing of personal data concerning him or her to the extent that that processing 'is necessary for the performance of a task carried out in the public interest or in the exercise of official authority vested in the controller' (Art 6(1)(e)). Under the GDPR, the term 'processing' includes dissemination; Art 4(2). Article 6(1)(e) of the GDPR will cover a public authority required to answer a request under FOIA or FOI(S)A. The disapplication of the duty to comply with the requirement to disclose the information is qualified by the coda to Art 21(1) of the GDPR, which provides that upon receipt of such a request from the data subject 'the controller shall no longer process the personal data unless the controller demonstrates compelling legitimate grounds for the processing which override the interests, rights and freedoms of the data subject or for the establishment, exercise or defence of legal claims.' The Art 21(1) right to object is considered further in §10– 015. Where an individual has made such an objection to a public authority, the starting point is that a public authority proposing to disclose personal information relating to that individual must invite the views of the individual before doing so in order for the public authority to consider properly whether the coda to Art 21(1) applies. The right to object does not apply to manual unstructured data held by a public authority: DPA 2018 s 24(2)(b)(iv).

affected third party may be able to bring an action in damages.[174]

22– 041 Personal information

Where compliance with a request for information may entail disclosure of personal information about a third party there are specific provisions to protect the interests of that individual. A distinction is drawn between:

(1) requests for access to personal information about the person making the request (ie subject access requests) which also entail the disclosure of personal information about a third party; and

(2) requests that result in the disclosure of personal information about a third party.

The latter are dealt with under FOIA and are considered in detail in Chapter 33. As already noted, the issue of consultation is addressed through the Code of Practice. The former are channelled through the GDPR/DPA 2018.[175]

22– 042 Confidential information

Where the disclosure of information to the public (otherwise than under FOIA) by the public authority holding it would constitute a breach of confidence actionable by a third party, that information will be rendered exempt information if it was that third party which supplied the information to the public authority.[176] It would seem that the exemption does not extend to information held by a public authority which it did not obtain it directly from that third party. Nevertheless, even in this situation other proscriptions against disclosure may apply, thereby rendering it exempt information.[177] Whilst in some situations it will be clear whether or not disclosure of the information to the public will constitute an actionable breach of confidence, in others it will not. A person by whom such a breach would be actionable may be well placed to contribute to the public authority's understanding of the qualities of the information. A public authority's failure to seek those views before releasing such information will expose the public authority to a claim for damages.

---

174 The action would be founded upon a breach of the underlying right. Damages for a breach of an underlying private law right could be sought as part of judicial review proceedings: Senior Courts Act 1981 s 31(7); CPR 54.3(2). A court may also order a public authority to pay damages under the Human Rights Act 1998 s 8, where that public authority has acted in a way that is incompatible with a right derived from the ECHR. In this case, the court will have to be satisfied that an award of damages is necessary to ensure just satisfaction for the person concerned, having regard to the other remedies granted and the consequences of the unlawful act: *R (Anufrijeva) v London Borough Southwark* [2003] EWCA Civ 1406, [2004] QB 1124; *R (N) v SSHD* [2003] EWHC 207, [2003] HRLR 20, [2003] UKHRR 546. In an egregious case it might be possible to mount a claim on the basis of misfeasance in public office.

175 See further: Ch 10 (in relation to general processing); Ch 12 (in relation to law enforcement processing); Ch 14 (in relation to processing by the intelligence services).

176 FOIA s 41; FOI(S)A s 36.

177 FOIA s 44(1); FOI(S)A s 26. See further §§35– 015 to 35– 026.

CHAPTER 23
Disentitlement

1. EXCESSIVE COST OF COMPLIANCE

23–001 Introduction

One of the risks of a freedom of information regime is that an applicant may make applications for information which would result in a public authority incurring disproportionate cost or in an unreasonable diversion of a public authority's resources.[1] FOIA does not require a public authority to comply with a request for information where the cost of complying with the request would exceed a specified limit.[2] However, where the cost of compliance does exceed the specified limit and the duty to disclose does not arise, a public authority nevertheless has a power to provide the information and may charge for the same.[3] As will be seen, the combined operation of the provisions has the result that:

— when a public authority is determining whether there is no duty to comply with a request for information because the cost of compliance would be excessive, it takes into account the cost of determining whether or not it holds the information, the cost of locating the information and the cost of retrieving it;

— however, once a public authority has properly determined that there is no duty to comply with a request for information because the cost of compliance would be excessive, but it nevertheless decides to exercise its power to do so, it may charge not just for the cost of determining whether or not it holds the information, the cost

---

[1] This was a potential problem identified in the White Paper: Cabinet Office, *Your Right to Know: The Government's Proposals for a Freedom of Information Act. White Paper* (Cm 3818, 1997) para 2.26. The concept of a 'substantial and unreasonable diversion of resources' is deployed expressly in the Australian legislation: Freedom of Information Act 1982 (Commonwealth of Australia) ss 24AA(1)(a).

[2] FOIA s 12(1); FOI(S)A s 12(1). There is no equivalent provision in the environmental information regime: see §18–015 and see *Mersey Tunnel Users Association v IC and Halton BC*, IT, 24 June 2009 at [90].

[3] FOIA s 13(1); FOI(S)A s 13(1).

of locating the information and the cost of retrieving it, but also for the cost of informing the applicant whether it holds the information and the cost of communicating the information to the applicant.

There is no provision for a public authority, in estimating the costs at either stage, to take into account matters such as the cost of considering whether the information is exempt information or the cost of considering public interest issues.

23– 002 Excessive cost: effect

Where a public authority estimates that the cost of complying with a request for information would exceed the appropriate limit,[4] then it is relieved of its two obligations under s 1(1) of FOIA.[5] This has been described as 'a guillotine which prevents the burden on the public authority from becoming too onerous under the Act.'[6] However, a public authority is only relieved of its duty to confirm or deny if the estimated cost of complying with that duty alone would exceed the appropriate limit.[7] It is notable that the Acts use the word 'would' rather than 'might'. This is likely to be of particular relevance where a public authority is unable to estimate the costs of compliance with any certainty. In such a case, if the public authority were to estimate that the cost of compliance would fall somewhere between a lower and an upper figure, it is unlikely that it would be able to take advantage of the provisions on excessive cost of compliance where the lower figure was below the appropriate limit. In such a case, it could not be said that the estimated costs 'would' exceed the appropriate limit. Where a request for information captures information some of which falls to be disclosed under the freedom of information regime and some of which falls to be disclosed under the environmental information regime, it is suggested that it is impermissible for a public authority to take into account the cost of complying with the latter. This is because the latter is not a request for information to which s 1(1) of FOIA would to any extent apply.[8]

23– 003 Estimating compliance cost

The Freedom of Information Act 2000 does not itself prescribe the type of costs which a public authority is entitled to take into account, or the manner of estimating those costs, when assessing whether the cost of complying with a request for information would exceed the appropriate limit. The Act makes provision for such matters to be prescribed by regulations.[9] Those regulations are the Freedom of Information and Data Protection (Appropriate Limit and Fees) Regulations 2004.[10] The Information Commissioner has produced guidance on the application of the Fees Regs 2004.[11] The Regulations provide that a public authority may, for the purpose of estimating whether the cost of complying with a request for information[12] would

---

4 FOIA s 12(1). Although the FOI(S)A does not invoke the concept of an 'appropriate limit', the effect of the relevant provisions is broadly the same (see the FOI(S)A s 12(1)). As to the 'appropriate limit', see §23– 006.

5 Or its obligation under s 1(1) of the FOI(S)A, as the case may be: *Quinn v IC and Home Office*, IT, 15 November 2006 at [50]; *Johnson v IC and MoJ*, IT, 13 July 2007 at [52]. As to a public authority's obligations under s 1(1) of the FOIA or s 1(1) of the FOI(S)A, see §1– 008(4).

6 *Quinn v IC and SSHD*, IT, 15 November 2006 at [50].

7 FOIA s 12(2).

8 Being the opening requirement in Fees Regs 2004 reg 5(1). Section 1(1) does not apply to environmental information because of FOIA ss 1(2), 2(1), 2(2) and 39. This will be the case regardless of whether the request for environmental information is contained within the same document as the request for information under the FOIA.

9 FOIA s 12(5); FOI(S)A s 12(4).

10 Abbreviated in this work as the 'Fees Regs 2004.' As to the position in Scotland, see §23– 005.

11 *Requests where the cost of compliance exceeds the appropriate limit*, 9 September 2015.

12 That is, a request for information to which s 1(1) of the FOIA would, apart from the appropriate limit, to any extent apply: Fees Regs 2004 reg 4(1) and (2)(b).

exceed the appropriate limit, take account only of the costs it reasonably expects to incur in determining whether it holds the information,[13] locating the information (or a document which may contain the information),[14] retrieving the information (or a document which may contain the information),[15] and extracting the information from a document containing it.[16] Further, where any of those costs are attributable to the time which persons undertaking any of those activities[17] on behalf of the public authority are expected to spend on those activities, those costs are to be estimated at the rate of £25 per person per hour.[18] Accordingly, the costs that may be taken into account at the stage when a public authority is determining whether or not the cost of compliance would exceed the appropriate limit do not include the costs of considering whether the information is exempt information, the costs of considering public interest issues, the costs of informing the applicant whether it holds the information, or the costs of communicating the information to the applicant.

23–004 Compliance estimates: case law

A number of Upper Tribunal decisions have addressed the appropriate approach to estimation for the purposes of FOIA section 12. First, the public authority must make an estimate as to what the costs of compliance would be. Section 12 operates predictively and does not require the public authority to embark on a search.[19] The estimate must be 'sensible, realistic, and supported by cogent evidence.'[20] The estimate is entirely subjective to the public authority concerned and is related to the way in which the public authority holds the relevant information.[21] The public authority is not obliged to exclude costs which it would not have been necessary to incur had it collated and stored information more efficiently[22] or even those which it would not have been necessary to incur had it complied with legal obligations relating to the holding of such information.[23] However, the estimate must be of costs which the public authority reasonably expects to incur related to the matters set out in regulation 4(3). The Upper Tribunal has emphasised that this is not a purely objective test as to what costs it would be reasonable to incur but that it introduces an objective, qualifying element, allowing the Information Commissioner and Tribunal to remove from the estimate any amount the authority could not reasonably expect to incur on account of the nature of the activity or its

---

13 Fees Regs 2004 reg 4(3)(a).

14 Fees Regs 2004 reg 4(3)(b).

15 Fees Regs 2004 reg 4(3)(c).

16 Fees Regs 2004 reg 4(3)(d). This does not include the cost of redaction if it is a simple task of redacting names from documents: *Jenkins v IC and DEFRA*, IT, 2 November 2007. It does, however, include the time spent in making a judgment about what should be disclosed, when balancing various criteria, as such a process is regarded as retrieving from each document the information which is required to be disclosed: *Morris v IC and Dept of Transport*, FTT, 7 June 2010 at [35]-[38]. Regulation 4(3)(d) focuses on extracting information which has been requested from a document which also contains information which has not been requested. It does not cover redacting exempt information which would otherwise form part of the information which has been requested: *Chief Constable of South Yorkshire Police v Information Commissioner* [2011] EWHC 44 (Admin), [2011] 1 WLR 1387 at [27]-[33].

17 That is, the activities referred to in Fees Regs 2004 reg 4(3).

18 Fees Regs 2004 reg 4(4). It should be noted that this is a fixed, not a maximum, figure.

19 *Kirkham v IC* [2018] UKUT 126 (AAC) at [16] noting, however that in some cases this may be the best, and appropriate, way to form an estimate. And see Information Commissioner's guidance, *Requests where the cost of compliance exceeds the appropriate limit*, 9 September 2015 at paras 28-36.

20 *Randall v IC and Medicines and Healthcare Products Regulatory Agency*, IT, 30 October 2007 at [12] approved by the Upper Tribunal in *Commissioner of Police for the Metropolis v Information Commissioner and Mackenzie* [2014] UKUT 479 (AAC) at [33].

21 *Kirkham v IC* [2018] UKUT 126 (AAC).

22 *Commissioner of Police for the Metropolis v IC and Mackenzie* [2014] UKUT 479 (AAC) at [37].

23 *Cruelty Free International v IC* [2017] UKUT 318 (AAC) at [1] and [19]-[34].

amount.[24]

23–005 Compliance cost: FOI(S)A

Section 12(4) of FOI(S)A enables regulations to be made which make provision for the costs to be estimated and the manner in which those costs are to be estimated. The Regulations make provision for the estimation of the 'projected costs' in relation to a request for information.[25] The projected costs are stated to be the total costs, whether direct or indirect, which the public authority reasonably estimates it is likely to incur in locating, retrieving and providing such information. The Regulations state that in estimating projected costs no account may be taken of costs in determining:

(a) whether the authority holds the information specified in the request;[26] and
(b) whether the person seeking the information is entitled to receive the requested information or, if not so entitled, should nevertheless be provided with it or should be refused it.[27]

The Scottish regime differs from that of the FOIA in that the public authority is not allowed to include the cost of determining whether it holds the information. Under both FOIA and FOI(S)A, public authorities are not allowed to take into account the cost of considering whether the information is exempt information. Under FOI(S)A the public authority is at liberty to take into account the costs of informing the applicant that it holds the information and the cost of communicating that information to the applicant.

23–006 The 'appropriate limit'

The Freedom of Information Act 2000 provides that the 'appropriate limit' is to be prescribed by regulations, which may provide that different limits apply in different cases.[28] Those regulations are, again, the Freedom of Information and Data Protection (Appropriate Limit and Fees) Regulations 2004. These provide that in the case of a public authority which is listed in Part I of Sch 1 to FOIA or in the case of a public authority in Scotland, the appropriate limit is £600.[29] In the case of any other public authority, the appropriate limit is £450.[30]

23–007 Cumulating multiple requests

The Freedom of Information Act 2000 anticipates the possibility that the provisions protecting public authorities from incurring excessive costs in complying with requests could be emasculated in a situation where several separate requests are submitted.[31] Accordingly, the Act makes provision for regulations to prescribe that in certain circumstances, where two or more requests for information are made to a public authority by one person, or by different persons who appear to the public authority to be acting in concert[32] or in pursuance of a

24 *Kirkham v IC* [2018] UKUT 126 (AAC) at [20].

25 Fees (Scot) Regs reg 3 (see further §22–017) and Fees (s 13) Regs reg 3 (see further §23–010).

26 Regulation 3(2)(a)(i).

27 Regulation 3(2)(a)(ii).

28 FOIA s 12(3). Although the FOI(S)A does not invoke the concept of an 'appropriate limit', the FOI(S)A s 12(1) provides that the relevant amount should be prescribed by regulations.

29 Fees Regs 2004 reg 3(2) and Fees (Scot) Regs reg 5. Although the FOI(S)A does not invoke the concept of an 'appropriate limit', the effect of the relevant provisions is the same.

30 Fees Regs 2004 reg 3(3). Under the FOI and DP (Limit and Fees) Regs, costs are to be estimated at the rate of £25 per hour: reg 4(4). Under the Fees (Scot) Regs any estimate of the cost of staff time in locating, retrieving or providing the information cannot exceed £15 per hour per member of staff: reg 3(2)(b).

31 This was a potential problem identified in the white paper (Cabinet Office, *Your Right to Know: The Government's Proposals for a Freedom of Information Act. White Paper* (Cm 3818, 1997) para 2.26.

32 A phrase normally associated with a criminal enterprise (see *DPP v Merriman* [1973] AC 584). It generally connotes

campaign,[33] the public authority may treat the estimated cost of compliance as being the estimated cost of complying with all of the requests.[34] Pursuant to the regulations, where two or more such requests relate, to any extent, to the same or similar information and they are received by the public authority within any period of 60 consecutive working days,[35] then the estimated cost of complying with any of the requests is to be taken to be the total costs which may be taken into account by the public authority of complying with all of them.[36] The guidance exhorts public authorities to be cautious about treating separate requests in this way, particularly where the cumulative cost of complying exceeds the appropriate limit by only a small amount.[37] It is suggested that in a case where the cumulative cost of complying with related requests is excessive, the public authority may wish to consider whether the information could be communicated in a more cost-effective manner, such as by publication on its website.

23– 008 Cumulative cost: FOI(S)A

The power of a Scottish public authority to refuse to comply with separate requests on grounds of excessive cumulative cost is much more limited than that of public authorities covered by FOIA. Where two or more requests are made to a Scottish public authority by different persons,[38] the public authority is only relieved of the duty to comply with either or any of those requests where the information sought in the requests covers the same subject or overlaps to a significant extent,[39] the authority estimates that the total cost of complying with both or all of the requests would exceed £600,[40] and, on the basis that it considers it reasonable to do so,[41] the public authority makes the information available to the public at large within the period of 20

---

a joining together of two or more persons to do what is sought to be done.

33 FOIA s 12(4); FOI(S)A s 12(2). The FOI(S)A differs slightly from the FOIA in this respect, in that it does not refer to different persons who appear to be acting in pursuance of a campaign, but refers to different persons whose requests appear to have been instigated wholly or mainly for a purpose other than the obtaining of the information itself: FOI(S)A s 12(2)(b). As to the position in Scotland, see §23– 008. The FTT has emphasised that it is only necessary under the Regulations for the public authority to be satisfied that that the different persons *appear* to be acting in the relevant way. The question is therefore whether the public authority reasonably took the view that it did: *HM v IC and Warwickshire CC*, FTT, 27 January 2015.

34 FOIA s 12(4); FOI(S)A s 12(2). The relevant regulations are the Fees Regs 2004 and the Fees (Scot) Regs.

35 In this context, a working day means any day other than a Saturday, a Sunday, Christmas Day, Good Friday or a day which is a bank holiday under the Banking and Financial Dealings Act 1971 in any part of the United Kingdom: Fees Regs 2004 reg 5(3). Because bank holidays under the Banking and Financial Dealings Act 1971 differ in the various parts of the United Kingdom, the effect of the regulations referring to a bank holiday under the Banking and Financial Dealings Act 1971 'in any part' of the United Kingdom is to exclude each of the following days: New Year's Day (or, if New Year's Day be a Sunday, January 3), January 2 (or if January 2 be a Sunday, January 3), March 17 (or if March 17 be a Sunday, March 18), Easter Monday, the first Monday in May, the last Monday in May, the first Monday in August, the last Monday in August, December 25, December 26 (if it not be a Sunday) and December 27 (in a year in which December 25 or 26 is a Sunday): see Banking and Financial Dealings Act 1971, Sch 1.

36 Fees Regs 2004 reg 5(1) and (2). Requests will be similar where there is an overarching theme or common thread running between them in terms of the nature of the information that has been requested: *Dedalus Ltd v IC and Arts Council of England*, FTT, 21 May 2010 at [104] and Information Commissioner's guidance, *Requests where the cost of compliance exceeds the appropriate limit*, 9 September 2012 at para 45. In *Harding v IC and London Borough of Camden*, FTT, 17 October 2011 at [27]-[51] the Tribunal cast doubt on the 'overarching theme' approach. In *Independent Police Complaints Commission v IC*, FTT, 29 March 2012 at [26] the Tribunal required only a 'very loose connection' between two sets of information.

37 See: www.justice.gov.uk/information-access-rights/foi-guidance-for-practitioners/procedural-guidance/foi-fees-aggregation

38 Fees (Scot) Regs reg 6.

39 Fees (Scot) Regs reg 6(a).

40 That is, the amount prescribed under the Fees (Scot) Regs reg 5 — see reg 6(b).

41 Fees (Scot) Regs reg 6(c).

working days of receipt by it of the first of the requests.[42] In addition to the significantly more restrictive criteria that must be met in the case of a Scottish public authority (as compared to public authorities governed by FOIA) which are expressly imposed by the relevant provisions, there is also a restrictive criterion which is implicit in them. Before a Scottish public authority may take advantage of the excessive cumulative cost of compliance provisions, it must have sent to each applicant the requisite notice within 20 working days of receipt by it of the first of the requests.[43] Accordingly, it may only take advantage of those provisions in relation to requests which are made within 20 working days of each other. This is a significantly shorter period than the period of 60 consecutive working days applicable to public authorities covered by FOIA.[44]

23– 009 Excessive cost notices

Where a public authority claims that it is not obliged to comply with its duties under s 1(1) of FOIA because the cost of complying with it would be excessive, it must within the time for compliance with that section give the applicant a notice stating that fact.[45]

23– 010 Excessive cost: fees

The Freedom of Information Act 2000 makes provision for public authorities to charge for the provision of information which might not otherwise be provided because of cost considerations.[46] In cases where a public authority is not obliged to comply with a request for information because the cost of complying with it is deemed to be excessive,[47] where the communication of the information is not otherwise required by law, and where no provision is made by or under another enactment for the charging of fees, then the public authority may charge a fee for the communication of that information.[48] A public authority is not under any obligation to accept an offer to pay the cost of providing the information in excess of the appropriate limit.[49] In such a case, however, the Code of Practice provides that public authorities should consider what advice and assistance can be provided to help the applicant revise or re-frame their request with a view to bringing it within the cost limit, which may include suggesting that the subject or the time-span is narrowed.[50] Merely suggesting to the applicant that the request is refined by reducing the amount of information requested may be insufficient: large sophisticated organisations can be expected to provide assistance specific to their computer systems by explaining to the requester how the most thorough search is likely to result in the financial limit being exceeded and to suggest a reformulation of search terms.[51] If a fee is to be charged, it is to be determined by the public authority in accordance with regulations, which prescribe a maximum fee.[52] The maximum fee which may be charged is a

---

42 That is, the period specified in reg 6(d) of the Fees (Scot) Regs — see reg 6(e). The public authority must, within the same period, notify each requester of this decision.

43 Fees (Scot) Regs reg 6(d).

44 Fees Regs 2004 reg 5(2)(b).

45 FOIA s 17(5); FOI(S)A s 16(4). As to notices in cases where the cost of compliance with a request for information would be excessive, see further §24– 010.

46 Explanatory Notes to the FOIA, para 58.

47 As to cases where the cost of compliance with a request for information would be excessive, see §23– 009.

48 FOIA s 13(1) and (3); FOI(S)A s 13(1) and (4).

49 *Dedalus Ltd v IC and Arts Council of England*, FTT, 21 May 2010 at [113].

50 Section 45 Code of Practice, para 6.9.

51 *McGoldrick v IC*, FTT, 30 October 2017 at [18].

52 FOIA s 13(1); FOI(S)A s 13(1). The relevant regulations are the Fees Regs 2004 and the Fees (s 13) Regs.

sum equivalent to the total of two categories of costs. First, the costs that the public authority is entitled to take into account when estimating the cost of complying with a request.[53] However, costs in this first category must not include any costs which the public authority is entitled to take into account solely by virtue of the provisions relating to the cumulative cost of complying with separate requests.[54] Secondly, the costs that the public authority reasonably expects to incur in informing the applicant whether it holds the information and in communicating the information to the applicant.[55] These costs include the cost of redacting exempt information.[56] Costs in the second category which may be taken into account include the costs of giving effect to any preference expressed by the applicant as to the means or form of communicating the information,[57] the costs of reproducing any document containing the information,[58] and the costs of postage and other forms of transmitting the information.[59] Where any of the costs which relate to informing the applicant whether the public authority holds the information and communicating the information to the applicant are attributable to the time which persons undertaking any of those activities[60] on behalf of the public authority are expected to spend on those activities, those costs are to be estimated at the rate of £25 per person per hour.[61] Where a Scottish public authority proposes to communicate information in a case where the cost of compliance with a request for information is excessive, it is subject to two restrictions. First, it must notify the fee to, and agree it with, the applicant before the information is communicated.[62] Secondly, the fee shall not in any case exceed the sum of £50 plus the amount by which the 'projected costs' exceed £600.[63] In this context, the 'projected costs' are the total costs, whether direct or indirect, which a public authority reasonably estimates that it is likely to incur in locating, retrieving and providing the information.[64] However, in estimating projected costs, no account may be taken of costs incurred in determining whether the public authority holds the information specified in the request or whether the applicant is entitled to receive it (or, if not so entitled, whether he should nevertheless be provided with it or refused it).[65] Further, any estimate of the cost of staff time shall not exceed £15 per hour per member of staff.[66] It is to be noted that both sets of provisions impose a maximum fee but make no other provision for the calculation of fees. Nevertheless, a public authority in exercising its discretion to charge a particular level of fee must do so in accordance with normal public law principles.[67] Accordingly, improper

53 That is, the costs which the public authority may take into account under reg 4 of the Fees Regs 2004: Fees Regs 2004 reg 7(2)(a). As to such costs, see §§23–003 to 23–005.

54 Fees Regs 2004 reg 7(3). As to the provisions on the cumulative costs of complying with separate requests, see §§23–007 to 23–008.

55 Fees Regs 2004 reg 7(2)(b).

56 See ICO guidance *Fees that may be charged where the cost of compliance exceeds the appropriate limit*.

57 Fees Regs 2004 reg 7(4)(a).

58 Fees Regs 2004 reg 7(4)(b).

59 Fees Regs 2004 reg 7(4)(c).

60 That is, the activities referred to in Fees Regs 2004 reg 7(2)(b).

61 Fees Regs 2004 regs 4(4) and 7(5). It should be noted that this is a fixed, and not a maximum, figure.

62 Fees (s 13) Regs reg 4.

63 Fees (s 13) Regs reg 4. This provides some continuity with the fees which may be charged in a case which does not involve excessive cost of compliance: see §23–006.

64 Fees (s 13) Regs reg 3(1).

65 Fees (s 13) Regs reg 3(2)(a).

66 Fees (s 13) Regs reg 3(2)(b).

67 For an example of a case where the Tribunal held that the fees charged by a public authority were unreasonable

discrimination between different types of requests or a lack of consistency in approach in relation to the level of fees may be unlawful.

23– 011 Late reliance on section 12

It is now firmly established that, subject to the Tribunal's case management powers, a public authority is entitled to invoke in tribunal proceedings exemptions contained in Part II of the Act (exemptions: ss 21-44) that had previously not been relied upon by the public authority in reaching its decision.[68] In *All Party Parliamentary Group on Extraordinary Rendition v IC and Ministry of Defence*, decided before the decision of the Court of Appeal in *Birkett,*[69] the Upper Tribunal held that, whatever the position in relation to late claiming of substantive exemptions contained in Part II of FOIA, the position under the statutory scheme in respect of the s12 costs-limit was different and raised particular considerations of its own.[70] Key considerations in reaching that conclusion were that the modest costs limit could yield to repeat requests in 60-day periods, an estimate of future costs was only meaningful at an early stage and that the statutory scheme requires dialogue to refine the request to what is realistically available within the limit. Those considerations meant that late reliance on section 12 was permissible only where this did not give rise to prejudice or material unfairness.[71] Subsequent FTT decisions adopted conflicting approaches to the question.[72] A differently constituted Upper Tribunal re-visited the question of late reliance on s12 and held that a public authority may rely for the first time before the FTT on the provisions of FOIA, apart from those contained in Part II, subject only to the tribunal's case management powers.[73] Insofar as the Upper Tribunal in *APPGER* considered that the FTT had a *discretion* to allow late reliance on s12, that was inconsistent with the Court of Appeal's decision in *Birkett.*[74] The reasoning of the Court of Appeal in *Birkett* and of the Upper Tribunal below,[75] and in particular the explanation of why there was no scope for a non-statutory discretion, applied equally to the question of late reliance on ss 12 and 14. The position is thus the same as for the exemptions contained in Part II FOIA.

2. VEXATIOUS REQUESTS

23– 012 Introduction

A public authority is not obliged to comply with a request for information[76] under FOIA if the

(in the context of the EIR), see *Markinson v IC,* IT, 28 March 2006.

68 *DEFRA v IC and Birkett* [2011] UKUT 39 (AAC), [2011] UKUT 17 (AAC); *Birkett v DEFRA* [2011] EWCA Civ 1606, [2012] PTSR 1299.

69 *Birkett v DEFRA* [2011] EWCA Civ 1606, [2012] PTSR 1299. The case was concerned with the EIR, rather than FOIA.

70 *All Party Parliamentary Group on Extraordinary Rendition v IC and Ministry of Defence* [2011] UKUT 153 (AAC).

71 *All Party Parliamentary Group on Extraordinary Rendition v IC and Ministry of Defence* [2011] UKUT 153 (AAC) at [84]-[86].

72 See, for example: *Sittampalam v IC and BBC,* FTT, 4 July 2011 (reliance not permitted for the first time before the Information commissioner); *Lee v IC and King's College Cambridge,* FTT, 19 December 2012 (following APPGER, no justification for relying on s12 at late stage); *Independent Police Complaints Commission v IC,* FTT, 29 March 2012 (following *Birkett,* public authority entitled to rely on s 12).

73 *McInerney v IC and Dept of Education* [2015] UKUT 0047 (AAC) at [28]-[42].

74 *Birkett v DEFRA* [2011] EWCA Civ 1606, [2012] PTSR 1299.

75 *DEFRA v IC and Birkett* [2011] UKUT 39 (AAC), [2011] UKUT 17 (AAC).

76 That is, the public authority is not obliged to comply with its duties under s 1(1) of the FOIA (or of the FOI(S)A, as the case may be).

request is vexatious.[77]

23– 013 Early case law

The Freedom of Information Act 2000 does not provide any assistance as to what is meant by 'vexatious'.[78] The Tribunal had, since 2005, been developing divergent approaches. The first was based on the five criteria set out in the Information Commissioner's guidance.[79] The second approach preferred a dictionary definition of 'vexatious', ie tending to cause trouble or harassment by unjustified interference.

23– 014 Current case law

In three related cases of *Dransfield*,[80] *Craven*[81] and *Ainslie*[82] the Upper Tribunal gave guidance on what vexatious means in this context.[83] It found that neither the dictionary definition nor the Information Commissioner's guidance provided the correct test, although both were useful starting points. The Commissioner's five factors were at best pointers to potentially relevant considerations, and a means to an end of the ultimate test. A holistic approach needed to be taken and 'vexatious' connoted a 'manifestly unjustified, inappropriate, or improper use of a formal procedure.'[84] The Upper Tribunal proceeded to provide guidance as to the appropriate approach to vexatiousness in this context by identifying four broad issues or themes by reference to which the question of whether a request is truly vexatious might be considered: (1) the burden on the public authority; (2) the motive of the requester; (3) the value or serious purpose of the request; and (4) any harassment and/or distress caused. Appeals from the Upper Tribunal's decisions in *Dransfield* and *Craven* were dismissed by the Court of Appeal.[85] The Court held that the Upper Tribunal was right not to attempt any comprehensive or exhaustive definition of 'vexatious.' The emphasis should be on an objective standard: consistently with the constitutional nature of the right in question,[86] public authorities face a high hurdle in establishing that a request is vexatious. The starting point is that vexatiousness:

> primarily involves making a request which has no reasonable foundation, that is, no reasonable foundation for thinking that the information sought would be of value to the requester, or to the public or any section of the public.

The decision-maker must 'consider all the relevant circumstances in order to reach a balanced conclusion as to whether a request is vexatious.'[87] The Upper Tribunal has on a number of

---

[77] FOIA s 14(1); FOI(S)A s 14(1). The EIR provide for a similar exception in the case of requests which are 'manifestly unreasonable': EIR reg 12(4); EI(S)R reg 10(4). As to manifestly unreasonable requests under the EIR, see §18– 022.

[78] The Australian Law Reform Commission rejected an amendment to the Australian Freedom of Information Act 1982 which would have allowed requests to be rejected on the basis that they were vexatious, arguing that vexatiousness is a vague concept likely to result in unpredictable implementation (Australian Law Reform Commission and Administrative Review Council, *Open Government: a Review of the Federal Freedom of Information Act* (Canberra, Australian Law Reform Commission, 1982) para 7.18).

[79] *When can a request be considered vexatious or repeated?* (ver 5, June 2012) and Information Commissioner's guidance on Vexatious or Repeated Requests (whether the request is (i) obsessive, (ii) harassing or distressing to staff; (iii) would impose a significant burden to comply; (iv) was designed to cause disruption or annoyance; and (v) lacks a serious purpose).

[80] *IC v Devon CC and Dransfield* [2012] UKUT 440 (AAC)

[81] *Craven v IC and DECC* [2012] UKUT 442 (AAC).

[82] *Ainslie v IC and Dorset CC* [2012] UKUT 441.

[83] As well as guidance on the related concept of 'manifest unreasonableness' under the EIR.

[84] *IC v Devon CC and Dransfield* [2012] UKUT 440 (AAC) at [27].

[85] *Dransfield v IC and Devon CC* [2015] EWCA Civ 454, [2015] 1 WLR 5316.

[86] As to which, see *Kennedy v Charity Commission* [2014] UKSC 20, [2015] AC 455 at [153].

[87] *Dransfield v IC and Devon CC* [2015] EWCA Civ 454, [2015] 1 WLR 5316 at [68].

subsequent occasions, observed that the Upper Tribunal's guidance was not challenged on appeal and the Tribunal has continued to refer to and apply it.[88]

23–015 Vexatiousness in practice

Since the question whether a request is vexatious depends upon all the circumstances of the particular case consideration of past cases is of limited value. However, the following points of principle are worthy of note.

(1) While the starting point is to consider the value of the request, even a compelling public interest in the disclosure of the information does not necessarily trump other factors, which can, in an appropriate case, tip the balance.[89]

(2) If complying with a request would impose a substantial burden on the public authority, a request may be considered vexatious even if it has some value to the public.[90] However, the hurdle for a finding of vexatiousness based only on this factor is high.[91]

(3) Requests must be considered in context. Previous dealings between a requester and a public authority may be taken into account when determining whether a request is vexatious, even if the request would not be vexatious when viewed in isolation.[92]

(4) The possible availability of the information through disclosure in other proceedings (eg before an employment tribunal) is irrelevant to the question of the seriousness of purpose for which the information was sought.[93]

(5) Circumstances arising after the date upon which the public authority was required to determine the request cannot be taken into account in determining whether the request was vexatious.[94] However, subsequent events can be taken account in deciding what steps – if any – to direct the public authority to make. Thus, if the requests have become vexatious as a result of subsequent events, the Information Commissioner and/or Tribunal can decide that the public authority is not obliged to answer.[95]

(6) When taking account of the extent of work required (ie the burden) to produce the necessary information, the time and cost of redacting any documents can (unlike FOIA s 12) be taken into account.[96]

23–016 Vexatious request notices

If a public authority is relying on a claim that it is not obliged to comply with a request for information because the request is vexatious, then it must (subject to one exception)[97] give a

88 *Oxford Phoenix Innovation Limited v IC and Medicines and Healthcare Products Regulatory Agency* [2018] UKUT 192 (AAC) at [63], [87]; *Soh v IC and Imperial College* [2016] UKUT 249 (AAC) at [45]-[55], [94]-[95], [110(g)]; *Cabinet Office v IC and Ashton* [2018] UKUT 208 (AAC); *Jephcott ('Y') v IC* [2016] UKUT 475 (AAC) at [34]-[40]; *Parker v IC* [2016] UKUT 0427 (AAC) at [22]-[30]; *Innes v IC and Buckinghamshire CC* [2016] UKUT 520 (AAC).

89 *Cabinet Office v IC and Ashton* [2018] UKUT 208 (AAC); *Home Office v IC and Cruelty Free International* [2019] UKUT 299 (AAC) at [18]-[19]. Further, a request can have a value or serious purpose even if the purpose it serves is entirely private: *Soh v IC and Imperial College* [2016] UKUT 249 (AAC) at [80].

90 *Innes v IC and Buckinghamshire CC* [2016] UKUT 520 (AAC) at [20].

91 *Soh v IC and Imperial College* [2016] UKUT 249 (AAC) at [92].

92 *Dransfield v IC and Devon CC* [2015] EWCA Civ 454, [2015] 1 WLR 5316.

93 *Soh v IC and Imperial College* [2016] UKUT 249 (AAC) at [88].

94 *Soh v IC and Imperial College* [2016] UKUT 249 (AAC) at [58]-[72] and [101].

95 *Stürmer v IC and Derbyshire DC* [2015] UKUT 568 (AAC) at [91]-[94].

96 *Innes v IC and Buckinghamshire CC* [2016] UKUT 520 (AAC) at [54] (note, however, that this was common ground).

97 As to the exception to the duty to give a notice to the applicant in cases where the request for information is vexatious, see §24–009.

notice to that effect to the applicant within the time for compliance with s 1(1) of FOIA.[98]

3. REPEAT REQUESTS

23–017 Introduction

A public authority is not obliged to comply with a request for information where it is a request for information[99] which is identical or substantially similar to a previous request made by the same applicant, where the public authority has already complied with that previous request and where a reasonable interval has yet to elapse between compliance with the previous request and the making of the current request.[100] The Information Commissioner has published guidance dealing with repeat requests under s 14 of FOIA.[101]

23–018 Identical & similar requests

The Freedom of Information Act 2000 does not give any guidance as to what is meant by 'identical' or 'substantially similar'. Whilst the former concept should not prove problematic for most public authorities, the concept of 'substantially similar' may provoke differences of opinion between public authorities and applicants. The Information Commissioner has emphasised that the scope of s 14(2) is fairly narrow and the circumstances in which it may be applied are unlikely to arise often.[102] An applicant may very properly restrict a request for information by reference to a period within which the information was created or first held by the public authority. Such a temporal restriction may be mutually advantageous, limiting the scope of the task for the public authority and helping to ensure that the cost of compliance does not exceed the applicable limit. It may be that this temporally-limited request does not yield the information anticipated or that it yields information that points to further information outside the original limit. Further information can quite properly be requested without falling foul of s14(2). The mischief to which the provision is directed is the wasting of a public authority's resources through the provision of information to an applicant who has already been provided with that information rather than to preclude a request the words of which may be substantially similar to a previous request but where the information that answers its terms is materially different.[103] It is notable that the provisions on repeat requests only apply where the requests are made by the same person, so its effect may be side-stepped by the expedient of placing a request through another person. Where identical or substantially similar requests are made by different persons, it may be appropriate to consider whether the later request is

---

98 FOIA s 17(5); FOI(S)A s 16(5). As to the time for compliance, see §§22–020 to 22–027. As to the requirement to give a notice in cases where a request for information is vexatious, see §24–009.

99 In other words, the public authority is not obliged to comply with its duties under s 1(1) of the FOIA or under s 1 of the FOI(S)A.

100 FOIA s 14(2); FOI(S)A s 14(2). The EIR regime has no specific provision to this effect. However, the same objective is arguably secured by it excluding manifestly unreasonable requests: EIR reg 12(4)(b); EI(S)R reg 10(4)(b); see §18–022.

101 *Information Commissioner guidance, Dealing with repeat requests (section 14(2)).*

102 *Information Commissioner guidance, Dealing with repeat requests (section 14(2)),* para 8.

103 The Home Office Freedom of Information Unit suggested that one of the factors which could be taken into account when assessing whether a request was 'substantially similar' to an earlier one was whether it was reasonable to expect that fresh information would be disclosed on the new request: House of Commons, *Public Administration Committee—Third Report* (Cm 4355, 1999) Annex 6, para 31 (see Ch 1 n 68). However, it would seem that this is a matter which goes to the reasonableness of the interval between the requests (as to which, see §23–019) rather than to the similarity of the requests.

vexatious.[104]

23– 019 Reasonable intervals

The Freedom of Information Act 2000 does not give any guidance as to what should be taken into account when determining whether a reasonable interval has elapsed. However, it is likely that similar considerations will apply, such as the nature of the information, the purpose for which the information is held and the frequency with which the information is altered.[105]

23– 020 Repeat request notices

If a public authority is relying on a claim that it is not obliged to comply with a request for information because the request is a repeat request, then (subject to one exception)[106] it must give a notice to that effect to the applicant within the time for compliance with s 1(1) of FOIA.[107]

104 As to vexatious requests, see §§23– 012 to 23– 016.

105 See the DPA 1998 s 8(4). During the debate in the House of Lords, the frequency with which the information is altered was put forward by the government spokesman as one of the factors which would affect the reasonableness of an interval: Hansard HL vol 617 col 1014 (17 October 2000).

106 As to the exception to the duty to give a notice to the applicant in cases where the request for information is a repeat request, see §24– 009.

107 FOIA s 17(5); FOI(S)A s 16(5). As to the requirement to give a notice to the applicant in cases where the request for information is a repeat request, see also §24– 009.

CHAPTER 24

The response

1. THE DUTY TO SEARCH

24–001 Determining the holding

The basic duties imposed by s 1 of FOIA apply to information held by the public body at the time that the request is received.[1] Whether information is 'held' will be a question of fact, applying a common sense and non-technical approach.[2] The Code of Practice advises that this includes information stored in off-site servers or cloud storage and information held by other organisations, including off-site storage or information provided to lawyers for the purposes of litigation.[3] Holding is not, however, simply a physical concept. There must be a recognised link between the information and the authority so that it can be properly said that it is 'held' by the authority.[4] The reasons why an authority was given, obtained or created information will inform whether it is held by the authority for the purposes of FOIA.[5] The Code of Practice provides that 'information is "held" by the public authority if it is retained for the purpose of the public authority's business' and contrasts 'purely personal, political, constituency, or trade union information,' which is not.[6] In certain cases, it will be important to determine the exact

---

1 FOIA s 1(1), (4); FOI(S)A s 1(1), (4).

2 *University of Newcastle upon Tyne v Information Commissioner and BUAV* [2011] UKUT 185 (AAC), see esp [27]-[44].

3 Section 45 Code of practice, para 1.9.

4 *University of Newcastle Upon Tyne v IC and BUAV* [2011] UKUT 185 (AAC) at [27]; *Dept of Health v IC and Lewis* [2017] EWCA Civ 374, [2017] 1 WLR 3330 at [54]; *Holland v IC and University of East Anglia* [2016] UKUT 260 (AAC) addressing the similar – but not identically worded – requirement under the EIRs, that the information is in the authority's possession and was 'produced or received' by it.

5 *Dept of Health v IC and Lewis* [2015] UKUT 0159 (AAC) at [97].

6 Section 45 Code of Practice, para 1.10. And see also Information Commissioner Guidance, *Information held by a public authority for the purposes of FOIA*, paragraphs 29-32.

nature of the legal relationship between a person holding information and the public authority, or to determine the legal structure pursuant to which information was created or held.[7] The information in relation to which the duties apply includes information held by another person on behalf of the public authority.[8] FOIA applies to information held in private email accounts (such as Hotmail, Yahoo and Gmail) and other media formats where that information is held on behalf of a public authority. If the information held in a private account amounts to public authority business it is very likely to be held on behalf of the public authority in accordance with s 3(2)(b) of the Act.[9]

24–002 Deleted information

Recorded information which has been destroyed before the request was received will self-evidently not be held by a public authority at the time of the request. However, determining whether information recorded in electronic form has been destroyed is not straightforward. The Tribunal has held that where deleted information can be recovered by various technical means, it will be a question of fact and degree as to whether it is held[10] and that simple restoration from a back-up tape should normally be attempted because information on such tapes is 'held' by the public authority.[11] If the information is difficult and expensive to retrieve the cost limit under FOIA section 12 may come into play.[12] The latest Code of Practice suggests that information deleted before the request was received which is only held in electronic back up files should generally be regarded as not being held,[13] but does not explain why. The Information Commissioner advises that it will be reasonable for public authorities to interpret most requests as relating to their current or 'live' records, unless the requester refers to an old version or makes it clear that they expect to be provided with deleted information.[14]

24–003 Extent of the search duty

Invariably a public authority will have to search through the information that it holds in order to respond to a request for information, whether in order to identify the information that it holds which answers the terms of that request or to establish that it does not hold any information answering the terms of that request. A public authority may require an applicant to provide further particulars in order to identify and locate the information requested.[15] The s 46 Code of Practice encourages public authorities to have record systems that include the capacity to search for information requested under FOIA.[16] The Act does not stipulate the extent to which a public authority must search for information answering the terms of a request, but the Code of Practice provides that searches should be conducted in a 'reasonable and intelligent way based on an understanding of how the public authority manages its records.' The Code advises that if a reasonable search in the areas most likely to hold the information

---

7 *Chagos Refugees Group v IC and FCO*, FTT, 4 September 2012 at [55]-[68], where following an analysis of the factual and legal relationship between the FCO and its external consultants, the Tribunal concluded that information authored and held by the consultants was not held on behalf of the FCO.

8 FOIA s 3(2)(b); FOI(S)A s 3(2)(b). See further §20–010.

9 See Information Commissioner Guidance, *Official information held in private email accounts*, 9 March 2017.

10 *Harper v IC and Royal Mail Group plc*, IT, 15 November 2005 at [21].

11 *Harper v IC and Royal Mail Group plc*, IT, 15 November 2005 at [27]. Applying the same approach to the EIR: *Keiller v IC and University of East Anglia*, FTT, 18 January 2012.

12 *Whitehead v IC*, FTT, 29 April 2014 at [16].

13 Section 45 Code of Practice, para 1.11.

14 Information Commissioner Guidance, *Information held by a public authority for the purposes of FOIA*, para 45.

15 FOIA s 1(3); FOI(S)A s 1(3). See further §22–011.

16 Section 46 Code of Practice para 9.3.

does not reveal it, the public authority may consider that on the balance of probabilities the information is not held.[17] These provisions reflect the approach which has consistently been taken by the Tribunal on the extent of the search required.[18] However, the time which a public authority spends, or would need to spend, locating and retrieving the information answering the terms of a request is relevant to whether the cost of compliance would be excessive.[19] On a complaint by an applicant, the Information Commissioner will investigate the adequacy of the search made by the public authority and will not accept the public authority's bare assertion that it has carried out an adequate search.[20] An applicant who is unsatisfied with the conclusion reached by the Information Commissioner may appeal to the Tribunal. The Tribunal will review the Commissioner's conclusion, if necessary hearing evidence on the issue.[21] The Tribunal does not demand certainty.[22] A public authority must carry out a reasonable search.[23] A search should be conducted intelligently and reasonably. An exhaustive search conducted in unlikely places is not required.[24] The Tribunal considers that, because of the cost involved, most of those who make a freedom of information request prefer a search delivering most relevant information to a hypothetically exhaustive search delivering more. In deciding whether the search has been a reasonable one, the Tribunal will consider all relevant factors, including the public authority's analysis of the request, the scope of its search, and the rigour and efficiency with which it conducted the search.[25] The measure of what is reasonable is coloured by the cost limit set by the Regulations.[26] It would seem that in reviewing the reasonableness of a public authority's search, the Tribunal will do so on the basis of the filing systems available to the public authority notwithstanding shortcomings in those systems.[27]

2. NON-SUBSTANTIVE RESPONSES

24–004 Introduction

A person's entitlement to receive information requested and to be informed whether the

[17] Section 45 Code of Practice, para 1.12.

[18] See, for example: *Bromley v IC and Environment Agency*, IT, 31 August 2007; *Ames v IC and Cabinet Office*, IT, 24 April 2008; *Malcolm v IC*, IT, 19 December 2008; *Dudley v IC*, IT, 20 April 2009; *Reed v IC*, IT, 3 July 2009; *Garrard v IC and Home Office*, FTT, 6 September 2010 at [20].

[19] Fees Regs 2004 reg 4(3). See §§23–001 to 23–010. There is no equivalent provision in the environmental information regime.

[20] *Berend v IC and LB of Richmond*, IT, 12 July 2007 at [84]. Where the critical issue is whether information is held, it is incumbent upon the Information Commissioner to analyse very carefully the searches the public authority claims to have undertaken: *Garrard v IC and Home Office*, FTT, 6 September 2010 at [20].

[21] *Bromley v IC and Environment Agency*, IT, 31 August 2007 at [13]; *Fortune v IC and National Patient Safety Agency*, IT, 16 April 2008 at [6]; *Ames v IC and Cabinet Office*, IT, 24 April 2008 at [10]; *Reed v IC*, IT, 3 July 2009 at [32]-[38].

[22] *Bromley v IC and Environment Agency*, IT, 31 August 2007 at [13]; *Dudley v IC*, IT, 20 April 2009 at [31]; *Innes v IC*, IT, 27 October 2009.

[23] *Reed v IC*, IT, 3 July 2009 at [42].

[24] *Muttitt v IC and Cabinet Office*, FTT, 31 January 2012; *Chagos Refugees Group v IC and FCO*, FTT, 4 September 2012 at [70].

[25] *Bromley v IC and Environment Agency*, IT, 31 August 2007 at [12]-[13]; *Ames v IC and Cabinet Office*, IT, 24 April 2008 at [107]; *Malcolm v IC*, IT, 19 December 2008; *Dudley v IC*, IT, 20 April 2009 at [24]-[47]; *Reed v IC*, IT, 3 July 2009 at [39]-[56]; *Garrard v IC and Home Office*, FTT, 6 September 2010 at [20].

[26] The FOI & DP (Limits & Fees) Regs: see *Francis v IC and South Essex Partnership Foundation NHS Trust*, IT, 21 July 2008. In other words, 18 hours or 24 hours (at £25 per hour), depending on the type of public authority.

[27] *Francis v IC and South Essex Partnership Foundation NHS Trust*, IT, 21 July 2008 at [18]-[19]; *Dudley v IC*, IT, 20 April 2009 at [24]-[47]; *Lee v IC and King's College Cambridge*, FTT, 19 December 2012 at [32]-[40]. But see §22–035 for a discussion of the duties for public authorities to search for 'deleted' information on computer systems.

information requested is held by the public authority[28] is made subject to certain other provisions of FOIA.[29] The bases upon which a public authority may refuse to comply with a request may conveniently be grouped into two broad classes:

(1) Procedural bases, where the form of the request is defective, cost of compliance is excessive or fees have not been paid.

(2) Substantive bases, where the information is exempt information, either by virtue of a provision conferring absolute exemption or where the information is exempt information by virtue of a qualified exemption and the public interest is on balance against disclosure.

The basis for refusal influences the form of the refusal notice that must be given to the applicant.

24–005 Procedurally defective requests

There are four types of 'procedural reason' that entitle a public authority to refuse or to place in abeyance a request for information:

(1) Inadequately particularised request: where a public authority reasonably requires further information in order to identify and locate the information requested, then, provided that it has informed the applicant of that requirement, it is not obliged to provide the information requested until it receives the further information that it requires to identify and locate that information.[30]

(2) Vexatious or repeat request: a public authority is not obliged to comply with a request for information if that request is vexatious.[31] Nor is a public authority obliged to comply with a request for information if it is a request which is identical or substantially similar to a previous request made by the same applicant, the public authority has already complied with the previous request, and a reasonable interval has yet to elapse between compliance with the previous request and the making of the current request.[32]

(3) Failure to pay required fee: where a public authority has given a fees notice to an applicant, it is not obliged to comply with the request for information unless the applicant pays the fee within the period of three months beginning with the day on which the fees notice was given to the applicant.[33]

(4) Excessive cost of compliance: where a public authority estimates that the cost of complying with a request for information would exceed the appropriate limit, it is not obliged to comply with that request.[34]

24–006 Revelatory requests

Where a request is made in respect of information in relation to which an absolute exclusion from the duty to confirm or deny applies, a public authority is not obliged to comply with the

---

28 Termed, in this work, 'the access right' and 'the existence right', respectively: see §1–008(4).

29 FOIA s 1(2); FOI(S)A s 1(6).

30 FOIA s 1(3); FOI(S)A s 1(3). As to requiring further particulars of a request for information, see §§22–010 to 22–011. An analogous exemptions applies in relation to environmental information: EIR reg 12(4)(c); EI(S)R reg 10(4)(c); and see §§18–013 to 18–014.

31 FOIA s 14(1); FOI(S)A s 14(1). As to vexatious requests, see §§23–012 to 23–016.

32 FOIA s 14(2); FOI(S)A s 14(2). As to repeat requests, see §§23–017 to 23–020.

33 FOIA s 9(2); FOI(S)A s 9(3). As to fees notices, see §§22–012 to 22–019.

34 FOIA s 12(1); FOI(S)A s 12(1). As to the situations where the cost of complying with a request for information would be excessive, see §§23–001 to 23–010.

request.[35] Where a request is made in respect of information in relation to which there is an exclusion (but not an absolute exclusion) of the duty to confirm or deny, a public authority is not obliged to comply with the request where the public interest in maintaining the exclusion of the duty to confirm or deny outweighs the public interest in disclosing whether the public authority holds the information.[36]

24– 007 Deferred decision

Where a request is made in respect of information in relation to which there is an exclusion (but not an absolute exclusion) of the duty to confirm or deny or in respect of information which is exempt information (but not by virtue of a provision conferring absolute exemption), a public authority may defer compliance with the request for such time as is reasonable in the circumstances pending a decision on where the public interest lies.[37]

3. REFUSAL TO COMMUNICATE

24– 008 Introduction

Where a public authority claims that it is not obliged to comply with a request for information, it is required to give the applicant a notice to that effect.[38] The purpose of a refusal notice is not just to ensure that an applicant is informed of the outcome of a request for information, but also to ensure that an unsuccessful applicant is aware of the reasons why his request has been refused and to enable him to decide on an informed basis whether to take the matter further.[39] The expectation is that the requirement to give such a notice will make it less likely that a public authority will make an unjustified claim that it is not obliged to comply with a request for information, as it will be required to apply its mind to the justification at the time.[40] The nature of a refusal notice and the time within which it is to be provided to an applicant depend upon the basis for refusal, as well as upon what is being refused. These may be divided into the following categories:

(1) refusal notices where a request is vexatious or is a repeat request;
(2) refusal notices where the cost of compliance is excessive;
(3) refusal notices where the information falls within Part II of the Act but no public interest balancing exercise is involved; and
(4) refusal notices where information falls within Part II of the Act and a public interest balancing exercise is involved.

An applicant may apply to the Information Commissioner under s 50 complaining that a refusal notice does not comply with the requirements of Part I of the Act.[41] The Commissioner may issue a decision notice that specifies whether the public authority has or has not complied with the requirements of s 17. A party dissatisfied with that decision notice may appeal to the

---

35 FOIA s 2(1)(a).

36 FOIA s 2(1)(b).

37 FOIA s 10(3). There is no equivalent provision in FOI(S)A.

38 FOIA s 17; FOI(S)A s 16.

39 In some jurisdictions, public authorities are subject to more onerous duties in relation to explaining their decisions. See, eg, the Freedom of Information Act 2014 (Republic of Ireland) s 13(2)(d), the Freedom of Information Act 1982 (Cth of Australia) s 26(1) and *Re Luton and Commissioner of Taxation* (1996) AAR 492.

40 See, eg, Australian Law Reform Commission and Administrative Review Council, *Open Government: A Review of the Federal Freedom of Information Act 1982*, ALRC 77, ARC 40 (Canberra, 1995) para 7.19.

41 See §45– 006.

Tribunal in relation to the finding as to the adequacy of the refusal notice.[42]

24– 009 Vexatious and repeat requests

Where a public authority is relying on a claim that it is not obliged to comply with a request for information because it is vexatious or a repeat request,[43] then (subject to one exception) it must give the applicant a notice stating that fact.[44] The exception is that the public authority need not give such a notice where it has previously given the applicant a notice in relation to a previous request for information stating that it is relying on such a claim[45] and, in all the circumstances, it would be unreasonable to expect the public authority to serve a further notice in relation to the current request.[46] FOIA does not impose upon a public authority a duty to state why it considers a request to be vexatious or a repeat request, although the Code of Practice suggests that public authorities may wish to do so as part of their s 16 duty to provide advice and assistance in this respect to the applicant.[47] As with other refusal notices, any such notice must contain particulars of the public authority's procedures for dealing with complaints about requests for information (or state that the authority does not have such a procedure)[48] and it must provide details of the right to apply for a decision by the Information Commissioner as to whether the request has been properly dealt with.[49] Any notice must be served within the time for compliance with s 1(1) of FOIA.[50]

24– 010 Excessive cost of compliance

Where a public authority is relying on a claim that it is not obliged to comply with a request for information because the cost of compliance would be excessive,[51] then it must give the applicant a notice stating that fact.[52] FOIA does not impose upon a public authority an express duty to state why it considers that the cost of complying with a request would be excessive, but it may be reasonable to expect a public authority which is faced with such a request to provide advice and assistance in this respect to the applicant.[53] As with other refusal notices, such a notice

---

42 See further §45– 012. For example: *Hogan and Oxford CC v IC*, IT, 17 October 2006 at [22]-[24].

43 Under FOIA s 14, or FOI(S)A s 14. As to vexatious requests, see §§23– 012 to 23– 016. As to repeat requests, see §23– 017.

44 FOIA s 17(5); FOI(S)A s 16(5).

45 The FOIA s 17(6)(b) refers to a previous notice that the public authority is relying on a claim that s 14 applies and not just a previous notice that the public authority is relying on a claim that a request was vexatious. Accordingly, it would seem that a public authority is entitled to rely upon the provisions of s 17(6) where it has previously served either a notice that a request is vexatious or a notice that a request is a repeat request. The Scottish provisions are slightly more restrictive, in that a public authority is only excused from giving a notice if it has previously given a notice in respect of an identical or substantially similar request: FOI(S)A s 16(5)(a).

46 FOIA s 17(6); FOI(S)A s 16(5). In relation to information held by Scottish public authorities, there is an additional requirement that the previous request was identical or substantially similar to the current request: FOI(S)A s 16(5)(a).

47 See the s 45 Code of Practice at para 7.17.

48 FOIA s 17(7)(a); FOI(S)A s 19(a).

49 That is, the right conferred by the FOIA s 50 or the FOI(S)A s 47: FOIA s 17(1)(b); FOI(S)A s 19(b). In relation to information held by Scottish public authorities, the notice must also contain particulars of the right to apply to the public authority for a review of its decision under s 20(1): FOI(S)A s 19(b).

50 FOIA s 17(5). In relation to information held by Scottish public authorities, the notice must be given within the time for compliance laid down by s 10 of the FOI(S)A: FOI(S)A s 16(5). As to the time for compliance, see §§22– 020 to 22– 027.

51 Under the FOIA s 12 or the FOI(S)A s 12. As to the situation where the cost of complying with a request for information would be excessive, see §§23– 001 to 23– 010.

52 FOIA s 17(5); FOI(S)A s 16(4).

53 Pursuant to the duty imposed by the FOIA s 16(1) or the FOI(S)A s 15(1). The Section 45 Code of Practice, para 6.9, suggests that where a request is refused under s 12, authorities should consider what advise and assistance can

must contain particulars of the public authority's procedures for dealing with complaints about requests for information (or state that the authority does not have such a procedure)[54] and it must provide details of the right to apply for a decision by the Information Commissioner as to whether the request has been properly dealt with.[55] The notice must be given within the time for compliance with s 1(1) of FOIA.[56]

24– 011 Exempt information

Where a public authority is to any extent relying on a claim that the requested information is excluded from the duty to confirm or deny (whether an absolute exclusion or otherwise) or a claim that information is exempt information, it must give the applicant a notice to that effect.[57] Such a notice must state that the public authority is relying on the relevant claim,[58] it must specify the exclusion or exemption in question[59] and it must state (if it would not otherwise be apparent) why the exclusion or exemption applies.[60] While the statement required by s 17(1) ought not itself disclose exempt information, that statement must describe the information sufficiently in order to state why an exemption applies. A misdescription or mischaracterisation of that information, particularly if it facilitates reliance upon an exemption, will not constitute a notice which 'states' why the exemption applies. Where there are a significant number of 'pieces' of information to which different exemptions apply, a statement is often most conveniently provided in tabular form, with a row for each discrete piece of information and a column for each exemption and explanations for the same. However, the public authority is not required to state why an exemption applies if, and to the extent that, that statement would involve the disclosure of information which would itself be exempt information.[61] As is the case with other refusal notices, such a notice must contain particulars of the public authority's procedures for dealing with complaints about requests for information (or state that

be provided to help the applicant reframe or refocus the request with a view to bringing it within the cost limit: for example, by refining the subject matter or reducing the timespan covered.

54 FOIA s 17(7)(a); FOI(S)A s 19(a).

55 In other words, the right conferred by s 50 in the FOIA and s 47 in the FOI(S)A: FOIA s 17(1)(b); FOI(S)A s 19(b). In relation to information held by Scottish public authorities, the notice must also contain particulars of the right to apply to the public authority for a review of its decision under s 20(1): FOI(S)A s 19(b). The applicant can further appeal to the Tribunal, and the Tribunal can inquire into the matters that have and have not been taken into account by the public authority in carrying out the estimate and and remove from the estimate any amount the authority could not reasonably expect to incur on account of the nature of the activity or its amount: see *Kirkham v IC* [2018] UKUT 126 (AAC) at [20].

56 FOIA s 17(5). In relation to information held by Scottish public authorities, the notice must be given within the time for compliance laid down by s 10: FOI(S)A s 16(4). As to the time for compliance, see §§22– 020 to 22– 027.

57 FOIA s 17(1); FOI(S)A s 16(1).

58 FOIA s 17(1)(a); FOI(S)A s 16(1)(b). In relation to information held by Scottish public authorities, subject to s 18 of the FOI(S)A, the notice must also state that the public authority holds the information: FOI(S)A s 16(1)(a). The difference in treatment presumably arises from the fact that s 16(1) of the FOI(S)A applies only to requests for information which the public authority holds, whereas s 17(1) of the FOIA applies to any request for information. Section 18 of the FOI(S)A disapplies s 16(1)(a) and (2) in a case where the public authority considers that to reveal whether the information exists or is held would be contrary to the public interest.

59 FOIA s 17(1)(b); FOI(S)A s 16(1)(c).

60 FOIA s 17(1)(c); FOI(S)A s 16(1)(d). In this context it is unlikely that it will be sufficient for the public authority merely to paraphrase the wording of the exemption. The addition of this requirement was a departure from the position in the Freedom of Information Bill 1999, cl 15. See also House of Commons, *Public Administration—Third Report* (Cm 4355, 1999) Annex 6, para 39B (see Ch 1 n 68) and House of Lords, *Draft Freedom of Information Bill—First Report* (Select Committee Report HL 97), Session 1998-1999, 27 July 1999, paras 51 to 54 (see Ch 1 n 43). This is the line that has been taken by the Tribunal: *Hogan and Oxford CC v IC*, IT, 17 October 2006 at [22]. Where a public authority relies on FOIA s 40 to refuse a request, it should refer to the applicable data protection principles: *Magherafelt District Council v IC*, FTT, 3 February 2010 at [56]-[57], upheld on appeal, *IC v Magherafelt DC* [2012] UKUT 263 (AAC).

61 FOIA s 17(4); FOI(S)A s 16(3).

the authority does not have such a procedure)[62] and it must provide details of the right to apply for a decision by the Information Commissioner as to whether the request has been properly dealt with.[63] The notice must be served within the time for compliance with s 1(1) of FOIA.[64]

24– 012 Contrary to the public interest

Where a public authority is to any extent relying on a claim that the requested information is exempt information (but not by virtue of a provision conferring absolute exemption) and that the public interest in maintaining the exemption outweighs the public interest in disclosing the information, then it must (subject to one exception)[65] state the reasons why it has so decided.[66] Similarly, where a public authority is to any extent relying on a claim that the requested information is subject to an exclusion (but not an absolute exclusion) from the duty to confirm or deny (but not by virtue of a provision conferring absolute exclusion) and that the public interest in maintaining the exclusion of the duty to confirm or deny outweighs the public interest in disclosing whether the public authority holds the information, then it must (subject to one exception)[67] state the reasons why it has so decided.[68] The exception in each case is that the public authority need not make such a statement if, and to the extent that, the statement would involve the disclosure of information which would itself be exempt information.[69] The reasons must be stated in the refusal notice or in a separate notice given within such time as is reasonable in the circumstances.[70] The provision for separate notice to be given is to allow for the situation where the public authority has deferred its decision on where the public interest lies.[71] Where a public authority has deferred its decision on where the public interest lies, then the notice given to the applicant[72] must:

(a) state that the public authority has not yet reached a decision as to where the balance of the public interest lies;
(b) contain an estimate of the date by which the public authority expects that it will have reached that decision;[73] and

---

62 FOIA s 17(7)(a); FOI(S)A s 19(a).

63 In other words, the right conferred by s 50 of the FOIA and s 47 of the FOI(S)A: FOIA s 17(1)(b); FOI(S)A s 19(b). In relation to information held by Scottish public authorities, the notice must also contain particulars of the right to apply to the public authority for a review of its decision under s 20(1): FOI(S)A s 19(b).

64 FOIA s 17(1). In relation to information held by Scottish public authorities, the notice must be served in accordance with the time allowed for compliance with the request by s 10: FOI(S)A s 16(1).

65 In relation to information held by Scottish public authorities, a second exception applies: see n 69.

66 FOIA s 17(3); FOI(S)A s 16(2). In this context it would be prudent for the public authority to specify the public interest factors, both for and against disclosure, that it has taken into account. Failure to do so may result in a finding by the Tribunal that the public authority has failed to provide a valid refusal notice: see, eg, *Hogan and Oxford CC v IC*, IT, 17 October 2006 at [22]-[24].

67 In relation to information held by Scottish public authorities, a second exception applies: see n 69.

68 FOIA s 17(3); FOI(S)A s 16(2). In this context it would be prudent for the public authority to specify the public interest factors, both for and against disclosure, that it has taken into account.

69 FOIA s 17(4); FOI(S)A s 16(3). In relation to information held by Scottish public authorities, FOI(S)A s 18, provides for a further exception in a case where the public authority considers that to reveal whether the information exists or is held would be contrary to the public interest.

70 FOIA s 17(3). As the FOI(S)A does not provide for a public authority to defer a decision on where the public interest lies in such a case, that Act contains no provision for a separate notice to be served at a time after the service of the refusal notice.

71 See the FOIA s 10(3) and §22– 025. As to the position in relation to information held by Scottish public authorities, see §22– 025 n 94.

72 That is, the notice given in accordance with s 17(1) of the FOIA.

73 These estimates should be realistic and reasonable, particularly as it is likely that public authorities will be expected to comply with their estimates. If an estimate is exceeded, the public authority should apologise and provide reasons for the delay.

(c) contain all the usual matters that must be included in a refusal notice where the information is exempt.[74]

24– 013 Partial refusal

It may be the case that a request for information will seek both information which a public authority is required to communicate to the applicant and information which it is not required to communicate, for example, because it is exempt information. In such a case, a public authority must communicate the information which it is required to communicate in the normal way and follow the normal procedures in relation to that information which it refuses to communicate.

24– 014 Redaction

The Freedom of Information Act 2000 provides for the communication of information to applicants and not for the provision of documents.[75] Accordingly, where an applicant requests information which forms part of a document and that document also contains other information which the applicant is not entitled to receive (for example, because the information is exempt information or because it is outside the terms of the request), the public authority must decide whether it will:

— provide the applicant with the entire document, thereby effectively waiving the exemption in relation to any exempt information[76] or providing the applicant with information that has not been requested;[77]
— redact the document so that the applicant only receives what he is entitled to and what has been asked for; or
— provide the information by a means other than the provision of a copy of the document (eg by the provision of a newly created document containing only those parts of the original document containing information to which the applicant is entitled or by the provision of a summary of the document).

Whichever option is adopted, the public authority is not entitled to avoid its obligations in relation to the requested information that is either not exempt information or is exempt information solely by virtue of a qualified exemption for which the public interest weighs in favour of disclosure.[78] Where the second or third option is chosen, a public authority should be careful to ensure that any new or redacted document does not create a misleading impression of the information which is held by the public authority. If there is a risk of such a misleading impression being created, then it might be more appropriate to consider providing

[74] FOIA s 17(2). As the FOI(S)A does not provide for a public authority to defer such a decision, that Act contains no similar provisions as to notices.

[75] This is in contrast to freedom of information legislation in all but one of the comparable jurisdictions. Where provision is made for access to documents, provision is also made for the redaction of those documents. See, eg, the Freedom of Information Act 1982 (Commonwealth of Australia) s 22(1) (substituted in 2010); Access to Information Act 1982 (Canada) s 25; Freedom of Information Act 2014 (Republic of Ireland) s 18.

[76] In other words, a discretionary disclosure: see §§5– 007 to 5– 014 and §§20– 036 to 20– 038.

[77] In Australia (where the unit of disclosure and exemption is a 'document'), the approach taken where disclosure of a single document would disclose information that would reasonably be regarded as irrelevant to a request, is to ask whether such disclosure would reasonably, as opposed to irrationally or absurdly, be considered or looked on as irrelevant and, if so, not include it in the response: *Re Russell Island Development Association Inc and Department of Primary Industries and Energy* (1994) 33 ALD 683.

[78] This is spelled out in the environmental information and data protection regimes: EIR reg 12(11); EI(S)R reg 10(7); DPA 1998 s7(5). This accords with the view expressed by the government spokesman in the House of Lords: Hansard HL vol 617 cols 930-931 (17 October 2000). The House of Commons Public Administration Committee had recommended that an express provision to this effect be included in the Act: House of Commons, *Public Administration—Third Report* (Cm 4355, 1999) para 120 (see Ch 1 n 68). This is the approach adopted in the Official Information Act 1982 (New Zealand) s 17.

the information in an alternative manner, such as by way of a summary.[79] In relation to statistical information, the House of Lords has held that perturbation of the information by a process of 'barnardisation'[80] is a matter of presentation of information, rather than altering the information.[81]

4. COMMUNICATION OF INFORMATION

24–015 Introduction

Section 1(1) of the Freedom of Information Act 2000 confers an entitlement on a person who makes a request for information, but it does not describe the correlative duty imposed on the public authority to which the request is made. That correlative duty is described in s 11 of the Act.[82] Where the request for information does not express a preference that the public authority communicate the requested information by one or more of the three means set out in s 11(1), then the public authority's duty is to comply with the request 'by communicating information by any means which are reasonable in the circumstances.' It is thus implicit in FOIA that the communication of requested information will not necessarily involve the provision of a copy of that information to an applicant.[83] Where a request for information does express a preference for one of those three means, then the public authority must, so far as reasonably practicable, give effect to that preference. However, while the applicant's entitlement under FOIA is to recorded information, rather than the record itself, there can be circumstances in which aspects of the record (for example a letterhead or logo) constitute part of the information sought rather than automatically being regarded simply as part of the record. In such circumstances a public authority cannot rely upon s11(4) to avoid providing that information since it is required by s1(1), which imposes an obligation independent of s11.[84] Where a request is made for information that is a dataset, or which forms part of a dataset, held by the public authority, and the applicant requests that information be communicated in an electronic form, then the public authority must, as far as is reasonably practicable, provide the information to the applicant in an electronic form that is capable of re-use, in other words, a re-useable format.[85] Any complaint against a decision of a public authority under s 50 is referable to the duty imposed by s 11.

24–016 No preference expressed

Where an applicant when making a request for information does not express a preference for the information to be communicated to him by one or more of the three means listed in s 11(1), a public authority may comply with that request by communicating information by any means

[79] It is likely that the difficulty of redacting information which an applicant is not entitled to see is one of the circumstances which a public authority would be entitled to take into account when deciding whether it is reasonably practicable to give effect to an applicant's preference as to the means of communication of the information: FOIA s 11; FOI(S)A s 11. As to the applicant's preference as to the means of communication of the information, see §24–018. See also *Craven v IC*, IT, 13 May 2008 at [29].

[80] That is, by expressly adding -1, 0 or 1 to very low values so as to make more difficult identification of the individuals reflected in those values.

[81] *Common Services Agency v IC* [2008] UKHL 47, [2008] 1 WLR 1550 at [15].

[82] Regulation 5(1) of the EIR and of the EI(S)R are drafted differently. Their animating provision – reg 5(1) – operates by imposing a duty, with the correlative entitlement to be inferred from that duty.

[83] See, for example: FOIA s 11(1)(b); FOI(S)A s 11(2)(c).

[84] See *IPSA v IC* [2015] EWCA Civ 388, [2015] 1 WLR 2879.

[85] FOIA s 11(1A), inserted by the Protection of Freedoms Act 2012 s 102, with effect from 1 September 2013.

which are reasonable in the circumstances.[86] Similarly, if an applicant has expressed a preference for communication of the requested information by one or more of the means set out in s 11(1) but, in whole or in part, it is not reasonably practicable for the public authority to give effect to that preference, that public authority will comply with the request 'by communicating information by any means which are reasonable in the circumstances.' The duty imposed by s 11(4) must be informed by the purpose of the Act, which is to facilitate rather than hinder the disclosure of information held by public authorities.[87] Accordingly, under s 11(4) compliance with a valid request for information is achieved by communicating the non-exempt requested information by any means which are reasonable in the circumstances. The Information Commissioner advises that where no preference is specified it will generally be reasonable for the form to be dictated by the manner in which the applicant has made their request: for example, where the request is submitted by email it would generally be reasonable to assume that they wish to receive a response electronically.[88] A public authority is not restricted to one of the three means set out in s 11(1). Nor is there any sensible reason why different 'pieces' of information answering the terms of a request should not be communicated by different means, if that is what is reasonable in the circumstances. In deciding whether the means of communication are reasonable in the circumstances, a public authority may take into account the form in which it holds the information, the volume of the information to be communicated, the cost of different means of communication and the applicant's ability to receive or read a particular means of communication. The House of Lords has held that, provided that it notifies the applicant that it has done so, a public authority can 'perturb' requested statistical information by a process of 'barnardisation'[89] and that this perturbation will simply be a matter of presentation of requested information, rather than constituting an alteration of the information held by the public authority.[90]

24– 017 Other relevant considerations

When considering how to communicate information, a public authority will need to take into account any relevant duties that it has under other legislation.[91] The view has been taken by the Information Commissioner that, without some other statutory duty, there is no obligation on a public authority to translate information from one language to another for the purposes of responding to a request for information.[92] It would nevertheless be prudent for a public authority to consider whether its duty to provide advice and assistance requires it to translate information for the benefit of an applicant.[93] Further, a public authority may wish to consider

86 FOIA s 11(4); FOI(S)A s 11(4). Where an applicant expresses a preference after having made a request for information, this will not engage FOIA s 11(1), although a late expression of preference might constitute a fresh request for information with a validly expressed preference: see *Innes v IC* [2014] EWCA Civ 1086, [2015] 2 All ER 560, [2015] 1 WLR 210 at [49]. Similarly, where an applicant expresses a preference when making a request for information but that preference is not one of the three listed in FOIA s 11(1), this will not engage s 11(1) and the public authority may proceed on the basis of no preference having been expressed. The FTT has used correspondence after the request for information in order to interpret a preference expressed in the request for information: *IPSA v IC and Leapman*, FTT, 29 April 2013.

87 See §§1– 015, 1– 017 and §§2– 016 to 2– 018.

88 See Information Commissioner Guidance, *Means of Communicating Information*, para 48.

89 That is, by expressly adding -1, 0 or 1 to very low values so as to make more difficult identification of the individuals reflected in those values.

90 *Common Services Agency v IC* [2008] UKHL 47, [2008] 1 WLR 1550 at [15].

91 For example, duties under the Equality Act 2010 or the Welsh Language Act 1993. A discussion of these duties is outside the scope of this work, but for examples of the guidance on this point, see the Scottish Ministers' Code of Practice, paras 7 to 8.

92 Information Commissioner Guidance, *Means of Communicating Information*, para 56.

93 As to the duty to provide advice and assistance, see §§21– 001 to 21– 006.

whether its duty to provide advice and assistance requires it to provide some warning to an applicant in an appropriate case that the information being provided to him or her is subject to copyright, data protection legislation or other constraints on the use of information.

24– 018 Preference expressed

Section 11(1) of FOIA provides that where an applicant, on making a request for information, expresses a preference for communication by one or more of three specified means, the public authority shall give effect to that preference so far as is reasonably practicable. The sub-section is notable in a number of respects. First, the obligation to give effect to a preference expressed by an applicant 'on making his request for information'[94] means that the obligation in subs (1) does not arise if the preference is expressed only after the request for information has been made.[95] Secondly, the entitlement to express a preference is limited to one or more of those means listed in subs (1). Any preference that is not one of the three means enumerated in s 11(1) will not engage the duty to comply with that preference, leaving the public authority to communicate the information by any means which are reasonable in the circumstances.[96] The three specified means are:

— the provision to the applicant of a copy of the information in a permanent form (or another form acceptable to the applicant);[97]
— the provision to the applicant of a reasonable opportunity to inspect a record containing the information;[98] and
— the provision to the applicant of a digest or summary of the information in a permanent form (or another form acceptable to the applicant).[99]

The right to choose a copy or summary in electronic form extends to choosing the particular software format in which the information should be communicated.[100] Thirdly, the use of the phrase 'one or more' indicates that the applicant is not limited to expressing a preference for only one of the specified means. There is no sensible reason why an applicant should not be able to specify a particular means of communication for certain information and another means for the remainder. Alternatively, an applicant may express a preference for a particular means if the information answering the terms of the request is less than a particular quantity and for a different means if it is more. Such a course may be sensible having regard to fees, the cost of compliance and copyright issues.

24– 019 Preference expressed: datasets

The Protection of Freedoms Act 2012 introduced section 11(1A) into FOIA.[101] Section 11(1A) provides that where a request is made for information that is a dataset, or which forms part of a dataset, held by the public authority and the applicant requests that information be

---

94 FOIA s 11(1). 'Request for information' is defined in FOIA s 8. The FOI(S)A refers to an applicant expressing a preference 'in requesting information': FOI(S)A s 11(1). And see *Glasgow City Council & anor v Scottish IC* [2009] CSIH 73 at [53]-[57]. The FTT has been prepared to look at post-request correspondence to intepret the preference expressed in a request: *IPSA v IC and Leapman*, FTT, 29 April 2013.

95 But a subsequent request to have the information communicated in a particular form might constitute a fresh request for information with a validly expressed preference: see *Innes v IC* [2014] EWCA Civ 1086, [2015] 2 All ER 560, [2015] 1 WLR 210 at [49]

96 FOIA s 11(4).

97 FOIA s 11(1)(a); FOI(S)A s 11(2)(a).

98 FOIA s 11(1)(b); FOI(S)A s 11(2)(c).

99 FOIA s 11(1)(c); FOI(S)A s 11(2)(b). The latter provision does not require that the digest or summary be in any particular form.

100 See *Innes v IC* [2014] EWCA Civ 1086, [2015] 2 All ER 560, [2015] 1 WLR 210 at [31]-[45].

101 Inserted by the Protection of Freedoms Act 2012.

communicated in an electronic form, then the public authority must, as far as is reasonably practicable, provide the information to the applicant in an electronic form that is capable of re-use.[102] A 'dataset' means information comprising a collection of information held in electronic form where all or most of the information in the collection:

(a) has been obtained or recorded for the purpose of providing a public authority with information in connection with the provision of a service by the authority or the carrying out of any other function of the authority;

(b) is factual information which is not the product of analysis or interpretation other than calculation (ie that it is the 'raw' or 'source' data), and is not an 'official statistic';[103] and

(c) remains presented in a way that (except for the purpose of forming part of the collection) has not been organised, adapted or otherwise materially altered since it was obtained or recorded.[104]

If an applicant does not want to have the dataset communicated in electronic form, because, for example, the applicant wants the dataset in hard copy only, then the duty in s 11(1A) will not arise. The public authority will still need to comply with the preference expressed by virtue of the existing duty in s 11(1)(a) of FOIA, and must provide the dataset in hard copy so far as it is reasonably practicable to do so. The obligation to give effect to a preference expressed under s 11(1A) arises only where the applicant expresses it 'on making the request for information.' The obligation does not arise if the preference is expressed after the request for information has been made.

24– 020 Reasonable practicability

The obligation to give effect to a preference expressed by an applicant for communication by way of one or more specified means only extends as far as it is reasonably practicable for the public authority to give effect to it.[105] In other contexts, the phrase 'reasonably practicable' has been equated to 'reasonable feasibility'.[106] Although this is a somewhat circular explanation, it is clear that the test of reasonable practicability falls somewhere between the two extremes of mere reasonableness and physical possibility.[107] A public authority may have regard to all the circumstances when deciding whether it is reasonably practicable to give effect to an applicant's preference, including the cost of doing so.[108] In addition to cost, such circumstances would normally include the form in which the relevant information is held by a public authority, the ease with which it can be converted from its existing form to the preferred form, the volume of the information to be communicated or summarised, and, where copies have

[102] The Explanatory Notes to the Protection of Freedoms Act 2012 state that a re-usable format is one where the information is available in machine-readable form using open standards which enables its re-use and manipulation: see para 389.

[103] Within the meaning given by Statistics and Registration Service Act 2007 s 6(1).

[104] The Explanatory Notes state that examples of the types of dataset which meet the definition (though not a comprehensive list) will include datasets comprising combinations of letters and numbers used to identify property or locations, such as postcodes and references; datasets comprising numbers and information related to numbers such as expenditure data; and datasets comprising text or words such as information about roles in a public authority: see para 394 of Explanatory Notes to Protection of Freedoms Act 2012.

[105] FOIA s 11(1); FOI(S)A s 11(1). Section 11(5) of the FOI(S)A expressly provides that a public authority cannot rely upon the 'reasonable practicability' test to side-step any duty to make reasonable adjustments imposed upon it by the Equality Act 2010.

[106] *Palmer and Saunders v Southend-on-Sea Borough Council* [1984] 1 WLR 1129, [1984] 1 All ER 945 (CA).

[107] *Edwards v National Coal Board* [1949] 1 KB 704 at 712 (a health and safety case); *Marshall v Gotham Co Ltd* [1954] AC 360 at 370 (a health and safety case); *Palmer and Saunders v Southend-on-Sea Borough Council* [1984] 1 WLR 1129, [1984] 1 All ER 945 (CA); *London Underground Ltd v Noel* [2000] ICR 109 (CA).

[108] FOIA s 11(2); FOI(S)A s 11(3).

been requested, any relevant copyright restrictions.[109] It is suggested that where it is difficult to provide the applicant with information in a particular form without also providing him with information to which he is not entitled (for example, exempt information or information outside the scope of the request), this will be a relevant circumstance for the public authority to take into account.[110] Where a public authority determines that it is not reasonably practicable to comply with an applicant's preference, it must notify the applicant of its reasons for that determination.[111] The public authority must then comply with the obligation imposed by s 11(4).[112]

24– 021 Practicability: dataset

The duty to provide the information in a re-useable electronic format applies only if it is reasonably practicable to provide it. There is no absolute duty for datasets to be provided in a re-useable format as it is recognised that, in some instances, there may be practical difficulties in relation to costs and information technology to convert the format of the information.

24– 022 Release of datasets for re-use

Under s 11A of FOIA a public authority must, in certain circumstances, make a dataset available for re-use. In order for the obligation to arise:

(1) a person must have made a request for a dataset;
(2) the dataset requested must include a 'relevant copyright work';
(3) the public authority is the only owner of the 'relevant copyright work' – in other words, it is not jointly owned with another party or owned in whole or in part by a third party; and
(4) the public authority is communicating the relevant copyright work to the requester under FOIA – in other words the dataset requested is not being withheld under one of the exemptions provided for in FOIA.[113]

When communicating such a dataset to an applicant, the public authority must make the dataset available for re-use in accordance with the terms of a specified licence. The obligation to make the dataset available for re-use does not apply to the extent that the relevant copyright work, or part of it, is a document to which the Re-use of Public Sector Information Regulations 2015 apply.[114]

24– 023 Fees: datasets

A public authority may charge fees for making datasets available for re-use.[115] Where a public authority intends to charge a fee, it must give the applicant a 're-use fee notice' stating the amount of the fee which must be paid before the dataset is available for re-use.[116] Where the public authority has given the applicant a re-use notice, it is not required to make the dataset

---

[109] The FTT has rejected an argument that where the public authority anticipated that the request was the first of many which it was likely to receive, the cost of treating like requests similarly was an irrelevant consideration: *IPSA v IC and Leapman*, FTT, 29 April 2013.

[110] As to redaction of documents, see §24– 014.

[111] FOIA s 11(3); FOI(S)A s 11(3).

[112] See §24– 016.

[113] The terms 'copyright owner', 'copyright work', 'database', 'database right', 'owner', 'relevant copyright work' and 'the specified licence' are defined in FOIA s 11A(8).

[114] FOIA, s11A(1A) and (1B).

[115] FOIA s 11A(3)-(7). The fee must be in accordance with regulations made under FOIA s 11B (subject to existing statutory powers for public authorities to charge a fee).

[116] FOIA s 11A(5).

available for re-use until the fee is paid in accordance with the notice. If the public authority is exercising any existing statutory power to charge, the authority may combine the re-use fee notice with any other notice in accordance with the relevant statutory power being exercised.[117]

24– 024 Deemed confirmation/denial

Where a public authority has complied with any obligation to communicate information to an applicant, then it is deemed to have complied with its duty to confirm or deny under FOIA.[118]

117 FOIA s 11A(6)-(7).

118 FOIA s 1(5).

Part V

Exemptions

CHAPTER 25
Information otherwise accessible

1. INFORMATION OTHERWISE ACCESSIBLE

25– 001 Introduction

Information that is reasonably accessible to the applicant otherwise than under FOIA is exempt information.[1] Unlike most exemptions in the Act, s 21 requires the circumstances of the applicant to be considered. The exemption is absolute, so that if information falls within s 21(1) it is not necessary to consider the public interest. The underlying rationale for the exemption would appear to be two-fold. First, where an applicant has a right under a specific legislative regime to obtain access to particular information, then that specific legislative regime should normally be used rather than FOIA. By this mechanism, the exemption ensures that an applicant does not circumvent the fees regime or other constraints of a specific legislative regime by using FOIA. Secondly, and more generally, the exemption prevents FOIA from being used as an alternative method of accessing information already available to the public, whether under a publication scheme or by other reasonable means. A broadly equivalent exemption is to be found in the freedom of information legislation of most of the comparative jurisdictions.[2] There is no equivalent exception in the EIR.[3] The exemption had a relatively

---

1 FOIA s 21(1); FOI(S)A s 25(1), which uses the phrase "reasonably obtainable" rather than "reasonably accessible."

2 There is no directly comparable exemption in the Freedom of Information Act, 1966 (USA). Although the Federal Court had suggested that an agency was not required to make requested records available by giving copies of them to a requester if the agency preferred to make the records available in one central location for examination (ie the reading room system) (*Oglesby v United States Department of the Army*, 920 F 2d 57, 70 (DC Cir 1990)), the Department of Justice recommends that such documents be copied to the requester: Freedom of Information Act Update, vol vol XII, No 2, at p 5. The Freedom of Information Act 1982 (Cth of Australia) s 12(1) removes the right of access to certain documents: '(a) a document, or a copy of a document, which is, under the Archives Act 1983, within the open access period within the meaning of that Act unless the document contains personal information (including personal information about a deceased person); or (b) a document that is open to public access, as part of a public register or otherwise, in accordance with another enactment, where that access is subject to a fee or other charge; or (ba) a document that is open to public access, as part of a land title register, in accordance with a law of a State or Territory where that access is subject to a fee or other charge; or (c) a document that is available for purchase by the public in accordance with arrangements made by an agency' — see §51– 011. The Official Information Act 1982 (New Zealand) s 18(d), provides a discretionary exemption for information that 'is or will soon be publicly available.' The Access to Information Act (Canada) s 68, provides that the Act does not apply to published

uneventful passage through Parliament.[4] The Information Commissioner has issued non-statutory guidance on the exemption.[5]

25–002 Scope of the exemption

The criterion for exemption is that the information be 'reasonably accessible to the applicant' otherwise than under FOIA. The exemption applies to information 'held' by the public authority. The authority must first establish, and confirm to the applicant in its reply to the request, that it holds the information sought. It may not seek to avoid the duty to ascertain whether it holds the information, even if it takes the view that the applicant should be seeking it from another source.[6] The provision[7] specifies certain situations in which information is deemed to be reasonably accessible and certain other situations where it is not. Where no deeming applies, in deciding whether information is reasonably accessible otherwise than under FOIA, consideration must be given to whether:

(a) the information sought[8] is freely available to the public or requires the applicant to take particular steps to access it;
(b) the information is available with or without charges;
(c) the access obligation is merely to make the information available for inspection or whether an applicant is entitled to obtain a copy of the information;
(d) the information that is available from another source will be subject to restrictions upon its use; and
(e) access to information is governed by the publication scheme of the public authority in question.

An applicant's preferred mode of access is irrelevant in determining reasonable accessibility.[9] Similarly, information in a document comprising or reproducing what is contained in another document (the latter document being reasonably accessible) will itself thereby be reasonably accessible.[10]

25–003 Available via enactment

material or material available for purchase by the public nor to library material: see §51–026(9). However, ss 2(2) and 19(2)(b) appear to specifically enable the Act to be used notwithstanding that the same material is available under other legislation or another source: see *Cyanamid Canada Inc v Canada (Minister of Health and Welfare)* (1992) 41 CPR (3d) 512 (FCTD). The Freedom of Information Act 2014 (Ireland) s 15(2), provides that the Act does not apply to a record that is available for inspection by members of the public, whether upon payment or free of charge, nor to a record where a copy is available for purchase or removal free of charge by members of the public, whether under an enactment or otherwise: see §51–035.

3 *Friends of the Earth v IC and ECGD*, IT, 20 August 2007 at [77].

4 The provision (cl 19) originally referred to information that was reasonably accessible to members of the public, but this was amended early on in its passage: see Hansard HC vol 347 col 1053 (5 April 2000). Another amendment that would have taken information reasonably accessible in one format (eg paper) but not in another format (eg electronic) out of the exemption was withdrawn: Hansard HL vol 617 cols 1011-1012 (17 October 2000).

5 Information Commissioner, *Information reasonably accessible by the applicant by other means (section 21)*, May 2013.

6 This follows from the fact that the exemption excuses the public authority from meeting the communication obligation in FOIA s 1(1)(b): it does not exclude the duty to confirm or deny under FOIA s 1(1)(a).

7 In *Glasgow City Council & anor v Scottish IC* [2009] CSIH 73 the Court of Session described the Scottish provision (which is modelled on FOIA s 21) as 'not a model of clarity' (at [59]).

8 The provision looks to the reasonable accessibility of the information sought. It is not concerned with whether a reasonable amount of the information requested is otherwise available: *England and LB of Bexley v IC*, IT, 10 May 2007 at [113]; *Ames v IC and Cabinet Office*, IT, 24 April 2008 at [18]. However, s 21 could be claimed for that part of the information which was reasonably accessible elsewhere.

9 *Glasgow City Council & anor v Scottish IC* [2009] CSIH 73 at [56].

10 *Glasgow City Council & anor v Scottish IC* [2009] CSIH 73 at [52].

The first category of information which is deemed to be reasonably accessible to the applicant is information which the public authority or any other person is obliged by or under any enactment[11] to communicate to members of the *public* on request, whether free of charge or on payment. The information must be available to all members of the public, not selected groups only. For the deeming to apply, there must be a right to be supplied with a copy of the information, not merely to inspect it.[12] An obligation to make information available for inspection only does not result in that information being automatically deemed to be 'reasonably accessible,'[13] but the public authority may still assess whether the circumstances are such that the information can be considered to be reasonably accessible to the applicant.[14]

25–004 Available via publication scheme

If a public authority is not obliged by or under any enactment to give access to information, it may nevertheless decide to make it available to members of the public under its publication scheme. If the publication scheme has been approved by the Information Commissioner,[15] and if payment required from the applicant has been prescribed by the scheme, then the information is to be regarded as reasonably accessible.[16] It is to be noted that for these purposes the information must be made available by the public authority to which the applicant has made his request: for the purpose of s 21(3) it is not enough that another public authority has made the information requested available through its publication scheme.[17] However, provided that these conditions are met, then availability under a publication scheme will be deemed to represent reasonable accessibility, even though this does not provide a practical means of access for a particular applicant. For example, the information will be regarded as 'reasonably accessible' even if the fees levied under the publication scheme are significant and are not affordable by the applicant.[18]

25–005 Otherwise reasonably accessible

If the information is not deemed reasonably accessible either under an enactment or because it is available under an approved publication scheme, an assessment must be made whether it is otherwise reasonably accessible to the applicant. This involves an assessment of the personal circumstances of the applicant. There are two aspects to this requirement:

(1) Some legislation gives a right of access to certain information only to a particular

---

11 As to the meaning of 'enactment', see §35–017. The exemption thus cannot be invoked where the only right of access is a common law right, eg a common law right enjoyed by a member of a council: see §37–009.

12 FOIA s 21(2)(b); FOI(S)A s 25(2)(b). For example, the Births and Deaths Registration Act 1953 s 33(1) provides that on payment of a fee, an applicant is entitled to a 'short-form' certificate of a person's birth. Contrast the building notice register kept by each local authority under the Building Act 1984 s 56, which does not include provisions granting a right to a copy of notices. If the obligation to communicate is limited to particular individuals (eg the applicant, because of certain attributes he possesses), FOIA s 21(2)(b) will not apply as the obligation is not to members of the public.

13 FOIA s 21(2)(b); FOI(S)A s 25(2)(b). The deeming applies only if the communication is 'otherwise than by making the information available for inspection.'

14 See §25–006.

15 See the definition of a publication scheme in FOIA s 19(1). See also *Davis v IC and Health and Social Care Information Centre*, FTT, 24 January 2013.

16 FOIA s 21(3); FOI(S)A s 25(3).

17 Assuming, of course, that the requested information is held by both public authorities.

18 *Glasgow City Council & anor v Scottish IC* [2009] CSIH 73 at [60]; *Davis v IC and Health and Social Care Information Centre*, FTT, 24 January 2013 at [26]. Although this may indicate that the publication scheme in question is not a reasonable one, such an issue is not a matter for the Information Commissioner to consider and does not fall within the Tribunal's jurisdiction when considering appeals from a decision notice approving reliance on FOIA s 21.

class of person.[19] In such a case, information may be reasonably accessible 'to the applicant' even if it would not be to another member of the public, if the applicant belongs to the class of persons which is entitled to exercise that right.[20] It will be necessary to assess whether it is reasonable to expect the applicant to take any procedural steps necessary to invoke his or her rights and whether there would be any restrictions placed upon the use of the information obtained as a result.

(2) The personal circumstances of the applicant may be relevant in determining whether information that is generally available to the public is not available to the applicant: for example, because of his or her personal characteristics. The public authority must consider the personal circumstances of the applicant in determining whether that information is reasonably accessible.[21] Factors affecting an individual applicant's ability to access information include the form in which the information is accessible (for example, digitally or otherwise), geographical restrictions or financial means. Thus, if the applicant's means are particularly limited or the fee payable for access to the information is excessively high, the information may not be reasonably accessible. Conversely, information may be significantly more accessible to a well-resourced applicant with access to all forms of information dissemination so that reliance on the exemption is justified. A public authority seeking to rely on the exemption will be required to address the applicant's individual circumstances in its response to the request.[22]

More generally, reasonable accessibility may depend upon the comparative ease with which an applicant may secure access to the information. For example, where an applicant seeks very specific information which is available on a website but only by much searching of it, the website access may well fall short of representing reasonable accessibility. However, difficulties of harvesting and re-use are not relevant to the issue of the accessibility of the information.[23] Information made available via inspection rather than by the supply of copies will generally be regarded as reasonably accessible.[24] An applicant's preferred mode of access[25] is irrelevant in deeming reasonable accessibility,[26] save insofar as his preferences may reflect his personal circumstances: that is, the difficulties which accessing the publicly available information would cause him.[27] If an applicant would be more restricted in the use that could be made of the information than would be the case under the Freedom of Information Act, the exemption may not apply.[28]

---

19 For example, rights of access to health records are given to executors and personal representatives under the Access to Health Records Act 1990 s 3(1). See §38– 002.

20 *Glasgow City Council & anor v Scottish IC* [2009] CSIH 73 at [67].

21 *MOJ v IC*, IT, 29 July 2008 at [34]. That is so even if the publication scheme allows a public authority to charge for the provision of information under it.

22 FOIA s 17(1)(c); FOI(S)A s 16(1)(d).

23 *Benson v IC and University of Bristol*, FTT, 10 November 2011 at [15].

24 Depending on the circumstances of the applicant, which must be investigated and taken into account: *Costello v IC and Northamptonshire County Council*, FTT, 3 July 2012. The determining provisions of s 21(2)(b) will not apply, but the Information Commissioner's view is that the availability of the information can still be considered under the remaining provisions of s 21 and that 'in most cases an applicant will need to present strong arguments that the information is not reasonably accessible': *Information reasonably accessible to the applicant by other means (section 21)*, 15 May 2013.

25 As provided for under FOIA s 11 and FOI(S)A s 11.

26 *Glasgow City Council & anor v Scottish IC* [2009] CSIH 73 at [56].

27 *Costello v IC and Northamptonshire County Council*, FTT, 3 July 2012, where the applicant's difficulties in attending to inspect the requested information was successfully relied upon.

28 *Newcastle Upon Tyne Hospital NHS Foundation Trust v IC*, FTT, 6 January 2012, where information disclosed by an

25–006 Available from another source

In order for s 21 to apply it is not necessary that the information be reasonably accessible to the applicant from the public authority to which the request under FOIA has been made. Section 21 is capable of applying irrespective of the identity of the alternative source of the information. Thus, information available from a public library, on a website or from a readily-available newspaper will generally fall within the terms of the exemption. Similarly, transcript of legal proceedings available on request from a court may be exempt information under the Act.[29] It should be noted that information contained in a historical record in the Public Record Office (ie The National Archives) or the Public Record Office of Northern Ireland cannot be exempt information by virtue of s 21.[30]

2. INFORMATION INTENDED FOR FUTURE PUBLICATION

25–007 Introduction

Under s 22(1) of FOIA[31] information held by a public authority is exempt information if:

(a) the information is held by it with a view to its future publication (whether by the public authority to which the request is made or any other person), whether or not the date for publication has been determined;

(b) at the time of the request, the information was already being held with a view to such publication; and

(c) it is reasonable in all the circumstances that the information should not be disclosed until the future date.[32]

Section 22(2) provides that the duty to confirm or deny does not arise if, or to the extent that, compliance with that duty would involve the disclosure of any information (whether or not already recorded) that falls within s 22(1).[33] Both exemption from the disclosure duty and exclusion from the duty to divulge are non-absolute. Thus, the duty to communicate information that falls within s 22(1) does not apply only if, or to the extent that, in all the circumstances of the case, the public interest in maintaining the exemption outweighs the public interest in disclosing the information.[34] Similarly, the duty to confirm or deny that such information is held remains excluded only if, in all the circumstances of the case, the public interest in maintaining the exclusion of that duty outweighs the public interest in divulging whether the public authority holds the information.[35] The EIR provide an exception to broadly

---

Employment Tribunal had restrictions placed on its use, with the effect that s 21 was inapplicable. Contrast *Armstrong v IC and HMRC*, IT, 14 October 2008, where the issue of restrictions on use on material obtained from a court does not appear to have been raised and s 21 was held to apply.

29 *Armstrong v IC and HMRC*, IT, 14 October 2008 at [37]-[57]. But see *Newcastle upon Tyne Hospital NHS Foundation Trust v IC*, FTT, 6 January 2012 on the relevance of any restrictions placed upon the use of information supplied by a court or other party.

30 FOIA s 64. There is no comparable provision in the FOI(S)A. In relation to historical records, see Ch 36.

31 FOI(S)A s 27(1).

32 The Information Commissioner has issued non-statutory guidance on this exemption: *Information intended for future publication and research (sections 22 and 22A)*. The exemption has been considered only rarely by the Tribunal, with a passing reference in *Lawton v IC and NHS Direct*, IT, 5 March 2008 at [11], but fuller consideration given to the exemption in *Queen Mary University of London v London and Courtney*, FTT, 22 May 2013.

33 There is no corresponding provision in the FOI(S)A.

34 FOIA s 2(2)(b).

35 FOIA s 2(1)(b).

similar effect.[36]

25– 008 Scope of the exemption

The principal purpose of the exemption is to spare a public authority that is, at the time of a request for information, engaged in the collation of information intended for future publication from being disrupted in that task by having to retrieve, edit and copy parts or all of that information in order to answer the request. In addition, the exemption may afford protection for a public authority from the harm resulting from the premature release of information or harm arising out of the context in which the information is disclosed if, for example, scientific data is published before verification and peer review.[37] However, when considering the harm caused by premature release, it will always be necessary to consider whether any anticipated harm is better analysed under one or more of the other exemptions contained in the Act.[38] It will be open to the applicant to re-submit his request for information at a later time when the harm from disclosure will have diminished or disappeared. In order to rely on the exemption, the public authority must show that the three conditions set out in paras (a)-(c) are met. The information must be held by the public authority with a 'view' to its publication at a future date. This connotes more than a mere hope or aspiration that the information will be published and suggests rather a concluded intention that the information will be published.[39] The point at which the public authority must assess whether it holds the information with a view to future publication is the moment at which the request is received. The public authority is not entitled to decide on receipt of a request that it will avoid disclosure by publishing the information. The information may be published by the public authority or a third party such as a commercial publisher or an internet service provider. Section 22(1)(a) does not require that a date is fixed for publication in order to allow reliance on the exemption, although the more uncertain the timetable for future publication, the less likely it is that the information is held with a view to its eventual publication and the less likely it is that it would be reasonable to withhold the information. The exemption applies to *information* held with a view to final publication. It will be a question of fact and degree whether the information contained in a draft *document*, which the public authority holds with a view to its publication once finalised, can properly be said to be held with a view to its future publication. In these circumstances, the degree to which the public authority anticipates the final version will include information not in the draft and vice versa is likely to be decisive. Finally, it must be reasonable in 'all the circumstances' for the information to be withheld until the proposed future publication. The test of reasonableness must be applied to the withholding of the information, not, for example, to some aspect of a public authority's policy on the early release of information. Whether or not it is reasonable to withhold the information must be assessed objectively, having regard to a wide range of factors. These will include the extent of the information requested, the imminence or otherwise of the future publication date, the significance of the information to the applicant, whether undue disturbance would be caused to any person or persons by the early release of information, the time and resources which must be devoted to answering the request, and the nature of and reasons for any further work relating to the information which it is envisaged will take place before it is published.[40] If a commercial price is to be obtained for the published

---

36 EIR reg 12(4)(d); EI(S)R reg 10(4)(d). The exception is considered more fully at §19– 011.

37 *Queen Mary University of London v London and Courtney*, FTT, 22 May 2013 at [9]. The Tribunal accepted that information collected in the course of a scientific study and intended for publication following peer review fell within the scope of FOIA s 22 and that premature publication would not be in the public interest.

38 For example, FOIA ss 35 and 36.

39 *Queen Mary University of London v London and Courtney*, FTT, 22 May 2013 at [11].

40 *Queen Mary University of London v London and Courtney*, FTT, 22 May 2013 at [13]-[14], examining the time taken for a process of peer review and submission to academic journals.

information, it is thought that loss of revenue could affect whether or not it is reasonable in all the circumstances for the information to be withheld although this will also depend on other factors. It is difficult to see why a single limited piece of information should be withheld, merely because it will at some point in the future form a small part of an expensive book.

25–009 The public interest

Even if information is exempt because it falls within the scope of s 22(1), an applicant will still be entitled to have the information communicated to him unless, in all the circumstances of the case, the public interest in maintaining the exemption outweighs the public interest in disclosing the information.[41] Similarly, even if the duty to confirm or deny does not arise as a result of the operation of s 22(2), an applicant will still be entitled to be informed that the public authority holds the information requested unless, in all the circumstances of the case, the public interest in maintaining the exclusion outweighs the public interest in divulging its existence.[42] The decision of the legislature not to make exemption under s 22 absolute contemplates some situations in which information falling within s 22(1) will have to be disclosed. The interplay between para 22(1)(c) and the public interest may be problematic. It may be a rare case in which a public authority determines that it is reasonable in all the circumstances for the information to be withheld, but determines that nonetheless it is in the public interest to disclose the information. Nonetheless FOIA appears to contemplate this possibility. It is possible to envisage situations where it is thought reasonable to withhold information because of time and resources considerations but those considerations are outweighed by the public interest in a significant piece of information being aired in public as soon as possible. In the case of scientific research, the public interest in allowing a peer review process to analyse and contextualise data has been accepted as a benefit outweighing the public interest in enabling rapid access to research findings.[43]

25–010 FOI(S)A scheme

The corresponding provision under FOI(S)A is both narrower and broader than its English equivalent. It is narrower in that as at the date of the request the information must be held with a view to publication at 'a date not later than 12 weeks after that on which the request for the information is made.'[44] Whether or not it is reasonable to withhold information is judged by reference to this date.[45] Thus, information intended to be published more than 12 weeks after the date of the request cannot be exempt from disclosure under these provisions. However, the Scottish Act also contains a specific exemption relating to information obtained in the course of, or derived from, a programme of research.[46] Such information is exempt information if the programme is continuing with a view to a report of the research being published, whether by a Scottish public authority or any other person[47] and publication of the information would or would be likely to lead to 'substantial' prejudice to the programme or the interests of those participating in it.[48] As in England and Wales, the exemption is a qualified one. Universities

41 FOIA s 2(2)(b).

42 FOIA s 2(1)(b).

43 *Queen Mary University of London v London and Courtney*, FTT, 22 May 2013.

44 FOI(S)A s 27(1)(a).

45 FOI(S)A s 27(1)(c).

46 FOI(S)A s 27(2).

47 FOI(S)A s 27(2)(b).

48 FOI(S)A s 27(2)(b). The protection also extends to this interests of those holding the information or, if it is the authority intending to publish the research information, the interests of the Scottish public authority: FOI(S)A s 27(2)(b)(iii) and (iv).

in Scotland have reported[49] that this exemption has been used effectively.

25– 011 Research information: FOIA

In July 2012, the House of Lords Justice Committee commended the greater clarity of the position in Scotland and recommended that FOIA be amended to give research carried out in England and Wales the same protection as in Scotland.[50] The recommendation was accepted by the Government,[51] which introduced a dedicated exemption to cover pre-publication research. The exemption[52] is prejudice-based, requiring prejudice or a likelihood of prejudice to the protected interest, namely a continuing programme of research with a view to publication of a report of that research. The exemption extends to prejudice or likely to prejudice to any individual participating in that programme or to the authority which holds the information for that programme. The exemption is qualified by the usual public interest test.

3. ENVIRONMENTAL INFORMATION

25– 012 Introduction

The right of access to 'environmental information'[53] held by a public authority is governed by the EIR and not, with one largely theoretical[54] possibility, FOIA.[55] The right of access to environmental information held by public authorities[56] is considered in detail in Part III (Chs 17-19) of this work. In very general terms, FOIA removes the s 1 rights[57] in relation to any information for which there is a right of access under the EIR. The practical difficulties in divining what is and what is not 'environmental information' are magnified by the unit of exemption (information) not being necessarily coincident with the unit in which information is normally recorded (a document or an electronic file). Within a single document or electronic file there may be both information that is 'environmental information' and other information that is not 'environmental information.' The public authority must identify which is which and, according to the applicable regime, decide whether particular material must be disclosed.[58]

25– 013 The exemption

Under s 39(1) of FOIA information is exempt information if the public authority holding it:

(a) is obliged by the EIR to make the information available to the public in accordance

49 See the report of the House of Commons' Justice Committee *Post-legislative scrutiny of the Freedom of Information Act 2000*, First Report of Session 2012-2013, 26 July 2012, p 79.

50 House of Commons' Justice Committee *Post-legislative scrutiny of the Freedom of Information Act 2000*, First Report of Session 2012-2013, 26 July 2012, p 80.

51 *Government Response to the Justice Committee's Report: Post-legislative scrutiny of the Freedom of Information Act 2000*, Ministry of Justice, November 2012, paragraph 48.

52 FOIA s 22A, introduced by the Intellectual Property Act 2014, s 20. FOI(S)A requires 'substantial prejudice.'

53 As to the meaning of which, see §17– 011.

54 Particularly theoretical since environmental information, if not exempted by FOIA s 39, may be exempted by FOIA s 21 (an absolute exemption): *Newbery v IC and Dept of Energy and Climate Change*, FTT, 3 September 2012 at [43]. See also *Rhondda Cynon Taff CBC v IC*, IT, 5 December 2007.

55 Similarly in relation to environmental information held by Scottish public authorities, it is governed by the EI(S)R and not the FOI(S)A.

56 The term 'public authority' has a wider meaning under the EIR/EI(S)R than it does under FOIA/FOI(S)A.

57 In other words, the right to have the requested information communicated and the right to know whether the requested information is held by the public authority.

58 *DBERR v IC and Friends of the Earth*, IT, 29 April 2008 at [29].

with the regulations;[59] or

(b) would be so obliged but for any exemption contained in the regulations.[60]

Section 39(2) provides that the duty to confirm or deny does not arise if, or to the extent that, compliance with that duty would involve the disclosure of any information (whether or not already recorded) that falls within s 39(1).[61] Both exemption from the disclosure duty and exclusion from the duty to divulge are non-absolute. Thus, the duty to communicate information that falls within s 39(1) does not apply only if, or to the extent that, in all the circumstances of the case, the public interest in maintaining the exemption outweighs the public interest in disclosing the information.[62] Similarly, the duty to confirm or deny that such information is held remains excluded only if, in all the circumstances of the case, the public interest in maintaining the exclusion of that duty outweighs the public interest in divulging whether the public authority holds the information.[63]

25– 014 Scope of the exemption

The purpose of the exemption is not to prevent or impede access to environmental information. Rather, its purpose is to give exclusivity to the EIR in so far as the information answering the terms of the request is 'environmental information.'[64] Unlike the system of precedence established by s 21 of FOIA (which does not disapply an applicant's s 1 rights where the information is exempted under the other access regime), s 39(1) also gives the EIR paramountcy in relation to its exceptions. Thus, if information falls within the scope of the EIR but is rendered exempt by those regulations, that information will be also exempt information for the purposes of FOIA.[65]

25– 015 The public interest

Even if information is exempt because it falls within the scope of s 39(1), an applicant will still be entitled to have the information communicated to him unless, in all the circumstances of the case, the public interest in maintaining the exemption outweighs the public interest in disclosing the information.[66] Similarly, even if the duty to confirm or deny does not arise as a result of the operation of s 39(2), an applicant will still be entitled to be informed that the public authority holds the information requested unless, in all the circumstances of the case, the public interest in maintaining the exclusion outweighs the public interest in divulging its existence.[67] As with all other qualified exemptions, the decision of the legislature not to make exemption under s 39 absolute contemplates some situations in which information falling within s 39(1) will have to be disclosed. Given that: (a) the only public interest in maintaining the exemption created by s 39(1) is the upholding of an exclusive, as opposed to a parallel, regime of access to environmental information; (b) that FOIA is itself an articulation of the public interest in the disclosure of information that is not exempt information under its own terms; and (c) that there is a particular public interest in the disclosure of environmental information, it is theoretically

---

[59] FOIA s 39(1)(a); FOI(S)A s 39(2)(a).

[60] FOIA s 39(1)(b); FOI(S)A s 39(2)(b).

[61] There is no corresponding provision in the FOI(S)A.

[62] FOIA s 2(2)(b).

[63] FOIA s 2(1)(b).

[64] In *Rhondda Cynon Taff CBC v IC*, IT, 5 December 2007 at [24] the Tribunal said that it was 'not quite correct to consider EIR and FOIA as mutually exclusive regimes.' It saw the two as running 'in parallel.'

[65] FOIA s 39(1)(b); FOI(S)A s 39(2)(b).

[66] FOIA s 2(2)(b).

[67] FOIA s 2(1)(b).

possible that information exempted under the EIR will be accessible under FOIA, provided of course that none of the other exemptions in FOIA applies.

CHAPTER 26

Security bodies, national security and defence

1. INTRODUCTION

26– 001 Overview – FOIA

Sections 23 to 26 of FOIA provide a series of exemptions and exclusions for information that, broadly speaking, relates to national security or defence matters.[2] Collectively, these provisions operate to exclude certain security bodies from FOIA regime and to prescribe three overlapping classes of exempt information.[3] Thus:

(1) Certain bodies dealing with security matters ('security bodies') are excluded from the definition of a 'public authority' in s 3 of, and Sch 1 to, FOIA and are thus institutionally excluded from the regime of the Act altogether. As a result, an effective request for information cannot be made to these bodies and they are not subject to any of the provisions or duties which otherwise apply to those listed or designated as public authorities by or under FOIA.[4]

(2) Information held by a public authority which was directly or indirectly supplied to it by, or which relates to, a security body is subject to an absolute exemption under s 23 of FOIA. In respect of such information, the duty to confirm or deny and the duty to communicate do not arise.[5]

(3) Information held by a public authority which was not directly or indirectly supplied to it by, and which does not relate to, any of the security bodies is subject to a qualified exemption under s 24 of FOIA if this is required for the purpose of safeguarding national security. In respect of such information, the duty to communicate does not arise if the public interest in maintaining the exemption outweighs the public interest in disclosing the information. Similarly, the duty to confirm or deny is excluded where or to the extent that the public interest in maintaining the exclusion outweighs the public interest in divulging whether the public authority holds the information.[6]

(4) Information whose disclosure under FOIA would, or would be likely to, prejudice the defence of the British Islands or of any colony or the capability, effectiveness or security of the armed forces of the Crown or of any forces co-operating with those forces is also subject to a qualified exemption under s 26 of FOIA. The duty to communicate does not arise in relation to such information if or to the extent that the public interest in maintaining the exemption outweighs the public interest in its

---

1 By Oliver Sanders QC, 1 Crown Office Row

2 See §26– 008 in relation to FOI(S)A s 31.

3 The government document *Factual and Background Material* published under *Your Right to Know: The Government's Proposals for a Freedom of Information Act* (Cm 3818, 1997) para 3.13 drew a distinction between 'two basic ways' of protecting specific bodies and types of information from the disclosure requirements of Freedom of Information legislation, namely, 'exclusions' (for bodies) and 'exemptions' (for types of information) (paras 24-30). Later parts of the document blurred the clarity of this distinction somewhat by referring to the 'exclusion' as well as the 'exemption' of types of information (paras 93-99).

4 See §§26– 011 to 26– 039.

5 See §§26– 040 to 26– 046, 26– 058, 26– 061 to 26– 064 and 26– 069.

6 See §§26– 058, 26– 061 to 26– 064, and 26– 069 to 26– 071.

disclosure. Similarly, the duty to confirm or deny does not arise in relation to such information if divulging whether the public authority holds it would, or would be likely to, prejudice the same defence interests and if the public interest in maintaining the exclusion of that duty outweighs the public interest in disclosure.[7]

The institutional exclusion of the security bodies outlined at (1) above and the exemptions outlined at (2)-(4) above potentially provide four layers of protection for sensitive security and defence information. The institutional exclusion of the security bodies is insurmountable and will conceal information regardless of its sensitivity. But other public authorities also hold security and defence information. This will be accessible unless one or more of the three exemptions is applicable and, in relation to the latter two exemptions, the public interest in maintaining the exemption is shown to outweigh the public interest in disclosure.

26– 002 Overview – DPA 2018

The DPA 2018 proceeds on the basis that all national security and defence related personal data processing falls outside the scope of the GDPR such that the imposition of connected legislative restrictions on the rights and obligations conferred thereunder would be otiose and is unnecessary.[8] The substantive provisions of the DPA 2018 regulating non-GDPR personal data processing contain a series of national security and defence exemptions and a freestanding regime governing personal data processing by the 'intelligence services':[9]

— s 26 exempts personal data from certain provisions of the applied GDPR and certain provisions of Pts 5-7 of the Act if this is required for the purpose of safeguarding national security or for defence purposes;[10]

— s 28 modifies the application of Arts 9 and 32 of the applied GDPR to personal data processing carried out for the purpose of safeguarding national security or for defence purposes;

— ss 44-45, 48 and 68 allow 'competent authorities' carrying out 'law enforcement processing' subject to Pt 3 of the Act to restrict, wholly or partly, the provision of certain information to data subjects where this is necessary to protect national security;[11]

— Pt 4 establishes the aforementioned intelligence services processing regime;[12]

— s 110 exempts personal data from certain provisions of the Pt 4 regime and various oversight and enforcement provisions in Pts 5-6 if this is required for the purpose of

[7] See §§26– 070 to 26– 071 and 26– 074 to 26– 079.

[8] GDPR Art 23 permits the imposition of legislative restrictions on the scope of certain rights and obligations provided for by Arts 5, 12-22 and 34 where these are a necessary and proportionate measure in a democratic society to safeguard, inter alia, national security, defence and public security. However, DPA 2018 does not contain any such restrictions (enacted under Art 23) on the basis that this is unnecessary because: the GDPR and the LED do not apply to the processing of personal data in the course of activities which fall outside the scope of EU law and national security and defence are outside the scope of EU law by virtue of the TEU Art 4(2) (GDPR recital (16) and art 2(2)(a) and the LED recital (14)); and the GDPR also does not apply to the processing of personal data in the course of activities which are carried out in relation to the common foreign and security policy of the EU or are within the scope of the LED (GDPR recital (16) and Art 2(2)(b) and (d)).

[9] DPA 2018 s 15(5). 'Intelligence service' means the Security Service, the Secret Intelligence Service ('SIS') or the Government Communications Headquarters ('GCHQ') (DPA 2018 ss 30(7) and 82(2)).

[10] DPA 2018 s 26(2). The listed provisions that may be disapplied include most of the data protection principles, the rights of data subjects, certain obligations on data controllers and processors and various oversight and enforcement provisions.

[11] DPA 2018 ss 44(4)(d), 45(4)(d), 48(3)(d) and 68(7)(d). DPA 2018 Pt 3 implements the LED and s 30(2) confirms that none of the intelligence services is a 'competent authority' for the purposes of its provisions.

[12] DPA 2018 Pt 4 is intended to give effect to the Council of Europe Conventions for the Protection of Individuals with regard to Automatic Processing of Personal Data of 1981 and 2018 which do apply in the national security context (ETS No.108 signed by the UK on 14 May 1981 and CETS No.223 signed by the UK on 10 October 2018). See the Explanatory Notes to the DPA 2018 paras 6-7, 41-42 and 58-61.

safeguarding national security;[13] and

— para 7 of Sch 11 disapplies the same provisions of the Pt 4 regime to the extent that their application would be likely to prejudice the combat effectiveness of any of the armed forces of the Crown.[14]

Although the aforementioned provisions appear much more extensive than the national security and defence exemptions in the DPA 1998, this is largely a result of the more complicated legislative picture at the EU level and the introduction of the intelligence services processing regime in Pt 4 of the DPA 2018 – the basic protection for national security and defence is essentially the same.[15]

26– 003Overview – EIR

Where (or to the extent that) a request for information relates to 'environmental information'[16] that request (or that part of that request) will fall to be determined by the EIR and not by FOIA.[17] The Regulations give the term 'public authority' a broader meaning than in FOIA. In particular, there are no institutional exclusions or exceptions for security bodies. Regulation 12 of the EIR provides an exception allowing for the non-disclosure of environmental information whose dissemination or disclosure would adversely affect international relations, defence, national security or public safety.[18] Disclosure may only be refused on this basis if, in all the circumstances of the case, the public interest in maintaining the exception outweighs the public interest in disclosing the information.[19] If doing so would involve the disclosure of information which would adversely affect international relations, defence, national security or public safety and would not be in the public interest, the relevant public authority may also refuse to confirm or deny whether the requested information exists and is held 'whether or not it holds such information'.[20] The reg 12 exception is itself made subject to a requirement that public authorities apply a presumption in favour of disclosure.[21]

26– 004Policy background

The Code of Practice on Access to Government Information contained an exemption for

---

13 DPA 2018 s 110(2) lists the provisions which may be disapplied by the s 110(1) exemption for the purpose of safeguarding national security.

14 DPA 2018 Sch 11 para 1 lists the provisions which may be disapplied by the para 7 exemption for the purpose of avoiding prejudice to the combat effectiveness of the armed forces.

15 DPA 1998 s 28 exempted personal data from the provisions of the data protection principles in, and Pts II-III and V and ss 54A and 55 of, that Act if exemption from the relevant provision was required for the purpose of safeguarding national security. DPA 1998 Sch 7 para 2 exempted personal data from the subject information provisions in that Act to the extent that the application of those provisions would have been likely to prejudice the combat effectiveness of any of the armed forces of the Crown. DPA 2018 Sch 20, paras 17-18 and 40 contain transitional provisions: saving the effect of the DPA 1998 s 28 and any certificates made thereunder with respect to the processing of personal data to which that Act applies (para 17); and continuing the effect of any such certificate as if it were a certificate made under one or more of the DPA 2018 ss 27, 79 and 111 for one year following the entry into force of the repeal of the DPA 1998 s 28 (para 18).

16 For the meaning of 'environmental information', see §§17– 008 to 17– 011.

17 FOIA s 39. Similarly, in relation to Scottish public authorities, it will fall to be determined by the EI(S)R and not the FOI(S)A; FOI(S)A s 39.

18 The more inclusive approach was dictated by the European Community Environmental Information Directive 2003/4/EC, which EIR were intended to implement. The exception from the obligation to disclose arises through: EIR regs 4(3), 5(1), 12(1)-(2) and (5)(a). See further §§19– 015, 26– 049 and 26– 068. Important differences between the environmental information regime and the regime under the FOIA are set out in Ch 6.

19 EIR reg 12(1)(b); EI(S)R reg 10(1)(b).

20 EIR reg 12(6)-(7); EI(S)R reg 10(6)-(7).

21 EIR reg 12(2); EI(S)R reg 10(2). See further §19– 003.

'information whose disclosure would harm national security or defence'.[22] The accompanying Guidance on Interpretation stated that the purpose of this exemption encompassed, so far as national security was concerned, the protection of 'information which could be of assistance to those engaged in espionage, sabotage, subversion or terrorism', 'individuals and sites which may be at risk' and 'the operations, sources and methods of the security and intelligence services' and, so far as defence was concerned, the protection of 'the operational effectiveness of the armed forces and their capacity to protect the country from external aggression' and 'servicemen and their civilian support staff, including those of friendly forces, and those under their protection'.[23] The White Paper, *Your Right to Know: The Government's Proposals for a Freedom of Information Act*, described 'national security, defence and international relations' as one of seven key 'specified interests' which could require non-disclosure if liable to be harmed by disclosure.[24] Both the White Paper[25] and the accompanying *Factual and Background Material*[26] went on to propose that a number of security bodies be excluded from the scope of any Act in order to preserve their effectiveness. When reporting on these proposals the House of Commons Public Administration Select Committee recommended against the institutional exclusion of the security bodies after noting that the comparable statutes in the USA, New Zealand and Canada contained exemptions for security and defence information but did not altogether exclude security bodies from the scope of their access regimes.[27]

26– 005 Legislative history – drafting

The provisions containing the security and defence exemptions in the draft Freedom of Information Bill published on 24 May 1999[28] underwent only minor revision before being included in the Freedom of Information Bill introduced in the House of Commons on 18 November 1999.[29] When reporting on the draft Bill, the House of Commons Public Administration Select Committee referred to arguments opposing the blanket exclusion of the security bodies put forward by a former Legal Adviser to the security and intelligence services[30] but ultimately accepted that the approach adopted was reasonable.[31] In relation to the security and defence exemptions, the introduction print of the Bill only differed from the draft version

---

22 *Open Government Code of Practice on Access to Government Information* (2nd edn, 1997), Pt II, para 1(a). Although the exemption referred to 'harm' there was nevertheless a presumption that such information should be disclosed unless the harm likely to arise from disclosure would outweigh the public interest in making the information available. See also: *White Paper on Open Government* (Cm 2290, 1993) paras 3.5-3.7 and Annex A, Pt II, para i; Scottish Executive's *Code of Practice on Access to Scottish Executive Information*, 2nd edn (2003) Pt II, para 1(a); and National Assembly for Wales *Code of Practice on Public Access to Information*, 3rd edn (2004), Annex B.

23 *Open Government Code of Practice on Access to Government Information: Guidance on Interpretation*, 2nd edn (1997) Pt II, para 1.3.

24 (Cm 3818, 1997) paras 3.8-3.11.

25 (Cm 3818, 1997) para 2.3.

26 Published under (Cm 3818, 1997) para 3.13. See para 96.

27 House of Commons Public Administration Select Committee Third Report Session 1997-1998 *Your Right to Know: the Government's Proposals for a Freedom of Information Act* (HC 398-I) 1998, paras 38-39. See also House of Lords Draft Freedom of Information Bill Select Committee First Report Session 1998-1999 *Report from the Select Committee Appointed to Consider the Draft Freedom of Information Bill* (HL 97) 1999, para 39 (see Ch 1 n 43).

28 *Freedom of Information: Consultation on Draft Legislation* (Cm 4355, 1999) Pt II, cls18 (information supplied by, or relating to, bodies dealing with security matters), 19 (national security), 20 (certificates under ss 18 and 19: supplementary provisions) and 21 (defence) (see Ch 1 n 68).

29 Clauses 21 (information supplied by, or relating to, bodies dealing with security matters), 22 (national security), 23 (certificates under ss 21 and 22: supplementary provisions) and 24 (defence).

30 That is, Mr David Bickford. See M Urban, *UK Eyes Alpha: The Inside Story of British Intelligence* (London, Faber & Faber, 1996), pp 85-86.

31 House of Commons Public Administration Select Committee Third Report Session 1998-1999 *Freedom of Information Draft Bill* (HC 570-I) 1999, paras 74-77 and Annex 6, paras 43-48.

in two respects: cls 21(5), 22(2) and 24(3) of the introduction print took a textually different approach to the engagement of the relevant exemptions and the non-application of the duty to confirm or deny;[32] and cl 22 on national security did not feature a 'jigsaw puzzle' exemption expressly ensuring the non-disclosure of apparently harmless information which might be harmful when looked at in conjunction with other pieces of a wider jigsaw puzzle.[33] Section 28 of the DPA 1998 was plainly the model for the clause which became s 24 of FOIA.[34]

26– 006 Legislative history – passage

The relevant clauses in the introduction print of the Freedom of Information Bill did not thereafter change on their way to enactment as ss 23-26 of FOIA, save for the inclusion in the list of security bodies of the Tribunal newly established under s 65 of the Regulation of Investigatory Powers Act 2000.[35] Indeed the security and defence exemptions in FOIA passed through Parliament with very little controversy. Amendments were put forward, but later withdrawn, which would have omitted the (s 23) exemption for information supplied by, or relating to, the security bodies altogether and made the operation of both that exemption and the (s 24) national security exemption dependent on the satisfaction of a prejudice or harm test.[36] These proposals were all partly justified by reference to the broader crime-related functions of some of the security bodies such as the Security Service[37] and the then-National Criminal Intelligence Service.[38] Amendments were also put forward which would have made the operation of the defence exemption dependent on the satisfaction of a 'substantial' prejudice

---

32 Compare draft Freedom of Information Bill published on 24 May 1999, cls 18(5), 19(2), 21(3).

33 Compare draft Freedom of Information Bill published on 24 May 1999, cl 19(3) which provided as follows 'Where, in relation to any information ("the information requested"), exemption from section 8(1)(b)-(a) is not required for the purpose of safeguarding national security, but (b) would be required for that purpose if any other information (whether or not held by the public authority and whether or not accessible, or likely to become accessible, to members of the public) became available at the same time or subsequently, the exemption shall be taken for the purposes of this section to be required for that purpose in relation to the information requested.' See House of Lords Draft Freedom of Information Bill Select Committee First Report Session 1998-1999 *Report from the Select Committee Appointed to Consider the Draft Freedom of Information Bill* (HL 97) 1999, paras 36-37 (see Ch 1 n 43). See also §26– 036(1).

34 Thus: 'The clause [which became FOIA s 24] is drafted in similar terms to s 28 of DPA 1998. The two provisions have the same purpose. It is therefore sensible for them to be drafted in similar language. Any difference of approach between the provisions could lead to them being interpreted differently. Clearly, that is not the intention.' — Hansard HC vol 347 col 1060 (5 April 2000) (Home Office Minister, Mr O'Brien, Report and Third Reading debate on the Freedom of Information Bill). Section 28 of DPA 1998 replaced the national security exemption in the DPA 1984 s 27 which provided that, '[A]ny question whether the exemption mentioned in subsection (1) above is or at any time was required for the purpose there mentioned [ie the purpose of safeguarding national security] in respect of any personal data shall be determined by a Minister of the Crown; and a certificate signed by a Minister of the Crown certifying that the exemption is or at any time was so required shall be conclusive evidence of that fact' (DPA 1984 s 27(2), see also s 27(3)). The 'required for the purpose of safeguarding national security' test was therefore the same under both Acts, the key difference being the addition of an appeal mechanism in DPA 1998 s 28: 'The right of appeal against a national security certificate is an important new safeguard. It represents an advance on the 1984 Act, which offered no appeal rights' — Hansard HC vol 315 col 586 (2 July 1998) (Home Office Minister, Mr Howarth, Report and Third Reading debate on the Data Protection Bill).

35 FOIA s 23(3)(e) (inserted pursuant to a government amendment): Hansard HL vol 619 cols 205-207 (14 November 2000).

36 In relation to the proposed omission of cl 21 (information supplied by, or relating to, bodies dealing with security matters) and the amendment of cl 22 (national security) see: Hansard HC vol 347 cols 1054-1062 (5 April 2000) (House of Commons Report and Third Reading). In relation to the proposed amendment of cl 21 (information supplied by, or relating to, bodies dealing with security matters) see: Hansard HL vol 617 cols 1256-1259 (19 October 2000) (House of Lords Committee Stage).

37 Including under the Security Service Act 1996 and the Security Service's 'management consultancy' type work advising other public bodies on matters such as security systems and controls.

38 Including, eg in relation to football hooliganism.

requirement but these were defeated on a vote.[39]

26– 007 Scottish public authorities

Under the Scotland Act 1998, the Scottish Parliament cannot make legislation which relates to or modifies the law on 'reserved matters'.[40] Corresponding restrictions apply in relation to the exercise of certain functions by the Scottish Ministers.[41] The following are in turn defined as 'reserved matters' for the purposes of the Scotland Act 1998: the functions of the Security Service, the Secret Intelligence Service and the Government Communications Headquarters;[42] the defence of the realm, the naval, military or air forces of the Crown (including reserve forces), visiting forces, international headquarters and defence organisations;[43] national security, the interception of communications, official secrets and terrorism;[44] and public access to information held by public bodies or holders of public offices other than certain Scottish public authorities.[45] In terms of the Scottish devolution settlement, it therefore follows that the Scottish Parliament had limited scope for creating access rights in relation to security and defence information in FOI(S)A.[46] More generally, the reservation of these matters in the Scottish devolution settlement (and their similar treatment in the Northern Ireland[47] and Wales[48] devolution settlements) derives from and reflects their national importance and may thus help to explain the cautious approach taken to them in FOIA.

26– 008 Overview – FOI(S)A

The Freedom of Information (Scotland) Act 2002 follows FOIA fairly closely in its approach to security and defence matters. Given the limitations on the legislative competence of the Scottish Parliament referred to above, the security bodies are inevitably excluded from the

---

39 Hansard HC vol 347 cols 1062-1071 (5 April 2000) (House of Commons Report and Third Reading).

40 Scotland Act 1998 ss 28-30, Sch 4, Pt I, paras 2, 3, Sch 5 (on 'legislative competence'). In the context of considering the Scotland Act 1998 (which has been said is to be interpreted on ordinary principles, the Supreme Court has held that the phrase 'relates to' indicates more than a loose or consequential connection or a touching upon the matter: *Martin v Most* [2010] UKSC 10, 2010 SC (UKSC) 40 at [49], [159]. And similarly: *Imperial Tobacco Ltd v Lord Advocate* [2012] UKSC 61, 2013 SLT 2 at [16]; *Re Agricultural Sector (Wales) Bill* [2014] UKSC 43, [2014] 1 WLR 2622 at [50]; *Recovery of Medical Costs for Asbestos Diseases (Wales) Bill* [2015] UKSC 3, [2015] AC 1016 at [25]; *Christian Institute v Lord Advocate* [2016] UKSC 51, [2016] HRLR 19 at [29] (concerning the Data Protection Act 1998).

41 Scotland Act 1998 ss 53-54 (on 'devolved competence').

42 Scotland Act 1998 s 30, Sch 5, Pt I, paras 1, 2(4).

43 Scotland Act 1998 s 30, Sch 5, Pt I, para 9(1)(a)-(d).

44 Scotland Act 1998 s 30, Sch 5, Pt II, s B8.

45 Scotland Act 1998 s 30, Sch 5, Pt II, s.B13. The subject matter of DPA 1998 and the European Community Data Protection Directive 95/46/EC ([1995] OJ L281/31) is also a 'reserved matter' under Scotland Act 1998 s 30, Sch 5, Pt II, s B2.

46 This is not to say that FOI(S)A as enacted is necessarily outside the legislative competence of the Scottish Parliament: it does not obviously contain any provisions which 'relate to' any 'reserved' security or defence 'matters' when the expression 'relates to' is read in accordance with the Scotland Act 1998 s 29(3); and the proviso to the Scotland Act 1998 Sch 5, Pt II, s.B13 would also appear to envisage legislation along the lines of FOI(S)A. See §3– 003.

47 Northern Ireland Act 1998 ss 4(1), 6(2), 14(5), Sch 2, paras 1, 4, 17.

48 Government of Wales Act 1998 s 22, Sch 2 and the Transfer of Functions Orders made thereunder, ie SI 1999/672 SI 2000/253, SI 2000/1829, SI 2000/1830, SI 2001/3679, SI 2004/3044, SI 2005/1958, SI 2006/1458, SI 2006/3334. The Government of Wales Act 2006 contains a saving for these Orders (s 162, Sch 11) and the reformed devolution settlement provided for thereunder took an identical approach to the non-devolution of security and defence matters (ss 58, 94, 108, Schs 3, 5, 7 (as enacted)). This approach was maintained when the Welsh devolution settlement was further reformed by the Wales Act 2004 and the Wales Act 2017 (Government of Wales Act 2006 ss 58, 58A, 82, 107, 108A, 114, Schs 3, 7A, 7B (as amended)).

definition of a 'Scottish public authority' in s 3 of, and Sch 1 to, FOI(S)A.[49] Information held by a Scottish public authority is subject to a qualified exemption under s 31 of FOI(S)A if this is required for the purpose of safeguarding national security or if its disclosure under that Act would, or would be likely to, prejudice substantially the defence of the British Islands or of any colony or the capability, effectiveness or security of the armed forces of the Crown or of any forces co-operating with those forces. These exemptions closely follow those in ss 24 and 26 of FOIA and both exclude the operation of the general entitlement to information in s 1 of FOI(S)A if or to the extent that the public interest in disclosing the information is outweighed by the public interest in maintaining the exemption.[50] FOI(S)A departs from FOIA model in relation to security and defence matters in two main respects: first, there is no express exemption for information held by a Scottish public authority which was directly or indirectly supplied to it by, or which relates to, a security body;[51] and, secondly, the exemption for defence information operates by reference to the 'substantial prejudice' test adopted elsewhere in FOI(S)A.[52]

26–009 Overview – EI(S)R

The Environmental Information (Scotland) Regulations 2004 apply to the same group of 'Scottish public authorities' as FOI(S)A together with a relatively small group of additional authorities and other persons with environmental functions of a public nature.[53] As with FOI(S)A, the security bodies fall outside this group and are not therefore subject to the requirements of the EI(S)R.[54] Regulation 10 of the EI(S)R provides an exception allowing for the non-disclosure of environmental information whose disclosure would prejudice substantially international relations, defence, national security or public safety.[55] A Scottish public authority may refuse to disclose such information if, in all the circumstances, the public interest in making the information available is outweighed by that in maintaining the exception.[56] In considering the application of this exception, Scottish public authorities are moreover required to interpret it 'in a restrictive way' and 'apply a presumption in favour of disclosure'.[57] In this regard, the EI(S)R closely mirror the EIR save that the exemption for security and defence information operates by reference to the 'substantial prejudice' test found in FOI(S)A rather than the 'adverse affect' test applied in the EIR.[58] If doing so would involve making information available which would, or would be likely to, prejudice substantially international relations, defence, national security or public safety and would not be in the public interest, the relevant Scottish public authority may also respond to a request by not revealing whether the requested

---

49 See also Scotland Act 1998, ss 29-30, Sch 5, Pt II, s B13.

50 FOI(S)A s 2(1)(b).

51 Compare FOIA ss 2, 23. Given the limitations on the legislative competence of the Scottish Parliament referred to above, it may have been felt unnecessary or even inappropriate to include an equivalent exemption in FOI(S)A and/or the omission may simply reflect the narrower responsibilities and competences of the Scottish public authorities and the limited extent to which they are likely to hold information supplied by or relating to the security bodies in practice. Having said this, a number of the Scottish public authorities (eg the Scottish Ministers and other authorities with criminal justice functions in relation to policing, prisons and parole) presumably hold some information within the terms of FOIA s 23(1). See further §3– 003.

52 FOI(S)A s 31(4); cf FOIA s 26(1). See further §3– 005(3).

53 EI(S)R reg 2(1).

54 See §26– 008.

55 EI(S)R regs 5(2)(b), 10(1)-(2), (5)(a).

56 EI(S)R reg 10(1).

57 EI(S)R reg 10(2).

58 EI(S)R reg 10(5)(a); cf EIR reg 12(5)(a).

information exists or is held 'whether or not it holds such information'.[59]

26–010 Comparative jurisdictions

National security exemptions are common to the freedom of information legislation of each of the comparative jurisdictions:[60]

(1) *United States of America*. 'Exemption 1' of the federal Freedom of Information Act 1966 (USA) exempts matters that are specifically authorised to be kept secret in the interest of national defence or foreign policy under criteria established by a Presidential Executive Order and are in fact properly classified pursuant to such an Order.[61] The Presidential Order for these purposes is currently Executive Order 13,526 which was issued by President Obama on 29 December 2009.[62] This Order provides that information may not be classified unless 'its disclosure reasonably could be expected to cause damage to the national security'.[63] The Order further provides that documents may only be classified by persons at certain designated levels[64] and that information may not be considered for classification unless it pertains to at least one of the following matters: (a) military plans, weapons systems or operations; (b) foreign government information; (c) intelligence activities (including covert action), intelligence sources or methods or cryptology; (d) foreign relations or foreign activities of the United States, including confidential sources; (e) scientific, technological or economic matters relating to the national security; (f) United States Government programmes for safeguarding nuclear materials or facilities; (g) vulnerabilities or capabilities of systems, installations, infrastructures, projects, plans or protection services relating to the national security; or (h) the development, production or use of weapons of mass destruction.[65] Classification generally lasts for 10 years but is subject to various provisions regarding review and declassification.[66] There is no institutional exclusion for security, intelligence or defence bodies.[67]

---

59 EI(S)R reg 10(8)-(9).

60 Freedom of Information Act 1966 5 USC 552 (2000 & Supp III 2003) (USA); Freedom of Information Act 1982 s 33(1)(a)(i) (Cth of Aust); Official Information Act 1982 ss 6(a), 31 (NZ); Access to Information Act (1982), ss 15(1), 16 (Canada); Freedom of Information Act 2014 s 33(1) (Ireland).

61 Freedom of Information Act 1966 5 USC 552(b)(1) s 6F(b) (USA). See also 5 USC 552(a)(3)(E), (b)(7)(D), (c)(3). See further §51–008(1). See also: S Dycus, A Berney, W Banks, P Raven-Hansen anf S Vladeck, *National Security Laws*, 6th edn (New York, Wolters Kluwer Law & Business, 2016) pp 1271-1283 (also covering the Presidential Records Act 1978 44 USC 2201-2207 (2000) USE, Privacy Act 1974 5 USC 552a (2000) (USA), Government in the Sunshine Act 5 USC 552b (2000) (USA) and Federal Advisory Committee Act 5 USC App (2000) (USA)).

62 Executive Order 13,526 replaced Executive Order 12,958 which was issued by President Clinton in 1995 and amended by President George W Bush in 2003 (see Executive Order 13,292). Executive Order 12,958 had itself replaced Executive Order 12,356, which was issued by President Reagan in 1982. According to its preamble, Executive Order 13,526 'prescribes a uniform system for classifying, safeguarding, and declassifying national security information'.

63 Under Executive Order 13,526: 'damage to the national security' means 'harm to the national defense or foreign relations of the United States from the unauthorized disclosure of information, taking into consideration such aspects of the information as the sensitivity, value, utility, and provenance of that information' (Pt 6 s 6.1(b)); 'the unauthorized disclosure of foreign government information is presumed to cause damage to the national security' (Pt 1 s 1.1(d)); there are three basic classifications, ie Top Secret, Secret and Confidential (Pt 1 s 1.2(a)); and these are applied according to the damage to national security that might reasonably be expected to result from disclosure, ie exceptionally grave damage (Top Secret), serious damage (Secret) and damage (Confidential).

64 Executive Order 13,526, Pt 1, s 1.3.

65 Executive Order 13,526, Pt 1, s 1.4. Agencies are required to identify exempt material on a page-by-page, section-by-section basis: *Allen v CIA*, 636 F 2d 1287, 1293 (DC Cir 1980).

66 Executive Order 13,526, Pt 1, s 1.5, Pt 3.

67 By way of exception to this general proposition, Freedom of Information Act 1966 5 USC 552(a)(3)(E) (inserted by the Intelligence Authorisation Act 2002 Pub L 107-306 provides that agencies which are 'an element of the

(2) *Commonwealth of Australia.* Section 33 of the Freedom of Information Act 1982 (Cth of Aust) exempts documents if their disclosure under the Act would, or could reasonably be expected to, cause damage to the security or defence of the Commonwealth.[68] The expression 'security of the Commonwealth' is in turn defined to extend to: (a) matters relating to the detection, prevention or suppression of activities, whether within or outside Australia, subversive of, or hostile to, the interests of the Commonwealth or of any country allied or associated with the Commonwealth; and (b) the security of any communications system or cryptographic system of the Commonwealth or of another country used for the defence of the Commonwealth or of any country allied or associated with the Commonwealth or the conduct of the international relations of the Commonwealth.[69] The Freedom of Information Act 1982 (Cth of Aust) also contains provisions which produce a similar effect to s 23 of FOIA and the institutional exclusion of the security bodies under that Act: the Australian Secret Intelligence Service, Australian Security Intelligence Organisation, Australian Signals Directorate, Inspector-General of Intelligence and Security, and the Office of National Assessments are exempt agencies which are deemed not to be 'prescribed authorities' for the purposes of the Freedom of Information Act 1982 (Cth of Aust);[70] the Australian Geospatial Intelligence Organisation and Defence Intelligence Organisation are deemed not to be included in the Department of Defence or to be agencies in their own right for those purposes;[71] and all agencies and ministers are exempt from the operation of the Freedom of Information Act 1982 (Cth of Aust) in relation to documents that have originated with, or have been received from, any of the Australian security or defence bodies already mentioned or (if in respect of operational intelligence or special access programs, under which a foreign government provides restricted access to technologies) the Department of Defence.[72]

(3) *New Zealand.* Sections 6 and 31 of the Official Information Act 1982 (NZ) provide that information may be withheld from disclosure under the Act if making it available would be likely to prejudice the security or defence of New Zealand.[73] There is no

---

intelligence community' (as defined by s 3(4) of the National Security Act 1957 50 USC 401(a)(4)) must not make any records available in response to requests for information submitted by non-US government entities (ie foreign governments and international organisations) or their representatives.

68 Freedom of Information Act 1982 s 33(1)(a)(i)-(ii) (Cth of Aust). See further §51–015(9). The section does not involve a consideration of whether disclosure would be contrary to the public interest: *Commonwealth of Australia v Hittich* (1994) 53 FCR 152 at 154. Rather, the section is an expression of the content of the public interest: *Re Mann and Australian Taxation Office* (1985) 3 AAR 261; *Re O'Donovan and Attorney-General's Department* (1985) 4 AAR 151 8 ALD 528; *Re Edelsten and Australian Federal Police* (1985) 4 AAR 220. See also the Archives Act 1983 s 33(1)(a) (Cth of Aust). Ministers previously had power to issue conclusive certificates specifying the relevant ground of exemption, the part or parts of the document covered and the particular kind of document in respect of which the exemption has been claimed under Freedom of Information Act 1982 s 33(2)-(4) (Cth of Aust), but these provisions were repealed with effect from 7 October 2009 by the Freedom of Information (Removal of Conclusive Certificates and Other Measures) Act 2009 s 3 and Sch 1 (Cth of Aust).

69 Freedom of Information Act 1982 s 4(5) (Cth of Aust). In *Re Slater and Cox* (1988) 15 ALD 20 it was held that damage to the security of the country would be found where disclosure would enable those engaged in espionage, sabotage, subversion, terrorism or similar activities to resist attempts by official security organisations to obtain information about their activities. In *Re Aarons and Australian Archives* (1986) 12 ALD 155 disclosure of symbols and expressions used by the security service ASIO was held to be contrary to national security.

70 Freedom of Information Act 1982 s 7(1), Sch 2, Pt I, Div.1 (Cth of Aust).

71 Freedom of Information Act 1982 s 7(1A), Sch 2, Pt I, Div.2 (Cth of Aust). Both Defence Organisations are parts of the Department of Defence (s 4(1)).

72 Freedom of Information Act 1982 s 7(2A)-(2D) (Cth of Aust).

73 Official Information Act 1982 ss 6(a), 31 (NZ). See §51–022(1). The Prime Minister may certify that disclosure would be likely to have this effect. Requests for personal information under Official Information Act 1982 s 24 (NZ) may also be refused if disclosure would be likely to prejudice the security or defence of New Zealand: s 27(1)(a).

institutional exclusion for security, intelligence or defence bodies: the New Zealand Security Intelligence Service is expressly subject to the provisions of the Official Information Act 1982 (NZ).[74]

(4) *Canada.* Sections 15-16 of the federal Access to Information Act (1982) (Canada) contain exemptions for information relating to international relations and defence (s 15) and law enforcement and investigations (s 16).[75] Under s 15 of the Access to Information Act (1982) (Canada) the head of a government institution has a discretion to refuse to disclose any record requested under the Act that contains information the disclosure of which could reasonably be expected to be injurious to the conduct of international affairs, the defence of Canada or any state allied or associated with Canada or the detection, prevention or suppression of subversive or hostile activities (including information relating to various specific defence and intelligence matters).[76] Section 16 of the Access to Information Act (1982) (Canada) confers a similar discretion to withhold information obtained or prepared by certain investigative bodies in the course of lawful investigations pertaining to criminal and law enforcement matters and activities suspected of constituting threats to the security of Canada. There is no institutional exclusion for security, intelligence or defence bodies: the Canadian Security Intelligence Service, the Office of the Inspector General of the Canadian Security Intelligence Service, the Security Intelligence Review Committee and the Department of National Defence are all listed in Sch 1 to the Access to Information Act (1982) (Canada) as 'government institutions' subject to the requirements of the Act.

(5) *Republic of Ireland.* Section 33 of the Freedom of Information Act 2014 (Ireland) provides that the head of a public body may refuse to grant a request under s 12 in relation to a record if, in the opinion of the head, access to it could reasonably be expected to affect adversely the security, defence or international relations of the State or matters relating to Northern Ireland.[77] Such a refusal must be issued in relation to records which contain information that was obtained or prepared for the purpose of intelligence in respect of the security or defence of the State or relate to specified security or defence interests.[78] The head of the public body must also refuse to confirm or deny the existence of any such records if satisfied that this would prejudice

---

[74] Official Information Act 1982 s 2, Sch 1 (NZ). See also the Privacy Act 1993 s 57 (NZ) as amended by the Intelligence and Security Act 2017 s 315 (NZ).

[75] Access to Information Act 1982, ss 15(1) and 16 (Canada). See §51– 032(1) and (11).

[76] On appeal, the court must form its own opinion in determining whether the explanations provided by the head of the government institution for refusing to disclose the requested records are reasonable but it is not entitled to order disclosure simply because it would have reached a different conclusion: *X v Canada (Minister of National Defence)* [1992] 1 FC 77 (TD); *X v Canada (Minister of National Defence)* (1992) 58 FTR 93 (FCTD). In this regard, the Canadian courts have shown themselves moderately deferential to respondent claims of exemption based on defence grounds: *Canada (IC) v Canada (Minister of National Defence)* [1990] 3 FC 22 (TD); *X v Canada (Minister of National Defence)* (1992) 58 FTR 93 (FCTD); *X v Canada (Minister of National Defence)* [1992] 1 FC 77 (TD); *Do-ky v Canada (Minister of Foreign Affairs and International Trade)* [1999] FCJ No 673, QL (FCA); *Dzevad Cemerlic MD v Canada (Solicitor General)* [2003] FCT 133, (2003) 228 FTR 1: 'In order to claim the exemption under section 21, the head of a government institution must demonstrate there is a reasonable expectation of injury' (at [24]). The Courts have accepted the 'mosaic' principle: *Ternette v Canada (Solicitor General)* [1992] 2 FC 75 at [35].

[77] Freedom of Information Act 2014 s 33(1) (Ireland). See §51– 039(4) and (13). Ministers can issue conclusive certificates in order to declare that a record is exempt by virtue of Freedom of Information Act 2014 s 33 (Ireland) provided that access to a record has been refused in reliance on this exemption and the minister is satisfied that the record is of 'sufficient sensitivity or seriousness' to 'justify' the issue of a certificate. While they remain in force, such certificates are conclusive in their effect subject to appeal to the High Court on a point of law under the Freedom of Information Act 2014 s 24(2) (Ireland). See: Freedom of Information Act 2014 s 34 (Ireland); and see further §5– 039(2).

[78] Freedom of Information Act 2014 s 33(1), (3) (Ireland).

any of these matters.[79] Without prejudice to the generality of s 33(1) of the Freedom of Information Act 2014 (Ireland), s 33(2) specifies categories of record which may 'in particular' fall within its terms including those containing 'information that relates to the tactics, strategy or operations of the Defence Forces in or outside the State'.[80] Although the main departments of state, the defence forces and other statutory bodies fall within the broad definition of 'public bodies' in s 6 of the Freedom of Information Act 2014 (Ireland), the Act does not apply to: records held or created by the Republic of Ireland Police Service (the Garda Síochána) that relate to, amongst other things, its Secret Service Fund or Security and Intelligence Section or its management and use of covert intelligence operations; or records held by the defence forces relating to specified security and defence enactments.[81]

2. THE SECURITY BODIES

26–011 The specified security bodies

As mentioned above, certain security bodies are excluded from FOIA regime altogether and information held by other public authorities is subject to an absolute exemption if it was directly or indirectly supplied to them by, or relates to, any of those bodies.[82] The excluded security bodies are specified in s 23(3) of FOIA[83] as:

(a) the Security Service;
(b) the Secret Intelligence Service ('SIS');
(c) the Government Communications Headquarters ('GCHQ');
(d) the special forces;
(e) the Regulation of Investigatory Powers Act 2000 Tribunal ('the RIPA Tribunal');[84]
(f) the Interception of Communications Act 1985 Tribunal ('the IOCA Tribunal');[85]
(g) the Security Service Act 1989 Tribunal ('the SSA Tribunal');[86]
(h) the Intelligence Services Act 1994 Tribunal ('the ISA Tribunal');[87]
(i) the Security Vetting Appeals Panel;
(j) the Security Commission;
(k) the National Criminal Intelligence Service ('NCIS');

---

79 Freedom of Information Act 2014 s 33(4) (Ireland).

80 The equivalent exemption in the former Freedom of Information Act 1997 (Ireland) s 24 did not contain an illustrative provision equivalent to the Freedom of Information Act 2014 (Ireland) s 33(2).

81 Freedom of Information Act 2014 (Ireland) s 42. The former Freedom of Information Act 1997 (Ireland) Sch 1 contained a list of 'public bodies' which included the main departments of state, the defence forces and the Garda Síochána, but it did not exempt any specific security or intelligence records held by them or name any security or intelligence bodies as such.

82 In the context of considering the Scotland Act 1998 (which has been said is to be interpreted on ordinary principles, the Supreme Court has held that the phrase 'relates to' indicates more than a loose or consequential connection or a touching upon the matter: *Martin v Most* [2010] UKSC 10, 2010 SC (UKSC) 40 at [49], [159]. And similarly: *Imperial Tobacco Ltd v Lord Advocate* [2012] UKSC 61, 2013 SLT 2 at [16]; *Re Agricultural Sector (Wales) Bill* [2014] UKSC 43, [2014] 1 WLR 2622 at [50]; *Recovery of Medical Costs for Asbestos Diseases (Wales) Bill* [2015] UKSC 3, [2015] AC 1016 at [25]; *Christian Institute v Lord Advocate* [2016] UKSC 51, [2016] HRLR 19 at [29] (concerning the Data Protection Act 1998).

83 There were originally twelve security bodies in FOIA as enacted. FOIA s 23(3)(m)-(o) and the thirteenth, fourteenth and fifteenth security bodes were added by way of subsequent amendments.

84 Established under the Regulation of Investigatory Powers Act 2000 s 65.

85 Established under the Interception of Communications Act 1985 s 7.

86 Established under the Security Service Act 1989 s 5.

87 Established under the Intelligence Services Act 1994 s 9.

(l) the Service Authority for NCIS;
(m) the Serious Organised Crime Agency ('SOCA');
(n) the National Crime Agency ('NCA'); and
(o) the Intelligence and Security Committee of Parliament ('ISCP').

The following paragraphs of this section deal with the institutional exclusion of the security bodies from FOIA regime, describe the identity and functions of each body and provide contextual information on the legal and constitutional framework within which they operate and the extent to which this achieves secrecy and accountability.[88]

26– 012Security bodies – exclusion

The 15 security bodies (seven of which have been abolished) are not expressly excluded from FOIA regime by reference to the list in s 23(3) of FOIA or any other list. Their exclusion is instead achieved through their omission from the list of 'public authorities' in Sch 1 to FOIA.[89] In this regard, s 1(1) only confers a general right of access to information held by a 'public authority' and in relation to requests for information made to a 'public authority'. The expression 'public authority' is in turn defined for present purposes by s 3(1)(a)(i) as 'any body which, any other person who, or the holder of any office which is listed in Sch 1'.[90] None of the security bodies specified in s 23(3) is 'listed in Schedule 1' and it follows that none of them is a 'public authority' for the purposes of the Act.[91] It is not clear whether any is exempt from the EIR. Arguably each of them 'carries out functions of public administration' and, on that basis, would be subject to the Regulations. What is clear is that none of the security bodies is institutionally excluded or exempted from the provisions of the DPA 1998: in so far as each security body is a data controller for the purposes of the GDPR or the DPA 2018, although s 147(6)a0 of that Act provides that the Information Commissioner may not give an assessment notice under s 146 to any of the security bodies.[92]

---

88 The former Intelligence Services, Interception of Communications and Surveillance Commissioners (appointed under the Regulation of Investigatory Powers Act 2000) were and their replacement the Investigatory Powers Commissioner (appointed under the Investigatory Powers Act 2016) is institutionally excluded from FOIA in the sense that none of them was or is listed as a 'public authority' in Sch 1. However, notwithstanding their oversight of and close involvement with a number of the 'security bodies' they are not specified as such in s 23(3) and are therefore treated as distinct from those bodies in this chapter: see §26– 037(2) and (3).

89 Furthermore, FOIA does not expressly bind the Crown and therefore only binds the Crown to the extent required by necessary implication: *Province of Bombay v Municipal Corporation of Bombay* [1947] AC 58 (PC); *AG of Ceylon v A D Silva* [1953] AC 461 (PC); *Madras Electric Supply Corp Ltd v Boarland* [1955] AC 667; *Ministry of Agriculture v Jenkins* [1963] 2 QB 317 (CA); *Wood v Leeds Area Health Authority* [1974] ICR 535; *Lord Advocate v Strathclyde Regional Council* [1990] 2 AC 580; and *R (Black) v Secretary of State of Justice* [2017] UKSC 81, [2018] AC 215. This 'doctrine of Crown immunity' is expressly saved and recognised by the Crown Proceedings Act 1947 ss 31(1), 40(2)(f). Following *BBC v Johns (Inspector of Taxes)* [1965] Ch 32 (CA) at 81 (Diplock LJ) the Crown's 'immunity' from the FOIA regime will also be enjoyed by the Crown's servants and agents to the extent that they are not brought under that regime by express provision or necessary implication (see also D Bailey and L Norbury, *Bennion on Statutory Interpretation*, 7th edn (London, LexisNexis, 2017) sec 4.14; W Wade and C Forsyth, *Administrative Law*, 11th edn (Oxford, Oxford University Press, 2014) pp 706-707). As FOIA does not expressly bind the Crown it therefore follows that the Crown's servants and agents are only bound to the extent that they are expressly listed as 'public authorities' in FOIA Sch 1 or to the extent that their being bound is required by necessary implication. See also s 81(3) and, in relation to the intelligence services and NCA, see the definition of 'government department' in s 84 at sub-paras (b) and (ba). The exclusion of those security bodies which are servants or agents of the Crown is thus doubly ensured through the operation of the presumption that statutes do not bind the Crown. The criminal offence provisions in FOIA s 77 and Sch 3, para 12 are nevertheless applied to all persons in the public service of the Crown as they apply to any other person: FOIA s 81(3).

90 For these purposes, 'body' includes an unincorporated association (FOIA s 84; FOI(S)A s 73) and 'person' includes a body of persons corporate or unincorporate (Interpretation Act 1978 s 5, Sch 1).

91 The intelligence services and NCA are excluded from the definition of 'government department' in FOIA s 84 (see sub-paras (b)-(ba)) and the House of Commons and House of Lords are not 'public authorities' in respect of information held by ISCP (FOIA Sch 1, Pt I, paras 2(e), 3(e)). None of the security bodies is a 'Scottish public authority' for the purposes of FOI(S)A s 3, Sch 1. See also the Scotland Act 1998 ss 29-30, Sch 5, Pt II, s.B13.

92 The application of the GDPR and the DPA 2018 to each of the surviving security bodies is dealt with in more

26– 013 The security bodies: order

The order in which the security bodies are listed in s 23(3) of FOIA would appear to be intentional. The security bodies are not listed in alphabetical order and they have not been ordered simply according to their size or practical importance, otherwise NCIS and SOCA would appear higher up the list.[93] Rather, the appearance of the Security Service, SIS, GCHQ and the special forces at the head of the list appears to reflect a certain primacy in terms of the nature and quality of the type of information which these bodies may supply to public authorities or which may relate to them: these four would appear to be the most important of the security bodies. Whether or not the final order was intended to convey a particular message or came about simply because the later entries were, in policy or drafting terms, just that,[94] the final order can be said to reflect a division between principal and ancillary security bodies as follows:

(1) The principal security bodies:
   (a) the three 'intelligence services', that is to say, the Security Service, SIS and GCHQ,[95] come first as the key operational bodies whose exclusion from FOIA regime is most important and most easily explained in policy terms;[96]
   (b) the special forces come next as an operational body, akin to a fourth intelligence service, whose exclusion from FOIA regime is seen as being equally important.[97]

(2) The ancillary security bodies:
   (a) the RIPA, IOCA, SSA and ISA Tribunals, the Security Vetting Appeals Panel and the Security Commission come next as a collection of non-operational oversight bodies whose exemption is, presumably, required by reason of their close connections with the principal security bodies or security and intelligence matters generally;[98]
   (b) NCA (the successor to, among others, NCIS and its Service Authority and SOCA) has an operational role but would appear to be the most borderline

detail as appropriate below.

93 FOIA adopts an alphabetical approach to the straightforward lists of 'other public bodies and offices' in Sch 1, Pts VI-VII but a more hierarchical approach in other areas where bodies are ordered according to their relative size or importance, with national bodies coming before devolved or regional bodies and with bodies from Scotland, Northern Ireland and Wales appearing in that order (eg FOIA ss 28(2), 59, 76, Sch 1 Pts I-III).

94 See §26– 014.

95 The compendious expression 'the intelligence services' is used in this chapter to refer to the Security Service, SIS and GCHQ in the same way as in, for example, the Regulation of Investigatory Powers Act 2000 s 81(1) and the Investigatory Powers Act 2016 s 263(1). The alternative expression 'the security and intelligence services' appears in the Official Secrets Act 1989 s 1 without further definition but there is no reason to think it goes any further than the three intelligence services. At the time the Official Secrets Act 1989 was enacted the Security Service Act 1989 (which would place the Security Service on a statutory basis upon coming into force) had only just been enacted and SIS and GCHQ still had no legal status: the Official Secrets Act 1989 received Royal Assent on 11 May 1989 and came into force on 1 March 1990 (see Official Secrets Act 1989 s 16(6) and Official Secrets Act 1989 (Commencement) Order 1990 SI 1990/199) while the Security Service Act 1989 received Royal Assent a fortnight before on 27 April 1989 and came into force on 18 December 1989 (see Security Service Act 1989 s 7(2) and Security Service Act 1989 (Commencement) Order 1989 SI 1989/2093). Although the Intelligence Services Act 1994 treated SIS as 'the Intelligence Service' (s 1(1)) its short title, coupled with its provisions relating to the Security Service, could be read as suggesting that it regarded all three services as 'intelligence services' (cf ss 8 and 10 in relation to the Intelligence Services Commissioner (originally distinct from the Security Service Commissioner) and the naming of the original and previous Intelligence and Security Committee with 'intelligence and security' in alphabetical order).

96 FOIA s 23(3)(a)-(c).

97 FOIA s 23(3)(d).

98 FOIA s 23(3)(e)-(j). Although it appears at the end of the list at FOIA s 23(3)(o), ISCP also falls into the category of non-operational oversight bodies.

of the security bodies and its exemption presumably came about by reason of the close connections with the Security Service which NCIS and then SOCA had and which NCA assumed.[99]

26– 014Security bodies: selection

The criteria by which the security bodies were selected for designation as such were never fully articulated prior to the enactment of FOIA. The exclusion of the principal security bodies, the intelligence services and the special forces, was proposed at the outset but the selection of the ancillary security bodies and the non-selection of other apparently similar bodies were not the subject of much scrutiny or debate. The White Paper, *Your Right to Know: The Government's Proposals for a Freedom of Information Act,* stated that the four principal security bodies would be excluded because they 'could not carry out their duties effectively in the interests of the nation if their operations and activities were subject to freedom of information legislation'.[100] Continuing this theme, the accompanying *Factual and Background Material*[101] referred again to the principal security bodies as candidates for exclusion 'requiring careful consideration' together with 'support provided to them by other bodies and information originating from them but held by other bodies'.[102] The government consultation paper *Freedom of Information: Consultation on Draft Legislation* first mentioned NCIS as a likely candidate for exclusion on the basis that its work is 'closely analogous' to that of the intelligence services.[103] The proposed exclusion of the IOCA, SSA and ISA Tribunals[104] was similarly explained on the grounds that 'their work is wholly concerned with security and intelligence matters' and 'they would not be able to carry out their work effectively if their activities, or even their administrative functions, were subject to freedom of information legislation'.[105] The designation of the Security Vetting Appeals Panel and the Security Commission as security bodies was not discussed at all in the policy and consultation documents which preceded and underlay FOIA.

26– 015Intelligence services: functions

The Security Service, SIS and GCHQ are specifically excluded from FOIA regime by s 84 which provides that they are not 'government departments' for the purposes of the Act.[106] Their identities and functions are prescribed and regulated primarily by the Security Service Act 1989, the Intelligence Services Act 1994, the Regulation of Investigatory Powers Act 2000

---

99 FOIA s 23(3)(k)-(m).

100 Cm 3818, 1997 para 2.3. This passage goes on to state, 'These organisations, and the information they provide, will be excluded from the Act, as will information about these organisations held by other public authorities.'

101 Published under Cm 3818, 1997 para 3.13.

102 Paragraph 96. This passage goes on to state, 'It is argued that reliance solely on a harm tested exemption would lead to the cumulative disclosure of a significant quantity of the agencies' records or of operational information. This would undermine confidence among those individuals and bodies on whose co-operation the effective functioning of the agencies relies, and would have a deleterious impact on the effectiveness of the Special Forces'.

103 Cm 4355, 1999 para 26.

104 The explanation is to be found in notes produced by the Home Office Freedom of Information Unit for the House of Commons Public Administration Select Committee on the clause in the draft Freedom of Information Bill published on 24 May 1999 which eventually formed the basis for FOIA s 23 (see *Freedom of Information: Consultation on Draft Legislation* (Cm 4355, 1999) Pt II, cl 18).

105 House of Commons Public Administration Select Committee Third Report Session 1998-1999 *Freedom of Information Draft Bill* (HC 570-I) 1999, Annex 6, para 43.

106 The intelligence services are not otherwise listed as 'public authorities' in FOIA Sch 1. Each one on the face of it satisfies the test of being a 'body or authority exercising statutory functions on behalf of the Crown', which would make it a 'government department' for the purposes of FOIA s 84, Sch 1, Pt I, para 1 but for the fact that each one is expressly excluded from the definition of 'government department' in s 84.

and the Investigatory Powers Act 2016.[107] Taking each service in turn:

(1) *The Security Service.* The Security Service (more commonly known as 'MI5') was 'placed on a statutory basis' by the Security Service Act 1989 which provides that 'there shall continue to be a Security Service'.[108] The Security Service is under the authority of the Home Secretary who appoints a Director General to control its operations and be responsible for its efficiency.[109] The Director General in turn makes an annual report on the work of the Security Service to the Prime Minister and Home Secretary and may at any time report to either of them on any matter relating to this work.[110] The Security Service has the following functions:[111] the protection of national security and, in particular, its protection against threats from espionage, terrorism[112]

---

107 See generally: *Halsbury's Laws of England*, 5th edn, 2014, vol 20, title 'Constitutional and Administrative Law', paras 243-248; I Leigh and L Lustgarten, 'The Security Service Act 1989' (1989) 52 *Modern Law Review* 801; L Lustgarten and I Leigh, *In From the Cold: National Security and Parliamentary Democracy* (Oxford, Oxford University Press, 1994); J Wadham, 'The Intelligence Services Act 1994' (1994) 57 *Modern Law Review* 916; M Urban, *UK Eyes Alpha: The Inside Story of British Intelligence* (London, Faber & Faber, 1996); A Bradley, K Ewing and C Knight, *Constitutional and Administrative Law*, 17th edn (London, Pearson, 2018) pp 518-531; O Hood Phillips and P Jackson, *Constitutional and Administrative Law*, 8th edn (London, Sweet & Maxwell, 2001) paras 19-038 to 19-040; S Twigge, E Hampshire and G Macklin, *British Intelligence: Secrets, Spies and Sources*, (Kew, The National Archives, 2009); C Andrew, *The Defence of the Realm: The Authorized History of MI5*, (London, Penguin Books, 2010); K Jeffery, *MI6: The History of the Secret Intelligence Service 1909-1949* (London, Bloomsbury, 2011); R Aldrich, *GCHQ: The Uncensored Story of Britain's Most Secret Intelligence Agency* (London, Harper Collins, 2011). See also the official government publications: Cabinet Office, *National Intelligence Machinery*, 5th edn (London, 2010); Intelligence and Security Committee, *Intelligence Oversight* (London, 2002); Home Office, *MI5: The Security Service*, 4th edn (2002); Cabinet Office, *Improving the Central Intelligence Machinery* 2009). Further information can also be found via the following websites: `www.gov.uk/government/organisations/national-security` (government website on 'National Security and Intelligence'); `www.mi5.gov.uk` (Security Service); `www.mi6.gov.uk` (Secret Intelligence Service); `www.gchq.gov.uk` (GCHQ).

108 Security Service Act 1989 s 1(1). This Act was passed against a background which had seen Lord Donaldson MR call for the Security Service to be placed on a statutory basis (comments made in the Court of Appeal on 10 February 1988 during the course of *AG v Guardian Newspapers Ltd (No 2)* [1990] 1 AC 109) and the commencement of *Hewitt and Harman v United Kingdom* (1992) 14 EHRR 657 (ECtHR). In ECHR terms, it had already been held in *Leander v Sweden* (1987) 9 EHRR 433 (ECtHR) that it is legitimate for member states to establish security or secret services to gather and disclose information about their citizens provided that such services are placed on a clear legal basis and made subject to adequate and effective safeguards against abuse (see also *Klass v Germany* (1979-80) 2 EHRR 214 (ECtHR)). The Security Service Act 1989 was itself modelled on the Interception of Communications Act 1985 which had been passed following *Malone v United Kingdom* (1985) 7 EHRR 14 (ECtHR). Prior to this the operation of the Security Service was governed by a directive issued by the Home Secretary, Sir David Maxwell Fyffe, to the Director General in 1952 as publicised by Lord Denning MR in his *Report on the Profumo Affair* (Cmnd 2152, 1963) and in his judgment in *R v SSHD, ex p Hosenball* [1977] 3 All ER 452 (CA). A great deal of the Maxwell Fyffe Directive found expression in the Security Service Act 1989 (Cabinet Office, *National Intelligence Machinery*, 2nd edn (London, HMSO, 2001) p 9). See also the House of Commons Home Affairs Select Committee Third Report Session 1998-1999 *Accountability of the Security Service* (HC 291) 1999.

109 Security Service Act 1989 ss 1(1), 2(1).

110 Security Service Act 1989 s 2(4).

111 According to Home Office, *MI5: The Security Service*, 4th edn (2002), the Security Service fulfils its functions by: 'collecting and disseminating intelligence, investigating and assessing threats and working with others to counter them, advising on protection and providing effective support for those tasks' (p 5); working 'closely' with SIS, GCHQ, the Home Office, the Foreign and Commonwealth Office, the Cabinet Office, the Northern Ireland Office, the Department of Trade and Industry, the Ministry of Defence and its Defence Intelligence Staff, law enforcement agencies (ie the United Kingdom's 56 police forces, the National Crime Squad, NCIS and HM Customs and Excise), the armed forces and various foreign security and intelligence services (pp 20 and 25-26); and by gathering intelligence through covert human intelligence sources, the interception of communications and directed and intrusive surveillance (p 22). See also Cabinet Office, *National Intelligence Machinery*, 5th edn (London, 2010) pp 10-12.

112 In May 1992, following the end of the Cold War, the Security Service acquired from the police responsibility for the collection of intelligence regarding Irish Republican terrorism in Great Britain: Hansard HC vol 207 cols 297-306 (8 May 1992); *Intelligence and Security Committee Report on Security Service Work Against Organised Crime* (Cm 3065, 1995); M Urban, *UK Eyes Alpha: The Inside Story of British Intelligence* (London, Faber & Faber, 1996), chs 15 and 21. In October 2007 the Security Service acquired the same responsibility in relation to Northern Ireland: Hansard HC vol 431 col 62WS (24 February 2005). The Security Service is largely responsible for two inter-departmental

and sabotage, from the activities of agents of foreign powers and from actions intended to overthrow or undermine parliamentary democracy by political, industrial or violent means;[113] to safeguard the economic well-being of the United Kingdom against threats posed by the actions or intentions of persons outside the British Islands;[114] and to act in support of the activities of police forces, NCA and other law enforcement agencies in the prevention and detection of serious crime.[115]

(2) *The Secret Intelligence Service.* SIS (more commonly known as 'MI6') was placed on a statutory basis by the Intelligence Services Act 1994 which provided that 'there shall continue to be a Secret Intelligence Service'.[116] SIS is under the authority of the Foreign Secretary who appoints a Chief of the Intelligence Service to control its operations.[117] The Chief makes an annual report on the work of SIS to the Prime Minister and Foreign Secretary and may at any time report to either of them on any matter relating to this work.[118] The functions of SIS are to obtain and provide information relating to the actions or intentions of persons outside the British Islands and to perform other tasks relating to the actions or intentions of such persons.[119] These functions are exercisable only in the interests of national security, with particular reference to the defence and foreign policies of Her Majesty's Government in the United Kingdom, in the interests of the economic well-being of the United Kingdom or in support of the prevention or detection of serious crime.[120]

(3) *GCHQ.* GCHQ was also placed on a statutory basis by the Intelligence Services Act 1994 which provided that 'there shall continue to be a Government Communications

---

bodies, the Centre for the Protection of National Infrastructure ('CPNI') (www.cpni.gov.uk) and the Joint Terrorism Analysis Centre ('JTAC') whose Heads are both accountable to the Director General of the Security Service. CPNI was established in February 2007 through the abolition and merger of the former National Security Advice Centre and the National Infrastructure Security Co-ordination Centre. JTAC was established in June 2003 through the expansion of the Counter-Terrorist Analysis Centre itself established in October 2001: *Government Response to the Intelligence and Security Committee Inquiry into Intelligence, Assessments and Advice Prior to the Terrorist Bombings on Bali 12 October 2002* (Cm 5765, 2003) para 11; *Intelligence and Security Committee Annual Report 2002-2003* (Cm 5837, 2003) para 62; *Government Response to the Intelligence and Security Committee's Annual Report 2002-2003* (Cm 5838, 2003) para 13; Cabinet Office, *National Intelligence Machinery*, 5th edn (London, 2010) p 16 where JTAC is listed as a separate 'intelligence and security agency' and a part of 'the United Kingdom's intelligence machinery'; Home Office, *Threat Levels: The System to Assess the Threat from International Terrorism* (London, TSO, 2006) pp 3, 5; HM Government, *Countering International Terrorism: The United Kingdom's Strategy* (Cm 6888, 2006) p 16.

113 Security Service Act 1989 s 1(2).

114 Security Service Act 1989 s 1(3). See §26– 074.

115 Security Service Act 1989 s 1(4) as inserted by the Security Service Act 1996 s 1(1) and amended by the Police Act 1997 s 134(1), Sch 9, para 60, the Serious Organised Crime and Police Act 2005 s 59, Sch 4, paras 55-56 and the Crime and Courts Act 2013 s 15, Sch 8, Pt 2, para 34. The Director General must also ensure that there are arrangements, agreed with the Director General of NCA, for co-ordinating the activities of the Security Service in pursuance of the Security Service Act 1989 s 1(4) with the activities of police forces, NCA and other law enforcement agencies: Security Service Act 1989 s 2(2)(c) as inserted by the Security Service Act 1996 s 1(1) and (3) and amended by the Police Act 1997 ss 12 and 134(1), Sch 9, para 61, the Serious Organised Crime and Police Act 2005 s 59, Sch 4, paras 55, 57 and the Crime and Courts Act 2013 s 15, Sch 8, Pt 2, para 35. Note also Cabinet Office, *National Intelligence Machinery*, 5th edn (London, 2010) p 11 — 'Since the establishment of [SOCA] the [Security] Service has suspended work on serious crime in order to concentrate more resources on counter-terrorism.'

116 Intelligence Services Act 1994 s 1(1). The Intelligence Services Act 1994 was modelled on the Security Service Act 1989 and the Interception of Communications Act 1985. (Indeed, the Security Service Act 1989 was itself modelled on the Interception of Communications Act 1985).

117 Intelligence Services Act 1994 ss 1(1) and 2(1).

118 Intelligence Services Act 1994 s 2(4).

119 Intelligence Services Act 1994 s 1(1). According to Cabinet Office, *National Intelligence Machinery*, 5th edn (London, 2010), SIS 'uses human and technical sources' and 'liaison with a wide range of foreign intelligence and security services' to fulfil its functions (p 6).

120 Intelligence Services Act 1994 s 1(2).

Headquarters'.[121] GCHQ is under the authority of the Foreign Secretary who appoints a Director of GCHQ to control its operations.[122] The Director makes an annual report on the work of GCHQ to the Prime Minister and Foreign Secretary and may at any time report to either of them on any matter relating to this work.[123] GCHQ has two main functions under the Intelligence Services Act 1994: first, to monitor, make use of or interfere with electromagnetic, acoustic and other emissions and any equipment producing such emissions and to obtain and provide information derived from or related to such emissions or equipment and from encrypted material;[124] and, secondly, to provide advice and assistance about languages (including terminology used for technical matters) and cryptography and other matters relating to the protection of information and other material to the armed forces of the Crown, Her Majesty's Government in the United Kingdom, Northern Ireland departments or, in such cases as it considers appropriate, to other organisations or persons, or to the general public, in the United Kingdom or elsewhere.[125] The first (monitoring) function is exercisable only in the interests of national security, with particular reference to the defence and foreign policies of Her Majesty's Government in the United Kingdom, in the interests of the economic well-being of the United Kingdom in relation to the actions or intentions of persons outside the British Islands or in support of the prevention or detection of serious crime.[126] The second (advisory) function is not subject to a specific purpose condition.[127]

26– 016Intelligence services: disclosure

Section 19 of the Counter-Terrorism Act 2008 establishes a broad statutory gateway authorising disclosures of information to and by each intelligence service where made for the purposes of the exercise of the functions of the receiving or disclosing service. Such disclosures are deemed not to breach any obligation of confidence or any other restricti[128]on on disclosure (however imposed), provided they do not contravene 'the data protection legislation' or Pts 1 to 7 or Ch 1 of Pt 9 of the Investigatory Powers Act 2016.[129] Section 20(1) of the Counter-Terrorism Act 2008 also preserves the effect of the duties with respect to the obtaining or disclosure of information imposed on the heads of each intelligence service by the Security Service Act 1989 and the Intelligence Services Act 1994. These duties oblige each such head to ensure that there are arrangements for securing that no information is obtained by his service except so far as necessary for the proper discharge of its functions, or disclosed by it except so

121 Intelligence Services Act 1994 s 3(1).

122 Intelligence Services Act 1994 ss 3(1), 4(1).

123 Intelligence Services Act 1994 s 4(4).

124 Intelligence Services Act 1994 s 3(1)(a).

125 Intelligence Services Act 1994 s 3(1)(b).

126 Intelligence Services Act 1994 s 3(2).

127 GCHQ's advisory functions has been in part fulfilled through a series of different 'information assurance' organisations. To this end, the National Cyber Security Centre ('NCSC') was established as 'a part of GCHQ' in October 2016 in place of its former 'information security arm', the Communications Electronics Security Group, together with the Centre for Cyber Assessment ('CCA'), the Computer Emergency Response Team UK ('CERT UK') and the cyber-related function of the Centre for the Protection of National Infrastructure ('CPNI') (www.ncsc.gov.uk).

128 Counter-Terrorism Act 2008 s 19(1), (3)-(5). Section 19(2) further provides that information obtained by an intelligence service in connection with the exercise of any of its functions may be used by it in connection with the exercise of any of its other functions.

129 Counter-Terrorism Act 2008 ss 19(6)-(7) and 20(2). As enacted, s 20(2) preserved the effect of prohibitions on disclosure in the DPA 1998 (s 20(2)(a)) and the Regulation of Investigatory Powers Act 2000 Pt 1 (s 20(2)(b)). Section 20(5) now adopts and applies the definition of 'the data protection legislation' found in DPA 2018 s 3(9).

far as necessary for that purpose, in the interests of national security, for the prevention or detection of serious crime or for the purpose of any criminal proceedings.[130] The provisions imposing these duties thus establish a statutory bar to the onward disclosure of information by the intelligence services other than for the purposes prescribed.[131]

26– 017 Intelligence services: processing

As already mentioned, Part 4 of the DPA 2018 contains a freestanding regime governing personal data processing by the intelligence services.[132] This marks a departure from the DPA 1998 which did not differentiate those services from other data controllers.[133] The Part 4 regime is intended to ensure compliance with the standards of the modernised Council of Europe Convention for the Protection of Individuals with regard to Automatic Processing of Personal Data of 2018[134] on the basis that this applies to national security matters while the GDPR and the LED do not.[135] The Part 4 regime is therefore somewhat less restrictive than the GDPR, but not significantly: Chapter 2 replicates the six data protection principles set out in Art 5(1) of the GDPR; s 86 and Schedules 9-10 broadly replicate the provisions on lawfulness, consent and the processing of 'special categories of personal data' in Arts 6-7 and 9 of the GDPR; and Chapters 3-4 on the rights of data subjects and the obligations of data controllers and processors broadly replicate corresponding provisions of the GDPR. Key points to note in relation to the Part 4 regime are as follows:

— where a third party provides an intelligence service with personal data, the abovementioned gateway in s 19 of the Counter-Terrorism Act 2008 (authorising disclosures of information to the intelligence services for the purposes of the exercise of their functions) will generally satisfy the first data protection principle requirement that personal data be obtained fairly and transparently;[136]

— if the intelligence services and their heads comply with the Security Service Act 1989

[130] Security Service Act 1989 s 2(2)(a) (in relation to the Security Service); Intelligence Services Act 1994 ss 2(2)(a) and 4(2)(a) (in relation to SIS and GCHQ respectively). See: Department for Constitutional Affairs, *Second Report to Parliament on the Review of Legislation Governing the Disclosure of Information* (November 2002); Lord Chancellor, *Freedom of Information Annual Report* (HC 6) 2002 s 5; Department for Constitutional Affairs, *Review of Statutory Provisions on Disclosure* (2005) p 50 referred to in Department for Constitutional Affairs, *Freedom of Information Annual Report 2005: Operation of the FOI Act in Central Government* (2006) p 13.

[131] The Interception of Communications Act 1985 s 6 provided, in similar terms, that the Secretary of State should make arrangements minimising the disclosure and use of material intercepted thereunder. In *R v Preston* [1994] 2 AC 130 (HL) it was held that this provision and the Interception of Communications Act 1985 s 2 entirely prevented the disclosure of such material in criminal proceedings despite the fact that they did not impose prohibitions or criminal sanctions in connection with the making or observance of the relevant arrangements (at 143 (Lord Jauncey) and 166, 168-169 and 172 (Lord Mustill)).

[132] DPA 2018 Pt 4 applies to the processing by an intelligence service of personal data wholly or partly by automated means and the processing by an intelligence service otherwise than by automated means of personal data which forms part of or is intended to form part of a 'filing system' (s 82(1)) and all such processing is in turn excluded from the scope of the applied GDPR in DPA 2018 Pt 2 Ch 3 (s 21(1)).

[133] DPA 1998 ss 1(1) and (4), 5. Each of the intelligence services was a data controller for these purposes: *Baker v SSHD* [2001] UKHRR 1275 at [4] and [9]; *Al Fayed v SSHD*, IT, 28 February 2002 at [3]; *Gosling v SSHD*, IT, 1 August 2003 at [2]; *Hitchens v SSHD*, IT, 4 Augusut 2003 at [2]; *Hilton v FCO*, IT, 28 June 2005 at [2]; *Stevenson v SSHD*, IT, 30 April 2009 at [3].

[134] Council of Europe Convention for the Protection of Individuals with regard to Automatic Processing of Personal Data (CETS No.223 signed by the UK on 10 October 2018 ('Convention 108 Mod')).

[135] See the Explanatory Notes to the DPA 2018 paras 6-7, 41-42 and 58-61. The GDPR and the LED do not apply to the processing of personal data in the course of activities which fall outside the scope of EU law (GDPR recital (16) and Art 2(2)(a) and LED recital (14)) and national security and defence are outside the scope of EU law by virtue of the TEU Art 4(2). The GDPR also does not apply to the processing of personal data in the course of activities which are carried out in relation to the common foreign and security policy of the EU or are within the scope of the LED (GDPR recital (16) and Art 2(2)(b) and (d)).

[136] DPA 2018 s 86(6) provides that data is to be treated as obtained fairly and transparently if it consists of information obtained from a person who is authorised by an enactment to supply it.

and the Intelligence Services Act 1994, their data processing should generally satisfy the 'necessary for the exercise of a public function' conditions for lawful processing and sensitive processing in para 5 of Sch 9 and para 7 of Sch 10 respectively;

— section 109 is much less elaborate than the corresponding provisions in Chapter V of the GDPR and effectively authorises the intelligence services to transfer personal data outside the United Kingdom if this is a necessary and proportionate measure carried out for the purposes of the relevant service's statutory functions; and

— sections 110 and 112 provide for exemptions which correspond with those applying in connection with data processing subject to the applied GDPR and Pt 3 of the DPA 2018, including in relation to national security.[137]

26– 018 The special forces: identity

The special forces are not themselves a 'public authority' for the purposes of FOIA and they are not a part of the wider 'public authority' comprising the armed forces of the Crown.[138] Section 84 of FOIA defines 'the special forces' to mean 'those units of the armed forces of the Crown the maintenance of whose capabilities is the responsibility of the Director of Special Forces or which are for the time being subject to the operational command of that Director'. The identities of the Director of Special Forces and of the units under his responsibility or command are not clarified further in FOIA. The only official statements made by the government on this topic in connection with the Freedom of Information Bill linked the special forces to the Special Air Service and the Special Boat Service.[139] More generally, the Government has elsewhere confirmed that the 'United Kingdom Special Forces Group' includes three Special Air Service Regiments (the regular 22 SAS Regiment and the Army Reserve 21 and 23 SAS Regiments), a number of Special Boat Service Squadrons (Regular and Reserve), a Special Reconnaissance Regiment, a regular Signal Regiment (18 (UKSF) Signal Regiment), a reserve Signal Squadron (63 (UKSF) Signal Squadron) and a Special Forces Support Group.[140]

---

137 See DPA 2018 ss 15, 26, 44, 45, 48, 68 and Sch 2. The list of provisions of Pt 4 set out in DPA 2018 s 110(2) which may be disapplied under DPA 2018 s 110(1) may at first blush appear more extensive and wide-ranging and subject to fewer exceptions than the corresponding list of provisions in DPA 2018 s 26(2). However, this largely results from differences between the applied GDPR in Pt 2 Ch 3 and the intelligence services processing regime in Pt 4 and the net effect is broadly comparable in substantive terms.

138 The 'armed forces of the Crown' are listed as a 'public authority' in FOIA Sch 1 Pt I para 6 but the special forces and units of the armed forces which are for the time being required by the Secretary of State to assist GCHQ in the exercise of its functions are expressly excepted from this provision by Sch 1 Pt I para 6(a)-(b). None of the armed forces is a 'data controller' for the purposes of the GDPR or DPA 2018 as such, but their processing of personal data is the responsibility of the Ministry of Defence which is a data controller for these purposes.

139 *Your Right to Know: The Government's Proposals for a Freedom of Information Act* (Cm 3818, 1997) para 2.3 and the *Factual and Background Material* (1997), para 96 (published under Your Right to Know, para 3.13), both contain explanatory references to the 'SAS' and 'SBS', after references to the special forces and a written answer to a Parliamentary Question about the clause in the Freedom of Information Bill which became FOIA s 4 confirmed that these initials stand for 'Special Air Service' and 'Special Boat Service': Hansard HL vol 612 col 124 (20 April 2000).

140 This information can be gleaned from: *Ministry of Defence Performance Report* 2001/2002 (Cm 5661, 2002) Annex E, table3; *'R' v AG for England and Wales* [2003] UKPC 22, [2003] EMLR 499 at [36] (Lord Hoffmann);
www.army.mod.uk/who-we-are/corps-regiments-and-units/special-forces-reserve/
www.army.mod.uk/who-we-are/corps-regiments-and-units/special-forces-reserve/63-uksf-signal-squadron/
www.army.mod.uk/who-we-are/corps-regiments-and-units/infantry/parachute-regiment/
www.royalnavy.mod.uk/our-organisation/the-fighting-arms/royal-marines/special-boat-service/special-boat-service
It is apparent that the Special Air Service and Special Reconnaissance Regiments are parts of the Army and the Special Boat Service Squadrons are parts of the Royal Marines. So far as concerns the establishment of the Special Reconnaissance Regiment (with effect from 6 April 2005) and the Special Forces Support Group (with effect from 3 April 2006), see the government announcements at: Hansard HC vol 428 col 1796 (16 December 2004); Hansard HC vol 432 col 130WS (5 April 2005); and Hansard HC vol 445 col 25WS (20 April 2006). There is also a Joint Special Forces Aviation Wing within the Royal Air Force which may not be part of 'the special forces' for the purposes of FOIA s 84 because it is 'under the peacetime command of the Station Commander of RAF Odiham' (www.raf.mod.uk/rafodiham/aboutus/jsfaw.cfm).

26– 019 The special forces: functions

There is very little publicly available official information about the special forces to explain their exclusion from FOIA regime.[141] This is largely attributable to the long-standing government policy of not commenting publicly on special forces matters.[142] However, a small number of public statements have been made. In 1996 the Government stated that the special forces have four primary roles, namely, reconnaissance, offensive action, the provision of support to indigenous forces and counter-terrorism.[143] During the course of the Strategic Defence Review begun in 1997, the government further stated that the special forces are involved in war-fighting operations and counter-terrorism work[144] and that they are a 'Spearhead' component of the 'First Echelon' of the United Kingdom's 'Joint Rapid Reaction Forces'.[145] In 2002, the Government also confirmed that it was planning to enhance the capabilities of the special forces and their 'enablers' in order to maximise their utility and flexibility.[146] And, in 2010, the Government stated that special forces 'have demonstrated their value across a broad spectrum of activity, from operating alongside our conventional forces in Iraq and Afghanistan to capacity building with our partners or hostage rescue;'[147] and 'contribute to a wide range of intervention operations and provide vital support to stabilisation operations and other commitments.'[148] Further information about the role of the special forces can be derived from: the introduction in 1996 of a Defence Council Instruction making the signing of a confidentiality contract a prerequisite to all service with the special forces;[149] and the issue in

---

141 Indeed, the exclusion of the special forces from the FOIA regime can itself be seen as a public pronouncement on the nature of their functions: *'R' v AG for England and Wales* [2003] UKPC 22, [2003] EMLR 499 at [36] (Lord Hoffmann).

142 *The Threat from Terrorism: Government Response*, para 39 at House of Commons Defence Select Committee, *Fourth Special Report of 2001-02* (HC 667), Appendix: 'The Government has in the past made it known that the UK has Special Forces which, as well as their war-fighting roles, are used in support of its counter-terrorist policy, and to provide assistance in this area to the law enforcement agencies. However, successive governments have adopted a policy of not commenting, save in exceptional circumstances, on Special Forces matters. The effectiveness of the Special Forces in the counter-terrorist role depends on maintaining secrecy about their operations, methods, capabilities (including numbers) and equipment. Moreover, we need to protect their identities because they and their families are at risk from terrorist groups. This therefore constrains what we can say in public about our plans for Special Forces.' See also *Statement on the Defence Estimates 1996* (Cm 3223, 1996) para 731, 'as a general rule, the government will not comment on matters which are judged to have an unacceptable impact on the successful conduct of operations or on the best interests of special forces personnel.' See also *In re Times Newspapers Ltd* [2008] EWCA Civ 2396, [2009] 1 WLR 1015 (Courts-Martial Appeal Court) at [18] 'the special forces have a justifiable policy of not disclosing the names of personnel whether they are active, that is badged members of the special forces, or ancillary staff' (Latham LJ giving the judgment of the Court). Cf the Prime Minister's announcement regarding the deployment of Special Forces in Afghanistan in 2009: Hansard HC vol 501 cols 835-836 (30 November 2009).

143 *Statement on the Defence Estimates 1996* (Cm 3223, 1996) para 727. See also the remainder of the section headed 'disclosure of information on the special forces' at paras 727-731.

144 *Strategic Defence Review* (Cm 3999, 1998). The conclusions of the *Strategic Defence Review* were approved by the House of Commons: Hansard HC vol 317 cols 1097-1177 (20 October 1998).

145 *Strategic Defence Review* (Cm 3999, 1998).

146 *Strategic Defence Review: A New Chapter* (Cm 5566, 2002), para 45.

147 Ministry of Defence, *Adaptability and Partnership: Issues for the Strategic Defence Review* (Cm 7794, 2010) p 19, para 2.1. It can also be noted that the draft House of Commons resolution proposed by the Government in March 2008 for the establishment of a new process for the Parliamentary approval of commitments of HM Armed Forces into armed conflict contained an exception for 'conflict decisions' involving members of the special forces or other members of the armed forces deployed only for the purpose of assisting the special forces: MoJ White Paper, *The Governance of Britain - Constitutional Renewal* (Cm 7342, 2008) pt I para 217, Annex A 'Draft Detailed War Powers Resolution' para 4.

148 HM Government, *Securing Britain in an Age of Uncertainty: The Strategic Defence and Security Review* (CM 7948, 2010) Pt 2, para 2.A.14.

149 *AG for England and Wales v Television New Zealand Ltd* (1999) 44 IPR 123 (CA) (NZ) at 124-126 (Henry J); *'R' v AG for England and Wales* [2003] UKPC 22, [2003] EMLR 499 at [2]-[10] (Lord Hoffmann) on appeal from *AG for England*

2000 of an amended 'DA-Notice' reiterating the counter-terrorist role of the special forces and suggesting that they are 'involved with' covert operations, sources and methods of the intelligence services.[150]

26– 020 The RIPA tribunal

In general terms, the RIPA Tribunal established under s 65 of the Regulation of Investigatory Powers Act 2000 deals with proceedings and complaints relating to the intelligence services and the use by those services and other public authorities of investigatory powers under the Intelligence Services Act 1994, the Regulation of Investigatory Powers Act 2000 and the Investigatory Powers Act 2016.[151] The RIPA Tribunal has effectively replaced the IOCA, SSA, and ISA Tribunals which are now defunct except in relation to complaints made before 2 October 2000.[152] None of these Tribunals is listed as a 'public authority' in Sch 1 to FOIA. Although the RIPA Tribunal is a 'data controller' for the purposes of the GDPR and DPA 2018, it is exempt from many of their regulatory provisions by reason of its status as a judicial authority. In particular, the RIPA Tribunal does not need to register as a data controller, designate a Data Protection Officer or comply with subject access requests, it is not subject to supervision or oversight by the Information Commissioner and complaints about its processing of personal data must instead be pursued with the Judicial Data Protection Panel established by the Lord Chief Justice and the Senior President of Tribunals pursuant to recital (20) to the GDPR.[153]

---

and Wales v 'R' [2002] 2 NZLR 91 (CA) (NZ) (see at [16]-[19] and [24] (Tipping J)); *MoD v Griffin* [2008] EWHC 1542 (QB); *MoD v MacLachlan* [2016] EWHC 3733 (QB). The Defence Council Instruction ('DCI') was issued on 4 October 1996 and provided, 'From the date of this DCI all Armed Forces personnel serving currently or in future on the establishment of units under the operational or administrative command of the Director of Special Forces will be required to sign a contract binding the signatory to a lifelong commitment not to disclose, without prior permission of the [Ministry of Defence], any information gained during service with Special Forces' (*AG for England and Wales v 'R'* [2002] 2 NZLR 91 (CA) (NZ) (see at [19] (Tipping J)).

150 Standing Defence Advisory Notice 5, 'United Kingdom Security and Intelligence Services and Special Forces' (DA-Notice 5) issued by the Defence, Press and Broadcasting Advisory Committee ('DPBAC') on 24 May 2000. See now DSMA Notice 03, 'Military Counter-Terrorist Forces, Special Forces and Intelligence Agency Operations, Activities and Communication Methods and Techniques' issued by the reformed Defence and Security Media Advisory ('DSMA') Committee in 2015 (www.dsma.uk). The Committee currently known as the DS<A Committee (and formerly known first as the 'DA Notice' Committee and then as the DPBAC)is a non-statutory advisory body which provides 'advice and guidance to the media about defence and counter-terrorist information the publication of which would be damaging to national security' on a voluntary and confidential basis (www.dsma.uk). The DSMA Committee itself comprises senior civil servants and editors from national and regional newspapers, periodicals, news agencies, television and radio and is chaired by the Ministry of Defence Director General Strategy and International. The DA-Notices cannot therefore be regarded as government statements as such but they are drafted within government and reviewed by the Secretary to the DSMA Committee before being agreed and issued by the DSMA Committee as a whole. See: Jaconelli, 'The D Notice System' [1982] *Public Law* 37; HC 773 (1979-1980); *The Protection of Military Information* (Cmnd 9112, 1983); Fairley, 'D Notices, Official Secrets and the Law' (1990) 10 OJLS 430; A Bradley, K Ewing and C Knight, *Constitutional and Administrative Law*, 17th edn (London, Pearson, 2018) pp 542-542; O Hood Phillips and P Jackson, *Constitutional and Administrative Law*, 8th edn (London, Sweet & Maxwell, 2001) para 26-011.

151 Regulation of Investigatory Powers Act 2000 ss 65-69, Sch 3; Investigatory Powers Tribunal Rules 2018 SI 2018/1334.

152 Interception of Communications Act 1985 s 7 and Sch 1 (establishing the IOCA Tribunal), Security Service Act 1989 s 5 and Schs 1-2 (establishing the SSA Tribunal) and Intelligence Services Act 1994 s 9 and Schs 1-2 (establishing the ISA Tribunal) were repealed except in relation to complaints made to those Tribunals before 2 October 2000 by the Regulation of Investigatory Powers Act 2000 ss 70, 82(2), Sch 5 and the Regulation of Investigatory Powers Act 2000 (Commencement No 1 and Transitional Provisions) Order 2000 SI 2000/2543.

153 See: GDPR arts 31, 33, 37(1)(a), 55(3), 58 and 83; DPA 2018, s 117, Sch 2 paras 5(3), 14(2); the Data Protection (Charges and Information) Regulations 2018 SI 2018/480 reg 2(1), Sch 1 para 2(2)(h); www.judiciary.uk/wp-content/uploads/2018/07/judicial-data-protection-panel-tor-20180515.pdf www.ipt-uk.com/content.asp?id=37

26– 021 RIPA tribunal – functions

So far as concerns the jurisdiction of the RIPA Tribunal:

— the Intelligence Services Act 1994 makes provision for warrants to be issued by a relevant Secretary of State authorising the intelligence services to enter on or interfere with property or wireless telegraphy or to do certain acts outside the British Islands;[154]
— the Regulation of Investigatory Powers Act 2000 makes provision in relation to the authorisation of the acquisition and disclosure of communications data[155] and the authorisation of directed surveillance (eg the covert monitoring of a target's activities, conversations and movements), intrusive surveillance (eg sound or video eavesdropping in a target's residential premises or private vehicle) and the conduct and use of covert human intelligence sources (ie under-cover officers and agents);[156]
— Parts 2-5 of the Investigatory Powers Act 2016 make provision for the targeted interception of communications and acquisition of communications data and targeted equipment interference by, amongst others, the intelligence services and NCA;[157] and
— Parts 6-7 of the Investigatory Powers Act 2016 make provision for the bulk interception of communications and acquisition of communications data, bulk equipment interference and the retention and examination of bulk personal datasets by the intelligence services.[158]

Any member of the public who is aggrieved by any conduct which they believe to have been carried out in relation to them by or on behalf of the intelligence services or who wishes to bring proceedings against them under s 7 of the Human Rights Act 1998 may make a complaint to

---

[154] Intelligence Services Act 1994 ss 5-7 (ss 5-6 replacing Security Service Act 1989 s 3). See also Regulation of Investigatory Powers Act 2000 ss 42, 44, 74 and the Investigatory Powers Act 2016 s 13.

[155] Regulation of Investigatory Powers Act 2000 Pt I, c II (acquisition and disclosure of communications data). The intelligence services and NCA are 'relevant public authorities' for the purposes of these provisions and certain of their members can therefore grant authorisations and engage in certain conduct in relation to communications data (s 25(1)). These provisions are due to be repealed and replaced by the Investigatory Powers Act 2016 Pt 3 (authorisations for obtaining communications data).

[156] Regulation of Investigatory Powers Act 2000 Pt II (surveillance and covert human intelligence sources). The intelligence services, NCA and any of Her Majesty's forces are 'relevant public authorities' for the purposes of ss 28-29 and certain of their members can therefore authorise directed surveillance and the conduct and use of covert human intelligence sources: s 30, Sch 1, paras 2 and 5-6 and Regulation of Investigatory Powers (Directed Surveillance and Cover Human Intelligence Sources) Order 2010 SI 2010/521. A relevant Secretary of State and the Director General of NCA are among those who can authorise intrusive surveillance on the application of the intelligence services, the Ministry of Defence and the armed forces (in the case of a Secretary of State) and NCA (in the case of the Director General of NCA) under the Regulation of Investigatory Powers Act 2000 s 32.

[157] Investigatory Powers Act 2016 Pt 2 (interception of communications), Pt 3 (acquisition of communications data) (not yet in force), Pt 4 (compulsory retention of communications data by communications service providers), s 13 and Pt 5 (equipment interference). Targeted interception warrants under Pt 2 may be applied for by the intelligence services, Metropolitan Police Service, Police Services of Northern Ireland and Scotland, HM Revenue and Customs and the Chief of Defence Intelligence and issued by the Secretary of State or Scottish Ministers, subject to Judicial Commissioner approval (ss 18-19, 21 and 30). Authorisations for obtaining communications data may be issued under Pt 3 by a wider range of public authorities (s 70 and Sch 4). Retention notices under Pt 4 may be issued by the Secretary of State, subject to Judicial Commissioner approval (s 87). Targeted equipment interference and examination warrants under Pt 5 may be applied for by the intelligence services, the Chief of Defence Intelligence and law enforcement officers and issued by the Secretary of State, Scottish Ministers or law enforcement chiefs, subject to Judicial Commissioner approval (ss 102-107 and Sch 6).

[158] Investigatory Powers Act 2016 Pt 6 Ch 1 (bulk interception of communications), Pt 6 Ch 2 (bulk acquisition of communications data), s 13 and Pt 6 Ch 3 (bulk equipment interference) and Pt 7 (retention and examination of bulk personal datasets). Bulk interception, acquisition and equipment interference warrants under Pt 6 may be applied for by the intelligence services and issued by the Secretary of State, subject to Judicial Commissioner approval (ss 138, 158 and 178). Class and specific bulk personal dataset warrants authorising the retention and examination of such datasets may be applied for by the intelligence services and issued by the Secretary of State, subject to Judicial Commissioner approval (ss 204-205).

or bring such proceedings before the RIPA Tribunal.[159] So far as concerns the RIPA Tribunal's handling of sensitive information, its Rules oblige it to carry out its functions 'in such a way as to secure that information is not disclosed to an extent, or in a manner, that is contrary to the public interest or prejudicial to national security, the prevention or detection of serious crime, the economic well-being of the United Kingdom or the continued discharge of the functions of any of the intelligence services.'[160] Having said this, it is important to note that the RIPA Tribunal is not solely concerned with security and intelligence matters or the conduct of other security bodies. It also has a wider remit to consider and determine complaints about the conduct of other public authorities exercising functions under the Regulation of Investigatory Powers Act 2000 and the Investigatory Powers Act 2016 in certain circumstances.[161]

26– 022 Security Vetting Appeals Panel

The creation of the Security Vetting Appeals Panel was formally announced in both Houses of Parliament on 19 June 1997 in written answers to two Parliamentary Questions asking 'what are the arrangements for hearing appeals from those who need to have access to protectively marked Government assets and have been refused security clearance or have had that clearance withdrawn?' These written answers read as follows:[162]

> An independent Security Vetting Appeals Panel, chaired by Sir Anthony May, will be established on July 1 to hear appeals against the refusal or withdrawal of clearance at Security Check (SC) or Developed Vetting (DV) levels and to advise the head of the organisation concerned. The Panel will be available to all those, other than recruits, in the public and private sectors and in the Armed Forces who are subject to security vetting at these levels, have exhausted existing appeals mechanisms within their own organisations and remain dissatisfied with the result. Separate arrangements are available to staff of the security and intelligence agencies. The establishment of the Panel therefore brings to an end the role of the Three Advisers who, since 1948, have been available to consider cases where security clearance was refused or withdrawn on the grounds of subversion.

The Security Vetting Appeals Panel is not listed as a 'public authority' in Sch 1 to FOIA and is not a 'government department' for the purposes of para 1 of that Schedule.[163] In formal terms, the Panel is an advisory non-departmental public body sponsored by the Cabinet

---

159 See *R (A) v Director of Establishments of the Security Service* [2009] UKSC 12, [2010] 2 AC 1 and *AJA v Commissioner of Police for the Metropolis* [2013] EWCA Civ 1342, [2014]1 WLR 285. The Regulation of Investigatory Powers Act 2000 s 62(2)(a) confers exclusive jurisdiction on the RIPA Tribunal to hear claims under the Human Rights Act 1998 s 7(1)(a) against any of the intelligence services.

160 Investigatory Powers Tribunal Rules 2018 SI 2018/1334 r 7. See also Regulation of Investigatory Powers Act 2000 s 69(6)(b).

161 Regulation of Investigatory Powers Act 2000 s 65(2)(b)-(d), (4)-(11). See, for example, *Gibbon v Rugby BC* UKIPT 06/31/CH; *Patton v Poole BC* [2010] UKIPT 09/01/C; *B v Department of Social Development* [2011] UKIPT 09/11/C; and *Davies v British Transport Police* [2018] UKIPT 17/93/H. The amendments made to the Regulation of Investigatory Powers Act 2000 by the Protection of Freedoms Act 2012 ss 37-38, 115(1), Sch 9, Pt 3 (with effect from 1 November 2012) restricted the exercise of powers thereunder by local authorities and the scope for related complaints to the RIPA Tribunal. However, it remains the case that the Tribunal may be called upon to determine complaints, references and proceedings within the Regulation of Investigatory Powers Act 2000 s 65(2)(b)-(d) which do not raise or involve any issues relating to security or intelligence.

162 Hansard HC vol 296 cols 245-246 (19 June 1997) (question by Mr Rooney MP, answer by the Prime Minister, Mr Blair); Hansard HL vol 580 col 123 (19 June 1997) (question by Lord Graham of Edmonton, answer by the Lord Privy Seal, Lord Richards). In March 1948 the Prime Minister, Mr Attlee, announced that all Communists and Fascists would be excluded from work 'vital to the security of the state' via a vetting system: Hansard HC vol 44 cols 3417-3426 (25 March 1948). This system evolved into the current Security Vetting Scheme which was last re-announced in a statement made by the Prime Minister, Mr Major Hansard HC vol 25 cols 764-766 (15 December 1994). See: Hennessy and Brownfield 'Britain's Coldwar Security Purge: the Origins of Positive Vetting' (1982) 25 *The Historical Journal* 4, pp 965-973; Joelson, 'The Dismissal of Civil Servants in the Interests of National Security' [1963] *Public Law* 51; A Bradley, K Ewing and C Knght, *Constitutional and Administrative Law*, 17th edn (London, Pearson, 2018) pp 533-535; White, 'Security vetting, discrimination and the right to a fair trial' [1999] *Public Law* 406; Cabinet Office, *HMG Personnel Security Controls*, version 4 (London, May 2018).

163 FOIA s 84.

Office.[164]

26– 023Security Commission

The creation of the Security Commission was formally announced by the Prime Minister, Sir Alec Douglas-Home, on 23 January 1964 after fears of possible security lapses that came to light after the resignation of Mr John Profumo MP.[165] The Commission's original terms of reference were:[166]

> If so requested by the Prime Minister, to investigate and report upon the circumstances in which a breach of security is known to have occurred in the public service, and upon any related failure in departmental security arrangements or neglect of duty; and, in the light of any such investigations, to advise whether any change in security arrangements is desirable.

The Security Commission is not listed as a 'public authority' in Sch 1 to FOIA and is not a 'government department' for the purposes of para 1 of that Schedule.[167] The Coalition Government announced the immediate abolition of the Security Commission in October 2010 as part of its 'Public Bodies Reform' programme.[168] The only statement made in relation to the Security Commission was as follows: 'for any breach of security the Government will consider the need for an inquiry and how it should be conducted.'[169] In formal terms, the Commission was an advisory non-departmental public body sponsored by the Cabinet Office.[170] There was some overlap between the respective remits of the Security Commission and the Intelligence and Security Committee originally established under the Intelligence Services Act 1994[171] and the demise of the Security Commission was arguably presaged by Intelligence and Security Committee statements expressing a desire to take primacy in cases of overlap.[172] As mentioned above, the basis for the Security Commission's specification as a security body was not

164 See the Cabinet Office, *Public Bodies 2016* (2016), Annex A, table 3B. On non-departmental public bodies generally see also *Halsbury's Laws of England*, 5th edn, 2014, vol 20, title 'Constitutional and Administrative Law', paras 311-314.

165 The actual basis for Mr Profumo's resignation was his having denied in Parliament that there had been 'impropriety' in his relationship with a Miss Keeler when, in fact, two years earlier for a period of weeks he had had a sexual relationship with her. The relationship was known to the Security Service and ended upon the advice of its Director General. See further: I Leigh and L Lustgarten, 'The Security Commission: Constitutional Achievement or Curiosity' [1991] *Public Law* 215; L Lustgarten and I Leigh, *In From the Cold: National Security and Parliamentary Democracy* (Oxford, Oxford University Press, 1994), pp 476-492.

166 Hansard HC vol 687 cols 1271-1275 (23 January 1964). The Security Commission was unflatteringly described as a 'lightning conductor' for security crises (*The Times*, 24 January 1964 cited in D Williams, *Not in the Public Interest: the Problem of Security in Democracy* (London, Hutchinson, 1965), pp 167-169) and a 'stable door operation' Hansard HC vol 145 cols 64-65 (16 January 1989). The terms of reference were twice expanded by the Prime Minister, Mr Wilson: Hansard HC vol 712 col 34 (10 May 1965) and Hansard HC vol 780 col 311 (26 March 1969).

167 FOIA s 84.

168 HM Government, *Public Bodies Reform – Proposals for Change*, (14 December 2011) p 8 and Cabinet Office, *Public Bodies 2012* (2012) Annex I.

169 HM Government, *Public Bodies Reform – Proposals for Change*, (14 December 2011) p 5.

170 See the Cabinet Office publications *Public Bodies 2009* (2009), p 17, annex A and *Cabinet Office Annual Report and Accounts 2008-2009* (HC 442, 2009) pp 105, 206. On non-departmental public bodies generally see also *Halsbury's Laws of England*, 5th edn, 2014, vol 20, title 'Constitutional and Administrative Law', paras 311-314. The Security Commission conducted 18 separate inquiries including: Cmnd 2722, 1965 on Bossard and Allen; Cmnd 3151, 1966 on Squadron Leader Reen; Cmnd 3365, 1967 on Helen Keenan; Cmnd 3856, 1968 on Chief Technician Britten; Cmnd 3892, 1969 on Clive Bland; Cmnd 5362, 1969 on Sub-Lieutenant Bingham and Leonard Hinchcliffe; Cmnd 5367, 1973 on Earl Jellicoe and Lord Lambton; Cmnd 8235, 1981 on John Wagstaff; Cmnd 8540, 1982 on civil service security procedures; Cmnd 8876, 1983 on Geoffrey Prime; Cmnd 9212, 1984 on Lance Corporal Aldridge; Cmnd 9514, 1985 on Michael Bettaney; Cmnd 9923, 1986 on security in Static Signals Units; Cm 2930, 1995 on Michael Smith; Cm 4578, 2000 on Steven Hayden; Cm 6177, 2004 on Ryan Parry and the security of the Royal Household.

171 See §26– 037(6).

172 Intelligence and Security Committee Annual Report 1997-1998 (Cm 4073, 1998) para 59; Intelligence and Security Committee Annual Report 1998-1999 (Cm 4532, 1999) para 75.

explained prior to the passage of FOIA, but it can be observed that some of its reports have never been published, or at least not wholly.[173]

26– 024 NCIS – abolition

NCIS and its Service Authority, together with the National Crime Squad and its Service Authority, were abolished and subsumed within SOCA with effect from 1 April 2006.[174] Both NCIS and its Service Authority nevertheless remain specified as 'security bodies' in s 23(3) of FOIA. As with the defunct IOCA, SSA, and ISA Tribunals, the logic of this is that other public authorities may still hold information which was supplied to them by, or relates to, NCIS or its Service Authority.

26– 025 NCIS – identities

NCIS was established in 1992 on a non-statutory basis as a common police service under the aegis of the Home Office before being placed on a statutory footing by the Police Act 1997 and becoming an executive non-departmental public body sponsored by the Home Office under the Criminal Justice and Police Act 2001.[175] The Police Act 1997 provided for the establishment of NCIS and its Service Authority (neither of which was listed as a 'public authority' in Sch 1 to FOIA)[176] as well as the National Crime Squad and its Service Authority (which were both listed as 'public authorities' for these purposes).[177] The NCIS Service Authority had legal personality as a body corporate consisting of 11 members,[178] whilst NCIS itself was a body consisting of its Director General together with police and civilian members.[179]

26– 026 NCIS – functions

The NCIS Service Authority operated under a Chairman and was charged with maintaining NCIS which in turn had the following functions: (1) to gather, store and analyse information in order to provide criminal intelligence; (2) to provide criminal intelligence to police forces in Great Britain, the Police Service for Northern Ireland, the National Crime Squad and other law enforcement agencies; and (3) to act in support of those bodies carrying out their criminal

---

173 For example the report on Sir Roger Hollis: see Hansard HC vol 1 cols 1079-1085 (26 March 1981). In lieu of the report's publication, Cmnd 8540, 1982 was issued containing a summary of certain action taken in response to some of the recommendations contained in the report. A large part of the report on Michael Bettaney also remains unpublished (see Cmnd 9514, 1985).

174 Serious Organised Crime and Police Act 2005 Pt 1.

175 See Cabinet Office *Public Bodies 2006* (2006), p 242. In relation to NCIS and its Service Authority see: Police Act 1997, Pt I; Criminal Justice and Police Act 2001 Pt V. Relevant provisions repealed with effect from 1 April 2006 by the Serious Organised Crime and Police Act 2005 ss 59, 174(2), Sch 4, paras 94-95, 162, 166, Sch 17, Pt 2.

176 It is plain that neither NCIS nor its Service Authority were meant to be 'public authorities' for the purposes of FOIA; contrast the approach taken to the similarly constituted National Crime Squad and its Service Authority which were both listed in FOIA Sch 1, Pt VI.

177 In relation to the National Crime Squad and its Service Authority see: Police Act 1997 Pt II; Criminal Justice and Police Act 2001 Pt V; FOIA Sch 1, Pt VI. Relevant provisions repealed with effect from 1 April 2006 by the Serious Organised Crime and Police Act 2005 ss 59, 174(2), Sch 4, paras 94-96, 162, 166, Sch 17, Pt 2. The original proposal that a National Crime Squad be established in place of the previous Regional Crime Squads was made in House of Commons Home Affairs Select Committee Third Report Session 1994-1995 *Organised Crime* (HC 18-11) 1995. The National Crime Squad thereafter came into being under the Police Act 1997 on 1 April 1998, its principal function being to prevent and detect serious crime which was of relevance to more than one police area. Like NCIS, the National Crime Squad was also an executive non-departmental public body sponsored by the Home Office: see the Cabinet Office publication *Public Bodies 2006* (2006), p 241.

178 Police Act 1997 ss 1, 46 and 90. Repealed by the Serious Organised Crime and Police Act 2005 ss 59, 174(2), Sch 4 paras 94-96, Sch 17 Pt 2.

179 Police Act 1997 ss 2, 9, 46, 90. Repealed by the Serious Organised Crime and Police Act 2005 ss 59, 174(2), Sch 4 paras 94-96, Sch 17 Pt 2.

intelligence activities.[180] In discharging its functions, the NCIS Service Authority was obliged to have regard to various objectives, targets, service plans, codes of practice and directions, ensure that NCIS was efficient and effective and produce service plans and reports on an annual basis.[181] NCIS was itself under the direction and control of a Director General with the rank of chief constable who was appointed by the Home Secretary and who was obliged to have regard to the Service Authority's service plan in discharging his functions and to produce an annual report.[182]

26– 027SOCA – abolition

SOCA was abolished and replaced by the NCA with effect from 7 October 2013.[183] As with NCIS and its service Authority, SOCA nevertheless remains specified as a 'security body' in s 23(3) of FOIA on the basis that other public authorities may still hold information which was supplied to them by, or relates to, SOCA.

26– 028SOCA – identity

SOCA was established as a body corporate with effect from 1 April 2006.[184] It consisted of a Board comprising a Chairman, a Director General and other members, who were all appointed by the Home Secretary, together with a capped number of internal *ex officio* members, themselves appointed by the Director General after consultation with the Chairman.[185] Although the Director General was appointed by the Home Secretary (following consultation with the Scottish Ministers and, in practice, the Northern Ireland Secretary) he maintained general operational control of SOCA on an independent basis.[186] SOCA had a nation-wide remit operating across the United Kingdom as an executive non-departmental public body sponsored and funded by the Home Office.[187] SOCA was a civilian body, not a police force, and it did not act on behalf of the Crown.[188] Police officers, Revenue and Customs officers and immigration officers seconded to work at SOCA automatically lost any special powers they had in their previous capacities as such and the Director General then had power to confer such powers on individual members of staff (whether permanent or seconded) by designation according to the business needs of the Agency.[189] SOCA is not listed as a 'public authority' in

180 Police Act 1997 ss 1, 2, 46 and 90. Repealed by the Serious Organised Crime and Police Act 2005 ss 59, 174(2), Sch 4, paras 94-96, Sch 17 Pt 2.

181 Police Act 1997 ss 2-5. Repealed by the Serious Organised Crime and Police Act 2005 ss 59, 174(2), Sch 4 paras 94-95, Sch 17 Pt 2.

182 Police Act 1997 ss 6 and 10-11. Repealed by the Serious Organised Crime and Police Act 2005 ss 59, 174(2), Sch 4 paras 94-95, Sch 17 Pt 2.

183 The Crime and Courts Act 2013, Pt 1.

184 Serious Organised Crime and Police Act 2005 s 1, Sch 1. For the policy background, see: the Home Secretary's announcement at Hansard HC vol 417 cols 58-60WS (9 February 2004); the Home Office White Paper *One Step Ahead: A 21st Century Strategy to Defeat Organised Crime* (Cm 6167, 2004). Relevant provisions repealed with effect from 7 October 2013 by the Crime and Courts Act 2013 s 15, Sch 8.

185 Serious Organised Crime and Police Act 2005 Sch 1 paras 1, 8-9.

186 Serious Organised Crime and Police Act 2005 s 21, Sch 1 para 9. The Security Service Act 1989 s 2(2)(c) was amended to place a duty on the Director General of the Security Service to ensure that there were arrangements, agreed with the Director General of SOCA, for co-ordinating the activities of the Security Service in pursuance of the Security Service Act 1989 s 1(4) with the activities of police forces, SOCA and other law enforcement agencies. Prior to the amendment of this provision by the Serious Organised Crime and Police Act 2005 s 59, Sch 4 paras 55, 57, arrangements of this kind had to be agreed with the Director General of NCIS.

187 SOCA, *SOCA Annual Plan 2013/14* (2013), p 6.

188 Serious Organised Crime and Police Act 2005 s 179, Sch 1 para 20.

189 Serious Organised Crime and Police Act 2005 ss 43-50.

Sch 1 to FOIA.[190]

26–029 SOCA – functions

SOCA not only replaced and assumed the functions of NCIS and the National Crime Squad, it also acquired certain functions of the Home Office and HM Revenue and Customs relating respectively to organised immigration crime and serious drug trafficking. SOCA's principal statutory functions were preventing and detecting serious organised crime and contributing to the reduction of such crime in other ways and to the mitigation of its consequences.[191] SOCA also acquired certain functions of the former Assets Recovery Agency in relation to the recovery of the proceeds of crime, with effect from 1 April 2008, and it absorbed the UK Human Trafficking Centre, with effect from 1 April 2010.[192] It also had ancillary functions as to the gathering, storing, analysis, disclosure and dissemination of information relevant to the prevention, detection, investigation, prosecution and reduction of all crime (not just serious organised crime) and 'general powers' to institute criminal proceedings and act in support of other police forces and law enforcement agencies.[193] In exercising its functions SOCA was obliged to have regard to its own annual plan, priorities and targets together with strategic priorities and codes of practice issued by the Home Secretary and publish an annual report.[194] In practical terms, SOCA was at least partially reliant on other police forces and law enforcement agencies for assistance and for the use and loan of staff, facilities, equipment, premises and services albeit that the provision of assistance might be mutual.[195] Given its remit, the inclusion of SOCA within s 23(3) of FOIA confers absolute exemption on types of information which were previously accessible under the Act through requests made to the National Crime Squad, Home Office and HM Revenue and Customs.

26–030 NCA – identity

The NCA was established with effect from 7 October 2013 and is a non-ministerial department comprised of NCA officers.[196] The NCA is under the direction and control of a Director General appointed by the Home Secretary after consultation with the Scottish Ministers and the Department of Justice in Northern Ireland.[197] The Director General (who is also an NCA officer) is operationally independent of ministers and is responsible for appointing the remaining NCA officers and for setting their terms and conditions.[198] The Crime and Courts Act 2013

[190] By confirming SOCA's status as a non-Crown body, Serious Organised Crime and Police Act 2005 s 179, Sch 1 para 20 precluded any argument to the effect that SOCA was a 'public authority' for the purposes of FOIA by virtue of its being a 'body or authority exercising statutory functions on behalf of the Crown' and therefore a 'government department' within the meaning of FOIA s 84, Sch 1, Pt I, para 1.

[191] Serious Organised Crime and Police Act 2005 s 2(1). There were limits on SOCA's power to act against revenue fraud or serious or complex fraud without the agreement of either HM Revenue and Customs or the Serious Fraud Office (s 2(3)-(4)).

[192] Serious Organised Crime and Police Act 2005 s 2A and Proceeds of Crime Act 2002 ss 2A-2B. Relevant amendments and transfers of functions were made by and under the Serious Crime Act 2007. The UK Human Trafficking Centre (now Unit) was (and still is) a non-statutory 'multi-agency centre' which was formerly sponsored by the Association of Chief Police Officers as part of the South Yorkshire Police.

[193] Serious Organised Crime and Police Act 2005 ss 3, 5, 32-36, 38.

[194] Serious Organised Crime and Police Act 2005 ss 4, 6-7, 9-10.

[195] Serious Organised Crime and Police Act 2005 ss 23-28.

[196] Crime and Courts Act 2013 s 1, Sch 1. Home Office and NCA, *Framework Document for the National Crime Agency* (London, TSO, 2013) para 3.1 and NCA, *NCA Annual Plan 2013-14* (2013), p 10. For the policy background, see: Home Office, *Policing in the 21st Century: Reconnecting Police and the People* (Cm 7925, 2010); statement by the Home Secretary, Mrs May, Hansard HC vol 529 cols 232-234 (8 June 2011); Home Office, *The National Crime Agency: A Plan for the Creation of a National Crime-Fighting Capability* (Cm 8097, 2011).

[197] Crime and Courts Act 2013 s 1(2), Sch 1, para 7.

[198] Crime and Courts Act 2013 ss 1(2), 4, Sch 1, para 9.

provides for the respective suspension and revival of the offices held by police constables, Revenue and Customs officers and immigration officers prior to and following a transfer to NCA and for secondments to and from NCA more generally.[199] NCA officers are under a statutory duty to co-operate with police constables, Revenue and Customs officers, immigration officers, members of the Serious Fraud Office, armed forces and coastguard and others for the purpose of assisting such persons in their activities to combat crime.[200] There are also provisions on the compulsory exchange of relevant information and the provision of assistance as between NCA, the Home Office, HM Revenue and Customs, the Serious Fraud Office and others charged with the duty of investigating organised crime or serious crime.[201] The NCA is not listed as a 'public authority' in Sch 1 to FOIA and it is excluded from the definition of 'government department' in s 84.[202]

26–031 NCA – functions

NCA has a United Kingdom-wide remit and is responsible for discharging functions conferred by the Crime and Courts Act 2013, the Proceeds of Crime Act 2002 and other enactments including, for example, witness protection functions under s 82 of the Serious Organised Crime and Police Act 2005. NCA's principal functions are the 'crime reduction function' of securing that efficient and effective activities to combat organised crime and serious crime are carried out (whether by the NCA, other law enforcement agencies or other persons) and the 'criminal intelligence function' of gathering, storing, processing, analysing and disseminating information that is relevant to activities to combat crime and recover the proceeds of crime.[203] The Home Secretary determines the NCA's strategic priorities (after consulting with others) and issues framework documents (agreed with the Director General) on its operation and administration and the Director General then issues annual plans and has regard to all of these when taking decision relating to operations.[204] NCA has four 'commands' (border policing; child exploitation and online protection ('CEOP'); economic crime; and organised crime, a national cyber crime unit and a national economic crime centre.[205] Various statutory prohibitions and gateways in the Crime and Courts Act 2013 regulate the disclosure of information to and by NCA.[206] Given that NCA has a wider remit than SOCA, incorporating functions previously exercised by the Police Central e-Crime Unit, the Criminal and Financial Investigations Borders Team within the former United Kingdom Border Agency and parts of the National Police Improvement Agency,[207] it follows that is specification as a security body within s 23(3) of FOIA has conferred absolute exemption on a wider range of information which might previously have been obtained from other public authorities.

---

199 Sch 1, paras 12-14.

200 Crime and Courts Act 2013 s 1(2), Sch 3, para 1.

201 Crime and Courts Act 2013 ss 1(5), 5, Sch 3, Pts 2-6.

202 This exclusion is necessary because the Crime and Courts Act 2013 Sch 1, para 1 provides that NCA functions, unlike SOCA functions, are exercisable on behalf of the Crown, ie NCA is a Crown body and it would therefore fall within the definition of 'government department' in FOIA s 84 were it not for the exclusion.

203 Crime and Courts Act 2013 s 1(4)-(5).

204 Crime and Courts Act 2013 ss 3-4, Sch 2. Home Office and NCA, *Revised Framework Document for the National Crime Agency* (London, TSO, 2015) and NCA, *NCA Annual Plan 2018-19* (2018).

205 NCA, *NCA annual Plan 2013-14* (2013) pp 12-14. It also incorporates a number of 'specialist' units: Proceeds of Crime Centre; Missing Persons Bureau; Modern Slavery Human Trafficking Unit; Central Bureau of the UK Protected Persons Service; Chemical Control Team; UK Financial Intelligence Unit; and Serious Crime Analysis Section.

206 Sections 7, 12, Sch 7.

207 NCA, *NCA Annual Plan 2013-14* (2013) p 12.

26– 032ISCP – identity

ISCP was established with effect from 25 June 2013 in place of the previous Intelligence and Security Committee established under the Intelligence Services Act 1994.[208] It is a statutory Committee of Parliament and not a Select Committee as such. ISCP consists of members who are drawn from the membership of and appointed by the House of Commons and the House of Lords,[209] provided that the relevant individuals have been nominated by the Prime Minister and are not Ministers of the Crown.[210] The ICSP members choose the Chair of the ICSP and hold office for the duration of the Parliament in question, subject to provisions as to the cessation of their eligibility and their removal and resignation.[211] The ICSP members are subject to the provisions of s 1(1) of the Official Secrets Act 1989 by virtue of notifications under s 1(1)(b) of that Act in order to allow them to have 'access to highly classified material.'[212] ISCP is not listed as a 'public authority' in Sch 1 to FOIA, information held by it is expressly excluded from the obligations of the Houses of Parliament as 'public authorities' under that Act and the 'data controller' in respect of personal data processed by ISCP is not the Corporate Officer of either House of Parliament for the purposes of the GDPR or DPA 2018.[213]

26– 033ISCP – functions

The main functions of ISCP are to examine and oversee the expenditure, administration, policy and operations of the intelligence services and such other activities of Her Majesty's Government in relation to intelligence or security matters as are set out in a memorandum of understanding.[214] The 'activities' included in the current memorandum of understanding

---

208 Justice and Security Act 2013 Pt 1. The Justice and Security Act 2013 s 19(1), Sch 2, para 1 abolished the previous Intelligence and Security Committee by repealing the Intelligence Services Act 1994 s 10 and Sch 3. However, the exercise was primarily one of reform, rather than replacement. The policy background can be found in HM Government, *Justice and Security Green Paper* (Cm 8194, 2011), Ch 3 and ISCP, *Intelligence and Security Committee of Parliament Annual Report 2012-2013* (HC 547) 2013, paras 126-131. The Justice and Security Act 2013 s 19(1), Sch 2, para 5 included ISCP as a specified security body in FOIA s 23(3)(o) and excluded information held by it from the provisions of Sch 1, Pt I, paras 2-3 listing the House of Commons and the House of Lords as 'public authorities' in respect of certain other information. As to the previous Intelligence and Security Committee established under the Intelligence Services Act 1994, see §26– 037(6).

209 Justice and Security Act 2013 s 1(2)-(3). The Justice and Security Act 2013 Sch 3 contained transitional provisions making the members of the previous Intelligence and Security Committee established under the Intelligence Services Act 1994 members of ISCP (see also the Justice and Security Act 2013 (Commencement, Transitional and Saving Provisions) Order 2013 SI 2013/1482 Art 3).

210 Justice and Security Act 2013 s 1(4). The Prime Minister must in turn consult the Leader of the Opposition before deciding whether to nominate a person for ISCP membership (s 1(5)).

211 Justice and Security Act 2013 s 1(6)-(7), Sch 1, para 1.

212 ISCP, *Intelligence and Security Committee of Parliament Annual Report 2012-2013* (HC 547) 2013, p 1.

213 FOIA Sch 1, paras 2(e) and 3(e) (definitions of 'House of Commons' and 'House of Lords') and DPA 2018 s 210(4). It does not follow from the latter provision that ISCP is exempt from, or not a 'data controller' for the purposes of, GDPR or DPA 2018. In this regard, DPA 2018 s 210(1) provides that Pts 1-2 and 5-7 of that Act 'apply to the processing of personal data by or on behalf of either House of Parliament' and the Explanatory Notes to the Justice and Security Act 2013 para 139 (on Sch 2 para 2 which amended DPA 1998 s 63A(2)-(3) to introduce corresponding provisions) made the following point:

> Since the [ISCP] will be composed of MPs and Peers (see section 1(2)) who are appointed by each House of Parliament (section 1(3)), and it will be a statutory Committee of Parliament, the DPA [1998] could be interpreted as applying to the [ISCP] as it applies to Parliament, with the data controller for the Committee being the corporate officer of the relevant House of Parliament (section 63A DPA [1998]). This would not be appropriate. The sensitivity of much of the data handled by the [ISCP] means that the corporate officers will not be entitled to have access to it, making it impossible for them to ensure that the requirements of DPA are followed. Paragraph 2 therefore amends the DPA [1998] to disapply s 63A DPA, so far as the [ISCP] is concerned.

214 Justice and Security Act 2013 s 2(1)-(2). The extension of these provisions to other activities of Her Majesty's Government in relation to intelligence or security matters was most directly intended to capture the Joint Intelligence Organisation and National Security Secretariat in the Cabinet Office, the Office for Security and

include the strategic intelligence activities of the Chief of Defence Intelligence, Ministry of Defence 'offensive cyber', the activities of the National Security Adviser, National Security Secretariat and Joint Intelligence Organisation within the Cabinet Office and the activities of the Office for Security and Counter-Terrorism within the Home Office.[215] However, 'particular operational matters' may only be considered in circumstances where: ISCP and the Prime Minister are both satisfied that the matter in question is not part of any ongoing intelligence or security operation and is of significant national interest; the Prime Minister has asked ISCP to consider the matter in question; or ISCP's consideration of the matter is limited to the consideration of information provided voluntarily by an intelligence service or government department.[216] In the exercise of its functions ISCP may request information from an intelligence services or government department and the relevant body is then obliged to disclose this, subject to a power of ministerial veto.[217] This veto may only be exercised where the relevant Secretary of State considers either that the information is 'sensitive' and its non-disclosure is in the interests of national security[218] or that the information is of such a nature that it could properly be withheld from a Departmental Select Committee of the House of Commons.[219] ISCP is required to make annual reports to Parliament on the discharge of its functions and may also make other such reports concerning any aspect of its functions on an ad hoc basis.[220] ISCP is required to send all its reports to Parliament in draft to the Prime Minister who may direct the omission of any matter that he considers would be prejudicial to the continued discharge of the functions of any intelligence service or any person carrying out activities of Her Majesty's Government in relation to intelligence or security matters.[221] The extension of ISCP's express powers to the wider government intelligence community, beyond the intelligence services, and to some operational matters and the creation of a default right to the disclosure of requested information, subject to a ministerial veto, represent an expansion of its remit when compared with the provisions in the Intelligence Services Act 1994 establishing the previous Intelligence Security Committee.[222] However, the case for the

Counter-Terrorism in the Home Office and Defence Intelligence in the Ministry of Defence (Cabinet Office and Home Office, *Justice and Security Act 2013 Explanatory notes* (2013) para 51 and ISCP, *Intelligence and Security Committee of Parliament Annual Report 2012-2013* (HC 547) 2013, p 1, para 134). The Justice and Security Act 2013 s 2(5)-(6) provides for the memorandum of understanding thereunder to be agreed between the Prime Minister and ISCP, published and laid before Parliament. The first and current iteration of this memorandum of understanding is set out in ISCP, *Annual Report 2013-2014* (HC 794) 2014, Annex A

215 ISCP, *Annual Report 2013-2014* (HC 794), 2014, Annex A, para 8. For the meaning of 'offensive cyber' see: ISCP, *Annual Report 2016-2017* (HC 655) 2017, pp 43-45.

216 Justice and Security Act 2013 s 2(3).

217 Justice and Security Act 2013 Sch 1, para 4. Any information disclosed under this provision is 'made available to [ISCP] subject to and in accordance with a memorandum of understanding under section 2' (Sch 1, para 4(2)(a), (3)(a)). There are also restrictions on the publication or onward disclosure of information received by ISCP in private in connection with the exercise of its functions (Sch 1, para 6).

218 Justice and Security Act 2013 Sch 1, para 4(4)(a). 'Sensitive information' is defined in Sch 1, para 5 as: (a) information which might lead to the identification of, or provide details of, sources of information, other assistance or operational methods available to the intelligence services or any part of a government departments or the armed forces which is engaged in intelligence or security activities; (b) information about particular operations which have been, are being or are proposed to be undertaken in pursuance of the functions of the intelligence services or any part of a government department or the armed forces which is engaged in intelligence or security activities; (c) information provided by, or by an agency of, the Government of a country or territory outside the United Kingdom where that Government does not consent to the disclosure of the information.

219 Justice and Security Act 2013 sch 1, para 4(4)(b). See Cabinet Office, *Giving Evidence to Select Committees: Guidance* (October 2014) ('the Osmotherly Rules').

220 Justice and Security Act 2013 s 3(1)-(2).

221 Justice and Security Act 2013 s 3(3)-(4).

222 In practice, the previous Intelligence and Security Committee established under the Intelligence Services Act 1994 heard evidence from and made recommendations in relation to the wider government intelligence community,

inclusion of ISCP as a specified security body within s 23(3) of FOIA is open to question given that the previous Intelligence and Security Committee was not so included, ISCP is not itself a public authority to which requests for information may be made and it appears likely that most information supplied by, or relating to, ISCP would fall within s 23 in any event.

26– 034 Importance of secrecy

In *Attorney-General v Guardian Newspapers Ltd (No 2)* Lord Griffiths advanced the following basic proposition: 'The security and intelligence services are necessary for our national security. They are, and must remain, secret services if they are to operate efficiently.'[223] This proposition has three limbs: first, the implicit point that national security is itself an important public interest objective;[224] secondly, the recognition that operationally effective intelligence services (and other security bodies) are essential to the achievement and maintenance of this objective; and, thirdly, the more practical point that their effectiveness is in turn dependent upon secrecy.[225] This secrecy is said to be necessary because of the 'special nature'[226] of the functions of the principal security bodies outlined above. In this regard, the principal security bodies deal in intelligence and surveillance and counter-intelligence and counter-surveillance and they undertake covert and clandestine operations: their activities, capabilities, equipment, methods, operations, organisation, personnel, plans, procedures, sources, systems and techniques must therefore remain secret, otherwise their targets will be able to adopt evasive or counteractive measures.[227] The importance of secrecy is, however, tempered by the recognition that the security bodies are not incapable of mistakes or misconduct which could have a profound and damaging impact on individuals, and that unrestricted secrecy is less likely to reveal any such mistakes or misconduct than some form of external disclosure.[228]

---

not just the intelligence services, and it occasionally considered operational matters, eg Intelligence and Security Committee, *Report into the London Terrorist Attacks on 7 July 2005* (Cm 6785, 2006). To a certain extent the Justice and Security Act 2013 therefore formalised and placed on a statutory basis ISCP's powers in this regard (Cabinet Office and Home Office, *Justice and Security Act 2013 Explanatory Notes* (2013), paras 51 and 57).

223 [1990] 1 AC 109 at 269, endorsed in *R v Shayler (David)* [2002] UKHL 11, [2003] 1 AC 247 at [25] (Lord Bingham). See also the reference to the Security Service needing to 'operate under and be protected by a cloak of secrecy' in order to carry out its functions effectively in *R v Shayler (David)* [2002] UKHL 11, [2003] 1 AC 247 at [98] (Lord Hutton).

224 This is because national security, properly performed, provides part of the foundation for a stable and democratic society in which human rights are protected and may be enjoyed. It is a matter of historic record that some of what has been done in the name of national security, even by democratic nations, has been done to destabilise governments, including those democratically elected.

225 It is important not to lose sight of the first of these limbs because the effectiveness and secrecy of the intelligence services are not simply ends in themselves, they are also means to the greater (but not ultimate) end of national security.

226 *R v Shayler (David)* [2002] UKHL 11, [2003] 1 AC 247 at [36] (Lord Bingham).

227 *R v Shayler (David)* [2002] UKHL 11, [2003] 1 AC 247 at [25], 'There is much domestic authority pointing to the need for a security or intelligence service to be secure. The commodity in which such a service deals is secret and confidential information. If the service is not secure those working against the interests of the state, whether terrorists, other criminals or foreign agents, will be alerted, and able to take evasive action; its own agents may be unmasked; members of the service will feel unable to rely on each other; those upon whom the service relies as sources of information will feel unable to rely on their identity remaining secret; and foreign countries will decline to entrust their own secrets to an insecure recipient' (Lord Bingham). See also the references in the same speech at [25]-[26] to: *AG v Guardian Newspapers Ltd (No 2)* [1990] 1 AC 109 at 118, 213-214, 259, 265 and 269; *AG v Blake* [2001] 1 AC 268 at 287; *Engel v The Netherlands (No 1)* (1979-80) 1 EHRR 647 (ECtHR) at [100]-[103]; *Klass v Federal Republic of Germany* (1979-80) 2 EHRR 214 (ECtHR) at [48]; *Leander v Sweden* (1987) 9 EHRR 433 (ECtHR) at [59]; *Hadjianastassiou v Greece* (1993) 16 EHRR 219 (ECtHR) at [45]-[47]; *Esbester v United Kingdom* (1994) 18 EHRR CD 72 (ECommHR) at [74]; *Brind v United Kingdom* (1994) 18 EHRR CD 76 (ECommHR) at [83]-[84]; *Murray v United Kingdom* (1995) 19 EHRR 193 (ECtHR) at [58]; *Vereniging Weekblad Bluf! v The Netherlands* (1995) 20 EHRR 189 (ECtHR) at [35], [40].

228 The point need not be laboured with illustrations, but some of the resultant tensions between interests are explored by the High Court of Australia in *A v Hayden* [1984] HCA 67, (1984) 156 CLR 532.

26– 035 Maintenance of secrecy

For information to remain secret it must be accessible to only a limited number of people. Once information becomes 'generally accessible'[229] it loses the quality of confidence and ceases to be secret. At a very basic level, information supplied by, or relating to, the security bodies only needs to be kept secret to prevent its being exploited to the disadvantage of national security. However, despite the fact that the vast majority of the general public would have neither the desire nor the ability to exploit information of this kind in such a way, it will normally need to be kept secret from them in order to prevent it becoming accessible to those who might. Apart from FOIA, the DPA 2018 and the EIR, various other statutory and non-statutory legal rules regulate the accessibility and disclosure of information supplied by, or relating to, the security bodies. These reflect a consistent approach by the courts, Parliament and the government to such issues and form the legal and policy background into which the relevant exemptions in the aforementioned enactments fit and must be understood. The most significant of these rules are mentioned in outline below:

(1) *Criminal law.* In criminal terms, the Official Secrets Act 1989 makes it an offence for serving or former members of the security and intelligence services, other Crown servants,[230] and government contractors to disclose certain types of information, documents or other articles without lawful authority.[231] Members of the security and intelligence services are thus prohibited from making any unauthorised disclosures of information, etc relating to security or intelligence.[232] Furthermore, all Crown servants and government contractors are prohibited from making 'damaging' unauthorised disclosures of information, etc relating to security or intelligence,[233]

---

229 *AG v Guardian Newspapers Ltd (No 2)* [1990] 1 AC 109 at 282 (Lord Goff); *Barclays Bank plc v Guardian News & Media Ltd* [2009] EWHC 591 (QB) at [22], [25]-[26].

230 As discussed above, it is not thought that 'the security and intelligence services' means anything other than the three intelligence services: §26– 013. The expression 'Crown Servant' includes Ministers of the Crown, civil servants, members of the naval, military or air forces of the Crown and any constable and any other person employed or appointed in or for the purposes of any police force or an NCA special (Official Secrets Act 1989 s 12(1)(a) and (c)-(e)). It also includes the Comptroller and Auditor General, the staff of the National Audit Office and the Parliamentary Commissioner for Administration (Official Secrets Act 1989 s 12(1)(g); Official Secrets Act 1989 (Prescription) Order 1990 SI 1990/200 Sch 2.

231 See generally: *Departmental Committee on Section 2 of the Official Secrets Act 1911, vols 1-4* (Cmd 5104, 1972) (The Franks Report); the Home Office White Paper *Reform of Section 2 of the Official Secrets Act 1911* (Cm 408, 1988); R Thomas, *Espionage and Secrecy: the Official Secrets Acts 1911-1989 of the United Kingdom* (London, Routledge, 1991); Palmer, 'The Government Proposals for Reforming Section 2 of the Official Secrets Act 1911' [1988] *Public Law* 523; Palmer, 'Tightening Secrecy Law: the Official Secrets Act 1989' [1990] *Public Law* 243; Bailin, 'The last Cold War Statute' (2008) 8 Crim LR 625. The ancillary offences provided for by the Official Secrets Act 1989 ss 5-6 and 8 and the other offences provided by the Official Secrets Act 1911 and 1920 are not dealt with further in this chapter, but see further *R v James (Daniel)* [2009] EWCA Crim 1261, [2010] 1 Cr App R (S) 57. The RIPA Tribunal can give 'official authorisations' and impose 'official restrictions' for the purposes of the Official Secrets Act 1989 (s 7(5)); Official Secrets Act 1989 (Prescription) Order 1990 SI 1990/200 Sch 3. The IOCA, SSA and ISA Tribunals were formerly prescribed for the same purposes but replaced by the RIPA Tribunal under the Official Secrets Act 1989 (Prescription) (Amendment) Order 2003 SI 2003/1918 Art 2(3), Sch 2.

232 Official Secrets Act 1989 s 1(1)-(2), (5) and (9). The information, document or article must be or have been in the person's possession by virtue of their position as a member of any of the security or intelligence services (s 1(1)). 'Security or intelligence' is defined to mean the work of, or in support of, the security and intelligence services or any part of them and references to information relating to security or intelligence are defined to include references to information held or transmitted by those services or by persons in support of them, or any part of them (s 1(9)). See *R v Shayler (David)* [2002] UKHL 11, [2003] 1 AC 247, confirming that Official Secrets Act 1989 s 1 is not incompatible with Convention rights.

233 Official Secrets Act 1989 s 1(3)-(5), (9). The information, document or article must be or have been in the person's possession by virtue of their position as a Crown servant or government contractor (s 1(3)). 'Security or intelligence' and references to information relating to security or intelligence have the same meaning as in s 1(1)-(2) (s 1(9)). For the purposes of s 1(3) a disclosure is damaging if it causes damage to the work of, or any part of, the security and intelligence services or would be likely to cause such damage (s 1(4)).

defence[234] or international relations.[235] There are also offences prohibiting all Crown servants and government contractors from making unauthorised disclosures of information, etc which have or would be likely to have certain effects in relation to the commission, prevention or detection of offences or the apprehension, prosecution or detention of offenders[236] or which are connected with interceptions of communications under, or other actions authorised by, warrants under various statutes.[237]

(2) *Civil law.* In civil law terms, actionable private law obligations not to disclose, without authority, information which is confidential to the Crown or which was acquired during the course of Crown service can arise at equity or common law under the general law of confidence,[238] contract[239] or fiduciary duties.[240] The Government can

---

[234] Official Secrets Act 1989 s 2. The information, document or article must be or have been in the person's possession by virtue of their position as a Crown servant or government contractor (s 2(1)). 'Defence' is defined to mean (a) the size, shape, organisation, logistics, order of battle, deployment, operations, state of readiness and training of the armed forces of the Crown, (b) the weapons, stores or other equipment of those forces and the invention, development, production and operation of such equipment and research relating to it, (c) defence policy and strategy and military planning and intelligence and (d) plans and measures for the maintenance of essential supplies and services that are or would be needed in time of war (s 2(4)). For the purposes of s 2(1) a disclosure is damaging if it (a) damages the capability of, or any part of, the armed forces of the Crown to carry out their tasks or leads to loss of life or injury to members of those forces or serious damage to the equipment or installations of those forces, (b) endangers the interests of the United Kingdom abroad, seriously obstructs the promotion or protection by the United Kingdom of those interests or endangers the safety of British citizens abroad or (c) would be likely to have any of those effects (s 2(2), see also s 3(2)). Serving members of the armed forces of the Crown are also subject to service discipline under the Armed Forces Act 2006, the Queen's Regulations for the Royal Navy, Army and Royal Air Force and the Manuals of Naval, Military and Air Force Law which themselves restrict unauthorised disclosures of information.

[235] Official Secrets Act 1989 s 3. See *In re Times Newspapers Ltd* [2007] EWCA Crim 1926, [2008] 1 WLR 234; *R v Keogh (David)* [2007] EWCA Crim 528, [2007] 1 WLR 1500. The offence covers information, etc relating to international relations (s 3(1)(a)) and confidential information, etc obtained from a state other than the United Kingdom or an international organisation (s 3(1)(b)). The information, document or article must be or have been in the person's possession by virtue of his or her position as a Crown servant or government contractor (s 3(1)). 'International relations' are defined to mean the relations between states, between international organisations or between one or more states and one or more such organisations and includes any matter relating to a state other than the United Kingdom or to an international organisation which is capable of affecting the relations of the United Kingdom with another state or with an international organisation (s 3(5)). For the purposes of s 3(1) a disclosure is damaging if it (a) endangers the interests of the United Kingdom abroad, seriously obstructs the promotion or protection by the United Kingdom of those interests or endangers the safety of British citizens abroad or (b) would be likely to have any of those effects (s 3(2), see also s 2(2)(b)-(c)). In relation to the exemption under FOIA for international relations, see §§27–001 to 27–016.

[236] Official Secrets Act 1989 s 4(1)-(2) and (4)-(6).

[237] Official Secrets Act 1989 s 4(1) and (3)-(6). The statutes in question are the Interception of Communications Act 1985, the Security Service Act 1989, the Intelligence Services Act 1994, the Regulation of Investigatory Powers Act 2000 and the Investigatory Powers Act 2016.

[238] For example, *AG v Guardian Newspapers Ltd (No 2)* [1990] 1 AC 109; *Lord Advocate v The Scotsman Publications Ltd* [1990] 1 AC 812; *The Observer & The Guardian v United Kingdom* (1991) 14 EHRR 153; *The Sunday Times v United Kingdom (No 2)* (1991) 14 EHRR 229; *AG v Shayler* [2006] EWHC 2285. It is also notable that the conventions governing the publication by former ministers of memoirs and other works relating to their experience as ministers (known as the 'Radcliffe Rules') provide that the consent of the Cabinet Secretary (with a right of appeal to the Prime Minister) is always required in relation to the publication of two categories of information, namely, information whose revelation would contravene the requirements of national security and information whose disclosure would be injurious to the United Kingdom's relations with other nations. See: the statement made to the House of Commons on behalf of the Prime Minister, Mr Attlee, by the Lord President of the Council, Mr Morrison, at Hansard HC vol 426 cols 1207-1208 (1 August 1946); the *Report of the Committee of Privy Counsellors [chaired by Lord Radcliffe] on Ministerial Memoirs* (Cmnd 6386, 1976) paras 79 and 91-92 produced following the 'Crossman Affair' and *AG v Jonathan Cape Ltd* [1976] QB 752; A Bradley and K Ewing, *Constitutional and Administrative Law*, 15th edn (London, Pearson Longman, 2011) p268; the reference to the Radcliffe Report in *Open Government Code of Practice on Access to Government Information: Guidance on Interpretation*, 2nd edn (1997) Pt II, para 2.3 in relation to the 'internal discussion and advice' exemption under that Code. The same restrictions apply, in relation to these two categories of information, to similar publications by former members of the Civil Service and Diplomatic Service under their respective Management Codes. See House of Commons, Public Administration Select Committee Tenth Report of Session 2008-09, *Leaks and Whistleblowing in Whitehall* (HC 83, 2009).

[239] For example: *AG v Barker* [1990] 3 All ER 257; *'R' v AG for England and Wales* [2003] UKPC 22, [2003] EMLR 499;

and does seek to enforce or vindicate such obligations through the pursuit of civil proceedings seeking any combination of injunctive relief, a declaration of right, an account of profits, damages, the delivery up or destruction of material and costs. Proceedings with similar objectives may also be brought to prevent or remedy infringements of intellectual property rights[241] or tortious interferences with other civil law rights and obligations.[242] Lastly, the Government can and does bring ancillary proceedings for contempt of court against those who have breached or undermined the purpose of related court orders.[243]

(3) *Public law.* In public law terms reference has already been made to the provisions of the Security Service Act 1989 and Intelligence Services Act 1994 putting the head of each intelligence service under a duty to ensure that there are arrangements for securing that no information is obtained by his service except so far as necessary for the proper discharge of its functions or disclosed by it except so far as necessary for that purpose, in the interests of national security, for the prevention or detection of serious crime or for the purpose of any criminal proceedings.[244] If and in so far as these provisions or the arrangements arrived at thereunder 'prohibit' other public authorities from disclosing the same information, s 44(1)(a) of FOIA confers a further absolute exemption on such information.[245]

(4) *Employment law.* In employment law terms, the 'whistle-blower' provisions inserted into the Employment Rights Act 1996[246] by the Public Interest Disclosure Act 1998 do not apply to employment for the purposes of the intelligence services or operate to protect disclosures which entail the commission of an offence under the Official Secrets Act 1989.[247] Section 202 of the Employment Rights Act 1996 also imposes more general restrictions on certain disclosures of information in the employment rights context which 'in the opinion of any Minister of the Crown' would be 'contrary to the interests of national security'.

(5) *Evidence, procedure and public interest immunity.* In evidential and procedural terms, it has

---

MoD v Griffin [2008] EWHC 1542 (QB); *MoD v MacLachlan* [2016] EWHC 3733 (QB)..

240 For example *IDC Ltd v Cooley* [1972] 1 WLR 443; *Island Export Finance Ltd v Umunna* [1986] BCLC 460; *AG v Shayler* [2006] EWHC 2285; cf *AG v Blake* [1998] Ch 439 (CA) at 453-455 (Lord Woolf MR) (in relation to existence of fiduciary duties after service; a point not considered on appeal in *AG v Blake* [2001] 1 AC 268).

241 For example under Copyright, Designs and Patents Act 1988 s 163; or on the grounds suggested in *AG v Guardian Newspapers Ltd (No 2)* [1990] 1 AC 109, Ch at 139-140 (Scott J) and HL at 263 (Lord Keith), 266 (Lord Brightman) and 275-276 (Lord Griffiths) and *Paragon Finance plc v Thakerar & Co* [1999] 1 All ER 400 (CA) at 409 (Millett LJ).

242 For example A Dugdale and M Jones (eds), *Clerk and Lindsell On Torts*, 22nd edn (London, Sweet & Maxwell, 2018) Ch 24; Sales and Stilitz, 'Intentional Infliction of Harm by Unlawful Means' (1999) 115 *Law Quarterly Review* 411.

243 *AG v Newspaper Publishing plc* [1988] Ch 333 (CA); *AG v Times Newspapers Ltd* [1992] 1 AC 191; *AG v Punch Ltd* [2002] UKHL 50, [2003] 1 AC 1046.

244 See §26– 016 above.

245 FOIA ss 2(3)(h), 44(1)(a). The wording of the absolute exemption in FOIA s 23 means that this point is unlikely to have any practical significance in relation to that Act. However, it could have a potentially greater significance in relation to FOI(S)A which does not contain an exemption for information supplied by, or relating to, the security bodies equivalent to FOIA s 23 but which does confer an absolute exemption on information whose disclosure by a Scottish public authority is prohibited by or under an enactment (FOI(S)A ss 2(2)(b) and 26(a)). See further §26–008. EIR reg 5(6) provides that 'any enactment or rule of law which would prevent the disclosure of information in accordance with these Regulations shall not apply' and EI(S)R reg 5(3) is in similar terms.

246 Employment Rights Act 1996, Pt IVA, ss 47B, 103A, 105(6A) and other provisions added by the Public Interest Disclosure Act 1998. These provisions protect workers from victimisation, dismissal and redundancy in the event that they make specified types of 'protected disclosures' relating to specified types of misconduct and malpractice.

247 Employment Rights Act 1996 ss 43B(3), 193. Those in Crown employment (including members of the intelligence services and the armed forces) are otherwise able to rely on the bulk of the employment rights conferred under that Act: see Employment Rights Act 1996 ss 191-193.

long been recognised that public interest immunity[248] may be claimed to prevent the disclosure and inspection of documents, the asking of written and oral questions and the admission of evidence in criminal and civil proceedings and inquests and inquiries before courts and tribunals[249] where this would cause harm or damage to, inter alia, national security and defence interests.[250] The European Court of Human Rights has held that the exclusion of similar material from public law proceedings regarding the validity of certain decisions taken on national security grounds can constitute an unjustifiable interference with Convention rights including the right of effective access to justice under Art 6 of the ECHR.[251] For this reason, a number of instruments now provide that documents and hearings dealing with sensitive material which must remain closed to parties in such proceedings should instead be handled in accordance with 'closed material procedures' involving 'special advocates' who will act in the interests of those parties but who will not disclose that material to them.[252] Sensitive

---

248 See generally: *Conway v Rimmer* [1968] AC 910; *Balfour v Foreign Office* [1994] 1 WLR 681 (CA); *R v Chief Constable of the West Midlands Police, ex p Wiley* [1995] 1 AC 274; *R v H* [2004] UKHL 3, [2004] 2 AC 134; *R v McDonald* [2004] EWCA Crim 2614; *R (Mohamed) v Secretary of State for Foreign & Commonwealth Affairs (No. 1)* [2008] EWHC 2048 (Admin), [2009] 1 WLR 2579 (DC); *R (Al-Sweady) v Secretary of State for Defence* [2009] EWHC 1687 (Admin) (DC); *R (Mohamed) v Secretary of State for Foreign & Commonwealth Affairs* [2010] EWCA Civ 65; *Al Rawi v Security Service* [2011] UKSC 34, [2012] 1 AC 531; *R (Secretary of State for Foreign & Commonwealth Affairs) v Assistant Deputy Coroner for Inner North London* [2013] EWHC 3724 (Admin) (DC), [2013] Inquest LR 258, [2014] ACD 43. Crown Proceedings Act 1947 s 28; Criminal Procedure and Investigations Act 1996, ss 3(6), 14-16, 21(2); CPR 31.19; H Woolf, J Jowell, A Le Suer and I Hare, *De Smith's Judicial Review*, 8th edn, (London, Sweet & Maxwell, 2018) paras 8-006 to 8-019; W Wade and C Forsyth, *Administrative Law*, 11th edn (Oxford, Oxford University Press, 2014) pp 711-720; O Hood Phillips and P Jackson, *Constitutional and Administrative Law*, 8th edn (London, Sweet & Maxwell, 2001) paras 33-022 to 33-028. Central government's current approach to public interest immunity issues is set out in identical statements made in both Houses of Parliament by the Lord Chancellor, Lord Mackay, and the Attorney-General, Sir Nicholas Lyell, on 18 December 1996: Hansard HC vol 287 cols 949-950 (18 December 1996) and Hansard HL vol 576 cols 1507-1508 (18 December 1996). These statements were made following a wide-ranging consultation exercise which itself followed the publication of the Scott Report (*Inquiry into the Export of Defence Equipment and Dual Use Goods to Iraq and Related Prosecutions* (HC 115) 1995-1996) and *R v Chief Constable of the West Midlands Police, ex p Wiley* [1995] 1 AC 274. The statements were accompanied by a detailed paper which was placed in the libraries of both Houses of Parliament and were endorsed by the incoming Labour administration in a written answer dated 11 July 1997: Hansard HC vol 297 cols 616-617 (11 July 1997). See M Supperstone and J Coppel, 'A New Approach to Public Interest Immunity' [1997] *Public Law* 211.

249 The doctrine of public interest immunity applies to both criminal and civil proceedings but its application may differ according to the nature of the proceedings and the differing considerations involved (eg if the liberty of the subject is at stake): *R v Governor of Brixton Prison, ex p Osman* [1991] 1 WLR 281 (DC) at 287 (Mann LJ). Public interest immunity rulings in civil cases are therefore not necessarily of direct relevance in criminal cases where the public interest in disclosure may be stronger and where the abandonment of the prosecution always remains a fall-back option in circumstances where both disclosure and non-disclosure are deemed unacceptable. In relation to public inquiries, see the Inquiries Act 2005 ss 19-21, 25(4)-(7).

250 In terms of domestic law see: *Duncan v Cammell Laird & Co Ltd* [1942] AC 624; *Asiatic Petroleum Co Ltd v Anglo-Persian Oil Co Ltd* [1916] 1 KB 822 (CA); *Balfour v Foreign Office* [1994] 1 WLR 681 (CA); *R v H* [2004] UKHL 3, [2004] 2 AC 134; *Al Rawi v Security Service* [2011] UKSC 34, [2012] 1 AC 531; *R (Secretary of State for Foreign & Commonwealth Affairs) v Assistant Deputy Coroner for Inner North London* [2013 EWCH 3724 (Admin) (DC). The European Court of Human Rights has endorsed public interest immunity claims upheld on such grounds in criminal proceedings provided the domestic courts exercise effective control and oversight: *Rowe and Davis v United Kingdom* (2000) 30 EHRR 1, 8 BHRC 325, [2000] Crim LR 584; *Jasper v United Kingdom* (2000) 30 EHRR 441, [2000] Crim LR 586; *Fitt v United Kingdom* (2000) 30 EHRR 480; *Edwards and Lewis v United Kingdom* [2003] Crim LR 891, (2005) 40 EHRR 24, (2003) 15 BHRC 189. See also the Investigatory Powers Act 2016 s 56 which prohibits the disclosure in legal proceedings of certain information about interceptions of communications.

251 *Chahal v United Kingdom* (1997) 23 EHRR 413, 1 BHRC 40 (ECtHR); *Tinnelly and Sons Ltd v United Kingdom* (1999) 27 EHRR 249, 4 BHRC 393 (ECtHR); *Al-Nashif v Bulgaria* (2003) 36 EHRR 655 (ECtHR).

252 An adjudicative process involving the use of closed material and special advocates is capable of being compatible with Convention rights under ECHR, Arts 5(4), 6 and 13: *A v SSHD (No.1)* [2002] EWCA Civ 1502, [2004] 1 QB 335 (CA) at [57] (Lord Woolf CJ) (decision reversed by House of Lords but not on this point, see [2004] UKHL 56, [2005] 2 AC 68); *A v SSHD (No 2)* [2004] EWCA Civ 1123, [2005] 1 WLR 414 at [51]-[52] (Pill LJ) and [235] (Laws LJ) (detention certificate proceedings under the Anti-terrorism, Crime and Security Act 2001) (decision reversed by House of Lords but not on this point, see [2005] UKHL 71, [2006] 2 AC 221); *SSHD v MB* [2007] UKHL 46, [2008] 1 AC 440; *RB (Algeria) v SSHD* [2009] UKHL 10, [2010] 2 AC 110; *A v United Kingdom* (2009) 49 EHRR 29 (ECtHR); *SSHD v F* [2009] UKHL 28, [2010] 2 AC 269; *Al Rawi v Security Service* [2011] UKSC 34,

identities and information can also be protected in legal proceedings through mechanisms which do not involve complete non-disclosure such as: private hearings;[253] orders and directions prohibiting the collateral and onward use of disclosed materials;[254] orders or directions requiring witnesses to give evidence anonymously or screened from public view;[255] and reporting restrictions.[256]

26– 036 Institutional exclusion

So far as concerns the treatment of the security bodies in FOIA, the key issue is whether and why the legitimate preservation of their secrecy should be pursued by absolute rather than qualified means: that is to say, does the need for secrecy require or justify the institutional exclusion of the security bodies from the regime of the Act and the absolute exemption of all information supplied by, or relating to, them irrespective of whether its disclosure might harm those bodies or national security? Many of the judicial pronouncements regarding the intelligence services and the importance of, and relationship between, their effectiveness and secrecy have been made in connection with decisions reviewing and affirming the need for a 'brightline rule' prohibiting all unauthorised disclosures by their members and former members.[257] Certain aspects of the rationale for this rule are not relevant in the freedom of information context, however, as disclosures under access to information legislation are not unauthorised and, provided they are controlled by reference to an adequate harm or prejudice test, they should not run the risk of damaging the trust of others in, or the morale of, the

[2012] 1 AC 531; *Tariq v Home Office* [2011]UKSC 35, [2012] 1 AC 452. Provision was first made for the appointment and appearance of special advocates and the adoption of closed material procedures in the Special Immigration Appeal Commission (Procedure) Rules 1998 SI 1998/1881. Similar context-specific legislative provisions followed in other areas and see now the general provisions in the Justice and Security Act 2013 Pt 2 and CPR 82. See more generally; Ip, 'The Rise and Spread of the Special Advocate' [2008] Public Law 717; Chamberlain, 'Special Advocates and Procedural Fairness in Closed Proceedings' (2009) 28 CJQ 314 and 'Update on Procedure Fairness in Closed Proceedings' (2009) 28 CJQ 448; Kavanagh, 'Special Advocates, Control Orders and the Right to a Fair Trial' (2010) 73 MLR 836; Tomkins, 'National Security and the Due Process of Law' (2011) 64 Current Legal Problems 215.

253 For example Administration of Justice Act 1960 s 12(1)(c); Official Secrets Act 1920 s 8(4); Criminal Justice Act 1988 s 159(1); Official Secrets Act 1989 s 11(4); Criminal Procedure Rules 2015 SI 2015/1490 Pts 24.2 and 25.2; Coroners (Inquests) Rules 2013 SI 1913/1616 r 11; CPR 39.2(3), CPR PD 39.1 see esp CPR 39.2(3)(b) 'a hearing, or any part of it, may be in private if it involves matters relating to national security'. See *R v Shayler (David)* [2003] EWCA Crim 2218, [2003] ACD 327 (CA) at [18]-[22] (Kennedy LJ); *In re A* [2006] EWCA Crim 4, [2006] 1 WLR 1361 (CA); *R (Malik) v Central Criminal Court* [2006] EWHC 1539 (Admin), [2006] 4 All ER 1141 (DC).

254 Criminal Procedure and Investigations Act 1996, ss 17-18; Criminal Procedure Rules 2015 SI 2015/1490 Pt 15; CPR 18.2, 31.22, 32.12; *Davies (Joy Rosalie) v Eli Lilly & Co (No 1)* [1987] 1 WLR 428 (CA) at 431-432 (Lord Donaldson MR).

255 For example: Coroners and Justice Act 2009 Pt 3, Ch 2; CPR 39.2(4), PD 39.1; *R v Lord Saville of Newdigate, ex p A* [2000] 1 WLR 1855, [1999] 4 All ER 860, [1999] COD 436 (CA); *R v Shayler (David)* [2003] EWCA Crim 2218, [2003] ACD 79 (CA) (permission to appeal) at [10]-[17] (Kennedy LJ); *R v Davis* [2006] EWCA Crim 1155, [2006] 1 WLR 3130; *R (Bennett) v HM Coroner for Inner South London* [2004] EWCA Civ 1439, [2005] UKHRR 44 (CA); *R v HM Coroner for Newcastle Upon Tyne, ex p A* (1998) *The Times*, 19 January 1998; *Re Ministry of Defence's Application* [1994] NI 279 (CA) (NI); *Doorson v The Netherlands* (1996) 22 EHRR 330 (ECtHR); *X v United Kingdom* (1993) 15 EHRR CD 113 (EcommHR); *In re Officer* [2007] UKHL 36, [2007] 1 WLR 2135; *In re Times Newspapers Ltd* [2008] EWCA Crim 2396, [2009] 1 WLR 1015.

256 For example Administration of Justice Act 1960 s 12; Contempt of Court Act 1981, ss 4 and 11.

257 *AG v Guardian Newspapers Ltd* [1990] 1 AC 109 at 269 (Lord Griffiths). Cited with approval in: *Lord Advocate v The Scotsman Publications Ltd* [1990] 1 AC 812 at 828 (Lord Jauncey); *AG v Blake* [2001] 1 AC 268 at 286-287 (Lord Nicholls); *R v Shayler (David)* [2002] UKHL 11, [2003] 1 AC 247 at [25] and [36] (Lord Bingham). See also: *The Observer & The Guardian v United Kingdom* (1991) 14 EHRR 153; *The Sunday Times v United Kingdom (No 2)* (1991) 14 EHRR 229; *AG v Shayler* [2006] EWHC 2285. A categorical or 'brightline' rule against unauthorised disclosures is imposed by the Official Secrets Act 1989 s 1 (on members of the intelligence services) and the general law of confidence (on members of the intelligence services and, arguably, others in a similar position). Membership of 'the intelligence services' is not necessarily an essential or exclusive pre-condition in this regard: note the reference to 'members or former members of those services who have had access to information relating to national security' in *R v Shayler (David)* [2002] UKHL 11, [2003] 1 AC 247 at [68] (Lord Hope).

intelligence services.[258] Moreover, it is well established that there are occasions when government can and should consider and authorise the disclosure of information supplied by, or relating to, security bodies. Such occasions may arise in relation to: the disclosure and inspection of documents in legal proceedings and the application of the doctrine of public interest immunity;[259] requests for authorisation to publish memoirs and books relating to service with the principal security bodies;[260] and the disclosure of information to, and the inclusion of material in the published versions of reports produced by, oversight bodies.[261] There would appear to be two main justifications for taking an absolutist approach to secrecy in the freedom of information context:

(1) *Mosaic prejudice.* First is the contention that any disclosure of information supplied by, or relating to, security bodies is necessarily harmful because it will contribute pieces to a public domain 'mosaic' or 'jigsaw' of information about those bodies. This argument gives rise to the theory that such disclosures cause 'mosaic prejudice' because apparently innocuous information connected with security and intelligence matters can prove to be acutely revealing when read in conjunction with other pieces of the mosaic or when used as the basis for deductions and inferences about gaps in the picture.[262] Most of the domestic judicial dicta dealing with the dangers of mosaic prejudice have arisen in relation to the need for the brightline rule mentioned above and have stressed the particular risks run by individuals who attempt to assess for themselves how an intended disclosure will add to the public mosaic.[263] It could therefore be argued that the force of these dicta diminishes in the freedom of information context, where decisions to disclose can be taken by or in consultation with the security bodies.[264] Against this, a pre-

258 *AG v Blake* [2001] 1 AC 268 at 287 (Lord Nicholls); *R v Shayler (David)* [2002] UKHL 11, [2003] 1 AC 247 at [100] (Lord Hutton); *AG v Shayler* [2006] EWHC 2285.

259 See §26– 035(5).

260 For example S Rimington, *Open Secret: The Autobiography of the Former Director General of MI5* (Hutchinson, London, 2001). Refusals of authorisation to publish are judicially reviewable see: *AG v Guardian Newspapers Ltd (No 2)* [1990] 1 AC 109 at 163 (Scott J, Ch); *R v Shayler (David)* [2002] UKHL 11, [2003] 1 AC 247 at [31]-[35] (Lord Bingham) at [72]-[85] (Lord Hope) and at [107]-[116] (Lord Hutton); *'R' v AG for England and Wales* [2003] UKPC 22, [2003] EMLR 499 at [36] (Lord Hoffmann); *AG v Shayler* [2006] EWHC 2285; *R (A) v Director of Establishments of the Security Service* [2009] UKSC 12, [2010] 2 AC 1.

261 See §26– 037(2), (3) and (6).

262 See §§6– 024 to 6– 025 for a general discussion of 'mosaic prejudice'. The Government certainly regarded mosaic prejudice as a live issue when it published the consultation paper *Freedom of Information: Consultation on Draft Legislation* (Cm 4355, 1999). As mentioned above, cl 19(3) of the draft Bill annexed to this paper contained an express 'jigsaw puzzle' exemption which would have ensured the non-disclosure of apparently harmless information which might be harmful when looked at in conjunction with other pieces of the wider puzzle: 'Where, in relation to any information ("the information requested"), exemption from section 8(1)(b)-(a) is not required for the purpose of safeguarding national security, but (b) would be required for that purpose if any other information (whether or not held by the public authority and whether or not accessible, or likely to become accessible, to members of the public) became available at the same time or subsequently, the exemption shall be taken for the purposes of this section to be required for that purpose in relation to the information requested'. This draft provision was criticised for being too broad (eg House of Lords Draft Freedom of Information Bill Select Committee First Report Session 1998-1999, *Report from the Select Committee Appointed to Consider the Draft Freedom of Information Bill* (HL 97) 1999, paras 36-37: see Ch 1 n 43) and was not repeated in the Freedom of Information Bill introduced in the House of Commons on 18 November 1999.

263 In relation to unauthorised disclosures see: *AG v Guardian Newspapers Ltd (No 2)* [1990] 1 AC 109 at 269, 'What may appear to the writer to be trivial may in fact be the one missing piece in the jigsaw sought by some hostile intelligence agency' (Lord Griffiths); *R v Shayler (David)* [2002] UKHL 11, [2003] 1 AC 247 at [101], 'such a decision [ie whether a disclosure would or would not be damaging] could not safely be left to that individual because he may not have a full appreciation of how that piece of information fits into a wider picture and of what effect the disclosure might have on other aspects of the work of the service of which he is unaware or of which he lacks a full appreciation' (Lord Hutton).

264 The courts in the US and Australia have usually endorsed the mosaic approach to prejudice in relation to national security exemption claims in the freedom of information context. Because the security bodies in the US (eg the CIA) do not enjoy the institutional exclusion enjoyed by their UK counterparts under the FOIA, 'mosaic prejudice'

disclosure assessment and authorisation process might not entail a particularly effective use of time and resources within the security bodies and it would not provide total immunity from mosaic prejudice in any event. While the security bodies can evaluate the pieces of the mosaic they know to be in the public domain and the extent to which a particular disclosure would add to the overall publicly accessible picture, they cannot know every piece of information held by hostile forces and individuals (which may not be in the public domain but may make the proposed disclosure more damaging) and they cannot predict the subsequent emergence of further pieces of information which will elucidate the picture even further.

(2) *Countervailing human rights.* A more defensive argument in support of the absolutist approach takes the need for secrecy and the risk of mosaic prejudice as its starting point before asserting that there is no human rights based reason for taking a more qualified approach. The need to act compatibly with 'Convention rights' within the meaning of the Human Rights Act 1998[265] or rights under European Community law that can be relied upon before the domestic courts,[266] may require that disclosures of information are considered

---

has been accepted by the courts in a way that secures a similar result to institutional exclusion. Because the absolute exclusion of security bodies has been otherwise secured in the UK, it is suggested that caution must be exercised before transposing the principles and reasoning of US decisions on 'mosaic prejudice' to information held by public authorities in the UK. The standard authorities on 'mosaic prejudice' in the US are: *Halperin v CIA*, 629 F 2d 144, 150 (DC Cir 1980) ('each individual piece of intelligence information, much like a piece of a jigsaw puzzle, may aid in piecing together other bits of information even when the individual piece is not of obvious importance in itself'); *Salisbury v United States*, 690 F 2d 966, 971 (DC Cir 1982) (referring to the 'mosaic-like nature of intelligence gathering'); *American Friends Services Committee v Department of Defense*, 831 F 2d 441, 444-45 (3d Cir 1987) ('compilation' theory); *Taylor v Department of the Army*, 684 F 2d 99, 105 (DC Cir 1982); *National Security Archive v FBI*, 759 F Supp 872, 877 (DDC 1991) (held that disclosure of code names and designator phrases could provide a hostile intelligence analyst with a 'common denominator' permitting the analyst to piece together seemingly unrelated data into a snapshot of specific FBI counter-intelligence activity); *Jan-Xin Zang v FBI*, 756 F Supp 705, 709-10 (WDNY 1991) (upholding classification of any source-identifying word or phrase, which could by itself or in aggregate lead to disclosure of an intelligence source); *Berman v CIA*, 378 F Supp 2d 1209 at 1215-1217 and 1222 (ED Cal 2005); *Edmonds v US Department of Justice*, 405 F Supp 2d 23, 33 (DDC 2005), holding that the mosaic theory 'comports with the legal framework'; *American Civil Liberties Union v Department of Justice*, 321 F Supp 2d 24, 37 (DDC 2004) where, in holding that the Department of Justice could withhold statistical intelligence-collection data, the court commented that 'even aggregate data is revealing', and concluded that disclosure 'could permit hostile governments to accurately evaluate the FBI's counterintelligence capabilities'; *Bassiouni v CIA*, 392 F 3d 244, 246 (7th Cir 2004) ('when a pattern of responses itself reveals classified information, the only way to keep secrets is to maintain silence uniformly'); *Center for National Security Studies v US Department of Justice*, 331 F 3d 918, 928 (DC Cir 2003) ('[a] complete list of names informing terrorists of every suspect detained by the government at any point during the September 11 investigation' could 'allow terrorists to better evade the ongoing investigation and more easily formulate or revise counter-efforts'; *ACLU v Dept of Justice*, 681 F 3d 61, 71 (2d Cir 2012). Mosaic prejudice is also now recognised in the USA by Executive Order 13,526, para 1.7(e). In relation to Australia see: *Re Low and Department of Defence* (1984) 2 AAR 142 at 149; *Re Actors' Equity Association of Australia and Australian Broadcasting Tribunal (No 2)* (1985) 7 ALD 584; *Re Robinson and Department of Foreign Affairs* (1986) 11 ALN N48; *Re Throssell and Australian Archives* (1986) 10 ALD 403 at 406-407; *Re Throssell and Department of Foreign Affairs* (1987) 14 ALD 296; *Re Slater and Cox (Director General, Australian Archives)* (1988) 15 ALD 20 at 27; *Re McKnight v Australian Archives* (1992) 28 ALD 95 at 112; *Re Ewer and Australian Archives* (1995) 38 ALD 789; *Re Dunn and Department of Defence* [2004] AATA 1040. A mechanical application or an unquestioning acceptance of all claims of mosaic prejudice will, of course, emasculate the rights given by FOIA. See Pozen, 'The Mosaic Theory, National Security and the Freedom of Information Act' (2005) 115 *Yale LJ* 628.

265 Human Rights Act 1998 s 1(1)-(3), Sch 1 define 'the Convention rights' for the purposes of that Act as the rights and fundamental freedoms set out in Arts 2-12 and 14 of the Convention for the Protection of Human Rights and Fundamental Freedoms (Cmd 8969, 1953) ('ECHR') and Arts 1-3 of the First Protocol and Arts 1-2 of the Sixth Protocol thereto. The ECHR, Arts 1 and 13 are notable omissions from 'the Convention rights'. Primary and subordinate legislation must, so far as possible, be read and given effect in a way which is compatible with the Convention rights (s 3) and it is unlawful for public authorities (including courts and tribunals) to act in a way which is incompatible with them unless left with no alternative by primary legislation (s 6).

266 In this regard, reliance can be placed on Community law in accordance with the doctrine of direct effect including the subsidiary or related doctrines of vertical, indirect and incidental direct effect: P Craig and G De Búrca, *EU Law: Text, Cases and Materials*, 6th edn (London, Oxford University Press, 2015) chs 7-9; D Wyatt and A Dashwood, *European Union Law*, 6th edn (Oxford, Hart, 2011) Ch 8. In particular, the doctrine of incidental direct effect requires that national law implementing Directives is interpreted and applied in accordance with Community law and norms and is therefore relevant to DPA 2018 (insofar as it supplements the GDPR and implements the LED)

by reference to a harm or prejudice test where such rights are in play. In this way, the following are capable of requiring a public authority to allow or authorise the disclosure of information:

- — the right to life under Art 2 of the ECHR;[267]
- — the right to a fair trial under Art 6 of the ECHR;[268]
- — the right to respect for private and family life under Art 8 of the ECHR;[269]
- — the right to freedom of expression under Art 10 of the ECHR;[270] and
- — corresponding rights under CFR, the GDPR and the LED.

Although none of these rights is absolute and each of them may have to give way to the requirements of national security,[271] their engagement effectively requires that the competing interests involved be weighed against each other before a final decision is taken on disclosure. The engagement of these rights thus precludes the adoption of an absolutist approach to secrecy and requires that non-disclosure be supported by some evidence of the harm that disclosure would cause.[272] When it comes to general requests for information under FOIA, however, there are unlikely to be any countervailing rights in play as neither the ECHR nor Community law confers a general right of access to information; an absolutist approach may therefore be seen as less objectionable.[273] It should also be

and EIR (implementing European Community Public Access to Environmental Information Directive 2003/4/EC): Case 14/83 *Von Colson v Land Nordrhein-Westfalen* [1984] ECR 1891; Case C-106/89 *Marleasing SA v La Comercial Internacional de Alimentacion SA* [1990] ECR I-4135; Cases C-240-244/98 *Océano Grupo Editorial v Rocio Murciano Quintero* [2000] ECR I-4491; Craig 'Directives: Direct Effect, Indirect Effect and the Construction of National Legislation' (1997) 22 EL Rev 519; see §5– 037. In relation to the interpretation of DPA 1998 see in particular: *Campbell v MGN Ltd* [2002] EWCA Civ 1373, [2003] QB 633 at [96] (Phillips MR); *Durant v Financial Services Authority* [2003] EWCA Civ 1746, [2004] FSR 28 at [3]-[4] (Auld LJ); *Common Services Agency v IC* [2008] UKHL 47, [2008] 1 WLR 1550 at [7], [20]-[27] (Lord Hope), [82] (Lord Rodger), [91] (Baroness Hale); *South Lanarkshire Council v Scottish IC* [2013] UKSC 55, [2013] 1 WLR 2421 at [7]-[8] (Baroness Hale, giving the judgment of the Court); *Vidal Hall v Google Inc* [2015] EWCA Civ 311, [2016] QB 1003; *Lloyd v Google LLC* [2019] EWCA Civ 1599, [2020] EMLR 2 at [40].

267 *Öneryildiz v Turkey* (2004) 39 EHRR 12 (ECtHR) at [84]; affirmed at (2005) 41 EHRR 20 (ECtHR) (GC) at [62], [90]. See further §4– 023.

268 *R (S) v Plymouth City Council* [2002] EWCA Civ 388, [2002] 1 WLR 2583; *McGinley and Egan v United Kingdom* (1998) 27 EHRR 1 (ECtHR). See further §4– 022.

269 *Gaskin v United Kingdom* (1989) 12 EHRR 36 (ECtHR) at [60]; *Botta v Italy* (1998) 26 EHRR 241 (ECtHR); *Guerra v Italy* (1998) 26 EHRR 357 (ECtHR) at [60]; *McGinley and Egan v United Kingdom* (1998) 27 EHRR 1, 4 BHRC 421, (1998) 42 BMLR 123 (ECtHR) at [101] and [103]; *R (S) v Plymouth City Council* [2002] EWCA Civ 388, [2002] 1 WLR 2583, [2002] 1 FLR 1177, [2002] BLGR 565; *MG v United Kingdom* [2002] 3 FCR 289, (2003) 36 EHRR 3 (ECtHR); *Craxi v Italy (No1)* (2004) 28 EHRR 47 (ECtHR); *Roche v United Kingdom* (2006) 42 EHRR 30 (ECtHR). See further §§4– 005 to 4– 010.

270 See fn 260 in connection with requests for authority to publish service memoirs by former members of the security bodies.

271 In relation to ECHR Art 6 see: §§4– 005 to 4– 010; *Fayed v United Kingdom* (1994) 18 EHRR 393 (ECtHR) at [65]-[67]; *Tinnelly and Sons Ltd v United Kingdom* (1999) 27 EHRR 249, 4 BHRC 393 (ECtHR) at [74]; *Lithgow v United Kingdom* (1986) 8 EHRR 329 (ECtHR) at [194]. In relation to ECHR, Arts 8 and 10 see: ECHR, Arts 8(2) and 10(2). In relation to personal data rights see: GDPR Art 23; LED recitals (44) and (62) and Arts 13 and 15-16; DPA 2018 ss 26, 28, 44-45, 48, 68 and 110.

272 Establishing a real risk of mosaic prejudice may or may not suffice in this regard, but there is no automatic presumption that it will and each case must be dealt with on its merits.

273 Although the right to freedom of expression under ECHR Art 10 includes 'the right to receive and impart information and ideas without interference,' the domestic courts have refused to recognise it conferring any right of access to information: *R (Persey) v Secretary of State for the Environment, Food and Rural Affairs* [2002] EWHC 371 (Admin), [2003] QB 794 (DC) at [52]-[53] (Simon Brown LJ); *R (Howard) v Secretary of State for Health (Note)* [2002] EWHC 396 (Admin), [2003] QB 830 at [103] (Scott Baker J); *BBC, Petitioners (No 2)* 2000 JC 521; *Sugar v BBC (No 2)* [2012] UKSC 4, [2012] 1 WLR 439 at [94]-[98 (Lord Brown); *Kennedy v Charity Commission* [2014] UKSC 20, [2015] AC 455 at [91]-[92], [96], [101], [144]]-[148] and [154}; *cf R (Wagstaff) v Secretary of State for Health* [2001] 1 WLR 292 (DC). Contrast the developing jurisprudence from the ECtHR which now recognises that right in certain circumstances (considered at §§4– 015-4– 021). See further Sir Stephen Sedley, 'Information as a Human Right' in J Beatson and Y Cripps (eds), *Freedom of Expression and Freedom of Information: Essays in Honour of Sir David*

remembered that in circumstances where countervailing rights operate in other contexts to require the disclosure of information supplied by, or relating to, the security bodies, it may nevertheless be possible to restrict the number of people to whom that information is disclosed, thus minimising the risk of mosaic prejudice;[274] such measures cannot be taken under FOIA.[275]

26– 037 Accountability & supervision

Having set out the high level of secrecy conferred on the security bodies, the wider institutional and constitutional context in which they operate needs to be understood. This context will help determine the practical consequences of the security bodies' exclusion from FOIA regime in terms of the effect it has on other public authorities and the accessibility of information more generally. The extent to which the security bodies are subject to authorities and mechanisms allowing for the oversight and regulation of their work is also critical to an evaluation of two interdependent issues: first, the effectiveness and transparency of their public accountability and, secondly, the justifiability of their institutional exclusion from FOIA regime. In terms of the ancillary security bodies, the RIPA, IOCA, SSA and ISA Tribunals, the Security Vetting Appeals Panel, the Security Commission and the ISCP are themselves oversight bodies, whilst NCA is subject to the complaints and misconduct regimes operated by the Independent Office for Police Conduct in England and Wales, the Police Investigations and Review Commissioner for Scotland and the Police Ombudsman for Northern Ireland.[276] In terms of the principal security bodies, an amount of accountability and supervision is provided by some of the ancillary security bodies, as has already been mentioned, together with (1) the Comptroller and Auditor General and National Audit Office, (2) the Investigatory Powers Commissioner, (3) the Parliamentary Commissioner for Administration and, in more limited circumstances, (4) the Privy Council. In addition to this, (5) the various Cabinet Office Committees have an oversight role in relation to the intelligence services.[277] A brief outline of the functions of the seven additional oversight bodies follows:

(1) *The Comptroller and Auditor General.* The Comptroller and Auditor General and the National Audit Office are listed as a 'public authorities' in Part VI of Sch 1 to FOIA and they supervise, and therefore hold information about, the security bodies and their sponsoring departments.[278] Since 1994 the government has brought forward in

---

Williams (Oxford, Oxford University Press, 2000).

274 Even where the disclosure of confidential information is required on public interest grounds, the courts recognise that this does not necessarily extend to publication to the world at large and may be limited to the police or appropriate regulators: *AG v Guardian Newspapers Ltd (No 2)* [1990] 1 AC 109 at 269 (Lord Griffiths) and 283 (Lord Goff); *Francome v MGN Ltd* [1984] 1 WLR 892; *Re a Company's Application* [1989] Ch 477; *ABC v Telegraph Media Group Ltd* [2018] EWCA Civ 2329, [2019] EMLR 5. *cf Initial Services Ltd v Putterill* [1968] 1 QB 396 at 405-406; *Lion Laboratories Ltd v Evans* [1985] QB 526; *Barrymore v News Group Newspapers Ltd* [1997] FSR 600 at 603; *London Regional Transport v Mayor of London* [2001] EWCA Civ 1491, [2003] EMLR 4. See also §26– 035(5) on the restrictions that may be placed on the collateral and onward use of materials disclosed in legal proceedings.

275 See §§6– 027 to 6– 028.

276 Police Reform Act 2002 Pt 2; Police, Public Order and Criminal Justice (Scotland) Act 2006 (Act of the Scottish Parliament) Pt 1 Ch 2; Police (Northern Ireland) Act 1998 Pt VII.

277 For a proposed set of standards in this regard, see generally the 'Principles of Oversight and Accountability for Security Services in a Constitutional Democracy' published in July 1997 by the Center for National Security Studies, Washington and the Helsinki Foundation for Human Rights, Warsaw. The special forces are not subject to any equivalent Committees or Commissions, although the House of Commons Defence Select Committee examines the expenditure, administration and policy of the Ministry of Defence: HC Standing Order, No 152; A Bradley, K Ewing and C Knight, *Constitutional and Administrative Law*, 17th edn (London, Pearson, 2018) pp 216-218; O Hood Phillips and P Jackson, *Constitutional and Administrative Law*, 8th edn (London, Sweet & Maxwell, 2001) paras 12-029 to 12-033.

278 National Audit Act 1983; *Halsbury's Laws of England*, 5th edn, 2014, vol 20, title 'Constitutional and Administrative Law', paras 492-494 and 496-497; O Hood Phillips and P Jackson, *Constitutional and Administrative Law*, 8th edn

a single published vote, known as the Single Intelligence Account, the aggregate expenditure and budget provision for the intelligence services in a form that is 'fully open to scrutiny by the Comptroller and Auditor General, apart from limited restrictions to protect the identities of certain sources of information and the details of particularly sensitive operations'.[279] The Single Intelligence Account is decided by Ministers through the biennial Spending Review mechanism and has the Prime Minister's National Security Adviser as its Accounting Officer.[280] The total allocation for the intelligence services is made known to Parliament and the public, but the details (including the apportionment to each service) are only revealed to the Comptroller and Auditor General, the ISCP and the Chairman of the House of Commons Public Account Committee.[281]

(2) *The Investigatory Powers Commissioner*. The Investigatory Powers Act 2016 established a new Investigatory Powers Commissioner in place of the former Intelligence Services Commissioner, Interception of Communications Commissioner and Surveillance Commissioners established by the Regulation of Investigatory Powers Act 2000.[282] Like each of his predecessors, the Investigatory Powers Commissioner is not listed as a 'public authority' in Sch 1 to the Freedom of Information Act 2000. The Investigatory Powers Commissioner and the other Judicial Commissioners who support him (known collectively for the purposes of the 2016 Act as 'the Judicial Commissioners') are appointed by the Prime Minister and exercise approval and oversight functions under various enactments in relation to the authorisation of specific uses of regulated investigatory powers.[283] The Investigatory Powers Commissioner must also keep under more general review (including by way of audit,

---

(London, Sweet & Maxwell, 2001) paras 12-018 to 12-019.

279 Hansard HC vol 233 col 52 (24 November 1993) (written answer by the Prime Minister, Mr Major, to a Parliamentary Question tabled by Mr Robinson). See: Cabinet Office, *National Intelligence Machinery*, 5th edn (London, TSO, 2010) pp 4-5; Cabinet Office, *Security and Intelligence Agencies Financial Statement 2017-18* (HC 1509) 2018 pp 3-9.

280 The Cabinet Secretary acted as Accounting Officer until 1 August 2002 when the role was transferred to the newly created Cabinet Office Security and Intelligence Co-ordinator. This post was renamed 'Permanent Secretary, Intelligence, Security and Resilience', and merged with the Chairmanship of the Joint Intelligence Committee with effect from the appointment to both positions of Sir Richard Mottram on 14 November 2005 (Cabinet Office, *National Intelligence Machinery*, 5th edn (London, TSO, 2010) p 22; *Intelligence and Security Committee Annual Report 2005-2006* (Cm 6864, 2006) paras 7-12). The Cabinet Secretary thenresumed responsibility for the Single Intelligence Account in 2007 when the functions of the Permanent Secretary, Intelligence, Security and Resilience were split between a separate Chairman of the Joint Intelligence Committee and Head of Intelligence Assessment, on the one hand, and a Security Adviser to the Prime Minister and Cabinet Secretary known as the Head of Intelligence, Security and Resilience, on the other; Intelligence and Security Committee Annual Report 2006-2007 (Cm 7299, 2008) paras 73-74; Intelligence and Security Committee Annual Report 2007-2008 (Cm 7542, 2009) paras 129-133. Following the general election in 2010, the Coalition Government further reformed the central government arrangements for co-ordinating and managing the national intelligence machinery. These reforms included the creation of a new ministerial National Security Council and the appointment of a National Security Adviser as its secretary. The first National Security Adviser was appointed on 12 May 2010 and he inherited the role of the Principal Accounting Officer for the Single Intelligence Account: see *Intelligence and Security Committee Annual Report 2010-2011* (Cm 8114, 2011) paras 125-129 and 135-139.

281 Intelligence and Security Committee, *Intelligence Oversight* (London, 2002), p 8; Cabinet Office, *National Intelligence Machinery*, 5th edn (London, TSO, 2010) pp 4-5. Security Service Act 1989 s 2(3A)(b) permits the disclosure of information by the Security Service to the Comptroller and Auditor General. Intelligence Services Act 1994 ss 2(3)(b) and 4(3)(b) permit the disclosure of information by SIS and GCHQ respectively to the Comptroller and Auditor General.

282 Investigatory Powers Act 2016 Pt 8 Ch 1 (see esp ss 227 and 240). The former Intelligence Services Commissioner had in turn replaced the Security Service Commissioner and the Intelligence Services Commissioner established by the Security Service Act 1989 and Intelligence Services Act 1994 respectively (Regulation of Investigatory Powers Act 2000 ss 59-60). The former Interception of Communications Commissioner had likewise replaced the identically named Commissioner established under the Interception of Communications Act 1985 s 8.

283 Investigatory Powers Act 2016 ss 227, 233.

inspection and investigation):

— the exercise by public authorities of statutory functions relating to the interception of communications, the acquisition or retention of communications data, the obtaining of related communications data and equipment interference; the acquisition, retention, use or disclosure of bulk personal datasets by the intelligence services;
— the giving and operation of national security notices under s 252 of the Investigatory Powers Act 2016;
— the exercise of certain functions relating to communications involving prisoners; the exercise by public authorities of functions by virtue of Pts 2-3 of the Regulation of Investigatory Powers Act 2000 (surveillance, covert human intelligence sources and investigation of electronic data protected by encryption etc.); the adequacy of security arrangements under s 55 of the Regulation of Investigatory Powers Act 2000;
— the exercise by public authorities of functions by virtue of the Regulation of Investigatory Powers (Scotland) Act 2000 (Act of the Scottish Parliament) (surveillance and covert human intelligence sources);
— the exercise by the police of functions under Pt 3 of the Police Act 1997 (authorisation of action in respect of property); and the exercise by the Secretary of State and Scottish Ministers of functions under ss 5-7 of the Intelligence Services Act 1994 (warrants for interference with wireless telegraphy, entry and interference with property etc).[284]

Many of the aforementioned functions are exercisable by or empower the intelligence services, armed forces and NCA, amongst others. Section 230 of the Investigatory Powers Act 2016 further empowers the Prime Minister to issue directions requiring the Investigatory Powers Commissioner to keep under review the carrying out of any aspect of the functions of the intelligence services or, so far as engaging in intelligence activities, the armed forces or the Ministry of Defence.[285] The Commissioner may also accept referrals from ISCP recommending a specific investigation, inspection or audit.[286] Sections 235 and 237 of the Investigatory Powers Act 2016 empower the Judicial Commissioners to carry out investigations, inspections or audits, oblige public

[284] Investigatory Powers Act 2016 s 229.

[285] The Investigatory Powers Act 2016 s 230 replicates the Regulation of Investigatory Powers Act 2000 s 59A (additional functions of the Intelligence Services Commissioner) inserted by the Justice and Security Act 2013 s 5 with effect from 25 June 2013. The Prime Minister is obliged to publish directions issued under the Investigatory Powers Act 2016 s 230 (and any revocation thereof) save in so far as this would be contrary to the public interest or prejudicial to national security or related interests (s 230(4)). Two such directions dated 22 August 2017 were announced by the Prime Minister Mrs Theresa May in a written statement to Parliament (Hansard HC vol 636 col 34WS (1 March 2018)): the Investigatory Powers Commissioner (Additional Directed Oversight Functions) (Consolidated Guidance) Direction 2017 (instructing the Commissioner to keep under review compliance with the Consolidated Guidance on Detainees dated 6 July 2010 by the intelligence services and armed forces and, so far as they are engaged in intelligence activities, members of the Ministry of Defence, see *R (Equality and Human Rights Commission) v Prime Minister* [2011] EWHC 2401 (Admin), [2012] 1 WLR 1389 (DC)); and the Investigatory Powers Commissioner (Additional Directed Oversight Functions) (Security Service Agent Participation in Criminality) Direction 2017 (instructing the Commissioner to keep under review the application of the Security Service guidelines on the use of agents who participate in criminality and the authorisations issued in accordance with them). Oversight by the former Intelligence Services Commissioner of compliance with the Consolidated Guidance began on an extra-statutory basis in 2009 (see written statement to Parliament of the Prime Minister Mr Gordon Brown, Hansard HC vol 489 cols S5WS-S6WS (18 March 2009) and *Report of the Intelligence Services Commissioner for 2010* (HC 1240) 2010 para 28) and was placed on a statutory basis under the Regulation of Investigatory Powers Act 2000 s 59A in 2014 (see the Intelligence Services Commissioner (Additional Directed Oversight Functions) (Consolidated Guidance) Direction 2014, written statement of the Prime Minister Mr David Cameron, Hansard HC vol 588 col WS33 (27 November 2014) and *Report of the Intelligence Services Commissioner for 2014* (HC 225) (2015) Appendix 8).

[286] Investigatory Powers Act 2016 s 229.

authorities and others to provide information, assistance and access and create an 'information gateway' authorising disclosures of information, provided these do not breach 'the data protection legislation'.[287] The Investigatory Powers Commissioner must make annual and (on request or as he considers appropriate) other reports to the Prime Minister and she must in turn publish and present to Parliament the Commissioner's annual reports, excluding any parts whose publication would be contrary to the public interest or prejudicial to national security or related interests.[288]

(3) *The Parliamentary Commissioner for Administration.* The Parliamentary Commissioner for Administration[289] has a limited role to play in relation to the oversight of the security bodies: none of the security bodies is directly subject to his investigative remit (save for NCA which may only be investigated in respect of the exercise of certain asset recovery functions);[290] and, although their sponsoring departments are subject to such investigation,[291] various security and defence related matters are nevertheless excluded.[292] As a 'public authority' listed in Part VI of Sch 1 to FOIA, the Parliamentary Commissioner for Administration may be asked to disclose information, but his ability to do so will be subject to the exemptions in Part II of that Act and the provisions on onward disclosure in s 11 of the Parliamentary Commissioner Act 1967.[293] The Parliamentary Commissioner for Administration may also exchange certain types of information with the Information Commissioner[294]

---

287 The Judicial Commissioners are likewise obliged to give the RIPA Tribunal all such documents, information and other assistance as the Tribunal may require in connection with its investigation, consideration or determination of any matter (Investigatory Powers Act 2016 s 232(1)).

288 Investigatory Powers Act 2016 s 234.

289 Parliamentary Commissioner Act 1967; A Bradley, K Ewing and C Knight, *Constitutional and Administrative Law*, 17th edn (London, Pearson, 2018) pp 629-637; O Hood Phillips and P Jackson, *Constitutional and Administrative Law*, 8th edn (London, Sweet & Maxwell, 2001) paras 34-005 to 34-014.

290 Save for NCA, none of the security bodies is listed as a government department, corporation or unincorporated body subject to investigation by the Commissioner in the Parliamentary Commissioner Act 1967, Sch 2 and it follows that action taken by or on behalf of the security bodies in the exercise of their administrative functions cannot be investigated under the Parliamentary Commissioner Act 1967 s 5. In relation to the limited coverage of NCA, see Parliamentary Commissioner Act 1967 Sch 2 n 14.

291 Parliamentary Commissioner Act 1967 Sch 2. The list includes the Cabinet Office (not including any of the Secretariats (including intelligence and security functions carried out by the Chairman of the Joint Intelligence Committee and the Prime Minister's Security Adviser respectively) or the office of the Secretary of the Cabinet: Parliamentary Commissioner Act 1967, Sch 2, n 3), Foreign and Commonwealth Office, Home Office and Ministry of Defence (including the Defence Council, Admiralty Board, Army Board and Air Force Board: Parliamentary Commissioner Act 1967 Sch 2, n 11).

292 Parliamentary Commissioner Act 1967 s 5, Sch 4, paras 1-5. The Parliamentary Commissioner Act 1967 s 11(3) does envisage the Commissioner having access to documents or information whose disclosure might be prejudicial to the safety of the State or otherwise contrary to the public interest and if he did investigate or obtain security or defence information he could, in theory, disclose it to others but only for certain specified purposes (including the purposes of the investigation in question and of any report to be made thereon) and subject also to any notices in writing given by a Minister of the Crown specifying documents or information or classes of documents or information whose disclosure would, in the opinion of the Minister, be prejudicial to the safety of the State or otherwise contrary to the public interest (s 11(2)-(3)).

293 These provisions effectively prevent the disclosure under FOIA of any information obtained by the Parliamentary Commissioner for Administration in the course of or for the purposes of an investigation under the Parliamentary Commissioner Act 1967. See also FOIA s 44. The provisions on ministerial notices in Parliamentary Commissioner Act 1967 s 11(3) do not apply in relation to disclosures made by the Parliamentary Commissioner for Administration under FOIA, as they only operate to prevent the Parliamentary Commissioner Act 1967 from being construed as authorising or requiring the disclosure of any document or information specified in a relevant notice. This is unlikely to be significant, however, as FOIA, Pt II and Parliamentary Commissioner Act 1967 s 11(2) will almost inevitably prevent the disclosure of any information that might have been covered by a ministerial notice under Parliamentary Commissioner Act 1967 s 11(3).

294 FOIA s 76(1) (disclosure by the Information Commissioner) and Parliamentary Commissioner Act 1967 s 11AA (disclosure by the Parliamentary Commissioner for Administration) (inserted by FOIA Sch 7 para 2 and amended by the DPA 2018 Sch 19(1) para 3). The Information Commissioner may disclose to the Parliamentary

and provide him with information which relates to certain matters within the Information Commissioner's remit or the commission of certain offences under FOIA or the DPA 2018.[295]

(4) *The Privy Council.* Issues of constitutional importance, including issues connected with security and defence matters, are sometimes referred to ad hoc committees of the Privy Council for advice. In this way, public service security arrangements,[296] the legal basis for and practice relating to telephone tapping,[297] government policy towards the Falkland Islands prior to Argentina's invasion in 1982,[298] intelligence on weapons of mass destruction[299] and the use of intercepted material as evidence in court[300] have been reviewed by such committees. One reason for referring such matters to the Privy Council is that Privy Counsellors take an oath on appointment binding them not to disclose anything said or done 'in Council' without the consent of the Sovereign and sensitive information can therefore be disclosed to them on 'Privy Counsellor terms'.[301] A further reason is that committees of the Privy Council can be political and yet non-partisan and can also examine the work of past administrations.[302] It would appear that the Privy Council is not a 'public authority' for the purposes of FOIA.[303]

(5) *Cabinet Office Committees.* Previous editions of this work referred at this point to a

Commissioner for Administration information obtained by, or furnished to, him under or for the purposes of FOIA or 'the data protection legislation' if it appears to him to relate to a matter which could be the subject of an investigation by the Parliamentary Commissioner for Administration (FOIA s 76(1)). Information obtained by the Parliamentary Commissioner for Administration by virtue of this provision is nevertheless subject to Parliamentary Commissioner Act 1967 s 11(2)-(3) on onward disclosure and ministerial notices: Parliamentary Commissioner Act 1967 s 11(5), inserted by FOIA Sch 7 para 1.

295 Parliamentary Commissioner Act 1967 s 11AA (inserted by FOIA Sch 7 para 2). The disclosure of information by the Parliamentary Commissioner for Administration under this provision is nevertheless subject to Parliamentary Commissioner Act 1967 s 11(3) on ministerial notices (Parliamentary Commissioner Act 1967 s 11AA(2)). While such disclosure need not be made for a purpose specified in Parliamentary Commissioner Act 1967 s 11(2), a Minister of the Crown may prevent it by giving the Parliamentary Commissioner for Administration notice in writing under Parliamentary Commissioner Act 1967 s 11(3) that disclosure would, in his or her opinion, be prejudicial to the safety of the State or otherwise contrary to the public interest (see also FOIA s 44).

296 A committee, convened in the aftermath of the Burgess and Maclean defections, was in fact referred to as a conference of Privy Counsellors. For the background see Hansard HC vol 545 col 1609 (7 November 1955) and Hansard HC vol 546 col 1462 (23 November1955). Its report was not published, but a summary was made public (Cmnd 9715, 1956).

297 *Report of the Privy Councillors appointed to inquire into the interception of communications* (Cmnd 283, 1957) (Birkett Report).

298 *Falkland Islands Review: Report of a Committee of Privy Counsellors* (Cmnd 8787, 1983). The Prime Minister, Mrs Thatcher, consulted five former Prime Ministers to secure their consent to the committee on Falkland Islands policy having access to the papers of previous governments and secret intelligence assessments. See: A Bradley, K Ewing and C Knight, *Constitutional and Administrative Law*, 17th edn (London, Pearson, 2018) p 283; Lord Hunt, 'Access to a Previous Government's Papers' [1982] *Public Law* 514; Hansard HC vol 26 col 1039 (1 July 1982); Hansard HC vol 27 col 469 (8 July 1982).

299 *Review of Intelligence on Weapons of Mass Destruction* (HC 898) 2004 (Butler Report).

300 *Report of the Privy Council of Intercept as Evidence* (Cm 7324, 2008).

301 *Halsbury's Laws of England*, 5th edn, 2014, vol 20, title 'Constitutional and Administrative Law', para 269; A Bradley, K Ewing and C Knight, *Constitutional and Administrative Law*, 17th edn (London, Pearson, 2018) pp 282-284; O Hood Phillips and P Jackson, *Constitutional and Administrative Law*, 8th edn (London, Sweet & Maxwell, 2001) para 16-003.

302 I Leigh and L Lustgarten, 'The Security Commission: Constitutional Achievement or Curiosity' [1991] *Public Law* 215 at 216.

303 The Privy Council is not listed in FOIA Sch 1 and it cannot easily be described as a 'body or authority exercising statutory functions on behalf of the Crown' and thus a 'government department' for the purposes of s 84, Sch 1, Pt I, para 1. However, the Privy Council Office which, under the Lord President of the Council, is responsible for preparing business for the Privy Council and its committees has been described as, to a certain extent, 'a real administrative department': *Halsbury's Laws of England*, 4th edn, 1996 re-issue, vol 8(2), title 'Constitutional Law and Human Rights', para 526 (language not repeated in 5th edn). See also §26– 012, n 89 on the 'immunity' of certain Crown bodies from the provisions of FOIA.

Ministerial Committee on the Intelligence Services chaired by the Prime Minister, which comprised the Deputy Prime Minister, the Defence, Foreign and Home Secretaries and the Chancellor of the Exchequer and had the following terms of reference: 'to keep under review policy on the security and intelligence services'.[304] This Ministerial Committee was itself assisted by a Permanent Secretaries' Committee on the Intelligence Services, which was chaired by the Cabinet Office Permanent Secretary, Intelligence, Security and Resilience, and which provided advice periodically on intelligence collection requirements, the intelligence services' programmes and expenditure and other issues related to intelligence.[305] The non-statutory management and supervision by central government, particularly the Cabinet Office, of the intelligence services and matters of 'intelligence policy' has since undergone significant administrative reform. First there was a Ministerial Committee on National Security, International Relations and Development with an Intelligence Sub-Committee (comprising the Prime Minister, Chancellor of the Exchequer and Foreign, Home and Defence Secretaries) and a corresponding Permanent Secretaries' Committee and Sub-Committee at official level. These were in turn supported by a National Security Secretariat and a Security and Intelligence Directorate within the Cabinet (itself established in 2007).[306] Further reforms were initiated by the Coalition Government immediately following the general election in 2010.[307] A ministerial National Security Council and a non-ministerial National Security Adviser now 'oversee all aspects of national security.'[308] The Prime Minister chairs the National Security Council[309] and appoints the National Security Adviser, who acts as the Secretary to the Council and heads the National Security Secretariat which supports the Council. The National Security Council agrees an Intelligence Coverage and Effects ('ICE') Plan on an annual basis, determining the priorities for SIS and GCHQ.[310] None of these Committees is excluded from FOIA regime (they would appear to be parts of the Cabinet Office, which is a public authority for the purposes of Sch 1 to that Act)[311] and their practical importance is difficult to judge.

26–038 Other intelligence machinery

One notable feature of the approach taken to the security bodies is the omission from the list specified in s 23(3) of FOIA of two other bodies which undoubtedly deal with security matters

---

304 Cabinet Office, *National Intelligence Machinery*, 4th edn (London, TSO, 2006) p 17.

305 Cabinet Office, *National Intelligence Machinery*, 4th edn (London, TSO, 2006) p 18. The Cabinet Secretary acted as Chairman of the Committee until 1 August 2002, when the duty was transferred to the newly created Cabinet Office Security and Intelligence Co-ordinator. This post was renamed Permanent Secretary, Intelligence, Security and Resilience and merged with the Chairmanship of the Joint Intelligence Committee with effect from the appointment to both positions of Sir Richard Mottram on 14 November 2005 (Cabinet Office, *National Intelligence Machinery*, 4th edn (London, TSO, 2006) p 22; *Intelligence and Security Committee Annual Report 2005-2006* (Cm 6864, 2006) paras 7-12).

306 Cabinet Office, *The National Security Strategy of the United Kingdom: Security in an Interdependent World* (CM 7291, 2008); Cabinet Office, *The National Security Strategy of the United Kingdom: Update 2009: Security for the Next Generation* (CM 7590, 2009), Cabinet Office, *Improving the Central Intelligence Machinery* (2009) paras 35-36, Annex 1.

307 Cabinet Office, *National Intelligence Machinery*, 5th ed (London, 2010) pp 16-21; *Intelligence and Security Committee Annual Report 2010-2011* (Cm 8114, 2011) paras 125-129 and 135-138; *Intelligence and Security Committee Annual Reports 2011-2012* (Cm 8403, 2012) paras 22-24.

308 *Intelligence and Security Committee Annual Report 2010-2011* (Cm 8114, 2011) para 125.

309 Although styled a 'Council' and not a 'Committee', the National Security Council is effectively a Cabinet Office Committee. The most important Cabinet Ministers are permanent members of the National Security Council and it has ministerial sub-committees covering various subjects.

310 ISCP, *Annual Report 2016-2017* (HC 655) 2017, pp 47-48.

311 FOIA s 84, Sch 1, Pt 1, para 1. See also FOIA s 35(4) on 'committees of the Cabinet'.

and which complete the government's 'national intelligence machinery',[312] namely, the Defence Intelligence Staff ('DIS') and the Joint Intelligence Committee ('JIC'):[313]

(1) *The Defence Intelligence Staff.* In the official government publication *National Intelligence Machinery* the DIS is dealt with under the heading, 'the intelligence and security agencies', but treated not as an additional intelligence service as such, but as 'an essential element' of the national intelligence machinery.[314] The DIS is a part of the Ministry of Defence funded out of the Defence Votes that was created in 1964 by the amalgamation of the Navy, Army and Air Force intelligence staffs and the civilian Joint Intelligence Bureau.[315] The DIS does not have any statutory basis or identity but its tasks are to analyse information, from both overt and covert sources, and to provide intelligence assessments, advice and strategic warning to the JIC, the Ministry of Defence, military commands and deployed forces.[316] The DIS also has responsibility for two separate organisations, Defence Geospatial Intelligence and the Defence Intelligence and Security Centre, which are responsible for providing imagery, geographic products and intelligence training.[317] The Defence Secretary is responsible for the DIS and its operations are controlled by the Chief of Defence Intelligence who reports to the Chief of the Defence Staff and the Permanent Secretary of the Ministry of Defence and who is also a Deputy Chairman of the JIC.[318]

(2) *The Joint Intelligence Committee.* The JIC is a part of the Cabinet Office which also has no statutory basis or identity.[319] The JIC is chaired by a Chairman who is also the Professional Head of Intelligence Analysis and it comprises: senior officials in the Foreign and Commonwealth Office, Home Office, Ministry of Defence, Department of Business, Innovation & Skills, and HM Treasury; the heads of the intelligence services; the Chief of the Assessments Staff; and its Deputy Chairman, the Chief of Defence Intelligence.[320] The JIC is designed to bring an overall coherence to the

---

312 *Intelligence and Security Committee Annual Report 1999-2000* (Cm 4897, 2000) paras 17-23; *Government Response to the Intelligence and Security Committee's Annual Report 1999-2000* (Cm 5013, 2000) paras 5-9; Cabinet Office, *National Intelligence Machinery* (4th edn, TSO, London, 2006); *Intelligence and Security Committee Annual Report 2001-2002* (Cm 5542, 2002) paras 8-12.

313 For these purposes, references to the JIC should be read as a compendious short-hand for the entirety of the central intelligence machinery within the Cabinet Office which comprises the JIC itself, the Chairman of the JIC and Head of Intelligence Assessment, and their supporting staff.

314 Cabinet Office, *National Intelligence Machinery*, 5th edn (London, 2010) pp 13-14. See: Ministry of Defence, *The Defence Intelligence Staff* (2005); *Inquiry into the Export of Defence Equipment and Dual Use Goods to Iraq and Related Prosecutions* (HC 115) 1995-1996, para C2.26 (Scott Report); A Bradley, K Ewing and C Knight, *Constitutional and Administrative Law*, 17th edn (London, Pearson, 2018) pp 522-523. ICSP, *Annual Report 2016-2017* (HC 655) 2017, para 278 said 'there might be an argument for [DIS] becoming the fourth agency alongside MI5, SIS and GCHQ, but that DIS was itself opposed to this.

315 Cabinet Office, *National Intelligence Machinery*, 5th edn (London, 2010) p 14. This followed the enactment of the Defence (Transfer of Functions) Act 1964 and the creation of a unified Secretary of State for Defence and Ministry of Defence: *Halsbury's Laws of England*, 4th edn, 1996 re-issue, vol 8(2), title 'Constitutional Law and Human Rights', paras 439-447.

316 Cabinet Office, *National Intelligence Machinery*, 5th edn, (London, 2010) p 13.

317 Cabinet Office, *National Intelligence Machinery*, 5th edn, (London, 2010) p 13; Ministry of Defence, *The Defence Intelligence Staff* (2005), p 6.

318 Cabinet Office, *National Intelligence Machinery*, 2nd edn (London, HMSO, 2001) pp 11-12.

319 Parliamentary Commissioner Act 1967 Sch 2 n 2 formally acknowledges the existence of the Joint Intelligence Committee in providing that the Cabinet Office does not include, for the purposes of its being a department subject to investigation by the Parliamentary Commissioner for Administration, 'any of the Secretariats (including the intelligence and security functions carried out by the Chairman of the Joint Intelligence Committee and the Prime Minister's Security Adviser, respectively) or the office of the Secretary of the Cabinet': revised wording substituted by Parliamentary Commissioner Order 2008 SI 2008/3115 Sch 2 with effect from 12 November 2009.

320 Cabinet Office, *National Intelligence Machinery*, 5th edn, (London, 2010) p 23.

tasking of the intelligence services, the assessment of their product and the determination of their resource needs and performance.[321] To this end, the JIC's main outputs are intelligence assessments and briefs produced using secret intelligence and open-source material for ministers and officials and, secondly, it establishes the Government's requirements and priorities for secret intelligence.[322] The JIC thus advises on priorities for intelligence gathering and provides ministers and senior officials with assessments of the resulting intelligence in the fields of security, defence and foreign affairs and is supported by the Assessments Staff.[323]

Neither the DIS nor the JIC is listed as a 'public authority' in Sch 1 to FOIA but, as already mentioned, they are parts of the Ministry of Defence and Cabinet Office respectively which are both 'public authorities' for these purposes.[324] It follows that neither the DIS nor the JIC is institutionally excluded from FOIA regime.

26– 039SCOPE programme

According to the previous Intelligence and Security Committee's annual report for 2005-2006:

> SCOPE is a major IT programme designed to enable organisations across the intelligence community to improve fundamentally the way they work together, by transferring data electronically in a secure and timely manner. SCOPE has ten departmental and agency partners who contribute to its costs and share oversight of its development. The programme is directed and managed by the Cabinet Office, while support services will be provided from two locations outside London.[325]

The 'partners' referred to were the three intelligence services, the former SOCA and six

---

321 Cabinet Office, *National Intelligence Machinery*, 5th edn, (London, 2010) pp 22-26 and 36-38; *Review of Intelligence on Weapons of Mass Destruction* (HC 898) 2004 (Butler Report); *Review of Intelligence on Weapons of Mass Destruction: Implementation of its Conclusions* (Cm 6492, 2005); Hansard HC vol 432 col 432 (23 March 2005); *Intelligence and Security Committee Annual Report 2012-2013* (HC 547) paras 97-100. Lord Butler's Review of Intelligence on Weapons of Mass Destruction, published in 2004, concluded that there should be a clear separation between the formulation of intelligence policy (which comes under the National Security Council and Secretariat) and intelligence analysis and assessment (which is led by the JIC).

322 On the current role and status of the JIC's requirements and priorities see: *Intelligence and Security Committee Annual Report 2010-2011* (Cm 8114, 2011) paras 139-142; *Intelligence and Security Committee Annual Report 2011-2012* (Cm 8403, 2012) paras 29-34.

323 The JIC's full terms of reference were revised in October 2009 in light of Cabinet Office, *Improving the Central Intelligence Machinery* (2009) (and related reforms) and now reads as follows: 'The role of the Joint Intelligence Committee is: To assess events and situations relating to external affairs, defence, terrorism, major international criminal activity, scientific, technical and international economic matters and other transnational issues, drawing on secret intelligence, diplomatic reporting and open source material; To monitor and give early warning of the development of direct and indirect threats and opportunities in those fields to British interests or policies and to the international community as a whole; To keep under review threats to security at home and overseas and to deal with such security problems as may be referred to it; To contribute to the formulation of statements of the requirements and priorities for intelligence gathering and other tasks to be conducted by the Intelligence Agencies; To maintain oversight of the intelligence community's analytical capability through the Professional Head of Intelligence Analysis; To maintain liaison with Commonwealth and foreign intelligence organisations as appropriate, and to consider the extent to which its product can be made available to them. Members of the Committee are to bring to the attention of their Ministers and Departments, as appropriate, assessments that appear to require operational, planning or policy action. The Chairman is specifically charged with ensuring that the Committee's monitoring and warning role is discharged effectively. The Committee may constitute such permanent and temporary sub-committees and working parties as may be required to fulfil its responsibilities.'

324 They are both 'government departments' within FOIA s 84 and Sch 1 Pt I para 1.

325 *Intelligence and Security Committee Annual Report 2005-2006* (Cm 6864, 2006) para 82. The Committee also said the following about SCOPE: 'This ambitious programme, which is aimed at fundamentally changing the way the UK Intelligence Community interacts through the introduction of a secure web-based information system, links the 10 main producers and consumers of intelligence' (*Intelligence and Security Committee Annual Report 2004-2005* (Cm 6510, 2005) para 70); 'The SCOPE programme will build on the current messaging system, the UK Intelligence Messaging Network (UKIMN), as well as delivering additional functionality, such as shared databases and the ability of the intelligence community to work across organisational boundaries' (*Intelligence and Security Committee Annual Report 2003-2004* (Cm 6240, 2004) para 116). See also *Intelligence and Security Committee Annual Report 2002-2003* (Cm 5837, 2003) paras 63-65.

government departments, namely, the Cabinet Office, the former Department of Trade and Industry, the Foreign and Commonwealth Office, the Home Office, HM Revenue and Customs and the Ministry of Defence.[326] Before becoming operational, the SCOPE system was hailed as marking 'the beginning of the end of hard copy intelligence distribution.'[327] However, although 'Phase 1' of its delivery was implemented in late 2007, 'Phase 2' was then abandoned in April 2008 and the previous Intelligence and Security Committee thereafter refrained from reporting further on its fate due to a 'contractual dispute process.'[328] Following the completion of this process, ISCP reported in 2013 that 'Phase 2' had been cancelled and the project abandoned in July 2008 after being 'beset by problems' in a 'rather sorry saga.'[329] If 'Phase 1' of SCOPE achieved any lasting practical effects, questions may arise whether a departmental partner 'holds' SCOPE information for the purposes of s 1 of FOIA and, if so, whether this was supplied by, or relates to, any of the security bodies for the purposes of s 23.

3. INFORMATION SUPPLIED BY, OR RELATING TO, THE SECURITY BODIES

26– 040 Section 23 FOIA – scope

As already indicated, information held by a public authority which was directly or indirectly supplied to it by, or which relates to, a security body is subject to an absolute exemption under s 23 of FOIA.[330] Section 1 of FOIA does not apply in respect of such information so that the duty to communicate does not arise.[331] So far as concerns the duty to confirm or deny, public authorities need not inform applicants whether they hold information covered by the s 23 exemption if, or to the extent that, this would itself involve the disclosure of information which was directly or indirectly supplied by, or which relates to, a security body, whether or not that information is already recorded.[332] In this regard, the expression 'whether or not already recorded' is significant because the term 'information' would otherwise be confined to information recorded in any form.[333] Having said this, a public authority must specify the

326 *Intelligence and Security Committee Annual Report 2005-2006* (Cm 6864, 2006) para 82.

327 *Intelligence and Security Committee Annual Report 2005-2006* (Cm 6864, 2006) para 88.

328 *Intelligence and Security Committee Annual Report 2007-2008* (Cm 7542, 2009) paras 147-150; *Intelligence and Security Committee Annual Report 2008-2009* (Cm 7807, 2010) paras 123-124; *Intelligence and Security Committee Annual Report 2009-2010* (CM 7844, 2010) pars 61-63.

329 ISCP, *Intelligence and Security Committee of Parliament Annual Report 2012-2013* (HC 547) 2013 Annex B, paras 136-142, P-Q.

330 Once a record containing particular information directly or indirectly supplied by, or relating to, a security body has been transferred to The National Archives or the Public Record Office of Northern Ireland in accordance with the Public Records Act 1958 or the Public Records Act (Northern Ireland) 1923, the exemption conferred on that information by FOIA s 23 ceases to be absolute. As a result, FOIA s 1 will not apply in respect of such information, and the duty to confirm or deny and the duty to communicate will not arise, only if the public interest in maintaining the exclusion of the relevant duty outweighs the public interest in divulging whether the public authority holds the information or in disclosing the information itself: s 64(2). The latter provision achieves this outcome by providing that, in relation to any information falling within s 23(1) which is contained in a historical record in The National Archives or the PRO of Northern Ireland s 2(3) shall have effect with the omission of the reference to s 23. In *Lownie v IC, National Archives and FCO*, FTT, 12 July 2018, the FTT found that these provisions allow for the possibility of cases where the public interest in disclosure is strong and indicate Parliament's judgment that some point the passage of time will dilute the importance of the interests protection by s 23 (at [89]). It is also important to bear in mind here that information contained in a historical record in The National Archives or the PRO of Northern Ireland cannot be exempt information by virtue of ss 21-22: s 64(1).

331 FOIA s 23(1) engages s 2(2)(a) and (3)(b) so as to prevent the duty to communicate from arising in respect of the exempt information. FOIA s 23(5) engages s 2(1)(a) and (3)(b) so as to prevent the duty to confirm or deny from arising in relation to the exempt information.

332 FOIA s 23(5).

333 FOIA s 84.

exemption relied upon when refusing to divulge or communicate information in reliance on s 23.[334] The exemption in s 23 of FOIA applies irrespective of whether the information in question is confidential, known to the applicant or wholly non-confidential.[335]

26– 041 Indirect information supply

For information supplied to a public authority by a security body to be caught by the exemption in s 23 of FOIA it need not have been obtained by the security body in the exercise of any particular function or supplied by it in writing or in confidence. The public authority holding the information need not have received it directly from the security body: it may have passed through a number of hands before indirectly reaching that authority. There is also no requirement that the information should have originated with the security body: it may simply have been supplied by that body to a third party on its way to the recipient public authority. The simple question posed in one appeal under s 57 of FOIA was 'how did the [public authority] come to have this information.'[336] One result of this is that where the same piece of information reaches authority 'A' via a security body and authority 'B' by some other non-security body route, it will be exempt from disclosure by authority 'A' under s 23 but available from authority 'B' as of right unless it relates to a security body or is subject to some other exemption in Part II of the Act. This is merely a concomitant of the institutional exemption afforded to information held by, emanating from or passing through the security bodies rather than a lapse in the protection provided by the Act. Another result is that a public authority which has received the same piece of information independently from security body and non-security body sources may nevertheless treat it as exempt under s 23. Lastly, there may be circumstances where a security body forwards information without assessing its contents or considering its dissemination in an active way or where the security body has no intention or desire that it should end up in the hands of the public authority in question: issues could then arise whether this has involved a meaningful act of 'supply to' that public authority 'by' the security body for the purposes of s 23.

26– 042 Meaning of 'relates to'

Whether information 'relates to' a security body will be a question of both fact and law.[337] The expression is conventionally used to require a link between subject and object.[338] In a number of appeals under s 57 of FOIA the Tribunal has emphasised that the expression 'relates to' should be given a 'broad interpretation.'[339] It has also offered the following definition:

---

334 FOIA s 17(1)(b) and (5). See further §§26– 058 to 26– 063.

335 See §26– 054 in relation to the relevance of confidentiality to the application of FOIA s 24. In *McCarthy v IC*, IT, 27 April 2007 at [11] the Tribunal rejected an argument that Art 2 of the ECHR (right to life) impinged upon the operation of s 23: 'Whether or not he saw the [requested information] could not affect the risk of the United Kingdom becoming involved in a conflict which might endanger his life, even if such a risk engaged his Art 2 rights, which it does not.'

336 *All Party Parliamentary Group on Extraordinary Rendition v IC and FCO*, FTT, 3 May 2012 at [59], [61] and [68]. The question falls to be answered on the balance of probabilities: *Metropolitan Police v IC*, FTT, 23 May 2010 at [20].

337 The question falls to be answered on the balance of probabilities: *Metropolitan Police v IC*, FTT, 23 May 2010 at [20].

338 In the context of considering the Scotland Act 1998 (which has been said is to be interpreted on ordinary principles, the Supreme Court has held that the phrase 'relates to' indicates more than a loose or consequential connection or a touching upon the matter: *Martin v Most* [2010] UKSC 10, 2010 SC (UKSC) 40 at [49], [159]. And similarly: *Imperial Tobacco Ltd v Lord Advocate* [2012] UKSC 61, 2013 SLT 2 at [16]; *Re Agricultural Sector (Wales) Bill* [2014] UKSC 43, [2014] 1 WLR 2622 at [50]; *Recovery of Medical Costs for Asbestos Diseases (Wales) Bill* [2015] UKSC 3, [2015] AC 1016 at [25]; *Christian Institute v Lord Advocate* [2016] UKSC 51, [2016] HRLR 19 at [29] (concerning the Data Protection Act 1998). See further the discussion and authorities at §31– 009.

339 See: *Cabinet Office v IC*, Information Tribunal, 4 June 2009 at [21]-[23] and [26]-[27]; *Dowling v IC and Police Service for Northern Ireland*, FTT, 22 February 2012 at [19]-[22] ('relates to' means more than 'identifies or in any way describe' and 'a broad interpretation of these words is therefore inevitable' subject to 'limits to be imposed by

> Applying the ordinary meaning of the words 'relates to', it is clearly only necessary to show some connection between the information and a s 23(3) security body; or that it touches or stands in some relation to such a body. Relates to does not mean 'refers to'; the latter is a narrower term.[340]

In *Corderoy v Information Commissioner*, the Upper Tribunal held that although the information contained in a record supplied to a security body for the purpose of the discharge of its statutory functions and to other non-security bodies for other purposes may be 'of interest to' and so 'relate to' the security body 'as a matter of language', it may nevertheless be possible to disaggregate parts of that information which do not 'relate to' that security body for the purpose of engaging s 23.[341] In that case, the disputed information was legal advice relating to the legality of overseas drone strikes and the Upper Tribunal held that the generic, non-operational building blocks of the legal analysis underpinning that advice did not 'relate to' the security bodies involved in specific drone strike operations. That said, the Upper Tribunal also emphasised that its conclusion rested on its understanding of the Parliamentary intention behind s 23 and the fact that the interest of security bodies in the disaggregated legal analysis was shared by Parliament and the public and the qualified exemptions in ss 35(1)(c) and 42 of the Freedom of Information Act 2000 were obviously engaged in any event.[342] The phrase 'relates to' (and cognate forms) has long been used to link the power of devolved or colonial legislatures to make laws on or about particular subject matters. In this regard s 4(1) of the Government of Ireland Act 1920 (now repealed) prevented the old Parliament of Northern Ireland from making laws 'in respect of' certain excepted matters. Phrases such as 'in respect of', 'in relation to' and 'dealing with' describe the nature and extent of the connection between a law and particular permitted or, more usually, prohibited subject matters. As a matter of ordinary construction, laws can 'relate to' more than one matter.[343] Applying these principles, one would say that information does not 'relate to' a security body if it merely 'touches on' the

---

common sense and, in a particular case, the probable ambit of the need for protection'); *All Party Parliamentary Group on Extraordinary Rendition v IC and FCO*, FTT, 3 May 2012 at [68] and [70] ('To sum up we consider that the Tribunal should adopt a broad, although purposive approach to the interpretation of s 23(1). However this should be subject to a remoteness test so that we must ask ourselves whether the disputed information is so remote from the security bodies that s 23(1) does not apply.'); *Home Office v IC and Cobain*, FTT, 30 January 2013 at [15]-[19]; *Callus v IC and Home Office*, FTT, 6 May 2014 at [39]-[41]; *University and Colleges Admissions Service v IC and Lord Lucas* [2014] UKUT 0557 (AAC) at [44]-[46] (meaning of 'relates to' in FOIA s 7(5)); *Home Office v IC and Cobain* [2014] UKUT 0306 (AAC) at [39]; *All Party Parliamentary Group on Extraordinary Rendition v IC and FCO* [2015] UKUT 0377 (AAC) at [14]-[33]; *Reprieve v IC and FCO*, FTT, 26 April 2016 at [37]-[39]; *Corderoy and Ahmed v IC and Attorney General* [2017] UKUT 0495 (AAC) at [51] [54] and [59]-[62]; *Department of Health v IC and Lewis* [2017] EWCA Civ 374, [2017] 1 WLR 3330 at [13] (Sir Terence Etherton MR) (meaning of 'relates to' in FOIA s 35(1)).

340 *All Party Parliamentary Group on Extraordinary Rendition v IC and FCO*, FTT, 3 May 2012 at [65].

341 *Corderoy and Ahmed v IC and Attorney General* [2017] UKUT 0495 (AAC) at [38]-[45] and [57]-[61].

342 *Corderoy and Ahmed v IC and Attorney General* [2017] UKUT 0495 (AAC) at [61]. The Upper Tribunal went on to find that the public interest in maintaining the exemptions in FOIA s 35(1)(c) (Law Officer advice) and s 42 (legal professional privilege) outweighed the public interest in disclosing the information comprising the disaggregated legal analysis.

343 See *R (Hume) v Londonderry Justices* [1972] NI 91(DC) at 110-113 (Lord Lowry CJ) (in relation to the Government of Ireland Act 1920 s 4) approving the analysis put forward in H Calvert, *Constitutional Law in Northern Ireland: a study in regional government* (London, Stevens, 1968) pp 187-196 and rejecting the approach taken in *Gallagher v Lynn* [1937] AC 863 where the 'doctrine of pith and substance' (applied in *Russell v The Queen* (1882) 7 App Cas 829 (PC) in relation to the Constitution Act 1867, formerly the British North America Act 1867) was applied at p 870 (Lord Atkin). The doctrine of pith and substance evolved in relation to the Constitution Act 1867 because that Act required that a law had to 'relate to' a particular matter within the exclusive area of either dominion or provincial legislative competence. A strained construction and search for each law's single pith and substance was thus required but in the absence of exceptional circumstances requiring such an approach, the doctrine of dual respection will ordinarily apply. Note the gloss on 'relates to' in the Scotland Act 1998 s 29(3) and the Government of Wales Act 2006, s 108A(2)(c) and (6), the general clarification of 'deals with' in the Northern Ireland Act 1998 s 98(2) and the specific qualification of 'deals with' in the Northern Ireland Act 1998, Sch 2, para 22 and Sch 3, para 42. The Supreme Court considered the relevant provisions in the Scotland Act 1998 in *Imperial Tobacco Ltd v Lord Advocate* [2012] UKSC 61, 2013 SLT 2, 2013 SCLR 121. See the discussion in §31–010, dealing with the same phrase in FOIA s 35.

body in question. However, the information need not be 'solely or mainly' concerned with or focused on that body or have that body as its 'pith and substance'. In this regard, information which relates to a security body's sources, methods, activities, plans or members, will generally relate to that body.

26– 043 Nil return information

In certain circumstances, the fact that a public authority does not hold information which was supplied to it by, or which relates to, a security body could itself reveal the lack of any security body involvement in the subject matter of the relevant information request.[344] The question may therefore arise whether the disclosure of requested information (without reference to or reliance on s 23) will thus involve the disclosure of exempt information falling within s 23 of FOIA. The answer to this may lie in the approach taken to the meaning of 'information' in s 23(1)-(2) and the effect of the reference to 'information (whether or not already recorded)' in s 23(5).[345] This can be demonstrated by reference to two hypothetical requests for information made to a government department or police authority regarding the involvement of the security bodies in a particular operation: request A asks for a list of every agency that was involved and request B asks for a list of every security body that was involved. If a security body was involved in the operation, the department or authority can respond to both requests with a partial list and a partial refusal notice which states that the authority is not obliged to confirm or deny whether it holds information relating to the involvement of the security bodies or to disclose any such information by virtue of s 23. If no security bodies were involved in the operation, however, the department or authority could only respond in the same fashion if: it holds information 'recorded in any form' which confirms the non-involvement of the security bodies;[346] or it does not hold any such information but the fact of security body non-involvement is nevertheless 'information (whether or not already recorded)' within s 23(5) and this would be disclosed if the applicant were informed that the requested information is not held. The Government takes the view that 'information (whether or not already recorded)' in s 23(5) is synonymous with 'unrecorded information' and extends to the absence of recorded information and the fact of security body non-involvement more generally.[347] It also considers that s 23(5) may therefore allow a neither confirm nor deny refusal to divulge, irrespective of whether the requested information is held and s 23(1) is engaged.

---

344 *Cabinet Office v IC*, Information Tribunal, 4 June 2009 at [15]-[22]; *All Party Parliamentary Group on Extraordinary Rendition v IC and FCO*, FTT, 3 May 2012 at [77].

345 FOIA s 84 gives 'information' the default meaning of 'information recorded in any form'. As to the meaning of 'information' as it is otherwise used in the Act, see §§20– 001 to 20– 008. FOIA ss 22(2), 23(5), 27(4)(b) and 42(2) all include references to 'any information (whether or not already recorded)' while FOIA ss 51(8) and 75(2) both refer to 'unrecorded information'. Although the two expressions would appear synonymous, it may be possible to discern some significance in the use of the different formulations, eg it could be argued that the use of 'already' confines 'any information (whether or not already recorded)' to information which is not yet recorded but which will or would be recorded at some point in the future or in the ordinary course of events.

346 FOIA s 1(4) would prevent the department or authority from generating a record of security body non-involvement (following receipt of the information request) simply to enable it to say that it therefore holds recorded information relating to the security bodies.

347 See MoJ, *Exemptions Guidance — Section 23: information supplied by, or relating to, bodies dealing with security matters*, March 2012: 'The fact that a public authority does not hold information supplied by one of the security bodies can itself be information relating to those bodies' (p 2); 'confirming that information is not held and thus that there is, or has been, no [security body] involvement in an issue can be as sensitive as confirming that there is or has been such involvement. Such information is itself information about a [security body] and is exempt under section 23' (p 3); 'The use of neither confirm nor deny may be undermined not only by confirming that there is information held (ie implying that the [security bodies] have an interest in the subject) but also by confirming that no information is held (ie implying that the [security bodies] do not have an interest. Thus, to protect from disclosure the fact that no information is held the use of section 23(5) alone or section 23(5) and section 24(2) together may be justified' (p 5). See also *Baker v IC & ors*, IT, 28 February 2007 at [34].

26– 044 GCHQ & special forces

The terms of FOIA allow scope for the composition of both GCHQ and the special forces to change over time as different units of the armed forces are transferred to or from duties assisting GCHQ or the remit of the Director of Special Forces.[348] Whether or not such transfers take place at all, questions could arise whether a unit of the armed forces was a part of GCHQ or the special forces at the time it supplied certain information or whether information relating to that unit relates to, or has ceased to relate to, GCHQ or the special forces for the purposes of s 23 of FOIA. The relevant references to units of the armed forces being part of GCHQ or the special forces 'for the time being' tend to suggest that what matters is their status as such when the information request is made. So far as concerns the supply of information, what matters for the purposes of s 23 is that the unit of the armed forces which directly or indirectly supplied the information to the public authority was a part of GCHQ or the special forces at the time it did so. The question which s 23 appears to pose, namely whether information currently relates to any of the security bodies, is capable of raising more complicated issues. On a straightforward reading, information relating to sensitive work done by a unit of the armed forces at a time when it was a part of GCHQ or the special forces will cease to be exempt under s 23 once that unit ceases to be a part of GCHQ or the special forces. By the same token, information relating to non-sensitive work done by a unit of the armed forces at a time when it was not a part of GCHQ or the special forces will be exempt under s 23 once it becomes a part of GCHQ or the special forces. These outcomes may seem counter-intuitive at first blush because the sensitive information is left unprotected and the non-sensitive information is exempt. However, past membership of GCHQ or the special forces, possibly for a very short period, cannot confer permanent 'security body' status under s 23 and the past modus operandi of a unit which has since assumed more sensitive duties may well require protection. In practice, of course, the type of information likely to be affected by such questions will very often 'relate to' the unchanging core of GCHQ or the special forces in any event and, if not exempted by s 23, there may yet be a role for ss 24 and 26 of FOIA.

26– 045 Holders of security information

Bearing in mind the functions of the security bodies set out above, it is to be expected that numerous public authorities listed in Sch 1 to FOIA will hold information which was supplied to them by, or which relates to, those bodies. Candidates include: major ministerial departments of state such as the Attorney-General's Office, Cabinet Office, Department for Communities and Local Government, Department for International Development, Department of Business, Innovation & Skills, Foreign and Commonwealth Office, Home Office, Ministry of Defence, Ministry of Justice, Northern Ireland Office and HM Treasury;

---

[348] In relation to GCHQ, see FOIA ss 23(4) and 84 (definition of 'government department') and Sch 1, Pt I, para 6(b) and note that by virtue of s 23(4) GCHQ in s 23(3)(c) includes units or parts of units of the armed forces which are 'for the time being' required to assist GCHQ. Although there is no obvious reason why FOIA s 23(4) (and the Intelligence Services Act 1994 s 3(3)) refer to units of the armed forces assisting GCHQ 'in carrying out its functions' while FOIA Sch 1, Pt I, para 6(b) refers to them assisting GCHQ 'in the exercise of its functions', it is submitted that the different formulations are intended to have the same meaning and effect. In relation to the special forces, see FOIA s 84 (definition of 'the special forces') and Sch 1, Pt I, para 6(a) and note that the special forces are those units of the armed forces (no allowance is made for parts of units) the maintenance of whose capabilities is the responsibility of the Director of Special Forces (the words 'for the time being' are not included) or which are 'for the time being' subject to the operational command of that Director. So far as concerns the words 'for the time being' being applied in relation to those units subject to the operational command of the Director of Special Forces but not in relation to those units the maintenance of whose capabilities is the responsibility of that Director, for the latter type of unit to be a part of the special forces it must nevertheless be true to say that the maintenance of its capabilities '*is* the responsibility of the Director of Special Forces'. It would therefore appear that the use or non-use of 'for the time being' is not of great significance and may simply reflect the fact that periods of 'operational command' can be of varying length whilst the maintenance of a unit's capabilities will tend to be a more long-term responsibility.

the armed forces of the Crown; non-ministerial departments and agencies such as HM Revenue and Customs, the Government Legal Department and the United Kingdom Security Vetting; law enforcement agencies and prosecuting authorities such as the police, Crown Prosecution Service and Serious Fraud Office; regulatory and financial bodies such as the Bank of England and the Financial Conduct Authority; oversight bodies such as the National Audit Office and the Parliamentary Commissioner for Administration; and a number of other public authorities such as the Armed Forces Pay Review Body, the Civil Service Appeal Board, the Defence Nuclear Safety Committee, the Diplomatic Service Appeal Board, the Imperial War Museum, the National Army Museum, the National Maritime Museum, the Royal Air Force Museum and the United Kingdom Atomic Energy Authority.

26– 046 The security & other bodies

The selection of the security bodies specified in s 23(3) of FOIA and the omission of other similar bodies raises some questions about the purpose and effect of s 23. In relation to the principal security bodies, the question arises as to why the DIS and JIC are not also institutionally excluded from FOIA regime. In relation to the RIPA, IOCA, SSA and ISA Tribunals, the Security Vetting Appeals Panel and the Security Commission, the question arises as to why information supplied by, or relating to, the Investigatory Powers Commissioner, (who has similar oversight functions and is also not a 'public authority' for the purposes of FOIA), is not also subject to the s 23 exemption. In relation to NCIS and its Service Authority, the question originally arose as to why the National Crime Squad and its Service Authority and the various police Special Branches were not also excluded from FOIA regime.[349] In constitutional terms, the answer must be that the selection of the security bodies and the treatment of other associated bodies in FOIA reflects an overall policy judgement as to the competing public interests involved. The difference of approach between, on the one hand, the ancillary security bodies, and, on the other hand, the DIS, JIC and Investigatory Powers Commissioner, is nevertheless difficult to explain: although it is easy to imagine in relation to the latter group that their designation as security bodies for the purposes of s 23 of FOIA would not have added much to its impact, it is more difficult to imagine that the non-designation of the former group would have diluted that impact to a significant degree.

4. INFORMATION WHOSE EXEMPTION IS REQUIRED FOR NATIONAL SECURITY PURPOSES

26– 047 Section 24 FOIA – scope

As already indicated, information held by a public authority which was not directly or indirectly supplied to it by, and which does not relate to, any of the security bodies is subject to a qualified exemption under s 24 of FOIA if this is required for the purpose of safeguarding national security. However, the detailed terms of the exemption require closer examination:[350]

(1) Section 24(1) renders information that does not fall within s 23(1) (ie information which was not directly or indirectly supplied by, and does not relate to, any of the security bodies) exempt information if or to the extent that exemption from the duty to communicate is required for the purpose of safeguarding national security. The

349 Albeit that the more recent inclusion in FOIA s 23 of first SOCA and now NCA has excluded the interests of the former, and now abolished, National Crime Squad from the FOIA regime, thereby expanding the scope of the institutional exclusion provided for by s 23. See §§26– 028 to 26– 029.

350 This analysis appeared in the first edition of this work and was set out in full and endorsed by the Tribunal in *Baker v IC & ors*, IT, 28 February 2007 at [30]-[33].

exemption is a qualified exemption, so that even if information falls within the description of the exemption (and is thus exempt information) it is then necessary to consider whether in all the circumstances the public interest favours disclosure of the information or maintenance of the exemption.[351] The fact that the exemption is qualified implies that there may be instances in which it will be in the public interest to disclose information, notwithstanding that exemption is required for the purpose of safeguarding national security.[352]

(2) Section 24(2) provides that 'the duty to confirm or deny does not arise if, or to the extent that, exemption from s 1(1)(a) is required for the purpose of safeguarding national security'. Unlike s 24(1), this limb of the national security exemption is not expressed to apply only to 'information which does not fall within s 23(1)'. Indeed s 24(2) is not expressed to relate to any particular category of information and it does not itself stand as a 'provision' which 'states that the duty to confirm or deny does not arise in relation to any information' for the purposes of s 2(1). As it was plainly not the intention that s 24(2) should operate independently of s 2(1),[353] s 24(2) must nevertheless be made to interact with s 2(1). This can be achieved by reading s 24 as a whole for the purposes of s 2(1), so that s 24 is itself a 'provision' which 'states that the duty to confirm or deny does not arise in relation to any information'.[354] On this basis, s 24 provides that the duty to confirm or deny does not arise in relation to information which does not fall within s 23(1) (ie information which was not directly or indirectly supplied by, and does not relate to, any of the security bodies) if, or to the extent that, exemption from s 1(1)(a) is required for the purpose of safeguarding national security. Again, the exclusion is a qualified one, so that even if the terms of s 24(2) are satisfied (and thus the duty to confirm or deny does not arise) it is then necessary to consider whether in all the circumstances the public interest favours confirmation or denial or maintenance of the exclusion.[355] As already mentioned, the fact that the exclusion is qualified implies that there may be instances in which it will be in the public interest to divulge the existence of information, notwithstanding that exclusion of that duty is required for the purpose of safeguarding national security.

26– 048Section 28 DPA 2018 – scope

As also indicated above, the DPA 2018 contains a number of exemptions which are applicable

351 FOIA s 2(2)(b).

352 Otherwise the exemption will be effectively metamorphosed into an absolute exemption.

353 The same can be said of all the other provisions in Pt II which state that the duty to confirm or deny does not arise without stating that this is the case 'in relation to any information', ie FOIA ss 22(2), 26(3), 27(4)(a), 28(3), 29(3), 31(3), 33(3), 34(2), 38(2), 41(2), 43(3) and 44(2); cf ss 23(5), 27(4)(b), 30(3), 32(3), 35(3), 36(3), 37(2), 39(2) and 42(2).

354 Reading FOIA ss 2(1) and 24(1)-(2) together in this way is consistent with s 2(3) in two respects: first, s 2(3) treats whole sections as 'provisions in Part II' for the purposes of s 2(1)-(2); and, secondly, s 2(3) does not designate s 24 as conferring absolute exemption and it is therefore clear that s 24 was intended to confer a qualified exemption subject to a public interest balancing test, which in turn requires that s 24(2) should engage s 2(1). It is further clear from FOIA s 24(3) that s 24(2) was not meant to operate independently of s 24(1): national security certificates under s 24(3) may certify that exemption from s 1(1)(b) is or was required for national security reasons (ie a duty to communicate certificate under s 24(1)) or that exemption from both s 1(1)(a) and (b) is or was required for national security reasons (ie a duty to confirm or deny and duty to communicate certificate under s 24(1) and (2)). The equivalent provision in the draft Freedom of Information Bill at *Freedom of Information: Consultation on Draft Legislation* (Cm 4355, 1999) Pt II (ie cl 19(2)) was more explicit in this regard: 'In relation to information which is exempt information by virtue of subsection (1), the duty to confirm or deny does not arise if, or to the extent that, exemption from section 8(1)(a) is required for the purpose of safeguarding national security.' The opening words '[I]n relation to information which is exempt information by virtue of subsection (1)' were not included in the equivalent provision in the Freedom of Information Bill introduced in the House of Commons on 18 November 1999 (ie cl 22(2)), but this change appears to have been a stylistic one made to all the exemptions based on the same template rather than a deliberate attempt to disengage s 2(1).

355 FOIA s 2(2)(b).

if required for the purpose of safeguarding national security: in connection with 'general processing' subject to Chapater 3 of Part 2 of the DPA 2018, s 26 disapplies various provisions of the applied GDPR and Parts 5-7 of the Act if exemption is required for the purpose of safeguarding national security;[356] in connection with 'law enforcement processing' subject to Part 3 of the DPA 2018, ss 44-45, 48 and 68 allow 'competent authorities' to restrict, wholly or partly, the provision of certain information to data subjects to the extent that and for so long as the restriction is, having regard to the fundamental rights and legitimate interests of the data subject, a necessary and proportionate measure to protect national security;[357] and, in connection with 'intelligence services processing' subject to Part 4 of the DPA 2018, s 110 disapplies various provisions of Parts 4-6 if exemption is required for the purpose of safeguarding national security.[358] Personal data may therefore be exempt from the subject access rights and other data subject rights otherwise conferred by the applied GDPR and the DPA 2018 and their other regulatory requirements if this is required for the purpose of safeguarding national security. None of these national security exemptions operates, or can be overridden, by reference to any public interest balancing test.

26–049 Regulation 12 EIR – scope

As already indicated, reg 12 of the EIR provides a qualified exception to the duty to disclose environmental information which allows public authorities to refuse to disclose information to the extent that its disclosure would adversely affect international relations, defence, national security or public safety.[359] Disclosure may only be refused on this basis if, in all the circumstances of the case, the public interest in maintaining the exception outweighs the public interest in disclosing the information.[360] If doing so would involve the disclosure of information which would adversely affect international relations, defence, national security or public safety and would not be in the public interest, the relevant public authority may also refuse to confirm or deny whether the requested information exists and is held 'whether or not it holds such information'.[361] The reg 12 exception is also made subject to a requirement that public authorities apply a presumption in favour of disclosure and this should arguably govern their

[356] The provisions listed in DPA 2018 s 26(2) are: chapter II of the applied GDPR (principles) (except for the lawfulness requirements of s 5(1)(a) and Art 6 and the special categories requirements of Art 6); all of chapter III of the applied GDPR (rights of data subjects); in chapter IV of the applied GDPR, Arts 33-34 on the notification and communication of personal data breaches; all of chapter V of the applied GDPR (transfers of personal data to third countries or international organisations); in chapter VI of the applied GDPR, Arts 57(1)(a) and (h) and 58 (functions of the Information Commissioner); chapter VIII of the applied GDPR (remedies liabilities and penalties) (except for Arts 83-84 on fines and penalties); and various provisions in DPA 2018 Pts 5-7 relating to the functions of the Information Commissioner, enforcement and supplemental matters, namely, s 115(9) (so far as it relates to Article 58(2)(i) of the applied GDPR) and ss 115(3) and (8), 119, 142-154, 170-173 and 187 and Sch 15). DPA 2018, s 28: disapplies Art 9(1) of the applied GDPR (prohibition on processing of special categories of personal data) to the extent that processing subject to the applied GDPR is carried out (a) for the purpose of safeguarding national security or for defence purposes, and (b) with appropriate safeguards for the rights and freedoms of data subjects (s 28(1)); and modifies the application of applied GDPR Art 32 (security of processing) to a data controller or data processor to the extent that it is processing personal data subject to the applied GDPR for the purpose of safeguarding national security or defence purposes (s 28(2)-(4)).

[357] DPA 2018 ss 44(4)(d), 45(4)(d), 48(3)(d) and 68(7)(d).

[358] The provisions listed in DPA 2018 s 110(2) are: Pt 4 Ch 2 (the data protection principles) (except for the lawfulness requirements of s 86(1)(a) and (2) and Schs 9-10; Pt 4 Ch 3 (rights of data subjects); in Pt 4 Ch 4, s 108 on the notification of personal data breaches; in Pt 5, s 119 and Sch 13 paras 1(a) and (g) and 2 (functions of the Information Commissioner); and in Pt 6, ss 142-154 and 170-176 on enforcement.

[359] EIR reg 12(1)(a) and (5)(a). See also EI(S)R reg 10(1)-(2) and (5)(a) applying the 'would, or would be likely to, prejudice substantially' test and an additional requirement that reg 10(4)-(5) are interpreted 'in a restrictive way' to an otherwise similarly worded national security 'exception'.

[360] EIR reg 12(1)(b). See also EI(S)R reg 10.

[361] EIR reg 12(6). See also EIR reg 12(7), 'For the purposes of a response under paragraph (6), whether information exists and is held by the public authority is itself the disclosure of information.' See also EI(S)R reg 10(8)-(9).

assessment of whether, first, disclosure would adversely affect one of the prescribed interests for the purposes of reg 12(1)(a) and, secondly, the public interest in maintaining the exception outweighs the public interest in disclosure for the purposes of reg 12(1)(b).[362] Regulation 4(3) of the EIR moreover provides that the general duty to disseminate environmental information does not extend to information which a public authority would be entitled to refuse to disclose under reg 12.

26– 050 Meaning of 'national security'

The expression 'national security' is not defined in FOIA, the DPA 2018 or the EIR and it has not been the subject of exhaustive definition in any other statutes or judicial decisions.[363] A number of general themes can, however, be extracted from a variety of sources:

(1) In 1985 the Home Office White Paper, *Interception of Communications in the United Kingdom*, stated that the interests of national security encompass 'terrorist, espionage or major subversive activity, or [the] support of the Government's defence and foreign policies.'[364]

(2) In 1988 the Prime Minister, Mrs Thatcher, stated in answer to a Parliamentary Question,

> National security is generally understood to refer to the safeguarding of the State and the community against threats to their survival or well-being. I am not aware that any previous administration has thought it appropriate to adopt a specific definition of the term.[365]

(3) The Security Service Act 1989 envisages that the protection of national security requires that it be protected against threats from espionage, terrorism and sabotage, from the activities of agents of foreign powers and from actions intended to overthrow or undermine Parliamentary democracy by political, industrial or violent means,[366] but that it does not itself extend to safeguarding the economic well-being of the United Kingdom against threats posed by the actions or intentions of persons outside the British Islands or preventing or detecting serious crime.[367]

(4) In 1991 the Report of the Security Service Commissioner for 1990 stated,

> The concept of national security however is wider than this and is not easily defined; indeed it is probably undesirable that I attempt an all-embracing definition. In my opinion it includes the defence of the realm and the government's defence and foreign policies involving the protection of vital national interests in this country and abroad. In this regard I would draw a distinction between national interest and the interests, which

---

362 EIR reg 12(2). By contrast, the 'presumption in favour of disclosure' in EI(S)R reg 10(2)(b) is to be applied by Scottish public authorities 'in considering the application of the exceptions referred to in paragraphs (4) and (5)', ie in considering whether disclosure would, or would be likely to, prejudice substantially national security for the purposes of reg 10(1)(a) but, arguably, not in considering whether the public interest in making the information available is outweighed by that in maintaining the exception for the purposes of reg 10(1)(b).

363 *Esbester v United Kingdom* (1993) 18 EHRR CD 72 (ECommHR); *Hitchens v SSHD*, IT, 4 August 2003 at [47]. See generally: L Lustgarten and I Leigh, *In From the Cold: National Security and Parliamentary Democracy* (Oxford, Oxford University Press, 1994), pp 3-35; I Cameron, *National Security and the European Convention on Human Rights* (The Hague, Kluwer Law International, 2000) pp 39-58; MoJ, *Exemptions Guidance—Section 24: National Security*, March 2012, p 3.

364 Cmnd 9438, 1985 para 21.

365 Hansard HC vol 126 col 7 (25 January 1988).

366 Security Service Act 1989 s 1(2).

367 Security Service Act 1989 s 1(3)-(4). The same distinction between the interests of national security, on the one hand, and the interests of the economic well-being of the United Kingdom and the prevention or detection of serious crime, on the other, is drawn in the Security Service Act 1989 s 2(2)(a) and the Intelligence Services Act 1994 ss 1(2), 2(2)(a), 3(2) and throughout the Regulation of Investigatory Powers Act 2000 and the Investigatory Powers Act 2016). This is also reflected in the separate provision made for the economic interests of the United Kingdom and law enforcement in FOIA ss 29-31. See further chs 19 and 20.

are not necessarily the same, of the government of the day. What is a vital national interest is a question of fact and degree, more easily recognised when being considered than defined in advance.[368]

(5) The European Commission of Human Rights and the European Court of Human Rights[369] have held that the following may pose a threat to national security and may therefore be countered in the interests of national security: disloyalty in the public services (in relation to security vetting procedures);[370] espionage;[371] inciting disaffection of military personnel;[372] indiscipline in the armed forces and the police;[373] separatist organisations;[374] subversion;[375] and terrorism.[376]

(6) *National Security and the European Convention on Human Rights* by Iain Cameron states:

> It would also seem clear that, in an era of global interdependence, the ordinary meaning of "national security" cannot be limited to the simple preservation of territorial integrity and political independence from external armed attack, or dictatorial interference by foreign powers. National security must also logically encompass espionage, economic or political, and covert (destabilising) action by foreign powers. Moreover, notwithstanding a lack of foreign involvement, purely internal threats to change the existing political order of the state by force (ie revolutionary subversion and terrorism) must also be covered. Certainly these are regarded by most if not all governments as legitimate national security concerns.[377]

(7) In *Secretary of State for the Home Department v Rehman*,[378] the House of Lords made the

---

368 Cm 1480, 1991 para 10.

369 In *Hewitt and Harman v United Kingdom* (1 September 1993) No 20317/92 (ECommHR) an application based on the ECHR Art 8 brought following the implementation of the Security Service Act 1989 was ruled inadmissible by the European Commission of Human Rights. In relation to the Security Service Act 1989 the Commission said 'the principles referred to above do not necessarily require a comprehensive definition of "the interests of national security"' and 'the Commission considers that in the present case the law is formulated with sufficient precision to enable the applicants to anticipate the role of the Security Service' (p 13).

370 *Glasenapp v Federal Republic of Germany* (1987) 9 EHRR 25 (ECtHR) at [86]-[87]; *Kosiek v Federal Republic of Germany* (1987) 9 EHRR 328 (ECtHR) at [79]-[80]; *Vogt v Federal Republic of Germany* (1996) 21 EHRR 205 (ECtHR) at [49]-[51].

371 *Klass v Federal Republic of Germany* (1978) 2 EHRR 214 (ECtHR) at [48]; *Hadjianastassiou v Greece* (1992) 16 EHRR 219 (ECtHR) at [43].

372 *Arrowsmith v United Kingdom* (1979) 19 DR 5 (ECommHR) at [24].

373 *VDSÖ and Gubi v Austria* (1995) 20 EHRR 56 (ECtHR); *Grigoriades v Greece* (1999) 27 EHRR 464 (ECtHR) at [41]; *Rekvényi v Hungary* (2000) 30 EHRR 519 (ECtHR) at [39]; *Smith and Grady v United Kingdom* (1999) 29 EHRR 493 (ECtHR); *Lustig-Prean and Beckett v United Kingdom* (2000) 29 EHRR 548 (ECtHR).

374 *United Communist Party of Turkey v Turkey* (1998) 26 EHRR 121 (ECtHR) at [39]-[41]; *Socialist Party v Turkey* (1999) 27 EHRR 51 (ECtHR) at [33]-[36].

375 *Leander v Sweden* (1987) 9 EHRR 433 (ECtHR) at [59].

376 *Klass v Federal Republic of Germany* (1978) 2 EHRR 214 (ECtHR) at [48]; *Zana v Turkey* (1999) 27 EHRR 667 (ECtHR) at [48]-[50].

377 I Cameron, *National Security and the European Convention on Human Rights* (The Hague, Kluwer Law International, 2000) p 43.

378 [2001] UKHL 47, [2003] 1 AC 153. The House of Lords approved the Court of Appeal's rejection of the narrower definition of 'national security' adopted by the Special Immigration Appeals Commission, namely, 'a person may be said to offend against national security if he engages in, promotes, or encourages violent activity which is targeted at the United Kingdom, its system of government or its people. This includes activities directed against the overthrow or destabilisation of a foreign government if that foreign government is likely to take reprisals against the United Kingdom which affect the security of the United Kingdom or of its nationals. National security extends also to situations where United Kingdom citizens are targeted, wherever they may be' (see the speeches of Lord Slynn at [2] and Lord Hoffmann at [43]). *SSHD v Rehman* [2001] UKHL 47, [2003] 1 AC 153 at [15]-[17] and [50] were referred to by the Information Tribunal under the heading 'definition of national security' in *Baker v IC & ors*, IT, 28 February 2007 at [26]. The First-tier Tribunal has adopted and applied the same definition, eg: *Kalman v IC and Dept for Transport*, FTT, 6 July 2010 at [34]; *Summers v IC and Metropolitan Police*, FTT, 24 February 2012 at [8]; *Camden Community Law Centre v IC and FCO*, 8 March 2012 at [42] ('The concept of national security is a wide one. It refers not only to actions which are aimed at, or against the United Kingdom, its system

following points: 'national security' means 'the security of the United Kingdom and its people';[379] the interests of national security are not limited to action by an individual which can be said to be 'targeted at' the United Kingdom, its system of government or its people;[380] the protection of democracy and the legal and constitutional systems of the state is a part of national security as well as military defence;[381] 'action against a foreign state may be capable indirectly of affecting the security of the United Kingdom';[382] and 'reciprocal co-operation between the United Kingdom and other states in combating international terrorism is capable of promoting the United Kingdom's national security'.[383]

(8) By way of contrast with the foregoing, the second of the 'Johannesburg Principles on National Security, Freedom of Expression and Access to Information' proposes a much narrower formulation:

> A restriction [on expression or information] sought to be justified on the ground of national security is not legitimate unless its genuine purpose and demonstrable effect is to protect a country's existence or its territorial integrity against the use or threat of force, or its capacity to respond to the use or threat of force, whether from an external source, such as a military threat, or an internal source, such as incitement to violent overthrow of the government.[384]

26– 051 Traditional approach

Throughout the twentieth century the domestic courts consistently held that national security is the primary responsibility of the executive, that the executive has the particular experience and expertise necessary to make assessments and decisions relating to national security, together with democratic responsibility for doing so, and that the courts are not in a position to question the executive in this regard once it has been shown, on credible evidence, that national security considerations are in play.[385] The degree to which these authorities suggested that national

---

of government or its people. It includes the legal and constitutional systems of this state as well as military activities. Indeed, actions against a foreign state are capable of indirectly, or directly, affecting national security.'). See also Tomkins, 'Defining and delimiting national security' (2002) 118 *Law Quarterly Review* 200 and Tomkins, 'National Security and the Role of the Court: a changed Landscape?' (2010) 126 *Law Quarterly Review* 543.

379 *SSHD v Rehman* [2001] UKHL 47, [2003] 1 AC 153 at [50] (Lord Hoffmann) and [64] (Lord Hutton). *R (Corner House Research) v Serious Fraud Office* [2008] UKHL 60, [2009] 1 AC 756 at [53] (Baroness Hale) treating national security as a threat to the safety of the nation as a nation state.

380 *SSHD v Rehman* [2001] UKHL 47, [2003] 1 AC 153 at [15] (Lord Slynn).

381 *SSHD v Rehman* [2001] UKHL 47, [2003] 1 AC 153 at [16] (Lord Slynn).

382 *SSHD v Rehman* [2001] UKHL 47, [2003] 1 AC 153 at [16]-[17] (Lord Slynn). See also at [53] and [62] (Lord Hoffmann) and [64] (Lord Hutton).

383 *SSHD v Rehman* [2001] UKHL 47, [2003] 1 AC 153 at [17] (Lord Slynn). See also *R (Corner House Research) v Serious Fraud Office* [2008] EWHC (Admin), [2009] 1 AC 756 (DC) at [139] 'National security is, to a significant extent, dependent upon co-operation with other states. That co-operation is dependent on fostering or maintaining good relations.' (Moses LJ, giving the judgment of the court) (reversed on appeal but not on this point [2008] UKHL 60, [2009] 1 AC 756).

384 Adopted on 1 October 1995 by a group of experts on international law, national security and human rights convened by Art 19, the International Centre Against Censorship, in collaboration with the Centre for Applied Legal Studies of the University of the Witwatersrand, Johannesburg: Art 19 and Liberty, *Secrets, Spies and Whistleblowers: Freedom of Expression and National Security in the United Kingdom* (London, Liberty, 2000), Appendix 1 and recommendation 4; S Coliver, 'Commentary on the Johannesburg Principles' in S Coliver (ed), *Secrecy and Liberty: National Security, Freedom of Expression and Access to Information* (Cambridge Mass, Martinus Nijdhoff, 1999). See also *SSHD v Rehman* [2001] UKHL 47, [2003] 1 AC 153 at [14] (Lord Slynn). A collective of organisations and academic centres facilitated by the Open Society Justice Initiative issued a set of 'Global Principles on National Security and the Right to Information' on 12 June 2013 (the 'Tshwane Principles'). These seek to build on the Johannesburg Principles but they expressly decline to define 'national security' and principle 2(c) states, 'It is good practice for national security, where used to limit the right to information, to be drafted precisely in a country's legal framework in a manner consistent with a democratic society.'

385 *The Zamora* [1916] 2 AC 77 (PC) at 107 'Those who are responsible for national security must be the sole judge

security was non-justiciable or that evidence of national security concerns could be demanded and reviewed to establish their bona fides and credibility varied a little from case to case, but the basic message remained the same: the courts would not interfere in the executive's assessment of national security matters.

26–052 **Proportionality approach**

The judicial organs of the ECHR[386] and the European Community[387] have taken a broadly similar approach, but, whilst they have expressly recognised and emphasised the wide margin of appreciation enjoyed by the executive in this area, they have also stressed the need for effective judicial control by means of judicial review on proportionality-based grounds. In the light of this jurisprudence, the domestic courts have recently restated and recast their approach in cases where human rights are engaged, whilst retaining the same basic respect and deference for the conclusions of the executive when it comes to national security matters.[388] In a different

of what the national security requires. It would obviously be undesirable that such matters should be made the subject of evidence in a court of law or otherwise discussed in public' (Lord Parker); *Chandler v DPP* [1964] AC 763 at 798 (Viscount Radcliffe) and 811 (Lord Devlin) (in relation to the defence of the realm); *R v SSHD, ex p Hosenball* [1977] 1 WLR 766 (CA) at 778 and 783 (Lord Denning MR) and 783-784 (Lane LJ); *Council of Civil Service Unions v Minister for the Civil Service* [1985] AC 374 at 402-403 (Lord Fraser), 404 and 406-407 (Lord Scarman), 410 and 412 (Lord Diplock), 420-421 (Lord Roskill) and 423 (Lord Brightman); *R v SSHD, ex p Ruddock* [1987] 1 WLR 1482, at 1490-1492 (Taylor J); *NHS v SSHD* [1988] Imm AR 389 (CA) at 395 (Dillon LJ); *R v Director of GCHQ, ex p Hodges* [1988] COD 123; *R v Secretary of State for Foreign & Commonwealth Affairs, ex p Everett* [1989] QB 811 (CA); *R v SSHD, ex p B, The Times*, 29 January 1991; *R v SSHD, ex p Cheblak* [1991] 1 WLR 890 (CA) at 902 and 906-907 (Lord Donaldson MR), 912 (Beldam LJ) and 916 (Nolan LJ); *R v SSHD, ex p Chabal* [1995] 1 WLR 526 (CA) at 531 and 535 (Staughton LJ); *R (Al Fawwaz) v SSHD* [2015] EWHC 166 (Admin) at [69]; *R v SSHD, ex p McQuillan* [1995] 4 All ER 400 at 424 (Sedley J); *Jahromi v SSHD* [1996] Imm AR 20 (CA) at 26 (Roch LJ). See also: Lee, 'GCHQ: Prerogative and Public Law Principles' [1985] *Public Law* 186; Morris, 'The Ban on Trade Unions at Government Communications Headquarters' [1985] *Public Law* 177; Sir Simon Brown, 'Public Interest Immunity' [1994] *Public Law* 579, 589-590; Dickson, 'Judicial Review and National Security' in B Hadfield (ed), *Judicial Review: A Thematic Approach* (Dublin, Gill & Macmillan, 1995). The same approach is taken in the USA: *Center for National Security Studies v Department of Justice* 331 F 3d 918 (DC Cir 2003) '...the courts must defer to the executive on decisions of national security...' (at 932, and see the general discussion of deference at 926-927); *LA Times Communications v Department of the Army*, 442 F Supp 880 at 899 (CD Cal 2006), stating that 'the Court defers' to army officers' evaluation of how release of information could benefit insurgents in Iraq; *Department of the Navy v Egan*, 484 US 518 at 527-530 (1988); cf Brandeis J (diss) in *Olmstead v United States*, 277 US 438 at 479 'Experience should teach us to be most on our guard to protect liberty when the Government's purposes are beneficent. Men born to freedom are naturally alert to repel invasion of their liberty by evil-minded rulers. The greatest dangers to liberty lurk in insidious encroachment by men of zeal, well-meaning but without understanding.' The Supreme Court of Canada has adopted a similar line to that taken in the United Kingdom: *Suresh v Canada (Minister of Citizenship and Immigration)* [2002] 1 SCR 3, 208 DLR (4th) 1, 37 Admin LR (3d) 159. The Australian courts, whilst acknowledging the special position of the executive in assessing matters of national security, reserve for themselves a supervisory role and have avoided express reference to their being 'deferential': *A v Hayden* [1984] HCA 67, (1984) 156 CLR 532; *Australian Communist Party v Commonwealth* [1951] HCA 5, (1951) 83 CLR 1, where Dixon J said at 188 'History and not only ancient history, shows that in countries where democratic institutions have been unconstitutionally superseded, it has been done not seldom by those holding the executive power. Forms of government may need protection from dangers likely to arise from within the institutions to be protected. In point of constitutional theory the power to legislate for the protection of an existing form of government ought not to be based on a conception, if otherwise adequate, adequate only to assist those holding power to resist or suppress obstruction or opposition or attempts to displace them or the form of government they defend.' Similar legislation was, on the other hand, upheld by a majority of the US Supreme Court in *American Communications Association v Dodds* (1950) 339 US 382.

386 *Ireland v United Kingdom* (1979-80) 2 EHRR 25 (ECtHR) at [206]; *Chahal v United Kingdom* (1997) 23 EHRR 413 (ECtHR) at [131] and [138]; *Tinnelly and Sons Ltd v United Kingdom* (1999) 27 EHRR 249 (ECtHR) at [78]; *R v Ministry of Defence, ex p Smith* [1996] QB 517 (CA) and *Smith and Grady v United Kingdom* (1999) 29 EHRR 493 (ECtHR).

387 Case 222/84 *Johnston v Chief Constable of the Royal Ulster Constabulary* [1987] QB 129 (CJEU); Case 175/94 *R v SSHD, ex p Gallagher* [1995] ECR I-4253, [1996] 1 CMLR 557 (CJEU); Case 273/97 *Sirdar v Secretary of State for Defence* [1999] ECR I-7403 (CJEU).

388 *SSHD v Rehman* [2001] UKHL 47, [2003] 1 AC 153 at [16] and [26] (Lord Slynn) and [49]-[50], [53]-[54] and [62] (Lord Hoffmann). See esp at [31], while 'issues of national security do not fall beyond the competence of the courts' it is 'self-evidently right that national courts must give great weight to the views of the executive on matters of national security' (Lord Steyn); at [50] 'the question of whether something is "in the interests" of national security is not a question of law. It is a matter of judgment and policy. Under the constitution of the United

but related context, national authorities have been given a wide, although not unfettered, margin of appreciation in determining whether there exists a 'public emergency threatening the life of the nation' so as to enable them to exercise their right to derogate from certain articles of the ECHR under Art 15(1) thereof.[389] In this context, it was stated that, 'Safeguarding national security is (with the possible exception of some questions of macro-economic policy and allocation of resources) the area of policy in which the courts are most reluctant to question or interfere with the judgment of the executive or (a fortiori) the enacted will of the legislature.'[390]

26– 053 Safeguarding national security

Based on the authorities mentioned in the two foregoing paragraphs, the executive's assessment of whether exemption from the relevant provisions of FOIA and DPA 2018 is required for the purpose of safeguarding national security will not generally be gainsaid.[391] The same goes for

Kingdom and most other countries, decisions as to whether something is or is not in the interests of national security are not a matter for judicial decision. They are entrusted to the executive' (Lord Hoffmann); and at [62] 'It is not only that the executive has access to special information and expertise in these matters. It is also that such decisions, with serious potential results for the community, require a legitimacy which can be conferred only by entrusting them to persons responsible to the community through the democratic process. If the people are to accept the consequences of such decisions, they must be made by persons whom the people have elected and whom they can remove' (Lord Hoffmann). See also: *R v DPP, ex p Kebilene* [2000] 2 AC 326 at 380-381 (Lord Hope); *Brown v Stott* [2003] 1 AC 681 (PC) at 834-835 (Lord Bingham); *A v SSHD (No 1)* [2004] UKHL 56, [2005] 2 AC 68 at [107]-[108] (Lord Hope), [154] (Lord Scott), [175]-[178] (Lord Rodger), [192]-[193] and [196]-[209] (Lord Walker diss); *R v Jones (Margaret)* [2006] UKHL 16, [2007] 1 AC 136at [30-[31] (Lord Bingham), [65]-[66] (Lord Hoffmann); *Huang v Secretary of State for Home Department* [2007] UKHL 11, [2007] 2 AC 167 at [16] (Lord Bingham giving the opinion of the Committee); *R (Corner House Research) v Serious Fraud Office* [2008] UKHL 60, [2009] 1 AC 756 at [54] (Baroness Hale); *Bank Mellat v Her Majesty's Treasury* [2013] UKSC 38, [2014] AC 700 at [21]; *R (Lord Carlile of Berriew QC) v SSHD* [2014] UKSC 60, [2015] AC 915 at [19]-[34] and [46]; *International Transport Roth GmbH v SSHD* [2002] EWCA Civ 158, [2003] QB 728 (CA) at [77] and [80]-[87] (Laws LJ); *R v SSHD, ex p Farrakhan* [2002] EWCA Civ 606, [2002] QB 1391; *Marchiori v Environment Agency* [2002] EWCA Civ 3 at [38]-[40]; *A v SSHD (No 1)* [2002] EWCA Civ 1502, [2004] QB 335 at [40] (Lord Woolf CJ) and at [66] and [81] (Brooke LJ); *R (Abbasi) v Secretary of State for Foreign & Commonwealth Affairs* [2002] EWCA Civ 1598, [2003] UKHRR 76 at [106] (Lord Phillips MR giving the judgment of the Court); *SSHD v MB* [2006] EWCA Civ 1140, [2007] QB 415; *R (Al Rawi) v Secretary of State for Foreign & Commonwealth Affairs* [2006] EWCA Civ 1279, [2008] QB 289 at [144]-[148] (Laws LJ); *R (Mohamed) v Secretary of State for Foreign and Commonwealth Affairs* [2010] EWCA Civ 65, [2011] QB 218 at [44]-[51] (Lord Judge CJ), [131]-[132], [137] (Lord Neuberger MR), [233] (Sir Anthony May); *R (Corner House Research) v Serious Fraud Office* [2008] EWHC (Admin), [2009] 1 AC 756 (DC) at [54]-[55] (Moses LJ giving the judgment of the Court) (reversed on appeal but not on this point); *Harrow Community Support Ltd v Secretary of State for Defence* [2012] EWHC 1921 (Admin) at [24]-[27] (Haddon-Cave J); *R (Secretary of State for Foreign & Commonwealth Affairs) v Assistant Deputy Coroner for Inner North London* [2013] EWHC 3724 (Admin) (DC) at [55]-[62]; *Re Freddie Scappaticci's Application* [2003] NIQB 56 at [17]-[19] (Carswell CJ) (NI); *Baker v SSHD* [2001] UKHRR 1275 at [76]; *Gosling v SSHD*, IT, 1 August 2003 at [44] and [48]. In relation to the language of 'deference' see now *R (Pro-Life Alliance) v BBC* [2003] UKHL 23, [2004] 1 AC 185 at [74]-[77] (Lord Hoffmann) and [144] (Lord Walker). Although these cases pre-date the creation of the new tribunal system, in these situations consideration does not appear to have been given to the appointment of an independent assessor to assist the tribunal evaluate matters. Section 27(1) of the Tribunals Courts and Enforcement Act 2007 provides:

> 'If it appears to the First-tier Tribunal or the Upper Tribunal that a matter before it requires special expertise not otherwise available to it, it may direct that in dealing with that matter it shall have the assistance of a person or persons appearing to it to have relevant knowledge or experience.'

389 See *Lawless v Ireland (No 3)* (1961) 1 EHRR15 (ECtHR) at para 28; *The Greek Case* (1969) 12 YB 1 (ECommHR) at [153]; *Ireland v United Kingdom* (1978) 2 EHRR 25 (ECtHR) at [207]; *Brannigan and McBride v United Kingdom* (1993) 17 EHRR 539 (ECtHR) at [43]; *A v SSHD (No 2)* [2004] UKHL 56, [2005] 2 AC 68 at [27]-[29] (Lord Bingham), [79]-[81] (Lord Nicholls), [107]-[108], [112], [115]-[119] (Lord Hope), [154] (Lord Scott), [165]-[166], [175]-[177] (Lord Rodger), [192], [196], [208] (Lord Walker) and [226] (Baroness Hale).

390 *A v SSHD (No 2)* [2004] UKHL 56, [2005] 2 AC 68 (Lord Walker, diss).

391 A need to attach 'due weight' to the executive's assessment of what is required for the purpose of safeguarding international relations and national security has been accepted in a number of appeals under FOIA, see: *All Party Parliamentary Group on Extraordinary Rendition v IC and Ministry of Defence* [2011] UKUT 153 (AAC) at [56]; *All Party Parliamentary Group on Extraordinary Rendition v IC and FCO*, FTT, 3 May 2012 at [131]; *Camden Community Law Centre v IC and FCO*, 8 March 2012 at [43]; *Transport for London v IC*, FTT, 28 February 2013 at [19]. *Blowe v IC, Home Office and Chief Constable of Greater Manchester*, FTT, 11 June 2018 at [21]. Despite this, the Information Tribunal had little difficulty in dismissing the Ministry of Defence's reliance upon s 24 in relation to an application for the directory (listing names, posts, work addresses, telephone numbers and email addresses) of the Defence Expert

its assessment of whether disclosure would adversely affect national security so as to engage the relevant exception in Part 3 of the EIR, albeit that this must be undertaken subject to a presumption in favour of disclosure.[392] In this regard, the executive may legitimately adopt a preventative or precautionary approach to the protection of national security and may consider not only direct or immediate threats but also the 'real possibility' of adverse effects on, and subsequent risks to, national security whether direct or indirect.[393] The Tribunal has accepted that 'required' in this context means 'reasonably necessary'[394] and it has posd the following alternative formulation: 'Put another way, is the exemption from the duty to disclose the requested information reasonably necessary to prevent a real and substantial increase in the risks of attack on national security.' [395] So far as concerns the communication of information or personal data under s 1(1)(b) of FOIA or the DPA 2018 the assessment to be made is simply whether non-disclosure is required for the purpose of safeguarding national security on the basis that disclosure would give rise to the real possibility of direct or indirect damage being done to national security. In relation to the dissemination or disclosure of information under regs 4(1)(a) or 5(1) of the EIR, a similar assessment is also required subject again to the presumption in favour of disclosure. However, a wider variety of factors may have to be taken into account in relation to confirmation or denial decisions under s 1(1)(a) of FOIA, the DPA 2018 or reg 12(6) of the EIR, as confirmation that a public authority holds or does not hold information or personal data of a particular description might be harmless in one case and yet give rise to damaging deductions and inferences if similar confirmation has to be withheld in another case. This may be accommodated on the basis that the public interest in disclosing whether the public authority holds information is, by itself, less compelling than the public interest in disclosing information.[396] Reference has already been made to the risk of mosaic prejudice being caused by the disclosure of information in the security and intelligence context and this will often be a factor in relation to national security assessments under s 24 of FOIA, ss 26, 44-45, 48, 68 and 110 of the DPA 2018 and reg 12 of the EIR.[397]

26– 054 Non-confidential information

Section 24 of FOIA, ss 26, 44-45, 48, 68 and 110 of the DPA 2018 and reg 12 of the EIR are all capable of conferring exemption on information or personal data that is known to the

---

Services Organisation: *Ministry of Defence v Information Commission and Evans*, IT, 20 July 2007 at [807]. *American Civil Liberties Union v Department of Defense*, 389 F Supp 2d 547 (SDNY 2005) offers a reminder of the limits to this, notwithstanding highly developed notions of deference in jurisprudence under the US Act: see §51– 008(1).

392 EIR, reg 12(1). See §26– 049.

393 *SSHD v Rehman* [2001] UKHL 47, [2003] 1 AC 153 at [16]-[17] and [22] (Lord Slynn) and [29] (Lord Steyn) (both approving *SSHD v Rehman* [2000] 3 WLR 1240 (CA) at [44] (Lord Woolf MR)); *Secretary of State for Defence v Guardian Newspapers Ltd* [1985] AC 339 at 355 (Lord Diplock), 371 (Lord Roskill) and 373 (Lord Bridge). The First-tier Tribunal has not required the threat to national security to be direct or immediate: *Kalman v IC and Dept for Transport*, FTT, 6 July 2010 at [33]-[34]; *Burt v IC*, FTT, 25 October 2011 at [39]-[40]; *Summers v IC and Metropolitan Police*, FTT, 24 February 2012 at [8]; *Transport for London v IC*, FTT, 28 February 2013 at [17]-[18]. MoJ, *Exemptions Guidance—Section 24: National Security*, March 2012, p 2 refers to the need to 'identify an undesirable effect on national security, or the risk of such an undesirable effect, that would occur if the information were released.' ICO, *Section 24: The National Security Exemption* (2012) para 9 says of the FOIA s 24 exemption: 'Required is taken to mean that the use of the exemption is reasonably necessary... "Necessary" in this context is taken to mean something less than absolutely essential but more than simply being useful or desirable...'

394 *Kalman v IC and Dept for Transport*, FTT, 6 July 2010 at [33]-[34]; *Burt v IC*, FTT, 25 October 2011 at [39]; *Summers v IC and Metropolitan Police*, FTT, 24 February 2012 at [8]; *Transport for London v IC*, FTT, 28 February 2013 at [17]-[18] and [105]. It is not easy to see how equating 'required' with 'reasonably necessary' should produce a surer result: both are evaluative and adherence to the statutory language is generally a surer course.

395 *Summers v IC and Metropolitan Police*, FTT, 24 February 2012 at [73].

396 See generally §6– 019.

397 See §26– 036(1) and references therein.

applicant or wholly non-confidential, just as much as on confidential information.[398] The question nevertheless arises whether the exemption of information which is already known to the applicant or in the public domain can realistically be required for the purpose of safeguarding national security or the disclosure of such information can be said to be capable of having an adverse affect on national security.[399] The first point to note here is that where information enters the public domain[400] without there being any official confirmation of its accuracy, it may nevertheless remain inherently unreliable.[401] Formal disclosure by a public authority will authenticate the information and thus entail the disclosure of an extra piece of information, namely, the fact that the information is true. It is therefore entirely possible for non-confidential information to attract the protection of s 24 of FOIA, ss 26, 44-45, 48, 68 or 110 of the DPA 2018 or reg 12 of the EIR. This is largely borne out by reference to the experience in the USA under the federal Freedom of Information Act 1966 (USA)[402] where the approach taken is that national security exemption claims are not undermined by a generalised allegation that classified information has been leaked to the press or otherwise made available to members of the public. Information is not considered to be in the public domain unless it has been the subject of an official disclosure.[403] Where a person seeks to defeat a national security claim for exemption on the ground that the information is in the public domain, the burden rests upon that applicant to point to specific information officially placed in the public domain that appears to duplicate[404] the withheld information.[405] Reports in the media, even

---

398 None of these provisions is expressly or implicitly confined to confidential information. See generally §6– 026.

399 DPA 2018 ss 26, 44-45, 48, 68 or 110 could require the exemption of such information, but it may be more difficult to justify this, particularly in relation to a data subject who, eg, is a former servant or agent of the intelligence services or has been subject to a prosecution involving evidence supplied by the intelligence services and who therefore knows that they hold personal data about him. In the context of the national security exemption in DPA 1998 s 33 the now-abolished Information Tribunal had recognised that establishing the need for a neither confirm nor deny response in such cases is not a foregone conclusion: *Baker v SSHD* [2001] UKHRR 1275 at [4] and [9]; *Gosling v SSHD*, IT, 1 August 2003; *Hitchens v SSHD*, IT, 4 August 2003; *Hilton v FCO*, IT, 28 June 2005.

400 In this regard, it has been said that for information to enter the public domain means 'no more than that the information in question is so generally accessible that, in all the circumstances, it cannot be regarded as confidential': *AG v Guardian Newspapers Ltd (No 2)* [1990] 1 AC 109 at 282 (Lord Goff). See also: *Northern Rock Plc v Financial Times Ltd* [2007] EWHC 2677 (QB) at [16] and [23]; *Barclays Bank plc v Guardian News & Media Ltd* [2009] EWHC 591 (QB) at [22] and [25]-[26].

401 At least while some doubt remains whether or not it is true, false or the product of speculation and that doubt is greater than that which ordinarily attaches to official information of the same kind. See the first instance judgment of Scott J in *AG v Observer Ltd* [1990] 1 AC 109 at 165: 'It is of importance to note that, save in the case of the Granada TV broadcast, none of the allegations that had previously been publicly made had been publicly made by an "insider". Mr Alexander is, in my view, entitled to say that allegations acquire, when made by an insider, a ring of authenticity that they did not previously possess.'

402 Freedom of Information Act 1966 5 USC 552(b)(1) (2000 & Supp III 2003) (USA).

403 For example, *Simmons v Department of Justice*, 796 F 2d 709, 712 (4th Cir 1986); *Abbotts v Nuclear Regulatory Commission*, 766 F 2d 604, 607-08 (DC Cir 1985); *Afshar v Department of State*, 702 F 2d 1125 (DC Cir 1983) (foreign government can ignore 'unofficial leaks and public surmise... but official acknowledgement may force a government to retaliate'); *Steinberg v Department of Justice*, 801 F Supp 800, 802 (DDC 1992) ('passage of time, media reports and informed or uninformed speculation based on statements by participants cannot be used... to undermine [government's] legitimate interest in protecting international security [information]'), affirmed at 23 F 3d 548, 553 (DC Cir 1994); *Frugone v CIA*, 169 F 3d 772 (DC Cir 1999) (disclosure by an employee of a different agency did not constitute a waiver of Exemption 1 protection); *Azmy v Dept of Defense*, 562 F Supp 2d 590, 598-599 (SDNY 2008) (although much known by the public about subject, no prior disclosure of specific information in question). cf *Lawyers Comm for Human Rights v INS*, 721 F Supp 552, 569 (SDNY 1989) (national security exemption is not available when the same documents were disclosed by foreign government or when the same information was disclosed to press in 'off-the-record exchanges').

404 It would appear that any material difference between that being requested and that which is in the public domain will allow the national security exemption to be maintained: *Public Citizen v Department of State* 11 F 3d at 199 (DC Cir 1993); *Public Citizen v Department of State*, 787 F Supp 12, 13, 15 (DDC 1992) (public Congressional testimony of the US Ambassador to Iraq did not constitute such a waiver so as to prevent the agency from invoking the national security exemption to withhold related records; his public testimony had not 'waived' Exemption 1

if widespread, about the general subject matter of the information requested will not defeat a claim for national security exemption for that type of information.[406] Public statements by former government officials do not constitute such an official disclosure,[407] 'generalised and sweeping comments' made by an official about WikiLeaks disclosures did not constitute official confirmation of their authenticity[408] and it would appear that even Congressional publications may not constitute an official disclosure.[409] Much the same conclusion has been arrived at in Australia in relation to information known to the applicant.[410]

26– 055Public interest

Even if information is rendered prima facie exempt or excepted (or if the duty to confirm or deny does not arise) for the purpose of safeguarding national security under s 24 of FOIA or because disclosure would adversely affect national security under reg 12 of the EIR, disclosure or divulgence will still have to take place under s 1 of the Act or regs 4-5 of the Regulations if, in all the circumstances of the case, the public interest in disclosure or divulgence outweighs, or is equal to, the public interest in maintaining the exemption or exception.[411] The legislative decision not to make exemption under these provisions absolute cannot properly be undone by giving the public interest in maintaining the exemption such weight as to make it automatically or intrinsically heavier than the public interest in disclosure.[412] However, whilst recognising that the exemption in s 24 of FOIA should not be seen as absolute,[413] the Tribunal has variously described the public interest in its maintenance as 'likely to be substantial'[414], as requiring 'a

protection because the context of the information in the documents was sufficiently different so as to not negate their confidentiality).

405 *Fitzgibbon v CIA*, 911 F 2d 755, 765 (DC Cir 1990); *Afshar v Department of State*, 702 F 2d 1125, 1130 (DC Cir 1983); *Billington v Department of Justice*, 11 F Supp 2d 45, 54-56 (DDC 1998); *Steinberg v Department of Justice*, 179 FRD 357, 361 (DDC 1998); *Pfeiffer v CIA*, 721 F Supp 337, 342 (DDC 1989).

406 *Schlesinger v CIA*, 591 F Supp 60, 66 (DDC 1984) (CIA records relating to Guatemala were properly classified despite the fact that the public domain contained significant information and speculation about CIA involvement in the 1954 coup in Guatemala: 'CIA clearance of books and articles, books written by former CIA officials, and general discussions in Congressional publications do not constitute official disclosures').

407 *Hudson River Sloop Clearwater, Inc v Department of the Navy*, 891 F 2d 414, 421-22 (2d Cir 1989).

408 *American Civil Liberties Union v Department of State*, 878 F Supp 2d 215, 224 (DDC 2012).

409 For example, *Salisbury v United States*, 690 F 2d 966, 971 (DC Cir 1982) (holding that inclusion of information in Senate report 'cannot be equated with disclosure by the agency itself'); *Military Audit Project v Casey*, 656 F 2d 724, 744 (DC Cir 1981) (publication of Senate report does not constitute official release of agency information).

410 *Re Reithmuller and Australian Federal Police* (1985) 8 ALN N92; *Re Robinson and Department of Foreign Affairs* (1986) 11 ALN N48 (inadvertent earlier disclosure by the agency); *Commonwealth of Australia v Hittich* (1994) 53 FCR 152; *Gersten v Minister for Immigration and Multicultural Affairs* [2000] FCA 1221, on app [2001] FCA 159.

411 FOIA s 2(1)(b) and (2)(b) and EIR reg 12(1)(b) and (6). DPA 2018 ss 26, 44-45, 48, 68 and 110 are not subject to an express public interest override provision but an assessment of the proportionality of any claim that their application is required for the purpose of safeguarding national security will nevertheless involve a similar balancing of national security interests, on the one hand, against the data subject's rights under DPA 2018 on the other hand: *Baker v SSHD* [2001] UKHRR 1275 at [63] and [83]; *Gosling v SSHD*, IT, 1 August 2003; *Hitchens v SSHD*, IT, 4 August 2003; *Hilton v FCO*, IT, 28 June 2005.

412 MoJ, *Exemptions Guidance—Section 24: National Security*, March 2012, p 5 states, 'There is obviously a very strong public interest in safeguarding national security. If non-disclosure is required to safeguard national security it is likely to be only in exceptional circumstances that consideration of other public interest factors will result in disclosure.'

413 *Kalman v IC and Dept for Transport*, FTT, 6 July 2010 at [47]; *Camden Community Law Centre v IC and FCO*, 8 March 2012 at [44].

414 *All Party Parliamentary Group on Extraordinary Rendition v IC and FCO*, FTT, 3 May 2012 at [113]; *Keane v IC* [2016] UKUT 461 (AAC) at [57]-[58]..

very strong public interest to equal or outweigh it'[415], as 'weighty'[416], as 'very weighty'[417] and 'inherently strong'[418] and as 'very great.'[419] The public interest balancing exercise must nevertheless be carried out in such a manner as to recognise that in some circumstances the public interest in disclosure will be sufficiently powerful to displace, or equal, an inherently compelling national security interest.[420] Were it assessed that the public interest in maintaining the relevant exemption and the public interest in disclosure were evenly balanced and in exact equipoise, the former could not be said to outweigh the latter and so disclosure would have to be the result: hence the above statement that disclosure must take place where the public interest in disclosure is equal to the public interest in maintaining the exemption.[421] The scales could also be made to tip in favour of disclosure or divulgence, for example, in relation to widely known non-confidential information whose exemption is nevertheless necessary for the purpose of safeguarding national security:[422] in such a case, the public interest in maintaining the exemption may have to be ascribed a more limited weight in accordance with the more limited effect it will have.

26– 056USA approach

In the US, once a document has engaged the national security exemption by being classified under the federal Freedom of Information Act 1966 (USA)[423] and the relevant Presidential Executive Order thereunder,[424] the focus of challenge becomes the propriety of this classification.[425] While the courts have over the years increased their preparedness to scrutinise claims for exemption on this ground, it remains an exemption in respect of which the courts are loath to substitute their judgment for that of the executive. In 1973 the Supreme Court[426] held that records classified under proper procedures were necessarily exempt from disclosure, without any possibility of judicial scrutiny.[427] Following this decision, Congress amended the

415 *Kalman v IC and Dept for Transport*, FTT, 6 July 2010 at [47].

416 *Summers v IC and Metropolitan Police*, FTT, 24 February 2012 at [80] and [90].

417 *Transport for London v IC*, FTT, 28 February 2013 at [115] ('Any risk to national security must be a very weighty public interest factor' even if the disputed information 'in itself is anodyne' and simply 'part of that mosaic of information which creates a real risk to national security').

418 *Dudgeon v IC and Police Service of Northern Ireland*, FTT, 3 May 2013 at [27].

419 *Dudgeon v IC and Police Service of Northern Ireland*, FTT, 3 May 2013 at [28].

420 A crucial factor here may be the engagement of legally recognised countervailing human rights (as against a more generalised public interest) favouring disclosure over non-disclosure. Such rights will not be absolute, and they are unlikely to be determinative in any event, but they will at least provide something extra of substance to go into the balance.

421 The presumption in favour of disclosure in EIR reg 12(2) could also have an effect in tipping finely balanced scales towards disclosure.

422 See §26– 054.

423 5 USC para 552(b)(1) s 6F(b) (USA).

424 Executive Order 13,526. See further §51– 008(1) and the footnotes therein. 'National security' means the national defence or foreign relations of the United States: Executive Order 12,958, para 6.1(cc).

425 Thus the issue on review is whether the classification was justified at the time that it was made and an agency may, as a matter of discretion, re-examine its classification decisions under a newly issued Executive Order in order to take into account changed international and domestic circumstances: *King v Department of Justice*, 830 F 2d 210 at 217 (DC Cir 1987). See also: *Lesar v Department of Justice*, 636 F2d 472, 481 (DC Cir 1980) (explaining that agency bears the burden of 'demonstrating proper classification under both the procedural and substantive criteria contained in the governing Executive Order'); *Schoenman v FBI*, 575 F Supp 2d 136, 151-52 (DDC 2008) (explaining that agencies must follow procedural requirements of the Executive Order in order to invoke Exemption 1); *Schoenman v FBI*, 841 F Supp 2d 69, 80 (DDC 2012) (information must be 'classified pursuant to the proper procedures and... substantively fall within the scope' of the Executive Order).

426 *EPA v Mink* 410 US 73 (1973).

427 *EPA v Mink*, 410 US 73 (1973) at 84.

Freedom of Information Act in 1974 to provide expressly for de novo review by the courts and for the in camera review of classified documents.[428] Despite these amendments, the courts, in the absence of evidence of bad faith on the part of an agency, routinely upheld agency classification decisions.[429] Although the courts subsequently increased their use of the in camera review procedures in order to facilitate full de novo reviews of national security claims even where bad faith was not an issue,[430] it was recognised that they should first 'accord substantial weight to an agency's affidavit concerning the details of the classified status of the disputed record.'[431] Provided an agency's affidavit evidence demonstrates substantive and procedural compliance with the requirements of the Executive Order and the requisite degree of particularity and does not disclose bad faith, examination of the documents by the court will either not be required or will be limited to sample documents.[432] The courts have also accepted 'mosaic' arguments and claims for exemption in relation to 'seemingly innocuous' information.[433] Claims for exemption can be supported by in camera affidavits[434] which the legal representatives of the person seeking access will not be allowed to see.[435] The courts will give substantial deference to agency expertise in national security matters[436] and have expressed

---

428 USC § 552(a)(4)(B).

429 For example, *Weissman v CIA*, 565 F 2d 692 (DC Cir 1977) at 698.

430 Starting with *Ray v Turner*, 587 F 2d 1187 (DC Cir 1978) at 1194-95.

431 *Ray v Turner*, 587 F 2d 1187 (DC Cir 1978) at 1194-95.

432 For example, *Doherty v Department of Justice*, 775 F 2d 49, 53 (2nd Cir 1985) ('the court should restrain its discretion to order in camera review'); *Hayden v National Security Agency*, 608 F 2d 1381, 1387 (DC Cir 1979) ('[w]hen the agency meets its burden by means of affidavits, in camera review is neither necessary nor appropriate'); *Public Education Center Inc v Department of Defense*, 905 F Supp 19, 22 (DDC 1995) (declining in camera review of withheld videotapes after according substantial weight to agency's affidavit that public disclosure would harm national security); *King v Department of Justice*, 586 F Supp 286, 290 (DDC 1983) (characterising in camera review as a last resort); *American Civil Liberties Union v Department of Justice*, 265 F Supp 2d 20 (DDC 2003), where the court held that the test for determining whether a document was properly classified 'is not whether the court personally agrees in full with the [agency's] evaluation of the danger – rather, the issue is whether on the whole record the Agency's judgment objectively survives the test of reasonableness, good faith, specificity, and plausibility in this field of foreign intelligence in which the [agency] is expert and given by Congress a special role'; *Larson v Department of State*, 565 F 3d857, 862 (DC Cir 2009) (holding that if agency affidavit contains 'reasonable specificity' and 'information logically falls within claimed exemption', then 'court should not conduct a more detailed inquiry to test the agency's judgment.').

433 *CIA v Sims*, 471 US 159, 179 (1985).

434 For example, *Patterson v FBI*, 893 F 2d 595, 599-600 (3d Cir 1990); *Simmons v Department. of Justice*, 796 F 2d 709, 711 (4th Cir 1986). The approach taken is that in such cases the agency is under a duty to 'create as complete a public record as is possible' before resorting to an in camera affidavit: *Phillippi v CIA*, 546 F 2d 1009, 1013 (DC Cir 1976). See also *Armstrong*, 97 F 3d at 580 (holding that when district court uses an in camera affidavit, even in national security cases, 'it must both make its reasons for doing so clear and make as much as possible of the in camera submission available to the opposing party' (citing *Lykins v Department of Justice*, 725 F 2d 1455, 1465 (DC Cir 1984)); *Patterson v FBI*, 893 F 2d 595 at 600 (3d Cir 1990); *Simmons v Department of Justice*, 796 F 2d at 710 (4th Cir 1986); *Scott v CIA*, 916 F Supp 42, 48-49 (DDC 1996) (denying request for in camera review until agency 'creates as full a public record as possible'); *Public Education Centre, Inc v Department of Defense*, 905 F Supp 19, 22 (DDC 1995) (ordering in camera review only after agency created 'as full a public record as possible').

435 *Phillippi v CIA*, 546 F 2d 1009, 1013 (DC Cir 1976).

436 For example, *Young v CIA*, 972 F 2d 536, 538-39 (4th Cir 1993) (finding district court properly deferred to agency because no evidence of bad faith); *Bowers v Department of Justice*, 930 F 2d 350, 357 (4th Cir 1991) (observing that '[w]hat fact... may compromise national security is best left to the intelligence experts'); *Doherty v Department of Justice*, 775 F 2d 49, 52 (2d Cir 1985) (according 'substantial weight' to agency declaration); *Miller v Casey*, 730 F 2d 773, 776 (DC Cir 1984) (same); *Taylor v Department of the Army*, 684 F 2d 99, 109 (DC Cir 1982) (holding that classification affidavits are entitled to 'the utmost deference') (reversing district court disclosure order); *Badalementi v Department of State*, 899 F Supp 542, 546 (D Kan 1995) (according substantial weight to agency's affidavit and granting motion for summary judgment in light of agency's expertise in national security matters); *Canning v Department of Justice*, 848 F Supp 1037, 1042 (DDC 1994) (describing how in according such deference, courts 'credit agency expertise in evaluating matters of national security by focusing attention primarily on whether affidavits are sufficiently specific and by ensuring that they are not controverted by contradictory evidence or evidence of bad faith'); *Abbotts v Nuclear Regulatory Commission*, 766 F 2d 604 (DC Cir 1985) overturning the district court's disclosure because it 'did not give the required "substantial weight" to the [agency's] uncontradicted affidavits;' ; *Edmonds v Department of Justice*, 405

a reluctance to substitute their judgment for that of the agency's 'unique insights' in the areas of national defence and foreign relations.[437] Even where the person requesting access has adduced expert evidence as to the security implications, this has not usually caused the courts to upset the agency's assessment of the national security implications of disclosure.[438] Thus, claims for exemption are generally upheld if the agency's affidavits are reasonably specific and there is no evidence of bad faith.[439] A similar degree of judicial deference to the assessments of the executive has also been shown by the Australian courts in the freedom of information context.[440]

F Supp 2d 23, 32 (DDC 2005) (explaining that '[t]his court must respect the expertise of the agency and stay within the proper limits of the judicial role in FOIA review'); *Cozen O'Connor v US Department of Treasury*, 570 F. Supp. 2d 749, 773 (ED Pa 2008) (noting that courts have 'neither the expertise nor the qualifications to determine the impact upon national security' and that a 'court must not substitute its judgment for the agency's regarding national defense or foreign policy implications'); *Miller v Department of Justice*, 562 F Supp 2d 82, 101 (DDC 2008) (noting that courts 'generally defer to agency expertise in national security matters'); *James Madison Project v CIA*, 605 F Supp 2d 99, 109 (DDC 2009) (reiterating that court grants deference to agency national security decisions and noting balance required between openness and national security); *Tarzia v Clinton*, No. 10-5654, 2012 WL 335668, at 12 (SDNY 30 January 2012) (restating court's responsibility to review agency determinations de novo while 'accord[ing] substantial deference to agency affidavits that implicate national security'); *Friedman v Secret Service*, 923 F Supp 2d 262 (DDC 2013) (acknowledging that courts 'generally defer to agency expertise in national security matters').

437 For example, *Miller v Department of State*, 779 F 2d 1378, 1387 (8th Cir 1985); *Maynard v CIA*, 986 F 2d 547, 556 n 9 (1st Cir 1993) (a court is 'not in a position to "second-guess"' agency's determination regarding need for continued classification of material); *Krikorian v Department of State*, 984 F 2d 461, 464-65 (DC Cir 1993) (where it was held that an agency has 'unique insights' in areas of national defence and foreign relations); *Willens v NSC*, 726 F Supp 325, 326-27 (DDC 1989) (where it was held that a court cannot second-guess agency's national security determinations when they are 'credible and have a rational basis'); *Azmy v Dept of Defense*, 562 F Supp 2d 590, 598-599 (SDNY 2008) (reiterating that agencies have 'unique insights' in areas of national security). But see *King v Department of Justice*, 830 F 2d 210, 226 (DC Cir 1987) (holding that trial court erred in deferring to agency's judgment that information more than 35 years old remained classified when Executive Order presumed declassification of information over 20 years old and agency merely indicated procedural compliance with Order); *Lawyers Comm for Human Rights v INS*, 721 F Supp 552, 561 (SDNY 1989) (reminding that such deference does not give agency *carte blanche* to withhold responsive documents without 'valid and thorough affidavit'). *Wolf v CIA*, 473 F 3d 370, 379 (DC Cir 2007), where the Court, in refusing to compel the CIA to confirm or deny whether it held information relating to Jorge Eliecer Gaitan (a Columbian presidential candidate who had been assassinated on 9 April 1948), said: 'it is logical to conclude that the need to assure confidentiality to a foreign source includes neither confirming nor denying the existence of records even decades after the death of the foreign national.' Similarly: *National Security Archive Fund, Inc v CIA*, 402 F Supp 2d 211, 216 (DDC 2005); *American Civil Liberties Union v US Department of Justice*, 429 F Supp 2d 179, 188 (DDC 2006), holding that 'the court must recognize that the executive branch departments responsible for national security and national defense have unique insights and special expertise concerning the kind of disclosures that may be harmful.'

438 For example, *Hudson River Sloop Clearwater, Inc v Department of the Navy*, 891 F 2d 414, 421-22 (2d Cir 1989) (retired admiral's opinion); *Gardels v CIA*, 689 F 2d 1100, 1106 n 5 (DC Cir 1982) (former agent of the CIA); *Pfeiffer v CIA*, 721 F Supp 337, 340-41 (DDC 1989) (retired CIA historian). Prior to 1986, no appellate court had ever upheld, on the substantive merits of the case, a decision to reject an agency's classification claim.

439 *Halperin v CIA*, 629 F 2d 144, 148 (DC Cir 1980); *Goldberg v Department of State*, 818 F 2d 71 (DC Cir 1987); *Schrecker v Department of Justice*, 74 F Supp 2d 26, 30 (DDC 1999); *Voinche v FBI*, 46 F Supp 2d 26, 29 (DDC 1999); *Billington v Department of Justice*, 11 F Supp 2d 45, 54, 58 (DDC 1998); *Canning v Department of Justice*, 848 F Supp 1037, 1 042-43 (DDC 1994); *Students Against Genocide v Department of State*, 257 F 3d 828 (DC Cir 2001). Thus, in *Rosenfeld v Department of Justice*, 57 F 3d 803, 807 (9th Cir 1995) the Court affirmed a district court disclosure order, finding the Government had failed to show with 'any particularity' why classified portions of several documents should be withheld. Similarly, *Wiener v FBI*, 943 F 2d 972, 978-79 (9th Cir 1991), where the applicant sought the FBI's files on John Lennon; these documented the FBI's role in the Nixon Administration's attempt to deport John Lennon in 1972; the FBI refused to disclose the information on national security grounds: Wiener, *Gimme Some Truth: The John Lennon FBI Files* (Berkeley, Univ of California Press, 2000). Also: *Oglesby v Department of the Army*, 920 F 2d 57, 66 n 12 (DC Cir 1990); *Scott v CIA*, 916 F Supp 42, 44-49 (DDC 1996).

440 *Re Maher and Attorney-General's Department* (1985) 3 AAR 396; *Re Stolpe and Department of Foreign Affairs* (1985) 9 ALD 104; *Re Fewster and Department of Prime Minister and Cabinet (No 2)* (1987) 13 ALD 139; *Re Wang and Department of Employment, Education and Training* (1988) 15 ALD 497; *Re Bayliss and Department of Health and Family Services* (1997) 48 ALD 443; *Gersten v Minister for Immigration & Multicultural Affairs* [2000] FCA 1221, [2001] FCA 159. See further §51– 015(9).

5. NATIONAL SECURITY CERTIFICATES AND THE OPERATION OF THE RELATED EXEMPTIONS

26–057 Conclusive certificates – overview

As is covered in more detail in the following paragraphs, FOIA, the DPA 2018 and the EIR all contain special provisions governing ministerial national security certificates which may be issued to certify conclusively that a national security exemption or exception applies to specified information or personal data. It is nevertheless important to recognise that the exemptions in ss 23 and 24 of FOIA and ss 26, 44-45, 48, 68 and 110 of the DPA 2018 and the exception in reg 15 of the EIR are all free-standing and may all be relied upon to justify the refusal of a request for information or personal data without recourse to a ministerial certificate.[441] The following paragraphs therefore contain general points of principle which are applicable to the operation of these provisions irrespective of whether they are engaged by way of a national security certificate.

26–058 Certificates – FOIA

National security certificates may be issued under ss 23 and 24 of FOIA as follows:

(1) Under s 23(2) of FOIA a Minister of the Crown may sign a certificate certifying that the information to which it applies was directly or indirectly supplied by, or relates to, any of the security bodies specified in s 23(3). Such a certificate will then stand as conclusive evidence of that fact (irrespective of whether it is a fact), thus confirming the engagement of the s 23 exemption, unless and until withdrawn or revoked[442] or quashed on an appeal under s 60(1) of FOIA. There is no provision allowing such a certificate to identify the information to which it applies by means of a general description or to be expressed to have prospective effect.[443] Such a certificate may only be signed by a Minister who is a member of the Cabinet or by the Attorney-General, the Advocate General for Scotland or the Attorney-General for Northern Ireland.[444]

(2) Under s 24(3) of FOIA a Minister of the Crown may sign a certificate certifying that exemption from the disclosure duty in s 1(1)(b) or from the divulgence and disclosure

---

[441] *Baker v IC & ors*, IT, 28 February 2007 at [5]: 'It should be noted that the Commissioner has reached an agreement with the Secretary of State for Constitutional Affairs acting on behalf of central government departments that a Ministerial Certificate under sections 23(2) and 24(3) would only be obtained in the event of a complaint to the Commissioner. In this case no such certificate was issued. In the Decision Notice the Commissioner welcomed the fact that the Cabinet Office had not made use of a Ministerial Certificate but, rather, had chosen to explain the reasons for its refusal in a letter to Mr Baker of 5th May 2006.' And see *Beam v IC and FCO*, IT, 12 May 2009 at [11] and [15]. See also MoJ, *Exemptions Guidance—Section 23: Information supplied by, or relating to, bodies dealing with security matters*, March 2012, pp 6-7 and MoJ, *Exemptions Guidance—Section 24: National Security*, March 2012, pp 7-8, Annexes A-B on the consequence of reliance or non-reliance on a certificate in terms of the consequences this will have for the applicable enforcement and appeals procedures.

[442] There is no obvious reason for construing FOIA ss 23(2), 24(3), 34(3) and 36(7), FOI(S)A s 31(2), DPA 2018 s 27(1), 79(1) or 111(1) or EIR reg 15(1) as preventing the withdrawal or revocation of certificates or rendering the signatories *functus officio*. Changes in circumstances may very well make the withdrawal or revocation of a certificate appropriate without the need (where this route is open) for an appeal to the Upper Tribunal. The existence of an implied power of revocation is confirmed by the language of DPA 2018 s 130(6) and Sch 20 para 17(3). See also: *Al Fayed v SSHD*, Information Tribunal, 28 February 2002 at [9] and [15]-[16]; W Wade and C Forsyth, *Administrative Law*, 11th edn (Oxford, Oxford University Press, 2014) pp 191-194; Interpretation Act 1978 s 12.

[443] Compare FOIA s 24(4), on the one hand, and DPA 1998 s 28(3) and DPA 2018 ss 27(2)(b), 79(4) and 111(2)(b), on the other.

[444] FOIA s 25(3).

duties in s 1(1)(a) and (b) is, or at any time was, required for the purpose of safeguarding national security.[445] Such a certificate will then stand as conclusive evidence of that fact (irrespective of whether it is a fact), thus confirming the engagement of the s 24 exemption subject to the application of the public interest balancing tests,[446] unless and until withdrawn or revoked or quashed on an appeal under s 60(1) or (4) of FOIA.[447] It is important to note here that such a certificate cannot certify for the purposes of s 2(1)(a) and (2)(a) of FOIA that, in all the circumstances of the case, the public interest in maintaining the exemption outweighs the public interest in divulging whether the public authority holds the information or in disclosing the information itself. The assessment and balancing of these competing facets of the public interest will therefore be subject to review by the Information Commissioner in the normal way. A national security certificate under s 24(3) may identify the information to which it applies by means of a general description and may be expressed to have prospective effect.[448] Such a certificate may only be signed by a Minister who is a member of the Cabinet or by the Attorney-General, the Advocate General for Scotland or the Attorney-General for Northern Ireland.[449]

26– 059Certificates – DPA 2018

A Minister of the Crown may sign a national security certificate under the DPA 2018 as follows: a certificate under s 27(1) certifying that exemption from all or any of the provisions of the applied GDPR or the DPA 2018 listed in s 26(2) of that Act is, or at any time was, required in relation to any personal data for the purpose of safeguarding national security; a certificate under s 79(1) certifying that a restriction on the provision of information to a data subject under ss 44(2), 45(1), 48(1)(b)(i) or 68(1) – imposed by a 'competent authority' carrying out 'law enforcement processing' subject to Part 3 of that Act - is a necessary and proportionate measure to protect national security for the purposes of ss 44(4)(d), 45(4)(d), 48(3)(d) or 68(7)(d);[450] a certificate under s 111(1) certifying that exemption from all or any of the provisions of Parts 4-6 mentioned in s 110(2) of that Act is, or at any time was, required for the purpose of safeguarding national security in respect of any personal data being processed by an intelligence service subject to Part 4. In this regard it should be noted that national security requirements may vary depending upon whether the concern is disclosure to a data subject under the DPA 2018 or disclosure to the Information Commissioner in the context of an information notice or assessment notice under ss 142 or 146 of that Act.[451] A certificate of the above kind will

---

445 FOI(S)A s 31(2)-(3). Under FOI(S)A s 31(2) a certificate may be signed by a member of the Scottish Executive and will stand as being conclusive of the fact certified (ie exemption from s 1(1) is required for the purpose of safeguarding national security): FOI(S)A does not expressly provide or allow for any appeal or review. Under FOI(S)A s 31(3), such a certificate may identify the information to which it applies by means of a general description and may be expressed to have prospective effect.

446 FOIA s 2(1)(b) and (2)(b).

447 As to appeals, see §45– 026.

448 FOIA s 24(4). Pursuant to FOIA s 60(4) a public authority may claim in proceedings under or by virtue of that Act that a certificate issued under s 24(3) which identifies the information to which it applies by means of a general description applies to particular information and, subject to any contrary determination by the Tribunal on appeal, the certificate will be conclusively presumed so to apply.

449 FOIA s 25(3).

450 Restrictions imposed under the DPA 2018 ss 44(4), 45(4), 48(3) or 68(7) may restrict the provision of information in whole or in part and to the extent that, and for so long as, necessary and proportionate having regard to the fundamental rights and interests of the data subject. DPA 2018 s 79(13) further provides that none of the enforcement powers conferred by Pt 6 of that Act may be exercised in relation to the imposition of a specific restriction in a s 79(1) certificate or a restriction falling within a general description in such a certificate.

451 See in connection with DPA 1998 s 28: *R (SSHD) v Information Tribunal* [2006] EWHC 2958 (Admin), [2007] 2 All ER 703 (DC) at [39]-[41] (Latham LJ); and the joint MoJ and ICO, *Memorandum of Understanding on National Security*

stand as conclusive evidence of the fact certified (irrespective of whether it is a fact), thus confirming the engagement of the relevant exemption, unless and until withdrawn or revoked or quashed on an appeal under s 27(3) or (5), s 79(5) or (7) or s 111(3) or (5).[452] Such a certificate: may identify the personal data to which it applies, or any restriction to which it relates, by means of a general description and may be expressed to have prospective effect;[453] and may only be signed by a Minister who is a member of the Cabinet or by the Attorney-General or the Advocate General for Scotland.[454] All national security certificates issued under ss 27, 79 and 111 of the DPA 2018 must be copied to the Information Commissioner who must then publish a record setting out the name of the issuing Minister and the date and text of each certificate, save for any text whose publication would, in the Minister's opinion, be against the interests of national security or contrary to the public interest or a risk to the safety of any person.[455]

26– 060 Certificates – EIR

Under reg 15(1) of the EIR a Minister of the Crown may certify that a refusal to disclose information under reg 12(1) is because the disclosure would adversely affect national security and would not be in the public interest.[456] For these purposes, Ministers of the Crown may designate persons to certify these matters on their behalf and a refusal to disclose information under reg 12(1) includes a neither confirm nor deny response under reg 12(6).[457] A certificate issued in accordance with reg 15(1) will then stand as conclusive evidence of the fact that disclosure would adversely affect national security and would not be in the public interest (irrespective of whether it would), unless and until withdrawn or revoked or quashed on an appeal under s 60 of FOIA.[458] A national security certificate under reg 15(1) of the EIR may identify the information to which it relates in general terms but there is no express provision allowing for such certificates to be expressed to have prospective effect.[459] The power to sign such a certificate or to designate another person to certify the relevant matters is only exercisable by a Minister who is a member of the Cabinet or by the Attorney-General, the Advocate General for Scotland or the Attorney-General for Northern Ireland.[460]

Cases (DPA) dated 2 September 2013 (setting set out guidelines on the handling and investigation by the Information Commissioner of complaints received about national security cases under DPA 1998 ss 42-43).

452 DPA 2018 ss 27(1) and (6), 79(3) and (8) and 111(1) and (6).

453 DPA 2018 ss 27(2), 79(2)(b) and (4) and 111(2). Pursuant to DPA 2018 s 27(5)-(7) a data controller may claim in proceedings under or by virtue of the applied GDPR or the DPA 2018 that a certificate under s 27(1) which identifies the personal data to which it applies by means of a general description applies to any personal data and, subject to any contrary determination of the Upper Tribunal on appeal, the certificate will be conclusively presumed so to apply. Pursuant to DPA 2018 s 79(7)-(9) a data controller may claim in proceedings under or by virtue of the DPA 2018 that a restriction under ss 44(4), 45(4), 48(3) or 68(7) falls within a general description in a certificate under s 79(1) and, subject to any contrary determination of the Upper Tribunal on appeal, the restriction will be conclusively presumed so to fall. Pursuant to DPA 2018 s 111(5)-(7) a data controller may claim in proceedings under or by virtue of the DPA 2018 that a certificate under s 111(1) which identifies the personal data to which it applies by means of a general description applies to any personal data and, subject to any contrary determination of the Upper Tribunal on appeal, the certificate will be conclusively presumed so to apply.

454 DPA 2018 ss 27(10), 79(12) and 111(10).

455 DPA 2018 s 130. As at 1 January 2019, it would appear that no such certificates have been published by the Information Commissioner.

456 See also EI(S)R reg 12.

457 EIR reg 15(2).

458 FOIA s 60 is applied for the purposes of the EIR with modifications by EIR reg 18(1), (3)-(4) and (7). As to appeals, see §45– 026.

459 Compare FOIA s 24(4) and DPA 1998 s 28(3).

460 EIR reg 15(6) giving the term 'Minister of the Crown' in reg 15(1)-(2) and (5) the same meaning as in FOIA s 25(3).

26– 061 Certificates – appeals

The circumstances in, grounds on and procedures by which national security certificates issued under ss 23(2) and 24(3) of FOIA, ss 27(1), 79(1) and 111(1) of the DPA 2018 and reg 15(1) of the EIR may be appealed to the Upper Tribunal under s 60(1) of FOIA or ss 27(3), (5), 79(5), (7) or 111(1), (3) of the DPA 2018 are dealt with elsewhere in this work.[461] For present purposes, however, the following points should be noted.

(1) The Tribunal may allow such an appeal and quash the relevant certificate if it finds: in relation to a certificate under s 23(2) of FOIA, that the information referred to in the certificate was not exempt information by virtue of s 23(1);[462] or, in relation to a certificate under s 24(3) of FOIA, s 27(1), 79(1) or 111(1) of the DPA 2018 or reg 15(1) of the EIR, that, applying the principles applied by the court on an application for judicial review, the Minister or the person designated by him did not have reasonable grounds for issuing the certificate.[463]

(2) A second type of appeal may be brought under s 60(4) of FOIA or s 27(5), 79(7) or 111(5) of the DPA 2018 by a party to any proceedings under or by virtue of the relevant Act if it is claimed by a public authority or a data controller that a certificate issued under s 24(3) of FOIA or s 27(1), 79(1) or 111(1) of the DPA 2018 which identifies the information, the personal data or the restriction to which it applies by means of a general description applies to particular information or personal data or a particular restriction. It is arguable that such an appeal may also be brought under s 60(4) of FOIA by a party to any proceedings under the EIR where similar claims are made by a public authority in relation to a certificate issued under reg 15(1) of the Regulations.[464] Appeals of this type are also dealt with elsewhere in this work, but it should be noted here that the Tribunal has power to determine that the certificate in question does not apply to the information, the personal data or the restriction referred to by the public authority or data controller.[465]

---

461 See §§5– 046, 45– 013 and 49– 016 to 49– 017. FOIA s 60 is applied for the purposes of the EIR with modifications by EIR reg 18(1), (3)-(4) and (7). Appeals under FOIA s 60, DPA 1998 s 28 and EIR reg 18(7) are governed by UT Rules.

462 FOIA s 60(2). The Tribunal is thus given full appellate jurisdiction to review the matter, unconstrained by any caveat that it 'apply the principles applied by the court on an application for judicial review' and assess only whether the minister had 'reasonable grounds for issuing the certificate' (cf FOIA s 60(3), DPA 2018 ss 27(4), 79(6) and 111(4) and EIR reg 18(7)).

463 FOIA s 60(3); DPA 2018 ss 27(4), 79(6) and 111(4); EIR reg 18(7). See further at §5– 041.

464 EIR reg 18(1), (3), (4)(a)-(b) and (7)(a). This assumes that EIR reg 18(7)(a) operates to apply FOIA s 60(4) as if the reference therein to a certificate under FOIA s 24(3) were substituted by a reference to a certificate issued in accordance with EIR reg 15(1). The interaction between these provisions is not perfect, however, as EIR reg 18(7)(a) refers to 'the reference' in FOIA s 60 to a certificate under FOIA s 24(3) when there are three such references. Moreover, EIR reg 15(3)(b) allows for a certificate to 'identify the information to which it relates in general terms' while FOIA s 60(4) applies to a certificate 'which identifies the information to which it relates by means of a general description.'

465 The Tribunal is thus given full appellate jurisdiction to review such matters unconstrained by any caveat that it 'apply the principles applied by the court on an application for judicial review' and assess only whether the Minister had 'reasonable grounds for issuing the certificate' (cf FOIA s 60(3), DPA 2018 ss 27(4), 79(6) and 111(4) and EIR reg 18(7)). The explanation for this is no doubt that the Minister can issue a new certificate with a much clearer application if dissatisfied with a determination made by the Tribunal under FOIA s 60(5) or DPA 2018 s 27(7), 79(9) or 111(7). In *Nasresfahani v SSHD and Data Controller* [2014] UKUT 0487 (AAC), the Upper Tribunal nevertheless took a more restrictive approach to the construction of its powers under the equivalent appeal provision in DPA 1998 s 28(6) given the wording of the relevant certificate under s 28(2). See at [27]: 'However, as under the certificate it is for the Security Services [sic] to determine whether or not the exemption is required for the purpose of safeguarding national security, in effect it is in our judgment a question whether the Security Services [sic] have lawfully made that determination. That is therefore also a question that is in effect to be determined on administrative law principles and in particular whether the determination failed to have regard to material considerations or was perverse or otherwise unlawful.' FOIA s 60(4) and DPA 2018 s 27(5), 79(7) and

26– 062 Neither confirm nor deny

Whether described as keeping a secret or concealing the truth, the exercise of withholding information is in substance the same. So long as questions are not asked about the information or its existence, the secret can be kept and the truth concealed, often without significant misinformation or evasion.[466] Once such questions are asked, however, the picture changes because truthful answers may betray the underlying secret. The only way to continue withholding the information is then by way of a misleading or evasive response. Where the reply must come from a public authority, a misleading response is rarely acceptable and an evasive response is therefore the only option consistent with continuing to keep the secret; this will inevitably take the form of a non-committal 'neither confirm nor deny' or 'no comment' response.[467] The picture becomes even more complicated once multiple questions may be asked, because it will then be possible to compare evasive and non-evasive responses and the questions which elicited them in order to deduce or infer the underlying existence or nature of withheld information. These complications in part stem from, and are intimately bound up with, the nature of mosaic prejudice.[468] Accommodating these considerations will tend to require that the neither confirm nor deny blanket be extended to cover all requests on a particular topic which are sufficiently specific that any variation in the use of evasive or non-evasive responses to them could give something away. Courts in the comparative jurisdictions have, in general terms, approved the adoption of a neither confirm nor deny response to statutory information requests where this is necessary to preserve the secrecy of information whose sensitivity is recognised and protected by the legislation in question.[469] The application of these principles to ss 23 and 24 of FOIA, s 26, 44-45, 48, 68 and 110 of the DPA 2018 and

111(5) only provide for the resolution by way of appeal of a dispute over a certificate's applicability where it arises, in relation to FOIA, 'in any proceedings under this Act', in relation to DPA 2018, 'in any proceeding under or by virtue of the applied GDPR or this Act' (s 27(5)) or 'under or by virtue of this Act' (ss 79(7) and 111(5)) and, in relation to EIR, 'in any proceedings under these Regulations' (see EIR reg 18(4)(a)(i)). The reason for the different formulations is unclear and their effect depends on whether the need for 'proceedings' is given a strict or generous construction; the latter would expand the scope for having disputes over a certificate's applicability resolved by the Tribunal without the procedural need for separate 'proceedings'.

466 The position may be different where there has been official disclosure of other information relating to the same subject and what is not released impinges upon the former's worth or reliability.

467 The alternative is not to answer at all, but it would then be uncertain whether the question or the answer has reached its intended recipient.

468 See §§6– 024 to 6– 025, and 26– 036(1). See also MoJ, *Exemptions Guidance—Section 24: National Security*, March 2012, Annex C and ICO, *Freedom of Information Act Awareness Guidance 21 – the duty to confirm or deny*, (2006), pp 4-5. For recent consideration of the reasons for adopting and adhering to a 'neither confirm nor deny' policy in the security and intelligence context see: *R (A) v Director of Establishments of the Security Service* [2009] UKSC 12, [2010] 2 AC 1 at [14] (Lord Brown); *DIL v Commissioner of Police of the Metropolis* [2014] EWHC 2184 (QB) at [25]-[39]; *R (Al Fawwaz) v SSHD* [2015] EWHC 166 (Admin) at [74]-[81]; *Re Freddie Scappaticci's Application* [2003] NIQB 56 at [6] and [15] (Carswell CJ) (NI); *In the matter of applications nos 187/01/62 and 107/01/77*, Investigatory Powers Tribunal. 23 January 2003 at [46]-[60]; *In the matter of applications no IPT/03/01/CH*, Investigatory Powers Tribunal, 31 March 2004 at [15]-[18]; *Frank-Steiner v Data Controller of the Secret Intelligence Service*, Investigatory Powers Tribunal, 26 February 2008 at [4] amd [45(iv)]; *Metropolitan Police v IC*, FTT, 23 May 2010 at [6], [16] and [21]-[24]; *Beasley v IC and Ministry of Defence*, FTT, 13 March 2012 at [14]-[15].

469 In the US such a response is known as a 'Glomar' response after the 'Glomar Explorer', a vessel involved in the leading case *Phillippi v CIA* 546 F 2d 1009 (DC Cir 1976). See also: Presidential Executive Order No 12,958 (as amended), para 3.6(a) 'An agency may refuse to confirm or deny the existence or non-existence of requested records whenever the fact of their existence or non-existence is itself classified under this order or its predecessors'; *Gardels v CIA* (1982) 689 Fed Rep (2d) Ser 1100. The security bodies in the USA are generally successful in defending their 'Glomar' responses: eg *Frugone v CIA*, 169 F 3d 772 (DC Cir 1999); *Wheeler v CIA*, 271 F Supp 2d 132 (DDC 2003); *Miller v Casey*, 730 F 2d 773 (DC Cir 1984); *Minier v CIA*, 88 F 3d 796 (9th Cir 1996). Somewhat atypically, in *American Civil Liberties Union v Department of Defense*, 389 F Supp 2d 547 at 561 (SDNY 2005) the Court observed that the 'danger of Glomar responses is that they encourage an unfortunate tendency of government officials to over-classify information, frequently keeping secret that which the public already knows, or that which is more embarrassing than revelatory of intelligence sources or methods.' See further §51– 013 (Australia); §51– 020 (New Zealand); §51– 028 (Canada); and §51– 037 (Ireland).

reg 12 of the EIR is dealt with below.[470]

26– 063 Exemption inter-relationship

Previous editions of this work suggested that ss 23 and 24 of FOIA should not be read as mutually exclusive and that such a construction would preclude simultaneous joint reliance on both, meaning that refusals citing one but not the other might be capable of having a 'tell-tale' or 'giveaway' effect revealing security body involvement or non-involvement. Following the publication of the first edition of this work, the then Department of Constitutional Affairs published non-statutory guidance notes on the various exemptions on Part II in FOIA which adopted a different interpretation of the relationship between ss 23 and 24.[471] In short, the Department accepted that ss 23(1) and 24(1) are mutually exclusive but contended that ss 23(5) and 24(2) are not and that simultaneous joint reliance on both is therefore possible in order to 'obscure' the fact of security body involvement or non-involvement.[472] The Information Tribunal adopted this approach in *Baker v Information Commissioner and Cabinet Office* without considering or deciding whether it was correct.[473] However, the First-tier Tribunal addressed the issue directly in *All Party Parliamentary Group on Extraordinary Rendition v Information Commissioner and Foreign & Commonwealth Office* and decided to maintain its endorsement of the Government's preferred interpretation.[474] As a matter of practice, this conclusion appears to have resolved the matter for the time being, pending any further consideration by the Upper Tribunal or a higher court. Furthermore, the Information Commissioner has issued guidance confirming that, notwithstanding the mutual exclusivity of ss 23(1) and 24(1) of FOIA he may accept them as being cited together 'in the alternative' in order to disguise which is in fact applicable.[475] In *Savic v Attorney-General* the Upper Tribunal did not dissent from but also expressly declined to confirm this approach without hearing argument. The Upper Tribunal set out four questions that 'merit consideration with the benefit of oral argument' and indicated that it saw 'some force in the generic assertion of the appellant that that the Commissioner and the [Cabinet Office] have taken an impermissibly broad approach to the NCND response based upon section 23(5) and section 24(2).'[476] For the record and in case the point is ever revisited, the alternative analysis originally set out in this work was as follows:

(1) Sections 23 and 24 confer very different types of exemption. Section 23 is absolute and applies in a mechanical way according to the satisfaction of factual criteria

[470] See §§26– 064 to 26– 068.

[471] DCA, *Exemptions Guidance – section 23*, undated, and DCA, *Exemptions Guidance – section 24*, undated. The same approach was taken in MoJ, *Exemptions Guidance – section 23: information supplied by, or related to, bodies dealing with security matters*, 14 May 2008. cf ICO, *Exemptions Guidance – section 23: Information supplied by or relating to security bodies* (2009) p 4 and ICO, *Exemptions Guidance - Section 24: The national security exemption* (2009) pp 3-4.

[472] DCA, *Exemptions Guidance – section 23*, undated, para 4.2, DCA, *Exemptions Guidance – section 24*, undated, para 4.4, MoJ, *Exemptions Guidance – section 23: information supplied by, or related to, bodies dealing with security matters*, 14 May 2008, p 4 and MoJ, *Exemptions Guidance – section 24: National Security*, 14 May 2008, p 6.

[473] *Baker v IC and Cabinet Office*, IT, 28 February 2007 at [34] and [43]-[45]. The appeal was determined on the papers and without an oral hearing and the relevant point was not argued. Interestingly, the Tribunal also endorsed (at [30]-[33]) the analysis at §26– 047 above, upon which the contrary view of the relationship between FOIA ss 23(5) and 24(2) was based. See also: *Metropolitan Police v IC*, FTT, 23 May 2010 at [15]-[16] describing simultaneous joint reliance upon FOIA ss 23(5) and 24(2) as 'accepted practice.'

[474] *All Party Parliamentary Group on Extraordinary Rendition v IC and FCO*, FTT, 3 May 2012 at [83] and [93]-[114] (point not considered by the UT on appeal in *APPGER v IC and FCO* [2013] UKUT 0560 (AAC) or *All Party Parliamentary Group on Extraordinary Rendition v IC and FCO* [2015] UKUT 0377 (AAC)). Followed in *Dudgeon v IC and Police Service of Northern Ireland*, FTT, 3 May 2013 at [22] and [32]. See also MoJ, *Exemptions Guidance - Section 23: information supplied by, or relating to, bodies dealing with security matters*, March 2012, pp 4-5 and MoJ, *Exemptions Guidance - Section 24: National Security*, March 2012, p 6. See also ICO, *Security bodies (section 23)* (2013) paras 11 and 23, ICO, *Safeguarding national security (section 24)* (2012) paras 17 and 24 and ICO, *How sections 23 and 24 interact* (2012).

[475] ICO, *How sections 23 and 24 interact* (2012) paras 21-33.

[476] *Savic v IC and Attorney General* [2016] UKUT 534 (AAC) at [41], [98]-[102] and [105]-[106].

regarding the historical supply and current content of the requested information. Section 23 thus leaves little scope for considering the desirability of a neither confirm nor deny approach in the particular circumstances of each case or as a matter of general policy for cases of the same type. By contrast, s 24 is qualified and applies in a purposive way where exemption is required for live and ongoing national security reasons. Section 24 therefore allows regard to be had not only to the content and sensitivity of the requested information, but also to the particular and general consequences of disclosure and, following on from this, the desirability of a neither confirm nor deny approach.

(2) Sections 23 and 24 are also mutually exclusive and do not overlap: s 24(1) only applies to information which does not fall within s 23(1); s 24(2) must be read as being subject to the same limitation in order to engage s 2(1); and s 24(3)-(4) must necessarily share the same limitation as well.[477] Moreover, s 23 takes precedence over s 24: it is not possible to rely on ss 23 and 24 in relation to the same information; and s 24 may only be relied upon if and to the extent that s 23 is not in play. One consequence of this is that reliance on s 23, which must be revealed under s 17(1)(b) of FOIA, will inevitably inform the applicant that his request has engaged information of the kind described in s 23 while reliance on s 24 instead, which must also be revealed under s 17(1)(b), will inevitably inform the applicant that his request has not had this effect: refusals based on ss 23 and 24 may therefore have a 'tell-tale' or 'giveaway' effect. A further consequence is that the effectiveness of s 24 and its ability to have regard to the desirability of the neither confirm nor deny approach are hampered by its confinement to information which does not fall within s 23(1).

(3) Having said this, it should be borne in mind that the amount of information revealed by the giveaway effect will always be limited. First, bare reference to s 23 under s 17(1)(b) will not identify the particular security body or bodies in question or reveal anything specific about their involvement, although this may be apparent from the context. Secondly, the institutional exclusion of the security bodies from FOIA regime means there is less scope for strategic sequential requests liable to yield variable responses and designed to flush out information through the giveaway effect. Thirdly, simultaneous joint reliance on ss 23 and 24 may be possible in relation to a single information request where different pieces of the information requested are subject to those provisions, and it may also be possible to rely on different exemptions in the alternative.[478] Fourthly, and as already discussed,[479] s 23(5) of FOIA allows a neither confirm nor deny response where divulgence would disclose unrecorded as well as recorded security body information and, because the fact that no such information is held is itself capable of being unrecorded information and may suggest that the security bodies did not and do not have any involvement in the subject matter of the request, there is considerable scope for reliance on FOIA, s 23 even in cases where the security bodies are not involved. This will also limit the giveaway effect because it may not be clear whether s 23(5) has been invoked by reason of security body involvement or the total absence thereof.

---

[477] The foundation of this analysis is set out at §26–047. Substantially the same text appeared in the first edition of this work and was repeated and endorsed by the Information Tribunal in *Baker v IC & Cabinet Office*, IT, 28 February 2007 at [30]-[33].

[478] In this latter regard, FOIA ss 23 and 24 may be exclusive but each is capable of overlapping with, eg ss 26 and 27. So, while there is no room for choosing between reliance on ss 23 or 24 (if s 23 is in play, s 24 is not), it is perfectly possible to rely on ss 26 or 27 in addition or in preference to either ss 23 or 24.

[479] See §§26–040 and 26–047.

26– 064 Section 23 – NCND

Under FOIA a neither confirm nor deny response may be given where the duty to confirm or deny does not arise by virtue of a Part II exemption which prevents the application of s 1(1)(a).[480] Reliance on s 23 of FOIA, but not s 24 or vice versa, might itself be thought to reveal something.[481] The extent to which this is thought to be the case will depend on the practical operation of s 23 in general and s 23(5) in particular[482] and the scope allowed thereunder for the use of neither confirm nor deny responses.[483] In this regard, further reference can be made to two hypothetical requests for information made to a government department or police authority regarding the involvement of the security bodies in a particular operation, namely, request A asking for a list of every agency that was involved and request B asking for a list of every security body that was involved.[484] As set out above, if a security body was involved in the operation the department can refuse to comment on this in reliance on s 23 and if no security bodies were involved it can adopt the same approach, provided the fact of this non-involvement is information held by it in recorded form or amounts to unrecorded information which relates to the security bodies for the purposes of s 23(5).[485] In relation to such a request, the use or non-use of s 23 will only prove revealing if it cannot be relied upon in cases of security body non-involvement.[486] However, if it can be used in such circumstances, so as to obscure the significance of the application of s 23, it might in practice need to be relied upon

---

480 During the passage of the Freedom of Information Bill, the Cabinet Officer Minister, Lord Falconer of Thoroton, gave the following example of a situation in which it might be necessary to give a neither confirm nor deny response to an information request: 'The clearest and easiest example is endangering the defence of the realm. You do not have to communicate information which endangers the defence of the realm. Nor do you have to confirm or deny whether such information exists when, if you did confirm or deny its existence, that in itself would endanger the defence of the realm. I give the obvious example. "Do you have detailed information concerning the chemical warfare capacities of the following countries?"; and then a list of countries is given. It could well damage the defence of the realm if one indicated the extent to which one had that information.' — Hansard HL vol 617 col 1252 (19 October 2000) (House of Lords Committee Stage). See also MoJ, *Exemptions Guidance—Section 23: information supplied by, or relating to, bodies dealing with security matters*, March 2012 pp 3-5; MoJ, *Exemptions Guidance—Section 24: National Security*, March 2012 p 4, Annex C.

481 The practice of allowing simultaneous joint reliance on FOIA ss 23(5) and 24(2) means that the potential impact of this issue is likely to be minimal.

482 FOIA s 23(5) prevents the duty to confirm or deny the existence or non-existence of recorded information from arising if, or to the extent that, compliance would involve the disclosure of any information, whether or not already recorded, which was supplied by, or relates to, a security body; see also s 17(4). Because s 23(1)-(2) does not include the formulation 'whether or not already recorded', national security certificates issued thereunder may apply only to recorded information unless it can be argued (by reference to the default definition of 'information' in s 84) that 'the context otherwise requires' a different construction of 'information' in s 23(2) (ie one that imports 'whether or not already recorded' because these words appear in s 23(5)). Not adopting such a construction would lead to the result that a national security certificate under s 23(1)-(2) could not be issued to support a refusal to confirm or deny the existence of recorded information to the extent that this refusal is based on a need to prevent the disclosure of unrecorded information which was supplied by, or relates to, a security body: the absence of a national security certificate in a s 23 case would then point to reliance on s 23(5) unrecorded information and this could itself be revealing. Nor does the additional category of unrecorded information which falls within s 23(5) present an area of possible overlap with s 24 even though it is not information falling within s 23(1): this is because s 24 itself only applies to 'information which does not fall within s 23(1)' in the default sense of 'information recorded in any form which does not fall within s 23(1)'.

483 The extent to which reliance on FOIA s 23 and not s 24 (or vice versa) will in practice be capable of revealing significant information will, in any event, be somewhat limited for the reasons given at §26– 063(3).

484 See §26– 043.

485 See §§26– 040 and 26– 043.

486 The more expansive and less revealing interpretation of FOIA s 23(5) was approved in *Beasley v IC and Ministry of Defence*, FTT, 13 March 2012 at [14]-[17] and the scope for obscuring security body involvement or non-involvement is enhanced by the practice of allowing simultaneous joint reliance on FOIA ss 23(5) and 24(2): see §26– 063.

in analogous situations.[487]

26– 065 Section 24 – NCND

Leaving to one side the effect which s 23 of FOIA has on the application of the exemption in s 24 of that Act, the basic purposive formulation of that exemption, and the equivalent exemptions in ss 26, 44-45, 48, 68 and 110 of the DPA 2018, leaves scope for all of these provisions to be applied in a way that has regard to the desirability of a neither confirm nor deny approach in comparable situations and the general risks of mosaic prejudice.[488] This is probably of more immediate significance in relation to subject access requests under, and other attempts to exercise or enforce other data subject rights conferred by, Ch III of the applied GDPR (in relation to 'general processing'), Ch 3 of Pt of the DPA 2018 (in relation to 'law enforcement processing') or Chapter 3 of Part 4 of the DPA 2018 (in relation to 'intelligence services' processing). In this regard, data controllers, particularly the intelligence services and NCA, may wish to avoid confirmation or denial that they are processing an individual's personal data (or disclosure of such data and related information) on the grounds that this may prejudice national security by revealing information about their investigations, operations, intelligence or sources. The intelligence services in particular have sought to pursue a neither confirm nor deny policy when responding to such requests and various national security certificates were issued and relied upon under the equivalent national security exemption in s 28 of the former DPA 1998 in order to allow them to do so. The history and success for them of this policy to date is outlined in the following two paragraphs.

26– 066 DPA 1998 certificates

Three national security certificates under s 28(2) of the DPA 1998 were originally issued by the Home Secretary (in relation to the Security Service) and the Foreign Secretary (in relation to SIS and GCHQ) in July 2000.[489] These certificates purported to confer a blanket exemption, allowing each intelligence service to respond with a vague and non-committal neither confirm nor deny reply to every subject access request made to it under s 7(1)(a) of the DPA 1998 without considering whether a different response might be acceptable in the particular circumstances of the case in question. On an appeal brought under s 28(4) of the DPA 1998 the Information Tribunal quashed the Home Secretary's original certificate on the basis that its effect was 'unnecessarily wide'[490] and the Foreign Secretary's original certificates were

---

[487] This is because the fact of security body non-involvement will arise as an implicit issue or piece of information in many situations. Returning to hypothetical requests A and B, the possibility that the only agencies involved in the operation might have been security bodies complicates the picture even further: if the fact of the operation is a matter of public record and no agencies are referred to in response to either request A or request B, it could be readily inferred that they must all have been security bodies. Avoiding this through adherence to the principle of neither confirming nor denying would, however, require a blanket refusal to comment on the involvement of state agencies in almost any security or defence type operation. MoJ, *Exemptions Guidance—Section 24: National security*, March 2012 p 6 may anticipate this difficulty when it talks in terms of information which 'could reasonably have been' supplied by or related to a security body. ICO, *Security bodies (section 23)* (2013) paras 19-21 suggest that the application of FOIA s 23(5) should be limited to requests which are 'in the territory of national security' meaning there is 'a realistic possibility' that a security body would be involved in the issue to which the request relates and the relevant public authority would hold information about this.

[488] See §26– 036(1).

[489] The Home Secretary's certificate was dated 22 July 2000 and the Foreign Secretary's certificates were dated 30 July 2000.

[490] *Baker v SSHD* [2001] UKHRR 1275, an appeal under DPA 1998 s 28(4). Having referred in general terms to the Council of Europe Convention for the Protection of Individuals with Regard to Automatic Processing of Personal Data dated 28 January 1981, the European Community Data Protection Directive 95/46/EC dated 24 October 1995 and the Human Rights Act 1998 ss 1, 3 and 6, the Tribunal asked itself whether the issue of the certificate was 'reasonable in the extended sense of proportionate by reference to the precepts of the ECHR' (at [63]) and concluded that the certificate had an 'unnecessarily wide effect' and should be quashed accordingly (summary, [14]).

subsequently withdrawn.[491]

26– 067 Replacement certificates

Three replacement certificates under s 28(2) of the DPA 1998 were then issued by the Home Secretary (in relation to the Security Service) and the Foreign Secretary (in relation to SIS and GCHQ) in December 2001, together with documents giving explanatory reasons.[492] The replacement certificates were expressed in broadly similar general and prospective terms and conferred exemption from different provisions of the DPA 1998 on personal data processed by the intelligence services depending on the purposes and types of data involved. The replacement certificates provided: first, that no data shall be exempt from s 7(1)(a) of the DPA 1998 if the intelligence service in question determines that adherence to the principle of neither confirming nor denying whether it holds data about an individual is not required for the purpose of safeguarding national security; secondly, that no data shall be exempt from s 7(1)(b)-(d) of the DPA 1998 if the intelligence service in question determines that the non-communication of such data or any description of such data is not required for the purpose of safeguarding national security; and, thirdly, that personal data processed by the intelligence services in the performance of their statutory functions were exempt from the (then) first, second and eighth data protection principles and potentially exempt from the sixth data protection principle. On appeals brought under s 28(4) of the DPA 1998 the Information Tribunal effectively upheld the format of all three certificates,[493] although it should be noted that it only did so in response to appeals founded on somewhat limited grounds.[494] In this regard, the Information Tribunal held that there were reasonable grounds for, in effect, delegating to the Security Service the power to determine the requirements of national security in relation to each request, bearing in mind the scope for challenging such determinations before the RIPA Tribunal under s 65 of the Regulation of Investigatory Powers Act 2000 or, possibly, by way of judicial review.[495]

26– 068 EIR – NCND

Regulation 12(6) of the EIR allows for a 'neither confirm nor deny' response to a request for

---

491 *Al Fayed v SSHD*, IT, 28 February 2002 at [9] and [15]-[16].

492 The Home Secretary's certificate was dated 10 December 2001 and the Foreign Secretary's certificates were dated 8 December 2001. Copies of the certificate and reasons document relating to the Security Service are annexed to the decisions of the Information Tribunal in *Gosling v SSHD*, IT, 1 August 2003 and *Hitchens v SSHD*, IT, 4 August 2003. The certificate and reasons document relating to GCHQ were also accompanied by a document headed 'GCHQ Arrangements' setting out the Foreign Secretary's policy in relation to requests made under DPA 1998 s 7 and the procedure to be followed by GCHQ when responding to them (*Hitchens v SSHD*, IT, 4 August 2003 at [48]). Copies of the certificates and reasons documents for all three intelligence services were also placed in the Libraries of both Houses of Parliament (*Intelligence and Security Committee Annual Report 2001-2002* (Cm 5542, 2002) para 50). The Foreign and Home Secretaries both signed a similar certificate under s 28(2) of DPA 1998 in relation to personal data processed by the previous Intelligence and Security Committee established under s 10 of the Intelligence Services Act 1994 or by its Secretariat, and the Committee in turn issued its own explanatory reasons document (*Intelligence and Security Committee Annual Report 2001-2002* (Cm 5542, 2002) paras 49-50 and Appendix 2). DPA 2018 Sch 20, paras 17-18 and 40 contain transitional provisions: saving the effect of the DPA 1998 s 28 and any certificates made thereunder with respect to the processing of personal data to which that Act applies (para 17); and continuing the effect of any such certificate as if it were a certificate made under one or more of the DPA 2018 ss 27, 79 and 111 for one year following the entry into force of the repeal of the DPA 1998 s 28 (para 18).

493 *Gosling v SSHD*, IT, 1 August 2003 followed in *Hitchens v SSHD*, IT, 4 August 2003 and *Hilton v FCO*, IT, 28 June 2005; *Stevenson v SSHD*, IT, 30 April 2009; *Nasresfahani v SSHD and Data Controller* [2014] UKUT 0487 (AAC); and see also *Re Ewing* [2002] EWHC 3169.

494 *Gosling v SSHD*, IT, 1 August 2003 at [28]; *Hitchens v SSHD*, IT, 4 August 2003 at [42].

495 *Gosling v SSHD*, IT, 1 August 2003 at [56]; *Hitchens v SSHD*, IT, 4 August 2003 at [49]; *Hilton v FCO*, IT, 28 June 2005. As to the scope for judicial review, see now *R (A) v Director of Establishments of the Security Service* [2009] UKSC 12, [2010] 2 AC 1.

environmental information, whether or not the public authority holds such information, if confirmation or denial would involve the disclosure of information which would adversely affect international relations, defence, national security or public safety.[496] As with s 24 of FOIA and ss 26, 44-45, 48, 68 and 110 of the DPA 2018, this provision allows the public authority to consider the desirability of a neither confirm nor deny approach in comparable situations and the general risks of mosaic prejudice when determining the risk of an adverse affect on any of those interests.[497] Having said this, the public authority must also apply the presumption in favour of disclosure imposed by reg 12(2) of the EIR and this could conceivably cause it to decide against adopting a neither confirm nor deny stance in circumstances where it might have done so under equivalent provisions in FOIA or the DPA 2018. It is clear from the inclusion of 'whether or not it holds such information' in reg 12(6) of the EIR and from reg 12(7), which provides that whether information exists and is held by a public authority is itself the disclosure of information, that neither confirm nor deny responses may be made thereunder irrespective of whether the public authority holds any sensitive information. If knowledge of the fact that the authority does not hold any such information could itself imperil one of the specified interests, a neither confirm nor deny response will be legitimate.

26– 069Relevant certificate date

National security certificates under s 23(2) of FOIA may certify that information was directly or indirectly supplied by any of the security bodies as a matter of historical fact or that it relates to any of those bodies as a matter of current fact.[498] National security certificates under reg 15(1) of the EIR may certify that the disclosure of information 'would' adversely affect national security and thus must mean if disclosure were to take place now or at any time in the future while the certificate remains in force.[499] However, national security certificates under s 24(3) of FOIA and s 27(1) and 111(1) of the DPA 2018 may certify that the exemption of the information or personal data to which it applies 'is or at any time was required' for the purpose of safeguarding national security. Similarly, national security certificates under s 79(1) of the DPA 2018 may certify that a relevant restriction on the provision of information to a data subject 'is or ant any time was a necessary and proportionate measure' to protect national security.[500] The past tense formulation 'or at any time was' is included to allow for national security certificates which are issued after the relevant exemption has been relied upon by the public authority or data controller or processor in question.[501] It does not enable a Minister to claim exemption where this is no longer required for the purpose of safeguarding national security, because the operative exemption provisions only apply in circumstances where exemption 'is required' for that purpose.[502]

[496] See EIR reg 12(7). See also EI(S)R reg 10(8)-(9).

[497] See §26– 036(1).

[498] See §26– 058.

[499] See §26– 060.

[500] DPA s 79(3).

[501] In relation to FOIA s 24, this was confirmed in House of Commons Public Administration Select Committee Third Report Session 1998-1999 *Freedom of Information Draft Bill* (HC 570-I), 1999, paras 74-77 and Annex 6, para 44.

[502] FOIA s 24(1)-(2); DPA 2018 ss 26(1)(a) and 110(1)).

6. INFORMATION PREJUDICIAL TO DEFENCE OR THE ARMED FORCES

26– 070 Introduction

As already indicated, information whose disclosure under FOIA would, or would be likely to, prejudice the defence of the British Islands or of any colony or the capability, effectiveness or security of the armed forces of the Crown or of any forces co-operating with those forces ('the s 26 defence interests') is also subject to a qualified exemption under s 26 of that Act. A similar exemption is to be found in the freedom of information legislation of each of the comparative jurisdictions.[503] The phrase 'would or would be likely to prejudice' is common to most of the prejudice-based exemptions in the Act. The nature of prejudice and the degree of likelihood which the phrase requires are considered elsewhere in this work.[504]

26– 071 Section 26 FOIA – scope

Section 26(1) of FOIA[505] provides that information is exempt information if its disclosure under the Act would, or would be likely to, prejudice any of the s 26 defence interests. Having reached that threshold, the duty to communicate will not apply where, in all the circumstances of the case, the public interest in maintaining the exemption outweighs the public interest in disclosing the information.[506] Section 26(3) provides a corresponding exclusion of the duty to confirm or deny where, or to the extent that, compliance with the duty to divulge the existence of information would, or would be likely to, prejudice any of the s 26 defence interests. Section 26(3) is not expressed to relate to any particular category of information and does not itself stand as a 'provision' which 'states that the duty to confirm or deny does not arise in relation to any information' for the purposes of s 2(1). However, for the reasons set out above in relation to s 24(2),[507] the whole of s 26 needs to be read as the 'provision' which 'states that the

---

503 In the United States, the Freedom of Information Act, 1966, 5 USC 552(b)(1) s 6F(b) (USA), exempts from disclosure national security information concerning national defence or foreign policy, provided that that information has been classified in accordance with the requirements of a Presidential Executive Order: see §51– 008(1). The Freedom of Information Act 1982 s 33(a) (Cth of Aust), provides an exemption where the disclosure of the requested document would, or could be reasonably be expected to, cause damage to (i) the security of the Commonwealth of Australia; or (ii) the defence of the Commonwealth of Australia: see §51– 015(9). The Act makes provision for neither confirming nor denying the existence of the requested documents where to do so would or could reasonably be expected to cause damage to these interests (see §51– 013). The Official Information Act 1982 ss 6(a), 7 and 27(1)(a) (NZ) and the Privacy Act 1993 ss 27(1)(a) and 27(2)(a)-(c) (NZ) provide absolute exemptions where the disclosure of the information would be likely to prejudice the security or defence of New Zealand or certain external dependencies: see §51– 022(1). The Official Information Act 1982 (NZ) provides for a conclusive certificate to be issued in relation to this exemption in connection with investigations by the Ombudsman (see §51– 021) and makes provision for neither confirming nor denying the existence of the requested documents where to do so would or could reasonably be expected to cause damage to these interests (see §51– 020). The Access to Information Act (1982) s 15 (Canada), provides a discretionary exemption for records the disclosure of which could reasonably be expected to cause injury to the defence of Canada or allied states: see §51– 032(11). 'Defence of Canada', etc is defined to include the efforts of Canada and of foreign states toward the detection, prevention and suppression of activities of any foreign state directed toward actual or potential attack or other acts of aggression against Canada or any state allied or associated with Canada: s 15(2). The Freedom of Information Act 2014 s 33(1) (Ireland), provides a discretionary exemption for records the disclosure of which could reasonably be expected to adversely affect the security or defence of the Republic of Ireland: see §51– 039(13). The public body must refuse to confirm or deny the existence of any record falling within the terms of the exemption if it thinks that to do either would be contrary to the public interest: Freedom of Information Act 2014 s 33(4) (Ireland): see §51– 037. A conclusive certificate may be issued in respect of this head of exemption: Freedom of Information Act 2014 s 32-34 (Ireland): see §51– 038.

504 See §§6– 020 to 6– 028.

505 FOI(S)A s 31(4).

506 FOIA s 2(2)(b).

507 See §26– 047(1).

duty to confirm or deny does not arise in relation to any information' and which therefore engages s 2(1). On this basis, if the s 26(3) description is met, the duty to confirm or deny does not apply only where, in all the circumstances of the case, the public interest in maintaining the exclusion of the divulgence duty outweighs the public interest in disclosing whether the public authority holds the information requested.[508]

26– 072 Defence – DPA 2018

As already indicated, s 26 of the DPA 2018 exempts personal data from certain provisions of the applied GDPR and Pts 5-7 of the Act if this is required for the purpose of safeguarding national security or for defence purposes.[509] The provisions that may be disapplied in such circumstances are listed in s 26(2) and include most of the data protection principles, the rights of data subjects, certain obligations on data controllers and processors and various oversight and enforcement provisions. The Government's Explanatory Notes to the DPA 2018 recorded that:

> The "defence purposes" element of section 26 is intended to ensure the continued protection, security and capability of the armed forces, and the civilian staff that support them, not just their combat effectiveness.[510]

Section 28 of the DPA 2018 also modifies the application of Arts 9 and 32 of the applied GDPR to the processing of personal data carried out for the same purposes: Art 9(1) (prohibition on processing of special categories of personal data) is disapplied to the extent that processing is carried out for one of those purposes and with appropriate safeguards for the rights and freedoms of data subjects;[511] and art 32 (security of processing) is disapplied to the extent that a controller or processor is processing personal data for one of those purposes and appropriate security measures are implemented.[512] So far as concerns defence purposes, the exemptions in ss 26 and 28 of the DPA 2018 more closely correspond with the exemption in s 26 of the Freedom of Information Act 2000 than the narrower exemption in Sch 7 to the former DPA 1998.[513] The latter only disapplied the subject access provisions of that Act from personal data to the extent that their application would have been likely to prejudice the combat effectiveness of any of the armed forces of the Crown.

26– 073 Regulation 12 EIR – scope

As already indicated, reg 12 of the EIR provides a qualified exception to the duty to disclose environmental information which allows public authorities to refuse to disclose information to the extent that its disclosure would adversely affect international relations, defence, national

---

[508] FOIA s 26(3) (read with s 26(1)) thus engages s 2(1)(b) so as to prevent s 1(1)(a) from applying and the duty to confirm or deny from arising in relation to the exempt information if the public interest balance favours non-divulgence.

[509] DPA 2018 ss 15(5) and 26(1). DPA 2018 Sch 11 para 7 enacts a similar exemption in relation to intelligence services processing subject to Pt 4 of the Act. The provisions of Pt 4 listed in Sch 11 para 1 do not apply to personal data processed by the intelligence services to the extent that their application would be likely to prejudice the combat effectiveness of any of the armed forces of the Crown.

[510] Para 165. This paragraph sets out a non-exhaustive list of 'examples of processing activities which might be considered defence purposes requiring the protection of the exemption' as follows:

> collection, consideration and utilisation of military or other defence related intelligence in support of current and future military operations; collation of personal data to assist in assessing the capability and effectiveness of armed forces personnel, including performance of troops; collection and storage of information, including biometric details, necessary to maintain the security of defence sites, supplies and services; management of data relating to former armed forces personnel who hold a reserve liability; sharing of data with coalition partners to support them in maintaining their security, capability and effectiveness of their armed forces.

[511] DPA 2018 s 28(1).

[512] DPA 2018 s 28(2)-(4).

[513] DPA 1998 s 37 Sch 7 para 2 (repealed).

security or public safety.[514] This exception operates in exactly the same way in relation to defence interests as it does in relation to national security interests and its terms do not require further description here.[515]

26– 074 British Isles & colonies

While s 24 of FOIA is concerned with safeguarding national security, meaning 'the security of the United Kingdom and its people',[516] s 26 of the Act might be thought to have a geographically wider purview in that it is overtly concerned with the defence of the British Islands and of any colony.[517] The significance of this should not be overstated, however, as it has been recognised that action overseas may be capable of indirectly affecting the security of the United Kingdom even if directed towards a foreign State.[518] For the purposes of s 26 of FOIA, the British Islands means the United Kingdom, the Channel Islands and the Isle of Man (but not the Republic of Ireland which could be said to fall within the British Isles).[519] The United Kingdom in turn means Great Britain (ie England, Scotland and Wales)[520] and Northern Ireland, while the Channel Islands means the Bailiwick of Jersey and the Bailiwick of Guernsey, Alderney and Sark and their respective dependencies.[521] Colony means any part of Her Majesty's dominions outside the British Islands,[522] except countries having fully responsible status within the Commonwealth[523] and their respective dependencies.[524]

26– 075 Armed forces of the Crown

The expression 'the armed forces of the Crown' is not defined in FOIA or the DPA 2018 but must include the regular, reserve and auxiliary naval, military and air forces of the Crown and the women's services of those forces.[525] Authority for the existence and maintenance of the

---

514 EIR reg 12(1)(a) and (5)(a). See also EI(S)R reg 10(1)-(2) and (5)(a) applying the 'would, or would be likely to, prejudice substantially' test and an additional requirement that reg 10(4)-(5) are interpreted 'in a restrictive way' to an otherwise similarly worded 'exception'.

515 See §26– 049.

516 *SSHD v Rehman* [2001] UKHL 47, [2003] 1 AC 153, at [50] (Lord Hoffmann) and [64] (Lord Hutton).

517 FOIA s 26(1); FOI(S)A s 31(4).

518 *SSHD v Rehman* [2001] UKHL 47, [2003] 1 AC 153 at [16]-[17] (Lord Slynn). See also at [53] and [62] (Lord Hoffmann) and [64] (Lord Hutton). It is at least conceivable that some colonies may be of little or no significance to the national security of the United Kingdom so that considerations relating to their defence could engage FOIA s 26 but not s 24.

519 Interpretation Act 1978 ss 5 22(1) Sch 1 Sch 2 para 4(2); D Bailey and L Norbury, *Bennion on Statutory Interpretation*, 7th edn (London, LexisNexis, 2017), sec 4.16.

520 Interpretation Act 1978 ss 5 22(1) Sch 1 Sch 2 para 5(a); Union with Scotland Act 1706 preamble Art 1.

521 D Bailey and L Norbury, *Bennion on Statutory Interpretation*, 7th edn (London, LexisNexis, 2017), sec 4.21.

522 Interpretation Act 1978 s 5 Sch 1; D Bailey and L Norbury, *Bennion on Statutory Interpretation*, 7th edn (London, LexisNexis, 2017), sec 4.22. MoJ, *Exemptions Guidance—Section 26: Defence* (14 May 2008), Annex A, lists the colonies as Anguilla, Bermuda, British Antarctic Territories, British Indian Ocean Territories, British Virgin Islands, Cayman Islands, Falkland Islands, Gibraltar, Montserrat, Pitcairn Island, South Georgia and South Sandwich Islands, Sovereign Base Area of Cyprus, St Helena and dependencies (Ascension Island and Tristan da Cunha), and Turks and Caicos Islands.

523 That is, countries other than the United Kingdom which are part of Her Majesty's independent dominions.

524 The statutory expression is 'territories for whose external relations a country other than the United Kingdom is responsible'. Associated states are also excluded from the definition of a colony, but this is now a defunct category as there are no longer any territories maintaining a status of association with the United Kingdom in accordance with the West Indies Act 1967.

525 This is supported by the definition of 'the armed forces of the Crown raised in the United Kingdom at the present day' at *Halsbury's Laws of England*, 5th edn, 2011, vol 3), title 'Armed Forces', para 301. The Armed Forces Act 1981 s 20(1) Sch 3 Pts I-II further provide that 'the armed forces of the Crown' (raised in the United Kingdom and excluding the Royal Navy) includes the women's services of those forces administered by the Defence Council: see also *Halsbury's Laws of England*, 5th edn, 2011, vol 3), title 'Armed Forces', para 318. On this basis, the armed forces

naval forces derives from the royal prerogative, while authority for the existence and maintenance of the military and air forces derives from statute.[526] In terms of the principal and most important statutes, regard should be had to the Armed Forces Act 2006, the Air Force (Constitution) Act 1917 and the Reserve Forces Act 1996.[527] The supreme government, command and disposition of all the armed forces by sea, land and air, and of all defence establishments, is ultimately vested in the Crown by prerogative right at common law and by statute.[528] However, these powers are now exercised on the advice of ministers and most matters relating to the armed forces are regulated by statute and administered by and through ministers, the Ministry of Defence, the Defence Council and the Admiralty, Army and Air Force Boards.[529]

26– 076 Other relevant forces

Although certain forces raised under the law of a colony, protectorate or trust territory and certain visiting forces can become subject to United Kingdom service law and discipline,[530] they are not 'armed forces of the Crown' for the purposes of FOIA.[531] Any forces co-operating with the armed forces of the Crown or any part of those forces are, however, relevant forces for the purposes of s 26 of FOIA.[532] Colonial, Commonwealth and other allied armed forces could fall into this category when co-operating with the armed forces of the Crown on operations or exercises on any kind of bilateral or multilateral basis or under the auspices of, for example, the North Atlantic Treaty Organisation or the United Nations.[533] There is also no express

of the Crown comprise: the regular forces (ie the Royal Navy, Army, Royal Air Force and Royal Marines); the reserve and auxiliary forces (including the Army Reserve); and the women's services and their reserves. The alternative expression 'Her Majesty's forces' is also used in some legislation, eg Armed Forces Act 2006, Pts 1, 3, 6, 14, 16-18. As to the armed forces more generally see: A Bradley, K Ewing and C Knight, *Constitutional and Administrative Law*, 17th edn (Pearson, London, 2018) p 262; O Hood Phillips and P Jackson, *Constitutional and Administrative Law*, 8th edn (Sweet & Maxwell, London, 2001) paras 19-002 to 19-018; FW Maitland, *The Constitutional History of England* (Cambridge, Cambridge University Press, 1919) pp 275-280, 324-329 and 447-462; W Anson, *Law and Custom of the Constitution*, 4th edn (Oxford, Oxford University Press, 1907) vol II(ii), pp 199-222; Rowe 'The Crown and Accountability for the Armed Forces' in M Sunkin and S Payne (eds), *The Nature of the Crown: a Legal and Political Analysis* (Oxford, Oxford University Press, 1999). The special forces and any unit or part of a unit which is for the time being required by the Secretary of State to assist GCHQ in the exercise of its functions are not excluded from the definition of the armed forces of the Crown for the purposes of FOIA s 26, cf Sch 1, Pt I, para 6. See also MoJ, *Exemptions Guidance — Section 26: Defence* (18 May 2008) Annex A.

526 Bill of Rights Act 1689 Art 1 prevents the Crown from raising or keeping a standing army within the United Kingdom in times of peace without the consent of Parliament; *Halsbury's Laws of England*, 5th edn, 2014, vol 20, title 'Constitutional and Administrative Law', paras 560-565; *Halsbury's Laws of England*, 5th edn, 2011, vol 3, title 'Armed Forces', paras 301-309.

527 The Army Act 1955, Air Force Act 1955 and Naval Discipline Act 1957 ('the Service Discipline Acts') were repealed and replaced by the Armed Forces Act 2006 and constitute the relevant provisions as to discipline in the armed forces in a harmonised and consolidated 'tri-service' format. Some parts of the Air Force (Constitution) Act 1917 remain in force. Some parts of the Reserve Forces Act 1996 and the whole of the Army and Air Force (Women's Service) Act 1948 were repealed and replaced by the Armed Forces Act 2006: see ss 378(2), 383(2), Sch 17. See generally: *Halsbury's Laws of England*, 5th edn, 2014, vol 20, title 'Constitutional and Administrative Law', paras 560-561.

528 *Halsbury's Laws of England*, 5th edn, 2014, vol 20, title 'Constitutional and Administrative Law', para 563.

529 Defence (Transfer of Functions) Act 1964; *Halsbury's Laws of England*, 5th edn, 2014, vol 20, title 'Constitutional and Administrative Law', paras 560-564 ; *Halsbury's Laws of England*, 5th edn, 2011, vol 3, title 'Armed Forces', paras 301-302.

530 Armed Forces Act 2006 ss 367-369; Visiting Forces (British Commonwealth) Act 1933 ss 4-5; Visiting Forces Act 1952; International Headquarters and Defence Organisations Act 1964; *Halsbury's Laws of England*, 5th edn, 2011, vol 3, title 'Armed Forces', paras 311, 322 and 405-421.

531 Note the exclusion of Commonwealth forces from the definitions of 'Her Majesty's air forces', 'Her Majesty's forces' and 'Her Majesty's military forces' in Armed Forces Act 2006 s 374.

532 FOIA s 26(2)(b); FOI(S)A s 31(5)(b)(ii).

533 The involvement of foreign States or international organisations might also engage the international relations exemption in FOIA s 27, FOI(S)A s 32(1).

requirement that these co-operating forces be either armed or foreign and so it might be argued that domestic or foreign police or security forces are included. One question arising in relation to other relevant forces is whether general prejudice to their capability, effectiveness or security is enough to engage s 26 or whether what matters is their capability, effectiveness or security whilst they are 'co-operating with' the armed forces of the Crown: the latter interpretation seems preferable, since otherwise account could be taken of prejudice to the capability, effectiveness or security of forces which co-operate only occasionally with the armed forces of the Crown.

26– 077 Defence of British Isles etc

Whether disclosure of particular information under FOIA would prejudice, or would be likely to prejudice, the defence of the British Islands or of any colony cannot properly be determined without some consideration of what the defence of the nation may reasonably require in the prevailing circumstances. Distinctions may be drawn between what is legitimately required for the defence of a nation in peacetime, during a time of preparation for war, during actual hostilities, upon the cessation of hostilities and in the transition to peace.[534] Prejudice to the defence of the nation will reflect those distinctions. The defence of the nation is not confined to the resistance of external threats to the nation, but extends to matters whose purpose is the protection of the nation.[535] Accordingly, there is bound to be some overlap between information whose disclosure would, or would be likely to, prejudice, on the one hand, the defence of the British Islands or of any colony and, on the other hand, the capability, effectiveness or security of any relevant forces, as well as a substantial overlap with information whose non-disclosure is required for the purpose of safeguarding national security. The s 26 defence interests are akin to the national security interests covered by s 24 of FOIA. The courts may therefore be expected to adopt an analogous approach to the executive's assessment of their protection and the type of disclosure which would be likely to cause them prejudice: the executive will thus be entitled to take a preventative or precautionary approach to the protection of the s 26 defence interests, taking into account the risks of mosaic prejudice,[536] and

[534] For a discussion of the fluctuating nature of what may legitimately be done under the aegis of the defence of the nation, see: *Stenhouse v Coleman* (1944) 69 CLR 457 at 471-472. The Constitution of Australia gives the Federal legislature the power to make laws with respect to the 'defence of the Commonwealth'. In general terms, the view taken is that in a period of stable and amicable international relations the extent of what may be done in the name of the defence of the Commonwealth is small: there can be no reasonable justification for interference with most ordinary civil activities. But at a period of international discord, the danger to the nation of becoming involved in war may be great and what may legitimately be done in the name of the defence of the nation is broader: *Farey v Burvett* (1916) 21 CLR 433 at 453; *Victorian Chamber of Manufacturers v The Commonwealth of Australia* (1943) 67 CLR 335 at 339; *Adelaide Company of Jehovah's Witnesses Incorporated v Commonwealth of Australia* (1943) 67 CLR 116.

[535] MoJ, *Exemptions Guidance—Section 26: Defence* (18 May 2008) Annex A states that defence, 'is achieved by maintaining the ability to use military force in support of legitimate political objectives, in particular the protection of the UK, overseas territories and national interests. Defence can therefore include self-defence, as well as measures taken in conjunction with other countries or under the auspices of an international organisation. Such measures may include steps for the detection, prevention and suppression of aggressive activities of any foreign state or party against the UK, overseas territories and national interests, and may include counter terrorist and resilience measures'. For the government line on prejudice to defence interests generally, see MoJ, *Exemptions Guidance — Section 26: Defence* (18 May 2008) pp 3-4.

[536] See §26– 036(1). This has been the approach taken by the High Court of Australia in determining whether a law is one with respect to the defence of the Commonwealth: 'It is not the duty or the function of the court to consider whether in its opinion such regulations are 'necessary' for defence purposes. Questions of legislative policy are determined by the legislature, not by the courts. If it can reasonably be considered that there is a real connection between the subject matter of the legislation and defence, the court should hold that the legislation is authorised by the power to make laws with respect to defence' (*Dawson v The Commonwealth* (1946) 73 CLR 157 at 173). However, the High Court has rejected the notion that the Parliament's or the executive's determination of the needs of defence can be conclusive: *Australian Communist Party v The Commonwealth of Australia* (1951) 83 CLR 1, where the Court held that a law *inter alia* dissolving the Australian Communist Party which, in its recital, was declared to be detrimental to the defence of the nation could not, in fact, be said to be related to the defence of the nation.

the courts can be expected to show a certain deference to its conclusions.[537] Section 2 of the Official Secrets Act 1989[538] provides some guidance as to the type of matters that may be relevant to 'defence'[539] and the type of effects which are 'damaging' to defence interests.[540]

26– 078 Capability of armed forces

So far as concerns the capability, effectiveness and security of any relevant forces, the Ministry of Justice has published its own guidance on the meaning of these terms:[541]

> Capability: Capability involves having the necessary skills to operate in a particular situation. In relation to defence it is derived from having trained manpower, serviceable equipment, the supporting systems and information needed to deploy to and conduct operations that meet the policy objectives set by government.
>
> Effectiveness: Effectiveness relates to the successful use of defence capability. This requires a readiness to undertake operations in a structured way that is appropriate to the situation, in conjunction with government departments and, where appropriate, other states and international organisations
>
> Security: Security is achieved through the protection of personnel from attack, both at a collective and at an individual level, and from the threat of compromise to the confidentiality, integrity and/or availability of defence assets.

The Information Commissioner has also issued guidance on this topic suggesting that information about the reliability of military equipment 'might' be exempt under s 26 of FOIA 'if it would enable an enemy to sabotage that equipment but not if the weakness was impossible to exploit or if it were one that was impossible to conceal.'[542] Finally, the former Ministry of

---

537 See §§26– 047 to 26– 056. See also: *R v Jones (Margaret)* [2006] UKHL 16, [2007] 1 AC 136 at [30], 'there are well-established rules that the courts will be very slow to review the exercise of prerogative powers in relation to the conduct of foreign affairs and the deployment of the armed services' (Lord Bingham citing: *Chandler v DPP* [1964] AC 763; *Council of Civil Service Unions v Minister for the Civil Service* [1985] AC 374; *Lord Advocate's Reference (No1 of 2000)* 2001 JC 143; *R (Marchiori) v Environment Agency* [2002] EWCA Civ 3, [2002] Eu LR 225 (CA)) and at [65]-[67] (Lord Hoffmann). For analogous wartime cases see: *Lipton Ltd v Ford* [1917] 2 KB 647; *Hudson's Bay Co v Maclay* (1920) 36 TLR 469; *John Robinson & Co Ltd v The King* [1921] 3 KB 183 at 197; *Fort Frances Pulp and Paper Co v Manitoba Free Press Co* [1923] AC 695 at 705-705; *Victorian Chamber of Manufactures v Commonwealth of Australia* (1943) 67 CLR 347 ('when a nation is in peril, applying the maxim *salus populi suprema lex*, the courts must concede to the Parliament and to the Executive which it controls a wide latitude to determine what legislation is required to protect the safety of the realm' at 400); *Hamilton v Kentucky Distilleries & Warehouse Co* (1919) 251 US 146 ('to the Congress, in the exercise of its powers, not least the war upon which the very life of the nation depends, a wide latitude of discretion must be accorded' at 163). For statements reiterating that decisions relating to defence procurement, training and operations in the defence context are not well suited to judicial determination and should be the subject of judicial caution and restraint: *R (Smith) v Secretary of State for Defence* [2010] UKSC 29, [2011] 1 AC 1 at [127] (Lord Rodger); *Smith v Ministry of Defence* [2013] UKSC 41, [[2014] AC 52 at [65] and [69] (Lord Hope), [128]-129 and [146]-[148] (Lord Mance, diss). In these situations consideration does not appear to have been given to the appointment of an independent assessor to assist the court or tribunal evaluate such matters. Section 27(1) of the Tribunals, Courts and Enforcement Act 2007 provides:

> 'If it appears to the First-tier Tribunal or the Upper Tribunal that a matter before it requires special expertise not otherwise available to it, it may direct that in dealing with that matter it shall have the assistance of a person or persons appearing to it to have relevant knowledge or experience.'

538 See §26– 035(1).

539 Official Secrets Act 1989 s 2(4) defines 'defence' to mean (a) the size, shape, organisation, logistics, order of battle, deployment, operations, state of readiness and training of the armed forces of the Crown, (b) the weapons, stores or other equipment of those forces and the invention, development, production and operation of such equipment and research relating to it, (c) defence policy and strategy and military planning and intelligence and (d) plans and measures for the maintenance of essential supplies and services that are or would be needed in time of war. See also MoJ, *Exemptions Guidance — Section 26: Defence* (18 May 2008) pp 3-4.

540 For the purposes of Official Secrets Act 1989 s 2(1) a disclosure is damaging if it (a) damages the capability of, or any part of, the armed forces of the Crown to carry out their tasks or leads to loss of life or injury to members of those forces or serious damage to the equipment or installations of those forces, (b) endangers the interests of the United Kingdom abroad, seriously obstructs the promotion or protection by the United Kingdom of those interests or endangers the safety of British citizens abroad or (c) would be likely to have any of those effects (s 2(2)).

541 MoJ, *Exemptions Guidance — Section 26: Defence* (18 May 2008) Annex A.

542 Information Commissioner, *Freedom of Information Act Awareness Guidance No 10: The Defence Exemption*, (2006), Pt C.

Defence publication *The Green Book: MoD Working Arrangements with the Media* provided guidance on procedures that the Ministry adopted 'in working with the media throughout the full spectrum of military operations.'[543] Under the heading 'Restrictions on Reporting' there was a list of 'Subjects that correspondents may not be allowed to include in copy, or radio or television reports without specific approval.'[544] These categories give a further indication of the types of information whose disclosure may be capable of prejudicing the capability, effectiveness or security of the armed forces.[545] The s 26 defence interests, of course, go much wider than this and are not confined to periods of operational activity.

26– 079 The public interest

Even if non-compliance with the duty to confirm or deny or the duty to communicate is required because divulgence or disclosure would, or would be likely to, prejudice any of the s 26 defence interests, divulgence or disclosure will still have to take place under s 1 of FOIA if, in all the circumstances of the case, the public interest in divulgence or disclosure is not outweighed by the public interest in preventing, or avoiding the risk of, such prejudice.[546] As with the safeguarding of national security interests under s 24 of FOIA, the decision of Parliament not to make exemption under s 26 absolute cannot properly be undone by giving the public interest in maintaining the exemption such weight as to guarantee that the public interest in disclosure will necessarily be lighter.[547] The exercise must be carried out in such a manner as to recognise that in some circumstances the public interest in disclosure will be sufficiently powerful to match an inherently compelling public interest in maintaining the

The remainder of this passage reads as follows: 'The timing of a disclosure is likely to be crucial. Information which might prejudice the effectiveness of a military operation that was either planned or underway might cause no harm once the operation had been concluded. This is not an absolute rule, and there will certainly be many cases where the disclosure of information about the tactics or weaponry involved in a successful operation might prejudice the chances of success in a similar operation in the future. When assessing whether disclosure would prejudice the purpose of defence, consideration should also be given to what information is already in the public domain. Where the same information is available from other, reliable sources, it will rarely be possible to argue that repeated disclosure would cause prejudice. By contrast, where the information available from elsewhere is of a more speculative nature (even though, in fact, true), then it will be easier to argue prejudice. Similarly, a public authority may legitimately decide to withhold information which is in itself relatively innocuous if that information would cause prejudice in combination with another piece of information which has already been put in the public domain.' See also, in similar terms, Information Commissioner, *Freedom of Information Act: Defence (section 26) (1 August 2016)* paras 21 and 36-38.

543 Ministry of Defence, *The Green Book: MoD Working Arrangements with the Media for sue throughout the Full Spectrum of the Conflict* (Joint Service Publication S80) (version 8, 31 January 2013. The Green Book was withdrawn on 24 May 2018 but can still be found at: www.gov.uk/government/publications/the-green-book

544 Ministry of Defence, *The Green Book: MoD Working Arrangements with the Media* (Joint Service Publication S80) (version 8, 31 January 2013 para 43.

545 The categories wee: (a) composition of the force and the locations of ships, units and aircraft; (b) details of military movements; (c) operational orders; (d) plans or intentions; (e) casualties; (f) organisations; (g) place names; (h) tactics, details of defensive positions, camouflage methods, weapon capabilities or deployments, force protection measures; (i) names or numbers of ships, units or aircraft; (j) names of individual servicemen; (k) prisoners of war, hostages or their familes. See also MoJ *Exemptions Guidance — Section 26: Defence* (18 May 2008) pp 3-4.

546 FOIA s 2(1)(b) and (2)(b). Similarly, if the disclosure of environmental information or the confirmation or denial of whether or not such information is held would adversely affect defence, an exception to the duty to disclose will arise under EIR reg 12 but only if, in all the circumstances of the case, the public interest in disclosure outweighs, or is equal to, the public interest in maintaining the exception (EIR reg 12(1)(b) and (6)).

547 MoJ, *Exemptions Guidance — Section 26: Defence* (18 May 2008) p 7 states, 'The public interest in avoiding prejudice to defence and the Armed Forces is strong and in most cases, will tend to outweigh the public interest in disclosing such information. However, where the risk of prejudice has been assessed as being minimal, or where the harm that is likely to result is of a trivial nature, or where the public interest in disclosure is itself particularly strong, this may tip the public interest balance in favour of disclosure.' In a similar vein, the Tribunal held that 'there would need to be very weighty countervailing considerations to outweigh a risk to security and safety of the forces which was of sufficient severity to have engaged section 26(1)(b)' in *Cole v IC and MoD* [2014] UKUT 0345 (AAC).

exemption.[548] For example, the public interest in complying with s 1 of FOIA may prevail where the degree of likelihood attaching to the apprehended prejudice is low. The United Kingdom public interest in defending a colony or protecting the capability, effectiveness or security of foreign forces may also deserve a lower weighting, particularly if the national security and international relations exemptions in ss 24 and 27 of FOIA are not engaged.[549] Moreover, it is generally recognised that the public interest in information about defence matters can be very great. The *Guidance on Interpretation* accompanying the *Code of Practice on Access to Government Information* stated in relation to the exemption for 'information whose disclosure would harm defence'[550] that this was not intended to prevent the disclosure of 'factual information relating to legitimate concerns on such matters as loss of life, or hazards and environmental intrusion arising from military operations or use of land.'[551] The guidance published by the Ministry of Justice states:[552]

> There is widespread interest in defence policy and the activities of the armed forces, and it is appropriate for the public to understand how and why key decisions are taken in these areas. The public interest will therefore be strong in relation to the disclosure of information that will inform debate and improve public understanding. Examples might include the disclosure of information relating to concerns on matters such as: national security; the safety of military personnel or loss of life; risks to the safety of civilians; the use of land or environmental impact of military activity (section 39 may also be relevant here); the factual and analytical basis used to develop defence policies; procurement; the use of public funds.
>
> On the other hand, the public interest is likely to weigh against the disclosure of information which could undermine the conduct of a specific military operation or have an adverse impact on security or safety. In addition, the disclosure of information in the face of an objection from an allied country, or in breach of a clear undertaking to preserve confidentiality, may well prejudice the UK's defence relations by restricting exchanges of information or by jeopardizing military co-operation.

548 See §26–055.

549 By way of a parallel, public interest immunity cannot be claimed by a foreign state or on the ground that disclosure would infringe the public interest of a foreign state: *Buttes Gas & Oil Co v Hammer (No 3)* [1981] QB 223 (CA) at 247, 251 and 262. However, it has been recognised that because the public interest of the United Kingdom requires continued co-operation, and recognises a convergence of interests, with foreign sovereign states, public interest immunity can nevertheless apply to various communications between British and foreign government departments or prosecuting authorities on international relations grounds: *Buttes Gas & Oil Co v Hammer (No 3)* [1981] QB 223 (CA) at 256; *R v Governor of Brixton Prison, ex p Osman* [1991] 1 WLR 281 (DC) at 285-286; *R v Horseferry Road Magistrates' Court, ex p Bennett (No 2)* (1995) 99 Cr App R 123 (DC) at 126; *R (Mohamed) v Secretary of State for Foreign & Commonwealth Affairs* [2010] EWCA Civ 65. Mention has already been made of the fact that action overseas may be capable of indirectly affecting the security of the United Kingdom, even if directed towards a foreign State: *SSHD v Rehman* [2001] UKHL 47, [2003] 1 AC 153 at [16]-[17] (Lord Slynn), [53] and [62] (Lord Hoffmann) and [64] (Lord Hutton).

550 *Open Government Code of Practice on Access to Government Information*, 2nd edn (1997) Pt II, para 1(a).

551 *Government Code of Practice on Access to Government Information: Guidance on Interpretation*, 2nd edn (1997) Pt II, para 1.1.

552 MoJ, *Exemptions Guidance — Section 26: Defence* (18 May 2008) pp 7-8.

CHAPTER 27

International and internal relations

1. INTERNATIONAL RELATIONS

27–001 Overview

Section 27(1) of FOIA[1] provides a four-limbed exemption in respect of information the disclosure of which, broadly speaking, would be likely to be prejudicial to relations between the government of the United Kingdom and a foreign state or which otherwise would be likely to be prejudicial to the interests of the United Kingdom abroad.[2] Section 27(2) of the Act provides a separate exemption for confidential information obtained from a foreign state, or from an international organisation or international court.[3] The s 27(2) exemption is purely class-based, with no requirement of harm or likelihood of harm resulting from disclosure. Both exemptions are qualified exemptions, so that whether or not there is a duty to disclose such exempt information will turn upon whether in all the circumstances of the case the public interest in maintaining the exemption outweighs the public interest in disclosing the information.[4] Section 27 also includes a corresponding exclusion of the duty to confirm or deny. Although a particular piece of information may readily fall within both sub-sections, the focus of each of

---

1 The FOI(S)A s 32(1)(a) is in similar terms, save that 'substantial prejudice' to the protected matters is required, rather than prejudice simpliciter. There is an argument that the Scottish provision relates to a matter outside the legislative competence of the Scottish Parliament. Under the Scotland Act 1998, the Scottish Parliament cannot make legislation which relates to or modifies the law on 'reserved matters' and corresponding restrictions apply in relation to the exercise of certain functions by the Scottish Ministers: Scotland Act 1998, ss 28-30, Sch 4, Pt I, paras 2, 3, Sch 5 (on 'legislative competence'), and Scotland Act 1998, ss 53-54 (on 'devolved competence'). The following are in turn defined as 'reserved matters' for the purposes of the Scotland Act 1998: (1) international relations, including relations with territories outside the United Kingdom, the European Communities (and their institutions) and other international organisations (under the heading 'foreign affairs etc'.): Scotland Act 1998 s 30, Sch 5, Pt I, para 7; and (2) public access to information held by public bodies or holders of public offices other than certain Scottish public authorities: Scotland Act 1998 s 30, Sch 5, Pt II, s.B13.

2 The provision echoes the language used in ss 3 and 6 of the Official Secrets Act 1989.

3 FOI(S)A s 32(1)(b) is in identical terms.

4 FOIA s 2(2); FOI(S)A s 2(1).

the two provisions is basically different. Section 27(1) is concerned to protect the interests of the United Kingdom in its dealings with and in other states. Section 27(2) is concerned to protect a facet of international comity. Whilst it can be said that any conduct that is potentially harmful to international comity is indirectly harmful to the interests of the United Kingdom, that harm may often be difficult to identify or measure at the time of proposed disclosure and it may have to compete with immediate interests that are clearly served by disclosure. Thus s 27(2) is capable of applying to information not captured by s 27(1). Moreover, determination of the applicability of s 27(2) is more straightforward, looking to the character of the information (ie whether it is confidential) and to the source of the information (ie whether it was obtained from a state other than the United Kingdom or from an international organisation or international court), rather than conjecturing about the effect of disclosure upon 'the interests of the United Kingdom abroad' and upon international relations. The issue of confidentiality and the scope of the s 27(2) exemption are considered in the main chapter on confidentiality.[5] The s 27(1) exemption, as well as the required sources of information for the s 27(2) exemption to operate, are considered in this chapter. With the exception of the US, similar exemptions of varying scope exist in each of the comparative jurisdictions.[6]

---

[5] See in particular §§34– 061 to 34– 064.

[6] In the United States, the Freedom of Information Act 1966 contains no specific exemption for information that might damage international relations or for information that was obtained from a foreign government in confidence. In practice, such information may be found to be exempt under Exemption 1 (national security information) provided that it has been earlier classified: see §51– 008(1) and Executive Order No 12,958 (as amended by Executive Order No 13,392), s 1.1(d). The amendment to the Executive Order instructed agencies to presume harm to the national security in releasing foreign government information. In order to be exempted, 'foreign government information' must be shown to have been provided to the US Government with an expectation of confidentiality and classified at the time as such: see *Weatherhead v United States*, 157 F 3d 735 (9th Cir 1998) and, on appeal, *Weatherhead v United States*, 527 US 1063 (1999), where a letter sent by the British Home Office to the Department of Justice was ordered to be disclosed because it had not been so classified. In *Weatherhead*, the British Government, upon being asked by the State Department whether it consented to release, stated that it was unable to agree because 'the normal line in cases like this is that all correspondence between Governments is confidential unless papers have been formally requisitioned'. If it has been classified, then exemption will generally be upheld. Thus, in *Krikorian v Department of State*, 984 F 2d 461 (DC Cir 1993) the court found that a telegram reporting discussion between an agency official and a high-ranking foreign diplomat regarding terrorism was properly withheld as foreign government information; release would jeopardise reciprocal confidentiality between governments. Differing views have been taken on whether the agency must demonstrate that the foreign state provided the information in confidence or whether that is to be presumed: *Steinberg v United States Department of Justice*, 179 FRD 357 (DDC 1998) and *Billington v Department of Justice*, 11 F Supp 2d 45 (DDC 1998) and 69 F Supp 2d 128 (DDC 1999). Exemption can also be secured under Exemption 7: §51– 008(7). The Freedom of Information Act 1982 (Cth of Australia) s 33, provides two exemptions that broadly correlate to the two provisions in FOIA s 27(1) and (2). Under Freedom of Information Act 1982 s 33(1)(a)(iii), a document is exempt where its disclosure would, or could be reasonably be expected to, cause damage to the international relations of Australia; under s 33(1)(b) a document is exempt if its disclosure would divulge any information communicated in confidence by or on behalf of a foreign government, etc: see §51– 015(9). The provision does not involve a consideration of the public interest. The Official Information Act 1982 (New Zealand), provides two separate absolute exemptions to cover analogous information. First, information may be withheld without a consideration of the public interest where disclosure would be likely to prejudice the international relations of the New Zealand Government: Official Information Act 1982 ss 6(b) and 27(1)(a); Privacy Act 1993 s 27(1)(b); and see §51– 022(1). Secondly, information may also be withheld without a consideration of the public interest where disclosure would be likely to prejudice the entrusting of information to the Government of New Zealand on a basis of confidence by the Government of any other country or any agency of such a government, or by any international organisation: Official Information Act 1982 ss 6(b) and 27(1)(a); Privacy Act 1993 s 27(1)(b); and see §51– 022(1). The Act provides for the Prime Minister to issue a conclusive certificate in support of the first: s 31. The Access to Information Act (Canada) s 15 provides a discretionary exemption for records the disclosure of which could 'reasonably be expected' to cause injury to the conduct of international affairs: see §51– 032(11). The Canada Evidence Act allows the Attorney-General to issue a certificate prohibiting the disclosure of information in connection with a legal proceeding for the purpose of inter alia protecting information obtained in confidence from foreign entities. The Freedom of Information Act 2014 (Ireland), s 33(1)(d) provides a discretionary exemption for records the disclosure of which could reasonably be expected to affect adversely the international relations of the State of Ireland and ss 33(2)(b)(ii) and 33(3)(c) provide a narrower mandatory exemption: see §51– 039(13). The Act provides for a conclusive certificate in support of the exemption: s 34.

27–002 Scope

Section 27(1) of FOIA[7] provides that where the disclosure of information under the Act would or would be likely to prejudice:

(a) relations between the United Kingdom[8] and any other state,

(b) relations between the United Kingdom and any international organisation or international court,

(c) the interests of the United Kingdom abroad, or

(d) the promotion or protection by the United Kingdom of its interests abroad,

then the information is exempt information. It is the relations and interests of the United Kingdom with which s 27(1) is concerned: it is not directly concerned with the interests of individual companies or enterprises as such.[9]

27–003 Likelihood of prejudice

The phrase 'would or would be likely to prejudice' is common to most of the prejudice-based exemptions in the Act. The nature of prejudice and the degree of likelihood which the phrase requires are considered elsewhere in this work.[10] The required probability of prejudice to the protected interests is that disclosure of the requested information be 'likely' to prejudice one or more of those protected interests. In considering s 27(1), the FTT has said that it:

> require[s] consideration of what is probable as opposed to possible or speculative. Prejudice is not defined, but we accept that it imports something of detriment in the sense of impairing relations or interests or their promotion or protection and further we accept that the prejudice must be real, actual or of substance.[11]

The Tribunal went on to effectively reduce the required level of probability by including 'risk of harm' as a species of 'prejudice.'[12] While the FTT noted that prejudice could include disclosure which 'makes relations more difficult or calls for [a] particular diplomatic response to contain or limit damage,' it went on to find that there would or could be prejudice to the interests of the United Kingdom if the consequence of disclosure was to create the risk of an adverse reaction from a foreign power. A similar approach was adopted in *Home Office v IC and John O*, where the Tribunal found that '[t]he risk of an adverse reaction by another State is enough…the prejudice would lie in the exposure and vulnerability to that risk.'[13] It is suggested, however, that the only point at which the probability of prejudice to a protected interest enters s 27(1) is through the words 'would be likely', and that a risk of prejudice and actual prejudice are not synonymous.[14]

7 And similarly the FOI(S)A s 32(1)(a), but with a requirement of substantial prejudice.

8 'United Kingdom' bears its ordinary meaning under the Interpretation Act 1978: in other words, Great Britain and Northern Ireland: s 5 and Sch 1. Great Britain consists of England, Scotland and Wales.

9 *Campaign against the Arms Trade v IC and MoJ*, IT, 26 August 2008, at [81].

10 See §§6–020 to 6–028. The Information Tribunal in *FCO v IC and Friends of the Earth*, IT, 29 June 2007 at [34] confirmed that the Tribunal's approach to prejudice in other exemptions was equally applicable to s 27.

11 *Campaign against the Arms Trade v IC and MoJ*, IT, 26 August 2008, at [80]. And similarly *Gilby v IC and FCO*, IT, 22 October 2008, at [23].

12 *Campaign against the Arms Trade v IC and MoJ*, IT, 26 August 2008, at [81]. And similarly *Gilby v IC and FCO*, IT, 22 October 2008, at [23].

13 *Home Office v IC and John O*, FTT, 10 April 2013 at [126]. See also: *Burt v IC*, FTT, 25 October 2011 at [31]; *All Party Parliamentary Group on Extraordinary Rendition v IC and FCO*, FTT, 3 May 2012 at [130].

14 Since 'risk' means the possibility of an adverse circumstance, by employing the formula 'would be likely to prejudice' a protected interest, s 27(1) already spells out the precise 'risk' that will engage the exemption. This is consistent with the manner in which the other exemptions employing the same prejudice formula have been applied by the Tribunal.

27– 004 The State and its organs

The Freedom of Information Act 2000 defines the word 'State' to include the 'government of any State and any organ of its government',[15] thereby alluding to its meaning in international law. There is no means of determining objectively the existence of a state: it is a matter of recognition by one state of another state, with recognition being largely presumed.[16] The stated view of the United Kingdom is:

> The normal criteria which the government apply for recognition as a state are that it should have, and seem likely to continue to have, a clearly defined territory with a population, a government who are able of themselves to exercise effective control of that territory, and independence in their external relations. Other factors, including some United Nations resolutions, may also be relevant.[17]

An entity unrecognised by the Foreign Office as a state will generally be treated by the courts as if it did not exist.[18] The constituent parts of a federated state, although often termed 'states' in their domestic law, are not states in the international law sense.[19] Whilst identification of a state itself will generally be straightforward, identification of the 'organs of its government' involves a consideration of the degree to which an entity is distinct from the executive elements of the government of the State.[20] The above starting-point has, in part, been displaced by the definition of 'state' given in s 27(5). Certainly so far as s 27(2) is concerned and seemingly so far as s 27(1) is concerned, the phrase 'State other than the United Kingdom' is defined to include references to any territory outside the United Kingdom. This is considerably wider than a state in its international law sense, and is sufficiently broad to include British territories.[21]

27– 005 International organisations

Section 27(5) of FOIA defines 'international organisation' to mean 'any international organisation whose members include any two or more states, or any organ of such an organisation',[22] thereby alluding to its meaning in international law. There is no fixed meaning in international law of the phrase 'international organisation.' However, the universal core attributes of an international organisation are:

---

15 FOIA s 27(5); FOI(S)A s 32(3).

16 See generally RY Jennings and AD Watts (eds), *Oppenheim's International Law*, 9th edn (Oxford, OUP, 2008) pp 120-123.

17 Hansard HC vol 102 col 977 (23 October 1986) (written answer). See also Hansard HC vol 169 cols 449-450 (19 March 1990) (written answer). This accords with the view taken in RY Jennings and AD Watts (eds), *Oppenheim's International Law*, 9th edn (Oxford, OUP, 2008), pp 120-123, where four conditions are identified as being necessary for the existence of a state: (1) a people, being an aggregate of individuals who live together as a community; (2) a territory in which the people are settled, even if its frontiers be disputed; (3) a government, meaning that there must be one or more persons who act for the people and govern according to the law of the land; and (4) a sovereign government, meaning that its domestic authority must not be dependent upon any other earthly authority.

18 *The Annette* [1919] P 105; *Luther v Sagor* [1921] 1 KB 456, [1921] 3 KB 532.

19 Such as the 50 states of the United States or the six states of Australia. Thus in *R (Alamieyeseigha) v Crown Prosecution Service* [2005] EWHC 2704, [2006] Crim LR 669 the Divisional Court held that Bayelsa State, a constituent part of the Federal Republic of Nigeria, did not conduct international relations.

20 *FCO v IC and Friends of the Earth*, IT, 29 June 2007 at [36(1)]. In *Coreck Maritime v Sevrybokholodflot*, 1994 SLT 893 (a state-owned shipping company held not to be an organ of the state on the basis that it was a commercial company, it had its own legal personality, it was substantially free of government control and it exercised no governmental functions).

21 That is: Anguilla, Ascension Island, Bermuda, British Antarctic Territory, British Indian Ocean Territory, British Virgin Islands, Cayman Islands, Falkland Islands, Gibraltar, Monserrat, Pitcairn Islands, St Helena, South Georgia and South Sandwich Islands, Tristan da Cunha, and Turks & Caicos Islands.

22 Similarly FOI(S)A s 32(3).

- that it is created by a treaty between two or more states;[23]
- possession of what might be called a constitution;
- that it is a legal entity in international law, in the sense of being a juridical person or having legal personality; and
- generally, but not always, having an exclusive membership of states or governments, or at any rate membership that is predominantly composed of states or governments.[24]

International organisations of which the United Kingdom is a member are readily identifiable as they are declared to be such by Order in Council[25] or, in a limited number of cases, by statute.[26] Some international organisations of which the United Kingdom is not a member are also readily identifiable by virtue of their having certain privileges and immunities conferred on them by Order in Council.[27] The list of international organisations that the United Kingdom has either recognised or upon which it has conferred privileges and immunities is extensive, but more notable inclusions are: the Asian Development Bank;[28] the Council of Europe;[29] the European Court of Human Rights;[30] the European Bank for Reconstruction and Development;[31] the European Space Agency;[32] the European Union and its organs;[33] the International Atomic Energy Agency; the International Bank for Reconstruction and

---

[23] *JH Rayner (Mincing Lane) Ltd v DTI* [1989] Ch 72 at 143 (Kerr LJ) where he also observed that most such treaties will be called a 'convention' or 'agreement'. Thus in *Westland Helicopters Ltd v Arab Organisation for Industrialisation* [1995] QB 282, [1995] 2 All ER 387, [1994] 2 Lloyd's Rep 608 the Arab Organisation for Industrialisation, which was created by treaty, whose members were states and which was given legal personality in each of its four member states, was recognised to be an 'international organisation'.

[24] See CF Amerasinghe, *Principles of the Institutional Law of International Organizations*, 2nd edn (Cambridge, Cambridge University Press, 2005) Ch 1; G Schwarzenberger, *International Law as applied by International Courts and Tribunals* (London, Stevens & Sons, 1976) vol III, pp 5-8.

[25] See the International Organisations Act 1968 s 1, replacing the International Organisations (Immunities and Privileges) Act 1950. Any such Order in Council must be laid in draft before Parliament and approved by a resolution of each House: s 10(1).

[26] Such as the Bretton Woods Agreements Act 1945 and the International Sugar Organisation Act 1973.

[27] For example, because the United Kingdom has entered into 'headquarters agreement' with an international organisation which has its headquarters in the United Kingdom. This includes: the International Cocoa Organisation; the International Coffee Organisation; the International Whaling Commission; the International Maritime Organisation; INTELSAT.

[28] Asian Development Bank (Immunities and Privileges) Order 1974 SI 1974/1251.

[29] General Agreement on Privileges and Immunities of the Council of Europe, Paris, 2 September 1949 (Cmd 8852, 1949).

[30] Second Protocol to the General Agreement on Privileges and Immunities of the Council of Europe, Paris, 15 December 1956 (Cmnd 579, 1957) (Commission of Human Rights); Fourth Protocol to the General Agreement on Privileges and Immunities of the Council of Europe, Paris, 16 December 1961 (Cmnd 4739, 1961).

[31] European Bank for Reconstruction and Development (Immunities and Privileges) Order 1991 SI 1991/757.

[32] European Space Agency (Immunities and Privileges) Order 1978 SI 1978/1105.

[33] Protocol on the Privileges and Immunities of the European Communities, Brussels, 8 April 1965 (Cmnd 5179, 1965) (as amended). In *Ryanair Ltd v IC and OFT*, FTT, 28 January 2013 the Tribunal upheld reliance upon FOIA ss 27(1)(b), 27(1)(c) and 27(2) on the basis that disclosure of the requested information would be likely to prejudice relations between the European Commission and the UK as a result of it breaching the Commission's reasonable expectation of confidentiality.

Development;[34] the International Court of Justice;[35] the International Monetary Fund;[36] the International Finance Corporation;[37] the North Atlantic Treaty Organisation;[38] the Organisation for Economic Co-operation and Development;[39] the United Nations (including various specialised agencies of the United Nations, such as the Food and Agriculture Organisation, the International Labour Organisation, the International Telecommunications Union, the United Nations Educational, Scientific and Cultural Organisation, the Universal Postal Union, the World Health Organisation, the World Meteorological Organisation, and the World Intellectual Property Organisation);[40] and the World Trade Organisation.[41] In addition to these readily recognisable international organisations, there exist many other international organisations (in the international law sense) including the Arab League, The Organisation of American States, The Organisation of African Unity, and The Association of South-East Asian Nations. So, too, the Commonwealth Secretariat.[42] These, too, will fall within the definition given by s 27(5), notwithstanding that these organisations do not enjoy any privileges and immunities in the United Kingdom.[43]

27–006 International courts

Section 27(5) of FOIA defines 'international court' to mean

> any international court which is not an international organisation and which is established: (a) by a resolution of an international organisation of which the United Kingdom is a member, or (b) by an international agreement to which the United Kingdom is a party.

A number of notable international courts are international organisations,[44] but the operation of s 27 is the same whether the body falls within the definition of 'international organisation' or within the definition of 'international court'. The phrase 'international court' has no fixed meaning in international law, but the essential attributes would appear to be that:

- it is created by a treaty between two or more states;
- it has a legal personality derived from international law;

[34] Articles of Agreement of the International Bank for Reconstruction and Development (Washington, 27 December 1945 (Cmd 6885, 1946) Art I. The International Bank for Reconstruction and Development was established by an agreement drawn up at the United Nations Monetary and Financial Conference held at Bretton Woods, New Hampshire, USA in July 1944: see the Bretton Woods Agreement Act 1945 preamble (repealed). See also International Bank for Reconstruction and Development (1988 General Capital Increase) Order 1988 SI 1988/1486.

[35] United Nations and International Court of Justice (Immunities and Privileges) Order 1974 SI 1974/1261.

[36] The International Monetary Fund was created at the Bretton Woods Conference in 1944. The constitution of the International Monetary Fund can be found in the Articles of Agreement of the International Monetary Fund (Washington, 27 December 1945 (Cmd 6885, 1946) (amended by TS 44 (Cmnd 7205, 1978); TS 83 (Cmnd 7331, 1978)). See also International Monetary Fund Act 1979 s 5.

[37] The International Finance Corporation is an affiliate of the International Bank for Reconstruction and Development: Articles of Agreement of the International Finance Corporation (Washington, 25 May 1955, TS 37 (Cmnd 1377, 1961) Art I. See also International Finance Corporation (1991 General Capital Increase) Order 1993 SI 1993/1059.

[38] Agreement on the Status of the North Atlantic Treaty Organisation, National Representatives and International Staff, Ottawa, 20 September 1951 (Cmnd 9383, 1951).

[39] Organisation for Economic Co-operation and Development (Immunities and Privileges) Order 1974 SI 1974/1258.

[40] Specialised Agencies of the United Nations (Immunities and Privileges) Order 1974 SI 1974/1260.

[41] World Trade Organisation (Immunities and Privileges) Order 1995 SI 1995/266.

[42] *Sukuman Ltd v Commonwealth Secretariat* [2006] EWHC 304 (Comm), [2006] 1 All ER (Comm) 621, [2006] 2 Lloyd's Rep 53.

[43] See *Arab Monetary Fund v Hashim (No 3)* [1991] 1 AC 114 at 167, which suggests that in such cases, in order to be recognised as an international organisation, the entity must be created not by treaty but by one or more of the member states.

[44] The European Court of Human Rights, see n 30; the International Court of Justice, see n 35; and the International Criminal Court.

- — it enjoys the usual immunities enjoyed by an international organisation; and
- — it has had conferred on it powers and duties that are essentially judicial, even if it also performs administrative acts.[45]

International courts vary in nature, but may be divided into:

(1) Courts of universal scope, which includes the International Court of Justice, the International Tribunal for the Law of the Sea, the Dispute Settlement System of the World Trade Organisation, and the International Criminal Court.

(2) Ad hoc criminal tribunals, which includes the International Criminal Tribunal for the former Yugoslavia and the International Tribunal for Rwanda.

(3) Regional Human Rights Courts, which includes the European Court of Human Rights, the Inter-American Court of Human Rights, and the African Court of Human and Peoples Rights.

(4) Judicial bodies of regional economic integration and the like, including the Court of Justice of the European Union (comprising the Court of Justice, the General Court and the Civil Service Tribunal), the Court of Justice of the European Free Trade Agreement, the Court of Justice of the Benelux Economic Union, the Central American Court of Justice, the Court of Justice of the Andean Community, the Court of Justice of the Common Market for Eastern and Southern Africa, the Common Court of Justice and Arbitration of the Organisation for the Harmonisation of Corporate Law in Africa, the Judicial Tribunal of the Organisation of Arab Petroleum Exporting Countries, and the Court of Justice of the Arab Maghrev Union.

27–007 International relations

There are basically two broad classes of information the disclosure of which may cause any of the types of prejudice identified in s 27(1)(a)-(b). The first class is information that has been supplied by a foreign State on the understanding or in the expectation that that information will not be further disseminated without the approval of the foreign State. In other words, the disclosure would break an understanding, whether express, implicit or arising from convention, and the breaking of that understanding by disclosure of the information would thereby result in a likelihood of harm to the protected interest. Whilst information in this class may, of course, also be rendered exempt information by s 27(2), there is the possibility of freestanding exemption under s 27(1). The second class embraces information the disclosure of which, on the basis of the particular information that would be disclosed, could be expected to cause prejudice to relations between the United Kingdom and another state or an international organisation or court. Here, the potential prejudice does not arise from the mere fact of disclosure of information that has been provided by a foreign state upon a particular understanding which would be broken: it arises from a likely effect of the disclosure of the particular information upon the international relations of the United Kingdom having regard to the information itself.

27–008 Breaking an understanding

The first class within s 27(1) needs to be approached with a degree of circumspection. In requiring harm or a likelihood of harm to the protected interest, s 27(1) is deliberately not framed as a pure class-based exemption. The contrast with s 27(2), which is purely class-based but narrower in the reach of that class, is readily apparent. Ready acceptance of generalised claims of a likelihood of harm so as to pick up all or most information within the s 27(1) class has the effect of converting the s 27(1) exemption into a pure class-based exemption. The FTT

---

[45] See P Sands *et al*, *Manual on International Courts and Tribunals* (London, Butterworths, 1999); CF Amersainghe, *Jurisdiction of International Tribunals* (The Hague, Kluwer Law International, 2003) pp 42-43.

has been alive to this and to the attraction for a public authority in making this claim, In *Foreign & Commonwealth Office v Information Commissioner*[46] the FTT rejected an argument that it should necessarily follow the assessment of the Foreign & Commonwealth Office of the likely prejudice to result from a disclosure of communications between officials of the United Kingdom and those of a foreign state, although it accepted that the FCO's view had to be taken into account. The Upper Tribunal has been more receptive to such claims, stating that appropriate weight must be attached to evidence from the executive branch of government about the prejudice likely to be caused to particular relations by disclosure of particular information.[47] In doing so it has transposed observations of the Master of the Rolls in *R (Mohamed) v Secretary of State for Foreign and Commonwealth Affairs* made in a different statutory context:

> In practical terms, the Foreign Secretary has unrestricted access to full and open advice from his experienced advisers, both in the Foreign Office and the intelligence services. He is accordingly far better informed, as well as having far more relevant experience, than any judge, for the purpose of assessing the likely attitude and actions of foreign intelligence services as a result of the publication of the redacted paragraphs, and the consequences of any such actions so far as the prevention of terrorism in this country is concerned.[48]

In *FCO v Information Commissioner v Plowden*[49] the Upper Tribunal went further, observing that members of the Tribunal do not have personal experience of the diplomatic consequences of disclosure and that, as a result, the Tribunal must in such cases rely more on the evidence and less on its own experience in assessing the balance of the public interest.[50] The Upper Tribunal is more likely to interfere with the FTT's judgment on where that balance lies than in the general run of cases.[51] In *Campaign against the Arms Trade v IC and MoJ*,[52] the Tribunal placed reliance upon evidence from diplomats of the anticipated reaction from the foreign government. Similarly, in *All Party Parliamentary Group on Extraordinary Rendition v IC and FCO*,[53] the Tribunal accepted the view of a member of the diplomatic service and a senior civil servant in the absence of any evidence seriously contradicting his view. In *Gilby v IC and FCO*,[54] the Tribunal readily concluded that disclosure of information concerning arms contracts with the Kingdom of Saudi Arabia would result in or would be likely to result in prejudice to relations between the United Kingdom and that State, as well as to the interests of the United Kingdom. In reaching this conclusion the Tribunal found that it was highly likely that any disclosure

---

46 *FCO v IC and Friends of the Earth*, IT, 29 June 2007 at [39].

47 *All Party Parliamentary Group on Extraordinary Rendition v IC and Ministry of Defence* [2011] UKUT 153 (AAC) at [56]. See also: *Plowden and FCO v IC*, FTT, 21 May 2012 at [20]-[21], overturned on different grounds in *FCO v IC and Plowden* [2013] UKUT 275 (AAC).

48 *R (Mohamed) v Secretary of State for Foreign and Commonwealth Affairs* [2010] EWCA Civ 65, [2011] QB 218 at [131].

49 *FCO v Information Commissioner and Plowden* [2013] UKUT 275 (AAC) at [13].

50 The Tribunal appears to be accepting 'expert' opinion evidence on one of the issues that the Tribunal is charged with determining. Given that the Legislature did not provide for a conclusive certificate in support of a claim for exemption under s 27(1) (in contrast to those which it provided to facilitate exemption under ss 23(2), 24(3) or 36(7)), the Tribunal's approach (which produces a result approaching the effect of a certificate) is questionable. In a situation such as this, it is suggested that the better course is for the Tribunal to enlist the assistance of a person or persons appearing to it to have relevant knowledge or expertise. Section 27(1) of the Tribunals Courts and Enforcement Act 2007 provides:

> 'If it appears to the First-tier Tribunal or the Upper Tribunal that a matter before it requires special expertise not otherwise available to it, it may direct that in dealing with that matter it shall have the assistance of a person or persons appearing to it to have relevant knowledge or experience.'

The Tribunals appear rarely, if ever, to have used the power. Lord Woolf recommended that greater use be made of assessors in his *Access to Justice: Final Report*, §§13.58-13.60. This has not happened (see Dwyer, 'The Future of Assessors under the CPR', *CJQ*, 219) and, in the public law sphere, there is an apparent preference for deference.

51 *FCO v Information Commissioner and Plowden* [2013] UKUT 275 (AAC) at [13].

52 IT, 26 August 2008, at [86]-[89].

53 *All Party Parliamentary Group on Extraordinary Rendition v IC and FCO*, FTT, 3 May 2012 at [134].

54 IT, 22 October 2008 at [42]-[44]. Similarly *Cole v IC and MoD*, FTT, 15 August 2017 at [71]-[74].

under FOIA would come to the attention of officials within the Kingdom of Saudi Arabia and that the damage would be distinct and greater than that caused by earlier unofficial ad hoc disclosures to similar effect.[55] Earlier Tribunal decisions showed a preparedness to question official say-so of harm to the protected interest.[56] In later decisions, however, the FTT has generally deferred to public authority claims that international relations would be likely to be prejudiced by the disclosure of a document, either sourced from or sent to a foreign state or recording meetings with representatives of a foreign state, provided that that claimed harm is supported by FCO evidence and that the information has not been formally otherwise disclosed.[57]

27– 009 Understandings: comparative law

Given that the harm sought to be avoided by the s 27(1) exemption relies to a significant extent on the reaction of a foreign state to the disclosure, comparative jurisprudence can provide a useful normative check upon the claims of prejudice. The jurisprudence of the comparative jurisdictions reveals that public authorities often maintain that disclosure of information in the first class would damage international relations. These claims have enjoyed a measure of success, although such claims have been approached with a degree of circumspection in order not to convert what is a prejudice-based exemption into a purely class-based exemption. In Australia, the Administrative Appeals Tribunal has been generally receptive to such claims.[58] In *Re Maher and Attorney-General's Department*[59] the President of the Tribunal upheld exemption on this basis for documents revealing negotiations that led to a treaty between Australia and United States on limiting the extra-territorial effect of anti-trust litigation in the United States. In *Re Slater and Cox (Director-General of Australian Archives)*[60] the Tribunal upheld non-disclosure of documents relating to the establishment of the Australian Secret Service and the Australian Secret Intelligence Service some 30 or so years before the making of the request. The necessarily generalised reasoning of the Tribunal[61] anticipated the approach taken by the FTT under FOIA:

> It is necessary to have some regard to differences in attitude, and to reflect the views, of foreign governments which provide information, etc to the Australian Government or its agencies. Failure to respect such views could lead to a diminution in co-operation and

---

55 See further §6– 026.

56 In *All Party Parliamentary Group on Extraordinary Rendition v IC and Ministry of Defence* [2011] UKUT 153 (AAC) the Upper Tribunal considered the possible disclosure of a memorandum of understanding between the United Kingdom and the Governments of Iraq, Afghanistan and the United States of America in respect of the treatment of persons detained in the conflicts in Iraq and Afghanistan (at [59]-[67]). The Upper Tribunal observed that protection of human rights was a fundamental duty of all state parties to the United Nations, and that the maintenance of the rule of law and protection of fundamental rights was known to be a core value of the Government of the United Kingdom. It accordingly found it difficult to see how any responsible government with whom the UK has friendly relations could take offence at disclosure of the terms of an agreement or similar practical arrangements to ensure that the law is upheld, and was unpersuaded that the exemption applied.

57 *Cole v IC and MoD*, FTT, 15 August 2017 at[55]; *Francis v IC and DFID*, FTT, 25 April 2014; *Jones v IC and FCO*, FTT, 29 April 2015 at [44]; *Cross v IC and Cabinet Office*, FTT, 7 January 2016 at [28]; *O'Hare v IC and Scotland Office*, FTT, 13 January 2017 at [35]-[36]; *Naseby v IC and FCO*, FTT, 3 May 2017 at [42]-[45].

58 The relevant principles as set out in guidelines published by the Australian Information Commissioner are summarised in *AA and Bureau of Meteorology* [2013] AICmr 46 at [13].

59 (1985) 7 ALD 731, 3 AAR 396 at [40]-[41]. Referred to in *Campaign against the Arms Trade v IC and MoJ*, IT, 26 August 2008, at [81], with seeming support.

60 (1988) 15 ALD 20. Later authorities have followed this reasoning: *Secretary, Department of Foreign Affairs & Trade v Whittaker* [2005] FCAFC 15; *Bui v Dept of Foreign Affairs and Trade* [2005] AATA 97; *Re O'Donovan & Attorney-General's Department* (1985) 8 ALD 528; *Commonwealth of Australia v Hittich* (1994) 53 FCR 152; *Wang v Department of Employment, Education and Training* (1988) 15 ALD 497.

61 As the Tribunal explained: 'The Scylla of disclosure of confidential material (or worse, of the contents of a document in issue), and the Charybdis of inadequate explanation must each be avoided.'

> consequently damage relations. Considerable weight should be given by the Tribunal to the views of objecting foreign governments since they are usually in the best position to assess the local, regional or international consequences of disclosure...If it can be anticipated that disclosure of the document would lessen the confidence which another country would place in the Government of Australia, that is sufficient ground for a finding that the disclosure of the document could reasonably be expected to damage international relations (though a mere allegation of damage or an expression of concern may not be sufficient).[62]

It is, of course, important to distinguish contrived prejudice (which may or may not be supported by the foreign government that supplied the information) or mere diplomatic irritation from true prejudice to relations between the United Kingdom and another state.

27– 010 Content prejudice

Quite apart from breaking any understanding with a foreign state, disclosure of certain information may risk souring relations between the United Kingdom and another state because of the very contents of that information. The FTT has found that the exemption was engaged both in relation to confidential exchanges between US and UK officials, and in relation to documents and communications commenting on US intentions and policy, or outlining steps that the UK would take in response to US requests.[63] The Tribunal has held that in assessing the effect on relations, it is relevant to take into account that the precepts of openness and transparency that underpin FOIA are alien to the foreign state in question.[64] However, the Upper Tribunal has similarly had regard to the fact that a particular foreign state is a constitutional democracy with its own well established traditions of free speech and freedom of information,[65] and the First-tier Tribunal has observed that a foreign state will be regarded as taking the United Kingdom as it finds it, including the effect of its domestic disclosure laws.[66]

27– 011 Content prejudice: comparative

The jurisprudence of the CJEU shows the court analysing the particular document(s) that would fall to be disclosed, paying regard to its type, its content and the wider context surrounding the information within it, so as to evaluate the harm that would be likely to result from its disclosure.[67] Of relevance will be the extent to which the information caught by the request related to facts that have already been made public or that are common knowledge.[68] The risk of the claimed harm may be reduced by factors such as political changes that have

---

62 At [35]-[36] and [50]. The Tribunal quoted with approval from the decision of Neaves J in *Re Throssell and Department of Foreign Affairs (No 2)* (1987) 14 ALD 296 at [16]: 'The material before the Tribunal tends to support the conclusion that the disclosure to the public of the records identified in the certificate could have the result of impairing the degree of trust and confidence which foreign governments place in the Government of the Commonwealth and, in consequence, of inhibiting the flow of information relating to security which might otherwise come to Australia from the overseas governmental agencies concerned and, possibly, similar agencies in other overseas countries. If such a result ensued, damage would be caused to the security and international relations of the Commonwealth. Whether such action on the part of the foreign governments and agencies would be a rational or otherwise proper reaction to the disclosure of these particular records is not to the point. The question is whether such action could reasonably be expected in the event of access being granted.'

63 *All Party Parliamentary Group on Extraordinary Rendition v IC and FCO*, FTT, 3 May 2012 at [133].

64 *Campaign against the Arms Trade v IC and MoJ*, IT, 26 August 2008, at [91]; *Gilby v IC and FCO*, IT, 22 October 2008, at [43]-[44].

65 *All Party Parliamentary Group on Extraordinary Rendition v IC and Ministry of Defence* [2011] UKUT 153 (AAC) at [65].

66 *Burt v IC*, FTT, 25 October 2011 at [36].

67 *Kuijer v EU Council (No 2)* [2002] 1 WLR 1941, Court of First Instance of the European Communities. This was a request for information under the access regime then applicable to institutions of the European Union: see further Ch 43. See also: *Sison v Council of the European Union* [2005] ECR II-1429, [2005] 2 CMLR 29.

68 At [63].

occurred since preparation of the document.[69]

27– 012 Interests of the UK

Paragraphs (c)-(d) of s 27(1) protect from disclosure information that would or would be likely to prejudice 'the interests of the United Kingdom abroad'. The phrase is sufficiently elastic to potentially embrace any financial, economic or proprietary interest abroad with which the United Kingdom (as a state) has some interest.[70] On the other hand, it is also susceptible to a narrower interpretation that confines it to matters of sovereign interest abroad.

27– 013 The public interest

As noted above, the exemption is qualified: it only applies if the public interest in maintaining the exemption outweighs the public interest in disclosing the information.[71] Its status as a qualified exemption means that likely prejudice to the protected interest from disclosure does not necessarily mean that the public interest balance will result in non-disclosure.[72] Depending on the information that stands to be disclosed, the following may be relevant to a consideration of the public interest:

(1) The recognised public interest in maintaining the confidentiality of diplomatic communications, in particular where the disclosure would interfere with the State's ability to negotiate delicate situations by stating different or even contradictory things to other states without the contradictions being too apparent.[73] The public interest will be particularly pressing if disclosure were to weaken the Government's bargaining position in negotiations with another state. Although the weight of this facet of the public interest will be time-sensitive, where the fragility of the negotiations is such there is a real risk that harm to future negotiations would result from merely revealing communications of the sort involved, the public interest in maintaining the exemption will subsist for a longer period.[74]

(2) The public interest in avoiding other forms of prejudice to relations between the United Kingdom and other states or international organisations or courts, such as might result from revealing previously undisclosed critical appraisals of foreign states or their institutions.[75]

(3) There is a public interest in avoiding a disclosure that would impede international negotiations, for example, by revealing a negotiating or fall-back position, or

---

69 At [66].

70 For examples of its application: *Campaign against the Arms Trade v IC and MoJ*, IT, 26 August 2008; *Gilby v IC and FCO*, IT, 22 October 2008; *Campaign Against Arms Trade v IC and Ministry of Defence*, FTT, 22 November 2011.

71 See: FOIA ss 2(1)(b) and 2(2)(b) and FOI(S)A s 2(1)(b). For a general discussion of this topic, see §§6– 001 to 6– 019.

72 *Cole v IC and MoD*, FTT, 15 August 2017 at [58], [91]; *O'Hare v IC and Scotland Office*, FTT, 13 January 2017 at [37]-[38].

73 *Gilby v IC and FCO*, IT, 22 October 2008, at [49]-[52]; *All Party Parliamentary Group on Extraordinary Rendition v IC and FCO*, FTT, 3 May 2012 at [170]. See the *White Paper on Open Government* (Cm 2290, 1993) paras 3.8-3.9 and Annex A, Pt II, para i; the Scottish Executive's *Code of Practice on Access to Scottish Executive Information*, 2nd edn (2003), Pt II; and the National Assembly for Wales's *Code of Practice on Public Access to Information*, 2nd edn (2001) Annex B. According to Harold Nicolson, *Diplomacy, a Basic Guide to the Conduct of Contemporary Foreign Affairs* (London, Thornton Butterworth, 1939) diplomats are 'sent abroad to lie for their country'.

74 This is the line that was taken by the Federal Court of Canada in *Do-Ky v Canada (Minister of Foreign Affairs & International Trade)* [1997] 2 FC 907. The difference with the 'candour' argument in relation to the development of government policy by officials (see §31– 015) is that the relationship is not one of master and servant, with the foreign State being under no obligation to convey information to the United Kingdom and potentially having an agenda of its own that may be compromised by the disclosure. See also *Besselink v Council of the European Union* (T-331/11) [2014] 1 CMLR 28 at [74]-[78].

75 *Campaign Against Arms Trade v IC and Ministry of Defence*, FTT, 22 November 2011 at [68]-[69].

weakening the Government's bargaining position.[76]

(4) Whether the disclosure would have an adverse impact upon the relationship between the Governments of the United Kingdom and of another State.[77]

(5) Whether the disclosure would have an adverse impact upon the protection and promotion of UK interests abroad.[78]

In practice, the approach of the FTT has been to regard these types of prejudice as serious, so that even if the likelihood of that risk becoming reality is slight, the public interest in upholding the exemption so as to contain that risk will often displace even a strong public interest in the disclosure of that information.[79] This, in effect, results in a de facto precautionary approach being taken once the terms of the exemption are found to have been met.[80]

27– 014 Foreign state reaction

In weighing the public interest in maintaining the exemption, it may be relevant to take into account the general attitude taken by the foreign state to the disclosure of official information.[81] For example, the public interest in maintaining exemption under s 27(1) in relation to a communication from the European Commission (which is an international organisation) where that exemption is founded upon likely prejudice to relations arising from the mere fact of disclosure is arguably diminished by the encouragement which various European Union instruments give to disclosure of official documents.[82] Although what is in the public interest of a foreign state is not directly relevant to an assessment of the public interest under FOIA, it may indirectly impinge upon that assessment.[83] On the other side of the balance, and underpinned by the rules of comity and international law, lies the principle that foreign states and organisations dealing with the public authorities in the United Kingdom must take the country as it is, including its laws relating to the disclosure of information.[84] Accordingly, the

---

76 *Open Government Code of Practice on Access to Government Information: Guidance on Interpretation*, 2nd edn (1997) Pt II, para 1.5. See also *Sophie in 't Veld v Council of the European Union* (T-529/09), 4 May 2012 at [88]; *Sophie in 't Veld v Commission* (T-301/10), 19 March 2013 at [123]-[125].

77 *Campaign against the Arms Trade v IC and MoJ*, IT, 26 August 2008 at [96]; *Gilby v IC and FCO*, IT, 22 October 2008 at [51]; *Campaign Against Arms Trade v IC and Ministry of Defence*, FTT, 22 November 2011 at [68]; *All Party Parliamentary Group on Extraordinary Rendition v IC and FCO*, FTT, 3 May 2012 at [166]-[168]; *All Party Parliamentary Group on Extraordinary Rendition v IC and FCO* [2015] UKUT 0377 (AAC) at [47].

78 *Campaign against the Arms Trade v IC and MoJ*, IT, 26 August 2008 at [96]; *Gilby v IC and FCO*, IT, 22 October 2008 at [51].

79 See, for example: *Naseby v IC and FCO*, FTT, 3 May 2017 at [46]-[47].

80 *All Party Parliamentary Group on Extraordinary Rendition v IC and FCO* [2015] UKUT 0377 (AAC) at [101]-[121].

81 *Campaign against the Arms Trade v IC and MoJ*, IT, 26 August 2008, at [91], [96]; *Gilby v IC and FCO*, IT, 22 October 2008, at [43]-[44], [51]; *All Party Parliamentary Group on Extraordinary Rendition v IC and Ministry of Defence* [2011] UKUT 153 (AAC) at [65]; *Home Office v IC and John O*, FTT, 10 April 2013 at [90]-[91].

82 Most notably Art 255 of the Treaty of Amsterdam and Art 42 of the Charter of Fundamental Rights of the European Union: see §§43– 003 to 43– 006. It will, in each case, be necessary to consider the general thrust of the legislative regime. cf *Ryanair Ltd v IC and OFT*, FTT, 28 January 2013 at [26]-[32] and [55].

83 *Burt v IC*, FTT, 25 October 2011 at [35]. By way of a parallel, public interest immunity cannot be claimed by a foreign state or on the ground that disclosure would infringe the public interest of a foreign state: *Buttes Gas & Oil Co v Hammer (No 3)* [1981] QB 223 (CA) at 247, 251 and 262. However, it has been recognised that because the public interest of the United Kingdom requires continued co-operation, and recognises a convergence of interests, with foreign sovereign states, public interest immunity can nevertheless apply to various communications between British and foreign government departments or prosecuting authorities on international relations grounds: *Buttes Gas & Oil Co v Hammer (No 3)* [1981] QB 223 (CA) at 256; *R v Governor of Brixton Prison, ex p Osman* [1991] 1 WLR 281 (DC) at 285-286; *R v Horseferry Road Magistrates' Court, ex p Bennett (No 2)* (1994) 99 Cr App R 123 (DC) at 126.

84 *Burt v IC*, FTT, 25 October 2011 at [36]. Just as the foreign entity would have to accept that if the information it conveyed to the public authority was personal information relating to the applicant, then that information would, notwithstanding that it had been conveyed to the public authority in confidence, have to be conveyed to the applicant if an application were made under s 7 of the DPA 1998, subject to any applicable exemptions under that Act.

usual public interest in securing openness and transparency will weigh in favour of disclosure, with the particular weight depending on what will be disclosed.[85] Thus, for example, the public interest in disclosing information that might reveal official corruption or that would enhance transparency in government transactions, especially where the subject matter is one of legitimate public concern (such as arms contracts), is particularly weighty.[86] There is also a strong public interest in disclosing the terms of arrangements with foreign governments relating to assurances to uphold fundamental rights.[87] Similarly, information which discloses serious corporate wrongdoing may outweigh any prejudice to international relations.[88]

27– 015 The duty to confirm or deny

Where, if a public authority were to inform an applicant that it holds or does not hold information of the description specified in the applicant's request, that revelation:

(a) would or would be likely to prejudice any of the matters set out in s 27(1); or

(b) would involve the disclosure of information (whether or not already recorded) which is confidential information obtained from a state other than the United Kingdom or from an international organisation or an international court,

then, to that extent, the duty to confirm or deny does not arise.[89] The precise terms of the request are critical to determining what would be revealed by confirming or denying that such information is held. A request that more specifically identifies the information sought will be more likely to fall within the exclusion than a request in general terms. The exclusion of the duty to confirm or deny is qualified. Accordingly, even if the request satisfies the terms of s 27(4) it will be necessary to consider whether, in all the circumstances, the maintenance of the exclusion of this duty is outweighed by the public interest in disclosing whether the public authority holds the information. This public interest balancing exercise is materially different from that employed for the purpose of determining whether the duty to communicate does not apply.[90]

27– 016 Confidential information– scope

Section 27(2) of FOIA[91] provides that 'confidential information' obtained by a state other than the United Kingdom[92] or from an international organisation[93] or international court[94] is exempt information. Section 27(3) defines what is meant by confidential information:

> For the purposes of this section, any information obtained from a State, organisation or court is confidential at any time while the terms on which it was obtained require it to be held in confidence or while the circumstances in which it was obtained make it reasonable for the

---

85 For example, in *All Party Parliamentary Group on Extraordinary Rendition v IC and FCO*, FTT, 3 May 2012 at [160]-[161], the Tribunal found that there was a strong public interest in transparency and accountability around the application of the Government's public policy opposing extraordinary rendition, in particular where Ministers had corrected statements made to Parliament about the application of the policy and in the face of claims that extraordinary rendition by the USA had helped to foil terrorist plots in the UK.

86 *Campaign against the Arms Trade v IC and MoJ*, IT, 26 August 2008 at [97]-[98]; *Gilby v IC and FCO*, IT, 22 October 2008 at [51], [55]-[57]; *Campaign Against Arms Trade v IC and Ministry of Defence*, FTT, 22 November 2011 at [67].

87 *All Party Parliamentary Group on Extraordinary Rendition v IC and Ministry of Defence* [2011] UKUT 153 (AAC) at [66].

88 *Sikka v IC and HMRC*, FTT, 11 July 2011 at [29]-[32].

89 FOIA s 27(4). Similarly: EIR reg 12(6); EI(S)R reg 10(8). There is no equivalent provision under the FOI(S)A. For an example of its application in this context, see *Ryanair Ltd v IC and OFT*, FTT, 28 January 2013 at [54].

90 See §§6– 018 to 6– 019 as to what it involves.

91 And FOI(S)A s 32(1)(b).

92 As to the meaning of 'a state other than the United Kingdom', see §27– 004.

93 As to the meaning of 'international organisation', see §27– 005.

94 As to the meaning of 'international court', see §27– 006.

State, organisation or court to expect that it will be so held.

The special provision of an exemption for confidential information emanating from foreign state bodies and the like (in addition to the general exemption for confidential information provided by s 41), reflects the particular sensitivities arising from the disclosure of such material.[95] The scope of the exemption is considered in the chapter dealing with confidential information.[96]

2. INTERNAL RELATIONS[97]

27– 017 Scope

Section 28(1) of FOIA provides that information is exempt information if its disclosure under the Act would, or would be likely to, prejudice relations between any administration in the United Kingdom[98] and any other such administration ('internal relations').[99] The phrase 'would or would be likely to prejudice' is common to most of the prejudice-based exemptions in the Act. The nature of the prejudice and the degree of likelihood which the phrase requires are considered elsewhere in this work.[100] Section 28(2) defines 'administration in the United Kingdom' for the purposes of the section to mean:

(a) the government of the United Kingdom ('the Westminster Government');
(b) the Scottish Administration;
(c) the Executive Committee of the Northern Ireland Assembly; or
(d) the Welsh Government.[101]

Section 28(3) provides that the duty to confirm or deny does not arise if, or to the extent that, compliance with s 1(1)(a) of FOIA would, or would be likely to, prejudice internal relations. The exclusion and the exemption in s 28 of FOIA are non-absolute: the duty to confirm or deny does not arise in relation to information prejudicial to internal relations only if, in all the circumstances of the case, the public interest in maintaining the exclusion of that duty outweighs the public interest in divulging whether the public authority holds the information;[102] and the duty to communicate in relation to such information does not arise only if, or to the extent that, in all the circumstances of the case, the public interest in maintaining the exemption outweighs the public interest in disclosing the information.[103] There is no equivalent exception

95 See §27– 007.

96 See §§34– 061 to 34– 064.

97 By Oliver Sanders QC, 1 Crown Office Row.

98 United Kingdom means Great Britain (ie England, Scotland and Wales) and Northern Ireland: Interpretation Act 1978 ss 5 22(1) Sch 1 Sch 2 para 5(a); Union with Scotland Act 1706 preamble Art 1.

99 FOI(S)A s 28 is identically worded save that it follows the slightly different drafting format and 'substantial prejudice' test adopted elsewhere in that Act. See *Scottish Ministers v Scottish IC* [2007] CSIH 8, 2007 SLT 274, 2007 SCLR 253 at [21]-[22]. Information contained in a 'historical record' (as to the meaning of which, see §36– 010) for the purposes of FOIA s 62 cannot be exempt information by virtue of s 28 and compliance with the duty to confirm or deny under s 1(1)(a) in relation to such a record is not to be taken to be capable of having any of the effects referred to in s 28(3): FOIA s 63(1)-(2).

100 See §§6– 020 to 6– 028.

101 As originally enacted, FOIA s 28(2)(d) referred to the (former) National Assembly for Wales. A reference to 'the Welsh Assembly Government' was substituted with effect from 25 May 2007 by way of an amendment made by the Government of Wales Act 2006 (Consequential Modifications and Transitional Provisions) Order 2007 SI 2007/1388 Sch 1 para 80. The reference to 'the Welsh Government' was then substituted with effect from 17 February 2015 by way of an amendment made by the Wales Act 2014 s 4(4)(a).

102 FOIA s 28(3) (read with s 28(1)) engages s 2(1)(b) so as to prevent s 1(1)(a) from applying and the duty to confirm or deny from arising in relation to the exempt information if the public interest balance favours non-divulgence.

103 FOIA s 28(1) thus engages s 2(2)(b) so as to prevent s 1(1)(b) from applying and the duty to communicate from

in the EIR. Where (or to the extent that) the information answering the terms of a request for information is environmental information, the request (or that part of the request) falls to be determined by the EIR and not by FOIA.[104] Accordingly, the fact that disclosure of environmental information would, or would be likely to, prejudice relations between any administration in the United Kingdom and any other such administration will not of itself remove the duty to disclose that information under the Regulations.

27– 018 The administrations in the UK

As already indicated, the administrations covered by s 28 of FOIA are the Westminster Government, together with the 'devolved administrations', namely, the Scottish Administration, the Executive Committee of the Northern Ireland Assembly and the Welsh Government. A brief outline of each devolved administration follows:[105]

(1) The Scottish Administration. The Scottish Administration was established under Part II of the Scotland Act 1998[106] and the reference in s 28(2)(b) of FOIA to the Scottish Administration must be construed as a reference to both its office-holders and their staff.[107]

(2) The Executive Committee of the Northern Ireland Assembly. The Executive Committee of the Northern Ireland Assembly was established under Part III of the Northern Ireland Act 1998.[108] The Committee consists of the First Minister and deputy First Minister and the Northern Ireland Ministers appointed under that Act.[109] Devolution in Northern Ireland was suspended with effect from 15 October 2002 before being restored on 8 May 2007.[110]

---

arising in relation to the exempt information if the public interest balance favours non-disclosure.

104 In the case of a request for information made of a Scottish public authority, it will fall to be determined by the EI(S)R and not by the FOI(S)A.

105 As to devolution generally see: O Hood Phillips and P Jackson, *Constitutional and Administrative Law*, 8th edn (London, Sweet & Maxwell, 2001) Ch 5; Mitchell, 'The Creation of the Scottish Parliament: Journey without End' (1999) 52 Parl Affairs 651; McAllister, 'The Road to Cardiff Bay: The Process of Establishing the National Assembly for Wales' (1999) 52 Parl Affairs 635.

106 The Scotland Act 1998 was passed to implement policy proposals set out in the government White Paper *Scotland's Parliament* (Cm 3658, 1997) and followed a referendum held in Scotland in September 1997 under the Referendums (Scotland and Wales) Act 1997. The Scottish devolution settlement was further reformed by the Scotland Acts of 2012 and 2016, passed either side of the Scottish independence referendum held on 18 September 2014 under the Scotland Act 1998 (Modification of Schedule 5) Order SI 2013/242 and the Scottish Independence Referendum Act 2013 (Scottish Act). The Scotland Act 2012 implemented certain recommendations contained in the report of the independent Calman Commission on Scottish Devolution, Serving Scotland Better: Scotland and the UK in the 21st Century. Final Report of Commission on Scottish Devolution dated June 2009. The Scotland Act 2016 implemented the all-party Smith Commission Agreement published in Report of the Smith Commission for further devolution of powers to the Scottish Parliament dated 27 November 2014.

107 Scotland Act 1998 s 126(6)-(7). The office-holders are the members of the Scottish Government (ie the Scottish Ministers including the First Minister and the Lord Advocate and Solicitor General for Scotland), junior Scottish Ministers and the holders of offices in the Scottish Administration which are not ministerial offices (ie the Registrar General of Births, Deaths and Marriages for Scotland, the Keeper of the Registers of Scotland, the Keeper of the Records of Scotland and certain other specified officers): Scotland Act 1998 ss 44-49, 126(7)(a), (8); Scottish Administration (Offices) Order 1999 SI 1999/1127. The former 'Scottish Executive' was renamed 'the Scottish Government' by the Scotland Act 2012 s 12.

108 The Northern Ireland Act 1998 was passed (together with the Northern Ireland (Sentences) Act 1998) to implement the Belfast Agreement (also known as the Good Friday Agreement) set out in the *Agreement Reached at Multi-Party Talks on Northern Ireland* (Cm 3883, 1998) and followed referendums held in Northern Ireland and the Republic of Ireland in May 1998. See also the related agreements between the United Kingdom and Republic of Ireland Governments: *Agreement Establishing Implementing Bodies* (Cm 4293, 1998); *Agreement Establishing a North-South Ministerial Council* (Cm 4294, 1998); *Agreement Establishing a British-Irish Council* (Cm 4296, 1998).

109 Northern Ireland Act 1998 s 20.

110 Pursuant to the Northern Ireland (St Andrews Agreement) Act 2006 s 2 Sch 2 (as modified by the Northern Ireland (St Andrews Agreement) Act 2007 s 1). As a result of that, the Northern Ireland (St Andrews Agreement) Act 2006 s 2 Sch 4 repealed the Northern Ireland Act 2000 with effect from 10 May 2007. See Burns, 'Devolution ... At

(3) As originally enacted, s 28(2)(d) of FOIA referred to the National Assembly for Wales which was established under Part I of the Government of Wales Act 1998[111] as a body corporate consisting of elected members.[112] The terms of the Welsh devolution settlement were then reformed with effect from 3 May 2007 by the Government of Wales Act 2006.[113] The National Assembly for Wales thereafter continued in being as a purely legislative elected body and devolved Welsh executive functions were assumed by the Welsh Assembly Government established under Part 2 of the Government of Wales Act 2006. Further reforms were enacted by the Wales Act 2014 and the Wales Act 2017.[114] The Welsh Assembly Government was renamed 'the Welsh Government with effect from 17 February 2015 as part of a further reform under the Wales Act 2014 and consists of the First Minister, Welsh Ministers, Counsel General and Deputy Welsh Ministers.[115] The reference in s 28(2)(d) of FOIA to the relevant devolved governmental body for Wales was updated first to 'the Welsh Assembly Government' in 2007 and then to 'the Welsh Government' in 2015 as part of the aforementioned reforms.[116]

It can therefore be noted that, for the purposes of s 28 of FOIA, the Scottish Administration includes staff as well as office-holders, whilst the Northern Ireland and Wales devolved administrations include only their elected ministers and not their staff.

27– 019 Background

No exemption equivalent to s 28 of FOIA was included in the *Code of Practice on Access to Government Information*[117] or proposed in the White Paper *Your Right to Know: The Government's Proposals for a Freedom of Information Act.*[118] This is not surprising as both documents preceded the establishment of the devolved administrations.[119] The draft Freedom of Information Bill published on 24 May 1999[120] and the Freedom of Information Bill introduced in the House of Commons on 18 November 1999 post-dated the original 1998 devolution statutes and both contained clauses equivalent to s 28 of FOIA.[121] During the passage of the Freedom of Information Bill two examples were given by the government of information held by a

Last?' (2007) 157 *New Law Journal* 248.

[111] The Government of Wales Act 1998 was passed to implement policy proposals set out in the government White Paper *A Voice for Wales* (Cm 3718, 1997) and followed a referendum held in Wales in September 1997 under the Referendums (Scotland and Wales) Act 1997. See also the Transfer of Functions Orders made under the Government of Wales Act 1998 s 22, Sch 2, ie SI 1999/672, SI 2000/253, SI 2000/1829, SI 2000/1830, SI 2001/3679, SI 2004/3044, SI 2005/1958, SI 2006/1458, SI 2006/3334.

[112] Government of Wales Act 1998 ss 1(2), 2.

[113] For the background to this reform, see the government White Papers *Better Governance for Wales* (Cm 6582, 2005).

[114] The Wales Act 2014 implemented much of the first report of the Silk Commission on Devolution in Wales, *Empowerment and Responsibility: Financial Powers to Strengthen Wales* dated November 2012 ('Silk I'). The Wales Act 2017 then implemented parts of the second report of the Silk Commission, *Empowerment and Responsibility: Legislative Powers to Strengthen Wales* dated March 2014 ('Silk II'), the Smith Commission Agreement published in *Report of the Smith Commission for further devolution of powers to the Scottish Parliament* dated 27 November 2014 and the government White Paper, *Powers for a purpose: Towards a lasting devolution settlement for Wales* (Cm 9020, 2015).

[115] Government of Wales Act 2006 ss 45-52, as amended by the Wales Act 2014 s 4.

[116] Government of Wales Act 2006 (Consequential Modifications and Transitional Provisions) Order 2007 SI 2007/1388 Sch 1 para 80; wales Act 2014 s 4(4)(a).

[117] *Open Government Code of Practice on Access to Government Information*, 2nd edn (1997).

[118] (Cm 3818, 1997).

[119] Note, however, the reference to devolution in the White Paper (Cm 3818, 1997) para 2.1.

[120] *Freedom of Information: Consultation on Draft Legislation* (Cm 4355, 1999) Pt II.

[121] Draft Bill, cl 23; Introduction Print of Bill, cl 26.

Westminster Government department which might be covered by the exemption, namely, 'a thumbnail sketch of the strengths and weaknesses of the individual members of an executive' and 'comments on a devolved administration's policy proposals or Acts'.[122]

27– 020 The comparative jurisdictions

Exemptions similar to s 28 of FOIA are provided for in the comparable legislation of Australia, New Zealand and Canada. Sections 26A and 47B of the Freedom of Information Act 1982 (Cth of Aust) contain a discretionary exemption for information whose disclosure would, or could reasonably be expected to, cause damage to relations between the Commonwealth and a State or divulge certain confidential Commonwealth-State communications.[123] As with s 28 of FOIA, the Australian equivalent is subject to a public interest override for information whose disclosure would, on balance, be in the public interest.[124] Section 7(b) of the Official Information Act 1982 (NZ) provides that information may be withheld if its disclosure would be likely to prejudice relations between any of the Governments of New Zealand, the self-governing state of the Cook Islands or the self-governing state of Niue. Section 14 of the federal Access to Information Act (1982) (Canada) contains a discretionary exemption for information which could reasonably be expected to be injurious to the conduct by the Government of Canada of federal-provincial affairs including information on federal-provincial consultations or deliberations and the strategy or tactics adopted or to be adopted by the Government of Canada relating to the conduct of federal-provincial affairs.

27– 021 Prejudice to internal relations

All the administrations have agreed a Memorandum of Understanding and a series of Supplementary Agreements 'setting out the principles which underlie the relations between them' and a series of bilateral agreements have also been agreed between various Westminster Government departments and their devolved counterparts.[125] Although these agreements are expressed to be non-binding statements of political intent, they reflect the way in which the administrations intend and would wish to relate to each other and may therefore provide a useful guide for what would and would not be liable to prejudice internal relations.[126] Although

---

122 Cabinet Office Minister, Lord Falconer of Thoroton, Hansard HL vol 617 col 1280 (19 October 2000) (House of Lords Committee Stage).

123 The words 'relations between the Commonwealth and a State' refer to the totality of their relationships at every level: *Arnold v Queensland* (1987) 6 AAR 463 at 472 (Wilcox J).

124 Freedom of Information Act 1982 s 47B (Cth of Aust).

125 See the Memorandum of Understanding and Supplementary Agreements Between the United Kingdom Government, Scottish Ministers, the Cabinet of the National Assembly for Wales and the Northern Ireland Executive Committee (Cm 5240, 2001) and successive versions of the Memorandum of Understanding and Supplementary Agreements between the United Kingdom Government, the Scottish Ministers, the Welsh Ministers and the Northern Ireland Executive Committee (Cm 7864, 2010, (September 2012)) and (October 2013). The principal agreement is the Memorandum of Understanding and there are four supplementary agreements: an Agreement on the Joint Ministerial Committee; and three Concordats on Co-ordination of European Union Policy Issues, Financial Assistance to Industry and International Relations. In very general terms, the importance of communicating and exchanging information between the administrations is stressed throughout, but there is also a recognition that some of this may need to take place on a confidential basis: see the Memorandum, paras 5-6, 12. In addition, central and devolved government departments also enter into subject-matter specific bilateral agreements and concordates relevant to their common interests and responsibilities. See also Information Commissioner, *Freedom of Information Act Awareness Guidance No 13: Relations within the UK* (2008) Pt B; and Welsh Assembly Government, *Code of Practice on Public Access to Information* (undated) Pts 1, 3, Annex A.

126 The Westminster government department with overall responsibility for devolution originally and (once again) is currently the Cabinet Office (formerly the Ministry of Justice, the Department for Constitutional Affairs and the Office of the Deputy Prime Minister). The Cabinet Office publishes Devolution Guidance Notes on various topics and these may be capable of providing some illumination in relation to the same issues: eg *Devolution Guidance Note No 6: Circulation of Inter-Ministerial And Inter-Departmental Correspondence*, 2005. In *Scotland Office (Stage 2) v IC*, IT, 10 March 2009, the Tribunal's approach to FOIA s 28 was 'informed by' its approach to FOIA s 27 (international relations) in *Campaign against the Arms Trade v IC and MoJ*, IT, 26 August 2008 (at [80], [81]). In other words, the

in legal terms each of the devolved administrations exercises its functions on behalf of the same Crown, their members may have very different political views and there is a constitutional distinction between the Crown in right of Her Majesty's Government in the United Kingdom, the Crown in right of the Scottish Administration, the Crown in right of Her Majesty's Government in Northern Ireland, and the Crown in right of the Welsh Government.[127] The logic of s 28 of FOIA is as follows: given that the Westminster Government and the devolved administrations do need to co-operate closely in a variety of areas, particularly in relation to the implementation of and compliance with the United Kingdom's obligations under European Community law, good internal relations are plainly a matter of great practical importance and they should not therefore be needlessly prejudiced or put at risk unless this is necessary on overriding public interest grounds. Whether the remaining exemptions in Part II of FOIA ought to suffice for these purposes is another matter, but the comparative jurisdictions at least show some consistency of approach to such issues and provide a precedent for s 28.

Tribunal considered whether prejudice was probable as opposed to possible or speculative, and it looked for something of detriment in the sense of impairing relations or interests or their promotion or protection (at [52]-[53]).

[127] See: Scotland Act 1998 s 99; Northern Ireland Act 1998 Sch 13 para 9(3); Government of Wales Act 1998 s 1(3); Government of Wales Act 2006 s 89.

CHAPTER 28
Economic and financial interests

28– 001 Introduction

By s 29(1) of FOIA information is rendered exempt information where its disclosure would prejudice, or would be likely to prejudice:

(a) the economic interests of the United Kingdom[1] or of any part of the United Kingdom; or

(b) the financial interests of any administration in the United Kingdom.[2]

An 'administration in the United Kingdom' is defined to mean the Government of the United Kingdom, the Scottish Administration, the Executive Committee of the Northern Ireland Assembly and the National Assembly for Wales.[3] The phrase 'would or would be likely to prejudice' is common to most of the prejudice-based exemptions in the Act. The nature of prejudice and the degree of likelihood which the phrase generally requires are considered elsewhere in this work.[4] Section 29(2) provides that the duty to confirm or deny does not arise if, or to the extent that, compliance with that duty would prejudice, or would be likely to prejudice, the interests protected by s 29(1). Both exemption from the disclosure duty and exclusion from the duty to divulge are non-absolute. Thus, the duty to communicate information whose disclosure would be prejudicial (or would be likely to be prejudicial) to the interests protected by s 29 does not arise only if, or to the extent that, in all the circumstances of the case, the public interest in maintaining the exemption outweighs the public interest in disclosing the information.[5] Similarly, the duty to confirm or deny that such information is held remains excluded only if, in all the circumstances of the case, the public interest in maintaining the exclusion of that duty outweighs the public interest in divulging whether the public authority holds the information.[6] A broadly equivalent exemption is to be found in the freedom of information legislation of most of the comparative jurisdictions.[7] The EIR do not provide

---

1 The United Kingdom means Great Britain (ie England, Scotland and Wales) and Northern Ireland: Interpretation Act 1978 ss 5 and 22(1) Sch 1 Sch 2 para 5(a); Union with Scotland Act 1706 preamble Art 1.

2 FOI(S)A s 33(2) is in similar terms, save that the prejudice must be substantial.

3 FOIA s 28(2); FOI(S)A s 28(2).

4 See §§6– 020 to 6– 028.

5 FOIA s 2(2)(b).

6 FOIA s 2(1)(b).

7 There is no directly comparable exemption in the Freedom of Information Act, 1966 (USA). The Freedom of Information Act 1982 (Cth of Australia) s 47H, provides an exemption where the disclosure of the requested document would, or could be reasonably be expected to, have a substantial adverse effect on the ability of the

for an analogous exception.

28– 002 Provenance of the exemption

Although the terms of the exemption are imprecise, the provenance of the exemption gives some clue as to its intended breadth. The exclusion of information whose disclosure could be harmful to the economy was in the Code of Practice. The amended version of the Code included an exemption for:

> information whose disclosure would harm the ability of the Government to manage the economy, prejudice the conduct of official market operations, or could lead to improper gain or advantage.[8]

The Explanatory Guidance on the Code gave a non-exhaustive list of examples of information that it considered fell within the exemption, as well as the underlying rationale for the exemption:

> Information about some types of proposals, or even the admission that certain possibilities are being considered, can lead to speculation, disturbance of the markets and even improper gain. It will therefore be necessary to consider the harm test set out in the exemption before releasing information regarding such matters as:
> — the currency, coinage or legal tender of the United Kingdom;
> — proposals for expenditure;
> — a contemplated change in the rate of bank interest or in Government borrowing;
> — a contemplated change in tariff rates, taxes, duties or any other revenue services;
> — a contemplated change in the conditions of operation of financial institutions;
> — a contemplated sale or acquisition of land or property; or
> — a contemplated sale or purchase of securities or of foreign or United Kingdom currency.[9]

The fact that information relates to one of these matters was not enough in itself: the exemption in the Code, as in FOIA now, was harm-based. The Explanatory Guidance simply sets out those classes of information that might, if disclosed, result in harm to the economy.

Commonwealth to manage the economy: see §51– 015(19). The exemption does not involve a consideration of the public interest. The AAT in *Re Waterford and Treasurer of Commonwealth of Australia (No 2)* (1985) 8 ALN N37 stated that if the document entitled Forward Estimates of Budget Receipts had the potential to have a significant impact on the government's ability to control the economy, then its disclosure would be contrary to the public interest and it would be exempt. The Administrative Review Council in its review of the Australian Act considered the exemption superfluous (because information could be exempted under other provisions) and recommended that it be repealed: Australian Law Reform Commission and the Administrative Review Council, *Open Government: a review of the Federal Freedom of Information Act 1982*, ALRC 77, ARC 40 (Canberra, 1995) para 9.28. The Official Information Act 1982 (New Zealand), ss 6(e) and 27(1)(a) provide absolute exemptions where the disclosure of the information would be likely to damage seriously the New Zealand economy by disclosing prematurely decisions to change or continue government economic or financial policies relating to: exchange rates or the control of overseas exchange transactions; the regulation of banking or credit; taxation; the stability, control, and adjustment of prices of goods and services, rents, and other costs, and rates of wages, salaries, and other incomes; the borrowing of money by the New Zealand government; and the entering into of overseas trade agreements: see §51– 022(5). The Official Information Act 1982 makes provision for neither confirming nor denying the existence of the requested documents where to do so would or could reasonably be expected to cause damage to the economy (see §51– 020). The Access to Information Act (Canada) s 18, provides a discretionary exemption for records the disclosure of which could reasonably be expected to cause injury to the financial or economic interests of Canada: see §51– 032(17). The Canadian Courts have required clear proof of a reasonable belief on the part of the Minister that there was a reasonable expectation of probable harm of the prescribed kinds: see *Canadian Council of Christian Charities v Canada (Minister of Finance)* [1999] 4 FC 245. In that case, the Federal Court held that the phrase 'injurious to the financial interests of the Government of Canada' in s 18(d) should not be interpreted as including revenue loss resulting from an increase in legitimate claims to deduction under the Income Tax Act. The Freedom of Information Act 1997 (Ireland) s 24(1), provides a discretionary exemption for records the disclosure of which could reasonably be expected to have a serious adverse effect upon the financial interests of the state or on the ability to manage the economy: see §51– 039(16).

8 *Open Government Code of Practice on Access to Government Information*, 2nd edn (1997) Pt II, para 6(a).

9 Cabinet Office, *Open Government: Code of Practice on Access to Government Information Guidance on Interpretation* 2nd edn (1997) para 6.1.

28– 003 Legislative history

The Bill leading to FOIA included an exemption[10] in substantially the same terms as s 29. An attempt was made to amend the Bill so that its terms would more closely resemble the exemption in the Code. Lord Mackay of Ardbrecknish argued:

> I can be brief on this, because it is a straightforward argument between the terms of the Bill and the code of practice. The Government thought the code of practice inadequate, but it is stronger than the Bill. The amendment would replace the provisions for a contents exemption in the Bill with the wording used in the code of practice. It would tighten up the Bill, ensuring that only information that would genuinely harm a specific economic interest would be exempt. At the moment, the clause would catch all information relating to the economy. The Government must not be allowed to include such catch-all exemptions, especially as they have drawn up the Bill in such a way that, if information is covered by an exemption, the public authority, rather than the information commissioner, decides whether it should be released. For those reasons, the exemptions should be worded as tightly as possible. The wording in the code is far superior in this regard to that in the Bill. The Government's supporters, who have just come so willingly to their aid in the Division, should ask themselves whether they believed that they fought the election for a Bill that is weaker than the code introduced by the previous Government.[11]

The response of Lord Bach was:

> I do not dispute that the interests identified in the amendment are important, but the Government do not believe that they are the only important economic or financial considerations in relation to which the inappropriate disclosure of information could lead to real harm being done to the economy.[12]

Lord Bach gave an example of information that would be captured by the proposed exemption but which would not be captured by the exemption in the code:

> Public authorities such as the DTI may hold documents which set out the advantages and disadvantages of investing in different regions. If that type of information were disclosed to an overseas business organisation which was contemplating setting up a factory in the UK, the organisation may be put off its proposed investment. However, if this amendment were carried, that would not exempt such information from disclosure.[13]

Other examples of information thought to be captured by s 29 but not by the Code were given by Lord Bassam of Brighton:

> I should like to assist Members of the Committee by providing some examples. First, the Treasury holds information about the performance of different sectors of the economy and information about whether it intends to raise or lower taxes—important information. Such information has an effect on the United Kingdom economy and its release needs to be carefully managed. Secondly, there exist research projects, the findings of which it would be unreasonable, impractical and inappropriate to publish before the project has been completed. Some research projects could easily run for longer than three months, but under this exemption they would have to supply information on request before the project was completed, with the possible effect of nullifying the results of that project.[14]

28– 004 Scope of the exemption

The terms 'economic interests' and 'financial interests' are capable of a considerable degree of overlap. However, the scope for overlap, as well as the ambit of the exemption itself, is reduced by these two interests being tied to different entities. In each case it is that entity whose interests

---

10 Clause 24.

11 Hansard HL vol 617 col 1286 (1 October 2000).

12 Hansard HL vol 617 col 1288 (1 October 2000).

13 Hansard HL vol 617 col 1288 (19 October 2000).

14 Hansard HL vol 617 col 1244 (19 October 2000).

are required to be prejudiced by disclosure. In order to be captured by s 29(1)(a), the economic interests required to be prejudiced by the disclosure are those of the United Kingdom or any part of the United Kingdom. It would seem that a city council is a 'part of the United Kingdom'.[15] In order to be captured by s 29(1)(b), the financial interests required to be prejudiced by the disclosure are those of any administration in the United Kingdom.[16] A further insight into the scope of the exemption comes from Part VI of the Act dealing with historical records.[17] It is not easy to conceive of information 30, 60 or 100 years old the disclosure of which would prejudice, or would be likely to prejudice, the economic interests of the United Kingdom or the financial interests of any administration of the United Kingdom. Nevertheless, the s 29 exemption is not removed where the information is contained in a historical record,[18] nor where it is contained in a record created 60 or 100 years earlier.[19] The decision to exclude s 29 from the exemptions that fall away with time can best be explained by the importance of the interest that is protected by the exemption, rather than by the nature of the information itself. While the quantity and type of information the disclosure of which would prejudice the economic interests of the United Kingdom, etc may be very greatly diminished when the information is, say, 60 years old, if that in fact is what the effect of its disclosure would be, then the desirability of avoiding the adverse effect is not lessened by the age of the information.

28–005 Economic interests

Not all information relating to the economy of the United Kingdom (or a part of the United Kingdom) will be exempted from disclosure by s 29. It is information prejudicing economic interests, rather than economic affairs, which is exempted by the section. Beyond the obvious instances of economic interests affecting the United Kingdom generally at a national level, such as forthcoming budgetary or fiscal policy decisions, the exemption would appear to cover information relating to a whole sector of the national economy.[20] As well as making strategic decisions, the State also acts as economic participant (buyer, seller, investor and lender) and as regulator and enforcer. It is arguable that, bearing in mind the scope of its activities in the economy and its corresponding interests, disclosure of information prejudicing or likely to prejudice these interests is also captured by the exemption.[21]

28–006 Financial interests

So far as financial interests are concerned, the exemption would appear to have a narrower application than in relation to economic interests. As noted above, the financial interests exemption may only be invoked if it relates to the financial interests of an administration as defined. A substantial part of the finances of such administrations are a matter of public record, as in the case of the public sector pay review, for example.

---

15 *Derry City Council v IC*, IT, 11 December 2006 at [29]. It is suggested that any unit significantly smaller than a local authority area cannot properly be characterised as a 'part of the United Kingdom': the word 'part' is here being used in its sense as a region, rather than as any portion of the whole.

16 As to the meaning of 'any administration in the United Kingdom' see §28–001.

17 See, more generally, Ch 6.

18 FOIA s 63(1).

19 FOIA s 63(3) and (4).

20 See *Norway v EFTA Surveillance Authority* [1999] 1 CMLR 851.

21 The Information Commissioner has accepted that the exemption in FOIA s 29(1)(b) applies to information which could be used to compromise the Land Registry's computer systems, since if those systems were significantly compromised it could have a knock-on effect on economic areas where the sale and purchase of land is a core activity and therefore impinge on the tax revenues which the UK government receives: Decision Notice References FS50208350, 4 May 2010.

28–007 The Bank of England

It is to be noted that, while 'any government department' is deemed to be a public authority[22] (and therefore the Treasury is a potential recipient of a request), the Bank of England is a public authority for the purposes of the Act only in respect of information held for purposes other than those of its functions with respect to:

— monetary policy,
— financial operations intended to support financial institutions for the purposes of maintaining stability, and
— the provision of private banking services and related services.[23]

Thus information relating to future or past interest rate changes or interventions to support a market sector is inaccessible as the Bank of England is not a public authority for the purposes of a request for such information. The Bank does, however, have obligations to publish certain information under the Bank of England Act 1998.

28–008 Actual or likely prejudice

Demonstrating the likely prejudice from a disclosure of information under the Act presents particular problems so far as this exemption is concerned. Tribunal decisions touching upon the exemption are rare and it has not generally met with success when invoked by a public authority. Where the disclosure of information would reveal a forthcoming government decision or announcement intended to benefit or protect the economy of the United Kingdom and that disclosure would be likely to result in pre-emptive behaviour that will reduce or negate the efficacy of the decision or announcement, it is suggested that the exemption will be satisfied. It is not in the economic interests of the United Kingdom that the government's power to regulate the economy be rendered ineffective or materially less effective. Beyond the more obvious examples, such as where premature disclosure could reasonably be expected to result in pre-emptive behaviour that makes it more difficult or expensive for the government to implement the decision or where premature disclosure will otherwise render the decision once made or announced less effective, engagement of the exemption is not straightforward. It is easy to assert the prejudice; but proof, even to a level sufficient for an administrative decision, will often be rather more difficult.[24] Expert evidence may be required to demonstrate the likelihood of such prejudice. The currency of the information will often be critical to the application of the exemption.

28–009 Market response as prejudice

The economic interests of the United Kingdom are shaped by its adherence to a free-market system. The response of that market, and its freedom to respond, to government decisions, whilst it may have adverse consequences for the Government, is not readily to be characterised as being prejudicial to 'the economic interests of the United Kingdom.' Since 1997, the Government has continued to publish the minutes of monthly meetings between the Chancellor of the Exchequer and the Bank of England. These minutes disclose sensitive economic and financial information. That this information is regularly made public without apparent damage makes it more difficult to contend that disclosure of other economic information has, or would be likely to have, the prejudicial effect required by s 29. However, the Information Commissioner has accepted that the Treasury is entitled to withhold detailed information used to 'underpin and inform' the Bank's quarterly inflation report, on the basis of the exemptions

[22] FOIA s 3(1)(a)(i) and Sch 1, para 1.

[23] FOIA Sch 1, Pt VI.

[24] See, for example: *Dept for Work and Pensions v IC*, FTT, 22 December 2014.

in s 29(1)(a) and (b).[25]

28–010 Impact of disclosed material

Some consideration must also be given to official information relating to the economy that is otherwise liable to be disclosed. Section 27 of the Industry Act 1975 provides that Ministers of the Crown and the Treasury must publish, make available and provide access to information and analysis as set out in Sch 5 to that Act. That Schedule provides:

> 1. For the purposes of this Schedule the Treasury shall keep a macro-economic model suitable for demonstrating the likely effects on economic events in the United Kingdom of different assumptions about the following matters, namely:
>   (a) government economic policies;
>   (b) economic events outside the United Kingdom; and
>   (c) such (if any) other matters as appear to the Treasury from time to time likely to have a substantial effect on economic events in the United Kingdom.
> 2. The model shall enable forecasts to be made:
>   (a) of any of the following, namely:
>   (i) the level of gross domestic product;
>   (ii) unemployment;
>   (iii) the balance of payments on current account;
>   (iv) the general index of retail prices; and
>   (v) average earnings; and
>   (b) of such (if any) other economic variables as are appropriate in the opinion of the Treasury from time to time.
>
> ...
>
> 6. Not less than twice in each year commencing with a date not later than one year from the coming into force of this Act, the Treasury shall publish forecasts produced with the aid of the model as to such matters and based on such alternative assumptions as appear to them to be appropriate.
> 7. Any forecast under this Schedule shall indicate, where possible, the margin of error attaching to it.
> 8. The Treasury shall from time to time publish an analysis of errors in such forecasts that would have remained even if the assumptions set out in the forecasts and on which they were based had been correct.

It is difficult to contend that disclosure of analogous information (for example, a micro-economic model) under FOIA would or would be likely to prejudice the economic interests of the United Kingdom if that class of information is liable to be disclosed under another Act of Parliament. The existence of this free-standing right to certain information that may impinge upon the economic interests of the United Kingdom is also relevant to the weighing exercise required by s 2 of the Act: it is difficult to see that the public interest in maintaining the exemption has particular force if another Act of Parliament gives a statutory entitlement to the disclosure of information of the same class.

28–011 The public interest

Even if information is exempt because it answers the terms of s 29(1), an applicant will still be entitled to have the information communicated to him unless, in all the circumstances of the case, the public interest in maintaining the exemption outweighs the public interest in disclosing the information.[26] Similarly, even if the duty to confirm or deny does not arise as a result of the operation of s 29(2), an applicant will still be entitled to be informed that the public authority holds the information requested unless, in all the circumstances of the case, the public interest

[25] Decision Notice Ref FS50474293, 10 June 2013.

[26] FOIA s 2(2)(b).

in maintaining the exclusion outweighs the public interest in divulging its existence.[27] The decision of the legislature not to make exemption under s 29 absolute cannot properly be undone by giving the public interest in maintaining the exemption such weight as to make the public interest in disclosure unable to outweigh it. The exercise must be carried out in such a manner as to recognise that in some circumstances the public interest in disclosure will be sufficiently powerful to displace an inherently compelling public interest in maintaining the exemption. In practice, the balancing exercise will comprise mainly weighing up the public interest in disclosure against the public interest in protecting the economic and financial welfare of the nation, the constituent parts of the nation, and the various national administrations. For information relating to past decisions involving the matters protected by s 29, it may be more difficult to find that the public interest in maintaining the exemption outweighs the public interest in disclosure.[28] So far as information relating to future decisions involving the protected matters, for example the imposition of exchange rate controls, the public interest in maintaining the exemption will, as a general rule, more readily outweigh the public interest in disclosure. The years since Black Wednesday have provided ample illustration of how entire markets and economic sectors can be destabilised by the acts of a very few speculators. Access to information which enables or informs such speculation cannot readily be characterised as being in the public interest. On the other hand, a potential investor seeking information about the future of a regional development will not necessarily be acting contrary to the public interest. Such an investor may well argue that a whole region will benefit from enhanced infrastructure and the creation of jobs by investment and that it is in the public interest that access to such information be provided.

27 FOIA s 2(1)(b).

28 Thus, in *Derry City Council v IC*, IT, 11 December 2006 at [29], although the information was held to fall within s 29, the passage of 6 years enabled the Information Tribunal to conclude that the public interest in maintaining the exemption was outweighed by the public interest in disclosure. Contrast the position taken by the European Court of Justice when considering the analogous exemption under Regulation 1049/2001: *Pitsiorlas v EU Council* (T-3/00) [2007] ECR II-4779, [2008] 1 CMLR 47 at [231]-[288].

CHAPTER 29

Investigation, audit, law enforcement and the courts

1. INTRODUCTION

29–001 Overview

This chapter is principally concerned with a group of provisions that exempt information from the disclosure obligations so as not to undermine the enforcement of the law (principally, but not exclusively, the criminal law) and the administration of justice. The exemptions take many different forms and often overlap in a haphazard way. Some depend on the purposes for which the information is (or has been) held, some on whether disclosure will cause prejudice (and some on a combination of the two);[1] some require the information still to be held for the relevant purpose, some that it was once so held; in some cases the current holder of the information must have had the relevant purpose, in others this is not required; in some the original source of the information or the purposes for which it was communicated to the public authority is relevant, in others not. In this chapter, this group of exemptions has been divided into seven sections. In each section, separate consideration is given to the scope of the exemption from the duty to communicate under the Freedom of Information Acts, to the role of the public interest, to the duty to confirm or deny, and to any equivalent exemption under the two sets of Environmental Information Regulations.[2] It is worth emphasising at the outset that neither the courts nor the courts service is a public authority, so that information held by them is not required to be disclosed under either FOIA or the EIR.[3]

29– 002 The public interest generally

The general purpose of these exemptions is set out in the White Paper which led to the introduction of FOIA:

> [freedom of information] should not undermine the investigation, prosecution or prevention of crime, or the bringing of civil or criminal proceedings by public bodies. The investigation and prosecution of crime involve a number of essential requirements. These include the need to avoid prejudicing effective law enforcement, the need to protect witnesses and informers, the need to maintain the independence of the judicial and prosecution processes, and the need to preserve the criminal court as the sole forum for determining guilt. Because of this, the Act will exclude information relating to the investigation and prosecution functions of the police, prosecutors, and other bodies carrying out law enforcement work such as the Department of Social Security or the Immigration Service. The Act will also exclude information relating to the commencement or conduct of civil proceedings.[4]

With the exception of provisions relating to court records,[5] none of the Freedom of Information Act exemptions in this group is absolute: they only apply if the public interest in maintaining the exemption outweighs the public interest in disclosing the information.[6] This public interest requirement must be satisfied even in cases where the test for exemption is whether prejudice will or is likely to be caused. Thus it is possible that although a particular disclosure would cause prejudice to the enforcement of the law or the administration of justice, nevertheless the information must be disclosed because the public interest in disclosure outweighs the prejudice. Nevertheless, there is a recognised public interest in maintaining these exemptions where disclosure would provide undesirable forewarning to the subjects of investigation or would prejudice confidential sources of information needed for such purposes.[7] As with the other qualified exemptions, in weighing the competing public interests, the relevant decision maker[8]

---

1 See §§5– 022 to 5– 023.

2 The EIR and the EI(S)R.

3 There is a free-standing right under the CPR to access certain documents held by the courts: see Chapter 42. See further §29– 033 below.

4 *Your Right to Know. The Government's Proposals for a FOI Act* (Cm 3818, 1997) §2.21. Although the form of the Act as enacted was quite different from that intended in 1997, the basic intention behind the provisions dealt with in this chapter is that revealed in the quotation.

5 FOIA s 32; FOI(S)A s 37.

6 FOIA ss 2(1)(b) and 2(2)(b); FOI(S)A s 2(1)(b); EIR reg 12(1)(b); EI(S)R reg 10(1)(b). For a general discussion of this topic, see §§6– 001 to 6– 019.

7 *DTI v IC*, IT, 10 November 2006 at [57], [60]-[61].

8 That is, the public authority from which information is sought, the Information Commissioner, the Tribunal or the courts.

will have to take into account all the circumstances of the case[9] and any relevant provisions of the ECHR.[10]

29– 003 Limits on exemptions

As with all exemptions under Part II of FOIA and Part 3 of the EIR, they only operate in relation to the obligations of disclosure provided by the relevant Act: they do not exempt a public authority from making disclosures required by other legislation or rules of law. Thus, they do not exempt a public authority from its obligations to disclose material to the accused in criminal proceedings or to the other party in civil proceedings and they do not affect its power to do so.[11]

2. INFORMATION HELD FOR PURPOSES OF CRIMINAL INVESTIGATIONS OR PROCEEDINGS

29– 004 Introduction

This and the following two sections involve three separate, but in practice largely overlapping, heads of exemption:

(1) information held for the purposes of a criminal investigation or criminal proceedings;
(2) information relating to the obtaining of information from confidential sources; and
(3) information whose disclosure might prejudice the enforcement of criminal law.

It will be noted that only the third involves a consideration of resultant prejudice. Similar exemptions are to be found in each of the comparative jurisdictions.[12]

29– 005 The exemption

Section 30(1) of FOIA exempts information held by a public authority if it has been held by it at any time for the purposes of any investigation which it has a duty to carry out with a view to it being ascertained whether to charge someone with an offence or whether a person charged is guilty,[13] or, if the authority itself has power to conduct criminal proceedings, for the purposes of an investigation carried out by it which may lead to criminal proceedings[14] or for the purposes of such criminal proceedings.[15] This is a class-based exemption: in spite of

---

9 FOIA ss 2(1)(b) and 2(2)(b); FOI(S)A s 2(1)(b); EIR reg 12(1)(b); EI(S)R reg 10(1)(b).

10 As to which, see Chapter 4.

11 See FOIA s 78; FOI(S)A s 66. See further Chapter 42.

12 In the United States, the Freedom of Information Act, 1966, 5 USC § 552(b)(7), exempts from disclosure records or information compiled for law enforcement purposes: see §51– 008(7). The Freedom of Information Act 1982 (Cth of Australia) s 37, provides an exemption where the disclosure of the requested document would, or could be reasonably be expected to, cause damage to law enforcement, confidential sources of information relating to law enforcement, fair trials, or methods of criminal investigation: see §51– 015(12). The Official Information Act 1982 (New Zealand), ss 6(c) and 27(1)(a), provides an exemption where the disclosure of the information would be likely to prejudice the maintenance of the law, including the prevention, investigation, and detection of offences, and the right to a fair trial: see §51– 022(3). The Access to Information Act (Canada) s 16(1)(c), provides a discretionary exemption for records the disclosure of which could reasonably be expected to cause injury to law enforcement or conduct of lawful investigations: see §51– 032(12). The Freedom of Information Act 2014 (Ireland) s 32, provides a discretionary exemption for records the disclosure of which could reasonably be expected to prejudice law enforcement and investigations or matters of internal security, or to reveal the name of a police informer: see §51– 039(12).

13 FOIA s 30(1)(a).

14 FOIA s 30(1)(b).

15 FOIA s 30(1)(c).

considerable parliamentary pressure,[16] and in contrast to the position in much of the comparative legislation,[17] there is no requirement for any prejudice to any investigation or proceedings to be shown for the exemption to apply. The exemption appears to be designed to relate to information held for the purposes of specific investigations or criminal proceedings, rather than to investigations or proceedings generally,[18] although the wording of the provision is possibly ambiguous.[19] It applies most obviously to information coming to the police,[20] the National Crime Agency, the Serious Fraud Office, the Crown Prosecution Service or the Director of Public Prosecutions in the course of specific investigations; but it may also apply to information held by many other bodies which have the power to conduct criminal proceedings of all sorts, including proceedings relating to quite minor offences.[21] For the exemption to apply the authority holding the information must be the same as the one which held it for the relevant purpose,[22] but it can have held it for that purpose at any time in the past,[23] it need not have obtained it for that purpose originally and the information does not have to be required any longer for that purpose.[24] Thus, information once coming within the exemption is always potentially exempt and the potential exemption applies even if a decision was made not to prosecute or if a prosecution has been completed, however long ago the investigation or prosecution was completed.[25]

29– 006 The public interest

If the information in question comes within the section, the duty to disclose does not apply if and to the extent that the public interest in maintaining the exemption outweighs the public interest in disclosing the information.[26] The weighing exercise necessitates an identification of the public interest in the maintenance of the exemption, always recognising that that public

---

16 For example: Hansard HL vol 617 col 1291 (19 October 2000).

17 See, eg Freedom of Information Act 1982 (Cth of Aust) s 37(1)(a); Freedom of Information Act 2014 (Ireland) s 32(1)(a).

18 As, eg, internal documents of the police showing investigation methods or procedures are likely to be covered by FOIA s 31(1)(a) and (b).

19 See the view of the Minister, Lord Falconer of Thoroton, in Hansard HL vol 612 col 827 (20 April 2000).

20 See, for example: *Digby-Cameron v IC and Bedfordshire Police*, IT, 26 January 2009; *Kelway v IC and Northumbria Police*, IT, 14 April 2009.

21 For example, local authorities which have numerous prosecutorial functions, the Health and Safety Executive (or inspectors appointed under s 19 of the Health and Safety at Work etc Act 1974), the Environment Agency, HM Revenue & Customs (see: *Armstrong v IC and HMRC*, IT, 14 October 2008 at [60]), the DBIS (see: *DTI v IC*, IT, 10 November 2006, involving an investigation under Companies Act 1985 s 447), DEFRA, the Food Standards Agency, the Financial Conduct Authority, the Competition and Markets Authority, the General Medical Council, but not, generally, the Independent Office of Police Conduct whose main function is to supervise the investigation by the police of alleged misconduct on the part of officers (rather than to conduct the investigation themselves). Note that FOIA s 30(5) expressly includes proceedings before courts-martial and other military courts within the concept of criminal proceedings.

22 The exemption is designed for prosecuting authorities as such.

23 *Toms v IC*, IT, 19 June 2006 at [6]; *Keely v IC*, IT, 19 May 2008 at [13]; *Wynn v IC and SFO*, FTT, 7 September 2012 at [27].

24 But the Tribunal has drawn a distinction between information 'used' for the purpose of an investigation and information 'held' for that purpose: *Benford v IC and DEFRA*, IT, 14 November 2007 at [61].

25 *Prince v IC and Devon CC*, FTT, 24 November 2017 at [17]. This appears to go further than was necessary to carry out the Government's expressed purpose for the provision, Lord Falconer of Thoroton stating that it was necessary 'to ensure that criminal proceedings are not jeopardised by the premature disclosure of information and to preserve the criminal courts as the sole forum for determining guilt': Hansard HL vol 612 col 827 (20 April 2000). But these issues may be relevant in assessing where the 'public interest' lies: see §29– 006.

26 FOIA ss 30(1) and 2(2)(b).

interest must be delineated in such a fashion that it is capable in practice of being outweighed.[27] Superficially, the public interest protected by this exemption might seem to be confined to protecting the successful investigation and prosecution of specific criminal offences.[28] However, this objective has numerous strands, a view supported by the Tribunal.[29] A more restrictive view would produce unfortunate consequences.[30] On this basis, it is thought that the public interest in maintaining the exemption will be taken to include the factors identified in the White Paper *Your Right to Know*, namely:

— the need to avoid prejudicing effective law enforcement;[31]

— the need to protect witnesses and informers;[32]

— the need to maintain the independence of the judicial and prosecution processes; and

— the need to preserve the criminal court as the sole forum for determining guilt.[33]

The force of the public interest in maintaining this exemption will depend in material part on the importance of the information to the investigation or proceedings,[34] the currency of the investigation or proceedings,[35] whether the information, or like information, has been earlier released and, if so, to whom, on what basis and for what purpose. The passage of time, the completion of a prosecution, the release of similar information into a public forum[36] and the inconsequentiality of the information can all be expected to weaken the public interest in the maintenance of the exemption.[37] There is likely to be a public interest in the disclosure of

[27] To avoid metamorphosing it into an absolute exemption.

[28] The advantage of non-disclosure in support of this public interest is obvious: to avoid warning those who are being investigated that this is the case and to avoid contamination of evidence, as to which see *R v Police Complaints Authority, ex p Green* [2004] UKHL 6, [2004] 1 WLR 725, [2004] 2 All ER 209, [2004] HRLR 19, [2004] UKHRR 939 at [71] (Lord Rodger). Once a prosecution is started the prosecutor will be obliged to disclose any relevant material to the accused (unless the court concludes that to do so is not in the public interest) under ss 3 and 7A of the Criminal Procedure and Investigations Act 1996; but the accused can only use or disclose such material for the purposes of the case or if disclosed in open court or with the court's permission (s 17 of the 1996 Act).

[29] See *Toms v IC*, IT, 19 June 2006, where the Information Tribunal upheld reliance on s 30(1) by the Royal Mail on the basis that the disclosure of the information requested would 'facilitate the commission of similar crimes [to those being investigated]' (at [9] and [23]).

[30] If s 30 applies to make information 'exempt,' s 31 (information whose disclosure would prejudice the prevention of crime) cannot apply: see s 31(1). Thus, if prejudice to the prevention of future crime was not relevant to the weighing of the public interest under s 30(1), it could result in information having to be disclosed once a particular investigation or prosecution was complete notwithstanding that its disclosure might prejudice the prevention of future crime.

[31] In which context account should be taken of the need for prosecutors to have a 'safe space' in which to make their decisions: *Public Prosecution Service for Northern Ireland v IC and Collins*, FTT, 3 June 2011 at [14]; *Cobain v IC and Crown Prosecution Service*, FTT, 8 February 2012 at [65]; *Wynn v IC and SFO*, FTT, 7 September 2012 at [32]-[35].

[32] Different considerations may apply in the case of police witnesses: see *McCluskey v IC and Public Prosecution Service for Northern Ireland*, IT, 21 December 2007 at [26]; *Armstrong v IC and HMRC*, IT, 14 October 2008 at [78].

[33] *Toms v IC*, IT, 19 June 2006; *Digby-Cameron v IC and Bedfordshire Police*, IT, 26 January 2009 at [14]; *Breeze v IC and Norfolk Constabulary*, FTT, 2 March 2012 at [26]-[27]; *Wynn v IC and SFO*, FTT, 7 September 2012 at [34]; *Stephens v IC and CPS*, FTT, 20 December 2012 at [11]; *Breeze v IC and NHS Business Services Authority*, FTT, 22 January 2014 at [32]; *Sittampalam v IC and CPS*, FTT, 9 July 2014 at [68]. See also the Information Commissioner's Guidance on Investigations and Proceedings (section 30) at paras 55-57.

[34] *Freebury v IC and Chief Constable of Devon and Cornwall Constabulary*, IT, 5 October 2009 at [40].

[35] *Kelway v IC and Northumbria Police*, IT, 14 April 2009 at [69]-[70]; *Digby-Cameron v IC and Bedfordshire Police*, IT, 26 January 2009 at [31].

[36] *Freebury v IC and Chief Constable of Devon and Cornwall Constabulary*, IT, 5 October 2009 at [37]; *Breeze v IC and Norfolk Constabulary*, FTT, 2 March 2012 at [32]-[34].

[37] See Hansard HL vol 618 col 274 (24 October 2000) and vol 619 cols 223-4 (14 November 2000). Note also s 16(1)(a) of the Access to Information Act 1982 (Canada) which that the corresponding exemption only applies to information less than 20 years old. In *Guardian Newspapers Ltd v IC and Chief Constable of Avon & Somerset Police*, IT, 5 April 2007 at [37] the Information Tribunal regarded the passage of 30 or so years from the creation of the documents sought (the complete files of a police force relating to the prosecution of Jeremy Thorpe for conspiracy

information about the commission of a criminal offence and the public interest in disclosure may, for example, be heightened:

— where disclosure would allay legitimate public concerns about an investigation or prosecution;[38]
— where it can be inferred from the documents that there has been a lack of vigour or proper vigilance in an investigation, irrespective of the vintage of that investigation;[39]
— where the information already officially released relating to an investigation or prosecution is unrepresentative of all such information held by the public authority;[40] or
— where some decision affecting the applicant has been made that is based, whether in whole or in part, on the information.[41]

29– 007 The duty to confirm or deny

Where the requested information is, or if it were held would be, exempt information under s 30(1), then the discrete duty to confirm or deny that that information is held by the public authority does not arise but, again, this is a qualified exclusion of duty.[42] It will therefore be necessary to consider whether, in all the circumstances, the maintenance of the exclusion of this duty outweighs the public interest in disclosing whether the public authority holds the information. Despite its superficial similarity, this public interest balancing exercise is materially different from that employed for the purpose of determining whether the duty to communicate does not apply.[43] As a general rule, the broader the terms of the request, the more difficult it will become for the public authority to contend that the public interest in excluding the duty to confirm or deny that such information is held by it outweighs the public interest in compliance with that duty, if only because it will be self-evident that the public authority does hold information of that description. But public authorities are likely to refuse to confirm or deny the holding of information relating to a particular investigation since even that limited disclosure might assist those who are under investigation.[44]

29– 008 FOI(S)A

The Scottish counterpart to s 30(1) is s 34(1) of FOI(S)A. The Scottish provision does not explicitly require the information to be held by the Scottish public authority which previously held it for the purposes of the investigation. Also, it does not cover the possibility of the authority which held the information itself having power to institute criminal proceedings;

---

to murder and for incitement to murder) and the date of the request as a 'double-edged sword'. Whilst it reduced the risk of prejudice to future investigations, it similarly weakened the legitimate public interest in knowing more of the background facts to the investigation.

38 Including a decision not to prosecute (*McCluskey v IC and Public Prosecution Service for Northern Ireland*, IT, 21 December 2007 at [27]) or a prosecution which collapsed due to a lack of evidence (*Breeze v IC and NHS Business Services Authority*, FTT, 22 January 2014 at [22] and [33]).

39 *Guardian Newspapers Ltd v IC and Chief Constable of Avon & Somerset Police*, IT, 5 March 2007 at [34].

40 See §§6– 012 and 6– 017.

41 The public interest can encompass the peculiar interest of an applicant in having access to information that touches upon or relates to that individual's rights or to matters of particular and legitimate concern to that individual: see §6– 015.

42 FOIA s 2(1)(b).

43 See §§6– 018 to 6– 019 as to what it involves.

44 FOIA s 30(3) accordingly allows for a generally consistent NCND policy to be followed, so as to avoid express or implied tip-offs as to whether information is held: *Maurizi v IC and CPS* [2019] UKUT 262 (AAC) at [84]-[85].

rather, it refers to an investigation which may lead to a report to the Procurator Fiscal.[45] There is also a special provision in s 34(2) of the Scottish Act making information exempt if it is held by a Scottish public authority for the purposes of an inquiry under the Fatal Accidents and Sudden Deaths Inquiry (Scotland) Act 1976[46] or if it has been held by such an authority for the purposes of any other investigation into the cause of death of any person. Apart from these differences, as well as the different manner in which the Scottish Act generally deals with the duty to confirm or deny,[47] the Scottish provision is materially the same as s 30(1) of FOIA.

3. INFORMATION RELATING TO THE OBTAINING OF INFORMATION FROM CONFIDENTIAL SOURCES

29–009 First requirement

Section 30(2) of FOIA contains specific provisions exempting information held by a public authority which was obtained or recorded for the purposes of the public authority's functions relating to criminal investigations or proceedings, as well as certain civil investigations or proceedings (relating, for example, to the disqualification of company directors). In each such case, however, there is an additional requirement that the information 'relates to the obtaining of information from confidential sources'.[48] In so far as this exemption relates to information obtained or recorded for the purpose of criminal investigation or proceedings, such information will very likely also be rendered exempt information by s 30(1).[49] However, s 30(2), unlike s 30(1), would seem not to require that the information has been held for the purpose of any particular investigation: it would seem to be enough that the information was obtained for the purposes of the public authority's functions relating to criminal investigations and proceedings generally.[50] In so far as this exemption relates to particular civil investigations and proceedings, it does not overlap with s 30(1).

29–010 Second requirement

The second requirement in s 30(2) is that the information 'relates to the obtaining of information from confidential sources'. This was said to be intended to protect the identity of particular sources of information,[51] but it is arguable that it is more limited. A neutral reading of the exemption results in it only applying to general information relating to the obtaining of information from confidential sources, and not a particular piece of information obtained from such a source in the course of a specific investigation or the identity of the particular source.[52]

---

45 There are similar provisions in the FOIA concerning the application of s 30 to Scottish public authorities: see s 30(6).

46 But if the inquiry is still continuing, see FOI(S)A s 34(2)(a).

47 See §3–005.

48 FOIA s 30(2)(b).

49 See: *Wynn v IC and SFO*, FTT, 7 September 2012 at [30].

50 See *Marriott v IC and Metropolitan Police Commissioner*, FTT, 6 October 2011 at [20].

51 See Lord Falconer of Thoroton in Hansard HL vol 619 col 220 (14 November 2000).

52 Compare the clearer and more explicit foreign legislation: Freedom of Information Act 1982 (Cth of Aust) s 37(1)(b); Official Information Act 1982 (New Zealand) s 9(2)(ba)(i); Access to Information Act 1982 (Canada) s 16(1)(c)(ii); exemption 7(D) in the Freedom of Information Act 1966 (USA) referred to in *Pope v USA* (1979) 599 F 2d 1383 and note not only the wording of FOIA s 30(2)(b) but also the use of the phrase 'for the purposes of its functions relating to….investigations [and]…proceedings' in s 30(2)(a). It is likely that the identity of confidential sources would be protected in any event by the very general prejudice based exemption in s 31(1)(a) and (b) or by s 30(1). The Tribunal has found that the identity of a particular source comes within the exemption: *Alcock v IC and Chief Constable of Staffordshire Police*, IT, 3 January 2007 at [35].

Whatever is precisely covered by the section, it is clear that it is not a requirement that the information itself is 'confidential' and it does not exempt any information simply on the grounds of confidentiality. Rather, it seeks to exempt information about the obtaining of information from confidential sources.[53] The phrase 'confidential sources' is likely to be construed as referring to sources who supply information 'on the understanding, whether express or implied, that his or her identity will remain confidential'.[54]

29– 011 The public interest

Exemption under s 30(2) is qualified.[55] An assessment of the public interest in maintaining this exemption should involve a consideration of both paragraphs of the exemption. So far as paragraph (a) is concerned, where the information relates to a criminal investigation or criminal proceedings, the relevant factors will be similar to those which arise upon an assessment of the public interest under s 30(1).[56] So far as paragraph (b) is concerned, the public interest in the maintenance of confidential sources of information will be of particular significance,[57] as will the ability of a person adversely affected by a decision based on the information to controvert it. The Tribunal has held that:

> the importance of the informant programme to modern policing work is so great that a very cautious approach should be taken before doing anything that those most closely involved with it consider might discourage informants or potential informants.[58]

Where disclosure would assist the subject of an investigation or the public in understanding an investigative decision taken by police, where disclosure would help in holding the police accountable for their actions and use of public funds, or where disclosure would assist the applicant or any member of the public in righting an injustice to a person investigated, the public interest in disclosure could be weightier.[59] If the public authority has a structured system for assessing the validity of information provided to them by informants, then these public interest factors will be reduced in weight as the public interest in disclosure will to some extent

---

53 Note not just the identity of such sources: it might include, eg, details of an investigation or surveillance operation associated with the management of external confidential sources.

54 See *Dept of Health v Jephcott* (1985) 62 ALR 421 at 426. See also *Luzaich v United States* (1977) 435 F Supp 31 at 35, which talks of a 'pledge of confidentiality'. Note the source does not have to be 'covert'; and the fact that a source is 'covert' does not necessarily make it 'confidential': eg, undercover police officers or concealed cameras are covert sources but they are not confidential sources; cf Information Commissioner's Guidance on Investigation and Proceedings (section 30) at para 42.

55 FOIA s 2(3).

56 As to which, see §29– 006.

57 *DTI v IC*, IT, 10 November 2006 at [57], [60], [61]; *Metropolitan Police v IC*, IT, 30 March 2009 at [17]-[20]; *Metropolitan Police v IC*, FTT, 9 July 2010 at [81], [87]; *Wynn v IC and SFO*, FTT, 7 September 2012 at [32]-[33]. See for a discussion of the public interest in preserving confidential sources in this and analogous contexts: *D v NSPCC* [1978] AC 171 (in particular 218C-F, 230A-B, 232F-G, 241C-D); *R v Police Complaints Authority, ex p Green* [2004] UKHL 6, [2004] 1 WLR 725 at [73] (Lord Rodger); *R v H* [2004] UKHL 3, [2004] 2 AC 134(Lord Bingham) at [18]: 'Circumstances may arise in which material held by the prosecution and tending to undermine the prosecution or assist the defence cannot be disclosed to the defence, fully or even at all, without the risk of serious prejudice to an important public interest. The public interest most regularly engaged is that in the effective investigation and prosecution of serious crime, which may involve resort to informers and undercover agents, or the use of scientific or operational techniques (such as surveillance) which cannot be disclosed without exposing individuals to the risk of personal injury or jeopardising the success of future operations.' See also *Pope v USA* (1979) 599 F 2d 1383 and *Jarvie v Magistrates' Court of Victoria at Brunswick* [1995] 1 VR 84 at 88: 'There is a public interest in preserving the anonymity of informers, since otherwise these wells of information will dry up and the police will be hindered in preventing and detecting crime; moreover, the public interest on which the need to protect informers rests is based in part on a regard for their personal safety, considered, not as a matter of expediency, but as an object in itself' (Brooking J).

58 *Marriott v IC and Metropolitan Police Commissioner*, FTT, 6 October 2011 at [46].

59 *Alcock v IC and Chief Constable of Staffordshire Police*, IT, 3 January 2007 at [38].

already have been served by that system.[60] There may be circumstances where the public interest in maintaining the exemption can be satisfied by the redacting of names, addresses and other details of confidential sources from information supplied by them but obviously this will not always be sufficient, since the very existence of that information may disclose too much about the identity or methods or mere fact of information being obtained from confidential sources.

29– 012 The duty to confirm or deny

Where the requested information is, or if it were held would be, exempt information under s 30(2), then the discrete duty to confirm or deny that that information is held by the public authority does not arise. The exclusion of this duty is a qualified one. It will be necessary to consider whether, in all the circumstances, the maintenance of the exclusion of this duty is outweighed by the public interest in disclosing whether the public authority holds the information. As noted above,[61] this public interest balancing exercise is materially different from that employed for the purpose of determining whether the duty to communicate does not apply.[62]

29– 013 FOI(S)A

Analogous provisions exist in FOI(S)A,[63] albeit slightly narrower in scope than under the Westminster Act.[64]

4. INFORMATION WHOSE DISCLOSURE MIGHT PREJUDICE THE ENFORCEMENT OF CRIMINAL LAW

29– 014 The exemption

By s 31(1)(a) and (b) of FOIA information which is not exempt under s 30[65] is nevertheless exempt if its disclosure under the Act would, or would be likely to, prejudice the prevention or detection of crime or the apprehension or prosecution of offenders.[66] The basic distinction between ss 30 and 31 is that:

— the former is concerned with information held by the public authority for the purpose of a specific investigation or criminal proceedings conducted by it, and with investigative material that relates to the obtaining of information from confidential sources;

— the latter is concerned with information, which although not held by the public authority for the purpose of a specific investigation or criminal proceedings conducted by it (nor relating to the obtaining of information from confidential sources), nevertheless would, if disclosed, prejudice or be likely to prejudice the

[60] *Alcock v IC and Chief Constable of Staffordshire Police*, IT, 3 January 2007 at [40].

[61] See §29– 007, where this duty is considered further.

[62] See §§6– 018 to 6– 019 as to what it involves.

[63] FOI(S)A s 34(3).

[64] The FOI(S)A does not include an equivalent of FOIA s 30(2)(a)(i) or (ii). FOIA s 30(2)(a)(iii) is equivalent to FOI(S)A s 34(3); FOIA s 30(2)(a)(iv) is equivalent to FOI(S)A 34(4), save that the second requirement is absent in relation to information held by Scottish public authorities.

[65] See §§29– 004 to 29– 008.

[66] FOIA s 31(1)(a) and (b).

enforcement of the law.[67]

The latter is, therefore, more concerned with adverse revelations of methodology.[68] Similar exemptions as to law enforcement procedures are to be found in the comparative jurisdictions.[69] The phrase 'would be likely to prejudice' in the context of this provision will be taken to mean that the prejudice must be a real possibility, or something which 'may well' result, as opposed to being 'more probable than not.'[70] Thus, not only insignificant harm but also fanciful or improbable risks of harm to the relevant interest are to be disregarded. Provided the relevant likelihood of prejudice is established, it does not matter which public authority holds the information[71] and it need not relate to a specific investigation or prosecution. Thus, the exemption might apply not only to information held for the purposes of a current investigation (assuming for some reason it was not in any event covered by s 30(1) of FOIA) but also to information disclosing methods and procedures for investigating or preventing crime.[72] Examples of information which might come within this exemption are as follows:

— policy documents setting out in what circumstances a public authority would prosecute for a breach of statute;[73]
— investigation manuals;[74]
— information about planned police or Border Agency operations or tactics;[75]
— intelligence about anticipated criminal activities;
— witness statements held by another public authority in relation to an anticipated

67 *England and LB of Bexley v IC*, IT, 10 May 2007 at [23]-[27].

68 It is questionable whether s 31 can be used to prevent the disclosure of confidential source information to any useful extent. First, the information will be exempt information by virtue of s 30 and therefore outside s 31. Secondly, a general assertion that the disclosure of such material will, or would be likely to, prejudice enforcement of the law is apt to metamporphose s 31 into a pure class-based exemption. This approach has been rejected elsewhere. In Canada, the Courts have required the public authority to identify a particular investigation that would be prejudiced, and have declined to uphold a refusal to disclose upon an assertion that investigative processes would generally be prejudiced: *Rubin v Canada (Clerk of the Privy Council)* [1993] 2 FC 391, TD, [1994] 2 FC 707, CA; (1996), 179 NR 320, SCC; *Lavigne v Canada (Commissioner of Official Languages)* [2000] FCJ 1412, QL FCA; *Information Commissioner v Minister of Citizenship and Immigration* [2002] FCA 270 ('chilling effect' argument rejected).

69 In the United States, the Freedom of Information Act, 1966, 5 USC § 552(b)(7)(E), exempts from disclosure records or information that would reveal techniques and procedures for law enforcement investigations or prosecutions or that would disclose guidelines for law enforcement investigations or prosecutions, provided that disclosure of the information could reasonably be expected to risk circumvention of the law: see §51– 008(7)(E). The Freedom of Information Act 1982 (Cth of Australia), s 37, provides an exemption where the disclosure of the requested document would, or could be reasonably be expected to, prejudice an investigation or enforcement of the law or to disclose confidential sources of information in relation to the enforcement or administration of the law: see §51– 015(12). The Official Information Act 1982 (New Zealand), ss 6(c) and 27(1)(a), provides an exemption where the disclosure of the information would be likely to prejudice the maintenance of the law, including the prevention, investigation, and detection of offences, and the right to a fair trial: see §51– 022(3). The Access to Information Act (Canada), s 16(1)(c), provides a discretionary exemption for records the disclosure of which could reasonably be expected to cause injury to law enforcement or conduct of lawful investigations: see §51– 032(12). The Freedom of Information Act 2014 (Ireland) s 32(1), provides a discretionary exemption for records the disclosure of which could reasonably be expected to prejudice law enforcement and investigations or matters of internal security, or to reveal the name of a police informer: see §51– 039(12).

70 See the Information Tribunal decisions in *Hogan and Oxford City Council v IC*, IT, 17 October 2006 at [34]-[36] and *John Connor Press Associates Ltd v IC*, IT, 25 January 2006 at [15], following the approach of Munby J in *R v Secretary of State for the Home Office ex parte Lord* [2003] EWHC 2073 (Admin). Generally, see §§ 6– 020 to 6– 028.

71 See, eg, *Hargrave v IC and National Archives*, IT, 3 December 2007, which related to the police file on a murder which took place in 1954 which had been passed to the National Archives but where the Tribunal found on the basis of closed evidence that there was still some prospect of the murderer being detected and prosecuted [34]-[37].

72 See the corresponding provision in the Freedom of Information Act 1982 (Cth of Aust), s 37(2)(b).

73 For a similar example in Australia, see: *Re Murphy and Australian Electoral Commission* (1994) 33 ALD 718.

74 For a similar example in Australia, see: *Re Arnold Bloch Leibler & Co and Australian Taxation Office (No 2)* (1985) 4 AAR 178, 9 ALD 7.

75 *Armitt v IC and Home Office*, FTT, 5 October 2012 at [27].

prosecution by the police or Crown Prosecution Service;[76]
— information about the criteria the police apply when considering the possible installation of secret surveillance equipment;
— information as to the registration numbers of unmarked police cars;
— information whose disclosure may facilitate the commission of an offence;[77]
— information as to the physical security of buildings or IT and telephone systems;[78]
— information as to numbers of police officers deployed in a particular area.

It should also be noted that the particular information in itself may appear innocuous but nevertheless come within the exemption because, when combined with other information which may be in the public domain or be otherwise accessible, its disclosure will or may result in the relevant prejudice.[79] There is an analogous exception in EIR regulation 12(5)(b), which covers 'information to the extent that its disclosure would adversely affect ... the ability of a public authority to conduct an inquiry of a criminal ... nature.' It is probably more limited than the FOIA exemption which includes information which is likely to prejudice '... the prevention ... of crime' as well as its investigation.

29– 015 The public interest

If the information in question comes within the section, the duty to disclose the information does not apply if the public interest in maintaining the exemption outweighs the public interest in disclosing the information. The general principles relating to the public interest weighing exercise are as for other exemptions:[80] the nature, degree and likelihood of the prejudice (to the prevention or detection of crime or the apprehension or prosecution of offenders) will need to be balanced against and to outweigh the public interest in disclosure of the interest in question.[81] As a general rule, the less significant the prejudice to the protected interest is shown to be, the greater the chance that the public interest balancing exercise will tilt in favour of disclosure.[82] The balancing exercise will be different according to which limb of the exemption

---

76 See, eg, *R v Police Complaints Authority, ex p Green* [2004] UKHL 6, [2004] 1 WLR 725 at [71], where Lord Rodger sets out the prejudice that can result from the disclosure of such witness statements and the public interest in their non-disclosure. In general criminal proceedings themselves should of course be open to public scrutiny: see Art 6 of ECHR.

77 For example: *Hogan and Oxford City Council v IC*, IT, 17 October 2006 (in which it was successfully argued that the disclosure of the vehicle information numbers (VINs) for vehicles kept by the Council would be likely to increase the risk of 'vehicle cloning'); *Hemsley v IC and Chief Constable of Northamptonshire*, IT, 10 April 2006 (in which it was successfully argued that disclosing details of all speeding offences recorded by a particular speed camera may encourage drivers to speculate as to when the camera was active and to speed when they thought it was not); *England and LB of Bexley v IC*, IT, 10 May 2007 (in which it was successfully argued that the addresses of vacant residential properties fell within s 31(1)(a)). See also *Voyias v IC and LB Camden*, FTT, 22 January 2013; *King v IC and DWP*, IT, 20 March 2008 at [58]-[59] (information that may increase the risk of identity fraud, knowledge of the security and operational management of an operational IT system, and the status of security controls); *Matheison v IC and Chief Constable of Devon and Cornwall*, FTT, 18 June 2012 at [6]-[7] (location of automatic numberplate recognition cameras).

78 See *King v IC and DWP*, IT, 20 March 2008, which concerned a risk assessment carried out for the Department of Work and Pensions when setting up a new system for claiming benefits by telephone.

79 The so-called 'mosaic' or 'jigsaw' principle. See §§6– 024 to 6– 025. This was effectively adopted by the IT in *Hemsley v IC and Chief Constable of Northamptonshire*, IT, 10 April 2006 at [23]. See also the Information Commissioner's Guidance on Law Enforcement (section 31) at paras 21-22.

80 See §§6– 010 to 6– 017.

81 Promoting public confidence in the security of a system and enabling the public to encourage public authorities to make them more robust are factors which can increase the weight of the public interest in disclosure: see *England and LB of Bexley v IC*, IT, 10 May 2007 at [62]. Conversely, a likelihood that disclosure would result in decreased compliance with the relevant legal regime will enhance the public interest in maintaining the exemption: *Bowditch v IC and BBC*, FTT, 30 November 2012 at [26].

82 *Hogan and Oxford City Council v IC*, IT, 17 October 2006 at [54]; *England and LB of Bexley v IC*, IT, 10 May 2007 at [29].

is relied upon. The public interest in maintaining the exemption will be stronger where disclosure would prejudice the prevention or detection of crime than where it is merely likely to have that effect.[83] The factors to be taken into account can include the consequences that accompany or follow criminal acts, including their direct or indirect financial or social consequences.[84]

29–016 The duty to confirm or deny

Where the requested information is, or if it were held would be, exempt information under s 31(1)(a) or (b), then the discrete duty to confirm or deny that that information is held by the public authority does not arise. The exclusion of this duty is a qualified one, and the principles relating to the public interest weighing exercise are likely to be similar to those in relation to s 30(1).[85]

29–017 FOI(S)A

The Freedom of Information (Scotland) Act 2002 contains provisions that are identical to those in FOIA, save that the relevant prejudice must be 'substantial'.[86]

29–018 EIR

Regulation 12(5)(b) of the EIR states that (subject to the public interest test in reg 12(1)(b)) a public authority may refuse to disclose environmental information to the extent that its disclosure 'would adversely affect…the course of justice…or the ability of a public authority to conduct an inquiry of a criminal…nature'.[87] These provisions are considered in more detail above[88] but are analogous to those in the Freedom of Information Acts considered in this section. One obvious difference is that the EIR require that disclosure 'would' cause the relevant adverse effect while the analogous provisions in the Freedom of Information Acts include cases where there is only a likelihood of prejudice.[89]

5. OTHER LAW ENFORCEMENT

29–019 Introduction

Both FOIA and FOI(S)A exempt information from disclosure if its disclosure is likely to prejudice[90] any of a large number of other law enforcement activities not directly concerned with crime in the narrow sense. They also expressly exempt information whose disclosure is likely to prejudice 'the administration of justice' in general. The most obvious difference of substance is that FOI(S)A requires substantial prejudice to be shown, as opposed to prejudice *simpliciter*.[91] The EIR similarly expressly allow public authorities to refuse to disclose environmental information to the extent that (subject to the public interest test) its disclosure

---

83 *Hogan and Oxford City Council v IC*, IT, 17 October 2006 at [54]; *England and LB of Bexley v IC*, IT, 10 May 2007 at [78].

84 *LB of Camden v IC and Voyias* [2012] UKUT 190 (AAC) at [10].

85 See §29–007.

86 FOI(S)A s 35(1)(a) and (b).

87 The equivalent Scottish public authority provisions are EI(S)R reg 10(1)(b) and 10(5)(b).

88 §19–026.

89 See §29–014.

90 For the meaning of 'prejudice' and the degree of likelihood required, see §§6–020 to 6–028 and 29–014.

91 As to the practical difference that the adjective 'substantial' makes, see §6–021.

would 'adversely affect the course of justice [or] the ability of a person to receive a fair trial' or the ability of a public authority to conduct an inquiry of a criminal or disciplinary nature.[92]

29– 020 Administration of justice

There is no definition of 'administration of justice' in the Freedom of Information Acts but presumably the phrase must be given a wide interpretation and the public interest in the administration of justice will be accorded considerable weight.[93] Justice must include not only justice as administered in the traditional courts but also justice administered in tribunals and by lay magistrates and even by arbitrators. It would also include non-contentious matters like inquiries and the business of coroners' courts. Prejudice in this context would include prejudice to a particular case and to the system of justice as a whole.[94] Thus, a disclosure which might prejudice a fair trial or prevent a judge or jury doing their job properly in a particular criminal case or which might discourage witnesses from coming forward to give evidence or from giving their evidence openly or frankly[95] would come within the exemption as would a disclosure which might undermine the ability of litigants to bring their cases to court generally or undermine the legal aid system or the judicial appointments system or the authority of individual judges.[96] There is considerable potential overlap between this exemption and others within ss 30 or 31 of FOIA and those provided by s 32 (court records), s 42 (legal professional privilege) and s 44 (contempt of court).[97]

29– 021 Tax and similar impositions

The two Freedom of Information Acts exempt information if its disclosure will or is likely to prejudice 'the assessment or collection of any tax or duty or of any imposition of a similar nature'.[98] This would cover not only information which might prejudice a particular investigation of a taxpayer's affairs but also internal HM Revenue & Customs information which showed, say, minimum financial limits below which they do not, as a matter of policy, investigate a self-assessment or details of plans to close tax 'loopholes'.[99]

29– 022 Immigration

The Freedom of Information Acts exempt information if its disclosure will or is likely to prejudice the operation of immigration controls.[100] This might cover, for example, statistical

---

92 See further §§19– 018 to 19– 018. The relevant provisions are EIR reg 12(1)(b) and 12(5)(b) and, in relation to Scottish public authorities, EI(S)R reg 10(1)(b) and 10(5)(b).

93 See ICO's Guidance *Law enforcement (section 31)* (2013) at §§25-27.

94 This includes the effectiveness of relationships between the different agencies involved in the administration of justice and the effectiveness of the operational elements of the judicial system and legal profession: *Sanders v IC*, FTT, 21 May 2014 at [33].

95 See in relation to witnesses generally *British Broadcasting Corporation, Petitioners (No 1)* 2000 SLT 845 at [25]-[27] and *R v Police Complaints Authority, ex p Green* [2004] UKHL 6, [2004] 1 WLR 725, [2004] 2 All ER 209, [2004] HRLR 19, [2004] UKHRR 939 at [71]-[73]. The trial itself will of course generally be held in the open: see Art 6 of ECHR.

96 See *Guardian News & Media Ltd v IC and MoJ*, IT, 10 June 2009 at [104]-[107].

97 Similarly FOI(S)A ss 26(c) (contempt of court), 36 (confidentiality) and 37 (court records).

98 See FOIA s 31(1)(d); FOI(S)A s 35(1)(d). In *Carins v IC and DVLA*, FTT, 2 September 2010 at [14] the Tribunal found that the exemption extends to a 'financial sanction imposed on those who fail to comply with a process for collecting information to determine whether or not the duty in question has fallen due' (in that case a penalty for failing to complete a Statutory Off Road Notification while not paying Vehicle Excise Duty).

99 In *Doherty v IC and HMRC*, FTT, 25 January 2012 at [9] the Tribunal observed that 'it is pretty much axiomatic that disclosure of HMRC's view that there is a loophole in tax legislation will lead to some taxpayers taking advantage of it.'

100 FOIA s 31(1)(e); FOI(S)A s 35(1)(e).

information relating to applications for and the grant of certain visas,[101] instructions to immigration officers as to how to conduct inquiries of those seeking entry to the country or information as to proposed changes to visa regimes (which usually take place with little or no notice).

29–023 Prisons

The Freedom of Information Acts exempt information if its disclosure will or is likely to prejudice the maintenance of security and good order in prisons and other lawful detention centres.[102] This would cover, for example, plans of the layout of prisons.

29–024 The public interest

If the information in question comes within the section, the duty to disclose it does not apply if the public interest in maintaining the exemption outweighs the public interest in disclosing the information.[103] The principles relating to the public interest weighing exercise are the same as those in relation to s 31(1)(a) and (b). The particular public interest in maintaining these various exemptions and the countervailing public interest in disclosure which must be outweighed will be largely self-evident.[104]

29–025 The duty to confirm or deny

Where the requested information is, or if it were held would be, exempt information under s 31(1), then the discrete duty to confirm or deny that that information is held by the public authority does not arise. The exclusion of this duty is a qualified one, and the principles relating to the public interest weighing exercise are likely to be similar to those in relation to s 30(1).[105]

6. OTHER INVESTIGATORY AND REGULATORY FUNCTIONS

29–026 Regulatory functions

Both FOIA and FOI(S)A exempt the disclosure of information if that is likely to prejudice the discharge of a wide range of investigatory and regulatory functions of public authorities.[106] The exemption in each of the Acts applies to the exercise of the relevant functions for specified purposes. These purposes include:

---

[101] *Raab v IC and Home Office*, FTT, 17 November 2014.

[102] FOIA s 31(1)(f); FOI(S)A s 35(1)(f). The exemption would cover young offender institutions, secure hospitals, secure training centres, local authority secure accommodation and immigration detention and removal centres: Information Commissioner's Guidance on Law Enforcement (section 31) at para 33. See, for example *Willow v IC* [2017] EWCA Civ 1876, where the Court of Appeal upheld the application of FOIA s 33(1)(f) to a training manual for the use of physical restraint against children and young people in custody.

[103] FOIA ss 31(1) and 2(2)(b). See §29–015.

[104] See *In re L (sexual abuse: disclosure)* [1999] 1 WLR 299 for an example of a balancing exercise carried out by a court analogous to the balancing exercise required in relation to the exemption based on likely prejudice to the 'administration of justice': the administration of justice in proceedings concerning the care of children requires non-disclosure of information arising in the proceedings in order to engender maximum frankness against which had to be weighed the public interest in the disclosure of child abuse in order to bring offenders to justice and protect other children.

[105] See §29–007.

[106] DPA 1998 s 31(1)-(3); FOIA s 31(1)(g) and (2); FOI(S)A s 35(1)(g) and (2). The public authority must adduce evidence to show that, if the information were disclosed, there is a substantial chance that the identified prejudice will result: *Boam v IC*, FTT, 16 May 2016.

— ascertaining whether any person has failed to comply with the law;[107]
— ascertaining whether any person is responsible for improper conduct;[108]
— ascertaining whether circumstances exist which would justify regulatory action under an enactment;[109]
— ascertaining a person's fitness or competence in relation to management of companies or in any professional activity;[110]
— ascertaining the cause of an accident;[111]
— protecting charities against misconduct and mismanagement and the loss of their property and recovering property which has been lost;[112] and
— securing the health safety and welfare of people at work[113] and protecting the public against risks to their health and safety from people at work.[114]

29–027 Regulatory function information

It is clear that this group of exemptions will cover information whose disclosure might prejudice inquiries into the causes of all kinds of matters which come within the purview of particular public authorities (eg local authorities, the Civil Aviation Authority, the Health and Safety Executive, the Official Receiver and NHS Trusts[115]). What is not so clear is whether, and if so

[107] FOIA s 31(1)(g) and (2)(a); FOI(S)A s 35(1)(g) and (2)(a). As to the meaning of 'ascertaining', see *Foreign and Commonwealth Office v IC*, FTT, 21 September 2011 at [32]-[34]; *Waugh v IC and Rotherham NHS Foundation Trust*, FTT, 28 December 2012 at [27].

[108] FOIA s 31(1)(g) and (2)(b); FOI(S)A s 35(1)(g) and (2)(b). See, for example, *Hepple v IC and Durham CC*, FTT, 26 February 2014 at [8]-[16].

[109] FOIA ss 31(1)(g) and 31(2)(c); FOI(S)A s 35(2)(c). In *Reith v IC and LB Hammersmith & Fulham*, IT, 1 June 2007, the Tribunal rejected an argument that disclosure of the local authority's policy on the towing away of vehicles under parking regulations would result in an increase in illegal parking. However, the paucity of the evidence should be noted: 'The Tribunal has not seen any evidence to suggest that this risk [ie a claimed significant risk that the overall deterrent effect in relation to illegal parking would be lost] has been demonstrated or is even likely. [The local authority] rely upon their parking enforcement expertise, however their evidence is not independent, and being unsupported amounts to bare assertion. Such examples as given by [the local authority] do not demonstrate anything more than an unsupported fear that disclosure might increase illegal parking' (at [32]). The Information Tribunal has decided that the enforcement of the penalty charge regime in connection with the congestion charge by Transport for London is clearly within s. 31(2)(c): see *Bangar v IC and Transport for London*, IT, 23 November 2009 at [7].

[110] FOIA s 31(2)(d); FOI(S)A s 35(2)(d). This would cover investigations by DfES into fitness of teachers under sections 141 and 142 of the Education Act 2002 and by DBIS in relation to orders under the Company Directors Disqualification Act 1986. See also *Thackeray v IC and Health Professions Council*, FTT, 30 March 2012 (complaints about health professionals) and *Mansfield v IC and Gambling Commission*, FTT, 18 August 2017 (gambling operator's fitness to provide gambling services).

[111] FOIA s 31(2)(e); FOI(S)A s 35(2)(e). This would cover investigations by the Health and Safety Executive into accidents at work, the Air Accident Investigations Branch of the Department for Transport in relation to air accidents and the police in relation to road traffic accidents.

[112] FOIA s 31(2)(f)-(h); FOI(S)A s 35(2)(f)-(h).

[113] FOIA s 31(2)(i); FOI(S)A s 35(2)(i). In *Stevenson v IC and North Lancashire PCT* [2013] UKUT 181 (AAC) at [72]-[76] the Upper Tribunal held that this was not limited to bodies responsible for enforcing health and safety legislation and was wide enough to cover the functions of Primary Care Trusts in monitoring and improving the standard of healthcare. However, it could apply only where protection of the public against health and safety risks are among the public authority's purposes.

[114] FOIA s 31(2)(j); FOI(S)A s 35(2)(j); DPA 1998 s 31(2)(f).

[115] See *Galloway v IC and NHS*, IT, 20 March 2009, where the Tribunal found that an inquiry into a 'serious untoward incident' came within s 31(2)(b), (e) and (j); also *Ryanair Ltd v IC and OFT*, FTT, 28 January 2013 at [58]-[59] (regulatory functions of the OFT relating to competition issues and mergers). In *Bousfield v IC and Alder Hey Children's NHS Foundation Trust*, FTT, 10 January 2013 at [9] the Tribunal held that the exemptions in section 31 FOIA 'concern public authorities with specific responsibilities for law enforcement and are not intended to engage, for example, anything a public authority might wish to do for the welfare of its employees.' Similarly, in *Crystal Windows and Doors v IC and OFT*, FTT, 16 December 2013, the Tribunal held that ss 31(1)(g) and (2)(d) do not apply to the regulatory functions of the OFT in promoting good practice and approving consumer codes. Compare, however, *Stevenson v IC and North Lancashire PC* [2013] UKUT 181 (AAC) at [72]-[80], where it was held that the

the extent to which, the prejudice need not relate to the specific inquiry for which the information has been obtained. The Canadian case *Rubin v Canada (Minister of Transport)*[116] neatly illustrates the issue. The applicant sought from Transport Canada a post-accident safety review report undertaken as a result of a Nationair aircraft crash in Jeddah, Saudi Arabia on 11 July 1991, in which 249 Nigerian passengers and 14 Canadian crew members were killed. It had been the worst airline disaster in Canadian history. Transport Canada refused the request. The trial judge ordered that Transport Canada should disclose only those parts of the report which could have been obtained through regulatory means or otherwise, without relying on confidential sources, but could refuse access to the remainder. He found a reasonable expectation of probable harm to the conduct of *future* accident safety reviews were the report to be disclosed, and that the public interest in maintaining confidential reviews outweighed the public right to access contemplated in the Canadian Act. Mr Rubin appealed and the Court of Appeal allowed his appeal, rejecting the trial judge's reasoning:

> to allow his judgment to stand, would protect from public review most non-regulatory investigations "past, present and future" on the nebulous ground that to disclose this information might have a chilling effect on future investigations. Given that the purpose of the Act is to broaden the public's access to government information, this cannot have been Parliament's intent.

The Court of Appeal was also influenced by the fact that such a broad interpretation of the exemption would render other exemptions in the Act practically superfluous. The Court of Appeal concluded that the exemption only referred to a specific, ongoing investigation or one that was about to be undertaken: it did not apply to the general investigative process. This line does not appear to have been followed in full by the Tribunal, which has accepted that possible apprehension by witnesses in future investigations of a similar type to the one in question may be relevant prejudice when the contents of an investigatory report are sought[117] and found similar prejudice where 'raw statements' themselves were sought.[118] The Tribunal has also found that disclosure of material about a particular matter which was likely to affect the voluntary flow of information in future to a financial regulator could in principle amount to prejudice to its investigatory function, although in that case the Tribunal was not persuaded on the facts that such was the likely effect given the incentives on financial institutions to make voluntary disclosure.[119]

29– 028 The public interest

If the information in question comes within the section, the duty to disclose the information does not apply if the public interest in maintaining the exemption outweighs the public interest in disclosing the information.[120] The broad principles relating to the public interest weighing

words 'law enforcement' in the sidenote to section 31 are intended only as a broad summary or indication of the scope of and reason for the exemptions), such that ss 31(1)(g) and (2)(j) could apply to monitoring and assurance functions, the exercise of which might lead to regulatory action being taken by another body.

[116] [1998] 2 FC 430, (1997) 154 DLR (4th) 414, Court of Appeal. The analogous provision is the Access to Information Act s 16(1)(c).

[117] See *HMRC v IC*, IT, 10 March 2009 at [55]-[60].

[118] See *Galloway v IC and NHS*, IT, 20 March 2009 at [57]-[68].

[119] See: *FSA v IC*, IT, 16 February 2009 at [18]-[25]; *Bangar v IC and Transport for London*, IT, 23 November 2009 at [9]-[12], where the relevant risk of prejudice was not established on the evidence; *Waugh v IC and Rotherham NHS Foundation Trust*, FTT, 28 December 2012 at [28], where the Tribunal accepted that the threshold in s 31(1)(g) of relevant prejudice was crossed where disclosure 'might well have made it more difficult for the Trust to engage appropriate investigators to look into potential clinical failings' and would mean that the evidence given to them 'might be less detailed and frank;' *Mansfield v IC and Gambling Commission*, FTT, 18 August 2017 at [33].

[120] FOIA ss 30(1) and 2(2)(b); FOI(S)A ss 2(1)(b) and 35(1). It is important to bear in mind that the mere finding of a relevant risk of prejudice is not the end of the matter; the public interest in avoiding that prejudice must outweigh the public interest in disclosure: see *Bangar v IC and Transport for London*, IT, 23 November 2009 at [13].

exercise have been considered above.[121] However, the nature of the investigations and regulatory activities with which the exemptions at hand are concerned will often be of wider public concern than the run-of-the-mill prosecution: accidents, particularly those involving trains or aircraft, invariably provoke public concern; so, too, maladministration that has been the subject of an official investigation of any sort. This particular public interest must be reflected in the balancing exercises that must be carried out under s 2 of FOIA. The particular public interest in disclosing information of this sort was recognised by the Canadian Court of Appeal in *Rubin v Canada (Minister of Transport)*:[122]

> Having stated the important role that post-accident safety reviews play in the overall safety of the aeronautics industry, I think it is also important not to underestimate the public's interest in disclosure and the positive impact disclosure may have on the regulation of the aeronautics industry. It should not be forgotten that in passing this Act, Parliament has specified the important role public scrutiny of government information plays in a democratic system. Indeed, as Justice La Forest recently affirmed in *Dagg*,[123] "The overarching purpose of access to information legislation... is to facilitate democracy. It does so in two related ways. It helps to ensure first, that citizens have the information required to participate meaningfully in the democratic process, and secondly, that politicians and bureaucrats remain accountable to the citizenry".

In a case where there has been an adequate report the public interest in disclosure of individual 'raw' witness statements may well be outweighed by the public interest in avoiding prejudice to future investigations, but the position may be different where an inadequate report has been prepared.[124]

29– 029 The duty to confirm or deny

Where the requested information is, or if it were held would be, exempt information under s 31(1), then the discrete duty to confirm or deny that that information is held by the public authority does not arise.[125] The exclusion of this duty is a qualified one, and the principles relating to the public interest weighing exercise are the same as those in relation to s 30(2).[126]

29– 030 EIR

The two sets of Environmental Information Regulations provide that, subject to the public interest test, a public authority may refuse to disclose environmental information if its disclosure would adversely affect '...the ability of a public authority to conduct an inquiry of a...disciplinary nature'.[127] Again, the public authority holding the information does not have to be the same as the public authority conducting the inquiry.

---

121 See §29– 006.

122 [1998] 2 FC 430, (1997) 154 DLR (4th) 414 (CA). The analogous provision in Canada is the Access to Information Act s 16(1)(c).

123 *Dagg v Canada (Minister of Finance)* [1997] 2 SCR 403 at 432-433.

124 *Galloway v IC and NHS*, IT, 20 March 2009 at [76].

125 FOIA s 2(1)(b); see eg: *Hampshire Constabulary v IC and Independent Police Support Group*, FTT, 13 Dcember 2011; *Thackeray v IC and Health Professions Council*, FTT, 30 March 2012.

126 See §29– 012.

127 EIR reg 12(1)(b) and 12(5)(b) and EI(S)R reg 10(1)(b) and 10(5)(b). See further §§19– 018 to 19– 018.

7. CIVIL PROCEEDINGS

29–031 Investigations

There are specific provisions in the two Freedom of Information Acts relating to information obtained by public authorities for the purposes of civil proceedings arising out of investigations of various sorts, although the details of the provisions in the two Acts differ. Section 30(2)(a)(iv) of FOIA exempts information obtained for the purposes of civil proceedings brought by or on behalf of the authority arising out of investigations conducted by it for any of the purposes set out in s 31(2),[128] provided the information relates to the obtaining of information from confidential sources.[129] Section 34(4) of FOI(S)A exempts information held by a Scottish public authority if it was obtained for the purposes of civil proceedings arising out of investigations conducted by it for any of the purposes set out in s 35(2) or out of criminal investigations, but there is no requirement that the information relates to confidential sources. In neither case is it necessary for there to be any prejudice shown.

29–032 Administration of justice

Both Freedom of Information Acts specifically exempt information held by a public authority the disclosure of which would or would be likely to prejudice 'the administration of justice':[130] this provision might include information held by the public authority in connection with civil proceedings being brought by or against it, although in general the paramount requirement for open justice would mean that no relevant prejudice would apply or the public interest in disclosure would prevail. Both Freedom of Information Acts also exempt information if its disclosure would or would be likely to prejudice any civil proceedings brought by any public authority and arising out of an investigation conducted for any of the purposes set out in s 31(2) of FOIA[131] by virtue of the royal prerogative or under statutory powers.[132] The Environmental Information Regulations provide that a public authority may refuse to disclose environmental information to the extent that its disclosure 'would adversely affect...the course of justice.'[133]

29–033 Information in court documents

Section 32(1) of FOIA[134] provides that information is exempt under the Act if it is held by a public authority only by virtue of being contained in: (a) a document filed or lodged with a court for the purposes of particular proceedings; (b) a document served on or by a public authority for the purposes of particular proceedings; or (c) a document created by a court or its administrative staff for the purposes of particular proceedings.[135] The exemption is absolute.[136]

---

[128] See §29–026.

[129] FOIA s 30(2)(b).

[130] FOIA s 31(1)(c); FOI(S)A s 35(1)(c). As to the phrase 'likely to prejudice', see §29–014.

[131] Or FOI(S)A s 35(2).

[132] See: FOIA s 31(1)(h); FOI(S)A s 35(1)(h). FOIA s 31(1)(i) contains a similar exemption if disclosure may prejudice an inquiry held under the Fatal Accidents and Sudden Deaths Inquiries (Scotland) Act 1976.

[133] EIR reg 12(5)(b) and EI(S)R reg 10(5)(b).

[134] FOI(S)A s 37(1)(a) provides a like exemption in relation to information held by Scottish public authorities. There is no equivalent under the environmental information regime.

[135] The words 'any document created by…a court' in s 32(1)(c)(i) were interpreted by the Tribunal as referring to documents created by a 'judge' as opposed to documents created by the court in the sense of an institution and therefore to include documents like draft directions and judgments produced by a judge personally but not to include a copy of a transcript of proceedings in a criminal trial in *Mitchell v IC*, IT, 10 October 2005 but the

The word 'court' is defined to include any tribunal or body exercising judicial power of the State.[137] A distinction falls to be drawn between those exercising judicial power (which are not subject to the Act) and the bodies that carry out the administration and support to the various courts and tribunals (which are subject to the Act).[138] Most documents filed with a court or tribunal will be held by one or other of those support bodies.[139] The word 'document' has been interpreted broadly so as to include audio recordings and transcripts,[140] electronic records of materials lodged in hardcopy form[141] and statistical data drawn from written court records.[142] The principal object of s 32(1) is to exempt information received or generated by a court in connection with proceedings in that court, but held by a public authority. Most commonly this will arise where the public authority is a party to court proceedings. The exemption will also cover information contained in documents generated or received by a public authority in the course of ongoing legal proceedings. The thinking behind the exemption is that the disclosure of information contained in court documents (which may include confidential information and which may have special restrictions upon its re-use) should be regulated by the procedure applying in the court or tribunal in question, rather than by the general freedom of information regime.[143] The Court, adopting an independent role, will better appreciate who should receive particular documents, when they should receive them and on what conditions they should receive them. The exemption will cover information contained in statements of case, application notices, witness statements, affidavits, skeleton arguments, and lists of documents

---

Tribunal has subsequently acknowledged that this decision was wrong: *MOJ v IC*, IT, 29 July 2008 at [32].

136 FOIA s 2(3)(c); FOI(S)A s 2(2)(d).

137 FOIA s 32(4)(a); FOI(S)A s 37(2). This would include, eg employment tribunals (see *DBERR v IC and Peninsula Business Services*, IT, 28 April 2009), the Employment Appeal Tribunal, mental health tribunals, Special Educational Needs Tribunals etc. It probably also encompasses the European Court of Justice and the European Court of Human Rights, which, though they do not exercise the judicial power of any state, are undoubtedly courts: Information Commissioner Guidance on Court, Inquiry or Arbitration Records (section 32) at para 15.

138 Although the Court Service falls within the definition of 'government department' in FOIA s 84 para 1 (by virtue of being a body that exercises statutory functions on behalf of the Crown) and, by virtue of Sch 1, Pt I, is thereby a 'public authority,' the courts themselves have a distinct personality as the bodies exercising the judicial power of the State. Although court files may be held by the Court Service, it may be that they are held on behalf of the court itself (at any rate while proceedings are being heard), in which case they would fall outside the operation of the Act: FOIA s 3(2)(a); FOI(S)A s 3(2)(a)(i). The position in relation to tribunals may be the same, given that their existence and functions are entirely statute-based. See: *Mitchell v IC*, IT, 10 October 2005 at [31].

139 But not documents such as a judge's notebooks.

140 *Mitchell v IC*, IT, 10 October 2005 at [21]; *Edem v IC and MoJ* [2015] UKUT 0210 (AAC) at [21]-[32].

141 *Kennedy v IC and Charity Commission*, IT, 14 June 2009 at [58] and upheld in the High Court in *Kennedy v IC and Charity Commission*[2010] EWHC 475 (Admin) at [78]-[79]; *Peninsula Business Services Ltd v IC and MoJ* [2014] UKUT 0284 (AAC) at [46] ('the term "document" in s 32 means no more than the form or format (paper, electronic, audio, video or otherwise) in which the information is recorded').

142 *Brown v IC and MoJ* [2016] UKUT 0255 (AAC) at [27] and [37] (the statistics 'take on the character of the [exempt] information from which they were derived').

143 See: *R (Guardian News and Media Ltd) v City of Westminster Magistrates' Court* [2012] EWCA Civ 420, [2013] QB 618 per Toulson LJ at [72]-[74]; *Kennedy v Charity Commission* [2014] UKSC 20, [2015] AC 455 per Lord Mance at [6]-[7] and [26], per Lord Toulson at [119]-[120] and per Lord Sumption at [156] (on appeal from *Kennedy v IC and Charity Commission* [2011] EWCA Civ 367); *Edem v IC* [2015] UKUT 210 (AAC) at [22]; *Brown v IC and MoJ* [2016] UKUT 0255 (AAC) at [25]. See also, in the EU context, *Sweden and API v European Commission* (C-514/07, C-528/07, C-532/07) [2011] 2 AC 359, [2010] ECR I-8533 at [77]ff. The relevant procedural rules can be summarised as follows: (a) copies of statements of case and any judgment or orders given or made in public can be obtained by non-parties without the need to seek the court's permission under CPR 5.4C(1); (b) any other document filed by a party, or communication between the court and a party or other person can be obtained by non-parties with the court's permission under CPR 5.4C(2) (with such applications being determined in accordance with the principles of open justice, and the default position being that the public should generally be allowed access: *Cape Intermediate Holdings Ltd v Dring* [2019] UKSC 38 at [41]-[47]); witness statements which have formed evidence-in-chief are open to inspection unless the court otherwise directs and in the circumstances set out in CPR 32.13(d); (d) access to transcripts of recordings of hearing before the High Court and County Court is governed by CPR 39.9; and (e) the dissemination of transcripts of criminal proceedings is governed by Crim PR 2015 rr 5.5, 36.9 and 42.9.

and disclosed documents served in the course of proceedings,[144] provided always that the information is held by the public authority only by virtue of being contained in such a document.[145] It will also include a transcript of proceedings held by a public authority for other reasons.[146] Where information contained in one of the sorts of document described in (a)-(c) is also held by a public authority for other reasons, that information will not be exempt information by virtue of s 32(1): but the fact that information which is within s 32(1) is used or processed by a public authority in other ways does not prevent the exemption applying.[147] The exemption may also apply in the context of criminal proceedings.[148]

29– 034 Inquiry and arbitration material

Section 32(2) of FOIA[149] provides that information is exempt information under the Act if it is held by a public authority only by virtue of being contained in: (a) a document placed in the custody of a person conducting an inquiry or arbitration, for the purposes of the inquiry or arbitration; and (b) any document created by a person conducting an inquiry or arbitration, for the purposes of the inquiry or arbitration.[150] It is irrelevant that the inquiry or arbitration is complete, provided that the information is still held only by virtue of being contained in the relevant documents.[151] It can even extend to documents first acquired by a public authority before the initiation of an inquiry if the public authority subsequently passes those documents to the inquiry.[152] 'Inquiry' in the subsection means an inquiry held under a statutory provision and an arbitration means an arbitration to which the Arbitration Act 1996 applies.[153] Inquiries within the subsection include an inquiry by the Charity Commission instituted under section 8 of the Charities Act 1993[154] and an inquiry by the Comptroller of Patents under the Register of Patent Agent Rules into alleged misconduct by a patent agent.[155] Other examples would be the Bloody Sunday Inquiry under the Tribunals of Inquiry (Evidence) Act 1921, the Marchioness Inquiry under section 268 of the Merchant Shipping Act 1995 and a planning

144 *Mitchell v IC*, IT, 10 October 2005 at [33].

145 As to the effect of the provision, see §29– 034.

146 *MOJ v IC*, IT, 29 July 2008.

147 *DBERR v IC and Peninsula Business Services*, IT, 28 April 2009 at [52]-[53].

148 'Cause or matter' is not defined in the FOIA but the Senior Courts Act 1981 s 151(1) defines cause to mean 'any action or any criminal proceedings'.

149 FOI(S)A s 37(1)(b) provides a like exemption in relation to information held by Scottish public authorities. There is no equivalent under the environmental information regime. There is no equivalent under the DPA 1998.

150 The phrase 'for the purposes of the inquiry' refers to the purpose for which the documents were placed in the custody of, or created by, the person conducting the inquiry, rather than the reason why they were being held by the public authority: *Kennedy v Charity Commission* [2014] UKSC 20, [2015] AC 455 at [28]. In this context 'inquiry' means an inquiry held under a provision contained in or made under an enactment (not, for example, the 1998 inquiry into inequalities in health requested by the Minister but not set up under a statute) and an arbitration means an arbitration under Pt I of the Arbitration Act 1996 (not, eg, under a consumer arbitration agreement under Pt II of that Act).

151 *Kennedy v Charity Commission* [2014] UKSC 20, [2015] AC 455 at [29]-[34].

152 *Kennedy v IC and Charity Commission*, IT, 14 June 2009 at [86]-[87] and [102], endorsed by the High Court in *Kennedy v IC and Charity Commission* [2010] EWHC 475 at [29] (despite those documents having been held, presumably for a purpose, prior to the inquiry).

153 FOIA s 32(4). Inquiries can be constituted: (1) under the Inquiries Act 2005; (2) under specific enactments (examples of which are given in the main text); or (3) by prerogative power of the Crown. Inquiries constituted under the Inquiries Act 2005 are provided with a complete procedural code. That code disapplies FOIA s 32(2) for those inquiries: see Inquiries Act 2005 ss 18(3) and 41. Where an inquiry is constituted under the Inquiries Act 2005, documents held by a public authority in connection or arising from that inquiry may nevertheless be exempt information under one or more other provisions in Pt II of FOIA.

154 See *Kennedy v Charity Commission* [2014] UKSC 20, [2015] AC 455.

155 *Szucs v IC and UK Intellectual Property Office*, IT, 26 February 2008.

inquiry under section 320(1) of the Town and Country Planning Act 1990, but not Lord Butler's review of the intelligence on weapons of mass destruction or Lord Phillips' inquiry into BSE. Information held by a Scottish public authority for the purposes of an inquiry under the Fatal Accidents and Sudden Deaths Inquiry (Scotland) Act 1976 is not covered by this exemption.[156] The exemption is absolute.[157] Save that it applies to inquiries and arbitrations, rather than court proceedings, the exemption is similar to that provided by s 32(1).[158]

29–035 The duty to confirm or deny

Where the requested information is, or if it were held would be, exempt information under s 32(1) or (2), then the discrete duty to confirm or deny that that information is held by the public authority does not arise.[159] The exclusion of this duty is an absolute one.[160]

8. AUDIT

29–036 The exemption

There are provisions in both Freedom of Information Acts exempting information held by public authorities which have functions[161] in relation to auditing the accounts of other public authorities or examining the economy, efficiency and effectiveness with which they use their resources if its disclosure would or would be likely to prejudice (or, in the case of Scottish public authorities, prejudice substantially) the exercise of such audit functions.[162] The likelihood of harm to the protected interest and the level of harm are the same as are required for the other harm-based exemptions in the Act.[163]

29–037 The bodies covered

The exemption only applies to information held by public authorities which have the relevant audit functions: this will most obviously cover information held by the National Audit Office but is likely also to cover HM Inspectorate of Court Administration, HM Inspectorate of Constabulary, HM Inspectorate of Prisons, Ofsted,[164] the Office of Government Commerce[165]

---

[156] FOI(S)A s 37(3).

[157] FOIA s 2(3)(c); FOI(S)A s 2(2)(d).

[158] See *Kennedy v Charity Commission* [2014] UKSC 20, [2015] AC 455 at [25].

[159] FOIA s 32(3).

[160] FOIA s 2(3)(c).

[161] The word 'function' in such a context is usually a reference to a specific statutory function.

[162] FOIA s 33; FOI(S)A s 40. There are similar exemptions in three of the comparative regimes. The Freedom of Information Act 1982 (Cth of Australia) s 47E, provides an exemption where the disclosure of the requested document would, or could be reasonably be expected to, prejudice the effectiveness of audits or tests or to have a substantial adverse effect upon the running of an agency: see §51– 015(14). The Access to Information Act (Canada) s 22, provides a discretionary exemption for records the disclosure of which could reasonably be expected to prejudice the use of audits or tests: see §51– 032(18). The Freedom of Information Act 2014 (Ireland) s 30(1) provides a discretionary exemption for records the disclosure of which could reasonably be expected to prejudice the effectiveness of audits or the procedures or methods employed for the conduct of them.

[163] See §§6– 021 to 6– 022. In *Office of Government Commerce v IC*, IT, 2 May 2007 the Tribunal specifically rejected an argument that a lesser likelihood of harm or a lesser degree of harm would suffice for the purposes of the exemption.

[164] See: *OFSTED v IC*, FTT, 20 February 2012; *Dept for Education (Northern Ireland) v IC*, FTT, 29 January 2013.

[165] This would appear to have been accepted by the Tribunal in *Office of Government Commerce v IC*, IT, 2 May 2007 (later consideration in *OGC v IC*, IT, 19 February 2009). The Office of Government Commerce is now part of the Efficiency and Reform Group within the Cabinet Office.

and the Care Quality Commission.[166] It does not relate to internal audits by public authorities. The Information Commissioner has also expressed the view that it would include *ad hoc* non-statutory audit functions.[167] Although private firms of accountants employed by public audit bodies are not themselves subject to the Freedom of Information Acts, the information generated by them in the course of carrying out work for a public authority may be information 'held' by the public authority even if it is in the physical possession of the private firm.[168]

29– 038 The information covered

The audit function of such bodies may be prejudiced by the disclosure of information in various ways. For example: relations with bodies being audited may be undermined by the disclosure of information supplied by them to auditors on a voluntary basis because such bodies may be less willing thereafter to supply information on that basis; audit methods may be disclosed in a way that undermines the effectiveness of the audit, either by revealing individual files to be audited beforehand or by disclosing methods to be used in future by auditors; or the disclosure of preliminary audit reports for discussion may create a misleading and unfair impression which is not borne out in the final report. The kind of information likely to be covered by the exemption would therefore comprise draft reports, audit methodology statements and correspondence between auditors and the bodies subject to audit. The applicability of the exemption is likely to be time-sensitive, with the risk of harm diminishing within even a fairly short span of time.[169] If information comes within the definition of 'environmental information' under the EIR or EI(S)R those regulations will govern the matter and since there is no equivalent to the public audit exemption under the regulations such information will be subject to disclosure under the regulations unless some other exemption applies.

29– 039 The public interest

If the information in question comes within the section, the duty to disclose the information does not apply if the public interest in maintaining the exemption outweighs the public interest in disclosing the information.[170] The principles relating to the public interest weighing exercise are the same as those in relation to s 31.[171] Given that the exemption is prejudice-based, the particular public interest in maintaining the exemption may be self-evident, but should be identified and analysed carefully before the weighing exercise is carried out.[172] It is unlikely that the public interest in maintaining the exemption would outweigh the public interest in disclosure in the case of standard audit methodologies or information already in the public domain and, once an audit is complete, it is obviously less likely that the public interest in maintaining the exemption would outweigh the public interest in disclosure. A public authority with audit functions may be well advised to consult an audited body from which information had come before making disclosure in order to have a full appreciation of the public interest issues.

---

166 See the Information Commissioner's Guidance on Public Audit Functions (section 33) at paras 7-8.

167 See Information Commissioner's Guidance on Public Audit Functions (section 33) at paras 6 and 9..

168 See *Chantrey Martin v Martin* [1953] 2 QB 286 at 293; *Gibbon v Pease* [1905] 1 KB 810; *Leicestershire County Council v Michael Faraday & Partners* [1941] 2 All ER 483; *Formica Ltd v ECGD* [1995] 1 Lloyd's Rep 692 at 703.

169 While the Tribunal in *Office of Government Commerce v IC*, IT, 2 May 2007 found that the 'gateway review' reports did fall within the exemption (ie the likely risk of prejudice was established) (at [52]), the age of the reports was also relevant to its consideration of the public interest in maintaining the exemption (at [85]). The decision was successfully appealed, although this point was not over-ruled: see *OGC v IC* [2008] EWHC 774 (Admin), [2008] ACD 54 at [84]-[91] and the subsequent consideration in *OGC v IC*, IT, 19 February 2009.

170 FOIA ss 33(2) and 2(2)(b); FOI(S)A ss 2(1)(b) and 40.

171 See §29– 015.

172 *OGC v IC* [2008] EWHC 774 (Admin), [2008] ACD 54 at [84]-[91].

29– 040 The duty to confirm or deny

The discrete duty to confirm or deny the existence of information provided by s 1(1)(a) of FOIA does not apply if and to the extent that compliance would or would be likely to prejudice the exercise by a public authority of its audit functions.[173] It is thought unlikely that there will often be such prejudice by the mere confirmation that such a public authority holds information but there may be cases where this would be so, for example if the authority was asked to confirm that information had been provided by a 'whistle-blower.'

[173] FOIA ss 33(3) and 2(1)(b).

CHAPTER 30
Privilege

1. PARLIAMENTARY PRIVILEGE

30– 001 Overview

Each House of Parliament is a 'public authority' within the meaning of FOIA.[1] Each House is accordingly subject to the information disclosure regime provided by that Act, as well as those of the EIR and the GDPR. Although the Houses of Parliament have submitted to these three regimes, respect for the special status of business conducted within the Houses of Parliament is maintained through an exemption for Parliamentary privilege. Specifically, to the extent that information captured by a request would, if communicated to the applicant, result in an infringement of the privileges of either House of Parliament, that information is exempt information for the purposes of FOIA.[2] There is a provision in the EIR that produces the same result in relation to 'environmental information'.[3] There is a similar exemption from the

---

[1] FOIA Sch 1 Pt I. They are thereby public authorities for the purposes of the EIR: EIR reg 2(2). The DPA 2018 applies to personal data processed (including held or stored) by or on behalf of the Houses of Parliament: DPA 2018 s 210.

[2] FOIA s 34(1). With the result that the duty to communicate the information under FOIA s 1(1)(b), does not apply.

[3] EIR reg 3(4). As to the meaning of 'environmental information' see §17– 011. Strictly, EIR reg 3(4) provides that the regulations shall not apply 'to either House of Parliament' to the extent required for the purpose of avoiding an infringement of the privileges of either House. The Information Commissioner's guidance suggests that the EIR 'will still apply to other public authorities holding environmental information relating to parliamentary proceedings' and prudently suggests that 'Public authorities should consult the authorities of the relevant House to clarify the position.' Information Commissioner, *Parliamentary privilege (section 34)*, para 34:
`ico.org.uk/media/for-organisations/documents/1161/section_34_parliamentary_privilege.pdf`
The wording of EIR reg 3(4) is unfortunate, but its purpose is clear and given the respect accorded by the courts to Parliamentary privilege and its constitutional importance, EIR reg 3(4) should be construed as saying that the EIR shall not apply to the extent required for the purpose of avoiding an infringement of the privileges of either House of Parliament, rather than in the limited way suggested in the Information Commissioner's guidance note.

subject access rights in the GDPR as supplemented by, or otherwise provided by, the DPA 2018.[4] The operation of these exemptions accordingly turns upon the scope of the privileges of Parliament. While these exemptions will principally apply to information held by either House of Parliament, they are not so confined, and the exemptions will apply equally to information held by other public authorities to the extent that its disclosure would infringe the privilege.[5] In all cases the exemption is an absolute one, so that there is no need to consider whether the public interest in disclosing the information outweighs the public interest in maintaining the exemption.[6] Similarly, in all cases where the mere confirmation or denial by a public authority that it holds the information requested would constitute an infringement of the privileges of either House of Parliament, the duty to confirm or deny will not arise.[7] There is no equivalent in relation to Scottish public authorities.[8] The privilege does not apply to proceedings in the National Assemblies of Northern Ireland or of Wales. Similar exemptions are to be found in each of the comparative jurisdictions except the United States and Canada.[9]

30– 002 Documents held by a House

As with all other public authorities, it is only information that is 'held' by one of the Houses of Parliament that is within the scope of the rights conferred by FOIA.[10] Members of Parliament and political parties are not 'public authorities' within the meaning of the Act. As such, papers held by them that are not 'in the custody of the House' are outside the right of access conferred by FOIA.[11] Information that is in the 'custody of the House' includes documents in the

---

4 DPA 2018 Sch 2, Pt 2, para 13 and Sch 11 para 4. See further §30– 012.

5 The Information Commissioner advises that as a matter of good practice, where a public authority other than one of the Houses of Parliament has received a request for information to which it thinks the exemption for parliamentary privilege may apply, it should contact the relevant House for advice: Information Commissioner, *Parliamentary privilege (section 34)*, para 28 ico.org.uk/media/for-organisations/documents/1161/section_34_parliamentary_privilege.pdf
Since disclosure of information in breach of parliamentary privilege is punishable by Parliament, where a public authority proposes to disclose information that might conceivably be covered by that privilege it is also good practice to contact the Freedom of Information Officer at the appropriate House of Parliament.

6 FOIA s 2(3)(d). This does not, of itself, mean that there cannot be discretionary disclosure of the information: see §§20– 036 to 20– 038.

7 FOIA s 34(2); EIR reg 3(4). The disapplication of this duty under FOIA is also absolute, so that it is not necessary to consider the public interest. Disapplication of the duty to confirm or deny is more likely to arise where the request is very specific, such that mere confirmation or denial is revelatory of the information sought. The EIR achieves the same result by disapplying the whole of the Regulations to the extent required for the purpose of avoiding an infringement of the privileges of either House of Parliament: EIR reg 3(4).

8 That is, under FOI(S)A or EI(S)R.

9 The Freedom of Information Act 1982 (Cth of Australia) s 46(c), provides an exemption where the disclosure of the requested document would infringe the privileges of the Commonwealth Parliament, State Parliaments and Territorial Assemblies: see §51– 015(6). The Official Information Act 1982 (New Zealand), ss 18(c)(ii) and 52(1), provides an absolute exemption where the disclosure of the information would constitute a contempt of the House: see §51– 022(7). This is a wider concept than Parliamentary privilege, and includes anything which has a tendency to obstruct or impede the House in its business, even something for which there is no precedent. The Freedom of Information Act 2014 (Ireland) s 31(1)(c), provides an exemption where the record consists of: (a) the private papers of a member of the European Parliament, or (b) the opinions, advice, recommendations, or the results of consultations, considered by either House of the Oireachtas or the Chairman or Deputy Chairman or any other member of either such House or a member of the staff of the Houses of the Oireachtas Service for the purposes of the proceedings at a sitting of either such House, or by a committee appointed by either such House or jointly by both such Houses and consisting of members of either or both of such Houses or a member of such a committee or a member of the staff of the Houses of the Oireachtas Service for the purposes of the proceedings at a meeting of such a committee: see §51– 039(3).

10 And similarly the EIR. See further §§18– 008 and 20– 009 to 20– 011.

11 House of Commons, *Public Administration Committee, Third Report, Session 1997-98*, 19 May 1998, para 37. Such papers are similarly outside the scope of the regime in Australia (see §51– 011), New Zealand (see §51– 018), Canada (see §51– 026) and Ireland (see §51– 035).

possession of officers of Parliament and officers of its Committees, and Members of Parliament, held for some function of the work of Parliament and its committees. The term may, depending on the circumstances, extend to any of the following types of material:

(a) records of committee proceedings held in private, where that record is held by another public authority;
(b) memoranda and draft memoranda submitted to committees;
(c) reports or draft reports of a Parliamentary Committee held by another public authority prior to that report's disclosure by the Parliamentary Committee itself;
(d) factual briefs or briefs of suggested questions prepared by the committee staff for the use of committee chairmen and members, and draft Reports which may be in the possession of a department as a result of a Minister being, or having been, a member of such a committee;
(e) internal papers prepared by Officers of either House, including advice of all kinds to the Speaker, briefs for the chairmen and other members of committees, and informal notes of deliberative meetings of committees;
(f) papers prepared by the libraries of either House, or by other House agencies such as the Parliamentary Office of Science and Technology;
(g) papers relating to investigations by the Parliamentary Commissioner for Standards;
(h) papers relating to the Registers of Members' Interests;
(i) bills, amendments and motions originating from Parliament or a Member rather than from parliamentary counsel or another government department;
(j) confidential legal advice of Law Officers or by the legal branch of any other Department to the Speaker, a committee chairman or a committee;
(k) any unpublished correspondence between Ministers and a member or official of either House, relating specifically to proceedings on any question, draft bill, motion or amendment, either in the relevant House, or in a committee;
(l) any correspondence with or relating to the proceedings of the Parliamentary Commissioner for Standards or the Registrar of Members' Interests.

30– 003 Privileges of Parliament

The House of Lords and the House of Commons claim for their members, both individually and collectively, certain rights and privileges which each House requires for the proper discharge of its functions and which exceed the rights possessed by other bodies and individuals. These are conventionally called the 'privileges of the Houses of Parliament'.[12] The privileges of the Houses of Parliament include the freedom of speech and debate in Parliament, the freedom from arrest (other than on a criminal charge or for contempt) and exemption from jury service. For present purposes, the privilege that is of greatest significance is the freedom of each House to control its own proceedings without external supervision, whether by the courts or otherwise. Each House is thus said to have 'exclusive cognisance' of its own 'proceedings'. That exclusive cognisance includes control over the disclosure of information within the custody of the House. The exemption in s 34 of FOIA operates to leave undisturbed the control by the Houses of Parliament over the disclosure of such information.

30– 004 Provenance and rationale

Parliamentary privilege is protected by Art 9 of the Bill of Rights 1689[13] and by common law

[12] Most of the privileges are common to both Houses, but some (not relevant for present purposes) are unique to each. For a fuller treatment of the privileges of the Houses of Parliament, see Joint Committee on Parliamentary Privilege, *Report*, July 2013, HL Paper 30, HC 100.

[13] 'That the freedom of speech and debates or proceedings in Parlyament ought not to be impeached or questioned in any court or place out of Parlyament.' Article 9 is not a comprehensive statement of the privilege, but is simply

authorities refusing to allow any challenge to what is said or done within the walls of Parliament in performance of its legislative function and established privileges.[14] The privilege is founded upon two principles:

— the need to avoid any risk of interference with free speech in Parliament; and
— the separation of powers, which requires the executive and the legislature to abstain from interference with the judicial function and requires the judiciary not to interfere with or to criticise the proceedings of the legislature.[15]

Although the courts are not bound by any views expressed by Parliamentary committees, by the Speaker or by the House of Commons itself as to the scope of Parliamentary privilege, the extent of which is ultimately a matter for the Court, its scope is a matter on which the court will pay careful regard to any views expressed in Parliament by either House or by bodies or individuals in a position to speak on the matter with authority.[16]

30– 005 Nature of the privilege

Parliamentary privilege prevents:

(1) the deployment in court or tribunal proceedings of statements made during proceedings in Parliament, but only where the object of the court or tribunal proceedings is to render the maker of the statement legally liable;[17]
(2) parties to litigation bringing into question anything said or done during proceedings in Parliament by suggesting (whether by direct evidence, cross-examination, inference or submission) that the actions or words were inspired by improper motives or were untrue or misleading;[18]
(3) a challenge to the veracity or accuracy of something said during proceedings in Parliament.[19]

Parliamentary privilege does not prevent reliance on evidence of what was said during proceedings in Parliament to show what was the motivation of the executive's action outside Parliament.[20] However, the reliance must not be such as to put another party to the proceedings at a disadvantage by that party being unable to contradict what was said during proceedings in Parliament. In particular, reliance upon an opinion or evaluative conclusion

---

a manifestation of the principle that the courts and Parliament are both astute to recognise their respective constitutional roles: *Prebble v Television New Zealand* [1995] 1 AC 321 (PC) at 332D; *OGC v IC* [2008] EWHC 774 (Admin), [2010] QB 98 at [31].

14 *Prebble v Television New Zealand* [1995] 1 AC 321 at 332. In a defence to a defamation action, Television New Zealand asserted justification and relied inter alia on statements by ministers in the House which Television New Zealand alleged were calculated to mislead the House or were otherwise improperly motivated. Mr Prebble, a government minister and plaintiff in the defamation action, applied to strike out that part of the defence said to rely on privileged material. The Privy Council upheld the striking out of pleadings, ruling that the privilege applied to the material in question. It was an infringement of the privilege for any party to question in legal proceedings words spoken or actions done in Parliament by suggesting they were untrue, misleading or done for improper motives, even when done in defence of proceedings brought by a member of the legislature.

15 *OGC v IC* [2008] EWHC 774 (Admin), [2010] QB 98 at [46].

16 *R v Chaytor* [2010] UKSC 52, [2011] 1 AC 684 at [15]-[16]. See also Joint Committee on Parliamentary Privilege, *Report*, July 2013, HL Paper 30, HC 100, para 31.

17 *OGC v IC* [2008] EWHC 774 (Admin), [2010] QB 98 at [32].

18 *Prebble v Television New Zealand* [1995] 1 AC 321 at 337A.

19 *Hamilton v Al-Fayed (No 1)* [2001] 1 AC 395 at 403; *OGC v IC* [2008] EWHC 774 (Admin), [2010] QB 98 at [39]-[40].

20 *Toussaint v The Attorney-General of Saint Vincent and the Grenadines* [2007] UKPC 48, [2007] 1 WLR 2825. In that case, the claimant had alleged that a compulsory purchase order constituted discriminatory or illegitimate expropriation. The claimant was entitled to rely on the Minister's statement to Parliament to show the true motivation for the compulsory purchase. The claimant did not allege that the Minister had misled Parliament; to the contrary, it was alleged that what he said to Parliament disclosed his true motivation. The allegedly wrongful act in that case was not the statement to Parliament, but the compulsory purchase to which it related.

expressed during proceedings in Parliament may effect an unfairness upon another party and may be impermissible on that basis.[21] It is thus always important to identify the purpose for which evidence of proceedings in Parliament is relied upon.[22]

30– 006 The exemption

So far as section 34 of FOIA is concerned, in making each House of Parliament a 'public authority' for the purposes of the Act, Parliament elected to submit itself to the obligations imposed by that Act: most notably, the obligation to provide a person with requested information held by it save to the extent otherwise prescribed by the Act. As such, where no exemption (apart from s.34) is applicable, the obligation to disclose requested information held by a House of Parliament will not normally constitute an infringement of the privileges of that House unless publication of that information has previously been restricted by a House. Each House of Parliament, should it deem it expedient, may prohibit the publication of its proceedings. In relation to proceedings of the House of Commons, it resolved in 1971 that:

> notwithstanding the resolution of the House on 3 March 1762 and other such resolutions, this House will not entertain any complaint of contempt of the House or breach of privilege in respect of the publication of the debates or proceedings of the House or of its committees, except when any such debates or proceedings shall have been conducted with closed doors or in private, or when such publication shall have been expressly prohibited by the House.[23]

Parliamentary privilege may be invoked to prevent the publication of evidence taken by a select committee before it has been reported to the House, including the publication of draft reports, in cases where such publication has not been authorised by the select committee or, in the Commons, if the select committee is no longer in existence, has not been authorised by the Speaker.[24]

30– 007 Proceedings in Parliament

Although the phrase has never been precisely defined in this jurisdiction,[25] 'proceedings in Parliament' have been said to comprise:

> The primary meaning of proceedings, as a technical parliamentary term, . . . is some formal action, usually a decision, taken by the House in its collective capacity. While business which involves actions and decisions of the House are clearly proceedings, debate is an intrinsic part of that process which is recognised by its inclusion in the formulation of article IX. An individual Member takes part in a proceeding usually by speech, but also by various

---

21 *OGC v IC* [2008] EWHC 774 (Admin), [2010] QB 98 at [58]-[59].

22 *Toussaint v The Attorney-General of Saint Vincent and the Grenadines* [2007] UKPC 48, [2007] 1 WLR 2825 at [19]; *OGC v IC* [2010] QB 98 at [49], [62]. See also *Gordon v IC and Cabinet Office*, FTT, 7 December 2012 at [78]-[79], itself referring to this paragraph in the 3rd edition of this work. In that case the Tribunal held at [83]-[85] that what was clearly in issue was a challenge upon the truth, motive and good faith of what was said in the course of Parliamentary proceedings, and that it was not going to take into account in any way whatsoever the facts, consequences or possible repercussions of an allegation that a Minister has misled Parliament.

23 226 Commons Journals 548-549.

24 Select committees are themselves empowered to publish evidence given to them, as is the Speaker if a select committee is no longer in existence: see HC Standing Orders (Public Business) (2018) no 135. When evidence has been given before a select committee meeting in public, no complaint of privilege will be entertained on the ground that it has been published before having been reported to the House: HC Standing Orders (Public Business) (2018) no 136.

25 In New Zealand, the Parliamentary Privilege Act 2014 has as one of its purposes the definition of 'proceedings in Parliament' for the purposes of Art 9 of the Bill of Rights 1688. S.10 of that Act sets out the definition applicable in New Zealand. As noted in D McGee, Parliamentary Practice in New Zealand, 4th edn (Auckland, Oratia Books, 2017), full text published online at: `parliament.nz/en/visit-and-learn/how-parliament-works/parliamentary-practice-in-new-zealand/` at 726. In Australia, a statutory definition of the term in Parliamentary Privileges Act 1987 s.16(2) has provided a detailed official exposition of what proceedings in Parliament might cover, but even that definition is not intended to be exhaustive.

> recognised forms of formal action, such as voting, giving notice of a motion, or presenting a petition or report from a committee, most of such actions being time-saving substitutes for speaking. Officers of the House take part in its proceedings principally by carrying out its orders, general or particular. Members of the public also may take part in the proceedings of a House, for example by giving evidence before it or one of its committees, or by securing presentation of a petition.[26]

It most obviously covers the various forms of business in which either House takes action and the whole process by which either House reaches a decision. Thus the courts may not challenge the means by which legislation was passed.[27] It also embraces things said or done by a Member of Parliament in the exercise of his functions as a member in a committee of either House and everything said or done in either House in the transaction of Parliamentary business, whether by a member of either House or by an officer of either House.[28] The phrase thus indisputably covers debates, motions, proceedings on bills, votes, parliamentary questions, proceedings within committees formally appointed by either House, proceedings within sub-committees of such committees, and public petitions, once presented. Similarly, statements made and documents produced in the course of these proceedings, notices of these proceedings, internal House or committee papers of an official nature directly related to the proceedings, and communications arising directly out of such proceedings (as where a member seeks further information in the course of proceedings and another member agrees to provide it), all constitute proceedings in Parliament.[29] So too are the steps taken in carrying out an order of either House. The workings of the Parliamentary Commissioner for Standards form part of the proceedings of Parliament.[30]

30–008 Matters outside proceedings

Certain activities of members are not 'proceedings in Parliament', even though they may take place within the House or a committee. A casual conversation between members in either House even during a debate is not a proceeding in Parliament.[31] Nor are the proceedings of

[26] Malcolm Jack (ed), *Erskine May's treatise on the law, privileges, proceedings and usage of Parliament*, 24th edn (London, Lexis Nexis Butterworths, 2011), pp 235-236, quoted in *R v Chator* [2010] UKSC 52, [2011] 1 AC 684 at [28].

[27] Joint Committee on Parliamentary Privilege, *Report*, July 2013, HL Paper 30, HC 100, para 29.

[28] *AG of Ceylon v de Livera* [1963] AC 103 (PC) at 120-121. For an instance of a case of mistaken encroachment on Parliamentary privilege through the cross-examination of a former Secretary of State to the effect that he had lied to a select committee, see *Weir v Secretary of State for Transport* [2005] EWHC 2192 (Ch) at [233]-[243]; at [242] the Judge apologised to Parliament.

[29] In *O'Chee v Rowley* [1997] QCA 401, (1997) 150 ALR 199 (dealing with the Parliamentary Privileges Act 1987 (Cth of Aust), which is said to be declaratory of some of the privileges of the Parliament of the Commonwealth of Australia) the Queensland Court of Appeal held that documents said by a Senator to have been created, prepared or brought into existence for purposes of or incidental to the transacting of Senate business were within the scope of Parliamentary privilege. The New Zealand Supreme Court ruled in *Attorney-General and Gow v Leigh* [2011] NZSC 106 that a briefing to the Minister from the Chief Executive of the Ministry of the Environment, given in order to enable the Minister to answer orally in the House of Representatives a written question posed, was not a proceeding in Parliament. To the extent that the decision suggests that in English law the privilege will only arise if it is 'truly necessary … in the sense of essential' for the proper and effective functioning of Parliament, it is wrong. In New Zealand, the decision promptly led the House of Representatives to pass the Parliamentary Privilege Act 2014, one of the express purposes of which is to 'define, for the avoidance of doubt, "proceedings in Parliament" for the purposes of Art 9 of the Bill of Rights 1688, and in particular to alter the law in the decision in *Attorney-General v Leigh*' (s 3(2)(c)). In *Makudi v Baron Triesman* [2014] EWCA Civ 179, [2014] QB 839 at [25]-[27], the Court of Appeal held that there may be instances where the protection of Art 9 extends to extra-parliamentary speech (though such cases 'will be infrequent, and the courts will look for a very strong case on the facts if Art 9 is to run'), generally where there is (1) a public interest in repetition of the parliamentary utterance which the speaker ought reasonably to serve and (2) so close a nexus between the occasion of his speaking, in and then out of Parliament, that the prospect of his obligation to speak on the second occasion (or the expectation or promise that he will do so) is reasonably foreseeable at the time of the first and his purpose in speaking on both occasions is the same or very closely related.

[30] *Hamilton v Al-Fayed (No 1)* [2001] 1 AC 395 at 406.

[31] Joint Committee on Parliamentary Privilege, *Report*, April 1999, HL Paper 43, HC 214, §101, citing *Coffin v Coffin*

committees not appointed or nominated by either House, such as backbench and party committees, or the Ecclesiastical Committee. A Member's correspondence, including correspondence with Ministers or other Members of either House, or their officers, is not privileged, unless it relates to actual or potential proceedings of the relevant House or committee.[32] In most such cases, however, it is unlikely that the information will be in the custody of a House of Parliament: as such, the information will not be within the grasp of FOIA.[33] Other examples of information within the custody of Parliament but that will not form part of the proceedings in Parliament (and so not be within s 34) are:

— Papers prepared by the libraries of either House, or other House agencies, intended to provide general or specific background information on matters not currently under examination, or expected or planned to be considered, in formal proceedings of either House or their committees.
— Members' correspondence and other communications not specifically related to proceedings of either House or of one of its formally constituted committees. For example, correspondence between a Member and a Minister about a constituency issue that is not the subject of proceedings.
— The deliberations of parliamentary bodies established by statute (although if they are discussing matters relating to the preparation of formal proceedings in parliament, those deliberations may well be privileged).
— Many administrative functions of Parliament, such as personnel matters, catering and other household activities.[34]

The principal matter to which Art 9 of the Bill of Rights 1689 is directed is freedom of speech and debate in the Houses of Parliament and in parliamentary committees. In considering whether actions outside the Houses and committees fall within parliamentary proceedings because of their connection to them, it is necessary to consider the nature of that connection and whether, if such actions do not enjoy privilege, that is likely to impact adversely on the core or essential business of Parliament. On that basis, the submission (for example) of claim forms for allowances and expenses does not qualify for the protection of privilege.[35] (Contrast judicial enquiry into whether a member should have registered an interest, which would trespass upon a proceeding in Parliament.[36]) In general, management functions relating to the provision of services in either House are only exceptionally subject to privilege, but occasionally management in both Houses may deal with matters directly related to proceedings which come within the scope of Art 9. For example, the members' pension fund of the House of Commons is regulated partly by resolutions of the House. Those resolutions are proceedings in

(1808) 4 Mass 1, HC (1938-39) 101.

32 See Information Commissioner, Parliamentary privilege (section 34), para 25 ico.org.uk/media/for-organisations/documents/1161/section_34_parliamentary_privilege.pdf and Joint Committee on Parliamentary Privilege, Report, July 2013, HL Paper 30, HC 100, paras 235-238.

33 See §30–002.

34 For example, *R v Graham-Campbell, ex p Herbert* [1935] 1 KB 594 (Court declining jurisdiction on a complaint that liquor was sold without a licence from the Parliamentary building). Also see the House of Commons, Research Paper 99/98, *The Freedom of Information Bill, 3 December 1999*, p 40. For the background on whether administrative functions were to be covered by the FOIA see pp 39-40. The House of Commons Select Committee on Public Administration stated that such information should not be protected from disclosure: see their *Third Report, Session 1997-98*, 19 May 1998, para 37.

35 *R v Chaytor* [2010] UKSC 52, [2011] 1 AC 684 at [47]-[48].

36 The first instance decision to the contrary in *Rost v Edwards* [1990] 2 QB 460 should not be followed. It was doubted in *Prebble v Television New Zealand* [1995] 1 AC 321 (PC) at 337 and see Joint Committee on Parliamentary Privilege, *Report*, July 2013, HL Paper 30, HC 100, paras 229-234 and the Government Response to the Joint Committee on Parliamentary Privilege (Cm 8771, December 2013) at 5, agreeing that the Registers in both Houses should be considered proceedings of Parliament.

Parliament, but their implementation is not.[37]

30– 009 Effect of the exemption

As noted above, the exemption in s 34 of FOIA operates to leave undisturbed the control by the Houses of Parliament over the disclosure of documents produced in the course of proceedings in Parliament, notices of these proceedings, internal House or committee papers of an official nature directly related to the proceedings, and communications arising directly out of such proceedings. Most such documents will be in the custody of one of the Houses of Parliament. However, the privilege can extend to information held by other public authorities, most commonly central government departments. Examples of information not in the custody of Parliament but the disclosure of which might infringe one of the privileges of Parliament are:

- Unpublished working papers of a select committee of either House, including factual briefs or briefs of suggested questions prepared by the committee staff for the use of committee chairmen and/or other members, and draft Reports. These are most likely to be in the possession of a central government department as a result of a Minister being, or having been, a member of such a committee.
- Legal advice submitted in confidence by the Law Officers or by the legal branch of any other Department to the Speaker, a committee chairman or a committee, or any official of either House.
- Drafts of motions, bills or amendments, which have not otherwise been published or laid on the Table of either House.
- Any unpublished correspondence between Ministers (or departmental officials) on the one hand, and, on the other hand, any member or official of either House, relating specifically to proceedings on any Question, draft bill, motion or amendment, either in the relevant House, or in a committee.
- Any correspondence with or relating to the proceedings of the Parliamentary Commissioner for Standards or the Registrar.

30– 010 Parliament published material

Most debates are conducted in public and most Parliamentary reports are available to the public. However Parliament retains the right to prohibit publication of its proceedings as it considers appropriate. Since 1971 this has been restricted to proceedings conducted in private or when publication has been expressly prohibited by the House, and the House allows publication of its proceedings which do not fall into those categories.[38] In 1980 the Commons resolved to allow its Official Report, published reports and public evidence taken by committees to be referred to in court proceedings without the need formally to petition the House for such permission.[39] Parliament has the right to prevent publication of the evidence taken by a select committee before it has been reported to the House.[40] So, for example, an application for disclosure of a Parliamentary Select Committee report, or of workings of that Committee, could not be sustained if such documents have not been released by Parliament itself. The same would apply to an unpublished draft report. Parliament also routinely publishes internal administrative documents and individual members' allowances and expenditure. Such

---

[37] See Joint Committee on Parliamentary Privilege, *Report*, April 1999, HL Paper 43, HC 214, para 248, quoted in *R v Chaytor* [2010] UKSC 52, [2011] 1 AC 684 at [73] and endorsed at [89].

[38] See 226 *Commons Journal*, 548-549.

[39] 236 *Commons Journal* 823.

[40] This would certainly be the case where Parliament has actively proscribed publication. It could arguably be otherwise where Parliament has merely taken no steps to publish committee evidence. However it is likely that the privilege applies in this latter situation as well, unless and until Parliament has taken a positive step to waive the privilege that would otherwise attach.

materials may remain privileged even following publication.[41] However disclosure of previously published information is unlikely to be an 'infringement' of the privilege. Further, such information is likely to be exempt information under s 21 of FOIA (information otherwise available).[42]

30– 011 Conclusive certificates

The Speaker of the House of Commons or, in relation to the House of Lords, the Clerk of the Parliaments may issue a conclusive certificate for the purpose of exempting a public authority from its disclosure duty or both its disclosure duty and its duty to confirm or deny that it holds any of the information requested. Such a certificate is conclusive evidence of the 'fact' that exemption from the duty or duties is, or at any time was, required for the purpose of avoiding an infringement of the privileges of either House of Parliament.[43] The effect of such a certificate in relation to information to which it applies is to remove practically all, if not all, an applicant's rights to challenge a decision not to communicate the information covered by the certificate and a decision neither confirming nor denying that the information requested is held by the public authority.[44] The Act provides no right of appeal against the issue of a certificate. Any attempt to seek to judicially review the decision to issue such a certificate is likely to be dismissed as itself contrary to the privilege.[45]

30– 012 GDPR and DPA 2018

To the extent that an individual asks a public body to be provided with a copy of the information that that public body holds about him or her, that request will fall to be decided by the GDPR and the DPA 2018 and not by FOIA.[46] The source of an individual's right of access to information about him or herself depends upon the purpose for which the requested person or organisation holds that information, or the identity of the organisation holding that information:

(a) Where the requested person or organisation is a 'competent authority'[47] and holds personal information for the law enforcement purposes,[48] the access right is

---

41 Publication by Parliament does not necessarily entail a waiver of privilege such as applies to the disclosure of material covered by legal professional privilege.

42 See Ch 25. There is no equivalent exemption or exception in the GDPR or the DPA 2018. There is a narrowed exception in EIR reg 6(1)(b).

43 FOIA s 34(3)-(4). Such certificates are seldom issued, but for an example of a case where one was issued, see ICO Decision Notice FS 50327178 of 1 February 2011, where a certificate was issued after the Information Commissioner's office began to look into a request for the names of any MPs under investigation by the Parliamentary Commissioner for Standards.

44 Appeals are considered generally in Chs 45-46. A potential avenue of challenge in relation to a s 34(2) certificate is considered at §45– 031.

45 However, query the situation if the Clerk of the Parliaments issued a certificate purporting to rely on a privilege of Parliament not previously recognised. Both Houses recognised in 1705 that they had no power to create new privileges (see 14 Commons Journal 555, 560, 17 Lords Journal 677). It may be that such a certificate would be ineffective as not being a claim to Parliamentary privilege.

46 FOIA s 40(1), FOI(S)A s 38(1). And, in relation to a request for environmental information, EIR reg 13(1) and EI(S)R reg 11(1).

47 Defined in DPA 2018 s 30(1) to mean a person specified in Sch 7 of that Act or any other person if and to the extent that that person has statutory functions for any of the law enforcement purposes, but not the intelligence services (as defined in DPA 2018 s 30(7)). The persons specified in Sch 7 include every Government department, other than a non-ministerial government department, chief officers of police and other policing bodies, other authorities with investigatory functions (including HMRC), authorities with functions relating to offender management, the DPP, courts and tribunals.

48 Defined in DPA 2018 s 31 to mean 'the purposes of the prevention, investigation, detection or prosecution of criminal offences or the execution of criminal penalties, including the safeguarding against and the prevention of threats to public security.'

conferred by the DPA 2018 and there is no exemption from the obligation to comply with a subject access request on the ground of Parliamentary privilege.[49]

(b) Where the requested person or organisation holds the information for intelligence service processing,[50] the access right is conferred by the DPA 2018 and an exemption is provided where compliance with a subject access request would breach Parliamentary privilege.[51]

(c) Where neither (a) nor (b) applies, and the processing of the personal information by the requested person or organisation is within the grasp of the GDPR (what is sometimes called 'ordinary processing'), it is the GDPR which provides the individual with a right of access to that information (ie to make a subject access request), but it is the DPA 2018 which provides for an exemption where compliance with that subject access request would infringe the privileges of either House of Parliament.[52]

(d) Where neither (a) nor (b) applies, but the processing of the personal information by the requested person or organisation is outside the grasp of the GDPR (what is sometimes called 'applied processing'),[53] it is the DPA 2018 which provides for the access right (by applying the GDPR right to that processing) and it is also the DPA 2018 which provides for an exemption where compliance with that subject access request would infringe the privileges of either House of Parliament.[54]

The right of an individual to require a public authority to provide a copy of the information it holds relating to that individual (ie one of the facets of a subject access request)[55] is dealt with in more detail in Part 2 (Chs 7-16) of this work. But to the extent that compliance with a subject access request is exempted on the ground that it would infringe the privileges of either House of Parliament, the principles in this section of this chapter apply.

2. LEGAL PROFESSIONAL PRIVILEGE

30– 013 Overview

Information in respect of which a claim to legal professional privilege could be maintained in legal proceedings is rendered exempt information under FOIA.[56] An analogous exemption is provided in the GDPR and the DPA 2018.[57] There is no express reference to legal professional

49 The right is conferred by DPA 2018 s 45.

50 Defined in DPA 2018 s 82 to mean processing by an intelligence service (ie by the Security Service, the Secret Intelligence Service or the Government Communication Headquarters).

51 The right is conferred by DPA s 94(1), and the exemption is provided for by DPA 2018 Sch 11, paras 1(1)(b) and 4.

52 The right is conferred by the GDPR Art 15, and the exemption is provided for by DPA 2018 Sch 2, Part 2, paras 1(a)(iii) and 13.

53 This is, processing to which Chapter 3 of Part 2 of the DPA 2018 (ss 21-28) applies. The processing to which Chapter 3 of Part 2 of the DPA 2018 applies is listed at DPA 2018 s 21.

54 The right is conferred by DPA 2018 s 22(1)-(2), applying GDPR Art 15 (for the purpose of conferring the right) and DPA 2018 Sch 2, Part 2, para 13 (for the purpose of providing the exemption).

55 Article 15(3) of the GDPR.

56 FOIA s 42(1).

57 DPA 2018, s 76(4); Sch 1, para 33; Sch 2, Pt 1, para 5(3); Sch 2, Pt 4, para 19; Sch 8, para 6; Sch 10, para 6; Sch 11, paras 3(3) and 9. In the GDPR, see Arts 9.2(f), 17.3(e). 18.2, 21.1 and 49.1(e) and recitals (50), (52), (65) and (111).

privilege in the EIR.[58] However, it has been held that reg 12(5)(b) – which allows a public authority to refuse to disclose information to the extent disclosure would adversely affect 'the course of justice, the ability of a person to receive a fair trial or the ability of a public authority to conduct an inquiry of a criminal or disciplinary nature' – supplies a similar (though not necessarily identical) exemption for the purposes of those Regulations.[59] The exemption under FOIA is not absolute, so that disapplication of the disclosure duty requires consideration of whether the public interest in the maintenance of the exemption outweighs the public interest in disclosure.[60] There is a correlative exemption from the duty to confirm or deny that information answering the terms of the request is held by the public authority.[61] Similar exemptions are to be found in each of the comparative jurisdictions.[62] Section 42 does not cover the privilege in aid of negotiations (commonly termed 'without prejudice privilege'), which is a separate and distinct rule. However such negotiations may be treated as confidential, and so be affected by the principles discussed in Chapter 25. Guidance on section 42 has been issued by the Information Commissioner.[63]

30– 014 Scope and meaning

'Legal professional privilege' is a rule or a collection of rules which seeks to protect the confidentiality of legal communications.[64] It comprises two limbs, 'legal advice privilege' and 'litigation privilege.'[65]

---

58 See §§19– 022 and 19– 008. Regulation 12(5)(d), (f) covers disclosure which would adversely affect confidentiality of proceedings where such confidentiality is protected by law, and the interests of persons providing information where that person was not under any legal obligation to so supply the information. The Scottish provisions are to the same effect: see the EI(S)R reg 10(5)(d), (f).

59 *DCLG v IC & WR* [2012] UKUT 103 (AAC) at [55]; *Hartles v IC*, FTT, 27 February 2013 at [21]-[40]; *DEFRA v IC and Portman*, FTT, 13 November 2012; *Kirkaldie v IC and Thanet DC*, IT, 4 July 2006 at [18]-[23]; *West v IC*, FTT, 25 October 2010 at [9]-[13]. Regulation 12(5)(b) covers disclosure which would adversely affect 'the course of justice, the ability of a person to receive a fair trial or the ability of a public authority to conduct an inquiry of a criminal or disciplinary nature.' This conclusion must be correct. Litigation privilege, for instance, has long been regarded as an aspect of the right to a fair trial in England and in other common law jurisdictions: see *Re Saxton* [1962] 1 WLR 968 at 972 (per Lord Denning); *Baker v Campbell* (1983) 49 ALR 385 at 427 (per Brennan J). The courts have emphasised that fairness requires a private and confidential sphere of preparation for litigation: see *Robert Hitchins Ltd v ICL*, CA, 10 December 1996 (per Simon Brown LJ); *Sumitomo Corporation v Credit Lyonnais Rouse Ltd* [2002] 1 WLR 479 at [46], CA (per Jonathan Parker LJ). Similarly *Archer v IC and Salisbury District Council*, IT, 9 May 2007 at [62]-[64]; *Mersey Tunnel Users Association v IC and Haiton BC*, IT, 11 January 2010 at [37]-[44]; *DEFRA v IC and Portman*, FTT, 13 November 2012 at [57]. See also *Williams v IC and Local Government Ombudsman*, FTT, 24 October 2012 at [21]-[24], where the rationale is explained as the risk of inhibiting the authority from seeking legal advice in confidence.

60 FOIA s 2(2).

61 FOIA s 42(2). See §30– 023.

62 In the United States, the Freedom of Information Act, 1966, 5 USC 552(b)(5), exempts from disclosure inter-agency or intra-agency memoranda or letters 'which would not be available by law to a party other than an agency in litigation with the agency', which has been interpreted to include records or information covered by attorney work-product privilege and attorney-client privilege: see §51– 008(5). The Freedom of Information Act 1982 (Cth of Australia) s 42, provides an exemption where the requested documents are subject to legal professional privilege: see §51– 015(4). In New Zealand, the Official Information Act 1982 ss 9(2)(h) and 27(1)(h), the Local Government Official Information and Meetings Act 1987 ss 7(2)(g) and 26(1)(h), and the Privacy Act 1993 s 29(1)(f), all provide a qualified exemption where non-disclosure is required to maintain legal professional privilege: see §51– 023(9). In Canada, the Access to Information Act, 1982 s 23, provides a discretionary exemption for solicitor-client privileged information: see §51– 032(8). The Freedom of Information Act 2014 (Ireland) s 31(1), provides an exemption where the record would be exempt from production in a court on the grounds of legal professional privilege: see §51– 039(3).

63 Information Commissioner, *The Exemption for Legal Professional Privilege* (version 1.2).

64 See generally: B Thanki (ed), *The Law of Privilege*, 3rd edn (Oxford, Oxford University Press), 2018; P Matthews and H Malek, *Disclosure*, 5th edn (London, Sweet & Maxwell, 2016) Ch 11; J Auburn, *Legal Professional Privilege: Law and Theory* (Oxford, Hart Publishing, 2000); C Passmore, *Privilege*, 3rd edn (London, Sweet & Maxwell, 2013); H Malek (ed), *Phipson on Evidence*, 19th edn (London, Sweet & Maxwell, 2017), Ch 23.

65 *Waugh v British Railways Board* [1980] AC 521 at 541-542, HL (per Lord Edmund-Davies). The distinction set out

(1) Legal advice privilege is concerned with confidential communications between lawyer[66] and client for the purpose of giving or receiving legal advice or assistance[67] in both the litigation and the non-litigation context.

(2) Litigation privilege is concerned with:

(a) confidential communications between a client or his lawyer and third parties; or

(b) other confidential documents

created for the dominant purpose of litigation (whether reasonably anticipated or commenced).

Confidentiality is therefore a necessary, but not a sufficient condition for both limbs of legal professional privilege.[68] The privilege belongs to the client and not to his lawyer or agent.[69] Only the client can invoke the privilege.[70] It is not open to a lawyer or other agent to do so unless acting on behalf of the client, and the lawyer or agent cannot invoke the privilege if the client has waived it.[71]

30–015 Nature of the privilege

The privilege is a bar to the compulsion of evidence. The confidentiality of legal communications has been recognised for some time as a human right under both Arts 6 and 8 of the ECHR.[72] Legal professional privilege is now afforded overriding importance in English law.[73] It is, however, a rule relating to immunity rather than admissibility,[74] since even improperly obtained privileged material may be admissible in evidence[75] It has now been characterised in English common law as both 'a fundamental human right'[76] and 'a fundamental condition on which the administration of justice as a whole rests.'[77] If it were

in Lord Edmund-Davies' speech was applied by the Court of Appeal in *Re Highgrade Traders Ltd* [1984] BCLC 151 at 164-165 (per Oliver LJ); and by the House of Lords in *In re L (a Minor) (Police Investigation: Privilege)* [1997] AC 16 at 24-5 (per Lord Jauncey) and *Three Rivers District Council v Bank of England (No 6)* [2004] UKHL 48, [2005] 1 AC 610, HL, at [65] (per Lord Carswell) and at [50]-[51] (per Lord Rodger).

66 The concept of a lawyer is essentially confined to solicitors, barristers, legal executives (and by extension foreign lawyers): *R (on the application of Prudential PLC) v HMRC* [2013] UKSC 1, [2013] 2 WLR 325. There are a number of statutory extensions to other professions: see Passmore, *Privilege*, 3rd edn (London, Sweet & Maxwell, 2013), para 1-218.

67 See B Thanki (ed), *The Law of Privilege*, 3rd edn (Oxford, Oxford University Press, 2018), para 2.02.

68 *Three Rivers District Council v Bank of England (No 6)* [2004] UKHL 48, [2005] 1 AC 610, HL, at [24] (per Lord Scott).

69 *R v Derby Magistrates' Court, ex p B* [1996] AC 487 at 504-5, HL.

70 Although the lawyer is under a professional obligation to assert the privilege on behalf of his client unless it has been waived: *R v Central Criminal Court, ex p Francis and Francis* [1989] AC 346 at 383, HL; *Bolkiah v KPMG* [1999] 2 AC 222 at 235-6, HL. The Court may also intervene to prevent a third party or even the client's lawyer making disclosure in breach of the client's privilege: *Harmony Shipping v Saudi Europe Line* [1979] 1 WLR 1380 at 1384-1385, CA.

71 *R v Peterborough Justices, ex p Hicks* [1977] 1 WLR 1371.

72 For example, *Golder v United Kingdom* (1979-80) 1 EHRR 524 (Art 6); *Niemietz v Germany* (1993) 16 EHRR 97 (Art 8). See the pre-incorporation House of Lords' decision in *R v SSHD, ex p Simms* [2000] 2 AC 115. Also see *Tamosius v United Kingdom* (2002) 35 EHRR CD323; *Foxley v United Kingdom* (2001) 31 EHRR 25; *McE v Prison Service of Northern Ireland* [2009] UKHL 15, [2009] 1 AC 908.

73 *R v Derby Magistrates Court, ex p B* [1996] AC 487 at 507-8, HL; *General Mediterranean Holdings SA v Patel* [2000] 1 WLR 272; *R (Morgan Grenfell & Co Ltd) v Special Commissioner of Income Tax* [2003] 1 AC 563 at [7].

74 *McE v Prison Service of Northern Ireland* [2009] UKHL 15, [2009] 1 AC 908 at [5], HL (per Lord Phillips).

75 *Calcraft v Guest* [1898] 1 QB 759, CA; *R v Tompkins* (1977) 67 Cr App R 181. The party to whom the privilege belongs might, of course, apply for an injunction to restrain its use: *Ashburton v Pape* [1913] 2 Ch 469, CA; *Goddard v Nationwide Building Society* [1987] QB 670, CA.

76 *R (Morgan Grenfell & Co Ltd) v Special Commissioner of Income Tax* [2003] 1 AC 563 at [7], HL (per Lord Hoffmann).

77 *R v Derby Magistrates' Court, Ex p B* [1996] AC 487 at 507 (per Lord Taylor CJ, with whom Lords Mustill and Lloyd

simply a rule of evidence, a client could only prevent disclosure in *legal* proceedings. There would be no guarantee that the same material could be kept from the police or some other agency, such as financial regulators, with the power to compel the production of documents or information. Hence, legal professional privilege can now generally be asserted in answer to any demand for documents by a public or other authority; it is not limited to a right which may be asserted only in the context of civil or criminal proceedings. Statutory powers requiring the production of documents are generally deemed to exclude the right to demand documents which are subject to legal professional privilege. Any exception to this rule would have to be explicitly supported by primary legislation.[78] In the absence of express abrogation, a necessary implication that Parliament intended to abrogate privilege arises only where the legislative provision would be rendered inoperative or its object largely frustrated in its practical application if the privilege were to prevail.[79] Any curtailment of privilege could only be to the extent reasonably necessary to meet the ends which justify the curtailment.[80] Consistent with this status, once privilege has been established, it is at common law absolute in the sense that it cannot then be overridden by competing considerations of public policy.[81] Furthermore, in accordance with the aphorism 'once privileged, always privileged,'[82] once a particular client's privilege has attached to a document or other privileged exchange, the privilege will persist, subject only to waiver or other types of loss, for his benefit and that of his successors in title for all time and in all circumstances.[83] The absolute nature of legal professional privilege has been subject to criticism and the Freedom of Information Act regime provides an unusual context where Parliament has in fact stipulated that the application of such privilege is not absolute but involves a public interest balancing exercise, described below.[84]

30– 016 Two types of privilege

The two limbs of legal professional privilege have been set out above.[85] Notwithstanding frequent misconceptions to the contrary, litigation privilege has no application to communications between lawyer and client, even where litigation is anticipated or has actually commenced: such communications will always fall within the realm of legal advice privilege.[86] Litigation privilege is thus both narrower (in terms of being confined to situations where documents or communications are made for the dominant purpose of litigation) and broader (in applying to a broader range of communications and documents) than legal advice privilege. The scope of legal advice privilege in England was for a short time thrown into doubt by the

agreed).

78 *R (Morgan Grenfell & Co Ltd) v Special Commissioner of Income Tax* [2003] 1 AC 563 at [8]; *General Mediterranean Holdings SA v Patel* [2000] 1 WLR 272; *R v Secretary of State for the Home Department, ex p Daly* [2001] 2 AC 532; *Bowman v Fels* [2005] 1 WLR 3083 at [70]-[91], CA. See also *Baker v Campbell* (1983) 153 CLR 52.

79 *Daniels Corporation International Pty Ltd v Australian Competition and Consumer Commission* (2002) 213 CLR 543 at [43] (per McHugh J).

80 *R v Secretary of State for the Home Department, ex p Daly* [2001] 2 AC 532, at [5] (per Lord Bingham) and at [31] (per Lord Cooke).

81 *R v Derby Magistrates' Court, Ex p B* [1996] AC 487 at 508-509 (*per* Lord Taylor CJ).

82 For examples of its use see *Calcraft v Guest* [1898] 1 QB 759 at 761, CA; and *Pearce v Foster* (1885) 15 QBD 114 at 119, CA.

83 Legal advice privilege will subsist after the dissolution of the company to which the advice was given: *Addlesee v Dentons Europe LLP* [2019] EWCA Civ 1600, [2019] 3 WLR 1255.

84 *Three Rivers DC v Bank of England (no 6)* [2004] UKHL 48, [2005] 1 AC 610, [2005] 4 All ER 948 at [26]; *Canada (Privacy Commissioner) v Blood Trive Department of Health* [2008] 2 SCR 574 (Sup Ct of Canada).

85 §30– 014.

86 See B Thanki (ed), *The Law of Privilege*, 2nd edn (Oxford, Oxford University Press, 2011), paras. 1.09-1.12.

Court of Appeal's decisions in the *Three Rivers DC v Bank of England* litigation,[87] but a more orthodox understanding of the principle was restored by the House of Lords in *Three Rivers DC v Bank of England (No 6)*.[88] Communications between parties with a common interest in litigation for the dominant purpose of informing each other of the advice received or of obtaining legal advice are also protected.[89] In England it appears that a corporate entity may be divided into constituent parts and correspondence within the corporation but not involving a lawyer, even for the purpose of seeking legal advice, will not benefit from legal advice privilege,[90] although litigation privilege might apply to such communications. The Court of Appeal has confirmed that only communications between a person or persons tasked with obtaining legal advice on behalf of a corporation and its lawyers will be protected by legal advice privilege. Communications with other employees will not be protected, even if such employees have factual information relevant to the legal advice sought.[91]

30– 017 Exceptions and qualifications

Certain communications that would otherwise fall within the general scope of the rule[92] are excepted from the privilege:

(1) Communications in furtherance of a crime or fraud are not communications within the ordinary scope of the professional lawyer-client relationship and so not privileged.[93]

(2) The privilege in the totality of a document may be waived or lost where part of that document has been disclosed such that it would be unfair for the disclosing party to continue to assert privilege over the remainder.[94] If privilege is waived there is no need to apply the public interest test and the information must be disclosed.[95]

---

87 *Three Rivers DC v Bank of England (No 6)* [2004] QB 916, [2005] 1 AC 610. In the latter case the Court of Appeal had accepted an argument that communications between the Bank of England and its lawyers was only covered by legal advice privilege to the extent that it was given in the furtherance of advice as to the Bank's legal rights and obligations, and did not extend to legal assistance for the dominant purpose of putting relevant factual material before an inquiry in an orderly and attractive fashion rather than for the taking of advice on such material.

88 [2005] 1 AC 610.

89 *Buttes Gas and Oil Co v Hammer (No 3)* [1981] QB 223; *Dadourian Group International Inc v Simms* [2008] EWHC 1784 (Ch); *R (Jet2.Com Ltd) v Civil Aviation Authority* [2020] EWCA Civ 35.

90 This is an application of the Court of Appeal decision in *Three Rivers DC v Bank of England (No 5)* [2003] EWCA Civ 474, [2003] QB 1556, concerning communications between the Bank of England's 'Bingham Investigation Unit' and other parts of the Bank for the purpose of seeking legal advice did not benefit from the privilege. In the subsequent case of *Three Rivers DC v Bank of England (No 6)* [2005] 1 AC 610 the House of Lords heard argument on this point but expressly declined to decide it: see Lord Scott at [47] and Lord Carswell at [118]. Doubts remain as to the correctness of *Three Rivers DC v Bank of England (No 3)* and it is unfortunate that the House of Lords did not take the opportunity to overturn it when the matter was squarely before them and had been fully argued, including by the Attorney-General, the Law Society and the Bar Council, all of whom had been permitted to intervene.

91 *Serious Fraud Office v Eurasian Natural Resources Corp Ltd* [2018] EWCA Civ 2006 , [2018] 9 WLUK 32. Had the Court of Appeal been free to depart from *Three Rivers DC v Bank of England (No 5)* [2003] EWCA Civ 474, [2003] QB 1556 it would have reached a different conclusion (at [130]).

92 See §30– 014.

93 *R v Cox and Railton* (1884) 14 QBD 153; *R v Central Criminal Court, ex p Francis & Francis* [1989] 1 AC 346; *Derby & Co v Weldon (No 7)* [1990] 1 WLR 1156; *Kuwait Airways Corp v Iraqi Airways Company* [2005] EWCA Civ. 286; The Times, 25 April 2006; *R v Gibbins* [2004] EWCA Crim 311; *C v C* [2007] WTLR 753. This exception can also apply in relation to litigation privilege, eg *R (Hallinan Blackburn) v Middlesex Crown Court* [2004] EWHC 2726 (Admin), [2005] 1 WLR 766.

94 *Great Atlantic Insurance Co v Home Insurance Co* [1981] 2 All ER 485; *Nea Karteria Maritime Co Ltd v Atlantic and Great Lakes Steamship Corp* [1981] Comm LR 138; *General Accident Corp v Tanter* [1984] 1 WLR 100; *Re Konigsberg (a bankrupt)* [1989] 3 All ER 289; *R v Secretary of State for Transport and Factortame Ltd* [1998] 1 All ER 736 (Note); *Somatra Ltd v Sinclair, Roche & Temperley* [2000] 1 WLR 2453. In *Kirkaldie v IC and Thanet DC*, IT, 4 July 2006 at [24]-[43] the Information Tribunal held that a Council had waived privilege over its legal advice by providing an oral summary of the principal conclusions of that advice during a public session of the Council.

95 *Kirkaldie v IC and Thanet DC*, IT, 4 July 2006 at [43].

(3) Privilege will also be waived where reference to a document is made in court documents, such as statements of case and witness statements[96] or where there has been reference to the content of legal advice received.[97]

(4) Privilege in a document will be waived where reference is made to it during the course of a trial, including in the course of advocate's speeches to the court, or by calling evidence of a privileged conversation[98] or having taken counsel's advice.

(5) Privilege does not extend to a copy of a privileged document in the hands of another party.[99] Nor does privilege extend to copies of non-privileged documents passed to or from a lawyer for advice, unless the selection might betray the contents of the legal advice.[100]

(6) In some jurisdictions (though not in England[101] or Australia[102]) the privilege may be taken to be overridden where the evidence may prove an accused innocent of a serious criminal charge.[103]

(7) There are various statutory exceptions to the privilege, such as s 291 of the Insolvency Act 1986, by which a bankrupt cannot withhold privileged documents from the Official Receiver. To the opposite effect it has been held that there was no express reference in s 20(1) of the Taxes Management Act 1970 to legal professional privilege and that section could not be construed as necessarily implying that a tax inspector could, by the issue of a notice, require the disclosure of documents which were subject to legal professional privilege.[104]

30– 018 Public interest concept

As stated above, the exemption for legal professional privilege in FOIA is a qualified one.[105] This is an unusual concept for an English common lawyer to deal with. It has been a defining feature of legal professional privilege at common law that it involves no such balancing exercise.

---

96 *Great Atlantic Insurance Co v Home Insurance Co* [1981] 1 WLR 529 at 538; *Derby v Weldon (No 10)* [1991] 2 All ER 908. The rule is based on the need to ensure the disclosing party has not misled the court by disclosing a selection of the document out of context or in a manner that is not properly representative of the whole. The material must be 'deployed' in court. Mere reference is usually insufficient. See also: *Expandable Ltd v Rubin* [2008] EWCA Civ 59, [2008] 1 WLR 1099.

97 Authorities on the issue are reviewed in *Dunlop Slazenger International Ltd v Joe Bloggs Sports Ltd* [2003] EWCA Civ. 901. Disclosure in a letter of the gist or conclusions of legal advice may waive privilege over all of that advice: *Bennett v Chief Executive Officer, Australian Customs Service* [2004] FCAFC 237, (2004) 210 ALR 220. Also see *Fulham Leisure Holdings Ltd v Nicolson Graham & Jones* [2006] EWHC 158 (Ch), [2006] 2 All ER 599, [2006] PNLR 23 (waiver of privilege over advice concerning one transaction did not necessarily lead to waiver over all advice relating to the dispute); *Raiffeisen Bank International AG v Asia Coal Energy Ventures Ltd* [2011] EWCA Civ 11.

98 *George Doland Ltd v Blackburn Robson Coates & Co* [1972] 1 WLR 1338.

99 *Calcraft v Guest* [1898] 1 QB 759; though the privilege-holder may seek an injunction under the principles in *Ashburton v Pape* [1913] 2 Ch 469.

100 *Ventouris v Mountain* [1991] 1 WLR 607, [1991] 3 All ER 472, [1991] 1 Lloyd's Rep. 441; *Lyell v Kennedy (No 3)* (1884) 27 ChD 1.

101 *R v Derby Magistrates' Court, ex p B* [1996] 1 AC 487.

102 *Carter v The Managing Partner, Northmore Hale Davy & Leake* (1995) 183 CLR 121.

103 *R v Gray* (1992) 74 CCC (3d) 267) (British Columbia Supreme Court); *S v Safatsa* (1988) 1 SA 868 (Appellate Division, South Africa). Also see *R v Craig* [1975] 1 NZLR 597 and *R v Dunbar and Logan* (1982) 138 DLR (3d) 221; *R v McClure* (2001) 195 DLR (4th) 513; *R v Brown* (2000) 210 DLR (4th) 341; *Goodis v Ontario* 2006 SCC 31, [2006] 2 SCR 32, 271 DLR (4th) 407.

104 *Three Rivers DC v Bank of England (No 6)* [2005] 1 AC 610; *R (Morgan Grenfell & Co Ltd) v Special Commissioner of Income Tax* [2002] UKHL 21, [2003] 1 AC 563. See also: *B v Auckland District Law Society* [2003] UKPC 8, [2003] 2 AC 736; *Woolworths v Fels* [2002] HCA 50, (2002) 193 ALR 1; *Daniels Corp v Accc* [2002] HCA 49, (2002) 194 ALR 561. As to whether provisions of the CPR override the privilege see *Lucas v Barking Havering and Redbridge Hospitals NHS Trust* [2003] 4 All ER 720; *Vasiliou v Hajigeorgiou* [2005] 3 All ER 17.

105 As is the case in New Zealand: see §51– 023(9).

Courts in England and in the rest of the Commonwealth have frequently stated that the concept of legal professional privilege is itself the result of a balancing process,[106] which was performed once and for all in the sixteenth century,[107] and that such arguments were either presumed[108] or considered and rejected[109] in the course of the development of the common law, and therefore once the rule applies no further balancing process should be carried out:[110]

> courts have for very many years regarded legal professional privilege as the predominant public interest. A balancing exercise is not required in individual cases, because the balance must always come down in favour of upholding the privilege.[111]

The use of a balancing test within the privilege would, it has been repeatedly said, fundamentally undermine the raison d'être of the privilege, namely a client's confidence in the sanctity of his legal communications:

> once any exception to the rule is allowed, the client's confidence is necessarily lost.[112]

Section 42 of FOIA cuts across these notions, but in a more measured fashion than a general consideration of the public interest would entail.

30– 019 Public interest balance

The balancing exercise imposed by s 2 of FOIA necessitates an identification of the public interest in the maintenance of the exemption, always recognising that that public interest must be delineated in such a fashion that it is capable in practice of being outweighed.[113] The burden of proof is on the public authority to satisfy the Tribunal that the public interest in maintaining the exemption outweighs the public interest in disclosure.[114] Cases concerning privileged information have largely involved claims of a general instrumental consideration underlying lawyer-client relationships in the abstract. For example, in *Bellamy v Information Commissioner* the public interest asserted was that in being able 'to receive disinterested and frank legal advice in order to assist [public bodies] in making appropriate decisions and there is less likelihood that they would receive such advice if those giving it knew it was to be made public…in order to allow legal advice to be provided unfettered by concerns about disclosure'[115] and the Tribunal applied this general instrumental public interest, stating that 'there is a strong element of public

[106] For example, *Waterford v The Commonwealth* (1987) 163 CLR 54 at 64-65; *Australian Federal Police v Propend Finance* (1997) 141 ALR 545 at 592, 609.

[107] *R v Derby Magistrates' Court, ex p B* [1996] 1 AC 487 at 508.

[108] *R v Uljee* [1982] 1 NZLR 561 at 576-577.

[109] *Carter v The Managing Partner, Northmore Hale Davy & Leake* (1995) 183 CLR 121 at 138.

[110] *Waterford v The Commonwealth* (1987) 163 CLR at 64, 74, 98-99; *AG (NT) v Kearney* (1985) 158 CLR 500 at 532; *Carter v The Managing Partner, Northmore Hale Davy & Leake* (1995) 183 CLR 121 at 128, 134 and 137; *Australian Federal Police v Propend Finance* (1997) 141 ALR at 592, 609.

[111] Lord Lloyd in *R v Derby Magistrates' Court, ex p B* [1996] 1 AC 487 at 509. Also see *Carter v The Managing Partner, Northmore Hale Davy & Leake* (1995) 183 CLR at 128-9, where Brennan J held that 'there is no occasion for the courts to undertake a balancing of public interests: the balance is already struck by the allowing of the privilege…if there can be no public interest which defeats the privilege, there can be no individual interest which does so.'

[112] *R v Derby Magistrates' Court, ex p B* [1996] 1 AC 487 at 508. In *Carter v The Managing Partner, Northmore Hale Davy & Leake* (1995) 183 CLR 121 at 139 the view expressed was that departure from this principle would mean that lawyers would become duty bound to recite the court's powers as to disclosure and this would intensify the chilling effect.

[113] To avoid metamorphosing it into an absolute exemption: *Kitchener v IC and Derby City Council*, IT, 20 December 2006 at [17]. The exercise is antithetical to orthodox privilege theory that 'once privileged, always privileged'. Thus, in *Calcraft v Guest* [1898] 1 QB 759 the privilege was asserted 110 years after the relevant communication. The House of Commons Select Committee favoured widespread disclosure of old opinions. Thus the House of Commons Public Administration Committee in its *Third Report, Session 1997-98*, 19 May 1998, stated at para 31: 'In the spirit of openness, the Government's vast storehouse of legal opinions on every conceivable subject should be made available to interested members of the public.'

[114] *Fisher v IC and Department for Work and Pensions*, FTT, 14 March 2012 at [15].

[115] *Bellamy v IC and DTI*, IT, 4 April 2006 at [24].

interest inbuilt into the privilege itself.'[116] That there is a strong public interest in non-disclosure in-built into legal professional privilege is accepted in a long line of Tribunal decisions starting with *Bellamy*. This has now been accepted by the High Court as being the correct approach:[117]

> In the light of the consistent line taken by the Tribunal as to the weight to be attached to the public interest against disclosure in-built into legal professional privilege (an approach which I have found to be the correct one) it was incumbent upon the Tribunal in the instant case to give significant weight to that interest. Further the Tribunal was obliged to consider whether the weight to be given to the public interest considerations militating against disclosure were countered by considerations of at least an equal weight which supported an order for disclosure.

It will therefore constitute a misdirection for a Tribunal not to acknowledge and give effect to the significant weight to be afforded to the exemption for information to which legal professional privilege applies.[118] While it would be wrong and involve an illegitimate re-writing of the statutory regime for the significance of legal professional privilege to be elevated to such a degree that the exemption could never be displaced in such cases,[119] a countervailing factor will inevitably have to be an interest of real weight and substance in order to displace the public interest in upholding the principle of legal professional privilege.[120] A proper weighing of the public interest in maintaining the exemption will involve both general and specific considerations.[121]

30– 020 Public interest generally

In relation to the general considerations, the general maintenance of the confidentiality of communications between any lawyer[122] and his client is a matter which is in the public interest.[123] It is recognised that care should be taken to ensure that freedom of information principles do not undermine the well established common law right to legal professional privilege, which enables a public authority to put all relevant facts before its legal advisers, and to receive advice based on them, without fear that either the facts or the advice will be disclosed to others without its consent.[124] Another factor is that the damage to this expectation will often not be matched by any tangible benefit from obtaining sight of confidential legal advice.[125] Here, the issue is not the effect that disclosure might have on particular information

---

116 *Bellamy v IC and DTI*, IT, 4 April 2006 at [35]; *Archer v IC and Salisbury DC*, IT, 9 May 2007 at [62]-[63]; *Rosenbaum v IC and House of Lords Appointments Commission*, IT, 4 November 2008 at [32]-[37].

117 *DBERR v O'Brien and IC* [2009] EWHC 164 (QB) at [48]. This judgment has been regarded as providing authoritative guidance for Tribunals: *Gordon v IC and Cabinet Office*, FTT, 7 December 2012 at [89].

118 *DBERR v O'Brien and IC* [2009] EWHC 164 (QB) at [53].

119 *Osland v Secretary to the Department of Justice* [2008] HCA 37 at [111]; *Crawford v IC and Department for Culture Media and Sport*, FTT, 10 July 2012 at [26]; *Home Office v IC and Yeo*, FTT, 15 April 2016 at [48].

120 *Osland v Secretary to the Department of Justice* [2008] HCA 37 at [152]. See, for example, *Crawford v IC and Lincolnshire CC*, FTT, 5 December 2011 at [12].

121 *Knight v IC and Newbury Town Council*, FTT, 4 April 2015 at [58]-[61]; *Home Office v IC and Yeo*, FTT, 15 April 2016 at [48].

122 No distinction is drawn between employed lawyers and lawyers in private practice: *Woodford v IC*, FTT, 21 April 2010 at [29].

123 For a more detailed analysis of the public interests advanced by the maintenance of the privilege, see J Auburn, *Legal Professional Privilege: Law and Theory* (Oxford, Hart Publishing, 2000) Ch 4. In the European Union context, see: *Turco v EU Council* (T-84/03) [2004] ECR II-4061, [2004] All ER (D) 363 (Nov); *Association de la presse internationale asbl v EC Commission* (T-36/04) [2007] ECR II-3201, [2007] 3 CMLR 51.

124 *Shipton v IC and National Assembly of Wales*, IT, 11 January 2007; *Gillingham v IC*, IT, 26 September 2007 at [16] and [36]; *Pugh v IC and MoD*, IT, 17 December 2007 at [28]-[33]; *Mersey Tunnel Users Association v IC and Merseytravel*, IT, 15 February 2008 at [26]-[34]; *Francis v IC and South Essex Partnership Foundation NHS Trust*, IT, 21 July 2008 at [45].

125 *Skinner v IC and North Somerset Council*, FTT, 1 March 2011 at [30]-[31].

or in a particular solicitor-client relationship: it is the effect that disclosure might have on future legal communications in general.[126] The assertion of this general type of concern for the detrimental effect of recognising an exception to the privilege is a highly speculative exercise at best. There is a strong argument that these factors weigh less heavily in the public sector because of the very existence of the freedom of information regime.[127] There are widely differing views on the effect of individual disclosures on the continued confidence of clients in the sanctity of their legal communications. On the one hand, it is often claimed that it is essential to the maintenance of continued candid lawyer-client relations that there are no new exceptions to the privilege.[128] An alternative view is that these concerns have been overplayed, and that the privilege could survive the recognition of exceptions without the collapse of lawyer-client relations.[129] There will, of course, be occasions when the public interest in disclosure will outweigh the public interest in maintaining privilege, such as where the harm likely to be suffered by the party entitled to privilege is slight or the requirement for disclosure is overwhelming.[130] However, the general trend has been to refuse disclosure, informed by the general interest in maintaining legal professional privilege.[131]

30– 021 Public interest specifically

The second aspect involves a consideration of the specific information captured by the request and that stands to be disclosed. One set of relevant factors may relate to the age of the relevant information:[132] when it was created; whether the purpose for which it was created is 'spent' in the sense that the information may no longer be relevant to present or future proceedings;[133] whether all limitation periods for an action based on the information have expired. Another relevant factor may be the official release by the requested or another public authority of other information on the same subject matter as the information which enjoys legal professional privilege: if the information officially released, particularly if released as a discretionary disclosure, is unrepresentative of the entirety of the information held, the public interest in maintaining the exemption may be weakened where disclosure would redress the situation.[134] The public interest in disclosure[135] will vary according to the information sought. Some clear, compelling and specific justification for disclosure must be shown so as to override the obvious

126 *Mercer v IC and MoD*, FTT, 11 July 2014 at [17]. See further §30– 018.

127 *Home Office v IC and Yeo*, FTT, 15 April 2016 at [48e].

128 For example, Lord Taylor CJ in *R v Derby Magistrates' Court, ex p B* [1996] 1 AC 487 at 508 'once any exception to the rule is allowed, the client's confidence is necessarily lost.'

129 For example, *Saunders v Punch* [1998] 1 WLR 986 at 996; *DEFRA v IC and Portman*, FTT, 13 November 2012 at [40].

130 *Shipton v IC and National Assembly of Wales*, IT, 11 January 2007 at [14(b)]; *Kessler v IC and HMRC*, IT, 29 November 2007 at [53] and [55]; *Bingham Centre for the Rule of Law v IC and Cabinet Office*, FTT, 9 December 2015 at [55]-[61].

131 See, eg: *Burgess v IC and Stafford BC*, IT, 7 June 2007; *Standerwick v IC*, FTT, 27 July 2010; *Fisher v IC and DWP*, FTT, 29 July 2010 at [14]; *Dept of Health and Social Security and Public Safety v IC and McDermott*, FTT, 13 November 2013 at [21].

132 *Kessler v IC and HMRC*, IT, 29 November 2007 at [57(8)]. As a general rule, the public interest in maintaining an exemption diminishes over time: *Mersey Tunnel Users Association v IC and Halton BC*, IT, 11 January 2010 at [48(x)].

133 Compare *Bellamy v IC and DTI*, IT, 4 April 2006 at [24]: The Commissioner also noted that the particular issue raised by the legal advice and exchanges sought remained 'live' which rendered it 'particularly sensitive'. The importance of currency was emphasised by the Information Tribunal in *Kitchener v IC and Derby City Council*, IT, 20 December 2006 at [18]. This is in contrast to the approach at common law, which treats legal professional privilege as permanent, but the Tribunal is reluctant to hold that this is a factor which will usually outweigh privilege: see *Williams v IC and Local Government Ombudsman*, FTT, 24 October 2012 at [49]; *Davis v IC*, FTT, 31 August 2011 at [18].

134 *Hayden v IC and Manchester Justice Centre*, FTT, 5 November 2013 at [32]-[42].

135 See §6– 011.

interest in legal professional privilege.[136] Circumstances where specific considerations may be in favour of disclosure despite legal professional privilege include:

— where the harm likely to be suffered by the party entitled to the privilege is likely to be slight;[137]
— where there is reason to believe that the authority is misrepresenting the advice that it has received;[138]
— where the public authority is pursuing a policy which appears to be unlawful or where there are clear indications that it has ignored advice that it has received;[139]
— where there is an overriding interest in openness and transparency on the facts or where advice on the topic has already been disclosed;[140]
— where the information protected by legal professional privilege shows evidence of malfeasance, fraud or corruption.[141]

The Tribunal has readily found that the public interest tilts in favour of maintaining the exemption where there is any degree of currency to a legal advice.[142] It is important that public authorities are not disadvantaged by disclosure, particularly in a litigation context.[143] However, in one case where the general public interest in accountability and transparency had been poorly served, disclosure was ordered to provide fuller reasoning as to how a particular conclusion had been reached.[144] A number of Commonwealth courts have developed a principle that the privilege may give way to a far weightier public interest where the privilege-holders no longer have a recognised interest to protect.[145] It may be that this principle, previously disfavoured (at least at common law) in England as well as Australia,[146] will now be relevant in weakening the case for continued confidentiality.

30–022 Public interest principles

The Tribunal[147] has more recently set out general guidelines, drawn from decided cases, while emphasising that each case turns on its own facts. These are encapsulated in the following ten principles:

(1) The 'default setting' is in favour of disclosure: information held by public authorities must be disclosed on request unless the statute permits it to be withheld.
(2) The balancing exercise begins with both scales empty and therefore level. The

---

136 *Mersey Tunnel Users Association v IC and Halton BC*, IT, 24 June 2009 at [48(ix)]; *Cabinet Office v IC and Aitchison* [2013] UKUT 0526 (AAC) at [58].

137 *Shipton v IC and National Assembly of Wales*, IT, 11 January 2007 at [14(b)].

138 *Osland v Secretary to the Department of Justice* [2008] HCA 37, (2008) 234 CLR 27 (High Court of Australia).

139 *FCO v IC*, IT, 29 April 2008 at [29].

140 *Maiden v IC and King's Lynn and West Norfolk BC*, IT, 15 December 2008 at [43]-[44].

141 *Mersey Tunnel Users Association v IC and Halton BC*, IT, 11 January 2010 at [50]; *Matthews v IC*, FTT, 15 August 2017 at [21]; *Holmes v IC and Cumbria CC*, FTT, 9 May 2017 at [28].

142 *Kitchener v IC and Derby City Council*, IT, 20 December 2006. But the fact that disclosure of legal advice may give rise to legal proceedings against the public authority is not a public interest factor in maintaining the exemption: *Kitchener* at [19].

143 *Savic v IC and Attorney-General* [2016] UKUT 534, 535 (AAC) at [35].

144 *Kessler v IC and HMRC*, IT, 29 November 2007 at [70].

145 *R v Craig* [1975] 1 NZLR 597 (NZ); *R v Dunbar and Logan* (1982) 138 DLR (3d) 221 at 252; *R v McClure* (2001) 195 DLR (4th) 513, [2001] 1 SCR 45; *R v Brown* [2002] 210 DLR (4th) 341 (Canada); *R v Ataou* [1988] QB 798, but over-ruled in *R v Derby Magistrates' Court, ex p B* [1996] AC 487; *Carter v The Managing Partner, Northmore Hale Davy & Leake*, (unreported) 15 July 1993, Supreme Court of Western Australia (Full Court) at 30-31 (Rowland J).

146 *Carter v The Managing Partner, Northmore Hale Davy & Leake* (1995) 183 CLR 121.

147 *Morris v IC and Dept for Transport*, FTT, 7 June 2010; *Szucs v IC*, FTT, 16 August 2011; *DEFRA v IC and Portman, FTT*, 13 November 2012.

public authority must disclose the information unless the public interest in maintaining the exemption outweighs the public interest in disclosing the information.

(3) Since the public interest must be assessed in all the circumstances of the case, the public authority is not permitted to maintain a blanket refusal in relation to the type of information sought.

(4) The mere fact that legal professional privilege applies to information is insufficient to justify non-disclosure. A public authority is only entitled to refuse to disclose such information if the public interest in maintaining the exemption outweighs the public interest in disclosure.

(5) The approach for the Tribunal is to acknowledge and give effect to the significant weight to be afforded to the exemption in any event, ascertain whether there were particular or further factors which point to non-disclosure and then consider whether the features supporting disclosure (including the underlying public interests which favour disclosure) are at the very least of equal weight.

(6) The public interest factors in favour of maintaining an exemption are likely to be of a general character. The fact that a factor may be of a general rather than a specific nature does not mean that it should be accorded less weight or significance:

> A factor which applies to very many requests for information can be just as significant as one which applies to only a few. Indeed, it may be more so."[148]

(7) Considerations such as openness, transparency, accountability and contribution to public debate are regularly relied on in support of a public interest in disclosure. This does not in any way diminish their importance as these considerations are central to the operation of freedom of information regimes and are likely to be relevant in every case where the public interest test is applied. However, to bear any material weight each factor must draw some relevance from the facts of the case under consideration to avoid a situation where they will operate as a justification for disclosure of all information in all circumstances.

(8) The 'public interest' signifies something that is in the interests of the public as distinct from matters which are of interest to the public.

(9) Some clear, compelling and specific justification for disclosure must be shown, so as to outweigh the obvious interest in protecting communications between lawyer and client, which the client supposes to be confidential.

(10) The age of the legal advice contained in the information is relevant. The passage of time would, as a general principle, favour disclosure. Legal advice is, however, still 'live' if it is still being implemented or relied upon as at the date of the request or may continue beyond that date to give rise to legal challenges by those unhappy with the course of action adopted.

30– 023 Duty to confirm or deny

Where or to the extent that a public authority, by confirming or denying that it holds the requested information, would thereby disclose exempt information under s 42(1), then the discrete duty to confirm or deny that that information is held by the public authority does not arise.[149] Confirmation or denial that information answering the terms of a request is held will only be likely to involve the disclosure of information in respect of which a claim to legal professional privilege could be maintained where the request is couched in very specific terms: for example, a request for advice to a particular effect. Again, this is a qualified exclusion of

---

148 *Home Office and Ministry of Justice v IC* [2009] EWHC 1611 (Admin) at [34] (per Keith J).

149 FOIA s 42(2).

duty. It will be necessary to consider whether, in all the circumstances, the maintenance of the exclusion of this duty is outweighed by the public interest in disclosing whether the public authority holds the information. Despite its superficial similarity, this public interest balancing exercise is materially different from and narrower than that employed for the purpose of determining whether the duty to communicate does not apply.[150] As a general rule, the broader the terms of the request, the more difficult it will become for the public authority to contend that the public interest in excluding the duty to confirm or deny that such information is held by it outweighs the public interest in compliance with that duty; if only because it will be self-evident that the public authority does hold information of that description.

30– 024 Scotland

The Scottish exemption is much wider, covering any information for which a claim to 'confidentiality of communications' could be maintained in legal proceedings.[151] In Scotland priests may have a form of privilege not recognised in England and Wales.[152] There already existed in Scottish law a general judicial discretion not to require answers that may betray confidences, even though the evidence is otherwise relevant and admissible.[153]

30– 025 Related FOI exemptions

There is a separate exemption for communications relating to advice given by Law Officers.[154] Law Officers include the Attorney-General, Solicitor General, Advocate General for Scotland, Lord Advocate, Solicitor-General for Scotland and the Attorney-General for Northern Ireland.[155]

30– 026 The GDPR and DPA 2018

To the extent that an individual asks a public body to be provided with a copy of the information that that public body holds about him or her, that request will fall to be decided by the GDPR and the DPA 2018 and not by FOIA.[156] The source of an individual's right of access to information about him or herself depends upon the purpose for which the requested person or organisation holds that information and/or the identity of the organisation holding that information:

(a) Where the requested person or organisation is a 'competent authority'[157] and holds personal information for the law enforcement purposes,[158] the access right is

---

150 See §§6– 018 to 6– 019 as to what it involves.

151 FOIA s 42(2).

152 ID Macphail, *Research paper on the Law of Evidence of Scotland* (Edinburgh, Scottish Law Commission, 1979) paras 18.38-18.40; D Field, *The Law of Evidence in Scotland* (Edinburgh, W Green, 1988) p 265. Compare the position in England: *R v Hay* (1860) 2 F & F 4; *Pais v Pais* [1971] P 119, though the waiver analysis in this case is questionable if there is no privilege recognised.

153 *HM Advocate v Airs* 1975 JC 64 at 70, SLT 177 at 180. However this is unlikely to be a sufficient explanation for the very different Scottish FOI exemption, as a similar discretion operated in England: *AG v Clough* [1963] 1 QB 773 at 792; *AG v Mulholland* [1963] 2 QB 477 at 489-490, 492.

154 FOIA s 35(1)(c).

155 FOIA s 35(5).

156 FOIA s 62(2).

157 Defined in DPA 2018 s 30(1) to mean a person specified in Sch 7 of that Act or any other person if and to the extent that that person has statutory functions for any of the law enforcement purposes, but not the intelligence services (as defined in DPA 2018 s 30(7)). The persons specified in Sch 7 include every Government department, other than a non-ministerial government department, chief officers of police and other policing bodies, other authorities with investigatory functions (including HMRC), authorities with functions relating to offender management, the DPP, courts and tribunals.

158 Defined in DPA 2018 s 31 to mean 'the purposes of the prevention, investigation, detection or prosecution of

conferred by the DPA 2018 and there is no exemption from the obligation to comply with a subject access request on the ground of legal professional privilege.[159]

(b) Where the requested person or organisation holds the information for intelligence service processing,[160] the access right is conferred by the DPA 2018 and an exemption is provided where compliance with a subject access request would breach legal professional privilege.[161]

(c) Where neither (a) nor (b) applies, and the processing of the personal information by the requested person or organisation is within the grasp of the GDPR (what is sometimes called 'ordinary processing'), it is the GDPR which provides the individual with a right of access to that information (ie to make a subject access request), but it is the DPA 2018 which provides for an exemption where compliance with that subject access request would breach legal professional privilege.[162]

(d) Where neither (a) nor (b) applies, but the processing of the personal information by the requested person or organisation is outside the grasp of the GDPR (what is sometimes called 'applied processing'),[163] it is the DPA 2018 which provides for the access right (by applying the GDPR right to that processing) and it is also the DPA 2018 which provides for an exemption where compliance with that subject access request would breach legal professional privilege.[164]

The right of an individual to require a public authority to provide a copy of the information it holds relating to that individual (ie one of the facets of a subject access request)[165] is dealt with in more detail in Part 2 (Chs 7-16) of this work. But to the extent that compliance with a subject access request is exempted on the ground that it would breach legal professional privilege, the principles in this section of this chapter apply.

criminal offences or the execution of criminal penalties, including the safeguarding against and the prevention of threats to public security.'

159 The right is conferred by DPA 2018 s 45.

160 Defined in DPA 2018 s 82 to mean processing by an intelligence service (ie by the Security Service, the Secret Intelligence Service or the Government Communication Headquarters).

161 The right is conferred by DPA s 94(1), and the exemption is provided for by DPA 2018 Sch 11, paras 1(1)(b) and 9.

162 The right is conferred by the GDPR Art 15, and the exemption is provided for by DPA 2018 Sch 2, Part 3, paras 18(c) and 19.

163 This is, processing to which Chapter 3 of Part 2 of the DPA 2018 (ss 21-28) applies. The processing to which Chapter 3 of Part 2 of the DPA 2018 applies is listed at DPA 2018 s 21.

164 The right is conferred by DPA 2018 s 22(1)-(2), applying GDPR Art 15 (for the purpose of conferring the right) and DPA 2018 Sch 2, Part 3, paras 18(c) and 19 (for the purpose of providing the exemption).

165 Article 15(3) of the GDPR.

CHAPTER 31
Policy formulation and public affairs

1. INTRODUCTION

31– 001 Overview

This chapter is concerned with two connected provisions of FOIA which exempt:

— information relating to government policy and ministerial communications;[1] and
— information the disclosure of which would be prejudicial to the conduct of public affairs.[2]

The first of these exemptions applies only to information held by government departments or by the National Assembly for Wales: it does not apply to information held by any other public authority.[3] This exemption is a purely class-based exemption, such that it does not matter that harm will not result from disclosure of the information concerned.[4] The exemption is a

1 FOIA s 35; FOI(S)A s 29.

2 FOIA s 36. The comparable provision in the FOI(S)A s 30, is in materially different terms: see §31– 027.

3 In relation to information held by Scottish public authorities, the comparable exemption is only applicable to information held by the Scottish Administration.

4 Though it may be relevant to a consideration of the public interest. In *DWP v IC*, IT, 5 March 2007, the Tribunal observed that 'the exemption in s 35(1)(a)… is a "class" exemption… in order for the exemption to be engaged the public authority does not need to demonstrate that any specific prejudice or harm would flow from the disclosure of the information in question… [in considering whether the public interest in maintaining the exemption

qualified exemption, however, so that even if information falls within the description of the exemption, it is then necessary to consider whether the public interest favours disclosure or the maintenance of the exemption. The second exemption can apply to information held by any type of public authority, but so far as information held by a government department or the National Assembly of Wales is concerned, those bodies may only rely on it if the first exemption is inapplicable. The second exemption is a prejudice-based exemption. It is only applicable if disclosure would, or would be likely to, prejudice the effective conduct of public affairs in any one or more of the ways specified in s 36(2). This exemption is an absolute exemption in the case where the information is held by the House of Commons or the House of Lords; but otherwise it is a qualified exemption.[5]

31–002 Inter-relationship

Where (or to the extent that) a request for information is for 'environmental information'[6] the obligation to disclose that information will fall to be determined by the EIR and not by FOIA.[7] The EIR provide no exception that is directly comparable to either the s 35 or 36 exemption. The EIR do, however, provide a qualified exception for 'internal communications'.[8] The exception is neither content-related (cf s 35) nor prejudice based (cf s 36), with the result that the principles relating to ss 35 and 36 cannot be readily transposed to the exception under the Regulations.[9] The internal communications exception is separately considered in Chapter 19.[10] The Regulations also provide for an exception to provide environmental information when 'the request relates to material which is still in the course of completion, unfinished documents or incomplete data.' This exception is also separately considered in Chapter 19. Information falling within the s 35 or s 36 exemption may also fall within another exemption. Exemptions that have been relied upon alongside s 35 and s 36 include s 14 (vexatious requests),[11] ss 23 and 24 (security matters)[12] and provisions based on prejudice to a particular interest such as s 26 (defence), s 27 (international relations),[13] s 29 (UK economy),[14] s 31 (law enforcement),[15] s 42 (legal professional privilege)[16] and s 43 (commercial interests).[17] Some exemptions have a very obvious overlap, for example s 35(1)(c) and s 42.[18] Where more than one exemption may apply

---

outweighs the public interest in disclosure of the information sought] it is relevant to consider what specific harm would flow from the disclosure of the particular information in question' at [23]-[24]. This statement was approved by Mitting J in *ECGD v Friends of the Earth* [2008] EWHC 638 (Admin) at [28].

5 FOIA s 2(3)(e); FOI(S)A s 2(2).

6 As to the meaning of which, see §§17–008 to 17–017.

7 *Department for Business, Energy and Industrial Strategy v Information Commissioner* [2017] EWCA Civ 844, [2017] PTSR 1644, affirming *Department for Business, Energy and Industrial Strategy v Information Commissioner* [2015] UKUT 671 (AAC). Where the request is made for information held by a Scottish public authority, it will fall to be determined by the EI(S)R and not by the FOI(S)A.

8 EIR reg 12(4)(e); EI(S)R reg 10(4)(e).

9 Although the public interest in maintaining the exception bears a similarity with the public interest in maintaining the exemptions.

10 §19–013.

11 For example *McInerney v IC and Dept of Education* [2015] UKUT 0047 (AAC).

12 For example *Dept of Health v Information Commissioner*, FTT, 19 July 2018.

13 For example *All Party Parliamentary Group on Extraordinary Rendition v IC and FCO* [2015] UKUT 0377 (AAC).

14 For example *Dept for Work and Pensions v IC*, FTT, 22 December 2014.

15 For example *Dunnett v IC and MoD*, FTT, 26 March 2014.

16 For example *Dunnett v IC and MoD*, FTT, 26 March 2014.

17 For example *Moorhouse v IC and DBIS*, FTT, 12 June 2014.

18 *Savic v IC and Attorney-General* [2016] UKUT 534 (AAC).

the question arises of whether a public authority (or the Commissioner or a Tribunal) should 'aggregate' those exemptions when conducting the public interest balance under s 2(2), discussed in Chapter 19 above.

31– 003 The public interest test

Apart from information held by the House of Commons or the House of Lords,[19] the exemptions considered in this chapter are all qualified. Accordingly, even if information falls within any of the descriptions in s 35 or s 36, the duty to disclose (and the duty to confirm or deny) will still apply unless the public interest in maintaining the exemption outweighs the public interest in disclosure (or the public interest in maintaining the exclusion of the duty to confirm or deny outweighs the public interest in disclosing whether the public authority holds the information). Thus, s 36 of FOIA allows for the possibility that the disclosure of information relating to public affairs is prejudicial to the interests described in s 35, but is nonetheless in the public interest. By contrast, policy information falling under s 35 of the Act is subject to a qualified exemption from the duty of disclosure irrespective of whether or not its disclosure would be 'prejudicial'. However, the fact that no prejudice would be caused to anyone by the disclosure of such information in any given case may well count as a significant consideration in favour of it being in the public interest that the exemption should not be maintained and that the information should be disclosed. As with the other qualified exemptions, the relevant decision-maker will have to take into account all of the circumstances of the case and any relevant provisions of the ECHR.[20] The weighing of the competing public interests poses particular problems in relation to information that falls within s 35(1). As noted previously,[21] on one side of the 'balance' introduced by s 2 is the public interest in *maintaining the exemption*: it is not the public interest in non-disclosure. A public authority must therefore identify the public interest that is expressed in the particular exemption and adjudge the extent to which disclosure of each item of information falling within the terms of the request would offend that public interest. The exercise requires the public authority to 'stand back and abnegate its own interests except and in so far as those interests are properly viewed as part of the public interest.'[22]

31– 004 Public interest: specific issues

For other prejudice-based exemptions, where what is at stake is national security, the defence of the realm, international relations, criminal investigations and so forth, the above public interest task is difficult, but may be achieved through a disciplined thought process. The public interest in maintaining an exemption for information held by a government department relating to 'the formulation or development of public policy' (to use the first of the limbs of exemption in s 35(1))[23] presents two additional challenges. First, there is nothing in the description itself that urges non-disclosure; or at least not without some rejection of the underlying premise of all freedom of information legislation.[24] This is further evidenced by the limited range of public authorities to which the exemption applies: if there is a public interest served by exempting information relating to the formulation or development of policy, it is not immediately obvious

19 But only in so far as the exemption provided by s 36 is concerned.

20 See Chapter 4.

21 §§6– 001 and 6– 010.

22 *DWP v IC*, IT, 5 March 2007 at [24].

23 The point applies equally to the other three limbs of exemption in s 35(1).

24 In *OGC v IC* [2008] EWHC 774 (Admin), [2008] ACD 54 Stanley Burnton J confirmed that s 35 does not create a presumption of a public interest in non-disclosure [75]-[79]. This was applied in *DBERR v IC and Friends of the Earth*, IT, 29 April 2008 at [103].

why that public interest stops with government departments and does not include the formulation or development of policy of, say, a local authority. Secondly and largely because of the first, a public authority's self-interest in non-disclosure of this class of information is apt to be presented or even perceived as the public interest in maintaining the exemption, with the public authority effectively determining its own cause. The exemptions therefore require government departments to steel themselves, and where required find that the public interest in maintaining these exemptions is outweighed by the public interest in disclosure.[25] The fact that information falls within one of the categories of qualified exemption under s 35 does not give it any 'inherent weight' or presumption in favour of non-disclosure when the public interest test under s 2(2) is applied; indeed, such a class, rather than contents, based approach to assessing the public interest in disclosure is 'arid'.[26] There is no 'sliding scale' of categories attracting greater or lesser weight in the public interest balancing exercise.[27] What matters is the content of the information and whether the 'actual harm or prejudice that the proposed disclosure would (or would be likely to or may) cause and the actual benefits its disclosure would (or would be likely to or may) confer or promote.'[28] Once a public authority has demonstrated that information falls within a category that attracts a qualified exemption, when it comes to the s 2(2) balancing exercise 'the scales stand empty at the outset of the analysis.'[29] It is less clear whether the 'scales stand empty at the outset' approach is appropriate in a s 36 case, as it is implicit in such a case that, for one of the qualified exemptions to arise, some specific prejudice to the public interest has already been established because a 'qualified person' must have provided a reasonable opinion that disclosure of information would have one of the adverse consequences provided for in s 36(2). That prejudice is likely also to be relevant to the public interest balancing exercise. In such a case, a 'scales stand empty at the outset' approach may be lawful as long as the decision-maker takes that prejudice into account at some stage in the s 2(2) balancing exercise.[30]

31– 005 Section 35-36 relationship

Apart from the restriction of s 35 to 'information held by a government department or by the National Assembly for Wales', the two provisions have a fair measure of overlap. In particular, the proceedings of the Cabinet, of the Executive Committee of the Northern Ireland Assembly and of the executive committee of the National Assembly for Wales are apt to be caught by

---

25 To do otherwise will effectively promote the exemptions into absolute exemptions. These propositions (as set out identically in the first edition of this text) were approved expressly by the Information Tribunal in *DWP v IC*, IT, 5 March 2007 at [31]-[32]. And more recently in *Department of Health v IC and Healey*, FTT, 5 April 2012 at [73]:

> We would observe that the DOH's position expressed in evidence is tantamount to saying that there should be an absolute exemption for risk registers at the stages the registers were requested in this case. Parliament has not so provided. Section 35 (and s 36) are qualified exemptions subject to a public interest test, which means that there is no absolute guarantee that information will not be disclosed, however strong the public interest in maintaining the exemption.

26 *Dept of Health v IC and Lewis* [2015] UKUT 0159 (AAC) at [22].

27 *Cabinet Office v IC and Aitchison* [2013] UKUT 0526 (AAC) at [60].

28 *Dept of Health v IC and Lewis (CA)* [2017] EWCA Civ 374, [2017] 1 WLR 3330 at [43], citing *APPGER v IC and FCO* [2013] UKUT 0560 (AAC) at [149].

29 *Cabinet Office v IC*, FTT, 12 November 2015 at [22]; *Baird v IC and Governing Body of the University of London*, FTT, 16 December 2013 at [42]; *Mitchell v IC & CPS*, FTT, 15 December 2014 at [46].

30 In *Dept for Work and Pensions v IC and Zola* [2016] EWCA Civ 758, [2017] 1 WLR 1 the 'qualified person' had given evidence (accepted by the FTT) that disclosure would prejudice the effective conduct of public affairs within s 36(2)(c). In approaching the s 2(2)(b) balancing exercise, the FTT adopted the approach that the 'scales stand empty at the outset of the analysis' (para 212). The UT considered this approach to be an error of law, although one that was not material to the outcome. In the Court of Appeal, Lloyd Jones LJ (with whom Richards LJ and Dyson MR agreed on his analysis of the law, although not its application to the facts) held that this was not an error of approach provided the qualified person's opinion was given proper weight at some point during the public interest balancing exercise: see [55].

both provisions. Similarly, it will often be open to certain public authorities to claim that the disclosure of information relating to the formulation or development of government policy (s 35(1)(a) or Ministerial communications (s 35(1)(b)) would, or would be likely to, inhibit the free and frank exchange of views for the purpose of deliberation (s 36(2)(b)) or prejudice the maintenance of the convention of the collective responsibility of Ministers of the Crown (s 36(2)(a)(i)). However, where information falls within s 35 the application of s 36 is explicitly excluded.[31] Although once thought that this might have far-reaching ramifications,[32] in practice this would appear to be treated as more theoretical than real. The approach taken is that the factors in s 36(2) are specific public interest factors that fall within, and are therefore protected by, the more general public interest categories in s 35(1). As such, prejudice to one of the specific factors in s 36(2) may be relevant to the assessment of whether the public interest in maintaining an exemption in s 35(1) outweighs the public interest in disclosure[33]. In such a case the outcome of the balancing exercise may turn out to be no different whether s 35 or s 36 is applied.

31– 006 Legislative history

The two kinds of information that are now dealt with separately in ss 35 and 36 of FOIA were not distinguished in the 1997 White Paper. Instead, they were both considered under the single heading of information relating to government decision-making and policy advice.[34] In the White Paper, the Government proposed that the question of whether or not such information would be disclosed should be determined by a test of 'harm', whereas the test to be applied in the great majority of cases would be one of 'substantial harm'.[35] The draft Bill published in May 1999 substituted the term 'prejudice' for that of 'harm' as the key term in the applicable test,[36] and made information now falling within the scope of s 35 of FOIA subject to a purely class-based exemption.[37] The 'prejudice' test and the introduction of a class-based exemption in respect of policy information held by government departments were also retained in the Bill

---

31 See FOIA s 36(1)(a). This does not apply under the FOI(S)A: information can be rendered exempt information upon both ss 29 and 30 of the Act.

32 This was the view expressed in the first four editions of this work on the basis that information falling within s 35(1) would have to be disclosed where the public interest in maintaining that exemption was outweighed by the public interest in disclosure notwithstanding the fact that, if s 36 could be relied upon, the outcome of the balancing exercise would be different.

33 For example, in *Cabinet Office v IC and Aitchison* [2013] UKUT 0526 (AAC), in assessing whether to disclose minutes of Cabinet meetings, which fell within the 'Ministerial Communications' exemption in s 35(1)(b), the Tribunal considered that the convention in relation to Cabinet collective responsibility (a s 36(2) factor) was a 'very weighty public interest factor' for maintaining the exemption. A similar approach was taken in *Bradford & Bingley Action Group v IC and Cabinet Office*, FTT, 10 June 2013 at [18]; *Home Office v IC*, FTT, 29 June 2015; *Cabinet Office v IC*, FTT, 22 July 2015 at [30]. In none of these cases did the Tribunal consider – or was it even argued - that this factor could not be taken into account under s 35(1) on the grounds that 'prejudice to the maintenance of the convention of collective responsibility of Ministers of the Crown' was a specific category of exemption under s 36(2).

34 Cabinet Officer, *Your Right to Know: The Government's Proposals for a Freedom of Information Act* (Cm 3818, 1997) para 3.12.

35 Cabinet Officer, *Your Right to Know: The Government's Proposals for a Freedom of Information Act* (Cm 3818, 1997) paras 3.7, 3.12. The decision to impose a simple 'harm' test on such information rather than a test of 'substantial harm' was explained on the basis that 'now, more than ever, government needs space and time in which to assess arguments and conduct its own debates with a degree of privacy. Experience from overseas suggests that the essential governmental functions of planning ahead, delivering solutions to issues of national importance and determining options on which to base policy decisions while still maintaining collective responsibility, can be damaged by random and premature disclosure of its deliberations under Freedom of Information legislation …': para 3.12.

36 This was done in order to make the Bill consistent in its terminology with other legislation including, notably, the DPA 1998 and the Local Government Act 1972: see House of Commons Select Committee on Public Administration, *Third Report* (Cm 4355, 1999) para 65.

37 Clause 28.

published in November 1999,[38] which later became FOIA.

31– 007 Passage of exemptions

The provisions of the Freedom of Information Bills concerning government information were recognised to be 'one of the especially difficult areas for freedom of information legislation'.[39] Both the introduction of a class-based exemption in relation to policy information held by government departments and the imposition of a test of 'prejudice' rather than 'substantial prejudice' in respect of information relating to public affairs were controversial. They were roundly criticised both at the Committee stage and in Parliament.[40] In particular, the introduction of a class-based exemption in respect of policy information held by government departments was objected to on the basis that the exemption was more restrictive than the provisions of the Code that applied in respect of this kind of information, according to which such information should only be withheld if its disclosure would harm the frankness and candour of internal discussion, and if that harm outweighed the public interest in openness.[41]

31– 008 Justification for the exemptions

The Government nevertheless insisted that the exemptions in respect of policy information and of information relating to public affairs were both justified. The imposition of a class-based exemption in respect of policy information was said to be necessary on the basis that, while the purpose of the Freedom of Information Bill was to increase openness in government, it was 'appropriate that policy-making should not take place in a goldfish bowl' and that there should be a process which allowed Ministers, public authorities and civil servants 'to exchange views in a way that they feel will be private to give them space to think and make decisions'.[42] The preference for a test of 'prejudice' as opposed to 'substantial prejudice' was explained on the basis that a public authority who sought to justify a decision to apply the exemption from the duty of disclosure to information relating to public policy on the basis that its disclosure would cause 'prejudice' of the relevant kind would in any event be required to show that the prejudice in question, or the risk of prejudice, was 'real, actual or of substance'. Consequently, there was nothing to be gained by including an additional requirement in the Bill that any 'prejudice'

[38] Clauses 33 and 34.

[39] House of Commons Select Committee on Public Administration, *Third Report* (Cm 4355, 1999) para 83.

[40] For criticism of the former class-based exemption, see, eg, House of Commons Select Committee on Public Administration, *Third Report* (Cm 4355, 1999) para 89; Mr Robert McLennan MP, Hansard HC vol 340 col 748 (7 December 1999); Lord Mackay of Ardbrecht, Hansard HL vol 618 col 275-276 (24 October 2000). For criticisms of the imposition of a test of 'prejudice' as opposed to 'substantial prejudice', see, eg, House of Lords, *Draft Freedom of Information Bill: First Report*, 27 July 1999, paras 32, 34-35.

[41] See eg, Lord Mackay of Ardbrecht, Hansard HL vol 618 col 275-276 (24 October 2000). It is to be noted that in the 1997 White Paper, the Government itself criticised the Code of Practice on the basis that the tests for harm contained therein were 'insufficient'. In particular, the exemptions contained in the Code of Practice, for the most part, gave 'no indication of the extent of harm against which the disclosure or withholding of the information should be judged'. In the Government's view, as expressed in the White Paper, 'the test to determine whether disclosure is to be refused should normally be set in specific and demanding terms. We therefore propose to move in most areas from a simple harm test to a substantial harm test, namely will the disclosure of this information cause substantial harm?' — *Your Right to Know: The Government's Proposals for a Freedom of Information Act*, paras 3.6-3.7. Note also that, whereas the White Paper proposed (in para 3.12) that a simple harm test should nevertheless be retained in respect of information relating to government decision-making and policy advice, the Government's final position, as explained by Lord Falconer of Thoroton, appears to be that the test of 'prejudice' applicable in respect of information relating to public affairs in fact requires a demonstration of 'substantial prejudice' before the exemption can be said to apply.

[42] Hansard HL vol 612 col 827 (20 April 2000) (Lord Falconer). The explanation of the rationale for the exemption illuminates the public interest weighing exercise: if the policy decision has been made by the time that the request is received there will be little public interest in maintaining the exemption; they will have had their space to think and make decisions. Moreover, so far as the existence duty is concerned, it is difficult to see how confirming or denying that information is held should stop anyone of normal sensitivity from having 'space to think and make decisions'.

should also be 'substantial'.[43] The fact that 'prejudice', when viewed properly, entails real, actual or substantial prejudice provides a further indication of the Government's rationale in subjecting policy-information to a class-based exemption, rather than a 'simple prejudice' exemption.[44]

2. INFORMATION RELATING TO THE FORMULATION OF GOVERNMENT POLICY, ETC

31–009 Introduction

Information held by a government department or by the National Assembly for Wales is exempt information if it relates to:

(a) the formulation or development of government policy;[45]
(b) Ministerial communications;[46]
(c) the provision of advice by any of the Law Officers or any request for the provision of such advice;[47] or
(d) the operation of any Ministerial private office.[48]

As noted at the outset of this Chapter, the exemption applies only to information held by government departments or by the National Assembly for Wales: it does not apply to information held by any other public authority.[49] The exemption has four discrete limbs, which need to be considered separately. So far as the first and second limbs of the exemption are concerned, special provision is made in relation to background statistical information.[50] So far as the first limb is concerned, special provision is also made in relation to background factual information.[51] The exemption is a qualified exemption,[52] and there is a corresponding exclusion of the duty to confirm or deny.[53] In relation to each of the limbs, the required connection is that the information 'relate to' what is described by the limb. The phrase 'relate to' and cognate expressions are notoriously vague.[54]

---

43 Lord Falconer of Thoroton, Hansard HL vol 612 col 827 (20 April 2000).

44 That is, in accordance with the approach taken in the White Paper *(Your Right to Know: The Government's Proposals for a Freedom of Information Act*, paras 3.6 to 3.7 and 3.12).

45 FOIA s 35(1)(a); FOI(S)A s 29(1)(a). 'Government policy' is defined in FOIA s 35(5), and in FOI(S)A s 29(4).

46 FOIA s 35(1)(b); FOI(S)A s 29(1)(b). 'Ministerial communications' is defined in FOIA s 35(5), and in FOI(S)A s 29(4).

47 FOIA s 35(1)(c); FOI(S)A s 29(1)(c). 'The Law Officers' is defined in FOIA s 35(5), and in FOI(S)A s 29(4).

48 FOIA s 35(1)(d); FOI(S)A s 29(1)(d). 'Ministerial private office' is defined in FOIA s 35(5), and in FOI(S)A s 29(4).

49 In relation to information held by Scottish public authorities, the comparable exemption is only applicable to information held by the Scottish Administration.

50 FOIA s 35(2); FOI(S)A s 29(2). See §31–022.

51 FOIA s 35(4); FOI(S)A s 29(3). See §31–023.

52 See §§31–001 to 31–003.

53 FOIA s 35(3). There is no separate duty to confirm or deny under the FOI(S)A. See §31–025.

54 The Supreme Court has held that the phrase 'relates to' indicates more than a loose or consequential connection or a touching upon the matter: *Martin v Most* [2010] UKSC 10, 2010 SC (UKSC) 40 at [49], [159]. And similarly: *Imperial Tobacco Ltd v Lord Advocate* [2012] UKSC 61, 2013 SLT 2 at [16]; *Re Agricultural Sector (Wales) Bill* [2014] UKSC 43, [2014] 1 WLR 2622 at [50]; *Recovery of Medical Costs for Asbestos Diseases (Wales) Bill* [2015] UKSC 3, [2015] AC 1016 at [25]; *Christian Institute v Lord Advocate* [2016] UKSC 51, [2016] HRLR 19 at [29] (concerning the Data Protection Act 1998). In the context of FOIA the meaning of the phrase 'relates to' has been considered in: *Home Office v IC and Cobain*, FTT, 30 January 2013 at [15]-[19]; *Callus v IC and Home Office*, FTT, 6 May 2014 at [39]-[41]; *University and Colleges Admissions Service v IC and Lord Lucas* [2014] UKUT 0557 (AAC) at [44]-[46] (meaning of 'relates to' in FOIA s 7(5)); *Home Office v IC and Cobain* [2014] UKUT 0306 (AAC) at [39]; *All Party*

31– 010 Exemption background

The first limb of s 35(1) renders material exempt information if it relates to the formulation or development of government policy. It has been said to reflect the public interest in maintaining a 'safe space' for participants to 'think the unthinkable' in order to test and develop ideas without external interference or distraction.[55] A broadly similar class of exemption is found in most of the comparable jurisdictions, with differences partly reflecting the differences in the systems of governance.[56] 'Government policy' is defined to include the policy of the Executive Committee of the Northern Ireland Assembly and the policy of the National Assembly for Wales.[57] The 1997 White Paper considered that there was a readily-identifiable core class of documents and materials that contain information falling within the exemption, including 'high-level' government records such as Cabinet and Committee papers,[58] as well as draft consultation papers and advice on policy prepared by civil servants for the benefit of Ministers. The House of Commons Select Committee on Public Administration, on the other hand, doubted that 'information relating to the formulation or development of policy' was a

---

Parliamentary Group on Extraordinary Rendition v IC and FCO [2015] UKUT 0377 (AAC) at [14]-[33]; *Reprieve v IC and FCO*, FTT, 26 April 2016 at [37]-[39]; *Corderoy and Ahmed v IC and Attorney General* [2017] UKUT 0495 (AAC) at [51] [54] and [59]-[62]; *Department of Health v IC and Lewis* [2017] EWCA Civ 374, [2017] 1 WLR 3330 at [13] (Sir Terence Etherton MR) (meaning of 'relates to' in FOIA s 35(1)). Contrast *R v Smith* [1975] QB 531 at 542B ('the words "relating to" are very wide. They are equivalent to "connected with" or "arising out of"') (Lord Denning). The active voice suggests that the required link to the protected interest may need to be apparent from the information itself. Thus, in *Tooheys Limited v Commissioner of Stamp Duties* (1961) 105 CLR 602 at 622 Taylor J said that 'the vital question is whether the instrument "relates" and not whether it may be "related" by an examination of extraneous circumstances.' Authorities considering the phrase in other contexts are illustrative of the interpretive technique used to resolve the flexibility inherent in the phrase: *Rein v Lane* (1867) LR 2 QB 144; *R v Sheffield Crown Court ex p Brownlow* [1980] QB 530 at 538G-539D; *re Smalley* [1985] AC 622 at 643D-644F; *R v Central Criminal Court ex p Randle* [1991] 1 WLR 1087; *Tooheys Limited v. Commissioner of Stamp Duties* (1961) 105 CLR 602 at 613-614, 617, 619 and 620-622; *PMT Partners P/L v. Aust National Parks and Wildlife Services* (1995) 184 CLR 301 at 313 and 330-331, where there is a survey of various other authorities; *All Party Parliamentary Group on Extraordinary Rendition v IC and FCO*, FTT, 3 May 2012 at [62]-[70], where the Tribunal considered the phrase in an information rights context; *EH v Information Commissioner* [2002] 3 IR 600; *Rotunda Hospital v Information Commissioner* [2009] IEHC 315; *Durant v FSA* [2003] EWCA Civ 1746. The last three are concerned with the meaning of the phrase in the context of a right to personal information. Generally, the authorities illustrate that resolution of any uncertainty is guided by an interpretation that will secure the object of the legislation without creating results that unnecessarily cut across existing legal rights or otherwise creating harsh results. See also: §§15– 021 and 26– 042.

[55] *Brain v IC and MoJ*. FTT, 15 September 2014 at [34]: 'In brief, s 35(1)(a) reflects the need for a safe space in which government policy can be formulated and developed in robust discussions where participants are free to 'think the unthinkable' in order to test and develop ideas, without fear of external interference or distraction, whether as a result of premature and lurid media headlines or otherwise. This short identification of the relevant interests served by the exemption may be supplemented by reference to the very useful discussion of arguments concerning safe space, chilling effect, record keeping, and protection of officials in paragraphs 194- 204 and 211-212 of the Commissioner's published guidance titled "Government policy (section 35)" version 1, 18 March 2013. We agree with those paragraphs of the Commissioner's guidance'. The 'need' supposes a certain unwillingness or inability on the part of those providing policy advice to do what they are engaged to do without this extra protection. See also *Dept of Health v IC and Lewis* [2017] EWCA Civ 374, [2017] 1 WLR 3330 at [15].

[56] In the United States, the Freedom of Information Act, 1966, 5 USC 552(b)(5), exempts from disclosure records that enjoy 'deliberative process privilege': see §51– 008(5). The Freedom of Information Act 1982 (Cth of Australia) s 47C, provides an exemption in relation to 'matter in the nature of, or relating to, opinion, advice or recommendation …in the course of the deliberative processes involved in the functions of an agency or Minister …and [the disclosure of which] would be contrary to the public interest': see §51– 015(11). The Official Information Act 1982 (New Zealand), ss 6(e) and 27(1)(a), provides a comparatively narrow, but absolute, exemption for information relating to decisions to change or continue government economic or financial policies: see §51– 022(5). The Access to Information Act 1985 (Canada) s 21(1), provides a discretionary exemption for records that contain advice or recommendations developed by or for a government institution or a minister of the Crown and for any account of governmental consultations or deliberations: see §51– 032(4) and (5). The Freedom of Information Act 1997 (Ireland) s 20(1), provides a discretionary exemption where the record contains matter relating to the deliberative process of the public body: see §51– 039(9).

[57] FOIA s 35(5).

[58] Cabinet Office, *Your Right to Know: The Government's Proposals for a Freedom of Information Act* (Cm 3813, 1997) para 3.12.

sufficiently well-defined class of information. It also took the view that such information should be included within the scope of the prejudice-based exemption contained in what is now s 36 of FOIA.[59]

31–011 Comparative jurisdictions

In each of the comparative jurisdictions there exists a similar exemption.

(1) In the USA, the Freedom of Information Act 1966 provides an exemption for inter-agency or intra-agency memoranda or letters 'which would not be available by law to a party other than an agency in litigation with the agency'.[60] This has been interpreted to mean records that would normally be privileged in civil proceedings. These privileges are broader than those that are enjoyed by a public authority in the United Kingdom and include deliberative process privilege, also known as 'executive privilege'. This protects records revealing the deliberative policymaking process of government. The Supreme Court has held that 'deliberative process privilege' exists to 'prevent injury to the quality of agency decisions'.[61] The injuries are thought to be occasioned by:

 (i) an impairment of open, frank discussions on matters of policy between subordinates and superiors;
 (ii) premature disclosure of proposed policies before they are finally adopted; and
 (iii) public confusion that might result from disclosure of reasons and rationales that were not in fact ultimately the grounds for an agency's action.[62]

(2) In Canada, the Access to Information Act provides a discretionary exemption for advice or recommendations developed by or for a government institution or a minister of the Crown.[63] In relation to this exemption, the Federal Court has held that:

> despite the importance of governmental openness as a safeguard against the abuse of power, and as a necessary condition for democratic accountability, it is equally clear that governments must be allowed a measure of confidentiality in the policy-making process. To permit or to require the disclosure of advice given by officials, either to other officials or to ministers, and the disclosure of confidential deliberations within the public service on policy options, would erode government's ability to formulate and to justify its policies. It would be an intolerable burden to force ministers and their advisors to disclose to public scrutiny the internal evolution of the policies ultimately adopted. Disclosure of such material would often reveal that the policy-making process included false starts, blind alleys, wrong turns, changes of mind, the solicitation and rejection of advice, and the re-evaluation of priorities and the re-weighing of the relative importance of the relevant factors as a problem is studied more closely. In the hands of journalists or political opponents this is combustible material liable to fuel a fire that could quickly destroy governmental credibility and effectiveness. On the other hand, of course, democratic principles require that the public, and this often means the representatives of sectional interests, are enabled to participate as widely as possible in influencing policy development. Without a degree of openness on the part of government about its thinking on public policy issues, and without access to relevant information in the possession of

---

59 House of Commons Select Committee on Public Administration, *Third Report* (Cm 4355, 1999) para 89.

60 5 USC 552(b)(5). Discussed further at §51–008(5).

61 *National Labor Relations Board v Sears, Roebuck & Co* (1975) 421 US 132 at 151.

62 *Russell v Department of the Air Force*, 682 F 2d 1045 (DC Cir 1982); *Coastal States Gas Corp v Department of Energy*, 617 F 2d 854 (DC Cir 1980); *Jordan v United States Department of Justice*, 591 F 2d 753 (DC Cir 1978).

63 Section 21(1)(a). Considered further at §51–032(4).

government, the effectiveness of public participation will inevitably be curbed.[64]

(3) In Australia, the Freedom of Information Act 1982 provides an exemption for documents that record the deliberative process of the federal government[65] the disclosure of which would be contrary to the public interest. In considering the public interest for the purposes of this provision, the Federal Court of Australia had held that disclosure of communications made in the course of the development and subsequent promulgation of policy tends not to be in the public interest and that the disclosure of such documents could inhibit frankness and candour in future pre-decisional communications as well as lead to confusion and 'unnecessary debate'. In particular, disclosure of documents that did not fairly disclose the reasons for a decision subsequently taken might be unfair to a decision-maker and may prejudice the integrity of the decision-making process.[66] This view, briefly held,[67] subsequently lost judicial favour,[68] although the argument continued to be run from time to time.[69] There remains a rift in judicial view, but with the majority taking the line that if the candour is to be successful, the public authority is obliged 'to demonstrate, as a factual rather than theoretical proposition, that disclosure would be contrary to the public interest.'[70]

(4) In New Zealand, the Official Information Act 1982 provides a discretionary exemption where the withholding of the requested information is necessary to maintain the effective conduct of public affairs, through the free and frank

---

64 *Canadian Council of Christian Charities v Canada (Minister of Finance)* [1999] 4 FC 245 at [30]-[32].

65 Freedom of Information Act 1982 s 47C. Considered further at §51–015(11).

66 *Re Howard and the Treasurer* (1985) 7 ALD 626, 3 AAR 169, in which the then Deputy Leader of the Opposition sought access to the documents provided by the Treasurer or his department to the Australian Council of Trade Unions during the government's bargaining session over the content and shape of the 1984/85 Budget. See also *Harris v Australian Broadcasting Corporation* (1983) 50 ALR 551, 78 FLR 236. These decisions were given early in the regime, with Davies J expressly acknowledging in *Re Howard* (at 635) that as time went on and with greater experience it might be necessary to revisit the principles he laid out. Later Australian decisions have been more circumspect in their acceptance of the candour argument: *Re Rae and Department of Prime Minister and Cabinet* (1986) 12 ALD 589; *Re Fewster and Department of Prime Minister and Cabinet (No 2)* (1987) 13 ALD 139; *Re Kamenka and the Australian National University* (1992) 26 ALD 585; *Re Cleary and Department of the Treasury* (1993) 31 ALD 214; *Re Eccleston and Department of Family Services and Aboriginal and Islander Affairs* (1993) 1 QAR 60. Even before *Re Howard* scepticism had been expressed, with a requirement that any such claim be supported by evidence: *Murtagh v Federal Commissioner of Taxation* (1984) 84 ATC 4516.

67 See §31–032 and §31–033.

68 In *General Manager, Workcover Authority of New South Wales v Law Society of New South Wales* [2006] NSWCA 84 at [154] the New South Wales Court of Appeal considered that the earlier decisions (such as *Re Howard*) were derived from Crown privilege authorities and that these 'were not an apt point of reference…Freedom of information legislation, as the earlier discussion reveals, was intended to cast aside the era of closed government and principles developed in that era may, with the benefit of twenty or more years of experience, be seen as anachronisms.'

69 *Accredited (Wholesale Tobacco) Distributors Pty Ltd v Griffiths* [2003] VSC 20. It has now been statutorily removed.

70 *General Manager, Workcover Authority of New South Wales v Law Society of New South Wales* [2006] NSWCA 84 at [158]. In *McKinnon v Secretary, Department of Treasury* [2006] HCA 45, (2006) 229 ALR 187 Callinan and Heydon JJ dismissed evidence from a former Secretary of the Attorney-General's Department (who had also served as President of the Australian Law Reform Commission and as a member of the Administrative Review Council) of his experience that disclosure of information, even very sensitive information, did not impede candid advice to a minister: 'One must question his, indeed anyone's, ability to express an opinion of that kind. We would, for ourselves, have given it little weight, as we would his rejection of other grounds relied upon by the respondent based upon his own personal experience' (at [116]). Nevertheless, they found no difficulty in accepting the Minister's assertion to the opposite effect: 'The second ground, which speaks of jeopardy to candour, and the desirability of written communications, obviously cannot readily be dismissed, and it seems to us that this is a matter upon which a Minister's opinion and experience are likely to be as well informed and valuable as those of anyone else, including senior officials' (at [121]). The Court did not identify the Minister's experience in these matters. In *McKinnon* there was a conclusive certificate under s 36(3), which rendered the question for the Tribunal one of whether there existed reasonable grounds for the claim that the disclosure of the document would be contrary to the public interest: cf FOIA s 36(2). Such certificates are no longer possible: Freedom of Information (Removal of Conclusive Certificates and Other Measures) Act 2009.

expression of opinions by or between or to ministers or members of a specified organisation or officers and employees of any department, organisation, or local authority in the course of their duty; or through the protection of such ministers, members, officers, and employees from improper pressure or harassment.[71]

(5) In Ireland, the Freedom of Information Act 1997 provides a discretionary exemption where the record contains matter relating to the deliberative process of the public body.[72]

31–012 Government policy formulation

Section 35(1)(a) of FOIA resembles one of the grounds of public interest immunity that the Crown used to rely upon to avoid what would otherwise have been its disclosure obligations in litigation.[73] That exemption enjoyed diminishing success in the Courts over the last half of the twentieth century, partly on the basis of the countervailing public interest in disclosure but also because the very notion that potential disclosure would inhibit candour was received with increasing scepticism.[74] It is fair to say that some judges were more receptive to the sentiment than others, but the preponderance of judicial view leaned increasingly against the notion that the potential of disclosure would adversely affect the candour of civil servants:

> The notion that any competent and conscientious public servant would be inhibited at all in the candour of his writings by consideration of the off-chance that they might have to be produced in a litigation is in my opinion grotesque. To represent that the possibility of it might significantly impair the public service is even more so. Nowadays the state in multifarious manifestations impinges closely upon the lives and activities of individual citizens. Where this has involved a citizen in litigation with the state or one of its agencies, the candour argument is an utterly insubstantial ground for denying him access to relevant documents.[75]

---

[71] Official Information Act 1982 s 9(2)(g); Local Government Official Information and Meetings Act 1987 s 7(2)(f). Considered further at §51–023(8).

[72] Freedom of Information Act 1997 s 20(1). Factual and statistical material is excluded from the scope of the exemption. The exemption is disapplied where the public interest is better served by disclosure than by non-disclosure: Freedom of Information Act 1997 s 20(3). The relevant minister may issue a conclusive certificate if he takes the view that the exemption applies. Considered further at §51–039(9).

[73] This class of exemption was referred to in *Smith v East India Co* (1841) 1 Ph 50 at 55 (Lord Lyndhurst): 'it is quite obvious that public policy requires…that the most unreserved communication should take place ….that it should be subject to no restraints or limitations; but it is also quite obvious, that if, at the suit of a particular individual, those communications should be subject to be produced in a court of justice, the effect of that would be to restrain the freedom of the communications, and to render them more cautious, guarded and reserved.'

[74] Starting with *Duncan v Cammell, Laird & Co* [1942] AC 642. In *Conway v Rimmer* [1968] AC 910 the House of Lords, whilst recognising that candour could be impaired by disclosure, rejected this as a class-claim. Lord Upjohn was more sceptical of the claim: '...the executive have relied upon the *Cammell, Laird* case to claim privilege in class cases on the ground that the public interest requires that the writings of every member of the executive from the highest to the lowest ….must be protected from production for the reason that the writer of the document must have a full, free and uninhibited right to pen his views without fear that they will ever be subject to the public gaze; in other words, secure in such knowledge he can then, and apparently only then, write with the complete candour necessary for the discharge of his functions as a member of the public service' (at 992). And later: 'I cannot believe that any Minister or any high level military official or civil servant would feel in the least degree inhibited in expressing his honest views in the course of his duty on some subject, such as even the personal qualifications and delinquencies of some colleague, by the thought that his observations might one day see the light of day' (at 994).

[75] *Burmah Oil Company Limited v Bank of England* [1980] AC 1090 at 1133 (Lord Keith). See also: *Sankey v Whitlam* (1978) 148 CLR 1 at 40 (Gibbs ACJ), 63 (Stephen J) and 96 (Mason J); *Williams v Home Office* [1981] 1 All ER 1151. Contrast with Lord Wilberforce in *Burmah Oil Company Limited v Bank of England* [1980] AC 1090 at 1112; *Air Canada v Secretary of State for Trade* [1983] 2 AC 394 at 437. The Tribunal in *Guardian Newspapers Ltd and Heather Brooke v IC and BBC*, IT, 8 January 2007 at [115] although questioning whether this statement was of particular assistance or relevance in the context of s 36, added that the passages served as 'a reminder that assertions of inhibition should perhaps not be too readily accepted.' In *DfES v IC and The Evening Standard*, IT, 19 February 2007 at [74] the Tribunal, after acknowledging different passages in *Conway v Rimmer* and *Burmah Oil*, said: '...we do not entirely ignore the fact that similar claims to those made to us have met with a degree of scepticism in much less transparent times than ours.'

Even before its formal abandonment, the position had been reached where the notion that those involved in the formulation or development of government policy would be legitimately inhibited in expressing their views or giving advice were it apprehended that those views or that advice might be disclosed enjoyed diminished respect in the higher courts.[76] The concept is no longer employed by government departments in support of public interest immunity claims.[77] Candour has, however, been successfully deployed in other contexts.[78] While there remain certain contexts in which the courts will restrain disclosure of relevant information to protect the public interest in ensuring the free and frank exchange of views between participants – 'candour'[79] – generally the public interest (at least in a litigation context) now supports disclosure of relevant information: the protection of 'candour' as a ground for non-disclosure has morphed into a duty of disclosure, termed the 'duty of candour.'[80] In any event, the Tribunal has repeatedly stated that it derives little assistance from these statements, which were made in a different era and in the context of civil litigation.[81]

---

76 Starting with Lord Radcliffe in the *Glasgow Corporation v Central Land Board* 1956 SC (HL) 1 at 20 who said that he would have supposed Crown servants to be 'made of sterner stuff', a view shared by Harman LJ in *Re Grosvenor Hotel, London (No 2)* [1965] Ch 1210 at 1255E. In *Rogers v Home Secretary* [1973] AC 388 at 413E-F Lord Salmon spoke of a 'candour argument' run by the Attorney-General as 'smack[ing] of the old fallacy that any official in the government service would be inhibited from writing frankly and possibly at all unless he could be sure that nothing he wrote could ever be exposed to the light of day.' See also *R v SSHD, ex p Duggan* [1994] 3 All ER 277 at 285e.

77 In a statement to the House of Commons on the future of public interest immunity in relation to Government documents, the Attorney-General (Sir Nicholas Lyell) spelled out that the new approach was to focus directly on the damage that disclosure would cause, with the former division between class exemptions and contents exemptions no longer being maintained: Hansard HC vol 287 cols 949-950 (18 December 1996); see also Hansard HC vol 297 cols 616-617 (11 July 1997). The Government's new approach was set out in a document that was placed in the libraries of both Houses of Parliament. Entitled *Annex C: Paper which Accompanied 1996 HMG Hansard Statement on PII*, it reiterates the abandonment of purely class-based claims (para.2.3), describing the distinction between class claims and contents claims as 'unhelpful and obscure' (para.3.3) and noting the particular difficulty with 'the advice to ministers class' (para.3.4). The new approach heralded is 'therefore based on the principle that PII can only ever apply where disclosure of material could cause real damage to the public interest' (para.4.1). In the section on 'Examples of the Government's approach', under the heading 'Internal discussion and advice' the paper states: 'The class is widely represented as reinforcing the executive's tendency to secrecy and unaccountability. In practice this type of PII claim is only considered, let alone made, on comparatively rare occasions, since it is only rarely that this kind of document is relevant to litigation. Government documents should not attract PII on the basis of any special privilege but merely on the basis, as for any other document, that in certain circumstances their disclosure would cause real harm. The Government accepts that an approach to PII which claimed a kind of blanket protection for pre-defined categories of documents would be wrong in principle…A claim will not be made simply because the document constitutes high level advice to ministers' (paras 5.5-5.6, 5.12). Wholly absent from the document was any suggestion that a claim might be made out on the basis that disclosure would inhibit the candour of civil servants or somehow prevent the free and frank exchange of ideas.

78 In *Cleveland County Council v F* [1995] 1 WLR 785, [1995] 2 All ER 236, [1995] 1 FLR 797 Hale J held that candour was a relevant consideration in determining an application to disclose material relating to wardship proceedings; see also *Oxfordshire County Council v L and F* [1997] 1 FLR 235, 251 (Stuart-White J) In *R (Persey) v Secretary of State for the Environment, Food and Rural Affairs* [2002] EWHC 371, [2003] 1 QB 794 the likely lack of candour of witnesses at a public inquiry into the outbreak of foot and mouth disease was a relevant consideration for the Secretary of State in determining that the inquiry into the disease should sit in private. *Compare R (Wagstaff) v Secretary of State for Health* [2001] 1 WLR 292, [2000] HRLR 646, [2000] UKHRR 875 the Divisional Court described the candour argument, which was there being used in support of the decision to hold in private an inquiry into a series of deaths caused by a NHS medical practitioner, as 'plainly now what might be described as a diminishing minority point of view, incapable in the circumstances of this case, where no vulnerable witnesses are apparently involved, of standing up to the weight of the arguments in favour of an open inquiry.'

79 The antiphrasis presumably unintentional.

80 For which see, for example: *Tweed v Parades Commission for NI* [2007] 1 AC 650 and see *Dept of Health v IC and Lewis* [2017] EWCA Civ 374, [2017] 1 WLR 3330 at [25]-[29].

81 *Lord Baker of Dorking v IC and DCLG*, IT, 1 June 2007 at [19]; *DfES v IC and The Evening Standard*, IT, 19 February 2007 at [74]; *Guardian Newspapers Ltd v IC and BBC*, IT, 8 January 2007 at [115].

31– 013 Government policy: scope

In earlier decisions, the tribunal took the view that the phrases 'relates to' and 'formulation and development of policy' should be given a reasonably broad interpretation.[82] By way of example, if a meeting or a discussion of a particular topic within it was as a whole caught by s 35(1)(a) activities, then everything that was said and done would be covered by s 35.[83] Further, the immediate factual background to policy discussions would itself be caught by s 35(1)(a).[84] The Court of Appeal has signalled a more restrictive approach, citing a later tribunal decision that the phrase 'should not be read with uncritical liberalism as extending to the furthest stretch of its indeterminacy, but instead must be read in a more limited sense so as to provide an intelligible boundary, suitable to the statutory context', and 'a merely incidental connection between the information and a matter specified in a sub-paragraph of section 35(1) would not bring the exemption into play; it is the content of the information that must relate to the matter specified in the sub-paragraph.'[85]

31– 014 Government policy: terminology

There are two grey areas in relation to the limb, at least at its extremities:

(1) in determining what is and what is not 'policy'; and

(2) in determining when the 'formulation or development' of policy starts and ends.

In relation to the first area, the wording of the limb appears to contemplate a dichotomy between 'policy' decisions and operational decisions made by government departments, with information relating to the latter falling outside of the scope of the exemption. As was recognised at the time of the Bill, however, the distinction will not always be clear,[86] and this is borne out by those occasions on which the word has been subject to judicial consideration.[87] In *Department for Education and Skills v Information Commissioner and Evening Standard*, the Tribunal recognised that s 35(2) appeared to envisage policy being formulated as a series of decisions

---

82 *DfES v IC and The Evening Standard*, IT, 19 February 2007 at [52]-[53]. In *O'Brien v IC and DBERR*, IT, 7 October 2008, the Tribunal held (at [20]) that information does not have to come into existence before the policy is formed for s 35(1)(a) to apply. See also *APPGER v IC and FCO* [2013] UKUT 0560 (AAC) at [125], [127], citing *OGC v IC* [2008] EWHC 774 (Admin), [2010] QB 98, [2008] ACD 54 and *HM Treasury v IC* [2009] EWHC 1811 (Admin), [2010] QB 563.

83 *DfES v IC and The Evening Standard*, IT, 19 February 2007 at [58].

84 A conclusion said to be supported by s 35(4): *DfES v IC and The Evening Standard*, IT, 19 February 2007 at [55].

85 *Dept of Health v IC and Lewis* [2017] EWCA Civ 374, [2017] 1 WLR 3330 at [13], citing *Dept of Health v IC and Lewis*, FTT, 17 March 2014 at [28]-[29]. The Upper Tribunal's decision is *Dept of Health v IC and Lewis* [2015] UKUT 0159 (AAC).

86 The breadth of the exemption under s 35(1)(a) was objected to in Parliament: see, eg, Hansard HL vol 618 col 276 (24 October 2000). The Campaign for Freedom of Information described the exemption under s 35(1)(a) of FOIA as a 'gigantic' class exemption: see col 278.

87 In *Bushell v Secretary of State for the Environment* [1981] AC 75, which involved consideration of the refusal by an Inspector at a public inquiry into the construction of certain motorways to permit certain questions by way of cross-examination, Lord Diplock (at 98B) said: '"Policy" as descriptive of departmental decisions to pursue a particular course of conduct is a protean word and much confusion in the instant case has, in my view, been caused by the failure to define the sense in which it can properly be used to describe a topic which is unsuitable to be the subject of an investigation as to the merits at an inquiry at which only persons with local interests affected by the scheme are entitled to be represented. A decision to construct a nationwide network of motorways is clearly one of government policy in the widest sense of the word.' Lord Edmund Davies said (at 115D)'…matters of policy are matters which involve the exercise of political judgment, and matters of fact and expertise do not become "policy" merely because a department of government relies on them.' In *Auckland Regional Council v North Shore City Council* [1995] 3 NZLR 18 at 23 the New Zealand Court of Appeal expressed similar sentiments in attempting to ascertain the meaning of the word 'policy' in the Resources Management Act 1991: 'It is obvious that in ordinary present-day speech a policy may be either flexible or inflexible, either broad or narrow. Honesty is said to be the best policy. Most people would prefer to take some discretion in implementing it, but if applied remorselessly it would not cease to be a policy. Counsel for the defendants are on unsound ground in suggesting that in everyday speech or in parliamentary drafting or in etymology, policy cannot include something highly specific.'

rather than a continuing process of evolution.[88] This was confirmed in *Secretary of State for Work and Pensions v Information Commissioner* which found that on the facts of that case the two stage decision and policy formulation process could be considered separately at each stage rather than as a continuum.[89] In relation to the second area, s 35(2) recognises that at some identifiable point a decision will be taken as to government policy such that it can no longer be said to be being formulated or developed. In *Department for Education and Skills v Information Commissioner and Evening Standard*, the Tribunal stated that when the formulation or development of a particular policy is complete is a question of fact.[90] The Tribunal concluded that:

> ... a parliamentary statement announcing the policy... will normally mark the end of the process of formulation. There may be some interval before development. We do not imply by that that any public interest in maintaining the exemption disappears the moment that a minister rises to his or her feet in the House... each case must be decided in the light of the circumstances. As is plain however, we do not regard a "seamless web" approach to policy as a helpful guide to the question whether discussions on formulation are over.[91]

More recently in *Department of Health v IC and Healey*, FTT, 5 April 2012 the Tribunal considered the Commissioner's revised Guidance on s 35 which accepted that:

> with the classic policy formulation process of turning a White Paper into actual legislation, the formulation of policy can be ongoing right up to the Bill receiving Royal Assent.[92]

The Tribunal concluded that:[93]

> We are prepared to accept that there is no straight line between formulation and development and delivery and implementation. ... a need for policy review and development may arise from implementation issues which in themselves require Ministers to make decisions giving rise to policy formulation and development. We therefore understand why the UCL report describes the process as a 'continuous circle' certainly until a Bill receives the Royal Assent.

Following from this, information relating to a review of the practical efficacy of a policy already in place may be characterised as representing information relating to the development of that policy.[94]

31– 015 Policy: public interest

As noted above, the public interest generally said to be embraced by this head of exemption is that disclosure of the deliberative process whilst it is being undertaken will cramp the ability of those engaging in it to freely explore the full range of options, including toying with the presently unthinkable.[95] The Tribunal recognised the need for 'a safe space' for government

---

88 *DfES v IC and The Evening Standard*, IT, 19 February 2007 at [57]. Similarly: *DWP v IC*, IT, 5 March 2007 at [56], [100]; *Office of Commerce v IC*, IT, 2 May 2007 at [56] (where the Tribunal drew a distinction between information relating to policy formulation or review and information concerned with implementation and delivery of those policies).

89 *DWP v IC*, IT, 5 March 2007 at [56].

90 *DfES v IC and The Evening Standard*, IT, 19 February 2007 at [75(v)].

91 *DfES v IC and The Evening Standard*, IT, 19 February 2007 at [75(v)]. See also §31– 015 below.

92 This is based on the research commissioned by the Commissioner from the Constitution Unit at University College London Understanding the Formulation and Development of Government Policy in the context of FOI June 2009 at [3.28] and [4.35] which noted that 'a strong trend in recent years has been to regard attention to delivery issues as an integral part of policy making and not something to be managed separately.....more attention is now paid in policy formulation to delivery issues and the managerial issues associated with policies are given far greater attention. Much modern theory of policy making also emphasises how far policy development is a continuous circle involving delivery and implementation as part of the process and not an afterthought.'

93 At [28]. The tribunal went on to say (at [28]): 'Critically the strength of the public interest for maintaining the exemption depends on the public interest balance at the time the safe space is being required.'

94 See, for example, *Plowden and FCO v IC*, FTT, 21 May 2012; on appeal *FCO v IC and Plowden* [2013] UKUT 275 (AAC).

95 See the quotations at §31– 008. The fact that the 'thinking' has been thought worthy of articulation and then of

officials to consider policy options:

> We consider that during the progress of a government introducing a new policy that the need for a safe space will change during the course of a Bill. For example while policy is being formulated at a time of intensive consultation during the initial period when policy is formed and finalised the need for a safe space will be at its highest. Once the policy is announced this need will diminish but while the policy is being debated in Parliament it may be necessary for the government to further develop the policy, and even undertake further public consultation, before the Bill reflects the government's final position on the new policy as it receives the Royal Assent. Therefore there may be a need to, in effect, dip in and out of the safe space during this passage of time so government can continue to consider its options. There may also come a time in the life of an Act of Parliament when the policy is reconsidered and a safe space is again needed. Such a need for policy review and development may arise from implementation issues which in themselves require Ministers to make decisions giving rise to policy formulation and development.
>
> ....the need for safe spaces during this process depends on the facts and circumstances in each case. Critically the strength of the public interest for maintaining the exemption depends on the public interest balance at the time the safe space is being required.[96]

The Government described the adverse effects said to flow from such disclosure as being the loss of frankness and candour, a danger of government by cabal, the damaging effect of disclosure on difficult policy decisions, an impact on record-keeping and damage to relations between civil servants and ministers and to the role of civil servants in the formation of policy.[97] These consequences are often referred to as the 'chilling effect' that such disclosure is claimed

---

being recorded in some form distinguishes it from the thinking and general discussion which generally precede the preparation of drafts, option statements and the like. It may be thought that the fact of something having been thought worthy of recording and official retention indicates that it has taken more definite form than the mere thoughts and discussion leading to it.

96 *Department of Health v IC and Healey*, FTT, 5 April 2012. The notion supposes some danger in the disclosure of the information from which the officials need protection.

97 *DfES v IC and The Evening Standard*, IT, 19 February 2007 at [35] (by way of evidence given by the former Cabinet Secretary and head of the civil service, Lord Turnbull). In *Office of Commerce v IC*, IT, 2 May 2007 Counsel for the public authority enumerated 14 types of adverse effect which were said would be likely to result should 'gateway review' reports become routinely discloseable soon after publication. A 'gateway review' is a review of a public delivery programme or procurement project carried out at a key decision point by a team of people independent of the team running the project: the objective of the review process is to secure best value for money in government procurement by examination of projects at critical stages through their life-cycle. The Tribunal (at [81]) rejected these collectively as being tantamount to a claim for absolute class exemption. Reiterating its stance in the *DWP* and *DfES* decisions in recognising 'that Government needs to operate in a safe space to protect information in the early stages of policy formulation and development', the Tribunal found (at [85]) that the public interest was not in the maintenance of the exemption because the critical decision (namely, to introduce identity cards) had already been taken, a Bill had been presented to Parliament and was being debated publicly: 'We therefore find that in the circumstances of this case it was no longer so important to maintain the safe space at the time of the requests.' That part of the Tribunal's decision was upheld by Stanley Burnton J in *OGC v IC* [2008] EWHC 774 (Admin), [2010] QB 98, [2008] ACD 54 at [100]-[101]. The Tribunal has declared itself unimpressed by claims that the risk of disclosure would have a chilling effect on the ability of Ministers to consider the full range of policy options and on the ability of civil servants to provide full and frank advice to Ministers: *HM Treasury v IC*, IT, 7 November 2007 at [61]-[63] and *ECGD v IC and Campaign Against Arms Trade*, IT, 21 October 2009 at [79]-[80]. The Tribunal has taken a similarly sceptical approach to assertions that a risk of disclosure would have an inhibiting effect upon lobbyists: see *MOD v IC and Evans*, IT, 20 July 2007 at [31], [33]-[34] and *DBERR v IC and Friends of the Earth*, IT, 29 April 2008 [113]-[134], and on non-civil servant Ministerial advisers, see *Cabinet Office v IC*, IT, 21 October 2008 at [29]-[30], and (in the context of the EIR) *SS for Transport v IC*, IT, 5 May 2009 at [124]-[126]. In *Cabinet Office v IC and Aitchison* [2013] UKUT 0526 (AAC) the Upper Tribunal said that 'it is open to argument at least in some contexts that the chilling effect is a positive, not a negative, point' (at [93], in a case in which the information related to a decision that was the product of a quasi-judicial function). On the other hand, Mitting J in *ECGD v Friends of the Earth* [2008] EWHC 638 (Admin), [2008] Env LR 40, [2008] JPL 1813 (at [38]) was readier to accept departmental prognostications in support of their claims for exemption, stating that 'there is a legitimate public interest in maintaining the confidentiality of advice within and between government departments on matters that will ultimately result, or are expected ultimately to result, in a ministerial decision. The weight to be given to those considerations will vary from case to case… But I can state with confidence that the cases in which it will not be appropriate to give any weight to those considerations will, if they exist at all, be few and far between' [38]. The notion of 'confidentiality of advice' within a public authority or between public authorities such as to weaken the rights conferred by FOIA is not without difficulty.

will have on government.[98] Whether because of their self-serving, counter-factual nature or otherwise, later tribunal decisions showed less inclination to accept these assertions. In *Department of Health v IC and Lewis*,[99] in upholding the Commissioner's decision to disclose the Ministerial Diary of the Secretary of State for Health, the Upper Tribunal highlighted what it called the 'weakness' in arguments for non-disclosure based on the need for candour:

> The lack of a right guaranteeing non-disclosure of information, absent consent, means that that information is at risk of disclosure in the overall public interest (ie when the public interest in disclosure outweighs the public interest in non-disclosure). As soon as this qualification is factored into the candour argument (or the relevant parts of the safe space or chilling effect arguments), it is immediately apparent that it highlights a weakness in it. This is because the argument cannot be founded on an expectation that the relevant communications will not be so disclosed. It follows that if he is properly informed, a person taking part in the discussions will appreciate that the greater the public interest in the disclosure of confidential, candid and frank exchanges, the more likely it is that they will be disclosed.

The Upper Tribunal went on to say that whenever any argument in favour of non-disclosure is relied upon then, without evidence addressing this 'weakness,' it is likely to be 'flawed.' There can be a public interest in withholding information relating to the formulation or development of government policy after completion of the policy formulation or development process.[100] But in that situation it will be for the public authority to provide evidence of the facts and circumstances to support the claim that disclosure of information relating to past policy-making will or might adversely impinge on current or future discussions.[101]

31– 016 Public interest technique

In *Department for Education and Skills v Information Commissioner and Evening Standard*,[102] the Tribunal set out the following principles to be applied to disclosure where information falls within s 35 and the public authority claims that the public interest in maintaining that exemption outweighs the public interest in disclosure:

> (i) The central question in every case is the content of the particular information in question. Every decision is specific to the particular facts and circumstances under consideration. Whether there may be significant indirect and wider consequences from the particular disclosure must be considered case by case.[103]
>
> (ii) No information within s 35(1) is exempt from the duty of disclosure simply on account of its status, of its classification as minutes or advice to a minister nor of the seniority of those whose actions are recorded.
>
> (iii) … the purpose of confidentiality, where the exemption is to be maintained, is the protection from compromise or unjust public opprobrium of civil servants, not

98 *ECGD v Friends of the Earth* [2008] EWHC 638 (Admin), [2008] Env LR 40, [2008] JPL 1813 at [38].

99 *Dept of Health v IC and Lewis* [2015] UKUT 0159 (AAC). The decision went to appeal: *Dept of Health v IC and Lewis* [2017] EWCA Civ 374, [2017] 1 WLR 3330.

100 *DEFRA v IC and Badger Trust* [2014] UKUT 0526 (AAC) at [52]-[53]; *Cabinet Office v IC and Webber* [2018] UKUT 410 (AAC) at [22].

101 *Cabinet Office v IC and Webber* [2018] UKUT 410 (AAC) at [33].

102 *DfES v IC and The Evening Standard*, IT, 19 February 2007 at [75]. The Tribunal (at [66]) expressly rejected a statement of Lord Falconer that 'information of this nature should be disclosed only where it is in the public interest to do so' on the basis that it inverted the public interest test in FOIA s 2(2)(b). The Tribunal has since applied the reasoning in the *DfES* decision: *HM Treasury v IC*, IT, 7 November 2007 at [58]-[64]; *Scotland Office v IC*, IT, 5 August 2008 [47]-[73]; *Cabinet Office v IC*, IT, 21 October 2008 at [35]-[38]; *Bowden Consulting Ltd v IC and Cabinet Office*, IT, 26 August 2009 at [46]-[54]. See also *O'Brien v IC and DBERR*, IT, 7 October 2008 [37]-[39], a decision upheld in part by Wyn Williams J (he rejected a challenge to the Tribunal's reasoning in relation to s 35) in *DBERR v O'Brien and IC* [2009] EWHC 164 (QB) at [21]-[33].

103 A passage approved by Mitting J in *ECGD v Friends of the Earth* [2008] EWHC 638 (Admin), [2008] Env LR 40, [2008] JPL 1813 at [28].

ministers … we were unable to discern the unfairness in exposing an elected politician, after the event, to challenge for having rejected a possible policy option in favour of a policy which is alleged to have failed.

(iv) The timing of a request is of particular importance to the decision. We fully accept the … argument … that disclosure of discussions of policy options, whilst policy is in the process of formulation, is highly unlikely to be in the public interest, unless, for example, it would expose wrongdoing within government. Ministers and officials are entitled to time and space, in some instances to considerable time and space, to hammer out policy by exploring safe and radical policies alike …

(v) If the information requested is not in the public domain, we do not regard publication of other information relating to the same topic for consultation, information or other purposes as a significant factor in a decision as to disclosure.

(vii) In judging the likely consequences of disclosure on officials' future conduct, we are entitled to expect of them the courage and independence that has been the hallmark of our civil servants … These are highly educated and sophisticated public servants who well understand the importance of their impartial role as counsellors to ministers of conflicting convictions …

(viii) … there may be good reason in some cases for withholding the names of… junior civil servants who would never expect their roles to be exposed to public gaze. These are questions to be decided on the particular facts, not by blanket policy…

(ix) ....

(x) ....

(xi) A blanket policy of refusing to disclose the names of civil servants wherever they appear in departmental records cannot be justified because, in many cases disclosure will do no harm to anyone, even if it does little good… There must… be a specific reason for omitting the name of the official where the document is otherwise disclosable. That reason may not need to be utterly compelling where, as will often be the case, there is little or no public interest in learning the name.

The Tribunal expressly rejected the notion that disclosing the names of the civil servants involved in making policy recommendations would prejudice them or their future role in the civil service.[104] Similarly, the Tribunal rejected the notion that the 'level' of a policy document could by itself provide support for the maintenance of the exemption:

> Is the very status of these minutes, the fact that they record meetings of the most senior officials discussing the funding issue, a factor which supports the maintenance of the exemption? In our view, it is not. It may, in some or many cases, increase the sensitivity of the matters minuted, disclosing, for example, whilst policy is being reviewed, that radical options are being discussed at a very high level. If it does, that will be a factor which can properly be taken into consideration when a government department is confronted with an FOIA request. To treat such status as automatically conferring exemption would be tantamount to inventing within s 35(1) a class of absolutely exempt information, for which

[104] At [68]. See also, in the context of FOIA s 36, *MoD v IC and Evans*, IT, 20 July 2007, in which the Tribunal stated 'those persons who expend public money must in general terms be expected to stand up and account for the activities they carry out in so doing' [60], and see [61]-[62]. But that does not mean that in all instances their names should be disclosed: see, eg, *DWP v IC*, IT, 5 March 2007 at [94]. In *DBERR v IC and Friends of the Earth*, IT, 29 April 2008 the Tribunal stated (at [101]):

> (a) Senior officials of both the government department and lobbyists attending meetings and communicating with each other can have no expectation of privacy.
>
> (b) The officials to whom this principle applies should not be restricted to the senior spokesperson for the organisation. It should also relate to any spokesperson.
>
> (c) Recorded comments attributed to such officials at meetings should similarly have no expectation of privacy or secrecy.
>
> (d) In contrast, junior officials, who are not spokespersons for their organisations or merely attend meetings as observers or stand-ins for more senior officials should have an expectation of privacy. This means that there may be circumstances where junior officials who act as spokespersons for their organisations are unable to rely on an expectation of privacy.
>
> (e) The question as to whether a person is acting in a senior or junior capacity or as a spokesperson is one to be determined on the facts of each case…

> the subsection gives no warrant and is a stance which the DFES quite rightly disclaimed. However, we do not consider that the matter ends there. We agree with the DFES submission that the weighing of the public interests involves in this case a consideration of any evidence of a wider impact on the conduct of government which might result from the Commissioner's decision – Lord Turnbull's "secondary signals." That conclusion seems to us to flow from the introductory words of s 2(2)(b) quoted above, "in all the circumstances of the case". They include indirect consequences.[105]

In *Secretary of State for Work and Pensions v Information Commissioner*[106] the Tribunal asked two questions in order to determine the public interest in the information being disclosed. First, what is the intrinsic value of the information? Where the intrinsic value of the information is greater, then the weightier is the public interest in maintaining the exemption.[107] Secondly, how relevant is the information to assist the public in understanding Government thinking on the relevant issue?[108]

31–017 Ministerial communications

The second limb of s 35(1) renders material exempt information if it relates to 'ministerial communications'. That phrase is defined to mean any communications between Ministers of the Crown; or between Northern Ireland Ministers, including Northern Ireland junior Ministers; or between Assembly Secretaries, including the Assembly Secretary.[109] The term also includes, in particular, proceedings of the Cabinet or of any committee of the Cabinet, proceedings of the Executive Committee of the Northern Ireland Assembly, and proceedings of the Executive Committee of the National Assembly for Wales. 'Northern Ireland junior Minister' is itself defined to mean a member of the Northern Ireland Assembly appointed as a junior Minister under s 19 of the Northern Ireland Act 1998.[110] It is to be noted that the exemption is for information that 'relates to' ministerial communications.[111] As the number of degrees of remove between the information in question and the original ministerial communication increases, it will become harder to maintain that the information 'relates to' the ministerial communication.[112]

31–018 Communications: public interest

This exemption has no analogous exemption in any of the comparative jurisdictions. The exemption presents peculiar difficulties so far as the public interest is concerned. Save for the effect of s 2, the exemption effectively takes out of the access regime all information relating to ministerial communications, irrespective of their content, irrespective of the harmlessness of their disclosure and irrespective of the origins of the information itself. This removal of a class of information that, on its face, has no characteristic requiring it to be cloaked in secrecy may be thought to be antithetical to the purpose of the Act.[113] The Secretary of State for the Home

105 At [69]-[70]. In *DWP v IC*, IT, 5 March 2007 at [82] the Tribunal reiterated that there is no necessary harm in the disclosure of information falling within s 35(1). In *FCO v IC and Friends of the Earth*, IT, 29 June 2007 a differently constituted Tribunal said that it was 'loath to regard that [ie that information could be exempt merely because of the seniority of those whose actions are recorded] as a principle of general application' at [42].

106 *DWP v IC*, IT, 5 March 2007.

107 *DWP v IC*, IT, 5 March 2007 at [85] and [108].

108 *DWP v IC*, IT, 5 March 2007 at [108].

109 FOIA s 35(5).

110 FOIA s 35(5).

111 See *O'Brien v IC and DBERR*, IT, 7 October 2008 at [20]; *Dept for Culture, Media & Sport v IC*, FTT, 22 February 2010 at [16].

112 See §31–009.

113 See §§1–014 to 1–020 and §31–015.

Department began the second reading speech for the Bill thus:

> Unnecessary secrecy in Government and our public services has long been held to undermine good governance and public administration, and my party has long been committed to change. At the last election, our manifesto stated: "We are pledged to a Freedom of Information Act, leading to more open government." The Bill will make that promise a reality. The Bill, by its first clause, lays down for the first time in our constitutional history that the public have a right to know about the work of Government and all other public authorities. Again for the first time, that right of access to information will be enforced by an independent Information Commissioner and an Information Tribunal with clear powers to override the decisions of Ministers or any other public authority as to whether information should be released. Moreover, the Bill will not only provide legal rights for the public and place legal duties on Ministers and public authorities, but will help to transform the culture of Government from one of secrecy to one of openness. It will transform the default setting from "this should be kept quiet unless" to "this should be published unless." By doing so, it should raise public confidence in the processes of government, and enhance the quality of decision making by the Government.[114]

A full reconciliation of this sentiment with the terms of s 35(1)(b) is only possible through the public interest balancing exercise prescribed in s 2 of the Act.[115] Against the backdrop of FOIA having set its face against non-disclosure of official information without objectively good reason and of s 35(1)(b) not having been made an absolute exemption, the decision-maker must identify the public interest which is served by maintaining an exemption for information whose only required attribute is that it relates to Ministerial communications. It will not be permissible to elevate the limb into a de facto absolute exemption by alighting on characteristics that invariably attend a Ministerial communication. In *Scotland Office v IC*, the Tribunal held that the principles established in *Department for Education and Skills v Information Commissioner and Evening Standard*[116] have 'considerable relevance' in the case of information falling within s 35(1)(b) as well as s 35(1)(a).[117] In *Cabinet Office v Information Commissioner* the Upper Tribunal held that there was no 'inherent weight' in favour of non-disclosure by reason of the fact that information fell within s 35(1)(b).[118] Any assessment of the significance of confidentiality in ministerial communications must be realistic:

> There is surely no one who believes that all ministers agree with all Government policy or that there are no compromises. It is a truth universally recognised that their collective responsibility is a stance...It is tempting to argue that any disclosure will undermine the confidentiality of ministerial communications. In a sense, that is right, but misses two points. First, it misses the point that the convention is now qualified by the possibility of disclosure. Second, it misses the point that section 2(2)(b) [of FOIA] requires a comparative exercise...[119]

31– 019 Cabinet: public interest

To the extent that such information would reveal the proceedings of the Cabinet, etc the public interest question may be fairly readily answered: the purpose served by the secrecy attaching to the records of Cabinet proceedings is long and widely recognised and reflects the need to protect the principle of collective responsibility,[120] which is also specifically protected in

---

114 Hansard HC vol 340 col 714 (7 December 1999).

115 See the introductory remarks at §31– 003.

116 IT, 19 February 2007 at [75].

117 IT, 5 August 2008 at [79]. See further §30– 013 above. The principles have also been applied to the EIR reg 12(4)(d)-(e): *Secretary of State for Transport v IC*, IT, 5 May 2009 at [105].

118 *Cabinet Office v IC* [2014] UKUT 0461 (AAC) at [69].

119 *Dept for Education v IC and Whitmey* [2018] UKUT 348 (AAC) at [12]-[14].

120 See *Cabinet Office v IC and Aitchison* [2013] UKUT 0526 (AAC) at [81]-[83]. The Tribunal should have regard to the Ministerial Code, quoted in *Aitchson* at [81]. In terms of its provenance, see *Conway v Rimmer* [1968] AC 910

s 36(2)(a)(i). This will be particularly compelling in relation to information that reveals the actual deliberations within Cabinet, but may be less compelling in relation to reports or submissions prepared for the assistance of Cabinet[121] or where the decision is known to be one for a Minister exercising a specific statutory function rather than one involving several Ministries or the Government generally.[122] Otherwise, however, the public interest in maintaining the exemption is not readily divined.[123] For these reasons it is very rare that the Tribunal will order the disclosure of cabinet minutes.[124] In one case where such minutes were ordered to be disclosed, the Tribunal[125] concluded:

- By reason of the convention of collective responsibility,[126] Cabinet minutes are always information of great sensitivity, which will usually outlive the particular administration, often by many years.
- The general interest in maintaining the exemption in respect of them is therefore always substantial. Disclosure within 30 years[127] will very rarely be ordered and then

at 952 and *AG v Jonathan Cape Ltd* [1976] QB 752. Similar statements are made in the comparative jurisdictions, apart from the USA: *AG v Hamilton* [1993] 2 IR 250 at 266; *Egan v Chadwick* [1999] NSWCA 176, (1999) 46 NSWLR 563 esp at 573-576 and at 589-592, which sets out a very useful history of the convention and its rationale.

121 *Commonwealth v Northern Land Council* (1993) 176 CLR 604; *Commonwealth v Construction, Forestry, Mining and Energy Union* (2000) 98 FCR 31; *Egan v Chadwick* [1999] NSWCA 176, (1999) 46 NSWLR 563; *Northern Australian Aboriginal Legal Service v Bradley* [2001] FCA 1080; *National Tertiary Education Industry Union v Commonwealth of Australia* [2001] FCA 610, (2001) 111 FCR 583. This is on the basis that disclosure of the actual deliberations will almost inevitably be inconsistent with the doctrine of collective responsibility, whereas disclosure of reports or submissions may not.

122 *Cabinet Office v IC and Aitchison* [2013] UKUT 0526 (AAC) at [62], [85].

123 This passage was considered by the Tribunal in *Scotland Office v IC*, IT, 5 August 2008. The Tribunal stated (at [78]): 'we do see some force in the argument... that the factors in favour of maintaining the exemption for some types of information in this category will, almost always, be strong and that "very cogent and compelling" reasons for disclosure would be needed before the balance tips in favour of disclosure in those situations. This is not to turn the public interest test around, or to say that just because the exemption is engaged that is a factor weighing against disclosure, but recognises the weight that should be given to the public interest factors for maintaining the exemption.'

124 In *All Party Parliamentary Group on Extraordinary Rendition v IC and FCO*, FTT, 3 May 2012 the Tribunal stated at [146] 'we consider Blake J [in *HM Treasury v IC* [2009] EWHC 1811 (Admin)] was referring to the combination of specificity and convention as establishing a strong weight in favour of maintaining the Law Officer exemption.' Both these ingredients seem to be applicable to this exemption where the convention on collective responsibility of ministers is relevant.

125 *Cabinet Office v IC*, FTT, 13 September 2010 at [46].

126 The convention is explained at [34]:

> It is a principle underlying cabinet government which has been recognised for at least one hundred and fifty years. Bagehot acknowledged its significance. Its importance grew as the Monarch's control of and influence over his or her ministers weakened and they closed ranks against royal attempts to weaken them by promoting division. It gained recognition as a fundamental requirement of effective and cohesive government. A useful recent account of its development and significance is to be found in House of Commons Library Research paper 4/82, published on 15 November 2004. Its requirements are set out today in the Ministerial Code, which has been published with modifications since 1992. Paragraph 2.1 provides :
>
> > The principle of collective responsibility, save where it is explicitly set aside, requires that ministers should be able to express their views frankly in the expectation that they can argue freely in private while maintaining a united front when decisions have been reached. This in turn requires that the privacy of opinions expressed in Cabinet and Ministerial Committees, including in correspondence, should be maintained.

The Tribunal considered at [35] the convention had two related aspects: The requirement that all ministers of every rank publicly support collective decisions of the Cabinet and Cabinet committees, suppressing any private dissent, whether or not they were party to such decisions ('the primary aspect'). The principle that the content of discussions, including the expression of divergent opinions, leading to such decisions will remain confidential. That imposes a duty of silence on ministers and others with access to the content of such discussions, notably special advisers and civil servants ('the secondary duty'). It is this latter aspect of the convention which is affected by s 1 of FOIA. See also §§31– 030 to 31– 031 below.

127 Now 20 years, subject to transitional arrangements: see §36– 010. In *Cabinet Office v IC and Aitchison* [2013] UKUT 0526 (AAC) the Upper Tribunal held that it was permissible when carrying out the public interest balancing exercise in relation to information more than 20 years old but caught by the earlier regime to take heed of the

only in circumstances where it involves no apparent threat to the cohesive working of Cabinet government, whether now or in the future.

– Such circumstances may involve the passage of time, whereby the ministers involved have left the public stage and they and their present and future successors know that such disclosure will not embarrass them during the critical phase of an active political career.
– Publication of memoirs and ministerial statements describing the meeting(s) concerned may weaken the case for withholding the information, especially where versions conflict, either factually ... or in their interpretation of what took place.
– The fact that the issues discussed in Cabinet have no continuing significance may weaken to a slight degree the interest in maintaining the exemption but the importance of the convention is not dependent upon the nature of the issue which provoked debate.
– There is always a significant public interest in reading the impartial record of what was transacted in Cabinet, no matter what other accounts of it have reached the public domain. Where the usual interest in maintaining confidentiality has been significantly weakened, that interest may justify disclosure.
– The public interest in disclosure will be strengthened where the Cabinet meeting had a particular political or historical significance, for example the discussion of the invasion of Iraq at the meeting under consideration in *Cabinet Office v IC & Lamb.*[128]

31– 020 Advice from a Law Officer

The third limb of s 35(1) renders material exempt information if it relates to the provision of advice by any of the 'Law Officers' or any request for the provision of such advice. The phrase the 'Law Officers' is defined to mean the Attorney-General, the Solicitor-General, the Advocate General for Scotland, the Lord Advocate, the Solicitor-General for Scotland and the Attorney-General for Northern Ireland.[129] This exemption will inevitably overlap with the exemption for information in respect of which a claim to legal professional privilege could be maintained.[130] It extends the scope of protection by picking up information that might not be privileged itself: for example, because it merely recounts or relays legal advice received. The public interest in the maintenance of this exemption is akin to the public interest in maintaining the exemption for information in respect of which a claim to legal professional privilege could be maintained.[131] It has long been a convention within Government that neither the fact of having sought the opinion of the Law Officers of the Crown, nor the content of that advice, is disclosed without the Law Officers' consent. In relation to the former, in *HM Treasury v IC*[132] Blake J held that 'Parliament intended real weight should continue to be afforded to this aspect of the Law Officers' Convention', and that 'the general considerations of good government underlining the history and nature of the convention were capable of affording weight to the interest in maintaining an exemption even in the absence of particular damage.'[133] Blake J held that the FOIA had preserved the Convention, but rendered it amenable to being outweighed by greater considerations of the public interest requiring disclosure of information in either limb

reduction in years for which Parliament now considers the exemption to apply (at [40]-[43]).

128 *Cabinet Office v IC and Lamb*, IT, 27 January 2009.

129 FOIA s 35(5).

130 FOIA s 42; FOI(S)A s 36(1); *Savic v IC and Attorney-General* [2016] UKUT 534, 535 (AAC) at [27]. See Chapter 30.

131 See §§30– 018 to 30– 021.

132 [2009] EWHC 1811 (Admin), [2010] 2 WLR 931. On appeal from the decision of the Tribunal in *HM Treasury v IC*, IT, 15 May 2008.

133 At [54].

of the Convention.[134]

31– 021 Private office operations

The final limb of s 35(1) renders material exempt information if it relates to the operation of any 'Ministerial private office'.[135] This phrase is defined to mean any part of a government department which provides personal administrative support to a Minister of the Crown, to a Northern Ireland Minister or a Northern Ireland junior Minister, or any part of the administration of the National Assembly for Wales providing personal administrative support to the Assembly First Secretary or an Assembly Secretary.[136] Most of the comparative jurisdictions remove such material from the operation of the legislation.[137] The policy underpinning this exemption is that information relating to the operation of a Minister's private office does not serve any of the purposes of the Act. On that basis, the public interest in disclosure of such information may be expected to be readily displaced by the public interest in maintaining the exemption.[138]

31– 022 Statistical information

Section 35(2) of FOIA provides that once a decision as to government policy has been taken, then any statistical information that has been used to provide 'an informed background' to that decision is to be taken out of the scope of the first two limbs of s 35(1).[139] In *Secretary of State for Work and Pensions v Information Commissioner*[140] the Tribunal approved the definition of 'statistical information' suggested in the MoJ Guidance, namely that it requires 'mathematical operations performed on a sample of observations or some other factual information'.[141] The fact that statistical information is at a certain point taken out of the scope of s 35 does not mean that that

---

134 At [54]. Applied in: *Cabinet Office v IC and Aitchison* [2013] UKUT 0526 (AAC) at [58]-[59]; *Savic v IC and Attorney-General* [2016] UKUT 534, 535 (AAC) at [36]-[37].

135 The phrase 'relates to' indicates more than a loose or consequential connection or a touching upon the matter: *Martin v Most* [2010] UKSC 10, 2010 SC (UKSC) 40 at [49], [159]. And similarly: *Imperial Tobacco Ltd v Lord Advocate* [2012] UKSC 61, 2013 SLT 2 at [16]; *Re Agricultural Sector (Wales) Bill* [2014] UKSC 43, [2014] 1 WLR 2622 at [50]; *Recovery of Medical Costs for Asbestos Diseases (Wales) Bill* [2015] UKSC 3, [2015] AC 1016 at [25]; *Christian Institute v Lord Advocate* [2016] UKSC 51, [2016] HRLR 19 at [29] (concerning the Data Protection Act 1998). In the context of FOIA the meaning of the phrase 'relates to' has been considered in: *Home Office v IC and Cobain*, FTT, 30 January 2013 at [15]-[19]; *Callus v IC and Home Office*, FTT, 6 May 2014 at [39]-[41]; *University and Colleges Admissions Service v IC and Lord Lucas* [2014] UKUT 0557 (AAC) at [44]-[46] (meaning of 'relates to' in FOIA s 7(5)); *Home Office v IC and Cobain* [2014] UKUT 0306 (AAC) at [39]; *All Party Parliamentary Group on Extraordinary Rendition v IC and FCO* [2015] UKUT 0377 (AAC) at [14]-[33]; *Reprieve v IC and FCO*, FTT, 26 April 2016 at [37]-[39]; *Corderoy and Ahmed v IC and Attorney General* [2017] UKUT 0495 (AAC) at [51] [54] and [59]-[62]; *Department of Health v IC and Lewis* [2017] EWCA Civ 374, [2017] 1 WLR 3330 at [13] (Sir Terence Etherton MR) (meaning of 'relates to' in FOIA s 35(1)).

136 FOIA s 5. The House of Commons Select Committee on Public Administration stated, in their *Third Report* (Cm 4355, 1999) para 89 that they did not believe that a class-based exemption for the operation of a private Ministerial office was appropriate. In their view, such information should be included within the scope of the prejudice-based exemption that is now to be found in s 36 of the FOIA.

137 In Australia, such material is excluded as a result of the definition of 'official document' in s 4 of the Freedom of Information Act 1982: see §51– 011. The definition of 'official information' in s 2 of the Official Information Act 1982 (New Zealand) excludes some, but not all, such information. The Freedom of Information Act 1997 (Ireland) s 46(1), treats such material as 'exempt records' and therefore outside the main operation of the Act: see §51– 035.

138 This may be illustrated by the decision of the Commissioner to order the disclosure of the ministerial diary of Andrew Lansley, the Secretary of State for Health, which was upheld by the FTT, Upper Tribunal and the Court of Appeal: *Dept of Health v IC and Lewis*, FTT, 17 March 2014; *Dept of Health v IC and Lewis* [2015] UKUT 0159 (AAC); *Dept of Health v IC and Lewis* [2017] EWCA Civ 374, [2017] 1 WLR 3330. A similar order for disclosure was made and upheld of the ministerial diary of Jeremy Hunt, another Secretary of State for Health: *Department of Health v IC*, FTT, 19 July 2018.

139 FOI(S)A s 29(2).

140 *DWP v IC*, IT, 5 March 2007 at [75]-[77].

141 MoJ, *Exemptions Guidance—Section 35*, 14 May 2008, p 9. Also adopted in *Makin v IC*, FTT, 24 January 2011 at [28].

information must be disclosed. Indeed, once exemption under s 35 drops away, the limitation imposed by the concluding words in s 36(1)(a) is disengaged, enabling the public authority to rely on this section to protect it from having to disclose to a member of the public any statistical information that it used to inform its policy decisions.[142] The subsection implies that statistical information can represent information relating to the formulation or development of government policy.

31– 023 Factual information

It is conventional for freedom of information legislation, when exempting policy deliberations from disclosure, to make some sort of exception for the factual material used in the course of those deliberations.[143] In introducing freedom of information legislation into Westminster, the Government indicated that it intended that as much as possible factual and background information gathered by public authorities in the process of devising policy and making decisions should be made publicly available.[144] Thus, the 1997 White Paper recorded that the protection which the Government envisaged would be imposed with respect to the disclosure of information relating to policy and public affairs was intended 'primarily to protect opinion and analytical information, not the raw data and factual background material which have contributed to the policy-making process'.[145] The White Paper promised that public authorities would be encouraged to make such information available, even where opinion and advice based upon it needed to remain confidential. Nonetheless, neither the draft Bill published in May 1999 nor the second draft introduced into Parliament on 18 November 1999 distinguished between policy information and advice, on the one hand, and factual or statistical background material on the other. Both versions of the Bill were heavily criticised for this. In its first Report on the May 1999 draft Bill, the House of Commons Select Committee on Public Administration recommended that the exemption for decision-making and policy formulation should 'specifically not be taken to apply to purely factual information held by public authorities, not to analysis, if that information has been created in order to inform policy decisions, and this distinction should be drawn clearly in the Bill.'[146] This position was also

---

142 See §31– 005. In relation to statistical information falling within the scope of s 36, the Commissioner has the power to review the decision not to disclose that information without being subject to the restriction that is applicable in respect of other kinds of information falling under s 36: namely, that that review must be limited to a consideration of whether the view of the relevant 'qualified person' that such information should not be disclosed was 'reasonable'. The Government conferred this broader power of review upon the Commissioner in respect of statistical information in order to underline its stated commitment to openness: Lord Falconer of Thoroton, Hansard HL vol 618 col 287 (24 October 2000).

143 In the United States, under the Freedom of Information Act, 1966, 5 USC 552(b)(5), the 'deliberative process privilege' does not include the underlying factual material: see §51– 008(5). The Freedom of Information Act 1982 (Cth of Australia) s 47C takes out of the 'deliberative process' exemption 'purely factual material:' see §51– 015(11). However, purely factual material within Cabinet records or records of the Executive Council remain within these exemptions: see §51– 015(1)-(2). The Official Information Act 1982 (New Zealand), bucks convention so as to retain an exemption for factual and statistical information. The New Zealand Law Commission, in its Review of the Official Information Act 1982, October 1997, saw no reason to change this. In Canada, factual material falls outside of the exemption provided by the Access to Information Act s 21(1): see §51– 032(4)-(5). The exemption provided by the Freedom of Information Act 1997 (Ireland) s 19(1), does not extend to factual material and the exemption provided by s 20 extends neither to factual information nor to statistical information: see §51– 039(1) and 51– 039(9).

144 Cabinet Office, *Your Right to Know: The Government's Proposals for a Freedom of Information Act* (Cm 3813, 1997) para 3.13.

145 Cabinet Office, *Your Right to Know: The Government's Proposals for a Freedom of Information Act* (Cm 3818, 1997) para 3.13.

146 House of Commons Select Committee on Public Administration, Third Report (Cm4355, 1999) para 93. The House of Lords Select Committee, in its *First Report on the Draft Freedom of Information Bill* (27 July 1999) accepted the arguments justifying a class-based exemption for policy advice, but agreed with the House of Commons Select Committee that policy advice should be distinguished from 'separable factual background' to that advice; and that 'such factual background should be exempt only if its disclosure "would substantially or would be likely substantially to prejudice the interests set forth in clause 28(3)"' — House of Lords, *Draft Freedom of Information Bill: First Report* (27 July 1999), para 34.

endorsed by the House of Lords Select Committee that commented on the Bill. Parliament, likewise, pressed strongly for a distinction between factual and statistical information, on the one hand, and policy information, on the other, to be made in the Bill, and for factual and statistical information to be excluded from the scope of the policy exemption.[147] The Government resisted these criticisms on the basis that, while factual material used to provide an informed background to decision-taking should be made available wherever possible, it could not be made available as of right, because:

> the dividing line between facts and opinions, or advice, is simply not that clear…There will be occasions where "facts" are part of the discussion or argumentation about options under consideration and where it will not be possible to disentangle facts from opinions or advice. On these occasions the disclosure of such information would, of itself, affect the decision-taking process. Thus there will be a need to withhold such information on a few occasions.[148]

The Government agreed, however, that greater openness could be achieved than the Bill allowed for[149] and amendments containing the provisions now to be found in ss 35(2)[150] and 35(4)[151] were introduced as a result.[152] It is to be noted that s 23(4) only comes into play when the first sub-section of s 35(1) is engaged (policy formulation) but does not apply to the other sub-sections.

31– 024 Factual information: technique

The approach taken by s 35(4) of FOIA is to exhort the decision-maker, when weighing the competing public interests in s 2, to have regard 'to the particular public interest in the disclosure of factual information which has been used, or is intended to be used, to provide an informed background to decision-making'.[153] This, of course, requires an identification of what is and what is not 'factual information'. As Wigmore observed at the outset of his treatise on evidence 'everything in the cosmos is a fact or a phenomenon'.[154] The phrase 'factual

---

147 Dr Tony Wright MP (Cannock Chase), for example, said in the course of the second reading of the second draft Bill 'We had discussions on the [first draft Bill] and the Home Secretary told the Select Committee on Public Administration that the "issue of factual or background information is important…and I think on the whole ought to be disclosed". Unfortunately, the Bill does not convert that desire into legislative provision, but I am heartened by the fact that it might still do that. …. We have a cumulative body of evidence which says that it is both desirable and practical to have such distinctions. However, the distinction is not made in the Bill, contrary to the developing practice to which I have pointed, and contrary to freedom of information regimes elsewhere, notably in New Zealand and Ireland. Hon members should be clear about what that means. It means that all information relating in any way to the development of policy—including purely factual background information—stands exempt. I simply do not believe that the House will allow that to be sustained. Clauses 33 and 34 [the precursors to ss 35 and 36] represent the hole in the centre of the Bill. At the very least, we need the facts, and an analysis of them...' — Hansard HC vol 340 col 753 (7 December 1999).

148 Lord Falconer of Thoroton, Hansard HL vol 612 col 827 (20 April 2000); Hansard HL vol 619 col 832 (22 November 2000). See also Jack Straw, Hansard HC vol 347 col 1027 (5 April 2000).

149 Lord Falconer of Thoroton, Hansard HL vol 618 col 287 (24 October 2000).

150 Lord Falconer of Thoroton, Hansard HL vol 618 col 287 (24 October 2000).

151 Hansard HL vol 619 col 147 (14 November 2000). The formulation contained in s 35(4) was preferred to various alternatives that were proposed which would have had the effect of excluding factual information altogether from the scope of the exemption now contained in s 35(1): see eg Hansard HC vol 347 col 997 (5 April 2000).

152 The amendment with respect to statistical information was welcomed in Parliament, but the majority of members of the House of Commons and House of Lords who spoke on the Bill continued to press for an exception from the exemption in respect of factual information, as well as statistical information: see, eg Hansard HL vol 618 cols 288–302.

153 In relation to information held by Scottish public authorities, FOI(S)A s 29(3). As an example of the provision in operation, see *DWP v IC*, IT, 5 March 2007 at [71]-[74], where the Tribunal noted that 'information can be characterised within a spectrum where pure advice was at one end of the spectrum and straight forward factual information at the other end of the spectrum....where information is firstly, so inextricably connected to the deliberative material that it is difficult to distinguish and secondly, where the vast weight of material is non factual information, we consider Parliament did not intend the sub-section to apply.'

154 JH Wigmore, *Treatise on the Anglo-American System of Evidence in Trials at Common Law*, 3rd edn (Boston, Little Brown,

information' is innately vague: whether an opinion is held is a matter of fact even if the opinion itself is not.[155] On the other hand, the choice of factual material and its presentation may constitute a matter of opinion,[156] just as the reaching of a conclusion or a view upon factual material may itself be a fact.[157] These complexities and distinctions are borne out by the comparative jurisprudence. In the United States, the Courts will normally allow agencies to withhold factual material in an otherwise 'deliberative' document in two situations. First, if a document comprises or includes a conscious selection of factual information out of a larger group of factual information, the act of selection of those facts is treated as deliberative in nature, entitling the selected facts to enjoy the deliberative process privilege exemption.[158] Secondly, factual information may be withheld in circumstances where it is so inextricably connected to the deliberative material that its disclosure would expose or cause harm to the agency's deliberations.[159]

31–025 The duty to confirm or deny

Section 35 also provides a corresponding qualified exclusion from the duty to confirm or deny.[160] The way in which the exclusion is worded is such that, if a given piece of information relating to the formulation of policy, etc is exempt information under s 35(1), then the corresponding duty to confirm or deny that the information is held does not arise. It should be noted that the public interest exercise differs for the two duties, so that even though the public interest may weigh in favour of maintaining the exemption from disclosure, it may nevertheless not weigh in favour of maintaining the exclusion of the duty to confirm or deny.

3. INFORMATION THE DISCLOSURE OF WHICH WOULD BE PREJUDICIAL TO PUBLIC AFFAIRS

31–026 Introduction

Section 36 of FOIA provides a further array of exemptions for what might loosely be described as information recording the deliberations of a public authority.[161] The scope and operation

---

1940), vol 1, p 1, para 1.

155 That there is no logical dichotomy between fact and opinion is recognised in the FOIA itself: s 36(2) and (7) involve a statutory transposition of fact and opinion.

156 The Federal Court of Australia in *Harris v Australian Broadcasting Corporation* (1984) 51 ALR 581 held that summaries of factual material could not be classified as 'purely factual material' for the purposes of s 47C (then, s 36) of the Freedom of Information Act 1982 if they were 'of such a character as to disclose a process of selection involving opinion, advice or recommendation for the purpose of the deliberative process'.

157 In *Harris v Australian Broadcasting Corporation* (1984) 51 ALR 581 the Federal Court held that 'conclusions expressed as findings' could be a statement of 'purely factual material notwithstanding it involves a conclusion based upon primary facts'.

158 *Montrose Chemical Corp v Train*, 491 F 2d 63, 66 (DC Cir 1974); *Mapother v Department of Justice*, 3 F(3d) 1533 (DC Cir 1993), where the Court held, in relation to a report which consisted of factual materials prepared for the Attorney-General's decision whether to allow former UN Secretary General Kurt Waldheim to enter the United States, that 'the majority of [the report's] factual material was assembled through an exercise of judgment in extracting pertinent material from a vast number of documents for the benefit of an official called upon to take discretionary action', and that it therefore fell within the deliberative process privilege. On the other hand, the Court held that a chronology of his military career was not deliberative, as it was 'neither more nor less than a comprehensive collection of the essential facts' and 'reflect[ed] no point of view'.

159 *Wolfe v United States Department of Health and Human Services*, 839 F 2d 768 (DC Cir 1988).

160 FOIA s 35(3).

161 Similarly, in relation to information held by Scottish public authorities, FOI(S)A s 30. The exemption is highly time-sensitive, in that the greater the passage of time between the creation of the information and the information request, the less force there is likely to be in an argument that the public interest in maintaining the exemption

of the provision varies according to the identity of the public authority holding the information:

— If the information is held by a government department or by the National Assembly for Wales and the information is exempt information by virtue of s 35, then s 36 is inapplicable.[162]
— If the information is held by the House of Commons or the House of Lords, then the exemption is an absolute exemption for the purposes of s 2(2)(a)[163] and provision is made for a conclusive certificate.[164]
— If the information is held by any other public authority, then the exemption is a qualified exemption and there is no provision for a conclusive certificate.

The section provides three overlapping heads of exemption, each of which requires a reasonable expectation of prejudice, or the likelihood of prejudice, to the interest protected by the head.[165] A similar exemption exists in each of the comparative jurisdictions except the United States of America.[166] Since the exemption in FOIA is prejudice-based as well as subject to a public interest override, it is the narrowest exemption of its type amongst the comparative

---

outweighs the public interest in disclosure: *Scottish Ministers v Scottish IC* [2007] CSIH 8, 2007 SCLR 253 at [16].

162 FOIA s 36(1)(a). As to the inter-relationship of the two provisions, see §31– 005. There is no equivalent restriction under the FOI(S)A.

163 FOIA s 2(3)(e). No analogous distinction is drawn in the FOI(S)A. The House of Commons Select Committee on Public Administration did not accept that the justification for the exclusion of Parliament from the right to official information had been made out. In their view, 'the exclusion of Parliament may well convey the wrong impression to the general public, given the purpose of this legislation' (*Third Report* (Cm 4355, 1999) para 37).

164 FOIA s 36(7). No provision is made for a conclusive certificate under s 30 of the FOI(S)A.

165 In *Guardian Newspapers Ltd and Heather Brooke v IC and BBC*, IT, 8 January 2007, the Tribunal interpreted the phrase 'would, or would be likely to' within s 36 (2)(b) as meaning 'inhibition would probably occur (ie on the balance of probabilities, the chance being greater than 50%) or that there would be a "very significant and weighty chance" that it would occur. A "real risk" is not enough; the degree of risk must be such that there "may very well be" such inhibition, even if the risk falls short of being more probable than not' (at [53]). See further §6– 022.

166 The Freedom of Information Act 1982 (Cth of Australia) s 34(1) provides a very broad exemption that embraces any record of Cabinet, a document brought into existence for the purpose of submission to Cabinet and so submitted, extracts from such documents, and any document that would disclose the deliberations or decisions of Cabinet other than an official document. An exception is made for purely factual material: s 34(1A). There is no public interest requirement or override and there is no requirement that prejudice result from the disclosure. The Official Information Act 1982 (New Zealand) s 9(2) (f)(ii) is in substantially identical terms to s 36(2)(a) of the FOIA. The provision has the effect of affording a good reason for non-disclosure for the purposes of s 5 of the Act unless 'the withholding of that information is outweighed by other considerations which render it desirable, in the public interest, to make that information available.' The New Zealand Law Commission, in its Review of the Official Information Act 1982, October 1997, para 217, noted that this had been interpreted to mean that 'the protection afforded is not a categorical one. It is not enough, for instance, to show that the relevant information is set out in a Cabinet document. Rather a judgment, involving an element of damage, is required: the person wishing to withhold must show that the withholding is necessary to maintain the particular interest. That phrase has been interpreted by the Ombudsmen as requiring that release would go 'to the heart' of the relevant interest. Factors such as the age of the information, or the timing of the request, may be relevant.' In Canada, s 69 of the Access to Information Act provides that the Act does not apply to confidences of the Queen's Privy Council for Canada (which includes the Cabinet and committees of Cabinet), including memoranda the purpose of which is to present proposals or recommendations to Council; discussion papers the purpose of which is to present background explanations, analyses of problems or policy options to Council for consideration by Council in making decisions; agenda of Council or records recording deliberations or decisions of Council; records used for or reflecting communications or discussions between ministers of the Crown on matters relating to the making of government decisions or the formulation of government policy; records the purpose of which is to brief ministers of the Crown in relation to matters that are before, or are proposed to be brought before, Council; and records that contain information about the contents of any record within any of the preceding classes of records. Section 19(1) of the Freedom of Information Act 1997 (Ireland), provides a mandatory exemption (it was, until the amendments made in 2003, a discretionary exemption) for any record: submitted, or proposed to be submitted, to the Government for their consideration by a Minister; containing information (including advice) for a member of the Government, the Attorney-General, a Minister of State, the Secretary to the Government or the Assistant Secretary to the Government for use by him solely for the purpose of the transaction of any business of the Government at a meeting of the Government; that consists of a communication between two or more members of the Government relating to a matter that is under consideration by the Government or is proposed to be submitted to the Government. 'Government' is defined in s 19(6) to be broadly akin to the Cabinet.

jurisdictions.[167] The meaning of 'prejudice' and the required probability of prejudice are generally considered earlier in this work.[168] The Government's preference for a test of 'prejudice', rather than substantial prejudice, was the source of some controversy during the passage of the Bill through Parliament. The decision to retain a test of 'prejudice' was, however, justified on the ground that, according to the Government, the test of prejudice was not a weak test; and the commissioner, who would have the power to overrule an authority if it was thought that any prejudice caused by a disclosure would be trivial or insignificant, would ensure that the authority was able to point to prejudice that was 'real, actual, or of substance'.[169] An argument that, although this provision does not per se provide for a class exemption, its application might in some circumstances involve the identification of documents by class, has been rejected in Scotland.[170] Finally, it should be noted that FOI(S)A requires 'substantial prejudice' for the purposes of this and other prejudice-based exemptions.

31– 027 Qualified person opinion

Section 36 is unique amongst the 23 sections of the Act conferring exemptions in its making the 'reasonable opinion' of a particular person determinative of its operation.[171] The 'reasonable opinion' criterion is not used in the regime applying to Scottish public authorities. Under that regime, the comparable exemption employs objective criteria, requiring substantial prejudice, or a likelihood of substantial prejudice, to the protected interest.[172] The reaching of a reasonable opinion is, in relation to each public authority, entrusted to a particular 'qualified person',[173] who is invariably at the highest level of accountability so far as that public authority

167 Although the information may independently be rendered exempt by s 35.

168 See §§6– 020 to 6– 028.

169 Lord Falconer of Thoroton, Hansard HL vol 612 col 827 (20 April 2000). Lord Falconer said 'I want to emphasise the strength of the prejudice test .... It is not a weak test. The commissioner will have the power to overrule an authority if she feels that any prejudice caused by a disclosure would be trivial or insignificant. She will ensure that an authority must point to prejudice which is "real, actual or of substance." We do not think that reliance on undefined words such as "substantial" or "significant" is a sensible way forward. We do not know how they will be interpreted by the commissioner or the courts. We can never deliver absolute certainty, but we can avoid making uncertainty worse by adding ill-defined terminology into the Bill.'

170 *Scottish Ministers v Scottish IC* [2007] CSIH 8, 2007 SCLR 253 at [14]. The correct approach, the Court held, was for each case to be assessed on its own facts and circumstances and that this will 'necessarily begin with the scrutiny of relevant individual documents and the ascertainment whether they contain particular information which, read in the context of related information, has or is likely to have the specified prejudicial effect…it is only after such scrutiny that it will be possible to say whether such information will have or is likely to have such an effect. The circumstance that one ends up with a "class", namely, with pieces of information of that particular kind, does not mean that a class-based approach to the exercise is ever legitimate' (at [13]).

171 Although, of course, there are provisions for conclusive certificates under ss 23, 24 and 34.

172 FOI(S)A s 30. The difference is further marked by the requirement under the FOI(S)A for substantial prejudice, rather than just prejudice. The experience of Scottish public authorities may be relevant to the FOIA s 2 balancing exercise in adjudging claims of the public interest in maintaining the exemption. In *Salmon v IC and King's College Cambridge*, IT, 17 July 2008 the Tribunal concluded that the acting provost of King's College, Cambridge was not a 'qualified person' for the purposes of section 36(5)(o) as that fell outwith the Minister's authorisation at the material time (although see the subsequent designation of 27 July 2007 which authorises the head of college by whatever title used of colleges within collegiate universities) [35].

173 In *Sugar v IC and BBC*, IT, 14 May 2009 the Tribunal concluded (at [10]) that the wording of s 36(2) did not require the opinion to be obtained at the time of the request. Rather, the section only requires that a reasonable opinion is obtained whether there would be, or would be likely to be, prejudice to the effective conduct of public affairs before the exemption is claimed. In *Thackeray v IC*, FTT, 2 December 2011 at [80] the Tribunal found that although the qualified person was not obliged to see the disputed information failure to inspect will not without more render the opinion redundant or unreasonable. The Tribunal stated that 'it follows that it is sufficient if it is shown the qualified person's opinion was based on a proper understanding of the disputed information.' In *Kikugawa v IC and Ministry of Justice*, FTT, 20 May 2012 at [20] to [23] the Tribunal expanded on the findings in Thackeray and stated 'it must be clear that the opinion must be that of the qualified person and she cannot simply sign a submission without reading it.' Also see *Surrey Police v IC*, FTT, 8 July 2010 at [54].

is concerned.[174] This unique aspect of the exemption was controversial and was criticised, both at the Committee stage and as the Bill went through Parliament, on the basis that the question of whether or not such information should be disclosed was one that the Commissioner should be free to determine on the merits, without being limited to a review of the qualified person's opinion.[175]

31– 028 Qualified person: practice

The role of the qualified person's opinion in determining whether a public authority is under a duty to disclose has two related limitations. First, the 'reasonable opinion' determinant is confined to deciding whether the disclosure of the information would have, or would be likely to have,[176] any of the effects set out in paras (a)-(c) of s 36(2). As noted above, except in relation to information held by the House of Commons or the House of Lords the exemption is a qualified exemption. Accordingly, the exercise prescribed by s 2(1) and (2) must then be carried out to determine whether the public interest in maintaining the exemption outweighs the public interest in disclosing the information.[177] The public interest in maintaining the exemption will, in part, be informed by the qualified person's *opinion* as to the prejudice that will or may be caused by the disclosure.[178] In this way, it may be that the extent to which the qualified person's opinion is borne out by the actuality will fall to be considered at this stage. Secondly, on its face, s 36 restricts the role of the Information Commissioner and of the Tribunal in any appeal to assessing whether the qualified person's opinion was reasonable: in other words, a review of the qualified person's decision akin to the *Wednesbury* irrationality test.[179] What matters is

---

174 The qualified person for each type of public authority is set out in FOIA s 36(5). For this reason, the s 36(2) opinion is not delegable: *Guardian Newspapers Ltd and Brooke v IC and BBC*, IT, 8 January 2007 at [26]. Qualified persons are listed at: www.foi.gov.uk/guidance/exguide/sec36/annex-d.htm

175 See the House of Commons Select Committee on Public Administration, *Third Report* (Cm 4355, 1999) para 90; the House of Lords, *Draft Freedom of Information Bill: First Report*, 27 July 1999, para 35; Hansard HC vol 340 col 782 (7 December 1999); Hansard HC vol 347 cols 1079-1088 (5 April 2000); Hansard HL vol 618 cols 303-313 (24 October 2000); and Hansard HL vol 619 cols 833-842 (22 November 2000). The Government justified the retention of the clause on the basis that 'the issues involved in the decision-taking process of public authorities are so near the heart of government that ...only a qualified person, as defined by the Bill, can have a full understanding of them. Although the issues in [s 36] are less sensitive than those in [s 35] and a class exemption is not justified, the Government do not believe that it would be right for the commissioner to substitute her view for that of the authority on the question of prejudice; hence the test of the reasonable opinion of a qualified person.' — Hansard HC vol 347 col 1085 (5 April 2000). This is the view taken by the Tribunal of its own role when reviewing a claim for exemption under s 36: *Guardian Newspapers Ltd and Brooke v IC and BBC* , IT, 8 January 2007 at [54].

176 As to the meaning of 'would, or would be likely to', see §6– 022. The same standard is required in s 36 as in other exemptions using this formula: *Guardian Newspapers Ltd and Heather Brooke v IC and BBC*, IT, 8 January 2007 at [53]. The Tribunal in *McIntyre v IC and MOD*, 4 February 2008, declined to find that the Information Commissioner could not find that the opinion of the qualified person was reasonable where the Minister failed to specify which limb of the prejudice test he relied upon [45]. The Tribunal concluded (at [45]) that 'where the qualified person does not designate the level of prejudice, that Parliament still intended that the reasonableness of the opinion should be assessed by the Commissioner, but in the absence of designation as to level of prejudice that the lower threshold of prejudice applies, unless there is other clear evidence that it should be at the higher level.'

177 *Guardian Newspapers Ltd and Heather Brooke v IC and BBC*, IT, 8 January 2007 at [69]. The 'qualified person' is not obliged to - although they can - address the public interest factors in favour of disclosure; their statutory role is limited to addressing the 'prejudice' that disclosure would cause, so a failure to address the public interest factors in favour of disclosure will not render their opinion 'unreasonable': *IC v E Malnick and The Advisory Committee on Business Appointments* [2018] UKUT 72 (AAC).

178 *Dept for Work and Pensions v IC and Zola* [2016] EWCA Civ 758, [2017] 1 WLR 1 at [55].

179 Thus Lord Falconer of Thoroton indicated that the Commissioner might overturn the qualified person's decision if she took the view that it was 'irrational' or 'perverse', or a view that 'no reasonable Minister or qualified person' would take; and he added that the Commissioner's review of the qualified person's decision would be conducted 'on a judicial review basis' — see Hansard HL vol 618 cols 305 and 306. See also Hansard HC vol 347 col 1085 (5 April 2000). This was the approach adopted by the Tribunal in *Guardian Newspapers Ltd and Heather Brooke v IC and BBC*, IT, 8 January 2007, although the Tribunal pointed out that as neither party sought to refer the Tribunal

whether the opinion was *substantively* reasonable: procedural flaws that might have rendered the decision unlawful in public law terms are not relevant to the assessment of the 'reasonableness' of the qualified person's opinion.[180] Again, however, even if the Commissioner does find that the qualified person's opinion is reasonable, he must then decide whether or not the information should be disclosed in accordance with the provisions of s 2 of FOIA.[181] In so doing, the Commissioner or Tribunal will have to determine how much weight should be given to the opinion of the qualified person that disclosing the information will have a prejudicial effect.[182] That task cannot properly be carried out without the Commissioner or Tribunal reaching its own view of whether the protected interests set out in paras (a)-(c) of s 36(2) would be, or would be likely to be, prejudiced by the disclosure of the information.[183] Respect and weight are normally given to the views of the qualified person, reflecting the relative

to *Hansard*, the Tribunal had not therefore taken into account Lord Falconer's statement (at [56]). The Tribunal was referred to the Information Commissioner's Awareness Guidance No 25 (revised), relating to s 36, and expressly stated that it did not endorse the view advanced in that Guidance that '...any opinion which is not outrageous, or manifestly absurd or made on the basis of irrelevant facts or without consideration of all relevant factors will satisfy the test [of reasonableness.].' The Tribunal considered that this was 'incorrect and should be disregarded' as an opinion could be objectively unreasonable without suffering from any of the defects cited in the Guidance. The Tribunal noted that it was not clear from the statutory wording the extent to which, if at all, in addition to being substantively reasonable, the opinion had to be reasonably arrived at; it concluded that in order to satisfy s 36(2) the opinion had to be both reasonable in substance and reasonably arrived at, stating that '...precisely because the opinion is essentially a judgment call on what might happen in the future, on which people may disagree, if the process were not taken into account, in many cases the reasonableness of the opinion would be effectively unchallengeable; we cannot think that was the Parliamentary intention' (at [64]). That the Tribunal may disagree with the qualified person's opinion does not mean that the qualified person's opinion was not a reasonable one for the purposes of s 36, see *MoD v IC and Evans*, IT, 20 July 2007 at [38]-[42]. See also *McKinnon v Secretary, Department of Treasury* [2006] HCA 45, (2006) 229 ALR 187 at [59], where the High Court of Australia, when considering whether there existed 'reasonable grounds for the claim that the disclosure of the document would be contrary to public interest' as required by s 58(5) of the Freedom of Information Act 1982 (Cth of Australia), stated that '...the expression "not irrational, absurd or ridiculous" is not synonymous with "reasonable grounds".'

180 *IC v E Malnick and The Advisory Committee on Business Appointments* [2018] UKUT 72 (AAC) at [56]; *Baird v IC and Governing Body of the University of London*, FTT, 16 December 2013 at [23].

181 The Tribunal has applied the principles established in *DfES v IC and The Evening Standard*, IT, 19 February 2007 at [75] (see §34– 011 above) to information falling within s 36: *Shipton v IC and National Assembly of Wales*, IT, 11 January 2007 at [16]-[17]; *MoD v IC and Evans*, IT, 20 July 2007 at [72]; *FCO v IC*, IT, 22 January 2008 at [24]-[28]; *SSHD v IC*, IT, 20 November 2008 at [41]-[67]; *Cabinet Office v IC*, IT, 27 January 2009 at [17]-[26]; *ECGD v IC and Campaign Against Arms Trade*, IT, 21 October 2009 at [62]-[115]; and *University of Central Lancashire v IC and Colquhoun*, IT, 8 December 2009 at [51]-[62].

182 In light of *Dept for Work and Pensions v IC and Zola* [2016] EWCA Civ 758, [2017] 1 WLR 1at [55], previous decisions in which the Tribunal refused to take the qualified person's opinion into account in the public interest balancing exercise are questionable. For example, in *Evans v IC and MoD*, IT, 26 October 2007 the Tribunal stated (at [36]) that 'we do not see the logic of then placing the Minister's opinion in the scales as a factor to be weighed in favour of maintaining an exemption whose engagement has been triggered by that very opinion. This seems to us like double counting the opinion which is a necessary safeguard to prevent inhibition being claimed without due cause ... we regard the opinion as a threshold condition, required to engage section 36, rather than a major piece of evidence in its own right.' The correct approach is illustrated by *Guardian Newspapers Ltd v IC and BBC*, IT, 8 January 2007, in which the Tribunal stated that the Commissioner, having accepted the reasonableness of the qualified person's opinion that the disclosure of the information would, or would be likely to, inhibit the free and frank exchange of views for the purpose of deliberation, 'must give weight to that opinion as an important piece of evidence in his assessment of the balance of public interest' at [92].

183 See Hansard HL vol 619 col 836 (22 November 2000) (Lord Falconer). Again, this is supported by the view of the Tribunal in *Guardian Newspapers Ltd and Heather Brooke v IC and BBC*, IT, 8 January 2007, which stated that '...when it comes to weighing the balance of public interest under s 2(2)(b), it is impossible to make the required judgment without forming a view on the likelihood of inhibition or prejudice' [88]. The Tribunal (at [91] and [92]) then proceeded: '...the qualified person has made a judgment about the degree of likelihood that such inhibition will occur. It does not necessarily imply any particular view as to the severity or extent of such inhibition or the frequency with which it will or may occur, save that it will not be so trivial, minor or occasional, as to be insignificant...in order to perform the balancing judgment required by s 2(2)(b), the Commissioner is entitled, and will need, to form his own view on the severity, extent and frequency with which inhibition of the free and frank exchange of views for the purposes of deliberation will or may occur.' Indeed, in reaching its conclusion that the material in question was not covered by the exemption contained within s 36, the Tribunal referred to the lack of evidence before it on the severity, extent and frequency of any future inhibition.

institutional competence of the witness and the Commissioner or Tribunal,[184] but undue deference is not to be accorded to the witness whose evidence must be carefully scrutinised.[185] This is the approach to be followed by both the Commissioner and the Tribunal on any appeal.[186]

31– 029 Statistical information

Section 36(4) of FOIA makes special provision in relation to the rendering of 'statistical information' into exempt information.[187] In relation to statistical information, the exemption created by s 36(2) operates like any of the other 22 provisions in the Act creating exemptions and a qualified person's opinion is not required. In other words, the statistical information is exempt information if its disclosure would have, or would be likely to have, any of the consequences set out in paras (a)-(c): it is not exempt information merely because, in the reasonable opinion of the qualified person, its disclosure would have, or would be likely to have, any of the consequences set out in paras (a)-(c).[188] On any review by the Information Commissioner, the question for the Commissioner will be similarly modified where the information in question is statistical information.

31– 030 Collective responsibility: scope

The first of the three limbs in s 36(2) describes information the disclosure of which would, or would be likely to, prejudice 'the maintenance of the convention of the collective responsibility of Ministers of the Crown'. This category of exemption is, in practice, invariably made as part of a claim for exemption under s 35(1)(a) or (b) and has been held to be a relevant factor in determining the public interest balance under those exemptions. In order to appreciate whether something would prejudice or would be likely to prejudice the convention, it is necessary to understand the exact nature of the convention and what end it is designed to serve. The matter was considered in *Attorney-General v Jonathan Cape Ltd*,[189] where the Attorney-General sought in 1975 to prevent the publication of a book, entitled *Diaries of a Cabinet Minister*, written by Richard Crossman, who had been a Cabinet Minister from 1964 to 1970, based upon a diary he had kept recording Cabinet discussions. The Attorney-General contended that publication of the book would undermine the doctrine of joint Cabinet responsibility, that it would represent a breach of the confidentiality and a breach of oath that every Cabinet Minister, as a Privy Councillor, is required to take, and that publication was therefore contrary to the public interest. Lord Widgery disagreed and the action was dismissed. The Court heard extensive evidence as to the nature of the convention, not all of it consistent, and concluded:

---

184 *All Party Parliamentary Group on Extraordinary Rendition v IC and FCO* [2015] UKUT 0377 (AAC) at [67]; *Dept of Health v IC and Lewis* [2015] UKUT 0159 (AAC) at [51]-[67].

185 *Baird v IC and Governing Body of the University of London*, FTT, 16 December 2013 at [43]-[44]; *FCO v IC and Plowden*, FTT, 28 January 2014 at [26].

186 *Guardian Newspapers Ltd and Heather Brooke v IC and BBC*, IT, 8 January 2007 at [64], [71]. The Tribunal in *MoD v IC and Evans*, IT, 20 July 2007 noted (at [14]) 'the question of whether the process of arriving at the opinion can be challenged is not without doubt.' The Tribunal in *McIntyre v IC and MoD*, IT, 4 February 2008 applied the approach in *Guardian and Brooke*, but with two caveats. First, where the opinion is overridingly reasonable in substance then, even though the method or process by which that opinion is arrived at is flawed in some way, this need not be fatal to a finding that it is a reasonable opinion. Second, the Tribunal should take a broad view of the way the opinion is arrived at, so that even if there are flaws in the process these can be subsequently corrected , provided that this is within a reasonable time period which would usually be no later than the internal review (at [31]). In *University of Central Lancashire v IC and Colquhoun*, IT, 8 December 2009 the Tribunal concluded (at [58]-[61]) that the 'perfunctory' process of forming the opinion supported a conclusion that it was not reasonably arrived at.

187 See *Cabinet Office v IC*, IT, 21 October 2008 at [39]-[40].

188 This special provision is, of course, not required for the regime applying to Scottish public authorities.

189 [1976] QB 752.

> It has always been assumed by lawyers and, I suspect, by politicians, and the Civil Service, that Cabinet proceedings and Cabinet papers are secret, and cannot be publicly disclosed until they have passed into history. It is quite clear that no court will compel the production of Cabinet papers in the course of discovery in an action, and the Attorney-General contends that not only will the court refuse to compel the production of such matters, but it will go further and positively forbid the disclosure of such papers and proceedings if publication will be contrary to the public interest.
>
> The basis of this contention is the confidential character of these papers and proceedings, derived from the convention of joint Cabinet responsibility whereby any policy decision reached by the Cabinet has to be supported by all members of the Cabinet whether they approve of it or not, unless they feel compelled to resign. It is contended that Cabinet decisions and papers are confidential for a period to the extent at least that they must not be referred to outside the Cabinet in such a way as to disclose the attitude of individual Ministers in the argument which preceded the decision. Thus, there may be no objection to a Minister disclosing (or leaking, as it was called) the fact that a Cabinet meeting has taken place, or, indeed, the decision taken, so long as the individual views of Ministers are not identified.[190]

The Attorney-General had argued that all Cabinet papers and discussions were *prima facie* confidential and that publication of them ought to be restrained if the public interest in concealment outweighed the public interest in a right to free publication: the court could, it was argued, restrain disclosure of Cabinet documents or proceedings that would reveal the individual views or attitudes of a Minister and confidential advice from civil servants (whether contained in Cabinet papers or not).[191] Lord Widgery CJ concluded:

> ...it seems to me that the degree of protection afforded to Cabinet papers and discussion cannot be determined by a single rule of thumb. Some secrets require a high standard of protection for a short time. Others require protection until a new political generation has taken over....I find overwhelming evidence that the doctrine of joint responsibility is generally understood and practised and equally strong evidence that it is on occasion ignored ...To leak a Cabinet decision a day or so before it is officially announced is an accepted exercise in public relations, but to identify the Ministers who voted one way or another is objectionable because it undermines the doctrine of joint responsibility.[192]

Lord Widgery CJ concluded that publication of the Crossman diaries would, as a matter of fact, not prejudice the maintenance of the convention of the collective responsibility of Ministers of the Crown:

> ...I cannot believe that the publication at this interval [ie 1975 in a volume relating to 1964-1966] of anything in volume one would inhibit free discussion in the Cabinet of today, even though the individuals involved are the same, and the national problems have a distressing similarity with those of a decade ago. It is unnecessary to elaborate the evils which might flow if at the close of a Cabinet meeting a Minister proceeded to give the press an analysis of the voting, but we are dealing in this case with a disclosure of information nearly 10 years later. It may, of course, be intensely difficult in a particular case, to say at what point the material loses its confidential character, on the ground that publication will no longer undermine the doctrine of joint Cabinet responsibility. It is this difficulty which prompts some to argue that Cabinet discussions should retain their confidential character for a longer and arbitrary period such as 30 years, or even for all time, but this seems to me to be excessively restrictive. The court should intervene only in the clearest of cases where the continuing confidentiality of the material can be demonstrated. In less clear cases—and this, in my view, is certainly one—reliance must be placed on the good sense and good taste of the Minister or ex-Minister concerned....The Attorney-General...has not satisfied me that

190 [1976] QB 752 at 764.

191 [1976] QB 752 at 765.

192 [1976] QB 752 at 767, 770.

publication would in any way inhibit free and open discussion in Cabinet hereafter.[193]

It is suggested that unless there is some measure of contemporaneity about the information or the subject matter of the information that falls to be released, it will be difficult to reasonably conclude that its disclosure would be likely to prejudice the maintenance of the convention of the collective responsibility of Ministers of the Crown.[194]

31–031 Responsibility: public interest

Lord Widgery's judgment in *Attorney-General v Jonathan Cape Ltd* also provides a useful insight into the public interest embodied in the exemption:

> I have already indicated some of the difficulties which face the Attorney-General when relied simply on the public interest as a ground for his actions. That such ground is enough in extreme cases is shown by the universal agreement that publication affecting national security can be restrained in this way. It may be that in the short run (for example, over a period of weeks or months) the public interest is equally compelling to maintain joint Cabinet responsibility and the protection of advice given by civil servants, but I would not accept without close investigation that such matters must, as a matter of course, retain protection after a period of years.[195]

Quite apart from its diminution in the likelihood of prejudice to the maintenance of the convention of the collective responsibility of Ministers of the Crown, the passage of time is likely also to diminish the public interest in the maintenance of the exemption.[196]

31–032 Inhibiting free advice etc

The second limb in s 36(2) describes information the disclosure of which would, or would be likely to, inhibit 'the free and frank provision of advice or the free and frank exchange of views for the purposes of deliberation'. The shortcomings in the 'candour argument' and its transformation into a 'duty of candour' in the context of public interest immunity in this country have already been noted in relation to the parallel exemption in s 35.[197] On the basis of these developments, it is suggested that, whatever might have been the position in past decades, it can no longer seriously be maintained that officials, either by dint of advising on

[193] [1976] QB 752 at 771. In *Cabinet Office v IC*, IT, 27 January 2009, the Tribunal noted (at [19]) that 'even assuming that there was a serious risk that the disclosure of [the information] would have led to the inference being drawn that there had been a disagreement between Ministers at the time it was prepared, we do not see how such an inference would have undermined the collective responsibility principle... The collective responsibility principle requires Ministers to support a decision once it has been reached, not to agree about everything before decisions have even been taken. The principle would only have been at risk of prejudice if specific views had been rehearsed in the paper which could then have been used to embarrass those holding them if a decision had gone against them.'

[194] Some further support for this proposition comes from the fact that such information in a 'historical record' cannot be exempt information: see FOIA s 63(1) and §36–011. In *Cabinet Office v IC and Lamb*, IT, 27 January 2009, a majority of the Tribunal concluded (at [78]) that the importance of maintaining the Convention was diluted by the extent to which some of the information had already been disclosed, both formally and informally, and the trend of important matters being discussed in small groups outside Cabinet.

[195] [1976] QB 752 at 768. In *Sankey v Whitlam* (1978) 148 CLR 1, Mason J, in referring to Lord Widgery's judgment, said: 'I also agree with his Lordship that the efficiency of government would be seriously compromised if Cabinet decisions and papers were disclosed whilst they or the topics to which they relate are still current or controversial. But I base this view, not so much on the probability of ill-formed criticism with its inconvenient consequences, as upon the inherent difficulty of decision making if the decision-making processes of Cabinet and the materials on which they are based are at risk of premature publication. Cabinet proceedings have always been regarded as secret and confidential' (at 98).

[196] In *Cabinet Office v IC and Aitchison*, FTT, 15 October 2012, a s 35(1)(b) case, the FTT (upheld in *Cabinet Office v IC and Aitchison* [2013] UKUT 0526 (AAC)) held that, while the maintenance of Cabinet collective responsibility was a 'very weighty' public interest factor against disclosure, 'at the time of the request the disputed information was 22 years old which in our view diminishes the weight to be given to this public interest in the circumstances of this case', at [68] (UT at [40]). The Tribunal considered it relevant that the duty to disclose historical records now arose after 20 years, not 30 years, following amendment by s 45 Constitutional Reform and Governance Act 2010.

[197] See §31–015.

matters of policy or of their seniority, would be likely to neglect their duty to give frank advice if that advice were to be released pursuant to a legislative obligation to do so.[198] Nevertheless, non-disclosure based on the inhibition of free and frank exchange of views and advice may be upheld where the public interest in disclosure is particularly limited[199] or where there is a particularly strong public interest in non-disclosure[200] or where other exemptions are also engaged.[201]

31– 033 Prejudicing public affairs

The last of the three limbs in s 36(2) describes information the disclosure of which would, or would be likely to, 'otherwise prejudice the effective conduct of public affairs'. Although it is not easy to imagine what prejudice, apart from undermining Cabinet secrecy and the questionable impact upon public officials' ability to advise candidly, would be likely to be caused to the effective conduct of public affairs from the 'disclosure of...information under [the Freedom of Information Act],'[202] this limb has proved an attractive sweep-up exemption. The Tribunal has found s 36(2)(c) engaged where disclosure:

— would create a risk that Home Office forensic pathologists would no longer provide information about the number of post mortems they had attended;[203]
— would inhibit CPS staff in conducting an internal investigation following a leak;[204]
— would discourage employers from participating in a scheme for encouraging the unemployed to return to work;[205]
— would create a risk of imposing an excessive burden on the exceptional hardship scheme for the HS2 rail extension;[206]
— would undermine the effectiveness of government tools for assessing the

[198] See, eg, *Cabinet Office v IC and Lamb*, IT, 27 January 2009 at [77]-[82].

[199] *Davies v IC and Cabinet Office*, FTT, 19 July 2017 (non-disclosure of internal discussions concerning a response to an individual complaint).

[200] For example, *Moore-Gilbert v IC & Department for Education* [2013] FTT, 23 September 2013 (where the FTT accepted that the disclosure of officials' discussions risked exposing the names of informants and discouraging third parties from providing information concerning 'extremists').

[201] For example: *Serewich v IC and Home Office*, FTT, 21 November 2016 (s 40 (personal information) also engaged).

[202] In *McIntyre v IC and MoD*, IT, 4 February 2008, the Tribunal found (at [25]) that the s 36(2)(c) exemption is intended to apply to those cases 'where it would be necessary in the interests of good government to withhold information, but which are not covered by another specific exemption, and where the disclosure would prejudice the public authority's ability to offer an effective public service or to meet its wider objectives or purposes due to the disruption caused by the disclosure or the diversion of resources in managing the impact of disclosure.' In *McIntyre v IC and MoD*, IT, 4 February 2008, the request was for information relating to the process for promotion in the Ministry of Defence, disclosure of which the Ministry of Defence contended would adversely affect the integrity of the promotion scheme. See also *Galloway v IC and NHS*, IT, 20 March 2009, where the exemption was successfully invoked by an NHS Trust in relation to the requested disclosure of witness statements from staff provided in the course of an investigation of a 'serious untoward incident' – see [96], [99]-[112]. In *Sankey v Whitlam* (1978) 148 CLR 1 a similar 'sweep-up' claim was made in support of a public interest immunity claim before the High Court of Australia. Mason J observed (at 97): 'They [the Executive] have sought refuge in the amorphous statement that non-disclosure is necessary for the proper functioning of the Executive Government and of the public service, without saying why disclosure would be detrimental to their functions, except for the reference to want of "candour." Perhaps affidavits in this form were acceptable in the days when it was thought that the court should uphold an objection once made by the Crown through its appropriate representative. But they are plainly unacceptable now that the court is to resolve the issue for itself, after an inspection of the documents when that is thought to be appropriate. An affidavit claiming Crown privilege should state with precision the grounds on which it is contended that documents or information should not be disclosed so as to enable the court to evaluate the competing interests.'

[203] *Workman v IC and Home Office*, FTT, 21 November 2017.

[204] *Mitchell v IC & CPS*, FTT, 15 December 2014.

[205] *DWP v IC and Zola*, FTT, 17 May 2013.

[206] *Helstrip v IC and High Speed Two (HS2) Ltd*, FTT, 29 January 2013.

effectiveness of policies;[207]

but not engaged where disclosure:

— would impose a disproportionate burden on a public authority (although such a request could amount to a 'vexatious' request under s 14).[208]

If the information has a further attribute (eg it is confidential information or it comprises sensitive national security material) then it may be that disclosure will result in prejudice to the effective conduct of public affairs: however, that additional attribute will invariably render the information exempt information under another provision of the Act.[209] It is suggested that resultant criticism cannot properly be characterised as representing prejudice to the effective conduct of public affairs.[210] The Tribunal has rejected a claim that disclosure might discourage proper minute-taking.[211]

31–034 The duty to confirm or deny

Section 36 also provides a corresponding exclusion from the duty to confirm or deny.[212] There is a subtle but important distinction in the operation of this exclusion from the exclusion given by s 35(3). Under s 35(3), if a given piece of information relating to the formulation of policy, etc is exempt information under s 35(1), then the corresponding duty to confirm or deny that the information is held does not arise. Under s 36(3), where information is exempt from the duty of disclosure under s 36(2), that is not determinative of whether the duty to confirm or deny arises under s 36(3).[213] Instead, the duty to confirm or deny does not arise where, in the reasonable opinion of a 'qualified person', informing the applicant that the public authority holds or does not hold the information requested would be, or would be likely to be, prejudicial

---

207 *Slater v IC and DWP*, FTT, 11 March 2016.

208 *McInerney v IC and Dept of Education* [2015] UKUT 0047 (AAC).

209 In *MoD v IC and Evans*, IT, 20 July 2007, the Ministry of Defence sought to rely on the exemption contained in s 36(2)(c) in the alternative to its reliance upon s 36(2)(b), deploying identical arguments for the former exemption as for the latter. The Tribunal noted (at [53]) that 'if the same arguments are to be advanced, then the prejudice feared is not "otherwise". Some prejudice other than that to the free and frank expression of advice (or views, as far as section 36(2)(b)(ii) is concerned) has to be shown for section 36(2)(c) to be engaged.'

210 In *Commonwealth of Australia v John Fairfax & Sons Ltd* (1980) 147 CLR 39 at 50-51 Mason J in granting an interlocutory injunction restraining the defendant on breach of copyright grounds from publishing but declining to grant an injunction on breach of duty-of-confidence grounds on the basis that disclosure was unlikely to injure the public interest said: 'The question then, when the executive government seeks the protection given by equity, is: What detriment does it need to show? The equitable principle has been fashioned to protect the personal, private and proprietary interests of the citizen, not to protect the very different interests of the executive government. It acts, or is supposed to act, not according to standards of private interest, but in the public interest. This is not to say that equity will not protect information in the hands of the government, but it is to say that when equity protects government information it will look at the matter through different spectacles. It may be a sufficient detriment to the citizen that disclosure of information relating to his affairs will expose his actions to public discussion and criticism. But it can scarcely be a relevant detriment to the government that publication of material concerning its actions will merely expose it to public discussion and criticism. It is unacceptable in our democratic society that there should be a restraint on the publication of information relating to government when the only vice of that information is that it enables the public to discuss, review and criticise government action…The court will not prevent the publication of information which merely throws light on the past workings of government, even if it be not public property, so long as it does not prejudice the community in other respects. Then disclosure will itself serve the public interest in keeping the community informed and in promoting discussion of public affairs. If, however, it appears that disclosure will be inimical to the public interest because national security, relations with foreign countries or the ordinary business of government will be prejudiced, disclosure will be restrained.' This authority was cited with approval in *AG v Observer Ltd* [1990] 1 AC 109 at 151-152 (Scott J), at 203 (Dillon LJ), at 218, 221 (Bingham LJ), at 258 (Lord Keith), at 270 (Lord Griffiths), at 283 'in a free society there is a continuing public interest that the workings of government should be open to scrutiny and criticism' (Lord Goff).

211 *Guardian Newspapers Ltd and Heather Brooke v IC and BBC*, IT, 8 January 2007 at [107].

212 FOIA s 36(3).

213 FOIA s 2(1).

to public affairs in one of the ways set out in s 36(2).[214] The exemption is qualified: the matters to be weighed, which are different from those weighed for the purposes of determining whether the duty to disclose applies, is treated elsewhere in this work.[215]

[214] The different ways in which the duty to confirm or deny has been disapplied under the FOIA is considered in §5–005.

[215] See §§6–018 to 6–019.

CHAPTER 32

Research, health and safety

1. OVERVIEW

32–001 Introduction

This Chapter is concerned with two sets of exemptions, each of which is designed to protect a specific interest from harm that would, or would be likely to, result from disclosure of requested information. The first is concerned with protecting (in broad terms) research that is in progress that would be likely to be prejudiced by early disclosure of information.[1] The second is concerned with information the disclosure of which would be likely to endanger the physical or mental health of an individual or that would endanger the safety of an individual.[2] There are two analogous exemptions in respect of the duty on a public authority to confirm or deny whether it holds information answering the terms of the request where that confirmation or denial would, or would be likely to, harm the protected interest.[3]

32–002 Public interest

Both sets of exemption are qualified exemptions, so that whether or not there is a duty to disclose information captured by one of the exemptions will turn upon whether in all the circumstances of the case the public interest in maintaining the exemption outweighs the public interest in disclosing the information.[4]

1 FOIA s 22A(1)); FOI(S)A s 27(2).

2 FOIA s 38(1); FOI(S)A s 39(1).

3 FOIA ss 22A(2) (research), 38(2) (health and safety). There is no separate duty to confirm or deny under FOI(S)A.

4 FOIA s 2(2); FOI(S)A s 2(2).

2. RESEARCH INTERESTS

32–003 Introduction

Section 20 of the Intellectual Property Act 2014 introduced a new exemption into FOIA (s 22A) which, in very broad terms, is designed to protect research that is in progress from harm that might result from the disclosure of information.[5] A like exemption had existed in FOI(S)A since its enactment.[6] The exemption is a qualified exemption.

32–004 Scope of the exemption

The exemption is limited in its reach by a definition that involves a narrowly described class of information, harm to a protected interest and a temporal limitation, before getting to a consideration of the public interest. In order for information to be captured by the exemption, four requirements must be met:

(1) First, the information has to have been obtained in the course of, or derived from, a 'programme of research.'
(2) Secondly, that programme of research must be a continuing programme.
(3) Thirdly, that programme of research must be one 'with a view to the publication, by a public authority or any other person, of a report of the research (whether or not including a statement of that information).
(4) Fourthly, disclosure of the information under FOIA before the date of publication would, or would be likely to, prejudice–
    (i) the programme,
    (ii) the interests of any individual participating in the programme,
    (iii) the interests of the authority which holds the information, or
    (iv) the interests of the public authority that it is proposed will publish the report of the research.

32–005 Programme of research

The only information captured by the exemption is information that has been 'obtained in the course of, or derived from, a programme of research.' A 'programme' of research will require that the research be pursuant to a plan or outline for that research. Since 'information' is defined as meaning 'recorded information,' it might seem that information that is recorded as part of the programme of research (eg observations recorded during the programme of research) is recorded information generated during the programme of research, rather than recorded information 'obtained in the course of, or derived from, a programme of research.' A programme of research is distinct from (for example) a course of study.[7]

32–006 A continuing programme

The programme of research must be a 'continuing' programme. Again, this stresses the need for there to be a plan or outline for the research in order for it to be within the reach of the exemption. It is only against such a plan or outline that it can be determined whether or not

5 The exemption took effect from 1 October 2014. The introduction of this exemption may have received some support from the disinclination of the Tribunal to uphold claims for exemption by research bodies (particularly those using animals as part of the research programme) based upon the health and safety exemption.

6 FOI(S)A s 27(2).

7 See, for example: Further and Higher Education Act 1992 ss 68, 76; Higher Education Act 2004 ss 12, 20; Higher Education and Research Act 2017 ss 101-102.

the programme is continuing, rather than having been concluded or having evolved into a further or different programme of research. It is suggested that the moment at which it is determined whether or not a programme is continuing is the moment at which the request is answered by the public authority, whether in the first instance or upon internal review. It is also suggested that a programme that has been discontinued or placed in abeyance before its conclusion is not a continuing programme.

32– 007 With a view to publication

The programme of research must be one 'with a view to the publication, by a public authority or any other person, of a report of the research.' Again, this points to the plan or outline setting the objectives and parameters of the programme of research including within it a stated intention of publishing a report of that research. However, it is not necessary that that statement of intent provide that the information captured by the request be included within the report.

32– 008 Protected interest prejudice

The fourth requirement of the exemption is prejudice, or a likelihood of prejudice, to the protected interests. There are four protected interests:

(i) the programme,
(ii) the interests of any individual participating in the programme,
(iii) the interests of the authority which holds the information, and
(iv) the interests of the public authority that it is proposed will publish the report of the research

The level of probability required by the exemption is the same as that used in other exemptions ('would or would be likely to'): this is considered elsewhere in this work.[8] The prejudice (or likely prejudice) that is required for engagement of the exemption is further narrowed by it being confined to prejudice to those interests resulting from disclosure of the information under FOIA before the date of publication of the report of the research. This might seem to exclude, for example, information obtained in the course of, or derived from, a publicly-known and controversial programme of research, unless it can be demonstrated that the disclosure of the particular information captured by the request will materially increase, or is likely to materially increase, prejudice to the protected interests.

32– 009 Public interest

The exemption is non-absolute: it only applies if the public interest in maintaining the exemption outweighs the public interest in disclosing the information.[9] As with the other qualified exemptions, in weighing the competing public interests, the relevant decision maker[10] will have to take into account all the circumstances of the case[11] and any relevant provisions of the ECHR.

---

[8] See §§6– 022 to 6– 027. In *MoD v IC and Evans*, IT, 20 July 2007 at [76], the Tribunal held that these principles applied to s 38.

[9] See: FOIA ss 2(1)(b) and 2(2)(b); FOI(S)A s 2(1)(b). For a general discussion of this topic, see §§6– 001 to 6– 019.

[10] That is: the public authority from which information is sought, the Information Commissioner, the Tribunal, or the courts.

[11] FOIA ss 2(1)(b) and 2(2)(b); FOI(S)A s 2(1)(b).

3. HEALTH AND SAFETY

32– 010 Introduction

Where the disclosure of information under FOIA would or would be likely: (a) to endanger the physical or mental health of any individual; or (b) to endanger the safety of any individual, then that information is exempt information by virtue of s 38(1).[12] The exemption is a qualified exemption, so that whether or not there is a duty to disclose such exempt information will turn upon whether in all the circumstances of the case the public interest in maintaining the exemption outweighs the public interest in disclosing the information. Similarly, to the extent that, if a public authority were to inform an applicant that it held information of the description specified in the applicant's request, that informing would or would be likely: (a) to endanger the physical or mental health of any individual; or (b) to endanger the safety of any individual, then the duty to confirm or deny does not arise.[13] The exclusion of this duty is also qualified, so that in such circumstances the public authority will be excused from informing the applicant that it holds the requested information only if the public interest in maintaining the exclusion outweighs the public interest in disclosing whether the public authority holds the information. Similar exemptions of varying scope exist in each of the comparative jurisdictions.[14] A substantial amount of information relating to health and safety is likely to be 'environmental information'[15] and therefore exempt under s 39 of FOIA. If this is the case, its disclosure falls

---

[12] FOI(S)A s 39(1), is effectively identical. EIR reg 12(5)(a) and EI(S)R reg 10(5)(a) provide for a qualified exception in respect of information the disclosure of which would adversely affect public safety.

[13] FOIA s 38(2). There is no separate duty to confirm or deny under the FOI(S)A.

[14] In the United States, the Freedom of Information Act, 1966, 5 USC 552(b)(7), exempts from disclosure records or information the production of which could reasonably be expected to endanger the life or physical safety of any individual: see §51– 008(7)(F). The Freedom of Information Act 1982 (Cth of Australia) s 37(1)(c), provides an exemption where the disclosure of the requested document would, or could be reasonably be expected to, endanger the life or physical safety of any person. Section 37(2)(c) provides a separate exemption for a document the disclosure of which would, or could reasonably be expected to, prejudice the maintenance or enforcement of lawful methods for the protection of public safety. Section 41(3) provides a special method of disclosure where it appears to the agency that the disclosure of the information to the applicant might be detrimental to the applicant's physical or mental health, or well-being. The Official Information Act 1982 (New Zealand) s 9(2)(c) provides a qualified exemption where disclosure would cause prejudice to measures protecting the health or safety of members of the public: see §51– 023(4). Sections 6(d) and 27(1)(a) provide an absolute exemption where disclosure would be likely to endanger the safety of any person: see §51– 022(4). The Access to Information Act (Canada) s 17 provides a discretionary exemption for records the disclosure of which could 'reasonably be expected' to cause a threat to an individual's safety: see §51– 032(14). There is no analogous exemption in respect of information the disclosure of which could reasonably be expected to threaten an individual's physical or mental health. The *Report of the Access to Information Task Force* (June 2002, Ottawa), p 56, recommended that one be included. The Privacy Act (Canada) s 28, provides discretionary exemption for any personal information that relates to the physical or mental health of the individual who requested it where the examination of the information by the individual would be contrary to the best interests of the individual. Section 25 of that Act provides a discretionary exemption where disclosure could reasonably be expected to threaten the safety of individuals. Section 20(6) of the Access to Information Act also specifically provides that the head of a government institution (being the primary decision-maker for the purposes of the Act) may disclose third party confidential information (which would otherwise be exempt) where disclosure under the Act 'would be in the public interest as it relates to public health, public safety or protection of the environment and, if the public interest in disclosure clearly outweighs in importance any financial loss or gain to, prejudice to the competitive position of or interference with contractual or other negotiations of a third party.' The Freedom of Information Act 1997 (Ireland), ss 23(1)(aa) and 28(3), respectively provide a discretionary exemption for records the disclosure of which might endanger the life or safety of any person or that might be prejudicial to the health of the applicant: see §51– 039(14). A separate exemption is provided for disclosures that could reasonably be expected to prejudice or impair lawful methods, etc for ensuring the safety of the public and of persons. Sections 27(2)(e) and 28(2)(e) provide a similar override to the Canadian Act in relation to confidential third party information the disclosure of which is 'necessary in order to avoid a serious and imminent danger to the life or health of an individual.'

[15] As to the meaning of which, see §17– 011.

to be considered under the EIR and not under FOIA.[16]

32– 011 Endangerment

The exemption is unique amongst the exemptions in FOIA in its requirement of 'endangering,' rather than 'prejudicing,' a protected interest.[17] Whilst some Tribunal decisions have held that there is no difference between the two terms,[18] it is suggested that the different terminology is deliberate and that it reflects the nature of the protected interest.[19] Specifically, it is suggested that 'endanger' will more readily be satisfied by any increased risk of the adverse consequence (harm to the physical or mental health or safety of any individual) but that it requires that the harm be more serious; whereas 'prejudice' places greater emphasis on the likelihood of the occurrence of that adverse consequence and less emphasis on the gravity of the adverse consequence. The level of probability required by the exemption is the same as that used in other exemptions ('would or would be likely to'): this is considered elsewhere in this work.[20]

32– 012 Physical or mental health

Consistent with the above analysis of the meaning of the requirement that disclosure 'endanger' the physical or mental health of an individual, Tribunal cases have repeatedly stated that the likely effect of disclosure must be more than 'stress or worry,' and that it must be 'real and not insignificant.'[21] In order for the exemption to apply, the Tribunal requires that it should be able to identify a specific risk to the physical or mental health of at least one individual.[22]

32– 013 Safety

Similarly, the Tribunal has not accepted generalised assertions that disclosure of the requested

---

16 And, in the case of information held by Scottish public authorities, under the EI(S)R and not the FOI(S)A. In relation to access to environmental information, see Chs 17-19.

17 As to the meaning of 'likely to prejudice' see §6– 022.

18 In *Hemsley v IC and Chief Constable of Northamptonshire*, IT, 10 April 2006 at [14] the Tribunal held that no practical distinction arose between prejudicing and endangering, at least for the purposes of that appeal. The same conclusion was reached in *People for the Ethical Treatment of Animals Europe v IC and University of Oxford*, FTT, 18 January 2010 at [30] and *Summers v IC and Metropolitan Police*, FTT, 24 February 2012. But in *British Union for the Abolition of Vivisection v IC and Newcastle University*, FTT, 13 July 2011 the Tribunal was not disposed to agree that 'prejudice' and 'endanger' meant the same thing, given that the language was not identical. Further, it was not persuaded that it would be right to read the word 'endanger' in a sense which would engage the exemption merely because of a risk of harm. It reasoned that there was always a risk that a researcher might become a target for persons opposing animal research by unlawful and violent means, but the researcher's physical health would not be endangered unless a specific attack were made. It was necessary to consider the likelihood of such an attack, and the likelihood of other conduct which would endanger mental health or other aspects of safety. There was also a causation requirement: the likelihood of persons being endangered was not to be considered in the round but as a consequence of the disclosure of the requested information. In a very different context, see *R v Whitehouse* [2000] Crim LR 172 which concerned the issue of whether the use of a mobile phone on an aircraft was an act 'likely to endanger an aircraft' contrary to Art 5 Air Navigation (No 2) Order 1995. The Court of Appeal concluded that 'likely to endanger' in this context would be satisfied if there was a real risk of endangerment. This case turned more on the meaning of 'likely' than of 'endanger'. In *R v Pearce* [1967] 1 QB 150 at 154-155 the Court of Appeal, again in a different context, spoke of endangering as being concerned with 'causing a source of danger'.

19 The ICO, in its guidance on s 38, takes the opposite view: 'Our view is that the use of the term 'endanger' equates to 'prejudice' and that section 38 is subject to the prejudice test.' The basis for this is not clear. It is a conventional canon of statutory interpretation that where the statutory drafter uses one word consistently and then chooses a different one, that is intended to signify a change in meaning, and that canon is particularly strong where the words were introduced into the statute at the same time, the statute is modern and is the product of close scrutiny.

20 See §§6– 022 to 6– 027. In *MoD v IC and Evans*, IT, 20 July 2007 at [76], the Tribunal held that these principles applied to s 38.

21 *Medical Justice v IC and Home Office*, FTT, 8 June 2016 at [42]-[58]; *Hepple v IC and Durham CC*, FTT, 26 February 2014 at [31]; *British Union for the Abolition of Vivisection v IC and Newcastle University*, FTT, 11 November 2011 at [16] (agreed between the parties).

22 *Hepple v IC and Durham CC*, FTT, 26 February 2014 at [31].

information might expose those employed within the public authority to abuse and threats.[23]

32– 014 Causation

The disclosure of information may endanger the health or safety of an individual:

(a) directly, that is without requiring any further step by a human agent in order for the danger to the health or safety to the individual to be capable of being realised into physical or mental harm to that individual; and

(b) indirectly, that is by increasing the likelihood of physical or mental harm to an individual, but which harm will not be realised without a further step by a human agent, whether the individual endangered or another individual.[24]

On an application of basis principles of causation, satisfying the link between the disclosure and the likelihood of the health of an individual being endangered will generally be easier in the first case than the second.[25] That said, both ultimately turn on an evaluative assessment of the content of the information, the facts and circumstances of the individual (or class of individuals) including that individual's existing physical and mental health, the source of the information and the basis on which the public authority acquired it, as well as whether other like information is publicly available. The exemption is directed to the likely consequences of *the disclosure* of the information, rather than the *likely use* that may or can be made of that information. The likely use that may or can be made of the information is an instance of indirect endangerment. Whether *the likely use* that will be made of disclosed information would endanger health or safety, is essentially a question of causation. On the usual principles of causation, if it is readily predictable that particular information, once disclosed, will be used in such a way as would risk harming the health or safety of an individual, then it may be said that the disclosure of the information will endanger the health or safety of that individual. On the other hand, where there is only a mere possibility that certain information may be misused in such a way as to endanger health or safety it becomes more difficult to say the disclosure of that information 'would or would be likely to endanger' health or safety.[26] This is particularly so if there is an obvious use that may be made of the information that would not be likely to endanger health or safety.

32– 015 Vulnerable individuals

Whether the disclosure of particular information would or would be likely to endanger the health or safety of an individual may depend upon whether that individual has vulnerabilities

[23] See, for example: *O'Hare v IC and Scotland Office*, FTT, 13 January 2017 at [52]-[54]; *Montague v IC and Tate Gallery*, FTT, 22 December 2014 at [41]-[42]; *British Union for the Abolition of Vivisection v IC and Newcastle University*, FTT, 11 November 2011 at [18], [48]-[49]; cf *Callus v IC and Home Office*, FTT, 6 May 2014 at [59]-[60].

[24] For an example of this: *Callus v IC and Home Office*, FTT, 6 May 2014 at [59]-[60].

[25] *British Union for the Abolition of Vivisection v IC and Newcastle University*, FTT, 11 November 2011 at [19]. In other areas of the law it is conventional to seek to identify the 'effective' or 'dominant' cause of an outcome: *Galoo v Bright Grahame Murray* [1994] 1 WLR 1360 at 1374-1375. Ultimately it will depend upon a commonsense interpretation of the facts. Intervening acts by third persons have always presented particular problems in relation to causation, and the following authorities provide useful illustrations, albeit in different contexts: *Weld-Blundell v Stephens* [1920] AC 956 (where the defendant, in breach of his contract, negligently left a libellous letter written by the plaintiff, where it was read by a third party, who was likely to, and did, communicate its contents to the persons libelled: the latter recovered damages for libel from the plaintiff, who then turned around and sued the defendant. The House of Lords, by a majority, held that the act of the third party, although foreseeable, was a 'new and independent' cause).

[26] The fact that disclosure might conceivably result in either harm is insufficient: *Keane v IC* [2016] UKUT 461 (AAC) at [50]. The Upper Tribunal rejected the less strict line taken in earlier FTT cases, for example: *Hemsley v IC and Chief Constable of Northamptonshire*, IT, 10 April 2006, where the Tribunal was prepared to find that a request for information relating to a specific speed camera, including times of its operation, would satisfy s 38(1); *Ministry of Defence v IC and Evans*, IT, 20 July 2007 at [76], where the Tribunal was satisfied that there was 'a sufficiently serious suggestion' of the requisite likelihood of prejudice to health from the publication of a directory of staff, notwithstanding a certain amount of external circulation of the directory.

or sensitivities particular to that individual. Where an individual already suffers from a physical or mental condition, in order for the exemption to engage the disclosure must be one that would, or would be likely to, worsen the condition or diminish the likelihood of its amelioration.[27] The public authority may be unaware of the particular vulnerabilities or sensitivities of an individual who becomes aware of or is otherwise affected by the disclosure. The terms of the exemption do not permit the public authority to guess at such vulnerabilities or sensitivities so as to invoke the exemption.[28] However, if the vulnerability or sensitivity is known to the public authority (because of other information that it holds or that has been brought to its attention), then the public authority will need to determine the application of the exemption on the basis of that knowledge. Where the applicant, or a person to whom the information can reasonably be expected to be conveyed, has a vulnerability or sensitivity, then it is conceivable that receipt of the information, if touching upon that vulnerability or sensitivity, may directly endanger that individual's mental or physical health.

32–016 Examples of applicability

The following are examples where a public authority has successfully invoked s 38:

(1) *Hemsley v Information Commissioner and Chief Constable of Northamptonshire*,[29] where the applicant sought information relating to a specific speed camera, including its times of operation. In upholding the claim for exemption, it is unclear whether the Tribunal considered that the information was exempt under s 38 or s 31(1) (prejudice to the prevention or detection of crime).

(2) *Lawton v IC and NHS Direct*,[30] where the applicant sought the local telephone numbers of the 22 NHS Direct call centres, so that he did not have to use the national 0845 number which carried a time-based fee for its use. The Tribunal accepted evidence that disclosure of the numbers would side-step the automatic routeing system that minimised call-waiting times and would prejudice the operation of the system. The Tribunal held that although the probability of an adverse health consequence was low (delayed access to medical advice), the health consequence itself could be severe, so that s 38 was 'clearly engaged.'

(3) *People for the Ethical Treatment of Animals Europe v Information Commissioner and University of Oxford*,[31] where the applicant sought information upon experiments on a macaque called Felix. The Tribunal accepted the University's evidence that disclosure would be likely to endanger the safety of University staff. It noted the need to establish that disclosure of the withheld information would *increase* the risk of endangerment in a situation which was already fraught. Contrast *British Union for the Abolition of Vivisection v Information Commissioner and Newcastle University*, where the evidence established only a 'relatively low level of risk from extremists' and the exemption was held not to be engaged.[32]

---

27 *Hepple v IC and Durham CC*, FTT, 26 February 2014 at [31]-[34]. Unless, of course, the exemption is satisfied by the disclosure causing, or being likely to cause, some other kind of endangerment to the physical or mental health of that individual or to that individual's safety.

28 For an example of a case in which it was argued (unsuccessfully) that release of information would be likely to endanger mental health, see *Phillips v IC and National Archives*, FTT, 15 February 2013 at [66]-[67].

29 IT, 10 April 2006.

30 IT, 5 March 2008.

31 *People for the Ethical Treatment of Animals Europe v IC and University of Oxford*, FTT, 18 January 2010.

32 At [48]. The House of Commons Justice Committee's *Post-Legislative Scrutiny of the Freedom of Information Act 2000*, 1st Report of Session 2012-2013, July 2012, has urged universities to use in full the protection that exists 'for the health and safety of researchers in section 38 of the Act, and expect[s] that the Information Commissioner will recognise legitimate concerns' (at para 222).

32– 017 Examples of inapplicability

The following are examples where a public authority has been unsuccessful in its attempt to invoke s 38:

(1) *Ministry of Defence v Information Commissioner and Evans*,[33] where the Tribunal rejected an argument that disclosure of a directory published by the Defence Export Services Organisation, listing names, job titles, work addresses, telephone numbers and e-mail addresses of its staff would be harmful to their health and safety. It was claimed that this information, used in conjunction with other information, could be deployed to harm them. Although the Tribunal acknowledged that there was some risk, it considered that it was too low to engage s 38.

(2) In *Bucks Free Press v Information Commissioner*,[34] the applicant sought the number of notices of intended prosecution arising from two particular speed cameras. The Tribunal held that since the information sought would not reveal enforcement patterns and so not affect driver behaviour, 'the connection between the incidence of speeding and the danger of accidents occurring is so obvious that it must follow that the section 38 exemption is ... not engaged.'

(3) In *Phillips v Information Commissioner and National Archives*,[35] files relating to a murder case in 1952 were sought from The National Archives. Parts of the file were withheld, with reliance placed on s 38. It was suggested that the release of graphic crime scene photographs or post-mortem reports would be likely to cause significant distress to the family of the deceased such that it would be likely to endanger its members' mental health. The Tribunal rejected this claim, noting that it had been provided with no objective evidence of the anticipated harm and that, since the case had been repeatedly publicly debated, the arguments did not stand up to reality.

32– 018 Comparative law

Although there is a considerable degree of potential overlap between the information caught by s 38(1)(a) (physical or mental health) and the information caught by s 38(1)(b) (safety), the comparative jurisprudence illustrates that their coverage is by no means identical. In particular, whereas the former exemption has greater potential direct application, the latter is only readily engaged by some predicted use of the information.

— In the US, under the safety exemption, where the applicant had previously threatened federal employees and third persons connected with law enforcement matters, the courts have upheld non-disclosure of the names and identifying information of persons in that class, provided that withholding that information is necessary in order to protect them from possible harm.[36]

— In Australia, exemption on the analogous safety ground has been upheld for documents relating to a surveillance operation carried out by the police into

33 IT, 20 July 2007 at [76]-[77].

34 IT, 18 January 2007 at [18].

35 *Phillips v IC and National Archives*, FTT, 15 February 2013 at [66]-[67].

36 *Blanton v United States Department of Justice*, 182 F Supp 2d 81 (DDC 2002), where, on the grounds of safety, the Court refused to order disclosure so as to protect the identities of FBI Special Agents and non-law enforcement personnel assisting in an investigation, even though the requester was incarcerated, on the basis that his threats against persons responsible for his arrest and conviction made it possible that those individuals could be targets of physical harm.; *LA Times Communications, LLC v Department of the Army*, 442 F Supp 2d 880 (CD Cal 2006) where it was held that disclosure of private security contractor company names operating in concert with US military forces in Iraq could endanger the life or physical safety of many individuals; *Brady-Lunny v Massey*, 185 F Supp 2d 928 (CD Ill 2002) where the court held that disclosure of a list of the names of detainees in a prison would endanger life and physical safety given security risks that always are present in inmate populations.

members of a sect, the Tribunal considering that release would give rise to a reasonable expectation that the life or physical safety of a person might be in danger.[37] Similarly, exemption has been upheld where disclosure of information such as a person's identity, views or whereabouts would make that person a potential target of violence by another person or group of persons. However, the Tribunal and Courts have required objective evidence to support a reasonable apprehension of danger.[38] Thus, where an applicant, who had four convictions for assault and who had been a recipient of a disability support pension that had been cancelled and then reinstated, sought access to the underlying documents for the cancellation decision, it was held not to be enough to engage the safety exemption that (a) the psychologist who had examined the applicant had requested that his report not be provided to the applicant because of his potential to react violently; (b) the applicant had made statements suggesting that he would act violently; and (c) when interviewed, the applicant had had a threatening demeanour, and the officer concerned had felt threatened by him.[39]

— Also in Australia, disclosure of a portion of an army manual concerning the tactical response to terrorism has been refused on safety grounds on the basis that if the relevant section of the manual were made public, there would be a significant risk to security.[40]

— In New Zealand, the disclosure of possible examination questions for pilots has been refused on safety grounds.[41] Other safety examples can be expected to include: the disclosure of plans of a prison,[42] and the disclosure of the new identity, or the location of, a recently released convicted child killer.[43] In each of these two cases it is difficult to see a legitimate need for the information sought by any applicant under the Act.

32– 019 The public interest

As noted above, the health and safety exemption is qualified or non-absolute: it only applies if the public interest in maintaining the exemption outweighs the public interest in disclosing the information.[44] This public interest must be satisfied even in cases where the endangerment of

---

37 *Re Anderson and Australian Federal Police* (1987) 11 ALD 356. But the Administrative Appeals Tribunal will scrutinise agency claims that disclosure of information to the applicant will result in physical danger: *Scholes v Australian Federal Police* (1996) 44 ALD 299 at [121]-[128].

38 *Re Boehm and Department of Industry Technology and Commerce* (1985) 7 ALN N186. On the other hand, the exemption has been held not to be satisfied where evidence was produced that one of several institutions where animal experiments were conducted had received a bomb threat. It was held that danger to lives or physical safety was only considered to be a possibility, not a real chance: *Re Binnie and Department of Agriculture and Rural Affairs* (1987) 1 VAR 361.

39 *Centerlink v Dykstra* [2002] FCA 1442. The Tribunal had taken into account that the medical evidence was two years old and that the applicant had never actually attempted to harm any official. Although the Federal Court allowed an appeal, that was on the basis that the Tribunal had failed to take into account relevant material, and it otherwise upheld the decision-making methodology of the Tribunal: in particular, that the fear of the officers could not be determinative of the issue.

40 *Re Hocking and Department of Defence* (1987) 12 ALD 554.

41 8 CCNO 78 and 9 CCNO 143.

42 In Australia, the Administrative Appeals Tribunal upheld an exemption in relation to a request by an applicant who had been interned during the Second World War on the grounds that the information referred to methods for protecting public safety during wartime: *Re Parisi and Australian Federal Police* (1987) 14 ALD 11 at 17. It is not clear how the Tribunal considered this continued to remain a threat to safety some 40 years later.

43 See *Venables v News Group Newspapers* [2001] Fam 430. In such circumstances Art 2 ECHR protecting the right to life is likely to be relevant when carrying out the balancing test relating to the public interest.

44 See: FOIA ss 2(1)(b) and 2(2)(b); FOI(S)A s 2(1)(b). For a general discussion of this topic, see §§6– 001 to 6– 019.

physical or mental health or safety is likely to occur. As with the other qualified exemptions, in weighing the competing public interests, the relevant decision maker[45] will have to take into account all the circumstances of the case[46] and any relevant provisions of the ECHR. Articles 2, 3 and 8 ECHR are all potentially engaged in relation to this exemption.[47] Relevant factors that will need to be considered no doubt include the risk and severity of any adverse effects on someone's health and the strength of the public interest in disclosure. It is suggested that the public interest in maintaining an exemption where it is the anticipated *use* of information that renders it exempt information will be liable to be displaced by the public interest in disclosure if there are legitimate uses for the information. Thus, the public interest in maintaining an exemption for information revealing the risks, however slight, in treatments or medicines on the basis that a proportion of the population will turn away from them (despite their beneficial effects), can only readily predominate over the public interest in disclosure of such information by rejecting the fundamental precepts of freedom of information legislation. In the parliamentary debates there was considerable discussion about withholding information about the risks of eating beef during the BSE controversy. Mr O'Brien, the Parliamentary Under-Secretary of State for the Home Department stated:

> Where public health is seriously at risk and information is held by the Government, it is difficult to see, on any reading of the Bill, how it could be justified for a Minister to take the view that the public interest was in favour of secrecy, unless a criminal investigation were about to be undertaken, in which case the public interest would have to be weighed very carefully. In circumstances where there is a clear view that public health would be at risk—particularly in the sort of situation in which BSE arose—under the Bill, it would always be in the public interest for that information to be in the public domain.[48]

32–020 Examples: non-disclosure

The following are examples where a public authority has successfully invoked s 38:

(1) *Hemsley v Information Commissioner and Chief Constable of Northamptonshire*,[49] where the Tribunal found that the public interest in maintaining the exemption outweighed the public interest in disclosure having regard to: the considerable quantity of information already available to the public in relation to safety cameras; the lack of legitimate utility in the particular information sought; the fear of misuse by others of the particular information sought by the applicant; and the fact that if it were provided in answer to this request, all such information would have to be disclosed.

(2) *Lawton v Information Commissioner and NHS Direct*,[50] where there was evidence that disclosure of the requested information would on occasions delay the public getting health advice, the Tribunal held that the public interest in maintaining the exemption outweighed the public interest in securing access to the information.

(3) *Summers v Information Commissioner and Metropolitan Police* involved a request for the total sum spent on the Royal Protection Unit in 2009-2010. The Tribunal

---

That there is particular public interest in the disclosure of information relating to health and safety of an individual is reflected in Pt IVA of the Employment Rights Act 1996, as inserted by the Public Interest Disclosure Act 1998, which recognizes a public interest in a disclosure by an employee tending to show 'that the health and safety of any individual has been, is being or is likely to be endangered' – s 43B(1)(d).

45 That is: the public authority from which information is sought, the Information Commissioner, the Tribunal, or the courts.

46 FOIA ss 2(1)(b) and 2(2)(b); FOI(S)A s 2(1)(b).

47 See Ch 4.

48 Hansard HC vol 357 col 723 (27 November 2000).

49 IT, 10 April 2006, outlined at §32–016.

50 IT, 5 March 2008, outlined at §32–016.

accepted, first, that the exemption was engaged, as the release of the information would be likely to endanger not only the safety of the figures protected but the public. The public interest in disclosing the information was 'heavily outweighed' by the public interest in maintaining the exemption.[51]

32– 021 Examples: disclosure

The following are examples where a public authority has been unsuccessful in its attempt to invoke s 38:

(1) *Ministry of Defence v Information Commissioner and Evans,*[52] in which the Tribunal found that even if s 38 had been engaged, the public interest in maintaining the exemption was 'easily outweighed' by the public interest in disclosure of the list.

(2) *Bucks Free Press v Information Commissioner,*[53] where the Tribunal held that since the requested information would not reveal enforcement patterns, the connection between it and driver behaviour was 'tenuous' such that 'the public interest in the undoubtedly important issues of speeding offences and public safety is not sufficiently strong to outweigh the public interest in informing the public debate on the fairness and efficiency of the management of the speeding camera facilities in the area.'

32– 022 The duty to confirm or deny

Where the requested information is, or if it were held would be, exempt information under s 38 (1), then the discrete duty to confirm or deny that the information is held by the public authority does not arise.[54] The exclusion of this duty is a qualified one. It will be necessary to consider whether, in all the circumstances, the maintenance of the exclusion of this duty is outweighed by the public interest in disclosing whether the public authority holds the information. This public interest balancing exercise is materially different from that employed for the purpose of determining whether the duty to communicate does not apply.[55] It will only be in limited circumstances that the decision maker will be exempted from confirming or denying that it holds such information. The need for an exemption to the duty to confirm or deny was debated by Parliament. Lord Goodhart, the Liberal Democrat peer, commented:

> There are certain possible circumstances in which the mere disclosure that information was held would be a potential danger, either to someone who would be seriously upset—mentally perhaps—by the realisation that such information was in the possession of a public authority, or to someone who had supplied the information. The fact that that was known might induce someone to take steps against him.[56]

Whilst, it is suggested, 'upset' — whether mental or otherwise — is not a sufficient reason for refusing to confirm or deny the existence of information, there may be certain circumstances where such disclosure could cause, or exacerbate, mental illness. Further, the disclosure of the existence of information, provided that the request is sufficiently narrowly formulated, might indicate the identity of an informer.

---

51 *Summers v IC and Metropolitan Police,* FTT, 24 February 2012 at [88], [95].

52 IT, 20 July 2007 at [76], outlined at §32– 017.

53 IT, 18 January 2007 at [24], outlined at §32– 017.

54 Not applicable under the FOI(S)R.

55 See §§6– 018 to 6– 019 as to what it involves.

56 Hansard HL vol 617 col 1250 (19 October 2000).

CHAPTER 33
Personal information

1. INTRODUCTION

33–001 Overview

Freedom of information legislation[1] provides two exemptions in relation to personal information in order to achieve two objectives:

(1) The first exemption applies to personal information concerning the individual who made the request for information – ie 'the applicant.'[2] The objective of the first exemption is to ensure that where (or to the extent that) an applicant's request for information captures personal data of which the applicant is the data subject, that request (or that part of the request) is taken out of the freedom of information regime, leaving it to be determined solely in accordance with the data protection regime.[3] The first exemption achieves this objective by rendering that personal information 'exempt information' for the purposes of freedom of information legislation,[4] while leaving in place that applicant's free-standing right of access under the data protection regime. This free-standing right, which the data protection

---

[1] By which is meant: FOIA; FOI(S)A; EIR; and EI(S)R.

[2] FOIA s 40(1); FOI(S)A s 38(1)(a); EIR reg 5(3); EI(S)R reg 11(1).

[3] The data protection regime means: (a) in relation to general processing, the GDPR supplemented by the DPA 2018; (b) in relation to law enforcement processing by competent authorities, Part 3 of the DPA 2018; and (c) in relation to intelligence service processing, Part 4 of the DPA 2018. In relation to which is which, see §8–002 and §§9–001 to 9–002.

[4] FOIA s 40(1); FOI(S)A s 38(1)(a); EIR reg 5(3); EI(S)R reg 11(1).

regime calls the 'right of access,' has its own set of exemptions and is considered elsewhere in this work.[5] Where personal information relates to both another individual and to the applicant – 'mixed personal information' – the first exemption does not apply, but the second exemption may apply.[6]

(2) The second exemption is concerned with personal information other than information of which the applicant is the data subject – third party personal information.[7] The objective of the second exemption is to ensure that where (or to the extent that) an applicant's request for information captures third party personal information, the applicant's right of access under freedom of information legislation is curtailed so as to respect the 'data integrity' of that third party.[8] The second exemption achieves this objective by rendering third party personal information 'exempt information' to the extent that disclosure of the third party personal information satisfies one or more of three conditions.[9] Those conditions borrow for the purposes of the second exemption the processing principles set out in the data protection regime, using those principles as the governing measure of data integrity.

For both exemptions, the first step in determining their applicability is identifying the extent to which information captured by the request for information constitutes 'personal data.' The two exemptions apply only to the extent that information captured by the applicant's request is 'personal data.' The freedom of information legislation also has correlative exclusions of the duty to confirm or deny.[10]

33– 002 Terminology

The personal information exemptions employ terminology used in data protection legislation:

— 'data subject,' which means the identified or identifiable living person to whom personal data relates;[11]

— 'personal data,' which means any information relating to a data subject;[12] and

— 'processing,' which covers all conceivable activities in the life-cycle of information, including receipt, recording, storage, holding, retrieval, adaptation, dissemination, publication and destruction of information.[13]

The DPA 2018 splits the regulation of data processing into three distinct streams:

(1) Intelligence service processing.[14] As a result of the absolute exemption in respect of information supplied by, or relating to, the intelligence services, and those bodies

5 In relation to general processing, see §§10– 014 to 10– 017; in relation to law enforcement processing by a competent authority, see §§13– 014 to 13– 017; and in relation to intelligence services processing, see §§14– 021 to 14– 029.

6 See §33– 001(2)(b) below.

7 FOIA s 40(2); FOI(S)A s 38(1)(b); EIR reg 13(1); EI(S)R reg 11(2).

8 Similarly: FOI(S)A s 38(1)(b); EIR regs 12(3) and 13; EI(S)R regs 10(3) and 11(2). The GDPR/DPA 2018 give an applicant no right of access to information of which he is not a data subject. 'Data integrity' includes an individual's right to the maintenance of privacy of certain sorts of information concerning him or herself.

9 FOIA s 40(3A)-(4A); FOI(S)A s 38(2)-(3); EIR reg 13(2)-(3); EI(S)R reg 11(3)-(4).

10 FOIA s 40(5). Similarly: EIR reg 13(5) (but only in relation to information relating to a third party); EI(S)R reg 11(6). There is no separate duty to confirm or deny under the FOI(S)A.

11 GDPR Art 4(1); DPA 2018 s 3(5). An 'identifiable person' means one who can be identified, directly or indirectly, in particular by reference to an identifier such as a name, an identification number, location data, an online identifier or to one or more factors specific to the physical, physiological, genetic, mental, economic, cultural or social identity of a natural person: GDPR Art 4(1). See further §8– 015.

12 GDPR Art 4(1); DPA 2018 s 3(2). See further §8– 016.

13 GDPR Art 4(2); DPA 2018 s 3(4). See further §8– 018.

14 DPA 2018 Part 4 (ss 82-113). This is dealt with in Ch 14.

not being public authorities within the meaning of freedom of information legislation, this stream is not referred to in the two personal information exemptions.[15]

(2) Law enforcement processing by a competent authority.[16] Where a request for information is made to a competent authority and it holds personal information answering the terms of the request as part of its law enforcement processing, application of the second exemption will fall to be determined by reference to the terms and principles of the law enforcement regime.

(3) All other processing – called 'general processing.'[17] Where a request for information does not fall within (2), application of the second exemption will fall to be determined by reference to the terms and principles of the general processing regime.

The general processing regime refers to 'processing principles,' whereas the law enforcement processing regime refers to 'data protection principles.'[18] The freedom of information legislation refers to them collectively as the 'data protection principles.'[19]

33– 003 More than one data subject

The second exemption covers two situations:

(1) Where the applicant is not a data subject of personal information, but another individual is – 'third party personal information.'

(2) Where both the applicant and one or more third parties are data subjects of personal information – 'mixed personal information.'

In the case of mixed personal information, the first exemption is inapplicable because it applies to personal data of which the applicant is *the* data subject (rather than to personal data of which the applicant is *a* data subject).[20] In the case of mixed personal information, an applicant may apply for access to that information under either the freedom of information regime or the data protection regime: the outcome is unlikely to differ materially.[21] In broad terms, data

---

15 FOIA s 23.

16 DPA 2018 Part 3 (ss 29-81). This is dealt with in Chs 12-13.

17 This is governed by the GDPR supplemented by DPA 2018. The range of processing covered by 'general processing' is set out in more detail at §8– 002 and §§9– 001 to 9– 002. General processing is dealt with in Chs 9-11.

18 These are set out in GDPR Art 5(1) and DPA 2018 s 34(1), respectively.

19 FOIA s 40(7); FOI(S)A s 38(5); EIR reg 2(4); EI(S)R reg 2(1).

20 FOIA s 40(1); FOI(S)A s 38(1)(a); EIR reg 5(3); EI(S)R reg 11(1). The Information Commissioner's publication *Personal data of both the requester and others (section 40 FOIA and regulations 5(3) and 13 EIR)*, ver 2.0, undated, states that 'where the request includes information which is both the personal data of the requester and a third party, and is so closely linked that it is not possible to separate it out, you should refuse that information under FOIA section 40(1) or EIR regulations 5(3) and consider it as a subject access request....' The authority cited in support of this statement (as it was in previous editions of this work) is *Fenney v IC*, IT, 26 June 2008, in which the unrepresented appellant in a matter decided on the papers appears not to have taken a point on the language of FOIA s 40(1). In the course of its decision the IT reasoned (at [13]):

> There is no basis for arguing that the DPA intended that the only data subject to be considered when assessing a document incorporating data on more than one individual is the one whose data is more extensive or more significant. If information incorporates the personal data of more than one person the data controller is not required to attempt an assessment as to which of them is the more significant and to then recognise the rights to protection of that individual and ignore any others. Its obligations are set out in sections 7(4) to 7(6) DPA, which require it to consider whether the information requested includes information relating to a third party and, if it does, to disclose only if that third party consents or it is reasonable in all the circumstances (by reference to the particular matters identified in subsection (6)) to comply with the request without his or her consent.

Closer analysis of the legislation has resulted in this work re-visiting its previous position.

21 Differences may include: fees; other applicable exemptions; further information that must be supplied under a GDPR/DPA request; and the consequences of non-compliance with the request.

protection legislation provides that the response to a data subject's access right may be restricted where that is a necessary and proportionate measure to protect the rights and freedoms of others.[22]

33– 004 The approach adopted

When freedom of information legislation was first proposed by the government of the day, it was intended that the two access schemes (ie under the then-DPA 1998 and FOIA) would run in parallel as a dual access regime, with their systems aligned as far as possible.[23] However, that proposal was abandoned when the Bill was drafted.[24] One alternative approach debated when the Bill received its third reading was to make the third party disclosure exemption under FOIA applicable when disclosure would be likely to result in a public authority breaching its obligation to respect the private life of individuals pursuant to Art 8 of the ECHR; but this did not find favour.[25]

33– 005 Rationale: first exemption

Access to personal information relating to oneself is a key element of any freedom of information regime. Individuals in the United Kingdom enjoyed rights of access to certain types of personal information about themselves well before the current freedom of information legislation came into force. From 1998 onwards the principal source of those rights was the DPA 1998 (which implemented the Data Protection Directive).[26] That Act, like the earlier DPA 1984, also provided safeguards in respect of the processing of personal data, most importantly by requiring data controllers to comply with eight data protection principles.[27] The advent of a comprehensive freedom of information regime, having at its core a general right of access to any information held by a public authority, gave rise to a potential overlap between the two Acts in relation to personal information held by public authorities. The solution arrived at was to channel a request by an applicant for information relating to himself through the DPA 1998 and to enhance the subject access right (but only in so far as it related to information held by a public authority) by enlarging the definition of 'data'.[28] The enlarged definition of 'data' captured information relating to an individual that was not part of a structured file relating to that individual. In this way the coverage of a subject access request, in so far as it related to personal data held by a public authority, resembled the coverage given by freedom of information legislation in relation to non-personal data held by a public authority. The amendments to freedom of information legislation made by the DPA 2018[29] continue the same regime – access to information that constitutes personal data of which the applicant is the data

---

22 GDPR Art 15(4), in relation to general processing; DPA s 45(4)(e), in relation to law enforcement processing by a competent authority. Under DPA 1998 this had been dealt with under s 7(4), which provided that where answering a request would disclose information relating to another identifiable individual the data controller was not obliged to do so unless that individual had consented to the disclosure or it was reasonable in all the circumstances to comply with the request without such consent: see further §15– 066.

23 Cabinet Office, *Your Right to Know. The Government's Proposals for a Freedom of Information Act. White Paper* (Cm 3818, 1997) paras 4.6-4.1; House of Commons Library, The Freedom of Information Bill: Data Protection Issues, Research Paper 99/99, 3 December 1999, p 7.

24 For example, from the Data Protection Registrar in her evidence to the Public Administration Committee: *Third Report of 1998-1999, Freedom of Information Draft Bill*, Vol II: HC 570-II of 1998-99, 16 August 1999, memorandum 2, p 18 para 4; *Third Report of 1998-1999, Freedom of Information Draft Bill*, Vol II: HC 570-I of 1998-99, 29 July 1999, para 98.

25 Hansard HC vol 347 col 982 (5 April 2000); Hansard HL vol 618 cols 409-412 (25 October 2000).

26 See Chs 15-16.

27 As to which, see §15– 036.

28 DPA 1998 s 1(1)(e), inserted by FOIA s 68(2)(a).

29 See further §33– 007.

subject must be sought under the GDPR/DPA 2018, and it is exempt information for the purposes of freedom of information legislation.

33–006 Rationale: second exemption

The second category of requests for personal information — requests for personal information about third parties — was placed within the province of freedom of information legislation. There is an inherent tension between the objective of freedom of information and the objective of protecting personal privacy and data integrity. These objectives will often conflict when an applicant seeks access to personal information about a third party. The conflict poses two related challenges for governments: first, to determine where the balance should be struck between those aims; and, secondly, to determine the mechanisms for dealing with requests for such information. The conflict between the right to personal privacy and the public interest in the disclosure of personal information was recognised by the Government when it first proposed freedom of information legislation[30] and there was continued recognition of that difficulty throughout the passage of the Bill.[31] As enacted, the balance was struck so as to give primacy to protection against intrusive disclosure of personal information by making personal information relating to another person exempt from disclosure under freedom of information legislation to the extent that that disclosure would offend the protection given by the DPA 1998.[32] The description adopted by the Tribunal is that the second personal information exemption:

> ... seeks to ensure that the interests of those requesting information from a public authority do not undermine, unnecessarily, the interests of those individuals whose personal data might find its way into the public domain as a result of the public authority complying with such a request.[33]

The interests of the person to whom the information relates are left with the public authority to advocate. Thus, while aspects of the scheme appear to favour a third party's privacy,[34] the United Kingdom's freedom of information legislation is alone amongst comparable legislation in not making provision for consulting a third party where information relating to that third party is sought by an applicant.[35] Nor is a third party given any right to initiate or to participate in appeal proceedings – permission needs to be sought from the FTT.

30 Cabinet Office, *Your Right to Know. The Government's Proposals for a Freedom of Information Act. White Paper* (Cm 3818, 1997) para 3.11(3).

31 See eg House of Commons, *Select Committee on Public Administration Third Report, Session 1997-1998*, 19 May 1998, paras 10-18.

32 FOIA s 40; FOI(S)A s 38; EIR regs 5(3), 12(3) and 13; EI(S)R regs 10(3) and 11. These are 'designed to preserve the application of the 1998 Act to that information': *Common Services Agency v IC* [2008] UKHL 47, [2008] 1 WLR 1550 at [5]. See also *LB of Camden v IC*, IT, 19 December 2007 at [22]. There is a further layer of complexity in Scotland, where the Information Commissioner, based in England, is responsible for the promotion and enforcement of the DPA 1998, even if the request is made in Scotland. The Scottish Information Commissioner and the Information Commissioner have signed a memorandum of understanding setting out the relationship between them in relation to freedom of information legislation, the intention being that they will co-operate with and provide assistance to one another.

33 *A v IC*, IT, 11 July 2006 at [11]; *Blake v IC and Wiltshire CC*, IT, 2 November 2009 at [24].

34 For example, in relation to personal information about public officials, where the FOIA draws no distinction between personal information that might be termed 'public' and that which is 'private'. The Data Protection Registrar had suggested that public officials should be afforded the same level of protection for information relating to their private lives as that enjoyed by others, but that there should be provision for greater disclosure of information relating to their public activities: *Third Report of 1998-1999, Freedom of Information Draft Bill, vol II*: HC 570-II of 1998-99, 16 August 1999, memorandum 2, p 19 paras 4.4-4.5. The Access to Information Act (Canada), s 3, definition of 'personal information', draws this distinction.

35 See further §§22–036 to 22–042.

33– 007 The 25 May 2018 changes

Until 25 May 2018 data protection was governed by the DPA 1998. On that date, the new regime comprising the GDPR and the DPA 2018 came into force. The DPA 2018 amended the second personal information exemption in the freedom of information legislation:[36]

(a) satisfaction of one of two conditions was replaced with satisfaction of one of three conditions; and

(b) satisfaction of the first condition by a contravention of any of the data protection principles in Part 1 of Sch 1 to the DPA 1998 was replaced by contravention of any of the processing principles in Art 5(1) of the GDPR (in the case of general processing) or the data protection principles in s 34(1) of the DPA 2018 (in the case of law enforcement processing by a competent authority).

Given that the content of the processing principles in Art 5(1) of the GDPR is different from the content of the data protection principles in Part 1 of Sch 1 to the DPA 1998, the amendment can have greater ramifications for the second personal information exemption than superficially might appear. It also means that jurisprudence considering the second personal information exemption in its pre-25 May 2018 form must be approached carefully.[37] Where a request for information was made before 25 May 2018, it is only to the extent that that request was dealt with by the public authority after 25 May 2018 that the amendments effected to the second personal information exemption have effect.[38] Accordingly, decisions on review may continue to be governed by the pre-25 May 2018 regime for some time after May 2018. In addition to the above changes, the new requirement of transparency in the first processing principle may impinge on the extent to which the public authorities are required to notify third parties what personal data of theirs has been disclosed.[39]

2. APPLICANT IS THE DATA SUBJECT

33– 008 Introduction

In freedom of information legislation, the first of the two personal information exemptions is for 'personal data' of which the applicant is the 'data subject.'[40] The exemption is an absolute exemption.[41] The result is that where (or to the extent that) an applicant's request for information captures information of which the applicant is the data subject (and that information has no other data subject), that information is exempt information under freedom of information legislation: the applicant must instead look to data protection legislation to obtain access to that information.[42] The first personal information exemption does not apply

---

36 DPA 2018 Sch 19 paras 58, 90(3), 307 and 312.

37 Specifically, the list of ways in which the lawfulness requirement in Art 5(1)(a) of the GDPR may be met (set out in GDPR Art 6(1)) is not identical to the list of conditions in DPA 1998 Sch 2, one of which had to be met in order to comply with the first data protection principle under DPA 1998. Many of the authorities concerning the second personal information exemption turned on whether the condition in DPA 1998 Sch 2 para 6(1) was met. The GDPR equivalent of DPA 1998 Sch 2 para 6(1) is Art 6(1)(f).

38 DPA 2018 Sch 20 paras 52, 56, 60 and 61.

39 The first processing principle is set out in GDPR Art 5(1)(a). As to transparency requirement within this principle, see §§9– 017 to 9– 022.

40 FOIA s 40(1); FOI(S)A s 38(1)(a); EIR reg 5(3); EI(S)R reg 11(1). As to the meaning of these terms, see §33– 002.

41 FOIA s 2(3)(f); FOI(S)A s 2(2)(e); EIR reg 12(1) and (3); EI(S)R reg 10(3). For an example where this exemption was applied, see *Edem v IC and FSA*, FTT, 16 April 2012 at [22].

42 In relation to general processing, the access right is provided for by GDPR Art 15: see further §§10– 014 to 10– 017. In relation to law enforcement processing by a competent authority, the access right is provided for by DPA

to information in which both the applicant and one or more third parties are data subjects – 'mixed personal information.' This is different from the situation where only part of the information captured by a freedom of information request constitutes personal data of which the applicant is the data subject. In the latter situation, only so much of the information captured by the request that is personal data of which the applicant is the data subject will be exempt under the first exemption; the remainder of the information captured by the request will fall to be considered under any other applicable exemptions.[43]

33– 009 The duty to confirm or deny

Freedom of information legislation grants a correlative exclusion of the duty to confirm or deny in relation to information which constitutes personal data of which the applicant is the data subject.[44] It is to be noted that the exclusion of the duty does not require that confirmation or denial would or might itself disclose the existence of the information or cause any particular prejudice.[45] The exclusion of the duty to confirm or deny is absolute.[46] Thus, where or to the extent that a public authority receives a request under freedom of information legislation for information that constitutes personal data of which the applicant is the data subject, the public authority need neither provide the information nor advise the applicant whether or not it holds the information. However, the public authority should, under s 16 of FOIA, offer advice and assistance by referring the applicant to the subject access rights under the applicable provisions of the data protection regime.

3. APPLICANT IS NOT THE DATA SUBJECT

33– 010 Introduction

The second personal information exemption deals with personal information that relates to one or more third parties.[47] The second exemption is engaged where three requirements are satisfied: the third requirement may be satisfied by meeting one (or more) of three conditions.

2018 s 45(1): see further §§13– 014 to 13– 017. Under the DPA 1998, such a request was termed a 'subject access request.'

43 See *Freeborn v IC and Sussex Police*, IT, 5 August 2008 at [1]-[8] and [19]; *Stevenson v IC and Chief Constable of West Yorkshire Police*, IT, 14 October 2008 at [1]-[24]; *Kelway v IC and Northumbria Police*, IT, 14 April 2009 at [55]-[61].

44 Similarly, EI(S)R reg 11(6), but not the EIR. *Comotto v IC*, FTT, 17 January 2013 at [19]. There is no separate duty to confirm or deny under the FOI(S)A. For the meaning of a 'duty to confirm or deny', see §1– 008.

45 See the distinctions drawn in §5– 005.

46 FOIA s 2(3)(f) and similarly EI(S)R reg 11(6).

47 FOIA s 40(2)-(7); FOI(S)A s 38(1)(b) and (2A)-(5); EIR reg 13(2A)-(5B); EI(S)R reg 11(2A)-(4A). In the context of considering the Scotland Act 1998 (which has been said is to be interpreted on ordinary principles, the Supreme Court has held that the phrase 'relates to' indicates more than a loose or consequential connection or a touching upon the matter: *Martin v Most* [2010] UKSC 10, 2010 SC (UKSC) 40 at [49], [159]. And similarly: *Imperial Tobacco Ltd v Lord Advocate* [2012] UKSC 61, 2013 SLT 2 at [16]; *Re Agricultural Sector (Wales) Bill* [2014] UKSC 43, [2014] 1 WLR 2622 at [50]; *Recovery of Medical Costs for Asbestos Diseases (Wales) Bill* [2015] UKSC 3, [2015] AC 1016 at [25]; *Christian Institute v Lord Advocate* [2016] UKSC 51, [2016] HRLR 19 at [29] (concerning the Data Protection Act 1998). In the context of FOIA the meaning of the phrase 'relates to' has been considered in: *Home Office v IC and Cobain*, FTT, 30 January 2013 at [15]-[19]; *Callus v IC and Home Office*, FTT, 6 May 2014 at [39]-[41]; *University and Colleges Admissions Service v IC and Lord Lucas* [2014] UKUT 0557 (AAC) at [44]-[46] (meaning of 'relates to' in FOIA s 7(5)); *Home Office v IC and Cobain* [2014] UKUT 0306 (AAC) at [39]; *All Party Parliamentary Group on Extraordinary Rendition v IC and FCO* [2015] UKUT 0377 (AAC) at [14]-[33]; *Reprieve v IC and FCO*, FTT, 26 April 2016 at [37]-[39]; *Corderoy and Ahmed v IC and Attorney General* [2017] UKUT 0495 (AAC) at [51] [54] and [59]-[62]; *Department of Health v IC and Lewis* [2017] EWCA Civ 374, [2017] 1 WLR 3330 at [13] (Sir Terence Etherton MR) (meaning of 'relates to' in FOIA s 35(1)).

33– 011 First & second requirements

The first requirement is that the information be 'personal data.'[48] Whether or not information is 'personal data' is determined according to ordinary data protection principles. The second requirement is that the data subject of the personal information not be the applicant. This will be satisfied where information makes no reference and is otherwise unconnected to the applicant. This requirement will also be satisfied by information of which the applicant is, with others, *a* data subject (ie 'mixed personal information');[49] but this requirement will not be satisfied by personal information of which the applicant is the only data subject.[50]

33– 012 Third requirement

The third requirement of the second exemption will be met to the extent that the information satisfies any one or more of three conditions.

(1) Where disclosure of the information to a member of the public (otherwise than under freedom of information legislation) would either contravene a 'data protection principle' or it would contravene a processing principle if the exemptions in s 24(1) of the DPA 2018 were disregarded.[51] The objective of the first condition is the protection of the data integrity and privacy of the person to whom the data relates. The first condition achieves this by borrowing the processing principles set out in Art 5(1) of the GDPR and using those principles as the yardstick by which to measure whether disclosure of the personal information under the freedom of information regime would or would not be an acceptable interference with the data subject's data integrity and privacy.[52] Where the first condition is satisfied, the exemption is absolute.[53]

(2) Where disclosure of the information to a member of the public (otherwise than under FOIA) would contravene Art 21 of the GDPR because the data subject has exercised his or her right to object to processing.[54] The objective of the second condition is to make specific provision for a situation in which the individual to whom the personal data relates has exercised his or her right to object to the processing of that data under Art 21 of the GDPR.[55] The second condition achieves this by importing into the FOIA regime the principles of Art 21 of the

48 As to the meaning of 'data subject,' see §33– 002.

49 See further §33– 003.

50 FOIA s 40(1), (2)(a) and (7); EIR reg 13(1); EI(S)R reg 11(2). The exemption in section 40(2) will not apply where the data relate both the to the applicant and to a third party. In this situation, the information will be rendered exempt information by FOIA s 40(1) and the applicant's right of access to this information will fall to be determined by the GDPR/DPA 2018. This is not a requirement under the FOI(S)A.

51 FOIA s 40(3A); FOI(S)A s 38(2A); EIR reg 13(2A); EI(S)R reg 11(3A). As to the meaning of the 'data protection principles' under the general processing regime, see §9– 006 (summary of principles) and §§9– 004 to 9– 039 (detail). In relation to law enforcement processing by competent authorities, the data protection principles are set out at §12– 011 (summary of principles) and §§12– 014 to 12– 036 (detail).

52 In the case of general processing by the public authority. In the case of law enforcement processing by a public authority that is a competent authority, the first condition achieves this by borrowing the data protection principles set out in DPA 2018 s 34(1). This condition is considered at §§33– 013 to 33– 023 below.

53 FOIA s 2(3)(f)(a); FOI(S)A s 2(2)(e)(ii); EIR reg 13(1)(a); EI(S)R reg 11(2)(b).

54 FOIA s 40(3B); FOI(S)A s 38(2B); EIR reg 13(2B)(a); EI(S)R reg 11(3B). In relation to GDPR Art 21 (right of data subject to object to processing), see §§10– 040 to 10– 044. There is no corresponding right for a data subject to object to law enforcement processing of personal data by a competent authority.

55 Prior to the DPA 2018 coming into force this was dealt with as part of the first condition by cross-references to DPA 1998 s 10.

GDPR.[56] Where information satisfies the second condition, the exemption is not absolute and the obligation to disclose will turn upon a consideration of the public interest.[57]

(3) Where, had the information been requested by the data subject under data protection legislation,[58] the information would be withheld on account of one of the exemptions applying to that request.[59] The objective of the third condition is to ensure that an applicant does not have a greater right of access to information relating to a third party than that third party would himself have had. The third condition imports the exemptions from disclosure under the data protection regime.[60] These are the exemptions that would apply to that third party were he to make a request under the data protection regime for data relating to himself. Where information satisfies the third condition, the exemption is not absolute and the obligation to disclose will turn upon a consideration of the public interest.[61]

Of the three conditions, it is the first that will most commonly be in issue.

33– 013 The first condition

The first condition applies where the disclosure of the information to a member of the public otherwise than under freedom of information legislation:[62]

(a) would contravene any of the data protection principles;[63] or
(b) would do so if the exemptions in s 24(1) of the DPA 2018 (manual unstructured data held by public authorities) were disregarded.

Of these two limbs, it is the first that will more commonly be in issue. The second limb will only apply to the extent that the information captured by the request: (a) is being held by the public authority in a manual, unstructured system;[64] or (b) is being processed in the course of an activity that is outside the scope of EU law or of an activity that is within Art 2(2)(b) of the GDPR.[65]

---

56 This condition is considered at §33– 024.

57 FOIA s 2(3)(f), (fa); FOI(S)A s 2(2)(e)(ii); EIR reg 13(1)(b); EI(S)R reg 11(2)(b).

58 In relation to general processing, a request is made under GDPR Art 15(1): see further §§10– 014 to 10– 017. In relation to law enforcement processing by a competent authority, a request is made under DPA 2018 s 45(1)(b): see further §§13– 014 to 13– 017.

59 FOIA s 40(4A); FOI(S)A s 38(3A); EIR reg 13(3A); EI(S)R reg 11(4A).

60 This condition is considered at §33– 025. The exemptions in relation to the general processing access right are provided for by DPA 2018 ss 15, 16 and 26, and Schs 2, 3 and 4: see further §10– 017 and Ch 11. The exemptions in relation to the law enforcement processing access right are provided for by DPA 2018 s 45(4): see further §13– 017.

61 FOIA s 2(3)(f); FOI(S)A s 2(2)(e); EIR reg 13(3); EI(S)R reg 11(4).

62 The inclusion of the phrase 'otherwise than under this Act' in FOIA s 40(3) makes it clear that the proposed disclosure has to be evaluated only under the data protection legislation as though FOIA or EIR did not exist. The culture of openness fostered by FOIA is thus subordinated to the protection of privacy as it finds expression in the data protection principles. Nor can the existence of FOIA fulfil any requirement of lawfulness or constitute a legal obligation under data protection legislation. See *House of Commons v IC and Norman Baker*, IT, 16 January 2007 at [46]-[50] (this point was not appealed).

63 These are identified in FOIA s 40(7) by cross-references to Art 5(1) of the GDPR (general processing) and DPA 2018 s 34(1) (law enforcement processing by a competent authority). Similarly: FOI(S)A s 38(5); EIR reg 2(4); EI(S)R reg 2(5). The processing principles for general processing are summarised at §9– 004. A more detailed analysis of them is set out at §§9– 006 to 9– 039. As to the meaning of 'general processing,' see §9– 001. The data protection principles for the law enforcement regime are summarised at §12– 011. A more detailed analysis of them is set out at §§12– 014 to 12– 036.

64 As to the meaning of which, see DPA 2018 s 21(4).

65 DPA 2018 ss 21(1), 24(1). Processing of personal data will be outside the scope of EU law principally where it is processing by an intelligence service, as defined in DPA 2018 s 82(2): see further §8– 036.

33– 014 Data protection principles

For the purposes of the first condition, the 'data protection principles' means:

- — in relation to general processing, the processing principles set out in Art 5(1) of the GDPR;[66] and
- — in relation to law enforcement processing by a public authority that is a competent authority, the data protection principles set out in s 34(1) of the DPA 1998.[67]

For each form of processing there are six principles. But the content of the six principles varies according to whether it is general processing or it is law enforcement processing. In determining whether there would or would not be a contravention of the 'data protection principles,' it is necessary to take account of the exemptions from those principles under the applicable processing regime. In other words, in considering whether there has been a contravention of any of the 'data protection principles,' those principles are not simply to be read in their 'raw' form as they appear in Art 5(1) of the GDPR or s 34(1) of DPA 2018, but all applicable exemptions must be taken into account.[68] Because the GDPR/DPA 2018 relate to all aspects of the 'processing' of data, the processing principles reflect the breadth of that term and do not always have an immediate application to the disclosure of data such as would result from a public authority providing information in answer to a request under freedom of information legislation. Nevertheless, as disclosure is one of the defined facets of 'processing', if disclosure of personal data of which the applicant is not the data subject contravenes any of the processing principles and none of the exemptions apply, this will render that data 'exempt information' for the purposes of freedom of information legislation. It is therefore necessary to consider each of the processing principles, recognising that some are inapposite to the disclosure of information by a public authority to an applicant.[69]

33– 015 The six principles

For the reasons set out below, it is suggested that in the majority of cases involving the second exemption, the only data protection principle which stands to be contravened by a disclosure under freedom of information legislation is the first principle.

(1) *First Principle*: Personal data must be processed lawfully, fairly and in a transparent manner in relation to the data subject.[70] Because of the intricacies of the first principle and its ready application to a disclosure under freedom of information legislation, it is considered separately below.

(2) *Second Principle*: Personal data must be collected for specified, explicit and legitimate purposes, and not further processed in a manner that is incompatible with those purposes.[71] The first part of the second principle relates to the collection of personal

---

66 The processing principles for general processing are summarised at §9– 004. A more detailed analysis of them is set out at §§9– 006 to 9– 039. As to the meaning of 'general processing,' see §9– 001.

67 The data protection principles for the law enforcement regime are summarised at §12– 011. A more detailed analysis of them is set out at §§12– 014 to 12– 036.

68 These exemptions are considered in chs 9-12.

69 Where a request is made of a public authority that is a competent authority that is holding the information for law enforcement purposes, it will be the data protection principles in Part 3 of the DPA 2018 that need to be considered. As to the meaning of 'competent authority.' see §12– 007. As to the meaning of 'law enforcement purposes,' see §12– 006.

70 A more detailed analysis of the first processing principle is set out at §§9– 006 to 9– 022 (general processing). In relation to law enforcement processing, see §§12– 014 to 12– 022.

71 A more detailed analysis of the second processing principle is set out at §§9– 023 to 9– 027 (general processing). In relation to law enforcement processing, see §§12– 023 to 12– 025. The 'purpose' does not have to be a core or operational purpose of the data controller; a data controller can process data for any lawful purpose: *Chief Constable of Humberside Police & ors v IC and SSHD* [2009] EWCA 1079 at [31], [56], [66] and [104]. Purposes can be notified

data: disclosure of personal information by a public authority is unlikely to result in a contravention of this part of the principle. The second part of the second principle is directed to all forms of processing, which will include disclosure. Given that for almost two decades public authorities holding information (including information supplied to or collected by them) have, under well-publicised freedom of information legislation, had a statutory duty when requested to disclose the information so requested (subject to cost and procedural issues, as well as the applicability of exemptions and public interest balance), it is difficult to characterise compliance with that statutory duty by disclosing that information as incompatible with the purposes for which it was collected. Further processing for archiving purposes in the public interest, scientific, historical or statistical purposes are not considered incompatible with the initial purposes. The disclosure of more extensive information on the same subject matter as that already disclosed does not constitute an additional 'purpose' or further processing of that information.[72]

(3) *Third Principle*: Personal data must be adequate, relevant and limited to what is necessary in relation to the purposes for which they are processed.[73] There is no definition of or guidance as to what is 'adequate', 'relevant' or 'excessive'.[74] As this principle is principally directed to the obtaining of data, it is difficult to see how disclosure of information under freedom of information legislation could by itself involve a contravention of this principle.[75]

(4) *Fourth Principle*: Personal data must be accurate and, where necessary, kept up-to-date; every reasonable step must be taken to ensure that personal data that is inaccurate having regard to the purposes for which it is processed, is erased or rectified without delay.[76] As this principle is directed to the holding or keeping of data, it is difficult to see how disclosure of personal information under freedom of information legislation could by itself involve a contravention of this principle.

(5) *Fifth Principle*: Personal data in a form that permits identification of data subjects must be kept for no longer than is necessary for the purpose or purposes for which it is processed.[77] As this principle is directed to the keeping of data, it is difficult to see how disclosure of personal information under freedom of information legislation could by itself involve a contravention of this principle.[78]

(6) *Sixth Principle*: Personal data must be processed in a manner that ensures appropriate security of the personal data, including protection against unauthorised

---

to the IC under broad heads: *House of Commons v IC and Norman Baker*, IT, 16 January 2007 at [98].

72 *Corporate Officer of the House of Commons v IC and Baker*, IT, 16 January 2007 at [97].

73 A more detailed analysis of the third processing principle is set out at §9– 028 (general processing). In relation to law enforcement processing, see §§12– 026 to 12– 027.

74 For an example of the application of this principle, see *Chief Constable of Humberside Police & ors v IC and SSHD* [2009] EWCA 1079.

75 In *Chief Constable of Humberside Police & ors v IC and SSHD* [2009] EWCA 1079 at [44], [57] and [66], the Court of Appeal was critical of the Information Tribunal for taking account of possible disclosure in determining whether the obtaining of data concerning criminal conviction and its retention on the Police National Computer breached the Third Principle.

76 A more detailed analysis of the fourth processing principle is set out at §§9– 029 to 9– 030 (general processing). In relation to law enforcement processing, see §§12– 028 to 12– 031.

77 A more detailed analysis of the fifth processing principle is set out at §§9– 031 to 9– 033 (general processing). In relation to law enforcement processing, see §§12– 032 to 12– 033.

78 In *Chief Constable of Humberside Police & ors v IC and SSHD* [2009] EWCA 1079 [44], [57] and [66], the Court of Appeal was critical of the Information Tribunal for taking account of possible disclosure in determining whether the obtaining of data concerning criminal conviction and its retention on the Police National Computer breached the Third Principle.

or unlawful processing and against accidental loss, destruction or damage, using appropriate technical or organisational measures.[79] It is difficult to see how a disclosure by a public authority under freedom of information legislation could by itself contravene this principle.

33– 016 First processing principle

On the above analysis, a public authority's disclosure (otherwise than under freedom of information legislation) of third party personal information will rarely contravene any data protection principle other than the first data protection principle. Accordingly, whether personal information relating to a third party is or is not exempt information will often turn on whether the disclosure of that information, otherwise than under freedom of information legislation, would contravene the first data protection principle. In relation to general processing, the first data protection principle involves three separate and cumulative requirements.[80]

— First, the personal data must be processed (ie disclosed) 'lawfully.' The lawfulness is to be adjudged on the basis of a disclosure otherwise than in compliance with any duty imposed by freedom of information legislation: in other words, but for the duty to disclosed imposed by freedom of information legislation, would it have been lawful for the public authority to have disclosed the personal data?

— Secondly, the personal data must be processed 'fairly.' In the present context, this means that the public authority's disclosure to an applicant of personal information relating to another person would be 'fair.' The 'fairness' is to be adjudged on the basis of a disclosure otherwise than in compliance with any duty imposed by freedom of information legislation: again, what this asks is whether, but for the duty to disclosed imposed by freedom of information legislation, would it have been lawful for the public authority to have disclosed the personal data?

— Thirdly, in the case of a public authority that holds the information as part of its general processing, the disclosure must be 'transparent' in relation to the data subject.[81]

Paradoxically, for freedom of information purposes the first processing principle is more readily satisfied for law enforcement processing than it is for general processing.

33– 017 Processed 'lawfully'

Where a public authority is holding personal information as part of its general processing, processing of that information will be 'lawful' if and to the extent that one of the following six bases is met:

(a) The data subject has given his consent[82] to the processing for a specific purpose.

(c) The processing is necessary for compliance with any legal obligation to which the data

---

79 A more detailed analysis of the sixth processing principle is set out at §§9– 034 to 9– 039 (general processing). In relation to law enforcement processing, see §§12– 034 to 12– 036.

80 GDPR Art 5(1); DPA 2018 s 34(1). In the case of a public authority holding information in its capacity as a competent authority engaging in law enforcement processing, the first data protection principle involves just the first two of these requirements: see §12– 014. But the content of these two requirements is quite different: in relation to the requirement that personal data be processed 'lawfully' for law enforcement purposes, see §12– 015; in relation to the requirement that personal data be processed 'fairly' for the law enforcement purposes, see §12– 014.

81 There is no requirement of transparency in relation to law enforcement processing by a competent authority: see §12– 014.

82 As to the meaning of 'consent' for general processing purposes, see §8– 024. Consent given in advance – a common feature of small print in many standard form contracts (particularly online) – will not be interpreted as consent to processing which is not proportionate: *Rugby Football Union v Consolidated Information Services Ltd* [2012] UKSC 55, [2012] 1 WLR 3333 at [50].

controller is subject.

(e) The processing is necessary for the purposes of a task carried out in the public interest or in the exercise of official authority vested in the controller.

(f) The processing is necessary for the purposes of legitimate interests pursued by the data controller or by a third party except where such interests are over-ridden by the interests or fundamental rights and freedoms of the data subject that require protection of personal data, in particular where the data subject is a child.

Point (f) of the first subparagraph shall not apply to processing carried out by public authorities in the performance of their tasks.[83]

Because the focus of the first condition is contravention of the data protection principles by the disclosure of information otherwise than under freedom of information legislation, that legislation cannot supply the legal obligation for the purposes of condition (c) nor the task or official authority for the purposes of condition (e).

33–018 Lawfully: competing interests

In setting out the circumstances in which processing will be lawful for the purposes of the first processing principle, Art 6(1) of the GDPR resembles the conditions listed in Sch 2 to the DPA 1998 (at least one of which had to be met in order for processing to comply with the first data protection principle under that Act). In particular, Art 6(1)(f) of the GDPR resembles – but is not identical to – condition 6(1) in Sch 2 to the DPA 1998. Many of the authorities considering the second personal information exemption as it read prior to 25 May 2018 turned upon the application of condition 6(1) in Sch 2 to the DPA 1998.[84] The following principles in relation condition 6(1) emerge from those authorities:

(1) If it can be shown that the disclosure of the information to the applicant was necessary[85] for the purposes of legitimate interests pursued by the public authority or the applicant,[86] then subject to the balancing exercise required for that condition, the condition will be satisfied.[87]

---

83 For the purposes of determining the lawfulness of the processing involved in the disclosure of the information, the coda to Art 6(1), ie beginning with the words 'Point (f)...' is to be disregarded: FOIA s 40(8); FOI(S)A s 38(5A); EIR reg 13(6); EI(S)R reg 11(7).

84 See, for example: *Goldsmith International Business School v IC and Home Office* [2014] UKUT 563 (AAC) at [34]-[42]; *Illingworth v IC and NHS Commissioning Board* [2016] UKUT 293 (AAC) at [22]-[24]; *UKIP v IC* [2019] UKUT 62 (AAC) at [28]-[29]; *Oxford Phoenix Innovation Limited v IC and Medicines and Healthcare Products Regulatory Agency* [2018] UKUT 192 (AAC) at [93]; *Morton v IC and Wirral MBC* [2018] UKUT 295 (AAC) at [35]-[38]; *IC v Halpin* [2019] UKUT 29 (AAC) at [10], [31].

85 The word 'necessary' carried with it connotations from the ECHR; ie whether a pressing social need is involved and whether the disclosure is proportionate to the legitimate aim pursued: *House of Commons v IC and Brooke, Leapman, Ungoed-Thomas* [2008] EWHC 1084 (Admin), [2009] 3 All ER 403 at [43]. Applied in *Davis v IC and Olympic Delivery Authority*, FTT, 4 January 2011 at [32] – disclosure of information about individual employees' performance-related pay would breach the first data protection principle. See also *R (Ellis) v Chief Constable of the Essex Police* [2003] EWHC 1321 (Admin) (DC), [2003] 2 FLR 566 at [29] and the authorities considered at §8–034.

86 In relation to this provision, it is the legitimate interests of the actual requester (who is the person who would have a right to receive the information under the Act) which must be considered; the fact that a disclosure under the Act is a disclosure 'to the world' is properly taken into account at the stage of considering the extent of the prejudice which would be caused to the data subject by the disclosure: *Digby-Cameron v IC and Bedfordshire Police*, IT, 26 January 2009 at [16].

87 In *A v Information Commissioner*, IT, 11 July 2006 the Information Tribunal found that the legitimate interests of a local education authority in disclosing the identities of two teachers who had expressed concern about a particular pupil being returned to class without additional teaching support to the parent of that child was outweighed by the legitimate interests of those teachers. In *Alcock v IC and Chief Constable of Staffordshire Police*, IT, 3 January 2007 at [32] the Information Tribunal held that even if an applicant were pursuing a legitimate interest in finding the name of an informant whose information had resulted in a damaging police investigation of the applicant, disclosure was nevertheless unwarranted by reason of the prejudice to the legitimate interest of the data subject, who had specifically requested that his identity be kept confidential. In *Evans v IC and MoD*, IT, 23 June 2008 the Tribunal held that it was necessary for a journalist to have access to raw data in order to publish a story about lobbyists' access to ministers, but that the prejudice caused to the lobbyist in question by release of the information

(2) 'Necessary' for the purposes of this condition means 'reasonably necessary,' and not absolutely or strictly necessary.[88] But in order for something to be necessary there must be no other reasonable means of meeting it.[89]
(3) Necessity is part of the proportionality test and requires the minimum interference with the ECHR Art 8 rights of the data subject that will achieve the legitimate aim pursued.[90]
(4) Public interest in the disclosure of official information can amount to a legitimate interest for the purposes of condition 6(1).[91]
(5) 'Legitimate interest' is a wider concept than 'public interest'.[92] For example, the pursuit of a legitimate business has been held to be a legitimate interest.[93]
(6) In order for condition 6(1) to be satisfied, the legitimate interests of those to whom the data would be disclosed (ie members of the public) must outweigh the prejudice to the rights, freedoms and legitimate interests of the data subject.[94]
(7) In carrying out the balancing exercise it is important to take into account that disclosure under freedom of information legislation would be free of any duty of confidence.[95]

33– 019 Lawful: special category data

To the extent that the data being processed falls within one or more of the special categories of personal data,[96] the processing will be prohibited (and therefore unlawful) unless one or more of the conditions in Art 9(1) of the GDPR, as supplemented by the further conditions in the DPA 2018, is met.[97] To the extent that information captured by a request is within one of the special categories of personal data and it relates to a person other than the applicant, this will operate to widen the circumstances in which that information will be exempt information by operation of the first condition.[98]

(concerning his business) outweighed the public interest in disclosure.

88 *South Lanarkshire Council v Scottish IC* [2013] UKSC 55, 2013 GWD 25-508, 2013 SLT 799, [2013] 1 WLR 2421. On the meaning of 'necessary' see further §8– 034.

89 *IC v Halpin* [2019] UKUT 29 (AAC) at [31].

90 *R (Ali & anor) v Minister for the Cabinet Office the Statistics Board* [2012] EWHC 1943 (Admin) at [76].

91 This follows from Recital 72 of Directive 95/46/EC: see *House of Commons v IC and Leapman, Brooke and Thomas*, IT, 26 February 2008 at [53]-[55]. See also *Davis v IC and Olympic Delivery Authority*, FTT, 4 January 2011 at [31(d)].

92 See *Evans v IC and MoD*, IT, 23 June 2008 at [20]: 'We recognise that legitimate interest is not the same as public interest: legitimate interest goes wider than the narrower concept of public interest: someone may have a legitimate interest in pursuing particular information which is of very little public interest.'

93 *Murray v Express Newspapers plc* [2007] EWHC 1908 at [76].

94 *Corporate Officer of the House of Commons v IC and Baker*, IT, 16 January 2007 at [90]; *England and LB of Bexley v IC*, IT, 10 May 2007 at [108]; *McTaggart v IC*, IT, 4 June 2007. The Tribunal in *Ministry of Defence v IC*, IT, 20 July 2007 at [79] held that disclosure of a directory of certain Ministry staff satisfied the conditions of para 6(1). However, a request for a full copy of an enforcement file concerning a property did not satisfy para 6(2) and was refused under EIR regs 12(5)(b) and 13: *Young v IC and Dept for Environment for Northern Ireland*, IT, 12 December 2007.

95 *Rodriguez-Noza v IC and Nursing and Midwifery Council* [2015] UKUT 449 (AAC) at [23]; *IC v Halpin* [2019] UKUT 29 (AAC) at [20].

96 Which, under Art 9(1) of the GDPR means personal data revealing: (a) the racial or ethnic origin of the data subject; (b) his political opinions; (c) his religious or philosophical beliefs; (d) whether he is a member of a trade union; (e) his health; (f) his sexual life or sexual orientation. A photograph of a person showing him to be Caucasian was held to constitute sensitive personal data under the DPA 1998 equivalent provision: *Murray v Express Newspapers plc* [2007] EWHC 1908 at [80].

97 A full consideration of the special categories of personal data is given in Ch 8.

98 FOIA s 40(3A); FOI(S)A s 38(2A); EIR reg 13(2A(a)); EI(S)R reg 11(3A)(a).

33– 020 Processed fairly

The second requirement of the first 'data protection principle' in general processing is that personal data be processed 'fairly.' For the purposes of the second personal information exemption, the processing in question is the disclosure of the personal information to a person other than a person who is the data subject of that information. Under the pre-25 May 2018 regime, the content of the requirement that personal data be processed 'fairly' was spelled out in some detail.[99] The content of the requirement that personal data be processed 'fairly' has not been spelled out in the post-25 May 2018 regime.[100] Nevertheless, certain considerations relevant to the notion of 'fair' processing do emerge from the GDPR. In summary, these provisions set out the information to be provided to the data subject where his or her data is collected from him or her or from other sources. Such information includes the purposes of the processing and the recipients or categories of recipients of the data. Such information can be given in reasonably generous terms.[101] However, if a public authority has stated that information provided to it will be used for a particular purpose, it will be more difficult to demonstrate that it would be fair to disclose that information in answer to a request for information.[102] This will be of particular importance where the person has volunteered the information, as opposed to supplying it under compulsion or in return for permission of some sort.[103] It has become increasingly common for public authorities to forewarn people supplying information to them (whether in completing a form or however) that that information may be disclosed under freedom of information legislation. Where information has been supplied to a public authority that has given such a warning, the requirement of fairness is more likely to be satisfied, and vice versa.[104]

33– 021 Processed fairly: categories

The wording of the first data protection principle in the DPA 1998 was held to mean that there was a general obligation to process data fairly, in addition to the requirement to comply with the detailed conditions that were listed in Schedule 2 of that Act.[105] This entailed an assessment of the nature of the data, the identity of the person to whom the information was to be disclosed and the possible implications for the data subject.[106] It did not, however, involve a consideration of the interests or motives of the person seeking the information. Over time, a consistent body of authority emerged in which the approach to certain, often-requested, categories of information became settled.

(1) *Public sector employees.* Where the data subject is or was an officer or an employee of a public authority, fairness may assume less importance:

---

99 DPA 2018 Sch 1 Part 2 paras 1-4.

100 See §9– 015.

101 See: *Grow with Us Ltd v Green Thumb (UK) Ltd* [2006] EWCA Civ1201; *House of Commons v IC and Norman Baker*, IT, 16 January 2007.

102 See, eg, *England and LB of Bexley v IC*, IT, 10 May 2007 at [106].

103 Although in *England and LB of Bexley v IC*, IT, 10 May 2007 certain information was required to be supplied by property owners in their Council Tax return, it was not mandatory to record that the property was empty and the evidence was that some owners did not include that information (at [103]).

104 In *England and LB of Bexley v IC*, IT, 10 May 2007 the Information Tribunal found at [106] that it would be unfair to disclose personal data (namely, the ownership of vacant properties in the area of the local authority) without the consent of the owner. Whether that line could be maintained for information received after the FOIA came fully into force and its effect widely known is not clear.

105 *Blake v IC and Wiltshire CC*, IT, 2 November 2009 at [28].

106 The inherent sensitivity of the information, the likelihood of identifiability of individuals from statistics, and by whom such individuals could be identified, is integral to the question of the fairness of disclosure: *Exeter City Council v IC and Guagliardo*, FTT, 24 September 2012.

> when assessing the fair processing requirements under the DPA…the consideration given to the interests of data subjects, who are public officials where data are processed for a public function, is no longer first or paramount. Their interests are still important, but where data subjects carry out public functions, hold elective office or spend public funds they must have the expectation that their public actions will be subject to greater scrutiny than would be the case in respect of their private lives. This principle still applies even where a few aspects of their private lives are intertwined with their public lives but where the vast majority of processing of personal data relates to the data subject's public life.[107]

There is a sliding scale of protection depending on where the data subject stands with regard to carrying out public functions and the public authority's duty to respect its employees' reasonable expectations of privacy.[108] There is a stronger expectation of privacy in the case of junior employees who are regarded as accountable to their employer and not directly to the public.[109] There is a strong expectation of privacy where personal data has been obtained for the purposes of an internal investigation during the course of a person's employment, even if the data subject is a senior member of staff.[110] However, in an appropriate case, redaction of names and other identifying details will permit a fair disclosure of the unredacted remainder.[111] Individuals who apply unsuccessfully for public sector jobs are entitled to expect that their job applications and the information they contain will be kept private.[112] Those who are paid from the public purse should expect some information about their salaries to be made public.[113] Disclosure of salary scales or bands is generally appropriate; disclosure of exact salaries will only be appropriate in exceptional circumstances.[114] The Information Commissioner has identified five non-exhaustive factors relevant to the determination of whether the disclosure of a public official's salary information would be fair:[115]

---

107 *House of Commons v IC and Norman Baker*, IT, 16 January 2007 at [78]. Applied in *Thackeray v IC and GMC*, FTT, 23 February 2010 at [63].

108 *Salmon v IC and King's College Cambridge*, IT, 17 July 2008 at [44].

109 *Gilbert v IC*, FTT, 21 March 2011 at [16]. See also: *Roberts v IC and DBIS*, FTT, 26 May 2010 at [25]; *Greenwood v IC and Bolton MBC*, FTT, 14 September 2010 at [48]; *Greenwood v IC and Bolton MBC*, FTT, 17 February 2012 at [26]; *Home Office v IC and Central London County Court*, FTT, 27 March 2012 at [30]; *Arts and Humanities Research Council v IC and Bimmler*, FTT, 4 December 2012 at [76]; *O'Hare v IC and Scotland Office*, FTT, 13 January 2017; *Ministry of Justice v IC and Le Vay*, FTT, 12 June 2017; *Cox v IC and Home Office* [2018] UKUT 119 (AAC).

110 *Salmon v IC and King's College Cambridge*, IT, 17 July 2008; *Waugh v IC and Doncaster College*, IT, 29 December 2008 at [40]; *Blake v IC and Wiltshire CC*, IT, 2 November 2009 at [34]; *Magherafelt District Council v IC*, First-Tier Tribunal, 3 February 2010 at [47]-[49]; *Bousfield v IC and Liverpool Women's Hospital NHS Foundation Trust*, FTT, 11 October 2010 at [50] (compromise agreements); *Guardian Newspapers Ltd v IC*, FTT, 8 November 2010 at [31] (de-registration of care providers); *Cubells v IC and General Medical Council*, FTT, 2 March 2016; *Waugh v IC*, FTT, 11 April 2016; *Foster v IC and GMC*, FTT, 30 May 2017; *Young v IC and NHS*, FTT, 7 July 2017 (position even clearer where information related to staff members' interaction with doctor falling short of complaints); but cf *Armitage v IC and Health and Care Professions Council*, FTT, 20 November 2017 (reasons for finding no case to answer against paramedic not exempt), and see similar reasoning in a related context *B v General Medical Council* [2018] EWCA Civ 1497 at [63]. The position may be different where the focus of the information is on the public authority, rather than an individual: *Bryce v IC and Cambridgeshire Constabulary*, FTT, 8 June 2010 at [74]; *Morton v IC and Wirral MBC* [2018] UKUT 295 (AAC) at [58]-[83] (whistleblowers).

111 *Dun v IC and National Audit Office*, FTT, 18 January 2011 at [55].

112 *Bolton v IC and East Riding Yorkshire Council*, FTT, 26 March 2012 at [20].

113 See Information Commissioner's Guidance *When Should Salaries be Disclosed?* (23 February 2009); *King's College London v IC*, FTT, 30 September 2014 at [97].

114 Information Commissioner's Guidance *When Should Salaries be Disclosed?* (23 February 2009) p 4.

115 This approach was endorsed by the Tribunal in *Gibson v IC*, First-Tier Tribunal, 22 January 2010 at [16] and [36]. See also: *Pycroft v IC and Stroud District Council*, FTT, 11 February 2011 at [21].

(a) what the individual in question was told at the commencement of, or during the course of, employment;
(b) the relevant contractual or non-contractual provisions and conditions surrounding the employment as well as the general surrounding circumstances;
(c) the level of the individual's grade and position within the public authority;
(d) the expectation and the degree to which other salary-related information was publicised and/or otherwise made available, eg salary/pay bands and other general information taking into account the contents of any published accounts;
(e) the need to strike a balance between information relating to the public position of the individual and the individual's private life.[116]

(2) *Elected representatives.* There are strong arguments in favour of disclosure where an individual has a role in the democratic process, even as a youth councillor, provided that their position is in the public domain (eg as a result of their facebook page).[117] Where information suggests that councillors or public officials have acted improperly or discreditably, the information is unlikely to be exempt.[118]

(3) *Others.* Although most of the decided cases concern information about officers or employees of public authorities, or about allegations of impropriety or discreditable conduct within such authorities, there are also decisions dealing with other situations such as the names of athletes who had undergone drug tests,[119] names of journalists identified in phone-hacking investigations,[120] and personal data relating to third parties in a convicted killer's statements to the police.[121]

33–022 Fairness by anonymisation

One means of disclosing personal information about a third party under freedom of information legislation while accommodating the requirement to process personal data fairly is by anonymising the personal data so that the third party can no longer be identified. In essence, if carried out to the point that the third party can no longer be identified from the information being disclosed, that information will cease to be personal data of which the third party is a data subject. Mere redaction of the name of a third party will not necessarily render information sufficiently anonymous to reach this point. The approach taken is to ask whether a 'motivated intruder' could identify the third party:

> The 'motivated intruder' is taken to be a person who starts without any prior knowledge but who wishes to identify the individual from whose personal data the anonymised data has been derived. This test is meant to assess whether the motivated intruder would be successful.
>
> The approach assumes that the 'motivated intruder' is reasonably competent, has access to resources such as the internet, libraries, and all public documents, and would

---

116 Citing *House of Commons v IC and Norman Baker*, IT, 16 January 2007, especially at [78].

117 *Morley v IC and Surrey Heath Borough Council*, FTT, 31 May 2012 at [76]-[77], overturned on the facts on appeal: *Surrey Heath BC v IC and Morley* [2014] UKUT 0339 (AAC).

118 See: *Haslam v IC and Bolton Council* [2016] UKUT 139 (AAC), where names of councillors summonsed to court for failing to pay council tax were not exempt; *Dedman v IC*, FTT, 9 January 2017, where a draft report into an investigation of serious complaints against the chair of a parish council were not exempt; *Vulliamy v IC*, FTT, 14 December 2017, former councillors, no general rule applies; *Simmonett v IC*, FTT, 9 October 2017, where a report into allegations of bullying and harassment against the chair of a parish council were not exempt.

119 *UK Anti-Doping Ltd v IC and Nourse*, FTT, 10 February 2014.

120 *IC v Colenso-Dunne* [2015] UKUT 471 (AAC).

121 *Corke v IC and West Yorkshire Police*, FTT, 28 June 2016.

> employ investigative techniques such as making enquiries of people who may have additional knowledge of the identity of the data subject or advertising for anyone with information to come forward. The 'motivated intruder' is not assumed to have any specialist knowledge such as computer hacking skills, or to have access to specialist equipment or to resort to criminality such as burglary, to gain access to data that is kept securely.
>
> Clearly, some sorts of data will be more attractive to a 'motivated intruder' than others. Obvious sources of attraction to an intruder might include … political or activist purposes, eg as part of a campaign against a particular organisation or person…[122]

33– 023 Processed transparently

As noted above, the first data protection principle as re-formulated under Art 5(1) of the GDPR contains a requirement to process data 'in a transparent manner in relation to the data subject.'[123] This may suggest that a public authority which discloses personal data of a third party under freedom of information legislation should make reasonable and proportionate efforts to notify the third party in advance and allow that third party to make representations, or at least notify the third party after the disclosure that it has been made.

33– 024 The second condition

Information satisfies the second condition where its disclosure to a member of the public would contravene Art 21 of the GDPR.[124] The second condition will rarely be satisfied. Under Art 21 of the GDPR an individual may give a notice to a data controller requiring the data controller to cease or not begin processing (which will include holding or disclosing) any personal data in respect of which he is the data subject on grounds relating to his or her particular situation. Where such a notice has been given, the data controller must no longer process the personal data unless it can demonstrate compelling legitimate grounds for processing that override the interests, rights and freedoms of the data subject or for the establishment, exercise or defence of legal claims. Thus information can only satisfy the second condition where the individual to whom that information relates has given the public authority a notice under Art 21 of the GDPR and disclosure of that information to the public would contravene Art 21 of the GDPR. The exemption is not absolute,[125] so that the public authority must weigh the public interest in upholding the exemption against the public interest in disclosing the information. There is a corresponding exemption from the duty to confirm or deny where giving to a member of the public a confirmation or denial that the requested information is held by the public authority would itself contravene Art 21 of the GDPR.[126]

33– 025 The third condition

Information satisfies the third condition where, had it been sought in a subject access request[127] by the person to whom it relates, it would have been withheld because of applicable exemptions

---

122 Taken from the Information Commissioner's *Anonymisation Code of Practice*, pp 22-23 and approved by the Upper Tribunal in: *IC v Magherafelt DC* [2012] UKUT 263 (AAC) at [37]-[40], [87]; *Information Commissioner v Miller* [2018] UKUT 229 (AAC); *Morton v IC and Wirral MBC* [2018] UKUT 295 (AAC) at [45]-[46].

123 See also recitals (39), (58), (60), (71) and (78) to and Art 13.2 and 14.2 of the GDPR, which provide some clues as to the content of 'transparency.' There is an expectation that the Information Commissioner's code of conduct will provide detail of what is required for transparency: Art 40.2.

124 FOIA s 40(3B); FOI(S)A s 38(2B); EIR reg 13(2B); EI(S)R reg 11(3B).

125 FOIA s 2(3)(f), (fa); FOI(S)A s 2(2)(e)(ii); EIR reg 13(1)(a); EI(S)R reg 11(2)(b).

126 FOIA s 40(5B)(b); EIR reg 13(5A); EI(S)R reg 11(6). Exemption from the duty to confirm or deny is absolute. There is no separate duty to confirm or deny under FOI(S)A and s 18 of that Act does not apply to exemption under s 38.

127 Whether under Art 15(1) of the GDPR or under DPA 2018 s 45(1)(b).

under the GDPR/DPA 2018 regime.[128] The third condition seeks to ensure that an applicant does not have a greater right of access to information relating to a third party than that third party himself would have. Freedom of information legislation achieves this objective by putting the person who made the request for information in the position that the person to whom the information relates would be in had the latter person made a subject access request under Art 15 of the GDPR. Thus, information is exempt information for the purposes of freedom of information legislation if that information, had it been sought under Art 15 of the GDPR by the data subject, would be exempt from communication to the data subject.[129] Exemption under the third condition is a qualified exemption, so that the public authority will need to go on and consider whether the public interest in maintaining this exemption outweighs the public interest in disclosure.[130] Similarly, the duty to confirm or deny is disapplied, where, had the person to whom the information relates made a subject access request, the public authority holding the information would not be required to inform that person whether it was holding or otherwise processing the information.[131]

33– 026 The duty to confirm or deny

In relation to the duty to confirm or deny, the position is similar to the disclosure duty: if the mere confirmation or denial of the holding of information answering the terms of the request would contravene any of the processing principles, then the duty to confirm or deny will be excluded.[132] Most of the decided cases under the former data processing regime concerned situations where confirmation would reveal the existence of complaints or allegations against individuals that have been dismissed or not pursued. Exclusion of the duty is qualified, so that it is necessary for a public authority to consider whether the public interest in maintaining the exclusion of the duty to confirm or deny outweighs the public interest in disclosing the information.[133] There is no duty to confirm or deny where giving such confirmation or denial would contravene an Art 21 GDPR notice,[134] or where the information would be withheld on a subject access request by the reason of the exemptions.[135]

4. PRE-25 MAY 2018 APPROACH

33– 027 Introduction

In order to understand the utility and limitations of authorities dealing with the pre-25 May

---

[128] FOIA s 40(4A); FOI(S)A s 38(3A); EIR reg 13(3A); EI(S)R reg 11(4A).

[129] FOIA s 40(4A); FOI(S)A s 38(3A); EIR reg 13(3A); EI(S)R reg 11(4A).

[130] FOIA s 2(3)(f), (fa); FOI(S)A s 2(2)(e)(ii); EIR reg 13(1)(a); EI(S)R reg 11(2)(b).

[131] The disapplication of the duty under the FOIA is effected by FOIA s 40(5B)(c). And similarly, EIR reg 13(5A)(b). The exemption from the duty to confirm or deny is, in the case of the FOIA, qualified.

[132] FOIA s 40(5B)(a)(i), (ii); EIR reg 13(5A); EI(S)R reg 11(6). There is no separate duty to confirm or deny under FOI(S)A and s 18 is inapplicable to this exemption. For the meaning of a 'duty to confirm or deny', see §1– 008. For cases on the duty to confirm or deny see: *Smith v IC*, FTT, 7 February 2014, appealed dismissed in *Smith v IC and Chief Constable of Essex Police* [2016] UKUT 455 (AAC); *Parker v IC and North Lincolnshire Council*, FTT, 26 February 2014; *Foster v IC*, FTT, 13 January 2014 at [18] (no inflexible rule that the existence of allegations of impropriety made against a professional person which have not become public should not be disclosed – upheld on this point on appeal: *Rodriguez-Noza v IC and Nursing and Midwifery Council* [2015] UKUT 449 (AAC)); *C v IC and Nursing and Midwifery Council*, FTT, 11 March 2015; *Mitchell v IC and Nursing and Midwifery Council*, FTT, 7 October 2015.

[133] FOIA ss 2(1), 2(3)(f) and 40(5B); EIR reg 13(5A). Exemption from the duty to confirm or deny is absolute under the EI(S)R.

[134] FOIA s 40(5B)(b); EIR reg 13(5b)(B). FOI(S)A and EI(S)R take a different approach – see EI(S)R reg 11(6).

[135] FOIA s 40(5B)(c), (d); EIR eg 13(5B)(c)-(e). FOI(S)A and EI(S)R take a different approach – see EI(S)R reg 11(6).

2018 amendments to the personal information exemptions, it is necessary to understand its similarities and differences from the legislation after that date. The first of the two personal information exemptions has not changed, and no more need be said about it. The second exemption, did change and more does need to be said about it before that change.

33– 028 Approach under DPA 1998

In the case of the second exemption, the pre-25 May 2018 regime provided exemption from the disclosure obligation if either of two (rather than any of three) conditions was satisfied. Putting to one side more esoteric situations, the first condition was satisfied whenever disclosure of the information to a member of the public otherwise than under FOIA would contravene any of the data protection principles in Sch 1 to the DPA 1998. The second condition was satisfied whenever the information would not have had to have been disclosed under a data subject request made under s 7 of DPA 1998. In practice, exemption under the second personal information exemption was invariably decided on the basis of the first condition, and the applicability of that condition tended to revolve around whether disclosure would breach the first data protection principle in DPA 1998. The first data protection principle required that personal data be processed fairly and lawfully, that at least one of the conditions in Sch 2 be met and, in the case of sensitive personal data, that at least one of the conditions in Sch 3 be met. As to these:

Fairly. Part 2 of Sch 1 to the DPA 1998 set out mandatory interpretational guidance to the meaning of 'fairly.' This guidance concentrated on the method by which the controller – in this case, the public authority – obtained the personal data. The case law in relation to fairness has been summarised above.[136]

Lawfully. It was unclear what the separate requirement of lawfulness was aimed at. Any disclosure of information proscribed by statute would certainly not be lawful processing.[137] The Tribunal suggested that 'lawful' meant not prohibited by law such that breach of an express contractual obligation of confidence would not constitute processing that was not lawful.[138] This position was impossible to reconcile with High Court authority which held that processing would be unlawful if it breached an equitable duty of confidence.[139] If a non-contractual, equitable obligation was relevant to whether processing was lawful, so too a contractual obligation of confidence had to be. Disclosure where data controllers knew that the disclosed data would be used for direct marketing purposes was unlawful if the data subject had made an objection under section 11 of the DPA 1998.[140] A disclosure of information that gave rise to a civil liability (eg because it is a breach of confidence) probably did not constitute lawful processing.[141] The question of whether disclosure was lawful also required a consideration of whether disclosure would breach

---

136 See §§33– 021 to 33– 021.

137 The Tribunal has suggested that disclosure which would be contrary to government guidance would also be unlawful: *England v IC*, IT, 10 May 2007. This is questionable, given that guidance is not legally binding.

138 *Gibson v IC and Craven District Council*, FTT, 22 February 2011 at [47]. cf *Kirkhope v IC and National Archives*, FTT, 15 January 2013 at [106].

139 *Campbell v Mirror Group Newspapers* [2002] EWHC 499 (QB) at [102]. See also: *Murray v Express Newspapers Ltd* [2007] EWHC 1908 at [72]; *Law Society & ors v Kordowski* [2011] EWHC 3185 (QB) at [78], [100].

140 *Robertson v Wakefield DC and SSHD* [2001] EWHC Admin 915, [2002] QB 1052. This case concerned a challenge under DPA 1998 and HRA 1998 to the practice of making information on the electoral register available to organisations, some of which would use the names and addresses on the register for the purposes of direct marketing. The claimant succeeded on all his grounds, including breach of his Art 8 right to private life and the right to free elections under Art 3 of Protocol 1 ECHR.

141 *Blake v IC and Wiltshire CC*, IT, 2 November 2009 at [37].

the Human Rights Act 1998.[142] Any disclosure that amounted to a breach of the data subject's Art 8 right to private life was not lawful.[143] The CJEU had held that communication of personal data to third parties amounted to an interference with Art 8, and that the provisions of Council Directive 95/46/EC permitting such communication had to be interpreted in accordance with Art 8.[144]

Schedule 2 condition. Although Sch 2 to the DPA 1998 provided six separate conditions, only one of which needed to be satisfied, invariably it was condition 6(1) that was invoked and proved contentious. This condition provided that:

> the processing is necessary for the purposes of legitimate interests pursued by the data controller or by the third party or parties to whom the data are disclosed, except where the processing is unwarranted in any particular case by reason of prejudice to the rights and freedoms or legitimate interests of the data subject.

This was said to involve a three-state approach in which the tribunal asked itself: (a) is the data controller or the third party or parties to whom the data are disclosed pursuing a legitimate interest or interests?; (b) is the processing involved necessary for the purposes of those interests?; and (c) is the processing unwarranted in the case by reason of prejudice to the rights and freedoms or legitimate interests of the data subject?[145]

142 Because there is no clear positive right to information or right to publish information, the consideration of lawfulness under HRA will likely be restricted to Art 8.

143 See *Dept of Health v IC and Pro-Life Alliance*, IT, 15 October 2009 at [71]-[72].

144 *Rechnungshof v Österreichischer Rundfunk* [2002] ECR I-4989, [2003] 3 CMLR 10 at [68] and [73]-[75].

145 *South Lanarkshire Council v Scottish IC* [2013] UKSC 55, [2013] 1 WLR 2421 at [18]; *Cox v IC and Home Office* [2018] UKUT 119 (AAC) at [20]-[21]; *Goldsmith International Business School v IC and Home Office* [2014] UKUT 563 (AAC) at [34]-[42]; *Illingworth v IC and NHS Commissioning Board* [2016] UKUT 293 (AAC) at [22]-[24]; *UKIP v IC* [2019] UKUT 62 (AAC) at [28]-[29]; *Oxford Phoenix Innovation Limited v IC and Medicines and Healthcare Products Regulatory Agency* [2018] UKUT 192 (AAC) at [93]; *Morton v IC and Wirral MBC* [2018] UKUT 295 (AAC) at [35]-[38]; *IC v Halpin* [2019] UKUT 29 (AAC) at [10], [31].

Chapter 34

Commercial and other confidentiality

1. BREACH OF CONFIDENCE: INTRODUCTION[1]

34– 001 The exemption

By s 41(1) of FOIA, information is rendered exempt information where it was obtained by a public authority from any other person (including another public authority)[2] and the disclosure of the information to the public (otherwise than under the Act) by the public authority holding it would constitute a breach of confidence actionable by that or any other person.[3] Similarly, the duty to confirm or deny does not arise if, or to the extent that, a confirmation or denial that the public authority holds the information specified in the request would (apart from the Act) constitute an actionable breach of confidence.[4] The exemption and the exclusion of the duty to confirm or deny are absolute.[5] Accordingly, disapplication of the duty to disclose and of the duty to confirm or deny does not expressly depend upon a balancing of the public interest in maintaining the exemption (or in excluding the duty to confirm or deny), on the one hand, against the public interest in disclosure (or in disclosing whether the public authority holds the requested information), on the other hand.[6] A public interest defence is, however, available to a claim for breach of confidence.[7] Therefore, a consideration of the public interest is required to determine whether disclosure would constitute an actionable breach of confidence. In addition, so far as government secrets are concerned, the Crown is not entitled to restrain disclosure or to obtain redress on confidentiality grounds unless it can establish that disclosure has damaged or would be likely to damage the public interest.[8] For these reasons, although the wording of the Act itself does not require any such evaluation to be made, the applicability of s 41 will involve in each instance some consideration of the public interest in disclosure and the public interest in maintaining the confidence. In balancing competing interests, the FTT has tended to take as a starting point 'the assumption that confidentiality should be preserved unless outweighed by countervailing factors'.[9] This approach is unobjectionable so far as concerns the cause of action for breach of confidence in its traditional form. It can be reconciled with the taxonomy of that cause of action as extended to accommodate claims relating to private information,[10] although the FTT has been criticised for failing to take proper account of the

---

1 For a more general treatment of the law of confidentiality, see: RG Toulson and CM Phipps, *Confidentiality*, 3rd edn (Sweet & Maxwell, 2012); T Aplin, L Bently, P Johnson and S Malynicz, *Gurry on Breach of Confidence. The Protection of Confidential Information*, 2nd edn (Oxford, Oxford University Press, 2012); P Stanley, *The Law of Confidentiality. A Restatement*, Hart, 2008; BC Reid, *Confidentiality and the Law* (London, Waterlow, 1986); L Clarke (ed), *Confidentiality and the Law* (London, Lloyd's of London, 1990); S Ricketson, *The Law of Intellectual Property: Copyright, Designs & Confidential Information*, 2nd edn (Sydney, Law Book Company, 1999); P Lavery, *Commercial Secrets: the Action for Breach of Confidence in Ireland* (Dublin, Round Hall, 1996).

2 But see §34– 006.

3 FOIA s 41(1); FOI(S)A s 36(2). For the position in relation to 'environmental information', see §34– 003.

4 FOIA s 41(2). In relation to Scottish public authorities, see §3– 005(1).

5 FOIA s 2(3)(g); FOI(S)A s 2(2)(c). Presumably because consideration of the public interest is inherent in determining whether there is an actionable breach of confidence.

6 FOIA s 2(1)-(2); FOI(S)A s 2(1).

7 *Derry City Council v IC*, IT, 11 December 2006 at [30]; *S v IC and General Register Office*, IT, 9 May 2007 at [26]-[28]; *McTeggart v IC and Dept for Culture*, Arts and Leisure, IT, 4 June 2007 at [28]-[29].

8 *AG v Guardian Newspapers Ltd (No 2)* [1990] 1 AC 109, 256, 265, 270, 282 and 293. See further §34– 028.

9 *Derry City Council v IC*, IT, 11 December 2006 at [35(m)], followed in *Anderson v IC and Parades Commission*, IT, 29 April 2008 at [31].

10 See §34– 038.

way the law of confidence has developed in the latter regard.[11] A similar exemption for confidential information is to be found in each of the comparative jurisdictions.[12]

34– 002 Private information

The cause of action for breach of confidence has been extended in recent years to cover misuse of private information. To accommodate this extension, the principles of confidentiality have been substantially adapted to the particular requirements of private information. As discussed in greater detail below,[13] the prevailing judicial analysis is that privacy claims have been accommodated by expanding (or, as some would say, distorting) the traditional cause of action for breach of confidence. Lord Nicholls has gone further, stating:

> As the law has developed, breach of confidence, or misuse of confidential information, now covers two distinct causes of action, protecting two different interests: privacy, and secret ("confidential") information.[14]

Whether the better view is that misuse of private information has come to be protected by radically modifying the traditional cause of action or due to the creation of a new and distinct cause of action, there seems no doubt that the basis on which such protection is provided is by a claim for breach of confidence. At the same time, because the elements of an actionable breach of confidence and the limitations that apply to that cause of action have undergone radical transformation in this extended territory, it is more convenient to consider separately the principles of confidentiality in relation to private or personal information.[15]

34– 003 Environmental information

Information to which a person has a right of access under the EIR is exempt information under s 39(1)(a) of FOIA.[16] Those regulations give a right of access to 'environmental information'.[17] To the extent that a request for information captures 'environmental information', the Act effectively routes that part of the request through the EIR.[18] Although those regulations do provide some protection for certain sorts of confidential information, they take a significantly different approach from the Act in relation to confidentiality. The protection they give is accordingly considered separately in this Chapter.[19]

---

11 See *British Union for the Abolition of Vivisection v SSHD* [2008] EWHC 892 (QB), Eady J at [27]-[35], a criticism adopted by the Court of Appeal in *British Union for the Abolition of Vivisection v SSHD*[2008] EWCA Civ 870, [2009] 1 All ER 44, [2009] 1 WLR 636 at [23], and heeded by the Tribunal in *Higher Education Funding Council for England v IC & anor*, IT, 13 January 2010 at [42].

12 In the United States, the Freedom of Information Act, 1966, 5 USC § 552(b)(4), exempts from disclosure records or information obtained from a person that is confidential: see §51– 008(4). The Freedom of Information Act 1982 (Cth of Australia) s 45, provides an exemption where the disclosure of the requested document would represent a breach of confidence other than that of the Commonwealth: see §51– 015(20). In New Zealand, the Official Information Act 1982 ss 9(2)(b)(ii) and 27(1)(c), the Local Government Official Information and Meetings Act 1987 ss 7(2)(b)(ii) and 26(1)(c) and the Privacy Act 1993 s 29(1)(b) provide a qualified exemption where the non-disclosure is required to protect information which is subject to an obligation of confidence: see §51– 023(3). The Access to Information Act (Canada) s 20(1)(b), provides a mandatory exemption for financial, commercial, scientific or technical information received in confidence from a third party: see §51– 031(5). The Freedom of Information Act 2014 (Ireland) s 35(1) provides a qualified exemption for information obtained in confidence: see §51– 039(5).

13 See §34– 031.

14 *OBG Ltd v Allan* [2007] UKHL 21, [2008] 1 AC 1.

15 At §§34– 030 to 34– 048.

16 In relation to Scottish public authorities, FOI(S)A s 39, similarly renders 'environmental information' exempt information for the purposes of that Act.

17 In relation to Scottish public authorities, a like right is given by the EI(S)R.

18 For a general treatment of the EIR and the EI(S)R, see Ch 6.

19 See §§34– 065 to 34– 067.

34– 004 Overview

A public authority faced with a request for information that includes confidential or commercial information or a trade secret will first need to identify which of that information captured by the request constitutes 'environmental information'.[20] In relation to requested information that is 'environmental information' the public authority will need to determine whether the special confidentiality exceptions that only apply to 'environmental information' are engaged.[21] In relation to the requested information that does not constitute 'environmental information', the public authority will need:

(1) To determine whether any of it constitutes a trade secret.[22]
(2) To determine whether the disclosure of any of it would, or would be likely to, prejudice the commercial interests of any person, including the public authority itself.[23]
(3) To determine whether any of the information was obtained from a State other than the United Kingdom or from an international organisation or international court.[24]
(4) To determine which of that information was 'obtained from any other person'[25] and, if so:
   (a) whether and to what extent that information falls within the ambit of the cause of action for breach of confidence in its traditional form;[26] and
   (b) whether and to what extent that information falls within the ambit of that cause of action as extended to private information.[27]

To the extent that the requested information falls within limb (b), that information will often also be rendered exempt information by s 40(2) of FOIA.[28] In those circumstances, s 40(2) will generally provide a more straightforward means of rendering information exempt information than s 41(1) in its application to private information.[29] Section 40(2)-(4) ensures that disclosure of personal information under the Act accommodates the data protection principles and, through them, the protection of an individual's privacy.[30]

34– 005 Internally-created information

The s 41 exemption only applies to information obtained by the public authority from another person.[31] The public authority therefore cannot rely upon the exemption as a basis for refusing to disclose information that it has itself created. Information that is obtained from an officer or employee of the public authority will not be obtained 'from any other person' if the officer or employee has disclosed the information in the course of his employment and acting solely

---

20 See §17– 011.

21 See §§34– 065 to 34– 067.

22 See §§34– 049 to 34– 056.

23 See §§34– 057 to 34– 060.

24 See §§34– 061 to 34– 064.

25 See §34– 005.

26 See §§34– 010 to 34– 029.

27 See §§34– 030 to 34– 048.

28 Similarly: FOI(S)A s 38(1)(b); EIR regs 12(3) and 13; EI(S)R regs 10(3) and 11.

29 FOIA s 40(2)-(4); FOI(S)A; s 38, EIR regs 12(3) and 13; EI(S)R regs 10(3) and 11.

30 Similarly: FOI(S)A s 38(1)(b); EIR regs 12(3) and 13; EI(S)R regs 10(3) and 11.

31 Similarly: FOI(S)A s 36(2); EIR reg 12(5)(f); EI(S)R reg 10(5)(f). This must be established on a balance of probabilities: *Dept of Business, Innovation & Skills v IC and Whyte*, FTT, 20 April 2015 at [36].

in his capacity as an officer or employee. No doubt this will generally be the case. It is, however, possible that information may be disclosed to the public authority by an officer or employee in a private capacity and in the expectation that it will be kept confidential. In those circumstances, the exemption contained in s 41 would potentially apply to it. Like considerations may apply where information is generated by contract workers who are engaged by a public authority and who may well carry out work within its buildings (eg doctors in an occupational health unit, supplied pursuant to a service agreement made between a public authority and a company which provides the public authority with occupational health services). The Tribunal has held that a concluded contract between a public authority and a third party does not constitute information obtained by that public authority from any other person for the purposes of s 41. The Tribunal went further and held on the facts that a document setting out the terms on which an airline company would use airport facilities provided by a public authority and by reference to which the parties had conducted themselves, even though not constituting a contract, was not information obtained by that public authority from any other person:

> We are aware that the effect of our conclusion is that the whole of any contract with a public authority may be available to the public, no matter how confidential the content or how clearly expressed the confidentiality provisions incorporated in it, unless another exemption applies (most probably, that one or both parties to the contract could show that its disclosure would be likely to prejudice its commercial interests, so as to bring section 43 into play). We are also conscious of the fact that contracts will sometimes record more than just the mutual obligations of the contracting parties. They will also include technical information, either in the body of the contract or, more probably, in separate schedules. Depending, again, on the particular circumstances in which the point arises, it may be that material of that nature could still be characterised as confidential information "obtained" by the public authority from the other party to the contract, (or perhaps a "trade secret" under section 43(1) of the Act) in which event it may be redacted in any disclosed version.[32]

Information included in a document provided by a contractor to an authority but which originates from the authority rather than the contractor, is not obtained from another person for the purposes of s 41.[33]

34– 006 Departmental information

The effect of s 81 of FOIA[34] is that, in general, the disclosure by one government department of information originating from another government department is not to be regarded as giving rise to an actionable breach of confidence, and so will fall outside the scope of the exemption contained in s 41. The reason for this is that, although s 81(1) provides that for the purposes of the Act each government department is to be treated as a person separate from any other government department, s 81(2) goes on to provide that s 81(1) does not enable:

(a) a government department which is not a Northern Ireland department to claim for the purposes of s 41(1)(b) that the disclosure of any information by it would constitute a breach of confidence actionable by any other government department (not being a Northern Ireland department); or

(b) a Northern Ireland department to claim for those purposes that the disclosure of information by it would constitute a breach of confidence actionable by any other Northern Ireland department.

---

32 *Derry City Council v Information Commissioner*, IT, 11 December 2006 at [32(e)]. See to similar effect: *Montague v IC and Tate Gallery*, FTT, 22 December 2014 at [27].

33 *Dept of Health v IC*, IT, 18 November 2008 at [33]-[37].

34 Although EIR reg 3(5) provides that each government department is to be treated as a person separate from any other government department, that particular regulation does not apply to Part 3, being the Part containing reg 12. There is no equivalent to s 81 under the FOI(S)A or to reg 3(5) under the EI(S)R.

As s 81(2) does not apply to information provided by a Northern Ireland department to a government department, and vice versa, the disclosure of such information may constitute an actionable breach of confidence, and it may fall within the scope of the exemption. This appears to have been the intention of the legislature. If the information supplied by a government department originates from a third party (in other words, it does not originate from another government department), then, subject to any loss of confidentiality resulting from the transmission between departments, it will retain the confidentiality that it had when held by the transmitting department.

34– 007 The meaning of 'actionable'

The exemption applies only to any disclosure by the public authority holding the information which would constitute a breach of confidence 'actionable' by the person who provided the information to that authority or by any other person.[35] One possible meaning of the word 'actionable' is that it will be satisfied whenever the circumstances afford 'grounds for an action at law'.[36] If that meaning applied here, the exemption would be available wherever there is in existence a claim for breach of confidence which satisfies the test of 'real prospect of success' or arguability.[37] Another possible interpretation is that 'actionable' means a breach of confidence that satisfies the essential elements for a successful breach of confidence claim,[38] but without a consideration of whether any of the public interest defences to the claim would defeat it.[39] A third interpretation is that the claim is only actionable if the claim would be successful, taking into account any public interest defences. The Tribunal has suggested a fourth meaning:

> which arises when the word "actionable" is used, not to indicate the test to be applied in assessing whether a possible cause of action should be taken into consideration, but for the purpose of indicating who has the necessary status to assert it.[40]

During the introduction of the Act into Parliament, Lord Falconer of Thoroton, Minister of State at the Cabinet Office, advised Parliament that an 'actionable breach' meant one that affords grounds for a claim for breach of confidence that will succeed: in other words, one that 'would be upheld by the courts'.[41] The Tribunal has taken the view that Lord Falconer's statement in promoting the legislation put the issue 'beyond doubt.'[42] This was the approach

---

35 One possible reason for the inclusion of the word 'actionable' was to avoid the uncertainties which the equivalent provision in the Freedom of Information Act 1982 (Cth of Aust) encountered before its amendment: see §51–015(20).

36 *Oxford English Dictionary*. That is, for example, the sense in which the word is used in the headnote to *Stephens v Avery* [1988] Ch 449, [1988] 2 All ER 477, [1988] FSR 510, in which Browne-Wilkinson VC refused to strike out a statement of case complaining of the misuse of information relating to a lesbian sexual relationship between the claimant and another woman, on the basis that it was arguable that the claimant's confidant and the editor and publisher of a newspaper to whom the confidant had imparted the information were bound by a duty of confidence with regard to the information.

37 Under CPR 3.4; or for resisting a claim for summary judgment under CPR 24. A claim satisfies that test if it is not merely fanciful: *Swain v Hillman* [2001] 1 All ER 91; *Krafft v London Borough of Camden* (2001) 3 LGR 37. In *Three Rivers District Council v Bank of England (No 3)* [2001] UKHL 16, [2001] 2 All ER 513 Lord Hope of Craighead observed that: 'The difference between a test which asks the question "is the claim bound to fail?" and one which asks the question "does the claim have a real prospect of success?" is not easy to determine.' For examples of claims and defences which were and which were not held to have 'a real prospect of success' under CPR 24 see *Celador Productions Ltd v Melville; Boone v ITV Network; Baccini v Celador Productions Ltd* [2004] EWHC 2362 (Ch), [2004] All ER (D) 298; and *Associated Newspapers Ltd v HRH the Prince of Wales* [2006] EWCA Civ 1776, [2007] 2 All ER 139.

38 See §34– 012.

39 See §§34– 024 to 34– 029.

40 *Higher Education Funding Council for England v IC & anor*, IT, 13 January 2010 at [25(c)].

41 Hansard HL vol 618 col 416; (25 October 2000); vol 619 cols 175-176 (14 November 2000).

42 *Higher Education Funding Council for England v IC & anor*, IT, 13 January 2010 at [26]-[27].

taken by the Upper Tribunal in *Evans v Information Commissioner*.[43] *Guardian* journalist Rob Evans had, over many years, sought disclosure from government departments of correspondence in which the Prince of Wales had sought to exert influence over government decision-making ("advocacy correspondence"). The Upper Tribunal accepted that:

> breach of confidence (which for these purposes includes a breach of privacy) will not be actionable if the defendant shows that the breach was justified in the public interest.[44]

The Upper Tribunal considered that the advocacy correspondence, other than in those parts containing "environmental information,"[45] contained confidential information obtained from the Prince for the purposes of s 41 of the Act.[46] But it considered that the public interest balance was clearly in favour of disclosure of the advocacy correspondence.[47] Following the Upper Tribunal's decision, however, the Attorney-General issued a certificate under s 53 of the Act stating that, contrary to the view of the Upper Tribunal, there had been no failure to comply with the relevant provisions of the Act or the 2004 Regulations. The departments did not therefore have to disclose the correspondence. A judicial review challenge to the certificate was ultimately resolved in favour of the journalist: the certificate was held to be invalid.[48] Certificates under s 53 are considered elsewhere in this work.[49] It is now tolerably clear, therefore, that s 41 requires a consideration of both:

(i) the elements of a claim for breach of confidence; and
(ii) the grounds on which such a claim may be defeated.

34– 008 The duty to confirm or deny

The duty to confirm or deny does not arise if, or to the extent that, a confirmation or denial that the public authority holds the information specified in the request would (apart from the Act) constitute an actionable breach of confidence.[50] This is an absolute exclusion of duty.[51] As a matter of practice, other than where the request is so specific that the mere confirmation that the information is held (without a disclosure of that information) would be to disclose the gist of the information, it is difficult to contemplate circumstances in which a public authority could properly refuse to confirm or deny that it held information under s 41(2).

34– 009 Consultation with others

There is no statutory obligation on the public authority to consult with persons to whom the information requested relates or whose interests are likely to be affected by the disclosure of information to the public pursuant to s 41 of FOIA. In accordance with s 45(2)(c) of the Act, however, consultation with such third parties is covered by section 3 of the 2018 Code of Practice issued by the Minister for the Cabinet Office pursuant to s 45(1) 'providing guidance to public authorities as to the practice which it would, in his opinion, be desirable for them to follow in connection with the discharge of the authorities' functions under Part 1' of the Act. The Code of Practice advises, amongst other things, that consultation will often be necessary because the third party better understands the sensitivity of the information and that such views

---

43 *Evans v IC and DBIS* [2012] UKUT 313 (AAC).

44 At [38].

45 *Evans v IC and DBIS* [2012] UKUT 313 (AAC) at [239].

46 *Evans v IC and DBIS* [2012] UKUT 313 (AAC) at [222].

47 *Evans v IC and DBIS* [2012] UKUT 313 (AAC) at [204] - [213].

48 *R (Evans) v Attorney-General* [2015] UKSC 21, [2015] AC 1787.

49 See §45– 011.

50 FOIA s 41(2). In relation to Scottish public authorities, see §3– 005(1).

51 FOIA s 2(3).

will be 'especially relevant' where is is necessary to consider public interest issues.[52] In practice, therefore, such persons are very likely to be consulted by the public authority before any disclosure is made. If the persons consulted consent to disclosure, and no other person is entitled to maintain any claim to confidentiality with regard to the information in question, then the public authority will be released from any obligation of confidence that it would otherwise have had, and it will not be able to rely on the exemption to resist disclosure. If the persons consulted do not consent to disclosure, and the public authority considers that disclosure would constitute a breach of confidence actionable by them, it is likely that the terms of their objection will bolster the public authority's stance. If the persons consulted do not consent to disclosure and claim it would constitute a breach of confidence actionable by them and the public authority disagrees with that view, the matter may well end up being resolved by the court either in proceedings brought by such persons for injunctive relief, or, conceivably, in proceedings brought against them by the public authority for declaratory relief. If any dispute is not resolved by those means, and the public authority decides to make disclosure in spite of such claims, any person whose rights of confidentiality are breached by the disclosure will be entitled to claim pecuniary relief in respect of such disclosure, subject to any common law defences that may be available to the public authority: these rights are not conferred by the Act, but arise at common law.

2. CONVENTIONAL BREACH OF CONFIDENCE[53]

34– 010 Sources of confidentiality

Obligations of confidentiality conventionally arise from contract, equity or statute.[54] The same facts may give rise to an obligation of confidentiality arising under more than one of these sources.[55] A contractual obligation of confidentiality may arise orally or in writing, and it may be express or implied. It is arguable that an express contractual duty of confidence carries more weight, at least when balanced against the restriction of the right of freedom of expression, than an implied duty of confidentiality.[56] Further, it is clear from the decisions of the Court of Appeal in *McKennitt v Ash*[57] and in *HRH the Prince of Wales v Associated Newspapers Ltd*[58] that a pre-existing confidential relationship is a matter of considerable importance when striking the balance between competing Conventions rights, such that:

---

52 See s 45 Code of Practice §§ 3.2-3.5. A failure to consult the third party, so that its position is not known, may also undermine the public authority's case that confidentiality-based exemption applies: *Montague v IC and Tate Gallery*, FTT, 22 December 2014 at [13] and [24].

53 In other words, breaches of confidence other than of private information, which are considered at §§34– 030 to 34– 048.

54 Prior to *Prince Albert v Strange* (1849) 1 Mac & G 25, (1849) 1 De G & Sm 652 where there was a misuse or a threatened misuse of confidential information, the courts would only intervene if it could be shown that that misuse constituted an infringement by the defendant of a right of property recognised at common law, a breach of contract by the defendant, a breach of trust by the defendant, or a use of information obtained by the defendant from a third party in the knowledge that that third party was in breach of contract or trust. See further: Lord Oliver, 'Spycatcher: Confidence, Copyright and Contempt', *Israel Law Review*, (1989) 23(4) 407.

55 *Robb v Green* [1895] 2 QB 315 (CA); *Nichrotherm Electrical Co Ltd v Percy* [1957] RPC 207 (CA); *Ackroyds (London) Ltd v Islington Plastics Ltd* [1962] RPC 97.

56 *HRH the Prince of Wales v Associated Newspapers Ltd* [2006] EWCA Civ 1776, [2008] Ch 57 at [69]; *Campbell v Frisbee* [2002] EWCA Civ 1374, [2003] EMLR 3 at [22], contrasting *London Regional Transport v Mayor of London* [2001] EWCA Civ 1491, [2003] EMLR 4 at [46] with *AG v Barker* [1990] 3 All ER 257 at 260.

57 *McKennitt v Ash v* [2006] EWCA Civ 1714, [2008] QB 73 (see, eg, Buxton LJ at [8(v)] and [15]-[24]).

58 *HRH the Prince of Wales v Associated Newspapers Ltd* [2006] EWCA Civ 1776, [2008] Ch 57 (see Lord Phillips CJ at, eg, [24]-[36], [48], [53], [65]-[68] and [74]).

> a significant element to be weighed in the balance is the importance in a democratic society of upholding duties of confidence that are created between individuals. It is not enough to justify publication that the information in question is a matter of public interest.... For these reasons, the test to be applied when considering whether it is necessary to restrict freedom of expression in order to prevent disclosure of information received in confidence is not simply whether the information is a matter of public interest but whether, in all the circumstances, it is in the public interest that the duty of confidence should be breached. The court will need to consider whether, having regard to the nature of the information and all the relevant circumstances, it is legitimate for the owner of the information to seek to keep it confidential or whether it is in the public interest that the information should be made public.[59]

In addition, the scope of express and implied obligations may be different.[60] Independently of contract, it is well established that there is free-standing jurisdiction in equity to protect confidence.[61] As Lord Walker put it in *Douglas v Hello! Ltd and others (No 3)*:

> If the person disclosing the information is in contractual relations with the claimant, the most natural claim will be for breach of an express or implied term in the contract. ...Where there is no contractual tie the cause of action is the equitable jurisdiction to restrain (or if it cannot be restrained, to award compensation or an account of profits for) breach of confidence.[62]

As no contract or privity is required, the equitable jurisdiction is of potentially wider application than the contractual jurisdiction. Where confidentiality arises by statute, the information will almost certainly be independently rendered exempt information by s 44(1)(a).[63]

34– 011 Breach of confidence

It is not clear whether s 41(1), in referring to 'a breach of confidence actionable by [the person from whom the public authority obtained the information] or any other person', is referring solely to confidences that are or would be actionable under the courts' equitable jurisdiction or whether it also covers all information deemed confidential (irrespective of whether it is commonplace) provided under a contract. It is suggested that the reference to a 'breach of confidence' (rather than to a 'breach of contract') and to it being actionable 'by that or any other person' point to the former. Plainly, however, the presence of such a contractual provision will be relevant to a determination of whether disclosure of the information would be protected by equity. If, contrary to this view, the phrase does extend to all information covered by a contractual prohibition on disclosure (including commonplace information), it will then be necessary to consider whether the contractual prohibition is actionable.[64]

34– 012 Actionable breach

The conventional starting point for considering the nature and scope of the equitable duty of confidentiality remains[65] the three-fold test identified in the judgment of Megarry J in *Coco v A*

---

59 *HRH the Prince of Wales v Associated Newspapers Ltd* at [67]-[68]. See also *Brevan Howard Asset Management LLP v Reuters* [2017] EWCA Civ 950, [2017] EMLR 28 at [63].

60 *Balston Ltd v Headline Filters Ltd* [1987] FSR 330 at 348.

61 The landmark authority is *Saltman Engineering Co Ltd v Campbell Engineering Co Ltd* (1948) 65 RPC 203, where, although there was a contract, the defendant's liability was found to rest on a breach of confidence.

62 *Douglas v Hello! Ltd and others (No 3)* [2007] UKHL 21, [2008] 1 AC 1 at [276].

63 Similarly, by FOI(S)A s 26(a). See further §§35– 015 to 35– 019.

64 It will be unenforceable where or to the extent that: (1) it would prevent an ex-employee from making proper use of his skills or otherwise constitutes an unreasonable restraint on trade; (2) it conflicts with competition law; (3) it would prevent publication that is in the public interest; or (4) it would otherwise be unlawful. Where the information is commonplace, there would 'be little' to weigh in the balance against any argument for disclosure in the public interest.

65 See *R v Department of Health, ex p Source Informatics Ltd* [2001] QB 424, [2001] 1 All ER 786 at [14]; *Douglas v Hello! Ltd (No 3)* [2006] EWCA Civ 595, [2006] QB 125 at [55].

N Clark (Engineers) Ltd:[66]

> In my judgment, three elements are normally required if, apart from contract, a case of breach of confidence is to succeed. First, the information itself, in the words of Lord Greene MR in *Saltman Engineering Co Ltd v Campbell Engineering Co Ltd*,[67] must "have the necessary quality of confidence about it". Secondly, that information must have been imparted in circumstances importing an obligation of confidence. Thirdly, there must be an unauthorised use of that information to the detriment of the party communicating it.

In *Attorney-General v Guardian Newspapers Ltd (No 2)*[68] Lord Goff of Chieveley stated the broad, general principle (non-definitively) as being:

> that a duty of confidence arises when confidential information comes to the knowledge of a person (the confidant) in circumstances where he has notice, or is held to have agreed, that the information is confidential, with the effect that it would be just in all the circumstances that he should be precluded from disclosing the information to others ... in the vast majority of cases ... the duty of confidence will arise from a transaction or relationship between the parties ... But it is well settled that a duty of confidence may arise in equity independently of such cases .

34– 013 Public policy considerations

The equitable jurisdiction is founded on obligations of conscience, and its essential basis is the duty to act in good faith.[69] It also rests on the notion that there is a public interest in the maintenance of confidences, and to this extent it is governed by public policy considerations. Such considerations mean that regard must be had to countervailing public interests. One such countervailing public interest is that of freedom of trade. Concern for this interest, coupled with the difficulties for employees of identifying what information of their employers is truly confidential, as opposed to forming part of the general stock of knowledge of those engaged in any particular line of business, has led the courts to observe that the proper way for employers to protect themselves:

> would be by exacting covenants from their employees restricting their field of activity after they have left their employment, not by asking the court to extend the general equitable doctrine to prevent breaking confidence beyond all reasonable bounds.[70]

Another countervailing public interest is that of freedom of expression. The fundamental right to freedom of expression has been recognised at common law for many years. Upon incorporation of the ECHR, including Art 10, into domestic law by the Human Rights Act 1998 this right became underpinned by statute.[71] There is also a public interest in promoting the accountability of government. As Lord Goff put it in the 'Spycatcher' case:

> although in the case of private citizens there is a public interest that confidential information should as such be protected, in the case of Government secrets the mere fact of confidentiality does not alone support such a conclusion, because in a free society there is a continuing public interest that the workings of government should be open to scrutiny and criticism.

---

[66] *Coco v A N Clark (Engineers) Ltd* [1969] RPC 41 at 47. The information in that case was technical information which was of value for commercial purposes; it was held not to be of a confidential nature because it was already in the public domain. See more recently: *Murray v Yorkshire Fund Managers Ltd* [1998] 1 WLR 96 (CA); *A v B plc* [2001] 1 WLR 2341, [2002] 1 All ER 449.

[67] *Saltman Engineering Co Ltd v Campbell Engineering Co Ltd* [1948] 65 RPC 203 at 215, [1963] 3 All ER 413 (Note).

[68] *Attorney-General v Guardian Newspapers Ltd (No 2)* [1990] 1 AC 109 at 281.

[69] See the discussion of the relevant principles of law by Bingham LJ in *AG v Guardian Newspapers Ltd (No 2)* [1990] 1 AC 109 at 214-216.

[70] *Printers & Finishers Ltd v Holloway* [1965] 1 WLR 1 at 6, [1963] 3 All ER 731; see also, to similar effect, *A T Poeton (Gloucester Plating) Ltd v Horton* [2000] ICR 1208, [2001] FSR 14 (CA). The employer is not obliged to point out to the employee the precise limits of what is sought to be protected as confidential information: see *Lancashire Fires Ltd v Lyons & Co Ltd* [1996] FSR 629 at 673-674.

[71] Lord Bingham in *R v Shayler* [2002] UKHL 11, [2003] 1 AC 247 at [21]-[22] and the cases cited therein.

Because of this, governmental bodies are not entitled to prevent disclosures about themselves and their activities unless there is a particular and sufficient public interest which requires that publication should be restrained.[72]

34– 014 Element 1 – circumstances

Where the person providing the information to the public authority expressly states that it is being provided in confidence, that will usually suffice to satisfy the first element.[73] Where a person is under a statutory duty to supply particular information to a public authority, that will often satisfy the first element, particularly if the public authority is under a statutory duty not to use the information other than in connection with its core functions. For example, a taxpayer who supplies to HM Revenue & Customs information relating to his income. Similarly, if a public authority received information in the exercise of its functions, although the provider is not obliged to supply it, that public authority will generally owe a duty to the provider not to use it for unrelated purposes.[74] The scope of the duty may vary from case to case according to the circumstances in which, and the purposes for which, the information was received.[75] Lord Goff's non-definitive formulation of the broad general principle makes clear that it is not essential that there should be a pre-existing relationship between the person seeking to enforce the duty and the person to whom the information was disclosed. The extent to which these principles will apply to information supplied to a public authority after the coming into force of the Freedom of Information Act is unclear and not without difficulty. First, although the cited decisions have relied on notions of confidentiality, often the outcome has turned on an analysis of the duties and powers of the public authority that acquired the information and whether the use to which the information has been put advances any of those functions. Those uses may be quite different from the purpose for which the person supplied the information to the public authority. Secondly, persons supplying information to a public authority after 2000 do so knowing that public authorities are subject to the disclosure obligations imposed by the Act and, more recently, the EIR. This should not affect the position of a person who is under a duty to supply information to a public authority (eg a tax return of a taxpayer). Where, however, a person volunteers information, the position may be different. A distinction may be drawn between the person who is required to provide information in order to secure a licence,[76] permission, grant, benefit, etc and the pure volunteer. In both cases, however, it is suggested that the stronger the potential requirement on the public authority, in the proper exercise of its functions, to share the information received (eg with a person who stands to be affected by it), the more difficult it will be to satisfy the first element.[77] In those circumstances, the public authority receives the information knowing that the due performance

---

[72] *Attorney-General v Guardian Newspapers Limited (No 2)* [1990] 1 AC 109, Lord Goff at 283. See §§6– 011 to 6– 016 for a discussion of the public interest considerations weighing in favour of disclosure.

[73] This will be most easily satisfied where a contract provides that all information received is received in confidence. As in *Dunford & Elliott v Johnson & Firth Brown* [1978] FSR 143.

[74] For example:*S v IC and The General Register Office*, IT, 9 May 2007, notes taken by the registrar of deaths during a question and answer session of a person registering a death held to be attended by an expectation of confidentiality.

[75] Thus in *Hellewell v Chief Constable of Derbyshire* [1995] 1 WLR 804 the court held that the police could make reasonable use of a 'mug shot' of an arrested person for the purposes of the prevention and detection of crime, investigation of alleged offences and apprehension of suspects. In *Marcel v Commissioner of Police* [1992] Ch 225 the court held that the police should not have allowed a party in civil proceedings to inspect documents seized by them in connection with a subsequently dropped criminal investigation. See also *Re Arrows Ltd (No 4)* [1995] 2 AC 75; *Taylor v Director of the Serious Fraud Office* [1999] AC 177; *R (Ingenious Media Holdings plc) v HMRC* [2016] UKSC 54, [2016] 1 WLR 4164.

[76] Such as the plaintiffs in *R v Licensing Authority established under Medicines Act 1968, ex p Smith Kline & French Laboratories Ltd* [1990] 1 AC 64.

[77] See, for example: *Webber v IC*, FTT, 22 March 2016 – claims for re-imbursement of expenses by former Prime Ministers, submitted to the Cabinet Office, were not confidential.

of its functions may require the dissemination of the information that it receives. It is suggested that this is consistent with the general principle that a person to whom confidential information has been disclosed may disclose that information where legitimate interests in disclosure outweigh those of protecting the confidence.[78]

34– 015 Element 2 – nature

The requirement that the information be of a 'confidential nature' is linked to the first element. The circumstances in which information is received will shape whether the information itself is of a confidential nature. The necessary quality is that 'the information must not be something which is public property and public knowledge.'[79] In other words, in order to be confidential the information must have about it 'the basic attribute of inaccessibility'.[80] Self-classification of the information as 'confidential', whether or not acquiesced to by the recipient public authority, does not give it the necessary quality of confidence.[81] The information must be such that a reasonable person would regard it as confidential.[82] Usages and practices of the industry or profession may be relevant.[83] So, too, may be the measures taken by the information provider to guard the information from wider dissemination.[84] In relation to certain classes of information the Courts have readily found that information has the requisite confidential nature:

— Correspondence between a person and his legal advisers.[85]
— Medical records relating to an individual, although readily characterised as part of a person's private life, have been held confidential on a conventional analysis of the cause of action.[86]

---

78 See *Webster v James Chapman & Co* [1989] 3 All ER 939 at 945. See further §34– 024.

79 *Saltman Engineering Co Ltd v Campbell Engineering Co Ltd* [1948] 65 RPC 203 at 215. In *Douglas v Hello! Ltd (No 3)* [2006] EWCA Civ 595, [2006] QB 125, [2005] 4 All ER 128 at [55] the Court of Appeal said: 'This is not the clearest of definitions. It seems to us that information will be confidential if it is available to one person (or a group of persons) and not generally available to others, provided that the person (or group) who possesses the information does not intend that it should become available to others.' In some cases, however, the courts use the expression 'quality of confidentiality' to describe a threshold requirement which information needs to satisfy in order to be capable of being confidential, and treat this requirement as embracing considerations which are different from, or additional to, the requirement of inaccessibility. See, for example, *Tillery Valley Foods v Channel Four Television* [2004] EWHC 1075; Ch, [2004] 101 (22) LSG 31, in which, following *Australian Broadcasting Corp v Lenah Game Meats Pty Ltd* [2001] HCA 63, Mann J held that an employee's filming of his workplace, workmates and their working activities did not necessarily result in the information captured on film having the quality of confidentiality.

80 *AG v Guardian Newspapers Ltd (No 2)* [1990] 1 AC 109 at 215. A document discussed at a public committee meeting of three local authorities was not considered to have this basic attribute of inaccessibility in *Case v IC and Colehill Parish*, FTT, 12 November 2013 at [89].

81 *Derry City Council v IC*, IT, 11 December 2006 at [34(a)], where the Information Tribunal held that the fact that some communication between the third party and the public authority was marked 'private and confidential' and that the agreement itself imposed an express obligation of confidence in relation to one piece of information, did not provide much assistance in determining whether the whole agreement was confidential. See also: *Worsley & Co v Cooper* [1939] 1 All ER 290; *Re Dalrymple* [1957] RPC 449; *Re Gallay Ltd's Application* [1959] RPC 141; *Drake Personnel Ltd v Beddison* [1979] VR 13; *Faccenda Chicken Ltd v Fowler* [1987] Ch 117 at 138; *Kone Elevators Pty Ltd v McNay* (1997) 19 ATPR 41-564; *cf Wright v Gasweld Pty Ltd* (1991) 22 NSWLR 317 at 333.

82 *Lancashire Fires Ltd v SA Lyons & Co Ltd* [1996] FSR 629 at 646, 656; *Dunford & Elliott v Johnson & Firth Brown* [1978] FSR 143 at 148.

83 *Thomas Marshall (Exports) Ltd v Guinle* [1979] Ch 227 at 248; *Weir Pumps Ltd v CML Pumps Ltd* [1984] FSR 33.

84 *E Worsley & Co Ltd v Cooper* [1939] 1 All ER 290 at 307; *Ansell Rubber Co Pty Ltd v Allied Rubber Industries Pty Ltd* [1967] VR 37 at 50.

85 *Watkins v SSHD* [2006] UKHL 17, [2006] 2 AC 395.

86 *Ashworth Security Hospital v MGN Ltd* [2002] UKHL 29, [2002] 1 WLR 2033; *R (B) v Stafford Combined Court* [2006] EWHC 1645, [2007] All ER 102, [2006] 2 Cr App R 34; *R (Axon) v Secretary of State for Health* [2006] EWHC 37, [2006] QB 539; *LB of Brent v N* [2005] EWHC 1676, [2006] 1 FLR 310; *Mersey Care NHS Trust v Ackroyd (No1)* [2003] EWCA Civ 663, [2003] EMLR 36; *A Health Authority v X (No1)* [2001] EWCA Civ 2014, [2002] 2 All ER 780, [2002] 1 FLR 1045.

— Statements made to the police in the course of a criminal investigation.[87]
— Tender documents for a commercial contract[88] and other documents received by a public authority from a counterparty in the course of commercial negotiations.[89]
— Information supplied to a public authority by a person under legal compulsion, such as a tax return.[90]
— Information supplied to a public authority which, although provided under legal compulsion, is of a highly personal and sensitive nature.[91]

34– 016 False information

A claim for breach of confidentiality, at least in a case involving personal information, may be successfully mounted even though the information is false.[92]

34– 017 Information to be published

A claim for breach of confidentiality may be successfully mounted to restrain the disclosure of information in advance of the time that the confider proposes to make public the information.[93]

34– 018 Death of the confider

In *Bluck v Information Commissioner and Epsom & St Helier University NHS Trust*[94] the appellant's adult daughter had died at a hospital. Five years later the appellant learned that the hospital had admitted liability for her daughter's death and had reached a settlement with her widower under which substantial compensation had been paid. The appellant's attempts at obtaining information from the hospital concerning her daughter's death were unsuccessful, because it refused to share such information without the consent of the widower, as the deceased daughter's next of kin. The appellant sought to overcome that refusal by making a request for information under the FOIA. The Information Commissioner upheld the hospital's claim that the information was exempt under s 41. The decision was upheld by the Information Tribunal. The Tribunal were right[95] (1) to agree with the authors of *Toulson & Phipps on Confidentiality*[96] that 'Equity may impose a duty of confidentiality towards another after the death of the original confider. The question is not one of property (whether a cause of action owned by the deceased has been assigned) but of conscience', (2) to agree also[97] with the authors' view that equity may in principle regard a doctor as owing a duty of conscience to a deceased's estate, in keeping with

---

87 *Taylor v Serious Fraud Office* [1999] 2 AC 177 at 211 (even though the material may be given in the knowledge that it will be made public in Court); *Woolgar v Chief Constable of Sussex Police* [2000] 1 WLR 25; *Commissioner of Police for the Metropolis and anor v Times Newspapers Ltd and anor* [2011] EWHC 2055 (QB).

88 *London Regional Transport v Mayor of London* [2001] EWCA Civ 1491, [2003] EMLR 4.

89 *Derry City Council v IC*, IT, 11 December 2006 at [34], where the Information Tribunal readily accepted that commercial negotiations between a third party and a public authority be subject to an expectation of confidentiality. That obligation would remain in place until the information in question had either passed into the public domain or had ceased to have commercial significance.

90 *Mount Murray Country Club Ltd & Ors v Commission of Inquiry into Mount Murray* [2003] UKPC 53, [2003] STC 1525, 75 TC 197, [2004] BTC 76.

91 For example: *S v IC and The General Register Office*, IT, 9 May 2007, notes taken by the registrar of deaths during a question and answer session of a person registering a death held to be attended by an expectation of confidentiality.

92 *McKennitt v Ash v* [2006] EWCA Civ 1714, [2008] QB 73.

93 *Khashoggi v Smith* (1980) 124 SJ 149; *Shelley Films Ltd v Rex Features Ltd* [1994] EMLR 134; *Creation Records Ltd v New Group Papers Ltd* [1997] EMLR 444.

94 *Bluck v Information Commissioner and Epsom & St Helier University NHS Trust* IT, 17 September 2007.

95 *Bluck v IC and Epsom & St Helier University NHS Trust*, IT, 17 September 2007 at [18]-[21].

96 Second edition, at para 11-953.

97 *Bluck v IC and Epsom & St Helier University NHS Trust*, IT, 17 September 2007 at [24].

the maxim that equity will not suffer a wrong to be without a remedy[98] and (3) to cite *Z v Finland*[99] in support of the proposition that medical data is of fundamental importance not only to the Art 8 rights of the individual but also to both the private and public interests of maintaining confidence in health services.[100]

34– 019 In the public domain

Confidential information will cease to be confidential once it has entered the public domain. This means:

> no more than that the information in question is so generally accessible that, in all the circumstances, it cannot be regarded as confidential.[101]

Whether information is so generally accessible that it is not confidential is a matter of fact and degree. Relevant considerations include the realities of accessibility, the nature of the information, and the lapse of time since dissemination took place.[102] For example, information in a library book filed under a specialised heading or on the website of a government department which would not be accessed without some degree of background knowledge may not be 'realistically accessible' or properly regarded as 'public knowledge'.[103] The disclosure of highly specific personal information (for example, carefully selected photographs of a wedding that had been sold on an exclusive basis) will not result in the loss of confidentiality for other information on the same subject matter (for example, other photographs of the same occasion taken surreptiously and offered for sale without the consent of the subjects).[104] In *BBC v Harper-Collins*[105] at least thirteen press reports of the information had made it public knowledge. General availability on the internet may also have this effect.[106]

---

98 See also *Armioniene v Lithuania* [2009] EMLR 7, (2009) 48 EHRR 53, 27 BHRC 389; *Webber v IC and Nottinghamshire NHS* [2013] UKUT 648 (AAC) at [46].

99 *Z v Finland* (1997) 25 EHRR 371 at [26].

100 Nevertheless, it is suggested that these principles did not compel the answer that the exemption should be upheld. The appellant's interest in the cause(s) of her daughter's death would appear to have been both understandable and reasonable. Moreover, she was only seeking disclosure to herself, not to the world at large. It was far from clear, therefore, whether it ought to have troubled the conscience of the hospital to make the disclosure that was sought; or, in Art 8 terms, whether the deceased had a reasonable expectation of privacy that her medical records would not be disclosed to her own mother by the hospital where she died, or whether that expectation should prevail over her mother's Art 10 rights. These considerations were strengthened on the facts by the circumstances that: the deceased had died some five years previously; the hospital had admitted negligence; and that part of the medical records had already been released in correspondence, press statements and court records disclosed to the appellant without restriction. As was the case in *W v Egdell* [1990] Ch 359 (CA), the real question before the Tribunal was not as to the existence of the duty of confidentiality but as to its breadth, and that the correct answer to the issue that was raised on the facts involved striking a balance between competing interests. The Tribunal should, perhaps, have been more hesitant to arrive at a conclusion that was contrary to its clear sympathy for the appellant (at [13]). It is also suggested that, both as a matter of principle having regard to equitable concepts that inform the law of confidence and in light of the result arrived at by the Tribunal in this case, it is not necessarily right to regard all requests for information in a manner that is 'applicant blind' and/or 'motive blind'. For similar cases with the same outcome, however, see *Redman v IC and Norfolk CC*, FTT, 13 November 2012 and *Trott and Skinner v IC*, FTT, 19 March 2013.

101 See *AG v Guardian Newspapers (No 2) Ltd* [1990] 1 AC 109, Lord Goff at 282.

102 In *S v IC and The General Register Office*, IT, 9 May 2007 the Information Tribunal found that a limited disclosure of the requested information did not cause it to lose its confidential character (at [70]-[73]).

103 *AG v Greater Manchester Newspapers Ltd* [2001] TLR 668, at [33]-[34]. Although it may be observed that in a modern society important information is often intelligible only to a limited number of people. On that basis, the issue is not that the information be generally accessible, but that it be readily accessible to a person interested in it.

104 *OBG Ltd v Allan* [2007] UKHL 21, [2008] 1 AC 1 at [122], [302], [329].

105 *BBC v Harper-Collins* [2010] EWHC 2424 (Ch), [2011] EMLR 6.

106 *Barclays Bank plc v Guardian News and Media Ltd* [2009] EWHC 591 [22]; *PJS v News Group Newspapers Ltd* [2016] UKSC 26, [2016] AC 1081 at [57].

34– 020 The effect of disclosure

The basic principle is that the duty of confidence is imposed not only on the person to whom information is confided but also on any third party who acquires the information and who knows that it is subject to an obligation of confidence. In this context, the question arises whether a recipient who is bound by an obligation of confidence can rely upon disclosure to the world at large, including as a matter of logic his own disclosure, to say that he is no longer bound by that obligation.[107] On one view, he can, because the consequence of any disclosure to the world at large, including a disclosure by the recipient, is that 'the secret, as a secret, has ceased to exist'.[108] The contrary view is that of the majority in *Schering Chemicals Ltd v Falkman Ltd.*[109] In that case Shaw LJ said:

> It is not the law that where confidentiality exists it is terminated or eroded by adventitious publicity. Nor is the correlative duty to preserve that confidentiality. The public interest may demand that the duty be gainsaid; but it cannot be arbitrarily cast aside.[110]

The significance of this approach to the exemption contained in s 41 of FOIA is that it cannot be assumed that the fact that information in the possession of the public authority which is subject to an obligation of confidence has been placed in the public domain releases the public authority from that obligation — particularly in the event that the information has been placed in the public domain in breach of the public authority's own obligation. The disclosure, or further disclosure, by the public authority of the information which it holds may still be actionable, in spite of the fact that the information is already in the public domain.[111]

34– 021 Element 3 – detriment

It is an open question whether detriment to the claimant is an essential ingredient of an action for breach of confidence.[112] If detriment does need to be established, however, it may well constitute sufficient detriment to the confider that information is to be disclosed to persons whom he would prefer not to know of it.[113]

34– 022 Limiting principles

In *Attorney-General v Guardian Newspapers (No 2) Ltd*[114] Lord Goff identified three limiting concepts to the broad general principle that he had stated. The first, that the principle of confidentiality does not apply to information that is generally accessible, has already been considered above.[115] The second is that the duty of confidence does not apply to information that is useless or trivial.[116] Although Lord Goff said that he did not need to develop this point, it has since assumed particular importance as a result of the extension of the law of confidence beyond its

---

107 The House of Lords alluded to the point in their speeches in *AG v Guardian Newspapers Ltd (No 2)* [1990] 1 AC 109, but it did not require to be resolved in that case because no relief was sought against Peter Wright, the author of 'Spycatcher', and he neither appeared nor was represented at any level in that litigation.

108 *O Mustad & Son v Dosen (Note)* [1964] 1 WLR 109, 111.

109 *Schering Chemicals Ltd v Falkman Ltd* [1982] QB 1, [1981] 2 All ER 321.

110 At 26-27, and see Templeman LJ at 37-38. See also *Exchange Telegraph Co Ltd v Central News Ltd* [1897] 2 Ch 48.

111 Further, as to personal information and 'public domain' see §34– 042.

112 *AG v Guardian Newspapers Ltd (No 2)* [1990] 1 AC 109 at 281-282. Similarly, *AG (UK) v Heinemann Publishers Australia Pty Ltd* (1987) 10 NSWLR 86 at 90; *Carindale Country Club Estate Pty Ltd v Astill* (1993) 42 FCR 307, 115 ALR 112.

113 *AG v Guardian Newspapers Ltd (No 2)* [1990] 1 AC 109 at 255-256.

114 *AG v Guardian Newspapers Ltd (No 2)* [1990] 1 AC 109 at 282.

115 See §§34– 019 to 34– 020.

116 This is dealt with at §34– 023.

traditional boundaries and into the realms of intrusion into personal autonomy.[117] The third limiting concept identified by Lord Goff is that in certain circumstances the public interest in maintaining confidence may be outweighed by the public interest in disclosure.[118]

34–023 Useless or trivial information

Where the information for which a claim for confidence is made is of a commercial nature, the claim will be defeated if the information is, from an objective standpoint, trivial or useless.[119]

34–024 Public interest defence

Public interest is available as a defence[120] to claims for breach of confidence, and it is a general defence[121] not limited to the refusal of equitable relief.[122] The basic principles are that:

(1) the public interest in disclosure may outweigh both private and public interests in the protection of confidences;

(2) where the balancing exercise comes down in favour of disclosure, it may favour only limited disclosure—either in the form of disclosure to less than the world at large or in the form of partial disclosure; and

(3) in the era of the Human Rights Act 1998, the Court, as a public authority, has a duty to act compatibly with Convention rights (as defined by section 1 of that Act), including the right to respect for private and family life, home and correspondence that is guaranteed by Art 8 and the right to freedom of expression that is guaranteed by Art 10, and where there is a tension between competing rights to carry out the parallel analysis mandated by the House of Lords in *Re S (Identification: Restrictions on Publication)*.[123]

This principle has been developed out of the more limited principle that there is no confidence in 'iniquity' (or wrongdoing). In *Attorney-General v Guardian Newspapers Ltd (No 2)*[124] Lord Goff of Chieveley summed the matter up as follows:

> The third limiting principle is of far greater importance. It is that, although the basis of the law's protection of confidence is that there is a public interest that confidences should be preserved and protected by the law, nevertheless that public interest may be outweighed by some other countervailing public interest which favours disclosure. This limitation may apply, as the learned judge pointed out, to all types of confidential information. It is this

117 See further §§34–030 to 34–048.

118 This is dealt with at §§34–024 to 34–027.

119 *AG v Guardian Newspapers Ltd (No 2)* [1990] 1 AC 109 at 282 (Lord Goff). At first instance, Scott J had given as an example *McNicol v Sportsman's Book Stores* (1930) McGCC 116, where the plaintiff was the originator of a betting system based on the age of the moon and had sought to restrain publication of his system.

120 This is how the point is characterised in, eg, *London Regional Transport v Mayor of London* [2003] EWCA Civ 1491, [2003] EMLR 4, by Robert Walker LJ at [35]. There is a school of thought that the true analysis is not so much that the public interest affords a defence but rather that the public interest principle is of relatively narrow application and that, where it does apply, it has the effect that no obligation of confidence arises at all. This characterisation has usually been preferred by the Australian courts: *Corrs Pavey Whiting & Byrne v Collector of Customs (Vic)* (1987) 14 FCR 434 at 451, 74 ALR 428 at 445 *et seq.*; *Smith Kline & French Laboratories (Aust) Ltd v Secretary, Department of Community Services and Health* (1990) 22 FCR 87 at 110, 95 ALR 87 at 124.

121 Although most of the reported cases have been concerned with the grant or refusal of an interlocutory injunction, it is submitted that the policy reasons given in the judgments apply with equal force to final injunctions and to pecuniary remedies.

122 Indeed, it now seems clear that essentially the same defence is also available to a claim for infringement of copyright (which, unlike a claim for breach of confidence, is clearly a claim that is based on a property right), and that the existence and scope of the defence is informed and bolstered by free-speech considerations in view of the effective incorporation into English law of Art 10 by the Human Rights Act 1998: see *Hyde Park Residence Ltd v Yelland* [2001] Ch 143; *Ashdown v Telegraph Ltd* [2002] Ch 149.

123 *Re S (Identification: Restrictions on Publication)* [2004] UKHL 47, [2005] 1 AC 593, Lord Steyn at [17].

124 *Attorney-General v Guardian Newspapers Ltd (No 2)* [1990] 1 AC 109 at 282.

> limiting principle which may require a court to carry out a balancing operation, weighing the public interest in maintaining confidence against a countervailing public interest favouring disclosure. Embraced within this limiting principle is, of course, the so called defence of iniquity.

The second basic principle is of the common law. It does not favour or encourage general publication, for example by the media or campaigning groups. But the obligation to act compatibly with the Convention right of freedom of expression (ie principle (3)) comes into play in such cases. Such cases are now rightly regarded as resting on a constitutionally protected right,[125] rather than the mere assertion of a competing public interest. The question here is whether there is justification on the facts for restricting publication in pursuit of one of the relevant legitimate aims specified in ECHR Art 10(2). These are 'the interests of national security...the protection of the...rights of others...preventing the disclosure of information received in confidence.' The restriction must be prescribed by law and must be 'necessary in a democratic society.' This requirement will not be met unless the relevant national authority (in a breach of confidence case, the court): (a) gives 'relevant and sufficient reasons' to justify the restriction; (b) the restriction on disclosure corresponds to a 'pressing social need'; and (c) it is 'proportionate to the legitimate aim pursued.'[126] The ECHR Art 10 right includes the right 'to receive and impart information and ideas.' In *Magyar Helsinki Bizottság v Hungary* the Grand Chamber of the ECtHR established the principles that the media and non-governmental organisations in particular had a presumptive right of access to state information under ECHR Art 10.[127] The Supreme Court had only shortly before doubted whether such a principle could be found in the jurisprudence of the Strasbourg court.[128] The right exists, more generally, whenever such access is instrumental for the exercise of that person's right to receive and impart information. The circumstances in which a public interest defence to a claim for breach of confidence may enjoy success can conveniently be considered under three headings, which may, of course, overlap:

— first, the public interest in the disclosure of iniquity;
— secondly, the public interest in the public not being misled;
— thirdly, the public interest in the disclosure of matters of public concern.

The extent to which it will be possible to make an assessment of these considerations for the purposes of s 41 of FOIA will vary from case to case. There is no hierarchy of categories of public interest and in any case the same question will arise: namely, whether the public interest in protecting the confidential information is outweighed by sufficiently significant matters of public interest.[129] The public authority may be able to make such an assessment from the information itself, or by having regard to a combination of the information, the nature of the request, and consultation with other persons. Where a journalist or a campaign group is requesting the disclosure under the Act for legitimate public interest reasons, s 41 will now have to be read and given effect to in a way which is compatible with its new right of access to information under ECHR Art 10.[130] Decisions as to whether disclosure should be given, when the s 41 exemption is relied upon, will have to be compatible with this right.[131]

---

125 See *R v Shayler* [2002] UKHL 11, [2003] 1 AC 247 at [22].

126 *Sunday Times v United Kingdom* [1979] ECHR 1, (1979) 2 EHRR 245 at [62]. The proportionality requirement is explained in detail by Lord Hope in *R v Shayler* [2002] UKHL 11, [2003] 1 AC 247 at [59]-[61].

127 *Magyar Helsinki Bizottság v Hungary* [2016] ECHR 18030/11 at [155]. This jurisprudence is considered at §§4– 010 ff.

128 See the majority in *Kennedy v Charity Commission* [2014] UKSC 20, [2015] AC 455 at [94].

129 *Brevan Howard Asset Management LLP v Reuters* [2017] EWCA Civ 950, [2017] EMLR 28 at [75].

130 See Human Rights Act 1998 ss 2 and 3.

131 In other words, to the extent that disclosure is refused, this will have to be justifiable under ECHR Art 10(2) as explained in *R v Shayler* [2002] UKHL 11, [2003] 1 AC 247.

34–025 Disclosure of iniquity

Although the defence of public interest is not confined to cases involving wrongdoing, that is the paradigm instance in which it operates. The courts have always refused to uphold the right to confidence when to do so would cover up wrongdoing: in the words of Wood VC in *Gartside v Outram*[132] there is 'no confidence as to the disclosure of iniquity'. In addition, in the era of the Human Rights Act 1998, such a public interest consideration may be an exception under Art 8(2) to the Art 8(1) right to respect for private and family life. The reason that exposure of wrongdoing should not be prevented, even if it is in breach of confidence, is that 'no private obligations can dispense with that universal one which lies on every member of society to discover every design which may be formed contrary to the laws of the society to destroy the public welfare'.[133] An allegation of wrongdoing will justify exposure in the public interest if it is a credible allegation from an apparently reliable source.[134] An illustration of the operation of the principle at the interim stage is provided by *Cream Holdings Ltd v Banerjee*,[135] in which the principal events related to tax evasion. The House of Lords held that these events were clearly matters of serious public interest such that restraint by interim injunction was inappropriate. In that case, the source of the information was an employee, and one of the arguments upon which the claimant employer relied[136] was that the situation was governed by, or at least should be appraised by reference to, express statutory provisions which applied to disclosures by employees. In rejecting this argument, Lord Nicholls, giving the leading speech with which the other members of the House of Lords agreed, stated that:

> The graduated protection afforded to "whistleblowers" by sections 43A to 43L of the Employment Rights Act 1996, inserted by the Public Interest Disclosure Act 1998, section 1, does not militate against this appraisal. Authorities such as the Inland Revenue owe duties of confidentiality regarding the affairs of those with whom they are dealing. The "whistleblower" provisions were intended to give additional protection to employees, not to cut down the circumstances where the public interest may justify private information being published at large.

34–026 Public not being misled

There is also a public interest in the public not being misled. Typically, this principle comes into play if a public figure misleads the public, where the media may be entitled to put the record straight.[137] The application of this principle to the facts of any particular case, and

---

132 *Gartside v Outram* (1857) 26 LJ Ch (NS) 113 at 114. The case is reported in differing terms in three other sets of reports: (1856) 3 Jur (NS) 39, 5 WR 35 and 28 LT(OS) 120.

133 *Annersley v Anglesea (Earl)* (1743) LR 5 QB 317n 17 State Tr 1139, cited by Lord Denning MR in *Initial Services v Putterill* [1968] 1 QB 396 at 405.

134 *AG v Guardian Newspapers Ltd (No 2)* [1990] 1 AC 109 at 283. In *S v IC and The General Register Office*, IT, 9 May 2007 the Information Tribunal, whilst holding that in relation to information found to be confidential 'the public interest would likely be in favour of disclosure if the disputed information provided evidence of criminal conduct, having regard to the contents of the letter the Tribunal is satisfied that it does not' (at [62]).

135 *Cream Holdings Ltd v Banerjee* [2004] UKHL 44, [2005] 1 AC 253, [2004] 4 All ER 617.

136 In the course of dealing with this argument, the House of Lords accepted that the Inland Revenue owed a duty of confidentiality to the claimant. This is supported by, for example, *Mount Murray Country Club Ltd v Commission of Inquiry into Mount Murray & Anr* [2003] UKPC 53 Lord Walker of Gestingthorpe at [33]: 'A taxpayer's returns of income are not covered by legal professional privilege. In the hands of the Revenue they are entitled to be treated as confidential, and subject to public interest immunity, because they relate to the taxpayer's personal affairs and are obtained by the Revenue under statutory compulsion.' It did not follow, however, that the defendants in *Cream Holdings Ltd v Banerjee* [2004] UKHL 44, [2005] 1 AC 253 (an employee and a local newspaper to which she revealed information) should not be permitted to publish information about the claimant's income and tax affairs, including its dealings with the Inland Revenue, where that disclosure was otherwise justified in the public interest.

137 See, eg, *Woodward v Hutchins* [1977] 1 WLR 760. See also *Theakston v MGN Ltd* [2002] EWHC 137, [2002] EMLR

especially one involving the media, is, also, informed by free speech considerations.

34–027 Matters of public concern

In *Initial Services Ltd v Putterill*,[138] the Court of Appeal held, first, that the exception allowing disclosure of information and documents obtained by an employee in the course of his employment extended to any disclosure that was justified in the public interest and operated with regard to a claim in damages; and, second, that disclosure to the press can fall within the principle. In *Fraser v Evans*[139] Lord Denning MR said:

> There are some things which are of such public concern that the newspapers, the Press, and, indeed, everyone is entitled to make known the truth and to make fair comment on it. This is an integral part of the right of free speech and expression. It must not be whittled away.

In *London Regional Transport v Mayor of London*[140] the Court of Appeal held that there was a public interest in enabling the general public to be informed of serious criticism from a responsible source of the value for money evaluation of the proposed public-private partnership involvement in the London Underground; and that this outweighed the preservation of commercial confidentiality in an interim report prepared by a firm of accountants which was based on commercially sensitive and confidential information that had been disclosed by private-sector bidders subject to express confidentiality agreements. An injunction to restrain the publication of a redacted version of that report was, accordingly, refused. The Court accepted the concession that there is a need for proportionality in any restraint of freedom of expression if the restraint is to be justifiable under Art 10(2) of the Convention.[141] Sedley LJ suggested that the concept of proportionality that formed the basis for deciding a variety of Convention issues in accordance with the jurisprudence of the European Court of Human Rights enabled the elastic concept of whether a reasonable recipient's conscience would be troubled to be replaced by a structured inquiry:

> Does the measure meet a recognised and pressing social need? Does it negate the primary right or restrict it more than is necessary? Are the reasons given for it logical? …for my part, I find it more helpful today to postulate a recipient who, being reasonable, runs through the proportionality checklist in order to anticipate what a court is likely to decide, and who adjusts his or her conscience and conduct accordingly.[142]

In *Jockey Club v Buffham*,[143] Gray J held that questions of the integrity and fairness of bookmaking to the betting public; the relationship of bookmakers to trainers and racing stables; and the effectiveness of the Jockey Club's regulatory role over the sport and industry of horseracing, were questions of proper and serious interest and concern to the public and, in particular, to the very many hundreds of thousands of people interested in horseracing, very many of whom will place bets from time to time. Accordingly, he ruled that the BBC should be allowed to broadcast information relating to such matters notwithstanding that it had been obtained from a 'whistleblower' who divulged it to the BBC in breach of express contractual obligations.[144]

22; *Campbell v MGN Ltd* [2004] UKHL 22, [2004] 2 AC 457; *Ferdinand v MGN Ltd* [2011] EWHC 2454 (QB).

138 *Initial Services Ltd v Putterill* [1968] 1 QB 396.

139 *Fraser v Evans* [1969] 1 QB 349 at 363.

140 *London Regional Transport v Mayor of London* [2003] EWCA Civ 1491, [2003] EMLR 4.

141 *London Regional Transport v Mayor of London* [2003] EWCA Civ 1491, [2003] EMLR 4, Robert Walker LJ at [49].

142 *London Regional Transport v Mayor of London* [2003] EWCA Civ 1491, [2003] EMLR 4, Sedley LJ at [57]-[58].

143 *Jockey Club v Buffham* [2003] QB 462.

144 In reaching this decision, Gray J had regard to what the Court of Appeal had said in *Grobbelaar v News Group Newspapers Ltd* [2001] 2 All ER 437 at [47], [201] about the public interest in whether there was corruption in football, to what Morland J had said in *Chandler v Buffham* [2002] EWHC 1426 on an earlier application for injunctive relief in relation to two of the documents with which the application before Gray J was concerned, and to what had been said by Sir Thomas Bingham MR in *R v Disciplinary Committee of the Jockey Club, ex p Aga Khan*

The Tribunal has applied the reasoning in *London Regional Transport v Mayor of London*[145] to s 41(1) of FOIA. In *Derry City Council v Information Commissioner*[146] it found that there was a public interest in disclosing commercial information where it shed light on a debate of wider concern (funding of an airport by a public authority). The Tribunal concluded that accountability of public funding for an airport used by private operators was sufficiently weighty to displace the confidentiality that attached to negotiations between the public authority and the airline operator. By contrast in *Zacharides v Information Commissioner and Sports Council* the FTT considered that the withheld information was of no relevance to the debate of public concern identified by the Appellant (the demise of grass-roots athletics in the UK).[147] In *Department for Business Innovation and Skills v Information Commissioner and Browning*[148] the FTT found there was a public interest in disclosure of the names of companies who had applied for export licenses to Iran, which were required to ensure compliance with international sanctions. But the evidence of likely detriment to the companies if their names were disclosed publicly was so compelling that the FTT had no difficulty in finding that disclosure would be an actionable breach of confidence. Even if trading lawfully with Iran any public identification would risk adverse measures against the companies by banks, other trading companies and the US Treasury.[149] This balancing exercise, involving as it does value judgments about competing public interests, can divide tribunals (as it sometimes does the appellate courts). In *Moss v Information Commissioner*[150] IBM had conducted and reported to the Home Office on competitive trials of biometric facial and fingerprint recognition technology offered by potential government contractors. Much public money had been, and might yet be, spent on such technology. Mr Moss doubted whether this technology could deliver the claimed benefits, and therefore justify the expenditure, and sought a copy of the report. The dissenting member of the FTT held that the public interest in disclosure of a redacted version of the report should prevail, applying the reasoning in *London Regional Transport v Mayor of London*.[151] The majority strongly disagreed, holding that there was an overriding public interest in maintaining the confidentiality of the report. The majority emphasised the risk of discouraging commercial organisations from participating in procurement exercises of this sort and the need for uninhibited assessment of technologies on which public money might be spent.[152]

34–028 Government secrets

Where confidential information is produced by the workings of government,[153] the question

---

[1993] 1 WLR 909 at 912, 914.

145 *London Regional Transport v Mayor of London* [2003] EWCA Civ 1491, [2003] EMLR 4.

146 *Derry City Council v Information Commissioner*, IT, 11 December 2006 at [35].

147 *Zacharides v IC and UK Sports Council*, FTT, 4 April 2011 at [71]-[79].

148 *Department for Business, Innovation and Skills v IC and Browning*, FTT, 22 September 2011, on appeal *Browning v Information Commissioner and DBIS* [2013] UKUT 236 (AAC) (20 May 2013).

149 *Department for Business, Innovation and Skills v IC and Browning*, FTT, 22 September 2011 at [60]-[62], [66]. The UT has dismissed an appeal against the FTT's decision. See *Browning v Information Commissioner and DBIS* [2013] UKUT 236 (AAC) (20 May 2013).

150 *Moss v IC and Home Office*, FTT, 24 April 2012.

151 *London Regional Transport v Mayor of London* [2003] EWCA Civ 1491, [2003] EMLR 4; *Moss v IC and Home Office*, FTT, 24 April 2012 at [122].

152 *Moss v IC and Home Office*, FTT, 24 April 2012 at [110]-[118].

153 Where government is not the source, but the recipient, of confidential information different considerations apply, for here the essential confidence is, or is likely to be, that of others, typically citizens. Broadly speaking, two different sets of circumstance are likely to arise. First, the information may have been imparted consensually, in which case it will be subject to ordinary principles, and confidence will not be lost unless, eg, the public interest in disclosure outweighs the public interest in maintaining the confidence: *London Regional Transport v Mayor of London*

arises as to the extent to which it is open to the government to rely upon the law of confidence to restrain use and disclosure of such information (whether by its own servants or agents, or by third parties to whom such information has been communicated). The reasons why a different approach is appropriate in the case of government secrets[154] from that which applies to private or commercial confidences were explained in *A-G (UK) v Heinemann Publishers Pty Ltd*[155] by McHugh JA in the following terms:

> ...the relationship between the modern State and its citizens is so different in kind from that which exists between private citizens that rules worked out to govern the contractual, property, commercial and private confidences of citizens are not fully applicable where the plaintiff is a government or one of its agencies. Private citizens are entitled to protect or further their own interests, no matter how selfish they are in doing so. Consequently, the publication of confidential information which is detrimental to the private interest of a citizen is a legitimate concern of a court of equity. But governments act, or at all events are constitutionally required to act, in the public interest. Information is held, received and imparted by governments, their departments and agencies to further the public interest. Public and not private interest, therefore, must be the criterion by which equity determines whether it will protect information which a government or governmental body claims is confidential.

34–029 Secrets: public interest

In *Attorney-General v Jonathan Cape Ltd*[156] the Attorney-General sought an injunction to restrain publication of Richard Crossman's book *Diaries of a Cabinet Minister*. Having said that 'when a Cabinet Minister receives information in confidence the improper publication of such information can be restrained by the court', Lord Widgery CJ went on to hold that the claimant had to establish not only (a) that publication would be a breach of confidence but in addition (b) that the public interest required that the publication be restrained, and (c) that there were no other facets of the public interest contradictory of and more compelling than that relied upon (by the claimant). In fact, the events described in the diaries were 10 years old, and there had been three general elections in the intervening period. In the result, Lord Widgery CJ refused an injunction, because:

> I cannot believe that publication at this interval of anything in volume one would inhibit free discussion in the Cabinet of today, even though the individuals involved are the same, and the national problems have a distressing similarity with those of a decade ago.

In *Commonwealth v John Fairfax and Sons Ltd*[157] Mason J proceeded on the basis that detriment was a necessary element of a cause of action for breach of confidence, and continued:

> The question then, when the executive government seeks the protection given by equity, is: What detriment does it need to show?
>
> The equitable principle has been fashioned to protect the personal, private and proprietary

---

[2003] EWCA Civ 1491 provides an illustration of how this might work in practice. Secondly, the information may have been imparted pursuant to an obligation imposed on the citizen (typically by statute), in which case the material legislation may stamp the information with confidentiality, and, in some instances, may expressly prohibit disclosure or restrict the uses to which the information may be put: the census and fiscal legislation provide examples.

154 In *British Steel Corp v Granada Television Ltd* [1981] AC 1096, the majority of the House of Lords held or assumed that the need for a different approach did not extend to statutory corporations, treated the claimant public authority as entitled to the same rights as a private organization, and regarded accountability to Parliament as a sufficient check. Contrast the approach taken in *Esso Australia Resources Ltd v Plowman* (1985) 183 CLR 10, 128 ALR 391 (HCA).

155 *A-G (UK) v Heinemann Publishers Pty Ltd* (1987) 10 NSWLR 86 at 191, 75 ALR 353 at 454, and subsequently adopted in *Coulthard v South Australia* (1995) 63 SASR 531 and in *Smith, Kline & French Laboratories (Aust) Ltd v Secretary, Department of Community Services and Health* (1991) 99 ALR 679, 23 FCR 291.

156 *Attorney-General v Jonathan Cape Ltd* [1976] QB 752 at 770-771.

157 *Commonwealth v John Fairfax and Sons Ltd* (1980) 147 CLR 39 at 51.

> interests of the executive government. It acts, or is supposed to act, not according to standards of private interest, but in the public interest. This is not to say that equity will not protect information in the hands of the government, but it is to say that when equity protects government information it will look at the matter through different spectacles. It may be a sufficient detriment to the citizen that disclosure of information relating to his affairs will expose his actions to public discussion and criticism. But it can scarcely be a relevant detriment to the government that publication of material concerning its actions will merely expose it to public discussion and criticism. It is unacceptable in our democratic society that there should be a restraint on the publication of information relating to government when the only vice of that information is that it enables the public to discuss, review and criticize government action.
>
> Accordingly, the court will determine the government's claim to confidentiality by reference to the public interest. Unless disclosure is likely to injure the public interest, it will not be protected.
>
> The court will not prevent the publication of information which merely throws light on the past workings of government, even if it be not public property, so long as it does not prejudice the community in other respects. Then disclosure will itself serve the public interest in keeping the community informed and in promoting discussion of public affairs. If, however, it appears that disclosure will be inimical to the public interest because national security, relations with foreign countries or the ordinary business of government will be prejudiced, disclosure will be restrained. There will be cases in which the conflicting considerations will be finely balanced, where it is difficult to decide whether the public's interest in knowing and expressing its opinion outweighs the need to protect confidentiality.

Mason J and Lord Widgery CJ accordingly adopted substantially the same approach. The passage from the judgment of Mason J set out above has been accepted as representing the law in England[158] and in Scotland.[159]

3. PRIVACY AND BREACH OF CONFIDENCE

34– 030 Introduction

By tying the exemption in s 41 to an actionable breach of confidence, FOIA imports the conceptual difficulties which surround the basis upon which the common law is prepared to offer protection against certain invasions of privacy. Because of these difficulties and the resultant uncertainties, it is convenient to give separate consideration to the concept of an actionable breach of confidence which concerns private information. Whatever the nomenclature used, information will only be exempt from the disclosure duty if that disclosure may properly be characterised as an actionable breach of confidence.[160] It is worth repeating the point made earlier: where or to the extent that personal information relating to a third person is captured by a request for information, s 40(2) will generally provide a more straightforward means of rendering information exempt information than will s 41(1).[161]

---

158 See *AG v Guardian Newspapers Ltd* [1987] 1 WLR 1248 at 1261-1262, [1987] 3 All ER 316 at 325-6; *AG v Guardian Newspapers Ltd (No 2)* [1990] 1 AC 109 at 150-2, 203, 218, 221-2, 257-8, 270, 283; *AG v Punch Ltd* [2001] QB 1028 at [40]; *R v Department of Health, ex p Source Informatics Ltd* [2001] QB 424 at [25]; *R v Shayler* [2001] 1 WLR 2206 at [71]-[72]. See also (in related litigation) the position in New Zealand *A-G for UK v Wellington Newspapers Ltd* [1988] 1 NZLR 129 at 176.

159 *Lord Advocate v Scotsman Publications Ltd* [1990] 1 AC 812 at 828, [1989] 2 All ER 852 at 862.

160 FOIA s 41(1); FOI(S)A s 36(2).

161 Unless the third person is deceased, in which case the data protection principles are inapplicable: DPA 1998 s 1(1), definition of 'personal data', and FOIA s 40(7). By way of example, see *Bluck v IC and Epsom & St Helier University NHS Trust*, IT, 17 September 2007.

34– 031 Privacy before the HRA 1998

The view that English law does not recognise invasion of privacy as an independent cause of action was clearly articulated by the Court of Appeal in *Kaye v Robertson.*[162] Even at that time, however, that starting point was subject to two significant qualifications. First, the facts of cases in which privacy issues arise often constitute another cause of action that is recognised by English law, most notably for a breach of confidence.[163] Secondly, even before the Human Rights Act 1998 came into force on 2 October 2000 it appeared that the law might be moving toward recognition of a discrete right of privacy of some description.[164] In *R v Khan,*[165] Lord Nolan said that there was no right of privacy in English law in terms similar to Art 8 of the Convention, and Lord Keith agreed with him. Lord Browne-Wilkinson, Lord Slynn and Lord Nicholls left open the question whether English law recognised a right of privacy, and, if so, what were the limitations of that right. Lord Nicholls referred to 'the important question whether the present, piecemeal protection of privacy has now developed to the extent that a more comprehensive principle can be seen to exist.'

34– 032 Convention rights

In accordance with s 1 of the Human Rights Act 1998, the Convention rights to which the Act applies include the rights and fundamental freedoms set out in Articles 8 and 10 of the Convention.[166] The rights set out in both Articles are qualified. In the case of Art 8, the qualifications include the Art 10 right to freedom of expression. In the case of Art 10, the qualifications include both the Art 8 right to respect for private and family life and the protection of information received in confidence.

34– 033 The HRA 1998

Section 6(1) of the Human Rights Act 1998 provides that it is unlawful for a public authority to act in a way which is incompatible with a Convention right. Obviously, this has the effect that a public authority which wrongly applies s 41(1) of FOIA may be in breach of this duty: the public authority may act incompatibly with Art 10 rights if it asserts that information is exempt when it is not; and, conversely, it may act incompatibly with Art 8 rights if it discloses private information which is in truth exempt information. In order to understand the process by which the Human Rights Act 1998 has had the effect of extending the boundaries of what constitutes an actionable breach of confidence, however, it is necessary to have regard to further provisions of that Act. First, s 2 requires any court or tribunal determining a question which has arisen in connection with a Convention right to take into account any relevant Strasbourg jurisprudence. Secondly, by virtue of s 6(3), a 'public authority' includes a court or tribunal. The effect of these provisions is that it is ordinarily the duty of the English courts, save where and so far as constrained by primary domestic legislation, to give practical recognition to the

---

162 [1991] FSR 62: 'It is well-known that in English law there is no right to privacy, and accordingly there is no right of action for breach of a person's privacy. The facts of the present case are a graphic illustration of the desirability of Parliament considering whether and in what circumstances statutory provision can be made to protect the privacy of individuals' at [66] (Glidewell LJ); 'This case nonetheless highlights, yet again, the failure of both the common law of England and statute to protect in an effective way the personal privacy of individual citizens' at [70] (Bingham LJ); 'This right has so long been disregarded here that it can be recognised now only by the legislature' at [71] (Leggatt LJ).

163 This was recognised by the Court of Appeal in its historical analysis of the law of confidence in *Imerman v Tchenguiz* [2010] EWCA Civ 908, [2011] Fam 116 at [54]-[67].

164 See, for example, the discussion of police powers exercised by various members of the Judicial Committee in *Morris v Beardmore* [1981] AC 446, [1980] 2 All ER 753, which were in terms of invasion of privacy.

165 *R v Khan* [1997] AC 558.

166 These are set out at §§4– 005 to 4– 034.

principles laid down by the Strasbourg institutions as governing the Convention rights specified in section 1(1) of the Human Rights Act 1998.[167] It may be open to an English court to hold that it is not bound by previous decisions of English courts which are incompatible with Convention rights, on the grounds that those previous decisions have not had regard to and given effect to relevant Convention rights and relevant Strasbourg case law.[168] A court which would ordinarily be bound to follow the decision of another court higher in the domestic curial hierarchy remains bound to follow that decision even if it appears to be inconsistent with a later ruling of the court in Strasbourg.[169]

34– 034 Application of the HRA 1998

Numerous commentators — both academics and judges speaking or writing in an extra-judicial capacity — have expressed varying degrees of criticism and concern about the efficacy of judicial attempts to expand and distort the cause of action for breach of confidence in order to provide a basis for privacy claims. In part, these views focus on the inadequacy of the incremental (case by case) evolution of an existing cause of action to cater for what would otherwise be the failure of the law to provide protection against invasions of privacy in a host of different factual situations; and in part on the suggested desirability of maintaining a distinction between breach of confidence on the one hand and privacy on the other. It is suggested that the incremental approach results in uncertainty, delay and costs. As Buxton LJ observed when comparing *Campbell v MGN Ltd*[170] and *Von Hannover v Germany*:[171]

> Had the House had the benefit of *Von Hannover's* case a shorter course might have been taken.[172]

This is particularly so because (as discussed above):[173]

> Put shortly, the precedential rules of English domestic law apply to interpretations of Convention jurisprudence.[174]

Accordingly, when, in *Murray v Express Newspapers plc*,[175] the Court of Appeal was asked to rule on whether there was a tension between the decision of the House of Lords in *Campbell v MGN Ltd*[176] and that of the European Court of Human Rights in *Von Hannover v Germany*,[177] the Court focussed on providing an exegesis of the decision of the House of Lords,[178] which it then applied to the presumed facts of the case before it. The Court did not consider it necessary to analyse *Von Hannover v Germany* in any detail:

---

167 *Kay v Lambeth London Borough Council* [2006] UKHL 10, [2006] 2 AC 465, Lord Bingham at [28]. And see more recently the comments of Lord Neuberger MR in *Manchester City Council v Pinnock* [2010] UKSC 45, [2011] 2 AC 104 at [48]-[49].

168 See, for example, *D v East Berkshire Community NHS Trust* [2003] EWCA Civ 1151, [2004] QB 558 in which the Court of Appeal held that the decision of the House of Lords in *X (Minors) v Bedfordshire County Council* [1995] 2 AC 633 could not survive the introduction of the Human Rights Act 1998; and *McKennitt v Ash v* [2006] EWCA Civ 1714, [2008] QB 73, especially per Buxton LJ at [62-64], in which the Court of Appeal held that the earlier decision of the Court of Appeal in *A v B plc* [2002] EWCA Civ 337, [2003] QB 195 'cannot be read as any sort of binding authority on the content of Articles 8 and 10'.

169 *Kay v Lambeth London Borough Council* [2006] UKHL 10, [2006] 2 AC 465, Lord Bingham at [43].

170 *Campbell v MGN Ltd* [2004] UKHL 22, [2004] 2 AC 457.

171 *Von Hannover v Germany* (2005) 40 EHRR 1.

172 *McKennitt v Ash v* [2006] EWCA Civ 1714, [2008] QB 73 at [39].

173 See §34– 033.

174 *McKennitt v Ash v* [2006] EWCA Civ 1714, [2008] QB 73.

175 *Murray v Express Newspapers plc* [2008] EWCA Civ 446, [2009] Ch 481.

176 *Campbell v MGN Ltd* [2004] UKHL 22, [2004] 2 AC 457.

177 *Von Hannover v Germany* (2005) 40 EHRR 1.

178 *Murray v Express Newspapers plc* [2008] EWCA Civ 446, [2009] Ch 481 at [21]-[35].

> Suffice it to say that, in our opinion, the view we have expressed is consistent with that in *Von Hannover* ... we have little doubt that, if the assumed facts of this case were to be considered by the ECtHR, the court would hold that David had a reasonable expectation of privacy and it seems to us to be more likely than not that, on the assumed facts, it would hold that the Art 8/10 balance would come down in favour of David.

34–035 Convention rights

The Convention is concerned on its face with human rights interferences by the state. These occur when public authorities or officials act in a way which penalises or restricts the exercise of the Convention right. In some circumstances, however, the Strasbourg court identifies what it calls a "positive obligation" on public authorities to act to protect human rights. This protection may be against interferences with the right by other individuals, not just the state. It has identified a positive obligation under ECHR Art 8 in various situations. In a leading Art 8 case it explained the principle at work thus:

> The Court recalls that although the object of Art 8 is essentially that of protecting the individual against arbitrary interference by the public authorities, it does not merely compel the State to abstain from such interference: in addition to this primarily negative undertaking, there may be positive obligations inherent in an effective respect for private or family life. These obligations may involve the adoption of measures designed to secure respect for private life even in the sphere of the relations of individuals between themselves.[179]

The measures adopted may include legislation to protect the right in the way envisaged by the Strasbourg case law. Or in our system they may include judge-made developments to the common law.[180] Under the Human Rights Act 1998 our judges have recognised a positive obligation to protect Art 8 rights against interferences by other persons such as journalists and media organisations. On this basis they have developed the common law of confidence so as to protect private as well as conventionally confidential information. These developments are discussed below. The ECHR rights of the defendant journalists have to be balanced, however, against the privacy rights being asserted. In *A v B plc*, Lord Woolf CJ explained that the court, as a public authority, was able to fulfil its duty under section 6 of the Human Rights Act 1998 Act 'by absorbing the rights which articles 8 and 10 protect into the long-established action for breach of confidence.'[181] He went on to say:

> There is a tension between the two articles which requires the court to hold the balance between the conflicting interests they are designed to protect. This is not an easy task but it can be achieved by the courts if, when holding the balance, they attach proper weight to the important rights both articles are designed to protect. Each article is qualified expressly in a way which allows the interests under the other article to be taken into account.[182]

This approach was endorsed by the House of Lords in *Campbell v MGN Ltd*,[183] where Lord Nicholls said:

> The time has come to recognise that the values enshrined in articles 8 and 10 are now part of the cause of action for breach of confidence. As Lord Woolf CJ has said, the courts have been able to achieve this result by absorbing the rights protected by articles 8 and 10 into this cause of action: *A v B plc* [2003] QB 195, 202, para 4. Further, it should now be recognised

179 *X and Y v The Netherlands* (1985) 8 EHRR 235 at [23].

180 This possibility was recognised by Dame Elizabeth Butler-Sloss P in an early case under the 1998 Act, *Venables v News Group Newspapers Ltd* [2001] Fam 430, [2001] 1 All ER 908 at [25]-[27].

181 *A v B plc* [2003] QB 195 at [4].

182 *A v B plc* [2003] QB 195 at [6].

183 *Campbell v MGN Ltd* [2004] UKHL 22, [2004] 2 AC 457. See, also, Baroness Hale at [132]-[133]: 'The 1998 Act does not create any new cause of action between private persons. But if there is a relevant cause of action applicable, the court as a public authority must act compatibly with both parties' Convention rights ... our law cannot, even if it wanted to, develop a general tort of invasion of privacy. But where existing remedies are available, the court not only can but must balance the competing Convention rights of the parties.'

> that for this purpose these values are of general application. The values embodied in articles 8 and 10 are as much applicable in disputes between individuals or between an individual and a non-governmental body such as a newspaper as they are in disputes between individuals and a public authority.
>
> In reaching this conclusion it is not necessary to pursue the controversial question whether the European Convention itself has this wider effect. Nor is it necessary to decide whether the duty imposed on courts by section 6 of the Human Rights Act 1998 extends to questions of substantive law as distinct from questions of practice and procedure. It is sufficient to recognise that the values underlying articles 8 and 10 are not confined to disputes between individuals and public authorities.[184]

In *Douglas v Hello! Ltd (No 3)*[185] the Court of Appeal carried out an extensive review of the case law, and concluded that:

> in so far as private information is concerned, we are required to adopt, as the vehicle for performing such duty as falls on the courts in relation to Convention rights, the cause of action formerly described as breach of confidence. As to the nature of that duty, it seems to us that sections 2, 3, 6 and 12 of the Human Rights Act 1998 all point in the same direction. The court should, in so far as it can, develop the action for breach of confidence in such a manner as will give effect to both Art 8 and Art 10 rights. In considering the nature of those rights, account should be taken of the Strasbourg jurisprudence. In particular, when considering what information should be protected as private pursuant to Art 8, it is right to have regard to the decisions of the European Court of Human Rights.[186]

Thus, Articles 8 and 10 are now 'the very content of the domestic tort that the English court has to enforce.'[187]

34–036 Privacy etc post-HRA 1998

Almost as soon as the Human Rights Act 1998 came into force,[188] the courts began grappling with the differences between the elements and parameters of the traditional claim for breach of confidence and the claim for protection of private information, and with whether this was any more than a labelling issue. In *Douglas v Hello! Limited*,[189] Sedley LJ said:

> What a concept of privacy does, however, is accord recognition to the fact that the law has to protect not only those people whose trust has been abused but those who simply find themselves subjected to an unwanted intrusion into their personal lives. The law no longer needs to construct an artificial relationship of confidentiality between intruder and victim: it can recognise privacy itself as a legal principle drawn from the fundamental value of personal autonomy.[190]

In the same case, Keene LJ said:

> The nature of the subject matter or the circumstances of the defendant's activities may suffice in some instances to give rise to liability for breach of confidence. That approach must now be informed by the jurisprudence of the Convention in respect of Art 8. Whether the resulting liability is described as being for breach of confidence or for breach of a right of privacy may be little more that deciding what label is to be attached to the cause of action, but there would seem to be merit in recognising that the original concept of breach of confidence has in this particular category of cases now developed into something different from the commercial and employment relationships with which confidentiality is mainly

---

184 *Campbell v MGN Ltd* [2004] UKHL 22, [2004] 2 AC 457 at [17]-[18].

185 *Douglas v Hello! Ltd (No 3)* [2006] EWCA Civ 595, [2006] QB 125.

186 *Douglas v Hello! Ltd (No 3)* [2006] EWCA Civ 595, [2006] QB 125 at [53].

187 *McKennitt v Ash v* [2006] EWCA Civ 1714, [2008] QB 73, Buxton LJ at [11].

188 On 2 October 2000.

189 *Douglas v Hello! Limited* [2001] QB 967.

190 *Douglas v Hello! Limited* [2001] QB 967 at [126].

concerned.[191]

Thereafter the courts began to give effect to privacy interests by expanding the boundaries of the law of confidence.

34– 037 Private matter confidential

The path which English law has chosen to follow has not made matters straightforward either for litigants or for the courts.[192] In this regard, the Court of Appeal in *Douglas v Hello! Ltd (No 3)*[193] remarked:

> We cannot pretend that we find it satisfactory to be required to shoehorn within the cause of action of breach of confidence claims for publication of unauthorised photographs of a private occasion.

As time has gone on, the practical effect of this process has been to create a cause of action relating to the misuse of private information that, in all but name, is distinct from the traditional cause of action of breach of confidence.[194] As is apparent from the discussion below,[195] when transposed to cases involving the use or disclosure of private information, both the essential elements of an actionable breach of confidence and the limiting principles that apply to that cause of action have either effectively been dispensed with or have undergone substantial qualification or metamorphosis. It is suggested that the principal reasons for this are not difficult to identify: essentially, the underlying values and interests (that is to say, personal autonomy and protection from intrusion) that are jeopardised by the misuse of private information differ in significant respects from the underlying values and interests that are recognised and protected by more traditional claims for breach of confidence.[196] And, where such differences exist, it is unsurprising that there should be differences as to the legal tests that are applicable, as to what is required before the law will grant protection, and as to the circumstances in which and the form in which the courts will be prepared to provide a remedy.

34– 038 Private information breaches

The unauthorised disclosure of information about a person's private life will be a violation of Art 8 of the ECHR where both:

(1) The disclosure relates to information in respect of which the person has a reasonable expectation of privacy, either because the information is obviously private or because its disclosure is one that would cause substantial offence to a reasonable person of ordinary sensibilities placed in the same position as that person.[197] This issue is determined objectively:

> The question is what a reasonable person of ordinary sensibilities would feel if she was placed in the same position as the claimant and faced with the same publicity.[198]

---

191 *Douglas v Hello! Limited* [2001] QB 967 at [166].

192 Or, of course, for the reasons given in §34– 030, for those concerned with interpreting and operating FOIA s 41.

193 *Douglas v Hello! Ltd (No 3)* [2006] EWCA Civ 595, [2006] QB 125 at [53].

194 In his Blackstone Lecture 'Sex, Libels and Video-surveillance' of 13 May 2006, Sedley LJ said that 'There are well-recognised constitutional objections to the creation by the courts of new torts. There are fewer such objections to the development, and even the renaming, of old causes of action to meet new conditions…Yet the situation we have now reached, where privacy is entitled to the protection of the law in everything but name, reduces the distinction between development and innovation to an abstraction.'

195 §§34– 038 to 34– 048.

196 See *Vidal Hall v Google Inc* [2015] EWCA Civ 311, [2016] QB 1003 at [25] where the Court of Appeal characterised misuse of private information as a cause of action in tort.

197 *Campbell v MGN Ltd* [2004] UKHL 22, [2004] 2 AC 457.

198 *Murray v Express Newspapers plc* [2008] EWCA Civ 446, [2009] Ch 481 at [35], quoting Lord Hope in *Campbell v MGN Ltd* [2004] UKHL 22, [2004] 2 AC 457 at [99].

(2) Having weighed the justification for interfering with the Art 8 right in issue, represented by the case advanced for the disclosure as a protected act of expression under Art 10, the court considers that the Art 8 right must nonetheless be protected. The issue here is:

> whether in all the circumstances the interest of the owner of the information must yield to the right of freedom of expression conferred on the publisher by Art 10?[199]

Typically this requires separate consideration to be given to different items or classes of information.[200]

A disclosure that meets both requirements will constitute an actionable breach of confidence.

34– 039 Private life

The first question which falls to be considered is: what constitutes part of an individual's private life in the eyes of the law? The European Court of Human Rights has taken a broad, open-ended approach to the meaning of private life. In *Niemetz v Germany*[201] the Court said:

> The Court does not consider it possible or necessary to attempt an exhaustive definition of the notion of "private life." However, it would be too restrictive to limit the notion to an "inner circle" in which an individual may choose to live his personal life as he chooses and to exclude entirely the outside world not encompassed within that circle. Respect for private life must also comprise to a certain degree the right to establish and develop relationships with other human beings.
>
> There appears, furthermore, to be no reason in principle why this understanding of the notion of "private life" should be taken to exclude the activities of a professional or business nature since it is, after all, in the course of their working lives that the majority of people have a significant, if not the greatest, opportunity of developing relationships with the outside world.[202]

In *Peck v United Kingdom*[203] the European Court of Human Rights held that 'private life' is a broad term not susceptible to exhaustive definition but includes the right to establish and develop relationships with other human beings, such that there is a zone of interaction of a person with others, even in a public context, which may fall within the scope of 'private life'.[204]

---

199 *Murray v Express Newspapers plc* [2008] EWCA Civ 446, [2009] Ch 481 at [27].

200 See, for example, *Lord Browne of Madingley v Associated Newspapers Ltd* [2007] EWCA Civ 295, [2008] QB 103.

201 *Niemietz v Germany* (1993) 16 EHRR 97 at [29].

202 See also: *Bensaid v United Kingdom* (2001) 33 EHRR 208 at [47]: '"Private life" is a broad term not susceptible to exhaustive definition. The Court has already held that elements such as gender identification, name and sexual orientation and sexual life are important elements of the personal sphere protected by Art 8…Mental health must also be regarded as a crucial part of private life associated with the aspect of moral integrity. Article 8 protects a right to identity and personal development, and the right to establish and develop relationships with other human beings and the outside world.' Personal telephone calls from an employee's workplace will prima facie be covered by the notion of 'private life' and 'correspondence' for the purposes of Art 8(1); personal emails sent from an employee's workplace and information derived from the monitoring of internet usage are similarly protected by Art 8: *Copland v United Kingdom* (2007) 45 EHRR 37, [2007] ECHR 253.

203 *Peck v United Kingdom (Application No 44647/98)* [2003] EMLR 15, (2003) 36 EHRR 41, 13 BHRC 669. Peck had been captured on closed circuit television when he had attempted suicide by cutting his wrists on a high street. Although the images used did not show the attempted suicide, they clearly identified Peck brandishing a kitchen knife in a public place. Although the police had attended the scene, Peck was not charged with any criminal offence. The images were used in a campaign to reflect the effectiveness of closed circuit television in combating crime. No attempt was made to mask Peck's identity. He subsequently appeared on a number of television broadcasts to discuss the publications of the footage and photographs, but nevertheless complained to the relevant media commissions about the disclosures. Peck tried unsuccessfully to obtain judicial review of the local authority's disclosure. Before the European Court, Peck complained: (1) that the disclosure by a local authority of closed circuit television footage and photographs which had resulted in images of himself being published and broadcast on a local and national level was a breach of his right to respect for family and private life under Art 8; and (2) that it had been a breach of Art 13 in that no effective domestic remedy existed in relation to the violation of his Art 8 right.

204 *Peck v United Kingdom (Application No 44647/98)* [2003] EMLR 15, (2003) 36 EHRR 41, 13 BHRC 669 at [57].

Disclosure of material to the public in a manner which could never have been foreseen may give rise to such an interference.[205] Recognised facets of an individual's private life include:

— a person's health;[206]
— a person's ethnic identity;[207]
— a person's personal relationships;[208]
— a person's sexual conduct;[209]
— a person's religious or philosophical convictions;[210] and
— a person's image.[211]

It will be noticed that these facets resemble what are 'special categories of personal data' within the meaning of the GDPR.[212] A person's private life is not confined to what takes place in the home or out of the public eye.[213] The fact that the subject is a public or political figure does not take information relating to that person out of the realm of private life. Thus, in *Standard Verlags GmbH v Austria (No 2)*,[214] the Court observed that:

> .... while reporting on true facts about a politician's or other public person's private life may be admissible in certain circumstances, even persons known to the public have a legitimate expectation of protection of and respect for their private life.

---

205 *Peck v United Kingdom (Application No 44647/98)* [2003] EMLR 15, (2003) 36 EHRR 41, 13 BHRC 669 at [60].

206 *Campbell v MGN Ltd* [2004] UKHL 22, [2004] 2 AC 457 (the position of the subject there was different on account of her having made public denials of the particular health aspect disclosed - see esp [56], [60]); *Z v Finland* (1997) 25 EHRR 371 at [71]; *S and Marper v UK* (2009) 48 EHRR 50 at [66]-[67].

207 *S and Marper v UK* (2009) 48 EHRR 50 at [66]-[67].

208 *Douglas v Hello! Ltd (No 3)* [2006] EWCA Civ 595, [2006] QB 125; *McKennitt v Ash v* [2006] EWCA Civ 1714, [2008] QB 73; *Standard Verlags GmbH v Austria (No 2)* [2009] ECHR 853.

209 *Mosley v News Group Newspapers Ltd* [2008] EWHC 687 (QB), [2008] EMLR 679; *S and Marper v UK* (2008) 48 EHRR 50 at [66].

210 *Folgero v Norway* [2007] ECHR 546 at [98]. But not a belief in fox-hunting: *Whaley & Anor v Lord Advocate* [2003] ScotCS 178.

211 *Sciacca v Italy* (2005) 43 EHRR 20 at [29]; *S and Marper v UK* (2009) 48 EHRR 50 at [66]. Where photographs are concerned, it is relevant to consider whether they relate to private or public matters and whether they were envisaged for limited use or likely to be made available to the general public: *Von Hannover v Germany* [2009] ECHR 853 at [61]. The Court held that disclosure to an extent which far exceeds the exposure to the public at the time may constitute a serious interference with the right to respect for private life (at [62]). In *Reklos & Davourlis v Greece* [2009] ECHR 200, [2009] EMLR 290, the European Court of Human Rights stated:

> A person's image constitutes one of the chief attributes of his or her personality, as it reveals the person's unique characteristics and distinguishes the person from his or her peers. The right to the protection of one's image is thus one of the essential components of personal development and presupposes the right to control use of that image.

For a photograph near the borderline of the reasonable expectation of privacy, see *Ferdinand v MGN Ltd* [2011] EWHC 2454 (QB) at [57].

212 GDPR Art 9(1). These were formerly 'sensitive personal data' under s 2 of the DPA 1998, as well as the European Directive which it implemented: see §33– 019. The DPA 1998 regulated the 'processing' of personal data. The term 'processing' covered holding, receiving, retrieval, dissemination and publication of personal data. The DPA 1998 restricted by reference to 'data protection principles' (set out in DPA 1998 Sch 1) the processing that the body could carry out: see Ch 33 generally. Schedules 2 and 3 of the DPA 1998 were linked to the first data protection principle. These Schedules, by giving paramountcy to certain matters, embodied a balance having similarities to that sought through the application of Articles 8 and 10 and the requirement of sufficient interference.

213 *Von Hannover v Germany* (2005) 40 EHRR 1, [2004] EMLR 21, 16 BHRC 545, where the claimant had been photographed in her daily outdoor life: playing tennis, on horseback, cycling, visiting a horse show and so forth. The Court held that although these activities occurred in public places, they were of a purely private nature and, accordingly, were within the scope of the claimant's private life.

214 *Standard Verlags GmbH v Austria (No 2)* [2009] ECHR 853 at [52]-[53]. This is not to say that the interference with privacy cannot be justified: see, for example, *Karhuvaara and Iltalehti v Finland* (2005) 41 EHRR 51, where the Court found that, even assuming the facts gave rise to an interference with the Art 8 rights of a politician, that interference was justified where a newspaper article printed a story concerning her husband's conviction for drunk and disorderly behaviour and affray.

34– 040 Sufficiency of interference

Not every disclosure relating to a person's private life will constitute an interference with that person's private life: it must be a 'sufficiently serious' disclosure. Strasbourg jurisprudence considers that the mere storing of data relating to the private life of an individual amounts to an interference within the meaning of Art 8 of the Convention. The Court will have regard to the manner of acquisition and retention, the nature of the records, the way in which it has been used and the results that may be obtained.[215] Examples provide the clearest guide to what will and will not suffice. In the following cases the Court held that the interference was sufficiently serious:

(1) *Douglas v Hello! Ltd (No 3)*,[216] which, as noted above, concerned photographs which had been taken surreptitiously at the wedding of two film stars.

(2) *Von Hannover v Germany*[217] which involved a complaint by Princess Caroline of Monaco that her Art 8 rights had been infringed by the publication in German magazines of photographs showing her engaged in family activities with her boyfriend and children in various public places.

(3) *McKennitt v Ash*[218] which concerned the publication of a book about a celebrated composer and performer of folk music. The book was written by a close friend of the claimant. The court upheld claims of confidentiality in relation to disclosures of the claimant's house:

> To describe a person's home, the décor, the layout, the state of cleanliness, or how occupiers behave inside it, is generally regarded as unacceptable. To convey such details, without permission, to the general public is almost as objectionable as spying into the home with a long distance lens and publishing the resulting photographs.[219]

Descriptions of the claimant's health, her relationship with her fiancé, her reaction to his death, and disclosure of the claimant's acquisition of property were all protected. On the other hand, a description of a shopping trip was not protected.

(4) *Mosley v News Group Newspapers Ltd*,[220] which concerned newspaper and online publication of a story and internet publication of video film relating to sex sessions which included sado-masochistic practices involving the head of Formula 1 and a number of women.

> Where the law is not breached, as I said earlier, the private conduct of adults is essentially no-one else's business. The fact that a particular relationship happens to be adulterous, or that someone's tastes are unconventional or 'perverted', does not give the media *carte blanche.*

(5) *Edward Rocknroll v News Group Newspapers Ltd*[221] concerning a series of photographs of the claimant semi-naked which had been taken by a fellow guest at a private fancy dress party.

34– 041 Insufficient interferences

In the following cases the Court held that the interference was not sufficiently serious:

---

215 *S and Marper v UK* (2009) 48 EHRR 50 at [66]-[67].

216 *Douglas v Hello! Ltd (No 3)* [2006] EWCA Civ 595, [2006] QB 125.

217 *Von Hannover v Germany* (2005) 40 EHRR 1, [2004] EMLR 21, 16 BHRC 545.

218 *McKennitt v Ash* [2005] EWHC 3003, [2006] EMLR 10.

219 *McKennitt v Ash* [2005] EWHC 3003, [2006] EMLR 10 at [135].

220 *Mosley v News Group Newspapers Ltd* [2008] EWHC 687 (QB), [2008] EMLR 679.

221 *Edward Rocknroll v News Group Newspapers Ltd* [2013] EWHC 24 (Ch).

(1) In *Mahmood v Galloway*[222] the court refused to restrain by interim injunction the publication on a website of two photographs of a journalist on the grounds (among others) that one of the photographs did not show him engaged in any activity which could be described as private but was 'simply a photograph of his face',[223] and that it could be assumed that he was aware that the other photograph was being taken when it was and that:

> As with anybody who consents to having his photograph taken [by a subject he was investigating or as part of a social occasion] he can be taken to have consented to its subsequent publication.[224]

(2) In *John v Associated Newspapers Ltd*[225] the court refused to restrain the publication in a newspaper of photographs that showed the claimant, Sir Elton John, standing in the street, outside his home in London, wearing a baseball cap and tracksuit, on the grounds (among others) that he had not established that he was more likely than not to obtain an injunction at trial, either on the basis that he had a reasonable expectation of privacy in the circumstances in which he found himself, or—if he did have such an expectation—on the basis that his Art 8 rights would prevail over the Art 10 rights of the newspaper.

(3) In *Ambrosiadou v Coward*[226] the Court of Appeal had to consider certain statements which had been made by a husband in a document in divorce proceedings. These included statements that the wife had obstructed his access to their son, that the wife's behaviour in their joint hedge fund business had damaged their relationship and that he had tried to save the relationship. The claimant was held to have no reasonable expectation of privacy in this information.[227]

(4) In *In re JR38* the Supreme Court held that children rioting in the street in Northern Ireland did not have a reasonable expectation of privacy in photographs of them which the police wished to disclose to the local media for publication (in the hope that the public would identify them).[228]

34–042 The public domain

The question of whether the material is in the public domain involves careful analysis of:

(1) the information's accessibility, and how general it is;

(2) the extent to which the information has, or is likely to have been, or continues to be, accessed in consequence;[229] and

(3) the extent to which the information can be said to have lost the necessary quality of confidentiality in light of (1) and (2) taking account of, amongst other things, the extent of further harm that may be caused by continued or further publication.

The need to adopt a more purposive examination of public domain in order to give effective protection in cases of private information has repeatedly been recognised in the decided cases. So far as personal information is concerned:

---

222 *Mahmood v Galloway* [2006] EWHC 1286, [2006] EMLR 26.

223 *Mahmood v Galloway* [2006] EWHC 1286, [2006] EMLR 26 at [19].

224 *Mahmood v Galloway* [2006] EWHC 1286, [2006] EMLR 26 at [20]. *Von Hannover v Germany* was said to be 'not in point' (at [19]).

225 *John v Associated Newspapers Ltd* [2006] EWHC 1611, [2006] EMLR 27.

226 *Ambrosiadou v Coward* [2010] EWCA Civ 409, [2011] EMLR 21.

227 *Ambrosiadou v Coward* [2001] EWCA Civ 409, [2011] EMLR 21 at [29]-[30].

228 *In Re JR38* [2015] UKSC 42, [2016] AC 1131.

229 For a case where the passage of time was a factor in finding a reasonable expectation of privacy, see *NT1 v Google LLC* [2018] EWHC 799 (QB), [2018] 3 All ER 581, esp at [223].

> the fact that a matter has once been in the public domain cannot prevent its resurrection, possibly many years later, from being an invasion of privacy. Whether in such a case there is an unwarranted invasion of privacy is a matter of fact and degree.[230]

In short, while the general position remains that public accessibility will deprive information that is placed in the public domain of the protection of the law of confidence, it may well not do so if the information is of a private or personal nature.[231] The touchstone will be whether such use or disclosure has an adverse impact on Art 8 rights. In *Douglas v Hello! Ltd (No 3)*[232] the Court of Appeal stated:

> Once intimate personal information about a celebrity's private life has been widely published it may serve no useful purpose to prohibit further publication. The same will not necessarily be true of photographs. In so far as a photograph does more than convey information and intrudes on privacy by enabling the viewer to focus on intimate personal detail, there will be a fresh intrusion of privacy when each additional viewer sees the photograph and even when one who has seen a previous publication of the photograph is confronted by a fresh publication of it…There is thus a further important potential distinction between the law relating to private information and that relating to other types of confidential information.[233]

The Court of Appeal rejected the argument that, as a result of their agreement to sell the story and photographs of the wedding to a magazine, the couple were precluded from contending that their wedding was a private occasion and, as such, protected by the law of confidence. Indeed, the Court of Appeal said[234] that, applying the reasoning of the decisions of the House of Lords in *Campbell v MGN Ltd*[235] and the European Court of Human Rights in *Von Hannover v Germany*,[236] 'the Douglases appeared to have a virtually unanswerable case for contending that publication of the unauthorised photographs would infringe their privacy'; and that, as there was no good reason for refusing an interim injunction (for example, on the basis that publication would be in the public interest), and as damages were not an adequate remedy for the Douglases, an injunction ought to have been granted to restrain publication. As against that, some cases concerning personal information contain statements to the effect that a person who has placed or allowed to be placed in the public domain information concerning a certain aspect or 'zone' of his private life may not be entitled to complain about the publication of other information concerning the same area — or, possibly, in an extreme case, any area — of his private life.[237] In *Campbell v MGN Ltd*,[238] however, the Court of Appeal sounded a note of

---

230 *R v BCC, ex p Granada Television Ltd* [1995] EMLR 163 at 168; *In Re JR38* [2015] UKSC 42, [2016] AC 1131. See also *Kinloch v HM Advocate* [2012] UKSC 62, [2013] 2 AC 93, esp [21], concerning police surveillance of suspects in public places.

231 *A v M (Family Proceedings: Publicity)* [2001] 1 FLR 562 (children likely to suffer harm if allegations already made public were repeated); *R (Robertson) v Wakefield MDC* [2001] EWHC 915 (Admin), [2002] QB 1052 and *R(Robertson) v SSHD* [2003] EWHC 1760 (restraint on use of addresses on electoral register for direct marketing); *X and Y (Children), Re* [2004] EWHC 762, [2004] EMLR 29 (restraint on republication of information already in the public domain, where it would have a significant effect on the Art 8 rights of children); *Green Corns Ltd v Claverley Group Ltd* [2005] EWHC 958, [2005] EMLR 31, [2005] 2 FCR 309 (restraint on newspaper publication of addresses of houses used to provide care for troubled children, including addresses which could be ascertained by a search of HM Land Registry). See also *Venables v News Group Newspapers Ltd* [2001] Fam 430, [2001] 1 All ER 908 and *AG v Greater Manchester Newspapers Ltd* [2001] TLR 668, (2001) 145 SJLB 279.

232 *Douglas v Hello! Ltd (No 3)* [2006] EWCA Civ 595, [2006] QB 125, [2005] 4 All ER 128.

233 *Douglas v Hello! Ltd (No 3)* [2006] EWCA Civ 595, [2006] QB 125, [2005] 4 All ER 128 at [105].

234 *Douglas v Hello! Ltd (No 3)* [2006] EWCA Civ 595, [2006] QB 125, [2005] 4 All ER 128 at [251]-[259].

235 *Campbell v MGN Ltd* [2004] UKHL 22, [2004] 2 AC 457.

236 *Von Hannover v Germany* (2005) 40 EHRR 1, [2004] EMLR 21, 16 BHRC 545.

237 *Theakston v MGN Ltd* [2002] EWHC 137, [2002] EMLR 398 at [68]; *A v B plc* [2002] EWCA Civ 337, [2003] QB 195 at [11(xii)]; *A v B, C and D* [2005] EWHC 1651, [2005] EMLR 851 at [16]-[23]; *Lennon v News Group Newspapers Ltd* [1978] FSR 573, 574-575.

238 *Campbell v MGN Ltd* [2002] EWCA Civ 1373, [2003] QB 633.

caution about the extent to which the courts will be prepared to adopt this approach in cases involving personal information:

> For our part we would observe that the fact that an individual has achieved prominence on the public stage does not mean that his private life can be laid bare by the media. We do not see why it should necessarily be in the public interest that an individual who has been adopted as a role model, without seeking this distinction, should be demonstrated to have feet of clay.[239]

The courts have been noticeably reluctant to discharge injunctions where the private information has entered the public domain through the social media or reporting of statements made under cover of Parliamentary privilege notwithstanding the existence of the injunction[240]. The significance of these considerations to the exemption contained in s 41 of FOIA is that whether, and to what extent, the fact that information has come into the public domain has the effect that it ceases to be confidential because it no longer has 'the necessary quality of confidence' depends upon the nature of the information. It is clear from cases such as *Campbell v MGN Ltd* and *Peck v United Kingdom*[241] that whether information is private or public does not depend upon whether it is accessible to the public. In short:

> ...it is not possible in a case about personal information to apply Lord Goff's test of whether the information is generally accessible, and to conclude that, if it is, then that is an end of the matter.[242]

34– 043 Offensive disclosures

Although certain information may not be obviously private – that is, not be information on one of the facets of an individual's private life[243] – nevertheless, if it is information the disclosure of which would cause substantial offence to a reasonable person of ordinary sensibilities placed in the same position as that person, that will constitute an actionable breach of confidence, subject to the weighing of legitimate interests in disclosure.[244] Again, examples provide the clearest guide to what will suffice:

(1) *Campbell v MGN Ltd*[245] where a newspaper published reports and pictures of a well-known fashion model attending meetings of a self-help group for drug addiction. The claimant had previously made public statements that she did not have a drug problem. She accepted that in those circumstances the newspaper was entitled to publish the fact that she was receiving treatment for her addiction, but successfully claimed that publication of the details of the meetings and of covert photographs of her attendance constituted a breach of confidentiality. Lord Hope said:

> Miss Campbell could not have complained if the photographs had been taken to show the scene in the street by a passer-by and later published as street scenes. But these were not just pictures of a street scene where she happened

[239] *Campbell v MGN Ltd* [2002] EWCA Civ 1373, [2003] QB 633 at [40]-[41]. Echoed in the House of Lords (where the decision of the Court of Appeal was reversed) by Baroness Hale of Richmond at [2004] UKHL 22, [2004] 2 AC 457 at [151]: 'It might be questioned why, if a role model has adopted a stance which all would agree is beneficial rather than detrimental to society, it is so important to reveal that she has feet of clay. But the possession and use of illegal drugs is a criminal offence and a matter of serious public concern. The press must be free to expose the truth and put the record straight.'

[240] See the judgments Eady and Tugendhat JJ respectively in *CTB v News Group Newspapers Ltd* [2011] EWHC 1326 (QB) and *CTB v News Group Newspapers Ltd* [2011] EWHC 1334 (QB). The reasoning in these judgments was identified as correct by the Supreme Court in *PJS v News Group Newspapers Ltd* [2016] UKSC 26, [2016] AC 1081 at [32].

[241] *Peck v United Kingdom* (2003) 36 EHRR 719.

[242] *Green Corns Ltd v Claverley Group Ltd* [2005] EWHC 958, [2005] EMLR 31, [2005] 2 FCR 309 at [78] (Tugendhat J).

[243] See §34– 039.

[244] See §§34– 048 ff.

[245] *Campbell v MGN Ltd* [2004] UKHL 22, [2004] 2 AC 457.

to be when the photographs were taken. They were taken deliberately, in secret and with a view to publication with the article. The zoom lens was directed at the doorway of the place where the meeting had been taking place. The faces of others in the doorway were pixilated so as not to reveal their identity. Hers was not, the photographs were published and her privacy was invaded.[246]

(2) *Murray v Express Newspapers plc*[247] which concerned a photograph of the infant son of a well known author taken without consent when his mother and father were pushing him in a buggy in a public street. The photograph was taken covertly with a long lens. It later appeared in a magazine. By his litigation friend the child sought an injunction to prevent further publication of the photograph, notwithstanding that the photograph showed nothing embarrassing or untoward. At first instance, Patten J found that the photographs were of innocuous conduct in a public place such as were not to give rise to a reasonable expectation of privacy, and he struck out the action. That decision was reversed in the Court of Appeal, where it was held:

> We do not share the predisposition identified by the judge … that routine acts such as a visit to a shop or a ride on a bus should not attract any reasonable expectation of privacy. All depends upon the circumstances.

Instances of what will not suffice have already been given.[248] In this context, the court is particularly sensitive to the potential offence caused by photographs:

> Special considerations attach to photographs in the field of privacy. They are not merely a method of conveying information that is an alternative to verbal description. They enable the person viewing the photograph to act as a spectator, in some circumstances voyeur would be the more appropriate noun, of whatever it is that the photograph depicts. As a means of invading privacy, a photograph is particularly intrusive. This is quite apart from the fact that the camera, and the telephoto lens, can give access to the viewer of the photograph to scenes where those photographed could reasonably expect that their appearances or actions would not be brought to the notice of the public.[249]

The courts are also astute to protect against disclosures involving children.[250]

34– 044 The balancing exercise

As indicated above, the second requirement for an actionable breach of confidence in respect of private information is that the case for protecting the privacy rights in play is stronger than the case for protecting the right to freedom of expression. When balancing Articles 8 and 10, the Court carries out a parallel analysis:

> First, neither article has *as such* precedence over the other. Secondly, where the values under the two articles are in conflict, an intense focus on the comparative importance of the specific rights being claimed in the individual case is necessary. Thirdly, the justifications for interfering with or restricting each right must be taken into account. Finally, the proportionality test must be applied to each.[251]

As the structure of Articles 8 and 10 of the Convention are the same, the like considerations apply to Art 8(2) as apply to Art 10(2):

> It is plain from the language of Art 10 (2), and the European Court has repeatedly held, that any national restriction on freedom of expression can be consistent with Art 10(2) only if it

246 *Campbell v MGN Ltd* [2004] UKHL 22, [2004] 2 AC 457 at [123].

247 *Murray v Express Newspapers plc* [2008] EWCA Civ 446, [2009] Ch 481.

248 See §34– 041.

249 *Douglas v Hello! Ltd (No 3)* [2006] EWCA Civ 595, [2006] QB 125 at [84], [104]-[107].

250 *Murray v Express Newspapers plc* [2008] EWCA Civ 446, [2009] Ch 481 at [45]. See also *Weller v Associated Newspapers Limited* [2015] EWCA Civ 1176, [2016] 1 WLR 1541 at [29]-[33].

251 *Re S (Identification: Restrictions on Publication)* [2004] UKHL 47, [2005] 1 AC 593 at [17].

> is prescribed by law, is directed at one or more of the objectives specified in the article and is shown by the state concerned to be necessary in a democratic society. 'Necessary' has been strongly interpreted: it is not synonymous with 'indispensable', neither has it the flexibility of such expressions as 'admissible', 'ordinary', 'useful', 'reasonable' or 'desirable': *Handyside v United Kingdom.*[252] One must consider whether the interference complained of corresponded to a pressing social need, whether it is proportionate to the legitimate aim pursued and whether the reasons given by the national authority to justify it are relevant and sufficient under Art 10(2).[253]

An interference with the right to respect for freedom of expression cannot be said to be 'necessary in a democratic society' unless:

(a) relevant and sufficient reasons are given by the national authority to justify the restriction;
(b) the restriction on protection corresponds to a 'pressing social need'; and
(c) it is proportionate to the legitimate aim pursued.[254]

34–045 Articles 8 and 10 factors

On the Art 8 side of the equation, 'the more intimate the aspect of private life that is being interfered with, the more serious must be the reasons for interference before the latter can be legitimate.'[255] Further, when striking a balance between competing rights, the Court is not restricted to considering the Art 8 rights of the immediate parties alone, but, where appropriate, can and should take account of the extent to which the threatened publication would adversely affect the Art 8 rights of others, such as close family members.[256] On the Art 10 side of the equation:

> There are undoubtedly different types of speech, just as there are different types of private information, some of which are more deserving of protection in a democratic society than others. Top of the list is political speech. The free exchange of information and ideas on matters relevant to the organisation of the economic, social and political life of the country is crucial to any democracy. Without this, it can scarcely be called a democracy at all. This includes revealing information about public figures, especially those in elective office, which would otherwise be private but is relevant to their participation in public life. Intellectual and educational speech and expression are also important in a democracy, not least because they enable the development of individuals' potential to play a full part in society and in our democratic life. Artistic speech and expression is important for similar reasons, in fostering both individual originality and creativity and the free-thinking and dynamic society we so much value. No doubt there are other kinds of speech and expression for which similar claims can be made. But it is difficult to make such claims on behalf of the publication with which we are concerned here. The political and social life of the community, and the intellectual, artistic or personal development of individuals, are not obviously assisted by pouring over the intimate details of a fashion model's private life.[257]

---

252 *Handyside v United Kingdom* (1976) 1 EHRR 734, 754 at [48].

253 *R v Shayler (David)* [2002] UKHL 11, [2003] 1 AC 247 at [23]. See also Lord Hope at [36].

254 See the decisions of the European Court of Human Rights cited and applied by Lord Bingham in *R v Shayler* in the passage cited above. In a concurring speech in *R v Shayler*, Lord Hope (at [61]) elaborated on the meaning of proportionality in this context and concluded that the following three stage test should be applied: (a) whether the objective to be achieved - the pressing social need - is sufficiently important to justify limiting the fundamental right; (b) whether the means chosen to limit that right are rational, fair and not arbitrary; and (c) whether the means used impair the right as minimally as possible. The same approach can be applied to conflicts involving other Convention rights, such as Art 6, or involving 'societal' interests, such as the duty of confidence.

255 *Douglas v Hello! Ltd (No 3)* [2006] EWCA Civ 595, [2006] QB 125 at [168].

256 See, for example, *CC v AB* [2006] EWHC 3083 (QB), [2007] EMLR 312 at [42]. There will have to be evidence of any such adverse effect: see *Ferdinand v MGN Ltd* [2011] EWHC 2454 (QB) at [50], [60]. See also *PJS v News Group Newspapers Ltd* [2016] UKSC 26, [2016] AC 1081, esp at [36], [37], [68] and [72]-[78].

257 *Campbell v MGN Ltd* [2004] UKHL 22, [2004] 2 AC 457 at [158]-[159].

In February 2012 the Grand Chamber of the European Court of Human Rights gave judgment in two important cases, *Von Hannover v Germany (No 2)*[258] and *Axel Springer AG v Germany.*[259] In each case the applicant complained that private information had been published by the media. In these judgments the Strasbourg court identified criteria laid down in its existing case law that were relevant to the balancing exercise.[260] These were:

(1) The contribution which the articles and/or photos in issue made to a debate of general public interest;

(2) How well known is the person concerned and what is the subject of the report?;

(3) The conduct of the person concerned prior to publication, in particular in discussing his/her private life with the press, or the fact that the material has already been published;

(4) The method/s by which the press of obtained the information in issue and its truth or otherwise. For example had photos subsequently published been obtained surreptitiously, through harassment or in other circumstances unfavourable to the person concerned?;

(5) The nature and severity of the sanction sought against, or (in the case of an application to Strasbourg) already imposed on the press. This is relevant to the proportionality of the interference with the free speech right.[261]

In *Von Hannover v Germany (No 2)*[262] the Strasbourg court had to consider a complaint by Caroline Von Hannover that the German courts had failed once again sufficiently to protect against the publication of photographs of her engaging in her private/family life (in fact on a skiing holiday). This time, however, the court considered that there had been no violation of her privacy rights. This was because the domestic courts had properly weighed the factors described above. In particular, the photographs had not been obtained in unfavourable circumstances and, alongside the accompanying articles, made a contribution to a debate apparently of general interest.[263] This debate was as to how the children of an ailing Prince Rainier of Monaco:

> reconciled their obligations of family solidarity with the legitimate needs of their private life, among which was the desire to go on holiday[264].

In *Couderc v France* the Grand Chamber considered an application by a news magazine that had published an interview with the mother of the illegitimate son of Caroline von Hannover's brother, the reigning Prince of Monaco. The French courts held that there had been a breach of the Prince's privacy, awarding him damages. The Grand Chamber found that the French courts had violated the publisher's ECHR Art 10 rights.[265] This was because, taken as a whole, the article could be understood as contributing to a public debate of public interest. At the time of the article, Prince Albert was single and childless and he had tried to keep the public in ignorance of the birth.

---

258 *Von Hannover v Germany (No 2)* [2012] ECHR 228, (2012) 55 EHRR 15.

259 *Axel Springer AG v Germany* [2012] ECHR 227, (2012) 55 EHRR 6.

260 *Von Hannover v Germany (No 2)* [2012] ECHR 228, (2012) 55 EHRR 15 at [107] and *Axel Springer AG v Germany* [2012] ECHR 227, (2012) 55 EHRR 6 at [89]-[95].

261 See §34– 044 above.

262 *Von Hannover v Germany (No 2)* [2012] ECHR 228, (2012) 55 EHRR 15.

263 *Von Hannover v Germany (No 2)* [2012] ECHR 228, (2012) 55 EHRR 15 at [114]-[126].

264 *Von Hannover v Germany (No 2)* [2012] ECHR 228, (2012) 55 EHRR 15 at [117]. The Court has since upheld the reasoning of the German courts in another case in which publication of holiday photos of the Princess was allowed: see *Von Hannover v Germany (No 3)* [2013] ECHR 835.

265 *Couderc v France* [2016] EMLR 19, (2016) 40 BHRC .

34– 046 Application to FOIA

Disclosure under FOIA will not necessarily engage the Convention right or any corresponding public interest. Disclosure under the Act is to the person who made the request. An applicant's motive in making a request for information is generally irrelevant to the processing of that request.[266] It is therefore suggested that where a request for information under the Act captures private information (ie the first condition is made out in respect of that information) that will ordinarily suffice to render that information exempt under s 41. It may be possible for an applicant to advance particular reasons why disclosure would be in the public interest or would otherwise justify the interference with a person's private life. These may be advanced by a journalist seeking to use the information in investigating and publishing to the general public in the public interest, and thereby in exercising important Art 10 rights.

34– 047 Private or personal life

It follows from these formulations that what is capable of being protected as part of an individual's private life may vary from case to case. In particular, whether or not use or disclosure of particular information infringes a person's privacy cannot be tested by asking whether, considered in isolation, the information is trivial or useless. On the contrary, that will depend upon all the circumstances, including, for example, where the information which is said to be private falls to be considered together with other material that would otherwise be of a private character, whether such material has already entered the public domain, when that other material entered the public domain, the extent to which that other material has been publicised, and whether that other material has been publicised with the consent or involvement of the claimant; and, with regard to the information which is said to be private, the manner in which and the purposes for which it was obtained, how it was stored or processed, the purposes for which it was or is intended to be published, and the consequences of publication. It is suggested that this appears from the cases considered above,[267] and may be especially true of photographs.[268]

34– 048 Privacy and false information

Traditionally, the law has drawn a clear distinction between the use or disclosure of true information on the one hand and the publication of false information on the other hand. The former can be the subject of a claim for breach of confidence, whereas (assuming it is injurious to the claimant's reputation) the latter is properly the subject of a claim for defamation. In *Campbell v MGN Ltd*,[269] Lord Hope said that 'there is a vital difference between inaccuracies that deprive the information of its intrusive qualities and inaccuracies that do not.'[270] In *McKennitt v Ash*,[271] Eady J described as 'somewhat simplistic' the proposition that 'a reasonable expectation of protection, or a duty of confidence, *cannot* arise in relation to false allegations', and continued

---

266 See §20– 017.

267 At §§34– 039 to 34– 044.

268 For the particular significance which may be attached to photographs taken without consent see (in addition to the cases cited in the main body of the text): *R v Broadcasting Standards Commission, ex p BBC (Liberty intervening)* [2001] QB 885, [2000] 3 All ER 989; *R v Loveridge* [2001] EWCA Crim 973; *Theakston v MGN Ltd* [2002] EWHC 137, [2002] EMLR 398 at [40]-[41]; *D v L* [2003] EWCA Civ 1169, [2004] EMLR 1at [23] (Waller LJ): 'A court may restrain the publication of an improperly obtained photograph even if the taker is free to describe the information which the photograph provides or even if the information revealed by the photograph is in the public domain. It is no answer to the claim to restrain the publication of an improperly obtained photograph that the information portrayed by the photograph is already in the public domain.'

269 *Campbell v MGN Ltd* [2004] UKHL 22, [2004] 2 AC 457.

270 *Campbell v MGN Ltd* [2004] UKHL 22, [2004] 2 AC 457 at [102].

271 *McKennitt v Ash* [2006] EMLR 10 at [178].

as follows:[272]

> As I observed in the case of *Beckham v Gibson*, 29 April 2005 (unreported), the protection of the law would be illusory if a claimant, in relation to a long and garbled story, was obliged to spell out which of the revelations are accepted as true, and which are said to be false or distorted: see also *W v Westminster City Council* [2005] EWHC 102, Tugendhat J.

In *W v Westminster City Council*[273] it was said that, in the event that the Council had received the false information that the claimant was the person of the same name who was a convicted paedophile and (acting entirely in good faith) had then kept that information on the family file, the claimant would have been able to rely on Art 8 to bring a claim under s 7 of the Human Rights Act 1998 against the local authority in order to establish that he was not the person of the same name who had been convicted of sex offending, without having to wait for publication of that information to occur, such as to found a claim in libel. The Court of Appeal in *McKennitt v Ash*[274] has now made clear that provided the matter in question is of a kind to which the law of private or confidential information applies, then it does not matter whether it is true or false – although falsity may be highly relevant to whether there is any or any arguable defence that it would be in the public interest for the matter to be published.[275] So far as concerns the applicability of s 41(1) of FOIA, therefore, disclosure of information of a private nature may be actionable as a breach of confidence even if that information contains inaccuracies, or even if it is entirely false.

4. TRADE SECRETS

34– 049 Introduction

Information that constitutes a trade secret[276] is rendered exempt information by s 43(1) of FOIA.[277] Where the information is 'environmental information', exemption from disclosure falls to be determined under the EIR and not FOIA.[278] Although those regulations do not provide an exception for 'trade secrets', some trade secrets may be excepted from disclosure under an analogous exception.[279] The trade secret exemption in FOIA is a class exemption, in that it applies to any information that amounts to a trade secret, irrespective of the consequences of disclosure. The exemption is not absolute, so that disapplication of the duty to disclose requires a weighing of the public interest in maintaining the exemption against the public interest in disclosure of the information.[280] There is no correlative disapplication of the

---

272 *McKennitt v Ash* [2006] EMLR 10 at [78].

273 *W v Westminster City Council* [2005] EWHC 102 at [288].

274 *McKennitt v Ash* [2006] EWCA Civ 1714, [2008] QB 73 at [78]-[80] (Buxton LJ), [82] (Latham LJ) and [85]-[87] (Longmore LJ).

275 If the information is true this may support the competing case under ECHR Art 10: see §34– 045 and, by way of example, see *Ferdinand v MGN Ltd* [2011] EWHC 2454 (QB) at [67]-[68].

276 For a more general treatment of the law of trade secrets, see: S Mehigan and A Kamerling, *Restraint of Trade and Business Secrets*, 6th edn (London, Sweet & Maxwell, 2010); AE Turner, *The Law of Trade Secrets* (London, Sweet & Maxwell, 1962); G Hughes (ed), *Dean's Law of Trade Secrets & Privacy*, 3rd ed (Sydney, Law Book Company, 2018); The Institute of Law Research and Reform, *Trade Secrets* (Edmonton, The Institute of Law Research, 1986); P Lavery, *Commercial Secrets* (Dublin, Round Hall, 1996).

277 In relation to Scottish public authorities, it is rendered exempt information by FOI(S)A s 33(1) (a). There is a limited exemption for trade secrets under DPA 1998 s 8(5): see §15– 059.

278 The disclosure regime under the EIR is considered in Chs 17-19. In relation to Scottish public authorities, disclosure of environmental information falls to be determined under the EI(S)R.

279 See §34– 067.

280 FOIA s 2(2)(b); FOI(S)A s 2.

duty to confirm or deny. A similar exemption is to be found in each of the comparative jurisdictions.[281]

34–050 Nature of a trade secret

The ambit of this exemption depends upon the scope of the concept of a trade secret in English law.[282] As there is no statutory definition of what constitutes a trade secret, guidance on the point needs to be sought in the case law.[283] Although the case law yields no exact definition of a trade secret, it does provide useful guidelines. In *Ansell Rubber Co Pty Ltd v Allied Rubber Industries Pty Ltd*,[284] Gowans J suggested the following guidelines:

> An exact definition of a trade secret is not possible. Some factors to be considered in determining whether given information is one's trade secret are: the extent to which information is known outside of his business; the extent to which it is known by employees and others involved in his business; the extent of measures taken by him to guard the secrecy of the information; the value of the information to him and his contemporaries; the amount of effort or money expended by him in developing the information; the ease or difficulty with which the information could be properly acquired or duplicated by others.

Similar guidelines are found in the judgment of Sir Robert Megarry VC in *Thomas Marshall (Exports) Ltd v Guinle*.[285] Although in the following passage he did not attempt to distinguish between trade secrets and other confidential commercial information, his criteria are of assistance in establishing the minimum requirements that must be met before information could properly be said to amount to a trade secret:

> If one turns from the authorities and looks at the matter as a question of principle, I think (and I say this very tentatively, because the principle has not been argued out) that four elements may be discerned which may be of some assistance in identifying confidential information or trade secrets which the court will protect. I speak of such information or secrets only in an industrial or trade setting. First, I think that the information must be information the release of which the owner believes would be injurious to him or of advantage to his rivals or others. Second, I think the owner must believe that the information is confidential or secret, ie, that it is not already in the public domain.[286] It may

---

281 In the United States, the Freedom of Information Act, 1966, 5 USC § 552(b)(4), exempts from disclosure trade secrets: see §51–008(4). The Freedom of Information Act 1982 (Cth of Australia) s 47, provides an exemption for trade secrets: see §51–015(5). The Official Information Act 1982 (New Zealand) ss 9(2)(b)(i) and 27(1)(a), provide a qualified exemption where the disclosure would disclose a trade secret: see §51–023(2). The Access to Information Act (Canada) s 20(1)(a), provides a mandatory exemption for trade secrets: see §51–031(4); s 18(a) provides a discretionary exemption for trade secrets belonging to the Government of Canada: see §51–032(3). The Federal Court has held that given the existence of other, restricted exemptions for confidential information, the term 'trade secrets' had to be given a reasonably narrow interpretation. It considered that a trade secret must be something probably of a technical nature which is guarded very closely and is of such peculiar value to the owner of the trade secret that harm to him would be presumed by its mere disclosure: *Société Gamma Inc v Canada (Secretary of State)* (1994) 56 CPR (3d) 58, 79 FTR 42. The Freedom of Information Act 2014 (Ireland) s 36(1)(a) provides a qualified exemption for trade secrets: see §51–039(6).

282 As to the meaning given to 'trade secret' in the context of freedom of information legislation in Australia, see: *Searle Australia Pty Ltd v Public Interest Advocacy Centre* (1992) 108 ALR 163, 36 FCR 111, where it was held by the full court of the Federal Court that the essential attributes of a trade secret were: (a) that it must be used in or usable in trade; in other words, an asset of the trade; (b) it must be used for the benefit of the owner's business; (c) it must not be in the public domain; (d) technicality is not required, but the more technical the information is, the more likely it is to be characterised as a trade secret. The Federal Court accepted that, in 'an appropriate case', the names of customers and the goods that they buy would be a trade secret, provided that these would be to the advantage of rivals to obtain.

283 The term has been used for over a century: in *Allsopp v Wheatcroft* (1872) Law Rep 15 Eq 59 at 64-65 Sir John Wickens referred to a 'clearly lawful restriction against divulging a trade secret'. See also: *Davies v Davies* (1887) 36 Ch D 359 at 385.

284 *Ansell Rubber Co Pty Ltd v Allied Rubber Industries Pty Ltd* [1967] VR 373.

285 *Thomas Marshall (Exports) Ltd v Guinle* [1979] Ch 227, [1978] 3 All ER 193, [1979] FSR 208.

286 Thus, under the equivalent provision under the Canadian Access to Information Act 1982, the Federal Court held that dosage information for a drug which was disclosed in a monograph available to health professionals was in

be that some or all of his rivals already have the information: but as long as the owner believes it to be confidential I think he is entitled to try and protect it. Third, I think that the owner's belief under the two previous heads must be reasonable. Fourth, I think that the information must be judged in the light of the usage and practices of the particular industry or trade concerned. It may be that information which does not satisfy all these requirements may be entitled to protection as confidential information or trade secrets: but I think that any information which does satisfy them must be of a type which is entitled to protection.

34– 051 Ordinary work knowledge

In *Faccenda Chicken Ltd v Fowler*[287] the Court of Appeal distinguished between trade secrets (which at common law may not be disclosed, quite apart from any contractual proscription against disclosure) and the information which an employee will inevitably acquire whilst employed (which is not subject to an implied obligation not to disclose). The correct characterisation of any particular item of information does not depend purely upon the attributes of the information, but will also depend upon the nature of the employment, the degree to which the employer impressed on the employee the confidentiality of the information, and whether the relevant information can be easily isolated from other information which the employee is free to use or disclose. When discussing those matters, the Court of Appeal said:

> In our judgment the information will only be protected if it can properly be classed as a trade secret or as material which, while not properly to be described as a trade secret, is in all the circumstances of such a highly confidential nature as to require the same protection as a trade secret *eo nomine* ... It is clearly impossible to provide a list of matters which will qualify as trade secrets or their equivalent. Secret processes of manufacture provide obvious examples, but innumerable other pieces of information are capable of being trade secrets, though the secrecy of some information may be only short-lived. In addition, the fact that the circulation of certain information is restricted to a limited number of individuals may throw light on the status of the information and its degree of confidentiality...though an employer cannot prevent the use or disclosure merely by telling the employee that certain information is confidential, the attitude of the employer towards the information provides evidence which may assist in determining whether or not the information can properly be regarded as a trade secret ... For our part we would not regard the separability of the information in question as being conclusive, but the fact that the alleged "confidential" information is part of a package and that the remainder of the package is not confidential is likely to throw light on whether the information in question is really a trade secret.

The distinction made by the Court of Appeal in *Faccenda Chicken Ltd v Fowler*[288] was considered by Hoffmann J in *Lock International plc v Beswick*:[289]

> There will be a good deal of ... information which an employee could not without breach of duty disclose while he was employed but which he is free to use as part of his own skill and knowledge after his employment has ceased...It would not, for example, be sufficient to say in general terms that they were extremely familiar with the way Metalcheck detectors worked with, as the plaintiff's witnesses repeatedly say, their "strengths and weaknesses." There may have been some particular strength or weakness which was indeed a trade secret, but general familiarity is pre-eminently the kind of skill and knowledge which the honest employee cannot help taking away with him...In the Technical Appendix I have considered all the alleged secrets and it seems to me that the only one in respect of which the plaintiff has even an arguable case is that relating to a particular weakness in the tuner diodes used in one circuit. Some of the claims to trade secrets, such as the use of marine ply or a common

---

the public domain: *Merck Frosst Canada Inc v Canada (Minister of Health and Welfare)* (1988) 20 FTR 73, 30 CPR (3d) 473; *Canada Post Corp v Canada (Minister of Public Works)* [1993] 3 FC 320, affirmed (1993) 64 FTR 62 (Fed. Court of Appeal); *Matol Botanical International Inc v Canada (Minister of National Health & Welfare)* (1994) 84 FTR 168.

287 *Faccenda Chicken Ltd v Fowler* [1987] Ch 117, [1986] 1 All ER 617, [1986] FSR 291.

288 *Faccenda Chicken Ltd v Fowler* [1987] Ch 117, [1986] 1 All ER 617, [1986] FSR 291.

289 *Lock International plc v Beswick* [1989] 1 WLR 1268 at 1274-1275, 1281, [1989] 3 All ER 373.

> microprocessor, I regard as frankly absurd...Many [employers] have great difficulty in understanding the distinction between genuine trade secrets and skill and knowledge which the employee may take away with him. In cases in which the plaintiff alleges misuse of trade secrets or confidential information concerning a manufacturing process, a lack of particularity about the precise nature of the trade secrets is usually a symptom of an attempt to prevent the employee from making legitimate use of the knowledge and skills gained in the plaintiff's service...Judges dealing with ex parte applications are usually also at a disadvantage in dealing with alleged confidential knowledge of technical processes described in technical language, such as the electric circuitry in this case. It may look like magic but turn out merely to embody a principle discovered by Faraday or Ampere.[290]

FSS Travel and Leisure Systems Ltd v Johnson[291] affords one example of a case in which a claim by an employer failed, essentially for the reasons discussed in the above passage. The Court of Appeal, agreeing with the decision of the deputy judge at first instance, held that the employer had not established an entitlement to any identifiable trade secrets, but, rather, was seeking to rely upon a restrictive covenant to lay claim, in effect, to the employee's skill, experience, know-how and general knowledge gained during the course of his employment.

34–052 Trade secrets – examples

The case law needs to be considered with care, as the distinction between confidential information and trade secrets is often unarticulated, if appreciated at all. Nevertheless, the following appear to have been characterised as trade secrets in the properly-understood sense:

— special methods of design and construction;[292]

— technical knowledge and experience connected with the manufacture of particular goods;[293]

— trade practices and processes which would be harmful if they fell into the hands of competitors;[294]

— information relating to sales, prices and customers which would be of advantage to a competing company;[295] and

— a financial model prepared by Atos as part of its successful bid for the contract to host and support the "Government Gateway" website and containing detailed information about Atos' pricing structure, treatment of costs, profit margin and so

---

290 See also: *Lansing Linde v Kerr* [1991] 1 WLR 251, where Staughton LJ referred to *Herbert Morris Ltd v Saxelby* [1916] 1 AC 688, *Faccenda Chicken Ltd v Fowler* [1987] Ch 117, *Balston Ltd v Headline Filters Ltd* [1987] FSR 330 and *Lock International plc v Beswick* [1989] 1 WLR 1268, and went on to say (at 259-260): 'It appears to me that the problem is one of definition: what are trade secrets, and how do they differ (if at all) from confidential information?' Staughton LJ considered a definition suggested by Counsel that 'a trade secret is information which, if disclosed to a competitor, would be liable to cause real (or significant) harm to the owner of the secret', and continued: 'I would add first, that it must be information used in a trade or business, and secondly that the owner must limit the dissemination of it or at least not encourage or permit widespread publication. That is my preferred view of the meaning of trade secret in this context. It can thus include not only secret formulae for the manufacture of products but also, in an appropriate case, the names of customers and the goods which they buy. But some may say that not all such information is a trade secret in ordinary parlance. If that view be adopted, the class of information which can justify a restriction is wider, and extends to some confidential information which would not ordinarily be called a trade secret.'

291 *FSS Travel and Leisure Systems Ltd v Johnson* [1999] FSR 505, [1998] IRLR 382, [1999] ITCLR 218.

292 *Reid & Sigrist Ltd v Moss and Mechanism Ltd* (1932) 49 RPC 461 (manufacture of aircraft turn indicators); *Standex International Ltd v CB Blades Ltd* [1976] FSR 114 (a unique mould engraving process).

293 *Cranleigh Precision Engineering v Bryant* [1964] 3 All ER 289 (a swimming pool); *Balston Ltd v Headline Filters* [1987] FSR 330; *Nordenfelt v Maxim Nordenfelt Guns and Ammunition Company* [1894] AC 535 (know-how in relation to machine guns); *Amber Size and Chemical Company, Limited v Menzel* [1913] 2 Ch 239.

294 *Malden Timber v McLeish* [1992] SLT 727; *Littlewoods Organisation v Harris* [1977] 1 WLR 1472; *Media Agency Group Ltd v Space Media Agency Ltd* [2018] EWHC 1434 (QB).

295 *Sir WC Leng & Co Ltd v Andrews* [1909] 1 Ch 763; *Harben Pumps (Scotland) v Lafferty* [1989] SLT 752; *Lansing Linde Ltd v Kerr* [1991] 1 All ER 418; *cf Faccenda Chicken Ltd v Fowler* [1987] Ch 117, [1986] 1 All ER 617, [1986] FSR 291.

on.[296]

It should be noted that the information that was held not to be capable of protection as a trade secret in *Faccenda Chicken Ltd v Fowler*[297] comprised the following sales information: the names and addresses of customers; the most convenient routes to be taken to reach individual customers; the usual requirements of individual customers; the days of the week and times of day when deliveries were made to individual customers; and the prices charged to individual customers. There is not necessarily any tension between this result and the approach suggested by Staughton LJ in *Lansing Linde v Kerr*,[298] who qualified his statement that the names of customers and the goods which they buy may amount to a trade secret by the words 'in an appropriate case'. The conclusion of the Court of Appeal in *Faccenda Chicken Ltd v Fowler*[299] that the sales information did not constitute a trade secret was reached by reference to the various matters (discussed above) that the court had held needed to be considered in order to determine whether any particular item of information fell within the implied term that was the subject of the decision of the court in that case.

34–053 Technical information

It is clear from the cases discussed above that it is neither a necessary nor a sufficient requirement for information to constitute a trade secret that it should be technical in nature, although technical information may — subject always to Hoffmann J's warnings about the danger of lawyers being blinded with science — more readily be held to amount to a trade secret. These conclusions are in line with the Australian cases. In *Searle Australia Pty Ltd v Public Interest Advocacy Centre*[300] the court observed that: 'It may be that the more technical the information is, the more likely it is that, as a matter of fact, the information will be classed as a trade secret. But technicality is not required.'[301]

34–054 Trade secrets – principles

In summary, therefore, in order for information to amount to a trade secret more is required than that it should be (a) trade information having a commercial value and (b) confidential to the person(s) claiming that it constitutes a trade secret.[302] What is required is a sufficiently high degree of confidentiality. Whether or not information is of such a high degree of confidentiality as to constitute a trade secret will depend on all the circumstances. Relevant considerations include: the value of the information, the investment made in developing the information, the extent to which it truly is secret, the extent to which access to it has been restricted or its secrecy and importance have been emphasised, and the extent to which it is separate and distinct from other information which cannot properly be regarded as a trade secret. Technicality is not required, although secret processes of manufacture, formulae and designs and so forth may more readily be regarded as trade secrets than information about costs, prices, sales and customers.[303] Technical information may have the appearance of distinctiveness and

---

296 *Department of Work and Pensions v IC*, FTT, 20 September 2010 at [55] and [82].

297 *Faccenda Chicken Ltd v Fowler* [1987] Ch 117, [1986] 1 All ER 617, [1986] FSR 291.

298 *Lansing Linde v Kerr* [1991] 1 WLR 251.

299 *Faccenda Chicken Ltd v Fowler* [1987] Ch 117, [1986] 1 All ER 617, [1986] FSR 291.

300 *Searle Australia Pty Ltd v Public Interest Advocacy Centre* (1992) 108 ALR 163, 36 FCR 111.

301 *Searle Australia Pty Ltd v Public Interest Advocacy Centre* (1992) 108 ALR 163 at 174.

302 Contrast the suggestion made by the House of Lords Select Committee which considered the draft Freedom of Information Bill that a trade secret is 'information of commercial value which is protected by the law of confidence' — *Report of the Select Committee*, 27 July 1998, para 45.

303 In Canada, in the equivalent provision of the Access to Information Act 1982, the Federal Court held that the term 'trade secret' should be reserved for more technical production information: *Merck Frosst Canada Inc v Canada*

sophistication, but in truth be trite or inseparable from a general stock of skill and knowledge which an employee may take away with him; in which case, it will not constitute a trade secret. Conversely, although it often may not do so, in an appropriate case financial and customer information may constitute a trade secret (eg where one or more of the following apply: dissemination of such information has been restricted; it is of great value; release of it would cause serious harm to the person from whom the information originates).

34– 055 The public interest

If the information in question constitutes a trade secret, the duty to disclose the information does not apply if the public interest in maintaining the exemption outweighs the public interest in disclosing the information.[304] The weighing exercise necessitates an identification of the public interest in the maintenance of the exemption, always recognising that that public interest must be delineated in such a fashion that it is capable in practice of being outweighed.[305] The public interest in the maintenance of this exemption should, it is suggested, involve an appreciation of:

— the maintenance of rights of intellectual property; and
— the potential of a chilling effect upon the provision to public authorities of information constituting trade secrets if such secrets are routinely disclosed upon a request being made under FOIA.[306]

34– 056 The duty to confirm or deny

The discrete duty to confirm or deny upon a public authority that it holds information of the description specified in a request[307] is not displaced on the ground that to comply with that duty would disclose a trade secret.

5. PREJUDICE TO COMMERCIAL INTERESTS

34– 057 Introduction

By s 43(2) of FOIA information is rendered exempt if its disclosure would, or would be likely to, prejudice the commercial interests of any person, including the public authority holding it.[308] Where the information is 'environmental information', exemption from disclosure falls to be determined under the EIR and not FOIA.[309] Those regulations provide an analogous exception (considered separately below)[310] for confidential commercial or industrial information the non-disclosure of which is provided by law to protect a legitimate economic interest. The exemption under FOIA is not absolute, so that disapplication of the duty to disclose requires a weighing of the public interest in maintaining the exemption against the public interest in disclosure of the information.[311] The duty to confirm or deny is similarly excluded where, or

(Minister of Health and Welfare) (1988) 20 FTR 73, 30 CPR (3d) 473.

304 FOIA s 2(2)(b); FOI(S)A s 2.

305 To avoid metamorphosing it into an absolute exemption.

306 See, for example, *Department of Work and Pensions v IC*, FTT, 20 September 2010 at [91].

307 FOIA s 1(1)(a). There is no separate duty to confirm or deny under the FOI(S)A.

308 In relation to Scottish public authorities, there is a similar exemption under FOI(S)A s 33(1)(b).

309 The disclosure regime under the EIR is considered in Chs 17-19. In relation to Scottish public authorities, disclosure of environmental information falls to be determined under the EI(S)R.

310 EIR reg 12(5)(e); EI(S)R reg 10(5)(e). See §34– 067.

311 FOIA s 2(2)(b); FOI(S)A s 2.

to the extent that, informing the applicant that the information specified in the request is or is not held would, or would be likely to, prejudice the commercial interests of any person.[312] The exclusion of the duty to confirm or deny is also not absolute.[313] Of the comparative jurisdictions, a similar exemption is to be found in the Australian, New Zealand and Irish regimes.[314]

34– 058 Scope

The exemption involves a consideration of:

— the notion of 'prejudice';
— the requisite degree of likelihood of prejudice; and
— the matter that is the proper subject of protection from that prejudice or likely prejudice.

The concept of 'prejudice' and the requisite degree of likelihood of prejudice are the same as those which are used for most of the other harm-based exemptions. These have been considered elsewhere in this work.[315] The object of the harm that forms the subject of the provision is the commercial interests of any person (including the public authority holding the information in question). This wording is of wide scope. In particular, there is no limitation on the nature or extent of the commercial interests that are material to the operation of the exemption. For example, there is no requirement that such interests should be serious or substantial;[316] nor is there any requirement that the protection of such interests should have any public interest element or justification. The phrase 'commercial interests' is apt to cover:

— the existing business of a person or organisation, including its know-how;[317]
— a proposed venture; and

---

312 FOIA s 43(3). There is no separate duty to confirm or deny under the FOI(S)A.

313 FOIA s 2(1)(b).

314 The Freedom of Information Act 1982 (Cth of Australia) s 47G provides an exemption in respect of information concerning a person in respect of his or her business or professional affairs or concerning the business, commercial or financial affairs of an organisation or undertaking, being information the disclosure of which would, or could reasonably be expected to, unreasonably affect that person adversely in respect of his or her lawful business or professional affairs or that organisation or undertaking in respect of its lawful business, commercial or financial affairs: see §51– 015(17). The Official Information Act 1982 (New Zealand), ss 9(2)(b)(i) and 27(1)(a), provides a qualified exemption where the making available of that information would be likely to unreasonably prejudice the commercial position of the person who supplied or who is the subject of the information: see §51– 023(2). The Freedom of Information Act 2014 (Ireland) s 36(1)(b) and (c) provides a qualified exemption for commercially sensitive information. In the other jurisdictions, protection from disclosure is provided through the confidentiality and trade secrets exemptions.

315 In relation to 'prejudice' generally, see §§6– 020 to 6– 028. In relation to the required degree of likelihood, see specifically §6– 022. In *John Connor Press Associates v IC*, IT, 25 January 2006, the Tribunal found that, because of earlier disclosures of similar information, there was no likelihood of harm.

316 This is, it seems, the deliberate intention of the legislature. The Select Committee had recommended that the phrase 'substantial prejudice' be used, but this recommendation was rejected: *Report from the Select Committee Appointed to Consider the Draft Freedom of Information Bill 1998-9*, July 1999, HL, para 32; *Select Committee on Public Administration, Third Report*, Sessions 1998-9, July 1999, HC 570-1, para 71. Contrast, also, the test of 'substantial harm' which had been proposed in *Your Right to Know. The Government's Proposals for a Freedom of Information Act. White Paper* (Cm 3818, 1997) para 3.7.

317 In Australia, under the equivalent provision in the Freedom of Information Act 1982, this exemption has been successfully invoked to exempt documents with information as to the nature of, techniques used in, and results of tests carried out into a pharmaceutical product *(Re Pfizer Pty Ltd and the Department of Health, Housing and Community Services* (1993) 30 ALD 647). See also: *Re Organon (Australia) Pty Ltd and Department of Community Services and Health* (1987) 13 ALD 588 at 595 (the fact that considerable time and money had been expended upon the compilation of statistical information supplied to the department and that the publication of the statistics would reduce the value of that investment was sufficient to meet the requirements of the exemption); *Gill v Department of Industry, Technology and Resources* [1987] VR 681 at 687; *Re The Staff Development and Training Centre and Secretary, Department of Employment, Workplace Relations and Small Business* (2000) 30 AAR 330 at 365-368; *Searle Australia v Public Interest Advocacy Centre* (1992) 36 FCR 111, 108 ALR 163 (the exemption does not apply to the compilation of material otherwise publicly available).

— the assets of a commercial enterprise, including its contracts.

The Tribunal has observed that the meaning of the word 'commercial' depends upon the context in which it is used, and in the present context it should not be tied to 'competitive participation in buying and selling goods and services'.[318] By way of example, the Tribunal has accepted as prejudicial to commercial interest a disclosure of the detail of certain commercially sensitive terms of the contract with Atos to host and support the "Government Gateway" website. The Tribunal accepted that disclosure of this information would be likely to prejudice the Department of Work and Pensions commercial interests in any future procurement of the Gateway service or any similar service systems.[319] By contrast, disclosure of details of a Department of Business, Innovation and Skills contract to provide a Business Growth Service did not prejudice the department commercially.[320] The imminence or otherwise of a re-tendering of a contract may be important to likelihood of prejudice. In *Cranfield University v Information Commissioner* the University's contract to provide courses for Ministry of Defence staff had another 18 years to run.[321] The contract had break and termination provisions. Although disclosure was sought of sensitive pricing information, which would be the price for a competitor 'to beat'[322] on such an exercise, it would not cause prejudice because, on the evidence, there was no foreseeable scenario in which re-tendering would occur.[323] In *King's College London v Information Commissioner* the college failed to persuade the Tribunal that the disclosure of the salaries of eight senior professional service (ie non-academic) staff would be likely to prejudice its commercial interests.[324] Arguments have been advanced by public authorities that disclosure under FOIA of information about an existing contract will damage their reputation and discourage prospective tenderers from bidding in the future. Such arguments may or may not succeed, depending on the facts.[325]

34–059 The public interest

If the information in question comes within the section, the duty to disclose the information does not apply if the public interest in maintaining the exemption outweighs the public interest in disclosing the information.[326] The weighing exercise necessitates an identification of the public interest in the maintenance of the exemption, always recognising that that public interest must be delineated in such a fashion that it is capable in practice of being outweighed.[327] Given the quintessentially private nature of the interest being protected by the exemption (the commercial interests of a person), it is difficult to see immediately what particular public interest there is in maintaining the exemption without importing interests that already stand to be protected by other provisions in Part II of the Act. It is suggested that it would be impermissible

---

318 *Student Loans Company Ltd v IC*, IT, 17 July 2009 at [42], endorsed in *University of Central Lancashire v IC and Colquhoun*, IT, 8 December 2009 at [31].

319 *Department of Work and Pensions v IC*, FTT, 20 September 2010 at [81]. The public interest in disclosure of this information outweighed that in maintaining the exemption, however, especially since Atos had been the only bidder for the contract. See at [104]-[108].

320 *Abbott v IC and DBIS*, FTT, 22 September 2016 at [52]-[55], though it would prejudice the contractor commercially.

321 *Cranfield University v IC and Peck*, FTT, 5 March 2012 at [1].

322 *Cranfield University v IC and Peck*, FTT, 5 March 2012 at [25].

323 *Cranfield University v IC and Peck*, FTT, 5 March 2012 at [29]-[44].

324 *King's College London* v IC, FTT, 30 September 2014.

325 Contrast *Patterson v IC and Dept of Education*, FTT, 12 July 2017 at [61] with *Conscape v IC*, FTT, 26 April 2017 at [10] and *Ministry of Justice v IC and Le Vay*, FTT, 12 June 2017 at [59]-[62].

326 FOIA s 2(2)(b); FOI(S)A s 2.

327 To avoid metamorphosing it into an absolute exemption.

to use the public interest weighing exercise for the purposes of s 43(2) effectively to reshape and enlarge the discrete exemptions provided elsewhere in the Act: most notably, the exemptions for confidential information and trade secrets. The public interest balancing exercise may be time-sensitive.[328] In *Department for Business Innovation and Skills v Information Commissioner and Browning*[329] the Tribunal identified the 'detriment' that would result to companies through the actions of third parties if their confidential status as applicants for export licenses to Iran were publicly disclosed as also being 'prejudice to their commercial interests' for the purposes of FOIA s 43(2). The high likelihood of such harm to the companies outweighed the public interest in disclosure of their names.[330] In *Department of Work and Pensions v Information Commissioner and Zola* the Tribunal was less impressed with an argument that workfare contractors and hosts, identified by the disclosures sought, would be targeted by opponents of the schemes and thereby suffer prejudice. Not only was the prejudice argument not made out[331] the high cost and controversial nature of the government schemes, in particular, gave rise to an overriding public interest in the participants being identified.[332] The Tribunal's decision has since been upheld by the Upper Tribunal and the Court of Appeal.[333]

34– 060 Duty to confirm or deny

Where compliance with the duty to confirm or deny would, or would be likely to, prejudice the commercial interests of any person (including the public authority holding the information), then the discrete duty to confirm or deny that that information is held by the public authority does not arise.[334] This is a qualified exclusion of duty.[335] It will therefore be necessary to consider whether, in all the circumstances, the maintenance of the exclusion of this duty is outweighed by the public interest in disclosing whether the public authority holds the information. As noted previously, despite its superficial similarity, this public interest balancing exercise is materially different from that employed for the purpose of determining whether the duty to communicate does not apply.[336] Short of a purely confirmatory request that, in its terms, sets out the information or the gist of the information sought, it is difficult to imagine any particular public interest in maintaining an exemption from the duty to confirm or deny that information is held. On the other hand, other than the public interest articulated through FOIA itself, it is also difficult to identify any particular public interest in confirming or denying the holding.

---

328 As in *Derry City Council v IC*, IT, 11 December 2006 where the Information Tribunal held that although the requested information was covered by s 43 'the risk of prejudice to the Council's commercial interests by the time the Complainant made his request was not sufficient to outweigh the public interest in having the Ryanair Financial Information disclosed' (at [28(b)]). The disclosure of pricing information in bids in a tendering exercise may be appropriate after some time has passed: *Palmer v IC and Royal Marsden Foundation Trust*, FTT, 6 February 2014 at [26]-[28]. Likewise, figures for an oil company's historic sponsorship of a public gallery: *Montague v IC and Tate Gallery*, FTT, 22 December 2014 at [36].

329 *Department for Business, Innovation and Skills v IC and Browning*, FTT, 22 September 2011; on appeal *Browning v Information Commissioner and DBIS* [2013] UKUT 236 (AAC) (20 May 2013) and see §34– 027.

330 *Department for Business, Innovation and Skills v IC and Browning*, FTT, 22 September 2011; on appeal *Browning v Information Commissioner and DBIS* [2013] UKUT 236 (AAC) (20 May 2013) at [69].

331 *DWP v IC and Zola*, FTT, 17 May 2013 at [188]-[206].

332 *DWP v IC and Zola*, FTT, 17 May 2013 at [208]-[222].

333 *Dept for Work and Pensions v IC and Zola* [2014] UKUT 0334 (AAC) and *Dept for Work and Pensions v IC and Zola* [2016] EWCA Civ 758, [2017] 1 WLR 1.

334 FOIA s 43(3). In relation to Scottish public authorities, there is no separate duty to confirm or deny under the FOI(S)A.

335 FOIA s 2(1).

336 See §§6– 018 to 6– 019 as to what it involves.

6. INTERNATIONAL CONFIDENCES

34– 061 Introduction

Section 27(2) of FOIA exempts information if it is confidential information obtained from a state other than the United Kingdom or from an international organisation or international court.[337] Where the information is 'environmental information', exemption from disclosure falls to be determined under the EIR and not FOIA.[338] Those regulations do not provide a separate exception in relation to confidential information obtained from another State or from an international organisation or international court. The exception provided in those regulations for certain confidential information (considered separately below)[339] may except the information from disclosure. The exemption in FOIA is a qualified exemption. What is confidential for the purposes of s 27(2) is statutorily defined by the Act as any information obtained from a State, organisation or court where (a) the terms on which it was obtained require it to be held in confidence or (b) the circumstances in which it was obtained make it reasonable for the State, organisation or court to expect that it will be held in confidence.[340] 'State', 'international organisation' and 'international court' are each statutorily defined by the Act.[341] The definitions are cast in wide terms.[342]

34– 062 Scope

This is a class exemption, so that it applies to any information that falls within this definition without regard to the consequences of disclosure. It is therefore potentially of wide scope. The exemption is capable of exempting information the disclosure of which would not 'constitute a breach of confidence actionable' by the supplier of the information or another person.[343] Its

337 In relation to information held by a Scottish public authority, exemption is provided by FOI(S)A s 32(1)(b). In the United States, exemption for information communicated by foreign governments in confidence is generally secured through Executive Order 13,526 and exemption 1: see §51– 008(1) and *Krikorian v Department of State* 984 F 2d 461 (DC Cir 1993). There must be a contemporaneous expectation of confidentiality: *Weatherhead v United States*, 157 F(3d) 735 (9th Cir 1998), concerning information from the British Government. The Freedom of Information Act 1982 (Cth of Australia) s 33(1) exempts a document the disclosure of which would divulge any information communicated in confidence by or on behalf of a foreign government, an authority of a foreign government or an international organisation to the Australian Government: see §51– 015(9). The Official Information Act 1982 (New Zealand), ss 6(b) and 27(1)(a), provides an absolute exemption where the disclosure of the information would be likely to prejudice the entrusting of information to the government of New Zealand on a basis of confidence by the government of any other country or any agency of such a government, or by any international organisation: see §51– 022(2). The Access to Information Act (Canada) s 13(1), provides a mandatory exemption for records containing information received in confidence from other governments: see §51– 031(1). The Freedom of Information Act 2014 (Ireland) s 33 provides a potentially wide exemption for information the disclosure of which would adversely affect international relations: see §51– 039(4).

338 The disclosure regime under the EIR is considered in Chs 17-19. In relation to Scottish public authorities, disclosure of environmental information falls to be determined under the EI(S)R.

339 EIR reg 12(5)(e); EI(S)R reg 10(5)(e). See §34– 066.

340 FOIA s 27(2); FOI(S)A s 32(2).

341 See FOIA s 27(5); FOI(S)A s 32(3).

342 See §§27– 002 to 27– 007 for a consideration of the exemption under FOIA s 27(1). The exemption may, in some circumstances, be able to be relied upon to exempt foreign confidential information on the basis that to disclose such information would be prejudicial to international relations.

343 Being the words used in FOIA s 41(1)(b) and FOI(S)A s 36(2)(b): *Campaign against the Arms Trade v IC and MoJ*, IT, 26 August 2008, at [57]. In Australia, where the Freedom of Information Act 1982 s 33(1)(b) provides an exemption where disclosure 'would divulge any information or matter communicated in confidence by or on behalf of a foreign government, an authority of a foreign government or an international organization to the Government of the Commonwealth, to an authority of the Commonwealth ...' It has been held that that exemption is not confined to communications which if disclosed would give rise to an action in breach of confidence. It extends to

practical operation is materially reduced by two considerations. First, although the focus of the definition is on the terms on which or the circumstances in which the information was obtained, and whether those terms or circumstances require it to be held or give rise to a reasonable expectation that it will be held in confidence, the definition also contains a temporal limitation. Information is only confidential within the meaning of the statutory definition for so long as that requirement or that expectation continues in effect.[344] For example, the terms on which the information was obtained may have the effect that if and in so far as it enters the public domain it is no longer required to be held in confidence by the public authority.[345] Similarly, the circumstances in which the information was obtained may mean that if and in so far as it enters the public domain there ceases to be a reasonable expectation that it will be held in confidence. Second, the section only applies to information that has itself been obtained from a foreign state or international organisation. Where the information sought originates from a public authority in the United Kingdom, but has been prepared using information from a foreign state or an international organisation, unless and to the extent that the former will reveal the latter, the domestic information will not be exempt information under this provision.[346] The Tribunal has nevertheless held that a memorandum of understanding could fall within the provision where a foreign State had provided the information for the purposes of that memorandum.[347] In *Campaign against the Arms Trade v IC and MoJ*,[348] the Tribunal upheld a claim for exemption under s 27(3) in relation to various memoranda of understanding between the Governments of the United Kingdom and of Saudi Arabia relating to the supply of defence equipment. The Tribunal, relying on s 27(3) and having regard to the subject-matter of the information and the consistent basis upon which the Saudi Arabian Government had supplied the source information to the United Kingdom Government, held that it was reasonable for the former to expect that the information would be held in confidence:

> the correct approach to that question is to consider what it would have been reasonable for the [Kingdom of Saudi Arabia] to have expected in all the circumstances. That does not justify imposing on the KSA our particular customs and principles as to transparency or democratic accountability. It should be judged against what would have been reasonable for the KSA to have expected....The concept of freedom of information and transparency is generally alien to their culture...To this extent the senior rulers and in particular the King could not be expected easily to accept or respond to the principles of disclosure and transparency to which we have referred in the context of the FOIA. We are satisfied on the evidence that these MoU were entered into on a basis on which the KSA would have

---

information which was communicated and received under an express or inferred understanding that it would be kept confidential: *Re Maher and Attorney-General's Department* (1985) 7 ALD 731 (it was enough that the information was supplied pursuant to a general understanding that communications of a particular nature would be treated in confidence); *Re Throssell and Australian Archives (No 2)* (1987) 14 ALD 296. Nor is it necessary that the agency make inquiries as to the motives of the person who supplied the information or whether it is based on false information: *Gersten v Minister for Immigration & Multicultural Affairs* [2000] FCA 1221. Nor, apparently, does it make any difference that the information is in the public domain: *Commonwealth of Australia v Hittich* (1994) 53 FCR 152, 35 ALD 717. The view taken in the comparative jurisdictions is that the evidence of the views of foreign governments should be afforded considerable weight, but is not determinative: *Re Slater and Cox*, (1988) 15 ALD 20; *O'Donovan and Attorney-General's Dept* (1985) 8 ALD 528 at 534; *Do-Ky v Minister for Foreign Affairs* [1997] 2 FC 907.

344 FOIA s 27(3); FOI(S)A s 32(2).

345 In the United States, a distinction is drawn between information that has unofficially 'leaked' into the public domain and that which has officially come into the public domain. Thus, in *Afshar v Department of State* 702 F 2d 1125 (DC Cir 1983) it was observed that a foreign government can ignore 'unofficial leaks and public surmise ... but official acknowledgment may force a government to retaliate.'

346 This is the approach which was taken by the Federal Court of Appeal in Canada in *Sherman v Canada (Minister of National Revenue)* [2003] FCA 202, where the applicant sought records containing statistics generated by the Canadian Revenue but derived from information obtained in confidence from the United States pursuant to a bilateral convention with respect to taxes on income and capital.

347 *Campaign against the Arms Trade v IC and MoJ*, IT, 26 August 2008 at [64].

348 *Campaign against the Arms Trade v IC and MoJ* IT, 26 August 2008.

> expected that each government would respect the confidentiality of those agreements at least in the absence of the other consenting to disclosure. The MoU were marked secret and regarded as confidential.[349]

A similar conclusion was reached in *Gilby v Information Commissioner and Foreign & Commonwealth Office.*[350] In *All Parliamentary Group on Rendition v Information Commissioner and Ministry of Defence,*[351] however, the Upper Tribunal doubted that a memorandum of understanding or similar agreement designed to ensure compliance with human rights in respect of those whose detention is transferred to another state could be perceived as confidential.[352] Moreover, one such memorandum of which disclosure was sought was with the United States. In contrast to the Kingdom of Saudi Arabia whose information was in issue in *Campaign Against the Arms Trade v Information Commissioner and Ministry of Justice* where:

> the Tribunal noted at [76] that the concept of freedom of information and transparency is alien to the culture, the USA is a constitutional democracy with its own very well established traditions of free speech and freedom of information[353]

The Upper Tribunal considered that cogent evidence would be required to show that s 27 was engaged in these circumstances.[354]

34– 063 The public interest

As noted above, the exemption is a qualified exemption. In other words, in each instance the exemption is subject to whether the public interest in maintaining it outweighs the public interest in disclosure.[355] Where no specific harm would result from the disclosure of the information, the public interest requirement may have the effect that the exemption does not apply. As against that, however, it may be argued that harm generally results from the disclosure of information in circumstances where that contradicts either the terms on which it was obtained or the reasonable expectation of the entity from which it was obtained, and that there is a public interest in upholding compliance with such terms or expectations and avoiding the harm in the shape of lack of trust (and, in all probability, a reduced flow of information) that results from not upholding compliance with the same:

> Parliament recognised and we accept that there is an inherent disservice to the public interest in flouting international confidence.[356]

Against that and underpinned by the rules of comity and international law, lies the principle that foreign states and organisations dealing with the public authorities in the United Kingdom must take the country as it is, including its laws relating to the disclosure of information. By conveying or transmitting information to a public authority in this country, the foreign entity must accept that that will be attended by certain loss of control over the further dissemination of the information.[357] Accordingly, a consideration of the public interest in maintaining the exemption will need to take into account:

---

349 *Campaign against the Arms Trade v IC and MoJ*, IT, 26 August 2008 at [75]-[77].

350 *Gilby v IC and FCO* IT, 22 October 2008, at [46], most of the reasons for which are apparently recorded in the closed part of its decision.

351 *All Party Parliamentary Group on Extraordinary Rendition v IC and Ministry of Defence* [2011] UKUT 153 (AAC).

352 *All Party Parliamentary Group on Extraordinary Rendition v IC and Ministry of Defence* [2011] UKUT 153 (AAC) at [59].

353 *All Party Parliamentary Group on Extraordinary Rendition v IC and Ministry of Defence* [2011] UKUT 153 (AAC) at [65].

354 *All Party Parliamentary Group on Extraordinary Rendition v IC and Ministry of Defence* [2011] UKUT 153 (AAC) at [66].

355 FOIA s 2(2)(b); FOI(S)A s 2(1)(b).

356 *Campaign against the Arms Trade v IC and MoJ*, IT, 26 August 2008 at [95].

357 Just as the foreign entity would have to accept that if the information it conveyed to the public authority was personal information relating to the applicant, then that information would, notwithstanding that it had been conveyed to the public authority in confidence, have to be conveyed to the applicant if an application were made under s 7 of the DPA 1998, subject to any applicable exemptions under that Act.

— whether the particular information or information of that class has been identified by the source as being confidential;[358]
— whether, quite apart from any formal identification, the information is of a sort conventionally considered to be confidential;
— whether, if the source of the information has designated it as confidential, that was done as a matter of course or perfunctorily;
— whether the other State understood that information of the class sought to be disclosed would be kept confidential;[359]
— whether the disclosure would have an adverse impact upon the relationship between the Governments of the United Kingdom and of another State;[360]
— whether the disclosure would have an adverse impact upon the protection and promotion of UK interests abroad;[361] and
— where the information emanates from the European Union, Art 255 of the Amsterdam Treaty;

On the other side of the balance, it is in the public interest to disclose information that might reveal corruption and that would enhance transparency in government transactions, especially where the subject matter is one of legitimate public concern (such as arms contracts).[362]

34–064 Duty to confirm or deny

The duty to confirm or deny does not arise if, or to the extent that, the confirmation or denial that would have to be given to comply with the duty would, or would be likely to, involve the disclosure of any confidential information (whether or not already recorded) which is obtained from a State other than the United Kingdom or from an international organisation or international court.[363] This disapplication of the duty to confirm or deny is only operative if, in all the circumstances of the case, the public interest in maintaining the exclusion of the duty outweighs the public interest in disclosing whether the public authority holds the information.[364]

7. ENVIRONMENTAL INFORMATION AND CONFIDENTIALITY

34–065 Introduction

Information to which a person has a right of access under the EIR is exempt information under s 39(1)(a) of FOIA.[365] In this way, whether or to the extent that a request for information captures 'environmental information', disclosure must be determined in accordance with the

358 In *Campaign against the Arms Trade v IC and MoJ*, IT, 26 August 2008 at [96], this was considered to be of paramount importance.

359 *Gilby v IC and FCO*, IT, 22 October 2008 at [54].

360 *Campaign against the Arms Trade v IC and MoJ*, IT, 26 August 2008 at [96]; *Gilby v IC and FCO*, IT, 22 October 2008 at [51].

361 *Campaign against the Arms Trade v IC and MoJ*, IT, 26 August 2008 at [96]; *Gilby v IC and FCO*, IT, 22 October 2008 at [51]. See also *Plowden and FCO v IC*, FTT, 21 May 2012 at [93]-[96] in relation to a record of the US President's comments during a phone conversation with the Prime Minister just before the Iraq war. This was reversed on appeal: *FCO v IC and Plowden* [2013] UKUT 275 (AAC) (15 June 2013).

362 *Campaign against the Arms Trade v IC and MoJ*, IT, 26 August 2008 at [97]-[98]; *Gilby v IC and FCO*, IT, 22 October 2008 at [51], [55]-[57].

363 FOIA s 27(4)(b). In relation to Scottish public authorities, there is no free-standing duty to confirm or deny.

364 FOIA s 2(1)(b).

365 Similarly, in relation to Scottish public authorities, FOI(S)A s 39.

EIR and not FOIA.[366] The disclosure regime under the EIR is considered in detail in Chapter 6. In summary, to the extent that a request for information captures information 'obtained from any other person' which is properly regarded as a request for 'environmental information', issues of confidentiality will be governed by the EIR.[367] The Regulations provide two exceptions from disclosure on confidentiality-related grounds. While the principles relating to confidentiality under FOIA[368] are also basic to the confidentiality-related exceptions in the EIR, the exceptions are materially narrower than their counterparts in the Act. It follows that where a request for information raises issues of confidentiality, it will be important to determine which (if any) of the information captured by the request is 'environmental information'.[369] Further, both exceptions are qualified by a public interest balancing test.[370]

34–066 Third-party information

Subject to the public interest test,[371] a public authority may refuse to disclose environmental information to the extent that its disclosure would adversely affect:

the interests of the person who provided the information where that person:

(i) was not under, and could not have been put under, any legal obligation to supply it to that or any other public authority,

(ii) did not supply it in circumstances such that that or any other public authority is entitled apart from these Regulations to disclose it, and

(iii) has not consented to its disclosure.[372]

The exception attempts to provide some protection for information held by a public authority that has been supplied to it by a third party. The list of conditions required for the exception to engage gives it a limited operation. First, the disclosure must adversely affect the interests of the person who provided the information. A mere likelihood of harm is not sufficient.[373] The regulations do not identify what sort of interests must be adversely affected, but it is suggested that any financial interest will qualify. Secondly, it must be information that was neither supplied under compulsion nor could have been obtained as a result of enforcement of any legal obligation. This is particularly limiting.[374] Thirdly, there are few circumstances in which information, other than personal information, held by a public authority may not lawfully be disclosed by it or any other public authority.[375] Unless another exception applies, even where the terms of this exception are met the public authority may only not disclose that part of the

---

[366] And, in relation to Scottish public authorities, the request must be determined in accordance with the EI(S)R and not the FOI(S)A.

[367] In the case of a request made to a Scottish public authority, issues of confidentiality will be governed by the EI(S)R.

[368] See §§34–010 to 34–029.

[369] See §17–011.

[370] EIR reg 12(1); EI(S)R reg 10(1). The provision is derived from Directive 2003/4/EC Art 4.2 (penultimate paragraph). See further §19–006.

[371] See §19–006.

[372] EIR reg 12(5)(f); EI(S)R reg 10(5)(f). Derived from Art 4.2(g) of the Directive and Art 4.4(g) of the Aarhus Convention. Regulation 4(3)(c) of the 1992 Regulations provided for a similar exception but without the public interest balancing test. In *R v Secretary of State for the Environment, Transport and the Regions, ex p Alliance against Birmingham Northern Relief Road (No 1)* [1999] Env LR 447, [1999] JPL 231, Sullivan J held that parts of the concession agreement fell within reg 4(3)(c). The exception does not apply to information on (or, possibly, relating to) emissions: EIR reg 12(9); EI(S)R reg 10(6).

[373] In *McIntyre v IC and University of East Anglia*, FTT, 7 May 2013 at [58] the FTT dismissed as 'speculation' a university's assertion that disclosure of a draft academic paper on climate change would adversely affect the interests of the authors.

[374] See the discussion in §19–026. See *Staffordshire County Council v IC and Sibelco (UK) Ltd*, FTT, 20 December 2010 for an example of a case where information was supplied voluntarily and the exemption applied.

[375] Again, see the discussion in §§19–026 and 20–034 to 20–035.

information in respect of which it is satisfied that in all the circumstances the public interest in maintaining this exception outweighs the public interest in the information's disclosure.[376] This exception does not apply to information on emissions.[377] What would seem to be left so as to engage the exception is information volunteered by a third person to a public authority, disclosure of which would constitute a breach of confidence[378] enforceable by the third party, provided always that the public interest in maintaining the particular exception outweighs the public interest in disclosure.

34– 067 Commercial etc information

Subject to the public interest test,[379] a public authority may also refuse to disclose environmental information to the extent that its disclosure would adversely affect 'the confidentiality of commercial or industrial information where such confidentiality is provided by law to protect a legitimate economic interest'.[380] The exception imposes two requirements. First, the information must enjoy the quality of confidentiality. This substantially imports the requirements of s 41(1) of FOIA.[381] Secondly, the information must be 'commercial or industrial information'. This takes out of the scope of the exception the private information limb of confidentiality.[382] The exception straddles three separate exemptions in FOIA.[383] While all trade secrets will be covered, non-confidential commercial information will not be covered. Nor will non-commercial or non-industrial confidential information be covered. The Directive provision from which it derived confirms its more limited scope, providing for refusal of a request for environmental information where disclosure would adversely affect 'the confidentiality of commercial or industrial information where such confidentiality is provided for by national or Community law to protect a legitimate economic interest, including the public interest in maintaining statistical confidentiality and tax secrecy'.[384] Unless another exception applies, even where the terms of this exception are met the public authority may only

376 EIR reg 12(1)(b); EI(S)R reg 10(1)(b). See §§19– 006 and 20– 036.

377 EIR reg 12(9); EI(S)R reg 10(6). Derived from Directive 2003/4/EC Art 4.2 (penultimate paragraph) and, more loosely, from the Aarhus Convention Art 4.4(d) (last sentence) and the last sentence of Art 4.4 itself.

378 As to which, see §§34– 010 to 34– 048.

379 See §19– 006.

380 EIR reg 12(5)(e); EI(S)R reg 10(5)(e). Derived from Art 4.2(d) of the Directive and Art 4.4(d) of the Aarhus Convention. The exception does not apply to information on (or, possibly, relating to) emissions: EIR reg 12(9); EI(S)R reg 10(6). Regulation 4(2)(e) of the 1992 Regulations provided for a similar exception but without the public interest balancing test. In *R v Secretary of State for the Environment, Transport and the Regions, ex p Alliance against Birmingham Northern Relief Road (No 1)* [1999] Env LR 447, [1999] JPL 231, the applicant sought access under the 1992 Regulations to a concession agreement, made under s 1 of the New Roads and Street Works Act 1991 between Midland Express Motorway Ltd and the Secretary of State, by which Midland Express was to design, build, finance and operate a motorway. After the agreement had been made, the required public inquiry concluded with the Secretary of State deciding to make the necessary orders. The applicant was concerned that the Secretary of State, in deciding to make the orders, might have been influenced by the prospect of having to pay compensation to Motorway Express if he decided otherwise. The Secretary of State refused to disclose the agreement, citing commercial confidentiality and reg 4(1)(a) and 4(2)(e) and the applicant challenged that refusal by way of judicial review. Sullivan J held that the issues of whether information was 'environmental information' and whether it was 'confidential' were objective issues to be determined in an objective manner (JPL at 247). He found that the concession agreement was not intrinsically confidential (JPL at 253) and rejected a submission that because it was a commercial document having financial implications all of it was confidential (JPL at 254). He accepted that information in the agreement relating to prices, costs, payment, compensation events and trade secrets should attract confidentiality (JPL at 255).

381 As to which, see §§34– 010 to 34– 015. See also *Office of Communication v Information Commissioner* [2010] UKSC 3 at [24] and *Jones v IC and Environment Agency*, FTT, 27 April 2012 at [38].

382 As set out in §§34– 030 to 34– 048.

383 Sections 41(1), 43(1) and 43(2); FOI(S)A ss 36 and 33(1).

384 Directive Art 4.2(d).

not disclose that part of the information in respect of which it is satisfied that in all the circumstances the public interest in maintaining this exception outweighs the public interest in the information's disclosure.[385] This exception does not apply to information on emissions.[386]

385 EIR reg 12(1)(b); EI(S)R reg 10(1)(b). See §19– 006.

386 EIR reg 12(9); EI(S)R reg 10(6). Derived from Directive 2003/4/EC Art 4.2 (penultimate paragraph) and, more loosely, from the Aarhus Convention Art 4.4(d)(last sentence) and the last sentence of Art 4.4 itself.

CHAPTER 35
Miscellaneous exemptions

1. COMMUNICATIONS WITH HER MAJESTY, ETC

35–001 Introduction

As originally enacted, s 37(1)(a) of FOIA provided that information relating to communications with Her Majesty,[1] other members of the Royal Family or the Royal Household was exempt information.[2] Similarly, the duty to confirm or deny did not arise in relation to such information.[3] Both the exemption and the exclusion were qualified.[4] Accordingly, even if information was exempt information under this provision, the public authority holding that information was obliged to disclose it unless the public interest in maintaining the exemption outweighed the public interest in disclosing the information.[5] The exemption in s 37(1) of

[1] The reference to Her Majesty fell to be construed as a reference to the Sovereign for the time being: Interpretation Act 1978 s 10.

[2] Similarly, FOI(S)A s 41. See §35–013.

[3] FOIA s 37(2) (as originally enacted). There is no discrete duty to confirm or deny under FOI(S)A.

[4] FOIA s 2(3) (as originally enacted); FOI(S)A s 2(2).

[5] Similarly, the duty to confirm or deny. FOIA s 37(1) and (2) engage s 2(2)(b) and (1)(b) respectively so as to prevent

FOIA for information relating to communications of this kind was strengthened with effect from 19 January 2011 by way of amendments effected by the Constitutional Reform and Governance Act 2010.[6] Section 37(1)(a)-(ab) now confer an absolute exemption[7] on information if it relates to communications with the Sovereign,[8] the heir or second in line to the Throne[9] or any person who has subsequently acceded to or become the heir or second in line to the Throne.[10] Section 37(1)(ac)-(ad) retain the original qualified exemption for information if it relates to communications with other members of the Royal Family[11] or with the Royal Household.[12] No equivalent amendments were made to s 41(a) of FOI(S)A, which remains in its original form. There is no equivalent exception in the EIR.[13] Accordingly, where (or to the extent that) information that answers the terms of a request for information is 'environmental

---

from arising, first, the duty to confirm or deny and, secondly, the duty to communicate, if the public interest in divulgence or disclosure (respectively) is outweighed.

6 The relevant amendments to FOIA ss 2(3), 37(1)(a) and 62-63 were made by the Constitutional Reform and Governance Act 2010 s 46, Sch 7, paras 1-5. Sch 7, para 6 also inserted a new FOIA s 80A which (insofar as it was brought into force) temporarily prevented the amendments to FOIA ss 2(3), 37(1)(a), 62-63 from having effect in relation to information held by Northern Ireland public authorities. However, the Constitutional Reform and Governance Act 2010 s 46, Sch 7, para 6 and FOIA s 80A were repealed with effect from 1 July 2012 by the Protection of Freedoms Act 2012 ss 104, 115(2), Sch 10, Pt 7, and the Northern Ireland position is no longer any different. The amendments to FOIA ss 2(3) and 37(1)(a) (which are of critical importance for the purposes of this chapter) were brought into force on 19 January 2011 by the Constitutional Reform and Governance Act 2010 (Commencement No. 4 and Saving Provision) Order 2011 SI 2011/46, Art 3, subject to a saving in Art 4 which provides:

> The 2000 Act continues to apply as it applied immediately before 19th January 2011 in respect of any request for information received by a public authority before that date.

The effect of the amendments to FOIA, ss 62-63 on historical records are discussed elsewhere in this work: see Ch 7. For the policy background to these reforms, which were enacted before and then brought into force after the 2010 general election see: P Dacre, *Review of the 30-Year Rule* (2009), para 8.8 ('the Dacre Review'); statement by the Prime Minister, Hansard HC vol 493 col 797 (10 June 2009); HM Government, *Government Response to the 30-Year Rule Review* (Cm 7822, 2010), paras 50-53; statement by the Secretary of State for Justice, Hansard HC vol 506, cols 834-835 (18 January 2011); statement by the Secretary of State for Justice, Hansard HC vol 521, col 35 WS (18 January 2011).

7 FOIA s 2(3)(ea).

8 FOIA s 37(1)(a). The reference to the Sovereign is to be construed as a reference to the Sovereign for the time being: Interpretation Act 1978 s 10. In the context of considering the Scotland Act 1998 (which has been said is to be interpreted on ordinary principles, the Supreme Court has held that the phrase 'relates to' indicates more than a loose or consequential connection or a touching upon the matter: *Martin v Most* [2010] UKSC 10, 2010 SC (UKSC) 40 at [49], [159]. And similarly: *Imperial Tobacco Ltd v Lord Advocate* [2012] UKSC 61, 2013 SLT 2 at [16]; *Re Agricultural Sector (Wales) Bill* [2014] UKSC 43, [2014] 1 WLR 2622 at [50]; *Recovery of Medical Costs for Asbestos Diseases (Wales) Bill* [2015] UKSC 3, [2015] AC 1016 at [25]; *Christian Institute v Lord Advocate* [2016] UKSC 51, [2016] HRLR 19 at [29] (concerning the Data Protection Act 1998). In the context of FOIA the meaning of the phrase 'relates to' has been considered in: *Home Office v IC and Cobain*, FTT, 30 January 2013 at [15]-[19]; *Callus v IC and Home Office*, FTT, 6 May 2014 at [39]-[41]; *University and Colleges Admissions Service v IC and Lord Lucas* [2014] UKUT 0557 (AAC) at [44]-[46] (meaning of 'relates to' in FOIA s 7(5)); *Home Office v IC and Cobain* [2014] UKUT 0306 (AAC) at [39]; *All Party Parliamentary Group on Extraordinary Rendition v IC and FCO* [2015] UKUT 0377 (AAC) at [14]-[33]; *Reprieve v IC and FCO*, FTT, 26 April 2016 at [37]-[39]; *Corderoy and Ahmed v IC and Attorney General* [2017] UKUT 0495 (AAC) at [51] [54] and [59]-[62]; *Department of Health v IC and Lewis* [2017] EWCA Civ 374, [2017] 1 WLR 3330 at [13] (Sir Terence Etherton MR) (meaning of 'relates to' in FOIA s 35(1)).

9 FOIA s 37(1)(aa).

10 FOIA s 37(1)(ab).

11 FOIA s 37(1)(ac). This provision excludes 'communications which fall within any of paragraphs (a) to (ab) [of s 37(1)] because they are made or received on behalf of a person falling within any of those paragraphs.'

12 FOIA s 37(1)(ad). This provision excludes 'communications which fall within any of paragraphs (a) to (ac) [of s 37(1)] because they are made or received on behalf of a person falling within any of those paragraphs.'

13 In *Evans v IC and DBIS* [2012] UKUT 313 (AAC) the Upper Tribunal noted at [50]:

> An interesting question may arise for the future as to whether, when the Regulations are applied to a particular case, the change in legislative policy under the Act may be relevant - for example as regards the public interest balance. It is unnecessary for us to express any view on that question and we do not do so.

information',[14] the fact that that information also relates to communications with Her Majesty, other members of the Royal Family or the Royal Household will not excuse the public authority from complying with the request.[15]

35–002 Background

The *Code of Practice on Access to Government Information* contained a similar, but narrower, exemption for 'information relating to confidential communications between Ministers and Her Majesty the Queen or other Members of the Royal Household, or relating to confidential proceedings of the Privy Council'.[16] The accompanying *Guidance on Interpretation* stated that that exemption was designed to protect confidences.[17] More long-standing restrictions have prevented parliamentary questions being asked of ministers regarding certain matters connected with the monarch, the Royal Family and the Royal Household.[18] As a matter of constitutional convention, the Sovereign must act on the advice of his or her ministers (usually provided by the Prime Minister on behalf of the government) ('the cardinal convention') and, in turn, he or she has a right and duty to be consulted by, to encourage and to warn those ministers ('the tripartite convention').[19] Confidentiality is generally seen as essential to the effective operation of these conventions in order to preserve the Sovereign's political neutrality and impartiality and to ensure that those involved are able to speak with frankness and candour and without fear of subsequent publicity.[20] Indeed, the amendments to ss 2(3) and 37(1) of FOIA may be said to recognise and reinforce the importance of confidentiality, at least in relation to the core constitutional functions mentioned above and the immediate relationship between Sovereign and government.[21] The relevant exemptions in the draft Freedom of Information Bill published on 24 May 1999[22] and the Freedom of Information Bill introduced in the House of Commons on 18 November 1999[23] were identically worded.

---

14 As to the meaning of which, see §17–011.

15 FOIA s 39; FOI(S)A s 39.

16 *Open Government Code of Practice on Access to Government Information*, 2nd edn (1997) Pt II, para 3. The exemption did not refer to harm or prejudice and it was not therefore subject to any balancing exercise weighing the public interest in disclosure against the public interest in non-disclosure. See also: the Scottish Executive's *Code of Practice on Access to Scottish Executive Information*, 2nd edn (2003) Pt II, para 3; and the National Assembly for Wales's *Code of Practice on Public Access to Information*, 3rd edn (2004) Annex B.

17 *Open Government Code of Practice on Access to Government Information: Guidance on Interpretation*, 2nd edn (1997) Pt II, paras 3.1 to 3.2.

18 M Jack (ed), *Erskine May's treatise on the law, privileges, proceedings and usage of Parliament*, 24th edn (London, LexisNexis, 2011) pp 360, 396. Although the *White Paper on Open Government* (Cm 2290, 1993) did not offer any additional commentary upon the exemption which eventually found expression in the *Open Government Code of Practice on Access to Government Information*, 2nd edn (1997) Pt II, para 3, it did propose a further exemption which was not taken further for 'information which could not be sought in a parliamentary question' (see Annex A, Pt II, para xv). Information Commissioner, *Freedom of Information Act Awareness Guidance No 26: Communications with Her Majesty and the Awarding of Honours*, (2006), Pt B(a) stated, 'It has been suggested by those with experience of royal matters that in practice very little additional information will become available under FOI – it will be a case of codifying and establishing more formal guidelines for the existing arrangements public authorities already have in place for dealing with information relating to royal communications' (omitted from the 2011 version, which was revised to reflect the amendments to FOIA s 37(1)).

19 *Evans v IC and DBIS* [2012] UKUT 313 (AAC) at [76]-[78]; *R (Evans) v Attorney-General* [2015] UKSC 21, [2015] AC 1787 at [35]-[36], [132]-[146], [164].

20 *Evans v IC and DBIS* [2012] UKUT 313 (AAC) at [87].

21 See the submissions made on behalf of the government in *Evans v IC and DBIS* [2012] UKUT 313 (AAC) at [59]-[62].

22 *Freedom of Information: Consultation on Draft Legislation* (Cm 4355, 1999) Pt II, cl 29(1).

23 Clause 35(1).

35– 003 The comparative jurisdictions

Section 9(2)(f)(i) of the Official Information Act 1982 (NZ) provides for the withholding of information where necessary to maintain the constitutional conventions that protect the confidentiality of communications by or with the Sovereign or her representative unless it is more desirable in the public interest that the information be made available.[24] Section 46(1)(d) of the Freedom of Information Act 1997 (Ireland) excluded and s 42(h) of the Freedom of Information Act 2014 (Ireland) excludes records relating to the President from the provisions of those Acts. None of the other comparative jurisdictions has any other exemptions in their access to information regimes equivalent to s 37(1) of FOIA.

35– 004 The Royal Family

Her Majesty and the other members of the Royal Family are not 'public authorities' for the purposes of FOIA[25] and are thus not subject to the regime established by the Act.[26] The expression 'the Royal Family' is not defined in FOIA and does not have any specific legal definition elsewhere. The monarch, his or her parents and grandparents, his or her spouse and their children, children-in-law and grandchildren are plainly members of the Royal Family.[27] How much further the Royal Family extends to others who are related to the monarch by blood or marriage falls to be answered by reference to convention, their styles, titles, forms of precedence and special privileges, their subjection to the monarch's general authority in relation to the supervision of minors and royal marriages, their inclusion in the Civil List and the applicability of special common law and statutory provisions.[28] While it will often be clear in

---

[24] See I Eagles, M Taggart & G Liddell, *Freedom of Information in New Zealand* (Auckland, Oxford University Press, 1992), pp 364-367.

[25] Her Majesty and the other members of the Royal Family are also not 'Scottish public authorities' for the purposes of FOI(S)A s 3, Sch 1 (see also the Scotland Act 1998 ss 29-30, Sch 5, Pt II, s.B13) or EIR reg 2(2) (*Cross v IC and Cabinet Office* [2016] UKUT 0153 (AAC) In *A-G for Prince of Wales v IC and Bruton* [2016] UKUT 0154 (AAC) it was held that the Duchy of Cornwall is not a 'public authority' for the purposes of EIR reg 2(2), but the Duke of Cornwall is in his capacity as the harbour and lighthouse authority for the harbour at St Mary's on the Isles of Scilly, but only in connection with environmental information by him in that capacity.

[26] Furthermore, FOIA does not expressly bind the Crown and therefore only binds the Crown to the extent required by necessary implication: *Province of Bombay v Municipal Corporation of Bombay* [1947] AC 58 (PC); *AG of Ceylon v A D Silva* [1953] AC 461 (PC); *Madras Electric Supply Corp Ltd v Boarland* [1955] AC 667; *Ministry of Agriculture v Jenkins* [1963] 2 QB 317 (CA); *Wood v Leeds Area Health Authority* [1974] ICR 535; *Lord Advocate v Strathclyde Regional Council* [1990] 2 AC 580; and *R (Black) v Secretary of State of Justice* [2017] UKSC 81, [2018] AC 215. This 'doctrine of Crown immunity' is expressly saved and recognised by the Crown Proceedings Act 1947 ss 31(1), 40(2)(f). Following *BBC v Johns (Inspector of Taxes)* [1965] Ch 32 (CA) at 81 (Diplock LJ) the Crown's 'immunity' from the FOIA regime will also be enjoyed by the Crown's servants and agents to the extent that they are not brought under that regime by express provision or necessary implication (see also D Bailey and L Norbury, *Bennion on Statutory Interpretation*, 7th edn (London, LexisNexis, 2017) sec 4.14, and W Wade and C Forsyth, *Administrative Law*, 11th edn (Oxford, Oxford University Press, 2014) pp 706-707). In practice, a great number of servants and agents of the Crown and other Crown bodies are brought under the FOIA regime by being expressly listed as 'public authorities' in FOIA Sch 1. The criminal offence provisions in FOIA s 77 and Sch 3, para 12 are also applied to persons in the public service of the Crown as they apply to any other person: FOIA s 81(3).

[27] MoJ, *Exemptions Guidance—Section 37*, undated, Annex A sets out a list of 'Members of the Royal Family since 1 January 1975 (as at November 2006)' which comprises 'Those entitled to use the title Majesty or Royal Highness and their spouses'. MoJ, *Exemptions Guidance—Section 37*, undated, Pt 1, para 1.2 states, 'The list will change over time, especially through marriage or birth. If an authority is in doubt as to whether someone should be included in the list (for example, not all those entitled to the title of Royal Highness may choose to use it) the Private Secretary to the Queen should be consulted.' Information Commissioner, *Freedom of Information Act Awareness Guidance No 26: Communications with Her Majesty and the Awarding of Honours*, (2006), Pt B stated, 'As a general rule the Royal Family will include all those individuals who hold or are entitled to hold the title of Majesty or Royal Highness and their spouses' (omitted from 2011 version, which was revised to reflect the amendments to FOIA s 37(1)).

[28] *Halsbury's Laws of England*, 5th edn, 2014, vol 29, title 'Crown and Crown Proceedings', paras 29-39. The Royal Family would certainly appear to extend beyond those entitled to the style of 'Royal Highness:' *Halsbury's Laws of England*, 5th edn, 2014, vol 29, title 'Crown and Crown Proceedings', para 37. Complications may arise in relation

practice whether a particular communication has passed from or to someone who is a member of the Royal Family for the purposes of s 37(1)(ac) of FOIA, formal membership for these purposes may depend upon questions of fact in the circumstances of each case. Once membership has been established, however, it is notable that s 37(1)(ac) of FOIA exempts all information regardless of whether the Family member in question was acting in a public or private capacity in relation to the relevant communication.[29]

35– 005 The Royal Household

The Royal Household is also not a 'public authority' for the purposes of FOIA[30] and is not subject to FOIA regime.[31] The expression 'the Royal Household' is not defined in FOIA and does not have any specific legal definition elsewhere.[32] The Royal Household assists the monarch in carrying out official duties and it includes the monarch's Household together with the Households of other members of the Royal Family who undertake public engagements. The Royal Household is under the overall authority of the Lord Chamberlain who is the senior member of the monarch's household and it is divided into five departments: the Private Secretary's Office; the Privy Purse and Treasurer's Office; the Master of the Household's Department; the Lord Chamberlain's Office; and the Royal Collection Trust.[33] While it will

to current members of the Royal Family who did not have their status as such when a particular communication took place and, conversely, in relation to former members of the Royal Family who have lost that status since a particular communication took place. It is notable that a less comprehensive protection from the regime is afforded to information that relates to communications with the Royal Family and Household than is afforded by s 23(1) to information supplied by or relating to the security bodies. Basic precepts of statutory interpretation suggest that some effect must be given to the use of different formulae. It is also significant that information contained in a 'historical record' (as to the meaning of which, see §36– 010) cannot be exempt information by virtue of s 37(1)(a)-(ad) after whichever is the later of the end of the period of five years beginning with the date of the death of the relevant Royal or the end of the period beginning with the date on which the relevant record was created (FOIA s 63(2E)-(2F)).

29 Each member of the Royal Family is, of course, a 'living individual' to whom personal data may relate for the purposes of GDPR art 4 and DPA s 3. Accordingly, the exemption in respect of personal information in FOIA s 40 may also be engaged in connection with their communications, particularly if conducted in a private capacity.

30 The Royal Household is also not a 'Scottish public authority' for the purposes of FOI(S)A s 3, Sch 1: see also the Scotland Act 1998, ss 29-30, Sch 5, Pt II, s.B13.

31 See also fn 25.

32 Note that the Sovereign Grant Act 2011 now makes extensive reference to 'the Royal Household.' MoJ, *Exemptions Guidance—Section 37*, undated, Pt 1, para 1.3 states that the Royal Household 'should generally be taken to include those individuals who are authorised to act on behalf of a member of the Royal Family (eg their employees, servants or agents) in fulfilling of [sic] public, official and constitutional roles'. The same passage continues: 'It will clearly include members of the Private Offices of members of the Royal Family. Contractors who supply goods and services to the Royal Household (such as holders of royal warrants) do not form part of the Royal Household. In cases of doubt, Departments should consult the private office of the member of the Royal Family to determine the precise role performed by the individual concerned when he or she was in communication with the Department.' Information Commissioner, *Freedom of Information Act Awareness Guidance No 26: Communications with Her Majesty and the Awarding of Honours*, (2011), Pt B states, 'The Royal Household comprises all the Households of members of the Royal Family. Each Household comprises the permanent members of the relevant private office and those who from time to time assist members of the Royal Family with their private and public duties. Contractors supplying goods and services to the Royal Household, including by royal warrant are not included in this definition.'

33 The respective heads of these five departments are: the Private Secretary (constitutional, official and political matters and media relations); the Keeper of the Privy Purse (financial, personnel, property and revenue matters and the management of the Civil List); the Master of the Household (domestic, hospitality and staff matters); the Comptroller (ceremonial and formal matters); and the Director of the Royal Collection (co-ordinating the work of the Surveyor of the Queen's Pictures, the Surveyor of the Queen's Works of Art and the Royal Librarian). The five heads of department meet under the chairmanship of the Lord Chamberlain as the Lord Chamberlain's Committee. The Private Secretary is also a Privy Counsellor: O Hood Phillips and P Jackson, *Constitutional and Administrative Law*, 8th edn (London, Sweet & Maxwell, 2001) para 14-011. The Royal Household also includes the Great Officers of State (eg the Earl Marshal and the Lord Great Chamberlain), other ancient officers together with numerous other domestic servants and staff who work for or on behalf of the Royal Family (eg ladies-in-waiting and footmen).

often be clear in practice whether a particular communication has passed from or to someone who is a member of the Royal Household for the purposes of s 37(1)(ad) of FOIA, the precise boundaries of that organisation may depend upon questions of fact in the circumstances of each case.[34] Furthermore, s 37(1)(ad) of FOIA only exempts information relating to communications 'with the Royal Household' (and not communications with its members) so that the exemption only applies to communications with Household members if and in so far as they were acting in their official capacity in relation to the relevant communication.[35] A possible complication could arise in this regard out of the fact that certain officers of the Household are *ex-officio* government whips who continue to be appointed on a political basis at the nomination of the Prime Minister.[36]

35– 006 Royal communications

The references in s 37(1)(a)-(ad) of FOIA to 'communications with' a member of the Royal Family or the Royal Household is broad enough to encompass all manner of written and oral transmissions and exchanges of information whether conducted directly or indirectly and whether passing from or to the Royal side.[37] The exemptions in s 37(1)(a)-(ad) of FOIA also apply irrespective of whether the public authority which holds the requested information, or indeed any public authority, is or was involved in or party to the communication in question. Information regarding the fact of such communications, details of the 'when, where, how, why, by whom, to whom' kind and the content of the information communicated can all 'relate to' those communications and so the exemption is of potentially broad application.[38] However,

---

[34] For example, Royal Collection Enterprises Limited is a trading subsidiary of the Royal Collection Trust which in turn funds the activities of the Royal Collection Department within the Royal Household. To this end, Royal Collection Enterprises Limited manages public access to certain castles and palaces, connected shops and certain image and intellectual property rights. The Keeper of the Privy Purse is Chairman of Royal Collection Enterprises Limited. The Director of the Royal Collection is responsible for its day-to-day operation but the company has its own Managing Director. It will be a question of fact in each case whether a particular communication with someone working for or on behalf of Royal Collection Enterprises Limited constitutes a communication with the Royal Household for the purposes of FOIA s 37(1)(ad). Although each Royal Household is formally dissolved upon the death of its monarch (signified by the symbolic breaking of the Lord Chamberlain's staff over the grave of the deceased monarch), information relating to prior communications with that Household may nevertheless benefit from the exemption in FOIA s 37(1)(ad). See also fn 25.

[35] Any information relating to a letter sent by Her Majesty is exempt under FOIA s 37(1)(a), but information relating to a private letter sent by someone who happens to be a member of Her Household is not exempt under FOIA s 37(1), unless sent on behalf of a member of the Royal Family or the Royal Household and in the course of their official duties.

[36] These are the Treasurer, Comptroller and Vice-Chamberlain of Her Majesty's Household in the House of Commons and the Captain of the Honourable Corps of the Gentlemen-at-Arms, the Captain of the Queen's Bodyguard of the Yeomen of the Guard and up to five Lords and/or Baronesses in Waiting in the House of Lords: *Halsbury's Laws of England*, 5th edn, 2014, vol 20, title 'Constitutional Law and Administrative Law', paras 151 (fn 16) and 283; O Hood Phillips and P Jackson, *Constitutional and Administrative Law*, 8th edn (London, Sweet & Maxwell, 2001) para 10-024. Strictly speaking, these whips are members of the Royal Household and it could be argued that information relating to communications with them is subject to FOIA s 37(1)(ad). However, they are paid their salaries out of money provided by Parliament as part of the expenses of the Treasury and the argument that communications with them should be regarded as 'communications with the Royal Household' for the purposes of FOIA s 37(1)(ad) is therefore weak: Ministerial and other Salaries Act 1975 s 3(1)(a) and (b), Sch 1 Pts IV and V para 2(f). MoJ, *Exemptions Guidance—Section 37*, undated, Pt 1 para 1.4 acknowledges that there is an issue here and states in relation to the relevant offices, 'Their activities as government whips are not covered by this exemption.'

[37] Such information could take the form of answers, assertions, claims, demands, ideas, messages, offers, opinions, propositions, questions, requests, responses or warnings and could be exchanged or transmitted by way of conversation, correspondence or discussion and on any basis ranging from one-off unilateral notification to fully inter-active dialogue. The choice of 'communications with' over 'communications between' leaves more room for the inclusion of one-sided or passive transmissions and exchanges. In this regard, the use of 'communications' in the plural should not be seen as requiring a sequence or series of communications — Interpretation Act 1978 s 6(c): 'words in the plural include the singular.'

[38] *Brown v IC and Attorney-General*, FTT, 26 August 2011 at [42]-[44].

it is also important to recognise its limitations: the exemption does not extend as far as all information directly or indirectly supplied by or relating to the Royal Family or the Royal Household;[39] it does not exempt information about the Royal Family or the Royal Household per se; and the precise meaning and limits of the expression 'communications with' will need to be established on a case-by-case basis. So far as the last point is concerned, it might be said that communicating 'with' someone requires that they be engaged to some degree so that unsuccessful or incomplete transmissions of information (eg a letter that is sent but recalled or not understood) do not count. Questions may also arise as to whether the copying or side-copying of documents to members of the Royal Family or the Royal Household necessarily entails any 'communication with' the relevant copy recipients.

35– 007 Public interest

As the exemptions conferred by s 37(1)(ac)-(ad) of FOIA are qualified exemptions, it is implicit that some information relating to communications with members of the Royal Family (other than the Sovereign or the heir or second in line to the throne) or with the Royal Household is to be disclosed under FOIA.[40] The task of weighing the public interest in maintaining an exemption that is purely class based (in other words, that does not have some type of prejudice as one of its composite elements) is always difficult. The task is particularly difficult where, as in s 37(1), the exemption does not reflect a well-understood proscription against disclosure: for example, safeguarding national security, legal professional privilege, trade secrets and so forth. Whereas in the latter cases it is always possible to assess the extent to which exemption is required in order to protect against that well-recognised harm, there is no such familiar protection to be secured by s 37(1), leaving the weighing exercise particularly prone to idiosyncratic views of the underlying public interest perceived to be protected by the exemption. With this caveat, it is suggested that the strength of the public interest in maintaining the exclusion of the duty to confirm or deny the existence of, or the duty to communicate, information relating to communications with members of the Royal Family (other than the Sovereign or the heir or second in line to the throne) or with the Royal Household will depend on the nature and public importance of that information. Members of the Royal Family fulfil public and official functions and are the recipients of public funds in return. The nature and content of their interactions with the outside world when they are acting in a public capacity and at public expense may therefore be of considerable public interest and the countervailing factors favouring non-disclosure will turn largely on the extent to which exposure to public scrutiny would prejudice the effective working of the Royal Family and the Royal Household given their status and importance.[41] Where communications have taken place with members of the Royal Family acting in their private capacities, however, the public interest in disclosure may be less strong and the legitimate interest in ensuring their privacy and dignity will acquire

[39] Compare FOIA s 23 on information directly or indirectly supplied by or relating to any of the security bodies: see n 25 and §§26– 040 to 26– 045.

[40] See §6– 011.

[41] MoJ, *Exemptions Guidance—Section 37*, undated, Pt 1, paras 3.3-3.8 place particular emphasis on the confidentiality of communications with the Sovereign and the heir to the throne in circumstances where the qualified exemption under FOIA s 37(1)(ac)-(ad) is now, and any related public interest balancing exercise will be, confined to information relating to communications with the more peripheral members of the Royal Family or Royal Household. See para 3.3: 'It is a fundamental constitutional principle that communications between the Queen and her Ministers and other public bodies are essentially confidential in nature and there is therefore a fundamental public interest in withholding information relating to such communications. That is so because the Sovereign has the right and the duty to counsel, encourage and warn her government. She is thus entitled to have opinions on government policy and to express them to her ministers. She is, however, constitutionally bound to accept and act on the advice of her ministers. Any communications which have preceded the giving of that advice remain confidential, because of the need to maintain the political neutrality of the Queen in public affairs (its reality and appearance); this itself is fundamental to the UK system of constitutional monarchy.'

more force.

2. HONOURS AND DIGNITIES

35– 008 Introduction

By virtue of s 37(1)(b) of FOIA, information that relates to the conferring by the Crown of any honour or dignity is exempt information.[42] Similarly, the duty to confirm or deny does not arise in relation to such information.[43] Both the exemption and the exclusion are qualified.[44] Accordingly, even if information is exempt under this provision, the public authority holding that information must disclose it unless the public interest in maintaining the exemption outweighs the public interest in disclosing the information.[45] There is no equivalent exception in the EIR. Accordingly, where (or to the extent that) information that answers the terms of a request for information is 'environmental information',[46] the fact that that information also relates to the conferring by the Crown of any honour or dignity will not excuse the public authority from complying with the request.[47]

35– 009 Background

The *Code of Practice on Access to Government Information* contained a similar, but narrower, exemption for 'information, opinions and assessments given in relation to recommendations for honours'.[48] The accompanying *Guidance on Interpretation* stated that the exemption was aimed at ensuring frankness, candour and honesty in the honours recommendation and selection process.[49] More long-standing restrictions have prevented parliamentary questions being asked

---

[42] FOI(S)A s 41 is identically worded save that reference is made to 'the exercise by Her Majesty of Her prerogative of honour' (FOI(S)A s 41(b)) instead of 'the conferring by the Crown of any honour or dignity' (FOIA s 37(1)(b)): see §35– 013. In the context of considering the Scotland Act 1998 (which has been said is to be interpreted on ordinary principles, the Supreme Court has held that the phrase 'relates to' indicates more than a loose or consequential connection or a touching upon the matter: *Martin v Most* [2010] UKSC 10, 2010 SC (UKSC) 40 at [49], [159]. And similarly: *Imperial Tobacco Ltd v Lord Advocate* [2012] UKSC 61, 2013 SLT 2 at [16]; *Re Agricultural Sector (Wales) Bill* [2014] UKSC 43, [2014] 1 WLR 2622 at [50]; *Recovery of Medical Costs for Asbestos Diseases (Wales) Bill* [2015] UKSC 3, [2015] AC 1016 at [25]; *Christian Institute v Lord Advocate* [2016] UKSC 51, [2016] HRLR 19 at [29] (concerning the Data Protection Act 1998). In the context of FOIA the meaning of the phrase 'relates to' has been considered in: *Home Office v IC and Cobain*, FTT, 30 January 2013 at [15]-[19]; *Callus v IC and Home Office*, FTT, 6 May 2014 at [39]-[41]; *University and Colleges Admissions Service v IC and Lord Lucas* [2014] UKUT 0557 (AAC) at [44]-[46] (meaning of 'relates to' in FOIA s 7(5)); *Home Office v IC and Cobain* [2014] UKUT 0306 (AAC) at [39]; *All Party Parliamentary Group on Extraordinary Rendition v IC and FCO* [2015] UKUT 0377 (AAC) at [14]-[33]; *Reprieve v IC and FCO*, FTT, 26 April 2016 at [37]-[39]; *Corderoy and Ahmed v IC and Attorney General* [2017] UKUT 0495 (AAC) at [51] [54] and [59]-[62]; *Department of Health v IC and Lewis* [2017] EWCA Civ 374, [2017] 1 WLR 3330 at [13] (Sir Terence Etherton MR) (meaning of 'relates to' in FOIA s 35(1)).

[43] FOIA s 37(2). There is no discrete duty to confirm or deny under FOI(S)A.

[44] FOIA s 2(3); FOI(S)A s 2(2).

[45] Similarly, the duty to confirm or deny. FOIA s 37(1) and (2) engage s 2(2)(b) and (1)(b) respectively so as to prevent from arising, first, the duty to confirm or deny and, secondly, the duty to communicate, if the public interest in divulgence or disclosure (respectively) is outweighed. Information cannot be exempt information by virtue of s 37(1)(b) after the end of the period of 60 years beginning with the year following that in which the record containing the information was created: FOIA s 63(3).

[46] As to the meaning of which, see §17– 011.

[47] FOIA s 39.

[48] *Open Government Code of Practice on Access to Government Information*, 2nd edn (1997) Pt II, para 8c. The exemption did not refer to harm or prejudice and it was not therefore subject to any balancing exercise weighing the public interest in disclosure against the public interest in non-disclosure: see Pt II.

[49] *Open Government Code of Practice on Access to Government Information: Guidance on Interpretation*, 2nd edn (1997) Pt II, paras 8.9-8.12. Paragraph 8.12 states that the exemption for information, opinions and assessments given in relation to recommendations for honours 'links in with' the restriction on the matters subject to investigation by the

of ministers regarding the granting of honours.[50] The relevant exemptions in the draft Freedom of Information Bill published on 24 May 1999[51] and the Freedom of Information Bill introduced in the House of Commons on 18 November 1999[52] were identically worded. The only difference between these provisions and s 37(1) of FOIA is the additional inclusion in the latter of a reference to the conferring by the Crown of dignities as well as honours.[53]

35– 010 Honours and dignities

There is an important distinction between honours and dignities which is maintained in numerous statutes.[54] Reference has already been made to the inclusion in s 37(1)(b) of FOIA of the reference to dignities (as well as honours) which was specifically achieved by way of amendment to the Freedom of Information Bill.[55] Awards, decorations and medals for bravery, gallantry, heroism and public service in the civilian and military spheres, the civic styles 'lord mayor', 'deputy lord mayor' and 'right honourable' and civic status as a city or royal borough are all conferred under the prerogative of honour.[56] In *Hazelwood v IC and Cabinet Office*, the Tribunal referred to the Oxford English Dictionary definition of 'honour' as 'a mark of respect or distinction', 'a privilege, a special right' and 'a source or cause of distinction' in holding that the exemption in s 37(1)(b) protects 'the honours system in its widest sense, including the system

---

Parliamentary Commissioner for Administration in the Parliamentary Commissioner for Administration Act 1967 s 5 Sch 4 para 11: 'the grant of honours, awards or privileges within the gift of the Crown, including the grant of Royal Charters.'

50 M Jack (ed), *Erskine May's treatise on the law, privileges, proceedings and usage of Parliament*, 24th edn (London, LexisNexis, 2011) p 360. The *White Paper on Open Government* (Cm 2290, 1993) did not offer any additional commentary upon the exemptions which eventually found expression in the *Open Government Code of Practice on Access to Government Information*, 2nd edn (1997) Pt II, para 8c.

51 *Freedom of Information: Consultation on Draft Legislation* (Cm 4355, 1999) Pt II, cl 29(1).

52 Clause 35(1).

53 FOIA s 37(1)(b). The words 'or dignity' were inserted pursuant to a government amendment moved by Lord Falconer of Thoroton at Committee Stage in the House of Lords: Hansard HL vol 618 col 315 (24 October 2000). The amendment was described as 'merely clarificatory' and explained as follows: 'The term "dignity" refers to peerages, and the amendment ensures that the exemption applies to the granting of peerages as well as meritorious awards' — Hansard HL vol 618 col 315 (24 October 2000). Compare FOI(S)A s 41(b).

54 For example, Honours (Prevention of Abuses) Act 1925 s 1; Adoption Act 1976 s 44; Legitimacy Act 1976 Sch 1, paras 3-4; Law Reform (Parent And Child) (Scotland) Act 1986 s 9; Family Law Reform Act 1987 ss 19 and 27; Human Fertilisation and Embryology Act 1990 s 29; Private International Law (Miscellaneous Provisions) Act 1995 s 6; Scotland Act 1998 s 30, Sch 5, para 2(3); Northern Ireland Act 1998 s 4, Sch 2, para 6; Adoption and Children Act 2002 s 71; Gender Recognition Act 2004 s 16; Human Fertilisation and Embryology Act 2008 s 48; Equality Act 2010 Sch 6 para 3; DPA 2018 Sch 2 para 15, Sch 11, para 6. It is notable that FOI(S)A s 41 refers to 'the exercise by Her Majesty of Her prerogative of honour' without mentioning the conferring of dignities.

55 See §35– 009. FOIA also amended DPA 1998 so as to exempt personal data processed for the purposes of the conferring of any dignity (as well as any honour) from the subject information provisions in that Act: DPA 1998 Sch 7, para 3 (now repealed) as amended by FOIA s 73, Sch 6, para 6 (this amendment having come into force on 14 May 2001 under FOIA s 87(3) and the Freedom of Information Act 2000 (Commencement No 1) Order 2001 SI 2001/1637 Art 2(d)). FOIA s 73, Sch 6, para 6 was itself inserted into the Freedom of Information Bill by way of amendment at the same time as the words 'or dignity' were added to what became s 37(1)(b) in order to ensure 'that the corresponding provision in the Data Protection Act is similarly amended.' — Hansard HL vol 618 col 315 (24 October 2000). Personal data processed for the purposes of the conferring by the Crown of any honour or dignity are similarly exempt from the GDPR provisions listed in DPA 2018 Sch 2 para 6 (see para 15) and the DPA 2018 Pt 4 provisions listed in DPA 2108 Sch 11, para 1 (see para 6).

56 *Prince's Case* (1606) 8 Co Rep 1a at 18b, 4 Co Inst 361 at 363, 1 Bl Com (14th edn) 271; *Halsbury's Laws of England*, 5th edn, 2014, vol 20, title 'Constitutional Law and Administrative Law', paras 567-570; *Halsbury's Laws of England*, 5th edn, 2014, vol 79, title 'Peerages and Dignities', para 801. Examples are the Victoria Cross, the Order of Victoria and Albert, the Albert Medal, the George Cross, the Imperial Order of the Crown of India, the Royal Red Cross, the Distinguished Service Order, the Order of Merit, the Imperial Service Order, the Edward Medal, the Territorial Decoration, the Order of the Companions of Honour and the Order of the British Empire. It is arguable whether the grant of borough status by royal charter under the Local Government Act 1972 ss 245-245A amounts to the conferring by the Crown of an honour for the purposes of FOIA s 37(1)(b).

for giving permission to companies to use the term "Royal".'[57] Although the Tribunal's acceptance that such permission constitutes a form of honour and that the system for its grant or refusal derives from the Royal prerogative may have been sound, it is submitted that its reliance on dictionary definitions was more dubious given that the reference in s 37(1)(b) to conferral by the Crown clearly points to a narrower, more specialist meaning.[58] Peerages, baronetcies, knighthoods, arms and precedence are conferred as dignities.[59] Appointment by the Crown as a Privy Counsellor or Queen's Counsel also carries with it certain consequences in terms of precedence and the right to use (as appropriate) the style 'right honourable' or the post-nominal initials 'QC.'[60] While the office of Queen's Counsel would not appear to constitute an honour or dignity as such, it has been suggested that the office of Privy Counsellor does constitute an honour.[61] That peerages are a type of dignity is probably the most important point to note here because, at least for the time being, the conferral of a life peerage carries with it the right to sit and vote in the House of Lords.[62] Whether the link between peerages and

---

57 *Hazelwood v IC and Cabinet Office*, FTT, 15 February 2017 at [26]-[27].

58 The point can be tested by asking whether reference to a dictionary definition of 'dignity' would prove useful in construing FOIA s 37(1)(b). The FTT also held that the purpose of the exemption is 'to protect the confidentiality of sensitive communications with the Royal Household on the subject of honours' (at [27]). If this were right then the purpose of FOIA s 37(1)(b) would be entirely coterminous with that of s 37(1)(a)-(ad) and the exemption itself would be otiose. The Upper Tribunal confirmed this in *Cabinet Office v IC and Morland* [2018] UKUT 67 (AAC) at [20]:

> Section 37(1)(a)-(ad), as noted in the previous paragraph, specifically protects the actual communications with the Sovereign and certain other members of the Royal Family and the Royal Household. Section 37(1)(b) must be concerned with activities other than communications with the Sovereign. The logical purpose of section 37(1)(b) is to ensure candour and protect confidences in the entire process of considering honours, dignities and medals.

59 *Ranger v House of Lords Appointments Commission* [2015] EWHC 45 (QB), [2015] 1 WLR 4324 at [16]-[19] and *Halsbury's Laws of England*, 5th edn, 2014, vol 79, title 'Peerages and Dignities', para 801. The right to bear arms is a dignity but the Crown's power to grant armorial bearings to individuals is delegated to the Kings of Arms: *Manchester Corporation v Manchester Palace of Varieties Ltd* [1955] P 133 (Court of Chivalry) at 147 (Lord Goddard); *Halsbury's Laws of England*, 5th edn, 2014, vol 79, title 'Peerages and Dignities', paras 801, 870-877. Arms are therefore not conferred on individuals 'by the Crown' for the purposes of FOIA s 37(1)(b). The position in relation to the conferring of arms on local authorities is more complicated: the power of grant was historically exercised by the Royal College of Arms (*Halsbury's Laws of England*, 5th edn, 2018, vol 69, title 'Local Government', para 143); but Her Majesty may by Order in Council authorise a new local authority to bear and use specified armorial bearings in certain circumstances under the Local Government Act 1972 s 247 and such grants arguably amount to the conferring 'by the Crown' of a dignity for the purposes of FOIA s 37(1)(b) (eg the Local Authorities (Armorial Bearings) Order 2006 SI 2006/3330). MoJ, *Exemptions Guidance—Section 37*, undated, Pt 2, para 2.2 states that 'some Crown appointments (both secular and ecclesiastical) will come within the category of 'honour or dignity' and so will come within this section. For example, some senior Church appointments (the appointment of archbishops, diocesan bishops, suffragan bishops, deans of cathedrals, deans and canons of the two Royal Peculiars and the First and Second Church Estates Commissioners) are dignities and so will fall within this section' (see also para 3.6).

60 *Halsbury's Laws of England*, 5th edn, 2014, vol 20, title 'Constitutional and Administrative Law', paras 268-269 and 271; *Halsbury's Laws of England*, 5th edn, vol 66, 2015, title 'Legal Professions', para 857.

61 See, eg A Bradley, K Ewing and C Knight, *Constitutional and Administrative Law*, 17th edn (London, Pearson, 2018) p 254 where membership of the Privy Council is described as a 'titular honour' and it is recorded that,'[T]he office is a recognised reward for public and political service, and appointments to it figure in the honours lists.' As to Queen's Counsel, see DPA 1998 s 37, Sch 7,para 3(a)-(b) and DPA 2018 Sch 2 para 14(1). In *A-G for Dominion of Canada v A-G for Province of Ontario* [1898] AC 247 (HL), Lord Watson said 'The position occupied by Queen's Counsel is in the nature of an office under the Crown, although any duties which it entails are almost as unsubstantial as its emoluments; and it is also in the nature of an honour or dignity to this extent, that it is a mark and recognition by the Sovereign of the professional eminence of the counsel' (at 252). MoJ, *Exemptions Guidance—Section 37*, undated, Pt 2, paras 2.1 and 2.3-2.4 exclude appointment to Queen's Counsel but include information relating to 'appointments to the Privy Council' (but not the Judicial Committee to the Privy Council) as covered by FOIA s 37(1)(b). See also Information Commissioner, *Freedom of Information Act Awareness Guidance No 26: Communications with Her Majesty and the Awarding of Honours*, (2011), Pt C.

62 *Norfolk Earldom Case* [1907] AC 10 HL (Committee for Privileges); *Wensleydale Peerage Case* (1856) 5 HLC 958 HL (Committee for Privileges); LJ 38; Life Peerages Act 1958 s 1(2)(b); *Halsbury's Laws of England*, 5th edn, 2014, vol 79, title 'Peerages and Dignities', para 824; House of Lords Act 1999. The House of Lords currently comprises the Lords Spiritual and the Lords Temporal. All of the Lords Temporal are entitled to sit and vote in the House of Lords by virtue of the conferring by the Crown of a dignity (ie their peerage) while the Lords Spiritual are not

membership of the House of Lords will survive further reform remains open to question.[63]

35– 011 Conferral of honours etc

The monarch is the fountain of all honour and dignity and enjoys the sole right of conferring all titles of honour and dignities.[64] By convention the monarch's powers in relation to titles of honour and dignities are exercised on the advice of the Prime Minister.[65] In relation to honours conferred on individuals for non-political reasons, a body known as the Main Honours Advisory Committee makes recommendations to the monarch via the Prime Minister.[66] In

---

because, while they are Lords of Parliament, they are not peers as such: *Halsbury's Laws of England*, 5th edn, 2018, vol 78, title 'Parliament', para 632; W McKay (ed), *Erskine May's treatise on the law, privileges, proceedings and usage of Parliament*, 24th edn (London, LexisNexis, 2011) p 12; O Hood Phillips and P Jackson, *Constitutional and Administrative Law*, 8th edn (London, Sweet & Maxwell, 2001) p 176, n 19; and *Standing Orders of the House of Lords Relating to Public Business* (HL 3) 2016, No 6. For these purposes, the Lords Spiritual are the archbishops and certain bishops of the Church of England and the Lords Temporal are life peers created under the Life Peerages Act 1958, and 92 hereditary peers given continued membership of the House of Lords under the House of Lords Act 1999 and relevant standing orders: *Halsbury's Laws of England*, 5th edn, 2018, vol 78, title 'Parliament', paras 632-639. Since the implementation of the House of Lords Act 1999, only the following 92 members of the House of Lords have been hereditary peers: 75 elected under that Act either by their own political party's hereditary peers or cross-bench grouping in proportion to that party or grouping's share of the hereditary peers, 15 elected under that Act by the House as a whole to act as Deputy Speakers or Committee Chairmen plus the hereditary Royal appointments of Earl Marshal and the Lord Great Chamberlain.

63 See: Report of the Royal Commission on the Reform of the House of Lords, *A House for the Future* (Cm 4534, 2000); Lord Chancellor's Department, *The House of Lords: Completing the Reform* (Cm 5291, 2001) paras 78-79 proposing to break the link; Department for Constitutional Affairs, *Constitutional Reform: Next Steps for the House of Lords* (CP 14/03), 2003, paras 21 and 24-28 abandoning the plan to break the link; and HM Government, *The House of Lords: Reform* (Cm 7027, 2007) paras 1.12, 1.15 and 9.36 reinstating the plan to break the link. However, note that the House of Commons and House of Lords came to different conclusions as to the appropriate composition of a reformed second chamber of Parliament in free votes on 7 March 2007 and 14 March 2007 respectively (see Hansard HC vol 457 col 1390 *et seq* (6 March 2007) and col 1524 *et seq* (7 March 2007) and Hansard HL vol 690 col 451 *et seq* (12 March 2007), col 571 *et seq* (13 March 2007) and col 741 *et seq* (14 March 2007). These votes were followed by a further White Paper (MoJ, *An Elected Second Chamber: Further Reform of the House of Lords* (Cm 7438, 2008)) and a response from the House of Commons Public Administration Select Committee (Fifth Report of Session 2008-09, *Response to White Paper: 'An Elected Second Chamber'* (HC 137)). The coalition government published a White Paper and draft bill setting out further proposals for reform of the House of Lords on 17 May 2011 (HM Government, *House of Lords Reform Draft Bill* (Cm 8077, 2011)). This was followed by: House of Lords and House of Commons Joint Committee on the Draft House of Lords Reform Bill, *Draft House of Lords Reform Bill Report Session 2010-12*, (HL 284/HC 1313) 2012; HM Government, *Government Response to the Report of the Joint Committee on the Draft House of Lords Reform bill* (Cm 8391, 2012); House of Commons second reading debate on the House of Lords Reform Bill on 9 and 10 July 2012; and government announced the abandonment of the Bill on 6 August 2012 and formally withdrew the Bill on 3 September 2012.

64 *Prince's Case* (1606) 8 Co Rep 1a at 18b, 4 Co Inst 361, 363, 1 Bl Com (14th edn) 271; *Halsbury's Laws of England*, 5th edn, 2014, vol 20, title 'Constitutional and Administrative Law', para 567; *Halsbury's Laws of England*, 5th edn, 2018, vol 69, title 'Local Government', para 141; *Halsbury's Laws of England*, 5th edn, 2014, vol 79, title 'Peerages and Dignities', para 801; O Hood Phillips and P Jackson, *Constitutional and Administrative Law*, 8th edn (London, Sweet & Maxwell, 2001) para 15-015(f).

65 However, the monarch reserves absolute discretion in conferring the Order of Merit, the Order of the Garter, the Order of the Thistle and the Royal Victorian Order: *Halsbury's Laws of England*, 4th edn, 1996 re-issue, vol 8(2), title 'Constitutional Law and Human Rights', paras 831-832. Thus Elizabeth II made the Governor of Southern Rhodesia a KCVO at the time of the Unilateral Declaration of Independence in November 1965: O Hood Phillips and P Jackson, *Constitutional and Administrative Law*, 8th edn (London, Sweet & Maxwell, 2001) p 316, n 4.

66 The Main Honours Advisory Committee was established as a non-departmental public body in October 2005 as part of the programme of reform set out in Cabinet Office, *Reform of the Honours System* (Cm 6479, 2005). However, it lost this status in 2010 and is now administered within the Cabinet Office (Cabinet Office, *Public Bodies 2012*, (2013) Annex I). See also: Public Administration Select Committee, Fifth Report of Session 2003-04, *A Matter of Honour: Reforming the Honours System* (HC 212-I) 2004; Sir Hayden Phillips, *Review of the Honours System* (2004); Public Administration Select Committee, Second Report of Session 2007-08, *Propriety and Peerages* (HC 153); and Cabinet Office, *Three Years of Operation of the Reformed Honours System* (2008). The Main Committee reviews the work of nine specialist Sub-Committees covering the subject areas: Arts and Media; Sport; Health; Education; Science and Technology; the Economy; Community, Voluntary and Local Services; Parliamentary and Political Science; and State. The former Honours Scrutiny Committee, established in 1923, was wound up with effect from 31 March 2005 (Cabinet Office, *Public Bodies 2006* (2006), p 330). See: *Report of the Royal Commission on Honours* (Cmd 1789, 1922) paras 24-28; 57 HL Official Report (5th series) 26 June 1924, col 1068; *Halsbury's Laws of England*, 5th edn, 2014, vol 20, title 'Constitutional and Administrative Law', paras 568, 574; O Hood Phillips and P Jackson,

relation to peerages and party-political honours, an independent House of Lords Appointments Commission recommends non-party-political persons for cross-bench life peerages and scrutinises the propriety and suitability of all nominations, first, to life peerages including those put forward by the political parties (excluding peers appointed to take on ministerial responsibility) and, secondly, for party-political and other honours proposed independently of the Main Honours Advisory Committee system.[67] Both the Political Honours Scrutiny Committee (now abolished) and the House of Lords Appointments Commission are listed as 'public authorities' in Sch 1 to FOIA.[68] Titles of honour are conferred by express grant in the form of letters patent and dignities are conferred by writ of summons in the case of peerages, by letters patent in the case of baronetcies and some knighthoods, by direct corporeal investiture in the case of most knighthoods or by warrants of precedence.[69] The expression 'the conferring by the Crown' in s 37(1)(b) of FOIA raises questions as to how far the exemption captures information relating to the earlier selection and recommendation process which precedes formal conferral by the Crown itself as well as information relating to non-conferral where a candidate is rejected, for whatever reasons, by the Crown or by those involved lower down. A Forfeiture Committee, comprising the Cabinet Secretary, Treasury Solicitor and the Permanent Secretaries to the Home Office and the Scottish Executive, makes recommendations on the cancellation of honours in the case of recipients convicted of criminal offences and it is likewise open to question whether related information is exempt under s 37(1)(b) of FOIA.[70] In *Cabinet Office v IC and Morland*, the Upper Tribunal held that while the 'statutory language of "the conferring by the Crown of any honour or dignity" undoubtedly creates a mental picture of the act of bestowing a medal or other honour', these words should not be given 'an unduly narrow interpretation' and 'the terms "relates to" and "any" both point to the breadth of the statutory language, which in turn suggests that the exemption covers both potential future honours as well as currently extant honours.'[71]

Constitutional and Administrative Law, 8th edn (London, Sweet & Maxwell, 2001) para 15-015(f). The Honours Scrutiny Committee was originally named the Political Honours Scrutiny Committee before being renamed in 2002 pursuant to a recommendation made in Committee on Standards in Public Life, Fifth Report *Standards in Public Life* (Cm 4057, 1998) pp 14 and 193, R100. Despite its abolition, the Political Honours Scrutiny Committee remains listed as a public authority in FOIA Sch 1.

67 The House of Lords Appointments Commission is an advisory non-departmental public body established by the Prime Minister on 4 May 2000 on a non-statutory basis pursuant to proposals set out in the government White Paper *Modernising Parliament: Reforming the House of Lords* (Cm 4183, 1999) Ch 6, paras 9-14. According to Cabinet Office, *Public Bodies 2006* (2006), p 4, the Commission's terms of reference are, 'To make recommendations on the appointment of non-party-political peers. The Commission also vets for propriety all nominations for life peerages, including those made by the political parties, and all individuals added to honours lists by the Prime Minister' (the Commission's Annual Report November 2015-October 2018 describes its role in similar terms (para 2)). In relation to cross-bench life peerages, the Prime Minister invites a fixed number of recommendations from the Commission and passes these on to Her Majesty for approval 'except in the most exceptional of circumstances'. The Commission acquired its functions relating to honours in April 2005 pursuant to the reforms set out in Cabinet Office, *Reform of the Honours System* (Cm 6479, 2005). The significance of this is likely to diminish following the Prime Minister's announcement in March 2006 that he will no longer add his own names to the twice yearly honours lists (Public Administration Select Committee, Fourth Report of Session 2005-06, *Propriety and Honours: Interim Findings* (HC 1119) 2006, paras 12-14). See also: O Hood Phillips and P Jackson, *Constitutional and Administrative Law*, 8th edn (London, Sweet & Maxwell, 2001) para 9-011; Report of the Royal Commission on the Reform of the House of Lords, *A House for the Future* (Cm 4534, 2000); Lord Chancellor's Department, *The House of Lords: Completing the Reform* (Cm 5291, 2001) paras 65-68; Department for Constitutional Affairs, *Constitutional Reform: Next Steps for the House of Lords* (CP 14/03), 2003, paras 29-43 and 53-60; Public Administration Select Committee, Fourth Report of Session 2005-06, *Propriety and Honours: Interim Findings* (HC 1119) 2006, paras 50-53; and HM Government, *The House of Lords: Reform* (Cm 7027, 2007) paras 8.11-8.20.

68 FOIA s 3 Sch 1 Pt VI.

69 Bl Com (14th edn) 272; *Halsbury's Laws of England*, 5th edn, 2014, vol 20, title 'Constitutional and Administrative Law', para 567; *Halsbury's Laws of England*, 5th edn, 2014, vol 79, title 'Peerages and Dignities', paras 814-815, 821-822, 829, 861 and 865; the Life Peerages Act 1958 s 1.

70 FOIA s 37(1)(a) may still be relevant in any event.

71 *Cabinet Office v IC and Morland* [2018] UKUT 67 (AAC) at [18].

35– 012 Honours etc: the public interest

The particular difficulties affecting the public interest so far as s 37(1) of FOIA is concerned have already been considered in relation to s 37(1)(a)-(ad), and these are equally applicable to s 37(1)(b).[72] While the conferring of honours and dignities is undoubtedly a matter of public interest,[73] it does not often carry any great practical consequences in legal, political or constitutional terms and the selection process often involves an evaluative assessment of personal information and the exercise of a very broad discretion. A public interest in maintaining the exclusion of the duty to communicate related information may therefore arise out of the need to protect confidences and to ensure frankness, candour and honesty in the recommendation and selection process[74] and the need to protect the feelings and privacy of those considered and their families particularly where it has been decided not to confer an honour.[75] A public interest in maintaining the exclusion of the duty to confirm or deny may also arise out of the same considerations, although this is less likely to be the case in circumstances where an honour or dignity *has* been conferred. So far as concerns information relating to the conferring of honours and most dignities (other than life peerages) on individuals, the public interest balance may therefore be thought normally to weigh in favour of non-disclosure rather than disclosure. The public interest balance may, however, be more likely to shift in favour of disclosure in relation to the conferring of honours on corporations or groups of people (where questions of privacy and personal distress are less likely to arise)[76] and in relation to the conferring of life peerages (where receipt of the dignity carries with it important consequences in terms of the right to sit and vote in Parliament and eligibility for ministerial office).[77]

---

72 See §35– 007.

73 The public interest in the fairness and transparency of the honours system has long been recognised: *Report of the Royal Commission on Honours* (Cmd 1789, 1922) paras 24-28; 57 HL Official Report (5th series) 26 June 1924, col 1068; the Honours (Prevention of Abuses) Act 1925. The public interest in the conferring of both honours and dignities more generally is also implicitly recognised by the inclusion of the Political Honours Scrutiny Committee (now abolished) and the House of Lords Appointments Commission in FOIA Sch 1, Pt VI as 'public authorities'.

74 See §35– 009 and *Open Government Code of Practice on Access to Government Information: Guidance on Interpretation*, 2nd edn (1997) Pt II, paras 8.9-8.12 on the equivalent exemption in the Open Government Code of Practice on Access to Government Information, 2nd edn (1997) Pt II, para 8c. In *Luder v IC and Cabinet Office*, FTT, 13 October 2011 the Tribunal summarised evidence heard from the Cabinet Office as to the importance of confidentiality to the honours process (at [20]) and concluded:

> There is therefore a substantive public interest in maintaining the confidentiality of the honours system. In support of this interest the Tribunal has seen evidence of the harm likely to be caused by the disclosure of the materials sought... (at [22])

The exemptions for personal and confidential information in FOIA ss 40-41 would protect a certain amount of personal information in any event.

75 See the remarks made by Lord Falconer of Thoroton at Committee Stage in the House of Lords in connection with a proposed government amendment to the relevant clause in the Freedom of Information Bill: 'The conferring of honours raises questions of personal confidentiality and the government believes that it should receive substantial protection under the Bill. The conferring of honours raises such questions not just in relation to the candidates for honours themselves and members of their families, but also in relation to those who contribute to the process of selection. Questions of confidentiality can arise just as easily in regard to posthumous awards. It will be obviously embarrassing, and potentially distressing, for surviving relatives to discover that the deceased was considered but rejected for an honour' — Hansard HL vol 618 col 315 (24 October 2000).

76 For example, the conferring of city or royal borough status on a local authority, the award of the George Cross to 'the Island Fortress of Malta' by George VI on 15 April 1942 and the award of the George Cross to the Royal Ulster Constabulary by Elizabeth II on 23 November 1999. Where a local authority has applied for and been refused city status it may well want to disclose information relating to its application in order to show it put forward the best case possible and in such cases it may make voluntary disclosure regardless of FOIA s 37(1)(b).

77 The greater 'constitutional significance' of peerages (which ought to represent appointments for future service) when compared with honours (which reflect past achievement) was emphasised throughout Public Administration Select Committee, Second Report of Session 2007-08, *Propriety and Peerages* (HC 153) (see paras 19, 35 and 39).

35– 013 Honours etc: FOI(S)A

Section 41 of FOI(S)A is the Scottish equivalent of s 37 of FOIA and, as mentioned above, it follows the wording of its Westminster counterpart save that reference is made to 'the exercise by Her Majesty of Her prerogative of honour' instead of 'the conferring by the Crown of any honour or dignity'.[78] Information held by Scottish public authorities which relates to the conferring by the Crown of any dignity will not therefore be exempt under the terms of s 41(b) of FOI(S)A. The only way of avoiding this conclusion is to argue that the conferring of dignities is an 'exercise by Her Majesty of Her prerogative of honour' but this is not a particularly persuasive proposition given the distinction drawn between honours and dignities elsewhere. The different approach in s 41(b) of FOI(S)A also raises two other questions which may lead to different results under the two regimes: first, whether there are any honours which may be conferred by the Crown other than in the exercise of Her prerogative of honour; and, secondly, whether there is any difference between the amount and type of honours-related information capable of 'relating to' the conferring by the Crown of any honour or dignity, on the one hand, and the exercise by Her Majesty of Her prerogative of honour, on the other.

35– 014 Honours etc: DPA 2018

The DPA 2018 binds the Crown and contains special provision for its application to the Royal Household, the Duchy of Lancaster and the Duchy of Cornwall.[79] Personal data processed for the purposes of the conferring by the Crown of any honour or dignity are also exempt from certain GDPR provisions.[80]

3. PROHIBITIONS ON DISCLOSURE

35– 015 Introduction

By s 44(1) of FOIA information is exempt from the disclosure obligation in s 1(1)(b) 'if its disclosure (otherwise than under [the Act itself]) by the public authority holding it (a) is prohibited by or under any enactment, (b) is incompatible with any EU obligation or (c) would constitute or be punishable as a contempt of court.' The exemption is an absolute one, so that

78 It might be argued that FOI(S)A is outside the legislative competence of the Scottish Parliament to the extent that it confers a qualified entitlement (subject to a public interest override) to information about honours and a general entitlement to information about dignities because the Scottish Parliament cannot enact provisions which 'relate to' 'reserved matters' (Scotland Act 1998 ss 28-30; 'honours and dignities' are defined as 'reserved matters' by the Scotland Act 1998 s 30, Sch 5, paras 1, 2(3)). This is not a strong argument for a number of reasons. First, FOI(S)A does not obviously contain any provisions which 'relate to' the conferring of honours or dignities when the expression 'relates to' is read in accordance with the Scotland Act 1998 s 29(3). Secondly, if and in so far as Scottish public authorities hold information about honours and dignities, it would be odd if the Scottish Parliament were unable to regulate public access to it particularly when FOIA regulates public access to such information when held by other (non-Scottish) public authorities. Thirdly, the proviso to the Scotland Act 1998 Sch 5 Pt II, s.B13 would appear to envisage legislation along the lines of FOI(S)A.

79 DPA 2018 s 209(4) provides: where the purposes for which and the manner in which any personal data is, or is to be, processed are determined by, inter alia, any person acting on behalf of the Royal Household, the data controller in respect of those data for the purposes of the GDPR and that Act shall be the Keeper of the Privy Purse.

80 Namely the GDPR provisions listed in para 6 of Sch 2 to the DPA 2018 (see para 15) and the provisions of Part 4 of the DPA listed in para 1 of Sch 11 (see para 6): see further §§11– 015 and 11– 034. The predecessor to these provisions was DPA 1998 s 37 Sch 7 para 3(b) as amended by FOIA s 73 Sch 6, para 6 (this amendment having come into force on 14 May 2001 under FOIA s 87(3) and the FOIA (Commencement No 1) Order 2001SI 2001/1637 Art 2(d)). In *Ranger v House of Lords Appointments Commission* [2015] EWHC 45 (QB), [2015] 1 WLR 4324 the High Court found DPA 1998 Sch 7 para 3(b) to be compatible with Directive 95/46 Arts 12-13 and the CFR Art 8.

no question of weighing competing public interests arises.[81] The duty to confirm or deny whether the public authority holds information requested provided by s 1(1)(a) of the Act does not arise if compliance with that duty would fall within any of paras (a), (b) or (c) above.[82] Section 26 of FOI(S)A contains a provision in almost identical terms to s 44(1) of the 2000 Act.[83] The basic position under the two Freedom of Information Acts is therefore that existing legal prohibitions on disclosure by the public authority 'trump' any rights given by the Acts and, where such prohibitions apply, not only is there no obligation to disclose under the Acts but there is no discretion to do so either. This is in contrast to the position under the EIR which oblige public authorities to disclose 'environmental information' regardless of any enactment or rule of law which would prevent such disclosure[84] and the DPA 2018, which provides that a data subject's access right has effect notwithstanding any enactment or rule of law prohibiting or restricting disclosure.[85]

35–016 General difficulties

Before considering separately these three categories of prohibition, it should be noted that although s 44 is on its face fairly straightforward, practical difficulties can arise in applying it.[86] In particular, although the section is likely to raise questions of law and issues particularly appropriate for decision by a court, the question whether the requested disclosure would be prohibited by any enactment or would be incompatible with an EU obligation or would constitute a contempt of court falls to be decided in the first instance by the public authority itself; and subsequently, if the applicant pursues the matter further, by the Information Commissioner.[87] It is only at the stage of the Tribunal[88] (or, in Scotland, the Court of Session)[89] that the decision-maker will necessarily be legally-qualified and sitting in a judicial capacity.[90] There is also a potential problem in that the decision whether the section applies involves (particularly in relation to contempt of court) a prediction of whether or not something which has not happened would infringe the law. Moreover, the assumed facts on which the prediction must be based are not made entirely clear by the section: thus, it is not made clear to whom, for what purpose and in what circumstances the disclosure whose legality is to be judged would be made (other than that it is otherwise than under the Act). This is in contrast to the position in the corresponding provision dealing with contempt of court under the Australian legislation which refers to 'public disclosure' of the relevant document.[91]

---

[81] FOIA s 2(1)(a), 2(2)(a), 2(3)(h).

[82] FOIA s 2(1)(a), 2(2)(a), 2(3)(h).

[83] See also FOI(S)A s 2(2)(b); the duty to confirm or deny whether the public authority holds requested information does not arise under the Scottish legislation.

[84] EIR reg 5(6); EI(S)R reg 5(3).

[85] DPA 2018 s 186. This provision is of benefit only to an applicant if he is the data subject of the information requested since the provisions referred to in s 186(2) only give rights to data subjects: GDPR Arts 12-23 and DPA 2018 ss 43-54 and 92-100.

[86] As it appears there were under the original s 38 of the Freedom of Information Act 1982 (Cth of Australia) which contained the corresponding provisions in relation to statutory prohibitions: *News Corp Ltd v National Companies and Securities Commission* (1984) 52 ALR 277; *Kavvadias v Ombudsman (Cth)* (1984) 1 FCR 80, 52 ALR 728; *Federal Commissioner of Taxation v Swiss Aluminium Ltd* (1986) 10 FCR 321.

[87] See §45–005.

[88] See §45–012.

[89] See §46–014.

[90] Even then, difficult issues of statutory construction might be better resolved by a court of record, as the FTT itself recognised in *PricewaterhouseCooper v Information Commissioner*, FTT, 4 March 2010 at [1].

[91] Freedom of Information Act 1982 (Cth of Australia) s 46.

4. PROHIBITIONS BY OR UNDER ENACTMENT

35–017 Definition of 'enactment'

In its ordinary sense, an 'enactment' is a legal proposition laid down in an Act or other legislative text with the effect that, when facts fall within an indicated area, specified legal consequences follow.[92] It seems clear that the word 'enactment' in section 44 is intended to include any enactment made by subordinate legislation,[93] although the word is not expressly defined in these terms for the purposes of section 44.[94] The relevant enactment can have been passed at any time as long as it prohibits the disclosure of the information at the time the question falls to be considered. It is thus possible in principle for rights under the Freedom of Information Acts to be removed by subordinate legislation made under different primary legislation without the Acts themselves being amended. However, the provision clearly does not cover departmental circulars or codes of practice even if issued under statutory authority;[95] nor does it cover any prohibition on disclosure provided by the common law, whether constituting a crime, tort or breach of contract.[96] However, the exemption applies not only to disclosures which would amount to criminal offences but also to those which are subject to regulatory or civil law enforcement, so long as the prohibition in question arises by virtue of an enactment.

35–018 Prohibitory enactments

There is a vast amount of legislation which potentially prohibits disclosure of information by public authorities.[97] Such legislation covers the whole range of government activities. There are numerous rationales for such prohibitions, although most commonly it is to preserve the confidentiality of information provided under compulsion by the citizen to public authorities. The following statutory provisions have been relied on in cases coming before the Tribunal:

— Abortion Regulations 1991 reg 5;[98]

— Animals (Scientific Procedures) Act 1986 s 24;[99]

---

92 This definition is taken from F Bennion, *Statutory Interpretation*, 5th edn (London, LexisNexis, 2008) p 396. As the author notes, the proposition containing the enactment may, as is most usual, be embodied in a single sentence of an Act or other instrument; or it may fall to be collected from two or more sentences, whether consecutive or not. The Interpretation Act 1889 s 35(1) appeared to take the view that an enactment was to be found within a single section or subsection. The provision is not repeated in the Interpretation Act 1978.

93 This was assumed by the Information Tribunal in *Meunier v Information Commissioner and National Savings & Investments*, IT, 5 June 2007at [64]-[78]. The Information Commissioner's *Guidance on Prohibitions on Disclosures* at para 11 states that the exemption covers disclosure which would breach primary legislation (an Act of Parliament) or secondary legislation (a Statutory Instrument).

94 See: FOIA ss 75(2)(b) and 84; FOI(S)A s 73, in which an 'enactment' includes an enactment comprised in, or in an instrument made under, an Act of the Scottish Parliament.

95 See *LB of Newham v IC*, FTT, 31 October 2012, where the Information Commissioner accepted that a statutory code, promulgated by the Secretary of State under the Gambling Act 2005, established a relevant prohibition 'under' an enactment.

96 Such disclosures may well be covered by another exemption (for example, breach of confidence which is dealt with at s 41 FOIA and s 36 FOI(S)A). Note also there is specific provision in s 79 FOIA (and s 67 FOI(S)A) giving immunity to public authorities from a defamation action arising from disclosure of information under the Acts unless the publication is made with malice.

97 The Department of Constitutional Affairs mentioned a total of 448 statutory provisions in its *Review of Statutory Prohibitions on Disclosure* (2005) although it also says that on investigation 122 of these do not operate as bars to disclosure under FOIA and that 116 had already been repealed or amended in the course of the review.

98 *Dept of Health v IC and Pro-Life Alliance*, IT, 15 October 2009.

99 *SSHD v British Union for the Abolition of Vivisection* [2008] EWCA Civ 870, [2009] 1 All ER 44, [2009] 1 WLR 636,

- — Census Act 1920 s 8;[100]
- — Civil Aviation Act 1982 s 23;[101]
- — Commissioners for Revenue and Customs Act 2005 ss 18 and 23;[102]
- — Communications Act 2003 s 393;[103]
- — DPA 1998 s 59;[104]
- — Enterprise Act 2002 s 237;[105]
- — Financial Services and Markets Act 2000 s 348;[106]
- — Health Service Commissioners Act 1993 s 15;[107]
- — Legal Aid Act 1988 s 38;[108]
- — Local Government Act 1974 s 32;[109]
- — Parliamentary Commissioner Act 1967 s 11;[110]
- — Premium Savings Bond Regulations 1972 reg 30;[111]
- — Police Act 1996 s 80;[112]
- — Public Audit (Wales) Act 2004 s 54(2);[113]
- — Public Service Contracts Regulations 1993 reg 30 and Public Contracts Regulations 2006 reg 43;[114] and
- — Statistics and Registration Services Act 2007 s 39.[115]

Other examples of relevant statutory provisions would be:

- — Police and Criminal Evidence Act 1984 s 64A(4) (which prevents the disclosure of a photograph taken by the police of someone in custody);

---

on appeal from [2008] EWHC 892 (QB), itself on appeal from Information Tribunal, 30 January 2008.

100 *Barrett v IC and Office for National Statistics*, IT, 23 April 2008.

101 *Hoyte v IC and CAA*, IT, 5 March 2008; *CAA v IC and Kirkaldie*, IT, 22 January 2010; *Phillips v IC*, IT, 10 February 2010.

102 *Allison v IC and HMRC*, IT, 22 April 2008; *HMRC v IC*, IT, 10 March 2009; *Waugh v IC and HMRC*, IT, 27 March 2009; *PricewaterhouseCooper v IC* [2011] UKUT 372 (AAC); *Lamb v IC*, FTT, 2 December 2010; *Ritchie v IC*, FTT, 26 July 2011; *IC v HMRC and Gaskell* [2011] UKUT 296 (AAC). See further *R (Privacy International and others) v HMRC* [2015] EWHC 1475 (Admin), [2015] 1 WLR 397 (judicial review of HMRC's refusal to disclose information about its export control functions).

103 *Morrissey v IC and Office of Communications*, IT, 11 January 2010.

104 *Friends of the Earth v IC and DTI*, 4 April 2007. The provision has since been repealed: see now DPA 2018 s 132.

105 *Dey v IC and OFT*, IT, 16 April 2007; *Dumfries and Galloway Council v Scottish IC* [2008] CSIH 12, 2008 SC 327.

106 *Slann v IC and FSA*, IT, 11 July 2006; *Craven v IC*, IT, 13 May 2008; *FSA v IC*, IT, 13 October 2008; *Calland v IC and FSA*, IT, 8 August 2008; *Rowland and FSA v IC*, IT, 3 April 2009; *FSA v IC* [2009] EWHC 1548 (Admin); *Wynn v IC and SFO*, FTT, 7 September 2012.

107 *Parker v IC and Parliamentary and Health Service Ombudsman*, IT, 15 October 2007; *Cubells v IC and Wrightington, Wigan & Leigh NHS Foundation Trust*, FTT, 30 May 2012.

108 *Stephen v IC and Legal Services Commission*, IT, 25 February 2009. This provision has since been repealed: see not Legal Aid, Sentencing and Punishment of Offenders Act 2012 ss 33, 34.

109 *Commission for Local Administration in England v IC*, IT, 11 March 2008; *Edmunds v IC*, IT, 20 May 2008; *Gore v IC and Local Government Ombudsman*, FTT, 23 March 2012.

110 *Bluck v IC*, IT, 7 October 2009.

111 *Meunier v IC and National Savings and Investments*, IT, 5 June 2007. This provision has since been repealed: see now National Savings (No 2) Regulations 2015 reg 82.

112 *Higginson v IC*, IT, 2 May 2006. This provision has since been repealed. The Police Reform Act 2002 ss 20-21 now require all complainants and other persons to be kept reasonably informed (but see s 21A which, when it comes into force, will restrict the disclosures of sensitive information).

113 *Thomas v IC*, FTT, 16 March 2011.

114 *Dept of Health v IC*, IT, 18 November 2008. These provisions have since been repealed: see no Public Contract Regulations 2015 reg 21, which applies 'without prejudice to' FOIA.

115 *Smyrl v IC and Statistics Board*, FTT, 3 April 2012.

— Representation of the People Act 1983 s 66(3) (which prohibits disclosure of information as to voting);
— Civil Procedure Rules 1998 rule 31.22 (which controls the subsequent use of documents disclosed in civil litigation).

The precise wording of all these statutory provisions varies substantially from enactment to enactment and it is essential that consideration is given to the precise terms of the prohibition in order to see whether it applies.[116] Often, legislation creates offences if certain categories of information are disclosed by members or employees of a public authority without lawful authority or excuse and/or otherwise than in the course of their duties and/or otherwise than for specified purposes and/or without the consent of specified persons and/or for prohibited purposes and such legislation often contains defences which apply if the defendant can show a subjective belief that he had lawful authority or that he did not know that the information came within the relevant category.[117] In many such cases it might be argued that the prohibition does not apply to a disclosure by the public authority at all or that if the public authority as a body was able to decide, in response to a specific request, that information should be disclosed notwithstanding the other exemptions in Part II, there would also be lawful authority for disclosure by an individual civil servant or officer on behalf of the public authority.[118] In some cases Ministers are given express powers effectively to prohibit the disclosure of information on the grounds of national security, or commercial confidentiality or simply the 'public interest'.[119]

35– 019 Jurisprudence

Where a statutory provision, in proscribing the disclosure of particular information, provides a saving for any power or duty to disclose that information, the information will nevertheless fall within s 44(1): the right conferred by s 1 is not shaped[120] to survive the proscription.[121] Equally, where a provision allows disclosure for the purpose of enabling a public authority to discharge its statutory functions, such functions will not be taken to include those under FOIA

116 For example, the definition of 'confidential information' must be considered by reference to the statute in question and cannot be equated with that in FOIA s 41: *British Union for the Abolition of Vivisection v SSHD* [2008] EWHC 892 (QB); *British Union for the Abolition of Vivisection v SSHD* [2008] EWCA Civ 870, [2009] 1 All ER 44, [2009] 1 WLR 636; *Rowland and FSA v IC*, IT, 3 April 2009 at [15]. See further *Cubells v IC and Wrightington, Wigan & Leigh NHS Foundation Trust*, FTT, 30 May 2012, where the prohibition on disclosure contained in the Health Service Commissioners Act 1993 s 15 was held to govern the actions of the Health Service Ombudsman only, and not to apply to those who had supplied information to the Ombudsman. In *R (Privacy International and others) v HMRC* [2015] EWHC 1475 (Admin), [2015] 1 WLR 397at [51] Green J observed that information 'is not exempt from disclosure under section 18(2) CRCA if and so far as it meets the test therein. In other words whether or not disclosure is to be made is governed by the CRCA 2005 not FOIA.'

117 See, eg, Census Act 1920 s 8; Finance Act 1989 s 182; Official Secrets Act 1911 s 1; Armed Forces Act 2006 s 17.

118 The DCA appears not to have appreciated this point when drafting the Freedom of Information (Removal and Relaxation of Statutory Prohibitions on Disclosure of Information) Order 2004 (SI 2004/3363): see eg s 59 of the Offices Shops and Railway Premises Act 1963 and s 154 of the Factories Act 1961 which clearly only apply to the actual individuals who have obtained information in the course of inspections and allow such an individual to disclose such information 'in the performance of his duty' but which were nevertheless the subject of amendment by SI 2004/3363 by the introduction of ss 59A and 154A respectively which disapply ss 59 and 154A where the disclosure is made by or on behalf of a public authority for the purposes of the FOIA. Both provisions have since been repealed. In *Meunier v Information Commissioner and National Savings & Investments*, IT, 5 June 2007, the Information Tribunal assumed there was no difference between a disclosure by the public authority and disclosure by a person employed by that public authority. In practice, the answer will often be that the public authority cannot have a disclosure save through an act of a member of its staff.

119 See, eg: Parliamentary Commissioner Act 1967 s 11(3); Environment Act 1995 s 113(3)(b); Airports Act 1986 s 30(7).

120 See §1– 003.

121 *Dey v Information Commissioner and Office of Fair Trading*, IT, 16 April 2007.

itself.[122] In the case of information which may only be disclosed with the consent of specified persons, the Tribunal has decided that, although public authorities may be expected to take steps to obtain such consent, if consent is required for disclosure and it has not been obtained the disclosure remains prohibited and s 44(1)(a) of FOIA applies to exempt the information from disclosure.[123] Where the statutory prohibition is subject to a discretion on the part of the public authority to disclose or involves an exercise of judgment on its part whether certain conditions enabling disclosure are properly met, the decision on the part of the public authority upon the application of the underlying statutory prohibition can only be challenged by way of an application for judicial review.[124] The Information Commissioner's powers do not include the power to assess whether or not a public authority's decision to exercise its powers in a particular way is unreasonable or otherwise unlawful. The Commissioner's powers are limited to verifying whether the exercise required by the Act has been correctly carried out by the public authority in question.[125] In turn, the Tribunal's powers on appeal are limited to assessing the legality of the Commissioner's decision.[126] Thus, an application for judicial review is the proper means of challenging the legality of a public authority's understanding and its application of its statutory powers and discretions.[127] In rare cases, a statutory bar may be enacted between the date at which an initial request is considered by a public authority and the date at which any complaint about the handling of the request is subsequently considered by the Information Commissioner. If the new statutory bar would have the effect that the public authority would be acting unlawfully in disclosing information in response to any decision notice from the Commissioner, then, even though the authority would not have been acting unlawfully had it made disclosure when originally requested, the Commissioner has a discretion not to require the public authority to take any steps in response to the request.[128]

---

122 *Slann v IC and FSA*, IT, 11 July 2006 at [37]-[38]; *Dumfries and Galloway C v Scottish IC* [2008] CSIH 12, 2008 SC 327; *Smyrl v IC and Statistics Board*, FTT, 3 April 2012 at [21]. Indeed, FOIA s 44 refers to 'disclosures otherwise than under this Act.'

123 See *Slann v Information Commissioner and Financial Services Authority*, IT, 11 July 2006, which dealt with a prohibition in s 348 of the Financial Services and Markets Act 2000.

124 There are many statutes which contain a general bar on the disclosure of information by a public authority unless that public authority considers that a particular test is met or a defined exception applies. An example is the Communications Act 2003 s 393, which prohibits the disclosure of information relating to a particular business obtained in the exercise of the statutory functions of the Office of Communications (OFCOM) unless the disclosure is 'for the purpose of facilitating the carrying out by OFCOM of any of [its] functions.' When assessing whether the statutory bar contained in a provision such as s 393 applies so as to engage the exemption under FOIA s 44, the question whether the conditions exist to bring the statutory exception into operation can be highly controversial. The requestor may wish to assert that the disclosure would further or 'facilitate' the carrying out of OFCOM's functions and, thus, the disclosure sought is not prohibited by the enactment relied upon. In *OFCOM v Morrissey and IC* [2011] UKUT 116 (AAC) at [47], [58], [62]-[63], the Upper Tribunal held that, in considering the Communications Act 2003 s 393(2), it was for OFCOM to decide whether disclosure would facilitate the exercise of one of its functions; if OFCOM decided that it did not, it was not within the powers of the Commissioner to assess whether that decision was irrational or otherwise unlawful.

125 See *OFCOM v Morrissey and IC* [2011] UKUT 116 (AAC) at [47], [58], [62]-[63], overruling *Hoyte v IC and CAA*, IT, 5 March 2008 in which the FTT had concluded that the Commissioner and the Tribunal could investigate whether the exercise of discretionary power to disclose, or to refuse to disclose, information was within the range of reasonable responses open to it or was Wedenesbury unreasonable: see *Associated Provincial Picture Houses Ltd v Wednesbury Corporation* [1947] EWCA Civ 1, [1947] 1 KB 223, [1947] 2 All ER 680. The Upper Tribunal noted in *OFCOM v Morrissey and IC* [2011] UKUT 116 (AAC) that the FTT in *Hoyte* had not been faced with any argument as to its jurisdiction to embark on a Wednesbury review of the public authority's discharge of its statutory discretionary powers.

126 FOIA s 58. The Tribunal must consider whether the notice against which the appeal is brought is not in accordance with the law or, to the extent that the notice involved the exercise of a discretion by the Commissioner, whether he ought to have exercised his discretion differently. See further §§45– 014 and 45– 014.

127 See, for example, *R (Privacy International and others) v HMRC* [2015] EWHC 1475 (Admin), [2015] 1 WLR 397.

128 *IC v HMRC and Gaskell* [2011] UKUT 296 (AAC), construing the Commissioner's powers under FOIA s 50(4).

35– 020 Human Rights Act 1998

It has been argued that the Human Rights Act may itself, through a combination of section 6 and Articles 6 or 8 of the ECHR, prohibit disclosure of certain information by public authorities. This argument was considered by the Information Tribunal in *Bluck v Information Commissioner*.[129] Although not necessary for its decision (because it found that the information was exempt under section 41 of FOIA), the Tribunal expressed the view that the general principles laid down by Art 8 of the Convention could not be elevated to the status of a specific legal prohibition of the type which section 44 was designed to uphold, and that the principles in Art 8 had already been taken account of in considering whether the information was confidential so that section 41 would apply to make it exempt.

35– 021 Comparative legislation

In contrast to the position in other jurisdictions, the section applies to 'any enactment' rather than to enactments that are expressly listed in the Act concerned.[130] There is no provision, as in Ireland, for particular enactments to be listed as not applying.[131] Nor, unlike the position in New Zealand, is there an express requirement for the decision-maker who relies on the section to specify the enactment relied on.[132] On the other hand, in some ways this exemption in the Freedom of Information Acts is narrower in scope than in some of the comparable legislation. Thus, the enactment must 'prohibit' the disclosure rather than 'restrict' it, as is the case in Canada and New Zealand;[133] and there is no scope for continued reliance on statutory provisions which give the public authority a discretion whether to disclose information or not, as is the case in the United States and Ireland.[134]

35– 022 Review, repeal or amendment

The Government stated during the passage of the Freedom of Information Bill that it would review all existing statutory prohibitions to disclosure and would repeal or amend any which on consideration could no longer be justified.[135] This intention found expression in s 75 of FOIA, which enables the Secretary of State to repeal or amend any enactment by order[136] if it appears that by virtue of s 44(1) the enactment is capable of preventing the disclosure of information under the Act.

35– 023 Removing statutory prohibitions

Section 75 of FOIA empowers the Secretary of State for Justice and the Minister for the Cabinet Office each to repeal or amend the enactment 'for the purpose of removing or relaxing the prohibition.'[137] Section 75(2) expressly defines 'enactment' for the purposes of the section

---

129 *Bluck v IC and Epsom & St Helier University NHS Trust*, IT, 17 September 2007 at [31]-[32].

130 Compare Access to Information Act (Canada) s 24(1) and Sch II and Freedom of Information Act 1982 (Cth of Australia) s 38(1)(b).

131 See Freedom of Information Act 2014 (Ireland) s 41(1).

132 See Official Information Act 1982 (New Zealand) s 18(c)(i). In practice this is very likely to happen in any event in the United Kingdom by reason of FOIA s 17(1)(c) and FOI(S)A s 16(1)(d).

133 See Access to Information Act (Canada) s 24(1); Official Information Act 1982 (New Zealand) s 52(3)(b)(i).

134 See: Freedom of Information Act, 5 USC 552(b)(3)(A)(i); Freedom of Information Act 2014 (Ireland) s 41(1)(b).

135 See Hansard, Standing Committee B, Freedom of Information Bill, 1 February 2000, col 385 per David Lock (Parliamentary Secretary, Lord Chancellor's Dept) and Hansard HL vol 617 col 905 (17 October 2000) (Lord Falconer).

136 Subject to approval by a resolution of each House of Parliament (FOIA s 82(2)(b)) or the Scottish Parliament (FOI(S)A s 72(2)(b)).

137 The Secretary of State's power is exercisable concurrently with the Chancellor of the Duchy of Lancaster: Transfer

as any enactment contained in an Act passed before or in the same Session as FOIA and any enactment contained in Northern Ireland legislation or subordinate legislation passed or made before the passing of the Act. It is therefore clear that the power does not relate to legislation passed after FOIA; this is presumably on the basis that Parliament and other legislators will be expected to take account of the principles enshrined in FOIA when passing new legislation. There is an ambiguity in s 75(2)(b) as to whether the subordinate legislation there referred to is only Northern Ireland subordinate legislation; it may be that the draftsman did intend this result on the basis that there would automatically be power to amend or repeal United Kingdom secondary legislation without the need for the express power[138] but this is unlikely to arise as an issue in practice. There is a similar power in FOI(S)A, which allows Scottish Ministers to repeal or amend an enactment for the same purposes 'in so far as it relates to any Scottish public authority.'[139] Subject to that limitation it is clear that the Scottish Ministers have power under the section to amend by order provisions in a United Kingdom Act of Parliament.[140] To date, the power to repeal or amend enactments under these provisions has only been exercised twice, by the Freedom of Information (Removal and Relaxation of Statutory Prohibitions on Disclosure of Information) Order 2004,[141] which deals with eight Acts of Parliament, and by the Freedom of Information (Relaxation of Statutory Prohibitions on Disclosure of Information) (Scotland) Order 2008[142] in relation to Scottish public authorities.

35– 024 Government review

The last word in relation to the Government's review was a report entitled 'Review of Statutory Prohibitions on Disclosure' which was published by the Department of Constitutional Affairs in June 2005. The report stated that there were 238 statutory provisions which had been identified as potentially operating as bars to disclosure but which on further consideration had been found not to operate in this way (in the case of 116 of them this was because they had been repealed or amended by other legislation in the course of the review).[143] 210 statutory provisions were identified as prohibiting disclosure under FOIA. Of these, 20 implement international confidentiality obligations and cannot therefore be removed; 7 were passed after FOIA and could not therefore come within s 75; 13 were amended or repealed by the Freedom of Information (Removal and Relaxation of Statutory Prohibitions on Disclosure of Information) Order 2004; 40 were to be amended or repealed and 19 time limited by further orders under s 75; the balance of 111 would be retained for reasons set out in the report or were still under review. The main expressed reasons for retaining prohibitions were as follows: the provision protects information obtained under compulsion (this not being a ground of exemption under the Freedom of Information Acts); the provision applies to organisations which are not subject to FOIA and it would not be practical to have different regimes in force; the provision implements an international obligation; the provision is limited and there is a partial access regime provided in the relevant legislation. Notwithstanding the expressed intention to amend, repeal or time limit a number of provisions, only the two orders mentioned in the preceding paragraph have been passed.

---

of Functions (Information and Public Records) Order 2015 art 3(2)(d).

138 See Interpretation Act 1978 s 14.

139 See FOI(S)A s 64.

140 See definition of 'enactment' in FOI(S)A s 64(2).

141 SI 2004/3363.

142 SI 2008/339.

143 Most notably by the Enterprise Act 2002 which according to the MoJ report at page 3 repealed or amended a large number of statutory prohibitions on disclosure and replaced them with a single coherent access regime for consumer information.

5. INCOMPATIBILITY WITH EU OBLIGATIONS

35– 025 Introduction

Section 44(1)(b) of FOIA confers an absolute exemption on information the disclosure of which (but for any obligation under the Act itself) is incompatible with any EU obligation.[144] 'EU obligation' is defined as any obligation created by or arising under the Treaties (as defined in the European Communities Act 1972), whether an enforceable EU obligation or not:[145] such obligations comprise any legal obligation in the Treaties or emanating from any of the European institutions whether or not they are directly enforceable without further enactment in the United Kingdom.[146] An example of such a provision is Art 19 of the European Council Directive of 23 April 1990 on the deliberate release into the environment of genetically modified organisms.[147] This Article provides that the competent authorities in the Member States (which would be 'public authorities' under the Freedom of Information Acts) shall not divulge to third parties any confidential information notified to them under the Directive[148] and that, if a notification under the Directive is withdrawn, the competent authorities must respect the confidentiality of information supplied.[149] If the relevant information comes within the terms of the prohibition in the Directive there is no question of applying the public interest test as there would be if the public authority were applying, say, the exemption in s 43 of Freedom of Information Act 2000 ('commercial interests'), though of course it must be recognised that the concept of 'confidentiality' itself is somewhat elastic and the decision whether information is confidential may itself involve public interest considerations.[150]

35– 026 EU Regulation 1049/2001

The House of Commons Public Administration Committee expressed concern about s 44(1)(b): the Committee said that they considered the European rules on disclosure of information to be too restrictive.[151] After the publication of the Committee's Report, the European Parliament and Council adopted Regulation 1049/2001 of 30 May 2001 regarding access to European Parliament, Council and Commission documents.[152] This is considered in more detail

144 See the remarks made at §§ 35– 015 to 35– 016.

145 See: Interpretation Act 1978 s 5 and Sch 1 and European Communities Act 1972 s 1 and Sch 1 Pt II.

146 See European Communities Act 1972 s 2(1) for definition of 'enforceable Community obligation'. Article 10 of the EC treaty requires Member States to abstain from any measure which jeopardises the attainment of the Treaty's objectives. Note that once the provisions of a directive have been enacted into UK law (eg the Financial Services and Markets Act 2000 (Disclosure of Confidential Information) Regulations 2001 SI 2001/2188 implementing provisions of the Investment Services Directive (93/22/EEC)) any prohibition on disclosure will come within s 44(1)(a) as well as s 44(1)(b).

147 Council Directive 90/220. Another example is the Medical Devices Directive 93/42/EC Art 20.

148 Article 19(1).

149 Article 19(5). European jurisprudence acknowledges that the protection of confidential business information is a general principle against which rights of access must be balanced: *AKZO Chemie BV v EC Commission* (C-53/85) [1986] ECR 1965, [1987] 1 CMLR 231, [1987] FSR 203 at [28]; *Samenwerkende Elektriciteits-Produktiebedrijven NV v EC Commission* (C-36/92 P) [1994] ECR I-1911 at [37]; *Varec SA v Belgium* (C-450/06) [2009] All ER (EC) 772, [2008] ECR I-581, [2008] 2 CMLR 24 at [49]; *Productores de Musica de Espana (Promusicae) v Telefonica de Espana SAU* (C-275/06) [2008] All ER (EC) 809, [2008] ECR I-271, [2008] 2 CMLR 17 at [43], [57], [61]-[63], [68]-[70].

150 See §§34– 024 to 34– 027.

151 See House of Commons *Public Administration Committee Third Report 1998-9 Session* (Cm 4355, 1999) para 111.

152 The Regulation entered into force on 3 December 2001 and is binding in its entirety and directly applicable in all Member States.

elsewhere in this work,[153] but in brief the Regulation provides a right of access to documents of the institutions subject to exceptions set out in Art 4. Article 5 of the Regulation provides a special regime for documents held by Member States which originate from a European institution. In view of the supremacy of European law, this special regime would apply in place of the provisions of the Freedom of Information Acts in relation to requests for access to such documents or information contained therein. Unless it is clear under the terms of the Regulation that a particular document or information should or should not be disclosed, the Member State must consult the institution concerned in order to take a decision on the matter or may simply refer the matter to the institution concerned. Articles 4(1), (2) and (3) provide that access to a document must be refused in the circumstances there set out. That proscription would therefore engage s 44(1)(b) of FOIA so as to defeat the domestic rights conferred by s 1. Although the exceptions in the Regulation are broadly similar to the exemptions provided in the Freedom of Information Acts, they are not identical.[154] Accordingly, the information that must be disclosed under the Regulation will not be exactly the same as the information that must be disclosed under FOIA. In particular, the question of where the public interest lies in a particular case will be a matter not for the public authority in the United Kingdom but for the Community institution and, ultimately, the European Court of Justice. It should also be noted that if disclosure is required under the Regulation it must be given even if under the Freedom of Information Acts it could have been refused.

6. CONTEMPT OF COURT

35– 027 Introduction

Information whose disclosure by the public authority holding it would constitute or be punishable as a contempt of court is exempt from disclosure under the Freedom of Information Acts.[155] This exemption appears to give precedence to the policy of preventing interference with the administration of justice (which is the underlying policy of the law of contempt of court) over the policy of free disclosure of information held by public authorities (which is the policy underlying the Freedom of Information Acts).[156] It should be noted that in many cases, the exemption provided by s 44(1)(c) of FOIA will also be provided by another provision in Part II, though generally the other provision will be subject to the public interest test in s 2.[157] There is no directly equivalent exception in the EIR. Accordingly, where (or to the extent that) information that answers the terms of a request for information is 'environmental information',[158] the fact that disclosure of that information would constitute or be punishable as a contempt of court will not excuse the public authority from complying with the request.[159] However, in such circumstances it may, depending on the facts, be arguable that disclosure would adversely affect 'the course of justice'.[160] In that case, subject to a consideration of the

153 See §§43– 016 to 43– 054.

154 See §43– 017.

155 FOIA s 44(1)(c); FOI(S)A s 26(c). See the introductory comments made at §§35– 015 to 35– 016.

156 See *AG v Times Newspapers Ltd* [1974] AC 273 at 294E (Lord Reid) for a discussion of the public policy underlying the law of contempt and its interaction with the public interest in freedom of speech.

157 This applies in particular to the exemptions provided by ss 30(1)(c), 31(1)(c), 32, 40, 41, 42 and 43; the same comment applies mutatis mutandis in relation to FOI(S)A ss 33, 34(1)(c), 35(1)(c), 36, 37 and 38.

158 As to the meaning of which, see §17– 011.

159 FOIA s 39; FOI(S)A s 39.

160 EIR reg 12(5)(b); EI(S)R reg 10(5)(b).

public interest balancing exercise, the public authority would be excused from its duty to disclose the information.[161] There are provisions similar to s 44(1)(c) in the freedom of information statutes in Australia,[162] New Zealand[163] and Ireland.[164] Although this exemption has not much featured in the jurisprudence arising out of FOIA,[165] a brief introduction of the relevant law and an account of how in practice it might apply to the Act follow.

35– 028 The law of contempt

The law of contempt can be highly technical and uncertain and is largely governed by common law rules.[166] The ECHR often plays an important role.[167] A person's guilt or innocence of contempt can depend on subjective knowledge and intent and on the practical effect of the act concerned and may be dependent on such questions as whether the legal proceedings concerned are civil or criminal, what stage they have reached, whether there is a jury, and the extent to which any information is already in the public domain. Proceedings are generally taken at the behest of the Attorney-General who has to make a fine judgment in the public interest as to whether they are appropriate.

35– 029 Classification of contempts

Contempt of court can arise in a myriad of ways. The traditional classification into 'civil' and 'criminal' contempts is no longer helpful. Of greater assistance is a re-classification into (a) conduct which involves a breach, or which assists in a breach, of a court order and (b) any other conduct which involves an interference with the due administration of justice, either in a particular case or, more generally, as a continuing process, the first category being a special form of the latter, with such interference being a characteristic common to all contempts. In general, breach of a court order is treated as a matter for the parties to raise by way of complaint to the court, whereas other forms of contempt are considered to be a matter for the Attorney-General to raise as guardian of the public interest in the administration of justice.[168] The Phillimore Report on the law of contempt[169] divided contempts between:

(a) 'contempt in the face of the court', for example, throwing missiles at the judge, insulting persons in court, demonstrating in court; and

(b) 'contempt out of court', subdivided into:

  (i) reprisals against witnesses after the conclusion of proceedings;

  (ii) 'scandalising the court', for example, abusing a judge *qua* judge or attacking his impartiality or integrity;[170]

---

161 EIR reg 12(1); EI(S)R reg 10(1).

162 Freedom of Information Act 1982 (Cth of Australia), s 46(a).

163 Official Information Act 1982 (New Zealand) ss 18(c)(ii) and 52(1).

164 Freedom of Information Act 2014 (Ireland) s 31(1)(b).

165 There appears to be a single Tribunal decision: *Nadarajah v IC*, FTT, 14 July 2015.

166 Notwithstanding the Contempt of Court Act 1981. For a more detailed account of the law of contempt, reference should be made to the authoritative texts: D Eady and A Smith, *Aldridge, Eady & Smith on Contempt*, 5th edn (London, Sweet & Maxwell, 2019); Borrie and Lowe, *The Law of Contempt*, 4th edn (London, LexisNexis, 2010); CJ Miller, *Contempt of Court*, 4th edn (Oxford, Oxford University Press, 2017). For a general account see *Halsbury's Laws of England*, vol 4 (2019) 'Contempt of Court.'

167 In particular, Arts 6 (fair trial), 8 (private life) and 10 (freedom of expression): see *Sunday Times v UK* (1979-80) 2 EHRR 245; *Goodwin v United Kingdom* (1996) 22 EHRR 123; *Omar v France* (2000) 29 EHRR 210; *Daltel Europe Ltd (In Liquidation) v Makki (Committal for Contempt)* [2006] EWCA Civ 94, [2006] 1 WLR 2704; *Hammerton v UK* (2016) 63 EHRR 23.

168 See *AG v Newspaper Publishing Ltd* [1988] Ch 333 at 362 (Donaldson MR).

169 Report of the Committee on Contempt of Court (Cmnd.5794, 1974).

170 This has since been abolished as a form of contempt: Crime and Courts Act 2013 s 33. Conduct which would

(iii) disobedience to court orders;

(iv) conduct, whether intentional or not, liable to interfere with the course of justice in particular proceedings.[171]

Disclosure of information by a public authority is only ever likely to constitute a contempt under (b)(iii) or (iv) in this classification, by being contrary to a court order or undertaking or by tending to prejudice proceedings or to undermine the administration of justice.

35–030 Application of s 44(1)(c)

As has been pointed out,[172] the application of this difficult area of law will have to be carried out in the first instance by the decision-maker in the relevant public authority or the Information Commissioner. This task is not made easier by the fact that the precise circumstances of the assumed disclosure by the public authority are not made clear by the section. What is clear, however, is that it is the act of disclosure by the public authority itself which must constitute the act of contempt (rather than possible acts by the recipient of the information,[173] although knowledge of the intentions of the recipient may be relevant). It is also clear that in order for the exemption to apply there must be almost certainty that a contempt will be committed.[174]

35–031 Practical examples

Cases where the exemption may apply are as follows:

(1) The most obvious and straightforward example would be a case where there is an order addressed directly to, or an undertaking[175] given expressly by, the public authority in question forbidding it from disclosing the relevant information:[176] in these circumstances there would clearly be no obligation to disclose it pursuant to a request made under Freedom of Information Act 2000 as to do so would almost certainly constitute a contempt of court.[177]

(2) If a public authority is a party to litigation it will be subject to the implied undertakings as to the use of disclosed documents which are now codified in CPR 31.22: to disclose a document or the information contained therein in breach of the terms of that rule would almost certainly constitute a contempt of court.[178]

(3) A public authority with the requisite knowledge and intent could also be in contempt of court if it disclosed information whose disclosure by another party was

---

previously have constituted 'scandalising the court' might still amount to contempt in the face of the court, or otherwise interfere with the course of justice in particulars proceedings.

171 See *The Sunday Times v UK* (1979) 2 EHRR 245 at 257.

172 See §§35–015 to 35–016.

173 See *Altman v Family Court of Australia* (1992) 15 AAR 236 (Administrative Appeals Tribunal) at [38].

174 The section requires that disclosure would constitute or be punishable as a contempt: see the discussion in relation to the New Zealand legislation in I Eagles, M Taggart & G Liddell, *Freedom of Information in New Zealand* (Auckland, Oxford University Press, 1992), at p 456.

175 As to undertakings, see *Halsbury's Laws of England*, vol 4 (2019) 'Contempt of Court,' para 83.

176 Such information is also likely to come within one or more other exemptions: eg under FOIA s 40 (personal information), s 41 (information provided in confidence), or s 43 (commercially sensitive information). See *Nadarajah v IC*, FTT, 14 July 2015 (where disclosure would have put the MOJ in breach of a court order designed to maintain the confidentiality of information disclosed in the course of judicial review proceedings brought against one of the MOJ's executive agencies).

177 Assuming, of course, that the public authority was aware of the order and its terms: see *Halsbury's Laws of England*, vol 4 (2019) 'Contempt of Court,' para 85.

178 See, eg: *Home Office v Harman* [1983] 1 AC 280; *Alterskye v Scott* [1948] 1 All ER 469. The information may well also be exempt information under FOIA s 41 and such disclosure would probably also be exempt under s 44(1)(a) as being prohibited by CPR 31.22.

in breach of an injunction or undertaking, on the basis either that it was aiding and abetting the third party's breach of the order or undertaking[179] or, in the case of an interlocutory order or undertaking preventing the disclosure of information which may be confidential, on the basis that the disclosure destroyed the confidentiality which it was the purpose of the order or undertaking to preserve and that there had therefore been an interference with the administration of justice.[180]

(4) It is a contempt of court under the 'strict liability rule' to publish information which creates a substantial risk that the course of justice in particular proceedings will be seriously impeded or prejudiced[181] if the proceedings are 'active' (regardless of intent):[182] however, it seems unlikely that a public authority complying with a request for information under the Freedom of Information Acts would be committing such a contempt since the disclosure of any such information would be unlikely to constitute a 'publication' for the purposes of the 'strict liability rule'.[183] It may be that if the public authority knew that a journalist or news organisation seeking formation intended to publish it in breach of the 'strict liability rule', disclosure by the public authority would amount to a contempt by aiding and abetting, which would allow the public authority to refuse disclosure under s 44(1)(c).[184]

(5) It is also a contempt of court to create a real risk of prejudice to the administration of justice (regardless of whether the proceedings are active) with the intention of doing so.[185] Since this form of contempt normally takes the form of a publication to the public and since it is hard to see how the public authority, if it had the relevant intent, would seek to rely on it in order to avoid the very disclosure which it intended to make, it seems most unlikely that this form of contempt would ever be relevant for the purposes of the Freedom of Information Acts.

(6) There are numerous specific statutory restrictions on the reporting of criminal and civil proceedings whose breach may also amount to a contempt of court.[186] Again, there will be a question whether disclosure of the information by the public authority itself pursuant to a request under the Freedom of Information Acts would

---

179 On aiding and abetting, see *Halsbury's Laws of England*, vol 4 (2019) 'Contempt of Court,' para 90.

180 See, on this form of contempt: *AG v Times Newspapers Ltd* [1992] 1 AC 191; *Jockey Club v Buffham* [2003] QB 462; *AG v Punch Ltd* [2002] UKHL 50, [2003] 1 AC 1046, [2003] 1 All ER 289. Note that information in this category is likely to be exempt under FOIA s 31(1)(c).

181 The forms of information which might have this effect are numerous, including: information inducing bias in the court (eg information on the personal character or antecedents of an accused which would tend to influence a jury, information as to alleged confessions, comments on the merits of litigation or the court by the Government); information prejudicing the court's ability to determine the true facts (eg comments tending to discourage witnesses or to affect the content of their evidence, information as to without-prejudice offers in civil litigation, reports of private investigations or interviews with witnesses); information tending to discourage or deter a litigant from pursuing litigation.

182 Contempt of Court Act 1981 ss 1-5.

183 A publication must be 'addressed to the public at large or any section of the public': see Contempt of Court Act 1981 s 2(1).

184 The factual hypothesis is perhaps unlikely; if these circumstances applied, the public authority would probably be able to rely on FOIA s 31(1)(b) or (c) and/or s 30(1)(c).

185 See Contempt of Court Act 1981 s 6(c) and *AG v News Group plc* [1989] QB 110; *AG v Hislop* [1991] 1 QB 514; *AG v Sport Newspapers Ltd* [1991] 1 WLR 1194: the precise scope of this form of contempt is not at all clear.

186 See *Halsbury's Laws of England*, vol 4 (2019) 'Contempt of Court,' paras 38-39; Magistrates' Court Act 1980 s 8C; Criminal Justice Act 1987 s 11; Sexual Offences (Amendment) Act 1992 s 1; Children and Young Persons Act 1933 s 39; Youth Justice and Criminal Evidence Act 1999 ss 44 and 45, Administration of Justice Act 1960 s 12. In theory, these statutory provisions might give rise to a prohibition on disclosure by or under an enactment for the purposes of s 44(1)(a) of FOIA, but the act of disclosure itself is unlikely to amount to publication (though if the journalist was known to have the relevant intention it might amount to aiding and abetting the relevant offence).

involve publishing it sufficiently widely so as to breach such a restriction, but knowledge of an intention to do so by a journalist or news organisation seeking the information is likely to mean that the public authority could rely on s 44(1)(c) on the basis that such disclosure would amount to aiding and abetting such a breach.[187] In this context it should also be noted that the court itself has various powers to make orders binding on the world which restrict the publication of information concerning criminal or civil proceedings[188] and that a breach of such orders would also constitute a contempt of court. The same comments apply in relation to such orders as to the statutory provisions mentioned above.

35– 032 Disclosure as contempt

Section 44(1)(c) of Freedom of Information Act 2000 also exempts information whose disclosure by the public authority would 'be punishable as a contempt of court'. Various statutes provide that where a person does anything in relation to a particular tribunal which, if it were a court, would amount to a contempt of court, the tribunal can certify that fact to a court and the court can investigate the matter and punish the person as if they had committed a contempt of court.[189] It is thought that the words 'punishable as a contempt of court' are designed to deal with actions which would be caught by this kind of provision. Given that the tribunals in question may have limited powers to grant injunctions and given that they are unlikely to be easily influenced by publications in the way that a jury would, it seems unlikely that this provision would arise for consideration very often.

[187] And no doubt it could also rely on FOIA ss 30 and/or 31.

[188] Note in particular Contempt of Court Act 1981 ss 4(2) and 11 (examples of information which the court has power to withhold from the public apart from those provided by statute are secret processes and the name of complainants in blackmail cases (*R v Socialist Worker* [1975] QB 637)), Children and Young Persons Act 1933 s 39 and the inherent power of the Family Division of the High Court in certain circumstances to make orders which protect children from publicity (see: *Re S* [2004] UKHL 47, [2005] 1 AC 593, [2004] 4 All ER 683).

[189] See, eg: Armed Forces Act 2006 s 311; Parliamentary Commissioner Act 1967 s 9.

Part VI

Other Rights to Information

CHAPTER 36

Historical records and public records

1. BACKGROUND

36–001 Introduction

A 'public record' may be described as a document created by a government or a department of government in the course of the business of government.[1] Such a description in a historical context necessarily begs a number of questions. The business of government varies over time: at some moments it may be thought to show an undue interest in men's souls; at other moments an indifference bordering on callousness. The historian AJP Taylor reckoned that until August 1914 a sensible, law-abiding Englishman could pass through life and hardly notice the existence of the State, beyond the post office and the policeman.[2] Since 1914 the position has changed dramatically. The extent of government business and the quantity of records generated by it

[1] A specific definition of 'public record' is given in the FOIA s 84, which picks up the definition in the Public Records Act 1958 s 10 and Sch 1: see §36–030.

[2] The opening line in AJP Taylor, *English History, 1914-1945*, Oxford History of England, vol 15, rev edn (Oxford, Oxford University Press, 1976) p 1.

have hugely increased. Furthermore, the means by which records can be maintained have also changed dramatically in the last 50 years. Nonetheless, what constitutes 'government' varies in context; for the mass of the population, until comparatively recently, what mattered in government was what occurred locally.

36–002 Medieval records

After the Norman Conquest there was, just as before 1066, no separation of records into those which might (according to later lights) have been classified as 'personal' to the King and those classified as 'public'.[3] All records were simply the King's personal records created in the course of the business of governing his kingdom. Likewise, such records as were kept by feudal lords derived from their position in feudal society or the maintenance of their estates and were their personal records which simply happened to have been created in the course of governing a feudal society. The King carried on his business in a peripatetic manner, taking with him his exchequer, personal belongings and records. Documents were conveyed in large chests.[4] The Domesday Book[5] (1086) was one such record of the King and is now regarded as the best-known public record in England. It was, in effect, a government survey of William's realm of England.[6] The Domesday Book, as a record of public inquisition or survey, remains admissible as evidence of boundaries.[7] It was compiled by royal commissioners and contains a general survey of most of the counties of England. It specifies the name and local position of every place, its possessor both in the reign of King Edward the Confessor and at the time of the survey with particulars,[8] quantities and descriptions of the land. It is, principally, manors which are described in the Domesday Book, England being at the time of the survey (and for some time thereafter) largely divided into manors.[9] Some northern counties and the cities of London and Winchester, which were not within manors, are not within the Domesday Book.

36–003 State records

Royal administration, which was inseparable from the governance of the State, came to develop and grow in complexity. It also became more centralised, with others (notably the King's justices) travelling on the King's business. Records, by way of copies, came to be necessary so that instructions (for example, by a writ) could be conveyed, but knowledge maintained centrally. In addition, records of the royal income and expenditure were maintained. In this regard it can be observed that the essential purpose of the Domesday Book was the

---

3 For a more comprehensive treatment of the history of public records in Great Britain, reference should be made to: CP Cooper, *An Account of the Most Important Public Records of Great Britain, and the Publications of the Record Commissioners: Together With Other Miscellaneous, Historical, and Antiquarian Information. Compiled From Various Printed Books and Manuscripts*, (London, Baldwin & Cradock, 1872); JD Cantwell, *The Public Record Office 1838-1958* (London, The Stationery Office, 1991); JD Cantwell, *The Public Record Office 1959-1969* (Richmond, The Public Record Office, 2000).

4 Some of which are preserved in The National Archives in Kew, near Richmond, Surrey TW9 4DU.

5 The document references for Domesday in The National Archives are E31/1 and E31/2. It consists of one folio volume of 382 pages and one quarto volume of 450 pages. The name 'Domesday' is from Old English 'Dom', meaning judgment.

6 However, it is not the oldest document held at The National Archives; that is an Anglo-Saxon land deed dated 974. However, if this and other such deeds are regarded as private records, then the Domesday Book is the oldest public record held by The National Archives.

7 *Iveagh v Martin* [1961] 1 QB 232 at 238; *Brackenborough v Spalding UDC* [1942] AC 310 at 313; *Nicholls v Ely Beet Sugar Factory* [1931] 2 Ch 84 at 89; *Harris v Earl of Chichester* [1911] AC 623 at 629, 632; *AG v Simpson* [1901] 2 Ch 671 at 688, 700; *Merttns v Hill* [1901] 1 Ch 842 at 850, 854; *Duke of Beaufort v John Aire & Co* (1904) 20 TLR 602; *Alcock v Cooke* (1829) 5 Bing 340.

8 The Anglo-Saxon Chronicle for 1085 records that no pig was left out.

9 C Jessel, *Law of the Manor* (Chichester, Barry Rose Law Publishers, 1998).

establishment of the terms of a new rating system to protect and enlarge the King's Revenue:[10] information is seldom obtained simply for the sake of obtaining information, no more than books are written simply for the sake of writing. Copies were made on parchment, that is to say on cleaned, dried and smoothed sheepskin. Copies were enrolled, ie sheets of parchment were sewn together to create rolls,[11] for easy carriage and storage. Departments of State gradually developed. The Exchequer was concerned with the financial side of medieval government and the Chancery was concerned with the administrative side. There was no systematic archiving of these records once their immediate use had passed. In the Tudor period the various secretaries of state retained many important state papers when they left office. In order to prevent this leakage and to make some permanent provision for the custody and arrangement of these papers, in 1578 the State Paper office was established. In the early eighteenth century the House of Lords established an inquiry into domestic records. As was the way, the inquiry proceeded through the reigns of Anne and George I. Before its conclusion, the House of Commons commenced its own inquiry, producing, some 30 years later, a report which observed that there were no indexes to the records and that such catalogues that did exist were incomplete. Another committee was appointed; but little was done over the following 40 years.

36– 004 Public record office: history

In all this time, no measures had been taken for the housing of the increasing mass of records. The casual or adventitious nature of storage created difficulties as to both access and maintenance. The usual places in which these records were stored,[12] such as the Chapter House at Westminster, the Tower of London and the stables in Holborn, were too small to contain the increasing mass of records, as well as being ill-suited to the purpose. That said, the purpose was not as it is today. From time to time, records might be consulted to resolve some legal controversy, but:

> ..except for these practical purposes they had hardly ever been consulted. Occasionally, indeed, historians had arisen who refused to base their story upon any but the best evidence. For the majority the study of the records under the then existing conditions was, to use Prynne's expression, too "heroic".[13]

The House of Commons committee, which had been appointed some 40 years earlier, produced a report; and the report prompted the appointment of a Record Commission in 1800 to investigate the state of the public records. Its minute book for June 28, 1809 has the following entry:

> On Wednesday the 28th of June, 1809, and the three following days, Mr Meaking of the Chirographer's Office brought and delivered into the Record Office at the Chapter House ten large cartloads of the transcript of Fines, each load being about one ton weight, and the number of bundles being about fourteen hundred.... Some of these bundles were brought from the Temple Church, where, from the dampness of the place, and a constant accumulation of filth and dirt, many of them are rendered almost completely useless, and many half-destroyed through lying in the wet, whereby they are become so fixed together as not to be separated without breaking them in pieces. The smell arising from the sad condition they were in rendered the arrangement of them etc very disagreeable and unhealthy.[14]

---

10 See C Platt, *Medieval England: A Social History and Archaeology from the Conquest to AD 1600* (London, Routledge and Kegan Paul, 1978). The 'Domesday Book' was for some time used as a term to denote any book containing a list of the rateable value of land: see *Lumsden v Inland Revenue Commissioners* [1914] AC 877 at 897, 900; *Commissioners of Inland Revenue v Herbert* [1913] AC 326 at 348, 351, 356.

11 Hence, the office of 'Master of the Rolls'.

12 There were over 60 such places by the beginning of the nineteenth century.

13 W Holdsworth, *A History of English Law in Sixteen Volumes*, vol 5, 4th edn (London, Methuen, 1936) p 601.

14 W Holdsworth, *A History of English Law in Sixteen Volumes*, vol 5, 4th edn (London, Methuen, 1936) p 600.

The Commissioners reported in 1819,[15] as did a Select Committee in 1822,[16] and their work led to the passage of the Public Record Office Act 1838. This was the first legislation to protect public records by the creation of an official archive.

36–005 The Public Record Office

Section 8 of the Public Record Office Act 1838 established the Public Record Office under the direction of the Master of the Rolls. The principal concern of the Public Record Office Act 1838 was to make provision for the records of the Exchequer, Chancery and other ancient courts of law. The Record Office when first constituted was supposed to exist for the sake of litigants who wanted copies of documents, rather than for historians.[17] The records were brought together in a single repository, administered by professional staff in a new government department. The site chosen was a place where records had since the thirteenth century been stored and was the redundant chapel of a hostel called Domus Conversarium. Situated in Chancery Lane, it had been a lodging house for Jews who had converted to Christianity. However, all Jews had been expelled from England in 1290 and the chapel, thereby superfluous, was then converted and used for storage of the rolls of Chancery. The Master of the Rolls came to live on the site, which became known as the Rolls Estate. The Public Record Office Act 1838 created no compulsion for the transfer of records to the Public Record Office. Many records were given to the Public Record Office, but no selection occurred and some material was worthless. The Public Record Office Act 1877 authorised the destruction of such documents, provided that they did not predate 1715.

36–006 The Public Records Act 1958

As the business of government developed over the next hundred years or so, there was a corresponding growth in the quantity of records. This necessitated a reconsideration of the regime which had been established in 1838. A parliamentary committee was established under Sir James Grigg.[18] The recommendations of that committee in 1954 led to the Public Records Act 1958, which remains the principal piece of legislation governing the operations of The National Archives. As its long title records, it was an Act to make new provision with respect to public records and the Public Record Office and for connected purposes. Accordingly, the 1958 Act repealed the Public Record Office Acts 1838 to 1898.[19] One of the matters dealt with in the Public Records Act 1958 was public access to public records. In general terms, the approach taken under the 1958 Act was to refuse access to records that were less than 50 years old (reduced in 1967 to 30 years old) held by the Public Record Office (ie The National Archives), but to extend the refusal period where disclosure 'could or might constitute a breach of good faith on the part of the Government.'[20] Whilst having a certain simplicity about it, the vagueness of such a determinant of access did not sit comfortably with a prescriptive scheme of disclosure created by the new regime that FOIA brought into effect from 1 January 2005. The FOIA regime replaced the access regime conferred by s 5 of the Public Records Act 1958.

---

15 Reports from the Commissioners Appointed to Execute the Measures Recommended by the Committee of the House of Commons, Respecting the Public Records of the Kingdom with an Account of their Proceedings.

16 Report from the Select Committee on Public Records of the Kingdom.

17 W Holdsworth, *A History of English Law in Sixteen Volumes*, vol 5, 4th edn (London, Methuen, 1936) pp 601-602.

18 Later, Lord Altrincham.

19 That being the collective title for the Public Record Office Act 1838, the Public Record Office Act 1877 and the Public Record Office Act 1898. The 1898 Act enabled worthless documents created between 1660 and 1715 to be destroyed.

20 Public Records Act 1958 s 5.

36– 007 Effect of FOIA: summary

The regime introduced by FOIA reinforced the distinction between the obligation on a public authority to provide access to official information and the obligation on a public authority to preserve certain information. In summary, with effect from 1 January 2005:

— rights of access to official information, and the corresponding duty on a public authority to disclose, are dealt with exclusively through FOIA, regardless of whether that information is contained in a public record, regardless of the age of the information, and regardless of whether it has been transferred to a records authority (such at The National Archives);

— obligations relating to the preservation of records remain governed by the Public Records Act 1958.[21]

In relation to an individual's right to access official information, the starting position is the ordinary one under FOIA: ie, the Act confers a right of access to information held by public authorities (which includes The National Archives), the profile of which right is shaped by a series of exemptions and, where an applicable exemption is not absolute, by a public interest balancing exercise. In the case of 'environmental information,'[22] the corresponding right of access and the correlative obligation on the public authority are to be found in the EIR. To this starting position, FOIA effects two important modifications in relation to information contained in a 'record.' The Act does not define what a 'record' is, but it contemplates that all recorded information will be 'contained in' a record.[23]

(1) First, FOIA introduces the concept of an 'historical record.' Under FOIA, a record becomes an 'historical record' at the end of the period of 20 years beginning with the year following that in which that record was created.[24] In this way, where a record has become an 'historical record' all the information contained in that record is to be treated under a modified FOIA regime, regardless of when that information was added to that record. The modified FOIA regime has a significantly reduced range of potential exemptions by comparison with the unmodified FOIA regime, and the range further reduces as the historical record gets older. This modified FOIA exemption regime is considered further below[25]

(2) Secondly, where a public authority has, at the time that a request for information is received, transferred information to a 'records authority,'[26] FOIA modifies the process by which that request will be responded to. Ordinarily, where a public authority receives a request for information, that public authority will decide for itself which exemptions apply to the information captured by the request, as well as the outcome of the public interest balancing exercise for the non-absolute exemptions. The public authority will do so regardless of the source of the information that it holds, including information sourced from another public authority. But for the modifications to the decision-making process, this would mean that if a request for information were received by a records authority (such as The National Archives), it would be that

---

21 Considered in §§36– 029 to 36– 042 below.

22 As to the meaning of which, see §17– 011.

23 FOIA ss 63, 64, 65. This appears to have been a nodding reference to the term 'record' as defined in the Public Records Act 1958, s 10. FOIA further contemplates that the collection of information that constitutes a 'record' might itself be be 'kept together in one file or other assembly': FOIA s 62(2). In this case, 'all the records in that file or other assembly are to be treated...as having been created when the latest of those records was created': FOIA s 62(2).

24 FOIA s 62(1).

25 At §§36– 008 to 36– 012.

26 This will most often be The National Archives.

records authority which would decide for itself whether to invoke an exemption and, in the case of an applicable non-absolute exemption, whether the public interest in upholding that exemption outweighed the public interest in disclosing the information. FOIA recognises that in this situation a records authority might not be best placed to evaluate which exemptions apply to information held by it or to determine the outcome of the public interest balancing exercise. Accordingly, in relation to a request for information received by a records authority, FOIA provides for a special consultative requirement and a special procedure for determining the public interest balancing exercise. The modified decision-making process is considered below.[27]

2. FOIA AND HISTORICAL RECORDS: EXEMPTIONS

36– 008 Introduction

The harm to a protected interest[28] that is likely to result from the disclosure of information will usually diminish with the age of that information. And, at some point, the level of harm or the likelihood of that harm resulting from disclosure will sufficiently diminish so as no longer to provide inadequate policy basis for the applicable exemption to defeat an applicant's entitlement to have access to the information. Rather than leave the determination of the moment at which this point is reached to individual decision-making, FOIA acknowledges the usual effect of time on the likelihood of resultant harm and on the degree of resultant harm by providing that certain exemptions in FOIA fall away according to the age of the information. However, rather than doing this by direct reference to the age of information itself – which could be difficult to ascertain[29] – FOIA does this by reference to the age of the 'record' containing the information.[30] Operation of the modified FOIA arrangement in relation to information contained in historical records thus involves identifying:

- what is a 'record';
- the moment at which a record becomes an 'historical record'; and
- whether a particular exemption that would otherwise be applicable has fallen away because of the age of the record containing the information.

The modifications effected by Part VI (ss 62-67) of FOIA vary according to the exemption that would otherwise be applicable to information captured by a request that is contained in an historical record. Further, the modifications to exemptions from the access right differ from the modifications from the existence right.[31] There is no comparable falling away of exceptions in relation to 'environmental information.'[32]

36– 009 'Record': meaning

FOIA does not define what a 'record' is, but it is apparent from ss 63-66:

- that information[33] will be contained in a 'record,'

[27] At §§36– 013 to 36– 020.

[28] That is, to an interest protected by an exemption in FOIA.

[29] For example, deciding whether time began from the moment of authoring the information, the moment when it was last amended, the moment when it was first acquired by the public authority etc.

[30] Defined in FOIA s 62(1).

[31] That is, the right conferred by FOIA s 1(1)(b) and 1(1)(a) respectively.

[32] As to the meaning of which, see §17– 011.

[33] That is, information recorded in any form: FOIA s 84.

- that a 'record' is something that is created on an identifiable date, and
- that a 'record' is something that can be transferred to a records authority.

It is also apparent that a record may 'for administrative purposes' be 'kept together in one file or other assembly.[34] In this way, FOIA taxonomizes what falls to be considered into 'information' (the smallest unit), 'records' (which by age can become 'historical records') and 'files or other assemblies' (being records created at different dates but which are for administrative purposes kept together). It is difficult to foresee any situation – apart from information held by a public authority recorded on a sheet of paper just left lying around in its premises – not being contained in a record. Whether that record forms part of one file 'or other assembly' should normally be apparent from the manner in which the record is arranged and, if at all, linked to another record or records.

36– 010 'Historical record': meaning

Section 62 of FOIA introduces the concept of 'historical record.' A record, for the purposes of Part VI of the Act, becomes a historical record at the end of 20 years beginning with the year[35] following that in which the record was created. Up until 1 January 2013 that period had been 30 years.[36] The original period of 30 years appears to have been selected in the light of the period that the Public Records Act 1958 had prescribed for the commencement of access under the regime it created.[37] Importantly, a record becomes an historical record regardless of whether it is a public record. Nor does transfer of the record to a records authority (eg The National Archives) have any bearing on whether it has become an historical record.[38] The sole determinant of whether a record has become a 'historical record' is the date on which the record was created. Thus, a record that has been accepted by The National Archives for preservation[39] will constitute a 'historical record' on ly if the age requirements of s 62 are met. Where records are created at different dates but are kept together in one file or other assembly, all the records are to be treated as having been created when the latest of those records was created.[40]

36– 011 Modified exemptions: access

So far as the access right is concerned, the modifications in respect of information contained in an historical record are as follows:[41]

Section	Exemption	Modification	Takes effect from	Source
21(1)	Otherwise available information	Not exempt information under this section	The record being held by the Public Record Office or the Public Record Office of Northern Ireland	64(1)

[34] FOIA s 62(2).

[35] A year is a calendar year: FOIA s 62(3).

[36] Section 46 of the Constitutional Reform and Governance Act 2010 effected the change. Transitional arrangements for records created between 1984 and 2001 (inclusive) are provided for in The Freedom of Information (Definition of Historical Records) (Transitional and Saving Provisions) Order 2012 SI 2012/3029.

[37] The subsections in s 5 of the Public Record Act 1958 that were repealed with effect from 1 January 2005.

[38] As is recognised by FOIA s 65.

[39] See §36– 033.

[40] FOIA s 62(2); FOI(S)A s 57(2).

[41] A reference to years in the table means the number of calendar years after the end of the calendar year of in which the record containing the information was created.

22(1)	Future publication	Not exempt information under this section	The record being held by the Public Record Office or the Public Record Office of Northern Ireland	64(1)
22A(1)	Research	No modification		
23(1)	Security bodies	Ceases to be an absolute exemption	The record being held by the Public Record Office or the Public Record Office of Northern Ireland	64(2)
24(1)	National security	No modification		
26(1)	Defence	No modification		
27(1)	International relations	No modification		
27(2)	International confidences	No modification		
28(1)	Internal relations	Not exempt information under this section	30 years	63(2C)
29(1)	The economy	No modification		
30(1)	Investigations & proceedings	Not exempt information under this section.	20 years	63(1)
30(2)	Confidential investigations material	No modification		
31(1)	Law enforcement	Not exempt information under this section.	100 years	63(4)
32(1)	Court records	Not exempt information under this section.	20 years	63(1)
32(2)	Inquiries & arbitrations	Not exempt information under this section.	20 years	63(1)
33(2)	Audit functions	Not exempt information under this section.	20 years	63(1)
34(1)	Parliamentary privilege	No modification		
35(1)	Government policy etc	Not exempt information under this section.	20 years	63(1)
36(2)	Prejudice to governmental work	Not exempt information under this section, apart from: (a) a case falling within s 36(2)(a)(ii); (b) a case falling within s 36(2)(c) where the prejudice or likely prejudice relates to the effective conduct of public affairs in Northern Ireland.	20 years	63(2A)
		Not exempt information in the two cases excepted above	30 years	63(2C)
37(1)	Royal family communications	Not exempt information under s 37(1)(a)-(ad)	The later of 5 years following the death of the person referred to in paragraphs (a)-(ac) or the reigning Sovereign (in the case of (ad)) and 20 years	63(2E)

		Not exempt information under s 37(1)(b)	60 years	63(3)
38(1)	Health & safety	No modification		
39(1)	Environmental information	No modification		
40(1)	Requester's personal information	No modification		
40(2)	Another's personal information	No modification		
41(1)	Information provided in confidence	No modification		
42(1)	Legal professional privilege	Not exempt information under this section.	20 years	63(1)
43(1)	Trade secret	Not exempt information under this section	30 years	63(2C)
43(2)	Prejudicial to commercial interests	No modification		
44(1)	Prohibition on disclosure	No modification		

36– 012 Modified exemptions: existence

So far as the existence right is concerned, the modifications in respect of information contained in an historical record are as follows:[42]

Section	Exemption	Modification	Takes effect from	Source
22(2)	Future publication	No modification		
22A(2)	Research	No modification		
23(5)	Security bodies	No modification		
24(2)	National security	No modification		
26(3)	Defence	No modification		
27(4)	International relations etc	No modification		
28(3)	Internal relations	Exemption disapplied	30 years	63(2D)
29(2)	The economy	No modification		
30(3)	Investigations & proceedings	No modification		
31(3)	Law enforcement	Exemption disapplied	100 years	63(5)
32(3)	Court etc records	No modification		
33(3)	Audit functions	Exemption disapplied	20 years	63(2)
34(2)	Parliamentary privilege	No modification		
35(3)	Government policy etc	No modification		
36(3)	Prejudice to governmental work	Disapplied, apart from: (a) a case falling within s 36(2)(a)(ii); (b) a case falling within s 36(2)(c) where the prejudice or likely prejudice relates to the effective conduct of public affairs in Northern Ireland.	20 years	63(2B)
		Disapplied in the two cases excepted above	30 years	63(2D)
37(2)	Royal family communications	No modification		
38(2)	Health & safety	No modification		

42 A reference to years in the table means the number of calendar years after the end of the calendar year of in which the record containing the information was created.

39(2)	Environmental information	No modification		
40(5)(a)	Requester's personal information	No modification		
40(5)(b)	Another's personal information	No modification		
41(2)	Information provided in confidence	No modification		
42(2)	Legal professional privilege	Exemption disapplied	20 years	63(2)
43(3)	Prejudicial to commercial interests	Exemption disapplied	30 years	63(2D)
44(2)	Prohibition on disclosure	No modification		

3. FOIA AND HISTORICAL RECORDS: DECISION-MAKING

36– 013 Introduction

Ordinarily, whenever a request for information is made of a public authority, it is that public authority which makes the disclosure decision in relation to all information answering the terms of the request which is held by it, irrespective of whether the information originated from another public authority. A request may be transferred by one public authority to another public authority: where this occurs, the receiving public authority will determine the request solely according to the information that it holds.[43] But for s 15 of FOIA, the ordinary position would have had the result that if a request for information were made of The National Archives,[44] it would have been The National Archives that would have determined the request in relation to all information held by it, including records previously transferred by a public authority to The National Archives under the Public Records Act 1958. As will be seen, FOIA, displaces the usual decision-maker only for the purposes of weighing the public interest and allocates decision-making responsibility on that point to the 'responsible authority'. There is thus a division of decision-making responsibility between The National Archives and the 'responsible authority'. It is first necessary to consider the four terms used by FOIA to secure this division of responsibility:

— 'transferred public record';
— 'responsible authority';
— 'appropriate records authority'; and
— 'open information'.

The EIR secures the same objective in relation to 'environmental information' contained in a historical record.[45]

36– 014 Designation: 'open information'

Where a public authority transfers a record (ie a set of recorded information) to The National Archives or another place of deposit, that public authority must consider whether that record should be released to the public: in other words, transferred as 'open'.[46] In reviewing a record for public release, a public authority must ensure that records become available to the public

---

43 In relation to transfers, see §§22– 033 to 22– 034.

44 Or another place of deposit appointed by the Lord Chancellor under the Public Records Act 1958 or the Public Records Office of Northern Ireland.

45 EIR reg 17; EI(S)R reg 15.

46 Section 46 Code of Practice, paras 18.1 and 18.3.

at the earliest possible time.[47] The public authority must consider which exemptions are applicable to the information in the record and whether the public interest supports the release of the information notwithstanding the applicability of an exemption.[48] If the outcome of the review is that records are to be transferred as open, the public authority should designate the records as 'open'. There is no formal review of this designation by The National Archives.[49] Where the public authority identifies specific information in the record which it considers ought not to be released under the terms of FOIA, it should prepare a schedule identifying this information precisely, citing the relevant exemption(s), explaining why the information may not be released and identifying a date at which either release would be appropriate or a date at which the case for release should be reconsidered.[50] A public authority must consider whether the exempt information could be redacted from the record and the remainder made open.[51] The public authority must then send its schedule to The National Archives for review and advice.[52] The Advisory Council then considers the case in favour of withholding the records for a period longer than 20 years.[53] The Advisory Council may respond: (a) by accepting that the information may be withheld for longer than 20 years and earmarking the records for release or review at the date identified by the authority; (b) by accepting that the information may be withheld for longer than 20 years but asking the authority to reconsider the later date designated for release or review; (c) by questioning the basis on which it is deemed that the information may be withheld for longer than 20 years and asking the authority to reconsider the case; (d) by advising the Lord Chancellor if it is not satisfied with the responses it receives from authorities in particular cases; e) by taking such other action as it deems appropriate within its role as defined in the Public Records Act.[54]

36– 015 'Transferred public record'

Section 15(4) of FOIA introduces the concept of a 'transferred public record'. The term is imported into the EIR for the purposes of 'environmental information'.[55] A 'transferred public record' is a public record[56] that has been transferred to The National Archives, to another place of deposit appointed by the Lord Chancellor under the Public Records Act 1958 or to the Public Record Office of Northern Ireland. Thus, when a public record is transferred from a public authority to The National Archives (or to another place of deposit, etc) it remains a 'public record' for the purposes of the Public Records Act 1958, but is labelled a 'transferred public record' for the purposes of FOIA. As noted earlier, not all information held by The National Archives is a public record: the Office can accept and hold material that is not a public record;[57] by definition such material will not be a 'transferred public record'.[58] In relation to

47 Section 46 Code of Practice, para 15.2.

48 Section 46 Code of Practice, para 18.1(a)-(b).

49 Section 46 Code of Practice, para 18.3.

50 Section 46 Code of Practice, para 18.4. And similarly in relation to 'environmental information' with the applicable exceptions in the EIR being identified.

51 Section 46 Code of Practice, para 18.5.

52 Section 46 Code of Practice, para 18.6.

53 The period was, until 1 January 2013, 30 years. Transitional arrangements apply in relation to records created between 1984 and 2001 (inclusive): see further §36– 039.

54 Section 46 Code of Practice, para 18.6.

55 EIR reg 2(1); but not EI(S)R.

56 'Public record' means public record as defined by the Public Records Act 1958: see §§36– 030 to 36– 031.

57 See §36– 033.

58 FOIA s 15(4). There is a broadly similar regime in FOI(S)A s 22.

this non-public record material held by The National Archives (or other place of deposit, etc), all decision-making for the purposes of FOIA remains with The National Archives (or other place of deposit, etc).[59] It should also be noted that the division of responsibility is not confined to 'historical records': it applies equally to public records that are not historical records but that have been transferred to The National Archives (or other place of deposit, etc).

36– 016 'Responsible authority'

Section 15(5) of FOIA defines 'responsible authority' by reference both to the party transferring the public record and to the destination of the transferred public record. The term is imported into the EIR for the purposes of 'environmental information'.[60]

(1) In the case of a public record transferred from a government department either to The National Archives or to a place of deposit appointed by the Lord Chancellor, the 'responsible authority' is the Minister of the Crown who appears to the Lord Chancellor to be primarily concerned.

(2) In the case of a public record transferred from any person other than a government department either to The National Archives or to a place of deposit appointed by the Lord Chancellor, the 'responsible authority' is the person who appears to the Lord Chancellor to be primarily concerned. Bearing in mind the wide definition given to 'public record',[61] it is readily apparent that that person may not be a public authority within the meaning of FOIA.[62] In this situation, that person is deemed to be a public authority, with certain consequential obligations which are discussed below.[63]

(3) In the case of a record transferred to the Public Record Office of Northern Ireland from a government department in the charge of a Minister of the Crown, the responsible authority is that minister of the Crown who appears to the appropriate Northern Ireland Minister[64] to be primarily concerned. If the transfer is from a Northern Ireland department then the responsible authority is the Northern Ireland Minister who appears to the appropriate Northern Ireland Minister to be primarily concerned. If the record was transferred from any other person then the responsible authority is the person who appears to the appropriate Northern Ireland Minister to be primarily concerned.[65]

36– 017 'Appropriate records authority'

Section 15(5) of FOIA identifies the Public Record Office (ie The National Archives) as 'the appropriate records authority' in relation to public records transferred to The National Archives. The term is imported into the EIR for the purposes of 'environmental information'.[66] In relation to a transferred public record transferred to a place of deposit appointed by the Lord Chancellor, the 'appropriate records authority' is the Lord Chancellor; if the record is in the Public Record Office of Northern Ireland, then 'the appropriate records authority' is the Public

---

59 On the basis that it will be treated as 'information held by a public authority' (ie The National Archives), but without the modifications effected by the FOIA in relation to transferred public records.

60 EIR reg 2(1); but not EI(S)R.

61 See §§36– 030 to 36– 031.

62 See FOIA ss 3-7.

63 FOIA s 66(6). As to those obligations, see §§36– 019 to 36– 020. The obligations can be lightened by simply designating all the information 'open information'.

64 That is, the Northern Ireland Minister in charge of the Department of Culture, Arts and Leisure in Northern Ireland: FOIA s 84.

65 The same remarks as in (2) apply in relation to a person that is not a 'public authority' within the meaning of the FOIA.

66 EIR reg 2(1); but not EI(S)R.

Record Office of Northern Ireland.

36– 018 'Open information'

Section 66 of FOIA contains the only reference in the Act to 'open information'.[67] The term is not defined,[68] but the operation of ss 15, 65 and 66 allows its meaning to be discerned. 'Open information' is information contained in a transferred public record that the responsible authority has, at some stage prior to the receipt by The National Archives of a request relating to that information, designated as 'open information'. The process by which this is done has already been described.[69] The designation of such information as 'open information' has the result[70] that The National Archives, when it receives a request for information contained in a transferred public record:

(a) need not consult the responsible authority in relation to a determination of whether that information is 'exempt information' (in other words, a determination whether the information falls within one or more of the provisions of Part II of the Act);
(b) need not consult the responsible authority in relation to a determination of whether the duty to confirm or deny that the information requested is held (or would be held) has been excluded by one or more of the provisions of Part II of the Act;
(c) retains for itself the task of balancing the public interest where the information is subject to a qualified exemption; and
(d) retains for itself the task of balancing the public interest where the exclusion of the duty to confirm or deny is a qualified exclusion.

It should be borne in mind that the designation of information as 'open information' by the responsible authority does not dictate the determination by The National Archives of matters (a)-(d). However, where the information has been designated as 'open information', then, if the information is contained in a historical record that is a public record, The National Archives must first consult the Lord Chancellor before refusing to disclose the information solely on the basis of a qualified exemption.[71]

36– 019 Request: first stage

Where The National Archives receives a request under FOIA that relates to information that is contained in a 'transferred public record', then, after satisfying itself as to the usual formalities for a proper request,[72] The National Archives must, within the usual time allowed for a public authority to answer a request:[73]

(1) identify the information held by it that answers the terms of the request;
(2) in relation to that information, having consulted the responsible authority,[74] determine whether it is 'exempt information' within the meaning of FOIA (in other words, determine whether it falls within one or more of the provisions of Part II of the Act, bearing in mind the age of the record in which the information is contained and the

67 Similarly, EIR reg 17(2).

68 Though it is in EI(S)R reg 15(8).

69 §36– 014.

70 Because the obligations in FOIA s 66(2)-(4) do not arise in relation to information contained in a transferred public record that the responsible authority has designated as open information: FOIA s 66(1). Similarly, EIR reg 17(2).

71 FOIA s 65(1); EIR reg 17(1). Reading ss 65(2) and 66(1) together, it is apparent that s 65 applies to, inter alia, information that the responsible authority has not designated as open information.

72 See §§22– 001 to 22– 011.

73 See §§22– 020 to 22– 027.

74 FOIA s 66(2)(b); EIR reg 17(2). The obligation to consult the responsible authority does not, however, arise if the responsible authority has previously designated the information as 'open information'.

removal of certain of those provisions in relation to a public record that is a historical record[75]);

(3) if any of the information that is determined to be exempt information is only so by virtue of a 'qualified exemption', send a copy of the request to the responsible authority;[76]

(4) where the information is 'exempt information',[77] and again having consulted the responsible authority,[78] further determine whether the duty to confirm or deny that information answering the terms of the request is held by The National Archives has been excluded by one or more of the provisions of Part II of FOIA, again bearing in mind the age of the record in which the information sought is contained and the removal of certain of those provisions in relation to a public record that is (or would be) a historical record;[79]

(5) if the duty to confirm or deny is only excluded by virtue of a 'qualified exclusion' and the request has not been sent under (3), send a copy of the request to the 'responsible authority';[80]

(6) communicate to the applicant any information that is not 'exempt information';[81] and

(7) in relation to any information that is 'exempt information':
   (i) give the applicant a notice under s 17(1); and
   (ii) in relation to any such information in respect of which it is necessary to weigh the public interest, give the applicant a notice as required under s 17(2).[82]

36–020 Request: second stage

By the end of the first stage, The National Archives will have dealt with all information answering the terms of the request, except information that is exempt information only by virtue of a provision conferring a qualified exemption. The second stage of a request received by The National Archives that relates to information contained in a 'transferred public record' is thus concerned with the weighing of the public interest. The way in which this task must be carried out varies according to whether the responsible authority has designated information in question as 'open information' and to whether the duty to confirm or deny has prima facie been excluded:

(1) If the information has been designated as 'open information' and it has been determined in the first stage that the information is exempt information (but only by virtue of a 'qualified exemption'), then The National Archives must determine whether in all the circumstances of the case, the public interest in maintaining the exemption outweighs the public interest in disclosing the information.[83] In so far as the outcome of this exercise is that the public interest weighs in favour of disclosure, then that information must be communicated to the applicant.[84] In so far as the outcome of this exercise is that the public interest weighs in favour of maintaining the exemption, then The National

75 See §36–010.

76 FOIA s 15(1)-(2). In the case of 'environmental information', the responsible authority decides where the public interest lies, having consulted the Lord Chancellor: EIR reg 17(3)-(4).

77 If it is determined not to be exempt information, it will have to be disclosed and the duty to confirm or deny will be taken to be complied with: FOIA s 1(5).

78 FOIA s 66(2)(a). The obligation to consult the responsible authority does not, however, arise if the responsible authority has previously designated the information as 'open information'.

79 See §36–010.

80 FOIA s 15(1)-(2).

81 FOIA s 10(1); EIR reg 17(3)(c).

82 See §24–011.

83 As to the general approach to this task, see §§6–010 to 6–017.

84 FOIA s 11.; EIR reg 5(1).

Archives must first consult the Lord Chancellor[85] and, if that consultation does not cause it to change its mind, give a notice to the applicant stating the reasons for that decision.[86]

(2) If the information has not been disclosed to the applicant under (1) above, then, if it has been designated as 'open information' and it has been determined in the first stage that the duty to confirm or deny does not arise in relation to it (but only by virtue of a 'qualified exclusion'), The National Archives must determine whether in all the circumstances of the case, the public interest in maintaining the exclusion of the duty to confirm or deny outweighs the public interest in disclosing whether The National Archives holds the information.[87] In so far as the outcome of this exercise is that the public interest weighs in favour of disclosing that The National Archives holds the information, then The National Archives must so inform the applicant. In so far as the outcome of this exercise is that the public interest weighs in favour of maintaining the exclusion, then The National Archives must give a notice to the applicant stating the reasons for that decision.[88]

(3) If the information has not been designated as 'open information' and it has been determined in the first stage that the information is exempt information (but only by virtue of a 'qualified exemption'), then the responsible authority[89] must determine whether in all the circumstances of the case, the public interest in maintaining the exemption outweighs the public interest in disclosing the information.[90] In so far as the outcome of this exercise is that the public interest weighs in favour of disclosure, then that information must be communicated to the applicant.[91] In so far as the outcome of this exercise is that the public interest weighs in favour of maintaining the exemption, then the responsible authority must first consult the Lord Chancellor[92] and, if that consultation does not cause it to change its mind, give a notice to the applicant stating the reasons for that decision.[93]

(4) On the footing that the information has not been disclosed to the applicant under (3) above, then, if the information has not been designated as 'open information' and it has been determined in the first stage that the duty to confirm or deny does not arise in

---

85 FOIA s 65(1)(a); EIR reg 17(1)(a).

86 FOIA s 17(3): unless, or to the extent that, the statement would involve the disclosure of information which would itself be exempt information (s 17(4)). Plainly, it would be sensible for the notice to record that the Lord Chancellor had been consulted.

87 As to the general approach to this task, see §§6– 018 to 6– 019.

88 FOIA s 17(3): unless, or to the extent that, the statement would involve the disclosure of information which would itself be exempt information (s 17(4)).

89 By virtue of FOIA s 66(4).

90 As to the general approach to this task, see §§6– 010 to 6– 017. In the case of 'environmental information' this determination is made by the responsible authority: EIR R17(3)(a).

91 FOIA s 11. It is not entirely clear whether it is the responsible authority, rather than The National Archives, that is responsible for informing the applicant of the decision and of communicating the information. Section 66(6) of the FOIA tends to suggest that it is the responsible authority who must do so: if this be correct, presumably it would simply pass over the copy which it had received from The National Archives under s 15(1) or a copy of that copy. On the other hand, s 15(3) tends to suggest that the responsible authority simply makes the determination, leaving execution of that determination to The National Archives. Either way, the responsible authority must inform The National Archives of the determination reached by it in relation to the weighing of the public interest. It is clear that in relation to 'environmental information' the appropriate authority must inform the applicant: EIR reg 17(3)(c).

92 FOIA s 66(5)(a); EIR reg 17(4)(a).

93 FOIA s 17(3): unless, or to the extent that, the statement would involve the disclosure of information which would itself be exempt information (s 17(4)). Plainly, it would be sensible for the notice to record that the Lord Chancellor had been consulted. As to whether it is the responsible authority or The National Archives that must carry into effect the determination, see §36– 013.

relation to it (but only by virtue of a 'qualified exclusion'), the responsible authority[94] must determine whether in all the circumstances of the case, the public interest in maintaining the exclusion of the duty to confirm or deny outweighs the public interest in disclosing whether The National Archives holds the information.[95] In so far as the outcome of this exercise is that the public interest weighs in favour of disclosing that The National Archives holds the information, then the responsible authority must so inform the applicant.[96] In so far as the outcome of this exercise is that the public interest weighs in favour of maintaining the exclusion, then the responsible authority must first consult the Lord Chancellor[97] and, if that consultation does not cause it to change its mind, give a notice to the applicant stating the reasons for that decision.[98]

In all cases, the task must be carried out within a reasonable time[99] and, in any event, within the time specified in the notice given in the first stage.[100]

4. PUBLIC RECORD BODIES

36–021 Public Record Office

The historical background to the Public Record Office (ie The National Archives) has already been outlined. The Public Record Office Act 1958 sets out the powers and duties of the Keeper of Public Records. These seemingly simple provisions belie the complexity of his functions. The National Archives[101] produces a manual, entitled Access to Public Records, which is intended to be a tool for use by those who need to understand the legal basis for the working of the public records system. As is there stated, from the moment of a record's creation to its final archiving in The National Archives, a complex web of legislative provisions, government policy instructions and departmental practices govern how it may be treated. It is the stated principal aim of The National Archives to assist and promote the study of the past in order to inform the present and the future. Whilst this work is not concerned with the preservation obligations as such, their inter-relationship with the rights of access necessitates some understanding of them. Before doing so, however, it is convenient to introduce the protagonists in the archiving of records.

36–022 Keeper of Public Records

Section 1 of the Public Records Act 1958 transferred direction of the Public Record Office from

---

94 By virtue of FOIA s 66(3).

95 As to the general approach to this task, see §§6–018 to 6–019.

96 As to whether it is the responsible authority or The National Archives that must so inform the applicant, see §36–020(3) fn 91.

97 FOIA s 66(5)(a). The astute reader will have noticed that the obligation to consult the Lord Chancellor in relation to a determination neither to confirm nor deny that the information is held does not apply where the information is open information: see s 65(1).

98 FOIA s 17(3): unless, or to the extent that, the statement would involve the disclosure of information which would itself be exempt information (s 17(4)). Plainly, it would be sensible for the notice to record that the Lord Chancellor had been consulted. As to whether it is the responsible authority or The National Archives that must carry into effect the determination, see §36–013.

99 FOIA s 10(3).

100 FOIA s 17(2). It would seem that if there were good, objective reasons why the decision-making body could not determine the matter within the time specified in the earlier notice, then, provided that the decision were nevertheless made within a reasonable time, this would be satisfactory.

101 On 2 April 2003 the Public Record Office and the Historical Manuscripts Commission joined together to form a new organisation called 'The National Archives'.

the Master of the Rolls to the Lord Chancellor. He was made generally responsible for the execution of the Public Records Act 1958 and required to supervise the care and preservation of public records. There was established by s 1(2) an Advisory Council on Public Records to advise the Lord Chancellor on matters concerning public records in general and, in particular, on those aspects of the work of the Public Record Office affecting members of the public who make use of the facilities provided by the Public Record Office (ie The National Archives). The Advisory Council on Public Records now operates within the Advisory Council on National Records and Archives. The Master of the Rolls is chairman of the Advisory Council on Public Records. The other members of the Council are appointed by the Lord Chancellor on such terms as he specifies. By s 1(2A), introduced by FOIA, the matters on which the Advisory Council on Public Records may advise the Lord Chancellor include matters relating to the application of FOIA to information contained in public records which are historical records within the meaning of Part VI of the 2000 Act. Every year the Lord Chancellor must lay before Parliament a report of the work of the Public Record Office. The report has to include any report made to him by the Advisory Council on Public Records. Section 2 of the Public Records Act 1958 empowers the Lord Chancellor to appoint a Keeper of Public Records. The Keeper of Public Records takes charge, under the direction of the Lord Chancellor, of the Public Record Office (ie The National Archives) and of the records in it. Further, the Lord Chancellor may with the concurrence of the Treasury as to numbers and conditions of service appoint such other persons to serve in the Public Record Office as he thinks fit. The Keeper of Public Records has, by s 2 of the 1958 Act, power to do all such things as appear to him necessary or expedient for maintaining the utility of the Public Record Office. In particular, he may:

(a) compile and make available indexes and guides to, and calendars and texts of, the records in the Public Record Office;
(b) prepare publications concerning the activities of and facilities provided by the Public Record Office;
(c) regulate the conditions under which members of the public may inspect public and other records or use the other facilities of the Public Record Office;
(d) provide for the making and authentication of copies of and extracts from records required as evidence in legal proceedings or for other purposes;
(e) accept responsibility for the safe keeping of records other than public records;
(f) make arrangements for the separate housing of films and other records which have to be kept under special conditions;
(g) where the Lord Chancellor gives his approval, lend records for display at commemorative exhibitions or for other special purposes; and
(h) acquire records and accept gifts and loans.

The Public Record Office (Fees) Regulations 2012[102] prescribe the fees which may be charged for inspection, authentication of records in the charge of the Keeper of Public Records and other services given by officers of the Public Record Office.

36– 023 Historical Manuscripts

The Historical Manuscripts Commission[103] was appointed by Royal Warrant dated April 2, 1869. The Commission's terms of reference were revised and extended by a further Royal Warrant given on 5 December 1959. Since then they have been:

— to make enquiry as to the existence and location of manuscripts, including records or

[102] SI 2012/1665 made under s 2(5) by the Lord Chancellor with the concurrence of the Treasury.

[103] The Historical Manuscripts Commission has offices in Quality House, Quality Court, Chancery Lane, London WC2A 1HP. It there provides access to the National Register of Archives and to the Manorial Documents Register.

archives of all kinds, of value for the study of history, other than records which are for the time being public records by virtue of the Public Records Act 1958;
— with the consent of the owners or custodians to inspect and report upon these;
— to record the particulars of such manuscripts and records in a National Register;
— to promote and assist the proper preservation and storage of such manuscripts and records;
— to assist those wishing to use such manuscripts or records for study or research;
— to consider and advise upon general questions relating to the location, preservation and use of such manuscripts and records;
— to promote the co-ordinated action of all professional and other bodies concerned with the preservation and use of such manuscripts and records; and
— to carry out in place of the Public Record Office the statutory duties of the Master of the Rolls in respect of manorial and tithe documents.

Since its inception, the Commission has, in summary, created and maintained:
— The National Register of Archives: a resource for those seeking information on the nature and location of records relating to British history. The National Register of Archives holds over 44,000 unpublished catalogues and listed manuscript collections and has been indexed. The indexes contain 150,000 references, with a further 300,000 connected records and these are available on the Historical Manuscripts Commission website.
— ARCHON: an up to date electronic directory of repositories in the United Kingdom and abroad and a portal to archival resources. ARCHON provides the framework for a virtual UK archival network.
— The Manorial Documents Register: an index to surviving manorial records in England and Wales. The Manorial Documents Register is administered by the Historical Manuscripts Commission on behalf of the Master of the Rolls. Some sections of the Manorial Documents Register have been stored on computer and are available on the Historical Manuscripts Commission website. The Manorial Documents Register records information on the whereabouts of manorial records excluding title deeds. Manorial records survive today in many national and local record offices and in some cases in private hands. The Historical Manuscripts Commission itself holds no manorial records. The Manorial Documents Register is not a register of title to manorial lordships and the Historical Manuscripts Commission does not collect or record information of this nature.
— Archives in Focus: an introduction to archives. It includes information on online archival resources designed for teachers, practical advice on what can be expected and what can be found when visiting a record office and guidance on how archives can be used for family, local and house history.

36–024 The National Archives

On 2 April 2003 the Historical Manuscripts Commission informally merged with the Public Record Office to form The National Archives. The National Archives is, in fact, an umbrella term, with the two bodies remaining distinct for legislative purposes. In October 2006 the Office of Public Sector Information, previously attached to the Cabinet Office, merged with the National Archives. The Office of Public Sector Information, which is responsible for Her Majesty's Stationery Office, performs its role from within the structure of the National Archives. The National Archives is a non-ministerial government department and an executive agency of the Ministry of Justice. Although the legal entity to which the various legal provisions applies remains the Public Record Office, since April 2003 the Public Record Office has functioned as part of The National Archives and has been known by that name.[104] For that reason,

[104] This is reflected in the s 46 Code of Practice.

normally this work uses The National Archives to mean the Public Record Office.

36– 025 Lord Chancellor

The Lord Chancellor is the government minister responsible for The National Archives. On normal policy matters concerning The National Archives, public and other records and the work of the Public Record Office and the Historical Manuscripts Commission he relies on advice from the Keeper of Public Records[105] and from his officials in the Lord Chancellor's Department. Since 1958, as minister responsible for the Public Record Office, he has had the benefit of independent advice on matters relating to public records from his Advisory Council on Public Records. For the moment he remains responsible for these, despite the transfer of certain functions formerly performed by him to the Secretary of State for Justice.[106]

36– 026 Advisory Council

The Advisory Council[107] on National Records and Archives was established by the Lord Chancellor on 2 April 2003. It has advisory functions of its own in relation to strategic and policy matters relating to the National Archives and archival policy. The Advisory Council on National Records and Archives embraces two further bodies, which advise on specific areas: the Advisory Council on Public Records (created by s 1(2) of the Public Records Act 1958) to advise on public records issues; and the Advisory Council on Historical Manuscripts to advise on matters relating to non-public records and manuscripts. All three bodies are chaired by the Master of the Rolls who sits with unpaid members, appointed by the Lord Chancellor, who represent a wide range of different interests, including Parliament, regular users of historical records and owners of private papers. The Council is independent of the Keeper of Public Records. The three Advisory Councils are all advisory Non-Departmental Public Bodies within the remits of the Parliamentary Commissioner for Administration (the Ombudsman), the Commissioner for Public Appointments and the Information Commissioner. None has any executive functions or powers.

36– 027 Role of Advisory Council

The Advisory Council's task is to advise the Lord Chancellor on any subject concerning archives and manuscripts, on issues relating to public access to the public records, and on the preservation of records, archives and manuscripts. It has no role in the day-to-day running of the National Archives, and no authority over the Keeper. The Council will normally meet four times a year, in February, June, October and December. Its most important task is to consider applications from departments for the extended closure of public records beyond the normal 20 years,[108] or for the retention of public records by departments. The Lord Chancellor's practice is never to sign an instrument approving extended closures or retentions until he has received advice on it from the Advisory Council. The reasons for applications are scrutinised closely, and departments may be asked for further justification. This reconsideration can lead to a document being made available after all. The Advisory Council also considers subjects such as the corporate plan of The National Archives and its performance against its objectives and targets; the acceptance by the nation of papers in lieu of tax; the sale and export of

---

[105] Appointed under s 2 of the Public Records Act 1958.

[106] See The Secretary of State for Justice Order 2007 SI 2007/2128. Up until 9 May 2007, the Secretary of State for Constitutional Affairs: see The Secretary of State for Constitutional Affairs Order 2003 SI 2003/1887.

[107] The legal entity is the Advisory Council on Public Records. Since 2003 the Council has functioned as The Advisory Council on National Records and Archives, and that term is used in the s 46 Code of Practice. The Advisory Council's address is: The Advisory Council on National Records and Archives, The National Archives, Kew, near Richmond, Surrey TW9 4DU.

[108] Previously 30 years, and still subject to transitional arrangements: see §36– 010.

historical manuscripts; public services provided by the National Archives and other UK archives; preservation policy for records and manuscripts of all sorts; and the level and fairness of fees. The Advisory Council reports to the Lord Chancellor every year in an annual report by the Master of the Rolls, which is published with the Keeper's Report. On matters of urgency or of particular importance it asks the Master of the Rolls to write to the Lord Chancellor directly.

36– 028 Master of the Rolls

Apart from his continuing responsibility in respect of the Chancery of England, the Master of the Rolls does not have charge and superintendence over, or custody of, any public records. Those public records which prior to the commencement of the 1958 Act were in the custody of the Master of the Rolls were thereafter (save for records of the Chancery of England) in the custody of the Keeper of Public Records or such other officer as the Lord Chancellor might from time to time appoint.

5. THE PRESERVATION OF PUBLIC RECORDS

36– 029 Introduction

The utility of much information, whether official or otherwise, is ephemeral. A public authority will wish to hold information for as long as it appears to have some relevance, or at least potential relevance, to the performance of that public authority's functions. The significance to a public authority of any information held by it will with time generally diminish. If for no other reasons than those of space and management, a public authority will ordinarily wish to cull the 'non-current' information held by it, either by destroying it or by archiving it. As will be seen in this section, the public record regime provides an orderly and defined methodology for doing so which recognises that information that has lost its contemporaneity to a public authority may nevertheless hold a different, residual interest for others. As will be seen in the next section, as particular information 'ages', the grounds for exempting the information from disclosure, which remain founded in FOIA, are reduced to a series of key exemptions.

36– 030 Public records: meaning

The Public Records Act 1958 distinguishes between public and other records. Section 10 provides that the phrase 'public records' has the meaning given by the first schedule to the Act and that the word 'records' includes not merely written records but records conveying information by any other means whatsoever.[109] The term 'records' in the 1958 Act and the term 'information' as defined in s 84 of FOIA are not synonymous.[110] When records for administrative purposes are kept together in one file they are, in consequence of s 10(2), treated for the purposes of the Act as having been created on the date of the last record. The provisions of Sch 1 of the Public Records Act 1958 have effect for determining what constitute public records. A comprehensive list is set out in the Schedule:

(1) The first category is administrative and departmental records belonging to Her Majesty,

[109] See s 46 Code of Practice, para 3, which uses the definition in BS ISO 15489-1:2001 Information and documentation – Records management – Part 1: General, namely 'information created, received and maintained as evidence or information by an organisation or person in pursuance of legal obligations or the transaction of business.'

[110] It is apparent from s 1(2A) of the 1958 Act that 'information' is contained in public records and from 10(1) that 'records' convey information. Further, the s 46 Code of Practice recognises that public authorities hold information other than and beyond the information contained in their records. It appears to suggest that inconsequential information recorded without any intention or expectation that it will be retained or form part of a set of information will not constitute or form part of a 'record.'

whether in the United Kingdom or overseas, in right of Her Majesty's Government in the United Kingdom.[111] This expressly embraces records of, or held in, any department of Her Majesty's Government in the United Kingdom or records of any office, commission or other body whatsoever under Her Majesty's Government in the United Kingdom. This first broad category is subject to a number of exemptions. These cover:

(a) the records of any government department or body which is wholly or mainly concerned with Scottish affairs, or which carries on its activities wholly or mainly in Scotland;

(b) registers, or certified copies of entries in registers, kept or deposited in the General Register Office under or in pursuance of any enactment, whether past or future, which provides for the registration of births, deaths, marriages or adoptions;

(c) except as provided by para 4 of the Schedule (which deals with records of court proceedings) records of the Duchy of Lancaster;

(d) records of the office of Public Trustee relating to individual trusts; and

(e) Welsh public records as defined in s 148 of the Government of Wales Act 2006.[112]

This first category will cover much of what is 'information held by a public authority' within the meaning of FOIA.

(2) The second category of public records is given by way of a table set out at the end of para 3 of the Schedule to the Act. This category is without prejudice to the generality of the first category and embraces the administrative and departmental records of the bodies and establishments set out in the table whether or not they are records belonging to Her Majesty. However, the provisions of para 3 of the Schedule are not taken as applying to records in any museum or gallery listed in the table which are part of its records acquired otherwise than by transfer from or under arrangements with a government department. The table (identifying public records), mentioned above, is divided into two parts. The first is a list of bodies and establishments under government departments and the second is a list of other establishments and organisations. Part I of the table, which has been substantially amended since 1958, includes such bodies as the Agricultural Wages Board

[111] Public Records Act 1958 Sch 1 para 2. For an example of the confusion that sometimes surrounds whether records 'belong' to Her Majesty, see *Kimanthi & ors v FCO* [2018] EWHC 1169 (QB).

[112] The following are defined by s 148(1) as 'Welsh public records':

(a) administrative and departmental records belonging to Her Majesty which are records of the Welsh Assembly Government,

(b) administrative and departmental records of the Auditor General,

(c) administrative and departmental records belonging to Her Majesty which are records of or held in any government department which is wholly or mainly concerned with Welsh affairs,

(d) administrative and departmental records belonging to Her Majesty which are records of any office, commission or other body or establishment under Her Majesty's Government which is wholly or mainly concerned with Welsh affairs in a field or fields in which the Welsh Ministers have functions, or the First Minister or the Counsel General has functions,

(e) administrative and departmental records of the bodies and establishments specified in subsection (2) (but not records of health service hospitals in Wales which are of the descriptions excepted from being public records for the purposes of the Public Records Act 1958 (c 51) in the case of health service hospitals in England), and

(f) any other description of records (other than records of the Assembly or the Assembly Commission or records of any court or tribunal or held in any department of the Senior Courts) which is specified by order made by the Lord Chancellor.

The bodies and establishments specified in s 148(2) are: (a) the Care Council for Wales, (b) the Countryside Council for Wales, (c) the Curriculum and Assessment Authority for Wales, (d) Family Practitioner Committees for localities in Wales, (e) the Further Education Funding Council for Wales, (f) the General Teaching Council for Wales, (g) health service hospitals, within the meaning of the National Health Service (Wales) Act 2006, in Wales, (h) the Higher Education Funding Council for Wales, (i) the Local Government Boundary Commission for Wales, (j) the National Council for Education and Training for Wales, (k) National Health Service Authorities for districts or localities in Wales, or for areas in or comprising Wales, including National Health Service trusts all of whose hospitals, establishments and facilities are situated in Wales, (l) the Qualifications, Curriculum and Assessment Authority for Wales, (m) the Wales Centre for Health, and (n) the Welsh Board of Health.

and the Legal Services Commission. Part II, likewise much amended since 1958, includes such bodies as the Adult Learning Inspectorate and the War Works Commission. The table in the Act should be consulted as necessary, having in mind that by para 3A of the Schedule the table may, by Her Majesty in Council, be amended by adding to either part of the table an entry relating to any body or establishment which is specified in Sch 2 to the Parliamentary Commissioner Act 1967 (ie departments or other bodies subject to investigation) or a body or establishment which could be added to Sch 2 to the Act of 1967.

(3) Records of courts and tribunals constitute the third category of public records.[113] This includes the records of, or held in, a department of the Supreme Court, including records of any proceedings in the court, such as writs and decrees: but it does not include skeleton arguments or trial bundles.[114] Excluded from the scope of this category are records of any court or tribunal whose jurisdiction is restricted to Scotland or Northern Ireland. Records for the purposes of this category include records of any proceedings in the court or tribunal in question and includes rolls, writs, books, decrees, bills, warrants and accounts of, or in the custody of, the court or tribunal in question. Paragraph 4 of the Schedule gives a list of courts and tribunals, which has also been amended since 1958. Further, the Lord Chancellor is given power to designate as public records those records of such other courts and tribunals as he specifies.[115] The list given by para 4 of Sch 1 to the 1958 Act includes records of the Supreme Court, records of, or held in, any department of the Senior Courts (including any court held under a commission of assize); records of county courts; quarter sessions; magistrates' courts; coroners' courts; courts-martial, whether held by any of Her Majesty's Forces in or outside the United Kingdom; naval courts in or outside the United Kingdom under enactments relating to merchant shipping; any court exercising jurisdiction held by Her Majesty within a country outside Her dominions; records of any tribunal having jurisdiction connected with any functions of a department of Her Majesty's Government in the United Kingdom or having jurisdiction in proceedings to which such a Government department is a party; records of the Lands Tribunal or of any Rent Tribunal or Local Valuation Court; of any Conveyancing Appeal Tribunal; of the Industrial Court; of umpires and deputy umpires appointed under the National Service Act 1948 or the Resumption in Civil Employment Act 1944; records of ecclesiastical courts when exercising certain testamentary and matrimonial jurisdictions; and of the Information Tribunal. The Lord Chancellor is, by s 8 of the 1958 Act, responsible for the public records of every court of record or magistrates' court which are not in the Public Record Office or a place of deposit appointed by him under the Act. With the exception of records held by the Supreme Court, the Lord Chancellor is given power to determine in the case of any such records the officer in whose custody they are for the time being to be placed. Under section 8(1A) of the 1958 Act, the chief executive of the Supreme Court has custody of the records of that Court. Section 124 of the Senior Courts Act 1981 requires all original wills and other documents which are under the control of the High Court in the Principal Registry or in any district probate registry to be deposited and preserved in such places as the Lord Chancellor may direct and, subject to the control of the High Court and probate rules, to be open to inspection. There is a particular saving (by s 8(5)) from the selection and transfer provisions of s 3 of the Act in respect of certain records of ecclesiastical courts but

---

113 Public Records Act 1958 Sch 1 para 4.

114 *GIO Personal Investment Services Ltd v Liverpool and London Steamship Protection and Indemnity Association Ltd* [1999] 1 WLR 984 at 992-993.

115 Public Records Act 1958 Sch 1 para 4(1)(o). The power is exercised by order in a statutory instrument.

the Lord Chancellor is able, after consulting the President of the Family Division, to direct their transfer to a place of deposit which he appoints.[116]

(4) Records of the Chancery of England are, other than any which are Welsh public records (as defined in s 148 of the Government of Wales Act 2006[117]), public records for the purposes of the Public Records Act 1958. Subject to the terms of s 7 of the Act, the Master of the Rolls continues to be responsible for, and to have custody of, the records of the Chancery of England and has power to determine where they should be deposited.[118] Section 3 of the Act, which deals with selection and preservation of public records, does not apply to the records of the Chancery of England; nor does s 6(4), which deals with consultation by the Lord Chancellor before appointing a place of deposit, apply. However, if records of the Chancery of England are deposited in the Public Record Office then they are in the custody of the Keeper of Public Records and subject to the directions of the Lord Chancellor, as in the case of any other records in The National Archives.

36– 031 Extension of 'public records'

Paragraphs 6, 7 and 8 of the First Schedule to the 1958 Act extend what is embraced by the definition of public records. Thus, public records include, other than any which are Welsh public records (as defined in s 148 of the Government of Wales Act 2006[119]):

— all records within the meaning of the Public Record Office Act 1838 or to which that Act was applied, which, at the commencement of the Public Records Act 1958,[120] were in the custody of the Master of the Rolls in pursuance of that Act;

— all records within the meaning of the Public Record Office Act 1838 or to which that Act was applied which at the commencement of the Public Records Act 1958 were in the Public Record Office and under the charge and superintendence of the Master of the Rolls; and

— all records forming part of the same series of documents as any series of documents falling under the previous heads. Paragraph 7 of the Schedule enables Her Majesty by order in Council to direct that any class of records (not being Welsh public records within the meaning of s 148 of the Government of Wales Act 2006[121]) not falling within the Schedule shall be treated as public records. No recommendation is to be made to Her Majesty for such an order unless a draft has been laid before Parliament and approved by each House.

Paragraph 7(2) provides that a question whether any records or class of records are public records for the purposes of the Act shall be referred to and determined by the Lord Chancellor who has to include his decisions on such questions in his annual report to Parliament. Furthermore, the Lord Chancellor has from time to time to compile and publish lists of the departments, bodies, establishments, courts and tribunals comprised in paras 2, 3 and 4 of the

---

116 There are certain public records, in the custody of the University of Oxford, included in an index a copy of which was transmitted to the principal probate registrar under s 2 of the Oxford University Act 1860 which are not required to be transferred. However, the Lord Chancellor has to make arrangements with the University of Oxford as to the conditions under which those records may be inspected by the public.

117 See n 112 above.

118 By s 73(1) of the Courts and Legal Services Act 1990 where the Master of the Rolls expects to be absent at a time when it may be appropriate for any relevant functions of his to be exercised he may appoint a judge of the Supreme Court to exercise those functions on his behalf. Relevant functions include functions under s 144A of the Law of Property Act 1922 (functions relating to manorial documents) and functions under s 7(1) of the Public Records Act 1958 (power to determine where records of the Chancery of England are to be deposited).

119 See n 112 above.

120 1 January 1959: Public Records Act 1958 s 13(3).

121 See n 112 above.

Schedule and lists describing more particularly the categories of records which are, or are not, public records as defined in the Schedule. Paragraph 8 of the Schedule declares that any class of government department, court, tribunal or other body or establishment in the Schedule by reference to which a class of public records is framed extends to a government department, court, tribunal or other body or establishment which has ceased to exist whether before or after the passing of the Public Records Act 1958. Further, by virtue of s 8(4) of the Public Records Act 1958 where private documents have remained in the custody of a court in England and Wales for more than 50 years without being claimed, the Keeper of Public Records may, with the approval of the Master of the Rolls, require their transfer to The National Archives, whereupon they become public records. Scotland and Northern Ireland have their own record offices and the National Assembly for Wales has the power to establish one for Wales. If one is established, the Lord Chancellor has power to impose (by statutory instrument) arrangements analogous to those in the Public Records Act 1958. The access regimes in Scotland and Northern Ireland mirror the access arrangements in England.

36– 032 Welsh public records

By s 146(1) of the Government of Wales Act 2006, Welsh public records are not public records for the purposes of the Public Records Act 1958. However, by subs.(2), the Public Records Act 1958 has effect in relation to Welsh public records until an order under s 147 imposes a duty on the National Assembly for Wales to preserve them. No such order has yet been made. Welsh public records are defined in s 148 of the Government of Wales Act 2006.[122]

36– 033 Preservation of other records

The Keeper of Public Records is empowered to accept records which are not public records. This is done where the Keeper is of the view that the records merit permanent preservation, and the body generating the records agrees to deposit them.[123] An agreement is entered into between the body and The National Archives. In relation to access and copying, the agreement renders the deposit similar to that by public record bodies. The organisation making the deposit must carry out the necessary selection and indexing work under the supervision of staff from The National Archives. The ownership of the records and their copyright status remain unaffected by the deposit. The Lord Chancellor is also able (in consequence of s 3(5)), if it appears to him in the interests of the proper administration of the Public Record Office, to direct that the transfer of any class of records shall be suspended until arrangements for their reception have been completed. As will be seen, although such records do not metamorphose into public records, they are 'historical records' with accompanying rights of access.

36– 034 Public records: management

The wide definition given to 'public records' covers the prosaic as well as the principal; and it will do so before any formal decision as to retention has been made by the public authority that brought the record into being. Inevitably, there must be some reduction in this mountain of material. The reduction process is spelled out in Part 1 of the s 46 Code of Practice and in the Public Records Act 1958 (in conjunction with Part 2 of the s 46 Code of Practice). The first secures the 'disposal' of material (including the destruction of day-to-day material that has no enduring significance). The second deals with material that has not been disposed of.

36– 035 Public records: disposal

---

122 See n 112 above.

123 Other records can be deposited with The National Archives, eg: manorial documents, under the Law of Property Act 1922 s 144A; instruments of apportionment, under the Tithes Act 1936 s 36(3); and orders of exchange by the Inclosure Commissioners, under the Inclosure Act 1857 s 5.

Paragraph 8 of the s 46 Code of Practice provides that public authorities must keep the records they will need for business, regulatory, legal and accountability purposes. In deciding what they keep, paragraph 8 requires a public authority to take into account:

— The legislative and regulatory environment within which it operates;
— The need to refer to authoritative information about past actions and decisions for current business purposes;
— The need to protect legal and other rights of the authority, its staff and its stakeholders;
— The need to explain, and if necessary justify, past actions in the event of an audit, public inquiry or other investigation.

Paragraph 12 of the Code provides that each public authority should define how long it needs to keep particular records, that it should dispose of them when they are no longer needed and that it should be able to explain why records are no longer held. 'Dispose' here means destroyed or transferred to an archives service for permanent preservation or presented under s 3(6) of the Public Records Act 1958.[124] The Code provides that a public authority should not keep records (ie the records should be destroyed) after they have ceased to be of use to the authority unless:

(a) The records are known to be the subject of litigation or a request for information. In this case, the public authority should delay destruction until the litigation is complete or, in the case of a request for information, all relevant complaint and appeal provisions have been exhausted.
(b) The records have long-term value for historical or other research and have been or should be selected for permanent preservation.
(c) The records contain or relate to information recently released in response to a request under the Act. This may indicate historical value and a public authority should delay destruction pending a re-assessment of that value.[125]

The Code suggests that disposal of records must adhere to the public authority's policies and disposal schedules.

36– 036 Public records: selection

Section 3 of the Public Records Act 1958 imposes a duty on every person responsible for public records of any description which are not in the Public Record Office or a place of deposit appointed by the Lord Chancellor under the 1958 Act to make arrangements for the selection of those records which ought to be permanently preserved and for their safekeeping. These duties are to be performed under the guidance of the Keeper of Public Records, who is responsible for the co-ordination and supervision of all action taken under s 3. The obligation imposed by the Public Records Act 1958 is in respect of those which ought to be permanently preserved.[126] Current practice has a two-stage selection process. Each government department has a Departmental Record Officer who is responsible for the management of its records.[127] He carries out the selection process under the guidance of The National Archives through the Central Records Management Department. The first review takes place, generally, five years[128] after a departmental file is closed. A public authority should have clearly established policies

[124] Presentation transfers ownership of the records to the receiving body and is undertaken by The National Archives in consultation with the public authority.

[125] Section 46 Code of Practice para 12.3.

[126] Section 3(3) of the Act requires that all public records created before 1660, ie the year of the restoration of the monarchy, be amongst those selected for permanent preservation.

[127] As explained by the National Archives System at: `www.nationalarchives.gov.uk/policy/act/system.htm`.

[128] This period of time is consistent with the policy of opening new files after five years of inactivity rather than adding to an existing file. If one merely added to the existing file, Public Records Act 1958 s 10(2) would, for the purposes of the Act, treat the record as having been created on the last date.

to assist in this task.[129] Records considered to be valueless are destroyed.[130] Those thought possibly necessary in the future for administrative or research purposes are kept for another 15 years. They are then assessed for permanent preservation on second review. Once selected for permanent preservation public records are, subject to a proviso, required to be transferred not later than 20 years after their creation either to The National Archives or to such other place of deposit appointed by the Lord Chancellor under the 1958 Act as the Lord Chancellor may direct.[131] Section 4 of the Act gives the Lord Chancellor power to appoint places of deposit. The proviso given by s 3(4) enables any records to be retained after 20 years if, in the opinion of the person responsible for them, they are required for administrative purposes or ought to be retained for any other special reason. If the person responsible is not the Lord Chancellor, then the Lord Chancellor must be informed of the facts and give his approval. The quantity annually transferred to The National Archives is about 1,830 metres.

36–037 Public records: destruction

Those public records which have been rejected as not required for permanent preservation are destroyed or, in the case of records for which some person other than the Lord Chancellor is responsible, subject to the approval of the Lord Chancellor, are disposed of in any other way. Any question arising under s 3 as to the person whose duty it is to make arrangements under the section with respect to any class of public records is required to be referred to the Lord Chancellor for his decision. If it appears to the Keeper of Public Records that as respects any public records in the Public Record Office (ie The National Archives) or any place of deposit appointed under the Act that they are duplicated by other public records which have been selected for permanent preservation or that there is some other special reason why they should not permanently be preserved, he may, with the approval of the Lord Chancellor and of the minister or other person, appearing to the Lord Chancellor as primarily concerned with public records of the class in question, authorise the destruction of those records or, with the same approval, their disposal in any other way.[132] Section 3 of the 1958 Act, which deals with selection and presentation of public records, does not render it unlawful for the person responsible for any public record to transmit it to the Keeper of the Records of Scotland or to the Public Record Office of Northern Ireland.

36–038 Public records: old regime

Section 5 of the Public Records Act 1958, as originally enacted, kept public records closed to public inspection for 50 years. This was reduced, subject to exceptions, to 30 years by the Public Records Act 1967 which amended s 5 with effect from 1 January 1968. The regime as given by s 5 of the 1958 Act was repealed by FOIA[133] from 1 January 2005. Up until then, access by the public to public records in The National Archives (other than those to which the public had access before their transfer to The National Archives) was not permitted for a period of 30 years beginning with the first day of January in the year next after that in which they had

---

[129] Section 46 Code of Practice, paras 12.4 and 16.1.

[130] Section 46 Code of Practice, paras 12.3 and 16.1.

[131] Public Records Act 1958 s 3(4). The period used to be 30 years. There is a transitional arrangement for records created between 1985 and 2001: see The Public Records (Transfer to the Public Record Office) (Transitional and Saving Provisions) Order 2012 SI 2012/3028.

[132] Public Records Act 1958 s 6.

[133] ss 67 and 86 and Sch 5 Pt I and Sch 8 Pt II.

been created.[134] However,[135] if it appeared to the person responsible[136] for any public records which had been selected by him for permanent preservation that they contained information which had been obtained from members of the public under such conditions that the opening of the records to the public after the 30-year period[137] might constitute a breach of good faith on the part of the Government or on the part of the persons who obtained the information, that person had to inform the Lord Chancellor accordingly so that those records were not available for public inspection after the expiration of 30 years or such other period as was determined except in circumstances as the person responsible for selection and the Lord Chancellor approved or after such further period of time as they approved. The 30-year closure period did not apply to records which had been open to the public prior to their transfer; they remained open. Further, s 5(1) gave the Lord Chancellor a discretion to open records, with the concurrence of the Minister concerned, earlier than the specified period. This was known as accelerated opening. Where a variation of the normal 30-year period occurred it was effected by a document signed by the Lord Chancellor and known as a Lord Chancellor's Instrument. The duty imposed on the Keeper of Public Records[138] was to arrange that reasonable facilities were available to the public for inspecting and obtaining copies of public records in the Public Record Office (ie The National Archives), subject to the time rule (ie the 30-year rule) and the good faith restraint, if applicable. It has been seen that the period of 30 years was capable of extension. This is illustrated by the records relating to the abdication in 1936 of King Edward VIII (later HRH the Duke of Windsor). Certain records were closed until after the death in 2002 of Her Majesty Queen Elizabeth, the Queen Mother.

36– 039 Non-disclosure pre-2005

The access right was, in addition, subject to those enactments set out in the Second Schedule to the 1958 Act which prohibited the disclosure of certain information obtained from the public except for certain limited purposes.[139] The Second Schedule listed a variety of enactments having this prohibitory effect, including the Coal Industry Nationalisation Act 1946 (s 56), the Statistics of Trade Act 1947 (s 9), the Industrial Organisation and Development Act 1947 (s 5), the Agricultural Statistics Act 1979 and the Film Levy Finance Act 1981 (s 8). Schedule 2 to the Act was repealed by FOIA, with effect from 1 January 2005.

36– 040 Public records: disposition

The National Archives has published a disposition policy providing a principled framework for the making of decisions to offer public records to archival institutions other than The National Archives. The power to appoint places of deposit was delegated by the Lord Chancellor to the Keeper of Public Records when, in 1992, the Public Record Office became an executive agency. There are about 235 archives, libraries, museums, galleries and government agencies which have been inspected by The National Archives and appointed to hold specified classes of public record. Throughout England and Wales local authority archive services have been appointed as places of deposit for public records of strong local interest. Many of the major national museums and galleries are appointed to hold their own administrative records or

134 Or such other period as the Lord Chancellor may, with the approval, or at the request, of the Minister or other person, who appears to him to be principally concerned, prescribe as respects any particular class of public records.

135 In consequence of the Public Records Act 1958 s 5(2).

136 Under the Public Records Act 1958 s 3.

137 Or other period determined under s 5(1).

138 By the Public Records Act 1958 s 5(3).

139 The duty is also subject to any other Act or instrument whether passed or made before or after the Public Records Act 1958 containing a similar prohibition.

specialist material which falls within their collecting policies. Places of deposit are periodically inspected by a member of staff from The National Archives. It is usual for a major place of deposit, such as a county record office, to be visited once every five years. All inspections are carried out by professionally qualified archivists with experience of working in a record office. The purpose of these inspections is to determine whether places of deposit offer conditions for the storage of records and facilities for public access which meet The National Archives' standards. These standards are largely based on BS 5454 relating to Records in Places of Deposit. From the year 2000 onwards, a checklist based on the Standard for Access to Archives, which has been developed by the Public Services Quality Group, will also inform The National Archives' inspections of places of deposit, so that access to records by users has the same weight as preservation.

36– 041 Other places of deposit

The preceding paragraphs have been substantially concerned with access to material in The National Archives. The Lord Chancellor is required, for all public records in places of deposit appointed by him outside The National Archives, to arrange that facilities are available for their inspection by the public comparable to those for public records in The National Archives.

36– 042 Public records: transfer

In addition to transfers of public records to places of deposit, s 3(6) of the Public Records Act 1958 allows the Public Record Office (ie The National Archives), under powers delegated by the Lord Chancellor to the Keeper of Public Records, to present government records which have not been selected for permanent preservation to places of deposit and other bona fide institutions. In this way such records are preserved and made publicly available as an alternative to their destruction. Presented records become the property of the recipient and cease to have public record status.[140] These records are transferred subject to conditions stipulated by The National Archives. Normal conditions will be a restriction on the disposal of the records without advance consultation with The National Archives and a 30-year closure period.

[140] Accordingly, they are not 'transferred public records' within the meaning of s 15(4) of the FOIA.

Chapter 37

Local government information

1. LOCAL GOVERNMENT INFORMATION

37– 001 Introduction

In addition to being subject to the main disclosure regimes,[1] information held by local government bodies[2] is also subject to disclosure obligations imposed by the common law and by specific statutory regimes. The applicability and the reach of these obligations depend upon:

(a) whether the person seeking the information does so as a member (eg as a councillor) of the local government body holding the information or does so as a member of the public; and

(b) whether the local government body is a local authority body operating executive arrangements or a committee system (see below).

A person seeking information as a member of the local government body has more extensive rights to information held by his or her local government body than a person seeking it as a member of the public. Common law rights are considered in section 2 of this chapter. Rights to information where a local authority is operating a committee system (or where it is operating executive arrangements but the information relates to a function that is not the responsibility of the executive) are considered in section 3 of this chapter. Rights to information where a local government body is operating executive arrangements and the information relates to a function that is the responsibility of the executive are considered in section 4 of this chapter.

37– 002 Local authority governance

In England,[3] a local authority[4] must operate one of:

(a) Executive arrangements. The term 'executive arrangements' means arrangements by a local authority for and in connection with the creation and operation of an executive of the authority, and under which certain functions of the authority are the responsibility of the executive.[5] Functions of a local authority operating executive arrangements that are the responsibility of the executive are regarded as exercisable by the executive on behalf of that authority and may not be discharged by the authority itself.[6] Functions of a local authority operating executive arrangements that are not the responsibility of the executive

1 That is, FOIA, the EIR (and, in relation to Scottish public authorities, their Scottish equivalents) and the Data Protection Act 2018.

2 For present purposes, a local authority body is any of the following: a county council, a district council, London borough council or any other principal council within the meaning of the Local Government Act 1972 s 270(1), a joint authority established by Part IV of the Local Government Act 1985, an economic prosperity board established under the Local Democracy, Economic Development and Construction Act 2009 s 88, a combined authority established under the Local Democracy, Economic Development and Construction Act 2009 s 103, Transport for London, a sub-national transport body established under the Local Transport Act 2008 s 102E, the Common Council of the City, the Broads Authority, a National Park Authority, a fire and rescue authority, parish and community councils, community health committees, the Assembly of the Greater London Authority and police and crime panels.

3 In Wales, the executive of a local authority must be one of: (a) an elected mayor of the authority and two or more councillors appointed by that mayor; (b) a councillor elected as executive leader by the authority and two or more councillors appointed by that executive leader; or (c) such form as prescribed in regulations by the Welsh Ministers. The manner in which functions are exercised, and the role of overview and scrutiny committees, is similar, but not identical, to that in England. Detailed consideration is beyond the scope of this book.

4 That is to say, a county council, a district council or a London borough council: Local Government Act 2000 s 9R(1).

5 Local Government Act 2000 ss 9B(4), 9R(1).

6 Local Government Act 2000 s 9DA(2)-(3).

are discharged in the usual way.[7] Executive arrangements by a local authority must include provision for the appointment by the authority of one or more committees known as 'overview and scrutiny committees.'[8] An overview and scrutiny committee will have power to review or scrutinise decisions made or other action taken in connection with the discharge of any functions that are or are not the responsibility of the executive, as well as to make reports or recommendations to the authority or the executive on such matters or on matters that affect the authority's area or the inhabitants of the area.[9] An overview and scrutiny committee of a local authority, or a sub-committee of such a committee, is treated as a committee or sub-committee of a principal council for the purposes of Part VA of the Local Government Act 1972 (ie access to the meetings and documents of certain authorities, committees and subcommittees).[10] An overview and scrutiny committee may require members of the executive and officers of the authority to attend before it to answer questions and may require other members of the authority to attend before it to answer questions relating to any specified function that is exercisable by the member.[11]

(b) A committee system. A 'committee system' means the arrangements made by a local authority that does not operate executive arrangements or prescribed arrangements, for or in connection with the discharge of its functions in accordance with the Local Government Act 1972 Pt VI (ss 101-109). Where a local authority operates a committee system, certain functions are non-delegable, either universally or in specified circumstances.[12] Unless otherwise specified, a function may be discharged by a committee, a sub-committee or an officer of the authority, or in some circumstances by another local authority.[13] Where a local authority operates a committee system, it, too, will have one or more committees as its overview and scrutiny committees.[14] These have similar powers and responsibilities as those of overview and scrutiny committees of a local authority operating executive arrangements.

(c) Prescribed arrangements. 'Prescribed arrangements' means such arrangements as may be prescribed in regulations made by the Secretary of State.[15]

37–003 Executive governance

The executive of a local authority may take one of two forms:

---

7 Local Government Act 2000 s 9DA(4).

8 Local Government Act 2000 s 9F.

9 Local Government Act 2000 s 9F. In providing a copy of a reports or recommendation to a member of the local authority, the overview and scrutiny committee may include any confidential information and any exempt information: Local Government Act 2000 s 9FD. 'Confidential information' has the meaning given by the Local Government Act 1972 s 100A(3) and 'exempt information' has the meaning given by the Local Government Act 1972 s 100I. The Secretary of State has made regulations prescribing the information that a relevant partner authority must provide to an overview and scrutiny committee and the information that must not be so disclosed: see Local Authorities (Overview and Scrutiny Committees) (England) Regulations 2012, SI 2012/1021 reg 4.

10 Local Government Act 2000 s 9FA.

11 Local Government Act 2000 s 9FA.

12 See Local Authorities (Committee System) (England) Regulations 2012, SI 2012/1020.

13 Local Government Act 1972 s 101.

14 Local Government Act 2000 s 9JA. Where a function of a local authority may be discharged by a committee, then, unless the local authority otherwise directs, the committee may arrange for the discharge of that function by a sub-committee or an officer of the authority; and where a function of a local authority may be discharged by a sub-committee of the authority, then, unless the local authority or the committee otherwise directs, the sub-committee may arrange for the discharge of that function by an officer of the authority: Local Government Act 1972 s 101.

15 Local Government Act 2000 s 9B(1)(c).

(a) an elected mayor[16] plus two or more councillors appointed to the executive by the mayor, (which form is called a 'mayor and cabinet executive'); or
(b) a councillor elected by the authority as the executive leader[17] plus two or more councillors appointed to the executive by that executive leader (which form is called a 'leader and cabinet executive').

Unless invited, a member of a local authority who is not a member of the authority's executive is not entitled to attend or speak at a meeting of the executive, or of a committee of the executive, which is held in private.[18] Regulations prescribe which functions must be the responsibility of the executive of an authority that has adopted executive arrangements, which functions may be the responsibility of that executive and which functions are not the responsibility of that executive but instead fall to be decided by the full council.[19] Any function that, under executive arrangements, is the responsibility of an executive of a local authority:

- is regarded as exercisable by the executive on behalf of the local authority;
- may not be discharged by the authority itself; and
- is not a function to which s 101 of the Local Government Act 1972 relating to discharge of an authority's functions by committees, sub-committees or officers or by another authority applies.

A function that is the responsibility of an executive of a local authority may, according to arrangements, be discharged by the executive, by a member of the executive, by a committee of the executive, by an area committee or by an officer of the authority.[20] A function that is not the responsibility of an executive of a local authority may be discharged by a committee, a sub-committee or an officer of the authority, or in some circumstances by another local authority.[21]

37–004 Overview

Beginning with modest rights conferred by the Public Bodies (Admission to Meetings) Act 1960 – introduced as a private member's bill by Mrs Margaret Thatcher and still in force – legislation has in a piecemeal fashion conferred, either on the public generally or on specific classes of person, rights to specific sorts of information held by local government bodies. These are in addition to the information rights conferred by FOIA, the EIR and the DPA 2018. In very broad terms the principal provisions in chronological order are:

(1) The Public Bodies (Admission to Meetings) Act 1960 gives a member of the press an entitlement to be supplied with a copy of the agenda and limited additional information relating to meetings of certain local government bodies that are required to be open to the public.[22]
(2) The Local Government (Records) Act 1962 confers on members of the public limited rights of access to records held by a local authority.[23]
(3) Part VA of the Local Government Act 1972 requires local authorities to make

16 That is to say, an individual elected as mayor of the authority by the local government electors the authority's area in accordance with the provisions made by or under the Local Government Act 2000 Part 1A: see ss 9H(1) and 9R(1). By being elected as mayor of an authority, an individual ceases to be a councillor of that authority.

17 The individual elected as executive leader remains a member of the authority during the period that that individual is the executive leader.

18 Local Government Act 2000 Sch A1 para 4.

19 Local Government Act 2000 s 9D(3), and see the Local Authorities (Functions and Responsibilities) (England) Regulations 2000, SI 2000/2853.

20 Local Government Act 2000 s 9E.

21 Local Government Act 1972 s 101.

22 §§37–043 to 37–044.

23 §37–045.

available for public inspection and copying the agenda, reports and background papers used at meetings of a wide range of local government bodies.[24] Part VA of the Act also confers on each member of a local authority a broad right of access to information held by that local authority. The rights of access conferred by Part VA were significantly widened by amendments effected in 2006.[25]

(4) Section 30 of the Local Government Act 1974 gives a right of public access to reports produced by the Local Commissioner into complaints of maladministration.[26]

(5) Sections 25-26 and 40 of the Local Audit and Accountability Act 2008 gives members of the public access to reports produced by an auditor which have been transmitted to a public body or its chairman.

(6) Section 22 of the Local Government Act 2000 and the regulations made under it provide similar rights of access as Part VA of the Local Government Act 1972, but in relation to information put to meetings of local authority executives.

These provisions are considered further in sections 3-5 of this chapter. In addition to these regimes, local authority bodies are required to maintain various registers and lists that contain more-or-less authoritative information on specific matters. Many of these registers and lists are, in whole or in part, open to the public, sometimes on payment of a fee. These registers include:

(7) Section 96 of the Local Government, Planning and Land Act 1980 gives members of the public access to a register of certain land holdings of local authority bodies.[27]

(8) Paragraph 8 of Sch 9 to the Local Government Finance Act 1988 gives members of the public a right of access to certain information in local non-domestic rating lists.[28]

(9) The Local Government Finance Act 1992 gives members of the public certain rights to access information relating to local domestic rating lists.[29]

The more important registers are considered in sections 6 and 7 of this chapter. It is beyond the scope of this book to deal with all of these registers, some of which are very specialised.

2. COMMON LAW RIGHTS OF ELECTED REPRESENTATIVES

37– 005 Introduction

Those elected to a local government body or an office have long had common law rights of access to information held by that body or office.[30] These are important rights that correlate with, and inform due performance of, the responsibilities of a person elected to a body or office. The rationale for these rights is that they enable those elected to a body or office to be fully informed about the matters for which the body or office is responsible, as well as generally to

---

[24] §§37– 011, 37– 011 to 37– 031.

[25] Effected by the Local Government (Access to Information) (Variation) Order 2006 SI 2006/88. Most notably, this replaced the existing Sch 12A with a new Sch 12A, reducing the number of exemptions and introducing a public interest balancing test in para 10.

[26] §37– 047.

[27] §37– 054.

[28] §37– 055.

[29] §37– 055.

[30] *R v Southwold Corporation, ex p Wrightson* (1907) 5 LGR 888, (1907) 97 LT 431; *R v Hampstead Borough Council, ex p Woodward* (1917) 15 LGR 309; *R v Barnes BC, ex p Conlan* [1938] 3 All ER 226; *R v Lancashire County Council Police Authority, ex p Hook* [1980] QB 603; *R v Birmingham City Council, ex p O* [1983] 1 AC 578, [1983] 1 All ER 497, 81 LGR 259; *R v Hackney London Borough Council, ex p Gamper* [1985] 1 WLR 1229, [1985] 3 All ER 275; *R v Sheffield City Council, ex p Chadwick* (1985) 84 LGR 563.

assist them carry out their responsibilities, whether as decision-makers or otherwise, and to facilitate accountability. More recently, legislation has reinforced the access rights of those elected to local government bodies, providing a free-standing, structured entitlement to information held by the body to which they have been elected. Elected representatives enjoy these common law and statutory rights in addition to those rights which they have as members of the public.

37– 006 Responsibility to constituents

Elected representatives in a local government body owe responsibilities to their constituents and to the body to which they have been elected. Those responsibilities include serving the public interest, acting with honesty and integrity, making decisions on the merits, being accountable and reaching his or her own conclusions.[31] Where a member of a local government body is involved in the making of a decision as part of that body's functions, whether because the decision is made by the body collectively or the member is on a committee to which has been assigned decision-making responsibility, that member must act diligently. Each member is under a common law duty to keep him or herself informed on all matters necessary to enable him or her to properly discharge his or her responsibilities as a councillor.[32] This duty is reiterated in the Localism Act 2011 s 27 and the codes of conduct that are required to be adopted thereunder.[33] Whether at common law or under statutorily sanctioned codes of conduct, this duty requires a member to take reasonable steps to inform him or herself about the matters relevant to a decision in which the member is involved.[34] Normally members will rely on officers to place before them the material that is needed for them to be sufficiently informed.[35] Members are not required to gather material that is not held by their body and that has not otherwise been brought to their attention.[36] But in informing themselves of matters relevant to their functions of their body, members are not restricted to relying on what has been supplied to them by officers or others.

---

31 See Local Government Act 2000 s 49 and The Relevant Authorities (General Principles) Order 2001 SI 2001/1401. Although it is permissible, and indeed both commonplace and desirable, for officers to prepare reports for councillors summarising the facts based on the information held by the council and making recommendations, it is the councillors alone who, unless they have delegated decision-making, make decisions. Regardless of how complete officers' reports may be, a councillor must be able to access the primary material held by the council upon which the reports have been based: *National Association of Health Stores v Department of Health* [2005] EWCA Civ 154.

32 See *R v Barnes BC, ex p Conlan* [1938] 3 All ER 226 at 230 (DC), quoted with approval by Lord Brightman in *R v Birmingham City Council, ex p O* [1983] 1 AC 578 at 593G.

33 Formerly under the Local Government Act 2000 s 50 and the Local Government (Model Codes of Conduct) Order 2007 (SI 2007/1159).

34 In the context of central government decision-making, Lord Diplock in *Secretary of State for Education and Science v Tameside MBC* [1977] AC 1014 at 1106A expressed the underlying principle: '[T]he question for the court is, did the Secretary of State ask himself the right question and take reasonable steps to acquaint himself with the relevant information to enable him to answer it correctly.' See further: *Edwin H Bradley & Sons Ltd v SSE* (1982) 47 P & CR 374 at 391-392; *R v Secretary of State for Environment, ex p Fielder Estates (Canvey) Ltd* (1988) 57 P & CR 424, [1989] JPL 39; *R (Q) v Secretary of State for the Home Department* [2003] EWCA Civ 364, [2004] QB 36 at [89]; *R v Merton* [2003] EWHC 1689 (Admin), [2003] 4 All ER 280 at [37]; *Patterson v London Borough of Greenwich* (1993) 26 HLR 159 at 164 (CA). The authorities were summarised most recently in *R (Plantaganet Alliance) v Secretary of State for Justice* [2014] EWHC 1662 (QB), [2015] 3 All ER 261, [2015] LGR 172 at [100], repeated in *R (Karia) v Leicester City Council* [2014] EWHC 3105 (Admin), 141 BMLR 163.

35 *R v Mendip DC, ex p Fabre* (2000) 80 P&CR 500 at 509. Members 'are not required to give personal detailed attention to every strand of fact and argument capable of bearing on the decision they are making. But they are required to have drawn to their attention the main lines of relevant debate': *R (007 Stratford Taxis Ltd) v Stratford-on-Avon District Council* [2011] EWCA Civ 160, [2011] LGR 404 at [11].

36 *Rhodes v Minister of Housing and Local Government* [1963] 1 All ER 300, [1963] 1 WLR 208; *Chris Fashionware (West End) Ltd v Secretary of State for the Environment* [1980] JPL 678; *Glover v Secretary of State for Environment* [1981] JPL 110; *Ynystawe, Ynyforgan and Glais Gypsy Site Action Group v Secretary of State for Wales and West Glamorgan County Council* [1981] JPL 874.

37–007 Function-relevant documents

Whether a member has a common law right of access to particular information held by his or her council is determined according to whether that member has a 'need to know' that information in order to perform his or her responsibilities as a councillor. In the case of a councillor who is a member of a committee or sub-committee, or where a council is to act in council, that councillor will necessarily thereby have a 'need to know' all information held by the council relevant to any issue before the meeting of the committee or sub-committee, or the meeting of the council, respectively.[37] The fact that such a councillor has already been provided with or has access to some information on such an issue does not diminish that councillor's entitlement to see all other information held by the council upon that issue: the councillor's right is to see all relevant information.[38] The fact that such a councillor has a collateral purpose in seeing the information does not negate the entitlement.

37–008 Other documents

In the case of a councillor who is not a member of a committee with a function to which the information relates, the common law right of access will exist only in relation to such information for which the councillor has demonstrable 'need to know' in order to perform his or her responsibilities as a councillor.[39] Mere curiosity or a desire to see and inspect documents by such a councillor will not be sufficient and, in the case of sensitive information, such a councillor will have to show compelling reasons for being shown the information.[40] The decision as to a councillor's need to know will be determined by the committee or sub-committee (or its delegate) having the function to which the information relates.[41]

37–009 Effect of confidentiality etc

Provided that a member of a local government body meets the 'need to know' common law threshold for access to information held by that body, the common law does not recognise any exemption or exception to that member's entitlement to access that information. Thus, where a local authority has been supplied with information on a confidential basis, it will not be a misuse of that information – and hence not a breach of confidentiality[42] – for that information

---

[37] *R v Birmingham City Council, ex p O* [1983] 1 AC 578, [1983] 1 All ER 497, 81 LGR 259 at 593E and 594B-C; *R v Lancashire CC Police Authority, ex p Hook* [1980] QB 603 at 617D-E, 624E-G, 627B; *R v LB Hackney, ex p Gamper* [1985] 1 WLR 1229 at 1237B, [1985] 3 All ER 275 at 281h-i (CA); *R v Broadland District Council, ex p Lashley* [2000] EWHC 358, [2000] LGR 708. This necessarily good reason appears to have been overlooked by the High Court in *R (Perry) v LB Hackney* [2014] EWHC 3499 (Admin).

[38] *R v Birmingham City Council, ex p O* [1983] 1 AC 578, [1983] 1 All ER 497, 81 LGR 259 at 594A-B.

[39] *R v Birmingham City Council, ex p O* [1983] 1 AC 578 at 594B; *R v London Borough of Hackney, ex p Gamper* [1985] 1 WLR 1229 at 1239A, 1240B, [1985] 3 All ER 275 at 283b. Thus in *R v Sheffield City Council, ex p Chadwick* (1985) 84 LGR 563 the exclusion of opposition councillor from a sub-committee on grounds of confidentiality was held unlawful. On this point too, *R (Perry) v London Borough of Hackney* [2014] EWHC 3499 (Admin) at [59] is at odds with the authorities.

[40] *R v Birmingham City Council, ex p O* [1983] 1 AC 578, [1983] 1 All ER 497, 81 LGR 259 at 594E-F; *R v Broadland District Council, ex p Lashley* [2000] EWHC 358, [2000] LGR 708. Information, including confidential information, before one committee can be relevant to the functions of another committee, especially one charged with considering efficiency or propriety: *R v London Borough of Hackney, ex p Gamper* [1985] 1 WLR 1229, [1985] 3 All ER 275. Thus, the right does not extend to documents that the member is merely curious to see: the member has to be actuated solely by the desire to discharge his public functions: *R v Hampstead BC, ex p Woodward* (1917) 15 LGR 309.

[41] *R v Birmingham City Council, ex p O* [1983] 1 AC 578, [1983] 1 All ER 497, 81 LGR 259 at 594F.

[42] Unless the confidentiality arises from statute. It is difficult to see how any council-function use by a councillor of confidential information provided to a council under a contract would constitute a misuse. Regardless of its confidentiality, it is doubtful that a council would have the vires to enter a contract that provided that information supplied by a contracting party to the council could not be shown to or relied upon by a councillor in the performance of his or her council functions. Nor could the provider of information relevant to a decision to be

to be provided to an elected member who has a right to know.[43] Protection of interests in that information is secured by limiting the use to which that member may put the information. An elected member who is given access to confidential information held by the body to which he or she has been elected will be under an equitable duty to maintain the confidentiality by not using – including disseminating – the information for any purpose other than, or associated with, the performance of the local government body's functions: anything else will be an unauthorised use of the information. This is because, to use the language of equity, from the perspective of a person of average intelligence and honesty, the member's conscience ought to be troubled by disclosing or otherwise using confidential information supplied to a local government body other than in connection with the performance of its functions.[44] Moreover, a member will normally be required to maintain the confidentiality of that information under standing orders of the council.[45] However, an unauthorised use of confidential information will not in equity amount to a breach of confidence where the elected member has a lawful excuse for that use. For example, it is not a breach of confidence (whether contractual or equitable) for a elected member of a local government body to disclose confidential information held by the body and to which the member has obtained access by virtue of his or her being elected to that body where:

— the disclosure is required by law;[46]

made by a local government body have a reasonable expectation that in providing it to that body it would be withheld from the elected members charged with and accountable for that decision of the body. See, generally, *R v Licensing Authority established under Medicines Act 1968, ex p Smith Kline & French Laboratories Ltd* [1990] 1 AC 64 at 103H-104B, 104E, 105C, F. It is the irreducible duty of councillors when performing their functions to properly inform themselves based on the material held by the council. This duty now finds statutory expression in the Local Government Act 2000 s 49 and The Relevant Authorities (General Principles) Order 2001 SI 2001/1401.

43 *R v Birmingham City Council, ex p O* [1983] 1 AC 578, [1983] 1 All ER 497, 81 LGR 259 at 594B-C, where Lord Brightman observed that 'there is no room for any secrecy as between a social worker and a member of the social services committee.' In *R v London Borough of Hackney, ex p Gamper* [1985] 1 WLR 1229 at 1239A, 1240B, [1985] 3 All ER 275 at 283b, Lloyd LJ found it 'difficult to imagine' that there could be information held by a council so confidential as to require redaction from members of the council having a need to know it. In *R v Sheffield CC, ex p Chadwick* (1985) 84 LGR 563 the exclusion of an opposition councillor from a sub-committee on grounds of confidentiality was held unlawful. On this point, *R (Perry) v LB Hackney* [2014] EWHC 3499 (Admin) at [59]-[61] appears to have mis-stated the test proposed by Simon Brown LJ in *R v Dept of Health, ex p Source Informatics Ltd* [1999] EWCA Civ 3011, [2001] QB 424 at [31]. The proper question in the case of disclosure of confidential planning information to members making a decision is whether the conscience of a reasonable member on the planning subcommittee, knowing that those members had an entitlement to the information for committee business, that those members had to take decisions having properly informed themselves from information held by their council and that those members would be bound to maintain the confidence, would be troubled by the disclosure of that information to those members for the purpose of determining whether to grant planning permission. In light of the responsibilities of a member and of the authorities, the answer to the question will be 'no.'

44 *R v Department of Health, ex p Source Informatics Ltd* [2001] QB 424 (CA). Or, putting it another way, the question is whether the reasonable person standing in the position of the recipient of the information, knowing the circumstances in which the information was imparted to and the circumstances in which it was obtained by the recipient, would perceive the particular use of the information (which use may be merely dissemination) as taking unfair advantage of the information: *Primary Group (UK) Ltd v Royal Bank of Scotland* [2014] EWHC 1082 (Ch), [2014] 2 All ER (Comm) 1121 at [236]-[237], endorsing *Smith Kline & French Laboratories (Australia) v Secretary of the Department of Health* (1991) 99 ALR 679. Thus, different uses of the information may yield different answers. In some cases, the circumstances may be such that a reasonable person in the position of the confidee would make further inquiries – and in particular would ask the originator of the information where that is not the person who supplied the information to the body, if he or she consented to it being given to the local government body – before making a particular use of the information. If the confidee makes that use without making those inquiries, then the confidee will be liable for breach of confidence: *Primary Group (UK)* at [240]; *Volkswagen Aktiengesellschaft v Garcia* [2013] EWHC 1832 (Ch) at [38].

45 *R v London Borough of Hackney, ex p Gamper* [1985] 1 WLR 1229 at 1239H, [1985] 3 All ER 275 at 283a.

46 *Tournier v National Provincial and Union Bank of England* [1924] 1 KB 461 (CA); *Parry-Jones v Law Society* [1969] 1 Ch 1 (CA). Care must be taken to consider whether the provision said to require the disclosure requires *confidential* information to be disclosed. Misprision of felony (but not misprision of treason) was abolished by the Criminal Law Act 1967. There are now statutory duties of disclosure in relation to certain terrorism offences and money laundering: see Terrorism Act 2000 ss 19, 21A and Proceeds of Crime Act 330.

— the original confidentiality in the information has since been lost;[47]
— the person supplying the information to the public body consents to the disclosure;[48]
— the interests of the local government body requires disclosure (or other use);[49] or
— there is a public interest in disclosure that outweighs the public interest underlying the maintenance of the confidentiality.[50]

The last of these is not an invitation to judicial idiosyncrasy by ad hoc decision-making, but is structured by reference to recognised facets of public interest. The facets of public interest that have been recognised as capable of outweighing the public interest in maintaining confidence are disclosures that assist the detection, investigation and prevention of crime or a serious civil wrongdoing,[51] or the protection human life and health,[52] or where disclosure is required for a fair trial or determination of civil rights and obligations,[53] or for the protection of national security.[54] A public interest in disclosure does not operate on an all-or-nothing basis, but will be shaped according to the public interest claimed to be served by the disclosure.[55]

---

47 *Saltman Engineering Co Ltd v Campbell Engineering Co Ltd* (1948) 65 RPC 203 at 215 (CA); *Attorney-General v Guardian Newspapers Ltd (No 2)* [1990] 1 AC 109 at 282; *Douglas v Hello!* [2007] UKHL 21, [2008] 1 AC 1. It is not always clear when confidentiality will be 'lost.' The courts have sometimes taken the view that it is sufficient that a person who wished to find the information could do so lawfully, albeit not readily: *Mustad v Dosen* [1964] 1 WLR 109 (HL); cf *AG v Greater Manchester Newspapers Ltd* [2001] EWHC 451 (QB); *Franchi v Franchi* [1967] RPC 149 at 152; *Stephens v Avery* [1988] Ch 449. More commonly, however, the courts will look at the type of information, the nature of the confidentiality interest, and the likely audience for the information, and ask whether its current availability is such that further protection will serve no useful purpose. Put another way, confidentiality can usually survive a certain amount of leakage: *PJS v News Group Newspapers Ltd* [2016] UKSC 26, [2016] AC 1081 at [86]. Where something becomes a matter of public record, such as conduct resulting in a criminal conviction or being referred to in open court, it will lose any confidentiality it might have had: *Hilton v Barker Booth & Eastwood* [2005] UKHL 8, [2005] 1 WLR 567 at [7]; *Long Beach Ltd v Global Witness Ltd* [2007] EWHC 1980 (QB).

48 *Tournier v National Provincial and Union Bank of England* [1924] 1 KB 461 (CA). Consent may be express or implied, and it is assessed on an objective basis, ie would a reasonable person think that the confidor had consented: *Sunderland v Barclays Bank Ltd* (1938) 5 Legal Decisions Affecting Bankers 163 (CA); *Turner v Royal Bank of Scotland* [1999] 2 All ER (Comm) 664 (CA); *Cornelius v de Taranto* [2001] EWCA Civ 1511, [2002] EMLR 6 at [27]. Consent must be given by a person having the authority and capacity to do so: *E v Channel Four Television* [2005] EWHC 1144 (Fam), [2005] 2 FLR 913.

49 *Tournier v National Provincial and Union Bank of England* [1924] 1 KB 461 (CA). The disclosure or use permitted is confined to what protection of those interests require: *Re C (a child) (care proceedings: disclosure of documents)* [2015] EWFC 79, [2016] 3 FCR 581 (2016) 151 BMLR 122 at [17]-[26]. The most common example will be where the information is required to help the local government body in legal proceedings.

50 *Attorney-General v Guardian Newspapers Ltd (No 2)* [1990] 1 AC 109 at 282.

51 *Gartside v Outram* (1857) 26 LJ Ch (NS); *Initial Services Ltd v Putterill* [1968] 1 QB 396 (CA), approved in *British Steel Corp v Granada Television Ltd* [1981] AC 1096 at 1169, 1201; *Malone v Metropolitan Police Commissioner* [1979] Ch 344 at 377; *Lion Laboratories Ltd v Evans* [1985] QB 526 at 537-538; *Woolgar v Chief Constable of Sussex Police* [2000] 1 WLR 25; *R (X) v Chief Constable of West Midlands Police* [2004] EWHC 61 (Admin), [2004] 1 WLR 1518; *Marlwood Commercial Inc v Kozeny* [2004] EWCA Civ 798, [2005] 1 WLR 104 at [42]. Minor violations of the criminal law will not suffice: *Mosley v News Group Newspapers Ltd* [2008] EWHC 1777 (QB), [2008] EMLR 679 at [111] (smoking cannabis in one's own home). Mere suspicions of the commission of a crime or other serious wrongdoing may not be enough: *Attorney-General v Guardian Newspapers (No 2)* [1990] 1 AC 109 at 283; *Corrs Pavey Whiting & Byrne v Collector of Customs* (1987) 74 ALR 428 at 450 per Gummow J. The public interest will permit disclosure to the relevant regulatory or investigative body, or some other public body with a proper interest to receive the information: *Francome v Mirror Group Newspapers Ltd* [1984] 1 WLR 892 (CA), disclosure to a jockey club and police; *Re A Company's Application* [1989] Ch 477, disclosure to the financial services regulator and the Inland Revenue. It may also be permissible to disclose to those who stand to be affected by the information or who might take protective measures in the light of that information: *Hellewell v Chief Constable of Derbyshire* [1995]1 WLR 804.

52 *Beloff v Pressdram Ltd* [1973] 1 All ER 241 at 260; *W v Egdell* [1990] Ch 359 at 416, 424 (CA).

53 *Price Waterhouse v BCCI* [1992] BCLC 583; cf *Marcel v Commissioner of Police of the Metropolis* [1992] Ch 225 (CA). The notion that the body holding the information should await a summons or subpoena presupposes that the party in the proceedings for which the information would be useful is aware that the body holds the information: cf *A Health Authority v X* [2001] 2 FCR 634; on app [2001] EWCA Civ 2014, [2002] 2 All ER 780 at [25].

54 *Weld-Blundell v Stephens* [1920] AC 956 at 965-6; *Hubbard v Vosper* [1972] 2 QB 84 (CA); *Beloff v Pressdram Ltd* [1973] 1 All ER 241 at 260.

55 *W v Egdell* [1990] Ch 359 at 398; *Attorney-General v Guardian Newspapers (No 2)* [1990] 1 AC 109 at 269, 283; *Re A*

37– 010 Multiple rights of access

Where a councillor has both a common law right to the information and another right to that information, that councillor is not required to exhaust the other avenue by which he or she might obtain the same information.[56]

3. RIGHTS UNDER PART VA OF THE LOCAL GOVERNMENT ACT 1972

37– 011 Scope

As noted above, Part VA of the Local Government Act 1972 applies where a local authority is operating a committee system (or where it is operating executive arrangements but the information relates to a function that is not the responsibility of the executive). In addition, statutory provisions apply Part VA to many other local government bodies, generally with bespoke adaptations. Although there is a separate regime that applies where a local authority is operating executive arrangements and the information relates to a function that is the responsibility of the executive, that regime adopts by reference certain of the definitions and techniques used in Part VA,

37– 012 Overview

Part VA of the Local Government Act 1972 confers on members of the public (including those who are councillors) three separate rights to inspect certain documents held by local authorities.[57] In addition, Part VA confers on councillors (but not members of the public) a separate and wider right to inspect documents held by their council. The rights revolve around meetings of a local authority, including meetings of its committees and sub-committees. In relation to county councils in England, district councils and London borough councils that operate executive arrangements under Part 1A of the Local Government Act 2000, public access to meetings and to information relating to decision of their executives and committees are governed by a separate statutory regime (see section 4 of this Chapter). The rights of access under Part VA are configured according to whether a document relates to business transacted at an open or a closed meeting of the council or one of its committees. As a general rule, a document relating to business transacted at a closed meeting will not be available to members of the public, but documents relating to other business of the council will be available to members of the public. In summary and subject to qualifications:

(1) Under s 100B, not less than 5 clear days before any meeting of a council, or any committee or sub-committee of a council, the council must make available for inspection by the public a copy of the agenda and of any report for that meeting.
(2) Under s 100C, for 6 years after any meeting of a council, or any committee or sub-committee of a council, the council must make available for inspection by the public a copy of the agenda and the minutes, as well as any report for, that meeting.
(3) Under s 100D, at the same time as a council makes reports available for inspection under s 100C or 100B, the council must also make available for inspection a list of the background papers for those reports, as well as the background papers

Company's Application [1989] Ch 477 at 481.

56 *R v Sheffield City Council ex p Chadwick* (1985) 84 LGR 563 at 575.

57 Pt VA of the Local Government Act 1972 comprises ss 100A to 100K and Sch 12. Pt VA was inserted by the Local Government (Access to Information) Act 1985. In the case of companies not at arms length controlled by a local authority, similar rights of access are conferred by the Local Authorities (Companies) Order 1995 SI 1995/849 para 10.

themselves.

(4) Under s 100F and in addition to his or her entitlements as a member of the public, each councillor is entitled to inspect any document held by the council containing material relating to[58] any business to be transacted at a meeting of the council or at any of its committee or sub-committee meetings.

The first three may be seen as obligations requiring disclosure to the public of information held by a council, whereas the last may be seen as a right by councillors to use information held by their council. Entitlement to inspect a document also entitles the person to have a copy of the document. Schedule 12A of the Act creates seven classes of 'exempt information.' Information within one of those classes is only exempt where in the circumstances of the case the public interest in maintaining the exemption outweighs the public interest in disclosing the information. Exemption is given to information in a document (rather than to the document itself), thus requiring partial disclosure where an exemption applies to only some information within a document. The rights conferred by Part VA are in addition to other access rights, including those arising under common law.[59]

37– 013 Applicable bodies

The obligations imposed by Part VA of the Local Government Act 1972 are imposed on 'principal councils.' As noted above, county councils in England, district councils and London borough councils that operate executive arrangements under Part 1A of the Local Government Act 2000, public access to meetings and to information relating to decision of their executives and committees are governed by a separate statutory regime (see section 4 of this Chapter). Section 100J in Part VA defines 'principal council', and other statutory provisions provide for certain further bodies to be treated as principal councils for the purposes of that Part. In summary, a 'principal council' means:

— in England, a council elected for a non-metropolitan county, a metropolitan district, a non-metropolitan district or a London borough;[60]
— in Wales, a council elected for a county or county borough;[61]
— a joint authority, ie an authority established by Part IV of the Local Government Act 1985;[62]
— the London Fire and Emergency Planning Authority;[63]

[58] In the context of considering the Scotland Act 1998 (which has been said is to be interpreted on ordinary principles), the Supreme Court has held that the phrase 'relates to' indicates more than a loose or consequential connection or a touching upon the matter: *Martin v Most* [2010] UKSC 10, 2010 SC (UKSC) 40 at [49], [159]. And similarly: *Imperial Tobacco Ltd v Lord Advocate* [2012] UKSC 61, 2013 SLT 2 at [16]; *Re Agricultural Sector (Wales) Bill* [2014] UKSC 43, [2014] 1 WLR 2622 at [50]; *Recovery of Medical Costs for Asbestos Diseases (Wales) Bill* [2015] UKSC 3, [2015] AC 1016 at [25]; *Christian Institute v Lord Advocate* [2016] UKSC 51, [2016] HRLR 19 at [29] (concerning the Data Protection Act 1998). The meaning of the phrase 'relates to' in an informational context is further considered at §31– 009. In the context of FOIA the meaning of the phrase 'relates to' has been considered in: *Home Office v IC and Cobain*, FTT, 30 January 2013 at [15]-[19]; *Callus v IC and Home Office*, FTT, 6 May 2014 at [39]-[41]; *University and Colleges Admissions Service v IC and Lord Lucas* [2014] UKUT 0557 (AAC) at [44]-[46] (meaning of 'relates to' in FOIA s 7(5)); *Home Office v IC and Cobain* [2014] UKUT 0306 (AAC) at [39]; *All Party Parliamentary Group on Extraordinary Rendition v IC and FCO* [2015] UKUT 0377 (AAC) at [14]-[33]; *Reprieve v IC and FCO*, FTT, 26 April 2016 at [37]-[39]; *Corderoy and Ahmed v IC and Attorney General* [2017] UKUT 0495 (AAC) at [51] [54] and [59]-[62]; *Department of Health v IC and Lewis* [2017] EWCA Civ 374, [2017] 1 WLR 3330 at [13] (Sir Terence Etherton MR) (meaning of 'relates to' in FOIA s 35(1)).

[59] Local Government Act 1972 ss 100F(5), 100H(7).

[60] Local Government Act 1972 s 270(1).

[61] Local Government Act 1972 s 270(1).

[62] Local Government Act 1972 ss 100J(1)(b), 270(1).

[63] Local Government Act 1972 s 100J(1)(bb).

— an economic prosperity board;[64]
— a combined authority;[65]
— Transport for London;[66]
— a sub-national transport body;[67]
— the Common Council;[68]
— the Broads Authority;[69]
— a National Parks authority;[70]
— a joint board or joint committee constituted under any enactment as a body corporate that discharges functions of two or more principal councils (within the meaning of the first five dashes or eighth dash above);[71]
— a fire and rescue authority constituted by a scheme under s 2 of the Fire and Rescue Services Act 2004 or a scheme to which s 4 of that Act applies;[72]
— the Homes and Community Agency so far as it is exercising functions conferred on it in relation to a designated area by virtue of a designation order;[73] and
— a Mayoral development corporation.[74]

An overview and scrutiny committee of a local authority, or a sub-committee of such a committee, is treated as a committee or sub-committee of a principal council for the purposes of Part VA of the Local Government Act 1972.[75] Part VA has effect as if the London Assembly were a principal council and any committee or sub-committee of the Assembly were a committee or sub-committee of a principal council, with certain modifications.[76]

37–014 Public attendance

As noted above, the public's rights of access under Part VA revolve around meetings of a local authority, including meetings of its committees and sub-committees. The starting position is that members of the public have a right under Part VA of the Local Government Act 1972 to attend meetings of principal councils and their committees.[77] Public notice of the time and place of the meeting must be given by posting it at the offices of the council at least five clear days before the meeting, or if the meeting is convened at shorter notice, then at the time it is convened.[78] While the meeting is open to the public, the council cannot exclude members of

64 Local Government Act 1972 s 100J(1)(bc).

65 Local Government Act 1972 s 100J(1)(bd).

66 Local Government Act 1972 s 100J(1)(be).

67 Local Government Act 1972 s 100J(1)(bf).

68 Local Government Act 1972 s 100J(1)(c).

69 Local Government Act 1972 s 100J(1)(cc).

70 Local Government Act 1972 s 100J(1)(cd).

71 Local Government Act 1972 s 100J(1)(d), (2).

72 Local Government Act 1972 s 100J(1)(f).

73 Local Government Act 1972 s 100J(1)(g).

74 Local Government Act 1972 s 100J(1)(h). 'Designated area' and 'designated order' have the meanings given to them in Pt I of the Housing and Regeneration Act 2008: Local Government Act 1972 s 100J(4B).

75 Local Government Act 2000 s 21(11).

76 Greater London Authority Act 1999 s 58(1).

77 Local Government Act 1972 s 100A(1). But there is no right to attend 'working parties': *R v Warwickshire DC, ex p Bailey* [1991] COD 284. Nor a 'homelessness board': *R v London Borough of Tower Hamlets, ex p Khalique* [1995] 2 FCR 1074.

78 Local Government Act 1972, s100A (6) (a). As regards representation hearings conducted by the Mayor of London, seven clear days are required: the Town and Country Planning (Mayor of London) Order 2008, Art 9(3)(c). In relation to meetings of a standards committee, the authority must give notice of the meeting to the

the public from the meeting.[79] A member of the public attending meeting is entitled to record, video and photograph the proceedings.[80] While the meeting is open to the public, accredited newspaper representatives attending the meeting for the purpose of reporting the proceedings must, so far as practicable, be afforded reasonable facilities for taking their report.[81]

37– 015 Public exclusion

The scope of the public's rights of access under Part VA is curtailed in respect of documents considered at meetings from which the public is likely to be, or has been, excluded. There are two provisions governing exclusion of members of the public from local authority meetings. First, under s 100A(2), the public must be excluded from a meeting during an item of business whenever it is likely, in view of the nature of the business to be transacted or the nature of the proceedings, that if members of the public were to be present during that item 'confidential information' would be disclosed to them in breach of the obligation of confidence. 'Confidential information' is given a narrower meaning than it has under the law of confidence and is defined to mean:

- — information furnished to a principal council by a government department upon terms (however expressed) that forbid the disclosure of the information to the public; and
- — information the disclosure of which to the public is prohibited by or under any enactment or by the order of a court.[82]

This definition of 'confidential information' does not include confidential information[83] which a local authority has received from a third party (other than that furnished by a government department) or which the council has itself generated.[84] Secondly, under s 100A(4), the public may be excluded from a meeting during an item of business whenever it is likely, in view of the nature of the business to be transacted or the nature of the proceedings, that if members of the public were to remain during the item there would be disclosure to them of 'exempt information'.[85] Information will only be exempt information if and so long as the public interest in maintaining the exemption outweighs the public interest in disclosure.[86] Accordingly, the council, committee or sub-committee must carry out the public interest balancing exercise before resolving to exclude the public. The resolution must identify the proceedings, or the part of the proceedings, to which it applies[87] and it must state the description, in terms of Sch 12A

parish council, in accordance with s100A(6)(a): Standards Committee (England) Regulations 2008, SI 2008/1085 reg 8(3)(a).

79 Local Government Act 1972 s 100A(6)(b). This does not preclude the body from excluding a member of the public for misbehaviour at a meeting: s 100A(8).

80 Local Government Act 1972 s 100A(7A)-(9).

81 Local Government Act 1972 s 100A(6)(c).

82 Local Government Act 1972 s 100A(3)(a). This is analogous to FOIA s 44, as to which see §35– 015.

83 As to the meaning of which, see §§34– 010 to 34– 029.

84 It would be open for a third party falling outside the exemptions in Part 12A to seek an order of a court upholding its contractual or equitable rights and thereby render the information 'confidential information' within the meaning of Part VA.

85 Local Government Act 1972 s 100A(4). The classes of exempt information are considered at §37– 021. For examples of the exercise of this power see *R v Kensington and Chelsea LBC, ex p Stoop* [1992] 1 PLR 58 (public excluded during a consideration of an application for the grant of planning permission); and *R v Wandsworth LBC, ex p Darker Enterprises Ltd* (1999) 1 LGLR 601 (public excluded during consideration of an application for a renewal of a licence for a sex establishment). Note that these cases pre-dated the changes to Sch 12A effected in 2006. This power does not extend to the Mayor of London when conducting representation hearings : Town and Country Planning (Mayor of London) Order 2008 Art 9(3)(a).

86 Local Government Act 1972 Sch 12A para 10. As to which, see §37– 024.

87 Local Government Act 1972 s 100A(5)(a).

to the Local Government Act 1972, of the exempt information giving rise to the exclusion of the public.[88] Where such a resolution is made, the meeting need not be open to the public during the proceedings to which the resolution relates.

37–016 Agendas and reports – s 100B

Section 100B of the Local Government Act 1972 imposes an obligation on a council to make available for public inspection, not less than 5 clear days[89] before any meeting of a council, or of any committee or sub-committee of that council:

— copies of the agenda for that meeting; and

— copies of any report for the meeting.[90]

Insofar as it relates to the agenda of a meeting, the s 100B obligation is absolute: the obligation is applicable regardless of whether the public will be excluded from the meeting when the item of business will be considered.[91] Insofar as the s 100B obligation relates to any report for the meeting, the obligation is subject to the power conferred upon the proper officer[92] by s 100B(2) to exclude, if he thinks fit, the whole or any part of a report which relates only to items during which, in his opinion, the meeting is likely not to be open to the public.[93] Thus, if a report relates to items during which the meeting is likely to be open to the public as well as to items during which the meeting is likely not to be open to the public, the proper officer has no power to exclude that report. Where the officer in question does take the view that the whole or part of any report should be excluded, every copy of the report, or part of the report, so excluded must be marked 'Not for publication',[94] and every copy of the whole or of the part of the report

---

88 Local Government Act 1972 s 100A(5)(b).

89 Where the meeting is convened at shorter notice, the copies of the agenda and reports must be open to inspection from the time the meeting is convened: Local Government Act 1972 s 100B(3)(a). The reference to 'five clear days' means five working days: *R v Swansea City Council, ex p Elitestone* [1993] 46 EG 181. In calculating the days, both the day of the meeting and the day on which notice is given are excluded: *R v Swansea City Council, ex p Elitestone* [1993] 46 EG 181. As regards representation hearings conducted by the Mayor of London, seven clear days are required: Town and Country Planning (Mayor of London) order 2008 Art 9(4). In Wales, the requirement is 3 clear days.

90 Local Government Act 1972 s 100B(1). In relation to the meetings of a standards committee, the authority must provide copies of the documents referred to in s 100B(1) to the parish council at least five clear days before the meeting: Standards Committee (England) Regulations 2008, SI 2008/1085 reg 8(3)(b). By s 100B(6), where a meeting of a principal council is required by s 100A to be open to the public during the proceedings or any part of them, a reasonable number of copies of the agenda, and subject to s 100B(8), of the reports for the meeting, must be made available for the use by members of the public present at the meeting. Section 100B(8) provides that s 100B(2) applies in relation to copies of reports provided in pursuance of s 100B(6)or 100B(7) as it applies in relation to copies of reports provided in pursuance of s 100B(1). In order to benefit from the rights of access to information under the Local Government Act 1972, it is sufficient that one is a local government elector, but it is not necessary that one should seek to obtain access to the information in question in that capacity. In *Stirrat v Edinburgh City Council* [1999] SLT 274 [1998] SCLR 971 the claimant, who was a partner in a firm providing a property enquiry service and also a council taxpayer in the City of Edinburgh, attended the Council's office in order to inspect documents in the exercise of his right to do so under s 101(1) of the Local Government (Scotland) Act 1973. Some documents were not available, and the Council refused the claimant access to them on the grounds of confidentiality and expense. The claimant presented a petition seeking a declaration that he was entitled to inspect the documents. The Council opposed the petition on the ground that the right to inspect the documents was linked to the right of the council taxpayer to object to the accounts, and did not apply where the inspection was for professional purposes. The Scottish Outer House granted the declaration, holding that the claimant had right and title to inspect the documents as a council taxpayer under s 101(1), and that the motive with which he sought to exercise that right was irrelevant.

91 Local Government Act 1972 s 100B(1).

92 'Proper officer' means an officer appointed for the purposes by the council: Local Government Act 1972 s 270(3)-(4).

93 As to which, see §37–015. In reaching his conclusion, the officer will also need to consider whether it is likely that the council, the committee or the sub-committee will conclude that the public interest in maintaining the exemption outweighs the public interest in disclosing the information to the public.

94 Local Government Act 1972 s 100B(5)(a).

so excluded must state the description, in terms of Sch 12A to the Local Government Act 1972, of the exempt information by virtue of which the council are likely to exclude the public during the item to which the report relates.[95] Where an item is added to an agenda, a copy of the revised agenda and, unless the public is likely to be excluded from the meeting when dealing with that item, a copy of any report for the meeting relating to that item, must be open to inspection from the time the item is added to the agenda.[96] Copies of any agenda or report that is open to inspection by the public need not be made available to the public until copies have been made available to members of the council.[97] An item of business may not be considered at a meeting of a principal council unless a copy of the agenda including the item (or a copy of the item) is open to inspection by members of the public for at least five clear days before the meeting or, where the meeting is convened at shorter notice, from the time the meeting is convened;[98] or unless, by reason of special circumstances, which must be specified in the minutes, the chairman of the meeting is of the opinion that the item should be considered at the meeting as a matter or urgency.[99]

37– 017 Minutes of meetings – s 100C

Once a meeting of a principal council, a committee or sub-committee, has been held, a council is for 6 years thereafter under an obligation to make available for public inspection:

— a copy of the agenda for the meeting;

— a copy of so much of any report for the meeting as relates to any item during which the meeting was open to the public;[100]

— the minutes of that meeting, or a copy of those minutes, excluding that part of the minutes of proceedings during which the meeting was not open to the public and which discloses exempt information;[101] and

— where applicable, a summary of the meeting.[102]

Whereas the proper officer[103] may have concluded for the purposes of s 100B of the Act that it was likely that part of the meeting would not be open to the public (with the consequence that reports for that part of the meeting were not made available for public inspection before the meeting), the council, committee or sub-committee may conclude that that part of the meeting should be open to the public, with the consequence that those reports will become available for public inspection. Where, as a result of the exclusion of parts of the minutes that would disclose exempt information, the minutes of the meeting that are made open to inspection do not provide members of the public with a reasonably fair and coherent record of the whole or part of the proceedings, the proper officer must make a written summary of those (or that part of

95 Local Government Act 1972 s 100B(5)(b).

96 Local Government Act 1972 s 100B(3)(b). The subsection is confusingly drafted, implying that items on an agenda have an existence separate from the agenda itself.

97 Local Government Act 1972 s 100B(3).

98 Local Government Act 1972 s 100B(4)(a). As regards representation hearings conducted by the Mayor of London, seven clear days are required: Town and Country Planning (Mayor of London) Order 2008 Art 9(4).

99 Local Government Act 1972 s 100B(4)(b).

100 Local Government Act 1972 s 100C(1)(c).

101 Local Government Act 1972 s 100C(1)(a). See the Standards Committee (England) Regulations 2008 reg 8(3)(c) for its application to meetings of a standards committee. Under the Local Government Act 1972 s 228(1), the minutes of proceedings of a parish or community council are open to inspection by any local government elector for the area, and the electors may take a copy of the minutes.

102 Local Government Act 1972 s 100C(1)(b).

103 'Proper officer' means an officer appointed for the purposes by the council: Local Government Act 1972 s 270(3)-(4).

the) proceedings.[104]

37– 018 Background papers – s 100D

If and so long as copies of the whole or part of a report for a meeting of a principal council are required by s 100B(1) or 100C(1) to be open to inspection by members of the public, then:

— those copies must include a copy of a list, compiled by the proper officer,[105] of the background papers for the report or the part of the report,[106] and

— at least one copy of each of the documents included in that list must also be open to inspection at the offices of the council.[107]

The s 100D obligation thus runs from the start of the s 100B obligation (normally 5 working days before the meeting) to the end of the s 100D obligation (4 years from the date of the meeting). If the proper officer has not correctly anticipated whether a meeting (or part of a meeting) will be open to the public, then background papers relating to the business of that meeting (or part of meeting) may be added to those made available to the public. Section 100D(1) does not require a copy of any document included in the list to be open to inspection after the expiration of a period of four years beginning with the date of the meeting.[108] The background papers for a report are those documents relating to the subject-matter of the report that disclose any facts or matters on which, in the opinion of the proper officer, the report or an important part of the report is based, and that have, in that officer's opinion, been relied on to a material extent in preparing the report.[109] The material to be disclosed need not include any confidential information the disclosure of which would be in breach of the obligation of confidence.[110]

37– 019 Councillor rights – s 100F

In addition to the rights conferred through sections 100B to 100D, members of principal councils also have a right to inspect any document that is in the possession or under the control of a principal council and contains material relating to any business to be transacted at a meeting of the council or a committee or sub-committee of the council.[111] The right applies to

104 Local Government Act 1972 s 100C(2).

105 'Proper officer' means an officer appointed for the purposes by the council: Local Government Act 1972 s 270(3)-(4).

106 Local Government Act 1972 s 100D(1)(a).

107 Local Government Act 1972 s 100D(1)(b). Section 100D(3) further provides that where a copy of any background papers for a report is required by s 100D(1) to be open to inspection by members of the public, the copy shall be taken for the purposes of Pt VA of the Local Government Act 1972 to be so open if arrangements exist for its production to members of the public as soon as is reasonably practicable after the making of a request to inspect the copy.

108 Local Government Act 1972 s 100D(2). In *Maile v Wigan MBC* [2001] Env LR 11, [2001] JPL 193 Eady J held that a database dealing with potentially contaminated sites in the Council's area did not form part of the committee report for the purposes of s 100C of the Local Government Act 1972, and was not a 'background paper' for the purposes of s 100D of that Act, because the Council's environmental health officer had not relied upon the database when drafting his report to committee. Consequently the claimant was not entitled to inspect the database under the provisions of the Local Government Act 1972.

109 Local Government Act 1972 s 100D(5). The background papers for a report do not, however, include any published works.

110 Local Government Act 1972 s 100D(4). As to the meaning of 'confidential information' in Part VA of the Local Government Act 1972, see §37– 015.

111 This right is in addition to any other rights that members of principal councils may have apart from s 100F: Local Government Act 1972 s 100F(5). At common law, a member is entitled to see any document which is in the possession of an authority of which he is a member if sight of the document is reasonably necessary to enable him to discharge his functions as a member of that authority: see *R v Barnes Borough Council, ex p Conlan* [1938] 3 All ER 226, 36 LGR 524, DC; *R v Lancashire County Council Police Authority, ex p Hook* [1980]QB 603; *Birmingham City District Council v O* [1983] 1 AC 578, [1983] 1 All ER 497, HL.

every councillor in the council, regardless of whether the document relates to business in respect of which the councillor has a decision-making function. In this respect, s 100F does not draw the distinction made by the common law power to inspect council documents.[112] Section 100F does not itself impose a supporting duty on a council to volunteer that it holds information, but nothing formal is required from a councillor to exercise his or her right to inspect. It appears to be implicit in the power 'to inspect' that the council have in place arrangements for councillors to inspect material relating to any business to be transacted. In relation to a principal council in England, this right is disapplied in respect of documents that appear to the proper officer to disclose 'exempt information.'[113] The disapplication of the right is itself disapplied (so as to restore the s 100F right of access) where the information falls within paragraph 3 of Schedule 12A (ie it is information relating to the financial or business affairs of any person including the authority, except to the extent that the information relates to[114] any terms proposed or to be proposed by or to the authority in the course of negotiations for a contract) or paragraph 6 of Schedule 12A (ie it is information that reveals that the authority proposes to give under any enactment a notice under or by virtue of which requirements are imposed on a person or make an order or direction under any enactment).[115] In relation to a principal council in Wales, s 100F(1) does not require the document to be open to inspection if it appears to the proper officer that it discloses exempt information[116] unless the information is of a description falling within paragraph 14 or 17 of Sch12A of the Local Government Act 1972.[117]

37–020 Exempt information

The starting position is displaced only where it appears to 'the proper officer'[118] that the document 'discloses exempt information.'[119] Information is 'exempt information' only to the extent that that information satisfies two requirements:

— it falls within one or more of the descriptions given in paragraphs 1-7 of Sch 12A; and

— in all the circumstances of the case the public interest in maintaining the exemption

[112] However, insofar as the document contains 'exempt information', a councillor's decision-making functions will affect the public interest balancing exercise: see §37–024.

[113] Local Government Act 1972 s 100F(2). The classes of exempt information are listed at §37–021. Information is 'exempt information' only where the public interest test is satisfied: see §37–024.

[114] In the context of considering the Scotland Act 1998 (which has been said is to be interpreted on ordinary principles, the Supreme Court has held that the phrase 'relates to' indicates more than a loose or consequential connection or a touching upon the matter: *Martin v Most* [2010] UKSC 10, 2010 SC (UKSC) 40 at [49], [159]. And similarly: *Imperial Tobacco Ltd v Lord Advocate* [2012] UKSC 61, 2013 SLT 2 at [16]; *Re Agricultural Sector (Wales) Bill* [2014] UKSC 43, [2014] 1 WLR 2622 at [50]; *Recovery of Medical Costs for Asbestos Diseases (Wales) Bill* [2015] UKSC 3, [2015] AC 1016 at [25]; *Christian Institute v Lord Advocate* [2016] UKSC 51, [2016] HRLR 19 at [29] (concerning the Data Protection Act 1998). In the context of FOIA the meaning of the phrase 'relates to' has been considered in: *Home Office v IC and Cobain*, FTT, 30 January 2013 at [15]-[19]; *Callus v IC and Home Office*, FTT, 6 May 2014 at [39]-[41]; *University and Colleges Admissions Service v IC and Lord Lucas* [2014] UKUT 0557 (AAC) at [44]-[46] (meaning of 'relates to' in FOIA s 7(5)); *Home Office v IC and Cobain* [2014] UKUT 0306 (AAC) at [39]; *All Party Parliamentary Group on Extraordinary Rendition v IC and FCO* [2015] UKUT 0377 (AAC) at [14]-[33]; *Reprieve v IC and FCO*, FTT, 26 April 2016 at [37]-[39]; *Corderoy and Ahmed v IC and Attorney General* [2017] UKUT 0495 (AAC) at [51] [54] and [59]-[62]; *Department of Health v IC and Lewis* [2017] EWCA Civ 374, [2017] 1 WLR 3330 at [13] (Sir Terence Etherton MR) (meaning of 'relates to' in FOIA s 35(1)). See further §31–009.

[115] Local Government Act 1972 s 100F(2A).

[116] Local Government Act 1972 s 100F(2C).

[117] Local Government Act 1972 s 100F(2D).

[118] That is, the officer appointed by the Council for the purposes of Part VA: s 270(3)-(4) of the LGA.

[119] Local Government Act 1972 s 100F(2).

outweighs the public interest in disclosing the information.[120]

The default position is thus disclosure of the information, with the onus on the proper officer to satisfy both requirements in order for that default position to be displaced. Even where the information satisfies those two requirements, to the extent that that information:

— relates to proposed development for which the local planning authority may grant itself planning permission or permission in principle pursuant to reg 3 of the Town and Country Planning General Regulations 1992; or

— is information that is required to be registered under certain legislation

it will not be 'exempt information' regardless of the public interest.[121]

37– 021 The exemptions

There are seven descriptions of information that, subject to satisfying the public interest requirement, are 'exempt information' for the purposes of Part VA of the Local Government Act 1972:[122]

(1) Information relating to any individual.[123]

(2) Information which is likely to reveal the identity of an individual.[124]

(3) Information relating to the financial or business affairs (whether contemplated, past or current) of any particular person (including the authority holding that information).[125] Where the information is sought by a member of the council, this exemption applies only to the extent that that information relates to any terms proposed or to be proposed by or to the authority in the course of negotiations for a contract.[126]

(4) Information relating to any consultations or negotiations, or contemplated consultations or negotiations, in connection with any labour relations matter arising between the authority or a Minister of the Crown and employees of, or office holders under, the authority.[127]

(5) Information in respect of which a claim to legal professional privilege could be maintained in legal proceedings.[128]

(6) Information that reveals that the authority proposes:

  (a) to give under any enactment a notice under or by virtue of which requirements are imposed on a person; or

  (b) to make an order or direction under any enactment.[129]

(7) Information relating to any action taken or to be taken in connection with the

---

120 Local Government Act 1972 s 100I(1) and para 10 of Sch 12A.

121 Local Government Act 1972 Sch 12A, paras 8 and 9.

122 Local Government Act 1972 s 100I(1). In relation to Wales, exempt information is that described in Part 4 of Sch 12A, subject to any qualifications in Part 5 and as interpreted in light of Part 6: Local Government Act 1972 s 100I(1A).

123 Local Government Act 1972, Sch 12A, Part 1, para 1.

124 Local Government Act 1972, Sch 12A, Part 1, para 2.

125 Local Government Act 1972, Sch 12A, Part 1, para 3, Part III, para 11(1). Information is nevertheless not exempt information by virute of paragraph 3 if it is required to be registered under: (a) the Companies Acts, as defined in the Companies Act 2006 s 2; (b) the Friendly Societies Act 1974; (c) the Friendly Societies Act 1992; (d) the Industrial and Provident Societies Act 1965 to 1978; (e) the Building Societies Act 1986; and (f) the Charities Act 2011, with the result that it must be disclosed.

126 Local Government Act 1972 s 100F(2A)(a).

127 Local Government Act 1972, Sch 12A, Part 1, para 4.

128 Local Government Act 1972, Sch 12A, Part 1, para 5.

129 Local Government Act 1972, Sch 12A, Part 1, para 6. Where the information is sought by a member of the authority, this exemption does not apply: Local Government Act 1972 s 100F(2A)(b).

prevention, investigation or prosecution of crime.[130]

Unlike many of the exemptions in freedom of information and data protection legislation, none of the exemptions depends upon a likelihood of resultant damage to a protected interest: they are purely class-based. Notwithstanding the exemptions, where the information relates to proposed development for which the local planning authority may grant itself planning permission pursuant to regulation 3 of the Town and Country Planning General Regulations 1992, then that information is not exempt information.[131] Apart from the above, under Part VA there is no exemption for information that would otherwise be protected by the law of confidence under contract or in equity.

37– 022 Effect of confidentiality

As noted above, commercial confidentiality is not a ground for non-disclosure to a member.[132] Where a local authority has been supplied with information on a confidential basis, it will not be a misuse of that information – and hence not a breach of confidentiality – for that information to be provided to an elected member who has a statutory right to inspect and copy it.[133]

37– 023 Maintaining confidentiality

Where an elected member exercises his or her statutory right to inspect information held by the body to which he or she has been elected, to the extent that that information is confidential information the member will be under an equitable duty to maintain the confidentiality by not using – including disseminating – the information for any purpose other than, or associated with, the performance of the local government body's functions or his or her other responsibilities as an elected representative of that body: anything else will be an unauthorised use of the information and a breach of confidence.[134] Where a member is given access to personal information, any use of that information other than performance of his or her responsibilities as a member must comply with the data protection principles.[135]

37– 024 The public interest

Information falling within one or more of the above seven descriptions is exempt information under Part VA of the Local Government Act 1972 only if and so long as, in all the circumstances of the case, the public interest in maintaining the exemption outweighs the public interest in disclosing the information.[136] This is not an invitation to an idiosyncratic assessment

---

130 Local Government Act 1972, Sch 12A, Part 1, para 7.

131 Regulation 3 provides that an application for planning permission by an interested planning authority to develop any land of that authority, or for development of any land by an interested planning authority or by an interested planning authority jointly with any other person, shall be determined by the authority concerned, unless the application is referred to the Secretary of State under section 77 of the Town and Country Planning Act 1990 for determination by him. However, regulation 3 does not apply where: (a) the interested planning authority does not intend to develop the land themselves or jointly with any person; and (b) to development involving certain sorts of demolition.

132 Save to the extent that it is information that falls both within paragraph 3 of Schedule 12A and outside the bracketed words in s 100F(2A)(a).

133 See further §37– 009 above.

134 See further §37– 009 above. Subject to any defences, it will be actionable at the suit of the confidor.

135 Although paragraphs 1 and 2 of Schedule 12A describe 'information relating to any individual' and 'information which is likely to reveal the identity of an individual' (respectively), there will often be a strong public interest in a member having this information for the performance of the member's responsibilities. The processing involved in providing to the member under s 100F will almost certainly comply with the data protection principles. Other uses of that personal information by the member will have to be considered according to the use and the nature of the information.

136 Local Government Act 1972, Sch 12A, Part 2, para 10.

of whether, in the decision-maker's personal conception of the public interest, disclosure would or would not be in the public interest. Rather, it demands that the decision-maker focus attention on the public interest embedded in the applicable exemption, weighing that public interest against the generally accepted public interest in transparency and accountable decision-making. Given that none of the exemptions is dependant upon a likelihood of resultant harm, it is to be expected that that likelihood will feature in an assessment of the public interest. Insofar as the information is sought by or would be disclosed to a member of the general public (ie to a person who is not an elected member of the authority disclosing the information) the exercise is similar to that which must be carried out in respect of qualified exemptions and qualified exceptions in FOIA and the EIR.[137] Insofar as the information is sought by or would be disclosed to an elected member of the disclosing authority, since:

— a disclosure to members is much more limited than a disclosure to the public;
— members are under duties to uphold any confidentiality in that information;[138] and
— members are under duties to inform themselves for the purposes of performing their functions,[139]

the public interest balance will be a different exercise from that undertaken where disclosure of these sorts of documents has been considered under FOIA and the EIR or to the public under Part VA of the Local Government Act 1972. Given the above three considerations, unless the member's interest in the information is unrelated to any of the member's responsibilities (including that of holding the body to account) where disclosure will be to a member of the authority as a general rule it should be significantly more difficult to show that the public interest in favour of maintaining the exemption outweighs the public interest in disclosure than where disclosure would be to a member of the public. Thus, the public interest in maintaining the exemption for information relating to the financial or business affairs of the local government body so far as concerns terms proposed by or to that body in the course of negotiations for a contract[140] will be substantially weaker where the disclosure is to members (who must uphold the confidentiality and who have a responsibility for those negotiations) than it will be where the disclosure is to a member of the public.

37–025 The arbiter

Under Part VA of the Local Government Act 1972 it is the 'proper officer' who is charged with deciding both whether information answers one or more of the descriptions in paragraphs 1-7 of Sch 12A and, if so, whether the public interest in maintaining the applicable exemptions outweighs the public interest in disclosing the information.[141] The 'proper officer' means the officer appointed by the 'principal council' for the purposes of Part VA.[142] From the propoer officer's decision there is no merit-review procedure or internal review process, but any decision (including a failure to decide) of the proper officer or a refusal of the a principal council to adhere to a decision of the proper officer may be dealt with by a claim for judicial review. As such, a proper officer would be expected to supply a person with a reasoned basis for any refusal, identifying the facets of the public interest taken into account and setting out the manner in which those facets have been weighed to reach the decision.

37–026 Timing, cost and copying

[137] As to which, see Chs 5 and 6. There are no absolute exemptions in Part VA of the Local Government Act 1972.

[138] See §37–023 below.

[139] See §37–006 above.

[140] See para 3 of Schedule 12A and s 100F(2A)(a).

[141] Local Government Act 1972 s 100F(2).

[142] Local Government Act 1972 s 270(3)-(4).

A document that, under the above provisions, is to be open to inspection must be so open at all reasonable hours[143] and without payment, except in the case of background papers for reports, where payment of a reasonable fee for inspection may be demanded.[144] Where a document is open to inspection by a person under the above provisions, the person may make copies of or extracts from the document,[145] or require the person having custody of the document to supply him with a photographic copy of the document or of extracts from it.[146] The rights so conferred are in addition, and without prejudice, to any such rights conferred by or under any other enactment.[147]

37– 027 Offences

It is a summary offence for a person having custody of a document which is required by s 100B(1), 100C(1) of 100EA(2) to be open to inspection under the above provisions to obstruct any person from exercising that right[148] or to refuse to furnish copies to any person entitled to obtain them.[149]

37– 028 Defamatory material

Where, in pursuance of s 100B(7), any accessible document for a meeting to which that section applies is supplied to, or open to inspection by, a member of the public, or is supplied for the benefit of any newspaper, the publication thereby of any defamatory matter contained in the document is privileged, unless the publication is proved to be made with malice.[150] This applies[151] to any meeting of a principal council and any meeting of a committee or sub-committee of a principal council. The 'accessible documents' for a meeting are:

- any copy of the agenda or of any item included in the agenda for the meeting;[152]
- any such further statements or particulars for the purpose of indicating the nature of any item included in the agenda;[153]
- any copy of a document relating to such an item which is supplied for the benefit of a newspaper in pursuance of s 100B(7)(c);[154]
- any copy of the whole or part of a report for a meeting;[155] and
- any copy of the whole or part of any background papers to a report for the meeting.[156]

---

143 Local Government Act 1972 s 100H(1).

144 Local Government Act 1972 s 100H(1).

145 Local Government Act 1972 s 100H(2)(a).

146 Local Government Act 1972 s 100H(2)(b). Section 100H(2) does not require or authorise the doing of any act which infringes the copyright in any work, except that, where the owner of the copyright is a principal council, nothing done in pursuance of s 100H(2) constitutes an infringement of that copyright: Local Government Act 1972 s 100H(3). Section 100H(3) has effect as if the Mayor of London were a principal council: Town and Country Planning (Mayor of London) Order 2008 Art 9(6).

147 Local Government Act 1972 s 100H(7).

148 Local Government Act 1972 s 100H(4)(a). The offence is punishable on conviction by the imposition of a fine not exceeding level 1 on the standard scale.

149 Local Government Act 1972 s 100H(4)(b).

150 Local Government Act 1972 s 100H(5).

151 By virtue of Local Government Act 1972 s 100H(6).

152 Local Government Act 1972 s 100H(6)(a).

153 Local Government Act 1972 s 100H(6)(b).

154 Local Government Act 1972 s 100H(6)(c).

155 Local Government Act 1972. s 100H(6)(d).

156 Local Government Act 1972 s 100H(6)(e).

37– 029 Enforcement

Enforcement of the above rights is by way of judicial review: there is no right of appeal to a tribunal or to the county court. Where the proper officer has decided to refuse to disclose the requested information, the proper officer should be named as a party to the proceedings. Whilst on conventional principles of judicial review the decision-maker is given evaluative latitude in making the decision, depending on the exemption invoked by the High Court on any such application for judicial review will generally be well placed to review that decision, resembling as it does decisions that are familiar to the court from consideration of claims for public interest immunity. A claim for judicial review of a decision refusing access may form one ground of a wider challenge to a decision made by the local authority body.

37– 030 Additional information

Principal councils are required to maintain a register stating:

— the name and address of every current member of the council and the ward or division which that member represents;[157]

— the name and address of every current member of each committee or sub-committee of the council.[158]

Principal councils must also maintain a list specifying those powers of the council which, for the time being, are exercisable from time to time by officers of the council in pursuance of arrangements made under the Local Government Act 1972 or any other enactment for their discharge by those officers and stating the title of the officer by whom each of the powers so specified is for the time being so exercisable.[159] Finally, principal councils are required to keep at their offices a written summary of the rights to attend the meetings of a principal council and of committees and sub-committees of a principal council, and of the rights to inspect and copy documents and to be furnished with documents which are conferred by Part VA of the Local Government Act 1972.[160] The above-mentioned register, list and summary must be kept open to inspection by the public at the offices of the council.[161]

37– 031 Relationship with FOIA

To the extent that one or other of the provisions of Part VA of the Local Government Act 1972 confers a right to information (whether directly or as extended to another body by a further statutory provision) that information will be exempt information under FOIA.[162] Although not entirely clear, it would seem that s 100H(7) will not operate to preserve the rights of access conferred by FOIA. This is because once a public authority is obliged by Part VA of the Local Government Act 1972 to communicate information to members of the public on request, that

157 Local Government Act 1972 s 100G(1)(a).

158 Local Government Act 1972 s 100G(1)(b). A substituted version of this paragraph (effected by the Local Government and Housing Act 1989 s 194, Sch 11 para 24), which would require additional information in relation to speaking rights at such committee and sub-committee meetings, has yet to be put in force.

159 Local Government Act 1972 s 100G(2). This section does not, however, require a power to be specified in the list if the arrangements for its discharge by the officer are made for a specified period not exceeding six months.

160 Local Government Act 1972 s 100G(3). The same written summary must also set out the rights to attend meetings and inspect, copy and be furnished with documents conferred by Pt XI of the Local Government Act 1972 and such other enactments as the Secretary of State by order specifies: Local Government Act 1972 s 100G(3). For the purposes of this subsection, references to the offices of every principal council have effect as if they were references to the principal office of the Mayor of London: Town and Country Planning (Mayor of London) Order 2008 Art 9(5)(a).

161 Local Government Act 1972 s 100G(4). This applies with modification to the Mayor of London: Town and Country Planning (Mayor of London) Order 208 Art 9(5)(b).

162 FOIA s 21(1). See §§25– 001 to 25– 006.

information becomes exempt information and the duty to communicate under FOIA does not apply.[163] There is, accordingly, no right remaining for s 100H(7) to add to. It should be noted, however, that FOIA draws a distinction for the purposes of this exemption between information that is required to be made available for inspection (to which the exemption will not apply) and information that is required to be communicated upon request (to which the exemption will apply).

4. RIGHTS IN RELATION TO EXECUTIVE DECISIONS

37– 032 Introduction

Where a county council in England, a district council or a London borough council operates executive arrangements under Part 1A of the Local Government Act 2000, access to information on decisions made or to be made[164] in connection with a function that is the responsibility of its executive is governed by regulations made under ss 9G and 9GA of that Act: namely, the Local Authorities (Executive Arrangements) (Meetings and Access to Information) (England) Regulations 2012.[165] Where the information is on a decision made or to be made in connection with a function which is *not* the responsibility of its executive, access to that information will be governed by Part VA of the Local Government Act 1972 – see section 3 of this chapter.

37– 033 Executive arrangements

Meetings of a local government executive and of its committees[166] must be open to the public except to the extent that the public are excluded.[167] The public must be excluded from a meeting during an item of business whenever:

(1) It is likely, in view of the nature of the business to be transacted or the nature of the proceedings, that if members of the public were present during that item, confidential information would be disclosed to them in breach of the obligation of confidence.[168] For the purposes of the 2012 Regulations, the term 'confidential information' bears a narrower meaning that it has under the law of confidence, namely:
   - information provided to the local authority by a government department on terms (however expressed) that forbid the disclosure of the information to the public; or
   - information the disclosure of which to the public is prohibited by or under any enactment or by the order of a court.[169]

   This is substantially the same meaning given to the phrase in Part VA of the Local

---

[163] By combination of FOIA ss 21(2)(b), 2(2)-(3) and 1(1)-(2), in that order.

[164] Whether by the executive of the local authority, a committee of the local authority executive, a joint committee all of whose members are members of a local authority executive (or sub-committee of the same), or an area committee within the meaning of the Local Government Act 2000 s 9E. For the purposes of the 2012 Regulations these are each termed 'the decision-making body.'

[165] For the purposes of this section of this chapter, hereinafter called the '2012 Regulations.' Different arrangements apply in Wales: see Local Government Act 2000 Part II, esp s 22, and Local Authorities (Executive Arrangements) (Decisions, Documents and Meetings) (Wales) Regulations 2001, SI 2001/2290.

[166] Committees include a joint committee, a sub-committee of a joint committee and an area committee of a local authority executive within the meaning of the Local Government Act 2000 s 9E: 2102 Regulations reg 2.

[167] Local Government Act 2000 s 9G; 2102 Regulations reg 4(1).

[168] 2012 Regulations reg 4(2)(a).

[169] 2012 Regulations reg 2.

Government Act 1972.[170] The 'obligation of confidence' means the obligation to uphold this narrower, statutory definition of confidential information.[171] The public may only be excluded for the part or parts of the meeting during which it is likely that confidential information (so defined) would be disclosed.[172]

(2) The decision-making body[173] concerned passes a resolution to exclude the public during that item of business on that basis that it is likely, in view of the nature of the item of business, that if members of the public were present during that item, exempt information would be disclosed to them.[174] The phrase 'exempt information' bears the same meaning given to it under Part VA of the Local Government Act 1972: for information to be 'exempt information' it must both be captured by one of the descriptions in Part I of Schedule 12A and be information for which the public interest in maintaining the exemption outweighs the public interest in disclosing the information.[175] The resolution must identify the proceedings or part of the proceedings to which it relates and state by reference to the descriptions in Schedule 12A identify by which of these it rendered exempt information giving rise to the exclusion of the public.[176] The public may only be excluded for the part or parts of the meeting during which it is likely that exempt information would be disclosed.[177]

(3) A lawful power is used to exclude a member or members of the public in order to maintain orderly conduct or to prevent misbehaviour at a meeting.[178]

37–034 Public meetings

Where the public is not excluded from a meeting (or part of a meeting) under any of the above provisions, the meeting (or that part of the meeting) is called a 'public meeting.'[179] On either 5 clear days' notice or upon the convening of the meeting, the decision-making body[180] must give notice of the time and place of the meeting by displaying those details at the offices of the local authority and, if the authority has a website, publishing them there.[181] All items of business to be considered at a public meeting must be included in an agenda available for public inspection not less than 5 clear days before the meeting.[182] In relation to 'key decisions' (that is, decisions likely to result in significant expenditure or savings to the local authority budget or likely to have a significant effect on communities living or working in two or more wards[183]), 28

[170] Section 100A(3).

[171] 2012 Regulations reg 2.

[172] 2012 Regulations reg 4(4).

[173] That is, the executive of the local authority, a committee of the local authority executive, a joint committee all of whose members are members of a local authority executive (or sub-committee of the same), or an area committee within the meaning of the Local Government Act 2000 s 9E.

[174] 2012 Regulations reg 4(2)(b).

[175] 2012 Regulations reg 2 in conjunction with the Local Government Act 1972 s 100I(1) and Sch 12A para 10. In relation to the meaning of 'exempt information' under Part VA of the Local Government Act 1972.

[176] 2012 Regulations reg 4(3).

[177] 2012 Regulations reg 4(4).

[178] 2012 Regulations reg 4(2)(c).

[179] 2012 Regulations reg 2.

[180] That is, the executive of the local authority, a committee of the local authority executive, a joint committee all of whose members are members of a local authority executive (or sub-committee of the same), or an area committee within the meaning of the Local Government Act 2000 s 9E.

[181] 2012 Regulations reg 6(1).

[182] 2012 Regulations reg 6(2), or on convening of the meeting if less than 5 days earlier.

[183] In *R (Friends of the Earth) v London Borough of Haringey* [2016] EWHC 1454 (Admin) the High Court held that the fact

days' notice must be given of it, setting out the documents to be considered in the making of it.[184]

37–035 Public meetings: inspection

A member of the public is entitled to inspect[185] and to have a copy of:

(a) the agenda of a public meeting; and
(b) every report (but not draft reports) for that meeting, other than those reports (or parts of report) that in the opinion of the proper officer relate to matters during which the meeting is likely to be a private meeting,[186]

apart from information in the agenda or a report that would disclose 'confidential information'[187] or that contains or is likely to contain 'exempt information.'[188] In this way, the bases for not making information in reports and agendas available to the public mirror those applicable to local authority decision-making covered by Part VA of the Local Government Act 1972.

37–036 Private meetings

Where the public is excluded from a meeting (or part of a meeting) under any of the above provisions, the meeting (or that part of the meeting) is called a 'private meeting.'[189] At least 28 days before a private meeting, a decision-making body[190] must make available at the council offices a notice to hold the meeting in private and, if it has a website, publish the same on that website.[191] The notice must set out the reasons for the meeting being private.[192] Representations may then be made on whether the meeting should be in private and, at least

that a decision would result in a council earning an income did not necessarily make it a key decision (at [70]).

184 2012 Regulations reg 9. An exception is provided where this is impracticable, and a procedure must be followed: 2012 Regulations reg 10.

185 If the authority has a website, it must be displayed there: 2012 Regulations reg 7(1)(b).

186 2012 Regulations reg 7(1)-(2). The 'proper officer' bears the same meaning that it does under Part VA of the Local Government Act 1972. Where a report, or part of report, is not available for inspection it must be marked 'not for publication' and must state that it contains confidential information or identify the description in Sch 12A of the 1972 Act that renders it exempt information: 2012 Regulations reg 7(5).

187 For the purposes of the 2012 Regulations, the term 'confidential information' bears a narrower meaning that it has under the law of confidence, namely it is confined to:
- information provided to the local authority by a government department on terms (however expressed) that forbid the disclosure of the information to the public; or
- information the disclosure of which to the public is prohibited by or under any enactment or by the order of a court.

188 2012 Regulations reg 20. As noted above, 'confidential information' under regulation 2 bears a narrower meaning than it has under the law of confidence, namely it means:
- information provided to the local authority by a government department on terms (however expressed) that forbid the disclosure of the information to the public; or
- information the disclosure of which to the public is prohibited by or under any enactment or by the order of a court.

The phrase 'exempt information' bears the same meaning given to it under Part VA of the Local Government Act 1972 and thus must both be captured by one of the descriptions in Part I of Schedule 12A and be information for which the public interest in maintaining the exemption outweighs the public interest in disclosing the information: 2012 Regulations reg 2 and Local Government Act 1972 s 100I(1) and Sch 12A para 10.

189 2012 Regulations reg 2.

190 That is, the executive of the local authority, a committee of the local authority executive, a joint committee all of whose members are members of a local authority executive (or sub-committee of the same), or an area committee within the meaning of the Local Government Act 2000 s 9E.

191 2012 Regulations reg 5(2). There is a let-out where the meeting is urgent and cannot reasonably be deferred: reg 5(6).

192 2012 Regulations reg 5(3).

5 clear days before the meeting, the decision-making body must publish a further notice of its intention to hold a private meeting and set out details of the representations received.[193] Unlike public meetings, a member of the public is not entitled to inspect or copy the agenda or the reports for a private meeting.

37– 037 Executive decision records

As soon as reasonably practicable after an executive decision has been made, a written statement must be prepared recording that decision, the reasons for the decision, the alternative options considered and rejected, and any conflict of interest.[194] A member of the public is entitled to inspect[195] and to have a copy of:

(a) the written statement recording the decision;

(b) any report (but not draft reports) considered at the meeting or by the individual making the decision other than those reports (or parts of report) that in the opinion of the proper officer relate to matters during which the meeting is likely to be a private meeting;[196] and

(c) the background papers to the report or part of report,[197]

apart from information in the written statement or in a report that would disclose 'confidential information'[198] or that contains or is likely to contain 'exempt information.'[199] In this way, the bases for not making information in written statements and reports available to the public mirror those applicable to local authority decision-making covered by Part VA of the Local Government Act 1972.

37– 038 Members' rights

Part 5 (regs 16-19) of the 2012 Regulations confers additional rights of access to documents for members of local authorities. In summary:

(1) Where a document held by a local authority contains material relating to business to be transacted at a public meeting, then, save to the extent that information in that document is captured by one of the descriptions within Part 1 of Schedule 12A to the Local Government Act 1972 or it discloses advice provided by a political adviser or it is

---

193 2012 Regulations reg 5(4)-(5).

194 2012 Regulations regs 12-13. The statement is prepared by the proper officer or, if the proper officer was not present at the meeting, the person presiding at the meeting; or, if the decision was made by an individual member, that member of the proper officer.

195 If the authority has a website, it must be displayed there: 2012 Regulations reg 14(1).

196 2012 Regulations reg 14.

197 2012 Regulations reg 15. A fee may be imposed for the inspection of these documents: reg 21(1)(c).

198 For the purposes of the 2012 Regulations, the term 'confidential information' bears a narrower meaning than it has under the law of confidence, namely it is confined to:
- information provided to the local authority by a government department on terms (however expressed) that forbid the disclosure of the information to the public; or
- information the disclosure of which to the public is prohibited by or under any enactment or by the order of a court.

199 2012 Regulations regs 14, 15 and 20. As noted above, 'confidential information' under regulation 2 bears a narrower meaning than it has under the law of confidence, namely it means:
- information provided to the local authority by a government department on terms (however expressed) that forbid the disclosure of the information to the public; or
- information the disclosure of which to the public is prohibited by or under any enactment or by the order of a court.

The phrase 'exempt information' bears the same meaning given to it under Part VA of the Local Government Act 1972 and thus must both be captured by one of the descriptions in Part I of Schedule 12A and be information for which the public interest in maintaining the exemption outweighs the public interest in disclosing the information: 2012 Regulations reg 2 and Local Government Act 1972 s 100I(1) and Sch 12A para 10.

confidential information,[200] a member of the local authority is entitled to inspect that document.[201] This information must normally be made available not less than 5 clear days before the meeting.[202]

(2) Where a document held by a local authority contains material relating to executive business to be transacted at a meeting (whether private or public) or transacted by an individual, then, save to the extent that information in that document:
   (a) is captured by one of the descriptions within paragraphs 1, 2 4, 5 or 6 or of Schedule 12A to the Local Government Act 1972,
   (b) relates to any terms proposed to be proposed by or to the authority in the course of negotiations for a contract,
   (c) discloses advice provided by a political adviser, or
   (d) is 'confidential information,'[203]

   a member of the local authority is entitled to inspect that document.[204] This information must normally be made available immediately after the decision has been made.[205] The distinction drawn between the unit of entitlement (a 'document') and the unit of disapplication ('information') means that where some (but not all) of the content of a document is information of a kind set out in (a)-(d) above, there will be partial disclosure of that document.

These rights are additional to any other rights that the member may have to that information.[206]

37– 039 Overview etc committees

Members of the overview and scrutiny committees are given a further right to request and be provided with documents held by the member's local authority: namely, a right of access to all documents that contain material relating to any business transacted by a decision-making body of that authority or to a decision made by an individual member of the executive or an officer in accordance with executive arrangements.[207] The only exceptions to this right are to the extent that such documents contain:

(1) Confidential information. The phrase 'confidential information' bears a narrower meaning than it has under the law of confidence, being confined to:
   – information provided to the local authority by a government department on terms (however expressed) that forbid the disclosure of the information to the public; or
   – information the disclosure of which to the public is prohibited by or under any

---

[200] For the purposes of the 2012 Regulations, the term 'confidential information' bears a narrower meaning than it has under the law of confidence, namely it is confined to:
   – information provided to the local authority by a government department on terms (however expressed) that forbid the disclosure of the information to the public; or
   – information the disclosure of which to the public is prohibited by or under any enactment or by the order of a court.

[201] 2012 Regulations reg 16(1).

[202] 2012 Regulations reg 16(2).

[203] For the purposes of the 2012 Regulations, the term 'confidential information' bears a narrower meaning than it has under the law of confidence, namely it is confined to:
   – information provided to the local authority by a government department on terms (however expressed) that forbid the disclosure of the information to the public; or
   – information the disclosure of which to the public is prohibited by or under any enactment or by the order of a court.

[204] 2012 Regulations reg 16(3).

[205] 2012 Regulations reg 16(3).

[206] 2012 Regulations reg 16(8).

[207] 2012 Regulations reg 17(1).

enactment or by the order of a court.[208]

(2) Exempt information. The phrase 'exempt information' bears the same meaning given to it under Part VA of the Local Government Act 1972 and thus must both be captured by one of the descriptions in Part I of Schedule 12A and be information for which the public interest in maintaining the exemption outweighs the public interest in disclosing the information.[209]

Again, the distinction drawn between the unit of entitlement (a 'document') and the unit of disapplication ('information') means that where some (but not all) of the content of a document is information of a kind set out in (a)-(d) above, there will be partial disclosure of that document. The documents must be provided to the member as soon as practicable after receipt of the request and, in any event, not more than 10 clear days after the request is received.[210] Apart from timing, the principal difference between the entitlement of members of the overview and scrutiny committees and those members who are not a member of either committee is that the former will be entitled to exempt information in the requested documents unless the public interest in upholding the exemption outweighs the public interest in disclosure to that member of the information. Given the important scrutiny functions performed by those who are members of the overview and scrutiny committees and the need to be properly informed in order to properly carry out that role, the public interest in upholding the exemption will, it is suggested, have to be overwhelming in order for the exemption to prevail.

37–040 Arbiter

Under the 2012 Regulations it is the 'proper officer' who is charged with deciding:

(a) what constitutes 'background papers';[211]
(b) the reports that should be excluded from being made available for public inspection on the basis that the meeting (or part of meeting) for which the report is prepared is likely to be a private meeting;[212]
(c) the other documents supplied to members of the executive in connection with an item in an agenda to be supplied to a member of the public or a journalist;[213]
(d) whether a document discloses exempt information of a description falling within Part 1 of Schedule 12 A of the Local Government Act 1972;[214]
(e) whether making a document available to the public would involve the disclosure of advice provided by a political adviser or assistant;[215]
(f) whether a document or part of document contains 'confidential information' within the meaning of the Regulations;[216] and
(g) whether a document contains exempt information.[217]

The 'proper officer' means the officer appointed by the 'principal council' for the purposes of

---

208 2012 Regulations reg 2.

209 2012 Regulations reg 2 in conjunction with the Local Government Act 1972 s 100I(1) and Sch 12A para 10.

210 2012 Regulations reg 17(2).

211 2012 Regulations reg 2.

212 2012 Regulations reg 7(2).

213 2012 Regulations reg 7(7(c).

214 2012 Regulations reg 16(5).

215 2012 Regulations reg 16(7), 20(2)(b) and 20(3)(b).

216 2012 Regulations reg 20(2)(a).

217 2012 Regulations 20(2)(b) and 20(3))(b). This includes a consideration of both whether information answers one or more of the descriptions in paragraphs 1-7 of Sch 12A and, if so, whether the public interest in maintaining the applicable exemptions outweighs the public interest in disclosing the information.

Part VA of the Local Government Act 1972.[218] From the proper officer's decision there is no merit-review procedure or internal review process, but any decision (including a failure to decide) of the proper officer, or a refusal of the principal council to adhere to a decision of the proper officer, may be dealt with by a claim for judicial review. As such, a proper officer would be expected to supply a person with a reasoned basis for any refusal, identifying the facets of the public interest taken into account and setting out the manner in which those facets have been weighed to reach the decision.

37–041 Offences

It is a summary offence for a person having custody of a document which is required to be open to inspection under the above provisions to obstruct any person from exercising that right or to refuse to furnish copies to any person entitled to obtain them.[219]

37–042 Enforcement

Enforcement of the above rights is by way of judicial review: there is no right of appeal to a tribunal or to the county court.[220] Where the proper officer has decided to refuse to disclose the requested information, the proper officer should be named as a party to the proceedings. Whilst on conventional principles of judicial review the decision-maker is given evaluative latitude in making the decision, depending on the exemption invoked the High Court on any such application for judicial review will generally be well placed to review that decision, resembling as it does decisions that are familiar to the court from consideration of claims for public interest immunity. A claim for judicial review of a decision refusing access may form one ground of a wider challenge to a decision made by the local authority body.

5. OTHER RIGHTS TO NON-REGISTER INFORMATION

37–043 Public Bodies etc Act 1960

The Public Bodies (Admission to Meetings) Act 1960 was passed at the instigation of Margaret Thatcher MP in 1960.[221] This Act opened up 'the meetings of certain bodies exercising public functions' to the press and other members of the public. The Act applies to the bodies listed in Sch 1 to the Act, including parish and community councils, the Welsh Development Agency, the Commission for Health Improvement, Strategic Health Authorities, Primary Care Trusts,[222] National Health Service Trusts established under s 5(1) of the National Health Service and Community Care Act 1990;[223] and, in Scotland, Health Boards constituted under the National Health Service (Scotland) Act 1978 (but only so far as regards the exercise of their executive functions), and National Health Service Trusts established under s 12A of the National Health Service (Scotland) Act 1978.[224] Section 1(1) of the Act provides that any meeting of a body

---

218 2012 Regulations reg 2 and Local Government Act 1972 s 270(3).

219 2012 Regulations reg 22(1).

220 *R (Friends of the Earth) v London Borough of Haringey* [2016] EWHC 1454 (Admin) illustrates the importance of making any such application as promptly as possible, and certainly before any decision is made founded upon the undisclosed document.

221 See further §1–002.

222 Except as regards the exercise of their functions under the National Health Service (Service Committees and Tribunal) Regulations 1992 or any regulations amending or replacing those Regulations: para 1(gg) of Sch 1 to the Public Bodies (Admission to Meetings) Act 1960.

223 Added by Art 2 of the Public Bodies (Admission to Meetings) (National Health Service Trusts) Order 1997.

224 Added by Art 2 of the Public Bodies (Admission to Meetings) (National Health Service Trusts) Order 1997.

exercising public functions to which the Act applies shall be open to the public.[225] Section 1(1) is, however, subject to a proviso contained in s 1(2), by virtue of which a public body may, by resolution, exclude the public from a meeting (whether during the whole or a part of the proceedings) whenever publicity would be prejudicial to the public interest by reason of the confidential nature of the business to be transacted or for other special reasons stated in the resolution and arising from the nature of the business or of the proceedings.[226] Where such a resolution is passed, the Act does not require the meeting to be open to the public during the proceedings to which the resolution applies. Section 1(3) of the Public Bodies (Admission to Meetings) Act 1960 further provides that a body may, under s 1(2), treat the need to receive or consider recommendations or advice from sources other than members, committees or sub-committees of the body as a special reason why publicity would be prejudicial to the public interest, without regard to the subject or purport of the recommendations or advice, but that the making by s 1(3) of express provision for that case shall not be taken to restrict the generality of s 1(2) in relation to other cases (including, in particular, cases where the report of a committee or sub-committee of the body is of a confidential nature). This provision covers advice from officers.

37–044 Rights under the 1960 Act

Section 1(4) of the Public Bodies (Admission to Meetings) Act 1960 provides that where a body is required by the Act to be open to the public during the proceedings or any part of them, then, on request and payment of postage, a copy of the agenda for the meeting as supplied to the members of the body must be supplied for the benefit of any newspaper. The agenda so supplied may, if thought fit, exclude any item during which the meeting is likely not to be open to the public. That person must also be supplied with a copy of such further statements or particulars, if any, as are necessary to indicate the nature of the items included, or, if thought fit in the case of any item, with copies of any reports or other documents supplied to the members of the body in connection with the item. This provision thus provides a limited class of person with a limited right to information in limited circumstances. For most local authority bodies, this right to information is overtaken by the right conferred by s 100B of the Local Government Act 1972.[227] To the extent that the Public Bodies (Admission to Meetings) Act 1960 confers a right to information, that information will be exempt information under FOIA.[228] Section 1(4)(c) of the Public Bodies (Admission to Meetings) Act 1960 provides that, while the meeting is open to the public, the body lacks the power to exclude members of the public from the meeting. Duly accredited representatives of newspapers attending for the purpose of reporting the proceedings for those newspapers must, so far as practicable, be afforded reasonable facilities for making their report and, unless the meeting is held in premises not belonging to the body or on the telephone, for telephoning the report at their own expense. Again, for most local authority bodies this provision is now overtaken by s 100A(7)-(9) of the Local Government Act 1972.[229]

37–045 Local Government Records

Section 1(1) of the Local Government (Records) Act 1962 confers on local authorities a broad

[225] This does not preclude the body from excluding a member of the public whose rowdiness is impeding business: *R v Brent Health Authority, ex p Francis* [1985] QB 869, [1985] 1 All ER 74; *R v Bude-Stratton Town Council, ex p Bennett* [2005] EWHC 2341; *R v London Borough of Brent, ex p Assegai* (1987) 151 LG Rev 891.

[226] The requirement to give reasons for excluding the public is, apparently, directory only: *R v Liverpool City Council, ex p Liverpool Taxi Fleet Operators' Association* [1975] 1 All ER 379.

[227] See §§37–011, 37–011 to 37–026.

[228] FOIA s 21(1). See §§25–001 to 25–006.

[229] See §37–014.

discretion do all such things as appear to them necessary or expedient for enabling adequate use to be made of records under their control. In relation to such records, a local authority may in particular make provision for enabling persons, with or without charge and subject to such conditions as the authority may determine, to inspect records and to make or obtain copies thereof.[230]

37– 046 Parish etc councils

The Local Government Act 1972 provides for the inspection by local government electors for the area of parish and community councils of the minutes of their proceedings, and such local government electors have the right, in addition, to make a copy of those minutes or an extract from them.[231] Orders for payments of money made by local authorities are also open to inspection by local electors,[232] while the accounts of local authorities, as well as those of any proper officer of a local authority, are open to inspection by the members of that authority, who may make a copy of those minutes or an extract from them.[233] These provisions apply to the minutes of proceedings and accounts of a joint authority, an economic prosperity board, a combined authority and police authorities established under s 3 of the Police Act 1996, as well as to the Metropolitan Police Authority, as if those authorities were local authorities and as if references to a local government elector for the area of the authority were references to a local government elector for any local government area in the area for which the authority is established.[234]

37– 047 Local Commissioner Reports

Where a Local Commissioner conducts an investigation, or decides not to conduct an investigation, into a complaint of maladministration, the Local Government Act 1974 requires him to send a report of the results of the investigation, or a statement of his reasons for not conducting an investigation to – amongst others – the authority concerned.[235] Subject to s 30(7) the authority must for a period of three weeks make copies of the report available for inspection by the public without charge at all reasonable hours at one or more of its offices; and any person shall be entitled to take copies of, or extracts from, the report.[236] The authority must supply a copy of the report to any person on request if he pays such charge as the authority may

[230] Local Government (Records) Acts 1972 s 1(1)(a).

[231] Local Government Act 1972 s 228(1). Section 228 also applies to the minutes of proceedings and accounts of a parish meeting as if that meeting were a parish council: Local Government Act 1972 s 228(8).

[232] Local Government Act 1972 s 228(2).

[233] Local Government Act 1972 s 228(3). Documents directed by s 228 to be open to inspection must be so open at all reasonable hours and, except where otherwise provided, without payment: Local Government Act 1972 s 228(6). It is an offence punishable upon summary conviction by a fine not exceeding level 1 on the standard scale for a person having custody of a document required by s 228 to be open to the public to obstruct any person entitled to inspect the document or to make a copy or extract, or to refuse to give copies or extracts to any person entitled to obtain copies or extracts: Local Government Act 1972 s 228(7).

[234] Local Government Act 1972 s 228(7A). In its application to the Broads Authority, those references in that section to a local government elector are to be construed as references to an elector for the area of any of the local authorities mentioned in s 1(3)(a) of the Norfolk and Suffolk Broads Act 1988. The authorities in question are Norfolk County Council, Suffolk County Council, Broadland District Council, Great Yarmouth Borough Council, North Norfolk District Council, Norwich City Council, South Norfolk District Council and Waveney District Council.

[235] Local Government Act 1974 s 30(1)(c).

[236] Local Government Act 1974 s 30(4). It is a summary offence for a person having custody of a report made available for inspection to obstruct any person seeking to inspect, or make a copy of, the report: Local Government Act 1974 s 30(6). The offence is punishable on conviction by the imposition of a fine not exceeding level 3 on the standard scale.

reasonably require.[237] Not later than two weeks after the report is received by the authority, the proper officer of the authority must give public notice, by advertisement in newspapers and other ways as he considers appropriate, that copies of the report will be available and shall specify the date, being a date not more than one week after public notice is first given, from which the period of three weeks will begin.[238] Section 30(7) limits the operation of the section, by providing that the Local Commissioner may, if he thinks fit after taking into account the public interest as well as the interests of the complainant and of persons other than the complainant, direct that a report shall not be made available for inspection or for copying.

37– 048 Accounts – introduction

Audit obligations have long provided individuals with a means of access to information held by public bodies. Typically, the right of access has been subject to three limitations: available only to local residents; being only for account-related documents; and being available only for a limited period each financial year. But once an individual satisfied those limitations, the right was remarkably free from the class and harm-based exemptions which ordinarily attend an access right. Section 33 of the Poor Law Act 1844, which dealt with the financial accountability of parishes, gave every person liable to be rated to the relief of the poor a right to inspect the parish books of accounts. Every such person was also given the right to make objections to those accounts before the auditor. These rights reflected 'the 19th Century concept that an audit was a public proceeding which any local government elector could attend.'[239] Section 122 of the Public Health Act 1848 gave 'persons interested'[240] a similar right in respect of the books of account of local boards of health. The Public Health Act 1875 consolidated and amended the earlier Acts, imposing similar accounting obligations on urban authorities that were not town councils. Section 247(4) of the 1875 Act extended the ratepayers' right of access beyond the accounts themselves so as to include contracts, deeds, receipts etc 'mentioned or referred to' in the books of account. That provision was replaced by s 224(1) of the Local Government Act 1933, which conferred a right on 'all persons interested'[241] to inspect every account subject to audit and all deeds, contracts, accounts, vouchers[242] and receipts 'relating to the accounts' for a period of 7 days before the audit. In replacing the conjunction 'mentioned or referred to' with 'relating to,' s 224(1) captured a wider range of documents than did its predecessor. Section 224 of the 1933 Act was replaced by s 159 of the Local Government Act 1972.[243] In turn, that section was replaced by s 17 of the Local Government and Finance Act 1982. None of the above Acts contained any express exemptions.[244] Section 17 of the 1982 Act was replaced by ss 14 and 15 of the Audit Commission Act 1998 and the Accounts and Audit

237 Local Government Act 1974 s 30(4A).

238 Local Government Act 1974 s 30(5).

239 *Lloyd v McMahon* [1987] 1 AC 625 at 641. And perhaps also preoccupation with disincentivising poverty.

240 A bankrupt living in the area was a 'person interested' as his estate could be liable for a surcharge: *Marginson v Tildsley* (1903) 67 JR 226.

241 Held to include a ratepayer, who could exercise his right through an agent: *R v Bedwellty UDC, ex p Price* [1934] 1 KB 333 and *R (HTV Ltd) v Bristol City Council* [2004] 1 WLR 2717, which consider the meaning of the phrase 'person interested.'

242 In *R v Monmouthshire County Council, ex p Smith* (1935) 51 TLR 435, 33 LGR 279 the Court held that application forms for the grant of bursaries for the higher education of students submitted to the Council were not 'vouchers' relating to the Council's accounts. Similarly *R v Glamorganshire CC, ex p Collier* [1936] 2 All ER 168.

243 In *London Borough of Hillingdon v Paulssen* [1977] JPL 518 it was held that under s 159 a ratepayer could inspect an architect's certificate and the documents authorising payments under a building contract to which his local authority was a party, but that that provision did not give the ratepayer the right to inspect the documents submitted by the contractor to the architect for the purposes of securing the architect's certificate.

244 Thus, in *Oliver v Northampton BC* (1986) 151 JP 44 the court held that an authority could not refuse to provide documents merely because they had been provided to it in confidence.

(England) Regulations 2011. Sections 14 and 15 of the Audit Commission Act 1998 provided two rights of access to account-related information. In both cases, the right of access was time-limited. The auditor was required to appoint a date from which the rights could be exercised[245] and the body had to give 14 days' notice of the date and the right.[246] The public right of inspection ran for 20 working days from that date.[247] Section 14 gave a local government elector for the area of a body subject to audit the right to inspect and make copies of any 'statement of accounts'[248] prepared under s 27 and of any report made to the body by an auditor.[249] There was no exemption from the s 14 right. Section 15 gave any 'person interested'[250] a right to inspect the 'accounts to be audited' and 'all books, deeds, contracts, bills, vouchers and receipts relating to them,' and to make a copy of any of them. Save, possibly, where the information was confidential,[251] the purpose of the person in seeking the information did not need to be audit-related.[252] The courts gave the phrase 'accounts to be audited' a broad meaning, so as to include the running record of financial movements that was used to make up the statement of accounts at the end of each financial year.[253] The courts also gave the conjunctive phrase 'relating to' a broad meaning, requiring only a factual connection between the accounts in question and not an express reference or mention by one to the other.[254] The only express exemption from the s15 right was in respect of so much of the accounts as contained 'personal information.' That was defined to mean information that identified, or enabled the identification of, a particular individual and which the auditor considered should not be inspected or disclosed.[255] In order not to offend Art 1 of Protocol 1 of the ECHR, the courts read down the right conferred by s 15, effectively making an exemption for commercially confidential information where the public interest in disclosure did not outweigh the public interest in maintaining the confidentiality.[256]

---

245 Accounts and Audit (England) Regulations 2011 reg 21.

246 Accounts and Audit (England) Regulations 2011 regs 10 and 24.

247 Accounts and Audit (England) Regulations 2011 regs 9, 14.

248 Or, in the case of a smaller body that chose otherwise, its income and expenditure account and the statement of balances.

249 The format and content of a 'statement of accounts' was not specified, other than that it had to be 'in accordance with proper practices in relation to accounts': Accounts and Audit (England) Regulations 2011 reg 7(1).

250 Although this did not mean anyone who expressed an interest, it did include a wider category of persons than simply local government electors or those who could make an objection at an audit. Thus, a corporate non-domestic ratepayer within the area was a 'person interested' in its accounts: *R (HTV Ltd) v Bristol City Council* [2004] 1 WLR 2717 .

251 *Veolia ES Nottinghamshire Ltd v Nottinghamshire County Council & ors* [2010] EWCA Civ 1214, [2012] PTSR 185 at [156]-[157] per Rix LJ. Etherton and Jackson LJJ expressly declined to decide the point.

252 *R (HTV Ltd) v Bristol City Council* [2004] 1 WLR 2717, where the information was sought for the purpose of making a television programme. Similarly, *Stirrat v City of Edinburgh Council* 1998 SCLR 973 and *Stirrat Park Hogg v Dumbarton DC* 1996 STL 1113, both dealing with the similarly-worded s 101 of the Local Government (Scotland) Act 1984.

253 *Veolia ES Nottinghamshire Ltd v Nottinghamshire County Council & ors* [2010] EWCA Civ 1214, [2012] PTSR 185 at [88]-[97].

254 The relationship could be established by the nature and function of the document. If a document recorded a payment and that payment was reflected in the body's accounts, the former related to the latter. Similarly, notes to the statement of accounts relating to the accounts: *Veolia ES Nottinghamshire Ltd v Nottinghamshire County Council & ors* [2010] EWCA Civ 1214, [2012] PTSR 185 [98]-[102].

255 So as not to offend Directive 95/46/EU.

256 On the basis that commercially confidential information was property and hence a 'possession' within the meaning of Art 1 of Protocol 1: *Veolia Veolia ES Nottinghamshire Ltd v Nottinghamshire County Council & ors* [2010] EWCA Civ 1214, [2012] PTSR 185 at [111] and [121]. Arguably, a similar reading down would be required to protect documents that are subject to legal professional privilege: *R (Morgan Grenfell & Co Ltd) v Special Commissioners for Income Tax* [2002] UKHL 1, [2003] 1 AC 563, [2002] 3 All ER 1.

37– 049 Accounts – current regime

The Local Audit and Accountability Act 2014 replaced the Audit Commission Act 1998. For accounting records, as well as for the documents from which they are derived, the rights conferred by the 2014 Act are potentially very extensive. Although the Act limits both the class of person entitled to access and the period of access, once a person is inside that class and that period, the potential exemptions from the obligation to disclose are far more limited than those under freedom of information, data protection, and local government legislation. The rationale for this would appear to be that accounting records, and the documents from which they are derived, are central to the financial accountability which the applicable body owes the class of entitled person and for which necessary access has long been recognised.

37– 050 Accounts – 'relevant authorities'

The regime established by the Local Audit and Accountability Act 2014 applies to 'relevant authorities.' These include: county councils, district councils, London borough councils, parish councils, joint authorities, Passenger Transport executives, the Greater London Authority, parish meetings, National Park authorities, police and crime commissioners, chief constables, fire and rescue authorities and combined authorities.[257] The reach of access rights to the accounting records and related documents of a relevant body varies:

(1) According to whether the relevant authority is or is not a 'smaller authority.' A relevant authority is a 'smaller authority' where, for the financial year in question or any of the two preceding financial years, either its gross income or gross expenditure did not exceed £6.5 million.[258]

(2) According to whether the relevant authority is a 'health service body.' A 'health service body' is a clinical commissioning group.[259]

(3) According to whether the relevant authority is a 'Category 1 authority' or a 'Category 2 authority.' A 'Category 1 authority' means a relevant authority that either is not a smaller authority or is a smaller authority that has chosen to prepare its accounts for the purpose of a full audit.[260] A 'Category 2 authority' is smaller authority that is not a Category 1 authority.

(4) If it is a smaller authority, according to:
   (a) whether it is an 'exempt authority'[261]; and
   (b) whether it is an 'opted in authority' or an 'opted out authority.'[262]

37– 051 Accounts – first access right

Two separate rights of access are conferred by the Local Audit and Accountability Act 2014. The first right is conferred only on a local government elector for the area.[263] Such a local

---

257 'Relevant authorities' are listed in the Local Audit and Accountability Act 2014 Sch 2.

258 Local Audit and Accountability Act 2014 s 6.

259 Local Audit and Accountability Act 2014 s 3(9). A clinical commissioning group means a body established under the National Health Service Act 2006 s 14D.

260 Accounts and Audit Regulations 2015 reg 2(1). The decision of a small authority to prepare its accounts for the purpose of a full audit is made under the Local Audit (Smaller Authorities) Regulations 2015 reg 8. Such a smaller authority is called a 'full audit' authority.

261 A smaller authority may certify itself as an exempt authority where it satisfies the requirements of the Local Audit (Smaller Authorities) Regulations 2015 reg 9.

262 Opting in and opting out is governed by Local Audit (Smaller Authorities) Regulations 2015 regs 11-12.

263 Local Audit and Accountability Act 2014 s 25. In relation to exempt authorities, see the Local Audit (Smaller Authorities) Regulations 2015 Schedule para 13. A local government elector means a person registered as a local government elector in the register of electors in accordance with the Representation of the People Act 1983: Local

government elector may inspect and make copies[264] of:

(a) the statement of accounts prepared by the authority;[265]
(b) the local auditor's certificate that the audit of the authority's accounts including that statement has been completed;[266];
(c) the local auditor's opinion on the statement of accounts;[A local auditor must give an opinion on the statement of accounts under the Local Audit and Accountability Act 2014 s 20(2)-(4). In relation to health service bodies, see s 21.]
(d) any public interest report relating to the authority or any entity connected with it;[267] and
(e) any recommendation relating to the authority or an entity connected with it.[268]

The first right is not time-limited, although it may not be exercised in respect of the above documents for a particular financial year until the audit has concluded and the relevant authority has published a notice to that effect.[269] Apart from being limited to documents prepared by the authority or that have been made available to the authority, there are no exemptions.[270]

37– 052 Accounts – second access right

The second right is conferred on 'any person interested' in an audit of accounts under the 2014 Act and on any 'journalist.'[271] Such a person may inspect and makes copies of:[272]

(a) the accounting records for the financial year to which the audit relates;[273] and
(b) all books, deeds, contracts, bills, vouchers, receipts and other documents relating to those financial records.[274]

The right to inspect is exercisable 'on reasonable notice at all reasonable times.'[275] The second

---

Audit and Accountability Act 2014 s 44(1). Special definitions apply to a relevant authority that is a Passenger Transport Executive, a National Park authority or the Broads Authority: Local Audit and Accountability Act 2014 s 44(6).

264 Inspection is without charge and all reasonable times; the copies must be provided on payment of a reasonable sum: Local Audit and Accountability Act 2014 s 25(2)-(3), Sch 7 para 4(5) and Accounts and Audit Regulations 2015 reg 10(3).

265 The content of the statement of accounts of a Category 1 authority is spelled out in the Accounts and Audit Regulations 2015 reg 7. The content of the statement of accounts of a Category 2 authority is spelled out in regs 10, 13(2), (4).

266 A local auditor must give a certificate under the Local Audit and Accountability Act 2014 s 20(2). In relation to health service bodies, see s 21.

267 A public interest report is prepared under the Local Audit and Accountability Act 2014 Sch 7 para 1(2).

268 A recommendation is prepared under the Local Audit and Accountability Act 2014 Sch 7 para 2(1).

269 Local Audit and Accountability Act 2014 s 16.

270 Local Audit and Accountability Act 2014 s 25(4).

271 Local Audit and Accountability Act 2014 s 26. 'Person interested' is the same phrase that was used in earlier like legislation and, presumably, is to be given the same meaning: see §37– 048. 'Journalist' is defined to mean any person who produces for publication journalistic material, whether paid to do so or not: s 26(1A). This is broad enough to include a person who privately investigates matters in order to post up articles on the internet, and the like.

272 Local Audit and Accountability Act 2014 s 26(1). The Act and Regulations do not specify who must bear the costs of copying, but the implication of s 26(3) might suggest that the relevant authority must bear the cost.

273 The responsible financial officer of the authority determines the form of that authority's accounting records, but these must contain entries from day to day of all sums of money received and expended by the authority and the matters to which its income and expenditure or receipts and payments relate, as well as a record of the assets and liabilities of the authority: Accounts and Audit Regulations 2015 reg 4(1)-(3).

274 This is the same phraseology as used in earlier legislation, and will almost certainly bear the same meaning: see §37– 048.

275 Accounts and Audit Regulations 2015 reg 14(3). The form of notice required should have been specified by the

right only exists within the 'period for the exercise of public rights.' This is a single period of 30 working days starting on the day following the day on which the responsible financial officer for the relevant authority publishes (including on the authority's website) the statement of accounts, the statement setting out the public's rights etc.[276] The second right is subject to two exemptions. First, the right does not entitle a person to inspect or copy any record or document containing information which is protected on the grounds of commercial confidentiality.[277] This exemption draws a distinction between 'information in a document' and the record or document itself. Provided that there is any information in a record or document that satisfies the definition of being protected on the grounds of commercial confidentiality, the entirety of the record or document will be exempt. Secondly, the right does not entitle a person to inspect or copy any part of a record or document that contains personal information.[278] Unlike the first exemption, the second exemption is not qualified on public interest grounds. But the presence of personal information does not exempt the entire document: it simply exempts the personal information itself. There may be occasions when the s 26 right will need to be read down in order not to transgress other rights protected by the ECHR.[279]

6. REGISTER INFORMATION: NON-PERSONAL MATTERS

37–053 Member functions

Where a member of a local authority discharges any function of the authority under section 236 of the Local Government and Public Involvement in Health Act 2007 (exercise of functions by local councillors in England), that member must—

(a) ensure that a record is made in writing of any decision made or action taken in connection with the discharge of that function; and

(b) within one month of the date on which the decision is made, or action taken, provide the record to the authority.[280]

Any written record provided to the authority under the Exercise of Functions by Local Councillors (Written Records) Regulations 2009, must be open to members of the public at the offices of the authority for a period of six years beginning with the date on which the decision was made or action taken.[281]

37–054 Local Government etc Act 1980

Under s 95 of the Local Government, Planning and Land Act 1980, the Secretary of State may maintain a register of land owned by the public bodies listed in Sch 16 to the Act. The

---

responsible financial officer when publishing the statement setting out the period for the exercise of public rights; reg 15(2)(b)(ii).

276 Accounts and Audit Regulations 2015 regs 14(1)-(2), 15.

277 Local Audit and Accountability Act 2014 s 26(4). Information is protected on the grounds of commercial confidentiality if its disclosure would prejudice commercial confidentiality and there is no overriding public interest in its disclosure: Local Audit and Accountability Act 2014 s 26(5).

278 Local Audit and Accountability Act 2014 s 26(6). Information is personal information if it identifies a particular individual or enables a particular individual to be identified other than being identified because it relates to a business carried on by an individual as a sole trader: Local Audit and Accountability Act 2014 s 26(7)-(8).

279 For example, so as to protect a document subject to legal professional privilege where the public interest in upholding legal professional privilege in the document outweighs the public interest in disclosing it: see fn 256. This is on the footing that 'bill' bears its meaning as a document.

280 Exercise of Functions by Local Councillors (Written Records) Regulations 2009, SI 2009/352, reg 2. The regulations were made pursuant to section 100EA(1) of the Local Government Act 2000.

281 Section 100EA (2) of the Local Government Act 2000.

Secretary of State must send to a Council in respect of whose area a register is maintained a copy of that register;[282] and such amendments as may be made to it.[283] A copy of a register sent to a council must be made available at the council's principal office for inspection by any member of the public at all reasonable hours.[284] If any member of the public requires a council to supply him with a copy of any information contained in such a copy of a register, the council must supply him with a copy of that information on payment of such reasonable charge for making it as the council may determine.[285] In addition, Part II of the Act imposes a general duty on local authorities to publish information relating to the discharge of their functions.

37– 055 Local Government Finance

The rating of real property in the United Kingdom is divided between non-domestic rating and domestic rating. Although a local authority is made responsible for the collection of both, in the former case all sums received are paid over to Central Government. In both cases, the regime involves rating lists containing all of the hereditaments (non-domestic or domestic, as the case may be) in the area of the local authority. The lists are amended from time to time to take account of changes in the nature and value of a hereditament. Schedule 9 to the Local Government Finance Act 1988 deals with various aspects relating to the administration of the non-domestic rating system. The non-domestic system provides for three types of lists: non-domestic rating lists; central non-domestic rating lists; and rural settlement lists. Paragraph 8 of Sch 9 confers a right on every person to request a valuation officer[286] or a billing authority[287] to provide him with such information as will enable him to establish the state of the non-domestic rating list. Access to the information must be provided free of charge, but a charge may be imposed for any copying requested. Information as to proposals and amendments to the list may be similarly accessed.[288] The Local Government Finance Act 1992 confers a corresponding right of access to local domestic rating lists. A person may require a listing officer to give him access to such information as will enable him to establish what is the state of a list, or has been its state at any time since it came into force, if the officer is maintaining the list;[289] and the list is in force or has been in force at any time in the preceding five years.[290]

37– 056 Environmental information

Although the EIR are the main instrument for obtaining access to 'environmental information',[291] there remain in place a series of provisions giving access to specific sorts of similar information, principally through publicly-accessible registers. While the EIR will often provide the readiest means of obtaining access to all such information, these more specific

---

282 Local Government, Planning and Land Act 1980 s 96(1)(a).

283 Local Government, Planning and Land Act 1980 s 96(1)(b).

284 Local Government, Planning and Land Act 1980 s 96(3).

285 Local Government, Planning and Land Act 1980 s 96(4).

286 A valuation officer is a person appointed by the Commissioners of Inland Revenue: Local Government Finance Act 1988 s 61.

287 Billing authorities are district councils, London borough councils, the Common Council of the City of London and the Council of the Isles of Scilly (in relation to England), and county councils and county borough councils (in relation to Wales): Local Government Finance Act 1992 s 1(2), applied by Local Government Finance Act 1988 s 144(2).

288 Local Government Finance Act 1988 Sch 9, para 9.

289 Local Government Finance Act 1992 s 28(1)(a). Section 91, which is materially identical to s 28, applies solely in relation to Scotland.

290 Local Government Finance Act 1992 s 28(1)(b).

291 As to the meaning of which, see §17– 011.

regimes generally have fewer exemptions and more limited scope for charging for provision of the information.

37–057 Food etc Act 1985

In order to ensure that food is not rendered unfit for human consumption by virtue of deposits into the sea, before any such deposit can be made, a licence is required. It is the duty of each licensing authority to maintain a register containing prescribed[292] particulars of or relating to:

(a) applications for licences made to that authority;
(b) the licences issued by that authority;
(c) variations of licences effected by that authority;
(d) revocations of licences effected by that authority;
(e) convictions for any offences under s 9;
(f) information obtained or furnished in pursuance of s 8(3), (4) or (5) of the Food and Environment Protection Act 1985;
(g) the occasions on which either of the responsible Ministers has carried out any operation under s 10 of the Food and Environment Protection Act 1985; and
(h) such other matters relating to operations for which licences are needed under Part II of the Act as may be prescribed.[293]

No information shall be included in any register which, in the opinion of either of the Ministers, is such that its disclosure on the register would be contrary to the interests of national security,[294] or would prejudice to an unreasonable degree some person's commercial interests.[295] A licensing authority is under a duty to secure that the register maintained by the authority is available, at all reasonable times, for inspection by the public free of charge;[296] and to afford to members of the public facilities for obtaining copies of entries, on payment of reasonable charges.[297] Registers may be kept in any form.[298]

37–058 Environment etc Act 1988

The right of access to information conferred by this Act is limited. It requires certain authorities to keep a register of certain notices served by the authority, to ensure that the register is indexed and to ensure that the register and the index are open to inspection by the public free of charge at all reasonable hours.[299] On request, and upon payment of any reasonable fee as the authority may require, a person inspecting the register can require the authority to provide him with a copy of the entry in the register.[300] The only authorities to which the Act applies and the only notices to which the Act applies are:

(1) notices issued by a fire authority[301] under Arts 29-31 of the Regulatory Reform (Fire Safety) Order 2005;

---

292 'Prescribed' means prescribed in regulations: Food and Environment Protection Act 1985 s 14(7). See, eg, Deposits in the Sea (Public Registers of Information) Regulations 1996.

293 Food and Environment Protection Act 1985 s 14(1).

294 Food and Environment Protection Act 1985 s 14(2)(a).

295 Food and Environment Protection Act 1985 s 14(2)(b).

296 Food and Environment Protection Act 1985 s 14(5)(a).

297 Food and Environment Protection Act 1985 s 14(5)(b).

298 Food and Environment Protection Act 1985 s 14(6).

299 Environment and Safety Information Act 1988 s 1(1). The register can be kept on a computer: s 1(4).

300 Environment and Safety Information Act 1988 s 1(1)(d). The authority can require the payment of a reasonable fee: presumably the cost of photocopying the page in the register.

301 As defined in the Regulatory Reform (Fire Safety) Order 2005 Art 25.

(2) notices issued by an enforcing authority[302] under ss 21 and 22 of the Health and Safety at Work etc Act 1974;

(3) notices issued by a local authority[303] under s 10 of the Safety of Sports Grounds Act 1975; and

(4) notices issued by the responsible authority[304] under ss 19(5) and 19(6) of the Food and Environment Protection Act 1985.

An exemption is provided where an entry would disclose a trade secret, but the provision requires the person upon whom the notice has been served to claim this exemption within 14 days of service.[305]

37–059 Town and Country Planning

Every local planning authority is required to keep a register containing prescribed information with respect to applications for planning permission.[306] The register must contain information as to the manner in which planning applications have been dealt with,[307] together with the type of information prescribed by a development order.[308] The register must be available for inspection by the public at all reasonable hours.[309] Each local planning register authority is also required to keep, in two parts, a register of every application for planning permission relating to its area.[310] A third part is also required to deal with local development orders. The register must contain information in respect of every application for a certificate of lawfulness of existing or proposed use or development made under s 191 or 192 of the Town and Country Planning Act 1990. The register must also record information about simplified planning zone schemes. To enable a person to trace any entry in the register, it must include an index together with a separate index of applications for development involving mining operations or the creation of mineral working deposits. The local planning register authority must also keep further a register under s 188 of the 1990 Act containing information with respect to enforcement notices and stop notices, and breach of condition notices. This register, too, must include an index for enabling a person to trace any entry in the register by reference to the address of the land to which the notice relates.

37–060 Hazardous Substances

Every hazardous substances authority must keep a register containing such information as may be prescribed with respect to applications for hazardous substances consent made to that

---

302 As defined in the Health and Safety at Work etc Act 1974 s 18(7)(a).

303 As defined in the Safety of Sports Grounds Act 1975 s 17(1).

304 As defined in the Food and Environment Protection Act 1985 s 2(2).

305 Environment and Safety Information Act 1988 s 4(1). As to trade secrets, see §§34–049 to 34–056.

306 The Town and Country Planning Act 1990 s 69(1). s 69(1) provides that the local planning authority must keep a register containing such information as is prescribed as to: a) applications for planning permission; (b) applications for permission in principle; (c) applications for non-material changes to planning permission under section 96A;(d) local development orders; (e) Mayoral development orders; (f) neighbourhood planning matters; and (g) simplified planning zone schemes.

307 Town and Country Planning Act 1990 s 69(2)(a).

308 Town and Country Planning Act 1990 s 69(2)(b).

309 Town and Country Planning Act 1990 s 69(5).

310 See: Town and Country Planning (Development Management Procedure) (England) Order 2015, SI 2015/595, Arts 40-43; Town and Country Planning (Development Management Procedure) (Wales) Order 2012, SI 2012/801, Arts 29-30.

authority;[311] to applications under s 17(1) of the Act made to that authority;[312] to hazardous substances consent having effect by virtue of ss 11 or 12 with respect to land for which that authority is the hazardous substances authority;[313] to revocations or modifications of hazardous substances consent granted with respect to such land;[314] and to directions under s 27 sent to the authority by the Secretary of State.[315] Every such register must be available for inspection by the public at all reasonable hours.[316]

37–061 Environmental Protection

The Environmental Protection Act 1990 makes detailed provision for public registers containing a variety of information. The information required to be recorded is information relating to:

— contaminated land;[317]
— litter;[318]
— genetically modified organisms;[319]
— stray dogs.[320]

In respect of all registers:

— Information is excluded from being in the register if in the opinion of the Secretary of State it would be contrary to the interests of national security.[321]
— No information relating to the affairs of any individual or business shall be included in a register maintained under the Environmental Protection Act 1990, without the consent of that individual or the person for the time being carrying on that business, if and so long as the information is, in relation to him, commercially confidential.[322]
— It is the duty of each enforcing authority to secure that the registers maintained by them under the section are available, at all reasonable times, for inspection by the public free of charge;[323] and to afford to members of the public facilities for obtaining copies of entries, on payment of reasonable charges[324] and places may be prescribed by the Secretary of State at which any such registers or facilities are to be available or afforded to the public in pursuance of the paragraph in question. Registers under the section may be kept in any form.[325]

37–062 Water Industry Act 1991

Various registers under Part II of the Water Industry Act 1991 must be maintained. The

311 Planning (Hazardous Substances) Act 1990 s 28(1)(a).

312 Planning (Hazardous Substances) Act 1990 s 28(1)(aa).

313 Planning (Hazardous Substances) Act 1990 s 28(1)(b).

314 Planning (Hazardous Substances) Act 1990 s 28(1)(c).

315 Planning (Hazardous Substances) Act 1990 s 28(1)(d).

316 Planning (Hazardous Substances) Act 1990 s 28(3).

317 Environmental Protection Act 1990 s 78R.

318 Environmental Protection Act 1990 s 95.

319 Environmental Protection Act 1990 s 122.

320 Environmental Protection Act 1990 s 149(8).

321 Environmental Protection Act 1990 ss 21(1), 78S and 123(1).

322 Environmental Protection Act 1990 ss 22(1)(a), 78T(1)(a) and 123(3)(a).

323 Environmental Protection Act 1990 ss 20(7)(a), 78R(8)(a), 95(4)(a), 122(2)(a), and 149(8).

324 Environmental Protection Act 1990 ss 20(7)(b), 78R(8)(b), 95(4)(b) and 122(2)(b).

325 Environmental Protection Act 1990 ss 20(8), 78R(9), 95(5) and s 122(3).

contents of the register must be available for inspection by the public at such times, and subject to the payment of such charges, as may be specified in an order made by the Secretary of State.[326] Any person may, on the payment of such fee as may be specified in an order so made, require the Authority to supply him with a copy of, or extract from, the contents of any part of the register, being a copy or extract which is certified by the Authority to be a true copy or extract.[327] Public registers must also be maintained by sewage undertakers and water undertakers. Registers must also be kept under the Water Resources Act 1991.[328]

37–063 Land registers

Section 96 of the Local Government, Planning and Land Act 1980 provides for registers of land holdings compiled and maintained under s 95 of that Act to be accessible by the public. In very general terms, the aim of the register is to list land holdings of local government bodies which, in the opinion of the Secretary of State, are being underutilised and to make that list open to the public. Under s 95(1), the Secretary of State is empowered to compile and maintain a register of land which satisfies certain conditions.[329] These conditions are:

— that a freehold or leasehold interest in the land is owned by a body to which Part X of the Act applies or a subsidiary of that body;[330]

— that it is situated in an area in relation to which Part X of the Act is in operation,[331] or is not so situated, but adjoins other land which is so situated and in which a freehold or leasehold interest is owned by a body to which Part X of the Act applies or a subsidiary of that body;[332] and

— that in the opinion of the Secretary of State the land is not being used or not being sufficiently used for the purposes of the body's functions.[333]

The Secretary of State has the power to enter on the register any such land satisfying the above conditions as he thinks fit.[334] He may also enter on the register any Crown land situated in an area in relation to which Part X of the Act is in operation or not so situated but adjoining other Crown land which is so situated.[335]

37–064 Part X bodies

Part X of the Local Government, Planning and Land Act 1980 applies to any body for the time being specified in Sch 16 to the Act.[336] The bodies specified in Sch 16 are:

---

326 Water Industry Act 1991 s 195(4).

327 Water Industry Act 1991 s 195(5).

328 Water Resources Act 1991 s 189.

329 These conditions are spelled out in s 95(2).

330 Local Government, Planning and Land Act 1980 s 95(2)(a).

331 The areas in relation to which Pt X of the Local Government, Planning and Land Act 1980 is in operation are determined by order made by statutory instrument by the Secretary of State in relation to the area of any district council or London borough council specified in the order: Local Government, Planning and Land Act 1980 s 94(2). See SIs 1980/1871 (in relation to certain specified areas of district and London borough councils); 1981/194 (in relation to certain specified areas of district and London borough councils); 1981/1251 (in relation to certain specified areas of district councils); 1981/1618 (in relation to all other areas of district councils in England, all other London Boroughs and the City of London); 1983/94 (in relation to certain specified areas of district councils); and 1984/1493 (in relation to all other areas of district councils in Wales).

332 Local Government, Planning and Land Act 1980 s 95(2)(b).

333 Local Government, Planning and Land Act 1980 s 95(2)(c).

334 Local Government, Planning and Land Act 1980 s 95(3).

335 Local Government, Planning and Land Act 1980 s 95(4). Section 95(5) further provides that the information to be included in the register in relation to any land entered on it shall be such as the Secretary of State thinks fit.

336 Local Government, Planning and Land Act 1980 s 93(1). The Secretary of State has the power to amend Sch 16

— a county council, a county borough council, a district council, a London borough council, and the Common Council of the City of London;
— a joint authority established by Part IV of the Local Government Act 1985;
— the London Fire and Emergency Planning Authority;
— a police authority established under s 3 of the Police Act 1996 and the Metropolitan Police Authority;
— an economic prosperity board established under section 88 of the Local Democracy, Economic Development and Construction Act 2009, or a combined authority under section 103;
— an authority established for an area in England under section 207 of the Local Government and Public Involvement in Health Act 2007;
— a development corporation established under the New Towns Act 1981 and an Urban Development Corporation established under the Local Government, Planning and Land Act 1980;
— a housing action trust established under Part III of the Housing Act 1988;
— the Regulator of Social Housing;
— the Civil Aviation Authority;
— British Shipbuilders, the Coal Authority, the British Broadcasting Association and the Environment Agency; and
— statutory undertakers, defined to mean any person authorised by any enactment to carry on any railway, light railway, road transport, water transport, canal, inland navigation, dock or harbour undertaking, or an undertaking for the supply of hydraulic power; provided that where a person carries on a business for a main purpose of which any such undertaking is merely ancillary, that person is treated as a statutory undertaker.

37–065 Public access to the register

The Secretary of State must send to a council in respect of whose area a register is maintained a copy of that register and such amendments to it as he may from time to time consider appropriate.[337] That council has a duty to incorporate those amendments.[338] A copy of the register must be available at the council's principal office for inspection by any member of the public at all reasonable hours.[339] If any member of the public requires a council to supply him with a copy of any information contained in such a copy of the register, the council must supply him with a copy of that information on payment of such reasonable charge for making it as the council may determine.[340]

37–066 Land Registration Act 2002

The register of title maintained under the Land Registration Act 2002 is open to inspection by any person. Any person may make copies of, or of any part of, the register of title; any document kept by the registrar which is referred to in the register of title; any other document kept by the registrar which relates to an application by him; or the register of cautions against

by order made by statutory instrument by adding an entry naming a public body not for the time being specified in that Sch or by amending or deleting any entry for the time being contained in the Schedule: Local Government, Planning and Land Act 1980 s 93(2). A statutory instrument containing an order under s 93(2) is subject to annulment in pursuance of a resolution of either House of Parliament: Local Government, Planning and Land Act 1980 s 93(3).

337 Local Government, Planning and Land Act 1980 s 96(1).

338 Local Government, Planning and Land Act 1980 s 96(2).

339 Local Government, Planning and Land Act 1980 s 96(3).

340 Local Government, Planning and Land Act 1980 s 96(4).

title.[341] This right is subject to rules which may provide for exceptions to the right and impose conditions on its exercise, including conditions requiring the payment of fees.[342] The registrar has a duty to keep an index for the purpose of enabling the following matters to be ascertained in relation to any parcel of land: whether any registered estate relates to the land; how any registered estate which relates to the land is identified for the purposes of the register; whether the land is affected by any, and if so, what, caution against first registration; and such other matters as rules may provide.[343] Rules may also make provision about how the index is to be kept, and may, in particular, make provision about the information to be contained in the index; the form in which information contained in the index is to be kept; and the arrangement of that information. Rules may make provision about official searches of the index.[344] Under s 69 of the Land Registration Act 2002, the registrar has a power to provide, on application, information about the history of a registered title;[345] and may arrange for the provision of information about the history of registered titles and may authorise anyone who has the function of providing information of the latter sort to have access on such terms as he thinks fit to any relevant information kept by him.[346]

37– 067 LGA 1972 – incidental power

Although much of the material held by a local authority relating to land is required to be made available under the above provisions, not all land information held by it falls within these provisions. Generally local authorities have considered that the provision of information about a property to prospective purchasers of that property was incidental to their statutory function of collecting and holding that information.[347] While a local authority may charge for the provision of this information,[348] it is not under a duty to provide that information. However, to the extent that such information is necessary for a property transaction, a refusal by a local authority to provide that information would almost certainly be an unlawful decision, capable of challenge by way of judicial review.[349]

7. REGISTER INFORMATION: PERSONAL INFORMATION

37– 068 Introduction

In addition to the right of access to personal information relating to the applicant conferred by the GDPR and to the restricted right of access to third-party personal information under FOIA,[350] a number of limited access rights to what might broadly be called personal

341 Land Registration Act 2002 s 66(1).

342 Land Registration Act 2002 s 66(2). The relevant rules are contained in the Land Registration Rules 2003 SI 2003/1417, Part 13. In particular, rule 136(1) provides that a person may apply for the registrar to designate a document as an exempt document if it contains prejudicial information.

343 Land Registration Act 2002 s 68(1). The relevant rules are contained in the Land Registration Rules 2003 SI 2003/1417.

344 Land Registration Act 2002 s 68(2). The relevant rules are contained in the Land Registration Rules 2003 SI 2003/1417.

345 Land Registration Act 2002 s 69(1). Section 69(2) provides that rules may make provision about applications for the exercise of the power conferred on the registrar by s 69(1): see the Land Registration Rules 2003 SI 2003/1417.

346 Land Registration Act 2002 s 69(3).

347 For which they were empowered under Local Government Act 1972 s 111 or Local Government Act 2000 s 2.

348 The Local Authorities (England) (Charges for Property Searches) Regulations 2008 (SI 2008 No 3248).

349 *Onesearch Direct Holdings Ltd (t/a Onesearch Direct) v City of York Council* [2010] EWHC 590 (Admin) at [83].

350 Restricted principally by FOIA s 40.

information exist in other statutory provisions. These are, in summary:

(1) a right of access to the register of disclaimers of peerage contained in the Peerage Act 1963;
(2) a right of access to certain information relating to marriage and civil partnership;
(3) a right of access to certain information relating to adoption;
(4) a right of access to certain human donor information; and
(5) a right of access to information as to licence conditions and supervision requirements of an offender exercisable by a victim of crime.

37–069 Hereditary peerages

A person who succeeds to a peerage in England, Scotland, Great Britain or the United Kingdom may, by an instrument of disclaimer delivered to the Lord Chancellor within the prescribed period,[351] disclaim that peerage for life.[352] Where the Lord Chancellor is satisfied that an instrument of disclaimer in respect of a peerage has been delivered within the prescribed time, he shall furnish to the person disclaiming a peerage a certificate to that effect, and shall cause particulars of the instrument and of his certificate to be entered into a register kept by him for the purpose, which shall be open to inspection by the public at all reasonable times.[353]

37–070 Marriage and civil partnership

The Marriage Act 1949, the Births and Death Registration Act 1953 and the Registration Service Act 1953, collectively govern the compulsory registration of births, deaths, marriages and civil partnerships. The Registration of Births and Deaths Regulations 1987[354] and the Registration of Marriage Regulations 2015[355] prescribe the information that must be recorded in the respective registers. Upon payment of the prescribed fee, a person may search the index of the register.

37–071 Adopted persons

The Adoption and Children Act 2002 provides adopted persons and others with certain rights of access to information where that adoption took place after 30 December 2005. The 2002 Act provides that there are two types of information: 'protected information'[356] and information which is not protected.[357] Section 57 of the 2000 Act provides that 'protected information' may only be disclosed to an adopted person in pursuance of sections 56 to 65.[358] Protected information is:

(1) Any 'section 56 information' kept by an adoption agency which is about an adopted person or any other person which is or includes identifying information[359] about the

351 That being the period set out in the Peerage Act 1963 s 1(3).

352 Peerage Act 1963 s 1(1).

353 Peerage Act 1963 Sch 1 para 3.

354 SI 1987/2088.

355 SI 1986/1442.

356 As defined in Adoption and Children Act 2002 s 57.

357 See Adoption and Children Act 2002 s 58.

358 Adoption and Children Act 2002 s 57(1) and (2). A registered adoption society which discloses any information in contravention of s 57 is guilty of an offence and is liable on summary conviction to a fine not exceeding level 5 on the standard scale: Disclosure of Adoption Information (Post-Commencement Adoptions) Regulations 2005 reg 21.

359 'Identifying information' about a person means information which, whether taken on its own or together with other information disclosed by an adoption agency, identifies the person or enables the person to be identified: Adoption and Children Act 2002 s 57(4).

person in question.[360]

(2) Any information[361] kept by an adoption agency[362] which the agency has obtained from the Registrar General[363] and any other information which would enable the adopted person to obtain a certified copy of the record of his birth or which is information about an entry relating to the adopted person in the Adoption Contact Register.[364]

37– 072 Registrar General

Where an adopted person who has attained the age of 18 years requests information from an adoption agency under s 60(2)(a) of the Adoption and Children Act 2002 that would entitle him to obtain a certified copy of the record of his birth and the agency does not have that information, the agency must seek that information from the Registrar General.[365] The Registrar General must disclose to any person (including an adopted person) at his request any information that the person requires to assist him to make contact with the appropriate adoption agency and disclose to the appropriate adoption agency any information that the agency requires, in relation to an application under s 60, 61 or 62 of the 2002 Act about any entry relating to an adopted person on the Adoption Contact Register.[366]

37– 073 Donor information

The Human Fertilisation and Embryology Authority is required to keep a register containing all information obtained by the Authority[367] that relates to the provision of treatment services for any identifiable individual, or the keeping or use of the gametes of any identifiable individual or an embryo taken from any identifiable woman, or if it shows that any identifiable individual was, or may have been, born in consequence of treatment services.[368] A person who has attained the age of 16 ('the applicant') may request the Authority to give the applicant notice stating whether or not the information contained in the register shows that a person other than a parent of the applicant would or might be a parent of the applicant and, if it does show that, giving the applicant so much of that information as relates to the person concerned as the Authority is required by regulations to give (but no other information) or stating whether or not that information shows that there are other persons of whom the donor is not the parent but would or might, but for the relevant statutory provisions, be the parent and if so the number of those other persons, the sex of each of them, and the year of birth of each of them.[369] There is a corresponding right conferred on an applicant to request the Authority to give the

360 Adoption and Children Act 2002 s 57(1).

361 'Information' means 'information recorded in any form': Adoption and Children Act 2002 s 144(1).

362 'Adoption agency' is defined in Adoption and Children Act 2002 s 2(1).

363 On an application pursuant to Adoption and Children Act 2002 s 79(5).

364 Adoption and Children Act 2002 s 57(2). The 'Adoption Contact Register' is defined in s 80(1) as a register maintained by the Registrar General at the General Register Office.

365 Disclosure of Adoption Information (Post-Commencement Adoptions) Regulations 2005 reg 19(1). Where the adoption agency seeks such information from the Registrar General, the agency must provide him in writing with the following information, so far as it is known, the name, date of birth and country of birth of the parents of the adopted person, the names of that person's adoptive father and mother, and the date of the adoption order. Disclosure of Adoption Information (Post-Commencement Adoptions) Regulations 2005 reg 19(2).

366 Disclosure of Adoption Information (Post-Commencement Adoptions) Regulations 2005 reg 20(1).

367 Human Fertilisation and Embryology Act 1990 s 31(1).

368 Human Fertilisation and Embryology Act 1990 s 31(2). Information does not fall within s 31(2) if it is provided to the Authority for the purposes of any voluntary contact register as defined in s 31F(1): Human Fertilisation and Embryology Act 1990 s 31(3).

369 Human Fertilisation and Embryology Act 1990 s 31ZA.

applicant information as to a person whom the applicant proposes to marry or enter into a civil partnership, or with whom the applicant is in (or proposes to enter in) an intimate physical relationship.[370] The Authority must comply with that request if the information contained in the register shows that the applicant was, or may have been, born in consequence of treatment services and the applicant is a relevant individual,[371] the Authority receives notice in writing from the specified person consenting to the request being made and that notice has not been withdrawn, and the applicant and the specified person have each been given a suitable opportunity to receive proper counselling about the implications of compliance with the request.[372] The information that the Authority is required by regulations to give is set out in the Human Fertilisation and Embryology Authority (Disclosure of Donor Information) Regulations 2004.

37–074 Victims of crime

If a court convicts a person ('the offender') of a sexual or violent offence and a relevant sentence[373] is imposed upon him in respect of the offence, the local probation board[374] for the area in which the sentence is imposed must take all reasonable steps to ascertain whether a person who appears to the board to be the victim[375] of the offence (or to act for the victim of the offence) wishes to receive information about any licence conditions or supervision requirements to which the offender is to be subject in the event of his release.[376] If a local probation board has ascertained that a person wishes to receive such information, the relevant local probation board must take all reasonable steps:

(1) to inform the person whether or not the offender is to be subject to any licence conditions or supervision requirements in the event of his release;
(2) if he is, to provide the person with details of any licence conditions or supervision requirements which relate to contact with the victim or his family, and
(3) to provide the person with such other information as the relevant local probation board considers appropriate in all the circumstances of the case.[377]

The Domestic Violence, Crime and Victims Act 2004 makes comparable provision for local probation boards to provide similar information (obtained from the Secretary of State and Mental Health Review Tribunal) to victims of persons subject to the Mental Health Act 1973. In general terms, the provisions require a local probation board to take reasonable steps to ascertain whether the victim wishes to receive information about any conditions to which the patient is to be subject in the event of his discharge from hospital. If so, the board is required to inform the victim of any such conditions, and with details of any conditions which relate to contact with the victim or his family.[378]

370 Human Fertilisation and Embryology Act 1990 s.31ZA.

371 Defined in section 31(4) of the Human Fertilisation and Embryology Act 1990 as '…an individual who was or may have been born in consequence of (a) treatment services, other than basic partner treatment services, or (b) the procurement or distribution of any sperm (other than partner-donated sperm which has not been stored) in the course of providing non-medical fertility services.'

372 Human Fertilisation and Embryology Act 1990 s 31ZB (3).

373 As defined in the Domestic Violence, Crime and Victims Act 2004 s 45(1).

374 Where the offender is to be supervised on release by an officer of a local probation board, that local probation board is the relevant probation board. In any other case, the relevant probation board is the local probation board for the area in which the prison or other place in which the offender is detained: Domestic Violence, Crime and Victims Act 2004 s 35(8).

375 As defined in Domestic Violence, Crime and Victims Act 2004 s 52(2).

376 Domestic Violence, Crime and Victims Act 2004 s 35(1), (3)(b) and (5).

377 Domestic Violence, Crime and Victims Act 2004 s 35(7).

378 Each provision should be examined for its precise terms. In relation to the case where the court convicts a person

CHAPTER 38
Medical records

1. HEALTH, MEDICAL AND CARE RECORDS

38–001 Introduction

Rights of access to medical information are to be found in various legislative provisions. The nature of the information is such that ordinarily the person seeking the information will be the subject of that information. To the extent that medical information held by a public authority relating to the applicant is 'data' that are 'processed' (which includes information that is held) the usual avenue of disclosure will be by request made under the GDPR/DPA 2018.[1]

38–002 Access to Health Records Act

The Access to Health Records Act 1990 provides a limited right of access to 'health records.' These are defined to mean a record which: (a) consists of information relating to the physical or mental health of an individual who can be identified from that information, or from that and other information in the possession of the holder of the record; and (b) has been made by or on behalf of a health professional in connection with the care of that individual.[2]

38–003 Limited scope of 1990 Act

So far as access to health records relating to a *living* individual is concerned, the rights of access are to be found:

(a) where the records are sought by the individual to whom the information in them relates — in the GDPR/DPA 2018; and

(b) where the records are sought by someone other than the individual to whom the information in them relates — in FOIA.

The Access to Health Records Act 1990 applies only to applications for access to records by the personal representative of a patient who has died or by a person who might have a claim arising

---

for a sexual or violent offence or makes a finding of insanity or unfitness to plead and then makes a hospital order with restrictions in respect of that patient: see Domestic Violence, Crime and Victims Act 2004 ss 36 and 38. In the case that the sentencing court makes a hospital direction and limitation direction in respect of an offender in addition to giving him a relevant prison sentence: see the Domestic Violence, Crime and Victims Act 2004 ss 39 and 41. Where an offender is transferred by the Home Secretary to hospital and restrictions are imposed under the powers in the Mental Health Act 1973: see Domestic Violence, Crime and Victims Act 2004 ss 42 and 44. In Northern Ireland: see Domestic Violence, Crime and Victims Act 2004 s 46 (amending the Justice (Northern Ireland) Act 2002).

[1] See Ch 10.

[2] Access to Health Records Act 1990 s 1(1). A 'health professional' bears the meaning given to it by the DPA s 204(1). 'Information' includes any expression of opinion about the patient; and 'care' includes examination, investigation, diagnosis and treatment: Access to Health Records Act 1990 s 11.

out of the patient's death.[3] Such a deceased person is not a data subject, and so falls outside the GDPR/DPA 2018. The access right is also conferred on a medical examiner stating or investigating the cause of the patient's death under section 20 of the Coroners and Justice Act 2009.[4] The right is exercised by an application in writing made to the holder of the record.[5] The 'holder' means (broadly speaking) the person who had performed primary medical services in respect of the deceased or, in other cases, the Health Authority, the NHS Trust, the NHS Foundation Trust etc.[6] Where an application is so made, the holder must give access to the record within 40 days (or 21 days where no new information has been added to the record in the preceding 40 days).[7] Access to the recorded is provided by allowing the applicant to inspect the record and, if the applicant so requires, supplying the applicant with a copy of the record.[8] The holder may not charge any fee for providing access (including providing the copy).[9]

38–004 Exemptions

The right of access is disapplied:

(1) Where the record includes a note, made at the patient's request, that he or she did not wish access to be given on such an application.[10]

(2) To the extent that it includes information included in the record before 1 November 1991.[11]

(3) To the extent that disclosure of information in the record would, in the opinion of the holder of the record, be likely to cause serious harm to the physical or mental health of any individual.[12]

(4) To the extent that information in the record relates to or was provided by an individual, other than the patient, who could be identified from the information;[13]

(5) To the extent that, in the opinion of the holder of the record, the patient expected that the information would not be disclosed to the applicant.[14]

(6) To the extent that compliance would disclose information showing that an identifiable individual was, or may have been, born in consequence of treatment

---

3 Access to Health Records Act 1990 s 3(1)(f).

4 Access to Health Records Act 1990 s 3(1)(g). Inserted by the Coroners and Justice Act 2009 s 177(1) Sch 21 Pt 1 para 29(1). The date on which this is to come into force is yet to be appointed: see the Coroners and Justice Act 2009 s 182(4)(e).

5 Access to Health Records Act 1990 ss 3(1), 11.

6 Access to Health Records Act 1990 ss 1(2), 11.

7 Access to Health Records Act 1990 s 2(2), (5).

8 Access to Health Records Act 1990 s 2(2).

9 Access to Health Records Act 1990 s 2(4).

10 Access to Health Records Act 1990 s 4(3). This would seem to mean that the deceased had in mind access being sought under a statutory entitlement, rather than a generalised request. But such a request would not need to identify the applicant.

11 Except insofar as the information therein is required to make sense of a later disclosed record, Access to Health Records Act 1990 s 5(1)(b).

12 Access to Health Records Act 1990 s 5(1)(a)(i). See *R v Mid Glamorgan Family Health Services, ex p Martin* [1995] 1 WLR 110, [1995] 1 All ER 356. For the operation of a similarly-worded provision in FOIA, see §§32–011 to 32–012.

13 Access to Health Records Act 1990 s 5(1)(a)(ii). This provision does not apply where the individual concerned has consented to the application, or where that individual is a health professional who has been involved in the care of the patient: s 5(2)(a)-(b). Such information would be redacted from the remainder: *Re AB (disclosure of medical records)* [2020] EWC 691 at [20].

14 Access to Health Records Act 1990 s 5(3)(a)-(b).

services within the meaning of the Human Fertilisation and Embryology Act 1990.[15]

(7) To the extent that, in the opinion of the holder of the record, it would disclose information that is not relevant to any claim which may arise out of the patient's death.[16]

38–005 Further rights

Where the health record is to be disclosed, but information therein is expressed in terms which are unintelligible without explanation, an explanation of terms must be supplied.[17] Where a person considers that any information contained in a health record, or any part of a health record, to which he has been given access is inaccurate, that person may apply to the holder of the record for the necessary correction to be made.[18] 'Inaccurate' means incorrect, misleading or incomplete.[19] Where such an application is made, if the holder of the record is satisfied that the information is inaccurate, the holder must make the necessary correction. If the holder is not so satisfied, then the holder must make in the part of the record in which the information is contained a note of the matters in respect of which the information is considered by the applicant to be inaccurate. In either situation, the holder must, without requiring any fee, supply the applicant with a copy of the correction or note.[20]

38–006 Enforcement

Where the holder of the record has failed to comply with the requirements of the Act, the applicant can apply to the High Court or a county court for an order compelling compliance.[21] Such an application would be made under CPR Part 8.[22] For the purpose of determining the application, a court may require the holder to make available the record for its own inspection.

38–007 Access to Medical Reports Act

An individual has a right of access to any medical report relating to him or herself which is to be or has been supplied by a medical practitioner for employment or insurance purposes.[23] In addition, medical practitioners have a duty to retain a copy of any medical report which they have supplied for employment or insurance purposes for at least six months from the date when it was supplied.[24] A medical practitioner, if so requested, must give an individual access to any medical report relating to him which the practitioner has supplied for employment or insurance purposes in the previous six months.[25]

---

15 Access to Health Records (Control of Access) Regulations 1993 (SI 1993/746) reg 2.

16 Access to Health Records Act 1990 s 5(4). This restriction only applies where the person making the request is a person who may have a claim arising out of the patient's death, and it does not apply to requests made by the patient's personal representative: *Re AB (disclosure of medical records)* [2020] EWC 691 at [46].

17 Access to Health Records Act 1990 s 3(3).

18 Access to Health Records Act 1990 s 6(1).

19 Access to Health Records Act 1990 s 6(3).

20 Access to Health Records Act 1990 s 6(2).

21 Access to Health Records Act 1990 s 8.

22 *Re AB (disclosure of medical records)* [2020] EWC 691 at [16].

23 Access to Medical Reports Act 1988 s 1.

24 Access to Medical Reports Act 1988 s 6(1).

25 Access to Medical Reports Act 1988 s 6(2). By s 6(3), the reference in s 6(2) to giving an individual access to a medical report is a reference to making a copy of the report available for his inspection, or supplying him with a copy of it.

38–008 NHS Foundation Trusts

The Independent Regulator of NHS Foundation Trusts must maintain a register of NHS foundation trusts.[26] The register must contain in relation to each NHS foundation trust:

(1) a copy of the current constitution,
(2) a copy of the current authorisation,[27]
(3) a copy of the latest annual accounts and of any report of the auditor on them,
(4) a copy of the latest annual report,
(5) a copy of the latest document sent to the regulator under para 27 of Sch 7 to the National Health Act 2006 (forward planning), and
(6) a copy of any notice given under s 52 of the 2006 Act (failing NHS foundation trusts).[28]

Members of the public may inspect the register at any reasonable time.[29] Any person who requests it must be provided with a copy of, or extract from, any document contained in the register on payment of a reasonable charge.[30]

26 National Health Service Act 2006 s 39(1).

27 As defined in National Health Service Act 2006 s 65.

28 National Health Act 2006 s 39(2).

29 National Health Act 2006 s 39(4).

30 National Health Service Act 2006 s 39(5).

CHAPTER 39

Business and financial information

1. ECONOMIC AND BUSINESS INFORMATION

39–001 Introduction

Although FOIA and the EIR are the main instruments for obtaining any information held by a public authority, including economic and business information, there remain in place a diminishing series of provisions giving access to specific sorts of economic and business information. While FOIA and, to a lesser extent, the EIR will often provide the readiest means of obtaining access to all such information, these more specific regimes generally have fewer exemptions and more limited scope for charging fees for provision of the information. In summary, these more limited regimes are:

(1) Under s 6 of the Nuclear Installations Act 1965, there is a right of public inspection of the list of sites in respect of which a nuclear site licence has been granted.

(2) Under s 42 of the Harbours Act 1964 and s 14 of the Pilotage Act 1987, there is a right of public inspection of the annual accounts prepared by a statutory harbour undertaker which relate to the harbour activities and to revenue derived from the provision of or the expenditure on pilotage services.

(3) Under the Railways Act 1993, there is a right of access to the Regulator's Register and the Franchising Director's Register.

(4) Under s 57 of the Coal Industry Act 1994, there is a right to a limited amount of information relating to the coal industry, held by the Coal Authority but generally supplied to it by those involved in that industry.

(5) Under s 48 of the Postal Services Act 2011, there is a right of inspection of the register maintained by OFCOM recording matters relating to the provision of postal operator licences.

(6) Under s 35 of the Transport Act 2000, there is a right to inspect the register maintained by the Civil Aviation Authority relating to licences granted companies to provide air traffic services.

(7) Various rights of access under the Communications Act 2003.

(8) Various rights of access under the Gambling Act 2005.

39–002 Nuclear Installations Act 1965

Under section 6 of the Nuclear Installations Act 1965, the Minister must maintain a list showing every site in respect of which a nuclear site licence has been granted and every site which is or was a relevant disposal site. This must include a map or maps showing the position and limits of each such site. The Minister must make arrangements for the list or a copy thereof to be available for inspection by the public and he shall cause notice of these arrangements to be made public in such a manner as may appear to him to be appropriate.

39–003 Harbours Act 1964 etc

Every statutory harbour undertaker must prepare an annual statement of accounts relating to the harbour activities[1] and to any associated activities carried on by him.[2] Copies of any statement of accounts identifying these matters shall be available for inspection by the public at all reasonable hours at the registered office of the competent harbour authority, and the competent harbour authority shall make copies available for purchase by members of the public at a reasonable charge.[3]

39–004 Railways Act 1993

The Office of Rail Regulation is required to maintain a register ('the Regulator's Register')[4] containing matters relating to the provision of licences (being licences authorising a person to be an operator of railway assets),[5] matters relating to access agreements, access contracts and installation access contracts,[6] matters relating to experimental passenger services,[7] closures[8] and the provisions of every railway administration order and of the discharge of such an order.[9] Similarly, the Secretary of State is required to maintain a register containing the provisions of every franchise exemption,[10] every franchise agreement,[11] every amendment of a franchise agreement[12] and other related matters ('the Franchise Director's Register').[13] The contents of the Regulator's register and the contents of the Franchise Director's register are available for inspection by the public, without payment of any fee, between 10.00am and 4.00pm on each working day.[14] Any person may, on the payment of such fee as may be specified in an order, require the Office of Rail Regulation to supply him with a copy of, or an extract from, any part of the Regulator's Register, being a copy or extract which is certified by the Office of Rail Regulation to be a true copy or extract.[15]

39–005 Coal Industry Act 1994

Provision for public access to information in respect of the coal industry is made under the Coal Industry Act 1994. Thus the Coal Authority is required to establish and maintain

1 'Harbour activities' means activities involved in carrying on a statutory harbour undertaking or in carrying out harbour operations: Harbours Act 1964 s 42(9).

2 Harbours Act 1964 s 42(1).

3 Statutory Harbour Undertakings (Pilotage Accounts) Regulations 1988 reg 5, and the Pilotage Act 1987 s 14.

4 Railways Act 1993 s 72(1).

5 Railways Act 1993 s 72(2)(a).

6 Railways Act 1993 s 72(2)(b).

7 Railways Act 1993 s 72(2)(d), 'experimental passenger services' being defined in Pt 4 of the Railways Act 2005.

8 Railways Act 1993 s 72(2)(da); see Pt 4 of the Railways Act 2005.

9 Railways Act 1993 s 72(2)(e).

10 Railways Act 1993 s 73(2)(a).

11 Railways Act 1993 s 73(2)(b).

12 Railways Act 1993 s 73(2)(c).

13 As contained in the Railways Act 1993 s 73(2)(d)-(ga). Section 73A imposes a similar obligation on the Scottish Ministers.

14 Railways (Register) Order 1994 Art 2; Railways Act 1993 s 72(7).

15 Railways Act 1993 s 72(8); Railways (Register) Order 1994 Art 3.

arrangements under which every person is entitled, on payment to the Authority of such fee and subject to such other conditions as the Authority may consider appropriate, to be furnished with certain information[16] and to have so much of the records maintained by the Authority as contain any such information, to be made available to him for inspection at such office of the Authority as it may determine and at such times as may be reasonable;[17] and also to make or be supplied with copies of or extracts from so much of the records maintained by the Authority as contain any such information.[18] For these purposes, 'records' includes registers, maps, plans and accounts, as well as computer records and other records kept otherwise than in documentary form.[19] The information that must be made available in this way is that contained in the register of licences and orders;[20] that contained in the register of rights;[21] and any of the following which is for the time being in the possession of the Authority: information about the geological or physiological features or characteristics of any land in which any unworked coal or any coal mine is situated or of any other land;[22] information about the identity of persons in whom interests and rights in any unworked coal or coal mine have been vested;[23] the contents of any plans of any coal mines or coal workings;[24] any other information about proposals for the carrying on by any person of any coal mining operations;[25] information about any subsidence or subsidence damage or about claims made under the Coal Mining Subsidence Act 1991;[26] and information about such other matters as the Secretary of State may prescribe by regulations.[27] In so far as the right of access conferred is one of inspection (and does not extend to being able to require the supply of a copy of the information), the existence of this right does not of itself cause the information to be exempt information under FOIA.[28]

39– 006 Postal Services Act 2011

OFCOM must maintain a register in which is recorded every notification given to them of persons carrying on business as a postal operator.[29] The Commission must ensure that the contents of the register are available for inspection by the public during such hours as may be specified in an order by the Secretary of State and subject to such reasonable fees (if any) as the Commission may determine.[30]

---

16 Coal Industry Act 1994 s 57(2)(a).

17 Coal Industry Act 1994 s 57(2)(b).

18 Coal Industry Act 1994 s 57(2)(c).

19 Coal Industry Act 1994 s 57(8). Records of the Coal Authority are public records for the purposes of the Public Records Act 1958: Coal Industry Act 1994 s 10.

20 That is, under Coal Industry Act 1994 s 35.

21 That is, under Coal Industry Act 1994 s 56.

22 Coal Industry Act 1994 s 57(1)(a).

23 Coal Industry Act 1994 s 57(1)(b).

24 Coal Industry Act 1994 s 57(1)(c). The Authority must maintain such records of information which comes into its possession and which falls into any of the preceding three heads as it considers appropriate: Coal Industry Act 1994 s 57(6).

25 Coal Industry Act 1994 s 57(1)(d).

26 Coal Industry Act 1994 s 57(1)(e).

27 Coal Industry Act 1994 s 57(1)(f).

28 See §25– 001.

29 Postal Services Act 2011 s 48(5).

30 Postal Services Act 2011 s 48(7).

39– 007 Transport Act 2000

The Civil Aviation Authority must maintain a register[31] containing details of licences[32] granted to a company authorising it to provide air traffic services in respect of an authorised area.[33] The CAA must ensure that the contents of the register are available for inspection by the public during such hours as may be specified in an order made by the Secretary of State.[34] If requested by any person to do so the CAA must supply him with a copy (certified to be true) of the register or of an extract from it.[35]

39– 008 Communications Act 2003

The Office of Communication must maintain a register for the purposes of s 33 of the Communications Act 2003[36] recording every designation by them, every withdrawal by them of a designation, every notification received by them under s 33 and any deemed notification received under s 33.[37] Information recorded in the register must be recorded in such manner as OFCOM consider appropriate.[38] The register is available for public inspection, subject to the payment of a fee.[39] OFCOM must also maintain a public register of information[40] relating to the issue, renewal or variation of wireless telegraphy licences or grants or recognised spectrum access.[41] Subject to such conditions (including conditions as to payment) as may be prescribed by regulations, the register is open to inspection by the public.

39– 009 Gambling Act 2005

The Gambling Commission must maintain a register of operating licences[42] containing such details of and relating to each licence as the Commission thinks appropriate.[43] The Commission shall make the register available for inspection by the public at all reasonable times,[44] and shall make arrangements for the provision of a copy of an entry in the register to the public on request.[45] A licensing authority[46] shall maintain a separate register of each of the

31 Transport Act 2000 s 35(1).

32 Namely those matters set out in the Transport Act 2000 s 35(3). This duty does not extend to anything of which the CAA is unaware: Transport Act 2000 s 35(4).

33 Transport Act 2000 s 5(1).

34 Transport Act 2000 s 35(7). No such order has been made.

35 Transport Act 2000 s 35(8). This provision does not apply if a charge required by a scheme or regulations made under s 11 of the Civil Aviation Act 1982, being a payment to be made to the CAA for the exercise of its functions, is not paid: Transport Act 2000 s 35(9).

36 Communications Act 2003 s 44(1).

37 Communications Act 2003 s 44(2).

38 Communications Act 2003 s 44(3).

39 Communications Act 2003 s 44(6).

40 Wireless Telegraphy Act 2006 s 31(1); Wireless Telegraphy (Register) Regulations 2004 reg 3.

41 Wireless Telegraphy (Register) Regulations 2004 reg 4(1).

42 The Commission may issue an operating licence, which is a licence which states that it authorises the user to operate a casino, to provide facilities for playing bingo, to provide facilities for betting, to act as a betting intermediary, to make gaming machines available for use, to manufacture, supply, install, adapt, maintain or repair a gaming machine, to manufacture, etc gambling software or to promote a lottery: Gambling Act 2005 ss 65(1) and (2).

43 Gambling Act 2005 s 106(1)(a).

44 Gambling Act 2005 s 106(1)(b).

45 Gambling Act 2005 s 106(1)(c).

46 As defined in s 2 of the Gambling Act 2005.

following:

(1) premises licences;[47]
(2) temporary use notices;[48]
(3) family entertainment centre gambling machine permits;[49]
(4) club gaming permits and club machine permits;[50]
(5) licensed premises gaming machine permits;[51]
(6) prize gaming permits.[52]

In relation to each of these registers, the authority shall make the register and the information contained in it available for inspection by members of the public at all reasonable times[53] and shall make arrangements for the provision of a copy of an entry in the register, or of information, to a member of the public on request.[54]

47 Gambling Act 2005 s 156(1). A premises licence is a licence which states that it authorises premises to be used for the operation of a casino, the provision of facilities for the playing of bingo, making gaming machines available for use, or the provision of facilities for betting: Gambling Act 2005 s 150(1).

48 Gambling Act 2005 s 234(1)(a). A temporary use notice is a notice provided by the holder of an operating licence which states his intention to carry on a prescribed activity for a period of less than 21 days in a period of 12 months: Gambling Act 2005 ss 214-218.

49 Schedule 10 to the Gambling Act 2005 para 23(1)(a).

50 Schedule 12 to the Gaming Act 2005 para 26(1)(a).

51 Schedule 13 to the Gaming Act 2005 para 22(1)(a).

52 Schedule 14 to the Gaming Act 2005 para 23(1)(a).

53 In relation to the register for premises licences: see Gambling Act 2005 s 156(1)(b). In relation to the register for temporary use notices: see Gambling Act 2005 s 234(1)(b). In relation to the register for family entertainment centre gambling machine permits: see Sch 10 to the Gambling Act 2005 para 23(1)(b). In relation to the register for club gaming permits and club machine permits: see Sch 12 to the Gaming Act 2005 para 26(1)(b). In relation to the licensed premises gaming machine permits: see Sch 13 to the Gaming Act 2005 para 22(1)(b). In relation to the register for prize gaming permits: see Sch 14 to the Gaming Act 2005 para 23(1)(b).

54 In relation to the register for premises licences: see Gambling Act 2005 s 156(1)(c). In relation to the register for temporary use notices: see Gambling Act 2005 s 234(1)(c). In relation to the register for family entertainment centre gambling machine permits: see Sch 10 of the Gambling Act 2005 para 23(1)(c). In relation to the register for club gaming permits and club machine permits: see Sch 12 to the Gaming Act 2005 para 26(1)(c). In relation to the register for licensed premises gaming machine permits: see Sch 13 to the Gaming Act 2005 para 22(1)(c). In relation to the register for prize gaming permits: see Sch 14 to the Gaming Act 2005 para 23(1)(c).

CHAPTER 40

Educational information

1. EDUCATIONAL INFORMATION

40–001 Introduction

The specific right to educational information differs somewhat from the other rights to official information in that it is in most part concerned with providing members of the public with general information relating to educational bodies, rather than information that is specifically addressed to answering the terms of a request. In brief terms, legislation places a duty to provide certain information on the governing body of each school, the head teacher of a school and each local education authority. Specific rights are, however, conferred on parents to access their child's educational record. Similarly, there are various rights of access in relation to reports of inspections of schools.

40–002 Education Act 1996

The Secretary of State is empowered to make regulations requiring the governing body of any institution that is maintained by a local education authority or a special school which is not maintained as such by such an authority, and the proprietor of every independent school to provide such information about the school as may be prescribed.[1] The regulations currently in force for England are the Education (School Information) (England) Regulations 2008.[2]

40–003 Governing bodies

The governing body of a maintained school must publish the report containing special needs information referred to in s 317(5) of the Education Act 1996 and any other general information relating to that school which they may decide to publish as a single document identified as the school prospectus.[3] Copies of the school prospectus must be made available at the school for distribution without charge to parents on request and for reference by parents and other persons.[4] The school prospectus must be published during the offer year and, except in the case of a special school, not later than six weeks before the date up to which parents may

1 Education Act 1996 s 537(1).

2 SI 2008/3093.

3 School Information (England) Regulations 2008 (SI 2008/3093), reg 10(1).

4 School Information (England) Regulations 2008 (SI 2008/3093), reg 10(2).

express a preference for a school in respect of the admission year.[5] In the case of a special school such information must also be published by copies being made available at the offices of the relevant authority for distribution without charge to parents on request and reference by parents and other persons.[6] In the case of any maintained secondary school, a copy of the school prospectus shall be provided without charge to the offices in the area served by the school of persons providing career services in accordance with arrangements made, or directions given, under section 10 of the Employment and Training Act 1973.[7]

40– 004 Head teachers

The head teacher of every maintained school must make available to parents of pupils at the school and other persons the following information:

— the times at which each school session begins and ends on a school day;

— particulars of the charging and remissions policies determined by the governing body of the school under s 457 of the Education Act 1996.

Copies of such information must be provided at the school for inspection by parents and other persons at all reasonable times on a school day and for distribution without charge to parents on request.[8] The head teacher of any school maintained by a local education authority must, prior to the end of the summer term of every school year, prepare a head teacher's report in respect of every registered pupil at the school containing the information referred to in Sch 1 of the Education (Pupil Information) (England) Regulations 2005 and provide a copy of each such report to the following persons free of charge:

— in the case of any pupil who is aged 18 or over at the time the head teacher's report is due to be provided and who is not proposing to leave school by the end of the school year to which the report relates, the pupil himself and, if the head teacher considers there to be special circumstances which make it appropriate, the parents of that pupil;

— in any other case, the parents of the pupil to whom the report relates.[9]

The head teacher of every maintained school must prepare a school leaver's report in respect of any pupil who has ceased to be of compulsory school age and is proposing to leave or has left the school, containing brief particulars of the pupil's progress and achievements in subjects and activities forming part of the school curriculum (other than in relation to any public examination or vocational qualification) in the school year during or at the end of which the pupil proposes to leave or has left school. The head teacher must provide a copy of the school leaver's report to the pupil concerned by no later than September 30 following the end of the school year during or at the end of which the pupil left the school.[10]

40– 005 Local education authorities

Local education authorities are also required to publish detailed information concerning schools in their area.[11] This information includes:

— the addresses and telephone numbers of the offices of the authority to which enquiries in respect of primary and secondary education in their area should be

[5] School Information (England) Regulations 2008 (SI 2008/3093), reg 10(3).

[6] School Information (England) Regulations 2008 (SI 2008/3093), reg 10(4).

[7] School Information (England) Regulations 2008 (SI 2008/3093), reg 10(5).

[8] Education (School Sessions and Charges and Remissions Policies) (Information) (England) Regulations 1999 reg 3.

[9] Education (Pupil Information) (England) Regulations 2005 reg 6(7).

[10] Education (Pupil Information) (England) Regulations 2005 reg 8.

[11] School Information (England) Regulations 2008 Pt 3 and Sch 3.

addressed;[12]

— the arrangements for parents to obtain the information specified in Sch 2 in the case of individual schools other than special schools;[13]

— as respects each school mentioned in the prospectus, other than a special school, the name, address and telephone number of the school and the name of a person to whom enquiries should be addressed, as well as the expected number of pupils at the school and their age range.[14]

Local education authorities must also publish the classification of each school maintained by them;[15] the authority's general arrangements and policies in respect of transport for pupils of compulsory school age and below to and from schools and institutions within the further education sector, including in particular the provision of free transport, the carriage on school buses of pupils for whom free transport is not provided, and the payment in whole or in part of reasonable travel expenses.[16] Local education authorities must publish their general arrangements and policies in respect of the provision of milk, meals and other refreshments including, in particular, the remission in whole or in part of charges. Such authorities must also publish details of their general arrangements and policies in respect of the provision of school clothing (including uniform and physical training clothes), and the making of grants to defray expenses in respect of such clothing and, in particular, the address from which parents may obtain detailed information about the assistance which is available and eligibility for it.[17] Local education authorities must also publish further details of their general arrangements and policies, in the case of pupils attending any school maintained by them, in respect of the making of grants to defray other expenses and the granting of allowances in the case of pupils of compulsory school age, including, in particular, the address from which parents may obtain detailed information about the assistance which is available and eligibility for it. Finally, local education authorities must publish: their general policy in respect of the entering of pupils for public examination; their general arrangements and policies in respect of special educational provision[18] for pupils with special educational needs[19] including, in particular, the arrangements for parents to obtain information about the matters referred to in Part 2 of Sch 3; and the arrangements for parents and others to obtain copies of and to refer to particulars of the charging and remissions policies determined by the authority under s 457 of the Education Act 1996.[20]

40–006 Special educational provision

Local education authorities have a further duty to publish the information specified in Part II

---

12 School Information (England) Regulations 2008 Sch 2, para 1.

13 As defined in s 337 of the Education Act 1996: School Information (England) Regulations 2008 Sch 3 Pt 1 para 2.

14 School Information (England) Regulations 2008 Sch 2 Pt 2.

15 That is, as a community, foundation, voluntary controlled or voluntary aided school or a community special or foundation school; a primary, middle or secondary school; a comprehensive, secondary modern or grammar school; a co-educational or single sex school; and as a day or boarding school or (as the case may be) a school taking both day and boarding pupils; in the case of a school with selection arrangements, a partially selective school or a grammar school; in the case of a school designated as having a religious character by an order under section 69(3) SSFA, the religious denomination, or denominations, of the school; in the case of a school with specialist status, its specialism: School Information (England) Regulations 2008 Sch 2 Pt 2 para 11.

16 School Information (England) Regulations 2008 Sch 3 Pt 1 para 11.

17 School Information (England) Regulations 2008 Sch 3 Pt 2 paras 3 and 4.

18 As defined in Education Act 1996 s 312: School Information (England) Regulations 2008 Sch 3 Pt 1 para 12.

19 As defined in Education Act 1996 s 312: School Information (England) Regulations 2008 Sch 3 Pt 1 para 12.

20 See also the School Information (England) Regulations 2008 Sch 3 Pt 1 para 8.

of Sch 3 to the School Information (England) Regulations 2008 concerning special educational provision.[21] This information includes the authority's detailed arrangements and policies in respect of the identification and assessment of children with special educational needs and the involvement of parents in that process; the provision made in community, voluntary and special schools maintained by them for pupils with special educational needs and the use made by them of such special schools maintained by other authorities; and special educational provision supplied otherwise than at school.[22] In addition, local education authorities must publish:

— their arrangements and policies in respect of the use of non-maintained special and independent schools;[23]
— the arrangements for parents who consider that their child may have special educational needs to obtain advice and further information;[24]
— the authority's arrangements and policies in respect of transport for pupils of compulsory school age and below to and from maintained and non-maintained special schools and independent schools;[25] and
— the arrangements for parents to obtain the information particularised in Sch 2 in the case of the special schools used by the authority which are maintained by them or other authorities.[26]

40–007 Publication of information

The information described in Sch 3 to the School Information (England) Regulations 2008 must be published by copies being made available for distribution without charge to parents on request, and for reference by parents and other persons at the office of the relevant authority and at every school maintained by the authority (other than nursery schools and special schools or a pupil referral unit).[27] Copies of the above-mentioned information must also be distributed without charge to parents of pupils at schools maintained by the relevant authority (other than nursery schools or special schools or a pupil referral unit) who, in the publication school year, are in the final year at such schools and who might transfer to other schools so maintained;[28] and by copies being made available for reference by parents and other persons at the public libraries in the area of the relevant authority.[29] Local authorities also have a duty, with respect to maintained schools,[30] to publish a composite prospectus containing the information specified in Sch 2 to the School Information (England) Regulations 2008 concerning those schools.[31]

40–008 Special educational needs

A local authority must publish specific information in relation to special educational needs provision.[32] The local education authority must publish this information by providing a written

21 As defined in s 312 of the Education Act 1996.

22 School Information (England) Regulations 2008 Sch 3 para 12.

23 School Information (England) Regulations 2008 Sch 3 para 13.

24 School Information (England) Regulations 2008 Sch 3 para 14.

25 School Information (England) Regulations 2008 Sch 3 para 15.

26 School Information (England) Regulations 2008 Sch 3 para 16.

27 School Information (England) Regulations 2008 reg 9(1)(b).

28 School Information (England) Regulations 2008 reg 9(1)(c).

29 School Information (England) Regulations 2008 reg 9(1)(d).

30 As defined by s 84(6) of the School Standards and Framework Act 1998.

31 School Information (England) Regulations 2008 reg 5(1).

32 Special Educational Needs (Provision of Information by Local Education Authorities) (England) Regulations 2001 reg 2 Sch 1.

copy of the information to any Primary Care Trust or social services authority which in the opinion of the local education authority has an interest in that information, making the information available on the internet and providing a written copy of the information to any person on request.[33] Any revisions to the information must be published by the local education authority as soon as reasonably practicable after a revision has been made by providing the revised information to a Primary Care Trust or social services authority previously provided with information by the local education authority, updating the website maintained by the authority on the internet to display the revised information and notifying the maintained schools in the authority's area of the revisions by post or by electronic communication.[34] The information must be published free of charge.[35]

40–009 Educational record

The governing body of any school maintained by a local education authority (other than a nursery school) and any special school not so maintained must make a pupil's educational record[36] available for inspection by the parent, free of charge, within 15 days of the parent's written request for access to that record.[37] The governing body must provide a copy of the pupil's educational record to the parent, on payment of such fee (not exceeding the cost of supply), if any, as the governing body may prescribe within 15 school days of receipt of the parent's written request for a copy of that record.[38] When complying with either request a governing body must not make available for inspection or provide a copy of any information which they could not lawfully disclose to the pupil himself under the DPA 1998 or in relation to which the pupil himself would have no right of access under that Act.[39]

40–010 Reports by Chief Inspector

A copy of a report sent to an appropriate authority[40] by Her Majesty's Chief Inspector of Schools in England concerning an inspection of a school[41] must be made available by it for inspection by members of the public at such times and at such places as may be reasonable. The appropriate authority must also provide a copy of the report free of charge (or in prescribed cases on payment of such fee as they think fit which does not exceed the cost of supply) to any person who asks for one and must take such steps as are reasonably practicable to secure that every registered parent of a registered pupil at the school receives a copy of the report within such period following receipt of the report by the authority as may be prescribed.[42] There are corresponding provisions for interim statements.[43]

[33] Special Educational Needs (Provision of Information by Local Education Authorities) (England) Regulations 2001 reg 3(1).

[34] Special Educational Needs (Provision of Information by Local Education Authorities) (England) Regulations 2001 reg 3(4).

[35] Special Educational Needs (Provision of Information by Local Education Authorities) (England) Regulations 2001 reg 3(5).

[36] 'Educational record' is defined in Education (Pupil Information) (England) Regulations 2005 reg 3.

[37] Education (Pupil Information) (England) Regulations 2005 reg 5(2).

[38] Education (Pupil Information) (England) Regulations 2005 reg 5(3).

[39] Education (Pupil Information) (England) Regulations 2005 reg 5(4).

[40] As defined in Education Act 2005 s 18.

[41] Namely a report issued pursuant to Education Act 2005 s 5.

[42] Education Act 2005 s 14. Where the school is a school other than a maintained school, the same duty falls on the proprietor of the school: Education Act 2005 s 16.

[43] Education Act 2005 ss 14A and 16A. Interim statements are defined in s 10A.

40–011 Reports by inspectors

A copy of any report and summary sent to an appropriate authority[44] by a registered inspector or member of the inspectorate concerning an inspection of a school[45] must be made available for inspection by members of the public at such times and at such place as may be reasonable. The appropriate authority must also provide a copy of the report and summary free of charge (or in prescribed cases on payment of such fee as they think fit which does not exceed the cost of supply) to any person who asks for one and must take such steps as are reasonably practicable to secure that every parent of a registered pupil at the school receives a copy of the summary within such period following receipt of the report by the authority as may be prescribed.[46] On receipt of such a report and summary, an appropriate authority must prepare a written statement of the action which it proposes to take in light of the report and the period within which it proposes to take it.[47] The appropriate authority must make any statement prepared by it under this section available for inspection by members of the public at such times and at such place as may be reasonable. The appropriate authority must provide a copy of the statement, free of charge (or in prescribed cases on payment of such fee as it sees fit which does not exceed the cost of supply) to any person who asks for one and must take such steps as are reasonably practicable to secure that every parent of a registered pupil at the school receives a copy of the statement as soon as reasonably practicable.[48] The latter requirement is taken to have been satisfied by the appropriate authority if it:

(a) takes such steps as are reasonably practicable to secure that every parent of a pupil at the school receives, as soon as is reasonably practicable, a copy of a document prepared by it which summarises the statement and contains a statement of the right to request a copy of it; and

(b) provides a copy of the statement to every parent of a registered pupil at the school who asks for one.[49]

40–012 Reports of religious education

It is the duty of a governing body of any voluntary or foundation school in England which has been designated under s 69(3) of the School Standards and Framework Act 1998 by the Secretary of State as having a religious character to secure that any denominational education given to pupils and the contents of the school's collective worship are inspected.[50] A person conducting such an inspection must report on these matters to the governing body.[51] The governing body must make any such report available for inspection by members of the public, at such times and at such a place as may be reasonable.[52] The governing body must take such steps as are reasonably practicable to secure that every parent of a registered pupil at the school for whom the school provides denominational education or who takes part in collective worship

---

44 As defined in Education Act 1996 s 43.

45 Namely a report issued pursuant to Education Act 2005 s 28.

46 Education Act 2005 s 38(4). Where the school is a school other than a maintained school, the same duty falls on the proprietor of the school: Education Act 2005 s 41(4).

47 Education Act 2005 s 39(1). Where the school is a school other than a maintained school, the same duty falls on the proprietor of the school: Education Act 2005 s 42(1).

48 Education Act 2005 s 39(7). Where the school is a school other than a maintained school, the same duty falls on the proprietor of the school: Education Act 2005 s 42(5).

49 Education Act 2005 s 39(8).

50 Education Act 2005 s 48(1).

51 Education Act 2005 ss 48(4), 49(2) and 49(3).

52 Education Act 2005 s 49(4)(a).

receives a copy of the report as soon as is reasonably practicable.[53]

53 Education Act 2005 s 49(4)(b).

CHAPTER 41

Common law rights and controls

1. COMMON LAW RIGHTS

41– 001 Traditional position

Until the Supreme Court's judgment in *Kennedy v Charity Commission*, courts in the United Kingdom had never recognised any person as having a common law right to request and inspect information held by a public authority.[1] The fact that a person had an easily recognisable interest in having access to the requested information or that its disclosure would cause no harm to the public authority was of no consequence to the common law. Occasionally, undesirable outcomes that resulted from the rigidity of this position appear to have been the catalyst for legislative intervention.[2] But until the enactment of FOIA, every such intervention was confined to conferring a right limited to a specific class of individuals and to specific sorts of documents. It was the absence of any effective wider right which left an unsatisfied need for a general entitlement to see information held by public authorities. That need was finally met through the FOI Act.[3] In *Kennedy v Charity Commission* the facts, as well as the findings of the First-tier Tribunal, suggested a gap in the coverage of the FOI Act that was difficult to reconcile with the object of the legislation – an exemption, the literal interpretation of which captured most of the requested documents, regardless of the public interest in their disclosure and regardless of the harmlessness of their disclosure, leaving no right of access to any of those documents. Having declined to use common law principles of statutory interpretation

---

1 *R v Mid Glamorgan Family Health Services, ex p Martin* [1995] 1 WLR 110, [1995] 1 All ER 356 (where it was held that a patient had no common law right of access to his medical records held by two public health authorities). It is also implicit in wider statements of principle in cases such as: *Entick v Carrington* (1765) 19 State Tr 1029 at 1063-1074, [1558-1774] All ER Rep 41; *Norwich Pharmacal Co v Customs and Excise Commissioners* [1974] AC 133; *Rice v Connolly* [1966] 2 QB 414 at 419. The only exception was for councillors and certain office-holders in respect of information held by the body for which they held office: see §§37– 005 to 37– 009. This may be seen as the common law's preparedness to imply an obligation on a public body so as to provide its office-holders with the means to perform their office. The common law's refusal, in the absence of some proprietary claim, to concern itself with information was similarly reflected in its refusal to recognise personal privacy: *Wainwright v Home Office* [2003] UKHL 53, [2004] 2 AC 406. The common law's ever-ready interest in anything proprietary may be seen behind the numerous claims that information was a species of property.

2 For example: the Public Bodies (Admission to Meetings) Act 1960, see §§37– 043 to 37– 044; Local Government Act 1972 Pt VA, see §§37– 011, 37– 011 to 37– 046; Access to Health Records Act 1990, see §§38– 001 to 38– 002.

3 In conjunction with the EIR, both taking full effect on 1 January 2005 See further §§1– 014 to 1– 017.

to give the exemption a meaning consistent with the policy of the legislation, the Supreme Court was left with the choice of acknowledging an ECHR Art 10 right to achieve a similar reading of the exemption or denying that right and opening the way to a claim in the ECtHR. The Supreme Court chose neither, instead divining in the common law a right of access to publicly-held information so as to make ECHR intrusion appear unnecessary.[4] Whether this illumination of the common law was prompted by a wish to protect its dominion from a non-domestic convention right which had shown greater acuity can only be speculated.[5] This chapter is concerned with trying to identify the bounds of and principles surrounding the common law right that made its appearance in the majority judgments in *Kennedy v Charity Commission.*

41– 002 Background to *Kennedy*

In *Kennedy v Charity Commission* Lord Mance, speaking for the majority of the Supreme Court, started his judgment by noting the importance of information to the processes of democratic government and to those who seek to hold it to account.[6] His description of the appeal as also concerning 'the relationship between the Freedom of Information Act and the statutory and common law position regarding the disclosure of information outside the scope of the FOIA,' was predicated on the common law being able to compel disclosure of information held by a public body in circumstances where that disclosure was not required by FOIA (and cognate legislation).[7] In *Kennedy*, a Times investigative journalist had requested disclosure of documents in a concluded Charity Commission inquiry into a controversial charity. The inquiry had been one of the most extensive ever carried out by the Charity Commission. The Charity Commission had published three brief reports under s 8(6) of the Charities Act 1993 which set out its findings but which did not set out any of the documentary basis for those findings. The journalist needed the underlying documents in order to understand the Commission's conclusions and to investigate whether the inquiry had been carried out properly. Most of the information he requested was in documents prepared by other public authorities or private persons or bodies for the purposes of the Charity Commission inquiry. The list of information falling within the terms of the request numbered over one thousand separate documents that had been submitted to the Charity Commission. It also included some pre-existing documents and communications between the Charity Commission, other public authorities, other entities or persons. It was common ground that the information was all of potential public interest.[8] The Charity Commission had decided that the information requested was caught by the class-based, absolute exemption in FOIA s 32(2)[9] as documents held by the Commission solely for

4 In *Wainwright v Home Office* [2003] UKHL 53, [2004] 2 AC 406 at [31] Lord Hoffmann, having observed that 'no one [had] suggested that freedom of speech is in itself a legal principle which is capable of sufficient definition to enable one to deduce specific rules to be applied in concrete cases,' declared that 'that is not the way the common law works.' In *Kennedy v Charity Commission* the Supreme Court demonstrated that the common law can work that way without even the need for submissions that it do so.

5 The common law had a similar conversion in relation to the protection of personal privacy. Again, the ECHR had earlier shown an ability to see the problem and to fashion a solution.

6 *Kennedy v Charity Commission* [2014] UKSC 20, [2015] AC 455 at [1].

7 At [2]. That this passage was not intended simply to be noting that a public authority might, without being compelled by FOIA, disclose information held by it, is apparent from the reasoning of the judgment (in particular, the rejection of the need to apply common law canons of construction to limit the scope of s 32 or to have recourse to Art 10 of the ECHR) and subsequent passages dealing with the common law 'principle' of disclosure: see [6], [9], [33]-[35], [45], [47] and [55]. Similarly Lord Toulson at [128], [131], [133], [135] and [140].

8 *Kennedy v Charity Commission* [2014] UKSC 20, [2015] AC 455 at [11].

9 This provides that information held by a public authority is exempt information if it is held only by virtue of being contained in (a) any document placed in the custody of a person conducting an inquiry or arbitration, for the purposes of the inquiry or arbitration, or (b) any document created by a person conducting an inquiry or arbitration, for the purposes of the inquiry or arbitration. See to the same effect FOI(S)A s 37(1)(b).

the purposes of the inquiry. In consequence there was no need for any consideration of whether the public interest in maintaining the exemption outweighed that which would be met by disclosure. Moreover, since s 32(2) does not describe a protected interest that would be or would be likely to be harmed by disclosure of the information, it was engaged regardless of the harmlessness of disclosure. It was argued on behalf of the journalist that the purpose of FOIA s 32(2) was to prevent interference with the process of an inquiry while it was continuing and that once the inquiry ended the exemption fell away. It was argued that the words of s 32(2) were capable of bearing this meaning and applying ordinary common law canons of statutory interpretation that reading should be preferred over one that resulted in the exemption applying until the documents had become an historical record. The Supreme Court rejected this submission.[10] In the alternative Mr Kennedy argued that an exemption that continued beyond the conclusion of the inquiry was an unjustifiable interference with his journalistic right of freedom of expression under ECHR Art 10.

41– 003 ECHR Art 10 in *Kennedy*

The journalist relied on the obligation of the court under the Human Rights Act 1998 to take account of, inter alia, judgments and decisions of the European Court of Human Rights.[11] Whilst this does not require domestic courts to follow those judgments, it has been accepted by domestic courts that generally they will follow any clear and constant jurisprudence of the Strasbourg court.[12] Mr Kennedy argued that there was such a body of Strasbourg case law establishing that societal 'watchdogs' including the press had a presumptive right under Art 10(1) to obtain information on matters of public concern from public authorities.[13] Put another way, there was a presumed positive obligation on the state to give access to information in this way. This duty arose even when there was no right under the relevant domestic law of the contracting state to receive the information.[14] He pointed to the FTT's decision in his appeal, which had found as a fact that there was no necessity in a democratic society under Art 10(2) for the Charity Commission's blanket refusal to disclose any of the information he was seeking.[15] This decision of the FTT showed that the refusal by the Charity Commission was disproportionate and so, he said, the refusal was a violation of his journalistic right. The court's obligation to read and to give effect to primary legislation 'so far as it is possible' in a way which is compatible with Convention rights[16] accordingly required it to read down s 32(2) in a way that gave him access to the material now that the inquiry had ended.[17] The Supreme Court, by a majority, also rejected this argument. If the appeal had turned on the journalist's argument for access under Art 10 the majority would have found in any event that earlier

---

10 *Kennedy v Charity Commission* [2014] UKSC 20, [2015] AC 455 at [28]-[30], [34], [102]-[104].

11 See Human Rights Act 1998 s 2(1).

12 See *R (Alconbury Developments Ltd) v Secretary of State for the Environment, Transport and the Regions* [2001] UKHL 23, [2003] 2 AC 295; *R (Ullah) v Special Adjudicator* [2004] UKHL 26, [2004] 2 AC 323; *R (Animal Defenders International) v Secretary of State for Culture, Media and Sport* [2008] UKHL 15, [2008] 1 AC 1312; *Secretary of State for the Home Department v AF (No 3)* [2009] UKHL 28, [2010] 2 AC 269; *Manchester City Council v Pinnock* [2010] UKSC 45, [2011] 2 AC 104. There has been slide back from this position: *Moohan v Lord Advocate* [2014] UKSC 67, [2015] AC 901 at [104].

13 Relying on: *Társaság a Szabadságjogokért v Hungary* (2011) 53 EHRR 3; *Kenedi v Hungary* (2009) 27 BHRC 335; *Gillberg v Sweden* (2012) 34 BHRC 247; *Shapovalov v Ukraine* (45835/05) [2012] ECHR 1665; *Youth Initiative for Human Rights v Serbia* (2013) 36 BHRC 687; *Österreichische Vereinigung zur Erhaltung v Austria* (2013) 36 BHRC 697.

14 *Kennedy v Charity Commission* [2014] UKSC 20, [2015] AC 455 at [93].

15 *Kennedy v Charity Commission*, FTT, 18 November 2011.

16 Human Rights Act 1998 s 3.

17 Or reading it in a case such as the present as a qualified exemption (requiring a balancing of the public interests for and against disclosure).

decisions of the Grand Chamber of the European Court of Human Rights, to the effect that there was no right of access to state material, should prevail: or at any rate that this was the case where there was no domestic law right to the material.[18] Accordingly there was no basis in the Strasbourg case law for reading down s 32(2) in the way contended for.[19] Lord Wilson, dissenting, considered that recent Strasbourg authority had made clear that a right to require an unwilling public authority to disclose information can arise under Art 10.[20]

41– 004 **Common law right in *Kennedy***

But the majority of the Supreme Court justices went on to hold that, even if Art 10 did give social watchdogs the presumptive right of access contended for, there was a common law right in exactly the same form. Therefore there would be no need to read down s 32(1) in the way suggested.[21] Although forming no part of the argument before the Court, the majority identified a previously unrecognised common law principle of open government which could be used to challenge decisions refusing access to state information, enforceable by judicial review proceedings.[22] This, however, was of no assistance to Mr Kennedy. His case was, and had only ever been, that the FOI Act, not the common law, gave him a claim to access.[23] The judgments of the majority are not clear as to when, beyond the case being considered by the Supreme Court, this principle might apply. In the case before the court the majority reasoned as follows. The relevant statutory provisions of the Charities Act 1993 identified the Charity Commission's objectives, functions and duties in terms that made clear the importance of the public interest in the operations of both the Charity Commission and the charities which it regulates. Its statutory functions included obtaining and disseminating information about its activities.[24] Importantly, the majority considered that there was also a common law presumption of openness in a context such as the present (namely public inquiries) akin to, though not the same as, the common law open justice principle applying to court proceedings.[25] In consequence, the Charity Commission had common law duties of openness, accountability and transparency.[26] The majority considered that FOI Act did not preclude this conclusion because FOI Act s 78 provides in terms that nothing in the Act is to be taken to limit the powers of a public authority to disclose information held by it.[27] Since the information sought was of genuine public interest and had been requested for legitimate journalistic purposes, the Charity Commission was under a presumptive common law duty to disclose. If it was to refuse to do so lawfully it had to show some persuasive countervailing considerations properly justifying a

18 As to the earlier decisions of the Grand Chamber on which this conclusion was based, see: *Leander v Sweden* (1987) 9 EHRR 357; *Gaskin v United Kingdom* (1989) 12 EHRR 36; *Guerra v Italy* (1998) 26 EHRR 357; *Roche v United Kingdom* (2005) 42 EHRR 599. And see *Kennedy v Charity Commission* [2014] UKSC 20, [2015] AC 455 at [94], [147].

19 *Kennedy v Charity Commission* [2014] UKSC 20, [2015] AC 455 at [94], [101], [145], [148].

20 *Kennedy v Charity Commission* [2014] UKSC 20, [2015] AC 455 at [189]. Lord Carnwath agreed with Lord Wilson [219].

21 *Kennedy v Charity Commission* [2014] UKSC 20, [2015] AC 455 at [35], [36], [101], [131].

22 Lord Carnwath JSC, dissenting at [202], noted that this approach though now adopted by the majority, was 'unsupported by any of the parties before us, in my view for good reasons…'

23 *Kennedy v Charity Commission* [2014] UKSC 20, [2015] AC 455 at [8], [101(i)]. Until the Supreme Court's judgment, it had never been suggested by any court that such a common law right existed and, indeed, the existence of such a common law right had been denied (see fn 1 above), providing the stated rationale for freedom of information legislation from the earliest inception of the bill to its enactment: see §§1– 002 to 1– 014 and §§2– 001 to 2– 018.

24 *Kennedy v Charity Commission* [2014] UKSC 20, [2015] AC 455 at [43], [126].

25 *Kennedy v Charity Commission* [2014] UKSC 20, [2015] AC 455 at [47], [48], [126], [132], [133].

26 *Kennedy v Charity Commission* [2014] UKSC 20, [2015] AC 455 at [51], [55].

27 *Kennedy v Charity Commission* [2014] UKSC 20, [2015] AC 455 at [39], [106], [156]. See also FOI(S)A s 66.

refusal.[28] Although not so expressed in the majority judgments, the principle in *Kennedy* may be seen as an extension or an adaptation of what has been characterised as the common law right of freedom of expression:

> The fundamental right of free expression has been recognised at common law for very many years... Modern democratic government means government of the people by the people for the people. But there can be no government by the people if they are ignorant of the issues to be resolved, the arguments for and against different solutions and the facts underlying those arguments.... But there can be no assurance that government is carried out for the people unless the facts are made known, the issues publicly ventilated....Experience...shows, in this country and elsewhere, that publicity is a powerful disinfectant. Where abuses are exposed, they can be remedied. Even where abuses have already been remedied, the public may be entitled to know that they occurred. The role of the press in exposing abuses and miscarriages of justice has been a potent and honourable one. But the press cannot expose that of which it is denied knowledge.[29]

41– 005 Common law enforcement

The majority in *Kennedy* envisaged that where the common law duties of openness, accountability and transparency were engaged on the facts, a request for the information could be made under both common law and the FOI Act:

> ...if for any reason the applicant was in doubt, he could ask the public authority to say whether it contended that the information was within section 32(2) and to explain its reason for saying so. If so, the public authority could not then complain about the applicant following the route of judicial review...[30]

The applicant would then ask the public authority to disclose the material under its general powers, rather than FOIA. This would force the public authority to consider the public interest considerations for and against disclosure that were relevant to the performance of its statutory functions. As Lord Sumption put it:

> ...the Charity Commission has never been asked to disclose the information under its general powers. It has only been asked to disclose it under a particular statute from which the information in question is absolutely exempt. This is not just a procedural nicety. If the commission had been asked to disclose under its general powers, it would have had to consider the public interest considerations for and against disclosure which were relevant to the performance of its statutory functions under the Charities Act. Its assessment of these matters would in principle have been reviewable by the court....[31]

In the event of a refusal and judicial review challenge the Administrative Court would approach the challenge applying principles of necessity and proportionality, rather than Wednesbury unreasonableness.[32] Thus:

> In any proceedings for judicial review of a refusal by the Charity Commission to give effect to such a request, it would be necessary for the court to place itself so far as possible in the same position as the Charity Commission, including perhaps by inspecting the material sought. Only in that way could it undertake any review to ascertain whether the relevant interests had been properly balanced. The interests involved and the balancing exercise would be of a nature with which the court is familiar and accustomed to evaluate and undertake. The Charity Commission's own evaluation would have weight, as it would under Art 10. But the Charity Commission's objectives, functions and duties under the Charities Act and the nature and importance of the interests involved limit the scope of the response

28 *Kennedy v Charity Commission* [2014] UKSC 20, [2015] AC 455 at [56], [128], [129].

29 *R v Shayler (David)* [2002] UKHL 11, [2003] 1 AC 247 at [21] per Lord Bingham of Cornhill.

30 *Kennedy v Charity Commission* [2014] UKSC 20, [2015] AC 455 at [135], Lord Toulson.

31 *Kennedy v Charity Commission* [2014] UKSC 20, [2015] AC 455 at [157].

32 *Kennedy v Charity Commission* [2014] UKSC 20, [2015] AC 455 at [54], [56], [132].

open to the Charity Commission in respect of any particular request.[33]

41–006 Domestic developments

There has not yet been a judicial review in which a refusal by a public authority to disclose information has been quashed by the High Court on the basis of the common law duty identified by the majority of the Supreme Court. The High Court has made clear that where the FOI Act is an available route to obtain disclosure of state material it is likely to be regarded as a suitable alternative remedy precluding permission to judicially review a refusal relying on the common law duty.[34] The courts have, however, given some consideration to the reasoning in *Kennedy* in other cases. In *R (Privacy International) v HMRC*[35] the High Court considered the powers and duties of HMRC to disclose information about its export control functions to the NGO, Privacy International. There was a dispute as to the breadth of the power of HMRC to disclose information about the exercise of these functions in circumstances where the NGO was concerned that malicious internet surveillance software was being supplied to oppressive governments in breach of export controls, and used to facilitate serious human rights abuses.[36] The court, having quashed an initial refusal by HM Revenue & Customs to exercise the power to disclose, drew on Lord Mance's opening observations in *Kennedy* in identifying the status of the requestor (as the media, a pressure group or an NGO) as a consideration which points towards some disclosure of material requested being required. In *R (D and another) v Parole Board* the Divisional Court considered the prohibition on publication of information about proceedings held in private before the Parole Board.[37] It held that the open justice principle, particularly the right of the public to receive information about judicial proceedings, applied to the proceedings of the Parole Board. Thus, it considered, some information about such proceedings, even though they took place in in private, might have to be put into the public domain, depending on the circumstances of the case.[38] In doing so it referred to an observation of Lord Toulson JSC in *Kennedy* that:

> The fundamental reasons for the open justice principle are of general application to any such body [viz a body exercising the power of the state], although its practical operation may vary according to the nature of the work of a particular judicial body.[39]

The Parole Board, it held, was such a body.[40] On this basis the common law open justice principle applied to it and the Divisional Court did not need to go on and consider an alternative argument advanced by a newspaper seeking information about the Parole Board proceedings that the common law duties of openness and transparency, identified by the majority in *Kennedy*, were engaged on the facts.[41]

---

33 *Kennedy v Charity Commission* [2014] UKSC 20, [2015] AC 455 at [56], Lord Mance. See also [132], Lord Toulson.

34 See *R (Good Law Project Limited, Molly Scott Cato Mep) v The Secretary of State for Exiting the European Union* [2018] EWHC 719 (Admin).

35 [2015] EWHC 1475 (Admin), [2015] 1 WLR 397.

36 *R (Privacy International and others) v HMRC* [2015] EWHC 1475 (Admin), [2015] 1 WLR 397 at [52]-[54]. HMRC accepted that it had a power to do so under s18(2) of the Commissioners of Revenue and Customs Act 2005.

37 *R (DSD) v Parole Board* [2018] EWHC 694 (Admin), [2018] 3 WLR 829. The prohibition was in r 25 of the Parole Board Rules 2016.

38 *R (DSD) v Parole Board* [2018] EWHC 694 (Admin), [2018] 3 WLR 829 at [175].

39 *Kennedy v Charity Commission* [2014] UKSC 20, [2015] AC 455 at [115].

40 *R (DSD) v Parole Board* [2018] EWHC 694 (Admin), [2018] 3 WLR 829 at [170].

41 *R (DSD) v Parole Board* [2018] EWHC 694 (Admin), [2018] 3 WLR 829 at [180].

41-007 ECtHR developments

In *Magyar Helsinki Bizottsag v Hungary*[42] – which post-dated *Kennedy v Charity Commission* – the Grand Chamber of the European Court of Human Rights had the opportunity to consider whether an NGO had a right of access to state information under Art 10, which information had been denied to it under domestic law. Magyar Helsinki Bizottság (the Hungarian Helsinki Committee) monitors the implementation of international human-rights standards in Hungary. Its initial research into the ex officio appointment of defence lawyers in the Hungarian criminal courts showed that the investigative authorities, in particular the police, were free to choose the defence lawyers in criminal cases. Defendants mistrusted the lawyers so selected, in particular, because many police departments used the same lawyers in most of their cases. This made the favoured lawyers dependent on the police appointments to earn a living. In order to pursue its research and campaigning on this issue, the Hungarian Helsinki Committee requested the names of the public defenders selected in the year 2008 from twenty-eight police departments, and the number of cases given to each of these lawyers. Two police departments refused to disclose the data. The Hungarian Supreme Court held that the data requested was personal data under section 2(1) of the Hungarian Data Act. Accordingly the Hungarian Data Act entitled the two departments to refuse the request. The Committee complained to the Strasbourg Court of a violation of its Art 10 rights. The Hungarian Government, and the United Kingdom Government intervening, argued that Art 10 was not engaged on the facts. They pointed in particular to the Grand Chamber decisions which the majority in the Supreme Court had relied on in *Kennedy* to deny the journalist's asserted right under Art 10.[43] The applicant relied on the recent Strasbourg case law at Chamber level, which the journalist had relied on in *Kennedy*.[44] Relying on this case law, the Hungarian Helsinki Committee argued that the Strasbourg court had now departed from the earlier Grand Chamber case law and had clearly taken the stance that a right of access to information held by public authorities fell within the ambit of Art 10. After a careful and detailed analysis of the history of the Convention and its case law, relevant international law and the relevant comparative law in the contracting states the Grand Chamber held that while Art 10 could not be interpreted as giving a general right of access to state information, such a right could exist in certain circumstances. It identified the considerations that would be relevant in identifying whether such a right existed as follows:

(1) The purpose of the information request

> 158. First, it must be a prerequisite that the purpose of the person in requesting access to the information held by a public authority is to enable his or her exercise of the freedom to "receive and impart information and ideas" to others. Thus, the Court has placed emphasis on whether the gathering of the information was a relevant preparatory step in journalistic activities or in other activities creating a forum for, or constituting an essential element of, public debate…
>
> 159 …in order for Art 10 to come into play, it must be ascertained whether the information sought was in fact necessary for the exercise of freedom of expression…

(2) The nature of the information sought

> 161. …the Court considers that the information, data or documents to which access is sought must generally meet a public-interest test in order to prompt a need for

[42] *Magyar Helsinki Bizottság v Hungary* [2016] ECHR 18030/11.

[43] See: *Leander v Sweden* (1987) 9 EHRR 357; *Gaskin v United Kingdom* (1989) 12 EHRR 36; *Guerra v Italy* (1998) 26 EHRR 357; *Roche v United Kingdom* (2005) 42 EHRR 599. And see *Magyar Helsinki Bizottság v Hungary* [2016] ECHR 18030/11 at [67], [69].

[44] Especially: *Youth Initiative for Human Rights v Serbia* [2013] ECHR 584, (2013) 36 BHRC 687; *Österreichische Vereinigung zur Erhaltung v Austria* (2013) 36 BHRC 697. And see *Magyar Helsinki Bizottság v Hungary* [2016] ECHR 18030/11 at [86].

disclosure under the Convention. Such a need may exist where, inter alia, disclosure provides transparency on the manner of conduct of public affairs and on matters of interest for society as a whole and thereby allows participation in public governance by the public at large…

(3) The role of the applicant

164. A logical consequence of the two criteria set out above – one regarding the purpose of the information request and the other concerning the nature of the information requested – is that the particular role of the seeker of the information in "receiving and imparting" it to the public assumes special importance…

165. While Art 10 guarantees freedom of expression to "everyone", it has been the Court's practice to recognise the essential role played by the press in a democratic society…

166. The Court has also acknowledged that the function of creating various platforms for public debate is not limited to the press but may also be exercised by, among others, non-governmental organisations, whose activities are an essential element of informed public debate. The Court has accepted that when an NGO draws attention to matters of public interest, it is exercising a public watchdog role of similar importance to that of the press …and may be characterised as a social "watchdog" warranting similar protection under the Convention as that afforded to the press..

167. The manner in which public watchdogs carry out their activities may have a significant impact on the proper functioning of a democratic society. It is in the interest of democratic society to enable the press to exercise its vital role of "public watchdog" in imparting information on matters of public concern…

168. Thus, the Court considers that an important consideration is whether the person seeking access to the information in question does so with a view to informing the public in the capacity of a public "watchdog". This does not mean, however, that a right of access to information ought to apply exclusively to NGOs and the press. It reiterates that a high level of protection also extends to academic researchers…and authors of literature on matters of public concern… The Court would also note that given the important role played by the Internet in enhancing the public's access to news and facilitating the dissemination of information… the function of bloggers and popular users of the social media may be also assimilated to that of "public watchdogs" in so far as the protection afforded by Art 10 is concerned.

(4) Ready and available information

…

170. … the Court is of the view that the fact that the information requested is ready and available ought to constitute an important criterion in the overall assessment of whether a refusal to provide the information can be regarded as an "interference" with the freedom to "receive and impart information" as protected by that provision.[45]

On the facts an interference was made out and the Hungarian government had failed to show sufficient reasons to justify the refusal.[46]

41–008 Common law right - in future

The *Kennedy* case is one of a group of recent Court of Appeal and Supreme Court cases in which the common law of open justice/open government has been accorded a form of primacy over Convention rights and the European proportionality standard of review has been adopted in the development of the common law.[47] In the other cases in the group, which concerned the courts, there was citation of precedent or legal principle from older cases. Not so in *Kennedy*.

45 *Magyar Helsinki Bizottság v Hungary* [2016] ECHR 18030/11 at [159]-[170].

46 *Magyar Helsinki Bizottság v Hungary* [2016] ECHR 18030/11 at [180], [200].

47 See also: *R (Guardian News and Media Ltd) v City of Westminster Magistrates' Court* [2012] EWCA Civ 420, [2013] QB 618; *A v BBC* [2014] UKSC 25, [2015] AC 588.

The majority did not see a problem with this, however. Indeed, Lord Toulson JSC said:

> To the extent that an enactment contains provisions about the disclosure of documents or information, such provisions have the force of law. But to the extent that Parliament has not done so, it must be for the statutory body to decide questions of disclosure, subject to the supervision of the court. I do not see the absence of a prior statement by the courts that in general the principle of openness should apply, subject to any statutory provisions and subject to any countervailing reasons, as a convincing reason for not saying so now.[48]

The minority did see a problem. As Lord Carnwath noted:

> …there is nothing in the *Guardian News* case, or any other existing authority to support the view that common law principles relating to disclosure of documents in the courts can be transferred directly to inquiries…[49]

Logically of course, in any strong and enduring development of the common law in a particular area, there must be one case in which the principle was first identified. *Kennedy* may prove to be such a case. Whether it will be remains to be seen. There are some obvious reasons why it may prove to be so. As the Supreme Court has recently observed of the common law open justice principle:

> …Its significance has if anything increased in an age which attaches growing importance to the public accountability of public officers and institutions and to the availability of information about the performance of their functions.[50]

Whether intentionally or otherwise, it may result in courts – which enjoy an absolute, pure class-based exemption under s 32(1) – finding themselves subject to common law requests. By parity of reasoning with *Kennedy v Charity Commission*, such requests may prove difficult to legitimately resist, certainly where made by journalists and other 'social watchdogs' with a legitimate interest in reporting on the legal proceeding to which the request relates. This increasing expectation of more governmental openness applies to public authorities other than courts. The courts will undoubtedly face more claims seeking information about the work of themselves and such authorities in years to come. If they want to meet this increased expectation, the open government principle identified by the majority in *Kennedy* is a flexible and attractive judicial tool where FOIA does not assist. They can also then attribute the constitutional progress to the common law rather than any Strasbourg jurisprudence, which some senior judges seem increasingly inclined to do. In *R (Osborn) v Parole Board*[51] the Supreme Court accepted that the importance of the Human Rights Act 1998 was unquestionable but it emphasised:

> ..It does not however supersede the protection of human rights under the common law or statute, or create a discrete body of law based on the judgments of the European court. Human rights continue to be protected by our domestic law, interpreted and developed in accordance with the Act when appropriate.[52]

There are also, however, reasons why it may not prove to be so. Some of these were identified in the dissenting judgments. The most important question is not how receptive the courts will be to such a development, but how receptive the public authorities (including the courts themselves), asked to disclose information outside of FOIA, will be.[53] Lord Wilson JSC put his finger on the point when he said:

> …the adequacy of a broadly discretionary power may be very different when exercised by

---

[48] *Kennedy v Charity Commission* [2014] UKSC 20, [2015] AC 455 at [128].

[49] *Kennedy v Charity Commission* [2014] UKSC 20, [2015] AC 455 at [241].

[50] *Khuja v Times Newspapers Limited and others* [2017] UKSC 49, [2017] 3 WLR 351 at [13] per Lord Sumption speaking for the majority.

[51] *R (Osborn) v Parole Board* [2013] UKSC 61, [2014] AC 1115.

[52] *R (Osborn) v Parole Board* [2013] UKSC 61, [2014] AC 1115 at [57] per Lord Reed speaking for the court.

[53] Something borne out by the pre-FOI Act Code of Practice, whose strong words of exhortation were not matched by departmental action: see §§2– 004 to 2– 013.

> a judge with no axe to grind rather than, albeit subject at any rate in theory to judicial review, by an executive authority requested to disclose documents which may justify criticism of it.[54]

In light of the Grand Chamber decision in *Magyar Helsinki Bizottsag*,[55] where a public authority refuses an FOI Act request of a journalist or NGO relying on a non-harm based absolute exemption, the better course for those acting for the journalist or NGO may be a challenge that takes the Art 10 issue to the First-tier Tribunal rather than a common law claim. Strasbourg has crafted a powerful and conceptually clear human right specifically for newsgatherers and social watchdogs, and has done so through a series of decided cases up to the highest level which explain how it works. By contrast, the strength and the reach of the emerging common law right remains unclear. Also, judicial review is more cumbersome and costly than the specialised procedures provided by the Act.[56] If the First-tier Tribunal follows *Magyar Helsinki Bizottsag* (which post-dates *Kennedy*), a reading down of exemptions in FOIA at tribunal level is an attractive option. If the obstructing provision is read down there will be full merits review before the First-tier Tribunal administering a regime that was carefully crafted after years of thorough consultation and debate. There will be no need for the arguments about the standard of review, identification and weighting of competing public interests, the drain on resources and so forth. These are debates that will inevitably arise in judicial review challenges based on the common law duty of openness.[57]

2. COMMON LAW CONTROLS

41–009 Misuse of private information

Since the coming into force of the Human Rights Act 1998 the courts have been compelled to accommodate claims for misuse of a person's private information.[58] Given that such a claim does not depend upon the existence of a prior agreement between the complainant and the misuser, the claim should logically have been classed as a tort recognised at common law. However, earlier clear statements from both the House of Lords and Court of Appeal[59] that the common law has never provided a general tort of invasion of privacy[60] would have necessitated an acknowledgment of the unthinkable. And so, breach of confidence – which, when not arising out of contract, has its roots in equity and not the common law – was pressed into service to fashion a solution.[61] Shoe-horning misuse of private information into breach of

---

54 *Kennedy v Charity Commission* [2014] UKSC 20, [2015] AC 455 at [199].

55 *Magyar Helsinki Bizottság v Hungary* [2016] ECHR 18030/11.

56 *Kennedy v Charity Commission* [2014] UKSC 20, [2015] AC 455 at [231], [234] per Lord Carnwath. The additional difficulties where the request is made of a court are considerable – something not adverted to in any of the judgments in *Kennedy v Charity Commission*.

57 *Kennedy v Charity Commission* [2014] UKSC 20, [2015] AC 455 at [247].

58 The House of Lords in *R v Khan (Sultan)* [1997] AC 558 at 571 had anticipated that compliance with the Convention, both in respect of the provisions of Art 8 and the requirement that there should be an effective remedy under Art 13, would necessitate a tort of invasion of privacy in English law. That followed identification of the lack of such a tort by the ECtHR in *Earl Spencer v United Kingdom* (1998) 25 EHRR CD 105 and *Peck v United Kingdom (Application No 44647/98)* [2003] EMLR 15, (2003) 36 EHRR 41, 13 BHRC 669. See further §§4–004 and 4–014.

59 *Wainwright v Home Office* [2003] UKHL 53, [2004] 2 AC 406; *Kaye v Roberston* [1991] FSR 62; *Douglas v Hello! (No 3)* [2001] QB 967, cf Sedley LJ at [125]-[126].

60 After surveying the authorities, Lord Hoffmann in *Wainwright v Home Office* [2003] UKHL 53, [2004] 2 AC 406 at [35] held: 'I would reject the invitation to declare that since at the latest 1950 there has been a previously unknown tort of invasion of privacy.' Lords Bingham, Hope and Hutton expressly agreed with Lord Hoffmann and Lord Scott delivered a judgment to the same effect.

61 *Douglas v Hello! Ltd (No 3)* [2006] QB 125 at [53]; *McKennitt v Ash* [2008] QB 73 at [8]-[11]; *Lord Browne of Madingley*

confidence, with its different origins and concerns, was never going to result in a comfortable fit.[62] After a suitable period, the charade was dropped and the courts recognised that misuse of private information is a tort, distinct from breach of confidence.[63] Misuse of private information has become an important cause of action in its own right. It is increasingly one which is pleaded in the alternative where a claim for breach of data protection principles may not succeed (at any rate succeed to the same extent). One reason why a data protection claim may not succeed is the statutory exemption from the operation of most of the data protection principles where personal data is processed solely for the special purposes of journalistic or academic, artistic or literary expression.[64]

41– 010 Elements of the tort

A person claiming misuse of private information must show:

(1) That their right to privacy under Art 8 of the ECHR was engaged by the use by the defendant of the information in issue. The touchstone for the engagement of Art 8 is whether the claimant has, on the facts, a reasonable expectation of privacy in relation to the subject matter of their complaint. This threshold test is objective and had to be applied broadly.[65]

(2) That their privacy right should outweigh the right to freedom of expression which the defendant was exercising in obtaining/using/disclosing the information in issue.[66] Again this is an acutely fact-sensitive question and all the circumstances of the case must be considered in resolving it.

It is not necessary that the misuse of private information has caused the claimant to be upset.[67] The remedies available in a claim for misuse of private information include interim relief in the

---

v Associated Newspapers Ltd [2008] QB 103; *Douglas v Hello! Ltd (No 3) sub nom OBG v Allan* [2007] UKHL 21, [2008] AC 1 at [255]; *Murray v Express Newspapers plc* [2009] Ch 481 *Imerman v Tchenguiz* [2011] Fam 116 at [65].

62 Equitable breach of confidence has its roots in unconscionability, with earlier cases principally concerned with restraining the publication of unpublished literary or artistic works, such as private letters or drawings: eg *Pope v Curl* (1741) 2 Atk 342, 26 ER 608; *Gee v Pritchard* (1818) 2 Swans 402, 36 ER 670; *Abernethy v Hutchinson* (1824) 1 H & Tw 28, 47 ER 1313; *Prince Albert v Strange* (1849) 1 Mac & G 25, 41 ER 1171, (1849) 1 De G & Sm 652. Equity was, on the claim of an employer, also able to restrain third parties from divulging or using information that that third party had received from an employee in breach of duty of the employer: *Tipping v Clarke* (1843) 2 Hare 383 at 389, 67 ER 157; *Lamb v Evans* [1893] 1 Ch 218 at 235; *Lord Asburnton v Pape* [1913] 2 Ch 469. Later in the twentieth century equity's role expanded to protecting confidentiality in purely industrial or business matters: *Saltman Engineering Co Ltd v Campbell Engineering Co Ltd* (1948) 65 RPC 203; *Seager v Copydex* [1967] 1 WLR 923; *Coco v AN Clark (Engineers) ltd* [1969] RPC 41; *Moorgate Tobacco Co Ltd v Phillip Morris Ltd (No 2)* (1984) 156 CLR 414. The latter development has sometimes been explained on the basis of unjust enrichment. The unconscionability of a disclosure could be informed by the public interest in the disclosure: *Gartside v Outram* [1856] 26 LJ Ch 113; *Weld-Blundell v Stephens* [1919] 1 KB 520; *Initial Services Ltd v Putterill* [1968] 1 QB 396; *Fraser v Evans* [1969] 1 QB 349; *Woodward v Hutchins* [1977] 1 WLR 760 – criticised somewhat in *Smith Kline & French Laboratories v Dept of Community Services & Health* [1990] FCA 151,(1991) 99 ALR 679 at [130]. Whilst unconscionability required a detriment to be suffered which equity would protect, in the sphere of personal information it was sufficient that disclosure of information relating to the claimant's affairs would expose his actions to public discussion and criticism: *Commonwealth v John Fairfax & Sons Ltd* (1980) 147 CLR 39 at 51-52.

63 *Vidal-Hall v Google Inc* [2015] EWCA Civ 311, [2016] QB 1003 at [43], [51]. Although permission to appeal was given by the Supreme Court, that was not pursued: [2015] 1 WLR 4934. It might also be observed that its close cousin, breach of the data protection principles, is a tort, ie breach of statutory duty.

64 See previously Data Protection Act 1998 s 32(4) and *Stunt v Associated Newspapers Ltd* [2017] EWHC 695 (QB), [2017] 1 WLR 3985; on app *Stunt v Associated Newspapers Ltd* [2018] EWCA Civ 1780. See now Schedule 2 Part 5 para 26 of the Data Protection Act 2018. These are considered further in chapters 7-15 above.

65 See *In Re JR38* [2015] UKSC 42, [2016] AC 1131. The attributes of the claimant will therefore be considered. The courts have recognised that there are considerations relevant to children, but not to adults, which might mean that in a particular case a child had a reasonable expectation of privacy where an adult did not. See *Weller v Associated Newspapers Limited* [2015] EWCA Civ 1176, [2016] 1 WLR 1541.

66 See generally §§34– 002 and 34– 020 to 34– 048.

67 *Gulati & ors v MGN Ltd* [2015] EWHC 1482 (Ch) at [143], affirmed in *Gulati v MGN Ltd* [2015] EWCA Civ 1291, [2017] QB 149.

form of prior restraint injunctions to prevent the use complained of. Damages can be substantial.[68]

41–011 Data protection relationship

Following the Court of Appeal's judgment in *Vidal-Hall v Google*,[69] claims for misuse of private information have had a mixed reception, with outcomes revealing less about governing principles than about differing judicial values and sympathies:

(1) In *Townsend v Google Inc*[70] Mr Townsend sought to serve Google in the USA with proceedings for misuse of private information, breach of confidence and breaches of the Data Protection Act 1998. His complaint was that a Google search against his name revealed press articles from the last six years referring to numerous unspent convictions, in open court proceedings, for sex offences. The judge found no serious issues to be tried in relation to any of the claims. In particular he concluded that on the facts there was no reason to displace the usual understanding that there could be no reasonable expectation of privacy in convictions which are not spent.

(2) In *Arthurs v News Group Newspapers Limited*[71] the eighteen year-old plaintiff had performed on an edition of a BBC television talent show and had been voted through to the next round of the competition. A newspaper then published an article revealing that he was the son of a convicted terrorist. He sought an interim injunction to prevent further publication of this information, claiming that the article was a misuse of his private information.[72] The judge concluded that the plaintiff was unlikely to establish a reasonable expectation of privacy at trial and refused the interim injunction.[73] The Northern Ireland Court of Appeal found no error of principle in the judge's decision that the Art 8 right was not engaged. This was so in particular since the:

> …father's convictions were in the public domain, as was his relationship with the applicant, who voluntarily entered the public domain[74].

(3) In *Ali v Channel 5*[75] the only claim was for misuse of private information. The defendant had broadcast a documentary showing High Court Enforcement Officers enforcing a possession order in respect of the claimants' home. The claimants were at home when the eviction was carried out and the footage had been shot both by a film crew and on the body cameras of the enforcement officers. After the eviction the claimants asked for the footage not to be broadcast.[76] The claim related only

---

[68] See the range of awards approved by the Court of Appeal in *Gulati v MGN Ltd* [2015] EWCA Civ 1291, [2017] QB 149, a group of cases where private information had been obtained repeatedly by phone hacking and used as the basis of numerous published tabloid articles about the claimants. Thirty such articles had been published about one claimant, Sadie Frost, and she received a total of £260,000 in general damages.

[69] [2015] EWCA Civ 311, [2016] QB 1003.

[70] *Townsend v Google Inc* [2017] NIQB 81.

[71] *Arthurs v News Group Newspapers Limited* [2017] NICA 70, [2018] EMLR 11.

[72] He also claimed interim relief at first instance on the basis that that the publication of the information about his father's conviction was unlawful processing of his sensitive personal data under s.2(g) and (h) of the Data Protection Act 1998, dealing respectively with information about the commission of criminal offences by the data subject and criminal proceedings against the data subject: *Arthurs v News Group Newspapers Limited* [2017] NICA 70, [2018] EMLR 11 at [2], [3], [17].

[73] *Arthurs v News Group Newspapers Limited* [2017] NICA 70, [2018] EMLR 11 at [12].

[74] *Arthurs v News Group Newspapers Limited* [2017] NICA 70, [2018] EMLR 11 at [46]

[75] *Ali v Channel 5 Broadcast Ltd* [2018] EWHC 298 (Ch), [2018] EMLR 17.

[76] *Ali v Channel 5 Broadcast Ltd* [2018] EWHC 298 (Ch), [2018] EMLR 17 at [124].

to the broadcasting of images of the claimants and their home during the eviction, and the details (rather than the fact of) the eviction.[77] The judge found a reasonable expectation of privacy in respect of the information, principally because of the protection from intrusion given by ECHR 8 to home and family life, and the visible shock and distress of the claimants that was apparent in the broadcast footage.[78] They had not consented to the broadcast of the material.[79] The programme contributed to a debate of public interest but the inclusion of the private information went beyond what was justified to this end.[80] Each of the claimants was awarded £10,000 in damages.[81]

(4) In *TLT & ors v SSHD* the department had accidentally published online a spreadsheet giving the name, age and nationality of TLT and information from which the general area in which TLT's family lived could be inferred.[82] TLT was the lead family member in a family also comprising TLU and TLV. The families on the spreadsheet had been returned to their country of origin as a result of having no right to remain in the United Kingdom. The Court of Appeal upheld the findings of the trial judge that TLU and TLV's private information had been misused while the spreadsheet was accessible online. Gross LJ[83] considered:

> …that TLU and TLV could readily be identified by third parties… Plainly, having regard to the law's policy of protecting the values underlying privacy … - and as is admitted by the Home Office in the case of TLT - TLU and TLV had a reasonable expectation of privacy and confidentiality in respect of their information in the spreadsheet. Without belabouring the point, that information went (inter alia) to their identities and their claims for asylum…[84]

Interestingly, the court considered that TLU and TLV also had valid claims for breaches of the Data Protection Act 1998, even though they were not named in the disclosed material. This was their personal data as it related to them and they could be identified directly or indirectly from it.[85]

(5) *Richard v BBC*[86] concerned a television news broadcast which revealed that there was a police investigation into an allegation against the famous entertainer of a sex offence against a boy under 16. The broadcast reported in real time on a search of the claimant's home by the police.[87] The claimant had not been, and never was, charged with any offence. The police investigation had been discontinued by the time the claim for misuse of private information was commenced.[88] A BBC journalist had received an unauthorised tip off about the investigation from a

---

77 *Ali v Channel 5 Broadcast Ltd* [2018] EWHC 298 (Ch), [2018] EMLR 17 at [143].

78 *Ali v Channel 5 Broadcast Ltd* [2018] EWHC 298 (Ch), [2018] EMLR 17 at [169].

79 *Ali v Channel 5 Broadcast Ltd* [2018] EWHC 298 (Ch), [2018] EMLR 17 at [172]-[178].

80 *Ali v Channel 5 Broadcast Ltd* [2018] EWHC 298 (Ch), [2018] EMLR 17 at [185] and [210].

81 *Ali v Channel 5 Broadcast Ltd* [2018] EWHC 298 (Ch), [2018] EMLR 17 at [220].

82 *TLT & ors v Secretary of State for the Home Department* [2018] EWCA Civ 2217, [2018] 4 WLR 101.

83 With whom McFarlane LJ and Coulson LJJ agreed.

84 *TLT & ors v Secretary of State for the Home Department* [2018] EWCA Civ 2217, [2018] 4 WLR 101 at [31].

85 *TLT & ors v Secretary of State for the Home Department* [2018] EWCA Civ 2217, [2018] 4 WLR 101 at [44]. The court was applying the definition of personal data in section 1 of the Data Protection Act 1998 which defined this as 'data which relate to a living individual who can be identified— (a) from those data, or (b) from those data and other information which is in the possession of, or is likely to come into the possession of, the data controller …'

86 *Richard v BBC* [2018] EWHC 1837 (Ch), [2018] HRLR 16.

87 *Richard v BBC* [2018] EWHC 1837 (Ch), [2018] HRLR 16 at [117].

88 *Richard v BBC* [2018] EWHC 1837 (Ch), [2018] HRLR 16 at [2].

confidential source and understood that the information originated from within the police. The investigating police force then confirmed the story to the journalist and provided him with information about the search on the understanding that the BBC would not publicise the investigation before the search.[89] A claim for breaches of the Data Protection Act 1998 was not pursued at trial on the basis that it added nothing to the claim in misuse of private information.[90] The judge found that the claimant had a right of privacy against the BBC which protected the information about him disclosed in the broadcast. This was not lost when the police force told the BBC about the search because the journalist had exploited his unauthorised tip off to manoeuvre the force into cooperating.[91] He also found that the harm to the Claimant's privacy rights through the BBC's disclosures outweighed the broadcaster's right to freedom of expression.[92] In particular he did not accept the BBC's case that there was a public interest in identifying the claimant as the subject of the investigation. He said:

> …It seems to me to be right to break this claim down into two parts. The first is whether the report of an investigation into (and search of the premises of) a well-known but unidentified celebrity would fall under Mr Millar's point. In my view it would….It does not follow that, because an investigation at a general level was a matter of public interest, the identity of the subject of the investigation also attracted that characterisation. I do not think that it did. Knowing that Sir Cliff was under investigation might be of interest to the gossip-mongers, but it does not contribute materially to the genuine public interest in the existence of police investigations in this area.[93]

The claimant was awarded £210,000 in general damages.[94]

41–012 A tort of invasion of privacy?

In *PJS v News Group Newspapers Ltd*[95] the Supreme Court had to consider whether an injunction preventing a tabloid newspaper from running a story should continue in force. The Court of Appeal had discontinued the injunction. The claimant and his partner were in the entertainment business and had two young children. The story was about the claimant's extra-marital sexual activities. During the currency of the injunction the story had been published in print in the United States of America, Canada, Scotland and elsewhere. Details of the story, including the names of those involved, were also easily accessible on internet websites and in social media. In deciding to continue the injunction the majority[96] approved the principles that had emerged from a series of first instance cases.[97] To this end they cited with approval the following observations of Eady J in one of the cases, *CTB v News Group Newspapers Limited*:[98]

> 23. It is important always to remember that the modern law of privacy is not concerned

89 *Richard v BBC* [2018] EWHC 1837 (Ch), [2018] HRLR 16 at [224].

90 *Richard v BBC* [2018] EWHC 1837 (Ch), [2018] HRLR 16 at [226].

91 *Richard v BBC* [2018] EWHC 1837 (Ch), [2018] HRLR 16 at [260].

92 *Richard v BBC* [2018] EWHC 1837 (Ch), [2018] HRLR 16 at [267]-[322].

93 *Richard v BBC* [2018] EWHC 1837 (Ch), [2018] HRLR 16 at [281]-[282].

94 *Richard v BBC* [2018] EWHC 1837 (Ch), [2018] HRLR 16 at [358].

95 *PJS v News Group Newspapers Ltd* [2016] UKSC 26, [2016] AC 1081.

96 Lord Neuberger, Lord Mance, Baroness Hale and Lord Reed.

97 *PJS v News Group Newspapers Ltd* [2016] UKSC 26, [2016] AC 1081 at [26]-[31]. The first instance cases were: *JIH v News Group Newspapers Ltd* [2010] EWHC 2818 (QB), [2011] EMLR 9: *Green Corns Ltd v Claverley Group Ltd* [2005] EWHC 958, [2005] EMLR 31; *CTB v News Group Newspapers Ltd* [2011] EWHC 1326 (QB); *CTB v News Group Newspapers Ltd* [2011] EWHC 1334 (QB).

98 *CTB v News Group Newspapers Ltd* [2011] EWHC 1326 (QB).

> solely with information or 'secrets': it is also concerned importantly with *intrusion* …[That] also largely explains why it is the case that the truth or falsity of the allegations in question can often be irrelevant…
>
> 24. It is fairly obvious that wall-to-wall excoriation in national newspapers, whether tabloid or 'broadsheet', is likely to be significantly more intrusive and distressing for those concerned than the availability of information on the Internet or in foreign journals to those, however many, who take the trouble to look it up. Moreover, with each exposure of personal information or allegations, whether by way of visual images or verbally, there is a new intrusion and occasion for distress or embarrassment. Mr Tomlinson argues accordingly that 'the dam has not burst.' For so long as the court is in a position to prevent some of that intrusion and distress, depending upon the individual circumstances, it may be appropriate to maintain that degree of protection. The analogy with King Canute to some extent, therefore, breaks down.
>
> 25. It may be thought that the wish of NGN to publish more about this 'story', with a view to selling newspapers and perhaps achieving other commercial advantages, demonstrates that coverage has not yet reached saturation point. Had it done so, the story would no longer retain any interest. This factor tends, therefore, to confirm my impression that the court's attempts to protect the claimant and his family have not yet become wholly futile.
>
> 26. In these circumstances, it seems to me that the right question for me to ask…is whether there is a solid reason why the claimant's identity should be generally revealed in the national media, such as to outweigh the legitimate interests of himself and his family in maintaining anonymity. The answer is as yet in the negative. They would be engulfed in a cruel and destructive media frenzy. Sadly, that may become unavoidable in the society in which we now live but, for the moment, in so far as I am being asked to sanction it, I decline to do so. On the other side … it has not been suggested that there is *any* legitimate public interest in publishing the story.

Taking their lead from these principles, the majority considered that the Court of Appeal had failed to give sufficient weight to:

> …the qualitative difference in intrusiveness and distress likely to be involved in what is now proposed by way of unrestricted publication by the English media in hard copy as well as on their own internet sites. There is little doubt that there would be a media storm. It would involve not merely disclosure of names and generalised description of the nature of the sexual activities involved, but the most intimate details. This would be likely to add greatly and on a potentially enduring basis to the intrusiveness and distress felt by the claimant, his partner and, by way of increased media attention now and/or in the future, their children…
>
> the media storm which discharge of the injunction would unleash would add a different and in some respects more enduring dimension to the existing invasions of privacy being perpetrated on the internet.[99]

The majority made repeated reference to the issue in the case as being one of 'invasion of privacy' through the past and (if the injunction was lifted) future coverage of the story, and also to the claim being for the 'tort of invasion of privacy.'[100] The terminology is striking, not least as the Court of Appeal had noted correctly that:

> The claimant issued proceedings against NGN in the Queen's Bench Division of the High Court, alleging that the proposed publication would be a misuse of private information and a breach of confidence.[101]

The language of the majority judgment may be simply a matter of form rather than substance. On this basis the tort identified in *Vidal Hall v Google Inc*[102] has acquired an alternative name, but

---

99 *PJS v News Group Newspapers Ltd* [2016] UKSC 26, [2016] AC 1081 at [35] and [45], Lord Mance, speaking for the majority.

100 See for example *PJS v News Group Newspapers Ltd* [2016] UKSC 26, [2016] AC 1081 at [1], [2], [3], [32], [33], [38], [43], [44].

101 *PJS v News Group Newspapers Ltd* [2016] EWCA Civ 393, [2016] Fam Law 962 at [11].

102 [2015] EWCA Civ 311, [2016] QB 1003.

is still to do only with one aspect of invasion of privacy, namely by misuse of private information. If it is a matter of substance, it is not yet clear what the difference of substance is. The principles on which the majority reached its decision were all well-established, albeit only at first instance. *PJS v News Group Newspapers Ltd* is a striking example of the distinction between breach of confidence and misuse of private information. It shows how and why the latter may require protection for the information by a prior restraint injunction, even when the information is widely known. Whether it is the first step towards a much broader, general tort of 'invasion of privacy' which the common law has so far failed to recognise, remains to be seen.[103]

[103] In the United States, the law has developed extensively since the publication of Warren and Brandeis 'The Right to Privacy' *Harvard Law Review*, vol 4 (1890), pp 193ff. The US Supreme Court in *Cox Broadcasting Corp v Cohn* (1975) 420 US 469 accepted the four separate facets of the tort of breach of privacy identified *The Restatement of Torts* (at 867) and by *Prosser and Keaton on The Law of Torts*: (i) intrusion upon a plaintiff's seclusion or solitude or his private affairs; (ii) public disclosure of embarrassing private facts about the plaintiff; (iii) publicity which places the plaintiff in a false light in the public eye; (iv) appropriation for the defendant's advantage of the plaintiff's name or likeness. That is not to suggest that this yields solutions to all the issues that may arise in relation to privacy, see, for example: *Carpenter v United States* (2018) 585 US; *United States v Jones* (2012) 565 US 400; *Zacchini v Scripps-Howard Broadcasting Co* (1977) 433 US 562.

CHAPTER 42
Court-held documents

1. GOVERNING PRINCIPLES

42–001 Introduction

This Chapter is concerned with access to and the use of documents held by a court, a tribunal or other similar body[1] in connection with proceedings before that court, tribunal or body. It addresses:

– the circumstances in which a non-party (including the media) may seek such documents from the court, tribunal or body, or from a party to the proceedings; and
– the uses that may be made of such documents.[2]

As will be seen, in relation to most such documents there is no right of access under FOIA or the EIR. Instead, the different courts, tribunals and like bodies administer their own access regimes. Access to documents in proceedings filed with or generated by them depends on the identity of the applicant, on the type of document for which access is sought and on the stage at which proceedings have reached. Once access to such a document is secured, there may be restrictions on the use that may be made of the information recorded in that document.[3]

42–002 **Courts as public authorities**

Courts, tribunals and the like are not public authorities within the meaning of the FOIA and the EIR.[4] As the right of access conferred by FOIA and by the EIR is a right in respect of recorded information held by a 'public authority,' there is no right of access under FOIA or the EIR to information held by courts, tribunals and the like. There is, however, a distinction between a court or tribunal – that is to say, those exercising judicial power of the state – and the organisation providing administrative support to those exercising judicial power of the state (eg HM Courts Service).[5] Documents for use in proceedings before a court, tribunal or like body will typically be filed with and be held by the organisation providing administrative support.[6] Normally, each supporting organisation is a 'public authority' within the meaning of FOIA and the EIR.[7] Although the right of access conferred by FOIA and by the EIR is a right to information 'held' by a public authority,[8] FOIA provides that:

> information is held by a public authority if it is held by the authority, otherwise than on behalf of another person...[9]

Since the coming into force of FOIA, the assumption has been that documents filed in proceedings or generated by those acting in a judicial capacity (eg judgments and orders) are

1 For the sake of convenience these are referred to generally as 'courts' meaning any body exercising the judicial power of the state.

2 There may be restrictions imposed by the criminal law or the law of contempt, for example: s 12(3) of the Administration of Justice Act 1960; s 97 of the Children Act 1989 (prohibition on identifying children subject to proceedings under the Children Act). And there may be restrictions arising from confidentiality or from court-imposed reporting restrictions or other limits on use.

3 Unlike documents disclosed pursuant to a request for information made under FOIA or the EIR.

4 There are some exceptions, for example the Parole Board of England and Wales. Under the EIR the corresponding exclusion is in Reg 3(3) which provides that the Regulations do not apply to any public authority to the extent that it is acting in a judicial or legislative capacity.

5 Thus, for example, the Court of Appeal consists of the ex officio judges (listed in s 2(2) of the Senior Courts Act 1981) and the ordinary judges (up to 39 in number): Senior Courts Act 1981 s 2(1). The High Court consists of those holding named judicial offices and up to 108 puisne judges: Senior Courts Act 1981 s 4(1). MH Cours Service was established in April 1995 as an executive agency of the Ministry of Justice. HM Courts Service is responsible for managing the Magistrates' Court, the Crown Court, the County Cours, the High Court and the Court of Appeal.

6 As opposed to, say, a judge's notebook, which will be personally held by that judge and thus outside FOIA and the EIR on any analysis.

7 HM Courts Service falls within the definition of 'government department' in FOIA s 84 (by virtue of being a body that exercises statutory functions on behalf of the Crown) and, by virtue of Sch 1, Pt I, is thereby a 'public authority.' The Northern Ireland Court Service is specifically included as a public authority: FOIA s 84, definition of 'government department.'

8 FOIA s 1(1); EIR reg 5(1).

9 FOIA s 3(2)(a). There is no equivalent under the EIR: see reg 3(2).

held by supporting organisations (such as HM Court Service) *on behalf of* the judicial entity.[10] As such, although the supporting organisations are 'public authorities' and although typically documents filed in proceedings or generated by those acting in a judicial capacity will be in the custody of the supporting organisation, those documents will not by 'held' by that supporting organisation, and so those documents will be outside of the reach of FOIA. To the extent that court documents are 'held' by a supporting organisation, s 32(1) of FOIA provides an exemption. The scope of this exemption is considered elsewhere in this work,[11] but for present purposes it is enough to observe that engagement of the exemption is purely class-based (ie it does not require a likelihood of harm to a protected interest) and it is absolute (ie it is not subject to a public interest balance). It would seem that the policy objective of taking documents filed in proceedings or generated by those acting in a judicial capacity outside the access right conferred by FOIA (whether on the basis that those documents are not 'held' by a public authority or because if they are so held they are exempted by s 32) is to leave disclosure of those documents within the control of the courts themselves.[12] This arrangement is not indicative of a policy intention that such documents should never be made publicly accessible. Rather, the intention is that disclosure of such documents is to be addressed through different, more specific schemes. These schemes are better adapted than FOIA to ensuring that the conduct of proceedings is not disturbed by requests for access to court documents. That such additional regimes may co-exist with FOIA is recognised by section 78 of FOIA.[13]

42– 003 The open justice principle

Regardless of its source, a court's power to permit access to documents by non-parties represents a facet of the common-law principle of open justice. This principle is said to be 'at the heart of our system of justice and vital to the rule of law.'[14] Although a review of the authorities on open justice conventionally starts with *Scott v Scott*, by the time of that judgment it had been the rule for some centuries that 'every Court of Justice is open to every subject of the King.'[15] That principle maintains to this day.[16] As a general rule, open justice requires that:

> ... courts must conduct their business publicly unless this would result in injustice. Open justice is an important safeguard against judicial bias, unfairness and incompetence, ensuring that judges are accountable in the performance of their judicial duties. It maintains public confidence in the impartial administration of justice by ensuring that judicial hearings are subject to public scrutiny, and that 'justice should not only be done, but should manifestly

---

10 See *Mitchell v IC*, IT, 10 October 2005 at [31].

11 See §29– 033

12 At any rate, while the proceedings are on foot.

13 *Kennedy v Charity Commission* [2014] UKSC 20, [2015] AC 455 at [6]-[7], [39], [123]; *Brown v IC and MoJ* [2016] UKUT 0255 (AAC) at [25]; *R (Guardian News and Media Ltd) v City of Westminster Magistrates' Court* [2012] EWCA Civ 420, [2013] QB 618 at [22]. To the extent that these other schemes fail to secure compliance with any ECHR right to access information, then the focus is on them and not on s 32: *Kennedy v Charity Commission* [2014] UKSC 20, [2015] AC 455 at [35]-[36], [133]-[142].

14 *R (Guardian News and Media Ltd) v City of Westminster Magistrates' Court* [2012] EWCA Civ 420, [2013] QB 618 at [1]-[2]; *R (O'Connor) v Aldershot Magistrates Court* [2016] EWHC 2792 (Admin), [2017] 1 WLR 2833 at [24]-[29].

15 *Scott v Scott* [1913] AC 417 at 440. And see: *A v BBC* [2014] UKSC 25, [2015] AC 588 at [23]-[26] for a description of history of the principle in Scotland; *Kennedy v Charity Commission* [2014] UKSC 20, [2015] AC 455. Courts may exclude persons where necessary to prevent disorder under their inherent jurisdiction and security officers may now exclude or remove persons from court premises in the circumstances described in s 53 of the Courts Act 2003. Where there is room for dispute about whether this section applies then the court should resolve the issue: *R (O'Connor) v Aldershot Magistrates Court* [2016] EWHC 2792 (Admin), [2017] 1 WLR 2833 at [34]-[37].

16 *A v BBC* [2014] UKSC 25, [2015] AC 588 at [23]-[26], [56]; *Kennedy v Charity Commission* [2014] UKSC 20, [2015] AC 455; *Dring (on behalf of the Asbestos Victims Support Groups Forum UK) v Cape Intermediate Holdings Ltd* [2019] UKSC 38, [2019] 3 WLR 429 at [41]-[50], upholding *Cape Intermediate Holdings Ltd v Dring (for and on behalf of the Asbestos Victims Support Group)* [2018] EWCA Civ 1795, [2019] 1 WLR 479 at [26]-[28]; *Chartered Institute of Arbitrators v B* [2019] EWHC 460 (Comm) applying the principle to the arbitral process.

and undoubtedly be seen to be done.'[17]

The principle has two aspects: (a) justice should be administered in public; and (b) nothing should be done to discourage fair and accurate reports of proceedings. These two aspects are not consistently recognised in the case law.[18] The principle requires that the evidence and argument deployed should be publicly known, so that society may judge for itself the quality of justice administered in its name, and whether the law requires modification.[19] The principle includes an obligation to place judicial decisions into the public domain, even where the hearing itself has adopted a private or closed material procedure.[20]

42–004 Open justice and documents

Access to documents, as opposed or in addition to access to court proceedings themselves, has become increasingly important in order to meet the demands of open justice. The modern practice is for courts, particularly the civil courts, to receive evidence and arguments in written form with the judge being invited to read them and with only limited reference being made in open court:

> As a matter of basic principle the starting point should be that practices adopted by the courts and parties to ensure the efficient resolution of litigation should not be allowed to adversely affect the ability of the public to know what is happening in the course of the proceedings.[21]

The starting point is that all documents are necessary and relevant for the purpose of ensuring open justice, and a court should not accede to general arguments that it would be possible to understand the trial without access to that document.[22]

42–005 Derogations from open justice

A derogation from open justice will only be permitted where strictly necessary to achieve justice. This is not a matter of discretion but 'a matter of principle…turning, not on convenience, but on necessity.'[23] It follows that where a decision whether or not to allow access is subject to review in a higher court then the test for review is not irrationality, but the reviewing court must itself consider what open justice requires.[24] Nor can the parties agree to depart from the general rule.[25] Some bases for limiting open justice are well established:

— cases relating to wards of court and lunatics as ones where the court is 'really sitting primarily to guard their interests' so that the general rule yielded to that paramount duty;[26]

— litigation as to secret processes where justice could not be done in public as it would destroy the subject matter;

17 *R (Guardian News and Media Ltd) v City of Westminster Magistrates' Court* [2012] EWCA Civ 420, [2013] QB 618 at [3], quoting from Law Commission of New Zealand, *Access to Court Records*, (2006) (Report 93) para 2.2.

18 *Khuja v Times Newspapers Limited and others* [2017] UKSC 49, [2017] 3 WLR 351 at [16]-[17].

19 *Home Office v Harman* [1983] AC 280 at 316.

20 *R (Mohamed) v Secretary of State for Foreign and Commonwealth Affairs* [2010] EWCA Civ 65, [2011] QB 218 at [37]-[41], [189].

21 *Barings Plc (in liq) v Coopers & Lybrand* [2000] 1 WLR 2353, [2000] 3 All ER 910 at [43]. The impact of the modern practice of pre-reading on open justice was discussed in *SmithKline Beecham Biologicals SA v Connaught Laboratories Inc* [1999] 4 All ER 498 at 511-513.

22 *Lilly Icos v Pfizer Ltd (No 2)* [2002] EWCA Civ 2, [2002] 1 WLR 2261 at [25].

23 *Scott v Scott* [1913] UKHL 2, [1913] AC 417 at 438.

24 *Kennedy v Charity Commission* [2014] UKSC 20, [2015] AC 455 at [132].

25 *Al Rawi & ors v Security Service & ors* [2011] UKSC 34, [2012] 1 AC 531at [84]; *R v Legal Aid Board, Ex p Kaim Todner* [1999] QB 966 at 977.

26 *Scott v Scott* [1913] UKHL 2, [1913] AC 417 at 437-8.

— to allow undercover police officers to give evidence anonymously and shielded from view so as not to jeopardise their effectiveness in future investigations, or to protect a party or witness from a risk to their safety (including their mental health if their identity is revealed).[27]

Beyond cases such as these it is impossible to anticipate all contingencies and the common law in this respect may change in response to changes in society and the administration of justice. Ultimately:

> the court has to carry out a balancing exercise which will be fact-specific. Central to the court's evaluation will be the purpose of the open justice principle, the potential value of the information in question in advancing that purpose and, conversely, any risk of harm which its disclosure may cause to the maintenance of an effective judicial process or to the legitimate interests of others.[28]

There is no general exception where confidentiality or privacy is in issue. Nor is the standard lowered in some classes of case, for example interim proceedings.[29] The burden lies on the person seeking a derogation to establish it by clear and cogent evidence.[30] Unwelcome publicity for a party is not a reason to refuse disclosure.[31] Where there are grounds to depart from the principle of open justice then any limitation should be kept to the minimum necessary so that, for example, a witness may be anonymized rather than exclude the public altogether. Where a hearing is held in private, then the judgment should be in public if that can be done consistently with the interests of justice.[32] Where the court grants an injunction to restrain the publication of private or confidential information, some restriction on access to information or the reporting of it may be required, since otherwise the injunction could be rendered ineffective.[33] Where an interim non-disclosure order is sought then it is subject to Practice Guidance, which contains a model order directing attention to the possible need to restrict access to documents.[34] Any restriction so ordered must still be minimized and this may require the court to make a choice between ordering anonymity, in which case more details of the case may be published without revealing the restrained information, and naming the parties, in which case little information can be disclosed without doing so.[35]

42–006 Open justice and human rights

The open justice principle is mirrored by the right in Art 6 of the ECHR to a 'fair and public hearing' in the determination of civil rights and obligations or of any criminal charge. Article 6 further requires that:

> Judgment shall be pronounced publicly but the press and public may be excluded from all or part of the trial in the interest of morals, public order or national security in a democratic

27 *A v BBC* [2014] UKSC 25, [2015] AC 588.

28 *R (Guardian News and Media Ltd) v City of Westminster Magistrates' Court* [2012] EWCA Civ 420, [2013] QB 618 at [85]. In *A v BBC* [2014] UKSC 25, [2015] AC 588 an order preventing disclosure of the identity of a sex offender in respect of whom a deportation order had been made was upheld. The order had been made on the basis that he was not at risk on return if his identity was protected.

29 See the review of the case law in *ABC v Y Ltd* [2010] EWHC 3176 (Ch), [2012] 1 WLR 537 at [18]-[20], [33].

30 *Practice Guidance (Interim Non-disclosure Orders)* [2012] 1 WLR 1003 at [10]-[14]; *Global Torch Ltd v Apex Global Management Ltd & Ors* [2013] EWCA Civ 819, [2013] 1 WLR 2993 at [34].

31 See eg *Global Torch Ltd v Apex Global Management Ltd & Ors* [2013] EWCA Civ 819, [2013] 1 WLR 2993 ('Public airing of the allegations may embarrass one side or the other. It often does, but that is not in itself a good reason to close the doors of the court').

32 *Department of Economic Policy Development of the City of Moscow v Bankers trust Co* [2004] EWCA Civ 314, [2005] QB 207.

33 The principles underpinning these kinds of injunctions engage the interplay between Arts 8 and 10 of the ECHR. This is considered in Chapter 4.

34 *Practice Guidance (Interim Non-disclosure Orders)* [2012] 1 WLR 1003.

35 *H v News Group Newspapers Ltd* [2011] EWCA Civ 42, [2011] 1 WLR 1645.

> society, where the interests of juveniles or the protection of the private life of the parties so require, or to the extent strictly necessary in the opinion of the court in special circumstances where publicity would prejudice the interests of justice.

The qualifications broadly reflect domestic common law or statute.[36] The underlying rationale is that it:

> ...protects litigants against the administration of justice in secret with no public scrutiny; it is also one of the means whereby confidence in the courts, superior and inferior, can be maintained. By rendering the administration of justice visible, publicity contributes to the achievement of the aim of Art 6(1), namely a fair trial, the guarantee of which is one of the fundamental principles of any democratic society ...[37]

Article 10 may be engaged where a person wishes to communicate or publish information derived from court proceedings. This is a qualified right and an interference with it can be justified where it is proportionate measure to pursue one of the legitimate aims in Art 10(2) including the protection of the rights and freedoms of others. Where disclosure presents a real and immediate risk to life that will engage Art 2 and since that is an unqualified right no balancing exercise arises and the court cannot order disclosure.[38] The same outcome will follow in the case of other unqualified Convention rights, such as Art 3[39] (freedom from torture or inhuman or degrading treatment) or Art 4 (freedom from slavery or forced labour and which includes human trafficking). Where Art 10 conflicts with a qualified right, such as Art 8, then the court must engage in a balancing exercise:

> First, neither article has *as such* precedence over the other. Secondly, where the values under the two articles are in conflict, an intense focus on the comparative importance of the specific rights being claimed in the individual case is necessary. Thirdly, the justifications for interfering with or restricting each right must be taken into account. Finally, the proportionality test must be applied to each. For convenience I will call this the ultimate balancing test.[40]

42-007 The inherent jurisdiction

The open justice principle applies to any body exercising the judicial power of the state although the practical application may vary according to the nature of the work of the particular judicial body.[41] Each of them has an inherent jurisdiction to determine how it should be applied, including when departures from the general rule are appropriate.[42]

> There can be no doubt at all that the court rules are not exhaustive of the circumstances in which non-parties may be given access to court documents. They are a minimum and of course it is for a person seeking to persuade the court to allow access outside the rules to show a good case for doing so. However, case after case has recognised that the guiding principle is the need for justice to be done in the open and that courts at all levels have an inherent jurisdiction to allow access in accordance with that principle. Furthermore, the open justice principle is applicable throughout the United Kingdom, even though the court rules may be different.[43]

---

36 *A v BBC* [2014] UKSC 25, [2015] AC 588 at [44].

37 *Werner v Austria* (1998) 26 EHRR 310 at [62].

38 *Marine A* [2013] EWCA Civ 2367 paras 68-76.

39 See *A v BBC* [2014] UKSC 24, [2015] AC 588 and *Khuja v Times Newspapers Ltd* [2017] 3 WLR 351 para 28.

40 *Re S (Identification: Restrictions on Publication)* [2004] UKHL 47, [2005] 1 AC 593 at [17].

41 *Kennedy v Charity Commission* [2014] UKSC 20, [2015] AC 455 at [115]; *R (DSD) v Parole Board* [2018] EWHC 694 (Admin), [2018] 3 WLR 829 where adjudications on matters of individual liberty were held to be 'paradigm examples of the exercise of a judicial function' [171] and where a rule that prevented making public any information about the proceedings was ultra vires (at [198]-[200]).

42 *A v BBC* [2014] UKSC 25, [2015] AC 588 at [27].

43 *Dring (on behalf of the Asbestos Victims Support Groups Forum UK) v Cape Intermediate Holdings Ltd* [2019] UKSC 38, [2019]

Thus the existence of court rules dealing with disclosure does not impinge upon the Court's inherent jurisdiction.[44]

2. THE GENERAL APPROACH

42–008 Introduction

As already noted, the statutory provisions governing access to court records vary according to the court concerned. The open justice principle, on the other hand, is applicable throughout the United Kingdom, even though the court rules may be different.[45]

> It follows that, unless inconsistent with statute or the rules of court, all courts and tribunals have an inherent jurisdiction to determine what that principle requires in terms of access to documents or other information placed before the court or tribunal in question. The extent of any access permitted by the court's rules is not determinative (save to the extent that they may contain a valid prohibition). It is not correct to talk in terms of limits to the court's jurisdiction when what is in fact in question is how that jurisdiction should be exercised in the particular case.[46]

As a result, there are certain common principles applicable to all courts. Some of these principles are universal, whereas others are common to all civil courts or to all criminal courts.

42–009 Documents in court: power

Formerly civil proceedings placed great emphasis on the 'orality' of those proceedings, enabling those attending the proceedings to hear everything put before the court. Thus, witnesses would be examined-in-chief by the party calling them, documents would be read onto the record, opening addresses and closing submissions would both be made orally and so forth. Open justice achieved its objectives by allowing any person to attend court and listen to the proceedings. Civil proceedings are no longer conducted on an entirely oral basis.[47] Witness statements have taken the place of examination-in-chief, and the judge is expected to have read them prior to the witness being called; trial bundles are pre-agreed and filed with the court before commencement of the trial; the judge should have read the parties' written openings before the case is formally opened; and skeleton arguments provide the backbone of parties' final submissions. On a trial of any length, the judge will have been allowed one or more

---

3 WLR 429 at [34]

44 *R (Guardian News and Media Ltd) v City of Westminster Magistrates' Court* [2012] EWCA Civ 420, [2013] QB 618 at [70], [75]; *Kennedy v Charity Commission* [2014] UKSC 20, [2015] AC 455 at at [188]; *Blue v Ashley* [2017] EWHC 1553 (Comm), [2017] 1 WLR 3630 at [9], [11]. Rules of Court can, provided they are not ultra vires for other reasons, go further than the common law requires but it is an open question how far they can restrict it. In *R (Pelling) v Bow County Court* [2001] EWCA Civ 122, [2001] UKHRR 165 Buxton LJ considered that if the CPR were inconsistent with the *Scott* principle then the 'potency and novelty' that Parliament intended by introducing the new regime could have demonstrated a sufficient intention to derogate from open justice. He found that there was no inconsistency and so the issue did not arise. Contrast earlier authorities: *Nestec v Dualit* [2013] EWHC 2737 (Pat) Birss J treated the lack of reference to certain classes of document in the rules as a reason not to allow access under the inherent jurisdiction (at [31]); *Chan U Seek v Alvis Vehicles Ltd* [2004] EWHC 3092 (Ch), [2005] 1 WLR 2965 where Park J found it 'very hard to imagine' invoking the inherent jurisdiction to order disclosure where the case was not covered by the CPR. In fact and following *Dring (on behalf of the Asbestos Victims Support Groups Forum UK) v Cape Intermediate Holdings Ltd* [2019] UKSC 38, [2019] 3 WLR 429 the documents he dealt with fell outside the CPR and so could only have been accessed through the inherent jurisdiction.

45 *Dring (on behalf of the Asbestos Victims Support Groups Forum UK) v Cape Intermediate Holdings Ltd* [2019] UKSC 38, [2019] 3 WLR 429 at [34], [41].

46 *Dring (on behalf of the Asbestos Victims Support Groups Forum UK) v Cape Intermediate Holdings Ltd* [2019] UKSC 38, [2019] 3 WLR 429 at [41].

47 *Lilly Icos v Pfizer Ltd (No 2)* [2002] EWCA Civ 2, [2002] 1 WLR 2261 at [7]; *Dring (on behalf of the Asbestos Victims Support Groups Forum UK) v Cape Intermediate Holdings Ltd* [2019] UKSC 38, [2019] 3 WLR 429 at [43].

'reading days' in order to absorb this material. Whilst these documents will all be before the judge deciding the matter and will have been exchanged between the parties, those attending court or reporting on court proceedings will be at a disadvantage in not having sight of that material. Accordingly, in order to achieve the same open justice objectives that were formerly secured by allowing a person to attend court and listen to proceedings, it has been necessary to recognise an entitlement of contemporaneous access to certain documents before the court. That such an entitlement exists is no longer doubted. The questions that have arisen have concerned the reach of that entitlement: what documents are within the entitlement, and at what moment does the entitlement arise? In relation to documents relied on in civil proceedings, a person who is not a party to the proceedings is generally entitled to have access to those documents that will put the person in the position that he or she would have been had the proceedings been conducted entirely orally and the person had been attending the proceedings.[48] The principle of open justice for these purposes is primarily concerned with monitoring justice as it takes place and not with reviewing the process long after the event.[49] Access will readily be granted to documents that would, under former practices, have been read out in open court or that put into writing submissions that would have been made orally but a more restrictive approach applies otherwise. The initial position taken by the courts was that:

> any member of the public who for legitimate reasons applies for a copy of counsel's written opening or skeleton argument, when it has been accepted by the judge in lieu of an oral opening, [should be regarded as] as prima facie entitled to it.[50]

Later cases at first instance drew a distinction between witness statements, expert reports and written submissions on the one hand, where disclosure would ordinarily be provided whether under Rules of Court or under the inherent jurisdiction and other documents where access would be denied.[51] In relation to criminal proceedings, the range of documents for which access would be given was extended, with the extension being justified on the basis that the purpose of the open justice principle was not simply to deter impropriety and sloppiness (which could be met by the simple fact of a hearing in public) but to enable the public to understand and scrutinise the justice system of which the courts are administrators:

> In a case where documents have been placed before a judge and referred to in the course of proceedings, in my judgment the default position should be that access should be permitted on the open justice principle; and where access is sought for a proper journalistic purpose, the case for allowing it will be particularly strong. However, there may be countervailing reasons...The court has to carry out a proportionality exercise which will be fact-specific. Central to the court's evaluation will be the purpose of the open justice principle, the potential value of the material in advancing that purpose and, conversely, any risk of harm which access to the documents may cause to the legitimate interests of others.[52]

In civil proceedings, the position as follows is that the court has an inherent jurisdiction to allow a non-party to inspect all documents before the court (apart from trial bundles where they have been marked up.[53] This extends to unmarked trial bundles, witness statements, expert reports,

48 *Lilly Icos v Pfizer Ltd (No 2)* [2002] EWCA Civ 2, [2002] 1 WLR 2261 at [9].

49 *Dian AO v Davis Frankel & Mead* [2004] EWHC 2662 (Comm), [2005] 1 WLR 2951 at [29]; *Dring (on behalf of the Asbestos Victims Support Groups Forum UK) v Cape Intermediate Holdings Ltd* [2019] UKSC 38, [2019] 3 WLR 429 at [42]-[43].

50 *GIO Personal Investment Services Ltd v Liverpool and London Steamship Protection and Indemnity Association Ltd* [1999] 1 WLR 984 at 996-7.

51 See eg: *Law Debenture Trust Corporation (Channel Islands) Ltd v Lexington Insurance Company & ors* [2003] EWHC 2297 (Comm); *British Arab Commercial Bank v Algosaibi Trading Services Limited and Ors* [2011] EWHC 1817 (Comm); *Nestec v Dualit* [2013] EWHC 2737 (Pat); *Sainsbury's Supermarkets Ltd v Mastercard Incorporated & Ors* [2016] CAT 6.

52 *R (Guardian News and Media Ltd) v City of Westminster Magistrates' Court* [2012] EWCA Civ 420, [2013] QB 618 at [85].

53 *Dring (on behalf of the Asbestos Victims Support Groups Forum UK) v Cape Intermediate Holdings Ltd* [2019] UKSC 38, [2019] 3 WLR 429. See also: *Chartered Institute of Arbitrators v B* [2019] EWHC 460 (Comm), dealing with an application for disclosure of various documents from the court records to enable their use in disciplinary proceedings brought

documents read out in court or which the court is invited to read, skeleton arguments, written openings and closings, and any other specific document which it is necessary for a non-party to inspect in order to meet the principle of open justice.[54]

42–010 Documents in court: discretion

In deciding whether to grant access the court will balance the non-party's reasons for seeking access against the parties' private interest in preserving their confidentiality. Relevant factors are likely to include:

(1) The extent to which the open justice principle is engaged, including the potential value in the information in question in advancing that purpose;
(2) Whether the documents are sought in the interests of open justice;
(3) Whether there is a legitimate interest in seeking copies of the documents and, if so, whether that is a public or private interest;
(4) The reasons for seeking to preserve confidentiality;
(5) The harm, if any, which may be caused by access to the documents to the legitimate interests of other parties, including national security, the protection of children and the disabled, and the protection of privacy, trade secrets and commercial confidentiality; and
(6) The practicalities and proportionality of granting the request.[55]

The non-party who seeks access will be expected to pay the reasonable costs of granting that access.[56] Given the importance of open justice the Court is likely to lean in favour of granting access to those documents available under the inherent jurisdiction where there is a legitimate interest in securing access to them.[57]

42–011 Public hearing: no judgment

The principle of open justice is engaged as soon as there is an effective hearing.[58] Thus, access to documents has been permitted where a case has settled part-way through the trial.[59]

42–012 Private hearing: no judgment

Where there has been no hearing then the open justice principle is not generally engaged. This might be, for example, because the case settles before there has been a hearing or because the documents were never referred to in an effective hearing. Access to documents in this situation

---

by and before the Chartered Institute of Arbitrators.

54 *Dring (on behalf of the Asbestos Victims Support Groups Forum UK) v Cape Intermediate Holdings Ltd* [2019] UKSC 38, [2019] 3 WLR 429, upholding to this extent the analysis of the Court of Appeal in *Cape Intermediate Holdings Ltd v Dring (for and on behalf of the Asbestos Victims Support Group)* [2018] EWCA Civ 1795, [2019] 1 WLR 479.

55 *Dring (on behalf of the Asbestos Victims Support Groups Forum UK) v Cape Intermediate Holdings Ltd* [2019] UKSC 38, [2019] 3 WLR 429 at [45]-[47]. The identity of the party seeking the information may be relevant to the exercise of the discretion: thus, the media may be better placed than others to demonstrate a good reason to be given access.

56 *Dring (on behalf of the Asbestos Victims Support Groups Forum UK) v Cape Intermediate Holdings Ltd* [2019] UKSC 38, [2019] 3 WLR 429 at [47].

57 *Cape Intermediate Holdings Ltd v Dring (for and on behalf of the Asbestos Victims Support Group)* [2018] EWCA Civ 1795, [2019] 1 WLR 479 at [127], [129]. Given the limited class of documents covered by the inherent jurisdiction and the express linkage to what would have been disclosed in open court proceedings it is difficult to see what room is left to balance confidentiality since that has already been lost. It may be that in practice the issue is unlikely to arise and the effective presumption of access in [129] will apply in most if not all cases. For an application of this principle, see: *Chartered Institute of Arbitrators v B* [2019] EWHC 460 (Comm).

58 *Cape Intermediate Holdings Ltd v Dring (for and on behalf of the Asbestos Victims Support Group)* [2018] EWCA Civ 1795, [2019] 1 WLR 479 at [126].

59 *Law Debenture Trust Corporation (Channel Islands) Ltd v Lexington Insurance Company & ors* [2003] EWHC 2297 (Comm), allowing access to submissions: see [28]-[35]. And see further: *NAB v Serco and Home Office* [2014] EWHC 1225 (QB) at [38]-[39].

will not be permitted unless there are strong grounds for thinking that it is in the interests of justice to do so.[60] For example, it was denied for documents filed in support of an application for summary judgment that was not pursued and where the nature of the case appeared sufficiently from documents to which access had been given.[61] Similarly, access was refused where documents had been referred to at an interim hearing but where the object of the application was to report in advance of trial evidence that it was proposed the witnesses would give.[62] However, access was given to documents filed in support of a summary judgment application before it was heard in order to assist them in other litigation arising out of the same transaction.[63] Some rules of court (notably CPR Part 5.4) allow access to documents even where there has not been a hearing. However, where permission is required then the principles on which that permission will be exercised are unlikely to differ from the principles applicable under the Court's inherent jurisdiction.[64]

42–013 Judgment: no public hearing

Where there has been a judicial decision without a hearing, such as where an application is determined on the paper, the court will lean in favour of allowing access to documents that were considered as part of the judicial decision-making process.[65]

42–014 Private hearing

A distinction is drawn between cases where the court sits in chambers as a matter of convenience and those where the public is formally and forcibly excluded. In the former case the principle of open justice applies in the same way as it does to public hearings, so that access is permissible under the inherent jurisdiction under the principles discussed above.[66] Where the public is formally excluded, that does not empty the open justice principle: it may still require information to be put into the public domain, usually by a reasoned decision or summary of it.[67] Where other information is sought following the court having decided that the public should be excluded from the hearing, then the same approach will apply as where documents have not been judicially considered at all: as such, there must be strong grounds for thinking that it is in the interests of justice to disclose them. The same applies where the court has considered the question of access to documents on the court file and has restricted access.[68]

42–015 Publicly-available documents

The power to order access to court documents ought not be used to obtain publicly available material.[69]

---

60 In *Sayers v Smith Kline* [2007] EWHC 1346 (QB) at [22] the court accepted that the standard should be no less exacting than would apply on an application under CPR 31.22 since an applicant should not be in a better position than would be a party seeking release from the implied undertaking and so had to show special circumstances.

61 *Dian AO v Davis Frankel & Mead* [2004] EWHC 2662 (Comm), [2005] 1 WLR 2951 at [57].

62 *Blue v Ashley* [2017] EWHC 1553 (Comm), [2017] 1 WLR 3630 at [13]-[16], [18], [23].

63 *HSH Nordbank AG v Saad Air* [2012] EWHC 3213 (Comm).

64 *Cape Intermediate Holdings Ltd v Dring (for and on behalf of the Asbestos Victims Support Group)* [2018] EWCA Civ 1795, [2019] 1 WLR 479 at [127]-[129].

65 *Dian AO v Davis Frankel & Mead* [2004] EWHC 2662 (Comm), [2005] 1 WLR 2951 at [56]; *Cape Intermediate Holdings Ltd v Dring (for and on behalf of the Asbestos Victims Support Group)* [2018] EWCA Civ 1795, [2019] 1 WLR 479 at [116]-[118].

66 *Dian AO v Davis Frankel & Mead* [2004] EWHC 2662 (Comm), [2005] 1 WLR 2951.

67 *R (DSD) v Parole Board* [2018] EWHC 694 (Admin), [2018] 3 WLR 829 at [174]-[177].

68 *ABC v Y Ltd* [2010] EWHC 3176 (Ch), [2012] 1 WLR 537 at [43]. The position might be different if the press sought documents from a private hearing in order to understand the proceedings or to report on them.

69 *Pfizer Health Ab v Schwarz Pharma Ag* [2010] EWHC 3236 (Pat), [2011] FSR 367 at [21], [34].

42–016 Interim hearings

The open justice principle is also in play in relation to interlocutory applications and the same principles apply. The court should then lean in favour of allowing access to documents that were judicially considered provided that the applicant has a legitimate interest in seeking them.[70]

42–017 Legitimate interest

Where the open justice principle is engaged then access to documents under the inherent jurisdiction or under permissive rules of court will still only be permitted to those persons with a legitimate interest in seeing the documents. Proper journalistic purposes have been recognised as an important interest. Similarly, where the object is to monitor that justice has been done, particularly as it takes place.[71] In other cases a legitimate interest has been shown where the applicant has sought access to documents that may have a bearing on other litigation in which they were involved,[72] or where an asbestos victims' support group wished to publish the material so that others could make use of it but without conducting analysis or research on the material themselves.[73] A party who is commercially active in a technical field to which a patent relates has a legitimate interest in seeing the grounds on which a patent had been attacked.[74]

42–018 The judgments register

Section 98 of the Courts Act 2003 requires that a register must be kept of judgments entered in the High Court or county court, administration orders or orders restricting enforcement under sections 112 and 112A of the County Courts Act 1984, sums payable by a conviction or order of a magistrates court and orders of the First-tier Tribunal, Upper Tribunal, Employment Tribunals or Employment Appeal Tribunal in respect of which any sums payable. The Register may be searched on payment of the appropriate fee.[75]

3. COURTS SUBJECT TO THE CPR

42–019 Claims registers and court files

Under CPR 5.4 a court or court office may keep a publicly accessible register of claims which have been issued out of that court or office. Any person paying the prescribed fee may search that register during office hours. The provision is permissive and registers are only currently

---

70 *Dian AO v Davis Frankel & Mead* [2004] EWHC 2662 (Comm), [2005] 1 WLR 2951 at [56] (a case decided under CPR Part 5.4C (2)) and as explained in *Cape Intermediate Holdings Ltd v Dring (for and on behalf of the Asbestos Victims Support Group)* [2018] EWCA Civ 1795, [2019] 1 WLR 479 at [122]. *Dian* refers to documents considered as part of the 'decision making process' but that must be understood in context and it is clear that no judicial decision is necessary for the open justice principle to apply.

71 *R (Guardian News and Media Ltd) v City of Westminster Magistrates' Court* [2012] EWCA Civ 420, [2013] QB 618 at [85]; *Dian AO v Davis Frankel & Mead* [2004] EWHC 2662 (Comm), [2005] 1 WLR 2951 at [30]; *Pfizer Health Ab v Schwarz Pharma Ag* [2010] EWHC 3236 (Pat), [2011] FSR 367 at [20]; *Chan U Seek v Alvis Vehicles Ltd* [2004] EWHC 3092 (Ch), [2005] 1 WLR 2965 at [37]. A similar conclusion was reached in *Various Claimants v News Group Newspapers* [2012] EWHC 397, [2012] 1 WLR 2545 at [78].

72 *Dian AO v Davis Frankel & Mead* [2004] EWHC 2662 (Comm), [2005] 1 WLR 2951; *Law Debenture Trust Corporation (Channel Islands) Ltd v Lexington Insurance Company & ors* [2003] EWHC 2297 (Comm).

73 *Cape Intermediate Holdings Ltd v Dring (for and on behalf of the Asbestos Victims Support Group)* [2018] EWCA Civ 1795, [2019] 1 WLR 479 at [131]-[136].

74 *Pfizer Health Ab v Schwarz Pharma Ag* [2010] EWHC 3236 (Pat), [2011] FSR 367 at [28].

75 See also the Register of Judgments, Orders and Fines Regulations 2005 (SI 2005/3595).

available at some offices of the Royal Courts of Justice. Details of the available registers are set out in CPR PD5A. The right to inspect the register does not extend to a right to inspect documents held on the court file. The file is not available for inspection except to the extent that the CPR so provide or the court so orders.[76] CPR 5.4A-D make provision for access to documents from court records. Those provisions do not apply in relation to 'any proceedings in respect of which a rule or practice direction makes different provision.'[77]

42–020 Court records: party access

CPR Part 5.4B provides that a party to proceedings may obtain from the records of the court the documents listed in paragraph 4.2A of the Practice Direction. This lists various documents that are filed with the court. If the court gives permission then that party may also obtain from the records of the court a copy of 'any other document filed by a party or communication between the court and a party or another person.'[78] Where necessary to protect the interests of justice and so far as compatible with open justice, the court may anonymise or redact documents to which a party may be given access under either part of this rule.[79] The documents listed in paragraph 4.2A include a judgment or order made in public (whether made at a hearing or without a hearing). However, they do not include a schedule to a *Tomlin* order so that even a party must seek permission to inspect such a schedule.[80]

42–021 Pleadings etc: non-parties

CPR Part 5.4C(1) establishes a general rule that a non-party may as of right obtain from court records:

(a) a copy of the statement of case but not any documents attached to it or served with it or

(b) a judgment or order given or made in public (whether made at a hearing or without a hearing).[81]

The court can limit access to a statement of case under CPR 5.4C(4). Statement of case is defined in CPR 2.3(a) and it includes particulars of claim, the defence and reply and any further information provided. It does not include other documents defining the issues, such as a notice to admit or response to it.[82] In judicial review proceedings, it includes summary and detailed grounds filed in accordance with CPR 54.8 and 54.14.[83] The definition is directed to proceedings at first instance and so does not include a notice of appeal or respondents notice, the effect being that these can only be accessed with permission.[84] A non-party may obtain a statement of case or judgment or order under this provision only if one of the conditions in

76 *Dobson v Hastings* [1992] Ch 394; *Dian AO v Davis Frankel & Mead* [2004] EWHC 2662 (Comm), [2005] 1 WLR 2951 at [20].

77 For example, the Rule does not apply to proceedings under CPR 76, 79, 80, 82 and 88 (various counter terrorism provisions and 5.4B is modified by PD8A para 23 in respect of a telecommunications restriction order).

78 CPR 5.4B(2).

79 *A v Chief Constable of Dorset* [2010] EWHC 1748 (Admin), [2011] 1 FLR 11.

80 *L'Oreal SA v eBay International AG* [2008] FSR 980.

81 This only applies in relation to a statement of case filed after 2 October 2006. Otherwise the rules previously in force still apply. Certain documents in connection with a mediation settlement enforcement order under CPR 78 are also excluded from this rule and may be inspected only with permission (CPR 5.4C(1B)). The right to obtain a copy of the statement of case is also subject to an order to the contrary under CPR 5.4C(4) considered below.

82 *Various Claimants v News Group Newspapers* [2012] EWHC 397, [2012] 1 WLR 2545 at [55]-[57]. The court went on to allow access to these documents under CPR 5.4C(2) subject to limited redactions necessary to avoid prejudice to criminal proceedings.

83 *R (Corner House Research) v Director of the Serious Fraud Office* [2008] EWHC 246 (Admin), [2008] CP Rep 20.

84 CPR PD52C para 33 requires represented parties to bring two extra copies of the skeleton argument for provision to accredited law reporters and accredited media reporters.

CPR 5.4C(3) is met, namely that the defendant has filed an acknowledgment of service or defence,[85] the claim has been listed for a hearing, or judgment has been entered in the claim. By CPR 5.4C(4) the court may, on the application of a party or of any person identified in a statement of case make an order restricting access to the statement of case.[86] Where such an order has been made then by CPR 5.4C(6) a non-party may apply on notice for access to the statement of case or a non-edited version. A decision to restrict access to the full statement of case is a derogation from open justice and must be limited in scope to what is required in the particular circumstances of the case.[87] In exercising this power, the starting point is that there should be a right to access an unredacted version and the reasons why the non-party wants that access are of little or no importance unless it can be said that the purpose is in some way improper.[88] The right to access to a judgment or order under CPR 5.4C(1)(b) only arises where it was given or made in public. Where the hearing is in private then a copy of the judgment is available with permission under Part 5.4C(2) (see below). Indeed, the fact that such an application may be made is a factor entitling the court to give judgment in private without breaching Art 6 of the ECHR.[89]

42–022 Other records: non-parties

CPR 5.4C(2) provides that 'any other document filed by a party, or communication between the court and a party or another person' may be obtained from court records with permission. It has been suggested that the court ought not to make a general order that non-parties may not obtain copies of documents on the court file because that gives the impression of pre-judging an application that has not yet been made.[90] The apparent breadth of this provision is limited by the fact that disclosure may only be made from 'the records of the court.' The term covers essentially documents kept by the court office as a record of the proceedings, many of which will be of a formal nature. The principal documents which are likely to fall within that description are those set out in paragraph 4.2A of CPR 5.4, together with 'communications between the court and a party or another person.' Other documents will only be 'records of the court' if they are of an analogous nature. They do not include disclosed documents, the trial bundle, trial witness statements, trial skeleton arguments or opening or closing notes or submissions, the trial transcripts or skeleton arguments.[91] The record may include witness statements and exhibits filed in relation to an application notice or Part 8 proceedings.[92] Where

85 If there are multiple defendants then either all must have done so or at least has done so and the court gives permission.

86 There is no power under this Rule to direct that only a redacted form of an Order should be supplied: *ABC v Y Ltd* [2010] EWHC 3176 (Ch), [2012] 1 WLR 537.

87 *G v Wikimedia Foundation Inc* [2009] EWHC 3148, [2010] EMLR 14 at [17], where anonymity having been granted, access to the statement of case was also to a version that did not disclose the identity of the claimant.

88 *Various Claimants v News Group Newspapers* [2012] EWHC 397, [2012] 1 WLR 2545 at [60]-[3] (where redactions were ordered to delete material that might prejudice criminal proceedings). See also *Global Torch Ltd v Apex Global Management Ltd & Ors* [2013] EWCA Civ 819, [2013] 1 WLR 2993 where the application under CPR 5.4C(4) failed for the same reasons that an application for a private hearing was unsuccessful. In *Associated Newspapers v Bannatyne & Ors* [2015] EWHC 3467 (Ch) redactions were made to preserve a confidentiality undertaking given to the applicant's wife in divorce proceedings but not in respect of misleading evidence that had been given (but later retracted) in those proceedings.

89 In *re Trusts of X Charity* [2003] EWHC 1462 (Ch), [2003] 1 WLR 2751.

90 *ABC v Y Ltd* [2010] EWHC 3176 (Ch), [2012] 1 WLR 537 at [9]. Despite this such orders are often made: see for example *DMK v News Group Newspapers* [2016] EWHC 1646 where inspection without permission was restricted to a redacted version of the pleadings in order to avoid undermining a non-disclosure injunction.

91 *Cape Intermediate Holdings Ltd v Dring (for and on behalf of the Asbestos Victims Support Group)* [2018] EWCA Civ 1795, [2019] 1 WLR 479 at [54], not following on this point *Chan U Seek v Alvis Vehicles Ltd* [2004] EWHC 3092 (Ch), [2005] 1 WLR 2965 and *NAB v Serco and Home Office* [2014] EWHC 1225 (QB).

92 *Cape Intermediate Holdings Ltd v Dring (for and on behalf of the Asbestos Victims Support Group)* [2018] EWCA Civ 1795,

documents do not fall within CPR 5.4C(2) then an application for access may be possible under the court's inherent jurisdiction. An application for access under CPR 5.4C(2) does not have to be made while the claim is in progress and can be made at any time. Delay in seeking access to an old file may be relevant to the exercise of the court's powers but the fact that the court no longer holds a copy of the document is not decisive because it can, for example, order a party to re-file it.[93] It also follows that an application for access to documents under this Rule can be made without the need for there to have been a hearing that causes the documents to have entered the public domain and without the documents having been considered as part of a decision-making process. However, in most cases disclosure will only be ordered in such case where there are strong grounds for thinking that it is in the interests of justice to do so.[94] Further guidance on the disclosure of documents and the media is given in guidance published by the court service.[95]

42–023 Procedure

Where permission is required to access a document from court records, a non-party must apply to the court.[96] The application may be without notice but the court may direct that notice be given by any person who may be affected by its decision.[97] The application notice must identify the document or class of document in respect of which permission is sought and the grounds relied upon.[98] Where permission is not required, a non-party makes a written request to the court for the document.[99] In both cases the prescribed fee must be paid. Similar requirements apply where the application is made under the court's inherent jurisdiction. An applicant may take copies of documents able to be inspected, but that person must bear the costs of and associated with the copying. Where documents are subject to the electronic working pilot in CPR PD51O then a person wishing to obtain a copy of a document available to a non-party must complete appropriate office copy request form and pay the appropriate fee. Where the court makes an order it may make it subject to conditions.[100] An order may include terms to protect the integrity of the documents to which access is allowed.[101] An application for an Order under CPR 5.4C(4) restricting access to a statement of case must be made by application

[2019] 1 WLR 479 at [41].

93 *Chan U Seek v Alvis Vehicles Ltd* [2004] EWHC 3092 (Ch), [2005] 1 WLR 2965 at [44]; *Blue v Ashley* [2017] EWHC 1553 (Comm), [2017] 1 WLR 3630 at [10].

94 *Dian AO v Davis Frankel & Mead* [2004] EWHC 2662 (Comm), [2005] 1 WLR 2951 at [57]. Where an application was made in a patent action by solicitors representing persons with a commercial interest, then that was held to be sufficient in *Pfizer Health Ab v Schwarz Pharma Ag* [2010] EWHC 3236 (Pat), [2011] FSR 367. The nature of the documents sought may also be relevant. For example in *Various Claimants v News Group Newspapers* [2012] EWHC 397, [2012] 1 WLR 2545 (where the documents had been referred to in open court) the documents included a notice to admit which was analogous to a statement of case.

95 https://assets.publishing.service.gov.uk/government/uploads/system/uploads/attachment_data/file/746849/HMCTS_media_guidance_-_Civil_Court_Guide.pdf

96 Pursuant to CPR 23.

97 CPR 5.4D(2) and para 4.3 of CPR PD5.

98 See also *Dian AO v Davis Frankel & Mead* [2004] EWHC 2662 (Comm), [2005] 1 WLR 2951 at [32]-[34], where it was held under predecessor provisions that an applicant cannot seek to inspect the entire file.

99 CPR 5.4D(1)(b).

100 This is under the general power CPR 3.1(3) or under the inherent jurisdiction, as well as being some parts of CPR 5.4C (eg 5.4C(4)(d)).

101 *Cape Intermediate Holdings Ltd v Dring (for and on behalf of the Asbestos Victims Support Group)* [2018] EWCA Civ 1795, [2019] 1 WLR 479 at [146]. See also *Various Claimants v News Group Newspapers* [2012] EWHC 397, [2012] 1 WLR 2545 where documents were disclosed but with redactions and *Sayers v Smithkline Beecham Ltd* [2007] EWHC 1346 (QB) where documents were anonymized.

notice.[102] However, this is not necessary where the application is included as part of an application for permission to apply for judicial review under CPR 54.[103] An application may be without notice, but the court may direct that notice be given to somebody who may be affected.[104] Specific guidance is given in relation to applications for redaction in procurement disputes by the Technology and Construction Court.[105]

42–024 Witness statements: non-parties

Where a witness statement forms part of the evidence adduced in support of an interlocutory application then it is part of the Court Record[106] and may be inspected by a non-party provided that the court gives permission.[107] The general rule is that at trial facts are proved by the oral evidence of witnesses.[108] However, a witness statement will stand as evidence in chief unless the court orders otherwise.[109] So far as inspection of witness statements by a non-party, the general rule is:[110]

> A witness statement which stands as evidence in chief is open to inspection during the course of the trial unless the court otherwise directs.

This is subject to the power to make a contrary order, including for redaction.[111] A witness statement 'stands as evidence in chief' only once the witness has been called to give evidence and confirms the accuracy of his or her witness statement. Thus, where a statement intended for use at trial was referred to at the hearing of an application to rely on expert evidence, that did not bring it within this rule.[112] Access to witness statements under this rule does not extend to access to documents referred to in a witness statement.[113] Those documents are not part of the court record (unless they fall within it for other reasons – for example if a statement refers to a pleading) and so can only be accessed under the court's inherent jurisdiction. A third party may be able to obtain a copy of a witness statement from a party to the proceedings, but this is subject to CPR 32.12 which states:

> (1) Except as provided by this rule, a witness statement may be used only for the purpose of the proceedings in which it is served.
> (2) Paragraph (1) does not apply if and to the extent that—
>   (a) the witness gives consent in writing to some other use of it;
>   (b) the court gives permission for some other use; or
>   (c) the witness statement has been put in evidence at a hearing held in public.

The reasoning behind this rule is that unless and until the witness is called, the statement is a

---

102 Pursuant to CPR 23.

103 *R (Corner House Research) v Director of the Serious Fraud Office* [2008] EWHC 246 (Admin), [2008] CP Rep 20 at [28].

104 CPR 5D(2).

105 *TCC Guidance Note on Procedures for Public Procurement Cases*, 17 July 2017.

106 It falls within the list in paragraph 4A of CPR PD5A.

107 Under CPR 5.4C(2).

108 CPR 32.2.

109 CPR 32.5.

110 CPR Part 32.13(1).

111 CPR 32.13(2)-(4).

112 *Blue v Ashley* [2017] EWHC 1553 (Comm), [2017] 1 WLR 3630 at [13]-[16], [18], [23]. Nor was it appropriate to order access under CPR 5.4C(2) (this would now have to be under the inherent jurisdiction following *Cape Intermediate Holdings Ltd v Dring (for and on behalf of the Asbestos Victims Support Group)* [2018] EWCA Civ 1795, [2019] 1 WLR 479. Until the witness gives evidence the statement is simply an indication of the evidence the witness will give if called. It assists preparation and open justice does not require access to it. Access was allowed to the witness statement prepared specifically for the expert evidence application but not to the expert report itself since the application to adduce it had failed.

113 *British Arab Commercial Bank v Algosaibi Trading Services Limited and Ors* [2011] EWHC 1817 (Comm) at [20].

confidential indication of the evidence to be given. In practice this rule raises similar issues to those that arise in connection with the use of documents obtained on disclosure.[114]

42–025 Judgments: non-parties

A different starting point applies in arbitration proceedings under CPR 62, with such proceedings normally being in private. This reflects the fact that the parties have initially chosen a private form of dispute resolution. However, even where the proceedings are private, the judgment need not be, particularly where the matter involves a point of principle or practice.[115] All hearings are tape recorded. Where the hearing is in public[116] or a judgment is given in public then members of the public are entitled to transcripts of the hearing or the judgment and a copy of an order on payment of authorized charges. Where the hearing or any part of it is in private then the right to a transcript of the hearing only applies if the court so orders. Where a judgment is given or an order made in private then the transcript or order will only be made available with the leave of the judge who gave the judgment or made the order.[117]

42–026 Access from a party

A party to litigation may generally disclose to a third-party, including the media, documents that they hold or that they have acquired or generated for the purposes of the proceedings subject to complying with any other restriction on disclosure to which they may be subject such as a duty of confidentiality[118] or so as not to commit a contempt of court or breach any other statutory duty that they may be under. However, it is a common feature of court proceedings that documents are obtained by one party from another, whether under an order for disclosure or otherwise. The common law recognises an implied undertaking that documents disclosed by one party to another can only be used for the purposes of the proceedings in which they have been disclosed unless the party whose documents were disclosed has consented or the court has given leave. The rationale for this implied undertaking is that since compulsory disclosure involves a serious invasion into a litigant's privacy and confidentiality, it ought not to be extended any further than strictly required for the purpose of securing that justice is done.[119] The principle is also said to promote openness and full disclosure.[120] Comparable undertakings are implied in other cases where documents were subject to compulsory disclosure or where they were provided voluntarily to pre-empt compulsion.[121] The implied undertaking continues even after documents has been referred to in open court such that passing them to a journalist after trial will constitute a contempt.[122] The common law implied undertaking does

---

[114] See §42–026 below.

[115] *Department of Economic Policy Development of the City of Moscow v Bankers Trust Co* [2004] EWCA Civ 314, [2005] QB 207.

[116] By CPR 39.2(1) the general rule is that a hearing is to be in public. However, a hearing, or any part of it, may be in private if the conditions in CPR 39.2(2) apply. These set out a series of cases where this may be necessary to protect such matters as confidential or private information, national security, or the interests of a child or protected party and concludes with the catch-all "the court considers this to be necessary, in the interests of justice". Further provision is made by CPR PD39A which identifies certain cases that shall be listed in private in the first instance.

[117] CPR PD39A para 1.11-12; 6.1-4.

[118] For an example of confidentiality restricting disclosure see *HRH Prince of Luxembourg v HRH Princess of Luxembourg* [2017] EWHC 3095 (Fam), [2018] 1 FLR 480, where an order was made restricting publication of an offer to settle financial remedy proceedings after balancing the competing Arts 8 and 10 rights at [80]-[117].

[119] *Home Office v Harman* [1983] AC 280 at 308, 322.

[120] *Crest Homes plc v Marks* [1987] AC 829 at 857, [1987] 2 All ER 1074.

[121] *Sybron Corp v Barclays Bank Plc* [1985] Ch 299 at 315; *Marcel v Commissioner of Police of the Metropolis* [1992] Ch 225 237.

[122] *Home Office v Harman* [1983] AC 280.

not apply to voluntary disclosure.[123] Following a successful challenge to the implied undertaking,[124] it has (so far as proceedings governed by the CPR) been codified and replaced with CPR 31.22:

> (1) A party to whom a document has been disclosed may use the document only for the purpose of the proceedings in which it is disclosed, except where—
> (a) the document has been read to or by the court, or referred to, at a hearing which has been held in public;
> (b) the court gives permission; or
> (c) the party who disclosed the document and the person to whom the document belongs agree.

This applies to any document that has been 'disclosed' and this disclosure occurs when a party states 'that the document exists or has existed.'[125] This does not require a list of documents: a reference in a witness statement is, for example, sufficient.[126] The provision applies to any document that has been disclosed and so, provided one of the parties is willing to allow access, the rule is significantly wider than 'court records' for the purposes of CPR 5.4C. The statutory test of being 'read to or by the court' or 'referred to' is wider than that applied under the inherent jurisdiction.

42–027 Documents read or referred to

Where a document is pre-read by the court and referred to by counsel in a skeleton argument that is spoken to in open court, or where a document is referred to (even though not read aloud) by counsel or by the court, CPR 31.22 will apply to that document provided that the judge has made a judicial decision on the basis of that material.[127] Where a document has been put before the court for the purpose of being read, then the burden lies on the party seeking to show that CPR 31.22(a) does not apply to establish that that document has not been referred to or read: for this purpose enquiry of the judge is not permissible.[128] By contrast, under the inherent jurisdiction in relation to access to documents for non-parties the presumption that documents have been read is limited to documents that the judge is specifically invited to read.[129]

42–028 Power to restrain use

The Court may, under CPR 31.22(2) order that a document should not be disclosed despite the

[123] For example *Brookfield Multiplex Ltd v International Litigation Funding Partners Pte Ltd (No 2)* [2009] FCA 449, (2009) 180 FCR 1, (2009) 256 ALR 416.

[124] *Harman v United Kingdom* (1985) 7 EHRR CD146, (1986) 46 Dr E Com HR 57.

[125] CPR 31.2.

[126] *SmithKline Beecham plc v Generics (UK) Ltd* [2003] EWCA Civ 1109, [2004] 1 WLR 1479 at [29]; *Index v Cloete* [2014] EWCA Civ 1128, [2015] ICR 254 at [45]; *Arcadia Group Ltd and others v Telegraph Media Group Ltd* [2019] EWHC 223 (QB) at [64]. The rule appears therefore to apply to disclosure that is voluntary. This conclusion has been subject to criticism: eg P Matthews and HM Malek QC, *Disclosure*, 5th Ed (London) Sweet & Maxwell, 2017, 8.01, 19.03; C Hollander QC, *Documetary Evidence*, 13th Ed (London), Sweet & Maxwell, paras 28-11-28-12.

[127] The court did not address the position if there had been a gratuitous reference to the documents – such as often happens when the parties announce a settlement and the judge comments on it, referring to the documents they have read. *Lily Icos Ltd v Pfizer Ltd (No2)* [2002] EWCA Civ 2, [2002] 1 WLR 2253 at [8] suggests that in such a case the implied undertaking would still apply. The court held that the '*Connaught* approach' is based on the assumed orality of a trial and so a settlement, even if announced in open court does not engage it.

[128] *Barings Plc (in liq) v Coopers & Lybrand* [2000] 1 WLR 2353, [2000] 3 All ER 910 at [53]. The statutory phrase in that case was whether the documents had become 'available to the public' but the case was treated as applicable to this rule in *Lily Icos Ltd v Pfizer Ltd (No2)* [2002] EWCA Civ 2, [2002] 1 WLR 2253 and applied in *NAB v Serco and Home Office* [2014] EWHC 1225 (QB). In *NAB* a report that was relevant to a claim against Serco was exhibited to a witness statement and remained in the bundle after the Serco claim settled and when it had no relevance to the remaining claim and was not referred to in skeleton arguments. The court held that CPR 31.22(a) applied even though the reference was 'marginal and gratuitous.'

[129] *Cape Intermediate Holdings Ltd v Dring (for and on behalf of the Asbestos Victims Support Group)* [2018] EWCA Civ 1795, [2019] 1 WLR 479 at [104].

fact that the implied undertaking would otherwise cease to apply to it. In deciding whether or not to exercise this power the court is guided by the open justice principle discussed above. It starts from the principle that very good reasons are required before departing from the normal rule of publicity:

> the court should take into account the role that the document has played or will play in the trial, and thus its relevance to the process of scrutiny referred to by Lord Diplock. The court should start from the assumption that all documents in the case are necessary and relevant for that purpose, and should not accede to general arguments that it would be possible, or substantially possible, to understand the trial and judge without access to a particular document. However, in particular cases the centrality of the document to the trial is a factor to be placed in the balance.[130]

42–029 Permission for collateral use

Where a document has not been referred to at a public hearing then the court may nevertheless grant permission for its use under CPR 31.22(b). It will be necessary to demonstrate special circumstances for release from the implied undertaking and that release or modification would not cause injustice to the person disclosing the document, with the burden lying on the person seeking release to demonstrate 'cogent and persuasive reasons.'[131] The exercise is a fact sensitive one, but where disclosure is sought for the benefit of a third party then they may face a particularly heavy burden and permission will 'virtually never' be given where the object is to allow a third party to bring a claim against the party giving disclosure.[132] On the other hand, where disclosure is sought to assist in the defence of a claim, the burden is lighter, and particularly if the disclosed document would reveal wrongdoing that supports the defence.[133]

4. COURT OF PROTECTION

42–030 Introduction

The Court of Protection is established by Part 2 of the Mental Capacity Act 2005. The Court of Protection Rules 2017 govern procedure in the court with effect from 1 December 2017.[134] The general rule is that hearings are in private but the court may authorize[135] particular persons or classes of persons to attend and may authorize publication or communication of information or material relating to the proceedings or publication of the whole or part of a judgment. It may also order that the hearing be in public. The court may only exercise its powers to depart from the general rule that the hearing be in private where there is 'good reason' to do so. Where it does so, it may restrict the identity of a party, witness or any other person and to restrict the publication of information.[136] These provisions mirror and re-articulate an

130 *Lily Icos Ltd v Pfizer Ltd (No2)* [2002] EWCA Civ 2, [2002] 1 WLR 2253 at [25]. See also *NAB v Serco and Home Office* [2014] EWHC 1225 (QB).

131 *Marlwood Commercial Inc v Koseny & Ors* [2004] EWCA Civ 798, [2005] 1 WLR 104 at [43], citing *Crest Homes plc v Marks* [1987] AC 829 at 859, 860, [1987] 2 All ER 1074. See also the summary in *Tchenguiz v Director of the Serious Fraud Office* [2014] EWCA Civ 1409 at [65].

132 *Milano Assicurazioni SpA v Walbrook Insurance Co Ltd and Another* [1994] 1 WLR 977 at 983, citing *Bibby Bulk Carriers Ltd. v. Cansulex Ltd* [1989] QB 155.

133 *Ex p Coventry Newspapers Ltd* [1993] QB 278; *Oxford County Council v P* [1995] Fam 161; *BDW Trading Ltd v Fitzpatrick* [2015] EWHC 3490 (Ch).

134 SI 2017/1035.

135 Where it does so then the effect is to disapply s 12 of the Administration of Justice Act which makes it a contempt to publish information relating to proceedings in private under the Mental Capacity Act 2005.

136 Rules 4.1-4. See also Practice Direction 4A which deals, among other things, with the procedure for notifying the press where a reporting restriction is sought and makes detailed provision as to the persons to whom and purposes

established common law exception to the principle of open justice.[137] Despite the general rule, the court will ordinarily, and without any application being made, direct that an 'attended' hearing be in public.[138] However, this will ordinarily also be subject to a reporting restriction restraining publication of the identity of the person lacking capacity.

42– 031 Documents from court records

A person who is not a party to proceedings may inspect or obtain from court records a copy of any judgment or order made in public.[139] The court may authorize a person who is not a party to inspect or take a copy of any other documents in court records. Before giving such an authorization, the court will consider whether the document should be provided on an edited basis. 'Court records' are not defined for these purposes, but a narrow meaning is likely.[140] The term will include a report ordered under s 49 of the Mental Capacity Act 2005.[141] Where an application for access to court documents is made by an accredited member of the press for journalistic purposes, a liberal approach will probably be taken on whether redaction is necessary, at least where there has been or is to be a public hearing. Restrictions on publication are a separate matter, but the press will ordinarily be trusted to act responsibly and not to publish matters in contempt of court.[142]

42– 032 Access to judgments

COPR confers a rights of access to a judgment whenever that judgment has been given in public. Where judgment has been given in private, then that judgment must not to be published (which includes disclosure to a non-party) unless the court gives permission. Publication without permission will be a contempt of court.[143] Where the judge concludes that publication of a judgment would be in the public interest, permission to publish that judgment will generally be given regardless of whether or not a request has been made by a party or by the media.[144] In some classes of case[145] permission to publish a judgment will be given unless

---

for which disclosure can be made of information relating to proceedings in private.

137 *A v Independent News & Media Ltd & ors* [2010] EWCA Civ 343, [2010] 1 WLR 2262 at [19], [27]. As to the principles applied when deciding whether to make a restricted reporting order: see *NHS Trust v FG* [2014] EWCOP 30 at [20]-[29]; *The NHS Acute Trust v C* [2016] EWCOP 17 at [53].

138 Practice Direction 4C.

139 COPR Rule 5.9. An application must be made using the procedure in Part 10 of the Rules.

140 See: *Cape Intermediate Holdings Ltd v Dring (for and on behalf of the Asbestos Victims Support Group)* [2018] EWCA Civ 1795, [2019] 1 WLR 479. Under the predecessor to this rule (Court of Protection Rules 2007 Rule 17) the CPS were granted access to a list of documents filed by the local authority in a case where there were allegations of sexual assault on a young woman with learning difficulties. An application for further access was adjourned when the CPS was unclear precisely for what purpose the material would be used and whether disclosure would irreversibly open the door to the defence to use the material within the trial itself: *LBX v TT (BY the Official Solicitor as her Litigation Friend) MJ, JJ, WT*, LT [2014] EWCOP 24, para 17.

141 See Public Guardian Practice Note PN6 01/2010 addressing the predecessor Rule 17 in the Court of Protection Rules 2007.

142 *A Healthcare NHS Trust v P* [2015] EWCOP 15, [2015] COPLR 147 holding that where an application for an injunction restraining publication was made then it was not necessary to anonymise the application. Publication in advance of the hearing would be a contempt because it would prejudice the outcome, making an application for a reporting restriction redundant.

143 Administration of Justice Act 1960 s 12.

144 See: *Practice Guidance on Transparency in the Family Courts and the Court of Protection—Publication of Judgments*.

145 The classes include matters such as giving or withholding serious medical treatment, deprivation of liberty, disputes about who should act as an attorney, moves into or from institutional care, sale of a home or property and affairs in excess of £1m, capacity to marry or have sexual relations, an application to restrain publication: *Practice Guidance on Transparency in the Family Courts and the Court of Protection—Publication of Judgments* para 17. This only applies to existing judgments or where the judge has ordered that it be transcribed. Thus this does not require the judge to generate a publishable judgment where he would not otherwise do so. For that an application must be made

there are 'compelling reasons' to the contrary. In all other cases 'the starting point is that permission may be given for the judgment to be published whenever a party or an accredited member of the media applies for an order permitting publication, and the judge concludes that permission for the judgment to be published should be given.' Where a judgment is published then public authorities and expert witnesses should be named unless there are compelling reasons why not: the person who is the subject of the proceedings and their family will not normally be named.

42–033 Access from a party

Where a hearing of proceedings under the Mental Capacity Act 2005 is in private, publication of information about the proceedings will generally be a contempt of court.[146] 'Publication' includes communication with a non-party. However, the court may authorize a communication, subject to such conditions as it thinks fit.[147] Documents obtained in proceedings are subject to an implied undertaking:

> Where a document has been filed or disclosed, a party to whom it was provided may use the document only for the purpose of the proceedings in which it was filed or disclosed, except where—
> (a) the document has been read to or by the court or referred to at a public hearing; or
> (b) the court otherwise permits.[148]

This is subject to any order of the court restricting publication of information.[149] It seems to follow that where documents have been referred to at a public hearing the court cannot, under this rule, prevent their further use as such (as it could do under the CPR) but can only prevent publication of identifying information or information relating to the proceedings. In practice there is probably little difference between the two powers.

5. FAMILY COURT

42–034 Introduction

The Family Court was established with effect from 22 April 2014 for the purpose of exercising powers under the Matrimonial and Family Proceedings Act 1984 and other legislation. It carries out the family law functions that were formerly vested in the County Court and Magistrates Court. The Family Procedure Rules 2010 — FPR — govern procedure in the Family Court and in the Family Division of the High Court (which continues to exercise the inherent jurisdiction and to deal with international cases). Proceedings are generally in private unless the court orders otherwise and it will not do so unless there are compelling reasons to the contrary.[150] Although the proceedings are private, 'duly accredited representatives of news gathering and reporting organisations' may be present for most hearings unless they are specifically excluded where it is necessary in the interests of a child concerned in or connected with the proceedings, the safety or protection of a party, witness or person connected with them, the orderly conduct of the proceedings or because justice will otherwise be impeded or

under para 18 and the person making the request must bear the cost (para 22).

146 Administration of Justice Act 1960 s 12.

147 COPR 4.2.

148 COPR 5.10.

149 COPR 4.3(2).

150 FPR 27.10. *DL v SL (Financial Remedy Proceedings: Privacy)* [2015] EWHC 2621 (Fam), [2016] 1 WLR 1259 at [13], not following *Luckwell v Limata (No2)* [2014] EWHC 536 (Fam), [2014] 2 FLR 1252 where Holman J considered that financial relief proceedings should normally be in open court.

prejudiced.[151] When the press attend in this way they do not do so as the 'eyes and ears' of the public but in order to report how the case is conducted 'in an abstract way.' The proceedings remain private and where the case concerns quintessentially private business then in 'almost every case where anonymisation is sought the right to privacy will trump the right to unfettered freedom of expression.'[152]

42– 035 General prohibition

There is no general rule permitting access by a third party to other documents in connection with family proceedings including those held by the court:

> no document...filed or lodged in the court office shall be open to inspection by any person without the permission of the court.[153]

Parties and their representatives may inspect and take copies but for non-parties the only exception in this rule is in respect of a copy of an order made in open court which will be made available to any person who requests it.[154]

42– 036 Judgments

The general prohibition on access extends to judgments given in private. This is subject to guidance, which identifies some classes of case in the Family Court or the inherent jurisdiction of the High Court where a judgment should be published unless there are compelling reasons to the contrary.[155] Although financial proceedings will ordinarily be held in private, judgments may be published where there has been serious misconduct: this is on the basis that it is in the public interest that it be exposed.[156]

42– 037 Witness statements

In matrimonial and civil partnership proceedings, witness statements that stand as evidence-in-chief are open for inspection during the course of the final hearing unless the court directs otherwise.[157] In matrimonial and civil partnership proceedings and in financial remedy proceedings a witness statement may be used only for the purpose of the proceedings in which it was served except and to the extent that either the court gives permission or the statement has been put in evidence at a hearing held in public.[158]

42– 038 Access applications

Application may be made to release documents, whether under the court rules or under the court's inherent jurisdiction.[159] Where a hearing has been in public, access to documents on the court file will normally be allowed if that access is sought for a proper journalistic

151 FPR 27.11. *DL v SL (Financial Remedy Proceedings: Privacy)* [2015] EWHC 2621 (Fam), [2016] 1 WLR 1259 at [10]-[11].

152 *DL v SL (Financial Remedy Proceedings: Privacy)* [2015] EWHC 2621 (Fam), [2016] 1 WLR 1259 at [10].

153 FPR 29.12.

154 FPR 29.12(2). The court office can and should supply this even if the applicant cannot state the name or case number if they can provide sufficient details of the case to allow the order to be located without undue difficulty such as the date and name of the judge: *Justice for Families Ltd v Secretary of State for Justice* [2014] EWCA Civ 1477, [2015] 2 FLR 321 at [25].

155 HMCTS, *Guidance on Transparency in the Family Courts: The Publication of Judgments*.

156 See for example the review of the cases in *Bloom v Bloom* (2018) 168 NLJ 7787.

157 FPR 22.19.

158 FPR 22.20.

159 FPR 29.12.

purpose.[160] Where a hearing has been in private, documents relating to it will not normally be disclosed to third parties. However, the judgment and associated documents may be provided for specific purposes such as for use in criminal proceedings. Where children are concerned, special principles will apply.[161] Any order for disclosure may be subject to restrictions limiting the use that may be made of any documents.[162]

42–039 Media access

While access to court documents in private proceedings is not generally necessary or desirable having regard to their confidential nature, it may be argued that access to certain documents is required in order fully to understand the proceedings. Where the media request access to documents, before acceding the court should first invite the consent of the parties to see any summaries, position statements and other documents that appear to the court to be reasonably necessary to secure a broad understanding of the issues in the case. Where necessary or appropriate, an application should be transferred to the High Court to ensure a consistent approach.

42–040 Access from a party

Where documents come into the possession of a party through participation in family law proceedings (ie they are not their own documents) then there are restrictions on the extent to which that party can provide those document to third parties. First, where the documents have been provided as a result of a court order for disclosure or in order to comply with a duty of full and frank disclosure (as for example in financial relief proceedings) then they are subject to an implied undertaking that they will be used only for the purposes of the proceedings in which they have been disclosed. The undertaking continues beyond the end of proceedings. The implied undertaking equally binds third parties or the press who come into possession of such documents or information recording the contents of the same.[163] However, the undertaking can be outweighed and will not prevent the Court from permitting publication where, for example, there has been iniquity or where it is necessary to protect rights under Art 10 of the ECHR. In this context, the undertaking is a weighty factor to be considered as is the fact that the Rules provide for financial remedy proceedings to be heard in private.[164] Secondly, where the proceedings relate to the inherent jurisdiction of the High Court with respect to minors, are brought under the Children Act or Adoption of Children Act 2002 or otherwise relate wholly or mainly to the maintenance or upbringing of a minor, it is a contempt of court to publish 'information relating to proceedings before any court sitting in private.'[165] 'Publication' has the same meaning as it has in defamation, thus covering most forms of dissemination of the information.[166]

---

160 *DL v SL (Financial Remedy Proceedings: Privacy)* [2015] EWHC 2621 (Fam), [2016] 1 WLR 1259 at [16].

161 *Re C (a minor) (care proceedings disclosure)* [1997] Fam 76; *Re X, Y and Z (children) anonymity of expert)* [2011] EWHC 1157 (Fam), [2012] 1 WLR 182; *Re C (a child) (care proceedings: disclosure of documents)* [2015] EWFC 79, [2017] 1 FLR 82; *Re X (adopted child: access to court file)* [2014] EWFC 33, [2015] 1 FLR 375.

162 *C (a child) (care proceedings: disclosure of documents)* [2015] EWFC 79, [2017] 1 FLR 82 at [34]-[36].

163 *Clliberry v Allen* [2002] EWCA Civ 45, [2002] Fam 261 at [54], [67]-[74], [82]; *Appleton v Gallagher* [2015] EWHC 2689 (Fam), [2016] 2 FLR 1 at [15].

164 *HRH Prince of Luxembourg v HRH Princess of Luxembourg* [2017] EWHC 3095 (Fam), [2018] 1 FLR 480 at [75]-[79], [80]-[118], where one party was restrained from publishing details of an open offer that made use of information disclosed by the other party. FPR 12.73 now allows for communications in certain classes of case (including with the permission of the court) and FPR 12.75 allows for certain communications for the purposes of the proceedings.

165 Administration of Justice Act 1960 s 12.

166 *Kent CC v B* [2004] EWHC 411 (Fam), [2004] 2 FLR 142. It does not prohibit disclosure to a Mackenzie Friend *Re O (Children)(Hearing in Private: Assistance)* [2005] EWCA Civ 759, [2006] Fam 1.

6. CRIMINAL COURTS

42–041 Introduction

Historically, although members of the public have always been able attend criminal proceedings there has been no corresponding right of access to documents or exhibits.[167] That changed in 2012, when the Court of Appeal established a default position that documents referred to in the course of proceedings in open court ought to be accessible.[168] Detailed provision is now made in the Criminal Procedure Rules 2015 — ie Crim PR.[169] Guidance has been published to support media access.[170] The same principles have been applied in Courts Martial, although there is no express procedure for access to documents.[171]

42–042 Reporting restrictions

Information obtained about criminal proceedings may be subject to reporting restrictions. Some apply automatically subject to a power on the part of the court to remove them,[172] while others apply automatically without any power to vary.[173] In other cases the court has a power to impose restrictions.[174]

42–043 Listing information

The court officer must publish listing details of cases if the information is available to the court officer, the hearing is due to take place in public and the publication is not prohibited by a reporting restriction.[175] The publication must be in the vicinity of the court room where the hearing is to take place and/or in accordance with directions given by the Lord Chancellor, including for publication by electronic means.

42–044 Non-party access

Limited information about cases by the court officer must be made available to a non-party.[176] A person who wants such information must apply to the court officer, specifying any information requested and paying the prescribed fee.[177] The court officer must provide that

---

167 *R v Waterfield* [1975] 1 WLR 711. The right of access may also be subject to restrictions. For example s 47 of the Children and Young Persons Act 1933 restricts access to a youth court without permission to persons directly concerned with the case and to bona fide representatives of the press.

168 *R (Guardian News and Media Ltd) v City of Westminster Magistrates' Court* [2012] EWCA Civ 420, [2013] QB 618.

169 And also: *Practice Direction (CA (Crim Div): Criminal Proceedings: General Matters)* [2015] EWCA Crim 1567.

170 *Jurisdictional Guidance to support media access to Courts and Tribunals*.

171 Rule 26 of the Court Martial Rules allows the court to have regard to the Criminal Procedure Rules: *R v Marine A* [2013] EWCA Crim 2367, [2014] 1 WLR 3326 at [49].

172 For example in respect of youth court proceedings under s 49 of the Children and Young Persons Act 1933 or the identity of a complainant of a sexual offence under s 1 of the Sexual Offences (Amendment) Act 1992.

173 For example: s 1 Judicial Proceedings (Regulation of Reports) Act 1992 – indecent or medical matters; s 1 Contempt of Court Act 1981 – risk of prejudice to active proceedings.

174 For example, by postponing a report of a public hearing. Part 6 of the Crim PR contains a list of provisions permitting a restriction on access to or reporting of proceedings and sets out the procedure for making an application for imposing or removing such a restriction.

175 Crim PR 5.8(9)-(11).

176 Crim PR 5.8.

177 The application need not be in writing if it is for the information listed in 5.8(6) (basic details about matters such as the dates of a hearing, charges, outcome, parties or the details of any reporting or access restriction ordered by the court).

information if it is available to the court, is not prevented by a reporting restriction and the trial has either not yet concluded or the verdict is not more than 6 months' old. In any other case the applicant must, unless the court otherwise permits, make an application in writing and explain for what purpose the information is required.[178] The application can be determined with or without a hearing and any hearing may be in public or in private. If the court so directs then the court officer must give the applicant other information about the case by word of mouth or allow them to 'inspect or copy a document, or part of a document, containing information about the case.'[179]

42–045 CPS protocol

Where the provision of information is not mandatory, an application should first be made to the party that supplied the information to the court. Where an application is made by a journalist or media organization, the application must first be made under the relevant CPS protocol.[180] If this is done and access has been denied, any application to the court should include reasons given for the refusal.[181] Under the CPS protocol each case will be dealt with individually taking account of the views of witnesses and those directly affected but with the overriding objective to provide an open and accountable prosecution service. Prosecution material that has been relied upon by the Crown in court should normally be released to the media, including maps, diagrams and other documents produced in court, videos showing scenes of crime, property seized or reconstructions, sections of transcripts or statements as read out, CCTV footage of the defendant (subject to copyright). Other prosecution material 'may' be released after consultation with the police and relevant victims, witnesses and family members. It includes: CCTV footage or photographs showing the defendant and victim, or the victim alone, that has been viewed by jury and public in court, subject to any copyright issues; video and audio tapes of police interviews with defendants, victims and witnesses; victim and witness statements. The same principles apply to a guilty plea but in that case material released to the media must reflect the prosecution case and must have been read out, or shown in open court, or placed before the sentencing judge.

42–046 Post-refusal application

If an application to the Court becomes necessary, the burden for justifying access will lie on the applicant. Considerations to be taken into account include:

i. whether or not the request is for the purpose of contemporaneous reporting; a request after the conclusion of the proceedings will require careful scrutiny by the court;
ii. the nature of the information or documents being sought;
iii. the purpose for which they are required;
iv. the stage of the proceedings at the time when the application is made;
v. the value of the documents in advancing the open justice principle, including enabling the media to discharge its role, which has been described as a 'public watchdog', by reporting the proceedings effectively;
vi. any risk of harm which access to them may cause to the legitimate interests of

---

178 Crim PR 5.8(3). In *R (Ewing) v Central Criminal Court* [2015] EWHC 2068 (Admin) the court left open the question whether an application under this Rule was civil proceedings with the result that a vexatious litigant needed permission to make it. The Rules do not require notice to the parties but this is expected by paragraph 5B.8 of the Practice Direction.

179 Crim PR 5.8(7). The Practice Direction makes clear that documents here include images in 'photographic, digital including DVD format, video, CCTV or any other form' - para 5B.3.

180 *Working together: Chief Police Officers, Chief Crown Prosecutors and the Media.*

181 Crim PR 5B.7

others; and

vii. any reasons given by the parties for refusing to provide the material requested and any other representations received from the parties.[182]

Where a document has been read aloud or treated as read aloud then access will normally be provided unless to do so would be disruptive to the court proceedings or place an undue burden on the court, the advocates or others. This will include the opening notes, statements agreed and read, admissions and skeleton arguments. Where a document is read out or summarised in part then the court should consider whether it is proportionate to provide a redacted version. Where access is sought to jury bundles or exhibits then the court should consider whether access is necessary in order to understand or effectively to report the case. It will also consider the privacy of third parties and any risk of prejudice to another case. Documents provided in confidence (for example pre-sentence reports, medical reports and victim personal statements) are unlikely to be disclosed, even where they have been referred to in open court. This applies equally to all members of the public but applications from an accredited member of the media will benefit from a greater presumption in favour of providing the requested material in view of the role of the press as a public watchdog. In that case the general principle is that documents should be supplied in response to a request from such a party, unless there is a good reason for not doing so. It is not for the judge to exercise an editorial judgment about the adequacy of the material already available to the paper for its journalistic purpose.[183]

42–047 Transcripts

Where someone may appeal to the Court of Appeal then proceedings in the Crown Court are recorded. Where the hearing is in public then a transcript must be made available to any person on payment of the prescribed fee. However, where the recording includes matters in respect of which there is a reporting restriction then a transcript containing that information may only be supplied to the Registrar or to a recipient to whom the supply will not contravene the restriction. Where the hearing was in private then the transcript may only be supplied to the Registrar or someone who was present at the hearing.[184]

42–048 Access from a party

An accused may use a document not relied upon by the Crown only for the proceedings in which it was disclosed or for other criminal proceedings (such as an appeal).[185] An accused may use or disclose an object 'to the extent that it has been displayed to the public in open court' or information to 'the extent that it has been communicated to the public in open court.' The Court may make an order giving permission for the use of information.

7. TRIBUNALS, INQUIRIES ETC

42–049 Introduction

The Tribunal system was re-organised by the Tribunals Courts and Enforcement Act 2007.

[182] Paras 5B.10-25.

[183] Para 5B.26 citing *Observer and Guardian v United Kingdom* (1991) 14 EHRR 153, (1991) ECHR 13585/88 and *R (Guardian News and Media Ltd) v City of Westminster Magistrates' Court* [2012] EWCA Civ 420, [2013] QB 618 at [82]. As pointed out in *R v Marine A* [2013] EWCA Crim 2367, [2014] 1 WLR 3326 at [56]: 'it is the activity of journalism for which the person seeks the material rather than status as an employee of a media organisation that is decisive'.

[184] Crim PR 5.5(2) and see Practice Direction 5B.32-36. 5.5.(3)/(4) provide for access to the recording with permission.

[185] Section 17 of the Criminal Procedure and Investigations Act 1996 limits the use to which an accused can put unused material given under sections 3, 4,7A, 14 or 15 or by an order under section 8.

Section 3 of that Act established the First tier-Tribunal and the Upper Tribunal. Some Tribunals continue to exist outside this structure notably the Employment Tribunals, and the Competition Appeal Tribunal.

42– 050 First-tier Tribunal

None of the chambers of the First-tier Tribunal has specific rules relating to access to documents by non-parties. In most cases hearings must be in public although there are some exceptions (for example special educational needs cases and disability discrimination in schools cases or criminal injuries compensation cases).[186] The rules for each of the chambers permit the Tribunal to make an order requiring disclosure of documents and they also enable the Tribunal to prohibit the disclosure or publication of (a) specified documents or information relating to the proceedings; or (b) any matter likely to lead members of the public to identify any person whom the Tribunal considers should not be identified. This is in addition to a specific power in some cases to prevent disclosure to a person if it would be likely to cause that or some other person serious harm, not proportionate or in the interests of justice.[187]

42– 051 Non-party access

The open justice principle is engaged by proceedings in the Tribunal. Accordingly, the Tribunal has an inherent jurisdiction to allow access to documents to non-parties that will be exercised in accordance with the usual open justice principles applicable to proceedings in the High Court. Guidance has been issued on applications for access.

42– 052 Access from a party

Documents produced pursuant to an order of the Tribunal are subject to an implied obligation not to use them for any collateral purpose, including other litigation, without the leave of the Tribunal or the express consent of the party disclosing or producing the document.[188] This probably does not apply to cases where documents have been disclosed voluntarily at least where there has been no qualification.

42– 053 Upper Tribunal

The Upper Tribunal – the UT – is established by section 3 of the Tribunals Courts and Enforcement Act 2007. The Rules make no express provision for access to documents by a non-party but, as with the First-tier Tribunal, they permit the Upper Tribunal to order that specified documents or information or identifying details not be disclosed or published. By section 25 of the 2007 Act the Upper Tribunal has, in relation to the production and inspection of documents and all other matters incidental to its functions, 'the same powers, rights, privileges and authority as the High Court.' As such, the Upper Tribunal has inherent power to grant a third party access to any documents relating to proceedings that are held in the UT records, and it has a duty under common law to do so in response to a request by an applicant

---

186 Tribunal Procedure (First-tier Tribunal) (Health, Education and Social Care Chamber) Rules 2008/2699 Rule 26; Tribunal Procedure (First-tier Tribunal) (Social Entitlement Chamber) Rules 2008/2685 Rule 30.

187 Rules 5 and 14 respectively of Tribunal Procedure (First-tier Tribunal) (Health, Education and Social Care Chamber) Rules 2008/2699, Tribunal Procedure (First-tier Tribunal) (War Pensions and Armed Forces Compensation Chamber) Rules 2008/2686, Tribunal Procedure (First-tier Tribunal) (Social Entitlement Chamber) Rules 2008/2685; Tribunal Procedure (First-tier Tribunal) (Tax Chamber) Rules 2009/273 (where the proviso for non-disclosure to a specified person does not apply); Tribunal Procedure (First-tier Tribunal) (General Regulatory Chamber) Rules 2009/1976; Rules 18 and 19 Tribunal Procedure (First-tier Tribunal) (Property Chamber) Rules 2013/1169; Rules 13 and 15 Tribunal Procedure (First-tier Tribunal) (Immigration and Asylum Chamber) Rules 2014/2604.

188 Tribunal Procedure (Upper Tribunal) Rules 2008/2698 Rule 14; Tribunal Procedure (Upper Tribunal) (Lands Chamber) Rules 2010/2600 Rule 15. *Menon v Herefordshire Council* [2015] EWHC 2165 at [53], [56]. In fact the order there was for production by a third party but similar principles applied.

unless the UT considers, on its own motion or on application by one or more of the parties, that any documents or information in them should not be disclosed to other persons.[189]

42–054 Employment Tribunals

Employment tribunals are established under the Employment Tribunals Act 1996. The Lord Chancellor must maintain a register containing (subject to the exceptions discussed below) a copy of all judgments of tribunals and reasons for them.[190] The Rules do not say how the Register can be accessed but it has, since 2017, been publicly accessible via its website. However, the Register only contains decisions and reasons and there is no express provision for access to documents corresponding to pleadings in the civil courts.

42–055 Witness statements

Any witness statement which stands as evidence-in-chief in Employment Tribunal proceedings must be available for inspection during the course of the hearing by members of the public attending the hearing.[191] This does not apply to the extent that the statement is ruled to be inadmissible and is subject to the powers of the Tribunal (see below) to restrict disclosure of any matter. This right of access is unlikely to be read as including documents referred to or exhibited to statements.[192] Nor is there any express provision allowing access to skeleton arguments or written openings. In principle, applications could be made under the inherent jurisdiction and/or under the Tribunal's general case management powers.[193]

42–056 Presidential guidance

Presidential Guidance on general case management requires the parties to prepare and bring a copy of the bundle and any witness statements to be shown to the media or public as appropriate.[194] The Tribunal will allow persons (including the press and media) present at the hearing to view documents referred to in evidence before it (unless it orders otherwise).[195] The Guidance does not expressly state that there is a right to take copies but the Tribunal can permit this and will have to do so if it is necessary to secure open justice. All documents and witness statements exchanged in the case may be used only for the hearing. Unless the Tribunal orders otherwise, they must only be shown to a party and that party's adviser/representative or a witness (insofar as is necessary). The documents must not be used for any purpose other than the conduct of the case. This restriction does not apply once the documents or statements have been referred to at a hearing. The implied undertaking in relation to disclosed documents also applies to the Employment Tribunals.

42–057 Reporting restrictions

An Employment Tribunal may, at any stage of the proceedings of its own motion or on an application make an order preventing or restricting public disclosure of any aspect of the proceedings so far as it considers necessary in the interests of justice or in order to protect the Convention rights of any person or in the circumstances identified in section 10A of the

---

[189] *Aria Technology Ltd v HMRC* [2018] UKUT 111 (TCC), [2018] 1 WLR 4377.

[190] Employment Tribunals (Constitution and Procedure) Regulations 2013 rules 14, 67.

[191] Rule 44 a.

[192] By analogy with the jurisprudence on CPR 32.22.

[193] Rule 29 Employment Tribunals (Constitution and Procedure) Regulations 2013.

[194] Guidance note 2 para 15; Guidance Note 3 para 19.

[195] Guidance Note 2 para 17; Guidance Note 3 para 24. This is subject to any order for redaction or non-disclosure.

Employment Tribunals Act 1996.[196] The orders that may be made include restricted reporting orders under sections 11 and 12 of the 1996 Act in cases involving allegations of sexual misconduct or sexual offences and in complaints relating to disability where case evidence of a personal nature is likely to be heard. However, the power also applies to other cases, provided that the Tribunal considers it necessary in the interests of justice or to protect convention rights and provided that full weight has been given to the principle of open justice.[197] In some cases reasons can be kept secret for national security reasons.[198]

42– 058 Access from a party

The Employment Tribunal has the same power with regard to disclosure and inspection as has the County Court.[199] Documents disclosed in Tribunal proceedings are subject to a restriction on collateral use. Where documents have been disclosed pursuant to an order of the Employment Tribunal it is implicit that the same restriction on disclosure by the recipient should apply as arises under CPR r 31.22[200] The implied undertaking also applies to voluntary disclosure.[201] It would appear that it is not open to the Employment Tribunal itself to grant permission for some collateral use, but the High Court may do so.[202]

42– 059 Competition Appeal Tribunal

The Competition Appeal Tribunal Rules[203] contain a provision that corresponds broadly to the implied undertaking under CPR 31.22 but with the qualification that where documents have been disclosed 'within a confidentiality ring' then the permission of the Tribunal is needed for their collateral use even if they have been referred to in open court.[204] Other than this, there is no specific rule dealing with access to documents by non-parties.[205] There is no general right to a copy of pleadings or correspondence with the CAT but where a 'pleading, skeleton argument, witness statement or expert report is referred to or quoted in open court' then a third party may apply to the Tribunal for a 'non-confidential' version if the relevant party does not agree to provide it.[206] Summaries of claims are available on the Tribunal website together with transcripts of hearings, orders, and decisions.

42– 060 Coroners

The law relating to coroners is now contained in the Coroners and Justice Act 2009.[207]

---

196 Statutory prohibition on disclosure, breach of confidence, or damage to the undertaking in which the witness works.

197 Employment Tribunals Act 1996 ss 11, 12, Employment Tribunals (Constitution and Procedure) Regulations 2013 Rule 50. Such Orders can extend beyond the promulgation of a Tribunal's decision if it is necessary in the interests of justice or to protect a person's convention rights: *Fallows v News Group Newspapers Ltd* [2016] ICR 801; *EF v AB* [2015] IRLR 619.

198 Employment Tribunals (Constitution and Procedure) Regulations 2013 Sch 2, para 6.

199 Rule 29 Employment Tribunals (Constitution and Procedure) Regulations 2013.

200 *IG Index v Cloete* [2014 EWCA Civ 1128, [2015] ICR 254 at [28].

201 *IG Index v Cloete* [2014 EWCA Civ 1128, [2015] ICR 254 at [45].

202 *IG Index v Cloete* [2014 EWCA Civ 1128, [2015] ICR 254 at [75]-[78].

203 Competition Appeal Tribunal Rules 2015/1648.

204 Rule 102.

205 See Competition Appeal Tribunal Guide 2015 para 9.63-7.

206 An example of the use of this power is *Sainsbury's Supermarkets Ltd v Mastercard Incorporated & Ors* [2016] CAT 6 where non-confidential documents were disclosed where they had been read by the Tribunal and referred to in open court.

207 Further provision is made in the Coroners (Investigations) Regulations 2019 (SI 2013 No 1629) and in the Coroners (Inquests) Rules 2013/1616.

Section 1 of the 2009 Act imposes a duty on the coroner to investigate certain deaths and schedule 5 confers powers to require evidence to be provided to the coroner. Where an inquest is held then it must be conducted in public unless the coroner directs otherwise for reasons of national security.[208] The Coroner must make the hearing details of all final inquest hearings publicly available in advance.[209] Hearings, including pre-inquest reviews are recorded and the recording is a document that must be retained by the Coroner. The Coroner must retain any document for at least fifteen years from the date on which the investigation is completed. The coroner may provide any document or copy of any document to any person who in the opinion of the coroner is a proper person to have possession of it.[210] The Chief Coroner has given guidance on the exercise of these powers, particularly in connection with disclosure to the media.[211] A member of the media requesting access may be required to show that they are a bona fide journalist and that they seek access for a proper journalistic purpose. They must specify precisely the document they require and why it is needed. In deciding whether to grant access the Coroner should be guided by the open justice principle. There must be a compelling reason not to accede to a media request.[212]

42– 061 Inquiries

Inquiries may be instituted under the Inquiries Act 2005, under specific statutory provisions or under the prerogative. Where an inquiry is held under the Inquiries Act 2005, there is a duty on the chairman to 'take such steps as he considers reasonable to secure that members of the public (including reporters) are able (a) to attend the inquiry or to see and hear a simultaneous transmission of proceedings at the inquiry; and (b) to obtain or to view a record of evidence and documents given, produced or provided to the inquiry or inquiry panel.'[213] Where an inquiry is not established under the 2005 Act, then, as an ordinary incident of holding documents, it will have power to disclose information and documents and, in making that decision, will be required to act in the public interest.[214] Whatever the source of the power to disclose information, a principle analogous to open justice may apply, at least where the inquiry is held in public or where a public report has been published. The freestanding power to disclose exists regardless of whether the person or body conducting the inquiry is or is not a public authority within the meaning of FOIA and of the applicability of exemptions under that Act. In deciding whether to disclose under this freestanding power, the person or body holding the inquiry must consider whether 'the public interest in disclosure is demonstrably outweighed by any countervailing arguments that may be advanced.'[215] If the matter is then challenged by way of judicial review then the court will itself decide whether open justice requires disclosure and will not apply a rationality standard.[216] Rule 18 of the Inquiry Rules 2006[217] requires that the chairman must, at the end of an inquiry under the 2005 Act, transfer the record of the inquiry to a government department or to the public record office, as the Minister directs. Where this is done then section 18(3) of the 2005 Act disapplies the absolute exemption in section 32(2) of

---

208 Coroners (Inquests) Rules 2013/1616 Rule 11.

209 Coroners (Inquests) Rules 2013 Rule 9(3).

210 Rule 27.

211 Guidance No 25. Coroners and the Media.

212 Guidance No 25. Coroners and the Media paras 28, 37-60.

213 Section 18.

214 *Kennedy v Information Commissioner* [2014] UKSC 20, [2015] AC 455 at [107].

215 *Kennedy v Information Commissioner* [2014] UKSC 20, [2015] AC 455 at [49], [121]-[132].

216 *Kennedy v Information Commissioner* [2014] UKSC 20, [2015] AC 455 at [132].

217 Inquiry Rules 2006 SI 2006/1838.

FOIA ceases to apply, such that access to the documents will be governed by the remaining exemptions in FOIA.

42– 062 Parole Board

Procedure before the Parole Board is governed by the Parole Board Rules.[218] Hearings are in private. Formerly, the rules provided for a blanket prohibition in terms that 'information about proceedings under these Rules and the names of persons concerned in the proceedings must not be made public.' This prevented disclosure of information, including reasons for decisions, to the public and even to victims of the person whose case was being considered by the Board. This was ruled ultra vires[219] by the Divisional Court, which held that the Board was a Tribunal to which the open justice principle applied. Following this judgment the Parole Board Rules were amended with effect from 22 May 2018.[220] The new rules provide that the Board is to supply a summary of the reasons for the decision to a victim where that person wishes to receive it unless the chair 'considers that there are exceptional circumstances why a summary should not be produced for disclosure.' The summary must be disclosed to 'any other person' if the chair 'considers that the public interest in the principle of open justice justifies disclosure.' Subject to this, information about proceedings under the Rules must not be disclosed except in so far as the Board chair directs. None of the provisions about disclosure permit disclosure of names of persons concerned in the proceedings apart from the parties.

218 SI 2016/1041.

219 *R (DSD) v Parole Board* [2018] EWHC 694 (Admin), [2018] 3 WLR 829 at [169]-[200].

220 Parole Board (Amendment) Rules 2018/541 rule 3.

CHAPTER 43

Information held by EU bodies

1. BACKGROUND

43– 001 Introduction

The institutions of the European Union have neither a strong nor a lengthy tradition of providing access to documents or information held by them. They are thus closer to the British model of government, with a predisposition towards secrecy and non-disclosure,[1] than to the openness long practised by the Scandinavian members of the EU. In the last 15 years, however, there has been a considerable opening up by the EU institutions. This chapter

[1] See generally: V Deckmyn and I Thompson (eds), *Openness and Transparency in the European Union* (Maastricht, European Institute of Public Administration, 1998); V Deckmyn, *Increasing Transparency in the European Union?* (Maastricht, European Institute of Public Administration, 2002).

focuses on the measures concerning access to documents held by and relating to the operation of EU institutions. This will include a discussion of the Code of Practice, Decisions 93/731 and 94/90 and the case law interpreting these decisions. Whilst the Code of Practice and decisions have now been repealed and replaced by Regulation 1049/2001, the case law under the earlier regime gives some indication as to how the General Court and the Court of Justice will interpret Regulation 1049/2001.

43– 002 Maastricht Treaty

The first express recognition of the importance of transparency and openness appeared in Declaration No 17 annexed to the Final Act of the Treaty of the European Union (the Maastricht Treaty), which stated:

> The Conference considers that transparency of the decision-making process strengthens the democratic nature of the institutions and the public's confidence in the administration. The Conference accordingly recommends that the Commission submit to the Council no later than 1993 a report on measures to improve the public access to the information available to the institutions.[2]

This stated commitment to openness was reiterated by the European Council in their declaration issued at the conclusion of the Birmingham meeting on 16 October 1992[3] and reaffirmed by the European Council at Edinburgh in December 1992.[4]

43– 003 Treaty of Amsterdam

Express provision for the right of access to documents was made in the Treaty of Amsterdam. Art 255 (formerly Art 191a) provided:[5]

> 1. Any citizen of the Union, and any natural or legal person residing or having its registered office in a Member State, shall have a right of access to European Parliament, Council and Commission documents subject to the principles and conditions to be defined in accordance with paragraphs 2 and 3.
> 2. General principles and limits on grounds of public or private interest governing this right of access to documents shall be determined by the Council, acting in accordance with the procedure referred to in Article 251 within two years of the entry into force of the Treaty of Amsterdam.
> 3. Each institution referred to above shall elaborate in its own Rules of Procedure specific provisions regarding access to its documents.

43– 004 Treaty of Lisbon

The Treaty of Lisbon which was signed on 13 December 2007 and came into effect on 1 December 2009 amended the Treaty Establishing the European Union (TEU) and the Treaty Establishing the European Community, renaming the latter the Treaty on the Functioning of the European Union (TFEU). Article 1 TEU notes that:

> This Treaty marks a new stage in the process of creating an ever closer union among the peoples of Europe, in which decisions are taken as openly as possible and as closely as possible to the citizen.

Article 10(3) TEU specifies that:

> 3. Every citizen shall have the right to participate in the democratic life of the Union. Decisions shall be taken as openly and as closely as possible to the citizen.

---

2 Declaration No 17 annexed to the Final Act of the Treaty of the European Union signed at Maastricht on 7 February 1992.

3 Birmingham declaration, 16 October 1992, para 3: '...We ask the Commission to complete by early next year its work on improving public access to the information available to it and to other community institutions.'

4 Conclusions of the Presidency, para 7.

5 The Treaty of Amsterdam came into force on 21 May 1999, so that the Regulation had to be adopted by 1 May 2001.

Article 15 TFEU is in the following terms:

> 1. In order to promote good governance and ensure the participation of civil society, the institutions, bodies, offices and agencies of the Union shall conduct their work as openly as possible.
> 2. The European Parliament shall meet in public, as shall the Council when considering and voting on a draft legislative act.
> 3. Any citizen of the Union, and any natural or legal person residing or having its registered office in a Member State, shall have a right of access to documents of the Union institutions, bodies, offices and agencies, whatever their medium, subject to the principles and the conditions to be defined in accordance with this paragraph.
>
> General principles and limits on grounds of public or private interest governing this right of access to documents shall be determined by the European Parliament and the Council, acting by means of regulations in accordance with the ordinary legislative procedure.
>
> Each institution, body, office or agency shall ensure that its proceedings are transparent and shall elaborate in its own Rules of Procedure specific provisions regarding access to its documents, in accordance with the regulations referred to in the second subparagraph.
>
> The Court of Justice of the European Union, the European Central Bank and the European Investment Bank shall be subject to this paragraph only when exercising their administrative tasks.
>
> The European Parliament and the Council shall ensure publication of the documents relating to the legislative procedures under the terms laid down by the regulation referred to in the second subparagraph.

In the sphere of the EU's Common Foreign and Security Policy, Art 39 TEU requires the Council to adopt a decision laying down rules relating to the protection of individuals and free movement of data with regard to the processing of personal data by the Member States when carrying out activities which fall within the scope of the Common Foreign and Security Policy. Compliance with these rules is subject to the control of independent authorities. Finally, Art 298(1) TFEU confirms that:

> In carrying out their missions, the institutions, bodies, offices and agencies of the Union shall have the support of an open, efficient and independent European administration.

43– 005 Post-Lisbon jurisprudence

The post-Lisbon case law has repeatedly underlined the importance of these ideas of openness and transparency as now underpinning the work of the EU institutions, with the Grand Chamber of the CJEU observing:

> The principle of transparency is stated in Articles 1 TEU and 10 TEU and in Art 15 TFEU. It enables citizens to participate more closely in the decision-making process and guarantees that the administration enjoys greater legitimacy and is more effective and more accountable to the citizen in a democratic system.[6]

The CJEU has summarised its case law to date on the way in which these general principles of transparency and openness inform the right of access to documents held by the EU institutions:[7]

> 73. ... Regulation No 1049/2001 reflects the intention expressed in the second paragraph of Art 1 TEU to mark a new stage in the process of creating an ever closer union among the peoples of Europe, in which decisions are taken as openly as possible and as closely as possible to the citizen: see, to that effect *Sweden and Turco v Council* (C-39/05, C-52/05)[8] at [34].
>
> 74 That core EU objective is also reflected in Art 15(1) TFEU, which provides that the institutions, bodies, offices and agencies of the European Union are to conduct their work as openly as possible, that principle of openness also being expressed in Art 10(3) TEU and

6 *Volker und Markus Schecke GbR v Land Hessen* (C-92/09) [2012] All ER (EC) 127, [2012] IP & T 513 at [68].

7 *ClientEarth v European Commission* (C-57/16 P) [2019] Env LR 19.

8 *Sweden and Turco v Council* (C-39/05, C-52/05) [2009] QB 269, [2009] 2 WLR 867, [2008] 3 CMLR 17.

in Art 298(1) TFEU, and in the enshrining of the right of access to documents in Art 42 of the Charter of Fundamental Rights of the European Union: see, to that effect, *Commission v Breyer* (C-213/15) at [52].

75 It can be seen from recital 2 of Regulation No 1049/2001 that openness enables the EU institutions to have greater legitimacy and to be more effective and more accountable to EU citizens in a democratic system. By allowing divergences between various points of view to be openly debated, it also contributes to increasing those citizens' confidence in those institutions: see, to that effect, *Sweden and Turco v Council* (C-39/05, C-52/05) at [45] and [59].

43–006 Article 6 of the Charter

Article 6(1)-(3) TEU provide:

1. The Union recognises the rights, freedoms and principles set out in the Charter of Fundamental Rights of the European Union of 7 December 2000, as adopted at Strasbourg, on 12 December 2007, which shall have the same legal value as the Treaties.
   The provisions of the Charter shall not extend in any way the competences of the Union as defined in the Treaties.
   The rights, freedoms and principles in the Charter shall be interpreted in accordance with the general provisions in Title VII of the Charter governing its interpretation and application and with due regard to the explanations referred to in the Charter, that set out the sources of those provisions.
2. .....
3. Fundamental rights, as guaranteed by the European Convention for the Protection of Human Rights and Fundamental Freedoms and as they result from the constitutional traditions common to the Member States, shall constitute general principles of the Union's law.

In theory, none of the rights set out in the Charter of Fundamental Rights – 'the CFR' – was being newly introduced to EU law by the fact of their inclusion in the Charter. All of them were said to have already been prefigured in the 'fundamental rights as general principles' jurisprudence of the CJEU. The rights now expressly set out in the CFR may therefore be understood and applied against the background of this earlier fundamental rights/general principles jurisprudence. The recognition of the rights, freedoms and principles set out in the CFR and according to them 'the same legal value as the Treaties' is not to be seen as marking a disruption or break from the CJEU's prior fundamental rights case law, but rather reflects the confirmation or codification of that case law.[9] This is consistent with the Declaration by all Treaty signatories concerning the CFR which was appended to the Lisbon Treaty in the following terms:

> The Charter of Fundamental Rights of the European Union, which has legally binding force, confirms the fundamental rights guaranteed by the European Convention for the Protection of Human Rights and Fundamental Freedoms and as they result from the constitutional traditions common to the member States. The Charter does not extend the field of application of Union law beyond the powers of the Union or establish any new power or task for the Union, or modify powers and tasks as defined by the Treaties.

There is, however, still force in the case law of the CJEU on fundamental rights as general principles. This has been given an express basis by Art 6(3) TEU which states that:

> fundamental rights, as guaranteed by the European Convention for the Protection of Human Rights and Fundamental Freedoms and as they result from the constitutional traditions common to the Member States, shall constitute general principles of EU law.

---

9 In *Criminal proceedings against Radu* (C-396/11) [2013] QB 1031, [2013] 3 WLR 681, [2013] All ER (EC) 410 the Advocate General noted (at [51]):

> Article 6(1) and (3) TEU merely represents what the United Kingdom terms in its observations a 'codification' of the pre-existing position. They encapsulate, to put it another way, a political desire that the provisions they seek to enshrine and to protect should be more visible in their expression. They do not represent a sea change of any kind.

Article 6(3) TEU thus gives express Treaty backing to the continuation by the CJEU of its more creative jurisprudence under which a whole range of fundamental rights and what might be called 'EU common law' general principles have been developed by that court, unconstrained by the letter of the Treaties or the limitations of the CFR.

43–007 Article 42 of the Charter

Article 42 CFR echoes, though without conditions, Art 15(3) TFEU in providing:

> *Right of access to documents*
>
> Any citizen of the Union, and any natural or legal person residing or having its registered office in a Member State, has a right of access to documents of the institutions, bodies, offices and agencies of the Union, whatever their medium.

Separately, Art 41 CFR echoes Art 298(1) TFEU in guaranteeing a 'right to good administration' in individuals' dealings with and within the EU, including the right of every person to have access to his or her file.[10] These procedural rights (and the implicit promise of an 'open, efficient and independent European administration') are now set out in Art 41 of the CFR, which guarantees a 'right to good administration' in the following terms (so far as relevant):

> 1. Every person has the right to have his or her affairs handled impartially, fairly and within a reasonable time by the institutions, bodies, offices and agencies of the Union.
> 2. This right includes:
>   (a) the right of every person to be heard, before any individual measure which would affect him or her adversely is taken;
>   (b) the right of every person to have access to his or her file, while respecting the legitimate interests of confidentiality and of professional and business secrecy;
>   (c) the obligation of the administration to give reasons for its decisions.

Article 41 of the CFR is sufficient in itself, and does not need to be made more specific by provisions of EU or of national law, to confer on individuals a right to an effective judicial remedy upon which they may rely directly before the courts of the Members States and of the EU.[11]

43–008 Article 52 of the Charter

Article 52(3) CFR ensures that the ECHR is a base-line for fundamental rights protection within the ambit of EU law:

> Insofar as this Charter contains rights which correspond to rights guaranteed by the Convention for the Protection of Human Rights and Fundamental Freedoms, the meaning and scope of those rights shall be the same as those laid down by the said Convention. This provision shall not prevent Union law providing more extensive protection.

As noted in Chapter 4 of this work, whilst there is no provision in the ECHR directly guaranteeing a right of access to personal or general information held by public authorities, the ECtHR has begun to fashion a right in respect of both – Art 8 being deployed for personal information and Art 10 being deployed for non-personal information sought by journalists or other 'social watchdogs.' This line of reasoning has not met with the same success in Luxembourg when dealing with access to documents under Regulation 1049/2001, the General

---

10 See *SGL Carbon AG v European Commission* (C-328/05) [2007] ECR I-3921, [2007] 5 CMLR 16 at [70]-[71].

11 *Egenberger v Evangelisches Werk für Diakonie und Entwicklung eV* (C-414/16) [2019] 1 CMLR 223, [2018] IRLR 762 at [78]-[79]. In *Max-Planck-Gesellschaft zur Förderung der Wissenschaften eV v Shimizu* (C-684/16) [2019] 1 CMLR 35 the court ruled that those provisions of the Charter which are expressed in mandatory and unconditional terms need not be given more concrete expression by the provisions of EU or national law in order to have direct effect. The CJEU further ruled in *Max-Planck-Gesellschaft* that such Charter provisions have direct effect in the same way as clear, precise and unconditional Treaty articles – ie they may be invoked both 'vertically' against EU institutions and 'emanations' of the Member State and also, unlike directives, 'horizontally' in disputes exclusively between private persons.

Court having rejected the applicability of this line of ECtHR jurisprudence.[12]

43– 009 Aarhus Convention

The European Community ratified the Aarhus Convention on 17 February 2005.[13] On 26 September 2006 the European Parliament and Council adopted Regulation 1367/2006: this is known as the 'Aarhus Regulation.' The Regulation came into force on 28 September 2006 and applied from 17 July 2007. In effect, the Aarhus Regulation applies Directive 2003/4/EC to all institutions, bodies, offices and agencies established by, or on the basis of, the EC Treaty.[14] Thus, in relation to 'environmental information' held by the European Parliament, the Council, the Commission, and all agencies and other bodies established by them, a person has a free-standing right of access to this information under the Aarhus Regulation.[15] There are certain additional considerations which are specific to the application of the Aarhus Regulation to environmental information held by EU institutions, bodies, offices and agencies, and these are considered in the next two paragraphs.

43– 010 NGOs

In addition to making provision for requests for environmental information to be made of the EU institutions by any natural or legal person, the Aarhus obligations of the EU institutions as set out in the Aarhus Regulation give an NGO the right to request internal review of any response to such a request and, if dissatisfied with that response, to bring an action before the CJEU. In order to benefit from these provisions the NGO has to show that:

(a) it is an independent non profit-making legal person in accordance with a Member State's national law or practice;

(b) it has the primary stated objective of promoting environmental protection in the context of environmental law;

(c) it has existed for more than two years and is actively pursuing the objective of environmental protection in the context of environmental law; and

(d) the subject matter in respect of which the request for internal review is made is covered by its objective and activities.

43– 011 Aarhus Regulation

The Aarhus Convention now forms an integral part of the legal order of the European Union.[16] The objective of the Aarhus Regulation is to ensure access to information concerning factors, such as emissions affecting or likely to affect elements of the environment, in particular air, water and soil: it is not confined to information concerning emissions actually or already released into the environment.[17] It includes a right to information on foreseeable emissions into the environment from particular products or active substances, under normal or realistic conditions of use of that product or substance, namely the conditions under which the authorisation to place that product or substance on the market was granted, and which prevail in the area where that product or substance is intended to be used. The CJEU takes a broad

[12] *Association Justice & Environment zs v European Commission* (T-727/15), 23 January 2017 at [73].

[13] See further Ch 17 of this work.

[14] The coverage of the Aarhus Regulation is thus broader than Regulation 1049/2001. That Regulation applies only to the European Parliament, the Council and the Commission and, by extension, to the Community agencies.

[15] The right of access to environmental information is considered in Chs 17-19 of this work. Although those chapters are directed to public authorities in the United Kingdom, the analysis is equally applicable to environmental information held by EU institutions, bodies, offices and agencies.

[16] *Lesoochranárske zoskupenie VLK vMinisterstvo životného prostredia Slovenskej republiky* (C 240/09) [2012] QB 606, [2012] All ER (EC) 1 at [58].

[17] *European Commission v Stichtung Greenpeace Nederland and another* (C-673/13) [2017] 2 CMLR 529.

view of the extent of the obligations under the Aarhus Regulation.[18] This will impinge on the interpretation of Regulation 1049/2001, with the effect that exceptions in that Regulation will be interpreted and applied strictly and narrowly in order to be limited derogations from the principle of the widest possible public access to documents.[19] The European Commission is not entitled to apply a presumption against disclosure in the case of documents drawn up in the context of an impact assessment on a proposal for legislation.[20] Access to general environmental information and monitoring is also a matter which falls within the remit of the European Environmental Agency, which is governed by and is tasked under the provisions of Regulation (EC) No 401/2009, among other things, to create an information network, provide a report on the state of the environment every three years, and otherwise collate, record and assess environmental data.

2. THE CODE OF PRACTICE AND DECISIONS 93/731 AND 94/90

43–012 General principles

The commitment to openness and transparency expressed in Declaration No 17 annexed to the Maastricht Treaty was realised on 6 December 1993 when, with the approval of both the Commission and the Council, a Code of Conduct concerning public access to Council and Commission documents was published.[21] The Council and Commission subsequently adopted this Code of Conduct by decision.[22] The Code of Conduct followed the conventional template for access legislation: a universal right of access, immediately qualified by exceptions, enforceable with a right of review. 'Document' was defined widely as including 'any written

---

18 *Bayer CropScience SA-NV and another v College voor de toelating van gewasbeschermingsmiddelen en biociden* (C-442/14), 23 November 2016, where the CJEU rejected the conclusion of the General Court and the submissions of the Member States and the Commission that a restrictive approach should be taken, by for example reading the reference to emissions affecting the environment as referring only to emissions emanating from industrial installations or processes.

19 *Saint-Gobain Glass Deutschland GmbH v European Commission* (C-60/15) [2018] Env LR 8, where the CJEU held that the concept of 'decision-making process' referred to in the first sub-paragraph of Art 4(3) of Reg 1049/2001 had to be construed as relating to decision-making, without covering the entire administrative procedure which led to the decision. That interpretation was consonant with Art 6 of the Aarhus Regulation and Art 4(4)(a) of the Aarhus Convention. The court held that although the administrative activity of the Commission did not require as extensive an access to documents as that concerning the legislative activity of a Union institution, the right of public access applied in principle to all documents whether drawn up or, received by and in the possession of, the Commission. Similarly, in *Protect Natur-, Arten-und Landschaftsschutz Umweltorganisation v Bezirkshauptmannschaft Gmünd* (C-664/15), 20 December 2017, the CJEU confirmed that although Art 9(3) of the Aarhus Convention (which provides that 'where they meet the criteria, if any, laid down in its national law, members of the public have access to administrative or judicial procedures to challenge acts and omissions by private persons and public authorities which contravene provisions of its national law relating to the environment') has of itself no direct effect in EU law, when read in conjunction with Art 47 of the Charter it imposes an obligation on the courts to ensure effective judicial protection of the provisions of EU environmental law, which might involve changes in their established rules on standing and time limits to allow the effective participation in the court process by interested environmental NGOs.

20 *ClientEarth v European Commission* (C-57/16) [2019] 1 CMLR 37, [2019] Env LR 11, where the environmental NGO ClientEarth was found to be entitled to see a draft impact assessment report relating to access to justice in environmental matters at Member State level in the field of EU environmental policy, as well an opinion of the Impact Assessment Board regarding that draft. The CJEU also annulled the Commission's refusal of ClientEarth's request for access to a Commission impact assessment report regarding a proposed binding instrument setting a strategic framework for risk-based inspection and surveillance in relation to EU environmental legislation (and the accompanying opinion of the Impact Assessment Board regarding that report).

21 93/730/EC [1993] OJ L340/41.

22 The Council adopted the Code of Conduct by Decision 93/731 on 20 December 1993 (93/731/EC, [1993] OJ L340/43). The Decision came into force on 1 January 1994. The Commission, on 8 February 1994, adopted Decision 94/90 which under Art 1 formally adopted the Code of Conduct. Decisions 93/731 and 94/90 have now been repealed and replaced by Regulation No 1049/2001 discussed at §§43–016 to 43–054.

text, whatever its medium, which contains existing data and is held by the Council or the Commission.'[23] However:

> [w]here the requested document was written by a natural or legal person, a Member State, another Community institution or body, or any other national or international body, the application must not be sent to the Council [or Commission][24] but direct to the author.[25]

Thus, the right of access to documents was limited to documents produced by the Council or Commission. The Commission and Council were obliged to inform applicants within one month whether the application was approved or rejected. The Code of Practice provided that a failure to reply within the period amounted to a refusal.[26] There was an obligation, if the request was refused, to give reasons for the refusal and set out further avenues of redress available, namely a complaint to the ombudsman under Art 195 and judicial proceedings under Art 230.[27]

43– 013 Exceptions

There were two types of exception to the general right of access. First, mandatory exceptions which provided that access to the document should not be granted where its disclosure could undermine:

(1) the protection of the public interest (public security, international relations, monetary stability, court proceedings, inspections and investigations);
(2) the protection of the individual and privacy;
(3) the protection of commercial and industrial secrecy;
(4) the protection of the Community's financial interests;
(5) the protection of confidentiality as requested by the natural or legal person who supplied any of the information contained in the document or as required by the legislation of the Member State which supplied any of that information.[28]

Secondly, a discretionary exception that provided that access to a Council or Commission document might be refused 'in order to protect the confidentiality of the Council's proceedings.'[29]

43– 014 Other European bodies

The Netherlands challenged the legal basis of the Decision permitting access to documents held by the Council.[30] The legal bases for the decision were founded in the rules of procedure and in Art 207(3) of the Treaty (vesting in the Council the power to adopt its own rules of procedure). The Netherlands Government argued that access to documents was a citizen's fundamental right and should therefore have a different legal basis. The European Parliament intervened in support of the Netherlands and argued that the Council had exceeded the powers conferred on it by Art 207. Advocate General Tesauro had some sympathy with the Dutch Government's arguments. The CJEU was less convinced. The court appeared to refuse to hold that access to information was a general principle of Community law, although it did indicate that the public's right of access to documents could not be deduced from the Council's

23 See Code of Conduct, General Principles 93/730 Council Decision 93/731/EC Art 1(2).

24 See Code of Conduct.

25 Decision 93/731/EC Art 2(2).

26 Decision 93/731/EC Art 7(1).

27 Decision 93/731/EC Art 7(3).

28 Decision 93/731 Art 4(1) and Code of Conduct exceptions (Commission).

29 Decision 93/731 Art 4(2) and Code of Conduct exceptions (Commission).

30 *Netherlands v Council of the European Union* [1996] ECR I-2169, [1996] 2 CMLR 996.

rules of procedure. But the court did not indicate what the legal basis was.[31] Whilst the Netherlands Government's arguments were rejected, the court has since consistently emphasised the importance of openness on the basis that it strengthens the public's confidence in the administration as well as enabling citizens to carry out genuine and efficient monitoring of the institution's exercise of its powers.[32] The CJEU subsequently held that the right of access extended to documents in the possession of the Council or Commission that related to both second pillar[33] (common foreign and security policy) and third pillar[34] documents (justice and home affairs). The Court of First Instance[35] also concluded that the right of access extended to confidential documents.[36] As a result of an inquiry by the European Ombudsman into access of documents held by institutions and bodies other than the Council and the Commission, the Ombudsman concluded that:

> failure to adopt and make easily available to the public rules governing public access to documents constitutes an issue of maladministration.[37]

As a result of this ruling all of the bodies to which it was addressed, with the exception of the CJEU, adopted rules governing public access to documents.[38]

43– 015 Interpretation

Both the Commission and Council initially adopted a narrow approach to disclosing documents under Decisions 93/731 and 94/90. In *Carvel and Guardian Newspapers Ltd v Council of the European Union*[39] a newspaper sought access to preparatory reports, minutes and attendance and voting

---

31 Numerous commentators have expressed the view that the only other legal basis for the decision is in a general principle of law, see: M Broberg, 'Access to documents: a general principle of Community law?' (2002) 27 *European Law Review* 194; U Öberg, 'EU Citizen's Right to Know: The Improbable Adoption of a European Freedom of Information Act' in A Dashwood and A Ward (eds), *Cambridge Yearbook of European Legal Studies*, vol 2 (Oxford, Hart Publishing, 2000) at p 315.

32 See, eg, *Interporc Im und Export GmbH v Commission of the European Communities* [1998] ECR II-231, [1998] 2 CMLR 82.

33 *Heidi Hautala v Council of the European Union* [2002] 1 WLR 1930, [2002] 1 CMLR 15, [2002] CEC 127, on appeal from [2001] ECR I-9565, [1999] 3 CMLR 528.

34 *Svenska Journalistforbundet v Council of the European Union* [1998] All ER (EC) 545, [1998] ECR II-2289, [1998] 3 CMLR 645 (refusal of various documents relating to the setting up of Europol). An application was made by Svenska to various Swedish bodies under Swedish legislation for twenty documents. The newspaper received 18 of the 20 documents. An identical application was made to the Council but only 4 out of the 20 were disclosed. The remaining 16 documents were refused on grounds of public interest (public security) and confidentiality because they disclosed positions taken by various Member States. The Court of First Instance annulled the decision because the Council had failed to give adequate reasons. It was unclear which exception applied to which document. The court further doubted that the disclosure would prejudice public security as the documents concerned negotiations on the adoption of the Europol Convention. In relation to the confidentiality exception there was no evidence that the Council had engaged in a balancing exercise.

35 The differing roles of the Court of First Instance and the CJEU are considered in §43– 054.

36 *Rothmans International BV v Commissioner of the European Communities* [1998] ECR II-2463, [1999] 3 CMLR 66, where the Court of First Instance rejected an argument that a 'comitology committee', composed of Member State representatives and chaired by a Commission representative, was not distinct from and independent of the Commission. The court held that the comitology committee, and others like it, were established to assist the Commission perform its functions and that since they had no individual resources they could not be viewed as 'another Community institution' nor as any other third party. The court held that exceptions to the right of access were to be narrowly construed so as to not to frustrate the proper operation of the right.

37 Decision of the European Ombudsman in his self-initiated inquiry into public access to documents (616/PUBAC/F/IJH), p 7.

38 Namely, the European Parliament, the Court of Auditors, the European Investment Bank, the Economic and Social Committee, the Committee of the Regions, the European Monetary Institute, the Office for Harmonisation of the Internal Market, the European Training Foundation, the European Foundation for the Improvement of Living and Working Conditions, the European Environment Agency, the Translation Centre for Bodies of the European Union, the European Monitoring Centre for Drugs and Drug Addiction, and the European Agency for the Evaluation of Medicinal Products.

39 [1996] All ER (EC) 53, [1995] ECR II-2765, [1995] 3 CMLR 359, [1996] CEC 282.

records of the Council of Ministers' meetings relating to social affairs, justice and agriculture. The Council refused disclosure of the documents relating to justice and agriculture on the grounds of confidentiality. This refusal was challenged by the newspaper with the support of the Danish and Dutch Governments and the European Parliament on the grounds that the decision amounted to a blanket refusal to release information. The newspaper contended that the Council had failed to exercise its discretion and balance the interests of the citizen in gaining access to its documents against any interests of its own in maintaining the confidentiality of its deliberations when making its judgment. The Court of First Instance annulled the decision on the grounds that the Council was obliged to balance relevant considerations and had failed to do so. *The Guardian* obtained the documents. The Court of First Instance indicated that the Commission was obliged to give reasons why it considered that the documents detailed in the request were within one of the exceptions.[40] The court indicated that Decision 94/90 was designed to provide 'for the widest public access possible' and as such any exception was to be interpreted strictly.[41] In *Hautala v European Union Council*[42] the appellant, a Finnish Member of the European Parliament, sought disclosure of a report on criteria for conventional arms exports. Disclosure was refused on the grounds that it was necessary for the protection of the public interest (international relations) as disclosure would harm EU relations with third countries. The decision was annulled because the Court of First Instance concluded that the Council was under a duty to consider partial access to the document excluding the parts of the report that risked damaging the EU's relations with third countries. The Council appealed unsuccessfully to the CJEU which reiterated its view that the exceptions were to be interpreted narrowly and laid down the following general principles:

(1) the Code of Practice related not only to access to documents but also to information contained in such documents;
(2) natural and legal persons had a right of access to information contained in a document not covered by one of the exceptions; and
(3) the general principle of proportionality required the Council to consider partial disclosure of a document when disclosure of the whole document would fall within one of the exceptions.[43]

3. REGULATION 1049/2001

43–016 Introduction

Regulation 1049/2001 marked a substantial enhancement of the right of access to documents held by the EU institutions.[44] The Regulation was adopted under the co-decision procedure and approved by the European Parliament on 3 May 2001 pursuant to Art 255 EC (now Art

---

40 See also *World Wildlife Fund UK v Commission of the European Union* [1997] ECR II-313, CFI (refusal to disclose documents relating to EU funded visitors' centre to be located in Ireland on grounds of the protection of the public interest as the documents related to possible infringement proceedings and as such were related to inspections and investigations). The Commission's decision was annulled on procedural grounds but the Court of First Instance also found that the Commission had failed to properly balance competing interests in respect of the confidentiality exception.

41 See also: *Van Der Wal v Commission of the European Communities* [2000] ECR I-1, [2002] 1 CMLR 16; *Bavarian Lager Company Ltd* [1999] ECR II-3217, [1999] 3 CMLR 544, [1999] CEC 543.

42 [2002] 1 WLR 1930, [2001] ECR I-9565, [2002] 1 CMLR 15, [2002] CEC 127.

43 [2002] 1 WLR 1930, [2002] 1 CMLR 15, [2002] CEC 127 at [23]-[27] and [31]-[32]. See also *Kuijer v Council of the European Union* [2002] 1 WLR 1941, [2003] All ER (EC) 276, [2002] 1 CMLR 42, [2002] CEC 238.

44 For a summary of the interpretative principles applicable to a regulation, see §§7–035 to 7–038.

15 TFEU). It came into force on 3 June 2001 and was applicable from 3 December 2001.[45] Its ambit is considerably wider than that of earlier EU schemes. On 5 December 2001 the European Commission amended its rules of procedure so as to incorporate Regulation 1049/2001.[46] The Regulation would appear to be fully retrospective: that is to say, it covers documents created before its coming into force.[47] As noted above,[48] there is a free-standing right of access to 'environmental information' held by EU institutions, conferred by the separate and more liberal regime implemented by Regulation 1367/2006.[49]

43– 017 Object of Regulation

Article 1 states that the purpose of the Regulation is:

(1) to define the principles, conditions and limits on grounds of public or private interest governing the right of access to institution documents provided for in artcile 255 of the EC Treaty in such a way as to ensure the widest possible access to documents;

(2) to establish rules ensuring the easiest possible exercise of this right; and

(3) to promote good administrative practice on access to documents.[50]

The introduction of the Regulation was greeted with considerable optimism, with the Commission suggesting that the new rules represented 'major progress.'[51] The Council stated that the Regulation was 'an important step towards more openness of the institutions and better accessibility of their documents.'[52] This change of approach has been recognised by the Court of Justice which has commented that:

> [the] regulation reflects the intention expressed in the second paragraph of Art 1 TEU of marking a new stage in the process of creating an ever closer union among the peoples of Europe, in which decisions are taken as openly as possible and as closely as possible to the citizen. As is stated in recital 2 to [the] regulation, the public right of access to documents of the institutions is related to the democratic nature of those institutions...[53]

The Regulation aims to facilitate the 'fullest possible public access' to EU documents [54] (particularly in cases where the EU institutions are acting in a legislative capacity), while at the same time seeking to preserve the 'effectiveness' of the institutions' decision-making processes, by preserving the secrecy of the institutions' internal consultations and deliberations where

---

45 See Art 19 of the Regulation 1049/2001.

46 The rules of procedure spell out the manner in which a request must be made, the manner in which the request is to be handled and the persons to be consulted before responding to the request.

47 See further §20– 011.

48 §43– 011.

49 Unlike the environmental information regime in its application to public authorities in the United Kingdom, the right conferred by Regulation 1049/2001 applies equally in relation to environmental information held by EU bodies: Art 2(6). Thus, a person seeking access to environmental information held by an EU body has rights under both Regulation 1049/2001 and under Regulation 1367/2006. In practice, because the latter is more liberal than the former, where there is no right to information falling within the terms of a request (or some of the information falling within the terms of a request) because of the applicability of an exception under Regulation 1367/2006 and/or upon an application of the public interest test in that Regulation, it is unlikely that the applicant will have a right to have that information disclosed under Regulation 1049/2001.

50 Regulation 1049/2001 Art 1.

51 European Commission, *European Governance. A White Paper*, Brussels, 25 July 2001 COM (2001) 428 at 11.

52 See 2346th Council meeting General Affairs, Brussels, 14-15 May, 2001, 8441/01 (presse 169).

53 *Council v Access Info Europe* (C-280/11) [2014] 2 CMLR 6 at [27].

54 *Sison v Council of European Union* [2005] ECR II-1429, [2005] 2 CMLR 29 at [61]; *IFAW gGmbH v European Commission* (C-64/05) [2008] QB 902 at [53]; *Commission of the European Communities v Technische Glaswerke Ilmenau GmbH* (C-139/07) [2011] 1 CMLR 3, [2010] ECR I-5885, [2011] Bus LR D81 at [51].

necessary to safeguard their ability to carry out their tasks: Art 4(3).[55] Somewhat tendentiously, it is claimed that the right of public access to documents of the EU institutions is related to the 'democratic nature' of those institutions.[56]

43–018 The register and publication

To make the citizen's right of access to documents as effective as possible, the institutions are obliged to provide public access in electronic form to a register of documents.[57] The institutions were obliged to have this register operational from 3 June 2002.[58] Each document must have a reference number, details of the subject matter and/or a short description of the content together with the date on which it was received or drawn up and recorded.[59] The institutions are under an obligation to make, as far as possible, documents publicly accessible in electronic form or through the register.[60] There is an obligation to make all legislative documents[61] directly accessible, subject to Arts 4 (exemptions) and 9 (sensitive information).[62] In addition to the register, a number of documents must, subject to Arts 4 and 9, be published in the official journal. Documents that must be so published include:

(1) Commission proposals;
(2) common positions adopted by the Council in accordance with the procedures referred to in Art 251-252 of the EU Treaty (now Art 294 of TFEU) and the reasons underlying those common positions, as well as the European Parliament's positions in these procedures;
(3) framework decisions and decisions referred to in Art 34(2) of the EU Treaty (now-repealed by the Lisbon Treaty);[63]
(4) conventions established by the Council in accordance with Art 34(2) of the EU Treaty (now-repealed by the Lisbon Treaty);
(5) conventions signed between Member States on the basis of Art 293 of the EU Treaty (now-repealed by the Lisbon Treaty); and
(6) international agreements concluded by the Community or in accordance with Art 24 of the EU Treaty (now-repealed by the Lisbon Treaty).[64]

In addition, the following documents must be published so far as possible:

(7) initiatives presented to the Council by a Member State pursuant to Art 67(1) of the EC Treaty or pursuant to Art 34(2) of the EU Treaty (now-repealed by the Lisbon Treaty);

---

55 *Borax Europe Ltd v European Commission* (T-121/05) [2009] ECR II-27 at [68], [70].

56 *Sweden and Turco v Council* (C-39/05, C-52/05) [2009] QB 269, [2009] 2 WLR 867, [2008] 3 CMLR 17 at [34].

57 Regulation 1049/2001 Art 10(2). The register is similar to publication schemes required of public authorities under the FIOA and FOI(S)A: see §§21–013 to 21–017.

58 Regulation 1049/2001 Art 11(3).

59 Regulation 1049/2001 Art 10(2).

60 Regulation 1049/2001 Art 12(2).

61 'Legislative documents' are defined in Art 12(2) as documents drawn up or received in the course of procedures for the adoption of acts which are legally binding in or for the Member States.

62 Regulation 1049/2001 Art 12(2).

63 A framework decision was a kind of legislative act of the European Union used exclusively within the EU's competences in police and judicial co-operation in criminal justice matters. Framework decisions were similar to directives in that they required member states to achieve particular results without dictating the means of achieving that result. However unlike directives, framework decisions were not capable of direct effect. Framework decisions were created in the Amsterdam Treaty and replaced joint actions, which were legal instruments available under the Maastricht Treaty. The Lisbon Treaty abolished framework decisions and the EU can now enact directives and regulations in the area of criminal justice by means of the ordinary legislative procedure.

64 Regulation 1049/2001 Art 13(1).

(8) common positions referred to in Art 34(2) of the EU Treaty (now-repealed by the Lisbon Treaty); and

(9) directives other than those referred to in Art 254(1)-(2) of EC Treaty (now Art 297(1)-(2) of TFEU), decisions other than those referred to in Art 297(1) of the TFEU, recommendations and opinions.[65]

43– 019 Assistance, reasons etc

Although Regulation 1049/2001 does not expressly impose a duty on the institutions to advise and assist a person making a request for information,[66] a similar result is achieved through various provisions in the Regulation. Article 14 places a duty on each of the institutions to take measures to inform the public of their rights under the Regulation. Member States are obliged to co-operate with the institutions in providing this information. Article 15 provides that the institutions must develop good administrative practices. Article 16 provides that the Regulation is without prejudice to any existing rules on copyright which may limit a third party's right to reproduce or exploit released documents. Each institution is obliged to publish an annual report which must include the number of cases in which the institution refused to grant access to documents, the reasons for such refusals and the number of sensitive documents not recorded in the register.[67]

43– 020 Persons entitled to the right

By Art 2(1) every citizen of the European Union and every natural or legal person residing or having its registered office in a Member State is given 'a right of access to documents of the institutions, subject to the principles, conditions and limits set out elsewhere in [the] Regulation.' There is no need to justify the request or explain why the request has been made.[68] As with all comparative freedom of information regimes, the motive of an applicant in seeking a document is largely irrelevant to the efficacy of the request.[69] The institutions have a discretion to grant access to documents, subject to the same principles, conditions and limits, to any natural or legal person not residing in or not having a registered office in a Member State.[70]

43– 021 Bodies subject to Regulation

The Regulation applies to 'the institutions.'[71] This is defined to mean the European Parliament, Council and Commission.[72] Recital (8) of the Regulation provides:

> In order to ensure the full application of this Regulation to all activities of the Union, all agencies established by the institutions should apply the principles laid down in this Regulation

On 30 May 2001 the institutions adopted a joint declaration to the Regulation in which they: (a) committed to extending the scope of this right to agencies and bodies created by the EU

---

65 Regulation 1049/2001 Art 13(2).

66 Compare the obligations imposed on public authorities in the United Kingdom: see §§21– 001 to 21– 006.

67 Regulation 1049/2001 Art 17(1).

68 Regulation 1049/2001 Art 6(1). *Petrie v Commission of the European Communities* [2002] 1 CMLR 18, [2002] CEC 57 at [26], a decision under Decisions 93/731 and 94/90; *Verein fur Konsumenteninformation v Commission of the European Communities* [2005] 1 WLR 3302, [2005] All ER (EC) 813, [2005] ECR II-1121, [2006] 2 CMLR 60, [2005] 4 CMLR 21 at [109]; *Sison v Council of European Union* [2005] ECR II-1429, [2005] 2 CMLR 29 at [50], [52]; *Franchet v Commission of the European Communities* [2006] 3 CMLR 37 at [81]-[82].

69 See §20– 017.

70 Regulation 1049/2001 Art 2(2).

71 Regulation 1049/2001 Art 2(1).

72 Regulation 1049/2001 Art 1(a).

legislature; and (b) encouraged institutions and bodies not created by the EU legislature to adopt internal rules on public access to documents which take account of the Regulation.[73] The regulations governing legislative agencies including the European Environment Agency and the European Agency for Safety and Health at Work were accordingly amended[74] and bodies including the European Central Bank, the European Investment Bank, the Economic and Social Committee, the Court of Auditors and the Committee of the Regions adapted their internal rules to reflect Regulation 1049/2001.

43– 022 Meaning of 'document'

The unit of disclosure in the Regulation is a 'document' rather than 'information.' However, the Court of First Instance has held that the Regulation 'applies to information generally and not simply to documents.'[75] A part-disclosure provision renders the difference largely insignificant.[76] 'Document' is defined widely to mean 'any content whatever its medium (written on paper or stored in electronic form or as a sound, visual or audiovisual recording) concerning a matter relating to the policies, activities and decisions falling within the institution's sphere of responsibility.'[77] As with all comparative access regimes, the right is a right to information that is recorded in some form: it does not impose upon an institution an obligation to record information.[78]

43– 023 Third-party information

Unlike the earlier Code of Practice and Decisions 93/731 and 94/90, Regulation 1049/2001 applies not only to documents created by the institutions but also to other documents held[79] by the institutions, including documents drawn up or received by them and in their possession, in all areas of activity of the European Union.[80]

43– 024 Court documents

Where a person who is not a party to proceedings before the CJEU makes a request to the CJEU under Regulation 1049/2001 for access to documents filed in the court by one or more of the parties to those proceedings, the CJEU will refuse that request: this is on the basis that the CJEU, in exercising its judicial (as opposed to its administrative) functions, is not an

---

73 [2001] OJ L 173/5.

74 European Environment Agency (Regulation No 1641/2003); European Food Safety Authority (Regulation No 1612/2003); European Aviation Safety Agency (Regulation No 1643/2003); European Maritime Safety Agency (Regulation No 1644/2003); Translation Centre for the bodies of the European Union (Regulation No 1645/2003); European Agency for Reconstruction (Regulation No 1646/2003); European Agency for the Evaluation of Medicinal Products (Regulation No 1647/2003); European Training Foundation (Regulation No 1648/2003); European Foundation for the Improvement of Living and Working Conditions (Regulation No 1649/2003); Community Plant Variety Office (Regulation No 1650/2003); European Monitoring Centre for Drugs and Drug Addiction (Regulation No 1631/2003); European Monitoring Centre on Racism and Xenophobia (Regulation No 1652/2003); OHIM (Regulation No 1653/2003); European Agency for Safety and Health at Work (Regulation No 1654/2003); European Centre for the Development of Vocational Training (Regulation No 1655/2003).

75 *World Wildlife Fund EPP v EU Council* (T-264/04) [2007] ECR II-911 at [67]. It is unclear what the court meant by this statement, as it made clear that the duty on the institution was not to provide information contained in documents in its possession.

76 Regulation 1049/2001 Art 4(6). See further *Sophie in 't Veld v Council of the European Union* (T-529/09), 4 May 2012 at [104]-[106].

77 Regulation 1049/2001 Art 3(a). The provision does not confer a right to interrogate the institution: *WWF European Policy Programme v European Union Council* (T-264/04) [2007] ECR II-911 at [75]-[76].

78 *World Wildlife Foundation v Council of the European Union* (T-264/04) [2007] ECR II-911 at [76].

79 As to the meaning of the term 'held' see §20– 009.

80 Regulation 1049/2001 Art 2(3). And see *Terezakis v European Commission* (T-380/04), 30 January 2008 at [38].

'institution' within the meaning of the Regulation.[81] Where, on the other hand, a person who is not a party to proceedings before the CJEU makes a request to an institution – for example, the European Commission – under Regulation 1049/2001 for access to documents it filed or received in those proceedings, that request must be granted save to the extent that disclosure of such a document engages one or other of the exceptions and subject to a consideration of the public interest.[82] That said, the CJEU has accepted the proposition that there exists a rebuttable presumption that disclosure of written submissions lodged by an institution or a Member State in court proceedings would undermine the protection of court proceedings within the meaning Art4(2) of the Regulation, provided that those proceedings are pending.[83] Parties in proceedings before the CJEU are, in principle, free to disclose their own written submissions (including appended documents).[84]

43– 025 The request

Applications for access to a document must be made in written form, which may be in electronic form, in one of the European Union's official languages and in a sufficiently precise manner to enable the institution to identify the document.[85] Article 6(2) of the Regulation provides that '[if] an application is not sufficiently precise, the institution shall ask the applicant to clarify the application and shall assist the applicant in doing so, for example, by providing information on the use of the public registers of documents.'[86]

43– 026 Third party consultation

Where information in a document captured by a request originates from a 'third party' (in other words, from a legal person other than the institution to which the request is addressed), then, unless it is clear that the document does or does not fall within one of the exceptions in Art 4(1) or (2), the institution receiving the request must consult that third party with a view to assessing whether any of the exceptions is applicable.[87] It is suggested that in this situation, the third party could properly make submissions that an exception other than that proposed to be relied upon by the institution was applicable. It could also make submissions whether there was or was not an overriding public interest in disclosure. The view of the third party once consulted does not bind the institution.[88]

---

81 *Sweden and API v European Commission* (C-514/07, C-528/07, C-532/07) [2011] 2 AC 359, [2010] ECR I-8533 at [81]-[82].

82 *European Commission v Breyer* (C-213/15) [2018] 1 CMLR 24, [2018] CEC 475 at [38], [49]

83 *European Commission v Breyer* (C-213/15) [2018] 1 CMLR 24, [2018] CEC 475 at [41]-[42].

84 *Germany v European Parliament* (C-376/98) [2000] ECR I-2249 at [10].

85 Regulation 1049/2001 Art 6.

86 See further *Williams v European Commission* (T-42/05), 10 September 2008 at [74] in which the CFI noted that 'the duty to provide assistance is therefore essential in order to ensure the effectiveness of the right of access established by Regulation No 1049/2001.'

87 Regulation 1049/2001 Art 4(4). In *IFAW Internationaler Tierschutz-Fonds GmbH v Commission of the European Communities* (T-168/02) [2005] 1 WLR 1252, [2005] 2 CMLR 28 the Court of First Instance said: 'consultation of the third party is, as a general rule, a precondition for determining whether the exceptions to the right of access provided for in Art 4(1) and (2) of the Regulation are applicable in the case of third-party documents' (at [55]). The consultation procedure is further spelled out in Commission Decision 2001/937/EC Art 5. The involvement of third parties is considerably stronger than that provided for under the FOIA and FOI(S)A: see §§22– 036 to 22– 042. The court has held that consultation of the third party is, as a general rule, a precondition for determining whether the exceptions to the right of access provided for in Article 4(1) and (2) of Regulation No 1049/2001 are applicable in the case of third-party documents: *ClientEarth v European Chemical Agency* (T-245/11), 23 September 2015 at [222]; *Jurašinović v Council of the European Union* (T-63/10), 3 October 2012 at [83]; *Bank Austria Creditanstalt AG v Commission* (T-198/03) [2006] ECR II-1429, [2006] 5 CMLR 10 at [71].

88 *ClientEarth v European Chemical Agency* (T-245/11), 23 September 2015 at [223]; *Jurašinović v Council of the European Union* (T-63/10), 3 October 2012 at [87].

43– 027 Member State consultation

A Member State has a free-standing power to request that an institution not disclose a document originating from that Member State without its prior agreement.[89] A Member State may lodge an objection at the time of proceedings without having earlier objected under Art 4(5).[90] Member States do not have a general, unconditional right to veto the disclosure of a document held by an a Community institution simply because it originated from that Member State.[91] In objecting to disclosure, a Member State is confined to the grounds in Arts 4(1)-(3) and, in particular, is not able to object on the basis of impairment of its own decision-making process.[92] The institution to which the request is made remains responsible for the lawfulness of its decision. Accordingly, the institution cannot accept a refusal from a Member State if it is given no reasons at all or if the reasons relied upon do not refer to Art 4(1) or (2). However, there is no requirement to carry out an exhaustive assessment of the Member State's decision – the review is limited to verifying the mere existence of reasons under the permitted exemptions.[93] Because of the expansive definition given to the word 'document', it is suggested that this will extend to a document (or that part of a document) generated within the institution but which reproduces information received from a Member State. If a Member State receives a request for a document in its possession that originates from an institution, the Member State must consult with the institution concerned prior to disclosure unless it is clear to the Member State whether or not the document should be disclosed.[94] Alternatively, the Member State may refer the request to the institution concerned.[95]

43– 028 The response: timing

An institution has 15 working days after registration of the application to either grant access to a document or provide reasons why access has been refused.[96] This period can be extended by another 15 working days if the request is for a very long document or a large number of documents, although the institution must give reasons in advance for this delay. Failure on the part of an EU institution to comply with the time-limits does not lead automatically to the annulment of the decision adopted after the deadline, but might give rise to compensation for any loss resulting from the lateness of the institutional response through an action for damages.[97]

---

89 Regulation 1049/2001 Art 4(5). The procedure is further spelled out in Commission Decision 2001/937/EC Art 5. See, eg: *Scippacercola v Commission of the European Communities* (T-187/03) [2005] 2 CMLR 54; *IFAW Internationaler Tierschutz-Fonds GmbH v Commission of the European Communities* [2005] 1 WLR 1252, [2005] 2 CMLR 28; *Terezakis v European Commission* (T-380/04), 30 January 2008 at [39].

90 *Pagkyprios organismos ageladotrofon (POA) Dimosia Ltd v European Commission* (T-74/16), 8 February 2018 at [33]-[34].

91 *IFAW GmbH v European Commission* (C64/05) [2007] ECR I-11389, [2008] QB 902; *France v Schlyter* (C-331/15) [2018] 1 WLR 1365; cf *Mara Messina v Commission of the European Communities* [2003] ECR II-3203, [2005] 2 CMLR 21; *IFAW Internationaler Tierschutz-Fonds GmbH v Commission of the European Communities* (T-168/02) [2005] 1 WLR 1252, [2005] 2 CMLR 28 (holding that where the originating Member State has requested that a document not be disclosed, the application for access to that document is governed by the relevant national provisions and not by the Regulation).

92 *Pagkyprios organismos ageladotrofon (POA) Dimosia Ltd v European Commission* (T-74/16), 8 February 2018 at [36], [41].

93 *IFAW Internationaler Tierschutz-Fonds gGmbH v Commission* (C-135/11), 21 June 2012) at [60]-[64].

94 Regulation 1049/2001 Art 5; see also Recital 15.

95 Regulation 1049/2001 Art 5.

96 Regulation 1049/2001 Art 7(1). From the reasons it must be possible to understand and ascertain, first, whether the document requested did in fact fall within the sphere of the exception relied on by the institution and, secondly, whether the need for protection relating to that exception was genuine, see *Sison v Council of European Union* [2005] ECR II-1429, [2005] 2 CMLR 29 at [61]; *Pagkyprios organismos ageladotrofon (POA) Dimosia Ltd v European Commission* (T-74/16), 8 February 2018 at [56]-[78], which sets out an analysis of the level of reasoning that is required.

97 *Co-Frutta Soc Coop v European Commission* (T-355/04, T-446/04) [2010] ECR II-1 at [71].

43–029 The response: examination

There has been considerable discussion in the case law as to the extent to which the institution has to undertake a concrete, individual examination of the documents before responding to a request. The Court of First Instance has concluded that there is, as a general rule, an obligation to examine each document referred to in the request to ascertain whether it should be disclosed or withheld.[98] Examination is, however, subject to the principle of proportionality.[99] The court has been prepared to find the examination obligation discharged on the basis of very limited evidence.[100] Further, in exceptional circumstances it may be possible to give a total refusal without individual examination of the documents if the administrative burden entailed by individual examination is too heavy.[101]

43–030 The response: reasons

The reasons for refusal can be brief.[102] The institution must also consider whether a document caught by a request can be disclosed without harm to protected interests by redacting parts of the document.[103]

43–031 Reconsideration request

If the institution makes a partial or total refusal of disclosure the applicant may, within 15 working days of receiving the institution's reply, make a confirmatory application asking the institution to reconsider its position.[104] If for whatever reason the institution fails to reply to the original request within the prescribed time limit an applicant is entitled to make a confirmatory application.[105] A confirmatory application must be decided within 15 working days from registration of the application, subject to the possibility of an extension of 15 working days if the request relates to a very long document or a large number of documents, although the institution must give reasons in advance for this delay.[106] The reconsideration procedure under the Regulation gives the institution concerned the chance to re-examine its position before taking a definitive refusal decision which could be the subject of an action before the EU courts. It is claimed that this procedure:

> makes it possible for initial applications to be dealt with more promptly and, consequently, more often than not to meet the applicant's expectations, while also enabling the institution to adopt a detailed position before definitively refusing access to the documents sought by the applicant, in particular where the applicant repeats the request for disclosure of those documents, notwithstanding a reasoned refusal by that institution.[107]

---

98 *Franchet v Commission of the European Communities* [2006] 3 CMLR 37 at [115]-[118].

99 See *Sophie in 't Veld v Council of the European Union* (T-529/09), 4 May 2012 at [105] in the context of partial access.

100 *Sison v Council of European Union* [2005] ECR II-1429, [2005] 2 CMLR 29 where the Court of First Instance concluded that a concrete assessment was demonstrated by the existence of a specific procedure for considering requests for sensitive documents together with the Council unanimously approving the refusal of access to such documents.

101 *Verein fur Konsumenteninformation v Commission of the European Communities* [2005] 1 WLR 3302, [2005] All ER (EC) 813, [2005] ECR II-1121, [2006] 2 CMLR 60, [2005] 4 CMLR 21 which concerned an application for an administrative file containing 47,000 pages.

102 *Sison v Council of European Union* [2005] ECR II-1429, [2005] 2 CMLR 29 at [62]-[65].

103 Regulation 1049/2001 Art 4(6). *World Wildlife Foundation v Council of the European Union* (T-264/04) [2007] ECR II-911 at [50]. See further *Sophie in 't Veld v Council of the European Union* (T-529/09), 4 May 2012 at [106].

104 Regulation 1049/2001 Art 7(3).

105 Regulation 1049/2001 Art 7(4).

106 Regulation 1049/2001 Art 8(2).

107 *Internationaler Hilfsfonds eV v European Commission* (C-362/08) [2010] 2 CMLR 1095 at [53]-[54].

Since the response to an initial application within the meaning of Art 7(1) of Regulation 1049/2001 is only the first position, it is not normally actionable since it does not produce legal effects. Where the response to the initial application is vitiated by a defect in that it failed to inform the applicant of its right to make a confirmatory application, it will be actionable.[108] An initial position will also be actionable (in the sense of being something which can be challenged before the CJEU) where an EU institution adopts a definitive position with a response to an initial application.[109]

43– 032 Reconsideration response

In the event of a partial or total refusal, the institution must write to the applicant setting out the reasons for the refusal and informing him of the remedies open to him, namely instituting court proceedings and/or making a complaint to the ombudsman.[110] Failure by an EU institution to respond to a confirmatory application for access to documents within the time limit will amount to a decision to refuse access and that implied decision will constitute the starting point for the period within which the applicant could bring an action for annulment.[111] A failure to reply within the prescribed period will also entitle an applicant to initiate court proceedings and/or complain to the ombudsman.[112]

43– 033 Reconsideration challenge

Any refusal of access to a requested document is subject to challenge by way of an action for annulment, whatever the reason relied on to refuse access, including that the requested document did not exist or was not in the possession of the institution concerned. The Regulation sets up a two-stage administrative procedure in relation to dealing with access to documents requests, with the additional possibility of court proceedings before the CJEU being taken by a disappointed applicant or a complaint being made to the European Ombudsman. Article 43 of the CFR states that:

> any citizen of the Union and any natural or legal person residing or having its registered office in a Member State has the right to refer to the European Ombudsman cases of maladministration in the activities of the institutions, bodies, offices or agencies of the Union, with the exception of the Court of Justice of the European Union acting in its judicial role.

43– 034 Mode of access and fees

If access to a document is granted, the applicant may either consult it at the institution in question or receive a copy, including, where available, an electronic copy according to his preference. Consultation on the spot, direct access in electronic form or through the register or copies of fewer than 20 A4 pages are free.[113] If the applicant is sent written documents exceeding 20 A4 pages the institution may charge the applicant, although any charge must be

---

108 *Brink's Security Luxembourg v European Commission* (T-437/05), 9 September 2009 at [74]-[75].

109 *Internationaler Hilfsfonds eV v European Commission* (C-362/08) [2010] 2 CMLR 1095 at [58]-[62]; *Strack v European Commission* (C-127/13) [2015] 1 WLR 2649 at [36].

110 Regulation 1049/2001 Art 8(1). Article 230 EC lays down the conditions for instituting court proceedings, whilst Art 95 EC lays down the conditions for making an application to the Ombudsman.

111 *Strack v European Commission* (C-127/13) [2015] 1 WLR 2649. The court also held that Regulation 1049/2001 did not allow for the derogation from the time limits laid down in Arts 7 and 8, which could not be varied by the parties and which were determinative in relation to the conduct of the procedure for access to documents. Accordingly if no express decision had been made by the expiry of the time limit for processing a confirmatory application laid down in Art 8 of Regulation 1049/2001, an implied refusal would be deemed to exist which could be the subject of an action for annulment.

112 Regulation 1049/2001 Art 8(3).

113 Regulation 1049/2001 Art 10(1).

limited to the real cost of producing and sending the copies.[114] To assist visually impaired individuals, documents must be supplied either in an existing version and format or in an alternative format such as Braille, large print or tape with full regard to the applicant's preference.[115] The Regulation does not expressly make provision for an institution to give a response that neither confirms nor denies that the requested document is held by it.[116]

43– 035 Exceptions – principles

Article 4 sets out the various exceptions to the general right of access to documents. Uniquely amongst the comparative regimes, all the exceptions are mandatory: an institution must refuse access if a document falls within the terms of an exception.[117] The exceptions are divided into absolute exceptions (in relation to which the public interest need not be considered) and qualified exceptions (which have a public interest 'override'). In addition, certain sorts of documents are classed as 'sensitive documents.' Disclosure of sensitive documents is governed by a special regime.[118] The majority of exceptions cannot be invoked in relation to documents more than 30 years' old. In the case of documents that are not 'sensitive documents', only those exceptions relating to privacy or commercial interest can be invoked thereafter. In the case of 'sensitive documents' all exceptions can be invoked irrespective of the age of the documents. The EU courts have frequently stated that the exceptions are to be interpreted and applied restrictively so as not to frustrate application of the general principle of giving the public the widest possible access to documents held by the institutions.[119] The onus is upon the institution to establish the applicability of an exception.[120] Furthermore, if an institution decides to refuse access it must first explain how disclosure could actually undermine the interest protected by the exception upon which it relies.[121] An EU institution may, in refusing a specific document access request, base its decisions on general presumptions which apply to certain categories of document, on the basis that considerations of a generally similar kind are likely to apply to applications for disclosure which relate to documents of the same nature.[122] A Member State may request the Commission or the Council not to communicate to third parties a document originating from that State without its prior agreement. But Member States do not have a

114 Regulation 1049/2001 Art 10(1).

115 Regulation 1049/2001 Art 10(3).

116 However, arguably such a response can be given where (or to the extent that) a request for information captures or would capture sensitive documents: see §43– 053.

117 *Sison v Council of European Union* [2005] ECR II-1429, [2005] 2 CMLR 29 at [51]; *World Wildlife Foundation v Council of the European Union* (T-264/04) [2007] ECR II-911 at [44].

118 Regulation 1049/2001 Arts 2(5) and 4(7); see §43– 053.

119 *ClientEarth v European Commission* (T-644/16) [2019] 1 CMLR 7 at [21]; *Sison v Council of the European Union* (C-266/05) [2007] ECR I-1233, [2007] 2 CMLR 17 at [61]; *Sweden and API v European Commission* (C-514/07, C-528/07, C-532/07) [2011] 2 AC 359, [2010] ECR I-8533 at [69]; *Council of the European Union v Access Info Europe* (C-280/11) [2014] 2 CMLR 6 at [28]).; *Petrie v Commission of the European Communities* [2002] 1 CMLR 18, [2002] CEC 57 at [66], a decision under Decisions 93/731 and 94/90; *Turco v EU Council* (T-84/03) [2004] ECR II-4061, [2004] All ER (D) 363 (Nov) at [60], [71]; *Verein fur Konsumenteninformation v Commission of the European Communities* [2005] 1 WLR 3302, [2005] All ER (EC) 813, [2005] ECR II-1121, [2006] 2 CMLR 60, [2005] 4 CMLR 21 at [106]; *Sison v Council of European Union* [2005] ECR II-1429, [2005] 2 CMLR 29 at [45]; *Franchet v Commission of the European Communities* [2006] 3 CMLR 37 at [84]; *Association de la presse internationale asbl v EC Commission* (T-36/04) [2007] ECR II-3201, [2007] 3 CMLR 51 at [51]-[53]; *Bavarian Lager Co Ltd v EC Commission* (T-194/04) [2007] ECR II-4523, [2008] 1 CMLR 35 at [94].

120 *WWF European Policy Programme v European Union Council* (T-264/04) [2007] ECR II-911 at [39].

121 *Council of the European Union v Access Info Europe* (C-280/11) [2014] 2 CMLR 6 at [31]. Similarly: *Council of the European Union v in't Veld* (C-350/12) [2015] 1 CMLR 11 at [64]; *Liga para a Proteccao da Natureza (LPN) v European Commission* (C-514/11, C-605/11) [2013] All ER (D) 197 (Nov) at [44]; *ClientEarth v European Commission* (C-612/13) [2015] All ER (D) 254 (Jul) at [68].

122 *Sweden and API v Commission* (C-514/07, C-532/07) [2010] EUECJ C-514/07, [2011] 2 AC 359 at [74].

general and unconditional right of veto on the disclosure of a document held by a Community institution simply because it originates from that Member State: requests for non-disclosure must be properly reasoned, identifying likely harm if reliance is placed on harm-based exceptions.[123]

43– 036 Likelihood and degree of harm

In order for a document to engage an exception in Art 4(1)-(2), the required level of harm to the interest protected by that exception is that disclosure of that document 'would undermine the protection' of either:

(a) the public interest encapsulated in the protected interest (in the case of public security, defence and military matters, international relations and the financial, monetary or economic policy of the Community or a Member State); or

(b) the protected interest itself (in all other cases).

In order for the exception in Art 4(3) to be engaged, the required level of harm to the interest protected by that exception is that disclosure of the document 'would seriously undermine the institution's decision making process.' The phrases 'would undermine' and 'would seriously undermine' used in Arts 4(1)-(3) arguably set a higher threshold of harm than the phrase 'would prejudice' as used in FOIA.[124] In terms of the likelihood of that harm, the courts have said that the:

> risk of a protected interest being undermined must be reasonably foreseeable and not purely hypothetical.[125]

The courts have made it clear that it will be necessary for the institution to show 'concretely and effectively', and not generally or in an abstract fashion, that disclosure would have the effect required to engage the exception.[126] Thus, unlike the harm-based exemptions in FOIA, for the engagement of any of the exemptions in Arts 4(1)-(3), a mere likelihood of harm would appear to be insufficient.[127] It must be shown that the access in question was likely specifically and actually to undermine the interest protected by the exception.[128] In each case, the likelihood of harm exercise must normally be carried out on a document-by-document basis to see whether disclosure of each would result in the required prejudice.[129] The Regulation expressly recognises that the likelihood of harm from the disclosure of a document may diminish with time.[130]

43– 037 Public interest balance

---

[123] For example, in *France v Schlyter* (C-331/15) [2018] 1 WLR 1365 the CJEU refused an appeal by France from the decision of the General Court (T 402/12, EU:T:2015:209) ordering the Commission to disclose the detailed opinion of the European Commission concerning a draft technical regulation from a Member State which had been notified to the Commission by the French authorities pursuant to Directive 98/34/EC laying down a procedure for the provision of information in the field of technical standards and regulations.

[124] For a further discussion of the level of harm required in the FOIA and the FOI(S)A, see §6– 021. And see *Muñiz v European Commission* (T-144/05), 18 December 2008 at [75].

[125] *Franchet v Commission of the European Communities* [2006] 3 CMLR 37 at [115]. Similarly *Technische Glaswerke Ilmenau GmbH v Commission of the European Communities* [2007] 1 CMLR 39 at [77] where the court said that the task for the institution was to determine 'whether access to the document would specifically and actually undermine the protected interest'.

[126] *ClientEarth v European Commission* (C-57/16) [2019] 1 CMLR 37, [2019] Env LR 11 at [51]; *Borax Europe Ltd v European Commission* (T-121/05) [2009] ECR II-27 at [71]. See further *EnBW Energie Baden-Wurttemberg v European Commission* (T-344/08) [2012] 5 CMLR 4 at [163]-[166].

[127] For a further discussion of the likelihood requirement in the FOIA and FOI(S)A, see §§6– 022 to 6– 025.

[128] *Muñiz v European Commission* (T-144/05), 18 December 2008 at [74]; *EnBW Energie Baden-Wurttemberg v European Commission* (T-344/08) [2012] 5 CMLR 4 at [162].

[129] *MyTravel Group Plc v European Commission* (T-403/05) [2008] ECR II-2027, [2008] 3 CMLR 49 at [74].

[130] Regulation 1049/2001 Art 4(7).

If the protection of an interest listed in Art 4(2)-(3) would be 'undermined' by disclosure of a document, the requested institution is required to refuse access to that document 'unless there is an overriding public interest in [its] disclosure.' The proviso contemplates that although disclosure of a document would (seriously) 'undermine the protection' given to an interest listed in Art 4(2)-(3), disclosure of that document might nevertheless be required. In other words, merely establishing that disclosure of a document would undermine the protection given to that interest will not of itself necessarily be sufficient to displace the obligation to disclose that document. Although expressed as a proviso, the jurisprudence makes clear that the institution must only refuse access 'where its disclosure would undermine the protection of one of the interests protected by that provision' and that undermining outweighs 'the public interest in the document being made accessible, having regard to the advantages of increased openness.'[131]

43–038 Documents establishing rights

The public interest has a special role to play where a person needs access to particular documents in order to establish that person's rights and to bring proceedings where those rights have been contravened:

> ... if the judicial review is to be effective the person concerned must be able to ascertain the reasons upon which the decision taken in relation to him is based, so as to make it possible for him to defend his rights and to decide, with full knowledge of the relevant facts, whether there is any point in his applying to the court with jurisdiction..[132]

Thus, even where an exception applies to a document – and thus disclosure might 'undermine' or 'seriously undermine' the protected interest – a demonstrated need for access to the document in order to establish or maintain rights may provide a recognisable basis for concluding that there is an overriding public interest in disclosure. Where a person is seeking compensation for the loss caused by a breach of an EU rule that has been investigated, that person may be able to secure disclosure of a document that satisfies the first two requirements on the basis of the public interest in a person being properly compensated, provided that that person establishes that it is necessary to be granted access to documents in the Commission's file in order to establish the breach.[133]

43–039 Absolute exceptions

Article 4(1) provides that the institutions shall refuse access to a document 'where disclosure would undermine the protection of:

(a) the public interest as regards:
- — public security;
- — defence and military matters;
- — international relations; or
- — the financial, monetary or economic policy of the Community or a Member State; or

(b) privacy and the integrity of the individual, in particular in accordance with Community legislation regarding the protection of personal data.'

Each of these exemptions is 'absolute' so that if disclosure would undermine the protected

---

[131] *Council of the European Union v Access Info Europe* (C-280/11) [2014] 2 CMLR 6 at [29], [32]. Similarly: *Sison v European Council* (T-47/03) [2007] ECR II-73, [2007] 3 CMLR 1022 at [62]; *Sweden and API v European Commission* (C-514/07, C-528/07, C-532/07) [2011] 2 AC 359, [2010] ECR I-8533 at [70]-[71]; *Sweden v My Travel Group plc* (C-506/08) [2011] ECR I-6237, [2012] All ER (EC) 968, [2011] 5 CMLR 18 at [74]-[76].

[132] *AlzChem AG v European Commission* (C-666/17), 13 March 2019 at [54]. Similarly: *Liga para a Proteccao da Natureza (LPN) v European Commission* (C-514/11, C-605/11) [2013] All ER (D) 197 (Nov) at [42]

[133] *European Commission v EnBW Energie Baden-Württemberg AG* (C-365/12) [2014] 4 CMLR 30 at [107].

interest, the exemption is engaged and the public interest does not fall to be considered.[134]

43– 040 Public security

European Union law does not impose on Member States a uniform scale of values as regards the assessment of conduct which may be considered to be contrary to 'public security':

> Member States essentially retain the freedom to determine the requirements of public policy and public security in accordance with their national needs, which can vary from one Member State to another and from one era to another, in particular as justification for a derogation from the fundamental principle of free movement of persons...[but]....those requirements must nevertheless be interpreted strictly, so that their scope cannot be determined unilaterally by each Member State without any control by the institutions of the European Union.[135]

Public security would appear to embrace both what, in domestic legislation, is termed national security and matters of law enforcement.[136] Documents in this category should normally be pre-classified as 'top secret' or 'secret' or 'confidential.'[137]

43– 041 Defence and military matters

It is conventional in freedom of information legislation to provide an absolute exemption for information the disclosure of which might reasonably harm defence and military matters. Given that defence and military matters are largely within the domain of individual Member States rather than the European institutions, the exception is less frequently invoked than the comparable exemption in FOIA. The interpretive principles followed in those other regimes are likely to be similarly applicable in relation to requests under the Regulation.[138] Documents in this category should normally be pre-classified as 'top secret' or 'secret' or 'confidential.'[139]

43– 042 International relations

Freedom of information legislation generally provides an exemption for information the disclosure of which is likely to harm international relations, and Art 4(1) exemplifies this.[140] Given that international relations will largely be carried out by Member States, the exception is less frequently invoked than the comparable exemption in FOIA. The CJEU has recognised that:

> ..in the context of international negotiations, the positions taken by the [European] Union are, by definition, subject to change depending on the course of those negotiations and on concessions and compromises made in that context by the various stakeholders. The formulation of negotiating positions may involve a number of tactical considerations on the part of the negotiators, including the Union itself. In that context, it cannot be precluded that disclosure by the Union, to the public, of its own negotiating positions, when the negotiating positions of the other parties remain secret, could, in practice, have a negative effect on the negotiating capacity of the Union.[141]

---

134 See §43– 037 above.

135 *PI v Oberbürgermeisterin der Stadt Remscheid* (C-348/09) [2012] QB 799, [2012] 3 CMLR 13 at [21]-[23].

136 *Sison v European Council* (T-47/03) [2007] ECR II-73, [2007] 3 CMLR 1022. See further §§26– 040 to 26– 046 and §29– 014.

137 Article 9(1).

138 See §§26– 070 to 26– 079.

139 Article 9(1).

140 See §§27– 001 to 27– 006 and §§34– 061 to 34– 064.

141 *Besselink v Council of the European Union* (T-331/11) [2014] 1 CMLR 28 at [72]. Similarly *Council of the European Union v in't Veld* (C-350/12) [2015] 1 CMLR 11 at [123]-[125].

43– 043 Financial, economic etc policy

Freedom of information legislation generally provides for an exemption for information the disclosure of which would prejudice financial, monetary or economic matters.[142] Provided that the documents emanate from or are sent to a body concerned with financial, monetary or economic regulation, the courts have shown themselves fairly ready to find this exception satisfied, both under the Regulation and under agency-specific analogues.[143] A similar exemption from disclosure exists in specific Community disclosure regimes, and the courts have shown themselves ready to find that it has been engaged.[144]

43– 044 Privacy and personal integrity

As with all disclosure regimes, the rights of public access to information held by public bodies may collide with the right of an individual not to have personal data unnecessarily disclosed.[145] The 'privacy and personal integrity' exception is an indivisible provision and requires that any undermining of privacy and the integrity of the individual be examined and assessed in conformity with the legislation of the European Union concerning the protection of personal data.[146] The fact that a document relates to an individual will not suffice for the engagement of this exception: what is required is that the document relate to the 'private sphere' of an individual (the volume of which may depend on the position held by that individual) and that there be a risk of prejudice to that individual's legitimate interests from the disclosure.[147] Thus, for example, disclosure of the opinions and views expressed by the participants at the meetings of an institution's decision-making body will not, by itself, fall within the sphere of the privacy of those participants, since those meetings will be professional meetings and disclosure of their views or opinions will not normally undermine the participants' privacy.[148] Similar exceptions are found in other European regulations.[149] This exception may be satisfied by redacting just the names of the individuals concerned.[150]

---

142 See *Pitsiorlas v Council of the European Union* (T-3/00, T-337/04) [2007] ECR II-4779, [2008] 1 CMLR 47. And see further §§28– 001 to 28– 011.

143 For example: *World Wildlife Fund EPP v EU Council* (T-264/04) [2007] ECR II-911.

144 For the application of the same phrase in the context of Decision 2004/258 and the right to documents, see: *Espírito Santo Financial Group SA v European Central Bank* (T-730/16), 13 March 2019; *Espírito Santo Financial (Portugal), SGPS, SA v European Central Bank* (T-251/15), 26 April 2018; *Versorgungswerk der Zahnärztekammer Schleswig-Holstein v European Central Bank* (T-376/13), 4 June 2014.

145 In *Borax Europe Ltd v European Commission* (T-121/05) [2009] ECR II-27 the Court of First Instance held that the Commission had unlawfully based a refusal to supply a recording of an experts meeting on the privacy and integrity exception. The court emphasised the requirement for the institution to explain how access to the document would specifically and effectively undermine the interest protected (at [37]). In that case, the Commission had relied on the privacy and integrity exception but had not pleaded specific ground pertaining to the risk of undermining the protection of privacy. Further, in relation to the protection of integrity, the court held that the Commission had made its decision 'on the basis of general grounds which are incapable of substantiating the existence' of a risk.

146 In other words, under the GDPR regime. *European Commission v Bavarian Lager Co Ltd* [2010] EUECJ C-28/08, [2010] ECR I-06055, [2011] Bus LR 867 at [59]; *Psara and others v European Parliament* (T-639/15, T-94/16), 25 September 2018 at [65].

147 *Dennekamp v European Parliament* (T-115/13), 15 July 2015 at [139]-[140]. The exception does not have the effect of creating a presumption in favour of the legitimate interests of a person whose personal data would be disclosed (at [127]).

148 *McCullough v European Centre for Development of Vocational Training* (T-496/13), 11 June 2015 at [87]-[88], [94]. Similarly: *Internationaler Hilfsfonds eV v European Commission* (T-300/10), 22 May 2012.

149 See for example Art 63 of Regulation 1107/2009, considered in *Arysta LifeScience Netherlands BV v European Food Safety Authority* (T-725/15), 14 December 2018.

150 See, for example: *Philip Morris Ltd v European Commission* (T-18/15), 15 September 2016 at [16].

43– 045 Qualified exceptions

Article 4(2) provides that the institutions shall refuse access to a document 'where disclosure would undermine the protection of:

— commercial interests of a natural or legal person, including intellectual property;

— court proceedings and legal advice,

— the purpose of inspections, investigations and audits,

unless there is an overriding public interest in disclosure.' Determining the applicability of each of these qualified exceptions involves four stages: (a) determining whether the content of the document involves or relates to the protected interest (eg is it legal advice or does it relate to legal advice): (b) determine whether disclosure of the document would undermine the protection of that interest; (c) determine whether there is nevertheless an overriding public interest in disclosure; and (d) to the extent that disclosure of information in the document would undermine the protection of that interest and there is no overriding public interest in its disclosure, determine whether some of the information in the document can be redacted and the balance of the document released.[151]

43– 046 Commercial interest exception

Article 4(2) provides that the institutions shall refuse access to a document where disclosure would undermine the protection of commercial interests of a natural or legal person, including intellectual property.[152] 'Business secrets' concern information of which not only disclosure to the public but also mere transmission to a person other than the one who provided the information may seriously harm the latter's interests.[153] Such information should be known only to a limited number of persons.[154] The exception is a qualified exception so that where the disclosure of a document would have the required level of harm, it is necessary to go on and consider where the balance of the public interest lies. In considering the public interest, the court will consider how significant the protected interest is to the applicant's request for the information.[155]

43– 047 Court proceedings exception

Article 4(2) provides that the institutions shall refuse access to a document where disclosure would undermine the protection of court proceedings.[156] The court's view is that the disclosure

---

151 See §43– 037 above.

152 In relation to the corresponding exemption applicable in relation to a request for information held by a public authority in the United Kingdom, see §§34– 049 to 34– 060.

153 *Postbank NV v Commission of the European Communities* [1996] All ER (EC) 817, [1996] ECR II-921, [1997] 4 CMLR 33 at [87].

154 *Systran SA and Systran Luxembourg SA v European Commission* (T-19/07), 16 December 2010 at [80]. See further *EnBW Energie Baden-Wurttemberg v European Commission* (T-344/08) [2012] 5 CMLR 4 at [135]-[143].

155 In *Co-Frutta Soc Coop v European Commission* (T-355/04, T-446/04) [2010] ECR II-1 at [133] the General Court noted in relation to this exception:

> The aim behind the application for access to the documents [in this case] is that of verifying the existence of fraudulent practices on the part of the applicant's competitors. The applicant thus pursues, amongst other objectives, the protection of its commercial interests. However, it is not possible to categorise the applicant's commercial interests as being an 'overriding public interest' which prevails over the protection of the commercial interests of traditional operators, the objective underlying the refusal of access to a part of the documents requested. In addition, the pursuit of the public interest in identifying cases of fraud in order to ensure the smooth operation of the banana market is not a matter for the operators, but for the competent Community and national public authorities, where appropriate following an application made by an operator.

156 In *Franchet v Commission of the European Communities* [2006] 3 CMLR 37 at [88]-[89] the Court of First Instance concluded that this exception precluded the disclosure of the content of documents drawn up solely for the purposes of specific court proceedings. The words 'documents drawn up solely for the purposes of specific court proceedings' should be understood to mean the pleadings or other documents lodged, internal documents

of pleadings lodged in pending court proceedings is presumed to undermine the protection of those proceedings – because of the fact that the pleadings constitute the basis on which the court carries out its judicial activities – and so a general rule can be applied to refuse access to court pleadings in open proceedings.[157] However, in closed proceedings no such general presumption can be applied, so that access to the pleadings in proceedings held behind closed doors can be refused by the Commission only after it undertakes a specific examination of the document to which access is requested and explains how disclosure of that document could specifically and effectively undermine the court proceedings in question.

43– 048 Legal advice exception

Article 4(2) provides that the institutions shall refuse access to a document where disclosure would undermine the protection of legal advice.[158] This is a qualified exception so that where the disclosure of a document would have the required level of harm, it is necessary to go on and consider where the balance of the public interest lies.[159] The fact that a document is headed 'legal advice/opinion' will not mean that it automatically comes within the exception.[160] The institution must examine whether disclosure of the parts of the document in question which have been identified as relating to legal advice 'would undermine the protection' of that advice.[161] Although the protection referred to is an institution's interest in seeking and receiving frank, objective and comprehensive legal advice,[162] it will be insufficient for an institution to refuse access to the legal advice in question merely by claiming a general need to maintain its confidentiality in order to be able to obtain full and frank legal advice.[163] To rely upon this exception effectively, the institution must show how disclosure of the legal advice in question would, on the facts of the particular case, constitute a genuine and reasonably foreseeable specific risk (rather than some purely hypothetical threat) to its legitimate interests.[164] If the institution takes the view that disclosure of a document would undermine the protection of legal advice as defined above, the institution must then go on to ascertain whether there is any overriding public interest justifying disclosure despite the fact that its ability to seek legal advice

---

concerning the investigation of the case, and correspondence concerning the case between the Directorate-General concerned and the Legal Service or a lawyers' office. The purpose of that definition of the scope of the exception was to ensure both the protection of work done within the Commission and confidentiality and the safeguarding of professional privilege for lawyers. In *Petrie v Commission of the European Communities* [2002] 1 CMLR 18, [2002] CEC 57 the Court of First Instance held that Member States are entitled to expect the Commission to guarantee confidentiality that might lead to infringement proceedings; this requirement of confidentiality remains even after the matter has been brought before the court. In relation to the corresponding exemption applicable in relation to a request for information held by a public authority in the United Kingdom, see Ch 20.

157 *Sweden and API v European Commission* (C-514/07, C-528/07, C-532/07) [2011] 2 AC 359, [2010] ECR I-8533.

158 In *Turco v EU Council* (T-84/03) [2004] ECR II-4061, [2004] All ER (D) 363 (Nov) the Court of First Instance rejected an argument from the applicant that only documents capable of undermining the protection of legal advice drawn up in the context of court proceedings are covered by the exception. The court said (at [62]): 'the words "legal advice" must be understood as meaning that the protection of the public interest may preclude the disclosure of the contents of documents drawn up by the Council's legal service in the context of court proceedings but also for any other purpose.' The court went on to observe (at [71]) that 'the fact that the document in question is a legal opinion cannot, of itself, justify application of the exception relied upon'. The court placed the burden of proof regarding the 'public interest override' on applicants, ruling also that the override could not be invoked in the general interest of transparency. In relation to the corresponding exemption applicable in relation to a request for information held by a public authority in the United Kingdom, see Ch 21.

159 See §43– 037 above.

160 *Sweden and Turco v Council* (C-39/05, C-52/05) [2009] QB 269, [2009] 2 WLR 867, [2008] 3 CMLR 17 at [38]-[39].

161 *Sweden and Turco v Council* (C-39/05, C-52/05) [2009] QB 269, [2009] 2 WLR 867, [2008] 3 CMLR 17 at [39].

162 *Sweden and Turco v Council* (C-39/05, C-52/05) [2009] QB 269, [2009] 2 WLR 867, [2008] 3 CMLR 17 at [42].

163 *European Commission v Agrofert Holding AS* (C-477/10) [2012] 5 CMLR 9.

164 *European Commission v Agrofert Holding AS* (C-477/10) [2012] 5 CMLR 9.

would thereby be undermined.[165]

43– 049 Investigations etc exception

Article 4(2) provides that the institutions shall refuse access to a document where 'disclosure would undermine the protection of the purpose of inspections, investigations and audits.'[166] In order to engage the exception, the first task is to identify whether the document relates to an inspection, investigation or audit. The term 'investigation' is not limited to searches carried out by an authority to establish an offence or irregularity, or to procedures aimed at bringing together and verifying information with a view to taking a decision: any structured and formalised European Commission procedure which has the purpose of collecting and analysing information in order to enable it to take a position in the context of its functions provided for by the EU and FEU Treaties will constitute an 'investigation.'[167] Documents relating to investigations carried out by the Commission in the context of infringement proceedings under Art 258 TFEU are not covered by this exception.[168] The institution concerned must also explain how access to that document could specifically and effectively undermine the interest protected by the exception.[169] The court will be prepared to presume that disclosure of the documents relating to an infringement procedure during its pre-litigation stage risks altering the nature of that procedure and changing the way it proceeds and, accordingly, that disclosure would in principle undermine the protection of the purpose of investigations.[170] The court has also been prepared to countenance 'chilling effect' arguments in relation to documents supplied to an institution conducting an investigation etc.[171] If the institution satisfies that requirement, the institution must go on to consider where the balance of the public interest lies.[172]

43– 050 Article 4(3) qualified exception

Article 4(3) provides a qualified exception for two classes of internal, deliberative documents:

(1) In the first class, access to a document is to be refused where the decision to which the document relates has not been taken and disclosure of the document would seriously undermine the institution's decision-making process.

(2) In the second class, even after the decision to which the document relates has been taken, access to a document is to be refused where that document contains 'opinions for internal use as part of deliberations and preliminary consultations' *and* disclosure would seriously undermine the institution's decision-making process.

All comparative freedom of information regimes include such a provision, although Art 4(3)

---

165 *Sweden and Turco v Council* (C-39/05, C-52/05) [2009] QB 269, [2009] 2 WLR 867, [2008] 3 CMLR 17 at [44].

166 *Franchet v Commission of the European Communities* [2006] 3 CMLR 37 at [104]-[113]. See further: *EnBW Energie Baden-Wurttemberg v European Commission* (T-344/08) [2012] 5 CMLR 4 at [125]-[126] in which a wide interpretation of 'investigations' put forward by the Commission was rejected as being incompatible with the object of providing the fullest possible effect to the right of access as required by recital 4 of the Regulation. In relation to the corresponding exemption applicable in relation to a request for information held by a public authority in the United Kingdom, see Ch 20.

167 *France v Schlyter* (C-331/15) [2018] 1 WLR 1365 at [46]-[52].

168 *Sweden and API v European Commission* (C-514/07, C-528/07, C-532/07) [2011] 2 AC 359, [2010] ECR I-8533; *Deutsche Telekom AG v European Commission* (T-210/15) [2017] 4 CMLR 30 at [27].

169 *Sumner v European Commission* (T-152/17), 5 December 2018 at [29]; *European Commission v Agrofert Holding AS* (C-477/10) [2012] 5 CMLR 9 at [97]. This is a true second requirement, see: *France v Schlyter* (C-331/15) [2018] 1 WLR 1365 at [61]-[85].

170 *Sumner v European Commission* (T-152/17), 5 December 2018 at [31]; *Deutsche Telekom AG v European Commission* (T-210/15) [2017] 4 CMLR 30 at [28]-[32]; *European Commission v EnBW Energie Baden-Württemberg AG* (C-365/12) [2014] 4 CMLR 30 at [66]-[68], [80]-[90].

171 *Deutsche Telekom AG v European Commission* (T-210/15) [2017] 4 CMLR 30 at [45];

172 See §43– 037 above.

would appear to impose a higher threshold of likely resultant harm than is required under the comparable provision in FOIA.[173] The principles specific to each class are considered in the following two paragraphs. With both classes, the required level of harm to the protected interest is 'seriously undermine', as opposed to merely 'undermine.' The exception is a qualified exception so that where the disclosure of a document would have the required level of harm, it is necessary to go on and consider where the balance of the public interest lies.[174] The public interest in a person having access to documents in order to establish and maintain rights – for example, by instituting proceedings – is of particular importance in relation to deliberative documents, partly because the documents will often by nature impinge upon a person's rights and partly because the harm from disclosure can be contained by restricting the use of the disclosed document.[175]

43– 051 Pre-decision documents

The first class in the Art 4(3) exception applies only to documents for internal use relating to an issue on which the EU institution concerned has not yet made a decision. The exception does not rule out the possibility of the disclosure of such a document. This part of the exception is concerned only with the decision-making process, and does not cover the entire administrative procedure that led to the decision.[176] Whether disclosure of a document prior to the making of a decision will 'seriously undermine' the protected interest will depend on factors such as the state of completion of the document in question, the precise stage of the decision-making process in question at the time when access to that document is refused, the specific context in which that process takes place, and the issues still to be discussed internally by the institution concerned.[177] Protection of the decision-making process from targeted external pressure may constitute a legitimate ground for restricting access to documents relating to the decision-making process.[178] If an institution wishes to rely on this exception, it will need to establish that access to the documents requested is likely to undermine specifically and actually the protection of the institution's decision-making process, and that the likelihood of that interest being so undermined is reasonably foreseeable and not purely hypothetical.[179] The courts have not readily accepted claims for exception under the first class of Art 4(3): in particular, 'candour' and 'blue-sky thinking' arguments have not been upheld.[180] Nor have the courts been ready to find that documents received by the institution from a third party are covered by the exception.[181] Where the document concerns environmental information, there will generally be a compelling public interest in its disclosure.[182]

---

173 See Ch 31 for comparative examples and for a detailed analysis of the provisions in FOIA and FOI(S)A.

174 See §43– 037 above.

175 See §43– 038 above.

176 *Saint-Gobain Glass Deutschland GmbH v European Commission* (C-60/15) [2018] Env LR 8 at [77]. Thus, the exception does not cover a document held by the institution that 'directly relates to matters dealt with as part of an administrative procedure pending before that institution' (at [77]).

177 *ClientEarth v European Commission* (C-57/16) [2019] 1 CMLR 37, [2019] Env LR 11 at [111]; *Saint-Gobain Glass Deutschland GmbH v European Commission* (C-60/15) [2018] Env LR 8 at [83].

178 *Pesticide Action Network Europe v European Commission* (T-51/15), 20 September 2016 at [30]; *MasterCard Inc v European Commission* (T-516/11), 9 September 2014 at [71].

179 *de Capitani v European Parliament* (T-540/15), 22 March 2018; *ClientEarth v European Commission* (T-424/14, T-425/14), 13 November 2015 at [63] at [52].

180 See, for example: *ClientEarth v European Chemical Agency* (T-245/11), 23 September 2015 at [159]-[163]; *Miettinen v Sweden* (T-395/13), 18 September 2015 at [59]-[73]; *Council of the European Union v Access Info Europe* (C-280/11) [2014] 2 CMLR 6 at [53]-[68].

181 See, for example: *MasterCard Inc v European Commission* (T-516/11), 9 September 2014 at [66].

182 *Saint-Gobain Glass Deutschland GmbH v European Commission* (C-60/15) [2018] Env LR 8 at [83]-[84].

43– 052 Post-decision documents

In order for a document to be captured by the second class of exception in Art 4(3) four requirements must be satisfied:

(a) the document must have certain attributes – namely, it must contain opinions for internal use as part of the deliberations and preliminary consultations within the institution;

(b) disclosure of the document would seriously undermine the institution's decision-making process;[183]

(c) the institution must have already taken the decision the process for which it is said would be seriously undermined; and

(d) there is no overriding public interest in the disclosure of the document.

The split in Art 4(3) between the first class (which is confined to where the decision has not been taken by the institution) and the second class recognises that once the decision has been taken the need to protect the decision-making process is less acute.[184] Moreover, the reach of the second class is narrower than the first class, extending only to 'documents containing opinions' and not including, for example, documents received by an institution from a third party.[185] As with the first class of Art 4(1), the courts have not accepted invocation of this exception on the institution's say-so that 'candour' and 'blue-sky thinking' would be damaged by disclosure.[186] Nor has the court been prepared to accept that third parties will be reluctant to provide the institution with information from which opinions are formed if those opinions are to see the light of day,[187] unless public access to the document would be particularly harmful to the institution in an activity that is self-evidently in the public interest – for example, combatting fraud etc.[188] Where a document relates to an ongoing investigation, with its own specific procedures for disclosure, the court has been prepared to uphold the Art 4(3) exception under this class where disclosure would impinge on the investigation and disturb the operation of its specific disclosure regime.[189]

43– 053 Sensitive documents

Sensitive documents are defined in Art 9 to be those documents originating from the institutions, or the agencies established by them, from Member States, third countries or International Organisations[190] that have been classified 'Très Secret/Top Secret', 'Secret' or 'Confidential' in accordance with the rules of the institution concerned. This system echoes

---

183 This is a distinct requirement from (a) and will not be satisfied by reiteration of (a): *McCullough v European Centre for Development of Vocational Training* (T-496/13), 11 June 2015 at [110].

184 *Sweden v My Travel Group plc* (C-506/08) [2011] ECR I-6237, [2012] All ER (EC) 968, [2011] 5 CMLR 18 at [78]-[80]; *EnBW Energie Baden-Wurttemberg v European Commission* (T-344/08) [2012] 5 CMLR 4 at [154].

185 *McCullough v European Centre for Development of Vocational Training* (T-496/13), 11 June 2015 at [99]-[100].

186 See, for example: *Espírito Santo Financial Group SA v European Central Bank* (T-730/16), 13 March 2019 at [172]-[188]; *Philip Morris Ltd v European Commission* (T-18/15), 15 September 2016 at [85]-[87]; *McCullough v European Centre for Development of Vocational Training* (T-496/13), 11 June 2015 at [109], [113]; *Sweden v MyTravel Group plc* (C-506/08) [2011] 5 CMLR 18, [2012] All ER (EC) 968 at [98] (the United Kingdom intervened in order to maintain a 'space for reflection' argument (at [63]), which failed).

187 *MSD Animal Health Innovation and Intervet international v European Medicines Agency* (T-729/14), 5 February 2018 at [108]-[115].

188 *Strack v European Commission* (T-221/08), 26 April 2016 at [148]-[153], [161]-[165].

189 *European Commission v Sweden* (C-365/12), 27 February 2014; *European Commission v EnBW Energie Baden-Württemberg AG* (C-365/12), 27 February 2014 at [114]-[119].

190 As to the meaning of 'international organisations,' see §27– 005.

that used in the United States pursuant to Executive Order.[191] The expectation is that such documents will be concerned with public security, defence and military matters. Applications for sensitive documents may be handled only by persons who have a right to acquaint themselves with those documents.[192] Sensitive documents shall be recorded in the register or released only with the consent of the originator.[193] Whilst an institution remains under a duty to give reasons if it refuses to disclose a sensitive document caught by the terms of the request, the reasons need only be provided in such a manner that does not harm the interests protected in Art 4.[194] It is suggested that this might enable a neither confirm nor deny response, on the basis that in some circumstances any other response would indeed harm the interests protected in Art 4.[195]

43– 054 Appeals

The Court of Justice of the European Union – the CJEU – is the institution that encompasses the whole judiciary of the European Union. It consists of two separate courts:

— The General Court (formerly the Court of First Instance[196]), which is the lower court. It deals with cases where individuals bring actions against the EU institutions. Because most appeals against refusal of access to documents involve an institution denying an individual access to documents, the majority are heard before the General Court (formerly the Court of First Instance).

— The Court of Justice (formerly the ECJ). This court hears appeals against the judgments of the General Court (by individuals, by EU institutions or by Member States). It also hears cases where one EU institution brings an action against another and cases between the EU institutions and the Member States. The Court of Justice also answers questions about EU law referred from national courts. The Court of Justice is assisted by Advocates General, who release a non-binding but influential Opinion about how to decide each case before the court gives judgment.

The courts cannot order the EU institutions to release documents. Instead, they have the more limited power to annul an institution's refusal to release them. This leaves the institution free to refuse access to the information requested on other grounds. The intensity of review of decisions by European institutions refusing access was considered by the CJEU in *Sison v Council.*[197] The CJEU dismissed Mr Sison's appeal against the Court of First Instance's rejection of his challenge to the Council's refusal to disclose certain documents on the grounds that they fell within the ambit of Art 4(1)(a). The court stated:

> ...the Court of First Instance...correctly held...as regards the scope of the judicial review of the legality of a decision of the Council refusing public access to a document on the basis of one of the exceptions relating to the public interest provided for in Art 4(1)(a) of Regulation No 1049/2001, that the Council must be recognised to have a wide discretion for the purpose of determining whether the disclosure of documents relating to the fields covered by those exceptions could undermine the public interest. The Court of First Instance also correctly held...that the Community Court's review of the legality of such a decision must therefore

191 See §26– 010(1).

192 Regulation 1049/2001 Art 9(2). See *Sison v Council of European Union* (T-110/03) [2005] ECR II-1429, [2005] 2 CMLR 29 which concerned sensitive documents. See further *Council of the European Union v European Commission* (C-539/10, C-550/10), 15 November 2012 at [53].

193 Regulation 1049/2001 Art 9(3).

194 Regulation 1049/2001 Art 10(4).

195 For a further discussion on the need in some circumstances for a neither confirm nor deny response, see §§26– 062 to 26– 065 and §26– 068.

196 Up until the coming into force of the Lisbon Treaty on 1 December 2009.

197 *Sison v Council of European Union* (T-110/03) [2005] ECR II-1429, [2005] 2 CMLR 29.

be limited to verifying whether the procedural rules and the duty to state reasons have been complied with, whether the facts have been accurately stated, and whether there has been a manifest error of assessment or a misuse of powers.[198]

[198] *Sison v Council of European Union* (T-110/03) [2005] ECR II-1429, [2005] 2 CMLR 29 at [47].

Part VII

Appeals, Remedies and Enforcement

CHAPTER 44

The Information Commissioner and the tribunals

1. THE FUNCTIONS OF THE INFORMATION COMMISSIONER

44– 001 Information Commissioner

The main responsibility for enforcing the GDPR, the DPA 2018, FOIA and the EIR lies with the Information Commissioner.[1] The office was originally established as that of the Data Protection Registrar.[2] It was renamed the Data Protection Commissioner by the DPA 1998[3] and later the Information Commissioner by FOIA.[4] The last name change coincided with the office being given responsibilities under that Act in addition to its responsibilities under the DPA 1998.[5] The Information Commissioner is now constituted as such under section 114 of DPA 2018, with Part 5 of the Act and Sch 13 setting out much of the law relating to her functions. The Information Commissioner is also responsible for the enforcement of the

1 Since July 2016 the Commissioner has been Elizabeth Denham. Her website is at www.ico.org.uk The Ministry of Justice is the sponsoring department within the Government. The functions of the Scottish Information Commissioner (who holds a corresponding position in relation to FOI(S)A and EI(S)R are dealt with at §§46– 001 to 46– 004.

2 Under the DPA 1984 s 3(1)(a).

3 DPA 1998 s 5(1).

4 FOIA s 18(1), with effect from 30 January 2001.

5 The combination of the two roles into one post was the source of some controversy in Parliament. The Government's justifications for combining the two roles were given in Hansard HC vol 347 cols 1040-1042 (5 April 2000) as: (1) the two roles were said by the then Commissioner to be complementary and she supported the idea; (2) consistent decisions would be made as to what should be disclosed; (3) the public would have a single point of contact when they sought information; (4) this was said to be the course adopted in Australia, New Zealand and Ireland. See also Hansard HL vol 617 col 1214 (15 October 2000).

Privacy and Electronic Communications (EC Directive) Regulations 2003, the INSPIRE Regulations 2009, the Re-use of Public Sector Information Regulations 2015, the Investigatory Powers Act 2016, the Electronic Identification and Trust Services for Electronic Regulations 2016 and the Network and Information Systems Regulations 2018.[6] She is also the 'supervisory authority' in the United Kingdom for the purposes of the GDPR and the 'designated authority' in the United Kingdom for the purpose of Art 13 of the 1981 Convention for the Protection of Individuals with regard to the Automatic Processing of Personal Data.[7] The Information Commissioner is subject to the supervision of the Tribunals and Inquiries Act 1992.[8] In addition to her specific statutory duties, the Commissioner sets herself the aims of providing a general inquiry service for individuals and organizations and influencing thinking on privacy and access issues.

44– 002 Terms of appointment etc

The Information Commissioner is appointed by the Crown by Letters Patent.[9] Schedule 12 to the DPA 2018 lays down the detailed terms of her appointment and powers. The Commissioner is a corporation sole and neither her nor her officers and staff are servants or agents of the Crown. The Commissioner's tenure is normally for one term of seven years and she can be removed from office only in pursuance of an address by both Houses of Parliament.[10] Provision is made for her salary and pension and for the appointment by her of one or two deputy commissioners and other officers and staff. She currently employs about 480 staff and handles more than 5,700 freedom of information complaints a year, along with 21,000 data protection concerns and 235,000 telephone calls. The funds required by the Commissioner are to be paid to her by the Secretary of State for Justice out of money provided by Parliament and she must pay all fees, charges, penalties and other sums she receives to the Secretary of State to be paid into the Consolidated Fund, although in practice it seems money she receives is retained under direction.[11] Her current budget is £27 million and her fee income is £21.3 million. She must keep proper accounts and records.[12] Each year she must lay before Parliament and publish a general report on the exercise of her functions.[13]

44– 003 FOIA and EIR functions

The main functions of the Information Commissioner under FOIA are investigating and determining whether public authorities have dealt with requests for information in accordance with Part I of the Act and issuing 'decision notices' on that issue, or are otherwise complying with Part I of the Act and the codes of practice issued by the Lord Chancellor and the Secretary of State under it, and enforcing such compliance.[14] She also has the general functions of:

---

6 SI 2003/2426, SI 2009/3157, SI 2015/1415, SI 2016/695 and SI 2018/506 respectively. The INSPIRE Regulations derive from European Directive 2007/2/EC.

7 DPA 2018 s 115(1) and 116(1)(b).

8 Tribunals and Inquiries Act 1992 s 1 and Sch I Pt I para 14(a).

9 DPA 2018 Sch 12 para 2(1).

10 DPA 2018 Sch 12 paras 2(3)-(4) and 3.

11 DPA 2018 Sch 12 paras 9-10.

12 DPA 2018 Sch 12 para 11.

13 DPA 2018 s 123(1). The reports are prepared for the year ending 31 March and can be accessed on the Information Commissioner's website.

14 FOIA Pt IV (ss 50-56). If there is a question whether the Commissioner has jurisdiction to determine a certain matter or exercise a certain power (eg where there is a question whether a body is a 'public authority' and thus subject to freedom of information legislation), the Commissioner must determine that matter first and in the affirmative before deciding any other matter: *E.ON plc v IC and Fish Legal* [2019] UKUT 132 (AAC) at [37]-[38]

— approving 'publication schemes' by public authorities;[15]
— preparing and/or approving 'model publication schemes';[16]
— promoting good practice by public authorities in following the provisions of the Act and the codes of practice;[17]
— disseminating information about the Act and about good practice;[18]
— assessing (with consent) whether public authorities are following good practice;[19]
— consulting the Keeper of Public Records about the promotion of the observance by local authorities of codes of practice issued by the Lord Chancellor under s 46;[20]
— giving recommendations to public authorities if it appears that their practice does not comply with such codes of practice;[21]
— disclosing information to the appropriate ombudsman if it appears to her that it could be relevant to an investigation by that ombudsman.[22]

The Lord Chancellor must consult the Information Commissioner before issuing or revising a code of practice under s 45(1) of FOIA providing guidance to public authorities in connection with the discharge of their functions under Part I or under s 46(1) in connection with the keeping, management and destruction of public records.[23] The Information Commissioner also has responsibility for bringing criminal proceedings against a public authority, or its officers and employees, which alters records to prevent disclosure pursuant to the Act.[24] She is also responsible for the enforcement of the EIR and has other functions under the regulations analogous to those under FOIA.[25] She is the respondent in appeals against a decision notice under FOIA or the EIR brought by the requester of information or the public authority.[26] In that capacity she is still acting as an independent regulator and has a role in assisting in and ensuring the proper administration of the FOIA regime. As such, her role in the tribunal is not to defend her decisions come what may. She keeps the merits of the decision under review and makes appropriate concessions even shortly before or during a hearing.[27]

44– 004 Data protection functions

The Commissioner's general functions under GDPR and DPA are set out in sections 115 and 116 of DPA 2018 and Schedule 13 thereto. The main specific functions provided by the DPA 2018 are:

— carrying out her various international roles in relation to data protection;[28]

---

15 FOIA s 19(1)(a). As to publication schemes, see Ch 21.

16 FOIA s 20(1).

17 FOIA s 47(1). As to codes of practice, see Ch 21. The Information Commissioner has issued numerous guides to the working of the FOIA in particular relating to the exemptions; they are available on the ICO website.

18 FOIA s 47(2).

19 FOIA s 47(3).

20 FOIA s 47(5). As to codes of practice under s 46, see §21– 012.

21 FOIA s 48.

22 FOIA s 76.

23 FOIA s 45(4) and 46(5)(b). See further §21– 007.

24 FOIA s 77(4). See also §50– 006.

25 See EIR regs 16(5) and 18.

26 There were about 284 such appeals in 2017/8 according to her annual report.

27 *Lubicz v IC and King's College London* [2015] UKUT 555 (AAC) at [51]; *British Union for the Abolition of Vivisection v IC and Newcastle University*, FTT, 11 November 2011 at [14(h)].

28 DPA 2018 ss 118-120.

— preparing codes of practice and guidance on numerous topics;[29]
— carrying out 'consensual audits'[30]
— carrying out other specific investigations by means of 'assessments', 'information notices', exercising powers of entry and search on warrant etc;
— enforcing compliance by data controllers and processors by imposing 'enforcement notices' and 'penalty notices';[31]
— dealing with complaints by data subjects in accordance with the GDPR and DPA 2018;[32]
— instituting criminal proceedings under the DPA 2018;[33]
— reporting annually to Parliament;[34] and
— reviewing compliance.[35]

When carrying out these functions the Commissioner is required to have regard to the importance of securing an appropriate level of protection for personal data, taking account of the interests of data subjects, controllers and others and matters of general public interest.[36]

44– 005 Other functions

As noted above, the Commissioner also has responsibility for enforcing other related Acts and Regulations, including the Privacy and Electronic Communications (EC Directive) Regulations 2003 (PECR). In relation to the PECR, the Commissioner has the power to apply to the courts under Part 8 of the Enterprise Act 2002 for an enforcement order in cases where breaches of the PECR are considered harmful to individual consumers.[37] She can also impose 'monetary penalty notices' under DPA 1998 ss 55A-E as modified by the PECR[38] if the relevant contravention was serious, of a kind likely to cause substantial damage or distress and the contravention was either deliberate or there was a risk of substantial damage or distress and reasonable steps to prevent a contravention were not taken.[39]

44– 006 Duties of confidentiality

The Information Commissioner has extensive powers and opportunities to obtain information in the course of enforcing the legislation for which she is responsible, including information held by public authorities. Further, no enactment or rule of law prohibiting or restricting the disclosure of information precludes any person from furnishing the Commissioner with any information necessary for the discharge of her functions.[40] The Commissioner and her staff are

29 See eg DPA 2018 ss 121-128, 160, 177, 200.

30 DPA 2018 s129.

31 DPA 2018 ss 149-153 and 155-157.

32 DPA 2018 s 165; see also s 166 which empowers the FTT to make orders to progress complaints if the Commissioner does not take appropriate steps to respond to a complaint.

33 DPA 2018 s 197(1).

34 DPA 2018 s 139.

35 See eg DPA s 178.

36 DPA 2018 s2(2.

37 Enterprise Act 2002 Part 8, s 213(2) and SI 2003/1399.

38 See SI 2003/2426 reg 31. Note that the relevant provisions of DPA 1998 remain in force for these purposes notwithstanding the new data protection regime which came into force in 2018: see DPA 2018 Sch 20 Part 9 para 58(1). A right of appeal against a monetary penalty notice to the First-tier (or Upper) Tribunal is given by DPA 1998 s 55B(5).

39 The application and interpretation of these provisions was considered by the FTT in *Scottish Borders Council v IC*, FTT, 21 August 2013 and by the Upper Tribunal in *IC v Niebel* [2014] UKUT 255 (AAC).

40 DPA 2018 s 131(1).

therefore potentially privy to much sensitive information, which may not in the event be made public. They commit an offence if they disclose, without lawful authority, any information which has been obtained in the performance of the Commissioner's functions which relates to an identified or identifiable individual or business and which is not available to the public from other sources, unless the disclosure is made with lawful authority.[41] There appears to be a lacuna in the English legislation, in that there is no provision making it an offence for the Commissioner or her staff to disclose information which comes to them under FOIA unless it relates to an identified or identifiable individual or business: there is no such lacuna in the FOI(S)A, which provides that the Scottish Commissioner or his staff or agents commit an offence (punishable on summary conviction by the maximum fine and on indictment by an unlimited fine) if they disclose without lawful authority any information which is received by them under the Act and which is not in the public domain.[42]

44–007 Human Rights Act 1998

The Information Commissioner is herself subject to the Human Rights Act 1998.[43] Articles 6, 8 and 10 of the ECHR are potentially relevant to the exercise of her functions.[44] Article 6 of the ECHR has very limited application to the work of the Commissioner in deciding whether applicants are entitled to information under the Acts since the rights granted are not 'civil rights'[45] within the meaning of the ECHR (although the civil rights of third parties may be affected), and, in any event, the various rights of appeal against their decisions probably mean that Art 6 will be satisfied. The Commissioner of course has a duty to act fairly in relation to her administrative decision-making. Formerly the European Court took the view[46] that Art 10 (which includes the right 'to receive information') only prohibited a government from restricting a person from receiving information from others who want to provide it and that it did not cast any obligation to provide information to an applicant against its will; but in the same case the Court decided that the failure by a public authority to disclose certain personal data might involve a breach of the right to respect for private and family life provided by Art 8. It seems likely that this decision would only impinge on applications for information under data protection legislation. The Commissioner is herself a public authority for the purposes of FOIA and the EIR[47] and potentially a 'controller' subject to data protection legislation, and she must accordingly comply with the provisions of all such legislation.

---

41 DPA 2018 132(1). The term 'business' will cover what is done by public authorities: *Lampert v IC* [2019] UKUT 60 (AAC) at [18].

42 FOI(S)A s 45(1), (3), (4).

43 See Human Rights Act 1998 s 6(1) and (3).

44 See Ch 4.

45 See the admissibility decision of the European Human Rights Commission in *Barry v France* (App No 14497/89) 14 October 1991 and *McGinley v United Kingdom* (1998) 27 EHRR 1 at paras 85-6. See, also: *Syndicat CFDT des Etablissements et Arsenaux du Val-de-Marne and Vesque v France* (App 11678/85) 7 December 1987; *Loiseau v France* (App No 46809/99) ECHR 18 November 2003; *Micallef v Malta* (App no 17056/06) ECHR 15 January 2008 at [39]. See further Ch 4.

46 *Gaskin v United Kingdom* (1990) 12 EHRR 36. The actual decision in *Gaskin* was that the failure to provide medical records relating to the applicant at his request was an interference with his Art 8 right to respect for his private and family life; this decision led to the enactment of DPA 1998 ss 68 and 69 which *inter alia* make health records, in whatever form they are kept, subject to the DPA 1998 and in particular the access rights provided by s 7, thereby potentially allowing individuals a right to obtain access to their own health records. See, further, Ch 4. See also in the English courts *R (Persey) v Environment Secretary* [2003] QB 794 at [51]-[52].

47 FOIA Sch 1 Pt VI.

2. THE FTT AND THE UPPER TRIBUNAL

44– 008 The Tribunals

Under the original scheme of the legislation, judicial supervision of information rights was primarily provided by the Information Tribunal[48] (although it had no jurisdiction in relation to FOI(S)A and no equivalent for it is provided under that Act).[49] The Information Tribunal was originally constituted as a statutory tribunal under the DPA 1984[50] as the Data Protection Tribunal. It was continued in existence by the DPA 1998[51] and its name was changed to the Information Tribunal by s 18(2) of FOIA,[52] which Act also extended its functions substantially. The jurisdiction of the Tribunal was purely statutory. However, by virtue of Art 2(3)(a) of the Transfer of Tribunal Functions Order 2010,[53] with effect from 18 January 2010 all the functions of the Information Tribunal were transferred to the FTT (and, to a limited extent, the Upper Tribunal) established under the TCEA 2007.[54] Cases formerly heard by the Information Tribunal ('information rights cases')[55] were assigned to the General Regulatory Chamber of the FTT and the Administrative Appeals Chamber of the Upper Tribunal.[56] The question as to which of the FTT and the Upper Tribunal deals with particular information rights appeals is determined by the Tribunal procedure rules: in summary, appeals involving national security certificates and very important or complex appeals are transferred to the Upper Tribunal.[57] Decisions of the First-tier Tribunal are not binding, whether on the tribunal itself or on the

[48] FOIA ss 57 and 60 and EIR reg 18. In relation to the DPA 1998, where no national security certificate had been issued under the DPA 1998, judicial supervision is provided by the County Courts and the High Court; where a national security certificate had been issued, judicial supervision is provided by the Tribunal (see §49– 016).

[49] Appeals from decisions of the Scottish Information Commissioner are heard by the Court of Session: FOI(S)A s 56.

[50] DPA 1998 s 3(1)(b).

[51] DPA 1998 s 6(3).

[52] With effect from 30 January 2001.

[53] SI 2010/22.

[54] Part 1 of this Act was designed to provide a new unified tribunals service by setting up the FTT and the Upper Tribunal under a new judicial office holder, the Senior President of Tribunals; it enabled the Lord Chancellor by order to transfer the jurisdiction of existing tribunals to the new tribunals; for the background see Sir Andrew Leggatt's report *Review of Tribunals* published in August 2001 and the Government's *White Paper Transforming Public Services: Complaints, Redress and Tribunals* published by the DCA in July 2004; the Upper Tribunal is a 'superior court of record': s 3(5). The Lord Chancellor is under a statutory duty to ensure that there is an efficient and effective system to support the carrying on of business by the Tribunals: see s 39 of the 2007 Act.

[55] That is, appeals under the DPA 1998, FOIA, the Privacy and Electronic Communications (EC Directive) Regulations 2003 and the EIR: see definition in the Practice Statement on composition of Tribunals issued by the Senior President of Tribunals dated 21 August 2009.

[56] The First-tier Tribunal and Upper Tribunal (Chambers) Order 2008 (SI 2008/2684) (as amended by SI 2009/1590) Arts 2(e), 5B(a), 6, 7(a)(vii).

[57] FTT Rules determine which cases are assigned to the Upper Tribunal: the relevant rule is r 19 of the FTT Rules: this provides that 'appeals' in relation to national security certificates must be transferred to the Upper Tribunal (r 19(1A)) and that other cases may be referred to the President of the General Regulatory Chamber and then transferred to the Upper Tribunal on his direction with the concurrence of the President of the Administrative Appeals Chamber of the Upper Tribunal (see rr 19(2) and (3)). Cases will only be suitable for transfer where some special feature merits this course: eg where the case is of considerable public importance or involves complex or unusual issues (as was the case in *Evans v IC and DBIS* [2012] UKUT 313 (AAC), concerning Prince Charles's correspondence with government ministers). At the time of writing, it does not appear that the Rules have been amended to replace references to appeals under DPA 1998 s 28 with references to appeals under DPA 2018 ss 27, 79 and 111, but it is a reasonable assumption that such appeals are intended to be covered by the FTT Rules r 19(1A).

Information Commissioner.[58] In addition to the Upper Tribunal's jurisdiction to hear appeals transferred to it under the rules, under s 11 of the TCEA 2007 there is a right of appeal on a point of law from the FTT to the Upper Tribunal, which in effect replaces the right of appeal from the Information Tribunal to the High Court provided by s 59 of FOIA. The Upper Tribunal is a 'superior court of record'[59] and (as well as being given the same powers as the High Court in relation to judicial review)[60] it is given the same powers, rights, privileges and authority as the High Court (and in Scotland, the Court of Session) in relation to the attendance of witnesses, the production of documents and all other matters incidental to its functions.[61]

44– 009 Membership of the Tribunals

Pursuant to section 6(4) of the DPA 1998, the Lord Chancellor had appointed members of the Information Tribunal. Prior to 18 January 2010, there were a chairman, 11 deputy chairmen and 34 other members. On that date, the chairman and deputy chairmen and the other members of the Information Tribunal became judges and other members of the FTT and the Upper Tribunal.[62] They were assigned to the General Regulatory Chamber and Administrative Appeals Chamber[63] with the intention that they should continue to hear information rights cases as before. New judges and other members of the FTT and the Upper Tribunal are appointed and assigned to those Chambers and to the information rights jurisdiction in accordance with the relevant provisions of the TCEA 2007 and secondary legislation and directions made thereunder.[64]

44– 010 Constitution of the Tribunals

The jurisdiction of the FTT and of the Upper Tribunal to decide information rights cases is to be exercised by a member or members of the General Regulatory or Administrative Appeals Chamber (as the case may be) chosen by the Senior President of Tribunals,[65] who can delegate that (and any other function) to any other judge,[66] in particular the relevant Chamber President or Principal Judge of the information rights jurisdiction. In practice, the judges chosen to hear information rights cases are those with experience of such cases (including those transferred-in from the Information Tribunal). The composition of Tribunals in the General Regulatory Chamber is now regulated by the Senior President's Practice Statement dated 27 February

---

58 *O'Hanlon v IC* [2019] UKUT 34 (AAC) at [17].

59 TCEA 2007 s 3(5). As to the meaning and significance of this, see *R (Cart) v Upper Tribunal* [2009] EWHC 3052 (Admin), [2010] 2 WLR 1012, where the Upper Tribunal was described as 'an alter ego of the High Court: it constitutes an authoritative, impartial and independent judicial source for the interpretation and application of the relevant statutory texts....It is a court possessing the final power to interpret for itself the law it must apply....[The Upper Tribunal's] role at the apex of a new and comprehensive judicial structure ought to be respected and given effect' (at [94]). The Divisional Court held that decisions of the Upper Tribunal were not generally amenable to judicial review (at [97]-[100]).

60 TCEA 2007 ss 15-21.

61 TCEA 2007 s 25(1) and (2).

62 See Art 4 and Schedule 1 to the 2010 Order. Note that the chairman and deputy chairmen designated to hear national security appeals under para 2 of Schedule 6 to the DPA 1998 became deputy judges of the Upper Tribunal and transferred-in judges of the FTT and other deputy chairmen became transferred-in judges of the FTT (Parts 3 and 4 of Schedule 1); all the other ('lay') members of the Information Tribunal are transferred-in other members of the Upper Tribunal and, as such, are automatically other members of the FTT (see: TCEA 2007 s 4(3)(c)).

63 Pursuant to paras 9 to 12 of Schedule 4 to the TCEA 2007.

64 See Schs 2 to 4 to the TCEA 2007.

65 Para 14 of Schedule 4 to the TCEA 2007.

66 Section 8(1)(a) of the TCEA 2007.

2015,[67] which provides that a decision that disposes of proceedings[68] or determines a preliminary issue must be made by a judge (who must preside) and two other members '... where each other member has substantial experience of data protection or of freedom of information (including environmental information) rights.'[69] but that any other decision (including striking out a case, giving directions, making an order by consent, or dealing with matters arising after a decision disposing of proceedings) must be made by one judge. There is an exception provided by paras 11(2) and (3) of the Practice Statement which allows such decisions to be made by one judge if the Chamber President considers it appropriate and the issue is whether the public authority holds information, whether it is in breach of time limits, whether the exemptions in section 12, 21 or 22 of FOIA apply or where the appeal is against an information or enforcement notice served under FOIA or the parties agree and the judge is familiar with the case. Any other decision (including striking out an appeal, giving directions, making an order by consent, or dealing with matters after a decision, costs) must be made by one judge.[70] Since 9 April 2013 there has been a Registrar of the General Regulatory Chamber who deals with most interlocutory matters. Her powers (which now include the power to strike out an appeal on the basis it has no reasonable prospects of success)[71] and those of FTT case-workers appointed under s 40(1) of the TCEA 2007 are provided by a Practice Statement made by the Senior President on 25 September 2017 under rule 4(1) of the FTT Rules. Any decision by a case-worker is considered afresh if a party applies within 14 days by the Registrar or a judge and any decision of the Registrar is likewise considered afresh by a judge.[72]

44– 011 The Upper Tribunal

In the Upper Tribunal, any decision is made by one judge unless the Senior President or Chambers President determines that it involves a question of law of special difficulty or an important point of principle or practice or that it is otherwise appropriate in which case the matter can be decided by two or three judges of the Upper Tribunal.[73] However, on a case transferred from the FTT to the Upper Tribunal where the Senior President or Chamber President considers it appropriate the case can be decided by one judge and two members or two judges and one member; the members concerned must have substantial experience of data protection or freedom of information (including environmental) rights.[74] The Upper Tribunal is not bound by decisions of the High Court where the Upper Tribunal is in effect exercising a jurisdiction formerly exercised by the High Court or where a co-ordinate jurisdiction is being exercised.[75]

44– 012 FOIA jurisdiction

The FTT and the Upper Tribunal have jurisdiction to determine the following appeals under FOIA:

---

67 Made under the First-tier and Upper Tribunal (Composition of Tribunal) Order 2008 (SI 2008/2835).

68 This does not include a decision to strike out a party's case under rule 8 of the FTT Rules: para 16 of the Practice Statement.

69 See paras 3, 11(1) of the Practice Statement.

70 Para 16 of Practice Statement dated 27 February 2015. In particular, costs decision can only be made by a judge sitting alone: *Brace v IC and Merseyside Fire and Rescue Authority* [2019] UKUT 305 (AAC) at [9]-[14].

71 See para 4(d) of Practice Statement dated 25 September 2017.

72 See paras 3 and 5 of the Practice Statement dated 25 September 2017.

73 Senior President's Practice Statement on the composition of the Upper Tribunal dated 26 March 2014 para 3(a).

74 Practice Statement dated 26 March 2014 paras 3(e) and 4B.

75 *Gilchrist v HMRC* [2014] UKUT 166 (TCC), [2015] Ch 183; *D v IC* [2018] UKUT 441 (AAC) at [32].

- — an appeal under s 57(1) by a complainant or a public authority[76] against a decision notice served by the Information Commissioner under s 50(3)(b) following a complaint under s 50(1) that the public authority had failed to deal with a request for information in accordance with Part I of the Act;[77]
- — an appeal under s 57(2) by a public authority against an 'information notice'[78] or an 'enforcement notice'[79] served on it;[80]
- — an appeal under s 60(1) by the Information Commissioner or any applicant whose request for information has been affected by a Minister's issue of a national security certificate under s 23(2)[81] or s 24(3);[82] and
- — an appeal under s 60(4) by a party to proceedings under the Act on the grounds that a certificate issued under s 24(3) identifying the information to which it applies by means of a general description does not apply to the particular information in question as claimed by the public authority holding it.[83]

44– 013 EIR jurisdiction

By virtue of regulation 18 of the EIR, the FTT and the Upper Tribunal have jurisdiction to hear appeals against decision notices served by the Information Commissioner in relation to applications for environmental information under the Regulations and by a public authority against an information notice or an enforcement notice as under s 57(1) and 57(2) of FOIA. By virtue of regulation 18(7) the Upper Tribunal also has jurisdiction to hear appeals relating to ministerial certificates made under regulation 15(1) equivalent to those provided by s 60(1) and 60(4) of the FOIA.[84] The Supreme Court has decided that regulation 18(6) (which purports to apply the 'executive override' provision in section 53 of FOIA in the context of environmental information) is not compatible with Art 6(2) of European Directive 2003/4/EC which was the basis for the EIR and that any such certificate issued in the context of EIR would be invalid.[85]

44– 014 DPA 2018 jurisdiction

The FTT and the Upper Tribunal have jurisdiction to hear appeals under DPA 2018 against

76 Or, in the case of 'transferred public records' (FOIA s 15(4)) within s 66 of the Act, the 'responsible authority' as defined in s 15(5) thereof: s 57(3).

77 This does not include determining whether a request for information made of a body to which the Act has limited operation falls or does not fall within the limited area of operation: *BBC v Sugar and IC* [2007] EWHC 905 (Admin), [2007] 1 WLR 2583. See further §20– 022.

78 FOIA s 51(1).

79 FOIA s 52(1).

80 Or, in the case of 'transferred public records' (FOIA s 15(4)) within s 66 of the Act, the 'responsible authority' as defined in s 15(5) thereof: s 57(3).

81 FOIA s 23(2) provides that a certificate signed by a Minister of the Crown certifying that information was supplied by or relates to any of the security bodies listed in s 23(3) is conclusive evidence of that 'fact' so as to make it 'exempt information' by virtue of s 23(1).

82 FOIA s 24(3) provides that a certificate signed by a Minister of the Crown certifying that exemption from s 1(1)(b) or ss 1(1)(a) and (b) is required shall be conclusive evidence of that 'fact' for the purposes of s 24(1) and (2) which provide exemption in those circumstances from the duties to state whether information is held and to communicate it pursuant to s 1(1)(a) and (b) of the Act respectively.

83 Appeals under s 60 must be transferred to the Upper Tribunal under rule 19(1A) of the FTT Rules.

84 There are similar provisions in relation to appeals under the INSPIRE Regulations 2009 (SI 2009/3157): see reg 11.

85 See *R (Evans) v Attorney-General* [2015] UKSC 21, [2015] AC 1787. Art 6(2) required an applicant refused disclosure of environmental information to have the right to review by a court or tribunal whose decision was final and binding on the public authority.

information, assessment, enforcement, penalty and penalty variation notices issued by the Commissioner.[86] There is also a right of appeal against a refusal of an application for the cancellation or variation of an enforcement notice under section 153 of DPA 2018 and a determination by the Commissioner under section 174 that data is not being processed for relevant purposes (journalism, academic, artistic or literary).[87] The grounds on which the Tribunal can allow an appeal are that the notice or decision was 'not in accordance with the law' or that it involved an exercise of discretion which the Commissioner ought to have exercised differently and the Tribunal can review any determination of fact on which the notice or decision was based.[88] If the appeal is allowed the Tribunal can substitute another notice which the Commissioner could have given or made.[89] The Tribunal also has jurisdiction on an application by a data subject to make an order requiring the Commissioner to progress a complaint made by the data subject about an infringement of the GDPR or Part 3 or 4 of DPA 2018 in relation to his personal data.[90]

44– 015 National security jurisdiction

The FTT and the Upper Tribunal also have jurisdiction to hear appeals against national security certificates issued by a Minister of the Crown under section 27, 79 or 111 of DPA 2018. These appeals are decided applying the principles applied in judicial review proceedings and the tribunal can quash the certificate if the Minister had no reasonable grounds for issuing the certificate. Each of those sections also provides for an appeal to the FTT and the Upper Tribunal by a party to proceedings in which a data controller is claiming that a certificate applies to particular data and gives the tribunal power to determine that the certificate does not apply to the data in question.[91] Which of the two tribunals hears the case is a matter for the Tribunal Procedure Rules.[92] In the context of appeals against national security certificates this means the Upper Tribunal hears the appeal.

44– 016 Practice and procedure

Section 22 of the TCEA 2007 makes provision for a Tribunal Procedure Committee to make rules governing the practice and procedure to be followed in the FTT and the Upper Tribunal. By section 22(4) the power is to be exercised to secure accessible, fair and quick and efficient justice and the rules are to be simple and simply expressed. They are to be interpreted in a manner that '... makes coherent sense of the rules as a whole.' There are two relevant sets of rules in force:[93]

— The FTT Rules[94] which govern all information rights appeals to the FTT;
— The Tribunal Procedure (Upper Tribunal) Rules 2008[95] which govern appeals

[86] DPA 2018 s 162(1).

[87] DPA 2018 s 162(2) and (4).

[88] DPA 2018 s 163(2) and (3): this is a 'full merits' appeal where the Tribunal stands in the shoes of the Commissioner and new evidence can be considered.

[89] DPA 2018 s 163(3): it is now firmly established by the jurisprudence on FOIA s 58 that the word 'or' in section 163(3) is to be read as 'and/or': see *IC v E Malnick and The Advisory Committee on Business Appointments* [2018] UKUT 72 (AAC) at [103].

[90] DPA 2018 s 166.

[91] See DPA 2018 ss 27(5)-(7), 79(7)-(9) and 111(5)-(7).

[92] See definition of 'Tribunal' in DPA 2018 s 205(1).

[93] Up-to-date versions of these Rules are reproduced in volume 2 of this work.

[94] SI 2009/1976 as amended by SI 2010/43, 2010/2653, 2011/651 and 2012/500.

[95] SI 2008/2698 as amended by SIs 2009/274, 2009/1975, 2010/43, 2010/44, 2010/747, 2011/651, 2011/3243, 2012/500, 2012/1363, 2012/2007, 2012/2890, 2013/477 and 2013/606.

transferred to the Upper Tribunal under rule 19 of the FTT Rules, in particular national security certificate appeals.[96]

Further, section 23 of TCEA 2007 enables the Senior President to give practice directions as to the practice and procedure in the two Tribunals with the approval of the Lord Chancellor, and the Chamber President to give practice directions as to the practice and procedure in the chamber of which she is President with the approval of the Lord Chancellor and the Senior President. A brief summary of the rules follows. More detail is provided where relevant in Chapter 45 (which deals with FOIA and EIR appeals against decision notices) and Chapter 47 (which deals with FOIA and EIR appeals against information notices and enforcement notices).

44–017 FTT Rules

The FTT Rules are of general application and not specific to information rights appeals. In accordance with modern practice, they contain an 'overriding objective' provision.[97] An appeal to the FTT must be brought within 28 days of the relevant notice. An appeal is initiated by a notice of appeal compliant with rule 22 and sent to the Tribunal.[98] The Rules make generous provision for parties to be added to an appeal.[99] Unless striking out a case under rule 8, the Tribunal must hold a hearing before making a final decision unless each party agrees to it being determined without a hearing and the Tribunal is satisfied that it can properly determine the case in that way.[100] Rule 8(3) confers power on the Tribunal to strike out the whole or any part of proceedings or bar a respondent to an appeal from taking further part in the proceedings in any case if:

(a) a party has failed to comply with a direction which stated that failure to comply could lead to striking out;

(b) the party has failed to co-operate with the Tribunal to such an extent that it cannot deal with the case fairly or justly; or

(c) the Tribunal considers that there is no reasonable prospect of the relevant party's case (or part of it) succeeding.

The power under rule 8(3) is a case management power but it should only be exercised as a matter of last resort when there is no alternative and after analysis and reflection.[101] Although the power to strike out can be exercised without holding a hearing, that discretion is a judicial one that should be exercised with care, particularly in the case of a litigant in person, and justified with reasons.

44–018 FTT procedural powers

The Tribunal has wide powers to govern the extent and nature of any submissions and evidence it requires to receive; it can admit any evidence regardless of its strict admissibility at a civil trial and it can exclude otherwise admissible evidence where it would be unfair to admit it.[102] Rule 14 governs prevention of disclosure or publicity of documents and information.

---

[96] That is, appeals under DPA 1998 s 28 and FOIA s 60 (see definition in UT Rules rule 1).

[97] Rule 2.

[98] There is a general jurisdiction to extend time: rule 5(3)(a).

[99] Rule 9.

[100] Rule 32: note 'hearing' is defined in rule 1. For an example of an appeal which was allowed on the basis that a party had been deprived of the right of a hearing under this provision, see *IICUS v IC and BIS and Ray* [2011] UKUT 205 (AAC).

[101] See *Wise v IC and Blackpool CC* [2013] UKUT 030 (AAC) at [7]-[11] for a statement of the principles under which the Tribunal should act. Rule 8(3)(a) should not be used to punish a party for the way in which it has conducted the appeal: *Dransfield v Information Commissioner and Devon CC* [2013] UKUT 0550 (AAC) at [12]-[15].

[102] Rule 15. Note the Tribunal's *Hearing Bundles - Good Practice Guide* relating to the presentation of bundles for information rights hearings.

Rule 14(6) is of particular significance in information rights cases in that it enables the Tribunal to direct that documents and information are disclosed to it without being disclosed to a party. The suggested procedure is contained in an important 'Practice Note.'[103] Rule 14(10) directs the Tribunal to conduct its proceedings and record its decision and reasons in such a way as not to undermine the effect of such a direction and rule 35(4) enables the Tribunal to exclude a party from any part of a hearing if necessary in order to give effect to rule 14(10). Rule 38(2) requires the Tribunal to provide the parties with written reasons for a decision which finally disposes of the case.[104] Part 4 of the Rules contains provisions whereby the Tribunal is given power on an application for permission to appeal to the Upper Tribunal under section 11 of TCEA 2007 to review a decision if it is satisfied that there was an error of law in it.[105] Although superficially attractive in many cases this is a provision which needs to be exercised with great care, having close regard to the relevant rules and to section 9 of TCEA 2007 or real problems are likely to ensue.[106]

44– 019 Upper Tribunal Rules

The Tribunal Procedure (Upper Tribunal) Rules 2008 (and, in particular, Part 3) govern appeals from the FTT to the Upper Tribunal. National security certificate appeals[107] and other appeals on the direction of the President of the General Regulatory Chamber with the concurrence of the President of the Administrative Appeals Chamber of the Upper Tribunal are transferred and determined by the Upper Tribunal.[108] Such appeals are not appeals from the FTT but are direct appeals from the relevant decision of the Information Commissioner or Minister. Part 3 of the Rules does not apply to them, but the Tribunal must give 'tailor-made' directions.[109] The Upper Tribunal Rules include an 'overriding objective' and case management powers similar to those in FTT Rules. They contain at rule 14(10) specific provision that the Upper Tribunal must ensure that information is not disclosed contrary to the interests of national security and consequential provisions in relation to hearings and decisions.[110] In contrast to the position in the FTT, the Upper Tribunal can make any decision without a hearing, although it must have regard to views expressed by the parties and, no doubt, exercise its discretion judicially and give reasons.[111] Schedule 2 to the Rules makes special provision in relation to national security certificate cases.

44– 020 Costs

The information rights jurisdiction of the tribunals is in general a 'costs-free zone.'[112] Costs can only be awarded in specific circumstances provided by legislation. In the FTT the only costs orders that can be made are (a) wasted costs orders under section 29(4) of TCEA 2007[113] or (b)

[103] Dated May 2012. See further *Browning v Information Commissioner and DBIS* [2013] UKUT 236 (AAC) (20 May 2013).

[104] See *Ainslie v IC and Dorset CC* [2012] UKUT 441 as to the requirements of reasons, including majority reasons.

[105] Rule 44(1).

[106] See case *Webber (GW) v IC and Cabinet Office* [2017] UKUT 229 (AAC) at [42].

[107] That is, appeals under FOIA s 60 or under that section as applied and modified by EIR reg 18 (and, it is thought, appeals under DPA 2018 ss 27, 79 and 111).

[108] Rule 19 of FTT Rules. Appeals other than national security appeals are likely to have some special feature, eg to be of considerable public importance or involve complex or unusual issues.

[109] See rule 26A of amd Sch 2 to the UT Rules.

[110] Rules 14(11), 37 and 40.

[111] Rule 34.

[112] *Kirkham v IC (Recusal and Costs)* [2018] UKUT 65 (AAC) at [61].

[113] Orders in relation to costs wasted as a result of the improper, unreasonable or negligent act or omission of a legal

if the Tribunal considers that a party has acted unreasonably in bringing, defending or conducting the proceedings.[114] In relation to proceedings transferred or referred by, or on appeal from, the FTT (which would include not only appeals from decisions of the Information Commissioner transferred to the Upper Tribunal but also appeals from the FTT under section 11 of TCEA 2007) the Upper Tribunal can make the same costs orders as the FTT.[115] There are also special costs provisions in relation to 'national security certificate' appeals: the Tribunal can make:

— a wasted costs orders under section 29(4);

— a costs order if it considers that a party or its representative has acted unreasonably in bringing, defending or conducting the proceedings;

— if a certificate is quashed, a costs order against the relevant Minister and in favour of the appellant; and

— if the appeal is against the application of a certificate, a costs order against the appellant if the appeal is dismissed, and in his favour if the appeal is allowed.[116]

Where the tribunals have a discretion to award costs, the starting point will usually be that if an order for costs is to be made at all, it will be that costs should follow the event, that is that the loser will pay the winner as fairness and justice would normally require.[117] Unless an application is hopeless, the Upper or FTT must give a 'paying' party an opportunity to make representations before a costs order is made.

44– 021 Contempt generally

Contempt of court is the term given for an interference with the course of justice.[118] The law relating to contempt of court derives both from common law and statutory sources.[119] Contempts divide into:

— civil contempts (ie breaches of a court order);[120] and

— criminal contempts (other conduct that interferes with the due administration of justice).[121]

There is a wide variety of conduct that will amount to a contempt:

(1) Words spoken, or acts done, in or in the precincts of a 'court'[122] which obstructs or interferes with the due administration of justice or that is calculated to do so. This

---

or other representative of a party.

114 See rule 10 of the FTT Rules which also lays down the procedure in relation to making costs orders. For examples of the Tribunal's approach to such an application, see: *Van Natta v IC and Metropolitan Police*, FTT, 3 October 2011; *Royal Mail Group Ltd v IC*, FTT, 8 September 2010.

115 Rule 10(1)(b) of UT Rules.

116 Rule 10(1A). As discussed above, it is not clear if the rules have yet been amended to include appeals under DPA 2018 ss 27, 79 and 111, but it is anticipated that they will be.

117 *Bastionspark LLP v HMRC* [2016] UKUT 425 (TCC) at [16]. In quantifying costs that the paying party should pay, the mobility component of disability living allowance should be ignored: *Brace v IC and Merseyside Fire and Rescue Authority* [2019] UKUT 305 (AAC) at [15]-[20].

118 *A-G v Punch* [2002] UKHL 50, [2003] 1 AC 1046 at [2].

119 The main statutory sources are: Contempt of Court Act 1981; Administration of Justice Act 1960 s 12; County Courts Act 1984.

120 Proceedings for civil contempt are generally instituted by an aggrieved party, who may waive the contempt. Proceedings for civil contempt are civil proceedings for the purposes of the admissibility of evidence. A writ of sequestration is available only in the case of civil contempt (because the writ is a method of enforcement of a civil judgment or order).

121 Proceedings for criminal contempt are instituted by the Attorney-General. The proceedings are criminal in nature.

122 The Upper Tribunal will certainly be treated as a 'court' and the FTT will probably be treated as a 'court': see §44– 021, 44– 022, 44– 023.

will include an assault or threat on any person in court during court proceedings;[123] disturbing and obstructing the court by insulting behaviour in its presence and at a time when it is actually sitting.[124]

(2) Making a sound recording of proceedings without the leave of the court.[125]

(3) Refusal of a witness to be sworn or to answer questions.[126]

(4) Publications that create a substantial risk that the course of justice will be seriously impeded or interfered with.[127]

(5) Publication of material in breach of tribunal order.[128]

(6) Interfering with a witness to a pending matter, the purpose or effect of which is to deter the witness from giving evidence or influence the nature of the evidence given.[129]

(7) To refuse or neglect to do an act required by a judgment or order of the court or tribunal within the time specified, or to disobey such an order of judgment requiring that a person refrain from doing an act.[130]

Examples (1)-(6) are criminal contempts, example (7) is a civil contempt.

44– 022 Contempt: FTT

In relation to a tribunal such as the FTT, contempt gives rise to two separate questions:

(a) whether the FTT is protected by the law of contempt at all; and

(b) if it is, whether the FTT itself has any power to deal with an alleged contempt or whether it can only be dealt with by some other court, either on reference to it or of its own motion.

The answers to these two questions depend on whether the FTT is a 'court of record' and, if it is a court of record, whether it is a superior court of record or an inferior court of record. The FTT is not declared by statute to be a 'court of record,' but its powers and procedural requirements point to it being a court of record.[131] If the FTT is a 'court of record', it is an inferior court of record.[132] For the purpose of the Contempt of Court Act 1981, the term 'court' includes any tribunal or body exercising the judicial power of the State.[133] It would appear that the FTT is a 'court' within the meaning of the 1981 Act (ie it exercises the judicial power of the State).[134] The FTT is not a 'superior court' within the meaning of the 1981 Act.[135] Any court

123 *Re Johnson* (1887) 20 QBD 68.

124 *R v Brompton County Court Judge* [1893] 2 QB 195; *Maharaj v AG for Trinidad and Tobago* [1977] 1 All ER 411; *Morris v Crown Office* [1970] 2 QB 114, [1970] 1 All ER 1079.

125 Contempt of Court Act 1981 s 9(1)(a).

126 *R v Phillips* (1983) 78 Cr App Rep 88; *AG v Mulholland* [1963] 2 QB 477, [1963] 1 All ER 767.

127 See Contempt of Court Act 1981 s 2.

128 *R v Horsham Justices, ex p Farquharson* [1982] QB 762 at 798.

129 *Re Johnson* (1887) 20 QBD 68.

130 The person must know of all the terms of the order: *Re W (Wards) (Publication of Information)* [1989] 1 FLR 246 at 261.

131 For example, its enforcement powers (TCEA 2007 s 27) and review of decisions (TCEA 2007 s 9). Ultimately it comes down to an impressionistic exercise based on a number of factors: see *AG v BBC* [1970] AC 303, [1980] 3 All ER 161.

132 On the basis that it is not mentioned in TCEA 2007 s 3(5).

133 Contempt of Court Act 1981 s 19.

134 In *Re Ewing* [2002] EWHC 3169 the High Court held that the predecessor tribunal, the Information Tribunal, was a 'court' within the meaning of the Contempt of Court Act 1981. It could be argued that the FTT is not exercising 'judicial power of the State' but simply the executive power of the State (since its jurisdiction under FOIA and EIR is to re-take the decision of the Information Commissioner, with power to 'substitute such other notice as could have been served' by the Information Commissioner - FOIA s 58(1)) albeit the FTT is required to go about it

of record, whether superior or inferior, has an inherent jurisdiction to deal summarily and of its own motion with a contempt committed in the face of the court.[136] In addition, the Queen's Bench Division of the High Court exercises a protective jurisdiction in relation to an inferior court of record and may act, whether on its own motion or otherwise, in respect of interference with the administration in proceedings in an inferior court.[137] To the extent that there is a shortfall in the powers of the FTT to compel attendance of a witness and to give evidence or produce documents, the FTT can refer any failure to comply with its orders to the Upper Tribunal and ask it to exercise its coercive powers.[138] It also seems likely that the FTT would also be considered a 'court' for the purposes of section 42 of the Senior Courts Act 1981 (which deals with vexatious litigants) in the same way as the Information Tribunal was.[139] It should be noted that the orders made by the FTT at the conclusion of information rights appeals will amount to the original or a substituted decision, information or enforcement notice of the Information Commissioner:[140] Such notices are enforceable at the instance of the Commissioner himself by certification to the High Court or Court of Session.[141] As for enforcement of monetary awards, sums payable under a decision of the FTT or Upper Tribunal are recoverable as if they were payable under an order of the county court or High Court, with analogous provisions in relation to Scotland and Northern Ireland.[142]

44– 023 Contempt: Upper Tribunal

The Upper Tribunal is a superior court of record.[143] It is a 'court' within the meaning of the Contempt of Court Act 1981[144] It is also almost certainly a 'court' for the purposes of the common law of contempt.[145] As such, the Upper Tribunal will have all the powers of the FTT[146] as well as power to deal summarily with a contempt committed outside the tribunal.[147] There are no rules relating to this jurisdiction and presumably the Upper Tribunal would follow the practice and procedure of the High Court as closely as possible.

---

judicially. However, the courts have elsewhere been quite ready to find such merit-review tribunals to be courts for the purposes of the 1981 Act: *P v Liverpool Daily Post and Echo Newspapers plc* [1991] 2 AC 370 at 417 (Mental Health Review Tribunal); *R (Mersey Care NHS Trust) v Mental Health Review Tribunal* [2004] EWHC 1749 (Admin), [2005] 1 WLR 2469; cf *General Medical Council v BBC* [1998] 1 WLR 1573, [1998] 3 All ER 426.

135 As it does not exercise powers equivalent ot those of the High Court.

136 *Balogh v St Albans Crown Court* [1975] QB 73, [1974] 3 All ER 283; *R v West Yorkshire Coroner, ex p Smith (no 2)* [1985] QB 1096, [1985] 1 All ER 100; *Re M (a minor)* [1999] Fam 263, [1999] 2 All ER 56.

137 *Balogh v St Albans Crown Court* [1975] QB 73, [1974] 3 All ER 283; *Bush v Green* [1985] 1 WLR 489, [1985] 3 All ER 721; *Re G (a child)* [2003] EWCA Civ 489, [2003] 1 WLR 2051.

138 See FTT Rules r 7(3). The Upper Tribunal's powers are under TCEA 2007 s 25.

139 See case *Re Ewing* [2002] EWHC 3169 at [40], but note that that case was, strictly speaking, only concerned with the Information Tribunal sitting on an appeal under DPA 1998 s 28(4).

140 FOIA s 58.

141 See discussion of this procedure below at §§50– 001 to 50– 003.

142 TCEA 2007 s 27.

143 TCEA 2007 s 3(5).

144 *R (MMK) v SSHD* [2017] UKUT 198 (IAC) at [11].

145 See the factors discussed in *AG v BBC* [1970] AC 303, [1980] 3 All ER 161.

146 See §44– 021, 44– 022, 44– 023 above.

147 This will include: assaulting, obstructing, threatening or otherwise interfering with persons officially connected with proceedings in the tribunal; attempting to suppress evidence by bribery; publication of words that are intended to interfere with the course of justice. It is also a contempt to make a witness statement containing a statement of truth without an honest belief in its truth: *Malgar Ltd v RE Leach Engineering Ltd* [2000] CP Reg 39, [2000] FSR 393; *Sony Computer Entertainment Inc v Ball* [2004] EWHC 1984 (Ch); *Solicitor General v Dodd* [2014] EWHC 240 (QB), [2014] FSR 27; *GB Minerals Holdings Ltd v Short* [2015] EWHC 1387 (TCC), [2015] TCLR 7.

44– 024 Human Rights Act 1998

The Tribunals themselves are subject to the Human Rights Act 1998.[148] However, the rights given by the FOIA do not give rise to 'civil rights and obligations' such as to require the Tribunals to comply with Art 6 of the ECHR in deciding cases under that Act,[149] but there may be occasions where Art 6 does apply: for example, where the civil rights of a third party are affected.[150] Furthermore, the Tribunals will obviously have regard to other provisions of the ECHR in exercising its jurisdiction (particularly in considering where the public interest lies when considering the applicability of any of the exemptions to disclosure in FOIA). Although the Tribunals are probably not public authorities for the purposes of FOIA, they may be 'controllers' for the purposes of the data protection legislation.

---

148 Human Rights Act 1998 s 6(1) and (3). See the discussion on the impact of the Human Rights Act in Ch 4.

149 *BBC v Sugar* [2008] EWCA Civ 191, [2008] 1 WLR 2289 at [41], [42] and [52] and *Browning v Information Commissioner and DBIS* [2013] UKUT 236 (AAC) (20 May 2013) at [82].

150 For example, a disclosure that will arguably breach contractual rights in relation to confidential information.

CHAPTER 45

FOIA and EIR appeals

1. FIRST STAGE: INTERNAL REVIEW

45–001 Internal review

A person who is dissatisfied with the response of a public authority to his or her request for information under FOIA or the EIR will normally first seek 'internal review' of that response by the public authority before resorting to the Information Commissioner, the tribunal system or the courts.

45–002 Section 45 code of practice

The code of practice issued under s 45 of FOIA states that it is best practice for public authorities to provide internal procedures for dealing with disputes about the handling by them of requests for information, which will usually be dealt with as a request for 'internal review.'[1]

[1] See FOIA s 45(2)(e) and Pt 5 of the Code. The current version of the Code was issued by the Cabinet Office on 4 July 2018.

Such disputes may arise from complaints by persons who have made requests for information about a failure to comply with s 1(1)(a) or (b) of the Act promptly[2] or objections to the contents of a notice of refusal by the public authority made under s 17(1), (3) or (5) relying on an exemption in Part II of the Act or stating that s 12 or s 14 apply to relieve it of the duty to comply with the request.[3] A notice under s 17 must, if appropriate, contain reasons for reliance on an exemption in Part II of the Act and reasons for claiming that the public interest in disclosure is outweighed by the public interest in maintaining the exemption[4] and must contain details of any complaints procedure and of the right to complain to the Information Commissioner under s 50.[5] The code provides that a request for an internal review should normally be accepted if made within 40 days of the public authority's decision. The internal review should provide for a fair and thorough review of procedures and decisions under the Act.[6] If possible, reviews should be undertaken by someone other than the person who took the original decision and they should 're-evaluate' their handling of the request.[7] Applicants should be informed of the outcome of the review and a record kept.[8] Reviews should be dealt with within targets which should normally be 20 days.[9] If the decision is that the information should be disclosed, it should be provided at the same time as the outcome of the review if possible.[10] In any event, the applicant should be informed of his right to apply to the Information Commissioner for a review of whether the public authority has met the requirements of the Act.[11]

45– 003 Statutory encouragement

The policy of the Act is to encourage attempts at resolving disputes by means of the internal complaints procedure. Thus, any notice of refusal of a request under s 17 of the Act must include particulars of any complaints procedure maintained by the public authority or state that it does not have one[12] and the Information Commissioner should not deal with an application under s 50 of the Act if it appears to the Commissioner that the complainant has not exhausted any complaints procedure which complies with the Code of Practice.[13]

45– 004 Environmental information

To the extent that a request for information captures 'environmental information',[14] the applicant has a right of internal review conferred by the EIR.[15] Where an applicant's request

---

2 Sections 1(1)(a) and (b) give the basic rights to be informed whether the public authority holds the information and to have it communicated; s 10(1) generally requires compliance within 20 working days of a request, but permits extensions in certain circumstances: see §§22– 020 to 22– 027.

3 Section 12 provides exemption where the cost of compliance would exceed an appropriate limit and s 14 provides exemption where the request is vexatious.

4 FOIA s 17(1)(c) and 17(3).

5 FOIA s 17(7).

6 Code of Practice para 5.8.

7 Code of Practice para 5.9.

8 Code of Practice para 5.10.

9 Code of Practice para 5.4.

10 Code of Practice para 5.11.

11 Code of Practice para 5.12.

12 FOIA s 17(7)(a).

13 FOIA s 50(2)(a).

14 As to the meaning of which, see §17– 011.

15 EIR reg 11; EI(S)R reg 16. No doubt by an oversight there is no modification to s 50(2)(a) of the FOIA provided

for information covers both 'environmental information' and other information, although the provenance of the applicant's right to internal consideration is different, the practical consequences are negligible.

2. SECOND STAGE: APPLICATION TO THE INFORMATION COMMISSIONER

45– 005 Application formalities

The second stage for a person who is dissatisfied with the response by a public authority to a request for information is an application to the Information Commissioner under s 50(1) of FOIA or that section as imported by the EIR.[16] The section is framed in such a way that it is only the person who made the original request for information who can apply. The application is for a decision whether, in any specified respect, the request for information has (or, by implication, has not) 'been dealt with in accordance with the requirements of Part I [of the Act]'.[17] There are no procedural requirements for making a complaint to the Information Commissioner. The Commissioner's website includes a standard complaint form for use in relation to the FOIA and EIR. This indicates that complaints will be dealt with on a 'first-come, first-served' basis. In investigating a complaint the Information Commissioner is entitled to make her own enquiries and to formulate a case on behalf of an applicant; the Commissioner has a duty to act fairly in the way he deals with an application, but this does not necessarily mean that every communication between her and an applicant or third party must be copied to the public authority.[18]

45– 006 Complaint: procedural grounds

The reference in s 50(1) to a request not having been dealt with in accordance with the requirements of Part I of the Act encompasses a wide range of potential complaints of a procedural nature. A complainant may apply to the Commissioner for a decision whether any of the following matters are in accordance with the Act:

(1) Whether a request for information made of a body to which the Act has limited operation (eg the BBC) falls or does not fall within the limited area of operation or whether the body is 'public authority' for the purposes of the EIR;[19]

(2) The level of fee sought by the public authority for complying with its duty to inform the applicant whether it holds information of the description specified in the request and for communicating that information to him;[20]

(3) The time taken by the public authority for complying with the request;[21]

(4) The means by which the public authority communicated the information to the

---

in EIR reg 18(4), although in the case of requests for environmental information the complaints procedure will be under reg 11 not the Code of Practice.

16 EIR reg 18. See further §18– 029.

17 FOIA s 50(1).

18 *South Lanarkshire Council v Scottish IC* [2013] UKSC 55, [2013] 1 WLR 2421 at [29]-[33]; *Fish Legal and anor v IC and ors* [2015] UKUT 52 (AAC) at [55].

19 *Sugar v BBC* [2009] UKHL 9, [2009] 1 WLR 430, [2009] 4 All ER 111 at [35]-[36].

20 FOIA s 9.

21 FOIA s 10. Even if there has been a breach of s 10, the Information Commissioner will have no power to specify any steps that must be taken by the public authority: *Harper v IC and Royal Mail Group plc* [2005], IT, 15 November 2005. The Commissioner can, however: (1) make a good practice recommendation under FOIA s 48; (2) mention the matter in her annual report under FOIA s 49; or (3) issue an enforcement notice under FOIA s 52, requiring adherence to time-limits.

applicant;[22]

(5) The refusal of a public authority to comply with a request on the basis of the cost of compliance being estimated to exceed the appropriate limit;[23]

(6) The refusal of a public authority to deal with a request on the basis that it is vexatious or is identical or substantially identical to an earlier request from the applicant;[24]

(7) The failure by an appropriate records authority upon receipt of a request to comply with its obligations under s 15 of the Act;

(8) The failure by a public authority to provide advice and assistance;[25] and

(9) The failure of a refusal notice to contain the information required under s 17 of the Act.

45– 007 Complaint: refusal grounds

Where none of the procedural matters are relevant and a public authority either:

— does not inform an applicant whether or not it holds information of the description specified in his request; or

— does not communicate to that applicant some or all of the requested information held by it,

the applicant's request will not have been dealt with in accordance with the requirements of Part I of the Act unless one or more of the qualifications introduced by s 1(2) and s 2 of the Act apply. An applicant may complain that, notwithstanding a public authority's denial that it holds information coming within the terms of the request,[26] it does in fact do so and that section 1(1)(a) and (subject to the effect of any exemptions) section 1(1)(b) have not been complied with. This raises a straight issue of fact which has to be determined on the balance of probabilities.[27] If the public authority seeks to rely on any of the exemptions in s 2, the Commissioner must consider:

(1) whether the information held by the public authority answering the terms of the request is exempt information by virtue of any provision in Part II (ss 21-44);

(2) if a provision by which the information is rendered exempt information does not confer absolute exemption, whether the public interest in maintaining the exemption outweighs the public interest in disclosing that information;

(3) whether the duty to confirm or deny that the public authority holds information of the description specified in the request has been disapplied by any provision in Part II; and

(4) if the duty to confirm or deny has been disapplied by any provision in Part II, whether the public interest in maintaining the exclusion of that duty outweighs the public interest in disclosing whether the public authority holds that information.

Depending upon the exemption, (1) and (3) involve considering, in relation to each piece of

---

[22] FOIA s 11.

[23] FOIA ss 12 and 13.

[24] FOIA s 14.

[25] FOIA s 16.

[26] The request must be read objectively in the light of the background circumstances: *Berend v IC and LB of Richmond*, IT, 12 July 2007 at [86]; *Dept for Culture, Media & Sport v IC*, IT, 22 February 2010 at [16].

[27] When such an issue is raised it is open to the Commissioner (and in due course the relevant Tribunal) to review the adequacy of the public authority's search for the information having regard if appropriate to the Lord Chancellor's Code of Practice on the keeping, management and destruction of records issued under FOIA s 46: see *Bromley v IC and Environment Agency*, IT, 31 August 2007 at [13]; *Babar v IC and British Council*, IT, 14 November 2007 at [31]; *Ames v IC and Cabinet Office*, IT, 24 April 2008 at [10]; *Weait v IC*, IT, 17 July 2007; *James v IC and DTI*, IT, 25 September 2007. See further §24– 003. It has frequently happened that additional information has emerged in the course of proceedings before the Information Commissioner or Tribunal.

information, whether the particular attributes identified in the exemption are present or the likely effects of its disclosure upon an identified interest. Where a conclusive certificate has been issued, (1) and (3) above will be answered to the extent that the information sought is covered by the certificate.

45– 008 Commissioner's function

On a section 50 application, the Information Commissioner is under a duty to consider whether a request has been dealt with in accordance with FOIA or EIR. That duty is performed by reference to the information available and arguments made to the Commissioner and limited by the terms of the request for information. But in performing her task she will have regard to the position of the complainant, the public authority and third parties and bear in mind that the complainant (and on occasions the public authority) may not be able to articulate all possible points. The Commissioner is entitled to consider any exemption or exclusion which seems to her to merit consideration even if not raised by the parties;[28] and, it follows, it is open to a public authority to seek to rely on new arguments and on exemptions or exclusions not previously invoked.[29] Further, the Commissioner can consider a case under the FOIA regime if she thinks that the public authority has wrongly identified information as 'environmental' and dealt with it under EIR and apply similar or equivalent exemptions or exclusions as appropriate, and vice versa.[30] If the Commissioner reasonably requires any information for the purposes of determining whether the public authority has complied with the requirements of Part 1 of the Act, the Commissioner can serve an 'information notice' on the public authority requiring it to furnish her with such information as is specified in the notice.[31] The Commissioner does not have to serve such a notice and is at liberty to use informal methods of investigation.[32] In a case involving a qualified exemption it is for the Commissioner to decide on the basis of all the material available to her where the public interest lies; this is a matter of judgment and not a discretionary decision.[33] Under section 50 of FOIA the Commissioner must consider whether the request for information has been dealt by the public authority in accordance with Part I of the Act, her decision must be based on the factual position as it existed at the date when the public authority made its decision (including any review decision) and any public interest balance must be assessed as at that date.[34] If circumstances have changed since the public authority's refusal to disclose information such that, for example, to do so has become unlawful, impossible or wholly impractical, it is open to the Commissioner to decide under s 50(4) that the public authority need take no steps notwithstanding the breach of the Act.[35] Obviously the Commissioner (and the Tribunal) can only require disclosure of

---

28 See *IC v Malnick and The Advisory Committee on Business Appointments* [2018] UKUT 72 (AAC) at [77], quoting extensively from *Birkett v DEFRA* [2011] EWCA Civ 1606, [2012] PTSR 1299.

29 *R (Evans) v Attorney-General* [2015] UKSC 21, [2015] AC 1787 at [73], [74].

30 *Fenning v IC and Christchurch BC*, FTT, 27 April 2015 at [19].

31 Information notices, including appeals against them, are considered at §47– 002 below. Note that the Commissioner is not confined to requiring the public authority to furnish her with recorded information: FOIA s 51(8). Thus it is open to the Commissioner to serve a public authority with an information notice that quizzes a public authority and requires it to reduce to writing what is currently unrecorded.

32 *King v IC and DWP*, IT, 20 March 2008 at [90].

33 *Lotz v IC*, FTT, 12 April 2017 at [9].

34 *All Party Parliamentary Group on Extraordinary Rendition v IC and FCO* [2015] UKUT 0377 (AAC) at [43]-[59]; *R (Evans) v Attorney-General* [2015] UKSC 21, [2015] AC 1787 at [72]-[73]. Whilst these authorities are binding, the logic of a merit-review tribunal making a fresh decision by reference to a historic temporal standpoint, particularly given the ability of the requester to make a fresh request for exactly the same information in order to have it re-determined by reference to later facts, is difficult to credit.

35 *IC v HMRC and Gaskell* [2011] UKUT 296 (AAC) at [15]-[31]; *All Party Parliamentary Group on Extraordinary Rendition v IC and FCO* [2015] UKUT 0377 (AAC) at [31]; *Home Office v IC and Cobain* [2015] UKUT 0027 (AAC) at [26];

information that comes within the terms of the relevant request.[36] The Commissioner has no power to modify the terms of a request for information.[37]

45– 009 Timing

Although the Act does not prescribe who bears the burden of persuading the Information Commissioner that the public authority has or has not acted in accordance with the Act,[38] the Tribunal has expressed the view that the Information Commissioner should normally communicate with the complainant and the public authority before reaching any decision, and not merely rely on the complaint notice and accompanying documentation.[39] Furthermore, the Commissioner should draw attention to any perceived breach of the duty to provide advice and assistance under s 16 of FOIA, notwithstanding that the complainant has not expressly raised that matter.[40] In a case where the Commissioner agrees with a public authority that information need not be disclosed, it is of particular importance that the Commissioner herself sees the disputed information and makes a full investigation.[41] The Commissioner can encourage the parties to settle, but if the parties cannot agree she must reach a decision on the complaint. Once a decision has been made and a decision notice has been issued, the Commissioner is functus: there is no sensible way of applying section 50 if it is construed as allowing more than one decision on the same complaint.[42]

45– 010 Commissioner's decision

Unless the Information Commissioner forms the view that the complainant has not exhausted an internal complaints procedure, that there has been 'undue delay' in making the application, that it is frivolous or vexatious or that it has been withdrawn or abandoned,[43] she must serve a 'decision notice' on the complainant and the public authority in question.[44] There is no set form for a decision notice: it is just a 'letter setting out the Commissioner's decision.'[45] If the decision is that the public authority has failed to communicate information or to confirm or deny whether it holds the information as required by s 1(1) of the Act or that it has failed to comply with any of the requirements of s 11[46] or s 17,[47] the decision notice must specify the steps to be taken by the authority to comply with its obligations and the period within which they must be taken.[48] The decision notice must also contain details of the right of appeal to the

---

Stürmer v IC and Derbyshire DC [2015] UKUT 568 (AAC) at [92].

36 *OGC v IC* [2008] EWHC 774 (Admin), [2010] QB 98, [2008] ACD 54 at [109]-[110].

37 *Home Office v IC and Cruelty Free International* [2019] UKUT 299 (AAC) at [14].

38 Compare the Australian Freedom of Information Act 1982 s 61 referred to in §45– 014. In relation to the burden of proof, see §§5– 024 to 5– 031.

39 See *Barber v IC*, IT, 20 February 2006 at [16]-[19].

40 *Barber v IC*, IT, 20 February 2006 at [16]-[19].

41 See: *Beam v IC and FCO*, IT, 12 May 2009 at [14]-[15]; and *Health Professionals Council v IC*, IT, 14 March 2008 at [52].

42 *IC v E Malnick and The Advisory Committee on Business Appointments* [2018] UKUT 72 (AAC) at [85]. Although the Upper Tribunal appears not to have taken into account the Interpretation Act 1978 s 12(1), the conclusion probably still holds good.

43 In any of which cases he must notify the complainant accordingly and let him know the grounds for not making a decision: FOIA ss 50(2) and 50(3)(a).

44 FOIA s 50(3)(b).

45 *Sugar v BBC* [2009] UKHL 9, [2009] 1 WLR 430, [2009] 4 All ER 111 at [37].

46 Obligations of public authority as to means by which information is communicated.

47 Obligations of public authority in relation to notices of refusal of requests for information.

48 FOIA s 50(4); but note the discussion above at §45– 008.

Tribunal provided by s 57 of the Act.[49] There is no express provision requiring that reasons be given, and there are arguments both for and against,[50] but the better view is probably that the Commissioner is under a duty to provide such reasons as he can.[51] In practice the Commissioner always gives reasons, sometimes quite substantial ones.

45– 011 Non-compliance certificates

There is a provision allowing a government department or the National Assembly for Wales (or any other public authority specified in an order made by the Secretary of State) to avoid the effect of a decision served on it relating to a failure to comply with s 1(1) in respect of exempt information[52] where within 20 days of the notice there is a certificate signed by an 'accountable person' given to the Information Commissioner stating that he has on reasonable grounds formed the opinion that there was no failure.[53] The 'accountable person' must give reasons to the complainant for the opinion he has formed unless that would involve the disclosure of exempt information.[54] An 'accountable person' (apart from special provisions about the National Assembly of Wales and the Northern Ireland Assembly) is a member of the cabinet or the Attorney-General and a copy of the certificate must be laid before Parliament.[55] This provision in effect purports to remove the supervision of the Tribunal as to where the public interest lies in relation to the disclosure of exempt information and represents a kind of 'trump card' in the hand of the higher executive.[56] The effectiveness of this provision was considered in detail *R (Evans) v Attorney-General*[57] (which concerned the Prince of Wales's letters to ministers), where the Supreme Court struck down the Attorney-General's certificate challenged by way of judicial review. In that case, the applicant journalist had appealed to the Upper Tribunal, and that Tribunal concluded that the requested information should be disclosed. The Attorney-General then issued a certificate, which the journalist challenged byway of judicial review. Part of the Supreme Court's reasoning in ruling against the certificate was that it was not open to the Attorney-General to seek to use a certificate to overturn a judicial decision such

---

49 FOIA s 50(5).

50 For example: *against*: (1) the fact that there is an express requirement to give 'grounds' when refusing to make a decision in FOIA s 50(3)(a); (2) the fact that in many cases there may be difficulties in giving reasons which do not themselves reveal the information which is the subject-matter of a request and the lack of any statutory guidance as to how this problem should be dealt with (compare in relation to the FTT: FTT Rules r 28; *for*: (1) the need for a party considering an appeal under FOIA s 57 to have some basis for deciding whether or not to appeal (2) in particular the provision at s 58(2) that the Tribunal can review 'any finding of fact on which the notice in question was based' and (3) the fact that the public authority in question must give reasons for deciding that an exemption under Pt II of FOIA applies and for claiming that the public interest in disclosing the information in question is outweighed by the public interest in maintaining the exemption (see FOIA ss 17(1)(c) and 17(3)).

51 *Scottish Ministers v Scottish Information Commissioner* [2007] CSIH 8, 2007 SCLR 253 at [17], dealing with the analogous FOI(S)A. Whether or not a claim for exemption is upheld, the Commissioner's ability to give reasons will be constrained by the need to avoid disclosing the information for which exemption is claimed.

52 In other words, information falling within one or more of the provisions in Pt II of the Act, irrespective of whether the public interest weighs in favour of disclosure: FOIA s 84.

53 FOIA ss 53(1), (2). Such a certificate was issued by Jack Straw, the Secretary of State for Justice on 24 February 2009 in respect of *Cabinet Office v IC and Lamb*, IT, 27 January 2009, upholding a decision of the Commissioner dated 19 February 2008, requiring the disclosure of minutes of Cabinet meetings of 13 and 17 March 2003 relating to the invasion of Iraq. A certificate was issued by Dominic Grieve, Attorney-General, on 16 October 2012 in respect of letters from the Prince of Wales to various Ministers which the Upper Tribunal had required the various departments concerned to disclose: see *R (Evans) v Attorney-General* [2015] UKSC 21, [2015] AC 1787.

54 FOIA s 53(6) and (7).

55 FOIA s 53(8) and (3).

56 The trumping effect of such certificates is a feature of freedom of information legislation in each of the Westminster-style comparative jurisdictions. See §§51– 014 (Australia); 51– 021 (New Zealand); 51– 030 (Canada); and 51– 038 (Ireland). In the USA, an equivalent is achieved with exclusions: see §51– 003.

57 *R (Evans) v Attorney-General* [2015] UKSC 21, [2015] AC 1787.

as that of the Upper Tribunal. What the position would have been had the certificate been issued at an earlier stage (eg following a decision notice by the Commissioner but before an appeal to the Tribunal) is not entirely clear from the judgment. In so far as requested information is 'environmental information' the position is somewhat clearer: the section 53 provision for an executive override incorporated into the EIR by reg 18(6) is not compatible with Art 6 of the relevant Directive (2003/4/EC) under which the Regulations were made (which requires provision for a full and final review by a court of any refusal to supply environmental information).[58]

3. THIRD STAGE: APPEALS AND THE FIRST-TIER TRIBUNAL

45– 012 Destinations for appeals

The tribunal or court with which an appeal should be lodged depends upon the decision that is being appealed against or otherwise challenged:

(1) Where a section 50 complainant or a public authority wishes to appeal against a decision notice of the Information Commissioner, that appeal is made to the FTT under section 57 of FOIA.[59] In suitable cases (eg where the appeal is of considerable public importance or involves complex or unusual issues), the appeal may be transferred to the Upper Tribunal.[60] Appeals against decisions made under FOIA and the EIR are allocated to the General Regulatory Chamber of the FTT.

(2) Where a person wishes to appeal against a national security certificate, that appeal must be made to the Upper Tribunal.[61]

(3) Certificates issued by the House Authorities under ss 34(3) and 36(7) of FOIA are not subject to any express appeal procedure.[62] Theoretically any challenge to such a certificate would have to be by way of judicial review.[63]

(4) Where a particular person has no right to appeal against an appealable decision (eg a third party who may be affected by a decision to disclose information and those who could appeal have chosen not to do so),[64] that person will need to challenge the decision by a claim for judicial review against the body making the decision.[65]

(5) Where a person has no right to appeal against a decision that is outside the appeal regime, that person will need to challenge the decision by a claim for judicial review against the body making the decision.[66]

45– 013 FTT practice and procedure

The relevant rules of procedure in relation to information rights appeals are the FTT Rules.[67] The general practice and procedure of the FTT has been considered above and reference

58 *R (Evans) v Attorney-General* [2015] UKSC 21, [2015] AC 1787 at [100]-[105] per Lord Neuberger.

59 See §44– 008 above for the statutory basis for the Tribunal's jurisdiction.

60 FTT Rules r 19(2)-(3).

61 See further §45– 026.

62 See further §5– 042. As to the effect of such certificates, see §§5– 033-5– 034.

63 See further §5– 043.

64 Where an appeal is initiated under (1) or (2), the third party can apply to join those proceedings.

65 See further §§45– 032-45– 034, 46– 018.

66 See further §45– 028. The First-tier Tribunal cannot decide common law right claims: *Home Office v IC and Cruelty Free International* [2019] UKUT 299 (AAC) at [27].

67 ie the 'FTT Rules'.

should be made thereto.[68] Particular points to note are as follows:

(1) There is no prescribed form of notice of appeal to the FTT, but the Tribunal Service provides a specimen form (T98) which it is sensible to use.[69] There is no requirement to accompany the notice of appeal with a skeleton argument. For that reason it is also sensible for the notice of appeal to have a more extensive narrative element and to develop the argument so as to make good the particular grounds of appeal.

(2) There is no requirement to serve the notice of appeal on the Information Commissioner or on the other party, but that too is a sensible course to follow.

(3) The notice of appeal must be received by the FTT within 28 days from the date on which the Information Commissioner's decision notice was sent to the appellant.[70]

(4) The practice and procedure in relation to parties to the appeal is considered below,[71] but it should be noted that the rules allow the Tribunal, instead of adding a party, to let any person attend and take part in a hearing or make written submissions.[72]

(5) In relation to decisions to strike out an appeal or response under r 8(3)(c) it should be noted that 'the appellant's case' is not the same as 'the grounds on which the appellant relies in his notice of appeal' and that in deciding to strike out on the grounds that the appeal has no reasonable prospect of success the Tribunal needs to take account of its power to review the whole position on an appeal and be satisfied that on no legitimate view of the facts or the law could the appeal succeed, bearing in mind that the grounds of appeal set out by an unrepresented appellant may be inarticulately expressed.[73]

(6) When deciding not to hold a hearing under rule 32(1) the Tribunal must be satisfied that it can properly determine the issues without a hearing even where the parties agree to this course: this must involve a consideration of whether an unrepresented appellant can properly formulate his appeal in writing, whether there are matters which may need to be explored further with the Commissioner or the public authority and whether holding a hearing is proportionate.

(7) Appeals to the Tribunal are not purely adversarial and there is an onus on the Tribunal to make allowances to enable appellants to participate fully in the proceedings.[74]

45– 014 Nature of an FTT appeal

The only basis for the appeal is that the relevant notice was 'not in accordance with the law' or was based on an exercise of discretion by the Commissioner which the Tribunal would exercise

---

68 See §§44– 016 to 44– 020 above.

69 A precedent completed form T98 with grounds is included in volume 2 of this work.

70 See FTT Rules, r 22(1). See the decision of the Court of Appeal in *Rana v LB Ealing* [2018] EWCA Civ 2074 for the meaning of the phrase "sent to [a party]" in the context of the Employment Appeal Tribunal Rules 1993. Note that the Tribunal has a general discretion to extend time under rule 5(3)(a) and would no doubt do so if a similar interpretation were adopted in the context of the FTT Rules which might cause injustice to an appellant who was unaware of a decision notwithstanding it had been "sent to" them. As to principles adopted on an application to extend time see also *X v IC* [2010] UKUT 236 (AAC) at [17]-[18].

71 See §45– 015.

72 FTT Rules, r 33(2).

73 *Jones v IC and Dept of Environment (Northern Ireland)* [2016] UKUT 82 (AAC).

74 *Jones v IC and Dept of Environment (Northern Ireland)* [2016] UKUT 82 (AAC) at [47]. While the Tribunal can raise legal points not taken by the parties (provided that it gives them adequate opportunity to address the Tribunal on those points), it is not open to the Tribunal to undertake its own search for evidence.

differently.[75] The Tribunal exercises a full merits appellate jurisdiction, and so stands in the shoes of the Commissioner when making its decision: if it disagrees with the Commissioner's decision, it must decide that her decision was not in accordance with the law even though it may not be vitiated by public law error.[76] The Tribunal may review any finding of fact on which the decision notice was based.[77] Although the Tribunal can take account of new evidence and of certain developments since the Commissioner's decision,[78] in relation to an appeal against a decision notice it, like the Commissioner,[79] must consider both the factual position and undertake the public interest balance as they existed at the date of the decision by the public authority.[80] The FTT is an 'experienced specialist jurisdiction' which routinely decides issues under FOIA[81] and it is entitled to and must therefore decide independently and afresh where the public interest lies if that is relevant to the question whether the public authority was required to disclose the requested information.[82] It is inherent in that task that the Tribunal must consider any relevant evidence or issue put to it by the parties, including a new exemption relied on by the public authority.[83] There is no special provision relating to the onus of persuading the Tribunal to allow an appeal.[84] The Tribunal has power to decide whether it has jurisdiction to deal with an appeal: thus, it can decide, for example, whether the body from whom information was requested is indeed a public authority.[85] There can be no appeal to the Tribunal where the Commissioner has decided not to issue a decision or other notice: but that refusal may found a claim for judicial review.[86]

45– 015 Parties to an FTT appeal

An appeal to a Tribunal may be launched only by the requester/section 50 applicant or the public authority.[87] The Information Commissioner is always a respondent to any appeal under s 57 and she will generally make submissions in support of the decision notice, but she is unlike other parties. She is an independent regulator and has a role in assisting in or ensuring the proper administration of the FOIA and EIR regimes. As such, her role is not to defend the decision come what may. She keeps the merits of the decision under review and makes

---

75 FOIA s 58(1).

76 *IC v E Malnick and The Advisory Committee on Business Appointments* [2018] UKUT 72 (AAC) at [90]; *E.ON plc v IC and Fish Legal* [2019] UKUT 132 (AAC) at [42].

77 FOIA s 58(2).

78 For example, changes in position of the parties or the discovery of information answering the request for information.

79 See §45– 008 above.

80 See: *Chagos Refugees Group v IC and FCO*, FTT, 4 September 2012 at [22]-[29] and cases therein cited; *Maurizi v IC and CPS* [2019] UKUT 262 (AAC) at [168], [184].

81 *Oxford Phoenix Innovation Limited v IC and Medicines and Healthcare Products Regulatory Agency* [2018] UKUT 192 (AAC) at [53].

82 Note that the exercise of balancing the public interest is not a matter of discretion but of evaluative judgment for the Tribunal: see *Lotz v IC*, FTT, 12 April 2017 at [9].

83 *IC v Malnick and The Advisory Committee on Business Appointments* [2018] UKUT 72 (AAC) at [45], [78], quoting from *Birkett v DEFRA* [2011] EWCA Civ 1606, [2012] PTSR 1299.

84 This is in contrast to the position in Australia, where it is expressly provided that in an appeal to the Australian Administrative Appeals Tribunal the burden of establishing that a decision to withhold information was justified lies on the public authority: Freedom of Information Act 1982 (Cth of Aust) s 61. The position is otherwise in relation to appeals against information and enforcement notices by public authorities: see rule 26 of the IT (EA) Rules which casts the onus of proof onto the Commissioner but which expressly excludes appeals under s 57(1).

85 See *Fish Legal and anor v IC and ors* [2015] UKUT 52 (AAC) at [55].

86 See §45– 028ff.

87 Or the putative public authority: *Fish Legal and anor v IC and ors* [2015] UKUT 52 (AAC).

appropriate concessions at any stage in the proceedings.[88] Where the appellant is a public authority, the person who made the request for information may apply to be joined as an additional party to the appeal.[89] Where the appellant is the person who made the request, the public authority may apply to be joined as an additional party to the appeal. The public authority will often be able to make a valuable contribution to the appeal, both in relation to the public interest and in adducing evidence of likely resultant harm to one of the interests protected by Part II of the Act. The Tribunal has invariably acceded to both sorts of joinder applications. The Tribunal may well regard a failure by a public authority to apply to join an appeal as 'not entirely sensible.'[90] In that situation the Tribunal may decide to join the public authority even though no application has been made.[91] Where both the person who made the request and the public authority to whom it was addressed are dissatisfied with a decision notice, they may both appeal to the Tribunal.[92]

45– 016 New grounds of exemption

After considerable doubt on the point and notwithstanding ss 10 and 17 of FOIA, it is now well established that a public authority is entitled to raise a new ground of exemption before the Tribunal.[93] The Tribunal can also consider a case under a different regime as between FOIA and EIR.[94] After much debate in the case law it is also now established that it is open to public authorities to rely on procedural exemptions like sections 12 and 14 of FOIA for the first time before the Tribunal.[95] Any late reliance will always be subject to the Tribunal's case management powers:[96] a public authority is not entitled as of right to raise a new exemption at any stage in the proceedings before the Tribunal, least of all at the last moment before a hearing.

45– 017 Evidence

Although proceedings before the Tribunal are not purely adversarial, the inquisitorial element of the proceedings does not extend to the Tribunal undertaking its own search for evidence. It is thus for each party to adduce such evidence as it considers will advance its case or weaken that of the other side. The Tribunal can (and almost invariably does) receive evidence that was not considered by the Commissioner in reaching her decision. The Tribunal has a large measure of discretion as to which evidence it should receive and the form it will take.[97] The public authority will, if it wishes, be able to use as evidence the information that is caught by

---

88 *Lubicz v IC and King's College London* [2015] UKUT 555 (AAC) at [51]. Unfortunately it is not always possible for the Commissioner to participate fully in all appeals or to instruct counsel where that may help because of limited resources which can create difficulties for the Tribunal.

89 FTT Rules r 9(3); UT Rules r 9(3). The Commissioner normally advises the requester of an appeal by a public authority and invites him to apply to join. The Tribunal would normally allow such joinder but whether fairness requires a requester who has not applied to join the appeal to be invited to do so at a later stage will depend on all the circumstances: *Lubicz v IC and King's College London* [2015] UKUT 555 (AAC) at [52].

90 *Webber (GW) v IC and Cabinet Office* [2017] UKUT 229 (AAC) at [7].

91 *IC v Bell* [2014] UKUT 106 (AAC).

92 See, eg: *Hogan and Oxford City Council v IC*, IT, 17 October 2006.

93 *DEFRA v IC and Birkett* [2011] UKUT 39 (AAC), [2011] UKUT 17 (AAC), upheld on appeal at *Birkett v DEFRA* [2011] EWCA Civ 1606, [2012] PTSR 1299; *IC v E Malnick and The Advisory Committee on Business Appointments* [2018] UKUT 72 (AAC) at [78].

94 *Fenning v IC and Christchurch BC*, FTT, 27 April 2015 at [19].

95 *McInerney v IC and Dept of Education* [2015] UKUT 0047 (AAC) at [2], [21]-[42].

96 *McInerney v IC and Dept of Education* [2015] UKUT 0047 (AAC) at [2], [31].

97 FTT Rules rr 15, 16.

the request. Such evidence will be taken in as 'closed material.'[98] The Information Commissioner will normally be able to see and make submissions on 'closed material.' In a 'closed session' the Information Commissioner will be able to make valuable submissions from a neutral standpoint that may be supportive of the person who made the request. The Tribunal may at any stage call for and inspect the information that is captured by the terms of the request, even if the parties themselves do not make the suggestion.[99] 'Closed material' may constitute the best evidence for the purpose of determining an appeal. The Tribunal routinely receives opinion evidence from civil servants and others relating in particular to the likelihood and extent of harm which will be caused to an interest protected by an exemption if information is disclosed. The Tribunal accords due respect to such opinions but is not bound by them. The Upper Tribunal with some justification has questioned the extent to which oral evidence of this nature is appropriate.[100]

45– 018 Closed material and hearings

The practice of the FTT in relation to 'closed material' being considered by the Tribunal (in particular, the information that answered the terms of the request for information and which gave rise to the appeal) is set out is set out in a 'Practice Note' dated May 2012 which the Upper Tribunal has stated should be taken into account by the FTT.[101] The Tribunal should always ensure that as much evidence as possible is given in open hearing.[102] Where a public authority proposes to rely on closed material, it should always make prior written application to do so.[103] The Tribunal draws a distinction between closed material that comprises the requested information itself and other closed material which is brought forward in order to uphold the claims for exemption. The Tribunal is more reluctant to allow the latter to be closed material and may only permit it where, were that material the subject of a FOI request, it would be covered by an exemption. Where the Tribunal permits the adduction of closed evidence, fairness will require the requester to be told as much as possible about the argument he has to address and of the evidence and the reasoning it is based on.[104] The FTT must keep a record of any closed session and provide a 'gist' of what happened to an excluded party at the earliest opportunity.[105] Even when there is no excluded party from a closed hearing because no-one choses to attend the hearing at all, the Tribunal should nevertheless canvass with the parties

98 The procedure to be followed if closed material is to be received in evidence is set out at §45– 018.

99 See, eg: *Bellamy v IC and DTI*, IT, 4 April 2006 at [32]. Note also FTT rule 5(3)(d) which enables the Tribunal to require any person to supply information or documents.

100 *APPGER v IC and FCO* [2013] UKUT 0560 (AAC) at [148]. The UT reasoned that 'the duty of candour [on the part of the public authority], documentary evidence and argument would provide an appropriate and sufficient process to fairly advance and test the risks of harm to the public interest being advanced, as it is in, for example, many PII claims.' It might also fairly be observed that ordinarily opinion evidence is only permitted from a witness with qualifications in a recognised field of expertise and who has expressed an overriding duty to the court or tribunal. It is very easy for such witnesses in FOI appeals (whose evidence is manifestly serving the interests of the public authority) to stray into arrogating to themselves the evaluative issue that is the exclusive domain of the Tribunal, ie what is the likelihood of disclosure of this information harming the interest protected by the exemption and what is the likely scale of that harm. The proper function of such witnesses is to put forward material from which the Tribunal can form the judgment as to the likelihood that disclosure of the requested information would harm the interest protected by the exemption and the likely scale and types of harm to that protected interest.

101 *Browning v Information Commissioner and DBIS* [2013] UKUT 236 (AAC) at [17]-[18].

102 *FCO v IC and Plowden* [2013] UKUT 0275 (AAC) at [10]; *D v IC* [2018] UKUT 441 (AAC) at [25], [33], [40].

103 The application is made under rule 14(6) of the FTT Rules.

104 *APPGER v IC and FCO* [2013] UKUT 0560 (AAC) at [154]; *FCO v IC and Plowden* [2013] UKUT 0275 (AAC) at [10].

105 *APPGER v IC and FCO* [2013] UKUT 0560 (AAC) at [147].

who are present what material should be made public.[106] A party which presents evidence on a closed basis cannot insist that it is not later disclosed in a decision of the Tribunal or by way of a 'gist':[107] nor, it seems, can a party seek to 'withdraw' evidence once adduced because the Tribunal later decides to disclose it.[108] Where the FTT gives 'closed reasons' these may need to be particularly detailed in order to inform the appeal court or tribunal of the reasoning process by reference to the contents of the document.[109] In very rare cases, which are likely to be both sensitive and of great public interest, it is open to the Tribunal (likely to be the Upper Tribunal) to order that a party excluded from the closed hearing and unable to see withheld material be represented by a 'special advocate'.[110] There are also special rules in relation to national security certificate appeals to the Upper Tribunal under section 60 of the FOIA which are considered further below in the context of such appeals under data protection legislation.[111]

45– 019 Relief on an FTT appeal

On an appeal under s 57:

- — if the Tribunal considers that the decision notice is 'not in accordance with the law'[112] or,
- — to the extent that the decision notice involved an exercise of discretion by the Information Commissioner, if the Tribunal considers that the Commissioner ought to have exercised his discretion differently,

the Tribunal must allow the appeal 'or' substitute an alternative notice such as could have been served by the Commissioner; but otherwise it must dismiss the appeal.[113] After much debate in the case law it is now established that the word 'or' must be read as 'and/or'[114] and that the Tribunal has the power to allow an appeal and issue a substitute decision notice: something that has been the normal practice of the FTT and Information Tribunal since the beginning of the jurisdiction.[115] After some debate it is also established that the Tribunal cannot remit matters to the Commissioner to decide.[116] Nor can it in effect remit matters to the public authority to review, even where the public authority has not considered the issue raised and did not participate in the appeal. Rather, the Tribunal must exercise its powers to reach a decision in relation to any issue which arises and will therefore on occasion simply have to adjourn and require the attendance and assistance of the Commissioner and/or the public authority where they have not participated previously.[117] The substitute decision notice must specify any steps

---

106 *Cabinet Office v IC* [2017] UKUT 229 (AAC) at [3].

107 *Cabinet Office v IC* [2017] UKUT 229 (AAC).

108 As appears to have been suggested in *APPGER v IC and FCO* [2015] UKUT 68 (AAC) though the point did not arise in practice: see [27].

109 *APPGER v IC and FCO* [2013] UKUT 0560 (AAC) at [43].

110 *Campaign against the Arms Trade v IC and MoJ*, IT, 26 August 2008 at [15] and [21]: this was a case concerning national security, although it was not a 'national security certificate appeal.' The basis for such an order is discussed in *Browning v Information Commissioner and DBIS* [2013] UKUT 236 (AAC) at [78]-[81]. The Upper Tribunal itself has express power to allow disclosure to a party's representative only (and not the party): UT Rules rule 14(5) and 14(6).

111 See Chs 47 and 48.

112 This will be referable to the request for information as it was submitted to and decided upon by the public authority: *Home Office v IC and Cruelty Free International* [2019] UKUT 299 (AAC) at [14].

113 FOIA s 58(1).

114 In other words, 'or' is being used to denote disjunction, not exclusive disjunction.

115 *IC v E Malnick and The Advisory Committee on Business Appointments* [2018] UKUT 72 (AAC) at [103]-[104]; *Richards v IC and Welsh Government* [2019] UKUT 379 (AAC).

116 See *IC v Bell* [2014] UKUT 106 (AAC) and *Clucas v IC*, FTT, 4 June 2014.

117 *Oxford Phoenix Innovation Limited v IC and Medicines and Healthcare Products Regulatory Agency* [2018] UKUT 192 (AAC)

to be taken by the public authority in the light of the Tribunal's decision in the same way as an original decision notice given by the Commissioner;[118] what steps are required may depend on events which have taken place since the request (eg the information may have been supplied in the context of the appeal). The Tribunal (like the Commissioner) retains a discretion not to order disclosure of information that ought to have been disclosed under FOIA or EIR: for example, where the request has become vexatious since it was made[119] or other exceptional circumstances like disclosure involving the law being broken or having become impossible,[120] notwithstanding that the 'default setting' must be in favour of disclosure. The substitute decision notice will be enforceable at the Commissioner's initiative in the same way as an original decision notice is under section 54(1) of FOIA. The Tribunal can also make a recommendation to the Information Commissioner that she use her powers under s 48 to make a practice recommendation to the public authority concerned.[121] A costs order may be made in limited circumstances.[122]

4. FOURTH STAGE: APPEALS TO THE UPPER TRIBUNAL

45–020 Appeals to the Upper Tribunal

Under section 11 of TCEA 2007 any party to a case has a right of appeal to the Upper Tribunal on any point of law arising from a decision made by the FTT other than certain 'excluded decisions.'[123] Such appeals are assigned to the Administrative Appeals Chamber of the Upper Tribunal and generally heard by a single judge of the Tribunal unless the Senior President or Chamber President considers that the appeal involves a question of law of special difficulty or an important point of principle or practice, or that it is otherwise appropriate, in which case it can be decided by two or three judges of the Upper Tribunal.[124] Section 11(5)(b) and (c) exclude from this right decisions of the FTT on appeals concerning national security certificates but such appeals are in any event automatically referred to the Upper Tribunal under rule 19(1A) of the Tribunal Procedure (FTT) (General Regulatory Chamber) Rules 2009. An appeal under section 11 of TCEA 2007 may only be brought with the permission of the FTT or the Upper Tribunal. The requirement for permission is not an additional requirement of the right to appeal: it is designed to filter out appeals which do not in fact raise any arguable point of law.

45–021 Appeal procedure

General practice and procedure in the Upper Tribunal and the UT Rules have already been considered in the previous chapter. Points of note in relation to FOIA and EIR appeals are as follows:

(1) In the first instance, permission to appeal to the Upper Tribunal against the decision of the FTT is sought from the FTT.[125] Unless otherwise specified in the

at [16]-[48].

118 FOIA s 50(4).

119 *Stürmer v IC and Derbyshire DC* [2015] UKUT 568 (AAC) at [91]-[95].

120 *Home Office v IC and Cobain* [2015] UKUT 0027 (AAC) at [24]-[31].

121 For an example, see *Bowbrick v IC and Nottingham City Council*, IT, 28 September 2006 at [70].

122 See further §44– 020.

123 As defined in TCEA 2007 s 11(5).

124 Practice Statement on Composition of the Upper Tribunal AAC para 3(a).

125 UT Rules r 21(2).

order of the FTT giving its decision, the application for permission to appeal must be received by the FTT no later than 28 days after the date on which the FTT sends the applicant the appealed decision or the final written reasons (whichever is the later, if they are separate).[126] If an applicant is out-of-time, the application for permission to appeal should include a request for an extension of time and should explain the reason that the application was not lodged within time.[127]

(2) There is no prescribed form for making application to the FTT for permission to appeal to the Upper Tribunal, but the Tribunal Service provides a specimen form (T96) which it is sensible to use.

(3) There is no requirement to accompany the application for permission to appeal with a skeleton argument. For that reason it is also sensible for the application to have a more extensive narrative element and to develop the argument so as to make good the particular grounds of appeal.

(4) There is no requirement to serve the notice of appeal on the Information Commissioner or on the other party, but that too is a sensible course to follow.

(5) The application and any ancillary matter arising under Part 4 of the FTT Rules is dealt with on the papers by the FTT judge unless, exceptionally, the Chamber President considers that it is appropriate for it to be decided by the same members who decided the appeal or a newly constituted Tribunal.[128] The issue for the judge is whether there is any arguable point of law disclosed by the application. If the judge refuses permission to appeal reasons must be given and the appellant must be notified of the right to apply to the Upper Tribunal for permission to appeal and the time limit for doing so.[129] If the judge decides that there is an error of law in the decision the Tribunal may undertake a review of the decision under section 9 of TCEA 2007 rather than giving permission to appeal, but this power is one to be exercised with great caution as it is full of procedural 'pit-falls.'[130]

(6) Where the FTT refuses to grant permission to appeal or does not admit the application for permission to appeal (ie because it is lodged out-of-time and the application for an extension of time is rejected), the applicant may apply to the Upper Tribunal for permission to appeal to it against the decision of the FTT.[131] In that situation:

(i) The application to the Upper Tribunal must be received by the Upper Tribunal no later than a month after the date on which the FTT sent its notice of refusal of permission to appeal (or to admit the application for permission to appeal) to the applicant.[132]

(ii) There is no prescribed form of application for permission to appeal, but the Tribunal Service provides a specimen form (UT13) that stands as both the application for permission to appeal and the notice of appeal, and it is sensible to use that.

(iii) There is no requirement to accompany the application with a skeleton

---

126 Rule 42(2). Note the decision of the Court of Appeal in relation to appeals to the Employment Appeal Tribunal relating to similar provisions in *Rana v LB Ealing* [2018] EWCA Civ 2074.

127 FTT Rules r 42(4).

128 Senior President's Practice Statement dated 27 February 2015 on composition of FTT para 15.

129 FTT Rules r 43(3).

130 See *Webber (GW) v IC and Cabinet Office* [2017] UKUT 229 (AAC) for a case where the FTT purported to exercise the power and ensuing problems.

131 UT Rules r 21(2).

132 UT Rules 21(3)(b). The Upper Tribunal can extend this time upon application being made: UT Rule r 21(6).

argument. For that reason it is also sensible for the application to have a more extensive narrative element and to develop the argument so as to make good the particular grounds of appeal.

(iv) The application must be accompanied by a copy of the FTT's decision and written statement of reasons, together with the reasons given by the FTT for refusing permission.[133]

(v) There is no requirement to serve the application for permission on the other parties.[134]

(vi) The application for permission is dealt with, in the first instance, on paper. The Upper Tribunal can strike out an application for permission to appeal.[135]

(vii) If the Upper Tribunal grants permission to appeal, it will send written notice of the permission and of the reasons for any conditions or limitations (if any) to each party, and the application for permission to appeal will stand as the notice of appeal.[136]

(viii) If the Upper Tribunal refuses permission to appeal (or imposes conditions or limitations on an appeal) without a hearing, then the appellant may within 14 days of the decision being sent apply for that decision to be reconsidered at a hearing.[137]

(7) Where the FTT grants permission to appeal to the Upper Tribunal and the appellant wishes to proceed with that appeal, then:

(i) The appellant must within one month of the date on which the FTT sent the permission decision lodge with the Upper Tribunal a notice of appeal.[138]

(ii) There is no prescribed form of notice of appeal, but the Tribunal Service provides a specimen form (UT13) which it is sensible to use.

(iii) The notice of appeal must be accompanied by a copy of the FTT's decision and written statement of reasons, as well as the FTT's notice of permission to appeal.[139]

(iv) It is not necessary for the appellant to serve the notice of appeal on the other parties. On receipt of the notice of appeal, the Upper Tribunal will itself send a copy of the notice of appeal and all the accompanying documents to each respondent.[140]

(8) A respondent may provide a response to a notice of appeal:[141]

(i) A respondent's response must be lodged with the Upper Tribunal no

---

133 UT Rules r 21(5).

134 The Upper Tribunal will do this automatically if permission to appeal is granted: UT Rules r 22(2)(b).

135 *Kirkham v IC* [2018] UKUT 303 (AAC).

136 UT Rules r 21(2)(b).

137 UT Rules r 22(3)-(5). The Upper Tribunal has decided that although it cannot strike out an appeal under rule 8(3)(c) it can strike out an application for permission to appeal, which would tend to undermine the right to a hearing; however, the Upper Tribunal would only exercise the jurisdiction to strike out with care and as a last resort and would need to consider whether it was right to decide to strike out the application without a hearing: see *Gaskin v IC and Norwich CC* [2016] UKUT 382 at [17] (quoting from *Dransfield v IC* [2016] UKUT 0273 (AAC).

138 UT Rules r 23(1)-(2). If out of time, the appellant can seek an extension of time by including an application for it in the notice of appeal, giving the reason why the notice was not lodged within time: UT Rules r 23(5).

139 UT Rules r 23(4).

140 UT Rules r 23(6)(a).

141 UT Rules r 24(1A).

later than one month after the respondent was sent notice that the Upper Tribunal had granted permission to appeal or, where the FTT granted permission to appeal, after the respondent was sent the notice of appeal to the Upper Tribunal.[142]

(ii) The respondent's response must state the grounds on which the respondent relies, including any grounds on which the respondent was unsuccessful in the FTT but intends to rely before the Upper Tribunal.[143]

(iii) The respondent's response must also state whether the respondent wants the case to be dealt with at a hearing.[144]

(iv) The respondent does not need to serve the other parties with a copy of the response, as the Upper Tribunal will do that.[145]

(v) The appellant may, within one month of receiving the respondent's response, lodge a reply with the Upper Tribunal, which the Tribunal will copy to the other parties.[146]

(9) The Upper Tribunal has power to require the FTT to provide it with 'reasons' or other information or documents in relation to the decision or the proceedings before it.[147]

(10) There are similar rules about disclosure to those applying in the FTT and, in particular, the Upper Tribunal has the power to order disclosure of documents or information by one party on the basis it will not be disclosed to other parties, which is obviously an important rule in the context of appeals in information rights cases.[148]

(11) The Upper Tribunal can admit any evidence it thinks fit[149] but is unlikely to do so often in information rights appeals given that an appeal is only on a point of law and the Upper Tribunal will respect the findings of fact of the FTT.[150]

(12) The Upper Tribunal can decide the final appeal without a hearing, although it must have regard to any view expressed by a party about whether to hold a hearing and the form thereof, and in doing so will have regard to the overriding objective[151] and (no doubt) to the needs of unrepresented litigants.[152]

(13) The Upper Tribunal has power to hold hearings in private excluding certain parties in the same way as the FTT.[153]

---

142 UT Rules r 24(2). An extension of time can be sought by making application for it in the response and explaining why it was not done in time: UT Rules r 24(4).

143 UT Rules r 24(3)(e).

144 UT Rules r 24(3)(f).

145 UT Rules r 24(5).

146 UT Rules r 25.

147 UT Rules r 5(3)(n): this power would enable the Upper Tribunal to seek additional or clarificatory reasons in a suitable case, or notes of evidence or comments from the members of the Tribunal in relation to an allegation of bias: this is analogous to the practice when the Employment Appeal Tribunal is hearing an appeal from the employment tribunal.

148 UT Rules r 14, in particular r 14(8).

149 UT Rules r 15.

150 An exception would be in a case where the public authority was maintaining that 'no steps' should be required under section 50(4) because of circumstances which have changed since the FTT hearing.

151 UT Rules r 2.

152 UT Rules r 34(1)-(2).

153 See UT Rules r 37(4)(c) and (d) in particular: the Upper Tribunal would be under the same obligations to disclose

45– 022 Grounds of appeal

An appeal on a 'point of law'[154] will most commonly be on the grounds:

(a) that the Tribunal misdirected itself in law or misunderstood or misapplied the law;
(b) that there was no evidence to support a particular conclusion or finding of fact made by the Tribunal; or
(c) that the decision was perverse in that it was one which the Tribunal, directing itself properly on the law, could not have reached or one which was obviously wrong.[155]

Other grounds of appeal include:

(d) actual or apparent bias on the part of the FTT
(e) some other procedural irregularity causing unfairness;
(f) a failure by the FTT to address all the issues identified by the appellant;[156] and
(g) the giving of inadequate reasons.[157]

Although in general procedural decisions within the discretion of the FTT will be respected, more scrutiny will be given to a decision to strike out an appeal under rule 8(3)(c) and the procedure surrounding it than ordinary case management decisions.[158] As a general rule, the UT will not entertain as a ground of appeal a point that was not made a matter of submission to the FTT, at least where that point was not so obvious that the FTT should have addressed it of its own motion.[159]

45– 023 General approach

In considering the FTT's decision, the Upper Tribunal must exercise a measure of judicial restraint. Not only should it not interfere in relation to permissible findings of fact, but it should consider any reasons given by the FTT 'as a whole', make due allowance for the 'exigencies of daily court room life' and not subject reasons to a narrow textual analysis to find an error so as to substitute their own judgment for that of the lower tribunal. The Upper Tribunal must also accord due respect to the fact that the FTT is an experienced specialist jurisdiction and assume, unless the contrary is shown, that it knew how to perform its function, even if every detail of a line of reasoning is not recorded.[160]

---

as much as possible to a party excluded from a hearing as the FTT in analogous circumstances: see §45– 018 above.

154 This right of appeal is similar to that formerly provided by section 59 of FOIA for appeals from the Information Tribunal to the High Court. What amounted to a 'point of law' under that section was considered in *BBC v Sugar* [2008] EWCA Civ 191, [2008] 1 WLR 2289 at [15], [17] (jurisdiction); *BBC v IC* [2009] EWHC 2348 (Admin), [2010] EMLR 6 at [52] (point of law equivalent to judicial review), [83]-[85] (respect for decisions of specialist tribunal: this point may not apply in the context of an appeal from the FTT to Upper Tribunal, which are both within the tribunal system and have access to specialisation); *HM Treasury v IC* [2009] EWHC 1811 (Admin), [2010] 2 WLR 931 at [54] (errors in tribunal's approach to public interest balance).

155 In short, an appellant will need to show that the outcome was wrong: *Highways England v IC and Manisty* [2018] UKUT 423 (AAC) at [6]. See, in relation to the analogous provisions about appeals from employment tribunals to the Employment Appeal Tribunal: *British Telecommunications plc v Sheridan* [1990] IRLR 27 at 30; *Melon v Hector Powe Ltd* [1981] ICR 43, [1980] IRLR 477; *Neale v Hereford and Worcester County Council* [1986] ICR 471, [1986] IRLR 168; *Watling v William Bird & Son (Contractors) Ltd* [1976] ITR 70.

156 *Bennis v IC and Stratford-upon-Avon DC* [2019] UKUT 317 (AAC).

157 The FTT's reasons must be adequate and, in the case of a dispute over a qualified exemption, comprise a clear statement of the competing public interests and an explanation of why the FTT came to the conclusion that it did: *Dept for Education v IC and Whitmey* [2018] UKUT 348 (AAC) at [17]-[19]. The FTT must not give the appearance of rubber-stamping a decision of the Information Commissioner by simply adopting what the Commissioner has said: *Adedeji v IC* [2019] UKUT 309 (AAC) at [10].

158 See, for example: *Jones v IC and Dept of Environment (Northern Ireland)* [2016] UKUT 82 (AAC); *Dransfield v Information Commissioner and Devon CC* [2013] UKUT 0550 (AAC) at [15].

159 *Cabinet Office v IC and Webber* [2018] UKUT 410 (AAC) at [39].

160 See: *Oxford Phoenix Innovation Limited v IC and Medicines and Healthcare Products Regulatory Agency* [2018] UKUT 192

45– 024 Disturbing findings etc

Although neither the findings of primary fact made by the FTT nor its evaluative conclusions based upon those findings can be challenged in the Upper Tribunal unless on the basis there was no evidence for them or that they were perverse, the Upper Tribunal does have some scope for reviewing decisions about the public interest balance. Its role is not to re-evaluate the material that was before the FTT and upon which it reached its conclusions, but to ensure that the FTT did not err in law in reaching those evaluative conclusions, including the public interest balance.[161] The boundaries of what is a question of law in this context are somewhat fluid: whether a particular factor is relevant to the public interest or not is clearly a question of law[162] but the relative weight to be given to different factors is more questionable. Although the Upper Tribunal will be particularly reluctant to gainsay the FTT's evaluative assessment of where the public interest lies, it may be more willing to become involved in a case relating, for example, to central government policy making (possibly) or an area where the expertise of the FTT 'does not reach', such as diplomatic matters.[163] As a specialist tribunal itself the Upper Tribunal is entitled to provide guidance on issues that arise on the public interest balance and its own decisions are binding authorities, so that it can review a decision of the FTT in the light of such guidance.[164]

45– 025 Relief on an appeal

If the Upper Tribunal finds that the making of a decision appealed involved the making of an error on a point of law it can (but need not) set aside the decision of the FTT.[165] Unlike the FTT, the Upper Tribunal has powers of remittal: if it decides to set aside the decision, it must either remit the case to the FTT for reconsideration or remake the decision itself;[166] since it is not a 'primary fact finder' the Upper Tribunal is likely to remit a case where new factual areas are likely to arise because a new exemption has been raised.[167] Where the Upper Tribunal remits a matter to the FTT on account of inadequate reasons by the FTT, it will require the FTT to re-conduct the appeal and not simply supplement the earlier reasons.[168] On a remittal it may give directions as to whether there should be a new FTT and give procedural directions.[169] If it allows an appeal and remakes the decision of the FTT it is open to the Upper Tribunal to substitute its own 'decision notice' for that of the Commissioner and to exercise the discretion which the Commissioner and the FTT have under section 50(4) of FOIA not to specify any steps to be taken by the public authority if that is appropriate;[170] in considering whether to do so the Upper Tribunal is entitled to take account of events which have occurred at any stage up to the making of the Upper Tribunal's decision even if it took place after the Commissioner's or the FTT's decision.[171]

(AAC) at [49]-[55] where the jurisprudence is helpfully set out; *Keane v IC* [2016] UKUT 461 (AAC) at [52]-[53].

161 *Cabinet Office v IC and Aitchison* [2013] UKUT 0526 (AAC) at [4].

162 See eg *IC v E Malnick and The Advisory Committee on Business Appointments* [2018] UKUT 72 (AAC) at [65].

163 *FCO v IC and Plowden* [2013] UKUT 0275 (AAC) at [12]-[13].

164 *Cabinet Office v IC and Aitchison* [2013] UKUT 0526 (AAC) at [3]-[11].

165 TCEA 2007 s 12(1) and (2)(a).

166 TCEA 2007 s 12(2)(b).

167 *IC v E Malnick and The Advisory Committee on Business Appointments* [2018] UKUT 72 (AAC) at [112].

168 *Coombs v IC and University of Durham* [2019] UKUT 119 (AAC) at [25].

169 TCEA 2007 s 12(3).

170 See §§45– 008 and 45– 019 as to the Commissioner's and FTT's discretion under section 50(4) of FOIA.

171 See *Stürmer v IC and Derbyshire DC* [2015] UKUT 568 (AAC) at [91]-[94].

45– 026 National security certificates

National security certificates issued under ss 23(2) and 24(3) of FOIA and reg 15(1) of the EIR may be appealed to the Upper Tribunal under an appeal mechanism provided for by ss 60-61 of FOIA and reg 18 of the EIR.[172]

(1) In relation to certificates issued under ss 23(2) and 24(3) of FOIA and reg 15(1) of the EIR, such an appeal may be brought by the Information Commissioner or any applicant whose request for information is affected[173] The Tribunal may allow the appeal and quash the certificate if it finds: in relation to a certificate under s 23(2) of FOIA, that the information referred to in the certificate was not exempt information by virtue of s 23(1);[174] or, in relation to a certificate under reg 15(1) of the EIR, that, applying the principles applied by the court on an application for judicial review, the Minister or the person designated by him did not have reasonable grounds for issuing the certificate.[175]

(2) A second type of appeal may be brought under s 60(4) of FOIA by a party to any proceedings under or by virtue of that Act if it is claimed by a public authority or a data controller that a certificate issued under s 24(3) of FOIA which identifies the information to which it applies by means of a general description applies to particular information. It is arguable that such an appeal may also be brought under s 60(4) of FOIA by a party to any proceedings under the EIR where similar claims are made by a public authority in relation to a certificate issued under

[172] As to the effect of a national security certificate, see §§5– 040 and 26– 057-26– 060.

[173] FOIA s 60(1) and EIR reg 18(7)(a). Similarly, DPA 2018 ss 27(3), 79(5) and 111(3). FOIA s 60 is applied for the purposes of the EIR with modifications by EIR reg 18(1), (3)-(4), (7). Appeals under FOIA s 60 and EIR reg 18(7) are governed by UT Rules.

[174] FOIA s 60(2). The Tribunal is thus given full appellate jurisdiction to review the matter, unconstrained by any caveat that it 'apply the principles applied by the court on an application for judicial review' and assess only whether the minister had 'reasonable grounds for issuing the certificate' (cf FOIA s 60(3), DPA 2018 ss 27(4), 79(6) and 111(4), and EIR reg 18(7)).

[175] FOIA s 60(3) and 111(4); EIR reg 18(7). Similarly DPA 2018 ss 27(4), 79(6). In determining whether the minister did or did not have reasonable grounds for issuing the certificate, the Tribunal will inevitably have to assess whether the minister did or did not have reasonable grounds for concluding: in relation to FOIA s 24(3), that exemption from the relevant provision is, or at any time was, required for the purpose of safeguarding national security; or, in relation to EIR reg 15(1), that disclosure would adversely affect national security and would not be in the public interest. See the discussion of the analogous 'reasonable grounds' provision in FOIA s 53(2) in *R (Evans) v Attorney-General* [2015] UKSC 21, [2015] AC 1787. It would appear that the Tribunal is thus confined to applying only one of the three heads of judicial review identified in *Council of Civil Service Unions v Minister for the Civil Service* [1985] AC 374 at 410 (Lord Diplock) (ie irrationality but not illegality or procedural impropriety): if the minister took into account an irrelevant consideration or failed to take into account a relevant consideration, made an error of law or failed to act fairly in a procedural sense this will only be relevant if and in so far as it led or contributed to him not having reasonable grounds for issuing the certificate. So far as concerns 'the principles applied by the court on an application for judicial review' in relation to 'reasonable grounds', the Tribunal will review whether the minister's decision was reasonable or so unreasonable that no reasonable minister could have taken it (*Associated Provincial Picture Houses Ltd v Wednesbury Corp* [1948] 1 KB 223 (CA)) and the intensity of its scrutiny will increase if it can be shown that 'fundamental rights' are engaged (*R v Ministry of Defence, ex p Smith* [1996] QB 517 (CA) at 554 (Bingham MR)). If satisfied that a 'Convention right' as defined by the Human Rights Act 1998 has also been affected by the minister's decision and the appellant may have been the 'victim' of this for the purposes of that Act, the Tribunal will also need to go further and determine whether the decision to issue a certificate was compatible with that Convention right and would thus have to apply a more intensive proportionality-based standard of review: *R (Daly) v SSHD* [2001] UKHL 26, [2001] 2 AC 532 at [26]-[27] (Lord Steyn); *Baker v SSHD* [2001] UKHRR 1275, at [63]; *Gosling v SSHD*, IT, 1 August 2003 at [48]. See also: *Kennedy v Charity Commission* [2014] UKSC 20, [2015] AC 455 at [51]-[55]; *R (Lord Carlile of Berriew QC) v SSHD* [2014] UKSC 60, [2015] AC 915 at [31]-[34]; *Pham v SSHD* [2015] UKSC 19, [2015] 1 WLR 1591 at [59]-[60], [98], [108]-[110]. The language used in FOIA s 60(3) might also be thought to suggest that the Tribunal must focus solely on the grounds which the minister had in his mind at the time he issued the certificate (to the exclusion of other grounds which he might now wish to rely upon). However, this will not affect the eventual outcome because there is nothing to prevent a minister from issuing a fresh certificate on new grounds to replace one that has been quashed.

reg 15(1) of the Regulations.[176] The Tribunal has power to determine that the certificate in question does not apply to the information referred to by the public authority.[177]

5. FIFTH STAGE: APPEAL FROM UPPER TRIBUNAL TO COURT OF APPEAL

45–027 Appeal to Court of Appeal

Section 13 of TCEA 2007 provides for an appeal from the decision of the Upper Tribunal to the Court of Appeal. Again, decisions in relation to national security certificates are excluded.[178] The appeal is with permission of the Upper Tribunal or the Court of Appeal on the application of any party,[179] but such permission may only be granted if the court or tribunal considers that the proposed appeal would raise some important point of principle or practice or there is some other compelling reason for the appellate court to hear the appeal.[180] The Court of Appeal has power on the appeal to set aside the Upper Tribunal's decision and either re-make it or refer the matter back to the Upper Tribunal or the FTT.[181] The application for permission must be received by the Upper Tribunal within one month of the sending of the Upper Tribunal's written reasons for its decision to the party appealing.[182] The Upper Tribunal can review its decision on receiving such an application but only if it has overlooked a legislative provision or binding authority or there is a new binding authority decided since the original decision.[183] The procedure in the Court of Appeal is governed by the Civil Procedure Rules

---

176 EIR reg 18(1), (3), (4)(a)-(b) and (7)(a). This assumes that EIR reg 18(7)(a) operates to apply FOIA s 60(4) as if the reference therein to a certificate under FOIA s 24(3) were substituted by a reference to a certificate issued in accordance with EIR reg 15(1). The interaction between these provisions is not perfect, however, as EIR reg 18(7)(a) refers to 'the reference' in FOIA s 60 to a certificate under FOIA s 24(3) when there are three such references. Moreover, EIR reg 15(3)(b) allows for a certificate to 'identify the information to which it relates in general terms' while FOIA s 60(4) applies to a certificate 'which identifies the information to which it relates by means of a general description.'

177 The Tribunal is thus given full appellate jurisdiction to review such matters unconstrained by any caveat that it 'apply the principles applied by the court on an application for judicial review' and assess only whether the minister had 'reasonable grounds for issuing the certificate' (cf FOIA s 60(3), DPA 2018 ss 27(4), 79(6) and 111(4) and EIR reg 18(7)). The explanation for this is no doubt that the minister can issue a new certificate with a much clearer application if dissatisfied with a determination made by the Tribunal under FOIA s 60(5) or DPA 2018 s 27(7), 79(9) or 111(7). In *Nasresfahani v SSHD and Data Controller* [2014] UKUT 0487 (AAC), the Upper Tribunal nevertheless took a more restrictive approach to the construction of its powers under the equivalent appeal provision in DPA 1998, s 28(6) given the wording of the relevant certificate under s 28(2). See at [27]: 'However, as under the certificate it is for the Security Services [sic] to determine whether or not the exemption is required for the purpose of safeguarding national security, in effect it is in our judgment a question whether the Security Services [sic] have lawfully made that determination. That is therefore also a question that is in effect to be determined on administrative law principles and in particular whether the determination failed to have regard to material considerations or was perverse or otherwise unlawful.' FOIA s 60(4) or DPA 2018 s 27(7), 79(7) or 111(5) only provide for the resolution by way of appeal of a dispute over a certificate's applicability where it arises, in relation to FOIA, 'in any proceedings under this Act', in relation to DPA 1998, 'in any proceeding under or by virtue of this Act' and, in relation to EIR, 'in any proceedings under these Regulations.' — see EIR, reg 18(4)(a)(i). The reason for the different formulations is unclear and their effect depends on whether the need for 'proceedings' is given a strict or generous construction; the latter would expand the scope for having disputes over a certificate's applicability resolved by the Tribunal without the procedural need for separate 'proceedings'.

178 TCEA s 13(8).

179 TCEA s 13(4).

180 The Appeals from the Upper Tribunal to the Court of Appeal Order 2008 (SI 2008/2834).

181 TCEA s 14.

182 UT Rules r 44(4): see *Rana v LB Ealing* [2018] EWCA Civ 2074 on analogous rules in relation to appeals to the Employment Appeal Tribunal as to when reasons are sent to a party. The application for permission to appeal must comply with rule 44(7).

183 UT Rules r 45(1).

Part 52. Appeals to the Supreme Court from the Court of Appeal will be governed by the normal rules governing such appeals.

6. JUDICIAL REVIEW

45–028 Limits to judicial review

FOIA and the EIR provide for numerous decisions and actions to be taken by 'public authorities', and by the Information Commissioner, the Secretary of State, and Ministers and others who are given power to sign certificates (in particular, the Speaker of the House of Commons and the Clerk of the Parliaments).[184] There is no provision in the Act expressly excluding the supervisory jurisdiction of the Administrative Court to grant judicial review under Part 54 of the Civil Procedure Rules 1998 in relation to such decisions and actions,[185] so that in principle they would be susceptible to judicial review. In most cases, however, the Act itself provides an appeal or other means of challenge[186] and the court would be unlikely to give permission for, or grant, judicial review in such cases unless there were exceptional circumstances.[187] There are, however, a few cases where judicial review by an applicant may be appropriate because of a gap in the appeal rights provided by the Act, for example the exercise by a Cabinet Minister or the Attorney-General of their power under s 53 of the Act to override a decision or enforcement notice of the Information Commissioner can be judicially reviewed, there being no other form of appeal.[188]

45–029 Information Commissioner

As for the Information Commissioner, the exercise of more general powers such as issuing codes of practice might in principle be open to judicial review, but decision notices, enforcement notices and information notices issued by the Commissioner, which are subject to the extensive rights of appeal given by s 57, are unlikely to be open to such review. There is one decision of the Commissioner, namely a decision not to pursue a complaint under s 50(2), however, which is not subject to any right of appeal under the Act and which would therefore be susceptible to judicial review.[189] A failure by the Commissioner to take a decision at all might also be the subject of a judicial review claim,[190] as might a failure to take one within a

---

184 See, eg: FOIA ss 23(2), 24(3), 34(3), 36(7) and 53(2).

185 Section 56(1) states that the Act 'does not confer any right of action in civil proceedings in respect of any failure to comply with any duty imposed by or under [it]' but is unlikely to be construed as excluding judicial review: compare similar (but stronger) exclusionary wording considered in, *ex p Waldron* [1986] QB 824, [1985] 3 All ER 775 (CA).

186 For example, the right to complain to the Information Commissioner under s 50(1) that a public authority has not complied with Pt I of the Act, the right to appeal against a decision of the Information Commissioner under s 57(1), the right to appeal against national security certificates under s 60, the right to appeal against the decisions of the Information Tribunal under s 59.

187 See: *Halsbury's Laws of England*, 5th edn , vol 61 (London, LexisNexis, 2010) para 657.

188 *R (Evans) v Attorney-General* [2015] UKSC 21, [2015] AC 1787.

189 For example, in the *Sugar* litigation, Mr Sugar commenced judicial review proceedings in the face of the Information Commissioner's assertion (upheld by the High Court and Court of Appeal but not the House of Lords: see *Sugar v BBC* [2009] UKHL 9, [2009] 1 WLR 430, [2009] 4 All ER 111 at [36]) that there was no appeal against his finding that the information requested was not held by the BBC in its capacity as a public authority since it did not amount to a decision under section 50 of FOIA. See now *Fish Legal and anor v IC and ors* [2015] UKUT 52 (AAC) at [23]-[55], which makes clear that the Commissioner has jurisdiction under FOIA s 50 to consider whether a body is a public authority and thus her decision on the point is susceptible to appeal under FOIA s 57.

190 *Tuckley v IC and Birmingham City Council*, IT, 28 February 2008 at [37].

reasonable time even though, in contrast to the position in Scotland,[191] there is no express time limit on the taking of a decision.

45– 030 The Tribunals

In principle decisions of both the FTT and the Upper Tribunal are susceptible to judicial review, notwithstanding that the Upper Tribunal is a 'superior court of record.'[192] However, there is a right of appeal on a point of law from the FTT to the Upper Tribunal, and from the Upper Tribunal to the Court of Appeal, so that the only case in which judicial review is likely to be available is where the Upper Tribunal refuses permission for an appeal to it from the FTT, being a decision from which there is no right of appeal. In considering an application for judicial review in such a case, the High Court will apply the test governing the allowance of second appeals in the Courts of England and Wales.[193] In relation to national security certificate appeals, where there is also no right of appeal from the Upper Tribunal,[194] it seems likely that decisions of the Upper Tribunal would also in principle be susceptible to judicial review by the High Court.

45– 031 Certificates

National security certificates are open to challenge under s 60 so there is unlikely to be any basis for a judicial review of the act of the relevant Minister in signing the certificate.[195] However, certificates signed under ss 34(3), 36(7) and 53(2) are not open to such challenge. As stated above, certificates signed by a Cabinet minister or the Attorney-General under s 53 of FOIA are open to judicial review. Those signed by the Speaker of the House of Commons or the Clerk of the Parliaments under ss 34(3) and 36(7) are probably not amenable to judicial review, on the basis of Parliamentary privilege.[196] However the scope of Parliamentary privilege is ultimately for the courts and not Parliament itself to define. Parliament cannot create new forms of privilege. Therefore a certificate may only be conclusive as to whether disclosure would infringe an established privilege. It would still appear to be open to an individual or the Information Commissioner to challenge non-disclosure on the basis that disclosure would not infringe any established form of privilege, and that the Speaker of the House of Commons or the Clerk of the Parliaments has misconstrued the ambit of Parliamentary privilege.[197]

---

191 See FOI(S)A s 49(3)(b).

192 *Cart v The Upper Tribunal* [2011] UKSC 28, [2012] 1 AC 663 at [87].

193 *Cart v The Upper Tribunal* [2011] UKSC 28, [2012] 1 AC 663 at [57] and [94]. The test is that the case would raise some important point of principle or practice or that there is some other compelling reason for the Court to hear it. This is the same test as is used for granting permission to appeal from the Upper Tribunal to the Court of Appeal: see §45– 027 above.

194 TCEA 2007, s 13(8)(a)-(b).

195 There is a suggestion in *Norman Baker MP* [2001] UKHRR 1275 at [48] that there may be a distinction between the Minister not having reasonable grounds for issuing a national security certificate and it being unlawful for him to have done so; in the latter case there is no express provision for an appeal to the Tribunal in s 60(3) so that, the Tribunal thought, in such a case it would be necessary (and presumably possible) to apply to the Administrative Court for judicial review. It is thought unlikely that this would arise in practice.

196 See on Parliamentary privilege *Halsbury's Laws of England*, 5th edn , vol 78 (London, LexisNexis, 2010) paras 1076-1093; *R v Parliamentary Commissioner for Standards, ex p Al Fayed* [1998] 1 WLR 669, [1998] 1 All ER 93 (CA). There may be a legitimate distinction to be drawn between s 34(3) certificates and s 36(7) certificates: s 34(3) certificates are to the effect that the relevant Parliamentary officer certifies that exemption is necessary to avoid an infringement of Parliamentary privilege (more likely to be privileged) whereas s 36(7) certificates relate to the opinion of such officer that disclosure of information by Parliament would prejudice the effective conduct of public affairs (an opinion which may be open to review without considering whether Parliamentary privilege is properly claimed).

197 However for a more restrictive interpretation of the court's powers in determining the ambit of Parliamentary privilege see Eagles, Taggart and Liddell, *Freedom of Information in New Zealand*, (Auckland, Oxford University Press, 1992) pp 469-470. Also see Lock [1985] *Public Law* 64.

7. THIRD PARTIES: INSTITUTION OF APPEALS AND PARTICIPATION IN APPEALS

45– 032 Introduction

As noted earlier,[198] a person or body other than the public authority to which a request for information under FOIA or the EIR is made may have a legitimate interest in seeing that some or all of the information answering the terms of a request is not communicated, either to that applicant or to anyone else.[199] That third party may be similarly concerned to see that any appeal against a refusal to communicate is adequately resisted and that the third party's interests in having the information not disclosed are properly articulated before the appellate body. As well as participating in any appeal, a third party may himself wish to initiate proceedings or an appeal where a decision has been or is proposed to be made by the public authority or by the appellate body to disclose information.

45– 033 Participation in appeals

Notwithstanding these legitimate interests a third party is given no right to participate in any decisions or appeals arising out of a request for information under FOIA or the EIR. Although a public authority, when making its original decision in relation to disclosure, may have informed the third party of the request and invited the third party's views on disclosure, there is nothing in either FOIA or the Code issued under s 45 of FOIA requiring the public authority to inform the third party either of the outcome of the request or of whether an appeal has been instituted[200] and a third party is given no entitlement to seek internal reconsideration. Likewise a third party has no entitlement to apply to the Commissioner for a decision whether a request has been dealt with in accordance with Part I of the Act, and there is nothing obliging the Information Commissioner, when an application has been made to her, to inform a third party of that application, to invite representations from the third party or to advise the third party of the outcome of it. There is no entitlement to appeal to the Tribunals; however, they have power to order any person to be joined as a party to an appeal under s 57 of FOIA, which may give third parties an opportunity to be heard.[201] The position of third parties has been treated more generously in comparative jurisdictions.[202]

45– 034 Institution of appeals etc

---

[198] See §22– 036.

[199] Disclosure under the Act is disclosure to the world: the public authority cannot itself restrict what the applicant does with the information once it is disclosed to him.

[200] Although the Code deals in Pt 3 with consultation with third parties it says only that, if a decision is made to release information following a consultation with a third party, it is generally best practice to inform the third party. It is arguable that in a case where s 40(2) FOIA is relevant, the public authority would be under an obligation under data protection legislation to inform the data subject of the request. And, in relation to commercially confidential material, a similar obligation may arise under Art 1 of Protocol 1 of the ECHR: see *Veolia ES Nottinghamshire Ltd v Nottinghamshire County Council & ors* [2010] EWCA Civ 1214, [2012] PTSR 185.

[201] FTT Rules r 9 and UT Rules r 9. If the decision is likely to affect the 'civil rights' of the third party it might be argued that the Human Rights Act 1998 and Art 6 of the ECHR would require the Tribunal to join him to the appeal so that such rights could be determined by an independent and impartial tribunal established by law: see *Zander v Sweden* (1993) 18 EHRR 175. Note also FTT Rules r 33(2), which enables the Tribunal to allow a third party to take a point in a hearing or make written submissions: but they would not have a right of appeal if that third party was not formally made a party of the appeal.

[202] As to the role of third parties in appeals can play in the comparative jurisdictions, see: §§51– 013 and 51– 014 (Australia); §§51– 031 and 51– 033 (Canada); §51– 038 (Ireland).

Although a third party's rights are therefore limited, a third party who has a recognised interest in seeing that information is not disclosed may well, on ordinary principles, be able to apply for a judicial review of a decision of a public authority, of the Information Commissioner or of the Tribunals that would result in the disclosure of that information.[203] Also, in certain circumstances a third party will be able to institute proceedings to restrain disclosure although there may be procedural difficulties if a court were to take a different view on an issue of confidentiality to that taken by the Information Commissioner or the Tribunals.[204]

[203] This is the route adopted in the USA: see §51– 009.

[204] See §34– 009.

CHAPTER 46
The Scottish Information Commissioner and FOI(S)A etc appeals

1. THE SCOTTISH INFORMATION COMMISSIONER

46–001 Appointment

The Scottish Information Commissioner is appointed by Her Majesty on the nomination of the Scottish Parliament.[1] A person is disqualified from being the Commissioner if that person is, or holds office in, or an employee or appointee of another Scottish public authority.[2] The Commissioner holds office for term not exceeding eight years, and that term may not be renewed.[3] Currently the Commissioner is appointed for a fixed term of 6 years. The Commissioner holds office for such salary and allowances and on such other terms as the Parliamentary corporation determines.[4] The Commissioner may only be removed from office if the Parliamentary corporation is satisfied that the Commissioner has breached the terms and conditions of office and the Scottish Parliament has resolved that the Commissioner should be removed for that breach; or where Parliament resolves that it has lost confidence in the Commissioner's willingness, suitability or ability to perform the functions of the office.[5] Other than in very limited respects, the Commissioner is not subject to the direction or control of the Parliament corporation, any member of the Scottish Executive or of the Parliament.[6] The Commissioner is entitled to take advice, assistance or any other service from a person who, in

1 FOI(S)A s 42(1).

2 FOI(S)A s 42(1A)-(1B).

3 FOI(S)A s 42(3), (5).

4 FOI(S)A s 42(2), (3A)-(3C).

5 FOI(S)A s 42(4A). The Commissioner may request Her Majesty to be relieved of office: FOI(S)A s 42(4)(a).

6 FOI(S)A s 42(7).

the opinion of the Commissioner, is qualified to give it[7] and may pay for the same.[8] The Commissioner may authorise others, including a member of the Commissioner's staff, to carry out any of the Commissioner's functions.[9] The Commissioner may appoint staff on terms and conditions as the Commissioner determines.[10] Neither the Commissioner nor his staff are regarded as servants or agents of the Crown.[11] The Commissioner has the usual suite of incidental powers.[12]

46– 002 Functions

The main functions of the Scottish Information Commissioner are:

(a) enforcing FOI(S)A by investigating and deciding whether Scottish public authorities have dealt with requests for information in accordance with Part 1 of the Act or are otherwise complying with Part 1;[13] and

(b) similarly enforcing EI(S)R by investigating and deciding whether those public authorities have dealt with requests for environmental information in accordance with the EI(S)R or are otherwise complying with the Regulations.[14]

The Commissioner also has the general functions of:

— being consulted upon regulations[15] and the code of practice;[16]
— approving publication schemes;[17]
— preparing model publication schemes;[18]
— promoting the following of good practice by Scottish public authorities in relation to the Act and the codes of practice issued under it and assessing whether they are following such good practice;[19]
— issuing practice recommendations to public authorities that appear to him not to be conforming with a code of practice under the Act;[20]
— disseminating information to and advising the public about the operation of the Act;[21]
— making proposals to the Scottish Ministers about their power under ss 4 and 5 of the Act to designate Scottish public authorities for the purpose thereof;[22]
— issuing practice recommendations to Scottish public authorities if he considers they are not following the codes of practice issued by the Scottish Ministers as to their

7 FOI(S)A s 42(9A).

8 FOI(S)A s 42(9B), but subject to the approval of the Parliamentary corporation: FOI(S)A s 42(9C).

9 FOI(S)A s 42(10).

10 FOI(S)A Sch 2, para 3(1).

11 FOI(S)A Sch 2, para 1(1). The Commissioner and his staff are based in St Andrews.

12 FOI(S)A Sch 2, para 6.

13 FOI(S)A s 43(1) and (3). As to codes of practice, see Ch 21.

14 The Commissioner's website emphasises the promotion of the public's right to know and the promotion of good FOI practice.

15 FOI(S)A ss 9(6), 12(5), 13(3).

16 FOI(S)A ss 60(4), 61(5).

17 FOI(S)A s 23(1), (5).

18 FOI(S)A s 24(1)-(4).

19 FOI(S)A s 43(1), (3), (7).

20 FOI(S)A s 44(1)

21 FOI(S)A s 43(2).

22 POI(S)A s 43(4).

functions under the Act and as to keeping, management and destruction of records issued under ss 60 and 61 thereof;[23] and

— issuing information notices and enforcement notices[24] and related enforcement functions.[25]

The Scottish Information Commissioner also has responsibility for enforcing the INSPIRE (Scotland) Regulations 2009 and other functions under those regulations analogous to his functions under FOI(S)A.[26]

46– 003 Human Rights Act 1998

The Scottish Information Commissioner is himself subject to the Human Rights Act 1998.[27] Articles 6, 8 and 10 of the ECHR are potentially relevant to the exercise of his functions.[28] Article 6 of the Convention has very limited application to the work of the Commissioner in deciding whether applicants are entitled to information under the Acts since the rights granted are not 'civil rights'[29] within the meaning of the Convention (although the civil rights of third parties may be affected), and, in any event, the various rights of appeal against their decisions probably mean that Art 6 will be satisfied. The Commissioner of course has a duty to act fairly in relation to their administrative decision-making. The ECtHR has decided[30] that Article 10 (which includes the right 'to receive information') only prohibits a government from restricting a person from receiving information from others who want to provide it and does not cast any obligation to provide information to an applicant against its will; but in the same case the Court decided that the failure by a public authority to disclose certain personal data might involve a breach of the right to respect for private and family life provided by Art 8. It seems likely that this decision would only impinge on applications for information under the GDPR and DPA 2018, and so impinge on the Information Commissioner rather than the Scottish Information Commissioner. The Scottish Information Commissioner is himself a public authority for the purposes of FOI(S)A and potentially a 'controller' subject to the GDPR and DPA 2018, and must accordingly comply with their provisions. In Scotland (unlike in England and Wales), since there is no appeal to a tribunal with power to decide issues of fact, the Commissioner has an enhanced duty of fairness.[31]

46– 004 Reporting and plans

Each year the Scottish Information Commissioner must lay a report each year before the Scottish Parliament on the exercise of his functions under the Act, which must include a record

---

23 FOI(S)A s 44. As to public records, see Ch 36.

24 Under FOI(S)A ss 50-51.

25 FOI(S)A s 53(1).

26 EI(S)R regs 17 and 18(5).

27 Human Rights Act 1998 s 6(1) and (3).

28 See Ch 4.

29 See the admissibility decision of the European Human Rights Commission in *Barry v France* (App No 14497/89) 14 October 1991 and *McGinley v United Kingdom* (1998) 27 EHRR 1 at paras 85-6. See, also,: *Syndicat CFDT des Etablissements et Arsenaux du Val-de-Marne and Vesque v France* (App 11678/85) 7 December 1987; *Loiseau v France* (App No 46809/99) ECHR 18 November 2003; *Micallef v Malta* (App no 17056/06) ECHR 15 January 2008 at [39]. See further Ch 4.

30 *Gaskin v United Kingdom* (1990) 12 EHRR 36. The actual decision in *Gaskin* was that the failure to provide medical records relating to the applicant at his request was an interference with his Art 8 right to respect for his private and family life; this decision led to the enactment of DPA 1998 ss 68 and 69 which *inter alia* make health records, in whatever form they are kept, subject to the DPA 1998 and in particular the access rights provided by s 7, thereby potentially allowing individuals a right to obtain access to their own health records. See, further, Ch 4. See also in the English courts *R (Persey) v Environment Secretary* [2003] QB 794 at [51]-[52].

31 *South Lanarkshire Council v Scottish IC* [2013] UKSC 55, [2013] 1 WLR 2421 at [29]-[33].

of the number of occasions on which he failed to reach a decision on a s 47(1) application within the four months specified by s 47(3)(b).[32] In addition, every four years the Commissioner must lay before the Scottish Parliament a strategic plan setting out how the Commissioner proposes to perform the Commissioner's functions during the 4-year period.[33] The strategic plan must set out the Commissioner's objectives and priorities during the period, how it is proposed to achieve them and the timetable and cost of doing so.

2. APPEALS

46–005 Introduction

There are five possible responses that a public authority may give to a request for information made under FOI(S)A:

(1) It may provide the applicant with all the information it holds answering the terms of the request.

(2) It may refuse to provide the applicant with some or all of the information it holds answering the terms of the request, claiming that that information is exempt information and, where an applicable exemption is a qualified exemption, that the public interest in maintaining that exemption outweighs the public interest in the disclosure of the information. To the extent that information requested is being refused on this basis, the response must be given by means of a 'refusal notice.'[34] That notice must disclose that the public authority holds the exempt information, state that it claims that that information is exempt information, specify the applicable exemption(s), state why each exemption applies and, if the exemption is not an absolute exemption, give its reasons for claiming that the public interest in maintaining the exemption outweighs the public interest in disclosing the information.[35]

(3) If the public authority estimates that the cost of complying with the request would exceed the amount prescribed,[36] it may serve a notice to that effect and not otherwise deal with the request.[37]

(4) If the public authority claims that the request for information is vexatious or that it has already recently[38] complied with the same request (or a request that is substantially similar), it may serve a notice to that effect and not otherwise deal with the request.[39]

32 FOI(S)A s 46(1) and (2).

33 FOI(S)A s 46A(1).

34 FOI(S)A s 16(1).

35 FOI(S)A s 16(1)-(2).

36 Currently £600, calculated at the rate of £15 per hour and excluding the cost of determining whether the public authority holds the information requested and whether the person is entitled to the information – in other words, it is the cost likely to be incurred by the public authority in locating, retrieving and providing the requested information: FOI(S)A s 12 and Fees (Scot) Regs regs 3, 5.

37 FOI(S)A s 16(4). It is open to a public authority to deal with the request even though it estimates that the cost of compliance exceeds the prescribed amount, and then serve a refusal notice. This may make sense where its estimate is borderline but the applicability of one or more exemptions is readily demonstrated.

38 See FOI(S)A s 14.

39 FOI(S)A s 16(5). It is open to a public authority to deal with the request even though it is vexatious or a repeat request, and then serve a refusal notice. This may make sense where the question of vexatiousness etc is time-consuming to prove or likely to be contentious, but the applicability of one or more exemptions is readily demonstrated.

(5) If the public authority does not hold any information to which the request relates, it must give the applicant notice that it does not hold the requested information.[40]

Apart from (1), an applicant may appeal against each of these responses. The appeal process is the same for each of the four response types. This section of this chapter is concerned with that appeal process and the analogous appeal process in respect of like responses to a request for environmental information under the EI(S)R.

46– 006 Timing and form of response

Each of four response types must be given by way of notice provided to the applicant not later than the 20th working day after the Scottish public authority receives the request for information or the payment of the fees sought by a fee notice (whichever is the later).[41] Each such notice must contain particulars:

(a) of the public authority's complaints procedures for the handling of requests for information;
(b) about the applicant's right under FOI(S)A[42] to require the public authority to review its actions and decisions in relation to the applicant's request for information;
(c) about the applicant's right under FOI(S)A[43] to apply to the Scottish Information Commissioner should the applicant be dissatisfied with the outcome of the public authority's review.[44]

The review and appeal procedures provided for in FOI(S)A and the EI(S)R are materially different from those provided for in FOIA and the EIR:

(1) Under FOI(S)A and the EI(S)R, an applicant must first require the public authority to review its own decision before applying to the Scottish Information Commissioner to look into the public authority's response.
(2) The Scottish Information Commissioner reviews the internal review decision, not the original decision.
(3) The Scottish Information Commissioner makes a full merit decision based on the facts, matters and circumstances as they stand at the time he makes his decision and upon the material before him.
(4) There is no appeal to a tribunal from the decision of the Scottish Information Commissioner. Appeal is instead to the Court of Session.

46– 007 First stage: review requirement

An applicant who is dissatisfied with the way in which a Scottish public authority has dealt with his or her request for information may require that public authority to review its actions and decisions in relation to that request: this is called a 'requirement for review.'[45] Importantly, an applicant cannot make an application to the Scottish Information Commissioner without having first sought a requirement for review.[46] The requirement for review procedure is distinct from any other procedure a public authority may have in place for dealing with general complaints about its service areas.

---

[40] FOI(S)A s 17(1).

[41] FOI(S)A ss 10(1), (3), 16(1), (4), (5), 17(1).

[42] FOI(S)A s 20(1).

[43] FOI(S)A s 47(1).

[44] FOI(S)A s 19.

[45] FOI(S)A s 20(1)-(2).

[46] FOI(S)A s 47(1). Internal review is not mandatory under FOIA.

46– 008 First stage: procedure

A requirement for review must be requested no later than 40 working-days after the date of receipt of a response from the authority, unless no response is received in which case the 40 working days runs after the end of the 20 working-day period for responding to the request.[47] Where a requirement for a review is made late an authority may comply with it, if it considers it appropriate to do so.[48] The review can be requested in writing or in a format that can be kept for future use, eg by email, fax, or a recording on an audio or video tape.[49] A requirement for review should give the applicant's name and an address for correspondence, details of the original request and explain why a review is requested.[50] So as to encourage the public authority to engage with the basis for review (rather than prompt a mere repeat of the original response) it is generally in the interests of an applicant to set out in the requirement for review all the facts and matters that would assist the public authority in reaching a different response, together with any perceived shortcomings in its original reasoning process. Specifically, where a public authority has relied on a non-absolute exemption, it is in the interests of an applicant to set out in his or her request for review as many facts and matters relevant to the public interest in the exemption(s) relied upon by the public authority and in the information being disclosed.[51] Unless the requirement for a review or the original request for information was vexatious,[52] the public authority must comply with a requirement for a review promptly and in any event not later than the twentieth working day after its receipt.[53]

46– 009 First stage: nature of review

On the review, the public authority can confirm (with or without modification), vary or substitute any decision or reach an original decision if the complaint is that no decision has been reached.[54] Although not expressly stated, it is a merit-review decision. The standpoint at which it considers both the factual position and at which it undertakes the public interest balance is the date of the review decision, not the date of the original decision. The public authority must thus take into account the facts, matters and circumstances that have come into existence since the original decision, as well as those that were present at the time of the original decision. The public authority must within 20 working days of receiving the requirement for review give the applicant a notice in writing setting out what it has done on the review and a statement of its reasons for so doing, or that it considers the requirement for review or the request for information to have been vexatious.[55] The notice must spell out the applicant's rights of application to the Scottish Information Commissioner and of appeal to the Court of Session.[56] Special provisions apply in relation to certain reviews when the relevant public

---

47 FOI(S)A s 20(5). The public authority may allow an applicant more time: FOI(S)A s 20(6). As to identification of the date on which it is made, see FOI(S)A s 74(1)(b).

48 FOI(S)A s 20(6).

49 FOI(S)A s 20(3).

50 FOI(S)A s 20(3).

51 So as to compel the public authority to engage with those facts and matters when reviewing its decision.

52 FOI(S)A s 21(8).

53 FOI(S)A s 21(1). Special provision is made for time limits in respect of information held by the Keeper of the Records for Scotland: FOI(S)A s 21(2). Similarly, special time limits apply in respect of certain schools: see the Freedom of Information (Scotland) Act 2002 (Time for Compliance) Regulations 2016/346, which deals with response time by reference to 'school days.'

54 FOI(S)A s 21(4).

55 FOI(S)A ss 21(5), (8) and (9).

56 FOI(S)A a 21(10).

authority is the Keeper of the Records of Scotland.[57] There is some further guidance on the requirements of a review in the Scottish Ministers' Code of Practice on the Discharge of Functions by Public Authorities Under the Freedom of Information (Scotland) Act.[58] The decision of the public authority set out in the notice supplants its original decision and forms the target for any further challenge by the applicant.[59]

46– 010 First stage: EI(S)R requests

A similar first stage review is provided for in respect of the response to a request for environmental information.[60] The time-limit for seeking the first stage of review is 40 working days after the applicant receives the decision or, if no decision is received, 40 working days after the last day within which the public authority was required to make the original decision.[61] The nature of the first stage review is the same as it is for a first stage review of a decision under FOI(S)A.[62] A public authority must response to a requirement for review by way of a notice to the appellant.[63] There is no express requirement for the public authority to give reasons for its decision on review, but its failure to do so can form the basis for a second stage appeal.

46– 011 Second stage: application

A person dissatisfied with the decision (or a failure or refusal[64] to take a decision) of a Scottish public authority on the first stage of review can apply to the Scottish Information Commissioner for a decision whether the request for information to which the requirement for review relates was dealt with in accordance with Part 1 of the Act.[65] This second stage of review applies equally to review decisions made in respect of requests for information under the EI(S)R.[66] In his guidance, the Scottish Information Commissioner terms an application under s 47 'an appeal,' and that terminology will be used in the following text.

46– 012 Second stage: procedure

Current guidance from the Scottish Information Commissioner recommends that an appeal be made online, on a form that can be downloaded, but does not require that route to be followed. If not online, the appeal must be in a format that can be kept for future use, eg in writing, by email or a recording on an audio or video tape.[67] An appeal must, as a general rule,

---

57 FOI(S)A ss 21(2) and 22.

58 See Code at paras 63 to 71.

59 FOI(S)A s 47(1).

60 EI(S)R reg 16. Although the review procedure is described in terms suggesting that it is discretionary, the application of Part 4 of FOI(S)A, which includes s 47, to appeals under the EI(S)R means that it is mandatory, since the later appeal stages pre-suppose completion of the first stage.

61 EI(S)R reg 16(2).

62 EI(S)R reg 16(3).

63 EI(S)R reg 16(4).

64 That is, one on the ground that the request is vexatious or repeated or there has already recently been an answer to the same or substantially the same request for information.

65 FOI(S)A s 47(1). The language is materially the same as the FOIA s 50(1): see §45– 005. The phrase 'dealt with in accordance with Part 1 of the Act' is sufficiently wide to cover a review decision dealing with any of the four types of reviewable responses identified in §46– 005.

66 EI(S)R reg 17.

67 The appellant should give his or her full name, an address for correspondence, details of the original request, set out why they were unhappy with how it was dealt with by the public authority and, finally, set out why they are unhappy with the outcome of the review. Copies of important documents (such as the original request, the response received (if any), the request for a review and any reply) should be included.

be brought six months from the date of the review decision.[68] There is no charge for an appeal. Following receipt of an appeal, an acknowledgement together with a copy of guidance for appellants must be provided. The Scottish Information Commissioner must make a decision on an application unless the impugned decision is an excluded decision[69] or he thinks it is frivolous or vexatious or it has been withdrawn or abandoned.[70] The Scottish Information Commissioner must invite the public authority's comments on the application and may endeavour to effect a settlement of the case.[71] Investigation will be undertaken by an investigating officer but decisions will be taken by the Commissioner (or a senior officer to whom he has delegated the responsibility). The Commissioner must (unless the appeal is settled) reach a decision on the appeal within four months of the receipt of the application.[72] The Commissioner must give both the applicant and the public authority a written notice of his decision: this is called a 'decision notice.'[73]

46– 013 Second stage: nature of review

The Act does not expressly spell out the nature of the 'appeal' to the Scottish Information Commissioner, but from the surrounding provisions it would appear to be a full merit review, so that the Commissioner stands in the shoes of the public authority and makes the decision afresh based upon the facts, matters and circumstances as they are at the time of the Commissioner's decision and upon the evidence he has.[74] Where the Commissioner decides that the public authority has, through its response to the request for information and the requirement for review, not dealt with the request in accordance with Part 1 of FOI(S)A, the decision notice must specify:

(a) the provision of FOI(S)A with which the public authority has failed to comply and the respect in which it has failed to comply;

(b) the steps which the public authority must take in order to comply; and

(c) the time within which it must take those steps.[75]

If the Commissioner allows an appeal against a failure to provide information, he will order the public authority to provide the information, usually within 45 days from the date of the decision notice – this is timed to arise after the time limit for any further appeal which is 42 days (see below). The Commissioner's decision is legally binding and can be enforced as if a contempt of court if the Commissioner has certified a failure to comply.[76] No civil right of action is

---

68 FOI(S)A s 47(2)-(7). The six months runs from the date by which the authority should have replied – being 20 working days after a review request was made. The Commissioner has the power to accept appeals after this time, if he considers it appropriate to do so: FOI(S)A s 47(5).

69 By s 48 FOI(S)A, which excludes decisions on a first stage review made by the Commissioner himself, the Procurator Fiscal and the Lord Advocate in his prosecutorial role. Such decisions will be open to challenge by way of judicial review, but only on a point of law.

70 FOI(S)A s 49(1), (2).

71 FOI(S)A s 49(3), (4).

72 Or such other period as is reasonable in the circumstances: FOI(S)A s 49(3), (5). Complex cases can take longer. The Commissioner must report annually to the Scottish Parliament on the number of decisions that take longer than four months.

73 FOI(S)A s 49(5).

74 Thus FOI(S)A s 49 speaks of the Commissioner making a 'decision' and, where he has received an application under s 47(1) is, under s 50, able to serve an information notice eliciting information from the public authority. Moreover, if there has been a material change of circumstances that impinges upon the applicability of an exemption or, more likely, the public interest balance in upholding an exemption, and if the Commissioner were to ignore that change that will simply prompt a fresh request of the public authority for the same information with the 'reasonable period of time' in FOI(S)A s 14(2) being informed by that material change of circumstances.

75 FOI(S)A s 49(5)-(7).

76 FOI(S)A s 53.

conferred in respect of a failure to comply with the Commissioner.[77] Where the Commissioner decides that the public authority has , through its response to the request for information and the requirement for review, dealt with the request in accordance with Part 1 of FOI(S)A, the decision must say so. The notice must contain particulars of the right of appeal to the Court of Session provided by s 56.[78] There is no express requirement on the Scottish Information Commissioner to give reasons in a decision but there is a common law duty to do so.[79] The Scottish Information Commissioner is under an 'enhanced duty' of fairness in reaching decisions as compared with the Information Commissioner, as he is the sole finder of facts with a right of appeal to the Inner House on a point of law only.[80] Once the Commissioner issues a notice, it cannot be changed. The Scottish Administration can be excepted from the duty to comply with any decision notice issued by the Commissioner in certain specified circumstances but only if the First Minister provides a certificate that there has been no failure as the Commissioner may have perceived to be the case and the information requested is of exceptional sensitivity.[81] No such certificates have yet been issued in Scotland.

46–014 Third stage: Court of Session

If an applicant or a public authority is unhappy with a decision of the Scottish Information Commissioner, each can appeal to the Court of Session but only on a point of law.[82] There is the same right of appeal in relation to decisions of the Scottish Commissioner under the EI(S)R.[83] An applicant may also make a complaint to the Scottish Public Services Ombudsman, although not on a matter that could have been taken to the Court or generally in respect of a properly made decision about which there is a simple disagreement over the result. An appeal to the Court of Session is to the Inner House, in broad terms the equivalent of the English and Welsh Court of Appeal, and whilst it can remit appeals to the Outer House, again broadly the equivalent of the High Court, that would be unusual.

46–015 Third stage: procedure

Procedure for an appeal to the Court of Session is provided for by Chapter 41 of the Rules of Court of Session. Part 1 of Chapter 41 deals with matters of urgency or competency of appeals, but the primary provisions for this kind of appeal are to be found in Part III. The appeal has to be made in a prescribed form (Form 41.25) and must be made within 42 days after the date on which the decision appealed against was intimated to the appellant, or if reasons are given later than the decision, then within 42 days after the date of the intimation of that statement of reasons.

46–016 Third stage: nature of appeal

The Inner House considered the restriction to appeals on a point of law in *Beggs v Scottish Information Commissioner*.[84] It identified four categories. First, it permits appeals on the general law: the content of its rules. Secondly, it permits appeals on the application of the law to the facts as found by the fact-finding tribunal or authority. Thirdly, it permits an appeal where

---

[77] FOI(S)A s 55.

[78] FOI(S)A s 56(9).

[79] *Scottish Ministers v Scottish IC* [2007] CSIH 8, 2007 SLT 274, 2007 SCLR 253 at [17]. Where the Commissioner decides that the request was frivolous or vexatious, there is a statutory duty to give reasons: s 49(1).

[80] *South Lanarkshire Council v Scottish IC* [2013] UKSC 55, [2013] 1 WLR 2421 at [31].

[81] FOI(S)A s 52.

[82] FOI(S)A s 56.

[83] EI(S)R reg 17(1).

[84] *Beggs v Scottish Information Commissioner* [2016] CSIH 23, 2016 SC 615, 2016 GWD 11-225 at [13].

there has been a fundamental error in the tribunal or authority's approach to the case: this would cover a decision that is *ultra vires*, or a case where the tribunal has taken account of irrelevant considerations, or a decision that no reasonable tribunal or authority could properly reach. It would also cover a perverse decision, or one that is irrational, or that contravened established principles of proportionality, or contravened Convention rights arising under the Human Rights Act 1998. Fourthly, an appeal on a point of law may be possible where the tribunal or authority makes finding of fat for which there is no evidence or which is inconsistent with the evidence and contradictory of it. But no appeal is possible in respect of the weight that the decision-maker has accorded to the various factors that are relevant to its decision, barring some fundamental error of approach. The Court also made clear that an appeal must not defeat the purpose of exemptions.[85] That may mean the deliberations of a Commissioner remain confidential. Moreover, there is no power for a court to review information on a confidential basis that was before the Commissioner. If the Commissioner decides that an exemption applies, the appeal will continue in ignorance of the underlying facts. Moreover, the Court also considered that it would accord a considerable degree of deference to the decisions of the Commissioner and would only interfere if there was a clear error of law.[86] In a further decision, *Welsh v Scottish Information Commissioner*,[87] the Inner House made clear it was not for it to review the merits of any decision of the Commissioner, and indeed that the Commissioner has no power or duty to go further than the role prescribed for him in the 2002 Act, section 47 in particular, such as to determine whether an officer of the public authority faced a conflict of interest. As with any decision of the Inner House, there is a possibility of an appeal to the Supreme Court , but only with permission either of the Inner House or of the Supreme Court.

46– 017 National security certificates

Under FOI(S)A and EI(S)R there is no provision for an appeal against ministerial certificates relating to national security issued under s 31(2) and reg 12(1) respectively.[88] It seems likely that such certificates would however be open to judicial review, with similar principles applying to conclusive certificates under FOIA.[89]

46– 018 Third-party appeals

A person or body other than the public authority to which a FOI(S)A request for information is made may have a legitimate interest in seeing that some or all of the information answering the terms of a request is not communicated, either to that applicant or to anyone else.[90] That third party may be similarly concerned to see that any challenge to a refusal to communicate is adequately resisted and that the third party's interests in having the information not disclosed are properly articulated before the court. As well as participating in those proceedings, a third party may himself wish to initiate the proceedings where a decision has been or is proposed to be made by the public authority or the Information Commissioner to disclose information. A third party is given no express right to participate in any decisions or appeals arising out of a request for information under FOI(S)A or the EI(S)R. Although a public authority, when making its original decision in relation to disclosure, may have informed the third party of the request and invited the third party's views on disclosure, there is nothing in FOI(S)A or the

85 At [14]-[15].

86 At [19].

87 *Welsh v Scottish Information Commissioner* [2015] CSIH 47, 2015 SLT 397, 2015 GWD 20-352.

88 Contrast the position under FOIA and the EIR: see §45– 026.

89 See §45– 031. As to the limits of judicial review in this area, see §§45– 032-45– 034, 46– 018.

90 Disclosure under the Act is disclosure to the world: the public authority cannot itself restrict what the applicant does with the information once it is disclosed to the applicant.

EI(S)R requiring the public authority to inform the third party either of the outcome of the request or of whether an appeal has been instituted[91] and a third party is given no entitlement to seek internal reconsideration. Likewise a third party has no entitlement to apply to the Commissioner for a decision whether a request has been dealt with in accordance with the Act, and there is nothing obliging the Information Commissioner, when an application has been made to him, to inform a third party of that application, to invite representations from the third party or to advise the third party of the outcome of it.[92] Although a third party's rights are therefore limited, a third party who has a recognised interest in seeing that information is not disclosed may well, on ordinary principles, be able to apply for a judicial review of a decision of a public authority or of the Information Commissioner that would result in the disclosure of that information.[93] Also, in certain circumstances a third party will be able to institute proceedings to restrain disclosure, although there may be procedural difficulties if a court were to take a different view on an issue of confidentiality to that taken by the Information Commissioner.[94]

---

91 In relation to commercially confidential material, a similar obligation may arise under Art 1 of Protocol 1 of the ECHR: see *Veolia ES Nottinghamshire Ltd v Nottinghamshire County Council & ors* [2010] EWCA Civ 1214, [2012] PTSR 185.

92 The position is the same under FOIA and the EIR: see §§45– 032-45– 034, 46– 018.

93 This is the route adopted in the USA: see §51– 009.

94 See §34– 009.

CHAPTER 47

Freedom of information: regulatory enforcement

1. FOI AND EIR

47–001 Introduction

In addition to her function of carrying out a second stage review whenever an applicant dissatisfied with the response of a public authority applies to her for such a review,[1] the Information Commissioner can initiate enforcement of the freedom of information regime by serving information notices and enforcement notices. The power to serve these notices is conferred on the Commissioner both to facilitate her carrying out of that second stage of review and to enable her to properly discharge her general function to promote observance of the Act and of the codes of practice issued under the Act.[2] These enforcement powers are carried over into the EIR.[3]

47–002 Information notices

The FOI Act confers power on the Information Commissioner to serve an 'information notice' on a public authority in two situations:

(1) Where the Commissioner has received a 'complaint' under s 50. In this situation, the Commissioner may serve an information notice requiring the public authority to furnish her with such information relating to the application as is specified in the notice.[4] The information notice must contain a statement that the Commissioner has received an application under s 50, but beyond this there is no requirement for the notice to give reasons for its service.[5] Such a notice can, for example, ask the public authority to describe the searches that it has carried out to locate the information that it holds answering the terms of a request for information. Or it

---

[1] That is, the second stage review initiated by a complainant under FOIA s 50 or as applied by EIR reg 18. See §45–005 above.

[2] FOIA s 47(1).

[3] EIR reg 18.

[4] FOIA s 51(1).

[5] *Aberdare Girls' School v IC*, FTT, 20 August 2010 at [35].

may be used to help determine whether the public authority's claim for exemption is well-founded.[6] Generally the Commissioner will seek the required information from a public authority without the need to serve an information notice; but public authorities are not always willing to comply voluntarily[7]. The Tribunal has stated that a public authority appealing against an information notice in this first type of situation would have a 'very high hurdle' to clear in convincing it that the Commissioner could and should carry out her functions under the Act without seeing the information in dispute.[8] In this way the Information Commissioner is able to compel the public authority to show her the information which is being sought by the applicant in order to form a judgment as to whether it or its existence ought to be disclosed under FOIA.[9]

(2) Where the Commissioner reasonably requires information for the purpose of determining whether a public authority has complied, or is complying, with the requirements of Part 1 of FOIA, or for the purpose of determining whether the practice of a public authority in relation to the exercise of its functions conforms with the codes of practice. In this situation the Commissioner may serve an information notice requiring the public authority to furnish her with such information relating to statutory compliance or to conformity with the code of practice as is specified in the notice.[10] The information notice must contain a statement that the Commissioner regards the specified information as relevant for either of the purposes referred to in that head, and of her reasons for regarding that information as relevant for that purpose.[11]

Each information notice must contain particulars of the right of appeal.[12] The time for compliance specified in an information notice must not expire before the end of the period within which an appeal can be brought against the notice and, if such an appeal is brought, the information need not be furnished pending the determination or withdrawal of the appeal.[13] An authority is not required to furnish the Commissioner with any information in respect of any communication between a professional legal adviser and his client in connection with the giving of legal advice to the client with respect to his obligations, liabilities or rights, or any communication between a professional legal adviser and his client, or between such an adviser or his client and any other person, made in connection with or in contemplation of proceedings (including proceedings before the tribunal) and for the purposes of such proceedings.[14] The

6 See, for example, *House of Commons v IC and Leapman, Brooke and Thomas*, IT, 26 February 2008 at [9].

7 See, for example: *Salmon v IC and King's College Cambridge*, IT, 17 July 2008 at [47]; *Francis v IC and GMC*, IT, 15 January 2009 at [13]; *Sittampalam v IC and BBC*, FTT, 4 July 2011 at [17]; *Muttitt v IC and Cabinet Office*, FTT, 31 January 2012 at [4]; *Wynn v IC and SFO*, FTT, 7 September 2012 at [7]. Sometimes the public authority does this on the basis of its own obligations of confidentiality, eg *Simmons v IC and Competition and Markets Authority*, FTT, 21 January 2015 at [19].

8 *Health Professionals Council v IC*, IT, 14 March 2008 at [52]. Such appeals have not met with much success, see, for example: *Swanage Town Council v IC*, Information Tribunal, 28 October 2009; *Aberdare Girls' School v IC*, FTT, 20 August 2010; *Norfolk Foster Care Association v IC and Norfolk Magistrates' Court*, FTT, 8 October 2013; *East Staffordshire Borough Council*, FTT, 29 December 2011.

9 See, in relation to the Commissioner's duties of confidentiality, §44– 006. Apparently, the Information Commissioner is able to substitute an information notice for a decision notice (ie a notice after receiving a complaint under s 50), thereby allowing the Commissioner to issue a fresh decision notice: *Clucas v IC*, FTT, 4 June 2014.

10 FOIA s 51(1).

11 FOIA s 51(2).

12 FOIA s 51(3).

13 FOIA s 51(4).

14 FOIA s 51(5). This was successfully relied on in *MoJ v IC*, IT, 6 August 2007.

Commissioner may cancel an information notice by written notice to the authority on which it was served.[15]

47– 003 Enforcement notices

Where the Information Commissioner is satisfied that a public authority has failed to comply with any of the statutory requirements in Part 1 of the Act,[16] the Commissioner may serve the authority with an enforcement notice requiring the authority to take, within such time as may be specified in the notice, such steps as may be so specified for complying with those requirements.[17] An enforcement notice must contain a statement of the requirement or requirements with which the Commissioner is satisfied that the public authority has failed to comply and her reasons for reaching that conclusion, and particulars of the right of appeal.[18] An enforcement notice must not require any of the provisions of the notice to be complied with before the end of the period within which an appeal can be brought against the notice and, if such an appeal is brought, the notice need not be complied with pending the determination or withdrawal of the appeal.[19] The Commissioner may cancel an enforcement notice by written notice to the authority on which it was served.[20] An enforcement notice will generally be served following an independent investigation by the Information Commissioner rather than following a complaint to her under s 50(1),[21] although there is nothing in Part IV of the Act to prevent an enforcement notice being served in respect of the same matter which is the subject of a decision notice.[22] One instance where the Commissioner might serve an enforcement notice is where there is a deliberate and persistent breach of time limits by a public authority.[23]

47– 004 Appeals against notices

A public authority on which an information notice or an enforcement notice has been served by the Information Commissioner may appeal to the tribunal against the notice.[24] There is no right to appeal against a refusal of the Commissioner to issue an enforcement notice or an information notice.[25] Nor is there any right of appeal by any person other than the person on whom the notice has been served.[26] The statutory basis for the Tribunal determining such an appeal is the same as that for determining an appeal against a decision of the Commissioner made on an application under s 50: namely, that the notice was not in accordance with the law or, if it involved the exercise of a discretion (which will cover almost all such notices), that the Commissioner ought to have exercised her discretion differently.[27] On such an appeal, the

---

15 FOIA s 51(7).

16 This would include in particular FOIA ss 1, 10, 11, 15, 16, 17 and 19.

17 FOIA s 52(1). This applies equally to the EIR through reg 18.

18 FOIA s 52(2).

19 FOIA s 52(3).

20 FOIA s 52(4).

21 See, for example, *Cabinet Office v IC and Lamb*, IT, 27 January 2009 at [32].

22 This was envisaged as a possibility in *Harper v IC and Royal Mail Group plc*, IT, 15 November 2005. The Upper Tribunal in *All Party Parliamentary Group on Extraordinary Rendition v IC and Ministry of Defence* [2011] UKUT 153 (AAC) at [42] described enforcement notices as 'by their nature a blunt instrument and are of no comfort to an individual requester whose particular request to a particular authority receives a delayed response.'

23 *Bowbrick v IC and Nottingham City Council*, IT, 28 September 2006 at [64]; *Home Office v IC*, FTT, 8 June 2010 at [38].

24 FOIA s 57(2).

25 *Brown v IC*, FTT, 30 December 2010 at [33]; *EJ v IC* [2011] UKUT 171 (AAC) at [22].

26 *Thornton v IC*, FTT, 22 May 2017 at [43].

27 FOIA s 58(1). For more detail, see §45– 014. The Tribunal has commented that s 58(1)(b) has a greater role in appeals concerning information notices and enforcement notices than it does in an appeal against a decision notice:

tribunal may review any finding of fact on which the notice in question was based.[28] In short, an appeal is a full merit-review of the facts by the FTT, but with the facts as they were at the moment at which the notice was issued. If on an appeal the tribunal considers that the notice against which the appeal is brought is not in accordance with the law, or, to the extent that the notice involved an exercise of discretion by the Commissioner, that he ought to have exercised his discretion differently, the tribunal must allow the appeal or substitute such other notice as could have been served by the Commissioner; and in any other case the tribunal must dismiss the appeal.[29] Where the FTT allows the appeal, it can also substitute a correct notice setting out what the public authority must do.[30]

47– 005 Non-compliance with notices

Where a public authority fails to comply with an information notice or an enforcement notice, the Information Commissioner may certify in writing to the High Court that the public authority has failed to comply with that notice.[31] A public authority which, in purported compliance with an information notice:

(a) makes a statement which it knows to be false in a material respect; or

(b) recklessly makes a statement which is false in a material respect,

is to be taken to have failed to comply with the notice.[32] Where a failure to comply is certified, the court may inquire into the matter and, after hearing any witness who may be produced against or on behalf of the public authority, and after hearing any statement that may be offered in defence, deal with the authority as if it had committed a contempt of court.[33] Non-compliance with an information notice or an enforcement notice is also a basis for the Information Commissioner obtaining a search and enter warrant.[34]

47– 006 Ministerial certificate

Where a government department or the National Assembly for Wales (or any other public authority specified in an order made by the Secretary of State) has been served with an enforcement notice that relates to its failure in respect of one or more requests for information to communicate exempt information (ie because the applicable exemption is (or all the applicable exemptions are) a qualified exemption and the public interest balance has been found to favour disclosure rather than a maintenance of that or those exemptions), it may avoid the effect of that enforcement notice by giving the Information Commissioner within 20 days of the notice a certificate signed by an 'accountable person' stating that that accountable person has on reasonable grounds formed the opinion that there has been no failure.[35] The

---

Lotz v IC, FTT, 12 April 2017 at [9].

28 FOIA s 58(2).

29 FOIA s 58(1).

30 *IC v E Malnick and The Advisory Committee on Business Appointments* [2018] UKUT 72 (AAC) at [103], declaring that *IC v Bell* [2014] UKUT 106 (AAC) at [26] was wrong to hold that all that the FTT could do was to allow the appeal and, in so doing, to identify the mistake in the notice.

31 FOIA s 54(1).

32 FOIA s 54(2).

33 FOIA s 54(3).

34 FOIA Sch 3 para 1(1)(a)(iii). Warrants under FOIA are considered further at §50– 004. These are also applicable to the EIR: see reg 18(2).

35 FOIA ss 53(1), (2). Such a certificate was issued by Jack Straw, the Secretary of State for Justice on 24 February 2009 in respect of *Cabinet Office v IC and Lamb*, IT, 27 January 2009, upholding a decision of the Commissioner dated 19 February 2008, requiring the disclosure of minutes of Cabinet meetings of 13 and 17 March 2003 relating to the invasion of Iraq. A certificate was issued by Dominic Grieve, Attorney-General, on 16 October 2012 in respect of letters from the Prince of Wales to various Ministers which the Upper Tribunal had required the various

'accountable person' must give reasons to the complainant for the opinion he has formed unless that would involve the disclosure of exempt information.[36] An 'accountable person' (apart from special provisions about the National Assembly of Wales and the Northern Ireland Assembly) is a member of the cabinet or the Attorney-General and a copy of the certificate must be laid before Parliament.[37] This provision in effect purports to remove the supervision of the Tribunal as to where the public interest lies in relation to the disclosure of exempt information and represents a kind of 'trump card' in the hand of the higher executive.[38] The effectiveness of this provision has been considered above.[39] In so far as requested information is 'environmental information' the position is somewhat clearer: the section 53 provision for an executive override incorporated into the EIR by reg 18(6) is not compatible with Art 6 of the relevant Directive (2003/4/EC) under which the Regulations were made (which requires provision for a full and final review by a court of any refusal to supply environmental information).[40]

2. FOI(S)A AND EI(S)R

47– 007 Introduction

In addition to his role in carrying out the second stage of review when application is made by an applicant, the Scottish Information Commissioner has free-standing enforcement powers. These powers are conferred on the Commissioner both to facilitate his carrying out of the second stage of review and to enable him to properly discharge his general functions:

(a) to promote the following of good practice by Scottish public authorities by promoting their observance of the Act and of the codes of practice issued under ss 60 and 61;[41] and

(b) to make practice recommendations to public authorities.[42]

The two principal instruments for such Commissioner-instigated enforcement are 'information notices' and 'enforcement notices.'

47– 008 Information notices

Section 50 of FOI(S)A confers power on the Scottish Information Commissioner to give a Scottish public authority an information notice.[43] The Commissioner may give an information notice in either of two situations. First, where an applicant has appealed to the Commissioner against a public authority's decision on a requirement for review.[44] Secondly, where the Commissioner reasonably requires information for the purpose of determining whether: (a) a Scottish public authority has complied or is complying with the provisions of FOI(S)A or

departments concerned to disclose: see *R (Evans) v Attorney-General* [2015] UKSC 21, [2015] AC 1787.

36 FOIA s 53(6) and (7).

37 FOIA s 53(8) and (3).

38 The trumping effect of such certificates is a feature of freedom of information legislation in each of the Westminster-style comparative jurisdictions. See §§51– 014 (Australia); 51– 021 (New Zealand); 51– 030 (Canada); and 51– 038 (Ireland). In the USA, an equivalent is achieved with exclusions: see §51– 003.

39 See §45– 011.

40 *R (Evans) v Attorney-General* [2015] UKSC 21, [2015] AC 1787 at [100]-[105] per Lord Neuberger.

41 The general functions of the Information Commissioner are set out in FOI(S)A s 43

42 These are provided for in FOI(SA) s 44.

43 Section 50 of FOI(S)A applies for the purposes of the EI(S)R, with references to the Act read as references to those Regulations: EI(S)R reg 17(1).

44 In other words, an application to the Commissioner under FOI(S)A s 47(1): FOI(S)A s 50(1)(a).

EI(S)R; or (b) the practice of a Scottish public authority conforms with the code of practice issued under FOI(S)A s 60 or s 61 or under EI(S)R reg 18.[45] In the second situation, an information notice will often be the first step in a longer enforcement process against the public authority. The Commissioner may serve more than one information notice and the response to one such notice may prompt the service of a subsequent information notice. An information notice must specify:[46]

(a) Whether it is being given following an appeal by an appellant to the Commissioner against a first-stage review decision, or whether it is being given for the purpose of the Commissioner determining whether the public authority has complied with the provisions of FOI(S)A or the EI(S)R or the various codes of practice issued under the same.[47]

(b) The information that the public authority must give the Commissioner.

(c) The form that the information must take.

(d) The time within which the public authority must give information to the Commissioner.[48]

(e) The public authority's right of appeal under FOI(S)A s 56 to the Court of Session against the information notice.

In responding to an information notice, a public authority is not obliged to provide information covered by legal professional privilege.[49] Apart from this, however, the public authority must provide all the information sought in the notice. In particular, neither the confidentiality that may subsist in information requested by the notice nor any obligation to maintain secrecy is not a basis for non-compliance with that notice.[50]

47– 009 Enforcement notices

Section 51 of FOI(S)A confers power on the Scottish Information Commissioner to give a Scottish public authority an enforcement notice.[51] The Commissioner may give an enforcement notice where he is satisfied that a Scottish public authority has failed to comply with a provision of Part 1 of FOI(S)A or the provisions of the EI(S)R: in other words, where he is satisfied that a Scottish public authority:

— has not provided information in response to a request where obliged to do so (or not done so within the prescribed time),

— has improperly given a notice that requested information is not held,

— has improperly claimed fees or refused to deal with a request on the ground of excessive cost of compliance, or

— has not properly carried out a requirement for review.

An enforcement notice must specify:[52]

---

45 FOI(S)A s 50(1)(b).

46 FOI(S)A s 50(1)-(3).

47 FOI(S)A s 50(2). In the latter case, the notice must include a statement of the purpose for which the notice is relevant and the reasons for so regarding the information.

48 In the case of an information notice served in the second situation, that time must not expire before the end of the period in which an appeal against the information notice under FOI(S)A s 56 may be brought, ie 42 days after the date that the information notice was served on the public authority.

49 FOI(S)A s 50(5).

50 FOI(S)A s 50(7). This is because information received by the Commissioner or his staff in response to an information notice must not be disclosed unless lawfully authorised: FOI(S)A s 45. It will be a criminal offence for the Commissioner or staff member to do so: FOI(S)A s 45(3).

51 Section 51 of FOI(S)A applies for the purposes of the EI(S)R, with references to the Act read as references to those Regulations: EI(S)R reg 17(1).

52 FOI(S)A s 51(1)-(2).

(a) The steps that the public authority must take.
(b) The time within which the public authority must take those steps.
(c) A statement of the provision that the Commissioner is satisfied that the public authority has failed to comply with and the respect in which it has failed to comply.
(d) The public authority's right of appeal under FOI(S)A s 56 to the Court of Session against the information notice.[53]

47–010 Appeals against notices

A public authority may appeal against an information notice or an enforcement notice to the Court of Session, but only on a point of law.[54] An appeal does not automatically operate to sist the information or enforcement notice. Where the Commissioner has given an enforcement notice to the Scottish Executive in respect of a refusal to answer a request for information relying upon certain exemptions, the First Minister of the Scottish Executive may give the Commissioner a conclusive certificate, the effect of which is to disapply the enforcement notice.[55]

47–011 Non-compliance with notices

Where a Scottish public authority has failed to comply with an information notice or an enforcement notice, the Commissioner may certify in writing to the Court of Session that the authority has failed to comply with the notice.[56] The Court may inquire into the matter and, after hearing any witness who may be produced against or on behalf of the public authority, and after hearing any statement that may be offered in defence, the Court may deal with the public authority as if it had committed a contempt of court.[57] If a sheriff is satisfied by evidence on oath supplied by the Information Commissioner that there are reasonable grounds for suspecting that a Scottish public authority has failed or is failing to comply with an information notice or an enforcement notice, and that evidence of such a failure to comply is to be found on any premises specified, the sheriff may grant the Information Commissioner a warrant that authorises the Commissioner or any member of his staff to enter and search the premises, to inspect and seize any documents that may constitute evidence and to inspect, examine, operate and test any equipment found in the premises in which information held by the public authority may be recorded.[58]

---

53 The time for compliance must not expire before the end of the period in which an appeal against the information notice under FOI(S)A s 56 may be brought, ie 42 days after the date that the information notice was served on the public authority: FOI(S)A s 51(3).

54 FOI(S)A s 56(c).

55 FOI(S)A s 52. There are various procedural requirements to be followed. The Commissioner could theoretically judicially review the conclusive certificate.

56 FOI(S)A s 53(1).

57 FOI(S)A s 53(3).

58 FOI(S)A Sch 3, para 1. Schedule 3 spells out the manner in which such warrants are to be executed, the matters exempt from inspection and seizure, and offences in connection with the execution of a warrant.

Chapter 48

GDPR and DPA 2018: private remedies and regulatory enforcement

1. OVERVIEW

48–001 Introduction

To make effective the applicable data processing requirements, the GDPR and the DPA 2018 enable a data subject to seek from a court private remedies against a contravening controller or processor, as well as enabling the Information Commissioner to undertake regulatory enforcement against a contravening controller or processor. A single breach of a requirement in the GDPR or the DPA 2018 may expose a controller or processor to both private remedies and regulatory enforcement, with the latter able to complement the former. A breach of a code of practice issued by the Information Commissioner does not of itself give rise to a private remedy, although it may be relied upon to initiate regulatory enforcement.[1] Regulatory enforcement may be instigated on the Information Commissioner's own motion or on a complaint by a data subject.[2] The scope of the remedies and regulatory enforcement that are available upon non-compliance with the requirements of the data protection regime depends upon whether the processing is by one of the intelligence services, by a competent authority for law enforcement purposes or whether it is general processing.[3]

48–002 Private remedies

The remedies that are available to a data subject depend upon:

— the particular continuing obligation or data subject right that has not been complied with;
— the consequences of non-compliance for the data subject;
— whether in relation to the processing for which a remedy is sought, the person against whom that remedy is sought is the controller or a processor of the personal data; and
— whether the processing is by one of the intelligence services, by a competent authority for law enforcement purposes or whether it is general processing.

The private remedies divide into:

— compliance remedies, where an order is sought that the defendant controller or processor be compelled to carry out specified remedial action within a prescribed time; and
— compensatory remedies, where an award of money is sought to compensate the data subject for a contravention of a right or principle.

A single claim may seek both types of remedy.

48–003 Regulatory enforcement

The Information Commissioner is responsible for regulatory enforcement under both the GDPR and the DPA 2018.[4] Where a data subject makes a complaint to the Commissioner, the Commissioner must investigate the subject matter of the complaint and inform the data

1 DPA 2018 s 127(2), (4). Nevertheless, a court or tribunal must, in any proceedings before it, take into account any relevant code of practice in force at the relevant time: DPA 2018 s 127(3). Similarly, a breach of the Framework for Data Processing by Government prepared under DPA 2018 s 191 does not of itself give rise to a private remedy, but is to be taken into account by a court or tribunal in any proceedings before it: DPA 2018 s 194.

2 DPA 2018 s 165(1)-(2).

3 On the division between processing by 'the intelligence services,' a 'competent authority for law enforcement purposes' and 'general processing', see further §8–002.

4 DPA 2018 ss 115-116; GDPR Arts 51, 57 and 58; LED Art 41.

subject of the outcome of that complaint.[5] The principal enforcement measures that may be taken by the Information Commissioner are:

(1) Issuing an information notice against either a controller or a processor or any other person.[6] An information notice will require the recipient to provide the Commissioner with particular information, or a category of information, that the Commissioner reasonably requires for the purposes of carrying out the Commissioner's functions under the data protection legislation.[7]

(2) Issuing an assessment notice against either a controller or a processor.[8] An assessment notice permits the Information Commissioner to assess whether the controller or processor has complied or is complying with the data protection legislation. An assessment notice may require a controller or a processor to permit the Commissioner to enter premises, to direct the Commissioner to particular documents, to assist the Commissioner to view documents, to provide copies of them, to direct the Commissioner to equipment or other material on the premises, to permit the Commissioner to inspect documents, information, equipment or material and to provide the Commissioner with an explanation of them, to permit the Commissioner to observe the processing of personal data and to make available for interview persons who process personal data on behalf of the controller.[9]

(3) Issuing an enforcement notice against a controller or processor.[10] An enforcement notice may be issued against a controller or processor where it has failed, or is failing, to comply with its continuing obligations or with a data subject's rights.[11] An enforcement notice will impose requirements that the Commissioner considers appropriate for the purpose of remedying the failure.[12] In this way, an enforcement notice may be used to achieve the same outcome as private proceedings brought by a data subject seeking compliance remedies.

---

[5] GDPR Arts 57(1)(f) and 77(2) (general processing); DPA 2018 s 165(5)-(6) (law enforcement processing and intelligence services processing). Where the Information Commissioner fails to take appropriate steps or fails to inform the data subject of the outcome of the complaint within 3 months of receipt, the data subject may apply to the First-tier Tribunal for an order requiring the Commissioner to take appropriate steps or to inform the data subject of the outcome within a specified time: DPA 2018 s 166. Provided that the Information Commissioner informs the data subject about the progress of the complaint within 3 months of receipt, the Commissioner is given a further three months within which to inform the data subject of the outcome: DPA 2018 s 166(1).

[6] DPA s 142(1); in relation to general processing, see also GDPR Art 58(1)(a) and DPA 2018 s 115(5). In relation to intelligence services processing, the power to issue an information notice is disapplied where that is required for the purpose of safeguarding national security: DPA 2018 s 110. The Commissioner may not give an information notice with respect to the processing of personal data for 'the special purposes' other than in very limited circumstances: DPA 2018 s 143(1). As to the meaning of 'the special purposes' see §11– 050.

[7] The 'data protection legislation' means the GDPR, the applied GDPR, the DPA 2018 and regulations thereunder, and regulations made under the European Communities Act 1972 s 2(2) that related to the GDPR or the LED: DPA 2018 s 3(9).

[8] DPA 2018 s 146(1); in relation to general processing, see also GDPR Art 58(1)(b) and DPA 2018 s 115(6). In relation to intelligence services processing, the power to issue an assessment notice is disapplied where that is required for the purpose of safeguarding national security: DPA 2018 s 110.

[9] DPA 2018 s 146(2).

[10] DPA 2018 s 149(1); in relation to general processing, see also GDPR Art 58(1)(c)(g), (j) and (h) and DPA 2018 s 115(8). In relation to intelligence services processing, the power to issue an enforcement notice is disapplied where that is required for the purpose of safeguarding national security: DPA 2018 s 110. Enforcement notices may also be issued against a monitoring body that has failed or is failing to comply with an obligation under GDPR Art 41 and against a certification provider: DPA 2018 s 149(3)-(4). The Commissioner may not give an enforcement notice with respect to the processing of personal data for 'the special purposes' other than in very limited circumstances: DPA 2018 s 152(1). As to the meaning of 'the special purposes' see §11– 050.

[11] DPA 2018 s 149(2). This also lists other circumstances in which an enforcement notice may be issued against a controller or processor.

[12] DPA 2018 s 149(6).

(4) Issuing a penalty notice against a controller or processor where it has failed, or is failing, to comply with its continuing obligations or with a data subject's rights,[13] or where there has been a failure to comply with an information notice, an assessment notice or an enforcement notice.[14]

There is a right of appeal against each of these types of notice.

48–004 Data subject complaints

A data subject has a statutory right to complain to the Information Commissioner if the data subject considers that, in relation to personal data relating to him or her, there has been an infringement of the requirements of data protection legislation.[15] This includes an infringement of any of the continuing obligations or any of the data subject rights.[16] Where the Commissioner receives such a complaint, the Commissioner must:

(a) take appropriate steps to respond to the complaint, including investigating and responding to it;

(b) inform the complainant of the outcome of the complaint;

(c) inform the complainant of the right to apply to the First-tier Tribunal for an order requiring the Commissioner to progress the complaint and inform the complainant of the progress and outcome of it; and

(d) if asked to do so by the complainant, provide the complainant with further information about how to pursue the complaint.[17]

If the Commissioner does not take appropriate steps to respond to it or, within three months of having received the complaint, has not provided the complainant with information about progress (or the outcome) of the complaint, the complainant may apply to the First-tier Tribunal for an order requiring the Commissioner to take, within a specified period, appropriate steps to respond to the complaint or to inform the complainant of progress or the outcome of the complaint.[18]

---

13 DPA 2018 s 155(1)(a); in relation to general processing, see also GDPR Arts 58(2)(i) and 83 and DPA 2018 s 115(9). In relation to intelligence services processing, there is no disapplication of the Information Commissioner's power to issue a penalty notice on the grounds of safeguarding national security: DPA 2018 s 110(2)(e)(i).

14 DPA 2018 s 155(1)(b); in relation to general processing, see also GDPR Arts 58(2)(i) and 83 and DPA 2018 s 115(9). In relation to intelligence services processing, there is no disapplication of the Information Commissioner's power to issue a penalty notice on the grounds of safeguarding national security: DPA 2018 s 110(2)(e)(i). The Commissioner may not give a penalty notice with respect to the processing of personal data for 'the special purposes' other than in very limited circumstances: DPA 2018 s 156(1). As to the meaning of 'the special purposes' see §11–050.

15 GDPR Art 77 (general processing); DPA 2018 s 165(1)-(2) (law enforcement processing and intelligence services processing). As well as being made by a data subject him or herself, the complaint may be made on behalf of a data subject by a body or association that is active in the field of protection of data subjects' rights and freedoms with regard to the protection of their personal data provided that that body or associates is required to apply all of its income and capital for charitable purposes, is prohibited from directly or indirectly distributing amongst its members any part of its assets (other than for charitable purposes) and has objectives that are in the public interest – called a 'representative body': GDPR Art 80 (in relation to general processing); DPA 2018 s 187 (in relation to law enforcement processing and intelligence services processing).

16 The continuing obligations are the obligations set out in Chapter 9 (in relation to general processing), Chapter 12 (in relation to law enforcement processing) and Chapter 14 (in relation to intelligence services processing). The data subject rights are those set out in Chapter 10 (in relation to general processing), Chapter 13 (in relation to law enforcement processing) and Chapter 14 (in relation to intelligence services processing).

17 GDPR Arts 57(1)(f) and 77(2) (in relation to general processing); DPA 2018 s 165(4)-(5) (in relation to law enforcement processing and intelligence services processing).

18 DPA 2018 s 166(1)-(2). If the Commissioner's consideration of the complaint is not concluded within 3 months, the Commissioner must, within each 3 months period until conclusion of the investigation, provide the complainant with information about progress of the complaint: DPA 2018 s 166(1). The application may be made to the FTT by a representative body on behalf of the data subject: GDPR Art 80 (in relation to general processing); DPA 2018 s 187(2)(b) (in relation to law enforcement processing and intelligence services processing).

2. PRIVATE REMEDIES

48–005 Introduction

All three types of data processing – that is, general processing, law enforcement processing and intelligence services processing – provide data subjects with private law remedies of varying scope. The potential remedies are coercive – called a 'compliance order'[19] – and compensatory.

48–006 Nature of the claim

In the taxonomy of private law claims, a claim by a data subject that a controller or processor, in processing his or her personal data, has not-complied with one or other of its continuing obligations[20] or the data subject's rights[21] is a claim in tort – namely, the tort of breach of statutory duty. As such, the limitation period is:

(a) Where the damages claimed consist of or include damages in respect of personal injuries[22] to the claimant or any other person – 3 years from the later of the date on which the cause of action accrued or the date of knowledge of the person injured.[23]

(b) Otherwise – 6 years from the date on which the cause of action accrued.[24]

To the extent that a claim involves a foreign element the Private International Law (Miscellaneous Provisions) Act 1995 means that the assessment of damages will be determined in accordance with the law of England and Wales.[25]

48–007 Jurisdiction

Private remedies are claimed in the civil courts, and not in the tribunals.[26] In relation to claims arising out of processing by a competent authority for law enforcement purposes and in relation to claims arising out of general processing, jurisdiction is exercisable by the High Court or a county court (in England, Wales and Northern Ireland) and by the Court of Session or the sheriff (in Scotland).[27] The choice between the High Court and the county court will be decided on the usual principles.[28] The High Court (in Scotland, the Court of Session) has

---

19 DPA 2018 s 167. A controller may be vicariously liable for employee breaches: *WM Morrisons plc v Various Claimants* [2020] UKSC 12 at [54]-[55].

20 That is, the obligations set out in Chapter 9 (in relation to general processing), Chapter 12 (in relation to law enforcement processing) and Chapter 14 (in relation to intelligence services processing).

21 That is, the data subject rights set out in Chapter 10 (in relation to general processing), Chapter 13 (in relation to law enforcement processing) and Chapter 14 (in relation to intelligence services processing).

22 'Personal injuries' includes any disease and any impairment of a person's physical or mental condition: Limitation Act 1980 s 38(1).

23 Limitation Act 1980 s 11(4). Date of knowledge is determined in accordance with Limitation Act 1980 s 14. A failure to notify a data subject of the right to apply to a court under DPA 2018 s 167 may be relevant for this purpose: see DPA 2018 s 44(5), 45(5), 48(1) and 51(5).

24 Limitation Act 1980 s 2. As damage is not necessary to bring a data protection claim, the cause of action will accrue from the date on which the breach occurred: Limitation Act 1980 s 2. Where a defendant has deliberately concealed from a claimant any fact relevant to the claimant's right of action, the period of limitation will not begin to run until the claimant has discovered the concealment or could with reasonable diligence have discovered it: Limitation Act 1980 s 32(1).

25 Private International Law (Miscellaneous Provisions) Act 1995 s 14(3)(b). The Rome II Regulation does not apply: see Art 1(2)(g).

26 DPA 2018 s 20.

27 DPA 2018 s 180(1); GDPR Arts 79(2) and 82(6).

28 In England and Wales, the default position is that proceedings (whether for damages or for a specified sum) may not be started in the High Court unless the value of the claim is more than £100,000: CPR PD7A para 2.1. This

exclusive jurisdiction to hear claims arising out of processing of personal data by the intelligence services.[29]

48–008 Pre-action practice: claimant

Before a claim is issued in the High Court, the pre-action protocol for media and communication claims should be followed.[30] This requires a claimant to give the defendant written notification of the claim – a 'letter of claim' – at the earliest opportunity, setting out the name of the claimant, the nature and basis for the entitlement to the remedies sought, any facts or matters relevant to England and Wales being the most appropriate forum for the dispute, and details of any funding arrangement in place.[31] In addition, the letter of claim should include the following information:

(a) any further information necessary to identify the data subject;
(b) the data controller to which the claim is addressed;
(c) the information or categories of information which is claimed to constitute personal data including, where necessary, the information which is said to constitute sensitive personal data or to fall within a special category of personal data;
(d) sufficient details to identify the relevant processing;
(e) the identification of the duty or duties which are said to have been breached and details of the manner in which they are said to have been breached, including any positive case on behalf of the claimant;
(f) why the personal data ought not to be processed/further processed, if applicable; and
(g) the nature and any available details as to any particular damage caused or likely to be caused by the processing or breach of duty complained of.[32]

Where a representative data protection claim is intended to be brought on behalf of data subjects, the letter of claim should also:

(h) set out the nature of the entity which intends to bring the claim and explain how it fulfils the relevant suitability criteria;
(i) include details of the data subjects on whose behalf the claim would be brought; and
(j) confirmation that they have mandated the representative body to represent them and receive compensation, where applicable.[33]

48–009 Pre-action practice: defendant

---

is subject to the requirements of any enactment. In relation to data protection claims, the only such requirements are DPA 2018 ss 94(13), 99(7), 100(6) and 180(3) requiring claims arising out of processing of personal data by the intelligence services to be brought in the High Court (in Scotland, in the Court of Session). The default position will be displaced, with the effect that a claim for less than £100,000 should be started in the High Court, where by reason of—

(1) the financial value of the claim and the amount in dispute, and/or
(2) the complexity of the facts, legal issues, remedies or procedures involved, and/or
(3) the importance of the outcome of the claim to the public in general,

the claimant believes that the claim ought to be dealt with by a High Court judge: PD7A para 2.4.

29 DPA 2018 ss 94(13), 99(7), 100(6) and 180(3).

30 The extent to which the protocol has been followed by the parties will be taken into account by a court in dealing with liability for costs and making other orders: Protocol para 1.3. The Protocol applies to cases within the scope of CPR r 53.1, but this does not extend to data protection claims initiated in the County Court unless the claim arises from activities of the media: see Protocol para 1.1 and the definition of 'media and communications claim' in CPR r 53.1.

31 Protocol para 3.1.

32 Protocol para 3.4. Where the letter of claim includes other causes of action, the protocol requirements for those causes should also be included.

33 Protocol para 3.4 and see GDPR Art 80.

The recipient of the letter of claim should provide a full response as soon as possible and, if more than 14 days is required, the recipient should immediately notify the claimant specifying the date by which the response will be provided.[34] The response should include the following:

(a) whether or to what extent the claimant's claim is accepted, whether more information is required or whether it is rejected;
(b) if the claim is accepted in whole or in part, the defendant should indicate which remedies it is willing to offer;
(c) if more information is required, then the defendant should specify precisely what information is needed to enable the claim to be dealt with and why;
(d) if the claim is rejected, then the defendant should explain the reasons why it is rejected, including a sufficient indication of any statutory exemptions or facts on which the defendant is likely to rely in support of any substantive defence; and
(e) where the claimant to a proposed action has indicated his or her intention to make an application to bring the claim anonymously, the defendant should indicate whether the defendant accepts such an order would be appropriate and give an indication of the basis for the defendant's position.[35]

48– 010 Court procedure

Where a claim initiated in the High Court includes allegations of a breach of the GDPR or the DPA 2018, that claim will fall within the definition of a 'media and communications claim' under the Civil Procedure Rules 1998.[36] A 'media and communications claim' must be issued in the Queen's Bench Division in the Media and Communications List.[37] In any 'media and communications claim' that includes allegations of breach of the GDPR or the DPA 2018, the claimant must specify in the particulars of claim:-

(a) the legislation and the provision that the claimant alleges the defendant has breached;
(b) any specific data or acts of processing to which the claim relates;
(c) the specific acts or omissions said to amount to such a breach, and the claimant's grounds for that allegation; and
(d) the remedies which the claimant seeks.[38]

48– 011 Representative actions etc

A single breach of the data protection principles may affect a group of data subjects. In relation to both general processing and law enforcement processing, special provision is made for a data subject to authorise certain bodies or other organisations to exercise the data subject's rights, both for compliance orders and for compensatory orders, as well as for a complaint to the Information Commissioner.[39] This is additional to the two procedures generally available in civil litigation for collective proceedings. There are thus three procedures potentially available for a breach of a data subject's rights to be brought by a claim other than in the data subject's own name:

---

34 Protocol para 3.6.

35 Protocol para 3.7.

36 CPR r 53.1(2)-(3). This will include a claim that is issued in the High Court and transferred to the County Court under CPR 53.4(2).

37 CPR rr 53.1(3)(b) and 53.4(1). This includes claims that also allege other causes of action, such as breach of confidence. See also para 19 of the Queen's Bench Guide.

38 Practice Direction 53B para 9. Although this is only mandatory in relation to claims that must be made in Media and Communications List, it is good general practice.

39 GDPR Art 80; LED Art 55; DPA 2018 ss 187-188.

(1) Representative proceedings.[40] Under the Civil Procedure Rules, where it is difficult or impossible for all persons affected by a claim to be parties to the proceedings, the court may order one or more persons to be made party to the claim as representative of persons who are not parties and to direct that orders made in the claim are to bind the represented persons. The critical requirement is that all the persons represented have 'the same interest' in the claim as the claimant. In a data protection claim, this will generally require the claim to be limited to one seeking compensation for the mere fact of a breach of the principles, rather than compensation that takes into account the particular circumstances of each of the data subjects.[41] It is not necessary for a representative claimant to obtain the authority of the represented person to bring the claim.[42] Nor is it necessary for a claimant to obtain the court's permission to issue a claim form as a representative of other claimants. A court has power to order that a person not act as a representative.[43] The representative claimant has full power to run the litigation on behalf of the represented class as the representative claimant thinks fit. Those represented are not parties to the litigation. Accordingly:

   (a) There is no disclosure against the represented parties, unless it is ordered as against a non-party.[44]

   (b) The represented parties are not liable for costs.[45]

(2) Under a group litigation order – a 'GLO.'[46] A GLO may be made where a number of claims give rise to common or related issues of fact or law. A GLO may be sought before or after the issue of a claim or claims. It may be sought by any party to a claim or on the court's own motion.[47] A GLO will identify the issues to be managed as part of the group litigation: for any individual claim to be captured by a GLO, it must raise these issues. It is a matter for the court to decide whether or not to make a GLO. Any judgment on a GLO issue will bind all the GLO claimants. Unlike representative proceedings, proceedings under a GLO allow for

---

40 Under CPR rr 19.6-19.7.

41 In *Lloyd v Google LLC* [2019] EWCA Civ 1599, [2020] EMLR 2, the claimant issued proceedings against the defendant Google on behalf of a class of more than 4 million Apple iPhone users, alleging that Google secretly tracked some of their internet activity, for commercial purposes, between 9 August 2011 and 15 February 2012. The claimant claimed a uniform amount by way of damages on behalf of each person within the defined class, without seeking to allege or prove any distinctive facts affecting any of them, save that they did not consent to the abstraction of their data. The judge at first instance had dismissed the claimant's application for permission to serve Google outside the jurisdiction inter alia on the basis that the members of the class did not have the 'same interest' within CPR 19.6(1) so as to justify allowing the claim to proceed as a representative action. This was overturned by the Court of Appeal on the basis that those whom the claimant sought to represent would all have had their browser generated information – something of value – taken by Google without their consent in the same circumstances during the same period, and were not seeking to rely on any personal circumstances affecting any individual claimant (whether distress or volume of data abstracted). The represented class were all victims of the same alleged wrong and had all sustained the same loss, namely loss of control over their browser generated information. The claimant had disavowed reliance on any facts affecting any individual represented claimant. That concession had the effect of reducing the damages that could be claimed to the lowest common denominator. Google could not raise any defence to one represented claimant that did not apply to all others. The wrong was the same and the loss claimed was the same. Therefore, the represented parties did, in the relevant sense, have the same interest. There was no injustice in the pleaded claim proceeding as a representative one (at [75]-[80]).

42 *Independiente Ltd v Music Trading On-line (HK) Ltd* [2003] EWHC 470 (Ch) at [32]; *Howells v Dominion Insurance Co Ltd* [2005] EWHC 552 (QB); *PNPF Trust Company Ltd v Taylor* [2009] EWHC 1693 (Ch) at [47].

43 CPR r 19.6(2).

44 *Ventouris v Mountain* [1991] 1 WLR 607, [1991] 3 All ER 472.

45 *Howells v Dominion Insurance Co Ltd* [2005] EWHC 552 (QB); *Smithkline Beecham plc v Avery* [2009] EWHC 1924 (QB).

46 Under CPR 19.11 and PD 19B.

47 PD 19B para 4.

divergences between the claimants: the judgment on the GLO issues leaves the other issues (eg quantification of compensation) to be decided on a claim-by-claim basis.

(3) Representation by a body or organisation pursuant to a data subject's authorisation.[48] This enables an individual data subject to authorise certain types of bodies or other organisations to exercise a data subject's rights, including the right to an effective judicial remedy. Unlike (1) and (2), there need be no other person apart from the single data subject with an interest in the claim or type of claim. In relation to non-General processing data protection claims, in order to be a 'representative body':

   (a) by enactment or its constitution, the body must be required (after payment of outgoings) to apply the whole of its income any capital it expends for charitable purposes, it must be prohibited from directly or indirectly distributing amongst its members any part of its assets (otherwise than for charitable or public purposes), and it must have objectives that are in the public interest; and

   (b) the body must be active in the field of the protection of data subjects' rights and freedoms with regard to the protection of their personal data.[49]

The Secretary of State may make regulations for a representative body to bring proceedings combining two or more such claims, but as yet no such regulations have been made.[50]

48– 012 Compliance orders

In relation to general processing and law enforcement processing (but not in relation to intelligence services processing),[51] where a court is satisfied that there has been an infringement of a data subject's rights under the data protection legislation in contravention of that legislation, it may make an order against the controller, or a processor acting on behalf of the controller, for the purposes of securing compliance with that legislation.[52] Such orders may be directed to non-compliance with the continuing obligations by a data controller or processor[53] or to a contravention of a data subject's rights.[54] A compliance order will require the controller, or a processor on behalf of that controller, to take the steps specified in that order or to refrain from taking the steps specified in that order, and it may specify the times within which each such step must be taken or desisted from.[55] The importance of compliance orders is

48 As provided for in DPA 2018 ss 187-188; GDPR Art 80, recital (142); LED Art 55. Such a body or organisation is called a 'representative body': DPA 2018 s 187(5).

49 DPA 2018 s 187(3)-(4) (in relation to law enforcement processing and intelligence services processing). In relation to General processing the requirements on the 'representative body' are substantially the same: GDPR Art 80(1).

50 DPA 2018 s 188. This does not apply to Scotland.

51 DPA 2018 s 167(4)(b). On the division between processing by 'the intelligence services,' a 'competent authority for law enforcement purposes' and 'general processing', see further §8– 002.

52 DPA 2018 s 167(1). The 'data protection legislation' means the GDPR, the applied GDPR, the DPA 2018 and regulations thereunder, and regulations made under the European Communities Act 1972 s 2(2) that related to the GDPR or the LED: DPA 2018 s 3(9). In relation to general processing, DPA 2018 s 167(1) embraces the right to an effective remedy against a controller or processor provided for by GDPR Art 79(1): DPA 2018 s 167(4)(a).

53 That is, the obligations set out in Chapter 9 (in relation to general processing) and Chapter 12 (in relation to law enforcement processing).

54 That is, the data subject rights set out in Chapter 10 (in relation to general processing) and Chapter 13 (in relation to law enforcement processing).

55 DPA 2018 ss 167(2)-(3).

underscored by the obligation on a controller to inform a data subject of the right to seek a compliance order.[56] In relation to intelligence services processing, a court may make the equivalent of a compliance order where:

(a) the controller has failed to comply with an access request;[57]
(b) the controller has not complied with a notice objecting to processing;[58]
(c) the personal data relating to the data subject is inaccurate;[59] or
(d) the processing infringes any of the six data protection principles applicable to intelligence services processing.[60]

48–013 Compensatory orders

Any person who has suffered damage as a result of contravention of the data protection legislation is entitled to compensation from the controller or processor for the damage suffered.[61] This applies to all four types of processing. 'Damage' covers both material (eg financial loss) and non-material damage, including distress.[62] Any controller involved in the contravening processing will be liable for the damage so caused.[63] A processor will be liable only in respect of the contravention of obligations that are specifically directed to a processor or where the processor has acted outside or contrary to lawful instructions from the controller.[64] A controller or processor has a defence where it proves that it was not in any way responsible for the event giving rise to the damage.[65] In relation to general processing, where more than one controller or processor, or both a controller and a processor, are involved in the same processing and are responsible for any damage caused by the processing, their liability is joint and several.[66] In relation to law enforcement processing and intelligence services processing, joint controllers are required to have determined in advance their respective responsibilities in

---

56 GDPR Art 12(4) (in relation to general processing); DPA 2018 ss 44(5)(e), 45(5)(e), 48(1)(b)(iv), 48(4)(d) and 51(5) (in relation to law enforcement processing by a competent authority).

57 DPA 2018 s 94(11)-(12).

58 DPA 2018 s 99(4)-(7).

59 DPA 2018 s 100(1).

60 DPA 2018 s 100(2). As to the meaning of the six data protection principles applicable to intelligence services processing, see §§14–007 to 14–015. In relation to the breadth of the court's discretion to make or decline to make an order, see §14–020.

61 GDPR Art 82(1) in relation to GDPR processing; DPA 2018 s 169(1) in relation to law enforcement processing and intelligence services processing; DPA 2018 s 22(1) in conjunction with GDPR Art 82(1) in relation to applied GDPR processing. On the division between 'intelligence services processing', 'law enforcement processing', 'GDPR processing' and 'applied GDPR processing', see §§8–002 and 9–002. The 'data protection legislation' means the GDPR, the applied GDPR, the DPA 2018 and regulations thereunder, and regulations made under the European Communities Act 1972 s 2(2) that related to the GDPR or the LED: DPA 2018 s 3(9).

62 GDPR Art 82(1) and DPA 2018 s 168(1) in relation to GDPR processing; DPA 2018 s 169(5) in relation to law enforcement processing and intelligence services processing; DPA 2018 s 22(1) in conjunction with GDPR Art 82(1) in relation to applied GDPR processing.

63 GDPR Art 82(2) in relation to GDPR processing; DPA 2018 s 169(2)(a) in relation to law enforcement processing and intelligence services processing; DPA 2018 s 22(1) in conjunction with GDPR Art 82(2) in relation to applied GDPR processing.

64 GDPR Art 82(2) in relation to GDPR processing; DPA 2018 s 169(2)(b) in relation to law enforcement processing and intelligence services processing; DPA 2018 s 22(1) in conjunction with GDPR Art 82(2) in relation to applied GDPR processing.

65 GDPR Art 82(3) in relation to GDPR processing; DPA 2018 s 169(3) in relation to law enforcement processing and intelligence services processing; DPA 2018 s 22(1) in conjunction with GDPR Art 82(3) in relation to applied GDPR processing.

66 GDPR Art 82(4) in relation to GDPR processing; DPA 2018 s 22(1) in conjunction with GDPR Art 82(4) in relation to applied GDPR processing. Where one or other has paid full compensation for the damage suffered, that controller or processor has a right of contribution from the other controller(s) or processor(s) according to the level of responsibility for the damage: GDPR Art 82(5).

a transparent 'arrangement.'[67] In those circumstances, a joint controller is only liable where that controller is responsible for compliance with the provision of the data protection legislation that has been contravened.[68] Damages awards under the previous data protection regime may provide some guidance to awards under the current regime, but the enlarged continuing obligations and data subject rights and the intervening recognition of a discrete fundamental right to the protection of personal data might result in higher awards than were previously the case.[69]

3. REGULATORY ENFORCEMENT

48–014 General processing

In relation to general processing,[70] the Information Commissioner (as the 'supervisory authority' for the purposes of the GDPR) is responsible for monitoring the application of the GDPR in order to protect the fundamental rights and freedoms of natural persons in relation to processing of personal data.[71] As such, the Commissioner can instigate regulatory processes without having received a complaint. On the other hand, where a data subject (or a body or organisation representative of one or more data subjects) lodges a complaint with the Information Commissioner in relation to general processing, the Commissioner must investigate it to the extent appropriate and must inform the data subject (or representative body) of the progress and outcome of the investigation within a reasonable period.[72] Unless manifestly unfounded or excessive, the Information Commissioner may not impose a charge on a data subject for dealing with such complaints.[73] As part of its regulatory powers in relation to general processing, the Information Commissioner may:

(a) Order the controller and the processor and, where applicable, the controller or

---

[67] DPA 2018 ss 58(2) and 61 in relation to law enforcement processing, s 104(2) in relation to intelligence services processing.

[68] DPA 2018 s 169(4). The 'data protection legislation' means the GDPR, the applied GDPR, the DPA 2018 and regulations thereunder, and regulations made under the European Communities Act 1972 s 2(2) that related to the GDPR or the LED: DPA 2018 s 3(9).

[69] As to damages under the DPA 2018, see §49– 008. In relation to the recognition of the fundamental right to the protection of personal data, see §§7– 019 to 7– 023. Initially, a superannuated approach to compensation had been taken under the DPA 1998, exemplified by Buxton LJ in *Johnson v Medical Defence Union* [2007] EWCA Civ 262, [2007] 3 CMLR 9, (2007) 96 BMLR 99 stating:

> There is no compelling reason to think that 'damage' in the directive has to go beyond its root meaning of pecuniary loss. Nor do I accept Mr Howe's contention that the fact that the directive envisages the protection of rights under art 8 of the European Convention (as to which, see [15] above) entails that compensation must be available in every case for loss of a type or category that would be covered by art 8: for example, damages for distress (at [74]).

Arden LJ dissented. In rejecting this passage as good law, the Court of Appeal in *Vidal Hall v Google Inc* [2015] EWCA Civ 311, [2016] QB 1003 was compelled to treat it as obiter (at [61]-[69]).

[70] On the division between 'GDPR processing', 'applied GDPR processing', 'law enforcement processing' and 'intelligence services processing' see §§8– 002 and 9– 002.

[71] GDPR Arts 51(1) and 57(1)(a) (in relation to GDPR processing) and DPA 2018 Sch 6 para 40(a)(i) in relation to applied GDPR processing; DPA 2018 s 115(1) in relation to both GDPR processing and applied GDPR processing. As to those fundamental rights and freedoms, see §8– 006.

[72] GDPR Art 57(1)(f) (in relation to GDPR processing) and DPA 2018 Sch 6 para 46 (in relation to applied GDPR processing); DPA 2018 s 165(1) in relation to both GDPR processing and applied GDPR processing. A data subject has a right to lodge a complaint with the Information Commissioner: GDPR Art 77 (in relation to GDPR processing) and DPA 2018 Sch 6 para 50 (in relation to applied GDPR processing). The Information Commissioner is required to facilitate the submission of complaints: GDPR Art 57(2).

[73] GDPR Art 57(3)-(4) (in relation to GDPR processing) and DPA 2018 Sch 6 para 46 (in relation to applied GDPR processing). Instead of charging a reasonable fee for a manifestly unfounded or excessive request, the Information Commissioner may refuse to act on the request: GDPR Art 57(4).

processor's representative to provide any information the Commissioner requires for the performance of the Commissioner's tasks – exercisable by an 'information notice.'[74]

(b) Notify the controller or the processor of an alleged infringement of the GDPR or applied GDPR regime – exercisable by an 'assessment notice.'[75]

(c) Order the controller or the processor to comply with the data subject's request to exercise his or her rights pursuant to the GDPR or applied GDPR regime, and/or to bring processing operations into compliance with the GDPR or applied GDPR regime – exercisable by an 'enforcement notice.'[76]

(d) Impose an administrative fine – exercisable by a 'penalty notice.'[77]

48– 015 Other processing

The Information Commissioner is the supervisory authority for the purposes of the Law Enforcement Directive.[78] In relation to law enforcement processing and intelligence services processing,[79] the Information Commissioner has enforcement duties and powers and duties that are similar to those owed and enjoyed in relation to general processing. Thus, the Information Commissioner must monitor and enforce the provisions of the DPA 2018 dealing with law enforcement processing and intelligence services processing.[80] Accordingly, the Commissioner can instigate regulatory processes without having received a complaint. On the other hand, where a data subject lodges a complaint with the Information Commissioner in relation to law enforcement or intelligence service processing, the Commissioner must investigate it to the extent appropriate and must inform the data subject of the progress and outcome of the investigation within a reasonable period.[81] Unless manifestly unfounded or excessive, the Information Commissioner may not impose a charge on a data subject for dealing with such complaints.[82] As part of the regulatory powers in relation to law enforcement processing and intelligence services processing, the Information Commissioner may:

(a) Order the controller and the processor and, where applicable, the controller or processor's representative to provide any information the Commissioner requires for the performance of the Commissioner's tasks – exercisable by an 'information notice.'[83]

(b) Notify the controller or the processor of an alleged infringement of the requirements of the law enforcement processing regime or the intelligence services processing

---

[74] GDPR Art 58(1)(a) (in relation to GDPR processing) and DPA 2018 Sch 6 para 47 (in relation to applied GDPR processing); DPA 2018 s 115(5) in relation to both GDPR processing and applied GDPR processing. The Commissioner is given further supportive powers in GDPR Art 58(1)(b)-(f), DPA 2018 s 115(7) and Sch 15.

[75] GDPR Art 58(2)(a)-(b); DPA 2018 ss 115(6) and 146.

[76] GDPR Art 58(2)(c)-(d); DPA 2018 s 115(8)(a). The Commissioner is given further supportive powers in GDPR Art 58(2)(e)-(h) and (j).

[77] GDPR Art 58(2)(i); DPA 2018 s 115(9). Further provision is made in GDPR Art 83. The factors identified in GDPR Art 83(2) as relevant to the amount of an administrative fine are largely replicated in DPA 2018 s 155(3).

[78] DPA 2018 s 116(1)(a) and LED Art 41.

[79] On the division between 'GDPR processing', 'applied GDPR processing', 'law enforcement processing' and 'intelligence services processing' see §§8– 002 and 9– 002.

[80] DPA 2018 Sch 13 para 1(1).

[81] DPA 2018 Sch 13 para 1(1)(g) in conjunction with s 165(4)-(5). A data subject has a right to lodge a complaint with the Information Commissioner: DPA 2018 s 165(2). The Information Commissioner is required to facilitate the submission of complaints: DPA 2018 s 165(3).

[82] DPA 2018 ss 134-135. Instead of charging a reasonable fee for a manifestly unfounded or excessive request, the Information Commissioner may refuse to act on the request: DPA 2018 s 135(1)(b).

[83] DPA 2018 s 142(1).

regime (as applicable) – exercisable by an 'assessment notice.'[84]

(c) Order the controller or the processor to comply with the data subject's request to exercise his or her rights pursuant under the law enforcement processing regime or the intelligence services processing regime (as applicable), and/or to bring processing operations into compliance with the law enforcement processing regime or the intelligence services processing regime (as applicable) – exercisable by an 'enforcement notice.'[85]

(d) Impose an administrative fine – exercisable by a 'penalty notice.'[86]

48–016 Service of notices

The Information Commissioner may give a notice under the DPA 2018 by delivering it to that individual, by sending it to that individual at his or her usual or last-known place of residence or business, or by leaving it for the individual at his or her usual or last-known place of residence or business.[87] A notice under the DPA 2018 may be given to a body corporate or unincorporate by sending it by post to the proper officer of the body at its principal office or by addressing it to the proper officer of the body and leaving it at that office.[88]

48–017 Guidance

The Information Commissioner is under a statutory duty to produce and publish guidance about how the Commissioner proposes to exercise the Commissioner's functions in connection with information notices, assessment notices, enforcement notices and penalty notices.[89] The Commissioner's guidance is contained in an undated document entitled *Regulatory Action Policy*. This is said to:

> sit under the umbrella of [the Commissioner's] Strategic Plan for 2017-2021 which sets out the Information Commissioner's mission to increase the trust the public has in government, public bodies and the private sector: trust in transparency, in the digital economy and in digital public service delivery.[90]

As well as being expressed to 'fulfil the obligation in the DPA 2018 to provide guidance' (p 5), the document covers the Commissioner's regulatory activity under numerous other statutory provisions.[91] The *Regulatory Action Policy* was laid before Parliament and there was no resolution not to approve it.[92]

48–018 Information notice (IN)

The Information Commissioner may give an 'information notice' to a controller, a processor

---

84 DPA 2018 s 146(1).

85 DPA 2018 s 149(1) and (2)(a)-(b).

86 DPA 2018 s 155(1) in conjunction with s 149(2)(a)-(b).

87 DPA 2018 s 141(2). This is in addition to any other lawful method of giving notice: DPA 2018 s 141(7). Where the notice is given by post, then, unless the contrary is proved, it is deemed to have been effected at the time at which the letter would be delivered in the ordinary course of the post: Interpretation Act 1978 s 7.

88 DPA 2018 s 141(3). In relation to a company registered under UK company law, the 'principal office' is its registered office: DPA 2018 s 141(6). As to the position of a partnership in Scotland, see DPA 2018 s 141(4). The 'proper officer' means the secretary or other executive officer charged with the conduct of the affairs of the company or other body: DPA 2018 s 141(6).

89 DPA 2018 s 160(1). The Act spells out in detail what the guidance must include: DPA 2018 s 160(3)-(7).

90 *Regulatory Action Policy*, p 4.

91 The statutory guidance under DPA 2018 s 160 is at pp 15-29.

92 See HL Secondary Legislation Scrutiny Committee, 40th Report of Session 2017-19, 11 September 2018, HL Paper 185, para 11. It is only the first edition of the guidance that is subject to Parliamentary approval.

or any other person.[93] The purpose of an information notice is to facilitate the Commissioner checking whether there has been compliance with data protection legislation.[94] The Commissioner's statutory guidance provides that the criteria for giving an information notice include:

- the risk of harm to individuals or the level of intrusion into their privacy potentially posed by the events or data processing under investigation;
- the utility of requiring a formal response within a defined time period;
- the utility of testing responses, by the fact that it is an offence to deliberately or recklessly make a false statement in a material respect in response; and
- the public interest in the response.[95]

Although there are limits to the content of an information notice, there are no statutory pre-requisites before the Commissioner may give a person an information notice.[96]

— An information notice addressed to a controller or processor may require the recipient to provide the Commissioner with information that the Commissioner reasonably requires for the purposes of carrying out the Commissioner's functions under the data protection legislation.[97]

— An information notice, whether addressed to a controller, processor or any other person, may require the recipient to provide the Commissioner with information that the Commissioner reasonably requires for the purposes of: (a) investigating a suspected failure to comply with one or other of the continuing obligations,[98] the data subject's rights,[99] or a suspected offence under the DPA 2018; or (b) determining whether general processing of personal data is carried out by an individual in the course of a purely personal or household activity.[100]

A person who is given an information notice may appeal to the First-tier Tribunal against it.[101]

---

93 DPA 2018 s 142(1).

94 The 'data protection legislation' means the GDPR, the applied GDPR, the DPA 2018 and regulations thereunder, and regulations made under the European Communities Act 1972 s 2(2) that related to the GDPR or the LED: DPA 2018 s 3(9). In relation to law enforcement processing, where a data subject requests the Commissioner to check that the controller's refusal of his or her data subject request was lawful or that the controller's restriction of the data subject's rights was lawful, the Commissioner must take appropriate steps, which may include an information notice, in order to respond to that request: DPA 2018 s 51(3).

95 *Regulatory Action Policy*, p 15.

96 The power to issue an information notice does not apply to personal data where exemption from the information notice power is required for the purpose of safeguarding national security or defence purposes: DPA 2018 ss 26(2)(h)(i), 110(2)(e)(i). The Information Commissioner may not give an information notice with respect to the processing of personal data for the 'special purposes' unless: (a) the Information Commissioner has under DPA 2018 s 174(3) made a written determination with respect to the data that has taken effect (or has reasonable ground to suspect that such a determination could be made and requires the information for such a determination); or (b) the processing has taken effect: DPA 2018 s 143(1). A determination under s 174(3) does not take effect until the later of the expiry of the appeal period or the conclusion of the appeal process: s 174(6). As to the meaning of 'the special purposes' see §11–050. In relation to such determinations, see §§48–056 to 48–058.

97 DPA 2018 s 142(1)(a). The Information Commissioner's functions includes all of those considered in §§48–014 to 48–055. The 'data protection legislation' means the GDPR, the applied GDPR, the DPA 2018 and regulations thereunder, and regulations made under the European Communities Act 1972 s 2(2) that related to the GDPR or the LED: DPA 2018 s 3(9).

98 That is, the obligations set out in Chapter 9 (in relation to general processing), Chapter 12 (in relation to law enforcement processing) and Chapter 14 (in relation to intelligence services processing).

99 That is, the data subject rights set out in Chapter 10 (in relation to general processing), Chapter 13 (in relation to law enforcement processing) and Chapter 14 (in relation to intelligence services processing).

100 DPA 2018 s 142(1)(b). As to the meaning of 'purely personal or household activity', see §8–038. This does not apply to applied GDPR processing, law enforcement processing or intelligence services processing: DPA 2018 s 3(14)(c) and s 142(10).

101 DPA 2018 s 162(1)(b). Subject to any extension of time granted by the FTT, the person named in the information notice has 28 days after the date on which the notice was sent to that person: FTT Rules r 22(1)(b). As to the nature of the appeal, see §48–053.

48– 019 IN limits

An information notice will not extend to information:

— that is subject to legal professional privilege but only if it is in respect of rights, liabilities, obligations or proceedings arising under data protection legislation;[102]

— the disclosure of which would breach a privilege of either House of Parliament;[103] or

— that would reveal evidence of the commission of an offence by the person to whom it is addressed.[104]

In relation to the processing of personal data for the special purposes, the circumstances in which the Information Commissioner has power to give an information notice are extremely limited.[105] Unless:

(a) a special purposes determination has taken effect (ie all appeal rights against the determination have been exhausted and failed); or

(b) the Commissioner has reasonable grounds for suspecting that a special purposes determination could be made and the Commissioner requires the information in the notice for the purposes of making that determination,

the Commissioner may not give an information notice with the respect to the processing of personal data for the special purposes.[106]

48– 020 IN formalities

An information notice must:

(a) state the legislative basis on which it is given;[107]

(b) state why the Commissioner requires the information;[108]

(c) provide information about the consequences of non-compliance with it;[109] and

(d) set out the rights of appeal against the notice.[110]

An information notice may:

(e) specify or describe particular information or a category of information;

(f) specify the form in which the information must be provided;

(g) specify the time or period within which the information must be provided;

---

[102] DPA 2018 s 143(3)-(5). The 'data protection legislation' means the GDPR, the applied GDPR, the DPA 2018 and regulations thereunder, and regulations made under the European Communities Act 1972 s 2(2) that related to the GDPR or the LED: DPA 2018 s 3(9).

[103] DPA 2018 s 143(2). As to the meaning of 'the privileges of either House of Parliament,' see Chapter 30.

[104] DPA 2013 s 143(6)-(9). Certain offences are excepted including offences under the DPA 2018.

[105] The 'special purposes' means any of: (a) the purposes of journalism; (b) academic purposes; (c) artistic purposes; (d) literary purposes. See further §11– 050.

[106] DPA 2018 s 143(1). As to the meaning of a 'special purposes determination', the circumstances in which it may be made and the list of appellate steps that must be completed before it takes effect, see §§48– 056 to 48– 059. In short, the circumstances are more theoretical than real.

[107] DPA 2018 s 142(2)(a). In other words, whether it is given under DPA 2018 s 142(1)(a), 142(1)(b)(i) or 142(1)(b)(ii).

[108] DPA 2018 s 142(2)(b). It is prudent for the Commissioner to spell out precisely and convincingly why the information is required, as it will facilitate enforcement of the information notice should there not be compliance.

[109] DPA s 142(4)(a). The consequences of non-compliance are: (i) an exposure to a court order under s 145; (ii) in the case of non-compliance by making a statement that the person knows to be false in a material respect or by recklessly making a statement that is false in a material respect, an exposure to prosecution under s 144; (iii) an exposure to a penalty notice under s 155; and (iv) in the case of non-compliance by destroying or otherwise disposing of, concealing, blocking or falsifying all or part of the information, or permitting the same, with the intention of preventing the Information Commissioner from viewing or being provided any of that information, an exposure to prosecution under s 148.

[110] DPA 2018 s 142(4)(b).

(h) specify the place where the information must be provided.[111]

48– 021 IN time for compliance

The default position is that an information notice may not require a person to do anything before the end of the period within which an appeal may be brought against the notice.[112] The Commissioner's statutory guidance provides that in specifying the period for compliance:

in particular whether or not to issue an 'urgent' information notice, we will have regard to what action is appropriate and proportionate and criteria including:

- the extent to which urgent investigation may prevent or limit the risk of serious harm to individuals or serious intrusion into their privacy. For example requesting an early report on a serious data security breach in order for the ICO to advise the controller on and validate appropriate notification to data subjects and appropriate mitigation of the breach.
- the extent to which urgent investigation may prevent the sanitisation, alteration, destruction, concealment, blocking, falsifying, or removal of relevant evidence of data processing;
- the scope of the notice, that is the scope of questions or requests in an information notice;
- the additional burden on the recipient in having to comply with a notice urgently;
- the impact on the rights of the recipient, should the ICO obtain information under an urgent information notice (which may be by court order), prior to an appeal being heard by the Information Tribunal [*sic*];
- the length of time of the investigation. For example, it may be appropriate and proportionate to issue an urgent information notice during a long running investigation where the questions are limited and the response may bring the investigation closer to completion; and
- the comparative effectiveness of other investigatory powers of the ICO.[113]

If an appeal is initiated against an information notice, that has the effect of staying the notice pending the determination or withdrawal of the appeal.[114] Where, however, an information notice states that in the Commissioner's opinion the information is required urgently and gives the Commissioner's reasons for that – an 'urgency statement' – the notice may require the information to be provided within a period of not less than 24 hours beginning with when the notice is given.[115] Where there is an urgency statement, the initiation of an appeal will not stay the notice.[116] A person may instead apply to a court either for the disapplication of the urgency statement or for a change to the time allowed for compliance with the requirements of the notice.[117] The Commissioner may cancel an information notice by giving written notice to the person to whom the information notice was given.[118]

---

111 DPA 2018 s 142(3).

112 DPA 2018 s 142(5). An appeal must be brought within 28 days of the date on which notice was sent to the person named in the notice: FTT Rules r 22(1)(b). See further §48– 053.

113 *Regulatory Action Policy*, pp 15-16.

114 DPA 2018 s 142(6).

115 DPA 2018 s 142(7).

116 DPA 2018 s 142(7).

117 DPA 2018 s 164. In England and Wales, the court is the High Court or the county court; in Scotland it is the Court of Session or the sheriff; and in Northern Ireland it is the High Court or a county court: DPA 2018 s 180(1). Where, however, the notice concerns intelligence services processing or the notice stated that the information was required urgently, it is only the High Court or the Court of Session: DPA 2018 s 180(3)-(4).

118 DPA 2018 s 142(8). There is no provision for the person to whom an information notice is given to apply to the Commissioner for a cancellation or variation of the notice: cf enforcement notices under DPA 2018 s 153(2)-(3).

48– 022 IN non-compliance

Where the Commissioner is satisfied that a person has failed to comply with an information notice, the Commissioner may give that person a penalty notice.[119] Alternatively, where the Information Commissioner considers that a person to whom an information notice has been given had failed to comply with a requirement in that notice, the Commissioner may apply to a court for an order requiring the person to provide information referred to in the notice – an 'information order.'[120] The Commissioner's statutory guidance states that:

> If a recipient of an information notice does not fully respond within the applicable time period, whether urgent or not, the Commissioner will promptly apply for a court order requiring a response. The Commissioner may decide not to make such application, having regard to criteria including:
>
> - the reasons for non-compliance with the information notice;
> - any commitments given by the recipient to responding to the information notice;
> - whether the information has been or is likely to be obtained from another source;
> - the comparative effectiveness of other investigatory and enforcement powers of the ICO. For example, the ICO may decide it has sufficient evidence to move to an enforcement action in any event; and
> - the public interest.[121]

48– 023 Information orders

Where, on an application by the Information Commissioner, the court is satisfied that a person has failed to comply with a requirement of an information notice, it may make an order requiring the person to provide the Commissioner with some or all of the following:

(a) information referred to in the information notice;

(b) other information that the court, having regard to the Commissioner's statement in the information notice as to why the Commissioner required the information, is satisfied the Commissioner does indeed require.[122]

The court is solely concerned with whether the recipient of the information notice has failed to comply with a requirement of that notice and, if so, which information the court should order the person to provide to the Information Commissioner.[123] An order so made is called an 'information order.' If the court does make an information order, the order must specify the time at which, or the period within which, the information must be provided.[124] An

[119] DPA 2018 s 155(1), following a notice of intent. Penalty notices are considered at §§48– 039 to 48– 052. The amounts that may be imposed in a penalty notice for non-compliance with an information notice are very significant: DPA 2018 s 157(4).

[120] DPA 2018 s 145. In England and Wales, the court is the High Court or the county court; in Scotland it is the Court of Session or the sheriff; and in Northern Ireland it is the High Court or a county court: DPA 2018 s 180(1). Where, however, the notice concerns intelligence services processing or the notice stated that the information was required urgently, it is only the High Court or the Court of Session: DPA 2018 s 180(3)-(4).

[121] *Regulatory Action Policy*, p 16, published under DPA 2018 s 160(1).

[122] DPA 2018 s 145(2). An application for an information order is made by a Part 8 claim form with a supporting application notice. This may be made to the applications court. The respondent to the application will be the person served with the information notice.

[123] DPA 2018 s 145(2). Given that the recipient of an information notice has a right to appeal to the FTT against it and that, unless there is an urgency statement, an application for an information order cannot be made before the time for appeal against the notice has expired, and that any appeal stays the information notice, the implication is that the FTT is the exclusive forum in which to challenge the Information Commissioner's decision to issue an information notice. If that facility is not invoked, then, other than where an information notice includes an urgency statement that has been challenged, on any application for an information order it will not be the function of the court to consider whether the notice should have been given: it will be treated as having been duly given.

[124] DPA 2018 s 145(3)(b). Where an information notice contains an 'urgency statement,' the person to whom the notice is addressed may apply to the court for a disapplication of the urgency statement in relation to some or all the requirements of the notice, and/or may apply for a change to the time at which, or the period within which,

information order may also specify the form in which the information must be provided and the place where the information must be provided.[125]

48– 024 IN offences

It is an offence for a person to make a statement in response to an information notice that that person knows to be false in a material respect, or recklessly to make a statement that is false in a material respect.[126] It is also an offence for a person who has been given an information notice to destroy or otherwise dispose of, conceal, block or falsify all or part of the information, or to permit the same, with the intention of preventing the Information Commissioner from viewing or being provided any of that information.[127] Where there are reasonable grounds for suspecting that an offence has been or is being committed, the Commissioner may apply to a court for a warrant to enter and search premises and to inspect, examine, operate and test any equipment found on the premises which is used or intended to be used for the processing of personal data.[128] It is an offence for a person intentionally to obstruct a person in the execution of such a warrant or to fail without reasonable excuse to give a person executing a warrant such assistance as the person may reasonably require for the execution of the warrant.[129]

48– 025 Assessment notice (AN)

The Information Commissioner may give an 'assessment notice' to a controller or a processor.[130] The purpose of an assessment notice is to permit the Information Commissioner to assess whether the controller or processor has complied or is complying with the data protection legislation, including by giving the Commissioner access to premises and equipment and by requiring the provision of documents and explanations.[131] It is by assessment notice that

---

a requirement in the notice must be complied with: DPA 2018 s 164(2). The court may disapply the urgency notice in part or in whole or it may vary its requirements in whole or in part: DPA 2018 s 164(3).

125 DPA 2018 s 145(3)(a), (c).

126 DPA 2018 s 144.

127 DPA 2018 s 148.

128 DPA 2018 s 154 and Sch 15 para 1(1)(a)(ii). In England and Wales, a warrant is sought from a judge of the High Court, a circuit judge or a District Judge (Magistrates' Court); in Scotland it is sought from a judge of the Court of Session, the sheriff or the summary sheriff; and in Northern Ireland it is sought from a judge of the High Court or a county court judge: DPA 2018 Sch 15 paras 2(1), 18 and 19.

129 DPA 2018 Sch 15 para 15.

130 DPA 2018 s 146(1). The Commissioner may not give an assessment notice:

(a) To a controller or processor with respect to the processing of personal data for the 'special purposes:' DPA 2018 s 147(5). This includes the 'purposes of journalism.' As to the full meaning of 'the special purposes' see §11– 050.

(b) To the Security Service, the Secret Intelligence Service, the Government Communications Headquarters, the special forces, the tribunals established under the Regulation of Investigatory Powers Act 2000 s 65, the Interception of Communications Act 1985 s 7, the Security Service Act 1985 s 5, the Intelligence Services Act 1994 s 9, the Security Vetting Appeals Panel, the Security Commission, the National Criminal Intelligence Service, the Service Authority for the National Criminal Intelligence Service, the Serious Organised Crime Authority, the National Crime Agency, or the Intelligence and Security Committee of Parliament: DPA 2018 s 147(6) in conjunction with FOIA s 23(3).

(c) To the Office for Standards in Education, Children Services and Skills in so far as it is a controller or processor in respect of information processed for the purposes of functions exercisable by HM Chief Inspector of Education, Children Services and Skills by virtue of the Care Standards Act 2000 s 5(1)(a).

131 The 'data protection legislation' means the GDPR, the applied GDPR, the DPA 2018 and regulations thereunder, and regulations made under the European Communities Act 1972 s 2(2) that related to the GDPR or the LED: DPA 2018 s 3(9). Whereas an assessment notice yields a non-consensual assessment, in relation to general processing the Information Commissioner also has the function of carrying out consensual assessments of the processing of a controller or a processor: GDPR Art 58(1); DPA 2018 s 129. 'Good practice in the processing of personal data' includes compliance with the requirements of data protection legislation: DPA 2018 s 128(5).

the Commissioner carries out data protection audits under the GDPR.[132] The Commissioner's statutory guidance states that in deciding whether to give an assessment notice:

> We will have regard to what action is appropriate and proportionate, and criteria including:
> - where we have conducted a risk assessment or other regulatory action, there is a probability that personal data is not being processed in compliance with the data protection legislation, together with a likelihood of damage or distress to individuals;
> - it is necessary to verify compliance with an enforcement notice;
> - communications with or information (eg news reports, statutory reporting or publications) about the controller or processor suggest that they are not processing personal data in compliance with the data protection legislation; and
> - the controller or processor has failed to respond to an information notice within an appropriate time.[133]

There are no statutory pre-requisites before the Commissioner may give a controller or a processor an assessment notice.

48–026 AN content

An assessment notice may require the controller or processor named in the notice to do any of the following:[134]

(a) permit the Commissioner to enter specified premises;

(b) direct the Commissioner to documents on the premises that are of a specified description;[135]

(c) assist the Commissioner to view information of a specified description that is capable of being viewed using equipment on the premises;

(d) comply with a request from the Commissioner for a copy (in such form as may be requested) of:

  (i) the documents to which the Commissioner is directed;

  (ii) the information which the Commissioner is assisted to view;

(e) direct the Commissioner to equipment or other material on the premises which is of a specified description;

(f) permit the Commissioner to inspect or examine the documents, information, equipment or material to which the Commissioner is directed or which the Commissioner is assisted to view;

(g) provide the Commissioner with an explanation of such documents, information, equipment or material;

(h) permit the Commissioner to observe the processing of personal data that takes place on the premises; and

(i) make available for interview by the Commissioner a specified number of people of a specified description who process personal data on behalf of the controller, not exceeding the number who are willing to be interviewed.[136]

---

[132] GDPR Art 58(1)(b); DPA 2018 s 115(6)-(7). In relation to law enforcement processing, where a data subject requests the Commissioner to check that the controller's refusal of his or her data subject request was lawful or that the controller's restriction of the data subject's rights was lawful, the Commissioner must take appropriate steps, which may include an assessment notice, in order to respond to that request: DPA 2018 s 51(3).

[133] *Regulatory Action Policy* p 17, produced and published under DPA 2018 s 160(1), (4)-(5).

[134] DPA 2018 s 146(2). A reference to 'the Commissioner' includes references to the Commissioner's officers and staff: DPA 2018 s 146(3).

[135] Examples of the sorts of documents that the Commissioner might require are given in the *Regulatory Action Policy* p 18 and include: strategies, policies, procedures, guidance, codes of practice, training material, protocols, frameworks, memoranda of understanding, contracts, privacy statements, privacy impact assessments, control data, job descriptions.

[136] The Information Commissioner's statutory guidance – *Regulatory Action Policy* – states (pp 20-21):

> We conduct interviews to develop further understanding of working practices and/or awareness of

For enforcement purposes, it is essential that the premises be specified in the assessment notice.[137] A person who is given an assessment notice may appeal to the First-tier Tribunal against it.[138]

48– 027 AN limits

An assessment notice will not require:

— disclosure of a communication that is subject to legal professional privilege but only if it is in respect of rights, liabilities, obligations or proceedings arising under data protection legislation;[139] or

— a person to do something that would involve an infringement of a privilege of either House of Parliament.[140]

In relation to the processing of personal data for the special purposes, the Information Commissioner has no power to give an assessment notice.[141] The Information Commissioner may, however, use the freestanding inspection power, which is unrestricted by reference to the special purposes, to similar end.[142]

48– 028 AN formalities

An assessment notice must:

(a) in relation to each requirement imposed by the notice, specify the time or times at which, or the period or periods by which, the requirement must be complied with;[143]

(b) provide information about the consequences of non-compliance with it;[144] and

---

regulatory obligations. Departmental managers, operational staff, support staff (eg IT staff, security staff) as well as staff involved with information and information governance may be interviewed.
Where possible we will schedule and agree interviews with the controller or processor before the on-site audit. We will give a schedule of areas to be covered before the audit, and will discuss and agree the level and grade of staff to be interviewed (eg managers, operational staff etc). Individuals should be advised by the target organisation in advance of their required participation.
We will use questions to understand individual roles and processes followed or managed, specifically referring to the handling of personal data and its security. Some questions may cover training and awareness, but they will not be framed as a test, nor are they intended to catch people out.
Interviews may be conducted at an individual's desk or in a separate room dependent upon circumstances, and whether there is a need to observe the working environment or examine information and records. Interviews will normally be 'one-to-one', but sometimes it may be appropriate to include a number of staff in an interview – where, for example, there are shared responsibilities. Auditors will take notes during the interviews.

137 DPA 2018 Sch 15 para 2(2).

138 DPA 2018 s 162(1)(b). Subject to any extension of time granted by the FTT, the person named in the assessment notice has 28 days after the date on which the notice was sent to that person: FTT Rules r 22(1)(b).

139 DPA 2018 s 147(2)-(4). The 'data protection legislation' means the GDPR, the applied GDPR, the DPA 2018 and regulations thereunder, and regulations made under the European Communities Act 1972 s 2(2) that related to the GDPR or the LED: DPA 2018 s 3(9).

140 DPA 2018 s 147(1). As to the meaning of 'the privileges of either House of Parliament,' see Chapter 30.

141 DPA 2018 s 147(5). The 'special purposes' means any of: (a) the purposes of journalism; (b) academic purposes; (c) artistic purposes; (d) literary purposes. See further §11– 050.

142 DPA 2018 s 119(1). See further §48– 055. Unlike the DPA 2018, Modernised Convention 108, while upholding the right and freedom of expression, requires it to be reconciled with, rather than cause it to trump, the fundamental freedoms of data subjects to which the Convention gives expression: see Arts 5(1), 6(2), 7(2), 9(1)(d), 9(2), 10(2), 10(4), 11(1)-(2), 14(4)(d), 14(6) and 20. Since the inspection powers of the Information Commissioner under DPA 2018 s 146 are non-existent in relation to processing of personal data for the special purposes, inspection under DPA 2018 s 119(1) will more readily be 'necessary' to discharge the international obligations in Modernised Convention 108.

143 DPA 2018 s 146(4).

144 DPA s 146(5)(a). The consequences of non-compliance are: (i) an exposure to a penalty notice under s 155; (ii) an exposure to a warrant under Sch 15; and (iii) in the case of non-compliance by destroying or otherwise disposing

(c) set out the rights of appeal against the notice.[145]

Where an assessment notice is given to a processor, the Information Commissioner must, so far as reasonably practicable, give a copy of that notice to each of the controllers for whom the processor processes personal data.[146]

48–029 AN time for compliance

The default position is that an assessment notice may not require a person to do anything before the end of the period within which an appeal may be brought against the notice.[147] The Information Commissioner's statutory guidance states:

> When deciding the period for compliance with assessment notices, in particular whether or not to issue an 'urgent', 'no-notice' or 'short-notice' assessment notice, we will have regard to what action is appropriate and proportionate, and criteria including:
>
> - the extent to which urgent investigation may prevent or limit the risk of serious harm to individuals or serious intrusion into their privacy;
> - the extent to which urgent investigation may prevent the sanitisation, alteration, destruction, concealment, blocking, falsifying, or removal of relevant evidence of data processing;
> - the scope of the notice, that is the scope of our requests in an assessment notice;
> - the additional burden on the recipient in having to comply with a notice urgently, on no-notice or on short-notice;
> - the impact on the rights of the recipient should the ICO gain access to its premises and data processing activities urgently, without notice or on short notice, and without the opportunity to appeal and/or for an appeal to be heard by the Information Tribunal [*sic*];
> - the length of time of the investigation. For example, it may be appropriate and proportionate to issue an urgent assessment notice during a long running investigation where the requests are limited and the response may bring the investigation closer to completion; and
> - the comparative effectiveness of other investigatory powers of the ICO.[148]

If an appeal is initiated against an assessment notice, that has the effect of staying the notice pending the determination or withdrawal of the appeal.[149] Where, however, an assessment notice states that in the Commissioner's opinion:

(i) there are reasonable grounds for suspecting that the controller or processor is failing, or has failed, to comply with any of the continuing obligations[150] or the data subject's rights,[151] or that an offence under the Act has been, or is being, committed; and

(ii) it is necessary for the controller or processor to comply with a requirement in the

---

of, concealing, blocking or falsifying all or part of the information, or permitting the same, with the intention of preventing the Information Commissioner from viewing or being provided any of that information, an exposure to prosecution under s 148.

145 DPA 2018 s 146(5)(b). A person who is given an assessment notice may appeal to the First-tier Tribunal: DPA 2018 s 162(1)(b). The notice should inform the recipient that an appeal must be brought within 28 days of the date on which notice was sent to the person named in the notice: FTT Rules r 22(1)(b).

146 DPA 2018 s 146(11).

147 DPA 2018 s 146(6). An appeal must be brought within 28 days of the date on which notice was sent to the person named in the notice: FTT Rules r 22(1)(b).

148 *Regulatory Action Policy*, pp 17-18, prepared and published under DPA 2018 s 160(1), (4)-(5).

149 DPA 2018 s 146(7).

150 That is, the obligations set out in Chapter 9 (in relation to general processing), Chapter 12 (in relation to law enforcement processing) and Chapter 14 (in relation to intelligence services processing).

151 That is, the data subject rights set out in Chapter 10 (in relation to general processing), Chapter 13 (in relation to law enforcement processing) and Chapter 14 (in relation to intelligence services processing).

notice in less than 7 days,

and the reasons for both are given in the notice, then provided that the notice does not specify domestic premises, the assessment notice may specify that lesser period for compliance and the initiation of an appeal will not stay the notice.[152] Where the Commissioner does not hold the opinion in (i) and (ii), or the notice specifies domestic premises, the Commissioner may instead include an 'urgency statement' in the notice. This is a statement that in the Commissioner's opinion it is necessary for the controller or processor to comply with the requirement in the notice urgently and it gives the Commissioner's reasons for that.[153] Where there is an urgency statement, at least 7 days must be given for compliance with the requirements, but the initiation of an appeal will not stay the notice.[154] A person may instead apply to a court either for the disapplication of the urgency statement or for a change to the time allowed for compliance with the requirements of the notice.[155] The Commissioner may cancel an assessment notice by giving written notice to the person to whom the notice was given.[156]

48– 030 Inspection during assessment

Central to the assessment process are the inspections and examinations that the Information Commissioner may carry out.[157] That process enables the Commissioner to identify object evidence of compliance with the requirements of the applicable data protection regime, and how policies and procedures have been implemented. The Commissioner's statutory guidance states:

> These reviews of personal data, and associated logs and audit trails, may consider both manually and electronically stored data, including data stored centrally, locally and on mobile devices and media.
>
> We use these reviews to evaluate how an organisation:
>
> - obtains, stores, organises, adapts or alters information (eg policies and procedures) or personal data;
> - ensures the confidentiality, integrity and availability of the data or service it provides;
> - retrieves, consults, or uses the information or personal data;
> - discloses personal data by transmitting or disseminating or otherwise making the data available; and
> - weeds and destroys personal data.
>
> The review may also cover management/control information, to monitor and record how personal data is being processed, and to measure how a controller meets their wider obligations under the legislation.
>
> The review may evaluate physical and IT-related security measures, including how personal data is stored and disposed of.
>
> The review and evaluation process may take place on site as part of a discussion with staff to demonstrate 'practice', or independently by way of sampling by auditors. If information is held electronically we may require the controller to provide manual copies or facilitate direct access.[158]

---

[152] DPA 2018 s 146(9). 'Domestic premises' means premises, or a part of premises, used as a dwelling: DPA 2018 s 148(12).

[153] DPA 2018 s 146(8).

[154] DPA 2018 s 146(8).

[155] DPA 2018 s 164. In England and Wales, the court is the High Court or the county court; in Scotland it is the Court of Session or the sheriff; and in Northern Ireland it is the High Court or a county court: DPA 2018 s 180(1). Where, however, the notice concerns intelligence services processing or the notice stated that the information was required urgently, it is only the High Court or the Court of Session: DPA 2018 s 180(3)-(4).

[156] DPA 2018 s 146(10). There is no provision for the person to whom an assessment notice is given to apply to the Commissioner for a cancellation or variation of the notice: cf enforcement notices under DPA 2018 s 153(2)-(3).

[157] See §48– 026.

[158] *Regulatory Action Policy*, pp 19-20, prepared and published under DPA 2018 s 160(1), (4)-(5).

48–031 AN non-compliance

There are two potential consequences that may follow from non-compliance with an assessment notice. First, where the Commissioner is satisfied that a person has failed to comply with an assessment notice, the Commissioner may give that person a penalty notice.[159] Secondly, where the Information Commissioner considers that a person to whom an assessment notice has been given has failed to comply with a requirement in that notice, the Commissioner may apply to a court for a warrant in relation to the premises specified in the assessment notice.[160] The Commissioner's statutory guidance states:

> If a recipient of an information notice does not fully respond within the applicable time period, whether urgent or not, the Commissioner will promptly apply for a court order requiring a response. The Commissioner may decide not to make such application, having regard to criteria including:
>
> - the reasons for non-compliance with the information notice;
> - any commitments given by the recipient to responding to the information notice;
> - whether the information has been or is likely to be obtained from another source;
> - the comparative effectiveness of other investigatory and enforcement powers of the ICO. For example, the ICO may decide it has sufficient evidence to move to an enforcement action in any event; and
> - the public interest.[161]

The warrant will authorise the Commissioner or any of the Commissioner's staff to enter the premises, to search the premises and to inspect, examine, operate and test any equipment found on the premises that is used or intended to be used for the processing of personal data.[162]

48–032 Publication of assessment

Although there is no express power conferred on the Information Commissioner to publish reports prepared setting out the process and outcome of an assessment, there is an incidental power to do so.[163] The Commissioner's statutory guidance states that the Commissioner will follow its separate policy on communicating its regulatory and enforcement activity.[164] The Commissioner's stated position is that the Commissioner's priority is:

> always to work to improve information rights practice and compliance among those we regulate. This will be our primary focus when deciding whether to publish information about our regulatory work.[165]

The regulatory communication policy lists the factors that the Commissioner will take into account for and against publication.

48–033 AN offences

It is an offence for a person intentionally to obstruct a person in the execution of such a warrant

---

159 DPA 2018 s 155(1)(b). Penalty notices are considered at §§48–039 to 48–052. The amounts that may be imposed in a penalty notice for non-compliance with an assessment notice are very significant: DPA 2018 s 157(4).

160 DPA 2018 s 154 and Sch 15 para 2(1). In England and Wales, a warrant is sought from a judge of the High Court, a circuit judge or a District Judge (Magistrates' Court); in Scotland it is sought from a judge of the Court of Session, the sheriff or the summary sheriff; and in Northern Ireland it is sought from a judge of the High Court or a county court judge: DPA 2018 Sch 15 paras 2(1), 18 and 19.

161 *Regulatory Action Policy*, pp 21-22, prepared and published under DPA 2018 s 160(1), (4)-(5).

162 DPA 2018 Sch 15 para 5(1). In relation to what such a warrant authorises and the sanctions for non-compliance, see Sch 15 paras 5-17.

163 See, by analogy: *R (Vote Leave) v Electoral Commission* [2019] EWCA Civ 1938, [2019] 4 WLR 157. But see DPA 2018 s 132 which sets limits on what the Commissioner may publish.

164 *Regulatory Action Policy*, p 21. That separate policy is entitled *Communicating our Regulatory and Enforcement Activity Policy* ver 1.0 (2019).

165 *Communicating our Regulatory and Enforcement Activity Policy* ver 1.0 (2019), p 3.

or to fail without reasonable excuse to give a person executing a warrant such assistance as the person may reasonably require for the execution of the warrant.[166] It is also an offence for a person who has been given an assessment notice to destroy or otherwise dispose of, conceal, block or falsify all or part of the information, or to permit the same, with the intention of preventing the Information Commissioner from viewing or being provided any of that information.[167]

48– 034 **Enforcement notice (EN)**

The Information Commissioner may give an 'enforcement notice' to a controller, a processor, a monitoring body or a certification provider.[168] As against a controller or processor, the purpose of an enforcement notice is to impose requirements on a controller or processor that is failing, or has failed, to comply with any of the continuing obligations[169] or the data subject's rights,[170] for the purpose of remedying the failure.[171] Prior to giving an enforcement notice, the Commissioner may have given the controller or processor an information notice for the purpose of investigating such a failure[172] or an assessment notice stating that in the Commissioner's opinion there has been such a failure.[173] It is by enforcement notice that the Commissioner carries out certain corrective powers under the GDPR.[174] Although there are limits to the content of an enforcement notice, the only statutory pre-requisite before the Commissioner may give a controller or a processor an enforcement notice is the Commissioner being satisfied that that controller or processor has failed, or is failing, to comply with any of its continuing obligations or the data subject's rights.[175] In deciding whether or not to give an enforcement notice where there has been a failure to comply with a provision of the GDPR or DPA 2018, the Commissioner must consider whether that failure has caused or is likely to cause any person damage or distress.[176] The Commissioner's guidance states that:

> The purpose of an enforcement notice is to mandate action (or halt action, such as

166 DPA 2018 Sch 15 para 15.

167 DPA 2018 s 148(1)-(2).

168 DPA 2018 s 149.

169 That is, the obligations set out in Chapter 9 (in relation to general processing), Chapter 12 (in relation to law enforcement processing) and Chapter 14 (in relation to intelligence services processing).

170 That is, the data subject rights set out in Chapter 10 (in relation to general processing), Chapter 13 (in relation to law enforcement processing) and Chapter 14 (in relation to intelligence services processing).

171 DPA 2018 s 149(2), (6).

172 DPA 2018 s 142(2)(b)(i).

173 DPA 2018 s 146(9). Where the Information Commissioner has reasonable grounds for suspecting that a controller or processor has failed, or is failing, to comply with the continuing obligations or a data subject's rights and that evidence of the failure is to be found on specific premises or is capable of being viewed using equipment on specified premises, the Commissioner may apply to a court for a warrant in relation to those premises: DPA 2018 Sch 15 para 1(1). In England and Wales, a warrant is sought from a judge of the High Court, a circuit judge or a District Judge (Magistrates' Court); in Scotland it is sought from a judge of the Court of Session, the sheriff or the summary sheriff; and in Northern Ireland it is sought from a judge of the High Court or a county court judge: DPA 2018 Sch 15 paras 1, 18 and 19. The warrant will authorise the Commissioner or any of the Commissioner's staff to enter the premises, to search the premises and to inspect, examine, operate and test any equipment found on the premises that is used or intended to be used for the processing of personal data. It is an offence for a person intentionally to obstruct a person in the execution of such a warrant or to fail without reasonable excuse to give a person executing such a warrant such assistance as the person may reasonably require for the execution of the warrant: DPA 2018 Sch 15 para 15.

174 Namely, those under GDPR Art 58(2)(c)-(g) and (j); DPA 2018 s 115(8).

175 DPA 2018 s 149(1)-(2).

176 DPA 2018 s 150(2). The distress or damage need not be substantial, since the requirement is not the higher one of 'substantial damage' or 'substantial distress' used in DPA 2018 ss 19(2), 25(1) and 41(2) and Sch 1 paras 8(4), 9(3) and 22(2). See also GDPR Art 82. As to what is within the grasp of the concepts of 'damage' and 'distress', see GDPR recitals (75), (83), (85), (86), (94) and (146).

processing or transfer) to bring about compliance with information rights and/or remedy a breach. Failure to comply with an enforcement notice invites further action, including the possibility of the ICO issuing a civil monetary penalty.

Enforcement notices will usually be appropriate where specific correcting action (or its prevention) may be required.[177]

Examples given in the guidance as to the circumstances in which the Commissioner may give an enforcement notice include:

- repeated failure to meet information rights obligations or timescales for them (eg repeatedly delayed subject access requests);
- where processing or transfer of information to a third country fails (or risks failing) to meet the requirements of the data protection legislation;
- there is a need for the ICO to require communication of a data security breach to those who have been affected by it; or
- there is a need for correcting action by a certification body or monitoring body to ensure that they meet their obligations.[178]

A person who is given an enforcement notice may appeal to the First-tier Tribunal against it.[179]

48– 035 EN limits

An enforcement notice will not require a person to do something that would involve an infringement of a privilege of either House of Parliament.[180] In relation to the processing of personal data for the special purposes, the circumstances in which the Information Commissioner has power to give an enforcement notice are extremely limited.[181] Unless:

(a) a special purposes determination has taken effect (ie all appeal rights against the determination have been exhausted and failed); and

(b) a court having jurisdiction has granted leave for the enforcement notice to be given,[182]

the Commissioner may not give an enforcement notice with respect to the processing of personal data for the special purposes.[183]

48– 036 EN formalities

An enforcement notice must state which provisions of the GDPR or DPA 2018 the Commissioner is satisfied the person to whom it is given has failed, or is failing, to comply with, and must give the Commissioner's reasons for reaching that opinion.[184] An enforcement notice may require the person to whom it is given to take the steps specified in the notice, to refrain from taking steps specified in the notice, or both.[185] In the case of an enforcement notice given

---

177 *Regulatory Action Policy*, p 22, prepared and published under DPA 2018 s 160(1), (6).

178 *Regulatory Action Policy*, pp 22-23.

179 DPA 2018 s 162(1)(c). Subject to any extension of time granted by the FTT, the person named in the notice has 28 days after the date on which the enforcement notice was sent to that person: FTT Rules r 22(1)(b).

180 DPA 2018 s 152(3). As to the meaning of 'the privileges of either House of Parliament,' see Chapter 30.

181 The 'special purposes' means any of: (a) the purposes of journalism; (b) academic purposes; (c) artistic purposes; (d) literary purposes. See further §11– 050.

182 In England, Wales and Northern Ireland, the court is the county court or the High Court, in Scotland it is the Court of Session or the sheriff: DPA 2018 s 180(1)-(2). A court will not give leave unless it is satisfied that the Commissioner has reason to suspect a failure to comply with the data processing requirements and that the controller or processor has been given notice of the application for leave or the case is urgent: DPA 2018 s 152(2).

183 DPA 2018 s 152(1). As to the meaning of a 'special purposes determination', the circumstances in which it may be made and the list of appellate steps that must be completed before it takes effect, see §§48– 056 to 48– 059. In short, the circumstances are more theoretical than real.

184 DPA 2018 s 150(1) in conjunction with s 149(1)-(2).

185 DPA 2018 s 149(1).

on the basis of non-compliance by a controller or processor with any of its continuing obligations or the data subject's rights, the Commissioner may impose a ban relating to all processing of personal data, or a ban limited to personal data of a specified description, processing for a specified purpose or in a specified manner, or processing at a specified time, or any combination of them.[186] Where the Commissioner gives an enforcement notice in respect of a failure by a controller or processor to comply with a data protection principle relating to accuracy[187] or to comply with a data subject's right to rectification, erasure or restriction of processing,[188] the notice may also require the controller or processor:

(a) to rectify or erase any other data that is held by the controller or processor which contains an expression of opinion that, in the opinion of the Commissioner, appears to be based on the inaccurate personal data;[189]

(b) in the case of inaccurate data provided by a data subject or third party but accurately recorded by the controller or processor, to take specified steps to ensure the accuracy of the data, to secure the data subject's view that the data is inaccurate and to supplement the data with a Commission-approved statement of the true facts relating to the matters dealt with by the data;[190] and

(c) in the case of a notice requiring rectification or erasure and where it is reasonably practicable, to require the controller or processor to notify third parties to whom the rectified or erased personal data has been disclosed of the rectification or erasure.[191]

48– 037 EN time for compliance

The default position is that an enforcement notice may not require a person to do anything before the end of the period within which an appeal may be brought against the notice.[192] The Information Commissioner's statutory guidance states:

> Timescales set out in an enforcement notice will usually reflect the imminence of proposed action that could lead to a breach of obligations, the severity and scale of any breach/failings, and the feasibility (including lead times) of any correcting measures or technology.[193]

If an appeal is initiated against an enforcement notice, that has the effect of staying the notice pending the determination or withdrawal of the appeal.[194] Where, however, an enforcement notice states that in the Commissioner's opinion it is necessary for a requirement in the notice to be complied with urgently and it gives the Commissioner's reasons for that, then it may specify a time for compliance that is not less than 24 hours after the notice is given.[195] The Commissioner's statutory guidance states:

> In addition, when deciding whether or not to issue an 'urgent' enforcement notice, and in

---

186 DPA 2018 s 150(3).

187 That is, non-compliance with the obligation under GDPR Art 5(1)(d) in relation to general processing, DPA 2018 s 38(1) in relation to law enforcement processing, and DPA 2018 s 89 in relation to intelligence service processing.

188 That is, non-compliance with a data-subject's request under GDPR Art 16, 17 or 18 (respectively) in relation to general processing, DPA 2018 ss 46 and 47 in relation to law enforcement processing, and DPA 2018 s 100 in relation to intelligence service processing.

189 DPA 2018 s 151(2).

190 DPA 2018 s 151(3). In setting the steps to ensure the accuracy of the data, the Commissioner must have regard to the purpose for which the data was obtained and further processed by the controller: DPA 2018 s 151(4).

191 DPA 2018 s 151(5)-(6). In determining whether it is reasonably practicable, the Commissioner must have regard in particular to the number of people who would have to be notified: DPA 2018 s 151(7).

192 DPA 2018 s 150(4), (6). An appeal must be brought within 28 days of the date on which notice was sent to the person named in the notice: FTT Rules r 22(1)(b).

193 *Regulatory Action Policy*, p 23, prepared and published under DPA 2018 s 169(1), (6).

194 DPA 2018 s 150(7).

195 DPA 2018 s 150(8).

deciding the period for compliance with such notice, we will consider whether urgent action by the recipient (to take specific steps or to stop specific processing of personal data) is appropriate and proportionate having regard to criteria including:

- the extent to which such urgent action may prevent or limit the risk of serious harm to individuals or serious intrusion into their privacy. For example requesting a controller stops using personal data for a specific purpose or takes action to protect personal data from security breaches;
- the scope of the enforcement notice;
- the additional burden or impact on the recipient in having to comply with an urgent enforcement notice within the period specified; and
- the comparative effectiveness of other enforcement powers of the ICO.[196]

Where there is an urgency statement, the initiation of an appeal against it will not stay the notice.[197] A person may instead apply to a court either for the disapplication of the urgency statement or for a change to the time allowed for compliance with the requirements of the notice.[198] The Commissioner may cancel or vary an enforcement notice by giving written notice to the person to whom the notice was given.[199] The person to whom an enforcement notice is given may apply to the Commissioner for the notice to be cancelled or withdrawn, but only after the time for appealing against that notice has expired.[200] A person who has been given an enforcement notice and who subsequently unsuccessfully applied to the Information Commissioner for its cancellation or variation, may appeal to the First-tier Tribunal against that refusal.[201]

48– 038 EN non-compliance

Where the Commissioner is satisfied that a person has failed to comply with an enforcement notice, the Commissioner may give that person a penalty notice: but an enforcement notice is not a pre-condition for giving a person a penalty notice.[202] The Information Commissioner's statutory guidance states:

> If a controller or processor fails to comply with an enforcement notice, the Commissioner will also consider whether or not to issue a Penalty Notice.[203]

Apart from a penalty notice, there are no other potential regulatory sanctions for non-compliance with an enforcement notice.

48– 039 Penalty notice (PN)

The Information Commissioner may give a 'penalty notice' to a controller, to a processor, and,

---

196 *Regulatory Action Policy*, p 23.

197 DPA 2018 s 150(8).

198 DPA 2018 s 164. In England and Wales, the court is the High Court or the county court; in Scotland it is the Court of Session or the sheriff; and in Northern Ireland it is the High Court or a county court: DPA 2018 s 180(1). Where, however, the notice concerns intelligence services processing or the notice stated that the information was required urgently, it is only the High Court or the Court of Session: DPA 2018 s 180(3)-(4).

199 DPA 2018 s 153(1).

200 DPA 2018 s 153(2)-(3). In other words, not before 28 days after the date on which the enforcement notice was sent to the person named in the notice: FTT Rules r 22(1)(b). This ability does not apply to information notices or assessment notices.

201 DPA 2018 s 162(2). Subject to any extension of time granted by the FTT, the person named in the notice has 28 days after the date on which the notice of refusal was sent to that person: FTT Rules r 22(1)(b).

202 DPA 2018 s 155(1). Penalty notices are considered at §§48– 039 to 48– 052. The amounts that may be imposed in a penalty notice for non-compliance with an enforcement notice are very significant: DPA 2018 s 157(4). Although a penalty notice does not require the controller or processor to have been previously given an enforcement notice, where such a notice has been given, the extent to which the controller or processor has complied with it will be relevant both to the decision whether to give a penalty notice and, if so, the amount of the penalty: DPA 2018 s 155(3)(i).

203 *Regulatory Action Policy*, p 23, prepared and published under DPA 2018 s 160(1), (6).

provided that a person who is neither the controller or processor of personal data has been given an information notice, to that other person.[204] Prior to giving a penalty notice, the Commissioner may have given the controller or processor an information notice, an assessment notice or an enforcement notice. But, where the Commissioner is satisfied that that controller or processor has failed, or is failing, to comply with any of the continuing obligations[205] or a data subject's rights,[206] an earlier notice of that kind addressed to the controller or processor is not required.[207] The only penalty is a monetary one. In certain circumstances the Commissioner may vary or cancel a penalty.[208] A person given a penalty notice may appeal against it, or against just the amount specified in it, to the First-tier Tribunal.[209]

48–040 PN guidance

The Information Commissioner's statutory guidance is required to include provision about the circumstances in which the Commissioner will consider it appropriate to issue a penalty notice, the appropriate circumstances for oral representations and how the Commissioner will determine the amount of penalties.[210] The Commissioner's stated aim in applying penalty notices is to ensure compliance with legislation and information rights obligations:

> To do this, penalties must provide an appropriate sanction for any breach of information rights or legislation, as well as act as an effective deterrent.[211]

As to the circumstances in which a penalty notice will be appropriate, the Commissioner's statutory guidance states:

> In the majority of cases we will reserve our powers for the most serious cases, representing the most severe breaches of information rights obligations. These will typically involve wilful, deliberate or negligent acts, or repeated breaches of information rights obligations, causing harm or damage to individuals. In considering the degree of harm or damage we may consider that, where there is a lower level of impact across a large number of individuals, the totality of that damage or harm may be substantial, and may require a sanction.
>
> This means that each case will be assessed objectively on its own merits. But our hierarchy and risk-based approach mean that it is more likely that a penalty will be imposed where, for

---

204 DPA 2018 s 155(1). In the GDPR, such penalties are called 'administrative fines:' GDPR Art 83. In days of yore, they were called 'mulcts.' The Commissioner may not give a penalty notice:

(a) With respect to the processing of personal data for the 'special purposes' (which includes the purposes of journalism) unless: (a) the Information Commissioner has under DPA 2018 s 174(3) made a written determination with respect to the data or the processing has taken effect; and (b) a court has granted leave for the notice to be given: DPA 2018 s 156(1). A determination under s 174(3) does not take effect until the later of the expiry of the appeal period or the conclusion of the appeal process: s 174(6). And before granting leave, the court must be satisfied that the Commissioner has reason to suspect that the failure to comply with the continuing obligations or a data subject's rights are of substantial public importance and the controller or processor has been given notice of the leave application: DPA 2018 s 156(2). As to the meaning of 'the special purposes' see §11–050.

(b) Where the purposes and manner of the processing are determined by or on behalf of either House of Parliament: DPA 2018 s 156(3).

(c) To the Crown Estate Commissioners or to a person who is a controller for the Royal Household (ie the Keeper of the Privy Purse), a controller for the Duchy of Lancaster or a controller for the Duchy of Cornwall: DPA 2018 s 156(4).

205 That is, the obligations set out in Chapter 9 (in relation to general processing), Chapter 12 (in relation to law enforcement processing) and Chapter 14 (in relation to intelligence services processing).

206 That is, the data subject rights set out in Chapter 10 (in relation to general processing), Chapter 13 (in relation to law enforcement processing) and Chapter 14 (in relation to intelligence services processing).

207 DPA 2018 s 155(1)(a).

208 See §48–051.

209 DPA 2018 s 162(1)(d), (3). Subject to any extension of time granted by the FTT, the person named in the notice has 28 days after the date on which the penalty variation notice was sent to that person: FTT Rules r 22(1)(b).

210 DPA 2018 s 160(7).

211 *Regulatory Action Policy*, pp 23-24.

example:
- a number of individuals have been affected;
- there has been a degree of damage or harm (which may include distress and/or embarrassment);
- sensitive personal data has been involved;
- there has been a failure to comply with an information notice, an assessment notice or an enforcement notice;
- there has been a repeated breach of obligations or a failure to rectify a previously identified problem or follow previous recommendations;
- wilful action (including inaction) is a feature of the case;
- there has been a failure to apply reasonable measures (including relating to privacy by design) to mitigate any breach (or the possibility of it); and
- there has been a failure to implement the accountability provisions of the GDPR.[212]

The guidance does not make express reference to the situation where the controller's breach stems from a criminal act of a third party that targeted data held by the controller.[213] The specified considerations that will inform the Commissioner's decision to impose a penalty and the quantification of penalty are the same:
- the nature, gravity and duration of the failure;
- the intentional character of the failure or the extent of negligence involved;
- any action taken by the controller or processor to mitigate the damage or distress suffered by the data subjects;
- the degree of responsibility of the controller or processor, taking into account technical and organisational measures implemented by the controller or processor in accordance with the GDPR and sections 57, 66, 103 and 107 of the DPA [2018];
- any relevant previous failures by the controller or processor;
- the degree of co-operation with the Commissioner, in order to remedy the failure and mitigate the possible adverse risks of the failure;
- the categories of personal data affected by the failure;
- the manner in which the infringement became known to the Commissioner, including whether, and if so to what extent, the controller or processor notified the Commissioner of the failure;
- the extent to which the controller or processor has complied with previous enforcement notices or penalty notices;
- adherence to approved codes of conduct or certification mechanisms;
- any other aggravating or mitigating factor applicable to the case, including financial benefits gained, or losses avoided, as a result of the failure (whether directly or indirectly); and
- whether the penalty would be effective, proportionate and dissuasive.[214]

48–041 PN limits

In relation to the processing of personal data for the special purposes, the circumstances in which the Information Commissioner has power to give a penalty are extremely limited.[215] Unless:

(a) a special purposes determination has taken effect (ie all appeal rights against the determination have been exhausted and failed); and

---

212 *Regulatory Action Policy*, pp 24-25.

213 Until that third-party act is known to the controller, it would be a misnomer to describe there as having been 'inaction' on the part of the controller. While inadequate security measures will be relevant, that inadequacy is not to be adjudged with the benefit of hindsight.

214 *Regulatory Action Policy*, p 24.

215 The 'special purposes' means any of: (a) the purposes of journalism; (b) academic purposes; (c) artistic purposes; (d) literary purposes. See further §11– 050.

(b) a court having jurisdiction has granted leave for the penalty notice to be given,[216]

the Commissioner may not give a penalty notice with respect to the processing of personal data for the special purposes.[217]

48–042 PN notice of intent

Before giving a penalty notice, the Information Commissioner must by written notice give the person a 'notice of intent' informing that person that the Commissioner intends to give a penalty notice.[218] The notice of intent must be given not less than 21 days and not more than 6 months before the penalty notice is given.[219] A notice of intent must contain:

(a) the name and address of the person to whom the Commissioner proposes to give the penalty notice;[220]

(b) the reasons why the Commissioner proposes to give a penalty notice,[221] including a description of the circumstances of the failure to comply with continuing obligations, the data subject's rights, an information notice, an assessment notice or an enforcement notice;[222]

(c) an indication of the amount of the penalty that the Commissioner proposes to impose, including any aggravating or mitigating factors that the Commissioner proposes to take into account;[223] and

(d) a statement that the person may make written representations about the Commissioner's proposal to give a penalty notice, a statement of the period within which those representations may be made.[224]

48–043 PN representations

A notice of intent must also state whether the Commissioner considers that it is appropriate for the person to have an opportunity to make oral representations about the intention to give a penalty notice, a statement that the person may make such representations and the arrangements for making them.[225] The Commissioner's guidance states oral representations will take place at the Commissioner's offices and that they are:

> ...only relevant in cases that are considered by us to be exceptional. It is likely that these could be appropriate in circumstances where:

---

216 In England, Wales and Northern Ireland, the court is the county court or the High Court, in Scotland it is the Court of Session or the sheriff: DPA 2018 s 180(1)-(2). A court will not give leave unless it is satisfied that the Commissioner has reason to suspect a failure to comply with the data processing requirements and that the controller or processor has been given notice of the application for leave or the case is urgent: DPA 2018 s 156(2).

217 DPA 2018 s 156(1). As to the meaning of a 'special purposes determination', the circumstances in which it may be made and the list of appellate steps that must be completed before it takes effect, see §48–056 to 48–059. In short, the circumstances are more theoretical than real.

218 DPA 2018 s 155(5) and Sch 16 para 2.

219 DPA 2018 Sch 16 paras 2(2), 3(4) and 4(1). The period for giving the penalty notice after the notice of intent may be extended by agreement between the Commissioner and the person to whom the notice of intent is addressed: DPA 2018 Sch 16 para 2(3).

220 DPA 2018 Sch 16 para 3(1)(a).

221 DPA 2018 Sch 16 para 3(1)(b).

222 DPA 2018 Sch 16 para 3(2)(a). In the case of a failure to comply with continuing obligations or data subject's rights, the notice must also include the nature of the personal data involved in the failure: DPA 2018 Sch 16 para 3(2)(b) in conjunction with s 149(2). The 'circumstances of the failure' may include any of the matters enumerated in DPA 2018 s 155(3).

223 DPA 2018 Sch 16 para 3(1)(c). 'Aggravating or mitigating factors' include any financial benefits gained, or losses avoided, as a result of the failure, whether directly or indirectly: DPA 2018 s 155(3)(k).

224 DPA 2018 Sch 16 para 3(3). The period for making written representations must be not less than 21 days beginning with when the notice of intent is given: DPA 2018 Sch 16 para 3(4).

225 DPA 2018 Sch 16 para 3(5).

- the central facts of any breach or failing are in dispute;
- the integrity of any technical witness evidence is in dispute;
- there is a requirement to make reasonable adjustments under the Equality Act 2010; or
- the consideration of 'harm' elements of a case would benefit from evidence from those affected.[226]

So far as suggesting that there be oral representations, the Commissioner's guidance states:

> If an organisation or individual thinks that their circumstances warrant oral representations of this nature, they can explain why they think this extra step is justified in their written representations. In particular, the [Information Commissioner] will need to understand what oral representations will add to the regulatory process. We will then decide whether or not to invite the target to a face-face meeting.
>
> However, it is unlikely that we will agree to take oral representations in a case that is principally technical in nature. In such cases, it is normally more appropriate to consider complex technical representations in writing.[227]

In terms of what may take place during an oral representations meeting, the Commissioner's guidance states that representatives of the 'target' of the notice of intent will be:

> ...able to explain in person how the privacy concerns and breaches occurred, submit mitigating factors, what they have (or plan to do) to achieve compliance and the reasons why they believe that the [Information Commissioner] should not take the intended regulatory action. A request for a reduction in the size of the penalty may also be submitted during the oral representations.[228]

48–044 PN deliberative process

The Information Commissioner may not give a penalty notice before the end of the period specified in the notice of intent for making oral or written representations.[229] In deciding whether to give a penalty notice and in determining the amount of the penalty, the Commissioner must consider any oral or written representations made by the person in accordance with the notice of intent.[230] The Commissioner's statutory guidance states:

> Where appropriate, we will also have regard to representations (including from any Concerned Supervisory Authorities elsewhere in the EU where the [Information Commissioner] is the lead Supervisory Authority or the Data Protection Board itself) under the cooperation and consistency mechanisms of the GDPR in setting the final amount of any penalty. These representations will be taken after the consideration of representations of the target of the penalty but before the final setting of any penalty level and following the procedures set out in relevant Data Protection Board rules of procedure.
>
> For very significant penalties (expected to be those over the threshold of £1M) a panel comprising non-executive advisors to the Commissioner's Office may be convened by the Commissioner to consider the investigation findings and any representations made, before making a recommendation to the Commissioner as to any penalty level to be applied. It will be the Commissioner's final decision as to the level of penalty applied. The panel may comprise technical experts in areas relevant to the case under consideration.[231]

48–045 Penalties: general processing

Where the penalty notice arises from general processing, when deciding whether to give a penalty notice to a person and the amount of the penalty, the Commissioner must in each case

---

226 *Regulatory Action Policy*, pp 25-26, prepared and published under DPA 2018 s 160(1), (7).

227 *Regulatory Action Policy*, p 26.

228 *Regulatory Action Policy*, p 26.

229 DPA 2018 Sch 16 para 4(1). And, presumably, any period extended by agreement under para 2(3).

230 DPA 2018 Sch 16 para 4(2).

231 *Regulatory Action Policy*, p 26.

ensure that the penalty is effective, proportionate and dissuasive, and must have regard to the following, so far as relevant:[232]

(a) the nature, gravity and duration of the infringement taking into account the nature scope or purpose of the processing concerned as well as the number of data subjects affected and the level of damage suffered by them;
(b) the intentional or negligent character of the infringement;
(c) any action taken by the controller or processor to mitigate the damage suffered by data subjects;
(d) the degree of responsibility of the controller or processor taking into account technical and organisational measures implemented by them;
(e) any relevant previous infringements by the controller or processor;
(f) the degree of cooperation with the supervisory authority, in order to remedy the infringement and mitigate the possible adverse effects of the infringement;
(g) the categories of personal data affected by the infringement;
(h) the manner in which the infringement became known to the supervisory authority, in particular whether, and if so to what extent, the controller or processor notified the infringement;
(i) where an enforcement order concerned with the same subject-matter has been given to the controller or processor, compliance with that order;
(j) adherence to approved codes of conduct or approved certification mechanisms; and
(k) any other aggravating or mitigating factor applicable to the circumstances of the case, such as financial benefits gained, or losses avoided, directly or indirectly, from the infringement.

48–046 Penalties: other processing

Where the penalty notice arises from a failure in law enforcement processing or intelligence service processing to comply with the continuing obligations or with a data subject right,[233] when deciding whether to give a penalty notice to a person and the amount of the penalty the Commissioner must have regard so far as relevant to:[234]

(a) the nature, gravity and duration of the failure;
(b) the intentional or negligent character of the failure;
(c) any action taken by the controller or processor to mitigate the damage or distress suffered by data subjects;
(d) the degree of responsibility of the controller or processor, taking into account technical and organisational measures implemented by the controller or processor;
(e) any relevant previous failures by the controller or processor;
(f) the degree of co-operation with the Commissioner, in order to remedy the failure and mitigate the possible adverse effects of the failure;
(g) the categories of personal data affected by the failure;
(h) the manner in which the infringement became known to the Commissioner, including whether, and if so to what extent, the controller or processor notified the Commissioner of the failure;
(i) the extent to which the controller or processor has complied with previous enforcement notices or penalty notices;
(j) adherence to approved codes of conduct or certification mechanisms;

[232] DPA 2018 s 155(2)(a); GDPR Art 83(1)-(2).

[233] The continuing obligations are those set out in Chapter 12 (in relation to law enforcement processing) and Chapter 14 (in relation to intelligence services processing). The data subject rights are those set out in Chapter 13 (in relation to law enforcement processing) and Chapter 14 (in relation to intelligence services processing).

[234] DPA 2018 s 155(3).

(k) any other aggravating or mitigating factor applicable to the case, including financial benefits gained, or losses avoided, as a result of the failure (whether directly or indirectly); and

(l) whether the penalty would be effective, proportionate and dissuasive.

48–047 PN formalities

A penalty notice must contain the following information—

(a) the name and address of the person to whom it is addressed;

(b) details of the notice of intent given to the person;

(c) whether the Commissioner received oral or written representations in accordance with the notice of intent;

(d) the reasons why the Commissioner proposes to impose the penalty, including a description of the circumstances of the failure to comply with any continuing obligations or data subject rights and the nature of the personal data involved in the failure;

(e) the reasons for the amount of the penalty, including any aggravating or mitigating factors that the Commissioner has taken into account;

(f) details of how the penalty is to be paid;

(g) details of the rights of appeal; and

(h) details of the Commissioner's enforcement powers.[235]

48–048 Maximum penalties

The maximum penalty depends upon:

— whether the processing from which it arises is general processing, law enforcement processing or intelligence service processing;

— whether the basis for the penalty notice is a breach of the continuing obligations, of a data subject right,[236] or non-compliance with an information notice, an assessment notice or an enforcement notice;

— in the case of a breach of the continuing obligations, the nature of the breach; and

— the size of the undertaking to which the notice is given.

In summary:

(1) In relation to requirements for general processing, the maximum amount of the penalty that may be imposed by a penalty notice is:

(a) where the infringement is of the continuing obligations (excluding child consent under Article 8 and the obligations in relation to processing that do not require identification under Article 11), of a data subject's rights or of the transfer obligations:

(i) in the case of an undertaking, the sterling equivalent of €20 million or 4% of the undertaking's total annual worldwide turnover in the preceding financial year, whichever is higher;

(ii) in any other case, the sterling equivalent of €20 million; and

(b) for all other infringements:

(i) in the case of an undertaking, the sterling equivalent of €10

[235] DPA 2018 Sch 16 para 5. As to the rights of appeal, see §48–053; as to the Commissioner's enforcement powers, see §48–052.

[236] The continuing obligations are those set out in Chapter 9 (in relation to general processing), Chapter 12 (in relation to law enforcement processing) and Chapter 14 (in relation to intelligence services processing). The data subject rights are those set out in Chapter 10 (in relation to general processing), Chapter 13 (in relation to law enforcement processing) and Chapter 14 (in relation to intelligence services processing).

million or 2% of the undertaking's total annual worldwide turnover in the preceding financial year, whichever is higher;

(ii) in any other case, the sterling equivalent of €10 million.[237]

(2) In relation to an infringement of the requirements for law enforcement processing, the maximum amount of the penalty that may be imposed by a penalty notice is:

(a) where the infringement is of the continuing obligations, a data subject's rights (other than of the automated decision safeguards) or the transfer obligations:

(i) in the case of an undertaking, €20 million or 4% of the undertaking's total annual worldwide turnover in the preceding financial year, whichever is higher;

(ii) in any other case, the sterling equivalent of €20 million; and

(b) for all other infringements:

(i) in the case of an undertaking, the sterling equivalent of €10 million or 2% of the undertaking's total annual worldwide turnover in the preceding financial year, whichever is higher;

(ii) in any other case, the sterling equivalent of €10 million.[238]

(3) In relation to an infringement of the requirements for intelligence service processing, the maximum amount of the penalty that may be imposed by a penalty notice is:

(a) where the infringement is of the continuing obligations, a data subject's rights (other than the rights relating to automated decision-making, and entitlements to information about decision making and to object to processing) or the transfer obligations:

(i) in the case of an undertaking, €20 million or 4% of the undertaking's total annual worldwide turnover in the preceding financial year, whichever is higher;

(ii) in any other case, the sterling equivalent of €20 million; and

(b) for all other infringements:

(i) in the case of an undertaking, the sterling equivalent of €10 million or 2% of the undertaking's total annual worldwide turnover in the preceding financial year, whichever is higher;

(ii) in any other case, the sterling equivalent of €10 million.[239]

(4) In relation to a failure to comply with an information notice, an assessment notice

---

[237] GDPR Art 83; DPA 2018 s 157(1). As to the meaning of an 'undertaking' see §9– 063. The amount must be specified in sterling: DPA 2018 s 155(1). The sterling equivalent must be determined by applying the spot rate of exchange set by the Bank of England on the day on which the notice is given: DPA 2018 s 157(7). 'Financial year' means the twelve months ending with 31 March: Interpretation Act 1978 Sch 1.

[238] DPA 2018 s 157(2). There is no definition of an 'undertaking' for these sorts of processing, but the Secretary of State may, by regulations, provide that a person of a description is or is not an undertaking: DPA 2018 s 159(1)(a). As at the date of writing, no such regulations have been made. The amount must be specified in sterling: DPA 2018 s 155(1). The sterling equivalent must be determined by applying the spot rate of exchange set by the Bank of England on the day on which the notice is given: DPA 2018 s 157(7). 'Financial year' means the twelve months ending with 31 March: Interpretation Act 1978 Sch 1.

[239] DPA 2018 s 157(3). There is no definition of an 'undertaking' for these sorts of processing, but the Secretary of State may, by regulations, provide that a person of a description is or is not an undertaking: DPA 2018 s 159(1)(a). As at the date of writing, no such regulations have been made. The amount must be specified in sterling: DPA 2018 s 155(1). The sterling equivalent must be determined by applying the spot rate of exchange set by the Bank of England on the day on which the notice is given: DPA 2018 s 157(7). 'Financial year' means the twelve months ending with 31 March: Interpretation Act 1978 Sch 1.

or an enforcement notice, the maximum amount of the penalty that may be imposed by a penalty notice is the higher maximum amount.

(a) in the case of an undertaking, the sterling equivalent of €20 million or 4% of the undertaking's total annual worldwide turnover in the preceding financial year, whichever is higher;

(b) in any other case, the sterling equivalent of €20 million.[240]

The EDPB has adopted guidelines issued by the Article 29 Working Party on the setting of administrative fines under the GDPR.[241]

48–049 Penalty quantification process

The Information Commissioner has set out in statutory guidance a five-step approach that the Commissioner will follow in setting a penalty:[242]

(1) The Commissioner will set an 'initial element' that does not include any financial gain from the breach

(2) The Commissioner will then '[add] in an element to censure the breach based on its scale and severity, taking into account the considerations identified at DPA s 155(2)-(4).'

(3) The Commissioner will then '[add] in an element to reflect any aggravating factors.'[243]

(4) The Commissioner will then '[add] in an element for deterrent effect to others.'[244]

(5) The Commissioner will then '[reduce] the amount (save that in the initial element to reflect any mitigating factors, including ability to pay.'[245]

Given that data subjects will generally be able to recover compensation for contravention of data protection requirements, including both continuing obligations and data subject rights, to avoid double penalisation it would seem that the quantification of the penalty should not reflect matters for which a data subject can secure an award of compensation.[246] On the other hand, disgorgement of benefits and cost-savings achieved from the contravention will not involve double penalisation.[247]

---

240 DPA 2018 s 157(4). There is no definition of an 'undertaking,' but the Secretary of State may, by regulations, provide that a person of a description is or is not an undertaking: DPA 2018 s 159(1)(a). As at the date of writing, no such regulations have been made. The amount must be specified in sterling: DPA 2018 s 155(1). The sterling equivalent must be determined by applying the spot rate of exchange set by the Bank of England on the day on which the notice is given: DPA 2018 s 157(7). 'Financial year' means the twelve months ending with 31 March: Interpretation Act 1978 Sch 1.

241 Guidelines WP 253, adopted on 3 October 2017.

242 *Regulatory Action Policy*, p 27.

243 It might be thought that, in taking into consideration the matters listed in DPA 2018 s 155(3) in step (2), aggravating factors had already been added in.

244 It is not clear what the difference is between adding in an element for 'deterrent effect to others' and the adding in under step (2) an element for a penalty being 'effective, proportionate and dissuasive' as required under DPA 2018 s 155(1).

245 Another consideration that should already have been reflected in the element yielded in carrying out step (2).

246 DPA 2018 ss 167-169. The factors point to the penalty being 'criminal' for the purposes of Art 6 of the ECHR: see, by analogy, *Jussila v Finland* [2009] STC 29; *Han v Customs & Excise Commissioners* [2001] EWCA Civ 1040, [2001] 1 WLR 2253; *Khan (t/a Greyhound Dry Cleaning) v Customs & Excise Commissioners* [2006] EWCA Civ 89, [2006] STC 1167; *Engel v Netherlands* (1976) 1 ECHR 647; *Oztruk v Germany* (1984) 6 EHRR 409; *Benham v United Kingdom* (1996) 22 EHRR 293; *Bendenoun v France* (1994) 18 EHRR 54.

247 The rationale for disgorgement of benefits is that of ensuring that the wrongdoer not be permitted to gain from the wrongdoing: *AG v Guardian Newspapers (No 2)* [1990] 1 AC 109 at 262. Disgorgement does involve questions of causation, albeit on equitable principles rather than common law, so that the fact that wrongdoer could have secured the same benefit or saving without the wrongdoing does not lessen the amount to be disgorged.

48–050 PN time for compliance

A penalty must be paid to the Commissioner within the period specified in the penalty notice and that period must be not less than 28 days beginning with the date on which the penalty notice is given.[248]

48–051 PN variation/cancellation

The Information Commissioner may vary a penalty notice by giving written notice to the person to whom it was given – a 'penalty variation notice.'[249] A penalty variation notice may not increase the amount of the penalty, reduce the period for its payment or otherwise be to the detriment of the person to whom the penalty notice was given.[250] A penalty variation notice must specify the penalty notice concerned and how it is varied.[251] Where a penalty variation notice reduces the amount of the penalty and, at the time when it is given, an amount has already been paid that exceeds the amount of the reduced penalty, the Commissioner must repay the excess.[252] The person to whom a penalty variation notice is given may appeal against the notice, or just the amount specified in the notice, to the First-tier Tribunal.[253] The Information Commissioner may also cancel a penalty notice by giving written notice to the person to whom it was given.[254] When a penalty notice is cancelled, the Commissioner may not take any further enforcement action and must repay any amount that has been paid under the penalty notice.[255]

48–052 PN non-compliance

Enforcement of penalties under a penalty notice or a penalty variation notice is achieved by engaging the provision in the Civil Procedure Rules for enforcement of decisions by a person other than the High Court or County Court as if the decision were a court order.[256] The Information Commissioner must not take action to recover a penalty unless the period for payment specified in the penalty notice (or the penalty variation notice) has ended or, where an appeal against such a notice has been lodged with the First-tier Tribunal, that appeal has been decided or otherwise ended.[257] In order to enforce payment of the penalty, the Commissioner must file in court an application notice using the relevant form.[258] The application may be made without notice.[259] Once the court determines the application and

---

248 DPA 2018 Sch 16 para 6.

249 DPA 2018 Sch 16 para 7(1).

250 DPA 2018 Sch 16 para 7(3).

251 DPA 2018 Sch 16 para 7(2).

252 DPA 2018 Sch 16 para 7(4).

253 DPA 2018 s 162(1)(e), (3). Subject to any extension of time granted by the FTT, the person named in the notice has 28 days after the date on which the penalty variation notice was sent to that person: FTT Rules r 22(1)(b).

254 DPA 2018 Sch 16 para 8(1).

255 DPA 2018 Sch 16 para 8(2).

256 DPA 2018 Sch 16 para 9(2)-(4). In England and Wales, CPR r 70.5.

257 DPA 2018 Sch 16 para 9(1).

258 The choice of court will depend on the amount sought to be enforced. The application notice is practice form N322A: see CPR PD 70 para 4.2. The application notice must include the name and address of the person against whom the order is sought and how much remains unpaid: PD 70 para 4.3. A copy of the penalty notice, or the penalty variation notice, must be included with the application notice. The application notice is filed in the court of the district in which the person by whom the sum is payable resides or carries on business. The application must be accompanied by the relevant fee.

259 CPR r 70.5(4)(a).

makes the order, it may be enforced as if it were an order of the High Court or the County Court (depending on which court determines the application).[260]

48– 053 Appeals against notices

A person who is given an information notice, an assessment notice, an enforcement notice, a penalty notice or a penalty variation notice, has a right of appeal to the First-tier Tribunal.[261] An appeal must be started within 28 days of the date on which notice was sent to the appellant.[262] An appeal starts at the moment that the notice of appeal is received by the First-tier Tribunal – not at the moment of sending that notice.[263] At a minimum, the notice of appeal must include:

- — the name and address of the appellant;
- — the name and address of the appellant's representative (if any);
- — an address where documents for the appellant may be sent or delivered;
- — the name and address of any respondent;
- — details of the decision or act, or failure to decide or act, to which the proceedings relate; and
- — the grounds on which the appellant relies.[264]

The appellant must attach to the notice of appeal a copy of the notice being appealed against, and any statement of reasons for that notice that the appellant has or can reasonably obtain.[265] In determining the appeal, the tribunal may review any determination of fact on which the notice was based.[266] Conventional tribunal practice and procedure apply for the determination of the appeal.[267] If, at the end of that procedure, the Tribunal considers that the notice is not in accordance with the law or that, to the extent that the notice involved an exercise of discretion by the Information Commissioner, that the Commissioner ought to have exercised that discretion differently, the Tribunal must allow the appeal or substitute another notice that the Commissioner could have given.[268] Otherwise the Tribunal must dismiss the appeal.[269]

---

260 The principal means of enforcement are: taking control of goods under TCPA 2007 ss 62-87 and Sch 12 and CPR rr 83-85; administration orders under the County Courts Act 1984 s 112; third party debt orders under CPR r 72; charging orders under the Charging Orders Act 1979 and CPR r 73; and insolvency proceedings under the Insolvency Act 1986. Where it is sought to enforce wholly or partially by execution against goods, where the sum which it is sought to enforce is £5,000 or more it must be enforced in the High Court, where the sum which it is sought to enforce is less than £600 it must be enforced in the County Court, and in any other case may be enforced in either the High Court or the County Court: High Court and County Courts Jurisdiction Order 1991 (SI 1991/724) art 8.

261 DPA 2018 s 162(1). In relation to a data subject who has made a complaint to the Information Commissioner and who is dissatisfied with the Commissioner's response, or lack of response, see §48– 004. Unless a data subject has made a complaint, it will be very difficult for that data subject to impugn the Commissioner's decision not to issue a notice, or the terms of a notice, since that will preclude complaint to the First-tier Tribunal and any application for judicial review is likely to be resisted on the basis that the data subject, by not making a data subject complaint, has not pursued an available alternative remedy.

262 FTT Rules r 22(1)(b).

263 FTT Rules r 22(1).

264 FTT Rules r 22(2).

265 FTT Rules r 22(3).

266 DPA 2018 s 163(2).

267 See §§45– 013 to 45– 019. Although a penalty under DPA 2018 is not described as being a penalty for an offence (and hence does not meet the domestic classification of a crime), for the purposes of Art 6 of the ECHR the sanction belongs to the criminal realm in that it is not intended to compensate or to deprive the recipient of a gain or saving, but is a sanction for misconduct: see GDPR Art 83(2); DPA 2018 s 155(2)-(3); *Jussila v Finland* [2009] STC 29. An appeal against a penalty may be characterised as criminal proceedings, attended by the procedural precepts of Art 6. Most notably, the burden of proof will be on the Commissioner, the standard will be the criminal standard, and the task for the Tribunal will be to determine for itself the correct penalty.

268 DPA 2018 s 164(3). The task for the Tribunal is identical to that on an appeal under FOIA under s 58(1) of that

The Tribunal is, generally speaking, a costs-free regime.[270]

48–054 Urgency disapplication

Information notices, assessment notices and enforcement notices may contain an 'urgency statement.'[271] An urgency statement has the twin effect of reducing the time for compliance with the notice and disapplying the stay which would otherwise apply on the lodgment of an appeal against that notice. Where a notice contains an urgency statement, the recipient of the notice may apply to the court for the disapplication of some or all of the requirements of the notice and for a change to the time at which, or period within which, a requirement in it must be complied with.[272] The court decides for itself whether to disapply the urgency statement or to vary its effect based upon the material before it: the court is not confined to reviewing the propriety of the Commissioner's decision to include an urgency statement.[273] On an application to disapply the urgency statement, the court may:

(a) direct that the notice is to have effect as if it did not contain the urgency statement;
(b) direct that the inclusion of the urgency statement is not to have effect in relation to a requirement of the notice;
(c) vary the notice by changing the time at which, or the period within which, a requirement of the notice must be complied with;
(d) vary the notice by making other changes required to give effect to a direction under paragraph (a) or (b) or in consequence of a variation under (c).[274]

The decision of the court is final.[275]

Act. In appeals under that provision, the FTT has rejected the proposition that on such appeals it is to make the decision afresh, based upon the facts, matters and evidence as they stand at the time of the determination of the appeal, preferring the notion that it is an historical exercise to be carried out by the Tribunal assuming as its temporal standpoint the moment at which the primary decision-maker – here, the Information Commissioner – made the appealed decision, and unconcerned by facts and matters since then. See further §§45–014 to 45–017.

269 DPA 2018 s 163(4). An appeal against a penalty may be capable of challenge on the basis of being disproportionate for the purposes of Art 1 of the First Protocol to the ECHR. This has been deployed in tribunal appeals against penalties imposed by HMRC for late payment of tax: *HMRC v Total Technology (Engineering) Ltd* [2013] STC 813; *Enersys Holdings UK Ltd v HMRC* [2010] UKFTT 20 (TC); cf *HMRC v Hok* [2013] STC 225.

270 See §44–020.

271 DPA 2018 s s142(7), 146(8), (9), 150(8) and 164(5).

272 DPA 2018 s 164(2). In England and Wales, the court is the High Court; in Scotland it is the Court of Session; and in Northern Ireland it is the High Court: DPA 2018 s 180(5). The application is distinct from an appeal against the notice itself (which is lodged with the FTT): the FTT has no jurisdiction to alter or revoke an urgency statement. In England and Wales, the application would be brought by a Part 8 claim form, with a supporting application notice using form N244. The respondent to the claim would be the Information Commissioner. Where the notice follows a complaint to the Information Commissioner by a data subject, the data subject should be given a copy of the claim and any other court papers, on the basis that the claimant is an interested party. Given the nature of the relief sought in such an application, there may be circumstances in which the application may be made before the commencement of the proceedings: see CPR r 25.2(2)(b). In such circumstances, the court will give a direction requiring a claim to be commenced: CPR r 25.2(3). Otherwise, an application will ordinarily need to be made on notice to the Information Commissioner: CPR r 23.4(1). Where the application arises in urgent circumstances such that there is no practical possibility of giving the required minimum three days' notice to the Commissioner, the application may be made without notice to the Commissioner: CPR r 23.4(2)(b) and PD 23A para 4.2. The application should be supported by evidence that both sets out why the order should be made and, in the case where notice has not been given, why notice has not been given: CPR r 25.3(3). The application will normally be held in public: CPR r 39.2. Where the application is heard without notice to the Information Commissioner, the legal representatives for the applicant are under a duty to provide a full note of the hearing to the Commissioner. This is to enable the Commissioner to make an informed decision whether to apply to discharge the order. Applications to set aside or vary are normally made back to the judge who made the original order.

273 On the basis the DPA 2018 s 164 does not constrain the function of the court in terms such as are in s 163(3)-(4).

274 DPA 2018 s 164(3).

275 DPA 2018 s 164(5). Since the only courts with jurisdiction are superior courts, this means that there is no appeal of any sort: *R (Privacy International) v Investigatory Powers Tribunal* [2019] UKSC 22, [2019] 2 WLR 1219 at [157]-

48– 055 Inspection power

The Information Commissioner may inspect personal data where the inspection is necessary in order to discharge an international obligation of the United Kingdom.[276] The power includes the ability to operate and test equipment that is used for the processing of personal data. Apart from where the Commissioner considers the case to be urgent, the Commissioner must give the controller or processor written notice before exercising the power.[277] Obstructing the Commissioner, or failing to give the Commissioner reasonable assistance, is an offence.[278]

4. SPECIAL PURPOSES PROCESSING

48– 056 Introduction

The term 'special purposes' is defined to mean one or more of the following:

(a) the purposes of journalism;
(b) academic purposes;
(c) artistic purposes;
(d) literary purposes.[279]

No further definition is given of any of those terms. The GDPR recognises that the rules governing freedom of expression and information – which include the special purposes – must be reconciled with the right to protection of personal data.[280] Nevertheless, under the DPA 2018 general processing for the 'special purposes' has been given plenary indulgence from compliance with the continuing obligations and the data subject rights.[281] The comprehensiveness of exemption effectively allows a controller processing personal data for special purposes to process personal data without regulation. As such, claiming to process personal data for the 'special purposes' presents great attractions, particularly to controllers whose processing would otherwise not bear scrutiny. Making and maintaining such claims is facilitated by the disapplication of most of the means of regulatory enforcement and the evisceration of private remedies that would otherwise test them. The only external control lies in a 'special determination,' which if it is made by the Information Commissioner and survives

[161]. However, the court retains its power to revoke or vary an order: CPR r 3.1(7). This will be more readily exercised where the application was heard without notice or with limited notice: *Collier v Williams* [2006] EWCA Civ 20, [2006] 1 WLR 1945; *Tibbles v SIG plc* [2012] EWCA Civ 518, [2012] 1 WLR 2591; *Thevarajah v Riordan* [2015] UKSC 78, [2016] 1 WLR 76 at [15]-[18].

276 DPA 2018 s 119(1). The power is exercisable only if the personal data is processed wholly or partly by automated means, or is processed otherwise than by automated means and forms part of a filing system or is intended to form part of a filing system: DPA 2018 s 119(2). This power does not apply to intelligence services processing of personal data where exemption is required for the purpose of safeguarding national security: DPA 2018 s 110(1)-(2). Nor does it apply to applied GDPR processing of personal data where exemption is required for the purpose of safeguarding national security or for defence purposes: DPA 2018 s 26(1)-(2).

277 DPA 2018 s 119(4)-(5). The most relevant obligations will be those in the Modernised Convention for the Protection of Individuals with Regard to the Processing of Personal Data (Convention 108) Arts 7(2), 10(1), 14(6) and 15. In relation to Convention 108, see further §§7– 007 to 7– 008, 7– 011 and 7– 031.

278 DPA 2018 s 119(6). The penalty is a fine: DPA 2018 s 196(1). It is a recordable offence: DPA 2018 s 199(1)(a). A person in the service of the Crown is liable to prosecution, but a government department is not: DPA 2018 s 209(6)-(7).

279 DPA 2018 s 174(1), Sch 1 paras 13(4), Sch 2 26(1). See also GDPR Art 85 and recital (153), which refer to 'journalistic purposes' and 'the purposes of academic, artistic or literary expression.'

280 GDPR Art 85 and recital (153).

281 The continuing obligations are those set out in Chapter 9 and the data subject rights are those set out in Chapter 10. See also §11– 050. The special purposes exemption does not apply to law enforcement processing or intelligence services processing.

a special appeal procedure, permits the claim of special purposes processing thereafter to be tested. The exemptions themselves are unassailable.[282]

48–057 Claiming special purposes

In order to disapply the continuing obligations and the data subject rights:

(a) the processing of the personal data must be carried out for the special purposes;
(b) the processing of that personal data must be being carried out with a view to the publication by a person (who need not be the controller or the processor) of journalistic, academic, artistic or literary material; and
(c) the controller must reasonably believe that publication of the material would be in the public interest.[283]

Where these conditions are met, then, to the extent that the controller reasonably believes that the application of the continuing obligations and data subject rights would be incompatible with the special purposes, they are disapplied.[284] The reasonableness of the controller's belief that it should not be subjected to any data regulation is facilitated by the requirement that the controller must take into account the special importance of the public interest in the freedom of expression and information.[285] A controller need only claim that the conditions are met and to hold the belief in order to pre-empt any proceedings seeking a private remedy.[286] The usual procedures:

— by which assertions and stated beliefs can be probed and tested (ie information orders and assessment orders),[287]
— by which compliance with the data protection regime can be enforced (enforcement orders and penalty notices),[288]
— for securing private remedies for non-compliance with data subject rights,[289]

are forestalled by the requirement for a prior 'special determination' from the Information Commissioner.[290] Unless and until a special determination has been made, and the avenues against it have been exhausted, and the determination has taken effect, regulatory enforcement and proceedings for a private remedy are placed in abeyance.[291]

48–058 Special determination

The Act does not state who may initiate the making of a special determination. In particular, it is not clear whether it may be initiated by a data subject making a complaint to the Information Commissioner, or on the Commissioner's own motion, or by a court where 'special purposes proceedings' have been stayed,[292] or any combination of these. Nor does the Act indicate the process leading to the making of a special purposes determination. A special

282 The exemptions are listed in DPA 2018 Sch 2 para 26(9).

283 DPA 2018 Sch 2 para 26(2).

284 DPA 2018 Sch 2 para 26(3). The full list of disapplied provisions is set out in DPA 2018 Sch 2 para 26(9).

285 DPA 2018 Sch 2 para 26(4). The controller must also have regard to codes of practice and guidelines that journalistic bodies have prepared for themselves: DPA 2018 Sch 2 para 26(5)-(6).

286 DPA 2018 s 176(1).

287 DPA 2018 ss 143(1)(a) and 147(5). An assessment notice may not be given regardless of any special determination.

288 DPA 2018 ss 152(1) and 156(1).

289 DPA 2018 ss 167(1), 169(1) and 174(2); GDPR Arts 79 and 82.

290 There is a very limited exception to this requirement in DPA 2018 s 143(1)(b)

291 DPA 2018 ss 174(2) and 176(1), (3) (in relation to claims for private remedies) and ss 143(1), 152(1) and 156(1) (in relation to regulatory enforcement other than assessment notices).

292 DPA 2018 s 176(1).

determination is a written determination by the Information Commissioner that, in relation to the processing of personal data, that personal data is not being processed:

(a) only for the special purposes;

(b) with view to the publication of journalistic, academic, artistic or literary material which has not previously been published by the controller.[293]

The Commissioner must give written notice of the determination to the controller and the processor, but is not statutorily required to give it to the data subject to whom the personal data relates.[294] The controller or processor may appeal against the determination to the First-tier Tribunal, but there is no provision for a data subject to appeal against the Information Commissioner declining to make a determination.[295] The only power conferred on the First-tier Tribunal on such an appeal is to cancel the Information Commissioner's determination.[296] A special determination is not effective until either the period for an appeal against the determination has ended without an appeal having been brought or an appeal has been brought against the determination and the appeal has been decided.[297]

48–059 Effect of special determination

A special determination has no effect other than to remove the bars to private law proceedings and to regulatory enforcement.

(1) In relation to regulatory enforcement, a special determination does not result in the restoration of the Information Commissioner's power to issue notices. Before the Commissioner may give a controller or processor an enforcement notice or a penalty notice with respect to processing of personal data for the special purposes, in addition to the special determination having taken effect, the Commissioner must also apply and secure from a court leave for that notice to be given.[298] A court must not grant leave for the notice to be given unless it is satisfied that the Commissioner has reason to suspect that the failure to comply with the continuing obligations or a data subject's rights is one of substantial public importance.[299] The court must also be satisfied that the controller or processor has been given notice of the

---

[293] DPA 2018 s 174(3). It is unclear whether the DPA 2018 requires the Information Commissioner to have determined both (a) and (b) before making a special determination, or whether the special determination may be of one or both of (a) and (b) and that that will suffice for the consequences of a special determination.

[294] DPA 2018 s 174(4).

[295] DPA 2018 s 162(4). The notice of the determination must provide information about the rights of appeal: DPA 2018 s 174(5). Subject to any extension of time granted by the FTT, the person named in the notice has 28 days after the date on which the notice of determination was sent to that person within which to appeal: FTT Rules r 22(1)(b). The refusal to make a determination might expose the Commissioner to a claim for judicial review on conventional public law grounds.

[296] DPA 2018 s 163(6).

[297] DPA 2018 s 174(6), ie 28 days after the date on which the notice of determination was sent to the controller. In the case where an appeal has been brought, the determination does not take effect until any further appeal has been decided or the time for appealing against the first appeal decision has ended without a further appeal being brought. A similar obstacle course under the DPA 1998 was never successfully completed in the 20 years of its existence: notwithstanding, for example, processing of personal data for the purposes of journalism that was the subject of investigation by the Leveson Inquiry.

[298] DPA 2018 ss 152(1) and 156(1). The Commissioner has no power at all to give an assessment notice with respect to the processing of personal data for the special purposes: DPA 2018 s 147(5).

[299] DPA 2018 ss 152(2) and 156(2). 'Substantial public importance' is not defined. In England and Wales, the court is the High Court or the county court; in Scotland it is the Court of Session or the sheriff; and in Northern Ireland it is the High Court or a county court: DPA 2018 s 180(1). In England and Wales, the application would be brought by a Part 8 claim form, with a supporting application notice using form N244. The respondent to the claim would be the controller or processor. an application will ordinarily need to be made on notice to the Information Commissioner: CPR r 23.4(1). The required minimum notice period is three clear days: CPR r 23.4(2)(b). The application should be supported by evidence that both sets out why the order should be made and, in the case where notice has not been given because of urgency, why notice has not been given: CPR r 25.3(3).

application or that the case is urgent.[300] Once these hurdles are overcome and the Information Commissioner gives the controller or processor an enforcement notice or a penalty notice, that controller or processor may appeal to the First-tier Tribunal against the notice in the conventional way.[301] It will be open to the controller or processor to found its appeal against the notice on the basis that there has been no failure to comply with the relevant data protection provisions[302] because those provisions have been disapplied.[303]

(2) In relation to legal proceedings against a controller for private remedies, a special determination merely lifts the stay on those proceedings.[304] Thereafter, it will be open to the controller or processor to defeat the claim on the basis that there has been no failure to comply with the relevant data protection provisions[305] because those provisions have been disapplied.[306] If the controller or processor is unable to defeat the claim on this basis, it may still seek to defend the claim as any ordinary claim where there is no issue of the personal data being processed for the special purposes.

5. NATIONAL SECURITY CERTIFICATE APPEALS

48–060 Introduction

The DPA 2018 contains special provisions governing ministerial national security certificates which may be issued to certify conclusively that a national security exemption applies to personal data. There are three separate provisions allowing for conclusive certificates:

(1) In relation to applied GDPR processing, a Minister of the Crown may sign a national security certificate certifying that exemption from all or any of the continuing obligations or data subject rights is, or at any time was, required in relation to any personal data for the purpose of safeguarding national security.[307]

---

300 DPA 2018 ss 152(2) and 156(2).

301 DPA 2018 s 162(1).

302 That is, the provisions listed in DPA 2018 s 149(2), and which comprise all the provisions founding the continuing obligations and data subject rights.

303 DPA 2018 Sch 2 para 26(3), (9). All that the controller or processor will need to show in order to be successful in its appeal is that: (a) the processing of the personal data was carried out for the special purposes; (b) the processing was or is being carried out with a view to the publication by a person (ie any person) of journalistic, academic, artistic or literary material; (c) the controller reasonably believes that the publication of the material would be in the public interest, having regard to the special importance of the public interest in freedom of expression and information; and (d) the controller reasonably believes that the application of the data protection provisions sought to be applied would be incompatible with the special purposes: DPA 2018 Sch 2 para 26(2)-(6). The special determination does not determine the question, or any part of the question, for the FTT.

304 DPA 2018 s 176(3).

305 That is, the provisions listed in DPA 2018 s 149(2), and which comprise all the provisions founding the continuing obligations and data subject rights.

306 DPA 2018 Sch 2 para 26(3), (9). All that the controller or processor will need to show in order to be successful in defeating the claim is that at the relevant time: (a) the processing of the personal data was being carried out for the special purposes; (b) the processing was being carried out with a view to the publication by a person (ie any person) of journalistic, academic, artistic or literary material; (c) the controller reasonably believed that the publication of the material would be in the public interest, having regard to the special importance of the public interest in freedom of expression and information; and (d) the controller reasonably believed that the application of the data protection provisions sought to be applied would be incompatible with the special purposes: DPA 2018 Sch 2 para 26(2)-(6). The special determination does not determine the question, or any part of the question, for the Court.

307 DPA 2018 s 27(1). Prior to the entry into force of the GDPR and the DPA 2018 - and the repeal of the DPA 1998 - DPA 1998 s 28(2) allowed a Minister of the Crown to sign a national security certificate certifying that exemption from all or any of the provisions of the data protection principles provided for by Pts II, III or V or ss 54A or 55

Such a certificate will then stand as conclusive evidence of that fact, thus confirming the engagement of the national security exemption in s 26(1)(a) of the DPA 2018, unless and until withdrawn or revoked or quashed on an appeal under s 27(3) or (5). Such a certificate may identify the personal data to which it applies by means of a general description and may be expressed to have prospective effect.[308] Such a certificate may only be signed by a Minister who is a member of the Cabinet or by the Attorney-General or the Advocate General for Scotland.[309]

(2) In relation to law enforcement processing, a Minister of the Crown may sign a national security certificate certifying that a restriction on the provision of certain information to a data subject is a necessary and proportionate measure to protect national security.[310] Such a certificate will then stand as conclusive evidence of that fact, thus confirming the engagement of the national security limb of the relevant provision, unless and until withdrawn or revoked or quashed on an appeal. Such a certificate may relate to a specific restriction or proposed restriction or identify any restriction to which it relates by means of a general description and may be expressed to have prospective effect.[311] Such a certificate may only be signed by a Minister who is a member of the Cabinet or by the Attorney-General or the Advocate General for Scotland.[312]

(3) In relation to intelligence services processing, a Minister of the Crown may sign a national security certificate certifying that exemption from all or any of the provisions on intelligence service processing is, or at any time was, required for the purpose of safeguarding national security in respect of any personal data.[313] Such a certificate will then stand as conclusive evidence of that fact, thus confirming the engagement of the national security exemption,[314] unless and until withdrawn or

of the DPA 1998 (which included the subject access rights conferred by s 7) was, or at any time had been, required for the purpose of safeguarding national security in respect of any personal data. Such a certificate then stood as conclusive evidence of that fact, thus confirming the engagement of the exemption in DPA 1998 s 28, unless and until withdrawn or revoked or quashed on an appeal under s 28(4) or (6). Such a certificate could: identify the personal data to which it applied by means of a general description and be expressed to have prospective effect (DPA 1998 s 28(3)); and be signed only by a Minister who was a member of the Cabinet or by the Attorney-General or the Advocate General for Scotland (DPA 1998 s 28(10)). DPA 2018 Sch 20, paras 17-18 and 40 contain transitional provisions: saving the effect of the DPA 1998 s 28 and any certificates made thereunder with respect to the processing of personal data to which that Act applies (para 17); and continuing the effect of any such certificate as if it were a certificate made under one or more of the DPA 2018 ss 27, 79 and 111 for one year following the entry into force of the repeal of the DPA 1998 s 28 (para 18).

308 DPA 2018 s 27(2). Pursuant to DPA 2018 s 27(5)-(7) a data controller may claim in proceedings under or by virtue of the applied GDPR or the DPA 2018 that a certificate under s 27(1) which identifies the personal data to which it applies by means of a general description applies to any personal data and, subject to any contrary determination of the Upper Tribunal on appeal, the certificate will be conclusively presumed so to apply.

309 DPA 2018 s 27(10).

310 DPA 2018 s 79(1). The information to which the certificate applies is that which would otherwise have to be provided to the data subject under s 44(2), 45(1), 48(1) or 68(1). Restrictions imposed under the DPA 2018 ss 44(4), 45(4), 48(3) or 68(7) may restrict the provision of information in whole or in part and to the extent that and for so long as necessary and proportionate having regard to the fundamental rights and interests of the data subject. DPA 2018 s 79(13) further provides that none of the enforcement powers conferred by Pt 6 of that Act may be exercised in relation to the imposition of a specific restriction in a s 79(1) certificate or a restriction falling within a general description in such a certificate.

311 DPA 2018 s 79(2) and (4). Pursuant to DPA 2018 s 79(7)-(9) a data controller may claim in proceedings under or by virtue of the DPA 2018 that a restriction under ss 44(4), 45(4), 48(3) or 68(7) falls within a general description in a certificate under s 79(1) and, subject to any contrary determination of the Upper Tribunal on appeal, the restriction will be conclusively presumed so to fall.

312 DPA 2018 s 79(12).

313 Exemption is from those provisions of DPA 2018 Part 4 listed in s 110(2).

314 That is, DPA 2018 s 110(2).

revoked or quashed on an appeal. Such a certificate may identify the personal data to which it applies by means of a general description and may be expressed to have prospective effect.[315] Such a certificate may only be signed by a Minister who is a member of the Cabinet or by the Attorney-General or the Advocate General for Scotland.[316]

48– 061 Appeal grounds

In relation to national security conclusive certificates under the DPA 2018, there are two kinds of appeal:

(1) The Tribunal may allow a certificate appeal and quash the relevant certificate if it finds that, applying the principles applied by the court on an application for judicial review, the Minister or the person designated by him did not have reasonable grounds for issuing the certificate.[317]

(2) Where, in any proceedings under the DPA 2018, the certificate identifies the personal data or the restriction to which it applies by means of a general description and the data controller claims that that certificate applies to personal data or a particular restriction, another party to those proceedings may appeal to the Tribunal on the ground that the certificate does not apply to the personal data.[318]

48– 062 ECHR and Charter

A conclusive certificate may engage rights under Article 8 of the ECHR and Community rights may also come into play by virtue of the fact that the DPA 2018 supplements the GDPR and implements the LED.[319] Article 8 of the ECHR, the GDPR, the LED and DPA 2018 do not confer absolute rights and all four expressly allow, where necessary and proportionate, for the curtailment and denial of these rights in the interests of national security.[320] The rights of

---

[315] DPA 2018 s 111(2). Pursuant to DPA 2018 s 111(5)-(7) a data controller may claim in proceedings under or by virtue of the DPA 2018 that a certificate under s 111(1) which identifies the personal data to which it applies by means of a general description applies to any personal data and, subject to any contrary determination of the Upper Tribunal on appeal, the certificate will be conclusively presumed so to apply.

[316] DPA 2018 s 111(10).

[317] DPA 2018 ss 27(4), 79(6) and 111(4). See further at §5– 041.

[318] DPA 2018 ss 27(5), 79(7) and 111(5). The Tribunal is thus given full appellate jurisdiction to review such matters unconstrained by any caveat that it 'apply the principles applied by the court on an application for judicial review' and assess only whether the Minister had 'reasonable grounds for issuing the certificate' (cf FOIA s 60(3), DPA 2018 ss 27(4), 79(6) and 111(4) and EIR reg 18(7)). The explanation for this is no doubt that the Minister can issue a new certificate with a much clearer application if dissatisfied with a determination made by the Tribunal under FOIA s 60(5) or DPA 2018 s 27(7), 79(9) or 111(7). In *Nasresfahani v SSHD and Data Controller* [2014] UKUT 0487 (AAC), the Upper Tribunal nevertheless took a more restrictive approach to the construction of its powers under the equivalent appeal provision in DPA 1998 s 28(6) given the wording of the relevant certificate under s 28(2). See at [27]: 'However, as under the certificate it is for the Security Services [sic] to determine whether or not the exemption is required for the purpose of safeguarding national security, in effect it is in our judgment a question whether the Security Services [sic] have lawfully made that determination. That is therefore also a question that is in effect to be determined on administrative law principles and in particular whether the determination failed to have regard to material considerations or was perverse or otherwise unlawful.' FOIA s 60(4) and DPA 2018 s 27(5), 79(7) and 111(5) only provide for the resolution by way of appeal of a dispute over a certificate's applicability where it arises, in relation to FOIA, 'in any proceedings under this Act', in relation to DPA 2018, 'in any proceeding under or by virtue of the applied GDPR or this Act' (s 27(5)) or 'under or by virtue of this Act' (ss 79(7) and 111(5)) and, in relation to EIR, 'in any proceedings under these Regulations' (see EIR reg 18(4)(a)(i)). The reason for the different formulations is unclear and their effect depends on whether the need for 'proceedings' is given a strict or generous construction; the latter would expand the scope for having disputes over a certificate's applicability resolved by the Tribunal without the procedural need for separate 'proceedings'.

[319] Indeed, the connection between rights to privacy (including under the ECHR Art 8) and data protection was strongly emphasised throughout the recitals to the European Community Data Protection Directive 95/46/EC and in Art 1, and it is similarly emphasised throughout the GDPR. See §§5– 037 to 5– 045 and especially 5– 044 on the way in which the Community law connection can engage rights to effective judicial oversight.

[320] See §5– 037 and §26– 036(2).

appeal against a conclusive certificate and the adequacy of the judicial oversight they provide will therefore be crucial if it is to be demonstrated that the use of national security certificates thereunder, and the application of the exemption therein, is compatible with Convention rights and Community law. In this regard, it is notable that in relation to the first substantive decision taken by the Information Tribunal under the equivalent predecessor provisions of the DPA 1998, a more intensive proportionality-based standard of review was applied and the certificate in question was quashed for having an 'unnecessarily wide effect.'[321]

6. JUDICIAL REVIEW

48– 063 Scope

The exercise of powers under the DPA 2018 will not generally constitute a public law function capable of challenge by judicial review, even where the controller is a public authority.[322] The only exceptions to this are:

(a) the special provisions relating to conclusive certificates, the issuing of which is a public law function; and
(b) decisions taken or not taken by the Information Commissioner.

The provisions of the DPA 2018 allowing for the issue of conclusive certificates are a species of ouster clause – namely, a partial ouster clause – because the certificates are themselves appealable. Unlike complete ouster clauses, partial ouster clauses have generally been upheld such that certificates under them do not give rise to claims for judicial review.[323]

48– 064 Information Commissioner

Where the Information Commissioner takes regulatory action against a controller or processor, that controller or processor generally has a right of appeal to the First-tier Tribunal.[324] On that basis, such decisions are not susceptible to judicial review.[325] Where a data subject lodges a complaint with the Commissioner that, in connection with personal data relating to him or her, there has been or is an infringement of data protection requirements, if the Commissioner fails to take appropriate steps, to keep the complainant informed about progress or fails to conclude an investigation within the prescribed time, the data subject may seek an order from the FTT spelling out remedial steps.[326] As a result, such failures on the part of the Information Commissioner will not normally provide a good basis for a claim for judicial review. On the other hand, in the following circumstances there is no right of appeal to the First-tier Tribunal

[321] *Baker v SSHD* [2001] UKHRR 1275. Note the emphasis on Convention and Community rights at [50]-[64] and, more generally, see §5– 037. In *Gosling v SSHD*, IT, 1 August 2003 a replacement certificate whose application depended upon a consideration of the requirements of national security in relation to the need for particular exemptions in each individual case was subsequently upheld by the Information Tribunal albeit upon limited grounds (at [28]) and the Tribunal again emphasised the relevance of Convention and Community rights when considering the appropriate intensity of its review (at [48]). This decision was followed in *Hitchens v SSHD*, IT, 4 August 2003, *Hilton v FCO*, IT, 28 June 2005, *Stevenson v SSHD*, IT, 30 April 2009 and *Nasresfahani v SSHD and Data Controller* [2014] UKUT 0487 (AAC).

[322] See: *Re McCord* [2020] NIQB 17.

[323] See further the authorities quoted at §5– 036.

[324] DPA 2018 s 162(1).

[325] If it were shown that such an appeal to the FTT would not adequately protect the interests of the controller or processor (eg because of delays within the FTT system), it is possible that the regulatory decision would be susceptible to judicial review. Similarly, if the sanction was effectively a criminal one (eg a penalty imposed by the Information Commissioner) giving rise to the protections required by Art 6 of the ECHR, but the FTT considered that, being a creature of statute, it could not give effect to them: eg *HMRC v Hok* [2013] STC 225.

[326] DPA 2018 s 166. See further §48– 004.

and, accordingly, there is the possibility of a judicial review claim:

(1) Where the Information Commissioner refuses to make a special determination.[327]

(2) Where a person is not the data subject or the controller or processor in respect of the personal data in respect of which the Information Commissioner has taken, or declines to take, regulatory action, but is affected by the processing or the regulatory step.

48– 065 The tribunals

In principle decisions of both the FTT and the Upper Tribunal are susceptible to judicial review, but the practical scope for such claims is very limited.[328]

7. THIRD PARTIES

48– 066 Introduction

The DPA 2018 specifically requires the Commissioner to take account of the interests of others and the public interest when carrying out functions under the GDPR and the DPA 2018.[329] Only data subjects are expressly given the right to make a complaint to the Information Commissioner.[330] As such, the duty on the Commissioner to act on a complaint is confined to complaints from a data subject.[331] The only persons who will normally have any potential involvement in regulatory measures or court proceedings will be the controller, the data subject to whom the processed personal information relates and the Information Commissioner. There is also scope for a processor to be involved or to be a party to such measures or proceedings. However, there may be circumstances in which a regulatory measure or court proceedings will also touch on the personal data of a third party or where the interests of a non-individual third party may be affected by a regulatory measure or court proceedings. In these circumstances, that third party may wish to be involved or influence the regulatory measure or court proceedings, or may wish to instigate proceedings in order to protect his, her or its interests.

48– 067 Regulatory measures

The Information Commissioner's power to give an information notice extends to persons who are not controllers or processors.[332] Where such a person is given a notice, that party has a right to appeal to the First-tier Tribunal against the notice.[333] The only persons to whom the Information Commissioner may give an assessment notice, an enforcement notice, a penalty notice or a special purposes determination are controllers and processors. In respect of such notices, where the interests of a third party stands to be affected by the notice, particularly as regards the protection of that third party's personal data, depending on the extent to which those interests are otherwise articulated, good practice may require the Commissioner to permit some involvement by the third party in the regulatory process.[334]

---

[327] See further §§48– 056 to 48– 058.

[328] See §45– 030.

[329] DPA 2018 s 2(2). The interests of 'others' in the processing of personal data is recognised in DPA 2018 ss 64(3)(d), 76(1)(a) and 128(5).

[330] DPA 2018 ss 44(1)(e), (5)(d), 45(2)(f), (5)(d), 48(1)(b), (4)(c), 93(1)(e), 94(2)(f), 165 and 187.

[331] DPA 2018 ss 165-166.

[332] DPA 2018 s 142(1).

[333] DPA 2018 s 162(1).

[334] DPA 2018 s 2(2).

48–068 Court and tribunal proceedings

Only the person who made a subject access request for information relating to him or herself may apply to a court for a compliance order.[335] Where such an order is made, a third party directly affected by such an order may apply to have the judgment or order set aside or varied.[336] A third party has no entitlement to appeal to the First-tier Tribunal. But a third party may be joined as a party to an appeal, whether on request by the third party or on the Tribunal's own initiative.[337]

335 DPA 2018 s 167; GDPR Art 79.

336 CPR r 40.9. For example, where the order will result in the disclosure of a third party's confidential business secrets: *IPCom GmbH v HTC Europe Co Ltd* [2013] EWHC 2880 (Ch). Another instance will be where the compliance order will impinge upon the personal data of the third party.

337 FTT Rules r 9 and UT Rules r 9. If the decision is likely to affect the 'civil rights' of the third party it might be argued that the Human Rights Act 1998 and Art 6 of the ECHR would require the Tribunal to join him to the appeal so that such rights could be determined by an independent and impartial tribunal established by law: see *Zander v Sweden* (1993) 18 EHRR 175. Note also FTT Rules r 33(2), which enables the Tribunal to allow a third party to take part in a hearing or make written submissions: but they would not have a right of appeal if that third party was not formally made a party of the appeal.

CHAPTER 49

DPA 1998: private remedies and regulatory enforcement

1. INTRODUCTION

49– 001 Introduction

Notwithstanding the coming into force of the GDPR and the DPA 2018, as a result of transitional provisions private, court-based remedies as well as regulatory enforcement available under the DPA 1998 will remain relevant for some time after 25 May 2018.[1] Moreover, given similarities between certain aspects of the DPA 2018 and the DPA 1998, the two decades of jurisprudence on the latter will serve to guide the operation of the former.

49– 002 Rights and duties

The DPA 1998 conferred on each individual (ie each data subject) four rights, each of which was triggered by the individual giving the data controller a notice:

(a) The right to know what personal data about the individual was being processed by the data controller and to have a copy of that personal data, which was exercised by a notice under s 7(1) - commonly called a 'subject access request.' If the data controller failed to comply with the notice, the individual could apply to a court for a coercive order: s 7(9). This was far and away the most commonly invoked right under the DPA 1998.

[1] Transitional provisions governing civil enforcement under DPA 1998 are in DPA 2018 Sch 20, Pt 7. In relation to private remedies for breaches of duty under DPA 1998, see Interpretation Act 1978 s 16.

(b) The right to prevent processing likely to cause damage or distress, which was exercised by giving the data controller a notice under s 10(1). If the data controller failed to comply with the notice, the individual could apply to a court for a coercive order: s 10(4).

(c) The right to prevent processing for purposes of direct marketing, which was exercised by giving the data controller a notice under s 11(1). If the data controller failed to comply with the notice, the individual could apply to a court for a coercive order: s 11(2).

(d) The right to prevent automated decision-making, which was exercised by giving the data controller a notice under s 12(1). If the data controller failed to comply with the notice, the individual could apply to a court for a coercive order: s 12(8).

In addition to these four rights, each of which required a notice in order to trigger a resultant duty upon the data controller, the DPA 1998 imposed a duty on the data controller to comply with the data protection principles set out in Part 1 of Schedule 1 to that Act. The imposition of this duty upon the data controller required no notice from the individual, but remained on a data controller for as long as the data controller was processing the individual's personal data. Non-compliance with this duty constituted a breach of statutory duty (a common law tort), actionable by the individual as an ordinary claim in the County Court or the High Court. On such a claim, the DPA 1998 provided specific remedies – compensation and erasure, destruction and correction etc orders. Such a claim could be made after the results of one of notice-invoked rights had been received. Alternatively, a person could claim a breach of one of the notice-invoked duties and seek a coercive order for compliance and, at the same time, claim a breach of the duty to comply with the data protection principles and seek compensation and erasure orders. An individual could seek relief on the former (eg an order that the data controller reveal the full extent of the individual's personal data being processed, the purposes for which it was being processed and the recipients of that personal data) before drafting the particulars of claim alleging breach of the data protection principles.

49– 003 Remedies and regulation

Although the DPA 1998 provided for both private, court-based remedies and commissioner-led regulatory enforcement, the latter gave the individual no remedy for past non-compliance by the data controller, but simply generated the hope that future processing by the data controller would comply with the precepts of the DPA 1998. It was quite common for an individual to initiate a complaint about a data controller with the Information Commissioner in order to obtain a normative analysis from the regulator of the processing complained of, before initiating a private law claim against the data controller founded on that processing.

2. PRIVATE REMEDIES: SUBJECT ACCESS REQUESTS

49– 004 Subject access rights

The means by which the subject access right under s 7 of the DPA 1998 was enforced were quite different from enforcement of the equivalent rights under FOIA. First, in contrast to the position under FOIA, there was no specific requirement for codes of practice issued or approved by the Commissioner under s 51(3) of the DPA 1998 to require authorities to institute internal complaints procedures. The Information Commissioner's Subject Access Code of Practice issued in August 2013 made no mention of internal complaints procedures.[2] Secondly, there was no involvement of the FTT: private remedies had to be sought through the courts.

[2] www.ico.org.uk/~/media/documents/library/Data_Protection/Detailed_specialist_guides/subject-access-code-of-practice.PDF

And thirdly, the Information Commissioner could encourage but ultimately not compel disclosure: compulsion required an application to court.

49– 005 Application under section 7(9)

The main remedy for an individual dissatisfied with the response to a request under s 7(1) of the DPA 1998 in relation to data of which he was the 'data subject' was by way of an application to a court under s 7(9). The approach to s 7(9) applications received detailed consideration in three major decisions of the Court of Appeal delivered in the two years before the repeal of the Act.[3] If the court on such an application was satisfied that the data controller in question had failed to comply with the request in contravention of any provision of s 7 it could, as a matter of discretion, order the data controller to comply with the request.[4]

49– 006 Practice and procedure

Both the High Court and a county court (or in Scotland the Court of Session or the sheriff) had jurisdiction to hear such an application.[5] The question for the court on such an application was whether the data controller had failed to comply with the request in contravention of the provisions of s 7 of the DPA 1998.[6] In a case where all of the data related to the data subject, determination of the application involved the court considering afresh the applicability of any exemption, unfettered by the decision of the data controller: it was not a review of the reasonableness of the data controller's decision or of the methodology applied by the data controller in reaching the appealed decision. In a case of 'mixed-data' – where the data related to the data subject and to one or more other individuals – the court would review the reasonableness of the data controller's discretion under s 7(4).[7] In determining whether an applicant was entitled to the information which he sought (including any question whether it was exempt from s 7 by virtue of Part IV of the Act) the court had power to require the information in question[8] to be made available for its own inspection but could not, pending a decision in the applicant's favour, require it to be disclosed to him whether by way of discovery or otherwise.[9] Subject to the rights of appeal to the Upper Tribunal mentioned below,[10] if a national security certificate had been issued under s 28(1) of the Act in relation to any data which was relied on by the data controller in the proceedings, this would constitute conclusive evidence that the exemption of that data from the provisions of s 7 of the Act was required for the purpose of safeguarding national security.[11] If the data controller claimed in the course of

[3] *Dawson-Damer v Taylor Wessing LLP* [2017] EWCA Civ 74, [2017] 1 WLR 3255; *Ittihadieh v 5-11 Cheyne Gardens RTM Co Ltd* [2017] EWCA 121, [2018] QB 256; *B v General Medical Council* [2018] EWCA Civ 1497.

[4] In early decisions such as *Durant v Financial Services Authority* [2003] EWCA Civ 1746, [2004] FSR 28 at [27] the courts indicated that where other legal proceedings are contemplated or in progress, they may be reluctant to allow individuals to use the subject access rights as a means of accessing information where disclosure should more appropriately be dealt with under the CPR. However, that approach has now been authoritatively rejected by the Court of Appeal in *Dawson-Damer v Taylor Wessing LLP* [2017] EWCA Civ 74, [2017] 1 WLR 3255 at [108]-[112] and *Ittihadieh v 5-11 Cheyne Gardens RTM Co Ltd* [2017] EWCA 121, [2018] QB 256 at [86]-[89].

[5] DPA 1998 s 15(1).

[6] DPA 1998 s 7(9). As the applicant's entitlement under s 7(1) is 'subject to the following provisions of ss 7, 8, 9 and 9A' of the Act, the court will have jurisdiction to consider whether the procedural requirements set out in those sections have been met in order to determine whether the failure to comply with the applicant's request is, in fact, in contravention of the applicant's entitlement.

[7] *B v General Medical Council* [2018] EWCA Civ 1497 at [104]-[105] ('the data controller is said to have a 'margin of assessment.')

[8] And information as to the logic involved in any decision-taking as mentioned in s 7(1)(d).

[9] DPA 1998 s 15(2).

[10] See §49– 016 for rights of appeal which are provided by DPA 1998 ss 28(4) and (6).

[11] DPA 1998 s 28(2).

the proceedings that a national security certificate in general terms applied to the personal data in question, the certificate would be conclusively deemed so to apply.[12] It was thought that if an applicant faced with such a certificate had indicated that he wished to appeal to the Upper Tribunal on either of those points, the court should grant an adjournment of the proceedings pending a decision of the Upper Tribunal. There were no specific rules of procedure relating to an application to the court under the DPA 1998 and, accordingly, the Civil Procedure Rules 1998 applied,[13] with most claims being brought under Part 8 of the CPR unless the claim also included a claim for breach of the duty to comply with the data protection principles. An appeal from the decision of the court dealing with the application could with leave be made to either the High Court or the Court of Appeal under Part 52 of the CPR.[14] It was not appropriate to seek a mandatory order requiring a public authority to comply with a subject access request in proceedings for judicial review, rather than under s 7(9) of the DPA 1998.[15]

3. PRIVATE REMEDIES: BREACH OF THE CONTINUING DUTY

49–007 Duty to comply with DPP

As noted above, in addition to the four, notice-invoked rights and resultant duties on the data controller, the DPA 1998 imposed a duty on the data controller to comply with the data protection principles set out in Part 1 of Schedule 1 to that Act. Non-compliance with this duty constituted a breach of statutory duty (a common law tort), actionable by the individual as an ordinary claim in the County Court or the High Court. On such a claim, the DPA 1998 provided specific remedies – compensation and erasure, destruction and correction etc orders.

49–008 Compensation

Under s 13 of the DPA 1998 as enacted, where a data controller contravened any of the requirements of the Act, an individual who suffered damage[16] or distress as a result was entitled to be compensated by the data controller.[17] Awards of compensation could only be made by the courts, and not by the Information Commissioner. The right to compensation for distress only arose if the individual also suffered damage by reason of the contravention, or if the contravention related to the processing of personal data for journalistic, artistic or literary purposes.[18] In 2016 the Court of Appeal held that this limitation was incompatible with EU

[12] DPA 1998 s 28(6).

[13] CPR 2.1.

[14] CPR 52.3; an appeal from the High Court is to the Court of Appeal; an appeal from the county court is normally to the High Court but is likely to be assigned to the Court of Appeal either on the basis that it has been allocated to the multi-track under rr 26.5 and 26.7(2) or if the court exercises its power under r 52.14 (see: CPR PD 52 paras 2A.1, 2A.2 and 2A.6).

[15] *R (Hussain) v Sec of State for Justice* [2016] EWCA Civ 1111, [2017] 1 WLR 761.

[16] In *Sofola v Lloyds TSB Bank plc* [2005] EWHC 1335 (QB), [2005] All ER (D) 299 (Jun), Tugendhat J commented at [43] that the refusal of banking facilities would arguably fall within the meaning of the word 'damage' in s 13. In *Johnson v Medical Defence Union* [2007] EWCA Civ 262, [2007] 3 CMLR 9, (2007) 96 BMLR 99 the Court of Appeal held that 'damages' means pecuniary damages only. That passage was followed by the High Court in *Murray v Express Newspapers Ltd* [2007] EWHC 1908 at [89]. However, the Court of Appeal expressed the view that 'the judge ha[d] construed 'damage' too narrowly, having regard to the fact that the purpose of the Act was to enact the provisions of the relevant Directive': *Murray v Express Newspapers plc* [2008] EWCA Civ 446, [2009] Ch 481 [at [63]. Elsewhere, the word 'damage' in s 13 has not been considered to be so constrained: *Lyons v Stephen House, QPM & anor* [2013] CSIH 46. In *Halliday v Creation Consumer Finance Ltd* [2013] EWCA Civ 333 it was conceded that 'damages' could include an award of nominal damages.

[17] DPA 1998 s 13. See also Directive 95/46/EC Art 23. Liability could arise vicariously: *WM Morrisons plc v Various Claimants* [2020] UKSC 12.

[18] DPA 1998 ss 3 and 13(2). As to heads of compensation under s 13 see *Johnson v Medical Defence Union (No 2)* [2006]

law and it was disapplied under Art 47 of the Charter.[19] It was a defence to a claim for damages for the data controller to prove that he took such care to comply with the requirement concerned as was reasonably required in all of the circumstances.[20] This appears to have been somewhat more generous than the defence for which the Data Protection Directive provided, namely that the data controller was not responsible for the event giving rise to the damage.[21] The right to compensation was conferred only on individuals.[22] There was, apparently, a de minis threshold below which compensation was not awarded.[23] Although it had been suggested that compensation should not be substantial,[24] this was not universally accepted[25] and the notion that the approach to quantum should diverge from that followed in other cases involving a violation of fundamental rights was questionable. Compensation for distress from the mere fact of non-compliance with the data protection principles was generally modest.[26]

49–009 Rectification and destruction

The court had a specific power to order rectification, blocking, erasure or destruction of personal data being processed by a data controller following a contravention of any of the requirements of the DPA 1998, including the subject access rights.[27] It may, on an application by the data subject, order the data controller to rectify, block, erase or destroy the personal data in question if it is satisfied both that the data subject has suffered damage by reason of the contravention, in circumstances entitling him to compensation under s 13, and that there is a substantial risk of further contravention in respect of those data in such circumstances.[28] Moreover, the court may additionally, if it considers it reasonably practicable, order the data controller to notify third parties to whom the data have been disclosed of their rectification, blocking, erasure or destruction.[29] This suite of powers was described as a 'toolbox of discretionary remedies.'[30] The question of reasonable practicability is to be assessed, in particular, having regard to the number of persons who would have to be notified.[31]

EWHC (Ch) 321, (2006) 89 BMLR 43 at [217]-[218].

19 *Vidal Hall v Google Inc* [2015] EWCA Civ 311, [2016] QB 1003.

20 DPA 1998 s 13(3). For an example of a claim where the defence under s 13(3) was made good, see *NT1 v Google LLC* [2018] EWHC 799 (QB), [2018] 3 All ER 581 at [227]-[228].

21 Directive 95/46/EC Art 23(2).

22 DPA 1998 s 13(1) and (2).

23 *TLT v SSHD* [2016] EWHC 2217 upheld on appeal at *TLT & ors v Secretary of State for the Home Department* [2018] EWCA Civ 2217, [2018] 4 WLR 101.

24 *Halliday v Creation Consumer Finance Ltd* [2013] EWCA Civ 333 at [33]-[35].

25 *CR19 v Chief Constable of Northern Ireland* [2014] NICA 54 at [22]. Damages will be awarded for loss of autonomy or loss of control, with the nature of the information disclosed and the degree of loss of control bearing on the assessment of compensation – the more intimate the information and the more extensive the disclosure, the treater the award: *Reid v Price* [2020] EWHC 594 (QB) at [51].

26 In *Halliday v Creation Consumer Finance Ltd* [2013] EWCA Civ 333 the Court of Appeal awarded £750 for a breach that did not lead to loss of credit or reputation, where the breach of principle resulted from a single technical error, with no manifestation of injury to feelings or of the distress.

27 DPA 1998 s 14(4). This remedy is independent of any claim for compensation. See *Sofola v Lloyds TSB Bank plc* [2005] EWHC 1335 (QB), [2005] All ER (D) 299 (Jun) at [47].

28 DPA 1998 s 14(4).

29 DPA 1998 s 14(5).

30 *NT1 v Google LLC* [2018] EWHC 799 (QB), [2018] 3 All ER 581 at [85]-[86].

31 DPA 1998 s 14(6).

4. REGULATORY ENFORCEMENT

49– 010 Information Commissioner

In relation to the access rights as against public authorities granted by s 7 of the DPA 1998, the roles of the Information Commissioner and the Tribunals are likely to be limited. Contravention of s 7 by a public authority by failing to supply information in accordance with that section would constitute a breach of the 'sixth data protection principle'.[32] Such contravention could be the subject of an 'enforcement notice' by the Information Commissioner pursuant to s 40 of the Act requiring the public authority to take steps to comply with its obligations, and could also in principle be the subject of a request for an assessment by the Information Commissioner under s 42 of the Act[33] and of an 'information notice' served by the Information Commissioner on the public authority under s 43[34] of the Act in connection with such an assessment or for determining whether the data protection principles had been complied with.[35] An information notice under s 43 is very similar to one under s 51 of FOIA save that s 43 includes an express provision, not found in s 51, that a person does not have to comply with an information notice if to do so would expose him to proceedings for an offence save for an offence under the DPA 1998 itself.[36]

49– 011 Request for an assessment

In addition to appealing to a court against any failure to comply with a subject access request, a data subject (or a person on his behalf) may request the Information Commissioner for an assessment as to whether it is likely that the processing has been or is being carried out in compliance with the provisions of the DPA 1998.[37] Such a request may include seeking an assessment by the Information Commissioner whether the data controller has disclosed under s 7 and in accordance with the Act information held by the data controller relating to the data subject.[38] Where such a request is made, the Information Commissioner is obliged to make an assessment in such manner as appears to him to be appropriate.[39] The Information Commissioner has a duty to act fairly towards the data controller and to follow the rules of

32 DPA 1998 s 4(4) Sch 1 Pt I para 6; Sch 1 Pt II, para 8(a).

33 The complaint made by the applicant in *R (SSHD) v* IT [2006] EWHC 2958 (Admin), [2007] 2 All ER 703 (DC) was treated as a request under DPA 1998 s 42. Such a request must be complied with by the Information Commissioner unless he has not been supplied with sufficient information to identify the person requesting the assessment and the 'processing' in question: DPA 1998 s 42(2).

34 Or, in theory, a 'special information notice' under s 44, though it is probably unlikely that a public authority will claim that 'personal data' were being processed by it for journalistic, artistic or literary purposes.

35 But note in this context DPA 1998 s 42(3)(c), which would suggest that the Commissioner would generally expect a data subject to seek to exercise his rights to apply to court under s 7(9) before proceeding with any assessment or serving an enforcement notice; presumably the failure of the Commissioner to carry out an assessment or serve an enforcement notice could in principle be the subject of an application for judicial review, but since a direct application under s 7(9) could be made against the real wrong-doer this is unlikely to be granted in practice.

36 DPA 1998 s 43(8).

37 DPA 1998 s 42(1).

38 DPA 1998 s 1(1), definition of 'processing', in particular para (c).

39 DPA 1998 s 42(2). In determining what manner is appropriate, the Information Commissioner may have regard to the extent to which the request appears to him to raise a matter of substance, whether there has been undue delay in making the request and whether the person is entitled to make an application under DPA 1998 s 7 in relation to the request: DPA 1998 s 42(3).

natural justice.[40] The advantage for a data subject in making a request for an assessment by the Information Commissioner is that, if an exemption on any of the specified grounds is relied upon by the data controller, the Information Commissioner will be able to call for the data relating to the data subject (as well as other information)[41] and, having examined those data (and other information), consider whether the exemption has been properly relied upon.[42] This can assume importance, as the data controller, in answering a subject access request, may have not informed the data subject that data relating to him had been withheld, the basis upon which it had been withheld or whether a national security certificate[43] is operating.[44] The minimum requirements of an assessment are that the Information Commissioner notify the person making the request whether he has made an assessment and, to the extent he considers appropriate, of the view he has formed or the action taken as a response to the request.[45] The action taken may include the service of an enforcement notice.

49– 012 Enforcement notice

Where the Information Commissioner is satisfied that a data controller has contravened any of the data protection principles, the Commissioner may issue an 'enforcement notice'.[46] The sixth data protection principle requires personal data to be processed in accordance with the rights of data subjects under the DPA 1998, and it is a breach of that principle to fail to supply information in accordance with section 7.[47] Thus, where the Information Commissioner is satisfied that a data controller has failed to comply with a subject access request, the Commissioner may issue a notice requiring the data controller to comply with the request.[48] Although in practice a request for an assessment will ordinarily be the catalyst for such an enforcement notice, the Information Commissioner can issue an enforcement notice whenever he is satisfied that a data controller has contravened or is contravening any of the data protection principles.[49] In deciding whether or not to issue an enforcement notice (and whether or not an information notice was served in considering the request for assessment), the

40 *South Lanarkshire Council v Scottish IC* [2013] UKSC 55, 2013 GWD 25-508, 2013 SLT 799, [2013] 1 WLR 2421 at [31]-[33].

41 By the service of an 'information notice' under DPA 1998 s 43(1). A person served with an information notice may appeal to the FTT against that notice: DPA 1998 s 48(1). Ordinarily, the information notice must not require compliance at a time sooner than the expiry of the time for an appeal: DPA 1998 s 43(4). However, if the Information Commissioner requires the information sought in the information notice as a matter of urgency, he may include in the information notice a statement to that effect: DPA 1998 s 43(5). In this case, the notice can require the information to be supplied 8 or more days after service of the information notice: DPA 1998 s 43(5). The data controller can include in an appeal against the information notice an appeal against the inclusion of such a statement: s 48(3). Appeals are governed by DPA 1998 Sch 6. The appeal is a merit-based appeal: DPA 1998 s 49.

42 The power of the IC to require the data holder to provide him with information extends to situations where the information is held by the Security Services: *R (SSHD) v Information Tribunal* [2006] EWHC 2958 (Admin), [2007] 2 All ER 703.

43 Under DPA 1998 s 28(2).

44 Thus, in *R (SSHD) v Information Commissioner* [2006] EWHC 2958 (Admin), [2007] 2 All ER 703 (DC), the Home Department responded to the data subject's request by stating 'We have processed your request and enclose copies of all the information which [the Immigration and Nationality Directorate] is required to supply under the DPA 1998.' The Home Department's response did not indicate whether there was any further information that it held relating to the applicant and, if so, upon what basis it declined to disclose it to him, including the existence of a national security certificate.

45 DPA 1998 s 42(4).

46 DPA 1998 s 40(1).

47 DPA 1998 Sch 1, Pt I and Pt II para 8(e).

48 DPA 1998 s 40(1). See, eg: *DCLG v IC*, IT, 23 April 2009.

49 DPA 1998 s 40(1).

Information Commissioner will be able to call for the data relating to the data subject (as well as other information)[50] and, having examined those data (and other information), consider whether the exemption has been properly relied upon. An enforcement notice must contain a statement of the data protection principle that the Information Commissioner is satisfied has been or is being contravened and the Commissioner's reasons for reaching that conclusion.[51]

49– 013 Cancellation or variation

The Information Commissioner may, after serving an enforcement notice, cancel or vary it.[52] At any time after the time for appeal against an enforcement notice has expired, the person on whom the notice has been served may apply to the Information Commissioner for a cancellation or variation of the enforcement notice on the ground that, by reason of a change of circumstances, the notice need not be complied with in order to ensure compliance with the data protection principles.[53]

49– 014 Regulatory appeals

Under s 48 of the DPA 1998[54] a data controller may appeal to the FTT or Upper Tribunal against an assessment, enforcement or information notice. Appeals to the FTT are merit-based.[55] The Tribunal must allow such an appeal if it considers that the notice was not in accordance with the law or if any discretion of the Information Commissioner ought to have been exercised differently and it may review any determination of fact on which the notice was based.[56] A person who has made a request for an assessment under s 42 does not have a right of appeal against the assessment notice.[57] Under s 55B(5) a person served with a monetary penalty notice may appeal against it, both against the notice itself and against the amount in the notice.[58] These appeals will be dealt with under the FTT Rules and the Tribunal Procedure (Upper Tribunal) Rules 2008 as appropriate.[59]

49– 015 Monetary penalty notice

Under s 55A of the DPA 1998, the Information Commissioner has the power to impose a monetary penalty notice on a data controller where there has been a serious contravention by the data controller of s 4(4) (the statutory duty to comply with the data protection principles) of a kind likely to cause substantial damage or substantial distress, and the contravention was deliberate or the data controller knew or ought to have known of the risk and failed to take

---

50 By the service of an 'information notice' under DPA 1998 s 43(1). See further n 41.

51 DPA 1998 s 40(6)(a).

52 DPA 1998 s 41(1).

53 DPA 1998 s 41(2).

54 Read with Transfer of Tribunal Functions Order 2010 (SI 2010/22) Art 2(3).

55 Appeals are governed by DPA 1998 Sch 6 and the Tribunal Procedure (First-tier Tribunal) (General Regulatory Chamber) Rules 2009 and, where there is a national security certificate, the Tribunal Procedure (Upper Tribunal) Rules 2008.

56 DPA 1998 s 49(1), (2).

57 Although the Information Commissioner must 'notify' the person who made the request, that person is not 'served' with the assessment notice: DPA 1998 ss 42(4), 48(1).

58 The Tribunal exercise a full merit jurisdiction, both in relation to the notice itself and the amount of the penalty: *Central London Community Healthcare NHS Trust v IC* [2013] UKUT 0551 (AAC) at [50]-[57]. If, on an appeal from the FTT to the UT, the UT concludes that the FTT erred in law, the UT has all the powers of the FTT, including the power to increase the penalty (at [82]-[87]).

59 See §§44– 017 to 44– 019. For an example of an appeal against an enforcement notice under the DPA 1998, though not in the context of a subject access request, see *Southampton City Council v IC*, FTT, 19 February 2013.

reasonable steps to prevent it.[60] The Commissioner can issue a monetary penalty notice even though the contravention of the Act comes to his attention by notification from the data controller.[61] In setting the penalty, it is permissible to offer the data controller a discount for prompt payment and forfeiting the right of appeal.[62] A person who receives a monetary penalty notice may appeal to the FTT. In such an appeal, the Tribunal does not simply exercise a supervisory jurisdiction but conducts a full merit review both of the decision to issue the notice and of the amount of the penalty.[63]

5. NATIONAL SECURITY CERTIFICATE APPEALS

49– 016 Appeal grounds

Where a national security certificate has been issued certifying in respect of some or all of any relevant data that exemption from the data protection principles or Parts II, III or V and/or s 55 of the DPA 1998[64] is, or at any time was, required for the purpose of safeguarding national security, then the certificate will be conclusive evidence of that 'fact'.[65] Although an applicant for data is not disentitled from appealing to a court where a conclusive certificate has been issued, the certificate will render the proceedings a foregone conclusion provided that it relates to the information sought. Instead, there are two discrete rights of appeal to the Upper Tribunal:[66]

(1) A person directly affected by the issuing of a conclusive certificate may appeal to the Tribunal against the decision to issue the conclusive certificate.[67] The task for the Tribunal on such an appeal is to consider whether, applying the principles applied by a court on an application for judicial review, the Minister did not have reasonable grounds for issuing the certificate: the Tribunal does not consider afresh whether exemption is in fact required for the purpose of safeguarding national security. Unless the Tribunal finds that the Minister did not have reasonable grounds for issuing the certificate, it must dismiss the appeal; if it finds that the

---

60 See *Central London Community Healthcare NHS Trust v IC* [2013] UKUT 0551 (AAC), on appeal from *Central London Community Healthcare NHS Trust v IC*, FTT, 15 January 2013.

61 *Central London Community Healthcare NHS Trust v IC* [2013] UKUT 0551 (AAC) at [20]-[24].

62 *Central London Community Healthcare NHS Trust v IC* [2013] UKUT 0551 (AAC) at [58]-[71].

63 *Central London Community Healthcare NHS Trust v IC* [2013] UKUT 0551 (AAC) at [50]-[51]. On appeal from the FTT to the Upper Tribunal, once the latter concludes that the former made an error of law in setting the penalty, the UT has all the powers of the FTT, including increasing the amount of the penalty (at [82]-[87]. See also: *LAD Media Ltd* v IC, FTT, 9 June 2017; *IT Protect Ltd v IC*, FTT, 24 August 2017.

64 These include the right of access under DPA 1998 s 7 and the enforcement provisions available to the Information Commissioner in Part V of the Act.

65 DPA 1998 s 28(2). A certificate may identify the personal data to which it applies by means of a general description; and it may be expressed to have prospective effect: DPA 1998 s 28(3). Conclusive certificates are considered further at §5– 046.

66 Assuming that an applicant in a particular case has a 'civil right' to disclosure of the data sought it seems that the Human Rights Act 1998 and Art 6 of the ECHR in particular would be satisfied by these arrangements (compare *Tinnelly & Sons Ltd v UK* (1998) 27 EHRR 249 where there was no independent or judicial scrutiny of the ministerial national security certificate). The Upper Tribunal has inherited this jurisdiction under the Transfer of Tribunal Functions Order 2010 SI 2010/22 Art 2(3) and the FTT Rules r 19(1A).

67 DPA 1998 s 28(4). A person directly affected can include not only the data subject but also the Information Commissioner: see *R (SSHD) v Information Tribunal* [2006] EWHC 2958 (Admin), [2007] 2 All ER 703 (DC) in which the Information Commissioner issued an information notice under s 43 of the Act in the course of an assessment under s 42 following a complaint by a data subject in response to which the Secretary of State issued a certificate to the effect that exemption from s 43 was required for the purposes of safeguarding national security and the Information Commissioner appealed to the Information Tribunal.

Minister did not have reasonable grounds for issuing the certificate, it may allow the appeal and quash the certificate.[68]

(2) Where a dissatisfied applicant has made a 'merit review' application to the relevant court against a failure to comply with a subject access request[69] and the data controller has claimed in those proceedings that a national security certificate that identifies information by means of a general description[70] applies to the information sought, then any other party to those proceedings may appeal to the Upper Tribunal on the ground that the certificate does not apply to the personal data in question.[71] The task for the Upper Tribunal is to consider whether the generally-worded certificate is apt to apply to all the information sought.

49– 017 Practice and procedure

Procedure in national security certificate appeals is governed by the Tribunal Procedure (Upper Tribunal) Rules 2008. The notice of appeal will be addressed to the FTT but, in accordance with rule 19(1A) of the FTT Rules, the appeal will automatically be transferred to the Upper Tribunal at which point the Upper Tribunal must give directions as to the consideration and disposal of the proceedings.[72] The Tribunal Procedure (Upper Tribunal) Rules 2008 are dealt with in general above[73] to which reference should be made but there are a number of special rules which should also be noted. First, schedule 2 to the Rules provides additional rules, relating to the notification and participation of the relevant Minister[74] and objections by the Minister to the publication of his response or any record of the Tribunal's decision. Rule 14(10) specifically enjoins the Upper Tribunal to ensure that information is not disclosed contrary to the interests of national security and the Tribunal must conduct proceedings and record its decision and reasons so as not to undermine the effect of that provision.[75] Rule 10(1A) makes special provision in relation to costs, in particular costs may be awarded against the relevant Minister if it allows an appeal against a certificate (without the usual requirement that he has acted unreasonably).[76] There is no provision for an appeal from a determination of the Upper Tribunal on an appeal relating to a national security certificate, so that judicial review of the

68 DPA 1998 s 28(5). In *Norman Baker MP v SSHD* [2001] UKHRR 1275 the Data Protection Tribunal (as the Information Tribunal was then known) held that a national security exemption certificate applying effectively a blanket exemption to files held by MI5 was unreasonably wide. The difficulty with the exemption was that the security service did not have to consider in any individual case whether responding to the request (even with a 'neither confirm nor deny' response) would harm national security. A revised form of the certificate was considered by the High Court in *Re Ewing* [2003] EWHC 3169 (QB), where it was held that the criticisms by the Information Tribunal had been addressed.: '... a general [neither confirm nor deny] policy, in response to requests for personal data, including as to the existence (or non-existence) of personal data, is in principle justifiable and cannot be criticised as unreasonable or unnecessary' (at [60]). In *R (SSHD) v IT* [2006] EWHC 2958 (Admin), [2007] 2 All ER 703 the Divisional Court upheld the decision of the Information Tribunal that the Secretary of State in issuing a certificate under s 28(2) of the Act was obliged to take account of the Information Commissioner's role under s 51(1) of 'checking' that an exemption had been properly claimed under s 28(1) as against the data subject and that, in failing to take account of the Information Commissioner's role, he did not have reasonable grounds for issuing the certificate as against the Information Commissioner. See also *Nasresfahani v SSHD and Data Controller* [2014] UKUT 0487 (AAC).

69 That is, under the DPA 1998 s 7(9).

70 Relying on DPA 1998 s 28(3).

71 DPA 1998 s 28(6).

72 UT Rules r 26A(2).

73 See §§44– 019 to 44– 021, 44– 022, 44– 023.

74 Rule 35(2) gives him a specific entitlement to attend any hearing, though note that rule 34(1) enables the Upper Tribunal to make any decision without a hearing.

75 See rule 14(11); see also rules 37(2A) and 37(4)(c) in relation to hearings and the exclusion of parties from them.

76 See rule 10(3)(d).

Tribunal's decision is likely, in principle, to be possible.[77]

6. JUDICIAL REVIEW

49–018 Judicial review

The position in relation to judicial review of acts and decisions under the DPA 1998 is similar to that under FOIA.[78] Again, there is no provision expressly excluding judicial review but, so far as an applicant is concerned, it will ordinarily be excluded by the principle that the court will not generally grant judicial review where there is some other remedy available. For this reason the court will not grant a mandatory injunction requiring a public authority to comply with a subject access request in judicial review proceedings, rather than a coercive order under DPA 1998 s 7(9).[79] This exclusion would not apply to decisions of the Upper Tribunal on national security appeals under s 28 of the DPA 1998[80] or to a failure to act on the part of the Information Commissioner on a request for an assessment under s 42(2) of the Act or an assessment notice that does not properly address an applicant's request.[81]

7. THIRD PARTIES AND APPEALS

49–019 Introduction

The issues which arise under the DPA 1998 in respect of third party participation in appeals are very similar to those which arise under FOIA.[82] However, the manner in which these issues have been addressed under the DPA 1998 is slightly different.

49–020 Role in appeals

Only the person who made a subject access request for information relating to him or herself could apply to a court for a coercive order under s 7 of the Act.[83] However, the DPA 1998 provides a free-standing right by any person who is, or believes himself to be, directly affected by any processing of personal data for an assessment by the Information Commissioner as to whether it is likely or unlikely that the processing has been or is being carried out in compliance with the provisions of the Act.[84] As 'processing' is defined to include the disclosure of information, this would appear to permit a third party who is, or would stand to be, directly affected by the disclosure of information to make application to the Information Commissioner for an assessment. The Commissioner is only required to provide the person making the

---

77 See above at §45–030.

78 See §§45–028 to 45–031.

79 *R (Hussain) v Sec of State for Justice* [2016] EWCA Civ 1111, [2017] 1 WLR 761.

80 See, eg, *R (SSHD) v Information Tribunal* [2006] EWHC 2958 (Admin), [2007] 2 All ER 703 (DC) where the Secretary of State brought an unsuccessful judicial review of the Information Tribunal's decision under DPA 1998 s 28(5) quashing a national security certificate issued by him. But note the position of the Upper Tribunal may well be different: see §45–030.

81 Since, in the last case, the person who made the request for an assessment does not have a right to appeal against the enforcement notice: DPA 1998 ss 42(4), 48(1).

82 See §§45–032 to 45–034, 46–018.

83 DPA 1998 s 7(9).

84 DPA 1998 s 42(1).

request with details of any view formed or action taken to the extent that the Information Commissioner considers appropriate.[85] Upon such an application being made, the Information Commissioner can issue an information notice,[86] a special information notice[87] or an enforcement notice.[88] The statutory right of appeal to the Tribunals only extends to a public authority against whom one or more of the above three notices has been served.[89] Outside these statutory rights of appeal, the position of a dissatisfied third party is akin to that under FOIA.[90]

[85] DPA 1998 s 42(2).

[86] DPA 1998 s 43.

[87] DPA 1998 s 44.

[88] DPA 1998 s 40.

[89] DPA 1998 s 48. These appeals are considered at §49– 014.

[90] See §§45– 032 to 45– 034, 46– 018.

CHAPTER 50
Warrants, offences and immunities

1. FOIA 2000 AND EIR 2004

50– 001 Regulatory contempt

The Information Commissioner has power to issue decision notices,[1] enforcement notices,[2] and information notices[3] requiring public authorities to take steps to comply with their obligations under the Acts or to supply information in order to determine whether they have complied with such obligations. If a decision notice, enforcement notice or information notice issued by the Information Commissioner (and not successfully appealed against)[4] is not complied with, she may certify that that is the case to the High Court.[5] The court may then inquire into the matter and, after hearing evidence and any statement which may be offered in defence, it may deal with the public authority 'as if it had committed a contempt of court.'[6]

1 FOIA s 50; FOIA s 56(1); EIR reg 18 (applying FOIA, Pt IV (ss 50-56), incl Sch 3). These are discussed in §45–010ff.

2 FOIA s 52; EIR reg 18 (applying FOIA, Pt IV (ss 50-56), incl Sch 3). These are discussed in §47– 003.

3 FOIA s 51; EIR reg 18 (applying FOIA, Pt IV (ss 50-56), incl Sch 3). These are discussed in §47– 002. Note that failure to comply with an information notice includes making a false statement in purported compliance with the information notice: FOIA s 54(2).

4 FOIA s 57; EIR reg 18 (applying FOIA, Pt V (ss 57-61)). An appeal can result in a substitute notice issued under FOIA s 58 which will operate and be enforceable as if it had been issued by the Information Commissioner.

5 FOIA s 54(1); EIR reg 18 (applying FOIA, Pt IV (ss 50-56), incl Sch 3).

6 FOIA s 54(3); EIR reg 18 (applying FOIA, Pt IV (ss 50-56), incl Sch 3).

50– 002 Contempt jurisdiction

If it was ever required in practice,[7] there may be difficulties in applying the provision for contempt of court. The normal ways of dealing with a person who has committed a civil contempt of court are by way of an order of committal to prison, a sequestration order, a fine, an injunction, an order that the contemnor pay the costs of the hearing (often on an indemnity basis) and (possibly) a declaration.[8] It seems unlikely that committal, sequestration or a fine would ever be appropriate in relation to a public authority (even assuming the public authority in question was an individual and therefore amenable to an order of committal) and, at least in relation to government departments, the House of Lords has expressed the view that a *finding* of contempt should suffice in any case.[9] Because the provision refers to dealing with the authority it does not seem that the court could make an order of committal or sequestration against individual officers who were personally responsible (even in a contumacious way) for the failure of the authority to comply with a notice by the Commissioner, as the court can normally do in the case of a breach of one of its own orders,[10] although it would presumably be open to the court to grant an injunction which could itself thereafter be enforced if still not complied with in this way.

50– 003 Contempt procedure

The procedure is laid down by CPR 81.15 and Practice Direction 81. The case would be heard by a single judge of the Administrative Court.[11] The form of certificate to be completed by the Commissioner is in Annex 1 to Practice Direction 81. There is an automatic right of appeal to the Court of Appeal against the making of a committal order by a High Court judge if that were the outcome.[12]

50– 004 Search warrants

Where there are reasonable grounds for suspecting:

- non-compliance with the requirements of Part 1 of FOIA or with the requirements of a decision, information or enforcement notice, or
- that an offence under s 77 of FOIA has been committed,

and there are grounds for suspecting that evidence of any of these is to be found on any premises, the Information Commissioner may seek a warrant from a circuit judge authorising her or her officers to enter and search premises, to inspect and seize documents or other material[13] which might be evidence of that non-compliance or offence, and to inspect, examine, operate and test equipment found there in which information may be recorded.[14] Save in cases

---

7 The Home Office's Freedom of Information Unit expressed the view that the provision was only there 'to give the Commissioner's notices the appropriate status': see Public Administration Committee, *Third Report*, 1998-99 Session, Annex 6, para 90.

8 *Halsbury's Laws of England*, 5th edn, Butterworths 2012, vol 22, para 94.

9 See *M v Home Office* [1994] 1 AC 377, [1993] 3 All ER 537 (Lord Woolf).

10 See CPR 81.4(3).

11 CPR 81.15(2).

12 CPR 52.3(1)(a)(i).

13 In relation to the power of a magistrate under s 8 of the Police and Criminal Evidence Act 1984 to grant a warrant to a constable to enter and search the premises (containing a like power to 'seize documents and other material'), the phrase 'other material' has been held to be wide enough to cover a computer and its hard disk: *R (Faisaltex Ltd) v Preston Crown Court* 2008] EWHC 2832 (Admin), [2009] 1 Cr App R 37; *R (Cabot Global Ltd) v Barkingside Magistrates' Court* [2015] EWHC 1458 (Admin), [2015] 2 Cr App R 26.

14 FOIA s 55 and Sch 3, para 1; EIR reg 18 (applying FOIA, Pt IV (ss 50-56), incl Sch 3). These powers are comparable to those given to the Inland Revenue Commissioners in relation to serious fraud by the Taxes Management Act 1970 s 20C and to constables by the Companies Act 1985 s 448, with the interesting result that,

of urgency or where this would defeat the object of the exercise, the occupier of the premises must have been given seven days' notice that access was required and have refused it and been warned of the application for a warrant and been heard on the matter.[15] This reflects a clear policy that agreement should be reached if possible, which no doubt also reflects the hope that public authorities will not normally destroy or hide evidence. Courts have consistently held that the issue of a search warrant is a very severe interference with individual liberty and is a step that should be taken only after mature consideration of the facts. The procedure that must be followed in order to obtain a warrant is never a mere formality.[16] In applying for a warrant, the Commissioner has a duty of full disclosure, including (it is suggested) advising the judge of whether any attempt has been made to obtain the documents or other material using an information notice (and, if so, the outcome of that attempt and why a warrant is nevertheless necessary)[17] and whether there has been any earlier search of the premises (and, if so, the details of that search).[18] The duty of candour requires disclosure of anything that might militate against the grant of the warrant.[19] The judge issuing the warrant is not simply reviewing the reasonableness of the decision of the Commissioner that the statutory criteria are met: before a warrant is issued, the judge must him or herself be satisfied that the statutory requirements have been established.[20] Where a warrant is sought in support of FOIA (or data protection and similar legislation), the statement of the supporting officer will, by its very nature, almost certainly require to be supported by the important underlying primary material and not just an account of them.[21] The warrant itself must properly identify the information and other material that may be searched for and seized.[22] Where the judge issuing the warrant was not provided with all the relevant information, the validity of the warrant will depend on whether the missing information might have led the judge to refuse to issue the warrant.[23]

50–005 Warrant execution

The warrant must be executed within seven days[24] and the person executing it can use

under the Freedom of Information Acts, it would be public authorities which are on the receiving end of the search and seizure order.

15 FOIA Sch 3 para 2; EIR reg 18 (applying FOIA Pt IV (ss 50-56), incl Sch 3).

16 *R (Redknapp) v Commissioner of the City of London Police* [2008] EWHC 1177 (Admin), [2009] 1 WLR 2091, dealing with a like power under the Police and Criminal Evidence Act 1984 s 8. Similarly: *R (Wood) v North Avon Magistrates' Court* [2009] EWHC 3614 (Admin), (2010) 174 JP 157; *Gross v Southwark Crown Court* [1998] COD 445.

17 Though, see: *R v Billericay Justices Ex p. Frank Harris (Coaches)* [1991] Crim LR 472, [1991] COD 188.

18 See, in relation to the analogous regime under the Police and Civil Evidence Act 1984 s 8: *R (Wood) v North Avon Magistrates' Court* [2009] EWHC 3614 (Admin), (2010) 174 JP 157.

19 *R (Energy Financing Team Limited) v Bow Street Magistrates' Court* [2005] EWHC 1626 (Admin), [2006] 1 WLR 1316; *R (Golfrate Property Management Limited) v Southwark Crown Court* [2014] EWHC 840 (Admin), [2014] 2 Cr App R 12 at [24]-[27].

20 *R (Bright) v Central Criminal Court* [2001] 1 WLR 662, [2001] 2 All ER 244; *R (Rawlinson and Hunter Trustees) v Central Criminal Court* [2012] EWHC 2254 (Admin), [2013] 1 WLR 1634 at [83]-[84].

21 See, by analogy: *R (Rawlinson and Hunter Trustees) v Central Criminal Court* [2012] EWHC 2254 (Admin), [2013] 1 WLR 1634 at [85]-[89].

22 *R (Lees) v Solihull Magistrates' Court* [2013] EWHC 3779 (Admin), [2014] Lloyd's Rep FC 233; *R (Cheema) Nottingham and Newark Magistrates' Court* [2013] EWHC 3790 (Admin), [2014] ACD 55.

23 See, in relation to the analogous regime under the Police and Civil Evidence Act 1984 s 8: *R (Dulai) v Chelmsford Magistrates' Court* [2012] EWHC 1055 (Admin), [2013] 1 WLR 220; *R (Goode) v Nottingham Crown Court* [2013] EWHC 1726 (Admin), [2014] ACD 6; *R (Mills) v Sussex Police* [2014] EWHC 2523 (Admin), [2015] 1 WLR 2199; cf *R (Golfrate Property Management Limited) v Southwark Crown Court* [2014] EWHC 840 (Admin), [2014] 2 Cr App R 12; *R (Rawlinson and Hunter Trustees) v Central Criminal Court* [2012] EWHC 2254 (Admin), [2013] 1 WLR 1634.

24 FOIA Sch 3 para 1(2); EIR reg 18 (applying FOIA Pt IV (ss 50-56), incl Sch 3).

reasonable force.[25] The warrant must be executed at a reasonable time unless this would mean the evidence would not be found.[26] The powers of inspection and seizure are not exercisable in respect of information which is exempt on national security grounds or communications subject to legal professional privilege in relation to advice or proceedings about obligations, rights or liabilities arising under FOIA or the EIR itself.[27] The Commissioner and her officers authorised by a warrant are 'relevant persons' within the meaning of section 51 of the Protection of Freedoms Act 2012.[28] As such, they must have regard to the Powers of Entry Code of Practice, dated December 2014.[29] The Code does not override the provisions in Schedule 3 but provides guidance and sets out considerations that apply before, during and after powers of entry. Under the Code:

(1) Relevant persons must consider whether the necessary objectives can be met by less intrusive means: §1.4. The Commissioner must consider all available intelligence before applying for a warrant, such as taking reasonable steps to verify that the information is accurate, recent and not provided maliciously: §12.1.[30] The application to the court for a warrant should generally be supported by a signed written authority from a senior official within the office of the Information Commissioner: §12.1.

(2) The authorised person should generally provide a Notice of Powers and rights in a standard format to the occupier, setting out that the entry has been conducted with a warrant, the powers of entry and associated powers used, the occupier's rights, any compensation or complaints procedures that exist and where a copy of the Code may be obtained: §7.1. The person authorised by the warrant should clearly identify him or herself to the landowner or occupier by showing his or her authorisation, their warrant and should explain clearly the purposes of the visit: §17.1.

(3) Unless it is not appropriate or practicable to do so (eg where it would not assist the purpose of exercising the power or where it is necessary to gain a genuine picture of day-to-day processes relating to the place being searched or where it is the aftermath of an incident), reasonable notice (usually not less than 48 hours) should be provided to the occupier or landowner of the intention before exercising the power of entry: §8.1. The notice should set out the date and time that it is proposed the power should be exercised: §8.2.

(4) The number of persons used to enter the premises should be reasonable and proportionate in the circumstances: §9.1.

(5) The power of entry should only be undertaken at reasonable hours (with reasonable hours being determined by reference to the normal working practices of the particular business concerned): §13.1 (see also para 5 of Sch 3 to FOIA).

(6) Where documents or other material are seized under the warrant, the person

---

25 As to the meaning of 'reasonable force' within the context of search warrants, see: *Swales v Cox* [1981] QB 849, [1981] 1 All ER 1115; *DPP v Meaden* [2003] EWHC 3005 (Admin), [2004] 1 WLR 945.

26 FOIA Sch 3 paras 4 and 5; EIR reg 18 (applying FOIA Pt IV (ss 50-56), incl Sch 3).

27 FOIA Sch 3 paras 8 and 9; EIR reg 18 (applying FOIA Pt IV (ss 50-56), incl Sch 3).

28 Protection of Freedoms Act 2012 (Code of Practice for Powers of Entry and Description of Relevant Persons) Order 2015 (SI 2015/240) Art 3.

29 Protection of Freedoms Act 2012 s 51(1). The Powers of Entry Code of Practice was laid before Parliament on 8 December 2014 and took force from 6 April 2015: see Protection of Freedoms Act 2012 (Code of Practice for Powers of Entry and Description of Relevant Persons) Order 2015 (SI 2015/240) Art 2. The Code is admissible in any proceedings and, in particular, a court or tribunal may take into account a failure by a relevant person to have regard to the powers of entry code in determining a question in any such proceedings: Protection of Freedoms Act 2012 s 51(3)-(4).

30

authorised by the warrant should provide the occupier of the premises with details of the items seized, procedures relating to the retention of property, appeal rights, how long items may be held before they are returned, and should explain any compensation procedures: §14.2.

(7) The occupier or his or her representative should be allowed supervised access to the seized property so as to examine or photograph it, unless this would prejudice the investigation of any offence or criminal proceedings: §15.3.

(8) The landowner or occupier may accompany the persons authorised by the warrant during the course of the visit unless that would interfere with the purpose of the visit, in which case the authorised person should give clear reasons for refusal: §17.5.

(9) The person in charge of exercising the warrant should make a record of the exercise of the power. The record should include the statutory provision under which the power was exercised; the name of the judge issuing the warrant; the date and time that the warrant was executed and, if present, the name of the occupier or person in charge of the premises; the address of the premises entered; whether the entry was with consent and, if not, whether consent was sought; the date time and duration that powers were exercised; the names of those involved in the exercise of the powers and of those present; grounds for refusal of any request by the landowner or occupier; a list of items seized; whether reasonable force was used to enter the premises and, if so, why; details of any damage caused and the reason and circumstances of that damage; whether a copy of the warrant was handed to the occupier or left on the premises and, if so, where; any information about obstructive conduct by the owner or occupier: §20.1-20.2.

50– 006 Criminal offences

Where a person has made a request for information, it is an offence for a public authority (or an officer or employee of that public authority or a person acting at its direction) to alter, deface, block, erase, destroy or conceal any record held by that public authority with the intention of preventing the disclosure by the authority of any of the information to which that applicant would have been entitled to have communicated to him or her.[31] Excepted from prosecution are Government departments (but not a person in the public service of the Crown),[32] the Welsh Assembly Government and a person acting on behalf of either House of Parliament, the Northern Ireland Assembly or the National Assembly for Wales.[33] It is a summary offence, punishable with a fine on level 5.[34] A prosecution can only be brought in England and Wales by the Information Commissioner or by or with the consent of the Director of Public Prosecutions.[35] It is also an offence to obstruct or to fail, without reasonable excuse, to give reasonably required assistance to a person executing a warrant under the procedure set out above.[36]

---

31 FOIA s 77(1); EIR reg 19(1).

32 As defined in FOIA s 84 (with certain exceptions, 'any body or authority exercising statutory functions on behalf of the Crown').

33 FOIA s 81(3); EIR reg 19(5).

34 FOIA s 77(3); EIR reg 19(3).

35 FOIA s 77(4); EIR reg 19(4).

36 FOIA, Sch 3, para 12; EIR reg 18 (applying FOIA, Pt IV (ss 50-56), incl Sch 3). See §50– 005.

2. FOI(S)A 2002 AND EI(S)R 2004

50– 007 Regulatory contempt

The Scottish Information Commissioner has power to issue decision notices,[37] information notices[38] and enforcement notices[39] requiring Scottish public authorities to take steps to comply with their obligations under FOI(S)A and EI(S)R or to provide specified information. If a decision notice, information notice or enforcement notice is neither complied with nor appealed against, the Scottish Information Commissioner may certify that that is the case to the Court of Session.[40] The Court may then inquire into the matter and, after hearing evidence and any statement that may be offered in defence, it may deal with the public authority as if it had committed a contempt of court.[41] The procedure for dealing with contempt is not materially different from that applicable under FOIA, and the commentary above is equally applicable.

50– 008 Search warrants

Where there are reasonable grounds for suspecting:

- non-compliance with the requirements of Part 1 of FOI(S)A or with the requirements of a decision, information or enforcement notice, or
- that an offence under s 65 of FOI(S)A has been committed,

and there are grounds for suspecting that evidence of any of these is to be found on any premises, the Scottish Information Commissioner may seek a warrant from a sheriff authorising him or his officers to enter and search premises, to inspect and seize documents or other material[42] which might be evidence of that non-compliance or offence, and to inspect, examine, operate and test equipment found there in which information may be recorded.[43] Save in cases of urgency or where this would defeat the object of the exercise, the occupier of the premises must have been given seven days' notice that access was required and have refused it and been warned of the application for a warrant and been heard on the matter.[44] The procedure for securing a warrant is not materially different from that applicable under FOIA, and the commentary above is equally applicable to warrants under FOI(S)A.[45] The Powers of Entry Code of Practice detailed above[46] applies to warrants under FOI(S)A.

---

37 FOI(S)A s 49(5); EI(S)R reg 17 (applying FOI(S)A Pt 4 incl Sch 3).

38 FOI(S)A s 50(1); EI(S)R reg 17 (applying FOI(S)A Pt 4 incl Sch 3).

39 FOI(S)A s 51(1); EI(S)R reg 17 (applying FOI(S)A Pt 4 incl Sch 3).

40 FOI(S)A s 53(1); EI(S)R reg 17 (applying FOI(S)A Pt 4 incl Sch 3).

41 FOI(S)A s 53(3); EI(S)R reg 17 (applying FOI(S)A Pt 4 incl Sch 3).

42 In relation to the power of a magistrate under s 8 of the Police and Criminal Evidence Act 1984 to grant a warrant to a constable to enter and search the premises (containing a like power to 'seize documents and other material'), the phrase 'other material' has been held to be wide enough to cover a computer and its hard disk: *R (Faisaltex Ltd) v Preston Crown Court* 2008] EWHC 2832 (Admin), [2009] 1 Cr App R 37; *R (Cabot Global Ltd) v Barkingside Magistrates' Court* [2015] EWHC 1458 (Admin), [2015] 2 Cr App R 26.

43 FOI(S)A Sch 3, para 1 ; EI(S)R reg 17 (applying FOI(S)A Pt 4 incl Sch 3). These powers are comparable to those given to the Inland Revenue Commissioners in relation to serious fraud by the Taxes Management Act 1970 s 20C and to constables by the Companies Act 1985 s 448, with the interesting result that, under the Freedom of Information Acts, it would be public authorities which are on the receiving end of the search and seizure order.

44 FOI(S)A Sch 3 para 2 ; EI(S)R reg 17 (applying FOI(S)A Pt 4 incl Sch 3).

45 See §§50– 004 to 50– 005 above.

46 See §50– 005.

50–009 Criminal offences

Where a person has made a request for information, it is an offence for a Scottish public authority (or an officer or employee of that public authority or a person acting at its direction) to alter, deface, block, erase, destroy or conceal any record held by that public authority with the intention of preventing the disclosure by the authority of any of the information to which that applicant would have been entitled to have communicated to him or her.[47] Members of staff, and those acting on behalf of, the Scottish Parliament, the Scottish Parliamentary Corporate Body and the Scottish Administration are specifically included within the reach of the offence, but the bodies themselves are excluded.[48] It is a summary offence, punishable with a fine on level 5.[49] It is also an offence to obstruct or to fail, without reasonable excuse, to give reasonably required assistance to a person executing a warrant under the procedure set out above.[50]

3. GDPR AND DPA 2018

50–010 Notice non-compliance

The final sanction in the hands of the Commissioner for a failure to comply with the DPA or the GDPR or an information notice, assessment notice or enforcement notice issued by her under DPA is a 'penalty notice,' which requires the payment of a penalty.[51] The sanction for non-compliance with such a notice is that the penalty can be recovered by the Commissioner as if it were payable under an order of the High Court or county court in England and Wales if the relevant court so orders.[52] The various means of enforcement of an order of the High Court and county courts are set out in Practice Direction 70 at paras 1.1-1.3: they would include insolvency proceedings. CPR 70.5 sets out additional procedural requirements where a body is seeking to recover a sum 'as if it were payable under an order' of the court.

50–011 Search warrants

Schedule 15 to the DPA 2018 contains detailed provisions about warrants to enter and search premises which can be obtained by the Commissioner from a High Court judge, a circuit judge or a District Judge (Magistrates Courts) where there are reasonable grounds for suspecting:

(a) that a controller or processor of personal data has failed to comply with the DPA or GDPR in any of the ways specified in s 149(2) of DPA or an offence has been committed under the DPA; or

(b) that evidence of the failure or breach is to be found on the premises.[53]

A warrant can also be granted when a controller or processor has failed to comply with an

---

47 FOI(S)A s 65(1); EI(S)R reg 19(1). The Scottish Information Commissioner has a Memorandum of Understanding with the Crown Office and Procurator Fiscal Service and Scottish police forces in relation to the investigation of criminal offences. This provides an agreed framework for the investigation and reporting of criminal offences under FOI(S)A s 65. The investigation is to be conducted jointly by the Scottish Information Commissioner and the relevant police force. The police force has responsibility for submitting reports of offences to the Crown Office and Procurator Fiscal Service. A formal investigation into an alleged offence under FOI(S)A s 65 will normally commence only when the allegation relates to a formal request for information under FOI(S)A or EI(S)R and the allegation is accompanied by evidence to indicate that an offence has taken place.

48 FOI(S)A s 68; EI(S)R reg 19(2)-(3).

49 FOI(S)A s 65(3); EI(S)R reg 19(2).

50 FOI(S)A, Sch 3, para 10 ; EI(S)R reg 17 (applying FOI(S)A Pt 4 incl Sch 3).

51 See DPA 2018 ss 155-157 and Sch 16 for the provisions relating to penalty notices.

52 Sch 16 para 9(2); paras 9(3) and (4) make provision in relation to Scotland and Northern Ireland.

53 Sch 15 para 1.

assessment notice.[54] The procedure for securing a warrant is not materially different from that applicable under FOIA, and the commentary above is equally applicable to warrants under the DPA 2018.[55] The Powers of Entry Code of Practice detailed above[56] applies to warrants under the DPA 2018. It is an offence to intentionally obstruct the execution of a warrant or to fail without reasonable excuse to give reasonably required assistance or to make certain false statements in response to certain questions.[57]

50– 012 Criminal offences

Sections 196-200 of the DPA 2018 deal with offences under that Act and their prosecution. Section 196 effectively lists the offences created by the DPA 2018. Those referred to in s 196(1) (basically offences involving the obstruction of inspections by the Commissioner, including the offence under para 15 of Sch 15 referred to above)[58] can only be the subject of summary conviction and a fine; those referred to in s 196(2) (eg breach of confidentiality requirements by the Commissioner's staff,[59] a false response to an information notice,[60] destroying records required by an information notice,[61] obtaining personal data unlawfully[62] and requiring disclosure of relevant records[63]) are triable either summarily or on indictment but are also only punishable with a fine. A prosecution for an offence under the DPA 2018 can only be instituted by the Commissioner or by or with the consent of the DPP.[64] An offence under s 173 (alteration of personal data to prevent disclosure) can only be prosecuted within 6 months after the date the prosecutor first knew of evidence sufficient to bring the proceedings and in any event no longer than 3 years after the offence was committed.[65] There is provision for the liability of directors and members of corporate bodies which are themselves guilty of such offences in certain circumstances.[66]

50– 013 Lawful authority defence

Disclosure with lawful authority is defined for the purposes of the offence under s 132 of the DPA 2018 as being only where:

(1) the disclosure is with consent of the individual or person carrying on the business concerned;
(2) the information was provided for the purpose of being made available to the public;
(3) the disclosure is made for the purposes of and is necessary for the discharge of the Commissioner's functions or an EU obligation;
(4) the disclosure is made for the purposes of any proceedings, whether criminal or civil; or

54 Sch 15 para 2.

55 See §§50– 004 to 50– 005 above.

56 See §50– 005.

57 Sch 15 para 15.

58 Offences under DPA 2018 ss 119 and 173.

59 See DPA 2018 s 132. This is the equivalent of DPA 1998 s 59(1): see §50– 020.

60 DPA 2018 s 144. This is the equivalent of DPA 1998 s 47(2).

61 DPA 2018 s 148.

62 DPA 2018 ss 170-171. These are the equivalent of DPA 1998 s 55: see §50– 015.

63 DPA 2018 s 184. This is the equivalent of DPA 1998 s 56(1): see §50– 019.

64 DPA 2018 s 197(1).

65 DPA s 197(3) and (4).

66 DPA s 198.

(5) the disclosure is necessary in the public interest having regard to the rights and freedoms or legitimate interests of any person.[67]

4. DPA 1998

50– 014 Search warrants

The DPA 1998 enabled the Information Commissioner to obtain a warrant authorising her or any of her officers or staff:

- to enter and search premises,
- to inspect, examine, operated and test any equipment found on the premises used or intended to be used for the processing of personal data,
- to inspect and seize documents and other material evidencing a contravention of the DPA 1998 or the commissioning of an offence under that Act,
- to require any person on the premises to provide an explanation of any document or other material so found, and
- to require any person on the premises to provide such other information as may reasonably be required for the purposes of determining whether the data controller had contravened, or was contravening, the DPA1998.[68]

In order to obtain the warrant, the Commissioner had to apply to a circuit judge or a district judge in a magistrates' court (or a sheriff in Scotland or a county court judge in Northern Ireland) with information on oath to satisfy the same: (a) that there were reasonable grounds for suspecting that a data controller had or was contravening any of the data protection principles or that an offence under the DPA 1998 had been or was being committed and that evidence of the same was to be found on the premises; or (b) that a data controller had failed to comply with a requirement of an assessment notice.[69] Other than in cases of urgency or where it would defeat the object of the entry, the Commissioner had to have given seven days' notice to the occupier demanding access which had been refused and notified the occupier of the application for the warrant.[70] The judge was given a discretion whether to grant the warrant. The procedure for securing and the criteria for getting a warrant was not materially different from that which is applicable under FOIA, and the commentary above is equally applicable to warrants under the DPA 1998.[71] The Powers of Entry Code of Practice detailed above[72] applied to warrants under the DPA 1998.

50– 015 Unlawful obtaining of data

In addition to the private rights of action and the civil enforcement regime, the DPA 1998 also created a number of criminal offences regarding the handling of personal data. The most important of these was s 55, which was directed at 'rogue third parties' obtaining or disseminating personal data without the consent of the data controller. More particularly, s 55:

(1) Made it an offence for a person knowingly or recklessly, without the consent[73] of the

---

67 DPA 2018 s 132(2).

68 DPA 1998 Sch 9 para 1.

69 DPA 1998 Sch 9 para 1.

70 DPA 1998 Sch 9 para 2.

71 See §§50– 004 to 50– 005 above.

72 See §50– 005.

73 A mistake as to the identity of the person to whom the data controller gave consent, eg because that person misrepresented who he or she was, would vitiate the consent: *R v Lineaker* [1995] QB 250, [1995] 3 All ER 69; *R*

data controller, either: (a) to obtain or disclose personal data or the information contained in personal data; or (b) to procure the disclosure to another person of the information contained in personal data.[74]

(2) Made it an offence for a person who obtained personal data in the above circumstances to sell that personal data.[75]

(3) Made it an offence for a person who obtained, or later obtained, personal data in the above circumstances to sell that personal data or to offer to sell that personal data.[76] An advertisement was deemed to be an offer to sell.[77]

The provision did not apply where the person was authorised to so act by enactment or order of court, or it was necessary to prevent or detect a crime, or the person acted in the reasonable belief that he had in law the right to do what he was doing or that he had the consent of the data controller to do what he was doing, or that in the particular circumstances it was justified as being in the public interest. The maximum penalty was a fine[78] and the court was given the power to order any personal data appearing to be connected with the offence to be forfeited, destroyed or erased.[79]

50– 016 Knowingly or recklessly

Two of the offences in the DPA 1998 had as an element of the offence that the conduct in question was done 'knowingly or recklessly': ss 55(1) and s 59(3). 'Recklessness' in this context was held to mean something in the circumstances that would have drawn the attention of an ordinary prudent individual to the possibility that the act was capable of causing the kind of serious harmful consequences that the section which created the offence was intended to prevent, and that the risk of those harmful consequences occurring was not so slight that an ordinary prudent individual would feel justified in treating them as negligible: it is only when this is so that the doer of the act is acting 'recklessly' if before doing the act, he or she either fails to give any thought to the possibility of there being any such risk or, having recognised that there was such risk, he or she nevertheless goes on to do it.[80]

50– 017 Notice non-compliance

It was not in itself an offence for a data controller to fail to comply with a subject access request. However, it was an offence for him to fail to comply with an enforcement notice that ordered the data controller to comply with such a request[81] or to fail to comply with an information

v Cort [2003] EWCA Crim 2149, [2004] QB 388; *R v Devonald* [2008] EWCA Crim 527.

74 DPA 1998 s 55(1).

75 DPA 1998 s 55(4). 'Information contained in personal data' meant that even if it were not possible to identify an individual from the information disclosed (eg because the names and other identifying information from which the remainder of the information could be linked) the offence would be made out: *R v Rooney* [2006] EWCA Crim 1841. For the purposes of s 55(4)-(6), the meaning of 'personal data' was enlarged to include 'information extracted from personal data': s 55(7). In this way, sale/offering to sell offences picked up where the seller had analysed the personal data to derive information about data subjects: ie the stuff of data analytics.

76 DPA 1998 s 55(5).

77 DPA 1998 s 55(6).

78 DPA 1998 s 60(2).

79 DPA1998 s 60(4).

80 *Data Protection Registrar v Amnesty International* [1995] Crim LR 633 (dealing with a like provision in the Data Protection Act 1984) and applying *R v Lawrence* [1982] AC 510, [1981] 1 All ER 974. See *Information Commissioner v London Borough of Islington* [2002] EWHC 1036, [2003] BLGR 38 also *Information Commissioner v LB of Islington* [2002] EWHC 1036 (Admin), [2003] BLGR 38 at [28]. The formula 'knowingly or recklessly' has been considered in other criminal, regulatory contexts: *R v X Ltd* [2013] EWCA Crim 818, [2014] 1 WLR 591.

81 DPA 1998 ss 40(1), 47.

notice issued by the Commissioner in relation to such a request.[82] The Act provided a defence where the person could prove that he exercised all due diligence to comply with the notice.[83] The maximum penalty was a fine.[84]

50– 018 Failure to notify

Under the DPA 1998, processing of personal data without registration was an offence.[85] Failure to keep up-to-date registration details was also an offence.[86] Based on the registration details of a data controller, the Information Commissioner could identify certain of that controller's processing as 'assessable processing'[87] and give the data controller notice that she was of the opinion that the processing was unlikely to comply with the provisions of the Act and that that processing could not be carried at any time 28 days thereafter.[88] Processing thereafter was a criminal offence.[89]

50– 019 Employment, etc offences

Under the DPA 1998, it was an offence for a person, in connection with the recruitment or continued employment of another person as an employee or with any contract for the provision of services to the first person by another person, to require that other person or a third party to supply the first person with a 'relevant record.'[90] A 'relevant record' meant records such as police and criminal records.[91] This prevented individuals from being forced to exercise their subject access rights in such circumstances. It was also an offence for a person concerned with the provision of goods, facilities or services to the public or a section of the public to require, as a condition of providing or offering to provide those goods, facilities or services, to require another person to provide a 'relevant record' for that person.[92] The offences did not apply where the requirement was mandated by statute, by any rule of law, by order of a court or that it was justified as being in the public interest.[93]

50– 020 Commission staff offence

It was an offence for the Information Commissioner, or anyone who had worked for her or on her behalf, knowingly or recklessly[94] to disclose any information obtained for the purposes of the DPA 1998 which related to an identifiable individual or business and which was not already within the public domain, unless he or she had lawful authority to make such a disclosure.[95]

---

82 DPA 1998 s 47.

83 DPA 1998 s 47(3).

84 DPA 1998 s 60(2).

85 DPA 1998 ss 17(1), 21(1).

86 DPA 1998 ss 20(1), 21(2).

87 Meaning that it was particularly likely to cause substantial damage or substantial distress to data subject or otherwise significantly prejudice the rights and freedoms of data subject: DPA 1998 s 23(1).

88 DPA 1998 s 23(5).

89 DPA 1998 s 23(6).

90 DPA 1998 s 56(1).

91 DPA 1998 s 56(6).

92 DPA 1998 s 56(2).

93 DPA 1998 s 56(3).

94 As to the meaning of 'knowingly or recklessly' see §50– 016.

95 DPA 1998 s 59(1), (3). 'Business' is to be given a broad interpretation, covering any identifiable organisation, government department, local authority, charity, other organisation or association, whether or not the body has a commercial or profit-making purpose or function: *Friends of the Earth v Information Commissioner and DTI*, IT, 4 April 2007 at [15], [22] and [40].

A disclosure was made with lawful authority if the data subject or person carrying on the business had consented; if it had been made pursuant to or for the purposes of certain statutory functions[96] or obligations, or of criminal or civil proceedings; or if it had been necessary in the public interest, having regard to the rights, freedoms and legitimate interests of others.[97] The prohibition on disclosure targetted unauthorised or reckless breaches of confidentiality: it did not preclude the Information Commissioner from the due performance of her functions where that required the disclosure of information supplied to her.[98]

50– 021 Director criminal liability

Where an offence under the DPA 1998 had been committed by a body corporate and it was proved to have been committed with the consent or connivance of, or attributable to any neglect on the part of, any director, manager, secretary or similar office holder of the body corporate (including those purporting to act in that capacity), that person (as well as the body corporate) was guilty of the offence and could be punished accordingly.[99] The provision required the prosecution to prove that the body corporate had committed an offence under the Act as a precondition of any secondary liability of the director, manager etc.[100] The intention of the provision was to fix criminal liability only on: (a) those who were in a position of real authority; and (b) decision makers in the company responsible for putting proper procedures in place.[101] The words 'attributable to,' whilst requiring proof of a causal connection between the neglect and the commission of the offence by the company, did not require that attribution to be entirely responsible for the commission of the offence by the company.[102] The term 'neglect' required proof of more than mere failure to see that the law is observed: it required an identification of a duty and either careless discharge of that duty or a failure to comply with that duty which was causative of the commission of the offence.[103] The provision required the prosecution to prove actual knowledge of the material facts or that the individual was, by reason of the surrounding circumstances, put on enquiry as to the material facts so as to require him to take steps.[104] 'Connivance' and 'neglect' may be established by inference:

> Where it is shown that the body corporate failed to achieve or prevent the result that those sections contemplate, it will be a relatively short step for the inference to be drawn that there was connivance or neglect on his part if the circumstances under which the risk arose were under the direction or control of the officer. The more remote his area of responsibility is from those circumstances, the harder it will be to draw that inference.'[105]

---

96 See *Roberts v IC and DBIS*, IT, 20 August 2009.

97 DPA 1998 s 59(2).

98 *Friends of the Earth v Information Commissioner and DTI*, IT, 4 April 2007 at [42].

99 DPA 1998 s 61(1). The formulation of words was substantially the same as that found in numerous other statutory provisions, eg: Adoption and Children Act 2002 s 143(1); Banking Act 2009 ss 83ZP, 83ZR, 221; Bribery Act 2010 s 14; Broadcasting Act 1990 s 195; Charities Act 2006 ss 65, 346; Communications Act 2003 s 404; Companies Act 2006 s 1255; Competition Act 1998 s 72; Customs and Excise Management Act 1979 s 171; Electricity Act 1989 s 108; Employment Rights Act 1996 s 180; Enterprise Act 2002 s 222; Environmental Protection Act 1990 s 157; Financial Services and Markets Act 2000 s 400; Fraud Act 2006 s 12; Health and Safety at Work etc Act 1974 s 37; Housing Act 1996 s 223; Water Resources Act 1991 s 217.

100 *R v Chargot Ltd* [2008] UKHL 73, [2009] 1 WLR 21 at [32], dealing with different legislation but with a like provision

101 *R v Boal* [1992] 1 QB 591 at 597H, dealing with a like provision in the Fire Precautions Act 1971; *R v Hutchins* [2011] EWCA Crim 1056.

102 *Wotherspoon v HM Lord Advocate* 1978 JC 74 at 78.

103 *Huckerby v Elliott* [1970] 1 All ER 189 at 194, 195.

104 *R v P* [2007] EWCA Crim 1937, [2008] ICR 96 at [14], dealing with a like provision in the Health and Safety at Work etc Act 1974 s 37; *Attorney-General's Reference No 1 of 1995* [1996] 1 WLR 970.

105 *R v Chargot Ltd* [2008] UKHL 73, [2009] 1 WLR 21 at [34].

50– 022 Application to Crown

Although the DPA 1998 bound the Crown,[106] government departments[107] nor the controllers of the Royal Household, the Duchy of Lancaster or the Duchy of Cornwall were liable to prosecution under the Act.[108] However, DPA 1998 s 55 (the unlawful disclosure of personal data etc) applied to a person in the service of the Crown as it applied to any other person.[109]

50– 023 Notice material admissibility

Information secured by the Information Commission pursuant to an information notice or a special information notice could not generally be used in evidence in a prosecution under the DPA 1998.[110]

50– 024 Institution of prosecution

Criminal proceedings for an offence under the DPA 1998 could only be brought by the Information Commissioner or with the consent of the Director of Public Prosecutions.[111] For all offences under the DPA 1998 the prescribed punishment, whether on summary conviction or on conviction on indictment, was a fine.[112]

5. IMMUNITIES

50– 025 Private claims

FOIA provides that it does not confer any right of action in civil proceedings in respect of a failure to comply with a duty imposed by or under FOIA.[113] The EIR includes a like provision.[114]

---

106 DPA 1998 s 63(1).

107 Government departments included any part of the Scottish Administration, the Welsh Assembly government, a Northern Ireland department and any body or authority exercising statutory functions on behalf of the Crown: DPA 1998 s 70(1).

108 DPA 1998 s 63(5).

109 DPA 1998 s 63(5).

110 DPA 1998 ss 43(8B), 44(9B).

111 DPA 1998 s 60(1).

112 DPA 1998 s 60(2), (3).

113 FOIA s 56(1). Note that the provision is worded so that the Act does not confer a right of action, rather than so as to protect public authorities or those working for them from any liability or claim – cf Public Health Act 1875 s 265, Local Government (Miscellaneous Provisions) Act 1976 s 39, Building Act 1984 s 115 etc. Section 56(1) thus makes clear that FOIA does itself not confer a private law right upon members of the public generally: see discussion in *Boyce v Paddington Borough Council* [1903] 1 Ch 109 and *Lonrho Ltd v Shell Ltd (no 2)* [1982] AC 173 at 185. Where a breach of statutory duty to an individual (as opposed to a statutory duty to members of the public generally) gives rise to a cause of action, that cause of action arises at common law rather than being conferred by statute: *Butler (or Black) v Fife Coal Co Ltd* [1912] AC 149 at 165; *Cutler v Wandsworth Stadium Ltd* [1949] AC 398 at 413. Whether Parliament intends that a breach of statutory duty to an individual should give not rise to a common law cause of action involves looking at the statutory scheme. The courts will readily read in an intention that a breach of statutory duty does not give rise to a common law cause of action where the statute provides a curial route for a person adversely affected by non-performance of statutory obligations to secure some form of relief. FOIA provides such a route, ultimately enforceable through FOIA ss 55(1) and 77(1). As such, a common law claim for breach of statutory duty that relies on breaches of FOIA or EIR is very unlikely to succeed. However, such a breach could form *an element* of a cause of action for misfeasance in public office or unlawful means conspiracy, as those torts require other elements before a right of civil action arises. It is doubtful that these provisions exclude judicial review proceedings: *Re Waldron (No1)* [1986] QB 824, [1985] 3 All ER 775 (CA).

114 EIR reg 18 (applying FOIA Pt IV (ss 50-56), incl Sch 3).

50– 026 Defamatory matter

There is also specific provision giving protection against proceedings for defamation brought in respect of information supplied to a public authority by a third party which is published to applicants under FOIA, unless the publication is made with malice.[115] The protection is conferred in relation to information communicated pursuant to the duty imposed by statute on the public authority. Accordingly, the statutory protection may not apply where a public authority discloses information to an applicant in response to a request but without being obliged to do so (eg because the information is exempt from the duty to communicate).[116] Similarly, the protection will not apply where a public authority volunteers information to a person other than the person who has made a request for that information (eg by posting the requested information onto the internet).

50– 027 Scotland: private claims

FOI(S)A provides that the Act does not confer a right of action in civil proceedings in respect of a failure by a Scottish public authority to comply with a duty imposed by, under or by virtue of the Act.[117] The provision is not materially different from its equivalent in FOIA, and the commentary above is equally applicable.[118] The EI(S)R includes a like provision.[119]

50– 028 Scotland: defamatory matter

Section 67 of FOI(S)A provides that where, pursuant to its obligations under s 1 of FOI(S)A, a Scottish public authority discloses to the requester information that was both supplied to the public authority by a third party and that is defamatory, that publication is privileged unless it is shown that that publication was made with malice. This is substantially the same as its equivalent in FOIA, and the commentary above is equally applicable.[120] The EI(S)R includes a like provision.[121]

50– 029 DPA: defamatory matter

The DPA 1998 did not, and the GDPR and DPA 2018 do not, give specific protection against proceedings for defamation in respect of material supplied by a (data) controller in response to a subject access request or the like. Since, by definition, most of that material will relate to the subject, this will not normally be a problem even if that material is defamatory.[122] Insofar as

---

[115] FOIA s 79. See also Defamation Act 1996 s 15(1). There is no direct equivalent in the environmental information regime, although EIR reg 5(6) may serve the same purpose. In this context, 'malice' means ill will or spite towards a person or any indirect or improper motive in the public authority's 'mind' which is its sole or dominant motive for publishing the words complained of: *Angel v HH Bushell & Co Ltd* [1968] 1 QB 813 at 831, [1967] 1 All ER 1018; *Horrocks v Lowe* [1975] AC 135 at 149-151, [1974] 1 All ER 662; *Branson v Bower* [2002] QB 737; *Joseph v Spiller* [2010] UKSC 53, [2011] 1 AC 852, [2011] 1 All ER 947. It is for the claimant to prove malice on the balance of probabilities: *Clark v Molyneux* (1877) 3 QBD 237; *Jenoure v Delmege* [1891] AC 73; *Joseph v Spiller* [2010] UKSC 53, [2011] 1 AC 852. The inclusion of defamatory matter unconnected with the duty or interest which gives rise to the privileged occasion may be evidence of malice as to the whole publication: *Adam v Ward* [1917] AC 309; *Clift v Slough Borough Council* [2010] EWCA Civ 1484, [2011] 3 All ER 118, [2011] 1 WLR 1774. In relation to internally generated material that is defamatory, see §20– 035.

[116] See §§20– 034 to 20– 038.

[117] FOI(S)A s 55(1).

[118] See §50– 025.

[119] EI(S)R reg 17 (applying FOI(S)A Pt 4 incl Sch 3).

[120] See §50– 026.

[121] EI(S)R reg 17 (applying FOI(S)A Pt 4 incl Sch 3).

[122] Since publication will not have been to a third person. See *Pullman v Walter Hill & Co Ltd* [1891] 1 QB 524 at 529.

it may reveal defamatory material about a third person, a data controller or controller would do well to redact that defamatory material. To the extent that redaction of defamatory material relating to a third person is not possible whilst complying with obligations under DPA 1998, GDPR or DPA 2018, the (data) controller may be able to rely upon defences in the Defamation Act 1996.[123]

[123] See section 15.

Part VIII

Comparative law

CHAPTER 51

The Comparative Jurisdictions

1. INFORMATION RIGHTS LEGISLATION ELSEWHERE

51–001 Introduction

The enactment of FOIA was preceded by extensive consideration of analogous legislation in Australia, New Zealand, Canada and Ireland:[1] comparative tables of exemption were prepared; the different types of harm that could engage an exemption were considered; the various approaches to the public interest were analysed; and so forth.[2] This is reflected in the final

[1] Freedom of Information Act 1982 (Cth of Australia); Official Information Act 1982 (NZ); Access to Information Act (1982) (Canada); Freedom of Information Act 1997 (Ireland). Although it has the most developed body of jurisprudence on the topic, reference to the Freedom of Information Act (1966) 5 USC 552 (USA) was more limited.

[2] See: Cabinet Office, *Your Right to Know—The Government's Proposals for a Freedom of Information Act. White Paper* (Cm 3818, 1997) paras 3-12, Annexes A and B (see Ch 1, n 66); *Background Material*, paras 33, 56-65, 70-71, 78, 108, 116-117, 125-129, 219. Hansard HC vol 340 cols 722, 728, 741, 746-749, 754, 759-761, 789 (7 December 1999); Hansard HC vol 347 cols 832, 837-839, 848-849, 922-926, 934 (4 April 2000); Hansard HC vol 347 cols 996, 1009, 1028, 1041, 1097, 1103 (5 April 2000); Hansard H vol 612 cols 830, 834, 838-839, 851, 867-868 (20 April 2000); Hansard HL vol 617 cols 888, 893, 939, 941, 946, 1010 (17 October 2000); Hansard HL vol 617 cols 1215,

product, whose structure and occasionally language resemble those employed in the legislation of the comparative jurisdictions.[3] The divergences are also pointed, with certain features of the comparative regimes having been considered but not adopted. An overview of each of the comparative regimes is given below. After a short history, the principal features of each regime are identified: the scope of the right; the approach to requests and permissible responses; the general treatment of exemptions, including classification by harm and by class; the role of the public interest; the specific heads of exemption; and the system of appeals and enforcement. These reveal certain universal issues, most notably the identification of those legitimate interests of an open, accountable and representative government that have paramountcy over the general right of access to government-held information. Elsewhere in this work, reference is made to authorities in these comparative jurisdictions where it is considered that it sheds light on FOIA, the EIR or the DPA 1998.

2. UNITED STATES OF AMERICA

51–002 Introduction

In 1966 the United States Congress passed the Freedom of Information Act.[4] It had evolved after a decade of debate among agency officials, legislators and public interest group representatives.[5] The Act was not, however, entirely novel. The Administrative Procedure Act of 1964[6] had included a public disclosure section, although this was thought to have fallen short of its goals. In 1974 significant amendments to the Freedom of Information Act were made[7] and the Privacy Act was passed.[8] The latter granted individuals enhanced rights of access to agency records maintained about themselves;[9] it restricted the rights of agencies to disclose personally identifiable records maintained by an agency; and it granted a right to individuals to seek amendment of agency records maintained on themselves. Further amendments to the

1256, 1279 (19 October 2000); Hansard HL vol 618 cols 438, 441-442 (25 October 2000); Hansard HL vol 619 col 619 (14 November 2000).

3 Most notably New Zealand and, to a slightly lesser extent, Australia.

4 5 USC 1002 (1964) (amended in 1966 and now codified at 5 USC 552). The Act took effect on 4 July 1967.

5 The main proponent of the legislation was a Californian Democrat Congressman, John Moss. A Republican Congressman, Donald Rumsfeld, signed as a co-sponsor. He explained the need for the Act: 'The unanimous action after years of delay results from the growing size and complexity of the federal government, of its increased role in our lives, and from the increasing awareness by Americans of the threat involved in Government secrecy in vital records affecting their fate…With the continuing tendency toward managed news and suppression of public information that the people are entitled to have, the issues have at last been brought home to the public...' (quoted in *The Arizona Republic*, 27 June 1966).

6 5 USC 1002. The Freedom of Information Act was in fact a revision of the public disclosure section of this Act.

7 The 1974 amendments considerably narrowed the overall scope of the Act's law enforcement and national security exemptions. It also broadened many of the Act's procedural provisions, including fees, time limits, segregability, and *in camera* inspection by the courts. President Ford vetoed the bill effecting the changes, calling it 'unconstitutional and unworkable', but both Houses overrode his veto.

8 5 USC 552a. The Act took effect on 27 September 1975.

9 5 USC 552a(d)(1). There is an overlap between the right of access bestowed by the Freedom of Information Act and that which is granted by the Privacy Act. The latter only applies to requests for personal information relating to the person making the request. Such a request need not state under which statute it is made. The technique is first to consider whether any exemption under the Privacy Act applies: if it does not, then the information must be released irrespective of the applicability of an exemption under the Freedom of Information Act. If an exemption under the Privacy Act does apply, then exemptions under the Freedom of Information Act must be considered: if none applies, the requested information must be released notwithstanding the applicability of an exemption under the Privacy Act: 5 USC 552a(t)(1); *Martin v Office of Special Counsel*, 819 F 2d 1181 (DC Cir 1987); *Savada v Department of Defense*, 755 F Supp 6 (DDC 1991); *Viotti v United States Air Force*, 902 F Supp 1131 (D Colo 1995), affirmed 153 F 3d 730 (10th Cir 1998).

Freedom of Information Act were made in 1976, 1986, 1996, 2002 and 2007.[10] On 21 January 2009, President Obama signed the 'Presidential Memorandum for the Heads of Executive Departments and Agencies on the Freedom of Information Act,'[11] which directed all agencies to administer the FOIA with a clear presumption in favour of disclosure, to resolve doubts in favour of openness, and to not withhold information based on 'speculative or abstract fears.' In addition, the President called on agencies to ensure that requests are responded to with 'a spirit of cooperation.'[12] In 2011 Congress passed the Faster FOIA Act, which was designed to improve FOIA processing.[13] In June 2016 President Obama signed into law the FOIA Improvement Act of 2016. The Act addresses a range of procedural issues, including requirements that agencies establish a minimum of 90 days for requesters to file an administrative appeal and that they provide dispute resolution services at various times throughout the FOIA process. The Act also codified the Department of Justice's 'foreseeable harm' standard, amended Exemption 5, and created a new 'FOIA Council.'

51–003 Scope of the right

Under the Freedom of Information Act, each federal 'agency'[14] is required to promptly make available its[15] 'records'[16] to any person[17] who makes a proper request for them.[18] The reason

---

[10] The 1976 amendment narrowed the Act's incorporation of the non-disclosure provisions of other statutes. The Freedom of Information Reform Act (1986) provided broader exemption protection for law enforcement information, special law enforcement record exclusions, and created a new fee and fee waiver structure. The Electronic Freedom of Information Act Amendments (1996) dealt with electronic records, electronic reading rooms, agency backlogs of requests, and other procedural provisions. The Intelligence Authorization Act of 2002 amended the Act to limit disclosures to foreign governments. The OPEN Government Act of 2007 effected amendments including the definition of news media requesters, the recovery of attorney fees and litigation costs, computing and tolling (or stopping) the time limits for responding to requests and treatment of agency records maintained by government contractors. Smaller changes were also made in 1978 and 1984.

[11] Available at: www.whitehouse.gov/the_press_office/FreedomofInformationAct/

[12] To similar effect, see Attorney-General Holder's *Memorandum for Heads of Executive Departments and Agencies Concerning the Freedom of Information Act* (19 March 2009), available at: www.justice.gov/ag/foia-memo-march2009.pdf. The FOIA Project, a research organization studying the FOIA policy of the Obama administration, has asserted that 'there is little evidence that these new standards have made any impact on actual Department of Justice practices in defending federal agency withholding': *Defensive Standards Hinder FOIA Openness*, the FOIA Project (1 Mar 2012), available at: http://foiaproject.org/2012/03/01/defensive-standards-hinder-foia-openness/#more-526. One issue has been the alleged use of personal e-mail accounts by agency leaders to avoid FOIA disclosures: *Landmark Legal Foundation v EPA*, No 12-1726 (DDC 2013).

[13] As at the date of writing, the Act awaits Presidential signature.

[14] This extends to agencies within the executive branch of the federal Government, including the Executive Office of the President and independent regulatory agencies: 5 USC 552(f)(1). However, the Act does not apply to entities that are not controlled by the federal Government. Thus, organisations which, although having a relationship with the federal Government, are autonomous, are outside the ambit of the Act: *Public Citizen Health Research Group v Department of Health, Education & Welfare*, 668 F 2d 537 (DC Cir 1981); *Irwin Memorial Blood Bank v American National Red Cross*, 640 F 2d 1051 (9th Cir 1981); *Gilmore v Department of Energy*, 4 F Supp 2d 912 (ND Cal 1998). Similarly, state Governments, municipal corporations, the courts, Congress and private citizens are not subject to the Act. Offices within the Executive Office of the President whose functions are limited to advising and assisting the President do not fall within the definition of 'agency': *Armstrong v Executive Office of the President*, 90 F 3d 553 (DC Cir 1996) (National Security Council not an agency); *Judicial Watch, Inc v Department of Energy*, 412 F 3d 125 (DC Cir 2005) (concluding that the National Energy Policy Development Group was not an agency subject to the Act, because 'its sole function [was] to advise and assist the President'). The Act does not cover Congressional documents: *United We Stand America v Internal Revenue Service*, 359 F 3d 595 (DC Cir 2004); *Dow Jones & Co v Department of Justice*, 917 F 2d 571 (DC Cir 1990).

[15] 'Agency records' are records that are (1) either created or obtained by an agency, and (2) under agency control at the time of the request: *Department of Justice v Tax Analysts*, 492 US 136 (1989). The OPEN Government Act 2007 made it clear that agency records do not lose their status as such when physically maintained by a government contractor for the purposes of record management. In determining whether an agency has sufficient control over a record in order for it to be an 'agency record', there are four factors to be taken into account: (1) the intent of the record's creator to retain or relinquish control over the record; (2) the ability of the agency to use and dispose of the record as it sees fit; (3) the extent to which agency personnel have read or relied upon the record; and (4) the degree to which the record was integrated into the agency's record-keeping system or files: *Lindsey v Bureau of Prisons*, 736 F 2d 1462 (11th Cir 1984); *Tax Analysts v Department of Justice*, 845 F 2d 1060 (DC Cir 1988), affirmed, 492 US

for the making of a request has no bearing on the merits of that request.[19] Nor does the initial right of access depend upon the existence or extent of public interest in the records sought.[20] The scope of the right was curtailed by an amendment to the Act in 1986 which introduced the concept of 'exclusions'.[21] Three provisions create record 'exclusions', the effect of which is to expressly authorise federal law enforcement agencies, in relation to especially sensitive records under certain specified circumstances, to treat the records as not subject to the requirements of the Freedom of Information Act 1966.[22] The application of one of the three record exclusions results in a response stating that no records responsive to the request exist, even though they may exist. These exclusions do not provide additional bases for an agency to withhold documents from the public: the exclusions only apply to records that are already exempt from disclosure.

51–004 Other rights

The Act does not speak of publication schemes, but contains two analogous provisions giving rise to automatic disclosure of certain agency information. Under the first, each agency is required to publish in the Federal Register certain information relating to itself for 'the

136 (1989). Personal records which are maintained by agency employees are not considered to be agency records: *Bureau of National Affairs Inc v Department of Justice*, 742 F 2d 1484 (DC Cir 1984); *Spannaus v Department of Justice*, 942 F Supp 656 (DDC 1996); *Fortson v Harvey*, 407 F Supp 2d 13 (DDC 2005).

16 The definition of 'record' was widened in 1996: see now 5 USC 552(f)(2). Before the inclusion of that definition, it had been held that 'records' did not include tangible, evidentiary objects: *Nichols v United States*, 325 F Supp 130 (D Kan 1971) (holding that archival exhibits consisting of guns, bullets, and clothing relating to the assassination of President Kennedy were not 'records'). However, 'record' had otherwise been given an expansive meaning to include: 'machine readable materials...regardless of physical form or characteristics' (*Forsham v Harris* 445 US 169 (1980)); an audiotape of Challenger astronauts on the basis that the Act 'makes no distinction between information in lexical and…non-lexical form' (*NY Times Co v NASA*, 920 F 2d 1002 (DC Cir 1990)); and a motion picture film (*Save the Dolphins v Department of Commerce*, 404 F Supp 407 (ND Cal 1975)). Presidential appointment calendars and visitor records are not 'agency records': *Judicial Watch v Secret Service* No 11-5282 (DC Cir 2013).

17 'Any person' includes foreign citizens, partnerships, corporations, associations, states and state agencies, and foreign or domestic governments: 5 USC 551(2). However, members of foreign legislatures are barred from making FOIA requests, since they are 'representatives of government entities': *All Parliamentary Group on Extraordinary Rendition v Dept of Defense*, 851 F Supp 2d 169, 174-177 (DDC 2012). Requests may also be made through an attorney or other representative on behalf of any person: *Constangy, Brooks & Smith v National Labor Relations Board*, 851 F 2d 839 (6th Cir 1988). However, fugitives may be denied access: *Doyle v Department of Justice*, 668 F 2d 1365 (DC Cir 1981).

18 5 USC 552(a)(3)(A). *Stone v Export-Import Bank of US*, 552 F 2d 132 (5th Cir 1977). In 2002 Congress amended the Act to prohibit requests to intelligence agencies from or on behalf of foreign intelligence services, whether friendly or hostile: 5 USC 552(a)(3)(E). 'Person' is defined at 5 USC 551(2).

19 *Environmental Protection Agency v Mink*, 410 US 73 (1973); *Department of Justice v Reporters Committee for Freedom of the Press*, 489 US 749 (1989).

20 *Jordan v Department of Justice*, 591 F 2d 753 (DC Cir 1978). It may, of course, impinge upon the applicability of an exemption.

21 5 USC 552(c).

22 The first exclusion may be used when a request seeks information that is exempt because disclosure could reasonably be expected to interfere with a current law enforcement investigation (ie exemption (7)(A)). There are three specific prerequisites for the application of this exclusion. First, the investigation in question must involve a possible violation of criminal law. Second, there must be reason to believe that the subject of the investigation is not already aware that the investigation is underway. Third, disclosure of the existence of the records, as distinguished from the contents of the records, could reasonably be expected to interfere with enforcement proceedings. When all these conditions are satisfied, an agency may respond to a request as if the records were not subject to the requirements of the Act. The second exclusion applies to informant records maintained by a criminal law enforcement agency under the informant's name or personal identifier. The agency is not required to confirm the existence of these records unless the informant's status has been officially confirmed. This exclusion helps agencies to protect the identity of confidential informants. The third exclusion only applies to records maintained by the Federal Bureau of Investigation that relate to foreign intelligence, counter-intelligence, or international terrorism. When the *existence* of these types of records is classified, the FBI may treat the records as not subject to the requirements of the Act. This exclusion does not apply to all classified records on the specific subjects. It only applies when the records are classified and when the *existence* of the records is also classified.

guidance of the public'. This includes a description of the agency's organisation, functions and procedures; its substantive rules; and statements of general policy.[23] This requirement provides the public with automatic access to basic information regarding the transaction of agency business. Under the second, certain types of internal records, such as final agency opinions and orders rendered in the adjudication of cases, specific policy statements, certain administrative staff manuals, and some records previously processed for disclosure under the Act, must be routinely made 'available for public inspection and copying'.[24] This is generally referred to as the 'reading room' provision of the Act.[25] A failure to comply with these requirements may provide a ground of challenge to an administrative decision that is related to information that ought to have been disclosed.[26] The effect of information falling within either provision is that it cannot be made the proper subject of a request under the Freedom of Information Act.[27] If an agency does not hold any record that answers the terms of a request, that agency is under no obligation to refer that request to any other agency where such records might be located. The Act contains no procedure entitling or enabling a third party to make representations before information relating to that third party is released to an applicant: this is dealt with, in part, by Executive Order.[28]

51–005 The request

A request must reasonably describe the records sought and it must be made in accordance with the agency's published regulations.[29] An agency is not required to create a record in order to respond to a request.[30] Nor is an agency required to answer a request for future information when it comes into existence.[31] However, an agency must undertake a search that is 'reasonably calculated to uncover all relevant documents'.[32] The Act provides for three levels

---

[23] 5 USC 552(a)(1).

[24] 5 USC 552(a)(2). The importance of pro-active disclosure was underscored in President Obama's 21 January 2009 FOIA Memorandum. The reading rooms must also include information requested under the Act but which the agency considers is likely to be requested by others as well: 5 USC 552(a)(2)(D). The rationale for this is to prevent the development of agency 'secret law', known to agency personnel but not to members of the public who deal with agencies. It is for this reason that records that have no precedent value and which do not constitute the working law of an agency are not required to be made available under this part of the Act: *National Labor Relations Board v Sears, Roebuck & Co*, 421 US 132 at 153-154 (1975); *Skelton v United States Postal Service*, 678 F 2d 35 at 41 (5th Cir 1982).

[25] Some of these records must be made available by agencies in 'electronic reading rooms'.

[26] *Checkosky v Securities and Exchange Commission*, 23 F 3d 452 (DC Cir 1994); *Kennecott Utah Copper Corp v Department of the Interior*, 88 F 3d 1191 (DC Cir 1996).

[27] 5 USC 552(a)(3)(A).

[28] A more detailed comparative treatment of third party rights of consultation and of 'reverse FOI' is given at §22–038.

[29] 5 USC 552(a)(3)(A). The request will 'reasonably describe' the records sought if it enables a professional agency employee familiar with the subject area to locate the record with a reasonable amount of effort. The scope of an answer to a FOIA request is limited to requests for records. Agencies do not have an obligation to answer questions posed: *Jean-Pierre v BOP*, 880 F Supp 2d 95 (DDC 2012), holding that requests for information such as 'who gave the order' and 'on what day' are not cognizable under FOIA because they ask questions calling for specific pieces of information rather than for records. Similarly, *Rodriguez-Cervantes v HHS*, 853 F Supp 2d 114 (DDC 2012). Each agency must publish in the *Federal Register* its procedural regulations governing access to its records under the Act. These regulations must inform the public of where and how to address requests; its schedule of fees for search, review, and duplication; its fee waiver criteria; and its administrative appeal procedures.

[30] *National Labor Relations Board v Sears, Roebuck & Co*, 421 US 132 (1975).

[31] *Mandel Grunfeld & Herrick v United States Customs Service*, 709 F 2d 41 (11th Cir 1983).

[32] *Weisberg v Department of Justice*, 705 F 2d 1344 at 1351 (DC Cir 1983). The adequacy of the search will depend upon the specificity of the request. The courts may review the adequacy of the search: *Krikorian v Department of State*, 984 F 2d 461 (DC Cir 1993).

of fees that may be assessed in response to a request according to categories of applicants.[33]

51–006 The response

Each agency is required to determine within 20 working days after the receipt of a proper request whether to comply with the request.[34] In 'unusual circumstances' an agency may have up to 10 days extra to answer.[35] The response must include a determination about what will be produced in response to the request.[36] The actual disclosure of records answering the terms of the request must follow promptly.[37] The agency can refuse to disclose if the applicant refuses to pay any fees.[38] An agency may charge an applicant three types of fee: the direct cost to the agency of searching for documents that answer the terms of the request; the direct cost to the agency in reviewing those documents to see what must be released; and duplication costs.[39] In permitting an agency to charge fees, the Act distinguishes records 'sought for commercial uses', requests made by 'an educational or non-commercial scientific institution whose purpose is scholarly or scientific research', requests from the media and requests from others. Provision is made for fee waiver or reductions where disclosure is in the public interest 'because it is likely to contribute significantly to public understanding of the operations or activities of government and is not primarily in the commercial interest of the requester'.[40] Disclosure must be in the form requested by the applicant.[41] If a request is refused in whole or in part, the agency must tell the applicant the reasons for the refusal.[42] The agency must also tell the applicant that there is a right to appeal.[43] If an agency fails to make a determination within the time limits, that may be treated as a constructive exhaustion of administrative remedies, entitling the applicant immediately thereafter to seek judicial review.[44] Where a record is not wholly comprised of exempt material the agency must, if it is reasonably practicable to do so, release any reasonably segregable portion that is not subject to an exemption.[45] The fact that supplying the records

33 5 USC 552(a)(4)(A)(ii).

34 5 USC 552(a)(6)(A)(i).

35 Defined to mean circumstances in which the agency: (1) needs to search for and collect records from separate offices; (2) needs to examine a voluminous amount of records required by the request; or (3) needs to consult with another agency or agency component: 5 USC 552(a)(6)(B)(iii). The agency is required to notify the applicant whenever an extension is invoked.

36 *Citizens for Responsibility & Ethics in Washington v Federal Election Commission*, 711 F 3d 180 (DC Cir 2013), holding that otherwise an agency would 'keep FOIA requests bottled up in limbo for months beyond the statutory deadline' and form an 'impermissible Catch-22.' Not all judicial circuits have followed this approach: *Dennis v CIA*, 2012 WL 5493377 at *2 (EDNY 2012), stating '[An] interim response informing [plaintiff] that [agency] is in the process of addressing [plaintiff's] inquiry is sufficient to satisfy the requirement that [agency] reply within the statutory time period'; *Carson v US Merit Sys Protect Bd*, 2012 WL 2562370, *2 (ED Tenn 2012), dismissing complaint that agency response was untimely when agency did not act in bad faith and agency answered request prior to commencement of litigation.

37 5 USC 552(a)(6)(C)(i). To improve FOIA processing speeds, the US Congress approved the 'Faster FOIA Act 2011.' This still awaits signature by the President.

38 *Trueblood v Department of the Treasury*, 943 F Supp 64 (DDC 1996).

39 5 USC 552(a)(4)(A).

40 5 USC 552(a)(4)(A)(ii)(II). Agencies can provide for the recovery of only the direct costs of search, duplication and review of records answering a request: 5 USC 552(a)(4)(A)(iv). Agencies are required to provide free of charge the first two hours of search time and the first 100 pages of duplication to all non-commercial requesters.

41 Unless it is not readily reproducible in that form or format: 5 USC 552(a)(3)(B).

42 5 USC 552(a)(6)(F).

43 5 USC 552(a)(6)(A)(i).

44 5 USC 552(a)(6)(C)(i)).

45 5 USC 552(b). The courts will scrutinise decisions to ensure that this obligation has been properly performed: *Trans-Pac Policing Agreement v United States Customs Service*, 177 F 3d 1022 at 1028 (DC Cir 1999). District courts have broad discretion to determine whether *in camera* inspection is necessary to evaluate the Government's claim that

in answer to a properly described request would be burdensome does not of itself provide a basis for non-compliance.[46]

51–007 Exemptions generally

An agency may refuse to disclose an agency record that falls within any of the nine statutory exemptions in the Freedom of Information Act. Generally speaking, the exemptions are discretionary in nature, so that it is open to an agency to grant disclosure to a record for which exemption could be claimed.[47] Access to a document that does not qualify as an 'agency record' may be refused on the basis that only agency records are available under the Act. Personal notes of agency employees may be refused on this basis. However, most records in the possession of an agency are 'agency records' within the meaning of the 1966 Act.

51–008 Specific exemptions

The right of access is disapplied to nine classes of matter:

(1) National security information concerning national defence or foreign policy, provided that that information has been classified in accordance with the procedural and substantive requirements of an executive order.[48] The information categories identified as proper bases for classification are:
 (a) foreign government information;[49]
 (b) vulnerabilities or capabilities of systems, installations, projects or plans relating

---

non-exempt material cannot be segregated from exempt material. There are limits to the obligation: see, generally: *Petroleum Information Corp v Department of the Interior*, 976 F 2d 1429 (DC Cir 1992); *Krikorian v Department of State*, 984 F 2d 461 (DC Cir 1993); *Solar Sources Inc v United States*, 142 F 3d 1033 (7th Cir 1998); *PHE Inc v Department of Justice*, 983 F 2d 248 (DC Cir 1993). Thus in *Students Against Genocide v Department of State*, 257 F 3d 828 at 837 (DC Cir 2001) the court held that an agency is not obliged to segregate and release images from classified photographs by 'produc[ing] new photographs at a different resolution in order to mask the [classified] capabilities of the reconnaissance systems that took them.' If, however, an agency determines that non-exempt material is so 'inextricably intertwined' that disclosure of it would leave only essentially meaningless words and phrases, the entire record may be withheld: *Neufeld v Internal Revenue Service*, 646 F 2d 661 at 663 (DC Cir 1981). In *Sherman v Department of the Army*, 244 F 3d 357 (5th Cir 2001) the court upheld the agency's decisions to require the requester to pay an estimated $350,000 to $1 million in costs for redacting social security numbers from a database of Vietnam medal awardees.

46 *Yeager v Drug Enforcement Administration*, 678 F 2d 315 (DC Cir 1982); *Ruotolo v Department of Justice*, 53 F 3d 4 (2d Cir 1995); *Nation Magazine v United States Customs Service*, 71 F 3d 885 at 892 (DC Cir 1995).

47 *Chrysler Corp v Brown*, 441 US 281 (1979); *Mobil Oil Corp v Environmental Protection Agency*, 879 F 2d 698 (9th Cir 1989); *Public Citizen v Department of State*, 11 F 3d 198 (DC Cir 1993); *Bartholdi Cable Co v Federal Communication Commission*, 114 F 3d 274 (DC Cir 1997); *Sherman v Department of the Army*, 244 F 3d 357 (5th Cir 2001). This was underscored in President Obama's 21 January 2009 FOIA Memorandum, which called on agencies to ensure that requests are responded to with 'a spirit of cooperation.'

48 5 USC 552(b)(1). Executive Order 13,526, made 1 January 2010. The Executive Order states that the information may not be considered for classification unless it concerns one of the following categories: military plans, weapons systems, or operations; foreign government information; intelligence activities, sources or methods; cryptology; foreign relations or foreign activities of the United States, including confidential sources; scientific, technological or economic matters relating to the national security; programmes for safeguarding nuclear materials or facilities; vulnerabilities or capabilities of systems, installations, projects or plans relating to the national security; or weapons of mass destruction. Additionally, compilations of unclassified information may be classified 'if the compiled information reveals an additional association or relationship that meets the standards for classification under [Executive Order 13,526': *ACLU v DOJ*, 681 F 3d 61 (2d Cir 2012). The Executive Order recognises three basic classifications according to the damage to the national security that might reasonably be expected to result from disclosure of the information to which the classification relates: top secret; secret; and confidential. The classification generally lasts for 10 years.

49 *Miller v Dept of Justice*, 562 F Supp. 2d 82, 102 (DDC 2008) (holding that disclosure of foreign government information would show that government's cooperation, capabilities and vulnerabilities, and would lead to negative diplomatic consequences and diminished intelligence capabilities); *Azmy v Dept of Defense*, 562 F Supp 2d 590, 600 (SDNY 2008) (holding that disclosure could be expected to 'impair [the Department's] ability to obtain information from foreign governments in the future, who will be less likely to cooperate with the United States if they cannot be confident that the information they provide will remain confidential').

to national security;[50] and

(c) intelligence activities, sources or materials.

This exemption can be used to give a response that neither confirms nor denies the holding of records answering the terms of the request.[51] The emergence of national security leaks by organisations like WikiLeaks also poses novel issues for FOIA.[52]

(2) Records that are 'related solely to the internal personnel rules and practices of an agency'.[53] This covers: (a) internal matters of a relatively trivial nature;[54] and (b) more substantial internal matters, the disclosure of which would risk circumvention of a statute or regulation.[55]

(3) Information prohibited from disclosure by another statute, provided that that statute either requires that the information be withheld from the public in such a manner as to leave no discretion on the issue or that that statute establishes particular criteria for

---

50 The courts have consistently declined to reject agency assessments of a threat to national security on the basis that they are not equipped to second-guess such assessments: *Ray v Turner*, 587 F 2d 1187 (DC Cir 1978); *Halperin v CIA*, 629 F 2d 144 (DC Cir 1980); *Goldberg v Department of State*, 818 F 2d 71 (DC Cir 1987); *Bowers v Department of Justice*, 930 F 2d 350 (4th Cir 1991); *Young v CIA*, 972 F 2d 536 (4th Cir 1992); *Students Against Genocide v Department of State*, 257 F 3d 828 (DC Cir 2001); *American Civil Liberties Union v Department of Justice*, 265 F Supp 2d 20 (DDC 2003); *National Security Archive Fund, Inc v CIA*, 402 F Supp 2d 211 (DDC 2005); *Edmonds v US Department of Justice*, 405 F Supp 2d 23 (DDC 2005); *American Civil Liberties Union v FBI*, 429 F Supp 2d 179 (DDC 2006). Agencies, it is thought, have unique insights into such matters: *Miller v Department of State*, 779 F 2d 1378 (8th Cir 1985); *Cozen O'Connor v Dept of Treasury*, 570 F Supp 2d 749 (ED Pa 2008); *Makky v Chertoff*, 489 F Supp 2d 421, 441 (DNJ 2007), affirmed, 541 F 3d 205 (3d Cir 2008); *Azmy v Dept of Defense*, 562 F Supp 2d 590 (SDNY 2008). Judicial deference to agencies' say-so on matters of national security has increased: *Morley v CIA*, 508 F3d 1108, 1124 (DC Cir 2007); *Larson v Department of State*, 565 F 3d857, 862 (DC Cir 2009) (noting that court need only examine whether agency's classification decision 'appears "logical" or "plausible"'); *Wolf v CIA*, 473 F 3d 370, 374-75 (DC Cir 2007); *Schoenman v FBI*, 575 F Supp 2d 136, 153 (DDC 2008); *James Madison Project v CIA*, 605 F Supp 2d 99 (DDC 2009); *Friedman v Secret Service*, 923 F Supp 2d 262 (DDC 2013), observing that courts 'generally defer to agency expertise in national security matters'; *Mobley v CIA*, 924 F Supp 2d 24 (DDC 2013) 'to the extent that plaintiffs ask this Court the judiciary is an extremely poor position to second-guess the executive's judgment' on national security. Similarly *ACLU v Dept of State*, 878 F Supp 2d 215, 222 (DDC 2012); *ACLU v Dept of Justice*, 681 F 3d 61, 71 (2d Cir 2012). The Executive Order expressly acknowledges the 'mosaic' basis for refusal to disclose a record. This has also been recognised in the Courts: *Halperin v CIA*, 629 F 2d 144 (DC Cir 1980); *Edmonds v Department of Justice*, 405 F Supp 2d 23 (DDC 2005); *American Civil Liberties Union v FBI*, 429 F Supp 2d 179 (DDC 2006) and authorities cited at §26–036(1).

51 This, in the United States, is called a 'Glomar response', based on the judgment in *Phillippi v CIA*, 546 F 2d 1009 (DC Cir 1976); *Amnesty International USA v CIA*, 728 F Supp 2d 479 (SDNY 2010), holding Glomar response regarding detention and treatment of detainees valid despite existing, limited public disclosures of their treatment, as the existing disclosures do not diminish the potential national security harm from release of information to the public; *Electronic Privacy Information Centre v National Security Agency*, 678 F 3d 926 (2012), upholding NSA issuance of Glomar response. Similarly *Moore v FBI*, 883 F Supp 2d 155, 164 (DDC 2012). It is frequently used in conjunction with exemption (1).

52 In general, the existence of leaked documents does not guarantee their accessibility under FOIA. The American Civil Liberties Union brought suit against the Department of Defense, seeking copies of documents leaked by WikiLeaks. The court held that the 'the WikiLeaks disclosure is no substitute for an official acknowledgment': *ACLU v Department of State*, No 11-01072, 4 (CKK) (DDC 2012).

53 5 USC 552(b)(2). As interpreted by the courts, there are two separate classes of documents that are generally held to fall within the second exemption. First, information relating to personnel rules or internal agency practices is exempt if it is a trivial administrative matter of no genuine public interest. Secondly, an internal administrative manual can be exempt if disclosure would risk circumvention of law or agency regulations. In order to fall into this category, the material will normally have to regulate internal agency conduct rather than public behaviour.

54 Often referred to as 'low 2' information. This covers routine internal personnel matters, such as performance standards and leave practices. The rationale for this part of the exemption is that the very task of processing and releasing these sorts of record would place an administrative burden on the agency that would not be justified by any genuine public benefit. The exemption does not apply where there is a genuine and significant public interest in disclosure of the records requested. In relation to the application of this provision: *Milner v Department of the Navy* 131 S Ct 1259 (2011); *Department of the Air Force v Rose*, 425 US 352 (1976); cf *Crooker v Bureau of Alcohol, Tobacco, Firearms and Explosives*, 670 F 2d 1051 (DC Cir 1981); *Dirksen v Department of Health and Human Services*, 803 F 2d 1456 (9th Cir 1986); *Maricopa Audubon Society v United States Forest Service*, 108 F 3d 1082 (9th Cir 1997).

55 Often referred to as 'high 2' information. This will extend to guidelines for conducting investigations, information that would reveal the identities of informants or undercover agents, information referring to the security techniques used in prisons, agency testing material, and so forth.

withholding or refers to particular types of information to be withheld.[56]

(4) Trade secrets[57] and commercial or financial information[58] obtained from a person that is privileged or confidential.[59] Information may also be withheld if disclosure would be likely to impair the Government's ability to obtain similar information in the future.[60] Only information obtained from a person other than a government agency qualifies under this exemption: information that an agency created on its own cannot normally be withheld under this exemption.[61] The provision protects the interests of both the Government and those who submit information to it.[62]

(5) Inter-agency or intra-agency[63] memoranda or letters 'which would not be available by law to a party other than an agency in litigation with the agency'.[64] This has been interpreted to mean records that would normally be privileged in civil proceedings.[65] These privileges are broader than those that are enjoyed by a public authority in the United Kingdom, and include: (a) deliberative process privilege, also known as 'executive privilege';[66] (b) attorney work-product privilege;[67] and (c) attorney-client

---

56 5 USC 552(b)(3). In relation to this provision, see: *American Jewish Congress v Kreps*, 574 F 2d 624 (DC Cir 1978); *Hayden v National Security Agency*, 608 F 2d 1381 (DC Cir 1979); *Halperin v CIA*, 629 F 2d 144 (DC Cir 1980); *Gardels v CIA*, 689 F 2d 1100 (DC Cir 1982); *CIA v Sims*, 471 US 159 (1985); *Cameranesi v Department of Defense*, No C 12-0595 PJH (ND Cal 2013).

57 'Trade secrets' has been given a narrower definition than given to it in tort law, so as to be confined to 'a secret, commercially valuable plan, formula, process, or device that is used for the making, preparing, compounding, or processing of trade commodities and that can be said to be the end product of either innovation or substantial effort.' *Public Citizen Health Research Group v Food and Drug Administration* 704 F 2d 1280 (DC Cir 1983). It requires that there be a direct relationship between the trade secret and the production process.

58 Provided that the information relates to business or trade, the courts have generally accepted that it is commercial or financial information: *Public Citizen Health Research Group v Food and Drug Administration*, 704 F 2d 1280 (DC Cir 1983); *Merit Energy Co v Department of the Interior*, 180 F Supp 2d 1184 (D Colo 2001). Detailed information on a company's marketing plans, profits, or costs can qualify as confidential business information.

59 5 USC 552(b)(4). In relation to confidentiality, a distinction is made between information submitted pursuant to obligation and information voluntarily submitted. In the former case, information is confidential for purposes of the exemption if it is 'private' or 'secret': *Food Marketing Institute v Argus Leader Media*, 139 S Ct 2356 (2019), overturning *National Parks & Conservation Association v Morton*, 498 F 2d 765 (DC Cir 1974). In the case of voluntarily submitted information, it is protected from disclosure provided it is not customarily disclosed to the public by the third party: *Critical Mass Energy Project v Nuclear Regulatory Commission*, 975 F 2d 871 (DC Cir 1992).

60 The Courts have drawn a sharp distinction between instances where a person has submitted information to an agency under compulsion and those cases where it has been volunteered to the agency: *Critical Mass Energy Project v Nuclear Regulatory Commission*, 975 F 2d 871 (DC Cir 1992); *Center for Auto Safety v National Highway Traffic Safety Administration*, 244 F 3d 144 (DC Cir 2001). The impairment must be significant: *Washington Post v Department of Health and Human Services*, 690 F 2d 252 (DC Cir 1982).

61 *Grumman Aircraft Engineering Corp v Renegotiation Board*, 425 F 2d 578 (DC Cir, 1970).

62 Although there is no formal requirement under the Act to do so, agencies will generally notify the person who submitted the business information that disclosure of the information is being considered.

63 These terms are not rigidly exclusive and can include some records generated outside an agency: *Department of the Interior v Klamath Water Users Protective Association*, 532 US 1 (2001); *Center for International Environmental Law v Office of US Trade Representative*, 237 F Supp 2d 17 (DDC 2002).

64 5 USC 552(b)(5).

65 *National Labor Relations Board v Sears, Roebuck & Co*, 421 US 132 (1975); *Federal Trade Commission v Grolier Inc*, 462 US 19 (1983).

66 The protection of records revealing the deliberative policymaking process of government is said to be founded upon three policy considerations: (1) the encouragement of open, frank discussions on matters of policy between subordinates and superiors; (2) the protection against premature disclosure of proposed policies before they are finally adopted; and (3) the protection against public confusion that might result from disclosure of reasons and rationales that were not in fact ultimately the grounds for an agency's action: *Coastal States Gas Corp v Department of Energy*, 617 F 2d 854 (DC Cir 1980); *Russell v Department of the Air Force*, 682 F 2d 1045 (DC Cir 1982); *Heggestad v Department of Justice*, 182 F Supp 2d 1 (DDC 2000); *Kidd v Dept of Justice*, 362 F Supp 2d 291, 296 (DDC 2005) (protecting documents on basis that disclosure would 'inhibit drafters from freely exchanging ideas, language choice, and comments in drafting documents'). In order to rely on the exemption, there are two requirements. First, the record must predate the decision to which it relates: *National Labor Relations Board v Sears, Roebuck & Co*,

privilege.[68] The exemption will be unavailable where the privilege has been waived by disclosure to third parties or non-federal agencies.[69]

(6) Information about individuals[70] in 'personnel and medical files and similar files',[71] provided that the disclosure of that information 'would constitute a clearly unwarranted invasion of personal privacy'.[72]

(7) Records or information compiled for law enforcement purposes.[73] In order to engage the exemption it must also be shown that one or more of six types of harm would flow from the disclosure of such records or information:

(A) The production of such records or information could reasonably be

---

421 US 132 (1975); *Access Reports v Department of Justice*, 926 F 2d 1192 (DC Cir 1991). Determining this is not always an easy task and there is much authority on the point. Secondly, the record must be a direct part of the deliberative process, in that it makes recommendations and expresses opinions on legal or policy matters: *Vaughn v Rosen*, 523 F 2d 1136 (DC Cir 1975). This second requirement excludes factual material: *Coastal States Gas Corp v Department of Energy*, 617 F 2d 854 (DC Cir 1980). The provision has been generously interpreted: *Coastal States Gas Corp v Department of the Environment*, 617 F 2d 854 (DC Cir 1980); *Skelton v United States Postal Service*, 678 F 2d 35 (5th Cir 1982); *Afshar v Department of State*, 702 F 2d 1125 (DC Cir 1983); *Access Reports v Department of Justice*, 926 F 2d 1192 (DC Cir 1991); *Wolfe v Department of Health and Human Services*, 839 F 2d 768 (DC Cir 1988); *Mapother v Dept of Justice*, 3 F 3d 1533 (DC Cir 1993). The courts have recognised that there is no straightforward dichotomy between deliberative material and factual material.

67 In other words, material prepared by a lawyer in contemplation of litigation. The privilege arises if litigation is probable: *Schiller v National Labor Relations Board*, 964 F 2d 1205 (DC Cir 1992). Privilege attaches provided that litigation was the primary factor in the decision to create the document: *Maine v Department of the Interior*, 285 F 3d 126 (1st Cir 2002).

68 In other words, confidential communications between a lawyer and his client relating to a legal matter for which the client has sought professional advice: *Mead Data Central Inc v Department of the Air Force*, 566 F 2d 242 (DC Cir 1977).

69 *Chilivis v Security & Exchange Commission*, 673 F 2d 1205 (11th Cir 1982); *Rockwell International v Department of Justice*, 235 F 3d 598 (DC Cir 2001).

70 The exemption requires that the record relate to an identifiable specific individual, and not merely a large class of unidentified individuals: *Arieff v Department of the Navy*, 712 F 2d 1462 (DC Cir 1983). It would seem that deceased individuals do not have privacy interests: *Na Iwi O Na Kupuna O Makapu v Dalton*, 894 F Supp 1397 (D Haw 1995).

71 The words 'similar files' have been construed to mean all information that 'applies to a particular individual': *Department of State v Washington Post Co*, 456 US 595 (1982); *Sherman v Department of the Army*, 244 F 3d 357 (5th Cir 2001).

72 5 USC 552(b)(6). The last words import into the exemption a requirement to balance the public's right to disclosure against the individual's right to privacy: *Department of the Air Force v Rose*, 425 US 352 (1976). The words 'clearly warranted' have been interpreted to mean that information falling within the opening words of the exemption will nevertheless not enjoy exemption under it except where there is a clearly demonstrable unwarranted invasion of privacy: *Getman v National Labor Relations Board*, 450 F 2d 670 (DC Cir 1971); *Avondale Industries Inc v National Labor Relations Board*, 90 F 3d 955 (5th Cir 1996). If it is shown that a protectable privacy interest would be threatened by disclosure of the record, the public interest in disclosure must be weighed against the privacy interest in non-disclosure. As to the manner in which this task is to be carried out, see: *Department of Justice v Reporters Committee for Freedom of the Press*, 489 US 749 (1989); *Department of State v Ray*, 502 US 164 (1991); *Department of Defense v FLRA*, 510 US 487 (1994) . As to what are protectable privacy interests, see: *Core v United States Postal Service*, 730 F 2d 946 (4th Cir 1984); *Nation Magazine v United States Customs Service*, 71 F 3d 885 (DC Cir 1995). The right to privacy of a public figure is a diluted one: *Fund for Constitutional Government v National Archives & Records Service*, 656 F 2d 856 (DC Cir 1981). The privacy interests of a public official are not as strong as those of a private citizen: *Lissner v Customs Service*, 241 F 3d 1220 (9th Cir 2001). While personal privacy normally concludes upon the death of the person to whom the information relates, relatives of the deceased may continue to have a privacy interest in the non-disclosure of information relating to the deceased: *National Archives & Records Administration v Favish*, 541 US 157 (2004). The onus is on the applicant to show that disclosure would be in the public interest of shedding light on an agency's performance of its statutory duties.

73 The exemption has, by amendments in 1974 and 1986, been broadened in its scope. The phrase 'law enforcement purposes' has been given a broad interpretation, to include the enforcement of state laws and of foreign laws: *Bevis v Department of State*, 801 F 2d 1386 (DC Cir 1986). Information not initially obtained or generated for law enforcement purposes may still qualify under this exemption if it is subsequently compiled for a valid law enforcement purpose at any time prior to invocation of the exemption: *John Doe Agency v John Doe Corp*, 493 US 146 (1989). A particularly generous application of the provision is allowed for criminal law enforcement agencies, although this tends to vary with circuit. The exemption does not apply to information compiled in an agency's general internal monitoring of its own employees to ensure compliance with its own procedures.

expected[74] to interfere with enforcement proceedings.[75]

(B) The production of such records or information would deprive a person of a right to a fair trial or an impartial adjudication.[76]

(C) The production of such records or information could reasonably be expected to constitute an unwarranted invasion of personal privacy.[77]

(D) The production of such records or information could reasonably be expected to reveal the identity of a confidential source.[78]

(E) The production of such records or information would reveal techniques and procedures for law enforcement investigations or prosecutions, or would disclose guidelines for law enforcement investigations or prosecutions, provided that disclosure of the information could reasonably be expected to risk circumvention of the law.[79]

(F) The production of such records or information could reasonably be expected to endanger the life or physical safety of any individual.[80]

(8) Matters that are contained in or related to examination, operating, or condition reports prepared by, on behalf of, or for the use of an agency responsible for the regulation or supervision of financial institutions.[81]

---

74 The 1986 amendment changed the required likelihood of harm from 'would interfere with' to 'could reasonably be expected to interfere with', thereby widening the scope of the exemption.

75 The protection afforded by the exemption only endures for so long as proceedings are pending or prospective: *National Labor Relations Board v Robbins Tire & Rubber Co*, 437 US 214 (1978). The types of harm which the courts have found might result from disclosure sufficient to engage the exemption include witness intimidation, fabrication of evidence, evasion of detection, premature revelation of evidence and revelation of strategies. A 'chilling' of witnesses will suffice: *Solar Sources Inc v United States*, 142 F 3d 1033 (7th Cir 1998). Recently the Courts have carried over into exemption (7)(A) the notions of deference conventionally reserved for assessments of national security: 'just as we have deferred to the executive when it invokes Exemption 1 and 3, we owe the same deference under Exemption 7(A) in appropriate cases, such as this one.' *Center for National Security Studies v Department of Justice*, 331 F 3d 918 (DC Cir 2003).

76 This exemption is rarely used, with agencies generally relying on (7)(A) instead. The only authority on it is *Washington Post v Department of Justice*, 863 F 2d 96 (DC Cir 1988).

77 Although there is an overlap between this exemption and exemption (6), the standard for engagement is different. Exemption (7)(C) protects against an unwarranted invasion of personal privacy, whereas exemption (6) protects against a clearly unwarranted invasion; exemption 7(C) allows the withholding of information that 'could reasonably be expected to' invade someone's privacy, whereas under exemption 6 information can be withheld only if disclosure 'would' invade someone's privacy. The exemption is given a generous interpretation: *Department of Justice v Reporters Committee for Freedom of the Press*, 489 US 749 (1989); *SafeCard Services v US Securities and Exchange Commission*, 926 F 2d 1197 (DC Cir 1991). It can also be relied upon to protect relatives of the person to whom the information relates: *National Archives & Records Administration v Favish*, 541 US 157 (2004).

78 A confidential source can include a state, local, or foreign agency or authority, or a private institution that furnished information on a confidential basis. In addition, the exemption protects information furnished by a confidential source if the data was compiled by a criminal law enforcement authority during a criminal investigation or by an agency conducting a lawful national security intelligence investigation. The courts have stated that the exemption must be given a 'robust' application in order to protect such sources of information: *Brant Construction Co v Environmental Protection Agency*, 778 F 2d 1258 (7th Cir 1985). What matters is not the nature of the information itself but the source of that information: *Department of Justice v Landano*, 508 US 165 (1993).

79 This only applies to techniques generally unknown to the public, and will not cover matters such as wire-tapping, eavesdropping, covert photography and so forth: *Albuquerque Publishing Co v Department of Justice*, 726 F Supp 851 (DDC 1989); *Jaffe v CIA*, 573 F Supp 377 (DDC 1983).

80 This has been interpreted as giving a very wide protection from disclosure of those involved in law enforcement: *Spirko v United States Postal Service*, 147 F 3d 992 (DC Cir 1998); *Rugiero v Department of Justice*, 257 F 3d 534 (6th Cir 2001).

81 5 USC 552(b)(8). This has been given a generous interpretation: *Gregory v Federal Deposit Insurance Commission*, 631 F 2d 896 (DC Cir 1980); *Public Citizen v Farm Credit Administration*, 938 F 2d 290 (DC Cir 1991). The provision has been said to have two purposes underlying it: (1) to protect the security of financial institutions by withholding from the public reports that contain frank evaluations of a bank's stability; and (2) to promote co-operation and communication between employees and examiners: *Berliner, Zisser, Walter & Gallegos v Securities and Exchange Commission*, 962 F Supp 1348 (D Colo 1997).

(9) Geological and geophysical information and data, including maps, concerning wells.[82]

51–009 Appeals and enforcement

An applicant has the right to an internal appeal on a merit basis against any adverse determination made by an agency.[83] If the agency upholds the decision, it must inform the applicant of its reasons and of the applicant's right of review in the federal courts.[84] Exclusive jurisdiction in relation to decisions under the Freedom of Information Act is vested in the United States district courts.[85] Before a district court will interfere with an agency's decision, the applicant must show that the agency has improperly withheld agency records.[86] In effect this means judges determine the propriety of agency withholdings *de novo*, with agencies bearing the burden of proof in defending the non-disclosure of records.[87] Agencies are required to prepare an index supported by an affidavit that itemises each withheld document (whether in whole or in part), identifying on a document-by-document basis the specific exemption relied upon and the facts and matters relied upon by the agency to justify non-disclosure.[88] Although the index will often comprise the only evidence produced by the agency, it may be supplemented or displaced by the court's *in camera* inspection of the requested documents.[89] If the court finds that an exemption does apply, it has no inherent or equitable power to order disclosure.[90] The court is empowered to consider the adequacy of the search made by an agency.[91] Appeals from the district courts are heard in the Court of Appeals. Third parties

---

82 5 USC 552(b)(9). This exemption is rarely used.

83 5 USC 552(a)(6)(A). The request must be answered within 20 working days: 5 USC 552(a)(6)(A)(i).

84 5 USC 552(a)(6)(A). Unless there has been no response within the 20 working day limit to a properly made request, the internal review (known as the 'administrative remedy') must be exhausted before applying to the Court: *Taylor v Appleton*, 30 F 3d 1365 at 1367 (11th Cir 1994); *Pollack v Department of Justice*, 49 F 3d 115 at 118 (4th Cir 1995). If, after the 20 working days but before a District Court suit is filed, the agency responds to the request, then the administrative remedy must be exhausted before applying to the court: *Oglesby v Department of the Army*, 920 F 2d 57 at 61 (DC Cir 1990).

85 5 USC 552(a)(4)(B).

86 *Kissinger v Reporters Committee for Freedom of the Press*, 445 US 136 at 150 (1980).

87 5 USC 552(a)(4)(B); *Natural Resources Defense Council v Nuclear Regulatory Commission*, 216 F 3d 1180 (DC Cir 2000). Although normally appeals are determined on a document-by-document basis, under certain circumstances courts have approved withholdings of entire, but discrete, categories of records which encompass all documents having similar contents: *National Labor Relations Board v Robbins Tire & Rubber Co*, 437 US 214 (1978). Before the court, the agency is not precluded from seeking to rely on an exemption that it did not rely upon at the administrative stage: *Young v CIA*, 972 F 2d 536 (4th Cir 1992). As to waiver of exemptions, see: *North Dakota* ex rel *Olson v Department of the Interior*, 581 F 2d 177 (8th Cir 1978); *Mobil Oil Corp v Environmental Protection Agency*, 879 F 2d 698 (9th Cir 1989); *Public Citizen v Department of State*, 11 F 3d 198 (DC Cir 1993); *Maydak v Department of Justice*, 218 F 3d 760 (DC Cir 2000).

88 This document is generally called the 'Vaughn Index' after the judgment of the Court of Appeals for the District of Columbia Circuit in *Vaughn v Rosen*, 484 F 2d 820 (1973). The index is required to be sufficiently detailed to enable the court to make a reasoned independent assessment of the claim of exemption. It must also be sufficiently specific to justify non-disclosure of the whole document, as opposed to just part of it: *Judicial Watch v Department of Health and Human Services*, 27 F Supp 2d 240 (DDC 1998); *Animal Legal Defense Fund Inc v Department of the Air Force*, 44 F Supp 2d 295 (DDC 1999). Where the documents are voluminous, a Vaughn Index may be prepared on the basis of representative samples: *Fensterwald v CIA*, 443 F Supp 667 (DDC 1977); *Weisberg v Department of Justice*, 745 F 2d 1476 (DC Cir 1984); *Bonner v Department of State*, 928 F 2d 1148 (DC Cir 1991); *Campaign for Responsible Transplantation v FDA*, 180 F Supp 2d 29 (DDC 2001).

89 Sometimes the Vaughn Index (because it is available to the applicant) will include less detail than is necessary to make good the claim for exemption, with the agency relying instead on an *in camera* inspection of the records sought: *Simon v Department of Justice*, 980 F 2d 782 (DC Cir 1992); *Department of Justice v Landano*, 508 US 165 (1993); *Maynard v CIA*, 986 F 2d 547 (1st Cir 1993); *Quiñon v FBI*, 86 F 3d 198 (DC Cir 1993); *Fiduccia v Department of Justice*, 185 F 3d 1035 (9th Cir 1999).

90 *Spurlock v FBI*, 69 F 3d 1010 (9th Cir 1995).

91 The agency must show that it made 'a good-faith effort to conduct a search for the requested records, using methods which can be reasonably expected to produce the information requested': *Weisberg v Department of Justice*, 745 F 2d 1476 (DC Cir 1984); *Truitt v Department of State*, 897 F 2d 540 (DC Cir 1990); *Oglesby v Department of the*

may bring proceedings to prevent an agency from disclosing records under the Act.[92]

3. COMMONWEALTH OF AUSTRALIA

51–010 Introduction

In 1982 the Federal Parliament of Australia passed the Freedom of Information Act 1982.[93] It was the first such piece of legislation in a Westminster system of government. The origin of the Act lay in a report of an inter-departmental committee tabled in the Federal Parliament in November 1976. The first Bill was introduced into the Senate by the Attorney-General in June 1978. That was referred to various committees and inquiries before taking its final form. Since its enactment, the Act has been significantly amended on five occasions,[94] most substantially in 2010.[95] The 2010 amendments saw the removal of conclusive certificates but, at the same time, the removal of a significant number of agencies from the operation of the Act, either entirely or in relation to certain functions.[96] The 2010 amendments also saw the introduction of an information publication scheme for agencies subject to the Act. The scheme commenced on 1 May 2011 and requires agencies to publish a plan showing how they will comply with the scheme requirements, publish specific categories of information and consider proactively publishing other government information.

51–011 Scope of the right

Section 11 of the Freedom of Information Act 1982 gives every person[97] a legally enforceable[98] right to obtain access in accordance with the Act to a 'document'[99] of an 'agency'[100] and to an

---

Army, 920 F 2d 57 (DC Cir 1990); *Campbell v Department of Justice*, 164 F 3d 20 (DC Cir 1998); *Rugiero v Department of Justice*, 257 F 3d 534 (6th Cir 2001). The court may use its powers to order discovery as part of the process: *Weisberg v Department of Justice*, 627 F 2d 365 (DC Cir 1980).

92 These proceedings themselves are not based upon The Freedom of Information Act but upon the *Administrative Procedures Act* (5 USC 701-706): *Chrysler Corp v Brown*, 441 US 281 (1979). As to reverse FOI generally, see: *CNA Finance Corp v Donovan*, 830 F 2d 1132 (DC Cir 1987); *McDonnell Douglas Corp v NASA*, 180 F 3d 303 (DC Cir 1999); *Campaign for Family Farms v Glickman*, 200 F 3d 1180 (8th Cir 2000); *McDonnell Douglas Corp v Department of the Air Force*, 375 F 3d 1182 (DC Cir 2004).

93 Since then each of the six states and one of the two internal territories has passed similar legislation: Freedom of Information Act 1982 (Vic); Freedom of Information Act 1989 (ACT); Government Information (Public Access) Act 2009 and, prior to that, the Freedom of Information Act 1989 (NSW); Freedom of Information Act 1991 (SA); Right to Information Act 2009 and, prior to that, the Freedom of Information Act 1991 (Tas); Right to Information Act 2009 and, prior to that, Freedom of Information Act 1992 (Qld); Freedom of Information Act 1992 (WA).

94 By the Freedom of Information Amendment Act 1983, the Freedom of Information Laws Amendment Act 1986, the Freedom of Information Amendment Act 1991, the Freedom of Information (Removal of Conclusive Certificates and Other Measures) Act 2009, and the Freedom of Information Amendment (Reform) Act 2010. The last is complemented by the Australian Information Commissioner Act 2010.

95 The 2010 amendments followed the report of the Administrative Law Review Council, *Open Government: A Review of the Federal Freedom of Information Act 1982*, ALRC Report No 77 (1996). A copy is available at: www.alrc.gov.au/report-77

96 Freedom of Information Act 1982 s 7 and Sch 2.

97 This has been held to extend to a foreign corporation: *Re Lordsvale Finance Ltd and Department of the Treasury* (1985) 3 AAR 301, AAT. And to convicted felons: *Re Ward and Secretary, Department of Industry and Commerce* (1983) 8 ALD 324. But in Victoria, not to a severely mentally retarded person: *Wallace v Health Commission of Victoria* [1985] VR 403. It refers to a single person, so that a firm cannot apply in its own name: *CKI Transmission Finance (Australia) Pty Ltd v Australian Taxation Office* (2011) 123 ALD 378; *Re Apache Energy Pty Ltd and National Offshore Petroleum Safety and Environmental Management Authority* (2012) 57 AAR 123.

98 Freedom of Information Act 1982 s 11A.

99 Document is defined broadly to include not only paper records but any other information which is capable of being reduced to written or visual form and which is capable of reproduction in that form: Freedom of Information Act

'official document'[101] of a Minister, other than an 'exempt document'. The phrase 'exempt document' is defined[102] to mean:

(1) A document that falls within one of the specific exemptions in Part IV of the Act;[103]
(2) A document that is held by or received from one of the bodies that is exempted from the operation of the Act;[104] and
(3) An official document of a Minister that contains some matter that does not relate to the affairs of an agency.

The right of access does not extend to documents that are publicly available independently of the Act,[105] to certain excluded bodies,[106] or to certain library, archive or museum collections.[107] An applicant is not required to demonstrate a need to know in order to exercise the general right of access.[108] The Act requires agencies to advise and assist those seeking to use its provisions.[109] The Act expressly encourages alternative access.[110]

1982 s 4(1). There is a specific provision in relation to computer-based information: Freedom of Information Act 1982 s 17. Apart from this, however, the Act does not require the generation of documents in order to answer a request: *Re Redfern and the University of Canberra* (1995) 38 ALD 457. It has been held that the Act does not extend to permit requests for documents that are received or created by the agency after the date of the request: *Re Edelsten and Australian Federal Police* (1985) 4 AAR 220 at 225, 9 ALN N65; *Re Lobo and Department of Immigration* (2011) 56 AAR 1. But the reviewing Tribunal can make a decision with respect to documents that have come into existence after the date of the request for access in certain circumstances: *Murtagh v Federal Commissioner of Taxation* (1984) 54 ALR 313.

100 'Agency' is defined to mean principally a Department of State of the Commonwealth and a prescribed authority (itself defined to mean a body corporate or unincorporated established by statute for a public purpose, a statutory office-holder and other bodies declared to be agencies): Freedom of Information Act 1982 s 4(1). A court is not an agency, except for documents that relate to matters of an administrative nature: *Bienstein v Family Court of Australia* [2008] FCA 1138. 'Document of an agency' is itself defined to mean a document in the possession of the agency, whether created in the agency or received in the agency: Freedom of Information Act 1982 s 4(1) and see: *Loughnan (Principal Registrar, Family Court of Australia) v Altman* (1992) 111 ALR 445; *Re Sullivan and Department of Industry, Science and Technology* (1996) 23 AAR 59 (in relation to custody of a document); *Beesley v Australian Federal Police* [2001] FCA 836 (importing notions of constructive possession). Personal documents can become documents of an agency: *Re Barkhordar and Australian Capital Territory Schools Authority* (1987) 12 ALD 332.

101 Defined to mean a document that is in the possession of a Minister in his capacity as a Minister, being a document that relates to the affairs of an agency or of a Department of State: Freedom of Information Act 1982 s 4(1). The effect of the definition is to exclude from the Act those documents which the Minister holds in a political, party or personal capacity. A document held by a Member of Parliament in his representative capacity does not become an official document of a Minister because the Member is, incidentally, a Minister. In relation to the Victorian equivalent, see *Birrell v Department of Premier and Cabinet* [1988] VR 73. The definition expressly excludes library material maintained for reference purposes and Cabinet notebooks.

102 Freedom of Information Act 1982 s 4(1).

103 As to which, see §51– 015.

104 Freedom of Information Act 1982 s 7. The bodies listed in Sch 2 to the Act are exempted from the operation of the Act. Documents emanating from security bodies, being the bodies listed in s 7(2A), render the agency holding the documents exempt from the Act so far as those documents are concerned: Freedom of Information Act 1982 s 7(2A). A minister is similarly exempt from the operation of the Act in relation to a document that has originated with or has been received from any of the security bodies: s 7(2B).

105 Freedom of Information Act 1982 s 12(1).

106 Certain bodies are wholly excluded and others are excluded only in relation to certain classes of documents: Freedom of Information Act 1982 ss 5, 6A, 7 and Sch 2. See further: *Kline v Official Secretary to the Governor-General* (2012) 295 ALR 398.

107 Freedom of Information Act 1982 s 13. The right of access to information officially held in the archives collection is dealt with under the Archives Act 1983.

108 Freedom of Information Act 1982 s 11(2). The Act can thus be used to achieve the same results as a *subpoena duces tecum* or discovery: *Johnson Tiles Pty Ltd v Esso Australia Ltd* (2000) 98 FCR 311.

109 Freedom of Information Act 1982 s 15(3)-(4).

110 Freedom of Information Act 1982 s 3A.

51–012 The request

A request must be in writing and must be sufficiently specific that the agency can identify the documents answering its terms.[111] If the request is made to the wrong agency, the recipient agency must direct the applicant to the correct agency.[112] Where an agency receives a request but does not hold the documents sought but either knows that another agency does or that the subject matter of the request is more closely connected with another agency, then the former agency may transfer the request to the latter agency.[113]

51–013 The response

The agency can refuse a request if there is a 'practical refusal reason', such as that dealing with it would involve an unreasonable diversion of the agency's resources[114] or the documents cannot be found, do not exist or have not been received.[115] The request must be answered within 30 days, but there is power to extend that by a further 30 days.[116] Provided that it is reasonably practicable, access must be given in the form sought by the applicant.[117] The agency may charge fees for dealing with the request, which must be paid in order to give rise to the obligation to disclose.[118] In the event of the agency refusing to disclose, whether in whole or in part, it must give reasons for the refusal.[119] In certain cases, the Act permits an agency neither to confirm nor deny the existence of a document.[120] The Act specifically provides for discretionary disclosure[121] and, in relation to certain exemptions, for third parties to be invited

---

[111] Freedom of Information Act 1982 s 15(2). The Tribunal has been reluctant to find that anything purporting to be a request is not a request: *Re Russell Island Development Association Inc and Department of Primary Industries and Energy* (1994) 33 ALD 683 at 692; *Re Redfern and University of Canberra* (1995) 38 ALD 457; *Re Collie and Deputy Commissioner of Taxation* (1997) 45 ALD 556 at 561.

[112] Freedom of Information Act 1982 s 15(4).

[113] Freedom of Information Act 1982 s 16. The Administrative Appeals Tribunal does not have a general power to look behind a decision to transfer a request: *Re Reith and Minister of State for Aboriginal Affairs* (1988) 14 ALD 430.

[114] Freedom of Information Act 1982 ss 24, 24AA, 24AB. See, for example: *Attorney-General v Honourable Mark Dreyfus* [2016] FCAFC 119, 242 FCR 472, 339 ALR 540. In relation to the use of multiple requests to evade the Victorian version of this provision, see: *Secretary, Department of Treasury and Finance v Kelly* [2001] VSCA 246. In addition, s 17(2) relates to the unreasonable diversion of resources with respect to electronic materials: see *Collection Point Pty Ltd v Commissioner of Taxation* [2013] 212 FCR 184.

[115] Freedom of Information Act 1982 s 24A. It is not for a court to say whether or not reasonable steps have been taken or if the agency is satisfied that the documents cannot be found: *Hamden v Campbell (No 2)* (2012) 57 AAR 189; *Chu v Telstra Corporation* (2005) 147 FCR 505.

[116] Freedom of Information Act 1982 s 15(5). If not made within this time, it is deemed to constitute a refusal: *Bienstein v Attorney-General* [2009] FCA 1501, *Bienstein v Attorney-General* [2010] FCAFC 45 and now s 15AC. Extra time is allowed for voluminous requests: s 15AB. Section 15AA deals with extension of time by agreement.

[117] Freedom of Information Act 1982 s 20.

[118] Freedom of Information Act 1982 s 29. The charges regime is set out in the Freedom of Information (Fees and Charges) Regulations 1982. Charges may be remitted or reduced, and there is an appeal process: s 29(4)-(11).

[119] Freedom of Information Act 1982 s 26. Global responses can be given: *Day v Collector of Customs* (1995) 130 ALR 106.

[120] Freedom of Information Act 1982 s 25. The Act uses the device of a notional document containing information as to the existence of documents answering the terms of the request. If that notional document would itself be an exempt document under s 33 (national security, defence and international relations), s 33A (Commonwealth/State relations) or s 37 (law enforcement), then the agency is not required to confirm or deny the existence of the actual documents. The Tribunal and Courts have not readily accepted agency claims based on this section: *Department of Community Services v Jephcott* (1987) 15 FCR 122. More recently, the Federal Court has held that, notwithstanding s 25, in a notice issued under s 26(1) the agency can deny the existence of any document covered by Part IV of the Act: *Secretary, Department of Health and Ageing v iNova Pharmaceuticals (Australia) Pty Ltd* (2010) 191 FCR 573.

[121] Freedom of Information Act 1982 ss 14 and 18(2). This does not enable the Administrative Appeals Tribunal to grant discretionary disclosure: *Re Waterford and Department of Health* (1983) 5 ALN N139; *Re Waterford and Department of Treasury* (1983) 5 ALD 193. It has been held that a discretionary disclosure cannot give rise to an estoppel in relation to the subsequent invocation of an exemption in relation to like documents: *Re Lordsvale Finance Ltd and*

to make representations before a decision is made to release documents.[122]

51– 014 Exemptions generally

Once a valid request has been made and appropriate charges are paid, a document that is subject to the Act must be disclosed: the only legal reason for not complying with this obligation is that the document is exempt.[123] The onus of proving that a document is exempt lies with the agency.[124] Resulting from its amendment in 2010, the Act divides exemptions into those that render a document unconditionally exempt[125] and those that render a document conditionally exempt.[126] Access need not be given to a document that is unconditionally exempt. Access must be given to a conditionally exempt document unless that would be contrary to the public interest.[127] The Act spells out the public interest factors, including matters that are not relevant.[128] Although the Act always had a purpose clause, it was significantly strengthened by the Freedom of Information Amendment (Reform) Act 2010.[129] Exemptions in Part IV of the 1982 Act are either class-based or require that a particular harm would or would be likely to result from disclosure of the document. The measure of likelihood employed for the harm-based exemptions is that disclosure 'would, or could reasonably be expected', to cause the identified harm.[130] The level or type of harm required in order to engage the harm-based exemptions varies: 'caus[ing] damage'; having 'a substantial adverse effect'; 'caus[ing] prejudice'; 'destroy or diminish'; being 'unreasonable disclosure'; 'unreasonably affect'; and 'likely to unreasonably expose to disadvantage.' Until removed in 2009, in relation to certain exemptions, a conclusive certificate could be issued where the relevant Minister had been

Department of Treasury (1985) 3 AAR 301.

122 Freedom of Information Act 1982 ss 26A (documents containing information that originated from a state), 27 (documents containing business information) and 27A (documents containing personal information). These provisions enable the third party to rely upon an exemption that is not sought to be engaged by the agency: *Re Parisi and Australian Federal Police* (1987) 14 ALD 11 at 15. However, the process need not be gone through if the agency is proposing to refuse access: *Motor Trades Association of Australia v Trade Practices Commission* (1993) ATPR 41-201 at 40-821. The pre-2010 amendment procedure was considered in *Mitsubishi Motors Australia Ltd v Department of Transport* (1986) 12 FCR 156, 68 ALR 626, where it was held that the reviewing Tribunal could, at the request of a third party, determine that a document treated by the agency as not exempt was exempt under s 43. A more detailed comparative treatment of third party rights of consultation and of 'reverse FOI' is given at §22– 038.

123 Freedom of Information Act 1982 s 11A.

124 Freedom of Information Act 1982 ss 55D and 61(1).

125 Freedom of Information Act 1982 ss 33-47A.

126 Freedom of Information Act 1982 ss 47B-47J.

127 Freedom of Information Act 1982 s 11A(5).

128 Freedom of Information Act 1982 s 11B.

129 Freedom of Information Act 1982 s 3. Under the earlier purpose clause, the courts had declined to interpret the exemptions by subject to any special restrictive presumptions: *News Corp Ltd v National Companies and Securities Commission* (1984) 1 FCR 64, 52 ALR 27; *Arnold v Queensland* (1987) 73 ALR 607; *Searle Australia Pty Ltd v Public Interest Advocacy Centre* (1992) 36 FCR 111, 108 ALR 163. In relation to the Victorian legislation, a contrary view had been taken by the High Court: *Public Service Board v Wright* (1986) 160 CLR 145 at 153-154. As to the new purpose clause, see *Re CKI Transmission Finance and Australian Taxation Office* (2011) 85 ATR 337.

130 Employed in Freedom of Information Act 1982 ss 33(1), 37(1), 47(1), 47B, 47E and 47G. The Tribunal and Courts have interpreted this as being something more than fanciful but which need not be more likely than not: *News Corp Ltd v National Companies and Securities Commission* (1984) 57 ALR 550; *Attorney-General's Department v Cockroft* (1986) 10 FCR 180 at 190, 64 ALR 97; *Arnold (on behalf of Australians for Animals) v Australian National Parks and Wildlife Service* (1987) 73 ALR 607; *Re Environment Centre NT and Department of the Environment, Sport & Territories* (1994) 35 ALD 765 at 778; *Re Lobo and Department of Immigration* (2011) 56 AAR 1 at [200]-[211] ('decision as to whether, when considered on a rational, as distinct from irrational, absurd or ridiculous basis, it is probable that the specified outcome will eventuate'); *Secretary, Department of Health and Ageing v Nova Pharmaceuticals (Australia) Pty Ltd* (2010) 191 FCR 573. The Tribunal and Courts have generally been prepared to accept at face-value agency claims of likely harm: *Arnold (on behalf of Australians for Animals) v Australian National Parks and Wildlife Service* (1987) 73 ALR 607.

satisfied that a document should not be disclosed.[131] The Act provides for severance of exempt material from a document that generally answers the terms of a request.[132] In certain circumstances, third parties are given rights to be informed that a request for access to documents has been made and to make submissions that access ought to be refused.[133] If, despite the representations of the third party, the agency decides that it will release the documents, the third party may seek internal review and thereafter apply to the Administrative Appeals Tribunal for a review of the agency's decision.[134]

51– 015 Specific exemptions

The exemptions may be grouped into 20 heads. The unconditional exemptions are:

(1) Documents that would divulge a foreign government confidence.[135]

(2) Documents the disclosure of which would, or could be reasonably be expected to, cause damage to the national security, defence or international relations of Australia.[136]

---

131 Removed by the Freedom of Information (Removal of Conclusive Certificates and Other Measures) Act 2009. The provisions were: s 33 (national security, defence and international relations), s 33A (Commonwealth/State relations), s 34 (Cabinet documents), s 35 (Executive Council documents) and s 36 (deliberative process documents). The role of the Administrative Appeals Tribunal in reviewing such a certificate had been limited to asking whether or not reasonable grounds existed at the time of the hearing for the claims made in the certificate. This prevented the Tribunal from weighing public interest factors in favour of disclosure against public interest factors favouring non-disclosure: *McKinnon v Secretary, Department of Treasury* [2006] HCA 45, (2006) 229 ALR 187.

132 Freedom of Information Act 1982 s 22(1). An agency is under a duty to consider whether some form of redacted document can be provided: *Day v Collector of Customs* (1995) 57 FCR 176 at 180, 130 ALR 106. The redacted document must not be misleading: *Re Carver and Department of the Prime Minister and Cabinet* (1987) 6 AAR 317 at 328, 12 ALD 447.

133 Thus, where a request is received by an agency for documents that contain information concerning a person's or organisation's commercial affairs, and it appears that the person or organisation might wish to contest the disclosure of the documents, then that person or organisation must be given notice of the request: Freedom of Information Act 1982 s 27. Similar third party provision is made in relation to documents containing personal information relating to a third party (Freedom of Information Act 1982 s 27A) and in relation to documents containing information that originated from a State (Freedom of Information Act 1982 s 26A).

134 Freedom of Information Act 1982 ss 26A, 26AA, 27, 27A and 60AA. Section 53C defines who is 'an affected third party.' That person is given a right to apply for internal review of an access grant decision (s 54A(2)), to be notified of a review application to the Information Commissioner (s 54P), to participate in that review (s 55A(1)(c)), to be given a copy of the Commissioner's decision (s 55K(6)), to appeal on a point of law to the Federal Court against the Commissioner's decision (s 56(1)), to apply to the Administrative Appeals Tribunal for merit review of the Commissioner's decision (s 57A) and to be notified of another person's appeal to the Tribunal (s 60AA(2)). A more detailed comparative treatment of third party rights of consultation and of 'reverse FOI' is given at §22– 038.

135 Freedom of Information Act 1982 s 33(b). This includes information communicated by an international organisation.

136 Freedom of Information Act 1982 s 33(a). This refers to Australia's ability to maintain good working relations with overseas governments and to protect the flow of confidential information between it and other governments: *Re Bui and Department of Foreign Affairs and Trade* (2005) 85 ALD 793. This head of exemption also exempts a document the disclosure of which would divulge any information communicated in confidence to the Australian Government by or on behalf of a foreign government, an authority of a foreign government or an international organisation. The information does not have to be confidential in nature: *Re Haneef and Australian Federal Police* [2009] AATA 51; *Gersten v Minister for Immigration and Multicultural Affairs* (2000) 61 ALD 445. Section 33 does not involve a consideration of whether disclosure would be contrary to the public interest: *Commonwealth of Australia v Hittich* (1994) 53 FCR 152 at 154; *Re Lobo and Department of Immigration* (2011) 56 AAR 1 at [85]-[89]. The section expresses an aspect of the public interest: *Re Mann and Australian Taxation Office* (1985) 3 AAR 261; *Re O'Donovan and Attorney-General's Department* (1985) 4 AAR 151, 8 ALD 528; *Re Edelsten and Australian Federal Police* (1985) 4 AAR 220. The Courts and Tribunal have been generally ready to accept agency assertions that this sort of harm would be caused: *Re Maher and Attorney-General's Department* (1985) 3 AAR 396; *Re Stolpe and Department of Foreign Affairs* (1985) 9 ALD 104; *Re Fewster and Department of Prime Minister and Cabinet (No 2)* (1987) 13 ALD 139; *Re Wang and Department of Employment, Education and Training* (1988) 15 ALD 497; *Re Bayliss and Department of Health and Family Services* (1997) 48 ALD 443; *Gersten v Minister for Immigration & Multicultural Affairs* [2000] FCA 1221, [2001] FCA 159. In this context, the Courts and Tribunal have been prepared to accept the 'mosaic theory' (see §§6– 024 to 6– 025): *Re McKnight and Australian Archives* (1992) 28 ALD 95. A document already in the public domain can still enjoy exemption under this section: *Commonwealth of Australia v Hittich* (1994) 53 FCR 152.

(3) Cabinet documents and records.[137]
(4) Documents the disclosure of which would, or could be reasonably be expected to, cause damage to law enforcement, confidential sources of information relating to law enforcement, fair trials, or methods of criminal investigation.[138]
(5) Documents and information the disclosure of which is proscribed by other statutes.[139]
(6) Documents subject to legal professional privilege.[140]
(7) Documents the disclosure of which would found an action (other than by the Commonwealth) for breach of confidence.[141]
(8) Confidential documents originating from the Parliamentary Budget Officer or from his office.[142]
(9) Documents the disclosure of which would be a contempt of Court or of the Commonwealth or a State Parliament.[143]
(10) Trade secrets.[144]

---

137 Freedom of Information Act 1982 s 34, considered in *Re Telstra Corp Ltd and Department of Broadband, Communications and the Digital Economy* [2010] AATA 118, (2010) 113 ALD 623. Purely factual material is generally exempted. The exemption applies to documents prepared for submission to Cabinet, even if not actually submitted to Cabinet: *Re Rae and Department of Prime Minister and Cabinet* (1986) 12 ALD 589; *Re Porter and Department of Community Services and Health* (1988) 14 ALD 403; *Re Reith and Minister for Aboriginal Affairs* (1988) 16 ALD 709. In relation to analogous legislation: *Department of Premier and Cabinet v Birrell (No 2)* [1990] VR 51.

138 Freedom of Information Act 1982 s 37. See generally: *Re Lobo and Department of Immigration* (2011) 56 AAR 1. This has been given a broad interpretation, covering: confidential sources of information (*McKenzie v Secretary to the Department of Social Security* (1986) 65 ALR 645); even if the information provided by the source is not in itself confidential (*Re Dale and Australian Federal Police* (1997) 47 ALD 417); policy documents setting out in what circumstances an agency would prosecute for a breach of statute (*Re Murphy and Australian Electoral Commission* (1994) 33 ALD 718); investigation manuals, even where large parts have been previously disclosed (*Re Arnold Bloch Leibler & Co and Australian Taxation Office (No 2)* (1985) 4 AAR 178, 9 ALD 7); any documents relating to public safety in a broad sense of the phrase (*Re Parisi and Australian Federal Police* (1987) 14 ALD 11); documents being used in an investigation (*News Corp Ltd v National Companies and Securities Commission* (1984) 57 ALR 550). But work accident investigation reports have been held not exempt under analogous Victorian legislation: *Accident Compensation Commission v Croom* [1991] 2 VR 322; nor is a police brief necessarily exempt: *Sobh v Police Force of Victoria* [1994] 1 VR 41.

139 Freedom of Information Act 1982 s 38. This provision gave rise to considerable litigation prior to its amendment in 1991. The principles were summarised in *Harrigan v Department of Health* (1986) 72 ALR 293 at 294-295. See also: *Kavvadias v Commonwealth Ombudsman* (1984) 52 ALR 728; *News Corp Ltd v National Companies and Securities Commission* (1984) 57 ALR 550; *Federal Commissioner of Taxation v Swiss Aluminium Australia Ltd* (1986) 66 ALR 159. In relation to analogous legislation: *Secretary to the Department of Premier and Cabinet v Hulls* [1999] 3 VR 331. See now *Mullen v Aged Care Quality and Safety Commissioner* [2019] FCA 1726.

140 Freedom of Information Act 1982 s 42. It has been held that for the purposes of the Act, legal professional privilege attaches to confidential professional communications between a Government agency and its salaried legal officers provided that it is undertaken for the sole purpose of seeking or giving legal advice or in connection with anticipated or pending litigation: *Waterford v Commonwealth* (1987) 163 CLR 54; see also *Austin v Deputy Secretary, Attorney-General's Department* (1986) 67 ALR 585; *Secretary, Department of Health v Proudfoot* (1993) 114 FLR 384; *Commonwealth of Australia v Dutton* (2000) 102 FCR 168; *Comcare v Foster* [2006] FCA 6. In relation to analogous legislation: *Director of Public Prosecutions v Smith* [1991] VR 63 (documents relating to the sufficiency of evidence). The sole purpose test has since been reduced to a dominant purpose test: *Esso Australia Resources Ltd v Federal Commissioner of Taxation* (1999) 168 ALR 123. It has been held that, for the purposes of the Act, privilege can be waived: *Bennett v Chief Executive Officer of the Australian Customs Service* [2003] FCA 53; *British American Tobacco Australia Ltd v Secretary, Dept of Health and Ageing* (2011) 195 FCR 123.

141 Freedom of Information Act 1982 s 45. This had been interpreted to capture information for which a common law breach of confidence would not succeed: *Baueris v Commonwealth of Australia* (1987) 75 ALR 327; *Corrs Pavey Whiting & Byrne v Collector of Customs* (1987) 14 FCR 434. Section 45 was subsequently amended to remove this possibility. The role of defences to an action in confidence and their applicability to the engagement of s 45 was considered in *Re Lobo and Department of Immigration* (2011) 56 AAR 1 and *Callejo and Department of Immigration and Citizenship* [2010] AATA 244, (2010) 51 AAR 308.

142 Freedom of Information Act 1982 s 45A.

143 Freedom of Information Act 1982 s 46.

144 Freedom of Information Act 1982 s 47(1)(a). This whole section is designed to protect the interests of third parties: *Harris v Australian Broadcasting Corp* (1983) 78 FLR 236, 50 ALR 551. As to the meaning of this provision, see: *Searle Australia Pty Ltd v Public Interest Advocacy Centre* (1992) 108 ALR 163, 36 FCR 111; *Secretary, Department of Workplace*

(11) Electoral rolls.[145]

The public interest conditional exemptions are:

(12) Documents the disclosure of which would, or could be reasonably be expected to, cause damage to relations between the Commonwealth and a state.[146]

(13) Documents that record the deliberative process of the federal Government[147] and its disclosure would be contrary to the public interest.[148]

(14) Documents the disclosure of which would have a substantial adverse effect on the financial or property interests of the Commonwealth of Australia or an agency.[149]

(15) Documents the disclosure of which would involve the unreasonable disclosure of personal information about any person (including a deceased person) other than the applicant.[150]

Relations & Small Business v The Staff Development & Training Centre Pty Ltd [2001] FCA 382, upheld at [2001] FCA 1375.

145 Freedom of Information Act 1982 s 47A.

146 Freedom of Information Act 1982 s 47B. This head of exemption also exempts a document the disclosure of which would divulge information communicated in confidence by or on behalf of the Government of an Australian state to the federal Government. The earlier version of this exemption (s 33A) had been given a broad interpretation: *Re Mickelberg and Australian Federal Police* (1984) 6 ALN N176; *Re Anderson and Department of Special Minister of State* (1984) 7 ALN N155; *Re Angel and Department of Art, Heritage and Environment* (1985) 9 ALD 113; *Arnold (on behalf of Australians for Animals) v Australian National Parks and Wildlife Service* (1987) 73 ALR 607; *Re Guy and Department of Transport* (1987) 12 ALD 358; *Re Birch and Attorney-General's Department* (1994) 33 ALD 675; *Re Environment Centre NT Inc and Department of the Environment, Sport and Territories* (1994) 35 ALD 765.

147 Freedom of Information Act 1982 s 47C. The Courts and Tribunal had given the first paragraph of the earlier version of this exemption (s 36(1)) a broad interpretation, capable of encompassing most documents held by an agency recording any form of consideration of a decision: *Harris v Australian Broadcasting Corp* (1983) 78 FLR 236, 50 ALR 551 (interim reports should not be released because they could mislead); *Re James and Australian National University* (1984) 2 AAR 327; *Murtagh v Federal Commissioner of Taxation* (1984) 54 ALR 313 (documents showing process of making an assessment of taxation); *Re Waterford and Department of the Treasury (No 2)* (1984) 1 AAR 1, 5 ALD 588; *Re Toohey and Department of the Prime Minister and Cabinet* (1985) 9 ALN 94; *Re Howard and the Treasurer (Cth)* (1985) 3 AAR 169 at 172-175; *Re Chapman and Minister for Aboriginal and Torres Strait Islander Affairs* (1996) 23 AAR 142, 43 ALD 139; *Re Subramanian and Refugee Review Tribunal* (1997) 44 ALD 435; *Re The Staff Development and Training Centre and Secretary, Department of Employment, Workplace Relations and Small Business* (2000) 30 AAR 330 at 354. In relation to analogous legislation: *Director of Public Prosecutions v Smith* [1991] VR 63 (documents considering whether to prosecute). Operational information (defined in s 8A, and which must be published in any event (s 8)), purely factual material, reports, etc are excluded from the exemption. The meaning of the earlier version (s 36) was considered in *Harris v Australian Broadcasting Corp (No 2)* (1984) 51 ALR 581.

148 In order for the exemption to engage, the agency must demonstrate that disclosure would be contrary to the public interest. As to the matters which the Courts and Tribunal have taken into account under the rubric of the 'public interest', see: *Murtagh v Federal Commissioner of Taxation* (1984) 54 ALR 313; *Burns v Australian National University (No 1)* (1984) 1 AAR 456 at 458; *Re Howard and Treasurer, Commonwealth* (1985) 3 AAR 169; *Re Swiss Aluminium and Department of Trade* (1985) 9 ALD 243; *Ryder v Booth* [1985] VR 869 (inability to get further similar information); *Re Reith and the Attorney-General's Department* (1987) 11 ALD 345; *Re Fewster and Department of Prime Minister and Cabinet (No 2)* (1987) 13 ALD 139; *Re Reith and Minister of State for Aboriginal Affairs* (1988) 16 ALD 709; *Re Kamenka and Australian National University* (1992) 15 AAR 297; *Re Chapman and Minister for Aboriginal and Torres Strait Islander Affairs* (1996) 23 AAR 142 at 155-159; *Re Bartle and Secretary, Department of Employment, Education, Training and Youth Affairs* (1998) 28 AAR 140. If this exemption is relied upon, the ground of public interest must be specified.

149 Freedom of Information Act 1982 s 47D.

150 Freedom of Information Act 1982 s 47F. Section 47F(2) prescribes matters that must be taken into account. Where the agency concludes that disclosure of the information would be detrimental to the health of the applicant, it may supply it instead to a medical practitioner, counsellor or social worker. It has been held that a company does not have 'personal affairs' within the meaning of the Act: *News Corp Ltd v National Companies and Securities Commission* (1984) 1 FCR 64, 52 ALR 277; *The University of Melbourne v Robinson* [1993] 2 VR 177. In New South Wales it has been held that the release of the name of a person is not necessarily information concerning the personal affairs of a person: *Commissioner of Police v District Court of NSW* (1993) 31 NSWLR 606. In Victoria, detailed references to the business affairs of victims of crime are not exempt where the victims had earlier disclosed them to the public: *Director of Public Prosecutions v Smith* [1991] VR 63. The words 'relating to' have been given a very wide interpretation: *Colakovski v Australian Telecommunications Corp* (1991) 29 FCR 429, 100 ALR 111; *Re Callejo and Department of Immigration and Citizenship* [2010] AATA 244, (2010) 51 AAR 308. 'Personal affairs' itself has also been given a wide meaning: *Re Williams and Registrar, Federal Court of Australia* (1985) 8 ALD 219, 3 AAR 529; *Young v Wicks* (1986) 13 FCR 85; *Department of Social Security v Dyrenfurth* (1988) 80 ALR 533; *Bleicher v Australian Capital*

(16) Documents the disclosure of which could reasonably be expected to destroy or diminish the commercial value of any information.[151]

(17) Documents the disclosure of which would, or could be reasonably be expected to, prejudice the effectiveness of audits or tests or to have a substantial adverse effect upon the running of an agency.[152]

(18) Documents the disclosure of which would be likely to result in an unreasonable exposure to disadvantage to specified agencies carrying out research that is incomplete.[153]

(19) Documents the disclosure of which would, or could be reasonably be expected to, have a substantial adverse effect on the ability of the Commonwealth to manage the economy.[154]

(20) Documents the disclosure of which would disclose information concerning the business, commercial or financial affairs of a person or organisation, the disclosure of which could reasonably be expected to have an unreasonably adverse effect upon that person or organisation or to prejudice the future supply of information to the Commonwealth of Australia.[155]

51–016 Appeals and enforcement

Where an agency refuses access to documents, the first right of appeal is one of internal review by someone other than the original decision-maker.[156] Generally, the applicant is required to lodge a request for an internal review within 30 days of receiving notification of the original decision.[157] The principal officer must review the decision within 30 days of receiving the request.[158] If the applicant either does not receive a response within that time or receives an unfavourable decision, he is entitled to apply to the Information Commissioner for a further review of the decision.[159] An application for review must generally be made within 60 days after the notice of the decision refusing access to a document was given to the applicant.[160] The power given to the Information Commissioner is to review any decision that has been made by an agency or minister with respect to a request for access to a document and to decide the

Territory Health Authority (1990) 12 AAR 246; *Colakovski v Australian Telecommunications Corp* (1991) 29 FCR 429, 100 ALR 111.

[151] Freedom of Information Act 1982 s 47(1)(b). The section is designed to protect third party interests: *Harris v Australian Broadcasting Corp* (1983) 78 FLR 236, 50 ALR 551. As to the meaning of information having a commercial value, see: *Gill v Department of Industry Technology and Resources* [1987] VR 681; *Secretary, Dept of Workplace Relations & Small Business v The Staff Development & Training Centre Pty Ltd* [2001] FCA 382, upheld at [2001] FCA 1375.

[152] Freedom of Information Act 1982 s 47E. In relation to the earlier version of this exemption (s 40), the Courts and Tribunal had required a substantial degree of gravity before finding a 'substantial adverse effect': *Harris v Australian Broadcasting Corp* (1983) 78 FLR 236, 50 ALR 551; *Re Dyki and Commissioner of Taxation* (1990) 12 AAR 544, 22 ALD 124 (completed job applications not exempt); *Searle Australia Pty Ltd v Public Interest Advocacy Centre* (1992) 36 FCR 111, 108 ALR 163; *Re Kamenka and Australian National University* (1992) 15 AAR 297, 26 ALD 585; *Re Murphy and Australian Electoral Commission* (1994) 33 ALD 718.

[153] Freedom of Information Act 1982 s 47H.

[154] Freedom of Information Act 1982 s 47J.

[155] Freedom of Information Act 1982 s 47G. See *Re Apache Energy Pty Ltd and National Offshore Petroleum Safety and Environmental Management Authority* (2012) 57 AAR 123.

[156] Freedom of Information Act 1982 ss 52-55E.

[157] Freedom of Information Act 1982 s 54B.

[158] Freedom of Information Act 1982 s 54C(3).

[159] Freedom of Information Act 1982 s 54L.

[160] Freedom of Information Act 1982 s 54M.

matter on the same basis as the agency or minister could have decided it. [161] A person may appeal against the Commissioner's decision, either to the Federal Court on a point of law or the Tribunal for merit review[162] The Tribunal may compel the production to it of the documents covered by the request in order to make its decision.[163] An appeal on a question of law lies from the Administrative Appeals Tribunal to the Federal Court.

4. NEW ZEALAND

51–017 Introduction

In New Zealand, the power to elicit official information originated in a 1962 statute establishing an ombudsman.[164] In May 1978 a Committee on Official Information was established to consider the extent to which official information could be made more readily available to the public. Following the Committee's reports,[165] the Official Information Act 1982 came into force on 1 July 1983. The State-owned Enterprises Act 1986 brought state-owned enterprises within the Official Information Act 1982. In 1987, the Act was amended by replacing the original ministerial veto of the Ombudsman's recommendations with a collective veto by Order in Council; by expanding the protection for information about competitive commercial activities; by imposing time limits; and by extending coverage to additional organisations. In that same year, a separate Act was passed providing analogous rights of access to information held by local authorities.[166] In 1993, the right of access to information where it related to a non-corporate applicant was transferred to the Privacy Act 1993. Thus, rights of access to official information are now split between three statutes:

(1) In relation to information relating to the individual requesting it, under the Privacy Act 1993;[167]

(2) In relation to other information held by local authorities, under the Local Government Official Information and Meetings Act 1987; and

(3) In relation to all other information, under the Official Information Act 1982.[168]

---

[161] Freedom of Information Act 1982 s 55K. The Commissioner's power on review are set out in ss 54Z to 55Q.

[162] The Tribunal is not restricted to the grounds of exemption relied upon by the agency: *Searle Australia Pty Ltd v Public Interest Advocacy Centre* (1992) 108 ALR 163; *Victorian Casino and Gambling Authority v Hulls* [1998] 4 VR 718 (relating to the analogous Victorian scheme). The Appellant's representative may be given access to documents upon appropriate undertakings: *Day v Collector of Customs* (1995) 130 ALR 106; *cf News Corporation Ltd v National Companies and Securities Commission* (1984) 57 ALR 550; *Department of Industrial Relations v Forrest* (1990) 21 FCR 93, 91 ALR 417 (a certificate case).

[163] Freedom of Information Act 1982 s 58E.

[164] The Parliamentary Commissioner (Ombudsman) Act 1962. That statute empowered the Ombudsman to obtain information from governmental agencies and to disclose in any report such matters as in the Ombudsman's opinion needed to be disclosed in order to establish grounds for any conclusions and recommendations made in the report.

[165] Committee on Official Information, *Towards Open Government: General Report* (vol 1, 1980); *Towards Open Government: Supplementary Report* (vol 2, 1981). The Committee is commonly referred to as the Danks Committee and the reports as the Danks Report. The Supplementary Report contained a draft Bill that was to become the Official Information Act 1982.

[166] The Local Government Official Information and Meetings Act 1987.

[167] As to the division between the Official Information Act 1982 and the Privacy Act 1993, see *Director of Human Rights Proceedings v Commissioner of Police* [2008] NZHC 1286.

[168] There is a limited inter-relationship between the statutes, so that where the applicant seeks information under the Official Information Act 1982 or under the Local Government Official Information and Meetings Act 1987 for information relating to a third party, the provisions of the Privacy Act 1993 are relevant: Official Information Act 1982 s 9(2)(a); Local Government Official Information and Meetings Act 1987 s 7(2)(a). A more detailed comparative treatment of third party rights of consultation and of 'reverse FOI' is given at §22–038.

In June 2012 the Law Commissioner published a review of the legislation.[169] It concluded that the coverage of the Official Information Act 1982 and the Local Government Official Information and Meetings Act 1987 should be combined in a single statute to facilitate administration and simplify the process. While the report suggests major changes to the regime, including a greater role for the Ombudsman, other central aspects – such as the operation of the public interest – it concluded it would maintain.

51– 018 Scope of the right

Section 12(1) of the Official Information Act 1982 enables citizens, residents and persons in New Zealand, as well as companies incorporated in New Zealand, to request a 'department or Minister of the Crown' to make available to the applicant any specified 'official information'.[170] It has been described as a 'constitutional measure.'[171] The term 'official information' is defined to mean 'information'[172] that is 'held'[173] by a department,[174] Minister of the Crown or organisation.[175] The right of access to personal information[176] (whether of an individual or a company) is provided separately from the general right to information.[177] The scope of the right varies according to the governing statute.[178] The access statutes require departments etc

169 *The Public's Right to Know: Review of the Official Information Legislation* (NZLC R 125), available at: http://r125.publications.lawcom.govt.nz/

170 In relation to information held by a local authority, the provision is the Local Government Official Information and Meetings Act 1987 s 10(1).

171 *Kelsey v Minister of Trade* [2015] NZHC 2497, [2016] 2 NZLR 218 at [19]-[22].

172 There is no definition of 'information'. As to the meaning given by the courts to 'information', see: *Commissioner of Police v Ombudsman* [1985] 1 NZLR 578 at 586, [1988] 1 NZLR 385 at 402 (CA) ('information' is 'that which informs, instructs, tells or makes aware'); *Ross v Tamaki City Council* [1990] DCR 11 (information under the Local Government Official Information and Meetings Act 1987 must be tangible or retrievable); *Aldous v Auckland City Council* [1990] DCR 385; *R v Harvey* [1991] 1 NZLR 242 at 246; *Herewini v Ministry of Transport* [1992] 3 NZLR 482 at 498; *Leach v Ministry of Transport* [1993] 1 NZLR 106 at 108. Excluded from 'official information' is certain information held by universities and information contained in library or museum material made or acquired and preserved solely for reference or exhibition purposes and certain other information: see Official Information Act 1982 s 2(1).

173 The Act does not define when information is 'held' by a department. See *R v Harvey* [1991] 1 NZLR 242 at 246.

174 Departments are those listed in Pt I of the First Schedule to the Ombudsmen Act 1975: Official Information Act 1982 s 2(1), but excluding the bodies listed in s 2(6).

175 Official Information Act 1982 s 2; Local Government Official Information and Meetings Act 1987 s 2(1). 'Organisations' are those named in Part II of the First Schedule to the Ombudsmen Act 1975 and those named in the First Schedule to the Official Information Act 1982. Certain organisations are excluded: see Official Information Act 1982 s 2(6).

176 That is, information that is about the person requesting the information. The distinction between 'personal' and 'non-personal' information has been described as 'both artificial and arbitrary': *Cornelius v Commissioner for Police* [1998] 3 NZLR 373 at 379; *cf Police v Keogh* [2000] 1 NZLR 736 at 742.

177 Requests for personal information by individuals about themselves are governed by the Privacy Act 1993. That Act provides that where an agency holds personal information in such a way that it can be readily retrieved, the individual about whom the information relates has a legal right, enforceable in a Court of law, to obtain confirmation from the agency of whether or not it holds such information and to have access to that information: s 6, principle 6(1) and s 11(i). This right applies to any individual who is a New Zealand citizen, or a permanent resident of New Zealand, or a person in New Zealand: Privacy Act 1993 ss 33 and 34 (s 2(1) defines 'individual' as a natural person). 'Personal information' is defined as being 'official information held about an identifiable person.' In *Commissioner of Police v Ombudsman* [1985] 1 NZLR 578 at 586, [1988] 1 NZLR 385 at 402 (CA), the Court took this to mean information about a person. Part IV of the Official Information Act 1982 (ss 24-27) is devoted to access to personal information by a body corporate. Section 24(1) bestows the right upon a body corporate to be given access to any personal information that is about that body corporate, subject ss 10 and 52. In relation to local authorities, the right of access by a company to information relating to itself is bestowed by the Local Government and Official Information Act 1987 s 23.

178 In the Official Information Act 1982 there is a 'principle of availability' (s 5) by which information held by a department should be made available unless there is a compelling reason not to. 'In contrast to the Official Information Act 1982, the focus of the Privacy Act 1993 is the protection of personal information, as opposed to the principle of availability under the Official Information Act 1982': *In the matter of C* [2005] NZFLR 56.

to give reasonable assistance to anyone using the Act.[179] The two main Acts also provide for publication schemes.[180]

51–019 The request

A request may be made orally or in writing, but it must have due particularity.[181] The department may refuse to answer a request that is frivolous or vexatious;[182] where the information requested is trivial;[183] where making the information available would involve substantial collation or research;[184] or where the information is or will shortly be publicly available.[185] Where a department receives a request but either does not hold the information sought and believes that another department does, or if it considers that the information requested is more closely connected with another department, then the former department may transfer the request to the latter department.[186]

51–020 The response

Within 20 working days of receiving a request, the department must inform the applicant whether access to the requested information is to be given and, if not, of the reasons for the decision.[187] The 20-working-day period may be extended for a reasonable period of time where the request is for a large quantity of information, requires searching through a large quantity of information, or requires consultations that cannot be completed within the original time limit.[188] If the requested information is not provided within the 20 working days or the extended period, the request is deemed to have been refused.[189] If the decision is to give access, that may take any of a number of forms: giving the applicant an opportunity to examine the

---

179 Official Information Act 1982 ss 13, 22(3), 23(3) and 24(3); Local Government Official Information and Meetings Act 1987 ss 11, 21(2), 22(2) and 23(2); Privacy Act 1993 s 38. The level of assistance that can be considered 'reasonable' under Privacy Act 1993 s 38 is subjective, and should take into account the ability of the person requiring access and the context: *Chief Executive of the Ministry of Social Development v Holmes* [2013] NZHC 672.

180 Official Information Act 1982 s 20. This requires the publication and updating of a document that describes the structure, functions, and responsibilities of all government departments and organisations subject to each of the Acts, as well as a description of the categories of documents held by each body and certain other details. Every person has a right of access to these last details: Official Information Act 1982 s 21.

181 Official Information Act 1982 s 12(2); Local Government Official Information and Meetings Act 1987 s 10(2). A request for personal information may be made by an agent: Official Information Act 1982 s 25(c); Local Government Official Information and Meetings Act 1987 s 24(c); Privacy Act 1993 s 45(c). A request for personal information made by a natural person under the Official Information Act 1982 is deemed to be a request under the Privacy Act 1993 s 6(1)(b).

182 Official Information Act 1982 s 18(h); Local Government Official Information and Meetings Act 1987 s 17(h); Privacy Act 1993 s 29(1)(j).

183 Official Information Act 1982 s 18(h); Local Government Official Information and Meetings Act 1987 s 17(h); Privacy Act 1993 s 29(1)(j).

184 Official Information Act 1982 s 18(f); Local Government Official Information and Meetings Act 1987 s 17(f); Privacy Act 1993 s 29(2)(a).

185 Official Information Act 1982 s 18(d); Local Government Official Information and Meetings Act 1987 s 17(d).

186 Official Information Act 1982 s 14; Local Government Official Information and Meetings Act 1987 s 12(b)(i); Privacy Act 1993 s 39. If the department in question has no grounds for believing either that another department possesses the requested information or that the requested information is more closely connected with another department, then the requested department may refuse the request: Official Information Act 1982 s 18(g).

187 Official Information Act 1982 ss 15(1), 22(3), 23(3) and 24(3); Local Government Official Information and Meetings Act 1987 ss 13 and 23(2); Privacy Act 1993 s 40(1)(a).

188 Official Information Act 1982 ss 15A(1)(a) and 24(3); Local Government Official Information and Meetings Act 1987 ss 14(1)(a) and 23(2); Privacy Act 1993 s 41(1)(a).

189 Official Information Act 1982 s 28(4) (in relation to a s 12 request). Where the request is made in such a form that the department does not recognise it as a request for information under the Act, then the deemed refusal provisions will not be engaged: *Chief Executive of the Ministry of Social Development v Holmes* [2013] NZHC 672.

document containing the information; providing a copy of it; providing information about a document's contents, etc.[190] If the decision is to refuse access, the department, etc must give reasons for the refusal and, if requested, the statutory grounds for that refusal.[191] A department, etc may only refuse to disclose information answering the terms of a proper request if it falls within one of the grounds of exemption.[192] In refusing a request, the department is not required to confirm or deny whether any information answering the terms of the request actually exists if to do so would be likely to damage security, defence, international relations, represent a breach of confidence, endanger individuals, reveal a trade secret or damage the economy.[193] A charge may be imposed for the disclosure of information, depending upon: the statute under which access is sought; whether the information sought is personal information; and whether the body to which the request is made is a public sector agency or a private sector agency.[194] Specific provision is made for excision of exempt information contained in a document.[195] Although there is no express power enabling a conditional release of information, there would appear to be an implicit power to do so, as the ombudsman is given power to investigate such conditions.[196] There is nothing proscribing the discretionary release of information that is exempt under the Act.[197]

51– 021 Exemptions generally

Exemptions under the New Zealand legislation divide into two broad classes: those that are engaged upon their terms being satisfied;[198] and those that will be disengaged if, in the circumstances, the withholding of particular information is outweighed by other considerations which render it desirable in the public interest to make that information available.[199] The exemptions may also be categorised into prejudice-based exemptions, which require that

---

[190] Official Information Act 1982 ss 16(1)(a)-(f) and 24(3); Local Government Official Information and Meetings Act 1987 ss 15(1)(a)-(f) and 23(2); Privacy Act 1993 s 42(1). The form of access must be that preferred by the applicant unless to do so would impair efficient administration and so forth: Official Information Act 1982 s 16(2); Local Government Official Information and Meetings Act 1987 s 15(2); Privacy Act 1993 s 42(2). This includes a requirement to make the information readable where it is stored in a way that is not visible to the applicant: *Commissioner of Police v District Court at Manukau* [2007] NZHC 101.

[191] Official Information Act 1982 s 19; Local Government Official Information and Meetings Act 1987 s 18.

[192] Official Information Act 1982 ss 18 and 27(1); Local Government Official Information and Meetings Act 1987 ss 17 and 26; Privacy Act 1993 s 30. This includes that a document containing the requested information cannot be found; Official Information Act 1982 s 18(e).

[193] Official Information Act 1982 s 10; Local Government Official Information and Meetings Act 1987 s 8; Privacy Act 1993 s 32.

[194] Official Information Act 1982 ss 15(2) and 24(3); Local Government Official Information and Meetings Act 1987 s 13(1A); Privacy Act 1993 ss 35, 36 and 59.

[195] Official Information Act 1982 ss 17(1), 22(4) and 24(3); Local Government Official Information and Meetings Act 1987 ss 16(1) and 23(2); Privacy Act 1993 ss 21(3) and 43(1).

[196] Official Information Act 1982 s 28(1)(c); Local Government Official Information and Meetings Act 1987 s 27(1)(c); Privacy Act 1993 s 66(2)(a)(iii), where the power is vested in the Privacy Commissioner. Examples of conditions imposed are: (1) where information was released on the condition that the information could only be published together with a statement or explanation from the holder of the information; (2) where information was to be used for Court proceedings on the basis of undertakings by the parties that the information would not be made available to the media.

[197] Although where its disclosure breaches the privacy principles set out in the Privacy Act 1993 this may give rise to a complaint either under that Act or to the Ombudsman. Discretionary disclosure does not attract the protection given by the Official Information Act 1982 s 48.

[198] Official Information Act 1982 ss 18(c)(i) and 52(3); Local Government Official Information and Meetings Act 1987 ss 17(c)(i) and 44(2); Privacy Act 1993 s 7.

[199] Official Information Act 1982 ss 18(c)(ii) and 52(1); Local Government Official Information and Meetings Act 1987 ss 17(c)(ii) and 44(1); Privacy Act 1993 s 29(1)(i).

disclosure 'be likely to prejudice' an identified interest,[200] and pure class-based exemptions, which do not require that prejudice flow from disclosure of the requested information. The applicability of exemptions varies according to whether the information sought is personal information and, if so, whether the person is a corporate person. In considering exemptions, the overarching principle is that information is to be made available unless there is good reason for withholding it.[201] Certificates may be issued by the Prime Minister or the Attorney-General on the grounds that disclosure of the requested information would be likely to prejudice: the defence or security of New Zealand or one of its dependencies; international relations; or the investigation, etc of offences.[202] The effect of a certificate is that the Ombudsman may not recommend the disclosure of the information to which the certificate relates.

51–022 The absolute exemptions

Information may be withheld without a consideration of the public interest where:

(1) Disclosure would be likely to prejudice the security or defence of New Zealand or certain external dependencies or the international relations of the New Zealand Government.[203]

(2) Disclosure would be likely to prejudice the entrusting of information to the Government of New Zealand on a basis of confidence by the Government of any other country or any agency of such a government, or by any international organisation.[204]

(3) Disclosure would be likely to prejudice the maintenance of the law, including the prevention, investigation, and detection of offences, and the right to a fair trial.[205]

(4) Disclosure would be likely to endanger the safety of any person.[206]

(5) Disclosure would be likely to damage seriously the New Zealand economy by disclosing prematurely decisions to change or continue government economic or financial policies relating to: exchange rates or the control of overseas exchange transactions; the regulation of banking or credit; taxation; the stability, control, and adjustment of prices of goods and services, rents, and other costs, and rates of wages, salaries, and other incomes; the borrowing of money by the New Zealand government; and the entering into overseas trade agreements.[207]

(6) Disclosure would be contrary to the provisions of another enactment.[208]

---

[200] The High Court has held that the test to be applied in determining whether withholding the information is necessary to protect one of the specified interests is one of 'reasonable' necessity, rather than 'strict' necessity: *Television New Zealand Ltd v Ombudsman* [1992] 1 NZLR 106 at 118. The 'would be likely' test has been held not to mean 'more likely than not', but to involve a lesser threshold, namely: 'a serious or real and substantial risk to a protected interest, a risk that might well eventuate': *Commissioner of Police v Ombudsman* [1988] 1 NZLR 385 (CA).

[201] Official Information Act 1982 s 5. *Kelsey v Minister of Trade* [2015] NZHC 2497, [2016] 2 NZLR 218 at [118]. The Courts have rejected the notion that there is a general presumption that exemptions are to be narrowly construed: *Commissioner of Police v Ombudsman* [1988] 1 NZLR 385 (CA).

[202] Official Information Act 1982 s 31.

[203] Official Information Act 1982 ss 6(a), 7 and 27(1)(a); Privacy Act 1993 ss 27(1)(a) and 27(2)(a)-(c).

[204] Official Information Act 1982 ss 6(b) and 27(1)(a); Privacy Act 1993 s 27(1)(b).

[205] Official Information Act 1982 ss 6(c) and 27(1)(a); Local Government Official Information and Meetings Act 1987 ss 6(a) and 26(1)(a); Privacy Act 1993 s 27(1)(c). See *Nicholl v Chief Executive of the Department of Work and Income* [2003] 3 NZLR 426 at [17].

[206] Official Information Act 1982 ss 6(d) and 27(1)(a); Local Government Official Information and Meetings Act 1987 ss 6(b) and 26(1)(a); Privacy Act 1993 s 27(1)(d).

[207] Official Information Act 1982 ss 6(e) and 27(1)(a).

[208] Official Information Act 1982 ss 18(c)(i), 27(1)(a) and 52(3)(b); Local Government Official Information and Meetings Act 1987 ss 17(c)(i), 26(1)(a) and 44(2)(b); Privacy Act 1993 s 7(2)-(3).

(7) Disclosure would be a contempt of court or of the House of Representatives.[209]

51–023 The qualified exemptions

The remaining exemptions involve a two-stage process. First, a consideration of whether withholding the requested information is necessary in order to protect particular interests or to avoid particular prejudice. Secondly, if it is so necessary, to consider whether the withholding of the information is outweighed by other considerations that nevertheless render it desirable in the public interest to make that information available. So far as the first stage is concerned, this will be satisfied where the withholding of the information is necessary:

(1) To protect the privacy of natural persons, including that of deceased natural persons.[210]

(2) To protect information where the making available of that information would disclose a trade secret, or would be likely to unreasonably prejudice the commercial position of the person who supplied or who is the subject of the information.[211]

(3) To protect information which is subject to an obligation of confidence or which any person has been or could be compelled to provide under the authority of any enactment.[212]

(4) To avoid prejudice to measures protecting the health or safety of members of the public.[213]

(5) To avoid prejudice to the substantial economic interests of New Zealand.[214]

(6) To avoid prejudice to measures that prevent or mitigate material loss to members of the public.[215]

(7) To maintain the constitutional conventions for the time being which protect: the confidentiality of communications by or with the Sovereign or her representative; collective and individual ministerial responsibility; the political neutrality of officials; and the confidentiality of advice tendered by ministers of the Crown and officials (these reasons are not applicable in the case of local authorities).[216]

(8) To maintain the effective conduct of public affairs, through the free and frank expression of opinions by or between or to ministers or members of a specified organisation or officers and employees of any department, organisation, or local authority in the course of their duty; or through the protection of such ministers, members, officers, and employees from improper pressure or harassment.[217]

---

[209] Official Information Act 1982 ss 18(c)(ii), 27(1)(a) and 52(1); Local Government Official Information and Meetings Act 1987 ss 17(c)(ii), 26(1)(a) and 44(1); Privacy Act 1993 s 29(1)(i).

[210] Official Information Act 1982 ss 9(2)(a) and 27(1)(b); Local Government Official Information and Meetings Act 1987 ss 7(2)(a) and 26(1)(b); Privacy Act 1993 s 29(1)(a). Although not involving a request under the Act, *Mafart and anor v Television New Zealand* [2006] NZCA 183 is illustrative of privacy interests being subordinated to the public interest by making important Court proceedings accessible to the public (video-tape of the committal proceedings of the Rainbow Warrior bombers). See further: *Gravatt v Auckland Coroner's Court* [2013] NZHC 390 at [80].

[211] Official Information Act 1982 ss 9(2)(b) and 27(1)(a); Local Government Official Information and Meetings Act 1987 ss 7(2)(b) and 26(1)(a); Privacy Act 1993 s 28(1)(a)-(b).

[212] Official Information Act 1982 ss 9(2)(ba) and 27(1)(c); Local Government Official Information and Meetings Act 1987 ss 7(2)(c) and 26(1)(c); Privacy Act 1993 s 29(1)(b). The courts have rejected the notion that the contractual provisions requiring confidentiality to be kept necessarily protected the information from being disclosed under the Act: *Wyatt Co (NZ) Ltd v Queenstown-Lakes District Council* [1991] 2 NZLR 180.

[213] Official Information Act 1982 s 9(2)(c); Local Government Official Information and Meetings Act 1987 s 7(2)(d); Privacy Act 1993 s 29(1)(c).

[214] Official Information Act 1982 s 9(2)(d).

[215] Official Information Act 1982 s 9(2)(e); Local Government Official Information and Meetings Act 1987 s 7(2)(e).

[216] Official Information Act 1982 s 9(2)(f).

[217] Official Information Act 1982 s 9(2)(g); Local Government Official Information and Meetings Act 1987 s 7(2)(f).

(9) To maintain legal professional privilege.[218]

(10) To enable a minister, department, specified organisation, or local authority holding the information to carry out, without prejudice or disadvantage, commercial activities.[219]

(11) To enable a minister, department, specified organisation, or local authority holding the information to carry on negotiations without prejudice or disadvantage, including commercial or industrial negotiations.[220]

(12) To prevent the disclosure or use of official information for improper gain or improper advantage.[221]

51–024 Appeals and enforcement

The first stage of the appeal system lies with the Ombudsman, who, upon a complaint, may investigate and review any decision to refuse access or to refuse to confirm or deny the existence of requested information.[222] The Ombudsman has all the normal powers under the Ombudsmen Act 1975, including compelling the production of information. After investigation, the Ombudsman must make a report with recommendations, setting out whether it is considered that the original decision was wrong or unreasonable.[223] The department is obliged to observe a recommendation of the Ombudsman unless the Governor-General, by Order in Council, otherwise directs.[224] Where no Order in Council is made, a person dissatisfied with the Ombudsman's recommendation may have it and the original decision judicially reviewed. Where an Order in Council is made, an appeal may be made to the High Court on grounds that it was wrong in law[225] and, from there, to the Court of Appeal.[226] There is statutory protection for those who in good faith release official information under the access acts.[227]

5. CANADA

51–025 Introduction

In Canada, legislation giving a general right of access to government-held information originated in the provinces. In 1977 Nova Scotia became the first Canadian jurisdiction to pass such legislation, followed by New Brunswick in 1978, Newfoundland in 1981 and Quebec in 1982.[228] Federal legislation giving a general right of access to government-held information was

---

218 Official Information Act 1982 ss 9(2)(h) and 27(1)(h); Local Government Official Information and Meetings Act 1987 ss 7(2)(g) and 26(1)(h); Privacy Act 1993 s 29(1)(f).

219 Official Information Act 1982 s 9(2)(i); Local Government Official Information and Meetings Act 1987 s 7(2)(h).

220 Official Information Act 1982 s 9(2)(j); Local Government Official Information and Meetings Act 1987 s 7(2)(i).

221 Official Information Act 1982 s 9(2)(k); Local Government Official Information and Meetings Act 1987 s 7(2)(j).

222 Official Information Act 1982 s 28(1); Local Government Official Information and Meetings Act 1987 s 27(1).

223 Official Information Act 1982 s 30(1); Local Government Official Information and Meetings Act 1987 s 29(1).

224 Official Information Act 1982 s 32(1); Local Government Official Information and Meetings Act 1987 s 31(1).

225 Official Information Act 1982 s 32B; Local Government Official Information and Meetings Act 1987 s 34.

226 Official Information Act 1982 s 32C; Local Government Official Information and Meetings Act 1987 s 35.

227 Official Information Act 1982 s 48(1); Local Government Official Information and Meetings Act 1987 s 41(1); Privacy Act 1993 s 115(1). If the original supplier to the department did so in breach of confidence, that person will not enjoy the statutory protection where that information is disclosed under an access Act: *Attorney-General v Davidson* [1994] 3 NZLR 143 (CA).

228 The original Nova Scotia Act was replaced in 1993 by the Freedom of Information and Protection of Privacy Act 1993 (Nova Scotia); Right to Information Act 1978 (New Brunswick); Freedom of Information Act 1990

passed in June 1982. Called the Access to Information Act, it was enacted at the same time as the Privacy Act,[229] and they came into force on 1 July 1983. All of the remaining provincial and territorial jurisdictions subsequently introduced similar legislation.[230] Since its enactment, the Access to Information Act has been amended on three occasions, all of which have been of relatively minor significance.[231]

51– 026 Scope of the right

Section 4 of the Act gives Canadian citizens and permanent residents a right of access to records under the control of a government institution, subject only to specific exclusions[232] and exemptions.[233] The Act gives the Governor in Council power to extend this right to others, and in 1989 the access right was extended to include all individuals and incorporated entities present in the country.[234] The unit of disclosure under the Access to Information Act is a 'record',[235] as opposed to a 'document' or 'information'. In order for the right to arise, a record must be 'under the control'[236] of a 'government institution'.[237] Decisions granting or refusing

---

(Newfoundland); An Act respecting Access to documents held by public bodies and the Protection of personal information 1982 (Quebec).

229 The purpose of the Privacy Act is, broadly speaking, to protect the privacy of individuals with respect to personal information about themselves held by a government institution and to provide individuals with a right of access to that information: *Dagg v Canada (Minister of Finance)* [1997] SCJ 63 at [61]; *Canada (Attorney-General) v Canada (Information Commissioner)* [2002] FCT 128.

230 Freedom of Information Act 1998 (Manitoba); Freedom of Information and Protection of Privacy Act 1992 (Saskatchewan); Freedom of Information and Protection of Privacy Act 1988 (Ontario); Freedom of Information and Protection of Privacy Act 1996 (British Columbia); Freedom of Information and Protection of Privacy Act 1994 (Alberta); Freedom of Information and Protection of Privacy Act 2001 (Prince Edward Island); Access to Information and Protection of Privacy Act 1994 (Northwest Territories); Access to Information and Protection of Privacy Act 1996 (Yukon Territory).

231 In 1992, the Act was amended to deal with the provision of records in alternative formats to individuals with sensory disabilities. In 1999, it was amended to make it a criminal offence to intentionally obstruct the right of access by destroying, altering, hiding or falsifying a record, or directing anyone else to do so. In 2001, it was amended by the Anti-terrorism Act which provides that a certificate by the Attorney-General prohibiting the disclosure of information for the purpose of protecting national defence or national security will override the provisions of the Access to Information Act.

232 Published, library and museum material are generally excluded from the operation of the Act: Access to Information Act s 68. So, too, confidences of the Queen's Privy Council for Canada (ie cabinet material): Access to Information Act s 69. In relation to cabinet material generally, see: *Canada (Minister of Environment) v Canada (Information Commissioner)* [2003] FCA 68.

233 Exemptions, which are provided for by Access to Information Act ss 13-26, are considered at §§51– 029 to 51– 032.

234 Access to Information Act Extension Order No 1 (SOR/89-207).

235 Access to Information Act s 3 defines 'record' to mean any documentary material, regardless of medium or form. It has been held that 'software' does not constitute a record; a 'record' can include something not yet in existence but that can be assembled from data already held: *Yeager v Canada (Correctional Service)* [2003] FCA 30.

236 The Act does not define when a record is 'under the control' of an institution. The authorities indicate that any document that happens to be in the custody or in the hands of a government institution, regardless of how or upon what conditions, will be under its control: *Montana Band of Indians v Canada (Minister of Indian and Northern Affairs)* [1989] 1 FC 143 (TD), 51 DLR (4th) 306; *Ottawa Football Club v Canada (Minister of Fitness and Amateur Sports)* [1989] 2 FC 480 (TD); *Canada Post Corp v Canada (Minister of Public Works)* [1995] 2 FC 110, 30 Admin LR (2d) 242, affirming [1993] 3 FC 320, 19 Admin LR (2d) 230; *Rubin v Canada (Minister of Foreign Affairs and International Trade)* [2001] FCT 440 (a returned document is not 'under the control' of an institution); *Federation des Producteurs v Canadian Food Inspection Agency* [2007] FC 704. In relation to documents obtained by the institution from a third party through court disclosure or discovery, see *Andersen Consulting v Canada* [2001] 2 FC 324.

237 Access to Information Act s 3 simply defines a 'government institution' as any department or ministry, body or office listed in Sch I of the Act. Schedule I lists 19 departments and ministries and a number of other bodies and offices. It also applies to Crown corporations and wholly-owned subsidiaries. But the Canadian Broadcasting Corporation enjoys similar exemption to that enjoyed by the BBC in the United Kingdom: Access to Information Act s 68.1. As to ministerial offices, see: *Canada (Attorney-General) v Canada (Information Commissioner)* [2000] FCA 26. As to the meaning of the phrase 'government institution,' see *Information Commissioner v Minister for National Defence*

access must be made by the 'head' of each government institution, with the head of each institution being designated by regulation.[238]

51–027 The request

A request must be made in writing.[239] There is no power to refuse to answer a request that is frivolous, vexatious or abusive. The only control over burdensome requests lies in the fees regime.[240] Where a government institution receives a request but considers that another government institution has a greater interest in the record, the former institution may transfer the request to the latter institution.[241] The Act provides for a publication scheme.[242] The head of a government institution must give every reasonable assistance to a person making a request and to respond promptly.[243]

51–028 The response

Within 30 days of receiving a request, a government institution must inform the applicant whether access to the requested record is to be given and, if so, to provide it.[244] The 30-day period may be extended 'for a reasonable period of time' where the request is for a large number of records, requires a search through a large number of records, requires consultations that cannot be completed within the original time limit, or where notice has to be given to third parties.[245] If a record is not provided within the original 30 days or the extended period, the request is deemed to have been refused.[246] If, after processing a request, it is decided to give access, that access takes the form of an opportunity to examine the record or the provision of a copy of the record.[247] If the institution decides to refuse access, it must cite the statutory ground for refusing access or what it would be if the record existed.[248] In refusing a request, the institution is not required to confirm whether any record answering the terms of the request actually exists.[249] An institution must so far as practicable excise exempted portions of records

---

[2009] FCA 175, upholding [2009] 2 FCR 86 (considering the circumstances in which a record physically located in a Minister's office is nevertheless under the control of the government institution over which he presides); *Canada (Information Commissioner) v Canada (Minister of National Defence)* [2011] SCC 25.

238 Access to Information Act Heads of Government Institutions Designation Order SI 1983/113.

239 Access to Information Regulations (SOR/83-507) reg 4.

240 Access to Information Act s 11 and Access to Information Regulations (SOR/83-507) reg 7 provide for an applicant to be charged an application fee, not exceeding $25, and also to be charged for: reasonable search and preparation time in excess of five hours; the costs of producing a record in an alternative format; the production of a machine-readable record; and reproduction costs. In all cases, specific amounts are set by regulation. Heads of institutions can require applicants to pay deposits, or to waive or repay a fee. The ability to use the fees regime to control what are considered to be frivolous or vexatious requests would appear to be limited: *Rubin v Canada (Minister of Finance)* (1987) 9 FTR 317, 35 DLR (4th) 517.

241 Access to Information Act s 8; Access to Information Regulations (SOR/83-507) reg 6.

242 Access to Information Act s 5.

243 Access to Information Act s 4(2.1).

244 Access to Information Act s 7.

245 Access to Information Act s 9.

246 As to the review by the courts of decisions to extend the time within which to respond to a request, see: *Canada (Information Commissioner) v Canada (Minister of External Affairs)* [1989] 1 FC 3, 32 Admin LR 265; *Canada (Information Commissioner) v Canada (Minister of External Affairs)* [1990] 3 FC 514; *X v Canada (Minister of National Defence)* [1991] 1 FC 670.

247 Access to Information Act s 12(1); Access to Information Regulations (SOR/83-507) regs 5 and 8.

248 Access to Information Act s 10(1).

249 Access to Information Act s 10(2).

and provide access to the rest.[250] An institution must make reasonable efforts to give a third party that supplied information to it notice of its intention to disclose that information.[251]

51–029 Exemptions generally

The Access to Information Act divides exemptions into mandatory and discretionary exemptions.[252] Mandatory exemptions must be invoked; discretionary exemptions allow the head of a government institution to decide whether the exemption needs to be invoked. Each exemption is based on either an 'injury test' or 'class test'. Exemptions which incorporate an 'injury test' take into consideration whether the disclosure of certain information could 'reasonably be expected' to be injurious to a specified interest.[253] 'Class test' exemptions are those applying to a record that matches the description given in the statutory provision; in order to engage the exemption there is no need to demonstrate any likelihood of injury resulting from disclosure of the record. Two of the mandatory exemptions include public interest overrides. These allow the head of a government institution to disclose information where this would be in the public interest as defined in the provision.[254]

51–030 Onus, purpose clause and conclusive certificates

Although there is no specific provision in the Act specifying whether it is the institution or the applicant who must demonstrate the applicability or inapplicability of a ground of exemption, the courts have held that where there is a contest between disclosure and non-disclosure of a record, the burden rests upon the party resisting disclosure.[255] This approach is consistent with the Act's purpose clause, which includes a statement of principle that government information should be available to the public and that necessary exceptions to the right of access should be limited and specific.[256] Until late 2001, the Access to Information Act did not include any mechanism for taking particular documents outside of its operation or for reducing the ability to review a non-disclosure decision. The Anti-terrorism Act (2001) amended the Access to Information Act by adding a provision[257] which provides that a certificate by the Attorney-

---

[250] Access to Information Act s 25. See *Sheldon Blank & Gateway Industries v Canada (Minister of Environment)* [2001] FCA 374.

[251] Access to Information Act s 27(1). The party can make representations in relation to the proposed disclosure: s 28. Similarly, if the Information Commissioner proposes to recommend disclosure, notice must be given to the third party: s 35(2)(c). As to the nature of the obligation to give a third party notice, see *Canada (Minister of Health) v Merck Frosst Canada Ltd* [2009] FCA 166, affirmed by *Merck Frosst Canada Ltd v Canada (Minister of Health)* [2012] SCC 3.

[252] There are no mandatory exemptions in the FOIA.

[253] The courts have interpreted this to mean that there must be a reasonable expectation of probable harm: *Canada Packers Inc v Canada (Minister of Agriculture)* [1989] 1 FC 47. Mere assertions will not suffice: *Jacques Whitford Environment Ltd v Canada (Minister of National Defence)* [2001] FCT 556; *Wyeth-ayerst Canada Inc v Canada (Attorney-General)* [2002] FCT 133; *Geophysical Service Inc v Canada-Newfoundland Offshore Petroleum Board* [2003] FCT 507; *Merck Frosst Canada Ltd v Canada (Minister of Health)* [2012] SCC 3.

[254] Access to Information Act s 20(6) permits the head of an institution to disclose commercial information from a third party if this would be in the public interest as it relates to health, safety or protection of the environment, and the public interest in disclosure clearly outweighs any injury to the third party. Section 19 of the Access to Information Act provides a similar public interest override in relation to the exemption for personal information. The consideration of the public interest only as it concerns the specific exemption, rather than in general, is the model adopted in the FOIA.

[255] *Maislin Industries Ltd v Minister for Industry, Trade & Commerce* [1984] 1 FC 939; *Rubin v Canada (Canada Mortgage and Housing Corp)* [1989] 1 FC 265; *Canada (Information Commissioner) v Canada (Minister of External Affairs)* [1990] 3 FC 665. This also applies where a third party resists disclosure: *Wyeth-ayerst Canada Inc v Canada (Attorney-General)* [2002] FCT 133; *Cistel Technology Inc v Canada (Correctional Service)* [2002] FCT 253; *Blank v Canada (Minister of Environment)* [2006] FC 1253. Where proceedings are on foot, the position is governed by Access to Information Act s 48.

[256] Access to Information Act s 2.

[257] Access to Information Act s 69(1).

General prohibiting the disclosure of information for the purpose of protecting national defence or national security will override the provisions of the Access to Information Act. The certificates are subject to review by the Federal Court of Appeal.

51–031 Mandatory exemptions

There are seven class-based mandatory exemptions:

(1) Information received in confidence from other governments.[258]
(2) Information obtained or prepared by the Royal Canadian Mounted Police on provincial or municipal policing services.[259]
(3) Personal information.[260]
(4) Trade secrets of a third party.[261]
(5) Financial, commercial, scientific or technical information received in confidence from a third party.[262]

---

258 Access to Information Act s 13(1). The exemption becomes discretionary if the body from whom the information was obtained either consents to its disclosure or makes it public itself: s 13(1). See *Sherman v Minister of National Revenue* [2003] FCA 202 (tax information exchanged under convention).

259 Access to Information Act s 16(3).

260 Access to Information Act s 19. The personal information exception has been the most invoked: http://www.armaedfoundation.org/pdfs/Freedom_of_Information_in_US_UK_and_Canada.pdf. As to the division between the Access to Information Act and the Privacy Act and the meaning of 'personal information', see: *Canada (Information Commissioner) v Canada (Minister of Industry)* [2002] FCA 212, (2002) 284 DLR (4th) 293; *Information Commissioner v Royal Canadian Mounted Police* [2003] 1 SCR 66; *Yaeger v National Parole Board* [2008] FCA 13. The Act adopts the definition of 'personal information' given in the Privacy Act s 3, which is that it is 'information about an identifiable individual that is recorded in any form' and then proceeds to give a series of specific inclusions. Personal information has been held to extend to qualitative evaluations of an employee's performance (*Canada (Information Commissioner) v Canada (Solicitor General)* [1988] 3 FC 557) and to the remuneration levels of various chairmen, heads, and presiding officials of an agency (*Rubin v Canada (Clerk of the Privy Council)* (1993) 62 FTR 287); see also: *Canada (Information Commissioner) v Canada (Cultural Property Export Review Board)* [2001] FCT 1054; *Canada (Information Commissioner) v Canada (Royal Canadian Mounted Police)* [2001] 3 FC 70, [2001] FCA 56; *Canada (Information Commissioner) v Canada (Minister of Citizenship and Immigration)* [2002] FCA 270; *Canada (Information Commissioner) v Transportation Accident Investigation and Safety Board* [2006] FCA 157 [2007] 1 FCR 203 (holding that recordings of air traffic controllers did not constitute 'personal information'); *Canada (Information Commissioner) v Canada (Minister of National Defence)* [2011] SCC 25. An 'identifiable individual' does not include a corporation: *Geophysical Service Inc v Canada-Newfoundland Offshore Petroleum Board* [2003] FCT 507. As to the level of detail that makes information 'personal information', see: *Gordon v Minister of Health* [2008] FC 258; *Information Commissioner v Canada (Public Safety and Emergency Preparedness)* [2019] FC 1279. The exemption is subject to a public interest override: s 19(6).

261 Access to Information Act s 20(1)(a). The Courts have given this exemption a narrow interpretation: *Merck Frosst Canada Inc v Canada (Minister of Health and Welfare)* (1988) 20 FTR 73; *Canada Post Corp v Canada (Minister of Public Works)* [1993] 3 FC 320, affirmed (1993), 64 FTR 62; *Matol Botanical International Inc v Canada (Minister of National Health & Welfare)* (1994) 84 FTR 168; *Société Gamma Inc v Canada (Secretary of State)* (1994) 79 FTR 42; *PricewaterhouseCoopers, LLP v Canada (Minister of Canadian Heritage)* [2001] FCT 1040; *Wyeth-ayerst Canada Inc v Canada (Attorney-General)* [2002] FCT 133; *Cistel Technology Inc v Canada (Correctional Service)* [2002] FCT 253; *St Joseph Corp v Canada (Public Works and Government Services)* [2002] FCT 274; *Canada (Minister of Health) v Merck Frosst Canada Ltd* [2009] FCA 166, affirmed by *Merck Frosst Canada Ltd v Canada (Minister of Health)* [2012] SCC 3.

262 Access to Information Act s 20(1)(b). The courts have held that the information must still have its confidentiality at the time of the request in order for the exemption to operate: *Maislin Industries Ltd v Canada (Minister for Industry, Trade & Commerce)* [1984] 1 FC 939. The general approach of the courts has been to scrutinise carefully claims of confidentiality, whether these claims are made by the government institution or by the third party that supplied the information: *Noël v Great Lakes Pilotage Authority Ltd* [1988] 2 FC 77; *Intercontinental Packers Ltd v Canada (Minister of Agriculture)* (1987) 14 FTR 142; *Ottawa Football Club v Canada (Minister of Fitness and Amateur Sports)* [1989] 2 FC 480; *Canada Packers Inc v Canada (Minister of Agriculture)* [1989] 1 FC 47; *PricewaterhouseCoopers, LLP v Canada (Minister of Canadian Heritage)* [2001] FCT 1040; *Jacques Whitford Environment Ltd v Canada (Minister of National Defence)* [2001] FCT 556; *Canada (Minister of Health & Welfare) v Merck Frosst Canada & Co* [2005] FCA 215 (even if the format is different, once the information is in the public domain it can no longer be confidential); *Minister of Public Works and Government Services v The Hi-Rise Group Inc* [2004] FCA 99, (2004) 238 DLR (4th) 44 (the rent paid by a government agency for premises held not to be confidential: 'when a would-be contractor sets out to win a government contract through a confidential bidding process, he or she cannot expect that the monetary terms, in the event that the bid succeeds, will remain confidential'), and similarly *131 Queen Street Limited v Canada (Attorney-General)* [2007] FC 347; *Heinz Company of Canada Ltd v Canada (Attorney-General)* [2006] FCA 378 (rejecting a claim by Heinz that information supplied by it to government inspectors was confidential). See also *Merck Frosst Canada Ltd v Canada (Minister of Health)* [2012] SCC 3, finding that financial, commercial, scientific or technical information need not have an

(6) Information the disclosure of which is restricted by or pursuant to any provision set out in Sch II to the Act.[263]

(6A) Information held by the Information Commissioner, the Privacy Commissioner, the Auditor-General, the Chief Electoral Officer and certain other office-holders, created or obtained by them in the course of an investigation, examination or audit conducted by them.[264]

There are two injury-based mandatory exemptions:

(7) Records the disclosure of which could reasonably be expected to cause loss or gain to a third party or prejudice to competitive position.[265]

(8) Records the disclosure of which could reasonably be expected to cause interference with contractual or other negotiations of a third party.[266]

51–032 Discretionary exemptions

There are ten class-based discretionary exemptions. These grant exemption from disclosure for records that contain:

(1) Information obtained or prepared by listed investigative bodies.[267]

(2) Information on techniques or plans for investigations.[268]

(3) Trade secrets or valuable financial, commercial, scientific or technical information belonging to the Government of Canada[269] or to various government-related agencies.[270]

(4) Advice or recommendations developed by or for a government institution or a minister of the Crown.[271]

(5) Any account of governmental consultations or deliberations in which government

---

'inherent value' and that 'administrative details' such as page and volume numbering do no qualify under the category. The supply of information to a government institution on a confidential basis, while a relevant factor, will not be determinative, as a third party cannot trump the rights conferred by the Act: *Canadian Tobacco Manufacturers' Council v Canada (Minister of National Revenue)* [2003] FC 1037.

[263] Access to Information Act s 24. The courts have said that it was intended that the invocation of provisions in other statutes to limit disclosure was intended to be as restrictive as possible: *Canada (Information Commissioner) v Canada (Immigration Appeal Board)* [1988] 3 FC 477.

[264] Access to Information Act ss 16.1 - 16.5.

[265] Access to Information Act s 20(1)(c). The courts have treated claims for this exemption with circumspection, requiring real evidence to support the reasonable expectation and not just surmise: *Burns Meats Ltd v Canada (Minister of Agriculture)* (1987) 14 FTR 137; *Glaxo Canada Inc v Canada (Minister of National Health & Welfare)* (1992) 41 CPR (3d) 176; *Cyanamid Canada Inc v Canada (Minister of National Health and Welfare)* (1992) 45 CPR (3d) 390; *Prud'homme v Canada (Canadian International Development Agency)* (1994) 85 FTR 302; *Matol Botanical International Inc v Canada (Minister of National Health & Welfare)* (1994) 84 FTR 168; *Jacques Whitford Environment Ltd v Canada (Minister of National Defence)* [2001] FCT 556; *Brookfield Lepage Johnson Controls Facility Management Services v Canada (Minister of Public Works and Government Services)* [2004] FCA 214.

[266] Access to Information Act s 20(1)(d). The courts have required the negotiations to be on foot and for the interference to amount to actual obstruction: *Société Gamma Inc v Canada (Secretary of State)* (1994) 79 FTR 42; *Saint John Shipbuilding Ltd v Canada (Minister of Supply and Services)* (1990) 67 DLR (4th) 315.

[267] Access to Information Act s 16(1)(a).

[268] Access to Information Act s 16(1)(b). For an example of its application, see *Rubin v Canada (Solicitor General)* (1986) 1 FTR 157.

[269] Access to Information Act s 18(a).

[270] Access to Information Act s 18.1.

[271] Access to Information Act s 21(1)(a). As to the meaning of 'advice or recommendations', see: *Canada Inc v Canada (Minister of Industry)* [2002] 1 FC 421. There is an exception where the record relates to a decision that is made in the exercise of a discretionary power or an adjudicative function and that affects the rights of a person: Access to Information Act s 21(2). Factual information falls outside the exemption: *Canadian Council of Christian Charities v Canada (Minister of Finance)* [1999] 4 FC 245; *Canada (Information Commissioner) v Canada (Minister of the Environment)* [2007] 3 FCR 125.

employees or a minister participates.[272]

(6) Government negotiation plans.[273]

(7) Government personnel or organisational plans.[274]

(8) Solicitor-client privileged information.[275]

(9) Information that is likely to be published within 90 days.

(9A) Draft internal audit reports of a government institution.[276]

There are nine injury-based discretionary exemptions. These apply to records the disclosure of which could 'reasonably be expected' to cause:[277]

(10) Injury to the conduct of federal-provincial affairs.[278]

(11) Injury to the conduct of international affairs, or to the defence of Canada or allied states.[279]

(12) Injury to law enforcement or conduct of lawful investigations.[280]

(13) Harm in facilitating the commission of a criminal offence.[281]

(14) Threat to an individual's safety.[282]

(15) Prejudice to the competitive position of government or to interfere with contractual

---

[272] Access to Information Act s 21(1)(b). There is an exception where the account relates to a decision that is made in the exercise of a discretionary power or an adjudicative function and that affects the rights of a person: Access to Information Act s 21(2). The courts have not inquired into the reasons for invoking this exemption: provided that the record answers the description, that will suffice: *Canada (Information Commissioner) v Canadian Radio-television and Telecommunications Commission* [1986] 3 FC 413; *Re Rubin and President of CMHC* (1987) 36 DLR (4th) 22. Factual information falls outside the exemption: *Canadian Council of Christian Charities v Canada (Minister of Finance)* [1999] 4 FC 245; *Canada (Information Commissioner) v Canada (Minister of the Environment)* [2007] 3 FCR 125.

[273] Access to Information Act s 21(1)(c). There is an exception where the record relates to a decision that is made in the exercise of a discretionary power or an adjudicative function and that affects the rights of a person: Access to Information Act s 21(2).

[274] Access to Information Act s 21(1)(d). There is an exception where the record relates to a decision that is made in the exercise of a discretionary power or an adjudicative function and that affects the rights of a person: Access to Information Act s 21(2).

[275] Access to Information Act s 23. The common law test of privilege is applied, including concepts of waiver: *Weiler v Canada (Minister of Justice)* [1991] 3 FC 617; *Wells v Canada (Minister of Transport)* (1995) 63 CPR (3d) 201; *Professional Institute of the Public Service of Canada v Canadian Museum of Nature* (1995) 63 CPR (3d) 449; *Canadian Jewish Congress v Canada (Minister of Employment and Immigration)* [1996] 1 FC 268; *Stevens v Canada (Prime Minister)* [1998] 4 FC 89; *Sheldon Blank & Gateway Industries v Canada (Minister for Environment)* [2001] FCA 374 (whether privilege applies to documents incorporated by reference); *St Joseph Corp v Canada (Public Works and Government Services)* [2002] FCT 274; *Canada (Information Commissioner) v Canada (Minister of Public Safety and Emergency Preparedness)* [2013] FCA 104. Litigation privilege is treated as coming to an end at the conclusion of proceedings: *Minister of Justice v Blank* [2006] SCC 39, [2006] 2 SCR 319, (2006) 270 DLR (4th) 257. The Supreme Court held that even if the documents were covered by litigation privilege, that would not prevent disclosure of a party's abuse of process or similar blameworthy conduct.

[276] Access to Information Act s 22.1. But only for 15 years after its creation and not once the final report has been published.

[277] Access to Information Act s 26.

[278] Access to Information Act s 14.

[279] Access to Information Act s 15. This includes information relating to military strategy, weapons, military deployment, or intelligence. It also includes diplomatic correspondence and cryptographic systems. The courts have shown themselves comparatively deferential to respondent claims of exemption under defence grounds: *Canada (Information Commissioner) v Canada (Minister of National Defence)* [1990] 3 FC 22; *X v Canada (Minister of National Defence)* (1992) 58 FTR 93; *X v Canada (Minister of National Defence)* [1992] 1 FC 77.

[280] Access to Information Act s 16(1)(c). The courts have required that the respondent identify a particular investigation that would be prejudiced, and declined to uphold a refusal to disclose upon an assertion that investigations generally would be prejudiced: *Rubin v Canada (Clerk of the Privy Council)* [1993] 2 FC 391 [1994] 2 FC 707 (1996) 179 NR 320, SCC; *Information Commissioner v Minister of Citizenship and Immigration* [2002] FCA 270 (rejecting 'chilling effect' argument).

[281] Access to Information Act s 16(2).

[282] Access to Information Act s 17.

or other negotiations of a government institution.[283]

(16) Harm in depriving a government researcher of priority of publication.[284]

(17) Injury to the financial or economic interests of Canada or of a government institution.[285]

(18) Prejudice to the use of audits or tests.[286]

51–033 Appeals and enforcement

There is a two-tiered review process. Applicants have the right to complain to the Information Commissioner about an institution's handling of their request.[287] Following an investigation and report by the Commissioner to the head of the institution, both applicant and Information Commissioner have a right to seek a review of a denial of access in the Federal Court of Canada.[288] Third parties may also apply to the Federal Court in order to prevent disclosure of a record.[289] The appeal to the Federal Court is an appeal on judicial review grounds.[290] The Court is entitled to examine any record in dispute[291] and it is normally accepted practice to allow counsel for an applicant to see the disputed documents to enable the case to be properly heard, but on an undertaking not to disclose them to the client.[292]

6. REPUBLIC OF IRELAND

51–034 Introduction

In Ireland, the first proposal to provide a right for access to official information came from a

283 Access to Information Act s 18(b).

284 Access to Information Act s 18(c).

285 Access to Information Act s 18(d). This does not extend to information that would result in an increase in legitimate claims for deductions under tax legislation: *Canadian Council of Christian Charities v Canada (Minister of Finance)* [1999] 4 FC 245.

286 Access to Information Act s 22. For an example, see *Bombardier v Canada (Public Service Commission)* (1990) 44 FTR 39.

287 Access to Information Act s 30. There is a 60 day time limit: s 31.

288 Access to Information Act ss 41 and 42. There must be a denial of access, so that if the institution claims that it has no documents, the applicant has no right of appeal; a court will not intervene where there is mere assertion that documents are held: *Creighton v Canada (Superintendent of Financial Institutions)* [1990] FCJ No 353, QL (FCTD); *Sheldon Blank & Gateway Industries Ltd v Canada (Minister of Environment)* [2001] FCA 374. The appeal is against the refusal to grant access, not the Information Commissioner's review: *Bellemare v Canada (Attorney-General)* [2000] FCT 429. However, the Court may properly take into account the Commissioner's views: *Canadian Council of Christian Charities v Canada (Minister of Finance)* [1999] 4 FC 245; *Blank v Canada (Minister of Justice)* [2009] FC 1221. As to an institution's ability to invoke for the first time an exemption during the appeal process, see: *Canada (Information Commissioner) v Canada (Minister of National Defence)* [1999] FCJ No 522, QL FCA.

289 Access to Information Act s 44. A third party can invoke s 19 on a s 44 review: *Heinz Co of Canada Ltd v Attorney-General* [2006] 1 SCR 441, 2006 SCC 13.

290 *Canadian Jewish Congress v Canada (Minister of Employment and Immigration)* [1996] 1 FC 268. The role of the Court is more limited where the exemption relied on turns on the head of a governmental institution reasonably believing that disclosure will result in an identified harm: *X v Canada (Minister of National Defence)* (1992) 58 FTR 93.

291 Access to Information Act s 46. The purpose of this provision is to enable the Court to have the information and material necessary to ensure that the discretion given to the administrative head has been exercised within proper limits and on proper principles: *Rubin v Canada (Canada Mortgage and Housing Corp)* [1989] 1 FC 265; see also *Canada (Minister of Environment) v Canada (Information Commissioner)* [2000] FCJ No 480, QL FCA. Protection against disclosure by the Court is given in s 47.

292 *Maislin Industries Ltd v Minister for Industry, Trade & Commerce* [1984] 1 FC 939 (TD); *Robertson v Canada (Minister of Employment and Immigration)* (1987) 13 FTR 120 (FCTD); *Hunter v Canada (Consumer and Corporate Affairs)* [1991] 3 FC 186 (CA); *Bland v Canada (National Capital Commission)* [1991] 3 FC 325 (TD); *Sheldon Blank & Gateway Industries Ltd v Canada (Minister of the Environment)* [1999] FCJ No 571, QL (FCTD). Cross-examination of deponents of affidavits in support of exemptions is not normally allowed: *X v Canada (Minister of National Defence)* (1992) 58 FTR 93 (FCTD).

private member's Bill in 1985. It received little support and matters remained there until late 1994 when the Fine Gael/Labour Party made a commitment to introduce access legislation as part of their programme for government. The Freedom of Information Act 1997 was passed on 21 April 1997 and came into operation on 21 April 1998.[293] Significant amendments were effected in 2003, which generally increased the ability of public bodies to claim exemption both from disclosing records and from having to confirm or deny the holding of records.[294] The 1997 Act was repealed and replaced by the Freedom of Information Act 2014 which came into force on 14 October 2014.

51–035 Scope of the right

Section 11(1) of the Act gives every person[295] a right of access to any 'record'[296] 'held'[297] by a 'public body'.[298] Certain records are, however, taken entirely outside the operation of the Act. These are termed[299] 'exempt records' and include:

— most records held by a court or tribunal other than those of an administrative nature;[300]

— records held or created by the Attorney-General or the Director of Public Prosecutions, or their offices, other than those of a general administrative character;[301]

---

293 Freedom of Information Act 1997 s 1(2). In relation to local authorities and health boards, the Act came into force on 21 October 1998. Its significance was described by the Supreme Court in *Sheedy v Information Commissioner* [2005] IESC 35 in these terms: 'The passing of the Freedom of Information Act constituted a legislative development of major importance. By it, the Oireachtas took a considered and deliberate step which dramatically alters the administrative assumptions and culture of centuries. It replaces the presumption of secrecy with one of openness. It is designed to open up the workings of government and administration to scrutiny. It is not designed simply to satisfy the appetite of the media for stories. It is for the benefit of every citizen. It lets light in to the offices and filing cabinets of our rulers.'

294 Freedom of Information (Amendment) Act 2003. This Act effected amendments to the definition of 'record'; allowed access to personal information that predated the commencement of the Freedom of Information Act 1997; strengthened the provisions relating to the refusal to confirm or deny the existence of a record answering the terms of a request; converted the protection of records relating to meetings of Government from discretionary to mandatory; extended the non-disclosure period of records relating to meetings of Government from 5 to 10 years; generally widened the scope of the exemptions. The net effect of the amendments is to make the Freedom of Information Act 1997 the most restrictive of the comparative jurisdictions so far as a person's right of access to official information is concerned, notwithstanding the words in the long title of the Act. The High Court in *Deely v Information Commissioner* [2001] IEHC 91 and prior to the amendments, had described the Act as being 'on any view, a piece of legislation independent in existence, forceful in its aim and liberal in outlook and philosophy.'

295 'Person' is defined in the Interpretation Act 1937 to include a body corporate. The long title of the Freedom of Information Act 2014 suggests that the Act is principally intended to be for 'members of the public' rather than companies.

296 'Record' is defined to include: a book or other written or printed material in any form (including in any electronic device or in machine-readable form; a map, plan or drawing; a disc, tape or other mechanical or electronic device in which data other than visual images are embodied so as to be capable, with or without the aid of some other mechanical or electronic equipment, of being reproduced from the disc, tape or other device; a film, disc, tape or other mechanical or electronic device in which visual images are embodied so as to be capable, with or without the aid of some other mechanical or electronic equipment, of being reproduced from the film, disc, tape or other device; a copy or part of anything listed: Freedom of Information Act 2014 s 2(1).

297 The phrase 'held by a public body' is defined to include a record under the control of a public body: Freedom of Information Act 2014 s 2(5). It also extends to records in the possession of a person who is providing a service for a public body under a contract for services, provided that the records relate to the service: Freedom of Information Act 2014 s 11. 'Control' suggests 'a degree of authority/dominion/management of the records rather than mere access to the records': *Minister for Enterprise Trade and Employment v Information Commissioner* [2006] IEHC 39.

298 Public bodies are listed in s 6(1) and include governmental departments, higher education institutions in receipt of public funding, any entity that was a public body under the 1997 Act. Bodies exempted or partially exempted from the Act are listed in the First Schedule. It only applies to a limited extent to the state broadcaster: *RTE v Information Commissioner* [2004] IEHC 113.

299 Freedom of Information Act 2014 s 2(1).

300 Freedom of Information Act 2014 s 42(a).

301 Freedom of Information Act 2014 s 42(f).

— records relating to audits, to the President, or to any private papers of a member of either House of the Oireachtas;[302]
— records revealing the source of information relating to enforcement or administration of the law;[303] and
— records otherwise available to members of the public.[304]

With two exceptions, the right of access applies only to records created on or after the 'effective date'.[305] The Act makes limited provision for the giving of assistance to people who seek access to information.[306] Under the Act, each public body must publish a 'publication scheme' setting out its functions and duties, the classes of records held by it, together with certain information in relation to the making of a request for access to records.[307] In addition to these rights, the Act grants individuals the right to require amendment of incorrect government records containing personal information concerning them.[308]

51–036 The request

A request is normally to be made in writing and must be adequately particularised.[309] The reason for the request is irrelevant to the entitlement to obtain access.[310] A request that is frivolous or vexatious or which would cause a substantial and unreasonable interference with or disruption of the other work of the public body concerned need not be answered.[311] A request need not be answered if the required fee has not been paid.[312]

51–037 The response

The public body is required to take reasonable steps to ascertain the location of records answering the terms of the request.[313] If the public body does not hold records answering the

302 Freedom of Information Act 2014 s 42(g), (h), (k). These are also picked up by the second limb of the definition of 'exempt record' in s 2(1).

303 Freedom of Information Act 2014 s 42(m).

304 Freedom of Information Act 2014 s 15(2). 'Effective date' is defined in s 2(1). This does not extend to information available under the DPA 1988: Freedom of Information Act 2014 s 15(3).

305 Freedom of Information Act 2014. The first exception is where earlier records are needed in order to understand post-commencement records: Freedom of Information Act 2014 s 11(5)(a). The second exception is in relation to records containing personal information relating to the person making the request: Freedom of Information Act 2014 s 11(5)(b). As to the meaning of the latter, see *EH v Information Commissioner* [2001] IEHC 182, where it was held that the record could constitute personal information about the requester even though the requester is not named in the record.

306 Freedom of Information Act 2014 ss 12(6) and 15(4).

307 Freedom of Information Act 2014 s 8. In addition, internal guidelines on the making of any decisions by a public body must be published: Freedom of Information Act 2014 s 8(2)(e). No express provision is made for any sanction for non-compliance with s 8, but the Information Commissioner may examine and report in their annual report on the extent of compliance with s 8. The Information Commissioner also has the power to examine practices and procedures adopted by public bodies for the purposes of compliance with the Act: Freedom of Information Act 2014 s 44(1).

308 Freedom of Information Act 2014 s 9. Personal information can include records relating to a subject matter in which the applicant has a real and substantial interest, such as proceedings before a committee of the medical council: *EH v Information Commissioner* [2001] IEHC 182.

309 Freedom of Information Act 2014 s 12(1). The request must specify the form of access sought.

310 Freedom of Information Act 2014 s 13(4). Accordingly, the public body cannot impose restrictions on the purpose for which released records may be used or persons to whom they may be shown: *EH v Information Commissioner* [2001] IEHC 58, [2001] 2 IR 463.

311 Freedom of Information Act 2014 s 15(1).

312 Freedom of Information Act 2014 s 15(1)(h). The amount of the fee is set by Freedom of Information Act 2014 s 27. Fees can be waived: Freedom of Information Act 2014 s 27(3), (6).

313 Freedom of Information Act 2014 s 15(1). Where it is estimated that the cost of search and retrieval is likely to exceed the amount prescribed by the Freedom of Information Act 2014 (Fee 1)(No 2) Regulations 2014, the public

terms of the request but actually or constructively knows that another public body does, the request must be transferred to that latter public body within two weeks of the receipt of the request.[314] Within four weeks of receipt of the request, the public body must notify the applicant of the decision on the application, together with the fees that must be paid in order to obtain access.[315] Failure to notify within the prescribed period is deemed to constitute a refusal.[316] If the decision involves a refusal, reasons must be given together with a statement of appeal rights.[317] If the public body decides to give access to a record, it can do so in any number of ways.[318] Where part of a record contains exempt material but the remainder does not, the public authority must give disclosure to as much of the non-exempt material as is practicable.[319] The public body can, in a wide range of circumstances, refuse to confirm or deny that it holds records answering the terms of a request.[320] The Act specifically provides for discretionary disclosure.[321]

51–038 Exemptions generally

Certain exemptions are mandatory, the remainder are discretionary. Some of the exemptions are prejudice-based exemptions, others are purely class based. The likelihood of harm needed to engage the prejudice-based exemptions varies from 'could reasonably be expected' to occasion the identified harm,[322] to 'would be likely' to occasion the identified harm,[323] to 'could' occasion the identified harm.[324] Approximately half of the exemptions include a provision that disapplies the exemption where, in the opinion of the head of the public body, the public interest would on balance be better served by granting rather than by refusing the request for access.[325] The Act provides for conclusive certificates in relation to: records recording the deliberations of a public body; records whose access could be expected to prejudice law

---

body is entitled to seek a deposit and need not commence the search until such time as the deposit is paid: Freedom of Information Act 2014 s 27(5).

314 Freedom of Information Act 2014 s 12(3) and (5). Where the requested body holds some, but not all, of the records answering the terms of the request and the public body actually or constructively knows that another public body holds other records, the first public body must so notify the applicant: Freedom of Information Act 2014 s 12(4) and (5).

315 Freedom of Information Act 2014 s 13(1). The period can be extended where the records involved are voluminous or where there have been other requests for the same records: Freedom of Information Act 2014 s 14(1).

316 Freedom of Information Act 2014 s 19.

317 Freedom of Information Act 2014 s 13(2)(d), (f).

318 Freedom of Information Act 2014 s 17(1). Generally speaking, the public body must give access in the form sought by the applicant: Freedom of Information Act 2014 s 17(2). The public body cannot impose restrictions on the purpose for which released records may be used or the persons to whom they may be shown: *EH v Information Commissioner* [2001] IEHC 58, [2001] 2 IR 463.

319 Freedom of Information Act 2014 s 18(1). The resultant redacted record must not be misleading: Freedom of Information Act 2014 s 18(2).

320 Where to do so would be prejudicial to government business, s 28(5); where to do so would be prejudicial to parliamentary or court business, s 31(4); where to do so would be prejudicial to law enforcement, s 32(2); where to do so would be prejudicial to security, defence or international relations, s 33(4); where to do so would reveal confidential information, s 35(4); where to do so would reveal commercially sensitive information, s 36(4); and where to do so would reveal personal information about someone other than the applicant, s 37(7).

321 Freedom of Information Act 2014 s 11(8). It is not clear whether a mandatory exemption represents a prohibition of access by law.

322 Freedom of Information Act 2014 ss 30(1), 32(1), 33(1), 36(1)(b), 39(1)(b), 40(1) and 40(2)(n).

323 Freedom of Information Act 2014 ss 36(1)(a) and 39(1)(a).

324 Freedom of Information Act 2014 s 36(1)(b)-(c).

325 Freedom of Information Act 2014 ss 29(1), 30(2), 32(3)(b), 35(3), 36(3), 38(3), 37(5) and 40(3). The onus lies on the public authority: *Minister for Communications Energy and Natural Resources v Information Commissioner* [2017] IEHC 222 at [49]-[51].

enforcement, investigations, public safety, domestic or national security, defence and international relations; and records containing certain confidential information or that might reveal the identity of certain informants.[326] The effect of a conclusive certificate is to remove the right of merit review in relation to the decision to treat the record as exempt.[327] Where the information included in a record to which access has been sought includes information obtained in confidence, commercially sensitive information or personal information, a third party to whom the information relates is given the opportunity to make submissions on the disclosure of it.[328] In such cases the onus is upon the public body to justify non-disclosure.[329] The courts construe the exemptions restrictively.[330]

51–039 Specific exemptions

There are 16 heads of exemption, half of which are mandatory and half of which are discretionary. The public body must refuse access where:

(1) the record has been or is proposed to be submitted to the Government for consideration by a Minister and was created for that purpose, or the record contains information for use at a meeting of the Government or consists of a communication between two or more members of the Government relating to the same;[331]

(2) the record contains or reveals a statement made at a meeting of the Government;[332]

(3) the record would be exempt from production in a court on the grounds of legal professional privilege; disclosure of the record would constitute a contempt of court; the record consists of the private papers of a member of the European Parliament, a member of a local authority or of a health board; or the record consists of the opinions, advice, recommendations or results of consultations considered by either House of the Oireachtas or its committees;[333]

(4) the record contains information: obtained for intelligence purposes; relating to the security forces; revealing diplomatic communications; or revealing confidential communications from foreign state organisations;[334]

---

326 Freedom of Information Act 2014 s 34.

327 There remains the more limited right to challenge the issue of the certificate on a point of law: Freedom of Information Act 2014 s 24(2). See also the limited right of review under Freedom of Information Act 2014 s 34(7) and (8).

328 Freedom of Information Act 2014 s 38. A more detailed comparative treatment of third party rights of consultation and of 'reverse FOI' is given at §22–038.

329 Freedom of Information Act 2014 s 22(12)(b).

330 *Minister for Agriculture and Food v Information Commissioner* [2000] 1 IR 309 at 319; *Sheedy v Information Commissioner* [2005] 2 IR 272 at 275; *Health Service Executive v Information Commissioner* [2008] IEHC 298; *Rotunda Hospital v Information Commissioner* [2009] IEHC 315; *P v Information Commissioner* [2009] IEHC 574; *FP v Information Commissioner & Ors* [2016] IEHC 771.

331 Freedom of Information Act 2014 s 28(1). Factual material is excluded and the exemption becomes inapplicable 10 years after the decision is made to which the record relates. The public body can refuse to confirm or deny the existence of any record falling within the terms of the exemption if it thinks that to do either would be contrary to the public interest: Freedom of Information Act 2014 s 31(4). The exemption will apply even if the record was not actually submitted to the Cabinet, provided that it was created for that purpose: *Minister for Education & Science v Information Commissioner* [2008] IEHC 279.

332 Freedom of Information Act 2014 s 28(2).

333 Freedom of Information Act 2014 s 31(1). The public body can refuse to confirm or deny the existence of any record falling within the terms of the exemption if it thinks that to do either would be contrary to the public interest: Freedom of Information Act 2014 s 22(2). For the purposes of the contempt provision, any disclosure will suffice: *EH v Information Commissioner* [2001] IEHC 58, [2001] 2 IR 463.

334 Freedom of Information Act 2014 s 33(2). The relevant minister may issue a conclusive certificate if he takes the view that the exemption applies. The public body can refuse to confirm or deny the existence of any record falling within the terms of the exemption if it thinks that to do either would prejudice the security, defence or international relations of the state, or matters relating to Northern Ireland: Freedom of Information Act 2014 s 33(4).

(5) the record contains information given to the public body in confidence or the disclosure of which would constitute a breach of confidence;[335]
(6) the record contains trade secrets, financial, etc information or contractual negotiations;[336]
(7) disclosure would be of personal information not relating to the applicant;[337] and
(8) disclosure of the information is prohibited by another statute.[338]

The public body may refuse access where:

(9) the record contains matter relating to the deliberative process of the public body;[339]
(10) disclosure of the record could reasonably be expected to prejudice the effectiveness of tests, inquiries, audits, etc carried out by a public body or have a significant adverse effect on staff management or disclose a negotiating position;[340]
(11) the record relates to the appointment or business or proceedings of a tribunal or an inquiry;[341]
(12) disclosure of the record could reasonably be expected to prejudice law enforcement and investigations or matters of internal security, or to reveal the name of a police informer;[342]
(13) disclosure of the record could reasonably be expected to adversely affect the security or defence of the Republic of Ireland or its international relations;[343]

---

335 Freedom of Information Act 2014 s 35(1). This exemption is disapplied where the public interest is better served by disclosure than by non-disclosure. The public body can refuse to confirm or deny the existence of any record falling within the terms of the exemption if it thinks that to do either would be likely to prejudice future disclosure of further similar information or constitute a breach of a duty of confidence: Freedom of Information Act 2014 s 35. This will be satisfied where the provider and the recipient regarded it as being confidential at the time of receipt. See: *Minister for Communications, Energy and Natural Resources v Information Commissioner & ors* [2019] IECA 68.

336 Freedom of Information Act 2014 s 36(1). This exemption is disapplied where the public interest is better served by disclosure than by non-disclosure. The public body can refuse to confirm or deny the existence of any record falling within the terms of the exemption if it thinks that to do either could reasonably be expected to result in a material financial loss or gain to the person to whom the person relates, could prejudice the competitive position of that person, or could prejudice contractual or other negotiations of the person to whom the information relates: Freedom of Information Act 2014 s 36(4). See: *University College Cork v Information Commissioner & anor* [2019] IEHC 195.

337 Freedom of Information Act 2014 s 37(1). This exemption is disapplied where the public interest is better served by disclosure than by non-disclosure. The public body can refuse to confirm or deny the existence of any record falling within the terms of the exemption if it thinks that to do either would involve the disclosure of personal information: Freedom of Information Act 2014 s 37(6). See: *FP v Information Commissioner & Ors* [2016] IEHC 771.

338 Freedom of Information Act 2014 s 41.

339 Freedom of Information Act 2014 s 29(1). Factual and statistical material is excluded from the scope of the exemption. The exemption is disapplied where the public interest is better served by disclosure than by non-disclosure: Freedom of Information Act 2014 s 29(1). The relevant minister may issue a conclusive certificate if he takes the view that the exemption applies.

340 Freedom of Information Act 2014 s 30(1). This exemption is disapplied where the public interest is better served by disclosure than by non-disclosure. This was considered in *Minister for Education and Science v Information Commissioner* [2001] IEHC 116 in relation to a request for education league tables.

341 Freedom of Information Act 2014 s 31(2).

342 Freedom of Information Act 2014 s 32(1). The public body can refuse to confirm or deny the existence of any record falling within the terms of the exemption if it thinks that to do either would have an effect specified in s 32(1)(a)-(c): Freedom of Information Act 2014 s 32(2). A conclusive certificate may be issued in respect of this head of exemption: Freedom of Information Act 2014 s 34. This exemption is disapplied where the public interest is better served by disclosure than by non-disclosure.

343 Freedom of Information Act 2014 s 33(1). The public body can refuse to confirm or deny the existence of any record falling within the terms of the exemption if it thinks that to do either would prejudice the security, defence or international relations of the State, or matters relating to Northern Ireland: Freedom of Information Act 2014 s 33(4). A conclusive certificate may be issued in respect of this head of exemption: Freedom of Information Act 2014 s 34.

(14) disclosure might be prejudicial to the health of the applicant;[344]
(15) disclosure would reveal information about research in progress carried out by or on behalf of a public body;[345] or
(16) disclosure would have a serious adverse effect upon the financial interests of the state, on the ability to manage the economy, or might disturb business or could result in an unwarranted benefit or loss to a person or to a class of persons.[346]

51–040 Appeals and enforcement

The first stage of appeal is a merit review by the 'branch head' of the public body to whom the request is made.[347] The second stage of appeal is a merit review by the Information Commissioner.[348] The onus of proof lies upon the public body to justify the decision not to grant access.[349] A third party who would be affected by a disclosure will normally be entitled to have his views taken into account.[350] An appeal to the High Court on a point of law lies from a decision of the Information Commissioner[351] or from the decision to issue a conclusive certificate.[352] The Act provides for various enforcement provisions,[353] as well as granting immunity from legal proceedings for the disclosure of information pursuant to the Act.[354]

344 Freedom of Information Act 2014 s 37(3).

345 Freedom of Information Act 2014 s 39.

346 Freedom of Information Act 2014 s 40. This exemption is disapplied where the public interest is better served by disclosure than by non-disclosure.

347 Freedom of Information Act 2014 s 21(1). The review decision must be made within three weeks of the application for review having been received: Freedom of Information Act 2014 s 21(4). Failure to respond in that time is deemed to constitute a refusal: Freedom of Information Act 2014 s 19.

348 Freedom of Information Act 2014 s 22. The Information Commissioner can rely on exemptions not invoked by the public body: *Minister for Education and Science v Information Commissioner* [2001] IEHC 116; cf *Minister for Agriculture and Food v Information Commissioner* [1999] IEHC 66, [2000] 1 IR 309, [2001] 1 ILRM 40. The Information Commissioner also has power to review a decision to defer access; a decision to grant access in the face of opposition from a third party under s 58; a decision to give access in one particular form, rather than another. The Information Commissioner has inquisitorial powers: Freedom of Information Act 2014 ss 23 and 45. He can refer questions of law to the High Court: Freedom of Information Act 2014 s 24(6).

349 Freedom of Information Act 2014 s 22(12).

350 *South Western Area Health Board v Information Commissioner* [2005] IEHC 177, [2005] 2 IR 547.

351 Freedom of Information Act 2014 s242(1). The limited nature of such an appeal was considered by the High Court in *Deely v Information Commissioner* [2001] IEHC 91, [2001] 3 IR 349; *Sheedy v Information Commissioner* [2005] 2 IR 272; *Rotunda Hospital v Information Commissioner* [2009] IEHC 315; *Kruse v Information Commissioner* [2009] IEHC 286.

352 Freedom of Information Act 2014 s 24(2).

353 Freedom of Information Act 2014 s 45.

354 Freedom of Information Act 2014 s 49.

Index